HANDBOOK OF ABNORMAL PSYCHOLOGY

HANDBOOK OF
ABNORMAL PSYCHOLOGY

An Experimental Approach

EDITED BY

H. J. EYSENCK, Ph.D.

Professor of Psychology, University of London
Director of the Psychological Laboratories, Institute of Psychiatry
Psychologist, Maudsley and Bethlem Royal Hospitals

BASIC BOOKS, INC., Publishers
New York

This book is dedicated to the memory of

Emil Kraepelin,

who first applied the methods and theories of experimental
psychology to the problems of abnormal behaviour.

Fifth Printing

First Edition
Published in the United States of America
by Basic Books, Inc., 1961
© Pitman Medical Publishing Co. Ltd. 1960
Library of Congress Catalog Card Number 61-7077
PRINTED IN THE UNITED STATES OF AMERICA

Foreword

BY WILLIAM A. HUNT

Chairman, Department of Psychology, Northwestern University

THROUGHOUT the first quarter of this century the prevailing organic orientation of American psychiatry with its reliance upon relatively simple, somewhat naive physiological and behavioral referents was favorable to the development of an experimentally oriented abnormal psychology. With the subsequent acceptance of psychoanalysis and the attendant ascendancy of the dynamic, functional approach, however, the interest in experimentation was overshadowed by a tendency to substitute a method, largely rational, which placed its stress upon the interpretation of often inaccurate and uncontrolled clinical observations.

In part this was attributable to the anti-experimental attitude of classical psychoanalysis. In part it was attributable to the difficulty of translating the new and exceedingly complex dynamic concepts into any clear and univocal behavioral dimensions amenable to exact definition, accurate observation, and adequate control, and hence open to objective measurement and experimental manipulation. In addition there began a sizable diversion of psychological manpower away from experimentation and into purely service functions. Many psychologists were so busy practicing the conventional techniques of assessment and psychotherapy that they had little time to worry about matters of rationale and validation. Finally, it seems fair to say that the complexities of the functional dynamic approach burst in upon a relatively unsophisticated psychology that was by no means a fully mature behavioral science. It has taken us some time to grow up to our problems, and research has suffered.

The picture is changing, however. Psychology is coming of age as a behavioral science. It is increasingly sophisticated in tackling its problems of experimental design, behavioral recording, and statistical interpretation; and as its sister behavioral sciences have in turn developed, it has borrowed wisely from them. The atmosphere within organized psychiatry also has become more favorable for research, and psychology has been admitted to full partnership on the psychiatric research team. The renaissance in neurology reopens the possibility of still another research collaboration that psychology has found valuable in the past.

Finally, the postwar training programs in clinical psychology have made their own important contribution. While many trainees are still being drained off into service functions, the firm resolution of professional psychology in insisting that research training be made an important part of any clinical training program has provided a sizable pool of able, serious young scholars with a genuine research dedication. Moreover, the placing of these programs in the various and countrywide university centers of academic activity, either through necessary administrative contact, participation in student training, or mere physical and intellectual contiguity, has done much to break down the traditional isolationist attitude of classical experimental psychology. An increasing number of experimental psychologists is being seduced into a participation in research within the clinical area. This may be a reflection of an applied trend developing within experimental psychology as a result of the interest generated in human engineering by the military research effort during and since World War II, but in larger part I think it stems from the firm conviction that normal and abnormal behavior are but opposite ends of a continuum and that the understanding of one demands an understanding of the other.

It would certainly be unduly optimistic to state that psychology as an experimental science is now ready for the final solution of all its problems in the field of mental health, but it is no exaggeration to say that it has made a promising beginning. This *Handbook of Abnormal Psychology* formally marks that beginning, and should make its own important contribution to the movement.

It is an unusually good handbook. The coverage is wide and eclectic. There are omissions, but an attempt to decide whether they are minor or major would provide only a pointless argument. The individual chapters are well organized and the authors in general have managed to rise above a mere survey of the literature and achieve an integration that at times is genuinely creative. Moreover, the editor has resisted what must have been a strong temptation to restrict the orientation to his own theoretical interests. The familiar Eysenckian dimensions of Neuroticism, Psychoticism, and Introversion-Extroversion are dealt with here, as they would have to be in any adequate survey of contemporary work, but they are dealt with in their proper context and perspective. The basic orientation is a broad one which conceives of abnormal psychology as an experimental affair, is critical of the older nosological categories, and proposes a new look at abnormal behavior through its careful objective measurement along a series of pertinent and meaningful behavioral dimensions. This is an increasingly popular orientation in the field in line with what would appear to be a renewed interest in and modernization of descriptive psychiatry.

The major significance of this volume, however, lies not in its excellence as a handbook, but rather in the fact that a handbook of abnormal psychology (actually of *experimental* abnormal psychology) is being published at this time. It marks an auspicious coming of age of psychology, and should offer leadership and encouragement to a growing movement. Its publication thus achieves some genuine historical significance.

September, 1960

Contributors

H. Brengelmann, M.D., Ph.D. (London), D.Phil. (Göttingen) Research Associate, Department of Psychiatry

P. Broadhurst, M.A., Ph.D. Lecturer, Department of Psychology; Director, Animal Laboratory

D. Campbell, Ph.D. Research Associate, Department of Psychology; now Lecturer, University of Auckland, New Zealand

H. J. Eysenck, Ph.D. Professor of Psychology, University of London; Director of Psychological Laboratories, Institute of Psychiatry; Psychologist, Maudsley and Bethlem Royal Hospitals

Cyril M. Franks, M.A., Ph.D. Lecturer, Department of Psychology; now Chief Psychologist, New Jersey Neuropsychiatric Institute

W. D. Furneaux, Ph.D. Research Associate, Department of Psychology

G. Granger, Ph.D. Lecturer, Department of Psychology; Director, Perceptual Laboratory

J. Inglis, Ph.D. Lecturer, Department of Psychology; now Associate Professor, Departments of Psychology and Psychiatry, Queen's University, Canada

H. Gwynne Jones, B.Sc. Senior Lecturer, Department of Psychology

I. Martin, Ph.D. Research Associate, Department of Psychology

V. Meyer, Ph.D. Research Associate, Departments of Psychology and Neurosurgery; now Lecturer, Department of Psychology

N. O'Connor, Ph.D. Psychologist, Medical Research Council Social Psychiatry Research Unit, Maudsley Hospital

R. W. Payne, Ph.D. Lecturer, Department of Psychology; now Associate Professor, Departments of Psychology and Psychiatry, Queen's University, Canada

L. Rees, M.D., B.Sc., M.R.C.P., D.P.M. Physician, Maudsley and Bethlem Royal Hospitals

J. Shields, B.A. Lecturer, Genetics Unit, Department of Psychiatry

E. Slater, M.D. Senior Lecturer, Genetics Unit, Department of Psychiatry

D. Trouton, M.A., M.B., B.Ch. Research Associate, Department of Psychology

R. Willett, Ph.D. Lecturer, Department of Psychology

A. Yates, Ph.D. Lecturer, Department of Psychology; now Lecturer, Department of Psychology, University of New England, Australia

Contributors

Contents

Numquam ita quisquam bene subducta ratione ad vitam fuit,
Quin res aetas usus aliquid adportet novi
Aliquid moneat: ut illa quae te scisse credas, nescias,
Et quae tibi putaris prima, in experiundo ut repudies.

Terence

Physicians must know their science is impotent if they do
not apply to it the power of mathematics.

Roger Bacon (1214–86)

Introduction

TEXTBOOKS on psychology usually preface the text with an apology for the difficulty of defining psychology. A HANDBOOK OF ABNORMAL PSYCHOLOGY ought to begin with a triple apology, because in addition to the obvious difficulties of defining the major subject it is not at all easy to define the concept of "abnormality," and even the connotations of the word "handbook" are far from obvious. We shall not attempt to give any new meaning to the term "psychology," but shall take it to denote the scientific study of the behaviour of organisms. Nor shall we worry overmuch about the general designation of this book; handbook is as handbook does. But we shall devote a little time to a discussion of the meaning of "abnormal," if only because our use of the term will be found to differ somewhat from that often accepted in psychiatry and clinical psychology.

As has frequently been pointed out, the word "abnormal" is used in at least two quite distinct senses. It may be equated with the *statistically unusual*, or it may be equated with *deviations from the ideal norm*. Often the two are combined, so that deviations from the norm which are decidedly unusual are called "abnormal" only when they are in an undesirable direction. Thus an I. Q. of 50 is considered abnormal, but not one of 150; cowardice, but not bravery; neurosis, but not superior adjustment.

As used in psychology, the term has come to refer to certain *unusual* and *maladaptive* states, such as schizophrenia, hysteria, anxiety state, and the like; this usage appears to have been taken over from psychiatry, where these behaviour patterns are regarded as medical diseases. As will be shown later (Chapter 1), this usage is not really justified by the facts; mental abnormalities do not represent qualitative disease entities having specific "causes." They resemble rather such continuously varying features as height, intelligence, hair colour, and the like, and demand quite a different type of analysis from that appropriate to "diseases."

It is for this reason that we have rejected the traditional arrangement of books on abnormal psychology, which closely follows the psychiatric mould. Hunt (1951) has put the situation very well: "Clinical psychology in (the) methodological sense is a more mature science than psychiatry. It is definitely experimental, if at times somewhat shakily so. As an experimental science, it has much to offer psychiatry, as I think many psychiatrists realize. For once, however, I am not advocating the 'team' concept, although it is one of my firmest beliefs. I would rather suggest that psychiatry attempt to stand upon its scientific feet, if only because of the good example it would set us in clinical psychology; far too many of us clinicians, instead of bringing our experimental tradition to the assistance of psychiatry, flee to the empirical ambiguities of psychiatry in an attempt to escape the rigorous scientific demands of our own discipline." This is precisely what we have attempted to do here—bring the experimental tradition of psychology to bear upon the "abnormal" behaviour of the organism. For reasons which will become apparent, we have rejected the psychiatric framework outright, preferring not to be bound and constrained by diagnostic schemes of dubious validity and known unreliability. Where the experimental findings summarized by us were couched in terms of such a system, we have of course had to make such use of them as we could, but we have, whenever possible, translated these classificatory schemes into a more empirical framework along the lines of dimensional analysis, outlined in Chapter 1.

In thus attempting to break away from the traditional frame, we have encountered two main difficulties. In the first place, much discussion had to be devoted to methodological problems. As long as clinical and experimental psychologists are content to take psychiatric diagnosis as their criterion, so long will their experimental designs be of exemplary simplicity and elegance—and their results equivocal and unrepeatable! But once we begin to question the validity of psychiatric diagnosis, and demonstrate its obvious lack of reliability, we are cast adrift on rather more turbulent waters, and have to consider seriously the problem of experimental design and methodological adequacy.

In the second place, most of the published evidence was found to be useless for our purpose, and had to be discarded. Less than one-fifth of the papers and books examined have been included, and even so the reader will find that what remains often gives rise to critical discussion rather than to enlightenment. We have preferred the positive to the negative approach, leaving out whole areas which traditionally would have been included (the vast literature of the Rorschach technique is one example) because detailed investigation revealed all dross and no gold (Eysenck, 1958), and including instead much less well cultivated areas (such as dark adaptation, or conditioning) because these seemed to hold out a more definite promise of future usefulness. We have little doubt that our critical judgements, leading to *exclusion*, can be justified by factual reference; we have less confidence that the same would at present be possible with respect to those judgements leading to the *inclusion* of material about which there is as yet not very much evidence. The book as a whole presents a point of view; it is in recognition of the fact that this point of view may easily be mistaken that we have prefaced the book with a quotation from Terence which William Harvey included for a similar purpose in his *Exercitatio Anatomica de Motu Cordis et Sanguinis in Animalibus* (1628).

Our conception of abnormality, then, is not in terms of classes of people suffering from mental diseases produced by definite "causes"; it is rather in terms of the defective functioning of certain psychological systems. The delineation of these systems, and the mapping out of the laws according to which they work, is the task of experimental psychology. There is no pretence that all is known about these systems, or about the laws governing their working. We are only too well aware of the low level of knowledge, and the high degree of speculation, which are so characteristic of even the most developed parts of psychology. But poor as this may be as a base, it is all there is; good intentions cannot conjure up scientific knowledge, and it is better to rely on a small but secure base, than float on insubstantial clouds of putative and supposititious generalizations without reference in reality.

Whenever possible, we have supplanted the usual paradigm of psychiatric research—x members of class y showed behaviour z—by what to our way of thinking is a superior paradigm: change in the independent variable x effects a change y in function z. In this paradigm, change y might be in the direction of making function z more "abnormal," or it might be in the opposite direction; provided the experiment included abnormality of functioning as a referent, it was considered to be relevant to our endeavour. Thus an experiment in which a hundred schizophrenics had been given the Rorschach test, and their performance discussed and perhaps compared with that of other groups, would not be included; an experiment in which experimentally induced anoxia caused a decline in dark-vision performance would be included. Indeed, while nearly all of the material traditionally included in books on abnormal psychology would have been gathered from experiments on abnormal groups, such as neurotics and psychotics, much of our material comes from normal groups. Readers who do not feel

in sympathy with this approach may like to consider that there are many textbooks written along the lines we have criticized; with one or two partial exceptions there is none which treats the subject in the manner here advocated.

A word may need to be added about the phrase "change in the independent variable x." These words have their usual meaning when we deal with the effects of administering a drug, carrying out an operation on the brain, or giving a series of cerebral electroshocks. It carries a slightly different meaning when this change in variable x is effected by choosing different groups of subjects (human or animal) whose positions on a continuum presumed to be highly correlated with x differ significantly. Thus Spence and his colleagues have carried out a series of investigations into the effects of anxiety (x) on conditioning and learning by comparing the performance of different groups of students scoring respectively high and low on a questionnaire presumed to be a measure of anxiety. While we cannot afford to reject any method of testing our hypotheses, attention should be drawn to the dangers inherent in this procedure. The continuum in question may not in fact be isomorphic with the hypothetical variable x; the method used for allocating people to positions on the continuum may have low reliability and low validity; position on the continuum may be indicative of a chronic state which produces different effects from those consequent upon acute and sudden stimulation-produced increases in x. Fortunately, all these points are open to empirical study, and much interesting material should emerge from a detailed investigation of the advantages and disadvantages of this paradigm.

Another point arises in connexion with the use of factors or continua in this type of research. As will be seen in Chapter 1, it is often possible to show that certain psychiatric groups have clearly assignable positions in the dimensional framework produced by the combination of factors or continua (as an example *see* Fig. 1.7 in Chapter 1). The question is sometimes put whether the dimensional framework is not merely a restatement of the original psychiatric type of classification. The answer, of course, is simply that the degree of correspondence observed is of some interest in making possible the translation of experimental findings from one field to the other. It is not, however, used or intended in any sense as proof of the correctness of the dimensional system, which is derived independently from the empirical relationships between experimental and behavioural measures of an objective kind applied to groups of normal and abnormal subjects. Even if there were no correspondence at all with psychiatric diagnostic classifications, this would not in any way invalidate the empirical findings.

Accumulation of facts, while indispensable, is not

enough in science; "those who refuse to go beyond fact rarely get as far as fact." Hence we have been particularly concerned to do two things. We have tried to use the laws and hypotheses of general, experimental psychology to account for the facts presented; it will be noted, for instance, how the Yerkes-Dodson Law appears to integrate the superficially heterogeneous content of many different chapters. (A quick look through a score of textbooks of abnormal and clinical psychology shows that none of them even deigned to mention this law!) We have also tried, where this deductive process could not be used because of the absence of well-substantiated laws in a particular field, to form generalizations from the available data, and thus suggest certain general rules or hypotheses which are sufficiently precise to admit of experimental tests. Thus there is throughout this book a stress on *integration through theory*, an attempt to see abnormal psychology as a part of general, experimental psychology. The laws of learning theory, to take but one example, apply no less to neurotics than to rats and college students; should it not be the task of the psychologist to deduce the details of abnormal behaviour from such general laws? This attitude has governed our view on the problem of treatment also, and on the relationship between abnormal psychology, or psychopathology, and psychiatry. Jaspers has put the case very clearly in his classical *Psychopathologie*—

Psychiatry always deals with individual people in their totality . . . But while the work of the psychiatrist is entirely with individual cases, he nevertheless requires to be also a psychopathologist, to look for general concepts and rules, in order to solve the problems presented by the single case. If the psychiatrist in the course of his practical work . . . makes use of science as only one of his aids, to the psychopathologist this science is an end in itself. He wishes to know and understand, characterize and analyze, not the individual person, but the general case. He is not concerned with the therapeutic use of his science . . . but only with truth, with facts, with connexions, and with proof. Not for him are empathy and understanding as such; they only furnish him with material. He requires ideas which can be conceptualized, which can be communicated, which can be fitted into an orderly scheme and which can be systematized . . . Science requires conceptual thinking which is systematic and can be communicated. Only in so far as such thinking has been developed can psychopathology claim to be scientific. That part of psychiatry which is art and expertise, which cannot be communicated but at best handed over in personal contact to susceptible disciples, cannot be the subject of printed explanation. Psychiatric instruction is more than the communication of conceptualized knowledge and more than the teaching of scientific facts. A book which is concerned with psychopathology can only offer scientific knowledge, and is valuable only in so far as it does precisely that. With a full realization of the importance of experience for practical treatment, and for the analysis of individual cases, we will nevertheless restrict ourselves consciously to those matters which are properly the subject matter of scientific knowledge.

While we have thus concentrated on *facts*, and *laws* relating facts together into an organized whole, we have not tried to erect any kind of grand metaphysical system, all-embracing and all useless. As Robert Boyle said: "It has long seemed to me to be none of the least impediments of the real advancement of true natural philosophy that men have been so forward to write systems of it." And as Bacon said of such system builders, they had "with infinite agitation of wit, spun out of a small quantity of matter those laborious webs of learning which are extant in their books . . . To what purpose are these brain-creations and idle plays of power? . . . Everyone philosophizes out of the cells of his own imagination, as out of Plato's cave." In its present humble state, psychology can at best support on a factual basis certain low-order generalizations; to go beyond these is to court disaster. Such generalizations are the building stones for all future advance; hence the importance of deriving them from the facts in a proper quantified manner. "Just as the ears are made for sound and the eyes for colour, so the mind of man is meant to consider quantity, and it wanders in darkness when it leaves the realm of quantitative thought." Thus Kepler, and we may perhaps add Roger Bacon's dictum of seven hundred years ago: "Physicians must know their science is impotent if they do not apply to it the power of mathematics."

A point of overriding importance has always seemed to us to be the *choice of variables* to be measured in our attempts to describe abnormal behaviour. This choice has in the past been made too often in a haphazard manner, determined by fashion (Rorschach), ease of obtaining data (questionnaire), or whim. Measurement in science grows out of a theoretical system, and is an inseparable part of that system; alter the system, and you alter the meaning and process of measurement. Only measurements so anchored have scientific meaning, and are capable of interpretation which is not arbitrary, subjective, and indeterminate. I have tried to make this point in detail elsewhere (Eysenck, to be published), and will not reiterate the arguments in its favour. It is necessary, though, to insist on it because several chapters are devoted to detailed discussions of the correct choice of variables in the investigation of mental abnormality. Thus the chapter by Granger attacks in detail the choice of variables in the study of perception, and the chapter by Furneaux sets out a system of description of problem-solving behaviour which specifies the most relevant variables in that field. In the fields of learning and conditioning, a similar attempt has been made by the writer (Eysenck, 1957) elsewhere, and consequently less space had to be devoted to this aspect by the authors of these chapters.

Our general outlook has of course governed the way in which the book has been organized. Part I deals with the description and measurement of abnormal behaviour in terms of sensorimotor functions, perceptual functions, thought processes, ego functions, and so forth. Part II deals with the causes and determinants of abnormal behaviour, such as genetic factors, constitutional factors, conditioning and learning, childhood and other environmental factors, and the like. Part III deals with the experimental study and modification of abnormal behaviour, concerning itself with the effects of drugs, psychotherapy, electroshock, surgical treatment, and so on. Like most classifications, this one merely serves the practical purpose of organizing the experimental material; it does not aspire to have more than heuristic value.

Many readers will undoubtedly feel that certain topics ought to have been included which in fact have been omitted. Ought a book such as this not have a special chapter on old age, which is probably responsible for more types of abnormal behaviour than many factors included? Should hypnosis not have been given extensive treatment? The list is endless, and we have no defence. These and many other topics ought to have been included but were not. Perhaps if a second edition is called for the publishers will be less insistent on our not overstepping the total number of words allocated to this venture . . . The remedy is in the reader's hand.

We have tried, in selecting our material, to avoid overlapping with handbooks devoted to other fields of psychology. Stevens's *Handbook of Experimental Psychology*, Lindzey's *Handbook of Social Psychology*, Carmichael's *Manual of Child Psychology*, and Stone's *Comparative Psychology* mark out fields of study which are relatively separate from our own, and it will be seen that only a very small percentage of the references in this HANDBOOK will be found in these other volumes. This may serve as evidence that the field of "Abnormal Psychology" has indeed a separate and independent existence, even though its definition, as mentioned before, may be difficult and heuristic; indeed the contents of this HANDBOOK may have to serve as a kind of operational definition of the field covered.

A final word may be in order to explain the composition of the team of writers whom I asked to contribute the various chapters. Originally I conceived the notion of writing a book such as this fifteen years ago when the exigencies of the war threw me into contact with psychoneurotic patients at the Mill Hill Emergency Hospital. Having little knowledge of the field, I naturally turned to the available textbooks on psychiatry and abnormal/clinical psychology. The perusal of some fifty of these left me in a state of profound depression, as none of them contained any evidence of properly planned or executed experimental investigations, or even the realization of the necessity for such. Nor did I find that concise and consistent framing of theories and hypotheses which usually precedes experimental investigations; all was speculation and surmise, laced with references to "clinical experience." Michael Faraday's words seemed only too apposite: "They reason theoretically, without demonstrating experimentally, and errors are the result." It was not until I turned back to Kraepelin that I found an attitude of mind which was willing to carry on the traditional brick-by-brick accumulation of evidence on the basis of properly planned experimental inquiries, and I soon noticed that much interesting and important work had in fact been done and reported in the Journals, although it had not penetrated into the textbooks. What more obvious, then, than to plan to gather together all these widely separated facts and theories into a textbook of abnormal psychology on a factual basis?

Accumulating material at the rate of a thousand articles and fifty books a year, I finally came to the conclusion that I could only write this book if I gave up all hope of doing research for at least three years. Once I had faced this choice in a determined fashion, the obvious solution suggested itself. During those years, there had gathered in my department a group of people who had specialized in different aspects of the general field of psychopathology, who had mastered the literature in their special areas of competence, and who had carried out experimental investigations in these various disciplines. Instead of trying in vain to duplicate their expertise, why not make use of their ability and unique experience to make the project a reality? Their enthusiastic collaboration was readily secured, and the general shape of the book was hammered out in a series of meetings. One or two colleagues from the psychiatric staff of the Maudsley and Bethlem Royal Hospitals had to be called in to cover areas which they were more competent to review than anyone in the Department, but with this exception all the chapters were contributed in the event by members of the Psychology Department. Some of these have since left and gone to the ends of the earth—Australia, U.S.A., New Zealand; one died under tragic circumstances, and was much mourned by all of us. But the book finally reached completion, and it remains for me to thank all my colleagues for their co-operation and their help. Each is responsible for his or her own chapter; I have not considered it my duty to censor opinions, but merely to avoid too much duplication, and to advise when asked to do so. Nor have I tried to ensure uniformity of outlook or agreement on all controversial points; what unity there is is due to the integration achieved by living, working, and arguing together. On one point, however, there is no disagreement whatever; the absolute necessity, namely, of applying the highest standards of experimental design and statistical treatment to the complex and perplexing problems offered by this fascinating but difficult field. It is for this reason that the dedication is to E. Kraepelin, the first person to be trained in the psychological laboratory, and to apply experimental methods to abnormal pyschology. It is sobering to consider, if only his outlook had prevailed in psychiatry, how much farther advanced our knowledge would now be! And how much less occasion there would be for what Huxley has called "the great tragedy of Science—the slaying of a beautiful hypothesis by an ugly fact."

H. J. Eysenck
Maudsley Hospital
1st *January*, 1958

REFERENCES

Carmichael, L., *Manual of Child Psychology* (New York, John Wiley & Sons, Inc., 1946).

Eysenck, H. J., *Dynamics of Anxiety and Hysteria* (London, Routledge & Kegan Paul, 1957).

Eysenck, H. J., Personality tests: 1950–1955 in *Recent Advances in Psychiatry* (London, Churchill, 1958).

Eysenck, H. J., "Personality as an integrating concept in psychology" in *Psychology: a Study of a Science*, Ed. S. Koch, Study II, Vol. 2 (to be published).

Hunt, W. A., Clinical psychology—science or superstition? *Amer. Psychologist*, **6**, 683–687 (1951).

Jaspers, K., *Allgemeine Psychopathologie* (Berlin, J. Springer, 1913, 1948).

Lindzey, G., *Handbook of Social Psychology* (2 vols.) (Cambridge, Mass., Addison-Wesley, 1957).

Stevens, S. S., *Handbook of Experimental Psychology* (New York, John Wiley & Sons, Inc., 1951).

Stone, C. P., *Comparative Psychology* (New York, Prentice Hall, 1951).

Acknowledgements

PERMISSION to quote lengthy extracts, tables or figures has been granted by many authors; in the case of tables and figures acknowledgement has been made in the text. We are grateful to them, and to the following publishers, or organizations, for their help—

Grune & Stratton, Inc.
William Heinemann Medical Books, Ltd.
Paul B. Hoeber, Inc.
S. Karger
Routledge & Kegan Paul
University of California Press
University of Toronto Press
John Wiley & Sons, Inc.
Pergamon Press
M. D. Publications, Inc.
N.Y. Academy of Sciences
The Williams & Wilkins Company
Clarendon Press, Oxford
Foreign Languages Publishing House, Moscow
G. Thieme
Cassell & Co.
University of Chicago Press
Munksgaard
Sidgwick & Jackson
Macmillan & Co.
American Psychological Association
American Physiological Society
Her Majesty's Stationery Office
American Medical Association
American Association for the Advancement of Science
The Rockefeller Institute for Medical Research
Millbank Memorial Fund
Veterans' Administration, Washington
Acta Physiologica Scandinavica
American Journal of Optometry Publishing Association
Psychosomatic Medicine
British Journal of Psychology
Psychological Reports
Journal of Mental Science
Annual Review of Psychology
Annual of Human Genetics
American Journal of Psychiatry
Eugenics Review
Genet. Psychol. Monogr.
Hereditas
Ztsch. fur menschliche Vererbungs—und Konstitutionslehr
The *Observer*
Psychometr. Monogr.
J. Abnorm. (Soc.) Psychol.

CHAPTER 1

Classification and the Problem of Diagnosis

H. J. EYSENCK

THE importance of classification in the field of abnormal psychology is well indicated by Cattell's dictum (1940) that *nosology necessarily precedes aetiology*. Marzolf (1945) expresses the same thought when he says that the *establishment of syndromes is preliminary to the discovery of aetiologies*. Before we can reasonably be asked to look for the cause of a particular dysfunction or disorder, we must have isolated, however crudely, the dysfunction or disorder in question, and we must be able to recognize it and differentiate it from other syndromes. The very term "abnormal" implies a principle of classification; we could not look for causes of "abnormality" unless we had some conception of what we mean by "normal," and what kinds of deviations we would agree to consider "abnormal." Having once given a rough and ready answer to this problem, we would then find that our group of "abnormal" persons was still too heterogeneous to make the concept of a single general cause a reasonable one, and we would have to pursue our efforts at classification by recognizing such subgroups in our population as mental defectives, psychotics, neurotics, and so forth.

Traditionally, classification in the field of abnormal psychology has been by means of specific diseases or syndromes; we speak of hysteria, or schizophrenia, or manic-depressive psychosis in much the same way as we speak of tuberculosis, or neurosyphilis, or cancer. This is probably due to the medical tradition in this field; psychiatry has always paid more attention to the thought habits of general medicine than to the facts and methods of modern psychology. It is probably advisable to begin this chapter by investigating the rationale underlying current diagnostic systems, and to investigate also the question of whether better methods may not now be available for the solution of this fundamental problem.

Fig. 1.1 shows a diagrammatic view of a typical medical disease, namely tuberculosis. We have a "cause," namely the tubercle bacillus, acting on an organism predisposed by constitutional and environmental factors to react to the bacillus. The illness, when it develops, is characterized by various symptoms, some of which have been indicated in the figure. Methods of cure are available, and reasonable estimates of final outcome can often be made. In other

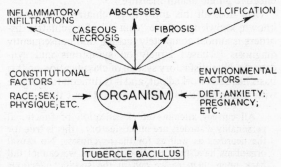

FIG. 1.1. DISEASE SYNDROME IN MEDICINE: TUBERCULOSIS

words, we have a rational system of aetiology, symptom-complex or syndrome, diagnosis, prognosis, and treatment. Diagnosis may be made on the basis of *either* the noxious agent which is designated the "cause" of the disease, *or* on the basis of the syndrome which is typical of the disease; which is done in practice depends on many factors which cannot be discussed here. Both methods may be used simultaneously.

This simple picture does not always correspond to reality. Neurosyphilis, for instance, is a term which includes all those disorders of the nervous structures, the envelopes surrounding them, and the blood vessels traversing them, which are caused by *treponema pallidum*. Its symptoms may be of almost any variety. "The symptoms of paretic neurosyphilis are protean in character and form almost any syndrome." (Cecil and Loeb, 1955). In other words, sometimes there is no close correspondence between "cause" and syndrome,

1

and it becomes difficult if not impossible to diagnose the former from the latter. This, however, is unusual, and most frequently there is some degree of correspondence between the two.

Historically, the discovery of the syndrome usually precedes the discovery of the "cause" of the disease (Mettler, 1947; Castigliani, 1941; Singer, 1928; Wittington, 1894). Thus the Roman writer Celsus (25 B.C.–A.D. 50) in his book *De Medicina* already discusses tuberculosis (Spencer, 1935), although the discovery of the tubercle bacillus did not take place until 1882. Nor did treatment always wait upon the discovery of the "cause"; Aretaeus the Cappadocian, who lived in the third century A.D., is credited with the advocacy of a milk diet in phthisis. "In the eighteenth century, the cause of scurvy was not known, but fresh fruit juices were used to prevent its occurrence. Jenner did not know the cause of smallpox, nor why vaccination should afford protection against the disease. John Snow died long before Koch saw the cholera vibrio under his microscope, but he knew that removing the handle of the Broad Street pump was an effective public health measure."

How does all this apply to psychiatry? As is well known, knowledge of the "causes" of psychiatric disorders is almost completely lacking and consequently diagnosis is based largely on symptoms and syndromes. No satisfactory system of classification on this basis has been worked out, and it is difficult to disagree with Cameron (1944) when he points out that—

All current attempts at classification of functional personality disorders are unsatisfactory; this is true for the neuroses as well as for the psychoses. No causal organisms have been implicated, hence we cannot fall back upon them as we can in the specific infectious diseases. There are no characteristic organic lesions, as there are in the systemic diseases; and the central nervous system exhibits no consistent changes that can be correlated with the syndromes as in neurological disorders. Physiological and biochemical studies do not support the older assumptions that fundamentally different metabolic processes underlie different forms of personality disorder. . . . It is important for persons working in the abnormal field to realize that the current official psychiatric classifications are not based upon final and convincing scientific evidence. They are children of practical necessities. Decisions as to the group in which a given behavior disorder shall fall depend upon schemata that actually were adopted, both in this country and in Great Britain, by a majority vote of the practising members of large associations. In some very fundamental respects these systems of classification represent frank compromises between dissident factions, as one can readily observe by reading the successive committee reports.

This interesting extension of the democratic process of majority rule into the scientific and medical fields

appears to be the final outcome of the method of classification devised by Kraepelin. As Degan (1952) points out—

His method of classification in its procedural aspects remains as the most popular, if not the only method of analyzing the complexities of psychiatric disease and synthesizing these into some type of order. His method may be described as the integrative resolution of the clinical observation of many cases with respect to their etiology, onset, symptomatology, course, and prognosis. Classificatory schemata derived in this manner are usually presented in the form of an essentially heuristic argument, and their ultimate validity is assessed in terms of the amount of agreement between the proposed system and the clinical experience and conceptions of the professional audience. Certainly, integrative clinical observation is well established as an exceedingly valuable method in medical research. However, the potential difficulties inherent in the communication of the subjective analytic and synthetic processes and criteria, and the absence of subsequent objective validation are obvious. . . . Official classifications follow fundamentally the same procedures as that of Kraepelin with only the additional formalization of the process of acceptance or quasi-validation. To say the least, this is a novel method of testing a scientific theory.

The failure of psychiatry to produce an acceptable classificatory system is obvious, not only in the necessity of introducing non-scientific criteria such as popular agreement, but also in the consistent lack of reliability shown in the actual use of the system by experienced psychiatrists. The evidence has been reviewed elsewhere (Eysenck, 1952), and it is clear that correlations between diagnoses made independently by different psychiatrists are too low to be readily acceptable as descriptive of the patients who are being examined. In part this is no doubt due to the low reliability of the ratings made of the symptoms which enter into the various syndromes. (Cattell (1957) reports a correlation of only 0·25 between experienced psychiatrists rating the symptom "anxiety" in eighty psychiatric patients!) but in part it undoubtedly reflects the faults of the general system which is being employed. No improvement is likely to occur until the basis of the present method is changed, and more modern methods substituted for those currently in use.

The first essential is probably the banishment of the notion of *disease* from the field of the functional mental abnormalities. Already in 1913, Jaspers pointed out that there are three *types* of psychiatric disorders. In the first group are those psychological abnormalities which are based on physiological and neurological disorders of the brain and the central nervous system—

The psychiatrist appears to be rescued from the difficulties presented by the concept of "disease" in those cases where he finds a *somatic* process to be responsible for the (psychological) disorder, a process which is objectively demonstrable and measurable. [In this connexion] psychopathology is only a means to an end, namely the discovery of physical symptoms. Physiology, not psychology, is the final aim of medical research. As physicians, we are concerned with the body alone. . . . Only those psychological processes are diseased which are produced by diseases of the brain.

Jaspers' second group contains the psychoses—

Which do not manifest somatic disorders of a kind which would enable us to diagnose psychosis by reference to them. Consequently the notion of disease is here primarily and exclusively related to psychological events. It is true that in many cases there occur somatic phenomena which suggest that perhaps some fundamental somatic cause may be at work and discoverable in the future. But in many cases these phenomena are absent. Hence it appears probable that certain definite somatic diseases will have to be excluded from this group and apportioned to the first group. Nevertheless, a clearly differentiated and independent group of disorders will remain, purified by this process of exclusion. Research into these disorders would be directed towards the discovery of psychological factors (*Grundfunktionen*) whose disturbance would render intelligible the manifold symptoms, rather in the same manner as in the first group.

In the third group of disorders we find the undesirable variants of humanity (*die unerwünschten Variationen des Menschseins*), and here there can be no question of somatic foundations for organic diseases. The body only enters the picture as it does in relation to healthy psychological development. Nor is the disease process . . . something quite novel compared with the preceding stage of health. We are dealing with fundamental properties of human existence (*Grundeigenschaften menschlichen Daseins*) . . . . Disorders in this group would be the neuroses, the character disorders, and criminal and other asocial propensities.

It may be possible to simplify this division even further. Eysenck (1957) has pointed out that the term "psychiatry" does not denote any meaningful grouping of problems or subjects of study, and that much of it is only of incidental relevance to psychology—

Few psychologists would probably disagree with the first of these two statements; anyone looking through the list of disorders officially falling under psychiatry will find it very difficult to find anything in common between G.P.I., schizophrenia, psychopathic behaviour, Alzheimer's disease, conversion hysteria, epilepsy, and Parkinsonism. From the point of view of the psychologist we may perhaps divide psychiatry into the *medical* part, dealing with the effects of tumors, lesions, infections, and other physical conditions, and the *behavioural* part, dealing with disorders of behaviour acquired through the ordinary processes of learning. Most neurotic disorders will come under this second heading, as well as possibly some or most of the schizophrenic and manic-depressive (functional) psychoses. Several related principles spring to mind, such as gross—as opposed to minute—changes

in the nervous system, or irreversible—as opposed to reversible—changes. The position, of course, is complex, and in the present state of ignorance no very clear-cut differentiations are possible; nevertheless, the distinction intended will be reasonably clear from what has been said, even though it cannot be claimed to be absolute, and even though borderline cases may have to be recognized.

Regarding the medical type of case, I believe that the contribution of psychology is secondary. Psychologists may occasionally be helpful in diagnosis, and even in relation to prognosis. . . . Similarly, psychological tests, particularly those of sensory dysfunction, may often give a timely warning of incipient neurological dysfunction and even help in its localization. . . . But these contributions, important though they may be, are secondary to the work of the neurologist, physiologist, and the surgeon. Psychology in this field is correctly conceived of as an ancillary. The position is quite different when we turn to the vast group of behavioural dysfunctions where there is no known neurological lesion or dysfunction.

Here, so the argument continues, psychology is the fundamental science, and rational methods of treatment have to be based on a thorough knowledge of modern psychological theory, particularly learning theory. This view is also explicitly put forward by Jaspers when he writes: "The study of psychology is indispensable for the psychopathologist as is the study of physiology for the somatic pathologist."

If psychology is of necessity secondary to other sciences in the investigation of the medical types of psychiatric disorder, it would also seem to follow that these disorders do not present any particular methodological difficulties in research and treatment, however complex in practical detail such investigations may be. In fact, one might reasonably ask why many of these disorders are usually dealt with by psychiatrists at all, seeing that in principle they are no different from other medical disease. It is true that psychological symptoms and changes play a prominent part in many of them, but these are secondary and are not really susceptible to psychological treatment. There are similar psychological changes in connexion with many diseases (depression associated with tuberculosis, for instance), yet these are not classed with the psychiatric disorders. It might be urged that the cortex and the C.N.S. underlie human behaviour in a very special sense, and that consequently it is reasonable to group diseases affecting these structures with those behaviour problems we call neuroses and psychoses. Hormonal secretions, however, or the autonomic system, equally determine behavioural reactions, yet disorders of these systems are not usually considered part of psychiatry. The answer is probably an historical one. The mental symptoms attending cortical disorders are much more obvious and more easily observed than are the physical ones, and consequently there was a very natural confusion between these states and the psychotic and neurotic ones. G.P.I. is a very obvious example of this. Only fifty years ago many psychiatrists still believed that this was due to psychological causes, and treated it by means of psychotherapy. As Bruetsch (1950) points out—

> The greater frequency of general paresis in males was explained by the preponderance of intellectual work in men, and by their more frequent contact with the strains of the world, with ambitions and frustrated hope. The small number of general paretics in the peasant class was explained on the grounds that they were relatively free from emotions and passions. . . . Krafft-Ebing, the famous Viennese professor of psychiatry, gave the following etiological possibilities for general paresis: dissipation in alcohol and love, heredity, smoking ten to twenty Virginia cigars, excessive heat and cold, trauma to the head, exhaustive efforts of making a living, weak nerves, and fright. Among women, the menopause was given as the most important factor because the onset was frequent between the ages of 40 to 50 years. . . . Among the first patients with general paresis, described by French psychiatrists, were many former soldiers and officers of the armies of Napoleon. In these it was speculated that the terrors of war were the precipitating factors. . . . It was not until the trend of investigations shifted from the clinic to the laboratory that the physical causation of general paresis was definitely established. . . . It is of the greatest therapeutic interest that the general paretic who during his illness is inadequately adjusted to his environment—as psychologists call it—becomes following malaria or penicillin therapy a well-adjusted personality without any psychotherapy whatsoever. Physical treatment and not mental healing, that is, talking or lecturing to the patient, relieves the patient of his abnormal behaviour, his emotional disturbances, and his delusions and hallucinations.

If the physical causation of G.P.I. and similar diseases had been known from the beginning, it is doubtful if these would have been classified as psychiatric disorders. It is historical accident, not logical classification, which causes psychiatry to split up into two fields, the medical and the behavioural, which have no underlying connexion with each other, and are as little related as are surgery and epidemiology, or otology and rhinoplasty. It is possible, of course, that the "behavioural" disorders may ultimately be swallowed up in the "medical" ones, and the case of G.P.I. certainly serves as a warning for us not to let speculation run too far ahead of knowledge, and to hold our hypotheses regarding the behavioural, as opposed to the medical, disorders tentatively and not dogmatically. Nevertheless, the distinction appears to be a fundamental one, and in the rest of the chapter we shall be concerned with the methodology appropriate to the "behavioural" disorders, and the main results produced to date by means of modern statistical and experimental methods.

What is the most noticeable and far-reaching difference between the medical and the behavioural disorders? It lies in the absence in the latter of the single "cause" characteristic of the former. In Fig. 1.1, it is the tubercle bacillus which lies at the basis of the whole series of symptoms which characterize the disease. In G.P.I., it is *treponema pallidum* which is the "cause" of all the variety of symptoms displayed. In the behaviour disorders, this single "cause" is absent, and we are left with what in Fig. 1.1 are merely contributory factors—the *constitutional* ones on the one side, the *environmental* ones on the other. This crucial difference between the two types of disorder makes it difficult to apply the term "disease" or "illness" to the behavioural disorders; it also necessitates a careful investigation of the appropriate statistical and experimental models to use in this connexion.

As Marzolf (1945) has pointed out—

> There are two ways . . . in which we try to order the phenomena of the natural world and thus explain them. . . . First, we classify phenomena as things or entities which have an invariant conjunction of properties or characteristics. It is this sort of ordering or explanation which is involved in organizing symptoms into syndromes, if and when this can be done. A second kind of explanation is the establishment of causal relations. In this case we likewise search for invariant relations, though they are between antecedents and consequents.

As Degan has pointed out, the first of these kinds of explanation gives rise to two types of analysis.

> Each individual or patient may be represented as a collection of the properties or characteristics of his behaviour. . . . The properties or characteristics in this case are the selected symptoms . . ., and the conjunction of these may be viewed either with respect to the individual as a whole or with respect to the relations between symptoms. In the first case, attention is centered on the groups of individuals who display identical, or less stringently, similar symptom patterns. This form of analysis inevitably results in a typology. The other mode of analysis relates each symptom to each of the other symptoms as to their mutual presence or absence, and in this way aggregates of symptoms may be found that display the required conjunction. The components of each of these aggregates are related through some common factor such as being manifestations of the same functional entity, consequent events of the same antecedent or complex of antecedents, etc.

Invariant conjunctions, as Degan and Marzolf recognize, are rare in biology; the presence of phenylpyruvic acid in the urine is always indicative of mental defect, although even here it must be admitted that mental defect is often present without the secretion. However, "relative conjunction is common in most biological research and is customarily evaluated in the probabilistic terms of modern statistical analysis.

Many . . . factors militate against a strict criterion of invariance. They emphasize the necessity for a statistical interpretation of syndrome formation and suggest the proper form of analysis to be statistical in nature."

As we shall see later, there are two main statistical models which are appropriate to the two types of analysis which Degan distinguishes. If we wish to view the conjunction of symptoms with respect to the individual as a whole, the preferred method of analysis is *canonical variate analysis*. If we wish to view the conjunction of symptoms with respect to their relation

These methods will be discussed in some detail later on; at the moment we must return to the distinction made by Marzolf between "explanation by conjunction" and "explanation by causal relation." These general models have given rise in psychology, and particularly in the study of personality, to two quite distinct schools, which have been named by Brand (1954) the "individual behaviour school" and the "general behaviour school" respectively. Eysenck (1958) has given a succinct presentation of the main differences between these two schools in the form of a Table, which is reproduced below (Table 1.1). As

TABLE I.1

	Individual behaviour	General behaviour
1. Type of theory	Individual behaviour	General behaviour
2. Aim of theory	Descriptive; cross-sectional	Causal, explanatory
3. Characteristic functions . . .	Static	Dynamic
4. Characteristic assumptions . . .	Non-specificity of behaviour	Specificity of behaviour
5. Characteristic method of analysis . .	Statistical	Experimental
6. Units of analysis	Traits, abilities, attitudes	D, $_sH_R$, $\bar{I}_R$, $_s\bar{E}_R$, etc.
7. Type of investigation . . .	Inductive	Hypothetico-deductive
8. Type of analysis	Correlational	Functional
9. Relationships analysed . . .	Interdependence	Dependence
10. Statistical paradigm . . .	Factor analysis	Analysis of variance
11. Type of generalization . . .	$\sigma a^2 = \sigma a_1^2 + \sigma a_2^2 + \ldots \sigma a_n^2 + \sigma a_s^2 + \sigma a_e^2$	$_sE_R = D \times {}_sH_R$
12. Field of application . . .	Social psychology	Physiological psychology

one to the others, the preferred method of analysis is *factor analysis*. The latter can be used with certain modifications to serve the former aim, as in the case of the analysis of correlations between persons (Eysenck, 1953), but the statistical requirements are too stringent to make this possible in any but exceptional cases.[1]

[1] Factor analysis is a method based on Mill's fourth canon, namely that "whatever phenomenon varies in any manner, whenever another phenomenon varies in some particular manner, is either a cause or an effect of that phenomenon; or is connected with it through some fact of causation." If we regard the concurrence of symptoms as covariation we may express it in terms of coefficients of correlation. Factor analysis then proceeds to find a solution for the minimum number of factors or parameters which can adequately account for all the experimentally obtained correlations. Among the assumptions made by this method of analysis is that the initial measures can be described as *linear functions* of the factors, an assumption which gives reasonable first approximations when the variables are monotonic functions of each other. In mathematical terms, what we do is to determine the rank of the correlation matrix; we end up with a system of *n* vectors in an *r*-dimensional space, where each of the vectors represents one of the initial variables (symptoms) and *r* is the number of factors. The correlations between the symptoms are given by the scalar products of the respective pairs of vectors. Factors so derived are seldom psychologically meaningful, and often require *rotation*; this leaves invariant the factor space and the positions within it of the variables, but changes the reference axes. (Thurstone, 1947; Burt, 1940; Thomson, 1939).

Canonical variate analysis deals with the relations obtaining between *r* groups of subjects, whether diagnostic, racial, or established on any other principle whatsoever, as shown on *n* tests or measures. The problem is the twofold one of establishing the dimensionality of the space required to accommodate the *r* groups, and of determining their respective positions

was pointed out in the paper from which this Table has been taken, these two approaches should be regarded as *complementary* rather than as *contradictory*; the analysis of interdependence ("conjunction") and the analysis of dependence ("causation") are both not only justifiable but also necessary methods of research in this highly complex and little understood field of psychological abnormality. No dogmatic assertions about the superiority of the one method should blind us to the usefulness of the other. We will return to this argument later on in this chapter.

There appears to be much confusion as to what can or cannot be done with analysis of interdependence, and particularly with factor analysis. Accordingly, a few examples will now be given of studies employing the technique of factor analysis, and illustrating certain misconceptions as well as certain advantages possessed by this method. Only a brief outline will be given; the reader will find detailed discussions of these and a large number of other studies in *The Structure of Human Personality* (Eysenck, 1953).

The first experiment to be discussed is the work of

to each other. The dimensionality of the space required cannot be higher than $r - 1$ or $n - 1$, whichever is the lower, but it may be lower, thus affording us a more parsimonious description. The probabilities of any individual whose test scores only are known and who belongs to any of the groups on which the analysis has been carried out, are also determined. Articles by S. B. G. Eysenck (1957) and H. J. Eysenck (1955) may be consulted for details and references.

Hewitt and Jenkins (1946). Taking their material from routine case histories, these authors studied five hundred problem children, the average age of whom was between 11 and 12, and the mean I.Q. 94. Forty-five traits were taken from the case histories, and inter-correlations calculated by means of tetrachorics. A cluster analysis was then performed (this is a simplified form of factor analysis), which revealed three factors or clusters of intercorrelated traits. The first one was

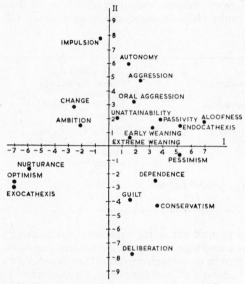

FIG. 1.2. PLOT OF FACTOR LOADINGS OF NINETEEN TESTS AS RELATED TO VARIABLE "EARLY WEANING"
(*From Goldman-Eisler*, 1948)

called "unsocialized aggressive behaviour"; the second was called "socialized delinquency behaviour"; and the third cluster was labelled "over-inhibited behaviour." Corresponding to these clusters of traits on the *child behaviour* side, there were three clusters on the *parental behaviour* side which were discovered in a similar manner. These three clusters were called "parental rejection," "parental negligence," and "parental repression." Having obtained these clusters on both the child behaviour and parental behaviour side, Hewitt and Jenkins now turn to their main hypothesis: "Children who differ from each other in expressing fundamentally different patterns of behaviour of maladjustment. . . . must have experienced fundamentally different patterns of environmental states; and conversely, children who are exposed to such fundamentally different patterns of situation, will exhibit fundamentally different patterns of maladjustment." Proof for this hypothesis is offered in the form of a table of correlations (Table 1.2) which shows that

parental rejection goes with unsocialized aggression, parental negligence with socialized delinquency, and parental repression with over-inhibited behaviour. These correlations are all relatively high and clearly significant (cf. also Lorr and Jenkins, 1953; Jenkins and Glickman, 1946; Lewis, 1954).

TABLE I.2

	Unsocial-ized aggression	Socialized delin-quency	Over-inhibited behaviour	Number of cases
Parental rejec-tion . .	0·48±0·07	0·02	− 0·20	101
Parental negli-gence .	0·12	0·63±0·07	− 0·17	78
Parental repres-sion . .	0·10	− 0·12	0·52±0·06	106

The second study to be mentioned is the work of Goldman-Eisler (1948, 1950, 1951). She has made an attempt to investigate the concepts of oral pessimism and oral optimism advanced by Abraham (1916, 1924, 1942), and Glover (1924, 1925). "Oral character traits are assumed to originate from repressed or deflected oral impulses which are determined during the nursing period, and which have undergone transformation into certain permanent behaviour patterns by the process of reaction formation, displacement, or sublimation. Two main syndromes of bipolar significance seem to emerge from Abraham and Glover's studies . . . . the basic conditions for the development and fixation in character of one or the other syndrome are assumed to be the experiences of gratification or frustration attached to the oral stage of libido development." On the one hand, we have the orally gratified type, which is described by analytic writers as being distinguished by imperturbable optimism, generosity, bright and sociable social conduct, accessibility to new ideas, and ambition accompanied by sanguine expectation. On the other hand, the orally ungratified type is characterized by a profoundly pessimistic outlook on life, sometimes accompanied by moods of depression and attitudes of withdrawal, a passive, receptive attitude, a feeling of insecurity, an ambition which combines an intense desire to climb with a feeling of unattainability, a grudging feeling of injustice, sensitiveness to competition and dislike of sharing.

Fig. 1.2 shows the result of a study in which self-rating scales for nineteen traits, each containing between six and ten items, were administered to one hundred and fifteen adult subjects and intercorrelated. Also included is another item, "early weaning" which was defined as "having been weaned not later than at the age of four months." It will be seen from the figure that the first factor to emerge from the analysis corresponds in broad outline to the hypothetical oral pessimism oral optimism factor, and that "early weaning" has a significant loading on oral pessimism. The second factor is irrelevant for our discussion here.

The third study to be considered was carried out by Eysenck and Prell (1951, 1952). Seventeen objective tests of neuroticism were given to fifty monozygotic and fifty dizygotic twins, all of whom were normal "in the sense of never having been patients at a Child Guidance Clinic, or in any other way suspected of mental disorders." The same tests were given to a group of twenty-one neurotic children, similar in age and intelligence to the normal twins. The factorial analysis of the intercorrelations of the tests for the normal children gave rise to a very clearly defined factor of neuroticism, and when factor scores were calculated on this factor, for the "normal" and the "neurotic" children, the two distributions were found to be differentiated at a very high level of significance ($p < 0.001$). A diagrammatical representation of the distribution of scores equated for a number of cases is given in Fig. 1.3.

On the hypothesis that neuroticism is inherited, we would expect factor scores on neuroticism to be much more alike in monozygotic twins than in dizygotic ones, and this deduction was in fact borne out. The intra-class correlation between monozygotic twins was 0·851; that between dizygotic twins 0·217. Calculation of Holzinger's h^2, which is presented by him as an estimate of the degree to which a given score is determined by hereditary factors, shows that $h^2 = 0·81$. While Eysenck and Prell are somewhat critical of this statistic, in view of the fact that some of the assumptions involved in its derivation are clearly not fulfilled in actual practice, there can be no doubt about the significance of the difference between the intra-class correlations in the two types of twins, establishing the fact that hereditary influences play a strong part in this field.

Having presented these three studies as examples of factor-analytic work in the field of personality abnormality, we must now proceed to a discussion of the logic underlying the argument. In so far as the three studies are concerned with the analysis of interdependence, and the isolation of factors, they clearly make a useful and valuable contribution. Subject to replication, these experiments demonstrate the existence of consistent response patterns of various kinds. We are on somewhat less secure ground when dealing with the question of interpretation. The names given to their clusters of factors by Hewitt and Jenkins are purely descriptive, and most readers of the detailed account that they give would probably agree that the terms are well chosen. In the case of Goldman-Eisler, the name chosen is probably somewhat question-begging, because it assumes that the pattern of correlated traits is in fact determined by early-weaning experiences. One might offer as an alternative hypothesis that the factor she has unearthed is nothing more than extraversion-introversion; indeed it will be noticed that among the items having high saturation on this factor are *endocathexis* and *exocathexis*, which appear to be simply the Greek equivalents of extraversion and introversion. In the case of the Eysenck and Prell

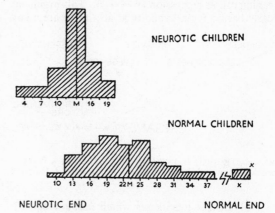

study it will be noticed that the factor is designated as one of "neuroticism," not only because of theoretical considerations or an inspection of the tests defining it, but mainly because of the experimentally demonstrated ability of the factor score to differentiate groups of normal and neurotic children. Such independent evidence regarding the nature of a factor has always seemed to the writer an indispensable part of the process of factor identification, and has indeed been made the basis of a special method of analysis called "criterion analysis" (Eysenck 1950).

It will be noted that the various authors of the papers here considered go beyond the analysis of interdependence, and believe that their work throws some light on the analysis of dependence as well. This is illustrated in Figs. 1.4 and 1.5 which depict diagrammatically the hypothesis underlying the Goldman-Eisler and the Eysenck and Prell study. (A similar diagram could also have been drawn for the Hewitt and Jenkins study.) It is important to consider the logic of this extension of the factor-analytic method because it does not appear to be justified in many cases. Let us first consider the kind of argument presented by Hewitt and Jenkins, or by Goldman-Eisler. This is illustrated in Fig. 1.6. In this figure P refers to the parental generation, F to the filial generation, x to a certain parental practice, and y to a certain filial practice. A single arrow denotes the use of a given practice by given representatives of a certain generation, while a double arrow denotes causation. The theories of Hewitt and Jenkins and Goldman-Eisler are illustrated in part A of Fig. 1.6. Put in words we get this kind of argument: Parents (P) practice early weaning (x); children (F) are aggressive (y) therefore early weaning causes aggression ($x \rightarrow \rightarrow y$). This argument clearly has no logical validity at all; there are many

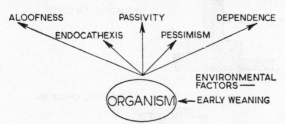

FIG. 1.4. DIAGRAM ILLUSTRATING THE ORIGIN OF A PSYCHOLOGICAL SYNDROME DEPENDENT ON ENVIRONMENTAL FACTORS

other alternative hypotheses which account equally well for the observed facts. One alternative hypothesis has been illustrated in Fig. 1.6, B; this may be called the hereditary theory. Using the same facts as before we may argue that aggressive parents wean their children early, and that the children inherit the parents' aggressiveness. Therefore, parents' aggressiveness is the genetic cause of the behaviour of the children, and x, the weaning behaviour of the parents, is irrelevant and supererogatory as far as the causal relations are concerned.

The second alternative hypothesis can be called the reaction theory. This is shown in Fig. 1.6, C, and again makes use of the same facts. According to this hypothesis, aggressive children behave aggressively to their mothers, reject the breast, etc. They therefore cause their mothers to wean them early. The origin of the child's aggressiveness is left indeterminate in this case; his early weaning is caused by his aggressiveness rather than the other way about.

Many other possibilities could be envisaged, but these two will suffice to show that the known facts cannot be used to support the environmental theory in any unequivocal manner. Essentially, the facts offered are *correlational*. A certain type of behaviour on the part of the parent is shown to be correlated with a certain type of behaviour on the part of the child. This is almost universally interpreted as proof of causation by modern psychologists with a bias in favour of environmental determination of behaviour, but once it is realized that we are simply dealing with correlation and nothing else, this assumption is

immediately seen to be untenable. It is one of the first lessons a student of statistics learns that *correlation does not imply direct causation*, and must not under any circumstances be so interpreted without *additional experimental proof*. It is curious that psychologists, almost without exception, have thrown this principle overboard and have interpreted the usually quite low correlations actually found as proof of environmental hypotheses without even considering hereditary or reactive hypotheses. This is all the more astounding

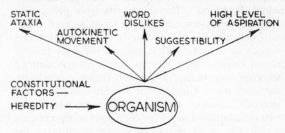

FIG. 1.5. DIAGRAMMATIC REPRESENTATION OF A PSYCHOLOGICAL SYNDROME DEPENDING MAINLY ON CONSTITUTIONAL FACTORS

as the same battle was fought out over thirty years ago in relation to intelligence. It will be remembered that the correlation between parental and familial intelligence was interpreted as evidence of the importance of *environment* by environmentalists and as evidence of the importance of *heredity* by hereditarians, until it was finally realized that the *fact* of a correlation of

(A) $P \rightarrow x$ ENVIRONMENTAL
          $F \rightarrow y$ THEORY
          $\therefore x \rightarrow \rightarrow y$

(B) $P \rightarrow x$ HEREDITARY
          $F \rightarrow y$ THEORY
          $\therefore P \rightarrow \rightarrow F \rightarrow \rightarrow y$

(C) $P \rightarrow x$ REACTION
          $F \rightarrow y$ THEORY
          $\therefore F \rightarrow \rightarrow P \rightarrow \rightarrow x$

FIG. 1.6. THREE DIFFERENT TYPES OF THEORY TO ACCOUNT FOR BEHAVIOUR RESEMBLANCES BETWEEN PARENTS AND CHILDREN

this kind was quite neutral with respect to the *causal explanation* favoured. Such an explanation must receive proof along quite different lines if it is to be acceptable.

What has been said here about the Goldman-Eisler study is, of course, equally true of the Hewitt and Jenkins one. There also the environmentalist hypothesis has been accepted unquestioningly, although the data do not enable us to choose between it and the "heredity" and the "reaction" hypothesis. It is possible that all the theories are correct up to a point, and even interaction factors may have to be considered.

How do these considerations affect the Eysenck-Prell study? The answer appears to be that here we have an attempt to go beyond the simple analysis of given elsewhere (Eysenck, 1957, and to be published) of the difficulties involved in causal research of this kind, and of the good points and imperfections of the models currently offered to psychologists by geneticists and environmentalists. For a further discussion the reader must refer to the chapter on genetics in this book.

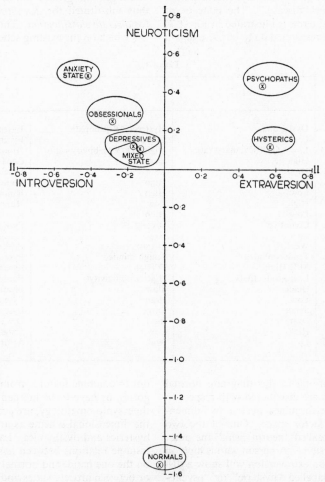

FIG. 1.7. POSITION OF ONE NORMAL AND SIX NEUROTIC GROUPS IN TWO-DIMENSIONAL FRAMEWORK DETERMINED BY CANONICAL VARIATE ANALYSIS OF OBJECTIVE TEST PERFORMANCES

interdependence and arrange an experiment in such a way that an answer becomes possible regarding the actual determination of the result by heredity factors. This, it will be remembered, was done by employing a research design featuring monozygotic and dizygotic twins. It is only this additional and vital step in the experimental procedure which makes it possible to draw any kind of conclusion from the results with respect to causation. A detailed discussion has been

These three examples have served as an introduction to the application of factor-analytic technique, and they have also revealed some of the difficulties which arise in research of this kind. We must now turn to its application in the wider field of the psychotic and neurotic disorders in general, and to a discussion of the main changes in our thinking which are required when we give up the psychiatric notion of the classical syndromes as *disease entities* and accept instead the factor-analytic notion of *dimensions of personality*. An example may illustrate the difference, as well as the relation between the two notions. The concept of *hysteria* as a disease entity, analogous to tuberculosis in Fig. 1.1, implies: (i) a single "cause" responsible for the symptoms observed, (ii) a homogeneity of all persons so diagnosed which sets them off qualitatively from all persons not so diagnosed, and (iii) a specific cure applicable to this "disease." The concept of hysteria in dimensional terms is illustrated in Fig. 1.7; this Figure summarizes research data to be presented in

concept extraversion-introversion objectively, and to measure a given subject's standing on the continuum.

The differences between this model and the psychiatric one will be obvious. Instead of a variable number of disease entities, differing from psychiatrist to psychiatrist, and diagnosed only with low reliability, we have two dimensions along which every person can be ranged and given a numerical score. *Continuity* is thus substituted for *discontinuity*[1], and *measurement* for *discrete classification*. The large number of neurotics which on the existing scheme of classification turn

TABLE I.3.

	I	E	Reference
Neurotic syndrome	Dysthymia	Hysteria: Psychopathy	Eysenck, 1947
Body build	Leptomorph	Eurymorph	Eysenck, 1947
Intellectual function	Low I.Q./Vocabulary ratio	High I.Q./Vocabulary ratio	Himmelweit, 1945; Foulds, 1956
Perceptual rigidity	High	Low	Canestrari, 1957
Persistence	High	Low	Eysenck, 1947
Speed	Low	High	Foulds, 1952
Speed/Accuracy ratio	Low	High	Himmelweit, 1946
Level of aspiration	High	Low	Himmelweit, 1947; Miller, 1951
Intra-personal variability	Low	High	Eysenck, 1947
Sense of humour	Cognitive	Orectic	Eysenck, 1947, 1956
Sociability	Low	High	Eysenck, 1956, 1957
Repression	Weak	Strong	Eriksen, 1954
Social attitudes	Tender-minded	Tough-minded	Eysenck, 1954
Rorschach test	M% High	D High	Eysenck, 1956
T.A.T.	Low productivity	High productivity	Foulds, 1953
Conditioning	Quick	Slow	Franks, 1956, 1957
Reminiscence	Low	High	Eysenck, 1956
Figural after-effects	Small	Large	Eysenck, 1955
Stress reactions	Overactive	Inert	Davis, 1948; Venables, 1953
Sedation threshold	High	Low	Shagass, 1956
Perceptual constancy	Low	High	Ardis and Fraser, 1957

detail later on. According to this diagram, normal and abnormal subjects are distributed with respect to behaviour and test performance over a two-dimensional continuum or factor space. One of the two continua or factors is called "neuroticism," the other "extraversion-introversion." A person who is high on neuroticism and high on extraversion will show a distinct tendency to be labelled "hysteric" or "psychopath" by an examining psychiatrist, while a person who is high on neuroticism and high on introversion will more likely be labelled "anxiety state" or "reactive depressive." The group of introverted neurotic symptoms has been labelled *dysthymia* by the writer (1947), and will be so designated throughout this book. A person high on neuroticism and intermediate with respect to extraversion-introversion is most likely to be labelled "mixed neurosis." An operational definition would, of course, be required of the dimensions involved: Table 1.3 shows some of the objective tests which would be used to define the

out to combine features from several diagnostic categories, or have to be lumped together as "mixed" in their symptomatology, are accommodated as easily in the dimensional scheme as are the "typical" but rare hysterics and dysthymics. Lastly, the scheme implies testable relations between hysterics and psychopaths, on the one hand, and normal extraverts on the other; or between anxiety states and reactive depressives, on the one hand, and normal introverts on the other. Shifts from one diagnosis to another, which should not occur on the hypothesis of discrete disease entities, are easily accommodated in the dimensional scheme if the facts demonstrate shifts along one dimension or the other in the course of time, or as the consequence of specific experimental or therapeutic manipulation. Indeed, as will be shown in later chapters, personality theories can be elaborated which predict such shifts on the basis of drug administration, brain operation,

[1] For attempts to prove experimentally and statistically the continuity hypothesis, *see* Eysenck (1950; 1952).

and other variables. The advantages of the dimensional system are considerable, and it may be noted that few psychiatrists are in fact willing to defend the old "disease entity" conception except in terms of its historical usefulness. Its early demise will be of considerable help in clearing the field and disabusing the minds of research workers of outmoded and erroneous notions.

There are many other advantages in explicitly adopting the statistical model associated with dimensional analysis. It enables us to do consciously and deliberately what psychiatrists have usually been doing unsystematically and haphazardly. A syndrome is fundamentally a statistical notion based on covariation; it seems obvious that its derivation will be placed on more secure grounds when it is carried out (i) on the basis of a properly formulated model, (ii) with awareness of the statistical requirements and difficulties involved, (iii) on the firm foundation of quantitative measurement of objective test performance, (iv) in relation to properly selected samples of the population in question, (v) in accordance with the rules of significance widely accepted in biological statistics. It is not implied that the syndromes isolated by psychiatrists in the last hundred years or so are inevitably imaginary and to be discarded; it seems more likely that such consensus as there is points to important and fruitful dimensions which could be validated by proper statistical research, and perhaps improved and sharpened. What does require discarding are the erroneous implications of "disease entities" implicit in psychiatric diagnoses, and the tacit assumption that subjectivity in the creation of systems of classification is a virtue. The psychiatrist typically bases his view on unsystematic observations of small and accidental samples of an undefined population; these observations are then integrated in accordance with unformulated canons of procedure along lines open to the influence of bias and preconceived opinion, and not subject to external safeguards and checks. No verification or duplication is possible, because none of the steps taken are made public; indeed, they are mostly inaccessible to the very person who is carrying out the analysis. It is not clear what assumptions are made, and no attempt is made to see whether the assumptions which appear to be implied are in fact justified. No doubt the psychologist working in the field also makes assumptions and commits errors; however, his assumptions are usually explicit and subject to experimental check. Even when they are not explicit, they can be deduced from the model, and another model substituted if the original one should prove to be contradicted by the facts. If he commits errors of sampling, of testing, of deduction, or of any other kind, these can be detected and corrected because the whole chain of argument and experiment is public and open to inspection. The "subjectivity" of the psychiatrist is often praised as likely to give rise to good hypotheses; this is possible, but science requires also a stage of verification, and this stage has no use for nonobjective methods of proof or argument, or for purely subjective *obiter dicta*. Science permits the investigator the greatest amount of freedom in *choosing* his hypotheses, but science also leaves little freedom in *proving* his hypotheses.

Much of what is said below with reference to the reaction patterns or factors isolated in empirical work by psychologists should be read in this context. Psychiatrists often point to the fact that factors are found which vaguely correspond to common diagnostic groupings, adding that nothing new has been contributed by the experimental and statistical work. This is incorrect. Some psychiatric hypotheses are supported, others are invalidated; it could not have been predicted beforehand which hypotheses would fall into which category. The writer's own work has supported Jung's typology, but not Kretschmer's; it could have been the other way round. There are so many psychiatric hypotheses, systems and syndromes that some of them are almost certain to be right; this does not mean that the task of deciding which in fact correspond to reality is one of supererogation. Futhermore, what was before mere surmise now has acquired operational definition and empirical standing; we can build on this newly acquired, firm foundation where previously there was nothing but shifting sand. Even so, it is not claimed that more has been done by experimental psychology than to make a beginning; with all its faults and crudities, this beginning contrasts with what went before in showing the essential feature of scientific work, namely, that it is *self-correcting*. Even if all the conclusions so far reached should turn out to be wrong, we would at least have the possibility of *proving* them to be wrong. This has never been possible with the traditional psychiatric approach.

In our survey of empirical studies, it will be useful if we begin with a brief summary of the main conclusions to which the evidence seems to lead. This is perhaps unusual, summaries by custom appearing at the end of a survey, but it will be found that the material under discussion is much more easily understood in terms of such a summary. The following then, are the main points to emerge: (i) There are two main, independent factors in the psychiatric field, associated with the *psychotic* and *neurotic* disorders respectively; these will be called *psychoticism* (P-factor) and *neuroticism* (N-factor). (ii) Both factors define continua which range all the way from extreme disorder to normality; there are no breaks or qualitative differences which would enable us to classify people into separate groups. (iii) Introversion-extraversion

TABLE I.4

ITEM SHEET ANALYSIS: VARIABLES INCLUDED IN THE FACTOR ANALYSIS

Number
of items
in Factor
Analysis

1		Age (16–39) v. (40–59)
2		Psychotic v. non-psychotic (i.e. neurosis and personality disorders)
3	Family History	Family history of psychosis
4	of Psychiatric	Family history of neurosis
5	Disorder	Family history of abnormal personality (e.g. psychopathy, alcoholism)
6		Unsatisfactory early life
7		Unsatisfactory adolescent adjustment
8		Work position falling and/or frequent unemployment due to instability of patient
9		Lacks confidence when in society
10	Previous	Unsatisfactory home life as an adult
11	Adjustment	Neurotic traits in childhood
12		Hysterical symptoms, lifelong or episodic
13		Obsessional symptoms, lifelong or episodic
14		Anxiety symptoms, lifelong or episodic
15	Previous	Definite mood variations before present illness
16	Symptoms	Energy output low, lacks effort for success and achievement
17		Symptoms of over 12 months' duration before admission
18		Gradual onset of illness
19		Constitutional causes important or dominant
20		Precipitating psychological and social (environmental) causes unimportant
21	Causes and	Functional disturbances in systems other than the nervous
22	Onset of	Retarded activity
23	Illness	Overactive, excited, manic or hypomanic, non-manic euphoria
24		Agitated
25		Impulsive and/or aggressive
26		Socially withdrawn
27		Compulsive acts and/or obsessional thoughts
28		Motor disturbances (e.g. posturing, grimacing and catatonic disturbances)
29		Depressed
30		Anxious
31		Mood disturbances (inappropriate or rapidly changing
32		Suspicious
33		Irritable
34	Symptoms	Suicidal feelings, intentions or serious attempts
35	of Present	Schizophrenic type of thought disorder
36	Illness	Psychogenic impairment of thought or memory
37		Delusions of guilt, self-reproach, unworthiness
38		Ideas of reference
39		Delusions (other than those included in 37 and 38)
40		Hallucinations
41		Severe insomnia at any time during illness
42		Gross disturbance of weight and/or food intake
43		Hypochondriacal attitude towards illness
44		Denial, indifference or unawareness of symptoms
45	Outcome in Hospital	Recovered or much improved at time of discharge

(I-factor) emerges as a third, independent factor which interacts with neuroticism in the manner suggested in Fig. 1.7, and possibly also with psychoticism. (iv) Intelligence is a fourth factor relatively independent of the other three, but interacting with all of them in complex and almost certainly non-monotonic ways. (v) When psychoticism is studied in isolation, several subfactors are discovered which are usually non-orthogonal and roughly correspond to traditional psychiatric groupings. These may be in part the projection into the psychotic dimension of neuroticism, intelligence, and extraversion-introversion.[1] (vi) Results are similar whether use is made of factor analysis or canonical variate analysis, and whether the material analysed consists of questionnaires, ratings, or objec-

[1] There is no evidence for the existence of a schizothymia-cyclothymia dimension as posited by Kretschmer (Eysenck, 1950, 1952). This is in good agreement with the genetic evidence, as shown in the chapter by Shields and Slater. There are however systematic differences in *inclusiveness of thinking* between patients diagnosed as schizophrenics and patients diagnosed as (endogenous) depressives (Eysenck, 1960); cf. the chapter by R. W. Payne in this book for a summary of the evidence.

tive personality tests. (vii) Distribution of individual scores on these factors reveals that no clusters corresponding to psychiatric disease concepts such as hysteria or schizophrenia exist; all distributions are continuous and without the clustering predicted in terms of any such theory. (viii) Descriptively, factor scores give a much more detailed and much more accurate picture of individual patients than does psychiatric diagnosis. (ix) Individual persons tend to have scores on all factors, not just on one; this shows the customary practice of allocating a patient to just one diagnostic group to be erroneous. Multiple diagnoses are more in accord with reality, but still less accurate and less descriptive than factor scores. (x) Some symptoms are more useful for factor measurement than others because they are relatively univocal; some, like "depression," have equally high loadings on several factors and consequently raise special difficulties of scoring.

We must now turn to a detailed consideration of some of the more important studies in this field, using factor analysis or canonical variate analysis. These will be taken seriatim and labelled according to the person or group of persons responsible for the given study or set of studies.

TABLE I.5

ORTHOGONAL ROTATED FACTOR LOADINGS

Variables	I	II	III	IV	V	VI	h^2
1	− 0·142	− 0·120	− 0·368	− 0·123	0·118	0·499	0·448
2	0·664	− 0·493	0·176	− 0·003	− 0·215	0·219	0·809
3	0·276	− 0·018	− 0·058	0·056	− 0·134	0·278	0·178
4	− 0·029	0·322	0·022	0·291	0·051	− 0·124	0·208
5	− 0·032	0·349	0·166	− 0·119	− 0·198	0·120	0·218
6	− 0·005	0·468	0·120	0·001	− 0·203	0·045	0·276
7	0·133	0·382	0·271	0·159	− 0·178	− 0·302	0·385
8	− 0·019	0·308	0·433	− 0·068	− 0·050	− 0·034	0·291
9	0·203	0·276	0·120	0·461	− 0·114	− 0·178	0·388
10	− 0·229	0·247	− 0·105	− 0·237	− 0·035	0·358	0·310
11	0·014	0·483	0·107	0·097	− 0·220	− 0·176	0·334
12	− 0·218	0·539	0·141	− 0·222	0·095	− 0·061	0·420
13	0·120	0·373	− 0·116	0·149	− 0·089	0·367	0·332
14	− 0·108	0·718	− 0·210	− 0·026	− 0·154	0·017	0·596
15	0·084	0·434	− 0·056	− 0·220	− 0·442	0·133	0·460
16	0·019	0·296	0·389	0·187	0·068	− 0·029	0·280
17	− 0·222	0·425	0·377	0·007	− 0·167	0·104	0·410
18	0·132	0·157	0·074	0·018	− 0·385	0·125	0·212
19	0·321	0·093	0·164	0·095	− 0·040	0·339	0·264
20	0·156	− 0·270	0·008	0·096	0·131	0·253	0·188
21	− 0·130	0·330	− 0·147	0·037	0·500	− 0·005	0·399
22	0·594	− 0·133	− 0·111	0·435	0·026	0·143	0·593
23	0·397	− 0·126	0·060	− 0·595	0·101	0·021	0·542
24	0·334	0·180	− 0·350	− 0·308	0·125	0·132	0·394
25	0·556	0·024	0·202	− 0·516	− 0·130	− 0·081	0·640
26	0·615	− 0·002	0·086	− 0·533	0·050	− 0·186	0·707
27	0·315	0·378	− 0·099	0·263	0·040	0·405	0·487
28	0·612	− 0·148	0·486	− 0·087	0·139	− 0·033	0·661
29	0·302	0·207	− 0·616	0·355	− 0·113	0·135	0·671
30	− 0·016	0·425	− 0·529	0·031	0·072	− 0·094	0·476
31	0·524	− 0·007	0·372	− 0·381	− 0·006	− 0·169	0·587
32	0·587	− 0·008	0·034	− 0·253	− 0·047	− 0·246	0·472
33	0·298	0·224	− 0·031	− 0·351	− 0·201	− 0·214	0·349
34	0·396	0·106	− 0·334	− 0·015	− 0·182	0·196	0·351
35	0·625	− 0·463	0·497	0·031	− 0·014	− 0·201	0·894
36	0·539	− 0·040	0·127	0·020	0·213	− 0·011	0·354
37	0·568	0·104	− 0·490	0·206	− 0·030	0·057	0·620
38	0·573	− 0·275	0·135	0·088	0·033	− 0·432	0·618
39	0·667	− 0·221	0·125	− 0·059	0·226	− 0·191	0·600
40	0·604	− 0·242	0·254	− 0·135	0·206	− 0·308	0·643
41	0·308	0·192	− 0·431	− 0·176	0·176	0·339	0·494
42	0·389	− 0·010	− 0·086	0·184	0·208	0·350	0·358
43	− 0·040	0·397	− 0·202	− 0·010	0·532	0·021	0·484
44	0·207	− 0·230	0·579	− 0·284	− 0·259	0·053	0·582
45	− 0·032	− 0·163	− 0·580	0·174	− 0·059	0·082	0·404

The Trouton-Maxwell Study

This experiment by Trouton and Maxwell (1956) makes use of an item sheet filled in by the psychiatrist responsible for the patient and which details the presence and absence of a large number of symptoms and traits, there being over five hundred items, intended to cover every psychiatrically significant aspect of the patient's history, symptoms and course of illness.

the presence of several misprints in the original article.)

Our main interest is in factors 1 and 2 which are shown in Fig. 1.8. These are clearly identifiable as *neuroticism* and *psychoticism* by virtue of the items defining each of the two factors; Trouton and Maxwell have no hesitation in labelling them accordingly. Factor 3 opposes schizophrenic symptoms (positive

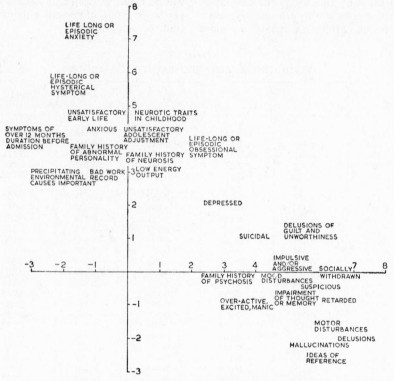

FIG. 1.8. ITEMS DEFINING NEUROTICISM AND PSYCHOTICISM FACTORS

Eight hundred and nineteen male patients aged between 16 and 59 inclusive, were selected at random from the population of The Maudsley and Bethlem Royal Hospitals, care being taken that all organic disorders were excluded. Forty-five items were selected from the total number, mainly on the basis of excluding items having such low frequencies that tetrachoric correlations could not be calculated for them. The forty-five items used are listed in Table I.4. Correlations were calculated between these items and a factor analysis carried out. Six factors were extracted and rotated with retention of orthogonality. The rotated factor matrix is given in Table I.5. (This table differs in some respects from that given in the original article; this is due to the omission of minus signs and

loadings) to symptoms characteristic of psychotic depression (negative loadings) and is, therefore, identified by Trouton and Maxwell with the well-known division in the psychotic field originated by Kraepelin and Bleuer. Factor 4 is labelled by Trouton and Maxwell as one of "inactivity-withdrawal." "Although not as well established as the preceding factors, the continuum is not only semantically satisfactory, but necessary to supplement other factors if some of the different variates of depression and schizophrenia are to be described." "The remaining factors contribute little to the variance and are probably unimportant. Five may represent hypochondriasis and six obsessionality (the latter is also descriptive of some of the features associated with involutional melancholia).

TABLE I.6

N = 266

Diagnosis	Psychotic +								Psychotic −							
	N+				N−				N+				N−			
	S+		S−		S+		S−		S+		S−		S+		S−	
	U+	U−	U+	U−	U+	U−	U+	U−	U+	U−	U+	U−	U+	U−	U+	U−
Schizophrenia	6	9	1	2	5	18	0	1	1	1	0	0	1	3	2	0
Mania	0	0	2	2	0	3	1	2	1	0	0	1	0	0	1	2
Depression	1	3	5	3	1	0	7	1	0	0	1	2	1	0	2	4
Involutional melancholia	0	0	4	2	0	0	6	9	1	0	0	0	0	0	0	1
Paranoia	0	0	0	0	0	6	1	1	0	0	0	0	0	2	0	0
							T = 102								T = 27	
Anxiety neurosis	1	0	1	1	0	0	1	2	2	2	2	4	1	4	2	7
Hysteria	1	3	1	2	0	1	1	0	0	4	3	5	1	10	2	1
Neurotic depression	1	0	0	0	0	2	1	2	0	2	1	1	0	4	6	11
Pathological and immature personality	2	0	0	0	1	6	0	0	4	15	0	1	2	8	0	2
							T = 30								T = 107	

There are, however, too few items with loadings on these factors for either of them to be identified with conviction."

It may be of interest to know just where in the dimensional system generated by this analysis patients of various orthodox diagnostic categories may be found. Table I.6 gives such a tabulation for two hundred and sixty-six unselected consecutive admissions at the Maudsley Hospital. On the left are nine diagnostic groups, divided into psychotic at the top and

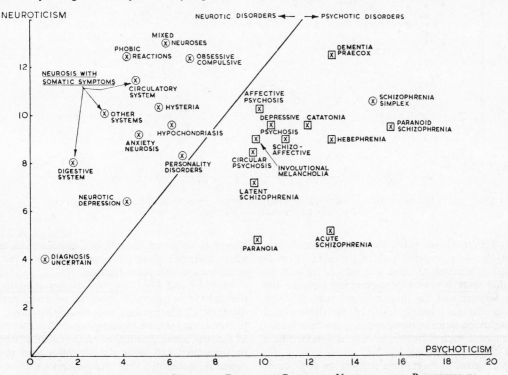

FIG. 1.9. POSITION OF VARIOUS CLINICALLY DIAGNOSED GROUPS OF NEUROTICS AND PSYCHOTICS IN TWO-DIMENSIONAL FRAMEWORK PROVIDED BY CANONICAL VARIATE ANALYSIS OF SYMPTOM RATINGS

neurotic at the bottom; on the right side of the table are numbers of patients in these groups falling into each of the sixteen categories produced by dichotomizing the first four factors. Thus, there are six schizophrenics who have an above mean score on psychoticism, neuroticism, schizophrenia and underactivity. Conversely, taking the last figure in the same row, there are no schizophrenics who are below the

is the mean factor score on these two dimensions of groups of patients. The oblique line running across the diagram gives a complete separation of the neurotic diagnoses and the psychotic diagnoses. There are many points of interest in this diagram, the most obvious one being perhaps that while the psychotic groups all have higher psychoticism scores than any of the neurotic groups, the psychotic groups also tend to

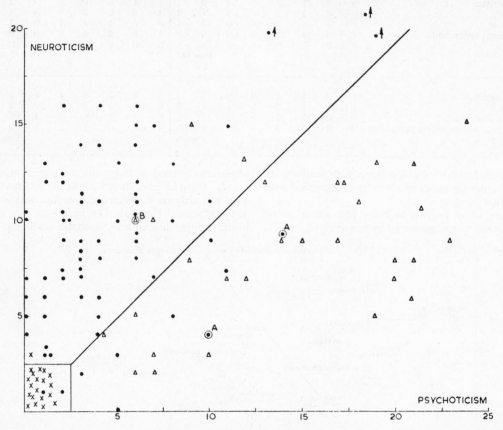

FIG. 1.10. PSYCHOMETRIC PROFILES OF THREE PATIENTS, PRESENTING THEIR SCORES ON FOUR FACTORS DETERMINED BY FACTOR ANALYSIS

mean on psychoticism, below the mean on neuroticism, depressive (at the negative pole of the schizophrenia-depression dimension), and overactive. It will be seen that there is reasonable agreement between the factor scheme and the diagnostic scheme, although even in this very rough form of the dimensional scheme, much more information is given than would be the case if each patient were only categorized by a single diagnosis.

Fig. 1.9 gives in diagrammatic form the position of various diagnostic groups in relation to neuroticism and psychoticism. What has been plotted in each case

have high scores on neuroticism, although not on the whole quite as high as the neurotic groups. We shall come back to this point later on.

Table I.7 and Fig. 1.10 give in diagrammatic form the individual scores of seventy neurotic patients, thirty psychotic patients and twenty normals. The picture is very similar to that given in Fig. 1.9. Nearly all the psychotics have higher psychoticism scores than the neurotics, but while the neurotics tend to have higher neuroticism scores than psychotics, there is no doubt that psychotics on the whole also have elevated scores on neuroticism. Normals, as might have been

expected, are very low on both neuroticism and psychoticism. There are two neurotics labelled A in the diagram whose scores fell well into the psychotic group; on readmission to the hospital these were re-diagnosed as psychotic. There is one psychotic patient marked B whose score falls well into the neurotic group; on readmission he was rediagnosed "neurotic."

TABLE I.7

FACTOR ALLOCATION

Analysis by Symptom Pattern Score: Comparison with Psychiatric Diagnosis

Diagnosis	Normal	Neurotic	Psychotic	Total
Normal ($\times$) .	19	1	0	20
Neurotic (•) .	2	60	8	70
Psychotic ($\triangle$) .	0	4	26	30
	21	65	34	120

The possibilities of dimensional description as op-posed to those of orthodox diagnostic procedures are illustrated in Fig. 1.11, where the scores of three patients (one anxiety neurotic, one agitated depres-sion, one schizophrenia) have been plotted with respect to the first four factors. The patterns are quite dis-tinct and probably more informative than any diag-nostic label could hope to be.

The Eysenck Canonical Variate Studies

The Trouton-Maxwell study made use of psychiatric ratings and employed the technique of factor analysis. There are obvious objections to both. Ratings are invariably highly subjective and may reflect nothing but the bias and prejudices of the rater. The authors argue strongly against the possibility that their results could be explained in these terms, but while their argu-ments have force, they nevertheless cannot completely eliminate this possibility. In a similar way the tech-nique of factor analysis can be criticized in its appli-cation to data of this kind which are unlikely to meet the underlying assumptions of this technique com-pletely, and may indeed make it quite inapplicable. It is fortunate, therefore, that we have available two studies using objective, quantitative tests applied to normal, neurotic and psychotic individuals, and em-ploying the technique of canonical variate analysis. If the results of such different studies should be similar to those of the Trouton-Maxwell study, then we can have much greater faith in the accuracy and validity of both.

The first of these studies, carried out by H. J. Eysenck (1955) employed twenty normal, twenty neurotic and twenty psychotic subjects. The tests used were measures of visual acuity, object recognition, mental speed and visual accommodation. The tech-nique of discriminant function analysis used for the study is very much like that of analysis of variance, but being in matrix form requires the calculation of several matrices. First, the total product-sum matrix (G) was computed for the four variables, then the between-groups product-sum matrix (B), the difference

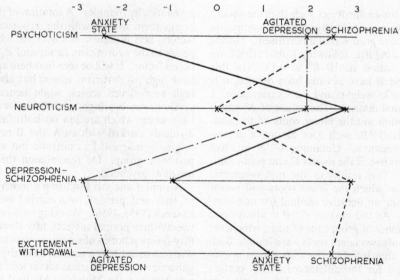

FIG. 1.11

between these giving us the within-groups product-sum matrix (*W*). (The latter was checked by an independent procedure). Hamilton (1950) and Rao and Slater (1949) in their analyses, proceeded to maximize the general distance function (*D²*); Eysenck followed instead Lubin's (1950) method of maximizing the square of the correlation ratio, given by

$$R^2 = \left(\frac{\text{deviance between groups}}{\text{total deviance}}\right)$$

In essence, the problem is this. We wish to find a set of weights in order to derive from our four tests a

ratio (*R*) between the three groups and the two variates is 0·84, a not unreasonably low figure when the unreliability of the criterion is borne in mind.

As a next step, scores were computed for each subject on both variates. This was done in the following way. The latent vectors furnish us with two sets of weights to apply to the scores, so that two measures can be calculated for each subject, one for each canonical variate. The scores Y_1 and Y_2 were found by multiplying the score of each subject by the appropriate weights and running them over the four tests. A plot of these scores is given in Fig. 1.12, where normals are represented by crosses, neurotics by dots and

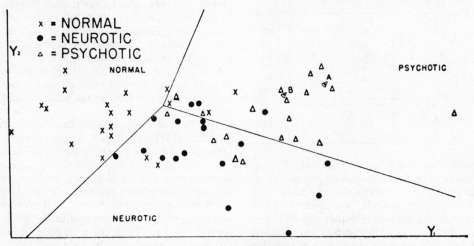

FIG. 1.12. VARIATE SCORES AND GROUP SEGREGATION USING VISUALLY FITTED LINES
(*From Eysenck*, 1955)

composite score for each subject such that the square of the correlation ratio (*R²*) between that composite variate and the three groups is at a maximum. Hence, if we take $R^2 = \acute{u}Bu/\acute{u}Gu$, following Lubin (1950), we arrive at the equation $(G^{-1}B - R^2 1)u = O$. (In this expression, *G* and *B* have already been defined, *u* is the column vector of weights and *ú* is its transpose. 1 is the unit diagonal matrix). The values of *R²* which satisfy this equation are the latent roots of the non-symmetric-matrix $G^{-1}B$, each root having a corresponding latent vector *u*. Obtaining $G^{-1}B$ involves calculating the inverse of the matrix *G* and post-multiplying it by *B*. This results in the non-symmetric matrix BG^{-1} from which the latent roots and vector are extracted using an iterative method for non-symmetric matrices. As the rank of $G^{-1}B$ is always one less than the number of groups (or of tests, whichever is the smaller), only two latent roots were found. Both were significant showing that two dimensions are required to account for the differences in test performance between the three groups. The correlation

psychotics by triangles. A rotation of the two variates brings them in line with the Trouton and Maxwell factors, and is shown in Fig. 1.13, where Z_1 corresponds to the neuroticism factor and Z_2 to the psychoticism factor. It will be seen that here again psychotics have high psychoticism scores, but also tend to have high neuroticism scores, while neurotics have low psychoticism but high neuroticism scores. Normals have scores which are low on both factors. Two individuals marked with an A and B respectively were originally diagnosed as neurotic but appeared in the psychotic group. On readmission they were rediagnosed as psychotic.

A similar analysis but using a much larger number of tests and persons, was carried out by S. B. G. Eysenck (1955, 1956). Working with one hundred and twenty-three normal subjects, fifty-three neurotics and fifty-one psychotics, she used six tests in all (an expressive movement test, a manual dexterity test, a psychogalvanic reflex test, a static ataxia test, a word association test and the Maudsley Medical Questionnaire).

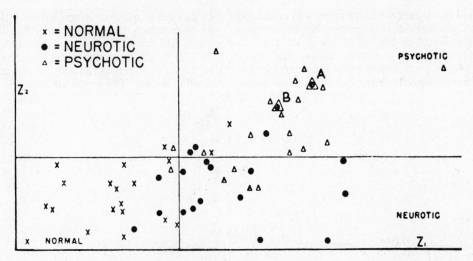

FIG. 1.13. RESULT OF "ROTATION" IN THE CASE OF THE PRESENT CANONICAL VARIATES
(*From Eysenck*, 1955)

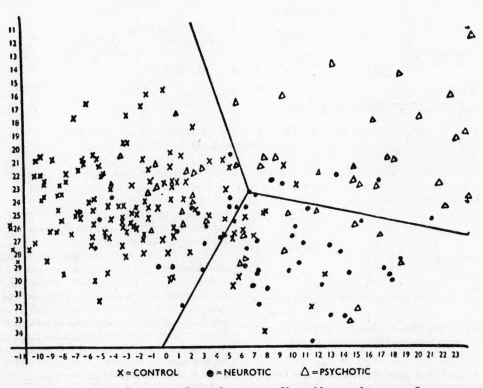

FIG. 1.14. VARIATE SCORES AND GROUP SEGREGATION USING MINIMUM LIKELIHOOD SOLUTION
(*From S. B. G. Eysenck*, 1956)

She found two significant latent roots, and calculated scores for the individual subjects of her experiments which are plotted in Fig. 1.14. We again note the same state of affairs as previously, namely, that neurotics are low on psychoticism whilst the psychotics are high on not only psychoticism, but also to some extent

now proceed to mention several studies which investigate more closely the subdivision within these great groups. The first of these was carried out by Eysenck (1947), in which thirty-nine symptomatic and descriptive items were intercorrelated for seven hundred neurotic patients. The results are shown in Fig. 1.15;

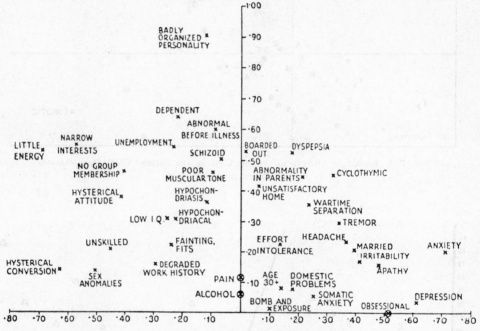

FIG. 1.15. ITEMS DEFINING NEUROTICISM AND EXTRAVERSION-INTROVERSION FACTORS
(*From Eysenck, 1947*)

on neuroticism. We may conclude, therefore, not only that the two canonical variate studies are in good agreement with respect to their conclusions, but also

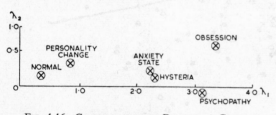

FIG. 1.16. CONFIGURATION OF DIAGNOSTIC GROUPS
(*From Rao and Slater*, 1949)

that they forcibly support the results of the Trouton-Maxwell study.

The Neuroticism and Extraversion-introversion Studies

Having shown the relatively clear-cut distinction between neurotic and psychotic disorders, we must

they support rather strongly Janet's hypothesis of hysterical disorders being opposed to dysthymic disorders. The results also seem to agree with Jung's hypothesis (cf. Fig. 1.3) of hysteria as characteristic of extraverted neurotics and the dysthymic disorders as characteristic of introverted neurotics.

The study just mentioned made use of factor analysis. Another experiment by Mayer-Gross *et al.* (1949) and Rao and Slater (1949), used the technique of canonical variate analysis. Two hundred and one neurotics and fifty-five normal officers were rated psychiatrically on thirteen main behaviour symptoms. These ratings were combined into three scores and canonical variate analysis carried out on these scores for five neurotic diagnostic subgroups and the normal subjects who constituted the sixth group. The results are shown in Fig. 1.16 where it will be seen that the first variate (neuroticism), opposes the normals to the neurotic individuals, while the second variate opposes the hysterics and psychopaths (extraverts) to the dysthymic groups, i.e. the obsessionals and anxiety states (introverts). The picture is in agreement with the Eysenck study but it should be noted that the second latent root in this study fell short of statistical significance.

Hildebrand (1958) has published a factorial study of the test performances of twenty-five conversion hysterics, twenty psychopaths, ten reactive depressions, ten obsessional neurotics, twenty-five anxiety states, fifty-five neurotics of mixed symptomatology, and a small sample of normal subjects. Twenty-five tests in all were used in this study, including questionnaires, performance tests, and measures of intelligence. Lawley's Maximum Likelihood Method was used for the extraction of factors. Three main factors emerged: neuroticism, extraversion, and intelligence. Factor scores were estimated for neuroticism and extraversion for all the subjects, and it was found: (1) that there were no significant differences among the neurotic population, as far as neuroticism was concerned, but that the normal group differed significantly from the total neurotic group; (2) that with respect to extraversion, "inspection of the means demonstrates clearly that the distribution follows the prediction. The hysterics and psychopaths are clustered at the extravert end of the distribution, and the dysthymics at the introvert end of the distribution, with the mixed neurotics occupying a central position." (Fig. 1.7 illustrates these findings.) Hildebrand also found that the sample of normal subjects used by him was atypical in being highly extraverted on a standardized scale. A more representative sample was substituted, and a canonical variate analysis performed by P. Slater (in Eysenck, 1960). The results of this analysis supported Hildebrand's conclusions on most points, but also added important information with respect to the dimensionality of the neurotic groups included; the data are too extensive, and the discussion too technical to be included here.

Far more impressive and convincing than Hildebrand's data is a more recent study by G. Claridge (in Eysenck, 1960). He based his selection of tests very largely on the experimental literature reviewed in Table I.3, as well as on certain direct deductions from Eysenck's *Dynamics of Anxiety and Hysteria* (1957); this theory was, of course, still in the process of construction when Hildebrand selected his battery of tests. Groups of sixteen hysterics, dysthymics, schizophrenics, and normals, equated for sex, age, and intelligence, were submitted to a very lengthy battery of tests and questionnaires, including measures of reminiscence, vigilance, disinhibition, massed practice effects, time error, time estimation, auditory flutter fusion, body sway suggestibility, rotating spiral after-effects, and tachistoscopic picture recognition, as well as measures of neuroticism and extraversion from the Maudsley Personality Inventory (Eysenck, 1959)

and the M.M.P.I. Precise predictions were made for each test with respect to its differentiating power between groups, and its likely factorial content in a correlational study between groups. The details are too numerous to be reviewed here in detail, but the outcome of the experiment on the whole was strikingly positive. In terms of both factor scores and canonical variate scores, it proved possible to differentiate the extraverted (hysteric) and the introverted (dysthymic) groups without, or with at most one error.

The improvement in efficiency of classification, clearness of outcome, and reliability of prediction from the Hildebrand to the Claridge study demonstrates the importance of theoretical considerations in designing factorial studies, as well as the possibilities of self-correction inherent in the factorial paradigm. It seems likely that an equal gain in clarity and validity will attend the further purification, both theoretical and experimental, of the present battery of tests.

Two further studies should be mentioned in this section. Both deal with the factorial analysis of anxiety and its symptomatology. Their interest arises from the fact that anxiety, from the theoretical point of view, is not a univocal variable but has loadings on both neuroticism and introversion; in other words, it is regarded as a conditioned fear reaction. Neuroticism is conceived of as an inherited autonomic over-reactivity, while introversion is characterized by strong conditionability (Eysenck, 1957); hence anxiety as a conditioned fear reaction appears most frequently in dysthymics, i.e. neurotic introverts. If, now, a factorial study were to be done of anxiety symptoms in patients suffering from anxiety, it should prove possible to separate out these two factors from each other, i.e. to obtain one factor of autonomic over-reactivity, and one characterized by the conditioned anxiety responses.

That this prediction is essentially correct has been shown by O'Connor, Lorr and Stafford (1956), and more particularly by Hamilton (1959). The latter intercorrelated thirteen variables, obtained through ratings made by several psychiatrists, and having reasonably high reliabilities; these were then inter-correlated and factor analysed, giving rise to two factors: (1) somatic anxiety, characterized by gastro-intestinal, genito-urinary, respiratory, cardiovascular, and general somatic and autonomic symptoms; (2) psychic anxiety, characterized by tension, fears, insomnia, cognitive changes, depression, behaviour, and anxious mood. These results agree reasonably well with those of O'Connor et al., and are in quite good agreement with its hypothesis. Unfortunately there is no direct study of the most direct deduction to be made from the hypothesis, namely that extraverted neurotics, i.e. hysterics and psychopaths, would be characterized by somatic anxiety, but not by psychic anxiety. This crucial experiment still remains to be performed.

Psychoticism and its Subdivisions

THE MOORE STUDY (1930; 1933)

This is probably the first to carry out "the empirical determination of certain syndromes underlying praecox and manic depressive psychoses." Three hundred and sixty-seven patients were rated for the presence or absence of forty-one symptoms, tetrachorics were calculated, and the resulting table analysed by a complex and cumbersome procedure. Eight factors in all were isolated; these, on being intercorrelated, gave rise to two "second-order factors" as they would be called nowadays. The first of these two was made up of the catatonic, cognitive defect, uninhibited and deluded-hallucinated syndromes; this appeared to be a *schizophrenic factor*. The second factor was made up of the retarded-depressed, constitutional-hereditary and manic components; this appears identifiable with *circular insanity*.

Thurstone (1947) reanalysed Moore's data with more modern methods and obtained five rather more clearly defined factors. Even more recent is another reanalysis of Moore's original correlations carried out by Degan (1952). He obtains the following main factors: A = hallucination-delusion (hyper-projection); B = depression; C = hyperexcitability; D = catatonia; E = schizophrenic dissociation; F = psychotic shock; G = hyperirritability; H = deterioration; I = neurasthenia.

These factors are themselves correlated and give rise to second-order factors. The first of these second-order factors, factor W, has high loadings on factors G, C and H and (negatively) I. According to Degan "factor W is quite obviously mania and seems to represent predominantly a condition of sustained hyperexcitability." Factor X has high loadings on E, F, A and H; "this factor is consistent with the current conception of hebephrenic schizophrenia and is so interpreted." Factor Y has positive loadings on I and B and negative ones on G and A. According to Degan "Factor Y . . . supports the proposal of a projective-introjective process at the basis of a paranoid-depression classification of psychosis." To the writer it seems possible that this factor may be similar to extraversion-introversion, although the lack of work done with that factor in the psychotic field makes it impossible to substantiate this interpretation. Factor Z has loadings on D, F, G and H, and (negatively) on B; it is interpreted as catatonic schizophrenia.

It is impossible in this brief space to give an adequate discussion or critique of the work of Moore, or the analyses done by Thurstone and Degan. Attention should be drawn, however, to the fact that the same matrix of intercorrelations gives rise to different numbers of factors, different numbers of second-order factors, and different interpretations of these factors in the three analyses. No criterion is offered for a choice between the different interpretations and it is not always obvious how in fact the interpretations given could be supported or disproved by further experimental work. This is a weakness of the factor-analytic approach which the writer has discussed in detail elsewhere (Eysenck, 1957) and to which attention must be drawn here in order to avoid too great confidence being placed in the results of any particular study.

THE WITTENBORN STUDIES

There are some thirteen studies reported by this author and various collaborators, details of which will be found in the references. What Wittenborn has done in effect is this: he has constructed fifty-five symptom rating scales, carefully drawn up and given in detail in a monograph by Wittenborn, Holzberg and Simon (1953). "The set of rating scales is considered to comprise a good sample of the descriptive aspects of mental hospital patients' behaviour currently considered by psychiatrists to be important in evaluating patients and in making diagnoses. Each rating scale describes only one extreme of a pathological manifestation. The scales are in such a form that they may be checked for every patient in order to reduce bias on the part of the raters, the scales being presented in a randomized, unlabelled manner. In order to minimize systematic differences between raters, due to their theoretical orientation, the scales are primarily descriptive and involve as little interpretation as possible."

These scales have been applied to many different groups of patients and several factor-analytic studies have been carried out. Nine clusters or factors emerge from these analyses, namely: (1) acute anxiety, (2) conversion hysteria, (3) manic state, (4) depressed state, (5) schizophrenic excitement, (6) paranoid condition, (7) paranoid schizophrenia, (8) hebephrenic schizophrenia, (9) phobic-compulsive. The individual items in the original scale are then weighted so that it becomes possible to give each patient a score for each of the nine factors or syndromes. The odd-even reliability scores for these cluster scores are reasonably high, ranging from 0·67 for depression to 0·92 for mania. They are not, however, independent of each other. Thus, for instance, there is a correlation of 0·88 between hebephrenic schizophrenia and schizophrenic excitement. There are several other correlations above 0·6, one of them between acute anxiety and phobic-compulsion (0·67) giving support to the concept of dysthymia. No second-order factor analysis appears to have been done by Wittenborn, which is unfortunate in view of these high correlations. (It must, of course, be remembered that the intercorrelations among the cluster scores are higher than intercorrelations among the clusters themselves would be; this is the probable result of the use of overlapping items and the rough system of weighting used.)

Wittenborn and Holzberg (1951) have compared the results of their rating scales with the Rorschach test, with the conclusion that "the present analyses cannot be taken as any evidence that descriptive aspects of the behaviour of psychotic patients may be identified with or predicted by a use of Rorschach scores." The same authors made an investigation into the use of the Wechsler-Bellevue score in this connexion and found all correlations with their descriptive rating scales to be very low. In another study Wittenborn and Mettler (1951) have studied the practical correlates of psychiatric syndromes by relating the Wittenborn scales to the kinds of socially practised behaviour observed in occupational therapy situations.

The problem of reliability has been attacked by Wittenborn et al. (1952) by having two different samples of patients rated by two different psychiatrists—

In order to maximize any difference in symptom clustering due to differences in psychiatrists, the psychiatrists who provided the ratings were selected in a way calculated to maximize the difference in their rating scales. It was possible to find two psychiatrists who were rating similar patients but who differed in age, cultural background, theoretical bias and training. . . . Clusters revealed by the two analyses were mutually consistent and similar to the clusters which had been found originally in large samples of patients rated by a variety of psychiatrists. The data did not challenge the claim that the qualitative behaviour significance of the cluster scores used in the quantified, multiple diagnosis, is relatively independent of ordinary differences between psychiatrists.

In spite of some contradictory evidence by Pumroy and Gogan (1955), who found relatively low coefficients of concordance between four observers of eleven patients for several of the scales, the data presented by Wittenborn and his colleagues are distinctly impressive, and from the practical point of view there seems to be no doubt that his scales are at the moment the most practical available method for quantitative dimensional description of abnormal behaviour. From the theoretical point of view, however, his failure to carry out a second-order factor analysis, and the relative lack of neurotic subjects and symptoms in his work, make it difficult to accept his conclusions as definitive.

THE GUERTIN STUDIES

There are eleven papers in this series which will be found in the bibliography under his name. Typical of his work is his 1952 "Factor Analytic Study of Schizophrenic Symptoms" in which he studied the intercorrelations between fifty-two symptoms in one hundred schizophrenics between the ages of 16 and 60. He obtained six factors which accounted for 58 per cent of the total variance: (1) excitement-hostility, (2) psychomotor retardation and withdrawal, (3) guilt conflict, (4) persecution-suspicion, (5) personality disorganization, (6) confusion-withdrawal. These factors are not independent; thus confusion-withdrawal correlates 0·49 with psychomotor retardation. Guertin finds that: "Several factors are required to describe most of the individuals in this study."

In some other studies, Guertin makes use of the Ferguson hospital adjustment scale. Working with unhospitalized schizophrenics he concludes that "approximately 63 per cent of the variance of the items samples could be described in terms of three oblique factors"; these he labels: (a) lack of general interest, (b) social withdrawal, (c) personal unconcern. (The correlations between these three factors are quite high, ranging from 0·5 to 0·7.) Guertin believes that his analyses provide some confirmatory evidence for Jenkin's hypothesis of the existence of three schizophrenic types (1952), which will be discussed presently.

Guertin also reports a number of inverted factor analyses, i.e. analyses in which correlations are run between patients rather than between symptoms. This technique, which has been discussed in some detail by the writer (Eysenck 1953) is difficult to justify for this type of material as there does not seem to exist a metric continuum over the different sets of symptoms. While Guertin's work is interesting therefore, it is rather difficult to evaluate. As regards his more orthodox studies it will be noted that the concordance of his results and those reported by Wittenborn is rather small. In part this may be due to differences in the respective samples and the total universe of ratings covered, but as both authors have sought a rather comprehensive coverage, this can hardly be the only reason. Such failure on the part of one author to verify the results of another, must make us doubtful about the validity of the results reported by either.[1]

[1] Similar objections apply to the work of Monro (1954, 1955, 1956), who has used R and Q methods of analysis on rating derived from two hundred mental patients. Monro follows in part Cattell's system of classification and analysis, and compares his findings with those of Cattell. In view of the importance and general interest of Cattell's work, it ought perhaps to have been treated here at some length. This has not been done for the following reasons. Cattell has worked almost entirely with normal subjects, and while he often uses psychiatric terminology in naming his factors, there is little independent evidence that this is justified, and that the presumed relationships with mental abnormality do in fact exist. Some recent and as yet unpublished Canadian work by

THE LORR AND JENKINS STUDIES

Jenkins (1952) has suggested a theory which he labels "schizophrenic sequence" and according to which there are three schizophrenic types, namely, the withdrawn, the disorganized and the type characterized by psychotic reorganization. Lorr and Jenkins have carried out several studies in recent years on the psychopathology and behaviour of hospitalized psychotics which may in part be looked upon from the point of view of their theory. In their 1955 article they describe the construction of eighty-one brief descriptive rating scales which were used on four hundred and twenty-three male psychotic patients. By a process of correlational analysis a 55-variable correlation matrix divisible into thirteen clusters was finally selected and subjected to multiple group factor analysis. Eleven factors were extracted and the first-order rotated oblique factor matrix is given as Table I.8. The authors group the factors for purposes of description and discussion "into those that appear to reflect affective disorders, those that may be considered indicative of schizophrenic processes, and those relating to disturbances of temperament or character which may be observable in non-psychotics as well as in psychotic patients."

Bipolar factor A "is retarded depression versus manic excitement . . . Wittenborn's bipolar manic-depressed factor bears close resemblance to A. Degan's unipolar factor, manic hyperexcitability, is very similar to the positive pole of A." Factor E "appears to be a melancholia-agitation. . . . Degan's 'depression syndrome' . . . resembles E. The agitated depressive picture repeatedly identified by Wittenborn also closely resembles factor E."

Factors I, K and G are related to Jenkins's hypothesis of the schizophrenic sequence. Factor I is regarded as one of *withdrawal* and is said to resemble Degan's factor H. Factor K is said to represent progressive personality *disorganization* and to resemble Degan's factor of schizophrenic dissociation. F and G respectively represent perceptual disorganization (Degan's factor of hyper-projection) and motor disorganization (with a possible resemblance to Degan's catatonia factor).

"An alternative to the pattern of disorganization is paranoid *reorganization* and stabilization . . . factor C appears to be descriptive of this paranoid pattern. . . . Wittenborn's paranoid schizophrenic factor is probably identical with it. . . . Paranoid suspicion is often paralleled or followed by grandiose expansiveness that appears to underlie factor J." Wittenborn's paranoid cluster is claimed to resemble J.

"The third group of factors consists of resistiveness (B), submissive versus belligerence (H), and activity level (D) . . . Degan's hyperirritability factor . . . may be the same as H but seems less well defined."

From the intercorrelations of these factors, three second-order factors are derived. The first (AA) denotes "a resistive withdrawal with motor disturbances." The second factor (BB) "appears to be a measure of schizophrenic disorganization, projection and distortion of thinking and perception." The third second-order factor (CC) "is a bipolar continuum of apathetic, confused withdrawal versus agitated hyperactivity." Lorr and Jenkins identify (AA) with Degan's second-order factor Z, (BB) with Degan's factor X, and one pole of the bipolar factor (CC) with Degan's factor W.

In a later study Lorr, O'Connor and Stafford (1956) attempted to verify the existence of the factors described and related them to the Wittenborn scales. They used thirty-nine of their own rating scales and sixteen of the Wittenborn ones, using a total of one hundred and sixteen psychotic patients. A total of fifty-two scales was used for the intercorrelations and the intercorrelations between these scales analysed by means of the multiple group method. The results of the analysis are similar to those reported previously and it is interesting to know that this time a second-order factor, similar to Degan's factor Y, appears. In the study previously mentioned this factor was the only one of Degan's four second-order factors which could not be duplicated.

The identification of factors attempted by Lorr and his colleagues is done entirely on the basis of inspecting the content of ratings having high loadings on each factor. This is known to be a difficult and unsatisfactory method, and it would have been preferable if a more objective technique such as that put forward by Ahmavaara (1956) had been used. However, it should be remembered that in a sense these are all pioneer studies, and that future work will undoubtedly incorporate such obvious improvements as this. As matters stand now, the reader has to form tentative conclusions on the basis of such material as is available, and on this basis the writer would suggest that while there are certain recurring clusters of similar implication running through this work, nevertheless, in most cases no confident identification can be made. This cautious conclusion with respect to the fundamental contribution these studies have to make, should not distract from their practical usefulness in identifying patients showing different reaction patterns. Regarded from this point of view, both scales and classifications are undoubtedly superior to the traditional psychiatric methods and systems.

N. Agnew and B. Craig on Cattell's factors 25 and 29 ("Accurate realism *v.* psychotic tendencies" and "Ready mobilization of energy") failed to find predicted relationships between test scores and psychiatric state, and also between factor score and psychiatric state. This is not necessarily fatal to Cattell's system, but it suggests caution in accepting it in so far as abnormal mental states are concerned.

TABLE I.8

FIRST ORDER ROTATED OBLIQUE FACTOR MATRIX V

Variable	No.	A	B	C	D	E	F	G	H	I	J	K
Loud in speech	5	83	04	21	−02	13	08	35	17	−02	−05	00
Overtalkative	4	67	23	09	−06	24	00	00	02	09	06	21
Moody	16	64	15	02	−03	40	26	27	13	08	14	07
Uninhibited	21	63	25	13	01	00	19	07	18	18	−02	15
Accelerated ideation	8	63	11	06	09	28	21	07	03	−04	25	−42
Overemotional	14	56	13	−06	−02	40	10	−06	11	02	08	05
Distractible	13	50	−19	03	−09	−05	−14	03	14	−09	−22	−38
Elated	15	46	08	−10	−42	−46	−02	00	00	05	16	05
Uncooperative	59	02	84	24	−05	05	−07	04	15	11	−06	15
Resistive	60	14	60	09	14	10	10	11	37	−05	11	−04
Swallows objects	50	−26	53	−10	14	12	−02	−03	−09	−02	37	02
Disoriented for place	32	−15	40	−13	20	−17	24	09	−06	−07	−05	30
Delusions of persecution	37	−09	−08	83	20	−02	−02	−09	06	−03	26	−09
Ideas of reference	35	05	07	73	−01	06	14	12	00	07	22	13
Delusions of influence	36	12	−05	69	00	−05	24	25	14	02	−14	23
No wetting	51	12	17	42	01	12	−24	00	−20	25	−13	02
Overactive	54	00	05	06	75	07	−03	−15	06	02	−03	03
Not anergic	78	20	−02	23	69	−02	22	20	15	09	03	−18
Accelerated activity	53	02	15	21	62	10	−07	06	−07	−03	00	06
Tense	18	05	03	−02	−06	66	−06	05	−08	−03	10	06
Anxious	17	−01	−09	08	−10	58	07	−06	06	16	−02	19
Hypochondriacal delusions	38	12	13	26	03	41	14	30	−15	02	15	37
Insightful	22	−06	−09	−08	11	37	20	−02	06	15	−16	−10
Visual hallucinations	43	01	07	14	04	02	74	−04	02	12	18	02
Auditory hallucinations	44	06	−06	24	09	02	68	00	07	−10	−16	14
Disoriented for self	34	−03	20	−01	−13	−08	64	47	12	27	29	27
Unreality feeling	30	−03	13	−01	−04	20	56	27	08	15	−05	36
Hostile impulses	28	18	−12	28	−06	33	50	35	19	22	31	−02
Not suicidal	24	28	23	17	−10	−23	−30	16	−01	−09	13	−12
Manneristic movements	48	−11	−05	09	−02	−05	−09	56	−09	−07	−04	04
Manneristic postures	47	−32	−04	06	09	−27	−07	45	01	03	12	04
Giggling or grimacing	20	−11	12	23	04	−36	−08	41	−07	03	−04	40
Obsessive thinking	27	06	−13	29	08	22	12	35	05	01	−33	21
Obscene	57	15	05	04	26	07	29	03	68	25	23	−01
Irritable	67	23	06	11	00	−04	−02	−07	65	−01	10	−06
Assaultive	66	21	12	38	14	13	07	35	64	−02	−03	23
Bullying	65	−07	37	−02	21	11	01	−02	59	34	18	06
Hostile	26	28	−17	−10	00	26	19	02	54	08	24	21
Assertive	63	29	10	17	18	04	03	11	52	09	00	07
Excessively busy	58	04	−03	−07	12	03	12	−04	10	57	09	−01
Overtalkative	55	07	11	11	26	−03	−03	00	15	53	07	01
Gregarious	61	04	26	09	34	04	02	11	−07	49	05	07
Neat	62	−11	−17	09	−04	−19	−05	14	−02	43	−01	00
Ideas of grandeur	39	03	13	08	−07	01	−07	−07	01	12	70	10
Conceited	23	14	−03	00	−08	−03	12	13	−04	03	69	−09
Feeling of sinfulness	40	−14	15	08	−01	22	10	20	−04	08	−43	19
Destructive	68	−02	25	−08	36	32	33	−01	15	−19	40	04
Irrelevant speech	10	−09	11	05	−09	−32	00	−07	16	04	07	72
Emotional disharmony	19	−34	10	−03	00	−42	11	−09	08	26	−05	61
Stereotyped speech	11	09	−01	00	02	00	14	37	06	12	12	60
Incoherent speech	9	−21	08	09	17	−27	03	11	−06	−16	00	59
Blocking	7	−28	05	−02	−06	10	−05	38	−04	27	−13	49
Bizarre delusions	42	13	00	02	04	04	04	37	24	−14	−12	38
Disoriented for time	33	−04	06	−11	03	−18	15	30	13	−16	−15	38
Elated	64	03	14	−03	15	−08	−04	09	−02	33	06	18

The Eysenck "Criterion Analysis" Study

There is one additional reason why the list of studies reviewed above is less certain and impressive than one might have wished. All the work done was carried out in terms of subjective ratings made by psychiatrists, clinical psychologists and others reared in a tradition which makes a point of regarding certain assumptions and relationships as relatively firmly established. It is possible, therefore, that such modest agreement between different analyses as has been found is nothing but a reflection of the common teaching received by the raters. It would require an experiment specially designed to make use of objective tests exclusively to overcome the inherent subjectivity of any kind of symptom rating schedule. Only one such study has been made (Eysenck 1952). In this experiment one hundred normal, fifty schizophrenic and fifty manic-depressive subjects took part. A large battery of objective tests was administered to the two hundred subjects; out of these twenty were selected for a correlational analysis. The method used was that of criterion analysis (Eysenck 1950) which requires the calculation of correlations separately for the normal and the abnormal group. Factors are then extracted from the two matrices separately. This is done in order to test the interpretation of the factors extracted in terms of the original dichotomy. For details the original publications should be consulted, but putting it very briefly, the argument runs like this: If, and only if, the differences between the normal and the psychotic groups are quantitative rather than qualitative, and the relations between each test and this continuum monotonic, and preferably linear, will the following relationship be obtained. (1) A factor will be found in the analysis of the matrix of correlations for the normal group which is identifiable as "psychoticism." (2) A factor will be found in the analysis of the matrix of correlation for the psychotic groups which is identifiable as "psychoticism." (3) The loadings on one of these factors will be proportional to the loadings on the other. (4) Both sets of loadings will be proportional to a set of index values denoting the adequacy of each test in separating the normal and psychotic groups from each other; the column containing these values is known as the "criterion column." The method of criterion analysis thus enables us to answer two questions simultaneously. It makes it possible for us to see whether or not the groups with which we are dealing are separated from each other on a quantitative or a qualitative basis, and it enables us to interpret the hypothetical factor of psychoticism in a unique and clear-cut fashion.

The results of the study are in good agreement with the hypothesis that psychoticism is a continuous variable responsible for separating the normal and other psychotic groups. The psychoticism factors extracted from the two groups correlated 0·871, and these two factors correlated with the criterion column 0·899 and 0·954 respectively. A second factor was found in both matrices and it was shown that this also was the same in both groups, the correlation between the two sets of factor loading being 0·768. It was hypothesized that this second factor might be one of schizothymia-cyclothymia, and this hypothesis was also capable of testing in terms of criterion analysis because of the inclusion of the schizophrenic and manic-depressive groups in the experimental design. A new criterion column was formed, based on the differentiating power of the tests as far as the two psychotic groups were concerned, but this was not found to be correlated with the second factor loadings, thus disproving this hypothesis.

This method of criterion analysis, which has also been applied with some success to the neurotic field (Eysenck 1950, 1952) has the obvious advantage of making the interpretation of factors more objective by relating them directly to diagnostic groups. This may appear to assume the correctness of the original diagnostic groupings, but this is by no means the case. Provision is made in the method for maximizing agreement between factor scores and criterion by means of a double process of rotation involving both the criterion and the factors. It is suggested that an application of this technique, together with the use of objective tests, would go far to clear the air of the inherent subjectivity of the more usual type of analysis, a subjectivity inherent not only in the choice of data, but also in the method of rotation.

Most of the studies so far considered would fall under the heading of "individual behaviour theories" in Table I.1; in other words, they are cross-sectional, descriptive, and essentially "static." However true and accurate the dimensional picture presented there might be, it could rightly be criticized for failing to provide a dynamic component, or any indication of *causal* relationships. To know a person's position on a given dimension is one thing; to know the reasons for his being there, and the methods for changing his position, is quite another. We require "general behaviour theories" to give us this type of information, and we require above all hypotheses linking these two types of theory together. As Hull (1945) has pointed out—

The natural science approach to behaviour theory presents two major tasks. The first is to make a satisfactory working analysis of the various behaviour processes; this consists in deriving, i.e. deducing, from the primary laws of the system the characteristic observable phenomena of the behaviour process in question as displayed by the modal or average organism under given conditions. . . . The second major task of the natural science approach to behaviour theory concerns the problem of innate behavioural differences under identical conditions between different species and between individuals within a given species. . . . Both types of task cry loudly and insistently for completion. But most neglected of all is the relationship between the two approaches.

An attempt to work out such an integration of the two approaches in the general field of abnormal psychology, and more specifically in that of the neurotic disorders, has been made by Eysenck (1957). Fig. 1.17 shows the general outline of the theory proposed to account for extraverted and introverted behaviour

conditioned responses, would also tend to be strongly socialized, while individuals with weak excitatory and strong inhibitory potentials, who would be expected on that basis to form weak and unstable conditioned responses, would also tend to be weakly socialized. The former group would thus tend to develop *introverted* behaviour traits (persistence, high level of aspiration, reliability, etc.), while the latter group would tend to develop *extraverted* behaviour traits (cf. Table I.3). Groups intermediate with respect to the excitation-inhibition balance would also be expected to be

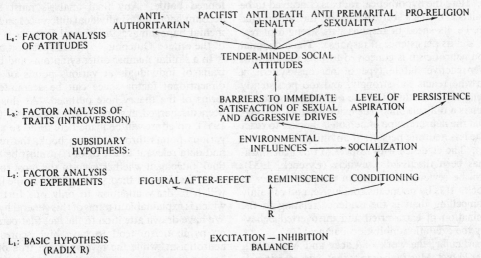

FIG. 1.17. DIAGRAMMATIC REPRESENTATION OF DIFFERENT LEVELS OF PERSONALITY ORGANIZATION AS DETERMINED BY INDIVIDUAL DIFFERENCES IN THE EXCITATION-INHIBITION BALANCE

respectively. At the base of the diagram we have the (presumably innate) balance between cortical excitation and inhibition, using these terms in the molar sense of Pavlov and Hull. Some persons are characterized by a nervous system predisposing them to develop exceptionally strong *inhibitory* potentials; others are characterized by a nervous system predisposing them to develop exceptionally strong *excitatory* potentials. Most people are intermediate between these extremes.

Certain phenomena observable in the psychological laboratory can be deduced from this hypothesis. Thus conditioning, reminiscence, figural after-effects, and many other phenomena are theoretically derivable from the concepts of excitation and inhibition, and consequently individual differences in these phenomena can be deduced from individual differences in the excitation-inhibition balance. If, in addition, we accept Mowrer's (1950) hypothesis that the socialization process depends on conditioning, then, under equal environmental pressure, individuals with strong excitatory and weak inhibitory potentials, who would be expected on that basis to form strong and stable

intermediate with respect to conditionability, and consequently with respect to socializability and extraversion-introversion. This analysis has been extended also to the field of attitudes and opinions (Eysenck, 1954), along the lines indicated in Fig. 1.17.

A causal scheme such as the one here suggested is susceptible of disproof along two lines. It mediates deductions which can be tested by means of analysis of *interdependence*, and it mediates deductions which can be tested by means of analysis of *dependence*. The first type of analysis suggests tests of the predicted relationships obtaining at each level of Fig. 1.17; thus we would predict correlations between the different attitudes at level L_4, the different traits at level L_3, or the different experimental phenomena at level L_2. The second type of analysis suggests tests of the predicted relationships between phenomena at one level and those at another; thus the theory predicts that extraverts (and hysterics) should be less easily conditionable than introverts (and dysthymics), or that introverts should have tender-minded attitudes, extraverts tough-minded ones. Many such tests have been carried out along both lines, and the results have on the whole supported the general hypothesis (Eysenck, 1957, 1960).

We thus see that "individual behaviour theories" and "general behaviour theories" are not essentially antagonistic, but can be integrated within the confines of a single scheme or system; "general behaviour theories" refer to the vertical type of deduction in Fig. 1.17, "individual behaviour theories" refer to the horizontal type. A complete explanation of any aspect of behaviour requires both types of theory, and both types of analysis.

A similar analysis is possible with respect to neuroticism. Here the hypothetical radix is conceived to be the balance or lack of balance of the autonomic system, i.e. its speed of response, its strength of response, and its persistence of response. The individual high on neuroticism is conceived to be a person with an over-reactive, labile type of nervous system, a person who reacts too strongly, and too persistently to strong external stimuli. (The question of speed of reaction is a difficult one. The evidence does not suggest that the neurotic type of person is quicker to react than the less neurotic person; if anything the opposite is true). The evidence with respect to this generalization has been discussed elsewhere (Eysenck, 1953), and will be reviewed in detail in another chapter in this book. It is by no means conclusive, and certainly less compelling than is the evidence relating to the determination of extraverted and introverted behaviour by the excitation-inhibition balance.

In particular, the work of Lacey and Malmo (cf. Chapter 11 by I. Martin) suggests that over-reactivity is not necessarily a property of the whole autonomic system, but may rather be the property of a particular subsystem. Nevertheless, however much the statement of the hypothesis may require to be qualified, it probably embodies a generalization which carries within itself the possibility of the successful mediation of many testable predictions.

Taking our two hypotheses together, we can certainly deduce the known facts about dysthymic and hysterical symptomatology and behaviour. As an example, let us consider the strong anxiety which is such a pronounced feature of the dysthymic personality. Anxiety may be defined as a conditioned fear reaction, and we would expect (other things being equal) that its strength would be determined by (i) habit strength as a function of the number of reinforcements received ($N \rightarrow {_S}H_R$), and (ii) incentive-reinforcement as a function of amount of reward ($w \rightarrow K$). Given equal amounts of N and w, i.e. equalizing environmental influences, we may substitute greater conditionability for greater N as giving rise to greater ${_S}H_R$, and greater autonomic reactivity for greater w as giving rise to greater K. Hence *under equal environmental pressure*, the person high on introversion and on neuroticism should develop strong conditioned fear responses as compared with persons having any other combination of scores on these two factors, due to his tendency to develop strong conditioned responses, and to react strongly to fear-producing stimuli with his autonomic system. It follows, of course, that differences in environmental pressure could overbalance these innate individual difference patterns; a dysthymic never exposed to pain or fear-producing situations would develop less anxiety than a normal extravert subjected to constant pain and fear-producing situations, as for instance during a prolonged battle. Any final analysis must take into account *both* innate individual differences and environmental happenings; the general formula is probably of the order: Outcome = f(Predisposition × Stress).

In a similar manner other symptoms and behaviour traits of individuals at various points of our two-dimensional factor space can be accounted for in terms of the theory here outlined. As this task has been discharged at some length previously (Eysenck, 1957), no effort will be made here to do so again. At various points throughout the book, the reader will find data relevant to the theory; it must be left to his final judgement whether even in the most rough-and-ready fashion our theory does justice to the facts. We will here draw attention to only one further point which is explainable in terms of this general hypothesis. We have drawn attention to the fact that persons high on psychoticism tend to have high scores also on neuroticism, while the reverse is not true of persons having high scores on neuroticism. If we conceive of psychoticism essentially as a disorder of the thought processes (cf. the chapters dealing with cognitive functions and thought disorders), then we might regard it as essentially a powerful *stress* which, when multiplied by an average *predisposition*, produces as the final outcome a strongly emotional and neurotic behaviour pattern. In other words, although the person high on psychoticism is not necessarily high on neuroticism, the strong stress produced by his disordered thought processes results in a high $w \rightarrow K$ sequence leading to strongly emotional reactions. This is, of course, no more than a hypothesis, and supporting evidence is largely lacking; however, the data reviewed in later chapters do give it some empirical support.

It is not to be thought that the general descriptive outline given in this chapter is immutable, or that it is complete. Nothing is more likely than that a much greater number of dimensions will be required to encompass this huge and complex field, and it is by no means unlikely that the final dimensions chosen will not be identical with those here presented. However, reviews are governed by the state of the evidence, not by the possible changes which will take place in a particular field which is being surveyed. At this writing, knowledge is lacking as to what these additional dimensions of personality might be, how they could be measured, or how they would be related to those described; Cattell's (1957) work indicates possible lines of development, but his work has not dealt with abnormal personality in sufficient detail to make it more than a detailed source of hypotheses. It is interesting to note that in his latest analysis of the relations obtained between his sixteen personality factors (1957) he discovers second-order factors which bear a striking similarity to neuroticism, extraversion, and psychoticism; such agreement between empirically derived systems of description which were based on quite different samples of the population and quite different samples of objective tests would go a long way towards the validation of the systems in question.

Even more convincing to the writer is the fact that these dimensions which were originally isolated by means of the analysis of interdependence correspond so well to reaction-systems which had been isolated independently, and without thought of individual differences, by physiologists and experimental psychologists. It is not unreasonable to expect individual differences in autonomic reactivity, or in the excitation-inhibition balance, to produce widespread behavioural effects which could not be overlooked in everyday life; it is equally reasonable to expect these effects to be recovered in the form of "factors" in the analysis of questionnaires and objective test reactions. The demonstration that such an analysis of dependence is not only theoretically possible but actually enables us to make testable predictions which empirical research has verified, speaks strongly against the possibility that the descriptive system in question is entirely based on statistical artefact, and has no relation whatever to reality. Such an integration of the laws of general psychology and the analysis of individual differences appears quite indispensable if statistical factors are to form part of modern experimental psychology, and not merely an esoteric game for the statistically-minded research worker. It also appears to be essential if the experimental psychologist is not to continue to disregard what is frequently the major source of variance in the phenomena he is observing —individual differences. Classificatory systems, in normal or in abnormal psychology, must pay equal attention to *general laws* and *reaction types*; they cannot afford the luxury of disregarding one half of the hard-won knowledge of modern empirical psychology.

REFERENCES

ABRAHAM, K., The first pregenital stage of the libido, in *Selected Papers* (London, Hogarth Press, 1916).

ABRAHAM, K., A short study of the development of the libido, viewed in the light of mental disorders, in *Selected Papers* (London, Hogarth Press, 1924).

ABRAHAM, K., The influence of oral eroticism on character-formation, in *Selected Papers* (London, Hogarth Press, 1942).

AHMAVAARA, Y., On the unified factor theory of mind, *Ann. Acad. Sci. Ferm.* (Helsinki, 1957).

ARDIS, J. A. and FRASER, E., Personality and perception: the constancy effect and introversion, *Brit. J. Psychol.* **48**, 48–54 (1957).

BRAND, H., *The Study of Personality* (New York, John Wiley & Sons, Inc., 1954).

BRUETSCH, W. L., Mental disorders arising from organic disease, in *The Biology of Mental Health and Disease* (New York, Milbank Memorial Fund, 1950).

BURT, C., *The Factors of the Mind* (London, Univ. of London Press, 1940).

CAMERON, N., The functional psychoses, in *Personality and the Behavior Disorders*, Ed. J. V. Hunt (New York, Ronald Press, 1944).

CANESTRARI, R., Sindromi psichiatrici e rigiditá percettiva, *Riv. exper. di Freniatria*, **81**, 1–10. (1957)

CASTIGLIONI, A., *History of Medicine* (New York, Macmillan, 1941).

CATTELL, R. B., The description of personality. I. Foundations of trait measurement, *Psychol. Rev.*, **50**, 559–594 (1940).

CATTELL, R. B., Second-order personality factors in the questionnaire realm, *J. Cons. Psychol.* **20**, 411–418 (1956).

CATTELL, R. B., The conceptual and test distinction of neuroticism and anxiety, *J. Clin. Psychol.*, **13**, 221–233 (1957).

CECIL, R. L. and LOEB, R. F., *A Textbook of Medicine* (London, Saunders, 1955).

DAHLSTROM, W. G., Research in clinical psychology: factor analytic contributions, *J. Clin. Psychol.*, **13**, 211–220 (1957).

DAVIS, D. R., *Pilot Error. Some Laboratory Experiments* (London, H.M.S.O., 1948).

DEGAN, J. W., Dimensions of functional psychosis, *Psychometr. Monogr.*, **6**, (1952).

ERIKSEN, C. W., Psychological defences and "ego-strength" in the recall of completed and incompleted tasks, *J. Abnorm. (Soc.) Psychol.*, **49**, 45–50 (1954).

EYSENCK, H. J., *Dimensions of Personality* (London, Routledge & Kegan Paul, 1947).

EYSENCK, H. J., Criterion analysis—an application of the hypothetico-deductive method to factor analysis, *Psychol. Rev.*, **57**, 38–53 (1950).

EYSENCK, H. J., Cyclothymia and schizothymia as a dimension of personality: II. Experimental, *J. Personality*, 345–384 (1951).

EYSENCK, H. J., *Scientific Study of Personality* (London, Routledge & Kegan Paul, 1952).

EYSENCK, H. J., *Structure of Human Personality* (London, Methuen, 1953; 2nd ed., 1959).

EYSENCK, H. J., *Psychology of Politics* (London, Routledge & Kegan Paul, 1954).

EYSENCK, H. J., Cortical inhibition, figural after effect, and the theory of personality, *J. Abnorm. (Soc.) Psychol.*, **51**, 94–106 (1955).

EYSENCK, H. J., Psychiatric diagnosis as a psychological and statistical problem, *Psychol. Rep.*, **1**, 3–17 (1955).

EYSENCK, H. J., Reminiscence, drive and personality theory, *J. Abnorm. (Soc.) Psychol.*, **53**, 528–333 (1956).

EYSENCK, H. J., The inheritance of extraversion-introversion, *Acta psychol.*, **12**, 95–110 (1956).

EYSENCK, H. J., *Dynamics of Anxiety and Hysteria* (London, Routledge & Kegan Paul, 1957).

EYSENCK, H. J., *The Maudsley Personality Inventory* (London, Univ. of London Press, 1959).

EYSENCK, H. J., Personality as an integrating concept in psychology, in *Psychology: a Study of a Science*, Ed. S. Koch, Study II, Vol. 2 (to be published).

EYSENCK, H. J. (Ed.), *Experiments in Personality* (London, Routledge & Kegan Paul, to be published).

EYSENCK, H. J. and PRELL, D., The inheritance of neuroticism: an experimental study, *J. Ment. Sci.*, **97**, 441–465 (1951).

EYSENCK, H. J. and PRELL, D., A note on the differentiation of normal and neurotic children by means of objective tests, *J. Clin. Psychol.*, **8**, 202–204 (1952).

EYSENCK, S. B. G., A dimensional analysis of mental abnormality, *Ph.D. Thesis, Univ. of London Lib.* (1955).

EYSENCK, S. B. G., Neurosis and Psychosis: an experimental analysis, *J. Ment. Sci.* **102**, 517–529 (1956).

FOULDS, G. A., Temperamental differences in maze performance, *Brit. J. Psychol.*, **42**, 209–217 (1951); **43**, 33–41 (1952).

FOULDS, G. A., A method of scoring the T.A.T. applied to psychoneurotics, *J. Ment. Sci.*, **99**, 235–246 (1953).

FOULDS, G. A., The ratio of general intellectual ability to vocabulary among psychoneurotics, *Internat. J. Soc. Psychiat.*, **1**, 5–12 (1956).

FRANKS, C. M., Conditioning and personality: a study of normal and neurotic subjects, *J. Abnorm. (Soc.) Psychol.*, **52**, 143–150 (1956).

FRANKS, C. M., Personality factors and the rate of conditioning, *Brit. J. Psychol.*, **48**, 119–126 (1957).

FREUDENBERG, R. K. and ROBERTSON, J. P. S., Symptoms in relation to psychiatric diagnosis and treatment, *Arch. Neurol. Psychiat. Chicago*, **76**, 14–22 (1956).

GLOVER, E., Notes on oral character formation, *Int. J. Psycho-Anal.*, **6**, 131–153 (1925).

GLOVER, E., The significance of the mouth in psychoanalysis, *Brit. J. Med. Psychol.*, **4**, 134–155 (1924).

GOLDMAN-EISLER, F., Breastfeeding and character-formation; the etiology of the oral character in psychoanalytic theory, *J. Personality*, **19**, 189–196 (1950).

GOLDMAN-EISLER, F., Breastfeeding and character-formation, *J. Personality*, **17**, 83–103 (1948).

GOLDMAN-EISLER, F., The problem of orality and its origin in early childhood, *J. Ment. Sci.*, **97**, 765–781 (1951).

GUERTIN, W. H., A factor analysis of the Bender-Gestalt test of mental patients, *J. Clin. Psychol.*, **8**, 363–367 (1952).

GUERTIN, W. H., An inverted factor analysis of schizophrenics, *J. Cons. Psychol.*, **16**, 371–375 (1952).

GUERTIN, W. H., A factor analytic study of schizophrenic symptoms, *J. Cons. Psychol.*, **16**, 308–312 (1952).

GUERTIN, W. H., A transposed analysis of the Bender-Gestalts of brain disease cases, *J. Clin. Psychol.*, **10**, 366–369 (1954).

GUERTIN, W. H., A transposed factor analysis of schizophrenic performance—the Bender-Gestalt, *J. Clin. Psychol.*, **10**, 225–228 (1954).

GUERTIN, W. H., A factor analysis of curvilinear distortions on the Bender-Gestalt, *J. Clin. Psychol.*, **10**, 12–17 (1954).

GUERTIN, W. H., A factor analysis of schizophrenic ratings on the Hospital Adjustment Scale, *J. Clin. Psychol.*, **11**, 70–73 (1955).

GUERTIN, W. H., A transposed analysis of the Bender-Gestalts of paranoid schizophrenics, *J. Clin. Psychol.*, **11**, 73–76 (1955).

GUERTIN, W. H., A factor analytic study of the adjustment of chronic schizophrenics, *J. Clin. Psychol.*, **11**, 174–177 (1955).

GUERTIN, W. H. and ZILAITIS, V., A transposed factor analysis of paranoid schizophrenics, *J. Cons. Psychol.*, **17**, 455–458 (1953).

HAMILTON, M., The assessment of anxiety states by rating, *Brit. J. Med. Psychol.*, **32**, 50–59 (1959).

HEWITT, L. E. and JENKINS, R. L., *Fundamental Patterns of Maladjustment* (Illinois, State of Ill., 1946).

HILDEBRAND, H. O., A factorial study of introversion-extraversion by means of objective tests, *Ph.D. Thesis, Univ. of London Lib.* (1953).

HILDEBRAND, H. O., A factorial study of introversion-extraversion, *Brit. J. Psychol.*, **49**, 1–11 (1958).

HIMMELWEIT, H. T., The intelligence-vocabulary ratio as a measure of temperament, *J. Personality*, **14**, 93–105 (1945).

HIMMELWEIT, H. T., Speed and accuracy of work as related to temperament, *Brit. J. Psychol.*, **36**, 132–144 (1946).

HIMMELWEIT, H. T., A comparative study of the level of aspiration of normal and neurotic persons, *Brit. J. Psychol.*, **37**, 41–59 (1947).

HULL, C. L., The place of innate individual and species differences in a natural-science theory of behaviour, *Psychol. Rev.* **52**, 55–60 (1945).

JASPERS, K., *Allgemeine Psychopathologie* (Berlin, J. Springer, 1913, 1948).

JENKINS, R. L., The schizophrenic sequence: withdrawal, disorganisation, psychotic reorganisation, *Amer. J. Orthopsychiat.*, **22**, 738–748 (1952).

JENKINS, R. J. and GLICKMAN, S., Common syndromes in child psychiatry: I. Deviant behaviour traits. II. The schizoid child, *Amer. J. Orthopsychiat.*, **16**, 244–261 (1946).

JENKINS, R. L. and LORR, M., Type-tracking among psychotic patients, *J. Clin. Psychol.*, **10**, 114–119 (1954).

LEWIS, H., *Deprived Children* (London, Oxford Univ. Press, 1954).

LORR, M. and JENKINS, R. L., Patterns of maladjustment in children, *J. Clin. Psychol.*, **9**, 16–19 (1953).

LORR, M., JENKINS, R. L. and O'CONNOR, J. P., Factors descriptive of psychopathology and behaviour of hospitalized psychotics, *J. Abnorm. (Soc.) Psychol.*, **50**, 78–86 (1955).

LORR, M., O'CONNOR, J. P. and STAFFORD, J. W., Confirmation on nine psychotic symptom patterns, *J. Clin. Psychol.*, **13**, 252–257 (1957).

LORR, M. and RUBINSTEIN, E. A., Factors descriptive of psychiatric outpatients, *J. Abnorm. (Soc.) Psychol.*, **51**, 514–522 (1955).

MALAMUD, P. I., Objective measurement of clinical status in psychopathological research, *Psychol. Bull.*, **43**, 240–258 (1946).

MARZOLF, S. S., Symptom and syndrome statistically interpreted, *Psychol. Bull.*, **42**, 162–176 (1945).

METTLER, C. C., *History of Medicine* (Toronto, Blakiston, 1947).

MAYER-GROSS, W., MOORE, J. V. R. and SLATER, P., Forecasting the incidence of neurosis in officers of the army and navy, *J. Ment. Sci.*, **95**, 80–100 (1949).

MILLER, D. R., Responses of psychiatric patients to threat of failure, *J. Abnorm. (Soc.) Psychol.*, **46**, 378–387 (1951).

MOORE, T. V., The empirical determination of certain syndromes underlying praecox and manic-depressive psychosis, *Amer. J. Psychiat.*, **9**, 719–738 (1930).

MOORE, T. V., The essential psychoses and their fundamental syndromes, *Stud. Psychol. Psychiat. Cath. Univ. Amer.*, **3**, 1–128 (1933).

MUNRO, A. B., A rating scale developed for use in clinical psychiatric investigations, *J. Ment. Sci.* **100**, 657–669 (1954).

MUNRO, A. B., Psychiatric types: a Q-technique study of 200 patients, *J. Ment. Sci.*, **101**, 330–343 (1955).

MUNRO, A. B., Behaviour patterns in mental disorder, *J. Ment. Sci.*, **102**, 742–752 (1956).

O'CONNOR, J. G., LORR, M. and STAFFORD, J. V., Some patterns of manifest anxiety, *J. Clin. Psychol.*, **12**, 160–163 (1956).

PUMROY, S. S. and KOGAN, W. S., The reliability of Wittenborn's scales for rating currently discernible psychopathology, *J. Clin. Psychol.*, **11**, 411–412 (1955).

RAO, C. R. and SLATER, P., Multivariate analysis applied to differences between neurotic groups, *Brit. J. Psychol., Stat. Sect.*, **2**, 17–29 (1949).

SHAGASS, C., Sedation threshold: a neurophysiological tool for psychosomatic research, *Psychosom. Med.*, **18**, 410–419 (1956).

SINGER, C. J., *Short History of Medicine* (London, Oxford Univ. Press, 1928).

SPENCER, W. G., *Celsus; De Medicina* (Cambridge, Univ. Press, 1935–1938, 3 Vols.).

THOMSON, G., *Factorial Analysis of Human Ability* (London, Univ. of London Press, 1951).

THURSTONE, L. L., *Multiple-factor Analysis* (Chicago, Univ. of Chicago Press, 1947).

TROUTON, D. S. and MAXWELL, A. E., The relation between neurosis and psychosis, *J. Ment. Sci.*, **102**, 1–21 (1956).

VENABLES, P. H., Change in motor response with increase and decrease in task difficulty in normal industrial and psychiatric patient subjects, *Brit. J. Psychol.*, **46**, 101–110 (1955).

WITTENBORN, J. R., HOLZBERG, J. D. and SIMON, B., Symptom correlates for descriptive diagnosis, *Genet. Psychol. Monogr.*, **47**, 237–301 (1953).

WITTENBORN, J. R., Patients diagnosed manic depressive psychosis—manic state, *J. Cons. Psychol.* **16**, 193–198 (1952).

WITTENBORN, J. R., A new procedure for evaluating mental hospital patients, *J. Cons. Psychol.*, **14**, 500–501 (1950).

WITTENBORN, J. R., Symptom patterns in a group of mental hospital patients, *J. Cons. Psychol.*, **15**, 290–302 (1951).

WITTENBORN, J. R. and HOLZBERG, J. D., The Rorschach and descriptive diagnosis, *J. Cons. Psychol.* **15**, 460–463 (1951).

WITTENBORN, J. R. and HOLZBERG, J. D., The Wechsler-Bellevue and descriptive diagnosis, *J. Cons. Psychol.*, **15**, 325–329 (1951).

WITTENBORN, J. R. and HOLZBERG, J. D., The generality of psychiatric syndromes, *J. Cons. Psychol.*, **15**, 372–380 (1951).

WITTENBORN, J. R. and METTLER, F. A., Practical correlates of psychiatric symptoms, *J. Cons. Psychol.*, **15**, 505–510 (1951).

WITTENBORN, J. R. and BAILEY, C., The symptoms of involutional psychosis, *J. Cons. Psychol.*, **16**, 13–17 (1952).

WITTENBORN, J. R., HESS, M. I., KRANTZ, K. H., MANDELL, W. and TATZ, S., The effect of water differences on symptom rating scale clusters. *J. Cons. Psychol.*, **16**, 107–109 (1952).

WITTENBORN, J. R., BELL, E. G. and LESSER, G. S., Symptom patterns among organic patients of advanced age, *J. Clin. Psychol.*, **7**, 328–331 (1951).

WITTENBORN, J. R., MANDLER, G. and WATERHOUSE, I. K., Symptom patterns in youthful mental hospital patients, *J. Clin. Psychol.*, **7**, 323–327 (1951).

WITTENBORN, J. R. and LESSER, G. S. Biographical factors and psychiatric symptoms, *J. Clin. Psychol.*, **7**, 317–322 (1951).

WITTINGTON, E. T., *Medical History from the Earliest Times* (London, 1894).

CHAPTER 2

Abnormalities of Psychomotor Functions[1]

AUBREY J. YATES

I. INTRODUCTION

THE term *psychomotor* is defined by Warren (1934) as "pertaining to the motor effects of mental or cerebral processes." Within this general concept, he distinguishes two subtypes of function. Sensorimotor activity involves "responses which follow directly upon sensory stimulation"; whereas ideomotor activity involves "responses which follow upon thought processes, even though of a fleeting character." The term sensorimotor, therefore, pertains to "neural activity, in which both the afferent and efferent segments of the neural arc are involved, or pertaining to the structure contained in such activity." The term ideomotor, on the other hand pertains to "the sequence of movements upon ideas."

This method of conceptualizing certain kinds of behaviour is obsolescent, but it has nevertheless a certain usefulness in bringing together for the purposes of this chapter a large variety of very different tasks. For instance, the classic example of a psychomotor task is the cancellation test, in which the subject is required to cancel certain letters only in a long series. In this situation, the motor act of cancellation follows the perception of the correct stimulus. Now it is clear that a large number of psychological tests can be defined in sensorimotor or ideomotor terms. In the reaction-time (R.T.) test, for instance, which superficially seems very different from a cancellation test, the subject is required to perform a motor act when, and only when, a given stimulus is present. Both of these tests are descriptively similar in that a sensation is followed by a response of a particular kind. On the other hand the best-known example of an ideomotor test is a simple fluency test in which the subject is required to say as many words as possible, beginning, for example, with the letter *C*.

In this case, although there is a general set, there is no specific external stimulus for each separate response —hence the term ideomotor.

It is clear, therefore, from these examples, that psychomotor tests are not in any way concerned as such with motor *ability*. The interest does not lie in the subject's skill in lifting his finger off the key in an R.T. experiment. It is, in fact, implicitly assumed in many psychomotor studies that all subjects are equal in their ability as far as the motor act itself is concerned. Psychomotor tests are simply a means of measuring the *speed* and *accuracy* of central functioning. Interest lies in what goes on *between* the objective onset of the stimulus (e.g. the light in an R.T. experiment) and the objectively observed motor response (e.g. lifting the finger). One major difficulty of course lies in the fact that a number of sequences take place between stimulus and observed response and differences, for example, between subjects in R.T. experiments may be related to differences within one or more of these sequences.[1] Even where records of complex psychomotor responses have been analysed (e.g. Luria, 1932; Davis, 1948), it has been assumed that these responses do not indicate impairment of the motor system itself (such as might follow injury to the motor cortex) but rather some kind of central disorganization which is *reflected* in the motor response.

It is clear that there will be a boundary where the change from a motor response which is used to reflect individual differences in speed and accuracy of central functions to a motor response which can be said to involve individual differences in the skill required to make the response itself will be difficult to detect. For example, it would be easy to analyse finger or manual dexterity in a way similar to that outlined above, i.e. as a constant interchange of stimulus-response mechanisms.

[1] Previous reviews of psychomotor functions (usually restricted to one or a few aspects of the subject) have been carried out by Hunt (1944), Espenschade (1947), Bayley and Espenschade (1950), Seashore (1951) and Canestrelli (1952). Bills (in Andrews (1948) Ch. 16) discusses methods of studying motor functions and efficiency.

[1] This problem, of course, is a very old one. It was, for instance, the subject of much research by Wundt (1873–4), following upon the original experiments of Donders (1865).

Hence the tests included in this chapter are somewhat arbitrary. After an examination of various possibilities it was decided to divide the tests into sections according to the type of response required. Three levels were found necessary to satisfy this criterion, the tests being allocated as follows—

A. *Simple motor response mechanisms*

1. Simple and complex R.T.
2. Cancellation
3. Tapping
4. Davis-type tests

B. *Complex motor response mechanisms*

1. Luria-type test
2. Mirror-drawing
3. Manual and finger dexterity
4. Rail-walking

C. *Continuous Motor response tasks*

1. Static ataxia
2. Body sway (suggestibility)
3. Steadiness
4. Perseveration
5. Fluency
6. Persistence
7. Continuous work

The present chapter will be organized into two sections, one attempting to summarize the facts concerning psychomotor functions, in so far as these have been clearly demonstrated, the other attempting to relate these facts in an orderly way and evaluate the various theories which have been put forward to account for the facts. Before this can be done, however, some of the general difficulties met with in the analysis will be briefly mentioned. These problems should be borne in mind when reading the chapter.

One of the major problems which has occupied workers in this field has been the puzzling question of the specificity or generality of the ability required to perform psychomotor tasks. The earlier studies in the field (e.g. Seashore, 1928, 1930) suggested that the ability to do one type of motor task was relatively independent of the ability to do any other. Many functional analyses have since been carried out[1] and the results are quite clear. For example, the analysis of thirty-eight psychomotor tests by Fleishman (1954) resulted in a matrix of almost uniformly positive, but largely low correlations.[2] Consequently although the

[1] Excellent reviews of these studies will be found in Seashore (1940, 1951), Fleishman (1953) and others.
[2] Calculations made by the author on available studies, e.g. Fleishman (1954), Rimoldi (1951), suggest that the first factor in an unrotated solution usually accounts for about 25 per cent of the total variance, a figure at least as high as that found for personality factors such as neuroticism.

existence of a general factor of psychomotor ability cannot be doubted, its importance has been generally rejected and a solution resulting in independent group factors preferred. Thus, Fleishman analysed his correlation matrix into ten independent group factors (Table II.1). The most interesting feature of this

TABLE II.1

SOME PSYCHOMOTOR FACTORS IDENTIFIED
BY FACTOR ANALYSIS

(*Adopted from E. A. Fleishman, "J. Exp. Psychol.," **48**, 437–454, 1954*)

I.	Wrist–finger speed
II.	Finger dexterity
III.	Rate of arm movement
IV.	Aiming
V.	Arm–hand steadiness
VI.	Reaction–time
VII.	Manual dexterity
VIII.	Psychomotor speed
IX.	Psychomotor co-ordination
X.	Spatial relations

table lies in the narrow abilities which are defined by each of the factors. The wrist-finger factor, for instance, is defined primarily by two simple tapping tests. The R.T. factor, on the other hand, is defined by visual and auditory R.T. only. The intercorrelation of these four tests (Table II.2) shows clearly that proficiency in R.T. bears little relationship to proficiency in tapping—a surprising finding in view of the apparent simplicity of the two tasks which appear to be measures of uncomplicated motor speed. Yet this finding has been repeated many times.

TABLE II.2

INTERCORRELATIONS OF FOUR
PSYCHOMOTOR TESTS

(*From E. A. Fleishman, "J. Exp. Psychol.," **48**, 437–454, 1954*)

	2	3	4
1. Visual R.T. . .	0·56	0·30	0·24
2. Auditory R.T. . .		0·20	0·17
3. Medium tapping .			0·72
4. Large tapping .			—

The factors isolated by Fleishman should not be regarded as definitive. The factors obtained by such analyses are dependent on the nature of the tests used, which have differed widely from study to study. Thus, Seashore, *et al.* (1940) factor-analysed a group of 21 tests and isolated five factors which they designated—

1. Speed of single reaction.
2. Finger, hand and forearm speed in restricted oscillatory movement.

3. Forearm and hand speed in oscillatory movements of moderate extent.

4. Steadiness or precision.

5. Skill in manipulating spatial relations.

The first factor was defined by four R.T. tests, horizontal tapping and rotation of speed drill, in contrast with Fleishman who found tapping and R.T. to be quite different abilities.

The majority of factorial studies carried out have little direct bearing on this chapter, since in most instances they were carried out on highly selected groups for special purposes[1] (for this reason also the group factors have been stressed more than the general factor). However, it is a fact that few investigations into psychomotor function in abnormal subjects have made any use of factorial methods or even of those results from factorial studies which are of general importance. One immediate difficulty, of course, would seem to lie in the very use of psychomotor tests in abnormals. If the correlations between tests are on the whole much lower than those found with intelligence tests then it would seem to be difficult to put forward any general theory to account for differences in psychomotor performance in abnormals as compared with normals; since poor performance on one test might be accompanied by good performance on another, if the correlation is low.

This leads to the second major problem. While intercorrelations between psychomotor tests tend to be low, though positive in normal groups, in abnormal groups the correlations tend to be very much higher, i.e. an abnormal who is poor on one test will tend to be poor on all other psychomotor tests. This difference can be seen clearly in data provided by Shapiro and Nelson (1955), whose figures are summarized in Table II.3.[2] The explanation of this curious and important fact has usually been given in terms of the small spread of scores shown by normal subjects, i.e. it is argued that the tests are much easier for normals than for abnormals. That this is not the correct explanation is shown quite clearly by the data provided by Fleishman (1954) in the study already referred to. He gives means and S.D.s for his normal group of subjects for all thirty-eight tests; on nearly all of these tests the distribution of scores is quite satisfactory for the purposes of correlation.[3] Furthermore, the reliability of Fleishman's tests is quite satisfactory, most of them being above 0·70. Although,

therefore, it is true that abnormal groups usually show a wider range of scores than do normal groups, the differences would not appear to be such as to account for the difference in correlations between the tests.

TABLE II.3

NUMBER OF SIGNIFICANT CORRELATIONS BETWEEN ERROR-FREE SPEED TESTS

(Total number of correlations in each sample = 45)

(From M. B. Shapiro and E. Nelson, "Brit. J. Med. Psychol.," 28, 239–256, 1955)

Sample	5 per cent level r = 0·44 to 0·55	1 per cent level r > 0·56
Normals . . .	3	1
Schizophrenics . .	8	19
Manic-depressives .	3	22
Organics . . .	8	12
Neurotics . . .	9	13

A further problem consists of the scattered and uncoordinated nature of many of the studies published on psychomotor functions in abnormals. The use of different kinds of tests to measure the same attribute (e.g. reaction-time), the use of criterion groups of abnormal subjects chosen in quite different ways (though bearing the same title) and the purely empirical nature of much of the research has led to results both confusing and discouraging. For this reason, stress has been laid in this chapter on those studies which have been most carefully performed and whose results are relatively unequivocal. In most cases, early and perhaps pioneering studies are neglected in favour of later, better controlled studies.[1] In view of the known unreliability of diagnosis, reference in general will be made only to differences between neurotics (and within neurotics, between dysthymics and hysterics), psychotics and normals.

A much neglected problem is that of the role of learning in psychomotor tests. In general, it has been assumed that practice or learning has little or no effect on performance, since the tasks involved (e.g. simple R.T., tapping, cancellation, etc.) are so simple that the subject works at his maximum right from the start. That this is not the case has most clearly been demonstrated quite recently by King (1954). Fig. 2.1 shows the improvement in score on three simple tapping and dexterity tests for schizophrenics and normals over a period of several trials. It is clear that there is a learning curve for even such a simple task.

---

[1] Most of the more sophisticated studies have been carried out in an attempt to devise tests for the selection of recruits for highly skilled posts in the American armed forces.

[2] These were a number of simple motor speed tests of the Babcock series on which no errors were made by the patients tested by Shapiro and Nelson.

[3] The argument concerning the distribution of "normal" scores has usually been put forward in those studies of a clinical nature where the numbers involved have been small.

[1] At the beginning of each section, reference will be made to recent reviews of the literature, where these exist.

In so far as differences in learning are known to exist they will not be treated in this chapter;[1] it should be remembered, however, that differences in learning may account for some of the puzzling findings with amount of learning. On the other hand, he includes a number of tasks (e.g. simple R.T., tapping) where the learning involved must be *relatively* small. Yet he calls all of these tests psychomotor tests. Fortunately,

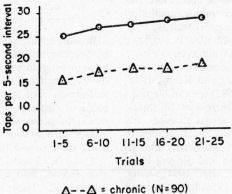

FIG. 2.1 (*a*). LEARNING CURVES ON THE TAPPING TEST FOR THE CHRONIC AND NORMAL GROUPS

Each point plotted represents the mean of five trials.

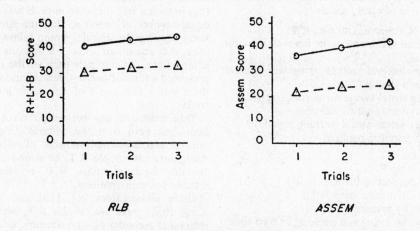

FIG. 2.1 (*b*). LEARNING CURVES ON THE DEXTERITY TESTS FOR THE CHRONIC AND NORMAL GROUPS

Each point plotted represents one trial.

(*From King*, 1954)

abnormal groups. This leads naturally to the problem of the relationship between skilled and unskilled motor tasks. Fleishman (1954), for instance, uses many tests which undoubtedly could be termed skilled tasks, i.e. tasks which involve a very considerable

[1] *See* Chapter 13 by G. Jones.

the problem is solved by the fact that very few tests involving *motor skills* have been given to abnormal groups. These include manual and finger dexterity and mirror-drawing, which will be included in this chapter. The choice of measures to be discussed is, however, somewhat arbitrary.

II. PSYCHOMOTOR FUNCTION OF NORMALS AND ABNORMALS

Simple Motor Response Mechanisms

REACTION-TIME (R.T.)[1]

The R.T. experiment has perhaps been more frequently used in the study of psychomotor function in abnormal subjects than any of the other tests we shall study; also a vast array of information is available for comparative studies on normal subjects.

The early experiments on abnormal subjects (e.g. Saunders and Isaacs, 1929; Wells and Kelley, 1922; Scripture, 1916; Bevan-Lewis, 1892) were of the most simple kind, involving the measurement of simple reaction-time to an auditory or visual stimulus and were carried out on miscellaneous, small groups of psychiatric patients. Later work (especially that of Huston and Senf, 1952; Huston and Singer, 1945; Rodnick and Shakow, 1940; Knehr, 1954; King, 1954; and Tizard and Venables, 1956) has been more concerned to test the validity of certain theories concerning responsiveness in abnormal (usually schizophrenic) patients.

The methodology adopted by the different investigators has been very variable. Some of the factors which have been controlled include—

   (i) Simple R.T. versus complex R.T.
  (ii) Short interval versus long interval between stimuli.
 (iii) Regular interval versus irregular interval between stimuli.
 (iv) Warning signal versus no warning signal.
  (v) Auditory versus visual stimulus.
 (vi) Auditory versus visual warning signal.
(vii) Type of response required—

   (a) simple lift R.T.;
   (b) simple jump R.T.;
   (c) simple disjunctive lift R.T.;
   (d) simple disjunctive jump R.T.;
   (e) reaction by pressing;
   (f) reaction by lifting and pressing in own time;
   (g) movement in own time from one key to another.

(viii) Musculature involved—

   (a) hand—left or right;
   (b) foot—left or right;
   (c) other limbs.

 (ix) Groups used. These include—

   (a) normals;
   (b) schizophrenics (acute and chronic);

   (c) manic-depressives (in manic or depressed state);
   (d) organics;
   (e) neurotics;
   (f) pseudoneurotic schizophrenics.

Broadly speaking, however, the technique developed by Shakow and his colleagues is that now used by most investigators—principally with the aim of testing the hypothesis set up by Shakow. His technique was as follows. The stimulus to which the response was required (usually a sound, but sometimes a light) would be presented at regular or irregular intervals after a warning sound. When the regular interval was used, there would be ten trials for each interval of 1, 2, 4, 7·5, 15 and 25 seconds, each set of trials for a given interval being completed before the next interval was started. There was a 5-second interval between each trial and a rest of one minute after each series of ten trials. In effect, the subject knew how soon after the warning bell, the stimulus would appear. In the irregular method, however, the interval between the warning bell and the stimulus was varied at random (but in such a way that each interval was presented an equal number of times) so that the subject did not know whether the stimulus would follow the warning after one second or after 7·5 seconds or after 25 seconds, etc. In this part each of the intervals was presented a total of twelve times in random order and there was a rest pause of 3 minutes after thirty-six trials.

This technique has been used on a number of occasions, both with and without drugs, and with normal and abnormal subjects. Practically all investigators use simple R.T. to sound or light, presumably because choice R.T. is considered too difficult for many patients.[1]

Other investigators (e.g. Hall and Stride, 1954; King, 1954), have used simple R.T. with a standard interval (5 seconds) with no warning, or delayed R.T. with a long interval (10 seconds) but with warning. A few investigators (Hall and Stride, 1954; King, 1954) have investigated the practice effect of repeated trials on R.T. It is obvious that the number of different ways of investigating R.T. in abnormals is legion.

The results obtained by these methods present a rather confused picture, but the following results would seem to be relatively clear-cut—

   (i) Undifferentiated schizophrenic groups are significantly slower than depressives and neurotics (Hall and Stride, 1954); normals (Huston *et al.*, 1937; Huston and Singer, 1945; Rodnick and

---

[1] Various aspects of R.T. and factors which influence it have been reviewed by Michon (1939), Chocholle (1948), Teichner (1954) and Woodworth and Schlosberg (1954). The work of Shakow and his colleagues has been brought together in Shakow (1946).

[1] But cf. Pascal and Swensen (1952).

Shakow, 1940; Tizard and Venables, 1956); and defectives (Tizard and Venables, 1956).

(ii) Chronic schizophrenics are significantly slower than acute schizophrenics, depressives and neurotics (Huston and Senf, 1952) and normals (King, 1954). Chronic psychotics are poorer than acute psychotics on a complex R.T. test (Windle and Hamwi, 1953; King, 1954).

(iii) Acute schizophrenics are *not* significantly slower than depressives, but are significantly slower than neurotics (Huston and Senf, 1952).

(iv) Neurotics are significantly faster than depressives (Hall and Stride, 1954; Huston and Senf, 1952), chronic and acute schizophrenics (Huston and Senf, 1952), and are not significantly slower than normals matched for age (King, 1954; Hall and Stride, 1954).

(v) Depressives are not significantly different from normals if the groups are roughly matched for age (Hall and Stride, 1954).[1]

These results are not very clear-cut. It is not easy to divide the various groups into psychotic and neurotic, since both Hall and Stride, and Huston and Senf employed psychotic depressives who apparently behave quite differently from schizophrenics, while the latter can be split into acute and chronic. Again the results with regard to neurotics are equivocal, but the differences which exist would seem to be much less than for groups of psychotics. The one clear-cut result would seem to be that patients diagnosed as chronic schizophrenics have consistently been found to be significantly slower than all other psychiatric groups, and than normals.[2]

Sex differences assumed some importance in the study by Hall and Stride, but were found to be minimal in most other studies, especially the large-scale one of King. With regard to age differences, Hall and Stride found that in the neurotic and depressive groups, subjects under 40 tended to be significantly faster than subjects over 40, while King found that subjects showed significant slowing with age but that old schizophrenics tended to be faster than young ones.

Research, however, has not been confined to the investigation of group differences only. Certain other aspects of R.T. have been investigated, with the following main results—

(i) Schizophrenics show more inter- and intra-individual variability in their R.T. responses than do normals (Huston *et al.*, 1937; Huston and Senf,

1952; Huston and Singer, 1945; King, 1954; Knehr, 1954; Rodnick and Shakow, 1940; Tizard and Venables, 1956) and this increased variability is apparent both under normal testing conditions and under the influence of drugs.

(ii) When the regular procedure is compared with the irregular procedure, schizophrenic patients show a curious reversal of behaviour. For short intervals of time the irregular procedure leads to a longer R.T. than does the regular procedure (for the same intervals). With longer intervals, the pattern is reversed, the change in behaviour appar-

TABLE II.4

CHANGE IN R.T. UNDER VARYING PREPARATORY INTERVALS FOR REGULAR AND IRREGULAR PROCEDURE IN NORMALS AND SCHIZOPHRENICS

(From E. H. Rodnick and D. Shakow, "Amer. J. Psychiat.," 97, 214–225, 1940)

Interval (seconds)	Regular procedure mean	Irregular procedure mean
	A. 25 SCHIZOPHRENICS	
	Milliseconds	*Milliseconds*
1	668·7	722·5
2	544·4	665·6
4	531·0	619·5
7·5	648·5	583·0
15	639·3	587·9
25	653·5	560·8
	B. 10 NORMAL CONTROLS	
1	262·7	315·2
2	239·2	290·7
4	261·1	296·6
7·5	275·5	303·6
15	278·1	296·0
25	312·3	305·3

ently taking place somewhere between the intervals of 4 seconds and 7·5 seconds. The validity of this finding seems undoubted (Rodnick and Shakow, 1940; Tizard and Venables, 1956).[1] In Rodnick and Shakow's data there is some suggestion that

---

[1] These results refer to studies using R.T. to sound or light; Huston (1935) found no differences between schizophrenics and normals on patellar tendon reflex.

[2] The negative results of Wells and Kelley (1922) and Saunders and Isaacs (1929) cannot be taken too seriously because of the small numbers involved.

[1] The negative findings of Knehr (1954) can be disregarded on a number of grounds, the principal objection to his study being that he used only two intervals (2 seconds and 10 seconds). This meant, of course, that the "irregular" presentations were such in name only; since the patient would soon realize that if the irregular interval were not 2 seconds, it could only be 10 seconds, whereas in Rodnick and Shakow's study, it might be 4, 7·5, 15, or 25 seconds. For other criticisms of Knehr's study, *see* Tizard and Venables (1956).

the same phenomenon may occur *later* (in terms of intervals) in normals.[1] The figures are shown in Table II.4.

Huston and Senf (1952) found that the Set Index was not significantly affected by the degree of co-operation, duration of illness and change of affect with drugs. These findings do not agree with those of King (1954). Although he found no relationship between R.T. and *duration* of illness, he did find a clear relationship between R.T. and *severity* of illness.

CANCELLATION

The cancellation test is a classic example of a psychomotor task. It is clearly analogous to a choice R.T. test in that the subject has to adopt a set and respond to the correct stimulus when it appears at irregular intervals by making a simple motor response. Although this test was extensively used by earlier workers in its many different forms[2] surprisingly little systematic use has been made of it in abnormal psychology. Mohr and Gundlach (1927) found no differences between asthenics and pyknics when intelligence was partialled out, a finding confirmed by Klineberg, Asch and Block (1934). More recently, Bonnet (1953) investigated changes in speed and accuracy on a cancellation test in psychotic patients who were given five to twenty repetitions of the test over a period of eight months.

TAPPING

Even such a simple test as tapping may be administered in a number of forms. Some investigators, for instance, have been interested in the simple speed of tapping on a single plate; others have studied oscillatory tapping alternately on two plates; others, again, have measured the spread or scatter of the taps. Again, preferred speed has been studied in contrast with maximum speed; while ability to repeat or copy a certain rhythm has been investigated.

Even with such a simple function, the results obtained on abnormal subjects are inconsistent—

(i) It is largely agreed that *speed* or *rate* of tapping does not discriminate between normals and neurotics (H. J. Eysenck, 1952a; S. B. G. Eysenck, 1955; Wulfeck, 1941; Himmelweit and Petrie, 1951). King (1954) found that his neurotics were significantly slower than his normals, but his neurotic group was small (N = 23) and the mean difference very small.

(ii) While H. J. Eysenck (1952a) found that two measures of *scatter* discriminated significantly between normals and neurotics on the one hand (neurotics showing more scatter) and between dysthymics and hysterics on the other (dysthymics showing more scatter), these results were not repeated by S. B. G. Eysenck (1955) who found no difference in scatter between normals and neurotics.

(iii) Shakow and Huston (1936) found that psychotics were significantly *slower* in tapping rate than normals (with schizophrenics slower than manic-depressives within the psychotic group). This finding was confirmed by King (1954) for *chronic* schizophrenics who were slower than both normals and neurotics. S. B. G. Eysenck (1955) found that while individual left- or right-hand speed scores did not differentiate between normals, neurotics and psychotics, the latter were slower than either of the other two groups on a combined score. The only contrary evidence here is that of Wulfeck (1941) who found no differences between normals, schizophrenics, depressives and neurotics.

(iv) S. B. G. Eysenck (1955) found that psychotics did not differ in amount of scatter from normals or neurotics.

We may conclude that *rate* of tapping does not discriminate between normals and neurotics but that there is a suggestion that scatter may do so. On the other hand, rate of tapping does discriminate between psychotic and other abnormal or normal groups, whereas scatter does not.[1]

CONTROL MOVEMENTS (DAVIS)

Davis (1946a, 1946b, 1947, 1948, 1949a, 1949b) carried out a series of experiments on the causes of pilot error. In some experiments he used a simulated cockpit in which instruments on a panel respond realistically to movements of the controls; in other experiments, he used an apparatus in which a pointer could be moved to a given position to the right or left of it.

He observed two types of errors; errors of *over-action* and errors of *inertia*. Subjects who were over-active "obtained large scores on control movements . . . responses to instrument deviations were excessive, the extent and gradient of the movements being greatly increased and over-correcting frequent. Numerous restless movements were observed . . . subjects felt excited and under strain, tense and irritable and sometimes frankly anxious." Subjects who were inert, on the other hand, made "errors which were large and of long duration, whereas

---

[1] A puzzling feature of Rodnick and Shakow's data is the consistently faster R.T. for longer preparatory intervals under the irregular procedure in the schizophrenic group.

[2] Whipple (1924) gives a summary of the different kinds of cancellation tests and the problems involved in measurement.

[1] Penrose and Wilson (1942) describe a peculiar spatial distribution of responses which they claim are found in psychotic patients when asked to tap on the table with a stylus. Various examples are given but no methods of measurement are described, nor any statistical results.

activity, represented by scores of control movements, was relatively little. . . . The individual responses were less hurried and less disturbed by restless movements than were those of the pilots showing the over-activity reaction, but they were often more extensive than at the beginning of the test. . . . Subjects reported that their interest had flagged and that their concentration had failed. A feeling of strain had now given way to one of mild boredom, tedium or tiredness."

Davis (1948) went on to show that if responses in the test are classified into three categories (normal, overactive, inert), then only 33 per cent of neurotic pilots showed a normal reaction, compared with 75 per cent of normals. Further, pilots suffering from anxiety states showed a strong tendency to make overactive responses; whereas pilots suffering from hysteria tended to display inert responses. (Table II.5.)

TABLE II.5

TEST RESULTS OF NORMAL AND NEUROTIC PILOTS

(*From D. R. Davis, "Pilot Error. Some Laboratory Experiments"* (H.M.S.O., 1948))

	Normal		Overactive		Inert		Total N
	N	Per centage	N	Per centage	N	Per centage	
Normal pilots .	268	75	59	17	28	8	355
Neurotic pilots .	13	33	11	28	15	38	39
Acute anxiety state	6	43	7	20	1	7	14
Hysteria . .	1	12·5	1	12·5	6	75	8
Other . . .	6	35	3	18	8	47	17

In another experiment (Davis, 1946b) 355 fit pilots were classified by two psychiatrists with regard to predisposition to neurosis as: nil, slight, moderate; and further classified on the Cockpit test as normal, over-

TABLE II.6

ASSOCIATION OF NEUROTICISM AND TEST SCORE

(*From D. R. Davis, "J. Neurol. Psychiat.,"* 9, 119–124, 1946b)

Predisposition	Type of response			
	Normal	Over-active	Inert	Per cent normal
Nil . . .	130	13	12	84
Slight . . .	113	32	9	73
Moderate . .	25	14	7	54
Per cent moderate .	9	24	25	

active, inert. The results (Table II.6) indicate a significant association between grade of predisposition and test class, the percentage of normal responses decreasing with increasing predisposition to neurosis. Fit pilots who were rated as obsessional tended to fall into the overactive class.

In an experiment (Davis, 1949a) using a simple pointer apparatus instead of the Cockpit, healthy, acutely anxious and hysteric pilots were given "extent" scores (ranging from 3–8) on the test. The results (Table II.7) showed clearly that the acutely anxious pilots tended to make more extensive responses than did normals; the hysterics showing the opposite tendency. Further, the response time of the hysterics was significantly *longer* than that of the normals, the latter being similar in this respect to the acutely anxious.

TABLE II.7

DEGREE OF ERROR OF NORMAL, ANXIOUS AND HYSTERIC PILOTS

(*From D. R. Davis, "Quart. J. Exp. Psychol.,"* 1, 22–28, 1949a)

	Distribution of cases (Extent scores in arbitrary unit)						
	3	4	5	6	7	8	Total
Healthy pilots . .	1	3	21	29	14	1	69
Acutely anxious .	1	1	2	3	6	2	15
Hysterics . .	4	5	2	1	0	0	12

Davis's experiments may be summarized in the following way—

1. Neurotics tend to make more errors of judgement compared with normals.
2. Within the neurotic group, dysthymics tend to make errors of overactivity, hysterics errors of inertia.
3. Similar tendencies are found within normal groups.

Davis (1946) also noted that "the errors in the instrument readings increased in size towards the end of the test . . . and there were few large errors in place of many small ones." Similarly, the number of errors in resetting the "fuel contents" indicator fell from the first to the third period but then increased significantly. These phenomena, which Davis called "late effects" indicate that, in general, errors of inertia tend to predominate over errors of overactivity *in all subjects* provided the test is continued for a long enough period.

Complex Motor Response Mechanisms

The Luria Technique[1]

This technique is a development by Luria (1932) of the original work of Nunberg (1918) who combined the Word Association test with measurements of hand movement at the time of and between verbal responses. The underlying rationale is that the internal conflict thought to occur when the subject is required to respond to an emotionally disturbing stimulus[2] will be reflected in motor movements which, being overt, can be recorded. Many studies have been published which support this general hypothesis.[3] A large number of variables have been recorded which may be classified generally as follows—

1. Reaction-time measures—

(a) time of verbal response;
(b) time of manual response (Speer, 1937; Eysenck, S. B. G., 1955);
(c) variability of time of response.

2. R-hand response (usually voluntary, made at time of verbal response)—

(a) regularity and duration of response (Malmo et al., 1951);
(b) height (Speer, 1937);
(c) number of disturbances (Speer, 1937).
(d) number of double depressions;
(e) number of depressions omitted; } (Eysenck, S. B. G., 1955)
(f) three longest—three shortest responses.

3. L-hand response (usually involuntary, both at time of R-hand response and between R-hand responses)—

(a) height, length, number of changes in direction, number of items producing L-hand response (Speer, 1937);
(b) number of reversals; } (Eysenck, S. B. G., 1955)
(c) maximum distance from base line.

4. Length of base line, i.e. actual length of the kymographic record (Eysenck, S. B. G., 1955).

Little attention has been paid to the degree of relationship between these variables. Malmo et al. (1951), Albino (1948), Krause (1937) and Sharp (1938) give figures which indicate low positive correlations between L- and R-hand disturbance, but indicate no relationship between amount of motor disturbance and speed of response (R.T.). Clarke (1950) showed that it was important to partial out differences in intelligence between psychiatric groups before group differences could be examined.

The results obtained on psychiatric groups may be summarized as follows—

(i) R-hand voluntary response is significantly more disturbed in neurotics than in normals (Clarke, 1950; Malmo et al., 1951; Eysenck, S. B. G., 1955).

(ii) L-hand involuntary response is significantly more disturbed in neurotics than in normals, provided the apparatus used is sufficiently sensitive (Albino, 1948; Clarke, 1950; Malmo et al., 1951; Eysenck, S. B. G., 1955).

(iii) Both local and general motor disturbance is greater in neurotics than in normals (Barnacle et al., 1935; Ebaugh, 1936).

These conclusions are further supported by the work of Morgan and Ojeman (1942) who found significant differences between groups rated as having low, intermediate and high degrees of conflict.

(iv) There is some evidence that the motor disorganization shown by dysthymics is different from that shown by hysterics (Barnacle et al., 1935; Malmo et al., 1951). Speer (1937) related introversion-extraversion to amount of L-hand disturbance and concluded that introverts tended to respond more than extraverts with the L-hand (i.e. showed more involuntary disturbance). Ebaugh's (1936) study indicated that anxiety cases showed more *general* disturbance than hysterics; and possibly more *local* disturbance.[1]

(v) Results obtained with psychotics indicate that they show at least as much disorganization as neurotics (Malmo et al., 1951), if not more (Eysenck, S. B. G., 1955).[2] Shuey (1937) distinguished four types of motor reaction with the R-hand (small, large, mixed, chaotic) and attempted to relate these to specific psychotic groups (manic-depressive, paranoid, catatonic) without much success.

The above general findings have been confirmed by the recent well-controlled study of S. B. G. Eysenck (1955). Using one hundred and twenty-three controls, fifty-five psychotics and fifty-five neurotics and a number of response categories, she obtained the results shown in Table II.8. From these data she concluded that R-hand disturbance differentiates better

---

[1] There is no adequate published summary of work on this test since the publication of Luria's (1932) book; unpublished reports may be found in Eysenck, S. B. G. (1955) and Clarke (1950).
[2] Clarke (1950) also used an electric shock as a stimulus.
[3] Olson and Jones (1931); Huston et al. (1934); Burtt (1936); Runkel (1936); Brandt (1937); Gardner (1937); Krause (1937); Reymert and Speer (1939); Morgan and Ojeman (1942).

---

[1] Ebaugh's results are difficult to interpret since he provides no measures of dispersion.
[2] Malmo et al. (1951) considered disorganization was primarily a function of severity of illness.

than L-hand disturbance, and that psychotics show even greater disorganization than do neurotics.

TABLE II.8

DIFFERENCES BETWEEN NORMALS, NEUROTICS AND PSYCHOTICS ON THE LURIA TEST

(From S. B. G. Eysenck, Ph.D. Thesis, 1955)

Variables	Controls (N = 123)	Neurotics (N = 55)	Psychotics (N = 55)	F	p
	M	M	M		
1. *Motor R.T.*					
No. of delays .	22·7	27·0	29·1	16·61	0·001
Σ total delays .	112·2	233·3	294·5	20·13	0·001
2. *R-hand disturbances*					
No. double depressions . .	2·0	4·7	5·9	11·71	0·001
No. omitted depressions .	0·1	0·3	1·8	9·79	0·001
Σ 3 longest − Σ 3 shortest R.T. .	14·2	16·7	18·6	5·21	0·01
3. *L-hand disturbances*					
No. reversals .	8·2	8·4	13·5	4·18	0·01
Max. distance from base line .	1·5	1·9	2·2	3·69	0·05
4. *Length of baseline*	297·9	406·9	503·2	21·74	0·001

MIRROR DRAWING[1]

Results obtained on the mirror-drawing test which has been extensively used with normal and abnormal groups are not so clear-cut as those obtained on the Luria test. Earlier studies suggested that speed and error scores in this test discriminate between "stable" and "unstable" individuals (Ball, 1929; Brower, 1948); that there is a negative correlation between mirror-drawing ability and inadequacy of social adjustment (Louttit, 1943); that psychotics and delinquents are significantly slower than normals (Peters, 1946); and that anxiety cases are significantly slower than normals (Wechsler and Hartogs, 1945).

Two carefully controlled studies throw light on these suggestions (in both cases a diamond-shaped figure was used compared with the more common star-shape). Using the groups of normals, neurotics and psychotics already referred to, S. B. G. Eysenck (1955) found that psychotics were significantly poorer than either neurotics or normals on five speed measures (first time, longest time, shortest time, average time, and first minus third time). The neurotics were also slower than the normals, but the main differences were much smaller.[2] These results are in agreement with those of Eysenck (1952a) who found

[1] Early studies are reviewed in Whipple (1924); later studies in Brower (1948); Clarke (1950); Waters and Sheppard (1952); and Eysenck, S. B. G. (1955).
[2] *Average* time for controls was 44·27 seconds; for neurotics 62·60; for psychotics 98·00 (*p* < 0·001). Clarke (1950) found no difference between normals and neurotics or between hysterics and dysthymics with respect to time scores.

highly significant differences on time taken between normals and psychotics.

We may conclude that the mirror-drawing test discriminates at a high level between normals and psychotics and possibly between normals and neurotics. No reliable information is available concerning errors.

MANUAL AND FINGER DEXTERITY

Relatively little work on abnormal subjects has been reported with this type of test. Lubin (1951) found a correlation with the normal-neurotic dichotomy of about + 0·60, while O'Connor (1951), testing high grade mental defectives obtained a neurotic factor saturation of 0·43 on manual and finger dexterity tests.

S. B. G. Eysenck (1955) found that parts M, N, O and P of the USES battery all discriminated significantly between psychotics and normals, while neurotics fell in between, but were significantly poorer than normals. These results support those by Eysenck (1952a) who compared normals with neurotics, the neurotics being significantly poorer on all four parts of the test. A comparison of the two studies is shown in Table II.9.[1] Tizard and O'Connor (1951) also found that manual and finger dexterity tests had significant loadings on a factor of neuroticism.

TABLE II.9

A COMPARISON OF TWO STUDIES ON MANUAL AND FINGER DEXTERITY TESTS

(From H. J. Eysenck, "Scientific Study of Personality," 1952, and S. B. G. Eysenck, Ph.D. Thesis, 1955)

	S. B. G. Eysenck, (1955)		Eysenck (1952)	
	Controls	Neurotics	Controls	Neurotics
	M	M	M	M
Part M .	75·45	72·62	77·29	71·87
Part N .	88·60	86·75	83·06	75·58
Part O .	27·76	25·29	26·22	23·60
Part P .	25·65	23·95	25·56	22·90
Total . .	217·36	208·61	212·13	193·95

Petrie (1948) found that dysthymics were significantly better than hysterics in the O'Connor Tweezers Test.

RAIL-WALKING TEST

This test, which was devised by Heath (1942, 1943, 1944, 1946, 1949) usually employs two 9 ft long rails,

[1] The results are remarkably consistent. The scores obtained by Eysenck (1952a) are slightly lower all round, presumably because the amount of pre-test practice was curtailed by him.

one 4 in. and one 2 in. wide, and one 6 ft long rail, 1 in wide. The test is given in an untimed form, the subject being required to walk along it in his stockinged feet (Heath, 1942). It has been extensively standardized (Heath, 1942, 1944, 1949) and has a high reliability.

Heath (1946) discovered an adjustment syndrome, characterized by poor motor co-ordination among other things, and the possible relationship of this lack of motor co-ordination to neuroticism was confirmed by the work of Tizard et al. (1950) and Tizard and O'Connor (1951). Using it along with a number of other tests, they found that it had a significant loading on the neuroticism factor which resulted from their factorial analysis. Unfortunately little work has since been carried out with this test on psychiatric groups.

Continuous Motor Response Tests

STATIC ATAXIA[1]

In this test the subject is told simply to stand still and relax, with the eyes closed and the hands hanging down the side, feet together. The test lasts for 30 seconds, usually, and maximum sway either forward or backward is the score. Data for one hundred and twenty normal controls and 1,230 neurotics (Eysenck, 1952a) show that 81 per cent of normals swayed less than 1 in., compared with only 32 per cent of neurotics; no normals swayed more than 2 in., while 31 per cent of neurotics did so. In another study (Eysenck, 1944), four times as many neurotics swayed more than 1 in. when compared with normals.

BODY SWAY (SUGGESTIBILITY)[2]

Two main problems have confronted workers on suggestibility. The first of these concerns the question whether or not suggestibility tests have anything in common (i.e. define one or more factors). The second concerns the relationship between suggestibility and abnormality.

(a) Types of Suggestibility

Early investigations produced conflicting reports. Thus Aveling and Hargreaves (1921) and others believed they had demonstrated the existence of general and group factors of suggestibility whereas Estabrooks (1929) reported zero or very low correlations. Still other writers believed in the existence of group factors of suggestibility—Hull (1933), for example, distinguished "prestige" and "non-prestige" suggestion. A considerable amount of light was thrown on this

problem by the researches of Eysenck. In one study, for example (Eysenck, 1943) he used eight tests of suggestibility and intercorrelated the resultant scores, with results shown in Table II.10. Two clear-cut independent factors emerged.[1]

TABLE II.10

FACTOR ANALYSIS OF 8 TESTS OF SUGGESTIBILITY

(From H. J. Eysenck, "J. Neurol. Psychiat," 6, 22–31, 1943)

Test	Loadings	
	Factor I	Factor II
1. Weights (personal)	+ 0·509	− 0·371
2. Lines (personal)	+ 0·772	− 0·002
3. Weights (impersonal)	+ 0·558	+ 0·048
4. Lines (impersonal)	+ 0·386	+ 0·016
5. Pendulum	+ 0·094	+ 0·386
6. Body sway	− 0·041	+ 0·623
7. Levitation up	− 0·194	+ 0·370
8. Levitation down	− 0·100	+ 0·546

(i) *Primary Suggestibility:* This factor is revealed by tests of the ideomotor type, i.e. psychomotor tests in which a motor movement is executed by the subject following the repeated suggestion by the experimenter that such a movement will take place, without conscious participation in the movement on the subject's part. The test which most satisfactorily defines this factor is Hull's Body Sway Test which has been extensively used for this purpose. The factor is also defined by the Chevreul Pendulum Test, the Arm Levitation Test and the Press-Release Test.[2]

(ii) *Secondary Suggestibility:* This factor is defined by tests other than motor tests and need not be considered further.[3]

The main characteristics of primary suggestibility are as follows (Eysenck, 1943)—

1. It is distributed in the experimental population as a U-curve (this U-curve being, however, an artefact of the method of measurement (Eysenck and Furneaux, 1945)).

2. It correlates in a significantly non-linear way with intelligence (subjects of average I.Q. being most suggestible).

3. It may manifest itself in a positive or negative response.

4. It is a highly reliable phenomenon.

---

[1] Edwards (1942) has reviewed the literature prior to 1942, and the factors which must be controlled in any study of static ataxia (Edwards 1942, 1946a, 1947). *See also* Travis (1945) and Eysenck (1947, Appendix B).
[2] For reviews of the literature, *see* Eysenck (1947, 1953).

[1] The results were repeated in a subsequent, more extensive study (Eysenck and Furneaux, 1945).
[2] *See* Eysenck (*Dimensions of Personality*, p. 166, 1947) for a description of these tests.
[3] Eysenck (1947) thinks there is some evidence for a third factor of suggestibility (prestige).

It is clear, therefore, that primary suggestibility is an important trait in that it can be clearly differentiated from other traits, can be measured by a group of objective tests and is a reliable phenomenon. Its relationship to personality differences is, therefore, of great interest.[1]

(b) Suggestibility and Personality

Early studies[2] considered that suggestibility is related to neuroticism but that it bears a special relationship to hysteria in that in this disorder an increased and exaggerated state of suggestibility can usually be found. However, Eysenck's researches showed conclusively that—

1. There is a close relationship between primary suggestibility and neurosis. In one study (Eysenck, 1944) one hundred and ten neurotics were compared with one hundred and ten normals (paired for Matrices I.Q.) on the Body Sway and Static Ataxia test. It was found that on the Body Sway test 63 per cent of male and 42 per cent of female neurotics were suggestible compared with 7 per cent of male and 8 per cent of female normals; sixteen neurotics fell outright, whereas no normal did. The correlation between primary suggestibility and neuroticism was 0·66.[3] The study of Messer et al. (1938) found a correlation between amount of sway and tendency to give neurotic responses on the Bernreuter Inventory in normal subjects.

2. Later researches showed clearly that there is a strong correlation between amount of sway and amount of neuroticism. Fig. 2.2 shows the average amount of suggestibility (on a Body Sway test) for six groups of neurotic patients, a total of nine hundred and sixty males and three hundred and ninety females. It is clear that sway increases steadily with increase in severity of illness (Eysenck, 1947).

3. Contrary to the earlier suggestions in the literature, there is some evidence that while neurotics as a group are more suggestible than normals, dysthymics are most suggestible of all. Eysenck

(1947) reports that correlations between anxiety as a symptom and suggestibility are 0·26 for men and 0·33 for women, while for conversion hysteria the correlations are 0·12 for men and −0·08 for women. Figures for hysterical personality and anxious personality are similar.[1]

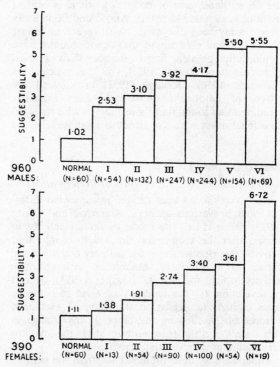

FIG. 2.2. AVERAGE SUGGESTIBILITY OF NORMALS AND NEUROTICS, SHOWING INCREASE IN SUGGESTIBILITY CORRELATED WITH INCREASE IN "NEUROTICISM"

(From Eysenck, 1947)

4. There is some evidence that suggestible patients are of two kinds in relation to tests of primary suggestibility. On the one hand there are suggestible subjects who constitute an active, alert group; on the other there are suggestible subjects who constitute a passive, lethargic group (Eysenck, 1943). The similarity of these two groups to the overactive v. inert dichotomy found by Davis will be readily apparent.[2]

5. There is some evidence that catatonic schizophrenics are negatively suggestible; paranoid

[1] Benton and Bandura (1953) found no evidence for a general factor of primary suggestibility (average r of four tests = −0·07) in a group of fifty normal university students. Their conclusions are open to serious objection in that (a) they used a highly selected group, particularly with regard to I.Q. (all University students), although Eysenck had shown that subjects of average I.Q. are most suggestible; (b) such a group would certainly restrict the range of scores on suggestibility tests and hence lower the correlation; (c) although attempting to replicate Eysenck's results, they omitted the Heat Illusion test and replaced it with the Vibration test.

[2] Eysenck (1947) reviews these studies.

[3] Since static ataxia tests (i.e. swaying without suggestion) discriminate powerfully between normals and neurotics, it is clearly necessary to allow for differences in "natural tendency to sway" in order to estimate the true effects of suggestibility. This was done by Ingham (1954, 1955) who confirmed the findings on body sway tests, even when differences in static ataxia were allowed for.

[1] An earlier study by Eysenck, however, (1943) using very carefully matched groups of conversion hysterics and dysthymics found no significant differences on primary suggestibility tests. Similarly Roach (1947) found no differences between introverted and extraverted normals.

[2] It does not seem to make any difference if hetero- or auto-suggestion is used (Baumgartner, 1931; Berremann and Hilgard, 1936; Eysenck, 1947).

schizophrenics positively suggestible; while manics are non-suggestible (Williams, 1932).

FINGER TREMOR[1]

In this type of test, the intention is to measure the amount of involuntary movement which appears when the finger, hand, arm or body as a whole is held as motionless as possible. Static Ataxia and Body Sway have already been discussed. With regard to Finger Tremor, it has been found that schizophrenics have significantly greater finger tremor than normal (Edwards and Harris, 1953),[2] as have defectives (Edwards, 1950). Kellogg (1932) investigated the effects of emotional excitement upon muscular steadiness and found that those subjects who reported emotional upset were less steady than those who did not.

PERSEVERATION[3]

(a) Dimensional Analysis of Tests of Perseveration

Perseveration has been defined in somewhat different ways by various authors. Cameron and Caunt (1933) define it as "the tendency for an activity to persist after the subject has decided to change that activity, this persistence in the primary activity being shown by a transitory interference with the new activity which follows it." Jasper (1931) defined perseveration as "the tendency of a set of neurons, once excited, to persist in the state of excitation autonomously, showing resistance to any change in this state." Both of these authors stress the involuntary nature of perseverative activity.[4]

Other authors have preferred to stress the behavioural acts which may be said to define perseveration. Thus, Kleemeier and Dudek (1950) define flexibility (the obverse of perseveration) "simply as the ability (a) to shift from one task to another or (b) to break through an established set in order to perform a task," i.e. their definition makes no assumptions concerning brain processes (cf. Jasper above). Scheier and Ferguson (1952), similarly, define rigidity and flexibility in terms of negative transfer effects.

The concept of perseveration derives originally from clinical observations, which were first systematized by

Gross (1902) in terms of primary and secondary function. Primary function was defined by Gross as the *intensity* of any stimulus. The intensity of the primary function would determine how long it would perseverate after the stimulus had been removed. The *duration* of the response was called the secondary function. An intense primary response would be followed by a long secondary response, a weak primary response by a short secondary response.

Gross then proceeded to relate type of function to type of personality, again basing his ideas on clinical experience. A person showing strong primary and long secondary responses would be deep-narrow (i.e. would suffer from a restriction of conscious awareness) or *introverted*; a person showing weak primary and short secondary responses would be broad-shallow (i.e. suffer from wide conscious awareness) or *extra-verted*. The deep-narrow person would tend to perseverate and have difficulty in switching from one task to another; the broad-shallow person would tend to flit from one subject to another and hence show little perseveration.

Most of the work carried out subsequently on perseveration derives directly or indirectly from the original work of Gross. Secondary function could manifest itself in at least four ways—

(i) the perseveration of a response after the stimulus has ceased, e.g. the length of time an after-image persists after the stimulus has been withdrawn.

(ii) the spontaneous reappearance of a response in consciousness after the original stimulus and response have both ceased. For example, a subject responding to successive stimuli A, B, C, D, etc., might respond with response A, to A; B, to B; C, to C, and then A, to D.

(iii) the extent to which the perseveration of a response to stimulus A *interferes with* (delays or prevents) the response to stimulus B, e.g. the extent to which writing S interferes with writing Z immediately afterwards.

(iv) the extent to which an ingrained (through repetition) response-habit interferes with a new response, although the interfering response may not itself be performed, e.g. mirror-writing.[1]

The complicated nature and differing interpretations of perseveration tests may be shown by brief consideration of one of the simplest of such tests: the S-Z tests. In this test, three steps are usually taken—

(i) writing S as quickly as possible for 1 minute;

---

[1] Whipple (1924) has reviewed the earlier literature. Edwards (1946b) has discussed the factors influencing tremor.

[2] In an earlier study, Huston and Shakow (1946) found similar results, using two indices of steadiness. Their subjects were one hundred and thirty-five male schizophrenics and sixty-four normals (with repeated testing over time for forty-nine schizophrenics and twenty-one normals). However, they found no difference in steadiness if co-operative subjects only were compared.

[3] Burri (1935), Rogers (1935a, 1935b), Kendig and Shevach (1937), Cattell (1946a, 1946b), Eysenck (1947, 1953) and Rim (1953) have reviewed this subject.

[4] The involuntary nature of the perseverative process has been contrasted with the essentially voluntary nature of persistence and forms the principal distinguishing feature.

[1] It may be noted in passing that Gross postulated that the length of secondary function is directly determined by the *strength* of the primary function, i.e., there should be a high correlation between primary and secondary function. Most investigators have used *speed* of response as a measure of both rimary and secondary function, not *strength*.

(ii) writing ƨ as quickly as possible for 1 minute;

(iii) writing SƨSƨ, etc., as quickly as possible for 2 minutes.

Such a test has been scored in a number of ways, each method intended as a measure of perseveration—

(a) The score (i − ii) may be regarded as a measure of the interference of the ingrained habit of writing S on a new, unfamiliar habit (such a measure may of course be obtained without (i) above being given at all).

(b) The score (i + ii) − iii may be regarded as a measure of the interference of writing S immediately before ƨ and vice versa, compared with writing either S or ƨ alone without interference.

Alternatively, the test may be given in the form—

(i) writing S
(ii) writing ƨ
(iii) writing S

in which case (i − iii) would indicate the amount of interference of (ii) on (iii).

Cattell (1935a) attempted to elucidate the nature of perseveration by giving many different kinds of "p" tests and intercorrelating the scores. Stephenson (1934) had pointed out three kinds of "p" tests—

(i) alternation tests;
(ii) creative effort tests;
(iii) direct "p" tests.

Using a large number of such tests Cattell intercorrelated the results obtained on fifty-two adults. As a result of this and later work he distinguished (1946a)—

(i) *Inertia of mental processes*, shown in "alternation tests" in which the subject has to switch to and fro between two interfering, alternate ways of performing tasks, the tasks being otherwise equivalent.

AAAA, etc.
BBBB, etc.
AB AB AB AB, etc.

Here the X and Y activities must follow in rapid temporal succession, producing interference by their momentum, inertia or after-effect.

(ii) *Disposition rigidity* or inertia of structural disposition. This shows itself in "creative effort" tests in which the score is measured as the difference between performing a task in some old, accustomed fashion and performing it in some new fashion, e.g.

SSSSS
ƨƨƨƨƨ

Here immediate temporal contiguity of the X and Y tasks is not essential, i.e. there is no question of inertia of functioning process.

Cattell argued that most of the published studies showed no evidence for the first type of perseveration; those which appeared to, did so because of the scoring technique—when this was corrected, no "p" factor was present. He concluded that there was a general factor proved only for motor "creative effort" tests and that this factor was best called "disposition rigidity." He reported a study of his own in which six tests involving solely the "creative effort" principle and confined largely to motor performance tests were given to one hundred women students. From the resultant analysis, a general disposition rigidity factor emerged which accounted satisfactorily for the variance.

The conclusions at which Cattell arrived remained unchallenged for some time as they seemed to account adequately for most of the published findings. Thus Jasper (1931), using sensory and motor tests on normal subjects had found no evidence for an overall factor of perseveration but concluded that there was some evidence for the existence of a narrow group factor of motor perseveration. Jones (1928), using sensory, motor and ideational tests on manics and depressives, had found evidence in the test intercorrelations of a "general" factor covering ideational and motor tests in the melancholics but not in the manics. Pinard (1932a) had found evidence of a group factor covering tests of both the alternation and creative effort type (all motor tests). Rethlingshafer (1942) in a factor analysis of twenty-nine variables on normal college adults of high I.Q. found (among others) a factor she named perseveration which had significant loadings on six tests (time the subject worked at a task; length of time hand grip is maintained; preferred motor tapping rate; effect of a slower intervening rate on preferred rate of tapping; and answers to questions on the Maller-Elkin Attention test).

Notcutt (1943) gave a number of tests purporting to measure the four supposed kinds of perseveration (sensory; motor creative effort; motor alternation; associative, i.e. tendency for ideas to occur involuntarily). Of the eighty correlations between individual tests, thirty-nine were positive and forty-one negative, the mean $r = 0.005 \pm 0.011$, i.e. the results were precisely what would be expected by chance fluctuations in the scores. With regard to the four types, he concluded that there was no evidence for a factor of sensory perseveration; that the evidence for a creative factor was inconclusive; that the alternation tests had a mean r of 0.181 (if one test was omitted), indicating a genuine though very small common factor; and

that there was no evidence for associative perseveration. Nor did he find any correlation between the
two motor groups of tests.

The situation was further reviewed by Walker *et al.*
(1941, 1943) who concluded that the evidence for a
general "p" factor was in all studies either decidedly
negative or, at best, only weakly positive. They
further pointed out that the tests used, by their very
nature, made it impossible to distinguish (even if a
general factor did exist) whether perseveration was
due to mental inertia (as in the alternation-type test)
or disposition rigidity (as in the creative-effort tests)
since the latter usually entered into the former.

In spite of Cattell's efforts to elucidate the field,
therefore, the evidence for either a general, or unrelated group factors, of perseveration remained
extremely tenuous. However, a new light was thrown
on the matter by Kleemeier and Dudek (1950) who
carried out an obvious (but until then unthought-of)
study. They used simple psychomotor tests which
previous studies had shown would result by factorial
analysis in numerical speed, perceptual speed and
verbal factors. Within each set one task involved
shifting. If these latter tests appeared on an independent axis in a factor analysis, there would be
evidence for a factor of flexibility. Thirteen paper and
pencil tests were used on two hundred and five college
students. Four factors accounted satisfactorily for
the variance. These were factors of perceptual speed,
verbal, single-digit number, and two-digit number.
The flexibility tests did not group themselves along an
independent axis but could be accounted for in terms
of the other factors. They concluded that "no factor of
flexibility need be postulated to account for differences
in performance on these simple alternation tasks."

While the study of Kleemeier and Dudek does not
entirely solve the "riddle of perseveration" (they did
not, for example, include any of the classical "p"
tests) it does suggest that the classical "p" tests may
be measuring factors other than perseveration and
that a factor of perseveration, even if it genuinely
exists, may contribute little to the total variance of the
test. This conclusion was, of course, implicit in the
previous findings which, even when positive, indicated
a relatively unimportant factor and was supported by
a recent careful study by Rim (1955). He used
twenty-one tests of perseveration on both normal and
neurotic subjects, and derived three factors of perseveration. With intelligence controlled, these factors
were defined as—

(i) Disposition-rigidity, operating in motor and
perceptual tasks—the rigidity of old-established
habits in the presence of new demands.
(ii) Creative-effort rigidity—carrying out a new
task never done before.

(iii) Cognitive or ideational rigidity—this was
defined by tests similar to those used by Kleemeier
and Dudek (1950).

The interesting point about Rim's study is that the
amount of variance accounted for by the three factors
of perseveration was as follows—

Factor I— 5·8 per cent
Factor II— 7·8 per cent
Factor III— 8·8 per cent.

These three factors together accounted for only
about 23 per cent of the total variance of the tests,
other factors and specifics presumably accounting for
the remainder.

It would seem reasonable to suppose, therefore,
that a combination of the approach of Kleemeier and
Dudek on the one hand, and of Rim on the other
would yield fruitful results. This was carried out,
more or less, by Scheier and Ferguson (1952) who
included tests of reasoning ability, cognitive rigidity,
motor speed and motor rigidity in a battery given to
sixty students. They identified three factors—

Factor A—a reasoning factor, involved in all
tests to some extent.
Factor B—a motor speed factor with high loadings on the motor speed *and motor rigidity tests.*
Factor C—a non-motor rigidity factor.

However, they also concluded that "the motor
rigidity tests used . . . have a factorial composition
which is very largely reasoning and motor speed."

It seems reasonable to conclude from the evidence
reviewed above that the most recent careful work
confirms the existence of two forms of motor perseveration—alternation "p" and creative effort "p"
(Rim, 1955); that these two factors nevertheless
account for only a small proportion of the total
variance attributable to the tests which are the best
measures of perseveration (Rim, 1955); and that
when suitable reference tests are included in a battery
of perseveration tests, the amount of variance attributable to the factors of motor perseveration is
negligible when compared with that attributable to
other factors, especially the factor of motor (perceptual-motor) speed (Kleemeier and Dudek, 1950;
Scheier and Ferguson, 1952).[1,2]

(b) *Perseveration and Personality*

Many attempts have been made to relate the supposed factors of perseveration with personality
factors. Early studies suggested that low "p" scores
were characteristic of manics (Jones, 1928; Pinard,

[1] This conclusion is largely supported by recent work of
Biescheuvel and Pitt (1955).
[2] More recently, interest has centred on the investigation
of rigidity The study of Cattell and Tiner (1949) suggested
that rigidity is a kind of "ideational" perseveration, to be
distinguished from "motor" perseveration.

1932*b*; Stephenson, 1932*a*). High "p" scores, on the other hand, were said to characterize depressives (Stephenson, 1932*a*); schizophrenics (Pinard, 1932*b*; Stephenson, 1932*b*); stutterers (Eisenson, 1937); "emotionality" (Cattell, 1956) and various traits such as "youngest child in the family, being brought up indulgently, being more ailing as a child, being socially isolated, poorer prognosis with therapy" (Cattell, 1950).

In a series of studies Kendig (1937*a*, 1937*b*, 1937*c*, 1937*d*) found high "p" scores to be associated with induced failure in the task and with acceptance of the task as a test, rather than as a casual affair.

Jasper (1931) found effectively zero correlations between perseveration scores and introversion-extra-version scores (as measured by Conklin's E-1 Interest test); however, as he also found a significant correlation between introversion and depression it seems likely that this scale was measuring neuroticism rather than introversion.

perseverators. Thus, neurotics seemed to be abnormal perseverators, but to fall into two clear-cut and opposite groups.

In a later study (Pinard, 1932*b*) he attempted to relate perseveration to introversion. Patients were interviewed and rated themselves on a scale covering all points related to introversion by previous investi-gators. He found that "the extreme perseverators and non-perseverators have in common lack of self-control and perseverance to a marked degree and they are unreliable, obstinate, 'touchy' and difficult. They differ from each other in that the extreme perseverator tends to be effeminate, 'nervous,' sensitive, senti-mental, serious, shy and solitary, whereas the extreme nonperseverator tends to be suspicious, inconsiderate, critical, impatient of criticism, tactless, silent and anxious and in a state of general tension with ups and downs in mood." Pinard's diagram summarizing his findings resembles Eysenck's dimensional system very closely.

NEUROTIC

Lacks self control and perseverance, unreliable, obstinate, touchy, difficult

EP Rebellious Serious Shy and solitary More intelligent	*EN* Irritable Selfish Silent and anxious Less intelligent
MP Effeminate, nervous Sentimental, sensitive	*MN* Inconsiderate, critical Tactless, ups and downs in mood, suspicious
Considerate Harmonious Reflective	Courageous, jovial good mixer

Self controlled, persevering, reliable
Practical, reticent, self-reliant

I   *E*

NORMAL

In his first study Pinard (1932*a*) appeared to relate extreme "p" scores to different types of neurosis. Thus, in a study on children, he found that 75 per cent of the most difficult and unreliable children were either over- or under-perseverators while the opposite was true of the self-controlled children, i.e. they showed moderate perseveration. The extremely perse-verative children were the real rebels, irritable, bad-tempered and moody; the non-perseverators were "petty," nagging and whining.[1] These results were confirmed for adult neurotics, 75 per cent of the most difficult and unreliable patients being over- or under-

Notcutt (1943) found a correlation of only − 0·03 between alternation "p" scores and introversion, using normal subjects, but this is not surprising since he found no clear-cut factor of perseveration.

Cattell (1946*b*) found a negative correlation between "w" and "p" in neurotics, supporting the earlier finding by Brogden (1940) whose first factor was identified as one of perseveration and was said by Brogden to bear "a considerable resemblance to Webb's 'w' factor." This would suggest a relationship between perseveration and neuroticism (since Eysenck (1953) has shown that Webb's "w" factor is the normal pole of a normal-neuroticism dimension).[1]

[1] Also using children (delinquents and normals), Clarke (1934) concluded that extremes of perseveration are associated with opposition to authority.

[1] Weisgerber (1954) has also related perseveration to neuroticism.

However, Cattell also found that "p"-scores were negatively correlated with his own E-factor (Dominance-Submission) which seems to be similar to Eysenck's I-E factor (Eysenck, *The Structure of Human Personality*, p. 64, 1953). In a further study on two hundred men and one hundred women, the correlation between dominance and rigidity was — 0·44. Furthermore, he found, like Pinard, that the relation of "p"-score to dominance was curvilinear—

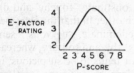

He concludes that "the factor of rigidity . . . is simply a relative inability to mould old habits, in one performance, to new ones . . . this means slowness of learning under the usual conditions of repetition of training . . . we shall assume that rigidity means a general slowness of learning." This *schema* also fits closely Eysenck's recent formulations characterizing the *introverted* neurotic as a rapid learner or over-socialized and the *extraverted* neurotic as a slow learner, or under-socialized. Cattell's final position, however, is far from clear.

It is clear from the definitions of primary and secondary function and their relationship to the deep-narrow and broad-shallow personality types that it would be predicted that high perseveration would be characteristic of introversion and low perseveration characteristic of extraversion in Eysenck's dimensional system; and that such a pattern would be expected to be found in normal subjects as well, since it is characteristic of introverts and extraverts, rather than neurotics. The findings of Cattell (1946*b*) and Pinard (1932*b*) in particular appear to support this hypothesis, especially in their suggestion of a curvilinear relationship indicating distinct groups of high and low perseverators.[1]

However, the careful study by Rim (1955) failed to reveal any evidence of a non-linear relationship between perseveration and neuroticism; failed to reveal any significant differences among neurotic subgroups which included hysterics and psychopaths, anxiety states and obsessives, and a mixed group of neurotics; and failed to reveal any correlation between perseveration and neuroticism on the one hand, or between perseveration and introversion-extraversion on the other. Similarly Petrie (1948) found no differences between hysterics and dysthymics on four tests of perseveration.

We must, therefore, conclude that factors of perseveration are of little importance in defining differences either between neurotics and normals or between extraverts and introverts. This is not surprising in view of the small amount of variance of the tests used to measure perseveration accounted for by the factors.[1,2]

FLUENCY[3]

Fluency tests constitute a classic example of the ideomotor type of psychomotor test, i.e. a verbal response following upon an "idea." The principal findings with respect to tests of fluency may be summarized as follows—

(i) The major variance of a battery of fluency tests can be accounted for by a general factor, which Rogers (1953) identifies as "g" plus Vernon's "v: ed" factor (verbal-educational).

(ii) Two orthogonal factors (in addition to the general factor) have been identified by Rogers (1953). The first factor is one of *oral* fluency; the second, a factor of *written* fluency. In independent studies, Rogers (1953, 1956) found that these three factors were extraordinarily stable, both as regards the tests which define them and the factor loadings of these tests.

(iii) Two further factors have been suggested by Rim (1955). One factor in his study defined three tests of oral verbal fluency where relatively *less constriction* is given in the instructions, viz. "towns," "trees" and "animals." This factor is the same as Rogers' factor of oral fluency. Rim's second factor defined three tests of oral verbal fluency where *more constriction* was given in the instructions, viz. "first letter A," "suffix -ion," and "anagrams." This factor is similar to a factor found by Rogers (1953) which he defined as "dealing with words in which one or more formal restrictions were placed on the response." The factor, however, cuts across the previous factors of oral and written fluency, since Rogers's study showed it was defined by both oral and written tests.[4] These results agree with earlier studies by Carroll (1941), Gewirtz (1948) and others.

(iv) Psychotics are significantly less fluent than either normals or neurotics. S. B. G. Eysenck

---

[1] Misiak and Pickford (1944), however, found results diametrically opposite; asthenic boys tended to be *low* perseverators; pyknic boys *high* perseverators.

[1] Mittenecker (1953) has recently proposed a new method for measuring perseveration, which is applicable to spoken or written language, 500–1,000 syllables in length; and has analysed the productions of cyclothyme and schizothyme normals, and psychotics.
[2] A similar conclusion was arrived at by Walker *et al.* (1945) and by Yule (1952), partly as a result of a logical examination of the nature of "p" tests and partly on the basis of the results of studies reviewed above.
[3] *See* Vernon (1950), Eysenck (1953), Rim (1953) and Rogers (1953, 1956) for reviews of the literature.
[4] Rim (1955) used only *oral* verbal tests.

(1955) found psychotics significantly poorer than either neurotics or normals (using three tests of relatively *less* constriction); while Eysenck (1952*a*) found similar results in a comparison of psychotics and normals only.

(v) The evidence for neurotic's being less fluent than normals is of doubtful significance. S. B. G. Eysenck (1955) found that they were, but to a much less degree than psychotics; while Rim (1955) could find no differences between normals and neurotics on six tests of fluency.[1]

(vi) Earlier suggestions that fluency may be related to differences in introversion-extraversion have not been confirmed. Petrie (1945) found no differences in fluency between hysterics and dysthymics, nor did Himmelweit (1946) and Rim (1955). Petrie (1945), however, did find that hysterics tend to make more *errors* than dysthymics under appropriately controlled test conditions.[2]

While the existence of various factors of fluency has clearly been demonstrated, therefore, it must be concluded that they have not been very useful in the analysis of differences in behaviour of different psychiatric groups.

PERSISTENCE[3]

(a) Dimensional Analysis of Persistence Tests

Like perseveration, persistence tests have been subjected to a great deal of experimentation in an effort to discover whether a unitary factor of persistence can be demonstrated or not. Much of the work has been unsatisfactory and inconclusive but on the whole appears to point to the existence of a general factor. However, the position was clarified considerably by the work of MacArthur (1951).[4] He intercorrelated twenty-two measures of persistence from which the influence of intellectual differences had been partialled out; 75 per cent of the correlations were positive, with 29 per cent significant. A factor analysis using simple structure revealed four factors: (1) a general persistence factor;[5] (2) a bipolar factor contrasting individual with group (prestige) persistence; (3) a bipolar factor contrasting reputation for persistence with objective evidence of persistence; (4) a factor of

persistence in a group of physical tests—holding foot over chair (leg persistence), maintained hand-grip (dynamometer), time of holding breath, and arm extension.

This last factor is relevant to the present chapter since it is measurable by tests of a psychomotor nature, particularly leg persistence and maintained hand-grip. The existence of such a factor has been demonstrated by other writers in addition to MacArthur. Thornton (1939) described a factor of "ability and/or willingness to withstand discomfort in order to achieve a goal" with high loadings on "time holding breath," "time standing shock," "time standing pressure," "maintained hand-grip."[1] Likewise Rethlingshafer (1942) described a factor of "willingness and/or ability to endure discomfort." As Eysenck (1953) points out the group factors of persistence demonstrated by MacArthur "are subject to measurement with a degree of validity probably not much below general persistence itself."

(b) Persistence and Personality

1. *Leg Persistence:* This test has been most commonly employed in studies with abnormals. The test is a very simple one, the subject usually being required to hold the leg outstretched one inch above the seat of a chair for as long as he can. The results obtained are conflicting and may be summarized as follows—

(i) Careful studies have shown that neurotics are not differentiated from normals in terms of persistence. Thus Eysenck (1952*a*) compared several groups of neurotics with normals; although all the neurotics had *lower* mean scores than the normal group, the differences were not significant. Similarly, S. B. G. Eysenck (1955) compared neurotics with normals and found no difference, as did Himmelweit and Petrie (1951) with neurotic and normal children. Ryans (1939) concludes from his review of the literature that non-persistent subjects "may show more pronounced leanings towards neuroticism and introversion than persistent persons" (introversion here is probably to be equated with neuroticism). However, this conclusion cannot be said to apply to motor persistence.

(ii) Several studies also suggest that there are no significant differences between hysterics and dysthymics on leg persistence (Eysenck, 1952*a*; S. B. G. Eysenck, 1955). Petrie (1948) on the other hand, found that dysthymics persevered over twice as long as hysterics.[2]

---

[1] Unfortunately, Rim's control group was small (N = 25) and rather unsatisfactory in its composition. Eysenck's (1955) results may be more reliable, therefore, in indicating a small but significant difference between neurotics and normals.

[2] In a recent study, Rogers (1956) found a significant relationship between fluency in dealing with words and Eysenck's introversion-extraversion factor. This finding would not appear to vitiate the conclusions arrived at above.

[3] *See* Ryans (1938*a*, 1939), Kremer (1942) and Eysenck (1953) for reviews of this topic.

[4] A detailed account of MacArthur's unpublished thesis is contained in Eysenck (pp. 288–290 *op. cit.*).

[5] Crutcher (1934) and Ryans (1938*b*) also found a general factor of persistence.

[1] Thornton did not think that this was a true persistence factor though he considered it might be related to persistence.

[2] Test instructions appear to play an important role in leg persistence tests. Thus S. B. G. Eysenck's (1955) neurotics showed very much greater persistence than did those tested by Petrie and Eysenck; but in the S. B. G. Eysenck (1955) study, the subjects were allowed to flex the leg if they wished.

(iii) Eysenck (1952*a*) found no differences between normals and psychotics in leg persistence.

2. *Dynamometer Persistence:* In this test, strength of grip is usually measured first and the subject then required to squeeze for as long as possible at half or two-thirds the maximum strength.

The major findings with this test are as follows—

(i) S. B. G. Eysenck (1955) reported that neurotics showed significantly less persistence than normals. As, however, the neurotics showed a much weaker initial maximum grip, it is possible that this affected their subsequent persistence. Similar results for normal *v.* neurotic children were reported by Himmelweit and Petrie (1957).

(ii) No comparisons are available for dysthymics and hysterics separately.

(iii) S. B. G. Eysenck (1955) also reported that psychotics showed significantly less persistence than normals (with the same reservations as to initial strength of grip). The psychotics did not differ from the neurotics in persistence.

WORK DECREMENT[1]

The "curve of work" (Thorndike, 1912) (i.e. the changes occurring in performance under conditions of prolonged performance of mental or physical work) has mediated a large amount of research on normal subjects. The work studied may be either physical in nature (e.g. ergographic) or "mental" (e.g. continual addition, naming colours, etc.). Among the major trends noted in the objective work curve are (*a*) warm-up effect; (*b*) practice effect; (*c*) spurts and rhythms; (*d*) general (work) decrement; (*e*) blocking. The two latter phenomena are of particular importance. Work decrement refers to the decline in amount of work done per unit time during a period of continuous practice. Blocking refers to temporary complete stoppages of work under the same conditions of practice. Such blockages and work decrements have been observed in both physical and mental work but are more easily observed in the former since the phenomena appear to be directly related to the lack of rest pauses. Such rest pauses are naturally more common in "continuous" physical work than in "continuous" mental work. However, under appropriate conditions of forced continuous mental work (such as naming colours) the involuntary blockages can be readily observed.

Both phenomena have been considered to be functions of fatigue[2] induced by continuous work.

Blockings could be obviated by enforcing rest pauses at about the same rate; while they could be increased by making the material more homogeneous. Thus, where conditions of work were most homogeneous, the average blocks per minute were 2·1; where they were least homogeneous, only 1·4 per minute (Robinson and Bills, 1926).[1]

The phenomena involved in the work curve have, of course, long attracted the attention of psychologists (Thorndike, 1912). However, little attention has been paid to the possibilities such phenomena offered in the investigation of abnormal subjects. Apart from the early work of Kraepelin (1902) and Hoch (1901) little information was available until very recently. Kraepelin had found that the performance of schizophrenics on a simple ten-minute addition test was characterized by rapid deterioration; if a rest was introduced after five minutes, performance increased markedly on the sixth minute, but then deteriorated rapidly again in the remaining four minutes. Hoch, on the other hand, reported that manic-depressives increased in strength of performance on the ergograph in the early stages of performance before showing the usual fatigue effects.

Since these early studies, little work has been done in this field. Mailloux and Newburger (1941) presented patients with a task involving four coloured lights with corresponding keys. Depression of the appropriate key extinguished a light and served to activate another. Thus continuous work was carried on for ten minutes. Patients were classified into six groups according to speed and type of response activity. Compared with the normal rate of seventy-two responses per minute, psychotics averaged a response rate of only 52·5, only one psychotic exceeding the normal mean. Psychotics averaged five blocks per minute compared with three for the normal group. Mailloux and Newburger found no relationship between work curve and blocking on the one hand and type of psychosis on the other.

More recently, using a very similar method, Venables and Tizard (1956*c*) and O'Connor *et al.* (1956) have repeated the study of Mailloux and Newburger. Venables and Tizard found an initial rise in performance (probably due to practice effects) followed by a fall, a further rise after rest and subsequent deterioration in schizophrenics. Long-stay schizophrenics performed consistently below short-stay schizophrenics at all stages of performance. A group of endogenous depressives were intermediate between the two schizophrenic groups but showed no

---

[1] *See* Bills (in Andrews *Methods of Psychology*, Chap. 16, 1948), and Robinson (1934) for excellent reviews of this subject.

[2] It has been shown conclusively that such "fatigue" is not entirely peripheral, i.e. muscular.

[1] The main work on this topic has been carried out by Bills (1931, 1935, 1937, 1943), Bills and Shapiro (1936), Robinson (1926), Robinson and Bills (1926). *See also* Poffenberger (1927), Freeman and Wonderlie (1935), Warren and Clark (1937), Huxtable *et al.* (1946) and Philip (1939*a*, 1939*b*, 1939*c*, 1940).

deterioration in performance, either before or after the rest pauses.[1]

It seems clear, therefore, that schizophrenics do show blockings and rapid work decrement compared with normals. This conclusion is supported by a recent study of Baruk *et al.* (1953). No information is available concerning the performance of neurotics.[1]

III. DISCUSSION

THE bewildering and often contradictory results brought together above do not mediate any obvious theories concerning the behaviour on psychomotor tests of neurotics and psychotics as compared with normals. For reasons which will be discussed below this is not surprising. However, some tentative suggestions will be made concerning possible reasons for those differences which are generally clear-cut.

Four relatively definite statements may be made concerning the psychomotor behaviour of abnormals and normals.

1. Compared with normal subjects, neurotics show no significant disorganization on *simple* psychomotor tasks (and may actually be better than normals). They do, however, show marked disorganization compared with normals on *complex* psychomotor tasks. This disorganization is not a function of lower intelligence or poorer special abilities.[2]

2. Within the total neurotic subgroup, there is evidence that introverted neurotics (i.e. dysthymics) show a different kind of motor disorganization compared with extraverted neurotics (i.e. hysterics); this difference is found also in normal extraverts and introverts.

3. Compared with normal subjects, psychotics show significant disorganization on both *simple* and *complex* psychomotor tasks.

4. There is some evidence that psychomotor tests which discriminate best between neurotics and normals are different from those which discriminate best between psychotics and normals, i.e. that psychosis and neurosis represent different dimensions.

In the following discussion, four important points should be borne in mind—

1. The differences outlined above refer to differences in *performance*, not to differences in *learning*. This distinction has become an important matter in theories of behaviour in recent years. The frequent failure to control for differences in learning ability before measuring differences in level of performance (i.e. when learning has been maximized) is extremely unfortunate and has undoubtedly contributed to much of the confusion prevailing in this field.

2. The method adopted above of summarizing the main findings in terms of type of response required (e.g. reaction-time, tapping, etc.) was dictated by the prevailing method of experimenting on two groups by comparing their performance on a single task. This method is particularly inappropriate in this field, since psychomotor tests are often short and correspondingly unreliable. It is extremely dangerous, therefore, to draw conclusions from studies using a single test. Psychomotor tests should be used as one strand among others in the investigation and testing of theories concerning abnormalities of behaviour. They can rarely be used satisfactorily on their own.

3. A major difficulty in interpreting the results of diverse studies in relation to a given theory is that the analysis of results of earlier studies may be quite inappropriate. A good example of this is the interpretation of the work of Davis (1948) outlined above. Davis showed that introverted neurotics gave a characteristically different kind of manual response as compared with extraverted neurotics. Now it would seem reasonable to suppose that similar results would be expected from the Luria (1932) test. Unfortunately, although much valuable work has been done on the Luria and although it is clear that neurotics do show motor disorganization in this test, it is difficult from the earlier studies to determine whether introverted and extraverted neurotics showed different kinds of responses comparable to those found by Davis, since no precise analysis of this kind has been carried out.[2] Thus it is possible only to point out that such differences would be expected if the Luria results were analysed in a particular way.

4. Very similar to this difficulty is the problem of negative results. The often repeated dictum that one negative result invalidates a theory is only a half-truth. It is true only if the experiment is sufficiently precisely controlled that a negative result will have an unequivocal interpretation. Now this is seldom true in the field of psychology. Let us suppose our theory

---

[1] This study of Venables and Tizard is open to serious criticism on the grounds of a failure to separate their endogenous depressive group into a short-stay and long-stay group. It is possible that, had they done so, the performance of the two groups would have been similar to those of the short-stay and long-stay schizophrenics, in which case the effects obtained could be due to either (*a*) length of stay; (*b*) psychoticism as such; or (*c*) an interaction of these two variables.

[2] Psychomotor tests have proved among the most useful measures for defining the factor of "neuroticism" by factorial methods. *See*, for example, the study by Himmelweit *et al.* (1946).

[1] The study by Christensen (1945) on neurotics has not been available for consultation.

[2] As pointed out earlier, several studies do, however, suggest that such differences exist.

predicts that extraverted neurotics will have a slower rate of tapping than introverted neurotics due to the more rapid growth of reactive inhibition in the former group. The analysis of the results in terms of number of taps per unit time may show no significant differences between the groups. This does not necessarily mean that the hypothesis has to be abandoned. The failure to find significant differences may be in the method of analysis adopted. A study by Boder (1935) is relevant. He showed that even such a simple activity as tapping has at least four components (movement up, upper reversal, movement down and bottom reversal). By means of oscillograph recordings he found that between both progressions there is a definite stop, which, in finger tapping, lasts from twice to four times as long as the progressions. He found that concomitant activities led to reduced speed, alterations in pattern of tapping, *differences in duration of arrested movement*, and reduction in tapping excursion. Now it is possible that taking an overall tapping rate as score on this test obscures significant differences in duration of arrested movement since extraverted neurotics may well "catch up" on other aspects of performance. In other words the prediction is relevant only to one aspect of performance and failure to isolate that aspect may lead to negative results in relation to the theory. This point should be remembered in all instances where negative results are obtained, especially where the theory is supported by other evidence.[1]

With these cautions in mind a brief review will be given of some theories which have been advanced to explain the results summarized above.

Psychomotor Performance of Neurotics

The following postulates help to account for the observed differences between neurotics and normals in psychomotor tasks and mediate new predictions which support the general theory—

1. Performance in the test situation may be conceptualized as dependent upon the interaction of drive strength and task complexity.[2]

2. Neurotics are characterized by high drive.

3. High drive may also be defined in terms of the strength of a stimulus. Thus a strong stimulus will have high drive value; a weak stimulus low drive value.[3]

4. Where the response required is simple, it will be facilitated by high drive.

5. Where the response required has to be chosen from among others (i.e. discrimination is involved), it will be impeded in its appearance by high drive.

The above postulates would mediate the following predictions—

(*a*) Neurotics will show psychomotor disorganization compared with normal subjects on complex but not simple tasks. The evidence in favour of this has been reviewed at length above.

(*b*) An increase in the strength of the stimulus will lead to an increased amplitude and speed of response in normal subjects. This prediction has been abundantly verified particularly in the field of reaction-time studies. Thus Johnson (1922) in an early study showed that increasing the strength of the stimulus led to a faster R.T., as did Chocholle (1945); Steinman and Veniar (1944) found that faster reactions to a constant stimulus ratio were obtained at the stronger of two levels of visual intensity. Higher muscular tension levels (Travis and Kennedy, 1947), increased motivation (Hipple, 1954) and mild electric shock (Henry, 1951) all facilitate speed of simple reaction-time. Above a certain intensity, however, a stimulus ceases to facilitate response and begins to inhibit it. This was shown by Johnson (1922) and by Pascal (1953) who found that when a loud disturbing noise was given with the ready signal for reaction-time, some subjects showed complete disruption of performance. This result would be expected from the Yerkes-Dodson law since it specifies *optimal* levels of intensity for most adequate performance.

Henry (1951) also showed that mild electric shock significantly speeded up speed of snatching a ball and speed of treadle pressing.

(*c*) An increase in induced anxiety in normals (usually by means of some stressful situation) will facilitate amplitude and speed of simple responses.[1] Thus, Ross *et al.* (1954) found that speed of tapping increased significantly with an increase in anxiety just before the subject engaged in a boxing match. An important study relevant here is that by Castaneda (1956) which links anxiety as drive and stimulus intensity as drive. His subjects were high- and low-anxiety[2] high-school boys and girls; the stimulus a buzzer with two intensities; the response, squeezing a dynamometer; and the scores recorded, amplitude and speed of reaction. On the theory

---

[1] Similarly, Earle and Gaw (1930) analysed manual and finger dexterity into three types of movement.

[2] This is, of course, a reformulation of the Yerkes-Dodson law (Yerkes and Dodson (1908); Dodson (1915)) that the optimum intensity of drive (shock) varies inversely with the difficulty of discrimination.

[3] The second postulate could also be written in these terms, i.e. that high drive in neurotics means that a stimulus having low drive value for normals will have high drive value for neurotics.

---

[1] There is no clear-cut division between this section and the previous one. *See* Lazarus *et al.* (1952) for a discussion of the effects of stress upon performance.

[2] Determined by scores on the Taylor Anxiety Scale (Taylor, 1953) which Franks (1956) has shown is mainly a measure of neuroticism.

that differences in intensity produce differences in relevant drive and differences in anxiety produce differences in irrelevant drive he predicted that (1) speed of reaction of anxious subjects should be faster than that of non-anxious subjects; and (2) the increase in speed of reaction attributed to increased stimulus intensity should be relatively greater for non-anxious subjects, thus reducing the difference between anxious and non-anxious subjects. With regard to amplitude Castaneda found that anxious subjects did indeed show significantly higher amplitude at weak intensities and that there was a greater increase with the more intense stimulus in non-anxious as compared with anxious (though the latter finding held only for boys). With regard to speed of reaction, Castaneda found no difference at the weaker intensity between anxious and non-anxious subjects and contrary to prediction found a greater increase in speed at the higher intensity for the anxious subjects.[1]

(d) Whereas increasing stimulus strength, inducing anxiety or stress in normals appears on the whole to facilitate response amplitude and speed in normals where the response required is simple in nature, it is predicted from the theory that the same factors would disrupt performance where the response required had to be selected from a range of possible choices or where the response itself is of a complex nature. There is a reasonable amount of evidence indicating the correctness of this prediction. Thus, a study by Grice (1955) indicates a significant increase in discrimination response time under conditions of induced anxiety or stress[2] and this is supported by the work of Patrick (1934a, 1934b).

Several studies on induced conflict (stress) indicate that "the probability of blockage as a reaction to conflict increases with the approach of the strengths of the conflicting responses to equality" (Sears and Hovland, 1941) and this conclusion is supported by several other studies (Hovland and Sears, 1938; Cartwright, 1941a, 1941b; Festinger and Wapner, 1947).

Similarly, it has been shown that complex motor reactions deteriorate markedly under stress in normal subjects. This holds for steadiness (Edwards, 1948; Kellogg, 1932; Parsons et al., 1954; Seashore and Koch, 1938; Ross et al., 1954); the work curve

(Burghmann, 1939) and more complex tasks (Lofchie, 1955; Russell, 1932; Starer, 1942; Hill, 1954; Canestrelli, 1941).

Thus we may reasonably conclude with Davis (1947) that in normal subjects "under conditions . . . in which . . . anticipatory tension was increased, skilled responses were more extensive, more precipitate, more disturbed by restless movements and less accurate than single conditions (simple stimuli) in which anticipatory tension was normal." The above results and those reported in the body of the chapter do seem to support the hypothesis that neurotics are characterized by a high state of drive which facilitates the correct response in a simple situation but impedes the correct response in a complex situation.

Psychomotor Performance of Introverts and Extraverts

Little can be said about this aspect of performance in psychomotor tasks, except to repeat that it seems to be clearly established that the *type* of motor response on a given task will differ for extraverts as compared with introverts where the appropriate experimental conditions are set. Within the neurotic disorganization apparent on complex tasks, hysterics will tend to react differently as compared with dysthymics. The main evidence for this proposition derives from the work of Davis (1946a, 1946b, 1947, 1948, 1949a, 1949b), which has been discussed above in detail, but similar differences could no doubt be obtained on tests such as those of the Luria, under appropriate conditions.[1]

That there are two major types of psychomotor response within both normal and neurotic groups is also suggested in the work of Chorus (1942, 1943) on abnormal children (that arising from diffusion of attention and that arising from lethargy); Fauville et al. (1937) (who distinguished the impulsive from the precise mode of motor reaction); Schleier (1939) (who distinguished extraverted from introverted types of movement); and Yarmolenko (1930) who distinguished the excitable type of child (rapid irregular movement) from the inhibited type (slower, more regular and more intense motions). The similarity of these types to those of Davis is clear.

Eysenck (1955) has postulated that differences between introverts and extraverts are due to differences in the rate of growth, magnitude and persistence of reactive inhibition, hysterics being characterized by rapid growth of inhibition, dysthymics by slow growth of inhibition. A number of experiments are reported by him which support this hypothesis, as does work by Broadbent (1953, 1956), including his interpretation

---

[1] Similar studies have been carried out by Wenar (1954) and Farber and Spence (1956) with conflicting results. They indicate neatly the problems involved in testing hypotheses of this nature. Thus, in the work of both Castaneda, and Farber and Spence, two major problems make negative results difficult to interpret, i.e., the adequacy of the strength of the anxiety (induced or otherwise) and the adequacy of the differences in intensity of stimulation.

[2] Grice, however, attributes the differences between his high and low anxiety groups to differences in intelligence.

[1] Descriptively, Davis's differentiation of hysterics as "inert" and dysthymics as "overactive," corresponds with Himmelweit's (1946) differentiation of hysterics as preferring speed to accuracy from dysthymics as preferring accuracy to speed.

of the results of Mackworth (1948) on errors in continuous watch-keeping. However, Eysenck's specific predictions made on the basis of his inhibitory-excitatory potential differences in extraverts and introverts have not so far included psychomotor tests. These tests would, it is clear, be eminently suitable for precise predictions in terms of the theory, particularly those tests involving continuous performance such as is involved in the study of the work decrement. There is here a rich field of investigation, which remains to be explored.[1]

Psychomotor Performance of Psychotics

Three explanatory models will be mentioned and briefly discussed in connexion with the psychomotor performance of psychotics.

1. The dissociative-integrative hypothesis of Kretschmer has mediated a large amount of experimental work.[2] By dissociation Kretschmer means the ability to form separate and partial groupings within a single act of consciousness; from this results the ability to dissect complex material into its constituent parts. Normal schizothymes (and schizophrenics) are said to be characterized by dissociative capacity; normal cyclothymes (and manic-depressives) by integrative capacity. In efforts to demonstrate the validity of this thesis, Kretschmer and his students made extensive use of psychomotor tests. Thus, on the basis of the theory it was predicted (and experimental evidence was brought forward in support) that leptosomes[3] would be superior to pyknics in the following tasks—

(a) Simultaneous performance on more than one psychomotor task, e.g. addition of numbers and calling out of numbers (Enke, 1928; Enke, 1930; Gurewitsch and Oseretzky, 1930; Schorn, 1928).[4]

(b) Motor activities, e.g. manual dexterity, quality of handwriting, bimanual co-ordination, fine steadiness test (Enke, 1929, 1930).

(c) Speed of motor activity, e.g. tapping (Enke, 1930).

(d) Speed of reaction-time under distraction (Kibler, 1925; Van der Horst, 1924).

Subsequent work, however (which overcame most of the obvious defects of the above studies, such as lack of statistical analysis of results, tests of significance and control of relevant factors such as sex, I.Q., age, etc.) has refuted Kretschmer's theory. Two lines of evidence may be quoted.

(i) Payne (1954) has shown conclusively that the tests used by Kretschmer as a measure of dissociative differences between schizothymes and cyclothymes do not define a factor of "dissociation" (the correlations between a large number of measures, including many specified by Kretschmer and others derived from the theory, clustered about zero and were distributed in accordance with the null hypothesis that there was no general factor). Hence it follows that these tests cannot be used to support Kretschmer's hypothesis and, indeed, refute it as an explanatory principle.[1]

(ii) In a number of studies, Eysenck (1952a, 1952b) has shown that there is no evidence for the existence of a dimension of cyclothymia-schizothymia, such as is required by Kretschmer's theory; but that there is evidence for a dimension of psychoticism-normality. In other words, on tests of the type used by Kretschmer, manic-depressives do *not* tend to fall at one end of a distribution of scores, schizophrenics at the other, and normals in the middle, as would be expected if Kretschmer's theory were correct. Rather *both* manic-depressives and schizophrenics tend to do *worse* than normals on those tests which distinguish the three groups, with schizophrenics falling in between normals and manic-depressives.

It would seem, therefore, that Kretschmer's concept of "dissociation" must be abandoned as an explanatory principle and research directed towards the solution of the problem that psychotics as a whole perform more poorly than normals on certain psychomotor tests.[2]

2. A hypothesis which has received surprisingly little attention since it was originally proposed is that of Shakow (1946) and his colleagues who account for

---

[1] It seems likely that research in this field will prove to be extremely complex. Thus, in the simple leg persistence task, performance may be a function of at least two drives and rate of growth of inhibition in neurotics. Hence, dysthymics will have a strong drive to avoid discomfort, a strong drive to carry out the instructions, and a slow rate of growth of inhibition; while hysterics would have a strong drive to avoid discomfort, a weak drive to conform with instructions and a rapid growth of inhibition.

[2] The literature has been reviewed in detail by Eysenck (1950) and by Payne (1954), the latter with respect to the hypothesized trait of *Spaltungsfähigkeit*.

[3] As Eysenck (1950) points out, Kretschmer tried to show the general validity of the concept of schizothymia-cyclothymia beyond the psychotic realm by using body build as a *tertium quid*; his method of proof was to show that normal people of leptosomatic or pyknic body build react to certain psychological experiences in a manner similar to that of schizophrenes and manic-depressives, who are known to be also leptosomatic or pyknic.

[4] Schorn's study was one of the few of Kretschmer's school which obtained negative results.

[1] This is not, of course, to say that the *differences* found by Kretschmer between e.g. schizophrenics and manic-depressives do not exist; but simply that such differences cannot be accounted for in terms of the postulated mode of reaction.

[2] But not on all such tests. As Eysenck (1952a) has shown, "those tests which had in past work been shown to have high correlation with neuroticism, or to discriminate well between neurotics and normals, do not show even a tendency to discriminate between normals and psychotics." Such tests include persistence, body sway, perseveration and work curve inversions.

the poor performance of schizophrenics on psycho-motor (and many other) tests in terms of failure of set. Table II.11 shows the results obtained for two groups of schizophrenics (selected and total) and normal controls on tests of steadiness, tapping, reac-tion-time (simple auditory and discriminatory visual) and prodmeter which illustrates quite clearly the highly significant results obtained. With regard to differences obtained under conditions of regular and irregular preparatory intervals in the reaction-time

3. Three recent studies by Venables and Tizard (1956a, 1956b, 1956c) have attempted to account for differences between schizophrenics and normals in terms of the growth of reactive inhibition. They base their hypothesis chiefly on the work of Pavlov (1941) who showed that dogs with weak inhibitory, nervous systems in whom pathological disturbances of the cortex are induced by means of functional interference tend to respond to conditioned stimuli with "para-doxical" responses (in which weak stimuli call forth a

TABLE II.11

SCORES OF SCHIZOPHRENICS AND NORMALS ON PSYCHOMOTOR TESTS

(From D. Shakow, "The Nature of Deterioration," 1946)

Variable	Normal			Total Schizophrenics			Selected Schizophrenics			CRs		
	N	M	σ	N	M	σ	N	M	σ	N/TS	N/SS	TS/SS
Steadiness score . . .	64	120·0	65·1	135	62·3	54·3	25	67·9	42·5	6·1	4·5	0·6
Tapping mean . . .	60	28·9	4·2	125	19·5	5·6	25	21·4	5·2	13·2	6·7	1·7
R.T. Simple auditory .	25	167	30	38	357	182	25	325	54	5·5	12·6	1·0
Discriminatory visual .	25	373	51	38	676	253	24	627	258	5·8	4·1	0·7
Prodmeter time . .	62	24·6	3·2	125	34·9	12·0	24	31·5	6·0	8·0	5·5	1·5
Errors	62	32·6	4·1	125	43·0	14·6	24	43·6	7·1	7·5	7·0	0·3

experiments, Rodnick and Shakow (1940) concluded: "Although the patients are able to maintain a com-paratively high preparatory set during the shorter intervals of the regular as compared to the irregular procedure, they have greater difficulty than do normals in maintaining the advantage. As a result they fall back upon a lower level of preparation at the longer intervals. This simpler adaptive level is essentially the same as that used in reacting in the irregular proce-dure, the conditions of which do not favour an optimal level of response." The Set Index derived by Rodnick and Shakow from their results discriminated without overlap between schizophrenics and normals in that study.

Recently Tizard and Venables (1956) repeated the work of Rodnick and Shakow and obtained as striking results using the Set Index. They discuss alternative theories to account for the results, such as blocking, differences between fast and slow responders among the schizophrenics, and differences between normals and schizophrenics in the rate of build-up of reactive inhibition. No evidence was found in the data to support any of these alternative hypotheses. Hence, the findings of Shakow and his colleagues and their hypothesis to explain them remains a challenge which should stimulate much more investigation than it has so far done.

larger conditioned response than do strong stimuli) and "ultraparadoxical" effects (in which excitatory stimuli are converted into inhibitory ones and in-hibitory stimuli into excitatory ones). Such stimuli are said to be of ultramarginal strength. According to Pavlov schizophrenic withdrawal and negativism are examples of paradoxical and ultraparadoxical pheno-mena. In two studies (1956a, 1956b) using different intensities of visual stimulus, Venables and Tizard did indeed find that chronic schizophrenics responded more quickly to weak stimuli than to strong.[1] In another study (1956c) they showed that on a repetitive task chronic schizophrenics fell away more quickly than did normals. These results are interpreted as due to the more rapid growth of reactive inhibition in schizophrenics. This hypothesis also helps to account for the recovery shown after rest, since this would be due to the dissipation of reactive inhibition.[2]

The results obtained by Venables and Tizard are striking and merit intensive further research in spite of the criticisms levelled earlier at the deficiencies of experimental control. However, it should be remem-bered that Tizard and Venables (1956) failed to obtain

[1] Compare the effects found with neurotics and normals above.

[2] The duration of the task is too short to enable normal subjects to develop significant amounts of reactive inhibition.

evidence that reactive inhibition had anything to do with the results obtained in the Rodnick-Shakow type of experiment;[1] that the differences they refer to may be a result of *basal* level of inhibition rather than differences in rate of growth of inhibition; and that, in view of Eysenck's work reported above (*see also* S. B. G., Eysenck, 1956), their differences may well be related to *psychoticism* rather than to schizophrenia *per se*.[2] Finally, attention should be drawn to the fact that Venables and Tizard (among others) have consistently obtained significant differences between acute and chronic schizophrenics and it is at least possible, therefore, that these differences are not related to the specific illness as such, but to an interaction effect between illness and length of stay in hospital.

It is clear from the above review that psychomotor tests have had a long and fruitful history in abnormal psychology. They have, however, proved to be of most value when used for testing specific hypotheses. In view of the recent tendency in this field for theory to assume a more significant role, there is no reason to doubt that they will prove even more useful in the future.

REFERENCES

ALBINO, R. C., The stable and labile personality types of Luria in clinically normal individuals, *Brit. J. Psychol.*, **39**, 54–60 (1948).

ANDREWS, T. G. (Ed.), *Methods of Psychology* (London, Chapman & Hall, Ltd., 1948).

AVELING, F. and HARGREAVES, H. L., Suggestibility with and without prestige in children, *Brit. J. Psychol.*, **12**, 53–75 (1921).

BALL, R. J., An objective measure of emotional stability, *J. Appl. Psychol.*, **13**, 226–256 (1929).

BARNACLE, C. H., EBAUGH, F. G. and LEMERE, F., Association-motor investigations of the psychoneuroses, *Amer. J. Psychiat.*, **91**, 925–937 (1935).

BARUK, H., LIFSCHITZ, A. G. Y. and MELZER, R., Étude de l'initiative psychomotrice et de la mise en train volontaire chez le sujet normal et en psychopathologie, *Encéphale*, **42**, 193–218 (1953).

BAUMGARTNER, M., The correlation of direct suggestibility with certain character traits, *J. Appl. Psychol.*, **15**, 1–15 (1931).

BAYLEY, M. and ESPENSCHADE, A., Motor development and decline, *Rev. Educ. Res.*, **20**, 367–374 (1950).

BENTON, A. L. and BANDURA, A., "Primary" and "Secondary" suggestibility, *J. Abnorm. (Soc) Psychol.*, **48**, 336–340 (1953).

BERREMAN, J. V. and HILGARD, E. R., The effects of personal hetero-suggestion and two forms of auto-suggestion upon postural movement, *J. Soc. Psychol.*, **7**, 289–299 (1936).

BEVAN-LEWIS, W., Reaction times in certain forms of insanity, in Tuke: *Dictionary of Psychological Medicine*, **2**, 1063–1067 (1892).

BIESHEUVEL, S. and PITT, D. R., The relationship between secondary function and some aspects of speed and tempo of behaviour, *Acta Psychol.*, *Hague* **11**, 373–396 (1955).

BILLS, A. G., Blocking: a new principle of mental fatigue, *Amer. J. Psychol.*, **43**, 230–245 (1931).

BILLS, A. G., Fatigue, oscillation and blocks, *J. Exp. Psychol.*, **18**, 562–573 (1935).

BILLS, A. G., Blocking: mental and anoxaemia compared, *J. Exp. Psychol.*, **20**, 437–452 (1937).

BILLS, A. G., *Psychological Efficiency* (New York, Harper & Bros., 1943).

BILLS, A. G. and SHAPIRO, K. J., Mental fatigue under automatically controlled rates of work, *J. Gen. Psychol.*, **15**, 335–347 (1936).

BODER, D. P., The influence of concomitant activity and fatigue upon certain forms of reciprocal hand movement and its fundamental components, *Comp. Psychol. Monogr.*, **11**, 4 (1935).

BONNET, D., L'apprentissage d'un test de barrage; aspects significatifs des courbes obtenues chez des malades mentaux, *Encéphale*, **42**, 101–136 (1953).

BRANDT, H., Evasion and a manifold association test, *Univ. Ia Stud. Child Welf.*, **13**, 25–50 (1937).

BROADBENT, D. E., Classical conditioning and human watch-keeping, *Psychol. Rev.*, **60**, 331–339 (1953).

BROADBENT, D. E., Inhibition and extraversion, *Quart. Bull. Brit. Psychol.*, *Soc.*, (1956).

BROGDEN, H. E., A factor analysis of forty character tests, *Psychol. Monogr.*, **52**, 3 (1940).

BROWER, D., The relations of visuo-motor conflict to personality traits and cardiovascular activity, *J. Gen. Psychol.*, **38**, 69–99 (1948).

BURGHMANN, J., The effect of distraction, both manual and mental, on the ergograph curve, *Austr. J. Psychol.*, *Phil.*, **17**, 273–276 (1939).

BURRI, C., The present status of the problem of individual differences in alternating activities, *Psychol. Bull.*, **32**, 113–139 (1935).

BURTT, H. E., Motor concomitants of the association-motor reaction, *J. Exp. Psychol.*, **19**, 51–64 (1936).

CAMERON, D. E. and CAUNT, T. G. B., Studies in perseveration, *J. Ment. Sci.*, **79**, 735–745 (1933).

CANESTRELLI, L., (Aspects of personality revealed by the processes of psychomotor adaptation. Psychological analysis of a reactive voluntary act with the photocyclographic method), *Arch. Psicol. Neur. Psich.*, **2**, 272–379 (1941).

CANESTRELLI, L., La psicometricita ed i suoi attributi essenziali, *Arch. Psicol. Neur. Psich.*, **13**, 349–371 (1952).

CARROLL, J. B., A factor analysis of verbal abilities, *Psychometrika*, **6**, 279–307 (1941).

CARTWRIGHT, D., Decision time in relation to the differentiation of the phenomenal field, *Psychol., Rev.*, **48**, 425–442 (1941*a*).

CARTWRIGHT, D., Relation of decision time to the categories of response, *Amer. J. Psychol.*, **54**, 174–196 (1941*b*).

---

[1] Here again, however, it should be remembered that the experimental conditions may not have been very appropriate for the development of reactive inhibition which is best seen under conditions of *massed*, i.e., very continuous work.

[2] It will be recalled that the supposed differences between schizophrenics and manic-depressives referred to by Venables and Tizard were criticized above.

CASTANEDA, A., Reaction time and response amplitude as a function of anxiety and stimulus intensity, *J. Abnorm. (Soc.) Psychol.*, **53**, 225–228 (1956).

CATTELL, R. B., On the measurement of perseveration, *Brit. J. Educ. Psychol.*, **5**, 76–92 (1935a).

CATTELL, R. B., Temperament tests in clinical practice, *Brit. J. Med. Psychol.*, **16**, 43–61 (1935b).

CATTELL, R. B., Perseveration and personality. Some experiments and a hypothesis, *J. Ment. Sci.*, **61**, 151–167 (1935c).

CATTELL, R. B., The riddle of perseveration: I. "Creative effort" and disposition rigidity, *J. Personality*, **14**, 229–238 (1946a).

CATTELL, R. B., The riddle of perseveration: II. Solution in terms of personality structure, *J. Personality*, **14**, 239–267 (1946b).

CATTELL, R. B. and TINER, L. G., The varieties of structural rigidity, *J. Personality*, **17**, 321–341 (1949).

CHOCHOLLE, R., Variations des temps de la réaction auditive en fonction de l'intensité à diverses fréquences, *Année Psychol.*, **41–42**, 65–124 (1945).

CHOCHOLLE, R., Quelques remarques sur les variations et la variabilité des temps des réactions auditives, *J. Psychol. norm. path.*, **41**, 345–358 (1948).

CHORUS, A., (The diagnostic value of the so-called personal rhythm.) *Alg. neder. tijdschr. wijsbegeert Psychol.*, **35**, 173–179 (1942).

CHORUS, A., (The personal rhythm and the rhythm of work in unstable children.) *Z. Kinderpsychiat.*, **10**, 40–51 (1943).

CHRISTENSEN, B. C., Studies on the effort syndrome; the patient's capacity for work and the variations in the arterial pressures and pulse rate during muscular work, compared with the condition found in normals, *Acta med. scand.*, **121**, 194–216 (1945).

CLARKE, A. D. B., The measurement of emotional instability by means of objective tests. An experimental inquiry, *Unpubl. Ph. D. Thesis, Univ. of London Lib.* (1950).

CLARKE, G., Some character traits of delinquent and normal children in terms of perseveration factor, *Aust. Counc. Educ. Res. Serv.*, No. 29 (1934).

CRUTCHER, R., An experimental study of persistence, *J. Appl. Psychol.*, **18**, 409–417 (1934).

DAVIS, D. R., The disorganization of behaviour in fatigue, *J. Neurol. Psychiat.*, **9**, 23–29 (1946a).

DAVIS, D. R., Neurotic predisposition and the disorganization observed in experiments with the Cambridge cockpit, *J. Neurol. Psychiat.*, **9**, 119–124 (1946b).

DAVIS, D. R., Disorders of skill: an experimental approach to some problems of neurosis, *Proc. Roy. Soc. Med.*, **40**, 583–584 (1947).

DAVIS, D. R., *Pilot Error. Some Laboratory Experiments* (London, H.M.S.O, 1948).

DAVIS, D. R., Increase in strength of a secondary drive as a cause of disorganization, *Quart. J. Exp. Psychol.*, **1**, 22–28 (1949a).

DAVIS, D. R., The disorder of skill responsible for accidents, *Quart. J. Exp. Psychol.*, **1**, 136–142 (1949b).

DODSON, J. D., The relation of strength of stimulus to rapidity of habit formation, *J. Anim. Behav.*, **5**, 330–336 (1915).

DONDERS, F. C., *On the Physiological Characteristics of Psychic Processes* (1865).

EARLE, F. M. and GAW, F., The measurement of manual dexterities, *Nat. Inst. Industr. Psychol.*, Rep. No. 4 (1930).

EBAUGH, F. G., Association motor investigation in clinical psychiatry, *J. Ment. Sci.*, **82**, 731–743 (1936).

EDWARDS, A. S., The measurement of static ataxia, *Amer. J. Psychol.*, **55**, 171–188 (1942).

EDWARDS, A. S., Body sway and vision, *J. Exp. Psychol.*, **36**, 526–535 (1946a).

EDWARDS, A. S., The finger tremometer, *Amer. J. Psychol.*, **59**, 273–283 (1946b).

EDWARDS, A. S., Body sway and non-visual factors, *J. Psychol.*, **23**, 241–254 (1947).

EDWARDS, A. S., Finger tremor and battle sounds, *J. Abnorm. (Soc.) Psychol.*, **43**, 396–399 (1948).

EDWARDS, A. S., Measurement of involuntary movement in the feeble minded, *Psychol. Serv. Cent. J.*, **3**, 153–155 (1950).

EDWARDS, A. S. and HARRIS, A. C., Laboratory measurements of deterioration and improvement among schizophrenics, *J. Gen. Psychol.*, **49**, 153–156 (1953).

EISENSON, J. A., Note on the perseverating tendency in stutterers, *J. Genet. Psychol.*, **50**, 195–198 (1937).

ENKE, W., Experimentalpsychologische Studien zur Konstitutionsforschung (Sinnes-und Denkpsychologische Untersuchungen), *Z. ges. Neurol. Psychiat.*, **114**, 770–794 (1928).

ENKE, W., Experimentalpsychologische Studien zur Konstitutionsforschung (Psychomotorische Untersuchungen), *Z. ges. Neurol. Psychiat.*, **118**, 798–817 (1929).

ENKE, W., Die Psychomotorik der Konstitutionstypen, *Z. angew. Psychol.*, **36**, 237–287 (1930).

ESPENSCHADE, A., Motor development, *Rev. Educ. Res.*, **17**, 354–361 (1947).

ESTABROOKS, G. H., Experimental studies in suggestion, *Ped. Sem.*, **36**, 120–139 (1929).

EYSENCK, H. J., Suggestibility and hysteria, *J. Neurol. Psychiat.*, **6**, 22–31 (1943).

EYSENCK, H. J., States of high suggestibility and the neuroses, *Amer. J. Psychol.*, **57**, 406–411 (1944).

EYSENCK, H. J., *Dimensions of Personality* (London, Routledge & Kegan Paul, 1947).

EYSENCK, H. J., Cyclothymia and schizothymia as a dimension of personality: I. Historical review, *J. Personality*, **19**, 123–152 (1950).

EYSENCK, H. J., *The Scientific Study of Personality* (London, Routledge & Kegan Paul, 1952a).

EYSENCK, H. J., Schizothymia-cyclothymia as a dimension of personality: II. Experimental. *J. Personality*, **20**, 345–384 (1952b).

EYSENCK, H. J., *The Structure of Human Personality* (London, Methuen, 1953).

EYSENCK, H. J., A dynamic theory of anxiety and hysteria, *J. Ment. Sci.*, **101**, 28–51 (1955).

EYSENCK, H. J. and FURNEAUX, W. D., Primary and secondary suggestibility: an experimental and statistical study, *J. Exp. Psychol.*, **35**, 485–503 (1945).

EYSENCK, S. B. G., A dimensional analysis of mental abnormality, *Unpubl. Ph. D. Thesis, Univ. of London Lib.* (1955).

EYSENCK, S. B. G., Neurosis and psychosis: an experimental analysis, *J. Ment. Sci.*, **102**, 517–529 (1956).

FAUVILLE, A., DEWYN, M. and CELIS, S., Aptitudes motrices et aptitudes perceptives, *Année Psychol.*, **37**, 17–57 (1937).

FESTINGER, L. and WAPNER, S., A test of decision time: reliability and generality, *CAA Div. Res. Rep.* No. 48 (1945).

FLEISHMAN, E. A., Testing for psychomotor abilities by means of apparatus tests, *Psychol. Bull.*, **50**, 241–262 (1953).

FLEISHMAN, E. A., Dimensional analysis of psychomotor abilities, *J. Exp. Psychol.*, **48**, 437–454 (1954).

FRANKS, C. M., Conditioning and personality, *J. Abnorm. (Soc.) Psychol.*, **52**, 143–150 (1956).

FREEMAN, G. L. and WONDERLIE, E. F., Periodicity of performance, *Amer. J. Psychol.*, **47**, 149–151 (1935).

GARDNER, J. W., An experimental study of the Luria technique for detecting mental conflict, *J. Exp. Psychol.*, **20**, 495–505 (1937).

GEWIRTZ, J. L., Studies in word fluency. I. Its relationship to vocabulary and mental age in young children, *J. Genet. Psychol.*, **72**, 165–176 (1948).

GRICE, G. R., Discrimination reaction time as a function of anxiety and intelligence, *J. Abnorm. (Soc.) Psychol.*, **50**, 71–74 (1955).

GROSS, O., *Die cerebrale Sekundärfunktion* (Leipzig, 1902).

GUREWITSCH, M. and OSERETZKY, N., Die konstitutionellen Variationen der Psychomotorik und ihre Beziehungen zum Körperbau und zum Charakter, *Arch. Psychiat. Nervenkr.*, **91**, 286–312 (1930).

HALL, K. R. L. and STRIDE, E., Some factors affecting reaction times to auditory stimuli in mental patients, *J. Ment. Sci.*, **100**, 462–477 (1954).

HEATH, S. R., Rail-walking performance as related to mental age and etiological type among the mentally retarded, *Amer. J. Psychol.*, **55**, 240–247 (1942).

HEATH, S. R., The military use of the rail-walking test as an index of locomotor co-ordination, *Psychol. Bull.*, **40**, 282–284 (1943).

HEATH, S. R., Clinical significance of motor defect with military implications, *Amer. J. Psychol.*, **57**, 482–499 (1944).

HEATH, S. R., A mental pattern found in motor deviates, *J. Abnorm. (Soc.) Psychol.*, **41**, 223–225 (1946).

HEATH, S. R., The rail-walking test: preliminary maturational norms for boys and girls, *Mot. Skills Res. Exch.*, **1**, 34–36 (1949).

HENRY, F. M., Increase in speed of movement by motivation and by transfer of motivated improvement, *Res. Quart. Amer. Ass. Hlth. Phys. Educ.*, **22**, 219–228 (1951)

HILL, H. E., An experimental study of disorganization of speech and manual responses in normal subjects, *J. Speech Dis.*, **19**, 295–305 (1954).

HIMMELWEIT, H. T., Speed and accuracy of work as related to temperament, *Brit. J. Psychol.*, **36**, 132–144 (1946).

HIMMELWEIT, H. T. and PETRIE, A., The measurement of personality in children. An experimental investigation of neuroticism, *Brit. J. Educ. Psychol.*, **21**, 9–29 (1951).

HIMMELWEIT, H. T., PETRIE, A. and DESAI, M., An experimental investigation of neuroticism, *J. Personality*, **15**, 173–196 (1946).

HIPPLE, J. E., Racial differences in the influence of motivation on muscular tensions, reaction time and speed of movement, *Res. Quart. Amer. Ass. Hlth. Phys. Educ.*, **25**, 297–306 (1954).

HOCH, A., On certain studies with the ergograph, *J. Nerv. Ment. Dis.*, **28**, 620–628 (1901).

HOVLAND, C. I. and SEARS, R. R., Experiments on motor conflict: I. Types of conflict and their modes of resolution, *J. Exp. Psychol.*, **23**, 477–493 (1938).

HULL, C. L., *Hypnosis and Suggestibility* (New York, Appleton-Century, 1933).

HUNT, J. McV., *Personality and the Behavior Disorders. Vol.* 2. (New York, Ronald Press, 1944).

HUSTON, P. E., The reflex time of the patellar tendon reflex in normal and schizophrenic subjects, *J. Gen. Psychol.*, **13**, 3–41 (1935).

HUSTON, P. E. and SENF, R., Psychopathology of schizophrenia and depression: I. Effect of amytal and amphetamine sulphate on level and maintenance of attention, *Amer. J. Psychiat.*, **109**, 131–138 (1952).

HUSTON, P. E. and SHAKOW, D., Studies of motor function in schizophrenia: III. Steadiness, *J. Gen. Psychol.*, **34**, 119–126 (1946).

HUSTON, P. E., SHAKOW, D. and ERICKSON, M. H., A study of hypnotically induced complexes by means of the Luria technique, *J. Genet. Psychol.*, **11**, 65–97 (1934).

HUSTON, P. E., SHAKOW, D. and RIGGS, L. A., Studies of motor function in schizophrenia: II. Reaction time, *J. Gen. Psychol.*, **16**, 39–82 (1937).

HUSTON, P. E. and SINGER, M. M., Effect of sodium amytal and amphetamine sulphate on mental set in schizophrenia, *Arch. Neurol. Psychiat. Chicago.*, **53**, 365–369 (1945).

HUXTABLE, Z. L., WHITE, M. H., and McCARTOR, M. A., A re-performance and re-interpretation of the Arai experiment in mental fatigue with three subjects, *Psychol. Monogr.*, **59**, 5 (1946).

INGHAM, J. G., Body sway suggestibility and neurosis, *J. Ment. Sci.*, **100**, 432–441 (1954).

INGHAM, J. G., Psychoneurosis and suggestibility, *J. Abnorm. (Soc.) Psychol.*, **51**, 600–603 (1955).

JASPER, H. N., Is perseveration a functional unity participating in all behaviour processes? *J. Soc. Psychol.*, **2**, 28–52 (1931).

JOHANSON, A. M., Influence of incentive and punishment upon reaction time, *Arch. Psychol. N.Y.*, **8**, 54–93 (1922).

JONES, L. W., An investigation into the significance of perseveration, *J. Ment. Sci.*, **74**, 653–659 (1928).

KELLOG, W. N., The effect of emotional excitement upon muscular steadiness. *J. Exp. Psychol.*, **15**, 142–166 (1932).

KENDIG, I., Studies in perseveration: II. Determining factors in the development of compulsive activity, *J. Psychol.*, **3**, 231–246 (1937*a*).

KENDIG, I., Studies in perseveration: III. The upper limen for perseveration and repetition, *J. Psychol.*, **3**, 247–251 (1937*b*).

KENDIG, I., Studies in perseveration. IV. Selective perseveration and repetition, *J. Psychol.*, **3**, 253–259 (1937*c*).

KENDIG, I., Studies in perseveration: V. Theoretical significance of the perseveration and repetition of conative activity, *J. Psychol.*, **3**, 261–264 (1937*d*).

KENDIG, I. and SHEVACH, B. J., Studies in perseveration: I. A survey of researches in perseveration, *J. Psychol.*, **3**, 223–230 (1937).

KIBLER, M., Experimentalpsychologischen Beitrag zur Typenforschung, *Z. ges. Neurol. Psychiat.*, **98**, 524–544 (1925).

KING, H. E., *Psychomotor Aspects of Mental Disease* (Commonwealth Fund, Harvard Univ. Press, 1954).

KLEEMEIER, R. W. and DUDEK, F. J., A factorial investigation of flexibility, *Educ. Psychol. Measmt.*, **10**, 107–118 (1950).

KLINEBERG, O., ASCH, S. W. and BLOCK, H., An experimental study of constitutional types, *Genet. Psychol., Monogr.*, **16**, 139–221 (1934).

KNEHR, C. A., Schizophrenic reaction time responses to variable preparatory intervals, *Amer. J. Psychiat.*, **110**, 585–588 (1954).

KRAEPELIN, E., Die Arbeitskurve, *Philos. Stud.*, **19**, 459–507 (1902).

KRAUSE, L. S., Relation of voluntary motor pressure (Luria) to two other alleged complex indicators, *J. Exp. Psychol.*, **21**, 653–661 (1937).

KREMER, A. H., The nature of persistence, *Stud. Psychol. Psychiat.*, **5**, 40 (1942).

LAZARUS, R. S., DEESE, J. and OSLER, S. F., The effects of psychological stress upon performance, *Psychol. Bull.*, **49**, 293–317 (1952).

LOFCHIE, S. H., The performance of adults under distraction stress: a developmental approach, *J. Psychol.*, **39**, 109–116 (1955).

LOUTTIT, C. M., The mirror-tracing test as a diagnostic aid for emotional instability, *Psychol. Rec.*, **5**, 279–286 (1943).

LUBIN, A., Some contributions to the testing of psychological hypotheses by means of statistical multivariate analysis, *Unpubl. Ph.D. Thesis, Univ. of London Lib.* (1951).

LURIA, A. R., *The Nature of Human Conflicts* (New York, Liveright, 1932).

MACARTHUR, R. S., An experimental investigation of persistence and its measurement at the secondary school level, *Unpubl. Ph.D. Thesis, Univ. of London Lib.* (1951).

MACKWORTH, H., Researches in the measurement of human performance, *M.R.C. Spec. Rep.* No. 268 (London, H.M.S.O., 1948).

MAILLOUX, N. M. and NEWBURGER, M., The work curves of psychotic individuals, *J. Abnorm. (Soc.) Psychol.*, **36**, 110–114 (1941).

MALMO, R. B., SHAGASS, C., BELANGER, D. J. and SMITH A. A., Motor control in psychiatric patients under experimental stress, *J. Abnorm. (Soc.) Psychol.*, **46**, 539–547 (1951).

MESSER, A. L., HINCKLEY, E. D. and MOSIER, C. I., Suggestibility and neurotic symptoms in normal subjects, *J. Gen. Psychol.*, **19**, 391–399 (1938).

MICHON, P., *Le Temps de Réaction. Techniques. Applications Cliniques* (Paris, Masson, 1939).

MISIAK, H. and PICKFORD, R. W., Physique and perseveration, *Nature*, **153**, 622 (1944).

MITTENECKER, E., Perseveration und Persönlichkeit, *Z. exp. angewand. Psychol.*, **1**, 5–31, 265–284 (1953).

MOHR, G. J. and GUNDLACH, R. H., The relation between physique and performance, *J. Exp. Psychol.*, **10**, 117–157 (1927).

MORGAN, M. I. and OJEMAN, R. H., A study of the Luria Method, *J. Appl. Psychol.*, **26**, 168–179 (1942).

NOTCUTT, B., Perseveration and fluency, *Brit. J. Psychol.*, **33**, 200–208 (1943).

NUNBERG, H., On the physical accompaniments of association processes in Jung, C. G., *Studies in Word Association* (London, Heinemann, 1918).

O'CONNOR, N., Personality variables which affect the vocational and social efficiency of high grade defectives, *Unpubl. Ph.D. Thesis. Univ. of London Lib.* (1951).

O'CONNOR, N., HERON, A., and CARSTAIRS, G. M., Work performance of chronic schizophrenics, *Occup. Psychol.*, (1956).

OLSON, D. M. and JONES, V., An objective measure of emotionally-toned attitudes, *J. Genet. Psychol.*, **39**, 174–196 (1931).

PARSONS, O. A., PHILLIPS, L. and LANE, J. E., Performance on the same psychomotor task under different stressful conditions, *J. Psychol.*, **38**, 457–466 (1954).

PASCAL, G. R., The effect of a disturbing noise on the reaction time of mental defectives, *Amer. J. Ment. Defic.*, **57**, 691–699 (1953).

PASCAL, G. R. and SWENSEN, C., Learning in mentally ill patients under conditions of unusual motivation, *J. Personality*, **21**, 240–249 (1952).

PATRICK, J. R., Studies in rational behaviour and emotional excitement: I. Rational behaviour in human subjects, *J. Comp. Psychol.*, **18**, 1–22 (1934a).

PATRICK, J. R., Studies in rational behaviour and emotional excitement: II. The effect of emotional excitement on rational behaviour in human subjects, *J. Comp. Psychol.*, **18**, 153–193 (1934b).

PAVLOV, I. P., *Conditioned Reflexes and Psychiatry*, Trans. W. H. Gantt (London, Lawrence & Wishart, 1941).

PAYNE, R. W., An investigation into the possibility of defining "dissociation" as a personality trait by means of objective tests, *Unpubl. Ph. D. Thesis, Univ. of London Lib.* (1954).

PENROSE, L. S. and WILSON, D. J., The spatial dispersion of psychotic responses in the tapping test, *J. Abnorm. (Soc.) Psychol.*, **37**, 131–133 (1942).

PETERS, H. N., The mirror-tracing test as a measure of social maladaption, *J. Abnorm. (Soc.) Psychol.*, **41**, 437–448 (1946).

PETRIE, A., The study of experimental methods of assessing personality. *Unpubl. Ph.D. Thesis, Univ. of London Lib.* (1945).

PETRIE, A., Repression and suggestibility as related to temperament, *J. Personality*, **16**, 445–458 (1948).

PHILIP, B. R., Studies in high speed continuous work: I. Periodicity, *J. Exp. Psychol.*, **24**, 499–510 (1939a).

PHILIP, B. R., Studies in high speed continuous work: II. Decrement, *J. Exp. Psychol.*, **25**, 307–315 (1939b).

PHILIP, B. R., Studies in high speed continuous work: III. Initial spurt and warming-up, *J. Exp. Psychol.*, **25**, 402–413 (1939c).

PHILIP, B. R., Studies in high speed continuous work: V. Pain, blocking and tiredness, *J. Exp. Psychol.*, **26**, 322–336 (1940).

PINARD, J. W., Tests of perseveration: I. Their relation to character, *Brit. J. Psychol.*, **23**, 5–19 (1932a).

PINARD, J. W., Tests of perseveration: II. Their relation to certain psychopathic conditions and to introversion, *Brit. J. Psychol.*, **23**, 114–128 (1932b).

POFFENBERGER, G. I., The effects of continuous mental work, *Amer. J. Psychol.*, **39**, 283–296 (1927).

RETHLINGSHAFER, D., Relationship of tests of persistence to other measures of continuance of activities, *J. Abnorm. (Soc.) Psychol.*, **37**, 71–82 (1942).

REYMERT, M. L. and SPEER, G. S., Does the Luria technique measure emotion or mere bodily tension? *Character & Pers.*, **7**, 192–200 (1938).

RIM, Y., Perseveration and fluency as measures of introversion-extraversion in abnormal subjects. *Unpubl. Ph.D. Thesis, Univ. of London Lib.* (1953).

RIM, Y., Perseveration and fluency as measures of introversion-extraversion in abnormal subjects, *J. Personality*, **23**, 324–334 (1955).

RIMOLDI, H. J. A., Personal tempo, *J. Abnorm. (Soc.) Psychol.*, **46**, 283–303 (1951).

ROACH, J. H. L., Autosuggestion in extroverts and introverts, *J. Personality*, **15**, 215–221 (1947).

ROBINSON, E. S., Principles of work decrement, *Psychol., Rev.*, **33**, 123–134 (1926).

ROBINSON, E. S., Work of the integrated organism, in *Handbook of General Experimental Psychology*, Ed. C. Murchison (Worcester, Clark Univ. Press, 1934).

ROBINSON, E. S. and BILLS, A. C., Two factors in the work decrement, *J. Exp. Psychol.*, **9**, 413–433 (1926).

RODNICK, E. H. and SHAKOW, D., Set in the schizophrenic as measured by a composite reaction time index. *Amer. J. Psychiat.*, **97**, 214–225 (1940).

ROGERS, C. A., The structure of verbal fluency, *Brit. J. Psychol.*, **44**, 368–380 (1953).

ROGERS, C. A., The orectic relations of verbal fluency, *Aust. J. Psychol.*, **8**, 27–46 (1956).

ROGERS, K., Perseveration, *J. Ment. Sci.*, **81**, 138–144 (1935a).

ROGERS, K., Perseveration and personality, *J. Ment. Sci.*, **81**, 145–150 (1935b).

ROSS, S., HUSSMAN, T. A. and ANDREWS, T. G., Effects of fatigue and anxiety on certain psychomotor and visual functions, *J. Appl. Psychol.*, **38**, 119–125 (1954).

RUNKEL, J. E., Luria's motor method and word-association in the study of deception, *J. Gen. Psychol.*, **15**, 23–37 (1936).

RUSSELL, J. T., Relative efficiency of relaxation and tension in performing an act of skill, *J. Gen. Psychol.*, **6**, 330–343 (1932).

RYANS, D. G., The meaning of persistence, *J. Gen. Psychol.*, **19**, 79–96 (1938a).

RYANS, D. G., An experimental attempt to analyse persistent behaviour: I. Measuring traits presumed to involve persistence, *J. Gen. Psychol.*, **19**, 333–353 (1938b).

RYANS, D. G., The measurement of persistence: an historical review, *Psychol. Bull.*, **36**, 715–739 (1939).

SAUNDERS, E. B. and ISAACS, S., Tests of reaction time and motor inhibition in the psychoses, *Amer. J. Psychiat.*, **9**, 79–112 (1929).

SCHEIER, I. H. and FERGUSON, G. A., Further factorial studies of tests of rigidity, *Canad. J. Psychol.*, **6**, 18–30 (1952).

SCHLEIER, R. P., (Motor behaviour and total personality), *Z. Psychol.*, **47**, 38–64 (1939).

SCHORN, M., Experimentelle Untersuchungen über die Mehrfachhändlung. *Z. Psychol.*, **108**, 195–221 (1928).

SCRIPTURE, E. W., Reaction time in nervous and mental diseases, *J. Ment. Sci.*, **62**, 698–719 (1916).

SEARS, R. R. and HOVLAND, C. I., Experiments on motor conflict: II. Determination of mode of resolution by comparative strengths of conflicting responses, *J. Exp. Psychol.*, **28**, 280–286 (1941).

SEASHORE, H. G. and KOCH, G., Postural steadiness under conditions of muscular tension and fatigue. *Psychol. Rec.*, **2**, 319–332 (1938).

SEASHORE, R. H., Stanford motor-skills unit, *Psychol. Monogr.*, **38**, Whole No. 178 (1928).

SEASHORE, R. H., Individual differences in motor skills, *J. Gen. Psychol.*, **3**, 38–65 (1930).

SEASHORE, R. H., Experimental and theoretical analysis of fine motor skills, *Amer. J. Psychol.*, **53**, 86–98 (1940).

SEASHORE, R. H., Work and motor performance, in *Handbook of Experimental Psychology*, Ed. S. S. Stevens (New York, John Wiley & Sons, Inc., 1951).

SEASHORE, R. H., BUXTON, C. E. and McCOLLOM, I. N., Multiple factorial analysis of fine motor skills, *Amer. J. Psychol.*, **53**, 251–259 (1940).

SHAKOW, D., The nature of deterioration in schizophrenic conditions, *Nerv. Ment. Dis. Monogr.*, New York, (1946).

SHAKOW, D. and HUSTON, P. E., Studies of motor function in schizophrenia. I. Speed of tapping, *J. Gen. Psychol.*, **15**, 63–103 (1936).

SHAPIRO, M. B. and NELSON, E. H., An investigation of the nature of cognitive impairment in co-operative psychiatric patients, *Brit. J. Med. Psychol.*, **28**, 239–256 (1955).

SHARP, D. L., Group and individual profiles in the association-motor test, *Univ. Ia Stud. Child Welf.*, **15**, 97–171 (1938).

SHUEY, H., An investigation of the Luria technique with normal and psychotic subjects, *J. Abnorm. (Soc.) Psychol.*, **32**, 303–313 (1937).

SPEER, G. S., The measurement of emotions aroused in response to personality test items, *J. Psychol.*, **3**, 445–461 (1937).

STARER, E., The effects of two simultaneous cognitive and affective stimuli, *J. Clin. Psychol.*, **8**, 402–405 (1952).

STEINMAN, A. and VENIAR, S., Simple RT to change as a substitute for the disjunctive reaction, *J. Exp. Psychol.*, **34**, 152–158 (1944).

STEPHENSON, W., Studies in experimental psychiatry. II. Some contact of p-factor with psychiatry, *J. Ment. Sci.*, **78**, 318–330 (1932a).

STEPHENSON, W., Studies in experimental psychiatry. III. p-score and inhibition for high-p *praecox* cases, *J. Ment. Sci.*, **78**, 908–928 (1932b).

STEPHENSON, W., An introduction to so-called motor perseveration tests, *Brit. J. Educ. Psychol.*, **4**, 186–208 (1934).

TAYLOR, J. A., A personality scale of manifest anxiety, *J. Abnorm. (Soc.) Psychol.*, **48**, 285–290 (1953).

TEICHNER, H., Recent studies of simple reaction time, *Psychol. Bull.*, **51**, 128–149 (1954).

THORNDIKE, E. L., The curve of work, *Psychol. Rev.*, **19**, 105–194 (1912).

THORNTON, G. R., A factor analysis of tests designed to measure persistence, *Psychol. Monogr.*, **51**, 1–42 (1939).

TIZARD, J. and O'CONNOR, N., Predicting the occupational adequacy of certified mental defectives: an empirical investigation using a battery of psychological tests and ratings, *Occup. Psychol.*, **25**, 205–211 (1951).

TIZARD, J., O'CONNOR, N. and CRAWFORD, J. M., The abilities of adolescent and adult high-grade male defectives, *J. Ment. Sci.*, **96**, 888–907 (1950).

TIZARD, J. and VENABLES, P. H., Reaction time responses by schizophrenics, mental defectives and normal adults, *Amer. J. Psychiat.*, **112**, 803–807 (1956).

TRAVIS, R. C., An experimental analysis of dynamic and static equilibrium, *J. Exp. Psychol.*, **35**, 216–234 (1945).

TRAVIS, R. C. and KENNEDY, J. L., Prediction and automatic control of alertness. I. Control of lookout alertness, *J. Comp. Physiol. Psychol.*, **40**, 457–461 (1947).

VAN DER HORST, L., Experimentellpsychologische Untersuchungen zu Kretschmer's *Körperbau und Charakter*, *Ztschr. ges. Neurol. Psychiat.*, **93**, 341–380 (1924).

VENABLES, P. H. and TIZARD, J., The effect of stimulus light intensity on the reaction time of schizophrenics, *Brit. J. Psychol.*, **47**, 144–145 (1956a).

VENABLES, P. H. and TIZARD, J., Paradoxical effects in the reaction time of schizophrenics, *J. Abnorm. (Soc.) Psychol.*, **53**, 220–224 (1956b).

VENABLES, P. H. and TIZARD, J., Performance of functional psychotics on a repetitive task, *J. Abnorm. (Soc.) Psychol.*, **53**, 23–26 (1956c).

VERNON, P. E., *The Structure of Human Abilities* (London, Methuen, 1950).

WALKER, K. F., STAINES, R. G. and KENNA, J. C., Is there a general factor of perseveration? *Aust. J. Psychol. Phil.*, **19**, 58–75 (1941).

WALKER, K. F., STAINES, R. G. and KENNA, J. C., P-tests and the concept of mental inertia, *Character & Pers.*, **12**, 32–45 (1943).

WALKER, K. F., STAINES, R. G. and KENNA, J. C., The influence of scoring methods upon score in motor perseveration tests. *Brit. J. Psychol.*, **35**, 51–60 (1945).

WARREN, H. C., *Dictionary of Psychology* (Boston, Houghton Mifflin, 1934).

WARREN, N. and CLARK, B., Blocking in mental and motor tasks during a 65-hour vigil, *J. Exp. Psychol.*, **21**, 97–105 (1937).

WATERS, R. H. and SHEPPARD, R., The mirror-drawing experiment: a brief historical note, *J. Gen. Psychol.*, **46**, 63–72 (1952).

WECHSLER, D. and HARTOGS, R., The clinical measurement of anxiety, *Psychiat. Quart.*, **19**, 618–635 (1945).

WEISGERBER, C. A., The relationship of perseveration to a number of personality traits and to adjustment, *J. Gen. Psychol.*, **50**, 3–13 (1954).

WELLS, F. L. and KELLEY, C. M., The simple reaction in psychosis, *Amer. J. Psychiat.*, **2**, 53–59 (1922).

WHIPPLE, G. M., *Manual of Mental and Physical Tests*. Part I. Simple Processes (Baltimore, Warwick & York, Inc., 1924).

WILLIAMS, G. W., A study of the responses of three psychotic groups to a test of suggestibility, *J. Gen. Psychol.*, **7**, 302–310 (1932).

WINDLE, C. and HAMWI, V., An exploratory study of the prognostic value of the complex reaction time test in early and chronic psychotics, *J. Clin. Psychol.*, **9**, 156–161 (1953).

WOODWORTH, R. S. and SCHLOSBERG, H., *Experimental Psychology* (London, Methuen, 1954).

WULFECK, W. H., Motor function in the mentally disordered. I. A comparative investigation of motor function in psychotics, psychoneurotics and normals, *Psychol., Rec.*, **4**, 271–323 (1941).

WUNDT, W., *Principles of Physiological Psychology*. 2 Vols. (Macmillan, 1873–4).

YARMOLENKO, A., (Motor characteristics of reflexological types in school children.) *Nov. refl. fiziol. nerv. Sist.*, **3**, 304–326 (1929). (*Psychol., Abstr.*, **4**, 4,218 (1930)).

YERKES, R. M. and DODSON, J. D., The relation of strength of stimulus to rapidity of habit formation, *J. Comp. Psychol.*, **18**, 459–482 (1908).

YULE, E. P., The classification of motor perseveration tests: some criticisms and deductions, *Brit. J. Psychol.*, **43**, 42–52 (1952).

CHAPTER 3

Expressive Movements and Abnormal Behaviour

J. C. BRENGELMANN

INTRODUCTION

As reviewed in the present chapter, *expressive movement* deals with the relationship of individual differences of involuntary motor behaviour to personality and abnormality, whether occurring during spontaneous or purposeful movements.

Psychogenic or organic motor disturbance, or disorganization, is not dealt with. The effects of abnormality are discussed in so far as abnormals behave with regard to variables which are traditionally registered under "expressive movement" in normal personality. For that reason, the classification used disregards systems employed in psychiatry, whether of the observational or inferred, anatomical-neurophysiological or psychoanalytical kind.

Results discussed are based on experimental evidence. Originally, between World Wars I and II, most of the links connecting expressive movement with personality were not directly measured. The widely used methods of ratings and matching of rated characteristics are, because of a number of inadequacies, disappearing from the scientific stage. They consequently will be given much less space than in the past. Instead, some of the more recently developed methods, promising far more favourable prospects, are discussed in greater detail. This implies the opinion that research in expressive movement, having reached the end of a stimulating cul-de-sac with rating techniques, will flourish again under the guidance of objective measurement. Trends of this kind are indicated. But, as they are only trends, the relative emphasis in this report will be placed on methodology and measurement.

The formulation of a general theory of expressive movement appears premature. It would not furnish predictions of unique consequence, nor be capable of specifying the conditions under which certain modes of expressive movement occur. However, a number of limited suggestions with possibly wider applications and considered fruitful for the advancement of research, will result from the discussions.

In the present rather exploratory stage of the objective analysis of expressive movement classifications are bound to be tentative. Since Allport and Vernon's *Studies in Expressive Movement* (1933) no appreciable improvement in description, or factorial classification, appears to have been made. In the present review, the first section deals with various forms of gross motor expression. In the remaining three sections, for reasons indicated above, methods of assessments, or tests, have been treated in an order, not obligatory, of "objectivity" in assessment. The entire report is divided as follows—

I. Complex bodily expression
   1. Gait
   2. Gesture
   3. Posture
   4. Facial expression
   5. Judgement of expression
   6. Voice
   7. Speech
   8. Language

II. Complex products of arts and drawing
   1. Artistic productions
   2. Free drawing
   3. Drawing completion
   4. Evaluation

III. Semi-objective techniques
   1. Copying of designs
   2. Manipulative tests
      (a) Mosaic Test
      (b) Colour Pyramid Test
      (c) Colour-star Test
      (d) Bunch-of-grapes Test
      (e) Evaluation
   3. Handwriting

IV. Objective tests

1. Writing pressure
2. Prismatic tracing
3. "Kinaesthetic" drawing

    (a) The Mira "myokinetic" test
    (b) Simple blindfolded drawing
    (c) Other movement tests

4. Figure Reconstruction Test

Finally, two more explanations are necessary. *Firstly*, certain aspects of expression, which are not of the motor type, have been discussed for reasons of completeness or immediate theoretical importance. *Secondly*, motor activities of the kind discussed in other chapters of the present volume have been dealt with when the reviewer felt satisfied about the usefulness of additions from the expressive movement point of view. Direct overlap in the content, it is hoped, has been avoided.

I. COMPLEX BODILY EXPRESSION

The subjects discussed under this heading vary to a considerable degree in the attention devoted to them; this appears largely to be a function of ease of measurement. Three points should be noted before discussing these subjects in detail; (a) although originally heavily favoured against other fields, research of the kind discussed in this section has become rare; (b) apparatus construction appears to have been in advance of research problems (objective measurement of complex movements, for example, has been described for decades without the implementation of corresponding personality research (Bernstein, 1927; Schleier, 1939; Voigt, 1939; Kretsinger, 1952); (c) where direct measurement of objective movement appeared difficult, as in the case of facial movement, traditional emphasis on "expression," or judgement of movement, has been retained. Although this has led to a distinction between the measurement of actual expressive movement and of individual differences regarding attitudes in judgement and perception, joint treatment still appears to be indicated.

Gait

Three papers of great originality have not been able to stimulate a systematic experimental investigation into personality characteristics of gait (Bogen and Lippmann, 1931; Wolff, 1935; Kietz, 1948). Objective methods of analysis have been known for decades but no publication relevant to the present subject can be quoted. (Anders, 1928; Schwartz and Vaeth, 1928; Liberson, 1936; Kreezer and Glanville, 1937; Glanville and Kreezer, 1937; Loucks, 1941.)

Gesture

Descriptions and classifications of gestures, supposedly expressive of personality rather than of cultural or conventional influences, have been frequently compiled (Allport and Vernon, 1933; Krout, 1935, 1954a, 1954b; Efron, 1941; Efron and Foley, 1947; Leonhard, 1949), but, pending experimental clarification, they are of little consequence. As long as there is no direct attack on personality correlates of gestures,

the vague belief will remain that most gestures are motor expressions of "feeling" and "emotion." A recent methodological improvement, however, may be recorded. Sainsbury (1954a, 1954b, 1955), extending Olson's (Young, 1947) method of time-sampling, used slow-motion film analysis of high reliability (split-half reliability of 0·93) to score nervous habits. Twelve patients were investigated under conditions of stressed and unstressed interviews, and gestural movements were found to increase with stress. Scores derived from the film sample correlated 0·998 with corresponding observational counting, and 0·87 with electromyographic scores. Emotionally disturbed patients, recommended for leucotomy, showed significantly more spontaneous nervous movements than did normal controls (1954a). This is consistent with other reports on increased gestural movement under stressful conditions (Jones, 1943a, 1943b).

The main merit of these studies appears to lie in the improvement of technique. The meaning of "stress" remains undefined and no differential effects between personality or abnormality criteria are known.

Posture

Psychiatrists and psychoanalysts alike have stressed that posture, as much as other gross bodily expressions, is characteristic of illness or unconscious psychological complexes (Deutsch, 1947). However, despite the fact that measurement of posture has shown individual differences to be both significant and reliable (Sollenberger, 1937; Travis, 1944; Allen, Taylor and Hall, 1945; Jones and Narva, 1955), the techniques developed have not been applied to measurement of personality and abnormality. A number of clinical observations on induced postural changes have been described but not systematically applied (Matthaei, 1924; Eidelberg, 1926). Schilder (Takala, 1953), for example, had his subjects stand with their eyes closed and their arms raised horizontally and extended sideways. It turned out that persons with neurotic tension tended unconsciously to let their arms come forward, while the tendency among the normals was rather the opposite. Results relating to standing steadiness (Lee, 1931), or static ataxia, are reported in Chapter 2.

Facial Expression

Facial expression as the "principal focus of emotional expression" has assumed a "strategic position among the expressive agents of the body" (Allport, 1938). Despite this "one is confronted with the fact that the expressions of the human face have contributed least

movements of various face muscles in over two hundred patients. Schizophrenics, for example, were said to have "well differentiated" forehead muscles, but to find it difficult to "screw up" their eyes.

The fact that, in humans, the assessment of facial muscle movement has not been developed beyond a rudimentary level has resulted in an almost exclusive preference for dealing with "expression proper," i.e., that portion of perception which evokes immediate

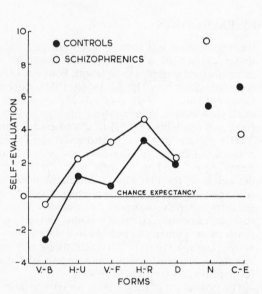

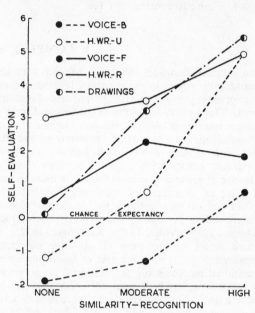

FIG. 3.1. *Left:* SCHIZOPHRENICS RATE THEIR OWN EXPRESSIONS MORE FAVOURABLY DURING UNCONSCIOUS, BUT LESS FAVOURABLY DURING CONSCIOUS (C-E), EVALUATION

Right: DURING UNCONSCIOUS SELF-EVALUATION, JUDGEMENT BECOMES MORE FAVOURABLE WITH INCREASED RECOGNITION OF SIMILARITY WITH PERSONAL EXPRESSION

(From Epstein, 1955)

to the detection of practically useful points of view but most to the theory of expression effect" (Rohracher, 1948). One good reason for this is that the analysis of facial expression has been predominantly dependent on judgement, the unreliability and bias of which have been discussed a number of times (Allport, 1938; Vernon, 1953; Taft, 1955; Mühle, 1956; Gage, Leavitt and Stone, 1956).

Direct measurement of face muscle movement has, on occasion, been attempted (Lynn, 1940; Coleman, 1949), but has not progressed to the stage of assessing individual differences. From the point of view of measurement, Wörner's (1940) time sequence analysis of facial movements recorded from monkeys appears to be of outstanding importance.

In order to assess constitutional differences along Kretschmer's lines Oseretzky (1932) described the

emotional attitudes and judgements not present in, but attributed to, the stimuli (Rohracher, 1948). These are dealt with in the following section.

Judgement of Expression

Instead of dealing with expressed movement *per se*, we are now analysing a mixture of stimulus movement and the attitudes of the observer towards such movement.

This medium, though complex, holds out great promise for the study of personality, as Wolff (1933, 1943) has demonstrated on a number of occasions. Given suitable experimental conditions, subjects fail to recognize their own face, voice, hands, writing, gait, etc., but may react "unconsciously" to such exposures with emotions varying in intensity and quality. When subjects were asked to evaluate their own unrecognized expressions, most of the judgements were found to be highly favourable, others were highly unfavourable and only a few were objective. These results were later confirmed by Huntley (1940).

Epstein (1955) in a most intriguing experiment investigated self-judgement of voice-backwards (V-B), handwriting-upside-down (H-U), voice-forwards (V-F), handwriting-right-side-up (H-R), names (N) and drawings (D) in normals and schizophrenics. The results are shown in Fig. 3.1.

This figure shows that self-evaluation is negative with highly disguised material. As the disguise decreases, self-judgements become increasingly favourable up to the point where complete identification occurs (i.e. drawings, or D), whereupon self-ratings become more modest. During *unconscious* evaluation, schizophrenics rated their own expressions significantly more favourably than did normals. In *conscious* evaluation (C-E), however, the opposite effect was found. Furthermore, Fig. 3.1 shows in a striking manner that during the period when subjects actually did not recognize expressions to be their own, favourable judgement increased with the degree of judged similarity with their own expression.

This experiment, although not strictly falling into the realm of expressive movement, has been reported because of its potential value in this field. In Sect. IV of this chapter it will be shown that confidence in performance, as one form of self-evaluation, interferes *directly* with objective expressive movement scores. Similarly to Epstein, the present author has found that such confidence depends on exposure conditions as well as defines certain personality correlates varying with such conditions.

Judgement of facial expression has led to yet another line of research. Eysenck (1954) reports an experiment in which normals, neurotics and psychotics were asked to judge various facial expressions from twelve photographs of male and female persons. Standard judgement check lists were used and deviation from a normal norm was scored, with the result shown in Fig. 3.2. High score signifies high agreement with the control norm.

Differences between the three groups were significant at the 0·1 per cent level and it may be seen from the above figure that deviation from the norm was highest for the psychotics. Essentially similar results were subsequently obtained by Chambers (1957), who used Szondi pictures as a basis for judgements. This author concluded that "as mental pathology increases in severity, conformity with the perceptual judgement of normals decreases."

The problem of variability in judgement of facial expression comes up again in the discussion of the Colour Pyramid Test (Sect. III). As this test is considerably different from the ones described above,

it may be suggested that the higher response variability in abnormals is of a fairly general kind.

This statement does not seem to add much to what is known already from other fields of personality research. However, there is a suggestion that judgement variability, as part of a more general response set, is of a heterogeneous nature. Eysenck, in his paper quoted above, states in a side remark that the judgements of neurotics were more *negative* and of

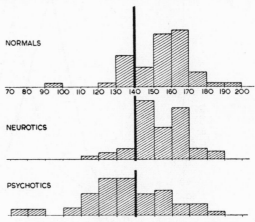

FIG. 3.2. AGREEMENT IN JUDGEMENT OF FACIAL EXPRESSION WITH A NORMAL STANDARD
This is high for normals and neurotics and low for psychotics.
(*From Eysenck*, 1954)

psychotics more *positive* than those of normals. This is consistent with the present author's recently published results obtained by investigating response set by means of an adjective check list. It was found that schizophrenics, as against normals and neurotics, scored highest on *positive* extremes; neurotics, however, highest on *negative* extremes (Brengelmann, 1958e; 1959a). It is suggested that these results agree with the finding of Epstein, reported above, that schizophrenics judge their own expressions rather favourably. Judgement of expression, response variability, confidence in performance and extreme response set may then be considered part of a general factor of self-esteem, which would be highly dependent on experimental conditions for its manifestation.

Voice

Since Pear's (1931) pioneer experiments, a number of investigations involving ratings and matching have been performed. Sanford (1942), in his extensive review, has presented evidence to indicate that "mainly at the level of impression" voice does express personality. However, as with other complex media of expression, such as facial and artistic expression, the flourishing times of early impressionistic studies have passed (compare other reviews: Rohracher 1948; Bell, 1951; Vernon, 1953). They have left us with the impression that voice appears an important means of studying individual differences in expression, without presenting any definite results. We are still left to rely on observational classifications such as those provided years ago by Newman and Mather

experiment (Table III.1) that, under stress, validity of intensity of voice may change. (These results are discussed further below.) Intensity correlated *positively* with "sensitiveness" and "emotional reticence," both of which can hardly be said to be typical of pyknic behaviour. Unfortunately, correlations for unstressed conditions were not given. At this point,

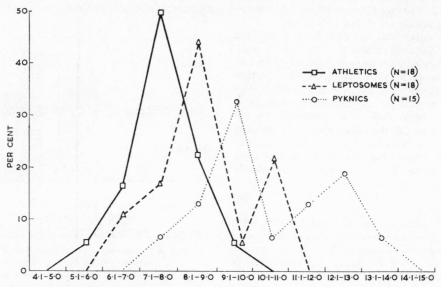

FIG. 3.3. LOUDNESS OF VOICE MEASURED BY THE DECIBEL RANGE
This increases in the order athletics—leptosomes—pyknics. Compare Fig. 3.11 for similar results on writing pressure.
(*From Grünewald*, 1957)

(1938) and Moses (1942), despite the fact that adequate equipment for phonometry (Murray and Tiffin, 1933; Zwirner, Maack and Bethge, 1955; Grünewald, 1957), and sound spectrography (Potter, Kopp and Green, 1947), etc., has been available for a long time.

Experimentally controlled work has been an exception. The frequently stated relationship between "melism" (Moses, 1942) and Kretschmer's somatotypes has been reaffirmed by Grünewald (1957), who found that pyknics manifested more melism than leptosomes and athletics. In addition, *loudness* of voice, as measured by its range, increased in the order athletics—leptosomes—pyknics (Fig. 3.3) similarly to writing pressure (Fig. 3.11). Both variables, it will be remembered, scored high loadings on Allport and Vernon's (1933) factor of emphasis. Grünewald's reference to the possibility of a factor of variability transcending various modes and media of expression receives some support. This, together with Allport and Vernon's suggestion of two independent types of variability, should be followed up.

In the light of Grünewald's results, the interesting suggestion may be derived from Korobow's (1955)

the pressing need for situational or conditional analysis may be underlined once again.

Speech

Although speech and language are not, strictly speaking, part of motor expression, their "emotional" aspects will be reported briefly so as to supplement the "cognitive" side discussed elsewhere in this volume. In a series of analyses, though on only a small number of subjects, Goldman-Eisler has investigated various basic conditions, some of which are referred to below. Certain relationships of time sequences of action and silence were found to be both characteristic of individuals and relatively constant (1951). While interviewers showed themselves consistent irrespective of the type of patient interviewed, they differentially modified patients' conversational activity (1952). In agreement with previous findings, speech rate was most consistent and sensitive in measuring differences between individuals (1954), as also was the rate of respiration and number of syllables spoken per respiration (1955).

Individual variations in speech activity are expected

clinically to correspond with fluctuations in tension and affect (Dollard and Mowrer, 1947; Kauffman and Raimy, 1949). Investigators have, accordingly, employed these conditions to analyse and vary such emotional states in a controlled manner. Korobow (1955), using three degrees of delayed auditory feedback as stress means, related a number of vocal elements to certain situational feelings and personality characteristics, as measured by questionnaires and check lists. Some results are shown in Table III.1. "Fracture" means stressing the individual syllables of words, i.e. ex'ten'u'a'ting, or stretching or slurring of words; "regression" the repetition of a word to correct either the whole word or a portion of it; "intrusion" the interpolation of ah's, eh's, um's, oh's, etc., between words and sentences.

TABLE III.1

CORRELATIONS BETWEEN VOCAL ELEMENTS AND PERSONALITY TRAITS FOR STRESS CONDITIONS OF DELAYED AUDITORY FEED-BACK

(From Korobow, 1955)

Responses	Personality category	r_{tet}
Intensity (db) . .	Sensitiveness	0·24*
	Emotional reticence	0·24*
Duration (sec) . .	Vindictiveness	− 0·29
	Disputatiousness	0·29
Per cent fractures .	Seclusiveness	0·24*
	Secretiveness	0·24*
	Irritability	0·27
	Unpleasant reminiscence	0·35
Per cent word regressions . . .	Co-operativeness	0·34
	Self-sufficiency	0·33
	Ambitiousness	0·36
	Morale	0·34
Per cent words omitted	Punctuality	− 0·22*
	Persistence	− 0·21*
	Emotional control	− 0·26
	Pleasant reminiscence	0·24*
Per cent intrusions .	Tempo	0·32

* Significant at 0·05 level; all other correlations significant at 0·01 level.

Results show that speech variables change significantly with stress and that stress effects are related to self descriptions of the "emotional" kind, whatever these may be. Similar types of speech disturbances in two patients were judged to be related to the degree of anxiety present during the interview (Mahl, 1956) without, however, a formal test of this assumption being conducted. Dibner (1956), analysing speech samples of thirty-nine patients, found two types of uncorrelated speech disturbance; one composed of indicators of speech disruption, the other of non-verbal reactions (sighing, laughter and voice change). These were considered indicators of situational anxiety,

aroused through the interview technique, rather than of a more permanent personality trait of anxiety, as measured by the G.S.R., ratings and self-reports.

Further experiments are bound to reveal relationships of greater complexity. Westrope (1953) and Benton, Hartman and Sarason (1955) have, for example, shown that the rate of verbal productivity in normals correlates positively with the Taylor Manifest Anxiety Scale which, in Eysenck's terminology (Franks, 1956), is known as a measure of neuroticism. On the other hand, although neurotics no doubt score higher on the M.A.S. than normals, their productivity appears to be considerably lower (Balken and Masserman, 1940; Lorenz and Cobb, 1953).

None of the experiments quoted in this section have been repeated. However, it appears safe to say that "emotional involvement" may be assessed by using diverse measures of speech activity and other peripheral signs accompanying speech. Experiments reveal the problem to be a complex one, requiring more experimental work before personality validation will offer lasting results.

Language

The use of language to measure expressive behaviour in psychiatric patients has been described a number of times in a systematic manner (Woods, 1938; Lorenz, 1952, 1955; Lorenz and Cobb, 1953). The main results of an experimental kind may be presented in three sections.

The *first section* deals with the *active/qualitative form of construction*, or the verb/adjective quotient (V.A.Q.) and the number of adjectives. The statistical analysis of these two scores is taken to have started with Busemann's (1925, 1926) finding in children that the V.A.Q. correlated positively, and "adjectives" negatively with ratings of "emotional instability." In other words, "activity" was indicative of instability and "qualitative" construction of stability.

Using responses to T.A.T. pictures, Balken and Masserman (1940) found that in neurotics, divided into conversion hysteria, anxiety and obsessive-compulsive states, hysterics used more adjectives and a smaller V.A.Q. than the other categories. Lorenz and Cobb (1953) found the V.A.Q. to be higher and "adjectives" to be lower in neurotics (all hysterics) than in normals. (Manics behaved similarly to neurotics.) Benton, Hartman and Sarason (1955), using normals, obtained a positive relationship between Taylor's Manifest Anxiety Scale, which is known to measure "neuroticism" (Franks, 1956), and the V.A.Q. The relationship to "adjectives" was negative, but acceptable significance was not reached in either case. Other results, consistent for spoken (Fairbanks, 1944) and written language (Mann, 1944), showed schizophrenics to vary similarly to other abnormals. The results are presented jointly in Table III.2.

This table shows that the V.A.Q. is lowest, and the adjectives score highest, for the stable/hysteric/normal/low anxiety types of personality. Firstly, it may be assumed that "activity" of language increases and "qualitative use" decreases with abnormality and/or neurotic tendencies. (Anxiety and obsessive-compulsive states tend to higher scores on neuroticism

higher than hysterics. So far, results on the use of pronouns are similar to those obtained using the V.A.Q. and the "adjectives" score. It is as well, however, to keep in mind that the pronouns score varies with the interviewer (Goldman-Eisler, 1954b).

"Because of the schizophrenic's self-preoccupation and his tendency to ignore his environment," pronouns, and in particular self-referrals, should be more frequent than in a normal person (Fairbanks, 1944).

TABLE III.2

"ACTIVE" AND "QUALITATIVE" LANGUAGE CONSTRUCTION IN NORMALS AND ABNORMALS

	Verb-Adjective quotient		Adjectives‡	
Score	High	Low	High	Low
Busemann* (1925) (normals) .	unstable	stable	stable	unstable
Balken and Masserman* (1940)	anxiety states (3·11) (medium: ob	conversion hysterics (1·35) s.-comp. 2·17)	hysterics (medium:	anxiety states obs.-comp.)
Lorenz and Cobb (1953) . .	hysterics (1·70) manics (1·68)	normals (1·07)	normals (12·2)	hysterics (10·6) manics (9·6)
Benton, Hartman and Sarason (1955)† (normals). . .	high anxiety (5·13)	low anxiety (4·97)	low anxiety (3·55)	high anxiety (3·38)
Fairbanks (1944) . . .	schizophrenics (4·90)	normals (3·43)	normals (6·69)	schizophrenics (5·37)
Mann† (1944) . . .	schizophrenics (2·38)	normals (1·98)	normals (9·45)	schizophrenics (8·33)

* Significance unknown.   † Not significant.   V.A.Q. of Fairbanks and Mann computed from mean scores.
‡ Percentage of total word sample.

questionnaires than hysterics.) Secondly, on account of Balken and Masserman's results, Eysenck (1950) has suggested that a "factor of dysthymia-hysteria" is involved. This aspect should also be explored.

Variations in score norms between investigators are considerable. As long as stimulus conditions are not standardized between groups, results cannot be assessed adequately.

In the second section, the use of pronouns, in which large individual differences have been found, is discussed (Conrad and Conrad, 1956). A high score is said to be associated with egocentric impulses or emphasis on communication. The incidence of the first person pronouns (for example, I, my, mine, me, myself) may mean rigidity in shifting from the subjective point of view; or a negative attitude to be disguised or dissimulated (Lorenz and Cobb, 1953); these authors found that abnormals, neurotics more than manics, had higher scores than normals. Within the neurotics, anxiety and obsessional-compulsive states scored

This was in fact confirmed, as far as spoken language is concerned. However, Mann (1944), using written language, obtained results of a contradictory kind. At the present time it appears difficult to say whether this is due to differences in the response mode (spoken versus written) or in the type of patient.

The third section of language characteristics deals with "vocabulary inflexibility." As it borders on the cognitive field rather closely it will be referred to only briefly. Johnson (1944), introducing a methodical and comprehensive study of language, devised the "type-token ratio" (T.T.R.). This is the ratio of the number of different words (types) to the total number of words (tokens) in a given passage. As might be expected, the mean T.T.R. of schizophrenics was significantly lower than that of normals in both spoken (Fairbanks, 1944) and written language (Mann, 1944). The latter author's results are shown in Fig. 3.4. It may be added that both authors accepted these results to be essentially independent of intelligence.

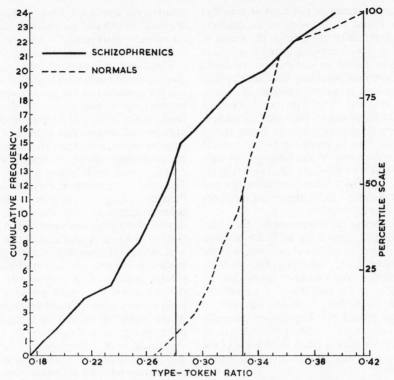

FIG. 3.4. CUMULATIVE FREQUENCY CURVES OF T.T.R.s FOR TWENTY-FOUR
SCHIZOPHRENICS AND TWENTY-FOUR NORMALS

Means are shown by vertical lines. High T.T.R. means great "flexibility."

(*From Mann,* 1944)

A somewhat similar experiment was performed by Mittenecker (1951). This author scored interview material obtained from normals and schizophrenics for (*a*) number of *repetitions of syllables*, (*b*) number of *syllables repeated*, and (*c*) mean *distance between repetitions*. Schizophrenics scored higher for (*a*) and (*b*) and lower for (*c*). A combination of all scores resulted in discrimination between the groups without overlap.

Results show consistently that the use of vocabulary is more "inflexible" in schizophrenics than in normals.

II. COMPLEX PRODUCTS OF ARTS AND DRAWING

Artistic Productions

Since Prinzhorn's (1919) monograph concerning *Das bildnerische Schaffen der Geisteskranken* interpretation of the artistic productions of mental patients has been extensive both in psychiatric and psychoanalytical work. Preference in treatment of such data goes to that derived from psychotics and the main conclusions reached were summarized by Mosse (1940) as follows: (1) the paintings of psychotics show a marked similarity to the drawings of children and of primitive peoples; (2) there are typical pathological signs such as stereotypy, mannerisms, symbolism, strange inaccessibility, etc.; (3) there is failure to achieve anything like realistic representation. If these conclusions could be accepted as they stand, one could indeed speak of progress in this field.

Anastasi and Foley (1940) were also impressed by the great claims made. It appeared, however, that interpretations were inflated by uncontrolled speculation, particularly of a psychoanalytic kind, and that clear clinical pictures did not, as a rule, emerge from the study of artistic productions.

Some examples of drawing characteristics, claimed to be typical of abnormals, are given. The choice of small paper for drawing was related to neurotic depression and anxiety. Aggressive patients preferred large paper. Unusual positions of drawings on a page were found in the work of depressives; *horror vacui*, or compulsive filling in of all spaces, in that of psychotics. Small drawing in relation to size of the paper was found in compulsion neurosis. Psychotics produced contaminating lines, overlapping functions of lines and criss-cross outlines of figures. Their drawings were also more repetitive and stereotyped. Some interpretations of lines may be quoted. Fuzzy and sloppy lines were taken to mean escape from rigidity, thin lines to mean repression, vertical lines greater assertiveness, circular lines greater submissiveness, spirals excitability, etc. Bell (1951) in his twenty-six-page summary table of drawing and painting characteristics provides these and hundreds of other alleged relationships.

Many of these appear quite reasonable. However, methods and interpretations vary so much between authors that an attempt to assess the consistency of the results must remain both frustrating and fruitless. More experimentally-minded authors, employing art productions mainly in the assessment of personality and adjustment, attempted a certain amount of standardization in procedure. The method generally used is demonstrated in the following three studies of personality, which are usually taken to be some of the best controlled ones in this field (compare the review by Precker, 1950).

Paula Elkisch (1945) selected the productions of eight children from a collection of 2,200 paintings and drawings made by a great number of children. They were rated for the following criteria of style: complexity-simplicity, expansion-compression, integration-disintegration and realism-symbolism. These criteria were related to sociometric ratings of "adjustment." These were as heterogeneous as were the art productions, and high correspondence was obtained.

Using the work of fifty-five freshmen or sophomore girls, Waehner (1946) drew up personality sketches from a series of "free" drawings, mainly from formal elements like size, format, distribution of form-elements, quality of lines, organization of form, perspective, shading, etc. Teachers then matched Rorschach interpretations with these sketches and correct matching is claimed in 87 per cent of the cases. The subjects were investigated in small groups of five to six.

In an extensive study of self-portraits, drawn by forty boys and forty girls, Stewart (1955) analysed thirty-one rated variables such as realism, skill, symmetry, qualities of line, etc. After factor analysis, the six clusters found were correlated with personal inventory scores, behaviour ratings, and ratings of inferred needs. Results which were of interest showed "skill quality" to be related to maladjustment and neurotic introversion in the boys' sample, but to

creativeness and "adjustive introversive tendencies" in the girls'. Width and variability of line correlated with "dominant extraversion" for the boys and with sociability and adjustment for the girls.

These three examples, selected for their outstanding quality, are in many ways typical of a great number of related studies in so far as they reveal a number of methodological weaknesses. Of these, only the most fundamental ones will be mentioned at present. It may be said, firstly, that criteria of art productions, whether of an impressionistic or analytic kind, and corresponding ratings, or other assessments, of personality have been largely *specific to investigators*. This makes comparison between investigators and, therefore, recognition of general trends in expressive behaviour difficult. The conclusion usually is that a certain investigator has made certain observations, the validity of which is restricted to that particular study.

A second criticism is directed against the *matching method*, predominantly used in studies discussed in the present section. It is now widely agreed that this method served as a "stop gap with little future," its main drawback being the impossibility of saying which of the numerous aspects of a personality sketch, a psychogram, or a case-study as a whole are the significant ones. Wrongly applied this method is also widely open to *contamination*. In most cases raters knew both the art productions and the subjects involved. They may, therefore, in their assessment have been influenced by extraneous cues. This would explain the numerous claims of positive results, which shrank to an insignificant degree when more rigorous methods of assessment were applied, as will be seen later on.

Free Drawing

Growing out of the assessment of artistic production a number of drawing techniques have been developed with varying limitations of instruction. This modification may be appreciated as one step towards standardization of procedure. Of the many techniques proposed, those which have received very little attention are not considered. Some of these are: the "Projective-Motor Test" (Rapkin and Wheeler, 1949); the "Most-Unpleasant-Concept Test" (Harrower, 1950); the "Family-Drawing Test" (Hulse, 1951); the "Baum Test" (Koch, 1951); the "Eight-Card-Redrawing Test" (Caligor, 1952); the "Rosenberg Draw-a-Person Test" (Levy, 1950); the "Inside-of-the-Body Test" (Tait and Ascher, 1955); the "Animal-Drawing Test" (Schwartz and Rosenberg, 1955); and the "Draw-as-an-idiot-would Test" (Ponzo, 1957).

Of the techniques classifiable under this heading, the "Draw-a-Person Test" (D.A.P., Fig. 3.5), derived from Goodenough (1926) and Machover (1949) has received greatest attention. It is discussed, here, jointly with Buck's (1948*a*, 1948*b*) "House-Tree-Person Test" (H.T.P., Fig. 3.5). Projective psychologists claim that results obtained by this technique are indicators of abnormal behaviour, as follows: "These psychomotor expressive productions reveal all components in the personality that revolve around the body-image, for example, acceptance of sexual role, anxiety or depressiveness in the sphere of interpersonal relations, anxiety relating to bodily processes or structures, relative degree of rigidity or flexibility of the personality, tendency to withdraw from reality, low sense of self-esteem or inferiority complex, etc." (Abt and Bellak, *Projective Psychology*, pp. 441–2, 1950). This is only a small portion of the great number of claims made by various projective psychologists. It may be all the more surprising to read in the same volume of *Projective Psychology* the following statement by Levy (1950): "In order to avert cynicism and disillusion it is well to emphasize that the technique of analysing drawings is without experimental validation, rarely yields unequivocal information, and frequently misleads the unwary into plausible misstatements about the personality of the person whose drawings are being studied."

When the evidence obtained has been examined, *correlations with abnormal* criteria have provided the following results.

It may be seen from this table that significant differences between normals and abnormals were obtained in every instance, but not between the various groups of abnormals. This statement, however, is not to be interpreted as a definite conclusion for at least three reasons. As a rule, the effect of interrelated scoring items was not analysed, cross-validation was not carried out and in most instances tester and scorer were identical, thus exposing scoring to contamination. Each one of these criticisms would suggest invalidity for almost the entire result.

This has in fact been demonstrated by more rigorously controlled studies. Having investigated human figure drawings by one hundred controls (dental patients) and eighty anxiety neurotics, Royal (1949) found that eight out of twenty-eight items tended to differentiate between the two groups. However, these eight items did not hold up under cross-validation. Similar results of cross-validation were reported by Michal-Smith (1953) and Kotkov and Goodman (1953). After matching controls (thirty-nine veterans awaiting dental treatment) and schizophrenics (N = 39) for age and school grades, Stonesifer (1949) obtained no significant differences between the groups, using the Goodenough point score. Having correlated human figure drawing scores with eight carefully prepared personality ratings of reasonable reliability (median of 0·82), Zimmer (1955) found very low coefficients (median of 0·16). In a

carefully designed study, Whitmyre (1953) found that adjustment, as rated from drawings of the human figure, did not discriminate between fifty psychiatric patients and fifty normals.

Successful results have been claimed in investigating the *prognostic value* of drawing techniques, similarly

FIG. 3.5. EXAMPLES OF RESPONSES TO THE DRAW-A-PERSON AND HOUSE-TREE-PERSON TESTS

to validation against abnormal criteria (Fiedler and Siegel, 1949; Ochs, 1950; Cowden *et al.*, 1955). These studies are open to the criticisms already made. Again, applying cross-validation to the psychiatric selection of flying personnel, Anastasi and Foley (1952) found considerable shrinkage in a number of significantly differentiating items, although a modest degree of success was retained. Certainly, more work is required to form a final judgement.

A third type of "validation," concerning the "content" of drawing expression, is mentioned only briefly. The analysis of "psychosexual adjustment" is taken as the outstanding example ever since

Machover's first reinterpretation, in terms of sexual adjustment, of the Goodenough intelligence test. In the H.T.P., for instance, some investigators insist that a tree or a chimney pot looks "phallic" and serves as an indicator of "psychosexual conflict" (Jolles, 1952a, 1952b). Sloan (1954) has already furnished reasonable

ratings of personality characteristics to D.A.P. scores, has already been mentioned as not successful.

On the surface, more promising results have been obtained by Witkin et al. (1954). Four graphic features: lack of body confidence, absence of struggle for sexual identity, lack of drive and a total drawing

TABLE III.3

PSEUDO-POSITIVE RESULTS AS AN EFFECT OF FAILURE TO CONSIDER ITEM-INTERCORRELATION, CROSS-VALIDATION AND CONTAMINATION

Author	Test	Subjects	Results
Anastasi and Foley (1944)	D.A.P.	340 C., 340 abnormals	61 per cent of 23 items differentiated at the 1 per cent level
Albee and Hamlin (1950)	D.A.P.	30 C., 21 anxiety neur., 21 schiz.	Pooled ratings. C–neur. (1 per cent); C–schiz. (1 per cent); Neur.–schiz. (N.S.)
Goldworth (Abstract 1950) . . .	D.A.P.	50 C., 50 neur., 50 schiz., 50 brain damage	13 per cent sign. differences of 306 comparisons between 4 groups
Holzberg and Wexler (1950) . . .	D.A.P.	78 C., 38 schiz., (of these: 18 paran., 12 hebephr., 6 cat.)	13 per cent of 174 items differentiated at 5 per cent level between C and abnormals. No sign. differences between abnormals
Singer (Abstract 1950) .	H.T.P.	40 C., 34 schiz.	28 per cent of 428 items differentiated at the 5 per cent level
Eigenbrode (Abstract 1951) . . .	D.A.P.	40 C., 40 schiz.	14 per cent of 184 items differentiated at the 5 per cent level
Gerard and Kornetsky (1955) . . .	D.A.P.	23 C., 33 opiate addicts	Maturational level (N.S.). Rigidity (1 per cent). Conventionality score (2 per cent)
Reznikoff and Tomblen (1956) . . .	D.A.P.	25 neur., 25 schiz.	18 items. Neur. v. schiz. (N.S.)

D.A.P. = Draw-a-Person.   H.T.P. = House-Tree-Person.   C = normal controls.   Neur. = neurotics.   Schiz. = schizophrenics.

criticism of such vague concepts which are "operationally indefinable" and "therefore intrinsically invalid symbols." As for the D.A.P., a competent review of the literature by Brown and Tolor (1957) has shown that "there is no convincing evidence that adequacy of psychosexual identification or adjustment is reflected in the choice of sex" and that "homosexuals do not draw a figure of the opposite sex first, contrary to widespread hypothesis."

This "muddied picture of the validity of human figure drawings" as Zimmer (1956) sees it, requires "experiments designed to yield definite answers." Steps have been taken in two directions. Drawings have been related to more objective criteria and the interference of some irrelevant factors has been defined. Zimmer's (1955) study, relating reliable

score were derived from the D.A.P. and yielded nearly consistently correlations significant at the 1 per cent level (in both males and females) with perceptual tests. Some kind of cross-validation is said to have taken place. These results may be regarded as encouraging in themselves. However, they in no way validate the postulated relationship between "field-dependent" performance and the "counterparts of personality characteristics" (D.A.P. scores), quoted above. Terms like "body confidence," "struggle for sexual identity" and "lack of drive" are meaningless until they are validated and operationally defined. In addition, as "personality" scores, they are much too complex to be used as dimensional measures and have no unitary meaning (Gruen, 1957).

One major source of error in making interpretations

has been uncovered. According to Goodenough's original intention, the D.A.P. was intended to serve as a measure of intelligence. Although results have remained inconclusive for reasons of unreliability in D.A.P. scoring, widely varying scoring items and types of subjects used, significant correlations between figure drawing, as well as H.T.P., and various types of intelligence tests have repeatedly been obtained (Buck, 1948b; Ansbacher, 1952; Murphy, 1956). This fact should compel investigators wishing to make personality inferences to assess and consider the role of intelligence. This has rarely been done and may in part have been favourable to the appearance of pseudo-successful results in relation to drawing techniques.

A further, and perhaps more important, source of error in making interpretations is interindividual variation in drawing proficiency, or artistic excellence. Albee and Hamlin (1949) indicated that the quality of the drawing may influence interpretation. Words and Cook (1954) produced evidence that placement of the hands in drawn representations of the human figure is a function of level of proficiency in drawing. The most important of all the papers quoted concerning drawing techniques is that of Whitmyre (1953). In a well-controlled study, this author asked twelve experts to rank the D.A.P. productions of fifty normals and fifty abnormals for degree of personal adjustment and artistic excellence. Further ranking for artistic quality was done by eight commercial artists. It was found that assessments for adjustment and artistic performance intercorrelated higher than 0·8 (sic). However, neither art nor adjustment ratings, made by psychologists and artists, were significantly related to the normal-patient dichotomy.

Drawing Completion

Of the various types of this test (compare the "Horn-Hellersberg Test," Hellersberg, 1945; Ames and Hellersberg, 1949; Frank and Rosen, 1949), only the "Wartegg Zeichentest (W.Z.T.)" (1939), predominantly used as a projective technique, has received sufficient attention to merit discussion. A theoretical system derived from the Leipzig Ganzheits-psychologie (Krüger-Sander) and including the following four basic functions, each accompanied by two more or less opposed characteristics, is used as a basis of interpretation (English version by Kinget, 1952)—

> *Wartegg Personality Functions* (Fig. 3.6)
> Emotion (outgoing—seclusive)
> Imagination (combining—creative)
> Intellect (practical—speculative)
> Activity (dynamic—controlled)

A great number of formal and expressive response categories are rated and represented configurationally, separately for the functions postulated (Fig. 3.6). In Germany, the W.Z.T. is extensively used by clinical psychologists both in normal and abnormal psychology, but validation apart from clinical impressions has not taken place. Where clinical groups have been used experimental controls are absent (Seiffert, 1951; Pfeiffer, 1951; Müller-Suur, 1952; Bauer, 1952; Luza, 1954).

It has, however, been found that Wartegg scores correlated significantly (0·79) with the Wechsler Scales (Anonymous, 1954; Stark, 1954), similarly to the drawing techniques described in the preceding section, and that primarily the W.Z.T. measures drawing ability and not personality (Mader, 1952). Both drawing skill and intelligence were found to interfere strongly with symptomatic traits (Takala and Hakkarainen, 1953). Intercorrelations of thirty-one scoring items with a variety of variables derived from personality questionnaires, interest inventories and ratings of situational behaviour and occupational success, yielded meagre results. A constructive proposition was, however, made by developing a multiple choice version of the W.Z.T., which would exclude the effect of drawing skill.

In a separate study by Takala (1953), only three of one hundred and fifty-four correlations between the W.Z.T. and a variety of questionnaire, psychomotor, expressive movement and projective technique scores were significant at the 5 per cent level (sic). It may safely be concluded that, at the present stage, personality and abnormality correlates of formal drawing characteristics of this kind are not known. Lossen's (1955) claim that "sequence analysis," instead of analysis of isolated items or drawings as a whole, measures "personality dynamics" and not traits cannot be accepted until proof is obtained. Sequence analysis, though logically a sound proposition, may merely reflect unspecific practice effects or unreliability.

Evaluation of Results

One may be in accord with the unanimous judgement of authors that artistic products and free drawing reveal very different aspects of personality and abnormality. This statement, however, is scientifically meaningless until we have demonstrated, *firstly*, that expressive movement *per se* is diagnostic of personality, and not via intelligence, artistic excellence, age, etc. *Secondly*, the basic measures of expressive movement, their functional conditions and personality correlates have to be defined in order to map out the field. The inescapable conclusion, after perusal of the literature, is that not one of these basic aims has even been approached during decades of analysis by some hundreds of investigators.

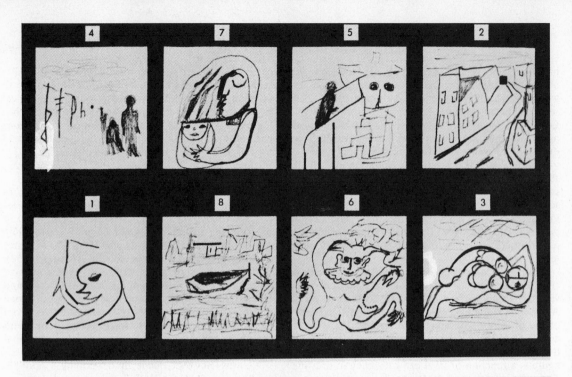

	CRITERIA	Total Score	1	2	3	4	5	6	7	8
NATURE	Animate	7	X/	X/	X		/		X	X/
	Physiognomy	4	/	/	/				XX	X
	Inanimate	1	/				/			
	Atmosphere	4	X		/	X		X/		
OBJECTS	Utility	4			X	X/		X/		
	Ornaments									
	Style					/				
COVERAGE	Movement	7	X	XX	X				XXX	
	Full	10	/	X	X	XX		XX	XX	X/
	Empty	1					X			
	Expanded	2			/			X		/
	Constricted									
	Organization	6	X		X	X/		/	X	X
	Detail	3		/	/	/			X	
LINES	Curved	6	/	X	/		X		X/	X/
	Straight	4	X		X/	X	/			
	Strong	7	X	XX	/		/	X	X	X
	Soft	3	X		/					

1	2	3	4	5	6	7	8	Total Score	CRITERIA	
									Fancy	**FANTASY**
	X	/		X		XX	/	5	Phantasm	
									Symbolism	
									Original	
									Symmetric	**ABSTRACT**
									Asymetric	
									Technical	
									Careful	
X	X							2	Casual	
									Light	**SHADING**
X/	X	X			X			5	Dark	
		/	/					1	Orientation	
									Closure	
									Parts	
	/	X	X	XX	X		/	6	Scribbles	
									Duplication	
									Repetition	
									Schematism	

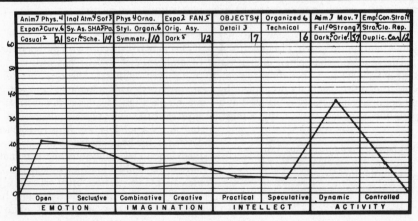

FIG. 3.6. RESPONSE AND EVALUATION OF THE WARTEGG DRAWING COMPLETION TEST

(From Kinget, 1952)

Before beginning detailed criticism, let us state the evidence agreed on between authors. Several reviews have already been quoted. Writers usually agree that *smallness and constriction* are expressive of neurotic signs of depression, anxiety and compulsion; of feelings of inferiority and timidity; of rejection and deprivation; of introversion and emotional dependence. *Large size and expansion* are taken to indicate outgoing, extraverted, aggressive and impulsive personalities. There is a back-door provided for observations which do not fit. "Over-controlled" persons, for instance, draw small or constricted, even when they don't fit the description given above. *Stereotyped rigid, repetitive and symmetrical arrangements* are claimed for a variety of categories like neurotic depression; maladjustment; self-centred, emotionally reacting and blocking personalities; paranoia; schizophrenia; psychotics in general and mental retardation.

There are some suggestions that *response variability* may be high in psychotics; *disregard of conditions* frequent with uncontrolled, asocial behaviour; *tendency to fill in* pronounced in schizophrenics and immature, aggressive, non-adaptive patients; consideration for *great detail* distinct in over-neat and pedantic personalities, and often in depressives; *odd responses* and *untidiness* more frequent in psychotics and feeble-minded; *sharp-edged versus smooth-curvy lines* more frequent in overtly aggressive persons with low adjustment and *good proportion* to be more prevalent in persons with initiative and a good measure of social adaptation.

Few clinicians, on the face value of these claims, would challenge their appropriateness. However, a *summary criticism* of these and other claims, some of which have already been indicated, should convince the reader of the actual poverty and lack of stringency in the conclusions. The following points are made—

1. Any investigator knows that odd, extreme, and poor responses are predominantly found in untestable, deteriorated, feeble-minded or brain-damaged persons. These most impressive characteristics are usually not found in testable functional abnormals, equated for intelligence, age and absence of brain damage with normals. If *deterioration* and *co-operation* is accounted for, a large proportion of otherwise discriminating characteristics remains useless.

2. Investigators have, with little effect, already been frequently criticized for insufficient or inappropriate *application of controls*, inadequacy of sampling, contamination, interference of irrelevant factors, and lack of formal testing of validity and reliability. The last has been found to be strongly influenced by artistic aspects of performance, rather than by actual movement characteristics.

3. There has been a great lack of empirical investiga-

tion and examination of testable hypotheses. *Loose theorizing* and interpretations of the analytical kind such as "psychosexual problems were freely projected," "broad spotting indicated regression to anal stage," "attempted to overcompensate with extra-large reinforced feet," or of the expressive kind such as: "rigid quality of lines," "intellectual realism of painting," "free floating anxiety" in curves, wobbly lines of "low security," high pressure as "vitality," jittery lines suggestive of "imitation," etc., have remained dominating but useless. There is complete absence of experimental justification for such pseudo-scientific terms, techniques being used as "maids-of-all-work."

4. *Clinical criteria* such as neurosis, psychosis, conduct disturbance and maladjustment have been accepted as ready-made psychiatric concepts without any further refinement. These criteria are bound to be heterogeneous. The suggestion, perhaps the most convincing, provided by the literature that depressed, anxious and compulsive neurotics draw smaller and more constricted than the outgoing, contact-seeking and aggressive personality has never been followed up by constructing corresponding objective criteria in an attempt to test the alleged relationships.

5. *Scores* used were too complex, or varied profoundly in number and nature between the investigators There has been no systematic item analysis between studies reported, nor was the effect of intercorrelated items assessed. This has resulted in a continued absence of meaning in the measures used.

6. Safeguarding *spontaneity of expression*, which is often invoked to defend neglect of experimental control and standardization, may well be an important point. It may, however, be argued that spontaneity would better be investigated by using *suitable* experimental controls to define its meaning instead of accepting any haphazard and incidental movements as scores. Subjects could be made to respond freely, visually as in the multiple choice proposition for the drawing completion test by Takala and Hakkarainen (1953), or else by manipulation, to all desired response types without artistic competence or intelligence interfering to a significant degree.

7. The *necessity of more objective scoring* procedures is shown by the high degree of error made in rating drawings. The agreement between various psychologists in rating such characteristics as paranoid signs, facial expression and stance was so low as to "suggest that it is precarious to accept most of the current assumptions regarding figure drawing analysis" (Fisher and Fisher, 1950). Moreover, experts agreed no more than untrained raters. Similarly, Blum (1954) exposed the "highly questionable validity" of the D.A.P. ratings from a number of other points of view.

III. SEMI-OBJECTIVE TECHNIQUES

Copying of Designs

Tests of copying and reproduction of designs have been used by Binet, Hetzer, Gesell and Kern, Rupp, Busemann, Ellis and Wolff (Wewetzer, 1956; Bell, 1951). The test of particular consequence for the

"good gestalt," etc. (Woltmann, 1950). These theoretical aspects, however, may be omitted from discussion as deviations in reproductions are so multivarious as not to follow the hypothesized gestalt laws.

The theory connected with the B.G.T., as expressed

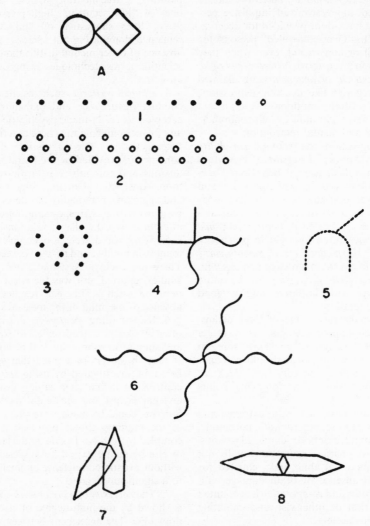

FIG. 3.7. FORMS OF THE BENDER VISUAL MOTOR GESTALT TEST

present discussion is the Bender-Gestalt Test, for short B.G.T. (original monograph, Bender, 1938; manual of instructions, 1946, 1949). This test consists of nine simple designs each of which is presented to a subject to copy on a sheet of paper (Fig. 3.7). Designs stem from Wertheimer and are supposed to embody principles of "gestalt" like "proximity," "continuity,"

by Pascal and Suttell (1951), is either too general or lacking in precise definition to be of great use, but may be mentioned because of its historical interest and reads as follows. "The greater the damage to the cortex through convulsive therapy, amentia, lack of maturation, trauma, etc., the greater the deviations from the stimulus. . . . Deviations in individuals without demonstrable brain damage reflect the individual's attitude toward reality. This attitude we believe to be a function of the integrative capacity of the organism, the ego."

As with free drawing, the B.G.T. has been used to assess a variety of things: maturation, intelligence, psychological disturbances, clinical improvement, age regression, brain damage and various kinds of physical treatments. Following the qualitative and interpretative phase of Bender, Hutt (1945), and others, more carefully controlled studies have been made as shown in Table III.4. In this context only the copying part of the B.G.T. is discussed, as drawing characteristics derived from the recall technique are known to be interfered with by memory. This would make separate assessment of "visuomotor" activity impossible, as movement and error aspects of the B.G.T. are difficult to separate. Results may now be inspected in the table below.

Because of repeated criticism, considerable efforts to improve objective scoring of the B.G.T. have been made. The results, however, have been contradictory from the beginning. Of the six studies accepting Pascal and Suttell's scoring system (5, 6, 8, 9, 10, 11 of Table III.4), two showed negative results. These were decidedly the better controlled studies, as Gobetz cross-validated his findings and Tamkin controlled for age, which was shown to be significantly related to the B.G.T. In general, the conclusion may be drawn that this test did not differentiate consistently between normals and abnormals, certainly not between neurotics and psychotics, regardless of scoring procedure.

Although the B.G.T. was not shown to be consistently correlated with functional abnormality it may nevertheless predict clinical improvement. Swenson and Pascal (1953) claimed correspondingly that those patients who subsequently recovered had a significantly lower mean z-score on the B.G.T. at the time of admission than those who did not recover. Unfortunately, none of the possibly important characteristics of the improved-unimproved dichotomy like type of

TABLE III.4

RESULTS USING THE BENDER GESTALT TEST

Differentiation between normals and abnormals has remained inconsistent. The test does not differentiate between abnormal categories

Author	Groups tested	Results
1. Billingslea (1948)	50 C., 100 neur.	63 indices, 25 test factors, results essentially negative
2. Pascal and Suttell (1951)	474 C., 187 neur., 136 psych.	Sign. differences between C and abnormals, not between neur. and psych. 102 items
3. Hanvik (1951)	14 patients with organic and 23 with functional back complaints (neur.)	No sign. differences using 3 scoring methods
4. Suttell and Pascal (1952)	278 C., 117 neur., 54 schiz.	4 of 12 items at 1 per cent level between C and schiz., none between neur. and schiz.
5. Addington (1952)	43 C., 32 schiz.	P and S score sign. differences
6. Gobetz (1953)	285 C., 108 neur., *cross-validation:* 54 C., 64 poorly adjusted	Failure of previous scoring systems. New system of 30 signs: sign. differences
7. Curnutt (1953)	25 C., 25 alcoholics	Sign. difference
8. Lonskin (1954)	37 neur., 36 psych.	P and S score, sign. differences
9. Bowland and Deabler (1956)	20 of each: C., neur., schiz., org.	P and S score between group sign., neur.–schiz. = N.S.
10. Sonder (1955)	40 C. with "normal" M.M.P.I. scores; 42 abnormals, mainly schiz.	P and S score, sign. difference
11. Tamkin (1957)	27 neur., 27 psych., *age* controlled	Neur. higher score than psych. (N.S.). No sign. correl. with M.M.P.I. scales

C. = normal controls.   Neur. = neurotics.
Schiz. = schizophrenics.   Psych. = psychotics.   M.M.P.I. = Minnesota Multiphasic Personality Inventory.

patients, chronicity, age and intelligence was stated. It is, therefore, impossible to say for what reason the subgroups differed. In addition, a correlation between *improvement* scores on the B.G.T. and in the clinical status might well have contradicted the conclusion, as improvement from error tends to be positively correlated with initial error level.

In a much better controlled experiment by Cowden, Deabler and Feamster (1955), two applications of the B.G.T. did not predict improvement consistently. At the same time, large discrepancies occurred between three other drawing tests (H.T.P., Self-Concept Drawing and Opposite-Sex Drawing). It may be considered a major fault in the design that functional and organic cases were mixed up apparently without any attempt to equate experimental and control groups for diagnostic label, nor any other important variable.

Sonder's (1955) outstanding experiment deserves greater attention and repetition with larger samples. This author, guided by indications from the literature, predicted that acute patients with good scores and chronic patients with poor scores will improve more than their opposites. Five tests, including the B.G.T., were administered within five days of admission to hospital. Patients admitted for the first time were classified as acute and those with previous admissions as chronic cases. Initial test results were then correlated with an independent psychiatrist's judgement of improvement at the end of a ninety-day period of hospitalization. The prediction was confirmed for both acute (6 per cent level) and chronic (1 per cent level) cases.

The results of these three studies are as heterogeneous as they can be, but provocative enough to call for validation under improved conditions.

An interesting attempt to test the psychoanalytic "regression" theory was made by Suttell and Pascal (1952). Fifty-four of each, schizophrenics, neurotics, adult normals and children of 6 to $9\frac{1}{2}$ and 10 to 14 years of age, were tested. Those signs which differentiated between the two groups of children did not differentiate between adult controls and schizophrenics. The authors concluded that regression, as measured by the B.G.T., is not peculiar to the schizophrenic.

Evaluating the experiments quoted, it may be said that some progress has been made when compared with free drawing technique. Scoring systems and number of items scored have varied less excessively. Administration and scoring has become more standardized and objectified, and has been followed by a considerable increase in reliability.

Scoring, however, is by no means objective and remains unnecessarily complicated. As was stated in the beginning, deviations do not follow the gestalt laws supposed to be underlying the various stimuli.

They are, in fact, rather specific to stimuli and subjects, with the result that distortions are numerous. A *parallel test* to the B.G.T. does not exist and is, in fact, extremely difficult to construct. If the same test is given twice, learning from greater familiarity may take place resulting in poor discrimination (Gobetz, 1953).

The *psychological nature* of the B.G. score is too complex, and inextricably lumps together heterogeneous movement characteristics or distortions (compare F.R.T., Sect. IV). To mention only one example, the reduction to one raw- or z-score does not permit differentiation between movement and error. This alone would explain lack of consistent differentiation between abnormal criteria.

The *choice of criteria* has not progressed beyond the traditional categories of neurotics, psychotics, or maladjusted. With the exception of Murray and Roberts (1956), who investigated expansion-constriction of one patient during his manic and depressed phases, no suggestion as to any functional properties or more specific validity has been made. Neurotics have never been split up into subcategories despite their divergences in movement, as was suggested by clinical description, assessments of drawings and art productions, as well as from objective expressive movement tests. Lonstein's (1954) neurotics, for example, consisted mainly of anxiety states, which explains his significant differences obtained between neurotics and psychotics, as differences in expressive movement are greatest between dysthymics and psychotics (compare F.R.T., Sect. IV).

Finally, individual differences of *skill in assessment* of drawings affect the B.G.T., as much as other drawing techniques. Mehlman and Vatovec (1956) submitted twenty-five paired protocols of organic and functional psychotics to three expert judges for "blind analysis." There were considerable differences between the judges, suggesting "a surprising heterogeneity of skill in the use of the B.G.T."

Manipulative Tests

The four tests described in this section have common elements in that they are primarily colour-reaction tests with the analysis of formal characteristics added, and that patterns are formed by manipulating a variety of stimulus items offered. The colour portion of the tests is largely associated with certain expectations of emotional reactivity. No particular *a priori* theory appears to have been set up for the structural, or formal portion. However, originators of the tests state, in general, that degree of abnormality correlates positively with poor structure.

Mosaic Test (Löwenfeld, 1949, 1954)

This test consists of two hundred and twenty-eight (small box), or four hundred and fifty-six (large box) standardized pieces of geometrical shapes, which may be of wood or other materials (Fig. 3.8). The small box contains twenty-four squares, forty-eight diamonds, forty-eight right-angled triangles, thirty-six equilateral triangles and seventy-two scalene triangles. The shapes are in six colours: black, white, red, green, blue, and yellow. The subject is asked to construct something on a wooden tray 13 in. × 10½ in. and the resulting patterns are recorded.

Löwenfeld felt that the type of pattern made, apart from the choice of colour, was indicative of the "personality structure." She also found certain patterns or elements to be related to various clinical categories. Many studies, claiming the usefulness of the Mosaic Test in the abnormal field, were descriptive or simply classified responses (Wertham and Golden, 1941; Diamond and Schmale, 1944; Wertham, 1950; Johnson, 1957). Reiman (1950) gave the test to controls and patients with "habit disturbance," "conduct disturbance" and "neurotic traits." Although the significance of the results was not computed, it appears from the data supplied that only very few of the thirty-three items would discriminate significantly. "Scatter," for example, would be greatest in subjects with conduct disturbance and productions would be largest from subjects with neurotic traits. These findings were not cross-validated, but resemble those found with free drawing.

The frequency with which certain types of designs occurred was determined by Kerr (1939) in a sample of over one thousand subjects. Using selected subjects, she obtained fairly high correlations between mosaic pattern interpretation and diagnosis. The results may, however, have been affected by contamination, as the interpretations were made by the experimenter giving the test. This, and other criticism made by Himmelweit and Eysenck (1944–6), throws doubt on the validity of the results. The latter authors, in a carefully designed matching experiment, confirmed however that experts could match mosaics and personality sketches and could write personality sketches from mosaics, which were made by doctors, with better-than-chance success. The experts failed, however, in giving significantly correct judgements on a personality questionnaire completed by the patients. The most important results are judged to be those obtained by the layout of test elements. Dysthymics (obsessionals, anxiety states and reactive depressives) tended to produce compact designs, while hysterics tended to produce scattered and intermediate designs. The results were not cross-validated.

In Levin's (1956) well-controlled and comprehensive study, a great number of mosaic scores, derived from the literature, were analysed for differentiation between (a) institutional and non-institutional groups, (b) normals and abnormals (fifty-two normals, four-teen "maladjusted," fourteen neurotic, thirty-four defective, twenty-nine paretic, and thirty-five schizophrenic subjects), (c) six diagnostic groups, and (d) between subjects with high and low scores on the clusters obtained from the Wittenborn Psychiatric Rating Scales. There is little need for further discussion, as the results were "sweepingly negative." The author suggests "that the discrepancies between clinical impressions and experimental findings may be

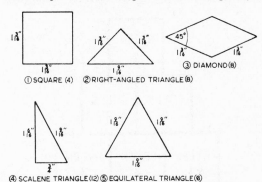

FIG. 3.8. THE FIVE SHAPES OF THE LÖWENFELD MOSAIC TEST

Number of shapes used is stated in brackets.

attributed to failure to recognize that diagnostic cues are obtained from interview aspects of the testing situation, rather than from the Mosaic Test itself."

COLOUR PYRAMID TEST (FARBPYRAMIDENTEST, HEISS AND HILTMANN, 1951)

Stimulated by the Swiss psychologist Pfister (1950), this test has been developed and rapidly expanded in the Freiburg (Germany) Department of Heiss. A pyramid consisting of fifteen squares of 2·5 cm side length (Fig. 3.9) is presented to the subject, together with square bits of paper in twenty-four colours (four shades each of red, blue, green, three of purple, two of yellow, orange and brown and, finally, one each of black, grey and white). The subject is instructed to choose from these colours and to complete a pyramid. Usually three such pyramids are requested in one session. More recently the instruction to make "ugly" pyramids has been added (Heiss, Hornsberg and Karl, 1955).

The far-reaching claims of this technique and its extensive use in clinical work have been swiftly followed by fundamental criticism (Luthe and Salman, 1953) and by experimental test. From the expressive movement point of view, a number of formal characteristics in pattern construction like "carpets" (unstructured layouts), arrangement in "layers" and "structures" have been studied. Another classification divides responses into "orderly" and "disorderly" arrangements. In the absence of statistical assessment, tests of significance were computed by the author where indicated.

Using neurotics, depressives, schizophrenics and controls Brengelmann (1953b), obtained no significant results, although means were in the predicted direction, indicating that abnormals, in particular schizophrenics, use fewer "structures" and construct in a more disorderly fashion. The effect of intelligence,

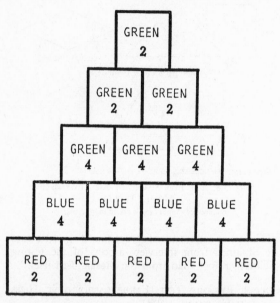

FIG. 3.9. STIMULUS FRAME OF THE COLOUR-PYRAMID TEST

age and sex was assessed. Frohoff (1953) reported highly significant differences between normals and controls, using norms published by Heiss as control data. Because he was not using his own controls, these data are not interpreted. When significance was assessed by the present author, no significant differences were found in Frohoff's data between four groups of schizophrenics (uncharacteristic, paranoic, hebephrenic and catatonic). The results were recomputed. In Seyfried's (1957) study, differences between seventy maladjusted boys and forty-five control subjects were significant at the two per cent level for both structuring (Chi-square of 9·099, 2 d.f.) and orderliness (Chi-square of 9·183, 2 d.f., results recomputed). Out of two hundred normals, Karl (1953) chose two groups characteristic of "strong" and "weak motivation" (Antriebsstruktur), using the upper and lower quartiles of responses to the Pauli Test (continuous arithmetic calculation). No significant differences in structuring were obtained (Chi-square of 1·636, 2 d.f., results recomputed). Conrad and Juncker (1954) first formed two extreme

groups of leptosomes and pyknics, which did not overlap on the Strömgren-Index of body build. Although no important relationship of this dichotomy to choice of colour was found, leptosomes structured considerably more than pyknics in the beginning.

Conrad (1954), being as critical about colour choice and abnormality as Brengelmann (1953a), proceeded to investigate differences in test attitude. His contention is that abnormals choose more at random and should therefore differentiate from normals regarding deviation from the stimulus colour norm (theoretical norm). This was criticized by Brengelmann (1956a), who obtained no significant differentiation with regard to deviations from the stimulus norm. Deviations from an independently established normal norm (empirical norm) were, however, significantly greater for neurotics, depressives and schizophrenics than for normals (Brengelmann, 1957c), indicating that abnormals follow test instructions in a more variable manner.

COLOUR-STAR TEST (FARBSTERNTEST, SEYFRIED)

This test, designed by the Austrian psychologist Seyfried, is very similar to the Colour-Pyramid Test. Instead of a pyramid form, a star-shaped pattern is used. This pattern consists of twenty equally large equilateral triangles. Highly significant differences were found between one hundred normals and thirty-five acute schizophrenics for both "structure" (Chi-square of 26·439, 1 d.f.) and "orderliness" (Chi-square of 27·068, 1 d.f.). However, an unidentified number of these patients was receiving electro-shock treatment (Bullinger and Seyfried, 1954).

A group of fifty normal girls was compared with twenty each of sexually and generally maladjusted girls (Bullinger and Seyfried, 1955). No significant differences were found in pattern construction. In yet another study, thirty depressed patients, eighteen of whom were "endogenous" depressions, were compared with fifty normals, all female subjects (Seyfried, 1955). No significant differences were obtained between groups with regard to carpets, layers, and structures (Chi-square of 3·349, 2 d.f.). A simple behavioural tendency was observed, namely the difference between subjects who turn stimulus elements with their fingers before putting them down versus those who put them down unhesitatingly, which discriminated at the one per cent level (Chi-square of 8·495, 1 d.f.). Depressives turned the stimuli more often. (All these results were recomputed by the present author.)

BUNCH-OF-GRAPES TEST (TEST "DEL GRAPPOLO D'UVA," SANGUINETI AND SIGURTA, 1951)

This is a modification of Lamparter's (Kroh School, Germany) colour-form reaction test, applied to abnormal psychology. It is similar to the two preceding tests; a number of circular shapes ("grapes"), varying in colour and size, and rectangular strips of paper ("branches") are offered to the subject to construct a bunch of grapes (Fig. 3.10). The number of shapes chosen and the space occupied by the subject to construct a pattern is not standardized.

EVALUATION

Differentiation between normals and abnormals, adjusted and maladjusted, or between clinical categories, has been partly significant, partly doubtful. The trends of means have been consistent. It may be said that these results have, though insufficient, been more encouraging than those reported in Sect. II. It

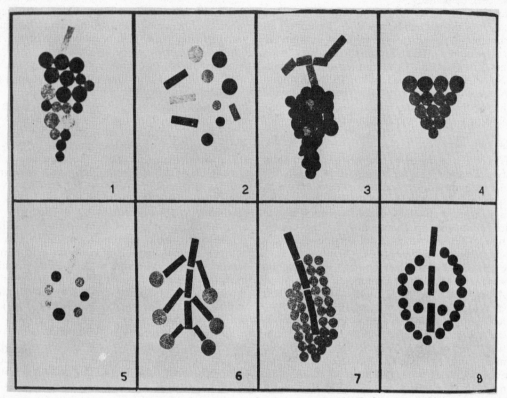

FIG. 3.10. RESPONSES TO THE BUNCH-OF-GRAPES TEST

Apart from colour choice, responses are mainly rated for symmetry, stereotypy, loss of form, circular shape, relief and size.

Considerable differences have been reported among neurotics, depressives, psychopaths, manics and various subgroups of schizophrenics by each of the following authors: Sanguineti and Sigurta (1951), Treves and Papo (1952), Lusso (1954), and Laricchia and Beretta (1954). The results were not assessed for significance, percentages only being given. These vary to a considerable degree between authors, but despite this, there has been no criticism of each other's work and the authors agree on the clinical usefulness of this test. As the scores depend on ratings whose reliability is unknown, no attempt was made by the present author to recompute the percentages given and assess them for significance.

may be argued that the rather stricter experimental limitations improved, if anything, the significance of results. In nearly all cases, however, sampling has been insufficiently controlled and final judgement must be reserved.

More or less incidental findings such as larger scatter in conduct disturbance, compared with other neurotic symptoms (Mosaic Test); greater variability of abnormals in response to the Colour Pyramid Test; and greater hesitation, or indecision, of depressives compared with normals in the Colour-star Test, are of interest and should be followed up.

The advantages of the manipulative tests described appear to be twofold: these are standardization of procedure and the restriction of number of scores taken. Though both these advantages are basically welcome, all the tests quoted have this in common, that no empirical development in construction has taken place. The tests were constructed rationally and have maintained their structure regardless of the results obtained. It appears unreasonable to expect a rationally conceived test to function at its optimum level. The same applies to the actual scores taken. Though few in number, no intercorrelations appear to have been computed.

It appears to be of distinct advantage that the application of the test can be repeated. This offers an opportunity of investigating response variability between sessions. Reliability itself has not been systematically assessed. Significant test-retest changes have, however, been reported for the Colour Pyramid Test (Conrad and Juncker, 1954). The psychological meaning of these is being investigated in the Heiss School using so-called "sequence analysis."

Handwriting

It is generally assumed by graphologists that form and style of handwriting are expressive of personality and that individual differences and changes vary with corresponding differences and changes in personality. If this is true, graphology should claim a unique position in diagnosing abnormality, as the change from normal to abnormal, and vice versa, could easily be studied from existing records.

The results of studies of handwriting have frequently been reviewed (Allport and Vernon, 1933; Lewinson and Zubin, 1942; Eysenck, 1945; Marum, 1945; Secord, 1949; Bell, 1951; Vernon, 1953). From the literature it appears that, on the European Continent, *a priori* theorizing (Pophal, 1949) and the non-statistical use of graphology (Heiss, 1950) still dominate the field. Methods adapted in Anglo-American countries have had little influence, as is shown by Klages' (1949a) 23rd edition of *Handschrift und Charakter*, which has hardly changed since 1916. In Anglo-American countries, the early enthusiasm of scientifically minded psychologists, which was aroused mainly through contact with displaced European graphologists, has been reduced to practically zero during the last decade. The *main results* to date, regardless of the methods used, are listed below.

By far the greatest number of studies has been completed in the field of *normal personality*, usually matching personality sketches, or case studies, with assessments from handwriting. Correlations between handwriting and personality questionnaires, or ratings, are of greater interest because these can be understood more easily in terms of dimensional measurement of personality. Slightly positive results were obtained in the assessment of personal values (Cantril, Rand and Allport, 1933); neuroticism and ascendance-submission (Harvey, 1934); neuroticism (Simon and Schönfeld, 1935; Eysenck, 1945) and emotionality-

introversion (Land, 1924). In the last experiment, small capital letters and extreme backhand and downhill writing were found to be significantly related to the trait quoted.

Middleton (1939, 1941) had untrained judges estimate dominance, neuroticism, self-confidence and sociability from handwriting. The results were largely negative. Pascal (1943b) obtained a number of significant correlations, which were not cross-validated, between handwriting and personality variables and these will be discussed below. The results of various other psychological tests have remained rather inconclusive (Enke, 1938; Schade, 1939; Super, 1941; Crider, 1941). Some significant correlations between handwriting and speech were obtained by Grünewald (1954), but again, these were not cross-validated.

In the field of *abnormality*, graphology has been applied to various psychiatric categories. Mayer-Benz (1929) achieved considerable agreement between the clinical diagnosis of psychopathy and handwriting analysis. In one study made by H. J. Eysenck (1945) a graphologist was able to match her analyses with personality diagnoses written by psychiatrists. In a later investigation by the same author, a different graphologist could not differentiate significantly between the handwriting of neurotics and normals. Lewinson predicted failure in college and maladjustment to a significant extent (Munroe, Lewinson and Waehner, 1944). Similar predictions of adjustment problems in students made by Wells (1946, 1949) were not very satisfactory.

Psychotic characteristics of handwriting were described by Lewinson (1940) as follows: (a) disturbed rhythm (irregularity or rigidity); (b) lack of balance between bond and release and (c) arrhythmic distribution (stereotype or beyond control). Further results suggestive of differences between psychotics and other groups are provided by Paskind and Brown (1940) and Mandowsky (1934). Schorsch (1939) believes that pre-psychotic writing differs from the corresponding writing of the same persons in the psychotic state. This was not confirmed by Legrün (1939).

The assessment of the *usefulness of handwriting analysis* is, for various reasons, an unrewarding task. If the opinion of eminent graphologists is followed, the claims are inconsistent and will lead us nowhere. If, in particular, Klages' (1949b) decision is taken seriously that psychological illness can "on principle not be detected from handwriting," most of the work quoted should not have been performed. If the actual results, regardless of the methods used, are taken as an indication little importance can be attached to graphology in the assessment of personality, or abnormality.

It has become a tradition with reviewers of handwriting to point to the difference between the *intuitive, subjective* or *holistic*, and the *analytic, objective* approach. An example of each of these two methods is given in Table III.5. It is noted that the intuitive approach makes use of a number of characteristics which are very difficult to measure directly, but may be of great importance.

In terms of results the holistic method has usually fared better. With the subjective method, the judge is presented with handwriting specimens and a set of character sketches, or other characteristics of personality, which are to be matched. With this technique even laymen can sometimes match slightly better than chance, and expert graphologists better still. This conclusion has been accepted for decades.

More significant, however, is the fact that *criticism of the matching technique*, on which the claims of intuitive graphology are almost entirely based, has increased. Apart from the meticulous precautions which must be taken to avoid the real danger of both artificial consistency and validity due to the effects of extraneous clues, the following are the main drawbacks of the matching technique. Success depends on the heterogeneity of subjects and tends to disappear with relatively homogeneous groups; not more than five or six subjects can be matched at a time; no continuous scores or reliable rankings can be obtained over larger groups; raters vary considerably in their use of cues and, finally, it is impossible to define which of the various traits of personality are assessed. Methodological criticism has thus increased out of proportion to the modest success claimed and has, for that reason, rendered the holistic-analytic controversy a pseudo-problem.

Any reviewer would feel more light-hearted about this statement if analytic handwriting analysis had shown greater promise. This is not the case. Lewinson and Zubin (1942) have elaborated a number of objectively scorable scales and certain combined ratio scores which are claimed to be more representative of the actual appearance of writing than simple analytical measures. This may be considered an important landmark. However, two experiments have been made since, using these or similar scoring procedures, with no demonstrable success.

Pascal (1943b) computed rank order correlations between twenty-two handwriting variables and each of thirty-six personality variables, derived from Murray's (1938) *Explorations in Personality*. Each of the twenty-two subjects had been investigated for thirty-six hours. Of the seven hundred and ninety-two intercorrelations, nine coefficients were significant at the one-per-cent level and thirty-two at the five-per-cent level. These results could easily have arisen by chance. Pascal then proceeded, helped by multiple correlations, to obtain a number of significant relationships between handwriting and personality. However, by selecting the highest coefficients, without cross-validation, he made capital of chance error and his results cannot be accepted as conclusive.

In the second type of analytical experiment made by Secord (1949), handwriting samples of fifty students were matched in sets of five with T.A.T. stories by five judges. On average, somewhat less than two matchings in each set of five were correct. In addition, Lewinson's claim of specific relationships between twenty-two handwriting and personality variables was tested (*Handwriting Analysis*, Chap. IX). No correlation was found to be significant at the five-per-cent level (N = 15).

The analytic approach, as it stands today, cannot claim to have added any positive result to the analysis of handwriting. While, however, the possibilities of intuitive handwriting analysis appear exhausted, objective procedures have hardly been applied properly. Cross-validation of Pascal's study, for example, may reveal a reasonable amount of consistency in results and may provide valuable hints for the selection of handwriting and personality variables.

The study of relationships between objectively measured handwriting and other expressive movement variables, appears to be of much greater promise, provided the personality and/or abnormality correlates of the latter are—to some extent at least—known. This approach which, with the construction of the F.R.T. (Sect. IV), is now feasible would remove the deficiencies in matching and rating. Additionally, more recently developed personality questionnaires of improved validity with respect to both personality and expressive movement, may be expected to be helpful. It is now known, for example, that when neurotics or neuroticism questionnaires have been used as criteria, no success has been obtained in the objective measurement of expressive movement, but that both extraversion and rigidity questionnaires have proved to be useful (Sect. IV). These latter two criteria, however, have not, so far, been used in handwriting analysis.

Some main points concerning handwriting analysis may now be *summarized*. *Intuitive analysis* has shown that handwriting can be diagnostic of normal and abnormal psychology. This method, however, is charged with a number of restricting deficiencies, already pointed out. In addition, *skill in analysis* is well known to vary widely even between experts. In the opinion of Vernon (1953), the amateur is "unlikely to give diagnosis of any value at all. Many so-called professionals are also inept, and there is no ready means of distinguishing the bad from the good."

Objective analysis has so far yielded no established correlates of handwriting. This approach, however,

TABLE III.5

PERSONALITY CORRELATES OF HANDWRITING

Upper part = intuitively conceived characteristics of various clinical categories (Marum, 1945).
Lower part = correlations between measured items and personality ratings, significant at the 5 per cent level
(Pascal, 1943*b*).

1. Depression	Failing or fluctuating lines; heavy pressure, or particularly thin, timid, and irregular pressure; slanting to left; signature placed toward middle or left of paper; small letters; diminished height of capital letters; corrections; slow writing. (At least two of these signs have been found in cases where depression is stated.)
2. Anxiety	Narrow distances between words; narrow distances between lines; words end abruptly; ellipses (in o, a, g, etc.) may be compressed by next letter; lines begin at extreme left without a margin; signatures may be on left half of paper; slant and flourishes may be to the left; pressure either heavy or there are irregular losses of pressure; writing small and slow with occasional abrupt loss of height.
3. Obsessional neurosis	Regularity and rigidity with some artificiality of style; narrowness; small letter formation; touched-up letters; perpendicular direction, or slant to left, or irregularity of slant; wide distances between words combined with narrow letters, or extremely small distances between words and lines.
4. Hysteria	Two types: (*a*) irregularity of height, width, and slant; fluctuation of lines; indistinct, mixed ligature; (*b*) grotesque slant to left; exaggerated flourishes; heavy pressure; covering strokes; irregular connectedness; lack of proportion in accentuation of some letters, particularly initials.
6. Schizophrenia	Rigid, unnatural writing; sloping to left; covering strokes in middle zone; some tendency to threadlike ligature; exaggerated loops in lower zone; discrepancy between text and signature; increased heights of letters in middle zone at ends of words; large distances and horizontal strokes between words.

Item	Personality correlate
4. Upper projection (b, h, k, l)	(−) anxiety, (+) affiliation, (−) projectivity, (−) understanding, (+) play, (−) radical sentiments, (−) narcissism
5. Lower projection (g, j, q, y, z)	(−) abasement, (−) succorance, (+) counteraction, (−) radical sentiments
6. Total vertical expanse	(−) projectivity, (+) play
8. Primary width (m, n, u)	(+) sentience
9. Primary width range (mid-zone range* divided by mean of 8)	(+) nurturance
10. Mid-zone size ratio (mean of 8 divided by the mean of mid-zone height)	(+) dominance, (+) rejective, (+) projectivity, (+) intensity
11. Distance between letters	(−) ego ideal
12. Distance between words	(−) understanding, (+) play
13. Mid-zone fullness (width of o)	(−) exocachexion
15. Lower zone fullness (lower loops of g, j, q, y)	(+) projectivity, (−) play
16. Width of pen-stroke	(+) infavoidance, (−) nurturance, (−) exocachexion, (+) harm avoidance
20. I dot distance (horizontal deviation from letter)	(−) infavoidance
28. Angular connexion of letters	(+) infavoidance
39. Balance of projection (5 minus 4)	(−) abasement, (+) defendance, (+) counteraction, (+) dominance, (−) radical sentiments, (+) super ego integration

* Mid-zone range = difference between highest and lowest measures of mid-zone.

is not considered to have been put to proper experimental test. The fact that there is no established set of signs, or any other communicable method of scoring, specific to any demonstrable personality aspect applies to both the subjective and the objective approach.

The advantages of handwriting, its frequent availability over long periods of an individual's lifetime and its relatively unintentional character, together with the suggestion that the objective analysis remains incomplete until more recently developed criteria are used, may guarantee continued interest in graphology for some time.

More systematic analysis of various conditions may contribute towards validation. The effect of "spontaneous" versus "copy" writing (Castelnuovo-Tedesco, 1948), the effect of writing under stress and distraction (Stracke, 1933; Pohl, 1936; Ostermeyer, 1937; Keyes and Laffal, 1953), the effect of drugs whose validity in connexion with other expressive movement measures are known (Rabin, 1953; Brengelmann, 1958a, 1958b, 1958c), microscopic measurement, relationship to muscle tension, and the assessment of response set, or attitude while writing are quoted as examples.

In addition to the difficulties already pointed out, it would be easy to criticize most previous experiments on the basis of poor experimental control, item analysis and choice of criteria. Much more serious, however, in view of future work, is the limitation, quoted from Vernon (1953), that "only about a quarter of the population are sufficiently fluent writers to have developed a mature, individual style." A further complication is the fact that many handwriting specimens are difficult to measure objectively, at least on a number of a comprehensive set of signs.

The prospects for graphology do not appear bright in the light of the well-known fact that comparatively simple objective measures of movement characteristics provide much more reliable and valid measures of personality. The practising charlatan will, however, continue to claim "good" results, as pointed out long ago by Krüger and Zietz (1933). These authors submitted the same character sketch to a number of subjects claiming the sketch to be an expert opinion of their character; all subjects were convinced that the sketch represented a description of their own character.

IV. OBJECTIVE TESTS

In this section, a number of heterogeneous motor tests are discussed which, at present, have this in common that, in the main, they are objectively scored. They are classified as writing pressure, prismatic tracing, kinaesthetic drawing and figure reconstruction. Their most important *aims* are, *first*, to demonstrate reliable correlates of expressive movement in both personality and abnormality and, *second*, to suggest definitions of the role which motor attitudes or styles play in the performance tasks from which they are derived.

Various types of expressive movement, essentially independent of performance abilities and related practice effects, are found in a number of motor tests of the reaction, co-ordination, agility, strength, steadiness, etc., type. In certain tests involuntary expressive features are more apparent than in others, as in track tracing and pursuit rotor performance of a sufficiently high level of difficulty, in the Luria-type of association-motor response and in the Porteus Maze Test (Q-score). It appears much too early to raise the question of the generality of such expressive functions, which implies that motor style is essentially constant for a particular individual over a number of tests. However, the definition of *some* personality correlates of style and of *some* conditions necessary for the manifestation of certain styles should at least

suggest a way out of the confused picture that characterizes expression research today.

Writing Pressure

For decades it has been a standard claim that "the hands . . ., being the most frequently used expressive mechanism of the individual, will afford the best indication of the general level of the individual's tension" (Johnson, 1928), that "it is a common experience that the individuality of people . . . can be distinguished through characteristic patterns of muscular activity" (Ruesch, Finesinger and Schwab, 1940), and that "it is common knowledge that the neuromuscular *tonus* of man is affected by, and in turn affects, his personality and behaviour patterns" (Goldzieher Roman, 1950).

With large individual differences specific to personality, what more could be asked for, particularly as considerable improvement in apparatus has taken place during the last thirty years? The results, however, have hardly come up to expectation.

Originally, variations in pressure were judged directly from handwriting of drawing characteristics, or from impressions left on the writing-pad. Anastasi and Foley (1941) reported that anxiety states, chronic schizophrenics, and advanced catatonics, drew faint lines, which were interpreted as little pressure. Heavy pressure was used by psychopaths and subjects suffering from various types of organic diseases. Uniform levels of pressure were typical of catatonics and the feeble-minded, whereas pressure variability was most frequently found in flexible and adaptable individuals. In children's paintings, according to Alschuler and Hattwick (1947), heavy strokes were said to be typical of assertiveness and light strokes of either low energy level, restraint, repression, fanciful imagination, or generous attitudes. Wolff (1946) preferred interpretation of the expressive kind. To him, oversharp lines revealed "definiteness," determined strokes "high security," high pressure "vitality" and low pressure "weakness."

Early attempts at the direct measurement of writing pressure included the *carbon copy method*. With this fairly reliable method, ten sheets of unglazed onion skin paper and ten sheets of light weight carbon paper are arranged alternately. Involuntary writing or drawing point pressure may then be scored as the number of sheets through which writing penetrates (Baxter, 1927). Using this method, some suggestive results were obtained by Clarke (1950) who investigated emotional instability in sixty-eight normals and one hundred and twenty-nine neurotics. Point-pressure penetration scores were derived from three rather heterogeneous tests: motor perseveration (SZ alternation), mirror drawing, and signature writing. There was an insignificant but consistent tendency for neurotics to press harder than normals. This difference was mainly due to the hysterics, pressure, on average, increasing in the order, anxiety states–normals–hysterics. This appears in keeping with the subjective observations already reported.

The introduction of *pneumatic recording* has led to a number of developments, which have been reviewed by Davis (1942) and Courts (1942). The most important technical development was the introduction of concurrent measurement of point- and grip-pressure. Relatively constant and considerable individual differences in pressure were found by Duffy (1932) who also obtained correlations of near 0·5 with ratings of children's excitability and emotionality. Later on, using twelve measures of pressure and four measures of fluctuation, reliable individual differences and a certain amount of generality of this type of muscle tension were found repeatedly by the same author (Duffy, 1936). Ruesch and Finesinger (1943) obtained results rather similar to those already reported. Grip- and point-pressure during continuous movement of handwriting were investigated using forty patients of various psychiatric and neurologic diagnoses and twelve controls. The patients' scores, both on grip-pressure and a questionnaire aimed at measuring feelings of tension, were significantly higher than those of the controls. Additionally, a significant positive

correlation was found in both the neurotic and psychotic patients between feelings of neuromuscular tension and point-pressure. No correlation was found between feelings of *general* tension and any of the pressure readings.

Pascal (1943a), among other scores, correlated pressure and pressure-range, obtained from twenty-one men, with five personality traits, as rated by seven psychologists. The following results were obtained which, it must be kept in mind, were not cross-validated.

Correlations	Energy	Expression	Impulsion	Dominance	Determination
Pressure Range	0·60	0·53	0·41	0·33	0·18
Average Pressure	0·54	0·54	0·39	0·20	0·01

$r = 0.55$ for 1 per cent., 0·43 for 5 per cent. level of significance

A number of correlations were significant, and this is provocative enough to be followed up. An interesting difference between sexes, which had already been observed by previous authors, was confirmed by Pascal. Adding ten female subjects to his male group, he found that men scored significantly higher on both average pressure and pressure range. Related findings derived from a different type of test are discussed under the heading "Figure Reconstruction Test" in this section.

The most extensive use of writing pressure since Kraepelin's *Schriftwaage* appears to have been made in Kretschmer's laboratory, judged from various summary reports (Steinwachs, 1950, 1952, 1953). Work was concentrated on constitutional and developmental problems. Only more recently does it appear that grip- and point-pressure have been related to neurotic disorders, as well as to brain damage and epilepsy (Steinwachs, 1955), but no actual results have been reported to date. It may be interesting to find out whether this departure from the usual somatic criteria results in new theoretical developments within Kretschmer's system. In Kretschmer's latest, 20th ed. of *Körperbau und Charakter* (1951) writing pressure is still treated in the same way as it was by Enke (1929) thirty years ago. After considerably improving the technique used by Steinwachs (1951), Kretschmer states: "Results are in principle comparable to those of Enke" (op. cit., p. 257). This implies greater pressure for leptosomes and athletics, against pyknics, and increase of pressure with writing time in the order leptosomes–pyknics–athletics, as seen in Fig. 3.11. Unfortunately, significance of differences was not assessed and no parameters other than means were supplied.

Pophal, a prominent research graphologist, who holds a chair in graphology at the University of Hamburg (Germany), may be expected to contribute to the field of personality. While he is, however, an outstanding theoretician of graphology, his experiments appear to be more generally of a psychological and physiological kind. His latest report was on methodological developments and the effect of excitant and depressant drugs, as well as glutamic acid, on writing speed and pressure (1956). Excitant drugs were stated to increase grip- and point-pressure.

In summary, it may be said that evidence has been quoted which shows: (*a*) that writing pressure is greater in abnormals than in normals; (*b*) that, in neurotics, writing pressure may be stronger in hysterics than in dysthymics; (*c*) that certain personality traits involving strongly expressive characteristics may correlate positively with writing pressure and (*d*) that

can be drawn as to its relationship to the basic dimensions of personality.

If results appear modest, activity in *apparatus construction* has been much more lively. Of the various reviews the most recent one by Luthe (1953) is

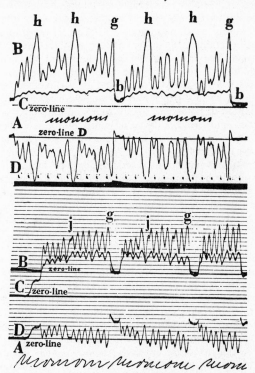

FIG. 3.12. TWO SAMPLE RECORDS OBTAINED FROM THE ELECTROSCRIPTOGRAPH

A = written test word *momom*; B = point-pressure; C = grip-pressure; D = pressure difference.
(*From Luthe*, 1953)

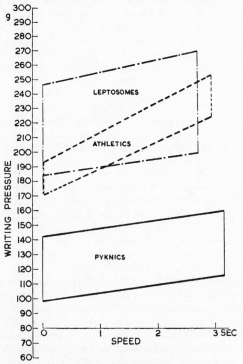

FIG. 3.11. WRITING PRESSURE AS RELATED TO CONSTITUTIONAL TYPES
(*From Kretschmer*, 1951)

writing pressure is lower in pyknics than in leptosomes and athletics. Surprisingly little is known about the writing pressure of psychotics despite the fact that motor disturbances are clinically much more characteristic of this category. Although there is a certain amount of evidence that pressure of the kind described is related to emotional tension, hardly any conclusion

mentioned. Mechanical-pneumatic recording appears to have lost its attraction, and electronic equipment to have taken its place. The method presented by von Bracken, Pungs and Riedel 1949 and von Bracken, 1952, enables micro-motoric speed and phase changes of pressure as well as the usual pressure scores to be analysed. Luthe's apparatus measures point- and grip-pressure, and also records the difference between these two measurements and claims advantage through the provision of an extra large writing plate. Both types of apparatus are very similar, using condenser capacity changes as equivalents of pressure exerted on stylus and writing plate, and recording these variations oscillographically. Sample records obtained with Luthe's "electroscriptograph" are shown in Fig. 3.12. To what extent these recent developments in apparatus construction will be reflected in validation remains to be seen.

Although *speed of writing* has been investigated many times it requires considerably more detailed analysis. This appears possible with the newer type of apparatus. At this point, Katz's (1948) "scripto-chronograph," which permits a different type of temporal analysis of individual letters directly from the written record, should be mentioned. The effect of various conditions, quoted in Sect. III on graphology, variability in letter writing and the effect of content on writing could be investigated with this apparatus. Essentially, the apparatus consists of a steel rod for writing, connected to a direct current source, writing paper impregnated with a colourless solution of potassium thiocyanate and an aluminium sheet underneath. The rod and aluminium sheet complete a circuit which is interrupted at predetermined intervals. Writing then appears not as a continuous line but as a series of dots or short lines, from which time sequence may be analysed.

There are a number of technical difficulties about measurement of writing pressure, as Luthe and others have already pointed out. Apart from these, it may be necessary and difficult to assess the effect of attitude, or set, on "involuntary" movement. In addition, as Pascal (1943*a*) has shown, pressure scores vary considerably with instructions to write with varying degrees of pressure, thus demonstrating the ease with which the results may be faked. It is also known that pressure varies significantly with the size of writing, with the type of stylus used and, presumably, also with the size of writing plate.

Although it has been much less investigated, writing pressure, or the "third dimension" of graphology, appears to hold out more promise than the analysis of handwriting itself. This may be due to the fact that scoring is objective and that pressure is far more independent of teaching and other environmental influences than are handwriting characteristics. It may also be a more sensitive measure of changes towards abnormality in comparison with overlearned handwriting performed under direct perceptual control.

Care must be taken to differentiate between *voluntary strength* and *involuntary pressure*. The former is recorded with ergographs, dynamometers, and the like. Strength has not been a very successful criterion in the assessing of personality (Moore and Sturm, 1952). It is said to be highly specific to tasks (Takala, 1953), and criticism has been made regarding reliability (Fautrel, 1954). The measurement of involuntary movement, as in writing pressure and the Luria type of apparatus, appears much more promising.

Prismatic Tracing

Experimental work on extent, magnitude and variability of error in motor performance has remained comparatively limited (Siddall, Holding and Draper, 1957), and corresponding personality correlates have hardly been established. It is the aim, in the present section, to point out expressive movement characteristics derived from, but essentially independent of, motor tracing, and to some of their meanings in terms of personality or abnormality.

Three points considered important will be made. *Firstly*, tests of the kind discussed, relying on performance *per se*, have not proved very successful in personality measurement. *Secondly*, expressive movement type of scores, derived from the same performance tests, can be shown to be powerful indicators of personality. *Thirdly*, the use of psychiatric criteria alone, as traditionally exercised, should be abandoned as a method unless personality criteria are used concurrently. These may, at present, be of the questionnaire type until standardized objective criteria, derived from apparatus tests, are available.

It has been known for a long time that motor *performance* scores represent relatively poor and inconsistent indicators of personality. Significant differences, if anything, were mainly obtained with schizophrenics under conditions where experimental controls were insufficiently applied. Huston and Shakow (1948), for example, showed that the inferior performance of schizophrenics was attributable to their poorer degree of co-operation rather than to schizophrenia *per se*. On the other hand, if we turn to the applications of motor performance it may be argued from the experiments of Davis (*see* Chapter 2) that expressive movement, or the style of motor attitude, is of importance. Motor behaviour of gross overaction versus inertia was found to be a most important source of pilot error in the cockpit. Similarly, Venables (1955), using a motor task involving the movement of a pointer in relation to stimulus lights, described performance which was seen to fall on a continuum of overactivity-inertia.

Lazarus, Deese and Osler (1952), in their review, described variability, stereotyped responses and changes in overt activity as effects which accompanied stressful motor performance. This suggests additional types of measurement of motor expression which are impressive enough to demand closer examination by the personality investigator. Furthermore, S. B. G. Eysenck (1955) points to the difference between motor disorganization and inadequacy of response in psychotics, and emotional irregularity in neurotics. The suggested division of inadequacy-irregularity may be considered an important pointer to an improvement of method, which might help to solve the present deadlock in measurement of association-motor response in abnormals.

These considerations are taken to suggest that scores dealing with overt bodily motor expression are more specific to personality than are performance measures. Accordingly, an experiment of motor tracing which was designed to measure apparently similar expressive variables was performed and may support this claim (Brengelmann, 1957b). In order to

largely independent questionnaire measures of personality, viz., extraversion, neuroticism and rigidity.

From other experiments, reported by H. J. Eysenck (1956a) and Star (1957), it is known that pursuit rotor performance and rate of increase in performance did

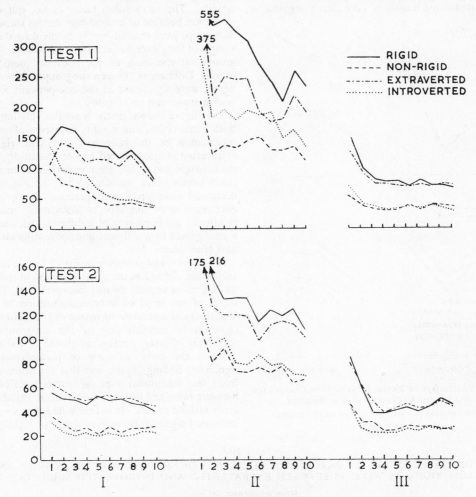

FIG. 3.13. RATIO ERROR-CORRECT TRACING WHILE WEARING PRISMATIC INVERSION LENSES
This is significantly related to extraversion and rigidity. I + III = left-right, II = upside-down
inversion. Ten trials of sixty seconds per section.
(*From Brengelmann, 1957b*)

produce the desired phenomena, prismatic inversion lenses were used as means of stress. They were set to cause left-right and upside-down inversion of the visual field. Under these conditions, forty-nine normal subjects were asked to trace a curvy stimulus line with a pencil. Scores of correct performance, magnitude of error, variability, and a complex quality of movement form were derived and related to three

not provide important or lasting relationships to extraversion and neuroticism. It may be added that performance, or rate of increase in performance, was consistently slightly lower for extraverts than for introverts in the beginning. With prolonged practice, differences in means between these groups tended to decrease. It is important to state this, as the prismatic tracing results, presently described, were exactly of the same nature as far as *correct* performance is concerned. (The pursuit rotor also provided a measure of correct performances.)

The important point is that, while correct performance on the prismatic tracing task yielded no significant correlations with any of the personality criteria used, all remaining measures were clearly significant

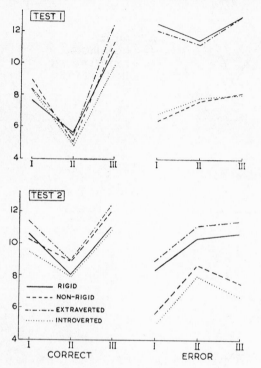

FIG. 3.14. VARIABILITY OF ERROR PERFORMANCE CORRELATES POSITIVELY WITH EXTRAVERSION AND RIGIDITY
Results for variability of correct performance are insignificant.
(*From Brengelmann*, 1957*b*)

in a rather specific manner. They could, with certain reservations, be repeated on retest after two or three days. The *first result*, showing the *ratio of error over correct performance*, is presented in Fig. 3.13. Correct performance itself was not, but error performance was, significantly related to both extraversion and rigidity. The neuroticism factor is left out of consideration because of insignificant results throughout. Subgroups were created simply by dividing the entire sample of forty-nine subjects into two practically equal groups on the basis of the relevant questionnaire scores. Differences between subgroups, shown in the figure, were significant at the one-per-cent level for both extraversion and rigidity.

This figure shows, firstly, a similar relationship of both extraversion and rigidity to excess of error, as represented by the ratio score. Highly rigid and extraverted subjects scored higher. Secondly, within the left-right and upside-down inversion performances, relationships were initially higher for rigidity and decreased more rapidly with practice. It appears that over-reaction of this type is particularly specific to rigidity at the beginning of a difficult task and when a changeover to a different and more difficult condition takes place.

A *second result* is shown in Fig. 3.14. It concerns variability, defined as the mean deviation of individual trials from a section mean. (Sections I, II, III consisted of ten trials of sixty-seconds duration each.) Variability of correct performance did not differentiate significantly between any of the subgroups; for variability of error, *t*-ratios are shown in Table III.6.

From the point of view of measurement, the significant finding, again, was that the score derived from the traditional type of correct performance measure remained insignificant, whereas variability of error yielded results. It is also noted that variability decreased significantly with practice for rigidity only.

TABLE III.6

VARIABILITY IN EXTENT OF ERROR DIFFERENTIATED SIGNIFICANTLY BETWEEN HIGH AND LOW RIGID, AS WELL AS BETWEEN EXTRAVERTED AND INTROVERTED SUBJECTS

(*From Brengelmann, 1957b*)

Variability of error	First test			Repeat test		
	I	II	III	I	II	III
24 High *v.* 25 low rigid .	3·69 (0·1 per cent)	2·37 (5 per cent)	2·48 (2 per cent)	N.S. (10 per cent)	N.S.	N.S. (10 per cent)
24 Extraverted *v.* 25 introverted . . .	3·08 (1 per cent)	2·09 (5 per cent)	2·53 (2 per cent)	2·75 (1 per cent)	N.S.	2·90 (1 per cent)

Significance levels in brackets.
I, II, III = sections of ten trials each of prismatic tracing.

During the repeat test, significant differences were obtained exclusively between the extraverted and introverted subjects (Sects. I and III).

Error and variability of error may be essentially related measures, judged by the similarity of their results. However, it has been possible to derive a score of complex movement quality which was specific to rigidity and not to extraversion and neuroticism. Because of its complex character, this score had to be assessed. As was shown above, extraverted and highly rigid subjects were similar in the extent of error made when following the direction of the stimulus track. Additionally, subjects varied widely in sideward movements or, roughly speaking, in the extent of error made at right angles to the stimulus track. This error type was rated as "angular-excessive" against "smooth-restrained." Although many extraverted subjects made excessive errors, they were preponderantly of the "smooth" kind, whereas rigid subjects were characterized by "angular" movements. This rating significantly differentiated between three degrees of rigidity, as shown in Table III.7, not however between the subgroups formed on the basis of the extraversion and neuroticism scores. Two raters were asked to choose one third of all subjects for each of the extreme reactions, leaving the remaining subjects as a medium group. The ratings proved to be adequately reliable.

TABLE III.7

"ANGULAR-EXCESSIVE" MOVEMENT FORM DISCRIMINATED SIGNIFICANTLY BETWEEN SUBGROUPS OF RIGIDITY, NOT HOWEVER BETWEEN THOSE OF EXTRAVERSION AND NEUROTICISM

(From Brengelmann, 1957b)

Movement form (sideward error)	Smooth-restrained	Medium group	Angular-excessive	N
High rigid . .	3	8	13	24
Low rigid . .	14	8	3	25
N	17	16	16	49

$\chi^2 = 13 \cdot 388$ (2 d.f.) Significant at 0·1 per cent level.

The results presented in this section may be *summarized* in the following statements. Scores of correct performance were not related significantly to three largely independent questionnaire criteria of extraversion, neuroticism and rigidity. Three scores derived from prismatic error tracing, error as such, variability of error and a rating of "smooth-restrained" versus "angular-excessive" movement form revealed differential relationships with both extraversion and rigidity.

These results are taken to throw new light on the widely used test of mirror tracing, which is described in Chapter 2 by Yates. The fact that mirror tracing has, for such a long time, not established any consistent results related to personality and abnormal criteria may have two explanations. Firstly, the type of mirror-tracing score traditionally used is unproductive. Scores of the kind described in the present section should be used instead. Secondly, the criteria of abnormality employed hitherto are insufficient. Because there was a lack of significant correlations between prismatic tracing and neuroticism, and because of the wrong choice of criterion groups, the frequently attempted differentiation between neurotics and normals may have failed. If abnormal groups are tested, personality questionnaires of the kind described in the present section should be employed.

In addition, the present results may be of use to investigators who study motor performance as a whole from a point of view excluding personality. This, in particular, may be true for research where complex motor functions are investigated by practice stages, as by Fleishman and Hempel (1954, 1955), because of an indication of specific time relationships between heterogeneous criteria of personality and certain aspects of behaviour in performance.

"Kinaesthetic" Drawing

Complex drawing techniques may have proved failures in the assessment of abnormality largely for the following three reasons: subjectivity of assessment, heterogeneity between the numerous items and dependence on artistic excellence in performance. If these sources of error are eliminated, considerable improvement may result and satisfy the usually agreed feeling of investigators that "there is something to expressive movement which is difficult to extract."

THE MIRA "MYOKINETIC" TEST (P.M.K.)

The demands of error control described above are, to a large extent though not entirely, met by the "myokinetic" type of test, or P.M.K., as constructed by Mira (1940).

Tests of this kind require the subject to start simple movement forms printed on the response paper, using full visual controls. After this, vision is blocked and the subject is required to continue the initiated movement which is now kinaesthetically guided.

Although the P.M.K. is, to a great extent, objectively scored, a substantial drawback is attached to it on account of the great number of subscores. This test requires the completion of the following types of drawings: lineograms, zig-zags, staircase-like forms, circles, chains of rings, parallels towards and away from the subject, and U-shaped figures. Each of these categories is drawn with both the right and the left hand. Records are then scored for "primary" and "secondary" deviations, and each of these records is again scored for vertical, sagittal and horizontal

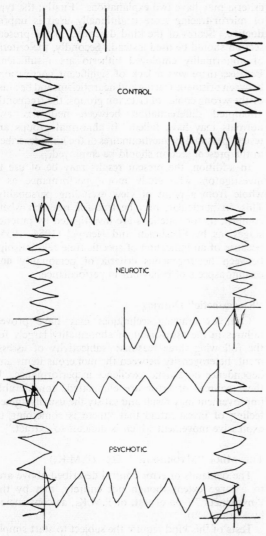

FIG. 3.15. SIMPLE BLINDFOLDED ("KINAESTHETIC") MOVEMENTS ARE LARGER FOR PSYCHOTICS THAN FOR NEUROTICS AND NORMALS

(*S. B. G. Eysenck, unpublished*)

deviations. Certain scores of size, density and axial deviation are added.

Takala (1953) has taken considerable pains to investigate the reliability and interrelations of test scores. As might be expected, a large number of reliabilities was doubtful. For sixty-eight categories

coefficients varied between 0·07 and 0·69. More than fifty were lower than 0·5 and only two higher than 0·6. Intercorrelations were, with few exceptions, positive and frequently significant. Factor analysis suggested that the numerous test scores might be profitably reduced to three factors. In practical application, this is far too complicated a task to be considered seriously. However, valuable hints for test reconstruction may be received from this study.

Takala also correlated P.M.K. scores with questionnaires, ratings and other personality assessments. The results were rather meagre and not cross-validated. As most of the original papers appeared in South American journals not accessible to the present author, the reader is referred to the reviews prepared by Takala (1953) and Stern (1954). In his most recently published test manual, Mira (1957) quotes about a hundred and thirty references. The investigations were mainly of the clinical, interpretative type. The relationships of scores to projective test results, occupational, intellectual and racial criteria are frequently discussed. Little emphasis has been placed on investigating experimentally the effects of clinical categories or objective personality criteria.

Mira claims, however, that his test measures the following characteristics: constitutional, genotypic reaction; transient, phenotypic reaction; intrapsychic coherence; aggression; depression-elation; extra-tension-introtension; constitutional emotivity; anxious impatience and constriction; excitation, inhibition and instability; constancy, or reaction rigidity; intellectual development; situational conflict and pathological alterations. As, with the exception of intelligence, no objective definition of the various personality characteristics mentioned has been given, the correctness of these claims cannot easily be assessed.

There are some points which require attention before more rigorously controlled research can be performed. As in Takala's work, reliability of test items varied extensively and was, on average, unacceptably low (0·5). Consequently, there is a considerable instability of norms between normal samples and the pattern of item intercorrelation appears to depart significantly from that found by Takala. No means and variances were provided for personality or abnormal functional criteria. The relationship to intelligence which, on a number of items is claimed to be high, requires a more objective and systematic treatment.

Like nearly all other tests described, the P.M.K. has not undergone any essential change since its initial conception. The technique requires, however, considerable revision by determining basic scores of high reliability which, in all likelihood, will be few in number.

SIMPLE BLINDFOLDED DRAWING

Simple drawing tests, depending on kinaesthetic guidance, were employed long before Mira constructed his P.M.K. (Allport and Vernon, 1933). In such tests, subjects were asked to draw three circles, waves, squares, etc., blindfolded. Reproductions were scored simply for size, amplitude, wave length, etc. The repeat reliability of this task was estimated to be 0·76 (Eisenberg, 1937). This is considerably higher than for Mira's P.M.K. Although it may be argued that this test is far too simple to be of great use in the face of the great complexity of expressive movement, it has stood its ground for what it measures extremely well. H. J. Eysenck (1952a, 1952b) and S. B. G. Eysenck (1956) consistently obtained highly significant differences between normals, neurotics and psychotics, as may be seen from Table III.8. Examples of test responses are given in Fig. 3.15. Further advantages are that this test is practically independent of intelligence and also very slightly related to age.

borated in various ways by the present author. Drawings of a square shape (1957a) and of a vase pattern (1955a), as used in a learning experiment, increased in size in the order normals–neurotics–psychotics. The same applied to a blindfolded test of tactual distance judgement of the Kundt type (1957a). Subjects were requested first to move slowly with their fingers over the "filled," or inspection, part of the stimulus and then to continue slowly on the "empty," or comparison, part until the size of the inspection part was subjectively equalled. Again, despite the fact that judgement was involved, scores increased significantly in the order normals–neurotics–psychotics. On two occasions, however, involving different types of tests, extent of movement increased in the order normals–psychotics–neurotics (Brengelmann, 1955a, Fig. 1; Brengelmann, 1957a, Table III.2). This time, no slow movement instruction was given. These results are simply shown to suggest that either type or test or instruction may affect movement responses.

TABLE III.8

SIMPLE EXPRESSIVE MOVEMENT TEST SERVING AS A RELIABLE MEASURE OF "PSYCHOTICISM"

(From S. B. G. Eysenck, 1956)

Average wave amplitude	Controls		Neurotics		Psychotics		F-ratio significance
	$\bar{x}$	s^2	$\bar{x}$	s^2	$\bar{x}$	s^2	
1	21·8	12·6	23·7	20·2	26·6	35·2	0·1 per cent
2	22·4	14·6	—	—	26·7	30·8	0·1 per cent
3	25·1	26·0	25·2	32·2	—	—	N.S.
Average wave length							
1	88·7	465·5	100·5	570·5	110·2	823·7	0·1 per cent
2	89·3	440·9	—	—	108·9	963·2	0·1 per cent
3	100·2	509·3	95·9	640·8	—	—	N.S.

1. = S.B.G. Eysenck, (1956); 2. = H. J. Eysenck, (1952a); 3. = H. J. Eysenck, (1952b).

The conclusion from this table would be that differences between groups were mainly due to the psychotics, as no consistent differences were obtained between normals and neurotics. Similarly, Crown (1953) failed to differentiate significantly between normals and tiqueurs. Within neurotics, anxiety states and hysterics were not found to be significantly different (Eysenck, 1952b).

OTHER MOVEMENT TESTS

An assortment of various types of tests is referred to because of a certain similarity of results. Firstly, findings reported in the previous section were corro-

The *significance of results*, presented in this section, is *assessed* in the following statements. *Firstly*, as shown by the Mira Myokinetic Test, it is not sufficient to construct an objectively scorable expressive movement test. Simplicity and reliability should be considered before everything else. *Secondly*, as regards simple, objectively scorable kinaesthetic drawing, it has been shown convincingly that this type of test measures "psychoticism" in a reliable manner. No significant differences were obtained between normals and neurotics, nor between neurotic categories. The reader should not overlook the fact that a test of greatest simplicity and short duration has achieved much better results than any of the complex drawing techniques discussed in Sects. II and III.

Figure Reconstruction Test (F.R.T.)

A number of considerations have led the present author to construct a test, called the Figure Reconstruction Test (F.R.T.), which largely meets the

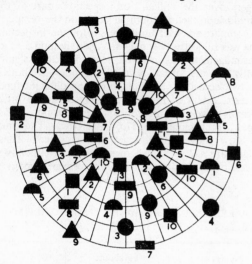

FRT IMMEDIATE RECALL
SET OF 10 PATTERNS

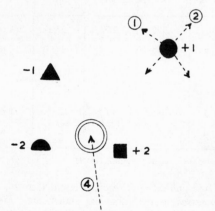

FIG. 3.16. *Top:* F.R.T. SET OF TEN PATTERNS OF
MODERATE LEVEL OF DIFFICULTY

Bottom: REPRODUCED PATTERN WITH STATEMENTS OF
POSITIVE OR NEGATIVE CONFIDENCE IN CORRECTNESS OF
PERFORMANCE

Two error scores; 1 = rotation, or axial displacement; 2 = distance, or radial error. *Two expressive movement scores:* 3 = size; 4 = distance of shapes from the centre.

(*Brengelmann,* 1958e, 1959a)

criticism levelled against other drawing techniques as follows. (*a*) The test items to be drawn are of the simplest kind, to exclude the effect of drawing skill. (*b*) Scoring is entirely objective. (*c*) The test is constructed so as to be repeatable and yield high degrees of reliability. (*d*) The test is disguised as a learning or recall test to divert attention from movement. (*e*) The test restricts the number of drawing scores to a minimum, yet permits comprehensive analysis of common score categories, including intra-individual measures of variability. This avoids that abundance of intercorrelated items which are difficult to combine directly (Mira, P.M.K., B.G.T.) as well as a too great simplicity with limited scope for analysis (e.g. draw a circle, square, etc.). (*f*) The test permits the scoring of expressive movement characteristics to be independent of accompanying error. (*g*) Portions of the test may be analysed separately to assess the effects of feelings of certainty, or confidence, connected with the performance aspect of the F.R.T., on movement characteristics.

The F.R.T. which measures learning, recall and recognition (Brengelmann, 1956*b*, 1958*e*, 1958*f*, 1959*a*), as well as expressive movement, requires reproductions of exposed patterns of simple geometric shapes (circle, triangle, square, etc.) to be drawn from memory. Shapes are reproduced around a central reference point provided on the response sheets, as shown in Fig. 3.16. This figure shows a recall version of moderate level of difficulty. One such test set consists of ten patterns of five shapes each, distributed evenly over the stimulus surface (upper portion of the figure). At the bottom, an example of a drawn reproduction is shown including a description of some basic scores, as well as one of four degrees of certainty (+2, +1, −1, or −2) added to each of the reproduced shapes. These marks indicate how certain subject felt about the correct placing from memory of the individual items.

There are two basic measures derived from such drawings, the actual *size* of the individual shapes and their *distance* from the central reference point; both measures are taken in millimetres. In addition, the *spread* of shapes between distances and the *variability* of size and distance between trials form important scores among a few others.

Some of the more important results, all cross-validated, are now described. *Firstly,* in the initial two experiments (Brengelmann and Marconi, 1958*d*), *size* was consistently larger in psychotics than in controls (Fig. 3.17). When the neurotics were divided into hysterics and dysthymics, hysterics drew consistently larger, but not significantly so. Both results are in agreement with Eysenck's findings from using a simple kinaesthetic test (Sect. IV). It will be noticed, however, that score norms varied considerably between these experiments; this occurred also in later tests. This difficulty was removed to a considerable extent by scoring *between trials variability* (Fig. 3.17), which provides essentially the same results at a much higher level of significance. Finally, by using the *ratio size variability/size* means were sufficiently identical between experiments for each of the four subgroups used, and significance of differences was retained

error) and *distance variability* (radial error). There is no reason to assume that axial error is differentially affected by individual differences in movement variability, as test items are equally spread over the stimulus surface and errors due to movements of this kind will cancel out. Systematic individual differences in radial expansion and variability, as determined by distance measures of the *non-error* type, have however

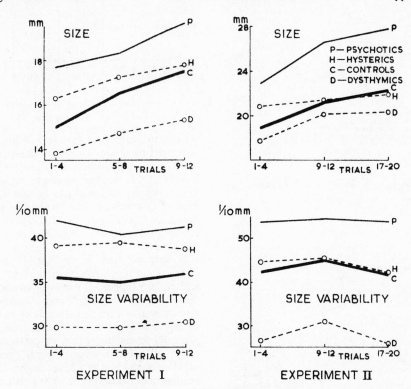

FIG. 3.17. THE SIZE OF REPRODUCED F.R.T. SHAPES IS DISTINCTLY LARGER FOR
PSYCHOTICS THAN FOR NORMALS
Some relationship to hysteria/dysthymia is found.
(*From Brengelmann and Marconi, 1958d*)

between hysterics and dysthymics, as well as between psychotics and dysthymics.

In general, the result was that size and measures derived from size were primarily indicative of "psychoticism" and, in the second instance, of hysteria/dysthymia. Similarly measures of distance were rather more related to hysteria/dysthymia than to psychoticism.

A *second* problem thought to be of fundamental importance is the *interaction between error and expressive movement* (Brengelmann, 1959b). This is demonstrated by comparing the two types of error variabilities (between trials variability), which may be derived from the F.R.T., *rotation variability* (axial

been found, the relevant scores being highest for hysterics and psychotics. Radial movement variability may correspondingly interfere with radial error. This is, in fact, shown in Fig. 3.18 and Table III.9.

The results show similar types of learning curves for both rotation and distance variability. However, considerable differences in subgroups are found between the two error scores. As to rotation variability, no significant differences between hysterics and dysthymics are found at any stage of practice. With distance variability, however, differences between hysterics and dysthymics are not only significant but, contrary to general expectation from the learning point of view, predominantly so in the early practice stages. This effect is, as predicted, also present in schizophrenics (compare trials 1–4 in Fig. 3.18) though not to a significant degree.

This result shows that, in drawing tasks, expressive movement may interfere significantly with correctness

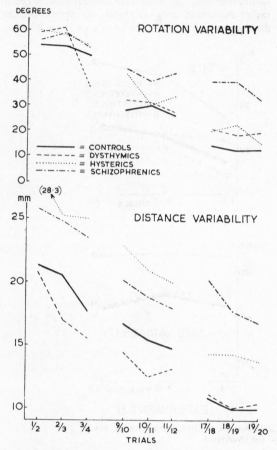

FIG. 3.18. SIGNIFICANT DIFFERENCES IN DRAWING VARIABILITY (ERROR MEASURE) BETWEEN HYSTERICS AND DYSTHYMICS, AS A FUNCTION OF ABSENCE (ROTATION) OR PRESENCE (DISTANCE) OF INTERFERENCE BY EXPRESSIVE MOVEMENT

(Brengelmann, unpublished)

of performance. With the F.R.T. such effects can be assessed. Error scores can be constructed which are either essentially free of such distortions or have been corrected for them. The criticism made of the Bender Gestalt Test that error and movement scores cannot be separated can now be better understood.

A *third* and a *fourth point* of further *steps in validation* are discussed jointly with Fig. 3.19. Careful inspection of results achieved with criteria hitherto used made a further reduction of the large variance, still unaccounted for, desirable. Two further criteria

TABLE III.9

SELECTIVE EFFECT OF EXPRESSIVE MOVEMENT ON DISTANCE VARIABILITY

(Compare Fig. 3.18)

t-ratios	Rotation variability		Distance variability	
	Trials 1–4	Trials 17–20	Trials 1–4	Trials 17–20
Hysterics *v.* dysthymics (28 d.f.) . . .	N.S.	N.S.	2·620 (2 per cent)	1·909 (10 per cent)
Schizophrenics *v.* normals (35 d.f.) . . .	N.S.	3·884 (1 per cent)	N.S.	3·329 (1 per cent)

2 — trials tests.

were introduced, the first one being "*rigidity*," as measured by a combination of scores of the Nigniewitzky (1955) (Brengelmann, 1959a) Scale and the Soueiff (1958) extreme response set score. By this means rigidity was found to be statistically independent of extraversion. The second new criterion was "*confidence*" (Brengelmann, 1959a) as described above (compare Fig. 3.16). Results are now shown in Fig. 3.19.

It may be seen *firstly* that, in neurotics, both distance and standard deviation of distance decreased with rigidity (upper left portion). *Secondly*, examining the effects of "*negative*" and "*positive confidence*," distance was not consistently related to the dichotomy of negative/positive confidence. However, it was generally found, regardless of personality type, that nearly all subjects spread shapes bearing marks of negative confidence to a lesser degree than those with positive confidence (upper right portion of Fig. 3.19). There are, however, significant individual differences to this effect, which are specific to personality (lower half of Fig. 3.19).

The lower left portion shows that, with one exception, *means of distance* increase with extraversion. There are no great differences between negative and positive confidence, but score norms differ widely between sexes. The relationship between SD-distance for *negative confidence* and extraversion is exactly contrary between the sexes. However, a consistent and significant relationship with perfect subgroup placings is found for *positive confidence*. It appears from this that the introduction of the criterion "confidence" considerably improved measurement and stabilized test norms.

The last few points are of sufficient importance to be described anew in terms of *correlations between personality criteria and distance scores*, which are presented in Table III.10.

DISTANCE

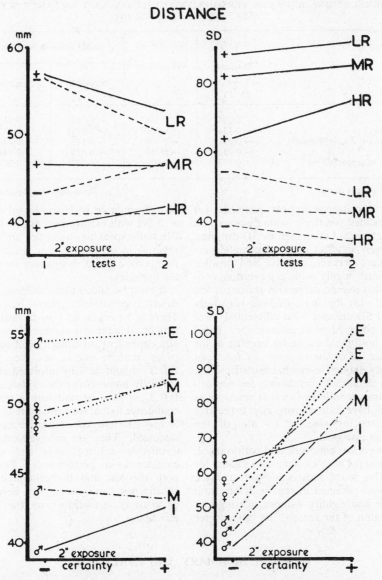

FIG. 3.19. *Top left:* DISTANCE DECREASES WITH DEGREE OF RIGIDITY ("CONSTRICTION"). *Top right:* STANDARD DEVIATION OF DISTANCE DECREASES WITH DEGREE OF BOTH RIGIDITY AND NEGATIVE CONFIDENCE. *Bottom left:* DISTANCE INCREASES WITH EXTRAVERSION, WITH MEANS VARYING TO A CONSIDERABLE DEGREE. *Bottom right:* BETWEEN THE SEXES, ONLY SD-DISTANCE OF POSITIVE CERTAINTY IS CONSISTENTLY RELATED TO EXTRAVERSION

(N = 8 per subgroup)

LR = low rigidity	+ = positive	E = extraverted
MR = medium rigidity	− = negative certainty in	M = medium group
HR = high rigidity	memory performance	I = introverted

(*Brengelmann, unpublished*)

97

TABLE III.10

CORRELATIONS BETWEEN PERSONALITY CRITERIA AND DISTANCE SCORES
(SPREAD, OR EXPANSION)

	Distance	SD-distance	SD-distance separate for confidence		
			negative	positive	diff. between neg. and pos.
Extraversion	0·398†	0·364*	− 0·083	0·480†	0·542†
Rigidity (Nigniewitzky)	− 0·424†	− 0·506†	− 0·471†	− 0·352*	− 0·059
Extreme response set (+ 2 only, Soueiff) .	− 0·347*	− 0·338*	− 0·191	− 0·275	− 0·158
Neuroticism	− 0·122	− 0·168	− 0·021	− 0·148	− 0·137
Negative confidence in reproduction .	0·177	0·074	0·533†	− 0·267	− 0·611†

N = 48 neurotics (24 male, 24 female).   Significance: † = 1 per cent, * = 5 per cent level.

The following conclusions appear justified. (a) *Extraversion* correlates positively with distance and SD-distance. High spread of shapes, or SD-distance, appears to be largely an effect of positive confidence. The difference score between negative and positive confidence correlates highly with extraversion considering the fact that questionnaire and apparatus test scores are related. (b) *Rigidity* correlates negatively with distance and SD-distance. No differential effect for confidence is observed as in extraversion. Rigid subjects contract both the distance for negative as for positive confidence. *Extreme response set* functions similarly to rigidity, though somewhat less effectively. (c) The reare no significant correlations for neuroticism. This is consistent with the fact that neurotics as a clinical group have not shown any expressive movement correlates as assessed by any of the drawing techniques discussed.

(d) The more *negative* confidence is in performance, the *greater* is spread for *negative* items and smaller for positive ones. This is the most significant and the most unusual result obtained in that it differs from both extraversion and rigidity without offering any immediate suggestion of the reason. Its large degree of independence is demonstrated by a correlation of − 0·298 with extraversion and − 0·183 with rigidity. Clinically speaking, neurotics are considerably more *negative* in confidence than schizophrenics. Within the neurotic group, dysthymics are more negative than the hysterics.

It must be added that confidence is greatly, though strictly systematically, affected by exposure conditions. There is, however, no time to deal with this here. It may be added that a number of results are systematically dependent on other conditions, such as size of paper, practice effects, sex, etc. Anyone using the F.R.T. should be fully informed about these.

Briefly *summarizing* the evidence obtained with the F.R.T., it may be said with a reasonable degree of confidence that at least five more or less heterogeneous factors interfere with expressive movement of the type discussed. They are extraversion, rigidity, hysteria-dysthymia, schizophrenia and verbally expressed confidence in performance. For reasons stated, both the test and the criteria employed, in their effectiveness and scope, go beyond the majority of findings established in the field of drawing techniques.

GENERAL SUMMARY AND EVALUATION

Section I

The areas of expressive movement research originally most heavily favoured have yielded relatively little worth reporting. This can hardly be explained as due to difficulties in measurement, as many aspects of voice, speech, and gross bodily movements are amenable to objective investigation. It may be argued that the emphasis on judgement of "expressive" qualities of movement has distracted attention from the actual measurement of movement. Although judgement of movement has opened up extremely fruitful avenues of research, emphasis on movement *per se* should be revived.

Abnormal or personality correlates of *gait, posture* and *facial movement* are practically unknown. *Gestures* are said to be expressive of "feeling" and "emotion." Particular types of gestures, nervous movements, are shown to be more frequent in neurotics than in normals. Nothing is known about *voice*, except for the suggestion that loudness and melism vary with body build, and intensity under stress with certain self-ratings of sensitivity. Various *speech* characteristics are also said to be indicative of emotional states. Statements using such vague non-operational terms as "emotionality" indicate how little advance has been made over mere clinical observation. However, a certain amount of analysis of relevant conditions has been performed which should aid validation considerably.

Judgement of expression, on the contrary, has produced rather suggestive results. This method, originally intended to serve as a rating substitute for objective measurement, has been shown to reveal quite specific individual differences in *self-evaluation*, as well as in evaluating others. Schizophrenics rate their own expression (voice, face, writing, drawing) more favourably than do normals, provided they do not recognize them as their own. Nothing is known about neurotics. However, in the use of language, neurotics, possibly more than schizophrenics, make more *self-references* (personal pronouns) than normals. They also score high on the verb-adjective quotient, which may be indicative of internal states of tension. These facts suggest that self-esteem plays an important role, possibly of a causative kind. It may be surmised that certain hitherto unconnected areas like unconscious self-evaluation, extreme response set, confidence in performance, level of aspiration, use of pronouns, etc., are closely related. In addition to such rationally and easily recognizable relations, movement itself (e.g. size) may be conjectured in order to give clues to the inner attitude toward dimension or to "ego evaluation" (Liss, 1938). In one case an expressive movement score (standard deviation of distance, F.R.T., Sect. IV) has already shown significance and, as regards personality, specific relationships existing between self-evaluation and movement.

Attention has been focused on neurotics. Psychotics, however, have sometimes been shown to vary similarly to neurotics. In the case of *"vocabulary inflexibility"* they may be expected to score relatively highly. Differential behaviour between abnormals has not been investigated extensively. Within the neurotic field it has, on occasion, been shown that the hysterics behave rather differently from the anxiety and obsessive-compulsive states.

Section II

On account of their complex and impressionistic nature *products of art* and *free drawing techniques* are difficult to evaluate. The application of controls in the assessment of personality by means of free drawing and drawing completion tests have revealed numerous previous claims of validity to be unfounded. As regards personality and abnormality, none of these techniques can claim to have established useful validity. It has been suggested that objectification, as for example, by using the multiple-choice technique,

might remove some major sources of error in the assessment.

Section III

The copying version of the Bender-Gestalt Test has not been shown to measure personality, nor to differentiate between abnormal categories. Results in assessing abnormality have remained inconsistent, and the dependence on rating with all its serious drawbacks, the difficulty of constructing parallel test forms and, perhaps most important, the heterogeneous nature of the assessed scores, discourage future use of this test.

Manipulative tasks, as the Mosaic Test, the Colour Pyramid Test, the Colour-star Test and the Bunch-of-grapes Test, have revealed some suggestive results in differentiating between various groups of abnormals, and between normals and abnormals. The results require cross-validation throughout. Tests of this kind could, in the writer's opinion, be fairly easily adapted to yield objective measures of style of movement, which could justify their further use.

Handwriting analysis has so far not provided any communicable method of measuring personality or abnormality to a reasonable degree. The suggestion has been made that this is partly due to the choice of inefficient criteria. The permanence of handwriting records appears to be one good reason to continue in search for validation.

Section IV

Although less frequently used, objective tests of expressive movement have provided more consistent results. On *writing pressure*, neurotics scored higher than normals. This may be considered to agree with their known higher degree of muscle tension. Additionally, hysterics, pyknics and energetic-expressive-impulsive types of personality press harder than their opponents. An investigation of what these groups have in common in this respect might be rewarding.

Error and variability in tracing while wearing *prismatic lenses* were significantly related to both extraversion and rigidity. A rated score called "angular-excessive" versus "smooth-restrained" movement discriminated between extraverted and rigid subjects.

Simple blindfolded *"kinaesthetic" drawing* differentiates significantly and consistently between psychotics on the one hand, and neurotics and normals on the other. Because of its simplicity, this technique is restricted in its application.

The *Figure Reconstruction Test*, objectively scored and disguised as a memory test, is known to be related to at least five criteria of both personality and abnormality, to wit, extraversion, rigidity, hysteria/dysthymia, schizophrenia and a measure of certainty.

It may be noted that neuroticism, as measured by clinical groups of neurotics or by means of a questionnaire, is not of great importance.

Choice of Criteria

A comparison between earlier sections and Sect. IV reveals that there has been considerable improvement in validation as criteria have been changed, but that this has varied between criteria. Extraversion, rigidity and certainty, as used in some of these studies, have not, in fact, been applied to expressive movement before. The repeated finding that neuroticism played no significant role seems to support the argument that poor results have, at least in part, been due to the choice of too complex, or inadequate, criteria such as "emotionality," "adjustment," "instability," etc., which are generally considered to be associated with neuroticism.

With the F.R.T., certain reliable differences have however been found using clinical categories of neurosis and psychosis as criteria, but there was a large overlap between groups.

It would seem, from these considerations, that the exclusive use of clinical criteria of any kind should be abandoned. There is, however, evidence strong enough to suggest that personality criteria of the kind employed are at least as important as clinical diagnosis and should be used in addition to the latter.

Empirical Test Construction

The inflation in test production has been justly criticized by many workers. Personality tests, however, with the exception of questionnaires, are as a rule constructed on "rational" grounds, i.e. without proper *empirical* development. This appears incongruous with scientific procedure in general and has been shown to be unsuitable in the field of expressive movement. Tables III.7 and III.10, for example, demonstrate the empirical derivation of fundamentally important variables which could hardly have been predicted on theoretical grounds. Evidence on two types of error variabilities, as presented in Fig. 3.18, shows the empirically derived distinction between expressive movement-free and movement-influenced error scores to be of great importance. If, for example, this distinction had been considered in the construction of widely applied tests like the Bender-Gestalt Test, the confusion resulting from relative emphasis on theorizing might have been avoided.

Functional Analysis

Greater flexibility in choice of criteria and emphasis on empirical test construction are important, though not sufficient. Alone they do not offer adequate control of variables. Suggestions have been made that change in conditions may change the validity of voice intensity (Sect. I), or of handwriting (Sect. III), or that exposure time may affect the effectiveness of movement scores (Brengelmann, 1958a). Striking examples of the modifying influence of task conditions have been discussed in connexion with unconscious evaluation of one's own expression (Epstein, Fig. 3.1) and with certainty, which is known to be intimately related to expressive movement (Table III.10; Brengelmann, unpublished results). Furthermore, movement variability could be shown to be both positively (Sect. IV) and negatively (Sect. IV) related to rigidity, a relation which may be a function of stressfulness of tasks. At the same time, correlations with extraversion were significantly positive throughout. From this evidence it is suggested that functional analysis, a method widely used in other biological sciences, should be introduced systematically to ascertain the conditions necessary to produce the phenomena studied.

General Recommendations

The last three points discussed, choice of inefficient criteria, use of heterogeneous test scores and disregard for conditional effects may explain why results have been so poor in a field rich in promise for personality work. Before other considerations, a higher regard for experimental procedures of the kind discussed appears necessary if basic functions of expressive movement and their personality or disease correlates are to be discovered.

The effect of such recommendations may be felt in fields where expressive movement is secondarily involved. Eysenck (1956a), Star (1957) and Brengelmann (1957b) found, for instance, that rate of improvement in tracking and tracing was, consistently, slightly negatively related to extraversion. This was taken to support Eysenck's learning theory involving certain assumptions concerning the cortical balance of excitation-inhibition (compare Eysenck, Casey and Trouton, 1957).

The tests used in the above studies involve, however, "expressive" movements of a kind likely to interfere with the actual motor performance, for which the theory was constructed. Both variability and extent of movement were demonstrated to be consistently and, as a rule, significantly related to extraversion. From this, it appears quite reasonable to assume that motor performance of extraverts tends to be less efficient than that of introverts solely on account of their higher variability and/or extent of movement. It has indeed, on a number of occasions, been shown that rate of improvement in performing the F.R.T., even using various levels of difficulty, was either the same for extraverts and introverts or, more often so, higher for extraverts (Brengelmann, 1958e; 1958f; Fig. 3.18). This statement applies only to test scores which are unlikely to be interfered with by expressive movement. In general then, the effects of expressive movement should be assessed whenever they are likely to interfere with other test scores or conditions investigated.

REFERENCES

ABT, L. E. and BELLAK, L. (Eds.), *Projective Psychology* (New York, Alfred A. Knopf, Inc., 1950).

ADDINGTON, M. C., A note on the Pascal and Suttell scoring system of the Bender-Gestalt Test, *J. Clin. Psychol.*, **8**, 312–313 (1952).

ALBEE, G. W. and HAMLIN, R. M., An investigation of the reliability and validity of judgments of adjustment inferred from drawings, *J. Clin. Psychol.*, **5**, 389–391 (1949).

ALBEE, G. W. and HAMLIN, R. M. Judgment of adjustment from drawings: the applicability of rating scale methods, *J. Clin. Psychol.*, **6**, 363–364 (1950).

ALLEN, S. C., TAYLOR, C. L. and HALL, V. E., A study of orthostatic insufficiency by the tiltboard method, *Amer. J. Physiol.*, **143**, 11–20 (1945).

ALLPORT, G. W., *Personality* (London, Constable, 1938).

ALLPORT, G. W. and VERNON, P. E., *Studies in Expressive Movement* (New York, Macmillan, 1933).

ALSCHULER, R. H. and HATTWICK, L. W., *Painting and Personality* 2 vols. (Chicago, Univ. of Chicago Press, 1947).

AMES, L. B. and HELLERSBERG, C., The Horn-Hellersberg test: responses of three- to eleven-year-old children, *Rorschach Res. Exch.*, **13**, 415–432 (1949).

ANASTASI, A. and FOLEY, J. P., A survey of the literature on artistic behaviour of the abnormal: III. Spontaneous productions, *Psychol. Monogr.*, **52**, No. 6. (1940).

ANASTASI, A. and FOLEY, J. P., A survey of the literature on artistic behaviour in the abnormal: IV. Experimental investigations, *J. Gen. Psychol.*, **25**, 187–237 (1941).

ANASTASI, A. and FOLEY, J. P., An experimental study of the drawing behaviour of adult psychotics in comparison with that of a normal control group, *J. Exp. Psychol.*, **34**, 169–194 (1944).

ANASTASI, A. and FOLEY, J. P., *Psychiatric selection of flying personnel: V. The human-figure drawing test as an objective psychiatric screening aid for student pilots* (San Antonio, Texas, U.S.A.F. School of Aviation Medicine, Randolph Field, October 1952. (Project No. 21–37–002, Report No. 5.)).

ANDERS, P., Über den individuellen Eigenrhythmus beim menschlichen Gange und seine Beziehungen zum Rhythmus der Herz- und Atemtätigkeit, *Pflüg. Arch. ges. Physiol.*, **220**, 287–299 (1928).

ANONYMOUS, Measuring intelligence by the Wartegg Drawing Completion Test. *Psychol. Res. Notes* No. 10 (Univ. of Detroit, 1954).

ANSBACHER, H. L., The Goodenough draw-a-man test and primary mental abilities, *J. Cons. Psychol.*, **16**, 176–180 (1952).

BALKEN, E. and MASSERMAN, J. H., The language of phantasy: III. The language of the phantasies of patients with conversion hysteria, anxiety state, and obsessional-compulsive neurosis, *J. Psychol.*, **10**, 75–86 (1940).

BAUER, L., Erfahrungen mit dem Warteggtest auf unserer Kinderstation, *Nervenarzt*, **23**, 52–55 (1952).

BAXTER, M. F., An experimental study of the differentiation of temperament on the basis of rate and strength, *Amer. J. Psychol.*, **38**, 59–96 (1927).

BELL, J. E., *Projective Techniques* (New York, Longmans, Green & Co., 1951).

BENDER, L., A visual motor Gestalt test and its clinical use, *Amer. Orthopsychiat. Assoc. Res. Monogr.* No. 3. (1938).

BENDER, L., *Instructions for the Use of Visual Motor Gestalt Test* (New York, Amer. Orthopsychiat. Assoc., 1946).

BENDER, L., Psychological principles of the visual motor Gestalt test, *Trans. N.Y. Acad. Sci.*, **11**, 164–170 (1949).

BENTON, A. L., HARTMAN, C. H., and SARASON, I. G., Some relations between speech behavior and anxiety level, *J. Abnorm. (Soc.) Psychol.*, **51**, 295–297 (1955).

BERNSTEIN, N., Kymozyklographion, ein neuer Apparat für Bewegungsstudium, *Pflüg. Arch. ges. Physiol.*, **217**, 782–792 (1927).

BILLINGSLEA, F. Y., The Bender-Gestalt: an objective scoring method and validating data, *J. Clin. Psychol.*, **4**, 1–27 (1948).

BLUM, R. H., The validity of the Machover D.A.P. technique, *J. Clin. Psychol.*, **10**, 120–125 (1954).

BOGEN, H. and LIPPMANN, O., Gang und Charakter, *Beih. Z. angew. Psychol.*, No. 58, (Leipzig, Barth, 1931).

BOWLAND, J. A. and DEABLER, H. L., A Bender-Gestalt diagnostic validity study, *J. Clin. Psychol.*, **12**, 82–84 (1956).

BRACKEN, H. VON., Recent trends in German psychology, *J. Gen. Psychol.*, **47**, 165–179 (1952).

BRACKEN, H. VON., PUNGS, L. and RIEDEL, H., Ein neues Gerät zum Registrieren des Schreibdrucks, *Abh. braunschw. wiss. Ges.*, **1**, 126–132 (1949).

BRENGELMANN, J. C., Farbwahl, Verlaufsform und Versuchsdauer des Farbpyramidentestes bei normalen und abnormalen Versuchspersonen, (Teil I). *Psychol. Rundschau*, **4**, 33–43 (1953a).

BRENGELMANN, J. C., Formale Gestaltungen im Farbpyramidentest als Funktion normaler und abnormaler Versuchsgruppen, (Teil II). *Psychol. Rundschau*, **4**, 165–173 (1953b).

BRENGELMANN, J. C., Grösse und Veränderung der Grösse von Reproduktionen als Mass des Bewegungsausdrucks, *Z. diagn. Psychol. u. Persforschg.*, **3**, 23–33 (1955a).

BRENGELMANN, J. C., Figurrekonstruktion: Grösse und Variabilität der Grösse von Reproduktionen als Bestimmer der Extraversion-Introversion, *Mschr. Psychiat. Neurol.*, **130**, 209–233 (1955b).

BRENGELMANN, J. C., Conrads Standardwahrscheinlichkeit in der Farbwahl: Eine Entgegnung, *Z. f. exp. u. angew. Psychol.*, **3**, 602–604 (1956a).

BRENGELMANN, J. C., Figurrekonstruktion: Rotationsfehler und Rotationsvariabilität als Indikatoren der Persönlichkeit, vorzüglich der Psychose, *Fol. psychiat. neerl.*, **59**, 230–254 (1956b).

BRENGELMANN, J. C., Complex perceptual processes, in *Perceptual Processes and Mental Illness. Maudsley*

Monographs, H. J. Eysenck, G. W. Granger and J. C. Brengelmann (London, Chapman & Hall Ltd., 1957a).

BRENGELMANN, J. C., Extraversion, neurotische Tendenz und Rigidität im Umkehrversuch (Prismenbrille), *Z. f. exp. u. angew. Psychol.*, **4**, 339–362 (1957b).

BRENGELMANN, J. C., Farbwahl und Variabilität der Farbwahl im Farbpyramidentest, *Arch Psychiat. u. Z. ges. Neurol.*, **196**, 297–306 (1957c).

BRENGELMANN, J. C., Differential effects of lysergic acid and Sodium Amytal on immediate memory and expressive movement, *J. Ment. Sci.*, **104**, 144–152 (1958a).

BRENGELMANN, J. C., d-amphetamine and amytal: I. Effects on memory and expressive movement, *J. Ment. Sci.*, **104**, 153–159 (1958b).

BRENGELMANN, J. C., d-amphetamine and amytal: II. Effects on certainty and adequacy of certainty in recall and recognition, *J. Ment. Sci.*, **104**, 160–166 (1958c).

BRENGELMANN, J. C., The effects of exposure time in immediate recall on abnormal and questionnaire criteria of personality, *J. Ment. Sci.*, **104**, 665–680 (1958e).

BRENGELMANN, J. C., Learning in neurotics and psychotics, *Acta psychol. Hague*, **13**, 371–388 (1958f).

BRENGELMANN, J. C., Abnormal and personality correlates of certainty, *J. Ment. Sci.*, **105**, 142–162 (1959a).

BRENGELMANN, J. C., Expressive movement and learning: a study of score complexity, *J. Ment. Sci.*, **105**, 81–92 (1959b).

BRENGELMANN, J. C. and MARCONI, J. T., Expressive movement in abnormals, with particular reference to extraversion and psychoticism, *Acta psychol. Hague*, **14**, 200–214 (1958d).

BROWN, D. G. and TOLOR, A., Human figure drawings as indicators of sexual identification and inversion, *Percept. Mot. Skills*, **7**, 199–211 (1957).

BUCK, J. N., The H-T-P test, *J. Clin. Psychol.*, **4**, 151–159 (1948a).

BUCK, J. N., The H-T-P technique: a qualitative and quantitative scoring manual, *J. Clin. Psychol.*, (*Monograph Supplement*), **4**, 317 (1948b).

BULLINGER, E. and SEYFRIED, H., Über den Farbsterntest (nach Seyfried). *Z. f. exp. u. angew. Psychol.*, **2**, 575–598 (1954).

BULLINGER, E., and SEYFRIED, H., Allgemein und sexuell verwahrloste Mädchen im Farbsterntest, *Praxis Kinderpsychol. u. Kinderpsychiat.*, **4**, 205–209 (1955).

BUSEMANN, A., *Die Sprache der Jugend als Ausdruck der Entwicklungsrhythmik* (Jena, Fischer, 1925).

BUSEMANN, A., Über typische und phasische Unterschiede der kategorialen Sprachform, *Z. pädag. Psychol.*, **27**, 415–420 (1926).

CALIGOR, L., The detection of paranoid trends by the eight card redrawing test. (8 CRT), *J. Clin. Psychol.*, **8**, 397–401 (1952).

CANTRIL, H., RAND, H. A. and ALLPORT, G. W., The determination of personal interests by psychological and graphological methods, *Character & Pers.*, **2**, 134–143 (1933–34).

CASTELNUOVO-TEDESCO, P., A study of the relationship between handwriting and personality variables, *Genet. Psychol. Monogr.*, **37**, 167–220 (1948).

CHAMBERS, J. L., Trait judgment of photographs by neuropsychiatric patients, *J. Clin. Psychol.*, **13**, 393–396 (1957).

COLEMAN, J. C. Facial expressions of emotion, *Psychol. Monogr.*, **63**, 1–36 (1949).

CONRAD, K., Über das Problem der Farbwahl im Farbpyramidentest bei normalen und abnormalen Versuchspersonen, *Z. f. exp. u. angew. Psychol.*, **2**, 33–50 (1954).

CONRAD, K. and JUNCKER, D., Über den konstitutionstypologischen Wert des Heiss-Hiltmannschen Farbpyramidentestes, *Z. menschl. Vererb. u. Konstit. Lehre*, **32**, 259–276 (1954).

CONRAD, DOROTHY C. and CONRAD, R., The use of personal pronouns as categories for studying small group interaction, *J. Abnorm. (Soc.) Psychol.*, **52**, 277–279 (1956).

COURTS, F. A., Relations between muscular tension and performance, *Psychol. Bull.*, **39**, 347–367 (1942).

CROWDEN, R. C., DEABLER, H. L. and FEAMSTER, J. H., The prognostic value of the Bender-Gestalt, H-T-P, TAT and Sentence Completion tests, *J. Clin. Psychol.*, **11**, 271–275 (1955).

CRIDER, B., The reliability and validity of two graphologists, *J. Appl. Psychol.*, **25**, 323–325 (1941).

CROWN, S., An experimental inquiry into some aspects of the motor behaviour and personality of tiqueurs, *J. Ment. Sci.*, **99**, 84–91 (1953).

CURNUTT, R. H., The use of the Bender-Gestalt with an alcoholic and nonalcoholic population, *J. Clin. Psychol.*, **9**, 287–290 (1953).

DAVIS, R. C., Methods of measuring muscular tension, *Psychol. Bull.*, **39**, 329–346 (1942).

DEUTSCH, F., Analysis of postural behavior, *Psychoanal. Quart.*, **16**, 195–213 (1947).

DIAMOND, B. L. and SCHMALE, H. T., The Mosaic Test: I. An evaluation of its clinical application, *Amer. J. Orthopsychiat.*, **14**, 237–250 (1944).

DIBNER, A. S., Cue-counting: a measure of anxiety in interviews, *J. Cons. Psychol.*, **20**, 475–478 (1956).

DOLLARD, J. and MOWRER, O. H. A., A method of measuring tension in written documents, *J. Abnorm. (Soc.) Psychol.*, **42**, 3–32 (1947).

DUFFY, E., The measurement of muscular tension as a technique for the study of emotional tendencies, *Amer. J. Psychol.*, **44**, 146–162 (1932).

DUFFY, E., Level of muscular tension as an aspect of personality, *J. Gen. Psychol.*, **35**, 161–171 (1946).

EFRON, D., *Gesture and Environment* (New York, King's Crown Press, 1941).

EFRON, D. and FOLEY, J. P., JR., Gestural behavior and social setting in *Readings in Social Psychology* Eds. T. M. Newcomb and E. L. Hartley, (New York, H. Holt, 1947).

EIDELBERG, L., Quantitative Untersuchungen der Lagebeharrung, *Mschr. Psychiat. Neurol.*, **61**, 101–108 (1926).

EIGENBRODE, C. R., Effectiveness of the Machover signs and others in differentiating between a normal group and a schizophrenic group by use of the projective drawing test, *Master's Thesis, George Washington University*, (1951).

EISENBERG, P., A further study in expressive movement, *Character & Pers.*, **5**, 296–301 (1937).

ELKISCH, PAULA, Children's drawings in a projective technique, *Psychol. Monogr.*, **58**, 1 (Whole No. 266) (1945).

ENKE, W., Experimentalpsychologische Studien zur

Konstitutionsforschung, (Psychomotorische Untersuchungen), *Z. Neurol.*, **118**, 798–817 (1929).

ENKE, W., Handschrift und Charakter im exakten Versuch, *Klin. Wschr.*, **17**, 1,624–1,627 (1938).

EPSTEIN, S., Unconscious self-evaluation in a normal and a schizophrenic group, *J. Abnorm. (Soc.) Psychol.*, **50**, 65–70 (1955).

EYSENCK, H. J., Graphological analysis and psychiatry: an experimental study, *Brit. J. Psychol.*, **35**, 70–81 (1945).

EYSENCK, H. J., *Dimensions of Personality* (London, Routledge & Kegan Paul, 1950).

EYSENCK, H. J., Schizothymia-cyclothymia as a dimension of personality: II. Experimental, *J. Personality*, **20**, 345–384 (1952a).

EYSENCK, H. J., *The Scientific Study of Personality* (London, Routledge & Kegan Paul, 1952b).

EYSENCK, H. J., Probleme der diagnostischen Untersuchung und Demonstration des Charakter-Interpretationstestes, *Z. f. exp. u. angew. Psychol.*, **2**, 1–32 (1954).

EYSENCK, H. J., Reminiscence, drive, and personality theory, *J. Abnorm. (Soc.) Psychol.*, **53**, 328–333 (1956a).

EYSENCK, H. J., The questionnaire measurement of extraversion and neuroticism, *Riv. Psicol.*, **50**, 113–140 (1956b).

EYSENCK, H. J., CASEY, S. and TROUTON, D. S., Drugs and personality: II. The effect of stimulant and depressant drugs on continuous work, *J. Ment. Sci.*, **103**, 645–649 (1957).

EYSENCK, S. B. G., A dimensional analysis of mental abnormality, *Ph.D. Thesis, Univ. of London Lib.* (1955).

EYSENCK, S. B. G., Neurosis and psychosis: an experimental analysis, *J. Ment. Sci.*, **102**, 517–529 (1956).

FAIRBANKS, HELEN, The quantitative differentiation of samples of spoken language: II. *Psychol. Monogr.*, **56**, 2, 19–38 (1944).

FAUTREL, M., Étude de la fidélité de la dynamométrie manuelle, *Bull. Cent. Étud. Rech. psychotech.*, **3**, 3–12 (1954).

FIEDLER, F. E. and SIEGEL, S. M., The free drawing test as a predictor of non-improvement in psychotherapy, *J. Clin. Psychol.*, **5**, 386–389 (1949).

FISHER, S. and FISHER, R., Test of certain assumptions regarding figure drawing analysis, *J. Abnorm. (Soc.) Psychol.*, **45**, 727–732 (1950).

FLEISHMAN, E. A. and HEMPEL, W. E., JR., Changes in factor structure of a complex psychomotor test as a function of practice, *Psychometrika*, **19**, 239–252 (1954).

FLEISHMAN, E. A. and HEMPEL, W. E., JR., The relation between abilities and improvement with practice in a visual discrimination task, *J. Exp. Psychol.*, **49**, 301–312 (1955).

FRANK, K. and ROSEN, E., A projective test of masculinity-femininity, *J. Cons. Psychol.*, **13**, 247–256 (1949).

FRANKS, C. M., L'échelle de Taylor et l'analyse dimensionelle de l'anxiété. *Rev. Psychol. appl.*, **6**, 35–44 (1956).

FROHOFF, W., Untersuchungen mit dem Farbpyramidentest (Pfister-Heiss) bei Schizophrenen, *Z. f. exp. u. angew. Psychol.*, **1**, 145–181 (1953).

GAGE, N. L., LEAVITT, G. S. and STONE, G. C., The intermediary key in the analysis of interpersonal perception, *Psychol. Bull.*, **53**, 258–266 (1956).

GERARD, D. L. and KORNETSKY, C., Adolescent opiate addiction: a study of control and addict subjects, *Psychiat. Quart.*, **29**, 457–485 (1955).

GLANVILLE, A. D. and KREEZER, G., The characteristics of gait of normal male adults, *J. Exp. Psychol.*, **21**, 277–301 (1937).

GOBETZ, W., A quantification, standardization and validation of the Bender-Gestalt test on normal and neurotic adults, *Psychol. Monogr.*, **67**, 6, 28 (1953).

GOLDMAN-EISLER, FRIEDA, The measurement of time sequences in conversational behaviour, *Brit. J. Psychol.*, **42**, 355–362 (1951).

GOLDMAN-EISLER, FRIEDA, Individual differences between interviewers and their effect on interviewees' conversational behaviour, *J. Ment. Sci.*, **98**, 660–671 (1952).

GOLDMAN-EISLER, FRIEDA, On the variability of the speed of talking and on its relation to the length of utterances in conversations, *Brit. J. Psychol.*, **45**, 94–107 (1954a).

GOLDMAN-EISLER, FRIEDA, A study of individual differences and of interaction in the behaviour of some aspects of language in interviews, *J. Ment. Sci.*, **100**, 177–197 (1954b).

GOLDMAN-EISLER, FRIEDA, Speech-breathing activity. A measure of tension and affect during interviews, *Brit. J. Psychol.*, **46**, 53–63 (1955).

GOLDWORTH, S., A comparative study of the drawings of a man and a woman done by normal, neurotic, schizophrenic, and brain-damaged individuals, *Doctoral Dissertation, Univ. of Pittsburgh*, (1950).

GOLDZIEHER-ROMAN, K., Tension and release. Studies of handwriting with the use of the graphodyne, *Personality, Sympos. No. 2*, 51–61 (1950).

GOODENOUGH, F. L., *Measurement of Intelligence by Drawings* (Yonkers, N. Y., World Book Co., 1926).

GRUEN, A., A critique and re-evaluation of Witkin's perception and perception-personality work, *J. Gen. Psychol.*, **56**, 73–93 (1957).

GRÜNEWALD, G., Studien zur vergleichenden Ausdruckskunde: Handschrift und Sprechweise, *Z. diagn. Psychol. u. Persforschg.*, **2**, 219–233 (1954).

GRÜNEWALD, G., Zur Schreib- und Sprechmotorik der Konstitutionstypen, *Z. Psychother. u. Med. Psychol.*, **7**, 165–176 (1957).

HANVIK, L. J., A note on the limitations of the use of the Bender-Gestalt Test as a diagnostic aid in patients with a functional complaint, *J. Clin. Psychol.*, **7**, 194 (1951).

HARROWER, M. R., The most unpleasant concept test. A graphic projective technique, *J. Clin. Psychol.*, **6**, 211–233 (1950).

HARVEY, O. L., The measurement of handwriting considered as a form of expressive movement, *Character & Pers.*, **2**, 310–321 (1934).

HEISS, R., Die diagnostischen Verfahren in der Psychologie. Das Graphologische Verfahren, *Psychol. Rdsch.*, **1**, 266–275 (1950).

HEISS, R. and HILTMANN, H., *Der Farbpyramidentest nach Max Pfister* (Bern, Huber, 1951).

HEISS, R., HONSBERG, I. and KARL, H., Vorläufige Mitteilung über die Verwendung von "hässlichen Pyramiden" im Farbpyramidentest, *Z. diagn. Psychol. u. Persfschg.*, **3**, 106–124 (1955).

HELLERSBERG, E. F., The Horn-Hellersberg Test and

adjustment to reality, *Amer. J. Orthopsychiat.*, **15**, 690–710 (1945).

HIMMELWEIT, H. T. and EYSENCK, H. J., An experimental analysis of the Mosaic projection test, *Brit. J. Med. Psychol.*, **20**, 283–294 (1944–46).

HOLZBERG, J. D. and WEXLER, M., The validity of human form drawings as a measure of personality deviation, *J. Proj. Tech.*, **14**, 343–361 (1950).

HULSE, W. C., The emotionally disturbed child draws his family, *Quart. J. Child Behav.*, **3**, 152–174 (1951).

HUNTLEY, W., Judgments of self based upon records of expressive behavior, *J. Abnorm. (Soc.) Psychol.*, **35**, 398–427 (1940).

HUSTON, P. E. and SHAKOW, D., Learning in schizophrenia: I. Pursuit learning, *J. Personality.*, **17**, 52–74 (1948).

HUTT, M. L., The use of projective methods of personality measurement in army medical installations. *J. Clin. Psychol.*, **1**, 134–140 (1945).

JOHNSON, B., Changes in muscular tension in co-ordinated hand movements, *J. Exp. Psychol.*, **11**, 329–341 (1928).

JOHNSON, T. F., The function of the Mosaic test in clinical practice, *J. Gen. Psychol.*, **56**, 51–58 (1957).

JOHNSON, W., Studies in language behavior: I. A program of research, *Psychol. Monogr.*, **56**, 1–15 (1944).

JOLLES, I., A study of the validity of some hypotheses for the qualitative interpretation of the H-T-P for children of elementary school age: I. Sexual identification, *J. Clin. Psychol.*, **8**, 113–118 (1952a).

JOLLES, I., A study of the validity of some hypotheses for the qualitative interpretation of the H-T-P for children of elementary school age: II. The "phallic tree" as indicator of psychosexual conflict, *J. Clin. Psychol.*, **8**, 245–255 (1952b).

JONES, F. P. and NARVA, M., Interrupted light photography to record the effect of changes in the poise of the head upon patterns of movement and posture in man, *J. Psychol.*, **40**, 125–131 (1955).

JONES, M. R., Studies in "nervous" movements: I. The effect of mental arithmetic on the frequency and patterning of movements, *J. Gen. Psychol.*, **29**, 47–62 (1943a).

JONES, M. R., Studies in "nervous" movements: II. The effect of inhibition of micturition on the frequency and patterning of movements, *J. Gen. Psychol.*, **29**, 303–312 (1943b).

KARL, H., Die Diagnostik der Antriebsstruktur im Farbpyramidentest, *Z. f. exp. u. angew. Psychol.*, **1**, 524–567 (1953).

KATZ, D., The scriptochronograph, *Quart. J. Exp. Psychol.*, **1**, 53–56 (1948).

KAUFFMAN, P. E. and RAIMY, V. C., Two methods of assessing therapeutic progress, *J. Abnorm. (Soc.) Psychol.*, **44**, 379–385 (1949).

KERR, MADELINE., The validity of the Mosaic Test, *Amer. J. Orthopsychiat.*, **9**, 232–236 (1939).

KEYES, E. J. and LAFFAL, J., The use of a graphomotor projective technique to discriminate between failure and success reactions in a level of aspiration situation, *J. Clin. Psychol.*, **9**, 69–71 (1953).

KIETZ, GERTRAUD., Der Ausdrucksgehalt des menschlichen Ganges, *Beih. Z. angew. Psychol. u. Charakterk.*, **93**, (1948). (Leipzig, J. A. Barth, 1948.)

KINGET, G. M., *The Drawing Completion Test* (New York, Grune & Stratton, 1952).

KLAGES, L., *Handschrift und Charakter. Gemeinverständlicher Abriss der graphologischen Technik* (Bonn, H. Bouvier & Co., 1949a, 257 Seiten).

KLAGES, L., Was die Graphologie nicht kann. Ein Brief, *Grenzgeb. Med.*, **2**, 47–52 (1949b).

KOCH, K., *Der Baum-Test* (Bern, Huber, 1951).

KOROBOW, N., Reactions to stress: a reflection of personality trait organization, *J. Abnorm. (Soc.) Psychol.*, **51**, 464–468 (1955).

KOTKOV, B. and GOODMAN, M., The draw-a-person tests of obese women, *J. Clin. Psychol.*, **9**, 362–364 (1953).

KREEZER, G. and GLANVILLE, A. D., A method for the quantitative analysis of human gait, *J. Genet. Psychol.*, **50**, 109–136 (1937).

KRETSINGER, E. A., An experimental study of gross bodily movement as an index to audience interest, *Speech Monogr.*, **19**, 244–248 (1952).

KRETSCHMER, E., *Körperbau und Charakter* (Berlin, J. Springer, 1951).

KROUT, M. H., Autistic gestures: an experimental study in symbolic movement, *Psychol. Monogr.*, **46**, 208 (1935).

KROUT, M. H., An experimental attempt to produce unconscious manual symbolic movements, *J. Gen. Psychol.*, **51**, 93–120 (1954a).

KROUT, M. H., An experimental attempt to determine the significance of unconscious manual symbolic movements, *J. Gen. Psychol.*, **51**, 121–152 (1954b).

KRÜGER, H. and ZIETZ, K., Das Verifikationsproblem. Experimentelle Untersuchungen über die psychologischen Grundlagen der Bestätigung von Charaktergutachten, *Z. f. exp. u. angew. Psychol.*, **45**, 140–171 (1933).

LAND, A. H., Graphology, a psychological analysis, *Univ. of Buffalo Stud.*, **3**, 81–114 (1924).

LARICCHIA, R. and BERETTA, P., Il "test" del grappolo d'uva di Sanguineti e Sigurta su di un gruppo di cento sogetti schizofrenici, *Neurone*, **2**, 307–316 (1954).

LAZARUS, R. S., DEESE, J. and OSLER, S. F., The effects of psychological stress upon performance, *Psychol. Bull.*, **49**, 293–317 (1952).

LEE, M. A. M., The relation of the knee jerk and standing steadiness to nervous instability, *J. Abnorm. (Soc.) Psychol.*, **26**, 212–228 (1931).

LEGRÜN, A., Schriften Geisteskranker aus ihrer Jugendzeit. *Z. pädag. Psychol.*, **40**, 85–91 (1939).

LEONHARD, K., *Ausdruckssprache der Seele* (Berlin—Tübingen, Haug, 1949).

LEVIN, M. L., Validation of the Löwenfeld Mosaic Test, *J. Consult. Psychol.*, **20**, 239–248 (1956).

LEVY, S., Figure drawing as a projective test in *Projective Psychology*, Eds. L. E. Abt and L. Bellak, 257–297 (New York, Alfred A. Knopf, Inc., 1950).

LEWINSON, T. S., Dynamic disturbances in the handwriting of psychotics, *Amer. J. Psychiat.*, **97**, 102–135 (1940).

LEWINSON, T. S. and ZUBIN, J., *Handwriting Analysis* (New York, King's Crown Press, 1942).

LIBERSON, W., Une nouvelle application du quartz piézoélectrique: piézoélectrographie de la marche et des mouvements volontaires, *Travail hum.*, **4**, 196–202 (1936).

LISS, E., The graphic arts, *Amer. J. Orthopsychiat.*, **8**, 95–99 (1938).

LÖWENFELD, M., The Mosaic Test, *Amer. J. Orthopsychiat.*, **19**, 537–550 (1949).

LÖWENFELD, M., *The Löwenfeld Mosaic Test* (London, Newman Neame, 1954).

LONSTEIN, M., A validation of a Bender-Gestalt scoring system, *J. Cons. Psychol.*, **18**, 377–379 (1954).

LORENZ, MARIA, Language concepts as related to psychiatry, *Quart. Rev. Psychiat.*, **7**, 123–138 (1952).

LORENZ, MARIA, Expressive behavior and language patterns, *Psychiatry*, **18**, 353–366 (1955).

LORENZ, M. and COBB, S., Language behavior in psychoneurotic patients, *Arch. Neurol. Psychiat. Chicago*, **69**, 684–694 (1953).

LOSSEN, H., Die Bedeutung der Verlaufsanalyse für den Wartegg-Zeichentest, *Z. diagn. Psychol.*, **3**, 142–154 (1955).

LOUCKS, R. B., Simplified photoelectronic recorder, timer, and stimulus control device, *J. Exp. Psychol.*, **28**, 443–453 (1941).

LUSSO, A. G. B., Sulla utilita' del test di Lamparter nella pratica clinica, *Arch. Psicol. Neur. Psich.*, **15**, 170–176 (1954).

LUTHE, W., An apparatus for the analytical study of handwriting movements, *Canad. J. Psychol.*, **7**, 133–139 (1953).

LUTHE, W. and SALMAN, D. H., Zur Struktur und Anwendbarkeit des Farbpyramiden-Tests nach Pfister, *Psychol. Rdsch.*, **4**, 207–217 (1953).

LUZA, S. M., La prueba de Wartegg en la esquizofrenia, *Rev. Neuropsiquiat.*, **17**, 162–194 (1954).

LYNN, J. G., An apparatus and method for stimulating, recording, and measuring facial expression, *J. Exp. Psychol.*, **27**, 81–88 (1940).

MACHOVER, KAREN., *Personality Projection in the Drawing of the Human Figure.* (*A method of personality investigation*) (Springfield, Ill., C. C. Thomas, 1949).

MADER, I., Die Anwendbarkeit des Wartegg-Tests bei der Persönlichkeitsbegutachtung im Pubertätsalter, *Psychol. Rdsch.*, **3**, 79–94 (1952).

MAHL, G. F., Disturbances and silences in the patient's speech in psychotherapy, *J. Abnorm. (Soc.) Psychol.*, **53**, 1–15 (1956).

MANDOWSKY, A., Beiträge zur vergleichend-psychologischen Untersuchung über die Handschrift. Physiognomische Untersuchungen über die Ausdrucksbewegung Geisteskranker unter besonderer Berücksichtigung der Schizophrenie, *Arch. f. Psychol.*, **91**, 49–96 (1934).

MANN, M. B., Studies in language behavior: III. The quantitative differentiation of samples of written language. *Psychol. Monogr.*, **56**, 2, 41–74 (1944).

MARUM, O., Character assessments from handwriting, *J. Ment. Sci.*, **91**, 22–42 (1945).

MATTHAEI, R., Nachbewegungen beim Menschen, *Pflüg. Arch. ges. Physiol.*, **202**, 88–111; **204**, 587–600 (1924).

MAYER-BENZ, L., Schriftdeutung jugendlicher Psychopathen, *Z. Kinderforsch.*, **35**, 637–649 (1929).

MEHLMAN, B. and VATOVEC, E., A validation study of the Bender-Gestalt, *J. Cons. Psychol.*, **20**, 71–74 (1956).

MICHAL-SMITH, H., The identification of pathological cerebral function through the H-T-P technique, *J. Clin. Psychol.*, **9**, 293–295 (1953).

MIDDLETON, W. C., The ability of untrained subjects to judge dominance from handwriting samples, *Psychol. Rec.*, **3**, 227–238 (1939).

MIDDLETON, W. C., The ability of untrained subjects to judge neuroticism, self-confidence, and sociability from handwriting samples, *Character & Pers.*, **9**, 227–234 (1941).

MIRA, E., Myokinetic psychodiagnosis: a new technique for exploring the conative trends of personality, *Proc. Roy. Soc. Med.*, **33**, 173–194 (1940).

MIRA Y LOPEZ, *Psicodiagnostico Miokinetico (PMK)* (Buenos Aires, Paidos, 1957).

MITTENECKER, E., Eine neue quantitative Methode in der Sprachanalyse und ihre Anwendung bei Schizophrenen, *Mschr. Psychiat.*, **121**, 364–375 (1951).

MOORE, J. E. and STURM, N. H., Relation of hand strength to personality measures, *Amer. J. Psychol.*, **65**, 111 (1952).

MOSES, P. J., The study of personality from records of the voice, *J. Cons. Psychol.*, **6**, 257–261 (1942).

MOSSE, E. P., Painting-analysis in the treatment of neuroses, *Psychoanal. Rev.*, **27**, 65–82 (1940).

MÜHLE, G. W., Neue Ansätze der Ausdrucksforschung und Ausdruckstheorie. Sammelreferat, 102–124, *Bericht 20. Kongress Deutsche Ges. f. Psychol.* (Göttingen, Hogrefe, 1956).

MÜLLER-SUUR, H., Psychiatrische Erfahrungen mit dem Wartegg-Zeichentest, *Nervenarzt*, **23**, 446–450 (1952).

MUNROE, R., LEWINSON, S. T. and WAEHNER, T. S., A comparison of three projective methods, *Character & Pers.*, **13**, 1–21 (1944).

MURPHY, M. M., A Goodenough scale evaluation of human figure drawings of three non-psychotic groups of adults, *J. Clin. Psychol.*, **12**, 397–399 (1956).

MURRAY, E. J. and ROBERTS, F. J., The Bender-Gestalt test in a patient passing through a brief manic-depressive cycle, *U. S. Forces Med. J.*, **7**, 1,206–1,208 (1956).

MURRAY, E. and TIFFIN, J., An analysis of some basic aspects of effective speech, *Arch. Speech*, **1**, 61–83 (1933).

MURRAY, H. A., *Explorations in Personality* (New York, Oxford Univ. Press, 1938).

NEWMAN, S. and MATHER, V. G., Analysis of spoken language of patients with affective disorders, *Amer. J. Psychiat.*, **94**, 913–942 (1938).

NIGNIEWITZKY, R. D., A statistical study of rigidity as personality variable, *M.A. Thesis, Univ. of London Lib.* (1955).

OCHS, E., Changes in Goodenough drawings associated with changes in social adjustment, *J. Clin. Psychol.*, **6**, 282–284 (1950).

OSERETZKY, N., Über die Mimik bei verschiedenen Konstitutionstypen, *Mschr. Psychiat.*, **83**, 95–127 (1932).

OSTERMEYER, GERDA., Die Beeinflussung der Handschrift durch gesteigerte Schreibgeschwindigkeit, Ärger und Verstellungslüge. (OSTERMEYER, G. and STERZINGER, O., *Graphologische Untersuchungen.* II). *Z. angew. Psychol.*, **52**, 6–23 (1937).

PASCAL, G., Handwriting pressure: its measurement and significance, *Character & Pers.*, **11**, 235–254 (1943a).

PASCAL, G., The analysis of handwriting: a test of significance, *Character & Pers.*, **12**, 123–144 (1943b).

PASCAL, G. R. and SUTTELL, B. J., *The Bender Gestalt Test* (New York, Grune & Stratton, 1951).

PASKIND, H. A. and BROWN, M., Constitutional differences

between deteriorated and non-deteriorated patients with epilepsy. IV. The handwriting, *Arch. Neurol. Psychiat.: Chicago*, **44**, 507–515 (1940).

PEAR, T. H., *Voice and Personality* (London, Chapman & Hall, 1931).

PFEIFFER, W., Der Zeichentest nach Wartegg in der psychiatrischen Diagnostik (unter besonderer Berücksichtigung der Reizverarbeitung), *Arch. Psychiat. u. Z. Neurol.*, **187**, 268–290 (1951).

PFISTER, M., Der Farbpyramidentest, *Psychol. Rdsch.*, **1**, 192–194 (1950).

POHL, U., Experimentelle Untersuchungen zur Typologie graphologischer Beurteilung, *Unters. Psychol. Phil. u. Päd.*, **11**, 3 (1936).

PONZO, E., An experimental variation of the draw-a-person technique, *Rorschach Res. Exch.*, **21**, 278–285 (1957).

POPHAL, R., *Die Handschrift als Gehirnschrift. Die Graphologie im Lichte des Schichtgedankens* (Rudolstadt/ Thür., Greifenverlag, 1949).

POPHAL, R., Über den Antrieb in der Handschrift, *Bericht 20. Kongress Deutsche Ges. f. Psychol.*, 186–187 (Göttingen, Hogrefe, 1956).

POTTER, R. K., KOPP, G. A., and GREEN, H. C., *Visible Speech* (New York, Van Nostrand, 1947).

PRECKER, J. A., Painting and drawing in personality assessment, *Rorschach Res. Exch.*, **14**, 262–286 (1950).

PRINZHORN, H., Das bildnerische Schaffen der Geisteskranken, *Z. ges. Neurol. Psychiat.*, **52**, 307–326 (1919).

RABIN, A. and BLAIR, H., The effects of alcohol on handwriting, *J. Clin. Psychol.*, **9**, 284–287 (1953).

RAPKIN, M. and WHEELER, W. M., A projective-motor test for personality analysis, *Rorschach Res. Exch.*, **13**, 87–91 (1949).

REIMAN, M. G., The Mosaic Test: its applicability and validity, *Amer. J. Orthopsychiat.*, **20**, 600–614 (1950).

REZNIKOFF, M. and TOMBLEN, D., The use of human figure drawings in the diagnosis of organic pathology, *J. Cons. Psychol.*, **20**, 467–470 (1956).

ROHRACHER, H., *Kleine Charakterkunde* (Vienna, Urban & Schwarzenberg, 1948).

ROYAL, R. E., Drawing characteristics of neurotic patients using a drawing-of-a-man-and-woman technique, *J. Clin. Psychol.*, **5**, 392–395 (1949).

RUESCH, J., FINESINGER, J. E. and SCHWAB, R. S., The electromyogram of handwriting, *Psychosom. Med.*, **2**, 411–437 (1940).

RUESCH, J. and FINESINGER, J. E., Muscular tension in psychiatric patients. Pressure measurements on handwriting as an indicator, *Arch. Neurol. Psychiat.: Chicago*, **50**, 439–449 (1943).

SAINSBURY, P., The measurement and description of spontaneous movements before and after leucotomy, *J. Ment. Sci.*, **100**, 732–741 (1954a).

SAINSBURY, P., A method of recording spontaneous movements by time-sampling motion pictures, *J. Ment. Sci.*, **100**, 742–748 (1954b).

SAINSBURY, P., Gestural movement during psychiatric interview, *Psychosom. Med.*, **17**, 458–469 (1955).

SANFORD, F. H., Speech and personality, *Psychol. Bull.*, **39**, 811–845 (1942).

SANGUINETI, I. and SIGURTA, R., Modificazione del test di Lamparter detto "del grappolo d'uva" e primi risultati della sua applicazione in neuro-psichiatria, *Arch. Psicol. Neur. Psich.*, **12**, 35–52 (1951).

SCHADE, W., Handschrift und Erbcharakter, *Z. angew. Psychol.*, **57**, 303–381 (1939).

SCHLEIER, R. P., Motorik und Gesamtpersönlichkeit. (Eine filmische Untersuchung zur Integrationstypologie). *Z. Psychol.*, **147**, 38–64 (1939).

SCHORSCH, G., Die prämorbide Persönlichkeit bei Schizophrenen, *Z. ges. Neurol. Psychiat.*, **167**, 154–157 (1939).

SCHWARTZ, R. P. and VAETH, W., A method for making graphic records of normal and pathological gaits, *J. Amer. Med. Assoc.*, **90**, 86–88 (1928).

SCHWARTZ, A. A. and ROSENBERG, I. H., Observations on the significance of animal drawings, *Amer. J. Orthopsychiat.*, **25**, 729–746 (1955).

SECORD, P. F., Studies of the relationship of handwriting to personality, *J. Personality.*, **17**, 430–448 (1949).

SEIFFERT, H. M., Testmethoden in der Psychiatrie, *Z. bl. Neurol.*, **112**, 1–27 (1951).

SEYFRIED, H., Depressionen im Farbsterntest, *Wiener Arch. Psychol. Psychiat. u. Neurol.*, **5**, 3–19 (1955).

SEYFRIED, H., Unauffällige und schwererziehbare Knaben im Farbpyramidentest (nach Max Pfister), *Z. f. exp. u. angew. Psychol.*, **4**, 245–273 (1957).

SIDDALL, G. J., HOLDING, D. H., and DRAPER, J., Errors of aim and extent in manual point to point movement, *Occup. Psychol.*, **31**, 185–195 (1957).

SIMON, W. and SCHÖNFELD, W., Vergleich der Intelligenzschätzung mit graphologischer und psychotechnischer Methode, *C.R.8. Conf. int. Psychotech.*, 700–701 (Prague, 1935).

SINGER, R. H., A study of drawings produced by a group of college students and a group of hospitalized schizophrenics, *Master's Thesis, Pennsylvania State College* (1950).

SLOAN, W., A critical review of H-T-P validation studies, *J. Clin. Psychol.*, **10**, 143–148 (1954).

SOLLENBERGER, R. T., A photographic study of tremor during postural contraction, *J. Exp. Psychol.*, **21**, 579–610 (1937).

SONDER, SYLVIA L., Perceptual tests and acute and chronic status as predictors of improvement in psychotic patients, *J. Cons. Psychol.*, **19**, 387–392 (1955).

SOUEIFF, M. I., Extreme response sets as a measure of intolerance of ambiguity, *Brit. J. Psychól.*, **49**, 329–334, 1958.

STAR, K., An experimental study of "reactive inhibition" and its relation to certain personality traits, *Ph.D. Thesis, Univ. of London Lib.* (1957).

STARK, R., A comparison of intelligence test scores on the Wechsler Intelligence Scale for children and the Wartegg Drawing Completion Test. *Master's Thesis, Univ. of Detroit Lib.* (1954).

STEINWACHS, F., Bericht über den I. Kongress der Gesellschaft für Konstitutionsforschung in Tübingen vom 27–29 April, 1950, *Psychol. Rundsch.*, **1**, 249–250 (1950).

STEINWACHS, F., Die verfeinerte mechanische Schreibwaage. Apparatives und Methodisches zur exakten Erfassung der Psychomotorik, *Arch. Psychiat. u. Z. Neurol.*, **187**, 521–536 (1951).

STEINWACHS, F., Bericht aus der "Forschungsstelle für

Konstitutions- und Arbeitspsychologie bei der Universität Tübingen," *Psychol. Rndsch.*, **3**, 71–72 (1952).

STEINWACHS, F., Beziehungen der puberalen konstitutionellen Entwicklung zur Psychomotorik und zur Leistungsstruktur, *Bericht* 19. *Kongress, Deutsche Ges. f. Psychol.* 198–201 (Göttingen, Hogrefe, 1953).

STEINWACHS, F., Möglichkeiten der schreibmotorischen Diagnostik bei psychogenen und zerebralen Störungen, *Bericht* 20. *Kongress, Deutsche Ges. f. Psychol.*, 191–193 (Göttingen, Hogrefe, 1956).

STERN, E., *Die Tests in der klinischen Psychologie* (Zürich, Rascher, 1954).

STEWART, L. H., The expression of personality in drawings and paintings, *Genet. Psychol. Monogr.*, **51**, 45–103 (1955).

STONESIFER, F. A., A Goodenough scale evaluation of human figures drawn by schizophrenic and non-psychotic adults, *J. Clin. Psychol.*, **5**, 396–398 (1949).

STRACKE, H., Über die Beeinflussung durch Ausführung einer Nebentätigkeit neben dem Schreibakt, *Arch. ges. Psychol.*, **89**, 109–138 (1933).

SUPER, D. E., A comparison of the diagnoses of a graphologist with the results of psychological tests, *J. Cons. Psychol.*, **5**, 127–133 (1941).

SUTTELL, B. J. and PASCAL, G. R., "Regression" in schizophrenia as determined by performance on the Bender-Gestalt Test, *J. Abnorm. (Soc.) Psychol.*, **47**, 653–657 (1952).

SWENSON, C. H. and PASCAL, G. R., A note on the Bender-Gestalt Test as a prognostic indicator in mental illness, *J. Clin. Psychol.*, **9**, 398 (1953).

TAFT, R., The ability to judge people, *Psychol. Bull.*, **52**, 1–23 (1955).

TAIT, C. D., JR. and ASCHER, R. C., Inside-of-the-Body Test: a preliminary report, *Psychosom. Med.*, **17**, 139–148 (1955).

TAKALA, M., Studies of psychomotor personality tests: I, *Ann. Acad. Sci. Fenn., Sarja-Ser. B.*, **81**, 2. (Helsinki, 1953).

TAKALA, M. and HAKKARAINEN, M., Über Faktorenstruktur und Validität des Wartegg-Zeichentests, *Ann. Acad. Sci. Fenn., Sarja-Ser. B.*, **81**, 1., (Helsinki, 1953).

TAMKIN, A. S., The effectiveness of the Bender-Gestalt in differential diagnosis, *J. Cons. Psychol.*, **21**, 355–357 (1957).

TRAVIS, R. C., A new stabilometer for measuring dynamic equilibrium in the standing position, *J. Exp. Psychol.*, **34**, 418–421 (1944).

TREVES, G. and PAPO, I., Risultati dell' applicazione del test "del grappolo d'uva" (modificato da Sanguineti e Sigurta) su di un gruppo di militari, *Arch. Psicol. Neur. Psich.*, **13**, 217–220 (1952).

VENABLES, P. H., Changes in motor response with increase and decrease in task difficulty in normal industrial and psychiatric patient subjects, *Brit. J. Psychol.*, **46**, 101–110 (1955).

VERNON, P. E., *Personality Tests and Assessments* (London, Methuen, 1953).

VOIGT, H., Gestaltpsychologische Untersuchungen zur menschlichen Motorik, *Arch. ges. Psychol.*, **103**, 231–265 (1939).

WAEHNER, T. S., Interpretation of spontaneous drawings and paintings, *Genet. Psychol. Monogr.*, **33**, 3–70 (1946).

WARTEGG, E., Gestalt und Charakter, *Beih. Z. angew. Psychol. u. Charakterk.*, (Leipzig, 1939).

WELLS, F. L., Personal history, handwriting, and specific behavior, *J. Personality*, **14**, 295–314 (1946).

WELLS, F. L., Adjustment problems at upper extremes of test "intelligence": Cases XIX–XXVIII, *J. Genet. Psychol.*, **74**, 61–84 (1949).

WERTHAM, F., The Mosaic test. Technique and psychopathological deductions, in *Projective Psychology*, Eds. L. E. Abt and L. Bellak, 230–256 (New York, Alfred A. Knopf, Inc., 1950).

WERTHAM, F. and GOLDEN, L., A differential-diagnostic method of interpreting mosaics and colored block designs, *Amer. J. Psychiat.*, **98**, 124–131 (1941).

WESTROPE, M. R., Relations among Rorschach indices, manifest anxiety, and performance under stress, *J. Abnorm. (Soc.) Psychol.*, **48**, 515–524 (1953).

WEWETZER, K. H., Der Visual Motor Gestalt Test als Hilfsmittel in der Klinischen Psychologie. *Bericht* 20. *Kongress, Deutsche Ges. f. Psychol.*, 193–195 (Göttingen, Hogrefe, 1956).

WHITMYRE, J. W., The significance of artistic excellence in the judgment of adjustment inferred from human figure drawings, *J. Cons. Psychol.*, **17**, 421–424 (1953).

WITKIN, H. A., et al., *Personality through Perception* (New York, Harper & Bros., 1954).

WÖRNER, R., Theoretische und experimentelle Beiträge zum Ausdrucksproblem, *Z. angew. Psychol. u. Charakterk.*, **59**, 257–318 (1940).

WOLFF, W., The experimental study of forms of expression, *Character & Pers.*, **2**, 168–176 (1933).

WOLFF, W., Involuntary self-expression in gait and other movements: an experimental study, *Character & Pers.*, **3**, 327–344 (1935).

WOLFF, W., *The Expression of Personality* (New York, Harper & Bros., 1943).

WOLFF, W., *The Personality of the Pre-school Child* (New York, Grune & Stratton, 1946).

WOLTMANN, A. G., The Bender visual-motor gestalt test, in *Projective Psychology*, Eds. L. E. Abt and L. Bellak, 322–356 (New York, Alfred A. Knopf, Inc., 1950).

WOODS, W. L., Language study in schizophrenia, *J. Nerv. Ment. Dis.*, **87**, 290–316 (1938).

WOODS, W. A. and COOK, W. E., Proficiency in drawing and placements of hands in drawings of human figure, *J. Cons. Psychol.*, **18**, 119–121 (1954).

YOUNG, F. M., The incidence of nervous habits observed in college students, *J. Personality*, **15**, 309–320 (1947).

ZIMMER, H., Prediction by means of two projective tests of personality evaluations made by peers, *J. Clin. Psychol.*, **11**, 352–356 (1955).

ZIMMER, H., Validity of sentence completion tests and human figure drawings, in *Progress in Clinical Psychology: II.*, Eds. D. Brower and L. E. Abt, 58–75 (New York, Grune & Stratton, 1956).

ZWIRNER, E., MAACK, A. and BETHGE, W., Vergleichende Untersuchungen über konstitutive Faktoren deutscher Mundarten, *Z. Phonetik*, **9**, 14–30 (1955).

CHAPTER 4

Abnormalities of Sensory Perception

G. W. GRANGER

I. INTRODUCTION

The Psychophysical Approach to Perception

IN preparing this chapter it seemed preferable to discuss a few well-investigated topics in some detail and from a definite point of view rather than attempt to say something briefly and eclectically about all aspects of the subject. The survey is restricted to *visual* perception where most of the research of interest to abnormal psychology has been carried out and, within this area, to processes which are usually classified as *sensory*.[1] The point of view which has influenced the selection of data is psychophysical. This approach to perception is not a novel one. On the contrary, it has been widely adopted in visual research for more than a century by sensory psychologists, physiologists and physicists. The psychophysical tradition was the "forerunner of the first genuinely experimental psychology" (Guilford, 1936) and it would be superfluous to mention it in a book devoted to experimental psychology were it not for the fact that a great deal of perceptual research in abnormal psychology has developed along quite different lines, under the influence of the mental-test movement, psychiatry and psychoanalysis. In consequence, the point of view adopted in this chapter may be unfamiliar to some clinical psychologists and needs to be stated explicitly and justified.

Developing as it did out of experimental physiology and the quantitative methods of the natural sciences, the psychophysical tradition is characterized by a search for quantitative laws (functional relations) between stimulus and response variables. In contrast to the psychometric approach to perception which (influenced no doubt by practical problems of selection and the need for diagnostic devices) has concerned itself with the amount of statistical association be-

tween individual differences in performance on perceptual *tests* under what may be termed "field" conditions, psychophysics has been primarily concerned with the *form* of the relationship between relatively isolated stimulus and response variables under controlled experimental conditions.

Before functional relations can be established between stimulus and response it is obviously necessary first to specify the stimulus. In the case of sensory research on vision this means specifying the quality and quantity of light entering the eye, its distribution in the field of view, duration, and similar characteristics. Next we have to specify relevant conditions of the organism, such as the state of light or dark adaptation, pupil size, retinal area stimulated, etc., and finally the response, verbal or otherwise.

The assumptions of a behaviourist[1] approach to perception have been expressed by Graham in the following general relation: $R = f(a, b, c, \ldots n \ldots t \ldots x, y, z)$, in which R refers to response, the first letters of the alphabet to properly specified aspects of stimuli, the last letters to properly specified conditions of the organism ("physiological and inferred, including the effects of instruction stimuli" (Graham, 1952, 62)), n to number of presentations and t to time. (Graham points out that the various terms are not always independent of one another.) In the classical type of psychophysical experiment we are interested specifically in R as a function of a single attribute of the stimulus, say intensity, all other conditions being held constant as far as possible. Graham's general equation then becomes $R = f(a)$.

To meet the requirements of the experimental programme implied by this formulation a great deal of research effort has been devoted to problems of photometry, colorimetry and applied optics, and to

---

[1] No rigid distinction is made in this chapter between sensation and perception for at the present time there seems to be no satisfactory basis, either behavioural or physiological for making such a distinction (cf. Graham, 1951; Gibson, 1948).

[1] In spite of the beliefs of some of the early psychophysicists that they were dealing with stimulus-*sensation* relations, the data of psychophysical experiments seem necessarily to be behavioural data.

the development of appropriate experimental techniques. Good examples of these techniques are Hecht and Shlaer's (1938) "fixation-and-flash" method for determining the absolute light threshold and dark adaptation, and Wright's (1946) binocular matching technique.

As a result of this emphasis on problems of specification and technique and the formulation of experimental problems in terms of functional relationships there now exists a body of well-established quantitative data and generalizations concerning some of the basic visual processes such as adaptation and intensity discrimination. These psychophysical functions, which define laws of perception, provide a firm experimental basis for investigating the effects of various abnormal conditions. It will be a thesis of this chapter that *such effects can best be assessed by recording their influence on the parameters of the basic psychophysical functions for the visual reception process.*

If we are to start from reproducible quantitative data it is difficult to see how there could be any other basis for discussing abnormalities of perception. Although in many cases suggestive for further research, data from clinical tests are not sufficiently reproducible or analytic to provide a basis for quantifying the effects of abnormal conditions. With few exceptions (as for instance in the case of Hecht and Mandelbaum's (1939) study of the relation between vitamin A deficiency and dark adaptation) where perceptual tests have been developed from previous psychophysical research, these data consist largely of correlation coefficients and analyses of variance between isolated and, from the viewpoint of sensory research, often quite arbitrary, test scores obtained under complex and inadequately controlled conditions.[1] With the reasons for the curious bifurcated development which mental measurement has undergone we cannot be concerned here (*see* Guilford, 1936, for a detailed discussion). Whatever the causes, the

fact remains that perceptual research using psychometric methods has been pursued independently of that in psychophysics and often without regard to the basic variables of visual experiments and the techniques that have been developed to handle them. This applies particularly to much of the research arising from the so-called "new look" movement in perception which has put so much emphasis on the role of personality factors, and to a great deal of perceptual research in clinical psychology directed towards the development of diagnostic tests.

In spite of their limitations, however, data from psychometric studies have been included in this chapter whenever they seemed to fulfil minimum requirements of specification and reproducibility. Data from so-called "projective" tests, like the Rorschach, have, on the other hand, been entirely omitted. The aims, methods and universe of discourse of advocates of these techniques are at present so far removed from those of experimental psychology that it was felt inappropriate to discuss such data in a book of this kind. The fact that experimental studies of after-images, contour and contrast effects, figural after-effects, apparent movement and other well-known perceptual phenomena have also been omitted should not be taken to imply that they have been omitted for the same reasons as have psychometric and projective test data. Such studies are of undoubted importance but, so far, experimental work in these areas has tended to be demonstrational rather than analytic, and adequate measuring techniques are in certain cases only just beginning to be developed (e.g. for measuring brightness changes in after-images (Padgham, 1953; 1957) and very few functional relations have been well established (*see*, for instance, Graham's (1951) excellent review of *Visual Perception*). In a chapter where considerable selection of topics has had to be made it seemed preferable to deal as far as possible with areas of perception in which our knowledge is most certain and where quantification is most highly developed.

The psychophysical point of view which has determined the choice of perceptual functions has also influenced the selection of abnormal conditions. Considerable space has been devoted to physiological stresses such as anoxia and very little indeed to functional psychiatric disorders, such as neuroses There are several reasons for this. First, experiments on physiological stresses have been concerned with functional relationships whereas studies of psychiatric patients have, with few exceptions, dealt only with rather arbitrary scores obtained from perceptual tests. Second, stimulus conditions have been carefully specified and controlled in studies of stresses whereas specification is much less precise in much of the psychiatric research. Third, in contrast to physiological stresses, functional disorders are, from an

[1] In pointing out this limitation there is no implication that the scores from such tests are worthless; only that the tests must be analysed experimentally before their sensory or perceptual significance can be known. Tests of "night-vision," such as the Livingston Rotating Hexagon test (Livingston and Bolton, 1943) have been shown to be of considerable value in practical situations even though it is not known to what extent the scores on these tests are determined by the absolute light threshold, scotopic acuity, pupil size, etc. Critics of some of the psychometric and factor-analytic work on perceptual tests have not always been clear on this point and have evaluated test scores as if they were intended to measure specific psychophysical functions when the intention of the test constructor was something quite different, viz. to assess certain operationally defined capacities (probably involving sensory, motor and other components) in an attempt to differentiate clinical groups, make predictions in personnel selection or measure traits of personality. Some of the psychologists who have adopted a psychometric and factor-analytic approach to perception have been well aware of the limitations of their method and emphasized the need for experimental analysis to reveal functional relationships (e.g. Thurstone, 1944; Eysenck, 1953).

experimental point of view, at present very difficult to specify and reproduce. Finally, reviews of the literature on neuroses and "functional" psychoses are already available elsewhere (Granger, 1953; Zubin *et al.*, 1957). To devote space to data which have no firm experimental basis seemed inappropriate in a handbook of *experimental* abnormal psychology.[1]

In spite of the inadequacy of the psychiatric data some readers may feel that by omitting them the author has left out almost the whole of abnormal psychology for there has been a tendency in some quarters to equate abnormal psychology with the study of psychological abnormalities in functional mental disorders. If, however, our approach to abnormal psychology is, as in this book, based on the psychological functions themselves rather than on psychiatric categories this definition is at once seen to be too narrow, for the so-called functional disorders represent only a fraction of the total number of abnormal conditions which affect perception. In addition to physiological stresses and drugs there are numerous organic conditions such as metabolic and cardiovascular disorders which must also be considered. From the practical viewpoint of experimental work on perception these organic conditions are of greater immediate interest for they can be specified more accurately.

It will be obvious to the reader that, apart from purely practical reasons of the type just considered, the psychophysical approach to perception can show no particular preference for one type of abnormal condition rather than another and makes no rigid distinction between "normal" and "abnormal" conditions. Although from certain points of view it may be useful to distinguish between "normal" and "abnormal"—or, as some sensory physiologists prefer to call them, "special" conditions (cf. Wald, 1954)—this distinction is of no fundamental importance. The chief concern of the psychophysicist is that the basic variables should be identified and specified as conditions of the organism in Graham's equation (page 108) and their quantitative effect assessed in terms of specific perceptual functions. This requirement applies also, of course, to the various personality factors about which so much has been written in recent years (Blake and Ramsey, 1951).

Psychophysics and Physiology

The psychophysical approach to the measurement of visual functions is associated in this chapter with a physiological point of view towards their analysis. This association between psychophysics and physiology is a traditional one which stems from their common origin in the physical sciences. The physiological method is well known but needs to be stated explicitly and justified for the same reason that it was earlier felt necessary to state the psychophysical approach to perception.

From the physiological point of view the visual system is considered to function as a physical mechanism, the eye being regarded as a complicated set of instruments for the detection of light stimuli. Stimulation of the eye by light causes a series of reactions in the subject's nervous system which spread from the photoreceptors to afferent nerve fibres, to the central system and then to effector systems (Pirenne, 1948). It is in this general way that physiology considers the chain of events in an experiment on the visual threshold in which a subject, say, presses a key to signal the detection of the light stimulus.

Although the psychophysicist may not be immediately concerned with the detailed analysis of the events occurring between stimulus and response, the physiological formulation of perceptual problems is essentially similar to the psychophysical. In both cases the subject's response is regarded as a neuromuscular reaction and in both cases an attempt is made to avoid the use of mentalistic concepts of sensation such as "seeing" and "vision." Where these terms are employed, they are used (or should be used) for convenience, as a mere manner of speech. In strict accordance with physiological method they should be replaced by more cumbersome phrases such as the "reaction of photoreceptors and nervous system to certain electro-magnetic radiations," as Pirenne (1948) has pointed out in a valuable discussion of the physiological point of view. This type of formulation may seem to some readers arbitrary or pedantic but it arises from a real desire to define perceptual problems in terms of the actual observables of visual experiments, to adopt a consistent attitude to all aspects of the S-R reaction, and to integrate perceptual research with physical science.

Although visual physiology concedes that the subject's response in a perceptual experiment is the outcome of a complicated series of reactions involving receptor, adjustor and effector mechanisms, it has in practice put a great deal of emphasis on peripheral receptor processes for it has always seemed a primary problem to ask how the quantitative characteristics of vision are limited and determined by the peripheral (and more accessible) reactions which occur when the eye is stimulated by light. In an extreme form the physiological point of view is exemplified particularly well by the work of Hecht and his associates, which provides much of the "normal" data against which

---

[1] Reference to these reviews, both of which have been written from a very different viewpoint from that of this chapter, reveals a mass of interesting observations and speculations concerning perceptual differences between normal and psychiatric groups that undoubtedly merit experimental study, but a paucity of reliable and definitive data.

the effects of abnormal conditions have been considered in this chapter.

Discussing the nature of the visual process in his 1937 Harvey Lecture, Hecht had the following to say—

A process such as vision in man represents a complicated series of events. It is not only the photoreceptor process itself which takes place in the outer end organs; but the nerve impulses which come from them, and which, when joined by other impulses, then pass through the various pathways to be transmitted, amplified, and perhaps altered until the final results at the cortex are achieved. Nor is the photosensory system of other animals much simpler. The receptor process is there, impulses are involved, ganglia have to be passed, and reflexes have to be initiated.

Since all these elements enter into the end result they surely influence its characteristics to some extent. The question is to what extent? And the answer can be secured only by experiment. Our own idea has been that no matter what enters in the chain of events, the ultimate place of origin of the impulses which pass along the optic tracts is in the initial action of light on the receptor cells in the sense organ. Therefore, for a number of years we have measured the different functions of vision and photoreception in man and other animals to ascertain how their quantitative properties depend on the characteristics of these very first reactions which must take place between light and the sensitive elements (Hecht, 1938, p. 37).

Elsewhere Hecht wrote—

The advantage of dealing with this first process is that it is photochemical, and that the properties of photochemical systems have been much studied and clearly formulated (Hecht, 1936, p. 17).

Although Hecht's extreme photochemical point of view has met with a good deal of opposition, most research workers in the physiology of vision have adopted a peripheralist method of study. While admitting that visual behaviour must be dependent in part upon processes occurring at the higher levels of the visual system it has seemed economical and necessary to first account for as many data as possible in terms of retinal events. In practice this approach has been dictated largely by the availability of experimental techniques and the relative ease with which peripheral events can be studied, as compared to more central processes.

In spite of its acceptance by visual physiologists and physicists, this point of view has had relatively few adherents among psychologists working in the field of perception. Instead of starting their analyses of visual processes in the periphery (i.e. with the stimulus and receptor mechanism) many psychologists, particularly of the Gestalt school, have either completely ignored the contribution of the periphery or made only passing and inadequate reference to it. This tendency, already apparent in much of the research on the general psychology of perception (see, for instance, Vernon's book, A Further Study of Visual Perception (Vernon, 1952)) and Tansley's (1953) critical review, made from a physiological viewpoint), has recently become very pronounced in perceptual research in differential psychology, personality study and clinical psychology. In their desire to reveal personality traits and to devise diagnostic tests of "central" disorders psychologists in these areas have devoted very little attention to peripheral events.

The limitations of what some sensory physiologists have (incorrectly) termed a "purely psychological approach," which starts by postulating hypothetical central mechanisms, and the fruitfulness of the peripheral method of analysis are brought out particularly well by some of the recent researches on problems of seeing at low illuminations. Contrary to what has often been supposed, a large part of the observed fluctuation in visual response at or near the absolute threshold of vision is due not to fluctuations in the subject's "attention," "central fatigue," or "inhibition" (see Guilford (1927) for references), but to unavoidable physical fluctuations in the light stimulus itself. At low illuminations no light source, however well controlled, is perfectly steady. The number of light quanta it emits fluctuates statistically from moment to moment about a mean value, as does the number of light quanta absorbed by the visual cells. Although biological variation may also be present it can only be assessed in relation to the physical variation; under certain conditions it is the physical variation which appears to dominate the S-R relationship (Hecht, Shlaer and Pirenne, 1942; Pirenne, 1956).

The discovery of regularities in visual behaviour due to the quantum nature of light (a direct outcome of the consistent application of the peripheralist method (Hecht, Shlaer, and Pirenne, 1942)) has implications not only for research on "simple" functions such as the absolute threshold but also for detail perception. Pirenne, Marriott and O'Doherty (1957) have shown, for instance, that under certain experimental conditions a close relationship must, for purely physical reasons, be expected to exist between the absolute light threshold and perception of detail not only in typical acuity objects such as Landolt Cs but also in complex reproductions of pictures. The relatively high positive correlation which Pirenne et al. were able to demonstrate failed to reveal itself in some of the more "psychologically-oriented" investigations (see, for instance, Craik and Vernon (1942)) due, apparently, to an omission on the part of investigators to give adequate attention to the specification, control and theoretical significance of peripheral variables in the visual process. In view of their results Pirenne *et al.* rightly (but perhaps a little too modestly!) point out that some of the rigid distinctions drawn between *sensory acuity* and *perceptual efficiency*, and conclusions about the allegedly poor predictive value of sensory threshold measurements as indicators of night visual efficiency in various wartime studies, "may not be quite as safely established as is often believed."

In spite of severe criticisms of the psychophysical and physiological approach to perception by some proponents of the personality via perception movement, clinical psychologists, and psychoanalysts (*see* for instance, Bruner and Krech, 1949), there seems to be nothing in recent research which invalidates this point of view. On the contrary, its proven usefulness in analysing normal perceptual processes encourages its application to abnormal conditions.

Rejection of this well-tried method may have been due in part to a misunderstanding of the claims of those who have used it. Contrary to what has often been supposed, even such extreme peripheralists as the photochemical theorists have never denied that visual thresholds can be influenced by the state of the central nervous system. As careful reading of the quotation from Hecht will show, there is plenty of scope in his scheme for all sorts of central influences and interactions to be considered, including individual variations in C.N.S. excitability which are the special object of study of personality psychologists.[1] That these central sources of variation must be measured and analysed under both normal and abnormal conditions before we can claim to have a complete understanding of visual mechanisms would be readily admitted by the photochemist and sensory physiologist.

Far from denying their influence, photochemical theorists such as Hecht and Wald have made some of the most precise measurements and analyses of these central factors under conditions of physiological stresses such as anoxia and insulin hypoglycaemia. These and similar studies by McFarland and his associates provide the framework for most of the discussion of abnormal conditions in this chapter not only because they are based on precise measurements

of well-defined psychophysical functions (*see* page 109) but also because they are considered to be of more fundamental importance to psychophysiology than are studies of specific clinical disorders. Their importance derives from three features of the experiments. First, they deal with basic discriminatory reactions of the organism's receptor mechanisms and may be expected to have implications for a variety of other perceptual functions. Second, the stresses which have been investigated cause disturbances of basic metabolic processes and neural effects similar to those observed in clinical disorders of several different bodily systems. Third, in contrast to much of the research in the clinical literature, the perceptual effects of these stresses have been systematically analysed within a framework of quantitative physiological theory.

Arrangement of Chapter: Content and Treatment

The chapter is arranged in six parts. Following this introduction, Part II deals with *Discrimination* and Part III with *Adaptation*, both basic properties of receptor systems. Part II is further subdivided into two sections, one dealing with the discrimination of intensity (brightness discrimination)[1] and spatial extent (visual acuity), the other with an aspect of temporal discrimination (critical flicker frequency). In discussing discrimination particular attention is given to the way in which it varies as a function of intensity of illumination for not only are the functional relationships well-established for all three aspects of discrimination, but quantitative theory has been particularly well developed in this area of research. Part III is entirely concerned with dark adaptation because most of the work relevant to abnormal psychology has been done on this aspect of adaptation.

Part IV of the chapter deals with a psychophysical and physiological analysis of the effects of the various abnormal conditions, while Parts V and VI deal with the implications of this analysis for other abnormal conditions and other perceptual functions.

Each visual function is discussed according to the following scheme: first, the basic psychophysical data are reviewed; second, theories and facts concerning physiological mechanism are discussed and, third, the effects of physiological stresses, drugs and other abnormal conditions are considered. Even

---

[1] In saying this the author has in mind a limited number of personality studies in which there is some reference, although often indirect, to neurophysiology, such as Eysenck's (1957) experiments on stimulant and depressant drugs. Most of the research on personality and perception is undertaken from a point of view so different from that of sensory physiology that it cannot be related to physiological research on vision. For a valuable discussion of the relation between physiological psychology and personality study, the reader is referred to Eysenck (1957). One of the major tasks of personality study, as Eysenck conceives it, is to analyse individual variation in factors which appear as constants in the physiological psychologist's equations. This point of view may be compared with that stated on page 109, namely, that the effect of abnormal conditions, variations in the state of the C.N.S., etc., can best be assessed by recording their influence on the parameters of psychophysical equations for the receptor process.

[1] Although it seemed preferable in a chapter of this kind to use these terms which are well known in the psychological literature, the thresholds to which they refer should, more properly, be designated as *luminance difference thresholds*, the experimental measurements referring to photometric quantities, It should be noted that some of the photometric terms and units used by investigators cited in this chapter are no longer in common use. For further information the reader is referred to the tables of conversion factors and discussion of photometric concepts given in the *Handbook of Experimental Psychology*, Ed. S. S. Stevens (John Wiley and Sons, Inc., New York, 1951).

though the chapter has been restricted to a few aspects of visual function, the psychophysical and physiological sections cover but a small fragment of the very extensive and specialized literature on vision. In selecting psychophysical material for inclusion the author has emphasized those features of the experimental data that seemed essential for evaluating the effects of the various abnormal conditions without burdening the reader with a detailed review of the literature. Considerations of a similar kind have determined the selection of experimental and theoretical material for the physiological section.

The particular choice and treatment of topics may appear, particularly to readers who are familiar with recent experimental and theoretical developments in visual research arising from the application of quantum and information theories, to give an inadequate and outmoded view of the psychophysiology of vision. In particular, it may appear that undue prominence has been given to the experimental and theoretical contributions of the late Selig Hecht and his associates. Some of the author's reasons for devoting so much space to Hecht's psychophysical work derive quite simply from the fact that Hecht provided what is probably the best critical synthesis of the early and basic psychophysical data on the functions dealt with in this chapter and, with his associates, verified, extended and analysed the data under rigorously-controlled conditions. Although recent measurements present a more complicated picture than appears from Hecht's analyses, these hardly affect those features of the data with which this review is concerned. The justification for dealing with Hecht's photochemical theory in some detail rests in part on the fact that Hecht provided a systematic quantitative treatment of visual data which served as a framework for the design and interpretation of some of the best researches so far undertaken on the effects of abnormal conditions. For this reason alone a fairly detailed discussion of his theory seemed necessary for the proper understanding and evaluation of the experiments.

To avoid giving the impression, which the sight of photochemical equations might convey, that the author is prejudiced in favour of an archaic theory (to which some of its harshest critics have applied the term "classical!"), he hastens to add and emphasize that the now widely-recognized limitations of simple photochemical theories of vision are accepted and discussed. What is advocated in this chapter is not the adoption of a photochemical (or, for that matter, any other) theory of vision but of the quantitative physiological method as exemplified by Hecht's researches, for it is considered that these provide a paradigm for the experimental investigation of abnormalities of sensory perception.

II. DISCRIMINATION

Brightness Discrimination and Visual Acuity

PSYCHOPHYSICAL DATA

(a) Brightness Discrimination

Early research by Steinheil (1837), Weber (1834) and others (*see* Hecht (1924c) for review) showed that the discrimination of intensity differences is relative and depends on the prevailing intensity. According to the early data, if I and $I + \Delta I$ are two intensities that can just be discriminated, the ratio $\Delta I/I$ is roughly constant. On the basis of inadequate measurements Fechner (1860) put forward the generalization that this fraction was constant (the Weber-Fechner law). This was shown to be invalid by Aubert (1865) whose results have been confirmed repeatedly by other workers (Hecht, 1924c, 1935).

The steady decrease in $\Delta I/I$ with increasing I is clearly shown in Fig. 4.1, based on Hecht and Wald's (1934) data for the eye of *Drosophila*. The curve drawn through the experimental points has the form

$$\Delta I/I = c(1 + 1/KI) \tag{1}$$

where c is a constant determining the position of the curve on the ordinate and K the constant determining

its position on the abscissa. Owing to the method of plotting the data on a double logarithmic grid their form and that of the curve are independent of the constants. Typical measurements for the bee by Wolf

FIG. 4.1. INTENSITY DISCRIMINATION OF *Drosophila*
(*Hecht and Wald*, 1934; *after Hecht*, 1935)

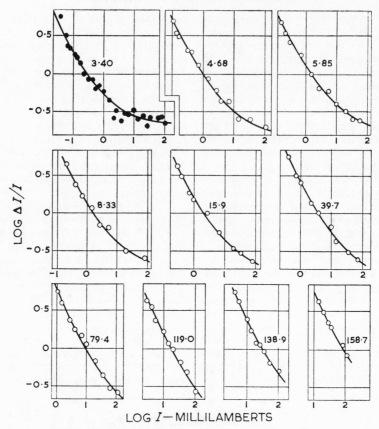

FIG. 4.2. INTENSITY DISCRIMINATION OF THE HONEY BEE

(*Wolf*, 1933a, b)

The filled circles are the data from the first paper; the open circles from the second. The numbers attached to the curves are the visual acuities multiplied by 1,000 and are inversely proportional to the size of the stripes used for the measurements.

(*After Hecht*, 1935)

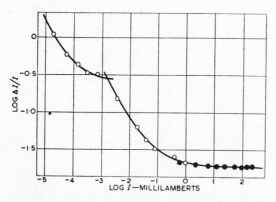

FIG. 4.3. INTENSITY DISCRIMINATION OF THE HUMAN EYE

Blanchard's (1918) measurements are the open circles; those of Lowry (1931) are the filled-in circles and have been raised 0·15 log unit along the ordinates to bring them into continuity with Blanchard's data.

(*After Hecht*, 1935)

(1933) are shown in Fig. 4.2. In this case the curve represents a somewhat different equation, though similar in form to equation (1), viz.

$$\Delta I/I = c[1 + 1/(KI)^{\frac{1}{2}}]^2 \qquad (2)$$

The same equation fits Hecht's (1924a) data for the clam *Mya*.

Whereas the relationship in the above instances is clearly a single continuous function, Aubert's (1865) data on the human eye and the later measurements of Blanchard (1918) and Lowry (1931) (obtained with "white" light) break into two parts, suggesting separate receptor systems. Fig. 4.3 shows the two sets of data plotted on the same graph. The high intensity portion of the data can be fitted by equation (2) while the curve for the low intensity portion is from equation (1), although either equation is satisfactory.

The dichotomy already apparent in the data of Fig. 4.3 obtained with "white" light, suggesting rod and cone function, has been brought out in other ways, by making use of light from different parts of the spectrum and employing different retinal locations. The early data of Koenig and Brodhun (1889) were obtained using red (670 mμ), orange (605 mμ) and yellow (575 mμ) light and show a single continuous function for the red and duplex curves for the orange and yellow. Fig. 4.4 is based on the more recent and reliable measurements of Hecht, Peskin and Patt (1938) for red, orange, yellow, green and blue light.

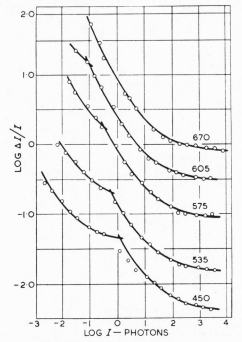

FIG. 4.4. HUMAN INTENSITY DISCRIMINATION FOR THE RED, ORANGE, YELLOW AND BLUE PARTS OF THE SPECTRUM

The labelling on the ordinate applies to the data for yellow (575 mμ). The orange and red curves have been raised 0·5 and 1·0 log unit, respectively, and those for green and blue have been lowered 0·5 and 1·0 log unit, respectively.

(Hecht, Peskin and Patt, 1938)

Fig. 4.5 shows the relation between log $\Delta I/I$ and log I for different retinal areas, as determined by Steinhardt (1936). The upper data were obtained with a field 56' in diameter falling largely within the rod-free area of the fovea and indicate a single function while the lower data, obtained from an area containing both rods and cones, show an inflexion point. Other data of Steinhardt's indicate a duplex curve when the test area is larger than 2° and a single curve similar to the curve for red light in Fig. 4.4 when small foveal fields are used (see Fig. 4.6.) Results essentially similar to those of Steinhardt have been obtained by Crozier and Holway (1939b) and

Holway and Hurvich (1938). The curves drawn through the data of Figs. 4.4, 4.5 and 4.6 are the same as those drawn through the measurements of Figs. 4.2 and 4.3. All the "cone" data are described by

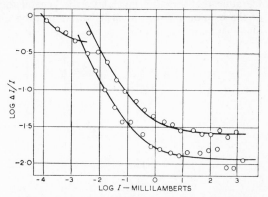

FIG. 4.5. INTENSITY DISCRIMINATION WITH DIFFERENT RETINAL AREAS, AND WITH WHITE LIGHT

(Steinhardt, 1936)

The upper data are with a field 51' in diameter; the lower with a field 3° 44' in diameter.

(After Hecht, 1935)

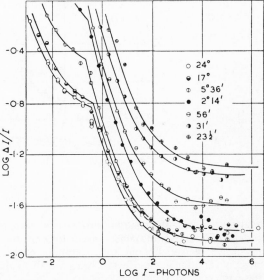

FIG. 4.6. INTENSITY DISCRIMINATION FOR THE HUMAN EYE AS INFLUENCED BY ILLUMINATION AND SIZE OF FIELD

(Steinhardt, 1936)

equation (2) while the more limited "rod" data can be fitted almost equally well by either equation.

The data of intensity discrimination are considerably more extensive than those that have been presented here and in any complete treatment of the topic other variables such as duration (Graham and Kemp, 1938), spatial separation of comparison areas

(Smith, 1936), state of adaptation of the eye (Wright, 1935), etc., would need to be considered. For the present purpose, however, the data are sufficient and there appears to be nothing in the psychophysical literature that seriously invalidates the general form of the relation between intensity discrimination and illumination, which results from Hecht's (1934a, 1937)

(1897) investigation was so thorough that his data have become classical. They show that the relationship between acuity and the logarithm of the intensity is sigmoid (*see* Fig. 4.7). The general form of this relation has since been confirmed repeatedly for the human eye (Löhner, 1912; Rice, 1912; Roelofs and Zeeman, 1919; Ferree and Rand, 1923; Lythgoe,

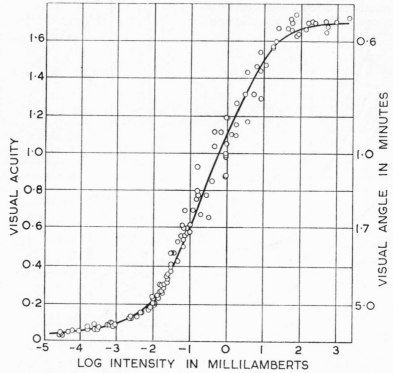

FIG. 4.7. RELATION BETWEEN HUMAN VISUAL ACUITY AND ILLUMINATION IN WHITE LIGHT
(Koenig's (1897) data, replotted by Hecht.)
The original intensities have been multiplied by 0·072 to convert them into mL.
(*After Hecht*, 1928)

analyses. The basic relation through the receptor systems of both rods and cones appears to be relatively unaffected by variation in area, duration, etc., the effect of variation in these factors being merely to alter the extraneous constants of this relation, as in Fig. 4.6.

(*b*) *Visual Acuity*

Visual acuity may be defined as "the reciprocal of the angular distance which must separate two contours in order that they may be recognized as discrete," the unit of separation being a minute of arc (Hecht, 1928). Like brightness discrimination, acuity is dependent among other things upon the intensity of illumination. Uthoff (1886, 1890) was the first to study this relationship over a wide range but Koenig's

1932; Wilcox, 1932, and others) and for the eyes of other animals (e.g. Hecht and Wolf, 1929; Hecht and Wald, 1934; Clark, 1935). Studies on the influence of spatial effects (e.g. Brown, 1946) and stimulus duration (Niven and Brown, 1944) have given results essentially similar to those for intensity discrimination, the basic form of the relation remaining unaffected.

The later studies have demonstrated that several factors not controlled in the earlier work (even in Lythgoe's often-quoted 1932 study) have an important influence on the results. They include pupil size, distance of the test object from the eye and the luminance and extent of the field surrounding the test object. To avoid these uncontrolled variables Shlaer (1937) designed an apparatus for presenting a test object that could be varied continuously in size over a range of about 1 : 100 at a fixed distance of one metre from the eye. This test object appeared in the centre of a 30° field and was observed through a 2-mm diameter artificial pupil. Means were provided for varying the illumination over a wide range (1 : 10¹⁰) in steps of about 0·3 log unit.

Two types of test object were used, a Landolt C and a grating. Data for both test objects show a break at a visual acuity of 0·15. Typical results are shown in Fig. 4.8 for the Landolt C. The curves drawn through the data are the same as those drawn through the similar data for intensity discrimination (Hecht, 1935).

As in the case of intensity discrimination, the dichotomy of acuity data becomes clearly apparent in

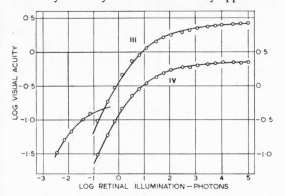

FIG. 4.8. HUMAN VISUAL ACUITY AND ILLUMINATION FOR WHITE LIGHT, USING THE MOST SENSITIVE PORTION OF THE RETINA
(*Shlaer*, 1937)

a double log plot and when colour and retinal location are varied. The effect of spectral variation was already apparent in Koenig's data which break into two parts when blue, green or white light was used but give a single function for red. Fig. 4.9 is based on the more accurate measurements of Shlaer, Smith and Chase (1942).

Pirenne, Marriott and O'Doherty (1957) have recently extended Shlaer's (1937) curves to include lower luminance levels. They measured the luminance levels required to resolve black Landolt Cs presented against a large circular "white" field subtending 47° at the eye. Eight test objects were used ranging between acuities of 1/3 and 1/295. Subjects were first dark adapted for half an hour and after their absolute thresholds had been measured the 47° field was exposed and the thresholds of visibility of the various Landolt Cs were determined binocularly using the natural pupil, one after the other, beginning with the largest C. A given C test object was presented in four positions with the gap facing up, down, right or left, in random succession, and the field luminance adjusted

in steps of 0·1 log unit until the subject judged correctly the position three times out of four trials. In Fig. 4.10 the results of this investigation are combined with those of Shlaer in the higher acuity range, in a double log plot. The horizontal broken line at acuity 1/3 indicates the upper limit of Pirenne, Marriott and O'Doherty's measurements.

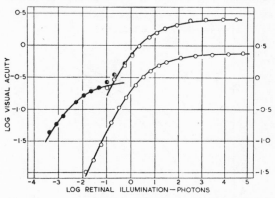

FIG. 4.9. HUMAN VISUAL ACUITY IN RED AND BLUE LIGHT
(*Shlaer, Smith and Chase*, 1942)

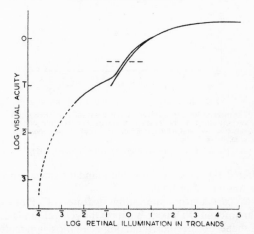

FIG. 4.10. DIAGRAM SHOWING THE GENERAL VARIATION OF VISUAL ACUITY WITH FIELD LUMINANCE, USING A LANDOLT C TEST OBJECT
(*Pirenne, Marriott and O'Doherty*, 1957)

The dotted line represents an extension of Shlaer's curve, based on Pirenne, Marriott and O'Doherty's data. Agreement between the two sets of data is very satisfactory over the range where they overlap (individual experimental points are shown in Fig. 1 of a paper by Pirenne and Denton, 1952). When pupil variation is taken into account agreement is even closer.

Some indication of the nature and extent of individual variation in acuity measurements at low luminance levels can be obtained from Fig. 4.11 which shows the mean log-acuity/log-luminance curve for twenty-two subjects. The curves on either side join the experimental values corresponding to twice the standard deviations. These vary between 0·142 and 0·240 log unit and are of about the same order of magnitude as the standard deviation for the absolute threshold; only one out of seven standard deviations

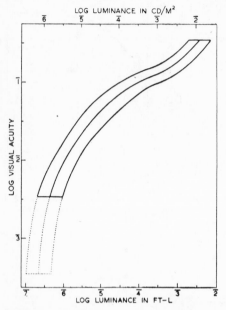

FIG. 4.11. ACUITY v. FIELD LUMINANCE

The main curves join the mean experimental values of twenty-two subjects for the C thresholds; the curves on either side join the values between which fall the results for the bulk of the population as explained in the text.

(*Modified from Pirenne, Marriott and O'Doherty, 1957*)

differed significantly from the standard deviation of the absolute threshold.

A particularly interesting feature of Pirenne, Marriott and O'Doherty's data is the general similarity in shape of the individual log-acuity/log-luminance curves at the lower acuity levels. The chief difference between individuals is in the position of their curves along the intensity axis, as illustrated by the three curves of Fig. 4.12. Correlations between luminance thresholds for the Landolt Cs and the absolute threshold ranged from 0·705 to 0·927 ($p < 0.001$).

PHYSIOLOGICAL DATA AND THEORIES

(a) Hecht's Photochemical Theory

(i) *The stationary state.* Hecht's (1937)[1] theoretical treatment of the data of brightness discrimination and

[1] Although Hecht's name is usually associated with photochemical theory, Pütter (1918) and Lasareff (1928) also contributed a number of ideas.

visual acuity is based on three simple chemical ideas concerning the photoreceptor process. First, there has to be a sensitive substance which absorbs the incident light and is changed by it into one or more active products. Second, a supply of this photosensitive material must be maintained if the process is to continue. These two processes Hecht terms the *primary light* and *primary dark* reactions, respectively. Third, the active products of the primary light reaction must do something the end result of which is the initiation of an impulse from the receptor cell. This is termed the *secondary dark reaction.*

Hecht then goes on to consider the properties of the *simplest* photochemical system which would correspond to the primary light and dark reactions. "Consider a photosensitive substance S whose total initial concentration is a. Let light of intensity I shine on it, and as a result let there be produced the photoproducts P, A, etc., whose concentrations at the moment t is given by x. The rate at which this primary light reaction $S \rightarrow P + A$ goes will be proportional to the intensity and to the concentration

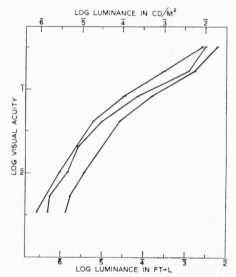

FIG. 4.12. VARIATION OF ACUITY WITH LUMINANCE

Individual C threshold values for three subjects.

(*Modified from Pirenne, Marriott and O'Doherty, 1957*)

$(a - x)$ of sensitive material" (Hecht, 1938). This rate may be written—

$$dx/dt = k_1 I(a - x)^m \qquad (3)$$

where k_1 is the combined absorption and velocity constant and m is an integral exponent which chemists term the order of the reaction, and may be 1, 2, etc.

Further suppose that the sensitive material S can

be regenerated (by the combination of some of the photoproducts, P, A, etc., with additional materials like vitamin A supplied by the retina). The velocity of this primary dark reaction $S \leftarrow P + A$ will be proportional to the concentrations x of the photoproducts and becomes—

$$- dx/dt = k_2 x^n \qquad (4)$$

where k_2 is a velocity constant and n the order of the reaction.

When this system is steadily exposed to light (corresponding to light adaptation to a given intensity), the velocities of the two reactions become equal and a *photostationary state* is reached. Setting equation (3) equal to (4) and solving for I, we get—

$$KI = x^n/(a - x)^m \qquad (5)$$

where $K = k_1/k_2$, which represents the relations between intensity and concentrations of photosensitive substance and photoproducts at the stationary state of the simple three-component system—

$$S \underset{\text{Dark}}{\overset{\text{Light}}{\rightleftharpoons}} P + A$$

In presenting this formulation Hecht emphasized that it is "too simple to correspond to what the photoreceptor process probably is" but at the same time brightness discrimination, visual acuity and various other visual functions all behave "as if they were controlled by just such a simple system as represented by the stationary state" (Hecht, 1938, p. 58).

(ii) *Brightness discrimination.* Having derived the stationary state equation Hecht considered the problem of brightness discrimination in the following way. The photochemical change produced by the intensity increment ΔI which can just be recognized when the eye is adapted to I is—

$$dx/dt = k_1 \Delta I(a - x)^m \qquad (6)$$

Assume that the *j.n.d.* in intensity is perceived when the number of impulses leaving the photoreceptor system is increased by a constant amount c'. This makes equation (6) equal to c' and gives $\Delta I = c'/k_1(a - x)^m$. Dividing this value of ΔI by the value of I obtained by solving equation (5) we get—

$$\Delta I/I = c'/k_2 x^n \qquad (7)$$

i.e. "intensity discrimination varies as some power of the concentration of photoproducts present at the stationary state."

x can be eliminated and comparison made between this general derivation and experimental data of $\Delta I/I$ against I only in terms of equation (5) when m and n are given specific values. When both the primary and light and dark reactions are monomolecular and m and $n = 1$, equation (7) becomes—

$$\Delta I/I = c(1 + 1/KI) \qquad (8)$$

where $K = k_1/k_2$ and $c = c'/ak_2$. When m and $n = 2$, i.e. when both reactions are bimolecular, equation (7) becomes—

$$\Delta I/I = c[1 + (1/KI)^{\frac{1}{2}}]^2 \qquad (9)$$

where $c = c'/a^2k_2$. When plotted on a double logarithmic grid, as in Fig. 4.13, the shapes of the curves

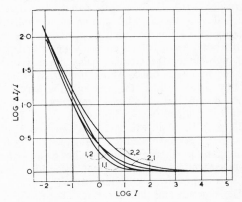

FIG. 4.13. THE RELATION BETWEEN $\Delta I/I$ AND I IN TERMS OF THE THEORETICAL DERIVATIONS OF HECHT

Drawn on a logarithmic grid, the curves have a form which is independent of any constants in the equations, but which is determined by the values of m and n representing the order of the primary photochemical and dark reactions in the photosensory system. The numbers attached to the curves show the value of m and n in order.

(*After Hecht*, 1937)

of these two equations are constant and independent of any constants in the equations. Only the values of m and n determine the shapes and slopes.

The curves drawn through the "cone" data of the human eye (Figs. 4.3, 4.4, 4.5 and 4.6, as well as the similar data of Hecht, Peskin and Patt (1938), Graham and Kemp (1938), Smith (1936), Hendley (1948), Mueller (1951)[1] and others), and those of the bee (Fig. 4.2) are from equation (9) while the curve drawn through the *Drosophila* data is that of equation (8). For the "rod" data of the human eye it is more difficult to decide which particular equation applies because the data are less extensive.

(iii) *Visual acuity.* Hecht's theoretical treatment of acuity developed in two stages, the first purely statistical and the second photochemical. According to the early formulation (Hecht, 1926, 1928) the increase in visual acuity with increasing illumination is due to the fact that individual receptors vary in sensitivity in a "statistical manner similar to that of other populations" so that more will be active at

[1] Mueller points out that a curve derived from Crozier's (1940) theory also fits his data equally well.

higher than at lower illuminations. Thus, a given region of the retinal mosaic will become functionally (not, of course, anatomically) finer at higher intensities, maximum acuity being attained when all receptors are active.

In later publications (Hecht, 1937) Hecht attempted to show that the assumption of a statistical distribution of light detectors in the retina is a necessary consequence of the photochemical system which he used to describe brightness discrimination. Following the earlier suggestions of Helmholtz (1896) and Hartridge (1918), Hecht suggested that "Two lines are resolved as a doublet when the space between them appears of a different brightness than in the lines themselves. An object is seen as a C or an O depending on whether the circular image formed on the retina contains a break whose brightness is recognizably greater than the rest of the circle. In other words, visual acuity may be intimately related to intensity discrimination. . . ." (Hecht, 1937, p. 277). With Mintz (Hecht and Mintz, 1939) Hecht later demonstrated that visual acuity is a form of brightness discrimination in the region of the diffracted retinal image and that the critical visual acuity α is directly proportional to $\Delta I/I$.

The experimental data show that both brightness discrimination and visual acuity vary with the intensity of illumination so that if they are related in some way they might be expected to show the same relation to intensity. Visual acuity should in fact vary inversely as the fraction $\Delta I/I$ does with intensity. In terms of equation (7), visual acuity should vary as some power of the concentration of photoproducts at the steady state. Putting V (visual acuity) equal to $bI/\Delta I$ and substituting in equation (7), Hecht obtains—

$$V = cx^n \qquad (10)$$

where $c = bk_2/c'$ as a lumped constant. Solving for specific values of m and n, the orders of the primary light and dark reactions, is the same as for brightness discrimination. On a double log plot the final curves are identical with those derived for brightness discrimination but are reversed in the sign of the ordinates.

(b) Alternative Theories, and Electrophysiological Data

Modifications of Hecht's theory, based on more recent information of events in the photochemical cycle have been proposed by Byram (1944, a, b) and Jahn (1946b). The theoretical curves which they derive certainly provide a better fit to some of the psychophysical data than do those of Hecht. Other modifications of Hecht's stationary state equation have been made by Bartlett (1942) and Bartlett and Hudson (1942) while alternative theories of a "neural"

nature have been proposed by Crozier and his associates (e.g. Crozier and Holway, 1939b). The essence of Crozier's theory, which has never been formulated explicitly, is that the sigmoid curves relating brightness discrimination and visual acuity to intensity are probability integrals in log I, reflecting the statistical distribution of receptor thresholds. At the lower intensities only the most sensitive elements (rods, cones, *and their associated neurones*) respond whereas at high intensities all elements respond. The assumed distribution of thresholds covers between four and eight log units and the thresholds themselves vary from one element to another and from moment to moment. Crozier's theory is a general "neurostatistical" theory of intensity discrimination which is supposed to apply to all the senses; the various senses ". . . are all controlled alike by a statistical mechanism which is an expression of the central nervous system" (Bartley, 1941, p. 44). A further example of a theory which assumes visual phenomena to be the expression of properties of hypothetical *central* nervous mechanisms is that of Householder (Householder, 1939; Householder and Landahl, 1945) who derives equations from assumptions about the dynamics of synaptic transmission that give a fairly satisfactory fit to some of the data of brightness discrimination.

An approach of an entirely different kind from those already considered is that of the quantum theorists. Following the successful application of quantum concepts to the absolute threshold (Hecht, Shlaer and Pirenne, 1942; Bouman and van der Velden, 1947; Baumgardt, 1950; Pirenne, 1956; *see* page 111), de Vries (1943), Rose (1948), Hendley (1948) and others have considered the increment threshold from the viewpoint of quantum theory. Although in the case of low field intensities it is clear that unavoidable fluctuations in the number of light quanta reaching the eye from the test area will lead to "frequency-of-seeing" curves similar to those obtained in absolute threshold experiments, it is more difficult to determine precise implications for the case where the field intensity is high or where it varies through a wide range of values. So far none of the proposed formulations has given a satisfactory account of the experimental data reviewed in the previous section. The simple formulations of Rose (1948) and de Vries (1943) can be dismissed, because they require a linear relation between log $\Delta I/I$ and log I, whereas in fact this is not observed.[1]

---

[1] Both de Vries and Rose suggested that the eye can be compared with an ideal detector, their physical model being a photocell without any dark current. Since there is some electrophysiological evidence which suggests that the human eye does not behave like an ideal detector with no intrinsic noise, Barlow (1957) has proposed an alternative model of a photocell with dark current which provides a better fit to some of the experimental data on the increment threshold.

Mueller (1951) has posed the question as to whether quantum concepts alone can be used to "predict" or "explain" the data of intensity discrimination, or whether additional neural and photochemical mechanisms will need to be invoked. While it is too early to decide how far quantum ideas will take us, it seems highly probable that part of the change both in intensity discrimination and visual acuity[1] with variation in light intensity is due to changes in neural interaction in the retina. Results of recent electrophysiological experiments by Barlow et al. (1957) suggest that part of the improvement in discrimination which occurs as the intensity of illumination increases may be due to the development of *lateral inhibition*. The authors suggest that this "may be one of the mechanisms which enables full use to be made of the information contained in the light absorbed in the retina" for "it seems admirably suited to preserve information about small differences in intensity between the neighbouring regions of the visual field," the function which Rose (1948) "claimed that the visual mechanism could perform almost to the limit set by the quantal fluctuations in the light absorbed." That inhibition has an important role in sensory discrimination has been suggested also by Granit (1947, 1951, 1955) on an analogy with its function in motor activity (cf. Sherrington, 1947). Its existence has been demonstrated in the retina and optic nerve (Granit and Therman, 1934, 1935; Hartline, 1935, 1938; Granit, 1947, 1952, 1955) and its possible function in simultaneous, successive and metacontrast, visual acuity and other aspects of discrimination has been considered by Hartline and his associates (Hartline, H. K., Wagner, H. G. and McNichol, E. F., 1952; Hartline, H. K., Wagner, H. G. and Ratcliff, F., 1956; Hartline, H. K. and Ratcliff, F., 1957), Graham and Granit (1931), Wright and Granit (1938), Granit (1947, 1955), Barlow (1953), Davson (1950), Alpern (1953), Asher (1950), Osgood (1953), Barlow et al. (1957), and others. A review of this literature is available elsewhere (Granger, to appear).

Until more data on "frequency-of-seeing" curves have been obtained to test the adequacy of quantum formulations, and until the electrophysiological results on retinal interaction can be related quantitatively to psychophysical data of human vision, the precise implications for visual theory of these recent

physical and physiological developments will be difficult to determine. As far as photochemical theories are concerned it now seems clear that any theory which postulates a progressive exhaustion of photosensitive substance in the end organs as the field intensity is increased, requires drastic modification simply because the rate of absorption of light quanta at the intensity levels in question is too slow a process (Baumgardt, 1950). Although the fraction of visual pigment which is bleached by light must be higher at higher intensities, and it may be that at any constant intensity a "stationary state" would be reached due to regeneration, it is clear that the amount of bleaching is very much smaller than Hecht supposed (cf. Rushton, 1958).

To say this is not to say that photochemical ideas should be entirely rejected; only that there are physical and physiological objections to a simple model of the type proposed by Hecht and to any *purely* photochemical theory. Although the formulation of a really adequate physiological theory remains a task for the future, it now seems certain that it will have to take account of factors both more peripheral (stimulus fluctuations) and more central (neural interaction in the retina) than did the photochemists.

In spite of the objections which can be raised against Hecht's simple scheme on physical, physiological and chemical (*see* Jahn, 1946b) grounds, from a purely psychophysical point of view this model may still have something to commend it in terms of its simplicity, and the precision with which the "stationary state" equation describes a large number of experimental data. As Hecht himself pointed out, even though complicating factors are undoubtedly present (and Graham has already considered some of these in his extension of Hecht's hypothesis to include effects of spatial and temporal interaction (e.g. Graham and Bartlett, 1940)), the equations which describe them must reduce to something like the stationary state equation in view of the precision with which it describes the data (Hecht, 1937, p. 281).

ABNORMAL CONDITIONS

Research on the effects of abnormal conditions on brightness discrimination is almost entirely confined to the study of two physiological stresses, anoxia and insulin hypoglycaemia, but these warrant detailed discussion in view of their methodological and theoretical importance.

Following the relatively uncontrolled observations of Schubert (1932) and Gellhorn (1936) that brightness discrimination was reduced by anoxia, McFarland, Halperin and Niven (1944) undertook a systematic study using Crozier's Visual Discriminometer (Crozier and Holway, 1939a). Differential thresholds were obtained for a square 1° test-field, presented against

[1] An interesting application of quantum concepts to visual acuity data is that of Pirenne (1946, 1948) and Pirenne and Denton (1952), who have shown that Hecht's hypothesis of variation in receptor sensitivity in a given retinal area is unnecessary. Because of quantum fluctuations occurring in the absorption of light by the retina these authors argue that the retinal mosaic must become functionally finer. Their theory casts doubt upon previous formulations of Lythgoe (1940) and von Buddenbrook (1940) who postulated changes in neural interaction, although it now seems (Pirenne, 1957) that in certain types of experiment interaction must be taken into account.

a large uniformly-illuminated background subtending 40°. The test-field was exposed for 0·1 sec just below a fixation point so as to appear in the centre of the larger field. Observations were made using the right eye. No artificial pupil was used as the diameter of the beam when it entered the eye was less than the minimum diameter of the eye pupil. The retinal illumination produced by the 40° field was 229 milliphotons.

the intensity (*I*) axis. The effect of anoxia is, apparently, greatest at the lower field intensities and becomes progressively less with increasing illumination. Data for each subject were plotted in a manner similar to that of Fig. 4.14 and the amount of displacement of each curve during anoxia determined graphically; the mean shift amounted to 0·356 log unit ($p < 0·01$). Of great interest was the fact that foveal dark adaptation curves obtained in the same

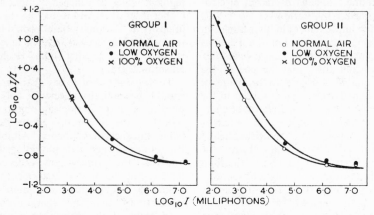

FIG. 4.14. THE EFFECT OF OXYGEN DEPRIVATION ON FOVEAL INTENSITY DISCRIMINATION
The curves are theoretical, derived from Hecht's equation, as explained in the text.
(*McFarland, Halperin and Niven,* 1944)

Intensity discrimination thresholds were made at increasing intensities of the larger field. Measurements were taken at a given intensity after the eye had been adapted for three to five minutes to the 40° field. Before obtaining differential thresholds subjects had previously been dark-adapted for fifteen minutes, the object of this preliminary dark adaptation being to enable comparisons to be made of the effect of anoxia on two different functions. The intensity of the test square was increased in steps of about 0·03 log unit until its outline could just be detected; at each field intensity, ten measurements were taken.

Data were obtained for nine trained subjects ranging in age between 18 and 26 years and are shown in Fig. 4.14 for one group of four subjects on the left and for the remaining five subjects on the right. The data were presented separately owing to differences in the light intensities employed. The "low oxygen" curves were obtained during a constant degree of oxygen deprivation (10·8 per cent oxygen) in a low oxygen chamber. The 100 per cent oxygen curves were obtained to demonstrate the reversibility of the effects of anoxia at the end of each experiment. The interesting feature of these data is that oxygen deprivation does not affect the *form* of the relationship between log $\Delta I/I$ and log *I*, but only its position on

experiment (*see* later discussion) were displaced upward along the log intensity axis by about the same amount, 0·354 log unit ($p < 0·01$). Control experiments were undertaken to see if pretended exposure to low oxygen tensions or subsequent administration of oxygen had any effect, but no changes were observed.

The curves drawn through the data of Fig. 4.14 are theoretical and are derived from Hecht's stationary state equation. McFarland, Halperin and Niven's (1944) interpretation of their data was suggested by Hecht and is essentially similar to that given in a paper by Hecht *et al.* (1946), to be discussed in Part IV.

In view of previous results which showed that glucose partially counteracted the effects of anoxia on dark adaptation (McFarland and Forbes, 1941; *see* section on dark adaptation), McFarland, Halperin and Niven (1945) decided to make a similar experiment with brightness discrimination. Under conditions similar to those of their previous experiment on anoxia they found that the ingestion of 50 g of glucose resulted in a considerable decrease in the impairment due to anoxia. At a simulated altitude of 13,800 ft glucose diminished the impairment to an amount corresponding to an altitude of only 8,000 ft in one subject, from 14,700 ft to about 11,000 ft in a second subject, and from 17,200 ft to about 9,000 ft in a third.

A further experiment by McFarland, Halperin and Niven (1946) in which they studied the effects of insulin on foveal brightness discrimination, was also based on the earlier dark adaptation studies, the apparatus being the same as that used previously. In four trained subjects, aged between 15 and 18, they found a rise in threshold if the blood sugar dropped below about 65 to 70 mg per cent (Folin Malmros method) following intravenous injections of insulin in amounts varying from 4 to 14 units. The curve relating visual thresholds to time paralleled the drop in blood sugar. Following inhalation of pure oxygen a reversal of a large part of the impairment occurred.

Plotting log $\Delta I/I$ against log I the authors found that hypoglycaemia caused a translation of the curve along the intensity axis toward higher intensities in all three subjects. The curves for one subject are shown in Fig. 4.15. As in the case of anoxia, the effect of hypoglycaemia is greatest at low intensities and declines at the higher intensities. For all three subjects the changes observed at the low and intermediate intensities were significant statistically ($p < 0.01$); at

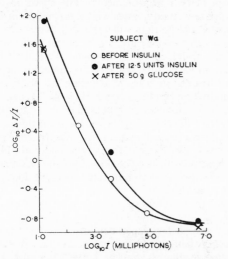

FIG. 4.15. THE EFFECT OF INSULIN HYPOGLYCAEMIA ON THE RELATION BETWEEN INTENSITY DISCRIMINATION AND ILLUMINATION

The curves are derived from Hecht's equation, as explained in the text.
(McFarland, Halperin and Niven, 1946)

the highest intensity the change was not significant in two cases and only just attained significance ($p < 0.01$) in the third.

Hecht, Hendley, Frank and Haig (1946) studied brightness discrimination with individuals breathing oxygen concentrations corresponding to seven different altitudes between sea level and 17,000 ft. Three luminance levels were used, 0·1, 0·01 and 0·001 mL, involving photopic vision only. The visual field

consisted of a large circular area subtending 27° visual angle, to which the subjects' eyes were light-adapted. In the centre of this field the illuminated image of a Landolt C could be projected for 0·2 sec. The position of the break in the circle was set by the operator and the subject's task was to discover this position by steadily increasing the luminance of the broken ring. In order to confine the study to brightness discrimination alone a large test object was used (7·5°) with a

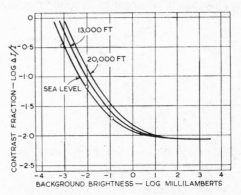

FIG. 4.16. THE RELATION BETWEEN THE CONTRAST FRACTION $\Delta I/I$ AND THE PREVAILING I

The curves are theoretical, from Hecht's equation. The effect of altitude (or oxygen lack) is merely to translate the curve along the abscissae.

(After Hecht, Hendley, Frank and Haig, 1946)

break of 1·5°, i.e. well above the visual acuity threshold at all intensities used. Red light was used "to insure the participation of daylight vision alone even at the lowest intensity." Fig. 4.16 shows the relation between the contrast fraction $\Delta I/I$ and the prevailing I, based on the average data of eight subjects. For all three background luminances, decreasing the oxygen concentration caused an increase in the amount of contrast which could be detected. The authors considered three aspects of this visual impairment. First, deterioration in brightness discrimination was obvious at a simulated altitude of 8,000 ft and became marked at 15,000 ft where at a low luminance level the contrast had to be twice as great as at sea level before it could be recognized. Second, a given increase in altitude caused a greater impairment at higher than at lower altitudes. In going from 12,000 ft to 15,000 ft the increase in brightness difference required for recognition of contrast was twice as great as that in going from 6,000 ft to 9,000 ft. Third, although impairment occurred at all luminance levels, the effect decreased as the luminance increased. The authors made extrapolations from their data to show what would be expected at higher intensities at 1 and 10 mL and it is interesting to note that these predictions have been realized in McFarland, Halperin and Niven's

(1944) study. As in that study, the quantitative form of the relation between brightness discrimination $\Delta I/I$ and I remained the same at all oxygen concentrations. The effect of anoxia was merely to shift the curve along the log I axis.

Following the earlier, inconclusive studies of Wilmer and Berens (1918), Bagby (1921), Berger and Boje (1937) and Furuya (1937) on the effects of anoxia on visual acuity, McFarland and Halperin (1940) carried out a systematic investigation in which they studied

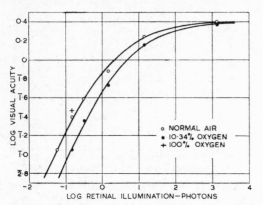

FIG. 4.17. THE EFFECT OF ANOXIA ON THE RELATION BETWEEN FOVEAL VISUAL ACUITY AND ILLUMINATION
(*McFarland and Halperin, 1940*)

the relation between foveal visual acuity and illumination over a wide range of intensities, using the apparatus devised by Shlaer (1937). The test object was a black Landolt C in which the width of the line and the gap was one-fifth of the total outside diameter of the letter. It appeared in the centre of a uniformly illuminated field 30° in diameter, which was illuminated by red light (670 mμ) so as to restrict measurements to the cones. The size of the test object was continuously variable over a range of 1:100 at a fixed distance of one metre from the subject's eye, which was placed immediately behind a 2-mm diameter artificial pupil. The letter could be rotated so as to be presented in eight different meridians, 45° apart.

Starting with a gap that was too small for the subject to perceive, this was gradually increased (in steps of about 0·010 to 0·020 log unit of visual acuity) until the subject could report the meridian in which the gap was located. Data were obtained in two experiments from eleven practised subjects, two in the first experiment and nine in the second. In the first experiment measurements were taken over almost the entire range of intensities mediated by cones in normal air and when the subjects were exposed to a low oxygen mixture (10·3 per cent oxygen). After ten minutes' dark adaptation measurements were started

at low intensities in normal air. Before making observations at a given intensity the eye was light-adapted to the field for three minutes and four readings were then obtained. After making observations for five minutes the subject rested and was then given three minutes' light adaptation to the field before observing again. When the intensity range had been covered the subject rested for twenty minutes and the procedure was repeated with the low oxygen mixture. Final observations were taken to determine the effect of breathing pure oxygen.

In the second experiment data were obtained for nine subjects at two intensities, one near the low end of the range (0·144 photon) and the other near the intensity value giving maximum acuity, at 1,320 photons retinal illumination. The procedure was similar to that of the first experiment but two different oxygen concentrations were used, 14·3 per cent, corresponding to 10,000 ft and 10·3 per cent, corresponding to 18,000 ft.

Data for one of the subjects in the first experiment are shown in Fig. 4.17; each datum represents the mean of four measurements. The curve on the left shows how acuity varies with illumination in normal air, that on the right when the subject was exposed to low oxygen. Evidently anoxia causes a displacement of the entire curve to the right along the intensity axis. In view of the shape of the curve this horizontal shift results in a large decrease of acuity at low illuminations and a progressively smaller decrease as intensity is increased. McFarland and Halperin point out that this may account for the inconclusiveness of the earlier experiments which were carried out at intensity levels where changes in acuity are likely to be relatively slight. The shift along the axis amounted to 0·38 for the data illustrated and 0·66 log unit for the other subject.

The mean values for the nine subjects of the second experiment are shown in Fig. 4.18. It is unfortunate that there are so few experimental points but these were carefully determined and may be considered "sufficient to locate the theoretical curve" (i.e. for Hecht's stationary state equation). This was drawn through the "normal air" data, then translated to the right to correspond with the point representing the measurements at the low intensity, at each of the conditions of decreased oxygen tension. This curve drawn through the lower point at 10·3 per cent oxygen concentration coincides with the upper point as well. The magnitude of the horizontal displacement was 0·24 log unit for 14·3 per cent oxygen and 0·46 log unit for 10·3 per cent oxygen. Mean differences due to anoxia were statistically significant ($p < 0.01$). In view of the lack of any appreciable vertical component in the displacement of the curve, the authors conclude that: "The maximum visual acuity is not affected by anoxia, although a higher illumination may be required to elicit it."

Using the same apparatus and procedure as that previously described (McFarland, Halperin and Niven, 1944), McFarland, Roughton, Halperin and Niven (1944) studied the combined effects of anoxia and carbon monoxide on intensity discrimination at sea level and at various simulated altitudes. Their results are of particular interest for earlier attempts to determine the least amount of carbon monoxide capable of producing impairment in behaviour had yielded no definite results with various psychological tests. They found that 5 per cent saturation of the blood with carbon monoxide depressed intensity discrimination to as great an extent as anoxia at 8,000 to 10,000 ft altitude and 15 per cent carbon monoxide saturation caused impairment equivalent to that at between 15,000 and 19,000 ft.

The sensitivity of intensity discrimination to carbon monoxide was so marked that even the effects of the small amounts of carbon monoxide absorbed from cigarette smoke could be demonstrated. After inhaling the smoke of three cigarettes the effect on sensitivity was equivalent to that of a simulated altitude of 7,500 ft (15·7 per cent oxygen). Absorption of a similar amount of carbon monoxide (4 per cent saturation) at a simulated altitude of 7,500 ft caused a combined loss of sensitivity equal to that at

efficiency." Using the procedure previously described (page 117), acuity and "flash" thresholds were obtained from a subject who had taken part in an experiment on dehydration. Comparing his luminance thresholds after "dehydration" with normal values obtained a month later an average increase of 0·25 log unit was found. The most interesting feature

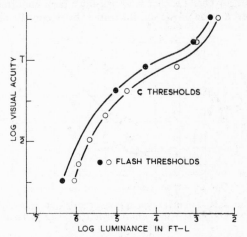

FIG. 4.19. THE EFFECT OF DEHYDRATION ON C AND "FLASH" THRESHOLDS

Open circles denote measurements made after experimental dehydration; filled-in circles denote measurements made under normal conditions.

(*Pirenne, Marriott and O'Doherty*, 1957)

about the results is that the whole acuity curve was displaced to higher intensities under the abnormal condition, as shown in Fig. 4.19.

Critical Flicker Frequency

PSYCHOPHYSICAL DATA

The sensation of flicker produced by regularly interrupted illumination disappears when the frequency of interruption is made sufficiently high. The frequency at which flicker can no longer be perceived is known as the *critical flicker frequency* (C.F.F.). Since Talbot undertook the first systematic experimental study of C.F.F. in 1834 an extensive literature has developed dealing with the basic psychophysical relationships. Talbot himself found that when the subjective fusion point was reached the sensation of brightness evoked is proportional to the luminance and duration, indicated by the ratio of the light:dark interval in the cycle (light–dark ratio or L.D.R.). Plateau (1835) confirmed and extended Talbot's findings and the result of their work is embodied in the Talbot-Plateau law, which appears to be perfectly exact provided, of course, fusion is obtained.

The most basic factor which determines C.F.F. is

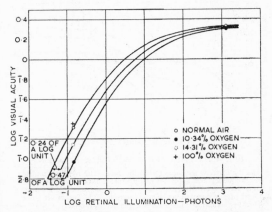

FIG. 4.18. THE EFFECT OF ANOXIA ON THE RELATION BETWEEN FOVEAL VISUAL ACUITY AND ILLUMINATION

Mean values of the data for nine subjects.
(*McFarland and Halperin*, 1940)

10,000 to 11,000 ft. Inhaling oxygen accelerated the elimination of carbon monoxide and also produced an improvement in visual sensitivity.

One final study which it seems important to mention, even though it is based on rather limited data, was undertaken by Pirenne, Marriott and O'Doherty (1957) as part of their investigation on "night-vision the intensity of illumination. This dependence was recognized by Plateau but it was Ferry (1892) who first proposed the formulation that C.F.F. varies directly with the logarithm of the intensity and Porter (1902) who made the first adequate measurements over a sufficiently wide range of intensities. The validity of the Ferry-Porter law (which is a variation of the Weber-Fechner law) has since been confirmed over a wide range of intensities by Kennelly and

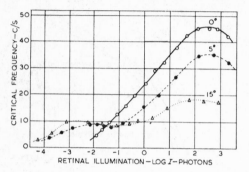

FIG. 4.20. THE RELATION BETWEEN CRITICAL FREQUENCY AND LOG I FOR WHITE LIGHT WITH A 2° FIELD IN THREE RETINAL LOCATIONS

These are at the fovea, and at 5° and 15° above the fovea. (The intensities shown must be multiplied by 40 to convert them to the correct intensities, owing to an error in the 1933 paper.)

(Hecht and Verrijp, 1933)

Whiting (1907), Ives (1912), Luckiesh (1914), Allen (1919, 1926), Lythgoe and Tansley (1929), Granit and Harper (1930), and many others. The later experiments by Hecht and Crozier and their associates (Hecht and Verrijp, 1933; Hecht and Smith, 1936; Crozier and Wolf, 1943, 1944; *see also* Landis (1954*a*) for numerous references to the work of Crozier, Wolf and Zerrahn-Wolf) indicate, however, that the exact relationship is sigmoid in form and that when large central areas are used, or regions in the parafovea, a break in continuity occurs, similar to that observed for other visual functions in accordance with the Duplicity Theory (Hecht, 1935, 1937).

Very complete data over a range of intensities sufficient to cover the entire functional range of the human eye have been obtained by Hecht and his collaborators and their curves provide a convenient basis for discussion. A very full description of their apparatus and the rationale underlying its design is given by Hecht, Shlaer and Verrijp (1933). It was designed to present to the subject a small field of light periodically interrupted and surrounded by a larger field continuously illuminated but otherwise identical with the flickering field. In the early experiments a 10° surround was used but this was later replaced by a 35° surround. Means were provided for controlling and recording the retinal position of the field, its

intensity, spectral composition and the frequency of interruption of its illumination. All measurements were made using an artificial pupil, 1·8 mm in diameter.

Fig. 4.20 shows Hecht and Verrijp's (1933) measurements made with a 2° field in three retinal locations, at the fovea and at 5° and 15° above the fovea. For the fovea, the relation is not rectilinear as was earlier supposed but sigmoid. However, over an intensity range of about two log units the data fall on a straight line with a slope of about the same magnitude as that found by earlier workers. Data for the peripheral fields fall into two parts, suggesting cone function for the high intensity section and rod function for the low intensity section.

Fig. 4.21, taken from Hecht and Smith (1936) shows on a double logarithmic grid the influence of the area of the test-field on the F-log I function, as determined for four centrally-located areas, 0·3°, 2°, 6° and 19° in diameter, using a 35° surround. Whereas the data for the two larger fields (6° and 19°) break into two parts, those for the smaller fields show a single continuous function. The same curve has been drawn through the cone portions of the 19° and 6° data as has been drawn through the 2° and 0·3° data, its equation being—

$$KI = f^2/(f_{max} - f)^2 \qquad (11)$$

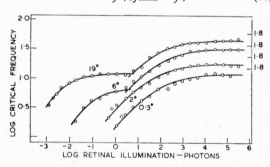

FIG. 4.21. AREA AND THE FLICKER RELATION

The log I axis is the same for all the data. The numbers on the log frequency axis apply to the uppermost data only; the other data have been displaced downward in steps of 0·2 log unit. Their precise position is given on the right. The curves are from Hecht's theoretical equations, as explained in the text.

(Hecht and Smith, 1936)

where I is the intensity, f the logarithm of the C.F.F. and K the dimensional constant which determines the position of the curve on the intensity axis just as f_{max} determines its position on the frequency axis. Neither K nor f_{max} affect the shape of the curve on the double log plot.

For the "rod" sections of the 19° and 6° data a somewhat different curve is required, its equation being—

$$KI = f/(f_{max} - f)^2 \qquad (12)$$

The identity of the curves for the rod data and also for the cone data suggests that the differences between the data for different sizes of field are not basic, under the conditions of Hecht and Smith's experiment. "Fundamentally the systems in the rods and cones which determine the relation between critical frequency and intensity remain the same regardless of

Lythgoe and Tansley (1929), Granit (1930), Granit and von Ammon (1931), Creed and Ruch (1932), Rose (1936), Miles (1950), Weekers and Roussel (1948), Riddell (1936), Phillips (1933), Hylkema (1942), Brooke (1951), Lloyd (1942), Monnier and Babel (1952) and Best (1953) show several apparently discrepant findings, some authors finding lower C.F.F.s

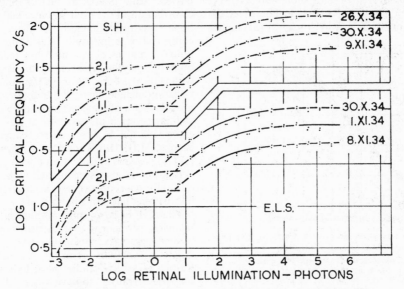

FIG. 4.22. INDIVIDUAL CURVES SHOWING THE RELATION BETWEEN CRITICAL FLICKER FREQUENCY AND RETINAL ILLUMINATION FOR A CENTRALLY LOCATED 19° FIELD

Each individual measurement as taken in the course of a run is shown as a dot. For convenience, the separate runs (dated to the right) have been spaced 0·2 log unit apart on the vertical axis; the values on the ordinate scale refer only to the topmost run for each subject. The numbers attached to the rod curves indicate the values of m and n in Hecht's equation used in drawing them. (*Hecht and Smith*, 1936)

area. Only the dimensional constants are changed by changing the area" (Hecht, Shlaer and Smith, 1935).

To confirm that the two sections of the F-log I data represent "rod" and "cone" function, a further experiment was undertaken with different parts of the spectrum (Hecht and Shlaer, 1936). As expected, for a "red" light of 670 mμ a single curve was obtained while the remaining wavelengths showed discontinuities corresponding, presumably, to the appearance of rod function. The 670 mμ data and the "cone" data for all other wavelengths could be fitted by the curve representing equation (11); those for the "rod" portions by the curve for equation (12).

The studies of Hecht and his associates form only a small part of the voluminous psychophysical literature on C.F.F. but there appears to be nothing in this literature which casts serious doubt upon the general form of the F-log I relation which they established for the human eye, although disputes have arisen concerning the effect of retinal location and area of test-field. Studies of regional variation in C.F.F. by

in the fovea than in the periphery, but these discrepancies appear largely due to failure to control pupil size, as Alpern and Spencer (1953) have shown. The better-controlled studies by Brooke (1951) and Lloyd (1942) give results essentially in agreement with those of Hecht and his associates. Lloyd's data on the effects of area also tend to agree closely with those of Hecht.

Other determinants of C.F.F. which cannot be discussed here in detail include the state of light or dark adaptation of the eye and surround illumination (Schaternikoff, 1902; Lythgoe and Tansley, 1929; Geldard, 1932; Fry and Bartley, 1936; Ryan and Bitterman, 1950), duration of exposure of the test-field (Granit and Hammond, 1931; Lythgoe and Tansley, 1929), wave-form (Luckiesh, 1914; Ives, 1922), L.D.R. (Crozier *et al.* (*see* Landis (1954a) for references); Cobb, 1934; Bartley, 1937; Porter, 1902; Piéron, 1928) and others. For a useful review the reader is referred to Landis (1954b). In general (and there are many discrepancies and complexities) it can be said that: (1) lower C.F.F.s tend to be obtained under conditions of dark adaptation than under conditions of light adaptation; (2) increasing the surround luminance causes an increase in foveal C.F.F. up to a maximum when surround and test-field luminances are equal, then declines; (3) C.F.F. decreases with an increasing L.D.R. (this is probably the most confused area of the whole subject); (4) larger areas give high C.F.F.s, but do not affect the Ferry-Porter law over a wide range; (5) higher

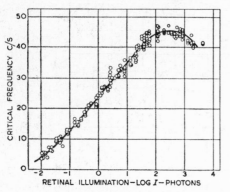

FIG. 4.23. RELATION BETWEEN FOVEAL CRITICAL FLICKER FREQUENCY AND ILLUMINATION

Data for S.H. recording the 176 separate measurements.
(*Hecht and Verrijp*, 1933)

C.F.F.s are obtained with increasing length of exposure from 0·1 to 1 second.

Measurements by Hecht and Crozier and their associates indicate that C.F.F. data are highly reproducible when made under carefully specified conditions. Thus marked similarity is found in the shape of the F-log I function obtained from different trained subjects and in the same subject on different occasions. Comparison of the curves for Hecht and Smith obtained on three different occasions is shown in Fig. 4.22. The slopes of the straight line portion of Hecht and Verrijp's (1933) curves are 11·1 and 11·0 respectively, and most of the carefully controlled experiments give values of about 11. Some indication of the scatter that occurs over a long period of time is given by Fig. 4.23 which shows the individual measurements made by Hecht for a foveal test-field over a year and a half. (The curve drawn through the data is the same one as is drawn through the average data in Fig. 4.20.)

Data on variation in larger groups of subjects relate only to a very restricted range of experimental conditions, e.g. to a single size of test-field, luminance level, retinal location, etc., but provided the experimental conditions are well-controlled, it is usually found that the range of variation is relatively small. Keys and Simonson (1952) for instance, found in a group of one hundred and three normal males (aged

52 ± 2·9 years) that the mean C.F.F. was 42·8 and the standard deviation 2·2. Retest data obtained by McNemar (1951) after one week correlated 0·97 with the original measures. Simonson and Brozek (1952) report a correlation of 0·98 over the same period of time.

Possible sources of individual variation include both physical and biological factors and their relative contribution to the total variance will vary depending upon experimental conditions. Thus, in the carefully controlled experiments of Hecht and Crozier purely physical sources of variation are reduced to a minimum but may be considerable in many of the studies with clinical groups. Possible physiological sources of variation include changes in pupil size and the transmission factor of the lens and ocular media. Variation in these components accounts at least in part for age changes in C.F.F. observed by Simonson, Enzer and Blankstein (1941a), Brozek and Keys (1945), Misiak (1947), Weekers and Roussel (1948) and Berg (1949). Within the sensory system itself variations may occur due to the effect of beverages such as coffee, alterations in breathing pattern, smoking, etc.

That C.F.F. is, as some authors suggest, related to relatively permanent characteristics of the individual which operate as personality traits in a variety of different functions remains to be demonstrated. Results of several studies have indicated a tendency for "perseverators" to have lower C.F.F.s than "nonperseverators" (Wiersma, 1906; Lankes, 1915; Biesheuvel, 1938) and "extraverts" to have lower C.F.F.s than "introverts" (Washburn et al., 1930; Madlung, 1935; Simonson and Brozek, 1952) but the operational definitions of these traits differ from one study to another and, with the possible exception of Simonson and Brozek's study, full details of which have not been published, experimental conditions are inadequately specified and controlled. An interesting study which bears on the interpretation of individual variation in terms of personality variables is that of McNemar (1951) who has shown the marked extent to which correlations can be reduced by relatively slight variations in stimulus conditions.

PHYSIOLOGICAL DATA AND THEORIES

(a) Photochemical Theories

Theories of C.F.F. are of two main types, those that put chief emphasis on peripheral (retinal) determinants and those which emphasize more central factors. Further subdivisions may be made in the case of retinal theories into photochemical and neural. Apart from the importance to visual theory of determining the critical structures and mechanism of C.F.F., elucidation of the part played by the retina, cortex and other components of the visual system is important also for the interpretation of changes in C.F.F. occurring in abnormal conditions.

Although theories of "intermittent vision" were proposed by Fick (1863), S. Exner (1870), K. Exner (1870), Ives (1922) and others, it was not until the publication of Hecht and Verrijp's (1933) paper that there was a really comprehensive theory available to describe the *quantitative* data of flicker. In presenting their theory Hecht and Verrijp stated quite explicitly that it was to be regarded only as a first approximation.

"The retina is a complicated structure, and not enough is known about it to furnish the material for an adequate formulation of so complex a phenomenon as flicker. However, no matter what else occurs in the retina, the very first step in vision must involve a photochemical change having certain fairly well defined characteristics. Since the products of this photochemical change serve only to *start* the complicated train of events which finally yield a series of impulses in the optic nerve, it cannot be expected that the behaviour of the photochemical system alone will yield a complete description of the receptor process. Nevertheless because quantitative ideas are available in photochemistry it is necessary to discover how far this very first photochemical transformation can go in characterizing the receptor process as a whole" (Hecht and Verrijp, 1933, p. 273). Later in the same article Hecht and Verrijp emphasize that, "The photochemical derivation is for a homogeneous system, and applies to a given cell or to a number of cells of identical properties" (*ibid.*, p. 278).

The derivation presented here is a later and simpler form of that given in the 1933 paper. In presenting it, reference will be made to equations discussed earlier in the section dealing with intensity discrimination.

Whereas brightness discrimination and visual acuity could be considered in terms of the stationary state of the primary light and dark reactions, in deriving equations for flicker Hecht had to take into account the secondary dark reaction which follows them. The velocity of the combined primary reactions as they occur under the influence of light is given by—

$$(dx/dt)_I = k_1 I (a - x)^m - k_2 x^n \qquad (13)$$

from equations (3) and (4). The rate at which the sensitive material is formed when, in the absence of light, the primary dark reaction proceeds alone, is given by equation (4).

When the illumination is intermittent the two reactions alternate rapidly and form a steady state. In the case where the L.D.R. is 1:1 the light and dark velocities will be equal. Putting equation (13) equal to equation (4) and solving gives—

$$KI/2 = x^n/(a - x)^m \qquad (14)$$

Except for the number 2 in the denominator which depends on the equality of light and dark periods this equation is identical with the stationary state equation. For other values of the L.D.R., 2 would be replaced by another number, this being the reciprocal of the fraction which the light duration is of the total light and dark cycle. Equation (14) is the basis of Talbot's law.

Hecht's treatment of C.F.F. is as follows. The effect of light on the sensitive material is carried forward by

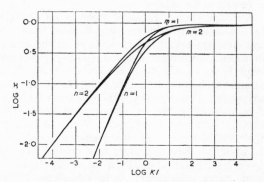

FIG. 4.24. THE STATIONARY STATE EQUATION PLOTTED WHEN m AND n ARE EACH 1 AND 2

Because of the double log plot the shape of the curves remains constant regardless of the values of K and a which merely locate the position of the curves on the axes.

(*Hecht and Smith*, 1936)

the secondary dark reaction which the photoproducts undergo. The concentration of these photoproducts is x (equation (14)), therefore the rate of the secondary dark reaction is—

$$(\Delta x/\Delta t)_{secondary} = k_3 x \qquad (15)$$

where k_3 is a velocity constant. C.F.F. represents the situation in which $\Delta x = c'$, that is, the change Δx in concentration in the dark time Δt is just too small to cause the physiological change that underlies the change in the visual brightness response. If the critical flicker frequency is f cycles of light and dark flashes per second, $f = 1/2\Delta t$. Substituting these values of Δx and Δt in equation (15) gives—

$$f = cx \qquad (16)$$

where $c = k_3/2c'$. Thus, C.F.F. is directly proportional to the concentration of photoproducts in the stationary state, as given by equation (14).

Fig. 4.24 shows a plot of the steady state equation when m and n are each 1 and 2; as in the case of the curves for brightness discrimination and visual acuity, their shape remains constant regardless of the values of K and a. The values of n determine the slope of the steep limb of the curves while *m* determines the curvature of the bend joining the steep limb with the horizontal one.

Reference to the experimental data on the *F*-log *I* function shows that the slope of the rod curve is always twice that of the cone curve and this determines the value of *n* in the two cases. The best fit to the cone data is always obtained when *m* and *n* are both equal to 2, as in the case of brightness discrimination and acuity. The rods tend to be more variable in respect of the value of *m*.

Although Hecht's equation accounts satisfactorily for a wide variety of flicker data obtained from man and other animals, it fails to account for the data of *Pseudemys*, *Sphaerodactylus* and *Asellus* (Crozier and Wolf, 1939; Crozier, Wolf and Zerrahn-Wolf, 1939*a*, *b*), and the observed shift in the *F*-log *I* curve following change in L.D.R. (Bartley, 1937; Crozier, Wolf and Zerrahn-Wolf, 1938*a*, *b*; Crozier and Wolf, 1940, 1941*b*, *c*) or temperature (Crozier, Wolf and Zerrahn-Wolf, 1937*a*) is opposite to that predicted from theory. To overcome these difficulties Jahn (1946*a*) has proposed a modification of Hecht's equation, based on more recent information about the events of the photochemical cycle. Jahn's equation has the same general form[1] as Hecht's so that it will fit all the experimental data that could be fitted by the old equation but the parameters of the two equations have a different significance. The new equation also accounts for the data on L.D.R., temperature, etc. An important difference between Jahn's theory and the earlier scheme of Hecht is that Jahn assumes that the value of the maximal C.F.F. is determined not by the photochemical cycle but by some other process which is unaffected by temperature.

(b) Neural Theories and Electrophysiological Data

Theories which assume that the shape of *F*-log *I* curves is determined by properties of the central nervous system rather than by the photoreceptors have been proposed by Crozier and his associates (*see* Landis (1954*a*) for references) and by Householder and Landahl (1945). From these theories, which rest on certain assumptions about the statistical and mathematical properties of central nervous activity (*see* section on Brightness Discrimination and Visual

Acuity), equations[1] can be derived which provide a reasonably good fit for some of the psychophysical data. To the extent that they predict S-R data the theories may be of value from a purely behaviourist point of view but from their very nature they cannot provide any detailed information on the relative contribution of specific structures to the phenomena of sensory flicker and fusion.

Information of this kind can only come from direct physiological analyses. Although they do not yet provide a basis for quantitative treatment of flicker data, electrophysiological experiments have already shown that retinal structures play a major part in the determination of sensory fusion. In the first place, the human electroretinogram, evoked by intermittent stimuli, shows a fusion of electrical responses at a frequency close to that of the C.F.F. determined by sensory methods (Dodt, 1951*a*) provided sufficiently intense stimuli are used. The upper limit is about 60 c/s in the light-adapted eye, while the fusion frequency recorded from the ERG of a dark-adapted eye is low, upper limit about twenty-five flashes per second, as found also in psychophysical research (Bernhard, 1940; Monnier, 1949). Further parallels between electrophysiological and psychophysical records appear when the effects of luminance[2], size of test-field, and state of adaptation are considered (Creed and Granit, 1933; Granit and Riddell, 1934; Granit and Therman, 1935). These results suggest that fusion is determined to a large extent in the retina. Moreover, as it now seems likely that the ERG is an almost pure receptor potential (Ottoson and Svaetichin, 1952, 1953; Noell, 1953; Brindley, 1956) the experiments on the human ERG would suggest that fusion may be determined in the receptors themselves.

Electrophysiological research has also contributed to our understanding of the mechanisms involved in flicker and fusion, in particular the part played by inhibition. According to Granit's component analysis of the ERG, PIII the negative component identified for various reasons with inhibition, plays an important part in determining the eye's responses to fast rates of intermittence, marked PIII activity being associated with a high C.F.F. and little or no PIII with a low C.F.F. (Granit, 1947). Granit's ERG analysis of flicker has been supplemented by more recent research on single retinal elements by Enroth (1952) in which she confirmed the earlier analysis and demonstrated in greater detail how flicker responses depend upon an interaction between excitation and inhibition.

---

[1] Jahn's equation for C.F.F. is—

$$F = \frac{k_4 P}{C'} \left[k_1 \, I(a - x) \right]^q (F_{max} - F)^r$$

where *F* is the critical flicker frequency, *x* is the amount of *P* or *A*, (*a* − *x*) is the amount of *S*, *I* is intensity, *P* is the fraction of the flicker cycle during which the light is on, k_4 is the velocity constant of the *LT* reaction (*see* page 139) *q* refers to the mechanism whereby the photoproduct *E* is utilized by the sense cells and *r* denotes a mathematical function of *F* (Jahn, 1946*a*).

[1] To describe some of his early measurements on the C.F.F./log intensity function Crozier used a logistic which was formally identical with Hecht's stationary state equation but he later found that a normal probability integral gave a somewhat better fit to both his animal and human data.

[2] *See*, especially, the results of recent research on the human retina reviewed by Granger and Ikeda (1959*b*).

Having analysed the fusion frequency of intermittent stimuli for single retinal elements she went on to study its relation to impulse frequency in a large assemblage of elements. The important generalization from this later work (Enroth, 1953) was that fusion frequency is directly proportional to impulse frequency. As fusion frequency is also a measure of brightness (the Ferry-Porter law), brightness now appears as a simple function of impulse frequency (cf. Adrian, 1928; Granit, 1955).

One further finding which may be mentioned is that of Svaetichin (1956). He observed a striking parallelism between the amplitude of the fish cone response for different light intensities (Fig. 4.25) and the "cone" portion of the sunfish's F-log I curve, as determined by Wolf and Zerrahn-Wolf (1936) using the optomotor response technique (Fig. 4.26). It will be observed that the two curves are very similar between 3 and 0 on the log mL scale. The significance of Svaetichin's finding for human vision comes from the fact that the F-log I curve for the sunfish is similar to the human curve (Fig. 4.26).

In the light of this recent electrophysiological research on the retina it is surely no longer "puzzling why the view of the exclusive or at least primary role of the retina has found such emphatic proponents" (Simonson and Brozek, 1952), although it was perhaps

more puzzling at the time when Simonson and Brozek made these comments. However, even though there is evidence that the primary mechanism of fusion is peripheral it is doubtful if anyone would maintain

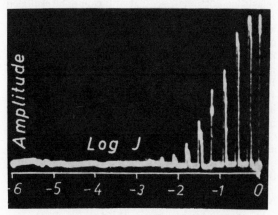

FIG. 4.25. THE RELATION BETWEEN AMPLITUDE OF THE FISH "L" CONE RESPONSE AND LOG INTENSITY OF THE LIGHT STIMULUS

"L" refers to one of three fundamentally different types of spectral response curve obtained from *Teleost* fish cones; it was labelled "L" "since it seems to correspond well to the luminosity mechanism."

(*Svaetichin*, 1956)

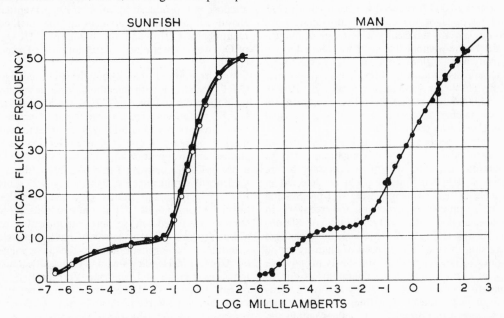

FIG. 4.26. THE RELATION BETWEEN CRITICAL FLICKER FREQUENCY AND LOG INTENSITY OF THE LIGHT STIMULUS

Left: curve obtained from the sunfish (*Lepomis*) using the optomotor response method.

(*Wolf and Zerrahn-Wolf*, 1936)

Right: curve for man obtained using the same method.

(*Crozier, Wolf and Zerrahn-Wolf*, 1937b; *after Bartley*, 1951)

that all the psychophysical data of flicker fusion are peripheral in origin. Having claimed that "the main characteristics of flicker and fusion are determined by the time constants of the photoreceptor responses," Svaetichin goes on to say that: "It cannot be excluded . . . that certain subtle phenomena noticed in the analysis of the perception of flicker and fusion may be caused by an activity at different levels of the visual pathways" (Svaetichin, 1956, p. 53). Svaetichin's comments apply particularly to phenomena noted by Bartley, such as brightness enhancement (Bartley, 1939, 1941). Evidence for central facilitation or inhibition comes from comparison of the results of binocular and monocular presentation (Ireland, 1950; Crozier and Wolf, 1941a) under conditions of in-phase and out-of-phase stimulation, and from various studies of cerebral action potentials (*see* Simonson and Brozek, 1952, for review).

ABNORMAL CONDITIONS

In contrast to the extensive data on brightness discrimination relatively few data are available dealing with the effects of physiological stresses on the F-log I function. Seitz (1940) investigated the effect of anoxia on the F-log I curve over an intensity range of about 4 log units for a centrally fixated 6° test-field and found that oxygen deprivation equivalent to that at 17,500 ft and 20,000 ft reduced C.F.F. for both cone and rod portions of the curve. Unfortunately his data do not cover a sufficiently wide range of intensities to determine whether the curve was shifted along the intensity axis or along both axes. Lowered foveal C.F.F.s were also found by Birren, Fisher, Vollmer and King (1946) at simulated altitudes of 10,000, 14,000, 15,000 and 18,000 ft. (The decrement in C.F.F. was uncorrelated with decrements on a visual field and body-sway test.)

Long latent periods in the C.F.F. response to anoxia were noted in both investigations. Up to thirty minutes' exposure was often necessary before the effect of 20,000 ft altitude could be detected in Seitz's investigation. Changes were still progressing after ninety minutes of exposure and recovery in atmospheric air took over thirty minutes. As Simonson and Brozek (1952) have remarked, these changes are surprising in view of the speed of changes in the blood gases. They suggest that the slowly progressive decrease of C.F.F. under these conditions is due to "a cumulative anoxic effect, possibly involving accumulation of metabolites." Breathing of pure oxygen can cause return to normal C.F.F. values within ten minutes.

Gellhorn and Hailman (1944) claim that parallel changes occur in C.F.F. and in the EEG during anoxia but unfortunately they do not provide sufficient information about the conditions of their C.F.F.

apparatus to enable the study to be properly evaluated. The results of various studies of anoxia have been conveniently summarized in Simonson and Brozek (1952, p. 11).

Rubinstein and Therman (1935) observed a significant increase in C.F.F. following two minutes of voluntary hyperventilation. The mean increase for a central area of 1° and a peripheral area of 4° was 3·5 flashes per second and for a 4° centrally-fixated area, 5·3 flashes per second. More recently Alpern and Hendley (1952) have attempted to determine whether the effect is due to changes in the hydrogen ion concentration of the blood or to a direct effect of carbon dioxide. Measurements were made using a test-field of 2·3° angular diameter, surrounded by an annular background 6° in diameter. The L.D.R. was 1:1 and observations were made through a 2-mm artificial pupil. The luminance of the surround was kept equal to the Talbot luminance of the flickering test-field. Metabolic acidosis was produced by the oral administration of ammonium chloride (4–8 mM/kg taken over a period of 24 to 36 hours) and metabolic alkalosis was produced by the oral administration of sodium bicarbonate (8–12 mM/kg taken over a period of 1 to 6 hours). Respiratory acidosis was produced by asking the subject to breathe a mixture of 7 per cent carbon dioxide and 93 per cent oxygen and respiratory alkalosis was produced by voluntary hyperventilation. Blood samples were taken using the method of Dautreband (1926) and the blood pH, HCO_3 and pCO_2 were determined according to Davenport (1950).

Results showed that although slight changes in C.F.F. occurred with metabolic acid-base changes (acidosis produced lowered C.F.F. and alkalosis raised C.F.F.) the effects were not significant. On the other hand, respiratory acidosis was associated with a marked decrease (4 c/s) at the two luminance levels studied and respiratory alkalosis was associated with a rise in C.F.F. between 3 to 5 c/s; both effects were statistically significant ($p < 0.001$). Fig. 4.27 shows, in a F-log I plot, the results obtained from twelve normal young adults.[1] It is unfortunate that these curves are based on so few experimental points although those plotted appear to have been reliably determined. The general form of the curve suggested by Alpern and Hendley's data is essentially similar to the F-log I curve of Hecht and Verrijp (1933) for a foveal test-field. (A depression in C.F.F. beyond the maximum was observed, when Hecht and Verrijp used a surround of 10°, which is of the same order as the size of the surround used by Alpern and Hendley.) The slope of the straight line portion of the curve (Ferry-Porter law) is 10, which also agrees fairly well

[1] The authors do not give a detailed account of their results but state that these will be published in full elsewhere.

with previous measurements. The data suggest that respiratory acidosis and alkalosis cause a shift of the entire curve along the frequency axis, downward in the former case and upward in the latter. From their results the authors conclude that the changes in C.F.F. are not due to changes in the blood pH *per se* but are indices of variation of the blood pCO_2.

Recent unpublished experiments by Granger and Ikeda confirm and extend Alpern and Hendley's findings concerning the effects of hyperventilation on the C.F.F./intensity relation and suggest that they are associated with the problems of areal variation in the C.F.F. and spatial summation in the visual system. Working with centrally-fixated fields ranging in size from a few minutes of arc to about 2° they found a pronounced increase of 2–3 c/s with the larger fields but none at all with the very small ones. Their suggestion that hyperventilation increases spatial integration is based on curves showing the relation between area and intensity for a fixed value of the C.F.F.

Studies of the effects of drugs are fairly consistent in showing that C.N.S. stimulants such as amphetamine (Simonson, Enzer and Blankstein, 1941b; Roback, Krasno and Ivy, 1952), caffeine (Schmidtke, 1951; Mücher and Wendt, 1951) and Dexedrine (Roback, Krasno and Ivy, 1952) raise C.F.F. while depressants such as barbiturates (Simonson and Brozek, 1952; Roback, Krasno and Ivy, 1952; Ideström, 1954) and alcohol (Enzer, Simonson and Ballard, 1944; Goldberg, 1943) lower C.F.F. Of the various drugs that have been used (for a review *see* Simonson and Brozek, 1952) alcohol is of particular interest because Goldberg has established that a quantitative relationship exists between C.F.F. changes and the blood-alcohol level.

Following its early application in ophthalmology (Braunstein, 1903) C.F.F. measurement has more recently been applied to problems in other branches of medicine. Lowered C.F.F.s have been reported in cardiovascular disorders (Enzer, Simonson and Blankstein, 1942; Krasno and Ivy, 1950), metabolic diseases such as hypothyroidism (Enzer, Simonson and

Blankstein, 1941), multiple sclerosis (Parsons and Miller, 1957) and lesions of the visual pathways (Phillips, 1933; Battersby, 1951; Battersby *et al.*, 1951). Claims that lesions of the frontal lobe lead to a depression of C.F.F. (Halstead, 1947) have not been substantiated (Battersby, 1951; Battersby, Bender and Teuber, 1951) although they may, under certain conditions, lead to transient changes (Young, 1949; Nolan, Lewis, Landis and King, 1956). Berg (1949)

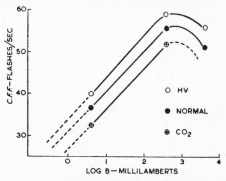

FIG. 4.27. THE EFFECT OF RESPIRATORY ACIDOSIS AND ALKALOSIS ON THE RELATION BETWEEN CRITICAL FLICKER FREQUENCY AND ILLUMINATION
(*Alpern and Hendley*, 1952)

and Akerlund (1953) found a lowering of C.F.F. under Evipan in cases of diffuse brain injury, but Blomberg (1955) has failed to confirm their findings. A detailed account of Berg's research is given in Zubin *et al.* (1957).

Possible psychiatric applications of C.F.F. measurement are suggested by the results of several studies in which "anxiety," variously defined, was associated with a lowered C.F.F. (Krugman, 1947; Goldstone, 1953, 1955; Bühler, 1954; Kubzansky, 1954), but Ricciuti (1948) found no differences between groups of neurotic, psychotic and normal subjects. More detailed accounts of the confused literature on psychiatric patients will be found elsewhere (Zubin *et al.*, 1957; Granger and Ikeda, 1959b).

III. ADAPTATION

PSYCHOPHYSICAL DATA

The term "dark adaptation" refers to the improvement in visual sensitivity which occurs during a stay in the dark after exposure to light. First described by Aubert (1865) it has since been investigated frequently in man and other animals (*see* Adams, 1929; Müller, 1932 and Hecht, 1934 for reviews of the early literature). Only a small fragment of the enormous literature, sufficient for an understanding of theories

of adaptation and the effect of abnormal conditions will be discussed here.

The earliest measurements were made by Piper (1903) using large test-fields, peripheral observation and white light. The data showed a continuous decrease in threshold extending for about thirty minutes and covering an intensity range of about 5,000:1. The increase in sensitivity was attributed to the rods owing to the peripheral nature of the measurements.

That adaptation can occur also in the cones was suggested by the early experiments of Nagel and Schaefer (1904), Inouye and Oinuma (1911) and Dittler and Koike (1912) and clearly demonstrated by Hecht (1921). Hecht found that following five minutes' exposure to a luminance of 90 mL the change in threshold of the fovea was of the order of 6 or 7:1 and dark adaptation was almost complete in four to

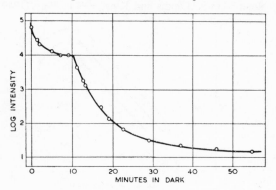

FIG. 4.28. DARK ADAPTATION OF THE EYE AS A WHOLE
Piper's (1903) data, re-plotted by Hecht.
(*Hecht*, 1937)

six minutes. His results have since been confirmed by Kohlrausch (1931), Crawford (1946), Graham (1930), Johannsen (1934) and others.

As both rods and cones show adaptation, data from the human eye as a whole display both phenomena as Kohlrausch (1922) first demonstrated in a retinal area containing both rods and cones. He found that the dark adaptation curve for this area showed two distinct segments apparently related to cone and rod function. A curve of this type is shown in Fig. 4.28. Such a curve has often appeared in textbooks as a "typical" dark adaptation curve but whether or not one of this type is obtained depends upon a number of conditions. Kohlrausch's (1922) data obtained for a 1° field situated 5° above the fovea show, for instance, that the colour of the test-light is important in determining the characteristics of the curve (Fig. 4.29). Of great importance also is the intensity and duration of the preceding light adaptation. Thus, even in the case of threshold data obtained with a "blue" test-light which show hardly any cone adaptation in Kohlrausch's study (lowest curve of Fig. 4.29) cone adaptation may become strikingly apparent provided the previous light adaptation has been sufficiently intense, as shown by Hecht and Haig (1936).

The effect of varying the intensity of light adaptation is brought out particularly well in Fig. 4.30, taken from Hecht, Haig and Chase (1937), which shows a family of dark adaptation curves following two-minute

exposures to various intensities of retinal illumination. (The filled-in circles indicate that the test-field appeared violet, while the open circles indicate that it appeared colourless.[1]) According to these results, the degree of adaptation which is reached in a given time varies inversely with the level of pre-adaptation; the cone-rod transition time is progressively delayed as the light adaptation is increased although the intensity of the test-field at which it appears is approximately constant.

According to Haig (1941), the effect of varying the duration of previous light adaptation is similar to that of varying the intensity. Increasing the degree of light adaptation, whether by varying intensity or duration, caused a reduction in the rate of rod adaptation in his experiments. The change of rate had two components, a decrease in slope and a displacement to the right along the time axis, the first effect being more marked after lower degrees of light adaptation, and the second after the higher ones. Haig suggested that his results were an expression of the Bunsen-Roscoe law.

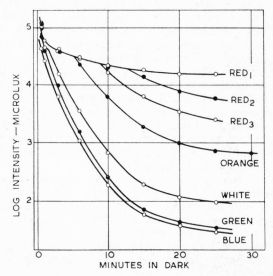

FIG. 4.29. THE DARK ADAPTATION OF AN AREA 1° IN DIAMETER, SITUATED 5° ABOVE THE FOVEA
(*Kohlrausch's* 1922, 1931 *data; after Hecht*, 1937)

Haig's results are at variance with earlier findings of Wald and Clark (1937) who found that duration and intensity were not interchangeable variables as far as subsequent dark adaptation is concerned. The problem has recently been investigated by Mote and Riopelle (1953) under a very wide range of intensity

[1] Use of a "violet" test-field is a valuable means for helping to make distinct the cone-rod transition point and is part of the standard procedure adopted in routine tests with the Hecht-Shlaer adaptometer.

and duration. They found that the reciprocity relationship holds in the case of the parafoveal dark-adaptation curve over a range of intensity and duration of the order of 1,000:1 but breaks down beyond that range. Limitations to the range of application of the reciprocity law have been observed also in studies of foveal adaptation (Crawford, 1946; Mote and Riopelle, 1951; *see also* Johannsen, McBride and

et al., 1953). Increasing the area or duration of the test-stimulus tends, within certain limits (but *see* Rushton, 1952) to shift both the cone and rod portions of the curve downward along the intensity axis, while stimuli making demands upon visual resolution or "form" perception tend to cause an upward displacement (Brown, 1954). In the latter connexion it should be noted that in certain cases the increase in luminance

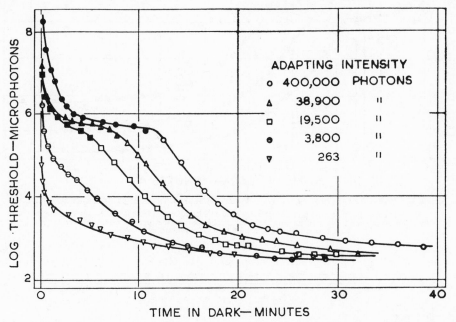

FIG. 4.30. THE COURSE OF DARK ADAPTATION AS MEASURED WITH "VIOLET" LIGHT
FOLLOWING DIFFERENT DEGREES OF LIGHT ADAPTATION
(*Hecht, Haig and Chase*, 1937)

Wulfeck, 1956). All these studies on the effects of varying degrees of light adaptation are of great importance in connexion with theories of dark adaptation (*see* later discussion).

Other studies with less direct bearing on the problems of this chapter concern the effects of variations in size of the adapting field (Honda, 1952), spectral distribution of the adapting-light (Hecht and Hsia, 1945; Smith, Morris and Dimmick, 1954), the influence of intermittent pre-adaptation (Mote, Riopelle and Meyer, 1950) and distribution of light in the adapting field (Baker, Debons and Morris, 1956).

In addition to the effects of wavelength already considered, other characteristics of the test-field that affect dark adaptation curves are area (Wald, 1938), duration (Wolf and Zigler, 1951) and stimulus pattern (i.e. whether a patch of light or more complex form is used for threshold measurement (Brown, J. L.

thresholds is due simply to a reduction in area illuminated (Miles, 1953; Granger, 1957). Taking quantum considerations into account (Pirenne, Marriott and O'Doherty, 1957) the distinction between "light sensitivity" and "form perception" at low intensities is not so sharp as has sometimes been supposed (cf. Craik and Vernon, 1942 and *see* page 111).

Provided adequate care is taken with the measuring technique, foveal and parafoveal dark adaptation curves for different individuals and for the same individuals at different times tend to be very similar in shape. The curves shown in Fig. 4.31 are taken from Hecht, Haig and Chase (1937) and those in Fig. 4.32 from Hecht (1921). Experiments made by other workers (e.g. Pirenne *et al.*, 1957; Granger, 1957c) confirm the high degree of reproducibility of the course of dark adaptation and the relatively small amount of individual variation when Hecht's "fixation-and-flash" technique is used (Hecht and Shlaer,

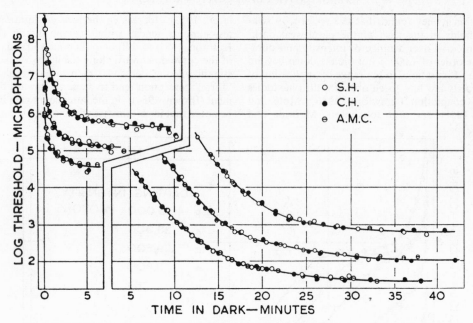

FIG. 4.31. DARK ADAPTATION FOLLOWING THREE DIFFERENT INTENSITIES OF LIGHT ADAPTATION

Coloured "cone" thresholds are plotted separately from colourless "rod" thresholds. The abscissae are the same for all the data; the ordinate scale, however, applies only to the topmost data, the other two sets have been displaced 0·5 and 1·0 log unit downward, respectively.

(*Hecht, Haig and Chase*, 1937)

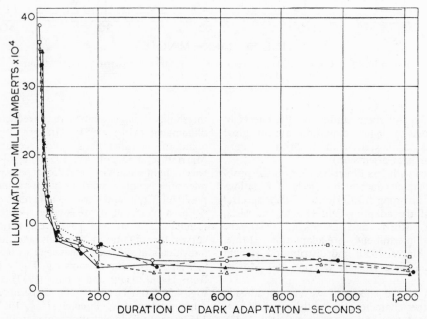

FIG. 4.32. INDIVIDUAL FOVEAL DARK ADAPTATION CURVES FOR FIVE SUBJECTS

Each point is the average of two readings, one for the left, and one for the right eye.

(*Hecht*, 1921)

1938). Less controlled methods of threshold determination, particularly the use of a fixation point with continuous viewing (Craik and Vernon, 1941) can lead to large individual variation due to the influence of "local adaptation" effects (Pirenne, Marriott and O'Doherty, 1957)[1] and regional variations in retinal sensitivity. Fig. 4.33, taken from Pirenne, Marriott and O'Doherty (1957) shows a fairly typical variation in cone-rod transition time between six and eight

0·80 log unit, and the variation in cone-rod transition time six to nine minutes. It is interesting to note that the range of variation in (mean) threshold values for the population of subjects in Hecht and Mandelbaum's (1939) study is of the same magnitude as the range of "uncertain seeing" in a single subject on a given occasion (Pirenne, 1956).

A tendency for final cone and rod threshold to vary in the same direction, as determined by correlating

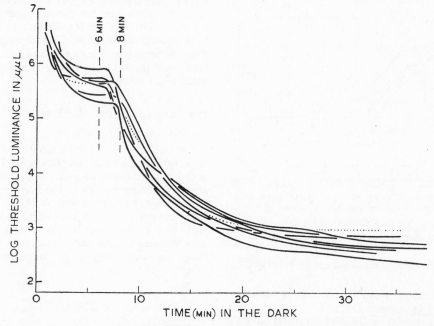

FIG. 4.33. INDIVIDUAL DARK ADAPTATION CURVES FOR EIGHT SUBJECTS, MEASURED BY THE
HECHT-SHLAER (1938) METHOD
(*Pirenne, Marriott and O'Doherty,* 1957)

minutes and a range of variation of 0·5 log unit at the final threshold.

Data from relatively unsophisticated subjects in large-scale clinical studies scatter more widely but the general similarity among individuals is still apparent. Fig. 4.34 is taken from Hecht and Mandelbaum's (1939) investigation of one hundred and ten normal subjects. Measurements were single readings and represented first performances. At the final rod threshold the range of threshold values is approximately 1 log unit, the range of cone thresholds about

[1] Hecht, Haig and Chase had the following to say about variation in dark adaptation data: "In our experience of over ten years, we have found that most of the variations in the data arise from failure to specify conditions of measurement. The major differences may be eliminated by fixing the intensity and duration of light adaptation, and the position, area and colour of the light used for measuring dark adaptation (Hecht, Haig and Chase, 1937, p. 841).

individual threshold values, has been observed in several investigations. Hecht and Mandelbaum found a product-moment correlation of 0·44, Sheard (1944) found a correlation of 0·63 and Birren and Shock (1950) one of 0·64, using similar techniques. Hammond and Lee (1941) reported a correlation of 0·39 between thresholds at ten minutes and forty minutes from the beginning of dark adaptation. The same authors found that the final rod threshold was independent of the rate of adaptation ($r = -0.06$) while Birren and Shock (1950) found that both the final cone and rod thresholds were independent of the rate of cone and rod adaptation ($r = 0.05$ and 0.18, respectively).

A maximum day-to-day variation of about 0·3 log unit in final threshold has been found by Hecht and his associates (Hecht and Mandelbaum, 1939), although smaller variation than this is commonly reported among trained observers under well-controlled conditions over considerable periods of time (Sheard, 1944). Sometimes, however, sudden changes of threshold may occur following a severe cold or "for no apparent reason" (Hecht and Mandelbaum, 1939). Variations of the order of 0·3 log unit have also been observed in tests carried out on the same

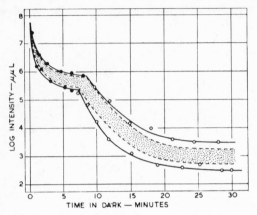

FIG. 4.34. THE COURSE OF DARK ADAPTATION IN
ONE HUNDRED AND TEN SUBJECTS

The points represent the single measurements made with two subjects yielding the highest and lowest values of the final threshold. The dotted area contains 80 per cent of the population. The "cone" adaptation is marked with filled circles, the "rod" with open circles.

(*Hecht and Mandelbaum*, 1939)

person at different times during the day (Pirenne, Marriott and O'Doherty, 1957).

Sources of normal variation of threshold values in well-controlled studies must include, in addition to changes due to quantum fluctuations in the stimulus, changes in the properties of the pre-retinal eye media, receptors, retinal synapses and visual pathways. Under other conditions, (e.g. many clinical investigations) to these factors must be added variations in physical conditions of the experiment, pupil size, eye movements and other non-sensory factors. The effect of age in raising rod and cone thresholds, though not apparently the *rate* of adaptation (Birren and Shock, 1950) is probably mediated by increasing opacity of the ocular media and reduced pupil size (this has not been controlled in some of the experiments) as well as by changes in the nervous system.

Physiological mechanisms responsible for producing day-to-day variation in the state of the visual system remain to be analysed but already some of the variables are known. McFarland and Forbes (1941) have, for instance, shown that variation in blood-sugar concentration is important (cf. experiments on insulin hypoglycaemia, page 142); comparing dark adaptation curves obtained before and after breakfast, when

the blood sugar varies from about 80 mg per cent to 100–120 mg per cent, they found a mean difference of 0·3 log unit; a decrease in threshold following breakfast was observed in nine out of ten subjects (*see* Fig. 4.35). The authors consider that "this degree of variation, the amount attributed by Hecht and Mendelbaum (1939) to intra-individual variation during the day or from day to day, may be accounted for by the variations in the blood sugar in relation to meals" (McFarland and Forks, 1941). This is perhaps somewhat optimistic but further experiments along the same lines (e.g. varying the amount and type of food ingested (Sheard, 1944), breathing pattern, etc.), if supplemented by animal experiments, should eventually lead to an understanding of the physiological mechanisms involved.

PHYSIOLOGICAL FACTS AND THEORIES

(a) Photochemical Theories

Theories of visual adaptation are of two types, those which claim that adaptation is photochemical in origin and those which maintain that changes occur also in neural mechanisms. The basic formulation of photochemical theory is due to Hecht (1919, 1920, 1921) and has already been considered both in general terms and in its application to intensity discrimination. Applied to visual adaptation, the photochemical theory states that during light adaptation rhodopsin

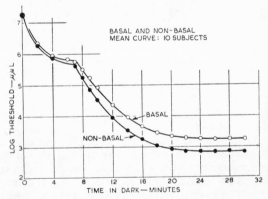

FIG. 4.35. THE MEAN DARK ADAPTATION CURVES FOR
TEN SUBJECTS IN THE BASAL AND NON-BASAL STATE
(*McFarland and Forbes*, 1941)

and other visual pigments are bleached and products formed which are insensitive to light. The effect of bleaching is to lower the concentration of sensitive material in the retina and, hence, the sensitivity of the visual mechanism to light. Recovery of sensitivity during darkness is due to the resynthesis of the sensitive material from its photoproducts. On this heory the absolute threshold is conceived as some simple function of the concentration of sensitive material in the photoreceptors. Following Hecht, the theory may be stated qualitatively as follows—

$$\xrightarrow{\text{Light}} S \left[\begin{array}{c} \text{light} \\ \rightleftharpoons \\ \text{dark} \end{array} P + A;\ L\,\|P + A\| \rightarrow I \right]^{\text{Impulse}} \rightarrow$$

Under stimulus of light a photochemical substance, S, is split into two photoproducts, P and A. Freshly formed $P + A$, denoted by $\|P + A\|$, catalyses a further reaction ($L \rightarrow T$) which is non-light sensitive and results in the formation of an active substance (T) from the inactive substance (L). T initiates the nerve impulse. P and A combine in the dark to reform the photosensitive material, S, and this reaction, plus the photochemical breakdown, is the basis of threshold changes that occur during light and dark adaptation. On this theory changes do not occur in the nervous system; the latter's role is merely that of a conducting mechanism which transmits the effects of photochemical changes to the brain. Following the general formulation of photochemical theory given on page 118, we may consider a situation where the degree of light adaptation is sufficient to bleach almost the whole of the photosensitive substance, S. Under these conditions the initial concentration a will equal x. After a period of time t in the dark when some regeneration has occurred, the concentration of S will be $(a - x)$, x being obtained by integrating equation (4) on page 119. It can then be shown that when the order n of the reaction is 1, $(a - x) = a(1 - e^{-k_2 t})$, and when $n = 2$, $(a - x) = ak_2 t/(1 + ak_2 t)$.

Although Hecht had some success in accounting for the dark adaptation data of various invertebrates such as *Mya*, on which his analysis was largely based, difficulties have arisen in attempting to apply the theory to direct measurements of the regeneration of rhodopsin[1] (Tansley, 1931; Zewi, 1940; Peskin, 1942) and to human dark adaptation data. Even when his initial assumption of direct proportionality between concentration and 1/log threshold intensity was discarded in favour of the assumption that concentration is proportional to 1/threshold (Wald, 1944) the experimental data could still not be satisfactorily fitted. Discrepancies arose particularly from experiments in which the degree of light adaptation was varied over a wide range. Whereas, according to Hecht's original theory, recovery curves following various degrees of light adaptation should retrace one another's paths and merely be displaced along the time axis, the actual data reveal marked differences in shape (*see* Thomson, 1950).

A modification of Hecht's theory has been proposed

[1] The second equation was found less unsatisfactory than the first one.

by Moon and Spencer (1945), in which they introduce various complications into the equations. Exponentials are introduced into equation (3) and several terms in equation (4), including an hysteresis integral which makes the rate of regeneration at any given time depend on the entire previous history of the process as well as its present state. Accepting Hecht's assumption that the threshold is reached at a given rate of decomposition, Moon and Spencer develop an elaborate mathematical structure from which they are able to derive expressions which agree with data not fitted by Hecht's equations (e.g. Haig's 1941 results).

A serious objection to both this and the earlier theory is that they rest on too simple a conception of the recovery mechanism: only the reversibility of the primary reaction is considered whereas it is now known to be more complicated than this. A modification of photochemical theory based on more recent information concerning the photochemical cycle has been proposed by Jahn (1946c), who assumes two reactions, one of which is bimolecular, starting from retinene and the other auto-catalytic, starting from vitamin A. In Jahn's view rhodopsin acts as a catalyst for the second of these reactions the speed of which is thus proportional to the product of the concentration of vitamin A and rhodopsin. From this modified theory Jahn can derive equations which provide a fairly satisfactory description of the family of recovery curves after different amounts of light adaptation (cf. Haig, 1941).

(b) Neural Mechanisms in Adaptation

Numerous objections have been raised against a purely photochemical explanation of visual adaptation by Lythgoe (1940), Granit, Holmberg and Zewi (1938), Elsberg and Spotnitz (1938), Granit, Munsterhjelm and Zewi (1939), Schouten and Ornstein (1939), Baumgardt (1950), Thomson (1949), Arden and Weale (1954) and many others. Of the various objections the most serious concerns the discrepancy between sensitivity changes and rhodopsin concentration. Granit and his associates (Granit, Holmberg and Zewi, 1938; Granit, Munsterhjelm and Zewi, 1939), were the first to show that large changes in the b-wave of the ERG in light and dark adaptation involve only very minor changes in the concentration of rhodopsin. According to their measurements, a large part of light and dark adaptation appeared to depend primarily upon the first fraction of rhodopsin to be bleached and the last to be resynthesized. They suggested that only a small fraction of the rhodopsin of a rod, probably concentrated at its surface, is directly involved in excitation and adaptation, the greater proportion representing a "store" from which the active surface material is replenished by diffusion (Granit, Hólmberg and Zewi, 1938).

Later Rose (1948) concluded that only a small fraction of the sensitivity changes occurring in light and dark adaptation can be ascribed to the capacity of visual pigments to absorb light, from his analysis of the behaviour of "ideal" picture pickup devices. Calculations by de Vries (1943), Baumgardt (1950) and Pirenne and Denton (1952), following the application of quantum theory to visual problems, also indicated that at moderate illuminations too little

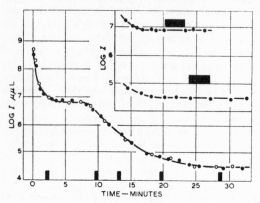

FIG. 4.36. THE INDEPENDENCE OF THE TWO EYES IN REGARD TO DARK ADAPTATION AND THRESHOLD MEASUREMENTS

The determinations were made with the right eye while the left was frequently exposed to light, as indicated by the black marks.

(*Mandelbaum,* 1941)

light reached the rods to produce sufficient bleaching of rhodopsin to accord with sensitivity changes. Experimental work by Hartline and his associates on light and dark adaptation in single receptors of the eye of *Limulus* indicates that although adaptation follows much the same course as in the vertebrate eye (Hartline and McDonald, 1947) little bleaching is apparently involved (Bliss, 1948).

Following the development of an ingenious technique for measuring the rhodopsin level in the living eye, Rushton and his collaborators have provided evidence that exposure of the human eye to a light which bleaches less than 2 per cent of its rhodopsin causes a fiftyfold increase in visual threshold, and at moderate room illuminations not more than 10 per cent of rhodopsin is bleached when equilibrium is reached. Following strong bleaching the subsequent return of the rhodopsin level to its full concentration follows an exponential curve with half-return constant of approximately 7 min. Rushton and Campbell (1954) conclude "that unless fairly bright photopic illumination is used, there is no appreciable change in the density of retinal rhodopsin."

In view of the above evidence it appears that a purely photochemical theory is no longer tenable,

even though Hecht's equations, as modified by Jahn (1946*c*) may still serve as a useful description of psychophysical data, so that the possibility of a neural component in adaptation should be considered. The question arises whether this component is central or peripheral (i.e. in the eye itself). Elsberg and Spotnitz (1938) claim that the central nervous system contributes to visual adaptation, citing evidence that adaptation of one eye affects the sensitivity of the other. Interocular effects of this kind have been claimed by several early authors although, as a review by Adams (1929) shows, opinions were divided on the subject. Helmholtz was one of those who held that the two eyes are independent.

The balance of evidence from the more carefully-controlled experiments is strongly in favour of Helmholtz's view. Mandelbaum (1941) could detect no difference between a dark-adaptation curve obtained in the normal way after light adaptation and another during which the opposite eye was exposed to a luminance of 6,000 mL through a 2-mm artificial pupil for several periods during the measurements (*see* Fig. 4.36). Crawford (1940) found no change in the value of the threshold energy of a fully dark-adapted eye when the light adaptation of the other eye was changed over a very wide range of intensities and the data of several other investigators support Helmholtz's opinion. It seems probable, as Crawford has suggested, that in experimental systems which have not employed Maxwellian view[1] some leakage of light may have occurred and affected the dark-adapted eye.

Although the matter is by no means settled (Wright (1946) for instance, has evidence to show that "adaptation of one eye can, under certain conditions, induce minor changes in the other"), the bulk of the evidence from interocular experiments is against Elsberg and Spotnitz's claim of a central component in adaptation (*see also* the later discussion of the effects of brain lesions).

Further support for the peripheral basis of adaptation comes from an experiment by Craik and Vernon (1941) in which they temporarily blinded one eye by applying pressure to the sclera. With a dark-adapted eye in this blinded condition they light-adapted it for three minutes to a luminance of 12,000 e.f.c. through a 2-mm pupil. At the end of light adaptation a dark adaptation curve was obtained from this eye. This curve was found to be the same as a curve obtained under similar conditions of light adaptation in a normal eye. The authors concluded that, "The normality of the dark adaptation curve obtained with an eye which has been blinded during the bright

[1] In the Maxwellian view (after the famous physicist, James Clerk Maxwell) an image of a light source is formed in the plane of the subject's pupil by means of a lens system. The method is frequently used in visual research where an extended test-field of high luminance is required.

adaptation period shows that light adaptation, both of rods and cones, is a retinal reduction of sensitivity and not a cortical one, since the primary stimulation never reached the higher centres."

From electrophysiological research comes further evidence in support of the peripheral nature of adaptation. The experiments already cited by Hartline[1] and MacDonald (1947) suggest that adaptation in man is determined in the retina while other evidence comes from studies of the ERG (Riggs, 1937; Wrede, 1937; Granit, 1947; Karpe and Tansley, 1948).

Accepting the evidence for the peripheral basis of dark adaptation and for a neural component, the question arises as to the nature of the neural mechanisms involved. Lythgoe (1940) suggested that a reorganization of neural connexions occurs during dark adaptation so that each fibre serves several elements by a spread of its synaptic connexions. The increased amount of convergence makes possible the integration of feeble light stimuli but at the same time there is a reduction in the eye's capacity for the finer discriminatory reactions which depend on the segregation of individual pathways. In other words, Lythgoe suggests that a type of "synaptic switching" occurs which has the effect of changing the properties of the retina from differentiating to integrative. A similar idea has been put forward by Adrian who considers that ". . . the interaction of nerve cells in the retina may change in degree or in sign, darkness favouring mutual summations over wider and wider areas" (Adrian, 1953, p. 110).

Although there is some evidence to show that the summation area increases during dark adaptation (Craik and Vernon, 1941; Arden and Weale, 1954) in the sense that an increase in area of test-field leads to a larger decrease in the value of the threshold energy in dark as compared with light adaptation, recent electrophysiological research by Barlow, Fitzhugh and Kuffler (1957) casts doubt upon Lythgoe's physiological speculations. Their work on changes in the organization of receptive fields suggests that although Lythgoe was correct in supposing that a change in retinal organization occurs in dark adaptation, he was doubly wrong on matters of detail. There appears to be a *decrease* rather than an increase in the degree of retinal interconnexion and the interconnexion which decreases is *inhibitory* rather than excitatory in type. However, in fairness to Lythgoe, it should perhaps be mentioned that he did seem to consider that part of the *initial* dark adaptation process must involve a recovery from inhibition for he regarded the uniformly-illuminated adapting-field as composed of a "multitude of contiguous glare sources" each producing inhibitory effects in the manner of Schouten and Ornstein's alpha-adaptation (Schouten and Ornstein, 1939).

Although there is an accumulating body of evidence for a neural component in adaptation it is incorrect to conclude, as some authors have done, that adaptation is entirely neural. Under certain conditions there is a striking parallelism[1] between the course of bleaching and resynthesis of rhodopsin and the course of dark adaptation as pointed out by Wald *et al.* (1957). The relative contribution and the time course of the photochemical and neural components remain to be determined. So far there are no electrophysiological data on neural mechanisms that can be related quantitatively to psychophysical data on human dark adaptation.

ABNORMAL CONDITIONS

Studies of the effect of anoxia on dark adaptation have been undertaken by Tanaka and Sekiguchi (1935), Fischer and Jongbloed (1935), Bunge (1936), Clamann (1938), McFarland and Evans (1939), McDonald and Adler (1939) and McFarland and Forbes (1941). Controls in several of the earlier studies are unsatisfactory but are adequate in the 1939 and later experiments. McFarland and Evans (1939) measured dark adaptation in twenty subjects under reduced oxygen tensions, at simulated altitudes of 7,400, 11,000 and 15,000 ft. Fig. 4.37 shows the composite dark adaptation curve at each altitude and also the effects of giving oxygen at the end of the experiment. The effects of anoxia are to increase the threshold by 0·10 log unit at 7,400 ft, by 0·22 log unit at 11,000 ft and by 0·40 log unit at 15,000 ft. At the highest simulated altitude a light intensity about two and a half times the normal is required in order to be seen. There was a rapid return to normal sensitivity when oxygen was administered. Changes of a similar order were obtained by McDonald and Adler (1939); in their experiment anoxia caused an equal elevation of rod and cone thresholds.

One of the most interesting results of these experiments is that anoxia shifts the whole dark adaptation curve upward along the intensity axis without changing its shape. The effect is equivalent to placing a neutral density filter in front of the eye, a greater amount of light being required to produce a given visual response.

McFarland and Evans' results were confirmed in a later, better-controlled study, by McFarland and Forbes (1941) in which the Hecht-Shlaer adaptometer

---

[1] Hartline had shown earlier (Hartline, 1930) that in the eye of *Limulus* dark adaptation occurred according to a chemical reaction of a second order, this being consistent with photochemical concepts.

[1] Wald has quite recently claimed that not only is there a qualitative parallelism, but also a measure of quantitative agreement if changes in the *logarithm* of the visual sensitivity (i.e. log 1/threshold) are compared with the rise of pigment concentration.

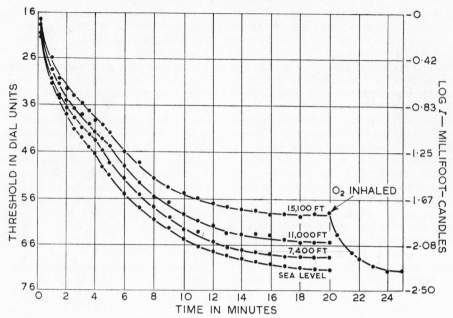

FIG. 4.37. THE EFFECT OF ANOXIA ON DARK ADAPTATION
(McFarland and Evans, 1939)

(Hecht and Shlaer, 1938) was used to measure dark adaptation and the effects of insulin hypoglycaemia were compared with those of anoxia. Following light adaptation to a large "white" adapting field of 35° angular diameter and 1,500 mL luminance for three minutes, thresholds were obtained for a 3° test-field situated 7° nasally in the right eye and exposed in 0·2 second flashes. The measuring light was from the extreme violet end of the spectrum.

Results for six practised subjects are shown in Fig. 4.38. The control curve is based on eighteen subjects. It will be seen that increasing degrees of anoxia cause an increased elevation of both rod and cone portions of the adaptation curve, the increase in threshold for 10·1 per cent oxygen being about 0·50 log unit for cones and 0·60 log unit for rods. The effects of insulin (5 to 8 units intramuscularly according to body weight) are shown in Fig. 4.39. Both control and

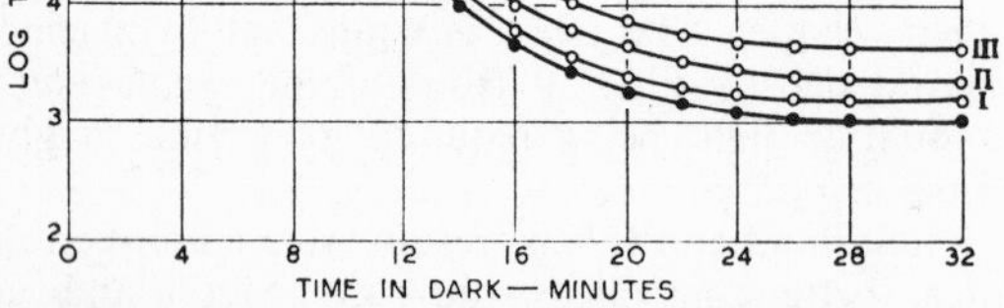

FIG. 4.38. MEAN DARK ADAPTATION CURVES SHOWING
THE EFFECT OF LOW OXYGEN TENSION

In the control curves each solid circle is based on the average of eighteen experiments; in the curves obtained at simulated high altitudes, each open circle is based upon the average of six experiments.

(McFarland and Forbes, 1941)

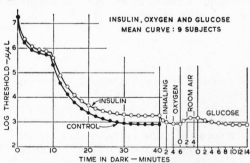

FIG. 4.39. THE EFFECTS OF INSULIN, OXYGEN AND
GLUCOSE ON LIGHT SENSITIVITY

The solid circles (control curve) are based on the average thresholds for nine subjects in air and the open circles for the same subjects also in normal air but after the injection of insulin, the inhalation of oxygen, and the ingestion of glucose. When the blood sugar was lowered by insulin the thresholds increased; when the subjects inhaled oxygen from a cylinder, the thresholds returned to normal; when the subjects were returned to room air the thresholds rose; and finally when the subjects ingested glucose the thresholds fell.

(McFarland and Forbes, 1941)

experimental curves are based on data for nine subjects. Insulin causes an upward displacement of the curve along the intensity axis by about 0·35 log unit.

Fig. 4.40 shows the combined effects of insulin and low oxygen for one subject. After obtaining a control curve the oxygen was reduced to 13·2 per cent and the subject was then given four units of insulin intra-muscularly. Fifteen minutes later a dark adaptation curve was obtained again. The increase in threshold was about 0·6 log unit, a change much greater than a similar degree of anoxia or hypoglycaemia would have produced separately and somewhat greater than the sum of their separate effects.

Upward displacements, similar to those observed by McFarland and Evans (1939) and McFarland and Forbes (1941) in their duplex dark adaptation curves obtained from areas containing both rods and cones, have also been obtained in foveal dark adaptation curves by McFarland, Halperin and Niven (1944) and Hecht *et al.* (1946) (*see* Fig. 4.41).

Of a somewhat different nature from the experi-ments already discussed are several very important studies dealing with the effects of physiological stresses on the absolute threshold of the fully dark-adapted eye. McFarland and Forbes (1941) deter-mined absolute thresholds for a 3° test-field situated

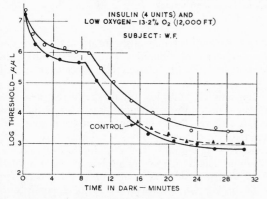

FIG. 4.40. THE COMBINED EFFECTS OF INSULIN AND LOW OXYGEN ON LIGHT SENSITIVITY

The solid circles (control curve) are based on measurements in normal air and the open circles in 13·2 per cent O_2 and after the injection of 4 units insulin. These effects were largely counter-acted (as indicated by the triangles) when glucose was ingested, the oxygen remaining at 13·2 per cent.

(*McFarland and Forbes*, 1941)

7° nasally and exposed in 0·2 second flashes to the fully dark-adapted eye. As in the usual Hecht-Shlaer procedure (Hecht and Shlaer, 1938), the test-field was illuminated by light from the extreme violet end of the spectrum. Several experiments were carried out to compare the effects of anoxia and hypoglycaemia. Oxygen concentrations of 13·3, 11·4 and 10·0 per cent

caused an average increase of 0·19, 0·36 and 0·61 log unit, respectively, in a group of six thoroughly prac-tised subjects. At the end of each test in low oxygen, subjects inhaled oxygen and, without exception, thresholds fell within two or three minutes to the normal level or even slightly below it. Changes in threshold could be detected after subjects had been inhaling oxygen for less than half a minute.

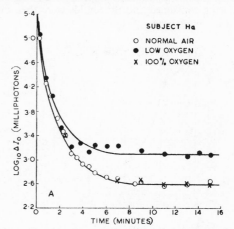

FIG. 4.41. EFFECT OF ANOXIA ON FOVEAL DARK ADAPTATION

(*McFarland, Halperin and Niven*, 1944)

In a second experiment McFarland and Forbes studied the effects of anoxia while the oxygen concen-trations were gradually decreasing. After a steady threshold value had been attained following forty minutes' dark adaptation, the air in the experimental room was diluted with nitrogen so that within about twenty minutes the percentage of oxygen was reduced from 21 to 13 per cent. During the following hour the threshold was determined every two to three minutes as the oxygen was being reduced by a slow but con-tinuous inflow of nitrogen. The final level averaged 10·2 per cent oxygen in experiments with five subjects and was lowered to 7·3 per cent for one subject. In each case the threshold rose as the oxygen concentra-tion decreased, the average increase being about five-fold at 10·2 per cent oxygen. Fig. 4.42 shows the mean curve for five subjects. Inhalation of oxygen caused a return to somewhat better than normal sensitivity within two to three minutes.

In view of experiments in which improvement in visual sensitivity has continued for several hours (Semeonoff, 1941; Hume and Krebs, 1949) measure-ments of the effects of anoxia and breathing of pure oxygen may be subject to a certain amount of error due to changes in the "control" threshold values but the size of this error seems likely to be negligible in relation to the experimental effect. For the subject who was exposed to an oxygen concentration of 7·3 per cent the threshold increase was about eightfold.

In a third experiment absolute thresholds were determined under normal conditions and then under anoxia. While the eyes remained in the dark-adapted state each subject drank a glassful of strong glucose solution (1 g glucose per kg body weight in 200 cc of water). Six to eight minutes elapsed while the glucose was being consumed and thresholds were then taken again in low oxygen.

"white" test-field, centred 13° below a red fixation point and exposed in flashes of one-fiftieth of a second. Observations were monocular through 1·6- or 2-mm artificial pupils in some of the experiments. These experiments were of two types, one in which the anoxia was of short duration and began and ended abruptly and another in which the anoxia was established gradually and maintained for several hours. Under the former conditions completely dark-adapted subjects, breathing through a mouthpiece,

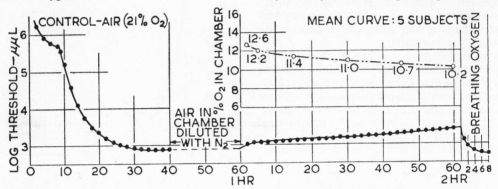

FIG. 4.42. THE EFFECT ON LIGHT SENSITIVITY OF ALTERING THE PERCENTAGE OF OXYGEN IN THE INSPIRED AIR

After the eye was dark-adapted (control curve) for forty minutes, the air in the chamber was diluted with nitrogen. Then the thresholds, which were determined every two to three minutes, gradually rose as the concentration of oxygen was reduced. At the end of each experiment, the subject inhaled oxygen from a cylinder and the threshold returned to normal. The curves are based on the mean values of five subjects.

(McFarland and Forbes, 1941)

Following the ingestion of glucose the blood-sugar concentration, which averaged 65 mg per cent and remained fairly constant during the low oxygen tests rose to 128 mg and thresholds returned to normal within six to ten minutes.

McFarland and Forbes next studied the effects of insulin, oxygen and glucose on the absolute threshold in that order. After about forty minutes' dark adaptation when a steady threshold value had been obtained, subjects were given 5 to 8 units of insulin intramuscularly according to body weight and final rod thresholds were obtained after a further period of forty minutes' dark adaptation. Subjects then inhaled pure oxygen for six minutes, were suddenly changed back to normal room air and finally ingested 70 mg of glucose in 200 cc of water. The sequence of threshold changes is shown in Fig. 4.39. It is seen that the threshold increase due to insulin could be counteracted by the inhalation of pure oxygen. Subsequent breathing of room air caused an increase in threshold while glucose caused a fall in threshold.

In an investigation of respiratory effects upon the visual threshold Wald, Harper, Goodman and Krieger (1942) confirmed the findings of Bunge (1936), McDonald and Adler (1939) and McFarland and Forbes (1941) on anoxia. They used a circular 1°

were switched instantaneously from room air to air-nitrogen mixtures containing 8 to 11 per cent oxygen. After twenty to thirty minutes the subject was returned abruptly to room air.

The simplest and most usual type of response was for the threshold to rise within one to ten minutes of anoxia to levels 0·2 to 0·5 log unit above normal. In repeated experiments with six subjects this change averaged 0·35 log unit. On returning to room air the threshold usually fell within a few minutes to normal level. (Certain subjects gave results which departed from this pattern in various ways, due apparently to variations in breathing patterns. These variations were later made the subject of special study.)

A second type of experiment was carried out in a gas chamber in which the air was diluted with nitrogen without change in total barometric pressure. Oxygen contents of 11 to 12 per cent, simulating altitudes of 15,000 to 17,000 ft, were attained within thirty to ninety minutes after the first introduction of nitrogen. They were maintained for about five hours. Results showed an increase in visual threshold with the first dilution of oxygen. Data for one subject are shown in Fig. 4.43. As the authors point out, the form of the relationship suggests that with further decrease in oxygen tension the threshold might rise beyond the maximum observed increase (0·35 log unit). However, the subject's behaviour indicated serious distress even at an 11 per cent oxygen level so that he probably could not have continued the experiment at lower oxygen pressures.

At the end of the experiment, after exposures of five, and six and a half hours to diminished oxygen tensions, the threshold returned to normal within five to six minutes. The magnitude of the changes observed in the long-term experiments agreed with those on sudden and short exposure to anoxia in the first experiment. Wald *et al.* comment on these results as follows: "The adjustment of central nervous structures to low oxygen tensions appears to be a rapid process. Anoxias of several hours' duration cause change in the threshold which neither exceed those recorded during the first few minutes nor persist longer after the return to room air" (Wald *et al.*, 1942, p. 897).

Wald *et al.* conducted further experiments on the effect of respiratory acid-base imbalance on the threshold. Subjects breathed to the beat of a metronome, as far as possible without change in amplitude and their rate and depth of respiration were recorded by pneumograph. For these experiments thresholds were measured in a 2° field centred 10° below the fixation point. Test flashes were of one-fiftieth of a second duration and 2-mm artificial pupils were used.

On increasing the rate of breathing room air by 50 to 100 per cent the threshold fell, within about five to ten minutes, to approximately half its normal value. In twenty-two experiments on two subjects the decrease ranged from 0·13 to 0·41 log unit and averaged 0·27 log unit (or a decrease of 47 per cent). Return to the normal threshold value occurred within two to three minutes. The increased sensitivity was not apparently due to increased oxygenation of the blood for oxygen tensions of 32 to 36 per cent did not appreciably affect the results. Instead it appears to be due to the alkalosis associated with hyperventilation. By adding carbon dioxide to the inspired gases it was possible to abolish or reverse the effect. The presence of 2 per cent carbon dioxide in mixtures containing 32 to 36 per cent oxygen did not affect the threshold when breathed at the normal rate but it completely abolished the decrease in threshold associated with rapid breathing. Increasing the carbon dioxide content to 5 per cent caused an increase of 0·2 to 0·5 log unit at both normal and rapid rates of ventilation. It appeared, therefore, that respiratory alkalosis and acidosis exert opposed effects upon the visual threshold, the former depresses and the latter raises the threshold by about equal amounts, averaging under the conditions of this experiment a factor of about 2.

Finally Wald *et al.* undertook experiments on the interaction of acid-base imbalance and anoxia upon

the threshold. As in the previous experiment, rate and depth of breathing were controlled and the test-field was viewed through an artificial pupil. The reaction to anoxia (10 per cent oxygen) was essentially similar to that observed in the first experiment (i.e. a doubling of threshold) but there was less individual variation due apparently to control of breathing. When oxygen was breathed at twice the normal rate a particularly interesting result occurred. Usually the threshold fell at first and always failed to rise for

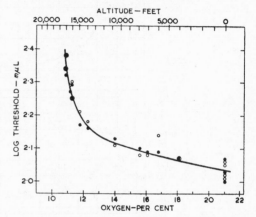

FIG. 4.43. VARIATION OF ABSOLUTE THRESHOLD WITH DECREASE IN OXYGEN TENSION OR RISE IN SIMULATED ALTITUDE

Open circles, right eye, solid circles, left eye.
(*Wald, Harper, Goodman and Krieger*, 1942)

several minutes. Finally it rose to values above normal although it could remain below the level attained at lower rates of breathing. Effects of rapid breathing apparently at first predominated over the effects of simple anoxia but after a time some of this advantage was lost.

In a later experiment Alpern and Hendley (1952) studied the effect of variation in acid-base balance on the absolute threshold using the Hecht-Shlaer adaptometer. The test-field was situated 3° above the fovea (the size is not given) and exposed in 0·2-sec flashes, using the method of constants. Frequency-of-seeing curves were determined for eight subjects after thirty minutes' dark adaptation and the threshold determined by taking the intensity of retinal illumination at which the stimulus was seen 60 per cent of the time. Details of the method of producing metabolic and respiratory acidosis and alkalosis have already been given in the section on critical flicker frequency. As in the case of C.F.F., significant changes in threshold occurred only with respiratory alkalosis and acidosis, the former lowering, the latter raising it. The mean decrease amounted to 0·16 log unit and the increase was 0·23 log unit ($p < 0.001$). It is unfortunate that the authors deal only with the effects on the statistically determined mean threshold value and do not present individual frequency-of-seeing curves.

In spite of several claims in the early literature (*see* Adams, 1929 for review) that the course of dark adaptation can be altered by the action of drugs,

Reviews of the literature by Rose and Schmidt (1947) and Segal (1953) provide further evidence of slight changes in threshold but very little indication of effects on the course of adaptation. However, the amount of well-controlled experimentation in this field is not yet large enough for final conclusions to be

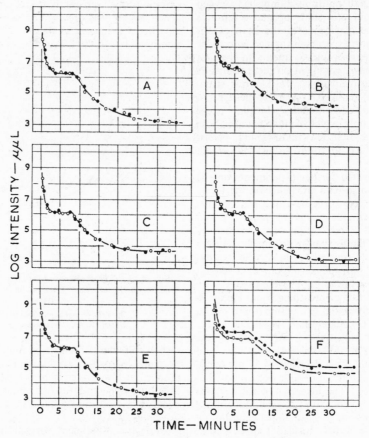

FIG. 4.44. THE EFFECT OF DRUGS ON DARK ADAPTATION

Control curves are indicated by open circles and experimental curves by filled circles. *A,* 20 mg of amphetamine sulphate orally; *B,* 5 mg of strychnine sulphate subcutaneously; *C,* 0·5 g of caffeine with sodium benzoate subcutaneously; *D,* 20 mg of morphine sulphate subcutaneously; *E.* 130 mg of phenobarbital orally; *F,* alcohol orally (whisky, equivalent to 180 cc of alcohol).

(*Mandelbaum,* 1941)

results of the more recent and carefully-controlled experiments are almost entirely negative. Using the Hecht-Shlaer adaptometer, Mandelbaum (1941) could detect no effect from strychnine, amphetamine, caffeine, phenobarbital, and morphine. Alcohol caused an increase of about 0·3 log unit in the final rod threshold and shifted the entire dark adaptation curve upward along the log-luminance axis but without changing its shape (*see* Fig. 4.44). The effects of alcohol are evidently similar to those of anoxia and insulin hypoglycaemia.

drawn. Apparently significant effects from caffeine (Segal, 1953) and amphetamine (Yudkin, 1941) on the cone-rod transition time, conflicting results on the effects of certain drugs (e.g. alcohol) and the insistence of Russian claims concerning the marked effects of sympathomimetic drugs[1] in increasing the rate of

[1] Marazzi (1943, 1953) found that adrenaline caused an inhibitory effect on the cat's optic cortex, and Rothan (1925) observed an increase in the visual threshold. Small increases in threshold have also been observed following the administration of ephedrine (Rose and Schmidt, 1947; Granger, 1954) but these were not statistically significant.

dark adaptation (Babskii, 1947; Babskii and Skulov, 1944) all indicate the need for further research. Investigation of the effect of various neurotropic drugs seems particularly necessary in view of the accumulating evidence for a neural component in adaptation.

Having considered the effects of physiological stresses and drugs it remains to consider the effects of various pathological conditions and "functional" disorders, in particular the condition known as night-blindness or nyctalopia· in which vision at low intensities is poorer than normal. Known since ancient days it has for long been associated with deficient rod vision (Parinaud, 1881). It exists in two forms, one of which is inherited and the other associated with vitamin A deficiency. Dark adaptation curves for permanently night-blind individuals show only the initial cone drop in threshold with no secondary rod drop during the first hour of dark adaptation (Dieter, 1929; Takagi and Kawakami, 1924). Other data indicate that nyctalopes possess only one luminosity curve corresponding to the high intensity cone curve of normal individuals.

Literature on the acquired form of night-blindness, shown to be associated with a diet deficient in vitamin A as a result of the researches of Holm (1925), Tansley (1931), Fridericia and Holm (1925), is voluminous (*see*, for instance, Jeghers (1937) review) although the number of well-controlled experiments is relatively small. Mention can be made here of only one of these, a study by Hecht and Mandelbaum (1939) in which the dark adaptation of seventeen subjects maintained on controlled vitamin-A-deficient diets was measured at frequent intervals. Following light adaptation to 1,500 mL for three minutes, thresholds were obtained for a 3° diameter field situated 7° nasally and exposed in 0·2 second flashes of "violet" light. Under conditions of vitamin A deficiency both cone and rod portions of the adaptation curve were displaced upward along the intensity axis although the general form of the curves remained the same. Fourteen out of seventeen subjects responded with an immediate increase in threshold which continued for the duration of the diet but the remaining three subjects required twenty-two, fifty-five and sixty days before showing a definite and continuous increase in threshold. Partial recovery was effected in some cases by giving single large doses of vitamin A but permanent recovery was slow, often requiring several months.

In a useful review, Sheard (1944) points out that in addition to inadequate intake of vitamin A, there are numerous conditions which can lead to a deficiency. "Fever, general infection· rapid growth, elevated basal metabolic rate, pregnancy, lack of bile or pancreatic secretions, changes in the gastro-intestinal tract, or hepatic disease may prevent or hinder the proper

absorption or storage of vitamin A." Cirrhosis of the liver is a good example of the operation of an aberrant factor in vitamin A metabolism and Haig, Hecht and Patek (1938) have provided data from fourteen patients suffering from this condition. They used a light-adapting field of 1,600 mL of four minutes' duration and obtained thresholds for a 4·5° diameter field situated 8·5° nasally in the right eye, and exposed in 0·2 second "violet" flashes. Thirteen subjects

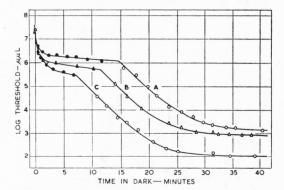

Fig. 4.45. The Dark Adaptation of a Patient with Alcoholic Cirrhosis of the Liver Determined at Different Times During Vitamin A Therapy

Curve *A* was obtained when the subject was on an ordinary diet; curves *B* and *C* were obtained after one hundred and five and one hundred and twenty-seven days, respectively, of vitamin A therapy. Measurements were made using a "violet" test light; those denoted by filled circles indicate that the light was seen as coloured, those shown as open circles were made when the light appeared colourless.

(*Haig, Hecht and Patek*, 1938)

showed a disturbance of dark adaptation. An interesting feature of the illustrative data shown in Fig. 4.45 is the decrease in cone-rod transition time, which occurred following a course of vitamin A therapy, as compared with its stationary position in experiments on dietary avitaminosis (Hecht and Mandelbaum, 1939).

The individual differences in response to vitamin-A-deficient diets observed in Hecht and Mandelbaum's experiment is a common feature of investigations of nutritional night-blindness, as is the marked variation in the time taken for recovery in patients undergoing vitamin A therapy. These two inconsistencies, which puzzled some of the early investigators, have been considerably clarified as a result of recent research. The first seems at least partially explicable in terms of the large individual variations in the amount of vitamin A stored in the liver. What appears to happen is that so long as stores of vitamin A remain in the liver, the blood vitamin A level is maintained above a certain value (about 50 I.U. per 100 ml of serum) and vision remains normal. When the liver stores become exhausted the blood level falls and the individual begins to show symptoms of night-blindness (Hume and Krebs, 1949; Moore, 1953).

Clarification of the second inconsistency results from a study by Dowling and Wald (1958) who have also made a major contribution to our understanding of the aetiology of night-blindness. By determining simultaneously the vitamin A content of the liver, the vitamin A of the blood plasma, the concentration of rhodopsin and of opsin (an additional component of

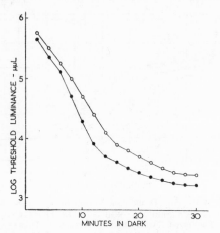

FIG. 4.46. MEAN DARK ADAPTATION CURVES OF TWENTY NORMAL AND TWENTY PSYCHIATRIC PATIENTS

Open circles denote psychiatric patients; filled-in circles denote normal subjects.

(*Granger*, 1957)

the visual pigments) in the retinae of rats kept on a vitamin-A-deficient diet, and recording ERG changes, they were able to present a clear and simple picture of the rise and fall of the disease. After vitamin A has left the blood due to depletion of the liver stores the retina is apparently no longer able to obtain sufficient vitamin A to occupy all its opsin, lower than normal amounts of rhodopsin are formed, and night-blindness ensues. At this stage when the retina contains all its opsin but insufficient supplies of vitamin A, it is possible to cure night-blindness very rapidly. By administering vitamin A as quickly as it can be acquired by the retina, rhodopsin is restored to its normal level and night-blindness ends. However, with further development of the deficiency the concentration of opsin itself begins to drop and at this stage anatomical deterioration of other tissues in the eye and elsewhere begins to occur. Under these conditions recovery from deficiency is much slower for time must be allowed for the structural repair of the eye tissues before a normal visual threshold can be obtained. Although their experiment was done on rats it seems probable that human night-blindness depends on very similar relationships.

Because the vitamin A studies represent an outstanding scientific contribution in which psychophysical measurements have figured prominently it seems necessary to say something briefly about their physiological and practical significance before going on to discuss other abnormal conditions. From a physiological point of view not only have they helped to elucidate the role of vitamin A in the biochemistry of visual excitation but they have also served to link the relatively isolated study of visual processes with the more general metabolism of vitamin A throughout the body and thus helped to make explicit some of the general "conditions of the organism" that affect visual response (see Graham's equation, page 108). From a practical viewpoint they provide an excellent example of the experimental investigation of the aetiology and therapy of a human deficiency disease.

The influence of various pathological conditions, including retinitis pigmentosa, glaucoma, syphilitic atrophy of the optic nerve and renal lithiasis, has been considered by Mandelbaum (1941). In none of these conditions is the rate of adaptation affected. Retinitis pigmentosa has an effect on the curve of rod adaptation, rod function becoming increasingly impaired until it apparently disappears completely leaving a cone curve of normal shape but situated at a higher intensity level. The same upward shift of the dark adaptation curve appears to a lesser extent in advanced glaucoma, optic nerve atrophy and the other disease conditions.

Clinical studies of dark adaptation curves in various types of brain lesion have been carried out by Ullrich (1943), Ruesch (1944), Krieger and Bender (1949, 1951) and Bender and Krieger (1951). All these authors claim various anomalies in threshold and in the course of dark adaptation but they do not provide sufficient information about experimental conditions and results for their conclusions to be assessed. Of the various studies Krieger and Bender's is the most suggestive for further research. It suggests, as would be expected, that lesions to the visual pathway beyond the retina result in raised thresholds. But although the authors claim that the rate of adaptation is affected, none of their published curves supports this claim. The threshold increases they observed can be accounted for in terms of a conduction block. It appears, however, that they have collected a large amount of unpublished data in which changes occurred in the shape of dark adaptation curves. Repetition of the experiment seems desirable.

Following a wartime observation that the incidence of "night-blindness" appeared to be higher among neurotics than among normal Service personnel, several studies have been undertaken in which the night-vision efficiency and dark adaptation of normal and psychiatric groups has been investigated. Results indicate (Granger, 1957a) that psychiatric disorder has no effect on the course of dark adaptation although there is a tendency for changes in threshold to occur with upward displacement of the entire "rod" dark adaptation curve along the intensity axis (Fig. 4.46).

Unfortunately the measurements are subject to some of the errors of the type discussed on page 137 so that one cannot conclude with any certainty that the absolute threshold is higher than normal (Granger, 1957b).

IV. PSYCHOPHYSICAL AND PHYSIOLOGICAL ANALYSIS OF STRESS EFFECTS

In view of their scope and the precise theoretical treatment of the data the studies of anoxia provide a convenient starting point for discussing mechanisms underlying the effects of physiological stresses. The most striking result of these studies is that anoxia does not apparently change the shape of the cone and rod dark adaptation curve or the curves relating brightness discrimination and visual acuity to illumination but merely affects their position on the intensity axis. The curves relating acuity and brightness discrimination to intensity are displaced to the right on the intensity axis while dark adaptation curves are displaced upward. If the absolute threshold for the dark-adapted eye is considered as the limiting value of the differential threshold when the field intensity is zero (McFarland, Halperin and Niven, 1944) the effects of anoxia on the absolute threshold can be shown to be similar both in direction and magnitude to the effect on intensity discrimination.

In all these experiments the effect of anoxia is, as McFarland et al. (1944) have pointed out, equivalent to placing a neutral density filter in front of the subject's eyes, a greater intensity of illumination being necessary to produce a given response. The analogy of the optical filter was current in Hecht's laboratory before the last war and "seems to have been shared by a number of other biologists" (Pirenne, Marriott and O'Doherty, 1957). Its application to "normal" data is nicely illustrated by a hypothesis suggested by Pirenne et al. (1957) in their research on "Individual differences in Night-vision Efficiency," referred to earlier in the chapter. With a view to accounting for individual variation in acuity and at the same time the general similarity in shape of log-acuity/log-luminance curves these authors put forward a "filter factor" hypothesis. The term *filter factor*[1] is used on analogy with the photographic filter factor which concerns the lengthening of exposure which becomes necessary when a given colour filter is used in a camera. In its simplest form the "filter factor" hypothesis "assumes that a subject A, behaves as if he had the same eyes, brain, mind, etc., as a subject B, but had in front of these eyes light filters of trans-

mission $1/k$, the value k being the filter factor. According to this hypothesis A would always need k times more *external* light than B to perform any given visual task" (Pirenne et al., op. cit., p. 27, 1957).

Applying this hypothesis to the acuity data in Fig. 4.12. A's and B's curves would be of the same shape

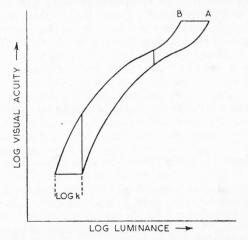

FIG. 4.47. DIAGRAM TO ILLUSTRATE THE FILTER FACTOR HYPOTHESIS

Subject *A* has the same acuity as subject *B* provided the luminance is multiplied by a constant factor *k* at all levels. The vertical lines indicate the variations of acuity at two fixed luminance levels.

(*Pirenne, Marriott and O'Doherty*, 1957)

but A's curve would be shifted horizontally as a whole to higher luminances by an amount equal to $\log k$, i.e. to the optical density[1] of the hypothetical filter. This horizontal shift is illustrated in Fig. 4.47 which gives curves for subjects A and B similar to the experimental curves of Fig. 4.12.

The hypothesis accounts for the experimental data in the range corresponding to rod vision; at the highest acuity and luminance levels, where acuity becomes constant and independent of luminance level the hypothesis has no meaning, as its authors point out. The predictive value of the hypothesis was tested in a further experiment on "perceptual efficiency" in

---

[1] Pirenne et al. point out that their use of the term *filter factor* probably originates from a report by Hartline and McDonald (1957). They also point out that, unlike the photographic filter factor which refers to change in exposure time, their filter factor refers to changes in light intensity.

[1] The optical density is defined as the negative logarithm, to base 10, of the fraction of light transmitted. Density $= \log \dfrac{I}{I_t}$, I being the incident light intensity and I_t the intensity transmitted.

which subjects were asked to perform a complex perceptual task (perceiving details in a Hogarth print) under conditions of low illumination. The authors were able to show that when the illumination falling on the picture was adjusted in accordance with the individual "filter factors," determined from their absolute thresholds in an earlier experiment, individual variation was almost completely eliminated.

As used by Pirenne et al. (cf. Hartline and McDonald, 1957; Hecht and Pirenne, 1940) the "filter factor" serves as a convenient "physical" descriptive device which leads to a number of predictions at the psychophysical level. However, it is also of interest to consider the possible physiological basis of the hypothetical filter in specific instances. An attempt has been made to do this by Hecht et al. (1946) in the case of anoxia experiments although these authors make no explicit reference to the filter factor analogy. Seeking a physiological basis for the effect of anoxia on brightness discrimination they propose a formulation in terms of Hecht's stationary state equation.

They point out that when setting up equations for the primary light and dark reactions Hecht (1937) introduced the fewest components required for quantitative description and explanation. In consequence, the stationary state equation involves light intensity and concentration "with only the most necessary constants to connect them with known chemical and physical laws." But the data of visual experiments refer not to concentrations of sensitive materials but to properties of the visual system which express neural activity resulting from the transformation of visual pigments. It becomes necessary, therefore, to formulate explicitly the relation between photochemically effective light and magnitude of visual function. In the earlier formulation Hecht (1937) assumed a one-to-one relation and included it in the constant k_1 (see page 118) but although this may be satisfactory for "normal" physiological conditions of the organism, abnormal conditions such as anoxia demand a more explicit consideration of the relation.

Hecht et al. then proceed to modify the original equations by introducing a factor α which, although they do not describe it thus, may be regarded as the physiological counterpart of the filter factor. "The simplest meaning to attach to α is that of a linear conversion factor from light absorbed to number of impulses leaving the particular sense organ, or ultimately reaching the cortex."

It is then possible to consider not merely the rate of photochemical change as in the original equations but the magnitude of the neural counterpart of the photochemical change. Hecht et al. write—

$$di/dt = \alpha dx/dt = \alpha k_1 I(a - x)^m \qquad (3a)$$

as representing the rate of impulse production i during the stationary state. The stationary state equation itself becomes—

$$\alpha k_1 I/k_2 = x^n/(a - x)^m \qquad (5a)$$

Under abnormal physiological conditions, such as anoxia, the conversion factor α which is normally constant and with k_1 forms a single constant, changes even though k_1 and k_2 may remain constant. Hecht et al. assume that α must become smaller under oxygen lack so that the same chemical change $k_1 I(a - x)^m$ will now produce a smaller effect in terms of visual function because it is multiplied by a smaller α.

Taking into account the conversion factor, the original equation (6), describing the increase in photochemical change which occurs when the intensity increment ΔI is added to the field intensity I, now becomes—

$$di/dt = \alpha k_1 \Delta I(a - x)^m \qquad (17)$$

which describes the neural effectiveness of the photochemical change, ΔI will now equal $c'/\alpha k_1(a - x)^m$ and equation (9), which is the appropriate equation for cone vision becomes—

$$\Delta I/I = C\left[1 + \frac{1}{(\alpha KI)^{\frac{1}{2}}}\right]^2 \qquad (18)$$

where $C = c/a^2 k_2$.

Plotted on a double logarithmic grid, the shape of the curve of equation (18) is constant and independent of C and αK which locate its position on the ordinate and abscissa, respectively. The experimental data indicate that anoxia affects neither the shape of the curve nor its position on the ordinate so that C is unchanged. Either α or K must be altered for the curve is shifted along the intensity axis to higher intensities.

Hecht et al. consider that as the constant C is not altered by anoxia, its components are also unchanged (it would be unlikely that a change in the numerator were balanced by a similar change in the denominator). Considering next the constant K, it seems unlikely that it is altered for it equals k_1/k_2, and k_1 has the dimensions of absorption (Hecht, 1924) and does not change with temperature or oxygen (Hecht, 1924b; Bruner and Kleinau, 1936; Chase and Hagan, 1943) while, from the previous argument, it appears that k_2 is unaltered. This leaves α as the only parameter likely to be affected.

From the data it is possible to determine how the conversion factor α varies with oxygen concentration, by considering the horizontal displacement along the log I axis for different concentrations. A constant $\Delta I/I$ requires αKI to be constant (from equation 18); since anoxia shifts the curve, increasing I, α must vary inversely with the intensity increment. Assuming α has a value of 1 at sea level (i.e. under "normal" physiological conditions) its value for any other oxygen concentration can be computed from the magnitude of the log *I* shift (log α will be 0 minus the increase in log *I* for a given concentration).

The relation between oxygen concentration and the conversion factor is shown in Fig. 4.48; at low oxygen concentrations the curve is steep and flattens out as sea level values are approached. Particularly interesting is Fig. 4.49 which shows the relation between the oxygen saturation of the blood and the intensity shift of the Δ*I*/*I* curve. (The saturation values represent average arterial saturation taken from the *Handbook of Respiratory Data in Aviation* (*see* Hecht *et al.* for reference, 1946). The straight line through the points has a slope of 4 so that the conversion factor α, corresponding to the log *I* shift, varies as the fourth power of the arterial saturation. As the authors rightly point out, much more knowledge about oxygen action is required before this relation can have much meaning but it is clear that relatively slight changes in oxygen saturation produce large changes in differential threshold. The interpretation which Hecht *et al.* suggest for the shift of the intensity discrimination curve can also be applied to McFarland,

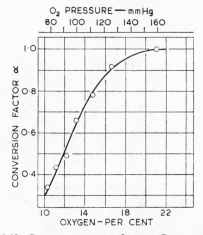

Fig. 4.48. Relation between Oxygen Concentration and the Conversion Factor α which "Translates Chemical Change into Physiological Magnitude"

The value of α is assumed unity at sea level.

(*Hecht, Hendley, Frank and Haig*, 1946)

Halperin and Niven's (1944) data and those of McFarland and Evans (1939).

Hecht *et al.* suggest that the "conversion factor" has a retinal locus, probably in the bipolar and ganglion cells. The reasons they provide for supposing that changes occur in the retina rather than the central nervous system are, first, the retina has a very high oxygen requirement, the highest rate of any tissue recorded by Warburg (1927) and, second,

"when flyers are subjected to centrifugal forces several times gravity they become temporarily blind before they become unconscious." The second of these reasons is less convincing than the first for there seems no reason why the visual cortex should not be affected before the brain centres associated with consciousness.

Available evidence indicates that Hecht *et al.* are correct in supposing that photochemical mechanisms are not involved but wrong in their emphasis on the

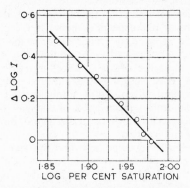

Fig. 4.49. The Relation between Oxygen Saturation of the Blood and the Intensity Shift of the Δ*I*/*I* Curve

(*Hecht, Hendley, Frank and Haig*, 1946)

exclusive role of the retina. The following considerations support a non-photochemical basis for the effect of anoxia. First, anoxia depresses sensitivity in the fully dark-adapted eye when regeneration of rhodopsin should be complete (Wald *et al.*, 1942). Second, anoxia produces an equal increase in cone and rod thresholds although different pigments are involved (McFarland and Forbes, 1941). Third, the rate of improvement in sensitivity when oxygen is reintroduced is too rapid to be explicable in terms of pigment regeneration (McFarland and Evans, 1939). Fourth, Vishinevskiy and Tsyrlin (1936) found that lowered atmospheric pressure caused a decrease in the electrical excitability of the eye as well as in its light sensitivity even though in the former case the photochemical system was by-passed.

That the retina itself may be affected, in accordance with Hecht's assumption, is shown by the results of experiments by Seitz (1940) and Seitz and Rosenthal (1941) who found that local application of strychnine to the conjunctiva counteracted the effects of anoxia on visual C.F.F. and the angioscotoma whereas no such changes occurred in the untreated eye. But evidence for the involvement of extra-retinal mechanisms comes from several sources. Clamann (1938) on the basis of limited data, suggested that central processes must participate because monocular thresholds were affected differently from binocular thresholds in his study of dark adaptation. Gellhorn and Hailman (1944) found that changes in visual C.F.F. were paralleled by typical anoxic changes in the brain, as evidenced by EEG records. The primary importance of the visual cortex is suggested by the electrophysiological observations of Noell and Chinn (1950) who found that inexcitability occurs in the visual system of the rabbit, under anoxia, in the following order: cerebral cortex, lateral geniculate bodies, retinal ganglion cells, retinal bipolar cells, and, lastly, the receptors.

In view of these considerations and the earlier criticisms of photochemical theory, the factor α can hardly be termed a conversion factor in the sense that it "converts" chemically-effective light into "impulses leaving the sense organ." A better term might be "central effectiveness" constant (cf. McFarland, Halperin and Niven, 1946), implying that it determines the central effectiveness of changes induced in the peripheral (photochemical *and* neural) mechanisms involved in reception.

The filter factor hypothesis and the above analysis also seem applicable to the effects of insulin hypoglycaemia on brightness discrimination and dark adaptation. There is, in fact, some reason to suppose that both conditions may produce their effect in the same way, by slowing the oxidative processes (McFarland *et al.*, 1946). Results of studies by Himwich and Fazekas (1937), Himwich, Frostig *et al.* (1939), Himwich, Hadidian *et al.* (1939), and many others indicate that as the blood glucose is decreased by insulin the oxygen consumption of the brain declines along with its glucose utilization. McFarland *et al.* (1946) have pointed to a strong parallelism between changes in the occipital potentials occurring during insulin hypoglycaemia and effects on visual thresholds. Brazier *et al.* (1944) found that blood-sugar levels below 70 mg per 100 ml, but not sufficiently low to impair consciousness, produced slowing of the dominant frequency and development of activity slower than alpha. The data of McFarland *et al.* (1946) show visual effects at blood-sugar levels below 65–70 m per 100 ml. High blood-sugar levels (above 130 mg per 100 ml) did not affect the EEG nor did they affect visual thresholds. Gellhorn and Kessler (1942) found, in accordance with the visual data, that the EEG changes induced by insulin hypoglycaemia could be off-set by inhaling pure oxygen. Himwich, Hadidian *et al.* (1939) found that EEG changes tended to lag behind the blood-sugar curve, a result paralleled by the occurrence of the maximum visual effect in McFarland, Halperin and Niven's experiments at a later stage than the minimum blood-sugar level. That insulin must exert its effect through central nervous metabolism rather than on the photochemical system of the eye is indicated by the lack of evidence that the breakdown of visual pigments involves glucose, as well as by the changes induced in the fully dark-adapted eye.

Data on the effects of respiratory acidosis and alkalosis on the absolute threshold (Wald *et al.*, 1942; Alpern and Hendley, 1952) may also be described in terms of the filter factor analogy, the former condition resulting in a high value of the filter factor and the latter condition in a low value. Alpern and Hendley[1] (1952) have attempted an explanation of their data at the photoreceptor level in terms of Fry and Alpern's (1946) extension of Jahn's (1946*a, b, c*) photochemical theory but other evidence suggests that changes occur central to the photoreceptors. Thus Dusser de Barenne, McCulloch and Nims (1937) showed in the cat that hyperventilation increased the pH of the cerebral cortex and simultaneously lowered its threshold for neural and electrical excitation while hypoventilation raised the threshold. Analogous results have been obtained with peripheral nerve (Lehmann, 1937).

Other data to which the filter factor analogy seems applicable include those from experiments on the effects of various pathological conditions (summarized by Mandelbaum, 1941), brain lesions, alcohol and, possibly, psychiatric disorders on the visual threshold and dark adaptation. In all these cases the psychophysical effect is the same and consists of an upward displacement of the adaptation curve along the intensity axis, although different physiological mechanisms may be involved. What these are can only be decided by further experiment. In the case of alcohol the mechanisms may be similar to those involved in anoxia, for there is some evidence that alcoholism is a form of anoxia (histotoxic) and that the tissue cells are poisoned in such a manner that they cannot use oxygen properly. Similar mechanisms may also be involved in the case of certain psychiatric disorders, such as schizophrenia in which oxygen deficiency has been reported from time to time (cf. McFarland, 1952) but the evidence for either raised visual thresholds or impaired oxidation in schizophrenia is far from satisfactory.

Although the analogy of the filter factor seems applicable to the effects of several different types of abnormal conditions, as well as to normal variation (e.g. Pirenne *et al.*, 1957; Hecht, Haig and Chase, 1937) its precise scope is difficult to determine in certain cases owing to lack of experimental data covering a sufficiently wide range of stimulus intensities. This is true of studies on the effects of certain physiological stresses and drugs on C.F.F. The data in Seitz's (1940) study of anoxia, for instance, are too limited to decide whether anoxia causes a shift in the F-log I curve along the intensity axis or along both

---

[1] Changes in the ERG during hyperventilation have been reported by Dodt (1951*b*) and Alpern *et al.* (1955).

axes. The upward displacement along the intensity axis of the entire dark adaptation curve by alcohol suggests that this drug may affect the F-log I curve in the same way. Goldberg (1943) has in fact described its effect in terms of the filter analogy but the experimental data are not sufficiently extensive to demonstrate this. More psychophysical data seem particularly desirable in the case of this drug for it has the interesting property of selectively blocking inhibition in the eye. Bernhard and Skoglund (1941) demonstrated this on the negative PIII component of the ERG and the "off" response from the frog's eye and suggested that this might be the mechanism underlying the drug's depressant action on sensory C.F.F. Bernhard (1941) found that the practically pure negative response of the cone eye of the tortoise (*Testudo graeca*) was also suppressed by alcohol and later studies by MacNichol and Benolken (1956) have shown that alcohol causes a blocking effect on inhibitory synapses in the lateral eye of *Limulus*. A further study which bears on the interpretation of C.F.F. changes is that of Svaetichin (1956) who found that a drop of diluted ethyl alcohol instilled into the fish retina lengthened the rise and decay times of the cone action potential. In spite of these results there is no reason to suppose that the effects of alcohol are exclusively on the retina. In fact the drug's depressant action on the absolute threshold during dark adaptation suggests that more central mechanisms may be affected for on the basis of Bernhard and Skoglund's results one might expect alcohol to lower the absolute threshold. The changes induced in the ERG by alcohol were essentially similar to those produced by dark adaptation. The depressant action of the drug at different levels might account for some of the discrepant findings reported in the literature.

Data which seem unlikely to be capable of description in terms of the filter factor analogy are those of Alpern and Hendley (1952)[1] on the effects of hyperventilation on C.F.F. for their curves suggest a "change in maximum discriminatory ability, rather than a shift to a higher or lower light level," even though they are based on very few experimental points. In spite of the limitations of the filter factor analogy it is interesting to note that neither anoxia nor hyperventilation affects the shape of the curve relating C.F.F. to intensity; only the dimensional constants appear to be changed. Taking into account the physiological data on the peripheral determination of dark adaptation and the curves showing the relation between the various differential thresholds and illumination the following generalization is suggested.

[1] The recent measurements of Granger and Ikeda (1959*a*) certainly cannot be explained in terms of a simple filter factor hypothesis.

Physiological stresses, drugs and other abnormal conditions do not affect the basic S-R relations through the receptor systems but merely alter the extraneous constants of those relations (cf. earlier discussion of the effects of area, page 127). Although visual thresholds (absolute and differential) are sensitive to various kinds of "physiological imbalance," functions such as dark adaptation and the improvement in discrimination which occurs when the illumination is increased, appear to be highly resistant to such changes. For instance, although under conditions of anoxia a threefold increase in the visual threshold can occur, the course of dark adaptation remains unaffected. The magnitude of the change induced by such a severe physiological stress, which is probably close to the limits of variation that can be expected from changes occurring in the central nervous system, is negligible in relation to the range of intensities covered in a typical dark adaptation experiment $(1:10^6)$ or the total range of intensities over which the eye can function $(1:10^{15})$.

However, even though the effects of anoxia and (what sensory physiologists are apt to call) other "special" conditions (cf. Wald, 1954) such as acidosis and alkalosis, are of only secondary importance to a physiology of the special senses concerned to explain the shape of dark adaptation curves or the relation between the incremental threshold and field intensity, the fact remains that fluctuations in visual thresholds can be induced by changes occurring in neural structures in the retina and central nervous system. Measurement and analysis of this variation by psychophysical and physiological methods is obviously necessary for a complete understanding of the visual process.

Analysis of threshold variation is important also from a broader viewpoint than that of Visual Physiology for, as Gellhorn has pointed out, the "sense organs (including the visual system) represent natural avenues of approach to the central nervous system" (Gellhorn, 1942). It was from this point of view that Cajal (1894) made his histological studies of the retina and Granit (1947) studied retinal physiology. The investigations of the effects of physiological stresses reviewed in this chapter have shown how psychophysical experiments on visual thresholds can reveal some of the fundamental metabolic characteristics of the central nervous system (cf. Gellhorn, 1942).

One of the chief reasons for the significance of visual threshold measurements arises from their sensitivity. Whereas it was formerly supposed that oxygen deprivation caused impairment only at high altitudes, visual thresholds revealed marked changes under relatively minor degrees of anoxia. In this respect they are more sensitive than tests of other sensory functions such as audition and some of the "higher" mental functions (McFarland, 1952). The further advantages of visual thresholds over other forms of psychophysiological test, which were pointed out by McFarland, Halperin and Niven (1944), are their independence of the effects of masking due to the subject's exerting additional effort, and their stability during control experiments when the physiological stresses are not applied and the precision with which the physical measurements can be made. Taking into account the results of their experiments on the absolute threshold Wald et al. (1942) considered that its advantage over other types of physiological measurement was that "it provides an index of net change in the central nervous system, usually the first to fail in physiological stress" (1942, p. 901).

V. IMPLICATIONS FOR OTHER ABNORMAL CONDITIONS

As one approach to the investigation of C.N.S. excitability and stresses involving the central nervous system, the measurement of visual functions already has a wide field of applications in medicine, as the clinical studies reviewed in this chapter have clearly shown. Significant changes in visual thresholds have been observed in metabolic disorders, diseases of the respiratory system, diseases of the blood, endocrine disorders, various intoxications, and disorders of the nervous system. Even though actual data are in certain cases available for only a few specific disorders in each of these areas, these data considered in relation to the studies of physiological stresses and drugs have implications for a variety of other pathological conditions. Changes in visual thresholds similar to those occurring in the experiments on anoxia would, for instance, be expected in a number of clinical disorders in which anoxia occurs in one of its several different forms. Any condition which results in mechanical interference with oxygen absorption, such as pneumonia, pulmonary oedema, pulmonary congestion, bronchial asthma and acute bronchitis, might produce measurable changes consequent to anoxic anoxia. Similarly the depression of visual sensitivity observed in anaemia would be expected to occur also in other conditions which lead to a diminution in the oxygen capacity of arterial blood due to a reduction in the amount of functioning haemoglobin. The decrease in C.F.F. found in circulatory failure associated with decompensated heart disease (Enzer, Simonson and Blankstein, 1942) might also be predicted to occur in conditions associated with vagoplastic phenomena such as Raynaud's disease, due to circulatory insufficiency and consequent "stagnant anoxia." Finally, any condition interfering with oxygen utilization by the tissues due to the poisoning of the tissue cells would be expected to have visual effects similar in part to those of alcohol.

The studies of insulin hypoglycaemia also have implications for various pathological conditions in which hypoglycaemia occurs, such as hepatic disease, adrenal cortical insufficiency, anterior pituitary insufficiency, various disorders of the central nervous system and miscellaneous conditions accompanied by severe grades of undernutrition, such as anorexia nervosa. Studies of hyperventilation have implications for many clinical conditions in which respiratory alkalosis occurs such as certain cases of encephalitis manifesting hyperpnoea over prolonged periods of time, fever (where hyperventilation can occur as a result of increased respiratory rate) and, possibly, hysteria, while the studies of respiratory acidosis have implications for clinical conditions in which the elimination of CO_2 through the lungs is retarded, as in pulmonary fibrosis. Even the very limited data on dehydration may have implications for conditions in which excessive loss of one or more of the body secretions or excretions occurs. Effects of these various stresses are not of course independent of one another, dehydration leading to a change in acid-base balance, etc.

Obvious implications for the study of psychotic and neurotic disorders (conditions of special interest to the practising clinical psychologist) arise from the experiments on stresses and drugs although these are clearer for the psychoses associated with metabolic, cardiovascular and endocrine disorders and intoxications than for the so-called "functional" psychoses and neuroses. Deviations from normal threshold values might be expected to occur in a wide variety of psychiatric patients suffering from functional disorders, in schizophrenics showing signs of oxygen deficiency (McFarland, 1952), in neurotics or psychotics with very high or very low "sedation thresholds" (Shagass and Naiman, 1955, 1956), in the so-called "cardiac" neuroses, and in "aeroneuroses" with symptoms of fatigue and exhaustion (Armstrong, 1936; Krugman, 1947), in severe anxiety attacks associated with the liberation of adrenalin into the blood stream (cf. studies of sympathomimetic drugs, page 133), and numerous other conditions. Available physiological and biochemical data do not, however, allow specific predictions to be made about all patients classified by psychiatrists into the general categories of schizophrenia, hysteria, anxiety state, etc., owing to the heterogeneity of physiological reactions within these groups.

Although there can be no doubt that the measurement of visual functions has a wide field of potential applications in psychiatry, neurology and other branches of medicine the fact that threshold variations are not specifically related to any particular abnormal condition means that in clinical applications "caution in the interpretation of results is necessary and, as a rule, additional information obtained by independent methods is desirable for more specific correlations" (Simonson and Brozek, 1952). To this cautionary note may be added the further requirement that experimental conditions in clinical research must be specified and controlled as carefully as is customary in Visual Psychophysics if data are to be reproducible and have unambiguous meaning in sensory terms. The need for precise controls is particularly important for the magnitude of the threshold changes induced by variations in the state of the central nervous system seem likely in many cases to be small in relation to other sources of variation.

The formidable array of requirements which sensory psychologists and physiologists consider must be met before psychophysical functions can be properly measured may seem to some clinical psychologists to introduce unnecessary complications into testing procedures. In fact, they serve to simplify description and analysis, as Mandelbaum has pointed out in a discussion of Hecht's rather elaborate "fixation-and flash" method for measuring dark adaptation: "One of the first principles in investigation is to isolate carefully the phenomenon being studied in order to remove as many extraneous influences as possible. If this procedure can be followed the results obtained are physiologically simple, for they describe the isolated phenomenon and are most readily capable of simple physiologic interpretation. However, simplicity in procedure—in this case inadequacy in the apparatus used and failure to meet the specifications to be outlined—can produce only the opposite effect. The no longer relatively isolated phenomenon of dark adaptation is obscured in a maze of complexities brought on by inadequate retinal fixation, altering color temperatures of the test light and many other uncontrolled factors" (Mandelbaum, 1941, p. 204). It is for this reason that those data on vitamin A deficiency and dark adaptation which have been obtained from "simple" and "rapid" tests have proved to be so unreliable and led to so much confusion regarding their interpretation.

VI. IMPLICATIONS FOR OTHER PERCEPTUAL FUNCTIONS AND CONCLUDING REMARKS

Having considered some of the implications of research on physiological stresses for other abnormal conditions, this final section will deal briefly with implications for other perceptual functions and with a few concluding remarks concerning further research. That severe physiological stresses such as anoxia and insulin hypoglycaemia and drugs such as alcohol and the barbiturates are likely to have a general depressant action on a wide range of functions is already clear from psychological and physiological research. What is not clear is precisely how and under what conditions other functions will be affected. Implications seem most obvious for anoxia and insulin hypoglycaemia for in both cases their effects can be described fairly satisfactorily in terms of the filter factor hypothesis. If this hypothesis is valid, it should be possible to make predictions about other perceptual functions which are known to be dependent on intensity of illumination.

Considering first other functions at what is traditionally regarded as the sensory level, anoxia and insulin hypoglycaemia might, for instance, be expected to cause changes in various spatial and temporal induction effects.[1] Limited data of McFarland,

Hurvich and Halperin (1943) suggest that the filter factor hypothesis may apply to the effects of anoxia on certain after-image phenomena. Following earlier research in which an inverse relationship[1] was found between the latency of the "tertiary" or Hess after-image and stimulus intensity, these authors found that the curve relating after-image latency to the intensity of retinal illumination was shifted along the horizontal (intensity) axis to higher intensities. The extent of this displacement appeared to be of the same order as in the case of the curves relating foveal visual acuity and brightness discrimination to illumination but their data are not sufficiently precise to decide whether the translation involves a slight vertical as well as an horizontal component. No experimental data are available on spatial induction but from electrophysiological and psychophysical data which suggest that simultaneous contrast is a function of intensity of illuminance (Wilcox, 1932; Barlow, 1953) one would expect a reduction in contrast effects following anoxia at certain lower levels of illumination.

Extending the hypothesis to more complex functions traditionally considered under the heading of Visual Perception (more specifically, Visual Space Perception), displacements would be expected to occur in the curves relating thresholds for monocular movement parallax (Graham, Baker, Hecht and Lloyd,

[1] The influence of one part of the retina on another is described as *spatial induction;* by *temporal induction* is meant the effect of a primary stimulus on the response of the retina to a succeeding stimulus" (Davson, *The Physiology of the Eye,* p. 88, 1950). Used in its broadest sense (Parsons, 1927) the term induction would cover the phenomena of adaptation and critical flicker frequency considered earlier in this chapter as aspects of discrimination.

[1] The general form of the function is curvilinear, latency decreases as intensity is increased, rapidly at first, then more gradually.

1948), and thresholds for stereoscopic vision (Mueller and Lloyd, 1948) to intensity. These few examples should be sufficient to give some idea of the possible scope of the hypothesis at different levels of visual functioning.

That the filter factor notion should apply to a number of different visual functions is not surprising when one considers that intensity of illumination is a fundamental stimulus variable in tasks making demands on visual discrimination. As the classical experiments on intensity discrimination, visual acuity and C.F.F. have shown, increasing the intensity of illumination has the effect of increasing the spatial and temporal discriminative ability of the visual system. Precise predictions about the extent of the effect for a given degree of oxygen deprivation and level of illumination could, of course, only be made in cases where the psychophysical functions themselves have been accurately defined over a wide range of stimulus intensities. This has been done for acuity, intensity discrimination and C.F.F., but only to a very limited extent for other aspects of perceptual discrimination. As Holway and Boring (1941) have so aptly remarked in another connexion, systematically determined functional relations are "wanted and wanting"; until they have been established, quantitative research on the effects of various abnormal conditions will be severely restricted in scope. From the limited data available one would expect many forms of visual discrimination to be greatly impaired under moderate degrees of anoxia at the lower levels of illumination whereas at the higher levels the effect would be negligible.

While the data reviewed in this chapter encourage application of the filter factor hypothesis to other visual functions it is already clear that changes in certain functions cannot be due solely to a reduction in the effective intensity of illumination. Thus, McFarland, Hurvich and Halperin (1943) found that administering oxygen for periods known to cause an increase in the apparent brightness of the visual field did not result in a recovery in after-image latency in subjects who had been exposed to low oxygen tensions. This suggested to them that other factors directly concerned with the velocity of the processes underlying the "eventuation" of the after-image are affected. Certain kinds of test-object used in experiments on acuity and anoxia have also revealed apparent discrepancies (Berger *et al.*, 1943) from a simple filter factor hypothesis.

These discrepancies, the apparent inability of the filter factor hypothesis to account for the effect of respiratory acidosis on C.F.F., the conflicting results of drug studies, the lack of well-established functional relationships in other areas of perception, and the paucity of knowledge concerning interrelations

between different sensory modalities make it premature to generalize very far beyond the rather narrowly-circumscribed area of visual discrimination. The immediate need is obviously for more extensive and, in certain cases (e.g. after-images and C.F.F.), more precise psychophysical data to specify the nature and extent of the effects of anoxia and other abnormal conditions. Having determined the psychophysical parameters which are affected, an attempt can then be made to determine the underlying physiological mechanisms.

Even when the psychophysical effect of different abnormal conditions appears to be the same, as in the case of the depressant action of anoxia, insulin hypoglycaemia, alcohol and the barbiturates, it cannot, of course, be assumed that the same physiological mechanisms are involved. Available data suggest that the mechanisms involved in anoxia and insulin hypoglycaemia may be similar. Both stresses are known to depress cerebral metabolism (Himwich, 1951) and the nature of the neurological changes as well as the order in which they occur, appear to be strikingly similar, but anoxia progresses on a much faster time-scale (Alexander and Himwich, 1939). In contrast to these stresses, the depressant action of alcohol on visual thresholds is probably mediated to only a very small extent by metabolic inhibition while the barbiturate group of drugs seems to exert its effect chiefly through direct interference with nervous activity by elevating the "synaptic threshold" and prolonging recovery time (Toman and Davis, 1949).[1] As Elliott, Page and Quastel have pointed out elsewhere, there is no reason to expect a common mode of action of central depressants "since there must be as many different ways of blocking central nervous activity as there are independent physiological parameters necessary for the normal maintenance of function in the central nervous system" (Elliott, Page and Quastel, 1955, pp. 516–517).

By integrating physiological research with psychophysical experimentation of a more analytic nature than has hitherto been carried out, it should be possible to obtain considerable insight into the finer mechanism of action of stresses and drugs, resolve some of the apparent discrepancies in the experimental data and provide information of great value to visual theory. Greater attention to the details of experimental conditions in dark adaptation studies and systematic variation of area/duration relationships of the test-field may, for instance, help to resolve some of the conflicting findings on drug effects and, at the same time, help to clarify the nature of the changes

---

[1] In view of recent research on centrifugal control of the sense organs (Granit, 1955), the barbiturates are a particularly interesting group of drugs owing to their marked effect on the reticular activating system (Goodman and Gilman, 1955).

in neural interaction which are supposed to occur during dark adaptation (Rushton, 1952). (Mandelbaum's (1941) entirely negative findings may have been partly dependent upon his particular choice of experimental conditions, in respect of stimulus size and duration (*see* page 141).)

The concluding remarks to this chapter must be essentially similar to those made earlier by Graham (1951) in his review of visual perception. The most pressing need in this field is for more experiments along the lines of those by Hecht, Wald, and McFarland and their associates, planned against a psychophysical and physiological background and designed to reveal functional relations. Only when more analytic data covering a wide range of values of relevant variables have been accumulated will it be possible to make really useful practical contributions to the solution of clinical problems or provide an adequate basis for the development of theory.

While it is perhaps too early to make pronouncements about the kind of theory which is most likely to advance our knowledge in this field, it would seem that to be useful a theory must make explicit the general relations implied in Graham's equation given on page 108. Theories of reception which deal with peripheral events and limiting conditions in the visual process provide an obvious starting point for further experimental and theoretical development but these and similar theories for other sensory modalities need to be supplemented by physiological and behaviour theories which can describe more central processes and conditions of the organism. Theories of the latter type and the experimental data which they describe will eventually provide a broader basis for sense organ theories by making explicit factors which are assumed to be secondary or constant in theoretical derivations for the receptor process. But for the present and probably for some time to come it seems that research will have to be guided by theories of the first type and, where these prove inadequate, by any relevant generalizations which have been formulated in psychophysics and sensory physiology for useful theories of the second type do not exist. Building upon the solid foundations laid by these two disciplines seems the surest way of advancing the psychophysiology of perceptual abnormalities toward scientific respectability and practical usefulness.

REFERENCES

ADAMS, D., Dark adaptation (a review of the literature), *M. R. C. Spec. Rep.* Ser. No. 127 (London, H.M.S.O., 1929).

ADRIAN, E. D., *The Basis of Sensation* (London, Christophers, 1928).

ADRIAN, E. D., The nervous reactions of the retina, *Trans. Illum. Engng Soc. Lond.*, **18**, 105–112 (1953).

AKERLUND, E., A study in acute head injuries examined with flicker-fusion determined under the influence of Evipan, *Acta chir. scand.*, Suppl. 174, (1953).

ALEXANDER, F. A. D. and HIMWICH, H. E., Nitrogen inhalation therapy for schizophrenia, *Amer. J. Psychiat.*, **96**, 643–655 (1939–40).

ALLEN, F., Some phenomena of the persistence of vision, *Phys. Rev.*, **28**, 45–56 (1909).

ALLEN, F., The persistence of vision of colours of varying intensity, *Phil. Mag.*, **38**, 81–89 (1919).

ALLEN, F., The variation of visual sensory reflex action with intensity of illumination, *J. Opt. Soc. Amer.*, **13**, 383–430 (1926).

ALPERN, M., Metacontrast, *J. Opt. Soc. Amer.*, **43**, 648–657 (1953).

ALPERN, M., FARIS, J., ESKILDSEN, P. and GARNETT, P., Effect of hyperventilation on the human electroretinogram, *Science*, **121**, 101–102 (1955).

ALPERN, M. and HENDLEY, C. D., Visual functions as indices of physiological changes in the acid-base balance of the blood, *Amer. J. Optom. and Arch. Amer. Acad. Optom.*, Monogr. 139 (1952).

ALPERN, M. and SPENCER, R. W., Variation of critical flicker frequency in the nasal visual field, *A.M.A. Arch. Ophthal.*, **50**, 50–63 (1953).

ARDEN, G. B. and WEALE, R. A., Nervous mechanisms and dark adaptation, *J. Physiol.*, **125**, 417–426 (1954).

ARMSTRONG, H. G., A special form of functional psychoneurosis, *J. Amer. Med. Ass.*, **106**, 1,347–1,354 (1936).

ASHER, H., Contrast in eye and brain, *Brit. J. Psychol.*, **40**, 187–194 (1950).

AUBERT, H., *Physiologie der Netzhaut* (Breslau, E. Morgenstern, 1865).

BABSKII, E. B., The significance of the sympathetic nervous system in regulation of the excitability of the visual analyser, *Probl. physiol. Opt. Leningr.*, **4**, 17–30 (1947).

BABSKII, E. B. and SKULOW, D. R., The effect of sympathectomy on visual adaptation to darkness, *Bull. Biol. Med. exp. URSS*, **18**, 7–8, 59–61 (1944).

BAGBY, E., The psychological effects of oxygen deprivation, *J. Comp. Psychol.*, **1**, 97 (1921).

BAKER, C. A., DEBONS, A. and MORRIS, D. F., Dark adaptation as a function of the intensity and distribution of light across the preadaptation field, *J. Opt. Soc. Amer.*, **46**, 401–404 (1956).

BARLOW, H. B., Excitation and inhibition in the frog's retina, *J. Physiol.*, **119**, 69–88 (1953).

BARLOW, H. B., Intrinsic noise of cones. Paper No. 28, 8th N.P.L. Symposium, *Visual Problems of Colour* (London, H.M.S.O., 1957).

BARLOW, H. B., FITZHUGH, R. and KUFFLER, S. W., Change of organization in the receptive fields of the cat's eye during dark adaptation, *J. Physiol.*, **137**, 338–354 (1957).

BARTLETT, N. R., The discrimination of two simultaneously presented brightnesses, *J. Exp. Psychol.*, **31**, 380–392 (1942).

BARTLETT, N. R. and HUDSON, G. H., Theory of the effects of light intensity and duration in determining visual responses, *Proc. Nat. Acad. Sci. Wash.*, **28**, 289–292 (1942).

BARTLEY, S. H., The neural determination of critical flicker frequency, *J. Exp. Psychol.*, **21**, 678–686 (1937).

BARTLEY, S. H., Some factors in brightness discrimination, *Psychol. Rev.*, **46**, 337–358 (1939).

BARTLEY, S. H., *Vision: a Study of its Basis* (New York, Van Nostrand, 1941).

BARTLEY, S. H., The psychophysiology of vision, in *Handbook of Experimental Psychology*, Ed. S. S. Stevens, 921–984 (New York, John Wiley & Sons, Inc., 1951.)

BATTERSBY, W. S., The regional gradient of critical flicker frequency after frontal or occipital lobe injury, *J. Exp. Psychol.*, **42**, 59–68 (1951).

BATTERSBY, W. S., BENDER, M. B. and TEUBER, H. L., Effect of total light flux on critical flicker frequency after frontal lobe lesions, *J. Exp. Psychol.*, **42**, 135–142 (1951).

BAUMGARDT, E. L. M., The quantic and statistical bases of the visual excitation, *J. Gen. Physiol.*, **31**, 269–290 (1948).

BAUMGARDT, E. L. M., *Les théories photochimiques classiques et quantiques de la vision et l'inhibition nerveuse en vision liminaire* (Paris, éditions de la Revue d'optique, 1950).

BENDER, M. B. and KRIEGER, H. P., Visual functions in perimetrically blind fields, *A. M. A. Arch. Neurol. Psychiat.*, **65**, 72–79 (1951).

BERG, O., A study of the effect of Evipan on the flicker fusion intensity in brain injuries, *Acta psychiat., Kbh.*, Suppl. 58, 1–116 (1949).

BERGER, C. and BOJE, O., Über den Einfluss von Sauerstoffmangel auf das Auflösungsvermögen des emmetropen Auges, *Skand. Arch. Physiol.*, **77**, 129–138 (1937).

BERGER, C., McFARLAND, R. A., HALPERIN, M. H. and NIVEN, J. I. The effect of anoxia on visual resolving power, *Amer. J. Psychol.*, **56**, 385–407 (1943).

BERNHARD, C. G., Contributions to the neurophysiology of the optic pathway, *Acta physiol. scand.*, **1**, (Suppl. 1), 1–94 (1940).

BERNHARD, C. G., Unpublished observation. Referred to in Bernhard, C. G. and Skoglund, C. R., *Acta physiol. scand.*, **2**, 10–21 (1941).

BERNHARD, C. G. and SKOGLUND, C. R., Selective suppression with ethyl alcohol of inhibition in the optic nerve and of the negative component PIII of the electroretinogram, *Acta physiol. scand.*, **2**, 10–21 (1941).

BEST, W., Die Abhängigkeit der Flimmerfrequenz von der Reizflächengrösse und dem Ort der gereitzten Netzhautstelle unter besonderer Berücksichtigung der Schwellenreizlichtstärke, *v. Graefes Arch. Ophth.*, **152**, 99–110 (1951).

BIESHEUVEL, S., The measurement of the threshold for flicker and its value as a perseveration test, *Brit. J. Psychol.*, **29**, 27–38 (1938).

BIRREN, J. E., FISHER, M. B., VOLLMER, E. and KING, B. G., Effects of anoxia on performance at several simulated altitudes, *J. Exp. Psychol.*, **36**, 35–49 (1946).

BIRREN, J. E. and SHOCK, N. W., Age changes in rate and level of visual dark adaptation, *J. Appl. Physiol.*, **2**, 407–411 (1950).

BLAKE, R. R. and RAMSEY, G. V. (Eds.), *Perception: an Approach to Personality* (New York, Ronald Press, 1951).

BLANCHARD, J., The brightness sensibility of the retina, *Phys. Rev.*, **11**, 81 (1918).

BLISS, A. F., The absorption spectra of visual purple of the squid and its bleaching products, *J. Biol. Chem.*, **176**, 563–569 (1948).

BLOMBERG, LARS, H., Clinical studies of nystagmus produced by Evipan, *Acta Psychiat. Neurol. Scand.*, Suppl. 97 (1955).

BOUMAN, M. A. and TEN DOESSCHATE, J., Nervous and photochemical components in visual adaptation, *Ophthalmologica, Basel*, **126**, 222–230 (1953).

BOUMAN, M. A. and VAN DER VELDEN, H. A., The two-quanta explanation of the dependence of the threshold values and visual acuity on the visual angle and the time of observation, *J. Opt. Soc. Amer.*, **37**, 908–919 (1947).

BRAUNSTEIN, E. P., Beitrage zur Lehre des intermittierenden Lichtreizes der gesunden und kranken Retina, *Z. Psychol.*, **33**, 171–206, 241–288 (1903).

BRAZIER, M. A. B., FINESINGER, J. E. and SCHWAB, R. S., Characteristics of normal electroencephalogram; effect of varying blood sugar levels on occipital cortical potentials in adults during quiet breathing, *J. Clin. Invest.*, **23**, 313–317 (1944).

BRINDLEY, G. S., Responses to illumination recorded by microelectrodes from the frog's retina, *J. Physiol.*, **134**, 360–384 (1956).

BROOKE, R. T., The variation of critical flicker frequency with brightness and various retinal locations, *J. Opt. Soc. Amer.*, **41**, 1,010–1,016 (1951).

BROWN, J. L., Effect of different pre-adapting luminances on the resolution of visual detail during dark adaptation, *J. Opt. Soc. Amer.*, **44**, 48–55 (1954).

BROWN, J. L., GRAHAM, C. H., LEIBOWITZ, H. and RANKEN, H. B., Luminance thresholds for the resolution of visual detail during dark adaptation, *J. Opt. Soc. Amer.*, **43**, 197–202 (1953).

BROWN, R. H., Spatial effects in human visual resolution, *J. Gen. Psychol.*, **35**, 77–86 (1946).

BROZEK, J. and KEYS, A., Changes in flicker-fusion frequency with age, *J. Cons. Psychol.*, **9**, 87–90 (1945).

BRUNER, J. S. and KRECH, D. (Eds.), *Perception and Personality* (Durham, N. C., Duke Univ. Press, 1949).

BRUNER, O. and KLEINAU, W., Zur Kenntnis des Sehpurpurs II. Über den Reaktionsmechanismus des Lichtbleichungsvorganges, *S. B. Akad. Wiss., Wien. Math.-naturwiss.*, **145**, Abt. IIb, 464 (1936).

BUDDENBROOK, W. von, *Grundriss der vergleichenden Physiologie* 2nd. ed., (Berlin, 1937).

BUHLER, R. A., Flicker fusion threshold and anxiety level, *Ph.D. Dissertation, Columbia Univ.*, (1954).

BUNGE, E., Verlauf der Dunkeladaptation bei Sauerstoffmangel, *Arch. Augenheilk.*, **110**, 189–197 (1936).

BYRAM, G. M., The physical and photochemical basis of visual resolving power. Part I: The distribution of illumination in retinal images, *J. Opt. Soc. Amer.*, **34**, 571–591 (1944a).

BYRAM, G. M., The physical and photochemical basis of visual resolving power. Part II; Visual acuity and the photo-chemistry of the retina, *J. Opt. Soc. Amer.*, **34**, 718–738 (1944b).

CHASE, A. M. and HAGAN, W. H., The photochemical and thermal reactions of visual purple in absence of oxygen, *J. Cell. Comp. Physiol.*, **21**, 65–76 (1943).

CLAMANN, H. G., Die Dunkeladaptation des Auges bei Sauerstoffmangel, *Luftahrtmed.*, **2**, 223–225 (1938).

CLARK, L. B., The visual acuity of the fiddlercrab, *Uca pugnax*, *J. Gen. Physiol.*, **19**, 311–321 (1935).

COBB, P. W., The dependence of flicker on the dark-light ratio of the stimulus cycle, *J. Opt. Soc. Amer.*, **24**, 107–113 (1934).

CRAIK, K. J. W. and VERNON, M. D., The nature of dark adaptation, *Brit. J. Psychol.*, **32**, 62–81 (1941).

CRAIK, K. J. W. and VERNON, M. D., Perception during dark adaptation, *Brit. J. Psychol.*, **32**, 206–230 (1942).

CRAWFORD, B. H., Ocular interaction in its relation to measurements of brightness threshold, *Proc. Roy. Soc.*, **128B**, 552–559 (1940).

CRAWFORD, B. H., Photochemical laws and visual phenomena, *Proc. Roy. Soc.*, **133B**, 63–75 (1946).

CREED, R. S. and GRANIT, R., Observations on the retinal action potential with especial reference to the response to intermittent stimulation, *J. Physiol.*, **78**, 419–440 (1933).

CREED, R. S. and RUCH, T. C., Regional variations in sensitivity to flicker, *J. Physiol.*, **74**, 407–423 (1932).

CROZIER, W. J., On the law for minimal discrimination of intensities. IV. ΔI as a function of intensity, *Proc. Nat. Acad. Sci. Wash.*, **26**, 382–389 (1940).

CROZIER, W. J. and HOLWAY, A. H., Theory and measurement of visual mechanisms. I. A visual discriminometer. II. Threshold stimulus intensity and retinal position, *J. Gen. Physiol.*, **22**, 341–364 (1939a).

CROZIER, W. J. and HOLWAY, A. H., Theory and measurement of visual mechanisms. III. ΔI as a function of area, intensity and wavelength for monocular and binocular stimulation, *J. Gen. Physiol.*, **23**, 101–141 (1939b).

CROZIER, W. J. and WOLF, E., The flicker response contour for the gecko (rod retina), *J. Gen. Physiol.*, **22**, 555–566 (1939).

CROZIER, W. J., and WOLF, E., Temperature and critical illumination for reaction to flickering light. VI. Flash duration period, *J. Gen. Physiol.*, **23**, 531–551 (1940).

CROZIER, W. J. and WOLF, E., Theory and measurement of visual mechanisms. IV. Critical intensities for visual flicker, monocular and binocular, *J. Gen. Physiol.*, **24**, 505–534 (1941a).

CROZIER, W. J. and WOLF, E., Theory and measurement of visual mechanisms. V. Flash duration and critical intensity for response to flicker, *J. Gen. Physiol.*, **24**, 635–654 (1941b).

CROZIER, W. J. and WOLF, E., Theory and measurement of visual mechanisms. VI. Wave length and flash duration in flicker, *J. Gen. Physiol.*, **25**, 89–110 (1941c).

CROZIER, W. J. and WOLF, E., Theory and measurement of visual mechanisms. IX. Flicker relations within the fovea, *J. Gen. Physiol.*, **27**, 119–138 (1943).

CROZIER, W. J. and WOLF, E., Theory and measurement of visual mechanisms. XII. On visual duplexity, *J. Gen. Physiol.*, **27**, 513–538 (1944).

CROZIER, W. J., WOLF, E. and ZERRAHN-WOLF, G., Temperature and critical illumination for reaction to flickering light. I. *Anax* larvae, *J. Gen. Physiol.*, **20**, 393–410 (1937a).

CROZIER, W. J., WOLF, E. and ZERRAHN-WOLF, G., Intensity and critical frequency for visual flicker, *J. Gen. Physiol.*, **21**, 203–221 (1937b).

CROZIER, W. J., WOLF, E. and ZERRAHN-WOLF, G.,

Critical illumination and flicker frequency, as a function of flash duration for the sunfish, *J. Gen. Physiol.*, **21**, 313–334 (1938a).

CROZIER, W. J., WOLF, E. and ZERRAHN-WOLF, E., Critical intensity and flash duration for response to flicker; with *Anax* larvae, *J. Gen. Physiol.*, **21**, 463–474 (1938b).

CROZIER, W. J., WOLF, E. and ZERRAHN-WOLF, E., The flicker response function for the turtle *Pseudemys*, *J. Gen. Physiol.*, **22**, 311–340 (1939a).

CROZIER, W. J., WOLF, E. and ZERRAHN-WOLF, G., The flicker response contour for the isopod *Asellus*, *J. Gen. Physiol.*, **22**, 451–462 (1939b).

DAUTREBAND, L., L'air alvéolaire obtend par la méthode Haldane-Priestley est l'air alvéolaire vrai, *C. R. Soc. Biol.*, **94**, 129 (1926).

DAVENPORT, H. W., *The A.B.C. of Acid-base Chemistry* (Chicago, Chicago Univ. Press, 1950).

DAVSON, H., *The Physiology of the Eye* (London, Churchill, 1950).

DIETER, W., Untersuchungen zur Duplizitätstheorie. III. Die angelborene, familiärerbliche, stationäre (idiopathische) Hemeralopie, *Pflüg. Arch. ges. Physiol.*, **222**, 381–394 (1929).

DITTLER, R. and KOIKE, I., Über die Adaptationsfähigkeit der Fovea centralis, *Z. Sinnesphysiol.*, **46**, 166–178 (1912).

DODT, E., Cone electroretinography by flicker, *Nature*, **168**, 738 (1951a).

DODT, E., Elektroretinographische Untersuchungen zur Analyse des Flimmerphänomens ein menschlichen Auge. *Z. d. Ophth. ges.*, **57**, 242–245 (1951b).

DOWLING, J. E. and WALD, G., Nutritional night blindness, *Ann. N.Y. Acad. Sci.*, **74**, 256–265 (1958).

DUSSER DE BARENNE, J. G., McCULLOCH, W. S. and NIMS, L. F., Functional activity and pH of the cerebral cortex, *J. Cell. Comp. Physiol.*, **10**, 277–289 (1937).

ELLIOTT, K. A. C., PAGE, I. H. and QUASTEL, J. H., *Neurochemistry* (Springfield, C. C. Thomas, 1955).

ELSBERG, C. A. and SPOTNITZ, H., The neural components of light and dark adaptation and their significance for the duration of the foveal dark adaptation process, *Bull. Neurol. Inst. N. Y.*, **7**, 148–159 (1938).

ENROTH, C., The mechanism of flicker and fusion studied in single retinal elements in the dark-adapted eye of the cat, *Acta physiol. scand.*, **27**, Suppl. 100 (1952).

ENROTH, C., Spike frequency and flicker fusion frequency in retinal ganglion cells, *Acta physiol. scand.*, **29**, 19–21 (1953).

ENZER, N., SIMONSON, E. and BALLARD, G., Effect of small doses of alcohol on the central nervous system, *Amer. J. clin. Path.* **14**, 333–341 (1944).

ENZER, N., SIMONSON, E. and BLANKSTEIN, S. S., State of sensory and motor centers in patients with circulatory insufficiency and in patients with hypothyroidism, *Amer. J. Physiol.*, **133**, 269P (1941).

ENZER, N., SIMONSON, E. and BLANKSTEIN, S. S., Fatigue of patients with circulatory insufficiency, investigated by means of fusion frequency of flicker, *Ann. Intern. Med.*, **16**, 701–707 (1942).

EXNER, S., Bemerkungen über intermittierende Netzhautreizung, *Pflüg. Arch. ges. Physiol.*, **3**, 214–240 (1870).

EYSENCK, H. J., *The Structure of Human Personality* (London, Methuen, 1953).

EYSENCK, H. J., *A Dynamic Theory of Anxiety and Hysteria* (London, Routledge & Kegan Paul, 1957).

FECHNER, G. T., *Elemente der Psychophysik* (Leipzig, 1860).

FERREE, C. E. and RAND, G., The effect of intensity of illumination on the acuity of the normal eye and eyes slightly defective as to refraction, *Amer. J. Psychol.*, **34**, 244–249 (1923).

FERRY, E. S., Persistence of vision, *Amer. J. Sci.*, **44**, 192–207 (1892).

FICK, A., Über den zeitlichen verlauf der Erregung in der Netzhaut, *Arch. Anat. Physiol. Lpz.*, 739–764 (1863).

FISCHER, F. P. and JONGBLOED, J., Untersuchungen über die Dunkeladaptation bei herabgesetztem Sauerstoffdruck der Atmungsluft, *Arch. Augenheilk.*, **109**, 432 (1935).

FRIDERICIA, L. S. and HOLM, E., Experimental contribution to the study of the relation between night-blindness and malnutrition. Influence of deficiency of fat-soluble A-vitamin in the diet on the visual purple in the eyes of rats, *Amer. J. Physiol.*, **73**, 63–78 (1925).

FRY, G. A. and ALPERN, M., Theoretical implications of the response of a photoreceptor to a flash of light, *Amer. J. Optom.*, **23**, 509–525 (1946).

FRY, G. A. and BARTLEY, S. H., The effect of steady stimulation of one part of the retina upon the critical frequency in another, *J. Exp. Psychol.*, **19**, 351–356 (1936).

FURUYA, G., The effects of low pressure on the human eye: visual acuity, *Acta. Soc. ophthal. jap.*, **41**, 42–49 (1937).

GELDARD, F. A., Foveal sensitivity as influenced by peripheral stimulation, *J. Gen. Psychol.*, **7**, 185–189 (1932).

GELLHORN, E., The effect of O_2-lack, variation in the CO_2-content of the inspired air and hyperpnea on visual intensity discrimination, *Amer. J. Physiol.*, **115**, 679–684 (1936).

GELLHORN, E., Anoxia in relation to the visual system, *Biol. Symp.*, **7**, 73–85 (1942).

GELLHORN, E. and HAILMAN, H., Parallelism in changes of sensory function and electroencephalogram in anoxia and effect of hypercapnia under these conditions, *Psychosom. Med.*, **6**, 23–30 (1944).

GELLHORN, E. and KESSLER, M., The influence of hypoglycemia and electroshock on the electroencephalogram, *Fed. Proc.*, No. 1, 11 (1942).

GIBSON, J. J., Studying perceptual phenomena, in *Methods of Psychology* 158–188, Ed. T. G. Andrews (New York, John Wiley & Sons, Inc., 1948).

GOLDBERG, L., Quantitative studies in alcohol tolerance in man, *Acta physiol. scand.*, **5** (Suppl. 16), 127 (1943).

GOLDSTONE, S., Flicker fusion measurements and anxiety level, *Ph.D. Dissertation, Duke Univ.*, 1953.

GOLDSTONE, S., Flicker fusion measurements and anxiety level, *J. Exp. Psychol.*, **49**, 200–202 (1955).

GOODMAN, L. S. and GILMAN, A., *The Pharmacological Basis of Therapeutics* (New York, Macmillan, 1955).

GRAHAM, C. H., An investigation of binocular summation: I. The fovea, *J. Gen. Psychol.*, **3**, 494 (1930).

GRAHAM, C. H., Visual perception, in *Handbook of Experimental Psychology*, Ed. S. S. Stevens, 868–920 (New York, John Wiley & Sons, Inc., 1951).

GRAHAM, C. H., Behaviour and the psychophysical methods: an analysis of some recent experiments, *Psychol. Rev.*, **59**, 62–70 (1952).

GRAHAM, C. H., BAKER, K. E., HECHT, M. and LLOYD, V. V., Factors influencing thresholds for monocular movement parallax, *J. Exp. Psychol.*, **38**, 205–223 (1948).

GRAHAM, C. H. and BARTLETT, N. R., The relation of size of stimulus and intensity in the human eye: III. The influence of area on foveal intensity discrimination, *J. Exp. Psychol.*, **27**, 149–159 (1940).

GRAHAM, C. H. and GRANIT, R., Comparative studies on the peripheral and central retina. VI. Inhibition, summation and synchronization of impulses in the retina, *Amer. J. Physiol.*, **98**, 664–673 (1931).

GRAHAM, C. H. and KEMP, E. H., Brightness discrimination as a function of the duration of the increment in intensity, *J. Gen. Physiol.*, **21**, 635–650 (1938).

GRANGER, G. W., Personality and visual perception: a review, *J. Ment. Sci.*, **99**, 8–43 (1953).

GRANGER, G. W., Effect of ephedrine on dark vision, *Nature*, **174**, 653 (1954).

GRANGER, G. W., Effect of psychiatric disorder on visual thresholds, *Science*, **125**, 500–501 (1957*a*).

GRANGER, G. W., Night vision and psychiatric disorders, *J. Ment. Sci.*, **103**, 48–79 (1957*b*).

GRANGER, G. W., Light and form thresholds during dark adaptation, *Acta Ophthal., Kbh.*, **35**, 361–371 (1957*c*).

GRANGER, G. W., Inhibitory interaction within the visual system (to be published).

GRANGER, G. W. and IKEDA, H., Effect of hyperventilation on critical flicker frequency, *Bull. Brit. Psychol. Soc.*, No. 38, p. 23a (1959*a*).

GRANGER, G. W. and IKEDA, H., Application of C.F.F. to psychiatry and neurology (to be published).

GRANIT, R., On interaction between distant areas in the human eye, *Amer. J. Physiol.*, **94**, 41–50 (1930).

GRANIT, R., *Sensory Mechanisms of the Retina* (London, Oxford Univ. Press, 1947).

GRANIT, R., Sight and the physiology of the retina, *Acta psychol. Fenn.*, **1**, 21–29 (1951).

GRANIT, R., Aspects of excitation and inhibition in the retina, *Proc. Roy. Soc. Lond.*, **140B**, 191–198 (1952).

GRANIT, R., *Receptors and Sensory Perception* (New Haven, Yale Univ. Press, 1955).

GRANIT, R. and AMMON, W. V., Comparative studies on the peripheral and central retina. III. Some aspects of local adaptation, *Amer. J. Physiol.*, **95**, 229–241 (1930).

GRANIT, R. and HAMMOND, E. L., Comparative studies on the peripheral and central retina. V. The sensation-time curve and the time-course of the fusion frequency of intermittent stimulation, *Amer. J. Physiol.*, **98**, 654–663 (1931).

GRANIT, R. and HARPER, P., Comparative studies on the peripheral and central retina. II. Synaptic reactions in the eye, *Amer. J. Physiol.*, **95**, 211–228 (1930).

GRANIT, R., HOLMBERG, T. and ZEWI, M., On the mode of action of visual purple on the rod cell, *J. Physiol.*, **94**, 430–440 (1938).

GRANIT, R., MUNSTERHJELM, A. and ZEWI, M., The relation between concentration of visual purple and retinal sensitivity to light during dark adaptation, *J. Physiol.*, **96**, 31–44 (1939).

GRANIT, R. and RIDDELL, L. A., The electrical responses of light-dark-adapted frogs' eyes to rhythmic and continuous stimuli, *J. Physiol.*, **81**, 1–28 (1934).

GRANIT, R. and THERMAN, P. O., Inhibition of the off-effect in the optic nerve and its relation to the equivalent phase of the retinal response, *J. Physiol.*, **81**, 47P (1934).

GRANIT, R. and THERMAN, P. O., Excitation and inhibition in the retina and the optic nerve, *J. Physiol.*, **83**, 359–381 (1935).

GUILFORD, J. P., Fluctuations of attention with weak visual stimuli, *Amer. J. Psychol.*, **38**, 534–583 (1927).

GUILFORD, J. P., *Psychometric Methods* (New York, McGraw-Hill, 1936).

HAIG, C., The course of rod dark adaptation as influenced by the intensity and duration of preadaptation to light, *J. Gen. Physiol.*, **24**, 735–751 (1941).

HAIG, C., HECHT, S. and PATEK, A. J., Vitamin A and rod-cone dark adaptation in cirrhosis of the liver, *Science*, **87**, 534–536 (1938).

HALSTEAD, W. C., *Brain and Intelligence* (Chicago, Chicago Univ. Press, 1947).

HAMMOND, E. C. and LEE, R. H., Criteria for scoring dark adaptation tests, *U.S. Nat. Inst. Health, Div. Indust. Hyg.*, July 10 (1941).

HARTLINE, H. K., The dark adaptation of the eye of *Limulus*, as manifested by its electrical response to illumination, *J. Gen. Physiol.*, **13**, 379–389 (1930).

HARTLINE, H. K., Impulses in single optic nerve fibers of the vertebrate retina, *Amer. J. Physiol.*, **113**, 59P (1935).

HARTLINE, H. K., The response of single optic nerve fibers of the vertebrate eye to illumination of the retina, *Amer. J. Physiol.*, **121**, 400–415 (1938).

HARTLINE, H. K. and MCDONALD, P. R., Light and dark adaptation of single photoreceptor elements in the eye of *Limulus*, *J. Cell. Comp. Physiol.*, **30**, 225–253 (1947).

HARTLINE, H. K. and MCDONALD, P. R., The frequency of seeing at low illuminations. Appendix C in Pirenne, M. H., Marriott, F. H. C. and O'Doherty, E. F., Individual differences in night-vision efficiency. *M.R.C. Spec. Rep.* Ser. No. 294, 70–81 (London, H.M.S.O., 1957).

HARTLINE, H. K. and RATCLIFF, F., Inhibitory interaction of receptor units in the eye of *Limulus*, *J. Gen. Physiol.*, **40**, 357–376 (1957).

HARTLINE, H. K., WAGNER, H. G. and MACNICHOL, E. F., The peripheral origin of nervous activity in the visual system, *Cold Spr. Harb. Symp. Quant. Biol.*, **17**, 125–141 (1952).

HARTLINE, H. K., WAGNER, H. G. and RATCLIFF, F., Inhibition in the eye of *Limulus*, *J. Gen. Physiol.*, **39**, 651–673 (1956).

HARTRIDGE, H., Chromatic aberration and resolving power of the eye, *J. Physiol.*, **52**, 175–246 (1918).

HECHT, S., Sensory equilibrium and dark adaptation in *Mya Arenaria*, *J. Gen. Physiol.*, **1**, 545–558 (1919).

HECHT, S., The dark adaptation of the human eye, *J. Gen. Physiol.*, **2**, 499–517 (1920).

HECHT, S., The nature of foveal dark adaptation, *J. Gen. Physiol.*, **4**, 113–139 (1921).

HECHT, S., Intensity discrimination and the stationary state, *J. Gen. Physiol.*, **6**, 355–373 (1924a).

HECHT, S., Photochemistry of visual purple. III. The relation between the intensity of light and the rate of bleaching of visual purple, *J. Gen. Physiol.*, **6**, 731–740 (1924b).

HECHT, S., The visual discrimination of intensity and the Weber-Fechner law, *J. Gen. Physiol.*, **7**, 235–267 (1924c).

HECHT, S., A quantitative basis for visual acuity and intensity discrimination, *Skand. Arch. Physiol.*, **49**, 146 (1926).

HECHT, S., The kinetics of dark adaptation, *J. Gen. Physiol.*, **10**, 781–809 (1927).

HECHT, S., The relation between visual acuity and intensity, *J. Gen. Physiol.*, **11**, 255–281 (1928).

HECHT, S., A theoretical basis for intensity discrimination in vision, *Proc. Nat. Acad. Sci. Wash.*, **20**, 644–655 (1934a).

HECHT, S., Vision: II. The nature of the photoreceptor process, in *A Handbook of General Experimental Psychology*, Ed. C. Murchison, 704–825 (Worcester, Mass., Clark Univ. Press, 1934b).

HECHT, S., A theory of visual intensity discrimination, *J. Gen. Physiol.*, **18**, 767–789 (1935).

HECHT, S., Intensity discrimination and its relation to the adaptation of the eye, *J. Physiol.*, **86**, 15–21 (1936).

HECHT, S., Rods, cones and the chemical basis of vision, *Physiol. Rev.*, **17**, 239–290 (1937).

HECHT, S., *The Nature of the Visual Process. The Harvey Lectures*, Ser. 33, 1937–8, 35–64 (Baltimore, Williams & Wilkins, 1938).

HECHT, S. and HAIG, C., Dark adaptation as influenced by intensity of light adaptation, *J. Opt. Soc. Amer.*, **26**, 304 (1936).

HECHT, S., HAIG, C. and CHASE, A. M., The influence of light adaptation on subsequent dark adaptation of the eye, *J. Gen. Physiol.*, **20**, 831–850 (1937).

HECHT, S., HENDLEY, C. D., FRANK, S. R. and HAIG, C., Anoxia and brightness discrimination, *J. Gen. Physiol.*, **29**, 335–351 (1946).

HECHT, S. and HSIA, Y., Dark adaptation following light adaptation to red and white lights, *J. Opt. Soc. Amer.*, **35**, 261–267 (1945).

HECHT, S. and MANDELBAUM, J., The relation between vitamin A and dark adaptation, *J. Amer. Med. Ass.*, **112**, 1910–1916 (1939).

HECHT, S. and MINTZ, E. U., The visibility of single lines at various illuminations and the retinal basis of visual resolution, *J. Gen. Physiol.*, **22**, 593–612 (1939).

HECHT, S., PESKIN, J. C. and PATT, M., Intensity discrimination in the human eye. II. Relation between $\Delta I/I$ and intensity for different parts of the spectrum, *J. Gen. Physiol.*, **22**, 7–19 (1938).

HECHT, S. and PIRENNE, M. H., The sensibility of the nocturnal long-eared owl in the spectrum, *J. Gen. Physiol.*, **23**, 709 (1940).

HECHT, S. and SHLAER, S., Intermittent stimulation by light. V. The relation between intensity and critical flicker frequency for different parts of the spectrum, *J. Gen. Physiol.*, **19**, 965–979 (1936).

HECHT, S., and SHLAER, S., An adaptometer for measuring human dark adaptation, *J. Opt. Soc. Amer.*, **35**, 269–275 (1938).

HECHT, S., SHLAER, S. and PIRENNE, M. H., Energy, quanta and vision, *J. Gen. Physiol.*, **25**, 819–840 (1942).

HECHT, S., SHLAER, S. and SMITH, E. L., Intermittent light stimulation and the duplicity theory of vision, *Cold Spr. Harb. Symp. Quant. Biol.*, **3**, 237–244 (1935).

HECHT, S., SHLAER, S. and VERRIJP, C. D., Intermittent stimulation by light. II. The measurement of critical flicker frequency for the human eye, *J. Gen. Physiol.*, **17**, 237–249 (1933).

HECHT, S. and SMITH, E. L., Intermittent stimulation by light. VI. Area and the relation between critical frequency and intensity, *J. Gen. Physiol.*, **19**, 979–991 (1936).

HECHT, S. and VERRIJP, C. D., Intermittent stimulation by light. III. The relation between intensity and critical flicker frequency for different retinal locations, *J. Gen. Physiol.*, **17**, 251–265 (1933).

HECHT, S. and WALD, G., The visual acuity and intensity discrimination of *Drosophila*, *J. Gen. Physiol.*, **17**, 517–547 (1934).

HECHT, S. and WOLF, E., The visual acuity of the honey bee, *J. Gen. Physiol.*, **12**, 727–760 (1929).

HELMHOLTZ, H., *Handbuch der physiologischen Optik* (Hamburg and Leipzig, Voss, 1896).

HENDLEY, C. D., The relation between visual acuity and brightness discrimination, *J. Gen. Physiol.*, **31**, 433–457 (1948).

HIMWICH, H. E., *Brain Metabolism and Cerebral Disorders* (Baltimore, Williams & Wilkins, 1951).

HIMWICH, H. E. and FASEKAS, J. F., The effect of hypoglycemia on the metabolism of the brain, *Endocrinology*, **21**, 800–807 (1937).

HIMWICH, H. E., FROSTIG, J. P., FASEKAS, J. F. and HADIDIAN, Z., The mechanism of the symptoms of insulin hypoglycemia, *Amer. J. Psychiat.*, **96**, 371 (1939).

HIMWICH, H. E., HADIDIAN, Z., FASEKAS, J. F. and HOAGLAND, H., Cerebral metabolism and electrical activity during insulin hypoglycemia in man, *Amer. J. Physiol.*, **125**, 578–585 (1939).

HOLM, E., Demonstration of hemeralopia in rats nourished on food devoid of fat-soluble A-vitamin, *Amer. J. Physiol.*, **73**, 79–84 (1925).

HOLWAY, A. H. and BORING, E. G., Determinants of apparent visual size with distance variant, *Amer. J. Psychol.*, **54**, 21–37 (1941).

HOLWAY, A. H. and HURVICH, L. M., Visual differential sensitivity and retinal area, *Amer. J. Psychol.*, **51**, 687–695 (1938).

HONDA, H., Effect of the stimulus area of previous light adaptation upon the course of dark adaptation, *Acta Soc. ophthal. jap.*, **56**, 519–524 (1952).

HOUSEHOLDER, A. S., A neural mechanism for discrimination, *Psychometrika*, **4**, 45–58 (1939).

HOUSEHOLDER, A. S. and LANDAHL, H. D., *Mathematical Biophysics of the Central Nervous System*, (Bloomington, Ind., Principia Press, 1945).

HUME, E. M. and KREBS, H. A., Vitamin A requirement of human adults. An experimental study of vitamin A deprivation in man, *M.R.C. Spec. Rep. Ser. No.* 264 (London: H.M.S.O.), 1949).

HYLKEMA, B. S., Examination of the visual field by determining the fusion frequency, *Acta Ophthal.*, Kbh., **20**, 181–193 (1942).

IDESTRÖM, C. M., Flicker fusion in chronic barbiturate usage, *Acta Psychiat. Neurol. scand.*, Suppl. 91 (1954).

INOUYE, N. and OINUMA, S., Untersuchung der Dunkeladaptation des einen Auges mit Hilfe des Helladaptierten Andern, *Arch. Ophth.*, Lpz., **79**, 145 (1911).

IRELAND, F. H., A comparison of critical flicker frequencies under conditions of monocular and binocular stimulation, *J. Exp. Psychol.*, **40**, 282–286 (1950).

IVES, H. E., Studies in the photometry of lights of different colours. I. Spectral luminosity curves obtained by the equality of brightness photometer and the flicker photometer under similar conditions, *Phil. Mag.*, **24**, 149–188 (1912).

IVES, H. E., A theory of intermittent vision, *J. Opt. Soc. Amer.*, **6**, 343–361 (1922).

JAHN, T. L., Visual critical flicker frequency as a function of intensity, *J. Opt. Soc. Amer.*, **36**, 76–82 (1946a).

JAHN, T. L., Brightness discrimination and visual acuity as a function of intensity, *J. Opt. Soc. Amer.*, **36**, 83–86 (1946b).

JAHN, T. L., The kinetics of visual dark adaptation, *J. Opt. Soc. Amer.*, **36**, 659–665 (1946c).

JEGHERS, H., Night blindness as a criterion of vitamin A deficiency, *Ann. Intern. Med.*, **10**, 1,304–1,334 (1937).

JOHANNSEN, D. E., The duration and intensity of the exposure light as factors in determining the course of the subsequent dark adaptation. I. The matching method, *J. Gen. Psychol.*, **10**, 4–19 (1934).

JOHANNSEN, D. E., McBRIDE, P. I. and WULFECK, J. W., Studies in dark adaptation. I. The pre-exposure tolerance of the dark-adapted fovea, *J. Opt. Soc. Amer.*, **46**, 67–71 (1956).

KARPE, G. and TANSLEY, K., The relationship between the change in the electroretinogram and the subjective dark adaptation curve, *J. Physiol.*, **107**, 272–279 (1948).

KENNELLY, A. E. and WHITING, S. E., The frequencies of flicker at which variations in illumination vanish, *Nat. Elect. Light Assn. Conv.*, **30**, 327–340 (1907).

KEYS, A. and SIMONSON, E., The flicker fusion frequency and its response to nitroglycerin in normal subjects and in patients with cardiovascular disease, *Circulation*, **5**, 215–224 (1952).

KOENIG, A., Die Abhängigkeit der Sehschärfe von der Beleuchtungsintensität. *S.B. Akad. Wiss.*, Berlin, 559 (1897).

KOENIG, A. and BRODHUN, E., Experimentelle Untersuchungen über die psychophysische Fundamentalformel in Bezug auf den Gesichtsinn, Zweite Mittheilung, *S.B. Akad. Wiss.*, Berlin, 641 (1889).

KOHLRAUSCH, A., Untersuchungen mit farbigen Schwellenprüflictern über den Dunkeladaptationsverlauf des normalen Auges, *Pflüg. Arch. ges. Physiol.*, **196**, 113–117 (1922).

KOHLRAUSCH, A., Tagessehen, Dämmersehen, Adaptation, *Handbuch der normalen und pathologischen Physiologie*. Eds. A. Bethe, G. v. Bergmann, G. Embden, and A. Ellinger, 12, Pt. 2, 1499 (Berlin, J. Springer, 1931).

KRASNO, L. R. and IVY, A. C., Response of the flicker fusion threshold to nitroglycerin and its potential value in the diagnosis, prognosis, and therapy of subclinical cardiovascular disease, *Circulation*, **1**, 1,267–1,276 (1950).

KRIEGER, H. P. and BENDER, M. B., Dark adaptation in lesions of the optic pathways, (Abstr.) *Fed. Proc.*, **8**, 89 (1949).

KRIEGER, H. P. and BENDER, M. B., Dark adaptation in perimetrically blind fields, *A.M.A. Arch. Ophthal.*, **46**, 625–636 (1951).

KRUGMAN, H. E., Flicker fusion frequency as a function of anxiety reaction; an exploratory study, *Psychosom. Med.*, **4**, 269–272 (1947).

KUBZANSKY, P. E., Visual discrimination and anxiety level under stress and non-stress conditions, *Ph.D. Dissertation, Duke Univ.*, (1954).

LANDIS, C. L., Crozier and Wolf on flicker-fusion, *J. Psychol.*, **37**, 3–17 (1954a).

LANDIS, C. L., Determinants of the critical flicker-fusion threshold, *Physiol. Rev.*, **34**, 259–286 (1954b).

LANKES, W., Perseveration, *Brit. J. Psychol.*, **7**, 387–419 (1915).

LASAREFF, P., Über die Beziehung zwischen der Empfindlichkeit des Auges bei der Wirkung schwelliger Reize und der Sehschärfe, *Z. Phys.*, **48**, 437–439 (1928).

LEHMANN, J. E., The effect of changes in pH on the action of mammalian A nerve fibers, *Amer. J. Physiol.*, **118**, 600–612 (1937).

LIVINGSTON, P. C. and BOLTON, B., Night visual capacity in psychological cases, *Lancet*, **244**, 263–264 (1943).

LLOYD, V. V., A comparison of critical fusion frequencies for different areas in the fovea and periphery, *Amer. J. Psychol.*, **65**, 346–357 (1942).

LÖHNER, L., Die Sehschärfe des Menschen und ihre Prüfung (Leipsic u. Wien, 1912).

LOWRY, E. M., The photometric sensibility of the eye and the precision of photometric observations, *J. Opt. Soc. Amer.*, **21**, 132 (1931).

LUCKIESH, M., On the growth and decay of color sensations in flicker photometry, *Physical Rev.*, **4**, 1–11 (1914).

LYTHGOE, R. J., The measurement of visual acuity, *M. R. C. Spec. Rep.* Ser. No. 173 (London, H.M.S.O., 1932).

LYTHGOE, R. J., The mechanism of dark adaptation: a critical résumé, *Brit. J. Ophthal.*, **24**, 21–43 (1940).

LYTHGOE, R. J. and TANSLEY, K., The relation of the critical frequency of flicker to the adaptation of the eye, *Proc. Roy. Soc. Lond.*, **105B**, 60–92 (1929).

MCDONALD, R. and ADLER, F. H., Effect of anoxemia on dark adaptation of normal and of vitamin A deficient subject, *Arch. Ophthal., N.Y.*, **22**, 980–988 (1939).

MCFARLAND, R. A., Anoxia: its effects on the physiology and biochemistry of the brain and on behaviour, in *The Biology of Mental Health and Disease*, 335–355, (New York, Hoeber, 1952).

MCFARLAND, R. A. and EVANS, J. N., Alterations in dark adaptation under reduced oxygen tensions, *Amer. J. Physiol.*, **127**, 37–50 (1939).

MCFARLAND, R. A. and FORBES, W. H., The effects of variations in the concentration of oxygen and of glucose on dark adaptation, *J. Gen. Physiol.*, **24**, 69–98 (1941).

MCFARLAND, R. A. and HALPERIN, M. H., The relation between foveal visual acuity and illumination under reduced oxygen tension, *J. Gen. Physiol.*, **23**, 613–630 (1940).

MCFARLAND, R. A., HALPERIN, M, H. and NIVEN, J. I., Visual thresholds as an index of physiological imbalance during anoxia, *Amer. J. Physiol.*, **142**, 328–349 (1944).

MCFARLAND, R. A., HALPERIN, M. H. and NIVEN, J. I., Visual thresholds as an index of the modification of the effects of anoxia by glucose, *Amer. J. Physiol.*, **144**, 378–388 (1945).

MCFARLAND, R. A., HALPERIN, M. H. and NIVEN, J. I., Visual thresholds as an index of physiological imbalance during insulin hypoglycemia, *Amer. J. Physiol.*, **145**, 299–312 (1946).

MCFARLAND, R. A., HURVICH, L. M. and HALPERIN, M. H., The effect of oxygen deficiency on the relation between stimulus intensity and the latency of visual after images, *Amer. J. Physiol.*, **140**, 354–366 (1943).

MCFARLAND, R. A., ROUGHTON, F. J. W., HALPERIN, M. H. and NIVEN, J. I., The effects of carbon monoxide and altitude on visual thresholds, *J. Aviat. Med.*, **15**, 381–394 (1944).

MCNEMAR, O. W., The ordering of individuals in critical flicker frequency under different measurement conditions, *J. Psychol.*, **32**, 3–24 (1951).

MACNICHOL, E. F. and BENOLKEN, R., Blocking effect of ethyl alcohol on inhibitory synapses in the eye of *Limulus*, *Science*, **124**, 681–682 (1956).

MADLUNG, H., Über den Einfluss der typologischen Veranlagung auf die Flimmergrenzen, *Untersuch. Psychol. Phil.*, **10**, No. 3, 1–65 (1935).

MANDELBAUM, J., Dark adaptation: some physiologic and clinical considerations, *Arch. Ophthal. N.Y.*, **26**, 203–239 (1941).

MARAZZI, A. S., The central inhibitory action of adrenaline and related compounds, *Fed. Proc.*, **2**, 33 (1943).

MARAZZI, A. S., Some indicators of cerebral humoral mechanisms, *Science*, **118**, 367–370 (1953).

MILES, P. W., Flicker fusion fields: II. Technique and interpretation, *Amer. J. Ophthal.*, **33**, 1,069–1,077 (1950).

MILES, W. R.. Light sensitivity and form perception in dark adaptation, *J. Opt. Soc. Amer.*, **43**, 560–566 (1953).

MISIAK, H., Age and sex differences in critical flicker frequency, *Science*, **37**, 318–332 (1947).

MONNIER, M., L'électroretinogramme de l'homme, *EEG. & Clinical Neurophysiology*, **1**, 87–108 (1949).

MONNIER, M. and BABEL, L., La fréquence de fusion de la rétine chez l'homme. I. Variations du seuil subjectif électrorétinographique selon le territoire rétinien stimulé, *Helv. physiol. acta*, **10**, 42–53 (1952).

MOON, P. and SPENCER, D. E., Visual dark adaptation: a mathematical formulation, *J. Math. Phys.*, **24**, 65–105 (1945).

MOORE, T. in *Symposium on Nutrition*, Ed. R. M. Herriott, 31–33 (Baltimore, Johns Hopkins Press, 1953).

MOTE, F. A. and RIOPELLE, A. J., The effect of varying the intensity and the duration of pre-exposure upon foveal dark adaptation in the human eye, *J. Gen. Physiol.*, **34**, 657–674 (1951).

MOTE, F. A. and RIOPELLE, A. J., The effect of varying the intensity and the duration of pre-exposure upon subsequent dark adaptation in the human eye, *J. Comp. Physiol. Psychol.*, **46**, 49–55 (1953).

MOTE, F. A., RIOPELLE, A. J. and MEYER, D. R., The effect of intermittent preadapting light upon subsequent dark adaptation in the human eye, *J. Opt. Soc. Amer.*, **40**, 584–588 (1950).

MÜCHER, H. and WENDT, H. W., Gruppenversuch zur Bestimmung der kritischen Verschmelzungsfrequenz beim binokularen Sehen. Anderungen unter Koffein und nach normaler Tagesarbeit, *Arch. exp. Path. Pharmak.*, **214**, 29–37 (1951).

MUELLER, C. G., Frequency of seeing functions for intensity discrimination at various levels of adapting intensity, *J. Gen. Physiol.*, **34**, 463–474 (1951).

MUELLER, C. G. and LLOYD, V. V., Stereoscopic acuity for various levels of illumination, *Proc. Nat. Acad. Sci. Wash.*, **34**, 223–227 (1948).

MÜLLER, H. K., Die Theorien der Adaptation, *Kurzes Handbuch der Ophth.*, **2**, 366 (1932).

NAGEL, W. and SCHAEFER, K. L., Über das verhalten der Netzhautzapfen bei Dunkeladaptation des Auges., *Z. Psychol.*, **34**, 271 (1904).

NIVEN, J. I. and BROWN, R. H., Visual resolution as a function of intensity and exposure time in the human fovea, *J. Opt. Soc. Amer.*, **34**, 738–743 (1944).

NOELL, W. K., Studies in the electrophysiology and metabolism of the retina, *U.S.A.F. Sch. Aviat. Med. Proj. No. 21-1201-0004, Rep.*, No. 1., 1953.

NOELL, W. K. and CHINN, H. J., Failure of the visual pathway during anoxia, *Amer. J. Physiol.*, **161**, 573–590 (1950).

NOLAN, D. C., LEWIS, C., LANDIS, C. L. and KING, H. E., *Studies in Topectomy* (New York, Grune & Stratton, 1956).

OSGOOD, C. E., *Method and Theory in Experimental Psychology* (New York, Oxford Univ. Press, 1953).

OTTOSON, D. and SVAETICHIN, G., Electrophysiological investigations of the frog retina, *Cold Spr. Harb. Symp. Quant. Biol.*, **17**, 165–173 (1952).

OTTOSON, D. and SVAETICHIN, G., Electrical activity of retinal receptor layer, *Acta physiol. scand.*, **29**, 31–39 (1953).

PADGHAM, C. A., Quantitative study of visual after images, *Brit. J. Ophthal.*, **37**, 165–170 (1953).

PADGHAM, C. A., Further studies of the positive visual after-image, *Optica Acta*, **3**, 102–107 (1957).

PARINAUD, H., L'héméralopie et les fonctions du poupre visuel, *C. R. Acad. Sci.*, **93**, 286 (1881).

PARSONS, J. H., *An Introduction to the Theory of Perception* (New York, Macmillan, 1927).

PARSONS, O. A. and MILLER, P. N., Flicker fusion thresholds in multiple sclerosis, *A.M.A. Arch. Neurol. Psychiat.*, **77**, 134–139 (1957).

PESKIN, J. C., The regeneration of visual purple in the living animal, *J. Gen. Physiol.*, **26**, 27–47 (1942–3).

PHILLIPS, G., Perception of flicker in lesions of the visual pathways, *Brain*, **56**, 464–478 (1933).

PIERON, H., Influence du rapport des phases sur la durée d'interruption d'une stimulation lumineuse périodique à la limite du papillotement, *C. R. Soc. Biol.*, **99**, 398–400 (1928).

PIPER, H., Über Dunkeladaptation, *Z. Psychol. Physiol. Sinnesorg.*, **31**, 161–214 (1903).

PIRENNE, M. H., On the variation of visual acuity with light intensity, *Proc. Camb. Phil. Soc.*, **42**, 78–82 (1946).

PIRENNE, M. H., *Vision and the Eye* (London, Chapman & Hall, 1948).

PIRENNE, M. H., Physiological mechanisms of vision and the quantum nature of light, *Biol. Rev.*, **31**, 194–241 (1956).

PIRENNE, M. H., "Off" mechanisms and human visual acuity, *J. Physiol.*, **137**, 48–49P (1957).

PIRENNE, M. H. and DENTON, E. J., Accuracy and sensitivity of the human eye, *Nature*, **170**, 1,039 (1952).

PIRENNE, M. H., MARRIOTT, F. H. C. and O'DOHERTY, E. F., Individual differences in night-vision efficiency, *M. R. C. Spec. Rep.* Ser. No. 294 (London, H.M.S.O., 1957).

PLATEAU, J., Betrachtungen über ein von Hrn. Talbot vorgeschlagenes photometrisches Princip. *Ann. Physik. Chem.*, **35**, 457–468 (1835).

PORTER, T. C., Contributions to the study of flicker. II. *Proc. Roy. Soc. Lond.*, **70A**, 313–329 (1902).

PÜTTER, A., Studien zur Theorie der Reizvorgänge: I-IV, *Pflüg. Arch. ges. Physiol.*, **171**, 201–261 (1918).

RAMON Y CAJAL, S., *Die Retina der Wirbeltiere* (Wiesbaden, 1894).

RICCIUTI, H. N., Comparison of critical flicker frequency in psychotics, psychoneurotics and normals, *Amer. Psychologist*, **3**, 276–277 (1948).

RICE, D. E., Visual acuity with lights of different colors and intensities, *Arch. Psychol. N.Y.*, **3**, 1–59 (1912).

RIDDELL, L. A., The use of the flicker phenomenon in the investigation of the field of vision, *Brit. J. Ophthal.*, **20**, 385–410 (1936).

RIGGS, L. A., Dark adaptation in the frog's eye as determined by the electrical response of the retina, *J. Cell. Comp. Physiol.*, **9**, 491–510 (1937).

ROBACK, G. S., KRASNO, L. R. and IVY, A. C., Drug effects of flicker fusion threshold, *J. Appl. Physiol.*, **4**, 566–574 (1952).

ROELOFS, C. O. and ZEEMAN, W. P. C., Die Sehschärfe im Halbdunkel, zugleich ein Beitrag zur Kenntniss der Nachblindheit, *Arch. Ophth., Lpz.*, **99**, 174–194 (1919).

ROSE, A., The sensitivity performance of the human eye on an absolute scale, *J. Opt. Soc. Amer.*, **38**, 196–208 (1948).

ROSE, H. W. and SCHMIDT, I., Factors affecting dark adaptation, *J. Aviat. Med.*, **18**, 218–230 (1947).

ROSE, R. T., The fusion frequency in different areas of the visual field. I. The foveal fusion frequency, *J. Gen. Physiol.*, **15**, 133–147 (1936).

ROTHAN, H., Über die Beeinflussung der Netzhautfunktion durch Adrenalin, *Klin. Mbl. Augenheilk*, **75**, 747 (1925).

RUBINSTEIN, B. and THERMAN, P. O., Influence of hyperventilation on the fusion frequency of intermittent visual stimuli, *Skand. Arch. Physiol.*, **72**, 26–34 (1935).

RUESCH, J., Dark adaptation, negative after images, tachistoscopic examination and reaction time in head injuries, *J. Neurosurg.*, **1**, 243–251 (1944).

RUSHTON, W. A. H., Chemical and nervous factors in dark adaptation, *Trans. Ophthal. Soc. U.K.*, **72**, 657–664 (1952).

RUSHTON, W. A. H., Kinetics of cone pigments measured objectively on the living human fovea, *Ann. N.Y. Acad. Sci.*, **74**, 291–304 (1958).

RUSHTON, W. A. H. and CAMPBELL, F. W., Measurement of rhodopsin in the living human eye, *Nature*, **174**, 1,096–1,097 (1954).

RYAN, T. A. and BITTERMAN, N. E., Investigations of critical flicker fusion frequency, *Report to Research Committee of Illum. Engng Soc.*, 1950.

SCHATERNIKOFF, M., Über den Einfluss der Adaptation auf die Erscheinung des Flimmerns, *Z. Psychol.*, **29**, 241–254 (1902).

SCHMIDTKE, H., Über die messung der psychischen Ermüdung mit Hilfe des Flimmertests, *Psychol. Forsch.*, **23**, 409–463 (1951).

SCHOUTEN, J. F. and ORNSTEIN, L. S., Measurements on direct and indirect adaptation by means of a binocular method, *J. Opt. Soc. Amer.*, **29**, 168–182 (1939).

SCHUBERT, G., Das verhalten des Zentralnervensystems bei rascher Rückkehr aus kritischem Unterdruck, *Arch. ges. Physiol.*, **231**, 1–19 (1932).

SEGAL, P., *Badanie adaptacji narządu wzroku do ciemności* (Warsaw: PZWL, 1953).

SEITZ, C. P., The effects of anoxia on visual function: a study of critical frequency, *Arch. Psychol. N.Y.*, **36**, No. 257, 1–38 (1940).

SEITZ, C. P. and ROSENTHAL, C. M., Effect of oxygen deprivation and strychnine administration on visual fusion: a study of the angioscotomas, *Arch. Ophthal.*, *N.Y.*, **26**, 276–287 (1941).

SEMEONOFF, B., Sensitivity of dark-adapted eye during a prolonged period of observation, *Nature*, **147**, 454–455 (1941).

SHAGASS, C. and NAIMAN, J., The sedation threshold, manifest anxiety, and some aspects of ego function, *Arch. Neurol. Psychiat. Chicago*, **74**, 397–406 (1955).

SHAGASS, C. and NAIMAN, J., The sedation threshold as an objective index of manifest anxiety in psychoneurosis, *J. Psychosom. Res.*, **1**, 49–57 (1956).

SHEARD, C., Dark adaptation: some physical, physiological, clinical and aeromedical considerations, *J. Opt. Soc. Amer.*, **34**, 464–508 (1944).

SHERRINGTON, C. S., *The Integrative Action of the Nervous System* (London, Cambridge Univ. Press, 1947).

SHLAER, S., The relation between visual acuity and illumination, *J. Gen. Physiol.*, **21**, 165–188 (1937).

SHLAER, S., SMITH, E. L. and CHASE, A. M., Visual acuity and illumination in different spectral regions, *J. Gen. Physiol.*, **25**, 553–569 (1942).

SIMONSON, E. and BROZEK, J., Flicker fusion frequency: background and applications, *Physiol. Rev.*, **32**, 349–378 (1952).

SIMONSON, E., ENZER, N. and BLANKSTEIN, S. S., The influence of age on the fusion frequency of flicker, *J. Exp. Psychol.*, **29**, 252–255 (1941).

SIMONSON, E., ENZER, N. and BLANKSTEIN, S. S., Effect of amphetamine (Benzedrine) on fatigue of the central nervous system, *War Med.*, **1**, 690–695 (1941b).

SMITH, J. R., Spatial and binocular effects in human intensity discrimination, *J. Gen. Physiol.*, **14**, 318–345 (1936).

SMITH, S. W., MORRIS, A. and DIMMICK, F. L., Effects of exposure to various red lights upon subsequent dark adaptation measured by the method of constant stimuli, *J. Opt. Soc. Amer.*, **45**, 502–506 (1954).

STEINHARDT, J., Intensity discrimination in the human eye. I. The relation of $\Delta I/I$ to intensity, *J. Gen. Physiol.*, **20**, 185–209 (1936).

STEINHEIL, C. A., Elemente der Helligkeits-Messungen am Sternhimmel, *Abhandl. math.-phys. Cl. K. bayer. Akad. Wissensch.*, **2**, 1 (1837).

SVAETICHIN, G., Receptor mechanisms for flicker and fusion, *Acta Physiol. scand.*, **39**, Suppl. 134, 47–54 (1956).

TAKAGI, R. and KAWAKAMI, R., Ueber das Wesen der Oguchischen Krankheit, *Klin. Mbl. Augenheilk.*, **72**, 349 (1924).

TALBOT, H. F., Experiments on light, *Phil. Mag.* (3rd. Ser.), **5**, 321–334 (1834).

TANAKA, H. and SEKIGUCHI, E., Influence of low atmospheric pressure on optic sensitivity, *Bull. Nav. Med. Ass., Japan* (Abstr. Sect.), **24**, 7 (1935).

TANSLEY, K., The regeneration of visual purple: its relation to dark adaptation and night blindness, *J. Physiol.*, **71**, 442–458 (1931).

TANSLEY, K., Review of Vernon, M. D., *A Further Study of Visual Perception*, *Brit. Med. Bull.*, **9**, 83 (1953).

THOMSON, L. C., The influence of variations in the light history of the eye upon the course of its dark adaptation, *J. Physiol.*, **109**, 430–438 (1949).

THOMSON, L. C., The nervous system in visual adaptation, *Brit. J. Ophthal.*, **34**, 129–146 (1950).

THURSTONE, L. L., *A Factorial Study of Perception* (Chicago, Univ. of Chicago Press, 1944).

TOMAN, J. E. P. and DAVIS, J. P., The effect of drugs upon the electrical activity of the brain, *Pharmacol. Rev.*, **1**, 425–492 (1949).

ULLRICH, N., Adaptationsstörungen bei Sehhirnverletzten, *Dsch. Z. Neuenheilk*, **155**, 1–31 (1943).

UTHOFF, W., Über das abhängigkeitsverhältniss der Sehschärfe von der Beleuchtungsintensität, *Arch. Ophth. Lpz.*, **32**, Abt. 1, 171–204 (1886).

UTHOFF, D., Weitere Untersuchungen über die Abhängigkeit der Sehschärfe von der Intensität sowie von der Wellenlänge im Spektrum, *Arch. Ophth. Lpz.*, **36**, Abt. 1, 33–61 (1890).

VERNON, M. D., *A Further Study of Visual Perception* (Cambridge Univ. Press, 1952).

VISHNEVSKIY, N. A. and TSYRLIN, B. A., Effect of decreased barometric pressure on dark adaptation, color vision and electric excitability of the eye, *Fiziol. zhur.*, **18**, 237 (1936).

VRIES, HL. DE, The quantum character of light and its bearing upon the threshold of vision, the differential sensitivity and visual acuity of the eye, *Physica*, **10**, 553–564 (1943).

WALD, G., Area and visual threshold, *J. Gen. Physiol.*, **21**, 269–287 (1938).

WALD, G., Vision: photochemistry, in *Medical Physics*, Ed. O. Glasser, 1658–1667, (Chicago, Year Book Publ., 1944).

WALD, G., On the mechanism of the visual threshold and visual adaptation, *Science*, **119**, 887–892 (1954).

WALD, G., BROWN, P. K. and KENNEDY, D., The visual system of the alligator, *J. Gen. Physiol.*, **40**, 703–713 (1957).

WALD, G. and CLARK, A. B., Visual adaptation and chemistry of the rods, *J. Gen. Physiol.*, **21**, 93–105 (1937).

WALD, G., HARPER, P. V., GOODMAN, H. C. and KRIEGER, H. P., Respiratory effects upon the visual threshold, *J. Gen. Physiol.*, **25**, 891–903 (1942).

WARBURG, O., Über die Klassifizierung tierischer Gewebe nach ihrem Stoffwechsel, *Biochem. Z.*, **184**, 484–488 (1927).

WASHBURN, M. F., HUGHES, E., STEWART, C. and SLIGHT, G., Reaction time, flicker, and affective sensitiveness as tests of introversion and extraversion, *Amer. J. Psychol.*, **42**, 412–413 (1930).

WEBER, E. H., De pulsu, resorptione, auditu et tactu: annotationes anatomicae et physiologicae. Leipzig: Köhler, 1834. Author's summary: Über den Tastsinn, *Arch. Anat. Physiol.*, 152 (1835).

WEEKERS, R. and ROUSSEL, F., La mésure de la fréquence de fusion en clinique, *Doc. Ophthalmologica*, **2**, 130–192 (1948).

WIERSMA, E., Die Sekundärfunktion bei Psychosen, *J. Psychol. Neurol. Lpz.*, **8**, 1–24 (1906).

WILCOX, W. W., The basis of the dependence of visual acuity on illumination, *Proc. Nat. Acad. Sci. Wash.*, **18**, 47–56 (1932).

WILMER, W. H. and BERENS, C., Medical studies in aviation. V. Effect of altitude on ocular functions, *J. Amer. Med. Assn.*, **71**, 1,394–1,398 (1918).

WOLF, E., The visual intensity discrimination of the honey bee, *J. Gen. Physiol.*, **16**, 407–422 (1933*a*).

WOLF, E., On the relation between measurements of intensity discrimination and visual acuity in the honey bee, *J. Gen. Physiol.*, **16**, 773–786 (1933*b*).

WOLF, E. and ZERRAHN-WOLF, G., Threshold intensity of illumination and flicker frequency for the eye of the sunfish, *J. Gen. Physiol.*, **19**, 495–503 (1936).

WOLF, E. and ZIGLER, M., Dark adaptation level and duration of test-flash, *J. Opt. Soc. Amer.*, **41**, 130–133 (1951).

WREDE, C. M., Time-course of dark adaptation in frog's eye as revealed by changes in electroretinogram, *Skand. Arch. Physiol.*, **77**, 93–94 (1937).

WRIGHT, W. D., Intensity discrimination and its relation to the adaptation of the eye, *J. Physiol.*, **83**, 466–477 (1935).

WRIGHT, W. D., *Researches on Normal and Defective Colour Vision* (London, Kimpton, 1946).

WRIGHT, W. D. and GRANIT, R., On the correlation of some sensory and physiological phenomena of vision, *Brit. J. Ophthal.*, Monogr. Suppl. 9, 1–80 (1938).

YOUNG, K. M., In *Selective Partial Ablation of the Frontal Cortex*, Ed. F. A. Mettler, 257–263 (New York, Hoeber, 1949).

YUDKIN, S., Vitamin A and dark adaptation; effect of alcohol, benzedrine and vitamin C, *Lancet*, **2**, 787–791 (1941).

ZEWI, M., Evidence for two phases in the regeneration of visual purple, *Acta physiol. scand.*, **1**, 271–277 (1940–1).

ZUBIN, J., BURDOCK, E. I., EDWARDS, R. E., HALL, K. R. L. and KING, H. E., *Experimental Abnormal Psychology* (New York, Psychiatric Institute, Columbia Univ. Press, 1957).

CHAPTER 5

Intellectual Abilities and Problem-solving Behaviour

W. D. FURNEAUX

THE INVESTIGATION OF "INTELLECT"

THE writer has for some years been concerned with the study of intellectual functions in humans, in particular with the examination of concepts such as those of *speed, power,* and *difficulty,* which in spite of the important role they must inevitably play in any theory of "intelligence," have been developed in a fashion so haphazard that even their definition is a matter for controversy. The results of these inquiries have circulated freely within the Institute of Psychiatry, but have not been widely reported elsewhere. The writers of some of the other sections of this HANDBOOK have thus found themselves in the difficult position of wishing to incorporate in their contributions a background of results and ideas with which their readers will not be familiar. The function of the present chapter is to sketch in this background, rather than to discuss in detail any aspect of abnormal function. It could well be regarded primarily as an introduction to the following chapter.

The study of the abnormal could proceed, in theory, in the absence of any clear understanding of normal mechanisms, but since these disparate fields must in the end be related in terms of concepts which are applicable to both, any change of outlook in the one will inevitably be reflected in the other. The point of view now to be described has been judged, by some, to be of value in connexion with the investigation of intellectual functions in patients demonstrating behaviour disorders, but it developed as a result of an attempt to investigate the normal determinants of score in so-called intelligence tests. The repeated demonstration that performance in "real-life" situations (e.g. success in examinations) can be predicted with reasonable accuracy from a knowledge of such scores provides ample justification for their use. The score given to a subject by such a test, however, describes his behaviour while taking it only very incompletely. This incompleteness does not arise because the score relates only to some *selected* aspect of the total behaviour, as do most scientific measure-

ments. It arises because it attempts to summarize the results of the interaction of several apparently complex processes. The possibility must therefore be considered that the empirically demonstrated relationship between test score and real-life performance really reflects an even closer relationship between such performance and some restricted part of the total test-solving activity, with the other determinants of test score serving only to introduce an unnecessary error variance. In order to minimize error variance an attempt must thus be made to maximize the number of categories into which the subject's total test-taking behaviour can be subdivided, and in terms of which it is to be scored. Obviously, types of response which are logically distinguishable might involve separate determinants, so that ideally, the process of dissection should continue until further subdivision within any category becomes impossible.

It thus appears that the only really satisfactory approach to the study of test-taking behaviour is that of the thorough-going logical-atomist. This approach does not involve the rejection of the important theoretical and experimental contributions to the study of cognition which have been made by proponents of the various kinds of field theory (among whom, for the purposes of this discussion, must be included Piaget), but rather a refusal to recognize that there is any essential antithesis involved in the two kinds of formulation, except in so far as field theorists tend also to stress the importance of the concept of emergence. Any field can be specified in terms of the interaction of a set of discrete determinants, to just the same extent as can the output of a binary computer, and field theories *per se* do no more than direct attention to a particular type of possible interaction among determinants.

If the determinant A is associated with behaviours $a_1, a_2, \ldots a_r$, etc., and determinant B with $b_1, b_2, \ldots b_r$, etc., then according to the doctrine of emergence the interaction of A and B may lead to behaviours of the order (a, b, Δ) and not (a, b), where Δ is some component which cannot be predicted from a knowledge of A and B. This being the case, behaviours (a, b, Δ) can be predicted by tests involving A and B in interaction, but not by the manipulation of scores derived from separate tests of A and B.

In a situation where one has the determinants and is examining the results of their interactions the concept of emergence may have its uses. Where the behaviour is known and its determinants are sought, however, the concept seems to border on the metaphysical. If tests A and B, between them, predict only a part of the variance associated with a behaviour, it is difficult to imagine any experiment which would show that the remaining part depended on interaction effects between determinants A and B rather than on the effects of, say, C. The relevance of any particular C could always be subjected to scrutiny, but not that of all possible Cs. It is quite certain, however, that any attempt to pursue the problem at all would require the existence of measures for the individual determinants A, B, C, D, . . ., etc., rather than mixtures of several of them in unknown proportions.

The concept of emergence, in so far as it is not simply an acknowledgement of ignorance, does no more than re-state the fact that the relationships with which science is concerned are descriptive, and not explanatory. If the interaction of A and B leads to events of an order (A, B, Δ) rather than (A, B) all that matters is to discover whether a specific interaction leads repeatedly to a particular event (E_i) or not. If it does not, even to a useful degree of approximation, then the phenomena concerned cannot be made the subject of any kind of scientific study. If it does, then the successful prediction that E_i will occur would seem to depend entirely on our ability to distinguish A, B, E_i and the interaction concerned, from the general background of other irrelevant phenomena, i.e. successful prediction presupposes adequate atomization.

The development of cognitive tests does not seem to have been guided, to any great extent, by considerations of the type which have now been advanced. Thorndike (1926) was clearly aware of, and critical of, this defect. He asserted that tests of intellect displayed "ambiguity of content, arbitrariness of units, and ambiguity of significance," and suggested that at least three scores, rather than one, were needed to describe intellectual ability. The first of these was to be a measure of the range of operations a particular intelligence could perform, the second was concerned with the rate at which these operations could proceed, and the third with the maximum level of difficulty at which satisfactory operation could be achieved. The present writer's whole approach to the measurement of human intellectual function has developed out of

ideas which found their earliest systematic presentation in this volume. Thorndike's development of them seems to have been hampered, however, by an approach that was at times over semantic, and by a failure to define his fundamental concepts with sufficient rigour. He was particularly concerned with an attempt to define an entity called "the intellect" (Thorndike, *The Measurement of Intelligence*, 1926; cf. the long discussion on p. 25 *et seq*.), rather than to develop the atomistic framework of description which would seem to have been the logical result of his own insights.

Spearman himself attempted to define three different components of intellect, but there seems to have grown up, among British psychologists at least, a very strong tendency to use "g" as an explanatory concept not itself amenable to further subdivision. The preconceptions of the majority of workers are well demonstrated by the titles under which they have reported their results, the archetype involving some such formulation as: "An attempt to find a factor of 'speed' as opposed to 'g.'" The danger of such preconceptions is well illustrated in a paper by Sutherland (1934), who examined the intercorrelations between three measures of the time taken to solve simple problems correctly, and one measure of g. He argued that, since score in the g test was not a speed measure, the existence of a factor of "speed" within the three time tests could only be assumed if their intercorrelations remained significant when the contribution of g was partialled out. As their average residual correlation with g eliminated was only about 0·12 he concluded that no speed factor existed. He does not appear to have noticed that the average correlation between time scores and g scores was about 0·57, while the average of the reliabilities of the time scores was about 0·57 also. The greater part of the non-chance variance of each of the time scores must thus have been determined by g. If, therefore, g is assumed to be independent of speed the ludicrous conclusion must be accepted that the time taken to solve problems is not a measure of speed.

It is, of course, possible, although rather unlikely, that the perfect g test is concerned only with the effects of some single determinant. It seems much more probable, however, that cognitive tests display positive intercorrelations because rather similar interactions of the same set of determinants play an important part in determining score in all of them, and the foundations of an adequate knowledge of the nature of test-taking behaviour must be based on the study of these individual determinants and of their modes of interaction.

It seems to the writer that the application of the statistical technique of factor analysis to large batteries of psychological tests (e.g. Holzinger,

1934–5 and Thurstone, 1939) with the object of defining group-factors in terms of which intellectual function can be described, has done less to advance our knowledge of intellectual mechanisms than is commonly assumed. It is difficult to resist the conclusion that all this work has been rather too empirical, and that most of it will eventually have to be repeated. It is often very useful to know how particular test-scores relate together, but if, as seems probable, most test-scores reflect the interaction of a set of attributes whose composition and relative importance are a function both of the exact details of construction of the test (e.g. the range of difficulty covered by the items it embodies) and also of the characteristics of the group within which it is used, then generalization from the findings of a particular investigation becomes almost impossible. It is not without significance that, after three decades during which test-scores of the conventional kind have been the basic data upon which factorial studies have been erected, nothing even remotely resembling an acceptable theory of cognition has been evolved. This is not the fault of the technique of factor analysis, which has in fact the unusual power of serving at the same time as a means of analysis and also of synthesis. It could perhaps be claimed that the factor-analysts have, on the whole, given very adequate answers to questions which have not always been very carefully formulated.

Within even the most carefully designed of existing "single-factor" tests analysis will reveal the existence of logically distinguishable categories of response whose possible effects on score demand separate consideration. Thorndike's subdivisions of "speed" and "altitude," for example, together with related concepts such as "accuracy," seem to be applicable to most of them. It follows that it is impossible to know just what significance can legitimately be assigned to these "factors." Vernon (1950), for example, has suggested that the "w" and "f" (fluency) factors of the Primary Mental Abilities studies are differentiated from the verbal factor "v" only in terms of the level of difficulty at which the two kinds of score were obtained. The following brief analysis will perhaps serve to direct attention to a further ambiguity of a similar kind.

Suppose that there are two relatively independent attributes, say "speed" and "accuracy," each of which affects test performance separately in a way which varies with the difficulty of the test and with the time allowed for completion, but not with test content. In any heterogeneous set, tests will vary in difficulty and in the time allowed for completion, and the correlations between tests could therefore reflect these differences as well as, or even rather than, those associated with content. In view of this possibility each of the fifty-seven tests used in the original P.M.A.

experiment was considered in turn, and a decision made as to whether it was likely to have served as a measure for speed or for accuracy in the experimental population used. In making this decision consideration was given to any experience the writer might have had in using the same, or a similar test within a British population of university students, to the method of scoring adopted, to the shape of the distribution of scores, to the time allowed, and to the apparent difficulty of the test items as gauged from a brief scrutiny. In respect of thirteen tests no decision could be made with even moderate confidence. Sixteen seemed to be concerned mainly with speed, ten with accuracy, and eighteen with both. In order to simplify the analysis the factors isolated from Thurstone's matrix by Eysenck (1939), using Burt's group-factor method, were used instead of the oblique solution favoured by Thurstone himself. In Eysenck's study only four factors were of any great importance, the remaining five each accounting for less than 2 per cent of the total variance. One of the four factors concerned was a general factor accounting for some 31 per cent of the total variance, the others being Verbal-Literary (5 per cent), Arithmetical (4·6 per cent), and Visuo-Spatial (6·6 per cent).

After the speed/accuracy dependence of all fifty-seven tests had been estimated the nine tests having loadings greater than 0·3 on the Arithmetical axis were examined. Six of them had been designated measures of speed, one of accuracy, one mixed, and one unclassified. Of the fifteen tests defining the Visuo-Spatial factor, five had been designated measures of accuracy, seven mixed, two speed and one unclassified. Both speed and accuracy are represented to an approximately equal degree within the Verbal-Literary tests, four being measures of speed, three mixed, and two accuracy. Of the seventeen tests having loadings above 0·65 on the General-Factor only one represents speed, while no less than six had been designated accuracy. At g saturations below 0·4, on the other hand, four of the nine classifiable tests measured speed, and only one accuracy.

It would be absurd to make too much of so cursory an examination. The evidence could, however, be interpreted as supporting the hypothesis that at least part of the apparent differentiation between Visuo-Spatial and Arithmetical tests is not due to differences of content at all, but to differences in the extent to which they measure speed as opposed to accuracy. The association of tests measuring accuracy with high loadings on the General-Factor is of interest in that it helps with the interpretation of the Factor. It is not however really relevant to the point under discussion, and in the present context the analysis will have served its purpose if it illustrates the difficulties which attend the use of the kind of complex test that still represents the psychologist's chief measuring instrument. It is rather as if the electrician had no means of measuring current and voltage independently, but could only use a wattmeter, to measure their product; or as if a tailor had to fit his customers from a knowledge of their weights.

In spite of its greater sophistication and range the monumental work of Guilford and his school, which is still proceeding, is of the same general kind as were the earlier studies (*see* Guilford, 1956, for a good summary of this work). The scores upon which the analyses are erected must all be based upon such complex interactions of material, operation, and context, that the disentangling of the true basic determinants, even with the aid of the most refined of correlational techniques, must be virtually impossible.

There has been an uneasy awareness of the unsatisfactory nature of psychological-test scores for several decades. It has been reflected in the work of Thorndike, and of the Factorists, but the approach of those who have participated in the speed-power controversy, although often extremely confused and unsatisfactory, seems to the writer to have displayed the most accurate assessment of the real nature of the problem. The search for a speed factor within intelligent behaviour began even before the first intelligence tests came into existence (e.g. J. Cattell's experiments at Columbia in 1894). Many workers, on the other hand, have denied the need for the separate measurement of speed, pointing to the high correlations between scores in timed and untimed tests in support of their contention. A paper by Sutherland was mentioned rather critically on a previous page (Sutherland, 1934), but its defects lay only in the initial acceptance of an unjustified assumption, in every other respect it displayed a standard of competence which could well have been taken as a model by the majority of participants in the controversy. Most studies have suffered from an astonishing degree of technical inadequacy. Speed was usually assessed by giving what was in part an accuracy score, such as the number of items solved correctly within a time-limit test. Alternatively, it was defined in terms of the total time required by the subject to complete a test, with complete disregard of the fact that correct and incorrect responses, as well as abandonments and omissions were thus assumed to be equivalent. Terms such as *power* and *level* seem sometimes to have been regarded as interchangeable, but at other times to involve important distinctions, while either might imply the total score under time-limit conditions, or alternatively under untimed conditions, at the whim of the author. Scores of these unsatisfactory types were then intercorrelated and the resulting coefficients interpreted with complete disregard of the part/whole

effects which they almost invariably incorporated. It is hardly surprising that the question as to whether speed of response demands separate consideration as a determinant of intelligent behaviour is still regarded by some as being an open one. The relevant literature cannot be reviewed here—it is far too voluminous—but two important studies are worthy of note. Slater (1938) has shown that within groups having a very small variance for score on a standardized intelligence test a very wide range of mental speeds (as measured by response-time per item correctly solved) can be demonstrated, and that these between-person differences in speed are associated with differences in school attainment. Tate (1950) has provided an able discussion of the problem of speed measurement, and has shown experimentally that such measurement can be accomplished with a very high degree of reliability and validity. Furneaux (1948) has also reported work which both supports and supplements that of Tate. Taken together these contributions suggest most strongly that the simple, unambiguous scores which result from properly considered measurements of response-rate are theoretically sound and also useful in practice. It occurred to the writer that they also have the merit of being scores of a kind which cannot easily be redefined in terms of sets of simpler determinants, and that they therefore satisfy the requirements elaborated in the opening paragraphs of this chapter. The question seemed to arise, therefore, as to whether it might not be possible and profitable to consider the human problem-solver (and thus the cognitive-test-taker) simply as a "black-box" whose input-output characteristics require to be specified in terms of unambiguously defined observations. This involves the setting on one side of the whole of the approach to cognitive function which originated with Binet and has come to be taken for granted ever since. Instead, we must approach problem-solving as if it were some kind of multiple-choice reaction, to be dealt with as far as possible by an extension of the classical stimulus-response approach which characterized the earliest days of systematized psychological research, and which was shown to be of value by such workers as Kirkpatrick (1900) and Kelly (1903). It is perhaps arguable that, if the orderly progress exemplified by such experiments had not been virtually halted following the publication of Binet's work in 1905, the whole field of psychometrics might by now have been far more soundly based than it is. This is not of course to argue that one should attempt to ignore the immensely valuable results which have been obtained by Binet and the mental-test movement which he founded. Binet's accomplishment in this field, however, was to devise a brilliant solution for an urgent practical problem, the solution involving the design of a novel form of school examination.

Psychologists have been feeling their cautious way back from this toward a genuinely scientific system of measurement ever since.

The relevance of the discussion, so far, to the study of abnormal (or normal) intellectual function can perhaps be illustrated by an example. At the present time one question frequently asked about the effects of psychoticism on intellectual function is something like: "Is the intelligence of psychotics reduced as compared with that of normals?" A very large number of studies has been made in an attempt to answer this question, with conflicting results. A typical experiment involves the administration of a standardized intelligence test to a sample of schizophrenics and to a sample of normals, followed by a comparison of the scores achieved by the two groups. The score a person achieves in a conventional intelligence test is a simple function of the number of problems which he can solve correctly, from a set which are given to him, in a particular specified time. His final score thus depends in part on how long he has to spend in obtaining those answers which prove to be right, in part on the amount of time he wastes in evolving answers which prove to be wrong, and in part on his ratio of right to wrong answers.[1] Unless these three determinants of score are highly correlated within both normal and schizophrenic groups it is impossible either to interpret the results of the experiment satisfactorily, or to generalize from them. If normals and schizophrenics achieve much the same scores, this may indicate that the problem-solving characteristics of both groups are virtually the same. The same result could arise, however, if schizophrenics were less accurate than normals but obtained both right and wrong answers more quickly. Alternatively they might be equally accurate, but might be quicker at arriving at incorrect solutions and slower at reaching correct ones. If this latter explanation were correct, then it would follow that if the experiment were repeated using an intelligence test in which the average difficulty of the problems was increased, then a different result would be obtained in that the schizophrenics would obtain higher scores than the normals. Even where the equality of scores arises from an identity of problem-solving performance between the two groups, it could not be assumed that a similar identity would arise in connexion with an easier or more difficult test, since this would be to assume that comparisons of performance made at one level of difficulty would be valid for problems at other levels. The methods of item analysis used in the construction of intelligence tests ensure that comparisons of accuracy made at one level of difficulty within normal groups bear some relation to those which would be made at another,[1] but they take no account of rate at all, and the item analyses made within normal groups are never repeated within the abnormal groups for which the tests are nevertheless assumed to be valid.

This list of shortcomings is far from exhaustive, but it will probably suffice to show that little useful information about intellectual functions can be obtained from the use of conventional intelligence tests in the absence of an adequate theoretical and experimental analysis of the ways in which a person's responses, first to single problems and then to carefully defined sets of problems, can legitimately be scored. An attempt will now be made to sketch in the bare skeleton of such an analysis and to report briefly on the results of some experimental work to which it has led, and to discuss some of the implications of both theory and experiment.

The Analysis of a Formalized Problem-solver

Scientific investigation has always to start with the brutal oversimplification of the phenomena with which it is concerned. In order to lay the foundations of the study of problem-solving behaviour it is necessary to ignore many attributes which undoubtedly influence problem-solving responses, and to concentrate at first on a few limited fields of study. It facilitates such an approach if we formalize the human problem-solver, regarding him simply as a problem-solving-box (PB) having only such characteristics as we may explicitly assign to it.

Let PB be a problem-box containing an unspecified mechanism, of such a nature that when it is supplied with an input I in the form of a problem, an output is produced which represents an attempt to solve the problem. Suppose that each such output is designated an *essay*,[2] and is represented by the symbol O_e.

This input/output relationship can conveniently be set out in symbolic form, i.e.—

$$I[PB] \rightarrow O_e$$

Suppose that a time, t_e elapses between the feeding in of the input and the production of the output. We can incorporate this additional information thus—

$$I[PB] \rightarrow O_e, t_e$$

After it has been produced any O_e can be inspected and a decision made as to whether it is right or wrong. Let any O_e which represents a right answer be reclassified as O_r, while O_w stands for a wrong answer, and let t_r and t_w be the values of t_e relevant

---

[1] This analysis is not really adequate, as will appear, but will serve for the present illustration.

[1] As will appear, even this statement is not strictly true.

[2] The term *essay* has been used, because, although archaic, it leads to the use of *e* in suffix positions rather than other letters of a more ambiguous connotation. Thus the use of *trial* would involve the suffix *t*, which is already widely used in connexion with measurements of time.

to O_r and O_w respectively. Thus all O_r and all O_w are also O_e, and all t_r and all t_w are also t_e.

Suppose now that it is observed that the repeated application of a particular input $_pI$ to a particular Problem-box $_\alpha PB$ is followed by O_r on the proportion of occasions q_r, but by O_w on the remaining proportion, q_w, the sequence of responses being unpredictable save in cases where q_r has the value zero or unity. We can designate this symbolically thus—

$$\{_pI\}[_\alpha PB] \rightarrow \{O_r\}^p + \{O_w\}^q$$

where the curly bracket has in each case the usual connotation of "a set of." Suppose further that even if attention is confined to $\{O_r\}$ the associated values of t_r are not all equal but vary in unpredictable sequence between the limits R_t and $(R_t + H_{tr})$, defining a distribution having a mean of $\bar{t}_r$ and variance V_{tr}. Similarly let the $\{t_w\}$ associated with $\{O_w\}$ define a distribution having the limits W_t and $(W_t + H_{tw})$, variance V_{tw}, and mean $\bar{t}_w$. Then we can write—

$$\{_pI\}[_\alpha PB] \rightarrow \{O_r\}^p, \{t_r\} + \{O_w\}^q, \{t_w\}$$

In order that the terms on the right-hand side of this relationship can unambiguously be associated with the results of applying a particular $_pI$ to a particular $_\alpha PB$, even when set down in the absence of the left-hand side, it is convenient to add appropriate suffixes, thus—

$$\{_pI\}[_\alpha PB] \rightarrow \{_{p\alpha}O_r\}^p, \{_{p\alpha}t_r\} + \{_{p\alpha}O_w\}^q, \{_{p\alpha}t_w\}$$

while the addition of similar suffixes to the distribution statistics, e.g. $_{p\alpha}V_{tr}$, shows to which problem and to which PB they relate. It will be convenient to use the symbol M to stand for the whole set of parameters of a particular kind, or for a particular distribution. Thus we have—

$_{p\alpha}M_{tr}$ comprises $_{p\alpha}\bar{t}_r$, $_{p\alpha}V_{tr}$, $_{p\alpha}R_t$, and $_{p\alpha}(R_t + H_{tr})$
$_{p\alpha}M_{tw}$ comprises $_{p\alpha}\bar{t}_w$, etc., etc.,

while

$_{p\alpha}M_{qr}$ comprises only q_r.

Since both O_r and O_w are special cases of O_e it follows that we also have $_{p\alpha}M_{te}$, where

$$_{p\alpha}M_{te} = _{p\alpha}M_{tr} + _{p\alpha}M_{tw}.$$

It is not necessary to give separate consideration to $_{p\alpha}M_{qw}$ since $q_w = 1 \cdot 0 - q_r$.

Our assessment of the problem-solving characteristics of $_\alpha PB$ must start with the collecting of sets of observations from which the values of these various "M-statistics" can be computed, all with reference to the inputs provided by a particular problem p. We can then collect similar data using the same input $_pI$

to other problem-boxes, $_\beta PB$, $_\gamma OB$, etc., and in this way compare their characteristics in respect of this one problem. Although, for a particular purpose, interest may centre on a particular statistic, say $\bar{t}_r$, we must not make the mistake of assuming that one statistic is of greater intrinsic importance than another, or of attempting to define the behaviour of a PB in terms of one statistic only in the absence of clear evidence that all are highly correlated. Nor must we compare, say, the value of $\bar{t}_r$ derived from one PB with the value of $\bar{t}_w$ or q_r derived from another, and imagine that the comparison has a meaning. It would be equally unwise to set up a score which was a more or less undefined function of a lumping together of several of the statistics and then to imagine that it could have more than an accidental significance. All these strange operations are involved in current mental-testing procedures, although often to a rather mild degree.

The value of any measurement of behaviour can be assessed only in terms of the extent to which it relates to other measurements of different kinds (for the purpose of theory construction) and to various kinds of "real-life performance." There is no *a priori* reason why the sets of M-statistics associated with each of a properly selected set of single problems should not turn out to represent a set of scores which have a greater value, thus assessed, than scores derived from tests made up of assemblages of problems.[1] In order to pick out the most useful set of single problems from among all possible problems it is necessary to find ways in which problems can be classified, and it is at this stage that concepts need to be introduced similar to those of "difficulty" and "type" which are in current use.

The concept of difficulty arose originally because, on introspection, the sense of effort associated with attempts to solve some problems is stronger than that associated with others. By analogy with the fact that, for example, differences in experienced brightness intensities can be related to a measurable property of the relevant stimuli, an attempt was made to relate differences in experienced effort to a measurable property of problems—their "difficulty." Unfortunately, on inspecting problems, no such property can be observed, nor can it unambiguously be associated with any of those properties of problems which can be observed such as the number of symbols which are required for their presentation. In spite of this the idea that a problem "has" a difficulty, the value of which can be discovered by suitable measurement, has persisted, and the procedure commonly employed

---

[1] Once the discussion moves from the consideration of *PB*s to that of actual human subjects it becomes necessary to reconsider the validity of this statement, because of complications arising from the effects of practice, etc., when a single problem is solved repeatedly.

in order to discover the difficulties of problems is to scale them in terms of the number of individuals in some defined group who fail in their attempts to achieve an acceptable solution. Recognizing that the "difficulty-values" thus allotted are a function of the group within which the calibration has been made, the more sophisticated approaches involve attempts to transform the values thus obtained into the values which would have been observed in some such group as "an unselected normal population," or even to define a scale having an absolute zero (Thorndike, 1926). Controversies have arisen from time to time as to whether the measurement of difficulty is most accurately carried out in terms of observations of the number of people who fail a problem, or of the time taken for satisfactory solutions to be achieved.

The notions underlying this approach may be well founded, and the development of information-theory concepts may eventually make it possible to scale problems for difficulty in terms of the right kind of analysis of their structure. So far, however, they seem to have led only to confusion. It seems better to accept the fact that problems can only be classified in terms of the differences in response characteristics which they evoke. We can justifiably scale them in terms of the values of $\bar{\imath}_r$, V_{tr}, q_r, etc., which are associated with them, but no useful purpose seems to be served by the choice of one particular statistic as being a measure of "difficulty," or by discussion as to which statistic affords the best measure of "difficulty." It is necessary to bear in mind, moreover, that any scale is intended to fulfil a particular limited classificatory function, and scales evolved in connexion with the responses evoked by problems must be constructed with this function in mind. Since all the components of response which have so far been discussed would seem to have much the same *a priori* importance, and since, in the absence of experimentation, their interrelationships are not known, it is necessary, in the first instance, to define a separate scale in connexion with each component, i.e. for our present purposes, in connexion with each of the M-statistics. It is convenient to call such scales "D-scales." That scale which is concerned with the ordering of problems in terms of the values of $\bar{\imath}_r$ which they evoke can usefully be designated the D_{tr} scale, and in terms of the same convention the D_{Vr} scale will relate to values of V_{tr}, D_{qr} to values of q_r, and so on.

To consider the D_{tr} scale as an example, the problem of scale construction is to assign to every problem a D_{tr} scale position such that if any $_{p\alpha}\bar{\imath}_r$ is measured then for any other input set $\{_{q\alpha}I\}$ the relevant value of $_{q\alpha}\bar{\imath}_r$ can accurately be forecast from a knowledge of $_{p\alpha}\bar{\imath}_r$, the scale position of p, and the scale position of q. If the scale position allotted to q is denoted by $_qD_{tr}$, then the requirement can be stated symbolically, and in a slightly modified form, thus—

$$\begin{aligned}_q\bar{\imath}_r &= f(_qD_{tr}, {}_\alpha K_{tr}) \\ &= f(D, K)_{tr}\end{aligned} \qquad (1)$$

where $_\alpha K_{tr}$ is an individual constant assigned to $_\alpha PB$ in terms of the value of $_{p\alpha}\bar{\imath}_r$ which is observed for it. The crucial requirement, of course, is that the form of $f(D, K)_{tr}$ must be the same for all individuals, only the value of K_{tr} differing from one person to another. Once the double task is completed of finding a form for $f(D, K)_{tr}$ and scale positions for p, q, etc., such that equation (1) is satisfied, all comparisons between individual PB's in terms of $\bar{\imath}_r$ can be made in terms of one measure per PB (i.e. K_{tr}) instead of in terms of all the values of $\bar{\imath}_r$ relevant to all possible problems.

Correlational studies using conventional test-scores have shown that performance in one kind of test cannot necessarily be forecast from a knowledge of performance in another kind. Such results suggest rather strongly that it may not be possible to arrange all possible problems along a single D_{tr} scale for use in conjunction with a particular form for $f(D, K)_{tr}$. We must be prepared to find that problems fall into sets (which may or may not involve differences of content analogous to the v, s, f, r, and other factors which result from the factor analysis of conventional test scores) for each of which a different D_{tr} scale and a different form for $f(D, K)_{tr}$ may be required. The members of any one set of problems may be said to define a particular *type* of problem. In the absence of experimentation it is impossible to say whether attempts at scale formation will lead to the discovery of a relatively small number of clearly discrete types, or to that of an infinite number which shade imperceptibly one into the other. In face of the latter eventuality it would be possible to define discrete types, for practical purposes, by assigning to the same type all those problems whose $\bar{\imath}_r$ values could be specified in terms of the same D_{tr} scale and the same form for $f(D, K)_{tr}$, within the limits of some specified degree of error. It is also possible that all attempts to construct D_{tr} scales, applicable without alteration to all PBs, might fail, but that subgroups of PBs could be defined within each of which all the members could be covered by a common scale. Although the construction of D scales can be carried out empirically and has a purely classificatory function it will be clear on reflection that the form of the function $f(D, K)$ which is relevant to a particular scale is contingent on the nature of the mechanism within PB whose functioning intervenes between the feeding in of an input and the appearance of an output. At this point the analysis thus has important implications in connexion with the study of abnormal behaviour. If it is found that the form of $f(D, K)$ relevant to a particular D scale is different in an abnormal group from that found for normal groups then it can be inferred that the actual nature of the problem-solving mechanism differs between normals and abnormals. If the $f(D, K)$ is common to both groups, however, then the nature of the mechanism is probably the same, although normals and abnormals might still be differentiated in terms of some of the Ks relevant to the M-statistics. So far as the writer knows there have as yet been no investigations of this kind.

The argument which has been conducted in terms of the D_{tr} scale is equally applicable to all the other scales implied by the statistics comprised within M_{tr}, M_{tw}, and M_{qr}. The primary concern of the psychometrician should thus be the construction of D scales, and in the absence of such scales there is no really satisfactory basis for the economical comparison of the problem-solving characteristics of different PB's or classes of PB. Given such scales, with each of which will be associated a particular $f(D, K)$, all comparisons will be made in terms of the K values relevant to the M-statistics associated with the types of problem which are being subject to study. Values of K can either be measured by the application of a particular $\{_{p\alpha}I\}$ or by computations based on the form of $f(D, K)$, following the single application of each of a number of problems which are members of the same D scale, and whose D positions are known.[1] Every kind of K value has an unambiguous meaning, however derived, in that it specifies the numerical value which would be observed for a particular M-statistic if a particular standard problem were applied to a particular PB. Questions of standardization, etc., do not therefore arise, although they are replaced, of course, by the problems involved in setting up D scales. As will appear, these latter are much more susceptible of solution than are those of defining, and collecting, a stratified sample from which can be deduced the characteristics of "an unselected normal population."

It is now necessary to modify the definition of a PB in order to take account of a property of the human problem-solver which has an important effect on his characteristics, although it seems never to be taken into account. When attempting a set of problems, as in a test, the subject is not willing to spend unlimited time on any one item. Faced with a difficulty which cannot be resolved within what, under all the circumstances seems to be a reasonable time, the reaction is to abandon the problem concerned, and to pass on to the next one. The length of time for which the subject continues to work at a particular problem has as one of its determinants his persistence, but this is

[1] Because of the effects of memory, this latter is the only feasible procedure with human subjects.

not the only factor involved, since the decision to abandon an item may sometimes be made on grounds which involve an intelligent assessment of the effects on score of attempting a lot of items rather than persisting with a few. It will be convenient, therefore, to designate the attribute as "Continuance," or C, a term free from any aetiological presuppositions. PB may be given characteristics analogous with those resulting from C by adding to it a device ST having the functions of a time-switch.

Let any input to PB be represented simultaneously at the input to ST. Let the normal state of ST be "off," but let it change to "on" immediately an input is received, and let it then remain in that state for a time t_s before reverting automatically to "off," at which time we can say that "Continuance has been exhausted." In the present context it is possible to consider only the simplest characteristics for ST, i.e. that it has no means of distinguishing between different problems as inputs, and that t_s varies between the limits S_t and $(S_t + H_{ts})$, defining a distribution M_{ts} of variance V_{ts} and mean $\bar{t}_s$, within which the sequence of t_s values cannot be predicted.

Let ST be coupled to PB, defining the composite device $(PB + ST)$, or PS. Let the ST relevant to $_{\alpha}PB$ be denoted $_{\alpha}ST$ and let the PS which results when they are coupled be $_{\alpha}PS$. Let the coupling be of such a nature that PB cannot start its problem-solving activity until ST is "on," and that the problem-solving process within PB is terminated as soon as it reverts to "off." Let such termination be signified by the appearance of an output O_s from PB, different in nature from the O_e which marks the production of an essay, and analogous to the entering of a dash or a question mark in the answer space on the part of a subject. If PB produces an O_e before C is exhausted, then ST moves to "off" immediately, and without the occurrence of O_s. A value of t_s which would have been observed if ST had not been coupled to PB is thus deleted from the M_{ts} distribution, whose characteristics are thus altered. In order that we can refer unambiguously and economically to the distributions which would have arisen in the absence of coupling and to those that are actually observed from the coupled device it will be useful to denote the former by M_{ts} as previously and the latter by M_{ts}. In a similar way, if C is exhausted before the value of t_e relevant to a particular input has elapsed, then an O_s will arise instead of the O_e which would have been observed in the absence of coupling, and a value of t_e will be lost from M_{te}. Let the resulting modified distribution be denoted by M_{te}. Any statistic relevant to any M can be distinguished from that relevant to the corresponding M in a similar way, e.g. by V_{te} instead of V_{te}. It will also be convenient to use the term "search" to denote the activity which is initiated within PB by an input I, and which terminates with the production of an O_e, or when ST moves to "off."

It is now possible to show that the evolution of D scales and the practical measurement of the various M statistics is considerably complicated by the effects of C. Unless these complications are taken into account, any attempt to compare normal and abnormal individuals, whether by using conventional tests or otherwise, may give rise to very misleading

never be switched off by the intervention of $_\alpha ST$, but always following the appearance of an O_e. In this region of D all M_{te} statistics are therefore unaffected. At D values greater than Z the $_\alpha PB$ will always be switched off by $_\alpha ST$ before an O_e can appear. In the region X to Y the number of O_e appearing after the lapse of times having values lying near to line B will be reduced, because on a proportion of occasions the $_\alpha PB$ will be shut off by $_\alpha ST$ before they have time to

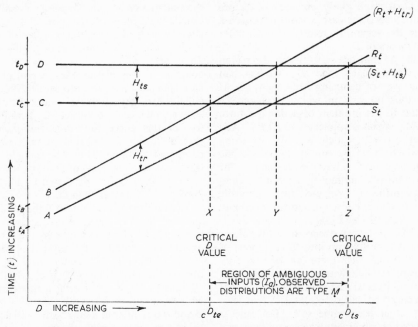

FIG. 5.1. THE INTERACTION OF SPEED AND CONTINUANCE, THEORETICAL

results. Terminological and other complications of considerable complexity result unless, in analysing the effects of C, the simplifying assumption is made that all types of D scale are identical. In the discussion which follows, therefore, the general term D scale will be used to cover all the scales D_{tr}, D_{tw}, D_{qr}, etc., unless the contrary is stated. Once the analysis has been completed in these terms the validity of the assumption can be tested experimentally.

Consider the relationships shown in Fig. 5.1 where the lines A and B, originating at t_a and t_b are supposed to define, for $_\alpha PB$, the longest and shortest times required for the production of an O_e at any value of D, there being no coupling between $_\alpha PB$ and $_\alpha ST$. The lines D and C define the longest and shortest values of t_s which relate to the uncoupled $_\alpha ST$, these values, $(S_t + H_{ts})$ and S_t, being the same at all values of D. If $_\alpha ST$ and $_\alpha PB$ are now coupled, the characteristics of the coupled device, PS, can be deduced from the diagram. At values of D less than X the $_\alpha PB$ will

appear. All those O_e appearing after times lying near to line A will however still arise. Between Y and Z the $_\alpha PB$ will always have been switched off before any O_e having $t_e > (S_t + H_{ts})$ can arise, so that for that small number of O_e that can emerge at all, values of t_e in the region of line A will predominate strongly. For D values greater than X, therefore, M_{te} will differ from M_{te} at all values of D, the difference becoming extreme at D values which approach Z.

It is important to realize that the actual values of D which correspond to the points X and Z will differ from one PS to another, depending in part on K_{te} and in part on $\bar{t}_s$. It will be useful to refer to problems having D values in the range $D = X$ to $D = Z$, for a particular PS, as problems which, for it, constitute *ambiguous-inputs*, or I_a. (Strictly speaking, of course it is not the inputs which are ambiguous, but the statistics based on their outputs.) The term I_u (unambiguous-input) will have the obvious complementary meaning. It will also be useful to use the term *critical-D-value* for values of D, such as those which have so far been denoted by X and Z, at which there is a transition from I_a to I_u, or vice versa. The critical value for the M_e statistics can be denoted by $_cD_{te}$, and that for M_s by $_cD_{ts}$.

If the characteristics of $_\alpha ST$ be considered, then for $D > {}_cD_{ts}$ all the M_{ts} statistics are identical with those of M_{ts}, for no O_e arise. For $D < {}_cD_{ts}$, on those occasions when the uncoupled t_s approaches the value $(S_t + H_{ts})$ an O_e is more likely to intervene before switch-off occurs than is the case when it approaches the value S_t. In this region, therefore, M_{ts} will differ from M_{ts} at all values of D.

Given only the M statistics (relevant to the region where D has a value greater than $_cD_{te}$ but less than $_cD_{ts}$) there is no way of deducing from them the M statistics, and thus no way in which data can be obtained relevant to the problem of defining a form for, say, $f(D, K)_{tr}$, which is applicable to all *PS*. Any comparison between *PS*s which is made by using problems for which $D > {}_cD_{te}$ can apply only to the particular D value, or values, concerned. The statistics being compared, moreover, are not the carefully defined quantities $\bar{t}_e$, V_{te}, etc., but composite measures depending in unknown proportions on both the statistics of M_{te} and also of M_{ts}.

A human subject is always observed in his role as a *PS*, and can never be split up into the components *PB* and *ST*. There may well, therefore, be very considerable ranges of D values within which attempts to compare sets of subjects will be unsatisfactory in that the problems concerned will represent I_a for at least some members of at least some sets. For such a subject the statistics observed when problems are administered will be M rather than M, and will thus be useless. It follows that tests designed to measure M_{te} statistics within heterogeneous groups will probably have to consist of rather "easy" problems. The only alternative is to try to raise $\bar{t}_s$ to such a high value that interaction of M_{te} and M_{ts} does not occur even at high D values. This would mean ensuring very high motivation for all individuals tested, and administering problems one at a time in a face to face situation so that problems were not abandoned as a result of a desire to attempt all those appearing on a test-sheet.

Fig. 5.1 has been used to illustrate the general case of O_e responses, but it could be applied equally well in connexion with the temporal characteristics of either O_r or O_w responses separately. Since the $f(D, K)$ relevant to D_{tr} and D_{tw} scales may differ, and since the M_{tr} statistics may have numerical values different from those for M_{tw}, it follows that an input which is I_u when it results in an O_r response might be I_a if it gave rise to an O_w. It is thus necessary to refer to inputs which are $I_{a(tr)}$ or $I_{a(tw)}$ to prevent ambiguity.

In the same way there will be one *critical-D-value*, $_cD_{tr}$, which is relevant to O_r responses, and another, $_cD_{tw}$, for O_w responses.

If O_r responses are now considered, then by analogy with the argument which has just been considered for O_e responses in general, a proportion of potential O_r responses will be lost when $I_{a(tr)}$ inputs are employed, being replaced by an equal number of O_s responses. Given a knowledge of the form of $f(D, K)_{tr}$ and of the statistics of M_{tr} and M_{ts}, it is possible to compute exactly what proportion of potential O_r responses can actually arise at any specified value of D_{tr} for a particular *PS*. This proportion will be unity at $D_{tr} < {}_cD_{tr}$, and zero at $D_{tr} > {}_cD_{ts}$, so that the complete curve relating the proportion of potential O_r responses arising (P_{sr}) to the D_{tr} value of the input will have a form bearing some relationship to that shown by the curve B in Fig. 5.2. It will be convenient to call this curve the *completion-characteristic*. It should be noted that this characteristic cannot be computed, as might at first be thought, by making a direct count of the ratio of O_r to O_s responses at each value of D, since any particular O_s may represent an unrealized O_w rather than O_r.

To problems at any value of D there will be a relevant value of q_r. Let the relationship between q_r and D be something like that shown by the *accuracy-characteristic* represented by the curve A of Fig. 5.2.

The probability (P_{srq}) that an O_r will actually be observed at any value of D is clearly the product of P_{sr} and q_r. If K_{qr} has only a moderate correlation with K_{tr} and $\bar{t}_s$ then for different *PS*'s the two curves A and B can differ in their relative and actual positions to a very considerable degree. Suppose that one untimed test of a conventional type involves items in the range P of D values (Fig. 5.2), while another covers the range Q. The curves A and B in Fig. 5.2 relate to a *PS* of low accuracy but high completion, and for it the only determinant of success in both tests is accuracy, since at D values such that completion is less than $1 \cdot 0$ all the responses would in any case be O_w. Suppose, however, that accuracy had been greater. Then the accuracy curve A would move to the right, towards the completion-curve. Accuracy would still be the only determinant of success in test P, but both accuracy and completion would be active in Q. If curve B moved to the left, indicating poorer completion, then test P would become a composite measure for both attributes, while if accuracy were a little greater and completion a little less then both tests would involve both determinants, but in different proportions.

Since completion is a function of the interaction of "speed" (as measured by K_{tr}) and "continuance" (as measured by $\bar{t}_s$) curve B will move to the left if either speed or continuance is reduced. The same mental test, if designed and scored in the conventional manner, will thus measure different combinations of speed, accuracy and continuance when applied to different *PS*s. Again, if a *PS* is fed with different tests, all of the same type, but all covering different ranges of *D*, then the score derived from each such test can relate to a different attribute or combination of attributes. It is an interesting corollary of this analysis that a test set without time-limit is not

these items are sufficiently "difficult" to lead to the production of some incorrect solutions by most members of the group, none are so difficult in relation to the range of mental speed existing within the group as to be given up as insoluble. If such a two-part test is set with time limit, the slowest members of the group will still be working on the N_e easy items when the time limit expires, and for them the determinants of success will be speed only. The moderately fast

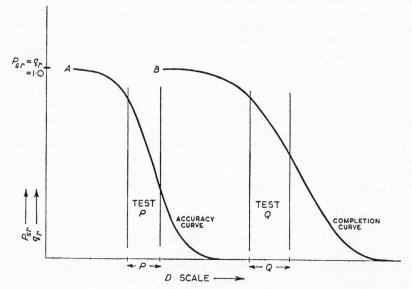

FIG. 5.2. THE INTERACTION OF COMPLETION AND ACCURACY, THEORETICAL

necessarily, or usually, a "speed-free" test. In any test which includes problems having *D* values which, for a particular subject, are greater than $_cD_{tr}$, score is determined in part by the completion characteristic, which is itself, in part, a function of speed (K_{tr}).

Some Implications

It seems that these conclusions, based on the analysis of a *PS*, must be applied equally to the human subject. Consider, as a further illustration, a test made up of items having such low *D* values that no individual in the population being examined returns any incorrect solutions. As the items are "easy" they will all be solved quite quickly, so continuance will not be a determinant of success. Under these circumstances the only factor influencing score if the test is timed will be K_{tr} for each subject, i.e. problem-solving speed. (If the test is untimed the group will of course exhibit zero variance.) Suppose now that following a set of N_e such easy items subjects have to proceed immediately to a set of N_m at higher values of *D*. To simplify the argument let us specify that although

individuals will all complete the N_e items, but at varying rates, so when the test finishes they will have been working for different times on the N_m items of moderate difficulty. During the time any individual is working on section N_m the rate at which his score will increase will be a function in part of his speed, but also in part, of his tendency to produce incorrect solutions. For this group of moderately fast individuals the final score attained will thus be determined in a fairly complex fashion both by speed and also by the frequency with which errors are produced. The very fast members of the group will all finish the test, but will be distributed in terms of their error tendencies. If, finally, a further set of N_d items, all at very high values of *D*, are added to the test, then the final score of the fast members of the group, who reach these N_d items within the time allotted will now depend in part on continuance, for those who are less continuant will lose possible increments of score through abandoning their efforts to obtain a solution before a sufficient time had elapsed for a solution to have a reasonable chance of emerging.

Any test can be regarded as consisting of $N_e + N_m + N_d$ items. If such a test is administered with time limit to a fairly homogeneous group it could measure mainly speed, mainly accuracy, or mainly continuance, depending on the interaction of the range of ability represented in the group, the time allowed for the test, and the numerical values of N_e, N_m, and N_d. In a fairly heterogeneous group the attributes measured, under certain conditions, could vary all the way from pure speed, for some individuals, and through various combinations of speed, accuracy and continuance. If unlimited time is allowed the manner in which these combine to determine the final score will be modified, but the same types of complication will arise as when a limit is imposed. It would thus appear that such a test cannot be said to measure any single, clearly defined trait, and that under some circumstances the same test will be comparing different subjects in terms of quite unrelated attributes. Conventional tests are therefore not very suitable for use in connexion with the comparison of normal and abnormal individuals, since if differences are demonstrated they will be as much a function of the range of D covered by the test items as of the attributes of the subjects.

If the same test measures different qualities in different individuals, it also seems to follow that each separate application of the same test to the same individual will tap different qualities if the intellectual powers are still developing during the period throughout which the test is repeated. Thus the determinants of score will be speed, accuracy and continuance in the case of (say) a ten-year-old child confronted with what is for him a rather difficult test. During the ensuing four or five years it is not unreasonable to assume that the child becomes more persistent, more accurate, and develops greater speed; although it does not appear that any measurements have as yet been made of the mode of development of these separate qualities. Should such changes in fact take place, the result would be to reduce the contribution made by the effects of continuance and accuracy to the test score, so that eventually the most important determinant becomes speed alone. The selection of tests for longitudinal studies, relating to the constancy, or otherwise, of "intelligence" and of cognitive structure in general, must inevitably be greatly complicated by the need to take such possibilities into account. Whether successive measurements are made in terms of the same test material or not there would seem to be a high probability that the various determinations are in fact concerned with different interactions of the three basic traits. If this should in fact be the case it would go a long way toward explaining the results obtained by Anderson (1939) who found that the intercorrelations of successive "intelligence"

scores reported for children were actually somewhat lower than those that would be expected on the basis of part/whole effects alone even if each successive yearly increment of score was completely uncorrelated with the score obtained at the beginning of that year. There certainly seems to be every reason to believe that developmental studies have little meaning unless they are carried out in terms of properly selected M-statistics, and that this demands a careful choice of D values for the problems that are to be utilized.

Since persistence will usually be one of the determinants of continuance, and may under some circumstances become its major determinant, it would seem to follow that persistence must be one of the factors influencing scores in so-called cognitive tests which embody problems for which $D > {}_cD_{tr}$ for those attempting them. That such a correlation would be observed was predicted by the writer (Furneaux, 1952, 1953) and subsequently confirmed by G. L. Mangan (Mangan, 1954) on the basis of a factor analysis of a battery which included both cognitive tests and measures of persistence.[1] Factor-analysing data reported by Bayley (Nelson, 1951), Hofstaetter (1954) too have suggested that persistence may affect cognitive test scores. In the writer's view no great weight can be given to Hofstaetter's findings, however, since as he himself is at pains to emphasize, the identification of the relevant factor as being one of persistence is based on a very tenuous argument. One would expect that in some forms of mental illness (such, perhaps, as the depressive psychoses) persistence might be greatly affected. The reduced cognitive-test scores sometimes reported as characterizing such illness might thus in reality be reflecting a change in an orectic attribute, as well as, or rather than, in a truly cognitive one.

The analysis also has other implications which are not directly relevant to the study of mental abnormality. For example, it would seem to follow that as the effective determinants of score are a function of the difficulty of the problems making up a test, then a factor analysis of inter-item correlations within a cognitive test should reveal one or more factors differentiating between items of different levels of difficulty. The emergence of such factors has in fact been reported from time to time (e.g. Guilford, 1941; Burt, 1942 and Vernon, 1950) and is clearly explicable in terms of the analysis here presented. It is only fair to add, however, that the cases so far reported might provide evidence for nothing of more significance than

[1] Readers of this chapter who also read Mangan's thesis may be puzzled to find that one or two of the arguments here presented also appear, word for word, in the thesis. Mangan was in fact quoting verbatim from material supplied to him by the present writer (Furneaux, 1953). The relevant acknowledgement was, unfortunately, accidentally omitted from his typescript.

a statistical artefact (Ferguson, 1941; Wherry, 1944 and Gourlay, 1951), so that too much significance should not be attached to them. The analysis is also obviously relevant to the theory and practice of item analysis, but as these are rather specialized topics they will not be discussed in the present context.

The discussion centred on Fig. 5.1 stressed the fact that for any particular $_\alpha PS$ numerical values for the M_{tr} statistics can only be obtained from the use of problems having D_{tr} values of less than $_cD_{tr}$ while the continuance statistics $\bar{\imath}_s$, V_{ts}, etc., have to be studied by using problems having D_{tr} values greater than $_cD_{ts}$. It may not be obvious that attempts to investigate the M_{qr} statistics too can only be useful if they are confined to observations of the outputs resulting from inputs having a restricted range of D. In the region $D_{tr} > {_cD_{tr}}$ a proportion of both potential O_r and potential O_w outputs will be lost because of the intervention of $_\alpha ST$, but the losses may be unequal if the numerical values of the M_{tr} statistics are different from those of M_{tw}. The ratio $N_r/(N_r + N_w)$ in this region does not necessarily define the statistic q_r, therefore, but only the interaction of the M_{qr} and M_{ts} statistics (where N_r and N_w are the number of O_r and O_w responses observed at a particular D_{tr} value). Data relevant to M_{qr} and $f(D, K)_{qr}$ can thus be collected only at D_{tr} values of less than $_cD_{tr}$ for each PS.

An Experimental Investigation

The discussion so far has rested on the logical development of a set of premises. It would lose most of its force if experiments should show, for example, that in the human problem-solver K_{tr}, K_{qr}, and $\bar{\imath}_s$, etc., were all very highly correlated; or that it was impossible to find forms for the various functions $f(D, K)$ which could be applied equally to all individuals (or at least to useful sets of individuals). At this stage it is therefore necessary to consider the results of some experimental work. Although a number of interim reports have been made, covering the gradual development of these experiments (Furneaux, 1948, 1950, 1952, 1955) no readily available account has previously been published. The exposition to be given here will therefore embody rather more detail than would usually be expected in a publication of this type. There appear to be no previous accounts of work directed to the kind of scaling problem which arises when the complications due to the effects of continuance are taken into account. The results of the analysis, moreover, are felt by some psychologists to be rather unexpected. Both these considerations reinforce the argument in favour of a reasonably detailed description.

The particular experiment which is to be discussed was performed with the help of two hundred and thirty-five soldiers, covering an age range of from 18 to 30 years, with a mean of 19·4. All had previously taken Anstey's Dominoes-Test, and the group had been selected to provide a roughly rectangular distribution between the limits of score defined by the points $+ 2·0\sigma$ and $- 1·5\sigma$, derived from the standardization distribution of this test. The upper limit was imposed by the failure to collect together a sufficient number of individuals having very high scores. The lower limit was deliberately chosen because of the need to use only subjects who were reasonably literate, and who could follow fairly complex instructions without too much difficulty. Each subject attempted letter-series problems of the kind used by Thurstone in his P.M.A. battery. Items had previously been scaled for "difficulty" in a rough-and-ready fashion, and were presented in cycles such that within any set of about five consecutive problems a very wide range of difficulty would be encountered. Instructions were designed to encourage high motivation, and the evidence suggests that this was achieved. Stress was laid on the need to persevere with items found to be difficult, rather than to attempt to reach the end of the test. All problems had to be worked through strictly in sequence, and once an item had been abandoned it could not be attempted again. An answer or a dash, signifying abandonment, was required in respect of each problem, and the time required for each response was measured to an accuracy of about two seconds, by using a device similar to that employed by Slater (1938). Testing was carried out in groups of about twenty, over a total time of three hours for each group. This was split up into two morning sessions of forty-five minutes each, separated by a fifteen minute rest period, followed by two similar periods after a break of one and a half hours for lunch.

Various corrections had to be made to the measured response times in order to eliminate the time spent recording answers and reading the timing device from the actual problem-solving time. These were made in terms of data derived from subsidiary experiments made on the same subjects. Corrected response times will be denoted by the symbols t_r, t_w, and t_s as heretofore. Of the two hundred and thirty-five problems available for presentation one hundred and twenty were attempted by every subject, and provided the basis for the analysis. A conventional item-analysis of these one hundred and twenty problems resulted in the rejection of forty. For the total experimental group the correlation between number right within the set of eighty surviving items, and Dominoes score, was 0·84.

If the investigation of the D_{tr} scale and its associated function $f(D, K)_{tr}$ are considered first, the object of the analysis must be to arrange as many as possible of the usable problems along a scale, and to find a function $f(D, K)_{tr}$, relating $\bar{t}_r$ and D_{tr}, which is equally valid for all subjects once each has been allocated his appropriate value for K_{tr}. In conducting this analysis we must take account only of responses at values of D_{tr} such that the observed M_{tr} statistics have not been affected by the interaction of continuance, i.e. all inputs considered must be $I_{u(tr)}$. We can only define such inputs rigorously, however, after a D_{tr} scale and a suitable form for $f(D, K)_{tr}$ have been evolved, and the associated M_{tr} statistics investigated. The escape from this circle of frustration lies via a series of iterations based on successive approximations. In order to simplify the description of the analysis the present tense will be used throughout.

Design of a D_{tr} Scale. Stage 1

For each of the eighty problems compute the proportion of the total experimental group who responded with O_r. Pick out, say, ten problems for which this proportion is highest, i.e. in conventional terms, the ten easiest problems, and assume that they will also have very low scale values for D_{tr}. These are thus problems which are unlikely to constitute $I_{a(tr)}$ inputs except in the case of subjects who have exceptionally poor continuance, or who are exceptionally slow. It will be convenient to refer to them as the *reference-problems.*

For each subject who has returned an O_r to at least five of the reference problems compute the mean of the values of t_r relevant to these problems. This is not a $\bar{t}_r$ measure, since it is unlikely that all the reference problems will turn out to occupy the same D scale position. It provides, in fact, a very rough-and-ready type of K_{tr} measure, say k_{tr}. A subject who has returned only a few O_r responses within the set of reference problems might well owe a high proportion of these successes to guessing, and would in any case receive only a very unreliable k_{tr} score from such a small number of responses—hence the rather arbitrary restriction with which this paragraph opens.

Let us now assume that for every subject, every type O_s response has equal status as a measure of t_s, contributing to an assessment of $\bar{t}_s$. Suppose that $\bar{t}_s$ is not a function of D_{tr}, and compute $\bar{t}_s$ for every subject. Pick out those whose continuance, thus computed, is above the mean. Other things being equal these subjects will have their values of critical-difficulty ($_cD_{tr}$) fairly high. There is thus a reasonable chance that the "easy" reference problems will all constitute type $I_{u(tr)}$ inputs for each of them.

From these continuant subjects pick out the forty with the lowest k_{tr} scores (i.e. the fastest) and designate these "Group F." Pick out the forty next in order, i.e. those of moderate speed, and designate these "Group M."

The most convenient function to use in defining a D scale calibrated in terms of t_r values is obviously of the form—

$$_a\bar{t}_r = mD_{tr} + {_aK_{tr}} \qquad (2)$$

where m has any convenient value. Assume that this function applies to each member of Group M, then it will follow that—

$$t_r(Av)_M = mD_{tr} + {_MC_{tr}} \qquad (3)$$

where $_MC_{tr}$ is the mean of all the values of K_{tr} relevant to the group members, and $t_r(Av)_M$ is the average value of t_r, within Group M, relevant to any problem which constitutes an input $I_{u(tr)}$ for all the members of the group. Since it is only the relative scale positions of items that are important, and not their absolute positions, we can decide to try the effects of adopting a scale such that in (3) above—

$$_MC_{tr} = 0$$
$$m = 1$$

i.e. we take the $t_r(Av)_M$ values as being also the D_{tr} values of the ten reference problems concerned.

Still on the assumption that the form of $f(D, K)_{tr}$ is identical for all subjects of Group M we can now compute the value of $_aK_{tr}$ for each subject, in terms of the nucleus of the D_{tr} scale provided by the ten reference problems. For each $_aS$ (subject) we have—

$$_aK_{tr} = \Sigma(_{p\alpha}t_r - {_pD_{tr}})/_a n \qquad (4)$$

where one value of $(_{p\alpha}t_r - {_pD_{tr}})$ is derived from each correctly solved item, p, from among the reference problems, and $_a n$ is the number of such correctly solved items. If we assume for the moment that the value of the range H_{tr} (Fig. 5.1) is not a function of D_{tr}, then the value relevant to each subject is estimated by subtracting his smallest value of $(_{p\alpha}t_r - {_pD_{tr}})$ from his largest value, while the value of $(R_t + H_{tr})$ is approximated, for each subject at $D_{tr} = 0$, by the largest of the values of $(_{p\alpha}t_r - {_pD_{tr}})$. It is easy to pick out the smallest observed value of t_s for each subject, and to assume that this gives an estimate of S_t (Fig. 5.1). The value of $_cD_{tr}$ for any subject is then that value of D_{tr} at which—

$$_{D=0}(R_t + H_{tr}) + {_cD_{tr}} = S_t \qquad (5)$$

i.e.
$$_cD_{tr} = S_t - {_{D=0}(R_t + H_{tr})} \qquad (6)$$

If, on computing this statistic, it were to turn out that for several subjects it had a value appreciably lower than the highest of the D values assigned to the reference problems, then it would follow that an appreciable proportion of the t_r data, derived from these problems, were relevant to $I_{a(tr)}$ inputs and not $I_{u(tr)}$. As has been explained, values of D_{tr} assigned to problems in terms of such data are quite useless for purposes of scale construction, and the observed

M_{tr} statistics are specific to the subject concerned, having no general validity.

In "Group M," however, the lowest value of $_cD_{tr}$ comes out to be 123, whereas the highest D value associated with a reference problem is 58. All inputs can therefore be assumed, with reasonable confidence, to have been of type $I_{u(tr)}$. If the form for $f(D, K)_{tr}$ assumed for equation (2) is universally applicable, it then follows that in any other group for which all the reference problems constitute $I_{u(tr)}$ inputs, the values of $t_r(Av)$ relevant to each of these problems, if plotted against their appropriate D_{tr} values, must define a straight line of slope $1·0$ within the limits of sampling error. Group F, which has already been defined, constitutes such a group, for the average value of $\bar{t}_s$ for its members turns out to be a little higher than that for group M, and, by definition, they are also appreciably faster. On plotting the relevant data the best-fitting straight line has a slope of $0·74$. A substantial part of the error variance of the array about this line is, of course, produced by the variance of K_{tr} between individuals. On subtracting this component and testing the significance of the difference between the two slopes we emerge with $p = 0·03$ (Snedecor, 1948). The plot strongly suggests, in fact, a curve having a negative acceleration. The form for $f(D, K)_{tr}$ assumed in equation (2) does not therefore provide an acceptable basis for the construction of the D_{tr} scale required.

Faced with such a result the next step must involve the formulation of a possible alternative form for $f(D, K)_{tr}$. The search is not, of course, a blind one, but can be guided by suitable graphical trials, and, in the present case, by hints obtained from other investigations. In 1948 (Furneaux, 1948) and 1950 (Tate, 1950) results were reported which showed that a logarithmic transformation of the response-time data relevant to problem-solving attempts resulted in improved homogeneity of variance between subjects. It seems reasonable therefore to try the effect of such a transformation in the case of the experiment now being reported, particularly as graphical inspection of the data suggests that it might be efficacious.

Design of D_{tr} Scale. Stage 2

Let $\log_{10} t_r = T_r$, then the revised form for equation (2) becomes—

$$_\alpha \bar{T}_r = mD_{tr} + {_\alpha}K_{Tr} \qquad (7)$$

The analysis now proceeds as from equation (2) in Stage 1, all statistics being concerned with values of T_r instead of t_r. The most suitable value for m, equations (2) and (3), is again $1·0$, and the crucial stage is again the final check as to whether this statistic comes out to have the same value in group F as was specified for it in group M.

In the experiment being discussed this test produces a numerical value of $1·08$. The analysis can therefore proceed on the assumption that equation (7) provides at least a reasonable approximation to the $f(D, K)_{tr}$ form required, over the range of K_{Tr} defined by groups F and M.

Design of D_{tr} Scale. Stage 3

For every subject in the experimental group a value of $_\alpha K_{Tr}$ can now be computed, using his O_r responses to reference problems according to the method described in Stage 1. His value of $_cD_{tr}$ is then calculated, again using the assumptions and methods of Stage 1. Those subjects for whom $_cD_{tr}$ is smaller than the largest D_{tr} value allotted to a reference problem are discarded, and analysis is continued with the remainder. For every subject retained there is an array of $_\alpha T_r$ values, relating to all the O_r responses made to the eighty problems being investigated. From each such value of $_\alpha T_r$ subtract the value of $_\alpha K_{Tr}$ relevant to the subject concerned. All arrays are thus superimposed at the point $D_{tr} = 0$, $\bar{T}_r = 0$, and if equation (7) is in fact of universal application the D value of any problem will be given by—

$$D = \dot{T}_r(Av) \qquad (8)$$

Where $\dot{T}_r$ is the value of $(T_r - K_{Tr})$ obtained from any one subject in respect of the problem concerned, and $\dot{T}_r(Av)$ is the mean value of $\dot{T}_r$ for the whole experimental group. The transformation from T_r to $\dot{T}_r$ is necessary to correct for the fact that the sample of subjects obtaining O_r responses differs from problem to problem in a way which is a function of the D_{tr} value of the problem.

By comparing the D_{tr} values thus allocated with the $_cD_{tr}$ values of each subject it will now be observed that for nearly all subjects some of the $\dot{T}_r$ values contributed to these determinations of D_{tr} were relevant to $I_{a(tr)}$ inputs. A series of iterations are thus necessary to remove such data, and their effects, from the analysis. At the conclusion of this process a D value of probably moderate accuracy will have been assigned to the majority of the eighty problems. Some, however, will have D values greater than the value of $_cD_{tr}$ relevant to even the fastest and most continuant of subjects, and thus can only be calibrated as having D_{tr} values greater than such and such. For a similar reason others will have to be calibrated in terms of only a very few data, and thus inaccurately.

Design of D_{tr} Scale. Stage 4

It is now possible to examine the statistics of M_{ts} in greater detail, with a view to improving the estimates of S_t, and thus of $_cD_{tr}$. Since some sort of D_{tr} scale position has been allocated to most items, and a value of K_{Tr} assigned to each subject, the value of

D_{tr} at which the time R_t becomes equal to the time $(S_t + H_{ts})$ can be computed. This gives the numerical value of $_cD_{ts}$ for each individual, and by taking account only of those t_s values relevant to O_s responses evoked by problems for which $D > {_c}D_{ts}$ it becomes possible to investigate M_{ts}.

Assume again that $\bar{t}_s$ is not a function of D_{tr}, and compute V_{ts} for each subject, using only $I_{u(ts)}$ inputs as defined above. The application of Bartlett's test now shows these variances to differ significantly from one individual to another ($\chi^2 = 310, p \simeq 0.01$ with 228 d.f.). On introducing the transformation $\log_{10} t_s = T_s$, however, homogeneity is achieved ($\chi^2 = 242, p \simeq 0.30$). Compute $\bar{T}_s$ for each subject, and then the values of $\dot{T}_s$ obtained by subtracting $\bar{T}_s$ from each available value of T_s. All M_{T_s} distributions are thus superimposed with $\bar{\dot{T}}_s = O$. Collect together all the values of $\dot{T}_s$ relevant to each particular problem, and compute their mean, $\dot{T}_s(Av)$, for the whole experimental group. On correlating $\dot{T}_s(Av)$ with D_{tr} over the whole set of problems we find a coefficient of 0.11 which with 31 d.f. is not significant. The assumption that T_s, and thus t_s, is not a function of D_{tr} seems therefore to be justified.

The method of timing used for the measurement of response times was such (Slater, 1938) that it is easy to find out how long a subject had already been working for when he attempted each problem. It is thus possible to plot each value of $\dot{T}_s$ contributed by each subject against this time already worked, and to see whether continuance varied appreciably during the time that testing was in progress. On plotting a single array including all $\dot{T}_s$ values derived from the whole group it becomes clear that no important variations occurred save during the concluding twenty minutes of both morning and afternoon testing periods. During each of these periods there is a steady fall in the values of $\dot{T}_s$, and an increase in the variance of the array. On further investigation this increase in variance is found to reflect the fact that subjects with high scores in the Dominoes test maintained their continuance virtually unchanged throughout the whole of each testing period, while those with low Dominoes scores were responsible for the general downward trend. The need to take account of variations in continuance would add formidable complications to the analysis, and to avoid these all data relating to the last twenty minutes of testing, in both morning and afternoon, are deleted from the analysis, for all subjects. After this has been done and revised values of V_{Ts} calculated, Bartlett's test gives $\chi^2 = 231$, $p \simeq 0.40$ with 220 d.f.[1], the best estimate of V_{Ts} being 0.0144 log sec.

The pooled distribution of $\dot{T}_s$, covering all subjects,

[1] At each stage of the analysis a few subjects fall out because of the nature of their test responses, scores, etc.

can now be taken as analogous to the M_{T_s} distribution that would result from a single subject of constant continuance who attempted a very large number of problems. There will be a small additional component of variance resulting from the sampling error associated with each individual determination of $\bar{T}_s$, but this will not be sufficiently large to produce any great distortion of the shape of the pooled distribution. On inspection this is clearly of normal type, so that it is reasonable to conclude that values of T_s which approach the extremes S_t and $(S_t + H_{ts})$ arise rather infrequently for any subject. The effective minimum value of T_s will in fact have a value of about $\bar{T}_s - 2\sqrt{V_{T_s}}$ for everyone, at all values of D_{tr}. Values of $_cD_{tr}$ computed in terms of this revised estimate of the minimum value of $\bar{T}_s$, for each subject, are of course higher than those resulting from the values of S_t, previously used, so that a larger number of $I_{u(tr)}$ become available for every subject. Iterations from this point result in revised values of D_{tr} for some problems, and in revised values of K_{Tr} for all subjects —all based on an increased number of data.

Design of D_{tr} Scale. Stage 5

If we take any two problems, p and q, and for each subject for whom they both constitute inputs $I_{u(tr)}$ compute $_{pa}T_r - {_{qa}}T_r = {_{(p-q)}}\dot{T}_r$, then if the value of V_{Tr} associated with each problem is equal, and is the same for all subjects, the variance of $_{(p-q)}\dot{T}_r$ within the whole group of subjects should equal $2V_{Tr}$. Starting with the problem having the lowest D value specify pairs of items of successive D_{tr} scale positions. For each pair compute the $_{(p-q)}\dot{T}_r$ variance within the total group, but taking account only of values derived entirely from inputs $I_{u(tr)}$.

Testing the resulting values for homogeneity the experimental data being considered give $\chi^2 = 45.7$, $p \simeq 0.04$ with 31 d.f. (Bartlett). The hypothesis that V_{Tr} has the same numerical value for all $I_{u(tr)}$ is thus untenable. On further investigation, however, it appears that the lack of homogeneity results from exceptionally large values of $2V_{Tr}$ associated with two particular problem pairs. On deleting these and repeating Bartlett's test on the remainder, we obtain a χ^2 of 36.1, i.e. $p \simeq 0.18$ with 29 d.f.

Now, compute separately within each subject, the variance of all the $_{(p-q)}\dot{T}_r$ values which arise from all those problem-pairs which constitute $I_{u(tr)}$ inputs, but ignore the two pairs deleted from the analysis above. On testing for homogeneity between subjects we find $\chi^2 = 227$, $p \simeq 0.4$ with 216 d.f. The variance estimate derived from the between-pairs-analysis was 0.1320, while the between-subjects-analysis gives a value of 0.1292. These clearly do not differ significantly, and their mean, 0.1306 log sec, provides an estimate of $2V_{Tr}$.

The analysis has provided no evidence inconsistent with the hypothesis of a numerical value for V_{Tr} which is constant over both subjects and problems, save in the case of one or both of the members of the two deleted problem-pairs. One can, however, imagine rather complicated (and unlikely) relationships between V_{Tr} and D_{tr} on the one hand and K_{Tr} on the other, which might also explain the results. No attempt will be made to dispose of them, in the present context, but the hypothesis of constancy will be accepted as being the simplest explanation of the data.

Up to the time of writing no rigorous analysis has been made of the exact form of the M_{Tr} distribution, but graphical inspections suggest that it is of normal type at all values of D_{tr} and for all subjects. Response times as long as $(R_t + H_{tr})$, at any value of D_{tr}, will therefore be rare, and the value of D at which any appreciable proportion of inputs turn out to be $I_{a(tr)}$ will therefore be rather higher than $_cD_{tr}$ as so far estimated. If the effective upper limit is taken to be $K_{Tr} + 2\sqrt{V_{Tr}} + D$, at any value of D, then a revised value of $_cD_{tr}$ can be computed for each subject. This revision will produce an increase in the

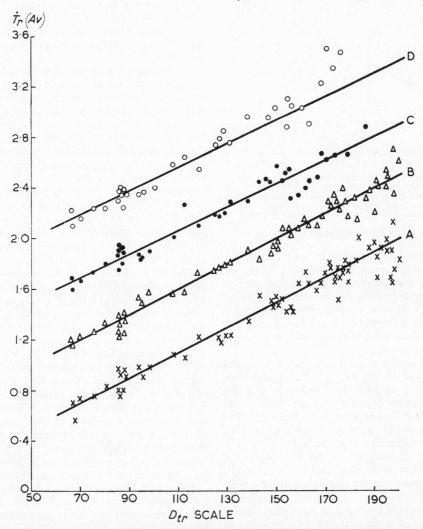

FIG. 5.3. $\dot{T}_r(Av)$ PLOTTED AGAINST $100D_{tr}$ FOR GROUPS OF VARYING SPEED

(*See* text.)

Note. The curves *A, B, C, D* show the relationships to which the data should conform: they are *not* the best-fitting straight lines. To facilitate the examination of this graph 1·5 log units have been added to each value of $\dot{T}_r(Av)$ in Group *D*, and values of 1·0 and 0·5 log units in Groups *C* and *B* respectively.

number of $I_{u(tr)}$ available for each person, and thus provides the starting point for further iterations. When these have been completed final values of K_{Tr} and $\bar{T}_s$ are available for all subjects, and final estimates of D_{tr} for each problem.

A crucial test is now possible to see whether equation (7) is acceptable as the form of a relationship between D and t_r which is equally applicable to all subjects. Divide all subjects into four approximately

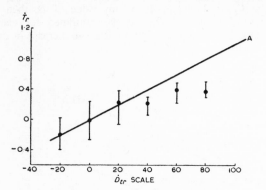

FIG. 5.4. DISCREPANCY BETWEEN RELATIONSHIP OF T_r TO D WHEN I_a INPUTS ARE USED, AND THAT APPLYING TO I_u

The straight line A gives the relationship applying in the case of I_u inputs. Each point plotted shows the median observed value of $\dot{T}_r$ which relates to the set of inputs I_a having values of $\dot{D}_{tr}$ within the range ± 10 of the central value shown. The vertical lines terminate at the values of the upper and lower quartiles.

Values of $\dot{D}_{tr}$ have been multiplied by 100.

equal subgroups in terms of their K_{tr} scores, the fastest being allocated to Group A, the slowest to D, and the remainder, in order, to the intermediate groups. For each subgroup compute the value of $\dot{T}_r(Av)$ relevant to each problem, and plot these values against the D values of these problems. For each subgroup separately the slope of the relevant best-fitting straight line should have a value of $1 \cdot 0$.

It will be clear from Fig. 5.3 that such a result was actually observed in the case of the experimental group concerned, so that the hypothesis that the relationship between D and $\bar{T}_r$ has the form set out in equation (7) for every subject is supported. The evidence presented in Stage 4 of the analysis also supported the hypothesis that the value of V_{Tr} is independent of $\dot{D}$, and identical for all subjects. It must be remembered, however, that this latter result was only demonstrated after two item-pairs had been deleted from the analysis. Subsequent examination showed that one item from one of these pairs should have been rejected at the stage of item analysis; a correlation of $0 \cdot 04$ with the criterion score had been wrongly computed as one of $0 \cdot 40$. It was hoped that this initial item analysis might define a set of items all more or less of the same type, using this last term in

the rather unorthodox manner suggested earlier in the discussion. The results of the analysis, and the accidental finding with the wrongly calibrated item, suggest that this was in fact accomplished. Since it will be shown, in the further analysis, that separately designed D_{tr} and D_{qr} scales correlate very highly, this is more or less what one would expect to find, since a conventional item-analysis is clearly an approximate method of classifying in terms of M_{qr} characteristics. It achieves this classification only approximately, however, since it makes no distinction between O_w and O_s responses.

In the second discrepant item-pair the non-homogeneous value of $2V_{Tr}$ was found, on investigation, to be associated with one of the two items, rather than both, but no explanation for the discrepancy has as yet been found.

It must now be shown that the deletion of $I_{a(tr)}$ responses was necessary, and that their retention would have produced the kind of complication predicted by the theoretical analysis of a PS. If $I_{a(tr)}$ inputs give rise to the same relationships between T_r and D_{tr} as have been demonstrated for $I_{u(tr)}$ inputs, then the effort to distinguish between the two kinds is clearly unnecessary, and the theory which calls for the distinction is unsound.

For every subject compute the values of $\dot{T}_r$ which relate to $I_{a(tr)}$ inputs in the same way as was used for type $I_{u(tr)}$. For each subject separately, compute the values of $\dot{D}_{tr}$ which apply to all these inputs, where $\dot{D}_{tr} = D_{tr} - {}_cD_{tr}$. All such inputs are thus re-scaled in terms of a D scale which has its zero at that point on the D_{tr} scale above which continuance should, in terms of the theory being examined, begin to distort relationships. On plotting $\dot{T}_r$ v. $\dot{D}_{tr}$ as a single array covering all subjects, the relationship graphed in Fig. 5.4 is obtained. If $I_{a(tr)}$ inputs behaved in the same way as do type $I_{u(tr)}$ this array would have defined a straight line of slope $1 \cdot 0$. As it clearly does not, the distinction between the two kinds of input appears to be justified. The nature of the array is in fact exactly of the kind that would have been predicted in terms of the discussion on pp. 175–176, both slope and dispersion decreasing as $\dot{D}_{tr}$ increases. When interpreting Fig. 5.4 it is important to bear in mind the fact that the problems which, as $I_{a(tr)}$ inputs, gave rise to this array are the same problems which, as $I_{u(tr)}$ inputs, led to the relationships shown in Fig. 5.3.

The results of the analyses justify the retention of the hypothesis that m, equation (7), and V_{Tr} are population constants. It is convenient to replace equation (7) by—

$$T_r = mD_{tr} + K_{Tr} + \varepsilon_i \qquad (9)$$

where ε_i is a positive or negative component arising on a particular occasion i, such that at every value of D the values of ε relevant to a large number of occasions are distributed with variance V_{Tr} about zero as mean.

Some psychologists, when discussing this hypothesis with the writer, have expressed surprise that such invariances should be found in a field where the discovery of substantial individual difference is the normal expectation. In the present study, however, such differences do not disappear, but are taken up in the individual-constants K_{Tr} and $\bar{T}_s$ which vary very considerably from one person to another. Equation (9) provides a form of relationship analogous to that embodied in, say, Fechner's law, which latter has served to clarify, rather than obscure, the study of individual differences in sensory thresholds. Equation (9) does, however, assert that there may be some cerebral mechanism involved in problem-solving activity, which is of the kind used in connexion with letter-series problems at least, and which has much the same form for at least a very wide range of individuals.

A Possible Problem-solving Mechanism

While the writer was speculating on the possible implications of these findings a report was published of a paper read by Hick (1950). In this paper Hick showed that the relationship between the time taken to react within a multiple-choice situation and the complexity of the choice situation could be expressed as—

$$RT = K \log M$$

where RT = choice reaction-time

$ K$ = an individual constant

$ M$ = a function of the complexity of the choice situation.

He developed the argument that this is the relationship one would expect to observe if multiple-choice activity involved successive binary classifications. As the brain seems to consist of a vast number of nearly identical units he argued that it might be permissible to posit that all its activities involve sequences of elementary operations of like kind and duration. Such a device might well function by carrying out successive binary switchings, with each "switch" taking the same time and involving the same sort of simple basic activity. This hypothesis of Hick's seems to imply that multiple-choice reaction-time is a measure of the time required for a search to be completed in the brain for the set of "connexions" which would initiate a required behaviour. It then occurred to the writer that problem-solving should perhaps be regarded as a special case of a multiple-choice reaction, and that it

would be interesting to see if the rather striking characteristics of equation (9) could be explained by postulating, within problem-solving processes, the repeated occurrence of some elementary activity which requires a substantially constant time for completion. The following hypothesis was eventually developed.

The brain structure of any individual, P, includes a set of $_pN$ neural elements which participate in problem-solving activities. It is not necessary at this stage to adopt any particular view as to the nature of these elements, which might be either single neurones or much more complex structures. The solution of a particular problem, h, of difficulty D, involves bringing into association a particular set, $_DN_h$, of these elements, interconnected in some precise order. (The terms "bringing into association" and "interconnected" should not necessarily be interpreted literally after the manner of, say, an electrical circuit. For example, the almost simultaneous firing of two otherwise independent units could constitute one method of bringing them into association, provided some device existed which could detect the simultaneity, while the exact order of firing might represent the mode of interconnexion.) When problem h is first presented single elements are first selected, at random, from the total pool $_pN$ and examined to see whether any one of them, alone, constitutes the required solution. A device must be postulated which carries out this examination—it must bring together the neural representations of the perceptual material embodying the problem, the rules according to which the problem has to be solved, and the particular organization of elements whose validity as a solution has to be examined. It must give rise to some sort of signal, which in the case of an acceptable organization will terminate the search process and will initiate the translation of the accepted neural organization into the activity which specifies the solution in behaviour terms. Alternatively, if the organization under examination proves to be unacceptable a signal must result which will lead to the continuation of the search process. It will be found useful to refer to this hypothetical device under the name of "the comparator."

If $D \neq 1$, the comparator will reject each of the $_pN$ trial solutions involving only a single element, and the search will then start for a pair of elements, which, when correctly interconnected, might constitute a valid solution. Suppose $D \neq 2$, then all possible organizations of the $_pN$ elements taken two at a time will also be examined and rejected, after which we can imagine that the search will continue among sets of three, four, five, etc. If $D = r$, then the comparator will reject in turn all the organizations involving from 1 to $(r - 1)$ elements, so that there will be a time

$\tau \sum_{r-1}^{1} E$ sec within which a solution cannot occur, where—

τ (Tosouton) = the time required for completing a single elementary operation within the search process.[1]

$\sum_{r-1}^{1} E$ = the number of elementary operations involved in the search process up to the level of complexity $(r - 1)$.

Similarly, after a time $\tau \sum_{r}^{1} E$ sec all possible organizations embodying r elements will have been examined, so that correct solutions to problems of difficulty r will always arise within the period defined by the two limiting times $\tau \sum_{r-1}^{1} E$ and $\tau \sum_{r}^{1} E$. In terms of such a hypothesis, therefore, V_{Tr} is in no sense a function of error of measurement but results mainly from the range of times required to set up all possible modes of neural organization at a particular level of complexity. It is perhaps worth noting, in passing, that within the framework of such a hypothesis error would be accounted for by positing that during the search process organizations arise at levels of complexity $r - \delta_1, r - \delta_2, \ldots$, etc.,[2] which satisfy most, but not all, of the requirements of a true solution to a problem of difficulty r. If the comparator has characteristics analogous to those of "band-width" in electrical and mechanical discriminators, i.e. if its discriminating powers are such that neural organizations which closely resemble the organization representing a correct solution may be accepted as the required organization, then the possibility of error arises. The frequency of error, thus conceived, will be a function of the band-width of the comparator, and since the number of "nearly-correct" organizations will increase as D is increased, the likelihood of error will increase with D.

This probability is clearly dependent on the exact nature of the search process. Finally, continuance is easily defined in terms of such a "search" hypothesis; it is a measure of the length of time during which, following the initiation of search, the comparator remains "set" for a particular problem.

As has been explained, the hypothesis thus summarized seemed to grow naturally upon the foundations laid down by Hick, working with reaction-time data. It has the merit that it can be checked experimentally in virtually all its aspects, relationships of

time against complexity which would characterize such a process can readily be computed, and compared with those actually observed. It can only be stated here that if it be considered that the search mechanism operates by setting up the orderly sequence of events outlined above, but takes account only of combinations rather than of possible permutations of neural organization, then time-complexity relationships approximating to those defined by equation (9) do in fact emerge. In the simplest, completely orderly case the observed distribution of log-times at a particular value of D should, of course, be rectangular rather than normal. This disparity between the requirements of the theory and observation can be removed by postulating that as time elapses after the initiation of the search for a particular solution the number of neural elements involved in successive interconnexions tends to increase steadily, but that interspersed with successive combinations involving a particular value of $_D N_h$ there also occur organizations involving either a larger or a smaller number of elements. In other words, an element of randomness must be imposed upon the type of order defined by the theory. It is interesting to note that if this is done then the theory predicts that with very low values of D, V_{Tr} should tend to increase as D decreases. This prediction from the theory has been confirmed by observations subsequently made. It is also of some interest that, if the theory is approximately true, then the solution of letter-series problems of such difficulty that they are correctly solved by only about 5 per cent of the unselected adult population involves the activity of less than one hundred neural elements.

A theory of this kind should not, of course, be taken too seriously. It might, for example, be objected that introspection during problem-solving reveals nothing comparable to the postulated search process, but then neither does visual experience in any way suggest the underlying complicated retinal and central processes. A more telling argument would be that it simply replaces the problem-solver by a little mannikin, the comparator. It could perhaps be claimed that it does serve the functions that a theory should, i.e. it accounts for such data as have been collected, suggests new experiments which could profitably be attempted, and predicts results for some of them.

One obvious prediction is that a change in the value of τ, such as one might expect to result from, say, an increase in drive, should leave unchanged the values of m and V_{Tr}, equation (9). A set of fifteen problems (set A) was therefore assembled, all having approximately the same low D_{tr} scale position, and a further set, B, all clustering around a slightly higher position. According to the theory, any group of subjects, no matter what their drive-state, should give rise to exactly the same value for $\bar{T}_r(Av)_B - \bar{T}_r(Av)_A$, where

---

[1] The Greek $\tau o\sigma o\tilde{v}\tau o\nu$ (Tosouton), meaning "so long," seems to be an appropriate name for this elementary period, particularly since τ is very appropriate as a symbol for a short period of time.

[2] If the possibility be accepted that the comparator might sometimes fail to respond to the "correct" organization, then response might also occur at levels of complexity $r + \delta$.

the two terms subtracted are the mean values of $\bar{T}$ relevant to the two sets of items, within the group concerned. This prediction has now been confirmed (within the limits of sampling error) for six different groups of university students, all comprising between thirty and seventy subjects, and covering a range of Faculties and ages. It has also been confirmed for one group of three hundred boys having a mean age of 14·4 years, in English grammar schools. For some of these groups the instructions given have stressed the fact that problems should be tackled at a comfortable, easy pace, while for others the fastest possible rate of work has been demanded. In every case adequate practice has preceded the actual testing.

V_{Tr} has behaved according to expectation in all those groups which have attempted the problems under what have come to be known as *unstressed* conditions, i.e. working at their own preferred pace. An appreciably discrepant value has been observed, however, in one of the groups of university students who were working under *stressed* conditions, i.e. at maximum rate. For this group the mean value of V_{Tr} among its members was significantly higher than expected. At the time of writing several lines of evidence appear to be converging to support the hypothesis that individuals who are working under a degree of drive in excess of that required for optimum performance in the task, display such exaggerated values of V_{Tr}. This single discrepancy may indicate an instability in the value of τ under such conditions.

The Investigation of M_{tw} and M_{qr}

Another prediction from the theory is clearly that the dispersion of the response-times arising in connexion with O_w outputs should be greater, at any value of D_{tr}, than that characterizing O_r outputs, since the former can arise at several levels of complexity, the latter only at one. Nothing has so far been said about the experimental investigation of the M_{tw} statistics, or of those of M_{qr}, nor of the problems which arise in connexion with the investigation of the associated functions $f(D, K)_{tw}$ and $f(D, K)_{qr}$. Space does not permit any detailed discussion of these topics. The general strategy used, a succession of iterations having the object of eliminating I_a inputs and of finding acceptable forms for the relevant functions $f(D, K)$, has been identical with that already described, but some of the detailed tactics have had to be modified. It must suffice to report of the M_{tw} statistics that values of $\bar{T}_w$ are smaller than values of $\bar{T}_r$ at the same D_{tr} value, the discrepancy increasing as D increases. Similarly, V_{Tw} is larger at all values of D_{tr} than is V_{Tr}, and again, the difference is greatest at high values of D. It is encouraging that these are just the characteristics which would be expected to arise from a device such as has been postulated. The numerical values of these statistics, however, seem to be subject to a degree of individual variation which it has not yet proved possible to describe in terms of a few simple $f(D, K)$ relationships. In view of this failure the M_{tw} statistics cannot as yet be summarized in terms of scores which have the same significance for all subjects. In the particular groups of soldiers studied the correlations between $\bar{T}_r$ and $\bar{T}_w$, at various low values of D_{tr}, ranged around 0·58. At high values they fell below 0·50. These values, and the differences between them, reflect in part the low reliability of the $\bar{T}_w$ scores; resulting partly from the high value of V_{Tw} and partly from the fact that, at low values of D_{tr}, a comparatively small number of O_w responses are available for the making of $\bar{T}_w$ assessments. They do serve to make it clear, however, that the temporal characteristics of incorrect responses do not provide a very good estimate of those for correct ones, and this underlines the unsatisfactory nature of some frequently used rate measures.

In connexion with M_{qr} the analysis has been more successful. Using the D_{tr} scale as a starting point it has been possible to specify a normal ogive which, given an appropriate value of K_{qr}, gives an acceptable fit to the data relating q_r and D_{tr} for each member of the experimental group which has been described. In evolving the relevant function only type $I_{u(tr)}$ inputs were of course taken into account. An attempt to reduce the SE_{est} of individual arrays about the best-fitting ogive, by altering the D scale values allotted to the various problems, met with very little success, the correlation between the D_{tr} scale which served as a starting point, and the D_{qr} scale finally evolved, being 0·92. There are thus strong grounds for believing that, with letter-series type problems at least, the ultimate determinants within problems of both response-time and response-quality, are much the same. The use of the term "difficulty" embracing both kinds of D scale, seems thus to be justified. What must not be done, however, is to attempt to calibrate for D by lumping O_w and O_s outputs together as "wrong" and using a simple index such as percentage of wrong answers in a defined group. It will be clear that this procedure will result in the formation of an unstable scale of a multi-dimensional kind, because of the intervention of the effects of continuance. In the group which has been described, a D scale thus derived exhibited a correlation of only 0·68 with the D_{tr} scale when computed within the Group D relevant to Fig. 5.3, whereas for Group A, pertaining to the same figure, the coefficient rose to 0·79.

Interrelationships among Scores

The demonstration that D_{tr} and D_{qr} scales are very closely related does not imply a similar high correlation between values of K_{Tr} and K_{qr} for individuals.

Data relating to this latter relationship, and to those involving $\bar{T}_s$ as well, are given for the experiment which has been described, in Table V.1. From this it will be clear that these are all relatively independent

TABLE V.1

INTERCORRELATIONS OF K_{Tr}, K_{qr}, AND $\bar{T}_s$

	K_{Tr}	$\bar{T}_s$
K_{qr}	-38	31
$\bar{T}_s$	-27	

Notes: (a) A high value of K_{Tr} implies low speed.
   (b) A high value of K_{qr} implies high accuracy.
   (c) A high value of $\bar{T}_s$ implies high continuance.
   (d) Of the total experimental group, only two hundred and nine could be scored for all three attributes.

scores which demand separate consideration. In more highly selected groups, such as university students, the coefficients concerned, as would be expected, are found to be considerably smaller. One cannot therefore justifiably talk of "letter-series test ability," but only of a person's standing in terms of each of the scores K_{Tr}, K_{qr} and $\bar{T}_s$. It seems difficult to resist the conclusion that results of a similar kind would be obtained if other types of problem material were investigated. Instead of intercorrelating conventional test scores, therefore, and describing cognitive structure in terms of such correlations, it seems that the foundation data for such analyses should be properly constituted measures of speed, accuracy and continuance, derived from each of the kinds of test material which it is desired to investigate.

It is very difficult to know whether K_{Tr} type scores derived from different kinds of problem material would display high intercorrelations, and thus define a useful speed-factor within all cognitive-test behaviour, since the speed scores used by nearly all those who have investigated this problem have been of the kind criticized in the earlier sections of this discussion. Rimoldi (1951), in a study remarkable for the range of activities it covered, showed that several fairly distinct speed factors were needed to describe his data, motor, perceptual, and cognitive rate measures each defining their own factor. His speed-of-cognition factor was a strong one, and included tests as disparate as "reasoning" and "space," together with measures of free-association rate, recognition rate, and speed of making judgements. On the other hand this cognition factor was only very slightly correlated with a perceptual-speed factor which included rate measures for reading, a verbal-meaning test, and a test of number. Nelson (1953), using reasonably well designed scores, found only very small intercorrelations

within a set of intellectual and motor speed-tests in a normal group, but as this group had a very restricted variance on the intellectual side, at least, this finding is of little significance. (With the "Nufferno" speed measures, for example, her group had a S.D. of about one quarter, of that characterizing an unselected normal population.) Nelson's abnormal groups, neurotics and psychotics, both of which displayed much larger variances than her normals, provided data which defined strong factors of mental and motor speed. In Thurstone's perceptual study (1949) a factor clearly analogous to Rimoldi's speed-of-cognition factor also emerged. There are in addition more than a score of correlational studies which have demonstrated intellectual-speed factors, but using unsatisfactory scoring methods.

The accuracy score (K_{qr}) derived from letter-series tests usually displays correlations with cognitive-test scores of the conventional kind which are higher than those associated with either speed (K_{Tr}) or continuance (C). This is not invariably the case, as everything depends on the relationship between the D values of the test items and the values of $_cD$ displayed by those taking them. In practice, however, accuracy does frequently emerge as the score which displays the closest relationships with those of the conventional kind. Since such conventional scores usually display quite high intercorrelations among themselves, this suggests that there may be quite a strong factor of accuracy underlying a wide variety of cognitive performances.

There would thus appear to be quite a strong justification for talking of a subject's *speed* and *accuracy* without making specific reference to the kind of problem-material in terms of which these attributes were measured. So far as continuance is concerned the position is less clear. In so far as test instructions can be designed in such a way that continuance becomes synonymous with persistence the results obtained from factorial studies of persistence tests are clearly applicable (e.g. Ryans, 1938). These investigators have shown that persistence tests do display intercorrelations which are sufficiently high to define a trait, or more probably two related traits. Unless instructions *are* so devised, however, continuance in a particular test will be affected by so many factors specific to that test that it would not be surprising if the continuance scores evoked by different instruments were only slightly related.

Until recently most psychologists have accepted the view that cognitive and orectic test-scores are relatively independent. A certain amount of evidence to the contrary has been available for some time, such as the work of Mandler (1952) who has shown that anxiety may reduce scores in certain kinds of test. Such demonstrations have usually been regarded as providing interesting exceptions, under rather unusual conditions, to well-established general rules. The analysis here presented, supported as it is by the results obtained by Mangan (1954) makes it difficult to accept such a viewpoint, since continuance will always involve orectic determinants. It is moreover quite obvious that speed in any problem-solving task will be a function of drive, and even if an increase in a subject's speed were always to be attended by just such a decrease in accuracy[1] as would serve to keep constant the overall score achieved in a conventional test, this would only serve to demonstrate rather clearly the inadequacy of such conventional tests for the purpose of making fundamental measurements.

The interdependence of cognitive and orectic traits seems to be demonstrated by the results of some experiments carried out by the writer in connexion with the relationship between stressed and unstressed speed. By subtracting K_{Tr} (stressed) from K_{Tr} (unstressed) for a particular individual one obtains a score which has been designated stress-gain, and which provides a measure of the extent to which he can improve his rate of production of O_r responses under the stressed instructions. This score was obtained for each of a group of seventy-five university students, who also completed the Guilford S.T.D.C.R. inventory. Taking the (D + C) score as providing a measure of neuroticism (Hildebrand, 1953) and the R score as a measure of extraversion, the whole group was divided up into four subgroups of approximately equal size—stable extraverts (SE), stable introverts (SI), neurotic introverts (NI), and neurotic extraverts (NE). The term neurotic is used here, of course, in a purely relative sense, and so far as is known no individual was actually neurotic in the overt, clinical sense. The mean values of stress-gain within each of these groups are displayed in Table V.2. The largest value is that associated with NE, whereas for NI a

TABLE V.2

RELATIONSHIP BETWEEN STRESS-GAIN
AND S.T.D.C.R. SCORES

		(D + C) score		
		⩽ 51	> 51	
R score	> 38	− 0·03	0·07	Stress/gain scores in log sec units
	⩽ 38	0·00	0·05	

Variance estimates: Between = 0·147 log sec units
Within = 0·036 log sec units
$F = 4·1$ with 3 and 71 d.f.
Sig. ≃ 0·01

[1] The writer knows of no evidence which indicates that this kind of compensation does in fact occur.

negative value was obtained, indicating a slower rate of work under stressed than under unstressed conditions. The simplest explanation of these results is probably that which assumes that introverted students, because of their greater intrinsic susceptibility to conditioning (Franks, 1957) have come to respond to any formal test or examination situation by generating a high drive. If neuroticism is in any case associated with a state of high drive, then the convergence of the two determinants, within the NI subgroup, will result in such a state of high drive, even under the unstressed conditions, that the further increase produced by the stressed instructions takes it to a value greater than the optimum postulated by the Yerkes-Dodson law, and actually results in a performance decrement. The NE group, on the other hand, will exhibit much less drive under unstressed conditions, increasing to a value nearer to the optimum during the stressed test.

Whatever explanation may be accepted, the results demonstrate clearly that performance in a cognitive-test situation is influenced in very important ways by orectic determinants. A rough distinction between the cognitive and orectic manifestations of a disorder may often be useful, but to use cognitive tests as if they gave information about some independent, encapsulated part of the personality would seem to be a quite unjustifiable procedure. One could in fact go so far as to suggest that the study of the way in which cognitive performance changes under the influence of testing régimes designed to vary such factors as stress, motivation, and the like, should form an essential part of psychometric practice.

The Measurement of "Level"

The detailed design of tests which can be used for making accurate measurements of such individual constants as K_{Tr} and K_{qr} will not be discussed here, since the question is considered elsewhere (Furneaux, 1953, 1956). It need only be stated that a set of tests of such kinds have been developed (Furneaux, 1953, 1956) and that the use of these instruments has led to results of the kind which are discussed by Payne in his contribution to this HANDBOOK. Little mention has as yet been made in the present contribution, however, of such attributes as *power* and *level*, nor of the techniques which have been used for their measurement.

There are no generally accepted definitions for either of these terms, and both are frequently used without any attempt at definition being made at all. They are normally treated as if synonymous, and usually as if they referred to scores in untimed tests. It will be clear from the discussion so far that if an untimed test is made up of items constituting $I_{u(tr)}$ inputs for the individual being assessed, then it will constitute a measure of accuracy alone, whereas if a proportion of the items are $I_{a(tr)}$, being difficult for the subject concerned, then the test will measure an interaction of speed, accuracy, and continuance specific to the combination of test and subject. The normal use of the terms power and level thus imputes to the subject nothing more fundamental than the ability to achieve a particular score in a particular test, which may or may not exhibit a high correlation with the score he would achieve in a different untimed test using the same kind of material.

The writer has found it useful to reserve the term *Level-Test* for use in connexion with tests which have deliberately been designed in such a way as to provide the subject with the maximum possible reward for persistent effort (Furneaux, 1953). The basic unit in such a test is a set of items comprising a cycle. The first problem in each cycle is very easy, each succeeding item is of greater difficulty than its predecessor, and the last is so difficult that few can solve it correctly even when given unlimited time. The number of items in a cycle is quite small, so that difficulty increases fairly rapidly from item to item. On the initial easy items, score will be a function of accuracy only, but speed and continuance in interaction play an increasingly important part as the later problems are attempted, even for highly able subjects. The total number of items correctly solved within one cycle will thus provide a score for effectiveness within a situation designed to reward high continuance, as well as speed and accuracy, and the test instructions are so designed that continuance depends almost entirely on persistence. The score provided by one cycle will be rather unreliable, being based on a small number of items. If, however, several such cycles are arranged in series, the mean score-per-cycle, computed over all items attempted, provides a measure of adequate reliability. The maximum score possible is the same no matter how few cycles have been completed, so that a time limit can be imposed without penalty to the slow worker. Such a subject, if he is also persistent and accurate, can in fact obtain a higher score than one who is fast but lacks persistence. The reliability of the measurement is the only thing that varies with the number of problems attempted. Level-scores, thus defined, are not altogether free from the kind of ambiguity which has been criticized in connexion with conventional-type intelligence tests, since different level-tests, incorporating different numbers of items per cycle, and covering different ranges of difficulty,[1] will still give rise to scores which are not altogether comparable. It will be clear, however, that this kind of assessment approximates, rather roughly, to a measurement of the maximum

level of difficulty at which the subject can function successfully when motivated to persevere with items experienced as difficult. In so far as this is the case such level-tests measure a reasonably invariant property of the individual. The design and use of such tests is dealt with in greater detail elsewhere (Furneaux, 1953 and 1956). They serve the function of indicating the subject's intellectual ceiling, without however providing any clue as to the relative size of the contributions to his effectiveness which are provided by the more fundamental attributes of speed, accuracy, and continuance. In the less disabling forms of schizophrenia, for example, there appears to be a phase during which patients achieve level scores of the same magnitude as those characterizing normal individuals. Their illness has thus not impaired their effectiveness in certain kinds of situation. Tests of speed, however, reveal a marked slowness in the same patients, which is compensated for by an increase in persistence. The latter kind of test thus reveals an important aetiological characteristic, while the former shows that the organism as a whole is able, at least for a time, to compensate for its effects. Both kinds of measuring device would therefore appear to have their part to play in the investigation of abnormal function.

SUMMARY

The thesis has been argued that a subject's score in a cognitive test of the familiar kind is determined by the interaction of a number of determinants which should really all receive separate consideration. A logical analysis of the nature of the problem-solving act suggests that three attributes, speed, accuracy, and continuance, are concerned in any kind of "intelligent" behaviour, and that the valid and unambiguous measurement of these traits can only be accomplished after the problem of classifying problems in terms of both "type" and "difficulty" has been solved. The problem of scaling for difficulty has been shown to be a more complex one than has in general been assumed, and an example has been presented showing the kind of experimental analysis which can be undertaken in an effort to achieve a valid difficulty scale. Once such a scale had been achieved, in the experiment described, it showed up the existence of characteristics of problem-solving behaviour which seem to be invariant as between all subjects, and this suggests that the "mechanisms" involved in problem-solving may have a particular form, which has been described.

Once valid methods of defining the basic attributes of speed, accuracy, and persistence have been evolved, it becomes possible to see how they must interact in different kinds of conventional test, and how these interactions must complicate attempts to understand the nature of cognitive abnormalities. The whole

---

[1] It should be stressed that, by definition, a level-test *must* include items in each cycle which are experienced as being very difficult by those for whom the test was designed.

chapter should be regarded as providing an introduction to the more detailed discussions presented by Payne, in that it serves to describe concepts and results used by him, but which have not previously been widely reported.

In defining the device *PS* the human problem-solver or subject has of course been grossly over-simplified. Continuance, for example, has been accounted for in terms of a switch *ST* which is either "on" or "off." During the course of a particular attempt to solve a particular problem, however, the subject will presumably manifest a drive state of systematically varying intensity, so that the appropriate analogy is more likely to be a continuously variable impedance interposed between *PB* and its power supply. Again, although the question of between-persons correlations among scores for such attributes as speed, accuracy, and continuance has been touched upon, nothing has been said of the consequences which would arise as a result of within-person correlations between the several kinds of event which participate in determining the nature and characteristics of a particular output. The complications which arise when attributes such as memory, fatigue, conditioned inhibition, and the like, are introduced into the analyses, have not been considered at all.

The early introduction of too great a degree of complication, however, is likely to defeat its own objects, useful trends being obscured by a mass of detail so complex as to defy analysis. At the present time only a few very tentative steps have been taken towards the evolution of a theory of human problem-solving activity, and the present paper represents no more than an attempt to provide the beginnings of a vocabulary, of a conceptual framework, and of a technique of analysis.

The writer believes that the human problem-solver is rather like a self-programming calculator. The effectiveness of such a device depends in part on the characteristics of the computing mechanisms, but also on the adequacy of the programming. If a subject is attempting a highly structured test, such as may be made up of letter or number series, nearly all the programming is, in effect, imposed from outside, by the instructions. Under these circumstances the subject is functioning almost exclusively as a computer, and the characteristics he displays in a "pure" test of this kind are likely to give information about some relatively simple cognitive mechanism. In a more complex situation, however, part of the subject's task is to decide how best to tackle his problem, i.e. how to programme himself. The outcome of his attempts to solve the problem will therefore probably depend on the interaction of several more or less independent computing mechanisms and on the effectiveness of the programming. It is thus very unlikely

that common descriptive functions $f(D, K)$ can be evolved which will describe the overall input/output characteristics of all subjects when they are attempting complex tasks, since the programming, and thus the computing mechanisms called into play and the order in which they are utilized, will vary from one subject to another. The analysis which has been attempted in the foregoing pages is thus applicable only to the computing aspects of human problem solving, and experimental work pertinent to the analysis can only be carried out by using highly structured tasks within which opportunities for differences of individual approach are as completely eliminated as may be possible. It may not be altogether fanciful to regard these computing mechanisms as making up an important part of "Intelligence A," as defined by Hebb (1949), while his "Intelligence B" would seem to result from the subject's gradual acquisition of sets of programmes suitable for bringing them into effective combination.

However this may be, it does seem probable that the investigation of both normal and abnormal cognitive function should take some account of the discussion here attempted, if it is to lead to fruitful results.

REFERENCES

ANDERSON, J. E., The limitations of infants and pre-school tests in the measurement of intelligence, *J. Psychol.*, **8**, 351–379 (1939).

BURT, C. and JOHN, E., A factor-analysis of Terman-Binet tests, *Brit. J. Educ. Psychol.*, **12**, 117–127, 156–161 (1942).

EYSENCK, H. J., Primary Mental Abilities, *Brit. J. Educ. Psychol.*, **9**, 3, 270–275 (1939).

FURNEAUX, W. D., The structure of "g" with particular reference to *speed* and *power*. *Proceedings of the 12th International Congress of Psychology*, Edinburgh (1948).

FURNEAUX, W. D., Speed and power in mental functioning, *Paper read before British Psychological Society*, London (1950).

FURNEAUX, W. D., Some speed, error, and difficulty relationships within a problem-solving situation, *Nature*, **170**, 37 (1952).

FURNEAUX, W. D., A note on the "Nufferno" tests of inductive reasoning abilities. Nuffield Research Unit (Inst. of Psychiatry) Internal Report F.1 (April, 1953).

FURNEAUX, W. D., The determinants of success in intelligence tests, *Proceedings of the British Association for the Advancement of Science*, Bristol (1955).

FURNEAUX, W. D., *The Nufferno Manual of Speed Tests*, and *The Nufferno Manual of Level Tests* (Publ. by the Inst. of Psychiatry, and distributed by the National Foundation for Educational Research, 1956).

FERGUSON, G. A., The factorial interpretation of test-difficulty, *Psychometrika*, **6**, 323–329 (1941).

FRANKS, C., Personality factors and the rate of conditioning, *Brit. J. Psychol.*, **48**, 119–126 (1957).

GOURLAY, N., Difficulty factors arising from the use of

tetrachoric correlations, *Brit. J. Statis. Psychol.*, **4**, 2, 65 (1951).

GUILFORD, J. P., The difficulty of a test and its factor composition, *Psychometrika*, **6**, 67–77 (1941).

GUILFORD, J. P., The structure of intellect, *Psychol. Bull.*, **53**, 267–293 (1956).

HEBB, D. O., *The Organization of Behavior* (New York, John Wiley & Sons, Inc., 1949).

HICK, W. E., Information theory in psychology, *Report of Proceedings of Symposium on Information Theory* (London, Ministry of Supply, 1950).

HILDEBRAND, P., A factorial study of introversion-extraversion by means of objective tests, *Unpub. Ph.D. Thesis, Univ. of London Lib.* (1953).

HOFSTAETTER, P. R., The changing composition of intelligence, a study in T-technique, *J. Genet. Psychol*, **85**, 159–164 (1954).

HOLZINGER, K. J., *Preliminary Reports on Spearman-Holzinger Unitary Trait Study*. (Chicago, 1935).

KELLEY, R. L., Psychophysical tests of normal and abnormal children, *Psychol. Rev.*, **10**, 345–352 (1903).

KIRKPATRICK, E. A., Individual tests of schoolchildren, *Psychol. Rev.*, **7**, 274–280 (1900).

MANDLER, G. and SARASON, S. B., A study of anxiety and learning, *J. Abnorm. (Soc.) Psychol.*, **47**, 2, 166 (1952).

MANGAN, G. L., A factorial study of speed, power, and related variables, *Unpubl. Ph.D. Thesis, Univ. of London Lib.* (1954).

NELSON, B., An experimental investigation of intellectual speed and power in mental disorders, *Unpubl. Ph.D. Thesis, Univ. of London Lib.* (1953).

NELSON, H., *Theoretical Foundations of Psychology* (New York, Van Nostrand, 1951).

RIMOLDI, H. J., Personal tempo, *J. Abnorm. (Soc.) Psychol.*, **46**, 283–303 (1951).

RYANS, D. G., An experimental attempt to analyse persistent behaviour, *J. Gen. Psychol.*, **19**, 333–353 (1938).

SLATER, P., Speed of work in intelligence tests, *Brit. J. Psychol.*, **29**, 1, 55 (1938).

SNEDECOR, G. W., *Statistical Methods* (327) (Iowa State College Press, 1948).

SUTHERLAND, J. D., The speed factor in intelligent reactions, *Brit. J. Psychol.*, **24**, 276 (1934).

TATE, M. W., Notes on the measurement of mental speed, *J. Educ. Psychol.*, **41**, 219 (1950).

THORNDIKE, E. L., *The Measurement of Intelligence* (Bureau of Publications, Teachers' College, Columbia University, 1926).

THURSTONE, L. L., *Primary Mental Abilities (Psychometric Monographs No.* 1) (Chicago, Univ. of Chicago Press, 1939).

THURSTONE, L. L., *A Factorial Study of Perception* (Chicago, Univ. of Chicago Press, 1949).

VERNON, P., An application of factorial analysis to the study of test items, *Brit. J. Statistic. Psychol.*, **3**, 1–15 (1950).

WHERRY, R. J. and GAYLORD, R. H., Factor pattern of test items and tests as a function of the correlation coefficient; content, difficulty, and constant-error factors, *Psychometrika*, **9**, 237–244 (1944).

The work described in Chapter 5 was carried out during the course of an investigation into the value of psychological tests as predictors of academic performance, and was financed under a Grant from the Nuffield Foundation.

CHAPTER 6

Cognitive Abnormalities

R. W. PAYNE[1]

I. GENERAL COGNITIVE LEVEL

Introduction

This chapter will attempt to summarize those research findings which deal with abnormalities of cognitive function, and the relationship between cognitive and other abnormalities. One large category of cognitive abnormality will not be dealt with, namely mental deficiency. Mental defectives are traditionally subdivided into the endogenous and the exogenous. The former category is held to be the result of heredity, and is thus more relevant to the discussion of genetically determined abnormalities given elsewhere. The latter disorder is held to be the result of brain damage, and this subject is also dealt with elsewhere.

Before attempting to theorize about cognitive abnormalities, it is useful to have some comprehensive theory about normal cognitive processes. Unfortunately no such theory exists. Furneaux has produced strong arguments against regarding "general intelligence" as a basic scientific concept. He points out that the g score derived from any cognitive measure is the result of interactions between a number of more fundamental processes. Similarly he regards Thurstone's "Primary Mental Abilities" or "factors" as principles of classification based on the content of the problem to be solved, but probably complicated by the fact that different basic processes may interact differently for each of these factors. It is not therefore proposed to regard either g or the P.M.A. factors as variables fundamental to a scientific analysis of cognition.

Some learning theorists have proposed "models" of problem-solving or cognition. They believe that cognition can be fitted into the general framework of learning theory, and that problem-solving is in essence the occurrence of internal mediating stimulus-response processes, which cannot be observed but only inferred. The postulated "response" provides the internal stimulus for subsequent observable behaviour.

By and large there are two schools of thought. For example, Maltzman (1955) believes that problem-solving is merely internalized "trial and error" learning, the reinforcing agent being the production of an "anticipatory goal response." This hypothetical construct is merely an internalized representation of the rewarding state of affairs which is to follow. In easy problems, the correct internal mediating response has a high habit strength (and probability of occurrence). In difficult problems the correct response has a low habit strength, and the solution of the problem must await the extinction (through lack of reinforcement) of the stronger but incorrect competing responses. (It is difficult to see why the correct response should produce this rewarding "anticipatory goal response." This presupposes an already existing connexion between the "correct" response and the "goal." In other words, it presupposes that the subject has already learned from past experience that this is the correct answer, an assumption for which there is little support in many cases.)

Other theorists (e.g. Maier, 1931a, 1931b, 1945), while accepting that cognition is the occurrence of some internal mediating process, deny that trial and error learning and reasoning can be identified. Maier (1931a) argues that reasoning as distinct from learning, involves a manipulation and reorganization of past experience and can be observed even in the rat. He believes that internal trial and error learning cannot account for the observed results, because the solution is perceived too quickly, and an intermediate stage is lacking (Maier, 1931b).

Perhaps the main fault of both types of theory is that they have produced no crucial experiments to decide between them. Neither theory appears capable of producing a precise enough prediction to disprove itself. This sort of theory, then, will be of little help in providing a frame of reference around which to order the considerable mass of data on cognitive abnormalities.

[1] Now Associate Professor of Psychology in Queen's University, Kingston, Ontario.

Guilford (1956) has produced an extremely elaborate analysis of cognition. He also proposes to discard "general intelligence" as a basic concept, and suggests that "intelligence" is much more complex than formerly imagined. He has subdivided problem-solving into various stages which he calls "cognition (discovery)," "production (convergent thinking)," "production (divergent thinking)," "evaluation" and "memory." Within each stage of problem-solving he has isolated numerous "factors" representing the type of material to be reasoned about (e.g. verbal), the type of reasoning required, and so on. This scheme has been evolved with the aid of a large number of factor analyses, this statistical tool being used in each study to test the hypothesis that a certain "mental process" can be identified. Guilford's analysis is not a theory in the sense that it explains the *mechanisms* of problem-solving. It does however provide a possible "cognitive map" with which to explore abnormalities of thinking. Guilford's theory has not been used in the present chapter as a frame of reference. This is mainly because it has never been applied in the study of mental abnormality, and is probably over elaborate for the purpose of classifying those data which exist at present. Nevertheless Guilford's analyses can probably provide some objective support for most of the principles of classification which *have* been adopted.

The frame of reference which will be used in the following discussion of cognitive abnormalities is based on Furneaux's analysis of problem-solving, although several extensions to Furneaux's scheme have been introduced. For the sake of clarity, this scheme is laid out below with a brief definition and description of each heading.

Frame of Reference

GENERAL INTELLECTUAL LEVEL

The majority of cognitive tests yield a score which is regarded as a measure of "general intelligence" or g. It is clear that g is conceived of as some sort of "average" intellectual score, and is usually measured by a single test most representative (factorially) of a wide group of tests administered (usually) without a time limit. While such scores are admittedly useful in predicting certain types of behaviour, as Furneaux demonstrates, they are not measures of fundamental psychological variables. The same g score can be produced by quite different interactions of fundamental variables. For example, a slow thinker who makes few errors and has low persistence might obtain the same g score as a fast thinker who makes many errors, but who has the same persistence. A single g score is not an adequate description of the cognition of the two individuals.

"General intelligence" or "general level" must inevi-tably be discussed since the bulk of the data in abnormal psychology is derived from such measures. It is clear, however, that any results which relate to general intelligence must remain ambiguous, as they do not tell us what difference in specific intellectual function yielded the observed difference.

VARIABILITY OF PERFORMANCE

It is known that an individual's level of performance on precisely the same reasoning task varies from day to day. Furthermore, there may be important individual differences in the amount of variability that occurs. Variability may partly be a function of the type of test material. Some people might be more variable on problems of some "content" than on others. Variability might in fact interact with any of the other variables to be discussed. The causes of such variability may themselves be numerous and complex, including variations in motivation, general health and so on. Hull (1943) believed that there is an irreducible core of inexplicable and unpredictable variation perhaps due to some property of the nervous system, and following Spearman, used the term "oscillation" to describe it.

CONTENT

Perhaps the first obvious division of cognitive tests is according to their content, or the nature of the data to be thought about. It is possible to differentiate between problems whose data are largely "numerical," "verbal," "spatial" and so on. It is clear that tests of different content do not intercorrelate perfectly, and this may be the main (but probably not the only) reason that relatively specific "factors" of intelligence can be demonstrated (e.g. Thurstone's Primary Mental Abilities). This principle of classification by content, of course, makes no reference to the type of *reasoning* the subject is required to do, nor to the mechanisms and thought processes involved.

TYPE OF PROBLEM

If any collection of cognitive tests is viewed dispassionately, perhaps the most surprising feature is the variety of types of problem the label refers to. Quite different types of reasoning are required for different problems. Some tests require nothing besides *inductive reasoning* (many sorting tests of concept formation are of this sort). Other tests involve straightforward *deductive reasoning* (e.g. some arithmetical problems). A large number of tests require a combination of these two processes for their solution (e.g. the Thurstone letter-series test). Some tests merely require the subject to produce as many curious "ideas" as possible, and Guilford (1956) calls them tests of *originality*. Some tests are nothing more than measures of *perceptual discrimination* (e.g. the tests which define the United States Employment Service (1955) General Aptitude Test Battery "P" factor). Rather different tests are those which require the subject to imagine what a visual pattern or diagram would look like if rotated (or otherwise altered in its spatial orientation). These are commonly called tests of *spatial reasoning*. Some tests merely assess the subject's *immediate memory span* (e.g. the Wechsler-Bellevue Digit Span subtest), some assess his capacity for *rote learning* (e.g. some subtests of the Babcock Levy (1940) test of "mental efficiency"), and finally there are some which assess nothing more than the long-term capacity for *retention* of items of information (e.g. the Wechsler-Bellevue Information subtest).

What is so surprising is not that these various "cognitive" measures intercorrelate imperfectly, but that they intercorrelate at all. Yet innumerable studies have clearly demonstrated a relationship between all these measures. Many tests of course involve combinations of these different mental operations.

It is obviously quite possible to classify tests in accordance with the type of reasoning required, and while such a principle of classification is not completely independent of the "content" of the problems, it is nearly so. Thus this "variable" may well interact with all the other variables to be discussed.

Thought Processes

The variables so far discussed all refer to methods of classifying the problems to be solved. They do not deal with the thought processes used in their solution. No attempt will be made to elaborate in detail a theory of cognition. However, the following headings all refer to aspects of thought which are known to be involved in solving cognitive tests.

(a) Speed

Furneaux has demonstrated that the speed of returning a *correct* solution to a problem may be one of the most fundamental variables in cognition. This is an important source of individual differences. However, speed may interact with any of the other variables discussed. For example, some people may be quick at solving problems with "verbal" content, but slow at other sorts of material. Speed by itself is only a partial determinant of score in most tests, and its importance will vary from test to test. Because people tend to "give up" extremely difficult problems rather than devote too much time to them, it can be a determinant of the score even in untimed tests.

(b) Persistence

A second determinant of the score on many tests is persistence. For most types of problem, the longer the individual is prepared to think about it, the greater the probability of obtaining a solution. Again this factor can interact with all the other variables. For instance, in an untimed test, persistence can compensate for slowness. Persistence may be partly a function of such variables as the content of the test. It may also be partly a function of "drive."

(c) Error

The tendency to give an incorrect solution in the belief that it is correct, in contradistinction to the "abandonment" of a problem, is another determinant of ultimate performance which is a source of individual differences. Again this variable can interact with the other variables discussed. Error also could partly depend on the "content" and the "type" of the problem.

(d) Distractibility

It is clear that in order to solve a problem, one must give one's attention to it. If the relevant thought processes are interrupted, the solution will be delayed, and the problem might even be abandoned before solution occurs. Individual differences in the ability to concentrate on the task in hand are clearly a factor in determining success. Again this variable can interact with the other variables mentioned.

(e) Memory Span

At first sight it is difficult to see why tests of immediate memory span (e.g. the Wechsler-Bellevue Digit Span Test) correlate so highly with other cognitive measures (Wechsler, 1944). On reflection this is perhaps not so unexpected. In order to solve any problem it is necessary to hold the test instructions in mind. People whose memory span is small will be handicapped if they forget part of the instructions. In orally administered tests, the data of the problem itself must be held in mind (e.g. in the Wechsler Arithmetic test) while possible solutions are considered. If any item is forgotten, a solution may become impossible. Even in written problems, where the test data can be referred back to, such checking could result in slowness which itself could lead to the abandonment of the item. Memory span is clearly relevant to "spatial" items (e.g. the Wechsler Block Design test where the subject must, at least temporarily, "retain" in his mind the design he is trying to build while he arranges the blocks).

(f) Learning

Individual differences in rote-learning capacity are clearly correlated with other cognitive measures (Ingham, 1949, 1952). This is probably because, for problems where the subject's immediate memory span is too small for all the relevant data to be retained on one repetition, some of the test data must be memorized before the process of finding a solution can begin.

Also in many cognitive problems (e.g. the Wechsler Block Design test) the subject must *learn* from the easier items what methods of manipulation are fruitful in order to solve the later more difficult items. This learning proceeds largely through trial and error, but individuals who are poor at learning will tend to get poor scores.

(g) Retention

Many cognitive problems depend for their solution on the utilization of items of information acquired in the past. It is obvious that arithmetic problems become extremely difficult if one has forgotten one's tables. In other words, one often brings to a problem certain possible solutions or partial solutions which one has learned in the past. If retention is poor, performance will tend to be impaired. Some test items of course consist in nothing more than asking the subject to recall solutions to problems he has learned in the past (e.g. many "comprehension" test items), or pieces of information he has learned by rote in the past (e.g. "information" test items).

(h) Drive

Since learning and cognition cannot be separated completely, drive will be a variable relevant to problem-solving if only because it affects rote learning. In addition, however, it probably affects persistence, and may also considerably influence the *speed* with which solutions occur (cf. Furneaux).

(i) Rigidity

If rigidity is the tendency to continue to pursue one line of thought after it ceases to produce correct answers, and if there are individual differences in rigidity, this variable will also directly affect problem-solving ability.

(j) Concept Formation

The "concept" is the manipulandum of thought. It is obvious that in any problem expressed verbally, if one person uses a word to denote one concept, and another person uses the same word to denote a different concept, even though both use identical reasoning processes, each will reach a different solution. An understanding of concept formation and the mechanisms on which it is based is clearly crucial to an understanding of thinking.

These then, are some of the variables which determine performance on cognitive tests. It is proposed to discuss *abnormalities* of cognitive function (and their associated abnormalities) under these general headings.

Intellectual Level during Mental Illness

The impairment of intellectual functioning in individuals who were once normal has long been regarded as a cardinal feature of insanity. Popular terms such as *lunatic*, *crazy*, and *insane* and medical terms such as *dementia praecox* suggest that intellectual deficit is the most striking feature of some types of illness. In the last century of course, many cases of dementia were undoubtedly due to organic diseases of the brain which have since been identified (e.g. G.P.I. resulting from syphilis of the central nervous system). Nevertheless most psychoses are still regarded as "functional" and no clear-cut causes have been demonstrated.

In spite of this, there has been an extremely unfortunate tendency for psychologists to regard psychiatric diagnostic labels as of fundamental importance to a scientific analysis of mental abnormality. Countless studies attempt to find objective correlates of these labels. Thus, instead of investigating, for example, the nature and causes of "slowness of problem-solving," a psychological variable which can be accurately defined and measured, and clearly related to other psychological variables, psychologists have concerned themselves with investigating the performance on batteries of tests of individuals whom psychiatrists have labelled "schizophrenic." They have never enquired closely into the meaning of the term schizophrenic, nor have they apparently been concerned to discover whether or not schizophrenia *can* be defined and detected accurately enough to make it a fundamental variable to which everything else must be related.

It is clear from Chapter I (H. J. Eysenck) that at least as far as the psychoses are concerned, psychiatric diagnostic categories do *not* have the status of scientific concepts, and therefore should *not* be regarded as in any way basic to an analysis of cognitive abnormality. However, the bulk of the literature relates test results to psychiatric labels, and not to specific symptoms rated independently by unbiased observers, nor to other unambiguous data about the patients. Therefore it will be difficult to interpret most of the studies. Even if some correlations with psychiatric labels *are* observed, the reasons for these will not be clear. The behavioural correlates of specific cognitive dysfunctions can only be speculated about from the data so far available in the literature.

One of the earliest studies investigating the general intellectual level of mental patients on a standard intelligence test was that of Wells and Kelley (1920). They administered the Binet test to one hundred and one psychotics and found a slightly lower than normal I.Q. The group included both schizophrenics and manic-depressives. Schott (1931) reports the results of a larger survey, also using the Binet test. He tested four hundred and fifty mental patients of all types, and reports "a moderately normal type of distribution skewed slightly toward the lower end of the scale." The median I.Q. was 92·4, the bottom quartile was 75·1 and the top quartile 103·87.

The earlier literature on general intelligence in mental patients has been well reviewed by Brody (1941) and Hunt and Cofer (1944). The latter authors point out that almost all the studies done up to that time used such tests as the Point-Scale or the Stanford-Binet, which were standardized on children. "This introduced age as an uncontrolled variable . . ." (Hunt and Cofer, p. 973, 1944). Therefore they regard their conclusions as tentative. Since then, the

Eysenck, 1947; Fey, 1951; Garfield, 1948 and 1949; Gilhooly, 1950; Gilliland, Wittman and Goldman, 1943; Hall, 1938; Harper, 1950a; Kogan, 1950; Lewinski, 1945a, 1945b and 1947; Olch, 1948; Rabin, 1941, 1944a, 1944b; Rapaport, Gill and Schafer, 1945; Rogers, 1951; Stotsky, 1952; Warner, 1950; and Webb and De Haan, 1951.)

This table needs considerable amplification and qualification. It is based almost entirely on the Wechsler-Bellevue scale, as this test is adequately standardized for age, and the I.Q. scores at each age

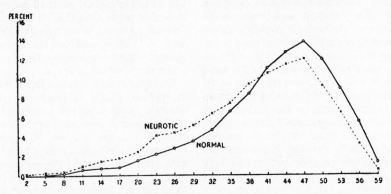

FIG. 6.1. DISTRIBUTION OF INTELLIGENCE-TEST SCORES OF 5,000 NEUROTIC AND 3,665 NORMAL SOLDIERS
(*From H. J. Eysenck, "Dimensions of Personality"*)

use of the Wechsler-Bellevue Scale (Wechsler, 1944) has become widespread, and many more data are available. Table VI.1 is based on a collection and

TABLE VI.1

INTELLIGENCE QUOTIENTS IN ABNORMAL GROUPS

(*Wechsler-Bellevue except where noted*)

Category	Mean I.Q.	No. of cases
Civilian neurotics . . .	105·01	987 (includes 145 on Matrices)
Neurotics (Army Service breakdowns)	93	5,000 (all on Matrices)
Epileptics	107·51	425
Schizophrenics . . .	96·08	1,284
Affective psychoses . .	94·87	65
Paranoid condition . .	118·3	7

combination of some of the more recently published data on the I.Q. levels to be found in various abnormal groups. (The table makes use of the data reported by Altus and Clark, 1949; Bannatyne, 1953; Carp, 1950; Cohen, 1950 and 1952a; Collins, 1951; Dana, 1957;

level are comparable (having a mean of 100 and a standard deviation of 15). However, in some cases additional I.Q. results obtained from Raven's Progressive Matrices test (Raven, 1950) were added. This was thought permissible since the Matrices test is also well standardized for age, and in the case of all the data included, the I.Q. quoted has a mean of 100 and a standard deviation of 15 for each age-group.

Perhaps the most interesting mean I.Q.s are those derived from individuals diagnosed neurotic. The civilian neurotic group includes only cases of breakdown in civilian life, although in many cases the subjects were war veterans (and indeed treated in "V.A." hospitals). The army service breakdown neurotic sample is one reported by Eysenck (1947), and consists of soldiers from the British Army who broke down during service in the 1939–45 war. The mean I.Q. level of the two groups is quite different. Eysenck gives the entire I.Q. distribution of his service breakdown neurotic group (based on the Matrices test). This is shown in Fig. 6.1.

In the same study, Eysenck (1947) compares the level of intelligence of the neurotic soldiers with the level of intelligence found in a group of matched soldiers who did not break down. The neurotic soldiers were significantly duller (average Matrix score for neurotics = 39·36 ± 9·90; for normals, average = 42·24 ± 9·77, C.R. = 14), although they had a higher proportion of extreme I.Q.s. He suggested that there might be a tendency for duller individuals to find army life more stressful and thus to break down more easily. He also suggested that the reverse might be true in civilian life, namely that in western societies the brighter people might find life more stressful and frustrating and thus tend to develop neurotic breakdowns more readily.

The mean I.Q. shown in Table VI.1 for civilian neurotics seems to bear out this suggestion. It was not possible to calculate a combined standard deviation from the entire nine hundred and eighty-seven civilian neurotic cases. However, it could be calculated from five hundred and eighty-eight of these cases. (This smaller group of five hundred and eighty-eight, all of whom had the Wechsler-Bellevue test, had a mean I.Q. of 105·27, which was very close to the mean of the entire group.) The standard deviation of this group was only 13·61. In other words, civilian neurotics are both brighter and more homogeneous than the normal population (as estimated from Wechsler's norms). Put in another way, these figures suggest that there are just as many very bright neurotic patients as very bright normal people, but whereas about 10 per cent of normal people have an I.Q. of 81 or lower, only about 3¾ per cent of the civilian neurotic population is as dull as this.

The mean I.Q. for epileptics was included in the table because it was once thought that epilepsy produced a progressive intellectual deterioration. The mean epileptic I.Q. of 107·51 given in Table VI.1 is perhaps misleading, as four hundred of the four hundred and twenty-five cases are derived from a single study by Collins (1951). She points out that the higher than average I.Q. of her group might be due to the fact that most were private patients from a relatively high socio-economic group. Collins's study suggests clearly that: "There is little evidence of deterioration except in organic cases." The average I.Q. for "essential epileptics" in this study was 111·20, for "traumatic epileptics" only 98·95, a difference significant at the 1 per cent level. Similar findings are reported by Winfield (1951) on sixty cases using the Wechsler, Thurstone's P.M.A. test, and the Matrices. These results are consistent with the bulk of the evidence in the literature according to a recent review by Jones (1953). It seems clear that epileptic seizures as such do *not* result in a general intellectual deterioration, although brain damage associated with epilepsy (or with any other set of symptoms) can in many cases produce a general intellectual deficit.

The mean I.Q. of 96·08 for a group of 1,284 schizophrenics is perhaps surprisingly high, as this disease is regarded, at least in many cases, as a dementing condition. It was not possible to calculate a standard deviation from all the cases. However, this was done for a smaller group of eight hundred and twenty-five cases (whose mean Wechsler I.Q. was 96·45, very close to the mean of the whole group). The standard deviation was 16·69. Thus schizophrenics would appear to be both duller and more heterogeneous than the general population. For example, while only 10 per cent of the general population have an I.Q. of 81 or lower, 17½ per cent of the schizophrenic population are as dull as this, or duller, according to these data. On the other hand, 8¼ per cent of schizophrenics have an I.Q. of 119 or higher, while 10 per cent of normals do as well or better than this. It is tempting to conclude that schizophrenia is not a single "illness" but a name used to cover a considerable variety of conditions, some of which have associated intellectual disturbances and some of which have not.

One important additional factor must be considered in relation to the schizophrenic data. While the neurotic group is probably reasonably representative of the general neurotic population, this is almost certainly not the case for the schizophrenic group. Fourteen of the studies from which the schizophrenic data are derived report the mean age of the schizophrenic group they tested. Except for two groups of paranoid schizophrenics (whose mean ages were 36·4 and 43·8) the highest mean age reported was 33·7 and the lowest 26·9. An examination of the age standard deviations (where given) reinforces the conclusion that almost *all* the schizophrenic data are derived from the age-group 20 to 40. Almost certainly there are large numbers of chronic schizophrenic patients over 40, resident in mental hospitals, and if it is true that at least a proportion of schizophrenics dement progressively, their scores must be lower than those reported, so that the present mean is probably unduly high. Probably a factor which introduces an enormous bias into this sample is that of testability. Many psychotic patients are so uncooperative or unresponsive that they are too difficult to test with the Wechsler-Bellevue, and the scores of this group, which may well be large, are clearly not represented. These patients may well include the more intellectually impaired.

That it is possible to select schizophrenic groups which have quite a low general intelligence when tested is clear from a number of studies. For example, Mainord (1953) tested a group of twenty-two schizophrenics judged to have deteriorated, and these obtained a mean I.Q. of only 84·5 on the Wechsler-Bellevue. Similarly Malamud and Palmer (1938) report a group of one hundred deteriorated schizophrenics who obtained a mean mental age of only 126·3 months (S.D. 14·4) on the Stanford-Binet.

The data available for affective psychosis are surprisingly few. The mean given in Table VI.1 is based on only sixty-five cases, and the studies on which it is based fail to provide enough information to make it possible to calculate a standard deviation that would be in any way representative. There is no real evidence that affective psychoses differ in tested I.Q. from schizophrenics in the older studies such as that of Barnes (1924), and the data reviewed by Hunt and Cofer (1944) generally support this conclusion.

Little can be said about the category of paranoid condition on the basis of the seven cases reported by Rapaport, Gill and Shafer (1945). Lack of contemporary data suggests that the use of this label has become out of date.

General intelligence has been related to two other large groups of behavioural abnormality. The first is delinquency. It is fairly well established that convicted delinquents, both adult and child, tend to have a mean I.Q. significantly below average. Taylor (1938) assessing 10,000 male adolescent prisoners (aged 16 to 22) on the Columbia group test, found a distribution of I.Q. skewed towards the lower end of the scale. Of the group three hundred and twenty-two were in fact illiterate. Mann and Mann (1939) report the same type of distribution of Binet test I.Q.s obtained from 1,061 delinquent boys and six hundred and seventy delinquent girls in their teens. They report a mean I.Q. for boys of 84·88 and for girls of 83·77. A similarly shaped distribution with a rather higher mean is reported for adults by Shakow and Millard (1935). These studies suggest that individuals of low intelligence are much more likely to get into trouble with the law. Whether low intelligence led them into crime, or merely caused them to get caught it is not possible to say.

Addiction to drugs is another category of abnormality which some earlier studies, often of rather few cases, related to low intelligence. For example, Hall (1938) tested thirty-seven female drug addicts, after withdrawal, on the Army Alpha, and found a mean I.Q. of 96·2 (S.D. 16·5). However, a fairly large study by Brown and Partington (1942) does not support this. They gave the Wechsler-Bellevue to three hundred and seventy-one narcotic drug addicts and found that "drug addicts range in intelligence from defective to very superior, with the largest percentages falling into the average and bright-normal classifications." However the addict group showed "a lower percentage of cases in defective and in the very superior intelligence classifications as compared with Wechsler's normal group."

The functional psychiatric diagnostic categories so far considered have been very broad. The data presented in Table VI.1 can to some extent be broken down. The results for the civilian neurotics are shown in Table VI.2.

TABLE VI.2

INTELLIGENCE QUOTIENTS IN SUBGROUPS
OF CIVILIAN NEUROTICS

(Wechsler-Bellevue except where noted)

Category	Mean I.Q.	No. of cases
Neurotic (not specified) . .	103·63	676
Mixed neurosis . . .	107·23	72 (includes 63 on Matrices)
Hysteric	106·11	43 (includes 25 on Matrices)
Psychopath	100·64	33 (includes 21 on Matrices)
Obsessive-compulsive . .	114·16	27 (includes 11 on Matrices)
Anxiety neurosis . . .	109·65	120 (includes 25 on Matrices)
Neurotic depression . .	109·28	72 (includes 63 on Matrices)
Total introverted neurotics .	110·36	163 (includes 36 on Matrices)
Total extraverted neurotics .	103·74	76 (includes 46 on Matrices)

Unfortunately most of the cases reported in the literature are not described in detail, or given any label other than neurotic. The cases which are subdivided have a higher overall mean intelligence, although this may be purely accidental. The main finding suggested by the table is that the neurotic groups classified by Eysenck as introverted (obsessive-compulsives, anxiety neurotics and neurotic depressives) have a higher mean I.Q. than those classified as extraverted (hysterics and psychopaths). Precisely the same observation was made by Eysenck (1945) on the 5,000 wartime army service breakdown neurotics. His results are presented in Fig. 6.2.

The mean raw Matrices score for the dysthymic neurotic group was 40·12 (S.D. 10·10). The mean score for the hysteric group was 37·12 (S.D. 12·08). The difference was highly significant (C.R. = 4·6). Bradford (1941) similarly reports a high incidence of hysterics among soldiers with very low test scores.

This apparently reliable finding is difficult to explain. Certainly extraverted neurotics are less common in mental hospitals than introverted neurotics. It is conceivable that extraverts find the same degree of neuroticism (and the symptoms resultant from it) less troublesome than introverts. Therefore they tend not to seek treatment. *Belle indifférence* is traditionally regarded as accompanying hysterical physical symptoms, and it is often claimed that these symptoms are unconsciously motivated, actually serving the purpose of making life more pleasant for the patient. Anxiety and obsessional symptoms on the other hand are seldom pleasant. It is conceivable that those hysterics who do become patients are more severely neurotic than their dysthymic counterparts. If we accept that a severe degree of neuroticism can produce some

At first sight, this breakdown is rather curious. The large bulk of cases are not given any label other than schizophrenic, and the two brightest groups are "schizophrenics" and "mixed schizophrenics." It is possible that many of these cases could have been labelled "early schizophrenics" or "acute schizophrenics." In other words, it is possible that these cases have been ill for a relatively short period of time, and do not present such severe or clear-cut symptoms.

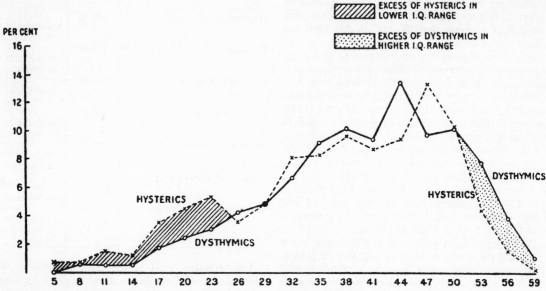

FIG. 6.2. DISTRIBUTION OF INTELLIGENCE-TEST SCORES OF 904 DYSTHYMICS AND 474 HYSTERICS
(*From H. J. Eysenck, "Dimensions of Personality"*)

intellectual impairment, the results could be explained. This suggestion, however, is extremely tentative and there is no other evidence to support it.

The breakdown of the schizophrenic group is given in Table VI.3.

TABLE VI.3

INTELLIGENCE QUOTIENTS IN SUBGROUPS OF SCHIZOPHRENIA
(*Wechsler-Bellevue I.Q.*)

Category	Mean I.Q.	No. of cases
Schizophrenic (not further specified)	97·53	928
Mixed schizophrenics . .	99·61	72
Paranoid schizophrenics . .	94·84	166
Simple schizophrenics . .	88·23	44
Catatonic schizophrenics . .	82·80	45
Hebephrenic schizophrenics .	80·60	29

For this reason they have not been further classified. If this group tends to be less severely ill, and contains many early cases of intellectual impairment which is progressive, it is not surprising that the group has the highest I.Q.

Where the patients have been further classified, it is interesting to note that those labelled paranoid schizophrenic are substantially brighter. This is even more striking since the average age of the "paranoid" subgroup is approximately 40, probably considerably older than the other subgroups (age data are unfortunately scanty for the other subgroups). In any event the paranoid schizophrenics have probably had at least as long to dement as the other subgroups. The data suggest, then, that schizophrenic patients with low levels of I.Q. are more likely to be labelled "catatonic" or "hebephrenic," and that those labelled "simple" are intermediate. Whether this is because the specific symptoms, to which these labels refer, are related to more severe intellectual impairment, or because these patients have always been dull, it is not possible to say from these figures. Nevertheless, the former explanation would probably be more generally accepted.

The breakdown of the affective psychoses is presented in Table VI.4.

TABLE VI.4

INTELLIGENCE QUOTIENTS IN SUBGROUPS OF AFFECTIVE PSYCHOSIS

(Wechsler-Bellevue I.Q.)

Category	Mean I.Q.	No. of cases
Manic-depressive (depressed state)	103·3	18
Depressive	91·0	8
Manic	90·0	32
Involutional depression . .	99·9	7

Were the numbers not so small, this table would suggest that involutional depressives do not apparently suffer from any impairment, while depressives and manics are roughly comparable in level to schizophrenics. It is clear, however, that firm conclusions cannot be drawn. The label "manic-depressive" traditionally refers to patients who have periods of mania and periods of depression alternating (just as the single labels "depressive" and "manic" imply recurring conditions of this sort *without* alternations between the two extremes). Modern usage, however, at least among psychologists, has probably become imprecise. All the manic-depressives reported were tested in a depressed phase, and it is possible that some psychologists use the term manic-depressive to include individuals with recurring depression who never show manic attacks. It would probably not be correct to conclude from this table that the cyclic disorders show no evidence of mental impairment.

DIRECT EVIDENCE FOR GENERAL IMPAIRMENT WITH MENTAL ILLNESS

All the results so far discussed are ambiguous in the extreme. No evidence has been presented to show that the intelligence of these patients (the psychotics especially) was not always at the same level. In other words, is psychosis a condition tending to occur more frequently among the dull, but itself producing no intellectual deficit, or do psychotic illnesses tend to produce intellectual impairment in people who were formerly normal? Few good studies have been carried out on this subject because of the obvious difficulty of obtaining and testing people who will later develop mental illnesses.

Probably the earliest study is one by Gardner

(1931) who examined the school records of one hundred adult schizophrenic patients and one hundred manic-depressive psychotics. He concluded that they were generally worse at school than their colleagues, but had more specific ability for art and music. No statistical analysis was performed and the study is not very informative. The same author later reported a different type of study (Gardner, 1940). A total of 3,500 normal children in Massachusetts was studied

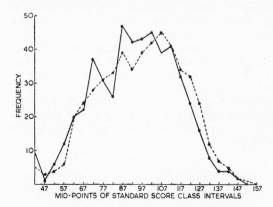

FIG. 6.3. DISTRIBUTION OF A.G.C.T. STANDARD SCORES FOR 510 PSYCHIATRIC IN-PATIENTS (SOLID) AND CONTROL DISTRIBUTION BASED ON DATA FOR 290,163 FIFTH SERVICE COMMAND INDUCTEES (BROKEN)

(From C. F. Mason, "Pre-illness Intelligence of Mental Hospital Patients")

year by year starting in 1922. Each year their intelligence was tested. By 1940, twenty-two had been admitted to a mental hospital. Their pre-illness I.Q. test scores were all below average, but since the group contained only six psychotics, few conclusions can be drawn.

A more satisfactory study is reported by Birren (1944). From the files of a child guidance clinic, the records were obtained of a group of thirty-eight children who had later become psychotic (schizophrenic, constitutional or organic, or miscellaneous, i.e. neurotic or psychotic reaction). He also examined fifty-three control cases who had not later become psychotic. The study suggested that "pre-psychotic cases as a group do not differ in intelligence from the general population studied by the Bureau of Child Study."

The only direct proof of intellectual deterioration with psychosis with which we are familiar is a study by Rappaport and Webb (1950). They found ten schizophrenic patients who had taken an I.Q. test in high school before they became ill. Each subject was given the *same* test again. The mean former I.Q. (in high school) was 97·60, while the mean present I.Q. (when psychotic) on the same tests, was only 63·90, a difference significant at the 1 per cent level.

The largest study of pre-illness I.Q. is reported by Mason (1956), who obtained a sample of five hundred and ten inductees of World War II, all of whom, as veterans, later broke down with some functional psychiatric illness. All had been given the American Army General Classification Test on being accepted for service. The pre-illness I.Q. scores of this group were compared with the scores obtained by a carefully matched control group consisting of 290,163 Fifth Service Command Inductees. Fig. 6.3 compares the pre-illness I.Q.s of the inductees, who later broke down, with the normal controls.

There is *no* statistically significant difference between the two distributions. At first sight these results would appear to support the contention that the below average I.Q. scores among psychotics are entirely a result of their illness. Mason, however, also gives the following table relating *type* of psychiatric illness to pre-illness level by comparing each group with the normal controls—

TABLE VI.5

DIFFERENCES IN PRE-ILLNESS I.Q. BETWEEN CONTROLS AND DIFFERENT DIAGNOSTIC GROUPS

(After Mason)

Group	N	d.f.	Chi square	p	Trend
All Patients . .	510[1]	16	22·32	0·14	
All schizophrenics .	368	16	32·60	0·02	low scores
Paranoid . .	66	3	3·10	0·39	
Catatonic . .	126	7	10·61	0·19	
Hebephrenic .	122	7	17·55	0·02	low scores
Simple . .	33	2	12·46	0·002	low scores
Other . . .	21	1	4·77	0·05	low scores
Non schizophrenics .	188	12	7·78	0·79	
Alcoholism . .	29	1	0·61	0·90	
Neurosis . .	79	5	1·93	0·20	
Manic-depressive .	25	1	17·65	0·001	high scores
Character disorder	55	3	4·21	0·25	

[1] This total is reproduced from the original article. The author does not explain how it is related to the subtotals below.

Unfortunately no I.Q. figures are given. Nevertheless the trends are interesting. It would appear that the "schizophrenics" as a group were below average in intelligence even before they became ill, while those labelled "manic-depressive" were above average. Both findings are consistent with the data in Tables VI.3 and VI.4. The finding that the pre-illness intelligence of hebephrenic schizophrenics is considerably below average is also consistent with Table VI.3. A lack in Mason's data, is any reference to depressives or manics, two groups whose I.Q. during illness is apparently well below average.

The conclusions which can be drawn from this study are limited, since the author did not retest the subjects on the same scales, and thus provide a direct measure of the amount of deterioration, if any, which had occurred. The finding, however, that the pre-illness I.Q. of schizophrenics is below average suggests that the amount of deterioration presumed to have occurred in many schizophrenic groups may have been overestimated. There is also a strong possibility that the label hebephrenic schizophrenic becomes attached to patients who have *always* been dull, just as the label paranoid schizophrenic may become attached to patients who have always been of about average intelligence.

Another method of demonstrating that psychosis produces impairment is by testing patients before and after recovery; but very few studies of this sort appear to have been made. Graham (1940) tested thirty-three schizophrenic patients on the Binet scale before and after insulin shock therapy. There was no significant difference in test score. We cannot, however, necessarily conclude that the insulin "cured" the patients, nor does the author claim this.

Davidson (1939) gave the Binet test to twenty-eight manic-depressive psychotics, and retested the same patients later. Eighteen had improved clinically, and in every case the Binet score improved. Two were judged worse by the doctors, and their Binet scores had declined. Davidson also tested and retested eighteen schizophrenics and the change in Binet score is reported as coinciding with the change in clinical status. In a second study, the same author tested twenty-five psychotics on the Matrices, and retested them later. Again the change in score is reported as coinciding with the change in clinical status.

Carp (1952) tested forty-two schizophrenic patients on the Wechsler-Bellevue before and after insulin therapy. There was a mean Wechsler I.Q. improvement of 4·7 points, but no control group was tested.

Callagan (1952) tested twenty-five depressive patients before treatment, one week after a course of E.C.T., and again five weeks after E.C.T., on a battery of tests. General intelligence was measured by five Wechsler-Bellevue subtests, both verbal and performance. A control group of twenty-five depressives who had had no E.C.T. was retested after similar intervals. While general intelligence improved after E.C.T., there was no significant difference between the control and experimental group. There was, however, a significant relationship between I.Q. improvement and clinical improvement rated by psychiatrists in *both* groups, so that the lack of significant differentiation in final I.Q. between the groups may partly have been because many of the untreated cases had also recovered considerably.

Another treatment claimed at least temporarily to

improve schizophrenics is the administration of sodium amytal. Several studies have investigated whether or not amytal also improves the general intellectual level of the schizophrenic. A fairly early study by Layman (1940) produced apparently quite striking results. Twenty schizophrenics were given the Binet and a form-board test before, during and after amytal. The Binet test results were much better for patients under amytal, but dropped back to their initial level on the third administration after the drug had been withdrawn. Similarly Mainord (1953) tested twenty-two deteriorated schizophrenics (who also had abnormal EEG records) before, during and after amytal, on the Wechsler-Bellevue. Their pre-amytal mean I.Q. was 84·5, their mean amytal I.Q., 100·6; and their post-amytal mean I.Q. only 86·4, a highly significant improvement being shown while the drug was being administered. A control group of eighteen non-deteriorated schizophrenics retested without the drug showed an average increase of only one I.Q. point.

Senf, Huston and Cohen (1955), however, obtained different results. They tested twenty-four chronic schizophrenics, twenty-two early schizophrenics, twenty-one depressives and twenty-one neurotics on a number of tests before and during amytal. General intelligence as estimated from three Wechsler Verbal Scale subtests did not alter significantly with amytal in any of the groups. Two recent studies by Ogilvie (1954) and Broadhurst (1957) criticize earlier work for failing to control several variables. In particular, a control group tested with a *placebo* was lacking in the earlier studies. Using the Nufferno test as a measure of general level, neither Ogilvie nor Broadhurst found changes in the general level of schizophrenics which they could attribute to amytal, in two large and extremely well controlled experiments. Both, however, observed fairly large improvements with practice. These studies suggest that the earlier results of Layman and Mainord *might* have been the result of the suggestion implicit in the administration of this drug. However, this alternative explanation is no less startling than the original observations.

One observation that is apparently uncontradicted, is that, by and large, a higher I.Q. score while ill is a better prognosis than a lower one, at least among schizophrenics. Carp (1950) investigated the response of forty-two schizophrenics to insulin treatment. Twenty-six were unimproved, and sixteen were improved. None of the improved group had a pre-treatment Wechsler I.Q. below 95, while fourteen of the unimproved group were lower than this. Stotsky (1952) gave the Wechsler to eighty-eight schizophrenics. After six months, forty-four had remitted and gone home, while forty-four were still in hospital. The remitted group had a mean I.Q. of 107·5 (S.D. 12·7), the unremitted group had a mean I.Q. of only 101·6

(S.D. 12·4), a difference significant at the 2 per cent level. A smaller group of twenty-eight schizophrenics who had remitted after only three months was compared with a group of twenty-eight who were still ill after three months. Again the remitted groups had obtained a mean I.Q. before recovery of 104·1 (S.D. 12·7), the unremitted group had a mean I.Q. of only 97·7 (S.D. 13.0), a difference significant at the 5 per cent level. There was a point-biserial correlation between I.Q. and remission of 0·21 for the first group and 0·24 for the second. These studies might suggest that the less seriously ill psychotic patients have less general intellectual impairment, and tend to recover quicker, although this is merely an unsupported inference.

The only study which gives direct evidence for progressive general deterioration with psychosis is one by Trapp and James (1937). Out of a large group of hospitalized schizophrenics, the authors found forty-one who had been given the Binet test within a week or two of admission, and who had remained in hospital without any remission. The length of this unbroken stay varied from four months to thirteen years. They were all retested on the Binet. If schizophrenia tends to produce a progressive deterioration, all these subjects should have become worse. Furthermore there should be a correlation between the length of the unbroken illness and the amount of deterioration. The authors do not calculate these figures, but fortunately they publish all the raw data, so that they can be worked out. The average Binet I.Q. for the whole group on admission was 82·8. The average retest I.Q. for the group was 75·2, representing a mean decline of 7·6 I.Q. points. The correlation between length of illness and drop in I.Q. for the whole group is 0·39. Both values are as predicted, and suggest that the longer the illness continues, the greater the I.Q. drop.

The authors also subdivide their cases according to type of schizophrenia. There were nineteen cases of paranoid schizophrenia whose mean age on admission was 32·1. Their mean length of illness was three years eight months, their mean admission I.Q. was 88·79, and their mean retest I.Q. 86·47, representing an average decline of only 3·32 I.Q. points. The paranoid group, as is usually the case, had the highest I.Q. on admission, and showed by far the smallest decline in I.Q. Nevertheless there was a correlation of 0·61 between length of illness and I.Q. drop. Since the mean I.Q. drop is small, this figure implies that the short stay cases actually improved their score (perhaps through practice), while the long stay cases were those whose I.Q. declined.

There were seven cases of simple schizophrenia, and, as is usual, these had an intermediate mean admission I.Q. of 79·71. Their mean admission age was 28·7, and their mean length of illness four years, seven months. Their mean retest I.Q. was 67·14, representing an average decline of 12·57 I.Q. points. The correlation between I.Q. decline and length of illness for this group was 0·57. Again, those who are ill longest, show the greatest decrease in score.

There were eleven cases of hebephrenic schizophrenia, and as is usual, these, along with the catatonics, had the lowest admission I.Q. The mean age of the hebephrenics on admission was 27·3 years, their mean length of illness four years, four months. Their mean admission I.Q. was 76·91, their mean retest I.Q. 63·36, representing an average decline of 13·55 I.Q. points. The correlation between I.Q. decline and length of illness for this group is only 0·03 (in the expected direction), probably because they were all ill a similar length of time and thus show no variation in length of illness.

The four catatonic cases had a mean age on admission of 28·5. Their mean length of illness was two years, ten months, their mean admission I.Q. 75·75 and their mean retest I.Q. 68·25. They show an average decline of 7·50 I.Q. points. The correlation between length of illness and I.Q. drop in this group is 0·48.

This study, then, suggests clearly that a schizophrenic illness without remission tends to produce a deterioration of general level which is progressive. The longer the illness, the more severe the deterioration tends to be. The one exception is that those diagnosed paranoid schizophrenic have a much higher initial I.Q., and while their deterioration also is a function of the length of their illness, it is much slower.

We can conclude from these studies that psychosis probably produces a general intellectual impairment, which deteriorates as psychotics get worse, and improves with recovery. However, direct and unequivocal studies are few.

INDIRECT STUDIES OF GENERAL INTELLECTUAL DETERIORATION

While there are few studies which give direct measures of general level before, during and after psychosis, there are a large number of studies which make use of indirect methods of estimating general intellectual deterioration. The main formal tests of general deterioration are the Babcock-Levy test for the measurement of efficiency of mental functioning (Babcock and Levy, 1940), the Shipley-Hartford test of deterioration (Shipley, 1940), the Hunt-Minnesota test for organic brain damage (Hunt, 1943) and the Wechsler-Bellevue Deterioration Index (Wechsler, 1944). All these tests except the Wechsler make use of the same principle. It is a well-known fact that vocabulary tests in normal people have a high correla-

tion with other tests of general intelligence (Wechsler, 1944). An impressive list of studies (Babcock, 1930, 1933, 1941a; Wells and Kelley, 1920; Altman and Shakow, 1937; Malamud and Palmer, 1938; Davidson, 1938, 1939; Simmins, 1933; Harbinson, 1937; Lidz, Gay and Tietze, 1942; Rabin, 1944; Klehr, 1949; Hunt and French, 1949; Hall, 1951; Rapaport et al., 1945; Wittman, 1933; Schwarz, 1932) suggest that, when normal and psychotic (or brain-damaged) groups are compared on a variety of tests, the test yielding the *smallest* mean difference is a vocabulary test. Usually the groups do not differ significantly in vocabulary score. The implication then is that vocabulary is the ability least affected by mental illness and deterioration. Thus the present vocabulary level of a psychotic subject will be a good measure of his pre-illness level of general intelligence. If the subject is also given a test of his *present* level of general intelligence, the discrepancy between the g score and the vocabulary score will provide a neat indirect measure of the amount of deterioration which has occurred. Babcock was the first psychologist to base a formal test of deterioration on this principle (Babcock, 1930, 1933, 1941a, 1941b).

While the general method would seem to have considerable "face" validity, it is obviously necessary to demonstrate that it works.[1] This would appear to be a simple matter. A group of patients could be given a good test of general intelligence on admission, and could then be retested after a period of time on the same test, and also given a test of deterioration. There should be a high correlation between the amount of deterioration demonstrated on retest, and the indirect deterioration score. Yet *none* of the common tests of deterioration mentioned have ever been validated in this way. The authors and subsequent investigators have been content to repeat the initial observation over and over again, i.e. that there is a larger discrepancy between g tests and vocabulary tests among psychotics (or organics) than exists among normals. Because of this lack of direct validation, data derived from these tests are less than conclusive.

The use of such tests in research has been criticized frequently (e.g. Solomon, 1939; Gerstein, 1949; Lewinski, 1948; Shapiro and Nelson, 1955; and Yacorzynski, 1941). Yacorzynski's (1941) main point is that vocabulary cannot be used as a measure of

---

[1] Crown (1949) reports the only study in which subjects known to have deteriorated organically were tested in this condition and actually retested on recovery. Four patients with myxoedema were tested while ill on the Mill Hill Vocabulary, the Progressive Matrices and the Shipley Hartford test. They were retested on recovery after treatment. There was a striking improvement on all the test scores. However their vocabulary scores improved just as much as the other scores. This study of course proves nothing about deterioration in functional disorders, but the same indirect measures have been widely used with organic cases.

pre-illness intelligence because it *does* tend to deteriorate with illness. He suggested that this could be demonstrated clearly if vocabulary tests were scored more accurately. That is, instead of scoring a definition correct or incorrect it should be rated for level of acceptability.

Capps (1939) and Shapiro and Nelson (1955)[1] found evidence that vocabulary is not unaffected by deterioration. Chodorkoff and Mussen (1952) administered a specially designed multiple-choice vocabulary test to fifty normals and fifty schizophrenics who were also given the Shipley-Hartford test. The schizophrenics selected a significantly greater number of inferior definitions (less "abstract," more "specific" and more "illustrative"). There was also a significant correlation between the Shipley-Hartford Conceptual Quotient and the type of definition chosen, the more "deteriorated" choosing the less "abstract" type of definition.

Harrington and Ehrmann (1954) gave the Wechsler-Bellevue Vocabulary test to twenty normals and twenty schizophrenics matched for age, sex and I.Q. Scored in the usual way, vocabulary did not differentiate the groups. However, the schizophrenics produced significantly more "concrete" responses as rated. Nevertheless, when both groups were given a special multiple-choice vocabulary test, there was *no* significant tendency for schizophrenics to select more concrete or more unsatisfactory answers.

Ackelsberg (1944) tested fifty senile patients classified by interview as "little deteriorated," "mildly deteriorated" and "marked deterioration." All were given a synonyms test, an antonyms test and a categorization test of classifying species words under the relevant genus word. They also had tests of word fluency and a test of homographs (giving as many meanings as possible to a word). *All* the tests differentiated the groups and the author concluded that all aspects of vocabulary deteriorate with general impairment. The main defect of the study is, however, that it may have been contaminated, as the original estimate of deterioration may have been based partly on the way the subjects used words in interview.

Feifel (1949) tested Yacorzynski's hypothesis by giving a vocabulary test to one hundred and eighty-five normal and one hundred and eighty-five abnormal subjects matched for age, sex, education and Binet vocabulary as scored in the usual way. Placing the vocabulary responses into five categories as had been suggested by Yacorzynski, he found that the abnormals gave significantly fewer synonym responses, and significantly more descriptive, inferior explanation, demonstration and illustrative responses.

An almost identical study was made by Moran, Moran and Blake (1952) on sixty-three schizophrenics also matched with sixty-three normals for age, sex, education and Wechsler vocabulary score. When Yacorzynski's method of analysis was used on the vocabulary responses, there were *no* significant differences between the groups in the number of synonym, use and description, explanation, inferior or error types of responses.

Rabin, King and Ehrmann (1955) tested twenty-five normals, twenty-five short-term schizophrenics and twenty-five long-term schizophrenics using the Wechsler vocabulary scale and the Ammon's Full Range Picture Vocabulary test. The latter test is non-verbal, and the answer is given by pointing to the appropriate picture. There was no differences between the normals and the short-term schizophrenics, but the long-term schizophrenics were worse on all the tests. They were *least* deteriorated on the Ammon's test although they were poor at explaining why they had pointed to the picture that they chose.

All these studies (except that of Moran, Moran and Blake, 1952) seem to be consistent with Yacorzynski's suggestions. Nevertheless, as a criticism of the use of vocabulary as a measure of past intelligence they are at least partly beside the point. It seems to be true that some deterioration in language function can be demonstrated among psychotics or deteriorated old people when special forms of vocabulary tests are devised, or when special systems of scoring are used for normal tests. However, this in no way disproves the often repeated original observation that vocabulary tests *scored conventionally* are not affected by mental disorder. It is probably safe to conclude that, if conventionally scored vocabulary tests are not unaffected, they are at least very little affected by mental illness.

The use of vocabulary tests as a measure of pre-illness level is perhaps the least important defect of indirect tests of deterioration, however. A much more important defect for their use with individual patients is their lack of standardization. Neither the Babcock, the Shipley-Hartford nor the Hunt-Minnesota test is adequately standardized. Babcock used the Binet vocabulary test, and relied on its standardization on children and very young adults. The standardization of the Shipley-Hartford is based almost entirely on normal people under twenty. It is well known that normal people continue to learn new words after twenty, just as they tend to perform less well on many non-verbal and speeded tests of intelligence. Thus, if the norms for eighteen-year-olds are used, the normal person of 50 will apparently have suffered a vast

[1] Shapiro and Nelson's study is typical of a few studies which have matched different diagnostic groups for age, and then found significant differences in vocabulary score. This does not prove, as the authors suggest, that vocabulary has deteriorated and is thus a poor measure of former level. As we have seen there is considerable evidence that different diagnostic groups did not have the same mean pre-illness general level in the first place.

amount of deterioration. That this is the case with the Shipley-Hartford scale has been demonstrated by Manson and Grayson (1947). Gilbert (1951) and Botwinick and Birren (1951) have demonstrated the same thing for the Babcock. This defect, however, does not make these tests useless for *comparative* studies between different abnormal groups provided the groups have been matched for age, so that not all the studies using these tests can be dismissed.

The Wechsler Deterioration Index is based on a different principle. It is merely the difference between those subtests which hold up with age, and those which decline with age in normal people. The rather curious assumption is that deterioration produced by psychosis or brain damage can be identified with the normal deterioration produced by age. The results of many of the early Binet studies make this unlikely (Wells and Kelley, 1920; Altman and Shakow, 1937; Malamud and Palmer, 1938; Davidson, 1938, 1939) since they found that only the *vocabulary* score failed to differentiate between normal and abnormal groups. Many Binet subtests similar to the Wechsler "don't-hold" tests *were* apparently affected by both psychosis and brain damage. By and large the Wechsler Deterioration Index has failed to produce consistent differentiation between normal and abnormal groups. For example, Schlosser and Kantor (1949) were unable to differentiate between fifty-six psychoneurotics, forty-two paranoid schizophrenics and forty-two residual non-paranoid schizophrenics. Garfield and Fey (1948), testing ninety-five cases, found no significant differences between six psychiatric groups, and no significant differences between psychotics and neurotics. Rappaport and Webb (1950) in the test-retest study of ten schizophrenics before and during illness already described, found a significant *negative* correlation between performance on the Wechsler "hold" tests and pre-illness I.Q. level, while the so-called "hold" test score was not significantly different from the I.Q. score obtained during illness. As one might expect, the deterioration index has such a high correlation with age (e.g. 0·60 reported by Johnson, 1947) that its practical clinical use would be impossible without age norms in any event.

Perhaps the most anomalous feature about the indirect measures of deterioration is the range of tests used to measure *present* general intelligence. One might imagine that the authors would all choose those tests which factorially were most representative of cognitive tests. Babcock, however, measures present level by means of a set of simple motor and mental speed tests, and tests of rote-learning ability because these tests were found to be *most* affected by psychosis. In other words, present general level is apparently equated with that aspect of impairment which is most marked. Shipley, on the other hand, uses a much

more conventional measure of g, a test of abstract reasoning using verbal material. Wechsler measures present-level only on those tests which are most affected by the ageing process. It would be surprising to find that these different indices of general deterioration were very highly correlated, and indeed they are not. Fox and Birren (1950), for example, found an insignificant negative correlation (− 0·16) between the Babcock index and the Wechsler deterioration index, in fifty normal old people. Garfield and Fey (1948) found a correlation of only + 0·13 between the Wechsler deterioration index and the Shipley-Hartford C.Q., using ninety-five cases with a wide range of psychiatric diagnoses, both neurotic and psychotic. Magaret and Simpson (1948), testing fifty mental patients, both psychotic and neurotic, found no significant correlation between the Shipley-Hartford C.Q. and the Wechsler deterioration index. Neither index correlated with a psychiatric rating of deterioration.

In spite of these shortcomings, the use of indirect measures of deterioration has produced a number of interesting findings. Although Babcock was the first to use vocabulary as a measure of former intelligence, the observation that vocabulary tends not to differentiate between normals and psychotics, while other tests do, was originally made on the Binet test. In 1920 Wells and Kelley gave the Binet test to one hundred and one psychotics (both schizophrenics and manic-depressives) and found that vocabulary was the highest subtest in the abnormal groups. This observation on the Binet test has been repeated many times. Altman and Shakow (1937) tested a number of groups of subjects matched for Binet mental age. The discrepancy between the vocabulary and the remaining tests was expressed as a difference between two standard scores. The results are shown in the following table—

TABLE VI.6

BINET STANDARD SCORE MINUS VOCABULARY
STANDARD SCORE

(After Altman and Shakow)

Group	Mean difference	S.D.
Matched for M.A.		
56 normals	− 0·220	0·735
56 delinquents	− 0·045	0·758
56 co-operative schizophrenics .	+ 0·265	0·750
Matched for M.A.		
30 normals	− 0·398	0·851
30 delinquents	− 0·292	0·908
30 non-co-operative schizophrenics .	+ 0·706	1·121

In both cases the schizophrenics differ from the normals at a very high level of significance. The two groups differ markedly in general level, so that the finding seems to hold good at two quite different M.A. levels.

Malamud and Palmer (1938) tested one hundred deteriorated schizophrenics, one hundred brain-damaged cases and one hundred normals all matched for Binet M.A. (the normals were mental defectives to obtain the matching). They found the following Binet-vocabulary discrepancies (in months of mental age)—

normal defective   = 0·84 (S.D. 0·141)

deteriorated schizophrenics = 38·44 (S.D. 1·507)

brain-damaged   = 42·42 (S.D. 1·367)

Davidson (1938) found an average difference of thirty months of mental age between vocabulary and Binet score in seventy-one schizophrenics, while two hundred and two normal controls showed a mean difference of only three months. The amount of the discrepancy was related to the doctors' ratings of deterioration for twenty-two cases studied.

Davidson (1939) found, as might be expected from the lack of age norms for the Binet, that the amount of discrepancy was also a function of age, with larger discrepancies occurring among the older. Nevertheless discrepancies still differentiated the different groups when age was controlled, as shown in the following table—

TABLE VI.7

VOCABULARY—BINET DISCREPANCIES IN M.A. UNITS

(After Davidson)

Group	Age		
	below 20	20–40	over 40
18 defective manic-depressives	+ 11	+ 3	− 12
215 non psychotic defectives .	0	− 1	− 6
172 defective epileptics . .	− 1	+ 3	− 12
18 defective schizophrenics .	− 2	− 17	− 12
21 psychotic epileptics . .	—	− 21	− 32
39 manic-depressives . .	− 12	− 24	− 26
50 non-psychotic epileptics .	− 12	− 27	− 17
27 schizophrenics . . .	− 45	− 44	− 59

This table agrees in some respects with the findings on present general level for these different groups, and it is plausible that the discrepancies are partly a function of general deterioration. The non-psychotic epileptics represent a slight anomaly as they are among the most deteriorated. However, we cannot be sure how many of these institutionalized cases were brain-damaged. It is also interesting that the two

defective psychotic groups are least deteriorated. Either the very dull deteriorate less, as they can't become appreciably worse on tests of this sort, or these groups have suffered an equal impairment on vocabulary and were thus judged always to have been defective.

Shakow (1946) also notes that the Binet-vocabulary discrepancy is a function of age, and reports a correlation of + 0·72 between age and discrepancy for a group of twenty-five schizophrenics.

We can conclude from these Binet studies that there is strong and consistent evidence for a large discrepancy between Binet vocabulary scores and Binet M.A. scores, which is not an artefact of age in psychotic groups, particularly schizophrenics. What this discrepancy is due to, ultimately, it is not possible to say. However, it is strong indirect evidence that some general intellectual deterioration is produced by psychosis.

Similar results have been obtained in a number of studies comparing vocabulary scores with other tests of general intelligence. Simmins (1933) tested two hundred mental patients and twenty controls on the Binet vocabulary test and a group of visual-perceptual g tests used by Spearman. She found no evidence for lower vocabulary scores among the abnormals. Using an arbitrary criterion for deterioration in terms of the magnitude of vocabulary − g discrepancies, she found the following proportions of deteriorated patients in different diagnostic groups; hysterics 0 per cent, anxiety neurosis 14 per cent, manic-depressives 41·5 per cent, *dementia praecox* 45 per cent, delusionals 56·5 per cent, melancholics 62 per cent. Harbinson (1937) using the same tests, found similar results except that, on these criteria, only about 30 per cent of schizophrenics are deteriorated whereas 80 per cent of melancholics are deteriorated. The failure, however, of either study to allow for age could clearly account for such discrepancies.

Lidz, Gay and Tietze (1942) used the discrepancy between the Koh's block score and the Binet vocabulary, and found evidence for deterioration in schizophrenics. Rabin (1944a) compared the Binet vocabulary score with the Wechsler-Bellevue I.Q. and found that psychotics had a much larger discrepancy than neurotics. Klehr (1949), using three Wechsler sub-tests, found that six out of twelve schizophrenics had both "comprehension" and "similarities" test scores below their vocabulary level. This was true of only 19 per cent of a small group of normals and defectives. Hunt and French (1949) report similar results for forty-two schizophrenics, three hundred and fifteen normals and fifty-eight defectives on the same tests.

Hall (1951) gave sixty-seven normals and thirty-six schizophrenics the Wechsler vocabulary test, and a large battery of tests of the "ability to abstract." The vocabulary score did not differentiate the groups, whereas the abstraction score differentiated at the 1 per cent level.

Himmelweit (1945) reports that, among the army service breakdown neurotics tested at Mill Hill, there was a significant tendency (based on 1,821 men and 987 women) for introverted neurotics to obtain higher vocabulary scores, and extraverted neurotics higher Matrices scores.

Although the Babcock-Levy test uses quite a different measure of present level (i.e. speeded mental and motor tests and tests of rote learning) a number of researches have found results very similar to those reported above. The findings on the Babcock Efficiency Index are best summarized by a table.

These results, taken at face value, again suggest that psychosis produces some degree of intellectual deterioration. There are no consistent differences between manic-depressives and schizophrenics. In these studies manics and depressives do not appear to have been treated separately from manic-depressives, but there is no evidence on this test that the cyclic disorders are free from deterioration.

Within the schizophrenic groups again there is a considerable range of results, and some of the undif-

TABLE VI.8

BABCOCK "EFFICIENCY INDICES" IN DIFFERENT DIAGNOSTIC GROUPS

Group	No. of cases	Mean index	Median index	S.D.	Range	Investigator
Normals	264	0·0	+ 0·1	1·18		Babcock, 1930
Normals	228		+ 0·5		— 3·4 to 3·2	Babcock, 1933
Normals	26	— 1·2			— 2·1 to 5·2	Wittman, 1933
Normals	54	— 0·6				Rapaport et al., 1945
Normals	20	— 0·25		0·86	— 3·5 to 1·5	Shapiro and Nelson, 1955
Normals aged 60–69 . . .	175	— 4·80				Gilbert 1935
Normals aged 60–70 . . .	50	— 5·3		1·6		Botwinick and Birren, 1951
Neurotics	4	— 0·6			— 0·8 to — 0·4	Wittman, 1933
Neurotics	40	— 1·0				Rapaport et al., 1945
Neurotics	20	— 2·82		1·92	— 6·1 to 1·2	Shapiro and Nelson, 1955
Psychoneurotics . . .	not given		— 1·2		— 8·7 to 5·2	Babcock and Levy, 1940
Psychoneurotics . . .	not given		— 1·2			Babcock, 1941
Psychopathic personality . . .	not given		— 1·9		— 7·2 to 1·9	Babcock and Levy, 1940
Psychopathic personality . . .	not given		— 1·9			Babcock, 1941
Epilepsy	54	— 0·81			— 5·0 to 5·0	Barnes and Fetterman, 1938
Epilepsy	26	— 5·4			— 10·2 to 1·1	Wittman, 1933
Drug addicts	27	— 1·2			— 3·9 to 2·0	Hall, 1938
Drug addicts	156	— 2·28		1·64		Partington, 1940
Alcoholics	66	— 2·3			— 4·2 to 1·4	Wittman, 1933
Manic-depressive . . .	not given		— 3·1			Babcock, 1941
Manic-depressive . . .	6	— 1·4			— 2·6 to — 0·3	Wittman, 1933
Manic-depressive . . .	20	— 5·48		2·92	— 10·7 to — 0·5	Shapiro and Nelson, 1955
Depressives	17	— 2·8				Rapaport et al., 1945
Schizophrenics . . .	42	— 2·2				Rapaport et al., 1945
Schizophrenics . . .	24	— 0·8			— 7·3 to 1·7	Wittman, 1933
Acute schizophrenics . . .	6	— 3·13		2·06	— 5·5 to — 0·9	Shapiro and Nelson, 1955
Dementia praecox . . .	110	— 3·4			— 8·3 to —	Schwartz, 1932
Simple schizophrenia . . .	not given		— 3·1		— 7·9 to 0·8	Babcock and Levy, 1940
Simple schizophrenia . . .	not given		— 2·7			Babcock, 1941
Catatonic schizophrenia . . .	not given		— 2·8		— 9·5 to 2·1	Babcock and Levy, 1940
Catatonic schizophrenia . . .	not given		— 3·0			Babcock, 1941
Paranoid schizophrenia . . .	not given		— 3·7		— 9·9 to 0·7	Babcock and Levy, 1940
Paranoid schizophrenia . . .	not given		— 3·3			Babcock, 1941
Hebephrenic schizophrenia . . .	not given		— 3·6			Babcock, 1941
Hebephrenic schizophrenia . . .	not given		— 3·8		— 12·1 to 0·8	Babcock and Levy, 1940
Chronic schizophrenia . . .	14	— 6·69		2·28	— 11·4 to — 2·5	Shapiro and Nelson, 1955
Senile psychosis	30	— 6·9		1·6		Botwinick and Birren, 1951

ferentiated cases are probably early schizophrenics. In these studies there are no striking differences between hebephrenics, simple schizophrenics, catatonics and paranoid schizophrenics. All seem about equally deteriorated. However, this is not really inconsistent with studies which suggest that hebephrenics have the lowest tested I.Q. when ill. If we accept that hebephrenics as a group are those who have always been duller, there is no reason to suppose that they *deteriorate* more. The main discrepancy lies in the paranoid subgroup, whose rate of deterioration was seen to be less than the other groups in previous studies.

The variable results quoted for epileptics are not surprising, as the presence or absence of brain damage is not controlled in these studies.

The Babcock test also suggests a fact which has *not* been suggested by the other studies, namely that neurotics show a mild degree of deterioration. Babcock (1940) reports a special investigation into the relationship between neuroticism and the efficiency index. She gave three hundred and thirteen normal subjects the Babcock test and the Bernreuter neurotic inventory. Correlations between the subtests of the Bernreuter and the efficiency index were in the expected direction, but insignificant. There was, however, a significant tendency for those scoring in the top quartile for neuroticism to be less efficient than those in the bottom (stable) quartile.

The fact that the Babcock test does not agree in detail with other studies of general deterioration is not surprising in view of the nature of the Babcock test items. The Babcock is largely a test of speed and differences in efficiency indices between groups may be due largely to this relatively specific function. This will be dealt with later.

Finally it should be noted that the efficiency index is clearly related to age, and that most of these studies found it especially important to match their groups for age. Normal old people show a great deal of deterioration on this test. It is clear that it could not be used as a clinical tool without age norms.

There have been relatively few studies investigating deterioration in functional groups using the Shipley-Hartford scale. Shipley and Burlingame (1941) tested three hundred and seventy-four patients, and obtained the following order for different clinical groups (from least to most deteriorated): normals, neurotics, depressives, manics, schizophrenics, involutionals. Unfortunately, unlike the better studies with the Babcock, the groups were not matched for age, and mean age differences could considerably affect the order of the groups. Garfield and Fey (1948) gave the Shipley-Hartford to thirty-five schizophrenics, sixteen neurotics, eight psychopathic personality cases, eight psychotics and twenty-three non-psychotic cases.

The C.Q. did not differentiate significantly between psychotics and neurotics, although the neurotics were slightly better.

The Hunt-Minnesota test (Hunt, 1943a, 1943b, 1944; Aita *et al.*, 1947; Armitage, 1946), while identical in rationale and general structure with the other tests of deterioration discussed, has so far been used only in the study of the effects of brain damage.

SUMMARY OF FINDINGS ON GENERAL INTELLECTUAL LEVEL

The data presented above suggest the following general conclusions—

1. Most studies suggest that neurotic disorders produce very little deterioration of general level. A small amount of impairment is however found on the Babcock test. While army service breakdown neurotics are below average in intelligence, civilian neurotics are both brighter and more homogeneous than the general population. Introverted neurotics tend to be brighter than extraverted neurotics.

2. Epilepsy as such produces no general deterioration, although if the convulsions are the result of brain damage, considerable general impairment can occur.

3. Psychosis produces a considerable degree of general deterioration, which is related to the severity of the illness and is probably progressive if the patient does not recover. Recovery, however, leads to considerable improvement.

4. By and large, affective disorders seem to have the same general level, when ill, as schizophrenics. However it is possible that manics and depressives suffer *more* general deterioration than the average schizophrenic group, since there is some evidence that their mean pre-illness I.Q.s are average or above. There is some very slight but conflicting evidence that cyclic forms of affective disorder (manic-depressive psychosis) do not produce deterioration. It is also possible that "Involutional Depression" produces very little general impairment, although data are few.

5. Schizophrenics in general are so heterogeneous that there is no real reason to regard them as suffering from a single disease entity, at least as far as cognitive results are concerned. On average, schizophrenics are duller than normal before becoming ill, and therefore on average may have deteriorated less than manics and depressives. Their mean illness level is just below average, and similar to that of the affective disorders. On average, without remission, schizophrenia produces a steady progressive deterioration.

Paranoid schizophrenics are of average I.Q. before illness, and while they, too, suffer a progressive deterioration in level if they do not recover, this deterioration is much slower than in other schizophrenics.

The term hebephrenia, when used, appears to refer

to a group of schizophrenics whose pre-illness I.Q. is low average to borderline defective. Hebephrenics also deteriorate as their illness progresses.

6. By and large, a high level of I.Q. while psychotic is a good prognostic indication.

From these findings we can only speculate about the relationship between general level and specific symptoms. Perhaps two or three guesses are possible. Systematic paranoid elusions and ideas of reference may occur mainly in people of average or above average pre-illness level (some involutional melancholics, some paranoid schizophrenics, some early, schizophrenics and a few depressives) who tend *not* to deteriorate rapidly with continued illness, nor to have very much below average levels while ill. It is

conceivable that the cognitive disability associated with these symptoms is relatively specific.

People of very low pre-illness intelligence, when they become psychotic tend to exhibit mood swings and silly, bizarre or grotesque forms of behaviour which in some cases leads to the label hebephrenic.

People who develop periodic catatonic stuperous conditions tend to have considerable associated intellectual deterioration.

The writer will attempt in the second section of the chapter to discover if possible what specific abnormality or combination of abnormalities of mental function could be responsible for these overall results for general level which are themselves completely ambiguous.

II. THOUGHT PROCESSES

VARIABILITY OF PERFORMANCE

It is quite possible to postulate individual differences with respect to "variability" of test performance. The more variable individuals would show a wider range of performance on the same test given on a number of occasions. Differences in variability would, however, be difficult to use as an explanation of *mean* differences in test performance. There is no reason why variable people should not produce as strikingly good performances on some occasions as they produce bad performances on others. Variability as used here is not equated with "distractibility," as the latter would produce a mean (if variable) decrease in performance.

Nevertheless variability has for many years been used as an explanation of general cognitive deterioration especially in schizophrenia.

A number of early studies investigated variability in different clinical groups by obtaining measures of "scatter" from the Binet test. Usually scatter was defined as the difference (in mental age units) between the Binet "basal" age (i.e. the age level at which *all* the tests were passed) and the age level at which the last item was passed. Thus variable people had large differences, while people with homogeneous performances had small differences. There were, however, minor variations in the method of assessing scatter.

Wells and Kelley (1920) were among the earliest to find that psychotics had an unusually large amount of scatter on the Binet test. Wallin (1927) reported similar results even earlier, and also found that neurotics had slightly more Binet scatter than had normals. Harris and Shakow (1937) reviewing the literature up to that time, point out that abnormally large Binet scatter has been claimed for the feeble minded, for *dementia praecox*, for alcoholism, for psychopaths, for manic-depressives and for organics.

They point out, however, that none of the early studies used an adult control group, but made use of the data for children. In 1938 Harris and Shakow themselves performed a large-scale study of Binet scatter using one hundred and fifty-four schizophrenics, one hundred and thirty-eight delinquents and one hundred and thirty-three normal controls. They found that Binet scatter was a function of mental age, and when this was controlled, the groups were not differentiated significantly. The implication is that Binet scatter is artificially reduced by the floor and ceiling of the test. Nevertheless Malamud and Palmer (1938) found that one hundred deteriorated schizophrenics had significantly more Binet scatter than one hundred defectives matched for mental age.

As the Wechsler-Bellevue became more popular, a number of studies of scatter on this test were reported. Olch (1948) defined Wechsler scatter as the average subtest deviation (ignoring direction) from the individual's mean subtest score. She reported that sixteen young schizophrenics had a scatter score of 9·8, and sixteen older schizophrenics had a score of 10·3. This was significantly larger than the mean scatter scores for young normals (3·2) and older normals (3·4). Magaret (1942), defining Wechsler scatter in the same way, found a mean scatter score of 11·2 for a group of eighty schizophrenics, much larger than the score of 2·7 obtained by normals of the same age. Schnadt (1952), reporting the results of one hundred neurotics, found that Wechsler scatter was a function of level of intelligence (a finding similar to Harris and Shakow's for the Binet).

Monroe (1952) defined Wechsler scatter as the individual's subtest standard deviation (about his own subtest mean). He tested one hundred and forty-four schizophrenics, one hundred and thirty-six psychoneurotics and seventy-two normals. Neurotics and normals did not differ in scatter, but schizophrenics of low intelligence had a large amount of scatter.

It seems probable then, that not all the differences found can be dismissed as due to differences in I.Q. There is evidence that schizophrenics have more scatter on the Wechsler and the Binet than normals, although it is doubtful if neurotics and normals differ.

This finding is, however, completely ambiguous. As Eysenck (1947) has pointed out, a larger scatter of subtest scores within a diagnostic group can be due to one of two things: either the individuals are more variable in their performance of all the tests, or the tests have much lower intercorrelations within the group. If the latter is the case, we might postulate some alteration in the relationships between mental functions in the group, but we could not say it is more variable in performance.

Fortunately there are a number of studies which investigate variability separately. Eysenck (1947) investigated the variability of test performance of large groups of neurotics and normals on the Matrices test. This test contains five sets of similar items. The index of variability used was the sum of each individual's deviations (regardless of direction) from the median score for each set obtained by individuals with the same total Matrices score. A group of one hundred normals had an average index of variability of 4·2, while a group of two hundred neurotics had an average index of 3·7. The difference is not statistically significant. A group of four hundred and seventy-five hysterics had an average index of 3·81, while nine hundred and four dysthymics had an average index of 3·72. Again the difference is insignificant. Thus there is no evidence that neurotics are abnormally variable, nor is there evidence of a difference in variability between introverted and extraverted neurotics.

Margaret Davies Eysenck (1945) administered twenty cognitive tests to eighty-four senile dementia patients, and retested them four months later. The coefficients of reliability were all high, and there was no evidence for greater variability among senile dementia patients than among normals.

Holzberg and Deane (1950) tested twelve schizophrenics and twelve neurotics matched for age, I.Q. and education on the Wechsler-Bellevue. Using a measure of *intra-test* scatter, they found that schizophrenics were significantly more variable than neurotics. This is, however, the only article reporting abnormal variability in schizophrenics. Derner, Aborn and Canter (1950), reviewing the literature on

TABLE VI.9

WECHSLER-BELLEVUE RELIABILITY COEFFICIENTS IN DIFFERENT CLINICAL GROUPS

Study	Groups	Method of assessment	Full scale I.Q.	Verbal scale I.Q.	Perf. scale I.Q.	Information	Comprehension	Arithmetic	Digit span	Similarities	Vocabulary	Picture arrangement	Picture completion	Block design	Object assembly	Digit symbol
Webb and De Haan (1951)	50 paranoid schizophrenics	split-half	—	—	—	0·72	0·57	0·68	0·37	0·58	0·83	0·46	0·68	0·75	0·36	—
	50 normals (matched for age and I.Q.)	split-half	—	—	—	0·69	0·36	0·69	0·28	0·59	0·88	0·17	0·27	0·61	0·20	—
Rabin (1944b)	30 schizophrenics	test-retest	0·55	0·78	0·52	0·89	0·12	0·75	0·62	0·38	—	0·54	0·32	0·71	0·31	0·34
	10 manic-depressive + 10 neurotic	test-retest	0·89	0·87	0·94	0·89	0·62	0·73	0·75	0·79	—	0·73	0·80	0·70	0·79	0·91
Rabin (1944c)	Total of 4 groups above (N = 60)	test-retest	0·84	0·89	0·76	0·99	0·44	0·68	0·77	0·62	—	0·67	0·60	0·74	0·65	0·57
Hamister (1949)	34 schizophrenics	test-retest	0·84	0·91	0·80	0·93	0·78	0·87	0·63	0·84	0·90	0·78	0·68	0·67	0·62	0·79
Derner, Aborn and Canter (1950)	38 normals (1 week retest)	test-retest	0·91	0·84	0·88	0·87	0·70	0·57	0·67	0·65	0·91	0·68	0·80	0·88	0·73	0·78
	60 normals (4 week retest)	test-retest	0·87	0·84	0·83	0·84	0·74	0·53	0·70	0·76	0·88	0·59	0·85	0·84	0·62	0·76
	38 normals (6 month retest)	test-retest	0·91	0·84	0·87	0·87	0·77	0·74	0·64	0·70	0·83	0·66	0·82	0·78	0·73	0·85

Wechsler reliability, conclude that there is no evidence that schizophrenics are more variable than normals in terms of test-retest reliability.

The reliability data for the Wechsler-Bellevue are summarized in Table VI.9.

Most of the reliability studies employing the Wechsler seem to have used normals or schizophrenics. The one study (Rabin, 1944b) using manic-depressives and neurotics unfortunately combines them. The best matched control group is that of Webb and De Haan (1951). The reliabilities they report for their paranoid schizophrenics and normals are lower than those of the other studies, because an uncorrected split-half coefficient was used. The two groups are very similar however. The normals reported by Derner, Aborn and Canter (1950) are not a very adequate control group for the Rabin (1944b, 1944c) and Hamister (1949) schizophrenic groups, because they were college students of above average intelligence. Nevertheless the differences are very small on the whole.

Although the literature is not extensive we can conclude then, that there is no evidence that the performance of any abnormal group is more variable than that of normals. It, therefore, seems clear that we cannot explain any of the differences in general level in terms of variability of performance.

If this is the case, the finding that schizophrenics have a greater Binet and Wechsler scatter than normals must mean that the subtests of these scales have a lower mean intercorrelation within the schizophrenic group.

There are very few studies of the comparative *size* of cognitive test intercorrelations within normal and abnormal groups. Rabin (1944a) correlated the Binet vocabulary with the Wechsler-Bellevue I.Q. within three groups of patients and a normal group. His findings are summarized in Table VI.10.

TABLE VI.10

CORRELATION (*r*) BETWEEN BINET VOCABULARY AND WECHSLER I.Q.

Group	Full scale I.Q.	Verbal I.Q.	Per-formance I.Q.
90 schizophrenics . .	0·75	0·83	0·54
18 manic-depressives .	0·77	0·79	0·67
24 neurotics . .	0·68	0·76	0·24
52 normals . . .	0·86	0·88	0·75

These correlations are lower for the schizophrenic group, as we would expect. It is surprising, however, that the neurotics produce the lowest correlations. There was no evidence for increased test scatter in

neurotics, and this finding may reflect some peculiarity of this rather small neurotic sample.

Decreased correlations between some cognitive tests among schizophrenics would suggest that a change in the functional interrelationships between the measures is produced by schizophrenia.

It has already been pointed out that one of the most anomalous facts in psychology seems to be that cognitive tests tend to have such high intercorrelations even though cognition refers to such a wide range of mental operations performed on such a wide range of test material. One explanation for this may well be that the average cognitive test is a very impure measure indeed. The ultimate score is determined by the interaction of a large number of different processes which tend to overlap between one test and another. Furneaux's work seems to demonstrate this clearly. For example, most cognitive tests are partly a function of "mental speed," but none of them are uncontaminated measures of speed. When tests are carefully designed to measure only *one* cognitive process, the size of their intercorrelations seems to decline sharply (e.g. the very low correlation between speed and error, cf. Furneaux).

It is possible then to account for a decrease in correlation within a schizophrenic group in the following way (assuming of course that the results are not merely an artefact of homogeneity of one of the variables among schizophrenics, an unlikely finding in view of the increased variances usually reported for this group). Let us suppose that in normals the score on Test 1 is equally determined by three unrelated functions A, B and C. Let us suppose the score on Test 2 is determined equally by three unrelated functions B, C and D. The two test scores are affected by B and C in common, and this will produce a substantial correlation within the normal group. One factor which could *decrease* the size of the correlation within the schizophrenic group would be the addition of a fourth determinant of the score on Test 2 for this group without any change in the determinants of the score on Test 1. The situation can be expressed diagrammatically as follows—

Test 1. A B C
Test 2.   B C D   normals $r = x$

Test 1. A B C
Test 2.   B C D E   schizophrenics $r < x$

The intrusion of function E into Test 2 for the schizophrenic group could easily be the result of some specific dysfunction. Let us suppose that E is an ability essential to the performance of Test 2. Let us suppose, however, that all normal people have very similar amounts of it, and are relatively homogeneous in this respect. Let us also suppose that, while a normal quantity of E is essential to do Test 2 perfectly, an excess of E is of no further help. If one has this critical amount of E (as all normal people do), test performance is *entirely* dependent on other factors (B, C and D). If, however, one drops *below* this critical amount of E ability, performance on Test 2 becomes increasingly affected. Thus E becomes an additional determinant of score in the schizophrenic group, and individuals within the group tend to vary in score depending on how much E they have. In other words, E is some specific disability in schizophrenics which, because of its severity, becomes an additional factor in the performance of many tests which are normally quite uninfluenced by this particular ability.

We should, therefore, find among schizophrenics at least two groups of tests, some influenced by a disability and some unaffected by it. It will be the correlations between the affected and the unaffected tests which will be reduced within the schizophrenic population. From the data so far discussed, it seems unlikely that vocabulary is much affected in schizophrenia. Therefore in Rabin's (1944a) study it is probably the Wechsler scores in schizophrenics which are influenced by some additional factor (a disability) not operative in the normal group.

Explaining abnormal scatter in schizophrenia has thus led us to postulate one (or more) specific intellectual disabilities among schizophrenics. Their possible nature will be discussed in later sections.

There is one factorial study of the Wechsler-Bellevue (Cohen, 1952a, 1952b) which supports the notion that intercorrelations are different within a schizophrenic group. Unfortunately the author does not give the matrix of correlations, so unusually *low* correlations cannot be demonstrated. Cohen performed separate factor analyses of the Wechsler-Bellevue subtests for one hundred neurotics, one hundred schizophrenics and one hundred brain-damaged cases. Using Thurstone's simple structure analysis he obtained a similar factor structure for each of the three groups. There were three main (oblique) factors which he labelled "Verbal," "Non-verbal" and "Freedom from Distractibility" (or "immediate memory span"). There was in addition, a second order factor which he labelled g. For the schizophrenic group, unlike the neurotics, "comprehension" is a poor g test (presumably showing reduced correlations with other variables). "Arithmetic" is also a poor g test for schizophrenics. However, "Digit Symbol" is a relatively good g test for this group. Other differences were found, and there is ample evidence for differences in the interrelationships between the tests when the schizophrenic group is compared with the neurotic group.

The other main factorial studies of cognitive tests in abnormal groups are concerned with patients with senile deterioration. In these studies, quite different findings have emerged. There is a tendency for the intercorrelations between the Wechsler subtests to *increase* in the senile age range (55+) (Balinsky, 1941; Birren, 1952). Parallel with this increased correlation there is a general change in the factorial composition of the Wechsler. Cohen (1957) discovered that: "In the 60–over 75 group the Memory factor undergoes a sharp increase in variance at the cost of the general factor. Thus, in aged subjects, intellectual performance, even on verbal tests, becomes dependent to a noteworthy degree on memory ability." This is consistent with findings by Balinsky (1941) and Birren (1952). There is evidence that the ability to memorize material is one determinant of cognitive score at all ages. However, it is likely that most young normals are sufficiently good at memorizing to make their cognitive performance dependent almost entirely on other factors. However, as the ability declines with age, older people find it increasingly difficult to memorize material. Thus they tend to be unable to learn new test instructions and new methods of manipulating material they have never seen before (e.g. Blocks). This becomes so handicapping that as the ability to memorize drops below a certain value it becomes an increasingly important determinant of many test scores. The situation can be illustrated by the following diagram (where A, B, C and M—memory—are relatively independent determinants of the scores of Tests 1 and 2)—

Test 1.	A	M	B			Young normals
Test 2.		M	B	C		$r_{12} = x$
Test 1.	A	M	M	B		Old normals
Test 2.		M	M	B	C	$r_{12} = x + \Delta x$
Test 1.	A	M	M	M	B	Senile dementia
Test 2.		M	M	M	B	C	$r_{12} = x + \Delta x + \Delta x$

As memory accounts for more and more of the variance of Tests 1 and 2, so the correlation between the two increases.

This general picture is consistent with the results of Margaret Davies Eysenck (1945) who uses the terms "fluid" and "crystallized" ability following Cattell (1943). She found a tendency for eighty-four senile dementia cases to do poorly on tests of fluid ability. If we can assume that learning is much more important in the latter tests (e.g. Raven's Matrices as contrasted with Vocabulary tests), the results are entirely consistent. Inglis (1957) has developed this theory in a recent paper and presents evidence in support of it which will be discussed later.

It is clear then, that a specific abnormality can lead to an increase in correlation between two tests which are both influenced by it, but a decrease in the correlation between two tests when the abnormality has become an important new determinant of the score on one, but not of the score on the other. We can expect considerable alterations in the intercorrelations of tests in abnormal groups. However, whether they decrease (as in the case of the tests discussed for schizophrenics) or increase (as in the case of some tests among seniles) depends *entirely* on the make up of the tests. No general prediction can be made about either group.

Summary and Conclusions

1. What evidence exists suggests that psychiatric groups, both neurotic and psychotic are no more variable in their test performance than normals. Differences in variability cannot explain the general cognitive abnormalities so far dealt with.

2. There is, however, evidence for an increased scatter of the subtest scores of the Binet and the Wechsler-Bellevue in schizophrenic groups. This must be due to a decrease in correlation between these subtests for this group. There is evidence that the correlation between a vocabulary test and the Wechsler I.Q. in a schizophrenic group is in fact reduced.

3. The cause of a reduced correlation within a psychotic group could be the influence of some specific disability which is not usually a determinant of test score, but which becomes so because of its severity. Tests affected by the disability thus show reduced correlations with tests unaffected by it.

4. A specific disability can lead to an increase in test intercorrelation when the disability affects all the tests concerned. This seems to be the case in old people and senile dementia patients. As they become very poor at rote learning, this becomes an increasingly important determinant of their score on all tests, and the intercorrelations between all the tests become higher.

CONTENT

There are no investigations which report differences between abnormal groups which are clearly due to differences in their ability to solve problems with different *content*. Those studies which have been made are inconclusive since content is only one of the variables which could produce differences between the tests given.

Most of the data available are concerned with differences in Wechsler-Bellevue subtest scores. There are many studies of Wechsler-Bellevue "profiles" in different groups (Altus and Clark, 1949; Carp, 1950; Collins, 1951; Brecker, 1946; Dana, 1957; Garfield, 1948, 1949; Gilliland *et al.*, 1943; Goldman *et al.*, 1946; Hamister, 1949; Harper, 1950a, 1950b; Jastak, 1953; Johnson, 1949; Klein, 1948; Kogan,

1950; Levine, 1949; Lewinski, 1945a, 1945b, 1947; Magaret, 1942; Olch, 1948; Patterson, 1946; Rabin, 1941, 1942, 1944a, 1944b, 1944c; Rapaport *et al.*, 1945; Senf *et al.*, 1955; Shoben, 1950; Sloan and Cutts, 1945; Stotsky, 1952; Warner, 1950; Webb and De Haan, 1951; Weider, 1943; and Wittenborn, 1956). Kogan (1950), reviewing eighteen of these studies concludes that there is no satisfactory evidence for specific Wechsler profiles for different clinical groups. Wittenborn (1949) agrees with this general conclusion. Both these and other authors (e.g. Jones, 1956) point out that even if clear cut "profiles" did exist for groups, they could not be used for "diagnostic" purposes with individuals because of the large error variance of Wechsler subtest scores. No one, however, appears to have computed weighted subtest means and standard deviations from the individual studies reported in the literature to determine to what extent profiles tend to cancel out when the data are combined.

Table VI.11 combines the data reported in the literature for Verbal I.Q.–Performance I.Q. discrepancies in different groups. (This table is based on the following studies: Altus and Clark, 1949; Carp, 1950; Dana, 1957; Harper, 1950a, 1950b; Lewinski, 1945b, 1947; Magaret, 1942; Olch, 1948; Rabin, 1944a, 1944b; Rapaport *et al.*, 1945; Stotsky, 1952; and Warner, 1950. Many studies had to be omitted because insufficient data were published.)

TABLE VI.11

WECHSLER VERBAL AND PERFORMANCE SCALE I.Q.s IN DIFFERENT PSYCHIATRIC GROUPS

Groups	N	Verbal I.Q.		Performance I.Q.	
		M	S.D.	M	S.D.
Schizophrenics	663	93·50	16·78*	92·67	16·36*
Mixed schizophrenics	29	94·90	—	91·20	—
Paranoid schizophrenics	90	91·52	—	93·93	—
Simple schizophrenics	35	87·29	—	84·49	—
Catatonic schizophrenics	45	86·42	—	81·93	—
Hebephrenic schizophrenics	29	82·28	—	79·14	—
Manic-depressives	18	104·0	—	102·6	—
Depressives	8	97·4	—	84·2	—
Neurotics (unspecified)	124	96·92	11·2*	98·92	13·5*
Introverted neurotics	127	110·10	10·96*	109·98	13·92*
Extraverted neurotics	18	112·1	—	111·1	—
Epileptics	25	98·64	13·10	100·76	11·34
Delinquents	53	82	—	98	—

* Based on fewer cases. The schizophrenic S.D. is probably a slight underestimate being based on two hundred and eighteen cases whose mean Verbal I.Q. was 100·3 and whose mean Performance I.Q. was 101·4. The neurotic S.D. is not as representative, being based on only a hundred cases (Mean Verbal I.Q. = 96·9, mean Performance I.Q. = 98·92). The introverted neurotic S.D. is based on only twenty-five cases (mean Verbal I.Q. = 101·68, mean Performance I.Q. = 103·32).

The largest differences tend to occur in the smallest and least representative samples. The 16-point difference for the delinquent group is the only strikingly large difference, and while it is based on a fairly small unrepresentative sample, it may indicate a tendency for the delinquents to have a low educational attainment, thus handicapping them on verbal items.

The large depressive difference of thirteen I.Q. points is based on only eight cases. For the rest, the difference seldom exceeds two I.Q. points, and while it may be statistically significant[1] in some cases because of the large numbers, it represents a very trivial difference indeed in terms of the comparative ability on the two sorts of material.

The simple schizophrenics, the catatonic schizophrenics and the hebephrenic schizophrenics have approximately a four-point difference in favour of the Verbal scale. These may be the most deteriorated of the schizophrenic groups, and it is possible that the Performance scale contains items which deteriorate slightly more rapidly with this disorder. Because of the large number of determinants of both Verbal and Performance I.Q. scores however, these findings are completely inconclusive.

One group not represented in the table is senile dementia. There is considerable evidence (Inglis, 1958) that these patients have a mean discrepancy in favour of the Verbal I.Q. However, since this is probably not a function of the "content" of the material as such, it will be discussed later.

Table VI.12 combines the data reported in the literature for Wechsler subtest performance. Beneath the results for each psychiatric group are the data for normals of the same age, as reported by Wechsler (1944). (This table is based on the following studies: Carp, 1950; Collins, 1951; Dana, 1957; Garfield, 1949; Gilliland et al., 1943; Hamister, 1949; Harper, 1950a, 1950b; Lewinski, 1945b, 1947; Magaret, 1942; Olch, 1948; Rabin, 1942, 1944b; Rapaport et al., 1945; Stotsky, 1952; Warner, 1950. Many studies had to be omitted because insufficient data were published.)

These "profiles" are surprisingly regular. The mean subtest differences appear to diminish as the number of cases on which the profile is based increases.

The most reliable data are for schizophrenics. Their highest subtest scores are on Vocabulary (9·73) and Information (9·32). Both tests merely involve the recall of information learned in the past, and while it is not surprising that these tests are least affected, there is no evidence that the *content* of the material as such as anything to do with it. The lowest subtest

scores in the schizophrenic group are Digit Symbol (7·07), Digit Span (7·53) and Arithmetic (7·55). While it is possible to postulate a specific inability to deal with numerical material, alternative explanations are possible. The difference between highest and lowest subtest score for this group is 2·66 weighted score points. The mean Vocabulary score for normals of this age is not available, but normals have a difference of 0·6 points between Information and Digit Span, suggesting that at least this much of the difference can probably be attributed to age.

The other schizophrenic groups are not dissimilar in that Information is always the highest subtest score (Vocabulary scores are lacking). Digit Symbol, Digit Span and Arithmetic tend to be the lowest test scores, although the order varies from group to group. Hebephrenics have relatively low Comprehension scores. Since the mean differences are so small, however, and the cases relatively few, much detailed speculation seems pointless.[1] By and large these findings are consistent with the subtest rank order reported by Jastak (1953) for eighty schizophrenics (unfortunately mean scores are not given). Johnson (1949) also found that Digit Span and Digit Symbol were among the lowest subtests in a group of sixty-nine schizophrenics (again means are not reported).

The number of cases in the affective groups are very small. However, test profiles are fairly regular. Information, Comprehension and Similarities tend to be higher than tests involving speed (e.g. Digit Symbol) or manipulation, but one cannot necessarily conclude that these groups find verbal problems easier.

Epileptics have a relatively regular profile, and their slight deviations are difficult to account for in terms of the "content" of the material.

The only large neurotic group is the Introverted one. Here the highest subtest score is Vocabulary (11·77) and the lowest, Digit Span (9·60), a difference of 2·17 weighted score points. Since normals at this age have a discrepancy of 0·95 between Information and Digit Span (Vocabulary data are lacking for normals), much of this can be attributed to age. The profile does not suggest a specific difficulty with any particular sort of test material.

Because of the fact that the Wechsler-Bellevue subtest scores are particularly "impure" factorially, it is one of the worst tests with which to assess the effect of test "content" as such. Some other studies are available however. Hunt and Older (1944) gave the revised Kent Emergency Test ("information" and "reasoning ability") a verbal "opposites" test, an

---

[1] No attempt has been made in any of these tables to assess levels of significance. The correct assessment of such levels involves the correlations between the tests for these groups, data which are seldom given.

[1] Again it is not possible to calculate levels of statistical "significance" through lack of data, particularly the test intercorrelations for each group. Even if these were available however, the number of mean comparisons possible would make a suitable statistical "null hypothesis" very elaborate indeed. Simple *t* tests would obviously be misleading.

TABLE VI.12

WECHSLER-BELLEVUE SUBTEST SCORES FOR DIFFERENT PSYCHIATRIC GROUPS

Group	N	Verbal I.Q.		Performance I.Q.		Age		Information		Comprehension	
		M	S.D.	M	S.D.	M	S.D.	M	S.D.	M	S.D.
Schizophrenics . . .	879	93·67*	16·8*	93·06*	16·4*	31·94*	—	9·32	3·19*	8·40	3·55*
Normals (same age) . . .	110	100·0	15	100·0	15	30–34	—	9·8	3·12	9·7	3·15
Mixed schizophrenics . .	29	94·9	—	91·2	—	30·45	—	10·0	—	9·0	—
Normals (same age) . . .	110	100·0	15	100·0	15	30–34	—	9·8	3·12	9·7	3·15
Simple schizophrenics . .	35	87·29	—	84·49	—	30·09	—	9·0	—	7·0	—
Normals (same age) . . .	110	100·0	15	100·0	15	30–34	—	9·8	3·12	9·7	3·15
Paranoid schizophrenics . .	90	91·52	—	93·93	—	36·4	—	9·0	—	8·0	—
Normals (same age) . . .	100	100·0	15	100·0	15	35–39	—	9·8	3·37	9·8	3·18
Hebephrenic schizophrenics . .	29	82·28	—	79·14	—	30·0	—	8·0	—	5·0	—
Normals (same age) . . .	110	100·0	15	100·0	15	30–34	—	9·8	3·12	9·7	3·15
Catatonic schizophrenics . .	45	86·42	—	81·93	—	26·87	—	8·0	—	7·0	—
Normals (same age) . . .	125	100·0	15	100·0	15	25–29	—	10·1	2·98	10·7	3·10
Manic	32	—	—	—	—	41	—	7·03	4·17	7·91	3·21
Normals (same age) . . .	75	100·0	15	100·0	15	40–44	—	10·1	3·70	10·0	3·32
Depressive	8	97·4	—	84·2	—	48·0	—	9·4	—	7·9	—
Normals (same age) . . .	60	100·0	15	100·0	15	45–49	—	9·5	3·21	9·5	3·33
Manic-depressive . . .	40	—	—	—	—	—	—	8·8	—	8·7	—
Normals (same age) . . .	—	—	—	—	—	—	—	—	—	—	—
Epileptic	425	98·64*	13·10*	100·76*	11·34*	24·41	—	10·87	3·19*	11·78	3·38*
Normals (same age) . . .	120	100·0	15	100·0	15	20–24	—	10·4	2·86	10·0	2·76
Neurotic	17	—	—	—	—	43	—	6·24	3·16	8·24	3·15
Normals (same age) . . .	75	100·0	15	100·0	15	40–44	—	10·1	3·70	10·0	3·32
Introverted neurotic . . .	127	110·09	10·96*	109·97	13·92*	33·27*	—	11·85	—	11·46	—
Normals (same age) . . .	110	100·0	15	100·0	15	30–34	—	9·8	3·12	9·7	3·15
Extraverted neurotic . .	18	112·1	—	111·1	—	32·2	—	11·6	—	12·0	—
Normals (same age) . . .	110	100·0	15	100·0	15	30–34	—	9·8	3·12	9·7	3·15

TABLE VI.12 (*contd.*)

Group	Arithmetic		Digit Span		Similarities		Vocabulary		Picture Completion	
	M	S.D.	M	S.D.	M	S.D.	M	S.D.	M	S.D.
Schizophrenics . . .	7·55	4·17*	7·53	3·15*	8·20	3·76*	9·73*	2·87*	8·16	3·53*
Normals (same age) . . .	9·2	3·31	8·95	3·41	9·5	2·76	—	—	9·6	3·30
Mixed schizophrenics . .	7·0	—	7·0	—	8·0	—	—	—	8·0	—
Normals (same age) . . .	9·2	3·31	8·95	3·41	9·5	2·76	—	—	9·6	3·30
Simple schizophrenics . .	4·0	—	7·0	—	7·0	—	—	—	7·0	—
Normals (same age) . . .	9·2	3·31	8·95	3·41	9·5	2·76	—	—	9·6	3·30
Paranoid schizophrenics . .	7·0	—	7·0	—	8·0	—	—	—	7·0	—
Normals (same age) . . .	9·1	3·08	8·7	3·12	9·4	2·67	—	—	9·0	3·39
Hebephrenic schizophrenics .	6·0	—	7·0	—	6·0	—	—	—	6·0	—
Normals (same age) . . .	9·2	3·31	8·95	3·41	9·5	2·76	—	—	9·6	3·30
Catatonic schizophrenics . .	6·0	—	7·0	—	7·0	—	—	—	6·0	—
Normals (same age) . . .	9·7	2·91	9·9	3·13	10·0	2·40	—	—	9·8	2·97
Manic	5·97	4·18	7·0	2·62	7·78	2·86	—	—	6·38	2·87
Normals (same age) . . .	8·9	3·84	9·0	2·92	9·7	2·67	—	—	9·0	3·05
Depressive	7·6	—	6·2	—	9·2	—	10·2	—	4·1	—
Normals (same age) . . .	9·2	2·94	7·8	2·52	9·3	2·90	—	—	8·2	2·80
Manic-depressive . . .	8·1	—	7·4		8·6		—		8·3	
Normals (same age) . . .	—	—	—	—	—	—	—	—	—	—
Epileptic	9·66	3·85*	9·08	3·32*	11·07	3·59*	11·08*	2·97*	10·68	3·06*
Normals (same age) . . .	9·8	2·60	10·1	2·96	10·2	2·06	—	—	10·3	2·86
Neurotic	6·24	2·26	6·71	3·07	8·54	2·95	—	—	6·53	3·03
Normals (same age) . . .	8·9	3·84	9·0	2·92	9·7	2·67	—	—	9·0	3·05
Introverted neurotic . . .	10·54	—	9·60	—	11·45	—	11·77*	—	10·99	—
Normals (same age) . . .	9·2	3·31	8·95	3·41	9·5	2·76	—	—	9·6	3·30
Extraverted neurotic . .	11·0	—	9·2	—	12·6	—	12·2	—	9·8	—
Normals (same age) . . .	9·2	3·31	8·95	3·41	9·5	2·76	—	—	9·6	3·30

TABLE VI.12 (*contd.*)

Group	Picture Arrangement		Object Assembly		Block Design		Digit Symbol	
	M	S.D.	M	S.D.	M	S.D.	M	S.D.
Schizophrenics	7·66	3·48*	8·86	3·61*	8·60	3·45*	7·07	2·97*
Normals (same age) . . .	9·2	3·28	9·7	2·86	9·7	3·30	9·2	3·31
Mixed schizophrenics . .	7·0	—	8·0	—	8·0	—	8·0	—
Normals (same age) . . .	9·2	3·28	9·7	2·86	9·7	3·30	9·2	3·31
Simple schizophrenics . .	7·0	—	7·0	—	7·0	—	7·0	—
Normals (same age) . . .	9·2	3·28	9·7	2·86	9·7	3·30	9·2	3·31
Paranoid schizophrenics . .	7·0	—	9·0	—	8·0	—	7·0	—
Normals (same age) . . .	8·7	3·42	8·7	3·39	9·0	3·61	9·2	3·17
Hebephrenic schizophrenics . .	7·0	—	7·0	—	7·0	—	5·0	—
Normals (same age) . . .	9·2	3·28	9·7	2·86	9·7	3·30	9·2	3·31
Catatonic schizophrenics . .	7·0	—	7·0	—	7·0	—	6·0	—
Normals (same age) . . .	10·2	3·17	9·7	2·74	10·3	2·98	10·4	3·23
Manic	6·13	3·10	6·31	3·02	7·87	3·90	5·90	2·76
Normals (same age) . . .	7·9	3·14	8·9	3·42	8·5	2·90	8·1	3·26
Depressive	6·4	—	4·8	—	4·9	—	5·5	—
Normals (same age) . . .	7·7	3·21	8·8	3·39	7·9	3·17	7·2	2·61
Manic-depressive . . .	8·3	—	8·6	—	8·7	—	7·1	—
Normals (same age) . . .	—	—	—	—	—	—	—	—
Epileptic	10·79	3·40*	10·61	3·61*	11·17	3·61*	10·05	3·15*
Normals (same age) . . .	10·5	2·83	10·4	2·93	10·7	2·89	10·7	2·79
Neurotic	5·94	2·65	6·71	2·58	7·46	3·34	5·06	3·27
Normals (same age) . . .	7·9	3·14	8·9	3·42	8·5	2·90	8·1	3·26
Introverted neurotic . . .	10·76	—	10·67	—	10·92	—	10·47	—
Normals (same age) . . .	9·2	3·28	9·7	2·86	9·7	3·30	9·2	3·31
Extraverted neurotic . . .	11·5	—	9·9	—	11·4	—	11·3	—
Normals (same age) . . .	9·2	3·28	9·7	2·86	9·7	3·30	9·2	3·31

* Based on fewer cases. The schizophrenic subtest standard deviations are based on an N of 516, except for the "Vocabulary" test, where the N is 258. The means of these smaller schizophrenic groups for the subtests are: Information = 9·3, Comprehension = 8·9, Arithmetic = 8·0, Digit Span = 7·6, Similarities = 8·5, Vocabulary = 9·5, Picture Completion = 8·6, Picture Arrangement = 7·9, Object Assembly = 9·3, Block Design = 9·2, Digit Symbol = 7·1. The epileptic subtest standard deviations are based on an N of 400. The means of this smaller epileptic group are: Information = 10·98, Comprehension = 11·88, Arithmetic = 9·66, Digit Span = 9·17, Similarities = 11·30, Vocabulary = 11·08, Picture Completion = 10·67, Picture Arrangement = 10·19, Object Assembly = 10·56, Block Design = 11·21, Digit Symbol = 10·10.

"easy directions" test and an "arithmetic reasoning" test to eighty-three cases of psychopathic personality, thirty-seven organics and thirty-one schizophrenics. The psychopaths did better on oral and worse on written tests. Otherwise there were no differences between the groups. There is no support for the hypothesis that schizophrenics find problems involving numerical material more difficult.

Penrose (1945) gave the Canadian Army "M" test to groups of affective disorders and schizophrenics. The results are shown in Table VI.13, which gives "standard scores" based on an army standardization sample of 9,000 males.

since other tests utilizing meaningful pictorial material are relatively well done. It is possible that the particular type of reasoning involved (inductive generalization) could be especially bad in this group. This will be discussed in the next section.

The author draws attention to one rather curious feature in these results. The male schizophrenic profile is very similar to the normal female profile. (Indeed the profiles correlate significantly.) It is as if male schizophrenics have a feminine pattern of aptitudes before they become ill and that illness merely reduces the general level. Since pre-illness studies are lacking, however, this must remain speculative. There

TABLE VI.13

"M" TEST PROFILE FOR PSYCHOTIC GROUPS

(*After Penrose*)

Subtest	Normal females (N = 50)	Schizophrenic females (N = 25)	Schizophrenic males (N = 55)	Affective females (N = 17)	Affective males (N = 35)
1. Picture completion	− 0·20	− 1·53	− 1·44	− 1·30	− 0·66
2. Pictorial absurdities	− 0·26	− 1·37	− 1·18	− 1·44	− 0·50
3. Figure construction	+ 0·15	− 0·80	− 0·94	− 0·79	− 0·76
4. Tool recognition	− 0·78	− 1·33	− 0·83	− 1·12	− 0·21
5. Mechanical information . . .	− 0·68	− 1·38	− 0·81	− 1·15	− 0·22
6. Arithmetic	+ 0·15	− 0·55	− 0·56	− 0·74	− 0·15
7. Vocabulary	+ 0·64	+ 0·11	− 0·13	+ 0·11	+ 0·11
8. Verbal analogies	+ 0·48	− 0·58	− 0·77	− 0·70	− 0·31
Mean	− 0·06	− 0·93	− 0·83	− 0·89	− 0·34

Unfortunately the author does not give the age of the groups, and age differences may not have been controlled. There are obvious sex differences on these tests, as seen from the results for normal females, and these must be allowed for in assessing the data for psychotic females.

As usual, schizophrenics do best on Vocabulary where their scores are very close to the normal average. They obtain below average, but very similar scores on Figure construction, Tool recognition, Mechanical information, Arithmetic and Verbal analogies. These tests differ both in content and the type of reasoning required, although all are timed. There is no evidence again that numerical content, as such, produces especially low scores among schizophrenics. They are, however, especially poor at Picture completion and Pictorial absurdities. It seems unlikely that this is due to the content of the tests,

is no tendency for schizophrenic females to have a particularly exaggerated female profile.

The affective groups also do best at Vocabulary. They obtain relatively poor, but similar scores on Tool recognition, Mechanical information, Arithmetic and Verbal analogies. There is no evidence that the affective group is better at tests using verbal material. Like the schizophrenics they are worse at Picture completion and Pictorial absurdities, perhaps for the same reason. However, they are also bad at Figure construction, a typical test of spatial reasoning. It is interesting that sex differences in aptitude are larger than the differences in profile between the two psychotic groups which are essentially very similar.

Perhaps the most satisfactory content study is one by Binder (1956) who gave the S.R.A. tests of Primary Mental Abilities (Thurstone) to one hundred and twenty male schizophrenics and a total of two hundred and fourteen normal controls. The groups did not differ significantly in age or years of education. The results are given in Table VI.14.

All these tests are timed. There are no striking differences between the tests, and no evidence that schizophrenics are better at tests involving one sort of content than another. At both age levels, normals have a fairly uniform superiority. (The only exception

sort of test content especially difficult. The differences in test scores discussed can be explained more easily in other ways.

TYPE OF PROBLEM

In the introduction it was pointed out that cognitive tests can require the subject to perform a wide range of different operations. Unfortunately data are not

TABLE VI.14

P.M.A. SCORE IN SCHIZOPHRENICS AND NORMALS

Younger Groups (Schizophrenic mean age = 29·2, S.D. = 5·6, N = 55, normal mean age = 27·8, S.D. = 5·2, N = 59)

Test	Schizophrenic	Normal	Mean diff.	S.E. of diff.	C.R.
Verbal meaning	20·0	30·0	10·2	2·1	4·8
Number	12·8	23·0	10·2	1·9	5·4
Word fluency	27·4	38·9	11·5	2·4	4·9
Space	11·4	21·5	10·1	2·0	4·9
Reasoning	7·4	13·2	5·8	1·2	4·7

For all differences $p < 0.0001$

Older Groups (Schizophrenic mean age = 53·6, S.D. = 7·9, N = 65, normal mean age = 52·0, S.D. = 8·0, N = 48).

Test	Schizophrenic	Normal	Mean diff.	S.E. of diff.	C.R.
Verbal meaning	16·2	21·3	5·1	2·1	2·5*
Number	13·6	17·6	4·0	1·9	2·1*
Word fluency	24·3	30·2	5·9	2·4	2·5*
Space	8·4	13·3	4·9	1·8	2·8†
Reasoning	5·2	5·6	0·4	0·8	0·5 N.S.

* $p. < 0·05.$ † $p < 0·01.$

is Reasoning which old schizophrenics evidently find easier.) These data, however, present one apparently discrepant finding. Older schizophrenics show much less general deterioration than young schizophrenics when compared with normals of the same age. None of the other studies discussed suggested that this would be the case. There is usually a tendency for deterioration to be progressive with uninterrupted psychosis. It is, of course, conceivable that the older schizophrenics were unrepresentative in that they all had atypical illnesses of short duration starting late in life. However this seems unlikely. This is apparently the oldest schizophrenic group reported in the literature, and if the finding is reliable, it would appear that after about age 45, schizophrenic deterioration slows down markedly so that the normal deterioration due to age begins to narrow the gap between schizophrenics and normals.

Summary and Conclusions

While unequivocal studies are lacking, there is no evidence that any psychiatric group finds any particular

available for all the different types of problem described, and only those for which abnormal data exist will be discussed.

(a) Perceptual Tests

Many cognitive tests merely require the subject to discriminate between simple visual patterns. Nevertheless they are usually correlated fairly highly with other cognitive measures. It is clear that cognition and perception cannot be separated completely. As Combs (1952) has pointed out, before we can think about any problem we must be able to perceive the elements of the problem. If we cannot differentiate these, we will be unable to solve it at all. Combs argues that: "The effectiveness of . . . behavior will necessarily be a function of the adequacy of . . . perceptions." He points out that people who have never learned to differentiate within certain perceptual fields through lack of exposure to them will never develop intelligence in this field.

Certainly perception is necessary to obtain the manipulanda of a problem, and it is not surprising that individual differences in the ability to discriminate are related to problem-solving ability. (Some studies even report a correlation between speed of discrimination of patterns of dots tachistoscopically presented, and vocabulary, cf. Kretch and Calvin, 1953; De Soto and Leibowitz, 1956; Pickrel, 1957.)

Abnormalities in perception have often been demonstrated in psychiatric groups and while this subject will be dealt with elsewhere, a few salient findings will be mentioned here.

Combs and Taylor (1952) attempted to demonstrate that anxiety (produced by "threat" or "stress") restricts the range of perception. A group of normal subjects were given the task of "coding" sentences. In one group neutral sentences were used, while in the other group the sentences contained a threat (e.g., "I said that my mother is a dirty whore," "Something is wrong with my sex organ"). Verbal threats by the examiner were also used in the second part of the experiment. As predicted, the "threat" sentences produced significantly more errors and took significantly longer to code.

The Bender-Gestalt test (Bender, 1938) merely requires the subject to copy a simple line drawing. Pascal and Suttell (1951) demonstrated that errors in reproduction, scored relatively objectively, differentiated between a large group of mainly neurotic out-patients, and a large group of mainly psychotic in-patients. The in-patient group made inferior reproductions. Gobetz (1953), testing one hundred and eight neurotics and two hundred and eighty-five normals, found that the neurotics reproduced the Bender-Gestalt drawings as accurately as normals. Lonstein (1954) found that forty-seven psychotic patients were significantly worse at reproducing the Bender-Gestalt drawings than forty-nine non-psychotics.

Niebiehr and Cohen (1956) tested ten normals, ten acute schizophrenics and ten chronic schizophrenics on the Bender-Gestalt test. Normals were best, acute schizophrenics worse, and chronic schizophrenics worst of all. These authors demonstrated that motor abnormalities alone could not explain the results, as they found a similar differentiation using a multiple-choice form of the test in which the subjects merely had to select the most accurate of six reproductions. Suttell and Pascal (1952) found that the errors in reproduction made by schizophrenics were quite unlike those made by children on this test.

Brengelmann in a series of studies (Brengelmann, 1953; Brengelmann and Pinillos, 1953) has demonstrated that abnormal groups are significantly poorer at recognizing pictures or objects presented tachistoscopically. Neurotics require significantly longer exposures than normals, and psychotics significantly longer exposures than neurotics. Alice Angyal (1948, 1952) found that schizophrenics make more errors in reproducing patterns of letters presented tachistoscopically than normals. Granick (1955) found evidence that neurotic children score less well than normal children in tests involving visual discrimination.

There seems to be considerable evidence then, that many psychotic patients are abnormally poor at tasks involving visual discrimination. The evidence for neurotics is less clear-cut. Brengelmann's and Granick's results suggest that some neurotics may also be poor at visual discrimination, and Combs and Taylor's findings suggest that this might be particularly related to high anxiety.

Penrose's (1945) results demonstrate that schizophrenics are below average in performing tests which merely involve visual discrimination (see Table VI.13, Tool recognition test). It is probable then, that the poor performance of psychotics on many performance tests involving visual material is partly due in some cases to visual perceptual abnormalities. The nature and possible causes of these will not be dealt with in this chapter.

There is less evidence for perceptual abnormalities in other modalities. One study (Trussell, 1939) even suggests that some schizophrenics may be better at auditory discrimination. A group of thirty-two schizophrenics were given the "verbal summator" test (a gramophone record of unintelligible speech played softly). Significantly more schizophrenics than normals when asked what the record said, gave a "meaningless" response. While there is some objective evidence (Wallace, 1956; De La Garza and Worchel, 1956) for some degree of disorientation in time among schizophrenics, it is not known what perceptual modality is involved.

These studies are all less than satisfactory, since perceptual abnormalities are merely related to broad diagnostic labels. It would be extremely interesting to know which psychotics (and which neurotics) suffer from perceptual abnormalities. It is always tempting to hypothesize that severe perceptual abnormalities will be found among those psychotics who suffer from hallucinations, and to expect these to occur in the same modalities. It is also conceivable that perceptual abnormalities, when found in neurotics, will be related to feelings of "unreality."

(b) Tests of Fluency

One of the earliest extensive investigations of fluency in abnormal subjects is reported by Studman (1935), who administered the eight fluency tests defining Spearman's "f" factor to a group of patients. Most fluent were nine manics who were well above average. Nineteen delusional patients, fifteen manic-depressives, seven anxiety neurotics and sixteen epileptics obtained average scores. Three groups were well below average in fluency, obtaining very similar scores: eighteen cases of *dementia praecox*, twenty-one melancholics and twenty hysterics.

Eysenck (1947), also using a group of fluency tests, found no significant differences between much larger groups of hysterics and dysthymics, and thus did not support this aspect of Studman's results. On the other hand, he found neurotics to be less fluent than normals, and a fluency test had a moderate saturation on a factor of neuroticism (Eysenck, *The Dimensions of Personality*, p. 256, 1947). In a later study Eysenck (1952) reports that a single fluency test (naming animals) differentiated between neurotics and psychotics, and had a fairly high loading on a factor defined by a number of tests differentiating these groups which he called "psychoticism." Psychotics were less fluent than neurotics.

Sybil Eysenck (1955), using three tests of fluency, found that, compared with one hundred and twenty-three normals, fifty-five neurotics had slightly lower scores, and fifty-five psychotics had much lower scores still. The overall results (*F* ratio) were significant at the 0·1 per cent level for each test. Within the psychotic groups, however, schizophrenics and depressives obtained nearly identical scores.

The evidence, then, is fairly consistent that neurotics are slightly below average in fluency, while both schizophrenics and depressives are considerably below average. Studman's early finding that nine manics were above average has not been repeated, as later studies did not investigate this group.

It is probable that fluency is not an important determinant of the score on most cognitive tests, so that it is difficult to account for general deterioration on other tests in these terms. What aspect of symptomatology is related to fluency is not known, although it could conceivably be related to the general level of activity of mental patients.

(c) Tests Involving Inductive Reasoning

In the last section it was pointed out that in Penrose's (1945) study, schizophrenics obtained their worst scores on two tests which apparently involve inductive generalization. (Picture completion and Pictorial absurdities, *see* Table VI.13.) These results are consistent with other reported findings.

Hausmann (1933) selected a group of one hundred and six patients (mainly psychotic) all of whom complained of being unable to think. He found that on two tests of absurdities and incongruities (one pictorial, one written), they obtained much lower scores than thirty-five school children and eighteen student nurses. Hunt (1935) showed that twenty-five schizophrenics were worse at detecting absurdities in a narrative than were eighteen organics, although the schizophrenics were better on other tests.

Hanfmann (1939a, 1939b) gave the Healy Pictorial Completion Test (Healy, 1921) to sixty-two schizophrenics, seventy normals and seventeen organics. The schizophrenics were much poorer than the normals. The piece selected to complete the picture was often incongruous with the action implied, and sometimes introduced a physical impossibility. Some pieces were selected as merely "symbolizing" the picture, and some solutions were quite incomprehensible. Normals made no absurd placements at all, while two-thirds of the schizophrenic group made one or more absurd placements.

Most of the studies on the ability to perform inductive reasoning utilize "sorting" tests and will be discussed later. Altogether there is considerable evidence that, for whatever reason, schizophrenics do especially poorly at tests which require inductive reasoning or the formation of an abstract generalization. Data for affective disorders are lacking.

Since inductive reasoning is required to some extent in a number of cognitive tests (e.g. Thurstone's letter series items), this disability may well be a factor in the impaired performance of some psychotics on these tests.

(d) Tests Involving Deductive Reasoning

Most problem arithmetic tests involve deductive reasoning almost exclusively. While there was some suggestion that Wechsler-Bellevue subtests involving "number" were low among schizophrenics it was pointed out that other studies suggest that schizophrenics are *not* especially bad at arithmetic problems. Indeed Malamud and Palmer (1938) found that the Binet items performed best by schizophrenics were vocabulary, information and problem arithmetic items. Shakow (1946) also found arithmetical reasoning least impaired in schizophrenics.

The most satisfactory deductive reasoning test was used in a study by O'Connor (1952). She gave a syllogisms test to a group of students, and even after general intelligence had been partialled out, obtained a significant correlation ($- 0·368$) between deductive reasoning ability and "ethnocentrism" (California "E" scale). Intolerant people obtained low reasoning scores.

Thus, while studies are few, there is no evidence that any abnormal group is particularly bad at deductive reasoning as such, although this specific ability may have other important correlates. The observed differences in general level cannot be explained in terms of a defect of this sort.

(e) Tests of Originality

While Guilford believes "originality" is an important cognitive factor, and a number of measures have been developed and shown to correlate fairly highly (Guilford *et al.*, 1951; Barron, 1955), there are no studies with abnormal subjects using these tests. There is, however, a large volume of data derived from studies using the "word association" technique, which provides a situation in some ways analogous to some of Guilford's tests.

No attempt will be made here to review the literature on word association. However, one finding is frequently reported (cf. Bell, 1948; Rapaport *et al.*, 1945). Schizophrenics tend to give highly original or unusual responses to the word-association test. Normal people behave as if they must keep within certain boundaries which are not usually mentioned in the instructions. In some ways schizophrenics are more "flexible," not assuming so many prohibitions. For example, Sybil Eysenck (1955) tested one hundred and thirty-five normals, fifty-five neurotics and fifty-five psychotics. She found that the psychotics: (*a*) repeated the stimulus word more frequently, (*b*) gave multiple responses more frequently, (*c*) perseverated the same response more frequently, (*d*) gave synonyms more frequently, (*e*) gave "cause-effect" responses more frequently, (*f*) more frequently had fewer than 10 per cent "popular" responses, and (*g*) gave fewer responses agreeing with the majority. All these differences were highly significant in differentiating the three groups, and in every case the neurotics were much more like the normals than the psychotics.

It is interesting that Smith and Raygor (1956) were able to produce unusual responses to a word association test in normals by "satiating" them on each stimulus word beforehand. This was done by having them fixate, and write the stimulus words· before doing the test. Presumably the more common (stronger) "associations" become satiated, allowing the weaker $S^H R$ links to become prepotent. This could provide a rationale for the growing practice in advertising of having "brain storming" sessions which last for many hours when there is a strong need for fresh or original ideas.

Quite possibly many psychotics would obtain relatively high scores on measures of originality. It is doubtful whether originality is an important determinant of the score on many cognitive tests. It is reasonable, however, to expect that it might be an asset in solving some "sorting" tests of inductive reasoning. This finding therefore is at first sight somewhat discrepant with the hypothesis that schizophrenics are especially poor at "induction."

Summary and Conclusions

1. There is considerable evidence that many psychotic patients have visual perceptual abnormalities which make them inferior at performing tests of visual discrimination. There is, however, no evidence for differences between schizophrenics and the affective disorders. Some neurotics may also have perceptual disabilities which might be related to anxiety. Perceptual abnormalities could partly account for the relatively poor scores obtained by psychotics on some performance tests of general intelligence. It is tempting also to relate them to the tendency in psychotics to develop hallucinations, and to feelings of unreality in neurotics, although no studies appear to have been done.

2. Neurotics are less fluent than normals and psychotics are less fluent than neurotics. Manics may be an exception in being more fluent than normal. It is difficult to account for many cognitive differences in terms of differences in fluency. It is conceivable that fluency might be related to the general level of activity although specific studies are lacking.

3. Schizophrenics appear to be especially bad at solving problems which require induction or the formation of abstract generalizations. This could contribute to their general cognitive disability.

4. There is no evidence that any abnormal groups have a specific disability for tests involving deductive reasoning.

5. There is some evidence that schizophrenics may be considerably above average in originality or the tendency to give unusual responses. It is doubtful whether this ability is important for the solution of many cognitive tests however.

COGNITIVE PROCESSES

(a) Speed

Furneaux has demonstrated that speed of problem-solving is one of the most important determinants of score, even on untimed tests. There is some evidence, however, that in normal people problem-solving speed is related to the type and content of the problem. For example, Rimoldi (1951) factor-analysed a large number of tests of "personal tempo," including speeded cognitive tests (Thurstone's P.M.A.). While no "pure" (i.e. error-free) speed measures were used, Rimoldi concluded that speed is not unitary. He suggested that speed of cognition, motor speed and perceptual speed are relatively independent. Even within the P.M.A. tests, speed of performing reasoning and space tests was relatively unrelated to speed of performing number and verbal tests.

Harriet Babcock (1930, 1933, 1941*a*) was the first psychologist to hypothesize that abnormal slowness among psychotics can account almost entirely for the general intellectual deterioration they demonstrate. Indeed, she believed that much of their general behaviour (unsociability, etc.) could be explained in terms of this relatively specific cognitive defect. As has been mentioned, Babcock demonstrated that a large number of very simple motor and mental speed tests differentiate well between normals and psychotics, and that psychotics obtain their lowest scores on such tests. Babcock used such measures almost exclusively to assess present level of efficiency in her test of deterioration. The data concerning the efficiency index have been discussed.

Shapiro and Nelson (1955) report an extensive investigation into Babcock's hypothesis. Twenty normals, twenty schizophrenics, twenty manic-depressives and twenty organics matched for age were given the Babcock test and other measures of speed (the Nufferno test). The authors predicted that if Babcock's theory were correct: "(a) Speed tests should significantly differentiate psychiatric groups and normals. (b) Speed tests should correlate negatively and significantly with degree of illness and prognosis. (c) Intercorrelations of the Babcock error-free speed tests should be consistent with the presence of a general factor of speed. Also, the Babcock speed tests should correlate significantly with other tests of speed." These predictions were nearly all verified. Normals were fastest on all the speed tests. Neurotics were usually slightly but significantly slower. Acute schizophrenics were slower than neurotics, manic-depressives slower still, and chronic schizophrenics and organics slowest of all. All the Babcock speed tests correlated with degree of illness and prognosis (of sixty-four correlations, only twelve were not significant).

The intercorrelations of the tests produced interesting results. As one might expect from Rimoldi's study, within the normal group the correlations were all low, "contraindicating the presence of one important general speed factor in normals." Within the three main abnormal groups the correlations were relatively high. When these were factor-analysed (Nelson, 1953) two relatively independent factors could explain the correlations. One was made up of mental speed tests, and the other was made up of motor speed tests. There is evidence, then, that in abnormal groups, motor retardation is relatively independent of slowness of reasoning. The higher intercorrelations between the tests in abnormals is due to the fact that they have a much wider range of speed scores. Normal subjects are relatively homogeneous on these measures.

Shapiro and Nelson's last test of Babcock's hypothesis was to match two groups (normal and abnormal) for psychomotor speed. These groups did not differ significantly on the Nufferno level test (an untimed letter series test) or on vocabulary. Again this was consistent with the theory that slowness is sufficient to account for differences in general level between normal and abnormal groups.

Campbell (1957) and Kessell (1955) also found that

several Babcock speed subtests differentiated well between normals and psychotics, thus confirming earlier results.

Many other studies have investigated speed of performing cognitive tests in abnormal groups. For example, Hausmann (1933) demonstrated that one hundred and six psychotic patients, all of whom complained of being unable to think, were slow on the substitution test of the Army Alpha. Senf, Huston and Shakow (1955) tested twenty-four chronic schizophrenics, twenty-two early schizophrenics, twenty-one depressives and twenty-one neurotics on the Army Alpha test with a ninety-second time limit, and on the same test with no time limit. When no time limit was given, there were no significant differences between the groups. On the timed test, the three psychotic groups were significantly worse than the neurotics, although there were no differences between the psychotic groups.

Eysenck (1947) found no tendency for five hundred neurotic soldiers to perform an untimed test any better than a timed test.

Foulds (1951) using a modified form of the Porteus Maze Test (allowing subjects to correct errors) found that both in "starting time" and total tracing time, introverted neurotics (anxiety states, reactive depressives and obsessionals) were significantly slower than extraverted neurotics (psychopaths and hysterics). Foulds (1952) also found that psychotic depressive patients were slow on the same measures. Kessell (1955) and Campbell (1957), repeating Foulds's work found that schizophrenics and depressives were significantly slower than normals in tracing time, although the two psychotic groups did not differ. "Starting time" results were less clear-cut, but the psychotic groups were always slower.

Unfortunately none of the studies so far mentioned are entirely conclusive. As Furneaux points out, to obtain time measures uninfluenced by other factors it is necessary to time every test item and to exclude the time taken for wrong items. Even Babcock's very simple error-free speed tests have been shown to produce errors in psychotic groups (Kessell, 1955).

Fortunately, there are a number of studies which make use of the Nufferno speed tests (cf. Furneaux). The results are very similar. Ogilvie (1954) compared a group of normal and schizophrenic subjects matched for age and general level (using Wechsler-Bellevue tests). The schizophrenics were significantly slower. Broadhurst (1957) obtained similar results using both schizophrenics and depressives.

Shapiro and Nelson (1955) report Nufferno speed and level test scores for groups of normal and abnormal subjects matched for age (mean age = 41, range = 20 – 50). Their results are summarized in Table VI.15.

TABLE VI.15

NUFFERNO SPEED AND LEVEL SCORES FOR DIFFERENT ABNORMAL GROUPS

(After Shapiro and Nelson)

Test	Number of cases	Normals	Acute schizophrenics	Chronic schizophrenics	Manic-depressives	Organics	Neurotics	F ratio	Significance
		20	6	14	20	20	20		
"Nufferno" level test	Mean . .	10·30	8·50	4·64	5·90	4·46	8·95	4·98	*
	S.D. . .	3·88	4·37	4·81	3·74	3·26	4·47		
	Range . .	9–17	3–13	1–16	1–14	1–10	3–19		
"Nufferno" uninterrupted speed (mean log times)	Mean . .	1·108	1·104	1·303	1·197	1·257	1·150	1·57	‡
	S.D. . .	0·168	0·249	0·286	0·189	0·259	0·221		
	Range . .	0·81–1·38	0·79–1·39	0·60–1·58	0·70–1·49	0·72–1·84	0·66–1·59		
"Nufferno" interrupted speed (mean log times)	Mean . .	0·986	1·090	1·195	1·151	1·202	0·991	2·56	†
	S.D. . .	0·164	0·156	0·179	0·262	0·172	0·168		
	Range . .	0·73–1·28	0·88–1·27	0·92–1·48	0·76–1·76	0·87–1·59	0·62–1·38		

* Significant at the 0·001 level
† Significant at the 0·05 level
‡ Not significant.

Eysenck reports an investigation in which one hundred and six normal male soldiers were compared with twenty psychotics and twenty neurotics (Eysenck *et al.*, 1957). The groups were not matched, although they are of similar age. The results are given in Table VI.16.

Although the speed-test score differentiates significantly, there are no significant differences between the groups on the Nufferno level test.

the groups significantly. The neurotics tended to be similar to the normals, or a trifle slower, while the two psychotic groups were both very much slower, there being little difference between the schizophrenics and the depressives. All the tests were intercorrelated, and factor-analysed for the combined group of subjects. A factor which was labelled "retardation" was obtained, on which nearly all the speed tests had high loadings. Factor scores were calculated and it was

TABLE VI.16

NUFFERNO SPEED AND LEVEL TEST SCORES IN NEUROTICS, PSYCHOTICS AND NORMALS

(After Eysenck)

Score		Control	Neurotic	Psychotic	Significance
Level	Mean	5·313	5·975	5·175	$F = 1·052$
	Variance	3·186	6·050	6·335	Not. sig.
Speed (mean log time)	Mean	0·961	0·969	1·166	$F = 15·042$
	Variance	0·020	0·029	0·041	Sig. at 0·1 per cent

Payne and Hewlett (to be published) administered a large battery of tests to carefully matched groups of twenty normals, twenty neurotics, twenty depressives and twenty schizophrenics. These tests included simple measures of mental and motor slowness (from Babcock's battery), the Nufferno Speed tests, tests of perceptual speed, tests of "overinclusive" thought disorder, tests of "concreteness" of thinking, and other measures. The results were consistent with earlier studies, in that the speed tests differentiated

shown that this factor significantly differentiated between the combined neurotic and normal groups, and the combined psychotic group. However, the schizophrenics were not significantly different from the depressives, both being equally retarded. In contrast to Nelson's (1953) finding, there was no tendency for motor and mental speed tests to be uncorrelated. Motor, mental and perceptual speed tests all differentiated the groups equally well, and had roughly equal loadings on the "retardation" factor. This factor of general retardation was correlated −0·38 with a factor labelled "overinclusive thinking." This was consistent with the hypothesis that abnormal slowness in schizophrenics is partly the result of this type of thought disorder. However, it was demonstrated that "overinclusion" could not entirely account for all the retardation shown by the schizophrenic group, and could account for none of the retardation shown by the depressives. It was concluded that in a psychotic group, abnormal slowness has at least two causes.

These studies yield consistent results. It is clear that even when the groups are matched for general level, psychotics tend to be significantly slower at problem-solving than neurotics and normals. There is apparently no difference in problem-solving speed between schizophrenics and manic-depressives. Even when manics as a group are treated separately, they obtain a similar mean score (Nelson, 1953) to the other psychotic groups. Early psychotic groups, however, are considerably faster (very near to normal), while chronic groups are considerably slower.

It is interesting that pure measures of speed of problem-solving (Nufferno speed tests) differentiate the groups less well than the Babcock tests of motor *and* mental speed. This may be because these tests also measure a third abnormality, "error," the effect of which will be discussed later. Motor speed will not be discussed further here, as it is dealt with elsewhere (*see* Chapter 2).

There is a considerable amount of overlap between psychotic and normal groups in problem-solving speed. In all the studies quoted, a proportion of psychotics obtain better than average scores. Indeed, Shapiro and Nelson's acute schizophrenics are not significantly slower than normals on one measure. It is thus fair to say that this abnormality is by no means uniformly present in psychosis. Ogilvie (1954) examined the *discrepancy* between speed and level in his schizophrenic group, and almost all his patients had speed percentile scores below their level percentile scores. This suggests that some "slowing down" of mental speed may be found in most psychotics, but there are very large individual differences in the amount of slowness produced.

On average, neurotics are a trifle slower than normals at problem-solving, but not as slow as psychotics. The neurotic range is apparently such that some neurotics get just as good (fast) scores as the best normals. However a small proportion are somewhat below the normal range. There are, however, significant differences *between* neurotic groups. Foulds (1951) found extraverted neurotics to be faster than introverted neurotics.

Foulds (1956) also followed up Himmelweit's (1945) finding that dysthymic neurotics get higher Mill Hill Vocabulary scores, while hysterics get higher Matrices scores. Foulds pointed out that in Himmelweit's study, a timed (twenty minute) version of the Matrices was used. When Foulds gave the Matrices test both timed and untimed, he found that, although hysterics were better at the timed test than dysthymics (thus producing a discrepancy in favour of the Matrices test) this was *not* true for the untimed test. Without a time limit, dysthymics considerably improve their scores, so that the Vocabulary-Matrices discrepancy no longer differentiates the groups. This study suggests clearly that extraverted neurotics are *faster* than introverted neurotics at problem-solving.

Furneaux has found similar results in normal students. If the Guilford-Martin "R" scale is used to measure extraversion-introversion in normals, and the "D" and C" scales are used to measure neuroticism, it is possible to compare subjects falling in the four "quadrants." It is the neurotic-extraverts who are fastest. Intermediate are the neurotic-introverts. The other two groups, normal-introverts and normal-extraverts are slowest, there being no difference between them. This does not coincide with the finding that neurotic patients are a trifle *slower* than normals on average. However the normal student group is relatively homogeneous with respect to neuroticism, and presumably only severely neurotic individuals have speed scores below (slower than) the normal range. The implication is that there is a curvilinear relationship between neuroticism and speed, people who are moderately neurotic being faster than the two extreme groups. This will be discussed further, later.

Clearly a combination of mental and motor slowness can account for much of the data discussed in earlier sections. The relative positions of different diagnostic groups on the Babcock efficiency index can be entirely accounted for in these terms, as Shapiro and Nelson have demonstrated. Mental and motor slowness can also account for many of the differences noted in subtest performance. On the Wechsler-Bellevue, Digit Symbol was the lowest subtest score in schizophrenics and among the lowest in other psychotic groups (*see* Table VI.12). This is the "purest" measure of speed in the Wechsler scale. The low Arithmetic score among schizophrenics may also be due to the fact that this is the only timed Wechsler Verbal subtest. The generally low level of psychotic groups on the P.M.A. tests (*see* Table VI.14) and the Canadian Army "M" tests (*see* Table VI.13) could also be due partly to the fact that these tests are timed. Conversely the tests *least* affected by speed (Wechsler Vocabulary, Information) are always highest in psychotic groups *unless* a time limit is imposed, as in the case of the Verbal meaning subtest of the P.M.A. (*see* Table VI.14). One fact, however, which *cannot* be explained by differences in speed is the fact that introverted neurotics have a higher general level than extraverted neurotics.

Since by no means all psychotic patients are extremely slow, it would be interesting to discover whether or not slowness is related to any specific symptom. A study by Wittenborn and Holzberg throws some light on this problem. Holzberg (1951a) gave Wittenborn's symptom rating scales (Wittenborn, 1951; Wittenborn and Holzberg, 1951b) and the Wechsler-Bellevue test to a mixed group of seventy-nine psychotics and neurotics. While rating scales of this sort have been criticized on the grounds that inconsistent results have been reported perhaps due to "rater-bias" (Trouton and Maxwell, 1956; Lorr, Jenkins and O'Connor, 1955), this study is at least suggestive. All nine "syndrome scores" were correlated with the Wechsler subtests. Very few correlations were significant. However, the Digit symbol subtest (the only relatively pure speed measure) correlated − 0·251 with the Paranoid Schizophrenia scale, and − 0·288 with the Paranoid Condition scale. The symptoms common to these two scales are persecutory ideas and delusions. It is conceivable that psychotics (both schizophrenics and manic-depressives) with these symptoms tend to be slow, while others do not. If this were accepted, however, we could not account for severe general deterioration purely in terms of slowness, since we have seen that patients with paranoid delusions probably do *not* deteriorate severely.

Harris and Metcalfe (1956) report a study of the symptom of "inappropriate affect" in psychotic patients. A group of forty schizophrenic patients were carefully rated for this symptom, and divided into three groups displaying "grossly flat" affect, "moderately flat" affect and "no flatness." These patients were given a battery of tests including the Wechsler-Bellevue, the Nufferno speed and level tests, analogies tests, sorting tests, proverbs tests, an "essential differences" test and an "absurdities" test. The results clearly suggested that *only* the tests involving mental speed (the Nufferno and the Wechsler—on account of the timed subtests) differentiated significantly. In each case the patients with "flat affect" were much slower. This symptom was also found to correspond highly with the general prognosis. The results confirm Shapiro and Nelson's finding that slowness is related to a poor prognosis. There was some tendency for inappropriate affect also to be related to severity of illness, and it is not certain that this factor alone might not have produced some of the differences in speed which were found.

Cognitive slowness, then, seems to be related to at least three variables. Extraverts tend to be fast, and introverts tend to be slow. There may well be a curvilinear relationship between speed and neuroticism.

Thirdly, there is a tendency for psychotics to be very slow. Since neuroticism and introversion-extraversion are unrelated, and since neither of these variables, probably, has any relationship with psychosis (Eysenck, 1952), it is highly likely that slowness can have several quite unrelated causes. Indeed this is highly probable *a priori*.

It is possible to conceive of problem-solving as some cerebral "search" process, where more difficult (complex) problems involve more cerebral "units," which have to be examined in all their permutations and combinations. Slowness could occur for a number of reasons. First of all, there could be important individual differences in the speed of the search process itself, very slow people for some reason or other having very slow "searching mechanisms." Slowness could also occur if, for some reason or other, the search process were interrupted, through distraction or blocking. Slowness could occur in some people if they found it necessary to repeat it a second time ("obsessional" checking). Finally, slowness could occur in some people if they misinterpreted problems in such a way that they made them needlessly complicated. Such people might consider data which normal people would regard as irrelevant, and thus considerably extend the length of the search process, since many more units would be involved, and many more permutations and combinations possible.

Various attempts have been made to account for abnormal slowness in different disorders. Most of these explanations will be treated in later sections. Two lines of approach, however, will be mentioned here.

Dispensa (1938) administered Thurstone's Psychological Test for college entrance to a large number of college women. Measures of basal metabolism were also taken. Three groups of women were obtained, seventy-eight with normal thyroid function, thirty-five with an overactive thyroid, and forty-one with an underactive thyroid. There was a significant tendency for the hyperactive thyroid group to be brighter, and the hypoactive thyroid group to be duller than the normal group. In fact even *within* the groups, measures of thyroid activity correlated significantly with intelligence. In view of other known effects of the thyroid, it is very tempting to attribute these differences to differences in mental speed. One might even suggest that the speed of the search process itself might ultimately be found to be partly a function of some such basic metabolic process.

The other line of investigation was entirely different. A study by Layman (1940) suggested that Sodium Amytal significantly increased mental speed in schizophrenics (as measured on form board tests). This could have accounted for the findings of Mainord (1953) and Senf *et al.* (1955) that amytal apparently increased the intellectual level of schizophrenics. Ogilvie (1954) and Broadhurst (1957) pointed out that these studies were relatively uncontrolled, as no *placebo* group had been tested. When Ogilvie repeated Layman's study *without* a *placebo* group, he found that amytal produced a significant speeding up in schizophrenics on the Nufferno tests. However when Ogilvie (1954) and Broadhurst (1957) later used a careful design in which a *placebo* group was tested, and the experimenter did not know whether the patient had been given amytal or *placebo*, no differences attributable to the drug were obtained. (Both groups, however, showed a considerable practice effect on retest.) These experiments do not "disprove" the earlier results. They merely suggest that they were not due to amytal. It is conceivable that the examiner's knowledge that the drug has been given and his (and the patient's) "faith" that it will produce striking results in some way produces an increased drive on the part of the patient. The evidence to be discussed later makes this at least a plausible hypothesis.

This line of inquiry has led to the interesting discovery by Campbell (1957) that by and large the slower the initial level, the greater the effect of subsequent practice in improving the speed of psychotic patients, at least on the Porteus Maze test. This is discussed elsewhere (by Jones) and will not be elaborated here.

Summary and Conclusions

1. Some psychotics are abnormally slow at performing mental and motor tests.

2. There is no evidence that schizophrenics, manics or depressives on average are differentiated by mental or motor speed tests.

3. Early psychotics are probably considerably faster, and not much slower than normals, while chronic psychotics are considerably slower on both types of speed tests.

4. In the psychotic groups, there may be a tendency for slowness to be associated with delusions of persecution, "inappropriate affect," and severe depression.

5. Motor and mental slowness can account for a good deal of the general deterioration noted in different groups, and can partly explain the subtest order produced on many tests of general intelligence.

6. There is probably a curvilinear relationship between cognitive speed and neuroticism, moderately neurotic individuals being faster than extremely stable or extremely neurotic individuals.

7. Extraverts tend to be faster than introverts on cognitive speed measures.

8. Cognitive slowness can probably be produced in a number of different ways, and different abnormal groups may be slow for quite different reasons.

(b) Persistence

Furneaux has demonstrated that persistence is another important determinant of score on cognitive tests, and that it becomes increasingly important when the tests are given with no time limit. It is obvious that individuals abnormally lacking in persistence would obtain reduced scores on most cognitive tests.

Factorial studies in normals (Ryans, 1938a, 1938b; Thornton, 1939; Rethlingschafer, 1942; Kremer, 1942; MacArthur, 1951) suggest that there may be two fairly well defined and relatively independent types of persistence, "ideational" and "physical." The former refers to the amount of time which is spent on very difficult or insoluble intellectual problems, the latter to the length of time people are prepared to submit to boring, fatiguing or uncomfortable physical tasks.

Unfortunately all the work with abnormal subjects appears to refer to tests of physical persistence. A series of studies (Eysenck, 1947, 1952; Sybil Eysenck, 1955) suggests that neurotics as a group may be less persistent than normals, and that extraverted neurotics are less persistent than introverted neurotics. While psychotics tend to be less persistent on some physical tests, the data are inconsistent. These findings would not necessarily apply to measures of intellectual persistence however.

One reason for the lack of data for intellectual persistence measures in abnormal groups may be the difficulties involved in collecting it. For example, Payne, Matussek and George (1959) recently attempted to measure the persistence of mental patients by using an insoluble problem. The problem at first sight looked simple enough, and the patients found it very interesting. This and other tests were given individually and all patients were warned not to discuss the tests with anybody else. After several patients had taken the test, however, the next refused to try it, saying it was impossible. He said that all the patients on his ward had spent half the night trying to do it, and they came to the conclusion that it was not possible. The test had to be abandoned.

If direct evidence is lacking, some inferences are possible however. In the study reported by Eysenck and summarized in Table VI.16 (Eysenck *et al.*, 1957) it was found that twenty psychotics were not significantly worse at performing the Nufferno level test than one hundred and six normals of similar age. The groups had not otherwise been matched, and the psychotics were significantly slower than the normals. Furneaux has shown that the score on the level test is determined almost entirely by three variables, speed, error and persistence. As will be mentioned later, there were no significant differences in "error" between the groups, although the psychotics made slightly *more* errors. In order to compensate for their slowness, therefore, it is clear that the psychotics must have been considerably more persistent than the normals, to have attained a similar level score.

Unfortunately similar deductions cannot be made from the data on neurotics. As it will be seen, however, other factors could account for the test performance of neurotics, and there is no need to postulate abnormally low persistence at intellectual tasks.

There is some slight evidence that introverted neurotics may be more persistent on cognitive tests than extraverted neurotics. Foulds (1956) demonstrated that on the untimed Matrices test, extraverted neurotics tend to do better at the beginning of the test and worse at the end of the test, while introverted neurotics tend to do better at the end of the test.

Summary and Conclusions

1. Early psychotic patients are probably more persistent than normals at cognitive tests, probably to compensate for their slowness.

2. There is no evidence about intellectual persistence in neurotics, but there is no reason to believe them abnormal in this respect.

3. There is some slight evidence that introverts may be more persistent than extraverts on cognitive tests.

(c) Error

Giving a wrong answer to a cognitive test in the mistaken belief that it is correct, is the most important single determinant of the score on many tests, especially untimed tests (cf. Furneaux). However, no satisfactory explanation of error has ever been advanced. Theories of problem-solving attempt to describe many stages in the process. Whether "thinking" is regarded as internalized trial and error learning, a search process or anything else, it is necessary to explain how the organism "knows" when the correct answer has been obtained. How is the answer "checked" when thought is completed, and how does this checking mechanism itself come to possess a criterion of the correct answer? Until this is explained, it is difficult to account for error, which is presumably some failure in the checking process.

There are obviously important individual differences in accuracy. Unfortunately few cognitive tests provide a measure of accuracy which is uncontaminated by other factors (abandonment, for example). The results are therefore ambiguous, and there are surprisingly few conclusive results for abnormal subjects.

One interesting series of studies relates to the Porteus Maze Test (Porteus, 1923). Poull and Montgomery (1929) gave this test to thirty-two girls and forty-two boys with "conduct disorder," and thirty-four girls and forty-seven boys who were well adjusted. The well-adjusted children obtained better Porteus Maze scores than Binet scores. The poorly-adjusted children obtained worse Maze scores than Binet scores. However the same groups showed no difference between Binet and Healy Completion Test II scores. This study was repeated in 1932 by Karpelles on one hundred and eighty-five normal boys and girls and one hundred and eighty-five maladjusted children who were "behaviour problems." Again there was a highly significant difference between the groups. The adjusted group had, on average, a higher Porteus I.Q. than Binet I.Q., while the behaviour problem group showed no differences. These studies suggest that the Maze test is not well standardized. However there is a consistent tendency for delinquent and problem children to get low Porteus Maze scores.

The reason for this difference soon became clear. The delinquent groups obtained low scores because they made more errors. However the errors were of a specific sort. The instructions clearly forbid going down blind alleys and retracing one's path, cutting corners, crossing lines, lifting one's pencil, and so on, while tracing through the mazes. The delinquent groups tended to be "impulsive" and disobeyed these instructions. This accounted for their poor performance when the test was administered and scored normally. Porteus (1942) produced a special scoring system, counting up errors of this sort, which he called the Qualitative (Q) score. He demonstrated that this score was even better for separating delinquent from normal children. This finding has often been repeated. It was repeated on children by Wright (1944), Doctor and Winder (1954), and Fooks and Thomas (1957). The Q score was also found to differentiate between adult delinquents and normal adults (Porteus, 1942; Purcell, 1956).

It is not surprising to find that delinquents or psychopaths are more impulsive and disobedient, even in the context of a simple test. Eysenck (1947, 1952) found such traits related to the personality dimension introversion-extraversion, and Hildebrand (1953) demonstrated that psychopaths were more extraverted than any other neurotic group. Hildebrand also demonstrated that the Porteus Maze Q score is a good measure of introversion-extraversion.

This research suggests that extraverts tend to make more errors than introverts probably because of such personality traits as impulsiveness and carelessness. That this is not confined to the Porteus Maze test is suggested by Furneaux, who demonstrated that the error score on the Nufferno speed and level tests is correlated with extraversion as measured by the Guilford-Martin R scale in normal students. Again, extraverts make more errors.

This fact is consistent with some of the data discussed in the first section. It was pointed out that I.Q.

appears to be related to introversion-extraversion within neurotic groups, the extraverts getting lower scores. It was also pointed out that delinquents usually get even lower I.Q. scores. If delinquents (psychopaths) are the most extraverted group of all, the correlation between error and extraversion can to some extent explain these differences.

In some ways, error through impulsiveness or carelessness could be regarded as "non-cognitive." That is, the assumption is that careless individuals could be made to reduce their errors if they could be made to change their attitude towards the test. Presumably these errors are *not* due to some basic abnormality of the checking process. If this is accepted, it is possible to make errors for more than one reason, since it is possible to imagine individuals whose checking mechanism is inaccurate, and who make a higher proportion of errors unavoidably. There is some evidence that this might be true of some psychotics.

Kessell (1955) found that more seriously ill psychotics made a substantial number of errors on the simple Babcock error free speed tests. Since Babcock's data suggest that normals do not make errors, and since this was the reason for selecting the tests, it is reasonable to conclude that psychotics are abnormal in this respect.

Eysenck examined the error scores of twenty psychotics on the Nufferno speed test (Eysenck *et al.*, 1957). The normal controls (N = 106) had a mean error score of 3·070 (variance = 8·490), twenty neurotics had a mean error score of 2·600 (variance = 8·884) and twenty psychotics had a mean error score of 4·450 (variance = 20·997). While psychotics made more errors, the difference was not significant (F = 1·707). However, Furneaux has combined these data with the data for schizophrenics collected by Ogilvie (1954) and Broadhurst (1957). He found a distinct tendency in all these studies for schizophrenics to make more errors than normals working at the same speed. Furthermore, if differences in variance are allowed for, the correlation between speed and error, normally low, becomes even lower in the psychotic group.

It is possible to speculate, then, that there is a disability which can be produced in psychotics which is independent of the disability which produces their slowness of thinking, and that this second disability leads them to make more errors in problem-solving. It is conceivably some abnormality in the checking mechanism. What specific symptom this might be related to it is not possible to say. It was pointed out earlier that abnormal cognitive slowness was probably not common enough or severe enough among pyschotics to account entirely for their low general level. An abnormal error tendency would help to explain the serious impairment of general level among the more deteriorated psychotics.

Summary and Conclusions

1. There are possibly two causes of "error" on cognitive tests in abnormal people.

2. Extraverts are more careless and impulsive, and tend to make more errors, probably for these reasons. This can in part explain why they perform tests of general level more poorly.

3. Psychotics may suffer from some disability, possibly unrelated to the cause of their intellectual slowness, which causes them to make more errors than normals. It is possible that this can account for some of their general intellectual deterioration, especially in chronic cases.

(d) Distractibility

It would seem reasonable to expect mental patients to be handicapped on cognitive tests by their other symptoms. People who are deeply depressed, who hear voices, or who are fearful of what others may do to them could not really be expected to concentrate on tests as well as normal people. One need not postulate abnormal distractibility, but merely an abnormal number of distractions. However, one carefully elaborated theory about the nature of schizophrenia rather surprisingly predicts that schizophrenics are peculiarly immune to distraction.

Bleuler believed that in schizophrenia mental processes become increasingly fragmented and unconnected. Kretschmer (1928, 1951) elaborated this theory considerably, and inspired a considerable amount of objective research. In essence Kretschmer holds that there is a fundamental "constitutional" variable schizothymia-cyclothymia which has numerous correlates both physical and mental. Schizothymes tend to be leptosomatic in body build, and also tend to develop schizophrenia. Cyclothymes tend to be pyknic in body build and tend to develop manic-depressive psychosis. Psychotic individuals in fact merely represent extremes on this constitutional continuum. The main psychological trait associated with schizothymia-cyclothymia is that of "dissociation" (*Spaltungsfähigkeit*). Dissociation is the ability to perform several mental activities (or to maintain several mental "sets") simultaneously with very little mutual interference or modification. Kretschmer interpreted a number of findings as supporting the theory that schizothymes and schizophrenics are extremely dissociated. For example, Van der Horst (1924) and Kibler (1925) found schizophrenics to be less distractible in a reaction-time situation, Kibler (1925) found schizophrenics better able to ignore "irrelevant" stimuli in a tachistoscopic perceptual test, Enke (1928) and Enke and Heising (1929) found leptosomes better at simultaneous mental additions, and Enke (1929, 1930) found leptosomes better able to do two physical tasks simultaneously. However, these findings did not arise out of carefully controlled studies, and indeed many of the early studies were probably contaminated in that the diagnosis was not made independently of the test results. Brengelmann (1954) in an extensive review of this literature concluded that there is no real evidence for any of these statements, since more carefully controlled studies (Mohr and Gundlach, 1927; Enke, 1928; Dambach, 1929; Reiter and Sterzinger, 1931; Klineberg *et al.*, 1934; Braat, 1936; Mountford, 1939; Kerck, 1940, 1944; and Eysenck, 1952) completely fail to support these results. Payne (1955) demonstrated that there is no evidence for the existence of a trait of dissociation in normal people, as a large number of Kretschmer's tests failed to reproduce more than an insignificant matrix of intercorrelations. In fact this study suggests that in normals, at least, the ability to perform two tasks simultaneously is very specific, and depends entirely on the nature of the tasks. Thus Kretschmer's theory must be discarded.

Norman Cameron (1951) has produced a hypothesis much more in line with common observations than Kretschmer's theory. He suggested that one factor which disturbs problem-solving in schizophrenic patients is the "interpenetration of personal themes." Their line of reasoning is distracted by some personal thought which intrudes itself and may even become mixed up with the problem itself. This disturbance also manifests itself in the form of "scattered speech," a disorganization of the logical sequence of speech, with long pauses and the use of inappropriate words. Cameron and Magaret (1949) were unable to produce scattered speech in normals who were doing a sentence completion test under ordinary conditions of distraction (listening to case reports played phonographically). However a "personal" distraction was effective. Hassol, Magaret and Cameron (1952) distracted normal subjects by playing them (through earphones) the recorded sound of their own voice giving a T.A.T. story while they were attempting to make up a story to a second T.A.T. card. Under these conditions their speech became disorganized, illogical, and full of pauses, and words were used inappropriately. Cameron and Magaret (1950) found that in normals, those who are "cheerful," "calm" and "non-introspective" are more prone to develop scattered speech with distraction than others. This suggests that extraverts may be more distractible than introverts.

Davis and Harrington (1957) report a rather different investigation. Fifty normal and fifty schizophrenic subjects were presented with sets of thirty-two pictures. They were given five pieces of information which would allow them to select only *one* picture in each set. Some sets contained human figures, while some were non-human. When a group of normals and a group of schizophrenics were matched for their ability to do the non-human problems it was found that the schizophrenic group was significantly worse at doing the human problems. On the other hand, two groups matched for ability on human problems did not differ on non-human problems. The study suggests that schizophrenics might well be distracted by human stimuli which produce disturbing personal thoughts which interfere with test performance.

Whiteman (1954) reported a similar investigation. Thirty-one schizophrenics and thirty-one carefully matched normal controls were given a Verbal analogies test, a Picture reasoning test and a Social Concept test. The Social Concept test consisted of a series of cards picturing human figures which together illustrated a concept such as "rescue." The schizophrenics were worse at all three tests than the normals, but they were worst at doing the Social Concept test, presumably due to the "interpenetration of personal themes" produced by the more distracting human content. The Social Concept test differentiated significantly when the differences between the two groups on the other measures had been partialled out.

Thought "blocking" has long been regarded as an important abnormality of schizophrenic thought. It is difficult, however, to demonstrate objectively on cognitive tests. Eysenck reports a rather interesting method of demonstrating it (Eysenck *et al.*, 1957). Twenty neurotics, one hundred and six normals and twenty psychotics were given the Nufferno speed test. The log time scores of normals are normally distributed on this test. "It was hypothesized that the familiar 'blocking' phenomenon in the thinking of psychotics might lead in this group to an excess of very long reactions, thus effectively causing a skew in the distribution of log time scores. This was done by calculating rough indices of skew . . ." "Skew" scores differentiated the groups at the 0·1 per cent level, the psychotics having much more skewed time distributions than the neurotics or the normals. It has never been proved that blocking is the result of some internal distraction, although this is a reasonable hypothesis.

It seems likely that the importance of the effect of distraction on the cognitive test performance of abnormal subjects has been underestimated. Cohen (1952b), separately factor-analysing the Wechsler-Bellevue subtest scores of one hundred neurotics, one hundred schizophrenics and one hundred brain-damaged patients concluded that the third important factor isolated could be labelled "freedom from distractibility." Wittenborn and Holzberg's (1951a) investigation relating the Wechsler-Bellevue subtests to the Wittenborn symptom rating scale has already been described. When nine "syndrome" scores were intercorrelated with the Bellevue subtest for seventy-nine mental patients, very few correlations were significant. The general intellectual superiority of the hysteric patients (as rated) compared with psychotics can account for six of the significant correlations obtained. The only other large group of correlations was that with the symptom cluster "excitement." The correlations were: − 0·252 with Digit Span, − 0·263 with Similarities, − 0·245 with Picture arrangement, − 0·268 with Block Design and − 0·281 with Digit Symbol. In each case "excited" patients did poorly. The sympton cluster Excitement refers to such symptoms as "spontaneous change in ideas, constant movement, compulsive acts, variations in rate of speech . . . unawareness of others, loudness, incontinence, delusional thinking and hallucinations" (Wittenborn, 1951). It seems likely that such patients would be extremely distracted while performing intelligence tests.

Wittman (1937) gave one hundred schizophrenics, thirty G.P.I. cases and thirty normals a number of cognitive tests. In the schizophrenic group, the correlations between test scores and a rating of co-operativeness ranged from 0·58 to 0·94. Rappaport and Webb (1950) report a correlation of 0·64 between the Elgin Test Reaction Scale and I.Q. for a group of ten schizophrenics. Rappaport (1951) reports a correlation of 0·89 between behavioural accessibility as measured by the Elgin Test Reaction Scale, and a vocabulary test score in two hundred and fifty-six schizophrenics. In a third study (Rappaport, 1953) on forty-two organics and eighty-five schizophrenics using seven cognitive tests, including the Wechsler-Bellevue, uncooperative subjects as rated by the Elgin scale were significantly worse than co-operative subjects on all the tests used. All these results are consistent with the hypothesis that the test scores of many psychotics are reduced partly because they are distracted by their symptoms.

Foulds (1951) reports an interesting attempt to bring distractibility under experimental control. Using a modified form of the Porteus Maze test, he found that a group of dysthymic neurotics was much slower than a group of extraverted neurotics both on "starting time" and "tracing time." Foulds hypothesized that the introverted subjects were especially distracted by their worries and anxieties. He argued that if some form of experimental distraction were given, the extraverted group should do much worse, while the introverted group should remain much the same. The distraction used was simply counting aloud while performing the mazes. As predicted the groups differed significantly in the effect of the distraction. In fact the dysthymic group actually became

faster on both measures. Presumably the second distraction (counting) prevented the occurrence of the first distraction (their thoughts) and was actually less handicapping. Foulds (1952) also demonstrated the same phenomenon in a group of depressed patients.

Kessell (1955) and Campbell (1957) were unable to repeat these results on groups of mainly psychotic patients (schizophrenics and depressives) and brain-damaged cases. They found that all the groups improved on retest with the distraction, and that this improvement could be attributed to practice. This lack of agreement may partly be due to the rather different patient groups used. Thus, while there is some doubt whether the effect of distraction can be controlled in the way suggested by Foulds, these studies do not disprove the contention that distraction is an important factor in the production of low test scores in many abnormal groups.

Summary and Conclusions

1. The effect of distraction on reducing scores on cognitive tests in mental patients has probably been underestimated. Very high correlations between ratings of co-operativeness and general distractibility, and the scores on a wide range of tests have been reported in psychotic groups.

2. Distraction probably affects timed tests much more than untimed tests.

3. A great deal of the deterioration found in cases of affective disorder on cognitive tests (which is as great or greater than that found in schizophrenia) may be due to distraction. Individuals whose main symptom is profound depression, with feelings of guilt and unworthiness from which they cannot free their minds, may obtain low test scores largely because they are unable to attend and concentrate.

4. Distraction may be the main cause of abnormal cognitive slowness in many depressed patients.

5. While few specific data are available, it is likely that manic patients are slow, and obtain poor g scores because they are abnormally excitable and distractible.

6. While dysthymic neurotic patients may be more distracted by their symptoms (anxieties, guilt feelings), extraverts may be more easily distractible than introverts.

(e) Memory Span

"Span of apprehension" or "immediate memory span" is in many ways a curious and complex phenomenon. Perhaps the most satisfactory account of it has been given by Broadbent (1957). If this theory is accepted, there is every reason to believe that immediate memory span is quite unrelated to learning and long term retention (see also Inglis, 1957). Broadbent believes that incoming information is held in temporary store until some action can be performed on it, by some form of mechanism which "circulates" it, feeding it back into the perceptual system at the end of each circuit. This circulating mechanism, however, can only hold (and circulate) a limited amount of information (a "bit" of information is not to be indentified with a "stimulus"). If information is held *without* circulating, it disappears after a short time has elapsed. Broadbent's "information theory" model, while simple, accounts for many known facts. If it is accepted, individual differences lie in the capacity of this circulating mechanism.

Unfortunately, tests of memory span have one grave drawback for use with abnormal subjects. It is never possible to discover whether the subject's memory span is small, or whether he merely failed to perceive the material in the first place simply because he was distracted. In fact Wittenborn and Holzberg (1951a), as has been mentioned, found the Digit Span subtest of the Wechsler-Bellevue to have a correlation of − 0·263 with the symptom cluster "excitement," a result already attributed to the distractibility of this group of patients. All the data discussed in this section are therefore ambiguous.

The reasons for believing immediate memory span to be an important determinant of score on many cognitive tests have been discussed in the first section. A poor memory span as such could clearly be a factor contributing to a reduction of general level in abnormal subjects.

The Digit Span subtest of the Wechsler-Bellevue scale is one of the most resistant to age in normal people (Doppelt and Wallace, 1955). However, it is influenced by other factors. Maher (1952) investigated the effect of set on digit span. Some series were given in a generally ascending order, some in a generally descending order, and some randomly. This introduced an expectancy which significantly determined the direction of errors. However normals and mental patients were not differentiated in terms of the type of error made.

Klugman (1948), testing three hundred neurotics, found a significantly reduced digit span when the test occurred at the *end* of the Wechsler-Bellevue, suggesting that fatigue conceivably reduces span of apprehension.

Moldawsky and Moldawsky (1952) found that normals have a decreased digit span when tested under anxiety-producing conditions, and Kaye *et al.* (1953) found that normals who complain of a high degree of test anxiety (on a questionnaire) have a lower immediate memory span than those who complain of very little test anxiety (when given group tests of memory span).

Anxiety in normals thus appears to reduce memory span, and there is some evidence that neurotic patients have a slightly below average memory span. Brengelmann (1958a) found no differences in memory span (using a five-second exposure of a pattern of figures) between two neurotic and two normal groups. However, the data from the Wechsler-Bellevue subtests presented in Table VI.12 show that Digit Span is the lowest subtest in the introverted neurotic and extraverted neurotic groups.

There is considerable evidence for a reduced memory span in psychosis. Van der Horst (1924) found psychotics to be poorer than normals. Eysenck (1952) and Sybil Eysenck (1955) found psychotics to be inferior to both normals and neurotics. Brengelmann (1958b) found psychotics to be inferior to neurotics only when a thirty-second exposure time was used, but not when a two-second exposure time was used. Cohen (1950) found psychotics to be inferior to neurotics on the Wechsler Memory Scale, a test containing many items of immediate memory span.

Although Kibler (1925) found manic-depressives to have a better memory span than schizophrenics, these results were not repeated by Braat (1936), Mountford (1939) or Eysenck (1952).

Cameron (1940) found that eighteen senile psychotic patients had an abnormally poor immediate memory span.

There are no studies relating memory span to introversion-extraversion as such. We have already seen that on the Nufferno (letter series) tests, extraverts are quicker, but make more errors than introverts. It is conceivable that this could be a function of memory span. Individuals (introverts) with a large memory span, might be able to hold the entire series in mind at once, and seek a solution which fits the entire series by examining all the possible permutations and combinations of the letters. Individuals with a small span (extraverts) might break the series in half, producing a solution based on two shorter, and in some cases indeterminate series. While this would be much quicker (there being fewer permutations and combinations to examine) it would be less accurate.

Summary and Conclusions

1. There is some evidence that memory span is reduced by anxiety in normal people.

2. Neurotics tend to have a lower memory span than normals.

3. Psychotics are lower than both neurotics and normals, although there are no differences between schizophrenics and manic-depressive psychotics.

4. These data are ambiguous, since they could be due to distraction or to true differences in the capacity of the mechanism of immediate memory. The differences are, however, strikingly similar to the differences between the groups produced by distraction.

(f) Learning

Although this subject is treated in detail by Jones, it is not possible to separate learning and cognition completely. Some cognitive tests such as vocabulary and information tests are merely measures of long-term retention, and are partly a function of the individual's past learning ability. Many other tests (e.g. some performance tests) are partly dependent on *present* learning ability, since new methods of manipulating material must be acquired during the course of the test. It has already been pointed out that in the older age groups, as learning ability declines, it probably becomes an increasingly important determinant of many test scores.

Inglis (1958), reviewing the literature on cognitive dysfunctions in elderly psychiatric patients, concludes that there is considerable evidence that some groups obtain lower scores on the Wechsler Performance Scale than the Wechsler Verbal Scale. He attributes this to their inability to learn new material. They do, however, tend to retain what they have learned in the past. Botwinik and Birren (1951) also conclude that senile psychosis is associated with defective rote-learning ability.

Inglis (1957) demonstrated that severe "memory impairment" in old people is probably due, not to an inability to retain information, but to a learning disability. In other words, these patients never register facts in the first place, so that they have nothing to forget. On the other hand, they tend to remember what they have learned in the past before they developed their learning defect.

Age is not the only factor which is related to learning however. Extraverts are poorer at learning than introverts. This fact can account to a large extent for the differences in general level discussed in the first section. Introverted neurotics, who have a higher learning ability also have high I.Q.s (*see* Table VI.2). Extraverted neurotics whose learning ability is worse, obtain lower I.Q.s. If we can regard delinquents or psychopaths as even more extraverted, it is not surprising to find that they have the lowest I.Q. of the three groups. These individuals tend to do poorly at school, and get low scores on tests involving the acquisition of information (e.g. Wechsler Verbal as opposed to Performance items—*see* Table VI.11).

Rote-learning ability as such is less clearly related to the test performance of psychotics. By and large, psychotics seem to derive as much benefit from practice when they are retested on intelligence tests as do normals (Rabin, 1944*b*; Hamister, 1949; Derner *et al.*, 1950). Learning in psychotics will be discussed again later.

Summary and Conclusions

1. Old people, and especially cases of senile psychosis are poor at rote learning and thus do worse on tests involving "present learning ability" (e.g. performance tests) than tests involving the retention of information learned in the past (e.g. information, vocabulary).

2. Memory disorders in the aged are probably learning disorders in the sense that facts are not remembered because they are not learned.

3. The relationship between learning and introversion-extraversion can partly account for the differences in general cognitive level between different neurotic groups. Dysthymics are best at learning, and have the highest I.Q. Hysterics are worse at both learning and intelligence test performance, and psychopaths are lower still.

(g) Retention

Hull pointed out as early as 1917 that in order to measure individual differences in long-term retention, it is essential to ensure that all subjects have learned the information to the same criterion. If this is not the case, retention scores will be a function of both the ability to learn, and the ability to retain, and will thus be quite ambiguous. Unfortunately there appear to be no studies of abnormal subjects in which retention has been adequately measured. Routine memory tests such as the Wechsler Memory Scale combine measures of rote learning, span of apprehension and long-term retention (inadequately controlled) as if they were identical functions, and thus produce completely inconclusive results.

There is some evidence in normal people that, just as some material may be harder to learn because it is "traumatic" and presumably produces conditioned avoidance responses (Cowen *et al.*, 1955; Jacobs, 1955), some material may be harder to recall once learned for the same reason (Garber, 1955; Klugman, 1956). There is also evidence that normal people may distort what they recall in ways which are related to specific personality characteristics (Davids, 1955). All these phenomena might be expected to occur in abnormal subjects, but no specific studies have been done.

The only generalization which appears warranted, is that those cognitive tests which appear to be least affected by any ability other than the capacity to recall information learned in the past (e.g. Vocabulary tests, the Wechsler Information subtest) seem least affected by mental illness. It is reasonable to conclude that apart from some organic conditions (e.g. aphasia), retention is not greatly affected by either psychosis or neurosis. Low scores on these tests could of course be obtained through uncooperativeness or extreme distractibility. It is curious that a large proportion of most routine psychiatric examinations of mental status is concerned with assessing long-term retention by means of personal information and general knowledge tests.

Summary and Conclusions

1. There are no adequate studies of long-term retention in abnormal subjects in which learning ability has been controlled.

2. What evidence there is suggests that retention may be almost completely unaffected in functional psychiatric disorders, although some patients may obtain low scores on information tests for other reasons (e.g. the inability to attend).

(h) Drive

In a previous section it was concluded that there is probably a curvilinear relationship between cognitive speed and neuroticism, individuals who are moderately neurotic being faster than very stable or very neurotic individuals. It is tempting to hypothesize that this is due to drive, there being some evidence for a curvilinear relationship between drive and learning (*see* Chapter 13). The "drive" concerned would probably be anxiety, since it is reasonable to regard neurotics as being more anxious than stable people.

There is a fairly large body of literature relating anxiety to cognitive test performance in normal people. Unfortunately the findings are somewhat contradictory, so that, although tentative generalizations can be suggested, no firm conclusions can be drawn.

Kerrick (1955) and Calvin *et al.* (1955) reported a consistent tendency on a wide variety of cognitive tests for anxiety as measured by the Taylor Anxiety Scale to be negatively correlated with test score. Anxious subjects were consistently poorer. Zweibelson (1956) reported that in children, situational anxiety produces a decrement in test performance.

On the other hand, Schulz and Calvin (1955) and Mayzner *et al.* (1955) found *no* significant correlation between the Taylor Anxiety Scale and I.Q. in normals, and Siegman (1956*a*) and Matarazzo (1955) found insignificant correlations in psychiatric patients. Shoben (1950) similarly found that anxiety as rated by the Cornell index appeared to have none of the usually expected effects on the Wechsler-Bellevue test.

These contradictory findings might, of course, be expected if the relationship between I.Q. and anxiety is curvilinear. Both very high and very low anxiety could produce a reduced score, and these studies could have selected groups at different anxiety levels. Such a relationship was in fact reported by Sarason and Mandler (1952) on two hundred and ninety-two students. While test performance was curvilinearly related to anxiety, moderately anxious students doing best, there was no relationship between anxiety and academic work over the year, where presumably stress factors were minimal. Sarason, Mandler and Craighill (1952) obtained a similar curvilinear relationship between the performance on a digit symbol test and

level of anxiety, in an experiment in which degree of stress was experimentally manipulated. Matarazzo and Phillips (1955) found a curvilinear relationship between the Taylor Anxiety Scale and digit symbol performance, but it was not statistically significant. Goodstein and Farber (1957), in a nearly identical study, also failed to obtain a significant curvilinear relationship.

One explanation for these positive and negative results might be that some element of *stress* is needed. It is not sufficient merely to correlate an anxiety scale with performance and expect to find a curvilinear relationship. This will only occur if, *during the test*, sufficient stress is applied (at least to normals) so that the people who report themselves anxious on a questionnaire are actually *made* anxious during the experiment. This was the case in the study by Sarason, Mandler and Craighill (1952), and some degree of stress probably operated in the study of Sarason and Mandler (1952). In both these experiments a significant curvilinear relationship was obtained.

One possible method of ensuring that potentially anxious subjects are made anxious during the test is to frustrate them. This was done in an experiment by Waterhouse and Child (1952). Normal subjects were given various cognitive tests under conditions of interference and non-interference. Subjects who claimed that interference upset them (on a questionnaire given previously) did worse (high anxiety group). Subjects who claimed that interference did *not* upset them actually did better in the stressful conditions (low anxiety group). The complexity of the cognitive tasks involved seemed to make very little difference in this experiment. A very similar study with very similar results was reported by Mohsin (1954), using as a cognitive measure the speed of performing the Passalong test.

McKinney *et al.* (1951) reported an experiment in which one hundred and ninety-six naval trainees were required to count different sorts of symbols as quickly as possible in normal conditions, and then with interruptions. The stress made them less accurate, but *faster* (in that more problems were attempted). The group's performance was relatively homogeneous, and uncorrelated with their response to a questionnaire, but, if it is assumed that this was a very stable group with low anxiety, these results are consistent with the hypothesis that it is *speed* which is curvilinearly related to drive level. That is, in the experiments discussed so far, the moderately anxious groups do better on tests than the extremely anxious or extremely stable groups merely because they work *faster*. This was clearly the case in Mohsin's (1954) experiment, and Mandler and Craighill's (1952) results were derived from a digit symbol test, where speed is extremely important. It is of interest that Castaneda (1956) found that reaction-time speed increases with increased stimulus intensity much more in an anxious than in a non-anxious group of normals.

Mandler and Sarason (1952a) found that a high anxiety group increased their speed of performing a Koh's Block test with practice much more than a low anxiety group. When stress was added, however (an intervening progress report—its nature did not matter), the high anxiety group became slower and the low anxiety group, faster. In a second study, however, the results before stress were not repeated although added stress still decreased the speed of the high anxiety group (Mandler and Sarason, 1952b).

Siegman (1956b), testing thirty-six medical and psychiatric patients, found that a high anxiety group (Taylor Scale) obtained poorer scores on the Matrices when it was given timed (stressed?), while a low anxiety group did better on the timed version of the test.

Furneaux has obtained very similar results with the Nufferno speed tests in normal students. The speed tests can be given in two ways. In the unstressed tests, subjects work at their own speed, and do not know that they are being timed. In the stressed tests, subjects are told to work as quickly as possible, and are aware they are being timed. The added stress *decreases* the speed of a very neurotic (high drive) group, but increases the speed of normal people (low drive group). Neuroticism in this case is assessed by the Guilford-Martin S.T.D.C.R. inventory.

It is possible then, to draw the following tentative conclusions from these studies. Individuals who are performing in a state of low drive *at the time of testing* tend to be slow at cognitive tests. Individuals who are in a state of medium drive tend to be fast. However, individuals in a state of very high drive tend again to be slow. Such evidence as exists, however, only relates to anxiety as a drive.

Maltzman (1955) argues from Hull's theory that high drive can in fact alter the *difficulty level* of cognitive problems. In hard problems, the correct response (an "internal" $S^H R$) has a lower habit strength than the incorrect responses. However, as drive level increases, the effective reaction potential ($S^E R$) of the wrong responses will become even greater than that of the correct response since $S^E R$ is a product of D and $S^H R$.[1] If this is the case, people

with high drive should find difficult tests much harder to do than easy tests, in comparison with people of low drive. While there is some evidence that this is the case for measures of learning (*see* Chapter 13), the only study investigating this relationship in cognitive tests (Waterhouse and Child, 1952) found no evidence that difficulty level and drive interact in this way. Child and Waterhouse (1953) prefer a different explanation, which perhaps fits the present data better. They argue that very high anxiety becomes distracting, as it produces conditioned responses of its own which interfere with the task.

This explanation is even more satisfying because it allows us to explain a fact discussed earlier. Extraverts (at the same average level of neuroticism) are considerably faster than introverts on cognitive tests. If we accept that introverts condition more easily than extraverts, it follows that they will have acquired more distracting conditioned responses to their anxiety than extraverts. These responses might be of two sorts. Some people might only have distracting thoughts (fears, etc.) which have become conditioned to a high anxiety level (anxious responses). Other people might have learned some ritual which serves the purpose of reducing their anxiety. This would probably be an obsessional tendency to check and recheck their answers (repeating the problem-solving search process). This would, of course, make their work more accurate, and we have already seen that introverts are more accurate than extraverts.

Indeed all the facts so far discussed about slowness in normals and neurotics could be included in the sort of framework discussed in detail in Chapter 13. The curvilinear relationship found between neuroticism (or anxiety as a drive) and speed might be an artefact produced by combining the data for extraverts and introverts. This would help to explain some of the earlier conflicting results, which

---

[1] Maltzman gives a rather unconvincing "quantitative" example of this, as follows—
For low drive, suppose for the *correct* response,
$$S^H R = 2, D = 1, S^E R = 2.$$
For the *incorrect* responses, $S^H R = 5, D = 1, S^E R = 5$.
Thus $S^E R$ incorrect minus $S^E R$ correct = 3.
However for high drive, for the *correct* response (if drive is doubled), $S^H R = 2, D = 2, S^E R = 4$.
For the *incorrect* responses, $S^H R = 5, D = 2, S^E R = 10$.
Thus $S^E R$ incorrect minus $S^E R$ correct = 6.

It might appear that in the high drive state, the wrong responses are twice as probable.

However, Maltzman nowhere defines the *units*. In the context of this argument the basic unit is clearly "probability of evocation of response." If we re-state the example in terms of *probabilities*, we get the following—

In the *low* drive state, for the *correct* response, $D = 1$, $S^H R = 0.2$, $S^E R = 0.2$ = probability of *correct* response occurring. For the *incorrect* responses, $D = 1$, $S^H R = 0.8$, $S^E R = 0.8$ = probability of *incorrect* responses occurring.

In the *high* drive state, for the *correct* response, $D = 2$, $S^H R = 0.2$, $S^E R = 0.4$ = probability of *correct* response occurring. For the *incorrect* responses, $D = 2$, $S^H R = 0.8$, $S^E R = 1.6$ = probability of *incorrect* response occurring. The second set of probabilities is obviously nonsense. In fact probabilities cannot be multiplied in this way. Note, however, that the *ratio* of correct $S^E R$: incorrect $S^E R$ remains the same at both levels of drive. The *proportion* of *right* to *wrong* responses thus remains the same at both drive levels. This example perhaps illustrates the dangers of quantification in psychology when the units are not specified. It must be noted that Spence (1956) is able to advance this sort of argument in such a way that the probabilities concerned do not add up to more than unity.

could be due either to a failure to produce real differences in drive *or* a product of the extent to which the subjects were introverted or extraverted.

It is conceivable that *unconditioned* anxiety is linearly related to speed. This could be because anxiety, like an overactive thyroid, in some way speeds up the mechanism of the search process at an unspecifiable physiological level. Were it not for *conditioned* anxiety responses, extremely neurotic subjects would be fastest of all. This leads to the prediction that the fastest group will be extremely extraverted neurotics. It is also possible that the number of conditioned anxiety responses produced is linearly related to the amount of anxiety present, and linearly related to the degree of *introversion* (conditionability) of the individual. Furthermore it is possible that a large number of conditioned anxiety responses produces a distraction (or an obsessional tendency) which outweighs the advantage of high drive. If all this were true, the slowest group of all would be the extremely introverted neurotic group who, as soon as a modest state of anxiety (drive) developed, would also develop a large number of distracting responses. The second slowest group would be the stable introverts, who would have less drive, and therefore would develop slightly fewer distracting responses than their neurotic counterparts. The second fastest group would be the very extraverted stable group, who would develop a little less drive than their neurotic counterparts, but who would also be free of any distracting conditioned anxiety responses.[1]

Curiously enough, Furneaux's analysis of speed-test results in normal students bears out all these predictions. If one measures the extent to which subjects speed up when asked to work as quickly as possible (on the stressed speed test), the highest "stress gain" scores are obtained by neurotic extraverts.[2] The second highest scores are achieved by stable extraverts. Lower still are stable introverts, and lowest of all, neurotic introverts, many of whom become much slower when stressed in this way.

This account must, of course, be regarded only as an hypothesis. A somewhat different hypothesis was discussed in the section on memory span in which it was stated as possible that introverts might solve letter series items in longer units, thus becoming

slower but more accurate. These two explanations are not entirely incompatible, as this is clearly a more thorough (obsessional) method of working which could serve to reduce the level of anxiety. The two hypotheses could, of course, be complimentary, both factors accounting for part of the observed differences.

Summary and Conclusions

1. The data relating drive to cognitive performance are somewhat conflicting, and only tentative hypotheses can be suggested.

2. There may be a linear relationship between *unconditioned* anxiety and speed of problem-solving, high anxiety producing high drive and fast performance. This could partly explain why neurotic subjects as a group are of above average general intelligence.

3. A high degree of introversion (conditionability) could produce a large number of distracting conditioned anxiety responses (or obsessional checking tendencies) themselves correlated with level of anxiety, which could slow down cognitive test performance more than high drive, by itself, speeds it up. These obsessional rechecking tendencies could, however, be responsible for the reduction in error found in introverted groups.

4. These two relationships when added together, could produce in a heterogeneous group a tendency for cognitive speed to appear to be related curvilinearly with neuroticism, or level of anxiety.

5. Because of these relationships, extraverted neurotics, when tested in a state of high drive (produced by "stress"), will work fastest, stable extraverts less fast, stable introverts slower, and introverted neurotics slowest of all.

(i) Rigidity

Rigidity has for many years been regarded by some writers as a personality variable of considerable importance. It was thought to account for a wide range of behaviour. As early as 1915, Lankes developed a questionnaire listing various rigid personality traits, which he administered to forty-seven normal subjects. He also gave them a wide range of tests, all of which he thought would be influenced in some way by rigidity (Lankes, like many earlier writers, uses the term perseveration). The tests included a cancellation test requiring a shift in the middle to another letter, a test of tapping speed (fast tappers he thought should perseverate), a colour wheel experiment to determine at what speed red and green blend to form grey (perseverators should see a blend at slower speeds), memory tests, a test of distractibility, word association tests, and even essays to write (perseverators should be good at long essays but poor at short ones). Lankes

---

[1] Another prediction follows from this explanation. In experiments in which introverts and extraverts are combined, and in which a "spurious" curvilinear relationship between anxiety drive and speed is found, the speed variance should increase enormously with increased anxiety. That is, the low drive group will be fairly homogeneous, but the high drive group, due to their heterogeneous reactions to high drive, should show very much variance about their mean.

[2] In each case these descriptions are based on responses to "extraversion" and "neuroticism" questionnaires (derived from the Guilford-Martin S.T.D.C.R. scales), the subjects being divided up into the four quadrants as they fall above and below the means of the two measures.

reported that *all* these measures correlated in the predicted direction with his rigidity questionnaire.

Lewin (1935, 1936) and Kounin (1941, 1948) believe that rigidity might be related to some fundamental property of the brain, which prevents one behavioural "region" from interacting with and modifying an adjoining region. This theory is very reminiscent of Kretschmer's theory of "dissociation" already discussed, and Goldstein's general theory of "isolation" (Goldstein, 1939, 1942). Kounin (1941, 1948) believes that rigidity increases with age, and performed several experiments using different measures of rigidity to demonstrate this.

Unfortunately, just as there is evidence (Payne, 1955) that different tests of dissociation have nothing in common, there is very strong evidence that there is no general factor of rigidity. In fact, no one has ever succeeded in repeating Lanke's (1915) results in detail. Studies by Jasper (1931), Shevach (1937), Notcutt (1943), Kleemeier and Dudek (1950), Goodstein (1953), Rim (1953), Forster *et al.* (1955), Davids (1955*b*) and Wolpert (1955) all report a complete failure to obtain a general factor of rigidity. Indeed, in many cases, none of the tests intercorrelated significantly. Even when rigidity tests are given under conditions of stress, a general factor fails to emerge. In fact stress does not alter the intercorrelations significantly (Applezweig, 1954; French, 1955).

There is some evidence that certain motor tests of rigidity produce two relatively specific factors (Cattell, 1946; Cattell and Tiner, 1949; Schaie, 1955) and some of these tests have been found to correlate with personality variables (Pinard, 1932; Eysenck, 1947, 1952).

The best factorial study of mental rigidity tests is reported by Guilford *et al.* (1957), who found evidence for two independent and relatively specific mental rigidity factors. One was labelled Adaptive flexibility, and was: "the ability to change a *set* in order to meet the requirements imposed by changing problems." The other was labelled Spontaneous flexibility, and was: "the ability to produce a diversity of ideas in a relatively unstructured situation."

The factor of adaptive flexibility is very similar to *Einstellung* rigidity, which Dunker (1945) described in his analysis of problem-solving. Dunker's analysis, while convincing, is mainly on a logical level and no experiments appear to have been performed to determine how important *Einstellung* rigidity might be in the solution of different types of standard cognitive tests.

By far the most frequently used measure of *Einstellung* rigidity is Luchins's "water-jar" test (Luchins, 1942, 1951; Luchins and Luchins, 1950). While Guilford did not use it in his factor analysis, it is very similar to tests of adaptive flexibility. In Luchins's

test (which has several variations), subjects are given a series of problems which require them to state how a given quantity of water might be measured out if they had three containers of known capacity. During a series of "set" problems, the subject finds that a certain complicated series of manoeuvres always produces an answer. These are followed by problems which can be solved very simply (by using two of the three containers), or by the complicated method which has been learned. Rigid people will continue to employ the complex method, while flexible people will change to the simple method. A very similar letter-maze test of *Einstellung* rigidity has been developed by Cowen *et al.* (1953), and shown to correlate significantly with the water-jar test.

There have been numerous attempts to relate *Einstellung* rigidity to other aspects of behaviour. Many investigators have tried to demonstrate that it is correlated with rigid behaviour in general as assessed by a questionnaire, but by and large the results are conflicting and inconclusive (Schmidt *et al.*, 1954; Rokeach *et al.*, 1955; Wolpert, 1954; Goodstein, 1953; Pitcher and Stacey, 1954; Cowen and Thompson, 1951). Similarly, attempts have been made to demonstrate that prejudiced people are especially rigid, by seeking correlations between *Einstellung* rigidity and the California Ethnocentrism scale. Again the results have been conflicting and inconclusive (Rokeach, 1948; Levitt and Zelen, 1953; Jackson *et al.*, 1957; Brown, 1953).

One line of research, however, has produced relatively consistent results. There is evidence that when normal subjects are tested under *stress* they become more rigid, both on some perceptual tests of rigidity (Smock, 1955*a*, 1955*b*; Erikson and Wechsler, 1955; Moffitt and Stagner, 1956) and on the Luchins test of *Einstellung* rigidity (Cowen, 1952*a*, 1952*b*; Maher, 1957).

This finding is perhaps not surprising. The development of *Einstellung* rigidity in Luchins's test is clearly a learned phenomenon, very similar to ordinary discrimination learning (i.e. some types of solution, and perhaps perceptions, are rewarded and some are not during the development of the set). It would seem probable that individuals who are better at learning would develop this set more easily. Since an increase of drive produces quicker learning, it is reasonable that an increase of anxiety produced by stress should make people more rigid on the Luchins test.[1] One might predict that for this reason introverted people would tend to be more rigid under stress than extraverted people. Indeed, psychiatrists often maintain

---

[1] Malmo and Wallerstein (1955) predicted that the "rigid" solution might ultimately extinguish through the development of "reactive inhibition" were it repeated often enough. However they did not test this prediction.

that introverted neurotics are more rigid in this sense. Unfortunately no studies investigating differences between neurotic groups or even between neurotic and normal groups appear to have been done with this test. It is interesting that Rokeach (1950) reports that, given longer over the test, normal people are less rigid, while Levitt and Zelen (1953) find the reverse, that speeded conditions produced flexibility. (Levine, 1955, found no relationship between *Einstellung* rigidity and speed of decision.)

There is much less work on the second sort of mental rigidity, Spontaneous flexibility. There is no evidence that it is related to stress in the same way. Ross *et al.* (1952), using the Wisconsin sorting test to determine how easy it was for normals to "shift" to a different method of sorting, found that the stress of being shocked had no effect on performance, and Wesley (1953) found the same measures of rigidity to be unrelated to the Taylor Anxiety Scale. McAndrew (1948) demonstrated that experience may be related to this sort of rigidity, as deaf children are much less able to shift (think of new methods of sorting) on a sorting test than normal children. Blind children, however, were normal in this respect.

Much has been written about rigidity in schizophrenia by Goldstein and his followers. Goldstein, while drawing a theoretical distinction between rigidity and concreteness (Goldstein, 1942), believes they both result from "isolation" in the nervous system (Goldstein, 1939), and in practice uses the same "concept formation" measures for both rigidity and concreteness (Goldstein and Scheerer, 1941). The discussion of the results from these tests will be left until the next section. It is interesting that Luchins (1951b), rating concreteness from the responses to a Similarities test, found no correlation with *Einstellung* rigidity as measured by the water-jar test.

While there are studies investigating motor rigidity and perceptual rigidity in psychotics (Stephenson, 1932a, 1932b; Pullen and Stagner, 1953), there are no satisfactory studies of adaptive flexibility in psychosis. Miller (1951) found that schizophrenics were more rigid in setting their level of aspiration in an experiment, than other groups. Jost (1955) found this true only of paranoid schizophrenics. There is no reason to believe that this sort of rigidity is related to either type of intellectual rigidity, however. Since the studies of rigidity in psychosis are inextricably bound up with studies of concept formation, this subject will be discussed further in the last section.

Summary and Conclusions

1. There is no general factor of rigidity, so that it is not possible to generalize about rigidity tests.
2. Guilford's analysis suggests that there are two independent kinds of intellectual rigidity, adaptive flexibility, or the ability to overcome a set, and spontaneous flexibility, or the ability to produce a diversity of ideas.
3. There is evidence that stress increases adaptive rigidity or *Einstellung* rigidity. This is probably because in *Einstellung* tests the set is learned, and high drive makes learning more rapid. It would be reasonable to expect introverts to be more rigid on this sort of problem than extroverts. This type of rigidity could account for part of the decrement in intellectual performance produced by stress in introverted neurotics.
4. Spontaneous flexibility has been very little investigated.
5. If rigidity and concreteness are not identified, and both logic and experimental results suggest they should not be, there are very few experiments on intellectual rigidity in psychosis. Rigidity in psychosis will be dealt with again in the final section.

(j) Concept Formation

(i) *Concreteness.* A concept might be defined as some symbol, usually a word, used to denote a large number of stimuli. These stimuli, however, may occur in quite different stimulus compounds. In other words, the concept often denotes an attribute common to a large number of different objects.

Thinking could be regarded as the internal manipulation of concepts, and in problem-solving, the units of the problem which the hypothetical search process examines in all their permutations and combinations could themselves be regarded as concepts.

Probably most of our concepts (words, etc.) are *learned*. It is possible to regard this sort of concept formation as a process of discrimination learning. Edna Heidbreder, in an extremely interesting series of studies on normal people, has demonstrated that concepts can be learned in this way, and that even though the same stimulus compound is never given more than once, the subject ultimately learns to associate the common attributes and to use some symbol to denote them (Heidbreder, 1946a, 1946b, 1947; Heidbreder, Bensley and Ivy, 1948; Heidbreder and Overstreet, 1948; Heidbreder, 1948, 1949a, 1949b). It is not surprising to find that in children, the capacity for rote learning is highly related to vocabulary. Those who learn quickest acquire the greatest number of concepts.

Many problems merely require us to manipulate concepts we already possess (most deductive reasoning tasks). If, however, we have not learned a concept crucial to the problem, we will fail. It is hardly surprising then, that rote-learning ability is correlated so highly with problem-solving ability.

Many other problems, however, can *not* be solved merely by manipulating concepts we already possess. These tasks involve a certain amount of induction.

In other words, some new concept must be formulated to denote some common aspect of the material, and the manipulation of this concept is crucial for success.

There is a good deal of controversy about whether or not *this* type of concept formation can be regarded as a process of internal learning, or whether it is more immediate—some form of sudden recognition ("insight"). Maier (1945) favours the latter point of view. Whatever the mechanism involved, however, the inability to form new concepts would be a considerable handicap in many types of problem-solving. This inability is usually called "concreteness," although the term is often not defined quite so specifically (e.g. Goldstein and Scheerer, 1941). Many psychologists (e.g. Goldstein, 1939b, 1940, 1946; Scheerer, 1946, 1953, 1954; Kasanin, 1945; Kasanin and Hanfmann, 1939) have come to regard concreteness as an important explanation of cognitive deficit, particularly in organic and schizophrenic patients.

Some of the evidence for this is derived from studies in which the Goldstein-Scheerer (1941) tests for concept formation have been used. Three of these are sorting tests. The Colour-Form test consists of a group of squares, triangles and circles of four different colours. The subject is asked to sort them into groups (form a concept) and then to resort them in a different way (form a second concept). They can be sorted for form or colour. The Object Sorting test is similar, but here a large number of everyday objects are used. The subject is asked to sort them into groups in as many different ways as he can (form as many concepts as possible). The Wool Sorting test is similar, except that the material used is skeins of coloured wool. Concepts such as "hue," "brightness" and "saturation" can form the basis of different methods of sorting. The last two tests are ordinary performance tests. One is a block design test in which various degrees of assistance are given, and the other is a test requiring the subject to reproduce patterns with small plastic sticks (the Sticks test). It is difficult to see what the last two tests have to do with concept formation unless a very broad definition indeed is used.

Goldstein and Scheerer, while developing a standard method of administering the tests, developed no standard scoring procedure. Concreteness is rated by the examiner, and a wide range of anomalies are called concrete, including an inability to sort at all, an inability to obtain more than one principle of classification, disobeying the instructions by failing to form the objects into groups, an inability to give a very precise verbal account of what has been done and why, and so on. Goldstein and Scheerer have never demonstrated that these anomalies are related in any way, nor that the tests themselves correlate.

Bolles and Goldstein (1938) gave this test battery to a group of sixteen schizophrenics, and reported that they were concrete. No control group of any sort was used, and it is not known how many normal people would have met their stringent criteria of an abstract performance. Hanfmann (1939c) reports concreteness in a single schizophrenic patient on a similar group of tests, and Cleveland and Dysinger (1944) also found that five schizophrenics were concrete on the Goldstein Object Sorting test. Again no control groups were tested.

Another group of studies makes use of the Vigotsky (1934) test of concept formation. This test consists of a number of wooden blocks of varying colours, shapes and heights. On the bottom of each block a nonsense syllable is printed. The examiner turns up the first block, and demonstrates that the name MUR is printed on the bottom. The subject is then asked to select all the blocks that can be grouped with this one. Each time an incorrect block is selected, it is turned upside down, to demonstrate that it has a different nonsense syllable on the bottom. This procedure continues until the subject correctly groups all the MUR blocks together. There are four different nonsense syllables, and four groups of blocks. The correct principle is neither colour, shape *nor* height, but volume, and the subject during the course of the test must formulate this concept. The only quantitative score used (Kasanin and Hanfmann, 1938; Hanfmann and Kasanin, 1937) is the "time-help" score, which is the number of times the examiner had to correct the subject, multiplied by five and added to the number of minutes needed to achieve the solution. This curious score obviously involves both speed of thinking and the ease with which the concept is acquired, and is necessarily ambiguous by itself.

Kasanin and Hanfmann (1938b) gave the Vigotsky test to fifty schizophrenics and forty-five normals of the same age. They found that the schizophrenics had significantly higher time-help scores than the normals, and that this probably was not due to educational differences.

In 1942, Hanfmann and Kasanin reported a larger study (Hanfmann and Kasanin, 1942; Kasanin, 1946) using the same test with sixty-two schizophrenics, ninety-five normal controls and twenty-four brain-damaged cases. In this study the time-help score was clearly a function of the amount of education of the subjects, but it still differentiated between schizophrenics and normals with the same education. The qualitative performance of the subjects was also rated on a variety of subjective criteria, and schizophrenics again were judged more concrete.

Fisher (1950) tested twenty normals, twenty conversion hysterics and twenty paranoid schizophrenics, using the Vigotsky test material as a sorting test to determine the number of different groupings the subjects could obtain. Normals had a mean of 16·1

(± 4·9), schizophrenics 11·3 (± 4·7) and hysterics 10·3 (± 3·9). While the normals are significantly better than the two abnormal groups, they are also brighter and considerably younger. The hysterics and the schizophrenics were not significantly different from each other.

The results using these tests of concept formation are thus almost entirely inconclusive. The Goldstein test studies are completely uncontrolled, and it is not possible to say that the Vigotsky test results were not merely due to slowness in the schizophrenic groups, since inadequate data are reported. Fisher's study certainly provides no evidence that schizophrenics are especially concrete in terms of the number of different sortings they can achieve.

McGaughran (1954) has developed a different system of scoring the Goldstein Object Sorting test. He believes that sortings can be assessed along two dimensions, a dimension of "open-closed" (conceptual freedom or concreteness) assessed by the number of objects the concept covers, and an unrelated "public-private" dimension, which is the extent to which the concept is usual or generally accepted. McGaughran and Moran (1956) administered an Object Sorting test to thirty-seven chronic paranoid schizophrenics and thirty-seven non-psychiatric hospitalized patients carefully matched for Wechsler vocabulary, educational level and age. When the test was rated in the usual way to assess concreteness, the groups were not differentiated significantly. In fact the paranoid schizophrenics were a trifle more abstract. These concreteness ratings were found to be significantly related to I.Q., as might be expected, the more abstract obtaining higher I.Q. scores. Paranoid schizophrenics however produced significantly more "private" responses and fewer "public" responses than normals. They also showed greater conceptual freedom, than the normals, incorporating more objects into their concepts, and in that sense generalizing more. Within the schizophrenic group, there was a strong tendency for private responses to be associated with a lower level of general intelligence, suggesting that the tendency to formulate unusual concepts may be a contributory factor to general cognitive impairment.

McGaughran (1957) in a further study contrasted thirty-seven schizophrenics and thirty-four brain-damaged subjects on the same test. The brain-damaged group produced significantly more "closed" (restricted) sortings, while the schizophrenics had significantly more private sortings. Again both variables correlated significantly with a vocabulary test, subjects with higher vocabulary scores having more public and fewer closed (restricted) sortings ($r = 0.42$ and -0.32 respectively).

McGaughran's series of studies suggests that schizophrenics are not concrete in the sense of being unable to form concepts. The concepts they form do, however, tend to be unusual. Brain-damaged patients, on the other hand, *do* tend to be concrete.

A quite different method of assessing concreteness has been by the use of proverbs. A concrete response to a proverb is usually said to be one which accepts the literal meaning, and does not generalize, or re-state it in the form of a general proposition. Wegrocki (1940) tested a group of schizophrenics with a proverbs test, and found them to be more concrete than children. Benjamin (1946) produced a standard series of proverbs. He too claimed that schizophrenics are concrete, although he published no adequate data. Becker (1956) found that concreteness as rated from the Benjamin proverbs correlated significantly (-0.682 with the Elgin Prognostic Scale in a group of twenty-four male schizophrenics, but insignificantly (0.048) in a group of twenty-seven female schizophrenics.

By far the most adequate study is one by Gorham (1956). In a "pilot" study, Gorham administered a set of twelve proverbs to seventy-eight normals and one hundred and eighteen chronic schizophrenics. The answers were rated in the usual way for concreteness. The subjects were also given a set of forty proverbs in the form of a multiple-choice test. For each proverb the subject had to select one of four alternative interpretations, some of which were "abstract" and some of which were concrete. Gorham found a significant correlation between concreteness measured in this way, and a test of verbal comprehension. The schizophrenics were significantly more concrete on the sets of proverbs. In a larger study, Gorham administered the same sets of proverbs to another group of one hundred chronic schizophrenics and one hundred normals matched for age, education and word knowledge. Both an abstraction score and a concreteness score derived from the multiple—choice test differentiated the groups significantly ($p < 0.001$ in each case). The ratings of both abstraction and concreteness derived from the ordinary proverbs test also differentiated at beyond the 0·001 level. All these results were cross-validated a third time on a fresh sample of eighty-nine schizophrenics and one hundred and five normals. There seems little doubt from this large scale and carefully controlled study that schizophrenics are abnormally concrete in their response to proverbs tests.

These findings are very similar to the results obtained with vocabulary tests. This literature was reviewed in the first section, and the general finding was that if definitions of words are rated as abstract or concrete, that schizophrenics as a group tend to produce concrete definitions.

All these studies are less than conclusive, however. There is little doubt that schizophrenics define words and interpret proverbs peculiarly. Their unusual use of language has been demonstrated objectively in other studies using different techniques (Ellsworth, 1951; Mirin, 1955). It is conceivable that this abnormality could be due to their inability to form new concepts. However there are equally probable alternative explanations. For example, curious definitions of words and proverbs could indicate not an inability to form new concepts, but a tendency to form *different* or unusual concepts. This would be more in keeping with McGaughran's results (McGaughran, 1954, 1957; McGaughran and Moran, 1956). It is also conceivable that, just as they tend to use and define words unusually, some schizophrenics may *interpret* words they hear unusually. They may misunderstand what they are told. Some schizophrenics may, for instance, interpret the instructions of the proverbs test as allowing either a general statement of the principle illustrated *or* the use of an apt (by their definition) concrete illustration of the meaning of the proverb.

A careful analysis of the use of language in schizophrenia has formed the basis of most psychiatric studies of thought disorder (Bleuler, 1950, 1951; Schneider, 1930). While these methods yield fruitful hypotheses, the hypotheses must be tested by more direct experiments. A conclusive answer can only arise from a study in which schizophrenics are actually required to form new concepts, and their ability to do this is assessed.

There are several studies which attempt to assess concept formation more directly. Rashkis, Cushman and Landis (1946) developed a test similar to the object sorting test, except that the "objects" to be sorted were words printed on cards. These had to be placed in blank squares on a large sheet of paper. Some of the squares already contained key words. The test, in fact, required the subject to build up a sort of "concept matrix" with the cards, the rows referring to different concepts. Afterwards, the subjects were required to verbalize their concepts, and then to shift by sorting all the cards differently. Results were obtained from nine children, eight schizophrenics, ten general paretics and nine normal adults. Only the normal adults performed the test perfectly. The paretics could attain no complex organization at all. The schizophrenics formed concepts but they were eccentric and unlike those used by the normals. These results are very similar to those reported by McGaughran and Moran (1956).

Rashkis (1947) reported a second, similar experiment. The same word sorting test was used, and a number sorting test was added. The subject was given numbers printed on cards, and required to complete a square matrix in which key numbers had been entered, and which also contained addition signs and equality signs—a sort of numerical "crossword puzzle." Ten schizophrenics, ten general paretics and ten arterio-

sclerotics were tested. The schizophrenics were best at both tests.

Feldman and Drasgow (1951) developed a test consisting of a set of cards. Each card pictured four objects in a row. For example, card 1 contained four circles. Three were large, and one small, and one of the large circles was coloured black. Three of the objects could be grouped together for one reason (e.g. all the large circles on card 1), but another group of three objects could be formed for another reason (e.g. all the white circles on card 1). Feldman and Drasgow gave the test to thirty-seven early schizophrenics and thirty-seven normals matched for age and education. The number of "single misses" (missing one of the two concepts) differentiated the groups at the 0·0001 level of significance, while the number of "double misses" (missing both concepts on a card) differentiated even better. All the schizophrenics had eight or more double misses while all the normals had seven or fewer double misses. These results are not unambiguous however. Schizophrenics could get poor scores either because they are unable to induce a concept at all (are concrete) or because they formulate an unusual concept which produces an unusual answer. The latter possibility must be taken seriously in view of the findings already discussed.

It is interesting that Payne, Matussek and George (1959) were unable to repeat Feldman and Drasgow's findings, on a small group of fourteen schizophrenics and thirteen neurotics, using a similar test scored identically. The groups were not differentiated significantly in terms of the total number of errors (and failures). The neurotics had slightly fewer double misses, but the difference was not significant. A one-minute time limit per card (as used by Feldman and Drasgow) was shown to have no influence on the results as the scores with and without the time limit were not significantly different.

A more satisfactory technique for investigating concept formation in abnormal subjects is the Wisconsin Sorting Test (Berg, 1948; Grant, Jones and Tallantis, 1949; Grant, 1951). This test is very similar to Heidbreder's technique for studying concept formation in normals. The test is composed of sixty-four cards. These have to be sorted one at a time with one of four stimulus cards. Each time the subject sorts a card, he is told "right" or "wrong." The first principle of sorting is based on colour. When the subject places ten cards consecutively with the correct stimulus card the principle is changed to "form." When the same criterion is reached for the second principle, it is changed again and the procedure continues. The test demands five shifts in all. The test is over when all the sixty-four cards are sorted *or* when all the concepts have been learned, whichever is first. Fey (1951) administered this test to twenty-two young schizophrenics and forty-seven young normals matched for age, tested intelligence, education and sex. Sixteen of the twenty-two schizophrenics failed to complete the test successfully, while only eight of the forty-seven normals failed. The schizophrenics who succeeded made more errors than the normals who succeeded. The correlation between success and I.Q. was insignificant in both groups. The overall performance on this test is unfortunately a function of both the ability to learn a concept and rigidity. The results would be more clear-cut if data had been reported on the number of trials needed to learn the *first* concept. There is, however (as will be discussed later), no reason for supposing schizophrenics to be abnormally rigid in this sense, so that some abnormality of concept formation is highly probable. Fey suggests that the schizophrenics obtained poorer scores not through difficulties in "initial" learning, but because they "seemed to experience more difficulty in holding the correct set, once having achieved it . . ." She also reports that when the groups were asked to *explain* the concepts, both normals and abnormals gave equally concrete explanations.

These studies then suggest that schizophrenics as a group are probably not abnormally concrete in the sense of being unable to form a new concept. They are, however, abnormal in the *type* of concepts they form. Their concepts tend to be unusual and often eccentric. They are able to learn normal concepts, but end to have difficulty in adhering to them when asked o employ them over a period of time.

There are remarkably few studies of concept formation in other disorders, particularly in the affective psychoses. Tong (1955) administered a sorting test to one hundred and sixty-one prison inmates. Some of the subjects failed to obey the instructions, and made patterns with the material instead of sorting it into groups. Slightly more of those who patterned than those who did not, were judged to be psychotic or brain-damaged.

Payne and Hewlett (to be published) in a study already referred to, administered a large number of tests of "overinclusive thinking," psychomotor, mental and perceptual slowness, and a number of miscellaneous measures to carefully-matched groups of twenty schizophrenics, twenty depressives, twenty neurotics and twenty normal people. Five measures of concreteness were also included. These were concreteness ratings derived from the Goldstein Colour-Form and Object Sorting tests, a concreteness rating derived from the Benjamin Proverbs test, and abstraction scores derived from an object classification test and the Shaw test of concept formation. It was predicted that the schizophrenics would be rated more concrete on the two Goldstein tests and the Proverbs test when the traditional criteria were used because unusual generalizations tend to be rated as concrete. This was the case for all three measures. The depressives were no different from the normals and neurotics on these three ratings. However, neither of the two abstraction scores produced significant differences between any of the groups. The entire battery of tests was intercorrelated and factor-analysed for the combined group. It was demonstrated that, as expected, the concreteness ratings from the Goldstein tests and the Proverbs test were loaded on a factor labelled "overinclusion." Factor scores of overinclusion significantly differentiated the schizophrenics from the other three groups, only schizophrenics being abnormal in this respect. Again this was consistent with the hypothesis that schizophrenics are rated as concrete merely because of their usual (overinclusive) generalizations. A factor labelled "general intelligence" was derived from the factor analysis. Factor scores for general intelligence did not differentiate the groups significantly. This was as expected, because the groups had been carefully matched for pre-illness level, and were not significantly different on the Nufferno "Level" test. All five measures of concreteness had very high loadings on this general intelligence factor (ranging from 0·57 to 0·83). It was suggested that concreteness as measured by these tests is mainly a measure of general intellectual level, although the concreteness ratings from the Goldstein tests and the Proverbs test are also affected by overinclusive thinking to some extent. It was concluded that there was no evidence that either of the two psychotic groups were concrete in the sense of being unable to produce abstract generalizations.

While an inability to develop new concepts as such is probably *not* a characteristic of any particular functional diagnostic group, it is possible that some individuals are abnormal in this respect. Several studies have investigated some possible causes of abnormal concreteness and some ways of altering it. Beier (1951) studied the effect of stress on concreteness. Sixty-two student teachers were given an abstract reasoning test and a test requiring them to formulate abstract explanations for groups of objects presented to them. A group tested under stress did worse than a group tested under normal conditions. It is not clear, however, whether the stress made them more rigid or whether it impaired their ability to form concepts.

Cohen, Senf and Huston (1954) gave a sorting test to a group of twenty-four chronic schizophrenics, twenty-two early schizophrenics, twenty-one depressed patients and twenty-one neurotics. The groups were not matched. Under normal conditions, the chronic schizophrenic group and the early schizophrenic group both produced "vague categories" and "chain associations." The depressives and the neurotics both produced more satisfactory categories, there being no differences between them. The groups were then retested under "affective conditions." Four common test objects were replaced by any four objects believed to be particularly emotionally disturbing to the individual patient. The normal test was repeated under the influence of Sodium Amytal, and finally the affective test was repeated under amytal. The drug by itself had a significant overall effect. All the subjects finished the test more quickly, especially the depressives who had initially been the slowest group. The drug reduced the quality of the answers given by the depressives, but improved the neurotics. The schizophrenics did not change. The affective condition of test administration by itself changed only the depressives, making their responses poorer. The affective conditions plus the drug made *all* the groups worse, the schizophrenics showing the greatest decline. For all the groups combined, the sorting test correlated + 0·34 with general intelligence.

This study suggests that an increase of affect, particularly when assisted by Sodium Amytal, may cause patients, and particularly psychotics, to become more vague in their concept formation, possibly due to the fact that these emotions have a distracting effect.

It is clear that a gross defect of rote learning could produce an inability to form new concepts, as most concept formation could be regarded as discrimination learning. As one might expect, there is some evidence from sorting tests (Inglis, 1958) that old people, and especially patients with senile dementia are abnormally concrete in the sense of being unable to sort at all. These studies are not as conclusive as it might appear, however. While *most* concepts are learned, the concepts which are "induced" in response to sorting tests are developed very quickly, and correspond better to the sort of concept formation described by Maier (1945) as *not* learned but immediately apprehended in some way. It is also rather anomalous that many of the concepts actually induced in these sorting tests are ideas like "size," "weight," or "colour." It is clear that old people must have learned, for example, the concept of size in the past. It is odd then, that they are unable to use such concepts to sort objects. The only reasonable explanation would seem to be that the *sorting test objects* were never incorporated into these learned concepts, because the test represents a new experience. In other words, *learned* concepts include *only* those "items" from which the concept has evolved. They do *not* extend to similar but entirely novel stimulus compounds. This is, in fact, quite compatible with the discrimination learning explanation for such concepts. It follows, however, that the extension of concepts into an entirely new situation may not be a process of learning at all, but some immediate "recognition." It is a failure in this second sort of concept formation

which causes the elderly to fail at sorting tests. As they *also* have learning defects, the implication is that they are poor at *both* types of concept formation, although the *cause* of their failure to "perceive" non-learned concepts is left unexplained.

The above studies suggest at least one possible cause of concreteness. There are also a few articles reporting investigations into other abnormalities which might be associated with abnormal concreteness. Rokeach (1951), assessing concreteness in one hundred and forty-four normal subjects by their ability to define words like "Buddhism" and "Capitalism" found that concreteness was correlated with ethnocentrism. Since intelligence was also correlated with ethnocentrism, however, the results are not conclusive. Mathews *et al.* (1953) found that among normal subjects, those more concrete on a sorting test tended to get higher "Pd" and "Ma" scores on the M.M.P.I. However, this could merely be another demonstration of the fact that extraverts tend to be duller than introverts.

Flavell (1956) gave a multiple-choice vocabulary test to twenty-four schizophrenics. They produced more concrete definitions than a normal group. There was a correlation of 0·60 in the schizophrenic group between the number of abstract responses and a measure of social interaction. The study suggests that schizophrenics with the most unusual concepts tend to be the least sociable, perhaps because they find communication with other people more difficult. It is interesting that Gollin and Rosenberg (1956) reported a similar finding for normal people. On the Rokeach test of concept formation, those who had high scores (were able to form concepts) tended to be less extreme in their social distances as assessed by a questionnaire.

(ii) *Overinclusion.* Norman Cameron (1944, 1947; Cameron and Magaret, 1951) has performed a number of investigations into the nature of concept formation in schizophrenia. In 1938 Cameron (1938a) administered an "incomplete sentences" test to twenty-five schizophrenic patients. He also (Cameron, 1938b) tested twenty-two patients with senile psychosis, twenty-nine normal children, and twenty normal adults. From an analysis of the way in which the subjects completed these sentence fragments, he concluded that schizophrenic's thought disorder is not a form of regression, as their sentences were unlike those of children. Their sentences were also unlike those produced by patients with senile dementia. The schizophrenic sentences had several peculiar characteristics, the most important of which he later attributed to overinclusion and the interpenetration of personal themes. In a further study Cameron (1939a, 1939b) gave the Vigotsky test to five of the most severely disorganized schizophrenics in the original group, and six of the most disorganized senile patients.

He concluded from a qualitative analysis of this material that the senile patients were unable to grasp the nature of the problem, and were rigid. The schizophrenics were not rigid. They showed, however, the same peculiarities of concept formation as those noted earlier. Their thought was distracted by the interpenetration of personal themes. They were also overinclusive. Cameron defines overinclusion as the inability to preserve conceptual boundaries. Ideas associated with, or distantly related to, concepts become incorporated into them, making them both more abstract and less precise. In the solution of a problem the schizophrenics "included such a variety of categories at one time that the specific problems became too extensive and too complex for a solution to be reached" (Cameron, 1939a).

A disorder of concept formation of this sort has been described by other writers such as Schilder (1954), Bychowski (1943) and Angyal (1946). Lovibond (1954) perhaps gives it the clearest general formulation.

Most concept formation can be regarded as a form of discrimination learning. For example, when a word is first heard in a certain context, it first comes to be associated with the entire situation ("stimulus compound"). As the word is heard again and again, only certain aspects of the stimulus compound are reinforced however. Gradually the extraneous elements cease to evoke the response (the word), having become inhibited through lack of reinforcement. This inhibition is in some sense an active process, as it suppresses a response which was formerly evoked by the stimulus. It is possible to imagine a disorder of the process whereby inhibition is built up to circumscribe and define the learned response (the word or concept). This disorder would result in overinclusion in the formation of the concept, and could be regarded as an extreme degree of stimulus generalization. We will use the term overinclusion for this postulated abnormality, although Cameron sometimes uses the term in a wider sense.

It is conceivable that when this abnormality develops (through some form of psychosis), concepts which are learned after the acquisition of the abnormality are the first to become affected, but that, gradually, recently acquired concepts, and, finally, older concepts are affected as the process of inhibition becomes weaker.

A number of studies have been reported which support the hypothesis that the main abnormality of concept formation responsible for the observations so far discussed, is abnormal overinclusion.

In 1948 Shneidman developed the Make-a-Picture-Story test, in which subjects are required to select human figures from a large group, place them on a background card (different backgrounds are used picturing outdoor and indoor settings) and then make up a story about the scene created. He administered

it to a group of fifty schizophrenics (72 per cent paranoid schizophrenics), and fifty normals. Among other differences in performance noted, the schizophrenics tended to use an abnormally large number of figures in their pictures. They seemed unable to restrict their attention to a few figures relevant to a simple theme. Balken (1943) similarly observed on the T.A.T. that schizophrenics tend to produce rather diffuse stories.

Zaslow (1950) developed a simple test to measure overinclusion. It consisted of fourteen cards. Card 1 depicts an equilateral triangle, and card 14 a perfect circle. In the intervening cards, the shape gradually changes from a triangle to a circle. In one part of the administration procedure the examiner places the cards in order, and asks the subject to indicate where the circles end, and where the triangles end. Zaslow predicted from Cameron's theory that schizophrenics would include more cards in each concept. The results obtained from twenty-four schizophrenics and sixteen normal surgical cases supported the hypothesis. Kugelmass and Fondeur (1955) repeating the study on forty-five early schizophrenics, twenty-three acute schizophrenics and twenty-three normals, failed to confirm these results at an acceptable level of significance. They found, however, that the test-retest reliability was so low as to be insignificant for some scores.

White (1949) tested twenty schizophrenics and twenty normals carefully matched for age, sex, education and background. They were given fifteen words printed on cards to group in any way they wished. The schizophrenics tended to form very large, vague categories, forming concepts such as "suspicion" or "having to do with God."

Daston, King and Armitage (1953) read two short stories aloud to twenty-five paranoid schizophrenics and twenty-seven matched normals. Afterwards the subjects were given a check list of thirty-six positive and thirty-six negative statements about the characters in the stories. The schizophrenic group checked off significantly more adjectives than the normals.

Moran (1953) tested several deductions from Cameron's theory on a group of forty schizophrenics and forty normals carefully matched for age, sex, vocabulary score and occupational level. The subjects were first given twenty-five words to define. There were no differences in the conceptual level of the definitions given, thus the hypothesis that "schizophrenics" are concrete was not supported. The subjects were then asked to give as many synonyms as possible for each word. As predicted from Cameron's theory, the schizophrenics gave more imprecise synonyms. The subjects were then given a test in which each word (printed on a page) was followed by eight response words, including neologisms. Some response words were an essential part of the concept denoted by the stimulus word, and some were words which were more or less associated. The subjects were asked to underline every word which they regarded as an essential part of the concept denoted by the stimulus word. As predicted, the schizophrenics did *not* underline significantly fewer correct words, but did underline significantly more of the distantly related words. When asked to free associate to the words, the schizophrenics produced more distant associations. When asked to incorporate the words into a sentence, their sentences were unclear, contradictory and ungrammatical. When the words were incorporated into a similarities and an analogies test, the schizophrenics produced significantly inferior performances. This study suggests strongly that the poor scores obtained by schizophrenics on such tests as similarities and analogies can be attributed to an overinclusive definition of the concepts involved.

Epstein (1953) developed a verbal test of overinclusion using a method very similar to that of Moran. Fifty stimulus words are each followed by six response words including the word "none." The subject is asked to underline all the response words which he considers a necessary part of the concept denoted by the stimulus word (or the word "none" if all are unnecessary). As predicted, a group of schizophrenics underlined significantly more words than a matched group of normals with the same level of vocabulary.

Rapaport *et al.* (1945), using an object sorting test, found that a group of schizophrenics were no more concrete than a group of normals. They did, however, tend to form more vague syncretistic concepts. Lovibond (1954) administered the Goldstein Object Sorting test to thirty-two schizophrenics and forty-five matched normal controls. He employed an elaborate rating system to assess the amount of overinclusion or failure in inhibition, which occurred in the sortings of the two groups. The scores differentiated significantly as predicted from Cameron's hypothesis.

An ingenious series of experiments by Chapman (1956) and Chapman and Taylor (1957) have provided the most convincing tests of the overinclusion hypothesis. Chapman (1956) investigated a group of forty schizophrenics and twenty-five matched normals. The subjects were shown three stimulus cards which had a picture or a symbol in each of the four corners. The subjects were asked to group a series of similar response cards with the relevant stimulus card. They were told to disregard *all* the pictures on the stimulus cards except the picture in the lower right-hand corner. A response card which contained anywhere among its four pictures an identical picture, or one of the same sort, as a stimulus card, was to be grouped with that stimulus card. Sixty response cards in all were used.

Response cards had varying numbers of items on them matching *irrelevant* items on the stimulus cards. It was predicted that the errors in the schizophrenic group would be produced by these distractor items. The results were exactly as predicted. Response cards with *no* distractor items did not differentiate the groups, normals and schizophrenics making an equal number of errors. Furthermore, as predicted, there was a strong relationship between the *number* of distractor items per card, and the number of mistakes made by the schizophrenic group. There was no such relationship within the normal group, all cards producing an equal number of errors. The schizophrenics' performance was not due to forgetting, as their errors did not increase during the test. The number of failures on this test within the schizophrenic group was correlated with a rating of severity of illness.

Chapman and Taylor (1957) in another experiment, investigated twenty-four mildly disturbed schizophrenics, twenty-four severely disturbed schizophrenics and twenty-four normals matched for age and education. As might be expected, the schizophrenic groups had lower tested I.Q.s. (It is obviously not desirable to match groups for present I.Q. since this is controlling for the disability one is seeking to explain in the experiment.) The subjects were given the name of a concept (e.g. fruit) and were asked to sort a number of cards, each bearing the name of a specific item (e.g. "apple," "fish"). Some of the cards bore the names of specific fruits, and therefore should be grouped in the "fruit" category. An equal number of cards bore the names of similar, but incorrect items (e.g. the names of vegetables). A third group of cards bore the names of quite different objects (e.g. birds). It was first predicted that the schizophrenics would overinclude by including the similar items (vegetables) with the correct items (fruits). The results were exactly as predicted. The normals made virtually no errors, while the schizophrenics included a significant number of similar cards incorrectly. There was no evidence for concreteness however, as the schizophrenics, like the normals, did not include the *dissimilar* cards. The two schizophrenic groups were not differentiated by the test. The test successfully differentiated between a group of normals and a group of schizophrenics matched for I.Q. In a second experiment, there was no evidence for abnormal "underinclusion" (the tendency to be abnormally restrictive in concept formation) in the schizophrenic groups.

These studies produce remarkably consistent results, which strongly support the hypothesis that schizophrenics display abnormal overinclusion in their concept formation.

It is conceivable (as Lovibond, 1954, has suggested) that overinclusion is only one aspect of a more general abnormality. Certainly one further prediction can be made from the hypothesis. In tests of adaptive rigidity, such as the Luchins test of *Einstellung* rigidity, a "set" is probably produced by the same process of discrimination learning believed to account for some concept formation. As some types of solution are consistently not reinforced, they become inhibited. Later, when the subject would find these solutions useful, he is "blinded" to them by the set he has developed. If schizophrenics are abnormal in their inability to develop this sort of inhibition, they should find it difficult to develop a set of this sort. This could be either an advantage or a disadvantage, depending on the sort of problem. They should, for example, be better at doing the Luchins *Einstellung* rigidity test. In fact, if this hypothesis is correct, schizophrenics should show an abnormal amount of adaptive flexibility. This prediction was tested by Payne and Hewlett (to be published), who compared twenty schizophrenics with a combined group of twenty normal, twenty neurotics and twenty depressives on a modified form of the Luchins *Einstellung* test. The schizophrenics were significantly less rigid following the establishment of the set.

Angyal (1946) seems to have been one of the first writers to suggest that schizophrenics are abnormal in their relative inability to develop a set. There are some other results consistent with this hypothesis. White (1949) investigated a group of twenty schizophrenics and twenty normals. The subjects were given a number of words printed on cards to read. Some were clearly printed, but some were so blurred that they were impossible to read (they were reproductions of very poor carbon copies). The subjects were told to guess what was on each card. On only three out of three hundred occasions, did any normal subject fail to give some word as a guess. Schizophrenics fairly frequently said that they did not know what was on the card, or tended to guess things other than words (e.g. "teeth" or "spots"). Presumably the normals, after seeing the first clear word, rapidly developed a set to perceive words whatever the card looked like, and failed to perceive the true nature of the stimuli. In a second experiment, the subjects were asked to make up sentences using the words. The normals, perhaps due to a preconceived set about what was required, never used the same sentence twice, and never used grammatically incomplete sentences. The schizophrenics frequently did both these things.

Payne, Matussek and George (1959) performed a different sort of experiment on a group of eighteen schizophrenics and sixteen neurotics. The subjects were shown a piece of paper on which circles containing letters or numbers were printed at random. Without verbal instructions, the examiner connected them with a pencil in the order 1—A—2—B, etc., numbers and letters alternating. The subjects were then given an identical sheet of paper, and motioned to do the same. No subjects made errors. Finally they were presented with a sheet of paper on which was printed many more circles containing letters and numbers, but this time in a quite different arrangement. Again the subjects were motioned to proceed. It was predicted that the neurotics would have no difficulty, since they would come into the test with a strong set that numbers and letters should be arranged in order. The first part of the test would confirm this set and they would subsequently completely ignore the other aspects, such as the spatial juxtaposition of the letters and numbers. Schizophrenics, on the other hand, should tend *not* to develop this set. In the final part of the test they should notice the altered arrangement of the letters, and the more complex and detailed explanation of the examiner's performance they had probably formulated during the first part of the test would no longer apply, since the same relationship between letter-number sequence and spatial arrangement no longer applied. It was predicted that in this conflict situation they would take very much longer, and would probably make a number of errors. Both predictions were verified significantly. The neurotics made an average of only 1·86 errors, while the schizophrenics made an average of 7·00 errors.[1] The two groups were also shown to differ significantly in overinclusion on the Epstein (1953) test. The schizophrenics were also more overinclusive in a measure derived from the Goldstein Object Sorting test. During the "handing over" part of this test (when the subjects are asked to select all the objects they would group together with a given object) the schizophrenics grouped together significantly more objects than did the neurotics.

It is possible to formulate the hypothesis of overinclusion in a more general way, so that it accounts for a number of other findings. All purposeful behaviour depends for its success on the fact that some stimuli are attended to and other stimuli are ignored. It is a well-known fact that when concentrating on one task, normal people are quite unaware of most stimuli irrelevant to the task. It is as if there were some filter mechanism (to use an information theory term) which cuts out those stimuli, both internal and external which are irrelevant to the task in hand, to allow the most efficient processing of incoming information. Many schizophrenics behave as if this filter had lost some of its inhibitory properties, and allowed irrelevant information to enter the processing mechanism. Abnormal intellectual slowness in some psychotics may well be due partly to this abnormality. Normal people only consider a certain amount of information as being relevant to the problem. Some psychotics

---

[1] The material used in this experiment was taken from the Leiter-Partington "Pathways" test. (Leiter and Partington, 1950.)

whose thought processes may be just as fast, might have more possible solutions to consider because they fail to exclude certain data which normal people judge to be irrelevant.

If this is the case, a number of predictions can be made. In a sorting test of inductive reasoning which has a large number of possible solutions, given no time limit, schizophrenics should be able to achieve many more solutions merely because they do not arbitrarily ignore some of the data as irrelevant, and are able to base extra methods of sorting on these additional aspects of the material (e.g. the unintentional scratches on the objects, their cleanliness, the shadows cast by the objects on the table, their personal associations to the objects, and so on). If schizophrenics are not essentially slow in thinking, they should be able to produce responses just as frequently as normals. They should however take much longer over the test, merely because they produce many more methods of sorting. They should present normal and abnormal sortings in a completely random order, because they should not distinguish between sortings based on relevant and sortings based on irrelevant aspects of the material.

Payne, Matussek and George (1959) verified some of these predictions on eighteen schizophrenics and sixteen neurotics. The sorting test used was a modification of Goldstein's Object Sorting test. The objects were squares, triangles and circles which varied in size, weight, thickness, density, material, and the hue, brightness and saturation of the colours. There were ten rational ways of sorting the objects. The schizophrenics obtained an average of 11·66 different methods of sorting, both rational and bizarre. The neurotics produced an average of only 7·07 methods of sorting. It is clear from these results that schizophrenics cannot be regarded as either concrete or rigid in the usual sense of the terms. In fact they are abnormal in their degree of spontaneous flexibility.

Payne and Hewlett (to be published) administered the same test to matched groups of twenty schizophrenics, twenty depressives, twenty neurotics and twenty normal people. As expected, the groups did not differ significantly in the number of rational responses, producing no evidence for abnormal concreteness in any of the groups. However, the schizophrenics produced many more unusual methods of sorting the material than did the other groups, and hence had a larger total number of responses. Similar results were obtained using the Shaw test of concept formation.

It is not surprising, if this hypothesis is accepted, that schizophrenics are original in their responses to word association tests, and that they do not adhere to the prohibitions which normal people assume are intended.

This general inability to develop an inhibitory set can account for some apparently diverse findings which have been reported. For example, Rodnick and Shakow (1940) attributed schizophrenic slowness and variability in reaction-time to an inability to maintain a set. (Huston and Senf, 1952; Huston and Singer, 1945; Knehr, 1954.) Pascal and Swensen (1952) found that when a very loud distraction is used, reaction-time measures no longer differentiate schizophrenics from other groups. (Presumably because all the groups are then equally distracted.) Venables (1958) reports a possible confirmation of this interpretation. He gave a multiple-choice reaction-time test in which the number of stimuli were varied from one to eight, to a group of normals, and a group of paranoid schizophrenics. When the relationship between the "bits" of information conveyed at each difficulty level, and reaction-time was examined, the curves suggested that the schizophrenics reacted at each level precisely as if the lights conveyed more information for them than for the normal subjects. That is, they reacted as if they were performing a more complex discrimination than the normals. This could possibly be because they have not only to distinguish between the lights, but also between the lights and the irrelevant stimuli they are unable to inhibit, or filter out. There is, however, one set of results which is difficult to reconcile with this hypothesis. Payne, Matussek and George (1959) found that a group of eighteen schizophrenics were neither significantly slower nor significantly more variable on a simple visual reaction-time test than a group of sixteen matched neurotics, although these same schizophrenics were significantly more overinclusive on a number of tests of concept formation than were the neurotics.

Most of the data so far discussed were derived from experiments on schizophrenics. There was no evidence that endogenous depressives are not equally overinclusive. Thus overinclusion might be an abnormality common to all psychotic patients. Indeed, Payne and Hirst (1957) in a small study found that eleven cases of endogenous depressives were significantly more overinclusive on the Epstein test than a matched group of fourteen normal people.

Payne and Hewlett (to be published) conducted a large scale study partly to determine whether overinclusion was an abnormality common to all psychotics, or specific to schizophrenics. A carefully matched group of twenty schizophrenics, twenty endogenous depressives, twenty neurotics and twenty normal people was given a number of tests of overinclusion, slowness (mental, motor and perceptual), and concreteness, along with other miscellaneous tests. In all twenty-three measures of overinclusion were obtained. Of these, thirteen were regarded as relatively "pure" measures, uncontaminated by other factors. The remainder were thought also to be measures of general psychomotor slowness. The tests from which these measures were derived included the Benjamin Proverbs test, the Goldstein Object Sorting test, the Shaw test, an object classification test, the Epstein test, the Luchins *Einstellung* test, and the Leiter-Partington Pathways test. All the measures of overinclusion produced mean differences in the expected direction. Only the schizophrenics had high (overinclusive) mean scores, the other three groups having very similar means. For the thirteen theoretically "pure" measures of overinclusion, six of these mean differences were significant.

All the tests for the combined group were intercorrelated and factor-analysed. It was predicted that the factor of overinclusion should be that factor which maximized the differences between the schizophrenics and the depressives. Such a factor was obtained by a suitable rotation in conjunction with a discriminant function analysis, and it was shown that the eight highest loadings were obtained by tests regarded as "pure" measures of overinclusion. Of the twenty-three measures of overinclusion, only four produced loadings on the factor opposite to prediction, and these were very small loadings indeed. Factor scores were computed for this overinclusion factor, and it was shown that schizophrenics were significantly more overinclusive than the other three groups, there being no significant differences between the depressives, the neurotics and the normals.

A factor labelled "retardation" was also obtained. This factor discriminated significantly between the combined psychotic group, and the combined normal and neurotic group, the psychotics being slower. There were no differences between the schizophrenics and the depressives, nor between the normals and the neurotics. The highest ten loadings on this factor were obtained by speed scores, and of the twenty-five loadings greater than ± 0.30, only six were not obtained by speed scores. This factor was a general factor of retardation, tests of mental, motor and perceptual slowness tending to have equally large loadings.

The correlation between the factor of retardation and the factor of overinclusion was -0.38. This was consistent with the hypothesis that an abnormal degree of overinclusion tends to produce slowness of thinking, presumably because overinclusive individuals have more data to think about for any given problem.

The third factor obtained was labelled general intelligence. It did not differentiate any of the groups significantly as they had been matched for pre-illness level.

This study suggested that the endogenous depressives, as a group, were abnormally retarded, but not overinclusive. They were relatively homogeneous with respect to retardation.

The schizophrenics, on the other hand, were extremely heterogeneous on both measures. While on average they were as retarded as the depressives, a large proportion was within the normal range, while a large proportion was more retarded than the average depressive. Similar results were obtained on the factor of overinclusion. Only about half the schizophrenics were abnormally overinclusive. Half were within the normal range, both on the factor score and on the individual tests. Half were completely outside the normal range. Schizophrenics' scores thus ranged from the most normal scores obtained, to the most abnormal scores obtained, on nearly all the measures of overinclusion. These results are consistent with most of the other studies reviewed. It is a common finding that schizophrenics as a group are extremely heterogeneous.

Payne and Hewlett concluded that schizophrenics should not be regarded as representing a single group. They suggested that there might be two groups of schizophrenics. One resembles the endogenous depressives, in that it is not abnormally overinclusive. Like the depressives, these schizophrenics are abnormally retarded. Indeed they are even slower than a depressive group. The reason for their abnormal slowness is obscure. It would be extremely interesting to discover what symptoms are found in this group. It is possible that these patients might show catatonic features and inappropriate affect (*see* Harris and Metcalfe, 1956); and might have a poor long-term prognosis.

The second group of schizophrenics are quite unlike depressives. They suffer from an abnormal degree of overinclusion. While they are slightly retarded, their slowness is merely due to their abnormal overinclusion, which causes them to over-elaborate most tasks, and thus take longer to do them. As a group, their speed scores are nearly all within the normal range. It is interesting to speculate what pattern of symptoms might be associated with this pattern of cognitive abnormality. It is tempting to relate overinclusion to paranoid delusions, and ideas of reference. Both these symptoms could be regarded as unwarranted generalizations from the facts. Patients with these symptoms often tend to perceive relationships where none exist, and to take as evidence for their views data which most people would not notice, or judge to be irrelevant (e.g. certain gestures). Payne and Hewlett (to be published) found that in their schizophrenic group, the two most overinclusive individuals, as judged by test scores, had been diagnosed as a paranoid schizophrenic, although they did not attempt to relate symptomatology to test scores systematically because of the small numbers in each group. It is possible that this group of schizophrenics suffers little general deterioration, and has a better long-term prognosis. Indeed, what general deterioration it demonstrates may be due solely to overinclusive concept formation.

It has been suggested that overinclusion is due to an abnormal degree of stimulus generalization. Mednick (1958) has independently formulated the same hypothesis, and has suggested that this might be due to an abnormally high drive level. Whatever the underlying cause, several studies have found evidence consistent with an abnormal degree of stimulus generalization in early schizophrenics (Garmezy, 1952; Bender and Schilder, 1930; Mednick, 1955). Carson (1958) failed to confirm these earlier findings, but none of these authors have attempted to relate stimulus generalization to any specific pattern of symptoms. Differences between the schizophrenic groups tested could account for such discrepancies. So far, no attempt appears to have been made to investigate the relationship between specific tests of overinclusion, and stimulus generalization gradient.

Summary and Conclusions

1. There is no evidence that schizophrenics or any other functional psychotic groups are abnormally concrete, or unable to form new concepts, although elderly demented patients are concrete in this sense.

2. Some schizophrenics may, however, have difficulty in adhering to new concepts when asked to employ them over a period of time.

3. There is considerable evidence that some schizophrenics form unusual and even eccentric concepts, and

that this abnormality is related to their low scores on tests of general intelligence. It is also associated with the severity of the illness, and with a lack of sociability, perhaps because it makes communication with others difficult. This abnormality can probably be exaggerated by a strong emotional disturbance, perhaps because of the distracting effect.

4. Some schizophrenics employ abnormally overinclusive concepts in the sense that they incorporate ideas which for normal people are only peripherally related, or irrelevant. Overinclusion makes their thinking both more abstract and more vague. It may be due to a specific learning disability, an abnormal degree of stimulus generalization perhaps caused by a defect in the ability to develop inhibition.

5. These abnormalities of concept formation may partly explain why some schizophrenics tend to make an abnormal number of errors on cognitive tests.

6. Overinclusion might be regarded as some failure of the mental filter mechanism which excludes stimuli which are irrelevant to the action of the moment. This could partly account for cognitive slowness in some schizophrenics, which could be due to the fact that these individuals consider aspects of cognitive problems excluded as irrelevant by normal people. This same abnormality might be the direct cause of the abnormal flexibility (both adaptive and creative) and originality of some schizophrenic patients.

7. It is not known what specific symptoms are related to abnormal overinclusion. It is conceivable, however, that it is responsible for the development of paranoid delusions and ideas of reference.

GENERAL SUMMARY AND CONCLUSIONS

It is difficult to produce a short comprehensive summary of the numerous facts and interrelationships which have been discussed. This summary is an attempt to bring together some of the main findings in a more integrated, but much more speculative form. The main difficulty throughout is that we have been forced to sidestep the central issue. There is no general theory of cognition, and those facts which were easiest to integrate and explain turned out in the main to be related to essentially non-cognitive processes like learning.

Problem-solving in normal people involves a number of probably independent processes. Perception is involved in the recognition of the data of the problem. Memory span is required to hold certain facts in mind temporarily while they are manipulated. Learning, with all its parameters, influences both the immediate ability to memorize additional vital facts too numerous for span of attention to incorporate and the ability to remember past experiences relevant

to the problem. It has even produced the concepts according to which the data are manipulated. At this point, however, cognition occurs. In some way, all these data are processed and an answer results. New concepts may spring suddenly to mind to assist this in a manner quite unexplained. People vary in the speed with which this processing occurs, in the accuracy of their answers, and in the time they are willing to devote to the task. Exactly how it is done, and what produces the error has never been satisfactorily explained.

Several apparently unrelated abnormalities seem to produce different "constellations" of cognitive abnormalities. Perhaps the most basic of all is a disorder of perception. This can interfere with the whole process from the very beginning, since the data of the problem are not obtained correctly. Errors in solution are therefore likely to occur. What causes this perceptual disability is not known, but it seems common in psychosis. It may be related to other misperceptions such as hallucinations, unreality feelings or even feelings of depersonalization.

An equally serious, but perhaps quite unrelated abnormality also occurs sometimes with psychosis. The mechanism of attention itself seems to become defective. Whatever filtering mechanism ensures that only the stimuli (internal or external) that are relevant to the task enter consciousness and are processed, seems no longer able to exclude the irrelevant. This has numerous repercussions. Thinking becomes distracted by external events. It also becomes distracted by irrelevant personal thoughts and emotions which may even become mixed up with the problem. Selective perception becomes impossible, so that instead of dealing with the essence of the problem, irrelevant aspects are perceived and thought about. Problem-solving becomes slower for that reason. When new concepts are learned, the individual is not able to learn to screen out the specific irrelevant stimuli which are occasionally associated with the common elements which define the concept. Thus an overinclusive concept is learned. Indeed, as the condition becomes more severe, ideas distantly related to concepts learned in the past no longer seem to be screened out and these concepts become contaminated so that all thought becomes more vague and imprecise, and errors of reasoning increase. These individuals may well develop paranoid delusions as the result of this disorder. The only advantage this state offers is that on those occasions when normal people *mistakenly* screen out certain aspects as irrelevant to a problem (adaptive rigidity), and fail to solve it, overinclusive individuals at least obtain all the data. In fact overinclusive individuals are excessively flexible and original and occasionally this is an asset.

A completely different set of cognitive abnormalities can result from rote-learning defects. In old age and especially senile dementia, the capacity for rote learning becomes so poor that cognition is affected for this reason. The *facts* of new problems cannot be learned, and the problem cannot be solved for this reason. Any task involving the acquisition of new motor skills is affected (performance tests). Memory disorders tend to occur, not through a retention defect, but simply because new facts are never learned. For most people this only occurs with great age, so that it does not affect learning in earlier life. However, a lifelong minor handicap of this sort is produced by extreme extraversion. Extremely extraverted people are less able to learn, so that the more the cognitive task is dependent on facts which have been learned in the past, or the acquisition of new facts, the worse they tend to be. When the facts of the problem are few enough to be held in their memory span, they can solve problems accurately. When the data are too numerous however, they may have to resort to splitting up the material and obtaining partial solutions, which they combine. They cannot learn the entire set of data so as to manipulate it simultaneously. This reduces their accuracy, although it increases their speed. Personality factors associated with extraversion also play their part. Such people tend to be less persistent and more impulsive, so that they tend not to check their thinking, tending to be fast but inaccurate. Extreme introversion produces the opposite effect. Here thought is slowed down by a tendency to check and be thorough, but accuracy is increased. Introverts also tend to display "adaptive rigidity" as they can quickly build up a set which may blind them to certain possibilities.

Physiological factors may play quite a different role. Anxiety and an excess of thyroid activity tend to increase the drive level of the individual, which for some reason speeds up the tempo of thought. This in itself is a considerable advantage, since it does not necessarily have any effect at all on accuracy. Unfortunately anxiety and introversion interact. When introverted people become too anxious, they tend to produce conditioned responses to the anxiety (fears, obsessional checking) which are so distracting that they slow down thinking much more than the higher drive speeds it up. Obsessional checking can, however, increase accuracy.

Since these main types of abnormality may be independent, various combinations of them are possible in individual cases. This could produce quite a complex pattern of disability. Individual differences in pre-illness level also complicate the picture.

This account is, of course, both speculative and incomplete. If more were known about the causes of error, no doubt other patterns of disability would be discovered. What is particularly lacking is any knowledge of the way *affective* disorders and cognitive abnormalities are related. There is every reason to believe that an affective illness can produce considerable cognitive impairment. Extreme excitability and distractability obviously produce poor performance, and depressive thoughts no doubt are equally distracting. However depression may do more than this. Like some catatonic conditions it may produce an extreme slowing of mental processes which possibly has a basic physiological cause. However this, like many other problems must remain a mystery at present.

REFERENCES

Ackelsberg, S. B., Vocabulary and mental deterioration in senile psychosis, *J. Abnorm. (Soc.) Psychol.*, **39**, 393–406 (1944).

Aita, J. A., Armitage, S. G., Reitan, R. M. and Rabinovitz, A., The use of certain psychological tests in the evaluation of brain injury, *J. Gen. Psychol.*, **37**, 25–44 (1947).

ALTMAN, CHARLOTTE H. and SHAKOW, D., A comparison of the performance of matched groups of schizophrenic patients, normal subjects, and delinquent subjects on some aspects of the Stanford-Binet, *J. Educ. Psychol.*, **28**, 519–529 (1937).

ALTUS, W. D. and CLARK, J. H., Subtest variation on the Wechsler-Bellevue for two institutionalized behavior problem groups. *J. Cons. Psychol.*, **13**, 444–447 (1949).

ANGYAL, A., Disturbances in thinking in schizophrenia, in *Language and Thought in Schizophrenia*, Ed. J. S. Kasanin (Berkeley and Los Angeles, Univ. of California Press, 1946).

ANGYAL, ALICE F., Speed and pattern of perception in schizophrenic and normal persons, *Character & Pers.*, **11**, 108–127 (1942–43).

ANGYAL, ALICE F., The Diagnosis of neurotic traits by means of a new perceptual test, *J. Psychol.*, **25**, 105–135 (1948).

APPLEZWEIG, D. G., Some determinants of behavioral rigidity, *J. Abnorm. (Soc.) Psychol.* **49**, 224–228 (1954).

ARMITAGE, S. G., An analysis of certain psychological tests used for the evaluation of brain injury. *Psychol. Monogr.* **60**, (whole No. 277) (1946).

BABCOCK, HARRIET, An experiment in the measurement of mental deterioration, *Arch. Psychol.*, *N.Y.*, **18**, No. 117 (1930).

BABCOCK, HARRIET, *Dementia Praecox, a Psychological Study* (The Science Press, 1933).

BABCOCK HARRIET, Personality and efficiency of mental functioning, *Amer. J. Orthopsychiat.*, **10**, 527–531 (1940).

BABCOCK, HARRIET, *Time and the Mind* (Cambridge, Mass., Sci-Art Publishers, 1941*a*).

BABCOCK, HARRIET, The level-efficiency theory of intelligence, *J. Psychol.*, **11**, 261–270 (1941*b*).

BABCOCK, HARRIET and LEVY, LYDIA, *Manual of Directions for the Revised Examination of the Measurement of Efficiency of Mental Functioning* (Chicago, Stoelting, 1940).

BALINSKY, B., An analysis of the mental factors of various age groups from 9–60, *Genet. Psychol. Monogr.*, **23**, 191–234 (1941).

BALKEN, EVA R., A delineation of schizophrenic language and thought in a test of imagination, *J. Psychol.*, **16**, 239–271 (1943).

BANNATYNE, A. D., An experimental study of introversion-extraversion by means of projective techniques, *Unpub. Ph.D. Thesis, Univ. of London Lib.* (1953).

BARNES, GERTRUDE, A comparison of the results of tests in the Terman Scale between cases of manic-depressive and *dementia praecox* psychoses. *J. Nerv. Ment. Dis.* **60**, 579–589 (1924).

BARNES, M. R. and FETTERMAN, J. E., Mentality of dispensary epileptic patients, *Arch. Neurol. Psychiat.*, *Chicago*, **40**, 903–910 (1938).

BARRON, F., The disposition towards originality, *J. Abnorm. (Soc.) Psychol.*, **51**, 478–485 (1955).

BECKER, W. C., A genetic approach to the interpretation and evaluation of the process-reactive distinction in schizophrenia, *J. Abnorm. (Soc.) Psychol.*, **53**, 229–236 (1956).

BEECH, H. R., An investigation of the performance on a perceptual-motor task by psychiatric patients with special reference to brain damage, *Unpubl. Ph.D. Thesis, Univ. of London Lib.* (1956).

BEIER, E. G., The effect of induced anxiety on flexibility of intellectual functioning, *Psychol. Monogr.*, **65**, No. 9. (Whole No. 326) (1951).

BELL, J. E., *Projective Techniques* (New York, Longmans, Green & Co., 1948).

BENDER, LAURETTA, *A Visual Motor Gestalt Test and its Clinical Uses*, Res. Monogr., No. 3, New York, (1938).

BENDER, LAURETTA and SCHILDER, P., Unconditioned reactions to pain in schizophrenia, *Amer. J. Psychiat.*, **10**, 365–384 (1930).

BENJAMIN, J. D., A method for distinguishing and evaluating formal thinking disorders in schizophrenia, in *Language and Thought in Schizophrenia*, Ed. J. S. Kasanin (Berkeley and Los Angeles, Univ. Calif. Press, 1946).

BERG, ESTA, A simple objective technique for measuring flexibility in thinking, *J. Gen. Psychol.*, **39**, 15–22 (1948).

BINDER, A., Schizophrenic intellectual impairment: uniform or differential? *J. Abnorm. (Soc.) Psychol.* **52**, 11–18 (1956).

BIRREN, J. E., Psychological examinations of children who later became psychotic, *J. Abnorm. (Soc.) Psychol.*, **39**, 84–96 (1944).

BIRREN, J. E., A factorial analysis of the Wechsler-Bellevue Scale given to an elderly population, *J. Cons. Psychol.*, **16**, 399–405 (1952).

BLEULER, E., *Dementia Praecox or the Group of Schizophrenias* (Trans. J. Zinkin) (New York, International Univ. Press, 1950).

BLEULER, E., Autistic thinking, in *Organization and Pathology of Thought*, Ed. D. Rapaport (New York, Columbia Univ. Press, 1951).

BOLLES, MARJORIE and GOLDSTEIN, K., A study of impairment of "abstract behaviour" in schizophrenic patients, *Psychiat. Quart.*, **12**, 42–65 (1939).

BOTWINICK, J. and BIRREN, J. E., The measurement of intellectual decline in the senile psychoses, *J. Cons. Psychol.*, **15**, 145–150 (1951).

BRAAT, J. P., Die experimentelle Psychologie und Kretschmers Konstitutionstypen, *Monatschrift Psychiatr. u. Neurol.*, **94**, 273–297 (1936).

BRADFORD, E. J. G., Performance tests in the diagnosis of mental deficiency, *Brit. J. Med. Psychol.*, **19**, 394–414 (1941–43).

BRECKER, S., The value of diagnostic signs for schizophrenia on the Wechsler-Bellevue Adult Intelligence test, *Psychiat. Quart. Suppl.*, **20**, 58–64 (1946).

BRENGELMANN, J. C., The effect of repeated electrical stimulation upon the capacity of depressed patients to learn visual patterns, *Ph.D. Thesis, Univ. of London Lib.* (1953*a*).

BRENGELMANN, J. C., Der visuelle Objekterkennungstest, *Z. f. exp. u. angew. Psychol.*, **1**, 422–452 (1953*b*).

BRENGELMANN, J. C., Spaltungsfähigkeit als Persönlichkeitsmerkmal (Kritischer Literaturbericht.) *Z. f. exp. u. angew. Psychol.*, **2**, 455 (1954).

BRENGELMANN, J. C., The effect of exposure time in immediate recall on abnormal and questionnaire criteria of personality, *J. Ment. Sci.*, **104**, 665–680 (1958*a*).

BRENGELMANN, J. C., Learning in neurotics and psychotics, *Acta Psychol.*, **13**, 371–388 (1958*b*).

BRENGELMANN, J. C. and PINILLOS, J. L., Bilderkennung als Persönlichkeitstest, *Z. f. exp. u. angew. Psychol.*, **1**, 480–500 (1953).

BROADBENT, D. E., A mechanical model for human attention and immediate memory, *Psychol. Rev.*, **64**, 205–215 (1957).

BROADHURST, ANNE H., Some variables affecting speed of mental functioning in schizophrenics, *Unpubl. Ph.D. Thesis, Univ. of London Lib.* (1957).

BRODY, M. B., A survey of the results of intelligence tests in psychosis, *Brit. J. Med. Psychol.*, **19**, 215–261 (1941–43).

BROWN, R. R. and PARTINGTON, J. E., The intelligence of the narcotic drug addict, *J. Gen. Psychol.*, **26**, 175–179 (1942).

BROWN, R. W., A determinant of the relationship between rigidity and authoritarianism, *J. Abnorm. (Soc.) Psychol.*, **48**, 469–476 (1953).

BUSS, A. H., Stimulus generalization as a function of clinical anxiety and direction of generalization, *J. Abnorm. (Soc.) Psychol.*, **50**, 271–273 (1955).

BYCHOWSKI, G., Physiology of schizophrenic thinking, *J. Nerv. Ment. Dis.*, **98**, 368–386 (1943).

CALLAGAN, J. E., The effect of electro-convulsive therapy on the test performances of hospitalized depressed patients, *Unpubl. Ph.D. Thesis, Univ. of London Lib.* (1952).

CALVIN, A. D., KOONS, P. B., BINGHAM, J. L. and FINK, H. H., A further investigation of the relationship between manifest anxiety and intelligence, *J. Cons. Psychol.*, **19**, 280–282 (1955).

CAMERON, D. E., Certain aspects of defects of recent memory occurring in psychoses of the senium, *Arch. Neurol. Psychiat. Chicago*, **43**, 987–992 (1940).

CAMERON, N., Reasoning, regression and communication in schizophrenics, *Psych. Monogr.*, **50**, No. 221, 1–33 (1938a).

CAMERON, N., A study of thinking in senile deterioration and schizophrenic disorganization, *Amer. J. Psychol.*, **51**, 650–664 (1938b).

CAMERON, N., Deterioration and regression in schizophrenic thinking, *J. Abnorm. (Soc.) Psychol.*, **34**, 265–270 (1939a).

CAMERON, N., Schizophrenic thinking in a problem-solving situation, *J. Ment. Sci.*, **85**, 1012–1035 (1939b).

CAMERON, N., The functional psychoses, in *Personality and the Behavior Disorders*, Vol. II. Ed. J. McV. Hunt (New York, Ronald Press, 1944).

CAMERON, N., *The Psychology of Behavior Disorders* (Boston, Houghton Mifflin, 1947).

CAMERON, N. and MAGARET, ANN, Experimental studies in thinking: I. Scattered speech in the responses of normal subjects to incomplete sentences, *J. Exp. Psychol.*, **39**, 617–627 (1949).

CAMERON, N. and MAGARET, ANN, Correlates of scattered speech in the responses of normal subjects to incomplete sentences, *J. Gen. Psychol.*, **43**, 77–84 (1950).

CAMERON, N. and MAGARET, ANN, *Behavior Pathology* (Boston, Houghton Mifflin, 1951).

CAMPBELL, D., A study of some sensory-motor functions in psychiatric patients, *Unpubl. Ph.D. Thesis, Univ. of London Lib.* (1957).

CAPPS, H. M., Vocabulary changes in mental deterioration, *Arch. Psychol., N.Y.*, No. 242 (1939).

CARP, A., Performance on the Wechsler-Bellevue Scale and insulin shock therapy, *J. Abnorm. (Soc.) Psychol.*, **45**, 127–136 (1950).

CARSON, R. C., Intralist similarity and verbal rote learning performance of schizophrenic and cortically damaged patients, *J. Abnorm. (Soc.) Psychol.*, **57**, 99–106 (1958).

CASTANEDA, A., Reaction time and response amplitude as a function of anxiety and stimulus intensity, *J. Abnorm. (Soc.) Psychol.*, **53**, 225–228 (1956).

CATTELL, R. B., The measurement of adult intelligence, *Psychol. Bull.* 40, 153–192 (1943).

CATTELL, R. B., The riddle of perseveration: I. "Creative effort" and disposition rigidity. II. Solution in terms of personality structure, *J. Personality*, **14**, 229–238, 239–267 (1946).

CATTELL, R. B. and TINER, L. G., The varieties of structural rigidity, *J. Personality*, **17**, 321–341 (1949).

CHAPMAN, L. J., Distractibility in the conceptual performance of schizophrenics, *J. Abnorm. (Soc.) Psychol.*, **53**, 286–291 (1956).

CHAPMAN, L. J. and TAYLOR, JANET, A., Breadth of deviate concepts used by schizophrenics, *J. Abnorm. (Soc.) Psychol.*, **54**, 118–123 (1957).

CHILD, I. L. and WATERHOUSE, I. K., Frustration and the quality of performance: II. A theoretical statement, *Psychol. Rev.* 60, 127–139 (1953).

CHODORKOFF, B. and MUSSEN, P., Qualitative aspects of the vocabulary responses of normals and schizophrenics, *J. Cons. Psychol.*, **16**, 43–48 (1952).

CLEVELAND, S. E. and DYSINGER, D. W., Mental deterioration in senile psychosis, *J. Abnorm. (Soc.) Psychol.*, **39**, 368–372 (1944).

COHEN, B. D., Motivation and performance in schizophrenia, *J. Abnorm. (Soc.) Psychol.*, **52**, 186–190 (1956).

COHEN, B. D., SENF, RITA and HUSTON, P. E., Effect of amobarbital (amytal) and affect on conceptual thinking in schizophrenia, depression, and neurosis, *A.M.A. Arch. Neurol. Psychiat.*, **71**, 171–180 (1954).

COHEN, J., Wechsler Memory Scale performance of psychoneurotic, organic, and schizophrenic groups, *J. Cons. Psychol.*, **14**, 371–375 (1950).

COHEN, J., Factors underlying Wechsler-Bellevue performance of three neuropsychiatric groups, *J. Abnorm. (Soc.) Psychol.*, **47**, 359–365 (1952a).

COHEN, J., A Factor-analytically based rationale for the Wechsler-Bellevue, *J. Cons. Psychol.*, **16**, 272–277 (1952b).

COHEN, J., The factorial structure of the WAIS between early adulthood and old age, *J. Cons. Psychol.*, **21**, 283–290 (1957).

COHEN, L. H., Imagery and its relations to schizophrenic symptoms, *J. Ment. Sci.*, **84**, 284–346 (1938).

COLLINS, A. LOUISE, Epileptic intelligence, *J. Cons. Psychol.*, **15**, 392–399 (1951).

COMBS, A. W., Intelligence from a perceptual point of view, *J. Abnorm. (Soc.) Psychol.*, **47**, 662–673 (1952).

COMBS, A. W. and TAYLOR, C., The effect of perception of mild degrees of threat on performance, *J. Abnorm. (Soc.) Psychol.*, **47**, 420–424 (1952).

COWEN, E. L., The influence of varying degrees of

psychological stress on problem-solving rigidity, *J. Abnorm. (Soc.) Psychol.*, **47**, 512–519 (1952*a*).

COWEN, E. L., Stress reduction and problem-solving rigidity, *J. Cons. Psychol.*, **16**, 425–428 (1952*b*).

COWEN, E. L., HEILIZER, F. and AXELROD, H. S., Self-concept conflict indicators and learning, *J. Abnorm. (Soc.) Psychol.*, **51**, 242–245 (1955).

COWEN, E. L. and THOMPSON, G. G., Problem-solving rigidity and personality structure, *J. Abnorm. (Soc.) Psychol.*, **46**, 165–176 (1951).

COWEN, E. L., WIENER, M. and HESS, JUDITH, Generalization of problem-solving rigidity, *J. Cons. Psychol.*, **17**, 100–103 (1953).

CROWN, S., Notes on an experimental study of intellectual deterioration, *Brit. Med. J.*, **2**, 684–685 (1949).

DAMBACH, K., Die Mehrfacharbeit und ihre typologische Bedeutung, *Z. f. Psychol.*, Erg.-Bd., **14**, 159–236 (1929).

DANA, R. H., Manifest anxiety, intelligence and psychopathology, *J. Cons. Psychol.*, **21**, 38–40 (1957).

DASTON, P. G., KING, G. F. and ARMITAGE, S. G., Distortion in paranoid schizophrenia, *J. Cons. Psychol.*, **17**, 50–53 (1953).

DAVIDS, A., Generality and consistency of relations between the alienation syndrome and cognitive processes, *J. Abnorm. (Soc.) Psychol.*, **51**, 61–67 (1955*a*).

DAVIDS, A., Some personality and intellectual correlates of intolerance of ambiguity, *J. Abnorm. (Soc.) Psychol.*, **51**, 415–420 (1955*b*).

DAVIDSON, MARSH, A study of schizophrenic performance on the Stanford-Binet scale, *Brit. J. Med. Psychol.*, **17**, 93–97 (1938).

DAVIDSON, MARSH, Studies in the application of mental tests to psychotic patients, *Brit, J. Med. Psychol.*, **18**, 44–52 (1939).

DAVIS, R. H. and HARRINGTON, R. W., The effect of stimulus class on the problem-solving behavior of schizophrenics and normals, *J. Abnorm. (Soc.) Psychol.*, **54**, 126–128 (1957).

DE LA GARZA, C. O. and WORCHEL, P., Time and space orientation in schizophrenics, *J. Abnorm. (Soc.) Psychol.*, **52**, 191–194 (1956).

DERNER, G. F., ABORN, M. and CANTER, A. H., The reliability of the Wechsler-Bellevue subtest scales, *J. Cons. Psychol.*, **14**, 172–179 (1950).

DE SOTO, C. and LEIBOWITZ, H., Perceptual organization and intelligence: a further study, *J. Abnorm. (Soc.) Psychol.*, **53**, 334–337 (1956).

DISPENSA, JOHNETTE, Relationship of the thyroid with intelligence and personality, *J. Psychol.*, **6**, 181–186 (1938).

DOCTER, R. F. and WINDER, C. L., Delinquent *v.* Non-delinquent performance on the Porteus Qualitative Maze Test, *J. Cons. Psychol.*, **18**, 71–73 (1954).

DOPPELT, J. E. and WALLACE, W. L., Standardization of the Wechsler Adult Intelligence Scale for older persons, *J. Abnorm. (Soc.) Psychol.*, **51**, 312–330 (1955).

DUNCKER, K., On problem solving, *Psychol. Monogr.*, **58**, No. 5 (1945).

ELLSWORTH, R. B., The regression of schizophrenic language, *J. Cons. Psychol.*, **15**, 378–391 (1951).

ENKE, W., Experimentalpsychologische Studien zur Konstitutionsforschung. (Sinnes-und denkpsychologische Untersuchungen), *Z. ges. Neurol. Psychiatr.*, **114**, 770–794 (1928).

ENKE, W., Experimentalpsychologische Studien zur Konstitutionsforschung. (Psychomotorische Untersuchungen), *Z. ges. Neurol. Psychiatr.*, **118**, 798–817 (1929).

ENKE, W., Die Psychomotorik der Konstitutionstypen, *Z. angew. Psychol.*, **36**, 237–287 (1930).

ENKE, W. and HEISING, L., Experimenteller Beitrag zur Psychologie der "Aufmerksamkeitsspaltung" bei den Konstitutionstypen, *Z. ges. Neurol. Psychiatr.*, **118**, 634–644 (1929).

EPSTEIN, S., Overinclusive thinking in a schizophrenic and a control group, *J. Cons. Psychol.*, **17**, 384–388 (1953).

ERIKSEN, C. W., Some personality correlates of stimulus generalization under stress, *J. Abnorm. (Soc.) Psychol.*, **49**, 561–565 (1954).

ERIKSON, C. W. and WECHSLER, H., Some effects of experimentally induced anxiety upon discrimination behavior, *J. Abnorm. (Soc.) Psychol.*, **51**, 458–463 (1955).

EYSENCK, H. J., *The Dimensions of Personality* (London, Routledge & Kegan Paul, 1947).

EYSENCK, H. J., *The Scientific Study of Personality* (London, Routledge & Kegan Paul, 1952).

EYSENCK, H. J., *The Structure of Human Personality* (London, Methuen, 1953).

EYSENCK, H. J., GRANGER, G. W. and BRENGELMANN, J. C., *Perceptual Processes and Mental Illness.* Maudsley Monographs No. 2 (London, Institute of Psychiatry, 1957).

EYSENCK, MARGARET D., An exploratory study of mental organization in senility, *J. Neurol., Psychiat.*, **8**, 15–21 (1945).

EYSENCK, MARGARET D., A study of certain qualitative aspects of problem-solving behaviour in senile dementia patients, *J. Ment. Sci.*, **91**, 337–345 (1945).

EYSENCK, S. B. G., A dimensional analysis of mental abnormality, *Unpubl. Ph.D. Thesis, Univ. of London Lib.* (1955).

FEIFEL, H., Qualitative differences in the vocabulary responses of normals and abnormals, *Genet. Psychol. Monogr.*, **39**, 151–204 (1949).

FELDMAN, M. J. and DRASGOW, J., A visual-verbal test for schizophrenia, *Psychiat. Quart. Suppl.*, part 1, 1–10 (1951).

FEY, ELIZABETH T., The performance of young schizophrenics and young normals on the Wisconsin card sorting test, *J. Cons. Psychol.*, **15**, 311–319 (1951).

FISHER, S., Patterns of personality rigidity and some of their determinants, *Psychol. Monogr.*, **64**, No. 1 (Whole No. 307) (1950).

FLAVELL, J. H., Abstract thinking and social behavior in schizophrenia, *J. Abnorm. (Soc.) Psychol*, **52**, 208–211 (1956).

FOOKS, G. and THOMAS, R. R., Differential qualitative performance of delinquents on the Porteus maze, *J. Cons. Psychol.*, **21**, 351–353 (1957).

FORSTER, NORA C., VINACKE, W. E. and DIGMAN, J. M., Flexibility and rigidity in a variety of problem situations, *J. Abnorm. (Soc.) Psychol.*, **50**, 211–216 (1955).

FOULDS, G. A., Temperamental differences in maze

performance. Part I. Characteristic differences among psychoneurotics, *Brit. J. Psychol.*, **42**, 209–217 (1951).

FOULDS, G. A., Temperamental differences in maze performance. Part II. The effect of distraction and electroconvulsive therapy on psychomotor retardation, *Brit. J. Psychol.*, **43**, 33–41 (1952).

FOULDS, G. A., The ratio of general intellectual ability to vocabulary among psychoneurotics, *Internat. J. Soc. Psychiat.*, **1**, 5–12 (1956).

FOX, CHARLOTTE, and BIRREN, J. E., Intellectual deterioration in the aged: Agreement between the Wechsler-Bellevue and the Babcock-Levy, *J. Cons. Psychol.*, **14**, 305–310 (1950).

FRENCH, ELIZABETH, G., Interrelation among some measures of rigidity under stress and non stress conditions, *J. Abnorm. (Soc.) Psychol.*, **51**, 114–118 (1955).

GARBER, R. G., Influence of cognitive and affective factors in learning and retaining attitudinal materials, *J. Abnorm. (Soc.) Psychol.*, **51**, 384–389 (1955).

GARDNER, G. E., The learning ability of schizophrenics, *Amer. J. Psychiat.*, **11**, 247–252 (1931).

GARDNER, G. E., Childhood physical and mental measurements of psychotic patients, *Amer. J. Orthopsychiat.* **10**, 327–342 (1940).

GARFIELD, S. L., A preliminary appraisal of Wechsler-Bellevue scatter patterns in schizophrenia, *J. Cons. Psychol.*, **12**, 32–36 (1948).

GARFIELD, S. L., An evaluation of Wechsler-Bellevue patterns in schizophrenia, *J. Cons. Psychol.*, **13**, 279–287 (1949).

GARFIELD, S. L. and FEY, W. F., A comparison of the Wechsler-Bellevue and Shipley-Hartford Scales as measures of mental impairment, *J. Cons. Psychol.*, **12**, 259–264 (1948).

GARMEZY, N., Stimulus differentiation by schizophrenic and normal subjects under conditions of reward and punishment, *J. Personality*, **20**, 253–276 (1952).

GERSTEIN, REVA A., A suggested method for analyzing and extending the use of Bellevue-Wechsler vocabulary responses, *J. Cons. Psychol.*, **13**, 366–370 (1949).

GILBERT, J., Mental efficiency in senescense, *Arch. Psychol.*, No. 188 (1935).

GILHOOLY, F. M., The relationship between variability and ability on the Wechsler-Bellevue, *J. Cons. Psychol.*, **14**, 46–48 (1950).

GILLILAND, A. R., WITTMAN, PHYLLIS and GOLDMAN, M., Patterns and scatter of mental abilities in various psychoses, *J. Gen. Psychol.*, **29**, 251–260 (1943).

GOBETZ, W., A quantification, standardization, and validation of the Bender-Gestalt test on normal and neurotic adults, *Psychol. Monogr.*, **67**, No. 6 (Whole No. 346) (1953).

GOLDMAN, ROSALINE, GREENBLATT, M. and COON, G. P., Use of the Bellevue-Wechsler scale in clinical psychiatry, *J. Nerv. Ment. Dis.*, **104**, 144–179 (1946).

GOLDSTEIN, K., *The Organism* (New York, American Book Co., 1939a).

GOLDSTEIN, K., The significance of special mental tests for diagnosis and prognosis in schizophrenia, *Amer. J. Psychiat.*, **96**, 575–578 (1939b).

GOLDSTEIN, K., *Human Nature* (Cambridge, Mass., Harvard Univ. Press, 1940).

GOLDSTEIN, K., Concerning rigidity, *Character & Pers.*, **11**, 209–226 (1942).

GOLDSTEIN, K., Methodological approach to the study of schizophrenic thought disorder, in *Language and Thought in Schizophrenia*, Ed. J. S. Kasanin (Berkeley and Los Angeles, Univ. of California Press, 1946).

GOLDSTEIN, K. and SCHEERER, M., Abstract and concrete behaviour, an experimental study with special tests, *Psychol. Monogr.*, **53**, No. 2, (1941).

GOLLIN, E. S. and ROSENBERG, S., Concept formation and impressions of personality, *J. Abnorm. (Soc.) Psychol.*, **52**, 39–42 (1956).

GOODSTEIN, L. D., Intellectual rigidity and social attitudes, *J. Abnorm. (Soc.) Psychol.*, **48**, 345–353 (1953).

GOODSTEIN, L. D. and FARBER, I. E., On the relation between A-Scale scores and digit symbol performance, *J. Cons. Psychol.*, **21**, 152–154 (1957).

GORHAM, D. R., Use of the proverbs test for differentiating schizophrenics from normals, *J. Cons. Psychol.*, **20**, 435–440 (1956).

GRAHAM, VIRGINIA T., Psychological studies of hypoglycemia therapy, *J. Psychol.*, **10**, 327–358 (1940).

GRANICK, S., Intellectual performance as related to emotional instability in children, *J. Abnorm. (Soc.) Psychol.*, **51**, 653–656 (1955).

GRANT, D. A., Perceptual versus analytic responses to the number concept of a Weigl-type card sorting test, *J. Exp. Psychol.*, **41**, 23–29 (1951).

GRANT, D. A., JONES, O. R. and TALLANTIS, BILLIE, The relative difficulty of the number, form and color concepts of a Weigl-type thinking and reasoning problem, *J. Exp. Psychol.*, **39**, 552–557 (1949).

GUILFORD, J. P., The structure of intellect, *Psychol. Bull.*, **53**, 267–293 (1956).

GUILFORD, J. P., FRICK, J. W., CHRISTENSEN, P. R. and MERRIFIELD, P. R., A factor-analytic study of flexibility in thinking, *Univ. S. Calif. lab. report*, No. 18 (1957).

GUILFORD, J. P., WILSON, R. C., CHRISTENSEN, P. R. and LEWIS, D. S., A factor-analytic study of creative thinking, *Univ. S. Calif. Lab. Report*, No. 4 (1951).

HALL, K. R. L., The testing of abstraction, with special reference to impairment in schizophrenia, *Brit. J. Med. Psychol.*, **24**, 118–131 (1951).

HALL, MARGARET, E., Mental and physical efficiency of women drug addicts, *J. Abnorm. (Soc.) Psychol.*, **33**, 332–345 (1938).

HAMISTER, R. C., The test-retest reliability of the Wechsler-Bellevue Test (Form I) for a neuropsychiatric population, *J. Cons. Psychol.*, **13**, 39–43 (1949).

HANFMANN, EUGENIA, Thought disturbances in schizophrenia as revealed by performance in a Picture Completion Test, *J. Abnorm. (Soc.) Psychol.*, **34**, 249–264 (1939a).

HANFMANN, EUGENIA, A qualitative analysis of the Healy pictorial completion test II, *Amer. J. Orthopsychiat.*, **9**, 325–330 (1939b).

HANFMANN, EUGENIA, Analysis of the thinking disorder in a case of schizophrenia, *A.M.A. Arch. Neurol. Psychiat.*, **41**, 568–579 (1939c).

HANFMAN, EUGENIA, A study of personal patterns in an intellectual performance, *Character & Pers.*, **9**, 315–325 (1941).

HANFMANN, EUGENIA and KASANIN, J., A method for the study of concept formation, *J. Psychol.*, **3**, 521–540 (1937).

HANFMANN, EUGENIA and KASANIN, J., Conceptual thinking in schizophrenia, *Nerv. Ment. Dis. Monogr.*, **67**, (1942).

HARBINSON, M. R., An investigation of deterioration of "General Intelligence" or "G" in psychotic patients, *Brit. J. Med. Psychol.*, **16**, 146–148 (1937).

HARPER, A. E. JR., Discrimination of the types of schizophrenia by the Wechsler-Bellevue Scale, *J. Cons. Psychol.*, **14**, 290–296 (1950a).

HARPER, A. E. JR., Discrimination between matched schizophrenics and normals by the Wechsler-Bellevue scale, *J. Cons. Psychol.*, **14**, 351–357 (1950b).

HARRINGTON, R. and EHRMANN, J. C., Complexity of response as a factor in the vocabulary performance of schizophrenics, *J. Abnorm. (Soc.) Psychol.*, **49**, 362–364 (1954).

HARRIS, A. and METCALFE, MARYSE, Inappropriate affect, *J. Neurol., Psychiat.*, **19**, 308–313 (1956).

HARRIS, A. J. and SHAKOW, D., The clinical significance of numerical measures of scatter on the Stanford-Binet, *Psychol. Bull.*, **34**, 134–150 (1937).

HARRIS, A. J. and SHAKOW, D., Scatter on the Stanford-Binet in schizophrenic, normal, and delinquent adults, *J. Abnorm. (Soc.) Psychol.*, **33**, 100–111 (1938).

HARWAY, N. I., *Einstellung* effect and goal-setting behavior, *J. Abnorm. (Soc.) Psychol.*, **50**, 339–342 (1955).

HASSOL, L., MAGARET, A. and CAMERON, N., The production of language disorganization through personalized distraction, *J. Psychol.*, **33**, 289–299 (1952).

HAUSMANN, M. F., A method to objectively demonstrate thinking difficulties, *Amer. J. Psychiat.*, **13**, 613–625 (1933).

HEALY, W., Pictorial Completion test II, *J. Appl. Psychol.*, **5**, 225–239 (1921).

HEIDBREDER, EDNA, The attainment of concepts: I. Terminology and methodology, *J. Gen. Psychol.*, **35**, 173–189 (1946a).

HEIDBREDER, EDNA, The attainment of concepts: II. The problem, *J. Gen. Psychol.*, **35**, 191–223 (1946b).

HEIDBREDER, EDNA, The attainment of concepts: III. The process, *J. Psychol.*, **24**, 93–138 (1947).

HEIDBREDER, EDNA, The attainment of concepts: VI. Exploratory experiments on conceptualization at perceptual levels, *J. Psychol.*, **26**, 193–216 (1948).

HEIDBREDER, EDNA, The attainment of concepts: VII. Conceptual achievements during card sorting, *J. Psychol.*, **27**, 3–39 (1949a).

HEIDBREDER, EDNA, The attainment of concepts: VIII. The conceptualization of verbally indicated instances, *J. Psychol.*, **27**, 263–309 (1949b).

HEIDBREDER, EDNA, BENSLEY, MARY L. and IVY, MARGARET, The attainment of concepts: IV. Regularities and levels, *J. Psychol.*, **25**, 299–329 (1948).

HEIDBREDER, EDNA and OVERSTREET, PHOEBE, The attainment of concepts: V. Critical features and contexts, *J. Psychol.*, **26**, 45–69 (1948).

HILDBRAND, H. P., A factorial study of introversion-extraversion by means of objective tests, *Unpubl. Ph.D. Thesis, Univ. of London Lib.* (1953).

HIMMELWEIT, HILDE T., The intelligence-vocabulary ratio as a measure of temperament, *J. Personality*, **14**, 93–105 (1945).

HOLZBERG, J. D. and DEANE, M. A., The diagnostic significance of an objective measure of intratest scatter on the Wechsler-Bellevue intelligence scale, *J. Cons. Psychol.*, **14**, 180–188 (1950).

HULL, C. L., The formation and retention of associations among the insane, *Amer. J. Psychol.*, **28**, 419–435 (1917).

HULL, C. L., *Principles of Behavior* (New York, Appleton-Century, 1943).

HUNT, H. F., *The Hunt-Minnesota Test for Organic Brain Damage* (test manual) (Univ. Minnesota Press, 1943a).

HUNT, H. F., A practical clinical test for organic brain damage, *J. Appl. Psychol.*, **27**, 375–386 (1943b).

HUNT, H. F., A note on the clinical use of the Hunt-Minnesota test for organic brain damage, *J. Appl. Psychol.*, **28**, 175–178 (1944).

HUNT, J. McV., Psychological loss in paretics and schizophrenics, *Amer. J. Psychol.*, **47**, 458–463 (1935).

HUNT, J. McV. and COFER, C. N., Psychological deficit, in *Personality and the Behavior Disorders*, Vol. II, Ed. J. McV. Hunt (New York, Ronald Press, 1944).

HUNT, W. A. and FRENCH, ELIZABETH, G., Some abbreviated individual intelligence scales containing non verbal items, *J. Cons. Psychol.*, **13**, 119–123 (1949).

HUNT, W. A. and OLDER, H. J., Psychometric scatter pattern as a diagnostic aid, *J. Abnorm. (Soc.) Psychol.*, **39**, 118–123 (1944).

HUSTON, P. E. and SENF, RITA, Psychopathology of schizophrenia and depression. I. Effect of amytal and amphetamine sulfate on level and maintenance of attention, *Amer. J. Psychiat.*, **109**, 131–138 (1952).

HUSTON, P. E. and SINGER, MARY M., Effect of Sodium Amytal and amphetamine sulfate on mental set in schizophrenia, *Arch. Neurol. Psychiat. Chicago*, **53**, 365–369 (1945).

INGHAM, J. G., An investigation into the relationship between memory and intelligence, *Unpubl. Ph.D. Thesis, Univ. of London Lib.* (1949).

INGHAM, J. G., Memory and intelligence, *Brit. J. Psychol.*, **43**, 20–32 (1952).

INGLIS, J., An experimental study of learning and "memory function" in elderly psychiatric patients, *J. Ment. Sci.*, **103**, 796–803 (1957).

INGLIS, J., Psychological investigations of cognitive deficit in elderly psychiatric patients, *Psychol. Bull.*, **55**, 197–214 (1958).

JACKSON, D. N., MESSICK, S. J. and SOLLEY, C. M., How "rigid" is the "authoritarian?" *J. Abnorm. (Soc.) Psychol.*, **54**, 137–140 (1957).

JACOBS, A., Formation of new associations to words selected on the basis of reaction-time—G.S.R. combinations, *J. Abnorm. (Soc.) Psychol.*, **51**, 371–377 (1955).

JASPER, H. H., Is perseveration a functional unit participating in all behavior processes? *J. Soc. Psychol.*, **2**, 28–51 (1931).

JASTAK, J., Ranking Bellevue subtest scores for diagnostic purposes, *J. Cons. Psychol.*, **17**, 403–410 (1953).

JOHNSON, ANNA P., Measuring mental deterioration by the "differential test score method," *Amer. J. Ment. Defic.*, **51**, 389–390 (1947).

JOHNSON, L. C., Wechsler-Bellevue pattern analysis in schizophrenia, *J. Cons. Psychol.*, **13**, 32–33 (1949).

JONES, H. G., Psychological factors in epilepsy: a review, *Rev. Psychol. appl.*, **3**, 209–227 (1953).

JONES, H. G., The evaluation of the significance of differences between scaled scores on the WAIS: the perpetuation of a fallacy, *J. Cons. Psychol.*, **20**, 319–320 (1956).

JOST, K. C., The level of aspiration of schizophrenic and normal subjects, *J. Abnorm. (Soc.) Psychol.*, **50**, 315–320 (1955).

KARPELES, LOTTA M., A further investigation of the Porteus Maze Test as a discriminative measure in delinquency, *J. Appl. Psychol.*, **16**, 427–437 (1932).

KASANIN, J. S., Developmental roots of schizophrenia, *Amer. J. Psychiat*, **101**, 770–776 (1945).

KASANIN, J. S., The disturbance of conceptual thinking in schizophrenia, in *Language and Thought in Schizophrenia*, Ed. J. S. Kasanin (Berkeley and Los Angeles, Univ. of California Press, 1946).

KASANIN, J. and HANFMANN, EUGENIA, Disturbances in concept formation in schizophrenia, *Arch. Neurol. Psychiat. Chicago*, **40**, 1276–1282 (1938a).

KASANIN, J. and HANFMANN, EUGENIA, An experimental study of concept formation in schizophrenia, *Amer. J. Psychiat.*, **95**, 35–52 (1938b).

KAYE, D., KIRSCHNER, P. and MANDLER, G., The effect of test anxiety on memory span in a group test situation, *J. Cons. Psychol.*, **17**, 265–266 (1953).

KEENE, M. and STONE, C. P., Mental status as related to puberty *praecox*, *Psychol. Bull.*, **34**, 123–133 (1937).

KERCK, ELISABETH, Mehrfacharbeit und Konstitutionstypus *Z. f. Menschlichen Verebungs u. Konstitutionslehre*, **24**, 337–347 (1940).

KERCK, ELISABETH, Spaltungsfähigkeit der Aufmerksamkeit und Konstitutionstypus, *Z. f. Menschlichen Verebungs u. Konstitutionslehre*, **28**, 167–176 (1944).

KERRICK, JEAN S., Some correlates of the Taylor Manifest Anxiety Scale, *J. Abnorm. (Soc.) Psychol.*, **50**, 75–77 (1955).

KERRICK, JEAN S., The effects of manifest anxiety and I.Q. on discrimination, *J. Abnorm. (Soc.) Psychol.*, **52**, 136–138 (1956).

KESSELL, ROSE, An investigation into some of the factors affecting speed of response in psychiatric patients with special reference to distraction, *Unpubl. Ph.D. Thesis, Univ. of London Lib.* (1955).

KIBLER, M., Experimental-psychologischer Beitrag zur Typenforschung, *Z. ges. Neurol. Psychiatr.*, **98**, 524–544. (1925).

KLEEMEIER, R. W. and DUDEK, F. J., A factorial investigation of flexibility, *Educ. Psychol. Measmt.*, **10**, 107–118 (1950).

KLEHR, H., Clinical intuition and test scores as a basis for diagnosis, *J. Cons. Psychol.*, **13**, 34–38 (1949).

KLEIN, G., An application of the multiple regression principle to clinical predictions, *J. Gen. Psychol.*, **38**, 159–179 (1948).

KLINEBERG, O., ASCH, S. E. and BLOCK, HELEN, An experimental study of constitutional types, *Genet. Psychol. Monogr.*, **16**, 139–219 (1934).

KLUGMAN, S. F., The effect of placement of the digits test in the Wechsler-Bellevue intelligence scale, *J. Cons. Psychol.*, **12**, 345–348 (1948).

KLUGMAN, S. F., Retention of affectively toned verbal material by normals and neurotics, *J. Abnorm. (Soc.) Psychol.*, **53**, 321–327 (1956).

KNEHR, C. A., Schizophrenic reaction time responses to variable preparatory intervals, *Amer. J. Psychiat.*, **110**, 585–588 (1954).

KOGAN, W. S., An investigation into the relationship between psychometric patterns and psychiatric diagnosis, *J. Gen. Psychol.*, **43**, 17–46 (1950).

KOUNIN, J. S., Experimental studies of rigidity. I. The measurement of rigidity in normal and feeble-minded persons. II. The explanatory power of the concept of rigidity as applied to feeble-mindedness, *Character & Pers.*, **9**, 251–272, 273–282 (1941).

KOUNIN, J., The meaning of rigidity: a reply to Heinz Werner, *Psychol. Rev.*, **55**, 157–166 (1948).

KREMER, A. H., The nature of persistence, *Stud. Psychol. Psychiat. Cath. Univ. Amer.*, **5**, 40 (1942).

KRETCH, D. and CALVIN, A., Levels of perceptual organization and cognition, *J. Abnorm. (Soc.) Psychol.*, **48**, 394–400 (1953)

KRETSCHMER, E., Experimentelle Typenpsychologie. Sinnes-und Denkpsychologische Resultate, *Z. ges. Neurol. Psychiatr.*, **113**, 776–796 (1928).

KRETSCHMER, E., *Körperbau und Charakter* (Berlin, Göttingen, Heidelberg: J. Springer, zwanzigste Aufl., 1951).

KUGELMASS, S. and FONDEUR, M. R., Zaslow's test of concept formation: reliability and validity, *J. Cons. Psychol.*, **19**, 227–229 (1955).

LANKES, W., Perseveration, *Brit. J. Psychol.*, **7**, 387–419 (1915).

LAYMAN, J. W., A quantitative study of certain changes in schizophrenic patients under the influence of sodium amytal, *J. Gen. Psychol.*, **22**, 67–86 (1940).

LEITER, R. G. and PARTINGTON, J., *Examination Manual for the Leiter-Partington Adult Scale* (Washington, D.C., Psych. Service Center Press, 1950).

LEVINE, D., Problem-solving rigidity and decision time, *J. Abnorm. (Soc.) Psychol.*, **50**, 343–344 (1955).

LEVINE, L. S., The utility of Wechsler's patterns in the diagnosis of schizophrenia, *J. Cons. Psychol.*, **13**, 28–31 (1949).

LEVITT, E. E. and ZELEN, S., The validity of the *Einstellung* test as a measure of rigidity, *J. Abnorm. (Soc.) Psychol.*, **48**, 573–580 (1953).

LEWIN, K., *A Dynamic Theory of Personality* (New York & London, McGraw-Hill, 1935).

LEWIN, K., *Principles of Topological Psychology* (New York & London, McGraw-Hill, 1936).

LEWINSKI, R. J., The psychometric pattern: I. Anxiety neurosis, *J. Clin. Psychol.*, **1**, 214–221 (1945a).

LEWINSKI, R. J., The psychometric pattern: II. Migraine, *Psychiat. Quart.*, **19**, 368–376 (1945b).

LEWINSKI, R. J., The psychometric pattern: III. Epilepsy, *Amer. J. Orthopsychiat.*, **17**, 714–722 (1947).

LEWINSKI, R. J., Vocabulary and mental measurement: a quantitative investigation and review of research, *J. Genet. Psychol.*, **72**, 247–281 (1948).

LIDZ, T., GAY, J. R. and TIETZE, C., Intelligence in cerebral deficit states and schizophrenia measured by Koh's Block Test, *Arch. Neurol. Psychiat. Chicago*, **48**, 568–582 (1942).

LONSTEIN, M., A validation of a Bender-Gestalt scoring system, *J. Cons. Psychol.*, **18**, 377–379 (1954).

LORR, M., JENKINS, R. L. and O'CONNOR, J. P., Factors descriptive of psychopathology and behaviour of hospitalized psychotics, *J. Abnorm. (Soc.) Psychol.*, **50**, 78–86 (1955).

LOVIBOND, S. H., The object sorting test and conceptual thinking in schizophrenia, *Austr. J. Psychol.*, **6**, 52–70 (1954).

LUCHINS, A. S., Mechanization in problem solving: the effect of *Einstellung*, *Psychol. Monogr.*, **54**, No. 6 (1942).

LUCHINS, A. S., Rigidity and ethnocentrism: a critique, *J. Personality*, **17**, 449–466 (1949).

LUCHINS, A. S., On recent usage of the *Einstellung*-effect as a test of rigidity, *J. Cons. Psychol.*, **15**, 89–94 (1951a).

LUCHINS, A. S., The *Einstellung* test of rigidity: its relation to concreteness of thinking, *J. Cons. Psychol.*, **15**, 303–310 (1951b).

LUCHINS, A. S. and LUCHINS, EDITH H., New experimental attempts at preventing mechanization in problem solving, *J. Gen. Psychol.*, **42**, 279–297 (1950).

McANDREW, H., Rigidity and isolation: a study of the deaf and the blind, *J. Abnorm. (Soc.) Psychol.*, **43**, 476–494 (1948).

McGAUGHRAN, L. S., Predicting language behaviour from object sorting, *J. Abnorm. (Soc.) Psych.*, **49**, 183–195 (1954).

McGAUGHRAN, L. S., Differences between schizophrenic and brain-damaged groups in conceptual aspects of object sorting, *J. Abnorm. (Soc.) Psychol.*, **54**, 44–49 (1957).

McGAUGHRAN, L. S. and MORAN, L. J., "Conceptual level" v. "Conceptual Area" analysis of object-sorting behavior of schizophrenic and nonpsychiatric groups, *J. Abnorm. (Soc.) Psychol.*, **52**, 43–50 (1956).

McKINNEY, F., HINES, RUTH R., STROTHER, G. B. and ALLEE RUTH A., Experimental frustration in a group test situation, *J. Abnorm. (Soc.) Psychol.*, **46**, 316–323 (1951).

MACARTHUR, R. S., An experimental investigation of persistence and its measurement at the secondary school level, *Unpubl. Ph.D. Thesis, Univ. of London Lib.* (1951).

MAGARET, ANN, Parallels in the behavior of schizophrenics, paretics and pre-senile non-psychotics, *J. Abnorm. (Soc.) Psychol.*, **37**, 511–528 (1942).

MAGARET, ANN and SIMPSON, MARY, A comparison of two measures of deterioration in psychotic patients, *J. Cons. Psychol.*, **12**, 265–269 (1948).

MAHER, B. A., Personality, problem solving and the *Einstellung* effect, *J. Abnorm. (Soc.) Psychol.*, **54**, 70–74 (1957).

MAHRER, A. R., A clinical study of set in intraserial learning, *J. Abnorm. (Soc.) Psychol.*, **47**, 478–481 (1952).

MAIER, N. R. F., Reasoning and learning, *Psychol. Rev.*, **38**, 332–346 (1931a).

MAIER, N. R. F., Reasoning in humans: II. The solution of a problem and its appearance in consciousness, *J. Comp. Psychol.*, **12**, 181–194 (1931b).

MAIER, N. R. F., Reasoning in humans: III. The mechanisms of equivalent stimuli and of reasoning, *J. Exp. Psychol.*, **35**, 349–360 (1945).

MAINORD, W. A., Some effects of Sodium Amytal on deteriorated schizophrenics, *J. Cons. Psychol.*, **17**, 54–57 (1953).

MALAMUD, W. and PALMER, E. M., Intellectual deterioration in the psychoses, *Arch. Neurol. Psychiat. Chicago*, **39**, 68–81 (1938).

MALMO, R. B. and WALLERSTEIN, H., Rigidity and reactive inhibition, *J. Abnorm. (Soc.) Psychol.*, **50**, 345–348 (1955).

MALTZMAN, J., Thinking: From a behaviouristic point of view, *Psychol. Rev.*, **62**, 275–286 (1955).

MANDLER, G. and SARASON, S. B., A study of anxiety and learning, *J. Abnorm. (Soc.) Psychol.*, **47**, 166–173 (1952a).

MANDLER, G. and SARASON, S. B., The effect of prior experience and subjective failure on the evocation of test anxiety, *J. Personality*, **21**, 336–341 (1952b).

MANN, C. W. and MANN, HELENE P., Age and intelligence of a group of juvenile delinquents, *J. Abnorm. (Soc.) Psychol.*, **34**, 351–360 (1939).

MANSON, M. P. and GRAYSON, H. M., The Shipley-Hartford Retreat Scale as a measure of intellectual impairment for military prisoners, *J. Appl. Psychol.*, **31**, 67–81 (1947).

MASON, C. F., Pre-illness intelligence of mental hospital patients, *J. Cons. Psychol.*, **20**, 297–300 (1956).

MATARAZZO, J. D. and PHILLIPS, JEANNE S., Digit symbol performance as a function of increasing levels of anxiety, *J. Cons. Psychol.*, **19**, 131–134 (1955).

MATARAZZO, RUTH G., The relationship of manifest anxiety to Wechsler-Bellevue subtest performance, *J. Cons. Psychol.*, **19**, 218 (1955).

MATHEWS, RAVENNA, HARDYCK, C. and SARBIN, T. R., Self-organization as a factor in the performance of selected cognitive tasks, *J. Abnorm. (Soc.) Psychol.*, **48**, 500–502 (1953).

MAYZNER, M. S., SERSEN, E. and TRESSELT, M. E., The Taylor manifest anxiety scale and intelligence, *J. Cons. Psychol.*, **19**, 401–403 (1955).

MEDNICK, S. A., Distortions in the gradient of stimulus generalization related to cortical brain damage and schizophrenia, *J. Abnorm. (Soc.) Psychol.*, **51**, 536–542 (1955).

MEDNICK, S. A., A learning theory approach to Schizophrenia, *Psychol. Bull.*, **55**, 316–327 (1958).

MIRIN, B., The formal aspects of schizophrenic verbal communication, *Genet. Psychol. Monogr.*, **52**, 151–190 (1955).

MILLER, D. R., Responses of psychiatric patients to threat of failure, *J. Abnorm. (Soc.) Psychol.*, **46**, 378–387 (1951).

MOFFITT, J. W. and STAGNER, R., Perceptual rigidity and closure as functions of anxiety, *J. Abnorm. (Soc.) Psychol.*, **52**, 354–357 (1956).

MOHR, G. J. and GUNDLACH, R., The relation between physique and performance, *J. Exp. Psychol.*, **10**, 117–157 (1927).

MOHSIN, S. M., Effect of frustration on problem-solving behaviour, *J. Abnorm. (Soc.) Psychol.*, **49**, 152–155 (1954).

MOLDAWSKY, S. and MOLDAWSKY, PATRICIA, C., Digit span as an anxiety indicator, *J. Cons. Psychol.*, **16**, 115–118 (1952).

MONROE, J. J., The effects of emotional adjustment and

intelligence upon Bellevue scatter, *J. Cons. Psychol.*, **16**, 110–114 (1952).

MORAN, L. J., Vocabulary knowledge and usage among normal and schizophrenic subjects, *Psychol. Monogr.*, **67**, No. 20 (Whole No. 370) (1953).

MORAN, L. J., MORAN, F. A. and BLAKE, R. R., An investigation of the vocabulary performance of schizophrenics: II. Conceptual level of definitions, *J. Genet. Psychol.*, **80**, 107–132 (1952).

MOUNTFORD, E. G., An experimental study of some German type-theories, *Character & Pers.*, **8**, 271–280 (1939–40).

NELSON, ELIZABETH H., An experimental investigation of intellectual speed and power in mental disorders, *Unpubl. Ph.D. Thesis, Univ. of London Lib.* (1953).

NIEBUHR, H. and COHEN, D., The effect of psychopathology on visual discrimination, *J. Abnorm. (Soc.) Psychol.*, **53**, 173–177 (1956).

NOTCUTT, B., Perseveration and fluency, *Brit. J. Psychol.*, **33**, 200–208 (1943).

O'CONNOR, PATRICIA, Ethnocentrism, "intolerance of ambiguity," and abstract reasoning ability, *J. Abnorm. (Soc.) Psychol.*, **47**, 526–530 (1952).

OGILVIE, B. C., A study of intellectual slowness in schizophrenia, *Unpubl. Ph.D. Thesis, Univ. of London Lib.* (1954).

OLCH, DORIS R., Psychometric pattern of schizophrenics on the Wechsler-Bellevue intelligence test, *J. Cons. Psychol.*, **12**, 127–136 (1948).

PARTINGTON, J. E., The comparative mental efficiency of a drug addict group, *J. Appl. Psychol.*, **24**, 48–57 (1940).

PASCAL, G. R. and SUTTELL, B. J., *The Bender Gestalt Test* (New York, Grune & Stratton, 1951).

PASCAL, G. R. and SWENSEN, C., Learning in mentally ill patients under conditions of unusual motivation, *J. Personality*, **21**, 240–249 (1952).

PATTERSON, C. H., The Wechsler-Bellevue Scale as an aid to psychiatric diagnosis, *J. Clin. Psychol.*, **2**, 348–353 (1946).

PAYNE, R. W., Experimentelle Untersuchung zum Spaltungsbegriff von Kretschmer, *Z. exp. u. angew. Psychol.*, **3**, 65–97 (1955).

PAYNE, R. W. and HEWLETT, J. H. G., Thought disorder in psychotic patients, in *Experiments in Personality*, Ed. H. J. Eysenck (London, Routledge, to be published).

PAYNE, R. W. and HIRST, HEATHER L., Overinclusive thinking in a depressive and a control group, *J. Cons. Psychol.*, **21**, 186–188 (1957).

PAYNE, R. W., MATUSSEK, P. and GEORGE, E. I., An experimental study of schizophrenic thought disorder, *J. Ment. Sci.*, **105**, 627–652 (1959).

PENROSE, L. S., Psychotic profiles and sex profiles shown by a test battery, *Amer. J. Psychiatr.*, **101**, 810–813 (1945).

PICKREL, E. W., Levels of perceptual organization and cognition: conflicting evidence, *J. Abnorm. (Soc.) Psychol.*, **54**, 422–424 (1957).

PINARD, H. W., Tests of perseveration: II. Their relation to certain psychopathic conditions and to introversion, *Brit. J. Psychol.*, **23**, 114–128 (1932).

PITCHER, BARBARA and STACEY, C. L., Is *Einstellung* rigidity a general trait? *J. Abnorm. (Soc.) Psychol.*, **49**, 3–6 (1954).

PORTEUS, S. D., *Studies in Mental Deviation* (1923, Training School Bulletin, Vineland, N. J., 75–116).

PORTEUS, S. D., *Qualitative Performance in the Maze Test* (Vineland, N. J., Smith, 1942).

POULL, L. E. and MONTGOMERY, R. P., The Porteus Maze Test as a discriminative measure in delinquency, *J. Appl. Psychol.*, **13**, 145–151 (1929).

PULLEN, M. S. and STAGNER, R., Rigidity and shock therapy of psychotics: an experimental study, *J. Cons. Psychol.*, **17**, 79–86 (1953).

PURCELL, K., A note on Porteus Maze and Wechsler-Bellevue scores as related to antisocial behavior, *J. Cons. Psychol.*, **20**, 361–364 (1956).

RABIN, A. I., Test score patterns in schizophrenia and non-psychotic states, *J. Psychol.*, **12**, 91–100 (1941).

RABIN, A. I., Differentiating psychometric patterns in schizophrenia and manic-depressive psychosis, *J. Abnorm. (Soc.) Psychol.*, **37**, 270–272 (1942).

RABIN, A. I., The relationship between vocabulary levels and levels of general intelligence in psychotic and non-psychotic individuals of a wide age-range, *J. Educ. Psychol.*, **35**, 411–422 (1944a).

RABIN, A. I., Fluctuations in the mental level of schizophrenic patients, *Psychiat. Quart.*, **18**, 78–91 (1944b).

RABIN, A. I., Test constancy and variation in the mentally ill, *J. Gen. Psychol.*, **31**, 231–239 (1944c).

RABIN, A. I., KING, G. F. and EHRMANN, J. C., Vocabulary performance of short-term and long-term schizophrenics, *J. Abnorm. (Soc.) Psychol.*, **50**, 255–258 (1955).

RAPAPORT, D., GILL, M. and SCHAFER, R., *Diagnostic Psychological Testing*, Vol. I. (Chicago: Year Book Publishers, 1945).

RAPPAPORT, S. R., The role of behavioral accessibility in intellectual function of psychotics, *J. Clin. Psychol.*, **7**, 335–340 (1951).

RAPPAPORT, S. R., Intellectual deficit in organics and schizophrenics, *J. Cons. Psychol.*, **17**, 389–395 (1953).

RAPPAPORT, S. R. and WEBB, W., An attempt to study intellectual deterioration by premorbid and psychotic testing, *J. Cons. Psychol.*, **14**, 95–98 (1950).

RASHKIS, H. A., Three types of thinking disorder, *J. Nerv. Ment. Dis.*, **106**, 650–670 (1947).

RASHKIS, H., CUSHMAN, T. F. and LANDIS, C., A new method for studying disorders of conceptual thinking, *J. Abnorm. (Soc.) Psychol.*, **41**, 70–74 (1946).

RAVEN, J. C., *Guide to Using Progressive Matrices* (1938) (London, H. K. Lewis, 1950).

REITER, O. and STERZINGER, O., Aufmerksamkeit und Konstitution, *Z. Psychol.*, **122**, 115–132 (1931).

RETHLINGSHAFER, D., The relationship of tests of persistence to other measures of continuance of activities, *J. Abnorm. (Soc.) Psychol.*, **37**, 71–82 (1942).

RIM, Y., Perseveration and fluency as measures of introversion-extraversion in abnormal subjects, *Unpubl. Ph.D. Thesis, Univ. of London Lib.* (1953).

RIMOLDI, H. J. A., Personal Tempo, *J. Abnorm. (Soc.) Psychol.*, **46**, 283–303 (1951).

RODNICK, E. H. and SHAKOW, D., Set in the schizophrenic as measured by a composite reaction time index, *Amer. J. Psychiatr.*, **97**, 214–225 (1940).

ROGERS, L. S., Differences between neurotics and schizophrenics on the Wechsler-Bellevue scale, *J. Cons. Psychol.*, **15**, 151–153 (1951).

ROKEACH, M., Generalized mental rigidity as a factor in

ethnocentrism, *J. Abnorm. (Soc.) Psychol.*, **43**, 259–278 (1948).

ROKEACH, M., The effect of perception time on rigidity and concreteness of thinking, *J. Exp. Psychol.*, **40**, 206–216 (1950).

ROKEACH, M., Prejudice, concreteness of thinking, and reification of thinking, *J. Abnorm. (Soc.) Psychol.*, **46**, 83–91 (1951).

ROKEACH, M., McGOVNEY, W. C. and DENNY, M. R., A distinction between dogmatic and rigid thinking, *J. Abnorm. (Soc.) Psychol.*, **51**, 87–93 (1955).

ROSS, B. M., RUPEL, J. W. and GRANT, D. A., Effects of personal, impersonal and physical stress upon cognitive behavior in a card sorting situation, *J. Abnorm. (Soc.) Psychol.*, **47**, 546–551 (1952).

RYANS, D. G., An experimental attempt to analyse persistent behavior: I. Measuring traits presumed to involve persistence, *J. Gen. Psychol.*, **19**, 333–353 (1938*a*).

RYANS, D. G., An experimental attempt to analyse persistent behavior: II. A persistence test, *J. Gen. Psychol.*, **19**, 353–371 (1938*b*).

SARASON, S. B. and MANDLER, G., Some correlates of test anxiety, *J. Abnorm. (Soc.) Psychol.*, **47**, 810–817 (1952).

SARASON, S. B. MANDLER, G. and CRAIGHILL, P. G., The effects of differential instructions on anxiety and learning, *J. Abnorm. (Soc.) Psychol.*, **47**, 561 (1952).

SCHAIE, K. W., A test of behavioral rigidity, *J. Abnorm. (Soc.) Psychol.*, **51**, 604–610 (1955).

SCHEERER, N., Problems of performance analysis in the study of personality, *Ann. N.Y. Acad. Sci.*, **46**, 653–678 (1946).

SCHEERER, M., Personality functioning and cognitive psychology, *J. Personality*, **22**, 1–16 (1953).

SCHEERER, M., Cognitive Theory, Chap. 3 in *Handbook of Social Psychology*, Ed. Gardner Lindzey (Cambridge, Mass., Addison-Wesley, 1954).

SCHILDER, P., On the development of thought, in *Clinical Psychiatry*, 233, W. Mayer-Gross, E. Slater, and M. Roth, (London, Cassell, 1954).

SCHLOSSER, J. R. and KANTOR, R. E., A comparison of Wechsler's deterioration ratio in psychoneurosis and schizophrenia, *J. Cons. Psychol.*, **13**, 108–110 (1949).

SCHMIDT, H. O., FONDA, C. P. and WESLEY, ELIZABETH, L., A note on consistency of rigidity as a personality variable, *J. Cons. Psychol.*, **18**, 450 (1954).

SCHNADT, F., Certain aspects of Wechsler-Bellevue scatter at low I.Q. levels, *J. Cons. Psychol.*, **16**, 456–461 (1952).

SCHNEIDER, CARL, *Die Psychologie der Schizophrenen* (Leipzig, Thieme, 1930).

SCHOTT, E. L., Superior intelligence in patients with nervous and mental illnesses, *J. Abnorm. (Soc.) Psychol.*, **26**, 94 (1931).

SCHULZ, R. E. and CALVIN, R. E., A failure to replicate the finding of a negative correlation between manifest anxiety and ACE scores, *J. Cons. Psychol.*, **19**, 223–224 (1955).

SCHWARTZ, R., Measurement of mental deterioration in dementia praecox, *Amer. J. Psychiat.*, **12**, 555–560 (1932).

SENF, RITA, HUSTON, P. E. and COHEN, B. D., Thinking deficit in schizophrenia and changes with amytal, *J. Abnorm. (Soc.) Psychol.*, **50**, 383–387 (1955).

SHAKOW, D., The nature of deterioration in schizophrenic conditions, *Nerv. Ment. Dis. Monogr.*, No. 70 (1946).

SHAKOW, D. and MILLARD, M. S., A psychometric study of 150 adult delinquents, *J. Soc. Psychol.*, **6**, 437–457 (1935).

SHAPIRO, M. B. and NELSON, E. H., An investigation of the nature of cognitive impairment in co-operative psychiatric patients, *Brit. J. Med. Psychol.*, **28**, 239–256 (1955).

SHEVACH, B., Studies in perseveration: VII. Experimental results of tests for sensory perseveration, *J. Psychol.*, **3**, 403–427 (1937).

SHIPLEY, W. C., A self-administering scale for measuring intellectual impairment and deterioration, *J. Psychol.*, **9**, 371–377 (1940).

SHIPLEY, W. C. and BURLINGAME, C. C., A convenient self administering scale for measuring intellectual impairment in psychotics, *Amer. J. Psychiat.*, **97**, 1313–1325 (1941).

SHNEIDMAN, E. S., Schizophrenia and the MAPS test: a study of certain formal psycho-social aspects of fantasy production in schizophrenia as revealed by performance on the Make-a-Picture-Story (MAPS) test, *Genet. Psychol. Monogr.*, **38**, 145–223 (1948).

SHOBEN, E. J. JR., The Wechsler-Bellevue in the detection of anxiety: A test of the Rashkis-Welsh hypothesis, *J. Cons. Psychol.*, **14**, 40–45 (1950).

SIEGMAN, A. W., Cognitive, affective, and psychopathological correlates of the Taylor manifest anxiety scale, *J. Cons. Psychol.*, **20**, 137–141 (1956*a*).

SIEGMAN, A. W., The effect of manifest anxiety on a concept formation task, a nondirected learning task, and on timed and untimed intelligence tests, *J. Cons. Psychol.*, **20**, 176–178 (1956*b*).

SIMMINS, CONSTANCE, Studies in experimental psychiatry: IV. Deterioration of "G" in psychotic patients, *J. Ment. Sci.*, **79**, 704–734 (1933).

SLOAN, W. and CUTTS, R. A., Test patterns of defective delinquents on the Wechsler-Bellevue test, *Amer. J. Ment. Defic.*, **50**, 95–101 (1945).

SMITH, D. E. P. and RAYGOR, A. L., Verbal satiation and personality, *J. Abnorm. (Soc.) Psychol.*, **52**, 323–326 (1956).

SMOCK, C. D., The influence of psychological stress on the "intolerance of ambiguity," *J. Abnorm. (Soc.) Psychol.*, **50**, No. 2, 177–182 (1955*a*).

SMOCK, C. D., The influence of stress on the perception of incongruity, *J. Abnorm. (Soc.) Psychol.*, **50**, 354–356 (1955*b*).

SOLOMON, R. S., Cognitive aspects of deterioration in mental patients, *J. Abnorm. (Soc.) Psychol.*, **34**, 497–517 (1939).

SPENCE, K. W., *Behaviour Theory and Conditioning* (London, Oxford Univ. Press, 1956).

STEPHENSON, W., Studies in experimental psychiatry: II. Some contact of p-factor with psychiatry, *J. Ment. Sci.*, **78**, 315–330 (1932*a*).

STEPHENSON, W., Studies in experimental psychiatry: III. P-score and inhibition for high p *praecox* cases, *J. Ment. Sci.*, **78**, 908–928 (1932*b*).

STOTSKY, B. A., A comparison of remitting and non-remitting schizophrenics on psychological tests, *J. Abnorm. (Soc.) Psychol.*, **47**, 489–496 (1952).

STUDMAN, L. GRACE, Studies in experimental psychiatry:

V. "W" and "f" factors in relation to traits of personality, *J. Ment. Sci.*, **81**, 107–137 (1935).

SUTTELL, BARBARA J. and PASCAL, G. R., "Regression" in schizophrenia as determined by performance on the Bender-Gestalt test, *J. Abnorm. (Soc.) Psychol.*, **47**, 653–657 (1952).

TAYLOR, F. H., Mental testing in male adolescent delinquents, *J. Ment. Sci.*, **84**, 513–523 (1938).

THORNTON, G. R., A factor analysis of tests designed to measure persistence, *Psychol. Monogr.*, **51**, 1–42 (1939).

TONG, J. E., Abstraction ability and impairment, *Brit. J. Med. Psychol.*, **28**, 19–28 (1955).

TRAPP, C. E. and JAMES, EDITH B., Comparative intelligence ratings in the four types of *dementia praecox*, *J. Nerv. Ment. Dis.*, **86**, 399–404 (1937).

TROUTON, D. S. and MAXWELL, A. E., The relation between neurosis and psychosis. An analysis of symptoms, and past history of 819 psychotics and neurotics, *J. Ment. Sci.*, **102**, 1–21 (1956).

TRUSSELL, MARY, A., The diagnostic value of the verbal summator, *J. Abnorm. (Soc.) Psychol.*, **34**, 533–538 (1939).

U.S. EMPLOYMENT SERVICE, *Guide to the use of General Aptitude Test Battery: Section III. Development* (Washington, D.C., U.S. Dept. of Labor, 1955).

VAN DER HORST, L., Experimentellpsychologische Untersuchungen zu Kretschmers *Körperbau und Character*, *Z. ges. Neurol. Psychiatr.*, **93**, 341–380 (1924).

VENABLES, P. H., Stimulus complexity as a determinant of the reaction time of schizophrenics, *Canad. J. Psychol.*, **12**, 187–190 (1958).

VIGOTSKY, L. S., Thought in schizophrenia, *Arch. Neurol. Psychiat. Chicago*, **31**, 1063–1077 (1934).

WALLACE, M., Future time perspective in schizophrenia, *J. Abnorm. (Soc.) Psychol.*, **52**, 240–245 (1956).

WALLIN, J. E. W., A further note on scattering in the Binet Scale, *J. Appl. Psychol.*, **11**, 143–154 (1927).

WARNER, S. J., The Wechsler-Bellevue psychometric pattern in anxiety neurosis, *J. Cons. Psychol.*, **14**, 297–304 (1950).

WATERHOUSE, I. K. and CHILD, I. L., Frustration and the quality of performance: III. An experimental study. *J. Personality*, **21**, 298–311 (1952).

WEBB, W. B. and DE HAAN, H., Wechsler-Bellevue split-half reliabilities in normals and schizophrenics, *J. Cons. Psychol.*, **15**, 68–71 (1951).

WEBB, W. W., Conceptual ability of schizophrenics as a function of threat of failure, *J. Abnorm. (Soc.) Psychol.*, **50**, 221–224 (1955).

WECHSLER, DAVID, *The Measurement of Adult Intelligence* (Baltimore, Williams & Wilkins, 1944).

WEGROCKI, H., Generalizing ability in schizophrenia: An inquiry into the disorders of problem thinking in schizophrenia, *Arch. Psychol. N.Y.*, **36**, No. 254 (1940).

WEIDER, A., Effect of age on the Bellevue Intelligence Scale in schizophrenic patients, *Psychiat. Quart.*, **17**, 337–345 (1943).

WELLS, E. L. and KELLEY, C. M., Intelligence and psychosis, *Amer. J. Insan.*, **77**, 17–45 (1920).

WESLEY, ELIZABETH, L., Perseverative behavior in a concept-formation task as a function of manifest anxiety and rigidity, *J. Abnorm. (Soc.) Psychol.*, **48**, 129–134 (1953).

WHITE, MARY A., A study of schizophrenic language, *J. Abnorm. (Soc.) Psychol.*, **44**, 61–74 (1949).

WHITEMAN, M., The performance of schizophrenics on social concepts, *J. Abnorm. (Soc.) Psychol.*, **49**, 266–271 (1954).

WINFIELD, D. L., Intellectual performance of cryptogenic epileptics, symptomatic epileptics, and post-traumatic encephalopaths, *J. Abnorm. (Soc.) Psychol.*, **46**, 336–343 (1951).

WITTENBORN, J. R., An evaluation of the use of Bellevue-Wechsler subtest scores as an aid in psychiatric diagnosis, *J. Cons. Psychol.*, **13**, 433–439 (1949).

WITTENBORN, J. R., Symptom patterns in a group of mental hospital patients, *J. Cons. Psychol.*, **15**, 290–302 (1951a).

WITTENBORN, J. R. and HOLZBERG, J. D., The Wechsler-Bellevue and descriptive diagnosis, *J. Cons. Psychol.*, **15**, 325–329 (1951a).

WITTENBORN, J. R. and HOLZBERG, J. D., The generality of psychiatric syndromes, *J. Cons. Psychol.*, **15**, 372–380 (1951b).

WITTMAN, PHYLLIS, The Babcock test in state hospital practice, *J. Abnorm. (Soc.) Psychol.*, **28**, 70–83 (1933).

WITTMAN, MARY P., An evaluation of opposed theories concerning the etiology of so-called "dementia" in *dementia praecox*, *Amer. J. Psychiat.*, **93**, 1363–1377 (1937).

WOLPERT, E. A., A new view of rigidity, *J. Abnorm. (Soc.) Psychol.*, **51**, 589–594 (1955).

WRIGHT, CLARE, The qualitative performance of delinquent boys on the Porteus Maze Test, *J. Cons. Psychol.*, **8**, 24–26 (1944).

YACORZYNSKI, G. K., An evaluation of the postulates underlying the Babcock deterioration test, *Psychol. Rev.*, **48**, 261–267 (1941).

YUKER, H. E., Group atmosphere and memory, *J. Abnorm. (Soc.) Psychol.*, **51**, 17–23 (1955).

ZASLOW, R. W., A new approach to the problem of conceptual thinking in schizophrenia, *J. Cons. Psychol.*, **14**, 335–339 (1950).

ZWEIBELSON, I., Test anxiety and intelligence test performance, *J. Cons. Psychol.*, **20**, 479–481 (1956).

CHAPTER 7

Abnormalities of Motivation and "Ego-functions"

JAMES INGLIS

INTRODUCTION

ANY account of human abnormal psychology must attempt to deal with the so-called "higher processes" not only in relation to intellectual or cognitive functions but also in relation to affective or orectic functioning.

It seems to the present author that certain consistencies may be traced in at least three adjacent experimental areas of considerable importance to abnormal psychology, which are referable to the interaction of such higher processes with stress and the arousal of affect or motivation on the one hand, and with individual differences on the other.

Before these interrelationships can be described, however, some consideration must be given to the terms which will be involved in the description.

The notion of higher process is invoked simply to take into account the fact that the adult human being is capable of behaving in relation not only to changes in external, and in simple internal, stimulation, but also is capable of behaving in relation to an immense, and an immensely complex, range of self-produced stimulations or "symbols."

Berlyne (1954) has discussed the usefulness of the notion of self-produced stimulation in, for example, relating experimental data concerned with "knowledge" within the framework of a stimulus-response psychology. He suggests that the way of talking about such self-stimulation, or "symbolizing," formulated by Osgood (1952) provides at least a good beginning.

Osgood states that, "a pattern of stimulation which is not the object is a sign of the object if it evokes in an organism a mediating reaction, this (a) being some fractional part of the total behaviour elicited by the object and (b) producing distinctive self-stimulation that mediates responses which would not occur without the previous association of non-object and object patterns of stimulation." (Osgood, 1952, p. 204.) Berlyne goes on to point out that, "Osgood's scheme thus follows this pattern—

$$\boxed{S} \mapsto r_m \ldots \ldots \ldots s_m \to Rx$$

where S is the sign, r_m the mediating reaction (a part of the response pattern made to the signified object), and Rx is the overt behaviour evoked by r_m. It will be seen that r_m is the behavioural equivalent of the 'concept' or 'meaning' which a sign, in traditional accounts of symbolization, 'conjures up' in the interpreter's 'mind.' " (Berlyne, 1954, p. 297.)

It is not only "knowledge," however, that can be conceived in these terms. Certain aspects of "emotional" or "orectic" behaviour can also be so conceived.

To put it at its simplest, when one "learns a word for X," one does *not* simply learn to connect noises or marks on a piece of paper with their referent in a neutral sort of way. A wide range of symbols are primarily emotive by nature. Even those which are ordinarily neutral can, of course, acquire emotional overtones by appropriate manipulation.

The need for recognizing *both* cognitive *and* orectic aspects of symbolizing has been pointed out, for example, by Morris (1946). He has suggested that symbolic processes may exist, not necessarily exclusively, in several different "modes of signifying."

Symbols in the "prescriptive" mode, for example, are of primary importance in human *cognitive* behaviour. These include symbols which are mainly concerned in arousing fractional anticipatory skeletal responses. The *orectic* aspect of behaviour is mainly the concern of symbols in the "appraisive" mode of signifying. In Osgood's terms, if the r_m initiates mainly drive-producing or emotional responses, it is an "appraisor."

In human abnormal psychology the appraisive content of symbolic processes (both verbal, pre-verbal and non-verbal) which are concerned with anxiety mediation are of very considerable importance. Such mediators, in the case of man, may not only be conditioned, "at the first level" so to speak, on simple tissue-injury-avoidance, as they may be with lower organisms. They may, in fact, be so remote from this

262

primary level as to appear as mediating many different "kinds of drive." Recently, however, Brown (1953) has suggested that there may, in fact, be a relation between anxiety drive and such higher-level motives as, for example, "self-esteem." He suggests that: "The important motivating component of many of the supposed acquired drives for specific goal objects is actually a learned tendency to be discontented or distressed or anxious in the absence of these goal-objects. On this view stimulus cues signifying a lack of affection, a lack of prestige, insufficient money, etc., would be said to acquire, through learning, the capacity to arouse an anxiety reaction having drive properties." (Brown, 1953, p. 12 *et seq.*)

This way of looking at human motivation is important on at least two counts. Firstly, it permits us to regard human motivational processes in the same light as the motivational processes of lower organisms. They may be different and more numerous in *kind*, especially in view of the vastly complex mediation systems used by man. We need not, however, regard them as being different in *source*, as is sometimes suggested by such expressions as "ego-involvement," and the like.

Secondly, it suggests that, in the consideration of individual differences, we may expect certain common elements to run through all aspects of, for example, "motivational intensity." In terms of personality structure some of the important individual differences may be, for example (i) neuroticism, which will determine the strength of the primary drives upon which anxiety may be secondarily conditioned and which will, in turn, then provide the basis for further learned drives; and (ii) introversion-extraversion, which, will determine the strength of the conditioning of the secondary, and other, drives.

The connexion between anxiety and socialization has been discussed by Mowrer (1950) while the importance of personality variables has been emphasized by Eysenck (1955). They have suggested that the process of socialization, i.e., the acquisition by the individual of a certain set of standards of conduct and behaviour may be considered to be mediated by a process of conditioning.

Now, if the process of socialization is based on a conditioning procedure, then the extreme introvert, subjected to a standard process of cultural indoctrination, should become over-socialized compared with the average sort of person. The extreme extravert, on the other hand, subjected to the same process, should become under-socialized compared with the average person. The contribution of neuroticism to this picture would be, perhaps, a basic "over excitability of the autonomic nervous system, particularly the sympathetic branch." (Eysenck, 1955, p. 53.) This would result, for the introvert, in an over-driven,

over-socialized individual; in other words in the tense, conflict-full dysthymic. The extravert would become over-driven and under-socialized; he would be typified, in fact, by the explosive hysterico-psychopathic individual.

It would follow from this argument that the appraisor elements related to "higher-level drives" in any individual's behaviour repertoire would be partly determined by his personality structure. In the introvert we would expect these to be strong and numerous, in the extravert, few and weak.

It is to be argued in this chapter that an important part of human orectic behaviour is related to the "handling" of such appraisive mediators, and that certain experimental data can be interpreted in terms of individual differences in dealing with such mediators under varying degrees of stress.

The principal consideration will be given to *that method of dealing with stress in which it may be said that individuals initiate avoidance reactions to their own anxiety-producing covert responses.*

It will become apparent that this formulation is akin to suggestions which have been put forward at various times, for example by Sears (1936), Angyal, (1941), and by Dollard and Miller (1950) and others, in an attempt to provide a behavioural interpretation of Freud's notion of "repression." Reviews of the evidence for such a formulation have been made by Sears (1943), Zeller (1950), and Farrell (1955).

There are, however, several important differences between previous adumbrations and the present chapter—

(i) In the first place, it is not the intention of the writer to review the evidence for, or against, "psychoanalytic theory" as such. It seems more worth-while to attempt to relate experimental data which have hitherto been more or less discrete rather than to recount attempts which have been made to evaluate virtually untestable "clinical hypotheses."

(ii) Secondly, previous authors have tended to discuss the elimination of anxiety-producing responses in terms of the more-or-less passive *inhibition* of such processes. The present writer wishes to emphasize rather the influence of active *avoidance* behaviour. It is to be suggested that the paradigm for the elimination of anxiety-producing mediating responses is to be found in experiments involving "escape-activity" rather than in experiments dealing with the simple exclusion of unrewarded responses.

Thus, in an animal like the rat, whose mediators are (comparatively speaking) few, anxiety-producing stimuli are mainly located, so to speak, externally. Hence they may be dealt with by straightforward. overt avoidance behaviour.

In man, however, both the anxiety-producing stimuli and the behaviour initiated for the reduction of anxiety may be much less overt, and may, in fact, consist in the suppression or avoidance of certain symbolic activities.

(iii) Thirdly, it must be taken into consideration that such avoidance-activity may have a more *or* less beneficial influence on the organism's repertoire of responses. Commonly symbols may fulfil both

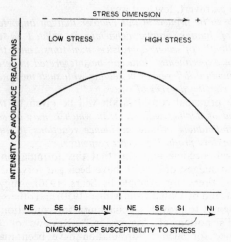

FIG. 7.1

"appraisive" (emotional) *and* "prescriptive" (cognitive) functions. By initiating *too much* avoidance, therefore, the individual may deprive himself of certain problem-solving "tools" and so may reduce the efficiency of his adjustment. On the other hand, insufficient avoidance may be equally maladaptive, since the consequent increase in the emotive properties of a situation may also be disruptive of efficient behaviour. Somewhat similar points have been made by Cameron (1947).

(iv) This latter view, that certain avoidance behaviour can be practised too little or too much leads to a fourth important consideration which has, in general, been ignored by previous writers. This relates to the interaction to be expected between *situations of differential stress* and *differential individual susceptibility to stress*.

It has emerged from several studies (cf. chapters by Jones in this HANDBOOK) that adequacy of performance may not be a simple linear function of drive-strength. There may, in fact, be an *optimum* level of drive for the execution of any task, and, in general, the more complex the task the lower the optimum drive level required for its efficient execution. The general form

of the relationship between drive and efficiency is curvilinear, taking the form of an inverted U-curve. (Cf. also Hebb, 1955 and Duffy, 1957.)

The avoidance of anxiety-mediating self-stimulation may be regarded as a kind of problem-solving task. It may be argued, therefore, that stress and the personality variables related to susceptibility to stress have a similar effect upon the achievement of an adequate "solution" involving the *avoidance* of anxiety-mediators, as they may have upon the efficient positive execution of other behaviours.

This notion agrees with the conclusion reached by Iverson and Reuder (1956) in their review of studies of "ego-involvement." They say: "Generalizing from their review, the writers propose the hypothesis that varying reactions to ego-involving conditions reflect, at least in part, a continuum of motivation. The relationship between degree of ego-involvement and efficacy of response appears to be a curvilinear one, inhibitive or disruptive at the extremes and optimally facilitative near the middle. There also appears to be a common personality dimension which is responsive to ego-involving conditions." (Iverson and Reuder, 1956, p. 175.)

In view of the working hypothesis adopted here it is suggested that their "continuum of motivation" may be regarded as one of differential "social stress" or "socialized-anxiety-production," and in terms of the propositions which have been put forward concerning the likely relevance of personality structure, their "common personality dimension," may be regarded as falling along a composite continuum comprising, in turn, neurotic extraverts (NE), stable extraverts (SE), stable introverts (SI), and neurotic introverts (NI).

The relations discussed may be conceived as illustrated in Fig. 7.1.

Thus, in situations of low objective "external" stress, individuals at the *NI* end of the composite continuum *NE–NI* may have already begun to initiate the avoidance of anxiety-mediators, since the motivational content of such reactions may, even at this stage, be sufficiently high for these individuals to be functioning "maximally" in respect of this avoidance activity. Such a process, under these circumstances of low objective stress may, however, be otherwise maladaptive since, as has been pointed out, it may concomitantly reduce access to other important cognitive aspects of these same mediators. Under the same circumstances of stress the individuals at the *NE* end of the continuum may not yet have begun to initiate avoidance behaviour.

On the other hand, in circumstances of high objective stress, the individuals at the *NE* end of the continuum will now initiate powerful avoidance behaviour. Individuals at the *NI* end, however, are now being subjected to so much stress that successful avoidance activity may be disrupted.

In such a situation both the powerful avoidance activity *and* the inability to avoid may be maladaptive, since the first leads to the diminished availability of possibly relevant cues and the second leads to the increase of anxiety in an already stressful situation.

It is suggested that this scheme may be used to relate data from three adjacent experimental areas, namely—

1. Studies concerned with "Perceptual Defence."
2. Studies concerned with the "Zeigarnik Effect" and
3. Studies of "Level of Aspiration" phenomena, which may now be considered in that order.

STUDIES IN "PERCEPTUAL DEFENCE"

Description of the Phenomena[1]

In 1947 Bruner and Postman used the notion of "perceptual defence," and its obverse, "perceptual sensitization" or "vigilance," to relate together results which they had obtained in an experiment designed to examine the connexion between associative reaction-times and recognition thresholds. In this study the association times of nineteen undergraduates were measured to ninety-nine words, some of these words being "neutral" in connotation (e.g., *clock*, *book*, etc.) and some "emotional" (e.g., *penis*, *hymen*, etc.). For each subject there were then selected the six words giving the longest, the six giving the median, and the six words giving the shortest reaction-time. A fortnight later the tachistoscopic exposure time necessary for each subject's recognition of the chosen words was examined. A correlation ratio was run for each subject and in seventeen out of the nineteen cases, a significant curvilinear relationship was shown to exist between the two measures. A generalized z-score function was plotted for the group (Fig. 7.2), the *eta* being 0·124 with a standard error of 0·054.

It can be seen from this figure that the relationships between association time and recognition time generate an inverted U-shaped distribution. The authors suggest that this is because, for most of their subjects, time of recognition increases as reaction-time; since, with the increase in emotionality of the stimulus, recognition is avoided as long as possible, as an anxiety-reducing technique, this constituting perceptual defence. Other subjects, however, tended to recognize more quickly words to which they had initially returned long reaction-times; they, in fact, showed perceptual vigilance or sensitization.

[1] This section will be concerned only with the results of experiments in perceptual defence in the visual modality. Those interested in similar work in the auditory modality are referred to further studies (by Cogan, 1956; Davids, 1955; Kleinman, 1957; Kurland, 1954; Lazarus, Eriksen and Fonda, 1951; Mason and Garrison, 1951; and Vanderplas and Blake, 1949). Studies of the effects of "positive values" (Allport, Vernon and Lindzey, 1951) on perception will not be examined although there are, of course, relations between these and the studies on "negative values" reviewed here (*see* Klein, Schlesinger and Meister, 1951; Postman, Bruner and McGinnies, 1948; Solomon and Howes, 1951; and Postman, 1953*b*).

A further demonstration of the defence phenomenon was then reported by McGinnies (1949). He presented sixteen student subjects with seven emotional and eleven neutral words and established their recognition thresholds for these words tachisto-

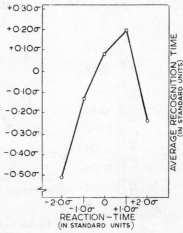

FIG. 7.2. AVERAGE RECOGNITION TIMES FOR WORDS ELICITING VARYING ASSOCIATIVE REACTION-TIMES

(From Bruner and Postman, 1947)

scopically. He also took readings of the subjects' galvanic skin responses. The subjects reacted with G.S.R.s of significantly greater magnitude during the pre-recognition presentation of the emotional words than they did during the pre-recognition presentation of the neutral words (*see* Fig. 7.3).

They also required longer exposures for the accurate recognition and report of the emotional words (*see* Fig. 7.4).

McGinnies concludes that: "The findings are interpreted as representing conditioned avoidance of verbal symbols having unpleasant meanings to the observer. The stimulus word serves as a cue to deeply embedded anxiety which is revealed in autonomic acitivity as measured by the G.S.R. Avoidance of further anxiety is contemporaneously aroused in

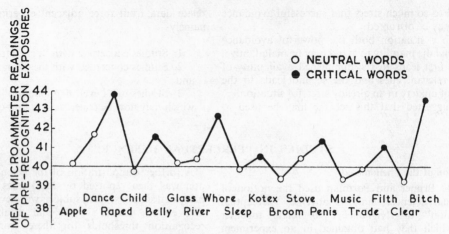

FIG. 7.3. GROUP AVERAGES OF GALVANIC SKIN RESPONSE TO NEUTRAL AND CRITICAL
WORDS DURING PRE-RECOGNITION EXPOSURES

(*From McGinnies*, 1949)

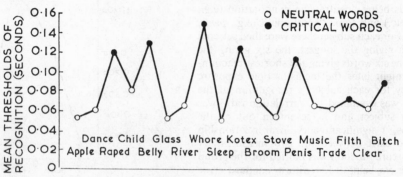

FIG. 7.4. MEAN THRESHOLDS OF RECOGNITION OF THE OBSERVERS TO THE NEUTRAL
AND EMOTIONALLY-CHARGED WORDS

(*From McGinnies*, 1949)

the form of perceptual defence against recognition of the stimulus object." (McGinnies, 1949, p. 251.)

Criticisms and Controversies

The notions of perceptual defence and vigilance have come in for a good deal of criticism, on several grounds. The main forms of criticism may be grouped, for convenience, under several heads and separately considered as follows—

LOGICAL DIFFICULTIES

One difficulty which has been seen to lie in the notion of perceptual defence comes from the apparent paradox that, in order to know what to avoid, the subject must first recognize the stimulus which is to be avoided. This difficulty has been recognized from the

beginning and was dealt with by Bruner and Postman in the following terms—

The paradox remains only so long as we (1) restrict the definition of *recognition* to one type of response—veridical report and (2) insist that all systematic responses to the stimulus depend on the *prior* occurrence of correct recognition. Neither of these restrictive assumptions is necessary. There can be tripped off, by the presentation of a stimulus, a multiplicity of response tendencies among which veridical reporting is only one, albeit a most important one. Other systematic reaction tendencies tripped off by the stimulus may be largely affective in nature and lead to various forms of avoidance responses. Each of these possible responses has its own threshold, determined by characteristics of the stimulus end and by the directive state of the organism (differential "availability" of the responses). Thus, veridical report has *its* threshold, and affective avoidance response has *its.* As our experiments suggest, the threshold for affective avoidance response is frequently lower than the threshold for veridical report. . . . If this rather reasonable assumption of the heirarchy of thresholds be accepted, a Judas eye notion of double-perception is not required to account for the phenomena of "defensive" perception in which avoidance responses seem to precede correct recognition. (Bruner and Postman, 1949, p. 26.)

Despite this proposal, which derives plausibility from work on "subception" (McLeary and Lazarus, 1949; Lazarus and McLeary, 1951) as well as the study by McGinnies already cited, the same type of difficulty has been raised by others including Howie (1952) and also by Allport (1955).

The former author has, however, been answered by Postman (1953*a*) and Allport has himself noted that—

> The term perceptual defence is misleading in that it suggests that defence is accomplished *through* perception (i.e. through the abortive character or self-retardation of the perceptual process) an interpretation that raises the dilemma of a subconscious, preperceiving perceiver. If we could consider that some fractional stimulus element in the situation, rather than the complete and meaningful stimulus pattern, can, in short exposures, lead the subject *to avoid perceiving anything further with respect to that stimulus pattern* until long exposures give him no escape from perceiving it, the matter could be more simply explained. It would not be a case of "perceptual defence," in the sense of raising the threshold, but simply of an inhibition of perceiving that has been conditioned to certain (actually perceived) cues. (Allport, 1955, p. 333.)

Studies by Bricker and Chapanis (1953) and by Murdock (1954) have provided evidence that, in fact, identification of words at near-threshold values is *not* necessarily an all-or-none matter so that it is not inconceivable that some such process as Allport suggests may, in fact, take place.

WORD FREQUENCY

A much more telling kind of criticism which has been levelled against the notion of perceptual defence is involved in the suggestion that the relative frequency of usage of words, as determined for example by the Thorndike-Lorge word-count (1944) is a more important determinant of recognition threshold than is the relative "emotionality-neutrality" of the words used in the experiments cited.

The principal proponents of the word-frequency criticism have been Howes and Solomon (1950). These authors examined the problem experimentally (1951) and were able to show that the visual recognition threshold of a word, as measured tachistoscopically, is an approximately linear function of the logarithm of the relative frequency with which the word appears in a word-count, the product-moment

correlations between the two variables ranging from − 0·68 to − 0·75.

An even more convincing study has been reported by Solomon and Postman (1952) which also examined the relationship between frequency of prior usage and recognition threshold. This latter study represented an advance on the Howes and Solomon experiments since it did not rely merely on an actuarial control of word-frequency. The undergraduate subjects in this experiment were required to read and pronounce different nonsense (actually Turkish) words. The number of times they were required to read the words ranged from once to twenty-five times. The subjects' recognition thresholds for these words were then compared with other words which they had *not* read before and it was found that thresholds varied inversely with frequency of prior usage. A similar experiment with equivalent results has been reported by King-Ellison and Jenkins (1954).

Goodstein (1954) has also reported the further analysis of a set of results obtained by Aronfreed, Messick and Diggory (1953). These authors had, in their study, confirmed that the mean visual recognition threshold for unpleasant words was significantly higher than the mean threshold for neutral and pleasant words. Goodstein was able to show that there was a parallel difference in frequency between the categories of words used.

Bresson (1955) in his brief review, also finds reasons for emphasizing the importance of frequency. His conclusion seems too facile, however, since he gives little or no consideration to those studies which provide evidence for the importance of other factors. In fact it has been recognized from the beginning that relative frequency might be an important determinant in the recognition situation. Bruner and Postman, for example, stated that—

> We do not believe, of course, that perceptual defence is the only factor responsible for the impairment in recognition associated with increased reaction time. Part of the correlation, particularly in the case of very fast reaction words, can be ascribed to familiarity. The positive correlation between popularity and speed of associative responses is a well established empirical fact (Marbe's Law). A familiar stimulus will not only elicit a quick and popular response, but it is also likely to be recognized readily, since familiarity will facilitate "closure" when only part of the stimulus word is seen under rapid exposure. *Some* of our fast reaction-fast recognition words are indeed among those which are known to give quick, popular responses. Familiarity, cannot, however, account in entirety for the correlation between speed of association and speed of recognition. Many words with relatively *fast* recognition and reaction times are not among those which normally yield quick, popular responses. And, conversely, among the *slow* and *medium* recognition and reaction words are many which, according to the convential norms, should have evoked

quick and popular responses. These discrepancies we attribute to the differential effect of perceptual defence in the face of emotionally charged stimuli. (Bruner and Postman, 1947, p. 75.)

Replies have been made, by other supporters of the notion of perceptual defence, to the charge that word frequency can account, by itself, for the phenomena observed in their experiments. McGinnies (1950), for example, attempted to rebut Howes and Solomon's

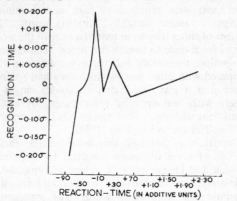

FIG. 7.5. CURVES OF RECOGNITION TIME CONSIDERED AS A FUNCTION OF ASSOCIATION TIME
(*From Delucia and Stagner*, 1953)

arguments on two grounds. In the first place he suggested that their assumptions, based on actuarial methods, of the frequency of usage of the emotional words were too low, and, secondly, he suggested that the correlations which Howes and Solomon (1951) reported between frequency and threshold were spurious since these authors drew a regression line through the two distributions represented by the emotional and neutral words, whereas such lines drawn *within* each distribution show no such marked relationship. The study by Solomon and Postman (1952), noted above, appears to answer both these counter-arguments of McGinnies since they obtained results consistent with the importance of word frequency *without* employing the word-count technique and using a *continuous* range of word frequency.

Cowen and Beier (1954) however, report an experiment with fifty-nine students who were required to decipher progressively less blurred carbon copies of words, some emotional, and some neutral. They found that significantly more trials were required to achieve the correct report of the former as compared with the latter. They also found *no* significant correlation between threshold and frequency ($r = + 0.003$).

Lazarus (1954) has pointed out that, after all, the two factors of familiarity and emotionality may interact; frequency itself may be partly a function of an individual's needs as well as experience.

A study has been reported by Delucia and Stagner (1953) who tested twenty members of the National Guard in an association time, and in a recognition threshold, situation in a way analogous to the method of the original study by Bruner and Postman (1947). Delucia and Stagner provide a graph (Fig. 7.5) of their results which show interesting similarities to the one given by Bruner and Postman (*see* p. 265, Fig. 7.2).

Delucia and Stagner point out that: "Both show an initial negative acceleration, a peak and a decline. The final segments of the two curves differ, perhaps because we have ten steps on the *x*-axis whereas Bruner and Postman have only five. The overall resemblance, however, seems noteworthy." (Delucia and Stagner, 1953, p. 302.) It should be noted that *even with frequency held constant*, these authors report that recognition time is still significantly related to association time and they conclude that: "Our data seem to support both the Bruner and Postman emphasis on emotional factors, and the Solomon-Howes stress on frequency." (Op. cit., p. 306.)

An ingenious experiment by Wiener (1955) used the *same* words as both threat and neutral stimuli by placing them in different contexts—for example, placing the word *fairy* in a context which emphasized its homosexual connotation and in a context which stressed its supernatural connotation. Differences in threshold were shown; in this case, however, the critical words were perceived *more quickly* when they had been in a threat context than when they had been in a neutral context.

From this review of criticisms and rebuttals it can be concluded that in any well-conducted experiment designed to elucidate further the phenomena of perceptual defence it is certain that there must be taken into account the important factor of word frequency, and also, in view of the findings of McGinnies, Comer and Lacey (1952) word-*length* should be controlled as well.

It is probably the case, however, that word frequency, by itself, cannot account for all the phenomena reported and that the notion of perceptual defence cannot be explained away in terms of this factor alone.

RESPONSE SUPPRESSION

Another kind of criticism which has been made of the apparent defensive phenomena is that they may, in fact, be due, at least in part, to the deliberate withholding of responses to emotional words by the subjects until it is abundantly clear what words are being shown, simply because of the embarrassment involved in reporting words like *penis, whore*, and the like, in an experimental situation.

This type of criticism has been put forward by Howes and Solomon (1950) who, it will be recalled, are also among the main proponents of the word-frequency argument.

Whittaker, Gilchrist and Fischer (1952) have published a note on data which they claim support the idea of "response suppression." When words derogatory to negroes were projected and the situation was conducted by a negro experimenter, these authors claim that the negro subjects' protocols showed evidence of "conscious suppression." Their case is somewhat weakened, however, by the fact that although this suppression effect was only noted with this S × E combination there was *no* significant difference between the mean illuminance threshold value for such words for this group of subjects and two other (white) groups also taken by a negro experimenter.

Postman, Bronson and Gropper (1953) report a more convincing study which was designed experimentally to vary the likelihood of response suppression. The subjects were ninety-six students; word frequency was controlled by the word-count method and thresholds were established by different levels of illuminance. Four different sets of instructions were used. Thus, one group was "uninformed," in that they were not warned to expect "taboo" words. A second group was "informed," i.e., they were told what to expect. A third group was "facilitated"; they were given instructions designed to discourage the withholding of taboo responses. A fourth group was "inhibited," being given instructions designed to encourage the withholding of responses. The results of this experiment showed that the thresholds for the taboo words were significantly *lower* than the thresholds for the neutral words. The relative thresholds for neutral and emotional words, however, varied significantly with the nature of the instructions, as would have been predicted from the response-suppression hypothesis.

The response-suppression hypothesis has also been favoured by Bitterman and Kniffen (1953). They used a tachistoscopic procedure with forty female students and they derive support for their hypothesis mainly on the basis of the fact that there was a significant decline in threshold for taboo words as a function of order of presentation (*see* Fig. 7.6).

These authors note that: "The fact that no order-effect is evident for the neutral words suggests that the order effect for the taboo words cannot be attributed to tachistoscopic practice. It must represent, instead, the development of insight into the essential nature of the situation. In the words of one subject, 'I caught on to what you were doing and then expected anything.' This result is precisely what might be anticipated on the assumption that differences in the threshold of taboo and neutral words (beyond those attributable to frequency of experience) may be

accounted for in terms of differential readiness to report rather than in terms of perceptual functioning." (Bitterman and Kniffen, 1953, p. 250.) It should be noted from Fig. 7.6 however, that the difference between taboo and neutral words was in fact significant even in the final position, a fact for which the authors' hypothesis does not seem to account.

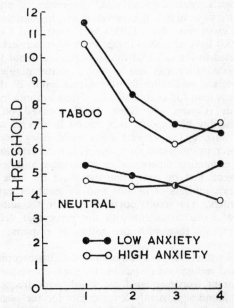

FIG. 7.6. MEAN THRESHOLDS (IN HUNDREDTHS OF A SECOND) FOR TABOO AND NEUTRAL WORDS AS A FUNCTION OF ORDER OF PRESENTATION
(*From Bitterman and Kniffen,* 1953)

Lysak (1954) also favours the response-suppression hypothesis, although it does not seem to the present writer that his investigation of the effect of shock on thresholds provides crucial evidence on this point.

In other studies in which the subjects were given instructions which led them to expect taboo words, Lacy, Lewinger and Adamson (1953) and Freeman (1954, 1955) have shown that this may, in fact, lead to *lower* recognition thresholds for the taboo than for the neutral words, a fact which will be discussed in more detail later (*see* pages 272 and 273).

In the meantime some of the data which have been produced by the supporters of perceptual defence in reply to the suggestion that their findings are explicable in terms of response suppression may be considered.

McGinnies and Sherman (1952) examined, tachistoscopically, the recognition thresholds of twenty male undergraduates for eight five-letter words of approximately equal frequency and of neutral meaning. Half of these task words were presented to the subjects immediately after the full exposure of a taboo word, half were presented following the exposure of a neutral word. These authors were able to show that the subjects' thresholds for the former were significantly higher than for the latter. They interpreted their findings in terms of *the generalization of an avoidance reaction* from the taboo to the neutral words. They argue that there can be no reason to suppose that subjects voluntarily withheld responses to stimuli which were, in fact, themselves neutral in connotation.

Cowen and Beier (1950) and Beier and Cowen (1953) have also shown that even when subjects are alerted to the fact that threat words are about to be exposed, they may still require a greater number of trials and more time for the correct report of threat words than for neutral words. These authors in one study (Cowen and Beier, 1954) checked on the possibility of response suppression in several ways; by warning the subjects what words they were to expect, by cross-examining them after the experiment, by estimating differences between male and female subjects and by comparing the effect on male and female subjects of like-sex and different-sex experimenters. The results obtained were, in the authors' view, more consistent with the perceptual defence hypothesis than with the notion of response suppression.

Newton (1955) has also examined tachistoscopically visual recognition thresholds for pleasant versus unpleasant words equated for word-count frequency. He found significantly fewer errors for the pleasant words. Response suppression would not seem to be an adequate explanation here since the unpleasant words (e.g., *shame*, *cruel*, etc.) were not such as to make it likely that the subjects would withhold verbal report simply from embarrassment.

It may be concluded, therefore, that the effect of response suppression, like the effect of word-frequency, must certainly be taken into account in any well-designed experiment concerned with perceptual defence. It seems, however, that when the possibility of withholding responses has been, as far as possible, eliminated or controlled, differences in threshold and/or in response time remain, and so remain to be explained.

Personalized Anxiety

Another general type of criticism has been made of some of the material employed in some perceptual defence experiments. Chodorkoff (1955) has pointed out that the use, for example, of taboo words does not guarantee their personal, anxiety-arousing relevance for every subject and that any adequate experiment must ensure the employment of such personally relevant threatening and neutral stimuli.

A search of the literature suggests that at least two main methods have been employed in attempts to secure items so that they contain a certain amount of personalized anxiety. In the first place, words have been employed which have elicited "complex-indicator" responses (e.g., delayed reaction-times) in word-association situations. Secondly, stimuli have been employed to which some anxiety-reaction has been experimentally secured (e.g., by association with electric shock). A brief review may be made of such studies under the separate heads.

1. *Word Association*

It will be recalled that this is the method initially used by Bruner and Postman (1947) to secure their "defended against" stimuli.

The same technique has been employed by Eriksen (1951) and by Chodorkoff (1954) who both obtained results consistent with the hypothesis of perceptual defence, and by Delucia and Stagner (1953) in the study already described (page 268).

A good recent study has been reported by Singer (1956) who also used the word association method.

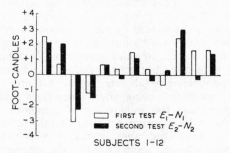

FIG. 7.7. Difference between Mean Threshold Values for Emotional and Neutral Words of Individual Subjects on Both Tests
(From Singer, 1956)

He estimated illuminance threshold for twelve young women on two occasions to two lists of eight neutral and eight emotional words respectively. He notes that: "From each of the two tachistoscopic tests, two mean recognition thresholds were obtained for each subject; the mean recognition threshold for the eight emotional words shown (E_1 and E_2) and the mean recognition threshold for the eight neutral words shown (N_1 and N_2). The differences $E_1 - N_1$ (in the case of the first test) and $E_2 - N_2$ (in the case of the second test), indicate the amount by which the mean recognition threshold for emotional words exceeds the mean recognition threshold value for neutral words. A positive value for this difference would indicate that the mean recognition threshold for emotional words was greater than the mean recognition threshold for neutral words. A negative value for this difference would indicate the reverse." (Singer, 1956, p. 307.) It can be seen from Fig. 7.7 that six subjects showed defensive reactions to the emotional words, while two showed vigilance reactions, and that most of the subjects showed consistency of reaction over the two occasions. Overall the defence effect was significant.

Mednick, Harwood and Wertheim (1957) secured five neutral and five disturbing words, controlled for frequency, for twenty-four students on the basis of word-association test responses. When it was suggested to the subjects that an apparently moving (but actually motionless) point of light in a dark room would trace out sentences containing the selected words, *fewer* of the disturbing words were reported, and when they were they showed a greater latency than did the neutral words.

It is interesting to note that all these studies took careful consideration of word frequency factors and, by ensuring the relevance of the stimuli, obtained results consistent with the perceptual defence hypothesis.

However, as Singer has cautiously put it: "In this experiment, and in several others, the objective criterion of the emotional connotation of a word has been the duration of reaction-time. Strictly speaking, the present experiment has only shown that higher thresholds (and the reverse) are obtained for words of a long reaction-time: that the words were actually emotional has not been unequivocally demonstrated. Our present knowledge indicates that two determinants are mainly responsible for the duration of reaction-time: the associative strength of the stimulus word and its emotional effect on the subject." (Singer, 1956, p. 308.)

2. Association with Shock

An experiment into the phenomena of "subception" (or "discrimination without awareness") by Lazarus and McCleary (1951) incidentally provided information of use in the examination of the problems of perceptual defence. In this study ten paralogs were presented to the subjects, and five of these were paired with an electric shock so that a conditioned P.G.R.s was obtained. When the ten paralogs were now exposed at speeds too rapid for the subjects accurately to report which stimulus was being presented, it could be shown that the syllables which had been previously paired with shock gave greater P.G.R.s than did the neutral syllables. It should be noted, however, that there was in this case *no* difference overall for the accuracy of report between shock and non-shock syllables.

An experiment by Reece (1954) used a factorial design to examine the effects of escapability and predictability of shock on the recognition thresholds

and learning of nonsense syllables by seventy undergraduate subjects. He was able to show that when he expressed his results as ratios between post- and pre-learning (i.e., shock-association) thresholds then there was a significant difference between these threshold ratios for the non-escape shock group compared with the escape shock group and also compared with the shock group.

Similar results have been reported by Rosen (1954) who argued that if the perception of a stimulus is painful to the organism and it cannot do anything directly to avoid it, then one consequence may be the raising of the recognition threshold for such a stimulus. This author was able to show, in accordance with prediction, that non-avoidable shock did raise the tachistoscopic recognition threshold of shock-associated words. The role of the learning process in the use of either defence or vigilance as the preferred mode of response to shock-associated stimuli has also recently been studied by Dulany (1957).

3. Other Methods of Securing Relevant Stimuli

Various other methods have been employed in order to secure personalized anxiety. For example, a study by Eriksen (1950) showed consistency between the handling of T.A.T. themes (as regards aggression, etc.) and the perceptual recognition of such relevant "theme" words. Those subjects who, for example, blocked or showed other emotional indicators in their stories as regards aggression also had higher tachistoscopic visual thesholds than those who did not.

Neel (1954) used groups chosen for being prone to conflict over sex or aggression and compared their recognition threshold for pictures containing mild or direct sexual or aggressive content with the corresponding thresholds of a "no-conflict" control group. Her results suggest that there may be differences in the kind of response made to different *kinds* of anxiety-provoking stimuli.

An interesting application of the notion of personalized anxiety applied to a single case has been reported by Walton (1954). Applying the method originally used by Rosenstock (1951) he was able to show that sentences containing material judged to be stressful on the basis of a patient's case-history were more defended against in terms of illuminance threshold than were similarly selected neutral items. Walton (1957) has also followed up these results on groups of patients.

A study by Carpenter, Wiener and Carpenter (1956) has shown that when anxiety-provoking words are individually chosen (from results on a "sentence completion" type of task) for subjects on the basis of their susceptibility to conflict in a particular area (e.g., sex, hostility, etc.) then the defence or vigilance behaviour in the perceptual situation is consistent with the behaviour in the sentence completion situation.

Smith (1953) however, failed to show differences in the recognition of hostile and neutral words in subjects rated as hostile or non-hostile on the basis of M.M.P.I. scores and a "hostility scale."

for emotional words may be *lower* than for neutral words.

In an article by Lacy, Lewinger and Adamson (1953) an experiment is reported (and its replication) in which thirty undergraduate subjects were tachistoscopically presented with neutral and obscene taboo words under three different conditions; i.e., (1) no knowledge; (2) general knowledge (in which each

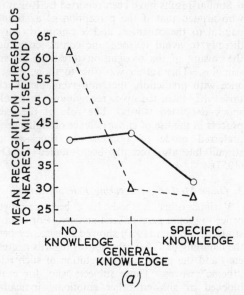

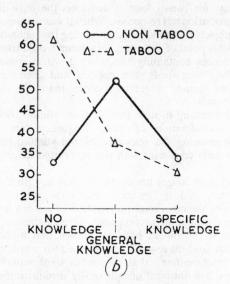

FIG. 7.8. (a) THE RECOGNITION THRESHOLDS FOR THIRTY SUBJECTS IN EXPERIMENT I TO THE FIRST WORD SEEN. (b) THE RECOGNITION THRESHOLDS FOR THIRTY SUBJECTS IN EXPERIMENT II TO THE FIRST WORD SEEN

(From Lacy, Lewinger and Adamson, 1953)

Spielberger (1956) reports on differences in oral and written recognition for stuttered words by stutterers and a control group of non-stutterers. There were differences in oral, but not in written, recognition thresholds. The author interprets his results as favouring the response-suppression hypothesis. This experiment is based on the assumption that stuttered words are emotionally loaded for stutterers. It should be noted, however, that recent work by Cherry and Sayers (1956) suggests that factors other than orectic may be of prime importance in stuttering behaviour.

Having discussed some of the main areas of controversy which are to be found in the work on perceptual defence, we may now turn back a little to examine some apparent contradictions which have arisen and which have appeared principally in studies concerned to elucidate the possible role of response suppression. It will be recalled that certain studies which permitted the subjects to *expect* the presentation of emotional or taboo words actually demonstrated that, under such conditions, the recognition thresholds

subject was told what *kind* of words to expect); and (3) specific knowledge (in which each subject was told exactly what words were to be shown). The found recognition thresholds for the two kinds of words are best described graphically (*see* Fig. 7.8).

The differences between conditions of knowledge were shown to be significant and the interaction Taboo × Knowledge was also significant. The small apparent differences between the experimental and replication results were not significant. The authors note in their discussion of these results—

The present experiment grew out of work which initially has been theoretically explained by the notion of perceptual defence. Competing with this conception is the explanation offered by Howes and Solomon which supposed that the slower times for the taboo words is due to the lesser frequency with which such words appear in visual experience. The present experiment enlarges the evidence with which these competing theories must deal. It is now necessary, not only to account for the longer reactions for taboo words seen under McGinnies' conditions, but also for the shorter reaction times seen under our "warning" conditions. In addition the competing theories must deal with the fact that differences in recognition thresholds involving taboo and non-taboo words disappear with habituation in experiments of this sort. The Howes-Solomon theory can account for the slowness with which taboo words are seen without warning, but it cannot explain the fact that such words are seen more quickly than non-taboo words when expectation exists. Further, the Howes-Solomon theory offers no grounds for explaining the habituation effects described above.

Looked at in the context of McGinnies' original theory the results suggest very strongly the bipolar character of the personal conditions which affect the speed with which perceptions are reported. In a sense, the experiment is a test of Bruner and Postman's views that these personal conditions are of such a nature that at some times they operate to defend against stimuli and at others to promote alertness to the reception of stimuli, whether defensiveness or alertness occurs depending upon the need prevailing in the receiver. (Lacy, Lewinger and Adamson, 1953, p. 173.)

These authors conclude that such differences with differing instructions are explicable in terms of changing dominance of "set."

Substantially the same results for forewarned subjects are reported by Freeman (1954). This latter author has also reported a study (Freeman, 1955) again using tachistoscopic recognition of taboo and neutral words by students. In one experiment, forewarning was used as one of the variables, and, in another, ego-involvement was employed. That is to say, the subjects were warned that the perceptual task they were about to do was related to academic success and aptitude. The effect of this forewarning was, as before, to reverse the speed of differential perception of taboo words. The effect of ego-involvement, on the other hand, was to speed up perception generally but to leave the neutral words as the faster perceived.

In fact, these findings illustrate what had been evident from Bruner and Postman's (1947) original study, that any notions designed to describe and explain the phenomena which exemplify perceptual defence must also make room for the obverse phenomena of perceptual vigilance.

Perceptual Defence and the Mediation-Motivation Hypothesis

The role of mediation-like processes in perception has been emphasized, from the "neuropsychological" point of view, by Hebb (1949) whose main concern has been to propose a model for perceptual processes which involves elements which are to some extent the neurological analogues of "mediators." Hebb adduces evidence mainly from the work of Senden (1932) and Riesen (1947) to show that apparently "simple"

perceptions are in fact complex; that they depend to a considerable extent on the self-stimulation provided, for example, by oculo-motor activity, and that their apparent simplicity and immediacy is only the end result of a long learning process.

Vernon (1955) has discussed the role of *schemata* in perception. Berlyne (1951), from the Hullian point of view, has made proposals suggesting that "perception" should, in behaviour theory, be introduced as an intervening variable, and be allotted the status of a stimulus-producing response.

Now the availability, to the organism, of such stimulus-producing responses in perceptual behaviour may be a function of several factors and among these the two most important are likely to be "habit strength" (e.g., as determined by word frequency) and "drive status"[1] (e.g., in terms of their role as, say, "anxiety mediators"), the latter quality depending not only on stimulus quality but upon susceptibility factors within the individual. (This is in agreement with the point made by Klein and Schlesinger (1949), by Lazarus (1955) and by Eriksen (1954b) among others, that one of the antecedent conditions which must be taken into account in such experiments is the "kind of individual" used as subject.)

Let us now consider what seems to happen in the situations of high and low stress such as were postulated at the beginning of this chapter.

1. *Low stress:* In a perceptual situation in which the habit strength of the mediators involved is held constant at approximately asymptotic value and the drive value of such mediators approaches a minimum, then individuals at the *NE* end of the suggested personality continuum may not be concerned to initiate any avoidance behaviour towards such mediators. Individuals at the *NI* end of the continuum, however, being much more susceptible to stress, may have already begun to initiate such avoidance (i.e., anxiety-reducing) activity. In terms of performance, then, individuals *NE* may appear to show perceptual vigilance whereas individuals *NI* are at this time showing evidence of perceptual defence.

2. *High stress:* In situations of similarly constant habit strength, but where the drive value is high, then, as in simple learning, the second part of the Yerkes-Dodson law effect becomes evident. Individuals *NE* now perform more markedly their mediation-avoidance activity; whereas, by reason of the fact that their drive component has now become excessive, individuals *NI* are now avoiding less adequately so that, in terms of performance, the vigilance and defence roles are now reversed.

---

[1] The effect of such determinants on perceptual behaviour has been examined experimentally by, for example, Engler and Freeman (1956), by Rockett (1956), by Newton (1956), and by Rigby and Rigby (1956).

These processes can be illustrated by their application to an earlier diagram (Fig. 7.9).

The advantages of this model seem to be as follows—

1. It permits the dismissal of "agency" notions (*see* Howie, 1952) since mediation may be triggered off, and presumably, therefore, *not* triggered off, by responses below the threshold of verbal report (Bugelski, 1956).

2. It takes into account both the components of word frequency and emotional value.

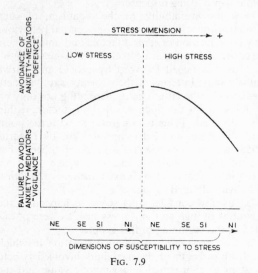

FIG. 7.9

3. It reduces the apparent gulf between response suppression and perceptual defence since the explanation may now be couched in terms of different levels of readiness to report. Thus, at one level we have the avoidance of the production of overt mediators towards other organisms and, at another, the avoidance of the production of covert mediators toward the organism itself.

4. It takes into account the apparently paradoxical phenomena of vigilance and defence and deals with such curvilinear relationships as were first noted by Bruner and Postman (1947).

It can also deal with the apparent vigilance effects which have been noted when the subjects have been warned to expect taboo words (as in the study of Lacy, Lewinger and Adamson, 1953) by suggesting that the effect of such instructions is to reduce anxiety, so producing indifference to avoidance.

5. Most important of all, this model explicitly states the parameters of individual differences which are expected to be relevant to performance in the perceptual defence situation.

Certain other studies which have been carried out in the investigation of perceptual defence phenomena may now be reviewed in order to see if they can be resolved with the model proposed.

Consideration of Some Further Evidence

It is evident that an ideal experiment, specifically designed to test the hypothesis put forward would, at least—

(*a*) control for such factors as word frequency and the likelihood of response suppression, and

(*b*) vary systematically such factors as personality structure and the anxiety arousing relevance of the stimuli used, and also take account of their interaction.

In default of such a single experiment the results of a number of further studies from the literature may be recounted which have commonly taken a few of these considerations into account.

It should be pointed out that, in the ordinary visual-threshold experiment it is likely that situations of low stress will be principally involved. That is to say, we shall be dealing mainly with the left-hand side of the postulated inverted U-distribution, and it will follow that these will mainly show a relationship between dysthymia and defence. This will arise from the fact that not only will the stimuli employed be only mildly stressful but also that the individuals used as subjects, even when they are selected as being at an extreme on some personality index, are usually students rather than, say, psychiatric patients.

There are, however, other studies which show the expected U-distribution of results. McClelland and Liberman (1949) showed such difference in threshold for "deprivation" words in subjects showing differences in "n-Achievement," (*see* Fig. 7.10).

Other relevant studies may be examined under headings provided by the principal factors taken into account in their design, as follows.

LOW STRESS AND PERSONALITY

An experiment by Chodorkoff (1954) used an "accuracy of self-description" test (which has been shown to be related to adjustment by Brownfain (1952)) and a Rorschach estimate of general adjustment to measure the personality variables. This study demonstrated that it was the less adequately adjusted individuals who showed defensive threshold phenomena. Another study by the same author, however, (Chodorkoff, 1956) attempted to relate anxiety to defensive phenomena with a negative outcome. It seems likely that such results are vitiated by the fact that the personality measures in this study were derived from Rorschach indices of very doubtful validity.

A study using a better measure of the relevant personality variables has been reported by Smock (1956a). He used two groups of twenty subjects;

one group chosen on the basis of high scores and one on the basis of low scores obtained on the Sarason Anxiety Scale (Sarason and Gordon, 1953). To estimate the effects of such anxiety on the perception of anxiety-arousing words Smock used a technique similar to that employed by McGinnies and Sherman (1952). The results obtained in this experiment confirm the present hypothesis in two respects. Firstly, anxiety level as measured by the Sarason test was positively associated with delayed recognition of words, and, secondly, the anxiety-arousing properties of the pre-task word also contributed to the elevation of recognition thresholds under all experimental conditions. The interaction which would have been expected on the present hypothesis was, however, not statistically significant.

Kissin, Gottesfeld and Dickes (1957) have also shown that persons who are inhibited (in the sense of "restrained" or "constricted") on projective tests may show raised thresholds for sexual, as compared with neutral words.

Pustell (1956) using shock-associated geometrical figures as tachistoscopic stimuli, found significant threshold differences between male and female students. The males showed vigilance, the females defence. Pustell claims that this was because the males found the shocks moderate, while the females found them severe.

High Stress and Personality

A study which appears to the present author to be illustrative of the situation to be expected on the right-hand side of the postulated inverted U-curve has been reported by Eriksen and Browne (1956). These authors experimentally manipulated the frequency of response strength of ten words for two groups of about twenty student subjects. For one of these groups they arranged that these ten words should also become conditioned stimuli for anxiety (through association with a failure experience). The groups were also divided in terms of high and low scores on the "Psychasthenia" scale of the M.M.P.I. Eriksen and Browne were able to show that while the variables of frequency and recency did, in fact, lower the perceptual recognition thresholds for the experienced words, this reduction was *less* in the case of the anxiety-conditioned words. They were also able to show that the group high on psychasthenia (or in our terms, in dysthymia) had a *lower* mean threshold on this occasion for the anxiety-related words than did the low psychasthenia group. Eriksen and Browne suggest that this difference in thresholds was due to the presumed fact that the failure-associated words were *less* anxiety-producing for the high psychasthenic group. The present writer would suggest, however, that the reverse may be the case and that, in the high-stress area in which

they were operating, the high psychasthenic groups were unable to avoid anxiety mediation and were therefore exhibiting vigilance. This latter interpretation would, in fact, seem to be more consonant with other results obtained by Eriksen (1952a, 1954a) discussed below (*see* pages 276 and 277).

Osler and Lewisohn (1954) using the Taylor Anxiety Scale and ingeniously employing paired stimuli as alike as possible, in which the difference in

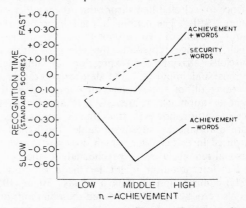

Fig. 7.10. Mean Recognition Times in Standard Scores for Achievement- and Security-related Words Plotted for the Upper, Middle and Lower Thirds of the n-Achievement Distribution as Obtained by Combining Ranks on the T.A.T. and Anagrams Measures of n-Achievement
(*From McClelland and Liberman, 1949*)

one letter alone made them acceptable or unacceptable (e.g., *tit-tot*, *bitch-botch*), also found *lower* thresholds for the unacceptable words in the high-anxiety group. The opposite difference, which would be predicted on the basis of the present hypothesis for the low-anxiety group, did not, however, appear.

Variation in Stress

In addition to the studies already quoted (e.g. Lacy, Lewinger and Adamson, 1953; Freeman, 1954, 1955) in which forewarning appears to have *reduced* anxiety, some studies have been made on the effect of the experimental increase of anxiety.

In one experiment which, however, attempted to vary the stressfulness of the task situation, Stein (1952) showed that under conditions of increased anxiety there was an accentuation of either sensitization *or* defence in twenty-four neurotic patients, rather than the progressive *change* from one to the other which would be predicted from the present hypothesis.

Zuckerman (1954) tried to see whether frustration-induced aggressive need had any effect on the tachistoscopic threshold for aggressive words compared with neutral words in groups of subjects in whom had been induced varying degrees of need-strength.

Higher thresholds were found for the aggressive words but these were not associated with the differing, presumably need-arousing, conditions. However, the experimental group *did* show greater *variability* in threshold phenomena than did the control group.

Blum (1954) demonstrated (in a study whose design, however, has been criticized by Smock, (1956*b*)) that, by increasing anxiety through two stages, subjects could be induced to show first vigilance and then defence for selected items from the "Blacky Pictures" (Blum, 1950). The author himself interprets these results in terms of two psychoanalytic hypotheses, in which vigilance represents the effect of "the unconscious striving for expression of underlying psychosexual impulses," and defence represents the "warding off of these threatening impulses as they begin to approach awareness." It appears to the present author, however, that Blum's results may be more economically subsumed under the hypothesis advanced in this chapter, which does not invoke the personalized agencies of psychoanalytic theory. A similar interpretation might be made of Nelson's (1955) confirmation of Blum's results. Blum (1957) has also cross-culturally validated these findings on a group of Italian subjects.

CONSISTENCY OF "RESPONSE STYLE"

Evidence for the current hypothesis should not only be traceable in studies which have used the same kind of situation (e.g., visual recognition) and which have attempted to control the relevant variables; further evidence should also be available from studies in which the process of "mediation avoidance" can be said to be at work in quite different kinds of situations.

For example, Blum (1955) has demonstrated relationships between such avoidance in *recall* and in recognition. In a situation which controlled the variables of "set," familiarity and selective verbal report, seventeen graduate student subjects were required to recognize tachistoscopically selected items from the Blacky Pictures. In the series of stimuli were included pictures to which the subject had previously shown both conflict and repression (i.e., avoidance tendencies such as forgetting the picture or its name in either of two recall procedures) and neutral pictures. Similar sets of scores were obtained for pictures which were *not* actually flashed (the subjects being unaware of this) so as to control for the actual avoidance within the perceptual situation. As Eriksen (1957) has pointed out, this is a very important kind of control to exercise, since it is necessary to show that the defence type of result is not obtained when subjects are tachistoscopically shown pictures other than the ones which are supposed to portray their conflicts. The results obtained in this experiment can be seen in Table VII.1.

There are an unequal number of subjects within each condition since all seventeen did not have pictures falling into all four conditions, for example, only six

TABLE VII.1

MEAN FREQUENCY OF PICTURE CALLS

(From Blum, 1955)

Conditions	No. of subjects	Mean No. of calls per picture
1. Present pictures (Conflict + repression) .	6	9·42 ⎫ $t = 3·83$
2. Present pictures (Neutral) . . .	14	17·12 ⎭ $p < 0·001$
3. Absent pictures (Conflict + repression) .	5	15·20 ⎫
4. Absent pictures (Neutral) . . .	14	16·69 ⎭ N.S.

subjects obtained "conflict plus repression" scores on one or more of the "present" pictures. Blum notes that—

Pictures representing areas of conflict and repression are significantly undercalled when the stimuli are actually present (Condition 1) in comparison to the same pictures unaccompanied by conflict and defence (Condition 2). This difference between disturbing and neutral pictures does not obtain when the stimuli are absent (Condition 3 *v.* 4). . . . Two interesting sidelights also deserve mention. Though the hypothesis deals only with the combined effect of conflict and repression, the data lend themselves to a further breakdown on the effect of conflict alone. Fourteen individuals showed conflict but no defence on present pictures. Their mean number of calls per picture is 17·68, which conforms closely to the chance expectancy. Therefore the conclusion is warranted that an avoidance response cannot be expected solely from the existence of conflict, but requires as an essential component, the predisposition to avoid, namely repression. (Blum, 1955, p. 27.)

Perhaps the best evidence concerning the consistency of response styles, and their relation to stress and personality factors, comes from the work of Eriksen. In one study Eriksen (1952*a*) compared the effect of individual differences in the response to ego-threat in a situation involving memory for incompleted tasks (*see* pages 280 *et seq.*) with the effect of these individual differences upon the perceptual recognition of ego-threatening stimuli. In the former situation college students were required simply to recall the names of tasks, half of which they had been allowed to complete and half of which they had been forced to leave unfinished. Half the subjects did the tasks under the guise of an intelligence test (i.e., they were made ego-involved, or, in our terms, they were made

TABLE VII.2

MEAN PERFORMANCE OF SUBJECTS AS RELATED TO THE TENDENCY TO SHOW SUPERIOR RECALL FOR SUCCESSFUL OR UNSUCCESSFUL SENTENCES

(From Lazarus and Longo, 1953)

Group	Learning by trials		Learning by number of correct syllables		Recall in terms of per cent of total*		Relearning by number of trials	
	S†	N	S	N	S	N	S	N
Superior recall of successes .	17·1	15·5	28·6	31·1	56·1	74·0	3·12	2·55
Superior recall of failures .	15·5	14·9	25·8	30·7	72·1	60·0	2·60	3·34

* This comparison results in a difference between groups by a Chi-square two-by-two analysis which is significant beyond the 0·01 level of confidence.
† S refers to shock syllables and N refers to non-shock syllables.

anxious). The other half did the tasks under much more relaxed conditions. It was found that the main effect of the ego-involvement procedure was greatly to increase the group variance on the recall of completed *v.* uncompleted tasks. That is to say, compared with the non-ego-involved group greater individual differences were apparent.

For the second part of this study individuals were selected from the ego-involved group in terms of their scoring either a high success-to-failure ratio or a high failure-to-success ratio in the recall of tasks. Eriksen then proceeded to determine the relation between association-time (on a word association test) and the recognition thresholds for "complex-indicating" words for these individuals. Comparison showed that individuals who had responded to threat in the first situation by forgetting their failures showed a similar avoidance reaction in their perception of threatening words. On the other hand, those who had a high failure-to-success ratio in the first situation perceived the threatening words as quickly as they did the non-threatening words.

Eriksen (1952*b*) was also able to show that subjects favouring successes over failures in the first type of situation described above also required longer to learn and to relearn paired associates when one of the pair was a word having a long reaction time in a word-association test. On the other hand, the subjects who favoured the incompleted tasks learned words with long association times just as quickly as words with short association times.

Spence (1957), on the other hand, failed to find such consistency in the learning and recognition of failure words. Absolute threshold difference rather than *direction* of difference was related to anxiety in his experiment.

However, Lazarus and Longo (1953) were also able to show that when individuals favouring successes to failures in the recall of interrupted tasks were required to learn and relearn pairs of nonsense syllables, some

of which had been associated with electric shock, then they recalled and relearned a higher percentage of the unshocked syllables. Those who had recalled more failures in the first situation, however, were able to recall and relearn a higher percentage of the shocked syllables (*see* Table VII.2.)

Lazarus and Longo note that—

The primary finding of this experiment is that subjects who recalled their successes in one situation also tended to recall material not associated with painful stimulation in another. This relationship occurs in spite of the fact that the two tasks employed are essentially different and the two experiments which are being compared utilized apparently different kinds of threat (viz. failure *v.* physical pain produced by electric shock). It is impossible to account for the correspondence in the performance of the subjects in the two situations in terms of task or ability variables. In order to explain the relationship, it appears reasonable to think in terms of some *intervening process* or some concept like habit or style of responding to threat. (Lazarus and Longo, 1953, p. 49.)

Such apparent "consistency of response" seems to the writer to be of considerable interest since it indicates, as has been noted by a number of authors, including Walton (1957), an important link between avoidance in simple perceptual tasks *and* in more complex ones. It also appears that the common mechanism of mediation avoidance, and similar effects of stress and personality on this mechanism, can also be adduced, for example in the work on memory for incompleted tasks, instances of which have been mentioned above. Such experiments have, of course, been commonly placed under the label of "studies in the Zeigarnik effect," and before the suggested relationships are further explored some of the findings made in this latter area may be briefly discussed.[1]

[1] A comparison of thresholds of recognition of normals and schizophrenic patients for neutral and taboo words has been reported by McGinnies and Adornetto (1952). Both groups showed higher thresholds for taboo words. The schizophrenic thresholds were generally higher than the normals for both types of words and they produced more "pre-recognition hypotheses."

STUDIES OF THE "ZEIGARNIK EFFECT"

Description of the Phenomena

In 1927 Zeigarnik reported a series of experiments concerning the performance and recall of simple paper-and-pencil tasks. In these experiments she allowed her subjects to complete some of the tasks but interrupted their performance on others before they had finished them. When they were later asked to recall the names of the tasks Zeigarnik found that most of her subjects recalled more of the uncompleted than of the completed items. This kind of differential recall has been labelled "the Zeigarnik effect."[1] This effect was originally measured in terms of the proportion

$$P = \frac{\text{Number of Interrupted } (I)\text{tasks}}{\text{Number of Completed } (C) \text{ tasks}}$$

and it can be seen that if $P = 1$ then there is no differential preference; if $P > 1$ then the interrupted I tasks are favoured in recall, and if $P < 1$ then the completed C tasks are favoured. The actual means of the ratios obtained by Zeigarnik in one experiment with thirty-two subjects averaged 1·9. This represented an advantage of 90 per cent to the I tasks. In another experiment with different items and fifteen different subjects the mean ratio was 2·0.

Following upon the work of Zeigarnik other investigators have criticized and have attempted to improve upon her methods and techniques.

Pachauri (1935a) argued the importance of better controls in the experimental study of the effect. This author reported a study (1935b) which took into account such variables as the nature and duration of the tasks (showing the longer the task the more likely it was to be recalled), and which also examined the effects of the difficulty of the tasks and the influence of repetition. On the whole, the results of this study were in remarkable agreement with Zeigarnik's original findings; I tasks being recalled on the average 90 per cent better than C tasks.

Other authors who have confirmed Zeigarnik's original findings include McKinney (1935) who studied the effect in relation to maze- and nonsense-syllable-learning; Martin (1940) who examined the effect of the time-span between task completion or incompletion and recall, and Cartwright (1942) and Gebhard (1948) who studied the effects of interruption on the rated "attractiveness" of activities.

Marrow (1938a, 1938b) used an experimental procedure with thirty subjects and twenty tasks taking

[1] Only the *recall* of tasks will be considered here, although some work has been similarly concerned with the *resumption* of interrupted tasks. Such work has been reported, for example, by Ovsiankina (1928) (*see* also Rickers-Ovsiankina, 1937), Freeman (1930, 1938), Rosenzweig (1933), Adler and Kounin (1939), Nowlis (1941), and Rethlingshafer (1941a, 1941b) among others.

into account such factors as serial position effect and individual differences in remembering. He was also able to show that the Zeigarnik effect was a function of "experienced failure" rather than of interruption or incompleteness *per se*. He also criticized the kind of ratio used in the first studies and suggested a more adequate measure in the form

$$\frac{\text{Average recalled } I \text{ tasks}}{\text{Average recalled } C \text{ tasks}}$$

De Monchaux (1952) showed that this reduced Zeigarnik's original ratio from 1·9 to 1·6. She also studied the effects on the recall ratio of the relation between item completion and serial isolation; showing the interaction between these factors to be significant.

Variations in the Phenomena

Despite the ample confirmation of the effect achieved by many investigators, certain variations and even contradictions have emerged from other studies. These have been commented upon by Prentice (1944), Boguslavsky and Guthrie (1941), Crafts, Schneirla, Robinson and Gilbert (1950), and Boguslavsky (1951) among others. The main contradiction has emerged from experiments which have found a preponderance of C over I tasks in recall. It should be noted, however, that Zeigarnik herself was aware of the possibility of obtaining such reversals. This happened in an experiment of hers when the subjects were fatigued (1927).

Rosenzweig and Mason (1934) however, secured more recall for C than for I tasks in subjects not suffering from fatigue. They used forty crippled children between the ages of 5 and 14 approximately. The tasks they gave them were jigsaw picture puzzles, and these were presented as a "test" with a prize for the one who did best. Each child was allowed to succeed on half the puzzles he attempted and prevented from completing the other half. At the end of the session each was asked to recall the names of the puzzles attempted. The scores obtained were "recall difference" scores, expressed as percentages from the formula

$$\frac{C \text{ recalled}}{C \text{ given}} - \frac{I \text{ recalled}}{I \text{ given}} \times 100$$

Altogether more C than I puzzles were recalled. The authors found, in fact, that the subjects could be divided into three groups—

    (i) those who remembered more C than I tasks;

    (ii) those who remembered more I than C tasks;

    (iii) those who remembered equal numbers of each.

They also found that those in group (i) were different from those in group (ii) in that they tended to have a higher M.A. and also a higher average rating, as made (fairly unreliably as it proved) by their teachers, in the trait of "pride."

Further work by Rosenzweig showed that this discrepancy with Zeigarnik's original results could be considered due, in part at least, to differences in ego-involvement, or, as the present writer would prefer to say, to differences in the amount of stress in, or to the amount of anxiety aroused by, the test situation. Thus, in one study (Rosenzweig, 1943) sixty college students were each given a series of jigsaw puzzles to solve but were only allowed to finish half of them. One half of these subjects were given the tasks under informal conditions (i.e., non-stressful) which were "task-oriented" in the sense that the experimenter implied that he wanted to find out certain facts about the material used. The remaining subjects had impressed on them that the results would reflect their own ability; that is to say, the conditions were formal, "ego-oriented," stressful, or anxiety-arousing. When the subjects were asked to recall what they had been doing, the results of this experiment, using the notation already described, could be tabulated as follows—

	$P < 1$	$P > 1$	$P = 1$
Informal conditions	7	19	4
Formal conditions	17	8	5

These results not only showed that the relative stressfulness of the situation plays a part in differential recall, but also that individual differences in reaction can be demonstrated.

The effect of such individual differences has received a good deal of attention from Alper. In one of her studies, Alper (1946) examined the general hypothesis that if in the completed-interrupted task situation the group of subjects is *unselected* for personality factors, then the ratio P will approximate unity. The subjects used in this study were twenty undergraduates (ten experimental, ten control). The main experimental tasks were the rearrangement of twenty-four twenty-word scrambled sentences; half of which were solvable in the time allowed and half of which were not. The control subjects were used only to measure performance on the tasks under *informal* conditions. The experimental group, on the other hand, were given twelve of the sentences (some solvable, some not) first under informal conditions, together with other tasks, and, second twelve different sentences (some solvable, some not) under the *formal*, "pseudo-intelligence-test" conditions, together with the other tasks. The control results served to ensure that the two sets of twelve sentences were of comparable difficulty.

For the experimental group it was shown that *fewer* sentences were solved under formal than under informal conditions; in other words, the ego-orienting circumstances were shown to be, in fact, more disrupting or stressful. Actual memory for the sentences was also found to be significantly poorer for the formal than for the informal conditions. There was, however, no significant difference in selective recall *within* the sessions. This finding Alper interprets as supporting the hypothesis that when subjects are unselected for personality factors then there will be no statistically significant difference between the incidental recall of an equal number of C and I tasks.

Alper (1948) then went on to examine two further hypotheses. The first of these stated that under conditions where equal numbers of I and C tasks are to be recalled, then subjects who recall more C tasks will show consistent differences in personality from subjects who recall more I tasks. This hypothesis was tested on the basis of data gathered in the previous investigation. It should be noted that the ten experimental subjects had, in that investigation, been intensively investigated, in terms of personality, at the Harvard Psychological Clinic, along lines similar to those recounted in Murray's *Explorations in Personality* (1938).

The second hypothesis examined by Alper was that the *direction* of selective recall would differ systematically between the formal and the informal situations.

Examination of the data permitted both these hypotheses to be upheld and Alper went on to suggest that the differences found could be explained in terms of "ego-strength." Those individuals characterized as strong egos preponderantly recalled I tasks in the informal situation and C tasks in the formal situation; while the converse was true of those with weak egos. According to the personality investigations conducted, those with strong egos were high on traits like self-confidence and low on dejection and pessimism; the opposite being true of those with weak egos.

Alper notes that—

Two major patterns of selective recall were isolated by studying the recall of the same Ss under two objectively different experimental conditions, a large body of personality data being available for interpreting the behaviour of each S. The recall of incompleted tasks when self-esteem is not objectively threatened is a pattern characteristic of the "strong ego" who needs to protect his self-esteem only when it is objectively threatened. The recall of completed tasks in an objectively non-self-esteem-involving situation and of incompleted tasks when self-esteem is objectively threatened is characteristic of the "weak ego" who can protect his self-esteem only when the threat is not objectively present. (Alper, 1948, p. 135.)

A critical review of these studies by Rosenzweig and by Alper has been written by Glixman (1948) who points out that the type of "recall ratio" used by these authors (i.e., of the type I/C) confounds a number of variables and makes interpretation of their results extremely difficult. For example, any decrease noted in the ratio I/C might be due to (i) a decrease in I task recall alone, or (ii) to an increase in C task recall alone, or (iii) to an increase in I task recall accompanied by a greater increase in C task recall. Glixman advocates instead the use of separate recall ratios for completed tasks $\left(\text{i.e. } \dfrac{\text{Number of } C \text{ tasks recalled}}{\text{Number of } C \text{ tasks performed}}\right)$ and for in-completed tasks $\left(\dfrac{\text{Number of } I \text{ tasks recalled}}{\text{Number of } I \text{ tasks performed}}\right)$ which avoids these difficulties.

Such points as he made have been further discussed by Rosenzweig (1952) and by Alper (1952).

Alper (1957) has recently reported further validating evidence for her hypotheses. Two groups of nine subjects were chosen as being, respectively, strong and weak egos. She demonstrated that it was then possible to predict correctly, significantly beyond chance, their ego-group membership from the direction of their recall patterns on I and C tasks over two sessions, one task- and the other ego-oriented.

The Zeigarnik Effect and the Mediation-Avoidance Hypothesis

Relationships between certain of the phenomena elicited in experiments on perceptual defence and recall of completed and incompleted tasks has already been traced (page 276 et seq.) for example, in the experiments of Eriksen (1952a, 1952b) and Lazarus and Longo (1953).

Postman and Solomon (1949) have also examined the notion that common motivational principles may govern behaviour in the two situations.

These latter authors conducted an experiment in order to ascertain the speed with which a subject would recognize stimuli representing C and I tasks. The subjects were eighteen students and they were required to solve a series of ten seven-letter anagrams, word-frequency being taken into account. The subjects were stopped, in each case, as soon as half of them had completed any given anagram. After this part of the experiment the recognition thresholds for these words were measured tachistoscopically. It was shown that, for the group as a whole, there was no significant difference in recognition thresholds for C and I tasks. Postman and Solomon note, however, that individual differences were evident in that the greater proportion of their subjects showed a significant difference of sensitivity for one or the other. In fact, this result is not inconsistent with Alper's

notion about the lack of differences which may be expected in such experiments when subjects are unselected for personality factors.

An interesting corollary of the suggested connexion between the Zeigarnik phenomena and perceptual defence is that the selective recall noted in the former may be due to faulty registration; whereas, of course, the explanation put forward in terms of "repression" usually emphasizes poor retention. A recent study by Caron and Wallach (1957) shows that the effects are, in fact, mainly due to selective learning rather than selective remembering.

Following the lead of these experimental attempts to unite these two areas it seems feasible to try to bring them together within the conceptual framework already employed in this chapter.

Since the main hypothesis has been expounded already, it will be sufficient to outline the main points here—

1. The conditions of differential ego-involvement (e.g., "formal v. informal" conditions of testing) may be regarded as lying on a continuum of differential stress.

2. The personality variables which are important are those which are related to susceptibility to stress (i.e., neuroticism) and to the development of socialized anxiety (i.e., introversion-extraversion).

It seems likely, therefore, that the relevant dimension described by Alper in terms of a dichotomy of strong ego and weak ego may well be a "continuum" through NE-NI.

3. Differential recall may be explained in terms of differences in efficiency of recall in situations of high, as compared with situations of low, stress. This is such that while it may be quite efficient to recall incomplete tasks in a low-stress situation it may be relatively inefficient (i.e., anxiety-provoking) to do so in situations of high stress, where the reduction of such anxiety-mediators may be preferable, while, on the other hand, too great avoidance may also be maladaptive.

These elements, and their interaction, may be represented in the familiar diagram (Fig. 7.11).

As before, the "Low Stress" half of the represented dichotomy is already a situation of differential stress for individuals of differing status on the personality continuum NE–NI. At the NE end individuals have not yet begun to initiate the avoidance of mediators involved in the recall of either C or I tasks. For the NI individuals, however, the situation has already come to be one of considerable stress so that they have already begun to suppress the recall of anxiety-producing mediators (i.e., the I tasks).

In the situation objectively involving high stress the NE individuals now avoid the recall of I tasks. Individuals at the NI end, however, have reached and passed such anxiety-level so that their avoidance behaviour breaks down and *I* tasks again preponderate in their recall.

Consideration of Some Further Evidence

The earliest experiments in the field were founded no theories of Lewin's, so that, implicitly at least, the notion of "personality" has had some part in the interpretation of experimental results. Perhaps the

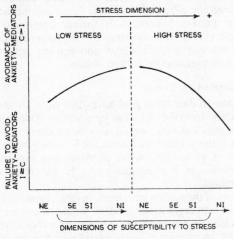

Fig. 7.11

earliest attempt to relate such results to independent, objective personality measurement was made by Pachauri (1936) who obtained no very conclusive results. More recently, however, studies using various techniques have elicited information which may be interpreted in terms of the hypothesis outlined.

As in the previous section of this chapter the relevant studies may be examined under headings provided by the principal factors taken into account in their design, as follows.

Stress and Personality

Eriksen (1954a) has reported an experiment which is almost equivalent to a direct test of the present hypothesis, which is, of course, fairly similar to his own way of conceptualizing the found relationships. In this study he set out to test three general hypotheses, as follows—

A. That "ego-strength" (measured in this experiment partly by a Rorschach conformity score not unlike that found by Eysenck (1947) to be a fairly good measure of neuroticism) should be *directly* related to the tendency to recall *I* tasks under task-oriented (i.e. "low stress") conditions and *inversely* related to the recall of *I* tasks under ego-oriented (i.e., "high stress") conditions.

B. That" hysteria," as measured by the M.M.P.I., should be inversely related to the recall of *I* tasks under ego-oriented conditions.

C. That "psychasthenia," also as measured by the M.M.P.I., should be directly related to *I* task recall under ego-oriented conditions.

Eriksen himself goes on to cite the relevance of these hypotheses to Eysenck's dimensional analysis of personality.

In fact, as can be seen from Table VII.3, the results of his experiment show, in line with the hypothesis advanced, that the *less* introverted the individual the more *I* tasks will he recall in a non-stressful situation; whereas the more *C* tasks will he recall in a stressful situation.

TABLE VII.3

CORRELATIONS BETWEEN THE EGO-STRENGTH SCALE AND COMPLETED-INCOMPLETED TASKS RECALL SCORE FOR THE EXPERIMENTAL AND CONTROL GROUPS

(From Eriksen, 1954a)

	Experimental (ego-oriented)	Control (task-oriented)
N	43	19
r	− 0·60	0·38
p	0·001	0·055

Analysis of the results of this experiment also showed that the higher the individual scores on the hysteria scale the *less* will be the tendency for him to recall more *I* tasks in the threatening (i.e., high stress) situation. Also, before neuroticism was partialled out of the psychasthenia score, the higher an individual's score was on this scale, the *greater* was the tendency to recall relatively more *I* tasks in the threatening situation.

Another study by Jourard (1954) failed to discover consistent relations (in terms of his own hypothesis) between certain Rorschach responses which were taken as measures of ego-strength and the recall of *I* tasks. However, the hypothesis outlined above would produce almost the opposite expectations from those predicted by Jourard. Thus, in terms of the notions outlined above, the present writer (like Alper) would expect little or no significant difference between the recall of *I* and *C* tasks in a population unselected for personality variables (since individual differences would tend to reduce the mean difference). Jourard, on the other hand, did predict differences, but his results were not in accord with his own prediction. Also, since the tests used were presented under formal, intelligence-test (and hence presumably stressful) conditions, the present author would predict that the strong egos would recall more *C* tasks, unlike Jourard, who predicted that they would recall more *I* tasks. In any case the Rorschach indices used by Jourard in this study have never been validated, whereas the one used by Eriksen (1954a) as has already been pointed out, was very similar to that derived from the multiple-choice Rorschach, which has been shown to be a valid test of neuroticism. It is therefore hardly surprising that Jourard was unable to report any consistent results arising from his study.

Two studies have been reported using the "Schneider index" which is an index of neurocirculatory efficiency, found to be low in neurotics, the results of which agree with the current hypothesis. Thus, Abel (1938) showed that, in a low stress situation requiring the recall of *I* and *C* tasks individuals with high Schneider indices (i.e., good neurocirculatory efficiency) recalled more *I* tasks, whereas those with low indices recalled more *C* tasks. Strother and Cook (1953) using the same index report results in striking agreement with Abel's in the performance of a test under conditions of differential stress. Those individuals with high neurocirculatory efficiency tended to show a gain in performance under conditions of increased stress while those with low efficiency showed a marked decrement.

The reaction to frustration, as represented by the Zeigarnik situation, has been explored by Rosenzweig and Sarason (1942) and Sarason and Rosenzweig (1942). These authors were concerned to evaluate Rosenzweig's "triadic hypothesis" which he had enunciated as follows: "Hypnotizability as a personality trait is to be found in positive association with repression as a preferred mechanism of defence and with impunitiveness as a characteristic type of immediate reaction to frustration," (Murray, 1938, p. 489).

The main measure of "repression" which these authors employed was the differential recall of *I* and *C* tasks in a situation of fairly mild stress. They were able to show that the correlations between the forgetting of *I* tasks and suggestibility (as measured by the "Body Sway" apparatus) in two groups for whom both these measures were available was 0·25 and 0·47 respectively. For another group for whom a correlation was obtained between forgetting of *I* tasks and ability to be hypnotized the correlation was 0.66.

Atkinson (1953) and Atkinson and Raphelson (1956) studied the relationship between "n-Achievement" as measured by responses to the T.A.T., to differential recall of *I* and *C* tasks under conditions differing in stressfulness. From previous formulations regarding the processes of socialization it is to be expected, on the present hypothesis, that those highest on n-Achievement will, in fact, be those individuals nearer the *NI* end of the *NE–NI* continuum. The

results of these experiments show that those subjects high in n-Achievement do, in fact, show an increasing tendency to recall more *I* tasks as stress increases and that the opposite is true of subjects low in n-Achievement who, as stress increases, tend to recall fewer *I* tasks. In addition, and again in line with the predictions of the present hypothesis, under conditions of relaxed orientation (i.e., low stress) the low n-Achievement group recalled *more I* tasks than the high n-Achievement group under the same conditions although the difference was only "near significance."

The present hypothesis is further confirmed by Alper's (1957) demonstration of an *inverse* relationship between n-Achievement and ego-strength in a group of twenty-eight college leaders.

VARIATIONS IN STRESS

Some studies have paid attention only to stress variables, ignoring factors of personality. Differences in the recall of tasks would only be expected in such cases if the subjects used were fairly homogeneous in terms of personality since, as Alper has suggested, the results of heterogeneity may be to cancel out differences.

Most of the studies have been, in fact, carried out on normal undergraduates and it would therefore be expected, in terms of the present hypothesis, that, overall, an increase in stress would produce the recall of a preponderance of *C* tasks, since most of such studies operate in the area of low-stress.

Such results have been reported by Walsh (1940, 1942) who investigated, in several experiments, the differential recall of various groups of school children. On the whole most of the work confirmed Zeigarnik's main finding, her general *I/C* ratio being 1·7. In view of the present hypothesis, however, it is interesting to note that one of the principal occasions when this ratio fell below unity, indicating superior recall of *C* tasks, was just after an air-raid when the children had been under considerable strain.

Lewis (1944) showed, in an experiment with fourteen students, each working with a "planted" co-worker in an "informal atmosphere," that co-operative completion was as good as "self-completion" so far as differential recall was concerned. She also went on to show (Lewis and Franklin, 1944) that an increase in stress (i.e., through ego-orientation) resulted in the recall of more *C* than *I* tasks.

A report by Sanford and Risser (1948) showed that, when twenty-five mothers were tested in the presence of their daughters, and were failed on six out of fifteen difficult tasks, recall produced a preponderance of *C* tasks. It should be noted that most of these women found the proceeding very embarrassing. A somewhat similar experiment with children, on the other hand, produced recall preponderance of *I* tasks, but the circumstances of administration were not nearly so stressful. Sanford and Risser conclude that such "self-defensive forgetting" is likely to occur when the need to regain self-respect is greatest and the possibility of doing this by constructive striving is at its lowest.

Glixman (1949) examined the recall changes for *I* and *C* tasks as a function of stress. This author showed in an experiment with college students, under three different degrees of anxiety arousing situation, that as stress increases the recall of *I* tasks decreases. He also showed, however, that there was no significant increase in the number of *C* tasks recalled with increase in stress. In another article (1948) he has presented his results as follows (*see* Table VII.4)—

The greater recall of *C* tasks under conditions of stress has also been confirmed by Kendler (1949) in a situation in which twenty-two college students were given sixteen jigsaw puzzles as an intelligence test and their recall compared with that of ten students given the same puzzles under neutral conditions. The former remembered more successful than unsuccessful tasks, to a significant degree, whereas the latter remembered more, though not significantly more, unsuccessful tasks.

Hays (1952) found that the effect, suggested here to be a function of stress, could be produced by interpolating a complex rather than a simple task between performance and recall.

Smock (1956) demonstrated differential recall of

TABLE VII.4

MEANS FOR RECALL RATIOS FOR COMPLETED AND INCOMPLETED TASKS AND FOR THE RECALL DIFFERENCE SCORE OVER SITUATIONS I, II, AND III, AND THE *F*-VALUES ASSOCIATED WITH VARIATIONS AMONG THE MEANS

(From Glixman, 1948)

	Situation I	Situation II	Situation III	F	F at 5 per cent
Recall Ratio: *C* . .	0·60	0·62	0·52	2·44	3·13
Recall Ratio: *I* . .	0·57	0·52	0·44	3·42	3·13
Recall Differences . .	0·03	0·10	0·08	0·50	3·13

These results can also be represented graphically, see Fig. 7.12.

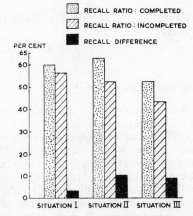

FIG. 7.12. MEANS FOR RECALL RATIO FOR COMPLETED AND INCOMPLETED TASKS AND FOR THE RECALL DIFFERENCE SCORE: SITUATIONS I, II and III

(From Glixman, 1948)

This table and graph show clearly that, as the stress increases so the recall of *I* tasks decreases. There can also be seen a tendency, as stress increases, for fewer tasks altogether to be remembered and for a greater proportion of these to be *C* tasks.

C and *I* tasks under different instructional conditions as shown in Fig. 7.13. He was also able to show that, under both conditions, recall of stimuli selected as likely to arouse anxiety were recalled to a lesser degree than were the neutral stimuli.

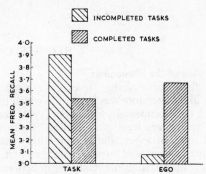

FIG. 7.13. FREQUENCY OF RECALL OF COMPLETED AND INCOMPLETED TASKS AS A FUNCTION OF INSTRUCTIONAL CONDITIONS

(From Smock, 1956)

An interesting cross-cultural verification of the effects of stress comes from a study by Ito (1957) who obtained with Japanese subjects the kind of results predicted.

As well as attempting to encompass such additional

evidence, the present formulation enables the resolution of an apparent discrepancy between the findings of Rosenzweig and Mason (1934) on the one hand, and those of Sanford (1946) on the other. It will be recalled (*see* page 278) that Rosenzweig and Mason found among their crippled children subjects that those of greater maturity tended to remember more *C* than *I* tasks. Sanford, however, using normal children, found the reverse, namely that those of more advanced M.A. tended to remember more *I* than *C* tasks. It should be noted, however, that in the first study the tasks were set under formal, test-like, competitive and presumably stressful (or ego-orienting) conditions, whereas in the second study the tasks were given under much less stressful conditions. Thus, if we suggest that those who appeared to be of greater maturity in each study were those nearer the *NE* end of the *NE–NI* continuum, then, given the differential stress, the results are as predicted by the present hypothesis and the contradiction vanishes.

One of the few studies examining the effect of *recall* of completed and uncompleted tasks in psychotic individuals is that by Winder (1952) who reports that while paranoid schizophrenics tend to recall more *I* than *C* tasks, non-paranoid schizophrenics show a slight but significant tendency to recall more *C* than *I* tasks.

Another study, by Tamkin (1957), showed that a group of schizophrenic subjects remembered more *I* than *C* tasks under ego-involved conditions.

It may be claimed, therefore, that in situations in which the anxiety component is provided by failure experience we find results which are consonant with

the hypothesis originally elaborated to relate findings in the adjacent field of perceptual defence.

Credence is further lent to this hypothesis by its ability to relate certain facts within this new area which at first seemed quite contradictory one to another.

It will be of considerable interest to see if the same hypothesis can be extended to relate together data from yet another adjacent area, namely that comprising studies in the phenomena known by the label of "Level of Aspiration." The tasks which are commonly used to elicit such phenomena are, of course, concerned to provide experience of performance in situations of success and failure so that it would seem reasonable to expect the current hypothesis to apply, at least in part.

Such a link has explicitly been suggested by Eriksen who notes that—

> Eysenck reports that in level-of-aspiration experiments Ss high on the extraversive pole tend to overestimate their performance and are little bothered by failure, while Ss falling on the introversive pole tend to underestimate their performance and are preoccupied by failure. Such reaction to failure and threat would, at least superficially, seem to be related to differential memory for completed and incompleted tasks. By emphasising the successful tasks and ignoring the failed ones, extraverted Ss would be expected to recall relatively more completed than incompleted tasks, while for the introversive Ss the tendency would be reversed. (Eriksen, 1954, p. 49.)

Some aspects of level of aspiration studies may now be considered.

STUDIES OF LEVEL OF ASPIRATION

Description of the Phenomena

The first reference to "level of aspiration" to appear in the literature was in a study which used the concept only incidentally. Dembo (1931) used the term "momentary level of aspiration" in an experimental study of anger, and Hoppe (1930) next took over this concept and experimented with it, being especially interested in the relationship between goal-setting and the feelings related to experience of success and failure.

The first objective definition of the notion, however, was provided by Frank, who defined it as: ". . . *the level of future performance in a familiar task which an individual, knowing his level of past performance in that task, explicitly undertakes to reach.* By *level of past performance* is meant *the goodness of the individual's past performance, as he knows it.*" (Frank, 1955a, p. 119.) The last phrase of this definition covers

the fact that the subject may, in certain experiments, be given a false score.

Rotter (1942b) has mentioned seven characteristics which such a task should have: it should be (1) novel, (2) neither too easy nor too difficult, (3) neither have too wide a variance, nor (4) be too stable; it should be (5) interesting, (6) not much influenced by learning, and, finally, (7) be convenient and adaptable. To these considerations Eysenck (1947) adds the suggestion that it should (1) show moderately high correlation between successive trials, so as to permit fair anticipation of future scores and that (2) success as shown in scores should not be too readily evaluated by the subject himself, but only by the experimenter.

Gardner (1940b) and Rotter (1942a) have further critically examined the use of the notion and methods employed for its study.

Eysenck (1947) has described in some detail one

piece of apparatus which has been used to derive level of aspiration scores. This is the "Triple Tester," which, he says, is—

> An adaptation of the pursuit meter, constructed by the late Dr. Craik of Cambridge University. The apparatus consists of a brass drum carrying an ivorine cover, rotating towards the subject. This ivorine cover is marked out as a helical "road" with holes punched in it. A "vehicle" in the form of a bronze ball moved sideways on a rack is steered along this road by a steering wheel. The purpose is to keep the ball on the line of holes; each "hit" is scored on an electric counter. The steering wheel operates the rack through an integrating gear instead of directly. Instantaneous deflection of the vehicle from its path is impossible with this method of transmission, and the subject is forced to anticipate the necessary moves. The more he anticipates, the smoother will be the path which he describes, whereas rapid movements made at the last moment will result in violent oscillation or wobbling of the vehicle which requires correction and leads to still worse scores. The test resembles in some ways the penny-in-the-slot machines seen at fun-fairs and has a certain fascination for most subjects which often makes them loath to abandon the machine after the testing session is over. (Eysenck, 1947, p. 129.)

A variety of other devices has, of course, been employed, prominent among them being the so-called "Aspiration Board" devised by Rotter (1942b). Some idea of the range of other methods employed may be gained from column 3 of Table VII.5.

The main "primary" measures which can be derived from such situations are represented in Fig. 7.14, which has been adapted from a figure provided by Lewin *et al.* (1944). For example, in the "Triple Tester" task described above, the Judgement Discrepancy Score (J.D.) is obtained as follows: after a few practice runs the subject may be told what the best possible score is and then given his initial test trial. He is then asked what he thinks his first score was. The difference between his actual score, and his judgement of it constitutes a J.D. score. He is now *told* his actual score and is then asked to say what he will get next time. The difference between this estimate and his past actual performance is his Goal Discrepancy (G.D.) score. The difference between what he says he will get next time and what he actually does get is his Attainment Discrepancy (A.D.) score.

Other secondary measures which have been used include the *Affective Discrepancy*, or difference between G.D. and J.D.; the *Index of Flexibility*, the sum of all shifts made in level of aspiration throughout the test, and the *Index of Responsiveness*, or the measure of typical response, i.e., the number of times bids are raised after success, and lowered after failure.

More detailed examination has been accorded to scoring practices and the measurement of interrelationships by Preston (1942), Lezak and Raskin (1950), Sutcliffe (1952a, 1952b, 1955), and by Siegal (1957), who relates the phenomena to a theory of games model.

It is evident that the notions employed can only be useful in so far as they have some kind of generality. They must, for example, be relatively independent of the actual tests employed. Examples of the range and

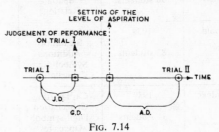

FIG. 7.14

J.D. = Judgement discrepancy
   = Difference between what you did get and what you then think you got.
G.D. = Goal discrepancy
   = Difference between what you did get and what you think you are going to get.
A.D. = Attainment discrepancy
   = Difference between what you think you are going to get and what you do, in fact, get.

(*After Lewin et al., 1944*)

types of generality which have been found are given, in chronological order, in Table VII.5.

As Eysenck has pointed out in his review: "The actual size of the correlation would appear to depend upon three points—

1. The similarity of the two tests, as regards the ability measured.

2. Similarity of the scale on which goodness of performance is measured.

3. Similarity of the experimental situation, i.e., whether the two tests are given in the same experimental session or not." (Eysenck, 1947, p. 133.)

Differences in aspiration expressions have also been noted between situations using different kinds of instructions. For example, Frank (1937) found that the achievement of subjects who were asked, "What do you think you will do?" were likely to be closer to their guesses than those who were asked, "What do you intend to do?" Festinger (1942a) also found that discrepancy scores of subjects who were asked, "What score would you like to make next time?" were likely to be significantly higher compared with those of subjects who were asked, "What score do you expect to get next time?" The influence of different kinds of instructions has also been examined in other studies (Preston and Bayton, 1941, 1942;

TABLE VII.5
SOME MEASURES OF THE GENERALITY OF LEVEL OF ASPIRATION PHENOMENA
(CHRONOLOGICAL ORDER)

Authors	Date and subjects	Tasks	Measures	Generality		
				1. Split-half: series of trials in one session	2. Test-retest: one experimental session to another	3. Intercorrelations over a variety of tasks
Frank	1935 36 students	Printing Quoits Spatial Relations	G.D.	—	0·26 to 0·75	0·37 to 0·62
Gould	1939 82 students	Synonyms Steadiness Additions Symbol-digit Cancellation	Average difference score	0·95 to 0·99	—	0·04 to 0·44
Gardner	1939 31 students	Card sorting Cancellation Digit symbol Opposites	G.D. (score No. 8)	—	—	0·38 to 0·70
Sears	1940 36 children	Reading Arithmetic	G.D.	0·91 to 0·94	—	0·74
Hilgard and Sait	1941 50 students	Card sorting Pursuit learning	J.D. G.D. A.D.	0·49 ± 0·11 0·71 ± 0·07 0·86 ± 0·04 0·95 ± 0·02 0·86 ± 0·04 0·69 ± 0·07	— — —	0·46 ± 0·11 0·66 ± 0·08 0·60 ± 0·09
Preston and Bayton	1941 60 negro students	Symbol-digits Cancellation Addition	Maximum actual and least estimates	—	0·32 to 0·99	0·31 to 0·99
MacIntosh	1942 60 students	Symbol-digits Cancellation Addition	Maximum actual and least estimates	—	− 0·15 to 0·52	− 0·09 to 0·79
Rotter	1942 205 various	Aspiration board	G.D. Shifts	0·73 to 0·85 0·70 to 0·86	0·32} 0·70} N = 32	—
Rotter	1943 45 students	Grade scores Aspiration board	G.D. G.D.	—	—	{0·61
Himmelweit	1947 40 neurotics	Pursuit meter Digit symbol	G.D.	—	—	0·25
Bills	1953 30 students	Dart throwing Target Marking-out Substitution Addition	G.D.	—	—	− 0·01 to 0·49
Harway	1955 88 students	Aspiration board Water-jar Problems Hidden word test	G.D.	—	—	0·14 to 0·46
Ausubel and Schiff	1955 50 students	Speed of reading Arithmetic Digit symbol Stylus maze	G.D.	0·54 to 0·89	—	0·38 to 0·71

Irwin and Mintzer, 1942; MacIntosh, 1942; Irwin, 1944; Preston, Spiers and Trasoff, 1947; Diggory, 1949; and Bayton and Whyte, 1950).

Variations in the Phenomena

From the beginning most studies have demonstrated high "Indices of Responsiveness" in most subjects. That is to say, the most "typical" responses have involved raising aspirations after success and lowering them after failure. For example, Jucknat (1937) showed that, in the case of children's performance on a maze task, 76 per cent shifted their aspirations upward following success and 84 per cent downward following failure.

However, besides such "typical" reactions, variations in level-of-aspiration phenomena have been described in the literature from time to time and it is these latter results which are of most interest in the present context. Such phenomena may be considered under two main headings—

(a) variations due mainly to *environmental* factors (principally changes in environmental *stress*) and

(b) variations due mainly to *personal factors* (principally differences in *susceptibility* to stress).

ENVIRONMENTAL FACTORS

This category may itself be subdivided as follows—

(i) *The Effect of "Reference Scales"*

It has been shown that the expressions of level of aspiration may be altered by making the subject aware of the status of his performance, either in relation to his own group (Anderson and Brandt, 1939) or in relation to members of other groups. An example of the latter kind of study is provided by Chapman and Volkmann (1939). These authors were able to show an inverse relation between level of aspiration and the social prestige value of the reference group. They gave eighty-six students a multiple-choice test of literary knowledge. These subjects were divided into four groups: (1) control subjects, who were given their own scores as a base-line for their aspirations; (2) subjects who were given their scores in terms of a comparison with a fictitious group of "literary critics"; (3) subjects given their scores in comparison with a fictitious group of students; (4) subjects given their scores in terms of a comparison with a group of "workers." The lowest discrepancy scores were obtained in the case of group 2, next for group 1, then for group 3, and the highest were obtained for group 4. That is to say, comparison with the "worker group" produced most "challenge to self-esteem," resulting in higher discrepancy scores. Similar effects of differential social prestige have been

observed elsewhere (Hertzman and Festinger, 1940; Gould and Lewis, 1940; Preston and Bayton, 1941; MacIntosh, 1942; Festinger, 1942*b*; and Hansche and Gilchrist, 1956). The effect of "intellectual prestige" has been neatly demonstrated by Gilinsky (1949). She attempted to make the position of the comparison group more precise in relation to the individual. Ten groups of ten students were each told the (fictitious) average I.Q.s and average scores of another group of students. They were then asked to state their I.Q. and

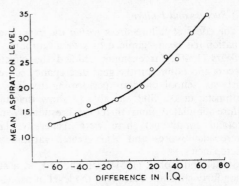

FIG. 7.15. ASPIRATION LEVEL AS A FUNCTION OF PERCEIVED DIFFERENCE IN ABILITY BETWEEN THE INDIVIDUAL AND THE COMPARISON GROUP

(From Gilinsky, 1949)

their level of aspiration on the test. The results (*see* Fig. 7.15) demonstrated that the greater the perceived difference in ability between the individual and the group, the further the level of aspiration diverged from the group norm.

(ii) *Social Factors*

Gould (1941) divided eighty-one students into two extreme groups showing high and low discrepancy scores respectively on six different tasks. She was able to show that members of the low discrepancy group had better economic and social backgrounds than the high discrepancy group. The author suggests that the latter group are subject to more social and economic stress than the former. A similar difference in social circumstance has been found between high and low discrepancy groups by Klugman (1948).

Differences between the sexes have been explained on similar grounds; less social pressure is put on women to "get ahead" so that they find a goal-setting situation less stressful. Smaller discrepancy scores for female normal and neurotic subjects have been reported by Himmelweit (1947), for negro women by Sumner and Johnson (1949), for schoolgirls by Walter and Marzolf (1951), and for female stutterers by Sheehan and Zelen (1955). Bruner and Rotter (1953) found differences in "shifting behaviour" between male and female Navaho Indians, the males shifting significantly more often. This difference was not confirmed in a study by Himelstein (1956) on white Americans.

That such social differentials may result in part, at least, from parental influence is demonstrated in a study by Little and Cohen (1950) who showed that a group of thirty asthmatic children who set high positive goals, compared with control children, had mothers who also set high positive goals for them, compared with the mothers of the control children.

(iii) Success and Failure

The effect of failure-stress *within* the experimental situation has been examined by several authors.

Sears (1940), for example, studied the effects of success and failure on the goal discrepancy scores of thirty-six school children performing reading and arithmetic tasks. She was able to show that under failure-stimulated (and therefore presumably more stressful conditions) there were, generally, larger discrepancy scores and also greater variability of discrepancies.

Steisel and Cohen (1951) also showed, in a study using forty students, that while the level of aspiration itself decreased markedly following severe failure, the discrepancy scores for their subjects under this condition were extremely high and positive. Somewhat similar results have been reported in a study of fifty students by Ausubel and Schiff (1955). They note that goal discrepancy scores were significantly more positive after cumulative than after variable failure.

PERSONAL FACTORS

The earlier workers who were concerned with level of aspiration phenomena, such as Hoppe (1930) and Frank (1935b) mainly attempted to *deduce* personality traits from the phenomena rather than to try to relate these effects to independent measures of personality. The first attempts to do this failed to show significant results. Gardner (1940a) using a digit-symbol substitution test on fifty-one adolescent subjects, correlated a version of the G.D. measure with ratings made on the subjects' personality traits by four independent judges. When the correlations between these variables were examined none were found to be significant. Gould and Kaplan (1940) correlated the G.D. scores of eighty-two students on various tasks with certain personality variables, including extraversion as measured by Guilford's S, E and M scales; only insignificant relationships were found.

Sears (1941) however, found more promising results in a further examination of data secured (Sears, 1940; *see* above) in her study of school-children under conditions of success and failure. She made what amounted to further "clinical" assessments or ratings of various discrepancy groups (these

were composed respectively of individuals showing low-positive, high-positive and negative discrepancies). At this descriptive level she found that the low-positive group were well adjusted socially, confident, adaptable, well oriented. The high-positive group, on the other hand, were not very well adjusted socially, tense, insecure, worried. The negative discrepancy group showed strong social reactivity and desire to impress others.

There is a suggestive relationship between these findings and Jucknat's (1937) earlier work. The latter author had three groups of subjects divided in terms of their school work into good, medium and poor students. The poor students tended to show either very low, or very high, aspirations, compared with the other two groups.

Contrary evidence, however, comes from a study by Hanawalt, Hamilton and Morris (1943) who found, in a study of forty college women, that it was the leaders and dominant individuals who tended to have the higher discrepancy scores.

Other workers have discriminated "patterns" of scores in which very high or very low discrepancy scores appeared to be related to personality difficulties. These include Gruen (1945) who found that, in adolescents, the maladjusted subjects tended either to keep their estimates *below* performance level or to make gross compensatory over-estimates. Ax (1947) divided twenty-five subjects into two groups, the "better integrated" and the "less integrated." The second group fell into two subgroups, one of these with high positive aspiration scores the other with large negative discrepancy scores. Klugman (1947, 1948) has reported positive correlation between a Psychosomatic Inventory and discrepancy scores, which he interprets as indicating that the more stable individuals tend to have lower discrepancy scores.

An interesting study by Berkeley (1952) related level of aspiration behaviour, on the Rotter Aspiration Board, to the activity of the adrenal cortex as measured by 17-ketosteroid excretion. He found the greater discrepancies were related to increase in steroid excretion (multiple $R = 0.70$). This author writes that: "The . . . response, in which a wide discrepancy is maintained between aspiration and achievement, is the response of the individual who is stressed by the situation, as indicated by increased activity of the adrenal cortex." (Berkeley, 1952, p. 448.) Cohen (1954) studied the relation, in fifty patients in a general hospital, between goal-setting behaviour and feelings of self-acceptance. He showed that there was a curvilinear relationship between the two; both very high and very low goal-setting being related to self-rejection, only those who could accept themselves were able to set low positive goals.

Bills (1953) and Steiner (1956) also report studies

concerned with relations between self-rating and level of aspiration behaviour.

Level of Aspiration and the Mediation-Motivation Hypothesis

It remains to be seen whether the level of aspiration phenomena already presented can be systematized in relation to an extension of the explanatory hypothesis already put forward in this chapter.

An attempt has been made to relate various performance and personality aspects diagramatically in Fig. 7.16.

ASPIRATIONS

It can be seen from this figure that there has been added to the conceptions which have so far been used another variable which is a curvilinear function related to the setting of the levels of aspiration with increase in anxiety (induced, for example, by experience of failure).

This notion derives plausibility from the findings of Steisel and Cohen (1951) who demonstrated that, whereas failure experiences were in general followed by *lowering* of the level of aspiration, this level, under several degrees of failure, does not continue to be reduced proportionately, thus resulting in *increase* in discrepancy scores with increasing failure. Similarly, Rao (1954) showed that the *rate* of decrease in level of aspiration, with an increase in the duration of failure stress, was not constant, but became negligible after a certain point.

JUDGEMENTS

It can be seen that this aspect of level of aspiration performance is held to be in accordance with the relationships presumed in the examination of the phenomena of both perceptual defence and the Zeigarnik effect.

Thus, at low levels of stress, recall is fairly indiscriminate. At moderate stress level it is focused on success mediation as an anxiety-reducing technique, which then at high stress levels breaks down, once more admitting the anxiety-mediating self-produced stimulation which in turn increases anxiety level even further.

PERFORMANCE

The evidence for the application of the "Yerkes-Dodson effect" to motor performance has been adduced elsewhere (*see* Chapter 2, by Yates).

The notion of a set of curvilinear relationships between performance and aspiration has previously been propounded by Holt (1946). This author points out that, "Bayton (1943) found some positive relation between levels of aspiration and achievement in the more ego-involved of two tasks, with previous

performance held constant. Yet when, in line with his suggestion, ego-involvement was increased considerably in this experiment, the relation fell back to zero. I have been able to reconcile his results and mine only by the hypothesis of a curvilinear relation between the degree of ego-involvement in a task and the extent to which levels of aspiration measure achievant

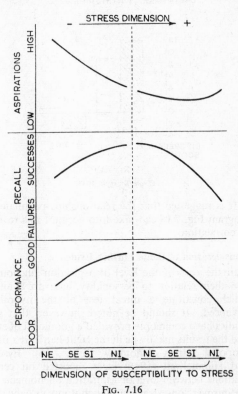

FIG. 7.16

motivation." (Holt, 1946, p. 412.) Holt describes this hypothesis in terms of three propositions—

"1. When ego-involvement is minimal, levels of aspiration have little motivational significance, being primarily rational judgments.

2. When ego-involvement is present but at low intensities, levels of aspiration have little defensive meaning, but reflect to some extent the intensity of motivation.

3. When ego-involvement surpasses a certain limit, defensive considerations become paramount, and the level of aspiration becomes more complexly determined." (Op. cit., p. 412.)

The same author (Holt, 1945) had previously reported a study in which after it had been empirically determined which of the two tests was the more ego-involving, subjects were given two level of aspiration tests. When he examined the correlation between aspiration and improvement for the less involved tasks the correlations were significant and *positive*. On the other hand for the more stressful task this correlation became *negative*.

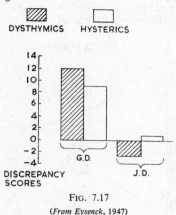

FIG. 7.17

(*From Eysenck*, 1947)

It is suggested that the relationships postulated in diagram Fig. 7.16 can take into account this reversal of correlation.

Consideration of Some Further Evidence

In the case of the level of aspiration phenomena and their relation to personality, data are available which constitute a direct test of the hypothesis advanced. It should be noted, however, that such studies have commonly provided a good deal of stress and the results mainly lie in the right-hand area of the proposed "stress dichotomy" (Fig. 7.16). Eysenck and Himmelweit (1946) have reported on certain relations between level of aspiration phenomena and the introversion-extraversion dichotomy as defined by two groups of fifty neurotic patients, dysthymics and hysterics respectively. The situation employed the "Triple Tester" described above. Although the two groups were quite comparable in age and intelligence, as well as in actual performance on the test, striking differences emerged in, for example, the G.D. and J.D. measures (Fig. 7.17).

As can be seen from the above diagram, dysthymics' aspirations are significantly higher, compared to performance, than are the aspiration scores of the hysteric group; also the judgement scores of the dysthymic group are significantly lower, compared to performance, than are the judgement scores of the hysterics. Similar differences have been reported for such groups by Himmelweit (1947) on a different test.

Differences between neurotics in general and normals in general have also been reported by Himmelweit. The principal difference between these groups lay in

the fact that the actual performance of the normals was significantly superior to that of the neurotics. Some of the most interesting results obtained, however, were concerned with *relationships* between various kinds of scores. For example, whereas the correlation between G.D. and J.D. scores was significantly *positive* for the normal groups, it was significantly *negative* for the neurotic groups. That is to say, while the members of both the neurotic and normal groups tended, on the whole, to overrate their future performance and underrate their past performance, in the normal group those who overrated their future performance more than others tended to underrate their past performance less. In the neurotic group, on the other hand, those who overrated their future performance more than others also underrated their past performance more. The findings of this study, in relation to the normal group, is in accordance with the results obtained by Hilgard and Sait (1941) who tested fifty students on a card-sorting and on a pursuit-learning task. In the case of

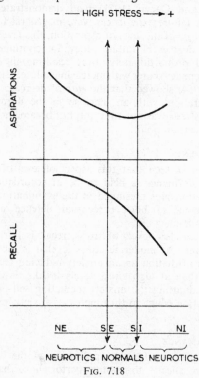

FIG. 7.18

both these tests the correlations, for this normal group, between G.D. and J.D. scores were significant and positive.

Given the relationships expressed between aspirations and recall, or judgement, expressed in Fig. 7.16, however, it may be suggested that the reversal of the sign of the correlation noted by Himmelweit may be a function of the part of the curve at which the various groups lie, as shown in Fig. 7.18.

Studies of the performance of psychiatric groups conducted independently of the above findings have been reported. For example, Hartogs (1949) studied the level of aspiration in two hundred and fifteen cases of anxiety neurosis and found an unduly high initial level in 81·2 per cent of these cases. Miller (1951) tested five groups of twenty-five patients including one group of conversion hysterics, one of neurasthenics, one of character disorders, one of paranoid schizophrenics and one of normal controls. On the basis of their G.D. scores on the Carl Hollow Square test Miller was able to divide these subjects into three groups. The neurasthenics, whom Eysenck would, of course, call dysthymics, obtained high discrepancy scores, while the character disorders and hysterics (i.e., neurotic extraverts) fell together with low discrepancy scores, the normals falling in between the two. Ausubel, Schiff and Goldman (1953) also found significantly higher level of aspiration and goal tenacity scores in a high-anxiety as compared with a low-anxiety group of college students in performance on a stylus maze test. A study by Raifman (1957) also suggests that patients suffering from peptic ulcer, who are commonly conceived as over-driven personalities, also show high goal-discrepancy scores.

Confirmatory data from normal subjects has also been provided by Gately (1954) who found level of aspiration behaviour was related to extraversion-introversion measures obtained from analysis of questionnaire and projective measures of personality. Here again the introverts showed the higher discrepancy scores.

Results on level-of-aspiration measures have also been obtained for abnormal groups of other kinds. So far as psychotics are concerned Escalona (1940) showed that manic patients demonstrated greater "mobility" than did depressed patients and were also more sensitive to success and failure. Miller (1951) found the scores of paranoid schizophrenics to lie nearer his normal control groups than did the groups of conversion hysterics, character disorders or neurasthenics. Winder (1952) found that paranoid schizophrenics showed positive, and non-paranoid small negative, discrepancy scores on a pursuit-rotor task. Jost (1955) found differences between a group of twenty-nine normal subjects and twenty-nine schizophrenics, carefully matched for age, occupation and education. The schizophrenics showed significantly higher reaction-times and frequency of high goal discrepancies. The response score mean on the other hand, was lower for the schizophrenics; they also forgot to make verbal statements of their goal more often than the normal subjects.

Level-of-aspiration phenomena have been examined in epileptic subjects by Arluck (1941) and in mentally defective persons by Shaw and Bensberg (1955), but in neither case did very striking results emerge.

CONCLUSION

A review of the results secured by various investigators in three adjacent experimental areas suggests that certain common elements may be distinguished in them.

An attempt has been made to trace the relationships in terms of interactions between stress and the susceptibility to stress, and the effect of such interactions upon mediation-avoidance behaviour.

The kind of investigations which have been considered form part of that body of data associated with the label ego-function. This examination of the literature has been conducted from that point of view which regards such a label as referring merely to one *kind* of behaviour rather than to a *source* of behaviour, as seems to be implied by some writers (e.g., Allport, 1943) or to an "upper member" in some hierarchy of behaviour, as seems to be suggested, for example, by McDougall (1936) in his notion of the "self-regarding sentiment."

In common with the general policy of this text attention has been focused on interrelationships among psychological data. Over twenty years ago J. McV. Hunt pointed out that—

> Almost blind acceptance of existing nosology has also been an unfortunate tendency (i.e. in psychological experiments with disordered persons). All too frequently this has led to the vain hope of supplying the psychiatrist with rule-of-thumb diagnostic tests for his own categories of disorder. As most of these diagnostic categories have been derived from rough clinical observation of gross symptoms, usually without even statistical check, they should not remain dogma. The experimental psychologist must proceed critically in his use of diagnosis. He should attack problems independently, achieving his own psychological classification inductively from experimental results. (Hunt, 1936, p. 47.)

The attack on "real life problems," through such inductive principles as have been presented, has, as yet, hardly begun; although, for example, Kleinman (1957) has attempted to relate the conceptions of perceptual defence to the phenomena of "psychogenic deafness." It may be hoped, however, that the practice of clinical psychology may benefit from such an approach to abnormal psychology at least as much as it has benefited from an uncritical acceptance of psychiatric models.

REFERENCES

ABEL, THEODORA, M., Neurocirculatory reaction and the recall of unfinished and completed tasks, *J. Psychol.*, **6**, 377–383 (1938).

ADLER, D. L. and KOUNIN, J. S., Some factors operating at the moment of resumption of interrupted tasks, *J. Psychol.*, **7**, 255–267 (1939).

ALLPORT, F. H., *Theories of Perception and the Concept of Structure* (New York, John Wiley & Sons, Inc., 1955).

ALLPORT, G. W., The ego in contemporary psychology, *Psychol. Rev.*, **50**, 451–478 (1943).

ALLPORT, G. W., VERNON, P. E. and LINDZEY, G., *A Study of Values* (Boston, Houghton Mifflin, 1951).

ALPER, THELMA G., Memory for completed and incompleted tasks as a function of personality: an analysis of group data, *J. Abnorm. (Soc.) Psychol.*, **41**, 403–420 (1946).

ALPER, THELMA, G., Memory for completed and incompleted tasks as a function of personality: correlation between experimental and personality data, *J. Personality*, **17**, 104–137 (1948).

ALPER, THELMA G., The interrupted task method in studies of selective recall; a re-evaluation of some recent experiments, *Psychol. Rev.*, **59**, 71–88 (1952).

ALPER, THELMA G., Predicting the direction of selective recall: its relation to ego strength and n-Achievement, *J. Abnorm. (Soc.) Psychol.*, **55**, 149–165 (1957).

ANDERSON, H. H. and BRANDT, H. F., A study of motivation involving self-announced goals of fifth grade children and the concept of level of aspiration, *J. Soc. Psychol.*, **10**, 209–232 (1939).

ANGYAL, A., *Foundations for a Science of Personality* (London, Oxford Univ. Press, 1941).

ARLUCK, E. W., A study of some personality characteristics of epileptics, *Arch. Psychol.*, *N.Y.* 37, No. 263, 1–78 (1941).

ARONFREED, J. M., MESSICK, S. A. and DIGGORY, J. C., Re-examining emotionality and perceptual defense, *J. Personality*, **21**, 517–528 (1953).

ATKINSON, J. W., The achievement motive and recall of interrupted and completed tasks, *J. Exp. Psychol.*, **46**, 381–390 (1953).

ATKINSON, J. W. and RAPHELSON, A. C., Individual differences in motivation and behavior in particular situations, *J. Personality*, **24**, 349–363 (1955).

AUSUBEL, D. P. and SCHIFF, H. M., A level of aspiration approach to the measurement of goal tenacity, *J. Gen. Psychol.*, **52**, 97–110 (1955).

AUSUBEL, D. P., SCHIFF, H. M. and GOLDMAN, M., Qualitative characteristics in the learning process associated with anxiety, *J. Abnorm. (Soc.) Psychol.*, **48**, 53–54 (1953).

AX, A. F., A validation study of the Rotter-Jensen level of aspiration test, *J. Personality*, **15**, 166–172 (1947).

BAYTON, J. A., Interrelations between levels of aspiration, performance, and estimates of past experience, *J. Exp. Psychol.*, **33**, 1–21 (1943).

BAYTON, J. A. and WHYTE, ESTHER, C., Personality dynamics during success-failure sequences, *J. Abnorm. (Soc.) Psychol.*, **45**, 583–591 (1950).

BEIER, E. G. and COWEN, E. L., A further investigation of the influence of "threat expectancy" on perception, *J. Personality*, **22**, 254–257 (1953).

BERKELEY, A. W., Level of aspiration in relation to adrenal cortical activity and the concept of stress, *J. Comp. Physiol. Psychol.*, **45**, 443–449 (1952).

BERLYNE, D. E., Attention, perception and behaviour theory, *Psychol. Rev.*, **58**, 137–145 (1951).

BERLYNE, D. E., Knowledge and stimulus-response psychology, *Psychol. Rev.*, **61**, 245–254 (1954).

BILLS, R. E., A comparison of scores on the Index of Adjustment and Values with behavior in level-of-aspiration tasks, *J. Cons. Psychol.*, **17**, 206–212 (1953).

BITTERMAN, M. E. and KNIFFEN, C. W., Manifest anxiety and "perceptual defense," *J. Abnorm. (Soc.) Psychol.*, **48**, 248–252 (1953).

BLUM, G. S., *The Blacky Pictures: a Technique for the Exploration of Personality Dynamics* (New York, Psychol. Corp., 1950).

BLUM, G. S., An experimental reunion of psychoanalytic theory with perceptual vigilance and defense, *J. Abnorm. (Soc.) Psychol.*, **49**, 94–98 (1954).

BLUM, G. S., Perceptual defense revisited, *J. Abnorm. (Soc.) Psychol.*, **51**, 24–29 (1955).

BLUM, G. S., An investigation of perceptual defense in Italy, *Psychol. Rep.*, **3**, 169–176 (1957).

BOGUSLAVSKY, G. W., Interruption and learning, *Psychol. Rev.*, **58**, 248–255 (1951).

BOGUSLAVSKY, G. W. and GUTHRIE, E. R., The recall of completed and interrupted activities: an investigation of Zeigarnik's experiment, *Psychol. Bull.*, **38**, 575–576 Abstract (1941).

BRESSON, F., Perception: fréquence de stimuli et motivation, *Année psychol.*, **55**, 67–78 (1955).

BRICKER, P. D. and CHAPANIS, A., Do incorrectly perceived tachistoscopic stimuli convey some information? *Psychol. Rev.*, **60**, 181–188 (1953).

BROWN, J. S., Problems presented by the concept of acquired drives, in *Current Theory and Research in Motivation: a Symposium* (Lincoln, Univ. of Nebraska Press, 1953).

BROWNFAIN, J. J., Stability of the self-concept as a dimension of personality, *J. Abnorm. (Soc.) Psychol.*, **47**, 597–606 (1952).

BRUNER, E. M. and ROTTER, J. B., A level-of-aspiration study among the Ramah Navaho, *J. Personality*, **21**, 375–385 (1953).

BRUNER, J. S. and POSTMAN, L., Emotional selectivity in perception and reaction, *J. Personality*, **16**, 69–77 (1947).

BRUNER, J. S. and POSTMAN, L., Perception, cognition and behavior, *J. Personality*, **18**, 14–31 (1949).

BUGELSKI, B. R., *The Psychology of Learning* (New York, Henry Holt & Co., 1956).

CAMERON, N., *The Psychology of Behavior Disorders* (New York, Houghton Mifflin, 1947).

CARON, A. J. and WALLACH, M. A., Recall of interrupted tasks under stress: a phenomenon of memory or of learning? *J. Abnorm. (Soc.) Psychol.*, **55**, 372–381 (1957).

CARPENTER, B., WEINER, M. and CARPENTER, J. T.,

Predictability of perceptual defense behavior, *J. Abnorm. (Soc.) Psychol.*, **52**, 380–383 (1956).

CARTWRIGHT, D., The effect of interruption, completion and failure upon the attractiveness of activities, *J. Exp. Psychol.*, **31**, 1–16 (1942).

CHAPMAN, D. W. and VOLKMANN, J., A social determinant of the level of aspiration, *J. Abnorm. (Soc.) Psychol.*, **34**, 225–238 (1939).

CHERRY, C. and SAYERS, B. McA., Experiments upon the total inhibition of stammering by external controls and some clinical results, *J. Psychosom. Res.*, **1**, 233–246 (1956).

CHODORKOFF, B., Self-perception, perceptual defense and adjustment, *J. Abnorm. (Soc.) Psychol.* **49**, 508–512 (1954).

CHODORKOFF, B., A note on Bitterman and Kniffen's "Manifest anxiety and perceptual defense," *J. Abnorm. (Soc.) Psychol.*, **50**, 144 (1955).

CHODORKOFF, B., Anxiety, threat and defensive reactions, *J. Gen. Psychol.*, **54**, 191–196 (1956).

COGAN, N., Authoritarianism and repression, *J. Abnorm. (Soc.) Psychol.*, **53**, 34–37 (1956).

COHEN, L. D., Level of aspiration behavior and feelings of adequacy and self-acceptance, *J. Abnorm. (Soc.) Psychol.*, **49**, 84–86 (1954).

COWEN, E. L. and BEIER, E. G., The influence of "threat expectancy" on perception, *J. Personality*, **19**, 85–94 (1950).

COWEN, E. L. and BEIER, E. G., Threat expectancy, word frequencies, and perceptual prerecognition hypotheses, *J. Abnorm. (Soc.) Psychol.*, **49**, 178–182 (1954).

CRAFTS, L. W., SCHNEIRLA, T. C., ROBINSON, ELSA, E. and GILBERT, R. W., *Recent Experiments in Psychology* (New York, McGraw-Hill, 1950).

DAVIDS, A., Generality and consistency of relations between the alienation syndrome and cognitive processes, *J. Abnorm. (Soc.) Psychol.*, **51**, 61–67 (1955).

DELUCIA, J. J. and STAGNER, R., Emotional *v.* frequency factors in word recognition, *J. Personality*, **22**, 299–309 (1951).

DEMBO, TAMARA, Der Ärger als dynamisches Problem, *Psychol. Forsch.*, **15**, 1–144 (1931).

DE MONCHAUX, CECILY J., The effect on memory of completed and uncompleted tasks, *Unpubl. Ph.D. Thesis, Univ. of London Lib.* (1952).

DIGGORY, J. C., Responses to experimentally induced failure, *Amer. J. Psychol.*, **62**, 48–61 (1949).

DOLLARD, J. and MILLER, N. E., *Personality and Psychotherapy* (New York, McGraw-Hill, 1950).

DUFFY, ELIZABETH, The psychological significance of the concept of "arousal" or "activation," *Psychol. Rev.*, **64**, 265–275 (1957).

DULANY, D. E., Avoidance learning of perceptual defense and vigilance, *J. Abnorm. (Soc.) Psychol.*, **55**, 333–338 (1957).

ENGLER, JEAN, and FREEMAN, J. T., Perceptual behavior as related to factors of associative and drive strength, *J. Exp. Psychol.*, **51**, 399–404 (1956).

ERIKSEN, C. W., Some implications for T.A.T. interpretation arising from need and perception experiments, *J. Personality*, **19**, 282–288 (1950).

ERIKSEN, C. W., Perceptual defense as a function of

unacceptable needs, *J. Abnorm. (Soc.) Psychol.*, **46**, 557–564 (1951).

ERIKSEN, C. W., Defense against ego-threat in memory and perception, *J. Abnorm. (Soc.) Psychol.*, **47**, 230–235 (1952a).

ERIKSEN, C. W., Individual differences in defensive forgetting, *J. Exp. Psychol.*, **44**, 442–446 (1952b).

ERIKSEN, C. W., Psychological defenses and "ego-strength" in the recall of completed and incompleted tasks, *J. Abnorm. (Soc.) Psychol.*, **49**, 45–50 (1954a).

ERIKSEN, C. W., The case for perceptual defense, *Psychol. Rev.*, **61**, 175–182 (1954b).

ERIKSEN, C. W., Personality, *Annu. Rev. Psychol.*, **8**, 185–210 (1957).

ERIKSEN, C. W. and BROWNE, C. T., An experimental and theoretical analysis of perceptual defense, *J. Abnorm. (Soc.) Psychol.*, **52**, 224–230 (1956).

ESCALONA, SIBYLLE, K., The effect of success and failure upon the level of aspiration and behavior in manic-depressive psychoses, *Univ. Ia Stud. Child Welf.*, **16**, 199–302 (1940).

EYSENCK, H. J., *Dimensions of Personality* (London, Routledge & Kegan Paul, 1947).

EYSENCK, H. J., A dynamic theory of anxiety and hysteria, *J. Ment. Sci.*, **101**, 28–51 (1955).

EYSENCK, H. J. and HIMMELWEIT, HILDE, T., An experimental study of the reactions of neurotics to experiences of success and failure, *J. Gen. Psychol.*, **35**, 59–76 (1946).

FARRELL, B. A., Some hypotheses of psychoanalysis, in *Experimental Psychology* Ed. B. A. Farrell (Oxford, Basil Blackwell, 1955).

FESTINGER, L., Wish, expectation and group standards as factors influencing the level of aspiration, *J. Abnorm. (Soc.) Psychol.*, **37**, 184–200 (1942a).

FESTINGER, L., A theoretical interpretation of shifts in level of aspiration, *Psychol. Rev.*, **49**, 235–250 (1942b).

FRANK, J. D., Individual differences in certain aspects of the level of aspiration, *Amer. J. Psychol.*, **47**, 119–128 (1935a).

FRANK, J. D., Some psychological determinants of the level of aspiration, *Amer. J. Psychol.*, **47**, 285–293 (1935b).

FRANK, J. D., A comparison between certain properties of the level of aspiration and random guessing, *J. Psychol.*, **3**, 43–62 (1937).

FREEMAN, G. L., Changes in tonus during completed and interrupted mental work, *J. Gen. Psychol.*, **4**, 309–333 (1930).

FREEMAN, G. L., The effect of inhibited micturition upon interrupted and completed acts of unrelated origin, *J. Gen. Psychol.*, **19**, 277–284 (1938).

FREEMAN, J. T., Set or perceptual defense? *J. Exp. Psychol.*, **48**, 283–288 (1954).

FREEMAN, J. T., Set versus perceptual defense; a confirmation, *J. Abnorm. (Soc.) Psychol.*, **51**, 710–712 (1955).

GARDNER, J. W., Level of aspiration in response to a prearranged sequence of scores, *J. Exp. Psychol.*, **25**, 601–621 (1939).

GARDNER, J. W., The relation of certain personality variables to level of aspiration, *J. Psychol.* **9**, 191–206 (1940a).

GARDNER, J. W., The use of the term "level of aspiration," *Psychol. Rev.*, **47**, 59–68 (1940b).

GATELY, G. M., The use of projection technique in an experimental study of level of aspiration, *Unpubl. Ph.D. Thesis, Univ. of London Lib.* (1954).

GEBHARD, M. E., The effect of success and failure upon the attractiveness of activities as a function of experience, expectation and need, *J. Exp. Psychol.*, **38**, 371–388 (1948).

GILINSKY, ALBERTA S., Relative self-estimate and the level of aspiration, *J. Exp. Psychol.*, **39**, 256–259 (1949).

GLIXMAN, A. F., An analysis of the use of interruption-technique in experimental studies of "repression," *Psychol. Bull*, **45**, 491–506 (1948).

GLIXMAN, A. F., Recall of completed and incompleted activities under varying degrees of stress, *J. Exp. Psychol.*, **39**, 281–295 (1949).

GOODSTEIN, L. D., Affective tone and visual recognition thresholds, *J. Abnorm. (Soc.) Psychol.*, **49**, 443–444 (1954).

GOULD, ROSALIND, An experimental analysis of "level of aspiration," *Genet. Psychol. Monogr.*, **21**, 1–116 (1939).

GOULD, ROSALIND, Some sociological determinants of goal striving, *J. Soc. Psychol.*, **13**, 461–473 (1941).

GOULD, ROSALIND and KAPLAN, N., The relationship of "level of aspiration" to academic and personality factors, *J. Soc. Psychol.*, **11**, 31–40 (1940).

GOULD, ROSALIND and LEWIS, HELEN B., An experimental investigation of changes in the meaning of level of aspiration, *J. Exp. Psychol.*, **27**, 422–438 (1940).

GRUEN, E. W., Level of aspiration in relation to personality factors in adolescents, *Child Developm.*, **16**, 181–188 (1945).

HANAWALT, N. G., HAMILTON, C. E. and MORRIS, M. L., Level of aspiration in college leaders and non-leaders, *J. Abnorm. (Soc.) Psychol.*, **38**, 545–548 (1943).

HANSCHE, J. and GILCHRIST, J. C., Three determinants of the level of aspiration, *J. Abnorm. (Soc.) Psychol.*, **53**, 136–137 (1956).

HARTOGS, R., The clinical investigation and differential measurement of anxiety, *Amer. J. Psychiat.*, **106**, 929–934, (1949).

HARWAY, N. I., Einstellung effect and goal-setting behavior, *J. Abnorm. (Soc.) Psychol.*, **50**, 339–342 (1955).

HAYS, D. G., Situational instructions and task order in recall for completed and interrupted tasks, *J. Exp. Psychol.*, **44**, 434–437 (1952).

HEBB, D. O., *The Organization of Behavior: a Neuropsychological Theory* (New York, John Wiley & Sons, Inc., 1949).

HEBB, D. O., Drives and the C.N.S., *Psychol. Rev.*, **62**, 243–254 (1955).

HERTZMAN, M. and FESTINGER, L., Shifts in explicit goals in a level of aspiration experiment, *J. Exp. Psychol.*, **27**, 439–452 (1940).

HILGARD, E. R. and SAIT, E. M., Estimates of past and future performances as measures of aspiration, *Amer. J. Psychol.*, **54**, 102–108 (1941).

HIMELSTEIN, P., Sex differences in shifting behavior in a level of aspiration experiment, *Psychol. Rep.*, **2**, 101–102 (1956).

HIMMELWEIT, HILDE T., A comparative study of the level of aspiration of normal and neurotic persons, *Brit. J. Psychol.*, **37**, 41–59 (1947).

HOLT, R. R., Effects of ego-involvement upon levels of aspiration, *Psychiatry*, **8**, 299–317 (1945)

HOLT, R. R., Level of aspiration: ambition or defense? *J. Exp. Psychol.*, **36**, 398–416 (1946).

HOPPE, F., Erfolg und Misserfolg, *Psychol. Forsch.*, **14**, 1–62 (1930).

HOWES, D. H. and SOLOMON, R. L., A note on McGinnies' "Emotionality and perceptual defense," *Psychol. Rev.*, **57**, 229–234 (1950).

HOWES, D. H. and SOLOMON, R. L., Visual duration threshold as a function of word probability, *J. Exp. Psychol.*, **41**, 401–410 (1951).

HOWIE, D., Perceptual defense, *Psychol. Rev.*, **59**, 308–315 (1952).

HUNT, J. McV., Psychological experiments with disordered persons, *Psychol. Bull.*, **33**, 1–58 (1936).

IRWIN, F. W., The realism of expectations, *Psychol. Rev.*, **51**, 120–126 (1944).

IRWIN, F. W. and MINTZER, MARCIA G., Effects of differences in instructions and motivation upon measures of the level of aspiration, *Amer. J. Psychol.*, **55**, 400–406 (1942).

ITO, M., The relationship between success-failure and completed-incompleted tasks—the effects of recall, *Jap. J. Psychol.*, **27**, 317–318 (1957).

IVERSON, M. A. and REUDER, MARY E., Ego-involvement as an experimental variable, *Psychol. Rep.*, **2**, 147–181 (1956).

JOST, K., The level of aspiration of schizophrenic and normal subjects, *J. Abnorm. (Soc.) Psychol.*, **50**, 315–320 (1955).

JOURARD, S. M., Ego-strength and the recall of tasks, *J. Abnorm. (Soc.) Psychol.*, **49**, 51–58 (1954).

JUCKNAT, M., Leistung, Anspruchsniveau und Selbsbewusstsein, *Psychol. Forsch.*, **22**, 89–179 (1937).

KENDLER, T. S., The effect of success and failure on the recall of tasks, *J. Gen. Psychol.*, **41**, 79–87 (1949).

KING-ELLISON, P. and JENKINS, J. J., The durational threshold of visual recognition as a function of word frequency, *Amer. J. Psychol.*, **67**, 700–703 (1954).

KISSIN, B., GOTTESFELD, H. and DICKES, R., Inhibition and tachistoscopic thresholds for sexually charged words, *J. Psychol.*, **43**, 333–339 (1957).

KLEIN, G. S. and SCHLESINGER, H., Where is the perceiver in perceptual theory? *J. Personality*, **18**, 32–47 (1949).

KLEIN, G. S., SCHLESINGER, H. J. and MEISTER, D. E., The effect of personal values on perception: an experimental critique, *Psychol. Rev.*, **58**, 96–112 (1951).

KLEINMAN, M. L., Psychogenic deafness and perceptual defense, *J. Abnorm. (Soc.) Psychol.*, **54**, 335–338 (1957).

KLUGMAN, S. F., Relationship between performance on the Rotter Aspiration Board and various types of test, *J. Psychol.*, **23**, 51–54 (1947).

KLUGMAN, S. F., Emotional stability and level of aspiration, *J. Gen. Psychol.*, **38**, 101–118 (1948).

KURLAND, S. H., The lack of generality in defense mechanisms as indicated in auditory perception, *J. Abnorm. (Soc.) Psychol.*, **49**, 173–177 (1954).

LACY, O. W., LEWINGER, NATALIE and ADAMSON, J. F., Foreknowledge as a factor affecting perceptual defense and alertness, *J. Exp. Psychol.*, **45**, 169–174 (1953).

LAZARUS, R. S., Is there a mechanism of perceptual

defense? A reply to Postman, Bronson and Gropper, *J. Abnorm.* (*Soc.*) *Psychol.*, **49**, 396–398 (1954).

LAZARUS, R. S., Psychology, *Progress in Neurology and Psychiatry*, Ed. E. A. Spiegel, **10**, 409–425 (1955).

LAZARUS, R. S., ERIKSEN, C. W. and FONDA, C. P., Personality dynamics and auditory perceptual recognition, *J. Personality*, **19**, 471–482 (1951).

LAZARUS, R. S. and LONGO, N., The consistency of psychological defenses against threat, *J. Abnorm.* (*Soc.*) *Psychol.*, **48**, 495–499 (1953).

LAZARUS, R. S. and MCCLEARY, R. A., Autonomic discrimination without awareness: a study of subception, *Psychol. Rev.*, **58**, 113–122 (1951).

LEWIN, K., DEMBO, TAMARA, FESTINGER, L. and SEARS, PAULINE S., Level of aspiration, in *Personality and the Behavior Disorders*, Ed. J. Mc.V. Hunt (New York, Ronald Press, 1944).

LEWIS, HELEN B., An experimental study of the role of the ego in work. I. The role of the ego in co-operative work, *J. Exp. Psychol.*, **34**, 113–126 (1944).

LEWIS, HELEN B. and FRANKLIN, M., An experimental study of the role of the ego in work: II. The significance of task-orientation in work, *J. Exp. Psychol.*, **34**, 195–215 (1944).

LEZAK, MURIEL D. and RASKIN, N. J., A new method of analyzing the data in an experiment on level of aspiration, *Amer. J. Psychol.*, **63**, 617–618 (1950).

LITTLE, SUE W. and COHEN, L. D., Goal setting behavior of asthmatic children and of their mothers for them, *J. Personality*, **19**, 376–389 (1950).

LYSAK, W., The effects of punishment upon syllable recognition thresholds, *J. Exp. Psychol.*, **47**, 343–350 (1954).

MACINTOSH, A., Differential effect of the status of the competing group upon levels of aspiration, *Amer. J. Psychol.*, **55**, 546–554 (1942).

MARROW, A. J., Goal tensions and recall: I., *J. Gen. Psychol.*, **19**, 3–35 (1938a).

MARROW, A. J., Goal tensions and recall: II., *J. Gen. Psychol.*, **19**, 37–64 (1938b).

MARTIN, J. R., Reminiscence and gestalt theory, *Psychol. Monogr.*, **52**, 235, 1–37 (1940).

MASON, H. M. and GARRISON, BARBARA K., Intelligibility of spoken messages: liked and disliked, *J. Abnorm.* (*Soc.*) *Psychol.*, **46**, 100–103 (1951).

MCCLEARY, R. A. and LAZARUS, R. S., Autonomic discrimination without awareness: an interim report, *J. Personality*, **18**, 171–179 (1949).

MCCLELLAND, D. C. and LIBERMAN, A. M., The effect of need for achievement on recognition of need-related words, *J. Personality*, **18**, 236–251 (1949).

MCDOUGALL, W., *Social Psychology* (London, Methuen, 23rd Ed., 1936).

MCGINNIES, E., Emotionality and perceptual defense, *Psychol. Rev.*, **56**, 244–251 (1949).

MCGINNIES, E., Discussion of Howes and Solomon's note on "Emotionality and perceptual defense," *Psychol. Rev.*, **57**, 235–240 (1950).

MCGINNIES, E. and ADORNETTO, J., Perceptual defense in normal and in schizophrenic observers, *J. Abnorm.* (*Soc.*) *Psychol.*, **47**, 833–837 (1952).

MCGINNIES, E., COMER, P. B. and LACEY, O. L., Visual recognition thresholds as a function of word length and word frequencies, *J. Exp. Psychol.*, **44**, 65–69 (1952).

MCGINNIES, E. and SHERMAN, H., Generalization of perceptual defense, *J. Abnorm.* (*Soc.*) *Psychol.*, **47**, 81–85 (1952).

MCKINNEY, F., Studies in the retention of interrupted learning activities, *J. Comp. Psychol.*, **19**, 265–296 (1935).

MEDNICK, S. A., HARWOOD, A. and WERTHEIM, J., Perception of disturbing and neutral words through the autokinetic word technique, *J. Abnorm.* (*Soc.*) *Psychol.*, **55**, 267–268 (1957).

MILLER, D. R., Responses of psychiatric patients to threat of failure, *J. Abnorm.* (*Soc.*) *Psychol.*, **46**, 378–387 (1951).

MORRIS, C., *Signs, Language and Behavior* (New York, Prentice-Hall Inc., 1946).

MOWRER, O. H., *Learning Theory and Personality Dynamics*, (New York, Ronald Press, 1950).

MURDOCK, B. B., Perceptual defense and threshold measurements, *J. Personality*, **22**, 565–571 (1954).

MURRAY, H. A., *Explorations in Personality* (New York: Oxford Univ. Press, 1938).

NEEL, ANN F., Conflict, recognition time and defensive behavior, *Amer. Psychologist*, **9**, 437, Abstract (1954).

NELSON, S. E., Psychosexual conflicts and defenses in visual perception, *J. Abnorm.* (*Soc.*) *Psychol.*, **51**, 427–433 (1955).

NEWTON, K. R., A note on visual recognition thresholds, *J. Abnorm.* (*Soc.*) *Psychol.*, **51**, 709–710 (1955).

NEWTON, K. R., Visual recognition thresholds and learning, *Percept. Mot. Skills*, **6**, 81–87 (1956).

NOWLIS, HELEN, H., The influence of success and failure on the resumption of an interrupted task, *J. Exp. Psychol.*, **28**, 304–325 (1941).

OSGOOD, C. E., The nature and measurement of meaning, *Psychol. Bull.*, **49**, 197–237 (1952).

OSLER, SONIA, F. and LEWINSOHN, P. M., The relation between manifest anxiety and perceptual defense, *Amer. Psychologist*, **9**, 446, Abstract (1954).

OVSIANKINA, MARIA, Die Wiederaufnahme unterbrochener Handlungen, *Psychol. Forsch.*, **11**, 302–389 (1928).

PACHAURI, A. R., A study of gestalt problems in completed and interrupted tasks: I., *Brit. J. Psychol.*, **25**, 365–381 (1935a).

PACHAURI, A. R., A study of gestalt problems in completed and interrupted tasks: II., *Brit. J. Psychol.*, **25**, 447–457 (1935b).

PACHAURI, A. R., A study of gestalt problems in completed and interrupted tasks. Part III., *Brit. J. Psychol.*, **27**, 170–180 (1936).

POSTMAN, L., On the problem of perceptual defense, *Psychol. Rev.*, **60**, 298–306 (1953a).

POSTMAN, L., The experimental analysis of motivational factors in perception, in *Current Theory and Research in Motivation: a Symposium* (Lincoln, Univ. Nebraska Press, 1953b).

POSTMAN, L., BRONSON, WANDA C., and GROPPER, G. L., Is there a mechanism of perceptual defense? *J. Abnorm.* (*Soc.*) *Psychol.*, **48**, 215–224 (1953).

POSTMAN, L., BRUNER, J. S., and MCGINNIES, E., Personal values as selective factors in perception, *J. Abnorm.* (*Soc.*) *Psychol.*, **83**, 148–153 (1948).

POSTMAN, L. and SOLOMON, R. L., Perceptual sensitivity

to completed and incompleted tasks, *J. Personality*, **18**, 347–357 (1949).

PRENTICE, W. C. H., The interruption of tasks, *Psychol. Rev.*, **51**, 329–340 (1944).

PRESTON, M. G., Use of the coefficient of correlation in the study of the D-score for the level of aspiration, *Amer. J. Psychol.*, **55**, 442–446 (1942).

PRESTON, M. G. and BAYTON, J. A., Differential effect of a social variable upon three levels of aspiration, *J. Exp. Psychol.*, **29**, 351–369 (1941).

PRESTON, M. G. and BAYTON, J. A., Correlations between levels of aspiration, *J. Psychol.*, **13**, 369–373 (1942).

PRESTON, M. G., SPIERS, ANNE and TRASOFF, JOYCE, On certain conditions controlling the realism and irrealism of aspirations, *J. Exp. Psychol.*, **37**, 48–58 (1947).

PUSTELL, T. E., The experimental induction of perceptual vigilance and defense, *J. Personality*, **25**, 425–438 (1956).

RAIFMAN, I., Level of aspiration in a group of peptic ulcer patients, *J. Cons. Psychol.*, **21**, 229–231 (1957).

RAO, K. U., The effects of stress on level of aspiration behaviour, *Unpubl. Ph.D. Thesis, Univ. of London Lib.* (1954).

REECE, M. M., The effect of shock on recognition thresholds, *J. Abnorm. (Soc.) Psychol.*, **49**, 165–172 (1954).

RETHLINGSHAFER, DOROTHY, Measures of tendency-to-continue: I. Behavior of feeble-minded and normal subjects following the interruption of activities, *J. Genet. Psychol.*, **59**, 109–124 (1941a).

RETHLINGSHAFER, DOROTHY, Measures of tendency-to-continue: II. Comparison of feeble-minded and normal subjects when interrupted under different conditions, *J. Genet. Psychol.*, **59**, 125–138 (1941b).

RICKERS-OVSIANKINA, MARIA, Studies on the personality structure of schizophrenic individuals: II. Reaction to interrupted tasks, *J. Gen. Psychol.*, **16**, 179–196 (1937).

RIESEN, A. H., The development of visual perception in man and chimpanzee, *Science*, **106**, 107–108 (1947).

RIGBY, W. K. and RIGBY, MARILYN, K., Reinforcement and frequency as factors in tachistoscopic thresholds, *Percept. Mot. Skills*, **6**, 29–36 (1956).

ROCKETT, F. C., Speed of form recognition as a function of stimulus factors and test anxiety, *J. Abnorm. (Soc.) Psychol.*, **53**, 197–202 (1956).

ROSEN, A. C., Changes in perceptual threshold as a protective function of the organism, *J. Personality*, **23**, 182–194 (1954).

ROSENSTOCK, I. M., Perceptual aspects of repression, *J. Abnorm. (Soc.) Psychol.*, **46**, 304–315 (1951).

ROSENZWEIG, S., Preference in the repetition of successful and unsuccessful activities as a function of age and personality, *J. Genet. Psychol.*, **42**, 423–441 (1933).

ROSENZWEIG, S., The experimental measurement of types of reaction to frustration, in *Explorations in Personality*, Ed. H. A. Murray (New York, Oxford Univ. Press, 1938).

ROSENZWEIG, S., An experimental study of "repression" with special reference to need-persistive and ego-defensive reactions to frustration, *J. Exp. Psychol.*, **32**, 64–74 (1943).

ROSENZWEIG, S., The investigation of repression as an instance of experimental idiodynamics, *Psychol. Rev.*, **59**, 339–345 (1952).

ROSENZWEIG, S. and MASON, GWENDOLYN, An experimental study of memory in relation to the theory of repression, *Brit. J. Psychol.*, **24**, 247–265 (1934).

ROSENZWEIG, S. and SARASON, S., An experimental study of the triadic hypothesis: reaction to frustration, ego-defense and hypnotizability. I. Correlational approach, *Character & Pers.*, **11**, 1–19 (1942).

ROTTER, J. B., Level of aspiration as a method of studying personality: I. A critical review of methodology, *Psychol. Rev.*, **49**, 463–474 (1942a).

ROTTER, J. B., Level of aspiration as a method of studying personality: II. Development and evaluation of a controlled method, *J. Exp. Psychol.*, **31**, 410–421 (1942b).

ROTTER, J. B., Level of aspiration as a method of studying personality: III. Group validity studies, *Character & Pers.*, **11**, 254–274 (1942c).

SANFORD, N., Age as a factor in the recall of interrupted tasks, *Psychol. Rev.*, **53**, 234–240 (1946).

SANFORD, N. and RISSER, J., What are the conditions of self-defensive forgetting? *J. Personality*, **17**, 244–260 (1948).

SARASON, S. B. and GORDON, E. M., The test anxiety questionnaire: scoring norms, *J. Abnorm. (Soc.) Psychol.*, **48**, 447–448 (1953).

SARASON, S. and ROSENZWEIG, S., An experimental study of the triadic hypothesis: reaction to frustration, ego-defense and hypnotizability: II. Thematic Apperception approach, *Character & Pers.*, **11**, 150–165 (1942).

SEARS, PAULINE S., Levels of aspiration in academically successful and unsuccessful children, *J. Abnorm. (Soc.) Psychol.*, **35**, 498–536 (1940).

SEARS, PAULINE, S., Levels of aspiration in relation to some variables of personality: clinical studies, *J. Soc. Psychol.*, **14**, 311–336 (1941).

SEARS, R. R., Functional abnormalities of memory with special reference to amnesia, *Psychol. Rev.*, **33**, 229–274 (1936).

SEARS, R. R., *Survey of Objective Studies of Psychoanalytic Concepts* (New York, Social Science Res. Council, 1943).

SENDEN, M. VON., *Raum-und Gestaltauffassung bei operierten Blindgeborenen vor und nach der Operation* (Leipzig, Barth, 1932).

SHAW, M. E. and BENSBERG, G. V., Level of aspiration phenomena in mentally deficient persons, *J. Personality*, **24**, 134–144 (1955).

SHEEHAN, J. G. and ZELEN, S. L., Level of aspiration in stutterers and non-stutterers, *J. Abnorm. (Soc.) Psychol.*, **51**, 83–86 (1955).

SIEGEL, S., Level of aspiration and decision making, *Psychol. Rev.*, **64**, 253–262 (1957).

SINGER, B. R., An experimental enquiry into the concept of perceptual defence, *Brit. J. Psychol.*, **47**, 298–311 (1956).

SMITH, J. G., Influence of failure, expressed hostility, and stimulus characteristics on verbal learning and recognition, *J. Personality*, **22**, 475–493 (1953).

SMOCK, C. D., The relationship between test anxiety, "threat expectancy," and recognition thresholds for words, *J. Personality*, **25**, 191–201 (1956a).

SMOCK, C. D., Replication and comments: "An experimental reunion of psychoanalytic theory with perceptual vigilance and defense," *J. Abnorm. (Soc.) Pyschol.*, **53**, 68–73 (1956b).

SMOCK, C. D., Recall of interrupted and non-interrupted tasks as a function of experimentally induced anxiety and motivational relevance of the task stimuli, *J. Personality*, **25**, 589–599 (1956c).

SOLOMON, R. L. and HOWES, D. H., Word frequency, personal values, and visual duration thresholds, *Psychol. Rev.*, **58**, 256–270 (1951).

SOLOMON, R. L. and POSTMAN, L., Frequency of usage as a determinant of recognition thresholds for words, *J. Exp. Psychol.*, **43**, 195–201 (1952).

SPENCE, D. P., A new look at vigilance and defense, *J. Abnorm. (Soc.) Psychol.*, **54**, 103–108 (1957).

SPIELBERGER, C. D., The effects of stuttering behavior and response set on recognition thresholds, *J. Personality*, **25**, 33–45 (1956).

STEIN, K. B., Perceptual defense and perceptual sensitization under neutral and involved conditions, *J. Personality*, **21**, 467–478 (1952).

STEINER, I. D., Self-perception and goal-setting behavior, *J. Personality*, **25**, 344–355 (1956).

STEISEL, I. M. and COHEN, B. D., The effects of two degrees of failure on level of aspiration and performance, *J. Abnorm. (Soc.) Psychol.*, **46**, 79–82 (1951).

STROTHER, G. B. and COOK, D. M., Neurocirculatory reactions and a group stress situation, *J. Cons. Psychol.*, **17**, 267–268 (1953).

SUMNER, F. C. and JOHNSON, E. E., Sex differences in levels of aspiration and in self-estimates of performance in a classroom situation, *J. Psychol.*, **27**, 483–490 (1949).

SUTCLIFFE, J. P., An evaluation of "A new method of analyzing the data in an experiment on level of aspiration," *Amer. J. Psychol.*, **65**, 465–469 (1952a).

SUTCLIFFE, J. P., The significance of some level of aspiration measures, *Aust. J. Psychol.*, **4**, 40–49 (1952b).

SUTCLIFFE, J. P., Responsiveness of the level of aspiration to success and failure as a function of task variability, *Aust. J. Psychol.*, **7**, 34–44 (1955).

TAMKIN, A. S., Selective recall in schizophrenia and its relation to ego strength, *J. Abnorm. (Soc.) Psychol.*, **55**, 345–349 (1957).

THORNDIKE, E. L. and LORGE, I., *The Teacher's Book of 30,000 Words* (New York, Columbia Univ. Press, 1944).

VANDERPLAS, J. M. and BLAKE, R. R., Selective sensitization in auditory perception, *J. Personality*, **18**, 252–256 (1949).

VERNON, M. D., The functions of schemata in perceiving, *Psychol. Rev.*, **62**, 180–192 (1955).

WALSH, TERESA, The memory of completed and uncompleted tasks: a study of volitional frustration, *Unpubl. M.A. Thesis, Univ. of London Lib.* (1940).

WALSH, TERESA, A further study of volitional frustration in respect of uncompleted tasks, *Unpubl. Ph.D. Thesis, Univ. of London Lib.* (1942).

WALTER, L. M. and MARZOLF, S. S., The relation of sex, age and school achievement to levels of aspiration, *J. Educ. Psychol.*, **42**, 285–292 (1951).

WALTON, D., An experimental study of a method of using perceptual errors as an aid in diagnosis, *J. Ment. Sci.*, **100**, 678–686 (1954).

WALTON, D., A further experimental study of using perceptual errors as an aid in diagnosis, *J. Ment. Sci.*, **103**, 556–580 (1957).

WHITTAKER, EDNA, M., GILCHRIST, J. C. and FISCHER, JEAN, W., Perceptual defense or response suppression? *J. Abnorm. (Soc.) Psychol.*, **47**, 732–733 (1952).

WIENER, M., Word-frequency or motivation in perceptual defense? *J. Abnorm. (Soc.) Psychol.*, **51**, 214–218 (1955).

WINDER, C. L., On the personality structures of schizophrenics, *J. Abnorm. (Soc.) Psychol.*, **47**, 86–100 (1952).

ZEIGARNIK, BLUMA, Über das Behalten von erledigten und unerledigten Handlungen, *Psychol. Forsch.*, **9**, 1–85 (1927).

ZELLER, A. F., An experimental analogue of repression: I. Historical summary, *Psychol. Bull.*, **47**, 39–51 (1950).

ZUCKERMAN, M., The effect of frustration on the perception of neutral and aggressive words, *J. Personality*, **23**, 407–422 (1954).

CHAPTER 8

Heredity and Psychological Abnormality

JAMES SHIELDS and ELIOT SLATER

In this chapter we shall consider how far the concepts of heredity can be used to explain some of the psychological abnormalities which have been described in this book. We are not speaking here of social heredity, in the sense in which a kingdom or a family business may be said to be hereditary. Our concern is the differences between individuals which arise from differences in their genetical make-up; and in this sense the hereditary are distinguished from the environmental causes of variation. Genetical and environmental factors interact with one another, and can never be completely disentangled. But by appropriate techniques it is possible to estimate how much of the total variance observed in a group of individuals, sharing a common environment, is contributed by genetical causes, though we are not thereby entitled to assume that the contribution would be the same if either the genetic constitution of the group, or the environment, were significantly changed.

Principles of Heredity

Before trying to deal with the extent to which psychological abnormalities may be said to be genetical, we must describe briefly the physical basis of heredity and what we know of the genes and their mode of action. In so far as psychological differences between individuals are genetically caused, they must be due to such differences between genes, i.e. to differences of a physical kind.

THE NATURE OF THE GENE AND ITS EFFECT ON DEVELOPMENT

The basic units of heredity are the genes. Chemically, they are thought probably to take the form of very large and elaborately constructed molecules of desoxyribonucleic acid (DNA). Fig. 8.1 may give some idea of the complexity of these molecules. Unless altered by mutation, the genes are transmitted from one generation to the next unchanged. They are capable of building up from the materials with which they are supplied other genes identical with themselves, so that one cell of the body can grow and divide into two, mother and daughter cells having the same genetical constitution. Mutation is a rare and rather haphazard event, which can be artificially brought about by the use of chemicals which will penetrate the nucleus of the cell without destroying it or by physical agents such as radiation. Apart from such experiments it is not likely to occur spontaneously much more frequently than once in every fifty thousand generations for any one gene. Such a change, when it does occur, will be a chemical one and consist in such an event as a rearrangement of a group of atoms, or the loss of a side-chain from a molecule. Differences so caused may be trifling or critical in their effects.

The genes exert their effects through their control of biochemical reactions, by speeding up some chemical reactions and retarding others, or by inhibiting some reaction until the chemical environment is such as to trigger it off. Their action resembles that of enzymes in that, though involved in chemical changes, they maintain their own identity. They control the development of the individual from the earliest stage of the fertilized ovum up to adult life and into old age. The variation due to some genetic differences may be seen very early, e.g. into a male or female constitution, but in other cases much later; and there is no point in life at which one can say that all latent genetic potentialities must have been manifested.

As a simple example of a genetic difference we may take the condition known as phenylketonuria which can be attributed to a single abnormal gene. Whereas the normal gene permits of normal body chemistry, the abnormal gene fails to provide an enzyme which converts the amino-acid phenylalanine into tyrosine, a foodstuff of vital importance to the brain. If the individual has one normal and one abnormal gene, he can still deal with the phenylalanine and can be mentally normal; if he has two abnormal

298

genes, he cannot carry out the essential chemical processes, and the phenylalanine is excreted in the urine as phenylpyruvic acid and can be identified by a simple colour reaction. The metabolic deficiency prevents normal development of the brain, and the abnormal individual is mentally defective.

We must think of these genetic-biochemical relationships as being ones of great complexity, involving many stages. H. J. Muller (1956) puts it—

> Whatever may be the nature of the primary chemical products of genes within the cell, these products must be of thousands of different kinds, corresponding with the thousands of different genes, and these products must interact with one another in innumerable ways to form secondary products, tertiary products and those ever further removed from the genes. It is usually only after a most intricate web of these inter-actions has been followed through that those end-products are at last found which we become aware of as the characteristics of the organism. . . . Because of the great indirectness of the route connecting the genes with these end results, it is evident that any given characteristic must be a resultant of the action of many genes, some playing a major role in its development but many more playing only a minor role.

Although the genes are transmitted as independent units, we must think of the genetic constitution as also largely acting as a whole. We shall find that the cumulative effects of the minor end results of many genes will be just as important in some fields as the major effects of single genes in other fields.

Once a major gene has produced its distinctive difference, this is not the end of the matter; for the specific abnormality so caused will become involved in a tangled web of secondary and tertiary consequences. Grüneberg (1947) has shown how, in the experimental animal though not in man, such complex problems of causation may be sorted out by tracking back through ever earlier stages in the development of the embryo. In the case of one particular gene in the rat (Fig. 8.2), the abnormality caused is quite simply an anomaly in the development of cartilage; the more distant effects, however, are of an extremely various kind, so that apparently clinically distinct diseases, liable to lead to death in quite different ways, can be traced back to this one cause.

Just as the effects of one gene may be many, so also the converse is true and the same end results can be brought about by different genes. There is a well-known form of blindness which is caused by a disease of the retina of the eye, *retinitis pigmentosa*. This condition can be watched by the oculist, with the aid of the ophthalmoscope, from its very earliest stages; and the actual pathological processes involved can be seen in all their detail. Nevertheless there are several different genes which can bring about this condition; and by an examination of the eye alone

it is impossible to say which of the genes is the one responsible.

The effect of the genes is not limited to early development. Both growth and regression in all stages from the embryonic to senile decay are under genetic control. Many genetically determined conditions—baldness in men, for example—do not usually become

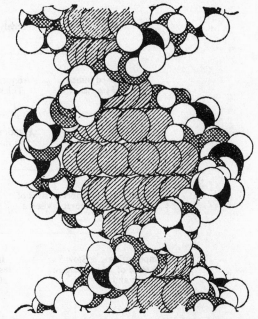

FIG. 8.1. PART OF A MODEL OF A GIANT MOLECULE OF DESOXYRIBONUCLEIC ACID (DNA)

DNA is found in the chromosomes, and (with minor exceptions) only in the chromosomes, of all living cells. A single molecule probably consists of at least a thousand turns of the helix shown above. The section shows how the groups of atoms are arranged in two intertwining spiral chains. Each chain consists of phosphate and sugar groups. Attached to the latter are various chemical "bases" which link one chain with the other. The varying sequence of the bases along the molecule may provide a kind of *code* by which hereditary characteristics are transmitted from one generation to the next.

(*By courtesy of the "Observer," 1956, and Dr. F. H. C. Crick*)

manifest until well on in adult life. In many of these the "pedigree of causes" will be more complex than in phenylketonuria, and allow, therefore, greater scope for variability in manifestation. *Diabetes mellitus* is a disease which is often genetically determined. It is due fundamentally to a deficiency of a circulating enzyme, insulin. Fig. 8.3 shows part of the network of consequences which can be set in motion by the failure to secrete sufficient insulin. Some of the end results are due to the impaired ability to burn sugar, others to the efforts of the organism to compensate for this. The course taken by the abnormality is influenced by secondary factors, some of them attributable to other genes, others the products of non-genetical factors, such as medical treatment, including the administration of insulin.

For an understanding of the way in which a genetical difference may manifest itself in an observable

may, indeed, suppose that the route from the gene to the end result will be more complex and indirect than ever; but we may still be able to show that certain effects can be put down to genetical causes.

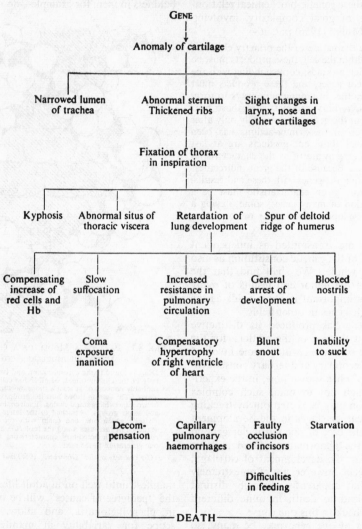

"PEDIGREE" OF CAUSES OF LETHAL CARTILAGE ANOMALY
IN THE RAT

GENE

↓

Anomaly of cartilage

Narrowed lumen of trachea   Abnormal sternum Thickened ribs   Slight changes in larynx, nose and other cartilages

Fixation of thorax in inspiration

Kyphosis   Abnormal situs of thoracic viscera   Retardation of lung development   Spur of deltoid ridge of humerus

Compensating increase of red cells and Hb   Slow suffocation   Increased resistance in pulmonary circulation   General arrest of development   Blocked nostrils

Coma exposure inanition   Compensatory hypertrophy of right ventricle of heart   Blunt snout   Inability to suck

Decompensation   Capillary pulmonary haemorrhages   Faulty occlusion of incisors   Starvation

Difficulties in feeding

DEATH

FIG. 8.2. "PEDIGREE" OF CAUSES OF LETHAL CARTILAGE ANOMALY IN THE RAT
(*After Grüneberg, 1947; by courtesy of Prof. H. Grüneberg and Messrs. Cassell*)

characteristic of the individual we depend on research and knowledge in many fields, such as embryology, biochemistry and physiology. Even in the best studied instances, our knowledge of the dynamic chain will be full of gaps. The application of genetics to the study of abnormal psychology is no different in principle from its applications in biology or medicine. We

though we can claim no detailed knowledge of the hypothetical genes involved or their mode of operation.

From what has been said it can be seen that it is the genes which are inherited, and not abnormalities or diseases themselves. The genes can only act in an environmental framework; and their effects will be influenced to a greater or lesser degree by the nature of that environment. One of the aims of genetical research is to discover how much of the total variance occurring in a given population can be attributed to genetical and to environmental differences between individuals. To understand how genetical variation can occur, we have to observe the way in which the

either chemically identical with its partner, or differing from it in some small though possibly important way. The genes are arranged along the length of the chromosomes, which are threadlike structures, often condensed in appearance because they are spirally twisted. The order in which the genes are arranged along the chromosome is largely held fixed, so that gene pairs lie

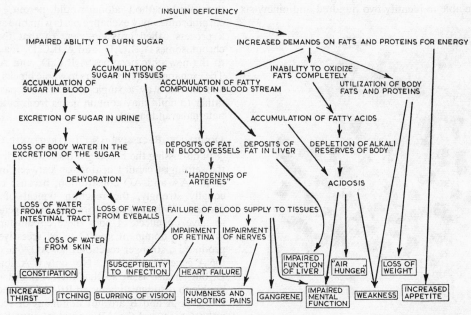

FIG. 8.3. SOME OF THE CONSEQUENCES OF THE RELATIVE DEFICIENCY OF INSULIN WHICH OCCURS IN DIABETES MELLITUS

(From Neel and Schull, 1954, after Anderson; by courtesy of Prof. J. V. Neel and the University of Chicago Press)

genes are distributed in their descent from parent to child.

LOCATION OF THE GENES ON THE CHROMOSOMES

The totality of the genes are organized into chromosomes, which are contained within the nucleus of the cell. Every species of living thing, with the exception of the most primitive, has its own characteristic number of chromosomes, there normally being twenty-three pairs in man (Tjio and Levan, 1956). Every cell in the body has its full complement of chromosomes, except for the sex cells, ova and spermatozoa which contain only half the normal number, one from each pair. The genes are too small to be seen individually— it has been estimated that in man each cell contains between 40,000 and 80,000 genes (Neel and Schull, 1954)—but the human chromosomes can be seen when suitably stained (Fig. 8.4). The chromosomes exist in pairs, each member of which is homologous to the other; the genes of which they consist are also homologous and paired, each member of a pair being

opposite one another in the chromosome pairs. In experimental animals, the gene can be identified both by its position along the length of a particular chromosome, and also by its effects, so that chromosome maps can be drawn. A particular gene can be shown to be capable of taking, in some instances, one of two or more alternative forms; and each of these forms will be likely to have a slightly different effect in development. Thus one of the genes which determines a man's blood group can take one of three forms, A, B and O. This gives the possibility of six different types of constitution—AA, AB, AO, BB, BO, and OO. The serologist can test for the presence or absence of an A or B gene, and so can distinguish some of these blood types from one another; but he has no way of testing for the presence of the O gene, so that some genetic types cannot be absolutely identified by serology alone.

These blood factors are representative of genes which cause no abnormality, and which are individually very common. Most of the severe conditions which have a simple genetical explanation are due to rare genes, i.e. the gene which is compatible with normality is extremely common, while its alternative form or allele is rare. Genetically man is extremely diverse, perhaps more so than any other species. To take a limited but practical illustration, Bertinshaw *et al.* (1950) tested the bloods of four hundred and seventy-five Londoners with eight groups of antisera, and were able to identify two hundred and ninety-six

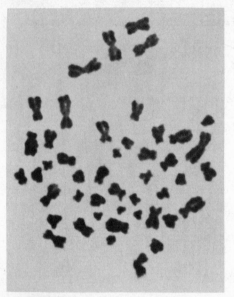

FIG. 8.4. THE HUMAN CHROMOSOMES

Colchicine-metaphase of human and embryonic lung fibroblasts grown *in vitro*.

(Tjio and Levan, 1956; by courtesy of Dr. J. H. Tjio and "Hereditas")

different combinations of blood groups. With the exception of identical twins, each individual is genetically unique. The existence of so much genetical diversity is a good reason to expect a genetical contribution to many modes of variation in which we are interested.

FORMATION OF THE SEX CELLS: FERTILIZATION

In the ordinary process of bodily growth and multiplication of cells, each chromosome builds up a duplicate of itself before the cell divides, so that each daughter-cell contains twenty-three pairs of chromosomes like the mother-cell. When the daughter-cell is to be a sex-cell (ovum or spermatozoon) the chromosomes do not build up duplicates but simply separate, so that the daughter-cell contains twenty-three single chromosomes. When spermatozoon unites with ovum in the process of fertilization the twenty-three pairs are re-established. The new individual therefore comes to have half his chromosomes from his father

and half from his mother; but of the chromosomes he obtained from his father, the proportion derived from his father's father and from his father's mother need not be equal at all. The process of selection within pairs of chromosomes is entirely random. In this way a great deal of mixing up of chromosomes, and therefore of genes, goes on from generation to generation; but the mixing is much more intimate than this method alone would permit. Pairs of chromosomes may exchange parts with one another by a process called crossing-over, so that the pair of chromosomes $A_1B_1C_1D_1$ and $A_2B_2C_2D_2$ may give rise to the new chromosomes $A_1B_1C_2D_2$ and $A_2B_2C_1D_1$. The exchange of genes occurs in whole blocks at a time; and in this way a single chromosome passed from father to child may contain genes from both the two paternal grandparents.

DOMINANT, RECESSIVE AND INTERMEDIATE GENES

In discussing the blood groups it was indicated that the serologist cannot distinguish between individuals of the AA and AO constitution, because both give, equally strongly, the reaction typical of A gene-carriers. If the A gene is present, the O gene appears to have no effect. Under these circumstances A is said to be dominant and O to be recessive. If AA produced a stronger reaction than AO, one could call the A gene intermediate. Not only is A dominant to O, but so also is B, so that the serologist is equally unable to distinguish between BB and BO individuals. However A and B are not dominant or recessive to one another, and the AB individual gives both the A and the B serological reactions.

From knowing what happens in the formation of the sex-cells and at fertilization, we can easily see what the offspring will be when individuals of the various types mate together. O is by far the commonest of the three genes, with A the next, while B is relatively rare. The commonest constitutions are therefore OO and AO. The first, having two genes of the same kind, is said to be homozygous for O, while the second is heterozygous. If an AO man mates with an OO woman, the child will be able to get either an A or an O gene from the father, only an O gene from the mother. The children of such a mating will tend to be AO and OO with an equal frequency. Suppose the dominant gene in which we are interested is not the normal A gene, but a gene which causes some abnormality or defect. Then, as this gene, *D* let us call it, will be rare compared with its normal allele *d*, the great majority of people will be of the *dd* constitution and normal, while there will be some people of the *Dd* constitution and abnormal. The *DD* constitution will be so very rare that it can be neglected (perhaps even incapable of surviving). A mating between normal and abnormal persons will be a mating of

Dd with *dd*, and half the children can be expected to be *Dd* and to show the same abnormality while the other half will be *dd* and normal. In this way the abnormality will appear to go down the generations from parent to child in a simple and direct way.

Let us take the case of two AO parents (Fig. 8.5). As their child could take either an A or an O gene from either parent, he would have one chance in four of being AA, one chance of being AO, one of being OA and one of being OO. One quarter of the expected children would, in fact, be of a different blood type, the O or not-A type, from both of their parents and from the rest of their brothers and sisters. Now let us suppose that the recessive gene, *d*, in which we are interested is one which causes abnormality, while the dominant gene *D* is now compatible with normality. Then two heterozygotes, or carriers, of the *Dd* type, though normal themselves, will have children one quarter of whom can be expected to be *dd* and abnormal. If such an abnormal person mates it will probably be with a person who is homozygous for the normal gene, of the type *DD*; all the children of this mating will be *Dd* and normal in appearance (though they carry the abnormal gene). In this case the abnormality, being due to a recessive gene, appears out of the blue in a family tree, is not apparently handed on from parent to child, but may easily strike more than one member of a sibship. An understanding of the simple principles enables one to work out the results of any particular mating for oneself.

Intermediate genes, neither dominant nor recessive, will frequently be found in cases where an effect can be shown to greater or lesser degree, instead of in an

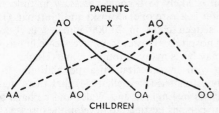

PARENTS

AO X AO

AA   AO   OA   OO

CHILDREN

FIG. 8.5. TWO PARENTS OF BLOOD-GROUP AO. POSSIBLE CHILDREN AND THEIR RELATIVE FREQUENCIES

all-or-none way. Quantitative genetic variation is almost the rule when we are concerned with normal and not pathological events.

SEX-LINKED INHERITANCE: COLOUR-BLINDNESS

One of the twenty-three pairs of chromosomes is anomalous in that the two members of the pair are not the same size and hence not strictly homologous. These are the sex chromosomes, of which the X-chromosome is of full size, while the Y-chromosome is hardly more than a fragment containing very little genetic material in proportion. In the case of man, it is

the female which is the homogametic sex, having two X-chromosomes, while the male is heterogametic and has one X- and one Y-chromosome. It will be seen that the female can only produce ova of one kind, with one X-chromosome, whereas the man can produce two kinds of spermatozoa, with an X- or with a Y-chromosome, which will in turn, after union with an ovum, produce respectively a female or a male.

As the X-chromosome is so much bigger than the Y-chromosome, the greater part of it in the male has no

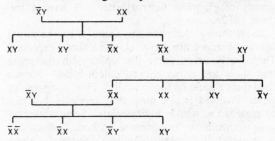

FIG. 8.6. POSSIBLE MATINGS AND TYPES OF OFFSPRING IN RECESSIVE SEX-LINKED INHERITANCE

$\bar{X}$ = abnormal sex-linked recessive gene
XX = normal female
XY = normal male
$\bar{X}$X = carrier female (unaffected)
$\bar{X}$Y = affected male
$\bar{X}\bar{X}$ = affected female (rare)

matching partner. Any gene, dominant or recessive, on this part of the X-chromosome, will have its full effect in the male, but if recessive will be liable to be suppressed in the female. Conditions so determined tend to show a very characteristic pedigree (Fig. 8.6), with transmission occurring through the female, but manifestation being practically confined to males. An affected male, mating with a normal female, will have nothing but normal children. His sons will have taken a Y-chromosome from him, without the abnormal gene; his daughters will have taken an X-chromosome carrying the abnormal gene, but will also have inherited from their mother a normal X-chromosome, with the normal dominant allele. If one of these heterozygous daughters marries a normal male, as one may readily see, all her daughters will be normal, though some of them will be heterozygous, whereas some of her sons will be abnormal. Those of them who inherit their grandmother's X-chromosome will be normal, those who inherit the grandfather's X-chromosome will get with it an abnormal gene which can now show its effect. For a female to show the abnormality, she must be the daughter of an affected father and a heterozygous mother.

Red-green colour-blindness is a relatively common perceptual anomaly, in which the affected person has difficulty in distinguishing red and green. Its dependence on a recessive sex-linked, or X-borne, gene is well established. In this country the gene frequency is over one in twenty, so that rather more than five per cent of males are colour-blind, while colour-blind females are rare. Clearly the frequency of the character in the female will be the square of the frequency in the male, i.e. something over one in four hundred. If p is the frequency of the abnormal gene, and q the frequency of the normal allele, then persons homozygous for the abnormal gene will have a frequency of p^2, persons homozygous for the normal gene a frequency of q^2, while heterozygotes will have a frequency of $2pq$.

So far theory. According to Stern (1950) the actual figures observed are fairly close to those expected. There is, however, some discrepancy, in the sense that there are rather more "colour-blind" women than there should be theoretically. First, the gene, or genes, involved is not absolutely recessive but can be regarded as weakly intermediate. Some heterozygous women have "poor colour aptitude," which can be mistaken for colour-blindness. Secondly, there are four main subtypes of partial colour-blindness: deuteranopia and protanopia which are dichromatic types, and deuteranomaly and protanomaly which are trichromatic types. Although all four subtypes are inherited in a recessive sex-linked way, two *loci* might be involved, each with the possibility of three alleles—

1. Gene for normal colour vision, which is dominant to the gene for deuteranomaly, which in turn is dominant to the gene for deuteranopia.
2. Gene for normal colour vision, which is dominant to the gene for protanomaly, which in turn is dominant to the gene for protanopia.

Total colour-blindness, or the ability to see no colours, distinguishing only shades of white and grey, is much rarer. It can be genetically determined by a recessive gene on the homologous part of the X- and Y-chromosomes (Haldane, 1936). Such so-called partially sex-linked genes are much less easily recognized as having a connexion with the sex chromosomes.

Sex-linked inheritance contributes little to the total of psychiatric abnormality. It was once suggested that a sex-linked dominant gene played a part in the causation of manic-depressive disorder, because this diagnosis is made more frequently in women than men. Clearly, women with two X-chromosomes would have twice the chance of receiving the gene that a man with one X-chromosome would have. However, it is easily seen that the fathers and mothers of affected females would have equal chances of being gene-carriers, whereas one would expect only the mothers of affected males to be gene-carriers. In fact, no such differential incidence is found, and other explanations have to be sought, e.g., in the difference between the male and the female constitution in the broad sense.

EXAMPLES OF DOMINANT INHERITANCE

Although it is probable that there are as many single genes of large effect causing psychiatric illness as other conditions such as metabolic disorders and eye disease, it is not surprising that so far very few have been identified. Nevertheless we have one excellent example in *Huntington's chorea*. This disease received its name from the fact that it was first satisfactorily described by an American country doctor of that name, whose father and grandfather, doctors before him in the same district of Long Island, had observed its appearance in generation after generation of certain local families. These families could be traced back to immigrants in a ship which had docked in Boston Bay some centuries before, and who had sailed from Bures in Suffolk.

In persons who carry the gene, nerve cells in the cortex and the basal ganglia of the brain are liable to die off prematurely. The first symptoms are usually shown in middle life, and the mean age of onset is 35. Men and women are equally liable. The characteristic symptoms are spontaneous jerky movements of the head, trunk and limbs, progressive personality changes, and progressive intellectual deterioration to severe dementia and eventual death, perhaps fifteen years after the onset. The personality changes are often the earliest signs of anything being wrong, and include such changes as increased irritability and aggressiveness, slovenliness, unreliability, lack of control and delinquency. Admission to a mental hospital is likely to become necessary in time. The condition is a rare one: Minski and Guttman (1938) found sixteen cases in 23,000 inmates in London mental hospitals. However, for every case in hospital, there may be as many as four at home (Hughes, 1925, dealing with an American rural population). It was recently estimated (Pleydell, 1954) that there may be 2,000 cases in England and Wales and perhaps twice as many persons destined to develop the disease.

As the condition is dominant and rare, affected persons will be heterozygous. They may pass on to their children either the chromosome with the normal gene, or the chromosome with the Huntington gene. One can expect, therefore, that 50 per cent of the children of a Huntington patient will develop the condition in time. Fig. 8.7 shows a pedigree of Huntington's chorea. A gene-carrier, however, may marry and have a family, and die of some other cause before the disease has had time to develop; in such a case, if some of his children develop the disease, the condition will have skipped a generation. Most gene-carriers do, in fact, have their families before they fall ill, so that the gene is not eliminated at all quickly from the population by the processes of natural selection. This sort of thing is rather the rule with dominant genes; the abnormalities they cause are often late in onset, or not very severe, or very variable in their gravity. Dominant genes which caused early death, before procreation could occur, would extinguish themselves on their appearance; and every new case would be due to a fresh mutation. The genetic nature of the abnormality would then be very difficult to

the ancestors in the family who had had the disease, rather than those who had not. They also thought it possible that subtle differences in muscular co-ordination and control might be found in heterozygotes. Leese, Pond and Shields (1952) studied a family in which it seemed possible that members who later became affected would show a definite type of abnormality in the EEG some years before other signs were detectable.

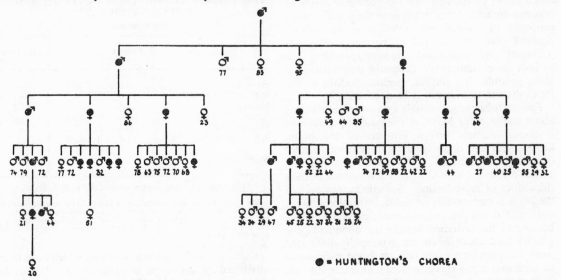

FIG. 8.7. DOMINANT INHERITANCE. FIVE GENERATIONS OF HUNTINGTON'S CHOREA

(After Sjögren 1935)

Extracts from a larger pedigree. None of the offspring of the normal members of the family have had Huntington's chorea. Spouses, all of whom were normal, are not shown, nor are children who died in infancy. The ages given for the unaffected members are those at death or when last heard of. It will be noted that many of the youngest generation still run considerable risk of being affected.

(By courtesy of Prof. T. Sjögren and the "Zeitschrift für menschliche Vererbungs- und Konstitutionslehre")

recognize as all cases would be sporadic. As a general rule, with genes which cause abnormality and disease, there is a balance between mutation on the one hand, causing the perpetual reappearance of the gene in the population, and natural selection on the other hand, removing it by the early death or reduced fertility it causes; gene frequencies tend to remain at an equilibrium.

With a condition of late onset as severe as Huntington's chorea the early detection of genetic carriers becomes important. Not only would this be helpful, especially for the genetic counsellor, in deciding which members of a family were and which were not liable to develop the disease, and to pass on the potentiality to children; but it could also lead to a better understanding of the pathology of the condition. No reliable indications have been found in Huntington's chorea. Minski and Guttmann have suggested that future choreic cases tend to resemble physically

Huntington's chorea can be classified among the presenile dementias. Another example of this group of conditions is *Pick's disease*. This is of rather later onset, and is clinically less well defined and less easily diagnosed; but there is evidence that it too is determined by a dominant gene (Sjögren 1952). Its manifestation rate is not as high as that of the Huntington gene, and modifying genes must play a more important part. Sjögren has calculated that 19 per cent of the parents and 7 per cent of the sibs of patients with Pick's disease were similarly affected, instead of the 50 per cent in each case required by theory. This would mean that the majority of gene-carriers were protected against developing the disease. Sanders (1941), has claimed (with doubtful reliability) that carriers can be detected by means of the Rorschach test some years before the onset of definite symptoms.

Another presenile dementia is *Alzheimer's disease*, pathologically quite distinct from Pick's disease although clinically often difficult to distinguish. Sjögren thinks that multifactorial inheritance is more likely than dominant inheritance in this case. The pathological changes are identical with those of ordinary senile dementia, though they are occurring unduly early; and the genetical basis may be the presence of a number of genes each favouring to some degree an early senility.

No gene, whose only effect is to cause deterioration and death at an age well after the normal cessation of procreation, will be eliminated from the population by processes of natural selection. It is accordingly probable that the changes of normal senility are primarily gene-determined. However, among the various forms that senile dementia may take, it is quite possible that further specific conditions, like Pick's disease, still remain to be discovered.

Epiloia (tuberose sclerosis) is a rare disease, affecting about one in every 30,000 of the general population; it causes multiple benign tumours of the brain, kidney, skin and other tissues and generally mental deficiency and epilepsy. It shows itself in childhood, and as a rule the individual is too abnormal to have the chance of reproduction. Sometimes, however, if the brain is not severely involved, institutional life is not required, and procreation can occur. Nevertheless, because of the restricted fertility the dominant gene which is the cause of the condition is rapidly eliminated from the population, the balance being maintained by fresh mutation; it is estimated that about one case in four is due to a mutation (Gunther and Penrose, 1935).

Of the commoner mental illnesses, the genetic basis of *manic-depressive psychosis* has been regarded as probably unifactorial and dominant (Slater, 1938; Kallman, 1950; Stenstedt, 1952). The gene would ordinarily show itself by causing a tendency to spontaneous variations of mood, probably only in some cases and at some times severe enough to need psychiatric treatment; in fact, the manifestation rate would be more like 30 per cent than 100 per cent, indicating the significance of aetiological factors other than the hypothetical specific gene. The main evidence to support this theory is the high incidence of severe disorders of a similar kind in parents, siblings, and children of manic-depressives. (Table VIII.1.)

Leonhard (1934), has investigated the families of patients with *atypical psychoses*. In many such families there appears to be a dominant form of inheritance, the same atypical features being shown in the mental illnesses of parents and children. Again, in some families schizophrenia appears to be related to a dominant gene of weak and variable manifestation. The schizophrenic illnesses observed by Böök (1953) in an isolated community in the north of Sweden were attributed by him to a gene which manifested itself fully in the homozygote, but also in 20 per cent of heterozygotes.

Although the genetics of affective and schizophrenic psychoses are obscure, it seems likely that a fair proportion of mental illness may be due to specific dominant genes with low penetrance.

TABLE VIII.1

EXPECTANCY (PER CENT) OF MANIC-DEPRESSIVE DISORDERS AMONG RELATIVES OF MANIC-DEPRESSIVE PROBANDS

(*After Stenstedt 1952*)

Investigator	Parents	Sibs	Children
Banse (1929) . .	10·8	18·1	—
Röll and Entres (1936) .	13·0	—	10·7
Slater (1938) . .	15·5	—	15·2
Strömgren (1938) .	7·5	10·7	—
Sjögren (1948) . .	7·0	3·6	—
Kallmann (1950) . .	23·4	23·0 \ *26·3 /	—
Stenstedt (1952) . .	7·4	12·3	9·4

* Dizygotic twins (equivalent genetically to full sibs).

The above risk figures, based largely on Stenstedt, are in most instances calculated after inclusion of some relatives with affective but not certainly manic-depressive disorders. Weinberg's abridged method of age-correction has generally been used. With the use of other methods higher figures would be obtained.

Other psychological abnormalities which have been attributed to dominant inheritance include *specific dyslexia* (congenital word blindness) and *tune deafness*. In the first condition, despite normal intelligence there is a marked difficulty in learning to read and write. Hallgren (1950), found that only twelve out of one hundred and sixteen unselected cases were isolated ones in the family, and that about 50 per cent of siblings having one affected parent were similarly handicapped.

Kalmus (1949), devised a battery of tests which discriminated persons who were unable to recognize commonly known melodies or to sing in tune. The trait showed bimodal distribution, and clear-cut differences were frequently shown between members of the same family, in such a way as to suggest that the variation might be caused by a single dominant gene. Kalmus suggested that the intrusion of such a gene into families of composers like Bach may have contributed to causes which disrupted long-standing musical traditions.

EXAMPLES OF RECESSIVE INHERITANCE

Rather less than 1 per cent of certified mental defectives suffer from *phenylketonuria* (PKU). As has been said earlier in this chapter, this condition is attributable to an inborn metabolic error. Individuals who carry two abnormal PKU genes are entirely unable to metabolize phenylalanine. These homozygotes are nearly always of very low intelligence, seldom being above imbecile level; and they very rarely propagate. It follows that practically all phenylketonurics will be derived from the mating of two heterozygotes, and in such sibships one in four will be expected to show the trait (cf. Fig. 8.5). Investigations by Fölling (1945), the Norwegian biochemist who discovered the condition in 1934, by Jervis (1939) in the U.S.A. and by Munro (1947) in Great Britain bear this out. In 1953 Jervis analysed all family data then available from these and other investigations Among two hundred and sixty-six sibships, four hundred and thirty-three persons out of a total of 1,527 were affected, or a little over 28 per cent. When allowance is made by appropriate methods for the fact that only families including at least one affected member are represented, figures closer to the expected 25 per cent are obtained.

In rare recessive conditions like this, one may expect an excess of cousin-marriage in the parents of affected persons. This has occurred in the illustrative pedigree given in Fig. 8.8. If p is the gene frequency, p^2 is the frequency of the homozygote, which may be roughly equated with the observed frequency of the abnormality. It has accordingly been calculated that in the case of PKU $p = 1/245$. The frequency of the heterozygote $= 2p(1 - p) = 1/123$; so we see that heterozygotes may be by no means uncommon even in the case of very rare conditions caused by a recessive gene. If one is a gene-bearer one runs no risk of producing a child with PKU unless one mates with another heterozygote; mating at random the chance of doing this would be 1/123, but only 1/8 if one were to mate with a first cousin. Hence it happens that there will be more cousin-marriage among the parents of persons suffering from rare recessive abnormalities than in the general population, and that the rarer the gene the higher the cousin-marriage rate will be. In Munro's series of forty-seven families, the parents were first cousins in five cases (10 per cent), against an expectation of 0·5 per cent for the general population. In the U.S.A. where p is estimated at the higher figure of 1/173, Jervis found that about 5 per cent of the parents of PKU patients were first cousins.

Unlike pathological dominant genes, recessive genes are quite widely spread in the population, being carried by heterozygotes who suffer no ill-effects; in this way they are protected against elimination by natural selection. Muller (1950) has opined that we all carry somewhere about eight pathogenic recessive genes. Recessive conditions, because of this immunity to selective processes, tend to be graver than dominant abnormalities, of earlier onset and less variable in their manifestations, and possibly also less open to environmental modification of their effects. This latter quality, however, depends very much on the degree of understanding of their mode of operation. There is evidence to suggest, for instance, that PKU subjects may be partly protected against excessive retardation of intellectual development by controlling their consumption of phenylalanine (Bickel et al., 1953; Blainey and Gulliford, 1956; Woolf et al., 1955).

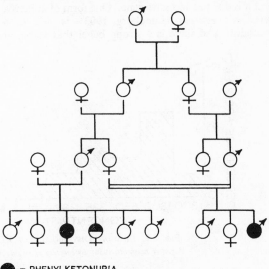

● = PHENYLKETONURIA

◖ = PROBABLY PHENYLKETONURIC, DIED YOUNG

⌐—⌐ = CONSANGUINEOUS MATING

FIG. 8.8. RECESSIVE INHERITANCE. PART OF A PEDIGREE OF PHENYLKETONURIA
(*After Fölling, Mohr and Ruud, 1945*)
Note the presence of the defect in collateral branches of the family but not among direct ascendants. In one instance the parents were first cousins.
(*By courtesy of Dr. A. Fölling*)

It is quite probable that the contribution of rare recessive genes, *in toto*, to the lower grades of mental deficiency is a significant one. This is most likely in the case of patients who show neurological abnormalities in addition to low intelligence. In his survey of all cases of mental deficiency in the Royal Eastern Counties Institution, Colchester, Penrose (1938) classified one hundred and twenty-eight patients as showing disease of the nervous system; of these eight, or 6·2 per cent had consanguineous parents. Even among the non-neurological patients there was an increased consanguinity rate of 3·1 per cent, suggesting that undifferentiated cases of defect include a proportion due to recessive genetic abnormalities. It is interesting that, until the discovery of the characteristic colour reaction in the urine, cases of PKU were indistinguishable from other defectives.

Other recessive conditions in mental deficiency

include *familial amaurotic idiocy*, both of the infantile and of the juvenile type, "true" *microcephaly*, and some cases of spastic paraplegia. These and other conditions are described by Penrose (1954).

Recessive defects are less well-known in the field of the *psychoses*. *Wilson's disease* (Bearn 1953), which is an error of metabolism causing the depositions of copper in the tissues, sometimes causes mental illness; and it is due to a recessive gene. One form of epilepsy, *myoclonic epilepsy* (Lundborg 1903), is due to a recessive; and there is a strong belief that some, at

INTERMEDIATE INHERITANCE

When PKU was first discovered, it was not possible to distinguish between the heterozygote and the normal homozygote, and the gene could be classified as recessive. However, this distinction is now possible (Hsia *et al.*, 1956); if the heterozygote is given a considerable amount of phenylalanine the percentage concentration of this substance in the blood rises to a higher level than in the normal homozygote, and is maintained at a raised level for a much longer time. It would therefore be more

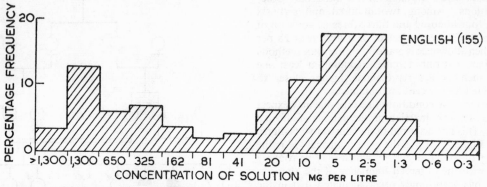

FIG. 8.9. BIMODAL DISTRIBUTION OF PTC TASTE THRESHOLDS IN ENGLISH MALES
(*After Barnicott*, 1950; *by courtesy of Dr. N. A. Barnicott and the "Annals of Human Genetics"*)

least, of the illnesses called schizophrenic are also recessively determined. The problem of the genetics of schizophrenia is discussed later.

In the field of *sense perception*, recessive genes make their own contribution to the total abnormality in a population. Many cases of deaf-mutism are caused in this way. A study of the offspring of cousins (Shields and Slater, 1956) revealed a relatively high proportion of persons who were blind or partially blind. The inability to taste phenylthiocarbamide (PTC), a substance which most people find distinctly bitter, can hardly be regarded as an abnormality, since about 30 per cent of British and white American people fail to taste the standard solution; but it is an example of a relatively objective and clear-cut variation in perception which behaves as a recessive trait (Snyder 1932). It is not the total inability to taste PTC which is due to a single pair of genes, but rather the taste threshold. When a group of people is tested with a series of solutions of PTC of different strengths, the lowest strength at which they taste a bitter being recorded, the resulting distribution is a bimodal one (Fig. 8.9). Analysis of the family data suggests that those who fall within the non-tasting part of the curve are homozygous for a recessive gene—though the genetics may be more complex than was at first thought, and there is some overlap between tasters and non-tasters.

strictly correct to regard the gene as intermediate between dominance and recessivity. The same can be said if, in the case of a dominant gene, it is found possible, to distinguish between the homozygous carrier of two abnormal genes and the heterozygote; in this case dominance would have to be reclassified as incomplete dominance, and the gene be better regarded as intermediate than dominant. Böök, Schut and Reed (1953) have suggested that the gene for recessive microcephaly might express itself in heterozygous form as moderate intellectual impairment, and Penrose (1938) has reported an excess of psychopaths among the relatives of microcephalics. Though microcephaly itself is a rare condition the gene frequency was estimated as between 1/162 and 1/230. Böök *et al.*, conclude that if this is the case borderline intellectual development in 0·5 to 1 per cent of the population might be due to the intermediate expression of the gene for genetic microcephaly. The evidence, however, is scanty so far and other interpretations are possible.

Sometimes it is found that the heterozygote possesses advantages over both types of homozygote. This is the case in the condition known as *sickle-cell anaemia*. The abnormal gene causes the production of a different haemoglobin from that produced by the normal gene. In persons homozygous for the abnormal gene, all the haemoglobin is of the abnormal kind, and the individual suffers from a severe anaemia and with difficulty survives childhood. The heterozygote has a mixture of normal and abnormal haemoglobins, and suffers only from a slight tendency to get anaemic if circumstances are such as to encourage such a tendency. On the other hand he has a biological advantage in being relatively much more resistant, than persons with only the normal haemoglobin are, to malignant types of malaria (Allison, 1954). Thus it is that in, for example, certain parts of Africa where malaria is common, the gene for the sickle-cell trait (as it is called in the heterozygote) is common too, despite its disastrous effects in the homozygote.

There is no certain case of intermediate inheritance in the field of psychological abnormality. Nevertheless it is possible that one or more of the genes involved in the causation of schizophrenia may be of this kind. It is often held that, if a recessive gene causes schizophrenia in the homozygote, in the heterozygote it may cause only a slight deviation of personality—the "schizoid" personality (Kallmann, 1938). If schizoid persons are, as it is often thought, cool, reserved, self-sufficient, then one can imagine circumstances in which they might have a considerable biological advantage over others. The high frequency of schizophrenia and of schizoid personality which Böök (1953) found in his north Swedish population could be regarded as related to the advantage conferred by schizoid traits in such a remote and hostile environment, in which opportunities for social life are reduced to a minimum. This idea approaches very near indeed to pure speculation. Nevertheless it bears thinking of when we try to explain why schizophrenia, which is biologically so disadvantageous, should also be so common.

PRINCIPLES OF POLYGENIC INHERITANCE

So far, largely for reasons of simplicity of exposition, we have dealt with conditions which are due to single pairs of genes. We now turn to multifactorial or polygenic inheritance.

The genes we have discussed so far show themselves by causing some single massive difference, by which they are, so to speak, labelled. But their effects do not end there. For instance, there is a recessive gene which in double dose causes the carrier to be an albino. But albinos differ from normal individuals not only in being unable to produce normal pigments in the hair, the skin and elsewhere, but also in being, on the average, smaller in stature, less fertile, less intelligent and shorter lived than others. There is no doubt that such fundamental biological variables as size, vitality and fertility are influenced, to some degree, by very great numbers of genes; these variables then show quantitative variation, and one is likely to find curves of distribution of the "normal" or Gaussian

kind, as is the case for instance with intelligence on the Binet scale. It is probable that the great majority of the genes which influence such graded characters do not have any single massive effect of their own; and to them the name of genes of small effect, or polygenes, is given. They are subject to the same laws of segregation as all other genes; but the description of the effects of segregation will be different. Thus Mendel bred races of tall and short peas, the difference depending on a single gene, and got tall and short progeny. In mankind, matings of tall and short parents will have a tendency to produce children of intermediate size, while two parents both of middle height are quite capable of producing both tall and short children. When we leave pathology for normal physiology and psychology, most of the characteristics in which we are interested are of a quantitatively variable kind, and, in so far as they are subject to genetical influence, regulated by multifactorial and not unifactorial inheritance.

Let us suppose that a particular characteristic, say that of height, is determined by three gene pairs, A and a, B and b, C and c. We will suppose that the capital letters tend to cause tallness, the lower-case letters shortness, that there is neither dominance nor recessivity, that all genes are equally common, and that mating is taking place at random. Then the tallest individual we can find, with the constitution AABBCC, will be relatively uncommon; for every one of him there will be six individuals one degree less tall: aABBCC, AaBBCC, AAbBCC, AABbCC, AABBcC, AABBCc. There will be fifteen combinations of four capitals with two lower-case letters, and in fact the population, graded by height, will be distributed according to the terms of the expansion of $(\frac{1}{2} + \frac{1}{2})^6 = (1 + 6 + 15 + 20 + 15 + 6 + 1)/64$. It is readily seen that the commonest group will be the middle group, with average height. It will also be seen that if we generalize, and write the expansion of $(p + q)^n$, in which $p + q = 1$, as n gets bigger and bigger we get a closer and closer approximation to the normal curve, which is skewed over the middle part of the curve very little, when n is big, even if p is bigger than q.

We may, in fact, say that where we find distributions of a normal kind we shall think of multifactorial inheritance, but not in cases where the distribution is not normal. The ability to taste PTC is, indeed, a graded character; but its distribution (Fig. 8.9) is not normal but bimodal with relatively little overlap in the middle part of the curve. Multifactorial inheritance will not do, therefore, in that case. However, even if the distribution is normal, this is no proof of a genetic and polygenic determination. A multiplicity of environmental or non-genetical factors, capable of operating additively, could conceivably result in the same sort of distribution; and a combination of polygenic and environmental factors could very easily do so. The proof of a genetical basis will depend on other observations.

Such a further observation, which may be made with a character showing normal distribution, is the demonstration of a regression equation linking the deviation from average values shown by a series of subjects with the deviation shown by their relatives.

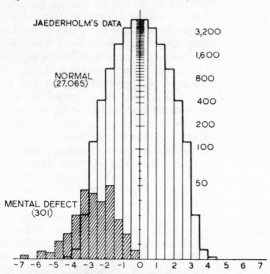

FIG. 8.10. DISTRIBUTION OF INTELLIGENCE

Estimate based on Binet test of three hundred and one defective and two hundred and sixty-one normal children. Jaederholm's data, from Pearson, 1931. Scores are shown in terms of standard deviations.

(By courtesy of "Annals of Human Genetics")

As an example, we may take the case of intelligence. As is well known, the Binet I.Q. is normally distributed, with mean at 100 and with a standard deviation of about 16 points. If we measure the intelligence of a series of schoolchildren, and also those of their sibs, it will be found that the correlated data are fairly well described by a linear equation: the I.Q. of the sib will tend to deviate from the mean in the same direction as that of the original subject or proband, though not so far. Similar regression equations will link I.Q.s of children with those of their parents, or those of parents with their children. In each case the "regression" is towards the mean. If we put the data in the form of correlation coefficients, they are of the order + 0·5 or rather more. This corresponds rather exactly with expectation on the genetical hypothesis, which involves the fact that pairs of sibs, or parent-child pairs, will have half their genetical equipment in common. Such a finding is very difficult indeed to explain on any environmental causation. The strength of the argument is to some extent reduced by the fact

that, in fact, people do not mate at random but preferentially with others of like intelligence to their own, and that there is a high positive correlation coefficient between the I.Q.s of spouses (as also of betrothed couples, and even friends). The existence of this homogamy would cause by itself some degree of positive correlation between sibs, but not enough to explain all that is found (Cattell and Willson, 1938; Conrad and Jones, 1940; Outhit, 1933; Fraser Roberts, 1940; Thorndike, 1944).

One need not be restricted to the closer blood relationships. A correlation coefficient of + 0·25 would be expected between probands and their grandparents, grandchildren, uncles, aunts, nephews and nieces; for first cousins the correlation should be + 0·125. These were in fact the order of the resemblances found between relatives in various physical measurements by Karl Pearson and the biometricians in the early years of the century, and were thought by them to be a disproof of Mendelism. The interpretation of the findings, on a Mendelian basis in terms of multifactorial inheritance, had to wait until the work of Fisher (1918) on stature. It was twenty years after that before the concept of polygenic inheritance was applied to intelligence, although its normal distribution was known.

LOW INTELLIGENCE

As long ago as 1912 Jaederholm made a survey of the intelligence of the great majority of all children in Sweden who were excluded from the ordinary schools on account of mental deficiency, together with a sample of normal schoolchildren. He used a modification of the Binet test. The results were analysed by Karl Pearson (1914). He showed that the distribution of scores corresponded reasonably well with the normal curve. The fit was three times better if the defective group was included along with the normal group. Not more than one-third of the defective group fell outside it, and there was a good deal of overlap between the scores of the brighter of the so-called defective children and those of the dullest children attending the ordinary schools. Fig. 8.10, taken from a later publication of Pearson (1931), shows this clearly. Later studies have given similar results. Thus Roberts, Norman and Griffiths (1935) made a survey during the 1930s of all children of school age in the city of Bath. Table VIII.2 shows part of the frequency curve of Stanford Binet I.Q.s which shows that about down to I.Q. 45 there is no excess of children with low scores. Below that level there was an excess of idiots and imbeciles.

Roberts (1950, 1952) made a special study of the siblings of the 8 per cent of the children with the lowest I.Q.s Their mean score was 77·4, that of their sibs 88·1, and the regression coefficient was 0·53. At the other end of the scale, Terman's (1947)

TABLE VIII.2

NORMALITY OF LOWER PART OF THE FRE-
QUENCY CURVE OF STANDFORD-BINET I.Q.s

(Based on a complete sample of 3,361 children)

(From Fraser Roberts, 1952)

Range of I.Q.	Expected No.	Observed No.
Above 73·78 . . .	3,193·0	3,195·2
73·78 — 67·57 . . .	100·8	94·9
67·57 — 44·97 . . .	66·5	58·4
Below 44·97 . . .	0·7	12·5

"superior children," with I.Q.s over 140, had offspring with mean I.Q. of 128. As has been said, these regressions are expected on the basis of polygenic inheritance, and are not compatible with single factor inheritance. However, when we come to persons of extremely low intelligence, idiots and imbeciles with I.Q. of 45 or less, comparable regressions are no longer observed. On Robert's small series, the I.Q.s of sibs of the imbeciles ranged from 88 to 117 with a mean of 99·9. This suggests that the occurrence of such grave defects is not accounted for by normal variation and polygenic inheritance, a conclusion which also follows from the fact that the curve of distribution deviates from normality at its negative extreme. What is suggested is the operation of special factors, such as injury, disease and, if genetical in nature, single dominant or recessive genes. A small part may also be played by incompatibilities of blood group between mother and unborn child such as may occur with respect to the Rhesus factor, or chromosomal anomalies as is now suspected in Mongolism. However, this whole class is not a numerous one, and not to be compared, as a social problem, with the very much larger numbers of the feeble-minded.

Personality as a Graded Character

The genetical background of intellectual abnormality can thus be regarded as determined polygenically for the greater part. The same is probably largely true on general grounds for the genetical background of personality abnormality. The situation, however, is more complex than in the case of intelligence. Personality is more difficult to assess or measure, it is a much less unitary character than intelligence and its manifestation throughout life is subject to quite wide fluctuations depending on a variety of circumstances. However, it is generally found helpful to regard personality traits as graded characters, and the same is true of major factors in personality, such as extraversion and neuroticism. When a group of persons is rated or measured on any personality scale it is generally found that, as in the case of intelligence, the scores tend to fall into the shape of the normal dis-

tribution curve. In so far as this distribution is reliable and is genetically determined it is likely to be due to the combined influence of many genes. In our opinion, that is certainly a likely hypothesis in the cases of neuroticism and extraversion, as described in this book, though there are certain points that will need clarification. Thus Eysenck finds it profitable to see the factor of neuroticism, as a psychological measure, as unitary in nature. The psychiatric geneticist would think rather of a predisposition determined by polygenic factors of somewhat heterogeneous kinds, though their effects, measured along a single dimension, could well fit in with Eysenck's findings.

In the psychotic dimension, matters are different again. A continuously graded factor of psychoticism would not account, by itself, for the specificities of inheritance in schizophrenic and manic-depressive families; but it might describe the non-specific variation in the susceptibility to these illnesses. Hypothetical specific schizophrenic and manic-depressive genes must both be supposed to have reduced rates of manifestation, and whether they are manifested or not could well depend on the intensity of a "psychoticism" factor. Such a conception would have consequences which could be tested by appropriate investigations.

Methods and Aims of Genetical Analysis

It is now the place to give an account of the research methods which may be used in psychiatric genetics, including those which help us to understand the mode of inheritance, such as family and population studies, and those which help to distinguish between the effects of heredity and environment, such as the study of foster-children and twins. A beginning must be made with work on animal behaviour.

Animal Studies

Although human beings are in some ways very favourable subjects for genetical study, there are ways in which they present particular difficulties. One cannot plan human breeding experiments; the size of the human family is small; and there is a time interval of some thirty years between one generation and the next. There are, therefore, advantages in pursuing psychological studies on laboratory-bred mammals such as rats and mice. This field of work has been dignified by the title of "psychogenetics."

A suitable technique is to select some characteristic of behaviour in which individual differences are shown and can, preferably, be measured. High scorers and low scorers are then separated and inbred with a view to producing distinct strains. If this is successful members of the two strains may then be cross-mated, and the capacities of their offspring measured. If genetical factors play a part, the two strains, with very different patterns of behaviour, can be built up; and the result of cross-mating is to reproduce individuals of intermediate performance.

Calvin S. Hall (1951), one of the leading American investigators in this field, has summarized the work that has been done on selective breeding up till 1951. His review shows that heredity is an important factor, not only in variations in maze-learning ability, but also in the choice of hypothesis (visual and spatial) adopted in maze-learning, in the preference for a high or low cage temperature, in the amount of voluntary activity displayed, in the speed of reaction, in wildness or tameness, in aggressivity, in emotionality, and in susceptibility to audiogenic seizures, which occur in some rats when the experimenter jingles a bunch of keys. This last trait was found to be inherited as a dominant in one strain and as a recessive in another.

In studies of aggression, black mice have been found to be more aggressive than albinos. One investigator (Ginsburg, 1942) tested the hypothesis that this difference might be caused by early environment, in that the mice might learn their behaviour from cues presented by their mother at an age when they were particularly susceptible. He did this by having some of his black mice reared by albinos, and some of his albino mice reared by black mothers. However, the young ones resembled their biological mothers, and not their foster-mothers or foster-sibs, in aggressiveness. This experiment supported the hypothesis that there are innate differences in aggressiveness in mice.

In a study of Hall's own (1951), emotionality was measured by the extent to which rats tended to defaecate or urinate when placed in a strange environment. Rats scoring high, on this definition, were bred together, as were the low-scorers. The emotional strain became increasingly emotional up to the ninth generation. Selection for non-emotionality yielded less systematic results, though the maximum effect was obtained in a single generation. When the emotional and non-emotional strains were eventually crossed, the offspring had a mean score and S.D. close to that of the heterogeneous parent population, from which they had been bred, but with an excess of low-scorers. Hall inferred that non-emotionality is dominant over emotionality. The emotional rats had significantly heavier thyroids (both sexes), adrenals (males only) and pituitary glands (females only).

Broadhurst (1956), working in the animal laboratory at Bethlem Royal Hospital, repeated parts of Hall's investigation, using more refined methods including brother-sister matings. He too was able to breed emotional and non-emotional strains from an originally mixed population. A cross-fostering experiment showed that maternal influence had no significant effect. There is thus strong evidence that emotionality in the rat, as measured by defaecation under stress, is under genetical control. Broadhurst has so far found it easier to select for non-emotionality than for emotionality. He has not investigated the mode of inheritance, but has gone on to use his pure strains to study the effect of emotionality on drive. The mode of investigation shows the value of making genetics the servant of psychology.

Hall looks forward to the time when the science of psychogenetics will make a real contribution towards our understanding of the *modus operandi* of the genes and of the environmental modifiability of innate behaviour patterns. "An understanding of psychogenetics," he concludes, "is a prerequisite of a dynamic psychology." A very similar viewpoint is adopted by Williams and his collaborators (1949). They and Mardones *et al.*, (1953) have succeeded in breeding strains of rats which are, and are not, liable to alcoholic addiction; on the basis of this work Williams develops the concept of genetotrophic diseases, in which the genetical deviation is merely the starting point of a chain of effects, into which environmental factors, such as nutritional ones, also enter.

PROBLEMS OF HUMAN GENETICS

The peculiar difficulties of genetical investigations in man have led to the elaboration of special techniques, particularly in the development and refinement of statistical methods. In the hands of mathematical geneticists, such as Sir Ronald Fisher, these have been brought to a level of power and refinement in advance of the observational knowledge to which only they can be applied. Special adjustments have to be made, in the analysis of data, for the fact that the likelihood of making some observations on an individual is affected by the age he has reached, for the fact that nearly all simple and practical methods of selection involve some kind of bias, and for other sources of error, some of which will emerge in what follows.

In genetical investigations on human families, much of the information required is likely to concern people who are dead or otherwise inaccessible, or who have little motive to co-operate. The readiness of contacts to provide information is affected by the theme of the investigation and by the climate of opinion. Owing to an increased liberality of opinion, such investigations in psychiatry are now a good deal easier than they used to be; but it is much easier to carry out research into pairs of twins than, say, into the children of parents both of whom have been mentally ill. It is, as a rule, easy to make a good contact with twins, owing to the fact that the public at large regards twinship as a matter of fascinating interest; it is easier to persuade a pair of twins to come to a psychological laboratory than a complete family.

Where medical records are involved, insurmountable

obstacles may arise, especially when members of a past generation are inquired about. Old, and sometimes even current, records from mental hospitals may be bare in the extreme, and insufficient for a reliable diagnosis. As has been said, sampling nearly always gives rise to problems. The investigator may have to make a choice between the carefully conducted personal study of a small group, with a possible sampling bias, and an unselected series which will include cases about which there is inadequate information. It is nearly always useless, at any rate in this country, to take investigation further than first-degree relatives; but even within this limited family group the obtaining of adequate information about personality and psychological abnormality will be very time-consuming. Parents cannot be equated with sibs or children, for not only do they belong to an earlier generation, but also they have been selected for health by the fact of having attained parenthood.

In studying the genetics of mental abnormality, psychological tests, desirable though they are on theoretical grounds, are often of no great value. Mental illnesses, both neurotic and psychotic, take a fluctuating course, and the state at any one time may be but a poor guide to the nature of a deviation which is best seen over a whole lifetime.

Psychiatric diagnoses, though extremely important for genetical studies, contain unfortunately a large subjective element; the very standards on which they are based vary to some extent from school to school. Efforts, not very successful ones, have been made to get away from diagnosis to single symptoms, to avoid this source of confusion or disagreement. A rather better method of by-passing the subjectivity of diagnosis was used by Leonhard and Schulz in an investigation into the families of schizophrenics: Leonhard diagnosed and classified the probands, and Schulz (1940) carried out the family investigations, each without any knowledge of the judgements of the other.

FAMILY INVESTIGATION

Pedigree Studies

The first attempts to study human heredity were by means of the inspection of single family histories that happened to catch the interest of the physician. In this form the family method was open to some rather obvious objections. Families that are obtained in this way are likely to be the unusual and heavily loaded ones; selected on account of their curiosity value, they are highly unrepresentative and tend to give an exaggerated view of the frequency with which abnormalities occur in the families of affected persons. However, when carried out systematically, on representative material and perhaps in combination with other methods, family studies remain the basic tool of the genetical research worker. They can take various forms and have various aims, as the following pages will show.

Empirische Erbprognose

By investigating all the parents, siblings and sometimes other more remote relatives of a complete and representative series of patients with a given clear-cut diagnosis one can obtain a reliable idea of what the facts are concerning the family incidence of the same and similar disorders. In some conditions—mostly rare ones—inspection or analysis of the pedigrees obtained in this way will reveal a simple mode of Mendelian inheritance. This was the case, as we have seen, with Huntington's chorea and phenylketonuria. With the commoner psychiatric abnormalities, such as schizophrenia, hereditary mechanisms are likely to be more complex and environmental factors to play a greater part. For these conditions family studies of the type described are nevertheless useful, even though the genetics of the condition may not be clear-cut. Empirical risk figures can be calculated which show the chances of different degrees of relative being similarly affected. The method, known as empirische Erbprognose, was first developed by the school of Rüdin in Munich during the 1920s and it has been used fairly extensively so far as the psychoses are concerned, in Germany, Scandinavia and other parts of the world. Not only do the results of adequately planned investigations of this kind often give valuable information on the probable mode of inheritance and the degree to which those persons who are presumed to be carrying the abnormal gene or genes responsible are likely to manifest the psychosis in question; but also the empirical risk figures are of particular value in estimating the genetic prognosis for other members of the family and their potential offspring. Thus the chance of a child of an epileptic developing epilepsy is about 5 per cent, the chance of the child of a manic-depressive developing a recognizable manic-depressive state is about 15 per cent, and the risk for the child of a schizophrenic has been estimated at figures from 9 per cent for some forms of the illness to 20 per cent for others. Estimates have similarly been obtained for siblings, nephews and nieces, and grandchildren in these and other clinical groupings. In recent years in the United States and elsewhere a number of heredity counselling clinics (Reed, 1955) have grown up, which rely heavily on the results of family investigations of this kind. The risks for relatives must of course be compared with those for the population in general, which are higher than might have been thought.

Because of the particular value of twins to genetical research, Kallmann (1953) in the United States has combined the twin and family methods, starting with a large series of patients who happened to be twins, and investigating their co-twins and other relatives. Table VIII.3 gives his principal findings in the case of

TABLE VIII.3

RISK OF SCHIZOPHRENIA FOR RELATIVES OF SCHIZOPHRENICS

(After Kallmann, 1946, 1950)

Class	Percentage risk of schizophrenia
Children of two non-schizophrenic parents (general population)	0·9
Relatives of adult schizophrenic index cases—	
Not consanguineous {Step-sibs . .	1·8
Not consanguineous {Spouse . .	2·1
First cousins	2·6
Nephews and nieces . . .	3·9
Grandchildren	4·3
Half-sibs	7·1
Parents	9·2
Full-sibs	14·2
Dizygotic co-twins . . .	14·5
Dizygotic co-twins of same sex .	17·6
Children with one schizophrenic parent .	16·4
Children with two schizophrenic parents	68·1
Monozygotic co-twins	86·2
Monozygotic co-twins living apart for at least five years	77·6
Monozygotic co-twins not so separated .	91·5

schizophrenia. It will be seen that the expectation of schizophrenia increases with closeness of blood-relationship to the proband, rather than with environmental similarity, though the latter has some effect, as is shown in the figures for step-sibs and for identical twins living together or apart.

Although in practice most family investigations of abnormalities start from hospital populations, others originate in surveys of schoolchildren or army conscripts. In some studies it has been possible to ascertain all cases of a specific abnormality in a defined area, and to start family investigations from there.

Among the earliest positive results of systematic family research was the elimination of some old and hoary misconceptions, such as the theory of anticipation. According to this, familial disorders tended to occur earlier and earlier in life in succeeding generations, until, mental deficiency taking the place of mental disorder, the morbid strain was eliminated. This has been shown to be a statistical artefact, caused by the fact that the most accessible information in a family study will be about the later disorders of the older generations, and the earlier disorders of the

younger generations. With this exploded theory went also the idea that the defectiveness of a human strain might show itself indifferently in a great number of forms, schizophrenia, epilepsy, psychopathy, criminality, prostitution, vagrancy, mental defect, etc., all arising from a single genetical cause. *Empirische Erbprognose* taught the lesson that different forms of psychiatric abnormality must be distinguished; and thereby it has become one of the foundation stones on which a scientific diagnostic classification will have to be based.

Genetical Analysis and Psychiatric Classification

It is a fashionable tendency in psychiatry to consider that there is no real difference between the "psychoses" and "neuroses," both these words being mere terms of convenience. This view is not supported by the results of family investigations. Such studies, in the hands of many workers, consistently confirm the existence of a real difference between conditions like schizophrenia or manic-depressive disorder, on the one side, and anxiety states, hysteria, etc., on the other. The difference between these two classes of conditions is not one of gravity but of specificity. Thus investigations of the relatives of schizophrenics have shown that they are more than normally liable to schizophrenia, but have no excessive risk of becoming manic-depressive or epileptic. On the neurotic side, the relatives of anxiety neurotics are more than normally liable to anxiety neurosis, but also are more than normally liable to hysterical illnesses, reactive depressions, and other neuroses (Brown, 1942). On the genetical hypothesis we are able to account for this class difference by supposing that in the aetiology of schizophrenia and manic-depressive disorder single genes of large specific effect are involved, whereas in the aetiology of anxiety states and hysteria, any genetical factors involved are probably polygenic and not very specific in their effects. This fits in well with the observation that neurotic modes of behaviour are within the compass of all of us, and can be regarded as non-pathological, whereas schizophrenic behaviour is beyond the normal range. If large numbers of individuals are subjected to physiological and psychological stress, such as occurs in war-time, the incidence of neuroses increases *pari passu* with the increase of stress, while the incidence of schizophrenia remains practically constant.

As a matter of historical fact, the classification most frequently used in genetical investigations in psychiatry has been derived from Kraepelin. This does not mean that psychiatric genetics is permanently wedded to it. Great improvements can be expected, and genetics can be expected to make its contribution. Kraepelin regarded the condition he called "paranoia" as being a syndrome in its own right; but his pupil Kolle (1931), who investigated the families of the patients whom Kraepelin himself had diagnosed as cases of paranoia, found that, from the familial genetical point of view, they did not distinguish themselves from paranoid schizophrenics. This investigation gave the death-blow to paranoia as a specific disease, and thereby solved a problem of classification which was beyond the reach of the unaided clinician.

Offspring of Two Psychotic Parents

By investigating the children of particular matings, light may be thrown both on the mode of inheritance of a predisposition and on its genetical homogeneity. An excellent example of what may be done in this way is provided by the work of Elsässer (1952). He collected, from his own material and from the work of others, one hundred and thirty-four pairs of husbands and wives, both of whom had suffered from an endo-genous psychosis. Most of these were either typical cases of schizophrenia or fairly typical manic-depressives, but as many as 29 per cent were sufficiently atypical, not to be readily classified in either of the two main diagnostic groups; they included paranoid involutional psychoses, confusional psychoses, etc., and Elsässer thinks that there were so many of them because psychotic parents are not a random selection of psychotic patients in general. There were four hundred and twenty-four children who passed the age of sixteen from these unions, and of these eighty-eight certainly and twenty-three probably had had psychotic illnesses by the time of the investigation. In his calculations Elsässer counts each of the doubtful cases as a half. Of course, a considerable part of the total number of children observed had lived through only a fraction of the life-span during which they would be liable to an endogenous psychosis (approximately fourteen to forty-five in the case of schizo-phrenia). When allowance is made for this, Elsässer could say that he had observed three hundred and twenty-nine life-expectancies for schizophrenia, two hundred and five for manic-depressive psychosis. Set against these denominators, the risks these children faced of developing schizophrenia or manic-depressive illness were two to three times as great as those facing children of one psychotic and one normal parent. This fact alone fits well with a genetical hypothesis of causation.

As will be seen from Table VIII.4, Elsässer cal-culated risks separately for the different combinations of psychotic parents. There were thirty-four families where both parents were schizophrenic; they pro-duced twenty certain and eight probable schizophrenics

TABLE VIII.4

THE CHILDREN OF TWO PSYCHOTIC PARENTS

Data of Elsässer, Schulz and Kahn

(*After Elsässer*, 1952)

Number of Parental pairs	Parental mating	Number of children over 16	Non-psychotic children			Psychotic children (doubtful cases shown as ½)					Corrected risk for endogenous psychosis (per cent)
			Normal	With psychiatric abnormality (mostly minor) or uncertain information*	Total	Schizo-phrenia	Manic-depressive psychosis	Atypical psychosis	Endogenous psychosis, ? nature	Total persons	
34	Schizophrenia × Schizophrenia	96	38	30	68	20¾	—	—	—	28	39·2
20	Manic-dep. × Manic-dep	47	28	5	33	1	9½	2	1	14	44·4
19	Schizophrenia × Manic-dep.	68	35	14	49	6¾	6½	1	2	19	31·2
23	Atypical × Schizophrenia	91	53	23	76	8	1½	3	½	15	21·3
21	Atypical × Manic-dep.	55	32	12	44	—	4½	4½	—	11	28·8
17	Atypical × Atypical	67	27	16	43	5	5½	10½	½	24	41·3
134		424	213	100	313	88 certain + 23 doubtful = 111					

* The hundred persons in this column consist of sixty-eight who are described as *mässig auffällig* (moderately conspicuous), fifteen psychopaths, ten persons with mental defect or neurological disease and seven about whom there was insufficient information.

in a corrected total of 61·3, equivalent to a percentage of 39·2. Not one of the children was manic-depressive. There were only twenty unions where both parents were manic-depressive; they produced nine certain and one probable manic-depressive children, and four other psychotics. One of these last, the daughter of two manic-depressives with not quite typical illnesses beginning in each case after the age of fifty, was a schizophrenic. The risk for psychosis was 44·4 per cent. The offspring of matings of schizophrenics with manic-depressives produced equal numbers of both major psychoses; the risk for psychosis was 31·2 per cent. The matings in which one or both parents had an atypical psychosis also resulted in a risk for the offspring of about the same magnitude. While analysis suggested that these atypical psychoses in the parents were in some instances, genetically, schizophrenic or manic-depressive, it also indicated that in others they were breeding true and appeared to be genetical entities in their own right. This is in keeping with the findings of Leonhard, which have been mentioned earlier.

It seems clear from these results that, if there is a genetical relationship between schizophrenia and manic-depressive psychosis, it cannot be a close one. It is interesting also that the illnesses of the children were not of any exceptional severity; if a child received two abnormal dominant genes, one from each parent, he might well show something of that kind, or perhaps a lethal or semilethal condition. There was one child of two schizophrenics who was born with supernumerary fingers and toes and died when a few days old—but this was probably coincidental.

Probably the most important finding is that not more than 40 per cent of the children of two schizophrenics were similarly affected, and that only some 16 per cent of their non-psychotic sibs could be described as schizoid personalities. If all schizophrenic illnesses depended on a single recessive gene, then all the children of two schizophrenics would themselves be homozygotes, and accordingly liable to the disease. On this theory, the fall from the expected 100 per cent to 40 per cent is difficult to explain; it becomes easier to suppose either that schizophrenia is heterogeneous, and that a variety of different specific genes are responsible from case to case, or that dominant inheritance with diminished penetrance plays a role. It is interesting, however, that in the only family where both parents had a deteriorating schizophrenia of hebephrenic or catatonic type with early onset, five out of the six children who survived infancy were schizophrenic and the sixth was an odd personality. It would seem likely that in this family, at least, parents and children were all homozygous for the same gene. This family was not used in Elsässer's statistics as, unlike the other families, it had

been selected through knowledge of the abnormal children.

Another highly important point is that of the non-psychotic children of these marriages 70 per cent were completely normal and only 5 per cent were regarded by Elsässer as psychopathic. On this ground any attempt to explain the high incidence of psychosis in the children as the result of the psychological effects of being brought up by a pair of psychotic or psychotic-to-be parents becomes very unconvincing; if the environment was as pathogenic as that, how were these normal children so completely spared?

Offspring of Consanguineous Matings

As we have seen in an earlier discussion, the heterozygous carrier of a rare recessive gene is much more likely to mate with another heterozygote if he marries a blood relative, such as a cousin, than if he marries at random. If he does, he will greatly increase his chances of producing a homozygous and abnormal child. The present authors, with their colleague W. L. B. Nixon (1957), investigated a series of three hundred and fifty-five mental hospital patients who were notified as the children of related parents, and compared them with a control series of equal size. There were significantly more schizophrenics in the proband than in the control series, ninety against sixty-three, the distribution of other diagnoses showing no significant difference. The existence of a so much higher incidence in the one series than in the other is what would be expected on the hypothesis of a recessive gene, but on this hypothesis alone one would have expected a greater difference. Taking into account the figures obtained, the best estimates available of the frequency of cousin marriage and the frequency of schizophrenia, the authors calculate that not more than one-sixth of the totality of schizophrenia could be attributed to a recessive gene. This is of course a provisional view, and would have to be modified if later workers found different incidences.

Linkage

If two genes are carried on the same chromosome, they are said to be linked, and the way in which each is handed on from parent to child will not be independent. Let us suppose that X has both the gene for Huntington's chorea and also the dominant gene for polydactyly, and that these two genes are linked. Now if X got both these genes from one parent, they will have come to him on the same chromosome, and any child he has will be liable to get from him either both of them or both of their normal alleles. If, however, X got one gene from his mother and the other from his father, then they will be on opposite members of the chromosome pair, and his children will be liable to get one or the other, but not both or neither. There is a certain amount of recombination of parts of chromosomes by "crossing over," so that the above rule is not absolute; the degree to which it approaches truth depends on how near the two genes are to one another on the chromosome. Family studies show whether or not two genes are linked, and if so how closely; so that by their aid it should theoretically be possible to build up a chromosome map. Very complete chromosome maps have been drawn up for experimental animals like *Drosophila*, but in man so far a beginning has only been made with the XY-chromosome pair. If it were possible to link rare pathological genes with common normal blood-group genes, a new and powerful technique of genetical analysis of the pathological condition would become available.

Detection of Carriers

Sometimes carriers can be detected more directly by means of family studies (Hsia, 1956; Neel, 1953). Suggestive findings have been made, for example, in diabetes (Pincus, 1934), where relatives are often found to have a low glucose tolerance; these persons may be potential diabetics. In the families of some patients with cystinuria the stone formation can be shown to be due to homozygosity for a gene which can be detected in its heterozygous form. By the technique of paper chromatography the expected proportion of relatives was found by Harris and Warren (1953) to have a raised excretion of cystine. The application of biochemical and other techniques to the relatives of psychiatric patients is perhaps a promising but no doubt complex field for future research and one which might have therapeutic possibilities. Already it has become possible to identify the carriers of phenylketonuria (*see* page 308). The relatives of epileptics frequently show abnormalities in their electro-encephalogram (Harvald, 1954) which suggest genetical interpretations, though not simple ones. Psychological tests could also be applied to relatives of psychiatric patients with a similar purpose in view.

Assortative Mating

A simplifying assumption which is very frequently made in theoretical genetics is that mating occurs at random. This is far from being even approximately true, and in man is even less true than in other species. In point of fact, the choice of a mate is limited in a great number of ways, so that the population can be, in a rough way, divided into separate inbreeding segments, or "isolates," along a number of dimensions. Thus there are geographical, economic, occupational, religious and many other divisions, within which most matings occur. In general, like tends to mate with like, Briton to marry

Briton, worker to marry worker rather than the Boss's daughter, clerk to marry clerk, Catholic to marry Catholic. This tendency to homogamy is seen also in psychological traits, both normal and pathological. It has already been mentioned that intelligent people tend to marry others of more than mean I.Q., and the stupid to marry those less than average. It is well known that deaf persons often marry one another, as do persons with other disabilities. If a number of genetically influenced conditions occur in one family, the most likely explanation is often neither genetical linkage, nor variability of manifestation, but assortative mating. In Huntington families (Leese *et al.*, 1952) one commonly finds other defects, such as eye conditions, tuberculosis, etc., which have probably entered the one family by selective mating. A study of assortative mating in respect of temperamental traits has shown the same tendency. Slater and Woodside (1951) investigated controlled series of normal and neurotic soldiers and their wives. The wives of the neurotics were themselves more neurotic and came from more neurotic families than those of the normal soldiers, and the dynamic factors involved could be partially clarified.

Homogamy in respect of genetically-determined traits has interesting consequences in increasing the variance shown by a population and in aiding the appearance of pure lines; homozygotes are favoured at the expense of heterozygotes. In itself homogamy is neither eugenic nor dysgenic, but makes the population more susceptible to change from selective influences of either kind. From the social point of view, it helps in the production of specialists of all kinds; we should probably have far fewer capable musicians if musical people did not tend to marry one another.

Fertility

The study of fertility is obviously another one of considerable genetical importance. It has a bearing on population genetics and is of relevance to the future health of the community. The possible consequences for the future of the negative correlation between intelligence and family size is one which has attracted a good deal of attention. A number of studies have shown that, both in the population as a whole and within single occupational groups, the more intelligent have fewer children than the less intelligent. A negative correlation of about 0·2 has been found by most investigators. On the assumption that intelligence is to a considerable extent inherited one would expect a gradual decline in the national intelligence. Summarizing the evidence Burt (1946) calculated that this would amount to 1·5–2 points in I.Q. per generation. If such a trend were to continue to the end of the present century, the proportion of persons with I.Q.s over one hundred and thirty in the population would fall to less than half the existing figure and that of the feeble-minded would be more than doubled. In 1947 an opportunity occurred to test the prediction that the I.Q. was falling. Fifteen years earlier all the eleven-year-old age group in Scottish schools had been tested with a group intelligence test. When the same age group was tested again with the same test in 1947 by a team of workers under Sir Godfrey Thomson (Scottish Council for Research in Education, 1949), instead of the feared fall in mean score there had been a slight rise. The association between family size and intelligence, however, was as marked as before. There seems to be general agreement that improved environmental conditions and increased test sophistication has contributed to the rise, but it is still an open question whether the improvement due to environment masks a decline in genetical quality. The decline, if real, would stop if the association between higher intelligence and lower fertility ceased to operate. There can be no doubt that the association is susceptible to cultural and psychological influences, and that secular changes occur. In Sweden, family limitation began many years ago in the best educated sections but has now permeated the entire population; the differential fertility, which was once very marked and alarming, is now practically zero. If the well-educated are open to suggestions of the desirability of family limitation, they are also open to the suggestion that the one- or two-child family is disadvantageous, psychologically for the children and perhaps also eugenically for the population. Recent studies of the fertility of university graduates and other favoured classes show a tendency to produce more rather than fewer children (Hubback, 1955; Hutton, 1953; Moberg, 1950; Nesbit, 1955).

In the field of psychological abnormalities, the usual finding is one of lessened fertility (Essen-Möller, 1935; Lewis, 1958). Thus many studies of schizophrenic families consistently show reduced fertility, and the work of Slater and Woodside already mentioned showed reduced rather than increased fertility among neurotics and psychopaths.

POPULATION STUDIES

The discussion of fertility has already led us from family studies to population investigations. It is obviously important from the medical and social points of view to assess the frequency with which different mental illnesses occur in the population as a whole, in different regions or social groups, and in the same region at different times. From the genetical point of view this information is important too. Without knowing the incidence of schizophrenia in the general population it is difficult to assess the significance of morbidity figures obtained for the relatives of schizophrenics. What is required here is

not the crude incidence at a given time, but the number of persons born who might be expected to have had the condition after having lived long enough for it to manifest itself.

Hospital admission statistics are not entirely suitable for calculating the general risk—only a proportion of psychotics and defectives reach hospital. However, Norris (1959) has been able to extract from hospital data a good deal of useful information regarding the incidence of mental disorders in London. By going further afield, estimates can be obtained along three rather different lines. These we may call: (1) the genealogical method, (2) the census method, and (3) the biographical method.

Genealogical Method

The first of these to be developed was the genealogical method. This is really no more than the family method applied to a selected group of persons who are supposed to be representative of the normal population. Hospital patients and their wives are comparatively accessible and have often been used in this kind of investigation. For example, Luxenburger (1928) studied the wives of patients with general paralysis (G.P.I.) in Munich and their families. As the disease is not genetical but due to syphilis, he assumed that these women were no more likely to be psychiatrically abnormal than others of the general population; in fact their families had rather more than their share of G.P.I. On the Danish island of Bornholm, Strömgren (1938) studied the sibs of general hospital patients and persons referred to a T.B. clinic.

Census Method

The samples chosen in the genealogical studies have in some ways not been very widely representative; and this method has been partly superseded by the cross-sectional census survey. The aim of this second method of population study is to ascertain all cases of psychiatric abnormality in a defined area at a given time. The families of the cases notified by official and unofficial sources can then be investigated too. This will bring to light further secondary cases and give information of genetical value. Thus Sjögren (1948) made an intensive cross-sectional study of a typical Swedish peasant population and supplemented it by genealogical research. He utilized for this purpose the very full information that can be obtained from old Swedish parish registers which go back to the seventeenth century.

Among other census-type investigations, we may mention that of Roth and Luton (1943) in Williamson County, Tennessee, and E. O. Lewis's (1929) well-known study of mental deficiency in two urban, two rural and two mixed areas in England. A more recent British example is Mayer-Gross's (1948) investigation of the incidence of mental disorders in Dumfriesshire. In this work a psychiatric Social Worker, Marjorie Brown, inquired about all patients discharged from the Crichton Royal Hospital during the previous ten years and about their families, and those of present patients. The co-operation of Public Assistance officers, teachers and social workers and ministers of the Kirk was then sought in an effort to ascertain other cases of mental abnormality; and children who had obtained an I.Q. of less than eighty in the eleven-plus examinations were investigated. It is perhaps the use of this last group that is the most distinctive feature of Mayer-Gross's study. It was interesting that the proportion of dullards and defectives among the schoolchildren was twice that found in the total material. The main explanation given for this was that subnormals can easily lead a useful life in that particular community, so that their handicap is hardly noticed after leaving school. In the whole population of 56,000 some 9 per cent were reckoned to be psychiatrically abnormal.

Mental health surveys are most frequently made in rural areas. Here populations are more static than in large towns; people are better known to one another and to those in authority; economic conditions are relatively more uniform. This is all to the good so far as genetic investigations are concerned. But it may be that results obtained in rural areas do not hold good for large towns. A town may perhaps contain less mental defect but more cases of neurosis.

One theoretical difficulty with the census method is that of calculating expectancy rates from the crude figures. Most persons in the population have not reached an age when one can say they will not develop a manic-depressive psychosis—let alone a senile one. Further, psychotics, and especially schizophrenics, have an excessive mortality rate and so will be underrepresented in a living sample.

Biographical Method

These difficulties can be met by the third method of population survey—the longitudinal biographical method. Here all persons born in a given year are taken as the starting point of the investigation and then followed up. With this there are even greater practical difficulties than in the census method. Klemperer (1933) was the first to try it out on persons born in Munich between 1880 and 1890, but he could trace only 70 per cent of them.

However, Fremming (1951) applied the biographical method to the Island of Bornholm. He succeeded in tracing 92 per cent of all those born there fifty-five or fifty-six years earlier, including most of those who had emigrated to the mainland. He paid some 2,000 visits to obtain information about over 4,000 persons. Fremming discovered some 12 per cent of them to have suffered from one or more kinds of mental abnormality, a rate strikingly similar to that calculated earlier for the same area by Strömgren using genealogical and census methods. The main difference in the two investigations was that Fremming's method brought to light a considerably higher proportion of manic-depressives, many of whom had never been in hospital and were quite well when seen. Slight drawbacks in the biographical method, apart from its practical difficulties, are: first, the fact that it will not represent present trends but those of a generation or two ago; and secondly no estimate can be given for involutional or senile psychoses unless an investigation group born some eighty years ago is taken.

Incidence of Psychosis and Neurosis

These three methods give estimates for the incidence of the psychoses and mental defect which are very close, considering the many differences between the different countries in which they have been tried out, the various standards of diagnosis and statistical methods used for calculating empirical risk figures. Thus schizophrenia is usually found to have a frequency of between 0·5 per cent and 1·0 per cent; epilepsy one of 0·3 per cent to 0·5 per cent. The rate for manic-depressive psychosis varies more considerably—between 0·2 per cent and 1·6 per cent—largely for methodological reasons. Mental defectives are generally thought to account for about 1 per cent of the population.

So far as neurosis and psychopathy are concerned, agreement is not so consistent, and most figures quoted are probably underestimates. Census studies give rates of about 2 per cent. Fremming gives 5 per cent, Ekblad (1948) who interviewed a large series of Swedish naval conscripts, claimed that 15 per cent of them were psychopathic; he uses the term to cover what in this country we would mostly call chronic neurosis or personality maladjustment. In spite of different methods of approach, high rates are found when the matter is gone into carefully. Russell Fraser (1947) examined a large sample of war-time workers in light engineering factories in the Midlands. He and his co-workers found that 10 per cent of them had lost work during the past six months on account of a temporarily disabling neurotic illness, and that a further 20 per cent had suffered from minor forms of neurosis during that period. Logan and Goldberg (1953) of the Medical Research Council Social Medicine Unit investigated seventy-four lads called up for National Service in a London suburb. Twelve were clearly disturbed with psychiatric treatment considered advisable, and a further nineteen, making 42 per cent in all, were also maladjusted at the time of the interview. One of the present writers (Shields, 1954), studied a sample of sixty-two pairs of ordinary twins from the L.C.C. Secondary Schools in which it was found that about the same proportion, or nearly half, had at some time or other been neurotic in a broad sense or had presented troublesome behaviour disorders.

While some recent trends in the assessment of mental health involve the intensive investigation of a few cases, Essen-Möller (1956) and three Swedish colleagues have recently shown what can be achieved in the assessment of health and personality traits by short single interviews supplemented by official records. Each psychiatrist averaged eleven to fourteen interviews a day over a period of two months, and together they succeeded in investigating personally 2,500 persons out of a total population of 2,550. The interview took the form of a conversation on the individual's medical and personal history. The area studied was a rural one which included a small municipality and the four investigators divided it equally between them. They assessed personality according to the concepts of Sjöbring. Each individual

was rated on a nine-point scale on each of the three constitutional variants of personality in the Sjöbring system—solidity, stability and validity—and also on capacity (intelligence). Each variant was found to be distributed not quite normally but roughly so. Part at least of the deviations from normality could be accounted for by differences between sexes, age groups and investigators. Some small correlations between the three variants and between these and intelligence were found. No correlation was larger than could reasonably be attributed to systematic diagnostic errors. The consistency between the findings of the four different investigators suggests a fair degree of reliability, especially when the method of investigation is considered. The results are in reasonable accordance with the concept of three mutually independent lines of variation in personality and a fourth, intelligence, each with a normal distribution. Essen-Möller and his colleagues also assessed the presence or absence of personality traits of a more pathological kind, asthenic states and various mental illnesses, past and present, and their inter-relations. We reproduce their cumulative table (Fig. 8.11) showing by sex

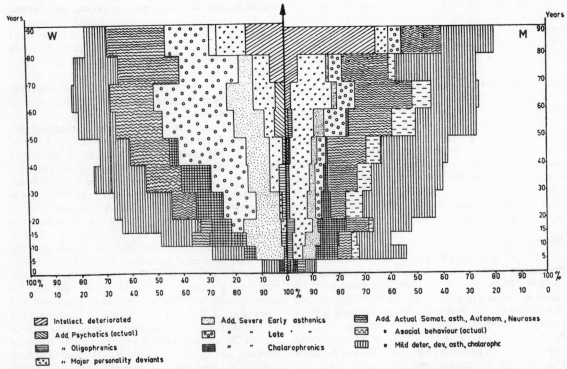

FIG. 8.11. CUMULATED PSYCHIATRIC DIAGNOSES, BY AGE AND SEX, IN A SWEDISH RURAL POPULATION

Note. W = women M = men. Among "major personality deviants" are included those who are markedly aggressive, restless, indolent or eccentric. "Asthenic" states are largely characterized by fatigue and nervousness. "Chalarophrenics," in Essen-Möller's terminology, are characterized by a persisting, objective mental and motor slackness or lack of energy. In the diagram "psychosomatic" complaints are grouped with neuroses. Alcoholism is included under asocial behaviour.

(From Essen-Möller, 1956; by courtesy of Prof. E. Essen-Möller and Messrs. Munksgaard)

and age groups the frequency with which the different major psychiatric groupings occurred, proceeding from the most severe to the more trivial. Each individual is counted once only, according to his most severe diagnosis if he had more than one. The reader is left to decide for himself where to draw the line between the normal and the abnormal part of the population. 67·2 per cent of the female and 60·4 per cent of the male living population had collected some psychiatric diagnosis. If we count as abnormal only oligophrenia (i.e. low grade mental defect), severe intellectual deterioration, present psychosis, major personality deviation (more frequent in males) and severe early asthenia (more frequent in females), then 14·9 per cent of the women and 12·3 per cent of the men would be regarded as showing psychological abnormalities. If a further group of persons, including those with severe late asthenia and present neurosis or alcoholism, is included as abnormal, the respective frequencies rise to 47·1 per cent and 34·5 per cent. The authors also make an attempt to estimate how much abnormality has a distinct pathology (including single genes) and how much is due to natural variation. Their analysis of resemblance within families is yet to be published.

Further work is needed to put population studies of personality and neurosis on a firm basis, and to allow the results of one study to be compared with those of another. Easily administered standardized personality tests, to supplement the history and personal observation and to introduce some quantitative measurement, would of course be very helpful, if they could be made reliable. Most tests, at present available, vary too much with the way the subject is feeling at the moment. It is important, also, that we should get to know the frequency, not only of neurosis, but also of those environmental factors, such as a "broken home," which are under suspicion. In researches of this kind there are good reasons for approaching the problem simultaneously from more than one point of view, genetical, social, psychiatric and psychometric.

Study of Isolates: Consanguinity Rate

Apart from surveys of the general urban or rural population, attention has also been given to isolates, or groups characterized by a high degree of in-breeding. One of the advantages of this work is that any genetically determined anomalies are likely to be homogeneous. Böök (1953) recently undertook the arduous task of studying three parishes in an isolated area in the north of Sweden, some thirty miles beyond the Arctic Circle. With the help of his wife, who had been born in the region, he gained the confidence of the population and was able to estimate the frequency and the genetics of the forms of mental disorder and

mental defect found there. Many of the cases of mental abnormality could be consolidated into one pedigree, traceable to thirty-one ancestral pairs. Some of his findings were referred to on pages 309 and 335.

Another investigation, with a primarily cultural orientation, was made by Eaton and Weil (1955) of the Hutterites, a religious sect living in communities of their own in the North of the United States and in Canada. Although these people appeared to be relatively free from neurotic troubles, perhaps because of their simple way of life, there was a high incidence of manic-depressive psychosis, for which the only simple explanation seems to be the genetical one.

In isolates there tends to be a high consanguinity rate in marriage, and this tends to favour the appearance of homozygotes; the result may be seen in a relative abundance of some rare recessive defect. The frequency of cousin marriage, both in the parents of trait-bearers and in the general population, is important to theoretical genetics in several ways. In the general population there are large differences between town and country. In Stockholm only about 0·4 per cent of marriages are between cousins, while in some isolated Swedish parishes the rate may be as high as 6 per cent. It is also likely to be high in minority religious groups. With the breakdown of isolates by the modern growth of communication cousin marriage is becoming less frequent.

HEREDITY AND ENVIRONMENT

The extent to which a given condition tends to run in families is no measure of the degree to which genetical factors are involved. On the one hand conditions with a genetic basis which are lethal at an early age, or are commonly caused by fresh mutation, or are so common as to be nearly universal (such as senile dementia), frequently show no conspicuous familial loading. On the other hand conditions which are independent of gene differences, such as for instance the presence of nits in the hair, may show a marked tendency to a familial distribution. The plausibility of a genetical or an environmental explanation will depend on one's existing knowledge and understanding; and the appearance in siblings of, say, an inborn error of metabolism or juvenile delinquency will be judged accordingly.

The genetical hypothesis can be rejected, if it can be shown that unrelated persons, subjected to similar environments, resemble one another as much as blood relatives. Environmental factors may also be brought out in individual case studies, and by giving special attention to social environment. Were the affected members of a given family subjected to a specific stress (such as separation from their mother at an early age) while the unaffected members were not? Spouses share a family environment, but differ genetically, and resemblances between them are likely to be environmentally caused, especially where the possibility of contagion, physical or psychological, arises. On this basis, Kallmann and Reisner (1943) included the examination of spouses in their family studies of tuberculosis. However, there are two kinds of material, foster-children and twins, which are particularly suited to the investigation of environmental causes of variation.

Foster-children

The study of fostered, adopted and orphanage children, who unlike other children are not brought up with their own biological parents, enables us, in theory at least, to disentangle the effects of heredity and environment in two complementary ways. On the one hand we can observe the effect of different environments on persons (or groups of persons) who are similar in heredity, as for instance when pairs of siblings are brought up in different homes. Alternatively we can observe the effects of similar environments on persons who are genetically unlike, for example, by comparing "own" and foster-children, or by observing the range of differences among children brought up in the relatively uniform atmosphere of an orphanage.

So far research on these lines has been done mostly in the United States and in the field of intelligence. Woodworth in his monograph entitled *Heredity and Environment* (1941) has summarized and discussed in a clear and fair-minded way the findings of research on foster-children carried out by Freeman and others (1928) in Chicago, Burks (1928) in California, Leahy (1935) in Minnesota, Skodak and Skeels in Iowa (1938, 1939, 1940, 1942) and others.

Attempts have also been made, in particular by the Iowa school to measure the improvement in I.Q. following adoption from an inferior into a superior home. However, the reliability of I.Q.s tested in the early years of life is notoriously low and an improvement in test score after some years might in part be due to the greater security of the child in its new home. Even if it is reliably estimated that adopted children have a higher I.Q. than their (often below-average) mothers, this might well be an instance of the expected "regression to the mean."

Other difficulties in planning and carrying out investigations into foster-children include the practical ones of following up an adequate sample of children placed away from home early in life; moreover, information about their own families is liable to be inadequate, especially in the case of the fathers of illegitimate children. The usefulness of this kind of research is limited too, because the range of foster-home environments tends to be limited. Among theoretical snags is selective elimination: when one investigates the adopted children of defectives, for example, one finds that their less promising children have not been adopted but retained in institutions, so that the adopted ones are not a fair sample. Selective placement is equally important: if the best children go to the best foster-homes, as is indeed intended when an attempt is made to match the child to the home, this would invalidate the findings. One investigator reports a correlation of 0·3 between "own" parent education and adoptive parent education.

Some investigators emphasize the fact that a good environment can raise by a few very worth-while points the I.Q. of children who come from an unfavourable background. The effect of different kinds of environment on the mean I.Q. of children, believed to be free from the effect of selective placement, is shown in the following findings of Freeman—

45 foster-children in *good* foster-homes scored an average of 112 points.

39 foster-children in *average* foster-homes scored an average of 105 points.

27 foster-children in relatively *poor* foster-homes scored an average of 96 points.

The following table from Leahy shows an apparent influence of the occupational level of the adoptive father on the intelligence scores of adopted children; but it will be seen that there was much less variation between the five adopted groups than between the five groups of "own" children, and that the children adopted into semi-skilled and relatively unskilled families actually did a good deal better on intelligence tests than children born into such families.

TABLE VIII.5

MEAN I.Q. OF FOSTER-CHILDREN AND OF "OWN" CHILDREN IN HOMES OF DIFFERENT OCCUPATIONAL CATEGORIES

(After Leahy, 1935)

Occupation of Father	Adopted children		Control ("own") children	
	Number	Mean	Number	Mean
Professional . .	43	113	40	119
Business management . .	38	112	42	118
Skilled trades and clerical . .	44	111	43	107
Semi-skilled . .	45	109	46	101
Relatively unskilled	24	108	23	102

The greater resemblance between parents and their own children than between parents and children adopted even early, is also borne out by the work of Burks, who gives her findings in the form of correlation coefficients—

	Foster group		Control group	
	Parents and adopted children		Parents and own children	
	r	N	r	N
Father's mental age .	0·07	178	0·45	100
Mother's mental age.	0·19	204	0·46	105

Burks concluded that heredity accounted for about 75 to 80 per cent of the variance in intelligence, under the environmental range from which her sample was taken. Woodworth is of the opinion that, despite their apparent differences, the various studies of the intelligence of adopted children have yielded comparable results; that the method is adequate to bring out any large differences due to the environment; but that scientific precision is not to be obtained.

We may end this section by referring to one of the rare studies of traits other than intelligence which have been studied by this method. It bears out the remarks of Woodworth. In 1945 Roe, Burks and Mittelmann reported on the emotional and social adjustment as adults of persons placed for adoption when under ten years of age by a large New York adoption society on account of their parents being alcoholic or psychotic. However, the majority of them either could not be traced or did not co-operate in the study. Over one-third of those seen showed evidence of various sorts of maladjustment, but with few exceptions they were living useful lives. Only very few were professional workers, though many of the foster-homes were of professional standing. This is probably not a bad result, all considered, and it is perhaps better than would have been expected if the children had remained in their unstable home environments. But as the persons with whom no contact was made may well have included an undue proportion of social failures, even so tentative a conclusion as that is hardly justified.

Twins, the Two Kinds

Twins can give us information both about specific environmental factors and about the relative importance of heredity. This is because there are two kinds of twins. There are the uniovular or monozygotic (MZ) pairs, which are derived from a single fertilized ovum, which has split into two (or sometimes more) individuals at a very early stage; and there are the

binovular or dizygotic (DZ) pairs, formed by the fertilization of two different ova by two sperms. The latter are no more alike genetically than an ordinary pair of brothers or sisters, and are often known as fraternal twins; they can expect to have no more than half their genes in common. Monozygotic twins, however, should be duplicates of one another in respect of each and all of their genes, and can be regarded as genetically "identical." MZ twins are sometimes rather different in appearance, and DZ twins can be extremely alike, so that it is occasionally difficult to allot a pair of twins to their correct biological class. The usual and best method of determining ovularity is to test the pair for similarities in respect of a number of traits, of a kind in which genetical causation predominates, such as eye colour, blood groups (Smith and Penrose, 1955) and fingerprints (Nixon, 1956). By such means the probability of an error in classification can be reduced to a level at which it can have no material effect in the comparison of two series.

Differences between Monozygotic Twins

When we compare MZ twins, we know that differences between them must be due to non-genetical causes. Some differences might be due to factors operating before birth, rather than to the post-natal environment. Influences of this kind are perhaps rather liable to occur in twins. Asymmetrical features, for example, such as the hair whorl going in opposite directions or one twin being left-handed and the other right-handed occur more frequently in twins than in the singly born (Newman, Freeman and Holzinger, 1937). With monochorionic pairs one twin may secure for himself more than an equal share of the placental circulation (Price, 1950) and this can lead to a significant difference between identical twins in birth weight. Both these factors should be borne in mind in interpreting the findings of twin studies. However, their influence in psychiatry is probably not very great; they might be more important in connexion with congenital abnormalities. Twins of both kinds, particularly MZ twins, have a lower birth weight and are less viable (Allen, 1955) than non-twins; the mean I.Q. of twin children is 5 points below the average for all sizes of family (Barclay and Maxwell, 1951). But if they survive the initial risks they probably grow up to form a fairly representative cross-section of the population; except possibly for certain forms of mental defect and epilepsy, the incidence of mental illness is not raised in twins. For instance, twins are no more often referred to the Maudsley Hospital than are singly-born persons (Shields, 1954). When we investigate a complete series of twins with a single condition we are probably making a fair sample of that condition.

Information about the post-natal environment can be obtained from identical twins in a number of ways.

Co-twin Control

According to Gesell's (Gesell, 1941) "co-twin control" method, one infant twin is trained in an activity such as stair-climbing, while the other twin is not given the training, and the effect of this is observed. The possibility of much direct experimentation in this way is of course limited, but the method could perhaps on occasions be applied, and not only to children (Glass, 1954). In cases where a pair of adult MZ twins have the same illness equally severely at the same time the effect of different treatments can be studied.

A less experimental application of the co-twin control method consists in making careful observations of twins in infancy and predicting the possible consequences of the similarities and differences and personal relationships noted at the time. In follow-up studies these predictions can then be tested.

Case Study

However, in psychiatric twin studies, as in ordinary clinical work, the retrospective case history method generally has to be used. Here the life histories of a pair of twins are compared and any differences between them in psychiatric status are related to their past experience or way of life (Slater, 1953). From the study of many pairs on these lines one can perhaps reach conclusions of general relevance to the causes and prevention of mental ill-health.

Twins Brought up Apart

One limitation of twin research as a means of assessing the influence of the environment is that we are normally confined to pairs who have been brought up in the same home and so have had similar experiences; and differences between MZ twins brought up together must often be attributed to the relations between them rather than to wholly external factors. However, twins brought up apart are very hard to come by. Over a period of years Newman, Freeman and Holzinger (1937) in America succeeded in investigating only nineteen such pairs of MZ twins, and to obtain this number many had to be bribed by a free visit to the World Fair in Chicago. Newman and his colleagues found that these twins, who were mostly adult, resembled one another in intelligence less closely than MZ twin schoolchildren who had been brought up together in Chicago, but they resembled one another more closely than DZ twin schoolchildren. There was a high correlation between the amount of formal education received and Binet I.Q. The difference between the MZ pairs brought up apart and those brought up together can be accounted

for very largely by a few pairs where there was a rather extreme difference in their backgrounds. Thus in one of these pairs, one twin had only two years' schooling while her partner had a college education and was herself a schoolteacher. They differed by 24 points in I.Q. Small inter-family differences had little effect on intelligence. In personality, correlations between twins were lower than in intelligence; this may have been largely because of the tests used, but here again the separated identical twins were on the whole no less alike than those brought up in the same home, and a number of clinical similarities were noted.

Craike and Slater (1945) have described a pair of MZ twins who were separated at nine months and who both developed paranoid schizophrenic illnesses later on. Kallmann (1938) has also described a pair of this kind, and yet another case has recently come to the notice of our Unit.

Through a television programme the B.B.C. recently brought to light a considerable number of normal MZ twins brought up apart, and some forty of these have so far been investigated at the Maudsley Hospital. They include all degrees of separation during childhood. Thus, there is a pair in which one twin was adopted by a well-to-do family in Chile and married a Frenchman. The other was brought up mostly in Denmark in poor circumstances with a psychopathic father, and she married an Englishman. In another pair, twin boys were brought up in separate homes from birth, but by different aunts living only next door to one another. It is interesting to compare the effects of different degrees of separation. The cases where the separations were not very extreme, such as those where one twin was brought up by mother the other by grandmother, are important for the opportunity which they give for assessing the significance of such factors as the age and personality of the mother, the presence of other children in the family, a town or country environment and the mutual influence of the twins.

From the results so far, age at separation does not appear to be of very great importance—the few pairs separated after the age of four differed as much in personality as the majority who were separated soon after birth. Nor does childhood contact with the twin appear to have made for greater similarity. One of the most strikingly similar pairs had no knowledge of one another until they were reunited by the research at the age of 36. On the whole the kind of home made a bigger difference than the degree of separation. In the pairs that differed most psychiatrically there was generally some definitely unsatisfactory feature in the early environment of the twin who had the poorer mental health. Differences in social class, though not marked in the series, could be seen to have an effect in causing differences of behaviour. However, the respective foster-parents of the two twins could differ quite a lot in age, personality and ideas of bringing up children, without this necessarily resulting in any obvious differences between the twins. Many striking similarities in speech, gesture, interests and temperament were noted. The results of a simple personality questionnaire, devised for us by Professor Eysenck, lend support to the observation that twins brought up in different homes can resemble one another closely in personality. For extraversion there was a positive correlation between twins of 0·60, for neuroticism one of 0·52. For intelligence the correlation was 0·77 on a non-verbal test. (Newman reported a correlation of 0·67 for Binet I.Q. between his separated MZ twins.) A preliminary account is given by Shields (1958).

Comparison of Resemblances within MZ and DZ Pairs

If MZ twins are alike in a particular respect, one cannot conclude that this is because of their possessing the same genes; it might be due to their similar environment. To help us decide this point we have the DZ—or hereditarily non-identical—pairs. If sex is a significant factor then the DZ pairs of the same sex can be compared with the MZ. One could hardly find individuals brought up in more similar environments than twins. Both kinds are born into the same home at the same time with all that this implies; they are more alike in this respect than ordinary siblings. If, in a representative series of pairs, the average resemblance between the MZ twins is markedly greater than that between the fraternals, then there is a strong case for the view that the genetical constitution has an important bearing on the condition in question, at least under present circumstances.

Psychological factors. An objection sometimes raised against a comparison of MZ with DZ twins is the fact that the former tend to go about together in childhood and are sometimes unusually closely attached to one another, while fraternal twins often develop more independently and so do not have quite so similar psychological environments. The influence of this might be quite important in some conditions, particularly in childhood; but in others it would be negligible. However, any difference of this sort between the two kinds of twins is largely a reflection of the innate needs of the twins themselves. Everyone tends to make his environment for himself, as well as to be influenced by it. One can, of course, test by observation whether those MZ twins who are most closely attached to one another are in fact more similar psychologically than the others. From our own (Shields, 1954) experience with normal London schoolchildren this did not seem generally to be the case. There is, however, another psychological factor

—one making for difference between MZ twins; this is the tendency with many of them for one to be the dominant partner, the other to be more submissive. Certainly it would be most implausible to explain any differences in resemblance between MZ and DZ twins entirely by external environmental factors, such as the ways mothers treat their twins. For this to be the true explanation, nearly all mothers would have to treat their MZ twins in exactly the same way, but handle DZ twins of the same sex very differently indeed. This does not appear to be the case at all. Some tendency of this kind may be forced on the parents by the twins themselves, but it is probably to a considerable extent offset by a reaction in the opposite direction. Mothers of MZ twins often like to think of their twins as different so that they may regard them as separate individuals. The mothers of DZ twins generally make the most conscientious efforts to give their twins the same of everything. Points such as these can often be clarified by actual case studies of twins. Further, as we have seen, the findings on twins brought up apart vindicate some of the presuppositions of the traditional twin method.

Unselected series. It is just as important in collecting a twin series as in other types of family investigation to guard against bias in selection. The field from which the collection is made must be defined, and within it the collection should be unselective and as comprehensive as possible. It has been shown (Luxenburger, 1930) that reliance on published case reports leads to a gross bias, as pairs of twins in which both members show the trait greatly preponderate. In any investigation in which there is any casualness or informality in ascertainment the same sort of bias is likely to arise; for some reason nearly everybody, including doctors, find twins who resemble one another much more interesting than twins who differ.

If an unselected series can be obtained, then estimates of *concordance rates* become interesting. A pair of twins is said to be concordant in respect of some trait if both members are alike in showing or not showing it, discordant if one shows it while the other does not. If the trait in question is wholly genetically determined, we shall expect all MZ twins to be concordant, but the concordance rate in DZ twins will depend on the mode of inheritance and frequency of the gene in the population. Thus, if we collect twins who (1) belong to blood group O, (2) have Huntington's chorea, (3) have phenylketonuria, the concordance rates which we shall expect to find in their DZ partners will be respectively (1) 70 per cent, (2) 50 per cent, (3) 25 per cent. From this it follows that no sound measure of degree of genetical determination can be obtained by simply setting the concordance rates in MZ and in DZ pairs in relation to one another. In the case of continuously distributed

TABLE VIII.6

TWIN RESEARCH: MZ AND DZ CONCORDANCE RATES IN A VARIETY OF CONDITIONS, MOSTLY PSYCHIATRIC

Condition investigated (author, year)	Number of pairs			Percentage positively concordant (to nearest 1 per cent) * = corrected for age	
	Total	Monozygotic	Dizygotic	Monozygotic	Dizygotic
Infectious diseases					
Measles (von Verschuer, 1932, and others, cited by Gedda, 1951)	1,163	600	563	97	94
Mumps (von Verschuer, 1932, and others, cited by Gedda, 1951)	190	92	98	78	73
Paralytic poliomyelitis (Herndon and Jennings, 1951)	47	14	33	36	6
Tuberculosis (New York) (Kallmann and Reisner, 1943)	308	78	230	62	18
Tuberculosis (England) (Simonds, 1957)	202	54	148	30	13
Mental deficiency (institutionalized cases)					
Rosanoff *et al.*, (1937)	366	126	240	91	53
Juda (1939) {"Endogenous" cases only	189	60	129	100	58
Juda (1939) {All cases	220	71	149	97	56
Schizophrenia					
Luxenburger (1928)	81	21	60	67	3
Rosanoff *et al.*, (1934)	142	41	101	67	10
Essen-Möller (1941)	31 (35)	7 (11)	24	22–71	17
Slater (1953)	156	41	115	{68 {76*	{11 {14*
Kallmann (original report, 1946)	{691	174	517	{69	{10
Kallmann (latest report to date, 1953)	{953	268	685	{86*	{15*
Kallmann and Roth (1956): Pre-adolescent schizophrenia	52	17	35	71–88†	17–23†
Manic-depressive psychosis					
Luxenburger (1942, cited by Gedda, 1951)	139	56	83	84	15
Rosanoff *et al.* (1935)	90	23	67	70	16
Kallmann (1950)	{75	23	52	96	26*
Kallmann (1953, latest report)	{85	27	58	100*	26*
Slater (1953): Endogenous affective disorder	38	8	30	{50 {c57*	29*
Da Fonseca (1959): Endogenous affective disorder	60	21	39	75	38
Involutional depression					
Kallmann (1950)	96	29	67	61*	6*
Senile psychosis					
Kallmann (1950)	108	33	75	43*	7*
Epilepsy					
Rosanoff *et al.* (1934)	107	23	84	70	24
Conrad (1935): Idiopathic	{161	{22	97	86	4
Conrad (1935): Symptomatic	{161	{8	34	13	0
Lennox and Jolly (1954): Without brain damage	{173	{51	47	88	13
Lennox and Jolly (1954): With brain damage	{173	{26	49	35	12

† The lower figure relates to co-twins with pre-adolescent schizophrenia, the higher to all schizophrenic co-twins.

TABLE VIII.6 (*continued*)

Condition investigated (author, year)	Number of pairs			Percentage positively concordant (to nearest 1 per cent) * = corrected for age	
	Total	Monozygotic	Dizygotic	Monozygotic	Dizygotic
Homosexuality, Crime, Behaviour Disorder, Neurosis, etc.			Same-sexed pairs		Same-sexed pairs
Male homosexuality (Kinsey Scale, 3 or more):					
Kallmann (1952)	63	37	26	100	12
Adult crime: Lange (1929), Rosanoff *et al.* (1934), Kranz (1936), Stumpfl (1936), Borgstroem (1939) —combined results	216	103	113	68	35
Juvenile delinquency: Rosanoff *et al.* (1934, 1941) .	67	42	25	85	75
Childhood behaviour disorder, etc.: Rosanoff *et al.* (1934, 1941): Behaviour disorder . . .	107	47	60	87	43
Kranz (1937): Juveniles with personality disorder requiring institutionalization . .	14	11	3	71	0
After Kent (1949): Emotional disorders (based on Child Guidance Clinic material) . . .	13	7	6	100	67
Shields (1954): Behaviour disorder or marked neurotic traits (based on 62 unselected pairs of twin-school-children)	41	23	18	74	50
Hysteria: Stumpfl (1937)	18	9	9	33	0
Neurosis, Psychopathic personality: Slater (1953) .	37	8	29	25	14
Neurosis, Psychopathic personality: Slater and Shields (1955): New series, provisional . .	70	38	32	53	25
Alcohol addiction : from series of 201 twin-pairs whose drinking habits were studied (*After* Kaij, 1957)	82	26	56	65	30

variables, the correlation coefficients within MZ and DZ pairs may be contrasted; and Holzinger has suggested his h^2 formula (*see* page 331) to combine both in an estimate of degree of genetical determination. This too cannot be regarded as fully reliable; and the best plan is to consider the meaning of the concordance rates found, in the total setting of the experiment.

From studies of twins alone one can obtain no information about the mode of inheritance. For this the twin and family methods can usefully be combined; a series of twins is obtained, and then not only their twin partners but other members of their families are investigated. Such a study will also provide information, through a comparison of probands with their singly born sibs as well as with their DZ partners, about early environmental influences; if these are important, DZ partners should be more alike than proband and sib.

Twin series of any useful size can only be obtained if the trait investigated is a common one; but within this field the method is a most useful one, particularly if the aetiology is obscure. A comparison of concordance rates in MZ and DZ twins provides a sensitive test of significant genetical causation. For this reason, such studies have proved particularly valuable in psychiatry, for psychiatric abnormalities tend to be very common, and also to be obscure. The table above shows some of the concordance rates which have been found in a great variety of conditions, from which a lesson may also be learned on how to interpret these figures (Table VIII.6). If, for instance, we contrast the rates in measles with those in mumps and in polio, a shift in the degree of genetical participation will be seen, even though in all three the specific cause of illness is a foreign agent. In the case of measles, it would seem that nearly everyone who meets the germ gets the illness, and that there is very little variation in individual susceptibility. In the case of mumps, there is much more variation in susceptibility, but, since there is little difference between MZ and DZ concordances, this variation must be largely non-genetical. Only in the case of polio, of these three, is there a strong suggestion that hereditary constitution may be a matter of moment.

Psychiatric Abnormality in Twins

Mental deficiency. The best investigation in the field of mental deficiency is that of Juda (for references *see* Table VIII.6). She studied the children attending

Special Schools in Munich, and made a complete ascertainment of the twins among them. Excluding cases where the defect was caused by birth injury or other possible exogenous causes, the MZ pairs showed 100 per cent concordance; that is to say, in every case the twin partner of the *propositus* or index case was also mentally defective to some extent. In fact, in fifty-five out of sixty twin pairs both had the same grade of deficiency. In the DZ pairs 58 per cent of the partners were concordant, but in only half of them were both twins affected to the same degree. The findings are consistent with the view that most cases of undifferentiated mental defect are of primarily genetical origin, and that environmental factors, at least those that can vary within the family, are of little significance. Juda's findings are in good agreement with those of Rosanoff in the U.S.A., who, without distinguishing cases of defect of known aetiology, found concordance rates of 91 per cent for MZ pairs, 53 per cent for DZ pairs, in a series of three hundred and sixty-six twin pairs.

Schizophrenia. The work of Luxenburger in this field is the pioneer work on psychosis in twins. In 1928 he drew attention to the necessity of working systematically, and recommended the ascertainment of the twins in a mental hospital population by checking in the birth registers. Doing this in a defined population of 16,000 schizophrenics, he discovered twenty-one who had MZ twin partners who had survived into an age of risk; in fourteen of these pairs both members were schizophrenic or probably so, in the other seven only one member was affected. Very similar figures have subsequently been found by Rosanoff, Kallmann and Slater; but in cases where a twin partner has not yet fallen ill allowance should be made for age at observation, and where this has been done age-corrected figures are given in the table.

A very large initial clinical material must be investigated before a large enough number of MZ twins with a given diagnosis and with a surviving partner can be assembled. Fraternal twins are of more frequent occurrence, but if the condition is one in which they are not often concordant, the sampling error of the concordance rate may be high. Thus in Luxenburger's series there were forty-eight DZ pairs, and in not one was the partner certainly schizophrenic. Kallmann and Slater, on larger material, have each found a concordance rate of 14 per cent, which is also given by Kallmann for the incidence in the sibs of schizophrenics. Kallmann's latest report is based on no fewer than nine hundred and fifty-three schizophrenic twins and their families. In accounting for the discordant MZ twins—only about 14 per cent—Kallmann lays great stress on body build and weight. He found that when one twin fell ill and the other did not, or when one twin was much more severely

ill than the other, it was the more asthenic twin who fared worse.

In the mental hospital material we have investigated from the Maudsley Hospital, we found a somewhat lower MZ concordance rate than Kallmann, one of 76 per cent; twenty-eight of the MZ partners of forty-one schizophrenics were also affected. Besides many close clinical similarities there were also some striking differences. For example, in one case one twin spent eighteen years in hospital, the other four months only. In about half the pairs the twins fell ill within two years of one another; but in one case one girl became schizophrenic at 16, her twin not until 47. This material was given a detailed analysis and description, so that some conclusions could be drawn about the features of the environment and of the personality associated with differences in mental health, and about the features of the illness which showed or did not show indications of genetical determination. The modern trend in twin research recognizes the value of detailed individual analysis, in addition to mass statistics.

Another detailed study is by Essen-Möller. He investigated a small but representative series of twins from a psychiatric clinic in Sweden, and brought to light many differences in severity. However, when both twins had some psychiatric disorder in which there were schizophrenic features in one, these tended to be present in the other too. He found it necessary to formulate the diagnosis in a more fluid way than the other workers mentioned, as many of the psychotic states were atypical. It is not easy to say just what the concordance rates were.

Affective psychoses. Studies on manic-depressive twins have not been carried out on such a large scale, but those that have been made give similar results. Kallmann found in twenty-three MZ pairs that twenty-two of the partners were similarly affected, against figures of 26 per cent for DZ twin partners and 23 per cent for sibs. Once again he found that the physical constitution was important, the less severely affected individuals being less obese. His work on involutional psychoses indicates that they should be distinguished from manic-depressive syndromes. MZ twin partners of involutional depressives were similarly affected in 61 per cent of cases; but he found also a raised incidence of schizophrenia among their relatives. In previously reported work from our Unit, we have had too small a number of manic-depressives to draw any conclusions. But in a recent series of sixty pairs, investigated here by da Fonseca and recently published in Portugal, results on the whole are in conformity with those of other studies. Da Fonseca's concordance rates as given in the table include partially concordant cases, i.e. those where the co-twin had an abnormal personality of a depressive or hypomanic kind. If overt illness is taken as the criterion the percentages concordant are reduced to 60 per cent and 31 per cent for MZ and DZ pairs respectively. Concordance for cyclothymic personality was higher than that for affective illness.

Senile psychoses and senility. It is once again to Kallmann that we are indebted for twin work in this field. He found a concordance rate in MZ twins of 43 per cent as against 6·5 per cent for DZ twins; and the incidence of such conditions in their other relatives was higher than in the general population. Studying a series of twins, selected only for having outlived the age of 60, he (1951, 1953) found that MZ pairs, even those who had lived apart for many years, showed a closer resemblance in intelligence, longevity and manner of ageing, than DZ pairs.

Epilepsy. The two principal investigators in this field have been Conrad in Germany and Lennox in the U.S.A. The work of the former is a model of thoroughness, but it is restricted to institutionalized epileptics. Lennox's material includes out-patients. In both studies a remarkably high concordance is reported for MZ twins, 86 and 88 per cent when cases of epilepsy due to acquired brain damage are excluded. Where there was a known or probable cause of local brain damage, the MZ rates were very much lower. This provides an example of the use of twin studies to throw light on the validity of diagnostic classification, and shows that the now somewhat suspect term "idiopathic epilepsy" does have a real meaning. It seems unlikely that, however far our methods of neurological investigation progress, we shall find a specific local cause for every case of epilepsy; in a considerable proportion of cases a constitutional instability must be the main factor.

Male homosexuality. A number of workers have reported single cases, or small series of cases, of homosexuality occurring in twins; however, Kallmann's series is the only thoroughly systematic one. He and his team had great difficulty in carrying it out, as their contacts showed the greatest reluctance to come to the Research Institute, and wished to be interviewed, if at all, in resorts which were familiar to them.

Out of Kallmann's (1953) eventual total of forty-five MZ twin pairs, only one was discordant; and in that case the homosexual twin was also, unlike his brother, schizophrenic. The other *propositi* in this series were confirmed homosexuals with a high rating on the Kinsey scale. A full classification of the DZ twin partners has only been given for the first twenty-six pairs (in 1952); of them one reached a grade of 5 or 6; two a grade of 3 or 4; eight a grade of 1 or 2; and fifteen were in the 0 grade. This is no higher an incidence of homosexual traits than Kinsey found for the white male American population on which he

worked. It is possible that Kallmann's material is influenced by a selection in favour of severity and constitutional predisposition, and that his figures would have been different if he had started with younger homosexuals. Nevertheless, the evidence is, of course, very strongly in favour of a genetical factor in the type of homosexuality which Kallmann studied.

Suicide. As a contrast with the above figures, we may mention Kallmann's (1953) work on suicide. A prolonged search of the literature disclosed no case of both of a pair of twins committing suicide—unless it were together in a suicidal pact; eventually one such case did come to his notice, and another has recently been reported by Dencker (1957). Though heredity may perhaps play some part in causing a melancholy disposition, suicide itself must require precipitation by accidental factors, such as sudden environmental pressures. This illustrates the relationship and the contrast between personality and behaviour, which have been more intensively investigated in the field of crime.

Crime. The first study of significance was carried out by Lange, who was so impressed by his findings that he entitled his report *Crime as Destiny*. Only three out of his thirteen MZ pairs were discordant, and in very few of the DZ pairs were both twins criminal. These results have not been subsequently confirmed, and later workers, such as Kranz and Stumpfl, have found concordance rates of about 60 and 40 per cent in MZ and DZ twins respectively.

The difference is not so great as to make one think that heredity plays any strongly preponderant role. The high concordance in DZ twins underlines the significance of early family background; and the 40 per cent discordance in the MZ twins supports the idea that special opportunities and temptations have to be regarded as important.

However, detailed clinical studies show that accident plays a smaller part, and personality a larger one, in the case of severe and persistent offenders. Some of the subjects were of a kind to drift naturally into a criminal career, and if so, the MZ twins generally resembled each other in this too. Crimes of violence in one twin would be matched by violence in the other; or both of the twins might be confidence tricksters or swindlers of a similar type, or petty larcenists, or sexually deviant. In some cases, behaviour, though similar, fell one side of the line of legality in one twin, on the other side in the other; or one might find the socially acceptable equivalent of what in the other became a transgression. By and large, it could be shown that whereas personalities resembled each other closely, the range of behaviour available to anyone of a given personality was surprisingly wide.

Included in Table VIII.6 are data from the first report of what should be an interesting study by Kaij of the *drinking habits* of twins. These were considerably more alike at all levels in MZ than in DZ pairs but the figures suggest that it can fairly often happen that one of the MZ twins is merely an above-average consumer, while the other ranks as an addict or chronic alcoholic.

Rosanoff's findings on *juvenile delinquency* show the very high concordance rate of 86 per cent for MZ twins—but an almost equally high one of 75 per cent for the same-sexed DZ twins. These findings resemble those of measles and mumps, rather than schizophrenia and epilepsy. Environmental factors have to be ranked high in importance, and among them, especially in juvenile delinquency, we have to take into account the influence of one twin on the other. On the borderlines of neurosis, we note that *behaviour disorders* in children are not so concordant in DZ pairs as is juvenile delinquency; such phenomena are likely to be a closer reflection of the personality than is delinquent behaviour in the young.

Neurosis. Twin studies in this field have been surprisingly deficient in number and scope. In published material from our Unit, in only two out of eight MZ pairs was the second twin likewise neurotic or psychopathic. In a subsequent study of schoolchildren, it was found that most MZ twins, while far from being replicas of one another psychologically, tended to be similar in temperament, and that when both had neurotic traits these were generally of the same kind. Even more striking were the differences within DZ pairs; if both of such a pair were neurotic, the symptoms were usually different. On the other hand, the appearance of behaviour disorders in a family was related to the poorness of the psychological environment. To over-simplify somewhat: type of reaction seemed to depend a good deal on constitutional factors, whilst severity was more closely related to the environment.

In continued work at our Unit, mainly on post-war Maudsley neurotic twins, we have found concordance rates of about 53 per cent in MZ twins and 25 per cent in DZ twins. This is using the objective but possibly somewhat trivial criterion of having been referred to a psychiatrist or, in the case of children, to a juvenile court. Such an arbitrary definition of "neurosis" does not have much meaning; and the crude concordance rates do not do justice to the personality resemblances.

These figures show that hereditary constitution is a factor of some significance in neurosis; and detailed case study can add information on the variability of expression of some constitutional characteristics. But such material is also interesting in providing the means by which one may analyse the environmental causes of neurosis, by investigating the histories of twins who have differed. Even the concordant pairs

are of use in this connexion, as there are frequently marked differences in the degree of a neurotic reaction. It would seem inapposite to classify all these reactions as pathological, or abnormal in more than a statistical or social sense. They are modes of behaviour which lie within the potentialities of the average normal person; and their causation is invariably multiple and complex. The twin method proves a very useful method of separating out some of the threads which enter into the tangle.

Psychology and Genetics

In the sections illustrating the various modes of inheritance and methods of research, we have made reference to many of the salient investigations in the field of psychiatric genetics. In this final section we propose to cover in a brief and synoptic way the present state of our knowledge of hereditary factors as they enter into particular types of psychological abnormality.

ABNORMALITIES OF PERCEPTION

Defects of *vision* may be caused by abnormalities of any part of the visual apparatus, from the cornea back to the higher association centres in the brain. Errors of refraction, long-sightedness, short-sightedness, astigmatism, are of course common, and frequently involve the participation of genetical factors. A man with a good "eye" may not necessarily be one who can see the moons of Jupiter, but rather one whose speed and accuracy in oculo-motor co-ordination enables him to excel at, say, tennis or cricket. The investigations of Galton (1869) have shown that proficiency in sports of many kinds runs in families, and this cannot be solely through a favouring family tradition. We have discussed colour-blindness under sex-linked inheritance; the defect is probably of a biochemical kind, involving the deficiency of a pigment in the retina. *Retinitis pigmentosa* is a disease affecting the retina, genetically determined, and leading to progressive loss of vision proceeding from night-blindness to total blindness. Alström (1957) found that about 10 per cent of the persons admitted to the Swedish government's school for the blind suffered from some form of blindness due to the same recessive gene. As an example of a defect in the highest nervous centres we have congenital *dyslexia* or word-blindness, which Hallgren (1950) has shown to be almost certainly due to a dominant gene.

Defects of *hearing* (Lindenov, 1953) are most commonly caused by infections of the middle ear, and so are essentially non-genetical. However a chronic disease of the middle ear, otosclerosis, tends to run in families, and is responsible for a large group of persons who become deaf in later life. Hereditary factors are more extensively involved in diseases of the inner ear and of the auditory nerves and their connexions, but little is known of their genetics. Among higher nervous abnormalities deaf-mutism when genetically caused is generally due to one of a number of different recessive genes (Stevenson and Cheeseman, 1956). Tune deafness (Kalmus, 1949) may be due to a dominant.

Of *other sense deficiencies* still less is known. Taste-blindness to phenylthiocarbamide (Snyder, 1932) is due to a recessive gene, and the inability to smell potassium cyanide is possibly due to a sex-linked recessive gene (Kirk and Stenhouse, 1953). According to Malan (1940), differences in the capacity for spatial orientation are largely inherited.

ABNORMALITIES OF INTELLIGENCE

We have already discussed in some detail the evidence that goes to show that the observed normal variation in intelligence can be satisfactorily accounted for by polygenic inheritance, with environmental factors playing a smaller but still substantial role. Variation of a pathological kind, in the I.Q. range below 50 per cent and including idiots and imbeciles, may also arise from genetical causes as well as from environmental ones such as birth trauma. Genetical factors are likely to be of the single-factor kind, such as the recessive gene of PKU. Twin studies have shown that genetical factors are important in cases of deficiency that find their way into institutions and special schools.

To this evidence we may add the results of twin researches in the physiological range, in which intelligence tests have been used. In the earlier work on these lines ovularity diagnosis was generally inadequate. However several workers (Thorndike, 1905; Merriman, 1924; Wingfield, 1928; Tallman, 1928; Verschuer, 1930; Herrman and Hogben, 1933; Newman, Freeman and Holzinger, 1937; Blewett, 1953, 1954; Strandskov, 1955; Thurstone, 1953; Vandenberg, 1956) have found that MZ twins show a closer resemblance in I.Q. than DZ twins. For instance, Newman *et al.* tested fifty MZ and fifty-two DZ pairs of schoolchildren with the Binet test, and obtained correlation coefficients of 0·88 for MZ and 0·63 for DZ twins.

Holzinger (1929) introduced the statistic h^2 as an index of heritability, the environment being held constant. This is calculated from the formula $(r_{MZ} - r_{DZ})/(1 - r_{DZ})$, a procedure which is not free from logical objection (May, 1951), although it has been much used. On Newman's material, h^2 was 0·68.

Eysenck has stated that correlations between the factor score derived from a battery of intelligence tests would give a truer picture than a single test.

Blewett (1953, 1954) carried out a study on these lines, using five scores from Thurstone's Primary Mental Abilities test (verbal, space, reasoning, number and fluency) and Furneaux's tests of speed and power. His factor scores gave rather lower correlations than those obtained by Newman, $0·76_{MZ}$ and $0·44_{DZ}$. The hypothesis that the factor score would prove to be more highly determined by heredity than any of the scores from single tests was not borne out. A higher h^2 was obtained for verbal (0·68), fluency (0·64), and reasoning (0·64) than for the factor score itself (0·58). However, Eysenck (1956), analysing the results of tests applied by both Blewett and McLeod to the same twins, found that tests of finger dexterity and rigidity had high loadings on intelligence. Including these tests, the factor score gave higher correlations, $0·82_{MZ}$ and $0·38_{DZ}$; $h^2 = 0·71$.

The use of a test such as Thurstone's P.M.A. should enable one to discover whether one aspect of intelligence is more highly inherited than another. Thurstone and his colleagues (1953) ranked the separate abilities in the order of the significance of the difference between the scores of forty-eight MZ and fifty-five DZ pairs; the order was space, verbal, fluency, number and reasoning. Vandenberg (1956) makes a rough comparison of the within-pair variance of forty-five MZ and thirty-seven DZ twins for a variety of psychological and other traits, diagrammatically and without giving numerical results. Of the traits probably related to intelligence the largest MZ-DZ difference was in P.M.A. sentence completion, followed successively by the Stanford spelling test, the W.I.S.C. vocabulary test, P.M.A. arithmetic, Raven's Progressive Matrices, and finally, with very little difference between the two kinds of twins, mechanical insight. The results of these investigations are not easily compared with one another, owing to the different ways in which the findings are presented. In all of them, however, verbal ability shows up as one of the most highly inheritable aspects of intelligence within the family.

Taking intelligence as a whole, a number of attempts have been made to estimate the proportion of the total observed variance which can be attributed to heredity on the one side and environment on the other. We have already mentioned Burks's (1928) estimate of 75 to 80 per cent attributable to heredity. Burt, in a paper published in 1943, summarizes extensive work done on this subject under his supervision; and more recently (1955) he has given his opinion that very nearly 90 per cent of the variance in intelligence exhibited by a complete age group is attributable to the genetic constitution of the various individuals, while approximately half of this could be predicted from the characteristics of near relatives. Godfrey Thompson, Hogben (1933) and others have estimated the contribution by heredity as rather lower, nearer to 60 per cent. In connexion with all such estimates, it must be remembered that only that degree of genetical and environmental variance which obtained in the circumstance of the experiment will be measured, and that this will be, on both sides, very much less than what obtains in the population at large. A group of L.C.C. schoolchildren, for instance, must come from a much more homogeneous environment than the population of Great Britain as a whole, not to speak of the population of the world. Generalizations on this subject must, therefore, be made only with great caution. Other authorities consider that the inter-action of heredity and environment is so complex that it is probably futile to try to inquire into the extent of hereditary determination (Anastasi, 1954; Carter, 1940; Jones, 1955; Langfeld, 1951; Thompson, 1954). Nevertheless much can be learned from attempts to do so.

ABNORMALITIES OF CHILD DEVELOPMENT

There is a wide range of normal variation in the rate and pattern of maturation. This is to a large extent genetically determined (Tanner, 1953). Twin studies show that MZ twins resemble one another more closely than DZ twins in the age at which they begin to talk (e.g. Bossik, 1934; Verschuer, 1927) and in the tests of development of Hetzer and Bühler (Lehtovaara, 1938). Russian studies on a small number of pairs showed that the height of jump attained by four-year-old twins was much more alike in MZ than DZ pairs (Mirenova, 1934). The Vineland Social Maturity Scale has been administered to twins by von Bracken (1939), Wilson (1941) and by Troup and Lester (1942). All report negligible differences between MZ twins and larger ones between DZ twins. There is probably an important genetical element controlling the rate of sexual maturation as shown for instance by the greater mean difference in age of first menstruation reported by Petri (1934) for DZ twins (12·0 months) than for MZ twins (2·8 months). However, mothers and daughters showed no closer resemblance in this respect than pairs of unrelated women, thus suggesting, as Stern (1950) points out, that differences in family environments and differences between one generation and the next are important too.

It is not suggested that any of the above developmental stages are entirely genetically determined or that they are simple, well-understood processes. But the combined influence of heredity on many aspects of development must be considerable and will play its part in determining many abnormalities of development, for example in psychosexual maturity. Luchsinger (1940) reports that speech development, especially retardation in speech, is largely hereditarily determined. We have already had occasion to refer to Hallgren's (1950) detailed study of backward readers. In her series of twins at Special Schools in Munich, Juda (1939) found three cases of MZ pairs where both were genuine late developers. In Kallmann's (1956) large twin material he discovered fifty-two cases of schizophrenia commencing before the age of 15. Twelve out of seventeen MZ co-twins also developed schizophrenia under the age of 15, and six out of thirty-five DZ co-twins. Preadolescent schizophrenia appeared to be a special case of adult schizophrenia, and three MZ and two DZ co-twins became schizophrenic after the age of 15.

Turning to minor disturbances of development, as seen for example in some of the commoner neurotic and behaviour disorders of children, the influence of the genes can perhaps be seen in the observation of Shields (1954) that when a pair of twins both have some trouble of this nature the symptoms are generally of the same kind in MZ twins but different in DZ twins. For instance, he reports six pairs where enuresis occurred in a MZ pair and in four of these both twins were similarly affected. There were ten DZ pairs where this symptom occurred and in none of them were both twins enuretic, though in some cases the twin partner had some other trouble. In a recent monograph Hallgren (1957) has attempted to clarify the part played by the constitution in this disorder, finding quite strong grounds for believing there to be a considerable genetical element in primary enuresis. However, childhood behaviour disorders are very common, often transient and often demonstrably reactive to unsatisfactory external circumstances. Faulty learning habits are also no doubt often to blame. The role of the genes will be relatively indirect.

PSYCHOPHYSIOLOGICAL TRAITS

In 1944 Jost and Sontag showed that similarities in autonomic response increased with the degree of genetic relationship. Earlier work on pulse-rate and blood-pressure in twins received confirmation and elaboration when Eysenck (1956) extracted an "autonomic" factor from the data of Blewett and McLeod. The scores of MZ twins on this factor had a correlation of 0·93, those of DZ twins of like sex one of 0·72; the factor was highly influenced by sex. Carmena (1934) tested the psychogalvanic reflex of thirty-six MZ and twenty-four DZ twins and concluded that nervousness and kindred temperamental traits were the result of hereditary influences. According to Kanaev (1938) MZ twins show striking similarities in the ease with which they can be conditioned. Similar abnormal electro-encephalographic records in relatives have been reported, though the work of

Harvald (1954) shows the mode of inheritance of EEG pattern to be a complex matter. Nevertheless, Lennox (1945) considers that in certain circumstances EEG patterns can be used as a criterion to distinguish MZ from DZ twins.

PERSONALITY

The relationship between autonomic factors, P.G.R., conditionability and EEG on the one hand, and personality characteristics, such as nervousness, extraversion and aggressiveness on the other, have been mentioned in the main body of the book. Body-build too, possibly through its relation with autonomic functioning, has well-known associations with personality and is genetically determined to a substantial degree. But the connexion between physiological make-up and personality is one of some fluidity. Thus Whelan (1951) reports a pair of MZ twins, both of whom had similarly abnormal EEGs of an epileptic kind; yet one behaved in an extremely psychopathic way, aggressive, antisocial and subject to fugues, while the other was psychologically and socially within normal limits.

When attempts are made, generally by means of the twin method, to investigate personality characteristics at the level of motor activity, positive findings as regards heredity are usually found. Thus Luchsinger (1940) found heredity to be an important determinant of posture, throwing movements and mimicry. Lehtovaara (1938) made cinematographic records of twins watching a film. The course, character and intensity of the mimical process was much more alike in the MZ pairs. Also using film studies of twins, Spindler (1955) found an important hereditary basis for emotional and expressive mobility in adults, but not for voluntary movements. MZ twins are frequently reported as having indistinguishable voices. Gedda and his colleagues (1955) have found that when recordings of their own voices and those of their twins were played back to a group of uniovular twins, they were as a rule unable to tell one from the other. Family resemblance in physique predisposes towards similar interests and abilities in sport and athletics such as are often found in father and son, in siblings, and particularly in MZ twins. Galton's observations on the subject have already been noted and Grebe (1955, 1956) has made some interesting observations on sporting abilities in twins and other relatives. MZ twins are more alike than DZ twins in tests of motor skill (McNemar, 1933) and mechanical ability (Brody, 1937). Thus expressive movements, speech characteristics and preferred activities—all of which are closely related to personality—appear to be largely genetically determined.

Questionnaire tests of neurotic tendencies, interests, etc. (Carter, 1932, 1933; Holzinger, 1929) generally

show lower levels of correlation (*see* Table VIII.7), but such tests often lack reliability, and validity. On the basis of such studies alone one cannot justifiably conclude, as has sometimes been done, that personality characteristics are much less highly determined genetically than intelligence.

TABLE VIII.7

TWIN RESEARCH: RESULTS, EXPRESSED IN THE FORM OF CORRELATION COEFFICIENTS, OF SELECTED PSYCHOLOGICAL TESTS APPLIED TO MONOZYGOTIC AND DIZYGOTIC TWINS REARED TOGETHER

(For references *see* text.)

Test	r_{MZ}	r_{DZ}
Intelligence tests		
Wingfield (National Intelligence Test and McCall's Multimental Scale) . . .	0·90	0·57
Herrman and Hogben (Otis) . .	0·84	0·48
Newman, Freeman and Holzinger (Binet) .	0·88	0·63
Blewett (factor score) . . .	0·76	0·44
Eysenck (data of Blewett and McLeod) (factor score)	0·82	0·38
Other psychological tests		
Mechanical aptitude (Brody) . . .	0·69	0·28
Motor skills (McNemar) . . .	0·79	0·43
Bernreuter's neurotic inventory (Carter) .	0·63	0·32
Woodworth-Matthews' neurotic tendencies (Holzinger)	0·56	0·37
Strong's vocational interests (Carter) .	0·50	0·28
Autonomic factor (Eysenck, data of Blewett and McLeod)	0·93	0·72
Neuroticism factor (Eysenck and Prell) .	0·85	0·22
Extraversion factor (McLeod) . .	0·77	0·03
Extraversion factor (Eysenck, data of Blewett and McLeod)	0·50	−0·33

Besides self-ratings, the opinions of others have been used to investigate similarities and differences between twins. According to Lassen (1931) teachers' ratings on a large number of social and moral characteristics have much higher correlations between MZ than DZ pairs. This may have been influenced by a halo effect. Similarly H. E. Jones (1955) reports that parents more often perceive personality differences in the case of DZ than MZ twins. However, Jones considers that these opinions of the parents of the twins may have the effect of producing an environment in which greater similarities come to be expected of MZ than of DZ twins. This stereotyping process might, he thinks, be of importance in maintaining or increasing the similarity of twins in certain traits.

Instead of using a single test, Eysenck and Prell (1951) used a variety of tests of different kinds, all purporting to discriminate between neurotic and normal subjects, and extracted the factor which they had in common. The tests were given to twenty-five pairs each of MZ and DZ twin schoolchildren and to a "criterion" group of children from a child guidance clinic. The score for the factor of neuroticism had a higher correlation between twins than the scores of any of the separate tests. r_{MZ} for factor score was 0·85, and r_{DZ} 0·22; h^2 was 0·82—even higher than h^2 for intelligence. The authors concluded that their factor of neuroticism was a biological reality and not just a statistical artefact, and that it was highly inheritable as a whole.

Two years later, Blewett (1953) repeated the experiment of Eysenck and Prell on a fresh sample of twins, using a largely different set of tests, but these did not intercorrelate in the expected way and no factor of neuroticism could be extracted. However, McLeod (1954) tested the same twins with tests designed to measure extraversion-introversion and found a very large difference between the two kinds of twin in their resemblance in factor score ($r_{MZ} = 0·77$, $r_{DZ} = 0·03$; $h^2 = 0·77$). Eysenck (1956) reanalysed the combined data of Blewett and McLeod and, in addition to factors for intelligence and autonomic function, extracted an extraversion factor which gave a r_{MZ} of + 0·50 and a r_{DZ} of − 0·33; the difference was significant at the 2 per cent level. The very low correlations between DZ twins in the study of McLeod and the negative one in that of Eysenck may possibly be attributable to the small size of the sample.

In 1953 Cattell devised an ingenious experimental design to analyse the contributions of heredity and environment, and of any correlation between them, to the variance of scores on personality tests. This makes use of (a) MZ twins in their own families, (b) siblings in their own families, (c) siblings, each member of a pair in a different family, (d) pairs of unrelated persons brought up in the same family, and (e) unrelated persons in different families. From their scores a series of equations can be solved for heredity and environment, both within and between families. Unlike other statistical methods hitherto proposed, such as Holzinger's h^2, this multivariate design takes into account any correlation between the single variances. Two years later Cattell and his colleagues (1955) reported on the first attempt to apply this design to the scores of schoolchildren on twelve personality factors from his "Junior Personality Quiz." He was, however, unable to obtain a sufficient number of pairs under group (c) above. The results are rather difficult to interpret. However, Tender-mindedness, General Neuroticism and Somatic Anxiety were among those factors found to be determined predominantly by the environment. Cyclothymic factors

and General Intelligence were predominantly determined by heredity.

Although considerable advances have been made in methodology, it cannot yet be claimed that objective tests of personality have given consistent results when applied to problems of heredity.

DEVIATIONS OF PERSONALITY

The relevance that findings based on measured personality factors would have to the genetics of neurosis and psychopathic personality lies, of course, in the widely held view that these conditions consist for the most part of deviations along one or a number of different dimensions of personality. The problem can, however, be approached more directly, though not in such a quantitative way, by investigating along more traditional lines.

Besides the twin studies referred to on pages 323–330, there have been a number of family studies, in which workers have investigated the incidence of all kinds of psychiatric abnormality among the relatives of persons showing some particular deviation of personality: von Baeyer (1935) on the relatives of pathological liars and swindlers, Brown (1942) on the families of anxiety neurotics, hysterics and obsessionals Cohen et al. (1951) on "neurocirculatory asthenia," Edith Rüdin (1953) on obsessional neurotics, and Ljungberg (1957) on conversion hysteria. All of these workers have found an excess of psychiatric abnormality, compared with the general population, among the relatives of these people, but not always of specifically the same kind. Thus von Baeyer found among the relatives of his pathological liars no large absolute number of swindlers of a similar kind, but rather an excess of persons showing similar personality traits, i.e., an excess of extreme extraverts, of cyclothymics, and people with marked hysterical traits. Brown found, among the relatives of the anxiety neurotics, an excess of anxiety neurotics, but also an excess of hysterics and of emotionally unstable people. Such findings as these led Slater and Slater (1944) to postulate not only a multifactorial but also a multi-dimensional genetical basis for the so-called neurotic and psychopathic deviations of personality. The hypothesis enables one to understand, on the basis of a simple working model, such facts as the shading off of the neurotic or psychopathic into the normal, and the clinical finding that most patients show weaknesses or handicaps of personality of more than one kind. The point has been effectively made by Williams (1956) that, if we take the 95 per cent level as the line of demarcation between "normal" and "abnormal," only 60 per cent ($0·95^{10}$) of people would be normal for all of ten characters, and less than 1 per cent for all of a hundred.

There is also a probability that specific genetic

factors may cause a deviation of personality not amounting to illness. Thus among the relatives of schizophrenics there is an excess of persons of schizoid personality, which might be explained if they were heterozygous for the hypothetical schizophrenic gene. A similar phenomenon may hold also in the families of manic-depressives. Personality deviations may also arise from purely environmental causes of many kinds, from birth trauma and organic illness in childhood, to defects in upbringing and conditioning in the widest sense.

Interesting studies of superior personalities and their families have recently been made by Juda (1953) and by Roe (1953). Roe studied sixty-four prominent American-born scientists and compared them with a control group of university faculty members of lesser distinction. As might have been expected, a combination of hereditary and environmental factors appeared to be responsible for the superiority of the *élite* group. Juda's material consisted of two hundred and ninety-four German-speaking men and women of the most outstanding achievement in the arts and sciences during the past three hundred years. Nearly all came from families with other signs of talent, and many were related to one another. The rate of mental abnormality in the relatives was raised by only a small amount; and though the incidence of abnormalities of personality among the subjects themselves was well above average expectations (about 20 per cent), yet one could still say that the great majority of them were healthy and normal. The view that practically all creative workers are psychopathic or insane is shown to be a travesty of the facts. Both Juda and Roe found an excess of first-born among their superior subjects.

PSYCHOSIS

We have already mentioned the hypothesis that a dominant gene with reduced manifestation plays an important part in the causation of *manic-depressive psychosis*. This theory, rather than one of multifactorial inheritance, is favoured by the fact that the tendency to endogenous mood swings seems to have a bimodal distribution. In the families of manic-depressives one rather frequently comes across persons who, though not necessarily psychotic, show marked depressive moods at times, or hypomanic phases, which occur spontaneously and without any clear environmental cause. Other members of the same families show no such tendency, and one can draw usually a fairly clear line between them. The presumption is that in those subject to endogenous mood swings, the temperamental deviation is attributable to the same gene as the psychosis, and that classification as a psychotic depends on the mood swing being long and severe enough to need psychiatric treatment.

Quite distinct, clinically, from the tendency to endogenous mood swings, is the tendency to overreact emotionally to strains and stresses of both a physical and psychological nature. The depression which may result is usually diagnosed as "reactive"; but some psychiatrists do not recognize the distinction between "reactive" and "endogenous."

It is probable that manic-depressive, or cyclothymic, disorders are not the only forms of affective psychosis which may have a hereditary basis. So-called involutional depression is probably a heterogeneous group of illnesses, including some manic-depressives, some schizophrenics, and perhaps also a nuclear group of a specific kind; this latter group would consist of people who fall insidiously ill on the basis of a rigid and obsessional, rather than a cyclothymic, personality. However, the most recent study of the genetics of involutional depression, that of Stenstedt (1959), failed to confirm this association between involutional depression and schizophrenia. While agreeing that involutional depression was aetiologically heterogeneous, environmental factors playing an important role in many cases, the results of his work were to support the older view that in so far as it was genetical it could not be distinguished from manic-depressive disorders. However, the milder (nonpsychotic) cases did not differ aetiologically from severe (psychotic) depressions.

While there is a great deal of evidence from twin and family studies that hereditary factors are of considerable importance in *schizophrenia*, there is still no general agreement on the mode of inheritance. Kallmann (1938, 1946, 1950), who has done more on the subject than anyone else, postulates a recessive gene whose effects are influenced by modifying genes, but a dominant gene with reduced manifestation has its supporters (Böök, 1953; Koller, 1939). There may not be as much difference between these views as might at first appear. Kallmann supposes that there is some degree of manifestation in the heterozygote, e.g., as a schizoid personality; and this would bring the mode of inheritance near to an intermediate type.

In his study of a North Swedish population, Böök calculated that his data could be explained by a gene manifesting itself in all homozygotes and in about one in every five heterozygotes. This hypothesis has been further examined by Slater (1958); and it was shown that the principal data supplied by Kallmann and Elsässer were in conformity with a gene of this intermediate type. At a gene frequency of 0·015, with manifestation in 26 per cent of heterozygotes, the theoretical expectancies of schizophrenia in the sibs of schizophrenics, the children of one schizophrenic, the children of two schizophrenics, and in the children of cousins were, respectively, 0·144, 0·143, 0·396, and

0·008. The corresponding observational findings are 0·142 (Kallmann), 0·164 (Kallmann), 0·392 (Elsässer), and 0·011 (Nixon and Slater). On this basis, some 70 per cent of all persons carrying an adequate genetical predisposition to schizophrenia would not fall ill, leaving therefore a considerable margin for the operation of environmental factors. The fact that schizophrenia is a relatively common disease as well as a biologically malignant one could be accounted for on this theory if there was some degree of heterozygotic advantage.

This is probably not the only genetical model which could be constructed to account for the available data, but it supplies an adequate working hypothesis. Attempts to demonstrate genetical heterogeneity for schizophrenia have not been entirely convincing so far. It seems unlikely that there will be any decisive answer to the problem without advances in other fields, e.g. the biochemical basis of schizophrenia.

Organic States and Epilepsy

Some forms of brain damage, including senile dementia and Huntington's chorea, are due very largely to the genetic constitution, and their psychological consequences depend closely on the extent of the brain damage. Genetical factors also play a part, but a more remote one, in the causation of arteriosclerotic dementia; they enter into the causes of arteriosclerosis, but other factors may determine how far the brain itself is damaged and hence how much psychological change there is. Most brain tumours are non-genetical. The psychological consequences of head injuries are of course primarily accounted for by the site and the amount of damage done; but brain injuries may also precipitate psychoses or bring out latent personality traits in predisposed persons.

One of the consequences of brain injury may be epilepsy, but in most epileptics no plausible external cause can be found. The genetical constitution is quite important in determining how easily a person develops epilepsy. This is probably a graded characteristic. The capacity to respond with a major convulsion to certain stimuli is universal in man, and this fact is made use of in the treatment of depression with E.C.T. But the threshold at which a fit occurs ranges from those who are most resistant down to those who suffer from "idiopathic" epilepsy. All investigations of the relatives of idiopathic epileptics have shown an increased incidence of epilepsy, and the genetical factor has also been demonstrated by twin studies. However, Ounsted (1955) has shown that the incidence of epilepsy in other members of the family is related to the nature of the fits; and the most trivial cases, such as infantile convulsions, often have the heaviest family loading. Ounsted found that 25 per cent of the sibs of the children who had had infantile convulsions had some form of convulsive disorder. When adult epileptics are investigated (e.g., by Alström, 1950), lower rates for the incidence of epilepsy in sibs have been found, usually around 4 per cent.

Studies with the EEG by Lennox (1939) and others indicate that electrical patterns of brain activity have a genetical constitutional basis. Lennox found that there was a high incidence of *cerebral dysrhythmia* in the parents of epileptics, and he postulated that this was connected with the possession of a dominant gene. Epileptics would then be constitutional dysrhythmics, who had suffered in addition some environmentally caused trauma sufficient to bring on epilepsy. However, there is too much individual variation in brain-wave patterns, even when taken under standardized conditions, for dysrhythmia to be a satisfactory unitary concept; and abnormalities of the pattern may also take a great number of different forms. The best measure of instability of brain physiology is obtained by submitting the subject to a graduated increasing dosage of a convulsant drug, given by intravenous injection; the level of dosage at which, first abnormalities in the EEG, and finally a convulsion, occur then becomes the required measure. Individual variation in this respect shows every sign of being a graded character, its genetical basis being then of a probably multifactorial kind.

CONCLUSION

In this chapter we have presented the genetical contribution to the study of abnormal psychology in very largely psychiatric terms. There are of course abundant reasons for this, into which we need not enter. One of them has been the fact that most of the genetical work on psychological abnormalities has been concerned with psychiatric syndromes, rather than with psychological concepts, such as perception, memory, emotion and learning. It is probable that those who are concerned with human genetics in the first place will continue to work along the same lines, for, as must have been seen, there are many pressing unsolved problems. Genetics, however, has another contribution to make, that of providing the framework for primarily psychological investigation, such as is seen in the work of Eysenck and his associates.

We began the chapter by asking in what sense and to what extent can physical heredity be offered as an explanation of psychological abnormality, or rather of various specific kinds of abnormality, for there can be no general answer. From the discussion which followed it can perhaps be seen that genetical studies try to answer three different but related kinds of question: the mode of inheritance (formal genetics), how the genes manifest themselves (developmental genetics), the relative share of heredity and environment (analysis of variance). The importance we attribute to heredity depends on which question we are most interested in, and this in turn depends on the nature of the condition under investigation and the point of view of the inquirer.

The first of these questions will be asked most often of specific non-normally distributed conditions. Ideally, the answer should be given in Mendelian terms, and with some estimate of the frequency and the distribution of the gene in the population. The influence of factors other than the specific gene, both those of a genetical and environmental kind, will appear in reduction of the manifestation rate or variabilities in expression. The greater the variability of expression, the more difficult the analysis becomes; and the lower the manifestation rate, the less important and less useful. Answers will be interesting to to the geneticist, and of relevance to the eugenist.

The second question relates to the mode of inter-action between heredity and environment. The work involved stretches from biochemical investigations on the action of single abnormal genes, over such work as Grüneberg's on embryo rats, to social and psycho-logical studies of twins. The results are of the greatest interest to the practical clinician; they may affect his work, from the theoretical side of the classification of diseases to the purely practical aspect of treatment. Ab-normalities due to single-gene differences will occupy pride of place; but deviations form the norm caused multifactorially will become increasingly accessible.

The third question is one which has dominated psychologists, particularly educational psychologists, in the past, as it has considerable social significance. Its importance, however, will diminish as our capacity to answer the first two questions improves. It has been, and still is, a battleground for debate, not always either dispassionate or sensible. The question is still worth asking about conditions which are graded in degree, can be measured with reasonable reliability and accuracy, and are universally distributed; and the answers obtained may be very important, though only in a limited field. They also suffer from being entirely provisional. As we have already mentioned, they can apply only to a limited population, extrapolation being more than usually dangerous, and they are rendered obsolete at once by any large and general change on either the genetical or environmental side. It is probable that, as our knowledge increases, we shall turn more and more in other directions.

GENERAL REFERENCES

General Genetics

DARLINGTON, C. D. and MATHER, K., *The Elements of Genetics* (London, Allen & Unwin, 1949 (446 pp.)).

DOBZHANSKY, T., *Evolution, Genetics and Man* (New York, John Wiley & Sons, Inc., 1955; London, Chapman & Hall, 1956 (398 pp.)).

GRÜNEBERG, H., *Animal Genetics and Medicine* (London, Hamilton; New York, Hoeber, 1947 (296 pp.)).

MATHER, K., *Biometrical Genetics: the Study of Continuous Variation* (London, Methuen; New York, Dover Publications, 1949 (167 pp.)).

Human Genetics

GEDDA, L., *Studio dei Gemelli* (Rome, Edizioni Orizzonte Medico, 1951 (1381 pp.)).

HARRIS, H., An Introduction to human biochemical Genetics (Cambridge, *Eugenics Laboratory Memoirs*, No. 37, 1953 (96 pp.)).

NEEL, J. V. and SCHULL, W. J., *Human Heredity* (Chicago, Univ. of Chicago Press, 1954 (361 pp.)).

RACE, R. R. and SANGER, RUTH, *Blood Groups in Man* (Oxford, Blackwell, 3rd edition, 1958 (377 pp.)).

ROBERTS, J. A. FRASER, *An Introduction to Medical Genetics* (London, Oxford Univ. Press, 2nd ed. 1959 (259 pp.)).

SORSBY, A. (Ed.) *Clinical Genetics* (London, Butterworth, 1953 (580 pp.)).
    Includes chapters on: the detection of carriers (Neel); polygenic inheritance (Mather); biometric evaluation of findings (Dahlberg); the inheritance of morpho-logical and physiological traits (Tanner); diseases of the nervous system (Pratt); oligophrenia (Böök); psy-chiatry (Slater); the sense organs (Sorsby and Lindenov).

STERN, C., *Principles of Human Genetics* (San Francisco, Freeman, 1950 (617 pp.)).

Psychiatry

MAYER-GROSS, W., SLATER, E. and ROTH, M., *Clinical Psychiatry* (London, Cassell, 1954 (652 pp.)).

PENROSE, L. S., *The Biology of Mental Defect* (London, Sidgwick & Jackson, 1949 (285 pp.) 2nd ed., 1954).

Genetics in Psychiatry and Psychology

(a) Books and Symposia

CONGRÈS INTERNATIONAL DE PSYCHIATRIE, PARIS, 1950. Rapports: VI. *Génétique et Eugénique* (Paris, Hermann, 1950 (192 pp.)).
    Reports on: the genetics of the psychoses (Kallmann); research methods (Penrose); the genetics of oligo-phrenia (Fraser Roberts); the genetical aspects of personality and neurosis (Slater); population studies in psychiatry (Strömgren).

HOOKER, D. and HARE, C. C. (Eds.) *Genetics and the Inheritance of Integrated Neurological and Psychiatric Patterns*, Research Publications, Association for Research in Nervous and Mental Disease, Vol. 33 (Baltimore, Williams & Wilkins; London, Baillière, Tindall & Cox, 1954 (425 pp.)).
    Includes chapters on: the principles of human genetics (David and Snyder); the inherited and acquired com-ponents of behaviour (Anastasi); the development of behaviour patterns (Gesell); the inheritance of intelli-gence (Thompson); personality development of the child (Senn); phenylketonuria (Jervis); epileptic twins (Lennox and Jolly); the familial occurrence of migraine (Goodell *et al.*); the genetics of psychotic behaviour patterns (Kallmann); genetic aspects of adaptability (Glass); the clinical applications of genetics (Neel).

KALLMANN, F. J., *Heredity in Health and Mental Disorder*

(London, Chapman & Hall; New York, Norton, 1953 (315 pp.)).
Based on the 19th Thomas W. Salmon Lectures: contains the most complete and recent account of Kallmann's comparative twin studies.

NATIONAL SOCIETY FOR THE STUDY OF EDUCATION. *Twenty-seventh Yearbook*, 1928. Part I: Nature and Nurture, their influence upon intelligence (460 pp.). Papers on: family resemblance in intelligence (Thorndike and Jones); the intelligence of foster children (Burks; Freeman *et al.*). (Bloomington, Public School Publishing Co.)

NATIONAL SOCIETY FOR THE STUDY OF EDUCATION. *Thirty-ninth Yearbook*, 1940. Intelligence, its Nature and Nurture. Part I: Comparative and critical Exposition (471 pp.). Reviews by: Carmichael, Carter, Cattell, Freeman, Goodenough, Terman, Wellman and others. Part II: Original Studies and Experiments (409 pp.) (Bloomington, Public School Publishing Co.).

Recent Progress in Genetics and its Implications for Psychiatric Theory, *Amer. J. Psychiat.*, **113**, 481–505 (1956). (Papers by: Bentley Glass, Franz Kallmann, H. J. Muller and Linus Pauling).

WOODWORTH, R. S., *Heredity and Environment* (Bulletin 47, Social Science Research Council, New York, 1941 (96 pp.)).

(b) Critical Reviews

COWIE, V. and SLATER, E., Psychiatric genetics, in *Recent Progress in Psychiatry*, Ed. G. W. T. H. Fleming (London, Churchill, 1957 (pp. 1–53)).

SLATER, E., Genetics in psychiatry, *J. Ment. Sci.*, **90**, 17–35 (1944).

SLATER, E., Psychiatric genetics, in *Recent Progress in Psychiatry*, Ed. G. W. T. H. Fleming (London, Churchill, 1950 (pp. 1–25)).

(c) Journals and Monographs

The following genetical journals sometimes contain papers relevant to psychology—

Acta Genetica et Statistica Medica (Basle and New York, Karger).

Acta Genetica Medicae et Gemellologiae (Rome, Instituto Gregorio Mendel).

Acta Psychiatrica et Neurologica Scandinavica (*Supplements*) (Copenhagen, Munksgaard).

American Journal of Human Genetics (Baltimore, American Society of Human Genetics).

Annals of Human Genetics (formerly *Annals of Eugenics*) (London, Cambridge Univ. Press).

Eugenics Quarterly (New York, American Eugenics Society).

Eugenics Review (London, Cassell).

Opera ex Domo Biologiae Hereditariae Humanae Universitatis Hafniensis (Copenhagen, Munksgaard).

REFERENCES

ALLEN, G., Comments on the analysis of twin samples, *Acta genet. med. gemell.*, **4**, 143–160 (1955).

ALLISON, A. C., Notes on sickle-cell polymorphism, *Ann. Hum. Genet.*, **19**, 39–51 (1954).

ALSTRÖM, C. H., A study of epilepsy in its clinical, social and genetic aspects, *Acta psychiat., Kbh.*, Suppl. 63 (1950).

ALSTRÖM, C. H., Heredo-retinopathia congenitalis monohybrida recessiva autosomalis, *Hereditas, Lund*, **43**, 1–178 (1957).

ANASTASI, A., The inherited and acquired components of behaviour, *Res. Publ. Ass. Nerv. Ment. Dis.*, **33**, 67–75 (1954).

BAEYER, W. VON, *Zur Genealogie psychopathischer Schwindler und Lügner. Sammlung psychiatrischer und neurologischer Einzeldarstellungen* (Ed. A. Bostroem and J. Lange), vol. 7. (Leipzig, Thieme, 1935).

BANSE, J., Zum Problem der Erbprognosebestimmung: die Erkrankungsaussichten der Vettern und Basen von Manisch-Depressiven, *Z. ges. Neurol. Psychiat.*, **119**, 576–612 (1929).

BARCLAY, G. and MAXWELL, J., The intelligence of twins, II, *Popul. Stud.*, **4**, 333–344 (1951).

BARNICOTT, N. A., Taste deficiency for phenylthiourea in African negroes and Chinese, *Ann. Eugen.*, **15**, 248–254 (1950).

BEARN, A. G., Genetic and biochemical aspects of Wilson's disease, *Amer. J. Med.*, **15**, 442–449 (1953).

BERTINSHAW, D., LAWLER, S. D., HOLT, H. A., KIRMAN, B. H. and RACE, R. R., The combination of blood groups in a sample of 475 people in a London hospital, *Ann. Eugen.*, **15**, 234–242 (1950).

BICKEL, H., GERRARD, J. and HICKMANS, E. M., Influence of phenylalanine intake on phenylketonuria, *Lancet*, **ii**, 812–813 (1953).

BLAINEY, J. D. and GULLIFORD, R., Phenylalanine-restricted diets in the treatment of phenylketonuria, *Arch. Dis. Childh.*, **31**, 452–466 (1956).

BLEWETT, D. B., An experimental study of the inheritance of neuroticism and intelligence, *Ph.D. Thesis, Univ. of London Lib.* (1953).

BLEWETT, D. B., An experimental study of the inheritance of intelligence, *J. Ment. Sci.*, **100**, 922–933 (1954).

BÖÖK, J. A., A genetic and neuropsychiatric investigation of a North Swedish population. I. Psychoses, *Acta genet.*, **4**, 1–100 (1953).

BÖÖK, J. A., SCHUT, J. W. and REED, S. C., A clinical and genetical study of microcephaly, *Amer. J. Ment. Defic.*, **57**, 637–660 (1953).

BORGSTROEM, C. A., Eine Serie von kriminellen Zwillingen, *Arch. Rass.-u. GesBiol.*, **33**, 334–343 (1939).

BOSSIK, L. J., The roles of heredity and environment in the physiology of childhood, *Proc. Maxim Gorki med.-biol. Res. Inst.*, **3** (1934) (Quoted by Stern, 1950).

BRACKEN, H. VON, Untersuchungen an Zwillingen über die Entwicklung der Selbstständigkeit im Kindersalter, *Arch. ges. Psychol.*, **105**, 217–242 (1939).

BROADHURST, P. L., Emotionality in the rat: a study of its determinants, inheritance and relation to some aspects of motivation, *Ph.D. Thesis, Univ. of London Lib.* (1956).

BRODY, D., Twin resemblances in mechanical ability with reference to the effects of practice on performance, *Child Developm.*, **8**, 207–216 (1937).

BROWN, F. W., Heredity in psychoneuroses, *Proc. Roy. Soc. Med.*, **35**, 785–790 (1942).

BURKS, B. S., The relative influence of nature and nurture

upon mental development. *National Society for the Study of Education*, 27th *Yearbook*, 1928, Part I, 219–318 (Bloomington, Public School Publishing Co.).

BURT, C., Ability and income, *Brit. J. Educ. Psychol.*, **13**, 83–95 (1943).

BURT, C., *Intelligence and Fertility. Occasional Papers on Eugenics*, No. 2 (London, Cassell, 1946).

BURT, C., The meaning and assessment of intelligence, *Eugen. Rev.*, **47**, 81–91 (1955).

CARMENA, M., Ist die persönliche Affektlage oder "Nervösität" eine ererbte Eigenschaft? *Z. ges. Neurol. Psychiat.*, **150**, 434–445 (1934).

CARTER, H. D., Twin similarities in occupational interests, *J. Educ. Psychol.*, **23**, 641–655 (1932).

CARTER, H. D., Twin similarities in personality traits, *J. Genet. Psychol.*, **43**, 312–321 (1933).

CARTER, H. D., Ten years of research on twins. *National Society for the Study of Education*, 39th *Yearbook*, 1940, Part I, 235–255 (Bloomington, Public School Publishing Co.).

CATTELL, R. B., Research designs in psychological genetics with special reference to the multiple variance method, *Amer. J. Hum. Genet.*, **5**, 76–93 (1953).

CATTELL, R. B., BLEWETT, D. B. and BELOFF, J. R., The inheritance of personality: a multiple variance analysis determination of approximate nature-nurture ratios for primary personality factors in Q-data, *Amer. J. Hum. Genet.*, **7**, 122–146 (1955).

CATTELL, R. B. and WILLSON, J. L., Contributions concerning mental inheritance. I. Intelligence, *Brit. J. Educ. Psychol.*, **8**, 129–149 (1938).

COHEN, M. E., BADAL, D. W., KILPATRICK, A., REED, E. W. and WHITE, P. D., The high familial prevalence of neurocirculatory asthenia (anxiety neurosis, effort syndrome), *Amer. J. Hum. Genet.*, **3**, 126–158 (1951).

CONRAD, H. S. and JONES, H. E., A second study of familial resemblance in intelligence; environmental and genetic implications of parent-child and sibling correlations in the total sample. *National Society for the Study of Education*, 39th *Yearbook*, 1940, Part II, 97–141 (Bloomington, Public School Publishing Co.).

CONRAD, K., Erbanlage und Epilepsie, *Z. ges. Neurol. Psychiat.*, **153**, 271–326 (1935).

CRAIKE, W. H. and SLATER, E., *Folie à deux* in uniovular twins reared apart, *Brain*, **68**, 213–221 (1945).

DENCKER, S. J., A twin study in mild organic deterioration. 1st int. Congr. hum. Genet., Part 5, *Acta genet.*, **7**, 434–437 (1957).

EATON, J. W. and WEIL, R. J., *Culture and Mental Disorders* (Glencoe, Free Press, 1955).

EKBLAD, M., A psychiatric and sociological study of a series of Swedish naval conscripts, *Acta psychiat.*, *Kbh.*, Suppl. 49 (1948).

ELSÄSSER, G., *Die Nachkommen geisteskranker Elternpaare* (Stuttgart, Thieme; New York, Grune & Stratton, 1952).

ESSEN-MÖLLER, E., Untersuchungen über die Fruchtbarkeit gewisser Gruppen von Geisteskranken, *Acta psychiat.*, *Kbh.*, Suppl. 8 (1935).

ESSEN-MÖLLER, E., Psychiatrische Untersuchungen an einer Serie von Zwillingen, *Acta psychiat.*, *Kbh.*, Suppl. 23 (1941).

ESSEN-MÖLLER, E., Individual traits and morbidity in a Swedish rural population, *Acta psychiat.*, *Kbh.*, Suppl. 100 (1956).

EYSENCK, H. J., The inheritance of extraversion-introversion, *Acta psychol.*, *Hague*, **12**, 95–110 (1956).

EYSENCK, H. J. and PRELL, D. B., The inheritance of neuroticism, *J. Ment. Sci.*, **97**, 441–465 (1951).

FISHER, R. A., The correlation between relatives on the supposition of Mendelian inheritance, *Trans. Roy. Soc. Edinb.*, **52**, 399–453 (1918).

FÖLLING, A., MOHR, O. L. and RUUD, L., Oligophrenia phenylpyruvica: a recessive syndrome in man, *Skr. norske Vidensk.-Akad.*, *I. Mat.-nat. Kl.*, **13**, 1–44 (1945).

FONSECA, A. F. DA, *Análise heredo-clinica das perturbaçoes afectivas atraves de 60 pares de gémeos* (Oporto, Faculdade de Medicina, 1959).

FRASER, R., *The Incidence of Neurosis among Factory Workers*, *Rep. Industr. Hlth Res. Bd.*, *Lond.*, 90 (1947).

FREEMAN, F. N., HOLZINGER, K. J. and MITCHELL, B. C., The influence of environment on the intelligence, school achievement and conduct of foster children. *National Society for the Study of Education*, 27th *Yearbook*, 1928, Part I, 102–217 (Bloomington, Public School Publishing Co.).

FREMMING, K. H., *Expectation of Mental Infirmity in a sample of the Danish Population. Occasional Papers on Eugenics*, No. 7 (London, Cassell, 1951).

GALTON, F., *Hereditary Genius, an Inquiry into its Laws and Consequences* (London, Macmillan, 1869).

GEDDA, L., *Studio dei Gemelli* (Rome, Edizioni Orizzonte Medico, 1951).

GEDDA, L., BIANCHI, A., and BIANCHI-NERONI, L. La voce dei gemelli. I. Prova di identificazione intrageminale della voce in 104 coppie (58 MZ e 46 DZ), *Acta genet. med. gemell.*, **4**, 121–130 (1955).

GESELL, A. L. and THOMPSON, H., Twins T and C from Infancy to Adolescence: a biogenetic study of individual differences by the method of co-twin control, *Genetic Psychology Monographs*, *No.* 24 (Provincetown, Journal Press, 1941).

GINSBURG, B. and ALLEE, W. C., Some effects of conditioning on social dominance and subordination in inbred strains of mice, *Physiol. Zoöl.*, **15**, 485–506 (1942).

GLASS, H. B., The genetic aspects of adaptability, *Res. Publ. Ass. Nerv. Ment. Dis.*, **33**, 367–377 (1954).

GREBE, H., Sport bei Zwillingen, *Acta genet. med. gemell.*, **4**, 275–295 (1955).

GREBE, H., Sportfamilien, *Acta. genet. med. gemell.*, **5**, 318–326 (1956).

GRÜNEBERG, H., *Animal Genetics and Medicine* (London, Hamilton, 1947).

GUNTHER, M. and PENROSE, L. S., The genetics of epiloia, *J. Genet.*, **31**, 413–430 (1935).

HALDANE, J. B. S., Search for partial sex-linkage in man, *Ann. Eugen.*, **7**, 28–57 (1936).

HALL, C. S., The genetics of behavior, in *Handbook of Experimental Psychology*. Ed. S. S. Stevens, 304–329 (New York, John Wiley & Sons, Inc., 1951).

HALLGREN, B., Specific dyslexia ("congenital wordblindness"): a clinical and genetic study, *Acta psychiat.*, *Kbh.*, Suppl. 65 (1950).

HALLGREN, B., Enuresis, a clinical and genetic study, *Acta psychiat.*, *Kbh.*, Suppl. 114 (1957).

HARRIS, H. and WARREN, F. L., Quantitative studies on the urinary cystine in patients with cystine stone formation and in their relatives, *Ann. Eugen.*, **18**, 125–171 (1953).

HARVALD, B., Heredity in epilepsy, an electroencephalographic study of the relatives of epileptics, *Opera ex Domo Biologiae Hereditariae Humanae Universitatis Hafniensis*, No. 35 (Copenhagen, Munksgaard, 1954).

HERRMAN, L. and HOGBEN, L., The intellectual resemblance of twins, *Proc. Roy. Soc. Edinb.*, **53**, 105–129 (1933).

HERNDON, C. N. and JENNINGS, A., A twin-family study of susceptibility to poliomyelitis, *Amer. J. Hum. Genet.*, **3**, 17–46 (1951).

HOLZINGER, K. J., The relative effect of nature and nurture on twin differences, *J. Educ. Psychol.*, **20**, 241–248 (1929).

HSIA, D. Y., The laboratory detection of heterozygotes, *Amer. J. Hum. Genet.*, **9**, 98–116 (1957).

HSIA, D. Y., DRISCOLL, K. W., TROLL, W. and KNOX, W. E., Detection by phenylalanine tolerance tests of heterozygous carriers of phenylketonuria, *Nature*, **178**, 1,239–1,240 (1956).

HUBBACK, J., The fertility of graduate women, *Eugen. Rev.*, **47**, 107–113 (1955).

HUGHES, E. M., Social significance of Huntington's chorea, *Amer. J. Psychiat.*, **4**, 537–574 (1925).

HUTTON, K., Intelligence quotients and differential fertility, *Eugen. Rev.*, **44**, 205–215 (1953).

JERVIS, G. A., The genetics of phenylpyruvic oligophrenia, *J. Ment. Sci.*, **85**, 719–762 (1939).

JERVIS, G. A., Phenylpyruvic oligophrenia (phenylketonuria), *Res. Publ. Ass. Nerv. Ment. Dis.*, **33**, 259–282 (1954).

JONES, H. E., Perceived differences among twins, *Eugen. Quart.*, **2**, 98–102 (1955).

JOST, H., and SONTAG, L. W., The genetic factor in autonomic nervous system function, *Psychosom. Med.*, **6**, 308–310 (1944).

JUDA, A., Neue psychiatrisch-genealogische Untersuchungen an Hilfsschulzwillingen und ihren Familien: I. Die Zwillingsprobanden und ihre Partner, *Z. ges. Neurol. Psychiat.*, **166**, 365–452 (1939).

JUDA, A., *Höchstbegabung* (Munich, Urban & Schwarzenberg, 1953).

KAIJ, L., Drinking habits in twins, 1st int. Congr. hum. Genet., Part 5, *Acta genet.*, **7**, 437–441 (1957).

KALLMANN, F. J., *The Genetics of Schizophrenia* (New York, Augustin, 1938).

KALLMANN, F. J., The genetic theory of schizophrenia, *Amer. J. Psychiat.*, **103**, 309–322 (1946).

KALLMANN, F. J., The genetics of psychoses: an analysis of 1,232 twin index families. *Congr. int. Psychiat.*, *Rapports:* **6**, 1–27 (Paris, Hermann, 1950).

KALLMANN, F. J., Comparative twin studies on the genetic aspects of male homosexuality, *J. Nerv. Ment. Dis.*, **115**, 283–298 (1952).

KALLMANN, F. J., *Heredity in Health and Mental Disorder* (London, Chapman & Hall; New York, Norton, 1953).

KALLMANN, F. J., FEINGOLD, L. and BONDY, E., Comparative adaptational, social and psychometric data on the life histories of senescent twin pairs, *Amer. J. Hum. Genet.*, **3**, 65–73 (1951).

KALLMANN, F. J. and REISNER, D., Twin studies and genetic variations in resistance to tuberculosis, *J. Hered.*, **34**, 293–301 (1943).

KALLMANN, F. J. and ROTH, B., Genetic aspects of preadolescent schizophrenia, *Amer. J. Psychiat.*, **112**, 599–606 (1956).

KALMUS, H., Tune deafness and its inheritance, 8th. int. Congr. Genet., *Hereditas, Lund*, Suppl. 605 (1949).

KANAEV, I. I., Physiology of the brain in twins, *Character & Pers.*, **6**, 177–187 (1938).

KENT, E., A study of maladjusted twins, *Smith Coll. Stud. Soc. Work*, **19**, 63–77 (1949).

KIRK, R. L. and STENHOUSE, N. S., Ability to smell solutions of potassium cyanide, *Nature*, **171**, 698–699 (1953).

KLEMPERER, J., Zur Belastungsstatistik der Durchschnittsbevölkerung, *Z. ges. Neurol. Psychiat.*, **146**, 277–316 (1933).

KOLLE, K., *Die primäre Verrücktheit* (Leipzig, Thieme, 1931).

KOLLER, S., Über den Erbgang der Schizophrenie, *Z. ges. Neurol. Psychiat.*, **164**, 199–228 (1939).

KRANZ, H., *Lebensschicksale krimineller Zwillinge* (Berlin, J. Springer, 1936).

KRANZ, H., Untersuchungen an Zwillingen in Fürsorgeerziehungsanstalten, *Z. indukt. Abstamm.-u. VererbLehre.*, **73**, 508–512 (1937).

LANGE, J., *Crime as Destiny* (London, Allen & Unwin, 1931).

LANGFELD, H. S., Heredity and experience, *Année psychol.*, **50**, 11–25 (1951).

LASSEN, M. T., Zur Frage der Vererbung sozialer und sittlicher Charakteranlagen, *Arch. Rass.-u. GesBiol.*, **25**, 268–278 (1931).

LEAHY, A. M., *Nature-nurture and Intelligence. Genetic Psychology Monographs*, No. 17 (Provincetown, Journal Press, 1935).

LEESE, S. M., POND, D. A. and SHIELDS, J., A pedigree of Huntington's chorea, *Ann. Eugen.*, **17**, 92–112 (1952).

LEHTOVAARA, A., Psychologische Zwillings untersuchungen, *Ann. Acad. Sci. fenn.B.*, **39**, (1938).

LENNOX, W. G., GIBBS, E. L. and GIBBS, F. A., The inheritance of epilepsy as revealed by the electroencephalogram, *J. Amer. Med. Ass.*, **113**, 1,002–1,003 (1939).

LENNOX, W. G., GIBBS, E. L. and GIBBS, F. A., The brainwave pattern; an hereditary trait, *J. Hered.*, **36**, 233–243 (1945).

LENNOX, W. G. and JOLLY, D. H., Seizures, brain waves and intelligence tests of epileptic twins, *Res. Publ. Ass. Nerv. Ment. Dis.*, **33**, 325–345 (1954).

LEONHARD, K., Atypische endogene Psychosen im Lichte der Familienforschung, *Z. ges. Neurol. Psychiat.*, **149**, 520–562 (1934).

LEWIS, A. J., Fertility and mental illness, *Eugen. Rev.*, **50**, 91–106 (1958).

LEWIS, E. O., *Report on an Investigation into the Incidence of Mental Defect in six Areas*, 1925–1927 (London, H.M.S.O., 1929).

LINDENOV, H., The ear, in *Clinical Genetics*, Ed. A. Sorsby 368–381 (London, Butterworth, 1953).

LJUNGBERG, L., Hysteria: a clinical, prognostic and genetic study, *Acta psychiat., Kbh.*, Suppl. 112 (1957).

LOGAN, R. F. L. and GOLDBERG, E. M., Rising eighteen in

a London suburb: a study of some aspects of the life and health of young men, *Brit. J. Sociol.*, **4**, 323–345 (1953).

LUCHSINGER, R., Die Sprache und Stimme von ein- und zwei-eiigen Zwillingen, *Arch. Klaus-Stift. VererbForsch.*, **15**, 462–523 (1940).

LUNDBORG, H., *Die progressive Myoklonus-Epilepsie* (Uppsala, Almquist & Wiksell, 1903).

LUXENBURGER, H., Demographische und psychiatrische Untersuchungen in der engeren biologischen Familie von Paralytikerehegatten, *Z. ges. Neurol. Psychiat.*, **112**, 331–491 (1928).

LUXENBURGER, H., Vorläufiger Bericht über psychiatrische Serien untersuchungen an Zwillingen, *Z. ges. Neurol. Psychiat.*, **116**, 297–326 (1928).

LUXENBURGER, H., Psychiatrische-neurologische Zwillingspathologie, *Z. ges. Neurol. Psychiat.*, **56**, 145–180 (1930).

LUXENBURGER, H., Das zirkuläre Irresein, in *Handbuch der Erbkrankheiten*, Ed. A. Gütt, Vol. 4 (Leipzig, Thieme, 1942).

McLEOD, H., An experimental study of the inheritance of introversion-extraversion, *Ph.D. Thesis, Univ. of London Lib.* (1954).

McNEMAR, A., Twin resemblances in motor skills, and the effect of practice thereon, *J. Genet. Psychol.*, **42**, 70–99 (1933).

MALAN, M., Zur Erblichkeit der Orientierungsfähigkeit im Raum, *Z. morph. Anthr.*, **39**, 1–23 (1940).

MARDONES, R. J., SEGOVIA, M. N. and HEDERRA, D. A., Heredity of experimental alcohol preference in rats. II. Coefficient of heredity, *Quart. J. Stud. Alc.*, **14**, 1–2 (1953).

MAY, J., Note on the assumptions underlying Holzinger's h^2 statistic, *J. Ment. Sci.*, **97**, 466–467 (1951).

MAYER-GROSS, W., Mental health survey in a rural area, *Eugen. Rev.*, **40**, 140–148 (1948).

MERRIMAN, C., The intellectual resemblance of twins, *Psychol. Monogr.*, **33**, 1–58 (1924).

MINSKI, L. and GUTTMAN, E., Huntington's chorea: a study of 34 families, *J. Ment. Sci.*, **84**, 21–96 (1938).

MIRENOVA, A. N., A comparative evaluation of methods for the development of combinative functions of preschool children: experiments with twin controls, *Proc. Maxim Gorki med.-biol. Res. Inst.*, **3** (1934) (Quoted by Stern, 1950).

MOBERG, S., Mental states and family size among matriculated persons in Sweden, *Popul. Stud.*, **4**, 115–127 (1950).

MULLER, H. J., Our load of mutations, *Amer. J. Hum. Genet.*, **2**, 111–176 (1950).

MULLER, H. J., Genetic principles in human populations, *Amer. J. Psychiat.*, **113**, 481–491 (1956).

MUNRO, T. A., Phenylketonuria. Data on 47 British families, *Ann. Eugen.*, **14**, 60–88 (1947).

NEEL, J. V., The detection of genetic carriers in inherited disease, in *Clinical Genetics*, 27–34, Ed. A. Sorsby, (London, Butterworth, 1953).

NEEL, J. V. and SCHULL, W. J., *Human Heredity* (Chicago, Univ. of Chicago Press, 1954).

NESBIT, J. D., The families of teachers, *Eugen. Rev.*, **47**, 115–116 (1955).

NEWMAN, H. H., FREEMAN, F. N. and HOLZINGER, K. J., *Twins: a Study of Heredity and Environment* (Chicago, Univ. of Chicago Press, 1937).

NIXON, W. L. B., On the diagnosis of twin-pair ovularity and the use of dermatoglyphic data, in *Novant' anni delle Leggi Mendeliane*, Ed. L. Gedda, 235–245 (Rome, Instituto Gregorio Mendel, 1956).

NIXON, W. L. B. and SLATER, E., A second investigation into the children of cousins, *Acta genet.* **7**, 513–532 (1957).

NORRIS, V., *Mental Illness in London, Maudsley Monographs No. 6* (London, Chapman & Hall, 1959).

Observer, The, *A hereditary code* (13th May, 1956).

OUNSTED, C., Genetic and social aspects of the epilepsies of childhood, *Eugen. Rev.*, **47**, 33–49 (1955).

OUTHIT, M. C., A study of the resemblance of parents and children in general intelligence, *Arch. Psychol.*, **149**, 1–60 (1933).

PEARSON, K., On the inheritance of mental disease, *Ann. Eugen.*, **4**, 362–380 (1931).

PEARSON, K. and JAEDERHOLM, G. A., *Mendelism and the Problem of Mental Defect* (London, Dulau, 1914).

PENROSE, L. S., A clinical and genetic study of 1,280 cases of mental defect, *M. R. C. Spec. Rep. Ser. No. 229* (London, H.M.S.O., 1938).

PENROSE, L. S., *The Biology of Mental Defect* (London, Sidgwick & Jackson, 1949, 1954).

PETRI, E., Untersuchungen zur Erbbedingtheit der Menarche, *Z. Morph. Anthr.*, **33**, 43–48 (1934).

PINCUS, G. and WHITE, P., On the inheritance of *diabetes mellitus*. III. Blood sugar values of the relatives of diabetics, *Amer. J. Med. Sci.*, **188**, 782–790 (1934).

PLEYDELL, M. J., Huntington's chorea in Northamptonshire, *Brit. Med. J.*, **ii**, 1,121–1,128 (1954).

PRICE, B., Primary biases in twin studies, *Amer. J. Hum. Genet.*, **2**, 293–352 (1950).

REED, S. C., *Counseling in Medical Genetics* (Philadelphia, Saunders, 1955).

ROBERTS, J. A. FRASER, *An Introduction to Medical Genetics* (London, Oxford Univ. Press, 1959).

ROBERTS, J. A. FRASER, Studies on a child population. V. The resemblance in intelligence between sibs, *Ann. Eugen.*, **10**, 293–312 (1940).

ROBERTS, J. A. FRASER, The genetics of oligophrenia, *Congr. int. Psychiat.*, Rapports **6**, 55–117 (Paris, Hermann, 1950).

ROBERTS, J. A. FRASER, The genetics of mental deficiency, *Eugen. Rev.*, **44**, 71–83 (1952).

ROBERTS, J. A. FRASER, NORMAN, R. M. and GRIFFITHS, R., Studies on a child population. I. Definition of the sample method of ascertainment, and analysis of the results of a group intelligence test, *Ann. Eugen.*, **6**, 319–338 (1935).

ROE, A., *The Making of a Scientist* (Toronto, Dodd Mead, 1953).

ROE, A., BURKS, B. S. and MITTELMANN, B., *Adult Adjustment of Foster-children of Alcoholic and Psychotic Parentage and the Influence of the Foster-home. Memoirs of the Section of Alcohol Studies*, Yale University, *No. 3* (New Haven, *Quart. J. Stud. Alc.*, 1945).

RÖLL, A. and ENTRES, J. L., Zum Problem der Erbprognosebestimmung: die Erkrankungsaussichten der Neffen und Nichten von Manisch-Depressiven, *Z. ges. Neurol. Psychiat.*, **156**, 169–202 (1936).

ROSANOFF, A. J., HANDY, L. M. and PLESSET, I. R., The

etiology of manic-depressive syndromes with special reference to their occurrence in twins, *Amer. J. Psychiat.*, **91**, 225–362 (1935).

ROSANOFF, A. J., HANDY, L. M. and PLESSET, I. R., The etiology of mental deficiency, *Psychol. Monogr.*, **216**, 1–137 (1937).

ROSANOFF, A. J., HANDY, L. M. and PLESSET, I. R., *The Etiology of Child Behavior Difficulties, Juvenile Delinquency and Adult Criminality, with Special Reference to their Occurrence in Twins.* Psychiatric Monographs, No. 1. (Sacramento, Department of Institutions, 1941).

ROSANOFF, A. J., HANDY, L. M., PLESSET, I. R. and BRUSH S., The etiology of so-called schizophrenic psychoses with special reference to their occurrence in twins, *Amer. J. Psychiat.*, **91**, 247–286 (1934).

ROSANOFF, A. J., HANDY, L. M. and ROSANOFF, I. A., Criminality and delinquency in twins, *J. Crim. Law and Criminal*, **24**, 923–934 (1934).

ROSANOFF, A. J., HANDY, L. M. and ROSANOFF, J. A., Etiology of epilepsy with special reference to its occurrence in twins, *Arch. Neurol. Psychiat. Chicago*, **31**, 1,165–1,193 (1934).

ROTH, W. F. and LUTON, F. H., The mental health program in Tennessee, *Amer. J. Psychiat.*, **99**, 662–675 (1943).

RÜDIN, E., Ein Beitrag zur Frage der Zwangskrankheit insbesondere ihrer hereditären Beziehungen, *Arch. Psychiat. Nervenkr.*, **191**, 14–54 (1953).

SANDERS, J., A family with Pick's disease, Proc. 7th internat. Genet. Congr., *Genetics*, Suppl., 254–255 (1941).

SCHULZ, B. and LEONHARD, K., Erbbiologisch-klinische Untersuchungen an insgesamt 99 im Sinne Leonhards typischen beziehungsweise atypischen Schizophrenien, *Z. ges. Neurol. Psychiat.*, **168**, 587–613 (1940).

SCOTTISH COUNCIL FOR RESEARCH IN EDUCATION, *The Trend of Scottish Intelligence*, (London, Univ. of London Press, 1949).

SHIELDS, J., Personality differences and neurotic traits in normal twin schoolchildren, *Eugen. Rev.*, **45**, 213–245 (1954).

SHIELDS, J., Twins brought up apart, *Eugen. Rev.*, **50**, 115–123 (1958).

SHIELDS, J. and SLATER, E., An investigation into the children of cousins, *Acta genet.*, **6**, 60–79 (1956).

SIMONDS, B., Twin research in tuberculosis, *Eugen. Rev.*, **49**, 25–32 (1957).

SJÖGREN, T., Vererbungsmedizinische Untersuchungen über Huntington's Chorea in einer schwedischen Bauernpopulation, *Z. menschl. Vererb.-u. KonstitLehre*, **19**, 131–165 (1935).

SJÖGREN, T., Genetic-statistical and psychiatric investigations of a West Swedish population, *Acta psychiat.*, *Kbh.*, Suppl. 52 (1948).

SJÖGREN, T., SJÖGREN, H. and LINDGREN, A. G. H., *Morbus Alzheimer* and *Morbus Pick*: a genetic, clinical and patho-anatomical Study, *Acta psychiat.*, *Kbh.*, Suppl. 82 (1952).

SKEELS, H. M., Mental development of children in foster homes, *J. Cons. Psychol.*, **2**, 33–43 (1938).

SKEELS, H. M., Some Iowa studies in the mental growth of children in relation to differentials of the environment: a summary. *National Society for the Study of Education*,

39th Yearbook, 1940, Part II, 281–308 (Bloomington, Public School Publishing Co.).

SKEELS, H. M., A study of the effects of differential stimulation on mentally retarded children; a follow-up report, *Amer. J. Ment. Defic.*, **46**, 340–350 (1942).

SKODAK, M., Children in foster homes: a study of mental development, *Univ. Ia Stud. Child Welf.*, **16**, (1) (1939).

SLATER, E., Zur Erbpathologie des manisch-depressiven Irreseins: die Eltern und Kinder von Manisch-Depressiven, *Z. ges. Neurol. Psychiat.*, **163**, 1–47 (1938).

SLATER, E., Psychotic and neurotic illnesses in twins, *M. R. C. Spec. Rep.* Ser. No. 278 (London, H.M.S.O., 1953).

SLATER, E., The monogenic theory of schizophrenia, *Acta genet.*, **8**, 50–56 (1958).

SLATER, E. and SHIELDS, J., Twins in psychological medicine. Paper read to the British Association, reported in: Relation of genetics to population studies, *Nature*, **176**, 532–533 (1955).

SLATER, E. and SLATER, P., A heuristic theory of neurosis, *J. Neurol. Psychiat.*, **7**, 49–55 (1944).

SLATER, E. and WOODSIDE, M., *Patterns of Marriage* (London, Cassell, 1951).

SMITH, S. MAYNARD and PENROSE, L. S., Monozygotic and dizygotic twin diagnosis, *Ann. Hum. Genet.*, **19**, 273–289 (1955).

SNYDER, L. H., The inheritance of taste deficiency in man, *Ohio J. Sci.*, **32**, 436–440 (1932).

SORSBY, A., *Genetics in Ophthalmology* (London, Butterworth, 1951).

SPINDLER, P., Ausdruck und Verhalten erwachsener Zwillinge, *Acta genet. med. gemell.*, **4**, 32–61 (1955).

STENSTEDT, A., A study in manic-depressive psychosis, *Acta psychiat.*, *Kbh.*, Suppl. 79 (1952).

STENSTEDT, A., Involutional melancholia, *Acta psychiat.*, *Kbh.*, Suppl. 127 (1959).

STERN, C., *Principles of Human Genetics* (San Francisco, Freeman, 1950).

STEVENSON, A. C. and CHEESEMAN, E. A., Hereditary deaf mutism, with particular reference to Northern Ireland, *Ann. Hum. Genet.*, **20**, 177–231 (1956).

STRANDSKOV, H. H., Some aspects of the genetics and evolution of man's behavioural characteristics, *Eugen. Quart.*, **2**, 152–161 (1955).

STRÖMGREN, E., Beiträge zur psychiatrischen Erblehre, *Acta psychiat.*, *Kbh.*, Suppl. 19 (1938).

STUMPFL, F., *Die Ursprünge des Verbrechens dargestellt am Lebenslauf von Zwillingen* (Leipzig, Thieme, 1936).

STUMPFL, F., Untersuchungen an psychopathischen Zwillingen, *Z. ges. Neurol. Psychiat.*, **158**, 480–482 (1937).

TALLMAN, G. G., A comparative study of identical and non-identical twins with respect to intelligence resemblances, *National Society for the Study of Education*, *27th Yearbook*, 1928, Part I, 83–86 (Bloomington, Public School Publishing Co.).

TANNER, J. M., Inheritance of morphological and physiological traits, in *Clinical Genetics*, Ed. A. Sorsby, 155–174, (London Butterworth, 1953).

TERMAN, L. M. and ODEN, M. H., *The Gifted Child Grows Up. Genetic Studies of Genius*, Vol. 4. (Stanford Univ. Press; Oxford Univ. Press, 1947).

THOMPSON, W. R., The inheritance and development of intelligence, *Res. Publ. Ass. Nerv. Ment. Dis.*, **33**, 209–231 (1954).

THORNDIKE, E. L., Measurements of twins, *Columbia Univ. Contr. Phil. Psychol. Educ.*, **13**, 1–64 (1905).

THORNDIKE, E. L., The resemblance of siblings in intelligence-test scores, *J. Genet. Psychol.*, **64**, 265–267 (1944).

THURSTONE, L. L., THURSTONE, G. T. and STRANDSKOV, H. H., A psychological study of twins. I. Distribution of absolute twin differences for identical and fraternal twins, *Research Report, No. 4. University of N. Carolina, Psychometric Laboratory* (1953).

TJIO, J. H. and LEVAN, A., The chromosome number in man, *Hereditas, Lund*, **42**, 1–6 (1956).

TROUP, E. A. and LESTER, O. P., The social competence of identical twins, *J. Genet. Psychol.*, **60**, 167–175 (1942).

VANDENBERG, S. G., The hereditary abilities study, *Eugen. Quart.*, **3**, 94–99 (1956).

VERSCHUER, O. VON, Die vererbungsbiologische Zwillings-forschung, *Ergebn. inn. Med. Kinderheilk.*, **31**, 35–120 (1927).

VERSCHUER, O. VON, Erbpsychologische Untersuchungen an Zwillingen, *Z. indukt. Abstamm.-u. VererbLehre.*, **54**, 280–285 (1930).

WHELAN, L., Agressive psychopathy in one of a pair of uniovular twins: a clinical and experimental study, *Brit. J. Delinqu.*, **2**, 1–14 (1951).

WILLIAMS, R. J., *Biochemical Individuality* (New York, John Wiley & Sons, Inc. 1956).

WILLIAMS, R. J., BERRY, L. J. and BEERSTRECHER, E., Individual metabolic patterns, alcoholism, genetotrophic diseases, *Proc. Nat. Acad. Sci., Wash.*, **35**, 265–271 (1949).

WILSON, M. T., Social competence of normal and defective twins, *Amer. J. Orthopsychiat.*, **11**, 300–304 (1941).

WINGFIELD, A. K., *Twins and Orphans* (London, Dent, 1928).

WOODWORTH, R. S., Heredity and Environment, *Bulletin 47, Social Science Research Council, New York*, (1941).

WOOLF, L. I., GRIFFITHS, R. and MONCRIEFF, A. A., Treatment of phenylketonuria with a diet low in phenylalanine, *Brit. Med. J.*, **i**, 57–64 (1955).

CHAPTER 9

Constitutional Factors and Abnormal Behaviour

LINFORD REES

THE study of human constitution has for one of its major objectives the discovery of stable organic correlations (integrated biological relations between the morphological, psychological and pathological characteristics of the individual) and eventually the precise numerical measurement of such correlations (Pearl and Ciocco, 1934).

The term constitution is variously used and most frequently in the limited sense of susceptibility to disease. In this work the term is used in its wider connotation and refers to the sum total of the morphological, psychological and physiological characters of an individual, all being mainly determined by heredity but influenced, in varying degrees, by environmental factors.

Physique lends itself more readily to exact measurement than other constitutional attributes, and provides a convenient starting point for the study of correlations between the various aspects of human constitution.

There is an infinite choice of morphological and other constitutional attributes for the study of human constitution. Attributes which show marked variability between individuals and relative constancy within the individual are more likely to be the most useful and relevant for human constitutional research. The choice of variable will ultimately be determined by practical results, viz. its usefulness, fruitfulness and validity in studying constitutional correlates. The concept of human constitution connotes predominant genetic determination and the relative constancy of constitutional attributes within the individual. Observable and measurable morphological characteristics are conveniently referred to as the morphophenotype. The morphophenotype is the resultant of the interaction of the morphogenotype (i.e. the sum total of the genetically determined morphological characteristics) and environmental influences.

The various aspects of human constitution which may be investigated can be classified into—

1. *Morphological.* Among various morphological characteristics studied in human constitutional research are general bodily configuration (physical type, bodily *habitus*, somatotype); body size; the distribution and relative development of tissue components, e.g. muscle, fat, skeletal and connective tissue; relative development of various physical attributes, e.g. disharmonious growth (dysplasia), the relative development of masculine and feminine characteristics (androgyny, gynandromorphy), etc.

2. *Physiological.* Particularly relevant in constitutional studies are the functional characteristics of the autonomic, central and peripheral nervous systems; cardiovascular and other visceral functions; anabolic-catabolic processes; biochemical characteristics; endocrine balance, etc.

3. *Psychological.* Aspects of human constitution include personality in its manifold aspects, temperament, character, intelligence, perceptive characteristics, psychomotor functions, etc.

4. *Immunological.* This classification includes relationships between various constitutional attributes and disease susceptibility, including physical illnesses, psychiatric and psychosomatic disorders.

The origin of concepts regarding possible relationships between physical and psychological characteristics and predisposition to diseases is rooted in antiquity and the present status of constitutional research can best be considered against the background of its historical development.

Historical Development of Concepts Relating Physical and Psychological Characteristics

The tendency to classify one's fellow beings into types according to physical characteristics is deep-rooted in human nature and has been carried out from ancient times.

Classification into types serves to bring the chaos of manifold individual differences into some degree of order.

The ancient Hindus classified men, according to physical and behavioural characteristics, into types designated the hare, the bull and the horse, and women, into types referred to as the mare, the elephant and the deer.

Physicians of ancient Graeco-Roman medicine described a number of different physical types with alleged specific susceptibility to certain diseases. Other writers attempted to correlate external lineaments of the body with mental and moral qualities.

The tendency to correlate physical and mental attributes can be described historically, in three main fields—

(a) Social-cultural notions of stereotypes, as exemplified by quotations from the literature.

(b) Medical. The attempt to discover correlations between various types of somatic *habitus*, temperament and susceptibility to diseases.

(c) Physiognomy, or the study of man's external lineaments, as a clue to his mental and moral qualities.

POPULAR NOTIONS OF PHYSICAL TYPE CORRELATES

In literature we find popular notions dating from antiquity that persons of certain physical types are associated with characteristic personality, character or degree of intelligence. In Plutarch's *Lives* (Chap. 62, Sect. 5) Julius Caesar exclaims: "I am not much in fear of those fat, sleek fellows but rather of those pale, thin ones." He refers to Anthony and Dolabella as the fat ones and to Brutus and Cassius as the thin ones. Shakespeare refers to relationships between physique and personality in a number of plays, the best example probably being in Caesar's remarks to Anthony (*Julius Caesar*, I, ii, 192)—

> Let me have men about me that are fat;
> Sleek-headed men and such as sleep o' nights.
> Yond' Cassius has a lean and hungry look;
> He thinks too much: such men are dangerous. . . . .
> Would he be fatter! but I fear him not:
> Yet if my name were liable to fear, I do not know the
>   man I should avoid
> So soon as that spare Cassius.

The idea of a relationship between physique and intelligence is expressed in the old Italian proverb *Capo grasso, cervello magro* (Fat heads, lean brains); in an old Greek proverb which states: "A gross belly does not produce a refined mind" and in Shakespeare's *Love's Labour's Lost* (I, i, 26)—

> Fat paunches have lean pates, and dainty bits
> Make rich the ribs but bankrupt quite the wits

The good humoured jollity and physical proportions of Falstaff are well known. Finally, the old English apothegm, "Fat and merry, lean and sad," may be quoted as it describes succinctly the popular notion of association between personality and physique.

Similarly, we can trace the concepts of the relationship between physical and temperamental characteristics right back to the time of the ancient Greek scholars and physicians. It is possible, as described by Ciocco (1936), to trace two parallel lines of development in the study of relationship between physical and mental attributes. The first is concerned with the humoral theories of the early Graeco-Roman writers, and the second is the science of physiognomy, founded by Aristotle.

HUMORAL CONCEPTS OF CONSTITUTION

Physical characteristics played a prominent part in the humoral theories of ancient Graeco-Roman medicine. Hippocrates (460–377 B.C.) thought sound health to be due to an optimum mixture of humours and disease to a disturbance of this relationship.

The humours were four in number, because, according to Empedocles and Pythagoras, there were four primary elements from which all substances were constituted, namely fire, water, earth and air, to which corresponded the four humours, blood, lymph and black and yellow bile. Galen (*c.* A.D. 129–199) gave detailed descriptions of nine temperamental types, which were considered to be determined by various mixtures of the humours. The various temperamental types were characterized by variations in the character of skin, hair, fat, skeleton, muscle, shape of chest, etc. The perfect temperament was characterized by physical symmetry. The Galenic doctrine of temperaments was, in fact, a general theory of disease causation as well as an attempt to explain individual differences in behaviour. Galen's teaching dominated medical thought and practice for many centuries. It was reproduced by Sir Thomas Elyot in 1534 in his book *Castell of Helth*. Stahl (1660–1734), being influenced by the then recent discovery of the circulation of the blood by Harvey, modified Galen's doctrine and attributed temperamental differences to the passage of various humours through channels of varying size. The fourfold classification of temperaments into sanguine, phlegmatic, choleric and melancholic types was reproduced in the eighteenth century, by Thomas Laycock, Professor at Edinburgh.

Parallel to the study of constitution in relation to disease was the study of physiognomy.

DEVELOPMENT OF THE STUDY OF PHYSIOGNOMY

Aristotle (384–322 B.C.) is regarded as the founder of the subject physiognomy, which attempted to justify popular and traditional concepts relating man's external lineaments with his mental and moral qualities. He published his beliefs in a book entitled *Physiognomonica*, in which he stated that the mental character is conditioned by the state of the body.

The study of physiognomy was carried on, as described by Ciocco (1936), in a similar fashion by Polemonis, a Greek writer of the third century A.D., and Adamantius, a Jewish physician of the fourth century A.D.

Della Porta (1536–1615) published a book *De humana physiognomonica*, in which he reported many facial characteristics which were alleged to accompany different moral and intellectual traits. This work is mostly speculation and based on a minimum of observation, as is Lavater's book on physiognomy (1841).

In the late eighteenth and early nineteenth centuries, the study of physiognomy was deflected by the work of Combe, Gall and Spurzheim (1809) into the now discredited science of phrenology, and later in the nineteenth century by the work of Lombroso (1891, 1911), who founded the doctrine of criminal anthropology, which postulated that the criminal as found in prison was an atavistic anomaly presenting morbid physical stigmata.

MODERN DEVELOPMENT OF KNOWLEDGE OF HUMAN CONSTITUTION

No significant progress was made in the study of the relationship between physical constitution, character and susceptibility to disease from the time of Hippocrates and Galen until the late nineteenth century, when Beneke (1878), a pathologist of Marburg, published data on the measurements of various internal organs, and the variations in size associated with age, disease and physical type. He described two main physical types: (1) the scrofulous-phthisical and (2) the rachito-carcinomatous, which roughly correspond to the modern distinction of the narrow and the broad types of body build.

Working round about the same time, was an Italian physician, Di Giovanni (1880) who made an extensive study of the relationship between physical constitution and susceptibility to diseases and who may be regarded as the founder of clinical anthropometry. He, however, went to the extreme of trying to prove that the cause of the special morbidity of an organ resided in its disproportionate development relative to that of other organs. He classified individuals by means of combinations of certain physical characteristics. His first and third combinations corresponded to the modern narrow and broad types. The Italian school of clinical anthropology, founded by Di Giovanni, was continued by Viola (1925 and 1932), who made extensive investigations into physical characteristics of the population of Northern Italy. He concluded that different physical types were due to differences in the relative development of the trunk and limbs. Viola's index has trunk volume (eight measurements) as the denominator and the length of the arm and leg

as the numerator. He recognized three morphological types—

1. the megalosplanchnic, characterized by a preponderance of the vegetative or digestive system, having a large trunk and short limbs;
2. the microsplanchnic, characterized by preponderance of the limbs over the vegetative or digestive system, having a small trunk and long limbs;
3. the normosplanchnic, which is midway between (1) and (2), having the harmonious relationship of trunk and limb.

Other workers of the Italian school included M. Boldrini (1931, 1935), who corroborated Viola's thesis of the fundamental relationship between trunk volume and limb length for discriminating physical types. He demonstrated statistically that chest circumference and stature could be substituted for the trunk volume and limb value of Viola's unwieldy index. Using an index consisting of $\dfrac{\text{circumference}}{\text{stature}}$ he found that brevitypes, corresponding to the megalosplanchnic type, tended to have numerous progeny, whereas longitypes, corresponding to the microsplanchnic type, tended to have a higher age of death and a smaller number of progeny.

Boldrini's system was statistically strong, but anatomically weak, whereas Viola's system was strong anatomically, but weak statistically.

The Work of Kretschmer

The modern revival of interest in the relationship between physical constitution, temperament, personality and psychiatric disorders was greatly stimulated by the work of Ernst Kretschmer, who, in 1921, published his book entitled *Körperbau und Charakter*.

Starting with the study of psychotic and potentially psychotic patients, he described, using a limited number of physical measurements, four main types of physique—

1. the asthenic or leptosomatic type, characterized by deficiency in thickness in all parts of the body. Length tends to preponderate in comparison with breadth and circumferential measurements;
2. the athletic type with a strong development of skeletal and muscular systems. The shoulders are wide, the chest is well developed and the trunk tapers in its lower part;
3. pyknic or pyknosomatic type is characterized by pronounced development of the body cavities and a tendency to increased fat deposition on the trunk. The extremities are short relative to circumferential measurements. The feet and hands tend to be broad and well upholstered with fat;

4. dysplastic group, which includes certain marked dysglandular syndromes.

He studied the distribution of these types in eighty-five manic-depressive patients and one hundred and seventy-five schizophrenics and concluded—

1. that there was a clear biological affinity between the psychic disposition of manic-depressives and the pyknic type of body build;
2. that schizophrenes exhibit, with many varieties of crossing and blending, the characteristic features of a diversity of physical types, the most common of which, are the leptosomatic, asthenic and certain types of dysplasia (viz. certain varieties of eunuchoid, polyglandular obesity, infantilistic and hypoplastic physiques);
3. that there was a weak affinity between schizophrenia and pyknic body build and likewise between manic-depressive psychosis and leptomsomatic, athletic and dysplastic types of body build.

Kretschmer extended his theory from the realm of psychotic types to normal personality types. He traced a gradation of temperamental characteristics from the pathological schizophrenic patient through schizoid psychopathy to the well-adjusted schizothymic personality. Likewise he traced a gradation of characteristics from manic-depressives through cycloid psychopathy, to normal well-adjusted cyclothymic personality. He contended that schizoid psychopaths and schizothymes tend to have leptosomatic, athletic and certain types of dysplastic physique and that cycloid psychopaths and cyclothymes tended to have a pyknic type of physique.

The work of Kretschmer must be accorded due importance, not only because he elucidated relationships between physical types and certain psychotic illnesses, but because of the tremendous amount of research which was stimulated by his theory. The value of his work was limited because of certain methodological difficulties, for example, his description of types was to a large extent based on clinical impression and only to a very limited degree defined by anthropometric measurements and indices. His classification tended to emphasize the existence of physical types as discrete and independent entities, although he does stress that the types described by him should be regarded as focal points around which a number of variations are distributed.

A large number of workers subjected Kretschmer's hypothesis to experimental investigation. Some investigators were unable to support Kretschmer's hypothesis from their findings, others only in part and some were able to give strong support to the theory; these will be discussed more fully later.

Much of the work that followed the publication of Kretschmer's (1921) theory was handicapped because the variations in body build in the normal population had not been ascertained by satisfactory objective inductive methods. Knowledge regarding factors underlying such variations was lacking and indices of body build, which were available, were not based on an inductive approach designed to determine which measurements in fact were likely to discriminate physical types.

Survey of Classifications of Physical Types

A large variety of typological classifications of physique have appeared since Hippocrates delineated the *habitus pthisicus* and the *habitus apoplecticus*.

A list of such classifications is given in Table IX.1.

The basis used for various classifications is diverse, varying from general body shape and other morphological characteristics to theories based on alleged physiological, immunological, dietetic and developmental features.

It is noteworthy that the majority of authors, many unknown to each other, have described more or less corresponding physical types as shown in the respective columns of Table IX.1. Generally a dichotomy of physique is described with contrasting antithetical types in columns 1 and 3, with a third type in some classifications.

The theory of physical types as disparate and mutually exclusive categories of body build has had to be abandoned in the light of more recent research and is now replaced by the concept of a continuous variation in body build (Rees, 1943).

During recent years a number of new techniques have been applied to the study of body build. These include—

1. factorial analysis and other statistical procedures for investigating variations in body build;
2. Sheldon's system of somatotypes;
3. Lindegard's method;
4. miscellaneous techniques such as analysis of tissue components, body disproportions, androgyny, etc.

Factorial Analysis of Human Physique

Until comparatively recently, constitutional research has been severely handicapped by the lack of reliable data concerning the variations in physique in the normal population and a lack of effective and economical description.

The problem was to develop a method which could deal inductively with the observed variations in physical dimensions, and which did not depend on preconceived ideas regarding the nature of the variations of body build and their determinants.

The technique of factorial analysis, which had proved fruitful in the study of intelligence, provided a

TABLE IX.1

TABLE IX.1

COMPARISON OF CLASSIFICATION OF PHYSICAL TYPES

	1	2	3
Hippocrates (460–400 B.C.)	*H. apoplecticus*	—	*H. pthisicus*
Rostan (1828)	Digestive	Muscular	Respiratory-cerebral
Beneke (1876)	Rachitic	Carcinomatous	Scrofulous-phthisical
di Giovanni (1880)	3rd Comb.	2nd Comb.	1st Comb.
Manouvrier (1902)	Brachyskeletal	Mesoskeletal	Macroskeletal
Virenius (1904)	Connective	Muscular	Epithelial
Stiller (1907)	—	Hypertonic	Atonic
Sigaud (1908)	Digestive	Muscular	Respiratory-cerebral
Bean (1912)	Hypo-entomorph	Meso-entomorph	Hyper-entomorph
Bryant (1915)	Herbivorous	Normal	Carnivorous
Mills (1917)	Hypersthenic	Sthenic	Asthenic
Viola (1919)	Macrosplanchnic	Normosplanchnic	Microsplanchnic
Kretschmer (1921)	Pyknic	Athletic	Leptosomatic
Bauer (1924)	Hypersthenic	Sthenic	Asthenic
Aschner (1924)	Broad	Normal	Slender
Bounak (1924)	Euryplastic	—	Stenoplastic
McAuliffe (1925)	Round	—	Flat
Stockard (1925).	Lateral	Intermediate	Linear
Draper (1925)	Gall bladder	—	Ulcer
Weidendreich (1926)	Eurysome	—	Leptosome
Pearl (1926)	Pyknic	Intermediate	Asthenic
Pende (1927)	Macrosplanchnic	Normosplanchnic	Microsplanchnic
Von Rohden (1928)	Endodermic	Mesodermic	Ectodermic
Boldrini	Brachytype	—	Longitype
Wiersma (1933)	Eurysomic	—	Leptosomic
Sheldon (1940)	Endomorph	Mesomorph	Ectomorph
Conrad (1941)	Pyknomorphy	Metromorphy	Leptomorphy
Burt (1947)	Pachysome	—	Leptosome
Martigny (1948)	Entoblastique	Mesoblastique	Ectoblastique
Hammond (1953)	Pachymorph	—	Leptomorph
Hammond (1957)	Eurysome	Mesosome	Leptosome
Rees and Eysenck (1945) and Rees (1950) .	Eurymorph	Mesomorph	Leptomorph
Lindegard (1953)	Fat factor high	Muscle and sturdiness factors high	Length factor high
Parnell (1957)	Fat factor (F) dominant	Muscle factor (M) dominant	Linear factor (L) dominant

relatively objective and inductive method of elucidating the variations in body build and their description in the most economical way.

Factorial analysis is concerned with the resolution of a set of variables in terms of a smaller number of categories or factors. Essentially it is a method which reduces a large number of correlations or covariations between variables to a small number of factors accounting for the correlations or covariations.

Factorial analysis is of particular advantage in the study of human physique as it provides a holistic representation of the human body far more comprehensive than that given by anthropometric measurements alone. Factorial analysis may be applied to the study of physique in two distinct ways, i.e. either applied to traits (anthropometric measurements) or to persons.

The majority of factorial studies on physique deal with traits as these studies provide an inductive method of ascertaining the nature of variations in physique. Factorial analysis of persons instead of traits provides, as indicated by Burt (1943), a method of determining how true an individual is to a particular type. It involves the specification of the type in question by a set of representative measurements expressed in standard measure. The correlation of a given individual with the standard pattern indicates how nearly he approximates to a perfect representative of the type.

The steps undertaken in the factorial analysis of anthropometric measurements are—

1. The calculation of correlations or covariations between all measurements for the entire group giving a matrix of correlations or covariations.

TABLE IX.2

Investigator	Group studied			Factor	
	Age in years	Sex	Composition	I per cent	II per cent
Cohen (1938)	Adults	M	British students	44	24
Cohen (1940)	Adults	M	British psychotics	46	19
Cohen (1941)	Adults	M	Jewish psychotics	35	25
Dearborn and Rothney (1941)	Children	—	American	59	8
Hammond (1942)	Adults	M	Irish	31	9
Burt (1944).	21	M	British students	} 50–60	—
	16	M	American		
Rees and Eysenck (1945)	Adults	M	British soldiers	35	25
Burt (1947) }				55	14
Burt (1949)	12–13	M	British schoolboys	45	13
Burt and Banks (1947) }					
Mullen (1940) (1)	7	F	American	43	5
(2)	9	F	American	41	5
(3)	11	F	American	48	4
(4)	13	F	American	39	9
(5)	15	F	American	32	11
(6)	17	F	American	29	12
Rees (1950)	Adults	F	British	—	—
Hammond (1957)	1	M	British schoolchildren	35	7
	1	F	British schoolchildren	35	5
	2	M	British schoolchildren	40	8
	2	F	British schoolchildren	50	8
	2	M	British schoolchildren	41	7
	3	F	British schoolchildren	50	8
	4	M	British schoolchildren	47	8
	4	F	British schoolchildren	43	8
	5	M	British schoolchildren	41	12
	5	F	British schoolchildren	47	8
	7–11	M	British schoolchildren	57	7
	7–11	F	British schoolchildren	53	9
	0–5	M	Aberdeen children	29	6
	0–5	F	Aberdeen children	43	4

2. Determining the factors underlying the observed correlations or covariations and removing the effect of each factor from the matrix before extracting the next factor; this process is repeated until the residual correlations are not significant statistically.

There are a number of different techniques of factorial analysis but, basically, each is concerned with analysing correlations or covariations in terms of factors which may refer—

1. to all the correlations or covariations in the matrix, i.e. general factors;

2. some of the correlations or covariations only, i.e. group factors;

3. specific or error factors which relate to separate measurements.

In the factorial methods usually employed in Great Britain, the factors extracted are independent or uncorrelated and are designated orthogonal factors.

Some factorial techniques involve rotation of factors in an attempt to get the best descriptions of groups of correlations, thus providing oblique or correlated factors.

The most frequently used factorial procedure is to extract a general factor first and then group factors relating to the shape of the body as a whole or of its constituent parts. Factorial analysis, whichever technique is used, provides a means of classifying body build with the fewest differentia covering the largest number of anthropometric data. The results of factorial analysis of physique also tell us which measurements help to discriminate and measure physical types. These may be combined in the form of a regression equation of weighted measurements, or in the form of suitably constructed ratios as indices of body build.

Factorial analysis was first applied to the study of physique by Spearman (1927); it was later employed by Cyril Burt (1938) and subsequently by Cohen

(1938, 1940, 1941) and Hammond (1942); there are more recent papers by Burt (1947, 1947, 1950, 1950), and by Burt and Banks (1947).

A description will be given of factorial studies of physique in adult men carried out by Rees and Eysenck (1945), and in adult women by Rees (1950) and the findings will be discussed in relation to those of

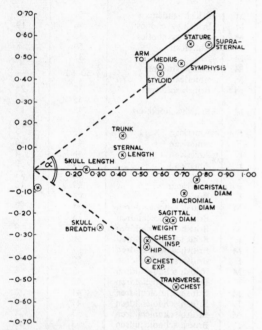

FIG. 9.1. SATURATION OF ANTHROPOMETRIC MEASURE-
MENTS WITH GENERAL AND TYPE FACTORS, MEN

a number of other workers who have employed factorial methods.

Some of the results are shown in Table IX.2 and will be referred to later.

FACTORIAL STUDIES OF PHYSIQUE IN ADULTS

Rees and Eysenck (1945) calculated the inter-correlations of eighteen variables (age and seventeen body measurements) for a group of two hundred soldiers successively admitted to Mill Hill Emergency Hospital. The measurements utilized in the study were taken according to the standardized procedures described by Hrdlicka (1939), Martin (1928) and Wilder (1920), and included stature, suprasternal height, symphysis height, breadth and length of skull, biacromial diameter, transverse chest diameter, sagittal chest diameter, bicristal diameter, trunk length, sternal length, arm length to radial styloid, arm length to tip of medius, chest circumference at inspiration, chest circumference at expiration, hip circumference and weight.

It was found that all the correlation coefficients between physical measurements were positive, indicating the existence of a general factor. A factorial analysis was carried out by Burt's (1940) summation method. Two main factors were extracted. The first factor, which had positive saturations throughout, contributed 34 per cent of the variance. The second factor was bipolar, having positive saturations with length measurements and negative saturations with breadth and circumferential measurements. This was clearly a factor of physical type, differentiating the *linear type* of physique at one extreme preponderating in length measurements in comparison with breadth and circumferential measurements, and a *broad type* at the other extreme, preponderating in breadth, width and circumferential measurements relative to length.

The factor saturations of body measurements are shown diagrammatically in Fig. 9.1.

A similar study was carried out by Rees (1950) on a group of two hundred female members of the Armed Forces suffering from neurosis, successively admitted to Mill Hill Emergency Hospital. The measurements taken in this group included stature, suprasternal height, symphysis height, breadth and length of skull, biacromial diameter, transverse chest diameter, sagittal chest diameter, bicristal diameter, length of sternum, length of arm, chest circumference at full inspiration and full expiration, hip circumference and weight.

Each of the fifteen variables was correlated with the others and the matrix of intercorrelation was analysed by Burt's (1940) summation method. Again it was found that all the measurements were positively correlated, indicating the existence of a general factor. When the effect of the general factor was removed, it was found that the residual coefficients were significant and varied from − 0·33 to + 0·59. The second factor extracted was bipolar having positive saturations for length measurements and negative saturations for breadth, width and circumferential measurements. This factor, as in the male group, accounts for the existence of two antithetical types of bodily architecture, viz. the narrow, linear or leptomorphic type at one extreme and its antithesis, the broad, lateral or eurymorphic type at the other.

The saturations of anthropometric measurements with the general and type factor in women are shown in Fig. 9.2.

These findings derived from factorial analysis of physique in British adult men and women are supported by a large number of other workers using factorial methods in groups of different ages, racial composition and socioeconomic status.

It was strikingly shown by Burt (1947), from an anthropometric study of 30,000 men of the Royal Air

Force, that in almost every age group and nationality the same two main factors emerged. Burt (1938) in his pioneering paper, describing factorial analysis of physical measurements in groups of British children and adults, also elicited a well-marked general factor and factors making for disproportionate growth in length, on the one extreme, and breadth, thickness, girth and weight on the other extreme.

Similar factors have been found from factorial studies on groups of different racial composition, e.g. Cohen (1941), in a group of one hundred Jewish patients in a mental hospital, Hammond (1942) in a group of one hundred adult Irishmen, and Burt (1944) in groups of young British and American men.

Thurston (1946) re-analysed data provided by Hammond (1942) consisting of twelve body measurements in a group of adult Irish males. He considered that there were four primary factors, two of these concerned with size and the other two concerned with length and breadth measurements, viz. (1) head size, (2) bone length, (3) transverse girth dimensions, and (4) a factor considered to be related to the size of the extremities.

The factors elicited from factorial analysis of body measurements will, of course, depend on the number and selection of the original measurements used. For example, Howells (1951) carried out a factorial analysis of physical measurements in one hundred and fifty-three university students. The data included a large number of head and face dimensions. There were three limb measurements and three facial length measurements. Howells elicited factors for limb and facial length and concluded that the factors extracted probably depended more on the measurements chosen than on growth patterns. He elicited, in all, seven factors, which he interpreted as relating to general body size, long bone length, cranial size, brain size, lateral facial cranial development, face length and ear size. These can be grouped into four size factors, two length factors and a breadth factor. Heath (1952) carried out a second order factorial analysis on twenty-nine measurements obtained on 4,128 women, taken in a study for women's clothing size standards. She extracted five first order factors, which were interpreted as length of bones, cancellous bone size, lower body girth, girth of extremities and upper body girth. Second-order factors were closely related to the usual length and breadth factors and the similarity between this solution and that obtained by the results of Rees and Eysenck (1945) and Rees (1950) was pointed out by Eysenck (1953).

Moore and Hsu (1946) carried out a factorial analysis of thirty-one measurements of head and body in a group of psychotic patients and found a general size factor; a factor of leptosomia, shown particularly in the length of hands, face, nose, long bones of the

limbs and stature; a factor of girth, or lateral type of body build, shown in chest, waist measurements and breadth of face; a factor of robustness, shown in forearm circumference, calf circumference and thickness of the neck. These can be grouped into a general

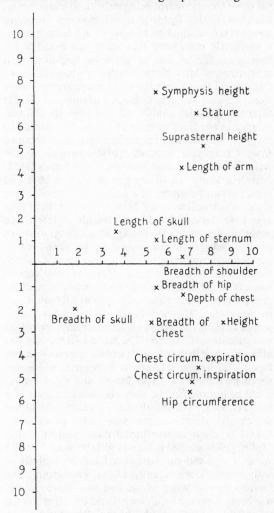

FIG. 9.2. SATURATION OF ANTHROPOMETRIC MEASUREMENTS WITH GENERAL AND TYPE FACTORS IN TWO HUNDRED WOMEN

size factor and a bipolar factor for leptosomia *v.* lateral and circumferential measurements.

FACTORIAL STUDIES OF PHYSIQUE IN CHILDREN AND ADOLESCENTS

The question arises whether the factors of physique elicited in adults are also found during the growth period of childhood and adolescence.

Carter and Krause (1936) analysed data provided

by Bakwen and Bakwen (1929) on neonates. A factorial analysis was carried out on groups of new-born babies, six hundred and eight male and six hundred and nine female. In both groups the results provided strong evidence of a general factor of size, the other factors elicited being difficult to characterize. Marshall (1936) factor-analysed eighteen measurements taken on children ranging in age from birth to 6 years. He considered that there was evidence for four group factors, one of which was identified with subcutaneous fatty tissue roughly corresponding to our general factor, but the other three group factors were difficult to characterize. Hammond (1957) reported factorial studies of physique in children ranging in age from birth to 18 years. In addition to his own data he used, for comparison, data obtained from Carter and Krause's (1936) analysis of the Bakwen's data and that provided from Low's (1952) Aberdeen study. In all age groups both in boys and girls, he found evidence of a general factor and a type factor which differentiated between the growth of long bones on the one hand and breadth of trunk and limbs on the other. He found, in addition, evidence of two subgroups corresponding to limb-breadth development and trunk-breadth development, which were related to some extent. Macloy (1940) carried out a factorial analysis on nineteen measurements on groups of boys and girls ranging in age from infancy to adult life. The first factor extracted was interpreted as being concerned with the development of fat and subcutaneous tissue. The second factor was one of linearity and the third was described as a cross-section type factor having saturations with girth, width and depth measurements. The second and third factors could be regarded as the opposite manifestations of a bipolar factor. The fourth factor extracted could not be clearly identified, but was most prominently related to chest measurements and shoulder width. Mullen (1940) studied groups of girls between 7 and 17 years of age and carried out a factorial analysis of anthropometric measurements in each age group. She found a general factor of size and two group factors, one being concerned with length and the other related to weight, bi-iliac width, bitrochanteric diameter, chest girth, chest width and chest depth.

Rees (1950) found that the results obtained by Mullen (1940) in American girls corresponded closely with the results of his investigation of two hundred adult British women. For example, there was a correlation of + 0·64 between the first factor saturation of the traits in Mullen's groups and Rees's group (Rees, 1950).

Burt (1949) gave further results derived from factorial analysis of four hundred and fifty-seven boys aged 12–13 years. The correlations between physical measurements were first analysed by the method of simple summation and subsequently by the method of subdivided factors. The results of analysis involving subdivided factors indicated that the leptomorphic factor had two subfactors, one for limb length and the other for trunk length, and the pyknic factor had two subfactors, one for transverse measurements and the other for sagittal measurements.

Classification of Physique in Terms of Orthogonal Subdivided Group Factors

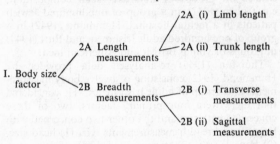

When it is considered that the various factorial studies of physique have differed not only in factorial method but in selection of measurements, and have dealt with groups differing in age, sex and racial status, there is a noteworthy consistency in the results. When marked differences occur in results they may be accounted for by: (1) particular choice of anthropometric measurements (e.g. Howells, 1951), (2) the factorial technique used, or (3) the interpretations of the factors extracted.

It is agreed with Hammond (1957) that the most direct method of analysis is that of extracting a general factor and then bipolar contrasting factors. Group factors need only be invoked if this method proves to be inadequate to express the relations satisfactorily, as for example, when there is evidence of an odd number of groups, or when relationships appear to apply to a small part of the correlation matrix.

Accurate comparison of the results of different workers is only possible if the body measurements are the same. Alternatively the analysis must be confined to those measurements which are common to the respective groups. This requirement would involve re-analysis from the correlation stage and has the twofold disadvantage of being laborious and limiting the data eligible for comparison.

It should be remembered that the factors elicited by factorial analysis are primarily statistical abstractions and further research will be needed to ascertain their relationship to genetic factors and growth processes and to endocrine, metabolic or other biochemical processes.

The importance and possible biological significance of the general and type factors are attested by their discovery at all ages during the growth period and in adult life, in each sex and also in different racial and social-cultural groups. Similar factors have been found in the animal kingdom, e.g. factorial analysis of physique of cows (Tanner and Burt, 1954), rabbits (Tanner and Sawin, 1953), and rats (Watson, 1956). The operation of the general and type factors in human physique is strikingly similar to the differential growth ratios determining body forms in the animal kingdom described by Huxley (1932).

INDICES FOR THE ASSESSMENT OF BODY BUILD DERIVED FROM FACTORIAL STUDIES

The results obtained from factorial analysis permit improvements to be made in the construction of indices for assessing body build. When the type factor has been isolated, it is possible to ascertain which measurements are correlated most highly with it and are therefore the ones most likely to be useful in the discrimination of physical types. There are a number of possible ways in which such information might be used to construct indices of body build. Undoubtedly, the best measure of body type would be given by a regression equation using body measurements as terms, weighted according to their correlation with the type factor. Such indices are, however, complicated, cumbersome and involve tedious calculations, thus limiting their practical usefulness.

Rees and Eysenck (1945) found that two measurements were highly correlated with the type factor, namely stature and transverse chest diameter. These measurements had similar saturations with the size factor and had similar saturations, but of opposite sign, with the type factor. The combination of these measurements in a ratio such as

$$\frac{\text{stature}}{\text{transverse chest diameter}}$$

would be free of the size factor and would tell us the individual's posit on the body-type continuum. In order to have a convenient figure without decimals, and a mean near 100, stature was multiplied by 100 and transverse chest diameter by 6. The Rees-Eysenck body-build index for males is therefore

$$\frac{\text{stature} \times 100}{\text{transverse chest diameter} \times 6}$$

Tables for the ready calculation of the index are provided by Rees and Eysenck (1945) and a nomogram has been devised by Hamilton (1950) to permit ready calculation of the index.

As stature and transverse chest diameter differ with regard to variability, it might be suggested, on statistical grounds, that standard measure (i.e. the measurement expressed in terms of standard deviation

units from the mean) rather than absolute measurements should be used in the index. In order to determine whether this was, in fact, necessary in practice, the index was calculated both in standard and absolute measure on a group of 1,100 soldiers and the correlation was found to be + 0·94. In view of this high correlation, the more convenient use of absolute measurements was considered fully justifiable.

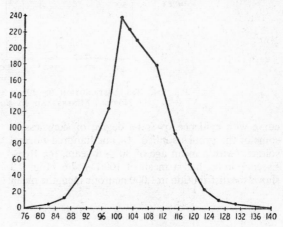

FIG. 9.3. FREQUENCY DISTRIBUTION CURVE OF
STATURE × 100
TRANSVERSE CHEST DIAMETER × 6
INDEX IN A GROUP OF 1,000 SOLDIERS SUFFERING FROM NEUROSIS

In men, the index of body build, derived from factorial analysis was, therefore, extremely simple. In women, however, it was not possible to produce a simple index and a regression equation was calculated. From Fig. 9.2 it will be seen that there are four measurements which show a high correlation with the type factor, namely stature, symphysis height, hip circumference and chest circumference. These four measurements were utilized to form a regression equation as follows—

Index of female body build = + 0·59 stature + 0·47 symphysis height − 0·31 chest circumference − 0·164 hip circumference. The measurements in the regression equation are expressed in standard measure. The pros and cons for ratios and partial regression equations for assessing body build will be considered in greater detail later.

DISTRIBUTION OF THE REES-EYSENCK BODY-BUILD INDEX FOR MALES AND FEMALES

The Rees-Eysenck index of body build for men was calculated for normal groups, neurotic groups and psychotic groups, and it was always found that body build was distributed along a unimodal frequency distribution curve, approximating the normal frequency

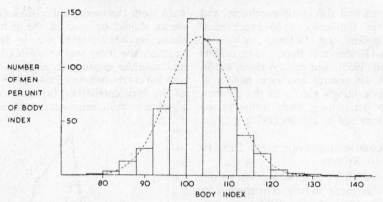

Fig. 9.4. The Distribution of Rees's and Eysenck's Body Index among 2,423
Normal Miners and Ex-miners in the Rhondda Fach

curve with evidence of some degree of skewness in some of the groups studied. In one hundred normal soldiers, with a mean age of 30 ± 6 years, the Rees-Eysenck index had a mean of 100·1 ± 7·6. Fig. 9.3 shows the distribution in 1,000 neurotic men, the mean

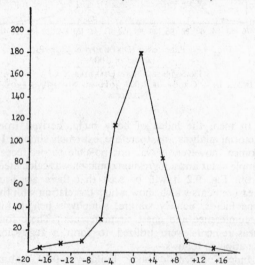

Fig. 9.5. Frequency Distribution Curve of a New Index of Body Build in a Group of Four Hundred Women

being 104·4 ± 7·9. The Rees-Eysenck index has also been calculated on 2,423 normal miners and ex-miners in the Rhonda Fach area of South Wales by members of the Medical Research Council Pneumoconiosis Unit (Fig. 9.4). It was found that the distribution in this group was slightly skewed to the right, showing that very high values of the index were relatively more frequent than very low values. It was found that the deviations from normality, though significant, were not marked.

The index of female body build consisting of the

regression equation, which is a function of stature, symphysis height, chest circumference and hip circumference was calculated for four hundred female Service neurosis patients successively admitted to Mill Hill Emergency Hospital. The mean was found to be + 0·385 and standard deviation ± 3·68. The frequency distribution curve of the index in this group is shown in Fig. 9.5. It will be seen that the distribution of the index of female body build approximates the normal frequency curve with some tendency to positive skewness. We find, as in the male group, a continuous variation in physique from the broad type, with high index values at one extreme, and a narrow type as its antithesis with low index values at the other.

We find, therefore, in both male and female groups a continuous variation in body build from one extreme to another, there being no evidence of bimodality or multimodality indicative of the existence of physical types in the sense of discrete and mutually exclusive categories. The male body-build index and the female body-build index, therefore, measure the position of the individual in the normal distribution curve of body build.

The extremes of the curve only, impress as well marked types. There are no natural dividing points and any demarcation of the curve into physical types, although convenient and at times necessary for purposes of research, will be arbitrary. Rees and Eysenck (1945) and Rees (1950), considered that statistically acceptable arbitrary demarcation points would be one standard deviation above and below the mean, dividing the curve into three classes—

1. Leptomorphs, with small breadth, width and circumferential measurements, relative to length;

2. Eurymorphs, with large circumferential measurements relative to length;

3. Mesomorphs with an intermediate relationship between lateral and linear measurements.

This division of the normal frequency distribution of body build is not intended in any way to convey the impression that these classes are disparate types. These categories of physique are ranges of body build objectively measured by new indices of body build and demarcated by statistical criteria for purposes of description and research.

An Evaluation of Anthropometric Indices in the Assessment of Body Build

Bodily measurements may be taken directly on the body or on standardized photographs or X-rays. From such measurements various indices of body build have been devised with the aim of providing objective methods of assessing physical type. A comprehensive list of such indices is given by Tucker and Lessa (1940).

It appears that, in the past, the construction of many of these indices has been based on an arbitrary selection of measurements which were combined in various ways in the hope that they would differentiate physical types.

Such arbitrary methods have hitherto been unavoidable, since inductively derived criteria for discovering which measurements were likely to be most discriminating in delineating and assessing physical types have, in the past, been lacking. Some indices were based on theories regarding the nature and origin of physical types; for example, the index of Viola, and its modification by Wertheimer and Hesketh (1926) is based on the theory of Viola (1925) that the relative growth of limbs and trunk volume are interdependent, in other words, the longer the limb the smaller the trunk volume, giving a microsplanchnic type; the shorter the limbs, the larger the trunk giving a macrosplanchnic (or megalosplanchnic) type.

A number of indices have been based on Kretschmer's (1921) description of types, using measurements thought to be useful in differentiating his types. Some studies have segregated contrasting types, such as the leptosomatic and pyknic types of Kretschmer, by visual impression. The two groups were then investigated anthropometrically and measurements showing the greatest differences between the groups used to form indices. This method has inherent disadvantages in that it merely provides an objective method of discriminating individuals, subjectively segregated into different physical types and cannot prove either the existence of the nature of physical types in the general population.

This method has been used to the best advantage by Strömgren (1937), who, by the method of least squares, was able to ascertain which measurements in combination most efficiently discriminated the leptosomatic types of physique from the pyknic types of physique. Strömgren's index is a function of stature, transverse chest diameter and sagittal chest diameter

according to the following equation: Strömgren's index $= -0.04$ stature $+ 0.12$ transverse chest diameter $+ 0.156$ sagittal chest diameter. Strömgren called the range $+ 0.15$ to $- 0.15$ the frontier zone and index value outside these were said to denote pyknic and leptosomatic types respectively. He said that the average values for pyknics is $+ 1$ and the average value for leptosomes is $- 1$. These index values imply that the *habitus* of the majority of individuals can be classified into leptosomatic or pyknic types with a narrow frontier range separating the two antithetical types. If we plot the frequency

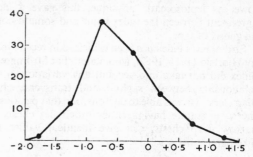

FIG. 9.6. FREQUENCY DISTRIBUTION CURVE OF STRÖMGREN'S INDEX

distribution curve of Strömgren's index for random samples of the normal population, neurotic groups and psychotic groups, as shown by Rees (1943), we find a continuous gradation from one extreme to the other. If physique were naturally divisible into leptosomatic and pyknic types, we would expect the frequency distribution curve to be bimodal, but in fact we find it is invariably unimodal and approximating normal frequency distribution curve (*see* Fig. 9.6).

Rees (1943) compared pyknic, intermediate and leptosomatic physical types assessed by impression with the types delineated by the index values given by Strömgren. The distribution of types assessed by visual impression, in a group of one hundred normal soldiers was pyknic 24 per cent, intermediate 53 per cent, leptosomatic 23 per cent. It is interesting to note that this corresponds closely to the distribution of macrosplanchnic, normosplanchnic and microsplanchnic types found in Northern Italy by Viola (1932). Out of the twenty-four pyknics determined somatoscopically, only nine would be pyknic according to Strömgren's criteria, nine were in the frontier zone and six had leptosomatic values. Forty-five out of the fifty-three individuals somatoscopically assessed as being of intermediate physique were leptosomatic according to Strömgren's criteria, only five were in the frontier zone and three would be called pyknics. There was, however, complete agreement regarding the leptosomatic type. Taking the group as a whole 74 per cent would be assessed as leptosomatic according to Strömgren's criteria, only 14 per cent intermediate and only 12 per cent pyknic. These findings do not necessarily mean that the index is thereby invalidated, but suggest that Strömgren's range of values for different physical types needs revision. Rees (1943) found that if one took the values of the 24th and 77th percentile as the upper and lower limits for the pyknic range and leptosomatic range respectively giving values of − 0·13 and higher as indicating a pyknic physique, values between − 0·133 and − 0·79 indicating intermediate range of physique and values − 0·79 and lower as leptosomatic physique, this gave a close agreement between the index value and somatoscopic diagnosis of type.

Strömgren's index has been criticized in recent years by Hjortsjo (1951, 1952), who stated that Strömgren's index did not take into account any variation in the relationship between sagittal and transverse chest diameters. He was able to demonstrate that persons of the same stature having either broad flat chests or narrow deep chests, can give identical values for Strömgren's indices.

CORRELATION BETWEEN VARIOUS INDICES

Ciocco (1936) pointed out that not only were we ignorant of the principles, which should underly the construction of various indices of body build or of the principles that had been utilized in the construction of indices in the past, but that we did not even know the degree to which they correlated with each other.

Rees (1949) pointed out that the correlation between various body-build indices was not only of intrinsic interest, but, under certain conditions, could provide a method of evaluating these indices. For example, if it were possible to take a number of body-build indices made up from different physical measurements on a random sample of the population and each index correlated with the others, this would provide a matrix of correlations which could be factor-analysed. If a general factor were found it would presumably relate to body type as this is what the indices are supposed to measure. It would then be possible to determine the saturations of the various indices with this general factor, and those indices having the highest saturation with it, should be the most valid ones for discriminating physical types.

This was done by Rees (1949) using thirteen body-build indices in a group of a hundred normal soldiers. Most of the indices were selected from the list given by Tucker and Lessa (1940) and were chosen because they contained the measurements available in the group (see appendix to this chapter). The list, therefore, does not necessarily comprise a representative sample and it will be seen that many of the indices are made up of similar measurements which would tend to result in high intercorrelations. The fact that stature and chest measurements are common to so many indices undoubtedly influences the size of the correlations found and will result in these body indices being highly correlated with the general factor. This method, in this instance, could not be used as a means of validation but only as a means of determining the degree of correlation between various indices.

It was found that the Rees-Eysenck body-build index correlated highly with other indices and had a correlation of 0·76 with the general factor. The following indices also correlated highly with other indices: Brugsch's index, Pignet's index, Wertheimer and Hesketh's index, B. Marburg's index and the ratio $\frac{stature}{sagittal\ chest\ diameter}$. Other indices had a very low correlation and clearly did not measure the same thing.

COMPARISON OF INDICES WITH SOMATOSCOPIC GRADING

Rees (1949) anthroposcopically classified one hundred soldiers into seven grades according to descriptions given by Kretschmer and others. The seven-point scale ranged from the extreme pyknic to extreme leptosomatic type. Various body-build indices were subsequently calculated independently and correlated with the anthroposcopic grading. The Rees-Eysenck index was found to have the highest correlation and had an index of forecasting efficiency of 73 (Rees and Eysenck, 1945).

It was concluded that the Rees-Eysenck index reproduces the subjective rating of the anthropometric worker more faithfully than other indices and therefore provides an objective method which effectively replaces anthroposcopic grading.

THE RELATIVE MERITS OF BODY-BUILD INDICES CONSTRUCTED IN THE FORM OF RATIOS AND REGRESSION EQUATIONS

As we have seen, the data obtained from factorial analysis of anthropometric measurements provide us with relevant information for the selection of measurements likely to be effective in discriminating physical types. The saturations of various anthropometric measurements with the leptomorphic-eurymorphic factor indicate which measurements are likely to be most effective in assessing physical types. The ideal method, undoubtedly, is one which uses all those measurements having a reasonably high saturation with the type factor in the form of a regression equation. To establish a regression equation utilizing a large number of measurements would, as already noted, be of limited practical usefulness in view of the fact that it would be extremely cumbersome and would involve tedious calculations.

Rees (1950) in his factorial analysis of physical constitution in women found that it was not feasible to devise a simple ratio as a body-build index as in the male group studied by Rees and Eysenck (1945), and utilized a regression equation consisting of four measurements having a high saturation with the type factor, namely stature, symphysis height, hip circumference and chest circumference. Burt and Banks (1947) found that a good multiple correlation with physical type could be obtained from stature, leg length, abdominal and shoulder girth and weight, which had a correlation of $+0.95$ with physical type as determined by 9 or more measurements.

Hammond (1953) calculated a series of regression equations for the type factors found in children. He points out that even with four or five measurements regression equations are rather cumbersome, since they require different weights for each age and sex group and possibly also social group to allow for the different means of standard deviations. He suggests, as an alternative simplification, the use of the ratio of measurements indicating opposite type tendencies. Hammond (1953) found that the ratio

$$\frac{\text{height}}{2 \times \text{chest circumference}}$$

had a correlation of 0·66 with the type factor in six-year-old boys and 0·73 in ten-year-old girls, and that it showed considerable constancy during the growth period. Another ratio, which he found useful was $\frac{\text{height}}{\text{hip girth}}$ which had a correlation with type of 0·83 for girls and also a high degree of constancy when calculated three years later.

The available evidence indicates that suitably constructed indices based on the results of factor analysis satisfactorily serve the purpose of providing a simple type assessment and have the great practical advantage of being more easily computed than indices consisting of regression equations.

Sheldon's Method of Classifying Varieties of Physique

Sheldon (1940) took standardized photographs of 4,000 college students. He sorted out these photographs and concluded that there were three main components in physique which he termed endomorphy, mesomorphy and ectomorphy. These terms were applied because it was considered that the three components of body build were derived from the three primary germinal layers, namely the endoderm, mesoderm and the ectoderm. Each individual was rated, by inspection, regarding each component on a 7-point scale, and the individual classified according to his rating in the three components.

Thus a 711 rating would be an extreme endomorph; this type would preponderate in breadth and circumferential dimensions. He has a round head, large, fat abdomen, weak arms with a great deal of fat in the upper arm and thigh but with slender wrists and ankles. He has, relative to his general size, a large liver, spleen, alimentary canal and lungs, and a great deal of subcutaneous fat.

A 171 rating would indicate the extreme in mesomorphy. This somatotype shows bone and muscle development, predominantly, he has a cuboid massive head, broad shoulders and chest, muscular arms and legs, with the distal segments strong in relation to the proximal, having a minimum amount of subcutaneous fat.

A person rated as 117 would be an extreme ectomorph. This somatotype is characterized by linearity having a preponderance of length measurements and a relatively poor development in breadth, width and circumferential measurements. He has a thin face with receding chin, thin narrow chest and abdomen, spindly arms and legs; the development of muscle and fat is small in relation to his size, with a relatively large skin area and nervous system. Sheldon (1940) described eighty-eight somatotypes of which about fifty are common.

Sheldon's method may be regarded as an advance on previous typologies which tended to emphasize physical types as disparate and mutually exclusive categories. The method, essentially, describes human physique as a continuous variation in three components of body build with the somatotype representing an arbitrary demarcation of the person's position in the continuous scale.

Sheldon's (1940) method of classifying physique aroused great interest and has been used in all parts of the world. The method has incurred criticism on the following grounds—

1. *Subjectivity of method.* It is essentially a subjective method based on anthroposcopy of standardized photographs.

Sheldon (1940) tried to provide a more objective assessment of somatotype for the age range 16–21 by a series of seventeen diameters taken from the photograph in relation to the height $\left(\frac{3 \times \text{weight ratio}}{\text{ponderal index}}\right)$. This, however, has not been found satisfactory and nowadays somatotype ratings are made from inspection of standardized photographs aided by reference to ponderal index values, which are now available for ages 16–35 years.

As the rating of components is a subjective procedure there is no certainty of agreement between different observers. It has, however, been demonstrated that the retest reliability of ratings is high with experienced workers. Brouwer (1956) found that ratings did not differ by more than half a unit by the same observer within an interval of some months. He also showed that two experienced observers did not differ on more than half a point in 81 per cent of cases. Tanner (1954) also provided evidence that the correlation between highly trained experienced somatotypers is high but that some differences do occur between observers, and should be taken into account when comparing results from different laboratories.

2. *Somatotype not necessarily constant.* Sheldon's somatotype, by definition, should not change with age, nutritional state, physical activity or training. However, Lasker (1947) found that the somatotype ratings of photographs taken before and after partial starvation are usually unlike. Furthermore Newman (1952) found significant somatotype changes with increase in age in adult men.

3. Sheldon's hypothesis that the three components of physique are derived from the three primary germinal layers has not been established scientifically and, in fact, is not generally accepted.

The validity of the number of primary components is also contested. Humphreys (1957), for example, found that the correlations between endomorphy, mesomorphy and ectomorphy on 4,000 individuals calculated from Sheldon's data provided evidence for the existence of only two independent (but not necessarily valid) types of physique.

Similarly, Howells (1952) found from a factorial analysis of persons (instead of traits) in a group of individuals who were markedly dominant in one of the three components, endomorphy, mesomorphy or ectomorphy, that the three factors or scale arrangements of the persons extracted did not correspond to Sheldon's three components. His results suggest that ectomorphy, and endomorphy are not independent factors, but are opposite manifestations of one underlying factor and basically one continuum. These results are confirmed by a similar investigation carried out by Ekman (1951) which also strongly indicates that two rather than three components are appropriate to account for Sheldon's data, and Sills (1950), who correlated somatotype ratings with a number of measurement ratios, also found that ectomorphy was the opposite of endomorphy, rather than a separate factor.

MODIFICATIONS OF SHELDON'S METHOD

Parnell (1954) pointed out that Sheldon's system had inherent practical disadvantages. Standards of somatotype dominance are subjectively determined; many people object to being photographed in the nude and there are technical difficulties, also, in finding the necessary accommodation for the photographic and other equipment required. He accordingly modified Sheldon's method and proposed in its place a deviation chart profile of physique. The chart gives a standardized scale for height, weight and the ponderal index, for (1) bicondylar measurements of the humerus and femur, (2) for maximal girth of the arm and calf, and (3) for the total of three skinfold measurements of subcutaneous fat. Parnell (1954) claims that the appropriate measurements for a given person recorded on the deviation chart give, at a glance, the main physical characteristics of the person and, with the aid of Sheldon's somatotype-ponderal index tables, a fairly accurate estimate of somatotype. Parnell (1957) further modified his technique and proposed ratings of the following: fat (F), muscularity (M), linearity (L) in place of Sheldon's endomorphy, mesomorphy and ectomorphy. He does not assert that the method is as suitable for somatotyping as photoscopy, but claims, in its favour, consistency and objectivity.

Parnell's (1954) modifications are criticized by Tanner (1954) on methodological and statistical grounds.

Hunt (1952) reports that Professor Hooton and his colleagues have attempted to devise a relatively fixed rating system, applicable to all adult ages and having an advantage of greater objectivity and simplicity than Sheldon's somatotyping technique. The system has three component 7-point scales. The first component is called fat and the second muscularity, both being rated from the inspection of nude photographs in much the same way as endomorphy and mesomorphy are by Sheldon's method. The third component is called attenuation and is derived from a 7-point scale based on the ponderal index $\left(\dfrac{stature}{3\sqrt{weight}} \right)$.

Hunt (1952) reviewing Hooton's approach, concluded that it expressed an unwillingness to dogmatize on the respective roles of heredity and environment, and is rather more operational than Sheldon's.

The existence of a high negative correlation between the first and third components (corresponding to endomorphy and ectomorphy respectively) in Hooton's system again raises the question whether they are opposite aspects of one continuum rather than a separate factor.

It will be noted that there is a marked similarity between Parnell's and Hooton's systems and both appear to acknowledge that one of the fundamental variations in body build appears to be linearity-laterality, corresponding to the leptomorphic-eurymorphic continuum, described by Rees and Eysenck (1945), with muscle and fat as additional factors determining variations in human physique.

Lindegard's Method of Assessing Body Build

Lindegard (1953) studied the variations in human body build, by means of anthropometric measurements, X-ray cephalometry and dynamometry, and concluded that there were four factors mainly responsible. These factors were designated length, sturdiness, muscle, and fat factors. The method operates with continuous variables and involves rating the position of a person in scales for each factor. The factors are assessed as follows—

1. Length factor, from length of radius and length of tibia;
2. Sturdiness factor, from the breadth of the femoral condyle, bimaleolar and bistyloid breadths, distance between the nasion and centre of *sella turcica*, as determined by X-ray cephalometry;
3. Muscle factor, from dynamometric recordings of handgrip and foot press;
4. Fat factor, from body weight and extremital girths.

Lindegard (1953) showed that the length and sturdiness factors were correlated with the morphology of the skeleton in different parts of the body. For example, an individual with a large length factor and an average sturdiness factor, is characterized by long extremities, a broad deep and long trunk, a flattened cranial base form, a high upper face and a long mandible.

An individual with a large sturdiness factor, but average length factor, would have long hands and long feet, a broad chest, large biacromial diameter and bi-iliac breadth, large cranium and large face length.

An individual with a large muscle factor tends to have large extremital girths and high urinary creatinine excretion. A large fat factor is associated with softness and roundness of the body. Lindegard (1953) claimed that these variables express not only the outer configuration of the body, but also its inner structure.

The length, sturdiness and muscle factors are determined directly on the individual. The fat factor is deduced by comparing the weight and extremital girths with the skeletal build and the muscle factor.

Lindegard (1953) plots the four factors on a graph in terms of standard deviation units and he claims that this gives a clear impression of the entire body build of an individual.

He finds that length, sturdiness and muscle factors are interdependent, and he attempts to deal with this by regression techniques giving a relative sturdiness factor and a relative muscle factor. The relative sturdiness factor expresses the skeletal sturdiness in relation to the length factor. The relative muscle factor is expressed by the dynamometric recording in relation to skeletal build as represented by stature.

Lindegard's (1953) method has been criticized because of the possibility that dynamometric recordings may be considerably altered within a short space of time by training and exercise, and may also be influenced by age, disease, etc. The method, however, has the great advantage of being objective.

Comparison of Factorial Types with Sheldon's Somatotypes

The results obtained from factorial analysis of groups which are different not only in age, sex and racial status, but also in selection of anthropometric measurements and technique of analysis used, exhibit a high degree of agreement in the factors elicited, but provide no factors comparable to Sheldon's somatotypes. Even when factorial analysis has been specifically carried out to validate Sheldon's somatotypes, e.g. the analysis of persons by Howells (1952) and Lorr and Field (1954), the results do not support Sheldon's threefold primary components of physique.

The available evidence suggests that endomorphy-ectomorphy is one continuum rather than two separate components.

Tanner (1952) demonstrated that ectomorphy is practically the same as Burt's leptosome factor, and Hammond (1957) considers that the pachysome pole of the type factor approximates to the endomorph. Parnell (1957) compared the Rees-Eysenck index with somatotype in a group of students. He found the highest index values were found in Sheldon's extreme ectomorphs and that Sheldon's ectomorphs and Rees and Eysenck's leptomorphs had much in common. He found that the lowest values of the Rees-Eysenck index were found in ectopenic mesomorphs, i.e. subjects who are low in ectomorphy, but who exhibit mesomorphy rather than endomorphy. Comparison is not really feasible as Parnell's types include assessments of muscle and fat, whereas the Rees-Eysenck index is based on skeletal measurements. Thus the results of factorial analysis do not provide support for Sheldon's threefold component somatotype system.

COMPARISON OF SHELDON'S AND LINDEGARD'S SYSTEMS

Lindegard (1956) compared his classification of physique with that of Hooton's modification of Sheldon's method and the results are given in Table IX.3.

It is noteworthy that here again we find evidence suggesting that ectomorphy-endomorphy is probably a continuum as it has high negative and high positive correlations respectively with the fat factor of Lindegard (1953). The validity of mesomorphy is sometimes questioned and Lindegard found that mesomorphy correlated with muscle but not with the sturdiness factor. This suggests that Sheldon's method is based on the outer configuration of the body rather than on its composition as implied by Sheldon (1940).

Tissue Component Analysis

The assessment of the relative development of tissues such as bone, connective tissue, fat and muscle is a newly developing and promising field of somatology. It is by no means a substitute for other systems or

TABLE IX.3

COMPARISON BETWEEN SHELDON'S (HOOTON'S) COMPONENTS AND LINDEGARD'S FACTORS

Sheldon's system (Hooton's modifications)	Lindegard's (1953) factors			
	Length	Sturdiness	Fat	Muscle
Endomorphy . . . . (Hooton's 1st component)	Low positive insignificant correlation (+ 0·05)	Not related	+ + + + (r = 0·96)	+ (+ 0·20)
Mesomorphy . . . . (Hooton's 2nd component)	Small negative correlation (− 0·19)	Not related	+ + (+ 0·32)	+ + (r + 0·29)
Ectomorphy . . . (Hooton's factor of attenuation)	+ + + (r = 0·21)	Not related	− − − High negative correlation (− 0·8)	− Small negative correlation (− 0·14)

methods of studying body build and could be complementary to factorial studies of physique, Sheldon's (1940) and Lindegard's (1953) systems.

The relative thickness of bone, fat and muscle can be measured by standardized X-rays of the calf (Stuart and Sobel, 1946; Reynolds, 1949; Reynolds and Askawa, 1950). It has been shown that the relative amounts of fat, muscle and bone in the calf are more or less independent of each other. Ectomorphs have the smallest amount of bone, muscle and fat, mesomorphs the largest amount of muscle and bone, and endomorphs the largest amount of fat (Reynolds, 1949; Reynolds and Askawa, 1950).

ASSESSMENT OF FAT

The development of adipose tissue can be assessed by a number of methods, in addition to the above X-ray method.

1. *Measurement of thickness of skinfolds* is described by Cureton (1947), Edwards (1950a and b), Brozek and Keys (1951), Brozek (1953), Tanner and Whitehouse (1955), Parnell (1954a, 1957).

Special calipers are used for this purpose and optimal requirements for such instruments are described by Edwards *et al.* (1955). A caliper designed to meet these requirements has been produced by Tanner and Whitehouse (1955).

Edwards (1950) took repeated skinfold measurements in some fifty different sites and was able to demonstrate that variation in body weight is accompanied by variation in the subcutaneous thickness of skinfolds.

2. *Physico-chemical methods.* McCance and Widdowson (1951) utilized physico-chemical methods for estimating body fat. The total body water was assessed by measuring the dilution of an introduced chemical substance, which is freely diffusible in all the body fluids (e.g. antipyrine) and from this the lean body mass is calculated. This subtracted from the total body weight leaves the weight of fat and bones. The weight of bones can be estimated from the weight of a comparable dry skeleton. This method is complicated and is of doubtful reliability.

3. *Specific gravity method.* Another method involves the calculation of the total amount of fat and water in the body. The amount of fat is directly related to the specific gravity which can be calculated by measuring the body volume by stereoscopic photographs, or by underwater weighing. The total body water content can be estimated by chemical means and it has been found that total body water and total body fat content are inversely proportional to each other.

4. Lindegard (1953) assesses the fat factor by eliminating the influence of bone and muscle tissues on body weight and from the girths of the extremities by partial regression calculations. He finds that the fat factor measured in this way correlated to the extent of + 0·55 with subcutaneous fat as measured by the technique of Reynolds (1950).

Brozek and Keys (1951) using the specific gravity method, found that age and sex factors influenced fat content in the body. Between ages 19–25 years 10 per cent of body weight was fat and between 45 and 55 years fat accounts for 21 per cent of body weight. The mean fat content was found to be about 10 per cent higher in normal females than in normal males of the same age.

THE MUSCLE FACTOR

An assessment of the development of muscular tissue in relationship to other morphological characteristics is included in the typological systems of Sheldon (1940), Parnell (1954, 1957) and Lindegard (1953). If muscular development is to be used for assessing body build and physical type, it is important to know its degree of constancy during a person's life. Muscularity is a factor which, theoretically, is capable of being modified by a number of conditions. Apart from disease, a number of conditions during normal active life may influence muscularity, e.g. the habitual level of physical activity which a person engages in during his occupational or recreational pursuits. Muscularity may also be altered by intensive physical activity over a comparatively short period of time. An attempt was made to assess the effect of habitual physical activity on the muscle factor by Lindegard (1956) in a group of two hundred and eight Swedish men who had left different occupations to enter military service. They were examined soon after entry to military service and subsequently after a period of six months during which time the men had been subjected to ordinary military training. The muscle factor was assessed by dynamometric recordings of the gross muscular strength of certain groups of muscles, viz. handgrip, shoulder thrust and shoulder pull. It was found that the dynamometric values initially recorded on entry for military service were highest in individuals belonging to the heavy or manual worker group, and were lowest in clerical workers. It was found that dynamometric measurements increased on the average by about 3 kg during the observation period of six months. Shoulder thrust and shoulder pull exhibited more variability than handgrip. These findings indicate that dynamometric measurements as an index of the muscular factor show considerable variability during a short space of time, and accordingly are less valid and reliable as measures of constitution. The effect of intense physical activity on a group of healthy men was studied by Tanner (1952). The group consisted of ten healthy men predominantly of mesomorphic physique who underwent a course of physical training by weight lifting over a period. The effect of the weight training on the physique was studied by means of anthropometric measurements and by standardized photographs from which further measurements were taken. These were taken twice before the onset of training, at intervals of three weeks during training and at four months after training had ceased. The largest increase was found in upper arm circumference in which every subject showed a significant increase. All measurements tended to revert to their pre-training values at four months after cessation of training. Tanner (1952) found that there were no significant changes in somatotype rating, but that the effect on regional somatotypes and dysplasia (as defined by Sheldon) was more marked. There were significant increases in strength in various tests ranging from 10 per cent to 80 per cent. Lindegard (1956) found that the muscle factor was positively correlated with the sturdiness factor to the extent + 0·26. This indicates that when the muscle factor is compared with other variables, it should be analysed independently of the sturdiness factor by means of partial correlation calculations. A positive correlation of 0·22 was found between muscle and length factors.

In conclusion, we may state that the muscle component of body build is difficult to measure satisfactorily. In addition to this disadvantage, it has been demonstrated that significant changes can occur with intensive exercise and as a result of habitual level of physical activity.

The available evidence indicates that muscle and fat are capable of showing marked variations in the individual during a comparatively short period of time and are far less constant than skeletal measurements for the study of the physical aspects of human constitution.

The Role of Genetic Factors in Determining Body Build

Body size, body shape, as well as many other morphological attributes such as the relative development of different organs and tissues, are a function of growth rates which in turn are largely determined by genes. Environmental factors, particularly nutrition and disease can modify, to some extent, these genetically determined characteristics, particularly if they occur during the growth period.

An assessment of the relative importance of genetic and environmental factors in determining various bodily dimensions can be made from the results of twin studies. Dalberg (1926) compared the variability of anthropometric measurements in identical and non-identical twins. The results showed that heredity accounted for 90 per cent of the variability of body length measurements and slightly less for the variability of body breadth, head and face dimensions. This finding is also supported by the results of Newman, Freeman and Holtzinger (1937), derived from a study of nineteen identical twins brought up apart from infancy. Newman et al. (1937), also found that there were no significant differences in height, weight, head length and head breadth in identical twins from a group of fifty pairs brought up together in the same environment.

The majority of bodily dimensions and the variations in body size and body shape have normal frequency distributions. This is in keeping with the hypothesis of multifactorial inheritance of these attributes. Davenport (1923) who classified individuals according to degree of linearity of body build for comparing physical type in parents and offsprings, produced results which also supported the view that multiple genetic factors are responsible for the inheritance of physical type. Palmer (1934) put forward evidence that the genes controlling the rate of physical growth are, to a large extent, independent in action from those controlling the final size achieved. It has also been shown that in animals general body size is largely determined by genetic factors. That this is true of mammals was shown by Castle (1922, 1941) and of birds by Walters (1931). It is interesting to note in this connexion that Gregory and Castle (1931) demonstrated that large and small races of rabbits exist which, as early as thirty hours after fertilization, show a difference in the number of blastomeres.

There is a great deal to be learnt about the genetics of the factors underlying body size, body shape and the relative development of different parts and tissues of the body, and this is a field which urgently merits the serious attention of genetic research workers.

The Relationship between Physical Type and Growth Processes

D'Arcy Thompson (1942) pointed out that the form of an organism is a function of growth, whose rate varies in different directions and must be regarded as an event in space-time and not merely a configuration in space.

Studies of growth in the human being and in animals have considerably elucidated the nature of the factors underlying the variations in human physique and promise to be a fruitful field for future research. Studies of growth in the human are of two main kinds—

1. Longitudinal studies which deal with the changes in an individual over a period of time. A number of longitudinal studies on growth and development during childhood, adolescence and later, are now in progress in various parts of the world, and the results should provide invaluable information for the science of somatology. A review of these projects is given by Garn (1957).

2. Cross-sectional studies which deal with individual differences at different ages. Most of the published work on growth utilizes this method.

In so far as the form of the human being is determined by the rate of growth in various directions, it is of fundamental importance to know how and when the types of physique found in the adult are determined. There is evidence that there are not only changes in growth resulting in increase in size of the body but also changes in differential growth, giving rise to changes in bodily configuration. D'Arcy Thompson (1942) from study of growth curves of weight and stature found differences corresponding to changes in the shape of the child as he grows. He states that the infant stores fat and the active child runs it off again. Between 4 and 5 years the increase of weight is at a minimum, but a fresh start is then made and the small schoolboy grows stout and strong. There is evidence

according to Tanner (1947a) of an increase in the rate of growth between $5\frac{1}{2}$ to $7\frac{1}{2}$ years, which has been referred to as the midgrowth spurt, and that the changes which appear to be mainly concerned with the midgrowth spurt are lateral dimensions. A person who exhibits a large midgrowth spurt and a small adolescent spurt will end up different in bodily form from a previously similar individual who had had a large adolescent but a small midgrowth spurt. The nature and significance of the midgrowth spurt is still *sub judice*, and it will probably be necessary to await the results of longitudinal studies of individuals from birth to adult life before its significance can be determined. The available evidence, however, indicates that all leptomorphic-eurymorphic differences found in adults cannot be attributed to differences between midgrowth and adolescent spurts.

Tanner *et al.* (1956) carried out an interesting study on a group of individuals who had been measured anthropometrically between 1925 and 1932 by the late Professor Alexander Low. Low (1952) measured a series of sixty-five boys and fifty-nine girls at birth and at subsequent birthdays up to and including age 5. Tanner and co-workers (1956) re-measured and somatotyped as adults aged 25 to 30 years, about two-thirds of the group. They found that the correlation of birth measurements with later measurements was much lower than the intercorrelation of later measurements between themselves. It was evident that the size of the new-born babe was only very slightly related to the size of the adult or even to the size of the two-year-old. They found evidence that the inherent growth characteristics of the child asserted themselves after birth, and the correlation between the childhood measurements and adult measurements rose sharply. They concluded that it was possible to predict adult size as reliably at the age of 3 years as it was at the age of 4 or 5 years.

Carter and Krause (1936) analysing the data of Bakwin and Bakwin (1929) on neonates, found evidence of a general factor and of a well-marked bipolar leptomorphic-eurymorphic factor, which accounted for 10 per cent or more of the variance. Bailey and Davis (1935) in a study of growth during the first three years of life also found evidence of a general growth factor which retarded rapidly at first then more slowly throughout the thirty-six months. They found that disproportionate growth rates occurred at certain periods, and corresponded to changes in body build. They found that lateral growth, giving rise to chubbiness, increased rapidly during the first eleven months, with a more gradual increase of longitudinal growth up to this age.

Mullen (1940) carried out a factorial analysis of anthropometric measurements in groups of girls, ranging in age from 7 to 17 years, and found in all age groups a general factor and two group factors corresponding to the bipolar leptomorphic-eurymorphic factor of Rees and Eysenck (1945). Similarly Macloy (1940) in a study of groups of boys and girls at various ages from birth to puberty, found evidence of a general factor as well as a type factor. Hammond (1957) carried out a factorial analysis of anthropometric data for individuals covering the period from birth to the age of 5. He included a group of infants from Leeds, data from Aberdeen, the infants collected by Professor Low referred to above, and also Carter and Krause's (1936) analysis of infants' measurements. He found that the evidence indicated length, girth and breadth types similar to those found in later life, and was uniform throughout the age range. He found that the type consistency was low in infancy and increased throughout the school ages. Hammond (1953) reported results of studies of groups of English children ranging in age from 5 to 18 years and consisting of groups differing in socio-economic status, comprising 1,430 private school children and 1,537 free school children. Measurements were repeated after three years in the children still attending the schools. He found in all groups a body size and a type factor indicating a pachysome-leptosome dichotomy corresponding to the leptomorphic-eurymorphic dichotomy of Rees and Eysenck (1945). He also found that the constancy of individual type values over periods of two or three years, as shown by the correlation between the first and second measurements, ranged from 0·65 to 0·92 for the different age, sex and racial groups, but the correlation tended to be lower about the time of puberty. He found that 11 per cent of the boys up to the age of 13 had changed their type, and up to the age of 14 this figure was 18 per cent. Among the girls, 8 per cent of those who had reached the age of 9 and 22 per cent of those who had reached age 10 to 13 years were found to have changed their physical type and after 14 years the figure fell to 12 per cent. He found the ratios $\dfrac{\text{height}}{\text{chest circumference}}$ and $\dfrac{\text{height}}{\text{hip girth}}$ were useful in the assessment of physical type and changed very little with age.

The available evidence suggests that the two main factors isolated by Rees and Eysenck (1945), and by Burt (1937 and his followers, occur in all age groups in both sexes.

The evidence also strongly indicates that physical type in a large proportion of individuals tends to remain relatively constant, as shown by the work of Hammond (1953, 1957).

Sex Differences in Body Build

A number of investigations have recently been devoted to the study of the differences in various morphological characteristics between males and females. These studies have utilized different methods, including—

1. anthropometric measurements treated by statistical techniques, such as factorial analysis and discriminant functions;
2. comparison of the distribution of physical types;
3. comparison of the distribution of the relative amounts of various tissue components, such as fat, muscle, bone, etc.;
4. anthroposcopy, including general appearance, contours of the body and ratings of specific features.

Anthropometric Differences and Differential Growth Rates between Sexes

Rees (1950) carried out a factorial analysis of anthropometric measurements on two hundred adult females and compared this anthropometric data with that of two hundred neurotic soldiers and one hundred normal soldiers of similar age distribution. It was found that the male groups exceeded the female group in all measurements except hip circumference. Females, however, were found to have a longer trunk relative to stature. There was considerable overlapping in all measurements. The variations in body build were found to be determined, as already indicated, by a general factor of body size and a type factor. In the female group, the anthropometric measurements having the highest correlation with the type factor were symphysis height, stature, chest circumference and hip circumference, whereas in the male group stature and transverse chest diameter had the highest saturations with the type factor.

Tanner (1951) used the statistical method of discriminant functions to ascertain the best possible discrimination between males and females with regard to biacromial diameter and bi-iliac diameter. He found that the best index for discriminating the sexes was 3 × biacromial diameter − bi-iliac diameter − 82. He found that this only misclassified 6 per cent of males and 20 per cent of females.

Lindegard (1953) compared a group of adult men and women anthropometrically. He found that the males were significantly greater in the mean value of the majority of measurements than the female group. Differences between the sexes were smallest regarding two measures of pelvic breadth, namely the bi-iliac and interspinous breadth. Tanner (1955) reports that the chief differences in body shape between men and women are that men have, on the average, broader shoulders, narrower hips and longer upper and lower extremities than women, which is in contradistinction to the findings of Lindegard (1953).

The differences found in physique between adult men and women can be explained by sex differentials in growth and growth rates. Thompson (1946) reviewing the relevant literature, concluded that boys exceed girls in mean weight until 11 years, and that from 11 to 14 years girls exceed boys and by 15 to 16 years superiority is regained by boys. By 20 years the mean weight of males exceeds that of females by 20 per cent. Girls, although smaller physically, tend to be more mature than boys in development, as shown by the earlier puberty and by the earlier pre-adolescent growth spurt. In males from puberty to maturity the growth in trunk and limbs is at first equal, then there follows a period of rapid trunk growth, circumferential growth continuing longer than growth in length. In females from puberty to maturity, the trunk elongates in the lumbar region and the pelvis enlarges, whilst the lower extremities cease to grow in proportion to the trunk. Tanner (1955) confirms that girls gain a temporary lead when their adolescent growth spurt starts and, for a time, are larger in all dimensions than boys. This lasts for the period 11 to 13 years, and then the boys' adolescent growth spurt starts and continues with greater intensity. Tanner (1947a) pointed out that the major relative growth velocity during the adolescent spurt is, of the hips in girls, and of the shoulders in boys.

Differences in physique have been observed between those who mature early and those who mature late. Baldwin (1921) found that boys and girls who were tall before puberty begin adolescence earlier than those who are short. Tanner (1955) demonstrated that somatotypes are related to the age of maturity. He found, for example, that ectomorphy increases steadily from a rating of 3·4 in the earliest maturers, to a rating of 4 in the latest maturers. Mesomorphy had the highest rating in the earliest maturers, whereas endomorphy showed no consistent trend at all. Barker and Stone (1936) and Worrell (1939) found that pyknic girls have the menarche eight months earlier than leptosomatic girls. Tanner (1955) states that early maturers, especially boys, are likely to be high in mesomorphy and low in ectomorphy. In girls early maturers may be somewhat high in endomorphy, but he states that these conclusions are tentative and that further data are required before definite conclusions can be reached.

SEX DIFFERENCES IN DISTRIBUTION OF PHYSICAL TYPES AND IN TISSUE COMPONENT ANALYSIS

The study of body types has, in the past, received far less attention in women than in men. Kretschmer (1921) pointed out that the types of physique described by him were less easily diagnosed in women, and Sheldon (1940) pays comparatively little attention to somatotypes in women. Sheldon, Dupertuis and McDermott (1954) discuss the sex factor in somatotypes and state that women are much more endo-

morphic than men and that all ages are heavier in proportion to stature. The mean $\dfrac{\text{height}}{3\sqrt{\text{weight}}}$ index for 4,000 college men was 13·19 and for 4,000 college women was 12·84, and the distribution of somatotypes in women was markedly different from that in men.

A comparison of the distribution in tissue components in males and females was carried out by Reynolds (1949) who utilized X-ray photographs of the calf and confirmed that females have on the average greater thickness of subcutaneous fat than men. Reynolds and Askawa (1950), claimed that the sex of a person X-rayed can be told with 90 per cent success from the relative amounts of fat and bone in the calf. Edwards (1950b) using skinfold calipers, found that skinfolds were one and a half times as thick in women as in men, and that this was due to subcutaneous fat.

Anthroposcopic Differences

Draper, Dupertuis and Caughey (1944) give descriptions of impressionistically determined morphological differences between males and females. They emphasize such features as the carrying angle of the upper extremity, the relative dimensions of pelvic and shoulder breadth, the characteristic outline of the space between the lower extremities when the heels are approximated, the silhouette of the outer part of the calf, the slope of the shoulders and the outward curve of the hip and thigh, all of which tend to show characteristic differences between males and females.

Androgyny (Gynandromorphy)

The terms androgyny and gynandromorphy refer to the degree of femininity of body build in the male and the degree of masculinity in body build of the female.

The study of androgyny and various other constitutional attributes has been the subject of a number of investigations recently. Androgyny has been assessed by two distinct methods—

1. Subjective procedures consisting of assessment of general appearance and ratings of special features. This method was used by Sheldon (1940), Seltzer (1945), Bailey and Bayer (1946), Draper, Dupertuis and Caughey (1944) and Parnell (1954).

2. Objective, anthropometric methods, as used by Tanner (1951).

Tanner (1955) considers that androgyny, in contrast to somatotype, is determined by events taking place at adolescence. Relationships between androgyny and various other attributes have recently been studied. Parnell (1954) studied the relationship between the relative incidence of masculine and feminine physical traits and academic and athletic performance. He found that academic distinction was associated with a significant trend towards a greater degree of feminine traits and that athletes, as would be expected, showed a higher incidence of strong masculine traits.

Lindegard and co-workers (1956) correlated various traits of masculinity with Sjobring's personality variables and with various endocrine functions, but found no significant relationships. Seltzer and Brouha (1943) found that a superior degree of physical fitness could only be achieved by persons with a strong masculine component in their body build, and that individuals having physiques weak in masculinity, tended to have poor effort tolerance. In a recent study by Coppen (1957), using Tanner's index in a study of toxaemia in pregnancy, it was found that patients who developed toxaemia had a higher incidence of masculine features in body build than those who did not develop toxaemia.

Dysplasia in Physique

Dysplasia is the term applied to the disharmonious development of one or more parts of the body and is assessed by the extent to which one part of the body fails to harmonize with another. The term is used differently by various workers who use different methods and criteria when they are making assessment.

Kretschmer (1921) described a number of dysplastic types of physique which he considered were due to glandular disturbances. He assessed these types anthroposcopically and considered that they had a biological affinity to schizophrenia.

Viola (1932) attempted to make a statistical assessment of dysplasia by finding the total of the percentage deviation of various bodily measurements from the average.

Sheldon (1940) uses the term dysplasia to denote the degree with which somatotype ratings for different parts of the body fail to agree with each other. Sheldon (1940) assesses dysplasia anthroposcopically and there are no objective methods available. The assessment of Sheldon's dysplasia is a complex task and probably can only be done with accuracy when the dysplasia is gross.

Howells (1952) from his factorial study of Sheldon's somatotypes, found that the results only supported the existence of two main components (or factors) underlying physique, and that therefore the whole concept of dysplasia, as expressed by Sheldon (1940), needed revision.

The causes of dysplasia are not known. The questions, whether genetic factors are the main determinants of the disharmonious growth of different parts of the body or whether disturbances interfering with the growth of certain parts of the body during the developmental period are predominantly responsible,

cannot be answered at present and must await further research.

Constancy of Body Type in Adult Life

The question of the degree of constancy of body type during adult life is of fundamental importance in studies on human constitution. Little research work has been carried out on the changes in physical dimensions and proportions during adult life and published results differ widely. Brugsch (1918) found that narrow-chested types developed into normal-chested types in one-third of all cases, between the age of 25 and 35 years, and that some normal-chested individuals can change with increasing age, to the wide-chested type.

Mills (1917), however, found in a study of 1,000 persons that no individual changed from one major class to another with increasing age, and that the only changes were in subtypes. Similarly Viola (1932) maintained that the types of *habitus* described by him, viz. the longitype and the brachytype, were not altered by age.

Bauer (1926), using Sigaud's (1914) classification of types, found that the broad type (the digestive type) occurred more frequently among subjects of advancing age.

The ideal method of investigating the effect of age on body type would be to carry out anthropometric investigations in a random sample of the normal population at regular intervals throughout infancy, childhood, adolescence, maturity and senescence. Results from such studies are not yet available. Another method which is available, but which must be regarded as second best, is to make a cross-sectional study of a random sample of adults of different ages.

Rees and Eysenck (1945) carried out a factorial analysis of seventeen anthropometric measurements in a series of two hundred soldiers. The age ranged from 19–55 years, with a mean of 34 years and standard deviation of 5·89. The Pearson product moment correlation coefficients between age and seventeen absolute physical measurements are shown in a table from which it will be seen that most of the traits show a negative correlation with age, indicating a slight tendency for individuals of the old-age groups to be smaller in these measurements. Chest and hip circumference, trunk and sternal length, show low positive correlations indicating a slight tendency for the older individuals to be larger in these measurements. The only correlations which are statistically significant are trunk, sternal length and sagittal chest diameter. The statistical significance is of a low order, the odds against the correlation being due to chance, being about 20:1.

Four body-build indices (*see* appendix to this

chapter for formulae) were calculated for the group and correlated with age—

1. The Morphological index
2. The Pignet index
3. Strömgren index
4. Brugsch's index.

The Morphological index showed the highest correlation, viz. − 0·245. Brugsch's index was next with a correlation coefficient of + 0·141. The correlation for Pignet index was − 0·098, and the Strömgren index + 0·097. All the correlations suggest a slight tendency for older individuals to be more broad in build. The correlation coefficient of the Morphological index is statistically significant at the 1 per cent level and Brugsch's index at the 5 per cent level.

Age was found to have a saturation of − 0·236 with the type factor, indicating a tendency for older members of the group to have relatively greater breadth, width and circumferential dimensions in contrast to length. The results obtained by Newman (1952) who studied the problem of stability in body build by examining a series of 40,000 individuals photographed by the U.S. Army and typed at Harvard University according to Hooton's modification of Sheldon's method are in conformity with these findings. The age range varied from 18–35 years. It was found that definite, although limited, changes associated with age occur in this group. The first and second components, corresponding with endomorphy and mesomorphy increased with age, while the third component corresponding to ectomorphy, decreased. The correlation between the first and second components, and the first and third components, increased with age, but the second and third components retained the same magnitude of association.

Lasker (1953) in a study of adult Mexican males, and Hooton and Dupertuis (1951) in a series of 10,000 Irish males, found that stature and sitting height reach a maximum in the thirties, and decline thereafter. Hooton and Dupertuis (1951) found a tendency for chest measurements to increase throughout adult life. These findings conform with our results. Increase in head measurements has also been reported by these workers and also by Buchi (1950) in a study of one hundred and ninety-six Swiss adults who were re-examined after an interval of nine years.

Lasker (1953) discussing the possible reasons for variation of anthropometric measurements with age, suggests that the change may occur mainly in the soft tissues, particularly cartilaginous and adipose tissues. The effect of adipose tissue on anthropometric measurements was clearly demonstrated by the work of Keys et al. (1950), who found a significant decrease in various bodily measurements during starvation.

Lasker (1953) believes there is strong evidence that the increased size of the face may, to some extent, be caused by oppositional growth of bone, although there may possibly be some changes in overlying soft tissue. He considers that it is probable that incremental growth changes continue for much longer than most anthropologists previously thought possible.

Environmental modifications of physique may occur as late as the third decade and subsequently. Lasker (1951) demonstrated the extent to which this was possible. Mexicans, who had resided in the United States, even temporarily, differed in size and proportions from their less perambulatory neighbours. He found that the differences were a function both of length of residence and age at emigration.

The available evidence, therefore, indicates that limited, but significant changes can occur in bodily dimensions and proportions with increasing age during adult life, and this emphasizes the extreme importance of controlling the age factor in constitutional studies in adults as well as in children.

Physiological Functions in Relation to Body Build

The physiological attributes of human constitution and their possible relationships to morphological, psychological and immunological features, have received comparatively little attention from research workers. The field of physiology, including endocrine and metabolic studies, is clearly an important one, as it might serve to bridge the gap between morphology, temperament and susceptibility to disease.

Tanner (1944) studied the relationship between Sheldon's components of physique and body temperature, cardiovascular functions and respiratory rate. He found that oral temperature and respiratory rate at rest, were correlated positively with ectomorphy and negatively with endomorphy. When he used an estimated leptosomic factor score instead of ectomorphy, the correlations were higher, + 0·32 with respiratory rate, and − 0·39 with oral temperature. Both ectomorphy and mesomorphy were found independently to have a tendency for higher oral temperature.

Gertler, Garn and Sprague (1950) and Tanner (1951a) have shown that the level of blood cholesterol is positively correlated with endomorphy. Kretschmer (1948) reported that serum albumin and serum antitrypsin are higher in leptosomes than pyknics.

The relationship between body build and the excretion rate of adrenal corticoids has been studied by a number of workers recently. Gertler et al. (1954), in a study of fifty individuals suffering from coronary disease, found that those with predominantly mesomorphic body build tended to excrete the highest amounts of 17-ketosteroids. The ectomorph, on the average, excreted the lowest amount of 17-ketosteroids, and endomorphic individuals were intermediate in this respect. Tanner (1955) found a correlation between increased excretion of androgens and the accelerated development of muscular strength in a longitudinal study of growth in adolescent boys. Genell, Jensen and Lindegard (1956) studied the urinary excretion of a number of different adrenal cortical hormones in one hundred and ninety-seven Swedish twenty-year-old healthy Army men and found that the muscle factor was positively correlated with secretion of 17-keto-steroids and 17-hydroxycorticoids.

Seltzer (1940) compared oxygen uptake and utilization in different types of physique and found that leptomorphic individuals had a lower level of mechanical deficiency as measured by oxygen-uptake experiments than those of broader body build. Seltzer and Brouha (1943) also found that the higher the androgyny the worse the exercise tolerance in normal men.

The study of relationships between physical type and physiological and biochemical functions is in its infancy and it remains to be seen whether the advent of improved techniques in physiology, biochemistry and body build assessment will reveal greater correlations.

Physique, Personality and Neurosis

The tendency to relate physical with psychological characteristics has its roots in antiquity and indeed formed a prominent part of the humoral theories of Graeco-Roman physicians. During recent times studies designed to investigate such relationships can conveniently be classified according to the physical characteristics or the particular physical typology used as the basis for investigating correlations with personality, temperament, character, behaviour, neurotic illness, etc.

STUDIES BASED ON VIOLA'S TYPOLOGY

Viola (1925) described three main types of physique; the macrosplanchnic type, possessing a large trunk, in comparison with the development of the limbs, having large development of horizontal and circumferential dimensions and relatively small development of vertical dimensions. The microsplanchnic type, its antithesis, has a small trunk and long limbs with vertical dimensions preponderating over horizontal dimensions. Intermediate between these types is the normosplanchnic type having a harmonious development of trunk and limbs. Viola considered that the macrosplanchnic type had an overdevelopment of the vegetative system, whereas the microsplanchnic type had an overdevelopment of the animal or locomotive system (viz. the body musculature, nervous system and skeleton). The macrosplanchnic and microsplanchnic types were believed to differ in intellectual capacity and temperamental characteristics attributable to differences in the relative development and activity of the vegetative and animal systems.

Pende (1928), a pupil of Viola, extended Viola's classification by introducing a number of endocrine variations. He considered that there were two main physiological biotypes—

1. The anabolic biotype, which he equated with megalosplanchnic body build, having specific temperamental and hormonal characteristics;
2. The catabolic biotype which was equated with microsplanchnic physique, having specific endocrine and neuro-vegetative characteristics.

However, these relationships are mainly speculative and lack scientific and experimental validation.

Naccarati (1934), using an index based on that of Viola, investigated the body build of one hundred male neurotic subjects. By means of the index he classified individuals into microsplanchnic, normosplanchnic and macrosplanchnic types. He found that the neurotic group had a higher proportion of extreme physical types than a normal group of similar sex and age distribution. He found that emotional neuroses (under which category he included both hysteria and anxiety states), were associated with a more macro-splanchnic type of physique than the normal group, whereas neurasthenic patients were more micro-splanchnic than both the normal and the emotional neurosis groups. Naccarati's work is difficult to assess because of his terminology and classification of neurosis. There would appear to be no valid reason for including such contrasting conditions as hysteria and anxiety state in the same diagnostic class. Similarly the term neurasthenia is extremely unsatisfactory, having for many years been ill-used and over-used. His findings are also unacceptable because of lack of statical treatment of the data.

Greenwood and Smith (1941), following the work of Boldrini (1925), who demonstrated that chest circumference and stature could be substituted for trunk volume and limb length in Viola's indices, used the ratio $\dfrac{\text{chest circumference}}{\text{stature}}$ as an anthropometric index. They correlated the index with intelligence, efficiency, neurotic manifestations such as anxiety and obsessional symptoms, and found all the correlations were in the realm of chance, the highest being $+ 0.23$.

INVESTIGATIONS BASED ON KRETSCHMER'S TYPOLOGY

A great deal of research was stimulated by Kretschmer's theory of an association between body types and temperamental types. A number of these studies selected well-defined types as described by Kretschmer and compared them with respect to a variety of psychological attributes by various methods. Thus van der Horst (1916) and Kibler (1925) utilized questionnaires, and their results confirmed the association between leptosomatic body build and schizothymic temperament on the one hand and pyknic body build and cyclothymic temperament on the other.

A series of investigations carried out by van der Horst (1916), Kibler (1925) and Enke (1928), indicated that persons of pyknic physique, compared with those of leptosomatic physique, were more easily distracted in reaction-time experiments, were able to remember a smaller number of differently coloured squares on a card given at a certain speed, were poorer in the tachistoscopic perception of nonsense syllables. In further experiments on the tachistoscopic perception of long unfamiliar words, leptsomatic individuals were found to use an abstractive, analytic dissociative method in which the total work was built up by reading successive letters and syllables and constructing the whole from the parts. Pyknic individuals on the other hand, tended to use a synthetic integrative method. Persons with athletic physique occupied an intermediate position in the results of these tests. There is also evidence that pyknics tended to respond predominantly to colour in tachistoscopic experiments, and also tended to react to colours on the Rorschach test.

Lindberg (1938) reviewing the relevant literature concluded that the evidence indicated that persons of pyknic physique had a distinct tendency towards colour reactivity, whereas schizothymes and leptosomatics showed a distinct tendency for form reactivity. Lindberg (1938), using his own special tests, was able to demonstrate that manic-depressives had a greater tendency to colour reactivity and schizophrenics a greater form reactivity. Using Strömgren's index, he was able to demonstrate significant relationships between pyknic body build, manic-depressive illness with a greater tendency to colour reaction on the one hand, and between leptosomatic body build and schizophrenic illness and form reactivity on the other. His evidence suggests, but not conclusively, that pyknics differ significantly from leptosomatics in colour-form reactivity. The work of Keehn (1953) has thrown doubt on the interpretation of the tests used as being measures of "colour-form reactivity."

Misiak and Pickford (1944) found that leptosomes react more to mental and physical stimuli on the psychogalvanic reflex and are more persevering and have a lower tendency to perseveration than pyknics. Smith and Boyarsky (1943) found that leptosomatic individuals have a higher tempo (as measured by tapping rate) and also a quicker reaction-time. Kretschmer (1941) showed that leptosomes had a more sudden onset of fatigue on the ergograph, and also showed more sudden and variable pressure in writing. Klineberg, Asch and Block (1934) compared a number of psychological tests on groups of leptosome and groups of pyknic subjects. Tests included cancellation of letters, intelligence tests, and tests of emotional adjustment and six tests specially designed to measure alleged characteristics of the two opposed constitutional types. They found no statistically significant differences between leptosomes and pyknics in these tests.

Similarly, Pilsbury (1939) and Kraines (1938) found no evidence to support Kretschmer's theory in a study of introversion-extraversion measured by personality inventories and physique measured by body-build indices.

More recently, Brattgård (1950) studied the relationship between personality attitude and physical make-up in a series of 1,000 patients attending a psychiatric clinic. This study is of special interest because the ratings of personality attitude had been made some time before the assessment of body build, and were not initially carried out with the intention of determining psychophysical correlates. He used Strömgren's index to assess body build, which was used for comparison with ratings previously made regarding patients' syntonic, psychasthenic and hysterical attitudes. He found that syntonic attitudes were associated with a pyknic physique, whereas psychasthenic attitudes were associated with leptosomatic physique.

Thus the results of investigations carried out to test Kretschmer's hypothesis of an affinity between personality and physical type are not all in agreement; some provide confirmation and others none.

FACTORIAL STUDIES OF THE RELATIONSHIP BETWEEN
PHYSIQUE AND TEMPERAMENT

1. *Children*

Burt (1938), in a study of physique and temperament in schoolchildren, found that there were comparatively low correlations between stoutness and cheerful emotions on the one hand and between thinness with inhibitive and repressive tendencies on the other. In adults he found that leptomorphic body build tended to be associated with repressive and introvertive temperament and eurymorphic body build with depression. Burt (1949), in a study of four hundred and fifty-seven boys aged 11 to 13 years utilized the method of subdivided factors and found that the leptomorphic factor included two subfactors, one for limb length and the other for trunk length. The pyknic factor also had two subfactors, one for transverse and the other for sagittal measurements. He carried out a similar analysis of temperament and his results, together with physical type correlates, are shown in Table IX.4.

2. *Adults*

Body-build indices derived from factorial analysis of physique were used for studying relationships between

TABLE IX.4

CLASSIFICATION OF PERSONALITY AND PHYSICAL CORRELATES BY ORTHOGONAL SUBDIVIDED GROUP FACTORS (BURT, 1949)

Factor	Designation	Attribute of disposition	Body size, physical types and subtypes
I	General factor of all round emotionality	Less emotionality	1. Small body size or 2. Pyknic—obese subtype
		More emotionality	Thin and slender physique (Leptomorph)
II	Extraversion versus introversion	Extraversion	1. Large body size 2. Pyknic—eurymorphic subtype
		Introversion	Leptomorphic physique
III	Euthymic versus dysthymic	Euthymic	Broader eurymorphic physique
		Dysthymic	Leptomorphic physique

physical type and personality and neurosis in adult men by Rees and Eysenck, first in a group of four hundred soldiers (Rees and Eysenck, 1945) and subsequently in a further group giving a total of one thousand soldiers (Eysenck, 1947). Physique was assessed by the Rees-Eysenck body-build index for men as already described.

Rees (1950) carried out a similar study in a group of four hundred women service patients suffering from

TABLE IX.5

	Lepto-morphs (150) per cent	Meso-morphs (730) per cent	Eury-morphs (120) per cent
Age 16–20	9	7	1
21–25	25	27	18
26–30	23	28	34
31–40	36	34	42
40 + ...	7	4	4
Hysterical personality . .	23	23	30
Hysterical attitude . . .	29	32	37
Hysterical conversion symptoms	29	33	40
Diagnosis conversion hysteria .	11	20	24
Intelligence average or below .	66	69	75
Vocabulary above average .	38	28	22
Anxious	67	60	56
Obsessional	35	23	15
Depressed	73	65	56
Diagnosis anxiety state . .	47	42	43
Reactive depression . .	20	18	13
Endogenous depression . .	1	2	4
Headaches	65	60	56
Dyspepsia	21	15	12
Tremor	31	36	25
Irritability	43	30	32
Loss of weight of more than ½ stone	20	12	4
Muscular tone good . .	20	30	40
Teetotal	50	52	39
Schizoid seclusive . .	39	32	31

neurosis, utilizing a new regression equation for classifying body build in women derived from factorial analysis. Table IX.5 gives a summary of the findings, given as percentages, in the male group, and Table IX.6 the results for the female group. It should be emphasized that the clinical ratings and assessments were made quite independently of the assessment of physique, and were part of the routine investigation and assessment by the medical staff of all patients admitted to Mill Hill Emergency Hospital. The results obtained in both male and female adult groups are very similar. Eysenck (1944) had previously found from a factorial study of neurotic symptoms and manifestations, that there was a dichotomy of clinical types into hysteria and dysthymia. Inspection of Tables IX.5 and IX.6 shows that in men and women, leptosomes tend towards dysthymic symptoms and traits, whereas eurymorphs tend towards hysterical traits and symptoms. Comparison of items relating to the introversion-extraversion dichotomy of Jung, and the schizothymic-cyclothymic dichotomy of Kretschmer (1934), shows that leptomorphs have a greater tendency to introversion or schizothyme tendencies, whereas eurymorphs tend to be more extraverted and cyclothymic. There is also evidence that leptomorphs tend to have a higher incidence of somatic manifestations of emotional tension and autonomic dysfunction than eurymorphs.

The results are similar to those found by Sandford et al. (1943) in normal children. Their tall-narrow type was found to be associated with autonomic dysfunction, good intelligence test results, satisfactory school progress and also with guilt feelings, remorse and other features indicative of dysthymia. Their wide-heavy type, on the other hand, correlated negatively with autonomic dysfunction and positively with secure feelings and lively self expression.

Our findings of an association between eurymorphs and extraverted and cyclothymic tendencies and between leptomorphs and introverted and schizothymic tendencies, lends support to Kretschmer's theory of an affinity between body build and personality type. The higher incidence of symptoms of autonomic dysfunction in leptomorphs corresponds to the results of a study "Physique and Effort Syndrome" by Rees (1945) in which it was found that, as a group, effort syndrome patients were more leptomorphic than normal controls, and the leptomorphic patients tended to have a lifelong history of symptoms of autonomic dysfunction in contrast to the eurymorphic effort syndrome patients in whom exogenous rather than constitutional factors were important.

STUDIES UTILIZING SHELDON'S SOMATOTYPES

Sheldon (1942) calculated correlations between a large number of psychological traits and found that

TABLE IX.6

	Lepto-morphs (60) per cent	Meso-morphs (263) per cent	Eury-morphs (77) per cent
1. Age			
16–20	12·2	17·5	20·2
21–25	61·1	51·2	45·9
26–30	10·7	19·6	24·3
31–40	7·7	9·8	8·1
41+	2·2	1·7	1·3
2. Hysteria versus dysthymia			
Hysterical personality . .	14·4	23·9	20·2
Very marked hysterical traits .	2	5	8
Hysterical, motor and sensory conversion symptoms . .	12	14	23
Headache	61	69	69
Anxiety, moderate and severe .	71	55	49
Depression, moderate and severe	52	41	33
Irritability	54	44	37
Diagnosis: anxiety state, acute, severe	14	10	8
Diagnosis: anxiety state (all types)	60	59	51·3
3. Personality			
Marked schizoid personality .	6·7	7	2·7
Very touchy and suspicious .	7	6	1·5
Weak, dependent . . .	89	55	46
Narrow interests . . .	63	52	54
Inert, apathetic . . .	15	6	9
Markedly cyclothymic . .	2·2	7	8·1
Hypochondriasis . . .	37	27	25
4. Autonomic dysfunction			
Autonomic symptoms (palpitations, sweating, etc.) . .	49	44	40
Effort intolerance . . .	65	62	55
5. Miscellaneous			
Duration of illness more than 1 year	40	45	27
Positive family history of marked neurosis	30	33	21
Childhood neurotic symptoms .	48	43	42
Backward in elementary school	5	6	13
Good past physical health .	57·7	71·7	22·9
Vocabulary test above average .	22	22	14
Matrices test above average .	13	10	12

they tended to form three clusters in which traits showed positive intracorrelations but had negative correlations with traits of the other groups. He considered these three groupings to be indicative of three primary components of personality which he termed viscerotonia, somatotonia and cerebrotonia. Viscerotonia is characterized by relative love of comfort, pleasure in digestion, greed for affection and approval and the need of people's company when in trouble. Sheldon states that the personality of viscerotonics seems to centre around the viscera. Somatotonia is characterized by an assertive posture, energy, a need of exercise, directness of manner, unrestrained voice and a need for action when in trouble. Cerebrotonia is characterized by restraint in posture, quick reaction, socio-phobia, inhibited social address, vocal restraint, youthful intentness and a need of solitude when troubled.

In a group of two hundred university men between the ages of 17 and 31 years, Sheldon (1942) found correlations between components of physique and temperament as follows: endomorphy and viscerotonia + 0·79, mesomorphy and somatotonia + 0·82, ectomorphy and cerebrotonia + 0·83. These correlations are much higher than those reported by other workers in the field of physical temperamental relationships.

Sheldon's (1942) findings have been criticized because of the possibility that a "halo" effect might have influenced the reported correlations as both physique and temperament were rated by the same observer.

Davidson, McInnes and Parnell (1957) investigated body build in a group of one hundred seven-year-old children with the object of determining what relationships existed between somatotype and psychiatric symptoms and psychological attributes. They found that symptoms of anxiety and emotional unrest were associated with ectomorphy. Among girls significant positive correlations were found between ectomorphy and meticulous, fussy and conscientious traits of personality. The results on the Rorschach test showed that ectomorphs tended to be associated with movement responses and endomorphs with colour responses, but the correlations were not statistically significant. In general the correlations between somatotype and psychological attributes were of a low order and none approached the high correlations reported by Sheldon 1942) between somatotypes and temperamental characteristics.

Parnell (1957) compared somatotype distribution in four hundred and five healthy students with that in a group of two hundred and eight students who were advised by their general practitioners to seek psychiatric care. It was found that the linear person with poor muscular development, and below average in fat, was six times more common in the patient group. The averagely fat, rather muscular short man was found to be five times more common in the healthy group than in the patient group.

Wittman, Sheldon and Katz (1948) studied the relationships between somatotype and psychiatric attributes based on Wittman's check-list. The first psychiatric component (designated manic-depressive) correlated 0·54 with endomorphy, 0·41 with mesomorphy, and − 0·59 with ectomorphy. The second psychiatric component (paranoid) correlated − 0·04 with endomorphy, 0·57 with mesomorphy, and

— 0·34 with ectomorphy. The third psychiatric component (hebephrenic) had a correlation of — 0·25 with endomorphy, — 0·68 with mesomorphy, and + 0·64 with ectomorphy. Sheldon *et al.* (1949) also attempted to correlate neurotic behaviour reactions with somatotype. Hysteria was found to be associated with ectopenia, neurasthenia with lack of development of mesomorphy, and psychasthenia with lack of development of endomorphy.

Humphreys (1957) severely criticized Sheldon's methods and states that the evidence provided by Sheldon supported not more than two independent (but not necessarily valid) types of temperament.

Child and Sheldon (1941) studied the correlation between somatotype and tests of verbal and numerical aptitude, ascendance-submission, and masculinity-femininity. The correlations were uniformly low, the highest being 0·21. Fiske (1944) found no significant correlation between somatotype and intelligence test score in a group of one hundred and thirty-three boys ranging in age from 13 to 17. Tanner (1957) refers to an investigation in which a group of boys aged 17 from an English boarding school were somatotyped by different observers from those assessing temperament by means of Sheldon's shortened scale. The results provided little to support Sheldon's claims for high correlations between somatotype and temperament. In so far as they go, the results of these studies are in good accord with those of Rees-Eysenck and of Burt, quoted above.

STUDIES BASED ON LINDEGARD'S METHOD OF ASSESSING PHYSIQUE

Lindegard and Nyman (1956) attempted to correlate personality attributes and physique in a group of three hundred and twenty men. Personality was assessed and rated according to the system of Sjobring and physique by Lindegard's (1953) method.

The results showed that the muscle factor correlated positively with "validity" (i.e. expansivity and self confidence versus unobtrusiveness). Both muscle and fat factors were negatively correlated with "stability" (i.e. emotional warmth versus emotional coolness and sophistication and proficiency of motor pattern).

Lindegard and Nyman (1956) considered that the findings of Rees and Eysenck (1945), that subjects of tall, narrow body build have a high vocabulary score, was compatible with their own findings of a significant negative correlation between vocabulary score and muscularity in their series. It is interesting that Wretmark (1953), in a study of personality in peptic ulcer patients and normal controls, using Sjobring's system for assessing personality and anthropometric indices for assessing body build, found that stability was the only factor to be correlated with body build. He found that substable individuals were relatively wide-heavy and that superstable individuals tended to be tall-narrow in body build.

Lindegard and Nyman's (1956) results were not wholly in conformity with either those of Kretschmer (1921) or those obtained by Sheldon (1942) regarding the physical make-up of the cyclothymic and viscerotonic individuals, but the criteria and methods used differ so widely that it is impossible to make a satisfactory comparison of results.

BODY SIZE IN RELATION TO PERSONALITY AND NEUROSIS

The significance of body size as opposed to bodily proportion, has received little attention by investigators of physical-psychological correlates.

1. *Index of Body Size*

Rees and Eysenck (1945) found that the following measurements had the highest saturation with the general factor of body size and were therefore likely to be the most useful measurements for the construction of size indices—

    (i) Suprasternal height
    (ii) Bicristal diameter
    (iii) Stature
    (iv) Transverse chest diameter

Stature and transverse chest diameter were the measurements chosen as these measurements had already been taken on a group of 1,100 soldiers, successively admitted to Mill Hill Emergency Hospital, and on whom detailed psychological data recorded independently were also available. The product of these two measurements gives a convenient index of body size. The mean stature for the group of 1,100 soldiers was 172·067 cm with a standard deviation of 6·69, and a coefficient of variation of 3·38. The mean transverse chest diameter was 27·63 cm with a standard deviation of 1·902 and a coefficient of variation of 6·98. It will be seen that the coefficients of variation of these two measurements differ considerably and therefore absolute measurements could not be used for inclusion in an index of body size. Each measurement was, therefore, converted into standard measure, that is expressed in terms of standard deviation, and the product of stature and transverse chest diameter expressed in standard measure was calculated on each patient. From Fig. 9.7 it will be seen that the index values are distributed along a normal frequency (Gaussian) curve with some positive skewness. The frequency curve shows no evidence of bimodality or multimodality, which would suggest the existence of disparate types of body size, but a continuous variation from one extreme to the other.

For the purposes of investigation it will be necessary to choose arbitrary points for classification of the group. The demarcation points chosen were one standard deviation above and below the mean, dividing the group into three classes—

1. Small size or microsomatics, individuals of index values of 1,683 and less.
2. Medium size or mesomatics, comprising individuals with index values between 1,684 and 3,110.
3. Large size or macrosomatics, individuals with index values 3,110 and over.

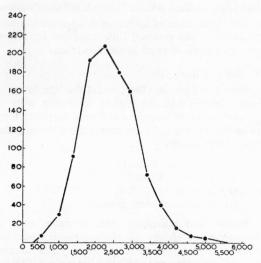

FIG. 9.7. FREQUENCY DISTRIBUTION CURVE OF THE BODY SIZE INDEX IN A GROUP OF 1,000 SOLDIERS

An item sheet on each patient in the hospital had already been completed quite independently of physical assessment and contained over two hundred items relating to social data, personal and family history, personality, symptomatology, etc. The distribution of various items for the microsomatic, mesosomatic and macrosomatic groups is given in Table IX.7. The significance of the differences in percentage incidence between the groups was tested by the critical ratio method and only ratios of 2 and over were taken as significant.

2. Body Size, Intelligence and Personality Traits

The results indicate that the microsomatic group tends to be lower in level of intellectual capacity than the macrosomatic group, as shown by the significantly higher proportion of individuals below average in intelligence in both progressive matrices and the vocabulary tests. Further evidence of a lower intellectual level in the microsomatic group is the higher proportion of individuals who failed to proceed beyond the second class from the top at primary school and the higher proportion of individuals who had unskilled

TABLE IX.7

SOCIAL DATA AND HISTORY

	Micro-somatics (156) per cent	Meso-somatics (688) per cent	Macro-somatics (156) per cent
Age			
16–20	7·7	7·3	3
21–25	25·6	25·4	26·9
26–30	25	28·3	30·1
31–40	37·2	34·7	36·5
41 +	4·48	4·2	3
Civilian occupation			
Unskilled	50·6	38·3	39·1
Semi-skilled	30·1	37·6	30·1
Skilled	12·1	20·5	23·7
Administrative or professional	5·8	4·5	4·5
Unduly frequent changes of employment	10·25	6·7	7·1
Civil state			
Married	55·8	65·8	62·8
Engaged	1·3	2·5	1·3
Single	37·1	26·2	30·1
Sexual activity			
Normal	73·7	80·7	76·3
Inhibited	17·3	11·2	8·9
Subject to worry	10·3	8·4	12·8
Education			
Elementary-poor	26·3	21·7	16·7
Elementary-good	58·9	63·1	59·6
Secondary or central	12·2	13·8	21·2
Higher	2·5	1·5	2·6
Past physical health			
Good	44·2	51·7	37·2
Medium	48·1	45·2	57·7
Poor	7·7	3·1	5·1
Alcohol consumption			
Teetotal	53·8	51·7	37·1
Moderate	44·2	45·2	57·7
Excessive	1·9	3	5·1
Family history			
Negative	12·8	11·4	12·2
Psychosis	5·1	4·9	6·4
Epilepsy	1·3	2·3	0·6
Mental deficiency	26·9	31·4	32·7
Pronounced neurosis	26·9	15	14·7
Slight neurosis	44·9	48·7	48·7

civil employment. The microsomatic group tends to be of inadequate personality make-up, as shown by the higher incidence of weak dependent, anxious and hypochondriacal traits of personality with narrow interests and hobbies. The macrosomatic group showed, in addition to greater body size, better musculature, tone and posture.

3. *Body Size and Neurosis*

Both microsomatics and macrosomatics show evidence of predisposition to a neurotic breakdown, as shown by the high incidence of childhood symptoms, by previous general behaviour indicative of a clear predisposition of mental illness and by the high proportion of individuals rated as being of unstable personality. The predisposition to neurosis in macrosomatics expressed itself differently from that in microsomatics in that they tended to be more active, rebellious and aggressive.

TABLE IX.8
PRESENT ILLNESS

Aetiology	Micro-somatics (156) per cent	Meso-somatics (688) per cent	Macro-somatics (156) per cent
Physical causes			
Unimportant	66·0	68·6	64·1
Precipitating	21·1	20·1	25·6
Important	12·2	10·2	10·9
Dominant	4·5	2·6	6·4
Psychological causes			
Unimportant	5·8	5·0	7·7
Precipitating	17·9	16·9	17·9
Important	39·1	40·0	44·2
Dominant	54·5	51·6	48·7
Stress of bombardment or exposure	20·5	26·5	25·0
War-time separation, regimentation	50·6	58·1	53·2
Unsuitable work . . .	17·9	15·4	16·7
Domestic problems . .	26·9	33·4	30·1
Duration of illness before admission			
0–3 months	6·4	4·7	4·5
3–6 months	11·5	10·6	13·5
6–12 months	16·0	19·5	18·6
1 year + ...	66·0	65·1	63·5

In symptomatology and psychiatric diagnosis, there was a general similarity between the three groups, a notable difference was the higher incidence of depression as a symptom in the macrosomatic group. The mesosomatic group usually occupies an intermediate position in the percentage incidence of those traits which show statistically significant differences.

Rees (1950), discussing these findings, concludes that the general picture emerging from the study is that neurotics of large body size tend to be more active, having more stable personalities, better musculature, a higher intellectual level and a better prognosis for return to military duties.

These findings are what one might expect on general considerations. The small person, apart from his constitutional make-up (i.e. his physical, psychological

TABLE IX.9
SYMPTOMATOLOGY AND DIAGNOSIS

	Micro-somatics (156) per cent	Meso-somatics (688) per cent	Macro-somatics (156) per cent
Somatic anxiety . . .	53·8	48·8	53·8
Headache—			
Mild	46·8	47·5	42·9
Severe	12·8	13·8	10·9
Lassitude, fatigue . .	53·2	51·3	50·1
Dyspepsia, vomiting .	18·6	14·8	13·5
Fainting	14·7	11·5	14·1
Pain not demonstrably organic in origin . . .	18·0	23·7	22·4
Tremor	30·1	25·0	26·9
Stammer	0·6	9·4	7·7
Enuresis	3·2	2·9	2·6
Sexual anomalies . .	12·8	13·5	15·4
Anxiety	85·9	83·0	94·4
Depression	71·8	90·0	58·3
Paranoid	0	0·6	1·3
Elation	0	0·6	1·3
Irritability	30·1	31·7	38·5
Apathy	21·2	31·7	19·9
Hypochondriasis—			
Mild	19·2	25·6	23·1
Moderate . . .	12·2	10·6	8·3
Severe	1·3	1·7	1·3
Hysterical attitude . .	28·8	33·4	28·8
Depersonalization . .	2·6	1·5	4·5
Hysterical conversion .	23·1	29·4	22·4
Symptoms . . .	10·3	5·7	3·8
Obsessive compulsive .	2·6	6·4	7·1
Muscular tone—			
Good	18·6	28·2	48·7
Poor	28·8	12·1	5·8
Average	52·6	59·7	45·5
Anxiety state . . .	57·7	66·0	63·5
Hysteria	25·0	23·5	19·2
Psychopathic personality .	9·6	9·3	14·1
Depressive state . .	20·5	19·2	23·1
Paranoid state . . .	2·6	1·7	1·3
Obsessional state . .	1·3	1·0	1·3
Mental deficiency . .	0·7	0	0·7
Epilepsy	1·3	0·6	1·3
Other mental disorders .	0·7	0·3	0
Physical disease . .	2·6	2·6	5·8
Intelligence—			
Progressive matrices—			
Above average . .	24·2	30·8	31
Below average . .	36·2	29·0	25
Vocabulary—			
Above average . .	20·0	27·0	37
Below average . .	20·0	27·0	11

and physical attributes, determined in main, genetically), might react in many ways to his smallness as Adler has indicated. A person may over-compensate for his smallness by assuming aggressive and dominating traits, or he may accept a more normal degree of compensation, or he may react by developing inferiority feelings. In our study we find little evidence

TABLE IX.10

	Micro-somatics (156) per cent	Meso-somatics (688) per cent	Macro-somatics (156) per cent
Clinically abnormal personality—			
General instability	45·5	48·8	52·6
Weak and dependent	57·7	49·7	37·8
Anxious	60·1	62·9	50·6
Touchy and suspicious	29·5	31·1	33·9
Cyclothymic	29·5	31·1	33·9
Schizoid	26·3	33·3	31·4
Hysterical	21·2	24·3	21·2
Obsessional	22·4	24·7	22·4
Hypochondriacal	26·9	32·7	16·7
Childhood neurosis	44·2	39·7	37·2
Positive family history	87·2	88·6	87·8
Poor work record	10·25	6·7	7·1
Repeated nervous breakdown	5·8	6·4	5·1

that neurotics of small body size tend to over-compensate by aggressive or dominating behaviour. It might be contended that a socially acceptable degree of compensation in this direction might have had a salutary affect in preventing neurosis. In fact, however, we find evidence of the opposite tendency, if anything, that is acceptance with feelings of inferiority, as shown by the high incidence of weak, dependent and timorous personalities, anxious highly strung types of personality (61 per cent), hypochondriacal tendencies (27 per cent), and the lack of such possible signs of over-compensation such as rebellious and aggressive tendencies (13 per cent) or conspicuous energy and activity (4·5 per cent).

While it is clear that there was little evidence of over-compensation for any feelings of physical inferiority in the microsomatic group, it would not be safe to assume that lack of such compensation, and the adoption of a defeatist attitude, and the surrender to feelings of inferiority, had played an important role in the development of neurosis in the micro-somatic group, although the adherent school would no doubt assume this to be the dominant factor. An aetiological study of this group showed that multiple aetiological factors were responsible, and that there was evidence of a high degree of assumed predisposition to neurosis or neurotic constitution, as defined by Slater (1943), in all groups as shown by the high incidence of clinically abnormal personality, positive family history, and the incidence of childhood neurotic symptoms.

It is interesting to note that the psychological correlates of body sizes are different from those associated with body type. Whereas the extreme types of body size show significant differences in the incidence of certain personality traits, the extremes of body type, the eurymorph and ectomorph, tend to be associated with hysterical and anxiety reactions respectively, which show no significant differences in groups classified according to body size.

Bodily Disproportions in Relation to Dominant Personality Traits

Seltzer (1946) described an investigation on a group of two hundred and fifty-eight Harvard under-graduates by means of anthropometric measurements and body-build indices. He paid particular attention to body disproportion, which he defines as values of an index which are extremely divergent from the mean, usually in one direction. Examples of such disproportions are a combination of wide shoulders and thin legs, or very broad hips relative to shoulder width, a very flat chest relative to shoulder width, very broad hips relative to chest breadth, broad face relative to chest width, etc. The term disproportion must not be confused with the term dysplasia. The term "disproportion" was not intended to carry a stigma of abnormality, and the ratios are simply normal deviates from the mean of the group as a whole. Seltzer (1946) found that disproportions were more frequent among individuals of unstable autonomic functioning than in the series as a whole. Individuals who were extremely linear were virtually twice as frequent in this trait grouping. In basic personality the less well integrated group was distinguished by a significant excess of individuals with extremely linear body builds, with flat chests relative to their shoulder breadths, and with small calf circumference relative to their shoulder breadths. He found significant excesses of one or more disproportions over the total series frequencies in the following trait groupings: unstable autonomic functions; less well integrated; mood fluctuations; sensitive affect; bland affect; meticulous traits; inhibited; self-conscious and introspective. Significant deficiencies, on the other hand, of one or more disproportions over the total series frequencies occurred in the following traits: well integrated; vital affect; practical organizing; humanistic and pragmatic.

The first list contains trait groupings indicating lesser stability and integration together with sensitivity; a complexity of the personality, with lower capacity for making easy social adjustment. The second list is diametrically opposite to the first. Here the traits are suggestive of stability, good integration and ease of making adjustments. Seltzer (1946) found that disproportions were most common in strong ectomorphs and least common in marked endomorphs and marked mesomorphs. He considered that the disproportions were constitutional and possibly indicated a genetic element in the determination of personality and behaviour.

INTELLIGENCE LEVEL AND PHYSICAL STATUS

Psychologists and educationalists have for many years tried to discover relationships between physical attributes and level of intelligence with the aim of obtaining objective aids for the assessment of the latter.

1. *Isolated Morphological Variables and Intelligence*

Investigations have been carried out to ascertain possible relationships between intelligence level and isolated anthropometric measurements of the skull and the body. Mead (1914) studied the relationship, in children, between height and weight and general intelligence and found that the lower the intelligence the more checked is physical growth, this being more evident with height than with weight. Doll (1916), from a study of three hundred and thirty-three children, reported a correlation of + 0·31 between stature and mental age and one of + 0·41 between standing height and mental age. Wheeler (1929) studied anthropometric data of the Harvard growth study on one hundred and fifty-four mentally dull boys and one hundred and nineteen mentally dull girls and found consistent, though slight, differences in stature, sitting height, sternal length, leg length, trunk length and bicristal diameter, which were smaller in the mentally dull groups than in normal children.

Somerville (1924), in a study of one hundred college students, found a correlation between intelligence and stature of + 0·1, sitting height + 0·13, weight + 0·1, chest girth + 0·01. None of the correlations was statistically significant.

Brooks (1928) studying groups of school and college pupils, reported that correlations between weight and intelligence varied between − 0·08 and + 0·31, and concluded that the results pointed to a zero correlation between weight and intelligence in adolescence.

Pearson and Moul (1925) conducted an elaborate biometric study of six hundred and sixteen boys and five hundred and eighty girls of Jewish origin, resident in London, and found a negligible correlation between estimated intelligence and height and weight.

Lee, Lorenz and Pearson (1903) studied honours and pass men at Cambridge using scholastic standing as a criterion of intelligence. They found a non-significant correlation between weight and intelligence of + 0·0502.

The product moment correlations between anthropometric measurements and intelligence level as measured by the Raven's progressive matrices in a group of two hundred soldiers is given below. All the correlations are low and none is statistically significant. The consensus of results there indicates a zero correla-

TABLE IX.11

Variate	Pearson product moment correlation coefficient
Stature	+ 0·111
Suprasternal height	+ 0·08
Symphysis height	+ 0·055
Breadth of skull	− 0·056
Length of skull	− 0·036
Biacromial diameter . . .	+ 0·012
Transverse chest diameter . . .	− 0·055
Sagittal chest diameter . . .	+ 0·055
Bicristal diameter	+ 0·11
Trunk length	+ 0·097
Sternal length	+ 0·125
Arm length to radial styloid . .	+ 0·055
Arm length to tip of medius . .	+ 0·073
Chest circumference at inspiration .	+ 0·051
Chest circumference at expiration .	+ 0·101
Hip circumference	+ 0·177
Weight	+ 0·172

tion between absolute anthropometric measurements and intelligence level.

2. *Physical Type and Intelligence Level*

Viola (1933) regarded the macrosplanchnic type as tending to be lower in intelligence level than the microsplanchnic and normosplanchnic types. In keeping with this, Naccarati (1921) found that bright children, during the growth period, tended to microsplanchny in contrast to less bright or dull children. In other investigations Naccarati (1924), Naccarati and Garratt (1924), found that correlations between $\frac{\text{height}}{\text{weight}}$ index and intelligence varied between + 0·1 and + 0·44, the average of thirteen correlation coefficients being + 0·256.

Stalnaker (1923) found that there were correlations of + 0·8 and + 0·3 between the $\frac{\text{height}}{\text{weight}}$ index and intelligence in groups of one hundred and fifty school pupils, whereas Heidbreder (1926), who studied a group of one thousand students and adequately controlled the data for sex distribution and reliability of intelligence tests, found that evidence pointed to a zero correlation.

Sheldon (1927) investigated four hundred and thirty-four college freshmen by means of Naccarati's index of body build and found that its correlation with intelligence rating was + 0·14 ± 0·03. Garratt and Kellogg (1928) also used the morphological index of Naccarati, calculated from photographs, and intelligence measured by psychological examination for college freshmen in a group of two hundred and six individuals and found a correlation of + 0·07 ± 0·05.

Sheldon (1942) found that the correlations between intelligence quotient and morphological types were low, but there were correlations of + 0·48 between "aesthetic intelligence" and mesomorphy and ectomorphy.

Parnell (1955) studied groups of three hundred and seventy-one boys and four hundred and twenty-one girls aged 11 and concluded that the less muscular children tended to pass the grammar school examination. He found that linear subjects with more than average fat for their weight were best at examinations.

He found that all-rounders in university students, viz. those who played games and got a first-class degree, were somewhat more muscular. Endomorphic ectomorphs obtained a significantly high proportion of first-class honours (35 per cent). Mesomorphs (65 per cent) obtained second-class honours. Ectomorphs were found to enjoy the widest range of possibilities for better or for worse. Mesomorphs were most consistent in obtaining a good level of performance with first- or second-class honours. Endomorphic ectomorphs who did exceptionally well in finals, received only a near average proportion of awards on entry.

BODY-BUILD INDICES AND INTELLIGENCE LEVEL

The following indices (see appendix to this chapter) were correlated with Progressive Matrices score in a series of two hundred successive soldiers admitted to Mill Hill Emergency Hospital: Morphological index + 0·118 ± 0·069, Pignet index + 0·161 ± 0·07, Brugsch index + 0·061 ± 0·07. All of these correlations are small and none is statistically significant.

A series of nine hundred and seventy-six successive soldiers admitted to Mill Hill Emergency Hospital were classified into leptomorph, eurymorph and mesomorphic physical types by means of the Rees-Eysenck index; 33 per cent of the leptomorphs were above average, that is Grades 1 and 2, compared with 25 per cent of the eurymorphs. 29 per cent were below average in the leptomorphs compared with 34 per cent in the eurymorphs. The mesomorphs were intermediate. On the vocabulary scale, 37·5 per cent of leptomorphs were above average, compared with 22 per cent of eurymorphs. The difference of 8 per cent in the above average intelligence grades in the Matrices tests is not statistically significant. The difference of 15·4 per cent in the above average intelligence grades in the vocabulary test is statistically significant at the 5 per cent level, and is in conformity with Lindegard's (1956) results.

In conclusion we may say that the correlation between physique and intelligence is so low that a knowledge of a person's physical status will be of no value in the prediction of intelligence in the individual case.

PHYSIQUE IN RELATIONSHIP TO DELINQUENCY AND CRIMINALITY

Investigators have, for many years, attempted to ascertain whether any significant relationships exist between physical type and various morphological characteristics and delinquency and criminality.

Lombroso (1911) studied morphological anomalies in criminals and founded the doctrine that the criminal, as found in prison, was an atavistic anomaly presenting morbid physical stigmata.

In more recent years, interest has turned away from the question of physical stigmata to other aspects of body build. Hooton (1939) studied 17,000 prison and reformatory inmates and reported significant differences in various body measurements between persons convicted of different types of crime. Among his findings were that both the shortest sixth and the heaviest sixth of the group headed the list of crimes for rape, sex offences and assault, but were lowest in murder, whereas the contrasting group consisting of tall and slender criminals had the highest incidence of murder and robbery, but the lowest or next lowest in crimes such as burglary, assault, rape and other sex offences.

Glueck and Glueck (1950) compared a group of delinquents, consisting of five hundred boys aged 11 to 18 years, with five hundred non-delinquent controls, matched for age, intelligence, racial origin and residence in under-privileged neighbourhoods. They compared anthropometric measurements and somatotype distribution and found that there was little difference in general body size, but that the delinquent group was considerably more mesomorphic and less ectomorphic than the non-delinquent group.

Sheldon et al. (1949), described a study of two hundred delinquent youths who were somatotyped according to Sheldon's system and were compared in respect of somatotype distribution with 4,000 college students. They found that the sample of delinquents differed sharply from the college somatotype distribution, having a distinct and heavier massing in the endomorphic-mesamorphic sector. They found that mesopenes were, on the whole, rare. Ectomorphs were rare and also ectomorphic-mesomorphs in comparison with endomorphic-mesomorphs. As a generalization, they concluded that the two hundred delinquent youths were decidedly mesomorphic and also decidedly ectopenic, but that there appeared to be no strongly defined tendency, either way, with regard to endomorphy.

Epps and Parnell (1952) studied a group of one hundred and seventy-seven young women, between the ages of 16 and 21, undergoing Borstal training. Anthropometric measurements were carried out on the delinquent group and compared with a group of one hundred and twenty-three university women aged between 18 and 21. They found that delinquents were heavier in body build and were more muscular and fat. In temperament they showed a predominance of somatotonia and viscerotonia. All these results are in good agreement with the Rees-Eysenck finding of a correlation between extraversion and eurymorph body build, and Eysenck's theory linking extraversion with psychopathy and criminality. (Cf. also Chapter 12.)

Physique and Type of Occupation

A good review of this subject is given by Damon and MacFarlane (1955), who point out that the first systematic study of physique of workers was carried out by Quetelet (1835), a Belgian statistician, who introduced the term anthropometry. Cathcart *et al.* (1935) found differences in strength and physique among individuals in different occupations. For example, they found that transport workers were taller, stronger and heavier than clerical workers. Coerter (1929) classified individuals in various occupations according to Rostan's constitutional types and found that locksmiths, transport workers and shoemakers tended to be of muscular type, and that lithographers, telegraphists, cabinet makers and weavers tended to have the respiratory type of body build.

Garn and Gertler (1950) found that a group of research workers was significantly less endomorphic, less mesomorphic and more ectomorphic than a group of factory workers in the same establishment.

MacFarlane (1946, 1953) and Damon (1935) found that civilian air pilots were smaller, heavier and stockier and generally more mesomorphic than the general population. Damon (1945) found that the more successful war-time aviators were more mesomorphic and masculine, with large chest girth, both relative and absolute to stature. Damon (1955), in a further study, utilizing techniques which included classical anthropometry, Seltzer's (1946) disporportions and an approximation of Sheldon's somatotyping, found that the more successful flyers were, on the average, more mesomorphic and masculine.

Woods, Brouha and Seltzer (1943) found that there was a significant association between masculinity of body build and high ratings for excellence as an officer. Seltzer (1945), in a study of two hundred and fifty-eight students, found significant relationships between choice of faculty and the masculinity component of physique. He found that in those individuals with low ratings of masculinity, there was a prediction towards arts and philosophy. Parnell (1953) found that students of engineering, dentistry and medicine were more mesomorphic and less ectomorphic than students of physics and chemistry. Tanner (1955) criticizes this work on the ground that many of the somatotypes have been obtained in an unconventional and an unwarranted manner, and also for its sketchy

statistical treatment. Tanner (1955) compared the physique of two hundred and eighty-seven officer cadets, one hundred and seventy-one Oxford University students, and one hundred and sixty-two medical students. He found that the officer cadets were much more mesomorphic and somewhat lower in endomorphy and ectomorphy than Oxford University students. The medical students were in between the other two groups in mesomorphy, but in endomorphy they were the lowest group. Both student groups exceeded the officer cadets in ectomorphy, but did not differ between themselves. In considering the possible determinants of these associations, Tanner (1955) discussed the possible role of (1) social background and early environmental effects; (2) self-selection by the individuals of their type of career; (3) institution selection; (4) physical changes after entry to the institution. He concluded that the type of occupation, social origin or educational attainment could not explain the differences and that self- and institutional-selection were undoubtedly the main factors involved.

In conclusion, one might say that the evidence suggests that there are tendencies for different types of physique to be associated with certain psychological characteristics, including personality traits and various neurotic symptoms, but the majority of investigations do not report any correlations as high as those reported by Sheldon (1942).

The available evidence suggests that the correlations between physical characteristics and personality traits, intelligence and neurotic symptomatology, although often statistically significant, are nearly always too small to be trusted for the needs of diagnosis.

Physique and Susceptibility to Disease

Physicians have, from time immemorial, attempted to establish correlations between constitutional attributes and tendency to develop various diseases. The dichotomy in physique described by Hippocrates (viz. the *habitus pthisicus* and the *habitus apoplecticus*) was followed by Galen's detailed differentiation of physical types associated with specific temperamental qualities and disease susceptibility.

John Hunter (1728–1793) was a strong proponent of the theory that susceptibility to disease varied with the type of constitution, but it was nearly a hundred years after his death before serious study of the relationships between morphological characteristics and disease was carried out by Beneke (1881) in Germany and Di Giovanni (1919) in Italy.

Interest in the constitutional aspects of medicine was relegated to the background as knowledge of bacteriology and pathology increased. In recent years greater interest has again been taken in the constitutional factors in disease, and this has been greatly stimulated by the marked prevalence at the present time of the so-called stress diseases or psychosomatic disorders in which constitution appears to play an important role.

There is a paucity of scientifically satisfactory investigations into the relationship between physical constitution and various diseases. Failure to utilize random samples of the disorder under consideration, and lack of satisfactory control groups and inadequate statistical evaluation of data, are some of the reasons for slow advance in this field.

PHYSIQUE AND PSYCHOSIS

Although Esquirol (1876) noted that the strong robust type had a tendency to be associated with an acute course of psychosis, with crises, whereas the lymphatic type tended to have a more chronic deteriorating course, Kretschmer (1921) must receive the main credit for elucidating relationships between physical type and psychotic type. The publication of his theory of a biological affinity between pyknic physique and manic-depressive psychosis on the one hand, and between schizophrenia and leptosomatic, athletic and certain dysplastic physiques on the other, stimulated research in all parts of the world.

The results of some of the investigations provide strong support for Kretschmer's hypothesis, others support it only in part, whereas some do not support it at all. Among the authors whose results supported Kretschmer's hypothesis, are Sioli and Meyer (1922), Olivier (1922), Jacob and Moser (1923), Michel and Weber (1924), Nenckel (1924), Weissenfeld (1925), Wyrsch (1924).

The work of Wertheimer and Hesketh (1926) merits more detailed consideration. They studied body build in sixty-five male patients by means of an index, based on that of Viola, which had leg length as the numerator and transverse chest diameter, sagittal chest diameter and trunk length as the denominator. They found that among patients with low index values (indicating a pyknic physique) there was a predominance of manic-depressives, whereas among patients with high index values (indicating more narrow type of body build) schizophrenic psychosis predominated. Schizophrenic patients were found to be scattered over a wider variety of body types, but the greater number fell into the leptosomatic and athletic groups.

Only partial support for Kretschmer's theory was given by the results of Raphael, Ferguson and Searle (1928), who compared a number of anthropometric measurements and body-build indices on sixty schizophrenics and sixty manic-depressives and Clegg (1935), who studied one hundred manic-depressives, one hundred normals and one hundred schizophrenics. Burchard (1936), who studied four hundred and seven male patients, including a group of one hundred and twenty-five schizophrenics and a group of one hundred and twenty-five manic-depressives, found that when the group was classified by impression into pyknic, athletic and leptosomatic types, there was an association between pyknic type and manic-depressive psychosis and between the leptosomatic type and schizophrenia. Comparison of anthropometric indices showed that transverse and sagittal chest diameters, bicristal diameter and certain body-build indices, showed statistically significant differences pointing to a more leptosomatic physique in schizophrenic patients. He found, however, that age influenced physical type. A more detailed analysis of the age factor on Burchard's data, carried out by Anastasi and Foley (1949), showed that there was a definite tendency towards a more pyknic body build with advancing age in each psychotic group as well as in the entire group. They found a correlation of − 0·256 between age and body-build index values for the entire group. The findings indicate that some of the difference observed between the two psychotic groups could be attributed to age, and suggest that the relationship between body build and types of psychosis, as indicated by the results of this study, is rather slight.

Farber (1938) studied the stature, weight and $\frac{height}{weight}$ ratio in eighty-one schizophrenics and eighty manic-depressive patients and considered that the tendency for pyknic type of physique to increase with age, and the greater tendency for physical deterioration in schizophrenia, would weaken if not entirely invalidate Kretschmer's theory. Connolly (1939) carried out an anthropometric study of one hundred male psychotic subjects and found that schizophrenic patients (excluding paranoid schizophrenics) were below the average for all measurements and paranoid schizophrenics and manic-depressives were above the average in body measurements. Using the Pignet index, he found that there was a preponderance of the leptosomatic type in the schizophrenic group and of the pyknic type in the paranoid schizophrenic and manic-depressives. This work therefore supports Kretschmer's theory, and in addition finds that paranoid schizophrenics are more akin to manic-depressives in bodily *habitus* than to other types of schizophrenia.

Cohen (1940), in a study of forty-seven English male patients, found a significant correlation of 0·413 between the combined weighted measure of arm length, leg length, waist circumference and manic-depressive psychosis and schizophrenia. In a group of fifty-one female Jewish patients, he found a significant correlation of 0·557 between a combined weighted measure of chest depth, pelvic breadth and manic-depressive psychosis and schizophrenia, thus supporting Kretschmer's theory. Betz (1942), in a careful study of the physical status of one hundred and ninety-three schizophrenic women, found that schizophrenes were small in general size, and showed a greater proportion of persons of asthenic build and a smaller proportion of persons of pyknic build than normal and non-schizophrenic groups. These findings were obtained both when the impressionistic method of assessing physical types and when anthropometric measurements were used.

Moore and Hsu (1946) carried out a factorial analysis on physical measurements in groups of psychotic patients and found significant relationships between body build and psychotic types at the 1 per cent level for the following relationships—

(a) Non-paranoid schizophrenics were below both manic-depressives and paranoid schizophrenics in the girth factor and were higher in the leptosomia factor and particularly high in the ratio of leptosomia, girth and robustness.

(b) Paranoid schizophrenics differed from manic-depressives in a lower ratio between the robustness factor and the girth factor.

An Anthropometric Study of Manic-depressive Patients

Rees (1953) carried out detailed anthropometric investigation of forty-two patients suffering from manic-depressive psychosis and compared the group with a group of one hundred normal subjects and forty-nine schizophrenic patients. The manic-depressive group was found to be significantly smaller in stature, suprasternal height and biacromial diameter, and was significantly larger in sagittal chest diameter than the normal group.

The Strömgren index significantly differentiated the manic-depressive group from the normal group indicating that the manic-depressive group was significantly more eurymorphic in body build.

Comparison of the manic-depressive and schizophrenic groups showed that the anthropometric measurement showing the greatest difference was sagittal chest diameter. The manic-depressive group was also significantly larger in bicristal diameter, hip circumference and transverse chest diameter. Various body-build indices showed significant differences indicating a greater tendency to eurymorphic build in the manic-depressive group, these included $\dfrac{\text{stature}}{\text{sagittal chest diameter}}$, the index showing the highest discrimination; the next was Strömgren index, followed by the following indices in order of degree of statistical significance of difference between the groups: $\dfrac{\text{trunk length}}{\text{sagittal chest diameter}}$, Pignet index, $\dfrac{\text{trunk length}}{\text{bicristal diameter}}$, the Boldrini index and the Morphological index. All

these indices, however, showed considerable overlapping and that the main differences between manic-depressive, normal and schizophrenic groups, were in the central tendency of a number of anthropometric measurements and body-build indices.

The Significance of the Age Factor in the Relationship between Physical Type and Manic-depressive Psychosis

As both manic-depressive psychosis and eurymorphic physique tend to occur more frequently in middle age, the question arises whether the alleged affinity between the two could be attributable to this temporal coincidence. In view of the increased incidence of manic-depressive psychosis in middle age, it is likely that a random sample will have a relatively high mean age. This was found to be the case in Rees's group which had a mean age of 50·47 years. It is of interest to compare the mean age of other manic-depressive groups investigated to test Kretschmer's theory. The following are some examples: Wertheimer and Hesketh (1926) 39·3 years; Raphael, Ferguson and Searle (1928) 47·5 years; Farber (1938) 44·5 years; Connolly (1939) 47·9 years. Thus all these groups have a considerably greater mean age than Rees's normal and schizophrenic groups. When only the younger members of the manic-depressive group were considered, they were found to be more pyknic in body build than the normal group, but the difference only just approached statistical significance. It was concluded that the age factor plays some part in the affinity between manic-depressive psychosis and eurymorphic body build, but that it did not account for the entire association and did not completely invalidate Kretschmer's theory.

In view of recent researches which indicate that in adult life increasing age determines changes of physique, it is of the greatest importance that in future researches on body build in manic-depressive psychosis, the age factor should be strictly controlled. The present investigation provides some support for Kretschmer's hypothesis between pyknic *habitus* and manic-depressive psychosis, but the correlation is not by any means as high as suggested by Kretschmer.

An Anthropometric Study of Schizophrenic and Normal Control Groups

In order to test Kretschmer's hypothesis of an affinity between schizophrenia and certain types of physique, Rees (1943) carried out a detailed anthropometric investigation of a random sample of forty-nine patients suffering from schizophrenia, and a control group of one hundred normal men of similar age distribution. The average age of the schizophrenic group was 28·75 years and did not differ significantly from that of the normal group (29·27 years). The schizophrenic group was found to be significantly smaller than the normal group in the following measurements: stature, chest circumference, hip circumference, biacromial diameter, suprasternal height and symphysis height.

The schizophrenic group was also significantly more leptosomatic than the normal group, as was shown by statistically significant differences in the Morphological, Boldrini and Pignet indices. The biserial coefficient of correlation between leptosomatic build, measured by the Boldrini index, and schizophrenia, was 0.64 ± 0.06.

Comparison of distribution of physical types objectively delineated by various body-build indices showed the schizophrenic group to have a lower percentage of persons of intermediate physique. The incidence of patients with eurymorphic body build did not differ significantly from the normal control group. The results correspond closely to those of Betz (1942) who carried out a careful study of the body build in a group of one hundred and ninety-three schizophrenic women and found that schizophrenics were smaller in general size and had a higher proportion of persons of leptosomatic body build than normal group.

BODY BUILD IN RELATIONSHIP TO TYPE OF SCHIZOPHRENIA

There is some evidence to suggest that paranoid schizophrenics tend to differ in physical constitution from catatonic, hebephrenic and simple types of schizophrenia. Connolly (1939) found that paranoid schizophrenics were above the average for all measurements, and were more pyknic in body build than the other types of schizophrenic patients. This was also borne out by the factorial studies carried out by Moore and Hsu (1946). The work of Mauz (1930), Kisselew (1931), Platner Heberlein (1932), Vanelli (1932), Langfeldt (1937) and Betz (1942), suggests that schizophrenics with a leptomorphic body build tend to have an early age of onset, show a greater degree of withdrawal, apathy and scattered thinking, whereas schizophrenics of eurymorphic body build tend to have a later age of onset, better preservation of personality, and better affective relations with the environment.

We have already seen that there is now considerable evidence that there is a tendency for pyknic body build to increase with age. The question arises therefore, whether the alleged association between paranoid schizophrenia and pyknic physique, and between leptomorphic physique and schizophrenia with an earlier age of onset, could be attributable largely or entirely to the age factor. There is a clear need for further research in this field utilizing diagnostic groups accurately matched for age, sex, socio-economic status and investigated by adequate anthropometric and statistical methods.

BODY BUILD AND PROGNOSIS IN SCHIZOPHRENIA

Kalman (1953) found that the tendency to extreme deterioration during the course of a schizophrenic illness, was correlated with the presence of high asthenic and low athletic components of physique. He found that schizophrenics with the high athletic (mesomorphic) and low asthenic (ectomorphic) component in physique showed the relatively strongest resistance and were usually of the paranoid type of schizophrenia. He found, in agreement with the observations of Klein and Oppenheim (1952), that the pyknic component, although unrelated to differences in deterioration, was associated with a relatively poor prognosis. Kalman (1953) also found that concordant, monozygotic twins, without significant somatotypic differences, tended to have similar types of schizophrenia, developing usually at the same age and having a similar outcome. When there were differences in physique and physical development in such twins, there were usually differences in the age of onset as well as in the severity of clinical schizophrenic symptoms. In the smaller group of monozygotic twins, discordant for schizophrenia, it was found that, as a rule, if one twin remained completely free from schizophrenic symptoms, a definite difference was found in physical strength and body weight from early childhood consistently in favour of the more resistant twin.

Bleuler (1948) produced evidence in support of his hypothesis that certain types of schizophrenia show certain physical attributes related to endocrine abnormalities. He found, for example, a certain type of schizophrenia associated particularly with the acromegaloid type of *habitus*. This type is distinguished by having large hands, feet and body size and a tendency to irritability and periodic exaggeration of the sexual urge. This type was frequently found to be associated with familial incidence of schizophrenia, and appeared to exert a favourable pathoplastic effect on the symptomatology of a co-existing schizophrenic illness. Schizophrenic illnesses associated with the acromegaloid *habitus*, were found by Bleuler (1948) to be characterized by a later onset and a particularly mild clinical course.

RELATIONSHIPS BETWEEN OTHER CONSTITUTIONAL ATTRIBUTES AND TYPE OF SCHIZOPHRENIA

The cardiovascular system studied both macroscopically and microscopically, has been extensively investigated in schizophrenic patients. Lewis (1936) reported that a hypoplastic circulatory apparatus was found consistently at autopsy in catatonic and hebephrenic types of schizophrenia. He found that the heart was approximately one-third smaller in these types of schizophrenia than in normal people, and he also found that heart size differentiated catatonic and hebephrenic patients from paranoid schizophrenics. This is of special interest in view of reports that paranoid schizophrenics differ from other types of schizophrenics in physique in that they have a greater tendency to eurymorphic physique. Capillary structure in schizophrenics has also interested research workers. Olkon (1939) found that schizophrenic patients showed striking deviations from the normal in their cutaneous capillaries. The differences found included a reduction in size in the number of capillaries per unit area, lack of uniformity, bizarre shapes and the appearances of haemorrhages. Olkon (1939) considered that the severity of the disease was correlated with the degree of derangement of capillary structure. Hauptman and Meyerson (1948) studied capillary structure in the nailfold and found characteristic differences between normal subjects, paranoid schizophrenics and non-paranoid schizophrenics. This work was extended by Wertheimer and Wertheimer (1955), who found that schizophrenic patients showed thicker capillary loops than the normal, and they regarded this as being due to stasis of the blood and engorgement of the capillaries. They found that schizophrenics were also characterized by a greater length and a greater degree of visibility of the sub-papillary plexus. This feature was considered to be due to an under-development of the mesodermal layer of the skin in which the capillaries lie. Paranoid schizophrenics were found to have capillaries more similar to the normal than catatonic, hebephrenic and simple schizophrenics. They found a negative correlation with mesomorphy and the degree of plexus visibility supporting the view that low mesomorphy and high plexus visibility are both manifestations of poor mesodermal development.

Shattock (1950) also found differences in vascular functions in catatonic schizophrenics compared with paranoid patients, and he found that improvement in systemic circulation coincided with the onset of remission.

To conclude, the available evidence on the whole lends confirmation, at least in part, to Kretschmer's theory of an affinity between schizophrenia and leptosomatic, athletic and certain dysplastic physiques. The incidence of pyknic or eurymorphic body build is, however, higher in schizophrenic patients than is suggested by Kretschmer's theory. There is evidence, which is suggestive but not conclusive, that body build in schizophrenia may be related to age of onset, clinical status, course and prognosis of illness, and that paranoid schizophrenics tend to exhibit constitutional differences compared with simple hebephrenic and catatonic schizophrenics. If further research establishes significant relationships between physique and onset of schizophrenia, its clinical forms and prognosis, the basis of such relationships may prove to be genetic, with the various genes of small effect, which determine body build, acting as modifiers to the schizophrenic gene or genes, as described by Rees (1957).

Physical Type in Relationship to Physical and Psychosomatic Disorders

PULMONARY TUBERCULOSIS

Although the description of the *habitus pthisicus* by Hippocrates clearly implied an affinity between narrow body build and tuberculosis, the association has usually been put down to the effect of the disease on body weight and physique generally rather than possibly indicating a predisposition to tuberculosis.

Recent work utilizing the findings obtained from mass radiography has helped to elucidate this age-old problem. Berry and Nash (1955) were able to demonstrate that the thickness of the skin and subcutaneous tissues measured from mass miniature radiographs, correlated to the extent of 0·86 with independent measurements of skinfold thickness made with fat calipers in the same series of individuals. They were thus able to show that subcutaneous fat may be estimated reasonably well from mass miniature radiographs and, in so doing, introduced a useful new technique for medical research.

These authors made a special study of a group of forty-nine people who had normal radiographs when first X-rayed and who later were found to have developed pulmonary tuberculosis. The interval between the first radiograph and that showing evidence of tuberculosis, ranged from two and a half to fifty-four months. They compared this group with a control group of similar age and sex distribution and matched as far as possible for occupation. They found that persons who developed tuberculosis had 17 per cent less fat than the controls.

They subdivided the groups into four types: Group 1, having long narrow chests, and Group 4, with short wide chests, with Groups 2 and 3 being intermediate. They found that individuals who developed tuberculosis had longer and narrower chests than the control subjects who did not develop tuberculosis, thus providing strong evidence in support of the *habitus phthisicus* of Hippocrates.

BODY TYPE AND ASTHMA

A number of investigators have, from time to time, claimed that there were special affinities between certain types of physique and the tendency to develop asthma. Hanse (1935) considered that asthmatics were predominantly of leptosomatic physique, and more recently Parnell (1954), using a modification of Sheldon's method in a group of university students, also considered that asthmatic patients were predominantly of ectomorphic physique. Horneck (1940), on the other hand, put forward the view that pyknic and muscular types were associated with asthma.

Rees (1957) studied a random sample of forty-two asthmatic men by means of the Rees-Eysenck body-build index. It was found that asthmatic subjects exhibited all ranges in physique, from the marked leptomorph to the marked eurymorph. Using the criteria of Rees and Eysenck (1945), the following distribution was found: eurymorphs 9, mesomorphs 21, leptomorphs 12. The mean value was identical to that of a normal healthy group of similar age distribution. The investigation yielded no evidence to suggest any significant relationship between asthma and body build. These conclusions are in agreement with those of Young (1953), who carried out anthropometric measurements both on a group of asthmatic children and a comparable control group, finding no significant differences in bodily measurements. The results are also in keeping with the work of Brouwer (1957), who used Sheldon's somatotyping method in groups of male and female asthmatic subjects. He found that asthmatics had a variety of somatotypes and did not differ significantly in somatotype distribution from the general population.

PEPTIC ULCER

During the present century a number of investigators have been interested in investigating the relationship between body build and the development of gastric or duodenal ulcers. Westphal (1914), Bauer (1918), Tscherning (1923), and Ruhmann (1926), reported that narrow types of body build were more common among ulcer patients. Draper and co-workers, in a series of publications since 1924, have reported relationships between body build and duodenal ulcer and gastric ulcer. They claimed that ulcer individuals had a smaller depth and breadth of the chest in relationship to height. They compared the physique of ulcer patients with those suffering from gall-bladder disease and stated that the index $\frac{\text{sagittal chest diameter}}{\text{length of the chest}}$ is lower in ulcer patients than those suffering from gall-bladder disease. This work is largely vitiated by the lack of satisfactory control groups and also because the age factor was not controlled. The average age for gall-bladder patients is 8·6 years higher than for the duodenal ulcer individuals, so that the difference in ages may have wholly or partly determined the differences in body measurements and bodily proportions. Feigenbaum and Howat (1934, 1935) compared sixty-seven ulcer individuals with seventy-nine diabetics and forty-six patients with gall-bladder disease. They studied these groups anthropometrically and found no significant differences between the diabetic and gall-bladder groups on the one hand and the peptic ulcer patients on the other. This work has been criticized by Wretmark (1953) both on grounds of methodology and with regard to the conclusions made. The work of many investigators has been partly vitiated because they did not separate duodenal ulcer from gastric ulcer patients.

A very carefully planned and well-controlled study of the relationship between personality, physique and peptic ulcer, was carried out by Wretmark (1953). This study is notable for the care with which a comparable control group was obtained, investigated and assessed by the same standards and criteria as the ulcer group. Body build was assessed by Strömgren's index and by indices described by Fürst (1933). It was found that duodenal ulcer patients had a more linear type of physique than the control group. The evidence regarding an affinity between gastric ulcer patients and similar types of physique was, however, not conclusive. The investigation also showed that there was a significant relationship between body build and the course of duodenal ulcer. The more leptomorphic the body build, the worse was the course of the illness.

Draper *et al.* (1944) found that peptic ulcer individuals showed more linearity of build, and that male duodenal ulcer patients were predominantly mesomorphic. Sheldon (1940) characterized duodenal ulcer and gastric ulcer patients as lacking in endomorphy (i.e. endopenic), but Brouwer (1956) points out that Sheldon's group of ninety-two male and twenty-five female duodenal ulcer patients had a strong tendency towards endomorphic mesomorphy which would indicate a heavy, stocky build but not endopenia. Brouwer (1956) found that his ulcer patients did not show mesomorphic body build as Draper *et al.* (1944) reported, nor endomorphic mesomorphy as Sheldon's figures suggest. He found, in conformity with Wretmark (1953), that duodenal ulcer patients were more inclined to leptosomatic body build, but did not differ significantly in ectomorphy from healthy male controls or from his total groups of male patients.

GALL-BLADDER DISEASE

Draper (1944) described a gall-bladder physical type characterized by thick, round, stocky body build. Sheldon (1940, 1949) confirmed Draper's findings, and that gall-bladder patients were usually mesomorphic-endomorphic.

Draper's gall-bladder group was found to be more thick, round and stocky than his peptic ulcer patients. However, his gall-bladder group is considerably older than his peptic ulcer group, and as the age factor is not adequately controlled, it is possible that some or all the physical differences may be a function of the age difference rather than indicating a biological affinity between gall-bladder disease and the broad, round, stocky body build.

Brouwer (1936), using Sheldon's method of somatotyping, also observed a preponderance of endomorphy in female gall-stone patients, but not significantly greater than that of a comparable healthy female control group.

CARDIOVASCULAR DISORDERS

The description of the *habitus apoplecticus* by Hippocrates suggested that the broad type of body build was associated with arterial disease and presumably high blood-pressure. Support for this is given by Robinson and Brucer (1940), who found that persons with arterial hypertension are usually of wide-heavy body build and often show a tendency to obesity.

Ciocco (1936) in a review of the literature, also states that there is evidence to indicate that the pyknic type has a tendency to hypertension and cerebral haemorrhage. During recent years attempts have been made to correlate cardiovascular functions in normal subjects with physical types and Sheldon's components of physique. Tanner (1947) investigated physiological functions in fifty healthy students and found no correlation between the components of physique on the one hand, and heart rate, cardiac output and blood-pressure on the other. Parnell (1955) found that the broadest hearts were found in pyknic types, and that in asthenic people the hearts were not only narrow but were also small in relation to their body size. He found that men of muscular build had the largest hearts and the slowest pulse rates. Recent investigations have brought forward evidence that coronary artery disease has a higher incidence in more mesomorphic men (Gertler, Garn and White, 1951; Spain *et al.*, 1955).

PHYSIQUE IN RELATIONSHIP TO EFFORT SYNDROME

Effort syndrome (synonyms: neurocirculatory asthenia, Da Costa's syndrome) is characterized by marked effort intolerance, by symptoms which unduly limit the patient's capacity for effort and by a number of signs depending on functional disturbance of the autonomic nervous system when such signs are not due to any organic disease. The cardinal symptoms are breathlessness, palpitations, fatigue, left chest pain, dizziness, and the cardinal signs are those of functional disturbances of the respiratory, vasomotor, muscular and sudomotor systems (Paul Wood, 1941).

It is convenient to divide the various possible causative factors into intrinsic (constitutional) and extrinsic. The role of physical constitution in patients suffering from effort syndrome was investigated by Rees (1944). Anthropometric measurements were carried out on groups of two hundred soldiers successively admitted to the effort syndrome unit at Mill Hill Emergency Hospital and groups of two hundred normal soldiers of comparable age and military status. A number of statistically significant mean differences in anthropometric measurements were found indicating that the effort syndrome group was significantly more narrow in body build than the control groups. Various anthropometric indices were also calculated and compared statistically. Significant differences were found in the Strömgren index and the Rees-Eysenck index, indicating that the effort syndrome group on the average was significantly more leptomorphic in body build than the normal groups.

Tanner (1951) considered that the data also provided evidence of marked differences in androgyny between the effort syndrome control group and a group of two hundred and thirty-seven Oxford students. He used formula 3 × biacromial diameter − bi-iliac breadth as a measure of androgyny and based his observations only on the mean value of the group. He remarks that the most striking features in the anthropometric data appear to be large hips, narrow shoulders and short legs (i.e. symphysis height). However, as Rees (1943) demonstrated, the leg length (as shown by symphysis height) was not significantly different between the effort syndrome patients and the normal control group, that hip width was, in fact, somewhat smaller in the effort syndrome group than in the control group, but that the difference was not statistically significant. In the second group of one hundred effort syndrome patients investigated, symphysis height was in fact greater than in the control group, but the difference was not statistically significant, and in the second hundred effort syndrome patients there was a greater hip circumference than in the normal group but the difference was again not statistically significant. The first hundred effort syndrome patients were significantly smaller than the control group in biacromial diameter; the second group was smaller in this measurement but not significantly so. Measurements showing the most significant differences in both groups of effort syndrome patients compared with the control groups were transverse and sagittal chest diameters, chest circumference and chest expansion. In the second hundred effort syndrome patients the most striking difference was found in sagittal chest diameter. Tanner's assumption that effort syndrome patients are more androgynic is not therefore substantiated by the data. Rees's (1944) findings are in keeping with the work of Seltzer (1940), who found that patients of leptomorphic physique showed a much lower mechanical efficiency when assessed by means of oxygen uptake experiments.

Patients classified under the category effort syndrome are heterogeneous both with regard to psychiatric symptomatology and in aetiological factors, showing varying proportions of intrinsic compared with extrinsic causative factors. The significance of leptomorphic physique in the genesis of effort syndrome becomes considerably elucidated when we compare effort syndrome patients with marked leptomorphic physique with effort syndrome patients with marked eurymorphic physique. This was done by Rees (1944), who found that 85 per cent of the leptomorphic effort syndrome patients had suffered from effort intolerance and symptoms of autonomic disequilibrium from an early age compared with 7 per cent in eurymorphic group; 66 per cent of the leptomorphic group had evidence of long standing personality traits of timidity, anxiety, and evidence of general neuroticism compared with 36 per cent in eurymorphic effort syndrome patients. The leptomorphic patients had a higher incidence of unsatisfactory factors in the family history of individuals with long-standing hypochondriacal tendencies. The eurymorphic effort syndrome patients were characterized by a comparatively short duration of illness. In 85 per cent the onset was less than two years before admission compared with 9 per cent in the leptomorphic group. Among the eurymorphic patients there was a higher proportion in whom exogenous factors were important aetiologically, for example, marked environmental stress, such as severe enemy action or precipitation by a febrile illness. It was, therefore, striking that leptomorphic effort syndrome patients had exhibited a predominance of constitutional factors in the aetiology as shown by the family history, longstanding symptoms of effort intolerance, autonomic disequilibrium, hypochondriasis and neuroticism. The eurymorphic effort syndrome patients on the other hand, tended to have effort intolerance of recent origin, which was often brought on by extrinsic factors such as traumatic experiences and febrile illness.

General Observations and Conclusions

The study of physical constitution has the respectable virtue of antiquity, but it is a field of investigation which has suffered from a surfeit of unverified hypotheses and a paucity of scientifically established facts. The majority of typological classifications which have from time to time been put forward, have lacked scientific basis and the entire concept of physical types in the sense of discrete and mutually exclusive categories has had to be abandoned in favour of a continuous variation ("dimensions") in body build. In order to facilitate the objective delineation of physical types, various anthropometric indices were devised, but most of these were not based on scientifically established criteria. Knowledge of the variations in human physique have been greatly advanced by modern methods, particularly factorial analysis and techniques introduced by Sheldon (1940), Lindegard (1954) and others. Factorial analysis and allied mathematical techniques have proved to be among the most fruitful scientific approaches to the study of variations in human body build. It should be noted that very few studies have utilized measurements specifically chosen for the purpose of factorial analysis. There is clearly a need for further research by factorial methods on well-selected and representative variables relating to all manifestations of physical constitution, including configuration of the body generally and of different regions, as well as the distribution of various tissues in the body.

Faulty methodology has in the past been responsible for failure to make more rapid progress in this field of research, e.g. failure to use random or representative samples of the disorder under investigation, failure to use satisfactory control groups, failure to control factors of age, sex, race and socio-economic status, etc. In some investigations the assessment of both psychological and physical attributes by the same observer has prevented the acceptance of the reported correlations at their face value in view of the possibility that bias or "halo" effect could be responsible for part or all of the alleged correlation. Improved objective techniques are also needed for the assessment, not only of physique, but of personality, mental and clinical status.

We have seen from the survey of available evidence that the correlations between physical and psychological attributes, although often statistically significant, are usually of a low order, and it remains to be seen whether in the future higher correlations will be found where improved research techniques and methodology are used. The very high correlations reported by Sheldon (1942) between somatotype and temperament, have not been confirmed by other workers. It is, therefore, possible that the correlations between the physical, psychological, and physiological aspects of human constitution and their relationship with disease susceptibility, although statistically significant and biologically important, may not be great enough to serve the needs of diagnosis.

If further research confirms or provides further evidence of significant relationships between physical attributes, personality and susceptibility to psychiatric, psychosomatic and physical disorders, the question will still remain regarding the precise nature of the factors or processes responsible for the associations. There appear to be two main possible explanations for correlations between certain physical and psychological attributes. Firstly the association could be due to life experiences, reactions and conditioning processes, linking different psychological attributes to different physical attributes. An alternative and more probable explanation is that they constitute integrated biological correlations between constitutional attributes. If this proves to be the case, the basis may be genetic, with the genes responsible for various aspects of body build exerting an influence on the manifestation of development of genetically determined aspects of personality and neurosis, psychosis or other illness. There is an urgent need for further genetic investigations in this field, especially in combination with longitudinal investigations of growth and development. Such investigations should, in due course, provide a body of scientifically established, valid data, regarding the interrelationships of physical, psychological, physiological disease susceptibility as integrated components of the total personality.

APPENDIX

Indices of Body Build

Pignet Index = Stature (cm) − [chest circumference (cm) + weight (kg)].

Morphological Index is a modification of that of Wertheimer and Hesketh (1926)—

$$\frac{\text{Symphysis height} \times 10^3}{\text{Transverse chest diameter} \times \text{sagittal chest diameter} \times \text{trunk length}}$$

Strömgren Index = − 0·04 stature + 0·127 transverse chest diameter + 0·56 sagittal chest diameter.

The following indices are quoted by Tucker and Lessa (1940)—

Bornhardt, A.

$$= \frac{\text{stature} \times \text{chest circumference}}{\text{weight}}$$

Brugsch's Index

$$= \frac{\text{chest circumference} \times 100}{\text{stature}}$$

Rohrer

$$= \frac{\text{weight} \times 100}{\text{stature} \times \text{shoulder breadth} \times \text{sagittal chest}}$$

Von Rohden

$$= \frac{\text{symphysis height}}{\text{chest circumference} \times \text{anterior trunk height}}$$

Lucas and Pryor

$$= \frac{\text{bi-iliac diameter} \times 1,000}{\text{stature}}$$

Pignet Ver Vaeck

$$= \frac{\text{weight} + \text{chest circumference} \times 100}{\text{stature}}$$

Martin

$$= \frac{\text{bicristal diameter}}{\text{shoulder breadth}}$$

Marburg, B.

$$= \frac{\text{leg length}}{(\text{transverse} + \text{sagittal chest diameter}) \times \text{trunk length} \times \text{shoulder breadth}}$$

REFERENCES

ADLER, H. M. and MOHR, G. J., Some considerations of the significance of physical constitution in relation to mental disorder, *Amer. J. Psychiat.*, **7**, 701–707 (1928).

ANASTASI, A. and FOLEY, J. P., *Differential Psychology* (New York, Macmillan, 1949).

ARISTOTLE, Physiognomonica. Trans. by T. Loveday and E. M. Forster, in *The Works of Aristotle* (Oxford, Clarendon Press, 1913).

ASCHER, B., Die Konstitution der Frau und ihre Beziehung zur Geburtsshilfe und Gynäkologie (Munchen: 1924).

BAKWIN, H. and BAKWIN, R. M., Types of body build in infants, *Amer. J. Dis. Child.*, **37**, 461–472 (1929).

BAKWIN, H. and BAKWIN, R. M., Body build in infants: V. Anthropometry of the newborn, *Hum. Biol.*, **6**, 612–626 (1943).

BALDWIN, B. T., The physical growth of children from birth to maturity, *Univ. Ia Stud. Child Welf.*, **1**, No. 1 (1921).

BAUER, J., *Die konstitutionelle Disposition zur inneren Krankheiten* (Berlin, J. Springer, 1917).

BAUER, J., *Vorlesungen über allegemeine Konstitutions-Vererbungslehre* (Berlin, J. Springer, 1923).

BAYLEY, N., Factors influencing the growth and intelligence of young children, 39th Yearbook, *Nat. Soc. Stud. Educ.*, Part II, 49–79 (1940).

BAYLEY, N., Size and body build of adolescents in relation to rate of skeletal maturing, *Child Develpm.*, **14**, 47–89 (1943).

BAYLEY, N. and BAYER, L. M., The assessment of somatic androgyny *Amer. J. Phys. Anthropol.*, **4**, 433–461 (1946).

BEAN, R. B., Morbidity and Morphology, *Johns Hopk. Hosp. Bull.*, **23**, 363–370 (1912).

BEAN, R. B., The two European types, *Amer. J. Anat.*, **31**, 359–371 (1923).

BEAN, R. B., Human types, *Quart. Rev. Biol.*, **1**, 360–392 (1926).

BENEKE, F. W., *Die anatomischen Grundlagen der Constitutionsanomalien des Menschen* (Marburg, 1898).

BENEKE, F. W., *Konstitution und Konstitutionelles kranksein des Menschen* (Marburg, Elwert, 1881).

BERNREUTER, R. G., The imbrication of tests of introversion-extraversion and neurotic tendency, *J. Soc. Psychol.*, **5**, 184–201 (1934).

BERRY, W. T. C. and NASH, F. A., Studies in the aetiology of pulmonary tuberculosis, *Tubercle*, **36**, 164–174 (1955).

BETZ, B., Somatology of the schizophrenic patient, *Hum. Biol.*, **14**, 21–47; 192–234 (1942).

BLEULER, M., Untersuchungen aus dem Grenz-gebiet zwischen Psycho-pathologie und Endocrinologie, *Arch. Psychiat. Nervenkr.*, **118**, 271–528 (1948).

BOLDRINI, M., Sivluppo corporeo e predisposizioni morbose, *Vita e Pensiero* (Milan, 1925).

BOLDRINI, M., La fertilita dei biotipi, *Vita e Pensiero*, (Milan, 1931).

BORCHARDT, L., Funktionelle und tropische Momente als Ursachen des gegensätzlichen Verhaltens von Pyknikern und Asthenikern, *Z. KonstLehre*, **16**, 1–7 (1931).

BRAAT, J. P., Die experimentelle Psychologie und Kretschmer's Konstitutionstypen, *Mschr. Psychiat. Neurol.*, **94**, 273–297 (1937).

BRATTGARD, S. O., Personality attitude and physical make-up, *Acta Psychiat. Neurol. scand.*, **354**, 339–354 (1950).

BROOKS, F. D., The organization of mental and physical traits during adolescence, *J. Appl. Psychol.*, **12**, 228 (1928).

BROUWER, D., Somatotypes and psychosomatic diseases, *J. Psychosom. Res.*, **2**, 23–34 (1957).

BROZEK, J., Measuring nutrition, *Amer. J. Phys. Anthropol.*, **11**, 147–180 (1953).

BROZEK, J. and KEYS, A., Evaluation of leanness-fatness in man: a survey of methods, *Nutr. Abstr. Rev.*, **20**, 247–256 (1951).

BROZEK, J. and KEYS, A., Evaluation of leanness-fatness in man, *Brit. J. Nutr.*, **5**, 194–206 (1951).

BRUGSCH, T., *Allgemeine Prognostik, oder die Lehre von der artzlichen Beurteilung des gesunden und kranken Menschen* (Berlin, 1918).

BRUGSCH, T., Die Morphologie der Person, in *Die Biologie der Person*, **2**, T. Brugsch, and F. H. Lewy, 1–114 (Berlin u. Wien: Urban & Schwarzenberg, 1926–1931, 1931).

BRYANT, J., Stasis and human efficiency, *Int. Abstr. Surg.*, 449 (May, 1914).

BRYANT, J., The carnivorous and herbivorous types of man, *Boston Med. Surg. J.*, **172**, 321–326; **173**, 384–387 (1915).

BUCHI, E. C., Anderung der Korperform beim erwachsensen Menschen, eine Untersuchung nach der Individual-method, Anthropologische Farschungen (Anthrop. Geselt. Wien, Ferdinand Berger, Horn. Heff. 1. 1950).

BURCHARD, M. L., Physique and psychosis, *Comp. Psychol. Mon.*, **13**, 84 (1936).

BURT, C., The analysis of temperament, *Brit. J. Med. Psychol.*, **17**, 158–188 (1937–38).

BURT, C., *Factors of the Mind* (London, Univ. of London Press, 1940).

BURT, C., Factorial analysis of physical growth, *Nature*, **152**, 75 (1943).

BURT, C., The factorial study of physical types, *Man*, **44**, 82–86 (1944).

BURT, C., A comparison of factor analysis and analysis of variance, *Brit. J. Psychol.* (Stat. Sect.), **1**, 3–26 (1947).

BURT, C., Factor analysis and physical types, *Psychometrika*, **12**, 171–188 (1947).

BURT, C., Subdivided factors, *Brit. J. Psychol.* (Stat. Sect.), **2**, 41–63 (1949).

BURT, C. and BANKS, CHARLOTTE, A factor analysis of body measurements for British adult males, *Ann. Eugen.*, **13**, 238–256 (1947).

CABOT, P. S. DE Q., The relationship between characteristics of personality and physique in adolescents, *Genet. Psychol. Monogr.*, **20**, 3–120 (1938).

CAMPBELL, J. K., The relation of the types of physique to the types of mental disease, *J. Abnorm. (Soc.) Psychol.*, **27**, 147–151 (1932).

CARTER, H. D. and KRAUS, R. H., The physical proportions of the human infant, *Child Developm.*, **7**, 60–68 (1936).

CARUS, C. G., *Symbolik der menschlichen Gestalt* (Orig. 1853; Edit. 1925, Celle).

CASTLE, W. E., Genetic studies of rabbits and rats, *Pub. Carnegie Inst.* No. 320 (1922).

CASTLE, W. E., Size inheritance, *Amer. Nat.*, **75**, 488–498 (1941).

CATHCART, E. P., HUGHES, E. R. and CHALMERS, J. G., The physique of man in industry, *M.R.C. Industrial Health Research Board, Rep.* No. 71 (London, H.M.S.O., 1935).

CATTELL, R. B., *Description and Measurement of Personality* (Yonkers-on-Hudson, World Books, 1946).

CHAILLOU, A. and MACAULIFFE, L., *Morphologie Medicale* (Paris, 1912).

CHILD, I. L. and SHELDON, W. H., The correlation between components of physique and scores on certain psychological tests, *Character & Pers.*, **10**, 23–34 (1941).

CIOCCO, A., The historical background of the modern study of constitution, *Bull. Inst. Hist. Med.*, **4**, 23–38 (1936).

CLEGG, J. L., The association of physique and mental condition, *J. Ment. Sci.*, **81**, 297–316 (1935).

COERPER, C., Personelle Beurteilung nach der practischen Lepenseignung (a) körperlich, in *Die Biologie der Person*, Ed. T. Brugsch, and F. H. Lewy (Berlin, Urban & Schwarzenburg, 1926).

COHEN, J. I., Determinants of physique, *J. Ment. Sci.*, **84**, 495–512 (1938).

COHEN, J. I., Physical types and their relation to psychotic types, *J. Ment. Sci.*, **86**, 602 (1940).

COHEN, J. I., Physique, size and proportions, *Brit. J. Med. Psychol.*, **18**, 323–337 (1941).

CONNOLLY, C. J., Physique in relation to psychosis, *Stud. Psychol. Psychiat., Cath. Univ. Amer.*, **4**, No. 5 (1939).

CONRAD, K., *Der Konstitutionstypus als genetisches Problem* (Berlin, 1941).

COPPEN, A. J., Psychosomatic aspects of pre-eclamptic toxaemia, *J. Psychosom. Res.*, **2**, 241–265 (1958).

CURETON, T. K., *Physical Fitness, Appraisal and Guidance* (London, 1947).

DAHLBERG, G., *Twin Births and Twins from an Hereditary Point of View* (Stockholm, Tidens, 1926).

DAMON, A., Physique and success in military flying, *Amer. J. Phys. Anthropol.*, **13**, 217–252 (1955).

DAMON, A. and MCFARLAND, R. A., The physique of bus and truck drivers, *Amer. J. Phys. Anthropol.*, **13**, 711–742 (1955).

DAVENPORT, C. B., Height-weight index of build, *Amer. J. Phys. Anthropol.*, **3**, 567 (1920).

DAVENPORT, C. B., Body-build and its inheritance, *Pub. Carnegie Inst.*, No. 329 (1923).

DAVIDSON, M. A., MCINNES, R. G. and PARNELL, R. W., The distribution of personality traits in seven-year-old children, *Brit. J. Educ. Psychol.*, **27**, 48–61 (1957).

DEARBORN, W. F. and ROTHNEY, J., *Predicting the Child's Development*, 360 (Cambridge, Mass., Sci.-Art. Publ., 1941).

DI GIOVANNI, A., *Clinical Commentaries Deduced from the Morphology of the Human Body* (London and New York, J. J. Eyre, 1919).

DOLL, E. A., *Anthropometry as an Aid to Mental Diagnosis* (New Jersey, Williams & Wilkins, 1916).

DRAPER, G., *Human Constitution* (Philadelphia, Saunders, 1924).

DRAPER, G., The emotional component of the ulcer susceptible constitution, *Ann. Intern. Med.*, **16**, 633 (1942).

DRAPER, G., DUNN, H. L. and SEEGAL, D., Studies in human constitution. 1. Clinical anthropometry, *J. Amer. Med. Ass.*, **82**, 431 (1924).

DRAPER, G., DUPERTUIS, C. W. and CAUGHEY, J. L., *Human Constitution in Clinical Medicine* (New York, Hoeber, 1944).

DRAPER, G. and MCGRAW, R. B., Studies in human constitution: V. The psychological panel, *Amer. J. Med. Sci.*, **174**, 299 (1927).

DRAPER, G. and TOURAINE, G. A., The man-environment unit and peptic ulcer, *Arch. Intern. Med.*, **49**, 616 (1932).

DUPERTUIS, C. W., Anthropometry of extreme somatotypes, *Amer. J. Physiol. Anthropol.*, **8**, 367–385 (1950).

DUPERTUIS, C. W., Body build and specific gravity, Proc. 19th Ann. Meeting of Amer. Ass. of Physical Anthropologists, *Amer. J. Phys. Anthropol.*, **8**, 260 (1950).

DUPERTUIS, C. W., PITTS, G. C., OSSERMAN, E. F., WELHAM, W. C. and BEHNKE, A. R., Relation of specific gravity to body build on a group of healthy men, *J. Appl. Psychol.*, **3**, 676–680 (1951*a*).

DUPERTUIS, C. W., PITTS, G. C., OSSERMAN, E. F., WELHAM, W. C. and BEHNKE, A. R., Relation of body water content to body build in a group of healthy men, *J. Appl. Psychol.*, **4**, 364–367 (1951*b*).

EDWARDS, D. A. W., Observations on the distribution of subcutaneous fat, *Clin. Sci.*, **9**, 259–270 (1950).

EDWARDS, D. A. W., Observations on the distribution of subcutaneous fat, *Clin. Sci.*, **9**, 305–315 (1950).

EDWARDS, D. A. W., HAMMOND, W. H., HEALY, M. J. R., TANNER, J. M. and WHITEHOUSE, R. H., Design and accuracy of calipers for measuring subcutaneous tissue thickness, *Brit. J. Nutr.*, **9**, 133–143 (1955).

EKMAN, G., On typological and dimensional systems of reference in describing personality, *Acta. Psychol.*, **8**, 1–24 (1951).

EKMAN, G., On the number and definition of dimensions in Kretschmer's and Sheldon's constitutional systems, *Essays in Psychology* (Uppsala, Almquist, 1951).

ENKE, W., Experimentalpsychologische Studien zur Konstitutionsforschung, *Z. ges. Neurol. Psychiat.*, **114**, 770–794 (1928).

ENKE, W., The affectivity of Kretschmer's constitutional

types as revealed in psycho-galvanic experiments, *Character & Pers.*, **1**, 225–233 (1933).

EPPS, P. and PARNELL, R. W., Physique and temperament of women delinquents compared with women undergraduates, *Brit. J. Med. Psychol.*, **25**, 249–255 (1952).

ESQUIROL, *Dictionnaire des Sciences médicales*, Vol. XVI (Paris, 1816).

EYSENCK, H. J., *Dimensions of Personality* (London, Routledge & Kegan Paul, 1947).

EYSENCK, H. J., *The Scientific Study of Personality* (London, Routledge & Kegan Paul, 1952).

EYSENCK, H. J., *The Structure of Human Personality* (London, Methuen, 1953).

FARR, C. B., Bodily structure, personality and reaction type, *Amer. J. Psychiat.*, **7**, 231–244 (1928).

FEIGENBAUM, J. and HOWAT, D., The relation between physical constitution and the incidence of disease, *J. Clin. Invest.*, **13**, 121 (1934).

FEIGENBAUM, J. and HOWAT, D., Physical constitution and disease: II. Absence of correlation between the anatomic constitution and predisposition to *diabetes mellitus*, cholecystitis and peptic ulcer, *Arch. Intern. Med.*, **55**, 445–456 (1935).

FISKE, D. W., A study of relationship to somatotype, *J. Appl. Psychol.*, **28**, 504 (1944).

FREEMAN, W., Psychological panel in diagnosis and prognosis; correlation of personality type with susceptibility to disease, based on 1,400 necropsies, *Ann. Intern. Med.*, **IV**, 29–38 (1930).

FÜRST, C. M., Eine Zahlenbezeichnung für die Kombinationen der Indices der drei Dimensionen des Schädels (Tr. I). *Anthrop. Anzeig.*, **10**, 209–214 (1933).

FÜRST, C. M., Grapische Darstellung der möglichen Kombinationen der indices der drei Dimensionen des Schädels (Tr. I), *Anthrop. Anzeig.*, **10**, 321–322 (1933).

GALL, F. J. and SPURZHEIM, J. G., *Recherches sur le Système nerveux* (Paris, 1809).

GARN, S. M., Research in human growth, *Hum. Biol.*, **29**, 1–11 (1957).

GARN, S. M. and GERTLER, M. M., An association between type of work and physique in an industrial group, *Amer. J. Phys. Anthropol.*, **8**, 387–397 (1950).

GARRETT, H. E. and KELLOGG, W. N., The relation of physical constitution to general intelligence, social intelligence and emotional stability, *J. Exp. Psychol.*, **11**, 113–129 (1928).

GARVEY, C. R., Comparative body-build of manic-depressive and schizophrenic patients, *Psychol. Bull.*, **30**, 567–568 (1930).

GENELL, S., JENSEN, C. C. and LINDEGARD, B., On the quantitative relationship between some steroid substances excreted in the urine by adult males, in *Bodybuild, Body-function and Personality* Ed. B. Lindegard (Lund, Gleerup, 1956).

GERTLER, M. M., GARN, S. M. and LEVINE, S. A., Serum uric acid in relation to age and physique in health and in coronary heart disease, *Ann. Intern. Med.*, **34**, 1,421–1,431 (1951).

GERTLER, M. M., GARN, S. M. and SPRAGUE, H. B., Cholesterol, cholesterol esters and phospholipides in health and coronary artery disease: II. Morphology and serum lipides in man, *Circulation*, **2**, 380–391 (1950).

GERTLER, M. M., GARN, S. M. and WHITE, P. D., Young candidates for coronary disease, *J. Amer. Med. Ass.*, **147**, 621–625 (1951).

GILDEA, E. F., KAHN, E. and MAN, E. B., The relationship between body build and serum lipides and a discussion of these qualities as pyknophilic and leptophilic factors in the structure of the personality, *Amer. J. Psychiat.*, **92**, 1247–1260 (1936).

GLUECK, S. and GLUECK, E., *Unravelling Juvenile Delinquency* (New York, Commonwealth Fund, 1950).

GREENWOOD, M. and SMITH, M., Some pioneers of medical psychology, *Brit. J. Med. Psychol.*, **14**, 1–30, 158–9 (1934).

GREGORY, R. W. and CASTLE, W. E., Further studies in the embryological basis of size inheritance in the rabbit, *J. Exp. Zool.*, **59**, 199–211 (1931).

GRUHLE, H. W., Der Körper der Normalen, *Arch. Psychiat., Nervenkr.*, **77**, 1–31 (1926).

HALL, W. S., Changes in the form of the body during the period of growth, *J. R. Anthrop. Inst.*, **25**, 21–45 (1896).

HAMILTON, M., Nomogram for the Rees-Eysenck body index, *J. Ment. Sci.*, **96**, 540 (1950).

HAMMOND, J., *Farm Animals. Their Breeding, Growth and Inheritance* (London, Arnold, 1940).

HAMMOND, W. H., An application of Burt's multiple general factor analysis to the delineation of physical types, *Man*, **52**, 4–11 (1942).

HAMMOND, W. H., Measurement of physical types in children, *Hum. Biol.*, **25**, 65–80 (1953a).

HAMMOND, W. H., Physique and development of boys and girls from different types of school, *Brit. J. Prevent. Soc. Med.*, **7**, 231–239 (1953b).

HAMMOND, W. H., Measurement and interpretation of subcutaneous fat, *Brit. J. Prevent. Soc. Med.*, **9**, 201–211 (1955a).

HAMMOND, W. H., Body measurements of pre-school children, *Brit. J. Prevent. Soc. Med.*, **9**, 152–158 (1955b).

HAMMOND, W. H., The constancy of physical types as determined by factorial analysis, *Hum. Biol.*, **29**, 40–61 (1957).

HAMMOND, W. H., The status of physical types, *Hum. Biol.*, **29**, 223–241 (1957).

HAUPTMAN, A. and MYERSON, A., Studies of finger capillaries in schizophrenia and manic-depressive psychosis, *J. Nerv. Ment. Dis.*, **108**, 91–108 (1948).

HEATH, C. W., *What People Are (a Study of Normal Young Men)* (Cambridge, Mass., Harvard Univ. Press, 1945).

HEATH, H. A., A factor analysis of women's measurement taken for garment and pattern construction, *Doctoral Dissertation, Dept. of Psychiat., Univ. of Chicago* (available on microfilm) 1950.

HEATH, H. A., A factor analysis of women's measurements taken for garment and pattern construction, *Psychometrika*, **17**, 87–95 (1952).

HEIDBREDER, E., Intelligence and the height-weight ratio, *J. Appl. Psychol.*, **10**, 52–62 (1926).

HENCKEL, K. O., Körperbaustudien an Schizophrenen, *Z. ges. Neurol. Psychiat.*, **89**, 82–106 (1924).

HENCKEL, K. O., Konstitutionstypen und europäische Rassen, *Klin. Wschr.*, **4**, 2145–2148 (1925).

HIPPOCRATES, *The Genuine Works of*, trans. from Greek with preliminary discourse and annotations by Francis Adams (New York, W. Wood & Co., 1891).

HJORTSJO, C. H., Eine neuer Index gemass dem "Tres-Indices"—Princip als Hilsmittel bei der Beurteilung der Korperkonstitution "Tri corp," *Lunds Universitets Årsskrift N.F.*, Avd. 2, Bd. 47, Nr. 4 (1951).

HJORTSJO, C. H., Stromgren's constitutional index and the "Tri corp." A comparison, *Acta. Psychiat. Neurol. Scand.*, **27**, 57 (1952).

HJORTSJO, C. H. and LINDEGARD, B., Critical aspects of the use of indices in physical anthropology, *K. Fysiogr. Sällsk. Lund, Förh.*, **23**, No. 8 (1953).

HOOTON, E. A., *Apes, Men and Morons* (New York, Putnam, 1937).

HOOTON, E. A., *Crime and the Man* (Cambridge, Mass., Harvard Univ. Press, 1939).

HOOTON, E. A., *The American Criminal* (Vol. I) (Cambridge, Mass., Harvard Univ. Press, 1939).

HOWELLS, W. W., Physical anthropology as a technique, *Amer. J. Phys. Anthropol.*, **1**, 355–361 (1943).

HOWELLS, W. W., Birth order and body size, *Amer. J. Phys. Anthropol.*, **6**, 449–460 (1948).

HOWELLS, W. W., Body measurements in the light of familial influences, *Amer. J. Phys. Anthropol.*, **7**, 101–108 (1949).

HOWELLS, W. W., Factors of human physique, *Amer. J. Phys. Anthropol.*, **9**, 159–191 (1951).

HOWELLS, W. W., A factorial study of constitutional type, *Amer. J. Phys. Anthropol.*, **10**, 91–118 (1952).

HRDLICKA, A., *Practical Anthropology* (Philadelphia, 1947).

HUMPHREYS, L. G., Characteristics of type concepts with special reference to Sheldon's typology, *Psychol. Bull.*, **54**, 218–228 (1957).

HUNT, E. E., (JNR.) Human constitution: an appraisal, *Amer. J. Phys. Anthropol.*, **10**, 55–74 (1952).

HUNTER, J., *The Works of John Hunter, with Notes*, Vol. 1. Ed. J. F. Palmer (London, Longman, 1835).

HUXLEY, J. S., *Problems of Relative Growth* (London, Methuen, 1932).

JACOB, C. and MOSER, K., Messungen zur Kretschmer's Körpersbaulehre, *Arch. Psychiat. Nervenkr.*, **70**, 93–108 (1923).

JOST, J. and SONTAG, L. W., The genetic factor in autonomic nervous system function, *Psychosom. Med.*, **6**, 308–310 (1944).

KALLMAN, F., *The Genetics of Schizophrenia* (New York, J. J. Augustin, Inc., 1938).

KALLMAN, F., The genetic theory of schizophrenia, *Amer. J. Psychiat.*, **103**, 309–322 (1946).

KALLMAN, F., *Heredity in Health and Mental Disorders* (New York, Norton, 1953).

KEEHN, J. D., An experimental investigation into the validity of the use of attitude to colour and form in the assessment of personality, *Ph.D. Thesis, Univ. of London Lib.* (1953).

KEYS, A. and BROZEK, J., Body fat in adult man, *Physiol. Rev.*, **33**, 245–325 (1953).

KIBLER, M., Experimental psychologischer Beitrag zur Typenforschung, *Z. ges. Neurol. Psychiat.*, **98**, 524–544 (1925).

KISSELEW, M. W., Der Körperbau und die besonderen Arten des Schizophreieverlaufs, *Z. ges. Neurol. Psychiat.*, **132**, 18–56 (1931).

KLINE, N. A. and OPPENHEIM, A. N., Constitutional factors in prognosis of schizophrenia, further observations, *Amer. J. Psychiat.*, **108**, 909 (1952).

KOLLE, K., Der Körperbau der Schizophrenen, *Arch. Psychiat., Nervenkr.*, **72**, 40–88 (1925).

KRETSCHMER, E., *Körperbau und Charakter* (Berlin, J. Springer, 1921).

KRETSCHMER, E., *Physique and Character* (New York, Harcourt & Brace, 1926).

KRETSCHMER, E., *Physique and Character*. An investigation of the nature of constitution and of the theory of temperament, 2nd Ed. K. Paul (London, Trench Trubner & Co., 1936).

KRETSCHMER, E., Tonus as a constitutional problem, *Z. ges. Neurol. Psychiat.*, **171**, 401–407 (1941).

KRETSCHMER, E., *Körperbau und Charakter* (19th Ed.) (Berlin, J. Springer, 1948).

KROGMAN, W. M., The physical growth of children: An appraisal of studies 1950–1955 *Monogr, Soc. for Res. in Child Developmt.*, Ser. No. 60, 1 (1956).

LANGFELDT, G., *The Prognosis in Schizophrenia and the Factors Influencing the Course of the Disease* (Copenhagen, Levin and Munksgaard, 1937).

LASKER, G. W., The effects of partial starvation on somatotype, *Amer. J. Phys. Anthropol.*, **5**, 323–341 (1947).

LASKER, G. W., The age factor in bodily measurements of adult male and female Mexicans, *Hum. Biol.*, **25**, 50–63 (1953).

LAVATER, J. C., *Essays on Physiognomy: For the Promotion of the Knowledge and the Love of Mankind*, Trans. Thomas Holcroft (London, Whittingham, 1804).

LAVATER, J. C., *L'art de connaître les Hommes par la Physiognomie* (Paris, 1835).

LAVATER, J. C., *La Physiognomie*. Traduction nouvelle par H. Bacharach (Paris, Librairie Française et Étrangère, 1841).

LAYCOCK, T., Physiognomical diagnosis, *Med. Times and Gazette*, **1**, 1–3, 51–54, 101–103, 185, 205–208, 287–289, 341–344, 449–451, 499–502, 551–554, 635–637 (1862).

LEE, A., LORENZ, M. D. and PEARSON, L., On the correlation of mental and physical characteristics in man, *Proc. Roy. Soc.*, **71**, 106–114 (1903).

LEWIS, N. D. C., The constitutional factors in dementia praecox, *Nerv. ment. Dis. Monogr.*, 39 (1924).

LEWIS, N. D. C., *Research in Dementia Praecox* (New York, National Committee for Mental Hygiene, 1936).

LINDBERG, B. J., Experimental studies of colour and non-colour attitude in school children and adults, *Diss. Acta. Psychiat. et Neurol.*, Suppl. 16 (1938).

LINDEGARD, B., *Variations in Human Body Build* (Copenhagen, Munksgaard, 1953).

LINDEGARD, B., (Ed.) *Body Build, Body Function and Personality* (Lund, Gleerup, 1956).

LINDEGARD, B., MORSING, C. and NYMAN, E. G., Male sex characters in relation to body build, endocrine activity and personality, in *Body Build, Body Function and Personality*, Ed. B. Lindegard (1956).

LINDEGARD, B. and NYMAN, E. G., Interrelations between psychologic, somatologic and endocrine dimensions, in *Body Build, Body Function and Personality*, Ed. B. Lindegard (1956).

LOMBROSO, C., *L'Uomo Delinquente* (Flli. Bocca, Torina, 1889).

LOMBROSO, C., *Crime, It's Causes and Remedies*, Trans. Horton (Boston, Little, Brown, 1911).

LORR, M. and FIELDS, V., A factorial study of body types, *J. Clin. Psychol.*, **10**, 182–185 (1954).

LOW, A., *Growth of Children* (Aberdeen, University Press, 1952).

LUCAS, W. P. and PRYOR, H. B., The body build factor in the basal metabolism of children, *Amer. J. Dis. Child.*, (Pt. II) **46**, 941–948 (1933).

LUCAS, W. P. and PRYOR, H. B., Physical measurements and physiological processes in young children, *J. Amer. Med. Ass.*, **97**, 1,127 (1931).

MACAULIFFE, L., Les origines de la morphologie humaine, *Bull. Soc. d'Étude des Formes Humaines*, Nos. 2 & 3, 155 (1925).

MCCANCE, R. A. and WIDDOWSON, E. M., A method of breaking down the body weights of living persons into terms of extra-cellular fluid, cell mass and fat and some applications of it to physiology and medicine, *Proc. Roy. Soc.*, **138**, 115–130 (1951).

MCCLOY, C. H., Appraising physical status and the selection of measurements, *Univ. Ia Stud. Child Welf.*, **12**, No. 2 (1936).

MCCLOY, C. H., An analysis for multiple factors of physical growth at different age levels, *Child Develpm.*, **11**, 249–277 (1940).

MCFARLAND, R. A., *Human Factors in Air Transport Design* (New York, McGraw Hill, 1946).

MCFARLAND, R. A., *Human Factors in Air Transportation* (New York, McGraw Hill, 1953).

MANOUVRIER, L., Étude sur les rapports anthropométriques en général et sur les principales proportions du corps, *Mém. de la Soc. d'Anth. de Paris*, Ser. 3, T. 2 (1902).

MARSHALL, E. L., A multiple factor study of 18 anthropometric measurements of Iowa City boys, *J. Exp. Educ.*, **5**, 212 (1938).

MARTIGNY, M., *Essai de Biotypologue Humaine* (Peyronnet, Paris, 1948).

MARTIN, R., *Lehrbuch der Anthropologie* (Jena, 1928).

MAUZ, F., *Die Prognostik der ergogensen Psychosen*, (Leipzig, Thieme, 1930).

MEADE, C. D., Height and weight of children in relation to general intelligence, *Ped. Sem.*, **21**, 394–406 (1914).

MICHEL, F. and WEBER, R., Körperbau und Charakter, *Arch. f. Psychiat.*, **71**, 265 (1924).

MILLS, R. W., The relation of body *habitus* to visceral form, position, tonus and motility, *Amer. J. Roentgenol.*, **4**, 155 (1917).

MISIAK, H. and PICKFORD, R. W., Physique and perseveration, *Nature*, **153**, 622 (1944).

MOHR, G. J. and GUNDLACH, R. H., The relation between physique and performance, *J. Exp. Psychol.*, **10**, 117–157 (1927).

MOLLENHOFF, F., Zur Frage der Beziehungen zwischen Körperbau und Psychose, *Arch. f. Psychiat.*, **71**, 98 (1924).

MOORE, T. V. and HSU, E. H., Factorial analysis of anthropological measurements in psychotic patients, *Hum. Biol.*, **18**, 133–157 (1946).

MULLEN, F. A., Factors in the growth of girls, *Child Develpm.*, **11**, 27 (1940).

NACCARATI, S., The morphological aspect of intelligence, *Arch. Psychol.*, No. 45 (1921).

NACCARATI, S., The morphologic basis of the psychoneuroses, *Amer. J. Psychiat.*, **3**, 527–545 (1924).

NACCARATI, S. and GARRETT, H. E., The relation of morphology to temperament, *J. Abnorm. (Soc.) Psychol.*, **19**, 3 (1924).

NEWMAN, H. H., FREEMAN, F. N. and HOLZINGER, K. J., *Twins: A Study of Heredity and Environment* (Chicago, Univ. of Chicago Press, 1937).

NEWMAN, R. W., Age changes in body build, *Amer. J. Phys. Anthropol.*, **10**, 75–90 (1952).

O'BRIEN, R., GIRSHICK, M. A. and HUNT, E. P., Body measurements of American boys and girls for garment and pattern construction, *U.S. Dept. Agric. Misc. Pub.* No. 366, 29–34.

OLIVIER, H. G., Der Körperbau der Schizophrenen, *Z. ges. Neurol. Psychiat.*, **80**, 489–498 (1922).

OLKON, D. M., Capillary structure in patients with schizophrenia, *Arch. Neurol. Psychiat. Chicago*, **48**, 652–663 (1939).

PALMER, C. E., Age changes in physical resemblance of siblings, *Child Develpm.*, **5**, 351 (1934).

PARNELL, R. W., Some notes on physique and athletic training with special reference to heart size, *Brit. Med. J.*, **1**, 1,292 (1951).

PARNELL, R. W., Physique and mental breakdown in young adults, *Brit. Med. J.*, **1**, 1,485–1,490 (1957).

PARNELL, R. W., Recording human constitution, *Eug. Rev.*, **XLIV**, 1, 20 (1952).

PARNELL, R. W., Physique and choice of faculty, *Brit. Med. J.*, **2**, 472–475 (1953).

PARNELL, R. W., Physical body measurements, *Trans. Assoc. Industrial Med. Officers*, **3**, 1 (1953).

PARNELL, R. W., The physique of Oxford undergraduates, *J. Hygiene*, **52**, 369–378 (1954).

PARNELL, R. W., Physique and performance: Honours class at Oxford, *Brit. Med. J.*, **2**, 491 (1954).

PARNELL, R. W., Somatotyping by physical anthropometry, *Amer. J. Phys. Anthropol.*, **12**, 209–240 (1954).

PARNELL, R. W., The relationship of masculine and feminine physical traits to academic and athletic performance, *Brit. J. Med. Psychol.*, **XXVII**, 4, 247 (1954).

PARNELL, R. W., Constitutional aspects of psychosomatic medicine, in *Modern Trends in Psychosomatic Medicine* (London, Butterworth, 1954).

PARNELL, R. W., Strength of body and strength of mind, *Brit. J. Physiol. Med.*, **18**, 7, 150–159 (1955).

PARNELL, R. W., DAVIDSON, M. D., LEE, D. and SPENCER, S. J. G., The detection of psychological vulnerability in students, *J. Ment. Sci.*, **101**, 425, 810–825 (1955).

PARNELL, R. W. and EPPS, P., Physique and temperament of women delinquents compared with women undergraduates, *Brit. J. Med. Psychol.*, **XXV**, 4, 249 (1952).

PARNELL, R. W., PEIERLS, G. E., STANDLEY, C. C. and WESTROPP, C. K., Physique and the Grammar school examination, *Brit. Med. J.*, **1**, 1,506–1,510 (1955).

PATERSON, D. G., *Physique and Intellect*, (New York, Appleton-Century, 1930).

PEARL, R., *Constitution and Health*, (London, Kegan Paul, 1933).

PEARL, R. and CIOCCO, A., Studies on constitution: II. Somatological differences associated with disease of the heart in white males, *Hum. Biol.*, **6**, 650–713 (1934).

PEARSON, K., Relationship of intelligence to size and shape of the head and other mental and physical characters, *Biometrika*, **5**, 105–146 (1906).

PEARSON, K. and MOULL, M., The problem of alien immigration into Great Britain, illustrated by an examination of Russian and Polish Jewish children, *Ann. Eugen.*, **1**, (Part II), 56–127 (1925–26).

PENDE, N., Le debolezze di Constituzione Collezione Bardi (Rome, 1922).

PENDE, N., *Constitutional Inadequacies* (Trans. by S. Naccarati,) (Philadelphia, Lea & Febiger, 1928).

PIGNET, L., Du coefficient de robusticité, *Bull. médicale*, 15 ann. 373–376 (1901).

PILLSBURY, W. B., Body form and success in studies, *J. Soc. Psychol.*, **7**, 129–139 (1936).

PILLSBURY, W. B., Body form and introversion-extraversion, *J. Abnorm. (Soc.) Psychol.*, **34**, 400–401 (1939).

PLATTNER, W., Körperbauuntersuchungen bei Schizophrenen, *Arch. Klaus-Stift. VererbForsch.*, (1932).

PLATTNER, W., Das Körperbauspektrum, *Z. ges. Neurol. Psychiat.*, **160**, 703–712 (1938).

PLATTNER-HEBERLEIN, F., Personlichkeit und Psychose asthenischer und pyknicscher Schizophrenen, *Z. ges. Neurol. Psychiat.*, **141**, 277–320 (1932).

QUETELET, A., Anthropometrie (Brussels, C. Muquardt, 1871).

QUETELET, A., Sur l'homme et le développement de ses facultés (1935, Eng. trans: A treatise on man (1842)). (Edinburgh, Chambers.)

RAPHAEL, T., FERGUSON, W. G. and SEARLE, O. M., Constitutional factors in schizophrenia, *Arch. Res. Neurol. Ment. Dis.*, **5**, 100–132 (1928).

REED, L. J., Biometric studies on U.S. Army officers, somatological norms in disease, *Hum. Biol.*, **5**, 61–93 (1933).

REES, L., Physical constitution in relation to effort syndrome, neurotic and psychotic types, *M.D. Thesis, Univ. of Wales* (1943).

REES, L., Physical constitution, neurosis and psychosis, *Proc. Roy. Soc. Med.*, **37**, 635–638 (1944).

REES, L., Physical and psychological aspects of constitution, *Eugen. Rev.*, **37**, 23–27 (1945).

REES, L., Physique and effort syndrome, *J. Ment. Sci.*, **91**, 89–92 (1945).

REES, L., The value of anthropometric indices in the assessment of body build, *J. Ment. Sci.*, **95**, 171–179 (1949).

REES, L., A factorial study of physical constitution in women, *J. Ment. Sci.*, **96**, 620–632 (1950a).

REES, L., Body build, personality and neurosis in women, *J. Ment. Sci.*, **96**, 426–434 (1950b).

REES, L., Body size, personality and neurosis, *J. Ment. Sci.*, **96**, 168–180 (1950c).

REES, L., Physical characteristics of the schizophrenic patient, in *Somatic Aspects of Schizophrenia*, Ed. D. Richter (London, Pergamon Press, 1957).

REES, L., The physical constitution and mental illness, *Eugen. Rev.*, **39**, 50–55 (1947).

REES, L. and EYSENCK, H. J., A factorial study of some morphological and psychological aspects of human constitution, *J. Ment. Sci.*, **91**, 8 (1945).

REYNOLDS, E. L., Degree of kinship and pattern of ossification, *Amer. J. Phys. Anthropol.*, **1**, 405–416 (1943).

REYNOLDS, E. L., The fat/bone index as a sex differentiating character in man, *Hum. Biol.*, **21**, 199–204 (1949).

REYNOLDS, E. L. and ASKAWA, T., A comparison of certain aspects of body structure and body shape in 200 adults, *Amer. J. Phys. Anthropol.*, **8**, 343–365 (1950).

ROSTAN, L., *Cours élémentaire d'hygiene* (Paris, 1828).

RUHMANN, W., *Der Uleuskranke*. Studien zur Konstitution und Symptomatik am gesamten Status bei chronischem Uleus Peptikum mit besonderer Verdauungskrankcheit (Berlin, Harger, 1926).

SANFORD, R. N., ADKINS, M. M., MILLER, R. B. and COBB, E. A., Physique, personality and scholarship, *Monogr. Soc. Res. Child. Develpm.*, **7**, No. 34, 73–174 (1943).

SCAMMON, R. E., The first seriatim study of human growth, *Amer. J. Phys. Anthropol.*, **10**, 329–336 (1927).

SCHWERIN, O., Rasse und Körperbau bei 100 Schizophrenen an Baden, *Allg. Z. Psychiat.*, **105**, 121–129 (1936).

SELTZER, C. C., Body build and oxygen metabolism at rest and during exercise, *Amer. J. Physiol.*, **129**, 1 (1940).

SELTZER, C. C., The relationship between the masculine component and personality, *Amer. J. Phys. Anthropol.*, **3**, 33 (1945).

SELTZER, C. C., Body disproportions and dominant personality traits, *Psychosom. Med.*, **8**, 75–97 (1946).

SELTZER, C. C. and BROUHA, L., The "masculine" component and physical fitness, *Amer. J. Phys. Anthropol.*, **1**, 95 (1943).

SELTZER, C. C., WELLS, F. L. and McTERNAN, E. G., A relationship between Sheldonian somatotype and psychotype, *J. Personality*, **16**, 431–436 (1948).

SHATTOCK, F. M., Somatic aspects of schizophrenia, *J. Ment. Sci.*, **96**, 32–142 (1950).

SHAW, F., A morphological study of the functional psychoses, *State Hosp. Quart.*, **10**, 413–421 (1925).

SHELDON, W. H., Morphological types and mental ability, *J. Personn. Res.*, **5**, 447–451 (1927).

SHELDON, W. H., Social traits and morphological types, *Personnel J.*, **6**, No. 1, 47–55 (1927).

SHELDON, W. H., Ability and facial measurements, *Personnel J.*, **6**, No. 2 (1927).

SHELDON, W. H., STEVENS, S. S. and TUCKER, W. B., *The Varieties of Human Physique* (New York, Harper & Bros., 1940).

SHELDON, W. H., HARTL, E. M. and McDERMOTT, E., *Varieties of Delinquent Youth* (New York, Harper & Bros., 1949).

SHELDON, W. H. and STEVENS, S. S., *The Varieties of Temperament* (New York, Harper & Bros., 1942).

SIGAUD, C., *Ma Forme Humaine* (Paris, A. Maloine, 1914).

SILLS, F. D., A factor analysis of somatotypes and their relationship to achievements in motor skills, *Res. Quart.*, **21**, 424–437 (1950).

SIOLI, F. and MEYER, A., Bemerkungen zur Kretschmer's Buch "Körperbau und Charakter," *Z. ges. Psychiat. Nervenskr.*, **80**, 439–453 (1922).

SLATER, E., The neurotic constitution, *J. Neurol.*, **6**, 1–16 (1943).

SLATER, E., The genetical aspects of personality and neurosis, *Congres Internat. de Psychiatrie, Paris*, 1950. *VI. Psychiatrie Sociale, Génétique et Eugenique*, p. 119.

SMITH, H. C. and BOYARSKY, S., Relationship between physique and simple reaction time, *Character & Pers.*, **12**, 46–53 (1943).

SOMMERVILLE, R. C., Physical, motor and sensory traits, *Arch. Psychol.*, No. 75, 108 (1924).

SPEARMAN, C., *Abilities of Man* (London, Macmillan, 1927).

SPURZHEIM, J. G., *Phrenology in Connexion with the Study of Physiognomy* (Boston, Capen & Lyon, 1933).

STALNAKER, E. M., A comparison of certain mental and physical measurements of school children and college students, *J. Comp. Psychol.*, **3**, 181 (1923).

STALNAKER, E. M. and ROLLER, R. D. (JNR.), A study of one hundred non-promoted children, *J. Educ. Res.*, **16**, 265–270 (1927).

STILLER, B., Die astenische Konstitutionskrankheit (Stuttgart, Enke, 1907).

STOCKARD, C. R., Human types and growth reactions, *Amer. J. Anat.*, **31**, 261–269 (1923).

STOCKARD, C. R., *The Physical Basis of Personality* (New York, Norton, 1931).

STONE, C. P. and BARKER, R. G., On the relationship between menarcheal age and certain aspects of personality, intelligence and physique in college women, *J. Genet. Psychol.*, **45**, 121–135 (1934).

STRÖMGREN, E., Über anthropometrische Indices zur Unterscheidung von Körperbautypen, *Z. ges. Neurol. Psychiat.*, **159**, 75–81 (1937).

STUART, H. C. and SOBEL, E. H., The thickness of the skin and subcutaneous tissue by age and sex in childhood, *J. Pediat.*, **26**, 637–647 (1946).

TANNER, J. M., Intercorrelations between cardiovascular variables in healthy men and the relation of physique to these and other variables. Proc. Physiol. Soc. Phila., *Amer. J. Med. Sci.*, **207**, 684 (1944).

TANNER, J. M., The morphological level of personality, *Proc. Roy. Soc. Med.*, **50**, 301–308 (1947).

TANNER, J. M., A guide to American growth studies, in *Yearbook of Physical Anthropology*, 1947 Ed. S. W. Lasker (New York: The Viking Fund, Inc., 1948).

TANNER, J. M., The relation between serum cholesterol and physique in healthy young men, *J. Physiol.*, **125**, 371–396 (1951a).

TANNER, J. M., The relationship between the frequency of heart, oral temperature and rectal temperature in man at rest, *J. Physiol.*, **125**, 391–409 (1951b).

TANNER, J. M., Some notes on the reporting of growth data, *Hum. Biol.*, **23**, 93–159 (1951).

TANNER, J. M., Current advances in the study of physique. Photogrammetric anthropometry and an androgyny scale, *Lancet*, **1**, 574 (1951).

TANNER, J. M., The physique of students: an experiment at Oxford, *Lancet*, **1**, 405–409 (1952a).

TANNER, J. M., The effect of weight-training on physique, *Amer. J. Phys. Anthropol.*, **10**, 427–462 (1952b).

TANNER, J. M., The assessment of growth and development in children, *Arch. Dis. Child.*, **27**, 10–33 (1952).

TANNER, J. M., Growth and Constitution, in *Anthropology Today*, Ed. Kroeber (Chicago, Univ. of Chicago Press, 1953).

TANNER, J. M., Growth of the Human at the time of adolescence, in *Lectures on the Scientific Basis of Medicine*, Ed. F. Frazer (London, Athlone Press, 1953).

TANNER, J. M., The inheritance of morpholoigcal and psychological traits, in *Clinical Genetics*, Ed. A. Sorsby (London, Butterworth, 1953*b*).

TANNER, J. M., *Growth at Adolescence* (Springfield, C. C. Thomas, 1955).

TANNER, J. M., Physique, character, and disease, *Lancet*, **2**, 635–637 (1956).

TANNER, J. M., The reliability of anthroposcopic somatotyping, *Amer. J. Phys. Anthropol.*, **12**, 257 (1954).

TANNER, J. M. and BURT, W. A., Physique in the infrahuman mammalia. A factor analysis of body measurements in dairy cows, *J. Genet.*, **52**, 37–51 (1954).

TANNER, J. M., HEALY, M. J. R., LOCKHARD, R. D., MACKENZIE, J. D. WHITEHOUSE, R. H., Aberdeen growth study: I. *Arch. Dis. Child*, **31**, 372–381 (1956).

TANNER, J. M. and SAWIN, P. P., Morphogenetic studies in the rabbit. Vol. XI. Genetic differences in the growth of the veterbral columns and their relation to growth and development in man, *J. Anat. London*, **87**, 54–65 (1953).

TANNER, J. M. and WEINER, J. S., The reliability of the photogrammetric method of anthropometry, with a description of a miniature camera technique, *Amer. J. Phys. Anthropol.*, **7**, 145–185 (1949).

TANNER, J. M. and WHITEHOUSE, R. H., The Harpenden skinfold caliper, *Amer. J. Phys. Anthropol.*, **13**, 743–746 (1955).

THOMPSON, D'A. W., *On Growth and Form.* (New Ed.) (Cambridge Univ. Press, 1942).

THOMSON, G. H., *The Factorial Analysis of Human Ability* (London, Univ. of London Press, 1946).

THURSTONE, L. L., Analysis of body measurements (The Psychometric Laboratory, Univ. of Chicago, No. 29, 1946*a*).

THURSTONE, L. L., Factor analysis and body types, *Psychometrika*, **11**, 15–21 (1946*b*).

THURSTONE, L. L., Factorial analysis of body measurements, *Amer. J. Phys. Anthropol.*, **5**, 15–28 (1947).

TIEDEMAN, D. V., The utility of the discriminant function in psychological and guidance investigations, *Harvard Educ. Rev.*, **25**, 2, 71–80 (1951).

TOURAINE, G. A. and DRAPER, G., The migrainous patient —a constitutional study, *J. Nerv. Ment. Dis.*, **80**, No. 1, 183 (1934).

TSCHERNING, R., Über die somatische und psychische Konstitution bei Uleus ventriculi, *Arch. Verdaukr.*, **31**, 351 (1923).

TUCKER, W. B., LESSA, W. A., Man: a constitutional investigation, *Quart. Rev. Biol.*, **15**, 256–289, 411–455 (1940).

VANELLI, A., La constituzione somatica degli schizofrenici, *Schizofrenie*, **1**, 3–14 (1932).

VIOLA, G., L'habitus phthisicus et l'habitus apoplecticus comme conséquence d'une loi qui déforme normale-

ment le type moyen de la race en ces deux type antithétiques. *Comptes rendus de l'Assoc. des anatomistes. Vingtième réunion* (Turin 6–8 April, 1925) p. 33 (of reprint) (1925).

VIOLA, G., *La Constituzione Individuale* (Bologna: Capelli, 1932).

VIOLA, G., Il mio metodo di valutazione della constitutione individuale, *Endocrinolgiae patalogia constituzate*, **12**, 387–480 (1937).

VON ROHDEN, F., Konstitutionelle Körperbauuntersuchungen an Gesunden und Kranken, *Arch. Psychiat.*, **79**, 786–815 (1927).

WALDROP, R. S., A factorial study of the components of body build (abstract), *Psychol. Bull.*, **37**, 578 (1940).

WATSON, R., Unpublished data, 1956: Library of Institute of Psychiatry, London.

WEIDENREICH, F., *Rasse und Körperbau* (Berlin, J. Springer, 1926).

WEISSENFELD, F., Körperbau und Charakter, *Z. ges. Neurol. Psychiat.*, **96**, 175 (1925).

WELLS, F., Relation between psychosis and physical type: a statistical study, *Amer. J. Psychol.*, **51**, 136–145 (1938).

WELLS, S. R., *How to Read Character* (New York, Fowler & Wells, 1869).

WENGER, M. A., An attempt to appraise individual differences in level of muscular tension, *J. Exp. Psychol.*, **32**, 213 (1943).

WERTHEIMER, F. I. and HESKETH, F. E. A., A minimum scheme for the study of the morphologic constitution in psychiatry with remarks on anthropometric technique, *Arch. Neurol. Psychiat. Chicago*, **17**, 93–98 (1925).

WERTHEIMER, F. I. and HESKETH, F. E. A., *The Significance of the Physical Constitution in Mental disease* (Baltimore, Williams & Wilkins, 1926).

WERTHEIMER, N. and WERTHEIMER, M., Capillary structure, its relation to psychiatric diagnosis and morphology, *J. Nerv. Ment. Dis.*, **122**, 14–27 (1955).

WESTPHAL, K., Untersuchungen zur Frage der nervosen Entstehung peptischer Ulcera, *Deutsch. Arch. f. Klih. Med.*, **114**, 327 (1914).

WHEELER, L. R., A comparative study of physical growth in dull children, *J. Educ. Rev.*, **20**, 273 (1929).

WIERSMA, E. D., Bodily Build, Physiological and Psychological Function, *Zerhand. d. Kon. Akad. Van Weten. Te. Amsterdam Afd. Naturlk.* (2de. Setc.) *deel.*, **30**, No. 2 (1933).

WIGANT, V., Attempts at anthropometric determination of the body types of Kretschmer, *Acta. Psychiat. Neurol.*, **8**, 465–481 (1933).

WILDER, H. H., *Laboratory Manual of Anthropometry* (Philadelphia, 1920).

WOOD, P., Da Costa's Syndrome, *Brit. Med. J.*, **1**, 767–772, 805–811, 845–850 (1941).

WOODS, W. L., BROUHA, L. and SELTZER, C. C., *Selection of Officer Candidates* (Cambridge, Mass., Harvard Univ. Press, 1943).

WRETMARK, G., The peptic ulcer individual, *Acta. Psychiat. et Neurol. Scand.*, Supp. 84 (Munksgaard, Copenhagen 1953).

WYRSCH, J., Beitrag zur Kretschmer's Lehre vom "Körperbau und Charakter," *Z. ges. Neurol. Psychiat.*, **92** (1924).

CHAPTER 10

Childhood Upbringing and other Environmental Factors

N. O'CONNOR and C. FRANKS

THE extensive literature on child development has often been recognized as a body of knowledge which should be integrated into general psychological theory. Inhelder (1957) draws attention to this situation and talks of some interdisciplinary studies which have made a contribution to the definition of standards of development. The attempts which are now being made to standardize criteria of developmental stages make the difficulties more apparent. Inhelder (1957), for example, talks of the failure of physiological growth stages to show a close correspondence with psychological stages. It can be said equally well that the explanatory hypotheses offered for supposed abnormalities of development are still very much at the stage of common-sense hunches. A glance at McV. Hunt's (1944) text and the chapters on child development suggests that considerable changes have been made since that time, but a review of our knowledge in any field other than the field of delinquency does not support the view that the psychology or psychiatry of abnormality in children has made notable progress. In learning studies, motivation and knowledge of social behaviour evidence is accumulating, but where neurosis and psychosis are concerned we are scarcely able to offer even a definition. Thus despite a change of emphasis we cannot claim any revelations in this field. The studies which were popular twenty years ago concerning breast feeding and oral character still appear but have not become an accepted part of general psychological theory and thus the foundation for more advanced research.

Instead, in this period, the pattern has shifted to different aspects of the mother-child relationship such as maternal deprivation and emotional dependency. But in this new field, studies continue to show a somewhat unsatisfactory set of contradictory results. Thus, although it has been shown that relationships between types of discipline and types of behaviour in

children are sometimes significant, the findings are not easily replicable. Similarly relationships between parental attitudes and psychosis in children are as frequently experimentally falsified (Nielsen, 1954) as verified (Wohl, 1954). Even the simple statement that for their later mental health the children need the affection and care of one mother, an "obviously true" statement, has turned out to be hard to prove.

It is because the field is one in which psychologists and psychiatrists have not adequately defined their problems that no complete and detailed exposition of behavioural abnormalities will be attempted in this chapter. Instead several topics have been selected either because they cover subjects which at present dominate the literature on children's mental ill health or because they represent new contributions to an established subsection of this field. In addition, one section concerned with the epidemiology of childhood disorders has been included, partly as a first attempt to draw attention to the lack of literature on this subject. No discussion of genetics or of the genetics $v.$ environment controversy is included in this chapter as the subjects are dealt with in other chapters. No detailed discussion of the large subjects of mental deficiency or delinquency is included.[1] Workers in the field may also notice the omission of any considerable discussion of dreams, phantasy and play. The decision not to include a section on this subject was made because of the relatively limited output in this field. The subjects discussed in subsequent sections are dealt with critically and the authors attempt to present a point of view concerning treatment in the last section. No attempt is made, however, to cover the field of childhood abnormality by giving an exhaustive

[1] Psychological problems connected with disturbance and maladjustment among mental defectives have been discussed by Hilliard and Kirman, et al. (1957), Clarke and Clarke (1958) and O'Connor and Tizard (1956).

exposition. The first section introduces material which psychologists often ignore as superficially outside their scope, and its relevance to psychological problems has often been undervalued.

In some sections in which, for example, parental attitudes are discussed, it may be questioned whether or not this topic is relevant to abnormality. The reason for discussing it is, however, that a connexion has been frequently claimed and that the stages in a child's development are often held to be "fixed" by parental attitude, and may later determine the type of breakdown even if they do not determine the breakdown itself.

What is an Abnormal Child?

Discussion of child development in the past has usually been carried out in one of two ways, either relatively systematically and empirically by such workers as Gesell (1945) and Munn (1955) or from the standpoint of an existing body of theory, as in the case of Susan Isaacs (1945, 1946), Anna Freud and Burlingham (1944) or Bowlby (1952).

In the psychological study of abnormal behaviour in children, development has tended to be derivative from psychiatry, as of childhood psychosis. In some instances psychology has apparently made a contribution of its own, as in the case of the diagnosis of mild backwardness with the aid of intelligence tests. However, this situation, i.e. one in which a relatively precise definition can be given to a group of disorders, is as rare in abnormal psychology as it is in psychiatry. For this reason, for example, in a recent symposium on juvenile schizophrenia, Kanner (1954) the leading psychiatric authority on the subject said: "There are those who do not believe in childhood schizophrenia, not having seen a case. At the best, none of us have seen very many cases in which we could make a definite diagnosis, not knowing the acceptable criteria." Subsequent discussion in the symposium tended to support this view despite the fact that two contributors felt that their secretaries could always differentiate between mental deficiency and childhood schizophrenia.

Because of diagnostic difficulties in such cases as psychosis and neurosis and because of the complication of social factors in cases of delinquency and mental deficiency, it is hard to present incidence or prevalence figures which are not misleading. Mayer-Gross, Slater and Roth (1954), refer to the difference between the proportions of the sexes seen at Juvenile Courts, Child Guidance Clinics and Psychiatric Out-patient Clinics. The ratios of males to females are respectively 5/1, less than 2/1 and 1/1 for the three years 1947–1949. The authors note that under present circumstances it is impossible to say whether the figures indicate a tendency to delinquency in boys

or a failure of psychiatrists to observe it in girls. They also draw attention to the loose generalizations so current in this field concerning both diagnosis and the outcome of treatment.

Blacker (1948) has estimated that about one to two per cent of children need psychiatric guidance each year. He warns that this figure is inadequate and not based on any consistent country-wide demand, but none the less making this assumption, he estimates that about four hundred Child Guidance Centres and about one hundred and fifty Child Psychiatric Clinics would be needed, roughly six times the provision existing in 1948. These centres are named according to the suggestion of the Feversham Committee wherein the first is conceived of as dealing with educational problems and the latter with problems of abnormal behaviour. Thus the former would deal with backwardness and mental deficiency and the latter with behaviour problems, neurosis and delinquency, although in practice both act as psychiatric clinics. The emphasis here is on early treatment with the aim of avoiding mental illness in later life. The assumed connexion, however, so strongly supported by common sense is not so easily verified by experiment either in relation to psychopathy or neurosis. One aspect of this problem is presented in another section of this chapter where the concept of maternal deprivation is discussed.

Turning from the uncertain situation of psychosis in children, which is rare, and childhood neurosis, which is as yet ill-defined, to the question of delinquency and backwardness, we are on much firmer ground even if the incidence of both depends to some extent on social provision and awareness. Thus it is likely that, although diagnostic errors may account for a percentage of misclassification, ineducability or extreme backwardness equivalent to I.Q. 50 or below, will be noticed and reported before the seventh year of life in most cases. Even here, however, the availability of private education might prevent the ascertainment of a percentage of imbeciles and idiots. In the table opposite (Table X.1) figures of ascertained ineducability in some counties and county boroughs in England and Wales are given for the year 1951. The same table gives figures for the incidence of educational subnormality and ineducability in the London County Council area in 1952 and 1953.

Penrose (1949) originally noted that backwardness showed an age distribution with a peak between 10 and 14 years of age. The table in which he presents this data indicates the extent to which backwardness is a problem of the social or educational demands made on the individual.

Admission to mental deficiency institutions follows another age pattern with a peak during the 16–19 year period according to the Registrar General's figures

TABLE X.1

THE INCIDENCE OF BACKWARDNESS

A. Incidence of Severe Backwardness
and Educational Subnormality in London

	1952	1953
Number of children on school rolls.	425,362	436,921
Number recommended as E.S.N. .	676	757
Number declared ineducable . .	73	93

B. Incidence of Ascertainment by Counties and
County Boroughs in England and Wales for 1951—
Selected Boroughs to Show Range of Ascertainment

County or County Borough	M.D. ascertainment per 1,000 population, December, 1951
Sunderland . . .	5·79
Grimsby	5·60
Rutland	4·53
West Ham . . .	4·37
Birmingham . . .	4·32
Anglesey	1·22
Blackpool . . .	1·10
Merioneth . . .	0·90
Carmarthen . . .	0·55
Cardigan	0·42

(1953). In a later publication (1955) he confirms this picture for the feeble-minded and presents further figures showing that cases of idiocy are hospitalized before the age of ten in about two cases out of three, whereas imbeciles are either hospitalized at this age or again during their later life from 35 onwards.

All such English studies as well as a recent study by Gruenberg (1957) in Onondaga County in New York State bring out the socio-economic distribution of feeble-mindedness with a greater prevalence in economically depressed and overcrowded regions. More severe forms of mental defect do not necessarily show this socio-economic weighting.

Overall it can be said that mental deficiency is subject to wide variation in disposal according to age, but that it is less subject to diagnostic disagreement and inconsistency over time than either childhood neurosis (maladjustment) or psychosis. As has been noted above, recent discussions show almost complete confusion on the subject of childhood schizophrenia and childhood neurosis is particularly intractable so far as definition and diagnosis are concerned.

Nevertheless, although diagnosis is often extremely difficult, children with behaviour problems and backward children come forward for treatment and their numbers are known. In 1946, for example, an estimate of E.S.N. children was given as 10 per cent of registered pupils in schools, and maladjusted children were thought to be 1 per cent of registered pupils. This compared with about 1·3 per cent suffering from all other physical handicaps listed, such as partially sighted, blind and deaf children, delicate and physically handicapped children, and those with speech defects.

Psychological Services for Schools

In 1956 UNESCO (1956) surveyed the need for psychological services and the services existing in several European countries. This review makes the following observations concerning the United Kingdom. After describing the provision of 10,000 special school places in Scotland where there are 830,000 children of school age (1·2 per cent) and 54,000 in England with above 6,000,000 (0·009 per cent) children it adds—

Official estimates of the proportion of children needing some form of special educational treatment—not necessarily in special schools or classes—vary between about 10 per cent to as much as 15–16 per cent of the school population. From these estimates the numbers of the delinquent are omitted. It will be seen that, even allowing for the fact that, for example, many of the largest group of all, the educationally subnormal, will be accommodated in ordinary schools with a specially adapted curriculum, there is still a considerable gap between what is considered desirable and what has so far been possible. In England it is estimated that some 20,500 children are awaiting places in special schools.

The significance of the comment is further emphasized by the following figures quoted from the Ministry of Education's Annual Report for 1954 (1954)—

	Number attending Special School	Number awaiting admission to Special School
E.S.N.	21,294	12,794
Maladjusted	3,294	804

Such figures would yield an estimate of less than 1 per cent backwardness, and less than 0·1 per cent maladjustment. Even at this very low figure and, despite the existence for the maladjusted of between two hundred and three hundred child guidance clinics and centres in England, the service falls very much below the need.

The most authoritative figure for maladjustment, however, is based on three surveys carried out by the Ministry of Education (1955). In these surveys made in Somerset in 1952, Birmingham in 1953, and Berkshire in the same year, samples of 883, 2,264, and 992 were selected from school populations of 57,000, 170,000 and 39,000 respectively, with attention to type of area and type of school but otherwise by random allocation.

Questionnaires to teachers were followed by interviews with children regarded as maladjusted. Parents were also seen and children allotted to one of five categories—

A—very maladjusted, excluding psychosis and mental deficiency;

B—probably maladjusted;

C—not maladjusted, but attention needed to schooling;

D—not maladjusted, but home conditions adverse;

E—not maladjusted.

The surveys yielded somewhat different percentages by diagnosis in the different areas. A summary of some of the findings is given in Table X.2.

TABLE X.2

PERCENTAGE DISTRIBUTION OF SCHOOL-CHILDREN BY DEGREE OF MALADJUSTMENT

	A	B	C	D	E
Somerset . . .	2·7	9·1	5·3	5·6	77·3
Berkshire . . .	0·8	4·6	1·3	1·8	91·4
Birmingham . .	0·8	15·0	6·7	1·9	75·5
Birmingham (converted score) . . .	0·5	11·6	0·8	0·6	86·5

It can be seen that there is little overall agreement. Birmingham's figures are based on school reports and different results appear if school and parents' reports are combined. As there is only agreement between school and home on 63·8 per cent of cases, a conversion of the agreed figures has been made to equal 100 per cent. These appear on row 4 of the table and are approximations. By correction in this way figures are made to fall between those of Somerset and Berkshire so far as Category E is concerned, the major group.

Altogether the figures disagree sufficiently to show that the factors affecting referral, apart from diagnosis are still too little understood. This fact is further emphasized when we compare one other study of children referred to (1955) as having been carried out by the Tavistock Clinic with the results quoted above. In this study a maximum estimate of 42 per cent and a minimum of 35 per cent neurosis was estimated. This percentage whilst more in line with studies made with adults, such as those of Russell Fraser (1947), who found 28 per cent of neurosis in men and 36 per cent in women, is a much higher estimate than the sum of any entries in columns A and B would indicate. It is likely that some of the maladjustment reported is situational and included some of those from column C of Table X.2.

The only conclusion one can fairly come to is that neurosis or maladjustment in children is very hard to ascertain. Attempts to assess it objectively have not met with conspicuous success. Thorpe and James (1957) report results of such an investigation which did not yield consistent objective measures presumably because of the variability of such measures with test conditions. Within the wide limits set by such deficiencies it might be guessed that a good deal of neurosis or maladjustment, apart from delinquency, exists in children possibly amounting to 15 or 20 per cent. This would lead us to expect about a million cases in a population of six million children. Even if this figure were wildly wrong and only 5 per cent were maladjusted, i.e. half the number of those known to be educationally subnormal, we would still have to consider treatment for about 300,000 children. In this area as in others it is likely that the demand will increase as more provision is made available.

The delinquent child is a further category over and above maladjusted, backward and psychotic children. In this case the nature of delinquency is such that figures are easily available. We can say, for example, that in England in 1954 there were 1,736 cases of detected crime among girls and boys aged between 14 and 17 years per 100,000 in this age group.

However, it is as well to remember that such figures, like accident figures, are partly a function of interpretation of the law and the severity with which it is enforced. It has been said that the appointment of a new chief of police in a town in the United States doubled the crime rate. For this reason it would be unwise to infer from the figures given that the delinquency rate is just over 1 per cent. It is further possible, for example, that delinquency figures overlap with maladjustment figures, just as Gittens (1952), among others, suggests that they overlap with figures for backwardness.

As little more can be attempted than a rough judgement, it would seem as if an adequate mental health service for children should be prepared to cope with 10 per cent of educational subnormality, 1 to 2 per cent of delinquency and an undetermined amount of maladjustment probably about 1 per cent of severe maladjustment and between 5 per cent and 20 per cent of milder disturbance. This means that, under present circumstances, one in three children need attention or care if they are not to suffer from their own handicaps or to fall foul of the law.

Although this section begins with a question, it may be thought by some that despite the presentation of many facts, an answer to this question has not been provided. The answer to the question is, however, implicit in the epidemiological information presented.

If, for example, opinions differ greatly from area to area about the percentage of neurotics in the population, this may be for one or more of the following reasons. Either conditions of case finding vary, or diagnostic criteria are different, or the incidence figures vary. Few sophisticated workers would offer the latter explanation before considering the two former, and in this case we have some indications that the diagnosis of even such a serious disorder as schizophrenia, presents difficulties in childhood.

If this is the case, it is likely that the diagnosis of disorders of lesser seriousness will present greater difficulties. If it is true of adults, as some maintain, that neurotic conditions remit in two-thirds of cases within two years of onset, this fact is likely to apply *a fortiori* to children where environmental factors apparently play some part in test diagnosis (Thorpe and James, 1957).

It seems likely, therefore, that clear-cut clinical entities are not apparent, and that the reason for the variability of estimates of incidence is not due to variability of incidence alone, but in a large degree to uncertainty of diagnostic criteria. It would be wrong, however, to give the impression that recognizable cases of childhood schizophrenia do not occur. They do in fact occur, although rarely. When found they are best recognized by applying criteria such as those of Bleuler (1911), for example, which would be appropriate for the diagnosis of the condition in adults. A general picture would include withdrawal, inactivity, seclusiveness and diminution of interests. Such clear-cut cases are, however, so rare that the observations made concerning the difficulties of ascertainment are relevant also to the question of definition. These are the views of Mayer-Gross, Slater and Roth (1954), although Bender (1947), stressing the importance of postural reflexes, claims to have described a clear-cut syndrome.

Natal and Pre-natal Factors Affecting Child Development

In recent years there has been a tendency for some students of child development to turn their attention to prenatal factors as distinct from those of the early environment. On the whole the literature on maternal attitudes and parental discipline, as indicated in the preceding section, although extensive, has failed to establish any hypotheses at an adequate level of proof, although in terms of learning theory, some gains have been made. It is interesting, even so, that paediatricians have begun to examine the connexion between damage due to stresses during pregnancy and at birth and subsequent aspects of behaviour. Psychologists themselves might do worse than turn their attention to this literature and try to devise the experiments which certainly remain to be done. The authors

know of very few psychologists in the British Isles (Stott, 1957; Rogers *et al.*, 1955), who have completed an investigation on this general question, although one or two others are in progress. Rather more studies have, of course, been made of one aspect of birth trauma, namely the consequences of brain injury in relation to mental defect. Discussion of the status of the literature on birth injury in this connexion can be found elsewhere (O'Connor, 1958).

This section is therefore intended to make available the findings of the very limited research programmes so far completed. Whilst extremely interesting they must, as yet, be regarded as tentative. Although the literature relative to psychological development is modern, as Rogers, Lilienfield and Pasamanick (1955) point out, associated studies date back at least to the work of Billard in 1839. Little's (1862) well-known paper on difficult labour, asphyxia and prematurity as causes of cerebral palsy and mental deficiency perhaps first revealed the importance of factors of this kind. There is no space here to discuss the development of the paediatric literature at the turn of the century concerning infant care, birth trauma and prenatal stress. Various factors have been primarily implicated as a result of different investigations. These include asphyxia, meningeal haemorrhages at birth and prematurity. However, while it was clear that such factors frequently caused death, many infants survived and their prognosis became a matter for investigation, especially in relation to neonatal asphyxia. So far results would appear to be conflicting. Many of them, however, were concerned with the intellectual development of apnoeic and premature children, and the relatively recent work of McPhail and Hall (1941) did not support the presumed association between mental retardation at school age and an apnoeic condition at birth. Whatever the prognosis for infants surviving birth accidents or intra-uterine stress, there was general agreement among investigators that such events put future mental development at risk.

Gesell and Armatruda (1947), among others, were responsible for the development of the theory of an underlying neuropathology in children suffering from dullness and personality disorders. However, whereas extensive literature exists concerning brain injury and mental defect the association with personality disorders is by no means so widely explored. In general, these have been associated with parental attitudes or other aspects of the post-natal environment.

There is only one properly controlled study of this kind available at present, that of Rogers, Lilienfield and Pasamanick (1955), mentioned above, although Stott (1957) in England has used similar methods of study to examine the antecedents of physical and mental handicap.

Rogers, Lilienfield and Pasamanick (1955), attempted

to study the birth records of behaviour-problem children in Baltimore schools. They listed behaviour problems under fifteen categories, general divisions of the descriptions of behaviour given by the teachers referring children to the Special Services Division of the Baltimore Department of Education. The percentage of children referred is usually about 4 per cent and the study reported investigated 1,800 children born on or after 1st January, 1940. Birth records were obtained for 1,151 of these children, and in about nine hundred cases they were matched with controls from the same classroom. As the labour to match the others seemed disproportionate, matching was discontinued and the groups compared as groups; four hundred and seventy-one cases and three hundred and fifty-nine controls for whom birth data were available were then compared on a number of variables. All these were single birth hospital deliveries with available birth histories and I.Q.s above 80. One hundred and thirty-three cases and fifty-seven controls, who differed from the selected groups only in having an I.Q. under 80, were studied separately.

Results from the selected groups are somewhat confused by their division into non-whites and whites, but this confusion can be lessened by reporting findings common to both the negro and white samples first and other findings later. For example, cases as distinct from controls were more frequently known to the Social Service Exchange. Cases tended to have a smaller birth weight than controls ($p > 0.05$ for whites, $p < 0.02$ for non-whites). Abnormalities of prenatal and para-natal periods were significantly greater among cases than controls ($p = 0.05$ for whites and $p < 0.01$ for non-whites).

When cases and controls with a history of abnormality of the prenatal and para-natal periods are compared, it is found that their families were registered with the Social Services Exchange significantly more often than families of cases without abnormalities.

In their general summary the authors give what may be presumed to be their most important conclusions. The appropriate inferences can be best summarized by quotation—

> Cases had a significantly larger proportion of premature births than did controls and abnormalities of the prenatal and para-natal periods occurred with significantly greater frequency among cases than among controls, regardless of race. The toxemias of pregnancy (pre-eclampsia, eclampsia, hypertensive disease) and bleeding (*placenta praevia*, premature separation of the placenta, bleeding before the third trimester) constituted those maternal complications largely responsible for differences found between white cases and controls in this area. Hyperactive, confused-disorganized cases had a larger proportion of abnormalities of the prenatal and para-natal periods than cases evidencing all types of behavior disorders. Cases and controls having I.Q.s

under 80 followed the same pattern as that found among those with I.Q.s over 80, but with an increased proportion of maternal and fetal complications among cases and controls respectively.

> When premature children were withdrawn from the white groups, full term white cases and controls did not differ in frequency of prenatal and para-natal abnormalities. Full term non-white children had a significantly higher proportion of abnormalities than did full term non-white controls. . . Abnormal conditions of the child at birth (asphyxia, cyanosis, convulsions, etc.) when unaccompanied by preceding maternal complications or prematurity did not differ in occurrence among cases and controls.

> Abnormalities of the prenatal and para-natal periods were found to be significantly associated with behavior disorders in children. The pattern of events found in association with behavior disorders has been noted previously in fetal and neonatal mortality, cerebral palsy and epilepsy. These latter entities have been postulated to constitute a "continuum of reproductive casualty." The findings in the present study suggest that some of the behavior disorders should be added to this continuum.

The authors are critical of their findings and draw attention to the limitation of the study, especially, for example, to the fact that neurological damage which did not lead to extreme backwardness, but only to behaviour disorders, would not be serious in itself, and therefore might be difficult to detect. Another and basic shortcoming is the retrospective character of the study, and a third the obviously subjective nature of the judgements concerning types of behaviour problem.

This study, however, has put forward some suggestive findings in a field as yet little explored. Further studies are needed, but have not been forthcoming so far. In Britain the study by Stott (1957) has attempted to show a connexion between reported pregnancy troubles and backwardness, malformation and early illness. The reported results were positive, but here again criteria of reported early illness may not be sufficiently precise.

It is regrettable that so little has yet been achieved in this field where one might expect child psychologists and paediatricians to have made extensive investigations. One current study which is based on a very large sample is that of the National Survey of Child Health and Development, directed by Douglas (1958). Its findings are based on a national sample and deserve to be quoted fully, but space will allow only a very brief catalogue of findings and the barest description of method. In this section we can confine our summary of findings to those concerning prenatal and birth conditions.

The sample was selected from 13,687 children born in the first week of March, 1946, and those used in the study were originally half this number. The sample was national in the sense that it covered the whole country. For this reason losses have been small, and losses from one area could be picked up in another so that in 1950, 5,386 children were enrolled, and in 1954, 4,452 were still taken into account. Unavoidable losses amounted to 8·9 per cent in 1950 and a further avoidable loss of 5 per cent was also recorded. According to Douglas the losses have not introduced any bias. Had the sample been local 45 per cent of the families would have been lost. Results are available by social class and at different ages.

Higher mortality in the first year of life due to pneumonia and gastro-enteritis was characteristic of lower socio-economic groups. Height followed a similar pattern with large families affecting height more adversely in the lower social groups, but not in the upper. In matters of general health, maternal care was found to be irrelevant. Other matters show a similar social gradient.

The main point of interest for this section is the comparison of the health of six hundred and seventy-six premature children with a control group born at term. The general finding was that the premature children spent more time in hospital during their first two years of life and were more susceptible to respiratory infections. Three of the premature children were mongols, two spastic and three had congenital cataract. Gross physical defects were not present in an unusual number of cases apart from these findings. Even these figures do not guarantee an unusual incidence rate for mongols for example. As one mongol would be expected in five hundred cases at the age of 10 and deaths would reduce the above quoted figures which are for the first six years of life only, it is uncertain whether or not they indicate an unusual incidence. However, the study suggests the need for further exploration.

What is very striking is that in such a field of study where results are likely to prove positive so few investigations have been made.

Parental Attitudes and the Development of Personality

One of the major controversies in this field centres around parental discipline. The question is asked: should the parents be strict or permissive? As with much of child development, expert opinions are offered and theories tenaciously held with little experimental foundation to support them.

One of the first empirical studies of this problem was made by G. Watson (1934), who examined the self-rating data obtained from two hundred and thirty graduate students. He found that those students who came from the strictest homes tended to be more hostile to parents, not submissive and dependent, to have more social and emotional problems and to be more worried and anxious and to have more guilt feelings. As Watson himself pointed out in a recent

publication (Watson, 1957), this study suffered from several serious defects: first, the "strict" category included homes where there was severe punishment and possibly rejection; second, the "lax" category included possible indifference and neglect as well as true concern for freedom; third, all data originated in self reports. Carpenter and Eisenberg (1938), however, came to essentially similar conclusions using a sample of five hundred college females. Myers (1935) found that adjustment in high-school children, both as measured by pupil questionnaires and by teachers' ratings, was totally unrelated to strictness of home discipline. On the other hand, Hatturck (1936) found that over indulged children from child-centred homes tended to be more babyish in that they tended to cry more readily, avoid risks and ask unnecessary help as judged by the independence expected at their age. Ayer and Bernreuter (1937) also found significant relationships between home discipline and general personality characteristics, the children from strict homes tending to "avoid reality." Symonds (1939), in a matched study which compared children from authoritarian homes with children from more permissive homes, found that the children of strict parents tended to be courteous, orderly and obedient, but at the same time they were timid and withdrawn, whereas the children of the permissive parents tended to be aggressive and less obedient but at the same time more self-confident and independent. The findings of Baldwin (1948) and Anderson (1940) confirm the latter finding. Radke (1946) studied forty-three nursery-school children by means of observation, picture interpretation tests and questionnaires to the parents. She found that children from autocratic homes showed less aggression and rivalry but were more passive and poorer in their social contact with other children, whereas children from less rigid homes were more active, showed more rivalry and were more popular with their associates. The researches of Shoben (1949) also confirm the general findings; he compared parents of children referred to clinics or brought before some juvenile authority with parents of non-problem children and found that the "problem children" parents tended to approve of strict discipline programmes and obedience much more than the non-problem parents. The study is of particular importance because it casts serious doubt on the popularly held belief that juvenile delinquency is in part caused by lack of parental discipline and punishment. More recently Watson (1957) compared children from strict homes with children from more permissive homes, using a number of measures of personality; he failed to find any clear personality trait which was associated with any particular home background, but the general tendency was for the children from permissive homes to have the more desirable personality characteristics.

Thus, the evidence although by no means conclusive, suggests that strict parents and training produce an obedient and conforming but passive and possibly inadequate child, whereas a more permissive environment results in greater aggression but more independence and possibly better social adjustment. No one as yet has shown to what extent the children of the more permissive parents are better adjusted because of the environmental training influences of the permissive atmosphere and to what extent hereditary factors are relevant; it may be that stable parents have stable children and that stable parents tend to produce permissive patterns of child-rearing behaviour.

It may be, too, that in a permissive environment the child gets rewarded for successfully coping with a new situation; the reward being both the allowance to carry on and to attempt a new task and the encouragement and approval at his success. The experiments of Harlow (1949) strongly suggest that successful learning facilitates further learning in animals, and it may well be that this applies to children also, i.e. learning itself becomes the reinforcement or reward.

It must be emphasized that many methodological shortcomings, even in the last work reported here, make any reliance on the findings extremely hazardous. This fact combined with the usual failure to control genetic factors because of the very great difficulty of doing so makes even these limited findings suspect; but, some experts consider that they are the best based of our recent findings concerning deviant behaviour in children.

Maternal Deprivation

If the study of child psychology and its abnormalities has begun to absorb a large percentage of the time of psychologists studying children, the study of the parent-child relationship has accounted for the largest expenditure of time and enthusiasm. Such theories are in part a movement away from the more genetic views such as those held, for example, in relation to mental deficiency by Tredgold (1908), Goddard (1923) and others in the early years of the century. In its present form the theory discussed below attributes some backwardness, some psychopathy and some emotional disturbances to "maternal deprivation." Bowlby (1952) in England and Spitz (1945, 1946) and Goldfarb (1943, 1945–6) in America have been the chief exponents of this theory and Bowlby's (1952) summary of the theory can be quoted. According to this theory "a warm, intimate and continuous relationship with his mother (or permanent mother-substitute)" in which both find satisfaction and enjoyment" is essential for the mental health of the child. Such a relationship can be considered absent when the mother is unable to give the small child the loving care he

needs, but the main controversy has been based on physical separation occurring over long periods during the first two years of the child's life and perhaps during the first five years.

The straightforward statement of a separation hypothesis is not as easy as it might seem at first. Most people agree about the truth of the common-sense assumption that feral children will be backward and abnormal or that neglected and cruelly treated children will be handicapped in various ways; but even this assumption, so commonly made, is not always true as Lewis (1954) has shown. When one goes further and seeks to establish one form of theory to account for the supposed facts, difficulties become much greater.

Bowlby relies very much on the work of Goldfarb in drawing his conclusions, but this work has been criticized (O'Connor, 1956) because of the subjective nature of many of the ratings on which Goldfarb relies. The chief reason for criticizing Bowlby's reliance on Goldfarb is because Goldfarb (1945–6) has a different set of opinions from Bowlby on the effects of maternal deprivation. Goldfarb, for example, believes that children in foster-homes present emotional problems as do children in institutions, but that they are different problems. Talking of home life and institution life, he says (1945–6): "It is probable that no matter how well both kinds of care are organized, there will be some groups of children most effectively reared in one kind of atmosphere as against another." It is also clear that Goldfarb regards rejected children living at home as in a different category from maternally deprived children, whereas Bowlby at the time his monograph was published, did not.

Another main source of criticism of Bowlby's conclusions concerns the permanency of the effects of deprivation. This doctrine has been criticized by Orlansky (1949), Murphy (1944), Beach and Jaynes (1954), and Stevenson (1957). The criticisms offered by these authors can be divided into three main groups. The first is criticism of the assumption that early experience has a permanent effect, more than, for example, later experience in childhood as distinct from infancy. The second is criticism of the fact that genetics are seldom adequately controlled and may explain effects which are sometimes assumed to be due to childhood experiences. A third criticism is that children may appear to show the consequences of deprivation as permanent effects because in later life their experience does not widen to include those aspects of experience which children do not usually meet. Effects may therefore be due to causes other than maternal deprivation.

Such views are supported by a great deal of critical evidence, some of which has been summarized elsewhere (O'Connor, 1956). Evidence is drawn from both sociological and clinical studies. For example, recovery of I.Q. following maternal deprivation has been shown by Wellman, Skeels and Skodak (1940), and recovery of self-confidence under similar circumstances by Page (1936), Clarke and Clarke (1954) have shown a rise of about 9 points of I.Q. over two years in patients who were admitted from cruel and neglectful homes and whose I.Q.s were recorded at a feeble-minded level on admission. Other studies, such as those of Lewis (1954) and Beres and Obers (1950) have shown that deprivation has by no means a consistent result in all cases. In Beres and Obers's study, deprived children followed up into late adolescence had made some sort of adjustment in all but one or two cases and half had made very satisfactory adjustments. Lewis's study examined the effect of lack of parental affection, parental neglect and a harsh depressive upbringing in children. More than one-fifth of all children admitted to a reception centre because of unsatisfactory homes were normal, although 45 per cent were definitely disturbed and nearly one-third mildly so. It was found that neglect and a dirty home do not lead to obvious psychological damage in children. Some of the figures presented show that a dirty home and a neglectful mother may be a positive advantage psychologically. The same is true of backwardness in the mother.

Several features of note were found to be associated with disturbances in the children. These were a neurotic or psychopathic mother, an affectionless mother or father, a prolonged stay in public care, and illegitimacy.

Lewis, in other words, found many factors significantly associated with disturbance in the child and not simply maternal deprivation. Of the latter she says: "Unless separation of child from mother had occurred before the age of two years and had been lasting, it bore no statistically significant relation to the normality or otherwise of the child's mental state at the time of admission." No clear connexion was evident between separation from the mother and a particular pattern of disturbed behaviour. Neither delinquency nor incapacity for affectionate relationships was significantly more frequent in the separated children.

Howells (1956) used the even more powerful technique of examining the histories of neurotics and controls for the incidence of maternal deprivation. He concludes in favour of the null hypothesis. This finding is similar to that of Ferguson and Cunnison (1951) in their review of the history of delinquent boys in Glasgow.

Several other interesting points have been made concerning the deprivation hypothesis. For example, the inconsistency of the outcome of child-rearing practices varying from extreme rigid rejection to extreme indulgence has been extensively recorded in the sociological literature. Orlansky (1949) reviews this material. Caplan (1954) has shown that, despite conditions of relative deprivation, Kikkuta children, although showing childhood problems such as thumb-sucking, appear to be well adjusted at adolescence. Douglas (1958) has suggested that his survey of children would lead to the conclusion that children become disturbed not because mothers leave them, but because the children are separated from familiar surroundings. It may be of course that surroundings should be understood to mean "places and people."

A number of authors have remarked on the lack of connexion between maternal attitude and later mental illness. The extensive studies of mother-child relations and their effects have provided many conflicting findings but no definite conclusions. It can only be inferred that such material leaves the issue undecided.

One point not made by previous workers arises from the male/female discrepancy in delinquency and neurosis figures. In the one case, as has been frequently shown, men exceed women by a ratio of 7:1 or 10:1 between the ages of 14 and 17 years (Ford, 1957). In the case of neurosis, women tend to exceed men in some forms by about 2:1, e.g., hysterical and neurotic depressive reaction, and equal them in others, e.g., anxiety reaction. In cases where the figures are different, the deprivation hypothesis requires that more deprivation should have occurred in the sex group with the highest mental disturbance. *Prima facie* it is unlikely that women should have shown a tendency to deprive or reject one sex rather than the other. However this may be, it is impossible to explain preponderances in opposite directions on such a theory. Deprivation can therefore only be regarded as causing a very small proportion of disturbance, otherwise it would be involved in a self-contradiction. While it would be incorrect to suggest that more has been claimed for the deprivation hypothesis the sex differences do require explanation.

One other main source of evidence which has recently been called in question is that of Spitz (1945, 1946). Spitz studied the effect of the deprivation of an emotional relationship between mother and child on the maturation and development of the child. This he attempted to do by comparing groups of children from two institutions, one in which the mothers were able to care for their children and the other in which they were not. The children were cared for in the latter case by nurses who each had charge of eight children and for this reason, although motherly, were unable to give the children very much attention. This study has been evaluated by Pinneau (1955). The question is further referred to in their replies to discussion (1955). Pinneau's objections to Spitz's studies amount to criticism of the latter's failure to take account of standardization, peculiarities of test measures and faults or subjectivity in judgement and interpretation. Such interpretations overlooked inconsistencies of statement, which leads Pinneau to assert that reported clinical symptoms supposed to be due to maternal deprivation could not have been occasioned by deprivation because it can be shown by internal evidence that the relevant time periods did not make this possible. Pinneau's main contentions are summarized (1955) as follows—

Some of the major vulnerabilities in Spitz's report of his studies may be summarized as follows: He fails to indicate the dates and places of the studies and neglects to indicate the composition and training of the research staff. He is inconsistent in his report of the number of children present in his studies, and his descriptions of their parents are contradictory. The groups which are compared as to mental and emotional development apparently differ in racial extraction, socio-economic background, and in heredity. He is inconsistent in his descriptions of their physical surroundings, of their care, and of their physical health. While most of his conclusions could only be considered plausible if based on longitudinal data, most of them are based on cross-sectional data, or at best on a mixture of the two. His reports regarding the average amount of time spent in observing the children are inconsistent, and other considerations indicate that there was a great deal of variability in the amount of time different infants were observed. He uses tests with means which apparently decrease with age. He assumes that test results at one age in infancy are highly related to test results several months later and that the same numerical quotient at different ages has the same relative significance, assumptions which are unwarranted in terms of our present state of knowledge.

The preceding conclusions make it clear that the results of Spitz's studies cannot be accepted as scientific evidence supporting the hypothesis that institutional infants develop psychological disorders as a result of being separated from their mothers.

Whilst much of Pinneau's criticisms are textual, he has raised a sufficient number of objections, especially concerning criteria of development, to call the material in question. This data, therefore, like that of Goldfarb (1943, 1945–6) and Bowlby (1952) needs further development before its conclusions can be unconditionally accepted.

Perhaps the last word on this general question should be left to Bowlby et al. (1956), who in recent works has considerably modified his earlier claims—

In the past, certain workers, notably Bowlby, Bender, Goldfarb and Spitz, have tended to underline both the similarities in the severely deprived children they have studied and the seriousness of the psychological damage for which they believe deprivation due to separation to be responsible. More recently others, notably Beres and Obers, and Lewis, whilst confirming that experience of separations are often pathogenic,

have emphasized the very varied clinical pictures presented by individuals who have had these experiences and the fact that a few appear to come through almost unscathed. In some of these cases, it is here argued damage of a hidden kind is probably present, although there may well be others where this is not so. Though this is a vital issue, it is one which cannot be settled without research of a far more refined character than has yet been done. Meanwhile it is clear that some of the former group of workers, including the present senior author, in their desire to call attention to dangers which can often be avoided, have on occasion overstated their case. In particular, statements implying that children who are brought up in institutions or who suffer other forms of serious privation and deprivation in early life *commonly* develop psychopathic or affectionless characters (e.g. Bowlby, 1944) are seen to be mistaken. The present investigation confirms the findings of Beres and Obers, and Lewis. Outcome is immensely varied, and of those who are damaged only a small minority develop those very serious disabilities of personality which first drew attention to the pathogenic nature of the experience.

The commendable recantation quoted here is both a tribute to the author's integrity and a demonstration of the weakness of the previous evidence from which firmer conclusions were originally expected.

Unfortunately not all workers are so ready to recognize the shortcomings of previous work and, whereas it might have been said that the weakness of developmental studies of forty to fifty years ago was their too ready reliance on genetical explanations, the besetting sin of present studies seems to be their willingness to fall back on the dynamics of mother-child relationships. In a subsequent section some aspects of early experience which may be relevant to subsequent development will be examined. These are examples of a form of deprivation of a different kind.

In concluding this section it must be noted that there is often confusion in the interpretation of reasons for the presumed effects of maternal deprivation. Some advance one kind of reason, some another. One of the more plausible explanatory hypotheses is that of too many substitute nurses. This hypothesis can be made to fit orthodox learning theory or psychoanalytic theory. It is discussed here in connexion with early manifestations of social responsiveness in the infant.

Social responsiveness begins in the first month of life when the baby begins to observe the face of an adult (Shirley, 1933).

Rheingold points out that the normative development of social behaviour has individual differences imposed on it and *in particular* environmental events modifying it. Other workers agree that social behaviour is especially susceptible to environmental events (e.g. Gesell and his associates, 1934, 1947). There is, for example, ample evidence that institutional babies depart from normal development, such babies being (not unexpectedly) in general less responsive to people (Freud and Burlingham, 1944; Gesell and Armatruda, 1947; Spitz, 1945).

Where babies brought up in families are concerned, little is known about the factors which modify their social responsiveness. In the well-known study of Dennis (1941), social responsiveness developed normally in a pair of twins reared under conditions of minimum social stimulation. This is the only experimental evidence—and rather inadequate, since the sample size is small and the adequacy of stimulus restriction dubious. Opinions and suggestions, even when made by people of acknowledged ability such as Bayley (1932) and Jersild (1954) are of value only in so far as they suggest hypotheses which remain to be tested. For example, Jersild (1954) suggests that a baby's awareness of a stranger is a function of the experiences he has previously had with people.

One of the most recent and well-designed studies is that of Rheingold (1956), who compared a group of institutional babies, aged about 6 months, being mothered by one person, with a group who were mothered by many, using both objective tests and systematic time sampling techniques. She found that although the "one mother" group did become more socially responsive to the "mother," they failed to show more discomfort with strangers than did the other group of babies. If anything there was a tendency for the "one mother" group to be *more* friendly to strangers. This might be explicable in the terms of the generalization of a learned response, the positive response of the new contacts providing the reinforcement. Such an hypothesis requires further investigation. The above experiment indicates that social behaviour in the infant is modifiable by changes in the environment, but does not tend to confirm the Spitz and Bowlby hypothesis.

In this respect therefore, as in the critique of the factual data, the maternal deprivation hypothesis has not received confirmation in experiment to a degree which would warrant its acceptance as a guide to action. It is none the less suggestive. Work like that of Bourne (1955), for example, which attempts to link conditions of mothering to imbecility breaks new ground and deserves replication. The importance of studying parent-child relations cannot be neglected and the topic is further discussed in the concluding section.

Bowlby's exploration of the field of maternal deprivation has been severely criticized; his investigations, however, have opened up a field which is important and demands further attention. It is always possible to fault work of this kind but in this case although many of the findings are self-contradictory, the underlying hypothesis makes such an appeal by reason of its common-sense nature that it would be ridiculous to ignore it.

Evidence Concerning Certain Psychoanalytic Hypotheses

Psychoanalytic hypotheses continue to attract much attention among students of child development. Among them the nature and effect of phases of development is popular. The first phase, the oral phase, is supposed to be dominant in the first year according to Freudian theory; the second phase, the anal phase, is supposed to be dominant from about the end of the first year until about the beginning of the fourth year, when the child is said to enter the third, or phallic, phase of his development. During this phase the child develops an interest in his genitals, begins to masturbate more frequently, to desire physical contacts more often, especially with members of the opposite sex and manifests exhibitionistic tendencies (*see* Blum, 1953). During this period the child is also supposed to have sexual fantasies, usually associated with masturbation. According to classical psychoanalytic theory, the core of this phase of personality development is the emergence of the Oedipus complex, in which the child's love for the parent of the opposite sex is confounded by hatred and jealousy of the parent of the same sex and in which the child in his fantasy life is supposed to usurp the place of his hated rival. Eventually the normal child resolves his Oedipal complex satisfactorily, the mechanisms by which this is brought about being different for boys and girls. The details of these mechanisms will be found in standard texts of psychoanalytic theory, such as those of Blum (1953) or Fenichel (1945). In both boys and girls the Oedipal desires, if satisfactorily resolved, are supposed to be replaced by *identification* with the parent of the same sex.

Critical reviewing of the evidence concerning such psychoanalytic hypotheses which are relevant to child development is an expanding task, but results of evaluative research may be reported as follows.

INFANTILE SEXUALITY

According to Levy (1928), over half a sample of forty-nine mothers reported that they had observed their (normal) children handling their genitals by the age of three. In another study of over three hundred problem children (Huschka, 1938), over half were reported by their mothers as having masturbated before, in many cases, the age of five.

Although orgasm or orgasmic equivalents are rare in small children, such responses are not unknown in boys and girls as young as two or three (Kinsey, Pomeroy, Martin and Gebhard, 1955; Kinsey, Pomeroy and Martin, 1952). It may well be, as

Dollard and Miller (1950) suggest in their learning theory treatment of masturbation, that the pleasure provides the reinforcement or reward for the practice to become a habit or learned response to certain stimuli. (A similar argument, of course, applies to adult sexuality of a more mature kind.) Certainly, there is much evidence to support the Freudian belief in infantile sexual curiosity; many children ask sex questions before the age of five (Hattendorf, 1932), and, according to the thorough observations of the late Susan Isaacs (1946) pre-school children are commonly curious about the sexual anatomy of the opposite sex.

It is, however, difficult to test the implications of the Oedipal complex theory since it is hard to see how the very real learned dependence of a small boy on his mother can be isolated from the hypothesized sexual desire of the boy for his mother. One aspect of the theory can be examined, however, and that is the supposed universality and inevitability of the Oedipal complex. Most anthropologists and social scientists can quote ample evidence of communities where there is no evidence of *any sort* of hostility towards the parent of the opposite sex (for example, among the Hopi Indians, *see* Eggan, 1953). The most recent and exhaustive review of the anthropological literature is provided by Honigmann (1954), who points out that when there is hostility towards the father it is more likely to be because the boy is more dependent upon the mother for his physical and emotional security.

According to orthodox psychoanalytic theory, identification takes place in the normal development of the child after the satisfactory resolution of the Oedipus conflict. Everyday experience would suggest that this is so, whatever the reason. Mowrer (1950) suggests that this is a learned habit pattern and not inevitable; according to Mowrer it is brought about by a system of selective rewards for the correct response. For example, the gratified father, pleased at seeing a miniature replica of himself in his son's behaviour pattern, rewards this pattern with praise and gifts and so the habit becomes learned. Sears and his colleagues (Sears, Pintler and Sears, 1946; Sears, P. S., 1951) have carried out extensive research on the role of the parent in developing learned behaviour in the child of the same sex. Assuming that the father provides the chief model for masculine behaviour patterns in his son, they hypothesized that his absence from home might delay the emergence of patterns such as aggression in his male children. However, since girls are hypothesized not to identify with the father but the mother, then the absence of the father should have little influence on his daughter's aggressive behaviour patterns.

To test this hypothesis they studied the aggressive doll play of twenty girls and twenty-two boys at each of three age levels (3, 4 and 5 years). At each level and within each group half the children came from homes with parents present, while half came from homes in which the father was away for some reason such as employment or military service. By and large, their findings confirmed the identification hypothesis, but the findings need confirmation. Other hypotheses concerning hunger and feeding have been investigated.

INFLUENCE OF THE HOME

According to reinforcement learning theorists it should be possible to predict the child's behaviour by considering the type of home he comes from. For example, if the approved (and hence reinforced) behaviour in the home is one of restriction and withdrawal, then the child should behave in a like manner outside the home. The studies of Baldwin and his colleagues at the Fels Institute of Human Development tend to confirm this. They developed a series of scales known as the Fels Parent Behaviour Rating Scales for the rating of children's homes on various dimensions, in many cases correlated, such as warmth, social adjustment, possessiveness, etc. They then compared the home rating on a personality attribute with the children's behaviour, as rated by nursery-school teachers and other observers, outside the home. In general, the findings supported the expectation in terms of reinforcement learning theory (Baldwin, 1948; Baldwin, 1949; Baldwin, Kalhorn and Breese, 1945; Baldwin, Kalhorn and Breese, 1949). If a learning theory rationale can be applied then one would expect the mechanism to be enhanced by some process of generalization. Bishop (1951) observed the behaviour of thirty-four children, ranging in age from 40 to 67 months, at first with their mothers, and, later, with a female adult whom the children had never seen before and who was carefully primed to react with each child in a standardized manner. Her findings strongly confirm the hypothesis that responses learned in one situation are likely to be generalized to a new situation.

It follows that, if a child can learn and carry over to new situations personality characteristics which are essentially normal, then he may equally learn and carry over neurotic characteristics. Levy (1943) made an intensive clinical study of twenty "overprotected" children. In approximately half of these cases the mothers indulged their children's every whim and the children tended to be disobedient, demanding and tyrannical at home; at school and in the playground they tended to behave in exactly the same manner. In the remaining half of the cases the "overprotection" took the form of maternal domination and overcontrol and the children tend to be withdrawn and docile; at school and in the playground they exhibited similar patterns of behaviour in their relationships with other children and adults.

In a similar manner it has been demonstrated that children's fears are, in many cases, learned from their parents and are in many cases of the same kind (Hagman, 1932). A common fear in small children is of the dark; according to Freudian theory this is supposed to be the most basic of all fears and directly related to mother separation; in other words, it is unlearned. The evidence casts grave doubt on this hypothesis. Thus Watson and Morgan (1917) found that a six-month-old baby was not afraid of the dark and Stern (1924) in a longitudinal study found that fear of the dark did not arise until the fourth year, i.e., until the child had *learned* that the dark was a thing to be feared. Of course, if children's fears are learned responses, then they should be capable of extinction like any other learned response. The well-known studies of Watson on the development, generalization and extinction of children's fears might appear to confirm this expectation.

HUNGER

There have been many conflicting counsels about the most advisable way to handle the infant's hunger drive, e.g. on schedule, on demand, with affection or in an impersonal manner.

Can almost any pattern be conditioned or learned? How early in life can this be effected? There is evidence that even the *foetus in utero*, and certainly the neonate, can be conditioned.

D. P. Marquis (1941) was interested in the problem of the learning of a feeding schedule within the first fortnight of life. Using restlessness measured by body activity as a criterion of adaptation to the feeding schedule concerned, she compared the body activities of two groups of infants who were on two different feeding schedules. Group A (N = 16) was on a three-hour feeding schedule for the first eight days but was shifted to a four-hour schedule on the ninth day. Both groups learned their respective schedules within a few days, their body activities increasing sharply shortly before the four- or three-hour periods were up. Furthermore, when Group B was abruptly shifted on the ninth day to a four-hour schedule it still began to register increased body movements after three hours. Thus it can be concluded that even new-borns can be conditioned to a particular, externally imposed, feeding schedule.

Despite this ability to learn, it could be, as dynamically inclined child psychiatrists maintain, that certain schedules and techniques are inherently better for the child. For example, Aldrich (1947) recommends breast-feeding on demand and at the same time giving the child much demonstrative affection. Such advice is usually based on some form of psychoanalytic

theory and it is the validity of these theories which must be considered next.

THE ORAL PHASE

According to Freud the oral phase is predominant in the normal individual during approximately the first year of life. It seems reasonable that the lips and mouth become erotogenic because of its conditioned association with hunger reduction (but *see* Sears and Wise, 1950). According to Freud, however, sucking represents the first expressions of sexuality (Freud, in Brill, 1938) and is not just an unconditioned food-getting response (and later a *conditioned* pleasure response), but a basic need in itself, i.e. sucking is an innate or unconditioned *pleasure-giving* response. Davis, Sears, Miller and Brodbeck (1948) compared the oral activities (both spontaneous and in response to specific stimuli) of three groups of neonates, each group being fed by cup, bottle and breast respectively. Of these three feeding methods, clearly cup-feeding is essentially non-sucking, bottle-feeding involves much sucking, while breast-feeding requires considerable and intensive sucking. The prediction is, therefore, that, if sucking is a learned drive associated with hunger reduction, then the cup-fed group should manifest less sucking drive *in general* than the other two groups and the breast-fed group should exhibit the maximum sucking drive. Their measure of non-feeding or pleasurable sucking was the amount of time spent by each infant in sucking the experimenter's finger placed in the mouth for a fixed period each day of a ten-day period. As predicted, they found that the breast-fed group yielded consistently more and more sucking responses as the ten-day training period progressed, while the scores of the other two groups were relatively unchanged. In learning theory terms, then, sucking in general had acquired much habit strength by reinforcement in the breast-fed group.[1] The present authors must conclude with Davis *et al.* (1948) that the drive to suck in general is at least a partially learned response. The sucking reflex is of course unlearned. Freudian theory would seem to be unconfirmed in that part which asserts that the generalized sucking drive, even in non-nutritional situations, is a completely unlearned or biologically pleasurable drive (whether a sexual expression or otherwise) but supported in that aspect which suggests that the pleasure derived from stimulation of the mouth and lips is a learned response derived from an original association with hunger reduction during feeding.

The child who is breast-fed has greater opportunity

---

[1] It has been pointed out that the experiment is not conclusive unless it was ascertained that the breast-fed babies were satisfied. If still hungry, their increased sucking would be due very much to drive rather than habit strength.

to learn this response, hence the physiological and psychological ability of the mother to breast-feed her baby is of direct relevance. Here there is some evidence to suggest that the maternal attitude is of significance in determining the adequacy of the milk supply (Newton and Newton, 1950).

As with any learned drive, it can be reduced by many methods, both direct and indirect. Most distress is likely to be suffered, presumably, in those infants (e.g., breast-fed) in whom the drive has been developed most strongly, when the drive is thwarted or inadequately satisfied. One might, therefore, expect different reactions to weaning in such children and, also, that in breast-fed children in particular the later the age of weaning the greater the sucking-pleasure habit strength built up and consequently the greater thwarting when this drive was no longer satisfied in the customary manner. Sears and Wise (1950) compared three groups of children aged under 10 years; an early-weaned group, weaned before they were a fortnight old; a middle-weaned group, weaned before they were three months old; and a late-weaned group, weaned after four months. They estimated the degrees of weaning disturbance from an interview with the mothers, the results being as predicted, there being a positive relationship between amount of disturbance and weaning and age of weaning. It is of interest that thumb sucking, which may be regarded as a measure of oral drive, also tended to be greater in the later weaned group who had had greater opportunity to build up a strong habit strength of sucking as a drive.

According to psychoanalytic theory (e.g., Fenichel, 1945), the future personality of the infant in childhood and in adulthood is very closely dependent upon the manner in which the infantile oral pleasure drive (said by analysts to be innate and biologically determined) is satisfied or thwarted; in particular it will (according to them) depend upon the stage and technique of weaning imposed. It will, therefore, be as well to examine the experimental evidence concerning the relationship, if any, between infantile oral experiences and later personality and behaviour. In psychoanalytic terms, one might predict that children deprived of adequate oral satisfaction as babes would seek and need oral satisfaction as older children and consequently become finger suckers. On the other hand, in terms of learning theory, one might expect those children who were given considerable oral reinforcement as babies to acquire the generalized oral habits and consequently to become habitual finger suckers.

One might expect that a positive relation exists between the learned habits of finger and dummy sucking. Levy (1928), however, found none of the children in his group who were allowed to use a dummy became finger suckers. When he studied his finger-sucking group he found that as small babies they had been nursed less often, and for briefer periods, than his non-finger-sucking group. In a much later study Levy (1934) split one litter of six puppies into three pairs. Over a period of three weeks one pair was given little opportunity for sucking and the feeds were made as short as possible by using a bottle with a large aperture in the nipple; another pair was given unrestricted opportunity to suck and the feeding bottles had tiny apertures in the nipple; the remaining pair was breast-fed by the mother. He found that the pair which had had little opportunity to suck during feeding sucked most of all in between meals, at each other's bodies and at offered fingers; the pair which were allowed unrestricted sucking at the bottle showed only a little non-restricted sucking behaviour and the breast fed pair showed none whatsoever.

Roberts (1944) found essentially similar results when he compared a thumb-sucking group with a control group of children and concluded that restricted sucking experience in infancy is a major determinant of habitual thumb sucking in later years. Thus the evidence confirms the prediction that oral deprivation in early life can lead to later oral habit patterns. Goldman-Eisler's (1951) study also confirms this finding. However, as G. Allport (1937) points out, the same results can be brought about by many different causes; there is good evidence to suggest that factors other than oral deprivation in infancy may result in thumb sucking (Simsarian, 1947).

It is also a basic assumption of many psychiatrists and diagnostically orientated psychologists that the method of early feeding (e.g., breast or bottle) produces general differences in later personality and adjustment. In many cases the clinician bases his theory on the subjective evaluation of his own case-material, and such observations have obvious shortcomings as scientific evidence. Many of the objective investigations of such theories suffer from serious methodological drawbacks. In particular, the data concerning the early infancy period are usually obtained by the introspection of some adult, and the samples studied have been both small and psychiatrically abnormal (e.g., Childers and Hamil, 1932; J. Hill, 1937). In the study by the Rogersons (1939), which successfully avoids these pitfalls, bottle-fed babies were compared with breast-fed infants in later years; the bottle-fed group was found to have a greater incidence of feeding and physical health difficulties and also to be more neurotic and to make poorer school progress. Although the sample size was unfortunately small, the data of Holway (1949) confirm these findings; she found that duration of breast-feeding was positively related to later good emotional adjustment. On the other hand, in a well-designed study, Peterson and Spano (1941) found no relationship between duration of breast-feeding and later childhood personality and adjustment. Similarly, Sewell and Mussen (1952), in a more ambitious study, aimed at relating three aspects of feeding behaviour to later adjustment, failed to obtain any clear-cut relationships between early oral experiences and later adjustment. It is thus not possible to arrive at any definite conclusions and more research is needed; in particular, the experimental design and techniques used need improvement. Introspective and subjective data must be avoided, only valid and reliable measuring instruments must be used and the data should be subjected to statistical analysis.

TOILET TRAINING

Toilet training would seem to be essentially an exercise in the development of a conditioned response, as the successful conditioning of a case of enuresis shows (Jones, 1956), inasmuch as an involuntary reflex has to become amenable to voluntary control. Dollard and Miller (1950) treat this problem at length in terms of a series of learned responses and come to similar conclusions, as do Mussen and Conger (1956). Most authorities agree, however, that the learning process should be delayed until the child is physiologically mature; thus the child should be able to understand and communicate with an adult fairly easily and he should be able to sit comfortably (English and Pearson, 1945; Gesell, Halverson, Thompson, Ilg and Costner, 1940; Huschka, 1942).

The learning theory approach is quite at variance with that of the psychoanalysts. According to the analysts, just about the age when it is agreed that a child is ready for toilet training (18–24 months), so he is in the second phase of personality development, namely the anal phase, as opposed to the earlier oral phase of the first year or so of life. In the anal phase the child is supposed to get pleasure primarily from anal activity. In the first phase of this stage pleasure is derived from expelling and in the second phase from retention. According to Freudian theory excessive indulgence or coercion during this phase may lead to fixation at this stage in later life and the development of what is called an anal character. As an adult the anal type is supposed to retain money as well as tend towards constipation; he tends to be mean, orderly, meticulous, cruel and aggressive (Fenichel, 1945).

Some of the implications of Freudian theory with respect to toilet training and personality development are difficult to test. For example, it seems impossible to tell with any degree of validity or reliability whether a two-year-old finds retention of his faeces pleasurable or whether he gets more enjoyment out of elimination. However, the existence of an anal character is easier to examine, since it can be considered in the older child or in the adult. Thus Sears (1936) has shown in male

students that the so-called anal character traits of orderliness, obstinacy and frugality are all positively intercorrelated. But there is little acceptable evidence concerning the relationship between these characteristics and early childhood toilet training.

It is known, however, quite apart from any theoretical considerations, that too strict toilet training or toilet training commenced too soon may actually *retard* the acquirement of bowel and bladder control (e.g., Whiting and Child, 1953). According to Despert (1944) toilet training is most readily achieved if the mother is calm and easy-going and herself exhibits no signs of distaste or disgust. An extensive study by Huschka (1942) of over two hundred children referred to a child guidance clinic as disturbed revealed that in over half of them bowel training had been too harsh or commenced too early, or both. She observed that in most of this subgroup the children had reacted almost immediately by maladaptive symptoms such as diarrhoea, constipation, fear, rage, guilt or excessive cleanliness. She also found that many of these children had been bladder trained far too early and had reacted adversely. It is difficult to generalize from these data to normal children, however, and there is a need for normative data.

There is some evidence which indicates that children toilet trained too early later tend to exhibit compulsive and rigid personality characteristics (Despert, 1944). There is other experimental evidence to indicate that over harsh toilet training is related to negativism and aggression (Sears, Whiting, Nowlis and Sears, 1953; Macfarlane, Allen and Honzik, 1954). A recent study by Beloff (1957) seems to provide evidence against the hypothesis that *anal* character results from method of toilet training although based on restrospective accounts of training. In a study of one hundred and twenty undergraduates, questionnaire responses were obtained to questions concerned with items corresponding to anal character traits. The traits chosen were obstinacy, "parsimony, orderliness, cleanliness, punctuality, procrastination, quasi-sadism in personal relations, conscientiousness, pedantry, feelings of superiority, irritability, desire to domineer, desire for personal autonomy."

Responses were compared with peer ratings of the one hundred and twenty subjects by four of their acquaintances. Responses of both when factor-analysed showed the emergence of only one significant factor. The correlation between the two factors was highly significant. It was therefore concluded that "a psychological functional entity" existed, corresponding to the character as described by psychoanalysts. However, this entity was not associated with toilet training experiences "but strongly to the degree of anal character exhibited by the mother." The procedure here was the comparison of age of completion of toilet training as a measure of coerciveness and the completion of the questionnaire by the mothers as a measure of anal character. A 2×2 analysis of variance established the significance of the latter. In this part of the experiment the subjects were forty-three graduates.

The study has the methodological weakness of retrospective studies of toilet training, but the results are of great interest in view of their statistical significance.

In general the evidence is inadequate to arrive at any conclusions with confidence; but although the precise mechanisms or consequences are obscure, there is good reason to believe that too early or too stringent toilet training may well produce adverse effects. Research is required into the nature and permanence of these effects, the likelihood of their occurring and under what circumstances these effects are most likely to occur. In this respect it is also necessary to relate the problems associated with various forms of toilet training to the personality and pathology of the children concerned.

These are only some examples of the conflicting evidence concerning psychoanalytic theories of children's behaviour problems. Many psychoanalytic propositions at first appear to be common-sense everyday observations which make an appeal for this reason, but when interpreted seem to be rather unusual observations of an exciting kind. In either form they are hard to verify. Writers such as Farrell (1951) have despaired of establishing psychoanalytic hypotheses in their original form. Its effectiveness as a rationale in therapy has been frequently disputed (Curran, 1937; Eysenck, 1952) and after many years, even the fundamental axioms remain unestablished. The results reported in this section do not lead the authors of this chapter to expect dramatic changes in the effects of treatment to result from a regime dictated by psychoanalytic theories. In saying this and in drawing attention to the difficulties of proving analytic hypotheses whether genetic or dynamic we have followed Farrell's criticisms. It would, however, be ungenerous and quite false to ignore the impact of Freud's contribution in directing attention to such matters as childhood sexuality and such plausible mechanisms as regression, projection and denial in relation to maladjustment. The consistent demand of analysts is that such phenomena should be explained. In calling for an explanation in terms of a meaningful interpretation it seems to us that they may be mistaken, just as it would be incorrect to try to interpret the verbal statements of some schizophrenics. However, such an opinion needs to be established and, so far, alternatives to psychoanalytic views have not been advanced. In this section we have tried to draw attention to the shortcomings of the analytic proposi-

tions. In the final section attention is drawn to some of the alternatives which learning theorists are beginning to advance.

Sensory Deprivation and Behaviour

Theses concerning isolation whether social, personal or physical have recently been resurrected after long neglect and their refurbishing has been undertaken in many different ways. Probably the foundation of these theories can be found in the stories of feral children and the classic study of the wild boy of Aveyron (Itard, 1932). However, more recently the inspiration for such work comes primarily from studies made by Hebb (1949), Thompson and Heron (1954) and others. Itard's study of the boy of Aveyron and Seguin's (1846) subsequent work with idiots have a link with this more recent work in so far as both have a similar opinion concerning the importance of sense training at an early stage.

Hebb (1949) makes early learning critical for later learning because he suggests that the entities of perception are themselves complex and not given as maintained by Köhler (1929) but based on experience. The justification for a statement of this kind has in recent years become more experimental than philosophical. In this section the experimental data will be reviewed with the intention of keeping in mind later disturbances of behaviour or other relatively permanent effects.

The impetus of this movement comes essentially from studies of children suffering social isolation. One of the earliest studies was that of Hill and Robinson (1929). Another source is undoubtedly the Iowa studies of the pre-war and post-war years. A study of the relevant material is that of Wellmann (1945). This school, despite certain earlier criticisms of their statistical procedures, has now succeeded in showing that some early loss of experience can be made up by education. Similar results have been reported by Clarke and Clarke (1954) with patients diagnosed originally as feeble-minded.

Theoretical development of learning and perception have made the biggest contribution. Hebb (1949) has laid great stress on early learning and its importance for later learning. His point is that even schemata may be learned and that such early learning is not only extremely slow and inefficient but also basic to later learning.

Hebb discusses the evidence for this conclusion and refers also to Hunt's (1941) experiment with the hoarding habits of rats and their connexion with earlier hunger experiences. The experiment referred to is only one of a number of similar studies which can be generally comprehended under the heading of deprivation. Maternal deprivation is discussed elsewhere in this chapter and might be said to be a special case of deprivation. To some extent, the confusion centring round this particular discussion has not prevented other theoretical issues from emerging clearly.

Since the studies at Iowa, a number of investigations have made apparent the disabling consequences of social, educational and emotional isolation with children and the effects of sensory deprivation with animals. Among the better examples of this work are the studies of Thompson and Heron (1954), Davis (1940), Bingham and Griffiths (1952) and Hebb (1947). A recent reappraisal of this work in the field of sensory perception is that of Zuckermann and Rock (1957).

The most succinct statement, however, of the relevant theoretical issues has been made by Hebb (1949) as follows—

> If the learning we know and can study, in the mature animal, is heavily loaded with transfer effects, what are the properties of the original learning from which these effects come? How can it be possible even to consider making a theory of learning in general from the data of maturity alone . . . transfer from infant experience may be much greater and more generalized.

G. A. Ferguson discussing this view in the *Canadian Journal of Psychology* for 1954 says: "In many adult learning situations, the most important variables exerting transfer effects on subsequent learning are the 'abilities'—the prior acquisitions that have attained their limit of performance." He goes on to argue the case for a theory in which learning depends on different combinations of abilities at different stages in learning and whereby some circumstances will completely prevent learning of some kinds: "An individual may possess the necessary ability to perform a task adequately, but may lack the ability to learn to perform the task under particular learning conditions." (Op. cit., p. 110).

The dispute concerning the origins of the basic abilities continues, and despite the extensive and good experimentation carried out in Canada, an article recently written by Zuckermann and Rock (1957) attempts to question the evidence for the effects of early experience in favour of a gestalt-oriented theory of innate perceptual processes. They say—

> One can hardly take a dogmatic position in an area where, as yet, there exists so little decisive experimentation. Nevertheless, it is important to determine the status of a scientific theory in relation to present knowledge. On the basis of logical analysis and an examination of relevant evidence, we have argued for the thesis that various aspects of the phenomenal world and, in particular, the segregation and shape of visual forms are given by innate organizing processes. Percepts may be modified and enriched by experiential factors, but

the effects of such factors presuppose the prior existence of visual forms.

> If the thesis defended in this paper is correct, perceptual organization must occur before experience (or personality factors which depend on experience such as need, purpose, and value) can exert any influence.

The case put forward in their article involves some special pleading, but also includes a reconsideration of some of the early work of von Senden (1932) producing arguments based on Michael Wertheimer's (1951) criticisms. These criticisms are presented as follows—

> On the human level, the data consist of observations made on cases of congenital blindness (due to cataracts) to whom vision was restored in later life by surgical operation. The literature on such cases has been analyzed by von Senden (1932) and his study is often cited in support of the empiricist theory. According to Hebb, for example, these patients could not immediately distinguish forms after vision was gained; a long, gradual, learning process was necessary to enable the patients to perceive. There are, however, serious deficiencies in this evidence (cf. Michael Wertheimer, who describes some of the flaws and, in addition, observes that von Senden has often been cited erroneously). The conditions and the exact time after operation of the observations were not adequately described; the extent of vision present before operation varied from case to case; some of the cases were young children whose reports are difficult to evaluate. Moreover, the patients, after operation, were faced with a strange new world and often the investigator (usually the surgeon) did not know what questions to ask, or what tests to perform, in order to elicit the subject's experience. In one case, for example, the patient "had great difficulty in describing her sensations in such a way as to convey any clear conception of them to another." Much of this evidence, therefore, is inconclusive.

This discussion is concerned primarily with the effect of early learning on later learning where actual skills are involved.

The question of the learning of emotional and dependent behaviour is more complicated and there is less available evidence with human beings.

What evidence there is suggests that isolation of a physical kind can be extremely disturbing. For example, the widely known work on adult isolation at the laboratories which has been reported by Bexton, Heron and Scott (1954) suggests that, "in other words, the maintenance of normal, intelligent, adaptive behaviour probably requires a continually varied sensory input. The brain is not like a calculating machine operated by an electric motor which is able to respond at once to specific cues after lying idle indefinitely. Instead, it is like one that must be kept warmed up and working," and that, in summary, this kind of deprivation resulted in "changes in intelligence-test performance and the hallucinatory activity, induced merely by limiting the variability of sensory input, providing direct evidence of a kind of dependence on the environment that has not been previously recognized."

The field is poorly developed, however, and has mostly centred around studies such as those of Spitz (1945, 1946, 1955) which are dealt with in detail in the section concerning maternal deprivation. It is interesting to observe that critics such as Pinneau (1955) draw attention to the conditions under which the children in Spitz's study lived. Not only were they deprived of the continuous attention of one mother, but in addition, by reason of staff shortage and because of physical isolation from one another, the children were actually prevented from exploring their environments. The field deserves considerable further exploration. There would seem to be the key to a much more adequate approach to educational backwardness in some deprivation experiments, but more information is needed. Some of the Russian work reported in Smirnov's (1957) collection of essays points to an interesting new technique of training students who have been deprived of the experience of some essential technique in a basic subject, such as counting mentally in arithmetic. The technique is based on a slow and elaborate reconstruction of the elements of the technique and their eventual internalization in thought. Such a process both comes in to line with Hebb's theories of basic learning abilities, takes account of the important effects of deprivation and suggests a solution.

Any reader who finds difficulty in seeing the relevance of these observations has only to consider the very common handicap of psychologists who lack adequate statistical and methodological training. The difficulties and "backwardness" to which such a lack of training has given rise are responsible for many of our current theoretical disputes.

Observations on the Effectiveness of Treatment

It is curious that so little work has been done to evaluate the effectiveness of treatment for maladjusted children. In view of such findings as those of Curran (1937), Miles, Barrabee and Finesinger (1951), and Eysenck (1952) with adults it is an odd fact that fewer evaluations have been attempted in the much more difficult field of child care. One of the few available was presented at the N.A.M.H. Ninth Child Guidance Inter-Clinic Conference (1951). The results reported are based on follow-up data from twenty-seven clinics with added information from five more. There are many shortcomings in returns which at this time were heterogeneous and very variable in the descriptive categories used. In addition, they cover a number of different periods, including part of the pre-war depression in England as well as the war years.

Overall, of course, as the conference delegates were well aware, was the shadow of subjectivity of judgement. In one of the reports, however, this was overcome to such an extent that five judges showed diagnostic agreement to the extent of intercorrelations of the order of 0·68 to 0·75.

The conference consisted of speeches and reports from clinics. It is interesting to note that of the one hundred and fifty clinics asked to co-operate, only thirty-four replied and submitted data although lack of time to compile data is given as the explanation for the small number of returns. The data presented by twenty-seven clinics enabled analysis by type of problem referred, diagnosis, cause of maladjustment ascribed and assessment of follow-up. The results from twenty clinics were summarized and cover 1,530 minors, 501 being girls and 1,029 boys, all between one year and 19 years of age. The type of problems noted were 462 behaviour problems, 262 psychosomatic cases, 370 personality problems, 247 educational problems and 36 unclassified cases. Diagnoses could not be tabulated because not all clinics replied and terminology differed considerably. Treatment, however, could be divided into five categories—

Play or psychotherapy	702
Parent guidance	592
Environmental adjustment	228
Remedial teaching	143
Group therapy	57

At the time cases were closed 895 cases were accounted for with 491 improved or symptom free, 64 improved and recovered, 172 unchanged or slightly worse and 14 unchanged or slightly better. The rest were accounted for in various ways irrelevant to the present discussion. The figures for recovery are impressive, but there is no way of evaluating particular treatment for the data. Follow-up showed 358 cases with no symptoms, 225 with slight symptoms, 106 showing no change and 16 showing deterioration.

Some further information can be obtained by referring to the individual reports from regional centres. For example, the conclusions of one Birmingham study are illuminating and are best quoted fully—

(a) Results were better for children in the younger age groups, where habits and parental influences had not been operative for so long a period.

(b) The better results in children of average or superior intelligence already alluded to are confirmed in the following which shows that the improvement is more lasting and progressive than in those whose intelligence is below average or dull.

(c) The relation between good results and degree of co-operation from the parents is most revealing, e.g.

when co-operation was "good" the 90 per cent which were found improved at closure, had maintained the improvement on follow-up, whereas with "bad" co-operation only 48 per cent had improved at closure, and only 66 per cent had maintained it.

(d) The children referred for "nervous" disorders are more likely on the whole to respond better, and these are really the more important cases, as the behaviour problems are more likely to be "grown out of" or yield to external circumstances, such as a change of environment.

Many other impressions emerge from the data presented, but it is doubtful whether any more definite conclusions could be sustained on the basis of the figures available because referral characteristics varied from region to region. Another chapter in this volume has been devoted to a more complete evaluation of treatment and those interested will find there a fuller analysis of the method used.

The Psychology of the Abnormal Child

It has not been possible to present a very detailed exposition of the psychology of the abnormal child in this chapter. Notably, discussion of delinquency and mental deficiency has been excluded and insufficient attention has been paid to fantasy fears and dreams. The authors believe, however, with these exceptions, that they have reflected the pre-occupations of child psychologists interested in abnormality.

There is no question that psychologists and psychiatrists in the last twenty years have been very much concerned with Freudian hypotheses about the later effects of early childhood experience. There is also little question that Mayer-Gross, Slater and Roth (1954) are correct when they point out that: "The hope of preventing, on a large scale, the psychological and social failures of adults by the psychiatric treatment of children, may well prove illusory; there are no present grounds other than optimism for thinking otherwise."

As was demonstrated in the early part of this chapter, the definition of maladjustment in children is not readily made. Symptoms which remain and refuse to yield to treatment are often minor deviations in an otherwise normal behaviour at a later stage of development. Similarly, acute maladjustment can disappear in children as readily as neurosis in an adult, and here as there, whether treated or not. Definition is just not so precise. It might be wise therefore to consider childhood maladjustment, either from the point of view of symptoms, or in completely different diagnostic groups from those applying to adults dependent on developmental arrest rather than by syndromes. The evanescent character of presenting symptoms as indicated by Thorpe and James (1957) makes diagnosis even more unreliable in the case of childhood neurosis than it is with neurosis in adults. In addition, the likelihood is great that the effect of one stage of development on another is less than has been claimed, as Orlansky (1949), Beach and Jaynes (1954) and, recently, Beloff (1957) have indicated.

Psychosis, except where defined as in the case of schizophrenia by Mayer Gross, Slater and Roth (1954), namely in terms of the symptoms of schizophrenia in adults, is just as difficult to define. So far the Registrar General's report for 1955 shows an admission rate for schizophrenia within the age group 10–15 years of 22 per million Home Population for males and 23 per million for females. This compares, for example, with 746 per million for men between the ages of 20 and 24, the highest figure, 23 per million, for men in the age group over 65 is the only other rate (except that for the over 75s) which is not double this expectation. The average figure for all ages is 260 per million for men and 232 for women. This reflects the tendency of psychiatrists not to diagnose schizophrenia before puberty and is part of the confusion on this point which may account for the inconclusive nature of the discussion in the symposium quoted earlier (Kanner, 1954).

Psychopathy, which has not been discussed in this chapter, has been no better defined by psychologists than psychiatrists. Psychiatrists such as Curran and Guttmann (1949) recognize a number of definitions of psychopathy and the recent report of the Royal Commission on the law relating to Mental Illness and Mental Deficiency (1957) succeeds only in reaffirming the present definition of the moral defective, calling this kind of person a psychopath and extending the definition to those with higher intelligence quotients. It is further suggested that the psychopathic personality is either aggressive or inadequate. So far most psychologists have not recognized the "inadequate" psychopath and definitions such as those offered by Eysenck (1957) classify psychopaths as extraverted neurotics with characteristically slow conditioning, poor persistance and a "tough minded" attitude. Eysenck's view is that the confusion of psychopathic definition can be resolved by considering the psychopath's social failure and inferring from this and his low conditionability, that the psychopath, like the hysteric, fails to learn readily. This accounts for his lack of moral and social standards. The dysthymic, on the other hand, conditions too readily. This theory is related to Mowrer's (1950) two-factor theory of learning and refers to autonomic "learning." The theory is discussed fully elsewhere, but, essentially, social conditioning is supposed to depend on autonomic conditioning, and this is supposed to be deficient in psychopaths. By definition, therefore, psychopathy cannot occur or be recognized until social conditioning has failed. It is therefore a condition which is likely to have a late onset. The Registrar General's Report (1955) notices twelve cases per million population for boys between 10 and 15 and eight per million for girls.

This kind of definition does not make the distinction made in the Royal Commission Report between inadequate and aggressive psychopaths. This is only one of many differences of definition, and hence of incidence, which have been noted by psychiatrists. At present aetiology is generally held to be unknown and definition is considered to be a matter of social convenience.

This confusion of definition in relation to neurosis, psychosis and psychopathy had left the field of childhood abnormality open to the extensive discussions of psychoanalytic theories of personality type referred to above. As we have emphasized, these suffer from a number of methodological weaknesses. Some of these have been already discussed, but one of considerable importance has not been mentioned. This is the need to control for genetic factors.

Methodologically, nearly all studies of child development neglect to control the genetic factor. This is scarcely surprising, as good control techniques would seem to be difficult to devise in the absence of a plethora of monozygotic twins reared apart, some according to strict, and some according to *laissez faire* disciplines. In a study such as that of Beloff (1957) but also in nearly all other studies, particularly those of Goldfarb (1943, 1945–6) the question of inheritance may play a part. Bodman (1950) referred to this possibility in his discussion of constitutional factors in hospitalized children. He tried to match children in two groups, according to parental history, for the disorder under study. This technique, whilst imperfect, is better than ignoring one important variable.

However, just as the Mill Hill studies during the last war revealed constitutional disposition to neurotic breakdown (Slater and Slater, 1944), they also showed, as did First World War experience, that neurotic breakdown could result from situational stress. This is just as likely to be true of children as adults. The possible error made by some workers, especially the analytically oriented, has been to regard environmental or training conditions during childhood as prognostic of later breakdown. If, however, we regard them as important for the child at the time, we can see that children's emotional disturbances might be studied as forms of reactions to situational stress irrespective of predisposing constitution. This short-term approach has not been investigated, because of the preoccupation with long-term hypotheses and also because of the findings of twin studies such as those of Eysenck and Prell (1951), which suggested that a high percentage of neurosis is inherited. However, the incidence of neurosis does increase during wars, and

neurosis has been shown to clear up even independently of treatment (Eysenck, 1952). In children, where the symptoms of neuroses are even less enduring than with adults, it would seem to the authors that further studies should be made by psychologists of situational stress in relationship to childhood maladjustment. It goes without saying that these should be controlled for parental histories.

It is true that in the field, situational factors are often presumed and thought to be too obvious to investigate. However, investigations of such obvious "facts" as the adverse effects of maternal deprivation are unusually difficult to prove. A possible reason for this is that, because of the complexity of environmental forces impinging on the individual, effects powerful at one stage may be combated by more powerful and irrelevant or opposite forces at the next. Whatever the cause, it seems desirable at this stage to examine the epidemiology of childhood maladjustment in an effort to elicit the extent to which such maladjustments are a social problem. This is likely to be a rewarding line of study because the incidence of severe psychotic disorders in children is known to be low and because the majority of maladjustments such as instability or neurosis are likely to be as transitory as they are in adults. For these reasons, irrespective of the aetiology of individual predispositions to breakdown, actual breakdown may be very much an end product of multiple factors of social stress. If we neglect the long-term effects of such factors and study them in their immediate results, we may make some advances on the interesting beginnings, now long past history, of Faris and Dunham (1939). At present, the clinic and the laboratory are separated by too great a gap. The possibility of closing this gap depends in part on enlarging the concept of maladjustment by a sociological study of behaviour. In part also, it depends on the developments of work like that of Miller and Dollard (1941), Mowrer (1950), and Eysenck (1957), which attempts to link laboratory learning theory with social learning, failure to learn and overlearning. Anthony (1957), Hindley (1957) and Gewirtz (1957) have recently attempted to integrate the work in this field. The attempt which has already been made to study parent-child relations will clearly continue, possibly influenced by learning theory. At present it is informed by an unfortunate mixture of basic Freudian theory and common-sense observations. The result is that its hypotheses are too vague to be verified by any experiment which has yet been devised. To get beyond this point the field must be critically reanalysed.

REFERENCES

ALDRICH, C. A., The advisability of breast feeding, *J. Amer. Med. Ass.*, **135**, 915–916 (1947).

ALLPORT, G., *Personality* (New York, Holt, 1937).

ANDERSON, J. P., *The Relationships between certain Aspects of Parental Behaviour and Attitudes of Junior High School Pupils* (New York, Teachers College, Columbia University, 1940).

ANTHONY, J., The system makers: Piaget and Freud, *Brit. J. Med. Psychol.*, **30**, 255–269 (1957).

AYER, M. E. and BERNREUTER, R., A study of the relationship between discipline and personality traits in young children, *J. Genet. Psychol.*, **50**, 165–170 (1937).

BALDWIN, A. L., The effect of home environment on nursery school behavior, *Child Developm.*, **20**, 49–62 (1949).

BALDWIN, A. L., Socialization of the parent-child relationship, *Child Developm.*, **19**, 127–136 (1948).

BALDWIN, A. L., KALHORN, J. and BREESE, F. H., Patterns of parent behavior, *Psychol. Monogr.*, **58**, No. 3 (1945).

BALDWIN, A. L., KALHORN, J. and BREESE, F. H., The appraisal of parent behavior, *Psychol. Monogr.*, **63**, No. 4 (1949).

BAYLEY, N., A study of the crying of infants during mental and physical tests, *J. Genet. Psychol.*, **40**, 306–329 (1932).

BEACH, F. A. and JAYNES, J., Effects of early experience upon the behavior of animals, *Psychol. Bull.*, **51**, No. 3, 239–263 (1954).

BELOFF, H., The structure and origin of the anal character, *Genet. Psychol. Monogr.*, **55**, 141–172 (1957).

BENDER, L., Childhood schizophrenia, *Amer. J. Orthopsychiat.*, **17**, 40–56 (1947).

BERES, D. and OBERS, S. J., The effects of extreme deprivation in infancy on psychic structure: a study in ego development. *Psychoanal. Study Child*, **5**, 212 (1950).

BEXTON, W. H., HERON, W. and SCOTT, T. H., Effects of decreased variation in the sensory environment, *Canad. J. Psychol.*, **8**, 70–76 (1954).

BILLARD, CHARLES-MICHEL, Diseases of children (Quoted Rogers *et al.*) *Acta Psychol. et Neurol. Scand.*, (1955, Supp. 102).

BINGHAM, W. E. and GRIFFITHS, W. J., The effect of different environments during infancy on adult behaviour in the rat, *J. Comp. Physiol. Psychol.*, **45**, 307–312 (1952).

BISHOP, B. M., Mother-child interaction and the social behavior of children, *Psychol. Monogr.*, **65**, No. 328 (1951).

BLACKER, C. P., *Neurosis and the Mental Health Services* (London, Oxford Univ. Press, 1948).

BLEULER, E., *Dementia Praecox or the Group of Schizophrenias* (Vienna 1911) Trans. Ziskin (New York, 1950).

BLUM, G., *Psychoanalytic Theory of Personality* (New York, McGraw-Hill, 1953).

BODMAN, F., Constitutional factors in institution children, *J. Ment. Sci.*, **96**, 245–253 (1950).

BOURNE, H., Protophrenia, *Lancet*, **2**, 1,156–1,163 (1955).

BOWLBY, J., Forty-four juvenile thieves, *Int. J. Psycho-Anal.*, **25**, 19–53; 102–128 (1944). (Also published as a monograph: London, Baillière, Tindall & Cox, 1946.)

BOWLBY, J., *Maternal Care and Mental Health*. W.H.O. Monograph Series 179 (Geneva, 1952).

BOWLBY, J., AINSWORTH, MARY, BOSTON, MARY and ROSENBLUTH, DINA, The effects of mother child separation: a follow-up study, *Brit. J. Med. Psychol.*, **29**, 211–247 (1956).

CAPLAN, G., Clinical Observations on the Emotional Life of Children in the Communal Settlements in Israel, in *Problems of Infancy and Childhood* (New York, Josiah Macey Found., 1954).

CARPENTER, J. and EISENBERG, P., Some relationships between family background and personality, *J. Psychol.*, **6**, 115–136 (1938).

CHILDERS, A. T. and HAMIL, B. M., Emotional problems in children as related to the duration of breast feeding in infancy, *Amer. J. Orthopsychiat.*, **2**, 134–142 (1932).

CLARKE, A. D. B. and CLARKE, A. M., Cognitive changes in the feebleminded, *Brit. J. Psychol.*, **XLV**, No. 3, 173–179 (1954).

CLARKE, ANN M. and CLARKE, A. D. B., *Mental Deficiency: the Changing Outlook* (London, Methuen, 1958).

CURRAN, D., The problem of assessing psychiatric treatment, *Lancet*, **2**, 1,005–1,009 (1937).

CURRAN, D. and GUTTMANN, E., *Psychological Medicine* (Edinburgh, Livingstone, 1949).

DAVIS, K., Extreme social isolation of a child, *Amer. J. Sociol.*, **45**, 554–565 (1940).

DAVIS, H. V., SEARS, R. R., MILLER, H. C. and BRODBECK, A. J., Effects of cup, bottle and breast feeding on oral activities of newborn infants, *Pediatrics*, **3**, 549–558 (1948).

DENNIS, W., Infant development under conditions of restricted practice and of minimum social stimulation, *Genet. Psychol. Monogr.*, **23**, 143–189 (1941).

DESPERT, J. L., Urinary control and enuresis, *Psychosom. Med.*, **6**, 294–307 (1944).

DOLLARD, J. and MILLER, N. E., *Personality and Psychotherapy* (New York, McGraw-Hill, 1950).

DOUGLAS, J. W. B. and BLOMFIELD, J. M., *Children under Fire* (London, Allen & Unwin, 1958).

EGGAN, D., The general problem of Hopi adjustment, in, *Personality in Nature, Society, and Culture*, Ed. C. Kluchkolm and H. A. Murray (New York, Knopf, 1953).

ENGLISH, O. S. and PEARSON, G. H. J., *Emotional Problems of Living* (New York, Norton, 1945).

EYSENCK, H. J., The effects of psychotherapy: an evaluation, *J. Cons. Psychol.*, **16**, 319–324 (1952).

EYSENCK, H. J., *The Dynamics of Anxiety and Hysteria* (London, Routledge & Kegan Paul, 1957).

EYSENCK, H. J. and PRELL, D. B., The inheritance of neuroticism. An experimental study, *J. Ment. Sci.*, **97**, 441–465 (1951).

FARRELL, B. A., The scientific testing of psychoanalytic findings and theory, *Brit. J. Med. Psychol.*, **24**, 35–41 (1951).

FARIS, R. E. L. and DUNHAM, H. W., *Mental Disorders in Urban Areas of Chicago* (Chicago, Chicago Univ. Press, 1939).

FENICHEL, O., *The Psychoanalytic Theory of Neuroses* (New York, Norton, 1945).

FERGUSON, T. and CUNNISON, J., *The Young Wage Earner. A Study of Glasgow Boys* (London, Oxford Univ. Press, for the Nuffield Foundation, 1951).

FORD, D., *The Delinquent Child and the Community* (London, Constable & Co. Ltd., 1957).

FRASER, RUSSELL, The incidence of neurosis among factory workers. 1947, *Rep. 2nd. Health Res. Bd.* (*Pink Reports*) *No.* 90 (London, H.M.S.O.).

FREUD, S., *Three Contributions to the Theory of Sex*, in

The Basic Writings of Sigmund Freud, Ed. A. A. Brill, 553–629 (New York, Modern Library, 1938).

FREUD, A. and BURLINGHAM, D., *Infants without Families* (New York, Int. Univ. Press, 1944).

GEWIRTZ, J. L., Social Deprivation: A Learning Analysis, in *Symposium, Dependency in Personality Development*, A.P.A. Congress, New York (1957).

GESELL, A., *The Embryology of Behavior* (New York, Harper & Bros., 1945).

GESELL, A. and ARMATRUDA, C. S., *Developmental Diagnosis* (New York, Hoeber, 1947).

GESELL, A., HALVERSON, H. M., THOMPSON, H., ILG, F. L. and COSTNER, C. S., *The First Five Years of Life: a Guide to the Study of the Preschool Child* (New York, Harper & Bros., 1940).

GESELL, A. and THOMPSON, H., *Infant Behaviour, its Genesis and Growth* (New York, McGraw-Hill, 1934).

GITTENS, J., *Approved School Boys* (London, Home Office, H.M.S.O., 1952).

GODDARD, H. H., *Feeblemindedness: its Causes and Consequences* (New York, Macmillan, 1923).

GOLDFARB, W., Infant rearing and problem behaviour, *Amer. J. Orthopsychiat.*, **13**, 249–265 (1943).

GOLDFARB, W., Psychological deprivation in infancy, *Amer. J. Psychiat.*, **102**, 19–33 (1945–6).

GOLDMAN-EISLER, F., The problem of "orality" and of its origins in early childhood, *J. Ment. Sci.*, **97**, 765–782 (1951).

GRUENBERG, E. M., *Technical Report of Mental Health Research Unit* (New York, New York State Depart. of Ment. Hyg., Syracuse Univ. Press, 1957).

HAGMAN, R. R., A study of fears of children of preschool age, *J. Exp. Educ.*, **1**, 110–130 (1932).

HARLOW, H. F., The formation of learning sets, *Psychol., Rev.*, **56**, 51–65 (1949).

HATTENDORF, K. W., A study of the questions of young children concerning sex: a phase of an experimental approach to parental education, *J. Soc. Psychol.*, **3**, 37–65 (1932).

HATTURCK, B. W., Interrelations between the preschool child's behavior and certain factors in the home, *Child Developm.*, **7**, 200–226 (1936).

HEBB, D. O., The effects of early experience on problem solving at maturity, *Amer. Psychol.*, **2**, 306–307 (1947).

HEBB, D. O., *Organization of Behavior* (New York, John Wiley & Sons, Inc., 1949).

HILL, J., Infant feeding and personality disorders. A study of early feeding in its relation to emotional and digestive disorders, *Psychiat. Quart.*, **11**, 356–382 (1937).

HILL, J. C. and ROBINSON, B., A case of retarded mental development associated with restricted movement in infancy, *Brit. J. Med. Psychol.*, **9**, 268–277 (1929).

HILLIARD, L. T. and KIRMAN, B. H. *et al.*, *Mental Deficiency* (London, Churchill, 1957).

HINDLEY, C., Contribution of associative learning theory to an understanding of child development, *Brit. J. Med. Psychol.*, **30**, 241–249 (1957).

HOLWAY, A. R., Early self-regulation of infants and later behavior in play interviews, *Amer. J. Orthopsychiat.*, **19**, 612–623 (1949).

HONIGMANN, J. J., *Culture and Personality* (New York, Harper & Bros., 1954).

HOWELLS, J. G., Day foster care and the nursery, *Lancet*, **2**, 1,254–1,255 (1956).

HUNT, J. McV., The effect of infant feeding-frustration upon adult hoarding in the albino rat, *J. Abnorm. (Soc.) Psychol.*, **36**, 338–360 (1941).

HUNT, J. McV., *Personality and the Behavior Disorders* (New York, Ronald Press, 1944).

HUSCHKA, M., The incidence and character of masturbation threats in a group of problem children, *Psychoanal. Quart.*, **7**, 338–356 (1938).

HUSCHKA, M., The child's response to coercive bowel training, *Psychosom. Med.*, **4**, 301–308 (1942).

INHELDER, B., *Developmental Psychology*. Annual Review of Psychology, Vol. 8 (Annual Reviews Inc. Palo Alto. Calif. 1957).

ISAACS, S., *Intellectual Growth in Young Children* (London, Routledge, 1945).

ISAACS, S., *Social Development in Young Children: a Study of Beginnings* (London, Routledge, 1946).

ITARD, J. M. G., *The Wild Boy of Aveyron*, trans. by George and Muriel Humphrey, (New York, Appleton-Century-Crofts, 1932).

JEPSILD, A. T., *Child Psychology* (4th ed.) (New York, Prentice Hall, 1954).

JONES, G., The application of conditioning and learning techniques to the treatment of a psychiatric patient, *J. Abnorm. (Soc.) Psychol.*, **52**, 414–419 (1956).

KANNER, L., *Neurology and Psychiatry in Childhood* (Ass. for Res. in Nervous and Mental diseases, Williams Wilkins, New York, 1954).

KINSEY, A. C., POMEROY, W. B., and MARTIN, C. E., *Sexual Behavior in the Human Male* (Philadelphia, Saunders, 1948).

KINSEY, A. C., POMEROY, W. B., MARTIN, C. E. and GEBHARD, P. H., *Sexual Behavior in the Human Female* (Philadelphia, Saunders, 1953).

KÖHLER, W., *Gestalt Psychology* (New York, Liveright, 1929).

LEVY, D. M., Fingersucking and accessory movements in early infancy: an etiological study, *Amer. J. Psychiat.*, **7**, 881–918 (1928).

LEVY, D. M., Experiments on the sucking reflex and social behavior of dogs, *Amer. J. Orthopsychiat.*, **7**, 881–918 (1934).

LEVY, D. M., *Maternal Over-protection* (New York, Columbia Univ. Press, 1943).

LEWIS, H., *Deprived Children* (London, Oxford Univ. Press, for the Nuffield Foundation, 1954).

LITTLE, W. J., On the influence of abnormal parturition, difficult labours, premature births and asphyxia neonatorum, on the mental and physical condition of the child, especially in relation to deformities, *Tr. Obst. Soc. London*, **3**, 293 (London, 1862).

MACFARLANE, J. W., ALLEN, L. and HONZIK, M. P., A developmental study of the behavior problems of normal children between twenty-one months and fourteen years, *Univer. Calif. Pub. Child Develpm.* **2** (Berkeley, Univer. Calif. Press, 1954).

MCPHAIL, F. L. and HALL, E. L., A consideration of the cause and possible late effect of anoxia in the new born infant, *Amer. J. Obstet. & Gynec.*, **42**, 686 (1941).

MARQUIS, D. P., Learning in the neonate. The modification

of behavior under three feeding schedules, *J. Exp. Psychol.*, **29**, 263–282 (1941).

MAYER-GROSS W., SLATER, E. and ROTH, M., *Clinical Psychiatry* (London, Cassell & Co. Ltd., 1954).

MILES, H. H. W., BARRABEE, E. L. and FINESINGER, J. E., Evaluation of psychotherapy, *Psychosom. Med.*, **13**, 83–105 (1951).

MILLER, N. E., and DOLLARD, J., *Social Learning and Imitation* (New Haven, Yale Univ. Press, 1941).

Ministry of Education Annual Report (London, H.M.S.O., 1954).

Ministry of Education Report of the Committee on Maladjusted Children (London, H.M.S.O., 1955).

MOWRER, O. H., *Learning Theory and Personality Dynamics* (New York, Ronald Press, 1950).

MUNN, N. L., *The Evolution and Growth of Human Behavior* (Boston, Houghton Mifflin, 1955).

MURPHY, L. B., in *Personality and the Behavior Disorders*, Ed. J. McV. Hunt (New York, Ronald Press, 1944).

MUSSEN, P. H. and CONGER, J. J., *Child Development and Personality* (New York, Harper & Bros., 1956).

MYERS, T. R., *Intrafamily Relationships and Pupil Adjustment* (New York, Teachers College, Columbia Univ. Press, 1935).

NEWTON, N. R. and NEWTON, M., Relationship of ability to breast feed and maternal attitudes towards breast feeding, *Pediatrics*, **5**, 869–875 (1950).

NIELSEN, C. K., The childhood of schizophrenics, *Acta psychiat. et neurol. scand.*, **414**, 281–289 (1954).

O'CONNOR, N., The evidence for the permanently disturbing effects of mother child separation, *Acta Psychol.*, **12**, 174–191 (1956).

O'CONNOR, N., *Brain Damage and Mental Defect in Mental Deficiency: the Changing Outlook*. Eds. Ann M. Clarke and A. D. B. Clarke (London, Methuen & Co., Ltd., 1958).

O'CONNOR, N. and TIZARD, J., *The Social Problem of Mental Deficiency* (London, Pergamon Press, 1956).

ORLANSKY, H., Infant care and personality, *Psychol. Bull.*, **46**, 1–49 (1949).

PAGE, M. L., Study in Child Welfare, *Univ. Ia Stud., Child Welf.*, **2**, 3-69 (1936).

PENROSE, L. S., *Biology of Mental Deficiency* (London, Sidgwick & Jackson, 1949).

PETERSON, C. H. and SPANO, FRANCES L., Breast feeding, maternal rejection, and child personality, *Character & Pers.*, **10**, 62–66 (1941).

PINNEAU, S. R., Infantile disorders of hospitalism and anaclitic depression, *Psychol. Bull.*, **52**, 429–452, (1955).

PINNEAU, S. R., Reply to Dr. Spitz, *Psychol. Bull.*, **52**, 459–462 (1955).

Proceedings of the Ninth Child Guidance Inter. Clinic Conference N.A.M.H. London, (1951). Follow-up on Child Guidance Cases.

Psychological Services for Schools. No. 3 Unesco Instit. for Educ. Ed. W. D. Wall (Hamburg, 1956).

RADKE, M. J., *The Relation of Parental Authority to Children's Behavior and Attitudes* (Minneapolis, Univ. Minnesota Press, 1946).

Registrar General's Statistical Review of England and Wales for 1949. Supplement on General Morbidity, Cancer and Mental Health (London, H.M.S.O., 1953).

Registrar General's Statistical Review of England and Wales for 1950–51. Supplement on General Morbidity, Cancer and Mental Health (London, H.M.S.O., 1955).

Royal Commission on the Law relating to Mental Illness and Mental Deficiency 1954–1957. Report (London, H.M.S.O., 1957).

RHEINGOLD, H. L., The modification of social responsiveness in institutional babies, *Monogr. Soc. Res. Child Developm.* **21**, No. 2 (1956).

ROBERTS, E., Thumb and finger sucking in relation to feeding in early infancy, *Amer. J. Dis. Child.*, **68**, 7–8 (1944).

ROGERS, M. E., LILIENFIELD, A. M. and PASAMANICK, B., Prenatal and postnatal factors in the development of childhood behaviour disorders, *Acta psychol. et neurol. scan.*, Suppl. 102 (1955).

ROGERSON, B. C. F. and ROGERSON, C. H., Feeding in infancy and subsequent psychological difficulties, *J. Ment. Sci.*, **85**, 1,163–1,182 (1939).

SEARS, R. R., Experimental studies of projection: I. Attribution of traits, *J. Soc. Psychol.*, **7**, 151–163 (1936).

SEARS, P. S., Doll play aggression in normal young children: influence of sex, age, sibling status, father's absence, *Psychol. Monogr.*, No. 65 (1951).

SEARS, R. R., PINTLER, M. H. and SEARS, P. S., Effect of father's separation on preschool children's doll play aggression, *Child Developm.*, **17**, 219–243 (1946).

SEARS, R. R., WHITING, J. W. M., NOWLIS, V. and SEARS, P. S., Some child-rearing antecedents of aggression and dependency in young children, *Genet. Psychol. Monogr.*, **47**, 135–236 (1953).

SEARS, R. R. and WISE, G. W., Relation of cup-feeding in infancy to thumb-sucking and the oral drive, *Amer. J. Orthopsychiat.*, **20**, 123–138 (1950).

SEGUIN, E., *Traitement Morale, Hygiene et Education des Idiots* (Paris, J. B. Battière, 1846).

SEWELL, W. H. and MUSSEN, P. H., The effects of feeding, weaning and scheduling procedures on childhood adjustment and the formation of oral symptoms, *Child Developm.*, **23**, 185–191 (1952).

SHIRLEY, M. M., *The First Two Years, a Study of Twenty-five Babies*. Vol. II. Intellectual development (Minneapolis, Univ. Minn. Press, 1933).

SHOBEN, E. J., The assessment of parental attitudes in relation to child adjustment, *Genet. Psychol. Monogr.*, **39**, 101–148 (1949).

SIMSARIAN, F. P., Case histories of five thumb-sucking children breast-fed on unscheduled regimes, without limitations of nursing time, *Child Developm.*, **18**, 180–184 (1947).

SLATER, E. and SLATER, P., A heuristic theory of neurosis, *J. Neurol., Psychiat.*, **7**, 49–55 (1944).

SMIRNOV, A. A., *Psychology in the Soviet Union*, Ed. Brian Simon (London, Routledge & Kegan Paul, 1957).

SPITZ, R. A., Hospitalism: an enquiry into the genesis of psychiatric conditions in early childhood, *Psychoanalyt. Study Child*, **1**, 53–74 (1945).

SPITZ, R. A., Anaclitic depression, *Psychoanalyt. Study Child*, **2**, 313–342 (1946).

SPITZ, R. A., Reply to Dr. Pinneau, *Psychol. Bull.*, **52**, 453–459 (1955).

STERN, W., *Psychology of Early Childhood*, trans. A. Barwell (London, Allen and Unwin, 1924).

STEVENSON, J., Is the human personality more plastic in infancy and childhood? *Amer. J. Psychiat.*, **14**, 152–161 (1957).

STOTT, D. H., Physical and mental handicaps following a disturbed pregnancy, *Lancet.*, **1**, 1,006–1,012 (1957).

SYMONDS, P. M., *Psychology of Parent-child Relationships* (New York, Appleton-Century-Crofts, 1939).

THOMPSON, W. R. and HERON, W., The effects of restricting early experience on the problem solving capacity of dogs, *Canad. J. Psychol.*, **8**, 17–31 (1954).

THORPE, G. and JAMES, D. P., Neuroticism in children, *Brit. J. Psychol.*, **48**, 26–34 (1957).

TREDGOLD, A. F., *Mental Deficiency* (London, Ballière, Tindall & Cox, 1908).

VON SENDEN M., *Raum-und Gestalt auffasoung bei operierten Blindgeboresien vor und nach der Operation* (Leipzig, Barth, 1932).

WATSON, G., A comparison of the effects of lax v. strict home discipline, *J. Soc. Psychol.*, **5**, 102–105 (1934).

WATSON, G., Some personality differences in children related to strict or permissive parental discipline, *J. Psychol.*, **44**, 227–249 (1957).

WATSON, J. B. and MORGAN, J. J. B., Emotional reactions and psychological experimentation, *Amer. J. Psychol.*, **28**, 163–174 (1917).

WELLMANN, BETH L., I.Q. changes in pre-school and non pre-school groups during pre-school years: A summary of the literature, *J. Psychol.*, **20**, 347–368 (1945).

WELLMANN, B. L., SKEELS, H. M. and SKODAK, M., Review of McNamar's critical examination of Iowa studies, *Psychol. Bull.*, **37**, 93–111 (1940).

WERTHEIMER, M., Hebb and Senden on the role of learning in perception, *Amer. J. Psychol.*, **64**, 133–137 (1951).

WHITING, J. W. M. and CHILD, I. L., *Child Training and Personality* (New Haven, Yale Univ. Press, 1953).

WOHL, C. W., Some antecedent factors in the family histories of 392 schizophrenics, *Amer. J. Psychiat.*, **110**, 668–676 (1954).

ZUCKERMANN, C. B. and ROCK, I., A reappraisal of the roles of past experience and innate organizing processes in visual perception, *Psychol. Bull.*, **54**, 269–296 (1957).

CHAPTER 11

Somatic Reactivity

IRENE MARTIN

THIS chapter will be concerned with experimental data on certain autonomic functions and on skeletal muscle activity assessed by recording muscle action potentials; these two classes together will be termed "somatic responses." Almost all these physiological variables are highly complex processes, requiring a degree of care in matters of instrumentation, controls, procedure, recording and measurement, rarely found in psychological experiments. It seems, moreover, to be curiously true that the more ambitious and complicated the project—and it is ambitious indeed to hope to establish the peripheral somatic concomitants of certain inner "feelings"—the more studied the neglect of a rigorous experimental technique.

Responses of this kind are obviously associated with many of the overt activities observed in the individual, but they very frequently follow many kinds of stimuli even when no movement is apparent. It is proposed to deal briefly in this chapter with the course of autonomic and skeletal muscle activity during the performance of particular tasks, and some evidence will be presented to show that the underlying physiological state is, as would be expected, of great importance in determining certain aspects of performance. The main concern will be, however, with the somatic responses of the resting individual when stimulated by controlled sensory stimuli to which he is required to make either no overt response or simple verbal responses.

There would appear to be every justification for first studying somatic responses under the simplest experimental conditions, since one of the fundamental tasks of an experimental approach to behaviour (and one which has received surprisingly little attention) would seem to be the determination of characteristic curves of responses as functions of input variation. Only in this way does it seem possible to understand the nature of the responses, their interrelations, and their functions under varying experimental conditions, on all of which could be based a systematic interlocking of facts.

This policy has not been explicitly stated in experimental work carried out within this field, with the notable exception of R. C. Davis, whose careful work well illustrates this outlook. Important, too, are the recent suggestions of Malmo (1958) linking physiological type measurements with learning theory. But the general approach in psychophysiological research has been confused and unformulated. Some specific guidance is urgently required to direct research in this field, and it will be argued in this chapter that one of the most fundamental ways of understanding human behaviour and its abnormalities will be via knowledge of the essential functions of the central nervous system.

Few of the hypotheses which have been mentioned in the literature merit really detailed comment (many of them appear to be ingenious and stimulating but are only loosely related to the specific experiments they purport to guide) but those which have been more persistently treated—Cannon's emergency arousal, and autonomic balance, for example—will be dealt with.

Most important, it is highly necessary to mention the real problems of recording responses: instrumentation, variables affecting the response, type of measurement to be made, etc. The data at present available can best be organized on the basis of the variables themselves—skin resistance, blood-pressure, peripheral vasomotor activity, skin temperature, heart rate, pupillary reactions, respiratory activity, and muscle action potentials—and the interrelation of these under some conditions will be considered in the following pages. So far as it is possible an attempt will be made within the individual sections to classify the available studies in accordance with response characteristics, i.e. into adaptation effects, varying amplitudes and latencies of response to different intensities of stimuli, and changing patterns of response. No complete consistency of this kind of classification is possible since, for some functions, such data have not been obtained; where this is the case an overall review of the available literature will be presented instead. The important function of conditioning, about which there is so much experimental evidence, will be treated fully in a separate chapter.

The present stage of development of research into somatic responses is such that it is still necessary to consider the usefulness of such topics as "emotion," within which a great part of the research using physiological measurements has been carried out. Psychologists in the past have been preoccupied with traditional categories of behaviour—instincts, emotions, motivation, and so on—which, in spite of the many objections to them, have been retained (sometimes redefined) and are in current use. Their reinstatement has frequently been accomplished simply by linking them to postulated physiological states; as Davis (1953) has commented, too often there has been simply a "physicalizing" of old concepts. The question to ask is: do concepts like motivation and emotion (with subcategories of anxiety, depression, etc.) provide a classificatory system within which to place the factual data obtained from objective measurements of physiological activity in human behaviour? The problem has particular relevance to studies of psychiatric patients, where emphasis is placed on emotional states such as anxiety. In view of the fact that our understanding of terms such as anxiety is largely derived from experiential analysis, the usefulness of introspective evidence will be considered first.

INTROSPECTIVE EVIDENCE

The simple reality of our experience is so evident to us that it is frequently argued that no complete account of emotion can ever be given without reference to private data. In a sense, of course, this is true, and it depends mostly upon personal views and aims whether such data are considered useful or not at the present.

The extensive and *wholly* introspective analysis by early psychologists was of little value: it led to no sound measurement, classification, or theoretical development. Yet introspective data of a sort continue to be used in many psychiatric studies where patients' judgements form the basis of clinical attempts to "objectify" symptoms. The interesting work of Shagass and Naiman (1956) on the sedation thresholds of different groups of psychiatric patients, might illustrate the type of clinical investigation which attempts to objectify clinical assessments of anxiety or tension, and Malmo and Shagass's work (1949b) the attempt to relate physiological activity of certain areas to subjects' complaints of symptoms. In contrast, many psychologists have despaired of attempts

to establish homologies between precise physiological events and vague and ill-defined emotional states assessed clinically or introspectively, and it has been argued that, if the concept of emotion is to be retained at all, it must be as a scientific inference rather than as a reality of experience (Brown and Farber, 1951). The experimental study of "anxiety" can possibly be made on this basis, but it is so far only a guess that specific responses defined operationally will relate to the anxiety constellation in clinical use.

A glance at the literature demonstrates that it is the different types of introspective evidence used which have led to confusion and argument about its value. Simple judgements—of intensity of sensory stimuli, or location of muscular aches—may form a useful basis for further experimentation, but the complex introspective analysis of higher mental activities seems to lend itself less readily to experimental control. It is predominantly this latter type of evidence which is used in psychiatric studies and which, coupled with clinical observation, has led to the development of a number of rather general hypotheses about the behaviour of psychiatric groups.

Hypotheses from such sources are necessarily couched in somewhat general terms, and offer little guidance when applied to specific experimental problems (cf. theories of autonomic balance and Cannon's emergency arousal discussed below). Not only is the classification of subjects in doubt, but so many different response measurements and stimulus conditions have been used that any integration or evaluation of the findings is (until they are repeated) both difficult and of doubtful value.

There remain a few careful, and some not so careful but interesting, experiments which will be described. The criticism which can be levelled against many of these is their lack of structuring within a useful framework: it is small wonder that, with so few facts available, there is little close guidance from existing theories, but there is less excuse for the absence of narrower hypotheses or aims to direct research towards a better understanding of these omnipresent psychophysiological functions.

The viewpoint, reached after considering the psychological literature, is that a detailed description of these somatic responses in relation to simple, quantified stimuli should lead towards a better description of the curves of basic processes, such as adaptation, and that the study of these response curves in relation to abnormal conditions (drug effects, for example) should prove more fruitful than the study of arbitrary measurements of responses to complex situations which cannot easily be brought within experimental control. Unfortunately, the desirability of objectivity and reproducibility of data, as well as of the quantification of stimuli, has not always been explicitly recognized in this field.

The measurement of "emotion" has frequently been attempted by means of physiological responses, and a glance at its status in psychology provides a useful starting point for considering research into autonomic and skeletal activities.

EXPERIMENTAL DEVELOPMENTS

From the early days of psychology a basis for the objective study of emotions was discerned in autonomic responses (see, for example, James, 1902). In Cannon's classical work with cats (1920) the importance of autonomic reactions in supporting muscular activity in states of defence and attack was clearly described, and terms such as fear and anger were applied to a class of behaviour fairly well defined, although not explicitly so, in stimulus-response terms.

In addition to the downward discharge from the thalamus, activating the sympathetic nervous system, Cannon pointed to the upward discharge from thalamus to cortex, which he supposed added the familiar emotional tone to incoming sensory impulses and reduced the inhibitory action of the cortex. Later research has tended on the whole to support and elaborate Cannon's thalamic theory. (Lengthier discussions may be found in Arnold, 1955; Gellhorn, 1953; and Lindsley, 1951.)

As is well known, Cannon's work with cats dealt with the usefulness of bodily changes as emergency functions, for example, the utility of the increased blood sugar as a source of muscular energy, of vascular changes favouring muscular exertion, of rapid coagulation in preventing loss of blood. In particular he laid stress upon reactions in states of fear and anger (considered to be dominant emotions) in which sympathetic nervous discharge was *diffuse*, involving acceleration of the heart, contraction of the arterioles, dilatation of the bronchioles, increase of blood sugar and sweating, inhibition of activity of the digestive glands and of gastro-intestinal peristalsis. On the other hand, Cannon believed that in conditions of thirst and hunger the general bodily need is signalled by more well-defined localized sensations, and so he drew a distinction between the appetitive and emergency functions of the autonomic nervous system.

The description of the emergency reaction appealed to psychologists, and Freeman's approach (1948) illustrates how Cannon's concepts were enthusiastically applied to the study of human behaviour. This writer advanced the thesis that all behaviour is an attempt to preserve organismic integrity by "homeostatic" restorations of equilibrium, and proposed a study of the typical homeostatic response curve from a basic energy level (relaxation) when the subject is "displaced" by an external stimulus of controlled intensity and duration. "The equilibratory sequence has three phases: (i) mobilization, wherein bodily energies are internally aroused to meet the stimulus-induced displacement; (ii) discharge, wherein the aroused energies are externally expressed by overt responses, and (iii) recovery, wherein the organismic energy system returns towards its pre-stimulus condition." Freeman believed that the major parameters whose interaction determines the personality pattern were discoverable through measurement of physiological reactions to common disturbing stimuli such as the noise of a pistol shot and frustration tests.

There followed a period of fairly intensive analysis of autonomic responses and their interrelations, leading to the description of many new facts; this, in turn, led to a modification of the original simpler viewpoint on autonomic functioning. Many years of research have followed Cannon's theory, and some of the subsequent physiological studies of subcortical mechanisms, such as the diencephalon, which have considerably enlarged our understanding of the higher-level organization of the autonomic nervous system, will be mentioned in the following sections.

The well-argued paper by Brown and Farber (1951) has recently discussed afresh the problem of emotion. They advocate that emotions can be most profitably conceptualized as hypothetical variables intervening between environmental conditions and responses, and that this should lead to "guesses at laws" concerning the functional relations between the hypothetical emotions and observable behaviour. "These guessed-at-laws would be of the general form 'behaviour is such and such a function of emotion or emotions'." Antecedent events, both external and internal, must be described, and any proposed theory must contain coherent statements of its relationship to the constructs contained in more general theories of behaviour. Brown and Farber illustrate this approach with anxiety and frustration. Anxiety, for example, is defined as the conditioned form of the pain-fear response (Mowrer, 1950) and it is widely assumed in learning experiments that the response involves autonomic arousal and skeletal motor discharge. (Mowrer, 1950; Solomon and Wynne, 1954.) This is a legitimate and potentially useful definition, but parametric studies of this state in man are still lacking.

Several psychologists, also rejecting the traditional concept of emotion, have argued that behaviour subsumed under this heading be placed along a continuum of energy mobilization (Duffy, 1951) or activation (Lindsley, 1951; Schlosberg, 1954). Various indices for assessing degree of arousal have been proposed, and Malmo (1957) has discussed the possible relationship between the intensity continuum and experimental investigations into anxiety and motivation.

There is a very great difference in outlook between the earlier psychophysiological research which concentrated on measuring "emotion" in its various forms, and the modern tendency to dismiss such concepts and to develop the usefulness of psychophysiological measurement within broader systems, such as the arousal continuum and learning theory (*see* Arnold (1955) for a recent survey of theories along traditional lines, and Malmo (1958) for newer proposals in relation to learning theory).

The task in hand is to determine in what sense the available data have laid the foundation of a systematic treatment of "emotions" and whether they have advanced our understanding of autonomic and skeletal muscle functions *per se*. The following sections will deal with experimental work on somatic responses first treated rather generally, and then more specifically considering the separate variables such as skin resistance and muscle action potentials.

A fairly wide cross-section of experimental studies will be reported since the field is not dominated by highly formulated aims and methods; unfortunately, very few studies have been repeated, so that a selection criterion of reproducibility of results can hardly be upheld. Discussion will be restricted to those studies where reasonably well-defined stimulus and response measures have been employed.

THE AUTONOMIC NERVOUS SYSTEM

Autonomic Balance

An early view on autonomic balance put forward by Eppinger and Hess (1910) has engaged the interest of many psychologists, who have made frequent attempts to measure autonomic balance, and to establish its personality correlates. Among the most serious and thorough investigations are those of Wenger (1941, 1948) who, differentiating on a chemical (i.e. adrenergic-cholinergic) rather than anatomical (sympathetic-parasympathetic) basis, aimed to test the hypothesis that autonomic imbalance, when measured in an unselected population, would be distributed continuously about a central tendency which he defines as autonomic balance.

A large-scale study (1948) was carried out upon aircrews during the war; it followed earlier work with children which had delineated a factor described in terms of a number of functions innervated by the autonomic nervous system and a second factor of muscular tension, and it seemed likely that these two factors might be of use in the elimination of unpromising men from the Army Air Force.

Careful preliminary investigations were made into effects of uncontrolled variables such as humidity and time of day, into the effects of different test administrators and methods of recording (e.g. different electrode jellies on skin conductance). Reliability coefficients were obtained for each test (*see* Table XI.1).

The 1948 monograph describes several studies, the results of which can briefly be summarized as follows—

1. a picture of sympathetic imbalance was found in the sample of operational fatigue patients, and the results were believed to support the contention that operational fatigue is characterized by excessive activity of the sympathetic branch of the autonomic nervous system.

2. from the second study it was concluded that autonomic imbalance in psychoneurotic patients, with functional predominance of the sympathetic nervous system, was indicated. The combined psychoneurosis test syndrome was seen to be similar to, but not identical with, that reported for operational fatigue.

TABLE XI.1

MEANS AND STANDARD DEVIATIONS OF NORMATIVE SAMPLE FOR ALL TEST VARIABLES AND TEST-RETEST RELIABILITY COEFFICIENTS FOR TWO SAMPLES

(*From Wenger*, 1948)

No.	Variables	Mean (N = 488)	σ488	γ34	γ39
10	Salivary output	4·2 cc	1·7	0·88	0·85
12	Salivary pH	7·2 pH	0·4	0·47	0·62
13	Dermographia latency	13·3 sec	4·5	0·35	0·42
14	Dermographia persistence	16·8 min	9·2	0·63	0·19
15	Palmar conductance	16·8 μmhos	7·1	0·70*	0·57
17	Log conductance change	30·1 log units	13·7	0·65*	0·70
19	Volar conductance	7·3 μmhos	2·2	0·67	0·27
21	Systolic blood-pressure	111·1 mm Hg	9·0	0·74*	0·33
23	Diastolic blood-pressure	70·0 mm Hg	7·4	0·67	0·33
25	Pulse pressure	41·1 mm Hg	10·0	0·64	0·44
27	Sinus arrhythmia	0·7 rating unit	1·1	0·25	0·45
28	Heart period	160·4 millimin/ 10 periods	23·5	0·73*	0·66
30	Sublingual temperature	99·0°F	0·4	0·11	0·28
32	Finger temperature (1st)	34·9°C	1·9	0·51	0·73
34	Finger temperature (2nd)	35·4°C	1·4	0·55	0·27
36	Lymphocytes	35·6 per cent	8·4	0·30	0·48
38	White blood count	7,500 per cu mm	1,680	0·36	0·05
39	Eosinophils	1·3 per cent	1·9	0·25	0·09
40	Blood sugar	94·0 mg/100 cc	18·0	0·22*	0·11
42	Respiration period	5·1 sec	1·4	0·65	0·68
44	Tidal air mean	21·8 mm	7·0	0·53	0·38
46	Tidal air sigma	4·5 mm	2·8	0·64	0·28
48	Oxygen consumption	50·4 cal per hr/ sq m	8·3	0·57*	0·10
50	Weight/Height	4·6 (10 step scale)	2·1		
51	Relaxation rating	5·1 rating units	1·4		
52	Pupillary diameter	5·3 mm	0·9	0·71	0·64

* Measurement influenced by the effect of a post-absorptive resting state.

3. Conclusions from separate investigations of asthmatic and peptic-ulcer patients were the same, in so far as no support was found for the hypothesis that these disorders are related to parasympathetic predominance as measured by the tests.

A factor which was satisfactorily defined as an autonomic factor arose from the analysis of the physiological data. This factor did not correlate to any extent with personality traits measured by Guilford's S.T.D.C.R. and G.A.M.I.N. scales (see, however, Eysenck, *The Structure of Human Personality*, p. 196, 1953, for a discussion of these results). Another factor was identified as "muscular tension," although it was less clearly defined.

Other attempts have been made to investigate autonomic balance (Darling and Darrow, 1938; Darling, 1940) all these attempts, however, carry the assumption that both sympathetic and parasympathetic systems act as a whole and in a generalized fashion, an assumption which has been amply criticized.[1] Darrow (1943) has pointed out that it is often difficult to determine whether an apparent change in the autonomic nervous system is due to increase of activity in one branch of the autonomic system, or to decrease of activity in the other. As he put it, the problem is literally to determine the weight on either side of a "balance," when that on neither side is known.

Some of the autonomic functions, such as sweat glands and peripheral blood vessels, used in early attempts to establish autonomic imbalance, were mistakenly believed to be innervated by both sympathetic and parasympathetic nerves. Autonomic innervation, either sympathetic or parasympathetic, of other variables is not proven; for example, Rothman (1945) argues that the phenomenon of red dermographism is a local response of the contractile elements of small vessels, not due to autonomic reactivity since it can be elicited in completely denervated areas with the same intensity as in normal innervated skin.

Even those organs with a clearly dual supply of parasympathetic and sympathetic nerves reveal, upon further study, a complex kind of innervation. Lacey (1956) cites an experiment in which the following simultaneous stimuli were applied to the peripheral cut ends of the appropriate nerves: a sympathetic stimulus, capable of increasing heart rate by 41 beats per minute, and a vagal stimulus capable of decreasing the heart rate by 34 beats per minute. The net result was a decrease of 30 beats per minute, illustrating the

importance of vagal tonus. Moreover, it is known that sympathetic excitation *potentiates* vagal inhibition: "thus, simultaneous stimulation of the cardiac-accelerator nerves or small doses of epinephrine makes the heart *even more sensitive to vagal stimulation.*" (Lacey, 1956.)

Such facts as these inevitably lead to caution in interpreting the results of experimental work which has been carried out on the concept of sympatheticotonia. At first glance it might be thought that a technique such as factor analysis could be of value in this field. But, as Darrow (1943) comments on Wenger's work, although factorial analysis may reveal relationships which otherwise might escape attention, it cannot "impart autonomic significance to tests which are not themselves valid according to acceptable physiological criteria."

Attempts to measure sympathetico- or vago-tonia of the autonomic nervous system by means of the reactions of the circulation to certain drugs have been attacked by Altschule (1953): "when the tests are carried out as described . . . they do not measure the reactivity of the autonomic nervous system. What they do measure are: the activity of enzymes that inactivate or destroy the drugs; the reactivity of the end organs (the heart and the blood vessels); and, in the case of acetyl-choline, the reactivity of some autonomic ganglia. All these phenomena occur at the same time, and any conclusion concerning the activities of the autonomic nervous system as a whole during the test is invalid."

Many years of investigations into autonomic functions have followed the publication of the Eppinger and Hess theory, and the need to modify the original conception of autonomic functioning is now widely recognized. Hess (1954) has stressed that classificatory terms having a *functional* significance are more appropriate than a separation based on morphologic criteria, such as the separation into sympathetic and parasympathetic systems: "this functional interpretation involves recognition of the fact that the antagonism between the sympathetic and parasympathetic systems really enables these two components to *supplement* each other in their effects."

Recent experimental work has also shown that, in arousal, individuals excite preferred organs rather consistently, and the type of organ or pattern aroused may differ from individual to individual. Lacey and his associates (1952, 1953) have carried out a series of investigations into differences in somatic response patterns to stress. A group of children in one study (1952) and adults in another (1953) were subjected to various stresses—mental arithmetic, hyperventilation, letter association, and a cold pressor test. Physiological variables recorded were (from children)

---

[1] It should be added that Wenger (1957) has recently described a modified approach to the problem of autonomic balance, based on fewer variables and aiming to differentiate hypo- and hyper-sympathetic or parasympathetic *syndromes*.

blood-pressure, heart rate, heart-rate variability and palmar conductance, and (from adults) heart rate, heart-rate variability and palmar conductance. They found that the patterns were fairly reproducible upon immediate retest, and in certain cases remained consistent for long periods. They also emphasized that patterning may appear in very similar functions, for example within cardiovascular variables themselves, as well as between say, the cardiovascular and sudomotor systems.

These authors take the view that the question "how reactive is this individual?" is not one that can be asked with respect to the autonomic system as a whole. For one measure he may be a marked hyporeactor, for another a marked hyperreactor. To determine the function showing truly maximal activation in a given individual would require simultaneous measurement of all autonomic functions, a task obviously impossible at present. They have formulated a principle of relative response specificity which states: "some individuals are so constituted that they will respond to a given hierarchy of autonomic activation whatever the stress: others will show greater fluctuation from stress to stress although they will exhibit one pattern more frequently than another; still other individuals will randomly exhibit now one pattern, now another. In addition, although the rank order of reactivity remains the same from stress to stress, the quantitative differences between the degree of activation of the different physiological measures will fluctuate considerably" (Lacey et al., 1953).

Malmo and Shagass (1949b) measuring autonomic and skeletal muscle functions in patient groups have postulated an allied principle of symptom specificity. They found that cardiac patients responded to stress with acceleration of heart activity, hypertensives by rise in blood-pressure, and that people with headache complaints had a higher level of muscle activity in the forehead than those without headaches. From these data it was hypothesized that "stress" situations do not activate all physiological systems, but only the specific physiological mechanism underlying the somatic complaint. Both these principles of specificity of response and symptom specificity, which seem to be reasonably well established under certain stimulus conditions are, of course, in disagreement with the concept of "mass action" of the sympathetic division of the A.N.S.

AUTONOMIC AND SKELETAL MUSCLE SYSTEMS

Freeman (in *The Energetics of Human Behaviour*, p. 261, 1948) has argued for the study of the relation of overt motor discharge to autonomic arousal processes during experimentally induced frustrations, on the basis of some preliminary studies which suggested that individuals who recover internal equilibrium quickly show a high degree of externalized activity. He further drew attention to the *appropriateness* of the motor discharge in regaining equilibrium, quoting results which indicated that subjects who discharge relatively more of their aroused energies through the motor channel specifically appropriate to the experimental displacement, tend to recover equilibrium quickly and to be left with only small amounts of residual tension. Freeman has depended very heavily upon measures of skin resistance and G.S.R. to indicate the arousal and recovery aspects of responses; unfortunately the specificity in patterns of autonomic responses which has been demonstrated must lead to scepticism of results based on a single measure to represent general responsiveness. The results of Freeman's factor-analytic studies (describing factors of discharge control, drive arousal and discriminative capacity) and their relation to other factor analyses of physiological measurements have been discussed by Eysenck (1953).

The study of the interaction of skeletal muscle and autonomic functions is obviously of importance, and an attempt has been made to elucidate their relationship in learning and conditioning experiments, where both components may be present (Solomon and Wynne, 1954). The physiological levels at which interaction between the systems may take place has been surveyed by Kennard (1947).

It is commonly believed (following Cannon) that under some "emergency" conditions, autonomic functions are organized to support the efficient activity of the muscles for attack or flight; however, the greater speed of transmission of motor than autonomic nerves, the shorter latencies of muscular reactions and (in the absence of reinforcement of the motor responses) their more rapid extinction, are facts which argue against a necessarily "supportive" role of autonomic responses, at least under certain simple conditions (*see* Davis et al., 1955, p. 21).

THE INHERITANCE OF AUTONOMIC FUNCTIONS

Jost and Sontag (1944) obtained measures of vasomotor persistence, salivary output, heart period, palmar and volar conductance, respiratory period and pulse pressure in groups of twins, siblings, and unrelated children. For these individual functions they derived difference scores between pairs of children (twins, siblings and unrelated). Only very small numbers of twins were seen, but some of the differences were significant, showing siblings to be less alike than twins, and unrelated children less alike than the siblings and the twins.

The inheritance in rats of certain elimination responses used as an index of "emotionality" is briefly discussed in Chapter 19 by Peter Broadhurst, and references given there.

ATTEMPTS TO DIFFERENTIATE EMOTIONS

The belief that separate emotions consist of particular patterns of autonomic and muscular responses has been widespread among psychologists, and several studies have been undertaken on this basis (Arnold, 1945, Ax, 1953). Such experiments involve complex stimulus conditions designed to arouse anger, fear, etc., or depend upon ratings of affective states or predominant needs, such as "anger out" or "anger in" (Funkenstein *et al.*, 1954). This means that their reproducibility is rather unlikely, and, in fact, the results of different experiments purporting to establish physiological concomitants of fear and anger have not in general confirmed one another (but *see* Funkenstein *et al.*, 1957).

It has been convincingly argued that the problem of determining how many basic emotions "exist" is similar to that of determining whether any emotion "exists"—

More progress might have been made if it had been asked instead whether observable behavior is most satisfactorily explained by the introduction of one or more constructs carrying an emotional label. If it appears desirable to have more than one each must be shown to have relations that are in some way distinctive with reference to the other elements of the theory and to each other. Different emotions exist as realities for psychology only if different defining operations and interrelations can be clearly specified for them. If such specifications cannot be made the superfluous terms are scientifically inadmissible and must be coalesced or deleted; appeals for their continuance on intuitive or phenomenologic grounds must be rejected. (Brown and Farber, 1951.)

FUNCTIONS OF THE AUTONOMIC NERVOUS SYSTEM

Skin Resistances and the Galvanic Skin Response (G.S.R.)

Of all psychophysiological measures, changes in skin resistance (or its reciprocal, conductance) and the psychogalvanic skin reflex have become the most popular with psychologists. This is partly due to the simplicity of the instrumentation required, but largely to the extreme sensitivity of the G.S.R. to sensory and ideational stimuli.

There are two methods of recording: (i) the Féré phenomenon (the more commonly used) in which the passage of a small external d.c. current is used to obtain a measure of apparent resistance, and (ii) the Tarchanoff phenomenon, where no external current is used and the potential difference of the skin between the two electrodes is used to deflect a galvanometer. A close agreement of results from the two methods has been reported (Jeffress, 1928) although at least one very modest correlation (0·35, significant at the 0·05 level) has been recently reported (Terry, 1953). Slow changes in levels of skin resistance may occur during measurement; upon this slow baseline drift a quicker variation, lasting some seconds and termed the G.S.R., is observed to follow certain types of stimuli.

Changes in polarization and permeability of the tissues (sweat glands in particular) are believed to underlie both the Tarchanoff and Féré effects. The physical nature of the phenomena has been discussed by Landis (1932) and methodology and circuits by Davis (1930). Results of the Féré effect are generally reported in ohms resistance or mhos conductance; as James and Thouless (1926) pointed out, the resistance of the subject when measured with direct current from an external source of voltage may be termed an "apparent resistance." The amount is actually greater than the subject's true resistance because of effects of the imposed E.M.F., and the E.M.F. of polarization; therefore unless the strength of the external current used, the characteristics of circuits, and area and composition of the electrodes are held constant from study to study, units of measurement from different experiments cannot be directly compared.

A method has been developed for the study of palmar sweating as such; this, a colorimetric technique, depends upon the interaction of a chemically treated paper with sweat containing a reactive salt, and the extent of the response can be graded according to the density of the stain (Silverman and Powell, 1944; *see also* Mowrer, 1953, for a further description of the technique and its application to the assessment of therapeutic treatment of psychiatric patients).

Wenger and Gilchrist (1948) obtained a correlation of 0·31 ($p < 0·01$), between palmar conductance and the stain index, although the palmar aspect of the fingers was used for the stain method, and the palm of the hand for conductance. They also obtained reliability coefficients of the two measures over different periods, and found that conductance measures were more reliable.

Factors which Affect Measurement

(i) *Electrodes.* This point is discussed by Landis (1932) and by Woodworth and Schlosberg (1954). Polarization, which may change either the voltage potentials or apparent resistance, may be reduced by the use of non-polarizing electrodes, for example, of silver-silver chloride, and by using a very small current. A detailed discussion of electrical phenomena within the skin and at the surface of electrode contact may be found in Rothman (1954).

The effect of the size of electrodes and cutaneous hydration on the electrical resistance of the skin has been investigated by Blank and Finesinger (1946) who found that the size of the electrode could be varied appreciably without changing the apparent skin resistance, as long as the area of skin moistened by the electrolyte solution was constant. As they pointed out, if an area of skin larger than the area of the electrode is accidentally wet with the electrolyte solution the apparent skin resistance will be low, and as the wet area outside the electrode dries the apparent skin resistance will increase. Any aqueous film such as sweat outside the area of the electrode but continuous with it acts to increase the size of the effective electrode.

(ii) *Temperature.* Kuno (1930) has argued that sweating caused by heating appears all over the body surface except the palms of the hands and soles of the feet. The effect of temperature on these regions has been investigated in several studies. No relationship was observed with basal resistance by Duffy and Lacey (1946) and Wenger (1948), but Conklin (1951) claimed positive findings and Venables (1955) found a sizeable relationship between temperature and conductance in a neurotic group above an effective temperature of 66°F, but not in a comparable normal group, a finding which S. B. G. Eysenck (1956) confirmed.

(iii) *Other factors.* The majority of studies has not established any relation between palmar resistance and humidity, although Venables (1955) obtained some evidence that humidity affects basal conductance level in both normal and neurotic groups.

Diurnal periodicity has been reported with resistance higher during the night than the day. Muscular tensions also influence the level of skin resistance (Freeman and Simpson, 1938; White, 1930; Wenger and Irwin, 1936). O'Connor and Venables (1956) have reported significant correlations between Binet I.Q. and resting conductance levels in imbeciles.

Measuring Units

The greatest complexity of handling skin resistance and G.S.R. results appears to lie in the treatment of measuring units. It is frequently stated that the magnitude of the response is related to the pre-stimulus level, i.e. the lower the degree of preceding activity the greater the response.

Lacey's article (1956) should be read on this topic. In general, the problem is to treat the raw data so that responses may be considered independently of basal readings, and so that scores yield a normal distribution. Some of the transformations in common use are the logarithm of the change in conductance, percentage conductance change, square root of conductance, and similar measures based on resistance units. New scoring systems have been proposed, among them the Paintal index (Paintal, 1951) and the recovery quotient (Freeman, 1942), but, as Lacey says, many of these proposals have turned out to be specific to the original data and unsatisfactory when applied to newly-obtained data. S. B. G. Eysenck (1956) showed that different correlations between responses and basal scores may be found in different groups of subjects (normals, neurotics, psychotics).

The term basal level is, of course, used in several ways. Many experimenters allow a few minutes of rest in order to establish a relatively stable basal activity before introducing stimuli and the reading immediately prior to the stimulus is used to assess relations between response and base.

Lacey (1956) has protested against many of the attempts to derive "base-free" response scores. He argues that the proposed solutions have not been rooted in physiological fact or theory, but have emerged entirely as a result of statistical manipulations and contends that: "a basic physiological error is involved in the common practice of quantifying the reactions of autonomically innervated structures by computing algebraic or percentage changes, and that additional error is committed by seeking arbitrary mathematical transformations that irrationally (by which I mean empirically, and without regard to physiological theory) remove the dependence of such computed changes upon pre-stimulus levels of physiological functioning in a specific experimental situation. I propose that such procedures in effect ignore the basic fact that one of the main functions of the autonomic nervous system and associated endocrine glands is to maintain a homeostatic norm."

Lacey adds an important corollary to the principle of the homeostatic restraint of response, namely that: "the recorded autonomic response is a function both of the induced magnitude of autonomic activation (as it would be seen in the absence of contrary changes) and of the promptness and vigour of secondarily induced autonomic changes that serve to restrain and to limit the effects of the initial disturbance."

He feels that whatever statistical technique is employed it should not obscure physiological phenomena, and so goes on to discuss what can be done about the dependence of change upon initial level. He proposes that a rational procedure would be to establish norms, i.e. frequency distributions, of responses at varying pre-stimulus levels of functioning for varying populations and stresses. Since this is manifestly impossible he proposes that the best statistical approximation to this ideal solution is attained by use of the technique of regression analysis. This involves the analysis of regression of stress level on initial level, and the resulting scores he terms autonomic lability scores.

Psychophysiological Functions of Palmar Sweating

Kuno's opinion, mentioned earlier, is that sweating in man is not uniform over all the body surface, in respect of either actual secretion or physiological significance. Whereas general bodily sweating appears to be temperature regulatory, palms of the hands and soles of the feet do not conform to this general rule. Kuno found that sensory stimulation and mental stress are able to provoke sweating of these parts, and suggested that this sweating may have a functional use inasmuch as moistening the surfaces of the palms would increase the friction between them and the objects with which they come into contact, thus improving tactile acuity. Sweating is apparently more profuse on those parts of the palms and soles which are protuberant and likely to touch objects on grasping or on walking.

Darrow (1936) has also argued that the galvanic skin response is preparatory and facilitative, Thouless (1925) that resistance level reflects the preparedness of the organism to react, and Mundy-Castle and McKiever (1953) quote Biesheuvel as suggesting that it is the somatic concomitant of Pavlov's investigatory reflex. Many investigations have been carried out on the basis that changes in skin resistance form part of the emergency reaction of the sympathetic nervous system, and this measure has also been used to indicate arousal, activation (Schlosberg, 1954) and energy mobilization (Duffy, 1951). Such conceptions are strengthened by the high resistance levels found during sleep and the rapid drop in resistance observed upon awakening.

Experimental work on skin resistance and the G.S.R. to various stimuli will now be reviewed. It is obvious, from what has been said, that careful control of many factors must be exercised. In addition, the response is notoriously sensitive to irrelevant and uncontrollable details such as coughing, changes in breathing, shifts in position, and movement of the hands.

Adaptation

One of the main characteristics of the G.S.R. is the ease with which it adapts to repeated stimuli; this effect may be shown within a single session or from day to day. Changes in level of resistance have also been observed within the initial resting period which is generally allowed in most experiments, and it has been suggested that these reflect level of arousal, as, for example, when the subject becomes alerted or adapted to the general experimental procedure. Auditory stimuli are usually employed in adaptation studies, but visual stimuli and electric shock have also been used. Unfortunately, some of the early studies, although well controlled, do not apply any statistical treatment to the data and it is difficult to judge the significance of diminished responses when presented in graphical form.

An example is a study by Davis (1934) who studied finger-tip resistance of eight subjects over five consecutive days, and found that the size of the reactions, both to a ready signal and to the stimulus tone (a 1,000 cycle tuning oscillator sound) was progressively smaller from day to day. The absolute level of each day's curve was also higher than on preceding days, which suggested that reaction to the general situation (which must have had some stimulating value at first) also decreased, as did the reaction to the tone. It was noticed that reactions to mental work and to music were slower than reactions to noise and that the response to mental work remained constant throughout the five-day period (i.e. no adaptation) while the response to the music increased.

Thus the nature of the stimulus may be important in curves of adaptation and, as Coombs (1938) points out, some other relevant factors may be the duration of the stimulus and time intervals between stimuli. He investigated adaptation to various types of auditory stimulation—horn, knocker, buzzer and gong—and the influence of time intervals on adaptation. His conclusions were: (i) that adaptation takes place more rapidly with a fifteen-second interval than with a thirty-second interval between stimuli; (ii) that adaptation proceeds rapidly at first and then slows down, and (iii) that there was evidence of a transfer effect since adaptation to successive series of new stimuli proceeded more rapidly. Again, results were presented in graphical and tabular form, with no statistical treatment.

Adaptation of general level of palmar skin conductance during periods of response rather than to discrete stimuli was studied by Duffy and Lacey (1946). They found decreasing conductance during the course of a two-and-a-half-minute rest period preceding the stimuli, and during the four repetitions of an auditory discrimination task which were required in a single experimental session. Statistical treatment of the data showed that these falls in conductance were significant. Significant day-to-day adaptation effects were also observed during period of rest and auditory discrimination.

A recent study investigated the differential adaptation rates of normals, psychotics and neurotics during an initial rest period. Neurotics were significantly higher in resistance than normals at the first minute, but not at the sixth. A comparison of the groups was then made by an analysis of variance on the first five minutes' scores, and it was found that both the actual resistance levels and the slopes of the curves differentiated the groups: the psychotics maintained a higher *level* of resistance than normals, and the neurotics evidenced a slower *rate of change* in resistance than normals during the five minutes (S. B. G. Eysenck, 1956).

It has been hypothesized that individual differences in G.S.R. adaptation rate may be related to temperamental factors underlying differences in excitatory-inhibitory balance. In a study based on this hypothesis the records obtained were classified into three groups according to the presence or absence of "endogenous" responses. The group with many

Decline in G.S.R. magnitude over ten repetitions (assessed by several statistical techniques) was found to be significant at the 0·03 level. Interestingly enough this decline in G.S.R. response occurred although basal resistance increased throughout the series of ten tones.

An increase in latency to repeated stimuli was noted, but it did not reach any adequate statistical significance level (see Table XI.2).

TABLE XI.2

SUMMARY OF RESULTS OF AN EXPERIMENT ON STIMULUS INTENSITY EFFECTS

(From Davis, Buchwald and Frankmann, 1955)

Variable	Response	Time (after stimulus of maximum response	Stimulus intensity effect	Repetition effect	Differential effect of repetition
M.A.P. (a-response)	Increase	1 sec	Significant	Decreases	Significant decrease for A* Non significant for B and C
(b-response)	Increase	3 sec (?)	Significant	Decreases	——
G.S.R.	Decrease in resistance	(Latency = 1·3 sec)	Significant	Decreases	——
G.S.R. latency			Significant	Increase	Significant decrease for A Significant increase for B and C
Breathing amplitude	Increase	15–20 sec for weaker stimuli	Significant for first presentation		Significant decrease for A Significant increase for B and C
Breathing cycle time	Increase	15–20 sec	Significant	Increase (Non significant)	——
Pressure pulse	Decrease Increase	12·5–15 sec	Significant		Significant decrease for A Not for B or C
Volume pulse	Decrease	5–10 sec	Significant	Decrease (Non significant)	——
Finger volume	Decrease	12·5–15 sec	Significant	Decrease (Non significant)	——
Chin volume	Increase	12·5 sec	Not significant	Decrease	——
Pulse time	Decrease Increase	2·5–5 sec 7·5–10 sec	Significant	Decrease (Non significant)	——

* A=120 db tone, B=90 db tone, C=70 db tone.

endogenous responses (the "labiles") tended not to adapt to the stimuli, whereas the group in whom G.S.R.s occurred only to the experimental stimuli (the "stables") did adapt (Mundy-Castle and McKiever, 1953). A subsequent study has also shown a very significant relationship between the frequency of "endogenous" (or spontaneous) responses and the ease of conditioning the G.S.R. (Martin, 1960). The significance of spontaneous autonomic responses has recently been discussed at length by Lacey and Lacey (1958).

A very thorough investigation of normal adaptation curves of skin resistance responses has been made by Davis, Buchwald and Frankmann (1955) using measures of G.S.R. magnitude and G.S.R. latency.

Stimulus Variation

The galvanic skin response can also be changed in amplitude by varying the intensity of the stimulus. Hovland and Riesen (1940) using both electric shock and auditory stimuli of varying intensities observed that galvanic reactions (Tarchanoff method) varied with the strength of shock stimuli in an approximately linear fashion, as did the logarithm of the response to intensity of tones (in decibels) except at extremely high intensities. A similar finding has been reported by Davis et al., (1955) using db values of 70, 90, and 120, i.e. that the log response is a linear function of the acoustic pressure (see Fig. 11.6). In their study, repetition effects interacted with intensities of stimulation; there was a significant decline between first and last presentation of the 120-db stimulus ($p < 0.01$) and for the 90-db stimulus ($p < 0.05$). For the 70-db stimulus the trends were in the same direction but did not reach statistical significance (*see* Table XI.3).

TABLE XI.3
MEAN MAGNITUDE (PER CENT) OF G.S.R. FOR VARIOUS INTENSITIES OF A 1,000-CYCLE TONE

(From Davis, Buchwald and Frankmann, 1955)

Intensity	Quarter of sitting				Mean
	1st	2nd	3rd	4th	
120 db (A)	37·4	24·7	24·3	24·1	27·6
90 db (B)	14·8	9·3	8·0	3·2	8·8
70 db (C)	9·3	3·7	4·7	6·7	6·1
Mean	20·5	12·6	12·3	11·3	—

Individual Differences

It can be readily appreciated that with so many variables and possible extraneous influence to take into account few studies carried out with the G.S.R. are likely to be entirely free from criticism. In addition, many personality studies have been carried out on small samples, often in a clinical context, and with no statistical treatment of results, so that evaluation of these is well-nigh impossible.

Landis summarized the available evidence in 1932, and drew attention then to the confused state of the findings concerning psychogalvanic activity in psychiatric patients, pointing out that there was no justification for using it as a measure of traditional psychological categories or personality traits. Since that time the topic has been vigorously pursued, and although additional results have hardly cleared the position a general impression appears to have emerged that schizophrenics frequently demonstrate high resistance levels and diminished responsiveness, while neurotics show a lowered resistance level and increased responsiveness. But it is doubtful whether any such general impression can be substantiated; what is urgently required is a careful specification of the stimulus conditions under which any discrepancy in physiological activity might be observed.

A very brief review of some recent findings will illustrate the present position. Freeman and Katzoff (1942) used a measure of G.S.R. recovery from different experimental frustrations which correlated with clinical ratings of emotional balance; Wenger's (1948) finding was that resting palmar conductance was significantly higher (i.e. lower resistance) in neurotic subjects and also that this measure was one of the best indicators of improvement in patients after a period of convalescence. Both Malmo and Shagass (1949a) and S. B. G. Eysenck (1956) have, however, reported higher initial resistance levels in neurotic subjects.

Malmo and Shagass (1949a) found no significant differences between various groups of patients and normals, using several measurements of the G.S.R. to pain stimulation, and Paintal (1951) confirmed this on a psychotic group but observed differences in the response to threat of shock (psychotics showing lower responsiveness). Jurko, Jost and Hill (1952), measuring G.S.R. to the Rosenzweig Picture Frustration study, found no differences between controls and neurotics, but a lowered response in schizophrenics.

Higher initial resistance of schizophrenics has been reported by Malmo and Shagass (1949a) Jurko, Jost and Hill (1952) and S. B. G. Eysenck (1956). This last author found that not only initial and final resistances were significantly higher in schizophrenics than other groups, but that this higher *level* was maintained throughout the experimental session. She concluded that basal conductance was the best discriminatory measure between schizophrenics and normals, and that change scores tended to discriminate between groups only to the extent that they were themselves correlated with basal conductance.

Physiology of Skin Resistance and the G.S.R.

The sweat glands are innervated by the sympathetic division of the A.N.S. but are dependent upon cholinergic transmission at the end-organs. A very comprehensive review of the physiology of skin resistance was made by Landis in 1932, and more recently by McCleary (1950).

Measurements of palmar sweating are often advocated as relatively uncomplicated indicators of sympathetic activity, but Darrow (1943) has questioned this assumption pointing out that, because of their cholinergic mediation, conditions altering cholinergic activity, whether by the amount of available acetylcholine, the concentration of cholinesterase, or the presence of adrenalin, may limit the level of secretory activity and the magnitude of response to stimulation. Another point is that although there is a common tendency to combine observations on both skin resistance and the G.S.R. and to treat them as though they have a common basis, the possibility must be considered that the G.S.R. and basal resistance result from partly separate mechanisms.

The nature of the mechanism producing changes in skin resistance has been discussed by McCleary (1950). He summarizes three possible physiological bases of the G.S.R. and shows that evidence is more or less equivocal in all cases. These are: (i) a vascular theory, i.e. that vasodilatation causes the G.S.R.,

(ii) that secretory activity of the sweat glands gives rise to changes in resistance level, and (iii) that the phenomenon arises from involuntary muscular activity.

He favours the view that the galvanic skin response depends upon a change in the sweat glands that precedes actual secretion (*see also* Thomas and Korr, 1957, who have presented evidence that the relation of skin conductance to the number of active sweat glands is very nearly linear).

Extensive physiological studies of the G.S.R. have been carried out by Wang (1957, 1958), who has reviewed his own and other work in this field from the standpoint of reflex physiology; he draws the conclusion that there are a number of inhibitory and excitatory influences on the G.S.R. operating from different levels of the central nervous system.

Summary: Skin Resistance

1. *General conclusions.* The G.S.R. is dependent upon pre-change level of resistance; the usual response to a stimulus (sensory or "ideational") is a decrease in resistance.

Both level of skin resistance and the G.S.R. show effects of adaptation, the speed of which is partly related both to the intensity and modality of the stimulus used. Latency of the G.S.R. is between one to two seconds, and may increase slightly to repeated stimuli.

Skin resistance level is much increased during sleep, and is low during active, alert states. For this reason, it has been used as a measure of arousal. Sympathetic innervation of the sweat glands (via cholinergic mediation) is believed to underlie the phenomenon.

2. *In relation to psychiatric disorder.* Pre-stimulus (or rest) conditions: the findings are variable in neurotics, a group which may have the same or slightly higher resistance than normals (although there are reports of lower resistance). Schizophrenics' resistance is reported as being significantly higher than normal in a number of studies, and this high level may be maintained throughout the experimental session.

Changes in basal level during initial rest: neurotics appear to show less change than normals (this may mean less adaptation to the situation) but findings in schizophrenic groups are variable.

The conflicting findings concerning *reactivity* are probably due to the variety of stimuli employed. There is a little evidence that recovery may be delayed in certain patient groups, and that schizophrenics' reactions to sensory stimulation are similar to normals'.

Circulatory Functions

Cardiovascular variables accessible to measurement include peripheral resistance, arterial pressure (systolic and diastolic), heart rate and stroke volume. The regulatory mechanisms and neural reflexes which operate to maintain homeostasis within the circulatory system have been well described in most physiology textbooks, as have some of the specific interactions between neural and hormonal effects.

Psychologists have been interested in the fact that cardiovascular responses take place in response to a wide range of stimuli including simple sensory stimuli and complex "emotional" situations and, as in the case of skin resistance, have supposed that measures of blood-pressure, heart rate, etc. may be related to certain psychiatric or psychological categories.

BLOOD-PRESSURE

There are many references in the literature to an increase of arterial pressure during emotional stress, but many of these consist of little more than uncontrolled observations, and only a few studies provide results which seem to be meaningful and which might be reproducible.

Factors which are believed to be responsible for the maintenance of blood-pressure are cardiac output, blood volume, peripheral resistance, and the elasticity of the arterial walls. Change of any one factor which might alter the pressure is generally offset by compensating mechanisms. Normally the peripheral resistance and cardiac output are adjusted so as to prevent any large change in mean arterial pressure, and failure to accomplish such an adjustment may in itself be indicative of arterial dysfunction (Hickam *et al.*, 1948).

Pressure declines from the aorta to the capillaries, and it is arterial pressure which has most often been investigated by psychologists; the average arterial pressure in man is given in physiology texts as about 120 mm Hg for systolic and 70-80 mm Hg for diastolic pressure. The difference between these two measurements is termed pulse pressure, and the arithmetic mean of systolic and diastolic pressure is called mean pressure.

Methods of Measurement

The commonest instrument for measuring systolic and diastolic blood-pressure is the standard mercury sphygmomanometer, but this instrument has many disadvantages; perhaps the most serious are the discomfort induced and the disturbance on the system being measured. Wenger (1948) also found that different examiners using this method obtained different mean readings for diastolic pressure.

Attempts have been made to produce continuous recorders which, to avoid the need for arterial punctures, employ a repetitive short-period occlusion cuff and usually record systolic pressure only. Such methods are of course indirect. Pickering (1955) has discussed some of the direct measures of arterial pressure in man and the results of several studies comparing direct with indirect measurements. Errors of measurement varied from study to study, but on the whole were quite considerable.

Factors Affecting Blood-pressure

Age, weight and the subject's sex may have an effect on blood-pressure. Systolic pressure seems to show some diurnal variation, being lowest during sleep (Kleitman, 1939) and highest at about 5 to 7 p.m. (Wenger, 1948, found it necessary to correct measures of systolic pressure against time of measurement). Arterial pressure may rise from distension of the bladder, and postural changes occasionally produce falls in pressure in some individuals. Blood-pressure readings may be influenced by variations in laboratory procedure and by different experimenters (Reiser *et al.*, 1955), and by place of testing (e.g. ward and laboratory, Malmo, Shagass and Heslam, 1951). It may also be abnormally high under certain pathological conditions (e.g. kidney disease).

In essential hypertension both systolic and diastolic pressures are raised, and this increase in pressure is attributed to high peripheral resistance resulting from a narrowing of the arteriolar bed. Arteriolar constriction may be induced both by sympathetic impulses and by circulating hormonal agents. Essential hypertension has been studied as a psychosomatic disorder (Katz and Leiter, 1939; Reiser, Ferris and Levine, 1954; and Hamilton, 1955). Many investigators have stated that hypertensive patients are particularly liable to an increase in blood-pressure in response to emotional stress.

Experimental studies

Quite large changes in blood-pressure (from 8 to 10 mm Hg) have been observed to follow a variety of simple sensory stimuli, and more complex forms of stimulation such as watching a film or participating in a psychiatric interview. A significantly larger diastolic reaction to an "anger" situation than to a fear situation has been reported by Ax (1953).

Hickam, Cargill and Golden (1948) found an increased mean arterial pressure (from 90 to 99 mm Hg) in normal subjects made anxious by an important examination. Heart rate, stroke volume, cardiac index and peripheral resistance, however, showed more marked changes, and these authors considered that the elevation in blood-pressure represented a relatively slight imbalance between a large increase in cardiac output and a large fall in peripheral resistance. They commented on the great variability of the circulatory response in anxiety.

A survey of the literature by Altschule (1953) led him to the conclusion that there is no evidence that chronic anxiety or any specific type of emotion, personality or conflict, causes lasting hypertension in normotensive persons. The available studies, which he considered, all referred to normal or slightly raised readings in most instances of neurosis and neurocirculatory asthenia, but patients in this latter category frequently demonstrate excessive rises in arterial pressure (especially systolic) when they exercise.

Arterial pressure in psychosis has also been discussed by Altschule (1953) who, after a comprehensive survey of the literature, considered that the evidence pointed to high blood-pressure in depressed (but not manic) patients. Although a few studies also describe high arterial pressure in schizophrenic patients, most readings reported in this group are in or below the normal range (*see* Altschule, 1953, for references). Shattock (1950) also reviewed a number of studies in which low blood-pressure was found in schizophrenics.

Since the appearance of these reviews there has been little enlightenment from subsequent studies, although some careful investigations of blood-pressure levels of psychiatric patients have been carried out by Malmo and his collaborators. As will be seen from the following descriptions, the variety of stimulus conditions and measures employed precludes a coherent organization of the results.

Measurements from psychiatric patients have often been made while the subjects rested, but as Malmo and others have stressed, response characteristics in addition to resting levels provide valuable data Another important factor may be the chronicity of the illness. Malmo and Shagass (1952) investigated the blood-pressure responsiveness of several psychiatric groups—chronic and acute schizophrenics and neurotics—and a normal control group, under three conditions: pain stimulation, rapid discrimination and mirror drawing. Auscultatory measurements were made with a standard mercury spyhgmomanometer and with a Cambridge recording sphygmotonograph (the authors referred to the latter as the machine method).

The mean machine scores of acute schizophrenics and neurotics were significantly higher for systolic pressure before and during the pain-stress than those of controls and chronic schizophrenics, but blood-pressure *changes* gave different results. Controls' and chronic schizophrenics' systolic pressure dropped during the pre-test periods, acute psychotics showed a small drop and neurotics failed to show a drop. Mean systolic and diastolic pressures increased with pain stimulation in all groups, but no significant differences were found between groups in respect of the amount of change. It was concluded that since chronic schizophrenics resembled normals in systolic blood-pressure reaction the evidence was inconsistent with the view that these patients are abnormally sluggish under stress.

During performance of a rapid discrimination and a mirror drawing task a greater rise in blood-pressure was shown by the psychoneurotic group (see Fig. 11.1). The increase between the first and last thirds of the neurotics' blood-pressure curve during mirror drawing

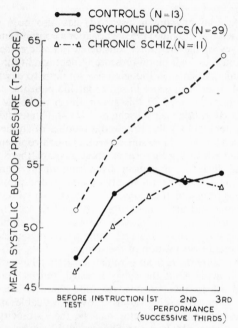

FIG. 11.1. MIRROR DRAWING TEST (CIRCLE)
Mean blood-pressure during second Mirror Drawing Test.
Note continuous rise in curve for psychoneurotics.
(*From Malmo and Shagass, 1952.*)

was statistically significant. Correlations of blood-pressure measurements during different situations showed that the highest degree of individual constancy in physiological reaction was to be found under conditions of stress.

The hypothesis that neurosis is characterized by defects in physiological regulation of reaction to stress was followed up in another study, by Malmo, Shagass and Heslam (1951). They suggested that defective physiological regulation may show itself in two main aspects of reaction—increased magnitude (or amplitude) and low degree of adaptation, and, therefore, studied the adaptation of the blood-pressure response to repeated brief stresses: the Porteus mazes, normal and inverted, and three cold pressor tests. The earlier finding of lower adaptation in patients was confirmed. Although reactions to the stimuli occurred in both groups, the controls' reactions tended to diminish as the session progressed,

while the patients' reactions tended to persist at the initial level.

It would obviously be of interest to obtain further information concerning the physiological response curves (gradients) of psychiatric subjects during the performance of motor tasks. Some work with normal subjects has been reported by Malmo and Davis (1956); they obtained highly significant gradients of blood-pressure during motor performance, and significant correlations between the steepness of the gradient and performance time, an important finding which requires substantiation.

In view of the interdependence of cardiovascular variables it would be highly desirable to obtain a broader picture of these functions by recording measures such as cardiac output and peripheral blood flow in addition to blood-pressure. Simultaneous measurement of widespread cardiovascular variables presents considerable technical difficulties, however, and Davis *et al.* (1955) found that the periodic application of occluding pressure seriously disturbed all the other variables of the circulatory system.

Summary: Blood-pressure

1. *General conclusions.* An *increase* in blood-pressure to stimulation is the general rule. Responses have been reported to a variety of sensory and "emotional" stimuli.

Adaptation occurs both to repeated stimulation, and in background level throughout the experimental session: on the other hand, accelerated gradients during performance of a motor task, related to performance time, have been demonstrated.

Relatively high degrees of individual consistency in blood-pressure measurements have been obtained in different situations.

2. *In relation to psychiatric disorder.* The general finding is that resting blood-pressure is normal or slightly elevated in neurotics. Most studies have reported low resting blood-pressure in schizophrenics; on the other hand, higher systolic pressure in acute schizophrenics and consistently higher diastolic pressure in chronic schizophrenics have been found.

With the stimulus conditions employed, changes in response to stimulation do not discriminate between psychiatric groups and normals. There is a little evidence that neurotics show anomalies of adaptation, i.e. they may persist at higher blood-pressure levels during performance.

PERIPHERAL VASOMOTOR CHANGES

The constriction and dilatation of the blood-vessels is one of the ways in which the redistribution of blood in accordance with the requirements of the organism may be achieved. Those vessels situated near the surface of the skin (and these are most accessible for measurement of changes in volume) are very directly concerned with the function of regulating body temperature both by exposing a variable blood surface and by altering the rate of flow. Peripheral vasomotor responses are also observed to follow external sensory stimuli, examples of which will be dealt with in this section.

Most measures of peripheral vasomotor activity in humans are indirect because it would be necessary to insert a cannula into the blood-vessels to obtain a direct estimate of the resistance offered by the peripheral blood-vessels to blood flow. The various available methods involve the measurement from the skin surface of such changes as colour, temperature, or volume (of a limb or digit), it being assumed that these are related to changes in the peripheral circulation.

On the assumption that vasoconstriction is accompanied by a diminution and vasodilatation by an increase in volume, the method of volume plethysmography has been developed; in the usual procedure an extremity (e.g. finger) is sealed in a rigid container filled with water or air, the volume displacement of which (following volume changes of the digit) can be recorded and interpreted as giving information on the amount of blood present in the region at the time. By occluding the venous return and measuring volume with respect to time, a measure of blood flow may be derived, viz. dv/dt.

Ackner (1956a) has reviewed some of the techniques for estimating peripheral blood flow, such as thermal methods and the photoelectric plethysmograph used by Hertzman et al. (1946). Davis (in Ellson et al., 1952) has described his attempt to use a modification of an electric impedance plethysmograph proposed by Nyboer (1947). The principle in Nyboer's plethysmograph consists of passing a low voltage radio-frequency current through a selected area and recording the changes in impedance of the tissues under different response conditions. In this method measurement is based on the comparison of an original signal with that observed after traversing the area under measurement. One drawback is that so far no satisfactory calibration of impedance plethysmographs with respect to the absolute volume being measured has been achieved (Davis et al. 1955).

Both volume and impedance plethysmographs record total volume changes of the area under measurement (e.g. tip of finger) as well as each peripheral pulse beat. The peripheral pulse beat appears superimposed on the total volume change, but these may be easily separated (see Ellson et al., 1952).

Some of the factors which influence peripheral blood flow are temperature, limb position, and interacting effects with other changes in the cardiovascular system. The size of the response following a stimulus is partly related to the pre-stimulus degree of dilatation; little in the way of reflex constriction can be expected if the vessels are not dilated beforehand (Ackner, 1956b). Vasoconstriction is controlled mainly by sympathetic nerves and also in part by hormones circulating in the blood; the distribution of vasodilator fibres throughout the parasympathetic nervous system is not generally conceded.

Vasomotor responses may be quite specific to particular regions and there is no evidence of a general vasoconstrictor effect under all stimulus conditions; indeed, constriction of one area (finger) and dilatation of another (chin) to identical stimuli have been found (Davis et al., 1955). Many authors have noted a relationship between mental tasks, alerting stimuli, and changes in volume of limb extremities.

Adaptation

It has frequently been observed that this response adapts to repeated stimuli, but there are few precise experimental data apart from the recent careful attempt to measure adaptation to a repeated tone which has been reported by Davis, Buchwald and Frankmann (1955). These authors (using an impedance plethysmograph) measured amplitude of response as the amount of decrease from the level prior to onset of each stimulus (a 98-db 800-cycle tone) to the maximum constriction following the stimulus, and converted these values to percentages of maximum response. The results of several statistical tests did not indicate the presence of a stimulus repetition effect, either in amplitude or latency of response, although a small decrease in the size of the response was noted. A significant decrease in magnitude of the volume pulse was, however, observed.

Latency and extinction of vasomotor functions were also studied in a further experiment, in which three levels of stimulus intensity were used: a 1,000 cycle tone of 70, 90 and 120 db (Davis et al., 1955). Volume pulse and finger volume showed a small increase in response size from 70 to 90 db and a much larger one (statistically significant) from 90 to 120 db, the log response being a linear function of the decibel values (a result similar to that obtained by Hovland and Riesen, 1940). Although decreasing response size upon repetition was noted, no adequate level of statistical significance was reached.

Somewhat different results for chin volume were obtained. Dilatation, rather than constriction, appeared to be the typical response and the latency was shorter than that of the finger volume response. When first and last quarters of the recording session were compared, there was a decrease in response, significant at the 5 per cent level, but there was no significant relation between response size and stimulus intensity. (These results are summarized in Table XI.2.)

Cutaneous Stimult

The intensity of certain forms of stimulation (electric shock, heat and sharp needles) and vasoconstriction and vasodilatation was investigated by Nafe and Wagoner (1936, 1938). These authors claimed a relationship between intensity of stimulation and amount of vasoconstriction, but gave no measurements.

A series of tactual stimuli—heat, heat "control," cold, pressure, prick and tickle—was applied to the skin of the left forearm in a study by Davis *et al.* (1955). The volume pulse response to the heat-control, cold, pressure and prick stimuli was a decrease in amplitude which reached its minimum about eight to twelve seconds after stimulus onset, and, except in the case of the prick stimulus, had returned to normal by the end of the period of measurement, which was about seventeen seconds. The most marked constriction effect was produced by the prick stimulus.

Right index finger and chin volume responses were both dilatation. During the seven seconds or so following stimuli only the pressure stimulus produced a significant finger dilatation; with the chin, the dilatation was significant for pressure and heat stimuli. *After* seven seconds following stimulation, finger dilatation was still significant for the pressure stimulus and chin dilatation significant for the heat stimulus.

The results indicated that some tactual stimuli produce a vascular *dilatation*, an effect which is opposite to the finger *constriction* effect observed to follow auditory stimulation.

Experimental Studies with Psychiatric Patients

There is an interesting literature, consisting mainly of observations but also a few experimental studies, on the presence of peripheral vasoconstriction in schizophrenic subjects. This may be associated with cyanosis, or cold, blue extremities, (which seems to be due to a constriction of the small arterioles of the skin) a condition which has long been described in psychotic patients and which may disappear on remission (Shattock, 1950 and Ackner, 1956a review this work).

There are also many scattered studies concerning excessive peripheral vasomotor responses of schizophrenics to external cooling (*see* Shattock, 1950, and Ackner, 1956a) and these have led to the opinion that schizophrenics show some impairment of the normal mechanism of vascular control (Richter, 1957) and that this circulatory defect may be located in the autonomic controlling centres situated in the hypothalamus (Gellhorn, 1953; Richter, 1957). It has been pointed out that the prolonged vasoconstriction appears to be necessary to preserve body-heat and is not a consequence of emotional disturbance since it is commonly observed in subjects who are withdrawn and manifest little emotional disturbance (Ackner, 1956a).

These general observations and impressions require precise experimental confirmation, and on the basis of existing evidence one would suppose that the careful study of cardiovascular responses of schizophrenics in relation to changes in external temperature would provide rewarding results.

There are few systematic studies which have aimed directly at relating vasomotor reactions to assessments of emotions such as "anxiety," but there are two interesting contributions to the topic. The first is a series of investigations carried out by Van der Merwe and Theron (1947), Theron (1948) and Van der Merwe (1948) using a Goetz finger plethysmograph. Measures obtained included rate of finger volume change with tasks (arithmetic problems), total reflex volume change with tasks, and variations in pulse volume.

Correlations of 0·409 (Van der Merwe and Theron, 1947) and 0·294 (Theron, 1948) were found between rate of finger-volume change with tasks and emotional stability as measured by the Bell scale, that is, those subjects who had high emotional adjustment scores tended to have a higher rate of change in finger volume (indicating greater degree of vasodilatation). These correlations were increased when adjustment was made for differences in initial pulse volume.

Similar measures were used in a subsequent experiment by Van der Merwe (1948) using the fifty subjects in Theron's (1948) experiment as a control group, and, in addition, twenty-one neurotic patients, eight with symptoms of anxiety and fifteen with hysterical and neurasthenic symptoms. Three measures—pulse volume before deep breathing, pulse volume before tasks, and rate of finger-volume change with a cold water test—were significantly *smaller* in the anxious patients than in the control subjects. *Larger* responses in the hysteric than in the normal group were obtained with all measures of pulse-volume and digital-volume change. Since both patient groups differed in opposite directions from the controls, a marked difference was found between the two patient groups: almost all the effects were significant at the 1 per cent level, indicating greater constriction or increased vasomotor tone in anxious patients than in hysterics.

The other study concerned with neurotic patients and their vasomotor responses has been reported by Ackner (1956b). His experiment utilized measurement of vasomotor activity while the subjects went to sleep because the tendency to vasodilatation rather than vasoconstriction should be observed when emotional factors are reduced or absent. It would follow that relaxed subjects, lacking apparent vasoconstriction, would manifest little change during sleep, but emotional subjects showing marked constriction would be expected to show greater changes. Seconal was used as a sleep-producing agent, because preliminary experiments with a short-acting barbiturate had shown that subjects did not vasodilate whilst awake.

In Ackner's plethysmographic study, volume changes of the finger tip were transmitted as changes in pressure applied to a beryllium copper bellows, constructed in the form of a variable condenser. The subjects lay on a bed with the left arm supported so that the arm remained at heart level. Three groups of subjects were used: (i) an anxiety group (N = 13, 10 female and 3 male); (ii) a non-anxiety clinical group (N = 10, 8 female and 2 male); (iii) a control group (N = 10, 3 female and 7 male). Average ages of the groups were similar.

Measurements of initial pulse-volume amplitude, and maximum pulse-volume amplitude during recording were obtained. The differences between the three groups in the pulse volume were not statistically significant, but changes occurring during sleep were highly significant (see Table XI.4). These measures of

TABLE XI.4

PULSE-VOLUME CHANGES IN CONTROLS, NON-ANXIETY PATIENTS AND ANXIETY PATIENTS DURING REST AND SLEEP

(From Ackner, 1956b)

	Mean initial pulse volume (cu mm)	Mean pulse-volume-increase (cu mm)
Resting tests		
Controls	9·4	1·0
Non-anxiety patients	5·8	1·6
Anxiety patients	3·4	1·0
Sleep tests		
Controls	10·1	0·55
Non-anxiety patients	6·3	2·3
Anxiety patients	4·9	12·3

Range of pulse-volume increase during sleep (cu mm)

Controls	0–2·5
Non-anxiety patients	0–5·0
Anxiety patients	6–23·0

change did not overlap at all between groups, the anxiety patients being completely differentiated from the other two groups by the magnitude of their vasodilatation. Similar results were obtained for pulse-rate changes during sleep, although the differences were not so significant. Two of the anxious patients who recovered from their disturbed emotional

state were found, on retest, to show little or no change in pulse volume during sleep.

Ackner concluded that: "vasoconstriction of the skin vessels on an emotional basis is part of a bodily alerting reaction to stress, which probably serves the function of diverting blood to areas which are becoming mobilized for offensive or defensive action." He considered that increased sympathetic activity along the vasomotor pathways seemed to be the most likely explanation of the maintained vasoconstriction.

Summary: Peripheral Blood Flow

1. *General conclusions.* The degree of constriction following a stimulus depends upon pre-stimulus level of dilatation. It has been found that constriction of the pulse and finger volume and dilatation of facial areas follow auditory stimuli, and dilatation of finger and chin volume follows certain cutaneous stimuli.

No adaptation of finger volume response and latency to a repeated tone was found by Davis *et al.* (1955) although adaptation was present in volume pulse measurements.

The finger volume decrease following a stimulus occurs somewhere between 5 and 7·5 seconds, reaching a maximum about 12 to 15 seconds after the stimulus with the method used by Davis *et al.* (1955).

Vasoconstriction is controlled by sympathetic nerves. Sleep is generally accompanied by increasing vasodilatation.

2. *In relation to psychiatric disorder.* There are many observations that schizophrenics are characterized by excessive peripheral vasoconstriction, but only a little precise experimental evidence to the effect that schizophrenics show excessive drops in skin temperature to cooling. These reactions are believed to be a consequence of the normal physiological preservation of body heat.

There is evidence of greater vasoconstriction in anxious patients, more clearly demonstrated during sleep. The rate of change in finger volume with commencement of certain tasks was found to correlate with a measure of emotional stability. One small group of hysterics was found to show greater vasodilatation than normals.

Skin Temperature

Skin temperature has been commonly used as an index of peripheral blood flow because in general the temperature of the skin depends upon the amount of heat brought to it by the blood-stream and upon the amount of heat lost from its surface (Plutchik, 1956; *see also* Ellson *et al.*, 1952, and Ackner, 1956a) but there are few detailed investigations of the actual relationship between changes in blood flow, vascular volume and skin temperature. There may be a complex interrelation under some conditions but independent variation under others (Fetcher, Hall and Staub, 1949).

Many studies have pointed to a diurnal temperature rhythm. Kleitman (1939) reviewed many of these investigations, most of which reveal a maximum value in the afternoon or evening hours, and a minimum in the early morning hours: he thought that this rhythm could be accounted for by the influences of food intake, muscular activity and sleep. Changes in vasomotor tone (such as could be induced by altering limb position) have also been found to affect skin temperature, finger volume and pulse volume (Goetz, 1950). It is obvious that many other variables will influence skin temperature; factors such as room temperature and humidity, time since ingestion of food, muscular activity and posture of the subjects as well as time of day must be reckoned with (see Sheard, 1947; Wenger, 1948; Flecker, 1951, and Ackner, 1956a).[1]

There are three main measuring techniques (Plutchik, 1956): (i) ordinary mercury thermometers, (ii) thermocouples or thermopiles attached to the surface of the skin, and (iii) radiometers. The latter measure heat radiation which, Plutchik suggests, depends not only on evaporation and blood flow in the skin directly under the instrument, but also on blood flow in deeper tissues. Both he and Ackner (1956a) have indicated advantages and disadvantages of the available instrumentation.

Although the literature on the psychophysiological functions of skin temperature in particular is scant and in general uncoordinated, a few observations emerge which, if corroborated, would deepen our understanding of this measure.

The relation of skin temperature changes to initial level has been considered by Plutchik and Greenblatt (1956) on very limited data obtained during psychiatric interviews. Finger temperatures were found to vary between the range 20° to 36°C.

The authors' tentative conclusions were that magnitude, rate and duration of subjects' temperature changes were related to initial (i.e. pre-change) temperature. They observed that larger rises occurred when the initial temperatures were low, that there was a tendency for temperature to rise at a faster rate from low than from high levels, that the lower the initial temperature the longer the rise would continue and that the fastest rate of change of skin temperature from any starting point was always an increase rather than a drop.

A certain time is required for warmth adaptation to room temperature; Flecker (1951), using a light

weight thermocouple attachment fitted to the subject's finger-tip, observed that the majority of his subjects' skin temperatures reached a maximum within the first twenty minutes. He also observed that the total range of measurements was approximately 22° to 35°C.

An early study by Helson and Quantius (1934) using a thermocouple held by the subject against the infra-orbital region near the nose, showed skin temperature changes as large as 4°F to a number of stimuli, including ice to neck, cold water, noise of a pounding hammer, a needle prick, etc., and also to verbal warning of these stimuli. Increases of temperature to the stimuli occurred more frequently than decreases (one hundred and thirty-three increases, sixty-six decreases) and there were sixty-three instances of no change. The authors claimed that slight change in the position of the thermocouple and bodily movements did not affect the readings. Variability in the direction of the response was also observed by Flecker (1951); most subjects in his study showed drops in skin temperature during a word-association test, and an increase during reading. In a learning situation twenty-three subjects showed a drop, four no change, and eleven an increase of finger temperature. These few studies are of some interest, but there are apparently no reports of research on skin temperature as the dependent variable measured in relation to stimuli varied in intensity, duration or number of repetitions.

Increase in skin temperature both to a spark stimulus and during induced tension (with a greater reaction to the spark) was recorded by Baker and Taylor (1954) by means of a thermistor placed against the palm of the left hand; the correlation table given by these authors shows that correlations between skin temperature and skin resistance vary under different conditions.

Many workers have reported excessive drops in skin temperature in schizophrenic subjects as a result of external cooling (see H. Freeman, 1939; Finkelman and Stephens, 1936) and such results have contributed to the view discussed in the previous section that temperature-regulatory centres may be less responsive in schizophrenia than in normal subjects.

In his studies on autonomic balance Wenger (1948) obtained two measures of resting finger temperature by means of a laboratory thermometer held by the subject between the fingers. The first reading (taken at the beginning of the session) gave an average of 34·9°C (S.D. 1·0) for four hundred and eighty-eight students and 34·1°C (S.D. 3·6) for two hundred and twenty-five operational fatigue patients ($p < 0.01$). The two variables which best reflected the improvement in patients after a period of convalescence were finger temperature (first reading) and palmar conductance. Finger temperature did not, however, discriminate between a group of anxiety states (N = 49) and a group of mixed neurotics (N = 49) but when

---

[1] It has been emphasized that there is no such thing as a "normal" skin temperature (as there is of mouth temperature) and that one must therefore define the conditions under which any measurement is obtained (Sheard, 1947).

all patients were combined and compared with a normal group, first finger temperature reading again discriminated significantly, patients having the lower finger temperature.

It is possible that this result may be related to the greater vasoconstriction (measured by means of a plethysmograph) which has been found in anxious patients, and simultaneous recordings of the two variables under different stimulus conditions should provide interesting data concerning the degree of similarity of their reactivity.

Summary: Skin Temperature

1. *General conclusions.* There is a little evidence that the magnitude, rate and duration of a subject's temperature changes are related to pre-change temperature. Rises in temperature were observed to have different characteristics from drops.

Skin temperature may increase or decrease following sensory stimulation, probably in part dependent upon the nature of the stimulus.

The modal rate of rise appears to be 0·6°–0·7°C per minute, and the response is fairly slow with a duration of generally less than one minute (Plutchik and Greenblatt, 1956).

2. *In relation to psychiatric disorder.* A few findings point to greater reactivity of schizophrenics to cool temperatures (*see* summary under peripheral blood flow). One study reports lower skin temperature of neurotics.

Heart Rate

The heart may increase its output in two ways, by increasing its output per beat, and by increasing beat frequency. The magnitude of the muscle potential occurring with each heart beat enables recordings to be made without difficulty; both the E.C.G. and the cardiotachometer (which counts beats) are in general use, but E.C.G. "artefacts" are commonly used from other recordings (e.g. skeletal muscle).

Diurnal curves of heart rate, closely following those of body temperature, have been described, and the individual's sex, degree of muscular activity and digestive state are factors which may influence heart rate.

Studies concerning cardiac changes in relation to emotional states are legion, but few provide precise data; in common with reports on other physiological variables, many deal with reactions during psychiatric interview, or other poorly-defined stimuli. Although the evidence appears to be overwhelming that many stimuli increase heart rate, the mechanism producing this reaction is likely to be complex. In addition to the direct effects on the circulation of "emotional" stimuli there may be indirect effects; for example a lowering of the peripheral resistance may cause a rise in cardiac output.

Some early investigations of cardiac effects following surprise stimulation led to the claim that changes in the wave-form of the electro-cardiogram were related to the point in the cardiac cycle at which the stimulus occurred, but it has since been demonstrated that these E.C.G. changes may be artefacts arising from extra-cardiac activity such as muscular activity of the arms and shoulders (Springer, 1935).

Using several surprise stimuli (a tipping chair and klaxon horn) Springer found a rapid increase in heart rate following stimulation which reached a maximum by the third or fourth beat and decreased almost to basal level by the end of ten seconds. Increments up to twenty-five beats per minute following a gun shot were reported by Berg and Beebe-Center (1941) and habituation effects noted. These authors give the repeat reliability of their index of cardiac startle as 0·53 (N = 33). They observed that a different stimulus or a lapse of time is sufficient for the disinhibition of the startle response.

Altschule (1953) reviewed the literature on the cardiovascular effects of emotional disorders and came to the conclusion that the cardiac rate is normal or only slightly accelerated in patients with neurosis or neurocirculatory asthenia, but that this latter group show excessive physiological and metabolic changes (such as severe increase in heart rate) when they exercise. When unselected psychiatric patients were separated on the basis of presence or absence of heart complaints (pre-cordial pain, palpitation, etc.) those with the symptoms were found to have a significantly higher heart rate than those without (Malmo and Shagass, 1949*b*). The results of two similar studies concerning heart rate of neurotic and normal subjects during pain stimulation are conflicting (Malmo and Shagass, 1949*a*, Malmo and Smith, 1955).

The findings in relation to schizophrenia are confusing. Malmo, Shagass and Smith (1951) found that mean heart rate of chronic schizophrenics was reliably higher than controls during pain stimulation, and increased markedly upon beginning a rapid discrimination task, in contrast to the relatively flat curve for normal controls. Jurko, Jost and Hill (1952) also found heart rates of schizophrenics higher than those of controls and neurotics, but they observed a *lower* change of rate on stimulation. Kivisto (1953) reported no differences in rate between psychotics and normals. There is almost certainly a marked variability of heart rate in an individual patient, irrespective of the type of psychosis present.

The Cardiovascular System: Organization of the Responses

No adequate integration can be made of the results of changes in cardiovascular variables without reference to their dynamic interaction within the circulatory system, within which regulatory mechanisms of great precision and sensitivity operate to maintain a homeostatic adjustment. To understand the widespread cardiovascular changes which occur following a stimulus it is necessary to have some knowledge of the underlying physiological mechanisms, a knowledge which could lead both to a more rational choice of the variables to record and a better

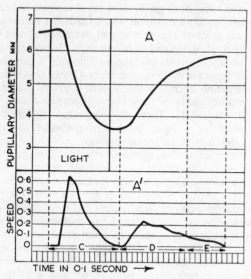

FIG. 11.2. PUPILLOGRAM (A) AND DIFFERENTIAL ANALYSIS (A¹) OF THE NORMAL REFLEX TO LIGHT IN MAN

(A) The pupillary diameter (in millimetres) is plotted against time (in 0·1 sec). After a latency period of about 0·2 sec, the pupil contracts in response to light, and redilates some time after the stimulus has come to an end. Contraction and redilatation consist of a faster primary and slower secondary phase.

(A¹) Contraction and redilatation within each successive tenth of a second are plotted (in 0·1 mm) against time (in 0·1 sec). Pupillary contraction and redilatation consist of different waves of increasing and decreasing speed of motion.

C-wave (contraction wave), the ascending branch corresponds to the "primary contraction phase," the descending branch to the slower "secondary contraction phase" of the pupillogram. D-wave (primary dilatation wave) and E-wave (secondary redilatation wave), in man the two redilatation waves tend to merge.

(*From Lowenstein and Loewenfeld, 1952a*)

interpretation of the observed responses (Davis *et al.*, 1955).

Some of the results obtained by Davis *et al.* (1955) in measuring specific cardiovascular responses to various stimuli have been described in the preceding sections. They have integrated their findings to describe an overall type of cardiovascular response, arising from auditory stimulation, the initial elements of which appear to arise predominantly from sympathetic activity. In summary, this is characterized—

by a first phase of cardiac acceleration, vasoconstriction, smaller pressure pulse, and probably increased diastolic pressure. The second phase is characterized by

continued vasoconstriction (with some recovery), stronger pressure pulse, subnormal heart rate, and probably increased systolic as well as diastolic pressure. The peripheral constriction of the first phase seems to bring on the second phase by acting in two directions: by increasing mean arterial pressure it activates the heart-slowing reflexes, and by increasing venous pressure and flow it returns more blood to the heart and increases the force of its beat and the amount of blood ejected.

Pupillary Reactions

The size of the pupil is varied by two smooth muscles working antagonistically: the dilator, which is activated by sympathetic nerves and produces the pupillary condition known as mydriasis, and the constrictor, which is activated by parasympathetic nerves to produce the state of miosis. The simple concept of reciprocal action of the two autonomic branches is widely held, but Gellhorn (1953) considers it too limited to give an adequate description of the mutual relations of sympathetic-parasympathetic innervation of the pupil.

A number of stimuli produce changes in pupillary diameter; for example, pain and nociceptive impulses arising from various parts of the body are followed by dilatation, and exposure of the retina to light produces pupillary constriction. Under normal conditions pupil size may vary with age, refractive errors, the state of light and dark adaptation, and numerous other factors. In the normal individual there are constantly small irregular fluctuations giving rise to a state of pupillary unrest which may be due to a combination of biological and physical causes.

With the development of the technique of infra-red pupillography (details of which are given by Lowenstein and Loewenfeld, 1950) it has become possible to measure pupillary reactions under conditions of both dark and light adaptation. By this means the shape of the pupillary response of man and other animals to a variety of stimuli, and under many conditions (e.g. experimental lesions at different levels of the C.N.S.) has been studied (Lowenstein, 1946, Lowenstein and Loewenfeld, 1950a, 1950b, 1951, 1952a, 1952b). These authors found that the reaction to light could be analysed into three stages, a primary contraction phase predominantly due to parasympathetic factors, and secondary and tertiary phases predominantly due to sympathetic factors. In normal human subjects the pupillary reflex to light consists of a contraction which is preceded by a latency period of between 0·2 and 0·3 sec, and is about 3 mm in extent. (*See* Fig. 11.2.)

Adaptation

It has been reported that when the light reflex of the pupil is elicited again and again (fifty to one hundred times or more) the latency period becomes longer, a refractory period develops, and the constriction becomes increasingly sluggish both in extent and duration. At some point (earlier with weak stimuli) the pupil no longer reacts to the light, but if a psychological or sensory stimulus is interposed between light stimuli, the pupil reacts again to the subsequent light stimulus, a phenomenon which Lowenstein and Loewenfeld (1952b) term "psychosensory restitution."

Restored reflexes can again be fatigued, but with each alternation of fatigue and restitution the number of stimuli necessary to reach exhaustion becomes smaller. It has also been claimed that the general fatigue produced by the stress of a working day adds to the fatiguability of the pupillary reflex to light (Lowenstein and Loewenfeld, 1952a).

The shape of each pupillary reflex to light is considered to indicate the degree to which the centres of control are disintegrated by fatigue. The various autonomic centres concerned with the integration of pupillary reflex activity show different degrees of fatiguability: sympathetic centres fatigue before parasympathetic centres, and cortical before subcortical (Lowenstein and Loewenfeld, 1952a, 1952b).

These authors have also studied the effects of experimental lesions placed along the pupillary pathways of rabbits, cats, and monkeys, with the purpose of providing a basis for pupillography as a diagnostic indicator of clinical lesions of the A.N.S. (Lowenstein and Loewenfeld, 1950a). The variety of pupillographic curves obtained has been fully described, and one of the conclusions reached is that all the pupillographic syndromes produced by such lesions in animals are observed in man as clinical manifestations of pathologic processes of corresponding sites.

Experimental Studies with Psychiatric Patients

Granger (1953) reviewing work on the pupillary responses of different psychiatric groups points out that it would hardly be surprising if such responses were found to be of value in the study of personality and functional disorders, in view of the multiple neural connexions of the pupillary pathways with different levels of C.N.S. functioning.

May (1948) observed a high incidence of diminished pupillary response to pain, light and muscular effort in schizophrenics, a finding which he connected with the general hypoactivity which schizophrenics show. This suggestive study should be followed up with a more objective method of measuring pupil size.

The analysis of pupillary reactions to light carried out by Lowenstein and Westphal (1933) led them to classify responses into four types: (1) a group which is rapid in both contraction and dilatation; (2) a group prompt in contraction and slow in dilatation (this type occurred most commonly); (3) a group

slow in contraction and prompt in dilatation, and (4) a group sluggish in both contraction and dilatation. These four types of responses are believed to represent four kinds of equilibrium of sympathetic-parasympathetic activity, and to be constitutionally determined. The authors claim a significant relationship between the first type of reaction and manic-depressive psychosis and between type (4) and certain schizophrenics (*see* Fig. 11.3.) In catatonic schizophrenics yet another type of reaction was observed,

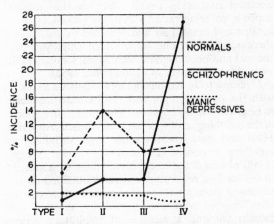

FIG. 11.3. THE DISTRIBUTION OF THE FOUR LIGHT-REACTION TYPES OF NORMALS, SCHIZOPHRENICS, AND MANIC-DEPRESSIVES

characterized by a long latency period, a rapid reaction to light and a long latency period for the redilatation followed by a full dilatation (*see also* Levine and Schilder, 1942). Such findings are of great interest, and merit further quantitative investigation in relation to selected groups of patients.

Pupil size of neurotics was investigated by Wenger (1948) in his study of autonomic balance; the measure obtained (of "static" pupillary diameter) failed, however, to correlate with other autonomic measures and to differentiate between groups. As Granger (1953) has pointed out in his review, the technique Wenger used was relatively crude, and the static type of record obtained was possibly not the most appropriate for investigating this type of problem.

Respiration

Woodworth and Schlosberg (1954) comment that respiration involves a reflex-automatic mechanism which primarily serves a metabolic function but which is also very responsive to changes in the organism's behaviour. Davis (in Ellson *et al.*, 1952) has discussed some of the mechanisms underlying respiratory movements, and has considered some of the "inputs to the breathing system" which initiate the changes.

Devices for recording breathing have been described by Woodworth and Schlosberg (1954) and by Davis (in Ellson *et al.*, 1952). There are two traditional methods, one depending on the volume of the inspired and expired air (using B.M.R. equipment) and the other (the pneumograph) depending on changes in girth of the chest and abdomen. A newer type of respiratory recorder has been described by Ackner (1956c); this is a rubber tube, filled with mercury, which constitutes a directly-varying resistance in an electrical measuring circuit. Yet another method depends on temperature variations picked up from inhaled and exhaled air and recorded by means of a thermocouple. In one study which employed both thermal and pneumograph techniques, similar results were obtained (Davis, in Ellson *et al.*, 1952).

Measures to an accepted index are difficult to obtain with the pneumograph, and results have inevitably to be given in terms of ratios. The extreme irregularity of the breathing amplitude has been stressed (Altschule, 1953) and data given on the high variability of breathing responses (Davis *et al.*, 1955). Wenger (1948) obtained test-retest correlations of about 0·5 to 0·6 for four respiratory measures obtained on two successive mornings (N = 54); three of these correlations dropped when the interval was three or four months but one, a measure of respiratory period, remained almost unaltered at $r = 0.65$.

Experimental Studies

The effect of various stimuli on respiratory changes is not clear. Altschule (1953) refers to some very early psychological experiments in which startle was reported to cause an immediate cessation of respiration followed by an increase of rate above normal. Stresses of various types may apparently give rise, in rather unpredictable fashion, to either increases or decreases in respiratory rate, although from the available literature Altschule considers increases to be more common.

Davis *et al.* (1955) have investigated breathing responses to a variety of simple stimuli. They found that breathing amplitude increased to a tone of 98 db and reached a maximum as late as 15 to 20 sec after the stimulus. They failed to observe adaptation effects to ten repeated stimuli; on the contrary, the means for the last half of the series tended to be higher than those for the first half, suggesting a facilitation rather than habituation of response to repeated stimuli. A tendency (not statistically significant) was also found for breathing cycle time to increase in response upon repeated stimulation.

Respiratory response also increased to auditory stimuli of increasing intensity (70, 90 and 120 db). The response to the stimulus of 120 db was significantly greater than that to the weaker tones; the difference between responses to the two weaker stimuli did not approach significance (*see* Table XI.2).

Repetition effects differed with the stimulus intensities employed; a *decrease* in response to the strong stimulus was found ($p < 0.01$) and an *increase* (just significant) to the weaker stimuli. The measurement of duration of breathing cycle during the 15–20-sec interval following stimulus showed an effect of stimulus intensity, significant in the case of the strongest stimulus.

The authors have suggested that the evidence indicates a certain amount of independence of the two respiratory measures (duration and amplitude changes) but it is worth noting that these particular variables were selected for statistical treatment from a number of rather complex response curves. An attempt was made to explain the changes in breathing observed in terms of physiological mechanisms such as decrease in vagal feed-back and increased arousal of the inspiratory centre.

Most of the work which has been carried out with respiratory measures of psychiatric patients has used vague stimulus conditions, such as "ideational" stimuli, psychiatric interviews, etc., and has paid little attention to the reliability, quantification or statistical treatment of the data obtained. It has been observed in several studies that the respiratory responses of neurotic and psychotic subjects differ from those of normals. Altschule (1953), however, considered that respiration is normal, or only slightly raised, in neurotic conditions, and shows no consistent pattern of change in patients with manic-depressive or schizophrenic psychoses. But most of the studies which he has reviewed in his book suffer from the lack of quantification observed above.

The significant findings of greater respiratory irregularity in anxious patients in response to painful stimuli reported by Malmo and Shagass (1949a) were not confirmed in a subsequent study (Malmo and Smith, 1955).

Muscle-action Potentials

A classification of the different techniques used to measure muscle tension has been made by R. C. Davis (1942). He favoured surface electromyography —the direct recording of action potentials from muscles—and with the advent of high-gain amplifiers this method has been quite widely used in psychological experiments. The present section will be confined to electromyographic (EMG) studies since these are most directly related to muscular activity; it should be pointed out that the relationship of measurements made by this method to other means of assessing muscle tension is largely unknown.

The difficulties attendant upon EMG recording and

the instrumentation required have been well discussed (J. F. Davis, 1952) in a monograph which also describes and considers the various bipolar surface electrodes in common use, and which gives details of the standard electrode placements used in the Montreal laboratories.

The signal obtained from surface electromyograms is compounded of many asynchronously firing motor units; from these arises the typical record of muscle spikes differing in amplitude and frequency. It is, of course, the electrical potential difference between the two electrodes which is fed to the amplifier as the input signal.

The quantification of the EMG record presents a formidable task, and, to overcome the difficulty, integrating devices are frequently used in conjunction with electromyographs. Most of the integrators described deal only with the magnitude of the signal (i.e. total charge), and do not discriminate between frequency and amplitude (R. C. Davis, 1948a; J. F. Davis, 1952; Sainsbury and Gibson, 1954). A basic assumption is that the amplitude of the EMG is highly correlated with increase of muscle activity. Travis and Lindsley (1931) have shown that with increasing intensity of contraction the frequency and voltage of the recorded waves increase, and Malmo, Shagass and Davis (1951) also found that their integrated measures of muscle potentials increased with the amount of pull exerted on a dynamometer. But, in another study relating the human EMG to muscle tension, differences were reported in the integrated output depending on whether isometric or isotonic tension was developed (Inman, Ralston et al., 1952). In this study the electrical output as revealed by the integrated EMG closely paralleled the tension in a muscle contracting isometrically, but not when the muscle was allowed to vary in length.

The modal frequency of muscle firing has been estimated at about 45 c/s (J. F. Davis, 1952) and sine waves of this frequency have been used as calibrating signals although higher frequencies are generally observed with needle electrodes and during muscle activity (with any form of electrode). Nevertheless, it is open to question whether the characteristics of the sine-wave signal are comparable with the spiky muscle signal which is to be integrated.

Units of measurement are generally reported in terms of microvolts, on the assumed basis of a constant relationship between peak and mean amplitude, but the term may be a little misleading (J. F. Davis, 1952, has discussed this problem). Only where standard equipment and procedures exist, for example, within a particular laboratory, is it possible to make direct comparisons of individuals' results.

Increased activity of the skeletal musculature has been reported in respect of a wide range of stimuli; obviously overt movements are accompanied by increases in motor unit discharge, but measurements obtained during situations where the subject is engaged in mental activities such as imaging (Jacobson, 1932; Shaw, 1938), listening (Wallerstein, 1954) and memorizing (Davis, 1939) also reveal changing levels of activity.

Muscle-action Potentials and Performance

There is an interesting literature on the relationship of muscle tension to performance, but much of this research, carried out many years ago, used a variety of tension measures other than electromyography. Any adequate summary of this sort of investigation would need to consider the many tension measures and their interrelationships, and so is beyond the scope of the present section. There remain, however, a number of EMG studies relating muscle-action potentials to various movements, tasks, etc. These have concentrated on different aspects of the total problem; some have considered the pattern of tensions—both focal and remote—in subjects engaged in a task, while others have considered the effects of these tensions upon quality of performance.

Meyer (1953) considered from the available evidence that muscle tension is typically generalized under most of the conditions commonly associated with difficult performance, e.g. lack of practice, prolonged work periods, distractions, complex materials and increased incentives. He has reviewed some of the studies dealing with changes in the distribution of muscle tensions during learning with, and without, artificially induced tensions. He pointed out that the sequence of elimination of tension during practice at a task is such that tension changes are from generalization to focalization. When induced tensions are used, facilitation appears most pronounced early in learning, while late-in-learning tension interferes with performance. In the natural learning situation (i.e. with no artificially induced tension) one of the conditions which produces generalized tension appears to be lack of practice, and Meyer has suggested that a positive role may be assigned to the tenseness of the individual who has just begun to learn, and that the optimal conditions for the novice are not the same as those for the skilled performer.

A review of the evidence led him to the conclusion that interacting responses are necessarily overlapping responses. To account for the way in which overlap is translated into interaction he suggested that simultaneous neural patterns may converge and summate to produce altered amplitude or latency of a response. Changes in the effects of induced muscular tension from facilitation to interference were assumed by Meyer to be related to greater excitation of inappropriate rather than appropriate motor neurons.

Interference with a movement of extension, for example, would be produced by "inappropriate" excitation of sufficient flexor cells to the point of threshold. On the basis of such arguments he developed a theory of efferent neural interaction to account for the effects of induced muscle tension upon both learned and unlearned responses.

Dealing with performance at a fairly simple level, R. C. Davis (1956b) has also hypothesized that the similarity of response patterns is the important factor in determining whether they will facilitate or inhibit each other, and he maintains that the rules of combination (or interaction) of simultaneous responses can best be ascertained by first finding the electromyographic pattern produced by single responses. These single patterns when combined with others might, of course, reinforce one another, neutralize one another, or have a mixed effect, according to the extent of their similarity.

Two completely independent patterns, having no overlap at all, would not be expected to interact but two responses requiring simultaneous actions of the same sort in the same place would be expected to produce the required vector sum more readily, and eventually facilitate the overt response by affecting its magnitude or latency.

Another aspect of the whole problem of the interaction of simultaneous "responses" is the relationship of existing muscle tensions (which are not themselves necessarily connected with overt movements) to performance. For example, Kennedy and Travis (1948) demonstrated that decreasing muscle-action potential output of the supraorbital muscles was accompanied by decreasing "alertness" and poorer reaction-times. R. C. Davis (1940) also found an inverse correlation between simple reaction-time and immediately preceding activity of the responding muscles; yet, as he points out, a high degree of muscle tension has hitherto been considered undesirable—a variable to be minimized for efficient performance.

It would seem likely that the conceptions used are probably too gross to lead to clear results, e.g. "good" performance is not likely to be a unitary affair, and tension produced by distraction or dynamometer gripping may well have different effects (R. C. Davis, 1956b). Several studies based on the simple hypothesis that the nature of the foregoing muscular activity will shape the developing response have been reported by R. C. Davis and his colleagues (summarized by R. C. Davis, 1956b). He has offered the suggestion that if *prior* excitation is in all respects like the desired response, its presence will be facilitative; if prior excitation is incompatible with the response to be made, inhibition and so poorer performance will occur.

Gradients of Muscle-action Potentials during Performance

A series of investigations on gradients of muscle-action potentials during a variety of activities has recently been reported. Gradients have been observed in the forearm during mirror drawing (Smith, 1953), in the chin and extensor muscles of both arms during listening (Smith, Malmo and Shagass, 1954), and in the forehead and chin while attending to several repetitions of a short story and an essay (Wallerstein, 1954). On this latter occasion gradients did not occur in the forearm extensors.

Bartoshuk (1955a) also investigated forearm and chin gradients of tension during mirror drawing, and showed that forearm EMG gradients were not paralleled by gradients in drawing speed, and so could not be attributed to them. He proposed the hypothesis that EMG gradients reflect the subject's motivation, and followed up this suggestion in a further study (Bartoshuk, 1955b). He argued from two assumptions—that both steepness of EMG gradients, and performance, are direct functions of the strength of motivation to perform a task—to the hypothesis that steepness of EMG gradients should be positively correlated with performance.

His results showed that the marked individual differences in gradient slope, when subjects were equated for amount of practice, were directly related to differences in quality of performance, measured by time and accuracy. In another study investigating the effects of incentive, difficulty and "goal structuring" on tracking performance it was found that the incentive was the primary factor in raising the EMG gradient but the relation of gradient slope to performance was not strongly substantiated (Surwillo, 1956).

Malmo and Davis (1956) have considered these EMG gradients as indicators of a dimension of arousal, along which states such as motivation might be placed; they use the term arousal to designate an intensity dimension of behaviour, following up the suggestion made by Duffy (1951) that two basic dimensions of arousal—intensity and direction—might replace the traditional classifications of psychology. These authors, using a procedure similar to Bartoshuk's, recorded right arm flexor and extensor muscle potentials, and also obtained measures of respiration, heart rate and blood-pressure. Highly significant gradients during performance were found in right arm muscles, heart rate and blood-pressure. Those for respiration and forehead muscles were less reliable but significant over a limited number of trials. Significant correlations between steepness of some of the physiological gradients (particularly blood-pressure) and performance time were obtained, the steeper the gradient the shorter the performance time.

Table XI.5 shows the intercorrelations among measures of gradient steepness.

It would seem from these findings that gradients of physiological functions other than skeletal muscles are related to overt performance, and the authors

below it (1950). Stimuli of 1,000 cycle tones, ranging within less than 10 db above and below the usual auditory threshold were used, and it was found that these weak subliminal stimuli produced muscular responses even when the subject thought that he had

TABLE XI.5

INTERCORRELATIONS AMONG MEASURES OF GRADIENT STEEPNESS (N = 43)

(From Malmo and Davis, 1956)

Physiological variable	Trials	Extensor 5–8	Flexor 1–4	Flexor 5–8	Heart rate 1–4	Heart rate 5–8	Blood-pressure 1–4	Blood-pressure 5–8
Extensor muscle . .	(1–4)	0·86	0·62	0·46	0·13	0·24	0·30	0·52
Extensor muscle . .	(5–8)		0·38	0·44	0·12	0·32	0·26	0·55
Flexor muscle . . .	(1–4)			0·67	0·02	0·26	0·05	0·34
Flexor muscle . . .	(5–8)				–0·01	0·47	–0·17	0·35
Heart rate . . .	(1–4)					0·53	0·25	0·35
Heart rate . . .	(5–8)						–0·18	0·20
Blood-pressure . .	(1–4)							0·42

have suggested, on the basis of the significant intercorrelations which were observed, that all these physiological functions may share, at least in part, some of the same mechanisms of central-neural control. They suggested that autonomic gradients may be used along with skeletal muscle gradients to provide a composite measure of arousal.

Adaptation

There is evidence that some kind of adaptation occurs during an experimental session. Davis has found in a large number of experiments that the *level* of tension between responses to stimuli declines through the session, and he has suggested that this diminishing tension might signify the initial presence of a response to the experimental situation which becomes extinguished as the session progresses. A significant decline in right forearm tension (but not in forehead tension) during a ten-minute rest period after connecting subjects to the electrodes has also been reported (Martin, 1956).

Auditory stimuli are known to produce muscular responses. R. C. Davis and his collaborators, in a series of studies (1948b, 1950, 1956a,c; Davis and Van Liere, 1949; Davis, Buchwald and Frankmann, 1955) have investigated adaptation effects to repeated auditory stimuli of different intensities, and their results will be presented in some detail since these experiments represent one of the best and most systematic attempts to relate response changes to stimulus variation. He has examined the question of how far down the scale of stimulus intensities such responses may be observed, by presenting sounds near the absolute threshold, some above and some

not heard the sound, although responses to unheard stimuli were smaller than to those reported heard.

The effects of various other factors were considered in this study, with the following results—

(i) repeated weak stimulation: a significant *increase* in response to the second stimulus was observed.

(ii) changes in stimulus intensity: responses showed little change with stimulus intensity up to the threshold, but above it they increased rapidly.

The sensitization of response to very weak auditory stimuli is in contrast to the responses to stimuli above 70 db to which varying amounts of adaptation were found (Davis *et al.*, 1955). Habituation appears to be a function of the size of the stimulus; very loud sounds (e.g. gunfire in the Davis and Van Liere, 1949, experiment) may not be followed by successive reduction in the amplitude of the response.

Two effects following strong auditory stimuli have been described by Davis (1948b); the *a* response and the *b* response. In this study, sound stimuli of 500 cycles were used at three intensity levels, 90, 95 and 99 db, each lasting four seconds, and recordings were obtained from the extensor muscles on the dorsal surface of both forearms.

The *a* response begins about 0·1–0·2 sec after the onset of the stimulus, reaches its peak about 0·1 sec later, and almost disappears by the next 0·5 sec. The *b* response seems to begin about 0·8 second after the onset of the stimulus, maintains this level for about another second, and then decays, rapidly at first and then slowly. The *a* response was found to show marked adaptation and had practically disappeared

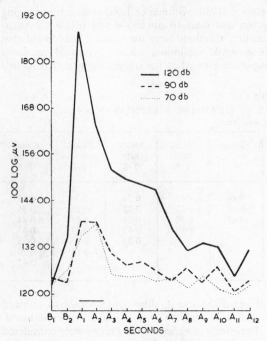

FIG. 11.4. MEAN MUSCLE-ACTION POTENTIAL (RIGHT FOREARM) RESPONSE TO 1,000-CYCLE TONE OF VARYING INTENSITIES

Horizontal line indicates stimulus duration.

(*From Davis, Buchwald and Frankmann,* 1955)

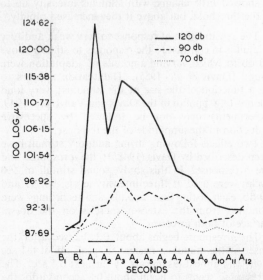

FIG. 11.5. MEAN MUSCLE-ACTION POTENTIAL (LEFT FOREARM) RESPONSE TO 1,000-CYCLE TONE OF VARYING INTENSITIES

Horizontal line indicates stimulus duration.

(*From Davis, Buchwald and Frankmann,* 1955)

after six or so repetitions of the stimulus; it was also affected by the intensity of the stimuli. The *b* responses were not so affected. Pre-stimulus tensions were found to be important both in determining the size and the spatial distribution of the *a* and *b* responses.

In a later experiment (Davis, Buchwald and Frankmann, 1955) a two-second 1,000 cycle tone of varying intensities (70, 90, and 120 db) was presented four times to subjects at one-minute intervals.

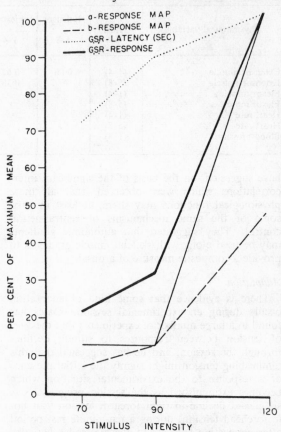

FIG. 11.6. MUSCLE-ACTION POTENTIAL (M.A.P.) RESPONSES AND GALVANIC SKIN RESPONSES (G.S.R.) PLOTTED AS A FUNCTION OF INTENSITY OF A 1,000-CYCLE TONE

(*From Davis, Buchwald and Frankmann,* 1955)

Figs. 11.4 and 11.5 show the responses for right and left forearm to the different intensities of stimulation. (These figures average the readings for all subjects for each measurement before and after the three stimulus intensities). The effects of stimulus intensity are given in Fig. 11.6 in which the *a* and *b* responses, both arms combined, are plotted as a function of stimulus intensity. The curves confirmed previous findings that the *a* response function undergoes a marked acceleration at a stimulus intensity of about

100 db and that the *b* response does not increase so rapidly.

The *a* response is significantly greater to the 120-db stimulus than to either of the two weaker stimuli; the difference between the effects of the weaker stimuli is non-significant. The general conclusions are the same for the *b* response, although the significance levels for the difference between strong and weak stimuli are somewhat lower.

Adaptation effects to the various intensities are seen in Fig. 11.7. For the *a* response, stimulus *A*, there is a significant decrease ($p < 0.01$) from first to last quarter of the sitting. For *B* and *C* stimuli combined, the successive quarters decline, but not significantly. For the *b* response, the slope of the adaptation curve for the strong stimulus is less steep, and the curve for the weaker stimuli follows it more closely. For both types of stimuli the difference between the first and last quarters is significant ($p < 0.05$). "Thus we have the rather complex situation that adaptation is a function of stimulus intensity for the *a* response, whereas for the *b*-response adaptation is less, and is not much affected by stimulus intensity." (Davis *et al.*, 1955.)

High intensity tones—100, 110, 115 and 117 db— of brief duration and presented to the subject at approximately 6-sec intervals, were used in a further experiment recording potentials from forearm muscles (Davis, 1956*a*). Each of the four stimulus intensities was delivered to each subject four times, in a Latin-square design. A progressive increment of response with increased stimulus intensity was clearly observed in the *a* response, the tension response within the range of stimuli used being approximately in proportion to the decibel level of the stimulus. On this occasion no *b* response was obtained, and Davis attributed its absence to the brevity of the tones used in this experiment (0·2 sec compared with 2·0 and 4·0 secs in the study previously described).

Again, adaptation to all stimulus intensities was apparent, and with its progress the effects of the several intensities remained, about as different from each other as they originally were. Davis (1956*a*) has summarized the findings on muscle action potentials in relation to auditory stimulation as follows—

   (i) the overall intensity response relation is probably curvilinear and positively accelerated.
   (ii) the persistent effects of noise are probably a prolongation of the *b* response.
   (iii) an instructed movement to a stimulus following quickly after a tension reflex will "reinforce" that reflex and prevent it from adapting.

As mentioned earlier, decline in background tension levels is a feature of all experiments. However, in two studies in which a steady continuous noise occurred, the level of muscle tension was sustained throughout (Davis, 1956*c*).

Studies Involving Psychiatric Patients

Several studies designed to objectify patients' complaints of symptoms apparently relating to certain muscle areas have been carried out. Tensional headache is a problem of this kind. Wolff (1948)

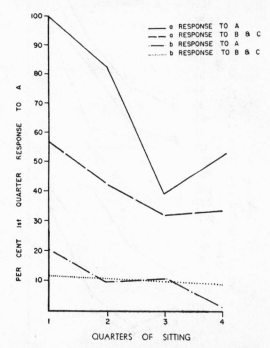

Fig. 11.7. Adaptation of Muscle-action Potential Responses (*a* and *b*) to Various Intensities of a 1,000-cycle Tone Presented in Mixed Order during a Sitting
A = 120 db, *B* = 90 db, *C* = 70 db
(*From Davis, Buchwald and Frankman, 1955*)

believed that head and neck muscles were frequently maintained at high levels of contraction and that this could be a cause of headache and other head sensations. Malmo and Shagass (1949*b*) showed that headache proneness was associated with increased muscle potentials of the neck during a standardized series of painful stimulations applied to the forehead, but was not associated with high heart rate, high heart-rate variability, or respiratory deviation. They put forward the principle of "symptom specificity" which stated that in psychiatric patients presenting a somatic complaint, the particular physiological mechanism of that complaint is specifically susceptible to activation by stressful experience.

Sainsbury and Gibson (1954) investigated the relation between symptoms reported by psychiatric patients and the activity of the skeletal muscles, and they also related the electromyographic measurement of skeletal activity from the left forearm and *frontalis* muscles to the patients' scores on an inventory

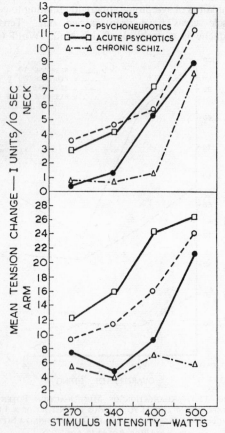

FIG. 11.8. MEAN CHANGE IN ARM AND NECK TENSION PLOTTED AGAINST INTENSITY OF THERMAL STIMULATON
(From Malmo, Shagass and Davis, 1951)

composed of items such as presence of worry, apprehension, inability to relax, etc. Their results may be summarized as follows—

(i) forehead (*frontalis*) tension, measured during rest, was significantly lower in a group of healthy normals than in a group of anxiety states.

(ii) when the patients were divided into two groups, one scoring high and the other scoring low on the "anxiety" inventory, mean muscle tension of forearm extensor and *frontalis* muscles was found to be significantly higher in the high-scoring group.

(iii) EMG measurements from specific symptom areas—headaches, aching of the arms, stiffness of the neck—were compared in patients with and without the symptoms: in each case there was a

significantly higher tension in the relevant muscle area in patients with the symptom.

(iv) Concurrent recordings were obtained from fifteen patients from *frontalis*, left forearm and left foot extensors, and posterior cervical muscles. A rank correlation of 0·45 was obtained ($p < 0·05$) a result which suggested that there was some degree of generalization of muscle tension.

A series of investigations into the skeletal-muscle response to stress of psychiatric patients has been carried out by Malmo and his colleagues. They have used a wide range of stimulus conditions: pain, administered by means of a Hardy-Wolff thermal stimulator (Malmo and Shagass, 1949*a*; Malmo, Shagass and Davis, 1951; Malmo and Smith, 1955) sound (Davis, Malmo and Shagass, 1954), perceptual and motor tasks (Malmo, Shagass and Davis, 1951) and psychiatric interview (Malmo, Shagass and Davis, 1950, Davis and Malmo, 1951, Shagass and Malmo, 1954).

Their early studies were prompted by the premise that the distinguishing feature of anxiety is that the patient reacts to ordinary everyday life situations as though they were emergencies. The first of the series (Malmo and Shagass, 1949*a*) employed a variety of physiological measures, including neck muscle potentials, recorded in association with thermal stimulation. Since anxiety has also been described as the expectation of trauma, recordings were also made during the anticipatory or preparatory phase prior to the application of the stimulus.

It was found that anxiety states and early schizophrenics were the most muscularly tense with the mixed patient group next and controls the lowest in tension. In the 1951 study (Malmo, Shagass, and Davis) EMG recordings were made from seventy-five patients: seventeen chronic schizophrenics, fourteen acute psychotics (mainly schizophrenics), forty-four psychoneurotics with pathological anxiety or tension, and twenty-one controls. Recordings of neck and right forearm flexor muscle potential were made under several conditions: pain stress, rapid discrimination test, and mirror drawing. The general conclusion here was that psychoneurotic and psychotic patients responded to stress with a greater degree of muscle tension than that found in control subjects; this finding was consistent for all the stress situations. Also, the general level of muscle tension was as high in schizophrenics under stress as in other psychiatric patients, except that they were tensionally underreactive to pain stimuli.

It can be seen from Fig. 11.8 which shows mean change in neck and arm tension plotted against intensity of thermal stimulation that, apart from the arm response of the chronic schizophrenics, the magnitude of the tension response increased as the stimulus intensity increased. Differences between patients and controls were most pronounced at the lower intensities and were not in fact statistically significant at the higher intensity levels. There was also evidence of a considerable individual consistency from one stress situation to another.

The patients showed a marked overreaction to the instructions in the preparatory period of the mirror drawing task; to account for this and similar results it was suggested that there may be a deficiency in the neurotics' central nervous system regulatory mechanism, such that immediate tensional output is too great.

Malmo and Smith (1955) have since reported further work using the pain stimulation procedures with measures of *frontalis*, neck, left and right forearm flexor and extensor muscles, obtained from a group of mixed patients (mainly anxiety states) and from normal controls. Mean tension values for each pre-stimulus period, warning, stimulation and post-periods were obtained. *Frontalis* muscle tension was found to be consistently successful in differentiating the patient from the control group, but on this occasion neck and forearm muscle potentials were only mildly successful in differentiating the groups.

The studies which have been described have mainly classified the neurotic subjects into two categories: anxiety states and mixed patients. The dimensional analysis of neurotic subgroups made by Eysenck (1952) showed that dysthymics (anxiety states, depressives, obsessional-compulsive states) were significantly differentiated from hysterics on a variety of tests. On this basis, therefore, an experiment was planned to investigate the levels and reactivity of muscle tension in two neurotic groups, one comprising anxiety states, the other mainly hysterics (Martin, 1956). Recordings were obtained from *frontalis* and right forearm extensor muscles during rest, and to various stimuli (delayed feed-back of speech during reading, and a motor frustration task). The anxiety states were significantly differentiated from the hysterics in both muscle areas during rest but not during stimulation. It was predicted that during the initial relaxation period lasting ten minutes differential relaxation rates of normals and neurotics would be observed, but although there was a downward trend in tension scores during the period the slopes of the curves were similar in both groups and failed to discriminate between them.

The electromyographic reaction to strong auditory stimulation was studied in groups of normals and psychiatric patients (ten neurotic and ten acute schizophrenic) by Davis, Malmo and Shagass (1954). Forearm extensor muscle potentials were recorded to ten stimuli (a burst of white noise lasting 0·125 sec

administered at one-minute intervals). Amplitude of responses at each tenth second period were measured for one second before and two seconds following each stimulus. (The curves of patients' and controls' responses are given in Fig. 11.9).

When the relation between background tension and amount of response was taken into account the patients were found to have a significantly higher response at 0·3 sec after stimuli than the controls ($p < 0.05$) and at 0·4 sec the significance of the

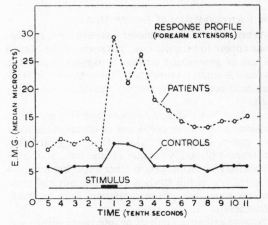

FIG. 11.9. COMPARISON OF PATIENTS AND CONTROLS IN FOREARM MUSCLE POTENTIAL AMPLITUDE FOR EACH TENTH-SECOND PRECEDING AND FOLLOWING STIMULATION
Each point on the curve is based on the averaged data from the first four stimulations.
(*From Davis, Malmo and Shagass*, 1954)

difference increased to the 1 per cent level. The authors considered their results within the framework of the startle pattern described by Landis and Hunt (1939); in the *immediate* reflex action which is of very brief duration there was no significant patient-control difference, but a delayed elevation of tension was observed in the patient group in the secondary or after-response. It would be of interest to repeat this study with a more homogeneous group of patients and with measurements from other muscle areas.

Marked adaptation of the response occurred in both psychiatric and normal groups. Adaptation effects in patients were also studied by Malmo and Wallerstein (1955) to a series of ten 3-sec heat stimulations applied to the forehead at 1-min intervals. The right forefinger rested on a button which the subject was instructed to press when he felt the heat was about to become painful (although it was explained that the pressure on the button would not terminate the stimulus).

Although a falling tension in the control subjects throughout the ten stimuli was noted, in contrast to the steady tension level maintained by the patients, the differences between the groups were not statistically significant. The patients significantly differed from the controls in the amount of change of mean latency of button pressure throughout the series (controls showed increased latency) and also in change of duration of button pressure, controls showing decreased durations. The results were interpreted as supporting the hypothesis that neurotics show less decrement in the strength of a voluntary response as a function of its repeated elicitation.

The Interrelationships of Tension Measures

When rather different motor tests are used, correlations appear to be quite low. However, if the clinical picture of generalized tension in certain psychiatric patients is correct, correlations between muscle areas measured electromyographically should be reasonably high.

As described earlier, Sainsbury and Gibson (1954) obtained a significant coefficient of concordance from four groups of muscles. This finding suggested that an increase of bodily tension in one area is reliably associated with an increase in other areas, but it should be noted that in this study selected anxious and tense patients were seen whose symptoms were probably rather severe.

A more extensive analysis of interrelationships was carried out by Malmo and Smith (1955) who factor-analysed ten variables: six were direct measures of muscle tension, from forehead, neck, left and right forearm extensor and flexor muscles, and the other four measures were EMG fluctuation, finger movement irregularity, head movement and body movement.

No factor of generalized muscle tension appeared; five of the muscle tension measures fell into a single factor of neck and bilateral-forearm tension while the sixth, *frontalis*, grouped itself with measures of movement and irregularity.

Summary: Muscle-action Potentials

1. *General conclusions.* All reported stimulus-induced changes have been an increase in muscle-potential; size of the response may depend upon pre-stimulus levels.

Adaptation of background tension levels throughout experiments is frequently observed, and the muscle-action potential response in general adapts quickly to repeated auditory stimuli. At extremes of stimulation R. C. Davis has reported increasing reaction to sounds near the auditory threshold, but little adaptation to sounds of very high intensity.

The response also increases as a function of increasing stimulus intensity: the overall intensity response relation is probably curvilinear and positively accelerated.

Latency is short (approximately 0·01 sec) and the response (Davis's *a* response) reaches a maximum within 1 sec following the stimulus.

2. *In relation to psychiatric disorder.* Most of the studies on psychiatric patients agree in one respect: that anxious patients demonstrate a *higher* level of muscle tension than normals. This seems to be consistently reported of *frontalis* muscles, and to a less extent with forearm and neck muscles. There is less information about the precise conditions under which the findings hold but there is agreement that the *frontalis* difference is apparent during rest (in anxious patients compared with controls) and also that forearm and neck muscle responses are slightly greater to certain forms of sensory stimulation, e.g. pain.

Strong auditory stimuli in one study also produced tensional responses of higher amplitude in a group of mixed psychiatric patients.

CENTRAL MECHANISMS

Many hypotheses may be found in the psychological literature concerning apparently central effects on the somatic responses which have been considered in the previous sections. Efforts are frequently made to underpin theoretical postulates (e.g. of the type that neurotics manifest a failure to adapt or a tendency to overreact) with reference to an assumed deficiency of functioning of some central regulatory mechanism such as the hypothalamus, the cortex, or the reticular activating system.

At the present time it is impossible to attribute either those aspects of total behaviour labelled "emotional," or particular somatic response functions, to any single central mechanism. Almost any kind of response is undoubtedly integrated from a number of different levels in the hierarchical arrangement, and the precise manner in which these centres interact and their relative contributions to the final response are largely unknown. The present section will give an idea of the sort of research which has been carried out with these problems in mind.

The assessment of behaviour consequences of central electrical stimulation or experimental ablation is frequently made by means of observations of total behavioural patterns such as "rage." The interpretation of such results is at best only suggestive (*see* Chapter 14 by Victor Meyer for a criticism of these techniques and experimental reports). Another more precise means is to record peripheral autonomic and skeletal muscle activity, although it has already been mentioned that these responses bear no clear-cut relationship in humans to different emotional states, and to infer the presence of an emotion from physiological arousal may not be justified. It would be more accurate, especially in studies with human subjects, to give results simply in terms of amplitudes and latencies of somatic responses (or other measurable responses).

The localization of function frequently attempted in experimental work employing techniques of electrical stimulation and ablation is a highly doubtful procedure (cf. Chapter 14) but some of the findings of this type of work may provide interesting clues for further investigation.

It has been found with lower animals (cats in particular have been studied) that decortication does not eliminate emotional expression; in fact decorticated animals respond rather readily and violently to rage-provoking stimuli. Such exaggerated responses, it has been suggested, result from the release of lower centres from cortical inhibition. Decerebration, however, is followed by a severe reduction in responsiveness.

Systematic exploration of the hypothalamus by means of electrical stimulation has shown that rage reactions, involving autonomic-somatic discharge, can be produced; the reaction usually ceases with cessation of the stimulus (but *see also* Hess, 1954). Bard (1934) found that animals with cortex and thalamus removed still showed rage if only the posterior part of the hypothalamus was left, but if the hypothalamus was completely removed the integrated rage pattern did not develop. (*See* Lindsley in *Handbook of Experimental Psychology*, p. 492, 1951, and Gellhorn, 1953, for discussions of this work.) Facts of this kind have emphasized the importance of subcortical mechanisms in the integration of emotional expression and in controlling autonomic reactions.

The careful work of Ranson (1937) and Hess (1954) using point by point stimulation of diencephalic regions with deeply embedded electrodes in freely-moving unanaesthetized cats, has furthered our understanding of the organization of autonomic and motor effects within the diencephalon. Hess's conclusions were that stimulation of the middle and posterior part of the diencephalon produces an effect of *general* sympathetic nervous system excitation, such as Cannon had described, in conditions of fear and rage. The rostral part of the hypothalamus, on the other hand, was found to be more intimately related to trophic processes such as digestion and elimination, via parasympathetic nervous mediation, and in this zone the arrangement is such that definite

mechanisms, e.g. lapping, vomiting, or defaecation, are evoked by the individual stimuli.

Not only autonomic effects but associated somatomotor signs appear to be mediated by the diencephalon. The distinction between autonomic and skeletal muscle systems, so clear at the peripheral level, is no longer maintained at the diencephalic level, where, Hess repeatedly emphasizes, organization is in *functional* rather than anatomical terms. He conceives of the diencephalon as co-ordinating many activities and functions in which autonomic organs are associated with somatomotor patterns, for example the assumption by the animal of the appropriate posture for defaecation and micturition, in which the functions of individual effector organs are united for the performance of a definite task. This functional integration of different organs and systems may be demonstrated *at all levels* of the nervous system.

The Cortex and Autonomic Functions

There is ample evidence of cortical autonomic representation (*see* Fulton, 1950; Gellhorn, 1953). Certain parts of the cerebral cortex appear to subserve both visceral and somatic functions (Kuntz, 1953; Gellhorn, 1953). This representation, in widespread cortical areas, permits of a functional grouping of autonomic processes to a greater extent than is possible in the hypothalamus and medulla (Hess, 1954). Examples are the sweating response of the palms following stimulation of the cortical motor area of the hand, the lachrymatory and pupillary changes which may follow the stimulation of the somatic cortical representation of eye movement (Kennard, 1947). Other cortical areas appear to be more concerned with visceral functions; these include among others the hippocampus, the amygdaloid area, and the rostral portion of the temporal lobe (Kuntz, 1953).

The relationship of cortex to diencephalon should be of great theoretical interest. Kuntz (1953) quotes experimental data in support of the assumption that interruption of the cortico-diencephalic fibre connexions liberates the subcortical emotional mechanisms from the inhibitory influences of cortical origin. It seems to be widely agreed that hypothalamic areas have the capacity for co-ordinating emotional and autonomic activity independently of impulses arising from the cerebral cortex.

Bard and Mountcastle (1948) found that removal of the neo-cortex leads to a state of "placidity": "in our placid cats the amygdala, the hippocampal formation, and the cortical field of the pyriform lobe had been left intact." When the amygdala and pyriform lobe were removed, a state of ferocity followed. These experiments seemed to indicate that the restraining influence on the hypothalamus is exerted in the cat through the phylogenetically oldest parts of the cortex (rhinencephalon) and their action opposed to that exerted by the neocortex (a conclusion which cannot be generalized to all species, *see* Fulton, 1950). More recent studies along these lines have been reviewed by Jasper, Gloor and Milner (1956).

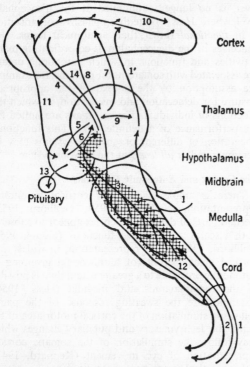

FIG. 11.10. SCHEMATIC REPRESENTATION OF PRINCIPAL CENTRAL NERVOUS STRUCTURES AND PROBABLE PATH-WAYS INVOLVED IN EMOTIONAL BEHAVIOUR

The diagram does not include the cerebellum and certain basal ganglia that may also participate.
Key. 1—somatic and cranial afferents; 1'—direct thalamocortical projections; 2—visceral afferent pathways; 3—centripetal projections of reticular formation; 4—diffuse thalamocortical projections; 5 and 6—interconnexions of hypothalamus and thalamus; 7 and 8—interconnexions between thalamus and cortex; 9—intrathalamic connexions; 10—intracortical connexions; 11—corticohypothalamic pathways; 12—visceral efferent pathways; 13—hypothalamohypophysical tract; 14—corticospinal pathways.
The crosshatched area represents the reticular formation.
(From Lindsley, 1951)

Lindsley (1951) and Jasper, Gloor and Milner (1956) have discussed the relationship of the limbic system to subcortical structures, including the hypothalamus; Maclean (1954) believes that this part of the primitive forebrain may provide a mechanism for the elaboration of emotions and emotional expression. Afferent connexions from the vagus to the anterior part of the formation have been demonstrated, and Maclean suggests that in this part of the brain there is a phylogenetically old cortical screen on which may be projected and fused a wide variety

of experiences derived from the visceral and external environment of the organism.

Some findings have recently been reported in connexion with the limbic system as a "reward" system. When rats with implanted electrodes were able to stimulate their own brains electrically by depressing a lever, "rewarding effects" (measured by the time spent pressing the lever) were observed. These rewarding effects were found in only particular areas of the limbic system (Olds, 1955).

Gellhorn (1953) has discussed the role of the cortex with respect to autonomic functions, and has suggested that—

(i) it inhibits autonomic centres, therefore its absence accounts for autonomic hyperactivity in sham rage.

(ii) it provides for a functional association of certain motor with appropriate autonomic effects.

(iii) it makes the activation of the autonomic centres in the hypothalamus possible through impulses reaching the brain via distance receptors of the visual, auditory, or olfactory apparatus. The biological significance of this process is obvious.

On the other hand it has been argued that the cortex plays an excitatory role in emotions and that this hypothesis could account for the reduction of anxiety after prefrontal lobotomy (Arnold, 1955). The general evidence from surgical cases, ablation experiments and local stimulation is that the cortex has both inhibitory and facilitatory effects upon diencephalic structures, and, as Gellhorn (1953) comments, while emotional response in man may be due to cortical excitation it is at the same time true that conditions leading to diminished (but not extinguished) cortical activity seem to predispose to emotional excitement.

Facts concerning the interaction of the cerebral cortex with subcortical structures, together with data from EEG recordings, have led Lindsley (1951) to propose an "activation theory" of emotion. EEG studies have shown that in relaxed individuals with no special stimulation, the dominant activity is the fairly rhythmic 10-per second alpha rhythm. They have also shown that an unexpected stimulus such as a light or a sound will block the alpha rhythm but that upon repetition of the stimulus adaptation will occur. The initial effectiveness of a stimulus in blocking the alpha rhythm thus appears to be its "arousal" aspect, and Lindsley considers the low-amplitude alpha waves of anxious subjects to be akin to this "activation" or "arousal" effect.

Fig. 11.10 illustrates the principal structures and interconnexions which are believed to be involved in the central regulation of emotional behaviour, and Lindsley argues that through these mechanisms varying degrees and complexity of activation are possible as a hierarchy of reflex responses progressively involves higher levels of the neuraxis.

Experiments with human subjects designed to elucidate the effects of various central mechanisms are hindered on several counts. Firstly, the relationship between somatic responses and "emotions" is not clear enough to allow any peripheral response to be indicative of emotional arousal. Secondly, there is so little knowledge about the behaviour of autonomic and motor responses as functions of stimulus variation that it is impossible to predict how normal response curves might be altered by central abnormalities.

The cortex and hypothalamus feature so prominently in discussions of both "emotions" and autonomic responses that one of the major problems awaiting attention is that of the relative contributions of these regions to psychological and psychophysiological functions. Although in lower animals the removal of certain cerebral areas may produce profound behavioural changes there is little evidence of clear-cut effects following brain damage in man. This may be due to the fact that analysis of quantitative alterations in specific functions has been neglected in favour of the examination of highly complex "qualitative" behavioural changes. The simultaneous advancement of both physiological and psychological knowledge should provide the material for an interaction of immense promise; what is required from the physiologist is an elucidation of the normal interrelationships of higher nervous mechanisms and more facts about the temporal and spatial effects of agents (such as drugs) which have a depressant or stimulant action on the central nervous system. Psychologists have still to determine more precisely normal behavioural response curves, for example those of adaptation, intensity functions, conditioning and learning. There can be no hard and fast division of labour between the two disciplines. The integration of fact and theory from both will almost inevitably be the outcome of common and frequently joint research effort.

SYNTHESIS AND CONCLUSIONS

The next important task of this chapter is to orientate these experimental data within the wider framework of psychological theory, but before attempting this there are several features which should be emphasized.

First, and of great importance, is the fact that few of the experiments have been repeated; and moreover, even the few repetitions do not invariably support earlier findings. There are three main hindrances to precise replication of the data: (i) the complex (and often highly specific) nature of the *stimuli* employed, (ii) the *measurements* ascertained, which are frequently derived in different ways and may be highly specific to the data, and (iii) the inadequacy of most measures or ratings which form the basis of the selection and grouping of *subjects*.

The unreliability of the measures of somatic systems may reflect the complexity of the physiological mechanisms underlying the functions being recorded but it may also indicate a poor specification of the conditions under which the measurements were obtained, and inadequate instrumentation, techniques and procedures. Such details have been discussed earlier in this chapter because in the absence of general concordance on these points they represent an important, time-consuming part of any experimental study.

The significance of the experimental data on somatic responses to psychology can now be considered in relation to classifications and theories which have already been formulated. The mutual benefit to theory and experimentation which would accrue from the forging of close links between them needs no emphasis. What is urgently required in much of the experimental work in psychophysiology is guidance and purpose; equally, most existing theories are sadly lacking in support from available facts.

Emotions. Sufficient has been said to indicate that the attempt to fit certain responses to particular emotions is, in the absence of any adequate definition of the emotion, fruitless from an experimental point of view. The individual's assessment of a feeling and the complex nature of the stimuli designed to arouse it are not easily brought within experimental control.

Physiological systems. The arguments against classifications based on the morphologic differentiation of nerves, e.g. sympathetic-parasympathetic systems, have been put forward. Some of the variables, e.g. skin resistance and peripheral vasomotor changes have been regarded as relatively uncomplicated indications of sympathetic activity, but even these are affected by many agents, and frequently sympathetic, parasympathetic and endocrine effects all combine and interact to produce an observed response.

Arousal theories, e.g. the continuum of "energy mobilization" proposed by Duffy (1951). The use of physiological measures which may serve as indicators of the intensity dimension, or "behavioural arousal" has recently been discussed by Malmo (1957) and he has extended this concept to integrate the results of investigations into pathological anxiety in psychiatric patients.

It would hardly be questioned that certain physiological variables do closely reflect the activity level of the organism, since lowered physiological levels during sleep and high levels during muscular activity have been repeatedly demonstrated. The attempt to differentiate anxious from non-anxious subjects on the basis of greater arousal in the former appears to be partly a restatement of the implicit assumption or hypothesis underlying most experiments which have already been carried out, although it proposes to extend the range of experimental *conditions*, e.g. from sleep to high arousal, under which measurements are obtained. In view of the rather moderate success of a large number of studies which have attempted to discriminate between anxious and non-anxious subjects on the basis of peripheral measures of autonomic and muscular activity it seems inappropriate to be too optimistic about the general importance of peripheral measures in the "anxiety" of man.[1]

Malmo has, however, drawn a distinction between pathological and transient states of anxiety, and it is possible that a great deal of the research which has been covered in the present review has failed to make such a distinction. He has suggested that, in *pathological* anxiety, some central inhibitory mechanism may be weakened such that stimulating situations will maintain constantly high physiological levels in the anxious subject. Anxiety is considered as a "disease of over arousal," and the critical neural change is thought of as being produced "by a process of attrition from excessive and extended overarousal" (Malmo, 1957).

The investigation of performance and response curves during different levels of physiological arousal is a most promising line of research, and the results of such studies should provide data of great value and interest.

The dimensional analysis of behaviour as carried out by Eysenck (1952). Eysenck has made certain suggestions concerning the underlying mechanism of the dimensions of "neuroticism" and "introversion-extraversion" which can usefully be considered in this context. He claims that neurotics as a group demonstrate over-reactivity of the sympathetic division of the A.N.S. in response to stressful stimuli, but that introverts and extraverts are characterized by the ease and difficulty respectively with which they form conditioned responses. An explanatory concept of inhibition-excitation has been put forward by Eysenck to account for the behaviour of introverts and extraverts, and the evidence for his proposals discussed in *The Dynamics of Anxiety and Hysteria* (Eysenck, 1957).

The inhibitory concept is defined in behavioural, rather than precise physiological terms, but the inhibitory-excitatory function of the cortex has been suggested as a likely central mechanism to integrate such widespread responses as conditioned, learned, and perceptual responses. There is evidence that the cortex does in fact influence somatic and autonomic functions, although there are few experimental data on the quantitative effects.

The results of investigations into physiological responses in psychiatric patients have already been summarized, and in general it can be concluded that few convincing and corroborated data have emerged. The exceptions are a consistently high level of muscle action potentials (particularly of the *frontalis* muscles) and a greater degree of vasoconstriction in anxious patients than in normals. These findings have been demonstrated during relaxation and sleep and also in response to certain sensory stimuli. There is also, perhaps, some evidence that blood-pressure is elevated under certain conditions in anxiety states.

In so far as there is evidence of *increased* physiological activity in anxious patients there may be support for the thesis of a greater excitatory potential (or weakened inhibitory potential) in these subjects. The data on hysterics are very few, but there are reports of lower muscle-action potential and greater vasodilatation in this group.

Explanatory hypotheses which incorporate the notion of inhibitory-excitatory mechanisms undoubtedly help to organize the unsystematic and uncoordinated findings; nevertheless, they suffer from the defect that they cannot bridge the gap between integrating diverse findings and offering reasonably precise guidance about what to expect of specific behavioural responses under specific experimental stimulus conditions. It is difficult, in these circumstances, not to agree with the rather empirical outlook expressed by R. C. Davis who has stressed the need which exists at the present to establish further facts simply about how various somatic responses are modified by stimulus variation. The extent to which these S-R relationships are affected by central mechanisms of inhibition-excitation would link this more empirical approach with the theoretical proposals of Eysenck and Malmo.

It has been strongly suggested that a fundamental experimental approach would *begin* with the analysis of characteristic response functions, and that existing categories such as "emotion" are of less value for the purpose of delineating classes of responses than some basic classification of the responses derived from experimental data. There is, of course, no reason why operational definitions (e.g. that of anxiety as the conditioned form of the pain-fear response) should not provide a useful conceptual framework. It is simply the case that, in the absence of experimental

---

[1] There is evidence (at least in dogs) that peripheral autonomic nerves can be blocked without drastically altering behaviour assumed to relate to anxiety (Wynne and Solomon, 1955). *See also* Cannon's discussion, *Bodily Changes in Pain, Hunger, Fear, and Rage*, Chap. 19 on the role of the viscera in emotional experience.

data on the concomitant autonomic and somatic responses such definitions can be only of potential value.

Learning theory. A great deal of experimental work has been carried out using various indices of "anxiety" in relation to conditioning and learning. Although Solomon and Brush (1956) have admitted that anxiety theories leave many questions open for investigation they maintain that avoidance of strong or noxious stimuli is of great interest because (among other reasons): "The emotion and motivation theorist sees the fear and anxiety concomitants of avoidance behaviour as possibly relatable to complex emotional disturbances in human subjects."

Although certain peripheral A.N.S. responses are considered to indicate a state of anxiety, there is evidence that the blocking of peripheral A.N.S. activity of dogs (Wynne and Solomon, 1955) and adrenalectomy in rats (Applezweig and Bawdry, 1955) do not eliminate escape and avoidance learning although it may be retarded. Solomon and Brush (1956) have proposed an ingenious explanation of findings such as these: they have suggested that the stimulus pattern from the viscera may serve as an important aversive stimulus pattern (drive) in its own right *early* in training: "Later on, when the avoidance response is quick, not so much goes on in the way of peripheral A.N.S. responding (the anxiety conservation principle)[1] but the reinforcing properties of proprioceptive stimuli and C.S. termination now are very important."

There has always been a traditional distinction between the categories of learning and emotion, but it would be argued today that there is no real justification for this. Malmo has recently made the proposal that measures of physiological activity may be usefully employed in the assessment of drive level (Malmo, 1958), and the general activity of the system being conditioned is a very important factor in the ease or difficulty with which conditioning is achieved (Martin, 1960).

Further, there is no basic division between the conditioning process and the phenomena of adaptation and disinhibition which have been discussed in the present chapter: they are all important functions which reflect changes in the C.N.S. to stimulus variation. Any theory which aims to account for these changes is likely to use familiar terms such as drive or arousal level, reactive inhibition, response strength, response latency and reaction threshold—concepts which may profitably be anchored to measurements of somatic responses.

The discussion so far has been based largely on reactions to sensory stimuli, as the simplest case to start with, although even in the case of these relatively

[1] *See* Chapter 13 of this HANDBOOK by Gwynne Jones.

simple stimuli the facts (concerning the responses obtained) are not clear. It is apparent that some qualitatively different stimuli produce reactions more readily than others, and the pattern of the response may differ with the modality of the stimulus employed.

It seems likely that it will be necessary at some time to study the responses which are provoked by *complex* stimulus constellations, not so much because of the sensory attributes of such stimuli but because of the specific significance attached to them by the individual.

In the case of sensory physiology and visual psychophysics the traditional approach has been to work with simple stimuli, the characteristics of which can be specified in terms of physical dimensions (e.g. wave length) and to understand complex functions in terms of what is known about the simple (*see* Chapter 4). This principle almost certainly can fruitfully be applied to the study of autonomic and muscular responses, and indeed there is scattered evidence about the differential reactivity of neurotics to simple sensory stimuli of sound and pain, and of schizophrenics to heat and cold stimulation, which suggests that promising results can be expected from this type of research.

This molecular approach does not, of course, preclude the molar one which seeks to relate complex stimulus constellations to measurable responses: they are mutually supporting rather than mutually exclusive. For example, "lie-detection," claimed by many to have immediate practical usefulness, depends upon the effect of complex stimulus conditions upon measures such as the G.S.R., heart rate and blood-pressure. In this case the immediate usefulness of the technique is undoubtedly related to the significance of the stimulus words. Again, certain test scores may differentiate groups of subjects (e.g. neurotics from normals, cf. the work of Wenger) and so have diagnostic value, or they may predict success and failure at particular jobs.

Promising tests may be discovered without prior analysis of the responses, but, as Eysenck (1952) points out, the responses must subsequently be experimentally analysed, purified, and the new measures used to isolate the relevant factors with greater accuracy.

The biological significance of many of the reactions to simple sensory stimuli remains unclear, but such stimuli have widespread somatic effects which obviously alert the organism, and which may facilitate performance. Many of the general arousing responses show rapid adaptation, while other, more segmental, reflexes are highly resistant to adaptation.

The avoidance reaction set up by stimuli of high intensity is of more evident biological utility. These traumatic stimuli might produce effects of a very different kind (a true "emergency" reaction to avoid tissue damage) from those of more mild stimulation:

there is evidence, for example, that such responses are more resistant to adaptation, and that even the anticipation of strong stimuli might be accompanied by measurable somatic reactions.

There are several hypotheses dealing with the reactions to less than traumatic stimuli. Their "arousal" or "alerting" value has been recognized. As Ackner (1956) has pointed out, in the case of sensory stimuli sensation *per se* is not the cause of the vasoconstrictor response; a cold stimulus does not maintain vasoconstriction, although it may be continuously recognized as cold.

Ackner's view that the vasoconstrictor response is part of an arousal or alerting reaction to a new stimulus situation is closely paralleled by the statements of Sokolov (1957) on what is termed the "orienting reflex." This author, using measures of skin resistance, plethysmograph, and the EEG, has measured changes produced by auditory, visual, tactile, thermal, proprioceptive and pain stimuli of varying intensity, duration and quality. In his discussion of the reaction obtained (the "orienting reflex") he comments: "The essential proof of the orienting nature of these reactions is the fact that they arise in response to every change in the environment, whether the stimulus is switched on or off, increased or decreased, or qualitatively changed."

It has been postulated (Milerian, 1957) that the cortex exercises an essential regulatory influence on the orienting reflex, inhibiting reflexes to stimuli which have no biological significance for the organism; although the physiological mechanisms of the orienting reflex are localized in subcortical centres, its normal function depends upon the interaction of cortex with subcortex.

It has frequently been claimed that the size of a response reflects differences in the conscious assessment of the significance of the stimulus, but in general it has proved difficult to relate different forms of responses to subjective assessments (particularly concerning "feelings") although some success has been claimed concerning degree of interest (Wallerstein, 1954) task difficulty (Davis, 1938) and, as would be expected, between judgements of intensity of stimuli and amplitudes of somatic responses.

Somatic responses may also be related to the quality of performance of certain tasks; it has been shown, for example, how gradients of muscular and other responses may be related to a measure of good performance, and Davis (1956b) has argued that overt responses may be influenced by the amplitude and distribution of pre-performance muscular tensions. The results of experiments dealing with quality or type of certain movements may, therefore, be partially understood in terms of the underlying physiological pattern.

The shape of this chapter has been dictated to a large extent by the paucity of explanatory concepts in a field abundant in detail: it has been guided by the purpose of presenting the available data on functional relationships between quantified stimuli and measurable somatic responses. So much has been done by so many investigators that the almost total lack of replication is not only a hindrance to the integration of "fact" into general theory but itself indicates the task for future research. The stage has been reached where the need for clearly formulated aims, and painstaking check and countercheck of experimental results, is paramount.

REFERENCES

ACKNER, BRIAN, Emotions and the peripheral vasomotor system: a review of previous work, *J. Psychosom. Res.,* **1,** 3–20 (1956a).

ACKNER, BRIAN, The relationship between anxiety and the level of peripheral vasomotor activity: An experimental study, *J. Psychosom. Res.,* **1,** 21–48 (1956b).

ACKNER, BRIAN, A simple method of recording respiration, *J. Psychosom. Res.,* **1,** 144–146 (1956c).

ALTSCHULE, M., *Bodily Physiology in Mental and Emotional Disorders* (New York, Grune & Stratton, 1953).

APPLEZWEIG, M. H. and BAWDRY F. D., The pituitary-adrenocortical system in avoidance learning, *Psychol. Rep.,* **1,** 417–420 (1955).

ARNOLD, MAGDA, Physiological differentiation of emotional states, *Psychol. Rev.,* **52,** 35–48 (1945).

ARNOLD, MAGDA, The status of emotion in contemporary psychology, in *Present-day Psychology*, Ed. A. A. Roback, 135–188 (New York, Philosophical Library, 1955).

AX, ALBERT F., The physiological differentiation between fear and anger in humans, *Psychosom. Med.,* **5,** 433–442 (1953).

BAKER, L. M. and TAYLOR, W. M., The relationship under stress between changes in skin temperature, electrical skin resistance and pulse rate, *J. Exp. Psychol.,* **48,** 361–366 (1954).

BARD, P., On emotional expression after decortication with some remarks on certain theoretical views, I and II, *Psychol. Rev.,* **41,** 309–329, 424–449 (1934).

BARD, P. and MOUNTCASTLE, V. B., Some forebrain mechanisms involved in the expression of rage with special reference to suppression of angry behaviour, *Res. Publ. Ass. Nerv. Ment. Dis.,* **27,** 362–412 (1948).

BARTOSHUK, ALEXANDER K., Electromyographic gradients in goal-directed activity, *Canad. J. Psychol.,* **9,** 21–28 (1955a).

BARTOSHUK, ALEXANDER K., Electromyographic gradients as indicants of motivation, *Canad. J. Psychol.,* **9,** 215–230 (1955b).

BERG, R. L., and BEEBE-CENTER, J. G., Cardiac startle in man, *J. Exp. Psychol.,* **28,** 262–279 (1941).

BLANK, I. H. and FINESINGER, J. E., Electrical resistance of the skin, *Arch. Neurol. Psychiat. Chicago.,* **56,** 544–557 (1946).

Brown, J. S. and Farber, I. E., Emotions conceptualised as intervening variables—with suggestions toward a theory of frustration, *Psychol. Bull.*, **48**, 465–495 (1951).

Cannon, W. B., *Bodily Changes in Pain, Hunger, Fear and Rage* (New York, Appleton-Century, 1920).

Conklin, J. E., Three factors affecting the general level of electrical skin resistance, *Amer. J. Psychol.*, **64**, 78–86 (1951).

Coombs, C. H., Adaptation of the galvanic response to auditory stimuli, *J. Exp. Psychol.*, **22**, 244–268 (1938).

Darling, R. P., Autonomic action in relation to personality traits of children, *J. Abnorm. (Soc.) Psychol.*, **35**, 246–260 (1940).

Darling, R. P. and Darrow, C. W., Determining activity of the autonomic nervous system from measurements of autonomic change, *J. Psychol.*, **5**, 85–89 (1938).

Darrow, C. W., The galvanic skin reflex (sweating) and blood pressure as preparatory and facilitative functions, *Psychol. Bull.*, **33**, 73–94 (1936).

Darrow, C. W., Physiological and clinical tests of autonomic function and autonomic balance, *Physiol. Rev.*, **23**, 1–36 (1943).

Davis, F. H. and Malmo, R. B., Electromyographic recording during interview, *Amer. J. Psychiat.*, **107**, 908–916 (1951).

Davis, J. F., *Manual of Surface Electromyography* (Montreal: Laboratory for Psychological Studies, Allan Memorial Institute of Psychiatry, (mimeo.) 1952).

Davis, J. F., Malmo, R. B. and Shagass, Charles, Electromyographic reaction to strong auditory stimulation in psychiatric patients, *Canad. J. Psychol.*, **8**, 177–186 (1954).

Davis, R. C., Factors affecting the galvanic skin reflex, *Arch. Psychol. N.Y.*, **18**, No. 115 (1930).

Davis, R. C., Modification of the galvanic reflex by daily repetition of a stimulus, *J. Exp. Psychol.*, **17**, 504–535 (1934).

Davis, R. C., Relation of muscle action potentials to difficulty and frustration, *J. Exp. Psychol.*, **23**, 141–158 (1938).

Davis, R. C., Patterns of muscular activity during "mental work" and their constancy, *J. Exp. Psychol.*, **24**, 451–465 (1939).

Davis, R. C., Set and muscular tension, *Ind. Univ. Publ.*, No. 10 (1940).

Davis, R. C., Methods of measuring muscular tension, *Psychol Bull.*, **39**, 329–346 (1942).

Davis, R. C., An integrator and accessory apparatus for recording action potentials, *Amer. J. Psychol.*, **61**, 100–104 (1948a).

Davis, R. C., Motor effects of strong auditory stimuli, *J. Exp. Psychol.*, **38**, 257–275 (1948b).

Davis, R. C., Motor responses to auditory stimuli above and below threshold, *J. Exp. Psychol.*, **40**, 107–120 (1950).

Davis, R. C., Physical Psychology, *Psychol. Rev.*, **60**, 7–14 (1953).

Davis, R. C., Response and adaptation to brief noises of high intensity, *School of Aviation Medicine, U.S.A.F. Report* No. 55–127 (1956a).

Davis, R. C., The relation of muscular tension to performance, *School of Aviation Medicine, U.S.A.F. Report* No. 55–122 (1956b).

Davis, R. C., Muscular activity during steady noise and its relation to instructed responses evoked by auditory signals, *School of Aviation Medicine, U.S.A.F., Reports* Nos. 55–124, and 55–126 (1956c).

Davis, R. C. and Van Liere, D. W., Adaptation of the muscular tension response to gunfire, *J. Exp. Psychol.*, **39**, 114–117 (1949).

Davis, R. C., Buchwald, Alexander M. and Frankmann, R. W., Autonomic and muscular responses, and their relation to simple stimuli, *Psychol. Monogr.*, No. 405, **69**, No. 20 (1955).

Duffy, Elizabeth, The concept of energy mobilisation, *Psychol. Rev.*, **58**, 30–40 (1951).

Duffy, Elizabeth and Lacey, O. L., Adaptation in energy mobilisation: changes in general level of palmar skin conductance, *J. Exp. Psychol.*, **36**, 437–452 (1946).

Ellson, D. G., Davis, R. C., Saltzman, I. J. and Burke, C. J., Report of research on the detection of perception, *Contract N6onr—18011, ONR*, 1952.

Eppinger, H. and Hess, L., *Die Vagotonie* (Berlin, 1910).

Eysenck, H. J., *The Scientific Study of Personality* (London, Routledge & Kegan Paul, 1952).

Eysenck, H. J., *The Structure of Human Personality* (London, Methuen, 1953).

Eysenck, H. J., *The Dynamics of Anxiety and Hysteria* (London, Routledge & Kegan Paul, 1957).

Eysenck, S. B. G., An experimental study of psychogalvanic reflex responses of normal, neurotic and psychotic subjects, *J. Psychosom. Res.*, **1**, 258–272 (1956).

Fetcher, E. S., Hall, J. F., Jr. and Shaub, H. G., The skin temperature of an extremity as a measure of its blood flow, *Science*, **110**, 422 (1949).

Finkelman, I. and Stephens, W. M., Heat regulation in dementia praecox. Reactions of patients with dementia praecox to cold, *J. Neurol. Psychopath.*, **16**, 321–340 (1936).

Flecker, R., Skin temperature as a psychophysical variable, *Austr. J. Psychol.*, **3**, 109–120 (1951).

Freeman, G. L., Methodological evaluation of the galvanic skin response, with special reference to the formula for R.Q., *J. Exp. Psychol.*, **31**, 239–248 (1942).

Freeman, G. L., *The Energetics of Human Behavior* (New York, Cornell Univ. Press, 1948).

Freeman, G. L. and Katzoff, E. T., Individual differences in physiological reactions to emotional stimulation and their relation to other measures of emotionality, *J. Exp. Psychol.*, **31**, 527–537 (1942).

Freeman, G. L. and Simpson, R. M., The effect of experimentally induced muscular tension upon palmar skin resistance, *J. Gen. Psychol.*, **18**, 319–326 (1938).

Freeman, H., Skin and body temperatures of schizophrenic and normal subjects under varying environmental conditions, *Arch. Neurol. Psychiat. Chicago*, **42**, 724–734 (1939).

Fulton, J. F. (Ed.), *A Textbook of Physiology*, 16th Edn. (Philadelphia, Saunders, 1950).

Funkenstein, D. H., King, S. H. and Drolette, Margaret, The direction of anger during a laboratory stress-inducing situation, *Psychosom. Med.*, **16**, 404–413 (1954).

FUNKENSTEIN, D. H., KING, S. H. and DROLETTE, MARGARET, *Mastery of Stress* (Cambridge, Mass., Harvard Univ. Press, 1957).

GELLHORN, ERNEST, *Physiological Foundations of Neurology and Psychiatry* (Minneapolis, Univ. of Minnesota Press, 1953).

GOETZ, R. H., Effects of changes in posture on peripheral circulation with special reference to skin temperature readings and plethysmogram, *Circulation*, 1, 56–75 (1950).

GRANGER, G. W., Personality and visual perception: a review, *J. Ment. Sci.*, 99, 8–43 (1953).

HAMILTON, MAX, *Psychosomatics* (London, Chapman & Hall Ltd., 1955).

HELSON, H., and QUANTIUS, L., Changes in skin temperature following intense stimulation, *J. Exp. Psychol.*, 17, 20–35 (1934).

HERTZMAN, A. B., RANDALL, W. C. and JOCHIM, K. E., The estimation of the cutaneous blood flow with the photoelectric plethysmograph, *Amer. J. Physiol.*, 145, 716–726 (1946).

HESS, W. R., *Diencephalon. Autonomic and Extrapyramidal Functions* (London, William Heinemann (Medical Books) Ltd., 1954).

HICKAM, J. B., CARGILL, W. H. and GOLDEN, A., Cardiovascular reactions to emotional stimuli: effect on the cardiac output, arteriovenous oxygen difference, arterial pressure, and peripheral resistance, *J. Clin. Invest.*, 27, 290–298 (1948).

HOVLAND, C. L. and RIESEN, A. H., Magnitude of galvanic and vasomotor response as a function of stimulus intensity, *J. Gen. Psychol.*, 23, 103–121 (1940).

INMAN, V. T., RALSTON, H. J., SAUNDERS, J. B. DE C. M., FEINSTEIN, B. and WRIGHT, E. W. JR., Relation of human electromyogram to muscular tension, *EEG & Clinical Neurophysiology*, 4, 187–194 (1952).

JACOBSON, E., Electrophysiology of mental activities, *Amer. J. Psychol.*, 44, 677–694 (1932).

JAMES, H. E. O. and THOULESS, R. H., A note on the effect of polarization in psychogalvanic experiments, *Brit. J. Psychol.*, 17, 49–53 (1926).

JAMES, WILLIAMS, *Principles of Psychology.* Vol. II (London, Macmillan, 1902).

JASPER, HERBERT, GLOOR, PETER and MILNER, BRENDA, Higher functions of the nervous system, *Annu. Rev. Physiol.*, 18, 359–386 (1956).

JEFFRESS, L. A., Galvanic phenomena of the skin, *J. Exp. Psychol.*, 11, 130–144 (1928).

JOST, H. and SONTAG, L. W., The genetic factor in autonomic nervous system function, *Psychosom. Med.*, 6, 308–310 (1944).

JURKO, M., JOST, H. and HILL, T., Pathology of the energy system: An experimental-clinical study of physiological adaptive capacities in a non-patient, a psycho-neurotic, and an early paranoid schizophrenic group *J. Psychol.*, 33, 183–198 (1952).

KATZ, L. N. and LEITER, L., The present conception of "essential hypertension," *Psychosom. Med.*, 1, 101–117 (1939).

KENNARD, MARGARET, Autonomic interrelations with the somatic nervous system, *Psychosom. Med.*, 9, 29–36 (1947).

KENNEDY, J. L. and TRAVIS, R. C., Prediction and automatic control of alertness. II. Continuous tracking, *J. Comp. Physiol. Psychol.*, 41, 208–310 (1948).

KIVISTO, P., Group differences in electrocardiographic responses, *Amer. J. Psychiat.*, 109, 858–860 (1953).

KLEITMAN, N., *Sleep and Wakefulness* (Chicago, Univ. of Chicago Press, 1939).

KUNO, Y., The significance of sweating in man, *Lancet*, 1, 912–915 (1930).

KUNTZ, A., *The Autonomic Nervous System* (Philadelphia, Lee & Febiger, 1953).

LACEY, J. I., The evaluation of autonomic responses: toward a general solution, *Ann. N.Y. Acad. Sci.*, 67, 123–164 (1956).

LACEY, J. I. and LACEY, BEATRICE C., The relationship of resting autonomic activity to motor impulsivity, *Res. Publ. Ass. Nerv. Ment. Dis.*, 36, 144–209 (1958).

LACEY, J. I. and VANLEHN, RUTH, Differential emphasis in somatic response to stress. An experimental study, *Psychosom. Med.*, 14, 71–81 (1952).

LACEY, J. I., BATEMAN, DOROTHY E. and VAN LEHN, RUTH, Autonomic response specificity. An experimental study, *Psychosom. Med.*, 15, 8–21 (1953).

LANDIS, C., Electrical phenomena of the skin, *Psychol. Bull.*, 29, 693–752 (1932).

LANDIS, C. and HUNT, W. A., *The Startle Pattern* (New York, Farrar & Rinehart, 1939).

LEVINE, A. and SCHILDER, P., The catatonic pupil, *J. Nerv. Ment. Dis.*, 96, 1–12 (1942).

LINDSLEY, D. B., Emotion, in *Handbook of Experimental Psychology*, Ed. S. S. Stevens, 473–516 (New York, John Wiley & Sons, Inc., 1951).

LOWENSTEIN, O., Clinical diagnosis of disturbance of the central sympathetic system by means of pupillography, *Arch. Neurol. Psychiat. Chicago.*, 55, 682–684 (1946).

LOWENSTEIN, O. and WESTPHAL, A., Experimentelle und klinische Studien zur Physiologie und Pathologie der Pupillenbewegungen mit besonderer Berücksichtigung der Schizophrenie, *Abh. Neurol. Psychiat. Psychol.*, 70, 1–81 (1933).

LOWENSTEIN, O. and LOEWENFELD, IRENE, The mutual role of the sympathetic and parasympathetic in the shaping of the pupillary reflex to light, *Arch. Neurol. Psychiat. Chicago.*, 64, 313–340 (1950a).

LOWENSTEIN, O. and LOEWENFELD, IRENE, The role of the sympathetic and parasympathetic systems in reflex dilatation of the pupil. *Arch. Neurol. Psychiat. Chicago*, 64, 341–377 (1950b).

LOWENSTEIN, O. and LOEWENFELD, IRENE, Types of central autonomic innervation and fatigue. Pupillographic studies, *Arch. Neurol. Psychiat. Chicago*, 66, 580–599 (1951).

LOWENSTEIN, O. and LOEWENFELD, IRENE, Disintegration of central autonomic regulation during fatigue and its reintegration by psychosensory controlling mechanisms: I. Disintegration. Pupillographic studies, *J. Nerv. Ment. Dis.*, 115, 1–21 (1952a).

LOWENSTEIN, O. and LOEWENFELD, IRENE, Disintegration of central autonomic regulation during fatigue and its reintegration by psychosensory controlling mechanisms: II. Reintegration, *J. Nerv. Ment. Dis.*, 115, 121–145 (1952b).

MACLEAN, P. D., Studies in the limbic system, in *Recent Developments in Psychosomatic Medicine*, Eds. E. D. Wittkower and R. A. Cleghorn (London, Pitman, 1954).

MALMO, R. B., Anxiety and behavioural arousal, *Psychol. Rev.*, **64**, 276–287 (1957).

MALMO, R. B., Measurement of drive: an unsolved problem in psychology, in *Nebraska Symposium on Motivation*, Vol. 6. Ed. M. R. Jones 229–265 (Lincoln, Nebraska, Univ. of Nebraska Press, 1958).

MALMO, R. B. and DAVIS, J. F., Physiological gradients as indicants of "arousal" in mirror tracing, *Canad. J. Psychol.*, **10**, 231–238 (1956).

MALMO, R. B. and SHAGASS, C., Physiologic studies of reaction to stress in anxiety and early schizophrenia, *Psychosom. Med.*, **11**, 9–24 (1949*a*).

MALMO, R. B. and SHAGASS, C., Physiologic study of symptom mechanisms in psychiatric patients under stress, *Psychosom. Med.*, **11**, 25–29 (1949*b*).

MALMO, R. B. and SHAGASS, C., Studies of blood pressure in psychiatric patients under stress, *Psychosom. Med.*, **14**, 82–93 (1952).

MALMO, R. B., SHAGASS, C. and DAVIS, F. H., Symptom specificity and bodily reactions during psychiatric interview, *Psychosom Med.*, **12**, 362–376 (1950).

MALMO, R. B., SHAGASS, C. and DAVIS, J. F., Electromyographic studies of muscular tension in psychiatric patients under stress, *J. Clin. Exp. Psychopath.*, **12**, 45–66 (1951).

MALMO, R. B., SHAGASS, C. and SMITH, A. A., Responsiveness in chronic schizophrenia, *J. Personality*, **19**, 359–375 (1951).

MALMO, R. B., SHAGASS, C. and HESLAM, R. M., Blood pressure response to repeated brief stress in psychoneurosis: a study of adaptation, *Canad. J. Psychol.*, **5**, 167–179 (1951).

MALMO, R. B. and SMITH, A. A., Forehead tension and motor irregularities in psychoneurotic patients under stress, *J. Personality*, **23**, 391–406 (1955).

MALMO, R. B. and WALLERSTEIN, H., Rigidity and reactive inhibition, *J. Abnorm. (Soc.) Psychol.*, **50**, 345–348 (1955).

MARTIN, IRENE, Levels of muscle activity in psychiatric patients, *Acta Psychologica*, Hague, **12**, 326–341 (1956).

MARTIN, IRENE, Variations in skin resistance and their relationship to G.S.R. conditioning, *J. Ment. Sci.* (to be published).

MAY, P. R. A., Pupillary abnormalities in schizophrenia and during muscular effort, *J. Ment. Sci.*, **94**, 89–98 (1948).

MCCLEARY, R. A., The nature of the galvanic skin response, *Psychol. Bull.*, **47**, 97–115 (1950).

MEYER, D. R., On the interaction of simultaneous responses, *Psychol. Bull.*, **50**, 204–220 (1953).

MILERIAN, E. A., Involuntary attention, in *Psychology in the Soviet Union*, Ed. Brian Simon (London, Routledge & Kegan Paul Ltd., 1957).

MOWRER, O. H., *Learning Theory and Personality Dynamics* (New York, Ronald Press, 1950).

MOWRER, O. H. *et al.*, *Psychotherapy. Theory and Research* (New York, Ronald Press, 1953).

MUNDY-CASTLE, A. C. and MCKIEVER, B. L., The psychophysiological significance of the galvanic skin response, *J. Exp. Psychol.*, **46**, 15–24 (1953).

NAFE, J. P. and WAGONER, K. S., The effect of thermal stimulation upon dilation and constriction of the blood vessels of the skin of a contralateral hand, *J. Psychol.*, **2**, 461–477 (1936).

NAFE, J. P. and WAGONER, K. S., The effect of pain upon peripheral blood volume, *Amer. J. Psychol.*, **51**, 118–126 (1938).

NYBOER, JAN, Plethysmograph: Impedance, in *Medical Physics*, Ed. O. Glasser, 736–743 (Chicago, Year Book Pub., 1947).

O'CONNOR, N. and VENABLES, P. H., A note on the basal level of skin conductance and Binet I.Q., *Brit. J. Psychol.*, **47**, 148–149 (1956).

OLDS, J., Physiological Mechanisms of Reward, in *Nebraska Symposium on Motivation*, Vol. 3, Ed. M. R. Jones, 73–139 (Lincoln, Nebraska, Univ. of Nebraska Press, 1955).

PAINTAL, A. S., A comparison of the galvanic skin responses of normals and psychotics, *J. Exp. Psychol.*, **41**, 425–428 (1951).

PICKERING, G. W., *High Blood Pressure* (London, Churchill, 1955).

PLUTCHIK, R., The psychophysiology of skin temperature: a critical review, *J. Gen. Psychol.*, **55**, 249–268 (1956).

PLUTCHIK, R. and GREENBLATT, M., Temperature changes of the skin: a function of initial level, *Amer. J. Psychol.*, **69**, 403–409 (1956).

RANSON, S. W., Some functions of the hypothalamus, *Harvey Lect. Ser.* 32 (Baltimore, Williams & Wilkins, 1937).

REISER, M. F., FERRIS, E. B. and LEVINE, M., Cardiovascular disorders, heart disease and hypertension, in *Recent Developments in Psychosomatic Medicine*, Ed. E. D. Wittkower and R. A. Cleghorn (London, Pitman, 1954).

REISER, M. F., REEVES, R. B. and ARMINGTON, J., Effect of variations in laboratory procedure and experimenter upon the ballistocardiogram, blood pressure, and heart rate in healthy young men, *Psychosom. Med.*, **17**, 185–199 (1955).

RICHTER, D., Biochemical aspects of schizophrenia, in *Schizophrenia. Somatic Aspects*, Ed. D. Richter (London, Pergamon Press, 1957).

ROTHMAN, S., The role of the autonomic nervous system in cutaneous disorders, *Psychosom. Med.*, **7**, 90–94 (1945).

ROTHMAN, S., *Physiology and Biochemistry of the Skin* (Chicago, Univ. of Chicago Press, 1954).

SAINSBURY, P. and GIBSON, J. J., Symptoms of anxiety and tension and the accompanying physiological changes in the muscular system, *J. Neurol. Psychiat.*, **17**, 216–224 (1954).

SCHLOSBERG, H., Three dimensions of emotion, *Psychol. Rev.*, **61**, 81–88 (1954).

SHAGASS, C. and MALMO, R. B., Psychodynamic themes and localised muscular tension during psychotherapy, *Psychosom. Med.*, **16**, 295–313 (1954).

SHAGASS, C. and NAIMAN, J., The sedation threshold as an objective index of manifest anxiety in psychoneurosis, *J. Psychosom. Res.*, **1**, 49–57 (1956).

SHATTOCK, F. M., The somatic manifestations of schizophrenia. A clinical study of their significance, *J. Ment. Sci.*, **96**, 32–142 (1950).

SHAW, W. A., The distribution of muscle action potentials during imaging, *Psychol. Rec.*, **2**, 192–215 (1938).

SHEARD, C., Temperature of skin and thermal regulation of the body, in *Medical Physics*, Ed. O. Glasser, 1,523–1,555 (Chicago, Year Book Pub., 1947).

SILVERMAN, J. J. and POWELL, V. E., Studies on palmar sweating: III. Palmar sweating in an army general hospital, *Psychosom. Med.*, **6**, 243–249 (1944).

SMITH, A. A., An electromyographic study of tension in interrupted and completed tasks, *J. Exp. Psychol.*, **46**, 32–36 (1953).

SMITH, A. A., MALMO, R. B. and SHAGASS, C., An electromyographic study of listening and talking, *Canad. J. Psychol.*, **8**, 219–227 (1954).

SOKOLOV, E. N., Higher nervous activity and the problem of perception, in *Psychology in the Soviet Union*, Ed. Brian Simon (London, Routledge & Kegan Paul, 1957).

SOLOMON, R. L. and WYNNE, L. C., Traumatic avoidance learning: the principles of anxiety conservation and partial irreversibility, *Psychol. Rev.*, **61**, 353–385 (1954).

SOLOMON, R. L. and BRUSH, ELINOR, S., Experimentally derived conceptions of anxiety and aversion, in *Nebraska Symposium on Motivation*, Vol. 4, Ed. M. R. Jones 213–305 (Lincoln, Nebraska, Univ. of Nebraska Press, 1956).

SPRINGER, N. N., Cardiac activity during emotion, *Amer. J. Psychol.*, **47**, 670–677 (1935).

SURWILLO, W. W., Psychological factors in muscle-action potentials: EMG gradients, *J. Exp. Psychol.*, **52**, 263–272 (1956).

TERRY, R. A., Autonomic balance and temperament, *J. Comp. Physiol. Psychol.*, **46**, 454–460 (1953).

THERON, P. A., Peripheral vasomotor reactions as indices of basic emotional tension and lability, *Psychosom. Med.*, **10**, 335–346 (1948).

THOMAS, P. E. and KORR, I. M., Sweat gland activity and electrical resistance of the skin, *J. Appl. Physiol.*, **10**, 505–510 (1957).

THOULESS, R. H., The causes of the continuous changes of resistance observed in psychogalvanic experiments, *Brit. J. Psychol.*, **16**, 5–15 (1925).

TRAVIS, L. E. and LINDSLEY, D. B., The relation of frequency and extent of action currents to intensity of muscular contraction, *J. Exp. Psychol.*, **14**, 359–381 (1931).

VAN DER MERWE, A. B., The diagnostic value of peripheral vasomotor reactions in the psychoneuroses, *Psychosom. Med.*, **10**, 347–354 (1948).

VAN DER MERWE, A. B. and THERON, P. A., A new method of measuring emotional stability, *J. Gen. Psychol.*, **37**, 109–124 (1947).

VENABLES, P. H., The relationships between P.G.R. scores and temperature and humidity, *Quart. J. Exp. Psychol.*, **7**, 12–18 (1955).

WALLERSTEIN, H., An electromyographic study of attentive listening, *Canad. J. Psychol.*, **8**, 228–238 (1954).

WANG, G. H., The galvanic skin reflex. A review of old and recent works from a physiologic point of view. Part 1, *Amer. J. Phys. Med.*, **36**, 295–320 (1957).

WANG, G. H., The galvanic skin reflex. A review of old and recent works from a physiologic point of view. Part 2, *Amer. J. Phys. Med.*, **37**, 35–57 (1958).

WENGER, M. A., The measurement of individual differences in autonomic balance, *Psychosom. Med.*, **3**, 427–434 (1941).

WENGER, M. A., Studies of autonomic balance in army air forces personnel, *Comp. Psychol. Mon.*, **19**, No. 4 (1948).

WENGER, M. A., Pattern analysis of autonomic variables during rest, *Psychosom. Med.*, **19**, 240–244 (1957).

WENGER, M. A. and GILCHRIST, J. C., A comparison of two indices of palmar sweating, *J. Exp. Psychol.*, **38**, 757–761 (1948).

WENGER, M. A. and IRWIN, O. C., Fluctuations in skin resistance of infants and adults in their relation to muscular processes, in *Studies in Infant Behaviour*. III. *Univ. Ia Stud. Child Welf.*, **12**, No. 1 (1936).

WHITE, M. M., The relation of bodily tension to electrical resistance, *J. Exp. Psychol.*, **13**, 267–277 (1930).

WOLFF, H. G., *Headache and Other Head Pain* (New York, Oxford Univ. Press, 1948).

WOODWORTH, R. S. and SCHLOSBERG, H., *Experimental Psychology* (London, Methuen, 1954).

WYNNE, L. C. and SOLOMON, R. L., Traumatic avoidance learning: acquisition and extinction in dogs deprived of normal peripheral autonomic functioning, *Genet. Psychol. Monogr.*, **52**, 241–284 (1955).

CHAPTER 12

Conditioning and Abnormal Behaviour

CYRIL M. FRANKS

INTRODUCTION

DESPITE half a century of experimental investigation and remarkable advances in laboratory technology there is as yet little agreement concerning the relative influences and importance of such fundamental parameters of the conditioning process as the intensity of the unconditioned stimulus or the relationship between conditionability and age. Furthermore, neither the neurophysiological mechanisms by which a conditioned response is established, nor even the site or sites of action have been determined with any degrees of confidence. It is not known whether it is meaningful to use the term "conditionability" at all with reference to any individual or animal, and the existence of a general factor remains yet to be demonstrated. There is little agreement concerning the delimitation of the term *conditioned response*, or what aspects of behaviour should be included in this category. For example, Konorski (1948) includes both classical and instrumental conditioning, whereas Thorpe (1956) limits his definition to the classical or Pavlovian variety. Bearing this situation in mind

and the fact that there is no universally recognized theory of learning, it is hardly surprising that the relationship between conditioning and learning is a matter of controversy and that no adequate or generally accepted theory of conditioning has yet emerged.

The primary purpose of this chapter is not to review such problems (this has been done elsewhere, Franks, 1958b), but to attempt an integration of a series of laboratory experiments into a theory of conditioning as it relates to personality and, in particular, as it relates to the aetiology, diagnosis and treatment of certain psychiatric abnormalities. The orientation of the author may be described as operational behaviourism; on the conditioning side, instigated by the vague and often internally inconsistent concepts of Pavlov and by the more precisely formulated, but also sometimes inconsistent, postulates of Hull; on the personality side, making considerable use of the dimensional system as described by Eysenck and his associates.

CONDITIONING AND PERSONALITY: DEVELOPMENT OF A THEORY

Previous Investigations

Before presenting a consistent theory of conditioning and personality it will be salutary to consider briefly the chaotic scene. In one form or another almost every aspect of temperament and mental abnormality has been presented as a consequence or malfunction of some conditioned response mechanism. For example, Freeman (1948) tried to treat negative adaptation in life situations as a kind of inhibitory conditioning and positive adaptation as a form of facilitatory conditioning, while Lovell and Morgan (1953) have managed to account for the development of a complex in similar terms. Murphy (1947) has even explained such deep-rooted personality traits as thrift as a result of conditioning, making use of an elaborate

system in which two processes, canalization and conditioning, account for all learned action patterns.

Gantt (1953b) has tried to formulate the principles that precipitate a neurotic breakdown in terms of a cleavage or dysfunction between the emotional, visceral and motor conditioned responses, while Liddell (1950) believes that the "choice" of neurotic breakdown induced in his animals is independent of breed or temperament. He believes that the intertrial intervals in the conditioning situation are the deciding factors; thus short intertrial intervals produced tonic immobility in his goats, whereas long intertrial intervals produced a chronic state of agitation or hyperexcitability. From these data Liddell somewhat vaguely speculated that the choice of neurosis is a

457

function of certain time constants in the central nervous system. Laughlin (1956) interprets adult neurosis as a product of earlier traumatic conditioning in childhood in a manner not too different from the psychoanalytic concept of the origins of traumatic neurosis, while Stogdill (1934) has made an interesting, but unfortunately largely anecdotal, attempt to formulate a theory of neurosis based almost entirely on learning and conditioning.

However, the conditioned response theory of neuroses which has the most influence on psychiatric thinking is undoubtedly that of Pavlov (1927, 1928, 1941, 1951, 1955), whose system is too well known to require elaboration here and, in any case, is too internally inconsistent and complex to describe in a few summary statements. Using one or more variations of Pavlov's techniques, experimental "neuroses" have been induced in all kinds of animals by numerous workers and it is remarkable how closely the abnormal behaviour symptoms induced artificially in animals resemble those obtaining in the neurotic human (e.g. Anderson and Liddell, 1935; Gordon, 1948; Liddell, 1956). It is of more relevant interest that similar techniques are also effective in producing experimental neuroses in humans (Freeman, 1940; Krasnogorski, 1925). (cf. Chapter 19 of this HANDBOOK by P. Broadhurst.)

One consequence of the inextricable confusion permeating Pavlov's writings, as presented in the English language, is the emergence of numerous and sometimes conflicting psychiatric systems supposed to be largely based on Pavlovian psychology. Of these probably the most well known, outside the Soviet Union, are Salter's desultory and superficial excitation theory (1949), Wolpe's reciprocal condition inhibition theory (1954), and, more recently, Sargant's (1957) admirable, if limited, extension to the treatment of various forms of war neuroses and the mechanics of political indoctrination and "brain-washing."

Of these three variations that of Wolpe is the least unsatisfactory. He regards neurotic behaviour as persistent, unadaptive conditioned or learned behaviour in which anxiety is almost always prominent; he presents considerable supporting evidence for his theory, and, unlike many psychiatrists, he is careful to state what he means by "anxiety." According to Wolpe, successful therapy depends upon the successful inhibition of these learned neurotic response patterns, and he presents detailed descriptions of the techniques by means of which this situation may be brought about. Like Dollard and Miller (1950), Wolpe leans heavily on Hullian learning theory but differs from these authors in several important respects. First, unlike Dollard and Miller, Wolpe does not accept the psychoanalytic account of what is supposed to happen to the patient during therapy. Second, he does not regard extinction as the main mechanism by means of which neurotic habits may be eliminated. Wolpe parts company with the more conventional Pavlovian therapists in his rejection of straightforward protective inhibition as a major therapeutic device. In its place he substitutes a complex and not very clear concept of reciprocal conditioned inhibition which is supposed to be the basis of most fundamental psychotherapeutic effects (cf. Chapter 20 of this HANDBOOK by H. Gwynne Jones).

It might be imagined that one essential prerequisite to the development of any conditioned response theory of personality and mental abnormality would be a detailed examination of the conditionability of various personality types and neurotic subgroups. Individual differences in conditionability have long been observed and there have been some attempts to describe different types of people according to the way they form conditioned responses, these experiments being carried out mainly with normal children (Cowan and Foulke, 1934; Ivanov-Smolensky, 1927a; Osipova, 1926; Pen, 1933). James (1934) differentiated twenty dogs into excitable and inhibitable types on the basis of their behaviour during the establishment of conditioned salivary discrimination. He believed that there must be a correlation between morphological form and behaviour type. In a similar manner Marinesco and Kreindler (1934), following Kretschmer's classification, noted corresponding patterns of conditioned response behaviour in children. But, with the exception of the anxious subject, remarkably few studies have been made of particular personality subgroups, and most investigators have confined themselves to the analysis of the conditionability of neurotics as a unitary group. This extensive concentration on studies of anxious states is possibly attributable to the ready availability of anxious individuals, both inside and outside psychiatric institutions, and also to the widespread interest which the problem of anxiety engenders both in clinical and research circles.

With the exception of Darrow and Heath (1932), who found no consistent relationship between neuroticism as measured by a personality questionnaire and P.G.R. conditionability, most investigators report that neurotic patients condition more readily and more strongly than normal subjects (e.g. Finesinger, Sutherland and McGuire, 1942; Fink, 1943; Schilder, 1929). Spence and Taylor (1952) compared eyeblink conditioning in normal, neurotic and psychotic subjects, predicting that because of the greater manifest anxiety both neurotics and psychotics would condition more easily than normals. However, they found that although the psychotics conditioned significantly more easily than the other two groups, the neurotic and normal groups differed insignificantly.

It is important to note that they neither related the amount of conditioning to the diagnosis of their neurotics, nor even stated what kinds of neurotics were included in their sample. A probable explanation of the finding that, in most, but not all, studies of conditioning in neurotics, the neurotics were found to condition more readily than normals will be offered shortly.

One of the few relevant facts that seem to be well established is that anxious subjects condition more easily than those who are relatively non-anxious. Welch (1953), in his review, concludes that pathological anxiety tends to produce more rapid conditioning and more slow extinction. This has been demonstrated for the P.G.R. (e.g. Schiff, Dougan and Welch, 1949; Welch and Kubis, 1947a, 1947b) and for the conditioned eyeblink response (e.g. Hilgard, Jones and Kaplan, 1951; Spence and Farber, 1953; Spence and Taylor, 1951; Taylor, 1951). The precise relationship between anxiety and conditioning apparently depends, among other things, on the measure of anxiety used. Thus Berry and Martin (1957) found no relationship between P.G.R. conditioning and the Sarason Test Anxiety Scale, whereas Welch and his associates found a positive relationship when clinical criteria were used to measure anxiety (Schiff, Dougan and Welch, 1949; Welch and Kubis, 1947a, 1947b).

The development of a reliable measure of individual differences in anxiety is of both practical and theoretical importance. One difficulty, as Kamin (1957) points out, is that the kind of threat manipulatable by experimentation and the anxiety of psychiatric patients may be mutually irrelevant. Jenkins and Lykken (1957) present further objections to the unitary concept of anxiety and there is little doubt that anxiety is a concept which is essentially further resolvable (Franks, 1956c).

Of the many attempts to provide objective measures of anxiety, reviewed elsewhere (Franks, 1956c), Taylor's scale is the best known. Taylor herself (1956) provides a recent review of the many uses of her scale, especially in relation to Hullian drive theory. In particular, her scale has been used by Spence and his associates to make predictions about eyelid conditioning. Working within a Hullian framework, in which behaviour is supposed to be a multiplicative function of a learning variable ($_sH_R$) and a motivational or drive variable (D), they have made certain predictions concerning the conditionability of anxious subjects. Arguing that total effective drive strength is, in part, a function of the manifest anxiety of the individual, they assume, like Miller (1948) and Mowrer (1939), that anxious subjects have a higher drive than less anxious subjects. Hence Spence and Taylor predicted that subjects scoring high on Taylor's Scale would

condition more readily than subjects who obtain only low scores (Farber and Spence, 1953; Spence and Farber, 1953; Spence and Taylor, 1951; Taylor, 1951; Spence, 1956).

In general their findings support this prediction, although the relationship obtained was often tenuous and sometimes even insignificant. Furthermore, in many cases this relationship became apparent only when extreme groups were compared. Nevertheless, despite these confusing and apparently conflicting results, there is adequate reason to assume that a positive relationship between anxiety and conditioning does exist. Some of this confusion, for example the occasional poor results of Spence and his colleagues, will become understandable at a later stage in this chapter.

Apart from the anxiety states, little attention has been paid to other kinds of neurotics. It is a remarkable fact that, although the aetiology of treatment of the hysterical disorders has evoked considerable attention from peripatetic psychiatrists interested in conditioning theory, the fundamental issue of the ease of the conditionability of the hysteric has, with very few exceptions, been ignored in favour of conjecture and supposition based on so called clinical experience. Some valuable experimentally derived data are, however, available.

Tinel and Michon (1928), in an intensive study of one case of hysteria, were able to demonstrate the role of the conditioned reflex based upon the occurrence of an initial trauma, (the evidence in favour of one trial learning will be presented at a later stage in this chapter). The experimental induction of a "conversion symptom" has been demonstrated by Liddell (1944) who, by the application of conditioning techniques, induced a limb rigidity in a sheep which persisted for several years after the animal was removed from the original situation. McGill and Welch (1947)[1] and Kennedy (1940) have produced a conditioned response theory of hysteria and its treatment; both projects unfortunately omitted first to investigate the basic conditionability of their hysteric groups. In view of data to be presented shortly to the effect that hysterics condition poorly, this makes the advocation of reconditioning therapy of limited value unless combined with the use of various drugs and other procedures which have been shown to modify the ability to form, retain and extinguish conditioned responses.

Although it is probably more difficult to establish conditioned responses in hysterics, there are many examples that such a procedure can become effective

[1] Welch, at least, is aware that the conditioning process in hysterics may well be "difficult and exceptional" and, in two of his publications (Welch and Kubis 1947a, 1947b), provides incidental comments to this effect.

under certain conditions. Sears and Cohen (1933) were able to establish a conditioned response in a case of hysterical anaesthesia, but *only* by utilizing the principle of irradiation from one sense modality to another; it could not be established by simple reinforcement or by irradiation within the same sense modality from one part of the body to another. Cohen and his colleagues (Cohen, Hilgard and Wendt, 1933) also succeeded in conditioning an hysterically "blind" eye to respond to a light stimuli. Warren and Grant (1955) found that conditioned eyeblink discrimination was less in a group of subjects scoring high on the psychopathic deviate (Pd) scale of the M.M.P.I. than in those subjects with low Pd scores. Lykken (1957), in a study to be considered in some detail at a later stage, made an important contribution to the meagre knowledge concerning the conditionability of various kinds of psychopaths. His otherwise excellent study is marred by a failure to compare his psychopaths and normals with a group of dysthymics.

Since little attention has been given to the conditionability of specific neurotic subgroups, it is inevitable that even less attention has been given to a *comparison* of the conditionability of various subgroups. Darrow and Heath (1932) report that their extraverts, as measured by a personality questionnaire, tend to form conditioned P.G.R. responses slightly more readily than their introverts. However, these findings are of almost no value since the questionnaire used is, at best, of doubtful validity. Their introversion-extraversion scale was that of Gilliland and Morgan (1931), for which the standardization group of "extraverts" consisted of manic-depressives!

Ericksen (1954), in two rather complex avoidance and non-avoidance conditioning experiments, found that a hysteric group of subjects showed significantly more stimulus generalization than a psychasthenic group, using the respective M.M.P.I. scores as criteria in all cases. Taylor and Spence (1954) compared the conditionability of anxious neurotics with "other neurotics" and failed to find any statistically significant differences. The group of "other neurotics" included alcoholics, general depressives, obsessives, compulsives and psychopaths. To account for the failure to differentiate these two groups by means of conditioning, it is necessary first to consider in some detail a theory which provides an alternative explanation of why anxiety is positively related to ease of conditioning.

Present Theory

Pavlov's theory of cortical functioning emphasizes two basic cortical processes, *excitation* and *inhibition*. It is impossible to define these terms without embark-

ing upon considerable and highly dubious speculation of a neurophysiological nature, and it is sufficient here to regard them as hypothetical molar constructs, both of which are positive in nature. Inhibition, it should be noted, is *not* regarded as merely the absence of excitation. (Considerable confusion is brought about, both in the works of Pavlov and other authors, by the unfortunate multiplicity of usages of the term "inhibition," which is widely used in at least three different senses. There is the general psychiatric usage to describe the behaviour of the introverted, withdrawn individual; there is the more precise, but not clearly understood, neurophysiological use; and there is the Pavlovian usage to describe a hypothetical positive molar cortical process. It should be stressed that cortical inhibition in the Pavlovian sense, which is, fundamentally, how the term is used here, should be associated with the *absence* of behavioural inhibition in the psychiatric sense.)

Following a plethora of experiments on the conditionability of dogs and the induction of experimental "neuroses" in animals, Pavlov likened the kinds of neuroses developed in his various types of dogs to those found in man. He made many speculations about the causes of various human mental disorders in terms of pathological variations in his two cortical processes, but, which is not surprising, in view of the many incompatible and certainly confusing statements concerning the central concomitants of neurotic abnormality, never followed up any of these observations. One such observation (Pavlov, 1927, p. 397 *et seq.*) was to the effect that neurasthenics possess an exaggeration of the central excitatory process, whereas hysterics possess an exaggeration of the central inhibitory process. Quite different statements have been made by Pavlov elsewhere in his works and this observation is of value chiefly as a starting point for the theory of conditioning and personality about to be presented here.

It is possible to deduce from Pavlov's statement that neurasthenics would form positive conditioned reflexes readily, and that, once formed, these reflexes would be slow to extinguish, whereas hysterics would form positive conditioned responses only with difficulty and that these responses would be extinguished fairly readily. However, the term *neurasthenia* is ill defined and rarely used in contemporary psychology, and it would seem germane first, to examine both *neurasthenia* and *hysteria* more carefully in an attempt to discover how they differ, and then, to utilize equivalent terms more in accord with contemporary nomenclature.

Neurasthenia and hysteria are generally regarded as two differing forms of neurosis, and consequently, if a dimensional personality framework be accepted, they must differ along some dimension other than neuroticism. Pavlov himself has implicitly suggested a possible dimension, namely the excitation-inhibition ratio, the neurasthenic being at the excitation-dominated end of the continuum and the hysteric at the inhibition-dominated end. As already indicated, such a dimension, being located centrally, is highly speculative, and its existence has to be inferred largely from peripheral observations made at the behavioural level. It is, therefore, necessary to seek a corresponding dimension of personality which may be described more directly and to which Pavlov's more hypothetical concepts may be related. In seeking such a dimension at the behavioural level the concepts of Jung seem most apposite. Jung (1924) has suggested that the characteristic neurosis of the extravert is hysteria whereas that of the introvert is psychasthenia; he also stressed the essential independence of introversion from neuroticism.

These ideas have been extended and systematized by Eysenck and his colleagues (1953) and, by the application of factor analysis, two orthogonal dimensions of personality have been isolated, namely, extraversion-introversion and neuroticism. (The existence of other orthogonal dimensions need not be of concern in the present discussion.) It has been shown that it is possible to describe neurotics classified in various ways in terms of their factor loadings on these two dimensions. Anxiety neurotics, obsessive-compulsives and reactive depressives, (collectively termed *dysthymics*) tend to have high scores on tests of neuroticism together with high scores on tests of introversion, but low scores on tests of extraversion, whereas hysterics and psychopaths have high scores on tests of neuroticism, but low scores on tests of introversion and high scores on tests of extraversion. These different kinds of neurotics differ essentially not along the dimension of neuroticism but along the dimension of introversion-extraversion.

Now the term "neurasthenic" is not a very definite entity and, from Pavlov's usage, would seem to embrace mild depressives, various fatigue states and some anxiety conditions; thus it seems reasonable to identify the concept of neurasthenia, associated with an exaggeration of the central excitation process, with Eysenck's concept of dysthymia. Similarly, it would seem reasonable to identify Pavlov's concept of hysteria, associated with an exaggeration of the inhibition process, with Eysenck's concepts of hysteria and psychopathy.

The behaviour of patients usually included in these categories lends strong support to the assumption that dysthymia is related to excessive *excitation*, and hysteria and psychopathy to excessive *inhibition*. Thus the dysthymic tends to present the following types of symptom; anxiety, compulsive thoughts and actions, oversensitivity to his environment, over-caution,

hesitancy, hyperactivity; he may be over-conscientious, irritable, introspective, ill at ease and agitated. All these characteristics are consistent with a presumed state of exaggeration of the central excitation process. Conversely the hysteric tends to be lacking in the above qualities; he is more likely to be impulsive, irresponsible and unreliable, to be insensitive to his environment and to the feelings of other people, and his responsiveness to his environment tends to be superficial and indiscriminatory. His abnormalities are more likely to be of a dissociative character such as fugues, escape mechanisms and other conversion symptoms. These characteristics would seem highly consistent with a presumed state of predominating cortical inhibition.

According to Eysenck's factorial studies, both the psychopath and the hysteric are extraverted and neurotic. By psychopath is meant the individual who has a history of asocial acts and who lacks the ability to control his immediate emotional responses. Superficially charming, he is nevertheless erratic and purposeless in his way of life and not truly responsive either to his general environment or to the feelings of other people. He is egocentric and lacking in moral qualities or a value system. Above all, he is highly unlikely to profit from past experience or to respond favourably to psychotherapy, love, discipline or intensive training. The striking similarity between the psychopath and the hysteric is discussed at length elsewhere (Franks, 1956a) and there would seem to be ample justification for regarding the psychopath, like the hysteric, as possessing an exaggeration of the central inhibitory process.

It seems, therefore, that both behaviourally and symptomatically neurotics differ from each other along the dimension of introversion-extraversion, and that the underlying central concomitant, presumably constitutional, may be found in the changing balance of the excitation-inhibition ratio, ranging from a predominance of excitation at the introverted (dysthymic) end to a predominance of inhibition at the extraverted (hysterico-psychopathic) end. If this is so, then an excitation-inhibition postulate should be tenable in accounting for many of the behavioural differences observed in normal introverts and extraverts.[1] It is the normal introvert who tends to possess the excitatory phenomena of hesitancy, conscientiousness, sensitivity and responsiveness to his environment; it is the normal extravert who tends to possess

[1] A neglected, but similar, theory is that originally propounded by McDougall to account for the differences obtained between introverts and extraverts in terms of a chemical theory of personality. McDougall (1929) postulated a mysterious substance which acts upon the nervous system so as to counteract the controlling activities of the cortex upon the more primitive lower levels of the brain. According to McDougall the extravert is the individual who is constitutionally provided with a large amount of this antidotal substance.

the inhibitory phenomena of impulsiveness, a lesser degree of conscientiousness and a certain lack of sensitivity to his environment.

The general hypothesis may now be stated that conditionability is related not to the degree of neuroticism present, but centrally to the postulated excitation-inhibition balance and behaviourally to the introversion-extraversion balance of the individual

and Withers, 1955). Using both eyeblink and P.G.R. reflexes it was found that anxiety states and other dysthymics (all introverted) conditioned significantly more easily than a group of hysterics and psychopaths (all extraverted) (Franks, 1956b). A group of normal subjects, being as a group neither extraverted nor introverted, tended to occupy an intermediate position (see Fig. 12.1). Furthermore, when the conditioning

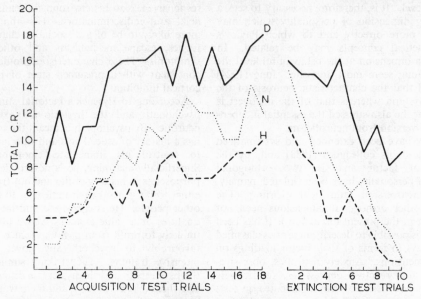

Fig. 12.1. The Total Number of Conditioned Eyeblink Responses Given by Twenty Dysthymics (D), Twenty Normals (N), and Twenty Hysterics and Psychopaths (H) at Each Test Trial

Note. The data reported in this and all other figures in this chapter, with the exception of Fig. 12.7, are obtained from a partial reinforcement conditioning schedule in which eighteen test or acquisition trials are interspersed irregularly among thirty reinforced trials; this is then followed immediately by a series of ten successive extinction trials.

concerned (Eysenck, 1957). An introverted subject, be he neurotic or normal, should form conditioned responses readily and these responses, once formed, should be difficult to extinguish; an extraverted subject, be he neurotic or normal, should form conditioned responses poorly and these responses, once formed, should extinguish readily.

Now, on both Spence's drive theory and on the above theory, anxious subjects would be expected to generate conditioned responses readily, hence a study confined to anxiety states would not provide a crucial experiment. A crucial experiment would have to examine both anxious and hysteric neurotics. On Spence's theory, since neuroticism is a drive, both groups should condition readily; on the present theory only the anxiety group should do so.

This crucial experiment was carried out in a soundproof conditioning laboratory especially designed for this purpose (Franks, 1954; Franks 1955; Franks

data were correlated with various personality questionnaires (see Franks, 1956b) the predicted relationship was found with introversion-extraversion (a high extraversion score indicating poor conditioning) and a marked lack of relationship with neuroticism.[1]

[1] The chimerical objection of Jenkins and Lykken (1957) that the three groups were not equal in the strength of the conditioned response on the very first trial, i.e. before any conditioning could have taken place, is unwarranted since only subjects who *failed* to give an original response to the conditioned stimulus were included in the experiment. In other words *all* subjects were equal in their strength of conditioning prior to any reinforcement being given. The fact that in some of the data reported the slopes of the curves are probably not significantly different for different groups suggests that, if confirmed, certain aspects of the theory, as presented, require substantial modification. It does not vitiate the general conclusions regarding the differential conditionability of introverts and extraverts. The suggestion of Jensen (1958) that differences in spontaneous eyeblink rate may account for the differences in eyeblink "conditionability" is plausible but inadequate to account for the obtained differences (see Franks, 1954). A similar and equally untenable argument is presented by Meyer (1953); based on the fact that induced general

These conclusions, especially those concerning the conditionability of dysthymics in general compared with hysterics in general, are limited by the method of selection of the patients included in the above experiment. The two neurotic groups were deliberately chosen to minimize overlap on the dimension of introversion-extraversion by selecting only those subjects who produced extreme scores on a questionnaire measure of extraversion. Hence the sample of

obtained (*see* Figs. 12.2 and 12.3). The only study to refute these findings is a dissertation of Das (1958), who failed to find significant correlation between conditioning and introversion-extraversion. (The correlation with extraversion is in the predicted direction.) On the other hand, Shagass and Kerenyi (1958), in Canada, obtained a highly significant correlation between ease of eyelid conditioning and introversion, using Guilford's questionnaires and a

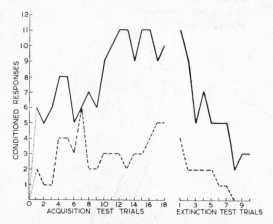

FIG. 12.2. THE TOTAL NUMBER OF CONDITIONED EYEBLINK RESPONSES GIVEN BY THE FIFTEEN MOST EXTRAVERTED SUBJECTS (BROKEN LINE) AND BY THE FIFTEEN LEAST EXTRAVERTED SUBJECTS (SOLID LINE)

These two extreme groups, as regards introversion-extraversion, were selected from a random sample of fifty-five male students who were all conditioned and given a personality questionnaire by two experimenters working independently.

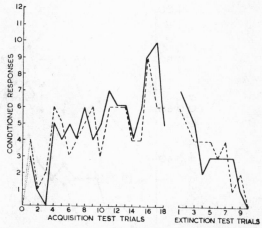

FIG. 12.3. THE TOTAL NUMBER OF CONDITIONED EYEBLINK RESPONSES GIVEN BY THE FIFTEEN MOST NEUROTIC SUBJECTS (BROKEN LINE) AND BY THE FIFTEEN LEAST NEUROTIC SUBJECTS (SOLID LINE)

These two extreme groups, as regards neuroticism, were selected from the same fifty-five subjects used to provide the data illustrated in Fig. 12.2.

patients finally accepted for conditionability cannot be considered as typical. That this limitation is not serious is apparent from the fact that only eight out of twenty-eight hysterics were initially rejected as not being sufficiently extraverted and seven out of twenty-seven dysthymics because of a corresponding lack of introversion. In any case, when a similar (Franks, 1957*b*) experiment was carried out with a much larger sample of normal subjects, similar results were

technique similar to that of Das and the present author.

In general then, the above experiments confirm the introversion-extraversion theory of conditioning and fail to support Spence's drive theory. They also make it possible to account for the fact that most previous studies which examined the conditionability of groups of neurotics found them superior to normals despite the fact that conditionability should be unrelated to neuroticism if the theory now being discussed is correct. The explanation is a practical one, rather than theoretical; among any unselected group of hospitalized neurotic patients the dysthymic variety are likely to preponderate; the psychopaths and hysterics are more likely to go to prisons or night clubs, or refuse to accept voluntary admission into a psychiatric hospital. In the one group where information about the neurotic sample is provided (Taylor and Spence, 1954) it will be recalled that no differences were found in conditionability between anxiety states on the one hand and a mixed selection of alcoholics, depressives, obsessives, compulsives and psychopaths,

muscle tension increases spontaneous blink rate and the assumption that a high score on the Taylor scale represents an "unusual amount of muscular activity," he argues that the superior conditionability of anxious subjects can be accounted for in terms of a greater "facilitation" of the eyeblink reflex. That the argument is untenable is apparent from an examination of the spontaneous blink rate of various neurotics and from the succinct observations of Bindra and his colleagues (1953). Jensen has also criticized the main conclusions on the ground that the relationship between introversion-extraversion and conditioning was obtained from one measure only, namely the eyeblink reflex. Apart from the fact that, as reported, similar results have been obtained for the conditioned P.G.R. response (Franks 1956*b*), Eysenck (1960) has recently presented evidence suggesting a reasonable degree of concomitance between a number of different conditioning measures and introversion-extraversion.

etc. on the other hand. Since both groups contained large numbers of introverted neurotics (dysthymics) it is hardly surprising that no differences in condition-ability were obtained!

It will be noticed that the introverted group in particular tend to achieve fairly well-established conditioning after as few as two reinforcements. This, of course, is no unusual phenomenon in conditioning experiments and cases of only one trial learning have

presents the results of a typical study (Franks and Trouton, 1958) in which normal subjects were allocated at random into one of three major groups, those receiving dexedrine, those receiving a *placebo* and those receiving Sodium Amytal. All three groups differed significantly from each other, the stimulant or excitatory drug increased conditionability and the depressant drug decreased. In earlier studies (Franks and Laverty, 1955; Laverty and Franks,

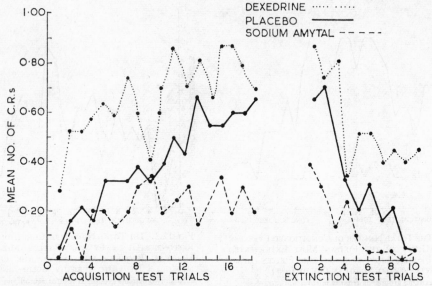

FIG. 12.4. MEAN NUMBER OF CONDITIONED EYEBLINK RESPONSES GIVEN BY GROUPS OF NORMAL FEMALE SUBJECTS RECEIVING DEXEDRINE, PLACEBO, OR SODIUM AMYTAL

Two experimenters were involved; one was responsible for giving the drugs or *placebo* and for other administrative arrangements, the other had no other contact with the subjects apart from operating the conditioning equipment.

not only been reported (e.g. Hudson, 1950) but have been given theoretical approval (Guthrie, 1952). The data provided by Kimble (Kimble, Mann and Dufort, 1955; Kimble and Dufort, 1956), as part of a series of experiments on the associative factor in eyelid conditioning, confirm the readiness with which eyelid conditioning takes place. He concludes that "the associative process in eyelid conditioning develops much more rapidly than the usual learning curve would lead one to believe."

In another series of experiments (Bartholomew, Franks and Marley, 1958; Franks and Laverty, 1955; Franks and Trouton, 1958; Franks, Trouton and Laverty, 1958; Laverty and Franks, 1956) drugs were used to produce central stimulant or depressive effects. (Eysenck (1957) has proposed a theory relating the effects of *stimulant* drugs to increases in introversion, and the effects of *depressant* drugs to increases in extraversion, cf. also Chapter 17 of this HANDBOOK, by Trouton and Eysenck.) Fig. 12.4

1956) it was found that a depressant drug reduced conditioning as predicted and, at the same time, increased the subjects' extraversion scores, while not altering their neuroticism measures.

The value of these findings is limited by a serious difficulty of interpretation. It is reasonable to believe that stimulant and depressant drugs have peripheral actions as well as central ones. Settlage (1936) gave cats a dose of amytal which was sufficient to prevent the performance of any conditioned response, while leaving the original unconditioned response unimpaired; after recovery from the drug, subsequent testing without any further reinforcement showed that a conditioned response had been successfully formed even though it never appeared during training and testing while the animals were under the influence of the drug. In the drug experiments cited above it is impossible to determine to what extent the findings reflect the peripheral motor consequences of the drugs concerned and to what extent they reflect any direct effects upon a central learning or connexion formation process. For example, the data illustrated in Fig. 12.4 would have been of much greater value had some additional testing of the degree of conditioning been carried out *after* the subjects had completely recovered from the effects of the drug. (For administrative reasons, this was impossible; however, an experimental investigation of this problem is almost complete at the time of writing.)

Despite this limitation it is instructive to compare the "conditioning curves" of normal subjects under the influence of drugs with the corresponding curves obtained from undrugged subjects belonging to various extreme groups. The similarity between the conditioned response behaviour of normal introverts, neurotic introverts (dysthymics) and subjects who have received a stimulant drug is very evident from the diagrams presented in this chapter. An equally striking parallel exists between the conditioned response behaviour of normal extraverts, neurotic extraverts (hysterics and psychopaths) and subjects who have received a depressant drug. The fact that it is possible to simulate certain aspects of neurotic behaviour by the application of centrally-acting drugs is of considerable theoretical and practical significance.

There is evidence in the literature (reviewed in Franks, 1956a; Franks and Trouton, 1958) to suggest that certain brain-damaged subjects (due either to natural or operative causes) tend to form conditioned responses only with difficulty, and that, in general, depressant drugs have a similar effect, whereas stimulants have the opposite effect upon conditioning. It is also remarkable how the theoretically predictable increase in extraversion tends to occur as a result of depressant drugs such as alcohol (Franks, 1958a) or of natural brain damage, or following certain forms of psychosurgery (Franks, 1956a). As Mayer-Gross, Slater and Roth (1954) point out, hysteric and psychopathic reactions are not uncommon following prefrontal leucotomy, and it is following certain physical illnesses, especially those involving the cortex, such as encephalitis lethargica, that hysteric and psychopathic symptoms sometimes occur. Kennedy (1954) also stresses the similarity between certain hysterics, brain-damaged subjects and psychopaths and postulates a constitutional similarity between these groups (cf. Chapter 15 of this HANDBOOK by R. Willett, for an extended discussion of the relation between brain damage and personality, cf. also Eysenck, 1957, for a general theory of personality change after brain damage).

It is now possible to account for the fact that, despite theoretical reasons why anxious subjects should condition more readily than non-anxious, many of those studies which made use of the Taylor scale as their measure of anxiety produced only slight

and sometimes insignificant confirmation of this relationship. The explanation seems to be that the Taylor scale is largely a measure of neuroticism (it correlates 0·92 with the Maudsley Medical Questionnaire and 0·86 with Guilford's D and C scales, which are all good measures of neuroticism) and only to a slight extent with measures of extraversion (Franks, 1954). Considerable experimental evidence from numerous studies by different authors is presented elsewhere (Franks, 1956c; Franks, Souief and Maxwell, 1959) to confirm that Taylor's Scale has a very considerable projection on to the neuroticism dimension and a relatively slight projection on to the introversion end of the introversion-extraversion dimension. This slight projection may account for the usually positive, always low and occasionally insignificant results obtained by Spence and his colleagues, and the fact that to get good results extreme groups have to be taken.

The failure of Bindra et al. (1955) to find any relationship between rate of salivary conditioning and scores on Taylor's Scale is hardly surprising. It should be pointed out that Bindra is a drive theorist and believes that his study gives support to an hypothesis originally proposed by Hilgard, Jones and Kaplan (1951). These authors state that anxious subjects, being more apprehensive, regard the air puff as a threatening stimulus. Therefore, since the eyeblink response is a protective one, anxious subjects are more likely to make the conditioned avoidance response than are non-anxious subjects. It must be noted that both Spence and Hilgard attribute differences in eyelid conditioning to differences in drive, but whereas Spence conceives of anxiety as part of a general heightened drive level, Hilgard appears to think in terms of a specific defence or protective drive. It is a pity that all of these authors used a measure only of neuroticism (the Taylor "anxiety" scale) and none of introversion-extraversion. The distinction between considering *relevant specific drives* and *drive in general*, including irrelevant drives, is a fundamental one and will be referred to again. (It is of interest to note that scores obtained from Taylor's scale do not even agree with psychiatric rating of "anxiety"; for example, both Bitterman and Holtzman (1952) and Franks (1954) failed to obtain significant correlations between ratings of anxiety obtained from Taylor's scale and ratings independently obtained by clinical assessments.)

Further evidence concerning the nature of Taylor's scale in relation to conditionability is to be found in a recent study by Lykken (1957). He found that psychopaths with a high score on Taylor's scale did not condition more readily than a group of subjects with significantly lower scores on her scale. If Taylor's scale is primarily a measure of neuroticism this result is in accord with the theory of conditioning presented in this chapter. Unfortunately, Lykken used no direct measure of extraversion: however, he did administer the Pd (psychopathy) scale of the M.M.P.I., which has been shown (Franks, Souief and Maxwell, 1959) to be to some extent a measure of extraversion, and he found that subjects who scored high on this scale tended to condition poorly *irrespective* of their position on the Taylor scale. Thus independent doubt is cast both on the nature of the Taylor scale and on the concept of drive as a conditioning variable under *all* circumstances.

The experiments cited, and arguments developed, all indicate that Taylor's anxiety scale is largely a measure of neuroticism and that individual differences in conditionability seem better accounted for in terms of introversion-extraversion than in terms of the Spence-Taylor theory of neuroticism or anxiety as a drive.[1] But before proceeding to a discussion of the clinical and practical implications of the intro-version-extraversion theory of conditioning, it is appropriate to consider briefly some further reasons why the drive theory of Spence and Taylor is believed to be partly erroneous.

As already indicated, their theory is based upon the assumption, taken from Hull's postulate system, that the total effective drive level is determined by the summation of all existent needs, both primary and secondary, and irrespective of their source and relevance to the nature of the reinforcement. If this is correct, then it should apply to variations in drives other than anxiety. It should hold for drives such as hunger and thirst. Experimentally these drives offer distinct advantages over that of anxiety, which is difficult to manipulate except in the indirect and crude method of group selection by means of a questionnaire or rating scale which is believed to be an adequate and valid measure of anxiety. It might be expected that the Taylor scale would at least be capable of yielding a meaningful quantitative score from which the amount of anxiety could be inferred; on the contrary, there is good evidence to believe that different scores on the Taylor scale do not represent different amounts of anxiety. (Sampson and Bindra, 1954.) The appetitive drives can be manipulated directly and with a far greater degree of certainty that the required modification is being effected. If the Spence-Taylor paradigm is correct then one would expect an increase in hunger and thirst to produce an increase in the ease of conditionability *whatever reflex is being measured.*

To test this prediction sixty normal male under-graduates were allocated at random to one of two groups, a "high drive" group who were rigorously deprived of any food, drink and tobacco throughout the day and a "low drive" group who were allowed to eat, drink and smoke in the usual manner (both groups contained approximately equal proportions of smokers.) At the end of the day all subjects were conditioned, using the frequency of conditioned eyeblink responses to a tone stimulus as the measure of conditioning (Franks, 1957a). The results, presented graphically in Fig. 12.5, indicate clearly that increasing D by food, drink and tobacco depriva-tion fails to produce any increase in the ease with which the eyelid response can be conditioned to a sound stimulus. Consequently the present study, like that of Buchwald and Yamaguchi (1955), who investigated the effects of water deprivation upon habit reversal in the rat, fails to give any support to the drive theory of conditioning as used by Spence. It is important to realize at this point that the above experiment only refutes the postulate that drive is relevant to conditionability *irrespective* of the rein-forcement and nature of the reflex used. Thus Bindra *et al.* (1955) failed to find any relationship between scores on Taylor's anxiety (or neuroticism) scale and the rate of salivary conditioning. But when the drive is a relevant one, such as hunger in a learning situation directly involving food, there is no doubt that it is also relevant to the efficiency of learning or condition-ing. Although hunger does not modify the learning of the conditioned eyeblink response, it certainly increases the ease and rate of conditioned salivation[1]. This has been demonstrated on both animals (Zener and McCurdy, 1939) and humans (Lashley, 1916; Winsor, 1928).

Even in those cases where the drive is relevant to the learning situation, the response strength is not as Spence would have his readers believe, a linear positive function of the intensity of the drive. Birch (1945) manipulated the relevant drive of food depriva-tion to investigate the effects of motivation in various problem-solving tasks in chimpanzees. Using six different degrees of deprivation ranging from two to forty-eight hours, he found that problem-solving

---

[1] Because Kamin (1955) found that his subjects' scores on a mechanical aptitude test were related to their learning he con-cluded that the superior conditioning of anxious subjects on tests of eyelid conditioning was a negative function of their familiarity with mechanical and electrical apparatus. Although it is premature to assume a causal relationship between the two measures on no further evidence than a correlation coefficient, this raises interesting possibilities concerning atti-tudinal and situational factors which may also modify condi-tionability.

[1] Hilgard, Jones and Kaplan (1951) argue that eyelid con-ditioning may be conceived of as an instrumental avoidance situation in which anxious subjects feel greater need to blink and thus avoid the noxious stimulus. In this case anxiety is a relevant drive to instrumental eyelid conditioning. However, in the series of eyeblink reflex experiments described in this chapter this seems to be an unlikely description of what happens; in the first place the air puff is scarcely noxious, a very mild stimulus being quite sufficient to produce a reflex blink; in the second place, the blink latency and duration are such that the air puff is not avoided.

efficiency was greatest under intermediate conditions of hunger. In short, Spence's use of Hull's postulate is too general and leads to erroneous deductions. A better formulation is that irrelevant drive is irrelevant to conditioning, the relevant variable being the postulated excitation-inhibition at the central level or introversion-extraversion at the behavioural level. When the drive is relevant to the conditioning or

certain circumstances, anxiety actually interfered with learning. As a consequence of this and other studies, Furber and Spence (1953) revised their theory and developed a rationale to predict that anxious subjects should perform more poorly than non-anxious subjects in situations involving competing responses. A recent carefully planned study by Saltz and Hoehn (1957) failed to confirm even this revised theory of

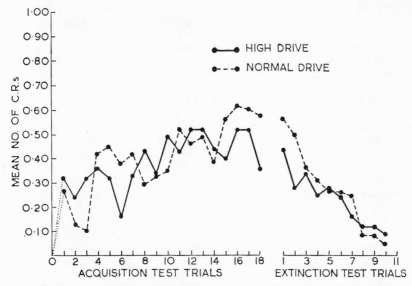

FIG. 12.5. Mean Number of Conditioned Eyeblink Responses Given by "High Drive" and "Normal Drive" Groups of Normal Male Subjects

learning situation then the strength of the response is relevant to the strength of the drive, with the proviso that the probable relationship is a curvilinear one rather than a positive linear function (cf. Chapter 19 by P. Broadhurst).

It is of interest to note that Spence's theory of manifest anxiety as a drive variable has been shown to be inadequate in other areas. Thus Montague (1953) found little evidence that anxiety facilitates verbal learning and strong indications that, under

anxiety as a drive in learning. Probably the clearest and most useful statement of the influence of relevant drives on learning and performance is given in the Yerkes-Dodson law: the more complex the task the lower the optimal drive level; the simpler the task the higher the optimal drive level. A discussion of this principle is beyond the scope of the present chapter and for an extended treatment the reader is referred elsewhere. (Eysenck, 1957; Young, 1936; also Chapter 19 of this book.)

CONDITIONING AND PERSONALITY: APPLICATION OF THE THEORY

The behaviour patterns of the dysthymic and of the hysteric have so far been considered largely in terms of an excess of the hypothetical processes of excitation and inhibition. If it be accepted that the dysthymic neurotic conditions readily and the hysteric poorly, it should be possible to proceed from the level of hypothetical constructs in the sense implied by McCorquodale and Meehl (1948) to a partly speculative, but certainly more direct, description of symptomatology and behaviour in terms of conditioning.

Through excessively strong and persisting conditioned response mechanisms, fear reactions in the dysthymic become conditioned response patterns to stimuli which are innocuous and neutral for other individuals. Thus the excessive anxiety which is so characteristic of dysthymia becomes a generalized and persistent response pattern. In a similar way the phobias, obsessions, compulsions and ruminations, etc. may be accounted for by taking into account the significant advances in the understanding of the methods by which verbal conditioning may be achieved. The fact that in many of these experiments the subject is *unaware* of the conditioned stimulus and of the fact that he is being conditioned is of importance. In certain circumstances particular situations have been shown to act as conditioned cues, highly specific to the patient and often without his awareness. There would seem to be no need to invoke psychoanalytic concepts to account for these phenomena.

In certain instances the individual receives only one traumatic reinforcement and it might be wondered whether this is sufficient, even in the most rapid of conditioners, to establish a persistent conditioned response. From laboratory experience many instances can be recalled of strong conditioning being established in very introverted neurotics after as few as two reinforcements. As already stated, experimental confirmation of single-trial conditioning has also been provided by Hudson (1953), and Guthrie (1952) has given a possible theoretical explanation of how such a situation might come about.

The hysterico-psychopath group has been described behaviourally in terms of some form of central inhibition or dissociation. If it is confirmed that such individuals form conditioned responses only with difficulty, and that these responses are readily relinquished, then it becomes possible to describe these individuals in terms of a difficulty in forming and ease in losing conditioned responses.

It is hardly necessary to labour the point by considering the behaviour patterns of the normal introvert and extravert in relation to their ability to form conditioned responses. The introverted normal and the dysthymic have similar behavioural characteristics, but the normal lacks the high neurotic (emotional) drive of the dysthymic; the extraverted normal resembles the hysteric but does not have his neurotic (emotional) drive.

It occasionally happens that a subject's questionnaire score of introversion-extraversion is diametrically opposed to his ease of conditioning as predicted in accordance with the theory of personality outlined above. Disregarding, for the moment, problems of errors in procedure or in matters of test reliability and validity, this apparent inconsistency can still be accounted for without vitiating the theory. Consider for example the person who conditions readily and yet gives a high extraversion score on questionnaires measuring his social behaviour pattern. It is at least possible that such an individual is an introvert and conditions readily, but is living in a cultural pattern where extraverted behaviour is the socially desirable and acceptable norm. Such a person would learn the pattern readily and consequently respond as an "extravert" on the questionnaires. If this hypothesis

is correct he should behave as an introvert on all measures of central excitation, such as sedation threshold, flicker fusion, Archimedes spiral, which are unaffected by social demands, and as an "extravert" on tests such as questionnaires or verbal interviews. It also follows, since the introvert on physiological tests can learn the extraverted pattern of social behaviour fairly easily if needs be, whereas the extravert on physiological tests can learn an introverted pattern of social behaviour only with much difficulty, that inconsistencies between conditioning and questionnaires should be greater for good conditioners than for poor. This is a testable prediction which may give rise to interesting research.

Delinquency

One of the most challenging and widespread problems in modern society is that of the *modus operandi* of the delinquent personality. At first impression it might seem feasible to subsume delinquency under the more general heading of psychopathy, but this would imply that all delinquents are extraverted, which is a simplification unwarranted by the facts. However, at least two studies (Gluecks, 1950; Miller, 1956) have shown that, although both introverts and extraverts can, and do, become delinquents, it is the extraverted children who tend to become the habitual juvenile and adult delinquents. It may be that behaviour which is commonly classified as psychopathic can be further resolved into two broad subgroups, a group of asocial offenders who just do not conform to society and another group of antisocial offenders who are against society (Franks and Willett, 1956).

This hypothesis is based on the finding that certain psychopaths find great difficulty in forming conditioned responses and that, once formed, these responses are soon extinguished. These psychopaths are also extraverted in personality. It is characteristic of such individuals that they are unable to learn from experience or punishment or to profit from help offered them, whatsoever its nature. Such individuals are those who become the "true" psychopaths; they are asocial in as much as they are unable to learn the rules of society. There may be, however, another group of delinquents who are very capable of conditioning and learning the rules of society. Unfortunately, the rules they acquired from their microcosmic section of the environment in which they exist are regarded as undesirable and antisocial by the vast majority of mankind. From their neighbourhood, family, friends and mass media such as the cinema they readily acquire a conditioned pattern of delinquent behaviour. If the theory of conditioning outlined here is correct, then such individuals would tend to be relatively introverted.

The concept of recidivism now takes on new attributes and a new complexity. In the search for the causes which contribute to recidivism many possible factors have been examined. For example, attempts have been made to relate the dimension of intelligence to the incidence and nature of recidivism, but, so far, no consistent relationships have emerged. (Franks, 1956*a*). When recidivism is examined in terms of the dimension of conditionability, i.e. of introversion-extraversion, two interesting possibilities arise. Some recidivists would have learned antisocial behaviour patterns from the undesirable environment in which they live. Even their repeated prison sentences, if largely custodial, would merely provide a reinforcement of the undesirable society whose patterns they learned so well. These recidivists, if the present theory is correct, could be detected by their tendency towards introversion and by their ease of conditionability in laboratory tests. They are the non-psychopathic recidivists who, if they are highly responsive to undesirable training, should be equally responsive to more desirable treatment in the form of psychotherapy and re-education, etc.

At the same time there might exist another group of recidivists, extraverted in personality and very poor at forming conditioned responses. These recidivists should be classified as truly psychopathic, i.e. asocial, rather than antisocial. They would not respond to any form of training or treatment and would be constitutionally largely unable to acquire the rules of the society in which they lived. In an era where an acute shortage of psychotherapists and facilities for skilled remedial training predominates a selection device based on personality and conditioning tests would be invaluable. An interesting, and readily testable, corollary is that the introverted delinquents should have come from emotionally or materially undesirable environments whereas the extraverted (psychopathic) delinquents, being indifferent to social learning, could have come from any sort of environment. None of the studies which have examined delinquents have related introversion-extraversion to home background in this way.[1]

Although this theory rests on slender evidence and must be regarded as speculative, there is some independent confirmatory evidence which lends support to these conjectures. Lykken (1957), using the P.G.R. as his measure of conditioning, also found that his psychopaths were more difficult to condition than his normal group. His study is extremely provocative in that it raises many fecund possibilities

and is well worth considering here in some detail. Lykken makes explicit a differentiation which has long been implied in clinical practice; he differentiates between the neurotic psychopath (presumably an individual who has high scores on tests of extraversion and on tests of neuroticism) and the sociopath (presumably with high scores on tests of extraversion but only moderate scores on tests of neuroticism). Since both are extraverted, both should condition poorly and this is what Lykken found, despite the fact that he conceived his experiment in an entirely different framework to that propagated here.

Conditioning as a diagnostic tool could be used in settings other than penological. For example, in industry the problem of the accident-prone worker has received much attention. There is some evidence (Petrie 1949) to suggest that certain post-leucotomized patients become more accident-prone, as well as more extraverted, sometimes psychopathic and possibly poorer at forming conditioned responses. It is possible that the increased proneness towards accidents in such patients is explicable in terms of loss of those acquired responses which previously enabled them to guard against the many hazards of twentieth-century living. A related observation which could be interpreted in a similar manner (except that it would be a lack of formation, rather than a loss, of conditioned reflexes) is that of Eysenck (1947), who noticed that the characteristic of "accident proneness" is ascribed to themselves more by extraverts than by introverts.

The Effects of Drugs

Psychopharmacology is becoming of growing importance, and every day new drugs, particularly stimulants and depressants, make their appearance. Now, if it is correct that stimulant drugs increase the ease with which new responses can be acquired and retained whereas depressants have the opposite effect, then psychotherapy (which may be reasonably regarded as an exercise in learning or conditioning) may profit from the judicious use of the correct drug at the correct stage in the proceedings. For example, a stimulant drug might be used when building up the new response pattern and a depressant drug when extinguishing an old and undesired pattern of behaviour. It is, however, an empirical fact that sufficient reliance cannot be placed on prediction of the effective dosage by utilizing such variables as lethal dose, age, sex or body weight. It is possible that this major difficulty might be overcome by an application of the theory of personality and conditioning presented in this chapter.

It has been postulated that introverts condition readily because of an effective exaggeration of the excitation process and that extraverts condition poorly because of an effective exaggeration of the inhibition

[1] From the point of view of the theory of personality and conditioning advanced in this chapter there is a considerable methodological advantage in working with such clearly recognized groups as delinquents and prostitutes, about whose behavioural "symptoms" there is no dispute (as contrasted with hysterics and dysthymics).

process. The resemblances between Figs. 12.1, 12.2, 12.3 and 12.4 strongly suggest that it is possible to simulate the conditioned response behaviour of normal or neurotic introverts and extraverts by giving any group of mixed subjects the appropriate stimulant or depressant drug.

One would expect a stimulant drug to increase excitation and consequently ease of conditioning, and at the same time make a subject more introverted;

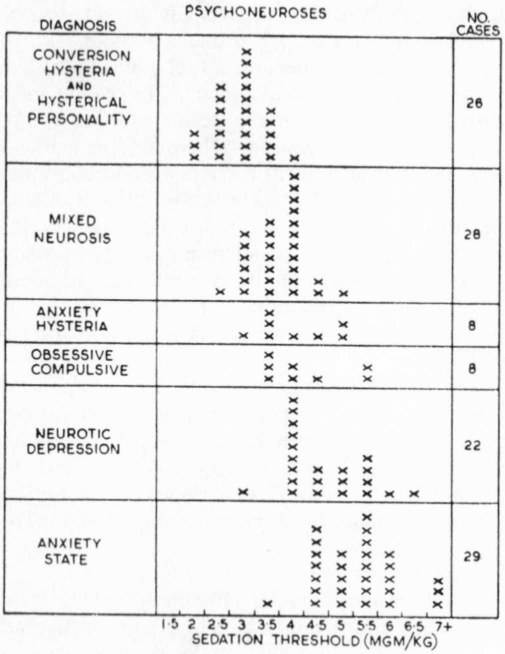

FIG. 12.6. SEDATION THRESHOLD DISTRIBUTION FOR VARIOUS NEUROTIC GROUPS
(*From Shagass*)

similarly, one would expect a depressant drug to increase inhibition, reduce ease of conditioning and at the same time, on the behavioural level, make the subject more extraverted (Eysenck, 1957). The experimental evidence cited supports these expectations. Furthermore, it follows that a subject who already conditions well and is introverted is presumably already in a state of cortical excitation; such a subject would require a very large dose of a depressant drug to sedate him. Conversely, it follows that a subject who already conditions poorly and is extraverted is presumably in a state of cortical inhibition; such a subject would require a very large dose of a stimulant drug to have a stimulant effect whereas only a relatively tiny dose of a depressant drug would be required to sedate him completely.

The confirmatory evidence stems both from clinical experience and from the data of various researches.

In this latter respect the many investigations of Shagass and his colleagues are of particular relevance. Unlike Pavlov, who was forced to infer the properties of central processes from observation of peripheral changes, Shagass was fortunate in having the well-established techniques of electroencephalography readily available for the more direct observation of central processes. Even before Shagass commenced his studies, there was reason to believe that a relationship exists between certain aspects of personality and the nature and amount of time the alpha rhythm is present in the record, and it now seems likely that such observations are associated with some form of central nervous excitability which is probably of a constitutional nature (Mundy-Castle 1955).

The technique evolved by Shagass (1956) for the measurement of depressant drug susceptibility depends on the fact that when Sodium Amytal is given intravenously at a fixed rate per kilogramme of body weight and the EEG is recorded continuously, the fast frequency (15–30 c/s) waves increase in amplitude. The curve of amplitude increase follows a typical sigmoid shape, eventually reaching a point of inflexion when it begins to level out. Shagass also noticed that this inflexion point coincides roughly with the onset of slurred speech and he claims to be able to measure both inflexion point and the onset of speech slur fairly accurately. The amount of Sodium Amytal required to produce these two phenomena is called by Shagass the "sedation threshold" for that drug and is supposed to be independent of age, sex and previous intake of sedatives (Shagass and Naiman, 1956).

Starting from the common clinical impression that effective sedation dosage is correlated with the degree of tension, Shagass developed the above technique as a measure of tension or manifest anxiety and eventually extended his investigation to include all types of neurotics. His principal findings are summarized in Fig. 12.6, from which it is apparent that hysterics require least Sodium Amytal to attain the critical sedation point and anxiety states most. Quite independently Shagass's results concur closely with the present theory: extraverts, already in a presumed state of central inhibition, require little extra inhibition to sedate them; introverts, in a state of presumed excitation, require a lot.[1]

[1] In a later publication (Shagass, Mihalik and Jones, 1957) Shagass presents, on the basis of somewhat jejune evidence, conclusions which are difficult to conciliate with the present theory of personality, which assumes (on good evidence) that the excitation-inhibition processes are constitutional and hence fairly permanent characteristics of the nervous system in its undrugged state. According to Shagass the sedation threshold is not fixed, but reflects "affective disturbance rather than enduring personality factors." Hence he regards the sedation threshold as a possible effective index of therapeutic effectiveness.

Although it seems unlikely that the stability of the excitation-inhibition balance is as ephemeral as Shagass suggests there is

This rationale is applicable to the findings of psychologists working within quite different frameworks. For example, Sheldon and Stevens (1945) have observed that high resistance to alcohol is listed as one of the criteria for their cerebrotonic temperament. Since cerebrotonics seem similar to dysthymics this is to be expected. It also accounts for the subjective impression of McDougall (1929) who, in discussing the phenomena of alcoholic intoxication, said that: "In a number of cases the markedly extraverted personality is very susceptible to the influence of alcohol. A very small dose deprives him of self-restraint and control and brings on the symptoms of intoxication, all of which are essentially expressions of diminished cortical control over the lower brain levels. The introvert on the other hand, is much more resistant to alcohol. He can take a considerable dose without other effect than that he becomes extraverted."

McDougall provides no objective measures of introversion-extraversion and without such a measure it is impossible to predict accurately any individual's susceptibility to stimulant and depressant drugs. As already stated, the more or less empirical rules developed for the estimation of effective drug dosages are of only limited value and it is sometimes found that different individuals vary apparently inexplicably in their responses to the same drug (Goodman and Gilman, 1941). A possible reason for such individual differences in the susceptibility of subjects of the same weight and age, etc. may lie in their individual differences in the excitation-inhibition balance. Weight and age data provide necessary but not sufficient criteria; it may also be essential to have some objective assessment of the subject's excitation-inhibition balance before an accurate prediction could be made about his susceptibility to any specific stimulant or depressant. The experimental findings and theoretical formulation presented in this chapter provide such a way. The dosage required would be predicted from the subject's position on the introversion-extraversion continuum, which is the behavioural concomitant of his excitation-inhibition balance, from his conditionability, which is another measure of this balance, and perhaps from a measure of his sedation threshold. Although *much* further research is required, these methods may eventually be of value both for the prediction of the dosages

required to produce certain desired effects and for the rational investigation of the effects of new stimulants and depressants upon behaviour (cf. Chapter 17 of this HANDBOOK, by Trouton and Eysenck).

There are many complicating factors, not least of which is the fact that many drugs have side effects which may be of sufficient strength to obliterate the predicted effect. Thus many excitants are also sympathomimetics and many sedatives depress autonomic activity to a marked degree. From the research point of view it is therefore better to use stimulants and depressants (using these much confused terms in the pharmacological sense, as categorized by Goodman and Gilman, 1941) with the minimum of side effects, as far as this is possible. If tests of conditionability are used it is sometimes difficult to evaluate whether the central concomitants of conditioning are being modified or merely the peripheral performance of certain activities. Sometimes it is possible to overcome these side effects by the use of other agents, but it is then incumbent upon the experimenter to demonstrate that these other agents are innocuous as far as the main predicted effect is concerned.

For example, the tertiary amine arecoline (an alkaloid found in the betel nut) has a pronounced inhibitory effect on the performance of an already learned response, but unfortunately produces undesirable effects. Atropine, also a tertiary amine, would prevent these peripheral effects, but it cannot be used since it would also protect the brain from the desired effects of these drugs. However, if methyl atropine, a quaternary analogue, is used in combination with the arecoline, then the subjects would be protected peripherally from the undesired side effects, leaving the central effects to be observed unimpaired (Pfeiffer and Jenney, 1957).

To demonstrate this experimentally with humans, four groups of subjects were conditioned to a high degree of responsiveness, then group *A* was given the arecoline-methyl atropine mixture, group *B* methyl atropine alone, and groups *C* and *D* were used as control groups. The results show clearly that the arecoline mixture had a pronounced inhibitory response on the conditioned reflex under investigation and that this effect could not be attributable to the methyl atropine. These findings are indicated graphically in Fig. 12.7, in which, for the sake of clarity, the control data, being almost exact replicas of the methyl-atropine data, are omitted. The arecoline inhibits the performance of the learned response at first, then, as its effects gradually wear off, the response gradually appears again and is finally extinguished in the normal manner (Franks, Trouton and Laverty, 1958). Thus considerable care is essential in investigating the effects of new drugs, each of which

---

reason to believe that it is subject to limited fluctuation. Thus Slavina (1936) studied salivary conditioning in children throughout the waking day over a period of nine days and found consistent diurnal variations, conditionability being less in the first and last periods of each day. It is of theoretical significance that these diurnal variations in susceptibility to conditioning broadly follow the variations in other measures such as the electric sensitivity of the eye or the sensitivity of teeth to pain (Kleitman, 1939). There is, of course, no *a priori* reason why constitutional elements should not in themselves be subject to some form of inherent variation; manic-depressive psychosis is a classical example of such an oscillation.

may require a specific method of study; it is dangerous, for example, to assume that all tranquillizers have a depressant effect upon the formation and performance of a learned response.

Another complicating factor, more difficult to resolve because of the many speculations involved, is that of the apparently contradictory effects sometimes reported when working with certain drugs. It has more than once been reported that the effects of

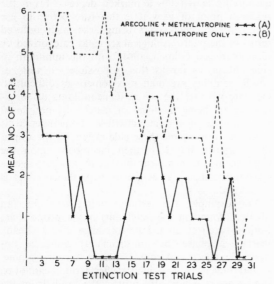

FIG. 12.7. THE EFFECT OF ARECOLINE UPON THE EXTINCTION OF THE CONDITIONED EYEBLINK RESPONSE

amphetamine are sometimes paradoxical (e.g. Reifenstein and Davidoff, 1939) and Carl and Turner (1939) repeatedly found, in their intensive studies of the psychological effects of amphetamine sulphate, that there was "a temporary period of lessened efficiency, actual retardation and perhaps even 'confusion' for a variable length of time after investigation, especially when the dosage is heavy." Recently, the present writer had occasion to suggest that a very introverted subject be given a fairly large dose of amphetamine sulphate by mouth. About half an hour later, much to everyone's surprise, the subject was fast asleep on a couch and it was not until much later that the more usual stimulant effects of the drug manifested themselves.

In order to account for these apparently paradoxical effects one must accept the theoretical relationship between drug action and personality developed here, together with a certain amount of speculation about the properties of the central processes involved and the effects of various drugs upon these processes. For example, it is logically possible to decrease any ratio

by increasing the denominator or by decreasing the numerator or by combining both operations. If the excitation-inhibition balance is regarded as a ratio this applies here also and considerable research is

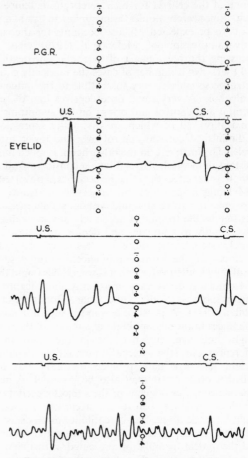

FIG. 12.8. SOME TYPICAL EYEBLINK RECORDS

U.S. = the occurrence of the unconditioned stimulus (an air puff) together with the conditioned stimulus (a tone).
C.S. = the occurrence of the tone alone.
The top record is that of a subject who gives very little spontaneous blinking. (Also included in this record are the P.G.R. responses to the two sets of stimuli). The middle record is the kind most frequently encountered, namely that of a subject who gives some spontaneous blinking. The bottom record is that of a subject who gives a considerable amount of spontaneous blinking. It should be noted that in all these records it is very easy to distinguish the conditioned and unconditioned responses.

required into the subtle modes of action of the drugs concerned.

Pavlov considered, possibly on inadequate evidence, that caffeine produced its stimulant effect by "destroying inhibition." One might expect amphetamine sulphate, unknown at the time Pavlov was carrying out his experiments, to be an even greater "destroyer of inhibition," but logically, at any rate, its mode of action could equally well be by increasing the excitation process. Whatever way the stimulant drug affects this ratio, the net result is a marked increase in the ratio in favour of excitation. So marked is this excitation, according to Pavlov, that a paradoxical phase of protective inhibition has to be established in order to preserve the cortical cells from damage. To discuss the possible mechanism by which this process is brought about would be both highly speculative and outside the scope of this volume. Perhaps the concepts of "induction" of Pavlov and Ischlondsky (1949) offer possible explanations. Whatever, the reason, there is some clinical evidence, e.g. the beneficial effects of sleep in times of stress and the effectiveness of various forms of sleep therapy (Korbikov, 1955), to suggest that some such mechanism might possibly apply. In the case of the introverted subject, already in a state of excitation, the increased excitation provided by the stimulant drug was presumably sufficient to produce a state of excitation so excessive that it was necessary to adopt sleep as a form of protective inhibition.

This theory helps to account for the data obtained in a series of experiments in which it was desired to investigate the effects of a stimulant drug upon conditioning by comparing a group of drugged subjects with a *placebo* group. It was found that in order to obtain the predicted significant increase in condition-ability it was necessary, with the intensity of dosage used, to allow two hours to elapse between the injection of the drug and the start of the experiment. When shorter intervals were maintained the drug failed to produce the predicted effects, even though the times were, pharmacologically, sufficient for absorption to have taken place. It would be interesting to investigate the production of paradoxical effects in a systematic manner by such means.

Throughout this chapter reference has been made to the use of drugs in the conditioning laboratory, both as experimental variables and as agents whose properties are to be investigated. Many of the inherent difficulties have been discussed already, but if the reader wishes to carry out such studies himself, or even to evaluate those studies which have been carried out by other workers, there are additional hazards of which he must be cognizant. Certain of these hazards are of particular importance because they indicate that the theory of drug action presented here is almost certainly a gross over-simplification.

Firstly the method of administration of the drug is of direct relevance to the effects produced, e.g. directly to the surface of the cortex, through intraventricular cannulae or systemically. Secondly, different doses of the same drug may produce differential effects which are not a linear or straightforward function of the size of the dose (Brown and Searle, 1938). Thirdly, the magnitude of the response depends, as one would expect, upon the conditioning technique and reinforcement schedule utilized; it is important to realize this when comparing the results of different workers. Fourthly, in working with depressants, despite the evidence presented throughout this chapter, it is unwise to assume too close a similarity between the postulated inhibitory effects of drugs, natural brain damage, disease, psychosurgery, sleep, hypnotism and the postulated inhibition pertinent to certain personality types. For example, it has been shown that conditioning under anaesthesia does not follow the same pattern as conditioning in the decorticated animal; the use of depressant drugs in the study of conditioning cannot justifiably be regarded as merely a convenient substitute for extirpation (Marquis and Hilgard, 1936; Sterling and Miller, 1941).

Fifthly, different aspects of behaviour may well be differentially affected by the same drug at the same or different times. Gliedman and Gantt (1956) found that both reserpine and chlorpromazine had most effect on unlearned reactivity, moderate effect on the retention of learned motor activity and least effect on the retention of learned autonomic activity. Therefore a battery of diverse conditioning techniques should always be used; only this type of approach will permit of a complete description of the drug's effects on learned and unlearned behaviour. It would be premature to reject a new tranquillizing drug as ineffective because it did not weaken any one response that happened to be tested. For example, Hunt (1956), after some provocative observations about the essential similarities between the mechanism of imprinting in birds, emotional disturbance in man and the conditioned emotional response, points out that Meprobamate may be an effective tranquillizer even though it does not block the sort of laboratory behaviour which most learning theorists would consider to depend upon a conditioned emotional disturbance or some form of aversive conditioning.

Sixthly caution must be exercised in the use and interpretation of *placebo* data. If, as has been suggested (Gliedman, Gantt and Teitelbaum, 1957; Trouton, 1957), a *placebo* response is a learned or conditioned response, then it is possible that the introvert will acquire and maintain *placebo* reactions more readily than the extravert. The confirmation of this interesting hypothesis would be of particular use to those interested in *placebo* effects as therapeutic measures. Seventhly, specific stimulants and depressants must be considered individually and their antagonistic effects must not be assumed without rigorous demonstrations. For example, the Newmans (1956) found that, in ordinary therapeutic doses, neither Dexamphetamine sulphate nor caffeine was effective in combating the depressant effect of alcohol as assessed by psychological and other tests.

Eighthly, many of the studies reported in the literature have been carried out on animals. Often the data were obtained from intensive investigations of a very few animals and often studies, which could otherwise be compared, have been carried out on different species. It is not surprising that, for these and other reasons, the findings are occasionally contradictory. This does not mean that animal research must invariably be suspect but merely that caution is required in making any generalizations. There are numerous examples of the value of such research and ample evidence that, despite an immense phylogenetic gap, the general principles of conditioning and learning under drugs apply in most species. Thus Dews (1956) found that central stimulants such as methamphetamine increased the pecking rate in pigeons in an operant conditioning situation, whereas phenobarbital tended to reduce this rate. And more recently, in the laboratory, Sinha, Franks and Broadhurst (1958), assuming alternation behaviour of rats in a maze to be a measure of inhibition, demonstrated clearly that this effect could be modified in the predicted directions by the administration of the appropriate amounts of stimulant and depressant drugs.

Differential Diagnoses

The use of conditioning techniques for descriptive, diagnostic and predictive purposes in the investigation of psychiatric disorders and treatment has been given insufficient attention outside the Soviet Union. Irrespective of any clearly formulated theory of conditioning it is possible to make good, if less efficient, use of conditioning procedures. In those few areas where the treatment takes the form of a direct application of conditioned response theory, the need for making use of conditioning in the selection of candidates and the prediction of success becomes even more apparent. Even if the assumption that an influential general factor of conditionability exists has eventually to be rejected, the possibility of predicting success in conditioning therapy by a particular test of conditioning need not be vitiated. However, in certain disorders treated along these lines, there is some slight empirical evidence to support the theoretical formulation that introverts condition well and extraverts poorly. Thus it has often been observed that psychopathy contraindicates success in conditioned aversion therapy with alcoholics. (Diethelm, 1955; Thimann, 1949.)

Gantt and his coworkers (Gantt, 1950; Reese, Doss and Gantt, 1953) used conditioning techniques to help establish a differential diagnosis between psychogenic and "organic" psychoses. There is much evidence to indicate that patients with organic brain disturbances find difficulty in producing and maintaining conditioned responses (Fleck and Gantt, 1951; Gantt, 1938; Gantt and Muncie, 1942; Rees, Doss and Gantt, 1953). This seems to apply whether the brain damage is a result of accident, disease or psychosurgery and is apparent in a wide variety of pathologies, e.g. Korsakoff's psychosis (Gantt and Muncie, 1942; Reese, Doss and Gantt, 1953), congenital idiots (Krasnogorski, 1933), cerebral palsy (Bordley, 1956). The fact that a catatonic, apparently out of all contact with the external world, is better able to form conditioned reflexes than a brain-damaged patient who is apparently in much better contact with reality, opens up exciting avenues for eventual therapy with certain forms of psychotics.

In general comparatively little is known about the conditionability of psychotics. According to Shipley (1934) schizophrenics are the slowest to acquire conditioned responses, followed by manic-depressives, neurotics and normals. According to Kaufman (1953), conditioned responses formed in the past in schizophrenics may persist but new ones cannot easily be formed. The poor conditionability of certain schizophrenics can be predicted in terms of Pavlovian concepts and there is some supporting evidence (e.g. Franks, 1954; Howe, 1952). On the other hand there is rather more experimental evidence that certain schizophrenics condition as well or better than normals in a variety of modalities (e.g. Pfaffman and Schlosberg, 1936; Bender and Schilder, 1930; Spence and Taylor, 1952). These conflicting findings are paralleled by an, at least, equal degree of confusion in the consideration of other aspects of the behaviour of psychotics; there is apparently no valid integrating principle which will account for the many ways in which different groups of schizophrenics have been reported to differ from normals and neurotics.

Numerous attempts have been made to develop a theory of schizophrenia consistent with Pavlovian concepts but none have been altogether successful (e.g. Ivanov-Smolensky, 1925, 1927, 1928, 1954; Gordon, 1948). Kempf (1953), without any experimental evidence, writes of schizophrenia as "a socially conditioned disintegrative emotional disease." Kanner (1943, 1951) provides a more fully substantiated discussion of the behaviour of autistic children in terms of excessive conditioning and Timmer (1931) has undertaken the enormous, and perhaps unrewarding, task of relating Kretschmer's theory of temperament and psychosis to brain physiology and conditioning. It is possible that considerable advances will be made when the experimental, free operant conditioning techniques of Lindsley (1956), which use what is essentially a glorified Skinner box, are more fully developed.

Sensory Measurements

Pavlov's original salivation method is useless for measuring the hearing acuity of small animals and consequently special conditioning techniques, often far removed from those originally devised by Pavlov, have had to be developed (e.g. Coller *et al.*, 1953; Elder, 1934; Horton, 1933; Wever, 1930). Probably the best technique, in that it is objective, readily quantifiable and suitable equally for small animals and all human subjects, is that of Dworkin and his associates (Dworkin, Kutzman, Hutchinson and McCabe, 1940.) They have investigated the hearing threshold and hearing range in normal animals and in those which have undergone operation and extended the method to the study of pitch and intensity discrimination. The study of sensory discrimination in children has, with very few exceptions (e.g. Kasatin and Levikova, 1935), been neglected; especially such aspects as the development of discrimination as a function of age and of individual differences in personality.

Under certain circumstances the ability to form a conditioned response may be the only evidence that a small baby is capable of responding to specific forms of sensory stimulation (Aldrich, 1938). It is often the only objective method of determining the hearing acuity of infants, mental defectives and certain psychotics. Recently attention has been focused on P.G.R. conditioning as an indication of auditory responsiveness (Bordley, 1956; Hardy and Bordley, 1956). Numerous investigators (e.g. Bloomer, 1942; Ewing, 1944; Keaster, 1947; Utley, 1949) have reported conditioning techniques in which the child is trained by various teaching devices to respond to auditory signals. Of particular importance is the "Peep Show," developed by Dix and Hallpike (1947), in which a child is conditioned to press a button whenever he hears a pure tone in order to be rewarded with an entertaining picture.

Such techniques are not without their dangers, as a valuable study by Goldstein *et al.* (1954) amply demonstrates. They found that auditory conditioning was difficult to establish in aphasic children, whereas it was readily established in non-aphasic children. It is probable that it would be equally difficult to establish a conditioned hearing response in hysteric and extraverted subjects, as well as in children suffering from other forms of brain damage. In brief, if it is not first established that a child is capable of forming conditioned responses fairly readily, negative results can be highly misleading. There is little doubt that in the past, because factors of conditionability and personality were ignored, children have been falsely diagnosed as suffering from defective hearing by means of incorrectly used conditioning techniques.

A similar difficulty arises when malingerers and hysterics are being examined. Only if the experimenter is successful in establishing a conditioned response to a stimulus affecting an hysterically anaesthetized sense modality, are the results of value (Sears and Cohen, 1933). Thus Cohen, Hilgard and Wendt (1933), in the case of a patient believed to be suffering from hysterical blindness, were able to establish a conditioned eyelid reaction to a light source flashed in the blind eye even though the subject did not report seeing the light. These workers even succeeded in establishing conditioned verbal responses to a light flashed into the blind eye. It is sometimes suggested that conditioning techniques would be of value in differentiating between patients suffering from hysteria and from some form of cerebral damage. Since both these categories are likely to condition poorly it is impossible to use conditioning techniques in an attempt to establish a differential diagnosis until more is known about the specific response patterns of hysterics in various conditioning modalities and about the specific conditionability of brain-damaged subjects as a function of the area and extent of the damage and the nature of the conditioning stimuli.

Emotional and Psychosomatic Aspects

The phrase "conditioned emotional reaction" can be traced back to Watson and his colleagues (Watson and Raynor, 1928). Together with many other independent investigators (e.g. Jones, 1930; M. C. Jones, 1924*a*; M. C. Jones, 1924*b*), they successfully developed and eliminated conditioned fear responses in children. (Gantt 1953*a*) gives a graphic account of the conditioned fear response of dogs in the real-life, as opposed to the laboratory situation. Masserman (1943), placing his cats in a situation where hunger impelled them towards food at the same time as an air blast drove them away, claims to have produced what he called an "experimental neurosis," but what is probably better described as a conditioned emotional response. It is of interest that the technique used by Masserman to dispel the "neurotic" symptoms greatly resembles the technique of extinction in an orthodox laboratory conditioning situation.

Critics of such laboratory experiments sometimes argue that in "real life" emotional reactions persist for much longer than laboratory-generated conditioned responses and that consequently these reactions must be attributable to factors other than conditioning. Such pundits ignore the plenitude of evidence derived from experiments based upon drive reduction theory, in which the drive reduction itself is hypothesized to act as a reinforcing agent and so perpetuate the conditioned response pattern of behaviour. In this way it is possible to account for the continual repetition of the apparently useless act of the obsessive compulsive, where the reduction of anxiety, itself a conditioned response, provides the necessary reinforcement to prevent the pattern from extinguishing itself. Another not incompatible possibility is that the conditioned response, by a process of stimulus generalization, gets reinforced in everyday life by numerous situations of varying degrees of similarity to the original conditioning stimulus. Watson is not alone in formulating a theory of conditioned emotions; similar is that of Skinner (1938), where emotion represents a change of reflex strength. Even Hull's concept is similar for, although he neither uses nor defines the concept of emotion, Hull apparently subsumes it under changes in drive strength.

Ample evidence has already been presented to suggest that anxiety is one of the most readily acquired and persistent conditioned reactions and one aspect of anxiety which has been most extensively investigated is the cardiac component. According to Gantt (1953a, 1953b), almost all conditioned responses possess a cardiac component which is more stable and more difficult to extinguish than the motor components of the conditioned response. This probably accounts, in part, for the wide pervasion of conditioned manifest anxiety; for example, conditioned tachycardia remains long after other components such as salivary conditioning have vanished. The fact that the "psychosomatic" aspects may be all that remains of an earlier conditioned response is regarded by Gantt as the basis of human conflict. The overt (motor) behaviour is adaptive, the cardiac and other autonomic conditioned components are not so easily extinguished. Thus there may be good *overt* adjustment to a situation but emotional conditioning from some previous situation is still present.[1]

For these reasons Gantt and his colleagues have given particular attention to a study of both cardiac conditioning and the specific changes in heart rate which are said to accompany the conditioning of all reflexes (Gantt 1944). It has been demonstrated that a close parallel exists between the intensities of conditioned motor responses and the amplitude of the heart-rate changes (Robinson and Gantt, 1947); these changes even parallel the time intervals between the various motor conditioning stimuli (Gantt, Gakenheimer and Stunkard, 1951). The changes in heart rate during the establishment of a conditioned response sometimes take the form of an acceleration and sometimes a deceleration, depending on the individual. Why this should be so or to what factors it is related are at present only partially resolved problems. Whatever the reasons, the fact

remains that the heart rate is one of the most sensitive and accurate physical indicators of what is commonly termed emotional stress or anxiety (Weiss, 1956).

The conditioning of cardiac responses can be readily induced in most normal subjects to a variety of originally innocuous stimuli (e.g. Garvey, 1933; Minut-Sarokhtina, Sarokhtin, and Turgel, 1934; Scott, 1930). Tigerstadt (1926) showed that a conditioned cardiac response (an increase in blood-pressure) could be produced in humans merely by bringing the subject back into a previously exciting situation under which blood-pressure measurements had originally been taken and Anderson, Parmenter and Liddell (1939) have demonstrated the development of an experimental neurosis and accompanying cardiac disorder in the sheep. When Beir (1940) conditioned various cardiovascular responses to a buzzer, using exercise as the unconditioned stimulus, he found that the conditioned cardiac response became more and more intense as the reinforcements continued. It is hardly surprising that it has been estimated that between 20 and 50 per cent of all patients who consult physicians for cardiac disorders show no organic lesions and that cardiac neuroses, i.e. functional heart disorders, have been found in almost every kind of neurotic to a greater or lesser degree (Wahl, 1932; Wyckoff, 1928). Beier (1940), as a result of his experiments, suggests that such cases could be treated by a process of reconditioning or of experimental extinction. The success of Maier's work (1939), in which he produced and cured experimental "neuroses" in rats by conditioning techniques, lends support to this suggestion.

There is some evidence to suggest that certain human involuntary processes can be made amenable to voluntary control by means of conditioned response techniques. Voluntary control can be initiated by a verbal or subvocal stimulus and, according to Menzies (1937), even by merely recalling a certain visual pattern.

Abnormal perception may also be produced in a similar manner and Leuba (1941) describes the production of what he calls "images" by means of sensory conditioning under hypnosis. A bell and a pin prick were paired for several trials and the subject told to forget on waking. Later, when he heard the bell he felt uncomfortable sensations in his hand. Ellson's (1941) studies support Leuba's contention that conditioned sensations and hallucinatory images are equivalent phenomena. Lundholm (1928) produced both positive and negative conditioned responses; in one study, after inducing posthypnotic deafness he was unable to condition a sound to an electric shock. Not everybody, however, has been successful in the field of sensory conditioning. Cason (1939), who introduced the term, failed to obtain any

---

[1] Gantt (1953a) reports in detail the case of a dog who had lost all traces of the salivary and motor conditioned responses to food established two years earlier, but the cardiac component of the response remained undiminished.

positive results; so did Kelley (1934), in a well-planned experiment specifically designed to produce conditioned hallucinations. On the other hand it has been reported possible to condition critical flicker fusion, thermal sensations and even changes in gustatory sensations (London, 1954).

Weitzenhoffer (1955) suggests that somatic changes such as blister formation induced under hypnosis may be regarded as conditioned physical reactions and it is possible that subjects can even be placed in, and withdrawn from, an hypnotic trance by conditioning procedures (Narbutovich, 1934). There would seem to be little doubt that words can become conditioned to both internal and external stimuli, and in this way can precipitate various physical reactions (Bechterev, 1906; Platonov, 1930). The self-induction of trance states, and other associated bizarre physical phenomena prevalent in certain oriental and primitive communities, may well be explicable along these lines, even though the precise mechanisms are not as yet fully understood. The application of conditioning theories to problems in anthropology is not novel; in the early part of this century Frazer (1922), and later Kempf (1931), suggested a conditioned response mechanism by which sympathetic magic and taboo might become an effective process.

Bykov (Bykov, 1957; Eagle, 1933 and Gantt, 1953a) is supposed to have produced conditioned bile and urinary secretions and even the constriction of the blood vessels and changes in blood sugar. He is also supposed to have produced conditioned leucocytosis. However, Gantt, Katzenelbogan and Leucks (1937) failed to condition the rise in blood sugar after an adrenalin injection was paired with either a buzzer or the "preparation for the injection." But these authors note that hyperglycaemia can be produced under hypnosis merely by the suggestion: "You have drunk a glass of sugared water." Gantt (1953a) later extended this work to the conditioning of autonomic activities such as the vestibular function of equilibrium.

There is also some evidence that the sedation effect of depressant drugs such as Sodium Amytal can be conditioned (London, 1953) and, if Wilczowski's (1954) untrustworthy conclusions are correct (his experiment lacked both adequate design and statistical treatment), it is possible to condition the physiological effects of alcohol. Kleitman and Crisler (1927) conditioned the retching behaviour originally produced by morphine to a sound stimulus. Metalnikov and Chorine (1928) succeeded in producing conditioned serological reactions in animals, but Razran (1933) criticized their experiments on methodological grounds. When Smith and Dalinger (1933) carried out a similar, but much better-controlled, experiment the positive results were confirmed.

Experiments such as the above are of considerable importance in the field of psychosomatic medicine, which is, unfortunately, one of the vaguest and most unscientific branches of psychology and psychiatry and one in which the literature is replete with anecdotal evidence, subjective impressions and dogmatic theory which rest on no adequate foundations. There is, however, a recent tendency in psychosomatic medicine to regard many somatic disorders such as allergies, peptic ulcers, mucous colitis, hypertension, etc. as conditioned response patterns of hidden origin (Friedman, 1951). The relationship between cortex and viscera is essential to an understanding of such disorders, and conditioned response techniques provide one of the most powerful tools for this purpose. Despite, in certain rare instances, egregious attempts to make their findings compatible with a rigid philosophic system, the data obtained by Soviet neurophysiologists are of primary significance. By combining electrophysiological and biochemical methods they have accumulated an impressive array of factual information which should not be overlooked on the above account (Liberson, 1957). It is claimed that bladder distension in man has been conditioned and also increases in metabolism; it is even claimed that conditioned diuresis has been established in a denervated kidney. There is ample evidence of EEG conditioning (*Proc. IV Int. Cong.*, 1957) and, more practically, of the conditioned inhibition of uncinate fits (Efron, 1957).

The wide variety of body functions which are capable of being readily conditioned has caused several workers to attempt to induce specific psychosomatic disorders by experimental means. There are for example, many indications that bronchial asthmatic attacks can be provoked by means other than direct contact with the specific noxious agent, i.e. various conditioned stimuli may be effectively substituted for the original agent (Kammerer, 1934; Mackenzie, 1885; Metsger, 1947). The Noelpps have carried out a recent series of experiments in which they provoked experimental asthmatic attacks in guinea-pigs by exposure to antigenic or histamine spray (1952, 1954). By pairing this procedure with a sound they were able to produce conditioned asthmatic attacks after as few as five reinforcements. Acting upon the observation that asthmatic attacks in humans often followed emotional events, Groen and his associates (Dekker and Groen, 1956; Dekker, Pelser and Groen, 1957) managed to induce asthmatic attacks by exposing their patients to artificially constructed emotional stimuli selected in each case from a survey of the specific clinical histories.

Despite progress such as the above, asthma still continues to be a subject of controversy and the building of a bridge between the psychogenic and the somatic schools of thought is far from complete

(Bastiaans and Groen, 1954). From recent reviews (Leigh, 1953; L. Rees, 1956) of the relevant literature, two facts clearly emerge. The first, that there is now considerable evidence that emotional factors are involved in the aetiology of certain cases of asthma and the second, that the relationships, if any, between fundamental personality attributes and dispositions towards asthma are still largely unestablished. Some investigators have claimed that asthmatic attacks have an hysterical basis while others report that the most common form of neurosis pertaining to asthma is that of anxiety (L. Rees, 1953).

Franks and Leigh (1958), in an attempt to throw light upon this problem in an objective manner, used the technique of conditioning coupled with personality questionnaires relating to introversion-extraversion. Although their asthmatic group was more neurotic than normal subjects, but less neurotic than non-asthmatic neurotics, they did not differ in condition-ability from the normal group or from the group of neurotics, of whom half were dysthymic and half were hysteric. These results are consistent with the pos-sibility, maintained by some allergists, that the common personality type assumed to be possessed by asthmatics is an effect and not a cause.

Psychogenic pain may be classed with the psycho-somatic disorders. It is possible that such pain is a form of conditioned "suffering" which is interpreted as pain by the patient because it was associated with pain at one time. For example, when a dog has been trained to respond to a bell in anticipation of a painful shock, it displays symptoms of anxiety or suffering when the conditioned stimulus is presented; but there is no reason to suppose that the animal is actually experiencing pain (Wikler, 1948, 1950). Thus Malmo and Shagass (1950) found that random movements during intervals between exposures of their subjects to head pain were reduced following prefrontal leucotomy, although head withdrawals to the actual painful stimuli were not. It may be that leucotomy, which is known to reduce conditionability in certain cases, reduces the strength of conditioning of responses to the suffering associated with pain. This may be the possible- mechanism underlying the effective reduction of intractable pain by surgical brain operations.

Conditioned Response Therapy

Sargant and Slater (1954) introduce their book with a sentence which is worthy of quotation: "It is a remarkable fact that, despite the popular notion that psychotherapy is the only method of treatment of psychological conditions, most of the big advances in psychiatric therapy have been along somatic lines." A frequent objection to such forms of treatment and, more specifically, to any application of conditioning

is that it is merely the symptom which is ameliorated and not the "underlying cause." Apart from the irrelevance of such a comment to a patient whose prime cause for complaint (and usually the initial reason for his referral) is reduced, there is an increas-ing body of experimental data which indicates that even the so-called "dynamic mechanisms" may be described and duplicated in a language system acceptable to the S-R learning theorist.

Probably the greatest contribution to the under-standing of unconscious processes has been made by the experimental psychologists using precise and readily quantifiable data, rather than by the more speculative clinicians. Schoenfeld (1950), defining anxiety in terms of the behavioural changes following a signal of forthcoming noxious stimuli, has given adequate arguments for the use of conditioning in the experimental study of anxiety. Often anxiety is an unconscious process in so far as it is impossible to verbalize. Lacey and Smith (1954), operationally defining anxiety in terms of the psychological changes that occur in anticipation of an electric shock, preceded this shock by a spoken word and showed that human subjects could develop a conditioned anxiety reaction in which the subjects were *unaware* of the nature of the conditioning signal. In another series of experiments, Lacey and his colleagues (Lacey and Smith, 1954; Lacey, Smith and Green, 1955) asked a group of normal subjects to chain associate for fifteen seconds to a list of forty different stimulus words. One of these words (differing for different subjects) was followed by an electric shock. They found that conditioned anxiety responses to verbal stimuli could be obtained often with as few as two reinforcements.

More recently the Staats (1957), testing an hypo-thesis that meaning itself is a kind of response and consequently capable of being conditioned, associated nonsense syllables with *different* words having a certain similarity of meaning. They were eventually successful in conditioning the common meaning components of the different words to the originally neutral nonsense stimuli. This study is of considerable importance for those who, with Mowrer (1954), view speech as a conditioning device and meaning as a conditioned response. It is significant that in the studies of Lacey a conditioned response appeared not only to the conditioned stimulus, but also to other stimuli meaningfully related to this stimulus. For example, if a conditioned response is obtained to the word "style" then semantic generalization may be found to both the homophone "stile" and the synonym "fashion."

Not only may meaning be conditioned without awareness but overt behaviour may be modified without the subject's knowledge. For example

McNair (1957) has shown that the rate of verbal responding can be influenced without the subject's awareness by altering the rate of reinforcement. Nuthmann (1957) found that the experimenter's saying "good" was able to function as a reinforcement for the conditioning of "acceptance of self" on a personality questionnaire relating to personal attitudes —this also without the subject's awareness. Hildin and Brown (1957) gave a questionnaire by telephone and obtained similar results using "good" as a reinforcer.

In a remarkable laboratory parallel of clinical repression, Ericksen and Kuethe (1956) extended these findings to show that conflict behaviour could be modified. They experimentally demonstrated avoidance conditioning without awareness by punishing certain arbitrarily selected words in a subject's chain association during a word association test by an electric shock and found that these words were "repressed" in the consequent test trials on the same word association test even when the threat of shock was absent. This study is atypical since it is one of the very few in which an experimental analogue of a dynamic concept successfully satisfies all the generally accepted criteria of the concept.[1]

Studies such as these are of importance in the application of conditioning principles to the treatment of patients by some form of psychotherapy since most psychotherapists work on the assumption that a behaviour reaction on their part can modify or influence their patient's behaviour. But this section is primarily concerned with the direct application of conditioning techniques in situations other than verbal. In this respect conditioned aversion therapy, in which a conditioned aversion is established by the use of some noxious unconditioned stimulus such as nausea or an electric shock, is probably the most widely recognized technique.

From a recent excellent review (Solomon and Brush, 1957) of avoidance conditioning and anxiety as the reinforcer for the learning of new responses it is clear that, apart from the treatment of alcoholism, electric shock is the most widely used aversion motivator. By this means all kinds of conditioned aversions can be produced in both animals and men. Probably because electric shock has many advantages, such as minimal adaptation properties and maximal control, the possibilities of utilizing in man other averting stimuli such as bright lights, loud noises,

heat spots and jets of air have been singularly neglected. Furthermore, the relative efficiencies of classical and avoidance types of aversion conditioning and the problems involved in the treatment of mental disorders by these means are still largely open questions.

Alcoholism is frequently treated by some form of conditioned aversion therapy, in most cases using apomorphine as the conditioned stimulus. Although there is a plethora of studies purporting to evaluate the effectiveness of such techniques (Franks, 1958a), the majority are of limited value in arriving at any conclusions. Firstly, despite minutiae of descriptive material, reports provide insufficient technical and procedural details of the methods used; secondly, although lip service is usually paid to the need for rigorous experimental techniques, few take this advice. It is consequently difficult to assess the potential value of conditioned aversion therapy for alcoholism carried out according to strict experimental schedules.

Many problems are associated with the use of apomorphine as the unconditioned noxious stimulus. For example, it has been demonstrated upon many occasions that centrally depressant drugs make the learning of new conditioned responses more difficult. If apomorphine is in this category (and no one has yet investigated this important problem) then it is clearly the most unsuitable drug to use alone as a noxious agent. Several solutions suggest themselves; it may be possible to find a noxious agent which is not a central depressant; it may be possible, prior to each session, to give the patient a stimulant drug such as caffeine to counteract the depressant, but not the nausea-producing action of the apomorphine. The concept of combining the apomorphine with some other agent is no new one, but the combinations suggested have not always been propitious; for example, Lemere and O'Hallaren (1949) propose to administer *sedatives* during the course of treatment to relieve tension.

It should be pointed out that the judicious use of additional pharmacological agents to augment the conditioning process apply equally to other forms of conditioned aversion therapy such as the treatment of fetishism (Raymond, 1956) or writer's cramp (Liversedge and Sylvester, 1955). Indeed, if psychotherapy is conceptualized as an exercise in learning and conditioning, then it might be considered advisable to give a depressant drug during the extinction of the undesired learning or habit pattern and a stimulant drug during the more positive or training part of the treatment. Sargant and Slater (1954) cite many examples of the use of Sodium Amytal for the reduction of manifest anxiety and in this context describe the drug as useful for "deconditioning to situations likely

---

[1] In the animal world regression has been demonstrated by, among others, Mowrer (1940) and Masserman (1943, 1946). An animal is first taught to obtain food by a simple reaction pattern. This conditioned pattern is then extinguished and a more complicated food-getting reaction pattern is developed in its place. If this more complex conditioned pattern is now associated with an electric shock or sudden blast of air the animal tends to "regress" back to the earlier and apparently extinguished learned pattern of response.

to produce anxiety." If anxiety is regarded as a conditioned response pattern of behaviour this would seem to be an admirable procedure. A preliminary attempt to make use of drugs in these ways is reported by Agostan (1944), although his theoretical orientation is extremely different to that presented here.

If apomorphine does behave as a depressant a quite different solution would be to make use of agents other than drugs as the noxious unconditioned stimulus, perhaps shock. Using this technique, Kantorovich (1929) was able to induce a conditioned aversion not only to the taste of alcohol, but also to its smell and sight and even to a photograph of a bottle.

Alcoholism and other addictions are frequently regarded as tension reducing and pleasure generating activities.[1] If it is correct that numerous physiological reactions, drug effects and internal secretions can be conditioned, then it might be possible to condition certain of the unconditioned physiological effects of alcohol and other drugs to innocuous conditioning stimuli. Furthermore, if many of the psychological effects of alcohol are conditioned responses to the sight, taste or smell of alcohol as a conditioned stimulus, then it should be possible to produce these same conditioned responses to more innocent and less harmful conditioning stimuli than alcohol. In this respect, Lindesmith (1947) comments that although the first stab of a hypodermic needle is painful to the morphine addict it rapidly becomes a conditioned stimulus to which the conditioned response is pleasure, and the subject then actually enjoys the entry of the needle. In one patient of Lindesmith's this response was so well established that he reacted to the injection of a saline solution as if it were morphine for as long as fifteen consecutive days. These techniques might be of value in counteracting the addiction withdrawal symptoms often experienced whatever form of therapy is used. Rubenstein (1931), using a similar procedure, was highly successful in the treatment of a chronic morphine addict.

After the treatment of alcoholism, the next most frequent use of direct conditioned aversion therapy is probably for the amelioration of various enuretic symptoms in children. Since the technique was reintroduced by the Mowrers (1938) many investi-

gators have reported successful results, but always with small samples. However, Martin and Kubly (1950) report a 74 per cent success with a total sample of one hundred and eighteen children. Most of the apparatus commercially available consists of some form of conductor, coiled or in two sections so that there is an insulating blanket or pad preventing the completion of the electrical circuit. When the child urinates the circuit is completed and a buzzer sounds. The buzzer acts as the unconditioned stimulus, waking is the unconditioned response which it is hoped to condition and bladder tension is the conditioned stimulus. The ultimate aim is for sphincter control, by a process of generalization, to become the eventual conditioned response. Although such a pattern can be established even before an infant can sit up, i.e. prior to effective voluntary muscle control, for a variety of reasons the technique is not advisable at this early age (Fleck, 1953; Kanner, 1943).

The aetiology and treatment of writer's cramp is currently a matter of much dispute. According to Liversedge and Sylvester (1955) the persistence of writer's cramp, whatever its origin, may be attributable to the formation of a conditioned response. Proceeding on this assumption they successfully treated a number of cases which had previously proved to be resistant to diverse kinds of psychotherapy. Whenever the subject's hand trembled in threading a metal stylus into a series of progressively smaller holes in a sheet of metal he received a mild electric shock, similarly whenever the subject was unable to trace various cursive patterns with a stylus, or whenever his muscles contracted and applied excessive pressure to the handle of a fountain pen, he also received a shock. The advantage of this type of therapy is that it can be given by anyone with sufficient understanding of the mechanical nature of the disorder to apply the various training exercises.

Considering the unimpressive record of psychotherapy, no possible techniques can be reasonably ignored, especially when the proposed techniques are based on some rational and testable formulation.[1] A particular example of the partial failure of the more conventional forms of psychotherapy is that of the treatment of the sexual disorders. As early as 1927 Kostyleff (1927) favourably contrasted conditioned reflex mechanisms with Freudian principles in the aetiology and treatment of sexual perversions. More recently, Gordon (1948) developed an extended conditioned reflex treatment of abnormalities such as incestuous attachments, fetishism, exhibitionism and scoptophilia, and Salter (1949), in his characteristically

---

[1] The case has been argued elsewhere (Franks, 1958a) that alcoholism is itself a conditioned disorder, the possible sequence of events being something like this: initially an individual drinks in a social setting and the alcohol, by a process of classical conditioning in accord with the principle of contiguity, becomes associated with the relief of tension and anxiety resulting from being with friends. Now, to account for the perpetuation of the habit in most situations, simple conditioning is inadequate and it is necessary to invoke a reinforcement theory; the alcohol reduces the anxiety and it is this drive reduction which provides the reinforcement for the pattern of drinking to perpetuate itself.

[1] The insuperable logical paradoxes of Freudian theory are presented nowhere more clearly than in the many publications of Mowrer (see Mowrer 1953). The false claims of the psychoanalysts were exposed in the American psychiatric literature as long ago as 1933 (Sachs 1933).

vigorous if flamboyant manner, attempted to explain how masochism may arise as a conditioned response and be treated accordingly. A striking apparent success is reported by Raymond (1956) who, after a discussion of fetishism as a conditioned disorder, treated and cured a chronic and severe fetishist by the use of a noxious conditioned aversion technique.

A novel area where the direct application of conditioned response techniques has been shown to be of some value is that of the treatment of bruxism (teeth grinding and gnashing during sleep). While the patient is in a deep hypnotic trance a conditioned response is established of waking from sleep as soon as the muscles of mastication begin to contract and start the grinding operation (Kuehner, 1956). Probably, as with enuresis and writer's cramp, it would be possible to develop a practical technique by means of which a conditioned aversion pattern of waking could be established without resort to hypnosis.

CONCLUSION

The methodology of conditioned reflexes has contributed much valuable information to the understanding of human behaviour and is a most promising tool in the formidable task of establishing an objective science of abnormal psychology. The many implications discussed in the major portions of this chapter bear witness to the exciting opportunities which this area of abnormal psychology can provide.

The contribution might have been greater had more concern been attached to those criteria which the present writer considers to be essential requisites of acceptable research (Franks 1957c). In this respect a marked contrast exists between the usually exemplary studies of the more academic investigators concerned with fundamental problems of learning theory or neurophysiology, and the quixotic, but frequently unsystematic and ill-conceived, experiments of the clinician and the applied psychologist. Many potentially important experiments are of limited value because of inadequate design and a lack of rigour in their execution; in some instances an insufficiency of technical or procedural details precludes any valid evaluations being made.

These are all necessary, but not sufficient, requirements for the emergence of a science of abnormal psychology which makes full use of conditioned response techniques and data. In addition, there is a need for some resolution of the problems fleetingly introduced in the first section of this chapter. In particular, the concept and inclusiveness of the term *conditioned response* requires much clarification. There is little doubt that the simple Pavlovian model, inviting as it is, is inadequate to account for all the facts, and it is probable that eventually conditioning and learning must be integrated into one comprehensive system.

The theory of conditioning and personality promulgated here suffers from many temporary weaknesses, not least of which are a present lack of extensive confirmatory data and the possibly premature assumption of a general factor of conditionability, the reality of which has yet to be demonstrated.

Although there is no *a priori* justification for this assumption (the principle of cortical equipotentiality no longer being tenable), the data presented in the present chapter are in agreement with the existence of either a general factor, or of several group factors, or even with both possibilities.

A further weakness, unfortunately common to almost all studies involving personality variables, is the diminutive magnitude of the obtained correlations between conditioning and those measures of personality to which conditionability is believed to be related; a possible explanation (when problems of test reliability, etc. have been excluded) is that the general factor, if it exists, is insufficient to account for an individual's ability to generate and retain conditioned responses. Other specific factors, at present unrecognized, may play a much larger role in the formation of conditioned responses than has hitherto been suspected. Another weakness of the present theory is that certain of the findings may relate not to classical conditioning, as it is generally (but not universally) defined, but only to behavioural changes at the peripheral levels. This is especially possible in those studies dependent on modifications induced by the actions of drugs and in those studies which attempt to relate largely peripheral phenomena, such as dark adaptation, to conditioning (Granger and Franks, 1958).

Nevertheless, the present theory provides many fundamental advantages which more than compensate for the existence of numerous weaknesses, none of which are devastating and all of which can be remedied. The theory is so formulated that it permits of predictions which may be explicitly tested in a variety of different situations and with a variety of conditioning techniques. Furthermore, it forms part of a much more extensive theory of human behaviour (Eysenck, 1957), in which the conditioned response is merely one aspect of the manner in which the central and autonomic nervous systems manifest their functions.

It is very likely that conditioning alone is insufficient

to account for all forms of normal and abnormal personality development. As Pavlov insisted, the conditioned response is one possible technique, certainly not the only one, for understanding the principles of central functioning and the ways in which the general laws of central activity manifest themselves. The findings derived from conditioned response experiments can therefore be integrated with the increasing number of predicted findings obtained in many different contexts and with many different techniques, beyond the scope of this chapter, but not of this volume.

In conclusion, it must be reaffirmed that both the general theory of personality and the specific aspects pertinent to conditioning will require much modification and much elaboration. However, the extreme probability that the theory, in its present form, is at best a simplified version of the true state of affairs, is not of necessity a disadvantage; the more complex the formulation in the initial stages, the more difficult it is to devise a series of crucial experiments. As Morris Cohen (1944, p. 182) puts it: "If, *per impossibile*, any theory were as complex as the actual facts, it would have no real value. All theory is a simplification and therefore incomplete."

REFERENCES

AGOSTAN, T., Experimental administration of Benzedrine sulfate and other central stimulants in psychoanalyses and psychotherapies, *Psychoanal. Rev.*, **31**, 438–452 (1944).

ALDRICH, C. A., A new test for hearing in the newborn, the conditioned reflex, *Amer. J. Dis. Child.*, **35**, 36–37 (1928).

ANDERSON, O. D. and LIDDELL, H. S., Observations on experimental neuroses in sheep, *A.M.A. Arch. Neurol. Psychiat.*, **34**, 330–354 (1935).

ANDERSON, O. D., PARMENTER, R. and LIDDELL, H. S., Some cardiovascular manifestations of experimental neuroses in sheep, *Psychosom. Med.*, **1**, 93–100 (1939).

BARTHOLOMEW, A. A., FRANKS, C. M. and MARLEY, E., Susceptibility to methylpentynol: 3. Eyelid conditioning and P.G.R. response, *J. Ment. Sci.*, **104**, 1167–1173 (1958).

BASTIAANS, J. and GROEN, J., Psychogenesis and psychotherapy of bronchial asthma: 242–268 in *Modern Trends in Psychosomatic Medicine*, Ed. D. O'Neil (London, Butterworth, 1954).

BECHTEREV, W. V., What is hypnosis? *J. Abnorm. (Soc.) Psychol.*, **1**, 18–25 (1906).

BEIER, D. C., Conditioned cardiovascular responses and suggestions for the treatment of cardiac neuroses, *J. Exp. Psychol.*, **26**, 311–321 (1940).

BENDER, L. and SCHILDER, P., Unconditioned and conditioned reactions to pain in schizophrenia, *Amer. J. Psychiat.*, **10**, 365–384 (1930).

BERRY, J. L. and MARTIN, B., G.S.R. reactivity as a function of anxiety, instructions, and sex, *J. Abnorm. (Soc.) Psychol.*, **54**, 9–12 (1957).

BINDRA, D., PATERSON, A. L. and STRZELECKI, J., On the relation between anxiety and conditioning, *Canad. J. Psychol.*, **9**, 1–6 (1955).

BIRCH, H. G., The role of motivational factors in insightful problem solving, *J. Comp. Psychol.*, **38**, 295–317 (1946).

BITTERMAN, M. and HOLTZMAN, W., Conditioning and extinction of the galvanic skin response as a function of anxiety, *J. Abnorm. (Soc.) Psychol.*, **47**, 615–623 (1952).

BLOOMER, H., A simple method for testing the hearing of small children, *J. Speech. Dis.*, **7**, 311–312 (1942).

BORDLEY, J. E., An evaluation of the psychogalvanic skin-resistance technique in audiometry, *Laryngoscope St. Louis*, **66**, 1,162–1,185 (1956).

BROWN, C. W. and SEARLE, L. V., The effect of variation in the dose of Benzedrine sulfate on the activity of white rats, *J. Exp. Psychol.*, **22**, 555–563 (1938).

BUCHWALD, A. M. and YAMAGUCHI, H. G., The effect of change in drive level on habit reversal, *J. Exp. Psychol.*, **50**, 265–268 (1955).

BYKOV, K. M., *The Cerebral Cortex and the Internal Organs*, Trans. W. H. Gantt (New York, Chem. Pub. Co., 1957).

CARL, G. P. and TURNER, W. D., The effects of Benzedrine sulfate (amphetamine sulfate) on performance in a comprehensive psychometric examination, *J. Psychol.*, **8**, 165–216 (1939).

CASON, H., Sensory conditioning, *J. Exp. Psychol.*, **19**, 572–591 (1936).

COHEN, L. H., HILGARD, E. R. and WENDT, G. R., Sensitivity to light in a case of hysterical blindness, studied by reinforcement-inhibition and conditioning methods, *Yale J. Biol. Med.*, **6**, 61–67 (1933).

COHEN, M. R., *A Preface to Logic* (New York, Holt, 1944).

COWAN, E. A. and FOULKE, M., Variation in susceptibility to the conditioning of inhibition as an index of constitutional type, *Child. Developm.*, **5**, 201–236 (1934).

CULLER, E. A., FINCH, G., GIRDEN, E. and BROGDEN, W., Measurements of acuity by the conditioned-response technique, *J. Gen. Psychol.*, **12**, 223–227 (1935).

DARROW, C. W. and HEATH, L. L., *Reaction Tendencies Relating to Personality in Studies in the Dynamics of Behavior*, Ed. K. S. Cashley (Chicago, Univ. of Chicago Press, 1932).

DAS, J. P., An experimental investigation of the relation between hypnosis, conditioning and reactive inhibition, *Ph.D. Thesis, Univ. of London. Lib.* (1957).

DEKKER, E. and GROEN, J., Reproducible psychogenic attacks of asthma. A laboratory study, *J. Psychosom. Res.*, **1**, 58–67 (1956).

DEKKER, E., PELSER, H. E. and GROEN, J., Conditioning as a cause of asthmatic attacks: a laboratory study, *J. Psychosom. Res.*, **2**, 97–108 (1957).

DEWS, P. B., Modification by drugs of performance on simple schedules of positive reinforcement, *Ann. N.Y. Acad. Sci.*, **65**, 268–281 (1956).

DIETHELM, O. (Ed.), *Etiology of Chronic Alcoholism* (Springfield, Ill., C. C. Thomas, 1955).

DIX, M. R. and HALLPIKE, C. S., The peep show. A new technique for pure-tone audiometry in young children, *Brit. Med. J.*, **2**, 719–723 (1947).

DOLLARD, J. and MILLER, N. E., *Personality and Psychotherapy* (New York, McGraw-Hill, 1950).

DWORKIN, S., KATZMAN, J., HUTCHINSON, G. A. and

McCabe, J. R., Hearing acuity of animals as measured by conditioning methods, *J. Exp. Psychol.*, **26**, 281–298 (1940).

Eagle, E., Conditioned inhibition of water diuresis, *Amer. J. Physiol.*, **103**, 362–366 (1933).

Efron, R., The conditioned inhibition of uncinate fits, *Brain*, **80**, 251–262 (1957).

Elder, J. H., Auditory acuity of the chimpanzee, *J. Comp. Psychol.*, **17**, 157–183 (1934).

Ellson, D. G., Hallucinations produced by sensory conditioning, *J. Exp. Psychol.*, **28**, 1–20 (1941).

Eriksen, C. W., Some personality correlates of stimulus generalization under stress, *J. Abnorm. (Soc.) Psychol.*, **49**, 561–565 (1954).

Eriksen, C. W. and Kuethe, J. L., Avoidance conditioning of verbal behavior without awareness: a paradigm of repression, *J. Abnorm. (Soc.) Psychol.*, **55**, 203–209 (1956).

Ewing, I. R. and Ewing, A. W. G., The ascertainment of deafness in infancy and early childhood, *J. Laryng.*, **59**, 309–333 (1944).

Eysenck, H. J., *Dimensions of Personality* (London, Routledge & Kegan Paul, 1947).

Eysenck, H. J., *The Structure of Human Personality* (London, Methuen, 1953).

Eysenck, H. J., *The Dynamics of Anxiety and Hysteria* (London, Routledge & Kegan Paul, 1957).

Eysenck, H. J., *Experiments in Personality* (London, Routledge & Kegan Paul, to be published).

Farber, I. E. and Spence, K. W., Complex learning and conditioning as a function of anxiety, *J. Exp. Psychol.*, **45**, 120–125 (1953).

Finesinger, J. E., Sutherland, G. F. and McGuire, F. F., The positive conditional salivary reflex in psycho-neurotic patients, *Amer. J. Psychiat.*, **99**, 61–74 (1942).

Fink, D. H., *Release from Nervous Tension* (New York, Simon & Schuster, 1943).

Fleck, S., Vigilance (orientating behavior), conditional reactions, and adjustment patterns in schizophrenic and compulsive patients, *Ann. N.Y. Acad. Sci.*, **56**, 342–382 (1953).

Fleck, S. and Gantt, W. H., Conditional responses in patients receiving electric shock treatment, *Amer. J. Psychiat.*, **108**, 280–288 (1951).

Franks, C. M., An experimental study of conditioning as related to mental abnormality, *Ph.D. Thesis, Univ. of London Lib.* (1954).

Franks, C. M., The establishment of a conditioning laboratory for the investigation of personality and cortical functioning, *Nature*, **175**, 984–985 (1955).

Franks, C. M., Recidivism, psychopathy and delinquency, *Brit. J. Delinq.*, **6**, 192–201 (1956a).

Franks, C. M., Conditioning and personality, *J. Abnorm. (Soc.) Psychol.*, **52**, 143–150 (1956b).

Franks, C. M., L'Echelle de Taylor et l'analyse dimensionnelle de l'anxiété, *Rev. Psychol. appl.*, **6**, 35–44 (1956c).

Franks, C. M., Effect of food, drink and tobacco deprivation on the conditioning of the eyeblink response, *J. Exp. Psychol.*, **53**, 117–120 (1957a).

Franks, C. M., Personality factors and the rate of conditioning, *Brit. J. Psychol.*, **48**, 119–126 (1957b).

Franks, C. M., Personality theory in Britain, in *Perspectives in Personality Theory*, Eds. H. P. David and H. von Bracken (London, Tavistock Publ., 1957c).

Franks, C. M., Alcohol, alcoholism and conditioning: a review of the literature and some theoretical considerations, *J. Ment. Sci.*, **104**, 14–33 (1958a).

Franks, C. M., Some fundamental problems in conditioning, *Acta Psychologica*, **14**, 223–246 (1958b).

Franks, C. M. and Laverty, S. G., Sodium amytal and eyelid conditioning, *J. Ment. Sci.*, **101**, 654–663 (1955).

Franks, C. M. and Leigh, D., The conditioned eyeblink response in asthmatic and non-asthmatic subjects, *J. Psychosom. Res.*, in press.

Franks, C. M., Souief, M. I. and Maxwell, A. M., A factorial study of certain scales from the M.M.P.I. and the S.T.D.C.R., to be published.

Franks, C. M. and Trouton, D. S., Effects of amobarbital sodium and dexamphetamine sulfate on the conditioning of the eyeblink response, *J. Comp. Physiol. Psychol.*, **51**, 220–222 (1958).

Franks, C. M., Trouton, D. S. and Laverty, S. G., The inhibition of a conditioned response following arecoline administration in man, *J. Clin. Exp. Psychopath.*, **19**, 226–233 (1958).

Franks, C. M. and Willett, B. A., Algumas sugestoes sôbre a conduta delinqüente, *Rev. de Psicol. Norm. e Patol.*, **2**, 103–110 (1956).

Franks, C. M. and Withers, W. C. R., Photo-electric recording of eyelid movements, *Amer. J. Psychol.*, **68**, 467–471 (1955).

Frazer, J. G., *The Golden Bough*, Abridged edn. (London, Macmillan, 1922).

Freedman, B., Conditioning of respiration and its psychomatic implications, *J. Nerv. Ment. Dis.*, **113**, 1–19 (1951).

Freeman, G. L., A method of inducing frustration in human subjects and its influence on palmar skin resistance, *Amer. J. Psychol.*, **53**, 117–120 (1940).

Freeman, G. L., *The Energies of Human Behavior* (Ithaca, N.Y., Cornell Univ. Press, 1948).

Gantt, W. H., Impairment of the function of adaptability as measured by a simple conditioned reflex test in certain psychogenic contrasted with organic diseases, *Sth. Med. J. Nashville*, **31**, 1,219–1,225 (1938).

Gantt, W. H., *Experimental Basis for Neurotic Behavior* (New York, Hoeber, 1944).

Gantt, W. H., The Conditioned reflex function as an aid in the study of the psychiatric patient, in *Relation of Psychological Tests to Psychiatry*, Eds. P. H. Hoch, and J. Zubin (New York, Grune & Stratton, 1950).

Gantt, W. H., The physiological basis of psychiatry: the conditional reflex, in *Basic Problems of Psychiatry*, Ed. J. Watts (New York, Grune & Stratton, 1953a).

Gantt, W. H., Principles of nervous breakdown—schizokinesis and autokinesis, *Ann. N.Y. Acad. Sci.*, **56**, 143–163 (1953b).

Gantt, W. H., Gakenheimer, W. A. and Stunkard, A., Development of cardiac reflex to time intervals, *Fed. Proc.*, **10**, 47 (1951).

Gantt, W. H., Katzenelbogen, S. and Loucks, R. B., An attempt to condition adrenalin hyperglycemia, *Johns Hopk. Hosp. Bull.*, **60**, 400–411 (1937).

Gantt, W. H. and Muncie, W., Analysis of the mental defect in chronic Korsakov's psychosis by means of the conditioned reflex method, *Johns Hopk. Hosp. Bull.*, **70**, 467–487 (1942).

GARVEY, E. R., A study of conditioned respiratory changes, *J. Exp. Psychol.*, **4**, 471–503 (1933).

GILLILAND, A. R. and MORGAN, J. J. B., An objective measure of introversion-extraversion, *J. Abnorm. (Soc.) Psychol.*, **26**, 296–303 (1931).

GLIEDMAN, L. H. and GANTT, W. H., The effects of reserpine and chlorpromazine on orienting behavior and retention of conditioned reflexes, *Sth. Med. J. Nashville*, **49**, 880–889 (1956).

GLIEDMAN, L. H., GANTT, W. H. and TEITELBAUM, H. A., Some implications of conditional reflex studies for *placebo* research, *Amer. J. Psychiat.*, **113**, 1,103–1,107 (1957).

GLUECK, S. and GLUECK, E., *Unraveling Juvenile Delinquency* (Cambridge, Mass., Harvard Univ. Press, 1950).

GOLDSTEIN, R., LUDWIG, H. and NAUNTON, R. F., Difficulty in conditioning galvanic skin responses: its possible significance in clinical audiometry, *Acta Otolaryng. Stockh.*, **44**, 67–77 (1954).

GOODMAN, L. and GILMAN, A., *The Pharmacological Basis of Therapeutics* (New York, Macmillan, 1941).

GORDON, W. W., Cerebral physiology and psychiatry, *J. Ment. Sci.*, **94**, 118–132 (1948).

GRANGER, G. W. and FRANKS, C. M., Dark adaptation and conditioning: some observed correlations, *Amer. J. Psychol.*, **70**, 462–464 (1957).

GUTHRIE, E. R., *The Psychology of Learning* (2nd edn.) (New York, Harper & Bros., 1952).

HARDY, W. G. and BORDLEY, I. E., Evaluation of hearing in young children, *Acta Otolaryng. Stockh.*, **40**, 246–360 (1956).

HILDRUM, D. C. and BROWN, R. W., Verbal reinforcement and interview bias, *J. Abnorm. (Soc.) Psychol.*, **53**, 108–111 (1956).

HILGARD, E. R., JONES, L. V. and KAPLAN, S. J., Conditioned discrimination as related to anxiety, *J. Exp. Psychol.*, **42**, 94–99 (1951).

HORTON, G. P., A quantitative study of learning in the guinea-pig, *J. Comp. Psychol.*, **15**, 59–73 (1933).

HOWE, E. S., A theoretical and experimental investigation of the conditioned galvanic skin response in normals, anxiety states and functional schizophrenica, *Ph.D. Thesis, Univ. of London Lib.* (1952).

HUDSON, B. B., One-trial learning in the domestic rat, *Genet. Psychol. Monogr.*, **57**, 173–180 (1950).

HUNT, H. F., Some effects of drugs on classical (type S) conditioning, *Ann. N.Y. Acad. Sci.*, **65**, 258–267 (1956).

ISCHLONDSKY, N. E., *Brain and Behaviour: Induction as a Fundamental Mechanism of Neuro-Psychic Activity* (London, Kimpton, 1949).

IVANOV-SMOLENSKY, A. G., Die bedingten Reflexe bei der depressiven Phase des Manisch-depressiven Irresein, *Mschr. Psychiat. Neurol.*, **58**, 376–388 (1925).

IVANOV-SMOLENSKY, A. G., On the methods of examining the conditioned food reflexes in children and in mental disorders, *Brain*, **50**, 138–141 (1927a).

IVANOV-SMOLENSKY, A. G., Études experimentales sur les enfants et les alienés selon la méthode des réflexes conditionnels, *Ann. méd-psychol.*, **12**, 140–150 (1927b).

IVANOV-SMOLENSKY, A. G., The pathology of conditioned reflexes and the so-called psychogenic depression, *J. Nerv. Ment. Dis.*, **67**, 346–350 (1928).

IVANOV-SMOLENSKY, A. G., *Essays on the Patho-physiology of Higher Nervous Activity* (Moscow, Foreign Lang. Publ. House, 1954).

JAMES, W. T., Morphological form and its relation to reflex action and behavior, *Proc. Ass. Res. Nerv. Ment. Dis.*, **14**, 28–54 (1934).

JENKINS, J. J. and LYKKEN, D. T., Individual differences, *Annu. Rev. Psychol.*, **8**, 79–112 (1957).

JENSEN, A., Personality, *Annu. Rev. Psychol.*, **9**, 295–322, (1958).

JONES, H. E., The retention of conditioned emotional reactions in infancy, *J. Genet. Psychol.*, **37**, 487–498 (1930).

JONES, M. C., The elimination of children's fears, *J. Exp. Psychol.*, **7**, 382–390 (1924a).

JONES, M. C., A laboratory study of fear: the case of Peter, *Ped. Sem.*, **31**, 308–315 (1924b).

JUNG, J. C., *Psychological Types* (London, Kegan Paul, 1924).

KAMIN, L. J., Relations between discriminatory apparatus stress, and the Taylor scale, *J. Abnorm. (Soc.) Psychol.*, **51**, 595–599 (1955).

KAMIN, L. J., The measurement of anxiety: a methodological note, *Canad. J. Psychol.*, **11**, 71–74 (1956).

KAMMERER, H., *Allergische Diathese und allergische Erkrankungen* (Munich, J. F. Bergmann, 1934).

KANNER, L., Autistic disturbances of affective contact, *Nerv. Child*, **2**, 217–250 (1943).

KANNER, L., The conception of wholes and parts in early infantile autism, *Amer. J. Psychiat.*, **108**, 23–26 (1951).

KANTOVOVICH, N. V., An attempt at associative reflex therapy in alcoholism, *Nov. Refl. Fiziol. Nerv. Sist.*, **3**, 436–447 (1929) (*Psychol. Abstr.*, **4**, No. 4282 (1930).

KASATKIN, N. I. and LEVIKOVA, A. M., On the development of early conditioned reflexes and differentiation of auditory stimuli in infants, *J. Exp. Psychol.*, **18**, 1–19 (1935).

KAUFMAN, D. A., The physiology of schizophrenia dementia, *Zhur. nevropat. i Psikhiat.*, **5**, 259–267 (1953).

KEASTER, J., A quantitative method of testing the hearing of young children, *J. Speech. Dis.*, **12**, 159–160 (1947).

KELLEY, E. L., An attempt to produce artificial chromaesthesia by the technique of the conditioned response, *J. Exp. Psychol.*, **17**, 315–341 (1934).

KEMPF, E. J., The probable origin of sympathetic magic and taboo, *Med. J. Record.*, **133**, (1) 22; (2) 59; (3) 118 (1931).

KEMPF, E. J., Neuroses as conditioned, conflicting, holistic, attitudinal, acquisitive-avoidant reactions, *Ann. N.Y. Acad. Sci.*, **56**, 307–329 (1953).

KENNEDY, A., Recent hysterical states and their treatment, *J. Ment. Sci.*, **86**, 988–1,019 (1940).

KENNEDY, A., Psychopathic personality and social responsibility, *J. Ment. Sci.*, **100**, 873–881 (1954).

KERBIKOV, O. V., Treatment of mental disease by sleep, *Lancet*, **1**, 744–745 (1955).

KIMBLE, G. A. and DUFORT, R. H., The associative factor in eyelid conditioning, *J. Exp. Psychol.*, **52**, 386–391 (1956).

KIMBLE, G. A., MANN, L. I. and DUFORT, R. H., Classical and instrumental eyelid conditioning, *J. Exp. Psychol.*, **49**, 407–417 (1955).

KLEITMAN, N., *Sleep and Wakefulness* (Chicago, Univ. of Chicago Press, 1939).

KLEITMAN, N. and CRISLER, G., A quantitative study of a salivary conditioned reflex, *Amer. J. Physiol.*, **79**, 571–614 (1927).

KONORSKI, J., *Conditioned Reflexes and Neuron Organisaiton* (London, Cambridge Univ. Press, 1948).

KOSTYLEFF, N., L'inversion sexuelle expliquée par réflexologie, *Psychol. et Vie*, **1**, 8–18 (1927).

KRASNOGORSKI, N. I., The conditioned reflex and children's neuroses, *Amer. J. Dis. Child.*, **30**, 753–768 (1925).

KRASNOGORSKI, N. I., Conditioned reflexes in the psychopathology of childhood, *Amer. J. Dis. Child.*, **45**, 335–370 (1933).

KUEHNER, G. F., Hypnosis in dentistry, in *Hypnosis and its Therapeutic Applications*, Ed. R. M. Dorcus (New York, McGraw Hill, 1956).

LACEY, J. I. and SMITH, R. L., Conditioning and generalisation of unconscious anxiety, *Science*, **120**, 1,045–1,052 (1954).

LACEY, J. I., SMITH, R. L. and GREEN, A., Use of conditioned autonomic responses in the study of anxiety, *Psychosom. Med.*, **17**, 208–217 (1955).

LASHLEY, K., Reflex secretion of the human parotid gland, *J. Exp. Psychol.*, **1**, 461–493 (1916).

LAUGHLIN, H. P., *The Neuroses in Clinical Practice* (Philadelphia, Saunders, 1956).

LAVERTY, S. G. and FRANKS, C. M., Sodium Amytal and behaviour in neurotic subjects, *J. Neurol. Psychiat.*, **19**, 137–143 (1956).

LEIGH, D., Asthma and the psychiatrist: a critical review, *Int. Arch. Allergy*, **4**, 227–246 (1953).

LEMERE, F. and O'HALLAREN, P., Pentothal Sodium treatment of alcoholism, *A.M.A. Arch. Neurol. Psychiat.*, **48**, 482–484 (1949).

LEUBA, C., The use of hypnosis for controlling variables in psychological experiments, *J. Abnorm. (Soc.) Psychol.*, **36**, 271–274 (1941).

LIBERSON, W. T., Recent advances in Russian neurophysiology, *Annu. Rev. Physiol.*, **19**, 557–588 (1957).

LIDDELL, H. S., Conditioned Reflex Method and Experimental Neuroses, in *Personality and the Behavior Disorders*, Ed. J. McV. Hunt (New York, Ronald Press, 1944).

LIDDELL, H. S., Some specific factors that modify tolerance for environmental stress, *Res. Publ. Ass. Nerv. Ment. Dis.*, **24**, 155–171 (1950) (Life Stress and Bodily Disease).

LIDDELL, H. S., *Emotional Research in Animals and Man* (Springfield, Ill., C. C. Thomas, 1956).

LINDESMITH, A. R., *Opiate Addiction* (Bloomington, Indiana, Principia Press, 1947).

LINDSLEY, O. R., New techniques of analysis of psychotic behavior, *Ann. Tech. Rep. No. 3, Office of Naval Research, U.S. Navy* (1956).

LIVERSEDGE, L. A. and SYLVESTER, J. D., Conditioning techniques in the treatment of writer's cramp, *Lancet*, 1,147–1,149, June 4th (1955).

LONDON, I. D., Therapy in Soviet psychiatric hospitals, *Amer. Psychologist.*, **8**, 79–82 (1953).

LONDON, I. D., Research on sensory interaction in the Soviet Union, *Psychol. Bull.*, **51**, 531–568 (1954).

LUNDHOLM, H., An experimental study of functional anaesthesia as induced by suggestion in hypnosis, *J. Abnorm. (Soc.) Psychol.*, **23**, 337–355 (1928).

LYKKEN, D. T., A study of anxiety in the sociopathic personality, *J. Abnorm. (Soc.) Psychol.*, **55**, 6–10 (1957).

MACCORQUODALE, K. and MEEHL, P. E., On a distinction between hypothetical constructs and interviewing variables, *Psychol. Rev.*, **55**, 95–107 (1948).

MCDOUGALL, W., The chemical theory of temperament applied to introversion and extraversion, *J. Abnorm. (Soc.) Psychol.*, **24**, 293–309 (1929).

MCGILL, V. J. and WELCH, L., Hysteria as a conditioning process, *Amer. J. Psychother.*, **1**, 253–278 (1947).

MACKENZIE, M., *Hay-fever, its Aetiology and Treatment, with an Appendix on Rose Cold* (London, Churchill, 1885).

MCNAIR, D. M., Reinforcement of verbal behavior, *J. Exp. Psychol.*, **53**, 40–66 (1957).

MAIER, N. R. F., *Studies of Abnormal Behavior in the Rat. The Neurotic Pattern and an Analysis of the Situation which Produces it* (New York, Harper & Bros., 1939).

MALMO, R. B., and SHAGASS, C., Behavorial and physiologic changes under stress after operations on the frontal lobes, *A.M.A. Arch. Neurol. Psychiat.*, **63**, 1–12 (1950).

MARINESCO, G., and KREINDLER, A., Des reflexes conditionnels. III. Applications des réflexes conditionnels à certains problems clinique, *J. Psychol. norm. path.*, **31**, 722–791 (1934).

MARQUISS, D. G. and HILGARD, E. R., Conditioned lid responses to light in dogs after removal of the visual cortex, *J. Comp. Psychol.*, **22**, 157–178 (1936).

MARTIN, B. and KUBLY, D., Results of treatment of enuresis by a conditioned response method, *J. Cons. Psychol.*, **19**, 71–74 (1955).

MASSERMAN, J. H., *Behavior and Neurosis* (Chicago, Univ. of Chicago Press, 1943).

MASSERMAN, J. H., *Dynamic Principles of Psychiatry* (Philadelphia, Saunders, 1946).

MAYER-GROSS, W., SLATER, E. and ROTH, M., *Clinical Psychiatry* (London, Cassell, 1954).

MENZIES, R., Conditioned vasomotor responses in human subjects, *J. Psychol.*, **4**, 75–120 (1937).

METALNIKOV, S. and CHORINE, V., Rôles des réflexes conditionnels dans la formation des anticorps, *C.R. Soc.biol.*, **99**, 142–145 (1928).

METZGER, F. C., Emotions in the allergic individual, *Amer. J. Psychiat.*, **103**, 697–699 (1947).

MEYER, D. R., On the interaction of simultaneous responses, *Psychol. Bull.*, **50**, 204–220 (1953).

MILLER, C. C., Follow-up studies of introverted children. III. Relative incidence of criminal behaviour, *J. Crim. Law, Criminol. & Police Sci.*, **47**, 414–422 (1956).

MILLER, N. E., Studies of fear as an acquirable drive: I. Fear as motivation and fear-reduction as reinforcement in the learning of new responses, *J. Exp. Psychol.*, **38**, 89–101 (1948).

MINUT-SAROKHTINA, O., SAROKHTIN, J. and TURGEL, K. U., The conditioned vagotrophic heart reflex: II. Associated respiratory arrhythmia, *Zh.Fiziol. U.S.S.R.*, **17**, 707–717 (1934).

MONTAGUE, E. K., The role of anxiety in serial rote learning, *J. Exp. Psychol.*, **45**, 91–96 (1953).

MOWRER, O. H., A stimulus-response analysis of anxiety

and its role as a reinforcing agent, *Psychol. Rev.*, **46**, 553–566 (1939).

MOWRER, O. H., An experimental analogue of "regression" with incidental observations on "reaction-formation," *J. Abnorm. (Soc.) Psychol.*, **35**, 56–87 (1940).

MOWRER, O. H., *Psychotherapy—Theory and Research* (New York, Ronald Press, 1953).

MOWRER, O. H., The psychologist looks at language, *Amer. Psychologist*, **9**, 660–694 (1954).

MOWRER, O. H. and MOWRER, W. M., Enuresis—a method for its study and treatment, *Amer. J. Orthopsychiat.*, **8**, 436–459 (1938).

MUNDY-CASTLE, A. C., The relationship between primary-secondary function and the alpha rhythm of the electro-encephalogram, *J. Nat. Inst. Personnel Res.*, **6**, 95–102 (1955).

MURPHY, G., *Personality: a Biosocial Approach to Origins and Structure* (New York, Harper & Bros., 1947).

NARBUTOVICH, I. O., Possibility of inducing hypnotic sleep and dehypnotisation in man by means of indifferent stimulation according to the conditioned reflex method, *Arkh. biol. Nauk.*, **34**, 1–14 (1934).

NEWMAN, H. W. and NEWMAN, E. J., Failure of dexedrine and caffeine as practical antagonists of the depressant effect of ethyl alcohol in man, *Quart., J. Stud. Alc.*, **17**, 406–410 (1956).

NOELPP, B. and NOELPP-ESCHENHAGEN, I., Das experimentelle Asthma bronchiale des Meerschweinchens. III. Studien zur Bedeutung bedingter Reflexe. Bahrungsbereitschaft und Haftfahigkeit unter "stress," *Int. Arch. Allergy*, **3**, 108–136 (1952).

NOELPP-ESCHENHAGEN, I. and NOELPP, B., New contributions to experimental asthma, *Progress in Allergy*, **4**, 361–456 (1954).

NUTHMANN, A. M., Conditioning of a response class on a personality test, *J. Abnorm. (Soc.) Psychol.*, **54**, 19–23 (1957).

OSIPOVA, V. N., Associative-stimulative and associative-inhibitive child types, *Vopr. Izuch.Vospit. Lichn.*, **1**, 16–20 (1926) (*Psychol. Abstr.*, **1**, 2,276 (1927)).

PAVLOV, I. P., *Conditioned Reflexes* (Trans. by G. V. Anrep) (London, Oxford Univ. Press, 1927).

PAVLOV, I. P., *Lectures on Conditioned Reflexes*, Vol. 1. (Trans. by W. H. Gantt) (London, Lawrence & Wishart 1928).

PAVLOV, I. P., *Lectures on Conditioned Reflexes*, Vol. 2. *Conditioned Reflexes and Psychiatry* (Trans. W. H. Gantt) (New York, International Pub. Co., 1941).

PAVLOV, I. P., *Collected Works*, 2nd edn., (5 volumes) (Moscow, Akad.Nauk., 1951).

PAVLOV, I. P., *Selected Works* (Trans. by S. Belsky) (Moscow, Foreign Languages Publishing House, 1955).

PEN, R. N., The problem of typological characteristics of the reflex activities of children, *Vyssh. Nerv. Deyat. Reb.*, 173–189 (1933) (*Psychol. Abstr.*, **8**, 713 (1934)).

PETRIE, A., Personality changes after prefrontal leucotomy. Report 2, *Brit. J. Med. Psychol.*, **22**, 200–207 (1949).

PFAFFMAN, C. and SCHLOSBERG, H., The conditioned knee jerk in psychotic and normal individuals, *J. Psychol.*, **1**, 201–206 (1936).

PFEIFFER, C. C. and JENNEY, E. H., The inhibition of the conditioned response and the counteraction of schizo-phrenia by muscarinic stimulation of the brain, *Ann. N.Y. Acad. Sci.*, **66**, 753–764 (1957).

PLATONOV, K. I., The word as a physiological and therapeutic factor, *Psikhoterapiya*, **11**, 112–118 (1930).

Proceedings of IVth International Congress of Electro-encephalography and Clinical Neurophysiology, *Acta Medica Belgica*, Brussels, (1957).

RAYMOND, M. J., Case of fetishism treated by aversion therapy, *Brit. Med. J.*, ii, 854–856 (1956).

RAZRAN, G., Conditioned responses in animals other than dogs, *Psychol. Bull.*, **30**, 261–324 (1933).

REES, L., Physical and emotional factors in bronchial asthma, *J. Psychosom. Res.*, **1**, 98–114 (1956).

REESE, W. G., DOSS, R. and GANTT, W. H., Autonomic responses in differential diagnosis of organic and psychogenic psychoses, *A.M.A. Arch. Neurol. Psychiat.*, **70**, 778–793 (1953).

REIFENSTEIN, E. C. and DAVIDOFF, E., The psychological effects of Benzedrine sulfate, *Amer. J. Psychol.*, **52**, 56–64 (1939).

ROBINSON, J. and GANTT, W. H., The orientating reflex (questioning reaction): cardiac, respiratory, salivary and motor components, *Johns Hopk. Hosp. Bull.*, **80**, 231–253 (1947).

RUBENSTEIN, C., The treatment of morphine addiction in tuberculosis by Pavlov's conditioning method, *Amer. Rev. Tuberc.*, **24**, 682–685 (1931).

SACHS, B., The false claims of the psychoanalyst: a review and a protest, *Amer. J. Psychiat.*, **12**, 725–749 (1933).

SALTER, A., *Conditioned Reflex Therapy* (New York, Creative Age Press, 1949).

SALTZ, E. and HOEHN, A. J., A test of the Taylor-Spence theory of anxiety, *J. Abnorm. (Soc.) Psychol.*, **54**, 114–117 (1957).

SAMPSON, H. and BINDRA, D., "Manifest" anxiety, neurotic anxiety and the rate of conditioning, *J. Abnorm. (Soc.) Psychol.*, **49**, 256–259 (1954).

SARGANT, W., *Battle for the Mind* (London, Heinemann, 1957).

SARGANT, W. and SLATER, E., *An Introduction to Physical Methods of Treatment in Psychiatry* (Edinburgh, Livingstone, 1954).

SCHIFF, E., DOUGAN, C. and WELCH, L., The conditioned P.G.R. and the E.E.G. as indicators of anxiety, *J. Abnorm. (Soc.) Psychol.*, **44**, 549–552 (1949).

SCHILDER, P., The somatic basis of the neurosis, *J. Nerv. Ment. Dis.*, **70**, 502–519 (1929).

SCHOENFELD, W. N., *An Experimental Approach to Anxiety, Escape and Avoidance Behavior in Anxiety*, Eds. P. H. Hoch and J. Zubin (New York, Grune & Stratton, 1950).

SCOTT, H. D., Hypnosis and the conditioned reflex, *J. Gen. Psychol.*, **4**, 113–130 (1930).

SEARS, R. R. and COHEN, L. H., Hysterical anaesthesia, analgesia and astereognosis, *Arch. Neurol. Psychiat. Chicago*, **29**, 260–271 (1933).

SETTLAGE, P. H., The effects of Sodium Amytal on the formation and elicitation of conditioned reflexes, *J. Comp. Psychol.*, **22**, 339–343 (1936).

SHAGASS, C., Sedation threshold: a neurophysiological tool for psychosomatic research, *Psychosom. Med.*, **18**, 410–419 (1956).

SHAGASS, C. and KERENYI, A. B., Neurophysiological studies of personality, *J. Nerv. Ment. Dis.*, **126**, 141–147 (1958).

SHAGASS, C., MIHALIK, J. and JONES, A. L., Clinical psychiatric studies using the sedation threshold, *J. Psychosom. Res.*, **2**, 45–55 (1957).

SHAGASS, C. and NAIMAN, J., The sedation threshold as an objective index of manifest anxiety in psychoneurosis, *J. Psychosom. Res.*, **1**, 49–57 (1956).

SHELDON, W. H. and STEVENS, S. S., *The Varieties of Temperament* (New York, Harper & Bros., 1945).

SHIPLEY, W. C., Studies of catatonia: VI. Further investigations of the perseverational tendency, *Psychiat. Quart.*, **8**, 736–744 (1934).

SINHA, S. N., FRANKS, C. M. and BROADHURST, P. The effects of a stimulant and a depressant drug on a measure of reactive inhibition, *J. Exp. Psychol.*, **56**, 349–354 (1958).

SKINNER, B. F., *The Behavior of Organisms* (New York, Appleton-Century, 1938).

SLAVINA, E. E., On diurnal variations in the excitability of the cerebral hemispheres and the effect of lack of sleep, *Arkh. biol. Nauk.*, **41**, 9–12, (1936) (Engl. summ. p. 159).

SMITH, S. H. and DALINGER, R., Hypersensitiveness and the conditioned reflex, *Yale J. Biol. Med.*, **5**, 387–391 (1933).

SOLOMON, R. L. and BRUSH, E. S., Experimentally derived conceptions of anxiety and aversion, in *Nebraska Symposium on Motivation*, Ed. M. R. Jones (Lincoln, Nebraska, Univ. of Nebraska Press, 1956).

SPENCE, K. W., *Behavior Theory and Conditioning* (New Haven, Yale Univ. Press, 1956).

SPENCE, K. W. and FARBER, I. E., Conditioning of extinction as a function of anxiety, *J. Exp. Psychol.*, **45**, 116–119 (1953).

SPENCE, K. W. and TAYLOR, J. A., Anxiety and strength of the U.C.S. as determiners of the amount of eyelid conditioning, *J. Exp. Psychol.*, **42**, 183–188 (1951).

SPENCE, K. W. and TAYLOR, J. A., The relation of conditioned response strength to anxiety in normal, neurotic and psychotic subjects, *J. Exp. Psychol.*, **45**, 265–272 (1952).

STAATS, C. K. and STAATS, A. W., Hearing established by classical conditioning, *J. Exp. Psychol.*, **54**, 74–80 (1957).

STERLING, K. and MILLER, J. G., Conditioning under anaesthesia, *Amer. J. Psychol.*, **54**, 92–101 (1941).

STOGDILL, R. M., Neurosis as learned behavior, *Psychol. Rev.*, **41**, 497–507 (1934).

TAYLOR, J. A., The relationship of anxiety to the conditioned eyelid response, *J. Exp. Psychol.*, **41**, 81–92 (1951).

TAYLOR, J. A., Drive theory and manifest anxiety, *Psychol. Bull.*, **53**, 303–320 (1956).

TAYLOR, J. A. and SPENCE, K. W., The relationship of anxiety level to performance in serial learning, *J. Exp. Psychol.*, **42**, 161–164 (1952).

TAYLOR, J. A. and SPENCE, K. W., Conditioning level in the behavior disorders, *J. Abnorm. (Soc.) Psychol.*, **49**, 497–503 (1954).

THIMANN, J., Conditioned reflex treatment of alcoholism: II. The risks of its application, its indications, contra-indications and therapeutic aspects, *New Engl. J. Med.*, **241**, 406–410 (1949).

THORPE, W. H., *Learning and Instinct in Animals* (London, Methuen, 1956).

TIGERSTADT, C., Der Blutdruck des Menschen bei psychischer Excitation, *Skand. Arch. Physiol.*, **48**, 138–146 (1926).

TIMMER, A. P., Die schizothymen und zyklothymen Temperament Kretschmers im Lichte des Pavlovschen bedingte Reflexe betrachtet, *Z. ges. Neurol. Psychiat.*, **133**, 329–351 (1931).

TINEL, J. and MICHON, G., Étude d'un cas a'hystérie: association des troubles hystériques et d'une arythmie extra-systolique. Guérison parallèle de ces troubles et de l'arythmie. Réalité physiologique des accidents observés. Rôle probable des réflexes conditionnels, *Encéphale*, **23**, 891–900 (1928).

TROUTON, D. S., *Placebos* and their psychological effects, *J. Ment. Sci.*, **103**, 344–354 (1957).

UTLEY, J., Procedures for examining very young acoustically handicapped children, *Ear, Nose & Throat Mnthly.*, **28**, 590–595 (1949).

WAHL, E. F., Cardiac manifestation of the psychoneurotic state, *J. Med. Assoc. Ga*, **21**, 428–430 (1932).

WARREN, A. B. and GRANT, D. A., The relation of conditioned discrimination to the M.M.P.I. Pd personality variable, *J. Exp. Psychol.*, **49**, 23–27 (1955).

WATSON, J. B. and RAYNOR, R., Conditioned emotional reactions, *J. Exp. Psychol.*, **3**, 1–4 (1920).

WEISS, B., Electrocardiographic indices of emotional stress, *Amer. J. Psychiat.*, **113**, 348–351 (1956).

WEITZENHOFFER, A. M., *Hypnotism—an Objective Study in Suggestibility* (New York, John Wiley & Sons, Inc., 1953).

WELCH, L., Human conditioning and anxiety, *Ann. N.Y. Acad. Sci.*, **56**, 266–272 (1953).

WELCH, L. and KUBIS, J., Conditioned P.G.R. (psychogalvanic response) in states of pathological anxiety, *J. Nerv. Ment. Dis.*, **105**, 372–381 (1947a).

WELCH, L. and KUBIS, J., The effect of anxiety on the conditioning rate and stability of the P.G.R., *J. Psychol.*, **23**, 83–91 (1947b).

WEVER, E. G., The upper limit of learning in the cat, *J. Comp. Psychol.*, **10**, 221–233 (1930).

WIKLER, A., Recent progress in research on the neurophysiologic basis of morphine addiction, *Amer. J. Psychiat.*, **105**, 329–338 (1948).

WIKLER, A., Sites and mechanisms of action of morphine and related drugs in the central nervous system, *Pharmacol. Rev.*, **2**, 435–506 (1950).

WILCZKOWSKI, E., The presence of a natural conditioned response in the blood of alcoholics, *Neurol. Neuroch. Psychiat. Polska*, **4**, 321–324 (1954).

WINSOR, A. L., Conditions affecting human parotid secretion, *J. Exp. Psychol.*, **11**, 355–363 (1928).

WOLPE, J., Reciprocal inhibition as the main basis of psychotherapeutic effects, *A.M.A. Arch. Neurol. Psychiat.*, **72**, 205–226 (1954).

WYCKOFF, J., Psychogenic heart disease, *Bull. N.Y. Acad. Med.*, **4**, 487–540 (1928).

YOUNG, P. T., *Motivation of Behavior* (New York, John Wiley & Sons, Inc., 1936).

ZENER, K. and MCCURDY, H. G., Analysis of motivational factors in conditioned behavior: I. The differential effect of changes in hunger upon conditioned, unconditioned and spontaneous salivary secretions, *J. Psychol.*, **8**, 321–350 (1939).

CHAPTER 13

Learning and Abnormal Behaviour

H. GWYNNE JONES

INTRODUCTION

EXPERIMENTAL work on learning has given rise to a number of generalizations concerning lawful relationships between variables which, stated in neutral terms, would be accepted by proponents of most "theories," although their interpretation would vary from theorist to theorist. Unfortunately, the majority of these generalizations were derived from laboratory experiments with animals, particularly the rat, and their application to human behaviour is frequently an essentially unvalidated argument by analogy. The circumstances of human learning, however, even in a laboratory, are frequently so unlike those in experiments with animals that the analogy becomes obscure and predictions based on empirically established relationships may be transferred from one situation to the other only if the experimental variables be first translated into the terms of higher order theoretical concepts, which may then yield new first-order factual predictions in the new situation. Hull's theoretical system (Hull, 1943, 1951, 1952), by virtue of its ambitious scope, lends itself most easily to this process: his premature attempt at strict quantification, which has produced some of the most damaging criticism of his viewpoint (cf. Koch, 1954), is the least necessary aspect of his theory for this type of extrapolation. With some modifications, this chapter will be written largely in Hull's terms although it is hoped that its substance could be expressed in the terms of several alternative theories.

Two specific modifications of Hullian theory, adopted for the purposes of this chapter, need particular mention. The first relates to the concepts of "reactive inhibition" and "conditioned inhibition," which may be particularly relevant to abnormal psychology. Hull's systematic use of these concepts

is illogical in certain respects and the writer's modification of the basic Hullian equation (Jones, 1958b) is adopted in order to avoid these difficulties. Thus Hull would express the relationship between "net reaction potential" ($_S\bar{E}_R$), "habit strength" ($_SH_R$), "drive" (D), "reactive inhibition" (I_R) and "conditioned inhibition" ($_SI_R$) as—

$$_S\bar{E}_R = f(D \times {_SH_R}) - (I_R + {_SI_R})$$

whereas the present alternative is expressed as—

$$\begin{aligned}_S\bar{E}_R &= f(D - I_R) \times ({_SH_R} - {_SI_R}) \\ &= f(D \times {_SH_R}) - (D \times {_SI_R}) - (I_R \times {_SH_R}) \\ &\quad + (I_R \times {_SI_R})\end{aligned}$$

The second major modification relates to Hull's inclusion of classical conditioning and instrumental learning within the same theoretical framework. It is considered that evidence derived from experiments such as those of Mowrer and Solomon (1954) and Mowrer and Aiken (1954) is sufficiently strong to justify the adoption of a dualistic theory, as advocated by Skinner (1935), Schlosberg (1937) and Mowrer (1947, 1950), in which Pavlovian conditioning by contiguity is equally effective with trial-and-error learning reinforced by drive reduction. Mowrer's view that conditioning relates only to the learning of responses mediated by the autonomic nervous system is not essential to such a theory, nor is any other particular response classification, though Welch's (1955) argument that conditioned responses are essentially involuntary has considerable force. Classical conditioning as such, has been treated in the previous chapter but aspects of its interaction with other learning processes will need to be considered further.

LEARNING AND NEUROSIS

Aetiology

Genetic factors have been shown to play an important role in determining the vulnerability of an individual to neurotic breakdown (cf. Chapter 8 of this HANDBOOK by Slater and Shields) but the actual behavioural disturbance probably results from the imposition of some form of environmental stress on the individual concerned. Learning is essentially the modification of an organism's behaviour resulting from its interaction with a changing environment and, for any learning process, the nature of the behavioural change will be partly determined by the genetic constitution of the organism. Therefore, in a sense, a neurotic breakdown may be described as learned, or learning processes may be important in its development. Certainly an aetiological theory of neurosis expressed in terms of learning concepts provides valuable links between abnormal and general psychology, and the possibility of experimental validation in laboratory situations.

Some symptoms may well result from the conditioning of a naturally occurring somatic reaction to incidental stimuli. Russian studies, described by Bykov (1953), clearly indicate that reactions of the circulatory, respiratory, urinary and other systems do become conditioned in everyday life situations. Thus, for example, refrigeration workers adapt physiologically to the low temperature within seconds of entering their workroom. The same physiological changes occur with similar rapidity if the room is entered when at a normal temperature, but if these workers are subjected to cold conditions in novel surroundings their adaptation time is no shorter than that for individuals without their experience of cold conditions. In this example the conditioned responses are entirely adaptive but it is conceivable that similar processes may lead to the development of non-adaptive psychosomatic symptoms. In similar fashion, an abnormal or disease reaction may be brought under the control of a range of originally inadequate stimuli thus giving a truly somatic symptom a "psychic" overlay and enabling it to become "triggered off" by processes generally recognized as psychological in nature. Consistent with this analysis, Metcalfe (1956) and Dekker and Groen (1956) have experimentally demonstrated the conditioning of attacks of asthma to such diverse stimuli as the photograph of a horse and a patient's mother in patients who were also sensitive to allergens.

Other symptoms may result, not from the learning of an unadaptive response, but from the failure to learn an adaptive response. Thus, in the course of maturation, a child learns not to urinate whenever his bladder is full but to inhibit this response in all but certain fairly specific environmental situations. At a later stage, these conditioned inhibitions are sufficiently well established to continue functioning during sleep. For the nocturnal enuretic, however, this degree of learning is not achieved or breaks down relatively easily.

While some symptoms may be such functionally discrete entities it is probable that the majority represent one facet of a more general neurotic disorder, which several authors would account for in learning terms (Shoben, 1949; Dollard and Miller, 1950; Mowrer, 1950; Cameron and Magaret, 1951; Wolpe, 1952; Skinner, 1953; Eysenck, 1957; Jones, 1958a). The majority of these agree with Freud (1926) in allocating to anxiety a central role in the maintenance of neurosis but they conceive of anxiety as a conditioned fear reaction, including affective and respondent components and possessing aversive drive properties. In its role as an acquired drive, anxiety will energize, and by its reduction, reinforce various aversive instrumental responses of the organism. As a powerful and massive response involving central, skeletal, autonomic and hormonal systems, anxiety will disrupt the ongoing reactions of the organism. As pointed out by Schoenfeld (1950), the application of the term "anxiety" to this particular concept is unfortunate in that it already carries many different connotations (cf. May, 1950). A more neutral term such as "conditioned emotional response" (C.E.R.) or "conditioned avoidance drive" (C.A.D.) would be more appropriate and include many experientially different phenomena such as "anxiety," "guilt" and "disgust."

The mediating role of a C.A.D. is best illustrated by a consideration of traumatic avoidance learning in animals (Solomon and Wynne, 1954; Solomon and Brush, 1956). If an animal, confined in a suitable apparatus, is presented with a neutral stimulus followed by a powerful electric shock, a massive pain-fear response involving central, neuro-endocrine and autonomic reactions ensues and the animal makes various aversive skeletal responses, of which some, if the apparatus is appropriately constructed, will terminate the shock and may, therefore, be described as escape responses. If, after one or several such trials, the animal is replaced in the apparatus, indications of fear are evident in response to the conditioned stimulus and before the onset of shock. This indicates that the fear reaction has become conditioned to this previously neutral stimulus and the C.A.D. may be measured by its disorganizing effect on unlearned or previously learned responses. With further trials in the original situation the escape responses tend to occur in response to the conditioned stimulus: escape from shock gradually or suddenly becomes avoidance of shock. Avoidance responses developed in this way, unlike the more usual instrumental responses of learning experiments, may be maintained throughout hundreds of extinction trials without the readministration of shock. According to the mediation hypothesis, this derives from the fact that reinforcement does in fact occur owing to a reduction of the C.A.D. by escape from the conditioned stimulus. Murphy, Miller and Mirsky (Murphy et al., 1955;

Miller *et al.*, 1955; Murphy and Miller, 1956), by means of an ingenious series of experiments with monkeys, have shown that a C.A.D. can be acquired by animals with no personal experience of shock but by seeing a stimulus animal receive shocks. These workers also demonstrated the generalization of avoidance responses to social non-experimental situations by the modification of social dominance hierarchies.

To explain the failure of extinction of the C.A.D. itself Solomon and Wynne (1954) have adduced two additional principles. The first, the principle of *anxiety conservation*, postulates that, by an early avoidance reaction, the conditioned stimulus is removed before the long-latency C.A.D. recruits to its full amplitude, thus protecting it from extinction. If, from partial extinction, the avoidance response latency increases, the C.A.D. develops fully, reinforcement occurs and the avoidance latency again decreases. Secondly, they postulate that severe trauma causes irreversible physiological changes which bring about a *partial irreversibility* of the C.A.D. resulting from such traumata. This paper reports evidence consistent with the principle of anxiety conservation, but Solomon and Brush (1956) express less confidence in its validity owing to failures to observe the expected relationships between the latencies of avoidance responses and physiological measures of emotional arousal. Reactions such as accelerated heart rate, however, are likely to be only partial components of the complex drive state and not necessarily correlated with the strength of the aversive tendency. If valid, this principle would ensure that evocations of the C.A.D. could never be "massed" and are, therefore, less liable to extinguish. Selye (1955) has shown that the chains of responses to traumata include hormonal releases deleterious to the tissues of the organism. The conditioned reaction, if allowed to develop fully, might also include similar endocrine responses and thus reinstate the original reinforcement conditions. In this way a "vicious cycle" would be established, consistent with the irreversibility principle.

The animals in traumatic avoidance learning experiments do not usually develop behaviour which could be described as "experimental neurosis." This is to be expected because the escape and avoidance responses are successful and the C.A.D. is playing an adaptive mediating role. Wolpe (1952) and others have shown that, when animals are subjected to traumatic shock from which they are unable to escape, marked behavioural distrubances occur, which may be claimed to merit the title "neurotic" in that they are unadaptive and persist through a considerable period of time outside the experimental situation. These represent various persistent auto-

nomic and skeletal responses which originally occurred in response to the shock and which markedly increase when stimuli associated with the shock situation are presented to the animal. Mowrer and Viek (1948), by means of an ingenious experiment, have shown that such abnormal responses in animals are not a function of the increased duration of shock when avoidance or escape is impossible but rather of the fact that no effective avoidance response may be established on the basis of C.A.D. reduction.

Physical pain of traumatic dimensions may be used as an extreme and prototypal example of environmental stress and, hence, traumatic avoidance learning may serve as a paradigm of the dynamics of learning mediated by a C.A.D. Wolpe (1952) points out that a series of mild electric shocks have effects equivalent to a single powerful shock and postulates a mechanism whereby the strength of a C.A.D. may progressively increase (cf. Chapter 19 of this HANDBOOK by P. Broadhurst). The complexity of this summation effect is evident from the work of Bindra and Cameron (1953), who showed that for human subjects a rest interval, during which no shocks were received and the conditioned stimulus was removed, had an "incubation effect," leading to an increased C.A.D. as measured by galvanic skin responses and impaired discrimination between "shock" and "non-shock" signals after the interval.

In human development, of course, a large number of aversive situations other than direct painful stimulation are common as illustrated by reports on individuals with congenital insensitivity to pain. Cohen *et al.* (1955) describe such a person and report her startle responses to sudden stimuli. West and Farber (1957) consider several cases and conclude that pain is not the exclusive precursor of a C.A.D., nor of the control required for socialization. They comment that a child of this type cries just as hard when spanked as does a "painful" child. Similar points are made by McMurray (1955) from a review of many cases but he is inclined to reject secondary drive theories of human motivation. Many traumatic situations for humans derive from the socialization process wherein individuals undergo a training in which socially unacceptable aspects of their behaviour, which are often strongly motivated, are punished by parents and the formal agents of society. The conflicts between powerful but incompatible response tendencies involved in such situations may be important in the generation of stress. Miller (1944), on the basis of experimental studies of conflict, claims that these remain unresolved only when avoidance motivation is operative and when the subject is retained in the area of conflict by physical limitations and other sources of avoidance, or the avoidance stimuli are ubiquitous or internal to the subject. Frustration, in the sense of the blocking of a path to a goal or of consummatory responses at a goal situation, may also give rise to aversive "emotional" reactions (Brown and Farber, 1951) but the interpretation of experiments on frustration is as yet too controversial to permit of a ready application to problems of human behaviour (Marx, 1956; Seward, 1956).

From such situations C.A.D.s may well develop in a manner similar to that described for traumatic learning in animals. Childhood may be a particularly vulnerable period in that it is a period of intense socialization, the undeveloped nervous system is more reactive and plastic, the possibilities of effective avoidance are less and C.A.D.s may become attached to a wider range of conditioned stimuli owing to lack of learned perceptual discriminations and the absence of refined discrimination through language development. This is not to say that a C.A.D. may not, however, develop at any period of life when new stresses appear.

On the basis of such a theory, the behavioural disturbance described as neurotic may be analysed into two types of response; (1) the C.A.D. or anxiety response itself which will have visceral, skeletal and nervous components, and (2) various instrumental responses by which the conditioned stimuli are removed and hence the C.A.D. reduced. Both are learned behavioural responses and, as such, are symptoms of the neurosis: their division may parallel the Freudian distinction between the underlying neurosis and its symptoms.

With respect to the conditioned stimuli involved, these may derive from three sources: the punishing agent itself, for example the parent, when disturbances in relation to individuals in authority may result; the incidental environmental stimuli at the time of stress, when disturbances of the nature of phobias may be expected; the stimuli involved in the individual's own behaviour at the time of stress as, for example, when a neurotic subject fears to express aggressive impulses. The latter type of conditioned stimulus is the least likely to be avoided successfully as it is, in a sense, self-generated. As such, it may give rise to a type of neurosis particularly difficult to treat. This type of conditioned stimulation is the only one considered in their analyses by the most influential theorizers in this field: Dollard and Miller (1950) consider that, in these circumstances, the neurotic solution is to inhibit the offending behaviour whereas Mowrer (1950) believes that the illicit response occurs but the consequences are avoided by various devices. In reaching these conclusions these writers fail to note that either adjustment, or maladjustment, is possible and rely on their apparently conflicting clinical experience. Whichever solution does in fact occur in the particular situation may be due to the circumstances of original reinforcement, that is according to which of several responses made was effective in reducing the C.A.D. Alternatively, and more probably, in the light of recent work, innate individual differences may largely determine the nature of the response.

Whatever the original conditioned stimuli, by the well established process of stimulus generalization, a range of stimuli will later evoke the neurotic behaviour. If these present themselves with considerable frequency the disturbance may well become chronic. Frequently the eliciting stimuli on various specific occasions may appear to an observer to be entirely dissimilar and extremely unlikely to occur on any single generalization continuum. This may well result from secondary generalization (Hull, 1943). Thus, if an animal, via the mediation of a C.A.D., has learned to avoid a black circle, it will, by generalization, also avoid a white circle. The avoidance of the white circle will itself be reinforced by C.A.D. reduction, and by a second generalization, a white square will now be avoided, though this stimulus has neither its squareness nor its whiteness in common with the original conditioned stimulus. Verbal links may also, in human beings, produce similar effects (Lacey and Smith, 1954; Lacey, Smith and Green, 1955).

Many of these processes may be, in a sense, unconscious in that several experiments (e.g. Sidowski, 1954) have shown that a response may be conditioned to a stimulus or class of stimuli while the subject is unaware of any connexion or of any reinforcing process. Lacey and his co-workers (Lacey and Smith, 1954; Lacey, Smith and Green, 1955) have shown this to be true of C.A.D. responses and also that "unconscious" conditioning tends to produce less adaptive and more generalized C.A.D.s. Thus it is likely that a "dangerous" topic of conversation may be avoided just as experimental stimuli are avoided and this may also apply to symbolic responses or "thoughts," thus bringing phenomena such as "repression" within the same conceptual scheme. From this point of view, however, the unconscious does not acquire any special "dynamic" attributes (see Chapter 7, by J. Inglis).

Somatic reactions may play several roles in such a dynamic system. The total C.A.D. response involves somatic components and such psychosomatic symptoms as frequency of micturition may be direct expressions of a chronic or recurring C.A.D. state. Other somatic symptoms may represent avoidance responses which enable the patient to evade conditioned stimuli and, therefore, to reduce the C.A.D. Hysterical blindness or paralysis most obviously fit this pattern but similar dynamics may underlie a wide range of symptoms.

Individual Differences: Theory

Individual differences will greatly affect the course of events in any individual case but these have been largely ignored by most of the theorists previously mentioned, who tend to assume an extreme environmentalist viewpoint. Dollard and Miller, for example, consider the existence of neurosis an automatic criticism of child-rearing practices in our culture. There is, however, ample evidence for a wide range of relevant individual differences both physiological and psychological in nature. Lacey *et al.* (1953) have shown that individuals display a reliable pattern of autonomic responses to any particular experimental stress situation and that this pattern varies from situation to situation and from person to person. Malmo and his associates (Malmo and Shagass, 1949; Malmo, Shagass and Davis, 1950) report evidence consistent with the view that different physiological mechanisms (autonomic or motor) are specifically susceptible, in different individuals, to activation by stressful experiences and are related to the symptoms shown by such individuals when psychiatrically disturbed (cf. Chapter 11 by I. Martin).

The dimensional system of "neuroticism" and "introversion-extraversion," described in an earlier chapter, is a useful framework within which to consider individual differences of a psychological character and one which Eysenck and his co-workers (Eysenck, 1955, 1957) have linked to the type of general theory outlined here. Neuroticism, or vulnerability to neurosis, in terms of such a theory, implies low tolerance for stress, whether it be physical, as in painful situations, or psychological, as in conflict or "frustration" situations. In learning theory terms, an individual scoring high on the factor of neuroticism would be characterized by a high level of drive in avoidance situations. High appetitive drives are not necessary to the theory and it may be that the high drive of neurotics is aroused only in situations of threat or "ego-involvement." Evidence is lacking concerning the drive level of neurotics in reward situations but there is considerable evidence that, compared with normal subjects, they exhibit lowered response thresholds to painful stimulation (cf. Hall, 1953). The interpretation of pain-reactivity experiments is, however, difficult as the responses involved are frequently voluntary in nature and the thresholds measured do not necessarily correlate with physiological pain thresholds. To date, however, direct measures of the latter are not available. The presentation of a stimulus tending to evoke different, equally strong and incompatible responses might well be considered an experimental paradigm of a psychological conflict situation. Experimental work on "intolerance of ambiguity" is therefore relevant to the present argument. Hamilton (1957*a*, 1957*b*) reports that anxious, obsessional and conversion hysteric groups of neurotic patients, while showing intergroup differences in the extent and manner of their avoidance, were all more intolerant of ambiguity than was his control group of normal subjects.

Eysenck's (1955, 1957) dynamic interpretation of the introversion-extraversion dimension in terms of individual differences along a neurological dimension of excitation-inhibition has been discussed fully in the previous chapter. It will suffice here to comment that the formal postulates, though based on Pavlovian notions, are stated in terms of differential susceptibility to "reactive inhibition" as conceived of by Hull. Correlated tendencies to inhibition of a more widespread and prolonged character are, however, implied in his expectation that neurotic extraverts (hysterics) will display symptoms of an inhibitory nature such as paralysis, amnesia, and anaesthesia while neurotic introverts (dysthymics) will present excitatory symptoms such as rumination, rituals, tremors, etc.

If such an interpretation of neurosis and neuroticism in learning theory terms is valid, the individual differences postulated should be reflected in the responses of experimental subjects in learning situations but, for unequivocal predictions from the theory to be made, it is necessary for the design of an experiment to include the systematic variation or measurement of at least the following variables: (1) the avoidance value of the stimulation presented (degree of stress); (2) the subjects' positions on the neuroticism dimension; (3) the subjects' positions on the introversion-extraversion dimension. The latter measures are seldom both available and the first is not yet possible: despite an increasing general interest in stress situations in recent years no satisfactory "stressor" metric has yet been achieved. Thus, in most instances, experimental results can be examined only for general consistency with the theory and not for detailed validation. If the theory survives such a general examination, while its "construct validity" will be enhanced, it will still require refinement and precise validation from further carefully designed experiments.

Before examining the results of specific experiments it is necessary to formulate the general expectations in terms of group differences in "learning efficiency" as measured by such scores as the number of trials required to learn to a criterion. As, in most learning experiments with human subjects, the relevant drive is presumably related to social conformity and achievement, and the placing of the subject in the experimental situation is a form of threat, however mild, it is assumed that avoidance drive will invariably be evoked to some degree and, therefore, the postulated differences in drive arousal will be operative. The relationship between these differences and the degree of stress is expressed graphically in Fig. 13.1.

In considering the consequences of such drive differences, the relationship between strength of drive and efficiency of learning has to be taken into account. Much evidence indicates that, at least for complex learning and avoidance motivation, a very high level of drive decreases efficiency and the overall relationship between these two variables is curvilinear rather than linear. (Courts, 1942; Hebb, 1955; Malmo, 1957.) An excellent empirical example of this relationship is provided by the classic Yerkes-Dodson experiments on discrimination learning in mice and kittens (Yerkes and Dodson, 1908; Dodson, 1915), which are discussed fully in the chapter by P. Broadhurst and which clearly indicate that the optimum intensity of "shock" reinforcement varies inversely with the difficulty of the discrimination task. If this is a principle of general application to learning situations it may be stated in terms of two general laws—

1. "Efficiency of learning is a curvilinear function of drive strength, some intermediate level of drive being optimal."
2. "Optimal drive strength is an inverse function of the difficulty of a learning task."

These laws, which are expressed graphically in Fig. 13.2. are consistent with the major predictions made by the Iowa group (Farber, 1954; Taylor, 1956; Spence, 1956) concerning the relationship between

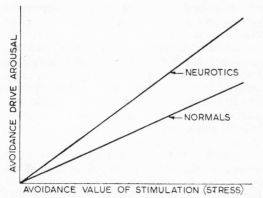

FIG. 13.1. GROUP DIFFERENCE IN AVOIDANCE DRIVE AROUSAL

drive strength and learning performance on tasks of varying complexity. It is surprising that Spence and his co-workers nowhere consider the Yerkes-Dodson principle though, for their theory to be valid, predictions from it concerning discrimination learning should be consistent with this finding.

Though the Iowa workers recognize the importance of the stimulus aspects of drive (cf. Farber, 1954, 1955) only its energizing effect is considered in their

theory which is based on the Hullian concept of excitatory potential as a multiplicative function of habit and drive strengths. In a situation in which only a single habit is evoked an increase of drive is expected to improve performance but, where competing response tendencies are operative, of which only one is scored correct by the experimenter, the effect of changes in drive strength is considered to depend on the number and comparative strength of the competing

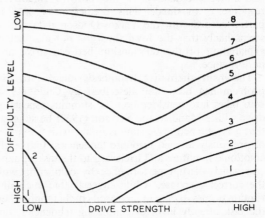

FIG. 13.2. ISOMETRICS OF LEARNING EFFICIENCY ON AN ARBITRARY SCALE OF 1 TO 8 (LOW TO HIGH)

tendencies. When the correct response is based on a relatively weak habit strength, increased drive is deleterious in that the stronger incorrect tendencies gain relatively more in excitatory potential and have, therefore, an enhanced probability of evocation. During learning, as the relative strength of the correct tendency increases, increased drive becomes progressively less injurious and ultimately advantageous when the correct response is pre-potent. In the complex situation, involving competing tendencies, increased drive may also lower efficiency by raising new incorrect competing responses above the threshold value of excitatory potential. This theory is dependent upon the range of oscillation of a response tendency being constant, as Spence (1956) assumes, or, if variable as Hull assumes, being a function of habit strength rather than reaction potential. Hull's statements on this point are unclear and little direct evidence is available. Buchwald and Yamaguchi (1955) submitted the theory to a fairly direct test by training rats in a T maze to a criterion of ten correct responses out of twelve and then with the maze reversed, retraining under low and high drive conditions. Contrary to the prediction derived from the theory, relearning was more rapid with high drive.

According to the algebraic summation theory of discrimination learning (Spence 1937; Jones, 1958b) the positive and negative responses to the negative (non-reinforced) stimulus compete during learning. The negative (correct) response is initially weaker and only gains minimal ascendancy at the end of training. Thus the Iowa theory would clearly yield the prediction that increased drive should tend to lower the efficiency of discrimination learning at all difficulty levels and throughout the range of drive but this effect should be most marked for difficult discriminations, when the initial ascendency of the positive (incorrect) response is maximal. This prediction is only in partial accord with the Yerkes-Dodson data and it seems likely that the Iowa theory is not a sufficient explanation of the relationship between drive and performance.

The main alternative hypothesis relevant to this problem has been well described by Child (1954) who takes into consideration the stimulus aspects of drive. Like Mandler and Sarason (1952) he suggests that a heightened drive state is linked with a number of previously learned response tendencies, frequently emotional in nature and irrelevant to the task in hand and which disrupt performance by competing with the correct response. Child suggests that such disruption occurs, owing to increased conflict, only when the task already involves competing tendencies, but the writer agrees with Taylor (1956) that to limit the theory in this manner is merely to complicate the Iowa hypothesis without adding to its predictive value. Nevertheless, there is considerable force in Child's arguments in support of interference, and it is likely that increased drive, particularly of an avoidance nature, is liable to set up task-irrelevant response tendencies. For these to affect scores in experimental situations, however, the irrelevant responses must be incompatible with the experimentally "correct" response and/or be included within the experimenter's scoring system. A muscular tremor may be considered as an example of the expected type of irrelevant response. In simple conditioning this is unlikely to be incompatible with the measured response and may even facilitate it. Only if such C.A.D. mediated responses become so massive as to force themselves on the experimenter's attention are they even recorded. In complex tasks, such as the serial learning of a stylus maze, the correct response is scored, as are certain specific predetermined incorrect responses. A movement determined by the tremor response, when the stylus is at a choice point, will be incompatible with all or all but one of the scored responses and, if randomly determined, will not affect the relative probabilities of these. The effects of a tremor would be to reduce the reliability of an individual's scores and to increase the time taken to traverse the maze. In a task such as target pursuit, any particular tremor response would be incompatible with "keeping on target" and, as the entire time spent off the target is usually involved in the scoring system, the tremor would materially affect a subject's score. Thus, the effect of task-irrelevant responses depends on their relevance to the scoring system and can only be evaluated when an adequate behavioural analysis of the task can be made.

A further possible effect of changes in drive has been neglected by both these theories. This is concerned with the stimulus properties of drive, as such, and can best be illustrated by reference to discrimination learning. Discrimination is most difficult to achieve when the positive and negative stimuli are most nearly alike, i.e. when they have most elements in common. The incidental experimental stimuli contribute to what they have in common and one of these is the drive stimulus. The stronger the drive, the more intense the drive stimulus, the greater its share of the stimulus complex, the greater the similarity between the positive and negative stimuli and, therefore, the greater the difficulty of discrimination. This effect would be opposed to any energizing value of increased drive and the interaction of the two effects would determine the optimal level of drive, thus producing a pattern of results similar to those reported by Yerkes and Dodson. In simple conditioning, where a single stimulus is linked with a single response, no deleterious effect would result but in trial-and-error learning of all types, discriminations between stimuli are as important as in discrimination learning though the additional factor of response selection is also involved. This hypothesis is akin to that advanced by Hilgard, Jones and Kaplan (1951) concerning the relationship between anxiety and discrimination learning. They suggest that anxious subjects perceive situations as more threatening than do non-anxious subjects and that "a person whose discriminations are dimmed by anxiety" is less likely to differentiate between the positive and negative stimuli.

A fourth possibility is that there exists a stable curvilinear relationship between drive and efficiency with a stable optimum drive value (Hebb, 1955) but that increasing task difficulty, irrespective of the degree and nature of response competition, increases drive in a manner analogous to the drive increment postulated as following frustration (Brown and Farber, 1951; Child and Waterhouse, 1953; Marx, 1956). If so, the optimum pre-task drive level would be lower the more difficult the task. This hypothesis is consistent with empirical studies of the relationship between task difficulty and such measures as muscle tension and palmar skin resistance (cf. Freeman and Giese, 1940) which tend to indicate that task difficulty is a stressor factor increasing drive.

The four hypotheses, outlined above, are not

mutually exclusive and all the postulated effects may contribute to the nature of the interaction between drive and performance. Their relative importance will vary from situation to situation but all are likely to produce the type of relationship reported by Yerkes and Dodson and postulated in the two general laws stated earlier.

In any learning situation an individual's performance will be determined, not only by his level of drive, but also by his position on the personality dimension of introversion-extraversion. The postulated effect of this factor alone is graphically illustrated in Fig. 13.3. but this will interact with the effects of drive according to the nature of the task. Thus, in the formation of a C.A.D. to an originally neutral stimulus, the imbalance towards excitation in introverts and towards inhibition in extraverts should ensure more effective conditioning in the former. The high unconditioned avoidance drive of neurotics, however, would tend to allow them to condition faster than normal subjects. Thus, while it may be predicted that neurotic introverts or dysthymics will condition most readily and stable extraverts least, no firm prediction can be made as to the comparative conditionability of stable introverts and neurotic extraverts (hysterics) unless the degree of stress is determined. As drive differences increase with degree of stress (Fig. 13.1.), while the difference between

predict. Eysenck (1956b) assumes that the development of conditioned inhibition, being a learning process, is slow in extraverts. As, however, the learning involved is the learning of a response of "not responding" and the postulated relevant drive is reactive inhibition, conditioned inhibition may well develop more readily in extraverts. For trial-and-error and other complex situations the interaction between drive and inhibitory effects is inevitably

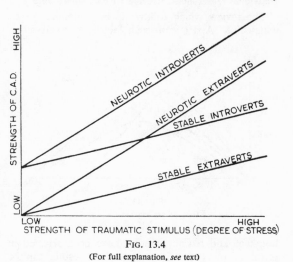

FIG. 13.4
(For full explanation, *see* text)

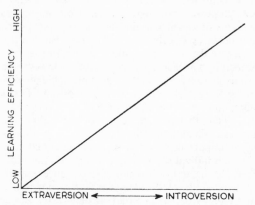

FIG. 13.3. LEARNING EFFICIENCY AS A FUNCTION OF INTROVERSION-EXTRAVERSION

excitatory and inhibitory potentials remains constant, stable introverts will be expected to condition faster than hysterics at low strength of the conditioned stimulus but at high stimulus strengths, the reverse would hold true. These expectations are graphically represented in Fig. 13.4.

The effects of introversion-extraversion on the growth of conditioned inhibition and, hence, on efficiency of discrimination, are more difficult to

complicated. At low levels of stress, when drive is below the optimum for all groups, dysthymics should be most efficient and stable extraverts least efficient, as in conditioning, but no firm prediction can be made of the relative efficiency of stable introverts and hysterics. At high levels of stress, when drive is above the optimum for all groups, both stable groups should be superior to both neurotic groups, with the introverted subjects superior within each category. In the intermediate range of stress, however, when drive is approximately optimal for one or other group, prediction of empirical results is virtually impossible. The intricacy of these interactions is illustrated in Fig. 13.5. which represents one of the possible sets of relationships consistent with our hypothesis. The interactions are further complicated when the stress involved in the task is not the result of the direct application of some unconditioned avoidance stimulus but results from some C.A.D. evoked by intrinsically non-traumatic stimuli in the situation. The conditionability differences shown in Fig. 13.4. then come into operation and the curves of Fig. 13.5. become distorted into those of Fig. 13.6. with the effect that their intercrossings in the range of moderate stress are further complicated and the extraverts are now superior to introverts at very high levels of stress.

From the Iowa hypothesis concerning the effects of intra-task response competition and the later hypothesis concerning the effect of task difficulty, increased response competition or increased task difficulty will have the same effect on group differences in learning efficiency as increased stress. Thus the abscissae of Figs. 13.5 and 13.6 represent both stress and task difficulty or some joint function of these.

Individual Differences: Review of Empirical Data

The review which follows is not intended to be exhaustive. Apart from such factors as availability,

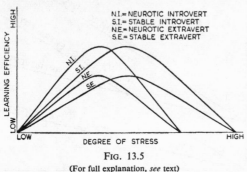

N.I.= NEUROTIC INTROVERT
S.I.= STABLE INTROVERT
N.E.= NEUROTIC EXTRAVERT
S.E.= STABLE EXTRAVERT

FIG. 13.5
(For full explanation, *see* text)

language and recency, studies have been selected in terms of the ease with which their results can be examined for compatability with the type of generalization concerning group or individual differences made in the preceding section. Only those studies which present data concerning learning, in the sense of improvement with practice, have been included; reports concerned with immediate memory have been omitted. Though greater weight must be attached to trends of demonstrable statistical significance, data exhibiting trends at an insignificant level are included. This is considered justifiable as an insignificant trend, if repeatedly observed, gains inductive power. It is hoped that no study has been omitted, the results of which run clearly counter to the theoretical biases which are no doubt evident throughout this chapter.

Ideally, the empirical evidence to be matched against our theoretical expectations should be derived from investigations employing neurotic subjects. Unfortunately, however, the majority of studies concerned with the psychodynamics of learning have utilized normal subjects. These are valuable and relevant to abnormal psychology when the personality variables taken into account are ones for which extreme values are characteristic of psychiatric patients. This is true of the many recent studies employing the Taylor Scale of Manifest Anxiety, or M.A.S., (Taylor, 1953). This scale was specifically

devised to test the Iowa hypothesis, described above, and it is assumed that M.A.S. scores are positively related to drive level and, according to Taylor (1956), any other specification of drive, e.g. hunger, would have been equally acceptable as an independent variable for their experiments. As both Taylor and Farber (1954) admit, anxious and non-anxious subjects differ in respects other than drive and these other differences are likely to influence performance but the Iowa researchers have deliberately neglected such additional factors. This standpoint would be defensible if the non-drive factors contributing to the

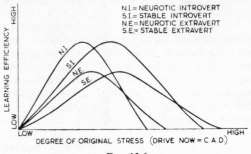

N.I.= NEUROTIC INTROVERT
S.I.= STABLE INTROVERT
N.E.= NEUROTIC EXTRAVERT
S.E.= STABLE EXTRAVERT

FIG. 13.6
(For full explanation, *see* text)

variance of M.A.S. scores were uncorrelated with the drive factor itself, which is unlikely. The M.A.S. has been discussed at length in the preceding chapter. In terms of Eysenck's dimensional system, it can be considered as largely a test of neuroticism and thus, in view of the theoretical interpretation of that factor, as mainly a measure of drive level. However, it is also likely to have a smaller but appreciable projection on the factors of introversion-extraversion. Furthermore, it is a scale of *manifest* or response-defined anxiety and therefore, indicative of habitual responses to stress. Finally, the stimulus aspects of anxiety may be of importance in the manner described above. Thus, an individual obtaining a high M.A.S. score is likely to have his learning performance enhanced by virtue of his relatively high excitatory potential and interfered with by habitual anxiety responses and impaired discriminations quite apart from the specific energizing effects of drive level, which may become masked or distorted.

Spence (1956) assumes, like Hull, that any drive present, whether relevant or not to the task in hand, will contribute to a "total effective drive state." This is acceptable in that it is one of the notions, whose implications are being tested in the researches. More difficult is the question whether an individual, scoring high on the M.A.S. and, presumably, having a history of manifestly anxious responses in a variety of circumstances, has a chronically high level of emotional arousal or whether the experimental situation has to be moderately novel, threatening or otherwise stressful in order to allow individual differences in emotional reactivity to become effective. Taylor (1956), reviewing evidence on this point, concludes that such individual differences are operative in most testing situations but that situational stress enhances their effects though not necessarily only by increasing differences in drive level. This problem is equally applicable to the individual differences in drive postulated as underlying the neuroticism dimension and Taylor's conclusion was implicitly assumed in the earlier theoretical discussion.

Most of the Iowa Studies and others making use of the Taylor scale employed groups of subjects, usually undergraduates, characterized by extreme M.A.S. scores and described as anxious or non-anxious. For experiments on differential conditioning, Spence and his co-workers (Spence and Farber, 1954; Spence and Beecroft, 1954) predict that anxious subjects compared with non-anxious will show greater excitatory strengths in response to the positive stimulus and to the negative stimulus and a greater difference in excitatory strengths. These predictions follow from their drive theory but, if the stimulus aspects as described earlier, are also considered, prediction becomes difficult in that the stimulus effects would tend to increase to a greater degree the excitatory strength to the negative stimulus for the anxious subjects and, therefore, tend to reduce their difference score. The overall effect on the difference would depend on the difficulty of the discrimination, i.e. the degree of similarity between the two stimuli. Spence and Farber explicitly assume that the internal drive stimuli have, for their groups, equal and relatively negligible habit loadings.

The authors' predictions were significantly confirmed for the responses to the positive stimulus, for four of five separate experiments, and they were generally supported by insignificant trends for the responses to the negative stimulus and the difference scores. This difference in predictive accuracy is consistent with the postulated stimulus effect. No predictions were made for the overall efficiency of discrimination learning but Restle and Beecroft (1955) reanalysed these data in terms of discrimination indices and found no differences between the subject groups.

In marked contrast to these findings are those of Hilgard, Jones and Kaplan (1951) who found that anxious subjects made an insignificantly greater number of responses to the positive stimulus than did non-anxious subjects but a similar difference was significant for the negative stimulus. This finding is contrary to Spence's predictions: for both groups of results to be consistent with the two-factor theory the

positive and negative stimuli should be more alike in the earlier study than in the Iowa experiments. In fact, different modes of stimulation and different dimensions of generalization were employed: whereas the Iowa workers used a 500-cycle tone as the positive stimulus and a 5,000-cycle tone as the negative stimulus, Hilgard et al. used equally illuminated windows to the right (positive) or left (negative) of a central fixation point.

Later investigations, while tending to support the two-factor theory, fail to settle the issue. This would require a repetition of the Iowa type of experiment but with experimental variation of the "distance" between positive and negative stimuli. Stevenson and Iscoe (1956) performed a discriminative learning experiment, using three squares of differing area and anxious and non-anxious subjects. The latter were significantly superior in learning and less variable. Bendig and Vaughan (1957) replicated this experiment but failed to cross-validate the finding at a significant level. Kamin (1955) found M.A.S. scores to be significantly and negatively correlated with the number of false responses to the negative stimulus in a discrimination situation but this finding failed to survive cross-validation and the original correlation lost significance when scores on a mechanical aptitude test were held constant. In a further experiment (in which mechanical aptitude was not measured) Kamin et al. (1955) report a similar correlation both with M.A.S. scores and intolerance of painful stimulation. The latter two measures were, however, uncorrelated and, as the pain tolerance scores were related to response latencies whereas M.A.S. scores were not, the authors suggest that high anxiety scores are related to impaired discrimination in this situation but low pain tolerance scores imply heightened avoidance tendencies producing higher probabilities and shorter latencies of response. The latter hypothesis implies a correlation between pain-intolerance and the number of correct positive responses but these data are not reported.

Stimulus generalization is theoretically akin to differential conditioning and the effect of increased drive, by virtue of both its energizing and stimulus properties, would be to increase responsiveness to generalized stimuli. Spence and Beecroft, in the paper already cited, report an insignificant trend in the reverse direction but Rosenbaum (1956), employing visual figures of differing height and a motor response, found that anxious, when compared with non-anxious subjects, showed significantly more generalization. This group difference was enlarged significantly when the subjects were given strong intermittent shocks during their performance of the task but not when weak shock or a buzzer was used. Wenar (1954) in a somewhat similar experiment, but testing temporal generalization, found that reaction-time tended (insignificantly) to be a function of both stimulus intensity (buzzer—weak shock—strong shock) and M.A.S. scores but there was no evidence of an interaction between these factors. Lacey, Smith and Green (1955) established conditioned cardiac responses to the word *cow* and report that subjects with high scores on a version of the M.A.S. show increased generalization to other words of rural connotation. This trend was consistent but insignificant. Farber and Spence (1956) failed to demonstrate any significant relationship between anxiety and generalization as measured by reaction-time but point out that the same is true of all investigations into generalization and discrimination when the criterion measure is response latency.

Serial learning tasks were employed by Taylor and Spence (1952) and Farber and Spence (1953) to test their theory concerning the effects of changes in drive on competing response tendencies. In the earlier study the task was a form of serial verbal "maze" and in the other a stylus maze. Assuming that errors on these tasks result from interference from response tendencies derived from remote associations, the authors predicted that anxious subjects would make more errors and take more trials to learn to a criterion than would non-anxious subjects. These predictions were confirmed at a significant level and, in an independent study by Matarazzo *et al.* (1955), a significant positive correlation was established between the number of trials to learn to a criterion on a stylus maze task and the full range of M.A.S. scores. In both Iowa studies, in accordance with a further prediction, a significant rank-order correlation was demonstrated between choice-point difficulty and differences in errors between the anxious and non-anxious groups. Even at the easiest choice-points, however, where errors were very few, the anxious subjects tended to be inferior whereas the reverse would be expected from the Iowa hypothesis. This is consistent with expectations derived from Fig. 13.5. provided that the overall difficulty-stress ratings of the tasks locate them to the right of centre along the abscissa. The validity of the finding has, however, been questioned by Axelrod, Cowen and Heilizer (1956) and, for the stylus maze task, when subgroups of anxious and non-anxious subjects were matched for total score, the anxious subjects were significantly superior at the easiest choice points and inferior at the most difficult. Axelrod *et al.* reanalysed the Farber and Spence data, allowing for overall differences in performance, and found the resulting correlation to be negative but insignificant. They also carried out a replication of the maze study but included subjects with middle-range M.A.S. scores. Though no significant differences were established in terms of errors, trials to criterion, or differential performance at choice-points of varying

difficulty, all trends were in the direction predicted on the basis of the Iowa hypothesis. Of considerable interest is these authors' finding that the "lie" scale of the M.M.P.I. (Hathaway and McKinley, 1943) was related more closely to learning performance than was the M.A.S.

Hughes, Sprague and Bendig (1954) failed to establish significant differences between groups with extreme M.A.S. scores on several serial verbal mazes as used by Taylor and Spence. They presented the stimuli, however, at intervals of four seconds whereas the former study had employed a two-second rate. Thus their tasks would be less stressful and located further to the left in Fig. 13.5. In these studies, consistent but non-significant negative correlations were found between choice-point difficulty and differential group performance as calculated in the Iowa studies.

Montague (1953) varied systematically the amount of interference in serial verbal learning by constructing three series of nonsense syllables with different extents of intra-list similarity and different association values. He reports a significant interaction between M.A.S. scores and interference values, anxious subjects being superior for the list with high association values and low intra-list similarity while non-anxious subjects were superior for the list of low association values and high similarity: difficulty level, as such, was uncontrolled in this experiment. Data most damaging to the Iowa hypothesis were obtained by Saltz and Hoehn (1957) in an investigation similar to Montague's but in which, by manipulation of the factors of intra-list similarity and association value, the authors selected "competing" and "non-competing" serial nonsense syllable lists which were empirically shown to be of equal difficulty for a group of non-anxious subjects. The performance of anxious subjects was very similar for both lists and the absolute difference was in the direction opposite to prediction. In a second experiment the performance of anxious and non-anxious groups was compared for easy-competing and difficult-non-competing material. Contrary to prediction there was no significant difference at the former task but the anxious group was significantly inferior at the difficult non-competing task. The authors conclude that M.A.S. scores are related to difficulty level rather than response competition and suggest that greater difficulty imposes greater stress and, therefore, releases potential anxiety. This view is consistent with our fourth drive-efficiency hypothesis.

Sarason (1956) found, under neutral conditions, that high scorers on the M.A.S. were superior to middle and low-anxious groups in the serial learning of nonsense syllables of high associative value but, with ego-oriented instructions to the effect that the task was a form of intelligence test, the latter two groups improved in performance whereas the high-anxious subjects deteriorated significantly. The effect of these instructions remained significant twenty-four hours later. Stress was further varied by making failure or non-failure reports on the subject's performance. Failure information resulted in lowered performance for all groups but this effect did not persist over twenty-four hours and affected all groups equally. In a later paper (Sarason, 1957a) a replication study is described using syllables of slightly lower association values (53 per cent), ego-oriented instructions as before, task-oriented motivating instructions and neutral control instructions. The results in general were consistent with those in the previous study with the task-oriented instructions being insignificantly less effective than the ego-oriented condition. In this study there is some evidence that low-anxious subjects responded differently from the middle-anxious group and in the same direction as the high-anxious group. Failure motivation was investigated further in a third study (Sarason, 1957b) employing high-and low-anxious groups. One group of each type was failed on a preliminary list of nonsense syllables similar to the experimental task. Other equivalent groups were failed on a dissimilar digit-cancellation task. Control groups, receiving no failure reports, showed no difference in performance but the low-anxious subjects were superior after both types of failure stimulation. Anxious subjects showed similar impairment of performance from both failure conditions but, whereas non-anxious subjects failed on the syllable task were no different from the non-anxious control group, the non-anxious group failed on the cancellation task were significantly superior to all other groups. As the experimental design ensured that the cancellation task was closest in time to the experimental task, this is consistent with Doris and Sarason's (1955) finding, for a non-learning task, that the nature of the interaction between anxiety and failure depends on the order of the tasks failed but is also consistent with more extensive generalization of failure effects for anxious subjects. The general pattern of all Sarason's results is consistent with our theoretical expectations but his detailed findings illustrate the complexity of the possible interactions of effects.

Beam (1955) investigated the interrelationships between serial nonsense-syllable learning, M.A.S. scores and stress, ingeniously induced by taking advantage of real-life stress situations. The scores of fifty-four subjects just prior to a doctoral examination, making an important oral report, or the "first night" of a dramatic performance were compared with those achieved in neutral conditions. On each occasion palmar sweat indices were recorded. The results indicate that stress had a highly significant and deleterious effect on learning efficiency, the magnitude of

which has correlated with increases in the amount of palmar sweating. M.A.S. scores, however, were not related to either effect. While stress impaired complex learning, G.S.R. conditioning was facilitated.

Silverman and Blitz (1956) threatened anxious and non-anxious groups with shock in two ways. Half the subjects were told, "You *may* receive a shock" and half, "You *will* receive a shock." The former instruction was considered an avoidance situation in that it implied that good performance would prevent shock and, consistent with this interpretation, non-anxious subjects decreased their errors on a serial rote-learning task in the avoidance situation and increased them in the non-avoidance situation. The anxious group slightly improved their scores in both conditions. There were no significant differences between anxious and non-anxious groups during preliminary training but on a test of the incidental learning of digits, the anxious group, presented with words to be learned, was significantly inferior. The experimental conditions had no effect on incidental learning. These results are clearly opposed to our theoretical expectations as no variants of Figs. 13.5 and 13.6 would portray declining normal performance through a range of stress within which neurotic performance improves. Hypotheses concerning failure, by the anxious subjects, to discriminate between the implications of the two forms of instruction might account for the differences but these would be very much *ad hoc*.

The results of Deese, Lazarus and Keenan (1953), obtained in a rather similar experiment are equally difficult to explain. Anxious and non-anxious subjects were divided into three groups, one receiving intermittent shocks, one receiving shocks when responding incorrectly and one under neutral conditions, while they were learning serial nonsense syllables of minimal similarity. For the combined conditions the anxious subjects were significantly superior but there was a significant interaction between anxiety and conditions to such an extent that the largest group difference occurred in the avoidance situation, owing to facilitation of performance in the anxious group and a decrement in the performance of the non-anxious group. Under the intermittent shock conditions, the group difference results entirely from deterioration of the performance of non-anxious subjects. The authors quote evidence to indicate that M.A.S. scores are related to the hysteria-psychasthenia continuum. This is in accord with the suggestion, made earlier, that the M.A.S. is related to introversion-extraversion as well as to neuroticism but Deese and his co-workers suggest that both extremes of M.A.S. scores reflect neurotic tendencies and anxiety but that low scorers have erected strong hysterical defences against their anxiety which break down under objective inescapable stress such as shock. The high scorers or psychasthenic (dysthymic) individuals, while generally displaying their anxiety, react to objective stress in a cool and intellectual manner. A hypothesis of this type would also account for Silverman and Blitz's results if threat of shock can be equated with shock, and would render both sets of results compatible with theoretical expectations. Lazarus, Deese and Hamilton (1954) report a further analagous experiment but using a more difficult list with high intra-list similarity. No significant differences were observed between the groups, nor between the stress-no-stress conditions but Taylor (1956) points out that all groups only averaged about one correct response per trial and, hence, the difficulty of establishing group differences in learning.

Consistently with Deese's interpretation of the M.A.S., Matarazzo, Ulett and Saslow (1955), when considering the total time taken to solve their maze, found a significant but curvilinear relationship with anxiety scores such that scorers in the mid-range were superior to both high and low scorers, but this is equally consistent with the curves of Figs. 13.5 and 13.6. It has been argued earlier that irrelevant competing responses are unlikely to affect error scores in a maze-learning situation but might well affect speed of performance. In conjunction with Matarazzo's *et al.* findings, this would suggest that both high and low M.A.S. scores are likely to be indicative of interference tendencies. Matarazzo *et al.* (1954) found a similar curvilinear relationship between M.A.S. scores and timed tests of intelligence, as did Siegman (1956), but no relationship with untimed intelligence tests but this was not confirmed in a later study (Matarazzo and Matarazzo, 1956). Discussing these findings, Matarazzo (1955) stresses the high negative correlation between the M.A.S. and the validity scale K of the M.M.P.I., which he interprets as a "defensiveness" scale.

Paired-associate techniques have been employed in several of the Iowa studies (Ramond, 1953; Taylor and Chapman, 1955; Spence, Farber and McFann, 1956; Spence, Taylor and Ketchel, 1956; Spence, 1956). Consistently, the performance of anxious subjects was superior for adjective pairs of high initial S-R associative strengths and minimal inter-pair similarity but non-anxious subjects were superior when stimulus members were similar or synonymous. In one experiment, the predicted superiority of anxious subjects was evident with an anticipation interval of 2·2 sec but disappeared with an interval of only 1·1 sec, which made "the learning problem . . . very difficult and quite stressful." This result is consistent with a move to the right along the abscissa of Fig. 13.5 and is used by Spence as evidence for task-interfering responses countering the greater energizing value of the high drive of anxious subjects.

Ramond's study is of particular interest. Each stimulus adjective was presented with a pair of response words, one of initially high and one of initially low associative linkage with the stimulus, from which the subject had to select the correct response e.g. $\text{tranquil} < \dfrac{\text{serene } (\surd)}{\text{rugged } (\times)}$. Elsewhere in the series a synonymous stimulus word was presented with the same response words but with the previously incorrect response now correct e.g. $\text{peaceful} < \dfrac{\text{serene } (\times)}{\text{rugged } (\surd)}$. As expected, non-anxious subjects were superior when the responses of low association value were correct. No significant difference was observed between groups when the high association responses were correct though there was a tendency for anxious subjects to be superior early in learning and inferior later. Though insignificant in extent, this trend was almost exactly duplicated in two of the later studies and is interpreted as resulting from growing interference, by generalization, from the gradually learned weak response. Though consistent with the Iowa hypothesis, in view of Saltz and Hoehn's results with serial learning, these results are ambiguous without adequate control of the difficulty factor.

Gordon and Berlyne (1954) introduced additional stress into a paired-associate task by informing the subjects that the task was a test of intelligence. Anxious subjects then tended, insignificantly, to require more trials to learn to a criterion. Half the subjects in each group were then told that their performance was above average and half that their performance was below average. Success information failed to produce differences in the performance of anxious and non-anxious groups in a second task but, with failure information, the anxious subjects were significantly inferior, though all groups took less trials to learn the second list than to learn the first.

Korchin and Levine (1957) varied difficulty and stress for two groups of normal subjects, anxious and non-anxious in terms of M.A.S. scores, and a group of hospitalized psychiatric patients with anxiety symptoms. All groups learned paired-associate tasks of two types, simple logically related word-pairs and incorrect multiplication formulae. Half the subjects in each group were tested with immediate (high stress) and half with delayed (low stress) inter-trial spacing. The non-anxious normal subjects were significantly superior to the anxious normal subjects for the false equations and a similar but insignificant difference was observed for the word-pairs: the different spacings had no effect on these trends. The patients were approximately equal in efficiency to the anxious normal subjects with delayed spacing but deteriorated with immediate spacing on both tasks. Both the high anxiety and patient groups tended to make more failures of response (no response rather than a false response) with immediate spacing.

Westrope (1953) tested anxious and non-anxious groups on a lengthened version of the Wechsler-Bellevue Digit Symbol test over eighteen trials in blocks of seven, five, three and three. Her results are represented graphically in Fig. 13.7 and display a consistent trend for the anxious to be superior to the non-anxious subjects over the first fifteen trials when conditions were neutral. The last three trials were administered in highly stressful conditions including observation, signals of "unsatisfactory" performance and impending shock, and actual shock. Performance declined during the stress period and the curves show a tendency for the non-anxious subjects to be superior to the anxious. The overall effect of stress was statistically significant while the interaction between anxiety and stress approached significance.

Fig. 13.7 clearly shows that in this study, as in others, though stress may effect learning, as such, its main effect is on performance, which falls well below the level already achieved. Carlson and Lazarus (1953), in a similar study, found that the slope of the improvement curve under stress was significantly and positively correlated with subject's scores on Winne's neuroticism scale, a measure highly correlated with the M.A.S.

Davidson, Andrews and Ross (1956) investigated the effects of anxiety and various types of stress on a continuous colour-naming task. They found no significant effect for the M.A.S. scores alone but various significant interactions between anxiety and stress. This suggests that M.A.S. scores indicate increased susceptibility to stress rather than chronic anxiety. In accordance with this notion, anxiety scores correlated positively with subjective experience of stress as reported on a questionnaire following the experiment.

Grice (1955) set a complex discrimination reaction-time task to two groups of airmen trainees, representing both extremes of M.A.S. scores. For both reaction-time and error scores the low-anxious group was significantly superior and showed significantly greater superiority on tasks of greater difficulty but, when analysis-of-covariance techniques were applied, it was shown that these differences could be accounted for in terms of general intellectual ability. This finding casts some doubt on the validity of other studies employing the M.A.S. but which do not control for intellectual factors. The correlations, however, between M.A.S. scores and most tests of intelligence are negligible (Taylor, 1955; Mayzner et al., 1955), at least for groups of students and, as Grice points out, the range of intelligence in his group is considerably wider than in most other studies.

Matarazzo and Matarazzo (1956), with the above result in mind, carefully controlled age, education and intelligence in an investigation into the relationship between M.A.S. scores and performance on a complex, double disc pursuitmeter, using as subjects psychiatric and non-psychiatric hospital in-patients. These authors failed to establish any significant relationship between performance and anxiety but report a trend for subjects with middle-range M.A.S.

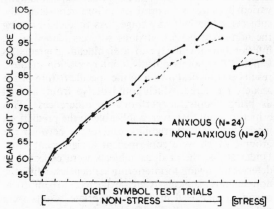

FIG. 13.7. DIGIT SYMBOL LEARNING OF "ANXIOUS" AND "NON-ANXIOUS" SUBJECTS IN STRESS AND NON-STRESS CONDITIONS

Data for both sexes combined.

(After Westrope, 1953)

scores to benefit most from practice. Maltzmann, Smith and Brooks (1956) found that subjects making relatively high numbers of target hits in a target-tracking task had significantly lower anxiety scores than those making relatively few hits.

Apart from the studies by Silverman and Blitz and by Deese, Lazarus and Keenan, all the studies reviewed, employing Taylor's scale, are consistent with the general expectation described in the earlier theoretical section. Two distinct possibilities emerge which merit further investigation: task difficulty, empirically determined, may be more important than the factors of response competition stressed by the Iowa group and many of the relationships between M.A.S. scores and other variables may be curvilinear rather than linear in nature.

Mandler and Sarason (1952) have employed a different type of anxiety questionnaire, intended to be a measure of "test anxiety," the anxiety evoked by such situations as formal examinations and psychological tests of ability. They make a formal statement of their hypothesis that subjects, scoring high on their questionnaire, respond to such tasks, not only with increased drive, but also with previously learned task-irrelevant responses to their anxiety, which interfere with performance. Predictions, derived from this hypothesis, are made concerning the results of an experiment involving repeated testing with items of Koh's Block Design Test and versions of the Wechsler Digit Symbol Test. Though these are essentially tests of intelligence, their repeated application produced typical learning curves. Scoring was mainly in terms of speed of performance and, as argued earlier, should therefore be affected by test-irrelevant responses. Stress was experimentally varied by success, neutral or failure reports to the subjects at the half-way stage. As predicted, during the non-stress period, anxious subjects tended to be inferior but not always to a significant degree. As Child (1954) points out, their interpretation of these results is equivocal owing to the specific nature of the anxiety measured, which could derive from, as well as bring about, the performance differences. This criticism is not, however, applicable to the predictions made concerning variability differences between the groups, which were confirmed at a significant level. Under stress, the anxious subjects were expected to deteriorate, owing to interfering tendencies, while the non-anxious subjects were expected to improve, owing to increased drive. Appropriate results were obtained for the Koh's Designs but no significant effects were observed on the Digit Symbol test. Success stimulation tended to produce effects similar to failure stimulation though to a lesser and insignificant degree.

Sarason, Mandler and Craighill (1952) made a similar digit symbol task sufficiently long to ensure that no subject could complete it in any one trial. Stress was varied by telling subjects that they either should or should not be able to finish in the time allowed. As predicted, anxious subjects were inferior but significantly so only for the stress condition. No absolute differences in variance were observed but the predicted trends of change in variance approached significance. Stress, as expected, improved the performance of non-anxious subjects but had no apparent effect on the anxious group. Child (1954) points out that these effects were of similar magnitude on the first and subsequent trials, when the subjects were aware that they would not complete the task. In the same paper, a second experiment is described in which ego-oriented or task-oriented instructions were given before performance on a stylus maze task, scored both in terms of errors and time. The results tended to fall in the predicted directions but most trends failed to achieve statistical significance.

In support of their view that test-anxious subjects, with repeated rewarded practice, should learn to modify their habitual responses to anxiety arousal so as to make them task-relevant and non-interfering, Sarason and Mandler (1952) report that individuals

scoring high on their questionnaire have relatively low scores on aptitude tests at the beginning of a college course but show slight relative superiority in terms of their later average college grades. As, presumably, the anxiety questionnaire was administered subsequently to the achievement of the relatively high grade averages, this finding cannot be explained in terms of the extinction of the anxiety response. In a further study, Mandler and Sarason (1953) show that test-anxious subjects tend, more than non-anxious subjects, to rate their performance as inferior. This subjective experience is an important factor in the performance of these subjects but its effect can be counteracted by specific success reports. Altogether, these investigations present strong evidence in support of the hypothesis of interference from task-irrelevant responses. The scores taken are, in general, such as would reflect such interference and the trends observed are consistent with the relationships portrayed in Fig. 13.5, provided that the stresses involved were only moderate, as seems likely.

A third personality questionnaire, the Interference Tendency Questionnaire (I.T.Q.) was employed by Waterhouse and Child (1953). This samples an individual's characteristic responses to frustration with particular reference to tendencies to respond in a manner likely to interfere with adequate performance of a task. Sarason and Mandler (1953) report a correlation of 0·47 between this measure and their own test-anxiety scale. Waterhouse and Child, and Williams (1955), demonstrated interrelationships between scores on this scale, motivating conditions, and performance on a wide variety of tasks very similar to those established in the investigations of Mandler and his associates. Except in two instances, however, these tasks were scored in terms of absolute score not in terms of learning and were, frequently, of an intellectual nature. It is of interest, however, that in most instances the scores taken were essentially speed scores.

Indices derived from the Rorschach test were used by Williams (1947) as measures of emotional and intellectual control and were shown to correlate highly with deterioration of performance on a digit symbol task under a combination of stresses such as shock, threat of failure and observation. Not surprisingly, in view of the general lack of validity of the Rorschach technique (Payne, 1955), this finding was not confirmed in a replication study by Carlson and Lazarus (1953) who also cite studies by Allee and by Stopol which also failed to relate performance under stress to Rorschach measures. Westrope (1953) also included Rorschach indices in the study described earlier but none of these were predictive of stress effects in the digit symbol task. The group Rorschach technique fared better in an investigation by Ausubel *et al.* (1953) into the mirror-drawing and blindfold stylus maze performance of two groups of subjects selected as scoring in the upper or lower fifths of a distribution of anxiety scores derived from this test. The groups also differed significantly in their responses to an anxiety inventory and evidence of the higher motivation of the anxious group was drawn from level of aspiration scores.

The main evidence concerning the learning ability of these groups derives from the maze task which was repeated over ten trials. At the first trial, the anxious subjects were significantly inferior both in terms of speed and errors. Their slower speed may be due to interference from competing responses but the initial difference in error scores is difficult to explain as, during the first trial, a subject has no basis, apart from chance trial and error, for choosing alleys and experience with early choice-points is no guide to later choices. During the course of the ten trials the anxious subjects increased their speed relatively more and were as fast as the non-anxious subjects on the tenth trial. They also gained more from practice on a simple trial maze and improved more in terms of error scores though this latter trend may well lose significance if the dubious difference in initial error scores is eliminated. When the task is relatively simple, requiring some fifteen to twenty trials for perfect performance, and the stressor elements in the situation are only moderate, the whole pattern of results is such as would be expected from placement of the task in a fairly central position along the abscissa of Fig. 13.5 with, possibly, increased stress during the early stages owing to the novelty of the situation.

Other investigators have employed no psychometric devices but have studied the effects on performance of anxiety induced experimentally in a variety of ways, many of which figured as supplementary variables in the studies already reviewed. Thus, McClelland and Apicella (1947) subjected two groups to failure stimulation and one to success stimulation (described as "neutral" by the authors) while learning a card-sorting task to a criterion. The success and one failure group then "rested" for four minutes, during which they practised a pursuit-meter task with success stimulation, and then completed ten further trials at the card-sorting task with no incentives. The remaining "failure" group proceeded to these additional trials immediately following their initial practice. Both failure groups were significantly impaired in their original learning. In the first of the final ten trials the rested failure group was superior to the rested success group and equal to the non-rested failure group. Thereafter, the non-rested failure group deteriorated whereas the other two groups improved slightly. The authors postulate that failure produced response conflict which lowered performance below the true level of learning. As failure and success groups were taken to the same performance criterion the failure groups actually learned more and this superiority became evident when the conflicts were removed by the rest period. The failure of the rested failure group to show reminiscence was explained in terms of retroactive inhibition produced by the interpolated task.

Bayton and Conley (1957) varied success and failure at a task requiring manual dexterity by level of aspiration techniques. Learning was measured in terms of speed scores. The experimental subjects were divided into three groups receiving five, ten or fifteen successful trials before experiencing failure. The shift to failure improved performance for the last two groups, but not for the group receiving only five success trials. Thus the effect of failure stimulation is partly governed by the background of reinforcement.

Sarason and Sarason (1957) gave fifteen trials at learning a serial nonsense-syllable list to subjects, half of whom then received ego-oriented instructions and half task-oriented instructions before fourteen trials on a second and equivalent list. Half of each group received failure stimulation and half was engaged in neutral conversation before proceeding with the fifteenth trial of the second list. Twenty-four hours later all groups carried out five more trials with the second list. The groups were compared by analysis of covariance techniques in terms of their performance on trials 15, 16, and 20 of the experimental list. Ego-oriented subjects were superior to task-oriented subjects on trial 16 and failed subjects were inferior to non-failed subjects on trial 15. There was also an insignificant trend for failure to have a greater detrimental effect in the task-oriented group. Thus failure appeared to have an immediate but temporary effect whereas high motivation from instructions had no immediate effect but facilitated later performance. From this and the preceding studies it is clear that the effectiveness of failure motivation depends on many factors but when effective it operates in a manner consistent with theoretical expectation.

Jones (1954), set his subjects a temporal maze task and varied stress in the form of frustration induced by varying fore-periods during which the maze was insoluble. Motivation was varied by giving ego-oriented or task-oriented instructions. His results indicate that short periods of frustration resulted in impaired learning efficiency and increased stereotypy of response but prolonged frustration did not increase this tendency. Ego-oriented instructions consistently exaggerated the effects of frustration but never to a significant degree.

Castaneda and Palermo (1955) tested the implications of the Iowa theory by varying habit strengths; this was done by varying periods of practice at a paired-associate task with five coloured lights as stimuli and five buttons as response manipulanda. The lists were relearned with three of the stimuli and response elements re-paired and, at this stage, stress in the form of speed instructions was introduced for half the subjects. The results, though trends were not always significant, were confirmatory of the predictions that performance would be impaired by stress when the dominant habit was incorrect, facilitated by stress when the dominant habit was correct and the trends would be magnified with increasing strength of the dominant habit. Castaneda (1956) reports similar findings from an analogous experiment. Though supporting the Iowa hypothesis these results may well derive from difficulty rather than competitional factors.

Silverman (1954) investigated the effects of threats of shock (unfulfilled after one demonstration shock) and auditory distraction on performance at a visual size-discrimination task. Both independent variables slightly, but insignificantly, improved performance whereas the combined stresses significantly impaired discrimination. As the task was learned to a criterion by all subjects, before the introduction of the experimental variables, this effect is not one on discrimination learning as such but may reflect changes in the stimulus generalization gradients consistent with the expectations described earlier. Rosenbaum (1953), as in the study previously described (Rosenbaum, 1956), demonstrated flattened generalization gradients with the administration of intermittent strong shock.

Eriksen and Wechsler (1955) studied the effects of random electric shocks on discriminative accuracy, which was tested by recording subjects' absolute judgements of size for a series of eleven squares of different sizes extending over a range within which control subjects had been shown to be capable of absolutely discriminating some four stimuli. When presented with a stimulus square, subjects responded with the number, from one to eleven, corresponding to their judgement. From an analysis of the results in terms of information theory it was concluded that there were no differences in accuracy of discrimination between the experimental and control groups but the stressed subjects were more biased in their use of the eleven categories and more stereotyped in their responses to specific squares. The authors, therefore, suggest that the effects of anxiety on discrimination result from changes in response thresholds rather than from any impairment of sensory discrimination. These findings do not constitute evidence against our hypothesis concerning the effects of a drive stimulus on discrimination learning which refers to response tendencies rather than sensory discrimination. Eriksen and Wechsler's ingenious experiment could well be adapted to form a direct test of this hypothesis but

doubt must be cast on the validity of this method of determining sensory discrimination, which depends on relationships within the response categories used by the subjects. In a somewhat similar experiment, but using a pseudo-E.S.P. situation, instead of absolute judgements, in order to free responses "from external stimulus determination," Kuethe and Eriksen (1957) demonstrated a significant relationship between anxiety on the one hand and stereotypy and bias in selecting numbers from one to eleven on the other. Yet in the earlier experiment category choices were the criteria of sensory discrimination.

Cowen, Heilizer and Axelrod (1955) controlled anxiety or emotional disturbance by selecting, for each subject, six adjectives considered to be related to personal conflicts by virtue of a large discrepancy between the subject's "actual" and "ideal" self-ratings on the traits described by these adjectives. These and six "neutral" adjectives, for which no such discrepancy was noted, were paired with nonsense syllables of low association value and formed a verbal learning task. The neutral pairs were learned significantly sooner than the conflict-related pairs and there was a significant positive correlation between the mean discrepancy score for a given adjective and the trials required to learn the pair in which that adjective figured. The same authors (Heilizer et al., 1956) later reported that there were no significant differences among groups, selected by M.A.S. scores, for the learning of the series as a whole or for the differential learning of conflict and non-conflict word pairs.

Jacobs (1955) found a similar significant tendency for words, considered, by virtue of long reaction-time in a free-association test, to be emotionally significant to a subject, to be learned less readily than neutral words when used as responses to nonsense syllables in a paired-associate list. This was accentuated when the words occurred in difficult serial learning positions. There was also some evidence that these trends were magnified for subjects considered maladjusted. Failure reports, however, tended to neutralize these effects. Merrill (1954) in an analogous experiment also found that "emotional" words were learned less easily by control subjects who showed no associative disturbances to any of the experimental words. An interpolated task, considered to be evocative of anxiety owing to its difficulty, and failure reports reduced efficiency of recall in both groups of subjects.

The Maudsley studies have, to date, been mainly concerned with the dimension of introversion-extraversion though the experimental results are inevitably related to neuroticism as well. The bulk of the work on learning, as distinct from conditioning, has been concerned with rotary pursuit tasks. Eysenck (1956b) reports on an experiment with fifty male students as subjects and which involved three five-minute "massed practice" periods of rotary pursuit separated by ten-minute rest periods. A measure of improvement throughout the test correlated negatively with both extraversion and neuroticism but neither correlation was significant. As the task is fairly difficult, these trends are in the direction which would be predicted but the main function of this study was to test the prediction that extraverts would show greater reminiscence than introverts owing to their postulated more rapid growth, higher maximum level and slower dissipation of reactive inhibition (I_R). Reminiscence scores were calculated by subtracting the mean time on target during the last three pre-rest ten-second periods from the time on target during the first post-rest ten seconds. There were two such scores for each subject corresponding to the two rest intervals: these were significantly intercorrelated $(r = 0.44)$. The first reminiscence scores (R_1) correlated significantly and positively $(r = 0.29)$ with subjects' extraversion scores (E) on the Maudsley Personality Inventory (M.P.I.) (Eysenck 1956a) while the correlation of E with the second reminiscence score (R_2) was insignificant. The neuroticism (N) scores of the M.P.I. also correlated significantly with R_1 $(r = 0.40)$ and, at a level approaching significance, with R_2 $(r = 0.27)$.

Eysenck argues that the lowered correlation between E and R_2, like the relatively low reliability of the R scores, derives from the contamination of the second reminiscence scores, resulting from the development of conditioned inhibition $(_sI_R)$ during the latter part of the pre-rest performance and its extinction during early post-rest performance. Although no prediction was made concerning correlations between R and N, these were to be expected from the concept of N as a drive variable. Increased drive increases I_R tolerance and, therefore, allows greater reminiscence. The lower correlation with R_2 was explained in terms of $_sI_R$ development, as before.

From this argument, it follows that the degree of correlation between R scores and both E and N should increase in conditions unfavourable to the development of $_sI_R$. Star (1957) aimed to achieve this by reducing the cycles of massed practice to ninety seconds, a time suggested by Eysenck (1956c) as approximating to that required for I_R to reach a critical level and initiate involuntary rest pauses. Four groups were selected in terms of E and N scores. One group (EN) included subjects scoring high for both E and N, one was low on both scales (en), one high on E and low on N (En) and one low on E and high on N (eN). These groups were given sixteen ninety-second cycles of massed practice separated by five-minute rest periods. It was predicted that group EN would show most reminiscence and en the

least with En and eN falling between. Similar predictions were made concerning relative depression of performance within cycles. These predictions would be valid only if appreciable $_sI_R$ development was prevented by the experimental conditions. Thus, on the basis of the theoretical argument outlined above and elaborated by Eysenck (1956c), two further predictions were made as a check on $_sI_R$ development. Firstly, it was predicted that no long-term warm up would be observed after rest-periods and, secondly, that all reminiscence scores would intercorrelate highly and a factor-analysis of the correlation matrix would suggest a single factor solution. Long term warm-up was, in fact, absent and, though the intercorrelations between R scores were low, they were non-random and generally positive and only a single common factor was extracted from the matrix. Thus Star considered that the development of any appreciable quantity of $_sI_R$ had been prevented. None, however, of the main predictions were confirmed at a significant level.

Star then replicated Eysenck's original experiment but added a fourth extended cycle of practice and employed his own apparatus. One hundred subjects were selected from a group of apprentices who were tested at their factory. There was again a significant correlation between E and R_1 and progressively smaller and insignificant correlations between E and R_2 and E and R_3. The correlation between N and R_1 was also significant but negative: the correlations of N with R_2 and R_3 were insignificant.

Das (1957) included rotary pursuit among a battery of tests administered to a group of normal subjects. He used ninety-second cycles of massed practice, as in Star's first study, but ten-minute rest pauses as in Eysenck's study. He failed to demonstrate any significant correlation between either E or N and reminiscence. The observed correlation between N and R_1 was, however, again negative and its size was just short of that required for significance $(r = -0.24)$. Star's analogous correlation was, in fact, identical in size but achieved significance owing to his larger experimental population. The same apparatus was used in Das's and Star's experiments and in a study by Bartholomew and Marley (1957) which replicated Star's original study both in its design and its results: no significant relationships were observed between reminiscence and M.P.I. scores.

Thus it appears that, for rotary pursuit, ninety-second cycles of massed practice and, possibly, five-minute rest periods are insufficiently prolonged to allow the demonstration of significant relationships between reminiscence and personality variables but with five-minute practice periods and ten-minute rest periods these relationships become evident. Extraversion, as measured by the M.P.I., is positively correlated with reminiscence but the latter's correlation with neuroticism may be either positive or negative, according to experimental factors as yet undefined. These relationships can only be demonstrated for the first reminiscence score, with which later reminiscence scores are only moderately correlated.

whereas performance at the beginning of the second practice period will be a function of—

$$D \times (_sH_R - _sI_R)$$

Reminiscence, the difference between these two values, will not be a function of I_R alone but of—

$$I_R \times (_sH_R - _sI_R)$$

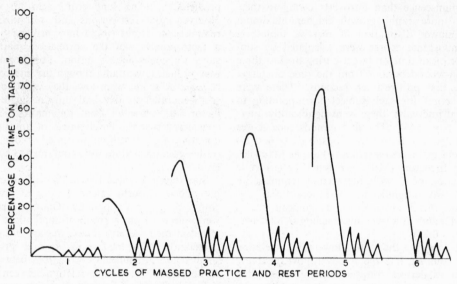

FIG. 13.8. THEORETICAL CURVES OF PERFORMANCE DURING MASSED PRACTICE OF ROTARY PURSUIT, ASSUMING HYPOTHESIS *A*

It seems to the writer that the predictions made by the authors of these studies are not based on a sufficiently elaborate theoretical analysis of the reminiscence phenomenon and, as the predictions depend as much on the learning theory as on the personality theory, it is considered justified to make such an analysis here. During an initial period of massed practice, $_sH_R$, I_R and $_sI_R$ will grow at independent rates and interact to produce a complex curve of performance. During the subsequent rest period I_R will dissipate but $_sH_R$ and $_sI_R$, being habit states, will remain relatively unchanged. Thus, at the beginning of the second period of massed practice, the initial $_s\bar{E}_R$ will be at a higher level than at the end of the first period of practice, the difference being reflected in the phenomenon of reminiscence. This reminiscence, however, while being a consequence of the dissipation of I_R is not, quantitatively, a function of I_R alone. From the equation described earlier, performance at the end of the first practice period will be a function of—

$$(D - I_R) \times (_sH_R - _sI_R)$$

$_sI_R$ and $_sH_R$ are minimal during the first of a series of massed practice periods and individual differences for these variables probably slight. I_R, if the rest period is sufficiently long to allow complete or near-complete dissipation, would be expected to develop to equal and considerable extents in each period. Thus the first reminiscence score should relate most closely to extraversion scores if the latter reflect individual differences in susceptibility to reactive inhibition.

$_sH_R$ would be expected to increase, according to the usual positive growth function, throughout the series until it reaches its asymptote. The same would be true of $_sI_R$ were it not for the discrimination process, resulting from fluctuations in the stimulus conditions, postulated by Eysenck (1956c) in explanation of the long-term warm-up phenomenon. $_sI_R$, according to Hull, is a negative habit, the acquisition of which is reinforced by drive reduction resulting from the dissipation of I_R during the period when the response is not made. Such drive reduction can only occur when I_R has accumulated to some extent, i.e. after a certain period of massed practice. During the early part of a later period of massed practice, when I_R is minimal, drive reduction can only occur in relation to positive drives and these are reduced by successful performance. Therefore, the negative reaction potential associated with an $_SI_R$ will tend to extinguish during the early period but $_SI_R$ is again reinforced later, as massed practice continues. This is essentially a discrimination learning situation and,

throughout, are graphically represented in Figs. 13.8 and 13.9. Fig. 13.8 is based on the additional assumption that the length of each massed-practice period is sufficiently long for I_R to accumulate to a level equal to that of drive and thus initiate a series of involuntary rest pauses (Hypothesis A), whereas Fig. 13.9 involves the contrary assumption (Hypothesis B) (*See* Fig.

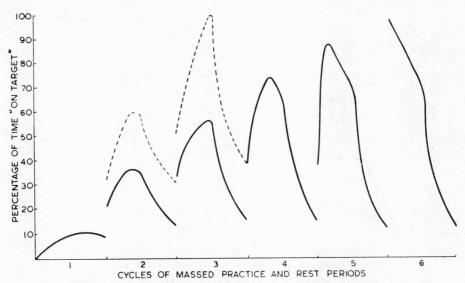

FIG. 13.9. THEORETICAL CURVES OF PERFORMANCE DURING MASSED PRACTICE OF ROTARY PURSUIT, ASSUMING HYPOTHESIS B

The broken lines represent performance at an increased ($\times 1 \cdot 5$) drive level.

after a series of massed-practice periods with intervening rest periods, $_SI_R$ would be expected to be operative when the drive stimulus corresponding to I_R is appreciable and inoperative when this stimulus is absent. Thus, while $_SI_R$, and the individual differences associated with it, will appreciably affect reminiscence scores for the middle cycles of a series, later scores will be relatively less affected. The same is true for individual differences associated with $_SH_R$. Subjects may differ in respect of their initial levels, rates of growth and asymptotes of $_SH_R$ but, when the asymptotes are reached, only the last of these can affect relative scores. Consistent with this argument, Eysenck (1956c) reports relatively high positive correlations within and between early and late reminiscence scores, positive correlations between the middle members of the series, and a low negative correlation between the two groups of scores.

Applying the above formula, theoretical curves of reaction potential during successive cycles of massed practice and rest, assuming the above theoretical analysis to be correct, applying arbitrary values to all the variables and assuming drive to be constant

13.10). It may be seen that the $_SE_R$ curves of Fig. 13.9 are of a form comparable to those empirically determined for the durations of practice used in the studies reviewed (Figs. 13.11 and 13.12), whereas the terminal low flat portion, inevitably associated with

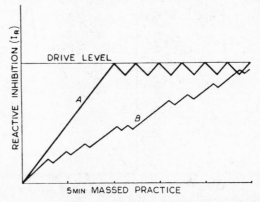

FIG. 13.10. GROWTH OF REACTIVE INHIBITION DURING FIVE MINUTES' MASSED PRACTICE OF ROTARY PURSUIT, ACCORDING TO HYPOTHESES A AND B

hypothesis *A*, is absent from the empirical curves though such a tendency was evident during the prolonged fourth practice period of Star's second experiment. Hypothesis *B* does not imply that no $_sI_R$ would be acquired. The probability of the correct response is by no means 100 per cent, particularly during the early stages of learning. Oscillation and

competing response tendencies ensure that involuntary rest pauses will occur and allow some dissipation of I_R with which to reinforce the growth of $_sI_R$.

Eysenck (1956c, 1957) suggests that hypothesis *A* is the more likely but, if I_R does in fact reach the level of drive and extraverts and introverts do not differ in their drive level, both groups would be expected to

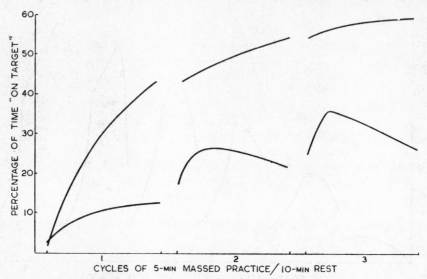

FIG. 13.11. EMPIRICAL CURVES OF PERFORMANCE DURING MASSED (LOWER CURVES) AND
DISTRIBUTED (UPPER CURVES) PRACTICE OF ROTARY PURSUIT
(*After Eysenck*, 1956c)

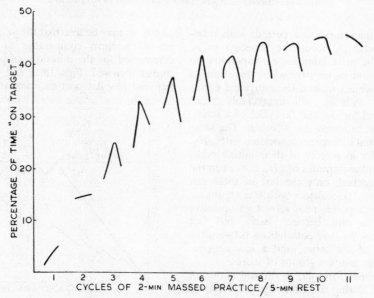

FIG. 13.12. EMPIRICAL CURVES OF PERFORMANCE DURING MASSED PRACTICE
OF ROTARY PURSUIT
(*After Eysenck*, 1956c)

end a period of massed practice with equal I_R. Then, if the rest period is sufficiently long for most of the I_R to dissipate, even for those (extraverted) subjects in whom such dissipation is slow, no group differences in reminiscence could be predicted, at least as resulting from differences in the rate and level of acquisition of I_R. If the rest period is shorter, introverts, whose I_R will have dissipated more rapidly, should show greater reminiscence than extraverts. On the basis of hypothesis B, however, the positive correlation between extraversion and reminiscence is directly explicable in terms of Eysenck's postulates.

There remains, however, the problem of the correlation between neuroticism and reminiscence. Neuroticism is conceived of as a drive variable but drive is not one of the postulated determinants of reminiscence (I_R, $_SH_R$, and $_SI_R$). The broken lines in Fig. 13.9 represent reaction potential for the second and third periods of massed practice with a drive value 1·5 times as great as that assumed in calculating the lower curves. Though the former curves are at an overall higher level the amount of reminiscence is identical with that for the lower level of drive. Empirically, however, reminiscence is scored from average performances during the latter part of one practice period and the early part of the next. The curves for high drive, compared with those for low drive, have a steeper initial and flatter terminal slope. Both these factors would tend to augment empirical measures of reminiscence and would be expected to give rise to a positive correlation between reminiscence and drive. Experimentally increased motivation has been shown to increase reminiscence in rotary pursuit tasks by Kimble (1950) and Wasserman (1951).

This is consistent with Eysenck's initial experiment. Star, however, reports a significant negative correlation between neuroticism and reminiscence scores for his replication experiment. From an examination of these authors' empirical curves, Star's subjects, as would be expected from the nature of their employment (engineering apprenticeship), reached a higher average level of performance, after equivalent practice, than did Eysenck's subjects (academic students). That this results from a generally higher level of $_SH_R$ is consistent, according to the above analysis, with the greater average reminiscence shown by Star's group. Within his group, Star reports a marked tendency for those subjects with high N scores to perform less well than those with low N scores, while Eysenck reports a lesser insignificant tendency in the same direction. In terms of our general expectations concerning learning efficiency (Fig. 13.5), this would suggest that Star's subjects were in a situation of higher stress and/or were more neurotic than Eysenck's subjects. From the earlier theoretical discussion of the effects of stress,

it would appear that $_SH_R$ is the component of the basic learning equation deleteriously affected by stress. Its value is functionally diminished, either by competition from incorrect or irrelevant habit tendencies, or by the enhanced effect of such competing tendencies owing to increased generalization resulting from a strong drive element in the stimulus complex. Within a group, even when the general $_SH_R$ level is high, those individuals with higher drive will tend to show functionally lower $_SH_R$ and, hence, lower reminiscence scores when the stress conditions are such that the general level of drive is above the optimum. Then, in such a group, a tendency for a negative correlation between reminiscence and drive would be set against the tendency for a positive correlation deriving from empirical methods of measurement.

For this theoretical explanation to account for all the findings described, it would be necessary to demonstrate that both Star's and Das's subjects were appreciably more neurotic than those of Eysenck, or that they were subjected to considerably greater stress. The mean N score of Star's apprentices was higher than that of Eysenck's students but this difference failed to achieve statistical significance and Eysenck employed the more difficult task in that his turntable made 72 r.p.m. whereas Star and Das used a speed of 60 r.p.m. The fact that Star's subjects were tested in the context of a training course and, though volunteers were requested, the response was 100 per cent, is, possibly, indicative of stress. He also comments on a continuous background hum of machinery during his testing. Both Eysenck's and Das's subjects were more truly volunteers but the latter were subjected to a battery of procedures which included a first experience as a hypnotic subject. Thus a case can be made in support of the present analysis but the argument must remain tenuous until experiments have been performed in which the stress variable is systematically controlled.

Treadwell (1956) tested Eysenck's postulates concerning the relationships between introversion-extraversion and motor learning by use of a track-tracing task and the "Thinking" (T) scale of the Minnesota T.S.E. Introversion-Extraversion Questionnaire (Evans and McConnell, 1941). Two groups of twenty subjects with extreme scores on this scale were employed in an experiment of $2 \times 2 \times 2$ factorial design in which practice periods of 108 and 459 sec and rest periods of 5 and 10 min were systematically varied. Significant results were obtained consistent with all the specific hypotheses tested. These were—

1. A group of extraverts will exhibit more reminiscence than will a group of introverts equivalent in initial learning ability and granted an equal rest period.

2. Because extraverts develop reactive inhibition more rapidly than introverts, this relative superiority in reminiscence scores will be proportionately greater after a short than after a long practice period.

3. Because reactive inhibition dissipates more slowly in extraverts, their relative superiority in reminiscence scores will be proportionately greater after a long than after a short rest period. The confirmation of the second of these predictions suggests that, for the longer of the two practice periods used in this experiment, which is appreciably longer than that used by Eysenck, reactive inhibition does reach the level of drive in the more extraverted subjects. The author quotes examples of rest pauses taken by some of her subjects, towards the end of this period, during which they ceased work completely.

Unfortunately, Treadwell's test of extraversion is different from that used in the Maudsley studies. The available evidence indicates that the two measures are unrelated in that Jensen (1957) found significant correlations between the E scale of the M.P.I. and the Minnesota S ($r = 0.81$) and E ($r = 0.21$) scales, but no correlation ($r = 0.05$) with the T scale. The subjects in Treadwell's study were also tested with the M.A.S. The "anxiety" scores, though correlating significantly with the Minnesota E Scale, ($r = + 0.26$) showed no significant correlation with the T scale or with the subjects' reminiscence scores ($r = 0.03$). This would be consistent with the previous theoretical analysis if the stress level in this experiment was intermediate between those in the Maudsley experiments. The author, however, suggests that there was little variance in neuroticism among her subjects and the scores obtained on the M.A.S. support this view.

Broadbent (1956) describes experiments on fatigue in human subjects demonstrating that repeated stimulation, without repetition of response, produces inhibitory effects on performance. Individual differences in such "fatigue" decrements, in subjects performing inspection or watch-keeping tasks, were found to be large and to correlate significantly with tests found to distinguish hysterics from dysthymics. These findings are consistent with Eysenck's theory and with his argument that reactive inhibition is a central rather than a peripheral phenomenon.

Eriksen (1954), using three different size squares as stimuli, related stimuli generalization to scores on the "Hysteria" (Hy) and "Psychasthenia" (Pt) scales of the M.M.P.I. Shock was administered to the subjects in one of two ways but all subjects received equal numbers of shocks. In the "avoidance" condition the subjects were told that failure to respond rapidly would be punished by shock, while the "non-avoidance" group were told that they would receive random shocks. The "avoidance" condition, as would be expected, resulted in greater generalization. The high Hy scorers exhibited more generalization than high Pt scorers in both conditions, a finding explained by the author in terms of breakdown of the defences against anxiety of the former group, as postulated by Deese, Lazarus and Keenan (1953). Taylor (1956) argues that these findings do not invalidate those of Rosenbaum, previously described, as the correlations between these scales and the M.A.S. is low. In terms of our dimensional framework, the Hy and Pt scales would both be expected to measure neuroticism, while Hy would also, to some extent, measure extraversion and Pt introversion. Neuroticism, as a drive variable, would be expected to increase generalization but there is no basis for deciding which group of subjects is the more neurotic. When the strength of the response tendency to the positive stimulus is controlled, as it was in Eriksen's study, there is, as described earlier, no clear theoretical basis for deciding whether introverts or extraverts will respond more to the negative stimuli.

Of related interest is the investigation by Warren and Grant (1955) into the relationship between conditioned eyeblink discrimination and the "psychopathic deviation" (Pd) scale of the M.M.P.I. In terms of Eysenck's theory, subjects scoring high on this scale would be expected to tend towards both high neuroticism and high extraversion. This is consistent with these authors' report of a correlation of $+ 0.51$ between this scale and the M.A.S. The positive and negative stimuli were similar to those used by Hilgard, Jones and Kaplan and described earlier. High and low Pd scorers showed no significant difference in their responses to the positive stimulus but the high scorers made significantly more responses to the negative stimulus and, therefore, achieved poorer discrimination. In terms of the neuroticism dimension the high Pd group would be expected to respond more to both stimuli and to discriminate less well but, for the positive stimulus, this would be offset by the poorer learning associated with extraversion. As stated above, the theoretical prediction concerning extraversion and the negative stimulus is uncertain but this study and that of Eriksen would suggest that extraverts discriminate less well than introverts. In Eriksen's study, however, shock was administered and the hypothesis of Deese et al. may apply.

All the studies reviewed so far have involved laboratory experimentation but similar relationships have also been shown to apply in real-life learning situations. Thus Lynn (1955) reports that scores on an anxiety questionnaire are positively and significantly correlated with reading achievement for children of ages from seven to eleven years. He acknowledges that anxieties to a degree beyond that characteristic of his group are likely to be related to scholastic retardation, as reported by authors such as Schonell (1942), and reports some confirmatory evidence from within his own data. Phillips and his associates (Gerard and Phillips, 1953; Phillips and Cowitz, 1953; Feffer and Phillips, 1953) present evidence indicating that individuals who perform inadequately under experimental stress conditions, irrespective of intellectual ability, are low in "social attainment" as measured by such factors as educational attainment, occupational status and acceptance of social responsibilities.

Sarason and Mandler's (1942) report concerning the relationship between scores on their questionnaire of "test anxiety" and performance in college examinations has already been mentioned. Furneaux (1956) found striking relationships between "neuroticism" and "introversion-extraversion" as measured by Guilford's D.C. and R. scales (cf. Eysenck, 1953), examination performance and measures derived from his cognitive tests (cf. Chapters 5 and 6 by W. D. Furneaux and R. W. Payne). When the four groups representing neurotic introverts (N.I.), stable introverts (S.I.), neurotic extraverts (N.E.) and stable extraverts (S.E.) were compared, it was found that the N.I. group was most successful in high level University examinations and the S.E. group least successful. Within the N.I. group, those who gave evidence of actual psychiatric disturbance did less well than those included only by reason of their test scores but remained superior to the other groups. This pattern was not evident for lower level examinations when, however, differences in cognitive ability were larger and accounted for more of the variation in examination marks. These findings are consistent with Figs. 13.5 and 13.6 and with those of Sarason and Mandler.

Janis and Feshbach (1953) presented illustrated lectures on dental hygiene to groups of High School students. The lectures were varied so as to evoke three intensities of fear motivation by including varying degrees of reference to and illustration of the tissue damage and pain resulting from dental caries. The degree of fear appeal correlated with the degree of affective reaction reported by the subjects on a questionnaire. All three levels of fear motivation were equally effective for teaching the facts of dental hygiene but, in terms of modification of actual behaviour, only the lecture with minimal fear appeal had any effect. In a later paper (Janis and Feshbach, 1954) these authors report the scores of these subjects on an anxiety questionnaire and their finding that anxious subjects, as compared with non-anxious, were consistently less influenced by the lecture with strong fear appeal but were more influenced by the lecture with minimal fear appeal. These results are entirely consistent with our theoretical expectations but a rather different follow-up study by Moltz and Thistlethwaite (1955) failed to reproduce the findings and showed that anxiety reduction, induced by reassurance, was not associated with increased learning or greater behavioural conformity with the "message" of the lecture.

The number of investigations into the learning characteristics of actual neurotic patients is unfortunately small and theoretical advances in this area will require far more studies of this type. Those concerned with classical conditioning were discussed in the previous chapter where Franks cites evidence to show that, whereas introversion-extraversion is related to conditionability, neuroticism is not so related. Strength of drive may well be irrelevant to the conditioning situations described but this should not be true of experiments concerned with the acquisition of conditioned drives, analogous to those described in the earlier discussion of traumatic avoidance learning in animals, but no experiments of this type have been carried out with neurotic subjects. Indeed, as Jensen (1958) pointed out, though a few experiments with human subjects have used a conditioned stimulus in avoidance situations, and measurements consistent with the development of a C.A.D. have been recorded (e.g. Wickens and Platt, 1954; Lacey, Smith and Green, 1955; Brothers, 1956) in no instance has the reduction of such a C.A.D., by the avoidance of the conditioned stimulus, been used to reinforce new instrumental learning in a different experimental setting. An empirical demonstration of this nature would do much to strengthen the bridge between experimental work on animals and theories of human learning.

Rosenbaum (1956) included in his study of stimulus generalization, described earlier, groups of psychiatric patients as well as normal subjects. These were divided into anxious and non-anxious subgroups in accordance with psychiatric ratings of anxiety. The results were, in the main, parallel to those for anxious and non-anxious normal subjects but, as many of the patients were diagnosed as schizophrenic, the implications are difficult to evaluate. Buss (1955) carried out a somewhat similar study with psychiatric patients of unspecified diagnosis but divided into two groups in terms of M.A.S. scores. With blocks of differing heights as stimuli, the anxious group made relatively more positive verbal responses at each test point and showed a flatter generalization gradient but these differences failed to achieve significance.

Matarazzo and Matarazzo (1956) and Korchin and Levine (1957) included psychiatric patients among their subjects for the experiments described earlier. The former authors found no difference in learning scores on their pursuit-meter task between psychiatric and other patients in their hospital sample. Korchin and Levine found that anxious patients behaved like anxious non-patient subjects but to an exaggerated degree, as would be expected. Diethelm and Jones (1947) studied the learning and retention of a stylus maze task by a group of depressive and psycho-neurotic patients displaying anxiety among their most prominent symptoms, and showed that their efficiency increased when their anxiety subsided.

Pascal and Swensen (1952) report that psycho-neurotic patients improved significantly less, during practice on a complex discrimination reaction-time task, than did normal control subjects. With the introduction, in an avoidance context, of a loud white noise, however, their performance improved to a level only slightly below that of the control subjects. If the noise is considered a stressor, this finding is inconsistent with expectations based on Fig. 13.5 and in a direction similar to the results of Silverman and Blitz (1956) and Deese, Lazarus and Keenan (1953) with anxious and non-anxious normal subjects. In this instance, however, an explanation in terms of an hysteria-psychasthenia dimension is inapplicable.

Taffel (1955) successfully modified the verbal behaviour of psychiatric patients by reinforcing with the word *good* any response sentence beginning with a pronoun of self-reference (I or We). Neither the relation between his responses and the experimenter's comments, nor the purpose of the experiment, was discovered by any of the subjects. The experimental group contained both psychotic and neurotic patients and was not subdivided in terms of diagnosis. All subjects were tested, however, on the M.A.S. and their scores were positively and significantly related to the measures of learning. This relationship tends to indicate that, among the neurotic subjects, the dysthymics learned most effectively.

Malmo and Amsel (1948) compared the learning of severely anxious patients and control subjects, using serial lists of eight nonsense syllables. Overall, the patients were inferior but, when serial position curves of error were examined, though these displayed the usual "bowing" effect, they were significantly higher in the patient groups only at the early positions in the series. The same was true of serial position curves of "oscillations at the threshold of recall" as measured by the mean number of presentations between the first success and last failure at each position. These findings are contrary to those which would be predicted from either the Iowa or the "frustration by difficulty" hypotheses described earlier: they are explained by the authors in terms of the hypothesis that patients show, in addition to intra-list interference effects, the effects of interference from anxiety mediated responses. They further suggest that this interference is maximal at the start of a trial but is voluntarily inhibited with an increase of drive resulting from failure with the early syllables. Willett

(1958), using normal subjects and concerned mainly with the effects of drugs on serial verbal learning, found that subjects with high N scores on the M.P.I. required more trials and made more oscillations than low N scorers but these differences led to increased "bowing" of the serial position error curves for the neurotic subjects, thus indicating maximal inter-ference with learning at the central positions in the series. The possible interrelationships between intra-series interference effects and personality variables are numerous and complex, and merit considerable further investigation. In view of the paucity of relevant data a theoretical analysis will not be attempted here.

Hall and Crookes (1952) compared the performance of normal and psychoneurotic subjects on two learning tasks. For a series of ten word-pairs, the normal group was significantly superior, both in terms of recall and for scores relating to the regularity of their individual learning curves. The second task involved the learning of a sequence of five position combina-tions for a bank of three switches operated by the subjects. Again the normal group was significantly superior on a learning score and tended to have more regular individual learning curves. A third score, "trial and error," referring to the number of switch movements made by the subject when the correct combination was incorrectly recalled, and a fourth score, the average time per response, failed to reveal any significant differences between the two groups. The neurotic subjects included thirty-nine patients with anxiety symptoms, nineteen with reactive depression, seven hysterics and six obsessionals, thus forming a mainly dysthymic group. Differences between the subgroups are difficult to evaluate, owing to differences in number, age and sex. On the verbal task the hysterics tended to improve least and pro-duced the least regular curves. On the performance task, the anxious patients were in all respects more similar to the normal group than were the depressives. The obsessionals employed most "trial and error" and hysterics the least. Compared with the control group, the neurotics showed, in general, less impair-ment on the motor than on the verbal task. Both tasks required the learning of series of associates, five triple motor associates and ten paired verbal associates. Internal interference factors and relative stress are difficult to assess.

Brengelmann (1954, 1958a, 1958b) carried out a series of investigations, employing his Figure Recon-struction Test (F.R.T.) (*see* Chapter 3 by J. C. Brengelmann), scores on which are relatively indepen-dent of age and intellectual level. In his major studies of learning (1957a) he used one of the most difficult versions of this test, which required the drawn reproduction of two patterns of shapes immediately following their successive exposure for five seconds. Among other scores, the mean angular displacement of the response shapes from their stimulus positions were calculated over a series of such trials (rotation error). Marked practice effects were evident and were consistently and significantly greater for the control group than for neurotic subjects, though the two groups were not significantly different during the early trials. When the neurotic patients were sub-divided into hysteric and dysthymic groups, there was no significant difference in learning ability between the subgroups but the hysterics, fairly consistently, tended to be slightly superior and in a later study (1957b), mainly concerned with "immediate memory" but including some data on learning, the hysterics were significantly superior to dysthymics when the exposure time was only two seconds, but no difference was evident with thirty seconds exposure. In these experiments, questionnaire measurement of neuroticism and introversion-extraversion within the control groups disclosed relationships with learning essentially similar to those described. For these relationships to be consistent with our theoretical expectations, the experimental conditions must be such as to merit placement to the extreme right of the abscissa of some variant of Fig. 13.6. The brief stimulus exposure would probably make the situation fairly stressful but scarcely to the required degree. In terms of difficulty, however, this version of the F.R.T. was specifically selected as extreme and, during the first trials, the subjects' error scores were scarcely superior to those for random responses. Furthermore, as described, the experimental variation of the exposure time and, therefore, of difficulty, produced changes in the relative efficiency of hysterics and dysthymics consistent with some version of Fig. 13.6.

Lykken (1957) included an ingenious shock-avoidance learning task in a battery of tests administered to patients diagnosed as psychopaths and to normal subjects. The former were subdivided into two groups: (1) "primary sociopaths" according to Cleckley's (1950) criterion of lack of the normal affective accompaniments of experience; (2) the remainder, described as "neurotic sociopaths." Both categories scored lower than the control group on a specially designed anxiety scale with no loading on a neuroticism factor and negligible correlations with the M.A.S. and the Welsh (1952) Anxiety Index. The latter scales, considered mainly measures of neuroticism, produced relatively high scores for the neurotic psychopaths and equal scores for the other two groups. In terms of Eysenck's dimensions, the primary sociopaths (group I) were presumably very extraverted and non-neurotic (very high inhibition, low drive), the neurotic sociopaths (group II) extraverted and neurotic (high inhibition, high drive) and the control

group (III) ambivert and non-neurotic (average inhibition, low drive). Consistently with Fig. 13.5 and moderate stress, group III showed most avoidance and group I least. The difference between groups I and III and that between II and III was statistically significant.

Conclusions

This study completes our review of the experimental literature. From the review it is abundantly clear that our preceding formulation of theoretical expectations was altogether too flexible for precise validation. Whereas the great majority of the studies reviewed produced results consistent with that formulation, this consistency was only achieved after a *post hoc* placement of the experimental situation along the stress-difficulty dimension. The relative difficulty of the experimental task is clearly of importance in determining the nature and direction of group differences in learning, and may well be the most important single factor. Furthermore, it is a factor which can be objectively and quantitatively controlled, as in the important experiment by Saltz and Hoehn (1957), but most investigators have failed to exercise this control.

Stress is, by contrast, a nebulous concept, the quantification of which is scarcely possible, but the stress situations devised by many investigators clearly affected the performance and probably the learning efficiency of their subjects, and differentially affected groups selected in terms of personality variables relevent to abnormal psychology. Indeed, it seems likely that the relatively mild stresses of laboratory situations have clearer and more predictable effects on psychological performance than on the physiological variables usually measured in experimental situations (cf. Chapter 11 by I. Martin). Psychological stress, induced by such devices as failure stimulation, generally interacted with personality variables in a manner consistent with our theoretical expectations, but the complexity of the factors contributing to "psychological stress" was evident in many studies. The main departures from expectation, and those most difficult to reconcile with current theories, resulted from the application of direct painful stimulation, such as electric shock, or the threat of such application. In three of the studies reviewed, situations of this type tended, in some circumstances, to improve the performance of subjects of presumably neurotic tendency and to impair that of more stable subjects. As mentioned in an early section of this chapter, a strong C.A.D. may derive from repeated mild traumata. The conditioned stimulus may then produce a stronger "punishment" effect than the reintroduction of the original trauma. It is possible that some mechanism of an analogous nature is responsible for the present aberrant findings, but it would be difficult to frame a testable hypothesis in these terms.

The imperfect consistency between the empirical results and our theoretical discussion undoubtedly derives, in part, from the fact that the latter was exclusively concerned with the personality dimensions of neuroticism and introversion-extraversion. This does not imply that the writer considers that other personality traits do not have important effects on learning. Indeed, the evidence reviewed indicates that the proportion of inter-individual variation accounted for by these factors may be relatively small. Deese and his co-workers (Lazarus, Deese and Osler, 1952; Deese and Lazarus, 1953) emphasize the importance of differences in individuals' perception of "threat"in stress situations and differences in *style*, as illustrated by Davis's (1948) experiments. Davis, using a simulated aircraft cockpit and other laboratory situations involving skills related to air pilotage, found that fast pacing tended to disorganize the performance of subjects displaying neurotic tendencies. Within this group, hysterics persisted in a slow but stable rate of response, thus achieving a moderate score by responding only to a proportion of stimuli. Dysthymics, however, tended to become overactive, ineffectively attempting to respond to every stimulus change, and thus achieving a lower score. As pointed out by Lazarus and Deese, the dysthymic style might, with a different task or different method of scoring, produce the higher score. Venables (1955) demonstrated the importance of such an overactivity-inertia continuum in a motor task, and its interaction with personality factors and task difficulty. Within a group of normal subjects, those scoring in the extraverted direction on a battery of tests showed a significant tendency to become more inert with increased difficulty of the task, while introverted subjects become more active. Similar tendencies were evident for hysteric and dysthymic groups of neurotic patients, except that the hysterics tended to show equal inertia at both difficulty levels. This particular trait may reflect the differences in the balance of neurological excitation and inhibition, postulated as underlying the introversion-extraversion dimension, and may account for some of the effects of stress on subjects with low M.A.S. scores demonstrated by Deese, Lazarus and Keenan (1953) and Silverman and Blitz (1956).

Brengelmann (1957b) reports significant relationships between scores on a test of "rigidity" and learning scores on the F.R.T. Wesley (1953) studied the relationships between scores on a rigidity questionnaire, M.A.S. scores and performance on a series of concept-formation tasks of the card-sorting type. The subjects were divided into a rigid group, with high

rigidity and low anxiety scores, an anxious group, with high anxiety and low rigidity scores, and a normal group with low scores on both scales. There was no significant relationship between the M.A.S. and rigidity scores but scores on each scale were related to learning efficiency. The anxious group required least trials to learn to the criterion on all four sorting tasks, required least trials to shift "set" and made least perseverative responses. Overall, these trends were not statistically significant but, when individual differences in initial learning were controlled, the rigid group required significantly more trials to shift set and made significantly more perseverative responses than the other groups. Grant and Patel (1957) used a similar task in an experiment involving shock and threat of shock. High scorers on the M.A.S. made relatively few perseverative and non-perseverative errors early in the series but, during the later stages when, presumably, the strength and number of competing responses were maximal, their relative performance deteriorated. Weiss (1957) made use of a specially designed test of perceptual rigidity, derived from the Lewinian concept of boundary impermeability, and found, as he predicted, that subjects who transposed in a size-discrimination learning task achieved low scores on this test, while those who failed to transpose achieved high rigiditiy scores.

Harley (1957) demonstrated a relationship between "achievement imagery" (A.I.) scores on the I.P.I. test (Hurley, 1955) and serial verbal learning, such that low A.I. scorers anticipated relatively few correct nonsense syllables with low motivation instructions, but low and high scorers were equally efficient with high motivation instructions. Performance also correlated negatively with hostility and insecurity scores derived from this test but, unlike the other findings, the correlation with insecurity was not confirmed in a second, more elaborate study. Johnston (1955) reports that high A.I. scorers were more efficient than low scorers in learning a stylus maze under neutral instructions but, with threat of shock, there was no significant difference between the groups. Similar significant difference between achievement imagery, learning efficiency and motivating instructions are reported by Williams (1955). Also related to Hurley's findings are those of Smith (1953) who reports an interactive relationship between expressed hostility, the paired-associate learning of words with hostile or non-hostile connotations and neutral or failure-stress conditions. Non-hostile subjects were impaired in their learning of hostile words after failure stress, whereas hostile subjects were similarly impaired in learning non-hostile words.

Individual differences in modes of defence against anxiety have already been mentioned and may have been important in the determination of the pattern of results in such studies as those by Deese, Lazarus and Keenan (1953), Eriksen (1954) and Hamilton (1957a). Other dimensions along which important individual and group differences may occur have been suggested by Lazarus, Deese and Osler (1952), Farber (1955) and others, but little evidence is available concerning the relationships between traits other than those considered and learning efficiency. Further experimentation is likely to produce such evidence and to throw light on the interrelationships between the traits already described. One advantage of the dimensional framework adopted here is that both neuroticism and introversion-extraversion represent differences at the type level and are derived from the intercorrelations between scores appertaining to many lower-order traits considered relevant to abnormal psychology (cf. Chapter 1 by H. J. Eysenck).

LEARNING AND PSYCHOSIS

The transition from the predispositional state of psychoticism into the state of manifest clinical psychosis seems much less dependent upon precipitating factors such as life-stresses than is that from neuroticism into clinical neurosis. It cannot then be argued that psychosis is a learned disorder, as was argued earlier for neurosis, nor are there strong theoretical reasons to postulate that individual differences in respect of learning variables play an important dynamic role in psychotic processes. Thus, in this section, the procedure adopted will be the reverse of that employed in the discussion of neurosis. The empirical results of investigations into the learning efficiency of psychotic patients will be examined for their theoretical implications and such generalizations as are possible made subsequently.

As impairment of learning is not generally regarded by clinicians as an important characteristic of functional psychosis, experimental studies of this function in psychotic patients are relatively few, at least in recent years. The more numerous studies during the early decades of this century were marred by several deficiencies such as inadequate control data, lack of statistical evaluation of the results and the inclusion within the same, usually small, experimental groups of patients from various diagnostic categories. Owing, presumably to a unitary concept of "insanity," the results were not usually examined for differential effects of different diseases and, as the groups frequently included a majority of brain-damaged subjects, the reported findings refer mainly to these. Because of these limitations, these early studies, which have been reviewed by such authors as Brody (1942), Hunt and Cofer (1944) and Campbell (1957), will not be described here but the most consistent or suggestive findings are noted below.

It is clear that both manic-depressive and schizophrenic patients are capable of learning, in that their performances improve with practice, but it seems likely that, despite this improvement, their learning ability is somewhat impaired compared with that of normal subjects. The latter finding is by no means universal and allowance was rarely made for the patient's initial performance, which was generally below that of control subjects. Simmins (1933) found a group of functional psychotics no worse than her control group on a series of short-term "memory" tests, when general ability (g) was controlled statistically. Hull's (1917) study of paired-associate learning suggests that any impairment observed tends to affect the impression rather than the retention stage of learning. Also of interest are the consistent early findings concerning continuous work (massed practice) at simple tasks, reported by such authors as Kraepelin, Hoch, Wells and Currie (cf. Hunt and Cofer, 1944). Schizophrenics, after an initial period of sustained performance, appear to reduce output at an abnormally high rate whereas manic-depressive patients, whether in manic or melancholic states, exhibit a reversal of the usual "fatigue effect" by improving in performance prior to a delayed decline.

Clinical testing procedures provide evidence that some degree of impairment of learning is characteristic of psychotic patients. Babcock and Levy (1940), for example, report lower scores for various groups of schizophrenic patients, when compared with normal subjects of similar vocabulary level and age, on a battery of tests of "mental efficiency," including tests of "initial learning" and "recall." The rationale for this type of test has been criticized by Shapiro and Nelson (1955) but these authors, with a more adequate test procedure, demonstrated impaired ability for learning the meanings of words in co-operative chronic schizophrenic and manic-depressive patients. A group of acute schizophrenics showed no learning impairment.

Hall and Crookes (1951) report on the performance of thirty-five schizophrenic patients, mainly in an early acute stage of their illness, while learning the verbal and motor tasks used in these authors' investigation of the effect of neurosis on learning, and described earlier in this chapter. Compared with normal subjects of comparable age and vocabulary level, these patients, despite considerable group overlap, were, on the average, significantly inferior in terms of learning scores and produced markedly irregular learning curves for both tasks. During their learning of the switch combinations, the schizophrenics tended to adopt a haphazard unsystematic trial-and-error approach and, during their learning of the word-pairs, words, commonly associated with the stimulus words, intruded among their responses. In general, the schizophrenic performance was suggestive of increased competition from previously learned responses and, possibly, of increased oscillation of response tendencies, though certain individuals showed perseverative trends. Bonnet (1953) similarly demonstrates a wide range of abnormalities in learning curves produced by psychotic patients working at a cancellation task.

Brengelmann (1958a), in the course of his experiments with the F.R.T., described earlier, tested forty-three psychotic patients in addition to the groups of neurotic and normal subjects. Seven of these were endogenous depressives and the remainder schizophrenics. For all the learning scores, the psychotics were significantly inferior to the control group and, frequently, they were significantly below the neurotics. Consistent with the level of difficulty of the task, there were no significant differences in error scores during the early trials.

Many of the early authors consider the difficulties in learning shown by psychotic patients to be secondary to more fundamental abnormalities of attention, co-operation or motivation. A similar view is advanced by Hunt and Cofer, who point out that the performance of schizophrenics is very variable but that increases of output can be obtained if the investigator makes efforts to gain the patients' confidence and co-operation. On the basis of this evidence and a variation in autonomic activity, concomitant with the variations in output, these authors consider that the deficit in schizophrenia is one of motivation rather than one of capacity.

Rather similar conclusions were reached by Huston and Shakow from the evidence of a long series of investigations into learning and other functions in schizophrenia. They noted that schizophrenics improved in terms of increased accuracy and decreased variance on pursuit-meter and prod-meter tasks (Huston, 1932; Shakow, 1932). A similar improvement occurred in speed of tapping over successive trials and widely separated sessions, while normal subjects failed to improve on the tapping task (Huston and Shakow, 1936). The major portion of the initial variance in speed was attributed to differences in the schizophrenics' co-operation as it was measured by behaviour ratings during the test sessions and which, therefore, are likely to be determined in part by the nature of the performance with which they are later correlated. In papers describing experiments on reaction-time (Huston, Shakow and Riggs, 1937,

Rodnick and Shakow, 1940) this concept of "lack of co-operation" was defined in terms of an inability to maintain an appropriate level of mental preparedness or set. Studies of manual steadiness (Huston and Shakow, 1946) produced results similar to those of other tasks. Compared with normal control subjects, schizophrenic patients were initially less steady and more variable but improved with practice, as did the control group. Ratings of co-operation showed an appreciable correlation ($r = +0.62$) with the steadiness scores and the initially least steady patients improved most with practice. In later studies (Huston and Shakow, 1948, 1949), schizophrenics, manic-depressives and normal control subjects practiced rotary pursuit for sessions of ten trials each at intervals of three months. Both the manic-depressive and normal groups improved significantly more than the schizophrenics, who had the poorest score initially. Again test scores were related to ratings of observed co-operation but those schizophrenics who merited the top rating for co-operation still failed to achieve scores equivalent to those of the normal subjects. When the apparatus was modified so that movement occurred only when the stylus was in contact with the target (prod-meter), the schizophrenics again showed impaired performance but improved considerably with practice. A group of schizophrenics, given prolonged practice at this task and aided by various motivational devices, finally achieved a level of performance only slightly below that typical of normal subjects.

Throughout this series of experiments, a consistent trend was noted for paranoid schizophrenics to behave most like normal subjects, both in terms of co-operation and test performance, while catatonics showed the greatest deficit and hebephrenics occupied an intermediate position. In general, Shakow (1946) considers that, while lack of co-operation is of major importance, psychosis has a specific effect on performance, particularly when the task is complex. Learning curves for schizophrenics are considered essentially similar in shape to those typical of normal groups and the characteristic lack of co-operation to derive from personal systems of incentives.

O'Connor, Heron and Carstairs (1956) investigated the motivation of schizophrenics more directly by setting a group of paranoid schizophrenics a button-sorting task for half an hour a day over twenty-eight days under various incentive conditions including encouragement, self-competition and payment by results. None of these conditions altered the rate of improvement but later studies (O'Connor, 1957a, 1957c; O'Connor and Topping, 1957) showed that money payments impaired the performance and learning of paranoid schizophrenics, both for laboratory tasks such as the learning of shapes by serial anticipation and the incidental recall of the colours of these shapes, and for normal subcontract industrial work. With normal subjects and other categories of chronic schizophrenics this type of incentive led to an improvement of performance.

Cohen (1956) compared the performance of schizophrenic and control groups on tasks involving the learning of a series of motor responses to successive visual stimuli. Under neutral conditions and in conditions of increased motivation, induced by a shock-avoidance technique, the schizophrenics showed impaired learning ability. The results indicated a differential facilitative effect on the schizophrenics of the motivational situation, but only for the second of the two tasks employed.

Peters (1953) compared the performance of chronic and acute schizophrenics on a series of multiple-choice learning problems of graded difficulty. The chronic patients took many more trials to learn to the criterion and, unlike the acute patients, tended to adopt stereotyped responses, repeated trial after trial, despite verbal guidance by the experimenter. Peters relates these stereotyped responses, in terms of their non-adaptiveness and difficulty of extinction, to those made by the rats in Maier's (1956) frustration studies and postulates that, although his subjects were ostensibly motivated by hunger from deprivation and insulin shock, they were unable to maintain a goal orientation, owing to frustration. An alternative hypothesis, suggested by Peters, relates to Pavlov's concept of "pathological inertia" in schizophrenia. In support of these hypotheses, Peters and his collaborators (Peters and Jenkins, 1954; Peters and Murphree, 1954) present evidence that guided problem-solving of the type described beneficially affected the performance of schizophrenics on other tasks and their clinical status.

The early findings concerning continuous work, described above, tend to suggest that schizophrenics are characterized either by low drive or by rapid development of reactive inhibition, while manic-depressives show the reverse pattern. As both groups tend to be worse than normal subjects in initial performance, a drive difference is the less likely. A differential susceptibility to reactive inhibition was earlier postulated as underlying the introversion-extraversion dimension but it has not been possible to separate the two psychotic groups in these terms (cf. Chapter 1 by H. J. Eysenck).

Venables and Tizard (1956b) followed up these early studies by comparing the performance of thirty non-paranoid schizophrenics and ten endogenous depressives on a continuous choice reaction-time task. The curves resulting from twenty minutes, massed practice, interrupted at the half-way stage by a one-minute rest period, are shown in Fig. 13.13. The

authors report a significant difference in level, but not in slope, between short- and long-stay schizophrenics the former being superior. The diagnostic groups differed significantly in slope, the depressives improving their performance steadily both before and after the rest period whereas the schizophrenics improved less before rest and their performance declined in the second period of practice. The schizophrenics also

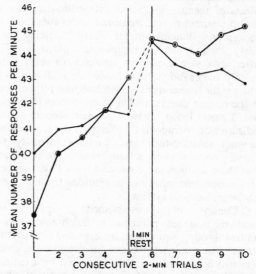

FIG. 13.13. PERFORMANCE OF SCHIZOPHRENIC (•—•) AND DEPRESSIVE (O—O) PATIENTS DURING MASSED PRACTICE OF A CONTINUOUS MULTIPLE-CHOICE REACTION-TIME TASK
(*After Venables and Tizard, 1956b*)

showed significantly more reminiscence than the depressive group.

Thus the findings are essentially confirmatory of the earlier studies and are interpreted by the authors in terms of differential susceptibility to reactive inhibition. This explanation was tested (Tizard and Venables, 1957) by applying an external distracting stimulus during a similar experiment, with the expectation that this would disinhibit the schizophrenics and improve their performance. A loud white noise was sounded from responses 21 to 30 during a series of fifty consecutive switching responses to a stimulus light. Without distraction, schizophrenics were characterized by a steady decline in reaction-time whereas control subjects improved. Distraction significantly improved the performance of non-paranoid schizophrenics but had no effect on paranoid patients. There was a positive correlation between ratings on a "social withdrawal" scale and the facilitating effect of distraction. Thus the hypothesis was supported but only for certain types of schizophrenia.

The authors also consider the alternative hypotheses that, in chronic withdrawn schizophrenics, the "central excitatory state" is lowered and increased sensory input has a non-specific facilitatory effect. Thus a generalized inhibitory state is postulated instead of the more specific reactive inhibition accumulated during the successive evocations of a response. This hypothesis was supported by the results of a further experiment designed so as to minimize the effects of reactive inhibition. Reaction-times to an auditory stimulus were measured under two levels of background illumination for thirty "sociable" and thirty "withdrawn" schizophrenic patients. The latter showed a significant tendency to react more quickly under bright than under dim illumination, whereas the former displayed an insignificant tendency in the reverse direction. The same authors (Venables and Tizard, 1956a, 1956c) elsewhere report results indicative of "paradoxical" effects on the relationship between reaction-time and stimulus intensity for chronic non-paranoid schizophrenics. It is argued that these findings are consistent with Pavlov's view of schizophrenic behaviour as resulting from a "weak inhibitory nervous system."

O'Connor (1957b) established groups of ten catatonic and ten paranoid schizophrenics and a control group, equivalent in age and intellectual status. These subjects worked for five minutes a day over two periods of five days, separated by a ten-day interval, at the task of underlining even numbers and cancelling odd numbers in lists of random numbers. As the task was practically error-free, this was essentially a speed test. There was no significant differences between the groups in respect of work decrement within trials, which occurred in all groups. Day-to-day improvement was greatest for the control group and least for the paranoid group. Reminiscence effects from the first to second set of trials were observable only for the control group. In this study the slope of the learning curves was linear in all groups but further work (O'Conner, 1957c) has consistently shown differences between the learning curves of paranoid and non-paranoid schizophrenics, the latter tending to display a negatively accelerated, curvilinear form and the former remaining linear over training periods of up to forty days.

The findings of Mailloux and Newburger (1941), who tested a large group of psychotic patients on a simple continuous choice reaction-time task similar to one used by Bills in a study from which Mailloux and Newburger derive their normative data are possibly related to some form of inhibition. Compared to the normal subjects of Bills's study, the patients displayed greater variability, a lower rate of response and more frequent and longer "blocks" in performance. No tests of significance were applied.

The investigation by Pascal and Swensen (1952), previously mentioned in the section on neurosis, is somewhat similar to that of Tizard and Venables though based on a different rationale. They report on practice effects for psychiatric patients and control subjects working at a complex discrimination reaction-time task over six trials of twelve responses each, separated by thirty-second rest intervals but with a longer interval between the fourth and fifth periods, during which a loud white noise was presented. This was subsequently sounded during the constant one-second fore-periods and terminated by a correct response. The schizophrenic subjects were insignificantly slower than matched control subjects at the commencement of training but improved significantly less until the introduction of the noise, which produced a marked increase in their speed of reaction and rendered their later performance little different from that of the control subjects. The schizophrenics were more variable than either the psychoneurotic or normal subjects. These authors interpret these effects by considering the noise a stressor and motivating device. Equally, it might be considered a disinhibitor, operating in the manner postulated by Tizard and Venables.

Bleke (1954) reports that, while no differences in learning or retention were observable between schizophrenic and control groups for a task requiring motor responses to a series of words analogous to the choice-points of a maze, those schizophrenics with an inadequate pre-morbid life adjustment showed greater reminiscence effects after a rest period than similar subjects with adequate pre-morbid adjustment or control subjects, but only in conditions of failure stress. Bleke considers that this cannot be due to increased reactive inhibition because no differences were observable in the pre-rest trials. Instead he postulates that the punishment condition produces interfering tendencies which inhibit effective performance and that these tendencies dissipate rapidly during the rest period. Bleke's own argument against reactive inhibition would be equally applicable to this explanation but the fact that the effect was only observed in punishment conditions contraindicates the reactive inhibition hypothesis. The fact that the effect only occurred with pre-morbidly inadequate patients suggests that the findings may not be related to psychosis as such but, possibly, to differences in neuroticism within the psychotic group. Similarly, as previously described, the usual relationships between M.A.S. scores and learning efficiency have been shown to apply within groups of psychotic patients. Robertson (1957), however, found no significant relationship between rated or admitted anxiety in the test situation and verbal learning scores for a hundred and twenty relieved and chronic psychotic patients.

Campbell (1957) made a thorough attempt to evaluate the learning behaviour of psychotic patients in terms of the various parameters of learning established in experimental work with normal subjects. His approach derives mainly from three sources—

1. Zeaman and Kaufman (1955), who considered the effects of individual differences in the various major constructs of Hullian theory on the shapes of learning curves.

2. Fleishman and Hempel (1954, 1955), who factor-analysed the matrices of correlations between scores on complex learning tasks and various reference tests at various stages of learning. For each of two tasks, there was a specific factor which increased markedly in importance during practice. Group factors accounted for an appreciable proportion of the variance at the beginning of practice but were negligible at the end. Thus, the learning curve tends to reflect a change in the combination of abilities used by the subject at different stages of learning and the growth in importance of the specific factor is analogous to the growth of habit strength.

3. Reynolds (1952), who reports findings similar to those of Fleishman and Hempel and also examined the intercorrelations between trials of the learning task. He found that, as practice proceeds, the correlations between the first and last trials decrease, whereas those between successive trials increase. These tendencies were reversed by a rest pause but were re-established with continued practice. These findings were interpreted as reflecting the reinforcement of correct habits and the extinction of incorrect habits during practice. During rest, the reactive inhibition associated with the incorrect responses would dissipate and these responses would again interfere until the extinction was re-established.

On the basis of a general review of the literature and an analysis of the findings concerning effects of practice from a series of investigations into speed of performance in psychotic patients, carried out by himself and other co-workers of Shapiro (Nelson, 1953; Shapiro and Nelson, 1955; Kessell, 1955; Broadhurst, 1957), Campbell makes the generalization that, for sensorimotor tasks, improvement in speed is greater for psychotic than for normal subjects, but suggests that this results from their initial slowness. Within both psychotic and normal groups, improvement in speed is correlated negatively with initial speed and follows an independent course from improvement in qualitative performance. Batteries of such tests produce generally higher intercorrelations within psychotic than within normal groups. This evidence, he considers, is consistent with three hypotheses, not mutually incompatible, concerning the nature of learning in psychotic patients—

1. When presented with a novel learning task, psychotics start from a lower initial habit strength than normal subjects, i.e. they start lower on a negatively accelerated growth curve and, therefore, derive greater benefit from the early stages of practice. The most likely cause of their initial low level is a low degree of positive transfer from similar tasks, implying a true impairment of learning in the sense that each reinforcement produces a relatively small increment of habit strength. This might still allow a rise to the same asymptote as normal subjects.

2. Psychotics embark on a novel task with a higher level of generalized conditioned inhibition. With practice, normal subjects might develop this to an equal degree.

3. As psychotic patients display a high degree of affective disturbance, they might be considered to possess high drive which would interact with learning in the manner discussed earlier.

Campbell attempted to verify these hypotheses in an experiment with twenty schizophrenic, twenty depressive and twenty normal subjects. These were given massed practice over twenty trials, with a five-minute rest pause between trials 12 and 13, at tracing open paper-and-pencil mazes at three levels of difficulty and a modified version of the Ammons (1955) Pathways Test. All subjects were also tested on a group of reference tests concerned with general intellectual ability, speed of problem-solving, spatial ability and motor speed. Unlike Ammon's finding, the pathways test produced no learning curves nor did the rest pause produce reminiscence. All three mazes produced marked practice effects, the mean learning curves for the simplest maze being reproduced in Fig. 13.14. For all mazes the abnormal subjects were slower throughout, but much more so at the commencement of practice. The depressives were, on the average, significantly slower than the schizophrenics. The rest pause slowed down performance in all three groups but with no significant differences between the groups, though the trend was more marked in the abnormal groups.

Each individual's learning curve for each of the three mazes was then assessed in terms of starting level, asymptote, and rate of approach to the asymptote (growth constant). The mean growth constant for the control subjects was significantly greater than that for the psychotics and the schizophrenics tended to produce higher constants than the depressives. The asymptotes differed significantly between all three groups, with normals highest and depressives lowest, even when the other two measures were controlled statistically. Campbell concludes that this analysis supports the view that the groups display different learning curves rather than different positions on the same curve. The similarity of the patterns at all three levels of difficulty contraindicates the drive hypothesis and the inhibition hypothesis was not supported. The correlations between trials were uniformly high for all

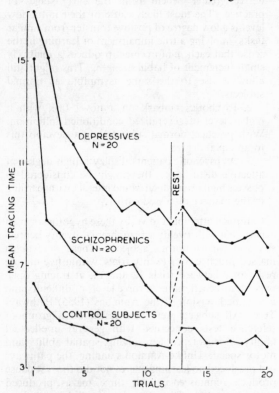

FIG. 13.14. PRACTICE GAINS IN SPEED OF MAZE TRACING
(After Campbell, 1957)

mazes and all groups. None of the expected trends of change were observed, even in the normal group. Similarly, the correlations between scores on the learning and reference tests remained high at every trial.

Campbell's study has been described in some detail not because special importance is attached to the results obtained, which were in many ways disappointing, but because of its methodological sophistication. The actual tasks used seem to have been inappropriate in that the phenomena observed by Fleishman and Hempel, Reynolds and Ammons were not reproduced, even by the normal group. This study would be well worth repetition, using tasks identical with those in the source studies. Careful description of psychotic learning in these terms would enable theory making to be placed on a sounder basis.

In this connexion, two parameters of learning, oscillation and stimulus generalization, rejected by Campbell as being unlikely to be of importance in psychotic performance, might well repay investigation by relating abnormalities of learning in psychotic patients with psychotic characteristics in other fields. One of the outstanding characteristics of psychotic performance is its variability, suggestive of an increased range of oscillatory potential $(_sO_R)$ and it is of interest that Hull (1917) found evidence of increased oscillation in abnormal subjects. In a simple learning situation involving a single stimulus-response connexion, as in conditioning, this would merely lead to lowered probabilities of response evocation during the early stages of learning and greater variability of response latency and amplitude throughout learning. In a complex situation, involving competing responses, enlarged ranges of fluctuation of response potentials would have an effect very similar to the diminished growth increment postulated by Campbell. Thus, from Fig. 13.15, it can be seen that, with a doubled range of oscillation, the difference in strength between two particular response tendencies needs to be twice as great to retain the same probabilistic advantage for the stronger tendency. It is also evident that increased oscillation will allow subthreshold tendencies to enter the competitional situation. These effects are very similar to those postulated by Spence and his colleagues as resulting from increased drive in complex

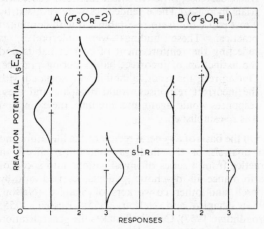

FIG. 13.15. COMPETING RESPONSES AT TWO RANGES OF OSCILLATION

tasks. The present hypothesis, however, generates different predictions concerning the relationships between simple and complex learning.

"Overinclusion" (cf. Chapter 6 by R. Payne) implies an inability to exclude irrelevant material, suggestive of a flattened gradient of generalization in psychotic patients. The effect of such an abnormality is illustrated in Fig. 13.16. If the distance S_2 to S_4 represents the range of stimulus generalization in normal subjects and S_1 to S_5 the equivalent range for psychotics it is clear that the presentation of S_3 will evoke many more response tendencies in psychotics than in normal subjects. Like the oscillation hypothesis, this would have the effect of increasing competition within a complex learning situation.

This hypothesis was tested specifically by Mednick (1955), who found a definite trend in this direction but this was significant for only one of the several measures used. He also found, however, that, within

of increased stimulus generalization in psychosis but to a degree scarcely sufficient to account for the relatively gross abnormalities of learning demonstrated in some situations.

Another promising approach to the objective description of learning in psychosis is that adopted by Lindsley, Skinner, and their associates (Lindsley, 1955; Raines, 1956), who apply Skinnerian methods of operant learning by adapting hospital rooms as man-size Skinner boxes. They have established high rates of lever-pressing responses with various schedules of reinforcement and a variety of incentives including

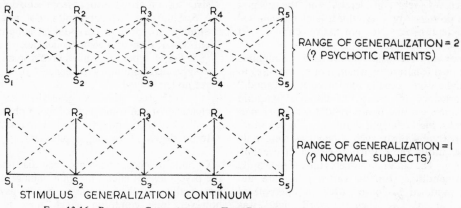

FIG. 13.16. RESPONSE COMPETITION AT TWO RANGES OF STIMULUS GENERALIZATION.

S —— R = Learned response tendency.
S ---- R = Generalized response tendency.

his schizophrenic group, measures of generalization were negatively and significantly related to the number of electroshock treatments received by the subject. As many had received such treatment this would tend to offset the overall trend. Garmezy (1951) also presents evidence of flatter generalization gradients in schizophrenic than in normal groups, both for geometric forms and for tones varying in pitch. The difference in gradients was minimal under reward conditions, but when failure stimulation was introduced, while the control subjects improved their discrimination, the schizophrenics made fewer responses to positive and negative stimuli and displayed a considerably flattened generalization gradient. Garmezy interpreted this finding as evidence of highly generalized withdrawal tendencies in schizophrenics. Chambers (1956) compared the performance of schizophrenic and non-psychotic patients on a "trial-and-error" sorting task and a task in which colour names were given to circles of different sizes. Only speed of performance differentiated the two groups on the former task but the schizophrenics made significantly more errors on the latter, and on several non-learning tasks also requiring discrimination. Thus, the available evidence supports the hypothesis

candy, cigarettes, coins, morsels of food, projected pictorial material and music. The reports to date are mainly concerned with the elaboration of the method but some tentative findings are reported. Among the more striking of these is the fact that, unlike normal controls, chronic schizophrenic patients tend to show occasional prolonged inter-response times and the frequency of these intervals appears to be correlated with the severity of psychosis. Very disturbed patients tend to continue at a low response rate despite reinforcement. Though performance in this situation is unrelated to verbal behaviour or to scores on psychometric tests, significant correlations with informal ratings of non-verbal ward behaviour and formal behaviour ratings have been demonstrated. In general, however, there is great variability in the response patterns produced by different patients, though small groups of patients may exhibit similar patterns. Some may display abnormalities of acquisition, some of extinction, while some may respond only to certain incentives or combinations of incentives. These groupings do not relate to psychiatric diagnostic categories. King et al. (1957), adopting this method, found that the operant response rates (pulling a plunger for candy and cigarettes) of thirty acute schizophrenics showed a significant curvilinear relationship with severity of illness. There was some evidence, though insignificant, that improved clinical status changed the response rate in a manner predictable from the initial severity of illness by use of this regression line.

The study by Salzinger and Pisoni (1957) who increased the proportion of statements expressing "affect" in the interview responses of schizophrenic patients by an operant conditioning technique, using verbal reinforcement of the now familiar *mmm-hm* type is of related interest. Individual differences in the learning curves were considerable and the steepest slope was produced by one subject later rediagnosed as manic-depressive. No normative data is yet available.

O'Connor and Rawnsley (1958) used a simplified technique of this nature by which motor responses to a signal light were verbally reinforced with "good." The performance of groups of chronic paranoid schizophrenics, chronic non-paranoid schizophrenics and normal subjects differed significantly in this situation, whereas previously such differences were only observable during the extinction period of eyeblink conditioning. The paranoid subjects took significantly longest to condition with the verbal procedure and displayed modified responses after an interpolated simple mental task and when the word "light" was used instead of an actual light. The authors suggest that these findings may imply abnormalities of the "secondary signalling system" in paranoid schizophrenics. None of the learning scores showed any significant correlation with scores on an introversion questionnaire.

The review of studies concerned with learning in functional psychosis, now completed, while disclosing many promising leads and much ingenious experimentation, reveals too many inconsistent and isolated trends and relationships to merit an attempt at a unifying theoretical analysis. At the same time, there is sufficient consistency within groups of findings to enable certain tentative generalizations to be made—

1. Psychotic patients of all types are capable of learning.

2. Despite this capacity, when compared with normal or psychoneurotic subjects, psychotics display impaired learning efficiency but individual differences are considerable and overlap between groups is large.

3. This deficit may not, or not entirely, derive from a true impairment of learning capacity but may be a secondary effect of abnormal motivational or other processes.

4. In terms of learning processes, manic-depressives form a group distinct from schizophrenics.

5. Similarly, schizophrenics do not form a unitary group and paranoid schizophrenics, in particular, display specific tendencies.

6. Some types of schizophrenia may result in exaggerated inhibitory tendencies of a character yet undetermined.

7. Increased stimulus generalization may be characteristic of some types of schizophrenia.

8. Chronicity and severity of psychosis are related to the degree of learning impairment.

Organic psychoses have not been discussed here as the psychological effects of brain damage are treated specifically in other chapters. Senile psychosis is, however, one condition which may result from structural damage to cerebral tissue but may, equally well, be the consequence of a more subtle functional deterioration. "Memory disorder" is frequently considered of especial importance in this condition. Inglis (1958) has recently reviewed the relevant literature and concludes that there is ample evidence that patients diagnosed as suffering from senile dementia exhibit learning disabilities both in respect of acquisition and reproduction, whether by recognition or recall. This writer presents empirical and theoretical evidence to support his view that the learning dysfunction, which has far-reaching effects on cognitive functions in general, is related to metabolic changes of blood content in old age.

CONCLUDING DISCUSSION

Although this chapter was intended to describe the effects of abnormal personality variables on learning processes, much of the discussion has necessarily been concerned with the nature of certain learning phenomena as such. Despite the ingenious hypotheses of learning theorists and the impressive output of experimental work on learning in recent years, theoretical explanations of the effects of such variables as task-complexity or the massing of practice remain uncertain. Clarification of many of the issues discussed here must await advances in learning theory as well as in personality theory. Recent elaborations of stochastic models and statistical learning theories promise such an advance but, at their present stage of development, they appear more useful for the description of behaviour in certain specific well defined situations than for the prediction of relationships over a wide range of behaviour. It would scarcely have been possible to assess the data reviewed in this chapter in the terms of any existing mathematical model, nor indeed, in those of information theory, another approach of considerable potentiality.

Despite the difficulties of precise evaluation, the majority of investigations reviewed produced evidence of lawful interrelationships between personality variables, learning variables and experimental conditions and, in many instances, a marked tendency was displayed for these relationships to be of a curvilinear rather than a linear nature. In view of the latter finding, future investigators would be well advised to employ experimental groups representative of a wide range of any particular personality variable rather than groups selected in terms of extreme scores. Statistical techniques of evaluation and description must also be adapted to deal with non-linear trends. Factor analytic techniques, for example, can only represent correlations of equal size throughout the ranges of dimensions such as neuroticism and introversion-extraversion. It seems possible, however, that, while these two dimensions may be orthogonal in their middle ranges, extreme introverts, by reason of unrealistic ambitions and standards, may create for themselves life-stresses which increase the risk of neurotic breakdown whereas extreme extraverts, with lower standards and a tendency to ignore or avoid difficulties, may reduce the stress to which they are subjected. Some explanation of this nature may account for the frequent finding of a small but significant positive correlation between neuroticism and introversion, when these are measured by questionnaire methods (Jensen, 1957).

The very complexity of the experimental findings accentuate the continuing need for careful and precise laboratory investigations. Clinical psychology cannot develop without experimental researches employing the methods of general psychology and these will inevitably lead to the mutual enrichment of both fields.

REFERENCES

AMMONS, C. H., An experimental study of temporary and permanent inhibitory effects associated with acquisition of a simple perceptual motor skill, *Ph.D. Thesis, Univ. of Kentucky*, (1955).

AUSUBEL, D. P., SCHIFF, H. M. and GOLDMAN, M., Qualitative characteristics in the learning process associated with anxiety, *J. Abnorm. (Soc.) Psychol.*, 48, 537–547 (1953).

AXELROD, H. S., COWEN, E. L. and HEILIZER, F., The correlates of manifest anxiety in stylus maze learning, *J. Exp. Psychol.*, 51, 131–138 (1956).

BABCOCK, H. and LEVY, L., *The Measurement of Efficiency of Mental Functioning* (Chicago, C. H. Stoelting, 1940).

BARTHOLOMEW, A. A. and MARLEY, E., Susceptibility to methyl pentynol: Personality and other aspects. Unpublished paper (1957).

BAYTON, J. A. and CONLEY, H. W., Duration of success

background and the effect of failure upon performance, *J. Gen. Psychol.*, 56, 179–185 (1957).

BEAM, J. C., Serial learning and conditioning under real-life stress, *J. Abnorm. (Soc.) Psychol.*, 51, 543–551 (1955).

BENDIG, A. W. and VAUGHAN, C. J., Manifest anxiety, discrimination, and transposition, *Amer. J. Psychol.*, 70, 286–288 (1957).

BINDRA, D. and CAMERON, LOIS, Changes in experimentally produced anxiety with the passage of time: incubation effect, *J. Exp. Psychol.*, 45, 197–203 (1953).

BLEKE, R., Reward and punishment as determiners of reminiscence effects in schizophrenic and normal subjects, *J. Personality*, 23, 479–498 (1954).

BONNET, D., L'apprentissage d'un test de barrage; aspects significatifs des courbes obtenues chez des malades mentaux, *Encéphale*, 42, 101–136 (1953).

BRENGELMANN, J. C., Learning in neurotics and psychotics, *Acta Psychol. Hague*, 13, 371–388 (1958*f*).

BRENGELMANN, J. C., The effects of exposure time in immediate recall on abnormal and questionnaire criteria of personality, *J. Ment. Sci.*, 104, 665–680 (1958*e*).

BRENGELMANN, J. C. and PINILLOS, J. L., Le test de reconstruction des figures, *Rev. Psychol. appl.*, 4, 187–202 (1954).

BROADBENT, D. E., Inhibition and extraversion, *Bull. Brit. Psychol. Soc.*, No. 29, inset p. 13. abstract (1956).

BROADHURST, ANNE, Some variables affecting speed of mental functioning in schizophrenics, *Ph.D. Thesis, Univ. of London Lib.* (1957).

BRODY, M. B., A survey of the results of intelligence tests in psychosis, *Brit. J. Med. Psychol.*, 19, 215–261 (1942).

BROTHERS, JOYCE D., An investigation of avoidance, anxiety, and escape behaviour in human subjects as measured by action potentials in muscle, *Genet. Psychol. Monogr.*, 53, 75–118 (1956).

BROWN, J. S. and FARBER, I. E., Emotions conceptualized as intervening variables—with suggestions towards a theory of frustration, *Psychol. Bull.*, 48, 465–480 (1951).

BUCHWALD, A. M. and YAMAGUCHI, H. G., The effect of change in drive level on habit reversal, *J. Exp. Psychol.*, 50, 265–268 (1955).

BUSS, A. H., Stimulus generalization as a function of clinical anxiety and direction of generalization, *J. Abnorm. (Soc.) Psychol.*, 50, 271–273 (1955).

BYKOV, K. M., New data on the physiology and pathology of the cerebral cortex, *Communication at the 19th International Physiological Congress*, Montreal, (1953).

CAMERON, N. and MAGARET, ANN, *Behaviour Pathology* (Cambridge, Riverside Press, 1951).

CAMPBELL, D., A study of some sensorimotor functions in psychiatric patients, *Ph.D. Thesis, Univ. of London Lib.* (1957).

CARLSON, V. R. and LAZARUS, R. S., A repetition of Meyer Williams's study of intellectual control under stress and associated Rorschach factors, *J. Cons. Psychol.*, 17, 247–253 (1953).

CASTANEDA, A., Effects of stress on complex learning and performance, *J. Exp. Psychol.*, 52, 9–12 (1956).

CASTANEDA, A. and PALERMO, D. S., Psychomotor performance as a function of amount of training and stress, *J. Exp. Psychol.*, 50, 175–179 (1955).

CHAMBERS, J. L., Perceptual judgement and associative

learning ability of schizophrenics and nonpsychotics, *J. Cons. Psychol.*, **20**, 211–214 (1956).

CHILD, I. L., Personality, *Annu. Rev. Psychol.*, **5**, 149–170 (1954).

CHILD, I. L. and WATERHOUSE, I. K., Frustration and the quality of performance: II. A theoretical statement, *Psychol. Rev.*, **60**, 127–139 (1953).

CLECKLEY, H., *The Mask of Sanity* (2nd ed.) (St. Louis, C. V. Mosby, 1950).

COHEN, B. D., Motivation and performance in schizophrenia, *J. Abnorm. (Soc.) Psychol.*, **52**, 186–190 (1956).

COHEN, L. D., KIPNIS, D., KUNKLE, E. C. and KUBZANSKY, P.E., Observation of a person with congenital insensitivity to pain, *J. Abnorm. (Soc.) Psychol.*, **51**, 333–338 (1955).

COURTS, F. A., Relations between muscular tension and performance, *Psychol. Bull.*, **39**, 347–367 (1942).

COWEN, E. L., HEILIZER, F. and AXELROD, H. S., Self-concept conflict indicators and learning, *J. Abnorm. (Soc.) Psychol.*, **51**, 242–245 (1955).

DAS, J. P., An experimental study of the relation between hypnosis, conditioning and reactive inhibition, *Ph.D. Thesis, Univ. of London Lib.* (1957).

DAVIDSON, W. Z., ANDREWS, T. G. and ROSS, S., Effects of stress and anxiety on continuous high-speed color naming, *J. Exp. Psychol.*, **52**, 13–17 (1956).

DAVIS, D. R., *Pilot Error. Some Laboratory Experiments* (London, H.M.S.O., 1948).

DEESE, J. and LAZARUS, R. S., The effects of psychological stress upon performance: a theoretical framework (John Hopkins Univ., mimeographed paper, Sept. 1953).

DEESE, J., LAZARUS, R. S. and KEENAN, J., Anxiety, anxiety-reduction, and stress in learning, *J. Exp. Psychol.*, **46**, 55–60 (1953).

DEKKER, E. and GROEN, J., Reproducible psychogenic attacks of asthma, *J. Psychosom. Res.*, **1**, 58–67 (1956).

DIETHELM, O. and JONES, M. R., Influence of anxiety on attention, learning, retention and thinking, *Arch. Neurol. Psychiat. Chicago*, **58**, 325–336 (1947).

DODSON, J. D., The relation of strength of stimulus to rapidity of habit-formation, *J. Anim. Behav.*, **5**, 330–336 (1915).

DOLLARD, J. and MILLER, N. E., *Personality and Psychotherapy. An Analysis in Terms of Learning, Thinking and Culture* (New York, McGraw-Hill, 1950).

DORIS, J. and SARASON, S. B., Test anxiety and blame assignment in a failure situation, *J. Abnorm. (Soc.) Psychol.*, **50**, 335–338 (1955).

ERIKSEN, C. W., Some personality correlates of stimulus generalisation under stress, *J. Abnorm. (Soc.) Psychol.*, **49**, 561–565 (1954).

ERIKSEN, C. W. and WECHSLER, H., Some effects of experimentally induced anxiety upon discrimination, *J. Abnorm. (Soc.) Psychol.*, **51**, 458–463 (1955).

EVANS, C. and McCONNELL, T. R., A new measure of introversion-extraversion, *J. Psychol.*, **12**, 111–124 (1941).

EYSENCK, H. J., *The Structure of Human Personality* (London: Methuen, 1953).

EYSENCK, H. J., A dynamic theory of anxiety and hysteria, *J. Ment. Sci.*, **101**, 28–51 (1955).

EYSENCK, H. J., The questionnaire measurement of

neuroticism and extraversion, *Rivista di psicologia*, **50**, 113–140 (1956a).

EYSENCK, H. J, Reminiscence, drive, and personality theory, *J. Abnorm. (Soc.) Psychol.*, **53**, 328–333 (1956b).

EYSENCK, H. J., "Warm-up" in pursuit rotor learning as a function of the extinction of conditioned inhibition, *Acta Psychologica*, **12**, 349–370 (1956c).

EYSENCK, H. J., *The Dynamics of Anxiety and Hysteria* (London, Routledge & Kegan Paul, 1957).

FARBER, I. E., Anxiety as a drive state, in *Nebraska Symposium on Motivation*, Ed. M. R. Jones, 1–46 (Lincoln, Univ. of Nebraska Press, 1954).

FARBER, I. E., The role of motivation in verbal learning and performance, *Psychol. Bull.*, **52**, 311–327 (1955).

FARBER, I. E. and SPENCE, K. W., Complex learning and conditioning as a function of anxiety, *J. Exp. Psychol.*, **45**, 120–125 (1953).

FARBER, I. E. and SPENCE, K. W., Effects of anxiety, stress and task variables on reaction time, *J. Personality*, **25**, 1–18 (1956).

FEFFER, M. and PHILLIPS, L., Social attainment and performance under stress, *J. Personality*, **22**, 284–297 (1953).

FLEISHMAN, E. A. and HEMPEL, W. E., Changes in factor structure of a complex psychomotor test as a function of practice, *Psychometrika*, **19**, 239–252 (1954).

FLEISHMAN, E. A. and HEMPEL, W. E., The relation between abilities and improvement with practice in a visual discrimination reaction task, *J. Exp. Psychol.*, **49**, 301–312 (1955).

FREEMAN, G. L. and GIESE, W. J., The relationship between task difficulty and palmar skin resistance, *J. Gen. Psychol.*, **23**, 217–220 (1940).

FREUD, S., *Inhibitions, Symptoms and Anxiety* (London, Hogarth Press, 1948 (1st publ. 1926)).

FURNEAUX, W. D., Some psychometric characteristics of university students seeking psychiatric help, *Bull. Brit. Psychol. Soc.*, No. 29, inset p. 7, abstract (1956).

GARMEZY, N., Stimulus differentiation by schizophrenic and normal subjects under conditions of reward and punishment, *J. Personality*, **20**, 253–276 (1951).

GERARD, D. L. and PHILLIPS, L., Relation of social attainment to psychological and adrenocortical reactions to stress, *Arch. Neurol. Psychiat. Chicago*, **69**, 352–354 (1953).

GORDON, W. M. and BERLYNE, D. E., Drive-level and flexibility in paired-associate nonsense-syllable learning, *Quart. J. Exp. Psychol.*, **6**, 181–185 (1954).

GRANT, D. A. and PATEL, A. S., Effect of an electric shock stimulus upon the conceptual behaviour of "anxious" and "non-anxious" subjects, *J. Gen. Psychol.*, **57**, 247–256 (1957).

GRICE, G. R., Discrimination reaction time as a function of anxiety and intelligence, *J. Abnorm. (Soc.) Psychol.*, **50**, 71–74 (1955).

HALL, K. R. L., Studies of cutaneous pain: a survey of research since 1940, *Brit. J. Psychol.*, **44**, 279–294 (1953).

HALL, K. R. L. and CROOKES, T. G., Studies in learning impairment: I. Schizophrenic and organic patients, *J, Ment. Sci.*, **97**, 725–737 (1951).

HALL, K. R. L. and CROOKES, T. G., Studies in learning impairment: II. Psychoneuortic patients, *J. Ment. Sci.*, **98**, 273–279 (1952).

HAMILTON, V., Conflict avoidance in obsessionals and hysterics, and the validity of the concept of dysthymia, *J. Ment. Sci.*, **103**, 666–676 (1957a).

HAMILTON, V., Perceptual and personality dynamics in reactions to ambiguity, *Brit. J. Psychol.*, **48**, 200–215 (1957b).

HATHAWAY, S. R. and McKINLEY, J. C., *The Minnesota Multiphasic Personality Inventory* (rev. ed.) (New York, Psychological Corp., 1943).

HEBB, D. O., Drives and the C.N.S. (conceptual nervous system), *Psychol. Rev.*, **62**, 243–254 (1955).

HEILIZER, F., AXELROD, H. S. and COWEN, E. L., The correlates of manifest anxiety in paired associate learning, *J. Personality*, **24**, 463–474 (1956).

HILGARD, E. R., JONES, L. V. and KAPLAN, S. J., Conditioned discrimination as related to anxiety, *J. Exp. Psychol.*, **42**, 94–99 (1951).

HUGHES, J. B., II, SPRAGUE, J. L. and BENDIG, A. W., Anxiety level, response alternation, and performance in serial learning, *J. Psychol.*, **38**, 421–426 (1954).

HULL, C. L., The formation and retention of associations among the insane, *Amer. J. Psychol.*, **28**, 419–435 (1917).

HULL, C. L., *Principles of Behavior* (New York, Appleton-Century, 1943).

HULL, C. L., *Essentials of Behavior* (New Haven, Yale Univ. Press, 1951).

HULL, C. L., *A Behavior System: an Introduction to Behaviour Theory Concerning the Individual Organism* (New Haven, Yale Univ. Press, 1952).

HUNT, J. McV. and COFER, C. N., Psychological deficit, in *Personality and the Behavior Disorders*, Vol. II, Ed. J. McV. Hunt (New York, Ronald Press, 1944).

HURLEY, J. R., The Iowa Picture Interpretation Test: a multiple choice variation of the T.A.T., *J. Cons. Psychol.*, **19**, 372–376 (1955).

HURLEY, J. R., Achievement imagery and motivational instructions as determinants of verbal learning, *J. Personality*, **25**, 274–282 (1957).

HUSTON, P. E., Eye-hand co-ordination in schizophrenic patients and normals as measured by the pursuitmeter, *Psychol. Bull.*, **29**, 662, abstract (1932).

HUSTON, P. E. and SHAKOW, D., Studies of motor function in schizophrenia: I. Speed of tapping, *J. Gen. Psychol.*, **15**, 63–106 (1936).

HUSTON, P. E. and SHAKOW, D., Studies of motor function in schizophrenia: III. Steadiness, *J. Gen. Psychol.*, **34**, 119–126 (1946).

HUSTON, P. E. and SHAKOW, D., Learning in schizophrenia: I. Pursuit learning, *J. Personality*, **17**, 52–74 (1948).

HUSTON, P. E. and SHAKOW, D., Learning capacity in schizophrenia, *Amer. J. Psychiat.*, **105**, 881–888 (1949).

HUSTON, P. E., SHAKOW, D. and RIGGS, L. A., Studies of motor function in schizophrenia: II. Reaction time, *J. Gen. Psychol.*, **16**, 39–82 (1937).

INGLIS, J., Psychological investigations of cognitive deficit in elderly psychiatric patients, *Psychol. Bull.*, **54**, 197–214 (1958).

JACOBS, A., Formation of new associations to words selected on the basis of reaction-time—G.S.R. combinations, *J. Abnorm. (Soc.) Psychol.*, **51**, 371–377 (1955).

JANIS, I. L. and FESHBACH, S., Effects of fear-arousing communications, *J. Abnorm. (Soc.) Psychol.*, **48**, 78–92 (1953).

JANIS, I. L. and FESHBACH, S., Personality differences associated with responsiveness to fear-arousing communications, *J. Personality*, **23**, 154–166 (1954).

JENSEN, A. R., The Maudsley Personality Inventory, *Acta Psychol.*, **14**, 314–325 (1958).

JENSEN, A. R., Personality, *Annu. Rev. Psychol.*, **9**, 295–322 (1958).

JOHNSTON, R. A., The effects of achievement imagery on maze learning performance, *J. Personality*, **24**, 145–152 (1955).

JONES, H. G., Neurosis and experimental psychology, *J. Ment. Sci.*, **104**, 55–62 (1958a).

JONES, H. G., The status of inhibition in Hull's system: a theoretical revision, *Psychol. Rev.*, **65**, 179–182 (1958b).

JONES, L. C. T., Frustration and stereotyped behaviour in human subjects, *Quart. J. Exp. Psychol.*, **6**, 12–20 (1954).

KAMIN, L. J., Relations between discrimination, apparatus stress, and the Taylor Scale, *J. Abnorm. (Soc.) Psychol.*, **51**, 595–599 (1955).

KAMIN, L. J., BINDRA, D., CLARK, J. W. and WAKSBERG, HELENE, The interrelations among some behavioural measures of anxiety, *Canad. J. Psychol.*, **9**, 79–83 (1955).

KESSELL, ROSE, An investigation into some of the factors affecting speed of response in psychiatric patients with special reference to distraction, *Ph.D. Thesis, Univ. of London Lib.* (1955).

KIMBLE, G. A., Evidence for the role of motivation in determining the amount of reminiscence in pursuit rotor learning, *J. Exp. Psychol.*, **40**, 248–253 (1950).

KING, G. F., MERRELL, D. W., LOVINGER, E. and DENNY, M. R., Operant motor behaviour in acute schizophrenics, *J. Personality*, **25**, 317–326 (1957).

KOCH, S., Clark L. Hull, in *Modern Learning Theories*, W. K. Estes, *et al.* (New York: Appleton-Century-Crofts, 1954).

KORCHIN, S. J. and LEVINE, S., Anxiety and verbal learning, *J. Abnorm. (Soc.) Psychol.*, **54**, 234–240 (1957).

KUETHE, J. L. and ERIKSEN, C. W., Personality, anxiety, and muscle tension as determinants of response stereotypy, *J. Abnorm. (Soc.) Psychol.*, **54**, 400–404 (1957).

LACEY, J. I., BATEMAN, D. E. and VAN LEHN, R., Autonomic response specificity, *Psychosom. Med.*, **15**, 8–21 (1953).

LACEY, J. I. and SMITH, R. L., Conditioning and generalization of unconscious anxiety, *Science*, **120**, 1,045–1,052 (1954).

LACEY, J. I., SMITH, R. L. and GREEN, A., Use of conditioned autonomic responses in the study of anxiety, *Psychosom. Med.*, **17**, 208–217 (1955).

LAZARUS, R. S., DEESE, J. and HAMILTON, R., Anxiety and stress in learning: the role of intraserial duplication, *J. Exp. Psychol.*, **47**, 111–114 (1954).

LAZARUS, R. S., DEESE, J. and OSLER, SONIA, F., The effects of psychological stress upon performance, *Psychol. Bull.*, **49**, 293–317 (1952).

LINDSLEY, O. R., Operant conditioning methods applied to research in chronic schizophrenics., *Psychiat. Res. Rep.*, **5**, 118–139 (1956).

LYKKEN, D. T., A study of anxiety in the sociopathic personality, *J. Abnorm. (Soc.) Psychol.*, **55**, 6–10 (1957).

LYNN, R., Personality factors in reading achievement, *Proc. Roy. Soc. Med.*, **48**, 996–998 (1955).

MAIER, N. R. F., Frustration theory: restatement and extension, *Psychol. Rev.*, **63**, 370–388 (1956).

MAILLOUX, N. M. and NEWBURGER, M., The work curves of psychotic individuals, *J. Abnorm. (Soc.) Psychol.*, **36**, 110–114 (1941).

MALMO, R. B., Physiological indicants of motivation and of "arousal." *Paper presented at the XVth. International Congress of Psychology*, Brussels, (1957).

MALMO, R. B. and AMSEL, A., Anxiety-produced interference in serial rote learning with observations on rote learning after partial frontal lobectomy, *J. Exp. Psychol.*, **38**, 440–453 (1948).

MALMO, R. B. and SHAGASS, C., Physiologic study of symptom mechanisms in psychiatric patients under stress, *Psychosom. Med.*, **11**, 25–29 (1949).

MALMO, R. B., SHAGASS, C. and DAVIS, F. H., Symptom specificity and bodily reactions during psychiatric interview, *Psychosom. Med.*, **12**, 362–376 (1950).

MALTZMANN, I., SMITH, W. M. and BROOKS, W. O., Some effects of different training conditions and manifest anxiety upon target tracking, *Psychol. Abstr.*, **30**, abstract No. 5,642 (1956).

MANDLER, G. and SARASON, S. B., A study of anxiety and learning, *J. Abnorm. (Soc.) Psychol.*, **47**, 166–173 (1952).

MANDLER, G. and SARASON, S. B., The effect of prior experience and subjective failure on the evocation of test anxiety, *J. Personality*, **21**, 336–341 (1953).

MARX, M. H., Some relations between frustration and drive, in *Nebraska Symposium on Motivation*, Ed. M. R. Jones (Lincoln, Univ. of Nebraska Press, 1956).

MATARAZZO, J. D., M.M.P.I. Validity Scores as a function of increasing levels of anxiety, *J. Cons. Psychol.*, **19**, 213–217 (1955).

MATARAZZO, J. D., ULETT, G. A., GUZE, S. B., and SASLOW, G., The relationship between anxiety level and several measures of intelligence, *J. Cons. Psychol.*, **18**, 201–205 (1954).

MATARAZZO, J. D., ULETT, G. A. and SASLOW, G., Human maze performances as a function of increasing levels of anxiety, *J. Gen. Psychol.*, **53**, 79–96 (1955).

MATARAZZO, RUTH G. and MATARAZZO, J. D., Anxiety level and pursuitmeter performance, *J. Cons. Psychol.*, **20**, 70 (1956).

MAY, R., *The Meaning of Anxiety* (New York, Ronald Press, 1950).

MAYZNER, M. S., JR., SERSEN, E. and TRESSELT, M. E., The Taylor Manifest Anxiety Scale and intelligence, *J. Cons. Psychol.*, **19**, 401–403, abstract (1955).

MCCLELLAND, D. C. and APICELLA, F. S., Reminiscence following experimentally induced failure, *J. Exp. Psychol.*, **37**, 159–169 (1947).

MCMURRAY, G. A., Congenital insensitivity to pain and its implications for motivational theory, *Canad. J. Psychol.*, **9**, 121–131 (1955).

MEDNICK, S. A., Distortions in the gradient of stimulus generalization related to cortical brain damage and schizophrenia, *J. Abnorm. (Soc.) Psychol.*, **51**, 536–542 (1955).

MERRILL, R. M., The effect of pre-experimental and experimental anxiety on recall efficiency, *J. Exp. Psychol.*, **48**, 167–172 (1954).

METCALFE, MARYSE, Demonstration of psychosomatic relationships, *Brit. J. Med. Psychol.*, **29**, 63 (1956).

MILLER, N. E., Experimental studies of conflict, in *Personality and the Behavior Disorders*, Vol. I., Ed. J. McV. Hunt (New York, Ronald Press, 1944).

MILLER, R. E., MURPHY, J. V. and MIRSKY, I. A., The modification of social dominance in a group of monkeys by interanimal conditioning, *J. Comp. Physiol. Psychol.*, **48**, 392–396 (1955).

MOLTZ, H. and THISTLETHWAITE, D. L., Attitude modification and anxiety reduction, *J. Abnorm. (Soc.) Psychol.*, **50**, 231–237 (1955).

MONTAGUE, E. K., The role of anxiety in serial rote learning, *J. Exp. Psychol.*, **45**, 91–96 (1953).

MOWRER, O. H., On the dual nature of learning: a re-interpretation of "conditioning" and "problem-solving," *Harv. Educ. Rev.*, **17**, 102–148 (1947).

MOWRER, O. H., *Learning Theory and Personality Dynamics* (New York, Ronald Press, 1950).

MOWRER, O. H. and AIKEN, E. G., Contiguity *v.* drive-reduction in conditioned fear: variations in conditioned and unconditioned stimuli, *Amer. J. Psychol.*, **67**, 26–31 (1954).

MOWRER, O. H. and SOLOMON, L. N., Contiguity *v.* drive-reduction in conditioned fear: the proximity and abruptness of drive-reduction, *Amer. J. Psychol.*, **67**, 15–25 (1954).

MOWRER, O. H. and VIEK, P., An experimental analogue of fear from a sense of helplessness, *J. Abnorm. (Soc.) Psychol.*, **43**, 193–200 (1948).

MURPHY, J. V. and MILLER, R. E., The manipulation of dominance in monkeys with conditioned fear, *J. Abnorm. Psychol.*, **53**, 244–248 (1956).

MURPHY, J. V., MILLER, R. E., and MIRSKY, I. A., Interanimal conditioning in the monkey, *J. Comp. Physiol., Psychol.*, **48**, 211–214 (1955).

NELSON, E. H., An experimental investigation of intellectual speed and power in mental disorders, *Ph.D. Thesis, Univ. of London Lib.* (1953).

O'CONNOR, N., The rehabilitation of chronic schizophrenics, *Bull. Brit. Psychol. Soc.*, No. 32, Inset p. 3 abstract (1957a).

O'CONNOR, N., Reminiscence and work decrement in catatonic and paranoid schizophrenics, *Brit. J. Med. Psychol.*, **30**, 188–193 (1957b).

O'CONNOR, N., Personal communication, (1957c).

O'CONNOR, N., HERON, A. and CARSTAIRS, G. M., Work performance of chronic schizophrenics, *Occup. Psychol.*, **30**, 153–164 (1956).

O'CONNOR, N. and RAWNSLEY, K., The acquisition of two types of conditioned response, *J. Abnorm. (Soc.) Psychol.*, **58**, 157–161 (1959).

O'CONNOR, N. and TOPPING, G., The response of chronic schizophrenics to incentives. Unpublished paper (1957).

PASCAL, G. R. and SWENSEN, C., Learning in mentally ill patients under conditions of unusual motivation, *J. Personality*, **21**, 240–249 (1952).

PAYNE, R. W., L'utilité du test de Rorschach en psychologie clinique, *Rev. Psychol. appl.*, **5**, 255–264 (1955).

PETERS, H. N., Multiple choice learning in the chronic schizophrenic, *J. Clin. Psychol.*, **9**, 328–333 (1953).

PETERS, H. N. and JENKINS, R. L., Improvement of chronic

schizophrenic patients with guided problem solving motivated by hunger, *Psychiat. Quart. Suppl.*, **28**, 84–101 (1954).

PETERS, H. N. and MURPHREE, O. D., The conditioned reflex in the chronic schizophrenic, *J. Clin. Psychol.*, **10**, 126–130 (1954).

PHILLIPS, L. and COWITZ, B., Social attainment and reactions to stress, *J. Personality*, **22**, 270–283 (1953).

RAINES, G. N. (Chairman), Discussion of paper presented by Ogden R. Lindsley, Ph.D., *Psychiat. Res. Rep.*, **5**, 140–153 (1956).

RAMOND, C. K., Anxiety and task as determiners of verbal performance, *J. Exp. Psychol.*, **46**, 120–124 (1953).

RESTLE, F. and BEECROFT, R. S., Anxiety, stimulus generalization, and differential conditioning: a comparison of two theories, *Psychol. Rev.*, **62**, 433–437 (1955).

REYNOLDS, B., The effect of learning on the predictability of psychomotor performance, *J. Exp. Psychol.*, **44**, 189–198 (1952).

ROBERTSON, J. P. S., Age, vocabulary, anxiety and brain damage as factors in verbal learning, *J. Cons. Psychol.*, **21**, 179–182 (1957).

RODNICK, E. H. and SHAKOW, D., Set in the schizophrenic as measured by a composite reaction time index, *Amer. J. Psychiat.*, **97**, 214–225 (1940).

ROSENBAUM, G., Stimulus generalization as a function of experimentally induced anxiety, *J. Exp. Psychol.*, **45**, 35–43 (1953).

ROSENBAUM, G., Stimulus generalization as a function of clinical anxiety, *J. Abnorm. (Soc.) Psychol.*, **53**, 281–285 (1956).

SALTZ, E. and HOEHN, A. J., A test of the Taylor-Spence theory of anxiety, *J. Abnorm. (Soc.) Psychol.*, **54**, 114–117 (1957).

SALZINGER, K. and PISONI, STEPHANIE, Reinforcement of affect responses of schizophrenics during the clinical interview. *Paper presented at the Eastern Psychological Association Meeting, N.Y. City* (1957).

SARASON, I. G., Effect of anxiety, motivational instructions, and failure on serial learning, *J. Exp. Psychol.*, **51**, 253–260 (1956).

SARASON, I. G., Effects of anxiety and two kinds of motivating instructions on verbal learning, *J. Abnorm. (Soc.) Psychol.*, **54**, 166–171 (1957a).

SARASON, I. G., The effect of anxiety and two kinds of failure on serial learning, *J. Personality*, **25**, 383–392 (1957b).

SARASON, I. G. and SARASON, B. R., Effects of motivating instructions and reports of failure on verbal learning, *Amer. J. Psychol.*, **70**, 92–96 (1957).

SARASON, S. B. and MANDLER, G., Some correlates of test anxiety, *J. Abnorm. (Soc.) Psychol.*, **47**, 810–817. (1952).

SARASON, S. B., MANDLER, G. and CRAIGHILL, P. G., The effect of differential instructions on anxiety and learning, *J. Abnorm. (Soc.) Psychol.*, **47**, 561–565 (1952).

SCHLOSBERG, H., The relationship between success and the laws of conditioning, *Psychol. Rev.*, **44**, 379–394 (1937).

SCHOENFELD, W. N., An experimental approach to anxiety, escape and avoidance behaviour, in *Anxiety*, Eds. P. H. Hoch and J. Zubin (New York, Grune & Stratton, 1950).

SCHONELL, F. J., *Backwardness in the Basic Subjects* (London, Oliver & Boyd, 1942).

SELYE, H., Stress and disease, *Science*, **122**, 625–631 (1955).

SEWARD, J. P., Comments on Professor Marx's paper, in *Nebraska Symposium on Motivation*, Ed. M. R. Jones, (Lincoln, Univ. Nebraska Press, 1956).

SHAKOW, D., A study of certain aspects of motor co-ordination in schizophrenia with the prod meter, *Psychol. Bull.*, **29**, 661, abstract (1932).

SHAKOW, D., The nature of deterioration in schizophrenic conditions, *Nerv. Ment. Dis. Monogr.*, No. 70 (1946).

SHAPIRO, M. B. and NELSON, E. H., An investigation of the nature of cognitive impairment in co-operative psychiatric patients, *Brit. J. Med. Psychol.*, **28**, 239–256 (1955).

SHOBEN, E. J. JR., Psychotherapy as a problem in learning theory, *Psychol. Bull.*, **46**, 366–392 (1949).

SIDOWSKI, J. B., Influence of awareness of reinforcement on verbal conditioning, *J. Exp. Psychol.*, **48**, 355–360 (1954).

SIEGMAN, A. W., The effect of manifest anxiety on a concept formation task, a nondirected learning task, and on timed and untimed intelligence tests, *J. Cons. Psychol.*, **20**, 176–178 (1956).

SILVERMAN, R. E., Anxiety and the mode of response, *J. Abnorm. (Soc.) Psychol.*, **49**, 538–542 (1954).

SILVERMAN, R. E. and BLITZ, B., Learning and two kinds of anxiety, *J. Abnorm. (Soc.) Psychol.*, **52**, 301–303 (1956).

SIMMINS, CONSTANCE, Studies in experimental psychiatry: IV. Deterioration of "G" in psychotic patients, *J. Ment. Sci.*, **79**, 704–734 (1933).

SKINNER, B. F., Two types of conditioned reflex and a pseudo type, *J. Gen. Psychol.*, **12**, 66–77 (1935).

SKINNER, B. F., *Science and Human Behavior* (New York, Macmillan, 1953).

SMITH, J. G., Influence of failure, expressed hostility, and stimulus characteristics on verbal learning and recognition, *J. Personality*, **22**, 475–493 (1953).

SOLOMON, R. L. and BRUSH, ELINOR S., Experimentally derived conceptions of anxiety and aversion, in *Nebraska Symposium on Motivation*, Ed. M. R. Jones (Lincoln Univ. of Nebraska Press, 1956).

SOLOMON, R. L. and WYNNE, L. C., Traumatic avoidance learning: The principles of anxiety conservation and partial irreversibility, *Psychol. Rev.*, **61**, 353–385 (1954).

SPENCE, K. W., The differential response in animals to stimuli varying within a single dimension, *Psychol. Rev.*, **44**, 430–444 (1937).

SPENCE, K. W., *Behaviour Theory and Conditioning* (London, Oxford Univ. Press, 1956).

SPENCE, K. W. and BEECROFT, R. S., Differential conditioning and level of anxiety, *J. Exp. Psychol.*, **48**, 399–403 (1954).

SPENCE, K. W. and FARBER, I. E., The relation of anxiety to differential eyelid conditioning, *J. Exp. Psychol.*, **47**, 127–134 (1954).

SPENCE, K. W., FARBER, I. E. and MCFANN, H. H., The relation of anxiety (drive) level to performance in competitional and noncompetitional paired-associates learning, *J. Exp. Psychol.*, **52**, 296–305 (1956).

SPENCE, K. W., TAYLOR, J. and KETCHEL, RHODA, Anxiety (drive) level and degree of competition in paired-associates learning, *J. Exp. Psychol.*, **52**, 306–310 (1956).

STAR, K. H., An experimental study of "reactive

inhibition" and its relations to certain personality traits, *Unpubl. Ph.D. Thesis, Univ. of London Lib.* (1957).

STEVENSON, H. W. and ISCOE, I., Anxiety and discriminative learning, *Amer. J. Psychol.*, **69**, 113–114 (1956).

TAFFEL, C., Anxiety and the conditioning of verbal behaviour, *J. Abnorm. (Soc.) Psychol.*, **51**, 496–501 (1955).

TAYLOR, JANET A., A personality scale of manifest anxiety, *J. Abnorm. (Soc.) Psychol.*, **48**, 285–290 (1953).

TAYLOR, JANET A., The Taylor Manifest Anxiety Scale and intelligence, *J. Abnorm. (Soc.) Psychol.*, **51**, 347 (1955).

TAYLOR, JANET, A., Drive theory and manifest anxiety, *Psychol. Bull.* **53**, 303–320 (1956).

TAYLOR, JANET A. and CHAPMAN, J. P., Anxiety and the learning of paired associates, *Amer. J. Psychol.*, **68**, 671 (1955).

TAYLOR, JANET A. and SPENCE, K. W., The relationship of anxiety level to performance in serial learning, *J. Exp. Psychol.*, **44**, 61–64 (1952).

TIZARD, J. and VENABLES, P. H., The influence of extraneous stimulation on the reaction time of schizophrenics, *Brit. J. Psychol.*, **48**, 299–305 (1957).

TREADWELL, EMER, Motor reminiscence and individual personality differences, *Unpublished dissertation, Queen's University*, Belfast (1956).

VENABLES, P. H., Changes in motor response with increase and decrease in task difficulty in normal industrial and psychiatric patient subjects, *Brit. J. Psychol.*, **46**, 101–110 (1955).

VENABLES, P. H. and TIZARD, J., The effect of stimulus light intensity on reaction time of schizophrenics, *Brit. J. Psychol.*, **47**, 144–145 (1956a).

VENABLES, P. H. and TIZARD, J., Performance of functional psychotics on a repetitive task, *J. Abnorm. (Soc.) Psychol.*, **53**, 23–26 (1956b).

VENABLES, P. H. and TIZARD, J., Paradoxical effects in the reaction time of schizophrenics, *J. Abnorm. (Soc.) Psychol.*, **53**, 220–224 (1956c).

WARREN, ANNE B. and GRANT, D. A., The relation of conditioned discrimination to the M.M.P.I. Pd personality variable, *J. Exp. Psychol.*, **49**, 23–27 (1955).

WASSERMAN, H. N., The effect of motivation and amount of pre-rest practice upon inhibitory potential in motor learning, *J. Exp. Psychol.*, **42**, 162–172 (1951).

WATERHOUSE, I. K. and CHILD, I. L., Frustration and the quality of performance: III. An experimental study, *J. Personality*, **21**, 298–311 (1953).

WEISS, E. S., "Absolute" and "relational" learning as a function of perceptual rigidity: a theory of discrimination learning and transposition, *Paper presented at the XVth International Congress of Psychology*, Brussels, (1957).

WELCH, L., The relationship between conditioning and higher learning, *J. Gen. Psychol.*, **53**, 221–229 (1955).

WELSH, G. S., An anxiety index and an internalization ratio for the M.M.P.I., *J. Cons. Psychol.*, **16**, 65–72 (1952).

WENAR, C., Reaction time as a function of manifest anxiety and stimulus intensity, *J. Abnorm. (Soc.) Psychol.*, **49**, 335–340 (1954).

WESLEY, ELIZABETH, L., Perseverative behaviour in a concept-formation task as a function of manifest anxiety and rigidity, *J. Abnorm. (Soc.) Psychol.*, **48**, 129–134 (1953).

WEST, L. J. and FARBER, I. E., The role of pain in emotional development, *Psychological Measurements Newsletter*, **3**, 10 abstract (1957).

WESTROPE, MARTHA, R., Relations among Rorschach indices, manifest anxiety and performance under stress, *J. Abnorm. (Soc.) Psychol.*, **48**, 515–524 (1953).

WICKENS, D. D. and PLATT, C. E., Response termination of the cue stimulus in classical and instrumental conditioning, *J. Exp. Psychol.*, **47**, 183–186 (1954).

WILLETT, R. A., The effect of a stimulant and a depressant drug on the serial rote learning of nonsense syllables. Unpublished paper (1958).

WILLIAMS, J. E., Mode of failure, interference tendencies, and achievement imagery, *J. Abnorm. (Soc.) Psychol.*, **51**, 573–580 (1955).

WILLIAMS, M., An experimental study of intellectual control under stress and associated Rorschach factors, *J. Cons. Psychol.*, **11**, 21–29 (1947).

WOLPE, J., Experimental neuroses as learned behaviour, *Brit. J. Psychol.*, **43**, 243–268 (1952).

YERKES, R. M. and DODSON, J. D., The relation of strength of stimulus to rapidity of habit formation, *J. Comp. Neurol.*, **18**, 459–482 (1908).

ZEAMAN, B. and KAUFMAN, M., Individual differences and theory in a motor learning task, *Psychol. Monogr.*, **69**, whole No. 391 (1955).

CHAPTER 14

Psychological Effects of Brain Damage[1]

V. MEYER

INTRODUCTION

ANYONE acquainted with the literature on the psychological effects of brain damage will agree that this field contains numerous controversial issues and that the findings do not permit a clear orientation. A vast number of isolated, disconnected studies have been reported, the results of which are equivocal, inconsistent, and very often contradictory; up to the present time no acceptable theory of brain organization and functioning has emerged from them and the diagnostic tests in this field show too high a degree of misclassification to be very useful for clinical use.

The main purpose of this chapter will be to examine critically the experimental designs and methodology, and the conclusions drawn from cognitive and orectic investigations of brain damage. An attempt will also be made to salvage from this mass of data and contradictory generalizations some unifying principles which may help to reduce the confusion within this area and to indicate a more fruitful approach to the problems.

Limited space does not allow a thorough review of the vast literature on this topic; objective experimental psychological test-findings on human material will be mainly considered here. Studies reported on single cases will be given little consideration because only limited generalizations can be drawn from them.

Findings of animal studies will not be discussed since these are of limited value in determining cerebral functions and their localization in man; but some data of animal investigations, which have particularly important implications for human material, will be referred to. Finally, the correspondence between some neurophysiological and psychological findings and theories will be discussed.

The greatest problem in reviewing the literature pertaining to some areas of investigation is to find a plan for arranging the references. References to a wide variety of studies in relative isolation and out of temporal context, without recourse to any plan, serve little purpose other than as a catalogue. It appeared to the author that the most adequate way of discussing the references, for his purpose, would be in terms of existing theories of brain organization and functioning. Thus the emphasis will be laid on the cerebral localization of functions with which these theories deal. Functions will be referred to in terms of test performance behaviour rather than in terms of psychological abilities or traits. The former term is preferred, since the latter implies a knowledge of the factorial composition of the psychological tests used and this information is not in fact available for all the tests.

THEORIES OF BRAIN FUNCTIONING AND ORGANIZATION

Following early observations that various disturbances are related to specific sites of brain lesions, the relationship between functions and the various parts of the brain has remained a clinical and a theoretical problem. Right from the start there have been two opposing schools with regard to "localization" of "higher mental functions" or rather "faculties," since the early investigators were dominated by a faculty psychology. Thus Gall (1813, as cited in Head,

Aphasia and Kindred Disorders of Speech, pp. 1–12, 1926) argued for an extreme form of localization of the "higher mental functions." On the other hand, Flourens (1824, as cited by Boring, *A History of Experimental Psychology*, pp. 62–67, 1950) upheld the view that the higher mental functions are not dependent on any particular part of the cerebrum. Both investigators agreed that primary sensory and motor functions are relatively well localized in the brain.

Despite the vast amount of experimental research aided by greatly improved techniques and methods,

[1] This chapter is based on a paper published by the author (1957).

the main issue, originated by Gall and Flourens, has not been settled. Recent notions put forward by neurophysiologists and psychologists, although rephrased in more sophisticated terms and supported by experimental findings, demonstrate that the original problem remains. Most of the exponents of theories of brain organization have attempted to take into consideration the findings of anatomy, neurophysiology and psychology in the development of their theories; at least they have endeavoured to avoid obvious contradictions. Thus a certain degree of correspondence can be found between the theories put forward by these disciplines. Readers interested in the detailed account of historical development of theories of brain functioning and organization may be referred to Morgan (1943) and Boring (1950).

Let us examine critically the three main theories based on neurophysiological data and then see to what extent the findings of psychological investigations of the effects of brain damage support these theories.

Associationism or Anatomical Theory

This theory gained support from early clinical findings and from the effects of stimulating the cortex electrically. Jackson (1932), studying patients suffering from focal epilepsy, and Fritsch and Hitzig (1870) and Ferrier (1873) using electrical stimulation, provided some evidence that certain parts of cerebral cortex along the precentral gyrus are associated with specific types of behaviour. Also Cushing (1909) produced similar patterns of functioning by stimulating electrically the post-central gyrus.

Partly on the basis of the above evidence and partly from studies of aphasic patients, Henshen (1920, 1922, as cited in Weisenburg and McBride, *Aphasia: a Clinical and Psychological Study*, pp. 29–31, 1935) and Kleist (1934, in op. cit., pp. 31–33) argued for a strict localization of function. Henshen presented evidence to show the exact location of the specific cells "endowed by nature" with the property of receiving specific impressions. Nielsen (1946) is the modern exponent of this theory. Corresponding to this view one finds the so-called molecular or switch-board theories in neurophysiology purporting to describe the mode of cortical activity. This model draws its analogy from an elaborate kind of telephone exchange with precise connexions. The exponents of this theory concern themselves with changes occurring in neurons during the process of learning, and they have a common premise that learning merely consists in the laying down of new pathways in the nervous system, between cells in the sensory and cells in the motor systems (Hebb, 1949).

These views have been severely criticized and are now hardly acceptable. Not only are the findings in support of this theory based on methods which have certain limitations, but new evidence renders it untenable. As regards electrical stimulation of the cortex, Penfield and Jasper (1954) demonstrated that the areas of the precentral and post-central gyri are related to different parts of the body and these can be mapped out. Continued application of the stimulus in the precentral gyrus, however, leads to further movements being added to whatever movement was produced first. Furthermore, not only do the foci for maximum effect change with time, but the effect of stimulation is dependent on the impulses arriving from other sources. Restimulation of the "same" spot often does reproduce the same sensation or movement. Frequently, however, it may produce a different sensation or movement, or it may be found that the behaviour originally produced can be reproduced by stimulation of another spot. Again, stimulation of the "same" spot which produces extension of the forearm, may produce flexion if the forearm is extended when restimulation of the "same" spot occurs. The stimulation technique confirmed these findings in the temporal and occipital areas of the cortex (Penfield and Jasper, 1954). Pampiglione and Falconer (1956) reported that clinical and electrographic features varied considerably from one point to another and even in the same patient for similar parameters of stimulation of the temporal cortex.

There is considerable evidence to indicate that the clear-cut demarcation between cortical sensory and motor areas can no longer be maintained. Twenty per cent of the stimulation experiments on the post-central gyrus result in movement rather than body sensation. Sensory representation in the motor cortex has been demonstrated (Malis, Pribram and Kreuger, 1953) and some findings suggest that each small area of the cortex is sensorimotor, with a preponderance of one or the other function (Lilly, Hughes and Galkin, 1956).

Electrical stimulation technique has been criticized for its considerable limitation as a method of investigating the localization of functions. First of all it produces some effects in so-called "excitable" areas, i.e. primary sensory and motor areas, and in the temporal lobes, but has no effects in the cortex, which lies anteriorly to the precentral gyrus and in the parietal cortex posterior to the post-central gyrus (Penfield and Rasmussen, 1950). Thus, the findings of the stimulation technique have been applied mainly to simple sensory and motor functions and it is impossible to generalize from these to the higher mental functions.

Secondly, such stimuli are essentially artificial (Mettler, 1949*b*; Fulton, 1947). Fulton pointed out that one cannot stimulate a single "spot" of the cortex without affecting other spots. Such stimulation is bound to affect some "simultaneous units," which generally discharge in definite temporal sequence: "One cannot excite a single muscle through cortical stimulation without affecting other—usually antagonistic—muscles groups" (Fulton, 1947, p. 274). Patterns of movements rather than isolated responses are usually evoked. Zeigler (1957), discussing problem of electrophysiological methodology pointed out that electrical stimulation presents various problems. Neural tissue is extremely sensitive to variations in the parameters of electrical stimulation, i.e. changes in frequency, intensity, duration, or wave-form may produce markedly different responses. The site of the stimulating electrode is not necessarily identical with the site of action of the stimulus current. Variations in impedance, threshold, and patterns of response to stimulation of chronic preparations, are frequent. Continued stimulation results in an injurious effect upon neural tissue. Characteristics of electrical stimulation are not necessarily equivalent to normal, physiological excitation of nerve fibres. These factors impose considerable limitations on the functional interpretations of results based on the electrical stimulation technique alone. It should be realized also that the application of this technique to the diseased brains of conscious human beings imposes even greater limitations on the interpretation of results.

It has been pointed out with regard to studies of aphasic patients, that Kleist's and Henschen's work was inadequate since the lesions in the brains of their subjects were not delimited so precisely as to justify the conclusions of neat relationships between lesions and speech dysfunctions; in addition, the examinations described were not sufficient to show the important characteristics of language and behaviour (Weisenburg and McBride, 1935). Not only do functional deficits produced by similar lesions show great individual variations, but Conrad (1954) also demonstrated, using two hundred and sixteen subjects with aphasic symptoms whose lesions were more satisfactorily localized, that damaged areas causing different types of aphasia are widely scattered over the dominant hemisphere and do not correspond to a strictly departmental or anatomistic view.

The findings of electrical stimulation of excitable areas of the cortex and naturally and artificially induced lesions in the sensory and motor cortex show that, while in a limited sense certain small parts of the cortex may be associated with specific types of behaviour, there is lability or plasticity inherent in cerebral tissue that prevents the attempt to localize functions at specific points. Denny-Brown (1950, p. 43), analysing motor dysfunctions resulting from cerebral lesions, concluded that many areas of the cerebral cortex are concerned with motor functions, and that the precentral gyrus has relative, not absolute, importance to all movements. Even though destruc-

tion of the precentral gyrus in man has a deleterious effect on movement of limbs of the opposite side, the loss is not absolute. He pointed out: "There is thus no 'centre' for spasticity, rigidity or involuntary movements nor may a pathway be expected for these functions. Each is the outcome of partial or complete release of a normal component in movement from its natural competitor."

A number of psychological studies on patients with naturally and artificially induced lesions, in "silent" parts of the cortex, provide additional evidence (to be presented later) that the anatomistic theory is untenable.

Lashley (1930, 1952) criticized the switchboard theory from a neurophysiological and psychological point of view. He was dissatisfied with the anatomistic theory since it did not account for certain properties of cortical activity, i.e. cortical integration (to be discussed later). Recent developments in neurophysiology also indicate that the molecular, telephone exchange theories of brain functioning are no longer acceptable (Lindsley, 1956). Hebb (1949, p. 41) points out that no one now believes that direct connexions are acquired between individual cells. The conception of gradients of neural activity, in the constantly active brain, has now been firmly accepted: "The question remaining is whether gradients and fields are the only mechanisms of selective neural actions or whether they are combined with an equally important mechanism of connexions and specialized conducting paths."

Field Theory or Theory of Equipotentiality

Over-reaction against the theory of neural connexions came from Gestalt psychologists (Koffka, 1935; Köhler, 1929, 1940) and Lashley (1930, 1938). The criticism was advanced against the old theory of linear, sensorimotor connexions, in which a single cell was held to be capable of exciting a second cell with which it was synapsed. The criticism of the Gestaltists was mainly based on the facts of perceptual generalization. Animals and human beings react in a specific manner to a range of objects that have only certain general or relational characteristics in common, and this reaction cannot be regarded as the result of the stimulation of identical nervous elements. A square is seen as a square, whatever its size, and in almost any setting; looking at it, fixation varies continuously, but we remain aware only of the single object. These undisputed facts of behaviour have been interpreted as suggesting that perception is independent of the *locus* of excitation.

Lashley (1929) presented other forms of evidence which make it difficult to accept the idea of a structural trace as the basis of memory. For example, removals of parts of the rat's cerebral cortex do not affect habits selectively. He concluded that the degree of impairment of maze learning and retention of such habits was proportional to the extent of cortical surface destruction (mass action) and unrelated to the *locus* of the damage (equipotentiality). According to him, all cells in a system acquire the same functions and distinct learning processes are not necessary for habits involving different stimuli or different parts of a cortical field.

On the basis of the above evidence, Lashley argued that all neurons of the cortex must be in constant activity and the integration must comprise complex patterns of interaction. He discarded the idea of conduction over relatively isolated paths (Lashley, 1942).

Köhler's position is similar to that of Lashley. In order to account for perceptual generalization, he postulated electrical fields in the cortex (Köhler, 1940; Köhler and Wallach, 1944). This is an alternative idea to Lashley's notion of irradiating waves of excitation and their interference patterns. Pavlov (1927) and Hull (1943) accepted the notion of a field action (irradiation and concentration, and the notions of gradients respectively), but did not specify the way in which perceptual generalization occurs.

Köhler and Lashley agree in their stress on patterning in the central nervous system as against *locus* of excitation, hence their doctrines are referred to as theories of equipotentiality. (Köhler does not use the term). The problem of patterning and form has been studied mainly in visual perception; it is only *assumed* that perception in other sense modes depends on the same principles. The law of equipotentiality generally holds that within functional areas of the cortex, the cortical cells are equipotential. Thus, the cortex does not function entirely in a unitary fashion, but the principle of mass action and equipotentiality, in effect, minimizes the role of so-called "trophic centers" in the cortex as organizers of behaviour. Lashley (1929) adopted an extreme position with regard to equipotentiality in the field of problem-solving and retention. Following an extensive series of experiments on maze learning and retention in rats, he concluded that any part of the rat's cortex is as good as another in its contribution to problem-solving of this sort. This view rests on the assumption that the sensory projection-areas have no critical sensory function in the maze running. (He adduced some evidence that the visual area of the cortex has an important non-visual function in retention of the maze habit (Lashley, 1931).) Maze running, he argued, is directed solely by some central nervous mechanism, and the various parts of the cortex are equipotential in their contribution to this central mechanism. Lashley's work continues to exercise considerable influence due to the extrapolated hypothesis that the human brain also

works in a unitary fashion, despite the fact that Lashley himself modified this view (Lashley, 1933).

The above findings initiated a considerable amount of theorizing about generalized effects of brain damage.

Köhler and Wallach (1944) have proposed a new treatment of perception which attempts to deal with certain obstacles for field theory (anatomical distortion of the cortical retina, *see* Hebb, 1949, pp. 51–58). The observed phenomenon of so-called figural after-effect showed that constant stimulation of parts of certain sensory surfaces of the retina sets up states of "fatigue" in corresponding areas of cortex which have measurable effects on the perception of stimuli projected subsequently on to the same region. These effects include fading of colour, apparent increase of distance from the observer, and displacement effects. Köhler and Wallach propose that the flow of electric currents in the cortex, aroused by visual excitation, increases the resistance of the quasihomogeneous volume of the tissue through which they flow. This increased resistance, which they call satiation, changes the course of current flow, which in turn results in the observed figural after-effects. Köhler and Fishback (1950) suggest that the injured tissue of brain-damaged patients may be regarded as comparable to a highly satiated part of normal tissue; that this area is polarized by the currents of test objects and that, as a consequence, such objects recede from the place of the defect as reported by Bender and Teuber (1947).

Klein and Krech (1952) reported that the brain-injured show greater figural after-effects than those whose brains are not injured. They used the kin-aesthetic test as a measure of figural after-effects. They drew a parallel between brain damage and satiation as produced by continuous stimulation. A suggestion was made by them that whereas satiation results in temporary and localized reduction of conductivity, brain injury produces a permanent and generalized state of lower conductivity. They pointed out that the properties of figural after-effects measure this conductivity so that the rate of appearance, extent and persistence of figural after-effects would be greater in brain-damaged cases than in normals.

A similar theory has been put forward by Shapiro (1951a, 1952, 1953, 1954a, 1954b). Using a model derived from Pavlov, and basing himself on the negative induction phenomena observed by Pavlov, he developed a theory exclusive to brain damage. According to this theory, brain-damaged subjects suffer from exaggerated inhibitory effects, and identical effects are produced by continuous stimulation. Excitation of one part of the brain by a sensory surface leads to the inhibition of other parts, and excitation of one stimulus-response sequence results in the inhibition of other stimulus-response sequences. He tested this theory on brain-injured and non-brain-injured patients, demonstrating that negative induction phenomena are more pronounced in the former than in the latter.

Eysenck (1955a, 1955b) identified *satiation* with Hull's concept of *reactive inhibition* (Hull, 1943). According to Eysenck's theory, in the sphere of personality, subjects, in whom strong reactive inhibition is generated rapidly and dissipated slowly, develop hysterical types of disorders in neurotic breakdown; conversely, individuals in whom weak reactive inhibition develops slowly and dissipates quickly, are predisposed to develop dysthymic disorders. Clinical evidence indicates that the pattern of symptoms of the hysteric is similar in many respects to the pattern of symptoms of the brain-injured person. Petrie (1952a) provided some evidence that brain injury (surgical interference by frontal leucotomy) produces a marked shift in the direction of greater extraversion as measured by objective tests. This finding, Eysenck argues, is in agreement with the hypothesis that brain injury produces an increase in speed and strength of reactive inhibition as a concomitant of the measured increase in extraversion. He pointed out that Reese's *et al.* (1953) findings on conditionability and Klein and Krech's (1952) results on kinaesthetic figural after-effects support his theory. The former investigation demonstrated that brain-injured patients are inferior in conditionability to non-brain-damaged subjects; the latter showed brain-damaged individuals to manifest greater figural after-effects than non-brain-damaged subjects.

The three notions, i.e. satiation, inhibition produced by negative induction and reactive inhibition, appear to have much in common. They all imply that a continuous excitation of a sensory surface leads to some kind of process in the cortex which causes subsequent responses to the same excitations to be altered. These alterations are much more pronounced in the brain-damaged than in the normal individual. Unfortunately, there is, at the moment, no direct neurophysiological or psychological experimental evidence regarding the identity or lack of identity of these notions. Thus, it would be premature to claim that the results reported in support of any one of these theories support another. Satiation rests on assumptions concerning processes in the central nervous system, i.e. polarization of cortical tissue by electrical currents; inhibition by negative induction assumes such cortical processes as irradiation and concentration of excitation and inhibition, as well as their mutual induction. Both notions imply spatial and temporal orderings of experience which correspond to spatial and temporal orderings of physiological processes. In Köhler's theory (1940, 1944) these orderings are predicted on the principle of "isomorphism," which,

apart from anything else, holds that a consciously perceived square must be paralleled by a corresponding squarelike excitation pattern at some place in the visual brain. Pavlov (1927) talks about *analysers* which denote the part of the nervous system dealing with a definite kind of stimuli. Reactive inhibition, on the other hand, does not rest on any processes in the cerebral nervous system and merely implies a temporal aspect of its functioning.

Goldstein (1939) developed a theory to account for the effects of brain damage which is based mainly on Gestalt psychology. He criticized localization theories based on symptomatological considerations. According to him—

> Localization of performance no longer means to us an excitation in a certain place, but a dynamic process which occurs in the entire nervous system, even in the whole organism, and which has a definite configuration for each performance. This excitation configuration has, in a certain locality, a specific formation ("elevation") corresponding to the figural process. This "elevation" finds its expression in the figure produced in the performance. A specific location is characterized by the influence which a particular structure of that area exerts on the total process, i.e., by the contribution which the excitation of that area, by virtue of its structure, makes on the total process (Goldstein, *The Organism*, pp. 260–261, 1939).

He reached the same conclusion with regard to the localization of sensory qualities. A perception is a specific pattern of the whole organism (Goldstein, op. cit., p. 268). In brain-damaged patients, certain cortical areas, through lesions, are isolated from the background of the rest of the central nervous system. ("Isolation" barriers can also be produced "functionally.") When such isolated areas are stimulated, they yield abnormal responses. The responses may be exaggerated and of abnormal duration. They may be primitive (less complex than normal), easily distracted, or there may be no response. Symptoms shown by brain-damaged patients can be easily understood in terms of these abnormal responses produced by isolation. The most important aspect of isolation for Goldstein is rigidity. Secondary rigidity, as distinguished from primary rigidity due to functional isolation, is regarded as being due to organic isolation and is dependent on the impairment of the higher mental processes, i.e. intelligence or abstraction (Goldstein believes that defective intelligence and defective abstraction-concreteness themselves are caused by organic isolation.) Brain-damaged patients exhibiting secondary rigidity are not rigid when they understand how to do the task. However, when they are forced to do a task they are unable to cope with by reason of their reduced capacity for abstraction (lack of intelligence), they become rigid. Their reaction to a problem which they cannot solve is to do something which they are able to do. Such rigid performance continues even though it is inadequate and they cannot shift even if asked to do so. Apart from that, these patients display concreteness which is to be regarded essentially as an inability to abstract (due to isolation).

Goldstein and Sheerer (1941), in a monograph on concrete behaviour, introduce a number of tests for concreteness. These tests generally require the subject to make an abstraction by sorting objects and explaining the principle of sorting, and then to shift to a different method of sorting, which requires a different principle of abstraction. It should be pointed out that the authors seem to lose sight of the previously made distinction between primary rigidity, secondary rigidity and concreteness. Concreteness means now an inability to abstract and an inability to shift.

Goldstein (1948) also concluded from the observations of aphasic patients with tumours that aphasia is associated with impairment of the attitude towards the abstract and categorical. This personality change is to be found especially in cases of lesions of the frontal lobes, but it may result to some extent in cases of lesions of other parts of the cortex. The author also maintained that this change is present to a greater degree in patients with lesions in the left hemisphere than with lesions in the right hemisphere.

Those workers, who may be called proponents of a "unitary" theory of brain functioning, still may be shown to differ somewhat in their conception of the effects of brain damage. The unitary nature of the process they discuss may in fact be shown to refer to two aspects of functioning which may, or may not, be related. In the first place, there are those who consider the effects of brain damage to be general *whatever* the actual site of the lesion. For example, Goldstein discusses concreteness due to organic isolation, Klein and Krech talk about lowered cortical conductivity due to satiation, Shapiro speaks of exaggerated inhibition produced by negative induction, Eysenck merely refers to increased reactive inhibition; Lashley takes a similar view with regard to maze learning in the rat. On the other hand, Köhler, for example, argues for generality of the kind of effect (increased satiation in areas adjoining pathological focus) but nevertheless such a theory lays emphasis on the actual situation of the damage. Pavlov (Shapiro based his theory on Pavlov's model) is concerned with the importance of analysers in behaviour. Lashley postulates a limited equipotentiality within functional regions for functions other than maze learning.

These theorists therefore may be labelled unitary theorists in so far as they emphasize mainly the general and generalized processes which result from brain injury and tend to play down the specific effects dependent on the site of the lesions. None of these

workers, with the exception of Lashley, has in fact tested his theory systematically in different sense modalities.

Let us see now to what extent the existing factual data support the above views. No specific attempt will be made to evaluate the theories from the viewpoint of data drawn from contemporary physiology of the central nervous system. Firstly, this is not within the scope of this chapter, and secondly, it is not all that important, since the above theories can be accepted as working hypotheses capable of explaining and systematizing the existing data derived from the behaviour of organisms and as such need not wait upon direct neurological confirmation.

Lashley's theory accounts in a general way for much of the behaviour and it does not conflict with the results of histological studies, nor does it contradict any physiological findings (Sholl, 1956). Like Köhler's theory, however, it does not account satisfactorily for learning and memory processes. Both theories stress the point that the pattern or shape of the sensory excitation determines learning and memory, and not the *locus* of stimulation. Such a position opposes the idea of the memory trace being a structural localized modification of the neurons. It is hard to see how Köhler and Lashley's dynamic reverberatory neuronal circuits could be stable enough to maintain memory indefinitely without becoming disorganized (Hebb, 1949, pp. 10–11; Sholl, 1956, p. 88). The fact that the cortex can be traumatized by concussion, epileptic seizure, or electroconvulsive therapy without having detectable effects on earlier memories strongly suggests that the repetition of a reverberatory activity tends to induce some lasting structural modification.

Lashley's principle of equipotentiality and mass action was developed from an extensive series of experiments on maze learning in rats. First of all there are some theoretical difficulties with this view as applied to human beings. The findings of animal studies are of little value in determining cerebral functions and their localization in man, because of the general trends of neural development towards encephalization. In lower animals the higher cortical centres display more generalized functions, and, as they gradually evolve phylogenetically from a relatively undifferentiated structure of tissue (pallium), they become gradually structurally differentiated, more complex and increasingly specialized with regard to functions which they take over from lower centres (Morgan, 1943). The advent of such higher intellectual functions as speech in human beings has resulted in a different organization of tracts in the central nervous system (Dandy, 1933). Osgood 1953, pp. 474–494), in his survey of neural functions in learning, concluded that with regard to maze learning in the rat there is evidence for localization of "higher functions" within the cortex and for Lashley's principles; however, these findings were derived from complex learning tasks performed by rats whose cortical structures are relatively undifferentiated. Performances similar to maze learning, after extirpation has been effected, have not been systematically investigated in monkeys and human beings; nevertheless the anatomical and neurophysiological evidence for the principle of encephalization strongly suggests that Lashley's model of brain functioning and organization is very unlikely to apply to human beings.

Hunter (1930) criticized Lashley's view on the ground that the maze learning had not been proven to be independent of sensory control. According to him, some evidence suggests that all sensory modalities contribute about equally to the control of maze performance and it is very likely that a lesion in any sensory projection area of the cortex would produce about the same deficit in sensory function, giving the appearance of equipotentiality. Pickett (1952) quotes additional experimental studies on rats to support this view and he himself tested Lashley's theory of equipotentiality by using a maze which can be run only on the basis of tactual and kinaesthetic cues. The results of the latter study are not consistent with the theory of equipotential function. Lansdell (1953), using a new type of intelligence test and rats reared in a complex environment, studied the effects of variously localized lesions; the results are regarded as inconsistent with the equipotentiality hypothesis.

As regards the human material, no direct systematic experimental work has been done to test Lashley's principles, since it is not possible to submit human subjects to direct experimental investigations, as it is the lower animals, and clinical material does not provide cases for crucial experiments. Several studies quoted by McFie and Piercy (1952) are in agreement with their own findings, and with other studies (Battersby, Krieger, and Bender, 1955; Zangwill, 1946), supporting Lashley's notion that retention and learning are functions of the brain as a whole. However, this evidence cannot be regarded as conclusive. Firstly, no study has been found which has investigated thoroughly and systematically learning and retentive abilities in a brain-damaged population, using the visual, auditory and tactual modalities, various materials and different modes of reproduction. Secondly, Ghent et al. (1955b) demonstrated that an impairment of a tactual learning discrimination was confined to the side opposite the lesion; these data emphasize the importance for some learning of that hemisphere which receives the main projections from the stimulated surface. Thirdly, the present author

(1956, 1959) showed that excisions of different parts of the brain may have different effects on learning ability tested in the three sense modalities using recall and recognition.

Apart from the above, the theory can be criticized on more general grounds. The formulation of the laws of cortical organization is difficult to test. The mass-action principle implies a positive correlation between behaviour and amount of tissue destroyed; the results obtained from one form of behaviour do not necessarily apply to the results of other forms of behaviour. Learning and retentive abilities are only two aspects of higher mental activity which are not necessarily highly correlated with other mental abilities such as general intelligence. Spearman (1932) and Thurstone and Thurstone (1941) regarded retention as a different process from intelligence, owing to low correlations obtained between it and other intelligence tests. (Lashley was aware of these limitations.)

The literature on human beings with brain damage has on the whole failed to substantiate the principle of mass action in general and even within limited functional regions, but some positive evidence has been presented. Halstead and Shure (1954) reported results which, in their opinion, indicate substantial confirmation of the principle of mass action. It is impossible to evaluate their statements because of insufficiency of data reported. The correlations between disturbance of the "abstraction factor" and the mass of frontal lobe tissue removed, and between the "power factor" and non-frontal areas are high. However, the correlation between the abstraction factor and non-frontal areas is reported to drop to 0·20; one would require a sample of about a hundred cases to make this value significant at the 5 per cent level. Apart from that, the authors pointed out that the various cortical areas are of "decidedly unequal importance for the mediation of various intellectual functions." Further evidence against the principle of mass action for various functions has been presented by many investigators (Hebb, 1942; Klebanoff, 1945; Landis, Zubin and Mettler, 1950; Zubin, 1952; Meyer, 1959).

The evidence for the equipotentiality principle provided by the studies quoted above (Ghent et al., 1955b; Meyer, 1956, 1957b) argues strongly against the extreme form of equipotentiality for learning ability in man. A considerable amount of evidence will be presented later which does not support Lashley's extreme form of equipotentiality for other functions. Even Lashley's modified view, i.e. equipotentiality of cortical cells within an anatomical region, is not consistent with some known facts (Hebb, 1949, pp. 38–54).

The main reason why Lashley's laws of cortical organization have, on the whole, found little support from experimental investigations is that, as stated, they lack precision and therefore are difficult to test. It may be that these principles hold under restricted conditions which must be rigidly defined.

Köhler's theory has been criticized on empirical and phenomenological grounds. Osgood (1953, pp. 236–243) pointed out that it is difficult to understand how Köhler's non-neural electrical currents, which seem to flow without regard to anatomy, can eventuate in behaviour. "At some point along the line we must transfer from direct currents in a field to impulses in nerve, since this is the way muscles are innervated" (op. cit., p. 237). He also disagreed with Köhler's emphasis upon figural after-effects which require, according to Köhler, a field theory for their understanding. These after-effects can be explained on the basis of known neurological mechanisms of the visual projection system and the postulation of a novel set of non-neural electrical forces in the brain is superfluous. Osgood and Heyer (1952) advanced an alternative explanation of figural after-effects in terms of satiation. Hebb (1949, pp. 58–59), following a critical examination of field theory and equipotentiality, concluded that there is no way of dealing with attention and attitude in terms of the configurational hypothesis and that it leaves too little room for the factor of experience. He also argued that some phenomena (displacement effects) seem inconsistent with the theory of figural after-effects and contended that the theory does not dispose of the difficulty related to the anatomical distortions of the cortical retina. Lashley et al. (1951) attempted to test the electrical field theory by placing a grid of strips of gold foil in contact with the visual cortex and by thrusting gold pins through the cortex in the macular area of monkeys. A variety of tests failed to reveal any disturbances of visual function resulting from either of these procedures. Similar findings were obtained more recently (Sperry and Miner, 1955; Sperry, Miner and Myers, 1955). These findings throw considerable doubt on the importance of the action of electric currents in cerebral integration as postulated by field theory. It must be remembered that there is no evidence that *cortical fields* were disrupted by the methods used in these studies. Howarth (1957) obtained some results which are contrary to the hypothesis of Köhler and Wallach; Seagrim (1957) concluded, on the basis of experimental results, that the whole topic of figural after-effects is more complex than has been assumed. Brenner (1953) reported findings which, according to her, are contrary to the conclusions of Deatherage and Bitterman (1952) and are inconsistent with the satiation hypothesis as an explanatory model. The latter workers reported that continuous visual stimulation in the path of movement altered the threshold and the nature of the apparent

movement perceived, which findings they cite as evidence for satiation hypothesis. Brenner, on the other hand, demonstrated that all forms of continuous stimulation have an identical effect on the perception of apparent movement; thus, an explanation which depends on a direct isomorphic relation between perception and cortical events is not tenable.

The methodological differences in various experiments testing Köhler's theory make it difficult to draw more than tentative conclusions. It would appear on the whole that the results fail to support the theory entirely and additional crucial experiments are needed to clarify the equivocal results obtained in these investigations.

The available evidence for the theories of brain damage, based on the hypothesis that brain damage is analogous to satiation, is, on the whole, equivocal and these theories are not fully acceptable. Here again, differences in experimental designs may account for the inconsistencies in the findings. Jaffe (1954) failed to confirm the results reported by Klein and Krech (1952); not only did brain-damaged subjects not differ from normals in the amount and persistence of kinaesthetic figural after-effects, but also these after-effects were not greater for the damaged hemisphere when compared with the undamaged one. This latter finding is particularly damaging to the theory of lowered conductivity in brain damage postulated by Klein and Krech. The author argued that his results are incompatible with the hypothesis of Köhler and Wallach.

Additional evidence on the perception of apparent movement makes it difficult to consider satiation as an analogue of brain damage. Brenner (1953, 1956) reported that in the perception of apparent movement the effects of brain damage and those of satiation are quite dissimilar. Continuous stimulation in four modalities resulted in a significant restriction of the range of time intervals over which apparent movement is perceived by normal subjects. Brain-damaged subjects did not differ markedly from normals in lower threshold values. The upper threshold was higher for the brain-damaged group than for normals. Brenner argued that the latter finding is in the opposite direction to that predicted on the basis of Shapiro's theory (1954b) and to that predictable from the theory of Klein and Krech (1952). She also demonstrated that after eight measurements of the thresholds there was no indication of a decrease in optimal time for apparent movement in brain-damaged subjects, such as might be expected on the basis of Eysenck's theory (1955a, 1955b). Teuber and Bender (1950), reported findings which are incompatible with the notion of isomorphism and the theories of brain damage based on a satiation hypothesis. The perception of apparent motion was obtained from patients with penetrating wounds in the visual cortex; thresholds of apparent movement were not significantly different under conditions where perception of apparent motion was obtained across a scotoma, nor under conditions where it was obtained in intact regions of the field. It should be pointed out that the above experiments are not crucial tests of the theories; they do, however, throw a considerable doubt on the validity of these theories.

Shapiro's theory of brain damage deserves to receive special consideration since several of the deductions derived from this theory in the field of visual perception were thoroughly and systematically tested and various relevant factors were put under control (Shapiro, 1951a, 1952, 1953, 1954a, 1954b). On the whole, the theory was supported by experimental findings and an independent verification of these findings was reported (Williams et al., 1956). The theory, however, has not been tested in other than visual modalities and the support for it was adduced on the basis of statistical significance of mean differences obtained between organics and non-organics; many brain-damaged patients did not behave as predicted from the theory. The other weakness of this theory is that it is based on a Pavlovian model of brain functioning. Konorski (1948, pp. 34–60), in his excellent critical evaluation of Pavlov's theory, pointed out that the whole style of this theory is foreign to contemporary physiological thought concerning the nervous system. What is more important, such concepts as excitation, inhibition, negative and positive induction are vaguely defined, the theory contains intrinsic contradictions and its statements are not in harmony with the experimental facts on which they are based.

Unless Shapiro's theory is tested further, using different modalities, and unless other relevant factors are incorporated in it and their relationship clarified, it cannot be fully accepted.

Goldstein's theory and his tests of concreteness have been criticized on general grounds. Hebb (1945) rightly pointed out that the theory is too broad and ill-defined to be meaningful, and is likely to lead to an *ad hoc* interpretation of symptoms. It explains at once too much and too little. Behaviour that seems to involve abstraction is called concrete and vice versa. The fact that amnesic aphasia (Goldstein, 1936) and schizophrenia (Balles and Goldstein, 1938) can be reduced to a "loss of the abstract attitude" demonstrates the vagueness and inconclusiveness of the term.

There has been no agreement concerning what Goldstein's tests measure. They generally require abstractions to be made by sorting objects and explaining the principle of sorting, and then to shift to a different method of sorting which requires a different principle of abstraction. It will be remembered that Goldstein and Sheerer (1941) did not maintain the original distinction between concreteness and secondary rigidity (Goldstein, 1939). "Abnormal concreteness" as "measured" by the tests seems to cover both inability to "abstract" and inability to "shift." Also, the tests seem to involve both sorts of rigidity, i.e. primary and secondary. Payne (1954) argued that Goldstein did not provide a proof for his assumption that the tests do measure concreteness, since he did not intercorrelate them. Thus, there is no reason to believe that they do have very much in common besides intelligence. Apart from that, he did not show that these tests measure anything more than general intelligence; if intelligence could account for a good deal of the test variance, the failure to do the test correctly would not necessarily indicate organic "isolation." Finally, the tests are qualitative and Goldstein did not standardize them on a normal population; he merely assumed that people of normal intelligence would be able to do them correctly. His emphasis on extensive studies of individual patients, without control data, affords no statistical information evaluable by standard methods, and lends itself to overgeneralization.

Goldstein's theory stimulated a great deal of investigation, the greater part of which attempted to discover whether or not Goldstein and Sheerer's tests discriminate between brain-damaged and non-brain-damaged subjects. Werner and Strauss (Werner, 1946; Werner and Strauss, 1940–41; Strauss and Werner, 1942–43a, 1942–43b) performed experiments into Goldstein's theory of isolation, comparing a number of brain-damaged children and a control group of non-brain-damaged children of the same intelligence; several differences, all postulated by Goldstein, were found. Many studies (Rylander, 1939; Halstead, 1940; Tooth, 1947; Lidz, Gay and Tietze, 1942; Sheerer, 1949; Grassi, 1953; Battersby, Krieger, Pollack and Bender, 1953) produced results, which, to some extent, support Goldstein's claims demonstrating that various tests of abstraction and shifting discriminate between brain-damaged subjects and various groups of non-organic individuals. However, none of these findings may be considered as conclusive, since either intelligence was not controlled, or neurotics and psychotics were not included. Boyd (1949) and Tooth (1947) demonstrated a strong relationship between the ability to do some of the tests used in the above studies and intelligence. The latter author showed that, when his brain-damaged and non-brain-damaged groups were matched for intelligence on Koh's block test, the test did not differentiate the groups significantly. Also, some evidence is available indicating that neurotics may perform as poorly as organics (Tooth, 1947) and psychotics may do even worse than brain-damaged patients (Boyd, 1949). Further studies failed to support Goldstein's theory. Armitage (1946) concluded that the Block Design Test cannot be used as a screening device between brain-damaged and non-brain-damaged subjects. Weisenburg and McBride (1935) opposed Goldstein's view because their cases showed no evidence, so far as the test findings were concerned, for assuming such fundamental, universal disturbance as Goldstein described. Meyers (1947) found that aphasic patients perform as well as their matched controls on non-verbal tests of inductive reasoning. McFie and Piercy (1952a, 1952b) reported that results obtained from testing patients with localized cerebral lesions on Weigl's Sorting Test do not support Goldstein's view that an impairment of abstraction results from a lesion irrespective of its location; neither do their results confirm the view that dysphasia is contingent upon impairment of abstraction. Brown (1955) showed that no significant difference in abstracting ability, as measured by Goldstein and Sheerer's tests, was found to exist between dysphasic patients and normal controls. Bauer and Becka (1954) demonstrated that aphasic patients did not show greater impairment of abstract ability than other brain-damaged cases and many of the aphasics displayed highly abstract behaviour. The results of the above studies, incomplete as they are, throw considerable doubt on the validity of Goldstein's theory. Research suggests that, while the ability to abstract may be impaired in some brain-damaged patients, there is no conclusive evidence that rigidity, as measured by Goldstein's tests, is produced by brain damage. There is, in fact, no clear evidence that the ability to abstract is anything more than general intelligence. Insufficient research has been performed to permit a clear-cut conclusion.

It is relevant to say a word about the work of Bender and Teuber (1949), since they indicated directions in which to search for a theory of brain functioning in the visual sphere, and these suggestions have been frequently taken at their face value as being applicable to the "unitary" theory of brain functioning. Describing various disturbances in visual perception following cerebral lesions, they drew attention to the following phenomena: on the one hand, it is known that circumscribed injuries in the visual cortex produce predictable regional losses of function in the field of vision; there is an approximate point-to-point correspondence between localized lesions in the structure and localized losses in function; on the other there is also evidence of generalized alteration of functions in those parts of the field where vision is unimpaired. Such radical alterations in the mode of visual functioning as fluctuation, obscuration, extinction, completion, and changes in perception of shapes,

spatial organization, flicker fusion, real and apparent motion have been reported.

It is sufficient to point out that all these alterations in function were observed in patients with posterior lesions (particularly occipital) performing on simple tasks involving visual perception, and that the phenomena reported may not be found in cases with lesions elsewhere. To take one phenomenon, i.e. C.F.F. (critical flicker frequency), Battersby (1951), Battersby, Bender and Teuber (1951) and Medina (1957) reported that under their experimental conditions, there was no alteration of the C.F.F. in patients with frontal lesions. The first two studies confirmed findings of other investigations that C.F.F. is decreased in patients with posterior lesions.

It should be pointed out that Teuber himself (1950) expressed the view that at the present stage of knowledge neither the assumption of regional localization of functions nor the postulation of a general factor are foregone conclusions. According to him, multifactor and general-factor hypotheses should be used only as a guiding frame of reference for the design of new tests and experiments which may lead to negative as well as positive evidence for either view.

Finally, it is pertinent to discuss briefly tests of brain damage, since designers of these assume explicitly or implicitly some generalized effects of brain injuries (unitary view) without taking into consideration the nature or the *locus* of lesions. A number of such generalized effects have been utilized, e.g. the already mentioned ability to abstract, learning and retention, perceptual abilities and intellectual deterioration (mental deterioration index). The reader interested in various tests of brain damage may be referred to Yates (1954, 1956), who described them and discussed their validity.

One of the greatest weaknesses of these tests is the lack of clear theory exclusive to brain damage behind them. Apart from this, most of them contain serious flaws and lack the basic requirements of a valid study. In addition, misclassifications reported are high and, frequently, claims of low misclassification are negated by cross-validation studies.

It appears that most investigators have been mainly concerned in developing tests which discriminate organics from non-organics at a high level of confidence, forgetting that despite high statistical significance of mean differences obtained, misclassification may still be too high for such tests to be sensitive enough for clinical use. Apart from that, alternative hypotheses are rarely considered and very seldom is any effort made to investigate why some brain-damaged patients do not behave as predicted. The evidence available from these studies can hardly be taken as a crucial proof for a unitary theory of brain damage.

It may be seen from the foregoing that none of the existing field theories of brain organization and functioning has been conclusively supported by the experimental evidence. Those theories which postulate an impairment of some cognitive ability, irrespective of the *locus* of the damage, are untenable. Those theories which postulate some general factor underlying various cognitive impairments have not been precisely stated nor adequately investigated to be acceptable in their existing forms.

Theory of Regional Equipotentiality or Functional Equivalence

This theory is intermediate between the two extreme ones which have been presented above. It argues for a limited form of localization. Weisenburg *et al.* (1936, p. 129), concluded that: "There are in all probability more or less independant groups of mental abilities. The typical normal adult does not show great differences in the development of these abilities . . . In cases of brain disease, however, or at least in cases of localized brain disease, they may be affected unequally." Lashley, as it has been pointed out, modified his own earlier theory and expounded the view of regional equipotentiality or "functional equivalence of parts within specific areas" (Lashley, 1933).

The so-called molar theories of connexionism in neurophysiology correspond more or less to the above view. Strictly speaking these theories are neither molar nor molecular. Like the molar, they are mainly concerned with the construction of general models describing neural activity in the learning process; however, they are connexionistic inasmuch as they assume that the changes occurring in learning are to be found in particular neurons and synapses and that new pathways are formed. Hebb's theory of cortical activity adopts such a model (Hebb, 1949). Hebb's theory of behaviour deserves special consideration since it leads to the most highly developed model that is based as far as possible on knowledge of the physiology of the central nervous system, and makes an attempt to find some correspondence between neurological and psychological conceptions.

Hebb adopted a half-way position between field and connexionistic theories, taking advantage of some of the obvious values in each theory and avoiding the difficulties connected with them. He pointed out that Köhler and Lashley deal adequately with the problem of perceptual generalization, but that they face great difficulty in their treatment of perception, learning, attention and attitude. According to Hebb, perception is not a unitary process, immediately given, but is slowly acquired through learning (Hebb, 1949, pp. 17–37). Secondly, the theory of

innate stimulus equivalence and equipotentiality is inconsistent with some experimental evidence (op. cit., pp. 38–54); for example, a learned response can be more readily elicited from one part of retina than another. Such evidence strongly argues against neural fields and gradients as the only mechanism of integration. Finally, since configuration theory requires the memory trace to be dynamic and dependent on activity in neuronal circuits, it is difficult to see how stable learning can occur and how autonomous central processes can exist and can influence behaviour (ibid., pp. 12–16).

In order to overcome the above difficulties, Hebb made the following assumptions: (1) a particular perception depends on the excitation of particular cells at some point in the central nervous system, (2) a separate learning process is necessary for the elicitation of the same response by stimulation of a separate region in a receptor surface, (3) the persistence or repetition of a reverbatory activity ("trace" underlying unstable memory) tends to induce some kind of growth process which leads to a permanent change in the connexions of the constituent neurons and so forms a basis for more permanent memory (ibid., pp. 60–66).

Impulses that arrive at a sensory area of the cortex may preserve certain topographical similarities with the pattern of stimulation, but these are soon lost among the complexities of neuronal interconnexions. A frequently repeated particular stimulation results in the slow development of a "cell-assembly" which consists of a diffuse structure of cells in the cortex, capable of acting briefly as a closed system and providing facilitation to other such systems. A series of such events constitutes a "phase sequence" which is the neural basis for thought process. The facilitation from one of these activities on the next constitutes the neural basis for "attention."

The theory is a form of connexionism; it does not, however, deal in direct connexions between afferent and efferent pathways. The connexions are merely utilized to establish autonomous central activities which eventually form the basis for further learning. The postulation of cell-assembly recognizes "a limited field action in the sensory projection areas, and something like a limited equipotentiality between cells that are in functional parallel in physiological systems" (ibid., p. 40). The concept of cell-assembly deals adequately with the problem of perceptual generalization.

Hebb's theory will easily account for much of the experimental data connected with perception, perceptual generalization, and learning. It also explains satisfactorily why destruction of part of the cortex will lead to an impairment of specific functions, why intelligence as measured by standard tests often remains unaffected following an injury to the brain (the evidence for these clinical facts will be presented in the next section of the chapter), and why some intellectual capacities are retained in old age when others are declining (Gilbert, 1935; Wechsler, 1944; Shaie *et al.*, 1953; Strother *et al.*, 1957).

Psychologists and neurosurgeons have frequently been puzzled to find intelligence level unaffected following the destruction of large parts of the human brain. Hebb (1949, pp. 294–299), analysing the nature of intelligence on clinical and theoretical grounds, draws a distinction between two components of intelligence. Intelligence *A* is an innate potential for learning, retaining and rearranging of perceptions and conceptual activities (in Hebb's theory cell-assemblies and phase sequences). It is an hypothetical concept and it refers to an innate capacity for acquisition of what is usually meant by intelligence. Intelligence *B* refers to the functioning of the brain in which development has occurred. It is related more to experience and can be recognized in everyday life and in the responses in I.Q. tests. Once a certain type of behaviour (phase sequence) has been established it does not depend on a particular amount of brain tissue and can persist when the amount available has been decreased. However, the innate capacity for elaborating and building new conceptual activities (intelligence *A*) is immediately diminished by damage to the brain. This aspect of intelligence has frequently been reported to be impaired in brain-damaged patients. A similar distinction between two components of intelligence has been drawn by Cattell (1943). His "fluid ability" refers to a "purely general ability to discriminate and perceive relations between any fundaments new or old." "Crystalized ability," on the other hand, consists of "discriminatory" habits long established in a particular field, originally through the operation of fluid ability, but no longer requiring insightful perception for their successful operation.

Both components enter into intelligence tests, but in adults the crystalized ability or intelligence *B* determines more the level of performance, whereas in childhood the fluid ability or intelligence *A* is predominant.

In support of this hypothesis Hebb (1949, pp. 289–294; 1942) and Strauss and Lehtinen (1950) provide a considerable amount of evidence showing that damage to the infant brain has much greater effect on subsequent generalized intellectual functioning than a similar damage to the adult brain. Weisenburg and McBride (1935), Rylander (1939) and Hebb (1942) support the hypothesis that brain-damaged adults (outside the speech area) are more impaired on tasks requiring logical solution of novel problems than on tasks involving problems of a familiar kind.

Meyer (1959) supported this view to some extent; he also showed, however, that certain kinds of learning of new solutions depend more on some brain regions than others. Inglis (1957) demonstrated that in elderly psychiatric patients with memory disorder, an impairment of learning ability seems to be associated with a disturbance in the solution of novel problems.

Another important aspect of Hebb's theory is the treatment of the memory trace. The activity of the cell-assembly does not depend on the maintenance of unique circuits. A trauma to the brain may leave much of the memory intact, since it has been established by process of growth and does not depend upon a dynamic reverbatory state that might be unstable.

Finally, the theory is possibly the only one that presents psychological problems in a manner which can be appreciated by the anatomist and the physiologist, and it is able to account for most of the facts as they are known today.

The acceptance of Hebb's theory demands three histological assumptions to be verified, i.e. the postulated growth process, the synchronization of activity in converging axons, and the anatomical convergence of the fibres themselves in the cell-assembly. Sholl (1956) pointed out that these assumptions are not in conflict with the facts. The histological information makes the occurrence of synchronization and convergence highly probable; the growth process, however, has not been verified. It should be pointed out that in recent years some data have been accumulated which support Hebb's notion that learning is a dual physiological process. Thus Boycott and Young (1955) showed that various ablations of parts of the brain of the octopus destroyed the capacity for permanent or long-term memory, but left immediate memory intact. Since immediate performance was normal it cannot be argued that the lesions produced defects in perception, attention, or motivation. Duncan (1949) and Thompson and Dean (1955) demonstrated that early electroconvulsive shock can destroy the changes produced by learning in rats, whereas learning and memory are not affected if shock is delayed for some period of time after acquisition. Here again, some evidence indicated that these deficits could not be produced by defects in perception, motivation nor attention. Finally, Scoville (1954) Milner and Penfield (1955) and Scoville and Milner (1957) reported cases of bilateral temporal damage who showed almost total loss of recent memory after an interval of five minutes. This loss affected recall as well as recognition, verbal as well as non-verbal material. Past memory, previous knowledge, personality, attention, concentration and I.Q. were relatively unimpaired.

These findings suggest that there is an initial and temporary physiological process, i.e. reverbertion, which maintains a short-lived memory and some time is required for the initial process to take place before it can produce a permanent, perhaps an anatomical, change which forms a basis for long-standing memory.

The main criticism that may be directed against Hebb's theory is that he relied to a great extent on data derived from experiments using the method of strychnine neuronography; these data are of dubious value (Sholl, 1956, p. 91). Apart from that, he did not attempt to quantify his theory. It is difficult to see in what way such a qualitative theory is predictive in the sense that precise expectations can be verified by experimental facts.

CLAIMS FOR LOCALIZATION OF FUNCTIONS

In this section a brief review of the literature on psychological studies which are concerned mainly with human material will be presented with the aim of illustrating inconsistencies in the various claims concerning localization of functions. Such a review will add further evidence for or against the theories of brain organization and functioning outlined above.

The literature is abundant in various claims for the localization of cognitive and orectic abilities within specific areas of the brain, indicating that the brain does not operate in a unitary fashion with respect to most functions, and supporting the theory of regional equipotentiality. The results, however, are frequently inconsistent and even contradictory as to what functions depend on which areas.

As a matter of convenience it is proposed to review the literature in terms of the respective lobes and cerebral hemispheres and then to discuss more important topics like intelligence, conditioning and learning, and personality. In the next section of the chapter the claims will be critically examined in general terms and the main causes of the disappointing results will be discussed.

Frontal Lobes

By far the greatest number of studies are concerned with the frontal lobes. This is partly due to the traditional view that the frontal lobes are the site of man's intellectual functions and partly because psychosurgery made such cases particularly available.

The literature on the frontal lobes is vast and most of the findings are based on cases of surgery for various pathologies and for the relief from mental disorders. It may be seen from various reviews of the literature on frontal lobe cases (Hebb, 1945; Crown, 1951; Klebanoff et al., 1954; and Chapter 15 of this HANDBOOK by R. Willett) that there is a complete lack of agreement as to what cognitive functions are impaired following an injury to the lobes. For practically every study showing impairment of some function, another study can be cited which failed to reveal any such impairment.

A number of workers reported various deficits and some of them attempted to interpret the observed defects in terms of a single concept, and thus to achieve a theoretical statement of the functions of the frontal association areas. Others, when confronted with the absence of evidence of intellectual deterioration argued that some aspect of intelligence, which is not measured by standard tests, is affected.

Goldstein (1944), Rylander (1939, 1943) and Halstead (1947) reported that frontal lobe cases manifested greatest impairment of intellectual ability and they expressed the notion that the more complex and integrative the function is the more dependent it is on the integrity of the frontal lobes. As regards the nature of the deficit, their opinions differed; Goldstein ascribed all defects to a loss of abstract attitude, Rylander maintained that the basic defect lies in reasoning, and Halstead argued that "biological intelligence is affected." Apart from these, such basic intellectual deficits as loss of the power of synthesis (Brickner, 1936), and creative ability (Hutton and Bassett, 1948) were advanced.

Other workers argued that there are no intellectual changes following frontal lobe injuries and it is possible that the frequently reported cognitive deficits are not directly produced by any pathology but are indirect results of personality changes. Thus, Karl and Elvidge (1955) maintained that the basic loss is lack of motivation, an inability to plan for and to maintain a goal. Freeman and Watts (1942, 1948) contended that frontal lobes are concerned with foresight with respect to self. Robinson (1946) tested and confirmed the hypothesis that there is a loss of capacity for prolonged attention which accounts for most of the deficits. Arnot (1952) argued that the basic function of the frontal lobes is "the persistence of emotional states, chains of thought, motor actions and motor inhibitions."

Several workers attempted to measure personality changes objectively (Crown, 1953; Tow, 1955; Petrie, 1949a, 1949b, 1952a). The main conclusions emerging from these studies were that, following leucotomy, patients showed a temperamental change from introversion towards extraversion and a conative change towards normality on the neuroticism dimension. Crown (1953) adduced some evidence that there is also a decrease in the factor of psychoticism.

Most of the above studies and a number of others,

not quoted here, fail to meet the basic requirements of a valid experiment. In most instances there is a lack of adequate normal controls, the data are rarely treated statistically, and the theoretical statements about the functions of the frontal lobes are not warranted by the findings. Apart from that, as it has been pointed out, most of the positive findings have not been confirmed. For instance, the Columbia-Greystone investigation (Mettler, 1949a, 1952) reported that, following ablations of prefrontal and orbital portions of the frontal lobes, there was no evidence of any permanent intellectual impairment. Such mental abilities as learning, memory, associations remained unchanged. The study also failed to show any regular alterations in Goldstein's ability to abstract, and no loss in creative ability, imagination, or high level of intellectual achievements was demonstrated. Finally no change or loss in social or ethical attitude was shown.

Hebb and Penfield (1940), and Hebb (1939, 1941, 1945) found little evidence of intellectual impairment on a series of cases with various frontal extirpations. Hebb (1945) also criticized some of the studies, demonstrating various defects on methodological grounds, and concluded that the various interpretations of the frontal lobe functions are too broad and ill-defined to be meaningful. Apart from that, some of the workers disregarded negative cases in their studies.

What is more important, from the point of view of localization of functions, is that no one has proved that any single form of behaviour is dependent on the frontal lobes or that a damage to this area has any effect on behaviour (Hebb, 1945). Various studies, showing positive results, are of interest in so far as various deficits may follow an injury to the frontal lobes, but inadequate information on the extent of anatomic destruction and pathologic dysfunction produced by injuries, and the frequent lack of adequate controls of other brain-damaged patients make untenable the conclusions that any of the functions reported are *solely* dependent on the frontal association area.

It is relevant to consider here the studies of Rylander (1939, 1943) and Halstead (1940, 1947) since both authors performed systematic mental testing following excision of frontal and non-frontal tumours and included normal controls. Both affirmed that lesions outside the frontal lobes cause no impairment comparable with that found in their frontal lobe cases. The value of their assertions may be questioned. First of all, precise anatomic and pathologic data are lacking; secondly, Rylander deliberately excluded from his control group patients with injury to language areas, and the age differences between the frontal and non-frontal groups in Halstead's study invalidate the

comparison between the two groups. Thirdly, some non-frontal patients showed intellectual impairment which was at least equal to the average for the frontal lobe group.

With respect to the assumption of the predominant importance of the frontal lobes for intellectual functioning, several studies (Battersby, Krieger, Pollack and Bender, 1953; Bauer and Becka, 1954; Battersby, Teuber and Bender, 1953; Teuber *et al.*, 1951; Teuber and Weinstein, 1954; Semmes *et al.*, 1954; Weinstein and Teuber, 1957; Aita *et al.*, 1947; Morrow and Mark, 1955) using various complex tasks, reported results which are incompatible with this notion. They showed that frontal lobe lesions, compared with lesions elsewhere, are not more disruptive of complex intellectual performance.

In conclusion, as Hebb pointed out (1945), it cannot be argued that the frontal association area has no function at all. The research so far available, however, has not conclusively established the dependence of any function on this area.

Left and Right Cerebral Hemisphere

Turning now to the non-frontal regions one finds more consistency in the reported findings, but these results are far from being unequivocal. The most consistent claims are that patients with the left hemisphere lesions (dominant side) are relatively poor at verbal tasks, while those with right sided lesions (non-dominant side) are worse at practical tasks, particularly the manipulation of spatial or spatio-temporal relationships. The possibility of such a differential pattern of functioning associated with the two hemispheres was raised by several studies (Weisenberg and McBride, 1935; McFie and Piercy, 1952a; Bauer and Becka, 1954; Patterson and Zangwill, 1944; McFie *et al.*, 1950; Milner, 1954; Morrow and Mark, 1955). Anderson (1951) and Reitan (1955a) tested this hypothesis and secured supporting evidence. Heilbrun (1956) confirmed that verbal deficits result from left-sided lesions, but this was true for an unselected population of left-sided cases, since the result indicated that this inferiority was largely a function of poor performance of patients with dysphasic symptoms. The non-language performance deficit associated with right hemisphere lesions was not entirely confirmed by his data. His left and right hemisphere groups produced almost identical scores on spatial tests; right-sided cases did more poorly on the spatial battery compared with their own verbal test performance.

In so far as these workers paid attention to the specific sites of the lesions, their findings indicate that the pattern of test performance is a function of the hemisphere in which the lesion occurs rather than its specific *locus*. McFie and Piercy's analysis of various deficits in terms of different lobes (McFie and Piercy, 1952a) and a number of other reports on the effects of lesions of the temporal and parietal lobes (to be presented later) appear to be inconsistent with the above findings. It is highly probable that the pattern of test performance associated with the two hemispheres may largely depend on the composition of the groups with respect to the specific sites of lesions. The lack of agreement between the findings of Heilbrun (1956) and those of Anderson (1951) and Reitan (1955a) could be explained if the last two authors included more cases with posterior lesions in their right hemisphere groups than Heilbrun did in his right-sided group.

The localization of speech functions in one hemisphere, usually the dominant one (the left hemisphere in a right-handed person) has been relatively well established. The dominant hemisphere appears to have some sort of executive and organizing role for speech. There is no agreement however, amongst students of aphasia about the nature of speech disorders, their classification, and their precise boundaries within the dominant hemisphere.

Generally speaking, there are three views on aphasia which are equivalent to the three theories of brain organization and functioning already described. On the one hand, Henschen (1920, 1922), Kleist (1934), and Nielsen (1946) classified aphasias functionally and anatomically into a multitude of various specific defects such as alexia, agraphia, amusia, amnesic aphasia, motor and sensory aphasia, and claim that each specific disturbance can be precisely localized within the dominant hemisphere. On the other hand, Goldstein (1948) and Head (1926) opposed the classification of aphasia into specific defects; they also opposed the doctrine that different language functions are differently localized in the left cerebral cortex. Roberts (1951) and Conrad (1954) provided evidence against extreme mechanical views of localization of various disturbances.

A more traditional view, which occupies an intermediate position between these two extremes, uses a loose functional and anatomical classification of aphasias, and maintains that some damaged areas cause one type of disorder more frequently than another, making the difference one of degree only. According to this view, aphasia seen in anterior parts of the dominant hemisphere is predominantly expressive, whereas in posterior parts it is predominantly receptive (Weisenburg and McBride, 1935; Conrad, 1954; Kennedy and Wolf, 1936; Schiller, 1947). There is a considerable amount of evidence that pure types of expressive and receptive aphasia are not frequently found. Weisenburg and McBride (1935), Conrad (1954) and Schiller (1947) demonstrated that the difficulty in word finding (amnesic or nominal

aphasia) can occur anywhere within the "speech areas" irrespective of the site of the lesion. Thus, Weisenburg and McBride pointed out that some expressive defect can always be found in aphasic patients; Schiller, demonstrated that in all cases with true aphasia there is difficulty in word finding. Schuell (1954) showed that no isolated pure disorders of speech were found on a thorough examination of aphasic patients. She postulated (1953; Schuell et al., 1955) that the basic difficulty of these patients is auditory impairment, i.e. difficulty to retain and evoke auditory patterns of language; all aphasic disturbances are believed to be secondary to this basic disorder.

It is clear from the foregoing that damage to the dominant hemisphere results in various speech disorders and deficits on verbal tasks, but it is not clear to what extent aphasic disturbances manifested clinically are responsible for verbal decrements on psychological tests and whether aphasia is purely a verbal disturbance or whether it implies more general intellectual loss.

It is difficult to give a clear-cut answer to these questions since the majority of studies did not exercise a rigorous control of aphasic disturbances. Some studies provided a considerable amount of evidence that verbal test deficits are attributable to aphasic symptoms (Meyer, 1959; Heilbrun, 1956). Others showed that such impairment can be demonstrated in cases with dominant hemisphere damage without clinically manifest aphasic disturbances (McFie and Piercy, 1952a; Rey et al., 1949; Meyer and Jones, 1957). Zangwill (1946) claimed that he could elicit dysphasic symptoms by means of specialized verbal tests in brain-damaged cases who did not show any disturbances of language on ordinary examination.

It appears that clinically manifested aphasic disturbances are responsible for impairment on verbal tests; however, such deficits can be also demonstrated to a lesser degree in cases with dominant hemisphere injury without clinically manifest aphasic disturbances. It is possible that the latter impairment may represent a subclinical condition on the same physiological continuum as clinically manifest aphasia.

With regard to the second part of the problem, there are three views. Goldstein (1948) regards various symptoms of aphasia as manifestation of a single more profound intellectual disorder; according to another, aphasia results in a mere loss of symbols leaving thought processes unimpaired (Kennedy and Wolf, 1936); a third view takes an intermediate position considering aphasia as a disturbance which affects all aspects of intelligence, although not to the same degree, so that performance on verbal tests of intelligence will be severely impaired and a milder deficit will be found on non-verbal tasks (Weisenburg and McBride, 1935; Hebb, 1942; Fox and German, 1935).

A crucial test for these theories demands the use of non-verbal tasks. The literature bearing on this problem is equivocal. Some workers presented evidence that aphasia is compatible with normal performance on some non-verbal tests (Meyers, 1947; McFie and Piercy, 1952b; Brown, 1955; Meyer and Jones, 1957; Meyer, 1959). Others, like Heilbrun (1956), Teuber and Weinstein (1956) supported Goldstein's view to some extent. Most of the empirical support has been provided for the third view (Weisenburg and McBride, 1935; Bauer and Becka, 1954; McFie and Piercy, 1952a).

The greatest weakness in these studies lies in the fact that many non-verbal tests involve verbal instructions, hence aphasics may be penalized on them because of difficulty in understanding what is required of them; unless it can be ascertained that the patient has grasped the instructions the results cannot be considered as valid (Kennedy and Wolf, 1936). In addition, Heilburn (1956) showed that different results may be secured from left-sided cases using non-verbal tests not requiring verbal responses. It is possible that those aphasics who show impairment on non-verbal tasks rely excessively upon verbal cues in solving problems and language disturbances may interfere with implicit verbalization which is used to elicit non-verbal responses.

It is pertinent to say a word about effects of hemispherectomy in man on psychological functioning. The overall evidence (Krynauw, 1950; Mensh et al., 1952; Uecker et al., 1954; Munz and Tolor, 1955) indicates that following excision of either hemisphere neither a pronounced improvement nor a marked decline of intellectual functioning can be found as a rule. Such evidence, however, does not add anything to the problem of localization. Firstly, most of the cases investigated were grossly deteriorated before the surgery and the frequently reported lack of deficits following the operation may be due to the removal of pathological tissue, which presumably exerted a deleterious influence on neighbouring cerebral areas and resulted in various clinical symptoms before the operation. Secondly, practically all cases suffered from congenital defects, hence it is doubtful whether the left hemisphere in right-handed cases was dominant for language functions.

In summary, the evidence adduced indicates conclusively that the dominant hemisphere governs language functions. As regards the non-dominant hemisphere it appears that non-verbal tasks depend more on it. The nature of the impairments associated with the respective hemispheres has not been investigated adequately, and the formulations, put forward by McFie and Piercy (1952a) and by Anderson (1951),

to account for these deficits are essentially speculative. Finally, it is untenable to maintain that a damage, irrespective of its site within a hemisphere, will produce the same test performance deficit commonly associated with that hemisphere.

Temporal Lobes

The present state of our knowledge of the functions of the temporal lobes is still fragmentary. This ignorance is due in part to a preoccupation, until recently, with the frontal lobes and in, part. to a lack of satisfactory clinical material, which mainly consists of cases with brain pathologies, the extent of which it is difficult to delimit. Apart from that, the rare occurrence of bilateral temporal injuries hinders our understanding of temporal lobe functions.

Several studies indicate that, following various abnormalities in the temporal lobes, specific abilities may be impaired. The most consistent finding is that temporal lobe epileptics manifest, as a group, an impairment on verbal tasks compared with non-verbal tasks (Rey et al., 1949; Meyer and Yates, 1955; Quadfasel and Pruyser, 1955). This is apparently inconsistent with the results in cases with hemispheric involvement presented in the previous section. If temporal lobe cases are randomly selected then such a sample should consist of some left- and some right-sided cases; hence one would not expect to find a differential pattern of verbal and non-verbal abilities for the total group, since the verbal decrements in one group would counterbalance the non-verbal decrements in the other group producing no significant discrepancy. None of the investigations into the effects of temporal lobe lesions quoted above, included a statistical analysis of results in terms of lateralization. A possible explanation of the discrepant findings is that epileptic foci tend to occur more frequently in the left than the right temporal lobe. Rey et al. (1949) found this in a sample of fifty-nine cases, irrespective of sex, and cited other evidence in support of this view. Hécaen and Piercy (1956) reported a significantly larger proportion of left-sided lesion cases with epileptiform auras and equivalents than similar right-sided cases. Possibly related to these findings are those of Busse et al. (1956) who showed focal disturbances of EEG of aged individuals to be almost exclusively temporal in locus and left in lateralization. On the evidence of these findings an unselected sample of cases with epileptic temporal lobe EEG abnormalities would consist of a greater proportion of left-sided cases, hence one would expect to find in such a sample a tendency to lower verbal than non-verbal scores. Also, a left-sided sample should show a highly significant verbal deficit, whereas a right-sided sample should produce lower non-verbal than verbal scores. This problem was investigated by

Meyer and Jones (1957) on a sample of temporal lobe epilepsy cases before and after temporal lobectomy for the relief of temporal lobe epilepsy and the findings supported the above hypotheses.

A number of investigators attributed memory functions to the temporal lobes. On the basis of the findings by means of electrical stimulation of the exposed cortex Penfield and Rasmussen (1950) attributed to the temporal lobes a role of perseveration of memory traces. The temporal lobe as a whole is concerned with memory functions and with judgements and assessments of current experience based on memory. The findings of several studies are consistent with Penfield's view (Milner and Penfield, 1955; Scoville and Milner, 1957; Quadfasel and Pruyser, 1955; Kolodny, 1928; Fox and German, 1935; Keschner et al., 1936; Scoville, 1954; Walker, 1957). These reported various deficits in memory processes following temporal lobe injuries. The situation, however, is far from being simple. The evidence from animal studies indicates that bilateral removal of the temporal lobes in monkeys does not result in a general loss of memory (Milner, 1954). The investigations previously quoted (Milner and Penfield, 1955; Scoville and Milner, 1957) reported that bilateral temporal damage in man, when the damage includes the anterior hippocampus and hippocampal gyrus, results in a persistent and generalized impairment of ability to record current experience, whereas the retention for past events remains unaffected. It appears then that past memory is not "stored" in the temporal lobes, but that these structures are important for the "recording of current experience." Quadfasel and Pruyser (1955) presented results which indicate that cases with psychomotor epilepsy and an EEG spike focus in the anterior part of the temporal lobes produced a memory deficit on test items involving verbal material and the auditory modality, but no such deficit was demonstrated on non-verbal items requiring the visual modality. These findings do not entirely support Penfield's view and the overall evidence indicates that only general registration of recent events is impaired following bilateral damage to the temporal lobes. Apart from that, unilateral damage appears to affect mainly registration of auditory material.

These studies, however, suffer from several defects which undermine the value of the conclusions drawn with respect to the nature of the deficits and their association with the temporal lobes. Firstly most of the reports are of a clinical nature with little or no attention paid to statistical evaluation of results. Secondly, they lack adequate normal and other brain-damaged controls. Thirdly, the extent of anatomical destruction and physiological dysfunction is not precisely determined. For instance, an attempt to localize the impairment of ability to record current experience, following bilateral medial resection, in specific regions of the temporal lobe (Scoville and Milner, 1957) is somewhat inferential, since the operations were done "blind." Fourthly, it is impossible to generalize from the limited findings to learning ability in all modalities for various types of materials. Finally, no attempt has been made to evaluate results in terms of the laterality of abnormalities and various relevant factors like intelligence and language disturbances have been left uncontrolled.

Milner (1954) pointed out, and adduced some evidence, that any evaluation of temporal lobe functions in man requires a breakdown into left and right temporal lobe lesions. In a preliminary study, Meyer and Yates (1955) reported results which are consistent in a way with the conclusions reached by Kolodny (1928), Fox and German (1935) and Keschner et al. (1936) in that temporal lobectomy cases demonstrated a pronounced impairment of learning verbal material presented auditorily. This impairment appeared to be associated with the operation on the dominant side only. Meyer (1959) attempted to investigate the nature of this deficit on a larger sample of dominant and non-dominant temporal lobectomy cases. Learning ability was assessed in the auditory, visual and tactile modalities for various types of material and methods of testing. Also, an attempt was made to determine to what extent nominal dysphasia contributed to the impairment of auditory learning manifested by the dominant group, and the possible influence of intelligence was taken into account. The findings indicated that dominant cases consistently showed a highly significant and persistent deficit on the auditory learning tests only. Since this impairment was in evidence on recall as well as on recognition mode of testing, it could not be accounted for solely in terms of nominal dysphasia. The difficulty was shown to be of acquisition and not merely of execution; the failure to learn following the operation was not correlated with intelligence level. The non-dominant group did not show any changes on any learning tests.

Since the aim of this study was to investigate the effects of temporal lobectomy on cognitive functioning and to define more closely the nature of any deficits detected, the results have no direct bearing on the problem of localization. It cannot be argued that auditory learning depends exclusively on the integrity of the dominant temporal lobe; but the findings indicate that this function does not depend on the integrity of the non-dominant temporal lobe and that visual and tactile learning abilities are independent of the integrity of either temporal lobe.

A number of results, probably related to those just discussed, indicated an impairment on various tests involving auditory modality, i.e. auditory pattern discrimination tests (Bauer and Becka, 1954), auditory flicker fusion test, auditory pattern association test, multisensory timing test (Halstead, 1955) and conditioning of EEG alpha response to a sound stimulus (Morrell, 1956). Halstead (1955) claimed that his new auditory tests detect unilateral temporal lesions at the 0·01 level. Some findings, however, are not consistent with those above, and it cannot be maintained that the auditory modality *per se*, irrespective of the nature of tasks, would be impaired as a result of injury to the temporal lobes. Thus Symmes (1955) using the multisensory timing test, concluded that the auditory problem does not discriminate between a group with the absence of tissue or the presence of focal epileptogenic lesion in the temporal lobe on the one hand and a group with the intact temporal cortex on the other. Chapman *et al.* (1955) reported that the degree of impairment on the auditory flicker fusion test appeared to be constant for several sites of cortical lesions studied. Morrell's cases with temporal epileptogenic lesions, manifesting an impairment in the ability to form a conditioned alpha response to a sound stimulus, did not show an impairment of the voluntary motor reaction to a tonal stimulus (Morrell, 1956).

The investigators discussed above failed to analyse the results in terms of laterality. Since the neurophysiological evidence "localizes" the auditory recognition within the dominant hemisphere (Nielsen, 1946) and since in the temporal lobe aphasia the auditory components of speech are impaired, with difficulty both in understanding and in retaining spoken language (Fox and German, 1935; Kennedy and Wolf, 1936; Nielsen, 1946; Schiller, 1947; Teitlebaum, 1942) one would expect to find impairment on various tests involving the auditory modality in cases with damage to the dominant temporal lobe only. Meyer's findings (1959) are consistent with this in demonstrating that only dominant temporal lobectomy cases manifested impairment on auditory learning tests, and in presenting some evidence that this deficit may be related mainly to the defective auditory modality resulting in a difficulty of registration and retention of auditorily presented material.

Apart from the above studies, various findings, related to the temporal lobes, have been reported. These are equivocal and inconsistent. Milner (1954) quoted studies of monkeys to show that bilateral removal of the temporal lobe severely impairs visual learning and retention. This deficit is particularly severe on tests of pattern discrimination. The critical area in this effect appears to be a small region on the ventral surface of the temporal lobe, damage to which is almost as detrimental to visual learning as is complete lobectomy. She also presented data on human

subjects which, according to her, are comparable with the animal studies and in agreement with them. Her temporal lobe cases, as a group, were inferior to the controls, both before and following unilateral temporal lobectomy, on visual tests involving complex pictorial material. She concluded that the deficit appears when "attention has to be given to many aspects of a complex picture, or when different pictures have to be arranged in a meaningful order on the basis of slight differences in detail." Reitan (1955), however, using the same test, detected similar defects only in cases with right temporal lesions. Bauer and Becka's (1954) results are inconsistent with Milner's and Reitan's findings since her visual discriminative tasks did not differentiate temporal lobe cases from cases with lesions elsewhere. Battersby *et al.* (1955, 1953) evaluated results on visual and tactile discriminative learning in the light of animal studies and in the light of Milner's claim attributing to the temporal lobes an integrative focus for the elaboration of visual impulses. Their findings failed to support such a view.

Consistent with the deficits found in cases with right hemisphere lesions, there are several studies which reported that right temporal lobe lesion cases manifest impairment on tests of a visuo-spatial nature. Hebb's case showed a defect of form perception, visual and tactual (Hebb, 1939); McFie *et al.* (1950) reported in their case of right temporal glioma a severe loss of "visuo-constructive ability." Milner's other finding was that the right temporal lobe group was inferior to the left temporal group and to frontal and parietal cases as a control group on tests of spatial patterning, both visual and tactual, the deficit being present before the operation but intensified afterwards (Milner, 1954). The most pronounced deficit was manifested by cases in whom the extirpation extended far back along the inferior surface of the temporal lobe. Probably related to these findings are those of Teuber and Weinstein (1954) who reported the right temporal group to show "negative transfer" on the Seguin-Goddard form board test rotated 180°. Meyer (1959), however, found little evidence for the above findings in his group of right temporal damage.

A further inconsistency, probably having some bearing on the visuo-spatial functioning, was added by two studies. Elithorn's findings suggested that a multiple-choice maze test is particularly sensitive to cerebral damage to the temporal lobes. His frontal group, submitted to the full type of leucotomy, performed significantly worse on this test also. Semmes *et al.* (1955) and Weinstein *et al.* (1956), on the other hand, demonstrated that the integrity of the temporal lobes is not important for spatial orientation (route finding) and that this ability is associated to some extent with the parietal lobes and most strongly associated with severe somaesthetic defect.

Finally, Semmes *et al.* (1954) reported her brain-damaged temporal group to be significantly inferior to other brain-damaged groups without temporal lobe lesions on complex tactual tasks. This, however, was not confirmed by Bauer and Becka (1954) and Battersby *et al.* (1955).

It is difficult to resolve the above inconsistencies since in most instances there is a lack of the relevant information to enable one to evaluate and to compare critically the reported findings. On the basis of the foregoing it can be concluded that damage to the dominant temporal lobe results in an impairment on verbal tests. This impairment is most likely to be partly due to a defective perception of auditory components of speech and partly due to nominal dysphasic disturbances. Apart from that, some evidence suggests that a deficit on various tests involving the auditory modality may be demonstrated, particularly on auditory learning tests. This deficit may be mainly related to an impairment of the auditory modality resulting in a difficulty in the registration and retention of auditory stimuli.

Non-dominant temporal lobe injury is most likely to result in a deficit on tasks of a visuo-spatial nature. Some evidence suggests that the more posteriorly the injury is placed the more severe is the deficit. The nature of this deficit has not been clarified.

Limited bilateral destruction of the temporal lobes has been demonstrated to result in a generalized and severe loss of ability to register recent events.

As regards the problem of localization the data do not provide a conclusive proof for the dependence on the temporal lobes exclusively of any of the functions reported.

Parietal and Occipital Lobes

These areas of the brain are not discussed separately in any detail, since it is difficult to obtain cases with damage to one without the other being affected. This is due to the fact that these areas are in close vicinity and merge into each other without a clear demarcation line.

A great many studies have directed attention to the effects which follow posterior lesions; the majority of these, however, contain clinical case reports and very few employ objective psychological tests and fulfil the basic requirements of a valid investigation. Semmes *et al.* (1955) quote some thirty such studies according to which disorientation in space is a prominent sequel of damage to the parietal lobes. A great number of such disturbances have been reported (Critchley, 1953). Some of these can be accounted for in terms of primary sensory and motor impairment or in terms of dementia; others are regarded as agnosias or apraxias since they are demonstrable in the absence of sufficient evidence for primary dysfunc-

tion or a general intellectual loss. The following defects of function have been reported: anosognosia (denial of illness), neglect of half of the body or of external space, difficulties in estimation of direction and distance of objects, confusion of right and left, apraxia for dressing, anomalies in constructional tasks, inability to follow habitual routes, and defects in place recognition. However, the evidence is equivocal as regards localization since many of the above alterations of functions have been reported to occur after damage to the occipital, temporal, and even frontal lobes (Weinstein and Kahn, 1950; Battersby *et al.*, 1956; Teuber and Mishkin, 1954; Teuber and Bender, 1949).

Several investigators have attempted to clarify the nature of space orientation, and to relate various disturbances to the left or to the right parietal lobe. Most of the conclusions are not based on objective facts and are essentially tentative. Weinstein *et al.* (1956) pointed out that discussions of the nature of the deficits centred around three hypotheses. The first regards spatial disorientation as a form of visual agnosia. The second suggests that the defect is confined to vision involving the primary aspect of sensation rather than the "higher organization" of sense data. The third maintains that spatial disorientation reflects general intellectual loss.

Some attempts have been made to test these theories more objectively by controlling relevant factors. Battersby *et al.* (1956) concluded that neither visual nor concomitant somatosensory defects could account for unilateral spatial inattention; those cases which showed the spatial deficit had, in addition to primary sensory defects, mental alterations. Ettlinger *et al.* (1957) concluded that disorders of visual space perception demonstrated by cases with right posterior lesions cannot be entirely accounted for in terms of impairment of differential visual sensitivity, unilateral visual extinction, central vestibular derangement, or in terms of a combination of these factors. Nor can such disorders be viewed as secondary to general intellectual impairment. The authors attempted to explain visuo-spatial disorders in terms of restriction of "the field of visual attention" associated with some degree of conceptual spatial loss. The best attempts in this field of research have been made by Semmes *et al.* (1955) and Weinstein *et al.* (1956). These investigators demonstrated that spatial disorientation (route finding) cannot be entirely explained as a loss of general intelligence, nor can it be regarded as visual or tactual agnosia. Also, they demonstrated that this deficit cannot be ascribed to the receptive difficulty in visual or tactile modality. Their data indicated that spatial disorientation is mainly related to severe somaesthetic defects, hence they play down the importance of the parietal lobes for mediating spatial functions. On the whole, these findings are consistent in so far as they do not support any of the hypotheses put forward to explain the nature of space disorientation.

Various clinical claims ascribe some disturbances of space orientation to both parietal lobes, some exclusively to the right or the left lobe. These claims have been summarized by Hécaen, Penfield, Bertrand and Malmo (1956). On the whole, the evidence is controversial and the differences between the lobes are not understood. There are some suggestions, supported to some extent by psychological test results, that right parietal lesions result in a failure on visuo-constructional tasks due to the lack of visual discriminative judgement (spatial agnosia) whereas damage to the left parietal lobe produces impairment on such tasks due to constructive apraxia (McFie and Piercy, 1952a; McFie et al., 1950; Zangwill, 1954).

Functions other than space orientation have been associated with the parietal lobes but the findings are rarely consistent. Since lesions to these areas are supposed to result in tactile deficits and tactile agnosia (Nielsen, 1946), one would expect cases with parietal-lobe damage to manifest greatest impairment on tasks involving the tactual modality. The following are consistent with this hypothesis, Jaffe's findings on tactual adaptation (Jaffe, 1955); Semmes et al. (1954) on transfer effect with regard to performance on complex tactual tasks, Bender et al., (1950) on barognosis, and Weinstein on negative time error in weight judgement (1955c). Weinstein, however, failed to demonstrate that parietal lobe cases showed greatest deficit on tests of barognosis (Weinstein, 1954), tactile size judgement (Weinstein, 1955a) and time error in tactile size judgement (Weinstein, 1955b). In addition performance on various complex tactual tasks did not discriminate parietal lobe cases from cases with lesions elsewhere (Bauer and Becka, 1954; Semmes et al., 1954; Battersby, Krieger and Bender, 1953; Ghent et al., 1955a; Battersby et al., 1955; Ghent et al., 1955b).

These results are further complicated in that Bender et al. (1950) and Weinstein (1955c) reported that deficits of weight judgement, related to parietal lobe damage, were not necessarily associated with concomitant somatosensory defects. Similarly, the defective performance of brain-damaged patients in general on various complex tactual tasks was demonstrated by some investigators to be independent of somatosensory defects in the hand involved (Battersby et al., 1955; Ghent et al., 1955b; Battersby, Krieger and Bender, 1953; Weinstein, 1954). On the other hand some evidence indicated that such impairments are related to somaesthetic defects (Ghent et al., 1955a; Weinstein, 1955a) and that the direction of the error may be determined by the presence of

somatosensory status (Weinstein, 1954). The results reported on size and weight judgements (Bender et al., 1950; Weinstein, 1954, 1955a, 1955b, 1955c) are further complicated by the bilateral and unilateral testing of hands.

Further inconsistency with regard to the parietal lobes may be found where arithmetic ability is concerned. Some investigators found that cases with right parietal lesions were inferior on arithmetic tasks (Weisenburg and McBride, 1935), others reported such impairment particularly in cases with left lobe damage (McFie and Piercy, 1952a; Strauss and Lehtinen, 1950).

The results are not clear as to what functions are dependent on the integrity of the occipital lobes. Changes on tasks in the field of vision have been shown to occur (Bender and Teuber, 1949; Teuber and Bender, 1949), which are consistent with the view that lesions to the visual cortex produce primary visual dysfunctions and disturbances of higher functions, i.e. visual agnosia (Nielsen, 1946). These have already been enumerated. Teuber and Bender (1949) pointed out that their cases did not contribute to the solution of the problem of localization, since many of them had other parts of the brain injured as well as the occipital lobe. Apart from this, some of the tests employed were measures of spatial orientation rather than of pattern vision proper, and it has already been pointed out that deficits on the former type of test are usually associated with the parietal lobes. Furthermore, deficits on various complex visual tasks frequently failed to discriminate cases with occipital lobe damage from cases with lesions elsewhere (Battersby et al., 1955; Bauer and Becka, 1954; Battersby, Krieger and Bender, 1953).

No direct light was thrown on the nature of impairment of visual tasks following damage to the occipital lobes. An investigation into the relation of such impairment to changes in primary sensory defects would present a considerable difficulty, since damage the geniculo-calcarine system not only produces circumscribed scotoma, but also impairs visual functions over the entire field of vision (Bender et al., 1951) Indirect evidence on brain-damage cases in general indicates that deficit on various visual tasks is relatively unaffected by the presence of primary sensory defects (Battersby et al., 1955; Battersby, Krieger and Bender, 1955; Weinstein et al., 1955). Surprisingly, some measures of tactual defects have been reported to be associated with defective performance on some visual tests (Weinstein et al., 1955). Finally, some indirect evidence shows that deficits on visual tasks cannot be described as visual agnosia since the same lesions that impaired performance on visual tasks interfered with performance on tactile tasks (Battersby et al., 1955; Battersby, Krieger and Bender, 1953).

Some of the studies described above, particularly

those by Semmes *et al.*, (1955) and Weinstein *et al.*, (1956), indicate that different results may be obtained with regard to localization of functions by means of analysis according to the *locus* of the lesion and by analysis according to concomitant defects. Thus the value of the available data on functions of the occipital and parietal lobes is further undermined by the fact that most of the investigators failed to examine systematically the relationship between performance on various tests to the presence or absence of other concomitant defects produced by the brain injury. Furthermore, those who did exercise such control did not attempt to localize concomitant defects.

When all the data have been taken into account, the only conclusion that can be drawn concerning the parietal and occipital lobes is that damage to the former is particularly apt to produce impairment on tasks involving spatial functions, and damage to the latter is to result in deficits on tasks making use of visual functions.

Intelligence

Despite sustained interest in the effects of cerebral lesions on general intelligence, there is no agreement on the localization of those injuries which might produce maximal deficits on tests designed to measure this function.

The results do not support Lashley's view on brain functioning, nor the claims which attribute to the frontal lobes the predominant importance for intellectual functioning. The uncertainty is enhanced by a number of reports which failed to detect deficits on tests of I.Q. following a destruction of large parts of the human brain (Hebb, 1949; Meyer, 1959; Hebb, 1945; Mettler, 1949a; Uecker *et al.*, 1954; Munz and Tolor, 1955).

Most of the information concerning changes in and localization of intelligence following brain injury is of limited and doubtful value. Firstly, it is based on samples of cases which are not representative of the brain-damaged population; these samples are mainly frontal lobe cases. Secondly, those investigators who used controls failed to equate them adequately with their brain-damage cases on all relevant variables. Thirdly, those who compared pre- with post-operative performance based their estimates of changes in intelligence on abnormal scores of both assessments. Since the premorbid scores are unknown, such estimates are rendered doubtful by the extent to which brain injury or mental disorder might have affected the patient's performance before the operation or continued to affect it after. It is particularly difficult to assess changes after psychosurgery since post-operative alterations in mental disorders complicate the issue, e.g. reported improvements may, frequently, compensate for deficits which would have been evident as a result of surgically induced damage.

The best information concerning the problem of localization of intelligence is provided by Weinstein and Teuber (1957). The authors compared scores on a standardized test of intelligence (Army General Classification Test) obtained from patients with penetrating brain injuries, approximately ten years after they had been wounded, with corresponding scores achieved before the injury. Controls, who have sustained peripheral nerve injuries, were also included in this study and tested in the same way as the experimental group. The pre-injury mean scores of both groups were practically identical. The brain-injured sample was subdivided into groups according to the estimated location of their lesions and the results were submitted to analyses of variance. The findings indicated that the group with left parietal or left temporal lesions exhibited a significant decrease, but that this decrease was mainly a function of aphasic disturbances. The most striking decrease in intelligence was produced by the group with left parieto-temporal injury compared with all other groups and a loss was still demonstrable when the aphasics were excluded from this group.

The main criticism which can be directed against this excellent study is that the localization of lesions was tentative, and intelligence was "narrowly" assessed. The previously quoted investigations (Meyer, 1959; Meyer and Yates, 1955) compel caution in drawing conclusions with regard to intelligence level following brain injury if assessment is restricted to one type of I.Q. test; the authors demonstrated that general intelligence may remain relatively unimpaired if assessed on tests not involving the patient's specific disabilities.

In view of the evidence adduced which associates damage to certain areas of the brain with deficits of various specific abilities, one may wonder why brain-damaged cases are frequently unimpaired on such I.Q. tests as the Wechsler, which is composed of subtests involving a wide variety of specific abilities. The main reason is that the test was designed for the measurement of general intelligence and, in accordance with this aim, the subtests were selected as valid measures of this ability and, as such, intercorrelate highly. Various attempts to discriminate organics from non-organics by means of Wechsler subtests have been unsuccessful (Yates, 1954). Specialized tests, designed to detect subtle cognitive changes, have been more successful than the standardized, more general tests. In view of this, it is dangerous to conclude that a patient is unimpaired following brain injury if the I.Q. level remains unchanged. This point is well illustrated by Hebb (1939) and Meyer (1959, 1955).

As with the other specific functions which have been discussed, no one has conclusively established the dependence of general intelligence on any one part of the brain.

Conditioning, Learning and Retention

The proposition that modifications in behaviour depend upon modifications within the central nervous system (C.N.S.) is acceptable to most contemporary psychologists. A great many of the studies which have been concerned with the problem of neurological changes following modifications in behaviour and attempts have been made to establish the *locus* in the C.N.S. essential for conditioning and learning. We shall restrict our discussion to the problem of localization.

Most attempts at localization have been performed on animals. Various reviews of the literature (Osgood, 1953; Harlow, 1953; Teuber, 1955; Stellar, 1957; Morgan, 1951; Zeigler, 1957) indicate that the findings, despite relatively well-controlled experiments, have their limitations and do not permit firm conclusions to be drawn with regard to localization and the principles of cortical functioning.

Since very little is known about human material, it may be useful to present briefly the conclusions obtained from animal studies. According to Osgood (1953, pp. 474–494), it appears that cortical tissue is not necessary for conditioning, as the subcortical centres are capable of eliciting conditioned reactions. The evidence suggests that conditioned reactions are organized simultaneously in the cortex and the subcortical centres. The cortex, however, does seem to have facilitating and inhibitory effects upon subcortically organized mechanisms. It also appears that, on the afferent side, the *locus* of the modifications necessary for association to occur is subjacent to the peripheral receptive and projective systems. As regards the efferent side of association, it is not clear whether occurrence of motor response in conjunction with conditioned stimulus is sufficient condition for learning to take place, nor whether motor response is a necessary condition for formation of associations. Culler's (1938) experiment is of great importance since he provided some evidence for localization of a formed association. He traced electrically a small spot in the cortex of a dog which evoked a motor response, previously established by means of conditioning to an auditory stimulus. This spot did not have such effect before conditioning nor after extinction. Its *locus* was not in the sensory nor motor projection areas, but was formed in a bordering "association" area.

As regards simple learning tasks, the evidence suggests that other regions (probably subcortical) may act vicariously for the destroyed parts of the cortex, and the more difficult tasks appear to depend on the cortical areas since they cannot be relearned after ablation of the areas responsible for the original learning. Learning functions are progressively more dependent on the cortex, and are accompanied by increasingly strict localization (equipotentiality within limited areas) as we move up the phylogenetic scale with increased encephalization.

A considerable amount of work has been done on monkeys in an attempt to discover neural correlates of modifications in behaviour. Morell *et al.* (1956) investigated the effects of epileptogenic lesions on the establishment of conditioned EEG rhythms to visual, tactile and auditory stimuli. The results showed a marked impairment only in the conditioned stimulus that involved the sensory area in which the lesion was produced. A lesion in the amygdaloid region produced a more general impairment affecting the establishing of conditioned reflexes to both auditory and visual stimuli. A focus in the frontal cortex had no effect at all. It is interesting and puzzling that the subsequent excision of the discharging lesions resulted in normal capacity for the formation of conditioned responses.

Chow and Hutt (1953) concluded that the most noteworthy results following ablation of the association cortex in monkeys are: impairment of delayed reaction after removal of frontal cortex; deficits of visual discrimination after damage to the rostral part of the middle temporal gyrus; deficit in taste discrimination following removal of the fronto-temporal cortex and insula. Apart from that, some evidence indicated that less pronounced deficits of somaesthetic discrimination and conditioned reactions can be found as a result of damage to the frontal, temporal and parietal association cortex. The authors pointed out that, owing to various flaws in most studies, the findings are of doubtful value with respect to localization. The greatest difficulty lies in defining and distinguishing the association cortex from the projection cortex; for this reason, studies using ablation techniques need to exercise more rigorous anatomical control. Also, the investigations are wanting in statistical analysis of behavioural data and in careful analysis of the nature of impairments.

Recent interest in the role of the reticular activating system and the rhinencephalon stimulated attention to the investigations of subcortical structures. Very few studies have been reported and the findings are not consistent. Thus some workers (Chow, 1954; Peters *et al.*, 1956) failed to demonstrate impairment of various discriminations, delayed reactions, and conditioned reactions following lesions to thalamic association neuclei (pulvinar and medialis dorsalis). Others (Schreiner *et al.*, 1953; Pechtel *et al.*, 1955) showed that larger lesions in the medialis dorsalis of cats produced impairment in various simple learning tasks.

There is some evidence that different aspects of learning may be differentially localized. Thus subcortical stimulation of the septal region markedly enhanced the performance of cats and rats on learning tasks, as if the shock constituted a reward (Olds and Milner, 1954; Sidman et al., 1955). Not all the areas explored were rewarding. Negative reinforcement was demonstrated in cats where the fear evoked by stimulation of certain subcortical regions could be used to motivate avoidance behaviour (Delgado et al., 1954; Delgado, 1955). For a detailed and critical review of the studies of the psychophysiology of learning and motivation using electrical stimulation of the brain the reader may be referred to Zeigler (1957).

Human material provides more complex data. This is due to the limited possibility of experimenting on human beings, and the lack of control over the locus and extent of lesions; at the same time it is possible to test and to determine more precisely than in animals the nature of a defect in function in a species which can communicate verbally.

A number of studies have been concerned with eliciting quantitative and qualitative differences in motor and autonomic conditioned responses in organic and non-organic patients. Since their ultimate aim was to use any discovered differences for differential diagnostic purposes, they provide little information on localization and neural correlates related to these functions. The results of these studies have been briefly summarized elsewhere (Reese et al., 1953) and the authors concluded that patients with various intracranial pathologies show marked deficiencies in learning motor, autonomic, and discriminative conditioned responses.

In a study previously quoted (Morrell, 1956) Morrell investigated cortical functions involving the auditory system in patients with sharply localized temporal lobe foci and with clinical symptoms suggesting a temporal lobe origin. The results indicated that while there was a marked impairment in the ability to form a conditioned alpha response to a sound stimulus, the motor reaction-time in these patients was unimpaired to both the tone and tactile stimulus.

It has already been pointed out that studies concerning learning ability are wanting in a systematic assessment of this ability, and that the findings are equivocal. Some investigations have indicated that the learning of various tasks is a function of the brain as a whole (McFie and Piercy, 1952a; Battersby et al., 1955; Zangwill, 1946), is related to the size of lesion (McFie and Piercy, 1952a) and unrelated to sensory defects (Battersby et al., 1955). The present author (Meyer, 1956, 1959), on the other hand, has

demonstrated impairment of auditory learning following temporal lobectomy of the dominant side, and this impairment was unrelated to the size of the injury. No such deficit was found in the non-dominant cases. Also, no visual nor tactile learning deficits could be elicited after the operation, on either side. Ghent's et al. findings (1955b) complicate the issue further, demonstrating that, regardless of the locus of the lesion and regardless of whether there were sensory defects in the hand tested, only the hand contralateral to the injury was inferior in learning a tactual discrimination.

Clinical experience with brain-damaged subjects indicates that defective retention, particularly for recent events, is a common symptom. Very few objective studies concerning the status of memory have been reported. McFie and Piercy (1952a) concluded that their results tended to confirm the view that impairment of retention, like impairment of learning, is related to the size rather than to the locus of cerebral lesions. Some findings indicated that the inability to estimate the duration of time after preceeding practice did not seem to be related to lesions in any particular cerebral area (Guthrie et al., 1955b; Weider et al., 1955). Williams and Pennybacker (1954), on the other hand, reported that memory impairment was most common when the area surrounding the floor and walls of the third ventricle was disturbed. The studies previously discussed which were concerned with the functions of the temporal lobes, ascribed the greatest impairment of memory for recent events to the bilateral damage to this region of the brain.

The criticisms, previously directed against studies on learning, hold for investigations of memory. As regards the latter, the greatest weakness lies in the lack of control for different stages of the memory process. Several authors have noted that the notion of memory contains within it several stages or phases which can in fact be considered common to the memory process (Hull, 1917; Ingham, 1949; 1952; McGeoch and Irion, 1953, p. 6).

In its broadest sense the process of memory is commonly divided into three sections: the phase of acquisition of material (the learning phase), the phase of retention, and the phase of reproduction or recognition (Ingham, 1949; 1952). This division is, of course, artificial, since all learning involves retention. It is customary to speak about learning when a short time elapses between acquisition and reproduction, and about retention when the interval is longer. Before retention proper can be tested adequately, it is important that learning to a criterion be established in order that differences in rate of learning may be controlled. Hull (1917) showed that patients of various clinical groups were significantly inferior to normal controls in the acquisition of material, but when the acquisition was controlled, and material learned to a criterion by controls and patients, the patients were not inferior to controls in reproducing material after a one-week interval. Thus, these results suggest that the memory impairment found in various clinical groups is caused by failure in the acquisition phase rather than that it is due to failure in retention. This finding throws doubt on the validity of so-called memory tests where the acquisition phase is not controlled. In addition, Eysenck and Halstead (1945) demonstrated that the practice of testing memory by the usual clinical tests is unsound, and that these tests measure intelligence rather than memory.

It is clear from the foregoing discussion that no conclusions can be drawn with regard to localization and neural principles underlying conditioning, learning and retention.

Personality

Most information concerning localization of orectic factors in the brain is based on animal studies. Various subcortical areas have been associated with the control of various emotional and motive states (Stellar, 1954). The reticular activating system has been implicated not only in the control of consciousness (Delafresnaye, 1954), but also in the control of emotional behaviour (Lindsley, 1951). Some have emphasized the importance of the rhinencephalic system in emotion, particularly the limbic system and hippocampus (McLean, 1954).

It is sufficient to refer the reader to two brief reviews of the recent literature on this topic (Teuber, 1955; Sprague et al., 1955) to show that many of the findings are equivocal and that they do not allow clear orientation. The main weakness of these attempts at localization is, first, that the nature of the orectic traits is undefined; and second, that the assessment by the experimenter may not be valid or reliable.

Investigations of personality changes in human subjects following brain lesions and surgical interventions have been based mainly on projective tests. Such studies are of little value in solving the problem of localization and brain functioning in relation to personality factors. Firstly, most experimenters assumed implicitly that the brain functions in a "unitary" fashion and accordingly their samples of brain-damaged cases were selected without consideration of the nature of lesions or their localization. Secondly, the main aim of these studies was to derive "signs" which would differentiate organics from non-organics. Thirdly, no effort was made to establish the reliability of these signs and there is little evidence that such tests as the Rorschach can be regarded as reliable and valid measures of personality factors (Payne, 1955). See also Chapter 15 of this HANDBOOK.

The only work, known to the author, that attempted objectively to measure personality changes following various types of frontal lobe operations, suggested that various parts of the brain may be contributing differentially to the different personality factors (Petrie, 1952b, 1954; Le Beau and Petrie, 1953a, 1953b, 1953c; Petrie and Le Beau, 1956).

The personality changes were measured by objective psychological tests which are related to Eysenck's dimensions of personality (Eysenck, 1947, 1952).

The authors claimed that all convexity operations, i.e. complete standard leucotomy, partial rostral leucotomy and circumscribed selective surgery in the region of the convexity (Brodman's area 9 and 10) were followed by a decrease in introversion and neuroticism. The more extensive the operation the more pronounced the changes which ensue. The greatest decrements along these continua were shown after the standard leucotomy and the least pronounced changes resulted after the most circumscribed operation involving Brodman's areas 9 and 10. Cingulectomy, on the other hand, presented a different picture; there was no evidence of decreased introversion, but psychoticism decreased. Circumscribed excisions in the orbital region resulted in changes which were intermediate between those after the selective surgery of areas 9 and 10 and those after cingulectomy. All the above operations decreased neuroticism, but this change was least marked after cingulectomy.

A limited finding suggested that unilateral left-sided operations may produce a pattern of changes closer to the effects of bilateral operations than was produced by unilateral right-sided operations.

These findings are of great interest and would be more convincing if normal controls had been used and more detailed statistical analysis of the data carried out. As they stand, they suggest that different frontal operations result in differential changes of personality variables, but the dependence of these variables on any area of the brain has not been conclusively established.

CRITIQUE

The main reasons for the inconsistencies of psychological findings and for the failure to develop an acceptable theory of brain functioning have been discussed at some length by Hebb, (1945) and in *The Organization of Behavior*, pp. 275–289 (1949) and by the present author (Meyer, 1957), and brief references to some of these reasons have been made in the previous sections of this chapter. It may, however, be helpful to recapitulate the main points and to present additional points which have not been mentioned previously.

Localization of Lesions. Anatomical and Physiological Sources of Error

The main cause of the disappointing results of psychological studies are difficulties and errors in localizing lesions. Before the presence or absence of a psychological function can be ascribed to a particular region of the brain, the extent of anatomical destruction and physiological dysfunction produced by the lesion must be accurately delimited.

PATHOLOGICAL LESIONS

An anatomical injury to the brain, whether atrophic, neoplastic or traumatic, does not affect only the region of the brain tissue that it occupies, but it can also induce alterations in distant parts of the brain. This may occur either from contiguous cerebral oedema, from transfer of intracranial pressure, or from the disruption of connexions between anatomical centres (Dandy, 1933). Apart from that, pathologically affected tissue may interfere physiologically with normal cerebral functioning in neighbouring tissue. This may be due to chemical changes in pathological cells which result in an alteration of the pattern of cell action and which, in turn, may affect adversely neighbouring cells, or even the rest of the brain, through abnormal cerebral activity (synchronous activity) (Hebb, 1945).

Degenerative processes and vaso-spastic episodes are of little value in the problem of localizing functions since the former are widespread (Dandy, 1933) and the latter are typically transient.

Errors in localization can be reduced by data obtained from pneumo-encephalographic and electro-encephalographic studies. These data, however, are far from precise. The amount of error may be reduced by data derived from histological studies after necropsy. Such studies are of infrequent occurrence, and since "dead brains" are the subject of the examination, the deleterious physiological effects of the pathological tissue cannot be determined.

SURGICAL LESIONS

The errors in localizing these are fewer since the amount of outright destruction is known, but one can never be certain that the removal constitutes the only lesion. In the case of tumours the brain is frequently so much distorted that it is difficult to determine anatomically the extent of excision, and in addition distant effects may be present. The removal of even small well circumscribed lesions or epileptogenic foci, where there are no underlying macroscopic abnormalities, often results in post-operative trauma (scars, oedema); and also the above mentioned physiological changes may occur. In all probability, neighbouring tissue will, subsequently, be adversely affected, and so add somewhat to the total volume of tissue removed.

It can, therefore, be seen that, in order to draw precise conclusions with regard to the problem of localization of functions, it is essential to know whether disturbances are due to (a) anatomical destruction (or surgical removal) restricted to the region of the brain involved, (b) permanent change in the remaining part of the brain, (c) permanent physiological dysfunctions induced by pathology on neighbouring tissue, or (d) transient physiological disturbances. Such information is very rarely available.

Disregard of the possible Differential Effects Following Various Types of Lesions

Another source of inconsistent findings is the tendency to lump together cases with various types of lesions, or to use a sample of cases with one kind of brain pathology and to generalize from the findings obtained to brain damage in general. The evidence indicates that not only can different types of lesions in the same *locus* produce quite different results, but also that apparently similar lesions, with respect to the type, *locus* and size, may have dissimilar effects—

(a) Hebb emphasized that the presence of diseased tissue may be more productive of symptoms than the mere absence of cerebral tissue (1939). Several findings are consistent with this view (Roberts, 1951; Fox and German, 1935; Morrell *et al.*, 1956; Nielsen and Raney, 1939; Kreuger *et al.*, 1954).

(b) Most of the marked changes in intellectual functioning are apt to occur with cerebral neoplasm, but this is not essential to produce such deficits (Battersby, Krieger, Pollack and Bender, 1953).

(c) The size of a lesion or its concentration is not the only important factor in producing symptoms (Hebb, 1945) and lesions apparently similar in most respects may result in different disturbances (Dandy, 1933).

(d) Psychological deficits may vary in accordance with the length of time a lesion has existed. The importance of differences with respect to this factor has been stressed by some authors (Karl and Elvidge, 1955; Bailey, 1955), and it has been pointed out that inconsistencies in findings on some psychological tests may be attributed to vast differences in the samples used with regard to the nature and duration of lesions (Battersby, Bender and Teuber, 1951b; Teuber and Mishkin, 1954).

The findings reported by Forgays (1952*a*; 1952*b*) are of particular importance in this connexion. He showed that no loss of function was detected immediately after cerebral injury in man, and in the rat, but that some time later there were delayed disturbances, while a partial or complete recovery from deficits occurred in a few weeks' time without special training.

Individual Differences

Another possible source of error may be due to individual differences in anatomical, physiological, and psychological organization and functioning of the brain—

(*a*) It is well known that brains differ from individual to individual in size and weight. Such variations have been noted with regard to particular lobes.

(*b*) Investigations of the dominant temporal lobe functions by means of electrical stimulation and lobectomies of various size indicate variations in clinical, electrographic and psychological functions according to *locus* (Pampiglione and Falconer, 1956; Penfield and Rasmussen, 1950; Meyer, 1959; Falconer *et al.*, 1955; Penfield, 1954).

(*c*) According to Klebanoff (1954), the literature on brain-damaged children suggests that they show more diffuse effects than brain-damaged adults. This may be due to an incomplete differentiation and integration of the cerebral organization and psychological functioning in children. Thus, greater compensation can occur through maturation, whereas in adults damage usually produces more lasting effects. It will be remembered that Hebb (1949; 1942), on the other hand, maintains that a damage to the child's brain has much greater effect on subsequent generalized intellectual functioning than a similar injury to the adult brain.

(*d*) Considerable amount of evidence shows that right-handers and left-handers differ in the cortical organization for language functions, and that children resemble left-handers in this respect. The notion that aphasia results from lesions of the dominant hemisphere as is indicated by contra-lateral handedness is undisputed with regard to clear-cut right-handed adults, but in the case of left-handed adults, and in the case of children, this rule does not apply (Hécaen and Piercy, 1956; Humphrey and Zangwill, 1952; Goodglass and Quadfasel, 1954; Roberts, 1955; Etlinger *et al.*, 1956). On the whole, there are more left-brain speakers than right-handers (Goodglass and Quadfasel, 1954; Etlinger *et al.*, 1956). The incidence and the persistence of language disturbances following unilateral lesions in left-handed

adults and in children, compared with the incidence and persistence in right-handed adults, strongly suggests that the former individuals lack fully developed dominance or specialization of one hemisphere for language functions.

Apart from this, it appears that one type of aphasia may occur more frequently in left-handers and another type of aphasia may be more common in right-handers (Hécaen and Piercy, 1956). Also, there is no fixed laterality for all functions and the laterality for speech and handedness does not determine the laterality for other functions (Goodglass and Quadfasel, 1954).

(*e*) According to Nielsen (1946), the extent to which the non-dominant hemisphere can recover the lost activity of the dominant hemisphere depends on individual differences in age, general health, the suddenness with which the major side fails, and potential. The older the patient, the more sudden the failure, the poorer the general health, and the greater the potential for language functions in the major side, the lower the chances for recovery to take place.

(*f*) Nielsen (1946) has pointed out that it is possible to find two different individuals with apparently identical lesions, confined to precisely the same area, who will manifest dissimilar after-effects due to different methods of training in acquisition of a particular ability. Conversely, differently localized lesions in two different individuals may produce identical disturbances due to the different level of development and the usage of abilities and modalities.

(*g*) The magnitude and even the direction of the previously discussed verbal-performance discrepancy, associated with left- and right-hemisphere lesions, may depend on the constitutional predisposition to have one ability "higher" than the other, on the educational background, and on the age of a patient. For instance, it has been demonstrated that the level of vocabulary and the level of non-verbal reasoning ability increase and decrease at different rates with age (Foulds and Raven, 1948); also, the median difference between Performance and Verbal I.Q.s of the Wechsler test varies with age and with the levels of I.Q.s (Wechsler, 1944).

The evidence adduced above argues against classifying brain-damaged cases together indiscriminately, against treating them as a homogeneous group and accepting findings uncritically.

Difficulties and Errors in the Interpretation of Results

One of the greatest failings in psychological studies on localization of functions is the lack of appreciation of the complexity of the problem and the misuse of the terms and concepts referring to cortical regions and to the nature of the dependence of functions on cortical areas (Osgood, 1953, pp. 475–477).

(a) It must be realized that the various regions of the brain do not constitute functional subdivisions in any sense. The lobes were originally named after the cranial bones under which they lie and as such represent a crude anatomical classification (Bailey, 1955).

The hypothesis that structural differences are correlated with functional specialization has not been supported. Dissimilar psychological functions do not necessarily imply architectonic differences (Lashley and Clark, 1946). The main difficulty with this hypothesis is that while histological studies of the cerebral cortex are in general agreement and show certain areas to be different with respect to histological organization, attempts to subdivide these regions have resulted in many different maps and a cleavage of opinions on various problems (Scholl, 1956, pp. 11–28).

Theoretically speaking, a "functional region" would refer to an area of the brain within which various parts are equivalent with respect to functional specialization. Practicing neurologists refer to functional regions in this sense. (In passing, it can be seen that if one defines a functional region in this way, then Lashley's statement of principle, that within a functional region the cortical cells are equipotential, is tautological.) All that is known is that there are small portions of the cortex which are mainly associated with the arrival of sensory impulses and others which are mainly concerned with the initiation of motor impulses. No other functional specialization can be ascribed to the remaining parts of the cortex subdivided into lobes or on the basis of histological organization, and no functional regions, as defined above, have been conclusively determined.

(b) In attempts to ascribe the possession of certain behavioural characteristics to the integrity of a specific part of the brain the pertinence of Jackson's dictum: "To locate damage which destroys speech and to localize speech are two different things" (Jackson, 1932, p. 130) is often overlooked.

It is commonly agreed that a function is "localized" when its permanent loss follows upon the focal damage of some circumscribed area of the brain, but such evidence does not prove that this area is a component which in any sense "contains" this function, but merely shows that this part of the neural connexions is essential for the behaviour concerned to occur. It is not legitimate to argue that a behavioural characteristic is represented in a region, centre, or spot (Penfield, and Jasper, 1954,

p. 240). It is clear that when the term localization is defined in this way, no function has been conclusively localized. In the first place, complete loss of function has seldom been reported, and in the second, there is a great deal of evidence to show that the cortex has an immense capacity to recover. In this connexion one should bear in mind Jackson's doctrine of deficiency and release phenomena relevant to lesions of the central nervous system (Jackson, 1932)

(c) It is presumed that, when a function whose loss is demonstrated over varying intervals after well-defined, localized damage, can be recovered by retraining, the first area is not essential for this function and some other area can take over the lost function (vicarious functioning of one area for another).

In order to trace the region of vicarious functioning one would have to demonstrate that damage to another area eliminates the possibility of retraining. This inference about brain functioning has been drawn from animal studies and there is no experimental evidence derived from human material either to support it or to reject it. It appears that language functions can be taken over by the non-dominant hemisphere, but such transfer does not occur as a rule, and there is little evidence of true substitution of function in the right hemisphere (Nielsen, 1946).

(d) If no loss of a given function can be elicited following an injury, it does not necessarily imply that this function is completely independent of the injured area. The function may be simultaneously organized in another area (replication of function), hence an injury to either region does not result in a loss. To show that the function is replicated one would require to demonstrate that damage to both regions results in a loss of the function. Here again, there is lack of experimental evidence from human material to support this inference.

(e) If the possibility of equipotentiality and mass action is to be verified, the *locus* and magnitude of the damage should be deliberately varied from subject to subject. Such experimental data from human subjects are lacking.

(f) Further difficulty in the experimental analysis of cerebral mechanisms arises from the fact that some functions, initially lost, particularly after lesions of sudden onset, manifest spontaneous recovery.

According to the theory of diaschisis (Monakow, 1914) a damaged area, not essential for a certain function, may withdraw facilitation from some other cortical or subcortical region, and so result in inadequate functioning of these regions. It is assumed that the area subject to the effects of diaschisis recovers in time and the lost function reappears spontaneously without training. Forgays's results (1952a; 1952b) appear to support the plausibility of this theory. He argued that the delayed disturbances could not be explained by the loss of cerebral tissue nor could the recovery take place through vicarious functioning. The deficits were most probably due to secondary pathological changes produced by the original injury. This study clearly illustrates that in order to arrive at valid experimental analysis of cerebral mechanisms, longitudinal assessment should be carried out and that one must make sure that no retraining has occurred between the testing periods.

It can be seen, therefore, that the complexity of the problem requires a rigorous experimental approach. Studies on human material do not show such an approach and most of the conclusions are not warranted by the data.

Flaws in Psychological Studies

CONTROLS

One of the most serious weaknesses in psychological investigations is the lack or misuse of control data. The premorbid level of psychological abilities is very rarely known; therefore, in order to detect the defective performance of a brain-damaged subject one requires data from normal controls. Evidence has been adduced to show that it is particularly dangerous to use unstandardized tests and to assume a "norm" for the normal population (Hebb, 1945; Pearson and Alpers, 1928; Shapiro and Nelson, 1955).

The nature of the problem under investigation determines what kind of controls are required. If the purpose is to determine the effects of a brain injury on a psychological test one must establish the level of performance on this test for normal subjects. Even if the aim is to assess the effects of a brain operation, normal controls must be tested and retested in the same way as patients, since the conditions, for which patients are being operated on, affect their pre-operative scores. Apart from that, test-retest data on normal subjects are essential for the adequate evaluation of results. If one wishes to find out whether one kind of injury is more effective than another in producing deficits, one must use clinical controls in addition to normal controls. Here again, the problem will determine what brain-damaged controls are needed. Those who study localization of functions and who design brain-damage tests must include a representative sample of brain-damaged population and normal controls; in the latter type of study psychiatric clinical groups should also be included.

Whatever controls are being used must be equated on any variable which might affect the test scores under investigation. The importance of the age factor is obvious, since various mental abilities decline with age (Gilbert, 1935; Wechsler, 1944; Shaie et al., 1953; Strother et al., 1957). Differences in intelligence can affect performance on various tasks differentially (Boyd, 1949; Beech, 1957). Beech (1957) reported that performance on a perceptual task was radically changed when allowance was made for the initial differences in intelligence. Also, the more intelligent brain-damaged patients were able to compensate for disabilities.

Other relevant factors have been referred to in the previous sections of the chapter.

NATURE OF DEFICITS

Most conclusions with regard to the effect of brain injuries or localization of functions are of doubtful value, since investigators have been preoccupied with demonstrating test deficits and ascribing them to specific lesions in given areas without proceeding to the analysis of the altered functions. As Teuber (1955) pointed out, the tendency is to stop when the "where" is discovered and the question of "what" to localize is left unanswered.

It must be realized that psychological tests are not pure measures of ability. Many of them involve primary motor and sensory functions and a variety of higher mental abilities difficult to define. Thus, performance on a test may be disrupted by cerebral lesions in different parts of the brain for different reasons (Zangwill, 1954; Williams and Pennybacker, 1954). Differently localized lesions may selectively impair different abilities involved in a test. To discover the "whereabouts" of localization, in the sense of damage to tissue disrupting test performance, cannot be regarded as a substitute for the analysis of abilities involved in test performance (Teuber and Weinstein, 1954). If the nature of a deficit is not precisely defined by a careful investigation, the only valid conclusion is that a lesion produces some complex dysfunction resulting in impairment on a test.

In order to determine why a patient failed on a test, or "what" to localize, one must analyse the nature of a deficit, taking into consideration any behavioural aspect which might affect test performance. There is evidence to show that if a test deficit is not analysed, wrong conclusions can be drawn with regard to the nature of impairment (Meyer and Yates, 1955; Semmes et al., 1955; Meyer 1959) and with regard to localization (Weinstein, et al., 1956). Several investigators indicate that impairments on various tasks may be related to various concomitant alterations of functions, e.g. somato-sensory (Weinstein, 1954; Weinstein et al., 1955; Weinstein, 1955a; Ghent et al., 1955a), aphasia (Weinstein et al., 1955; Teuber and Weinstein, 1956;

Meyer, 1959), and epilepsy (Ghent *et al.*, 1955*a*). Teuber's critical discussion (1955) of some animal and human studies shows that impairments following lesions in primary projection systems and so-called "association" areas are misleading as descriptions of the nature of underlying dysfunctions. He points out that one form of proof required to distinguish between, for example, a "hierarchy of functions" and "separate localization" needs the demonstration of a "double dissociation." Thus, it would have to be shown that, (*a*) one lesion might cause disturbance of a specific function in one modality without affecting this function as it is executed in other modalities; (*b*) that another lesion could disrupt the same function in other modalities without affecting its execution through the first.

EMPIRICAL APPROACH

The most common approach to the problem of brain damage is an empirical one. Such an approach is insensitive in the detection of deficits and in clarifying their nature. The lack of any hypothesis prevents the investigator from making deductions, constructing specific tests or using adequate experimental methods.

The literature on brain damage is abundant in information which can lead, if not to clear-cut hypotheses, at least to certain broad expectations.

STATISTICAL ANALYSIS

Frequently reports are inadequate in so far as the need for statistical tests of significance is ignored.

Concept of Brain Damage

Before the characteristics of any group can be explored, the criteria for the selection of the group must be clearly defined. It is commonly agreed that the only criterion of importance which determines whether or not a person is brain-damaged is the absence of cerebral tissue or the presence of pathological tissue. While such a definition is acceptable since it decides which people are brain-damaged, it has certain serious limitations. These have been thoroughly discussed elsewhere (Meyer, 1957) and only the salient points will be mentioned here—

(*a*) It must be realized that in the majority of cases pathology of the brain can only be inferred indirectly by various techniques. Each discipline has a specific concept of brain damage limited by the nature of its investigatory technique. The validity of diagnosis derived from each discipline is far from being perfect and the correspondence as to diagnosis is not very high. Psychologists rely on a final neurological diagnosis when selecting cases for investigation; this partly explains why psychological tests of brain damage show such a high degree of misclassification.

(*b*) As applied clinically, the definition given above has a descriptive, classificatory connotation without diagnostic implication. It groups together indiscriminately a vast variety of patients. The clinician is interested in diagnosis which implies aetiology, nature, *locus* of lesion, and prognosis.

(*c*) It refers in its scope to people with brain pathologies only and does not have regard to symptoms. Clinical knowledge of brain-damage cases and the test results characterizing them refer to cases with brain pathologies and symptoms.

(*d*) The emphasis on the importance of brain pathology as the only factor in producing symptoms is no longer fully acceptable. A high proportion of the "normal population" manifests certain abnormalities indicative of brain pathology (Busse *et al.*, 1956; Hill and Watterson, 1942; Williams, 1941). Certain pathologies have been shown to be neither the sole cause nor the sufficient condition for obtaining certain modifications of behaviour (Battersby *et al.*, 1956; Rothschild, 1945; Crome, 1955).

(*e*) The original definition implies a dichotomous qualitative difference between persons with and without brain pathology. In view of the fact that as the techniques and methods of ascertaining brain pathologies improve more cases are found to exhibit changes (Pampiglione and Kerridge, 1956), it is possible that eventually the alternative view of continuity based on quantitative differences will have to be accepted. Such a view has been expressed with regard to psychiatric diagnosis (Eysenck, 1955*c*).

(*f*) Since it is possible that brain pathology *per se* is not a relevant factor, and since it may not be a qualitatively differentiating variable, there is no point in attempting to ascertain its presence or absence alone. Instead, one should attempt to estimate its amount and to discover to what extent anatomic factors and, as Rothschild says (1945), "broader biologic or more personal factors" contribute to the appearance of symptoms.

CONCLUSIONS AND SUGGESTIONS FOR A MORE FRUITFUL APPROACH

The evidence presented does not enable this survey to be concluded with a clear-cut statement of definite principles with regard to brain functioning and organization. Neither the strictly "departmental" nor the strictly "unitary" views in their present form have been conclusively supported by experimental data. One finds the greatest support for the theory of "regional equipotentiality" in many psychological functions, but no one has conclusively and precisely established the dependence of any function on any brain region.

The field is abundant in isolated and disconnected studies which do not permit clear orientation. Closer examination reveals that frequent inconsistencies and contradictions may be only apparent and may be correctly interpreted as divergent findings which are due to differences in the samples used with regard to such factors as age of patients, age and type of injury and precise *locus* of lesions. They may be due also to the different tests, testing procedures and evaluation techniques. Various discrepancies, in fact, themselves suggest further lines of research which would throw light on the relevance of various factors.

The perennial controversy between the specific and general effects of lesions has not been settled conclusively. It may be that some general effects reported (Battersby, Krieger and Bender, 1953; Battersby, Krieger, Pollack and Bender, 1953; Bauer and Becka, 1954; Semmes *et al.*, 1954; Battersby *et al.*, 1955; Guthrie *et al.*, 1955a, 1955b; Weider *et al.*, 1955; Ghent *et al.*, 1955a; Teuber and Weinstein, 1956) are due to the complexity of the tasks employed. Adequate test performance depends on a number of different functions; any lesion may lead to a significant test impairment through disturbance of any of the functions involved in a test and for different reasons. Conversely, some underlying generalized effect may account partly for the appearance of specific effects. At the present stage of knowledge, exclusive preference should not be given to the notion either of general or of specific effects, since the nature of deficits has not been analysed (Teuber, 1955; Teuber and Weinstein, 1956).

A similar controversy between "specificity" and "generality" once prevailed in the field of intelligence and personality testing. The evidence based on factorial analysis supports a hierarchical view of cognitive factors (Vernon, 1950) and personality factors (Eysenck, 1947; 1952). It is plausible to postulate then that the functioning of the brain is also arranged in a hierarchical way. This view is supported by results, reported by Teuber and Weinstein (1955), which present a hierarchical finding for visual performance. Lesions which produce focal changes within the visual system also affect certain functions throughout this system, and the latter alterations are accompanied by more general deficits which occur irrespective of the *locus* of injury.

It is the writer's opinion that the first question to be answered is to what degree the effects of brain lesions are general and to what degree specific. Careful study of correlations between behavioural and neurological facts is both essential and basic to the development of a psychological theory of brain

functioning. This could be achieved by a study which would include a representative sample of brain-damaged patients and a sample of normal controls. The brain-damaged group should be given a large battery of tests which are known to be measures of well-defined orectic and cognitive factors. The results should be submitted to factorial analysis. In the next stage, more refined tests designed to assess the extracted factors should be administered to both the organic and the normal control groups. The results should be submitted to analysis of variance and the performance of each subgroup (subdivided according to the *locus* of the lesion) should be analysed in relation to those of the controls and of a complementary subgroup consisting, in each case, of the remainder of the brain-damaged group. Similar studies should be carried out on children of various age levels in order to define the nature of developmental aspects of brain organization and functioning. The use of large groups with variously localized lesions and the employment of statistical analysis will to some extent overcome the difficulty in the precise localization of lesions. In a number of studies, in an attempt to localize various functions, analysis of variance technique has been employed (Battersby *et al.*, 1955; Teuber and Weinstein, 1954; Semmes *et al.*, 1954; Weinstein and Teuber, 1957; Teuber and Weinstein, 1956; Semmes *et al.*, 1955; Weinstein *et al.*, 1956).

However, it would not be sufficient to stop at mere correlations and the research should proceed to clarify their significance. This would require an extensive and intensive study of the nature of each significant association between factors and *loci* of damage, controlling for all the relevant variables including the neurological mechanisms responsible for the negative and positive properties of functions. Such an approach would throw light on the nature of normal behaviour in the intact organism and it would also bring about co-ordination between neurology and psychology. What is most important, it would permit the development of a precise psychological theory on the basis of which sensitive diagnostic tests of brain damage could be constructed. Attempts to construct diagnostic tools at the present stage of knowledge are premature and doomed to failure. Eysenck (1955b; 1957) has demonstrated, in the field of personality, how an intensive study of statistically derived personality factors can be used to enable one to arrive at an explanatory theory to account for their existence.

It would appear that the clinical psychologist's contributions to the everyday problems of a clinic must be minimal if he lacks proper diagnostic tools, but the psychologist should never stress the diagnostic aspect of his work *alone*. Although the discovery of a lesion and its *locus* has important bearings on diagnostic and prognostic implications, in itself it does not explain the appearance of symptoms or elucidate the neurological mechanisms responsible for such behaviour (Skinner, 1938, p. 424).

The psychologist's main aim, as a student of behaviour, is to detect deficiencies, formulate explanations to account for them, and to test the deductions arising from his explanations. Such a method of investigation would lead to a thorough understanding of the patient's abnormality and, with the information available, an attempt could be made to retrain the patient. Such an approach has been applied to individual psychiatric cases (Shapiro and Nelson, 1955; Shapiro, 1951b; Payne, 1953). Some workers have demonstrated that brain-damaged patients are not necessarily passive carriers of morbid anatomical processes which have irreversible consequences; using acceptable theories to account for an abnormality, they designed successful treatment techniques (Schuell, 1953; Schuell et al., 1955; Birch and Lee, 1955; Efron, 1957).

Some of the clinical psychologist's findings will provide data for further fundamental research, and some of his results will be incorporated in the development of the theory of brain organization and functioning; but no matter how far fundamental research progresses, the clinical approach to individual cases is still likely to be of value. There are subtle individual differences which will still necessitate careful and precise investigation of each case on its own merit for the purposes of treatment and disposal.

In all types of work the clinical psychologist must bear in mind that, as in fundamental research, he will be of use precisely to the extent to which he can bring his training in scientific method and his knowledge of psychological principles to bear on the problems of the clinic.

REFERENCES

AITA, J. A., ARMITAGE, S. G., REITAN, R. M. and RABINO-WITZ, A., The use of psychological tests in the evaluation of brain injury, J. Gen. Psychol., 37, 25–44 (1947).

ANDERSON, A. L., The effect of laterality localization of focal brain lesions on the Wechsler-Bellevue subtests, J. Clin. Psychol., 7, 149–153 (1951).

ARMITAGE, S. G., An analysis of certain psychological tests used for the evaluation of brain injury, Psychol. Monogr., 60, No. 1, whole No. 277 (1946).

ARNOT, R., A theory of frontal lobe functions, Arch. Neurol. Psychiat. Chicago, 67, 487–495 (1952).

BAILEY, P., Discussion on papers on the temporal lobe in "Symposium on the temporal lobe," Arch. Neurol. Psychiat. Chicago, 74, 568–569 (1955).

BALLES, M. and GOLDSTEIN, K., A study of the impairment of "abstract behaviour" in schizophrenic patients, Psychiat. Quart., 12, 42–65 (1938).

BATTERSBY, W. S., The regional gradient of cortical flicker frequency after frontal or occipital injury, J. Exp. Psychol., 42, 59–68 (1951).

BATTERSBY, W. S., BENDER. M. B., POLLACK, M. and KAHN, R. L., Unilateral spatial agnosia (inattention), Brain, 79, 68–93 (1956).

BATTERSBY, W. S., BENDER, M. B. and TEUBER, H. L., Effects of total light flux on cortical flicker frequency after frontal lobe lesion, J. Exp. Psychol., 42, 135–142 (1951).

BATTERSBY, W. S., KRIEGER, H. P. and BENDER, M. B., The visual and tactile discrimination of complex stimuli by patients with cerebral neoplasm, Trans. Amer. Neurol. Ass., 78, 224–227 (1953).

BATTERSBY, W. S., KRIEGER, H. P. and BENDER, M. B., Visual and tactile discriminative learning in patients with cerebral tumors, Amer. J. Psychol., 68, 562–574 (1955).

BATTERSBY, W. S., KRIEGER, H. P., POLLACK, M. and BENDER, M. B., Figure-ground discrimination and the "abstract attitude" in patients with cerebral tumours, Arch. Neurol. Psychiat. Chicago, 70, 703–712 (1953).

BATTERSBY, W. S., TEUBER, H. L. and BENDER, M. B., Problem solving behaviour in men with frontal or occipital brain injuries, J. Psychol., 35, 329–351 (1953).

BAUER, R. and BECKA, D., Intellect after cerebro-vascular accident, J. Nerv. Ment. Dis., 120, 379–384 (1954).

BEECH, H. R., An investigation of the performance on a perceptual-motor task by psychiatric patients with special reference to brain-damage, Unpubl. Ph.D. Thesis, Univ. of London Lib. (1957).

BENDER, M. B. and TEUBER, H. L., Spatial organization of visual perception following injury to the brain, Arch. Neurol. Psychiat. Chicago, 58, 721–739 (1947).

BENDER, M. B. and TEUBER, H. L., Disturbances in visual perception following cerebral lesions, J. Psychol., 28, 223–233 (1949).

BENDER, M. B., TEUBER, H. L. and BATTERSBY, W. S., Discrimination of weights by men with penetrating lesions of parietal lobes, Trans. Amer. Neurol. Ass., 75, 252–255 (1950).

BENDER, M. B., TEUBER, H. L. and BATTERSBY, W. S., Visual field defects after gunshot wounds of higher visual pathways, Trans. Amer. Neurol. Ass., 76, 192–194 (1951).

BIRCH, H. G. and LEE, JOAN, Cortical inhibition in expressive aphasia, Arch. Neurol. Psychiat. Chicago, 54, 514–517 (1955).

BORING, E. G., A History of Experimental Psychology (New York, Appleton-Century-Crofts, 1950).

BOYCOTT, B. B. and YOUNG, J. Z., A memory system in Octopus vulgaris Lamarck, Proc. Roy. Soc., 143, 449–480 (1955).

BOYD, H. F., A provisional quantitative scoring with preliminary norms for the Goldstein-Sheerer Cube Test, J. Clin. Psychol., 5, 148–153 (1949).

BRENNER, MAY W., Continuous stimulation and apparent movement, Amer. J. Psychol., 66, 494–495 (1953).

BRENNER, MAY W., The effects of brain damage on the perception of apparent movement, J. Personality, 25, 202–211 (1956).

BRICKNER, R. M., The Intellectual Functions of the Frontal Lobes: A Study Based upon Observations of a Man after Partial Bilateral Frontal Lobectomy (New York, Macmillan, 1936).

BROWN, I., Abstract and concrete behavior of dysphasic

patients and normal subjects, *J. Speech Dis.*, **20**, 35–42 (1955).

BUSSE, E. W., BARNES, R. H., FRIEDMAN, E. L. and KELLY, E. J., Psychological functioning of aged individuals with normal and abnormal electroencephalograms, *J. Nerv. Ment. Dis.*, **124**, 135–141 (1956).

CATTELL, R. B., The measurement of adult intelligence, *Psychol. Bull.*, **40**, 153–193 (1943).

CHAPMAN, L. F., SYMMES, D. and HALSTEAD, W. C., Auditory flutter fusion in patients with cortical ablations, *J. Comp. Physiol. Psychol.*, **48**, 421–425 (1955).

CHOW, K. L., Lack of behavioral effects following destruction of some thalamic association neuclei in monkey, *Arch. Neurol. Psychiat. Chicago*, **71**, 762–771 (1954).

CHOW, K. L. and HUTT, P. J., The "association cortex" of *Macaca mulata*: A review of recent contributions to its anatomy and functions, *Brain*, **76**, 625–677 (1953).

CONRAD, K., New problems of aphasia, *Brain*, **77**, 491–509 (1954).

CRITCHLEY, M., *The Parietal Lobes* (London, Arnold & Co., 1953).

CROME, L., A morphological critique of temporal lobectomy, *Lancet*, **1**, 882–884 (1955).

CROWN, S., Psychological changes following prefrontal leucotomy: a review, *J. Ment. Sci.*, **97**, 49–83 (1951).

CROWN, S., Psychological changes following operations on the frontal lobes, *J. Cons. Psychol.*, **17**, 92–99 (1953).

CULLER, E. A., Observations on direct cortical stimulation in the dog, *Psychol. Bull.*, **35**, 687–688 (1938).

CUSHING, H., A note upon the faradic stimulation of the post central gyrus in conscious patients, *Brain*, **32**, 44–53 (1909).

DANDY, W. E., Physiological studies following extirpation of the right cerebral hemisphere in man, *Johns Hopk. Hosp. Bull.*, **53**, 31–51 (1933).

DEATHERAGE, B. H. and BITTERMAN, M. E., The effects of satiation on stroboscopic movement, *Amer. J. Psychol.*, **65**, 108–109 (1952).

DELAFRESNAYE, J. F. (Ed.), *Brain Mechanisms and Consciousness* (Springfield, Ill., C. C. Thomas, 1954).

DELGADO, J. M. R., Cerebral structures involved in transmission and elaboration of noxious stimulation, *J. Neurophysiol.*, **18**, 261–275 (1955).

DELGADO, J. M. R., ROBERTS, W. W. and MILLER, N. E., Learning motivated by electrical stimulation of the brain, *Amer. J. Physiol.*, **179**, 587–593 (1954).

DENNY-BROWN, D., Disintegration of motor function resulting from cerebral lesions, *J. Nerv. Ment. Dis.*, **112**, 1–45 (1950).

DUNCAN, C. P., The retroactive effect of electroshock on learning, *J. Comp. Physiol. Psychol.*, **42**, 32–44 (1949).

EFRON, R., The conditioned inhibition of uncinate fits, *Brain*, **80**, 251–262 (1957).

ELITHORN, A., A preliminary report on a perceptual maze test sensitive to brain damage, *J. Neurol. Psychiat.*, **18**, 287–292 (1955).

ETTLINGER, G., JACKSON, C. V. and ZANGWILL, O. L., Cerebral dominance in sinistrals, *Brain*, **79**, 569–588 (1956).

ETTLINGER, G., WARRINGTON, ELIZABETH and ZANGWILL, O. L., A further study of visual-spatial agnosia, *Brain*, **80**, 335–361 (1957).

EYSENCK, H. J., *Dimensions of Personality* (London, Routledge & Kegan Paul, 1947).

EYSENCK, H. J., *The Scientific Study of Personality* (London, Routledge & Kegan Paul, 1952).

EYSENCK, H. J., Cortical inhibition, figural after effect, and theory of personality, *J. Abnorm. (Soc.) Psychol.*, **51**, 94–106 (1955*a*).

EYSENCK, H. J., A dynamic theory of anxiety and hysteria, *J. Ment. Sci.*, **101**, 28–51 (1955*b*).

EYSENCK, H. J., Psychiatric diagnosis as a psychological and statistical problem, *Psychol. Rep.*, **1**, 3–17 (1955*c*).

EYSENCK, H. J., *Dynamics of Anxiety and Hysteria* (London, Routledge & Kegan Paul, 1957).

EYSENCK, H. J. and HALSTEAD, B. A., The memory function: I. A factorial study of fifteen clinical tests, *Amer. J. Psychiat.*, **102**, 174–180 (1945).

FALCONER, M. A., HILL, D., MEYER, A., MITCHELL, W. and POND, D. A., Treatment of temporal-lobe epilepsy by temporal lobectomy, *Lancet*, **1**, 827–835 (1955).

FERRIER, D., Experimental researches in cerebral physiology and pathology, *West Riding Lunatic Asylum Med. Rep.*, **3**, 1–50 (1873).

FLOURENS, M. J. P., *Recherches expérimentales sur les propriétés et les fonctions du système nerveux dans les animaux vertébrés* (Paris, Crevot, 1824).

FORGAYS, D. G., Reversible disturbances of function in man following cortical insult, *J. Comp. Physiol. Psychol.*, **45**, 209–215 (1952*a*).

FORGAYS, D. G., Reversible disturbances of function in rats following cortical insult, *J. Comp. Physiol. Psychol.*, **45**, 216–225 (1952*b*).

FOULDS, M. A. and RAVEN, J. C., Normal changes in the mental abilities of adults as age advances, *J. Ment. Sci.*, **94**, 133–142 (1948).

FOX, C. J. and GERMAN, W. J., Observations following left (dominant) temporal lobectomy, *Arch. Neurol. Psychiat. Chicago*, **33**, 791–806 (1935).

FREEMAN, W. and WATTS, J. W., *Psychosurgery: Intelligence, Emotion and Social Behavior Following Prefrontal Lobectomy for Mental Disorders* (Springfield, Ill., C. C. Thomas, 1942).

FREEMAN, W. and WATTS, J. W., Frontal lobe functions as revealed by psychosurgery, *Digest Neurol. Psychiat. Inst. Living*, **16**, 62–68 (1948).

FRITSCH, G. and HITZIG, E., Über die elektrische Erregbarkeit des Grosshirns, *Arch. Anat. Physiol. Lpz.*, 300–332 (1870).

FULTON, J. F., *Howell's Textbook of Physiology* (Philadelphia and London, Saunders, 15th edn, 1947).

GALL, F. J., *Cerveau. Dictionnaire des Sciences Médicales*, **4**, 447–479 (1813).

GERSTMAN, J., Syndrome of finger agnosia, disorientation for right and left, agraphia and acalculia, *Arch. Neurol. Psychiat. Chicago*, **44**, 398–408 (1940).

GHENT, LILA, SEMMES, JOSEPHINE, WEINSTEIN, S. and TEUBER, H. L., Tactile discrimination after unilateral brain injury in man, *Amer. Psychologist*, **10**, 408, abstract (1955*a*).

GHENT, LILA, WEINSTEIN, S., SEMMES, JOSEPHINE and TEUBER, H. L., Effect of unilateral brain injury in man on learning of a tactual discrimination, *J. Comp. Physiol. Psychol.*, **48**, 478–481 (1955*b*).

GILBERT, JEANNE, Mental efficiency in senescence, *Arch. Psychol. N.Y.*, No. 188 (1935).

GOLDSTEIN, K., The problem of the meaning of words based upon observation of aphasic patients, *J. Psychol.*, **2**, 301–316 (1936).

GOLDSTEIN, K., *The Organizm* (New York, American Book Co., 1939).

GOLDSTEIN, K., The mental changes due to frontal lobe damage, *J. Psychol.*, **17**, 187–208 (1944).

GOLDSTEIN, K., *Language and Language Disturbances* (New York, Grune & Stratton, 1948).

GOLDSTEIN, K. and SHEERER, M., Abstract and concrete behavior. An experimental study with special tests, *Psychol. Monogr.*, **53**, No. 2, Whole No. 239 (1941).

GOODGLASS, H. and QUADFASEL, F. A., Language laterality in left-handed aphasics, *Brain*, **77**, 521–548 (1954).

GRASSI, J. R., *The Grassi Block Substitution Test for Measuring Organic Brain Pathology* (Springfield, Ill., C. C. Thomas, 1953).

GUTHRIE, T. C., BERLIN, L., WEIDER, A., GOODELL, H. and WOLF, H. G., Studies on human cerebral functions: The capacity to terminate an adaptive pattern when it is no longer appropriate, *Trans. Amer. Neurol. Ass.*, **80**, 70–72 (1955*a*).

GUTHRIE, T. C., WEIDER, A., GOODELL, H., BERLIN, L. and WOLFF, H., Studies on human cerebral function: The capacity for retention as measured by the ability to estimate ten seconds, *Trans. Amer. Neurol. Ass.*, **80**, 201–202 (1955*b*).

HALSTEAD, W. C., Preliminary analysis of grouping behaviour in patients with cerebral injury by the method of equivalent and non-equivalent stimuli, *Amer. J. Psychiat.*, **96**, 1,263–1,294 (1940).

HALSTEAD, W. C., *Brain and Intelligence. A Quantitative Study of the Frontal Lobes* (Chicago, Univ. of Chicago Press, 1947).

HALSTEAD, W. C., Some fronto-temporal lobe relationships in "Symposium on the temporal lobe," *Arch. Neurol. Psychiat. Chicago*, **74**, 567 (1955).

HALSTEAD, W. C. and SHURE, G., Further evidence for a frontal lobe component in human biological intelligence, *Trans. Amer. Neurol. Ass.*, **79**, 9–11 (1954).

HARLOW, H. F., Higher functions of the nervous system, *Annu. Rev. Physiol.*, **15**, 493–514 (1953).

HEAD, H., *Aphasia and Kindred Disorders of Speech* (London, Macmillan, 1926).

HEBB, D. O., Intelligence in man after large removals of cerebral tissue; report on four left frontal lobe cases, *J. Gen. Psychol.*, **21**, 73–87 (1939*a*).

HEBB, D. O., Intelligence in man after large removals of cerebral tissue: defects following right temporal lobectomy, *J. Gen. Psychol.*, **21**, 437–446 (1939*b*).

HEBB, D. O., Human intelligence after removal of cerebral tissue from the right frontal lobe, *J. Gen. Psychol.*, **25**, 257–265 (1941).

HEBB, D. O., The effects of early and late brain injury upon test scores and nature of normal intelligence, *Proc. Amer. Phil. Soc.*, **85**, 275–292 (1942).

HEBB, D. O., Man's frontal lobes. A critical review, *Arch. Neurol. Psychiat. Chicago*, **54**, 10–24 (1945).

HEBB, D. O., *The Organization of Behavior. A Neuro-psychological Theory* (New York, John Wiley & Sons, Inc., 1949).

HEBB, D. O. and PENFIELD, W., Human behaviour after extensive bilateral removal from the frontal lobes, *Arch. Neurol. Psychiat. Chicago*, **44**, 421–438 (1940).

HÉCAEN, H. and PIERCY, M., Paroxysmal dysphasia and the problem of cerebral dominance, *J. Neurol. Psychiat.*, **19**, 194–201 (1956).

HÉCAEN, H., PENFIELD, W., BERTRAND, C. and MALMO, R., The syndrome of apractognosia due to lesions of the minor cerebral hemisphere, *Arch. Neurol. Psychiat. Chicago*, **75**, 400–434 (1956).

HEILBRUN, A. B., Psychological test performance as a function of lateral localization of cerebral lesion, *J. Comp. Physiol. Psychol.*, **49**, 10–14 (1956).

HENSCHEN, S. E., *Kleinische und Anatomische Beiträge zur Pathologie des Gehirns* (Stockholm, Nordiska Bokhandeln, 1920–1922).

HILL, D. and WATTERSON, D., Electro-encephalographic studies of psychopathic personalities, *J. Neurol. Psychiat.*, **5**, 47–65 (1942).

HOWARTH, E., Three experiments concerning the Köhler and Wallach hypothesis, *Aust. J. Psychol.*, **9**, 12–19 (1957).

HULL, C. L., The formation and retention of associations among the insane, *Amer. J. Psychol.*, **28**, 419–435 (1917).

HULL, C. L., *Principles of Behavior* (New York, Appleton-Century, 1943).

HUMPHREY, M. E. and ZANGWILL, O. L., Dysphasia in left-handed patients with unilateral brain lesions, *J. Neurol. Psychiat.*, **15**, 184–193 (1952).

HUNTER, W. S., A consideration of Lashley's theory of equipotentiality of cerebral action, *J. Gen. Psychol.*, **3**, 455–468 (1930).

HUTTON, E. L. and BASSETT, M., The effect of leucotomy on creative personality, *J. Ment. Sci.*, **94**, 332–350 (1948).

INGHAM, J. G., An investigation into the relationship between memory and intelligence, *Unpubl. Ph.D. Thesis, Univ. of London Lib.* (1949).

INGHAM, J. G., Memory and intelligence, *Brit. J. Psychol.*, **43**, 20–31 (1952).

INGLIS, J., An experimental study of learning and "memory function" in elderly psychiatric patients, *J. Ment. Sci.*, **103**, 796–803 (1957).

JACKSON, J. H., *Selected Writings of John Hughlings Jackson*, Vol. 2, Ed. J. Taylor (London, Hodder & Stoughton, 1932).

JAFFE, R., Kinesthetic after-effects following cerebral lesions, *Amer. J. Psychol.*, **67**, 668–675 (1954).

JAFFE, R., Tactile adaptation disturbances in lesions of the nervous system, *Arch. Neurol. Psychiat. Chicago*, **73**, 57–65 (1955).

KARL, V. A. and ELVIDGE, A. R., Four years' experience with prefrontal lobotomy, *Amer. J. Psychiat.*, **112**, 375–381 (1955).

KENNEDY, F. and WOLF, A., The relationship of intellect to speech defect in aphasic patients, *J. Nerv. Ment. Dis.*, **84**, 125–145, 293–311 (1936).

KESCHNER, M., BENDER, M. B. and STRAUSS, J., Mental symptoms in cases of tumour of the temporal lobe, *Arch. Neurol. Psychiat. Chicago*, **35**, 572–596 (1936).

KLEBANOFF, S. G., Psychological changes in organic brain lesions and ablations, *Psychol. Bull.*, **42**, 585–623 (1945).

KLEBANOFF, S. G., SINGER, J. L. and WILENSKI, H., Psychological consequences of brain lesions and ablations, *Psychol. Bull.*, **51**, 1–41 (1954).

KLEIN, G. S. and KRECH, D., Cortical conductivity in the brain-injured, *J. Personality*, **21**, 118–148 (1952).

KLEIST, K., Kriegsverletzungen des Gehirns in ihrer Bedeutung für die Hirnlokalisation und Hirnpathologie, Reprinted from *Handbuch der ärztlichen Erfahrungen im Weltkriege, 1922–1934*, **4**, 343–1,394.

KOFFKA, K., *Principles of Gestalt Psychology* (New York, Harcourt, Brace, 1935).

KÖHLER, W., *Gestalt Psychology* (New York, Liveright, 1929).

KÖHLER, W., *Dynamics in Psychology* (New York, Liveright, 1940).

KÖHLER, W. and FISHBACK, JULIA, The destruction of the Müller-Lyer illusion in repeated trials: I. An examination of two theories, *J. Exper. Psychol.*, **40**, 267–281 (1950).

KÖHLER, W. and WALLACH, H., Figural after-effects: an investigation of visual processes, *Proc. Amer. Phil. Soc.*, **88**, 269–357 (1944).

KOLODNY, A., The symptomatology of tumours of the temporal lobe, *Brain*, **51**, 385–417 (1928).

KONORSKI, J., *Conditioned Reflexes and Neuron Organization* (London, Cambridge Univ. Press, 1948).

KREUGER, E. G., PRICE, P. A. and TEUBER, H. L., Tactile extinction in parietal lobe neoplasm, *J. Psychol.*, **38**, 191–202 (1954).

KRYNAUW, R. A., Infantile hemiplegia treated by removing one cerebral hemisphere, *J. Neurol. Psychiat.*, **13**, 243–267 (1950).

LANDIS, C., ZUBIN, J. and METTLER, F. A., The functions of the human frontal lobe, *J. Psychol.*, **30**, 123–138 (1950).

LANDSELL, H. C., Effects of brain damage on intelligence in rats, *J. Comp. Physiol. Psychol.*, **46**, 461–464 (1953).

LASHLEY, K. S., *Brain Mechanism and Intelligence* (Chicago, Univ. of Chicago Press, 1929).

LASHLEY, K. S., Basic neural mechanisms in behavior, *Psychol. Rev.*, **37**, 1–24 (1930).

LASHLEY, K. S., Cerebral control versus reflexology. A reply to Professor Hunter, *J. Gen. Psychol.*, **5**, 3–20 (1931).

LASHLEY, K. S., Integrative functions of the cerebral cortex, *Physiol. Rev.*, **13**, 1–42 (1933).

LASHLEY, K. S., The mechanisms of vision: XV. Preliminary studies of the rat's capacity for detail vision, *J. Gen. Psychol.*, **18**, 123–193 (1938).

LASHLEY, K. S., The problem of cerebral organization in vision, in "Visual mechanisms," *Biol. Sympos.*, Ed. H. Klüver, **7**, 301–322 (1942).

LASHLEY, K. S., Functional interpretation of anatomic patterns, *Res. Publ. Ass. Nerv. Ment. Dis.*, **30**, 529–547 (1952).

LASHLEY, K. S., CHOW, K. L. and SEMMES, JOSEPHINE, An examination of the electrical field theory of cerebral integration, *Psychol. Rev.*, **58**, 123–136 (1951).

LASHLEY, K. S. and CLARK, G., The cytoarchitecture of the cerebral cortex of *Ateles:* a critical architechtonic study, *J. Comp. Neurol.*, **85**, 223–305 (1946).

LE BEAU, J. and PETRIE, ASENATH, A comparison of the personality changes after (1) prefrontal selective surgery for the relief of intractable pain and for the treatment of mental cases; (2) cingulectomy and topectomy, *J. Ment. Sci.*, **99**, 53–61 (1953a).

LE BEAU, J. and PETRIE, ASENATH, Étude psychologique des changements de la personalité produits par certaines opérations frontales sélectives, *Rev. Psychol. appl.*, **3**, 1–16 (1953b).

LE BEAU, J. and PETRIE, ASENATH, The psychological effects of selective frontal surgery including cingulectomy, *Proc. 5th int. Congr. Neurol.*, (Lisbon), **4**, 392, abstract (1953c).

LIDZ, T., GAY, J. R. and TIETZE, C., Intelligence in cerebral deficit states and schizophrenia measured by Koh's block test, *Arch. Neurol. Psychiat. Chicago*, **48**, 568–582 (1942).

LILLY, J. C., HUGHES, J. R. and GALKIN, THELMA, W., Some evidence for gradients of motor function in the whole cerebral cortex of the unanaesthetised monkey, *Proc. XX Int. Physiol. Congr.*, 567–568 (1956).

LINDSLEY, D. B., Emotion, in *Handbook of Experimental Psychology*, Ed. S. S. Stevens (New York, John Wiley & Sons, Inc., 1951).

LINDSLEY, D. B., Physiological psychology, *Annu. Rev. Psychol.*, **7**, 323–348 (1956).

MALIS, L. I., PRIBRAM, K. H. and KREUGER, L., Action potentials in motor cortex evoked by peripheral nerve stimulation, *J. Neurophysiol.*, **16**, 161–167 (1953).

McFIE, J. and PIERCY, M. F., Intellectual impairment with localized cerebral lesions, *Brain*, **75**, 292–311 (1952a).

McFIE, J. and PIERCY, M. F., The relation of laterality of lesion to performance on Weigl's Sorting Test, *J. Ment. Sci.*, **98**, 299–305 (1952b).

McFIE, J., PIERCY, M. F. and ZANGWILL, O. L., Visual-spatial agnosia associated with lesions of the right cerebral hemisphere, *Brain*, **73**, 167–189 (1950).

McGEOCH, J. A. and IRION, A. L., *The Psychology of Human Learning* (New York, Longmans, Green & Co., 1953).

McLEAN, P. D., The limbic system and its hippocampal formation, *J. Neurosurg.*, **11**, 29–44 (1954).

MEDINA, R. F., Frontal lobe damage and flicker fusion frequency, *Arch. Neurol. Psychiat. Chicago*, **77**, 108–109 (1957).

MENSH, J. N., SCHWARTZ, H. G., MATARAZZO, R. G. and MATARAZZO, J. D., Psychological functioning following hemispherectomy in man, *Arch. Neurol. Psychiat. Chicago*, **67**, 787–796 (1952).

METTLER, F. A. (Ed.) *Selective Partial Ablation of the Frontal Cortex* (New York, Hoeber, 1949a).

METTLER, F. A., Anatomy and Physiology. In *Selective Partial Ablation of the Frontal Cortex* (New York, Hoeber, 1949b).

METTLER, F. A., (Ed.) *Psychosurgical Problems* (London, Routledge & Kegan Paul, 1952).

MEYER, V., Learning changes following temporal lobectomy, *Bull. Brit. Psychol. Soc.*, **29**, inset 21, abstract (1956).

MEYER, V., Critique of psychological approaches to brain damage, *J. Ment. Sci.*, **103**, 80–109 (1957).

MEYER, V., Cognitive changes following temporal lobectomy for the relief temporal lobe epilepsy, *Arch. Neurol. Psychiat. Chicago*, **81**, 299–309 (1959).

MEYER, V. and JONES, H. G., Patterns of cognitive test performance as functions of the lateral localization of cerebral abnormalities in the temporal lobe, *J. Ment. Sci.*, **103**, 758–772 (1957).

MEYER, V. and YATES, A. J., Intellectual changes following temporal lobectomy for psychomotor epilepsy. Preliminary communication, *J. Neurol. Psychiat.*, **18**, 44–52 (1955).

MEYERS, R., The relationship between "thinking" and language. An experimental approach using dysphasic patients, *Trans. Amer. Neurol. Ass.*, **72**, 65–69 (1947).

MILNER, BRENDA, Psychological functions of temporal lobe, *Psychol. Bull.*, **51**, 42–62 (1954).

MILNER, BRENDA and PENFIELD, W., The effect of hippocampal lesions on recent memory, *Trans. Amer. Neurol. Ass.*, **80**, 42–48 (1955).

MONAKOW, C. VON, *Die Lokalisation im Grosshirn und der Abbau der Funktion durch Kortikala Herde* (Wiesbaden, J. F. Bergmann, 1914).

MORGAN, C. T., *Physiological Psychology* (New York, McGraw-Hill, 1943).

MORGAN, C. T., The psychophysiology of learning, in *Handbook of Experimental Psychology*, Ed. S. S. Stevens (New York, John Wiley & Sons, Inc., 1951).

MORRELL, F., Interseizure disturbances in focal epilepsy, *Neurology*, **6**, 327–334 (1956).

MORRELL, F., ROBERTS, L. and JASPER, H., Effects of focal epileptic lesions and their ablations upon conditional electrical responses of the brain in the monkey, *EEG & Clinical Neurophysiology*, **8**, 217–236 (1956).

MORROW, R. S. and MARK, J. C., The correlations of intelligence and neurological findings on twenty-two patients autopsied for brain damage, *J. Cons. Psychol.*, **19**, 283–289 (1955).

MUNZ, A. and TOLOR, A., Psychological effects of major cerebral excisions: intellectual and emotional changes following hemespherectomy, *J. Nerv. Ment. Dis.*, **121**, 438–443 (1955).

NIELSEN, J. M., *Agnosia, Apraxia, Aphasia: Their value in Cerebral Localization* (New York, Hoeber, 1946).

NIELSEN, J. M. and RANEY, R. B., Recovery from aphasia studied in cases of lobectomy, *Arch. Neurol. Psychiat. Chicago*, **42**, 189–200 (1939).

OLDS, J. and MILNER, P., Positive reinforcement produced by electrical stimulation of septal area and other regions of rat brain, *J. Comp. Physiol. Psychol.*, **47**, 419–427 (1954).

OSGOOD, C. E., *Method and Theory in Experimental Psychology* (New York, Oxford Univ. Press, 1953).

OSGOOD, C. E. and HEYER, A. W., A new interpretation of figural after-effects, *Psychol. Rev.*, **59**, 98–118 (1952).

PAMPIGLIONE, G. and FALCONER, M. A., Some observations upon stimulation of the hippocampus in man, *Paper read at E.E.G. Soc.*, London, May, 1956.

PAMPIGLIONE, G. and KERRIDGE, J., E.E.G. abnormalities from the temporal lobe studied with sphenoidal electrodes, *J. Neurol. Psychiat.*, **19**, 117–129 (1956).

PATTERSON, A. and ZANGWILL, O. L., Disorders of visual space perception associated with lesions of the right cerebral hemisphere, *Brain*, **67**, 331–338 (1944).

PAVLOV, I. P., *Conditioned Reflexes* (Trans. by G. V. Anrep) (London, Oxford Univ. Press, 1927).

PAYNE, R. W., The role of the clinical psychologist at the Institute of Psychiatry, *Rev. Psychol. appl.*, **3**, 150–160 (1953).

PAYNE, R. W., An investigation into the possibility of defining "dissociation" as a personality trait by means of objective tests, *Unpubl. Ph.D. Thesis, Univ. of London Lib.* (1954).

PAYNE, R. W., L'utilité du test de Rorschach en psychologie clinique, *Rev. Psychol. appl.*, **5**, 255–264 (1955).

PEARSON, G. H. J. and ALPERS, B. J., Aphasia: study of normal control cases, *Arch. Neurol. Psychiat. Chicago*, **19**, 281–295 (1928).

PECHTEL, C., MASSERMAN, J. H., SCHREINER, L. and LEVITT, M., Differential effects of lesions of the mediodorsal neuclei of the thalamus on normal and neurotic behavior in the cat, *J. Nerv. Ment. Dis.*, **121**, 26–33 (1955).

PENFIELD, W., Temporal lobe epilepsy, *Brit. J. Surg.*, **41**, 337–343 (1954).

PENFIELD, W. and JASPER, H., *Epilepsy and the Functional Anatomy of the Human Brain* (London, Churchill, 1954).

PENFIELD, W. and RASMUSSEN, T., *The Cerebral Cortex of Man: a Clinical Study of Localization of Function* (New York, Macmillan, 1950).

PETERS, R. H., ROSVOLD, H. E. and MIRSKY, A. F., The effect of thalamic lesions upon delayed response-type tests in Rhesus monkey, *J. Comp. Physiol. Psychol.*, **49**, 111–116 (1956).

PETRIE, ASENATH, Preliminary report of changes after prefrontal leucotomy, *J. Ment. Sci.*, **95**, 449–455 (1949a).

PETRIE, ASENATH, Personality changes after prefrontal leucotomy, *Brit. J. Med. Psychol.*, **22**, 200–207 (1949b).

PETRIE, ASENATH, *Personality and the Frontal Lobes* (London, Routledge & Kegan Paul, 1952a).

PETRIE, ASENATH, A comparison of the psychological effects of different types of operations on the frontal lobes, *J. Ment. Sci.*, **98**, 326–320 (1952b).

PETRIE, ASENATH, Effects on personality of excision in different regions of the brain, *Proc. 14th. Int. Congr. Psychol.*, Montreal, abstract (1954).

PETRIE, ASENATH and LE BEAU, J., Psychological changes in man after chlorpromazine and certain types of brain surgery, *J. Clin. Exper. Psychopath. & Quarterly Rev. Psychiat. Neurol.*, **17**, 170–179 (1956).

PICKETT, J. M., Non-equipotential cortical functioning in maze learning, *Amer. J. Psychol.*, **65**, 177–195 (1952).

QUADFASEL, A. F. and PRUYSER, P., Cognitive deficit in patients with psychomotor epilepsy, *Epilepsia*, **4**, 80–90 (1955).

REESE, W., DOSS, R. and GANTT, W. H., Autonomic responses in differential diagnosis of organic and psychogenic psychoses, *Arch. Neurol. Psychiat. Chicago*, **70**, 778–793 (1953).

REITAN, R. M., Certain differential effects of left and right cerebral lesions in human adults, *J. Comp. Physiol. Psychol.*, **48**, 474–477 (1955a).

REITAN, R. M., Discussion on papers on the temporal lobe in "Symposium on the temporal lobe," *Arch. Neurol. Psychiat. Chicago*, **74**, 569–570 (1955b).

REY, J. H., POND, D. A. and EVANS, C. C., Clinical and electroencephalographic studies of temporal lobe function, *Proc. Roy. Soc. Med.*, **42**, 891–904 (1949).

ROBERTS, L., Localization of speech in the cerebral cortex, *Trans. Amer. Neurol. Ass.*, **76**, 43–50 (1951).

ROBERTS, L., Handedness and cerebral dominance, *Trans. Amer. Neurol. Ass.*, **80**, 143–148 (1955).

ROBINSON, M. F., What price lobotomy? *J. Abnorm. (Soc.) Psychol.*, **41**, 421–434 (1946).

ROTHSCHILD, D., Senile psychoses and psychoses with cerebral arteriosclerosis, in *Mental Disorders in Later Life*, Ed. O. J. Kaplan, (Stanford Univ. Press, 1945).

RYLANDER, G., *Personality Changes after Operations of the Frontal Lobes* (London, Oxford Univ. Press, 1939).

RYLANDER, G., Mental changes after excision of cerebral tissue. A clinical study of 16 cases of resections in the parietal, temporal and occipital lobes, *Acta Psychiat. Neurol. Kbh.*, Suppl. 25 (1943).

SCHAIE, K. W., ROSENTHAL, F. and PERLMAN, R. M., Differential mental deterioration in late maturity, *J. Gerent.*, **8**, 191–196 (1953).

SCHILLER, F., Aphasia studied in patients with missile wounds, *J. Neurol. Psychiat.*, **10**, 183–197 (1947).

SCHREINER, L., RIOCH, D. MCK., PECHTEL, C. and MASSERMAN, J. H., Behavioral changes following thalamic injury in cat, *J. Neurophysiol.*, **16**, 234–246 (1953).

SCHUELL, HILDRED, Auditory impairment in aphasia: significance and retraining techniques, *J. Speech. Dis.*, **18**, 14–21 (1953).

SCHUELL, HILDRED, Clinical observations on aphasia, *Neurol., Minneapolis*, **4**, 179–189 (1954).

SCHUELL, HILDRED, CARROL, VIRGINIA and STREET, BARBARA STANSELL, Clinical treatment of aphasia, *J. Speech Dis.*, **20**, 43–53 (1955).

SCOVILLE, W. B., The limbic lobe in man, *J. Neurosurg.*, **11**, 64–66 (1954).

SCOVILLE, W. B. and MILNER, B., Loss of recent memory after bilateral hippocampal lesions, *J. Neurol. Psychiat.*, **20**, 11–21 (1957).

SEAGRIM, G. N., A further examination of non-satiational figural after-effects, *Aust. J. Psychol.*, **9**, 20–30 (1957).

SEMMES, JOSEPHINE, WEINSTEIN, S., GHENT, LILA, and TEUBER, H. L., Performance on complex tactual tasks after brain injury in man. Analysis by *locus* of lesion, *Amer. J. Psychol.*, **67**, 220–240 (1954).

SEMMES, JOSEPHINE, WEINSTEIN, S., GHENT, LILA and TEUBER, H. L., Spatial orientation in man after cerebral injury: I. Analyses by *locus* of lesion, *J. Psychol.*, **39**, 227–244 (1955).

SHAPIRO, M. B., Experimental studies of a perceptual anomaly: I. Initial experiments, *J. Ment. Sci.*, **97**, 90–110 (1951a).

SHAPIRO, M. B., An experimental approach to diagnostic psychological testing, *J. Ment. Sci.*, **97**, 748–764 (1951b).

SHAPIRO, M. B., Experimental studies of a perceptual anomaly: II. Confirmatory and explanatory experiments, *J. Ment. Sci.*, **98**, 605–617 (1952).

SHAPIRO, M. B., Experimental studies of a perceptual anomaly: III. The testing of an explanatory theory, *J. Ment. Sci.*, **99**, 394–409 (1953).

SHAPIRO, M. B., An experimental investigation of the Block Design Rotation Effect. An analysis of psychological effect of brain damage, *Brit. J. Med. Psychol.*, **27**, 84–88 (1954a).

SHAPIRO, M. B., A preliminary investigation of the effects of continuous stimulation on the perception of "apparent motion," *Brit. J. Psychol.*, **45**, 58–67 (1954b).

SHAPIRO, M. B. and NELSON, E. H., An investigation of

an abnormality of cognitive function in a cooperative young psychotic: an experiment of the application of experimental method to the single case, *J. Clin. Psychol.*, **11**, 344–351 (1955).

SHEERER, M., An experiment in abstraction testing form-disparity tolerance, *Confinia Neurologica*, **9**, 232–254 (1949).

SHOLL, D. A., *The Organization of the Cerebral Cortex* (London, Methuen, 1956).

SIDMAN, M., BRADY, J. V., BOREN, J. J. and CONRAD, D. G., Reward schedules and behavior maintained by intracranial self-stimulation, *Science*, **122**, 830–831 (1955).

SKINNER, B. F., *The Behavior of Organisms. An Experimental Analysis* (New York, Appleton-Century, 1938).

SPEARMAN, C., *The Abilities of Man* (London, Macmillan, 1932).

SPERRY, R. W. and MINER, N., Pattern perception following insertion of mica plates into visual cortex, *J. Comp. Physiol. Psychol.*, **48**, 463–469 (1955).

SPERRY, R. W., MINER, N. and MYERS, R. E., Visual pattern perception following subpial slicing and tantalum wire implantation in the visual cortex, *J. Comp. Physiol. Psychol.*, **48**, 50–58 (1955).

SPRAGUE, J. M., CHAMBERS, W. W. and STELLAR, E., Regional physiology of the cerebral nervous system, *Prog. Neurol. Psychiat.*, **10**, 57–92 (1955).

STELLAR, E., The physiology of emotion, *Psychol. Rev.*, **61**, 5–22 (1954).

STELLAR, E., Physiological psychology, *Annu. Rev. Psychol.*, **8**, 415–436 (1957).

STRAUSS, A. A. and LEHTINEN, L. E., *Psychopathology and Education of the Brain Injured Child* (New York, Grune & Stratton, 1950).

STRAUSS, A. A., and WERNER, H., Experimental analysis of the clinical syndrome "perseveration" in mentally retarded children, *Amer. J. Ment. Defic.* **47**, 185–188 (1942–43a).

STRAUSS, A. A. and WERNER, H., Comparative psychopathology of the brain injured child and the traumatic brain injured adult, *Amer. J. Psychiat.*, **99**, 835–838 (1942–43b).

STROTHER, C. R., SCHAIE, K. W. and HORST, P., The relationship between advanced age and mental abilities, *J. Abnorm. (Soc.) Psychol.*, **55**, 166–170 (1957).

SYMMES, D., Multisensory timing ability in persons with lesions of the temporal lobe, in "Symposium on the temporal lobe," *Arch. Neurol. Psychiat. Chicago*, **74**, 567 (1955).

TEITLEBAUM, H. A., The principles of primary and associated disturbances of higher cortical functions as applied to temporal lobe lesions, *J. Nerv. Ment. Dis.*, **96**, 261–273 (1942).

TEUBER, H. L., Neuropsychology, in *Recent Advances in Diagnostic Psychological Testing*, Ed. H. R. Harrower (Springfield, Ill., C. C. Thomas, 1950).

TEUBER, H. L., Physiological psychology, *Annu. Rev. Psychol.*, **6**, 267–296 (1955).

TEUBER, H. L., BATTERSBY, W. S. and BENDER, M. B., Performance of complex visual tasks after cerebral injury, *J. Nerv. Ment. Dis.*, **114**, 413–429 (1951).

TEUBER, H. L. and BENDER, M. B., Alterations in pattern vision following trauma of occipital lobes in man, *J. Gen. Psychol.*, **40**, 36–57 (1949).

TEUBER, H. L. and BENDER, M. B., Perception of apparent movement across acquired scotomata in the visual field, *Amer. Psychologist*, **5**, 271, abstract (1950).

TEUBER, H. L. and MISHKIN, M., Judgement of visual and postural vertical after brain-injury, *J. Psychol.*, **38**, 161–175 (1954).

TEUBER, H. L. and WEINSTEIN, S., Performance on a form board task after penetrating brain injury, *J. Psychol.*, **38**, 177–190 (1954).

TEUBER, H. L. and WEINSTEIN, S., General and specific effects of cerebral lesions, *Amer. Psychologist*, **10**, 408–409, abstract (1955).

TEUBER, H. L. and WEINSTEIN, S., Ability to discover hidden figures after cerebral lesions, *Arch. Neurol. Psychiat. Chicago*, **76**, 369–377 (1956).

THOMPSON, R. and DEAN, W., A further study on the retroactive effect of E.C.S., *J. Comp. Physiol. Psychol.*, **48**, 488–491 (1955).

THURSTONE, L. L. and THURSTONE, T. G., Factorial studies of intelligence, *Psychometric Monogrs.*, No. 2 (Chicago, Univ. of Chicago Press, 1941).

TOOTH, G., On the use of mental tests for the measurement of disability after head injury. With a comparison between the results of these tests in patients after head injury and psychoneurotics, *J. Neurol. Psychiat.*, **10**, 1–11 (1947).

TOW, P. M., *Personality Changes Following Frontal Leucotomy* (Oxford Med. Pub., 1955).

UECKER, A. E., FRENCH, L. A. and JOHNSON, D. R., Psychological studies of seven epileptic hemiparetics before and after hemispherectomy, *Arch. Neurol. Psychiat. Chicago*, **72**, 555–563 (1954).

VERNON, P. E., *The Structure of Human Abilities* (London, Methuen, 1950).

WALKER, A. E., Recent memory impairment in unilateral temporal lesions, *Arch. Neurol. Psychiat. Chicago*, **78**, 543–552 (1957).

WECHSLER, D., *The Measurement of Adult Intelligence* (Baltimore, Williams & Wilkins, 1944).

WEIDER, A., GUTHRIE, T. C., BERLIN, L. and WOLFF, H., Studies of human cerebral functions: The capacity for orientation as measured by the estimation of a minute, *Trans. Amer. Neurol. Ass.*, **80**, 226–228 (1955).

WEINSTEIN, A. E. and KAHN, R. L., The syndrome of anosognosia, *Arch. Neurol. Psychiat. Chicago*, **64**, 772–791 (1950).

WEINSTEIN, S., Weight judgement in somesthesis after penetrating injury to the brain, *J. Comp. Physiol. Psychol.*, **47**, 31–35 (1954).

WEINSTEIN, S., Tactile size judgement after penetrating injury to the brain, *J. Comp. Physiol. Psychol.*, **48**, 106–109 (1955a).

WEINSTEIN, S., Time error in tactile size judgement after penetrating brain injury, *J. Comp. Physiol. Psychol.*, **48**, 320–323 (1955b).

WEINSTEIN, S., Time error in weight judgement after brain injury, *J. Comp. Physiol. Psychol.*, **48**, 203–207 (1955c).

WEINSTEIN, S., SEMMES, JOSEPHINE, GHENT, LILA and TEUBER, H. L., Spatial orientation in man after cerebral injury: II. Analysis according to concomitant defects, *J. Psychol.*, **42**, 249–263 (1956).

WEINSTEIN, S. and TEUBER, H. L., Effects of penetrating brain injury on intelligence tests scores, *Science*, **125**, 1,036–1,037 (1957).

WEINSTEIN, S., TEUBER, H. L., GHENT, LILA and SEMMES, JOSEPHINE, Complex visual tasks performance after penetrating brain injury in man, *Amer. Psychologist*, **10**, 408, abstract (1955).

WEISENBURG, T. and McBRIDE, KATHARINE, *Aphasia: a Clinical and Psychological Study*, (New York, Commonwealth Fund, 1935).

WEISENBURG, T., ROE, ANNE and McBRIDE, KATHERINE, *Adult Intelligence: A Psychological Study of Test Performance* (New York, Commonwealth Fund, 1936).

WERNER, H., Abnormal and subnormal rigidity, *J. Abnorm. (Soc.) Psychol.*, **41**, 15–24 (1946).

WERNER, H. and STRAUSS, A. A., Causal factors in low performance, *Amer. J. Ment. Defic.*, **45**, 213–218 (1940–41).

WILLIAMS, D., The significance of abnormal electroencephalogram, *J. Neurol. Psychiat.*, **4**, 257–267 (1941).

WILLIAMS, H. L., LUBIN, A., GIESKING, C. and RUBENSTEIN, J., The relation of brain injury and visual perception to Block Design Rotation, *J. Cons. Psychol.*, **20**, 275–280 (1956).

WILLIAMS, M. and PENNYBACKER, J., Memory disturbances in third ventricle tumours, *J. Neurol. Psychiat.*, **17**, 115–123 (1954).

YATES, A. J., Validity of some psychological tests of brain damage, *Psychol. Bull.*, **51**, 359–379 (1954).

YATES, A. J., The use of vocabulary in the measurement of intellectual deterioration—a review, *J. Ment. Sci.*, **102**, 409–440 (1956).

ZANGWILL, O. L., Some qualitative observations on verbal memory in cases of cerebral lesion, *Brit. J. Psychol.*, **37**, 8–18 (1946).

ZANGWILL, O. L., Agraphia due to a left parietal glioma in a left-handed man, *Brain*, **77**, 510–520 (1954).

ZEIGLER, H. P., Electrical stimulation of the brain and the psychophysiology of learning and motivation, *Psychol. Bull.*, **54**, 363–382 (1957).

ZUBIN, J., Abnormalities of behaviour, *Annu. Rev. Psychol.*, **3**, 261–282 (1952).

CHAPTER 15

The Effects of Psychosurgical Procedures on Behaviour

R. A. WILLETT

INTRODUCTION

In a review which has become something of a classic, Hebb (1945) concludes that cerebral functions cannot be inferred from the observation of behavioural abnormalities accompanying tissue damage that has resulted from either trauma or disease processes. In these cases, he argues, the crucial information as to the extent and site of the lesion and its secondary effects is lacking and, he continues, can only be supplied where surgical lesions have been introduced into an otherwise intact cerebrum. Chow and Hutt (1953) have insisted on even more stringent control of these two variables, demanding in their review of the related work on *macaca mulata*, that only studies giving full histological details be accorded serious consideration in the identification of cerebral functions.

Such requirements as these can rarely be met in human subjects but the best approximation is certainly to be found in the various psychosurgical procedures carried out for the relief of psychiatric illnesses. Although, indeed, a number of neuro-pathological studies (Dax and Radley-Smith, 1943; Dax *et al.*, 1946; Greenwood, 1948; Mettler and Rowland, 1948; Yakovlev *et al.*, in Greenblatt *et al.*, 1950; Eie, 1954; Meyer and Beck, 1954 and Yokoi, 1957) have demonstrated that psychosurgical lesions tend to be inaccurately placed and their secondary degenerative effect widespread, we have considered that the measure of control, afforded by these techniques, warranted a treatment separate from that of "natural" brain damage, the aberrant condition dealt with in the preceding chapter.

Before coming to our review, several points of policy should be noted. Firstly, we shall use the term prefrontal leucotomy (or simply leucotomy) as that proper to describe procedures aimed at introducing lesions into the white matter of the frontal lobes. Where neurosurgically different techniques have been employed, terms, descriptive of the site or nature of

the lesions, as commonly found in the literature, will be used. Since all these surgical procedures have the common purpose of relieving psychiatric illnesses, the term in current use, psychosurgery, is adequate to describe them all and will be employed as the appropriate generic term throughout this review. "Lobotomy," although very frequently used in the literature in this connexion, is a misnomer and should be eschewed. Secondly, we have chosen Brodmann's reference system (1909) against the claims of more recent systems (e.g. Economo and Koskinas, 1925) as being that most frequently encountered in the literature.

Thirdly, our concern is with experimental studies and, from a consideration of the data that they provide, we shall see how far we can go towards presenting a coherent picture of the effects of psychosurgery on behaviour, and towards drawing substantial inferences about frontal lobe functions and their relationships to behaviour. While being aware of the objections to extrapolating from infra-human studies to human behaviour, we have regarded the data collected from these sources as having important implications for human studies and as being derived under conditions of experimental rigour which are probably optimal in the field. Just because of the difficulties arising in generalizing from one phylogenetic level to another, however, we have largely confined ourselves to studies on infra-human primates where physiological and neurological differences are probably minimal.

Finally, because we are primarily concerned with experimental data, we shall be minimally occupied with clinical reports where neither control observations nor objective measures have been employed. We have considered it a secondary purpose of our review to assess the therapeutic efficacy and rationale of psychosurgical procedures but, since we regard most of the reports that would usually be taken as central for such an assessment as being deficient in regard to both control observations and objectivity, our treatment of these topics may appear cavalier. The value of subjective uncontrolled clinical reports is that of all other raw observation; they are the source of hunches, hypotheses that lead to experimental and controlled observations and the elaboration of theories.

PSYCHOSURGERY: SOME GENERAL COMMENTS AND SUMMARY OF CLINICAL OBSERVATIONS

General Comments

The history of psychosurgery has been recounted too often before (Freeman and Watts, 1950; Greenblatt et al., 1950; Fisher, in Walker, 1951; Fulton 1951; Kalinowsky and Hoch, 1952) to be repeated here in any detail but a curious set of circumstances surrounding its reputed beginnings requires some comment.

Tradition has it that Egas Moniz, the noted Portuguese neurologist, conceived of the possibility of the operation as a treatment of psychiatric disorders after listening to papers by Brickner (1936) and by Fulton and Jacobsen (1935—see also Jacobsen, 1935; Crawford et al., 1947). The latter writers described the disappearance of experimental "neuroses" in two chimpanzees who had suffered extensive damage to the frontal areas. Brickner had given preliminary comments upon the behaviour and intellectual status of a single patient who had been subjected to extensive ablation of the frontal areas for the removal of a tumour. Now, if these papers did in fact suggest the possibility of a therapeutic surgical procedure at first, examination of the evidence, even slightly less than superficially, should have dispelled the idea at once.

In the first place, like procedures had been tried before without signal success (Burckhardt, 1890) and in the second, a closer consideration of the data upon which these papers were based would have revealed no grounds for encouragement. Jacobsen (1935), reporting on his and Fulton's observation, was at some pains to distinguish the rather restricted phenomenon of experimental neuroses from the equivalent term applied to psychiatric patients.[1] Moreover, the main burden of his and Fulton's paper was that a serious "intellectual" deficit followed frontal ablations in the chimpanzee observed.

Brickner reported on a single case, without having had the benefit of pre-operative assessments; for these crucial data he substituted the uncorroborated statements of the patient's relatives and friends. Basing himself on these and his own post-operative observations, he characterized the change in his patient in terms which were certainly mild enough to be reassuring but which, in fact, hardly represented

the gross aberrations in behaviour and cognition which his own protocols reveal (Brickner, 1936). So contrary are the indications for psychosurgery to be derived from these sources that one doubts the accuracy of the whole story. Moniz (1954) himself has relegated the influence of these papers to that of merely crystallizing certain ideas along lines he had already adumbrated at the time and, when one considers the matter, this does not seem unlikely. One cannot avoid the speculation that, at the time of the introduction of psychosurgery, psychiatry was ripe for a new therapeutic panacea and that, for a time at least, these procedures, enthusiastically espoused by a few workers at first, quickly took on the appearance of affording such a panacea.

Moniz's conception was not to reproduce the massive lesions effected in either the chimpanzee or Brickner's patient but to effect relatively circumscribed interruptions in the corticothalamic tracts in the frontal lobes. This has remained the basic aim of most later leucotomies and psychosurgical procedures.

These procedures have become very numerous indeed and, although it is not our business to trace their development in any detail, we shall have to mention some of the main innovations. Figs. 15.1 and 15.2, show diagrammatically the purposed lesion sites of some of the more commonly used techniques. More extensive descriptions than those intended here will be found in the original papers quoted and in Crook et al. (1949), and Kolb (1949), Fairman (in Greenblatt et al., 1950), Fulton (1951), Kalinowsky and Hoch (1952), Otenasek (1953), Le Beau (1954) and Schurr (1956).

As first used by Moniz (1936a and b) and the surgeon Lima the operation consisted of the destruction of corticothalamic pathways by the injection of alcohol through burr holes. This form of the operation was not retained for long, although proponents of it have reappeared from time to time (Fernandez-Moran, 1946; Soupault, 1954; Soupault and Bucaille, 1955). Moniz and Lima themselves replaced it by a procedure in which a "core" of tissue was removed by a special instrument, the leucotome, which they developed. It is interesting to note that the long-term assessment of these early operations has been unfavourable (Furtudo, 1949) but before any results could be properly assessed the procedure was applied,

[1] A comprehensive critique of the concept of experimental "neuroses" will be found in Chapter 19 of this HANDBOOK, by P. L. Broadhurst.

with various modifications in Italy (Rizzatti, 1937; Rizzatti and Borgarello, 1938; Fiamberti, 1937), Switzerland (Ody, 1938), America (Lyerly, 1939; Freeman and Watts, 1942, 1950) and England (McGregor and Crumbie, 1941).

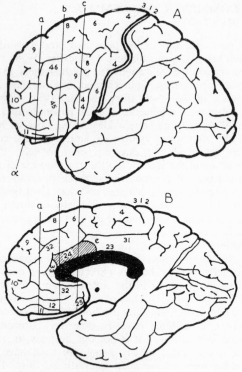

FIG. 15.1. *A.* LATERAL CONVEXITY VIEW OF THE FRONTAL CORTEX

Showing the planes of sections of—
(*a*) Anterior (Rostral) Leucotomy
(*b*) Standard Lobotomy
(*c*) Posterior Leucotomy
(*d*) Transorbital Lobotomy (approximate entry point of instrument)

B. MEDIAL VIEW OF THE FRONTAL CORTEX

Showing the planes of sections of—
(*a*) Anterior (Rostral) Leucotomy
(*b*) Standard Lobotomy
(*c*) Posterior Leucotomy
(*d*) (Shaded area, 24) Area involved in Cingulectomy

(*Adapted from Meyer and Beck*, 1954)

Undoubtedly the greatest impetus to the new psychosurgical procedures was given by the work of Freeman and Watts (1942, 1950) in America. Their original technique, the so-called standard lobotomy, is the basic operation from which most of the others have developed and, as can be seen from Figs. 15.1 and 15.2, was a relatively extensive procedure. Despite the enthusiasm of these two workers, this form of the operation also lost favour as various unfortunate *sequelae*, such as apathy, irresponsibility,

lack of initiative and energy, not to mention the commonly recorded high incidence of post-operative seizures, began to be reported (Rosenblum *et al.*, 1955; Walker *et al.*, in Thompson, 1955; Paul *et al.*, 1957). Moreover, the operation tended to be time-consuming in relation to the number of patients Freeman thought could benefit from it (in Thompson, 1955) and also—a serious practical consideration—patients treated by standard lobotomy frequently presented serious nursing problems for already under-staffed hospitals in the immediate post-operative period (Freeman and Watts, 1942, 1950). Consequently, much of the more recent history of psycho-surgery reduces to the establishment and investigation of new surgical procedures aimed at limiting the

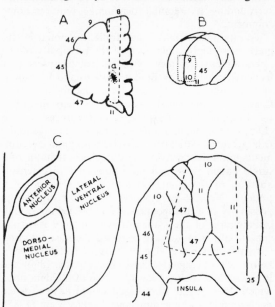

FIG. 15.2. *A.* CORONAL SECTION SHOWING THE APPROXI-MATE EXTENT OF THE BI-MEDIAL FRONTAL LEUCOTOMY (LYERLY-POPPEN TYPE)
(*a*) Fronto-Thalamic Bundle.

B. APPROXIMATE AREA EXCISED IN TOPECTOMY
C. CORONAL SECTION OF THE THALAMIC NUCLEI SHOWING THE RELATIVE POSITION OF THE DORSO-MEDIAL NUCLEUS INVOLVED IN THALAMOTOMY
D. ORBITAL VIEW OF FRONTAL LOBE SHOWING APPROXI-MATE AREA INVOLVED IN ORBITAL UNDERCUTTING (WITHIN BROKEN LINE)

(*Adapted from Meyer and Beck*, 1954)

supposed negative *sequelae* of standard lobotomy whilst retaining its reputed benefits.

At the present time almost every major neuro-surgeon in the field has his own version of a selective procedure, as the more circumscribed forms of psychosurgery have come to be called. Freeman

(1948, 1949) himself proposed transorbital lobotomy based on the pioneer work of Fiamberti (1937) in Italy. This technique differed from all others in that it involved no broaching of the cranium, an instrument being introduced into the orbital surface of the frontal cortex via the orbital plate, above the eyeball (Jones and Shanklin, 1950; Moore and Winkelman, 1950). The special advantages of this technique commonly claimed are, speed and facility (Freeman, 1948, 1949; Freeman *et al.*, 1954) and safety with fewer negative *sequelae* (Jones and Shanklin, 1950; Moore and Winkelman, 1950; Freyhan, 1954). Gardner (1957) has gone so far as to recommend the use of transorbital lobotomy in private practice.

Other modifications were introduced by Lyerly (1939)—Poppen (1948) has employed Lyerly's technique widely—Scoville (1949) and Scoville *et al.* (1951), McKissock (1951) and Grantham (1951). Both Pool (1951; Pool *et al.*, 1949) and Le Beau (1954) have been notable exponents of modified psychosurgical procedures and have introduced important variants of their own. Spiegel and Wycis *et al.* (1948), on the basis of their hypothesis that degeneration of the mediodorsal nucleus is largely responsible for the reported effects of psychosurgery, interrupt the corticothalamic tracts by stereotactic coagulation of the thalamic nuclei. Lindstrom (1954) and Fry (1956) have reported the production of very precise lesions by means of ultrasonic irradiation.

Again, because we do not wish to be led too far from our main path we shall not go into the various rationales for these separate procedures. One should note in passing, however, that frequently surgeons appear to have been prompted by hunches and empirical experience rather than by any clearly formulated hypotheses when proposing their various modifications. A number of accounts have been suggested for the effects of psychosurgery and these we shall briefly outline. They tend to be *ad hoc*, speculative and difficult to either prove or refute. Indeed, one is tempted to hazard the suggestion that few surgical procedures can be based on such tenuous grounds as those of psychosurgery.

Moniz (1936a), originally suggested that in mental illnesses, groups of cells formed abnormal "circuits" in the frontal lobes and became set in their patterns of activity so that the patient's associations became characteristically pathological. He therefore argued that the dysfunctioning frontal lobes should be severed from their connexions with the thalamus (regarded as the centre for the initiation of emotional responses) and thus isolated. Variants of this rationale for the operation have usually formed at least the core of later formulations.

Greenblatt and Solomon (1953b) for example, conceive that frontal lobe circuits, operating in a positive feed-back fashion, are the mechanisms sustaining emotional tension in psychotic individuals. The effect of psychosurgery is thus to cause great reductions in the cells and circuits of the frontal lobes, thereby reducing tension and the debilitating symptoms.

Puech *et al.* (1950)[1] summarize the views of a number of French writers whose notions share much in common with these better known formulations. Feuillett and Collin are quoted as writing—

> Pathological structures . . . suffer the same type of dissolution as the neuro-psychical edifice by which they are mediated. Their freed elements, at the time of the reorganization that follows, take their place in the plan of the whole, that of normal integration . . . surgical intervention could amount simply to the reduction of the active cerebral surface and, by this means, of its capacity to synthesize; this being in line with those authors like Lashley who posit a large degree of functional equipotentiality in the cortex. Certain facts give credence to such a quantitative factor; it is thus that the effects of lobotomy are more severe when carried out with varying cuts—larger or more posterior lesions increasing the area affected.

Sanchez and Camancho are quoted in the following terms—

> Lobotomy isolates a great area of intra-cerebral connexions; the remaining cortex being deprived of this area is forced to adapt new neuro-physical experiences to a new system of functional relationships.

Finally, Delay is quoted in these terms—

> The commonly found effects of leucotomy, particularly in the emotional sphere, can be explained by changes of cortico-basal interactions—between the frontal cortex on the one hand and the thalamus on the other and not so much the activity of the latter as such as in its role as a relay for the hypothalamic-hypophysico tract of the diencephalon.

A number of other such hypotheses have been offered. Greenblatt *et al.* (1950), for example, quote Cobb as also suggesting that leucotomy interferes with long circuiting.

One can note two main themes running through these speculations—a quantitative reductive factor being regarded as the principal determinant of change on the one hand and one of reformation of "circuits" or cell constellations on the other. Beyond such a comment it is not possible to go with these ideas. They presuppose the resolution of most of the problems besetting the neurology of the central nervous system, which resolution, as Meyer (Chapter 14) has pointed out, has by no means been achieved.

Hebb (1949) has offered an hypothesis rather different from these and one which is far more

---

[1] The writer is entirely responsible for any misrepresentation of these views through errors in translation.

TABLE XV.1
SELECTION OF CLINICAL STUDIES

Authors	Year	N	Type of patient	Operation	Problem of study	Findings and conclusions
Berliner et al.	1945	100	Chronic psychotics	Standard lobotomy	Clinical survey	Need for re-education stressed; good results with obsessionals, melancholics and schizophrenia.
McKenzie and Proctor	1946	27	Mixed psychotics and neurotic cases	Standard lobotomy	Clinical survey	Report 50 per cent social recovery rate; a mild hypersexuality noted in 25 per cent of cases.
Van Wagenen	1946	30	Mixed diagnoses	Standard lobotomy and corpus callosum lesions	Efficacy of lobotomy	Lobotomy relieves states of tension and depression. Result not achieved by dividing association fibres of corpus callosum.
Oltman et al.	1948	107	85 per cent schizophrenic diagnoses	Lyerly-Poppen type	Clinical survey	56 per cent of patients improved. Improvement rate higher for non-schizophrenic patients.
Rothschild and Kaye	1948	100	Schizophrenic diagnoses	Lyerly-Poppen type	Effects of leucotomy on schizophrenia	42 per cent of patients improved. Changes only superficial. No influence on the basic psycho-pathological processes.
Reitman, F.	1948	250	Mixed psychotic diagnoses	Various operations including a "low vertical orbital" procedure	Clinical survey and comparison of operations	Orbital procedure more effective. 24 per cent of patients recovered; prognosis poor for deteriorated cases.
Aldricht	1950	10	Mixed diagnoses	Standard lobotomy	Social adjustment in family life	The need for re-education and supervision in the presence of children stressed.
Drubin	1950	62	Psychotic male veterans	Modified standard lobotomy	Clinical survey	37 per cent greatly improved, 56 per cent improved, 7 per cent unimproved.
Edwards	1950	71	Mixed diagnoses	Transorbital lobotomy	Clinical survey	Operation good with anxiety and depression cases; not useful with schizophrenia. Few side-effects noted.
Hoffman	1950	78	Mainly schizophrenic diagnoses	Modified standard lobotomy	Clinical survey	Lobotomy operation of limited value. Should be used only as a last resort.
Lyerly	1950	127	Mixed diagnoses	Lyerly-Poppen type	Clinical survey	76 per cent greatly to moderately improved. 24 per cent unimproved.
Stengel	1950	330	Mixed diagnoses	Various procedures	Clinical survey	The nature and the extent of the change related to extent and site of the lesion and to premorbid personality.
Levine and Albert	1950	See text—subjects and operational procedures from the study by Greenblatt et al. (1950)		Effect of operations on sexual behaviour		No consistent changes noted. Changes related to the role played by anxiety in sex behaviour.
Moore and Winkelman	1950	110	Mixed diagnoses	Transorbital lobotomy	Clinical assessment of operation	Operation good with non-deteriorated psychotics and with psychoneurotic cases. Poor with deteriorated cases.
Johnson and Ehrenberg	1951	80	Mainly schizophrenic diagnoses	Lyerly-Poppen type	To determine the relationship of "reaction type" to improvement	The degree of recovery found to be inversely related to the degree of deterioration pre-operatively.
Pittman et al.	1951	200	Psychotic diagnoses	Standard lobotomy and transorbital lobotomy	Comparison of efficacy of two procedures	Transorbital lobotomy superior; some improvement in 69 per cent of cases.

Author	Year	No.	Diagnoses	Operation	Type of study	Findings
Sargant	1951		Psychosomatic disorders	Standard lobotomy	Clinical survey	Reduced anxiety in cases suffering from psychosomatic disorders.
Simon et al.	1951	33	Schizophrenic diagnoses	Unilateral and standard lobotomy	Comparison of two procedures	68 per cent of standard operation cases improved; 17 per cent of unilateral operation cases improved.
Worthing et al.	1951	600	Mainly schizophrenic diagnoses	Standard lobotomy	Clinical survey	Operation regarded as useful. 33 per cent of non-schizophrenics returned home.
Bonner et al.	1952	41	Intractible pain	Various procedures	Comparison of operations in pain cases	Standard lobotomy regarded as too drastic for pain cases.
Kane et al.	1952	122	Mixed diagnoses	Modified standard lobotomy	Clinical survey	63 per cent of cases benefited to some degree.
Margolis et al.	1952	13	Mixed psychotic diagnoses	Unilateral leucotomy	Assessment of operation	5 patients much improved; 4 moderately improved; 4 unimproved.
Swartzlander	1952	19	Schizophrenic diagnoses	Standard lobotomy	Clinical survey	Ward behaviour improved. Schizophrenic process unaffected. Some evidence of worsening after operation.
Stevenson and McCausland	1953	22	Recurring manic-depressive illnesses	Standard lobotomy	Effect of operation on the recurrent illness	Four year follow-up showed that the recurrent feature of manic-depressive disorder could be alleviated.
Greenblatt et al.	1954	85	See text—subjects from	Greenblatt et al. 1950	Work adjustment	Work level post-operatively below pre-morbid state.
Hoch et al.	1954	40	Pseudoneurotic schizophrenia	Topectomy, bimedial lobotomy and precoronal lobotomy	Clinical survey	88 per cent improved after 36–48 months. Period of "growth" necessary after operation.
Kraft	1955		Mixed diagnoses	Standard lobotomy	Changes in handwriting	No graphological changes noted.
Kral and Elvidge	1955	100	Mainly schizophrenic diagnoses	Bimedial leucotomy	Clinical report	73 per cent showed some improvement. 18 per cent developed seizures but these unrelated to recovery. Indifference and lack of drive noticed.
Newman	1955	25	Schizophrenic diagnoses	Modified standard lobotomy	Clinical survey	Superficial improvement. No change basic disease process.
Pippard	1955a	240	85 per cent neurotic and affective disorders; 15 per cent schizophrenic	Rostral leucotomy	Clinical survey	Improvement with reactive depressions, depressions, involutional melancholia and tension states.
Pippard	1955b	120	Non-psychotic diagnoses	Rostral and standard leucotomy	Comparison of the two operations	Little negative personality defect after rostral operation in 95 per cent; none in only 45 per cent after standard operation.
Lane	1956	19	Women, mixed diagnoses	Unspecified	Social adjustment in the family	Marital adjustment unchanged. Children disturbed either because of mother's indifference or "changed ways."
Schwarz	1956	46	Schizophrenic diagnoses	Various operations	Clinical survey	After six years, 27 per cent discharged, 73 per cent still in hospital. Operation of minimal value.
Freeman	1957	3,000	Mixed diagnoses	Standard and trans-orbital lobotomy	Clinical survey	70 per cent of schizophrenics, 80 per cent "affective disorders" and 70 per cent of psychoneurotics out of hospital in 5–10 year period. Transorbital lobotomy, found to be safer, more effective, more applicable to the needs of a modern state hospital.

elaborate and closely documented. In essence this hypothesis regards emotional disturbances as consisting of the disorganized firing of neural elements in the cerebral cortex. Leucotomy (or electroconvulsive-shock therapy) produces scar tissue and either this or "deafferentiation" in turn produces a state of hypersynchrony (the predominance of large potential slow waves) in the firing of the cerebral neurons. Such a hypersynchrony would then—

> provide a pacemaker . . . that would tend to pick up any neurons that are not incorporated in assembly activities and so substitute the "intrinsic" organization of cortical activity for the diffuse activity of the normal waking adult state.

It can be seen that the verification of this hypothesis is essentially conditional upon the demonstration of a concomitance between hypersynchrony and clinical improvement after psychosurgery. Taking this condition in two parts, it can be stated straight away that ample evidence is available to show that hypersynchrony very frequently follows psychosurgical procedures, which evidence we will outline in a later section dealing with electroencephalographic findings.

That Hebb's account is not entirely satisfactory, however, becomes evident when one considers that hypersynchrony after psychosurgery has been found in patients who have shown no clinical improvement —in the case of schizophrenic patients, for example. In a sense Hebb has allowed for this negative finding. He commences his account by observing, correctly we believe, that where improvement follows psychosurgery, the principal symptoms relieved are states of tension and anxiety and depressions. If these symptoms then comprise the emotional disturbances which consist of the disorganized firing of cerebral neurons, the hypothesis is much more limited in its application but much more defensible. This position also carries with it the not unreasonable implication that other forms of emotional disturbances are of a different nature from those relieved by psychosurgery and the presence of hypersynchrony, post-operatively, would be irrelevant for their course. The disproof of Hebb's hypothesis, would on this view, require that states of tension and anxiety and depressions be relieved without evidence of hypersynchrony in the EEG. records. A direct test of the hypothesis, along these lines has not been made but what evidence there is, will be presented in the later section mentioned.

We shall refer to other neurological hypotheses throughout our treatment of the data of psychosurgery but these, having more specific applications will be dealt with severally as the need arises. Likewise, the psychological hypotheses about the action of psychosurgical techniques will be treated separately.

Summary of Clinical Observations

As a preliminary to presenting the objective data with which we are primarily concerned, we wish to summarize the clinical findings of what we regard as a selection of the most reliable studies reported. A basically subjective method of assessment characterizes the studies to be reported here; the relevant sections from large-scale studies, employing objective measures additionally are included, together with animal investigations essentially subjective in method. Table XV.1 sets out examples of the sort of study with which we shall not be concerned, those which largely report the percentages of various categories of patients, judged to have recovered to greater or lesser extents after the operations to which they have been subjected.[1] Usually, these papers provide as well reflections on the functions effected by the procedures and the role played by the frontal lobes in behaviour.

Apart from the major texts in the field (Mettler, 1949, 1952; Lewis et al., 1956; Greenblatt et al., 1950; Greenblatt and Solomon, 1953; Freeman and Watts, 1942, 1950) excellent general reviews of clinical studies have been given by Partridge (1950), Crown (1951), Klebanoff (1945, 1954), Kolb (1949), and Kalinowsky and Hoch (1952). Freeman has provided a number of informative annual reviews of "Psychosurgery" (1951, 1952, 1953, 1954, 1955, 1956, 1957), to which reference can be made for short summaries of clinical results. Furthermore, a number of joint investigatory projects—apart from those we intend to discuss—have appeared and include interesting clinical data. Amongst these, the reports edited by Brigalow (1949), Overholser (1952, 1954) and Miller (1954) are perhaps the most important. Shevchenko (1954) has reported on Russian work in his monograph and presented the Russian view of prefrontal leucotomy.

As is evident from Table XV.1 any reviewer of this material has to face a multiplicity of aims and procedures that bedevils any attempt at generalization and astonishes with the versatility of the procedures and the industry of the investigators. Kolb (1953) brought a little light to bear on one aspect of this obscure complexity when he computed that, up to the date of his writing, the patients who were subjected to psychosurgery comprised: 60 per cent schizophrenics of divers classifications; 25 per cent "affective" disorders and 10 per cent psychoneurotic

---

[1] Two very relevant papers by Robins (1958, 1959) have appeared and must be mentioned. Robins compared recovery, discharge and remission rates for psychotic and epileptic patients after leucotomy, the subjects of control groups were matched on diagnosis, chronicity, age and sex. He could report no advantage for the leucotomy groups: categories of patients who recovered, recovered equally well in both treated and untreated groups; categories of patients who showed no improvement were equally present in both groups. These studies being well controlled are of the utmost importance.

patients. Even then, Kolb's list leaves out of account certain categories which cut across these psychiatric ones. Psychosurgery has been applied to epileptics (Baretto, Velasco *et al.*, 1949); very frequently for the relief of intractible pain (Scarff, 1948; Freeman and Watts, 1950; Le Beau, 1954); to cases of psychopathy (Kalinowsky and Scarff, 1948; Ackerly in Overholser, 1954); for the relief of affective disorders in old age (Scoville and Ryan, 1955) and has been applied in connexion with tuberculosis (Cheng *et al.*, 1956). The results with some of these dysfunctions—in the cases of epileptic conditions, in psychopathy and disorders in childhood, for example—have generally been regarded as failures (Kalinowsky and Hoch, 1952; Ackerly in Overholser, 1954) and, indeed, it is difficult to see how one procedure could possibly be beneficial for all these conditions and categories of patients, implying, as they frequently do, opposites in symptomatology.

Since the appearance of Freeman and Watts (1942) essentially clinical monograph reporting on their first eighty cases, a number of large-scale investigations have appeared which have included clinical investigations and deserve special mention. Apart from this first and the subsequent second editions of Freeman and Watts *Psychosurgery* (1950), those that we shall deal with are the two reports of the Columbia Greystone Associates (Mettler, 1949, 1952), the allied report of the New York State Associates (Lewis *et al.*, 1956) and the two reports by Greenblatt *et al.* (1950) and Greenblatt and Solomon (1953) from the Boston Psychopathic Hospital. All possess in common a belief in the "blunderbuss" approach, whereby a group of patients are investigated independently by the techniques of many disciplines and relatively discrete reports are presented on the results of the separate investigations. Each investigation, as far as one can make out, is largely empirical, that is, not hypothetico-deductive. Any piece of information concerning the effects of the operation is regarded as worth recording, no matter how unconnected with any other. To a certain extent one can sympathize with this desire for fact-gathering in the early stages of describing a phenomenon but the report of the New York Associates follows exactly the same methodology in most respects as was pursued by the first report of the Columbia Greystone Associates, albeit certain generalizations from the earlier works were followed up. One would have thought that enough random observations on psychosurgery would have been made by this time to encourage the beginnings of a more intensified, coherent and systematic series of studies.

The source reference for the succeeding studies and, in many respects the model for them, is the first edition of *Psychosurgery*, Freeman and Watts's report on their first eighty cases. The work is entirely clinical in approach but, to a greater degree than the succeeding studies, presents a commendable singleness of purpose. It reports about the same percentage of recoveries as became fashionable after it—about one third being greatly benefited, another third slightly improved and the remainder little, or not improved at all. One further fashion was set in that some attempt was made to characterize the essential nature of the change after the operations, the characterization carrying implications for the nature of frontal lobe functions. The conclusion of this first edition of *Psychosurgery* was that: "Psychosurgery alters the structure of the self through reducing self continuity" —self continuity being, presumably, some awareness of the continuity of oneself through the past, present and future. Hutton (1947) reports a similar interpretation for the changes of ten subjects studied pre- and post-operatively.

The second and greatly expanded edition of the work remains very much the same. Confirmatory clinical results are added but what meagre objective assessment was offered in the first volume is omitted from this second. Freeman makes one further addition when he introduces the technique of Transorbital Lobotomy and presents some preliminary results which, he claims, demonstrate that the method has those advantages we have previously mentioned.

One cannot really assess the worth of these two works by any accepted standards of scientific criticism. They are simply the massive accumulation of uncontrolled observation set out, often, in dramatic layout. A predilection of Freeman's for "before" and "after" photographs is indulged to the full and one senses that the authors' suspicion of objective methods of assessment, evident in the omission in the second edition of Hunt's original chapter on "Psychological Tests," is again reflected in the substituted chapter by Robinson. She describes her method of psychological assessment in the following terms—

> The method employed was uncomplicated but laborious and time-consuming. Divesting myself as completely as possible of all theories and preconceptions, I tried passionately to understand each person as I watched him and listened to him talk. Tests were made only to supplement observation. Later I went over my voluminous notes and made comparisons among individuals (in Freeman and Watts *Psychosurgery*, 1950).

The fruition of such "passionate endeavours" and a frequent by-product of many clinical investigations is a post-operative picture of the leucotomized patient. We have thought it fitting to include such a one at the end of this section.

The Columbia Greystone Associates (Mettler, 1949), listing some forty-three contributors in their first report, examined twenty-four operated patients and twenty-four matched controls. Their primary interest was to gather "information as to whether less drastic and technically improved neurosurgical approaches would produce results as satisfactory, or perhaps better than those obtained by lobotomy." To this end, the subjects selected for operation underwent the more or less circumscribed procedure of topectomy, a more drastic operation being proposed if the patient, within an appropriate interval, showed no improvement after this first.

All patients were psychotic, mainly of various schizophrenic diagnoses, and formed a group which the Associates came to realize was anything but homogeneous. Patients were allocated to the operations, subsumed under the term topectomy, in a non-random fashion as Tizard (1958) has pointed out, although when one considers that there were no less than nineteen operative procedures called topectomy, the randomness or otherwise of distributing twenty-four patients to operations becomes a matter of extremely limited meaning. Clinically the results appeared to be reasonably encouraging, a significantly greater number of operated subjects being rated as "improved" after three months, seven months and one year. Furthermore, the writers believed they had some evidence that areas (Brodmann) "9," "10" and "46" were most closely related to improvement. Finally, they suggested that the circumscribed procedure of topectomy was as effective as standard lobotomy and produced no noticeable deterioration of intellectual functions.

This first report of the Columbia Greystone Associates possesses the failings we pointed out at the beginning of this section to an extreme degree. One is impressed by its parts but perplexed by its almost total lack of coherence in design or use of controlled observations. The second report of these Associates (Mettler, 1952), listing thirty-six contributors (eleven of whom, including Mettler, Landis, Zubin, Curry and the surgeon Pool, were concerned in the first report) criticizes the first on a number of grounds and draws the general conclusion that its findings were unwarranted.

Two most telling criticisms are brought to bear upon the first report. Firstly, it is rightly pointed out that the fewness of the cases in each operative category completely invalidates any suggestion that areas "9," "10" and "46" could be of special importance. Secondly, the prognostic rating scale developed for the second study (the "Rocklands Investigation," Mettler, 1952) was applied to the subjects of the first. It was demonstrated thereby that the control group in the first study had much poorer (pre-operative) prognostic ratings; twelve of them having the lowest ratings and only one the highest, while of the operative group, twelve had the highest ratings and only one received the lowest. Thus they concluded that it was doubtful whether any of the improvements noted in the operated group could be attributed to the operation—they might as readily have been the result of the higher rate of recovery, likely for the operation group, over the course of time. The criticism does cast a grave doubt on the results of the first report but one must not lose sight of the unreliability of the ratings on prognosis themselves.

In form, the investigation reported in this second monograph of the Columbia Greystone Associates is very similar to the first except that the control of certain variables, particularly with respect to the cases selected, was much more satisfactory. Thirty-three cases comprised the subjects of this study, almost all being schizophrenic in symptomatology and of roughly equal numbers of the hebrephrenic, catatonic and paranoid subtypes. Information on the effects of two main operations was obtained, venous ligation (involving the interruption of the blood flow through the superior cerebral veins to the frontal lobes) and transorbital lobotomy (performed by Freeman). In addition to these, two cases were seen who received thalamotomy (Spiegel and Wycis's technique of cauterizing the dorsomedial nuclei of the thalamus) and two were subjected to thermocoagulation of the cerebral cortex, in particular, of areas "9" and "10."[1]

Twelve cases were seen who were subjected to venous ligation and nine were subjected to transorbital lobotomy. There were six controls but despite the many refinements introduced one cannot help feeling that a few cases have been again overburdened by the weight of too many operative procedures. The conclusions are more cautious than those of the first report and Mettler and Landis write that in none of the operations they have studied have they been able to demonstrate, unequivocally, any relationships between the psychosurgical procedures and rate of improvement. They consider the two reports together and note that as the period of hospitalization increased (a factor uncontrolled in the first investigation but taken care of in the second) the rate of improvement decreased and they incline to the belief that this factor together with the "total push" technique of post-operative treatment could well account for any improvement found amongst the operated group.

The most recent investigation, reported by many of the principals of the Columbia Greystone studies, is that of the New York Associates in Brain Research (Lewis et al., 1956) whose depleted ranks reach only thirty-one and who can manage only a much slimmer

[1] This procedure was based on the work, of Dusser de Barenne (1935) who demonstrated on monkeys that the application of different degrees of heat would destroy, quite discretely, layers of cortex, more being destroyed as more heat was applied.

volume. Sixty-six patients were seen, divided into subgroups rather arbitrarily on the basis of age and diagnoses and twenty-nine control patients, selected to match the two major operative groups. Two operations were employed this time, one involving the excision of the upper quadrants of the frontal areas (superior topectomy) and the other, the excision of the lower quadrants, an orbital procedure. The conclusions of these associates are very similar to those of the "Rocklands" group and contain some interesting observations about all three studies—

(a) Psychosurgery, if effective at all, is of minimal use with deteriorated patients and of maximum use with psychoneurotic patients and pseudoneurotic schizophrenics.

(b) The excision of any particular area results in no more improvement than in any other—either the larger number of fibres severed when the lesion is in area "9," "10" or "46" or the higher percentage of patients having good prognostic ratings in the first report, could account for the apparent greater success after the excision of these areas.

(c) Little adverse personality changes were noted —the major change appeared to be the reduction of excessive affect with no change in mental content.

(d) The comparative value of topectomy and standard lobotomy has not been decided, but no operation should be attempted until all other indicated treatments have been tried.

Before leaving this series one should point out that despite their shortcomings, they are probably the most valuable collection of papers on the topic that has so far appeared. Particularly in the latter two reports there is evidence of an acute awareness of the need for more objective methods and excellent methodological discussions by Mettler, Landis, Zubin and Hoch are included in both. The chapter on "Psychiatric Effects" by Hoch et al., in the New York State report, goes a long way towards rendering a psychiatric report objective, as objective as the method of subjective ratings will allow, and they present a plan for a properly controlled study of psychosurgery which would, once and for all, establish the connexion between operation and improvement rate, a connexion which remains, at the moment, tenuous.

The two reports from the Boston Psychopathic hospital possess at once virtues lacking in the Columbia Greystone and New York Associates reports and lack virtues possessed by them. Large numbers of patients were seen (five hundred in the first report, Greenblatt et al., 1950; one hundred and sixteen in the second, Greenblatt and Solomon, 1953) and relatively restricted and standardized operations were adhered to, but little awareness of the methodological problems of control and measurement, evident in the latter two reports of the Columbia group, is apparent.

The approach of the two Boston Psychopathic Hospital reports, like those of the former three, is that of the "blunderbuss," the juxtaposition of the efforts of large numbers of contributors being once again considered beneficial. Lyerly-Poppen type operations were applied to all patients of the first group in this series and the general clinical conclusion was drawn that 25 per cent of the operated cases could be discharged and that the symptoms most affected were: tension, agitation, excitement and aggression and the disturbing qualities of obsessional ideas and of hallucinations. The subjects were primarily schizophrenic and the improvement figure of 25 per cent is very similar to the one given by Hoch et al. for the New York State group, which figure the latter regarded as very low and probably due to factors other than the operations. In view of the lack of controls in this report from the Boston Psychopathic Hospital, we also incline to the belief that chance factors could account for such an improvement rate.

The second of the two reports from the Boston Psychopathic Hospital has serious omissions in point of controls similar to the first. It was also largely concerned with a schizophrenic population and was designed to compare the effects of bimedial lobotomy with a unilateral procedure and a full standard lobotomy. The "control" technique employed was to allocate subjects at random to the three procedures, thus trusting that any differences found between the operative groups would be due to the operations. Provided that the allocation was really random and that the post-operative treatment was the same for all groups, this does not seem an unreasonable device. An improvement would have been to employ a control group to account for factors of spontaneous recovery and the effect of the "total push" to which the patients were subjected following their operations.

The general conclusions of this second study are—

(a) neither bimedial nor unilateral lobotomy is as effective as full standard lobotomy;

(b) the patient loses drive, energy and force;

(c) the patient is less affected by past experience and more bound to immediate stimuli;

(d) the patient is less able to elaborate experiences and less able to sustain them.[1]

The investigations of both sets of "Associates," while clearly possessing certain serious weaknesses, represent advances on most of the purely psychiatric

[1] Paul et al. (1957) reporting on the long term follow-up of these patients claim that the bimedial procedure was superior. They quote improvement rates of 63 per cent for the bimedial operation, 44 per cent for the unilateral procedure and 31 per cent for standard lobotomy but do not statistically test for the significance of these figures.

investigations of the type illustrated in Table XV.1; they do present certain refinements in methodology.

One such refinement that should be mentioned briefly is that of the use of rating scales, either to assess behavioural changes directly or to develop a prognosis scale. Since we regard these techniques as essentially subjective, we include them here. Shrader and Robinson (1945) employed the Gardner Behaviour Chart (Wilcox, 1942) in the rating of sixteen schizophrenic patients before and after leucotomy (standard lobotomy) on fifteen scales. They concluded that the greatest change occurred in the appearance of patients and in their sociability. They also reported that the estimate of post-operative clinical improvement correlated (0·54) with pre-operative ratings and that the mean pre-operative rating of the fifteen scales was less favourable than the mean post-operative rating suggesting that the operations had produced an overall beneficial effect. The combination of ratings from different scales in this fashion could be a highly dubious procedure but, as they stand, Shrader and Robinson's findings agree with the observation made by the "Rocklands" group that the patient who is less seriously ill tends to improve. Bockoven and Hyde (1951) repeated Shrader and Robinson's earlier observation that sociability of patients was improved after psychosurgery. They applied a behaviour sampling technique to ten patients from the first Boston Psychopathic Hospital investigation before and after topectomy. They concluded that: "improvement consists of an increase of socialization accompanied by the development of a friendly, democratic attitude to other patients."

The studies of Sands and Malamud (1948) and of Becker and McFarland (1955) are primarily concerned with the development of prognostic scales as such, rather than with presenting information about the effects of psychosurgery. Sands and Malamud estimated the premorbid personalities of twelve schizophrenics and made ratings twice before operation and three times after operation. Their ratings were contrary to both independent estimates of improvement and the post-operative adaptation of the patient.

Becker and McFarland developed a twenty-three item rating scale battery from the records of the Columbia Greystone (Mettler, 1949) study, then applied it to the pre-operative records of three other groups of patients who had been subjected to psychosurgery. These authors then argued that, if their scales had been applied to these subjects before their operations, a considerable saving in operations and a proportionate increase in the percentage of improvements would have ensued. Unhappily no predictive as distinct from post-dictive validations are reported for their scales.

Freeman (1953b) derived ratings on the nineteen scales of the Malamud Rating Scale for 1,120 patients, of whom, six hundred and twenty-two had been subjected to standard procedures and four hundred and ninety-eight to transorbital lobotomy. Pre-operative ratings were made on the basis of case records and the relationship of these ratings to work and social adjustment, two years after operation, was examined. Freeman reported that the most favourable indications for psychosurgery were the presence of anxiety, obsessive thinking and self-directed violence as the principal symptoms complained of. Unfavourable indications were the presence of hallucinations, delusions, scattered thought disorders and externally directed violence. Despite the extreme subjectivity of this study, it would have been of considerable value, by virtue of the size of the sample alone if for no other reason, had some indication of the significance of the relationships been published. Unfortunately only frequency histograms have been given and mention made of chi-squares having been computed.

Another method of prognosis has been attempted by Kline and Tenney (1951) and by Kline et al. (1954) in terms of body types. The latter reported that of eighty-four patients, subjected to transorbital lobotomy, mesomorphic males and females with higher than average ratings in endomorphy showed the best prognosis in a three-year follow-up study. (Cf. Chapter 9 of this HANDBOOK by Linford Rees for a full consideration of the prognostic value of types of physique.)

Jackson and Jaco (1954) attempted to determine prognostic indicators for a group of five hundred and thirty-eight patients subjected to transorbital lobotomy. They reported that after remissions and unexpected recoveries, 52 per cent of the total improved group (57 per cent of all patients) were out of hospital while 96 per cent of the total unimproved group (47 per cent of all patients) were still in hospital. Chi-squares were computed between the improved and the unimproved group for a number of factors. They reported that sex (women), colour (negroes), involutional cases, paranoia, mixed schizophrenic diagnosis, a short duration of illness and of hospitalization, less than ten E.C.T.s, the absence of insulin therapy, being married, a higher education and a history of remission were all positive prognostic indicators and yielded significant chi-squares. Age, onset of illness, the presence of suicidal tendencies, birth order and the number of siblings yielded insignificant chi-squares and were judged to be unrelated to the likelihood of improvement after psychosurgery. Obviously many of the prognostic indicators these authors offer are intercorrelated, but their work contains important factual material.

Finally, we would like to refer to the more elaborate

investigations of Lorr *et al.* (1954, 1955) who employed factor analysis of ratings to identify the nature of the changes after psychosurgery in a group of schizophrenics. They made ratings on a number of "factors" of schizophrenia on a control group and an experimental group before and after the latter underwent psychosurgery. Two arrays of "change" scores were derived from the two sets of ratings—one for the control group, one for the experimental group. These two arrays were then factor-analysed to determine whether a single factor or several were required to characterize the change after operation. Their findings were that a single-factor of "improvement," more prominent in the operated group, was present together with a number of second order factors which, in an earlier study (Lorr, 1953) it had been shown, could be derived from their scales. Their conclusion was that psychosurgery accelerates a natural process of change. Clearly more elaborate procedures have their pitfalls as do those simpler ones with which we have heretofore been concerned.

In the first place, if we allow that the matrices of correlations, which appear to contain many significant coefficients, have not resulted purely from halo effects of the ratings, we are left wondering how change scores, from such unreliable measures as ratings, could produce anything other than completely insignificant matrices. In the second place, the inter-correlation of change scores as such is inappropriate on a number of grounds. It lacks generality of application in that, in the extreme cases of either no change at all or equal changes for each individual occurring, the correlation coefficients would be indeterminable and the analysis impossible. The fact that some significant correlations were found, merely suggests that some variation amongst the two groups of patients had occurred from test to retest and that the previous second-order analysis of the eleven factors of schizophrenia, held good. Nothing can be said about the direction of the change since concomitance towards worsening and towards improvement would contribute equally to the coefficients. The authors' identification of their first centroid as one of improvement, is thus completely unjustifiable.

Lastly, what interpretation one is going to put on the other three centroids, derived from the "change" score matrices, is quite obscure. Are they factors of change as such, as the authors suggest, or do they merely reflect the concomitance present in the earlier study (Lorr *et al.*, 1954)? What else would one expect to get out of matrices of change scores that was not in the basic scores? Certainly, if we allow that certain tests have been shown to change together, there is no possible way of showing that the togetherness was greater for the operated group than for the control group.

It is remarkable that the perfectly adequate table of pre- and post-operative scores (Table XV.3 of Lorr *et al.*, 1955) was not utilized in the discussion. Proper treatment of this table would have revealed all that the writers wanted to know, whereas the method they adopted, by its very nature, leaves these mean change scores out of account. As the table stands, it is interesting to note that mere inspection would suggest that both groups show slightly higher ratings post-operatively, the control group as much as the operated group.

Such studies as these, employing rating scales yield then very inconsistent information. As mentioned earlier, pen-portraits of the post-psychosurgery patient are a highlight of many clinical papers and, in fact, they do seem to perform the function of presenting the nature of the raw data at least vividly. To suggest then the nature of the raw data presented by post-psychosurgery patients, we would like to quote the pen picture given by Frankl and Mayer-Gross (1947) derived from their observations of sixty-eight leucotomized psychiatric patients—

> The patient is physically healthy, a good eater and sleeper with considerable euphoria. His prevailing mood is cheerfulness; he does not worry, is happy and contented and shows it. He may take his responsibilities too easily or shirk them altogether. He leads an active life, is restless and likes movement and change. His interests and hobbies are varied and variable with a preference for light entertainments and superficial past-times. He is easy-going, a good mixer and fond of social life and of being on good terms with everybody.
> On the other hand his relations with people around him are often without depth of feeling. He shows little sympathy or consideration for his next of kin or anybody else. He may be head-strong and unable to see the other person's point of view. He tends to quickly passing bursts of temper. He may attend to his work as before or he may do less well but invariably he thinks he does well, he is not a perfectionist.

Animal Studies Related to Clinical Investigations

Before concluding this section we would like to review briefly a number of investigations with animals, bearing directly upon the questions of the efficacy of psychosurgery and the nature of the changes wrought by it. The methods employed in many of these studies bear close resemblance to the subjective methods of the clinical studies we have been discussing, since the animals' behaviour has been frequently rated by the experimenters rather than measured objectively. For this reason we are including these studies here, rather than in that later section where investigations that have employed objective measures throughout are described.

It should be noted that the data being reported here have often been presented with observations on cognitive changes that have usually involved objective measures. These observations have been included, partly for convenience and partly because these cognitive changes appear to bear directly upon the orectic alterations, in a manner to be elucidated.

Masserman, for a long time, has been concerned with the investigation of the aetiological factors in neuroses through comparative studies and, in collaboration with others, has presented three papers which are of relevance here.

Pechtel et al. (1955) reported on the behaviour of seventeen cats which had been observed before and after they had been subjected to a stereotactic procedure similar to that of Spiegel and Wycis et al. (1948), an experimental neuroses having been established pre-operatively. These writers were partly interested in the effect of thalamic lesions on olfaction, which does not concern us here; their findings, germane to the matters we are discussing included—

(a) after stereotactic destruction of the mediodorsal nucleus, extensive amnesias for previous learning occurred in all animals;

(b) amelioration of acquired neurotic behaviour was noted;

(c) diminution in the speed and capacity for new learning was observed; motivation was retained at a pre-operative level but the animals were perseverative and stimulus-bound;

(d) intensified affective behaviour in relation to other animals and towards humans was observed;

(e) a change in characteristic social responses was seen, dependent upon the pre-operative experiences of the animals, i.e. cats who were made experimentally neurotic were significantly more aggressive after mediodorsal thalomotomy than were a group of normal controls after the same operative procedure.

Masserman and Pechtel (1956a) rated the behaviour of fifty cats and forty monkeys on thirty behaviour categories over periods of five months and measured their capacity to perform certain learning tasks. Approximately half the animals were then subjected to a procedure which induced experimental neuroses. The neurotic behaviour so established was allowed to stabilize over periods of between three and twenty-four months. The animals were then subjected to frontal excisions and their behaviour rated again. These writers record that the common effects of the lesions were—

(a) moderate or excessive amnesia;

(b) amelioration or disorganization of the neurotic patterns of behaviour;

(c) diminished adaptability in behaviour leading to (i) stimulus-bound perseveration, and (ii) impaired skill in problem-solving;

(d) affective changes, characterized by greater susceptibility to reactions indicative of startle and fear.

This second study, it can be seen, largely corroborates the findings of the first. Masserman and Pechtel (1956b) present some further corroborative evidence for these findings in a study which suggests that monkeys with brain lesions are slightly less resistant to and recover slightly less rapidly from procedures aimed at establishing experimental neuroses.

Each of these experiments is interesting but in respect of the light they shed on the changes wrought by psychosurgery their findings are equivocal. In both the first and second study quoted, some reduction of the neurotic behaviour patterns was reported but what patterns were labelled neurotic seemed rather arbitrary and any change in them would appear much more likely to be associated with some of the more general changes observed—the amnesias for instance, or the reported tendency towards being stimulus-bound. Indeed, on the contrary, some of the changes that were noted appeared to be of the type which, in human subjects would have been regarded as signs of increased neuroticism—for example, "increased affective behaviour," "greater susceptibility to reactions indicative of startle and fear."

Streb and Smith (1955) have reported findings similar to these, using rats as subjects. Fifty rats were trained to give a "crouching fear" response to the sound of a buzzer. Half of these animals were then subjected to partial ablations, the other half underwent sham operations. After recovery from the operations both groups were tested again and it was found that a significantly higher percentage of experimental animals who had suffered ablations, had lost the crouching response. The results suggest that, analogously, psychosurgery might well reduce anxiety in human subjects. Streb and Smith point out, however, that the same differentiation between the experimental and control group would have been achieved had mobility about the cage been the criterion and that, what measured reduction in "anxiety" did occur, occurred as part of a more general alteration of response tendencies.

Lichtenstein in two well controlled studies (1950a and 1950b) first outlined a method for inducing a "feeding inhibition" in dogs and, as in the succeeding studies reported above, utilized this neurosis in testing the efficacy of a psychosurgery-type procedure in dispelling such maladaptive responses. Through the controls he employed, Lichtenstein hoped to show that his results were not artefacts of the lapse of time occupied by the operation and the recovery from it, of the circumstances attendant upon the operative procedures—the anaesthetic for example—and that the results did not differ when different periods of time were allowed to elapse after operation. He reported, tentatively, that the experimental groups lost their feeding inhibitions to varying extents, depending on the animal.

Lichtenstein's final conclusions were, however, cautious. He pointed out that since the operations had resulted in widespread biological changes, the disturbance of established responses could have as readily been due to these changes as to the presence of lesions as such. If we couple this reservation with the smallness of his groups (four dogs in each of two experimental groups) and the fact that after the original operation one dog retained the feeding inhibition unimpaired and others retained it to a greater or lesser degree, we must conclude that Lichtenstein's results are completely equivocal. Lichtenstein reported one further interesting finding in that he suggested that after the frontal lesions the feeding inhibition could be established slightly less readily than before them. This finding is also tenuous in that it was based on the observation of only two animals.

Waterhouse (1957) stressed this element of re-training in a similar investigation employing monkeys. Eight animals were trained to make a five-second delayed response, a pattern discrimination and a colour discrimination. He further established a fear response to two kinds of auditory stimuli and avoidance responses to food. Four of the monkeys were then subjected to an operative procedure which severed some of the fibres in all of the corticothalamic tracts in the frontal lobes. Waterhouse reported that his post-operative monkeys showed a marked loss in the retention of their previously learned responses, although a fairly high level of performance was still evident. Relearning was possible nearly to the same level as was achieved pre-operatively.

Of direct interest to our concern in this section are the qualitative changes Waterhouse noted in the responses of the post-operative monkeys. He reported that they were both slower and less "forceful" in their responses. Again, also, a rapid extinction of learned responses was observed. Concerning the specific responses of conditioned fear and food avoidance, both these were reduced post-operatively and, although there was no significant difference in the extent to which these reductions occurred, the indication was that the fear response was more completely lost.

Considering these investigations together, their most clearly delineated feature is the probability that neurotic responses diminished as a function of some more general change. The present writer would like to suggest that the identity of this general change is a deficit in the formation and retention of conditioned responses. Waterhouse suggests very much the same conclusion and, with it in mind, draws the following implications from his investigation for psychiatric thinking around the problem of the effects of psychosurgery—

the following need close attention; (a) the extent to which lobotomy in humans leads to the extinction of fear and symptoms motivated by fear; (b) how far fear-based symptoms may be re-learned again if re-inforced in an unfavourable post-operative environment; it would also suggest careful study of any impairment of the alerting process in anticipation of danger and in the processes that sustain affective arousal; (c) finally, it poses the interesting more general problem of whether lobotomy leads to any deficit in the learning and retention of responses based on acquired motivation.

In addition to these reports bearing directly on the question of the efficacy of psychosurgery, there have been a number of comparative studies that have made more or less unsystematic observations of "emotional" behaviour following frontal ablations in animals. Such observations have not always been made with a view to drawing parallels with post-psychosurgical behaviour in human subjects but they have some relevance to this problem and to the original observations of Fulton and Jacobsen.

Harlow and Dagnon (1943) noted that their group of monkeys showed resistance to taming and habituation procedures and attempted to bite the experimenters after frontal lesions. There seems some parallel here with the frequently reported lack of emotional restraint after psychosurgical procedures and, possibly, also the behaviour is related to the suggested impairment of the acquisition and retention of fear-based responses previously noted.

The observation of Harlow and Dagnon was repeated by Harlow and Settlage (1947) and by Harlow et al. (1952). The latter conclude that—

in no observation of animals with anterior lesions has this laboratory been able to confirm the reports of emotional flattening and indifference to failure that were instrumental in the initiation of the technique of pre-frontal lobotomy. Instead the behaviour changes have been in the opposite direction.

It is possible that the cause of these discrepant reports might lie in the finding of Freudenburg et al. (1950). These writers repeated the observations of Fulton and Jacobsen (1935) on Rhesus monkeys, comparing the effects of lesions in the frontal areas with lesions in the dorsomedial nucleus. They reported that complete "taming" occurred when the lesions were placed in the coronal plane and were accompanied by degeneration of the dorsomedial nucleus; taming also occurred when the lesion was placed directly in this body. In the absence of the dorsomedial body being involved no taming was observed. It will be remembered that the lesions introduced by Fulton and Jacobsen were massive and almost certainly would have involved this body. If the lesions introduced by Harlow and his associates were more restricted the dorsomedial nucleus might not have been involved and, in agreement with the report of Freundenburg *et al.*, taming not have occurred.

A second commonly reported effect of frontal ablations in comparative studies which has some relevance to our purposes is the observation of hyperactivity. Richter and Hines (1938) give an excellent review of the early work in this field, including the most important studies carried out before 1938, during which period the phenomenon received a great deal of attention. A selection of studies since that date will serve to illustrate the nature of these data.

Richter and Hines had concluded from their review that both unilateral and bilateral removal of frontal lobes resulted in hyperactivity, the effect being heightened if the bilateral procedure followed the unilateral operation. They further concluded that areas "8," "9," "10," "11," "12" and the anterior ends of the caudate nucleus were the crucial areas involved. Kennard *et al.* (1941) largely confirmed these conclusions although they did not place so much stress upon area "9" or upon sections of the striatum. These latter workers utilized good control conditions and were thereby able to demonstrate that changes in metabolism and other autonomic disturbances were not causing the hyperactivity.

Wade (1952) compared the behaviour of monkeys following a leucotomy procedure with a lobectomy and an operation which severed some of the transectional fibres. She reported a consistent pattern of increased activity after both of the former two operations but none after the third. Her results would suggest, like those of Freudenburg *et al.*, that the mere presence of a lesion as such would not produce any dysfunction and that rather it was the severing of frontal association fibres at any of several sites that would effect the change.

One further general observation, of some relevance to this section and in line with studies already quoted, was made by Brody and Rosvold (1952). These writers investigated the effect of frontal lesions on social interaction amongst a group of *macacae mulatae*. Within this group, comprising six monkeys, a dominance hierachy was allowed to build up and become stabilized over a period of three months. Half of the monkeys were then subjected to frontal ablations and observations of the dominance hierarchy was continued for another seven months. The authors report that the hierachy was disturbed after the operation and was never re-established. They suggest that the breakdown occurred because of the lower-status monkeys' failures to retain or relearn their previously strong avoidance responses after the frontal excisions. This finding also is in line with our previous suggestion as to the nature of the orectic changes that occur after frontal lesions in animals.

The general conclusions that can be drawn from these comparative studies are thus clear. While amelioration of specific "neurotic" responses is suggested, the application of this finding to the matter of the efficacy of psychosurgery is rendered difficult by the concomitantly reported findings after ablations in animals of behaviour changes reminiscent of the disturbed affect of psychiatric patients. This apart, the reported reduction in experimental neuroses appears to be part of a more general deficit—one of decreased capacity to form conditioned fear responses.

General Conclusions Concerning Clinical Studies

From a consideration of the literature, the above description of sections of it and the data presented in Table XV.1, we would draw the following conclusions concerning the clinical studies of the effects of psychosurgery on behaviour—

(*a*) the therapeutic benefit of psychosurgical procedures remains essentially undetermined by clinical studies and the related comparative work, although many studies contain observations suggestive of certain changes;

(*b*) the changes that are suggested towards clinical improvement are much more evident for the nondeteriorated, largely non-psychotic patient;

(*c*) the nature of these putative changes appears to be a reduction in the intensity of affect; more particularly, in a reduction of the intensity of anxiety and tension states (conditioned fear responses in experimental animals), of compulsiveobsessional symptoms and reactive depressions, the disturbing quality of acute physical illnesses and of hallucinatory and delusional experiences;

(*d*) the superior benefits of any one procedure are also undetermined by these studies, although the negative *sequelae* of standard lobotomy, do seem to be rather more severe than those of more restricted operations.

Arising from these conclusions and the review of the clinical data upon which they are based, we wish, now, formally, to suggest an hypothesis as to the mode and type of change wrought by psychosurgical procedures, which hypothesis we shall examine whenever relevant data appear during the course of our subsequent general discussion.

Eysenck has described the structure of personality in terms of a number of factorially determined dimensions (1947, 1952, 1957a). These dimensions (*see* Chapter 1 of this HANDBOOK) are, neuroticism, introversion-extraversion and psychoticism. Neurological parameters have been suggested for the former two dimensions, which parameters should be regarded as hypothetical constructs. That parameter postulated as underlying neuroticism is a quality of lability in the autonomic nervous system and is often, in Eysenck's writing, regarded as manifest in anxiety and thought of as a drive state. That underlying introversion-extraversion has been postulated as a state of balance of the excitatory and inhibitory potentials of the central nervous system. In Eysenck's system the neurotic is characterized by an overly labile nervous system. The introvert is characterized by a predominance of *excitatory* potential while the extravert is thought of as being characterized by a predominance of *inhibitory* potential. Thus, when applied to psychiatric patients, this theory envisages the tense, anxious, compulsive, obsessive, phobic patient as possessing high degrees of both neuroticism and introversion. Conversely the hospitalized psychopath and the patient suffering from any of a variety of hysterical symptoms is seen as possessing high degrees of neuroticism and extraversion. Psychoticism refers to states where autisms and cognitive disturbances are pronounced—in those patients frequently labelled schizophrenic, for example.

Introversion-extraversion has been related to learning constructs (Eysenck, 1955a, 1955b, 1957a) and, in particular, Franks (1956) showed that a group of extraverts formed conditioned eyeblinks less readily than a group of introverts, when neuroticism was held constant (cf. Chapter 12 of this HANDBOOK).

Bearing this in mind, and the nature of the proposed dimensions, we would suggest the following hypothesis for the nature of the changes following psychosurgical procedures—

Those who advocate psychosurgical procedures seem, from their writing, to be striving to effect changes in the degree of neuroticism and psychoticism. The evidence reviewed above suggests that psychosurgical procedures result in a reduction of introversion.

The evidence for this hypothesis so far presented may be summarized briefly as follows: in those illnesses where the role of introversion is maximal—in anxiety states, in the presence of inappropriately learned responses (in phobias for example) or in states of tension—the benefit of psychosurgery seems to be maximal (Freeman, 1942, 1949; Hutton, 1947; Frankl and Mayer-Gross, 1947; Van Wagenen, 1946; Arnot, 1949; Cattell, 1950, 1953; Reiner and Sands, 1951; Allison and Allison, 1952, 1954; Kalinowski and Hoch, 1952; Freeman, 1953b; Greenblatt and Solomon, 1953; Hurt, 1947; Miller, 1954; Pippard, 1955a). Where extraversion is present to a high degree, in psychopathy for example, the benefits of psychosurgery are generally held to be minimal (Cattell, 1953; Kolb, 1953; Ackerly in Overholser, 1954). Likewise, where the disease process appears to involve fundamental structural or biochemical changes, as in the presence of psychoses, more particularly in the presence of psychotic deterioration, the operation also appears to be of little value (Johnson and Ehrenberg, 1951; Rothschild and Kaye, 1948; Mettler, 1952; Kalinowski and Hoch, 1952; Freeman, 1953b; Shevenko, 1954).

Finally, the comparative work so far reviewed—as has been intimated—strongly suggests that conditioned fear responses in experimental animals is reduced and this finding is congruent with that of Franks (1956) on human extraverts.

The status of the proposed hypothetical construct underlying introversion-extraversion is quite clear in the case of Franks's study—that extraverts should condition poorly follows directly from the proposal. That an increase in the relative dominance of the inhibitory potential should follow circumscribed lesions in the frontal cortex does not follow so obviously, although it would be possible to develop a plausible account in very general terms. The writer, however, feels that the very considerable advances that are being made in neurophysiology at the present time (Delafresnaye, 1954; Sprague and Chambers, 1955; Stellar, 1957) would immediately reveal the weaknesses of any such general account and it would seem best to tie any hypothesis about the action of psychosurgery closely to behaviour.

That extraverts condition more poorly than introverts is consistent with the hypothesis about extraversion and the predominance of cortical inhibition and, if it were shown empirically that post-leucotomy patients conditioned (to mention but one prediction) less readily than pre-leucotomy patients, this would be consistent with the proposal that the operation results in an increase of extraversion. It would also be consistent with the notion that an increase in the predominance of the inhibitory potential follows frontal lesions. These and other related findings might well form a nomological network of hypotheses having considerable explanatory power at the behavioural level. No direct prediction, however, carrying any high degree of conviction can be made, at the moment, from the introduction of frontal lesions into the cortex in terms of the neurological constructs Eysenck has proposed as underlying introversion-extraversion.

A full-scale investigation constructing such a nomological network by relating postulates involving the concept of inhibition (in, for example, learning and perception) and independent measures of introversion-extraversion to the effects of psychosurgical lesions is suggested by these notions. Such an investigation has not been carried out, hence most of the evidence we shall present in support of our hypothesis refers only to the behavioural pattern Eysenck has labelled extraversion. Little or none of this evidence directly involves the postulated underlying neurological construct.

STUDIES IN PERSONALITY CHANGES AFTER PSYCHOSURGERY

In turning, as we shall now do, to the assessment of personality changes after psychosurgery we must stress that the tools of measurement, commonly known or available to psychologists who have worked in this field, are most limited and of uncertain value. It is not surprising, then, that the general level of investigation in this area is rather lower than in the investigations of intellectual changes which we shall report in the next section.

Those studies we shall be concerned with here are of three main types: (a) investigations using the Rorschach Inkblot test or other projective devices; (b) investigations employing questionnaires and (c) investigations in which the use is made of batteries of performance tests thought to describe unitary factors of personality.

Projective Techniques: the Rorschach Test

The Rorschach Inkblot Test (Klopfer and Kelly, 1942, 1946) has found favour with many medical people and many clinical psychologists. It has been accredited with the twin virtues of being a "test" and thus seemingly objective, while in interpretation it is said to require those puissant faculties of clinical insight and intuition so dear to many clinicians. In spite of these qualities the validity of the Rorschach as a diagnostic tool has often been questioned (e.g. Payne, 1955) and in the absence of any final answer to this question, we cannot give too much credence to personality assessments based on it. It has, however, been employed very often with psychosurgical patients and we will make a report of some of the typical studies.

First, we shall summarize briefly the findings with the Rorschach from the large-scale studies referred to in the previous section. In the first report of the Columbia Greystone Associates, Zubin found no definite pattern of changes in scores following the operation, and what changes were suggested were equally prevalent amongst members of the control group. A statistical analysis of individual records revealed no significant differences between the control subjects and those who had undergone the operations. The only significant change was in the speed of reaction-time to the cards; the post-operative group was the slower.

No reference was made to the Rorschach Test in either of the later two reports connected with these workers, the "Rocklands" study (Mettler, 1952) or the report of the New York Associates in Brain Research (Lewis et al., 1956).

Hunt, in the first edition of Psychosurgery (Freeman and Watts, 1942) reported that the post-leucotomy patient showed a constriction of personality, some loss of "higher powers" and exhibited a greater preponderance of "popular" responses in their Rorschach responses. The earlier of the two reports from the Boston Psychopathic Hospital (Greenblatt et al., 1950) reached very similar conclusions from its application of this test. The authors in summarizing their findings with the Rorschach write—

Rorschach studies before and after lobotomy indicate slight but consistent impairments in abstraction capacity plus a great deal of indecision. The patients show more perseveration, more stereotypy, less fantasy and creative imaginativeness and reduced spontaneity and initiative. Freer emotional expression and fewer restrictions in the patients' affect were noted within the narrowed emotional range. These changes frequently interfered with judgement.

Greenblatt and Solomon (1953) found little reason to change this summary materially but added some observations concerning indications of anxiety. They reported for this second group of patients (some twenty-eight, tested between four and eight months after operation) that ratings of anxiety, derived from Rorschach protocols, remained the same as they were before operation and that the protocols after operation were still, characteristically, psychotic in kind. No further changes were noted on retest after twelve months, other than a reversion in some patients to a pre-operative level of emotional control and a marked increase in the amount of fantasy evident in the protocols of two patients. It was also concluded by these authors that the Rorschach protocols "had little if any relationship to clinical outcome."

Numerous other studies have employed the Rorschach Test to investigate the effects of psychosurgery on behaviour. Kisker (1944b) tested a group of severely psychotic patients before and after leucotomy on this test. He made only a "qualitative" judgement of his protocols because of the greatly disturbed character of his subjects. One can only suppose, that by "qualitative" judgement here was meant that the protocols were not scored according to one of the accepted systems (Klopfer and Kelly, 1942, 1946). The outcome of this rather unpromising beginning was rather along the lines of the other studies so far reported. Only very small changes were noted and it was claimed that their character was often anticipated in the pre-operative records.

Spiegel and Wycis (1949) were unable to demonstrate any consistent pattern of change in Rorschach responses in nine cases subjected to their stereotactic procedure although (a little forlornly one feels) they suggested that five of their nine cases showed some "improvement on the Rorschach criteria."

Crown (1952) in a well-controlled study of thirty-five, largely psychotic patients, reported a significant decrease in "F" scores, which decrease he suggested might be a reflection of the common clinical report of a "blunting" of tact and of a lessening of richness and originality in response.

Linford-Rees and Jones (1951) attempted to evaluate the effects of leucotomy and various other "active" therapies by means of the Rorschach Test. They reported that failures after leucotomy had significantly lower organic signs of Piotrowski although the test had little prognostic value. Their first mentioned finding is of some interest and accords well with the contention, found frequently in the literature, that too restricted a lesion is ineffective.

McFie, Piercy and Zangwill (1951) investigated a group of obsessional patients who had been subjected to psychosurgery and were likewise unable to demonstrate any change following the operation, or any consistent pattern of "obsessionality" for that matter, in the Rorschach protocols. They were able to report, however, that the obsessional patients tended towards "blocking" and exactitude in their pre-operative responses and that these tendencies disappeared from the immediate post-operative protocols although they became evident again in later testing periods. If any reliance at all can be placed on these latter observations they would suggest the somewhat tardy re-learning of disturbed patterns of response after psychosurgery which was suggested as a possibility by some of the previously reported animal studies.

Davidson (1952) obtained scorable Rorschach protocols on twenty-eight patients suffering from schizoid and "affective" disorders before and after they were subjected to leucotomies. He reported, once again, a poor correlation between Rorschach responses and clinical findings.

Wideman (in Miller, 1954) administered the Rorschach Test to sixty-one patients, after leucotomies, and reported that anatomical responses discriminated between an improved group and a non-improved group, such that 43 per cent of the former gave them and 73 per cent of the latter. This, however, was the only one of a number of Rorschach scores which did show any discriminatory power and could easily have been a chance finding.

Reitman (1955b) administered the Rorschach Test to a group of mixed brain-damaged patients, including some post-leucotomy patients. He compared the protocols of this group with those of a group of non-brain-damaged psychiatric and paraplegic patients. Contrary to the studies so far reported he found that all scores of the brain-damaged group other than w and F were significantly different from the scores of the psychiatric and paraplegic patients. He interpreted this difference as indicating that the brain-damaged group was characterized "by a general suppression of personality factors." This latter presumably means something the same as the "constriction" of personality reported by Hunt, although one cannot be at all sure of the implications of this description either.

Finally, we wish to report what is probably the best controlled study of its type in the field. Allison and Allison (1954) compared the pre-operative and post-operative Rorschach protocols of eight subjects undergoing transorbital lobotomy. Pre-operatively each subject was matched with a control on: diagnosis and treatment, period of hospitalization and duration of illness together with age and sex. One month prior to operation all subjects were given a Rorschach Test and henceforth lived together under the same closely supervised conditions up to the time of the operation. All subjects received the same pre-operative work-up and preparation, including the administration of a number of electroconvulsive shocks which served as the anaesthetic for the experimental group's psychosurgical procedure. All subjects received the same post-operative care and, after being tested post-operatively, their two sets of records were marked in random order and scored "blind."

The obtained sets of scores were then subjected to statistical analysis. Statistically significant decreases were found in m and FK scores and in the speed of responding to the cards (confirming Zubin's finding mentioned previously). A significant increase was found in w scores. Decreases in k, K and M scores and an increase in the frequency of the organic signs described by Dörken and Kral (1952) all approached significance. A non-parametric test of significance applied to the scores arranged according to the check lists of Harrower-Erickson (1942) and of Munroe (1945) also showed significant changes. These authors conclude, on the basis of these results, that the characteristic changes in their patients were—

(a) reduced tension and anxiety (lower m, k and K scores)

(b) loss of the ability to introspect (lower M scores)

(c) loss of enthusiasm (slower reaction-time)

(d) improved organizational ability (increased w)

(e) reduced creative ability (lower M).

They summarize their findings by claiming that their results corroborate many of the impressions that have been made clinically.

Despite the excellence of their design and execution of the work, one can, however, accept their findings only with reservations; particularly their interpretation of the change scores which is the only part of their study, albeit a crucial part, that is in any way subjective. To take only one patent example, one can see no compelling reason why slower reaction-time should be identified as loss of enthusiasm. One cannot but lament that such an excellently planned and executed piece of work should have utilized such a poor and suspect measure of personality as the Rorschach.

It will be noticed that one of the results of the above studies was interpreted as loss of creative ability. Many such references are to be found throughout the literature and should be mentioned here.

Hutton and Bassett (1948) used a number of techniques to demonstrate this putative deficit, including the orthodox Rorschach Test, the multiple-choice version of Harrower-Erickson (1942) and Murray's Thematic Apperception Test. They suggested that while the level of general intelligence remained high post-operatively (as measured by the Raven's Matrices and the Shipley Hartford Scales) originality and creative ability were considerably reduced. They took as measures of these latter the originality and number of the patients' responses to the various projective tests administered. Ashby and Bassett (1949) and Crown (1952) reached very similar conclusions although Reitman (1947) had described a contrary creative "spell" in a schizophrenic patient subjected to a psychosurgical procedure.

Zubin (in Overholser, 1952) has virtually settled this issue. He reported a number of systematic attempts to validate the Rorschach Test (number of M responses) as a measure of creativity by comparing the number of M responses given by groups of artistically gifted people with the number given by matched controls equally intelligent but less creatively gifted. In none of these attempts did the Rorschach discriminate between the two groups.

Zubin went on to characterize creative ability as being composed of, imaginativeness, problem-solving ability, skill and zeal and made a number of observations upon patients and their behaviour to determine whether any sign of any of these constituents being deficient, after psychosurgery, could be discovered. His observations were quite subjective, but such as his conclusions were he could find no evidence of any deficit in any of these factors.

Conclusions From Projective Test Studies

In general then we must conclude from this brief review of the projective test studies into the effects of psychosurgery, that, in point of the most objective aspects of the tests, only the study of Allison and Allison (1954) has unequivocally demonstrated any changes post-operatively. We have pointed out that we can accept their interpretations of their results only with reservations due to the subjectivity of these interpretations.

Questionnaires

Far fewer studies have utilized the much more objective method of measuring personality—the questionnaire. Vidor (1951) administered the M.M.P.I. scales to a group of leucotomy patients pre-operatively and post-operatively. She reported that the scales of "depression" and "psychasthenia" showed significant decreases. She also reported a decrease in the number of items which seemed to reflect the presence of anxieties, phobias, depression and hallucinations.

Darling and Sandall (1952) in a curious paper, report the administration of the M.M.P.I. to a group of eighteen hospitalized psychopaths who had undergone leucotomy. They do not burden the reader with scores or other cumbersome details but are happy, nevertheless, to conclude that their results support their convictions that psychopathic illnesses are as serious as psychoses and are caused by environmental stresses on hereditary predispositions; a conclusion which shows a most prudent regard for the complexity of the subject.

Reitman (1955c), using the same group as he did in his study of the Rorschach, administered the M.M.P.I. scales. He reported that the greatest differences here were that the brain-damaged group had *higher* scores on the "paranoia," "psychasthenia" and "schizoid" scales. The implications for psychosurgery from Reitman's studies must be tenuous since he used a mixed group. In particular we cannot conclude from his study that psychosurgery results in *increased* psychotic tendencies for we are given no pre-operative scores, nor do we know how well Reitman's control group matched his brain-damaged group in point of severity of psychiatric symptoms.

Conclusions from Questionnaire Studies

The conclusions from these questionnaire studies are clearly equivocal; they have yielded surprisingly little information.

Factorial Studies Using Objective Performance Tests

The dimensional approach to the analysis of personality has been referred to at length in a preceding chapter by Eysenck (Chapter 1). He, together with Cattell and Guilford, based partly on the pioneering work of Spearman, Thurstone and Burt, has been the principal proponent of this methodology which aims at reducing the multiplicity of response tendencies, that go to make up the totality we call personality, into a relatively small number of dimensions or factors. This is achieved by demonstrating broad bands of concomitances, amongst such response tendencies, through the technique of factor analysis or some related procedure. The principal studies that have utilized this approach in the field of psychosurgery are those of Crown (1952) and of Petrie (1952), both of whom have employed the framework provided by Eysenck (1947, 1952, 1957a).

Crown (1952) in the study already mentioned several times, predicted decreases in general intelligence, in neuroticism and in introversion. As measures of the latter two, he used batteries of performance tests by which Eysenck (1947, 1952) defined these factors. Crown's subjects were thirty-five psychotic patients of various diagnoses. He found that there was no consistent change post-operatively in either neuroticism or introversion. The absence of any marked decrease in neuroticism we would have expected; that no decrease in introversion occurred requires explanation since it apparently involves a direct contradiction of the hypothesis we have suggested for the nature of the change that takes place after psychosurgery.

In the first place, the tests Crown used, although the best available measures of the factor at the time, would not necessarily be those one would choose now if changes in introversion were being examined after leucotomy. More reliable measures would be derived from questionnaire scores (Eysenck, 1956) and various indices, taken from laboratory learning, perception and conditioning situations (Eysenck, 1957a), would be employed, rather than the earlier performance tests.

In the second place the subjects Crown used were psychotic, as has been described, and it seems probable that factors of attention, slowness, concentration, etc., frequently attendant upon psychotic disorders could have affected the performance test scores on which the measure of introversion-extraversion was based and if, as we suspect, psychotic elements remain unaffected by psychosurgical procedures, one would not expect any differences on test performances from the pre-operative occasion to the post-operative occasion.

This criticism of the choice of subjects for psychosurgery investigations has been made by Petrie (1952) and, more recently, by Tow (1955). Both accordingly drew their experimental samples from neurotic populations having well preserved personality structures. Petrie chose to test groups who were predominantly suffering from functional disorders such as compulsive-obsessional complaints, reactive depressions, anxiety states and, in general, those groups which Eysenck has termed dysthymic—those, in short, in whom we would predict the maximum change after psychosurgery.

In her original monograph (1952) Petrie presented the results of testing such groups of patients who were subjected to a standard lobotomy, a rostral procedure and a third smaller group who received only unilateral incisions. She has since published separately and with the collaboration of the French neurosurgeon Le Beau and his psychological associate, Maryse Choppy, a series of studies utilizing the same methodology on groups of patients subjected to various selective procedures (Le Beau and Petrie, 1953; Petrie and Le Beau, 1953; Petrie and Le Beau, 1956).

The subjects of the original monograph, which forms the basis of the work that followed, were tested approximately two weeks before operation and, in the case of standard lobotomy, at intervals of three and nine months after operation. In the case of the more anterior rostral operation, they were tested only once, six months after operation. In general, the same intervals have been adhered to in the investigations of the selective procedures, for purposes of continuity and comparison. Petrie summarized her findings from the first investigation as follows—

> the pattern of personality changes has been shown to be consistent in the four different types of operations examined and the alterations in the traits may be readily grouped so as to demonstrate changes in the dimensions of personality, viz.: a decrease in the strengths of traits associated with neuroticism and with introversion and a decrease in certain aspects of intelligence . . . alterations in personality are more pronounced after the posterior standard operation than the anterior rostral operation, particularly . . . in the sphere of intelligence.

Petrie's method of investigation has been the same for all groups of subjects tested. Table XV.2 shows the results from the original monograph rendered comparable with those of some later studies into the effects of selective procedures and including one group seen before and during the administration of the pseudo-leucotomizing drug, chlorpromazine. It will be noticed that one further factor, psychoticism, has been added to those factors originally studied. Many of the tests defining this factor were administered to Petrie's original group of subjects and these were later arranged to show changes along this dimension.

For a full description of the tests Petrie employed, reference should be made to her monograph (1952) but scrutiny of Table XV.2, as it stands, reveals a number of points for consideration.

TABLE XV.2

SHOWING PERFORMANCE TEST SCORES ARRANGED UNDER THE
RELEVANT FACTORS OF PERSONALITY

(Adapted from Petrie and Le Beau, 1956)

	Chlorpromazine 19 pain and mental patients		Cingulectomy 15 epileptic patients		Standard leucotomy 20 neurotic patients		Open rostral leucotomy 15 neurotic patients		Selective surgery of areas "9" and "10" 19 pain and mental patients	
	Mean diff.◯	Stand. dev. of diff.	Mean diff.◯	Stand. dev. of diff.	Mean diff.◯	Stand. dev. of diff.	Mean diff.◯	Stand. dev. of diff.	Mean diff.◯	Stand. dev. of diff.
Traits related to neuroticism										
Speed of writing	0·35	12·13	4·79	22·75	7·55*	13·56	13·43*	10·75	5·63	14·76
Disposition rigidity	−0·84*	0·80	−1·29	9·98	−0·72*	1·46	−0·72*	1·35	−0·69*	1·06
Self-criticism	−0·27	3·09	0·38	5·45	−6·84*	10·12	−5·00*	6·16	−0·82	6·15
Manual dexterity	−5·61*	10·54	−9·00*	13·00	−6·75*	7·43	−9·77*	13·35	−6·77*	8·79
Suggestibility	−0·03	1·14	−3·45*	4·22	−2·91*	3·99	−2·65*	4·21	−1·75	3·54
Traits related to introversion										
Self-blame	0·61	2·87	1·00	4·24	−7·84*	9·97	−2·33*	3·89	−1·65	5·59
Accuracy (number of mistakes)	−2·67	24·47	−14·36	46·97	5·55	18·25	4·92	27·38	2·46	14·23
Wechsler verbal I.Q.	4·21*	8·18	8·19	9·15	−7·51*◻	10·31	2·02◻	6·75	0·71◻	11·78
Wechsler perform-ance I.Q.	4·13*	4·46	8·21	5·75	1·49	6·05	5·02	11·35	0·82	9·20
Attitude to time	d.o.p.		n.c.		i.o.p.		i.o.p.*		i.o.p.	
Liking for sex humour	n.c.		n.c.		inc.		inc.*		inc.	
Traits related to psychoticism										
Fluency (I)	0·63	3·44	0·13	3·46	0·20	5·43	0·93	6·22	−0·36	4·13
Fluency (II)	0·33	2·79	1·20	2·30	1·16	7·14	1·15	3·41	−0·54	6·05
Tempo of tapping	5·61	15·01	9·18	39·04	1·11	18·62	−17·75	13·56	9·88	29·50
Concentration	1·67	7·32	0·67	5·27	1·95	7·90	1·92*	2·69	−0·78	5·05
Worst time score on track tracer	−7·61*	17·29	−25·95*	39·74	−15·00*	11·48	−17·63*	21·82	−16·21*	13·88
Worst error score on track tracer	0·10	5·10	−4·47	10·08	1·37	5·74	0·45	5·39	0·21	3·54
Passive fluctuation	4·00*	5·28	1·17*	1·80	−1·12	7·84	1·92	8·31	1·00	3·69

* Significant differences ($p = 0.05$ or higher).
† d.o.p. = decreased orientation to present; i.o.p. = increased orientation to present; n.c. = no change; inc. = increased.

◯   Mean difference scores derived by the subtraction of pre-operative scores from post-operative scores.
—   Changes in the direction of decreased neuroticism, increased extraversion, and decreased psychoticism.
◻   A relatively greater increase in performance I.Q. in comparison to verbal I.Q. taken as a change in the direction of increased extraversion.

First, it is clear that the most definite changes occurred with the original standard and rostral groups. In each of these groups the changes in the direction of decreased neuroticism are consistent and significantly different when compared pre-operatively and post-operatively. Also for these groups those tests related to introversion-extraversion change consistently in the direction of decreased introversion, half of the differences between pre-operative and post-operative scores being significant ones.

The position with respect to the selective procedures is not so clear. Consistent changes in both introversion-extraversion and neuroticism were recorded for the group subjected to selective surgery of areas "9" and "10" towards increased extraversion and decreased neuroticism and, as is in line with other reports in the literature, there was no consistent alteration in psychoticism. As can be seen, however, very few of the changes recorded reach statistical significance and some differences are extremely small.

TABLE XV.3

SHOWING PERFORMANCE TEST SCORES ARRANGED SO AS TO BE
COMPARABLE WITH TABLE XV.2

(Adapted from Tow, 1955)

Test		N	Post-op. mean	Pre-op. mean	Mean diff.	p value
Tests probably related to neuroticism						
1. Speed—						
(a) Letter cancellation (number	(i)	36	142·0	143·0	−1·0	N.S.
cancelled)	(ii)	36	135·0	137·0	−2·0	N.S.
(b) Track tracer (time for	(i)	36	98·0	103·0	−5·0	N.S.
completion in sec)	(ii)	36	87·0	98·0	−11·0	N.S.
(c) Porteus mazes (time in sec)	(i)	34	546·0	313·0	233·0	p = 0·01
2. Persistence—						
(a) Word formation (total number)	(i)	36	34·0	43·0	−9·0	N.S.
(b) Holding up leg (time in sec)	(i)	36	50·0	57·0	−7·0	p = 0·03
3. Troubles questionnaire—						
(a) Number of troubles ascribed						
to self	(i)	31	10·0	15·0	−5·0	N.S.
4. Disposition rigidity—						
(a) Easy alternations (ratio of	(i)	36	2·3	2·4	−0·1	N.S.
first to second task)	(ii)	36	2·8	2·9	−0·1	N.S.
(b) Difficult alternations (ratio	(i)	36	3·3	3·6	−0·3	p = 0·02
as in (i)	(ii)	36	3·6	3·4	0·2	N.S.
Tests probably related to introversion-extraversion						
1. Accuracy—						
(a) Letter cancellation (number	(i)	36	12·0	5·0	7·0	p = 0·01
of errors)	(ii)	36	9·0	4·0	5·0	p = 0·01
(b) Track tracer (number of	(i)	36	13·0	7·0	6·0	p = 0·01
errors)	(ii)	36	13·0	7·0	6·0	p = 0·01
(c) Porteus mazes (number of blind						
alley entries, once)	(i)	34	7·3	5·1	2·2	p = 0·01
(d) Porteus mazes (number of blind						
alley entries twice)	(i)	34	1·4	0·2	1·2	p = 0·01
Tests probably related to general intelligence						
1. Raven's matrices	(i)	36	34·0	38·0	−4·0	p = 0·01
2. Vocabulary (number correct,						
Terman, 1916)	(i)	36	68·0	73·0	−5·0	p = 0·01
Tests probably related to psychoticism						
1. Tempo (preferred)—						
(a) Counting forwards						
(time in sec)	(i)	36	13·5	14·0	−0·5	N.S.
(b) Counting backwards	(i)	36	20·5	21·0	−0·5	N.S.
(c) Reading easy prose	(i)	36	156·0	156·0	0·0	N.S.
(d) Reading difficult prose	(i)	36	128·0	135·0	−7·0	N.S.
(e) Dressing (time in min)	(i)	18	6·5	5·0	1·5	N.S.
(f) Undressing	(i)	18	12·0	9·0	3·0	N.S.
2. Fluency—						
(a) Tests of verbal fluency	(i)	36	15·0	22·0	−7·0	p = 0·01
(number of responses in	(ii)	36	21·0	35·0	−14·0	p = 0·01
one min)	(iii)	36	16·0	25·0	−9·0	p = 0·01
	(iv)	36	3·0	5·0	−2·0	p = 0·01
(b) Drawing test of fluency	(i)	36	11·0	13·0	−2·0	p = 0·01

— Changes in the direction of decreased neuroticism, increased extraversion and decreased psychoticism.

No consistent pattern is evident for the cingulectomy group in respect of introversion-extraversion or neuroticism, but a consistent decrease in psychoticism is noted for this group. Of seven scores defining this latter factor for the cingulectomy group only two changes reach statistical significance.

An examination of Petrie's work in detail will reveal many of the defects of pioneering studies, an enthusiasm that occasionally prompts the drawing of conclusions not strictly warranted by the data at hand being one of them, but the fact that her work represents the first thoroughly systematic attack on the problem of describing the behavioural changes after psychosurgery gives it a merit which must override all other characteristics it possesses.

Two other workers in the field of psychosurgery, one preceding that of Petrie and the other following it, have utilized similar objective tests, although neither has employed them in the systematic way in which Petrie has done. The earlier of these, Rylander (1939a and b, 1943, 1947, 1951), must be credited as being the first in the field of psychosurgery who applied objective tests in an effort to describe personality changes. Both Petrie and Tow have referred to Rylander's work extensively and we do not propose to repeat their comments here.

The work of Tow (1955) is in the same tradition as Petrie and Rylander. Like Petrie, Tow was careful to choose his subjects from amongst those patients suffering from "functional disorders," subjects who were not so ill as to yield equivocal scores on performance test. His subjects received a blind orbital type operation and were tested before and after operation at intervals similar to those employed by Petrie, with the difference that Tow tested post-operatively at one year. He saw thirty-six subjects in all.

Despite surprisingly little reference to Petrie's monograph, Tow administered many of the same tests. We have arranged his results in Table XV.3, to facilitate comparison between the two bodies of work, so that the scores of tests which are either the same or similar to those defining the personality dimensions in Petrie's table (XV.2) are grouped together. Under neuroticism may be grouped a number of speed of performance measures, four measures of disposition rigidity, two of persistence and one measure of the number of "troubles" ascribed by the patients to themselves. Under introversion-extraversion may be grouped four measures of accuracy, two Porteus Maze measures of Blind Alley entering, and the comparison of the change after operation between a performance test of intelligence and a verbal test. Under psychoticism may be grouped a number of measures of tempo (preferred) and of fluency. Detailed descriptions of these tests will be found in Tow's monograph.

Clearly no exact comparison is possible since the tests used have not been exactly the same in all cases but, nevertheless, it is instructive to consider the pattern of changes for this group of patients, as was done for Petrie's subjects. Three of the changes that we have grouped under neuroticism changed significantly although not in the same direction. All of the measures of speeded performance tended to show a reduction in speed (except the speed score on the Track Tracer), one measure of disposition rigidity changed towards increased rigidity and both measures of persistence showed a decrease in persistence. These scores suggest, if anything, an increase in neuroticism.

In the absence then of significant and completely consistent changes, no change towards decreased neuroticism is evident for this group, on the contrary there is more evidence for an increase in this factor.

All the tests which we have grouped under introversion-extraversion changed significantly and all of them, except the comparison of the two intelligence measures, towards an increase in extraversion. The comparison of the two intelligence scores is probably not particularly similar to the comparison Petrie made, since the Raven's Matrices is hardly a performance test in the same way as the Performance Scale of the Bellevue-Weschler Test.

Of the tests grouped under psychoticism, the measures of preferred tempo show no consistent trend nor are any of the changes significant ones. Contrary to Petrie's results all of the measures of fluency used by Tow showed significant changes after operation and, in terms of the dimensions employed by Petrie, all are in the direction of increased psychoticism.

Conclusions from the Factorial Studies

If we can be permitted the licence of considering these two studies together we can conclude—

(a) The most consistent changes are evident after standard lobotomy and rostral lobotomy, both towards indications of amelioration of psychiatric disturbances, and decreased introversion.

(b) The pattern of changes for the selective procedures reveals no clear trend but a decrease in introversion is evident in the scores of both groups of patients.

(c) Whether the amelioration of psychiatric disturbances, as indicated by changes in neuroticism and psychoticism, occurs after the selective procedures is uncertain. The two studies returned opposing findings for these factors in the sense that Tow's group appeared to have had a higher degree of psychoticism after operation than before.

These conclusions are to be thought of as suggestive only. The assumptions the foregoing treatment makes about the comparability of tests and what they measure are too tenuous to make decisive claims but, in general, it would appear that a reasonable summary of the two sets of findings would be that the question of whether changes in neuroticism or psychoticism occur remains unanswered but that the change towards increased extraversion is consistently evident.

STUDIES OF COGNITIVE CHANGES AFTER FRONTAL LOBE LESIONS IN ANIMALS AND PSYCHOSURGERY IN HUMAN SUBJECTS

Two influences have joined to make the study of cognitive changes after psychosurgery relatively much further advanced than those of personality with which we have so far been concerned. Firstly, the history of mental testing, with its tradition of objectivity, is a long one and has given rise to relatively well validated and reliable measures of intellectual capacities. Secondly the popular belief (probably at least partly without foundation) has been that increasing cognitive abilities (culminating in man) are related to the growth and complexity of the frontal cortex. Thus, runs the argument, any insult to these areas is likely to result in intellectual deficits and such deficits, or rather, such putative deficits, have prompted a large number of studies both in the comparative field and with the subjects of psychosurgical operations. Much of the animal work has also been directly concerned with the identification of the functions of the frontal lobes, as have some of the studies with humans, although these inquiries have usually been made incidentally within studies whose principal aim has been to assess the effects of a psychosurgical procedure.

Cognitive Changes after Frontal Lobe Lesions in Animals

An excellent general review of this topic has been presented by Chow and Hutt (1953); we intend to stress those studies, particularly the more recent ones, which bear directly upon the question of whether any intellectual deficits may be expected after psychosurgery. We will, as before, confine ourselves mainly to studies on the primates, those animals whose central nervous systems most closely resemble that of man. Even here the hazards of generalizing from one phylogenetic level to another are only too evident. One of the best established findings in the literature on frontal lobe lesions in primates is that while simple discrimination problems are not affected by lesions, delayed response and delayed alternation response type problems are, most markedly, so affected. There has been no such precise definition of a deficit obtained with human subjects in purely cognitive functions.

Historically, perhaps the most important workers in the field of animal extirpations and their effects upon behaviour have been Bianchi (1922) and Lashley (1929). The workers we will be largely con-

cerned with are, Jacobsen and his associates, Harlow and his associates, and Mishkin and Pribram and their associates. The animals involved in these studies have been commonly, rhesus monkeys, the species *macaca mulata*, baboons and chimpanzee. The tasks that have been commonly employed are—

(a) *Instrumentation*: the need to use, say rods, to obtain some goal object.

(b) *Sensory discrimination*: learning to choose one of two objects on the basis of some sensory difference; e.g. colour, form, roughness, etc.

(c) *Delayed response*: the animal is shown some goal object; the object is concealed in some way from the animal's view and, after a delay with the object out of the animal's sight, the subject is required to choose or identify the object.

(d) *Delayed alternation problems*: similar to (c) except that the animal has to reject the object indicated, after a delay, and is required to choose an alternative object that has been presented simultaneously, but not indicated.

(e) *Conditional reactions*: usually some variant of ordinary instrumental conditioning.

That the identification of frontal lobe functions is a dominant feature of these comparative studies, is evident from the earliest work. Jacobsen, for example, investigated the effects of frontal extirpations on monkeys in a series of experiments in the two decades from 1920 to 1940. He came to the conclusion that his results were in line with those of Brickner (1936) —that the deficit resulting from frontal lesions lay: ". . . in the synthesis into complex structures of the simpler engrammic products associated in the more posterior parts of the brain."

It is a little difficult to see just what is meant here and, in fact, such generalizations have tended to drop out of the more recent literature. Jacobsen himself (Jacobsen *et al.*, 1935) stays much closer to the data when he concludes from a series of extirpation studies that: ". . . after injury to the frontal association area, those activities which demand an integration over a period of time can no longer be effectively carried out."

On the basis of their numerous investigations into the effects of extirpations in monkeys, Jacobsen and his associates come to a number of more specific conclusions (Jacobsen, 1935; Jacobsen *et al.*, 1935; Jacobsen and Nissen, 1937)—

(*a*) Delayed response and delayed alternation type tasks show the most marked deficits after frontal lesions.

(*b*) Little or no deficit follows lesions on discrimination or instrumentation type tasks, unless they require temporal integration.

(*c*) The deficits of (*a*) are definitely associated with lesions in the frontal lobes since lesions in other areas (e.g. the parietal and occipital lobes) do not produce such deficits and unilateral frontal lesions produce less pronounced deficits than do bilateral lesions.

A great deal of the later work in this field has been directed towards testing and refining these findings. The work of Harlow, for example, overlapping that of Jacobsen, is very largely concerned with elaborating and duplicating his investigations. Harlow and Dagnon (1943) compared four bilaterally operated animals with six controls on discrimination problems. They concluded that, contrary to Jacobsen's finding, differences do exist between the operated animals and their controls in point of performance on this type of task although, with additional training, the former group could be raised to the level of the latter. Spaet and Harlow (1943) developed various delayed response problems that retained the essential feature of temporal delay while differing in make-up from the tasks used by Jacobsen. They used, for example, an interrupted "matching from sample" technique which required the animal to choose an object similar to one shown before a delay while a "sample" object remained in view during the delay. They employed also non-spatial delayed response problems where the choice objects had to be distinguished on other than purely spatial grounds and found, for all these variants, that their experimental groups performed as well as their controls.

These results of Harlow and Dagnon, and Spaet and Harlow are contrary to those of Jacobsen and his associates. The former writers account for these differences in findings by claiming that Jacobsen's animals were not allowed to form the crucial associations prior to the delay sufficiently well. They further conclude from their studies that no single ability seems to be destroyed in monkeys by frontal lesions and that when deficits in delayed response tasks are observed, they could be due to any of a number of factors; loss of speed of learning, loss of the effectiveness of the expected reward, etc. Harlow and Johnson (1943) provided an important control observation for these and all extirpation studies on the frontal lobes of monkeys, when they showed that operated monkeys would initiate behaviour to food when no new

associations were required to be formed, to the same extent as non-operated monkeys.

Harlow and Spaet (1943) and Campbell and Harlow (1945) modified the contradiction of Jacobsen's work somewhat and conceded that there was a characteristic deficit following frontal lesions in monkeys on delayed-response type problems, although they still emphasized that the operated monkeys could be trained readily to the level of the relevant control group, showing that the loss was not an absolute one. They also carried out further control studies which showed that test history, length of interval from operation to testing and the extent of lesions within the frontal lobes, had little effects upon the results. It should be noted that all the lesions employed in these studies were relatively extensive.

Campbell and Harlow (1945) summarize their findings as follows—

following the destruction of the frontal and prefrontal association areas, (monkeys) suffer a deficit in attending and fixating limited aspects of a test situation and this operates to reduce the effectiveness of the acquisition of complex problems such as the delayed reaction.

A summary of the earlier work of Harlow and his associates is to be found in Harlow and Settlage (1947) in which summary a wide variety of deficits, following frontal lesions in monkeys, are reported. The more recent work of these writers tends to be confusing. Contrary to the earlier finding of Harlow and Spaet, and Campbell and Harlow, Warren and Harlow (1951) showed that posterior lesions were more deleterious than more anterior ones. Harlow *et al.* (1952) cast a doubt on this revision by reporting that animals with anterior lesions tended to be poor on delayed response tasks but that animals with more posterior lesions were adequate on these tasks but poor on discrimination problems at which the former group had been adequate.

Finan (1939, 1940) analysed another important aspect of Jacobsen's work when he investigated whether the deficit associated with delayed response tasks was due to the absence of differentiating cues at the test choice-point, or whether the deficit only occurred "where the degree of influence exercised by repeated training in the establishment of their (i.e. the differentiating cues) corresponding habit is minimal." This suggestion is clearly similar to that made later by Spaet and Harlow, and Harlow and Dagnon that the animals in Jacobsen's study had not been allowed to form the relevant associates sufficiently strongly. Finan studied the performance of a group of operated monkeys on—

(*a*) A task which required the subject to move from one compartment of a cage to another, ten seconds after the raising of a dividing door; shock followed too early or too tardy reactions.

(b) A task where of two maze paths, one having a thirty-second delay chamber, the other a one hundred and twenty-second delay chamber, the first had to be learned.

(c) Delayed response tasks similar to Jacobsen's.

It will be observed that in both (a) and (b) the elements of delay are retained but the animal has constantly before him differentiating cues. Finan reported that there were no deficits in these two tasks but confirmed Jacobsen's finding that type (c) problems result in considerable deficits.

Wade (1947) also reported an important finding when she was able to show that injections of Nembutal (a sedative) into post-operative monkeys reinstated their capacities to perform delayed alternation tasks. Pribram (1950) repeated the observation in a study in which he examined the performance of a group of baboons who, over a period of six months, had shown consistently poor performances on delayed response tasks and were then subjected to a number of experimental conditions. One of these, the injection of Nembutal, confirmed Wade's finding. Pribram also reported that insulin, reduced environmental temperature and fasting resulted in improvements on the delayed response tasks, while no improvement resulted from the injection of Benzedrine, from increased environmental temperature or pre-feeding. Pribram's findings in this study, if nothing else suggest that no one factor of environment is crucial for the appearance of the deficit and that it is likely to occur only under quite precise conditions.

Blum et al. (1951) repeated Wade's and Pribram's investigation of the effects of Nembutal on delayed response task deficits and were unable to report their confirmation. Blum et al. suggested that improvement had occurred in the animals of the earlier studies because they had been tested at relatively short intervals after operation and had not performed better than chance during the initial post-operative period. The animals of Blum's et al. study differed from the subjects of the earlier studies in both of these respects and no improvement following Nembutal was observed.

Mishkin et al. (1953) proceeded from the above suggestions of Blum et al. and tested animals, at more than six-monthly intervals after operation, and which had scored above chance on delayed response tasks post-operatively. They concluded that improvement did in fact follow the injection of Nembutal, although they conceded that considerable re-training was required.

Wade (1947) had based her argument as to why any improvement in performance should follow the injection of Nembutal into post-operative monkeys on a suggestion of Malmo. Malmo (1943), subscribing to an interference theory of forgetting, suggested that the failure of operated animals upon delayed response tasks might be due to their being more liable to interference from irrelevant stimuli during the delay. Wade proposed that the administration of a sedative, depressant drug, would reduce the effective strength of these stimuli and so result in an improvement on the problem tasks.

It is worth noting at this point that, recently, Summerfield and Steinberg (1958) have made a similar observation with human subjects learning nonsense syllables. These authors required a group of subjects partially to learn lists of nonsense syllables then interrupted the learning process. During this interruption, employing appropriate controls, they administered nitrous oxide while the subjects were engaged in various tasks. They found that the administration of this depressant, nitrous oxide, significantly reduced the degree of forgetting evident during the subsequent resumption of the learning task. Their account of their findings is also in terms of the reduced efficacy of interfering stimuli during the interpolated interruption period, after the administration of the depressant drug.

The data on the effects of sedatives on performance after frontal lesions, in so far as they can be accepted, are relevant to the hypothesis we have suggested concerning the nature of the change frontal damage brings about. Because of the nature of the neurological parameter postulated as underlying introversion-extraversion, the relatively more extraverted person would be expected to be particularly prone to the effects of retroactive inhibition of the type analogous to that being proposed as responsible for the deficits in the performance of leucotomized monkeys on delayed response tasks. Since we have suggested that frontal lesions result in an increase in extraversion, the demonstrated deficit is thus consistent with this notion, as can be seen. If the hypothesis about an increase in extraversion following frontal lobe lesions were correct, and if the general hypothesis about the nature of the underlying neurological parameter of introversion-extraversion were also correct, then the found effect of Nembutal on delay response tasks would be expected. The finding forges another link in a nomological chain.

A great deal of the work of Mishkin and Pribram and their associates has also been concerned with analysing the putative deficit following frontal lesion in monkeys performing delayed response tasks. One general conclusion from their work confirms earlier findings in that they claim that the deficit tends to be maximal when the traditional left-right choice is used (see also Finan, 1940; Spaet and Harlow, 1943).

The various investigations of Mishkin and Pribram and their associates have resulted in these conclusions (Mishkin and Hall, 1955; Mishkin and Pribram, 1955; Pribram and Mishkin, 1955; Mishkin and Pribram, 1956; Pribram and Mishkin, 1956)—

(a) deficits follow when, instead of being placed side by side, the choice cups are placed one above the other;

(b) deficits follow when a "go-no-go" type of alternation is required;

(c) the deficit is definitely linked to lesions in the frontal lobes, since control groups with lesions in the infero-temporal region were able to perform the task adequately;

(d) the size of the deficit varies as some function of the stimulus conditions; for example, a group of frontal animals performed the task nearly as well as controls "whenever a single cue presented in one of two places was replaced by one of two cues presented in a single place." (Mishkin and Pribram, 1956.)

The basic observation of a deficit following frontal lesions has been studied in the light of various control situations some of which remain to be mentioned.

Forgays (1952), in a very important investigation, tested rats in a closed field apparatus at varying intervals after cerebral excisions had been made. He found that no drop in performance occurred if testing was carried out within two hours after operation. After this he reported the usual sharp decline in performance. Contrary to Jacobsen *et al.* (1935) he claimed that lesions in the parietal lobes seemed to be of importance for this task.

The important feature of Forgay's investigation is not this latter finding, of course, but the implication from the former that some rapidly occurring biochemical change or degenerative process following excisions might be responsible for the changes after frontal lesions.

Orbach (1956) has pointed out that the artificial production of the toxic action of cell degeneration and the mechanical distortion produced by pressure or diaschisis have not resulted in deficits in performance and he therefore doubted Forgay's results. In his own study, four monkeys were trained on delayed response tasks and trephine holes made. The animals were tested immediately after this procedure and for a further ten to fourteen days when frontal lesions were made "blind." The animals were then tested again between one and a half to six hours after the operation and for a further fourteen days. Orbach reported that no drop in performance followed the trephining procedure but that immediate deficits appeared after the introduction of frontal lesions, which deficit decreased with further testing but performance never reached the pre-operative level.

The discrepancy between the results of Forgays and Orbach may be due to either a difference connected to the different types of tasks employed or to a difference in response to injury of the more complex primate cerebrum.

Pribram (1955) demonstrated that the deficits were not due to lesions in the frontal eye-fields or due to the scarring of these areas, although he believed that the former were certainly somewhat involved in the production of deficits in delayed response tasks after frontal lesions. In his study monkeys were trained on visual pursuit tasks, visual discrimination tasks, visual field tests and delayed response tasks. Lesions were introduced into the frontal eye-fields, either surgically or by the implanting of ammonium hydroxide pastes which resulted in scarring of the tissues. Only the delayed response tasks were affected, showing that primary visual abilities were not the cause of the deficits. Scarring produced only slight temporary effects while the surgical lesions produced somewhat more marked deficits in performance on the delayed response tasks. Pribram concludes that the deficits he observed in this study were much less severe than those seen after anterior operations and could thus not be wholly responsible for deficits found after the latter.

Miles and Rosvold (1956) provided another control study when they showed that the deficit in delayed response behaviour of monkeys occurred whether the motivating conditions were food or electric shock.

One final study should be mentioned; that of Rosvold and Delago (1956). They implanted electrodes in various parts of the cortices of four *macaca mulata* monkeys and observed the effects of electrical stimulation and destruction by coagulation of these areas on visual discrimination and delayed response tasks. They found no consistent difference between the various effects of stimulation and coagulation but noted that the destruction of the *corpus striatum*, particularly of the caudate nucleus and its cortical projections, most regularly resulted in the changes in activity and gastronomical disturbances that have usually been ascribed to leucotomy and psychosurgical procedures in general. Miles and Rosvold, in the study quoted above, also concluded, after histological examination, that the caudate nucleus might well have been involved in the changes observed by them.

Conclusions from Animal Studies

As we pointed out at the beginning of this section, there is no necessary warranty for arguing from one phylogenetic level to another. If, however, we wish to apply these comparative findings to the cases of psychosurgery performed on human subjects, we could conclude that—

(a) a deficit in cognitive abilities, following psychosurgical procedures, might not be an absolute one, in the sense that manipulation of the form of the problem material could result in the disappearance of the deficit;

(b) the evidence, from these sources, as to whether degenerative biochemical processes or by-products result in cognitive deficits rather than the mere severing of tracts being responsible is inconclusive but generally does not support the first alternative;

(c) no deficit can definitely be ascribed to the frontal areas since, notwithstanding (b), some evidence points to the involvement of supracortical areas being involved, perhaps through neural degenerative processes.[1]

Cognitive Changes after Psychosurgery and Theories of Frontal Lobe Functions

Cognitive changes after psychosurgery in psychiatric patients have most usually been investigated with the very practical aim of describing what are essentially side-effects, albeit important ones, of the operative procedures. Most theories of frontal lobe functions have been based on the study of brain damage resulting from natural causes and, although these have been dealt with extensively in the preceding chapter, several of the most important should be mentioned here, as a preliminary to our discussion of cognitive changes, because they have influenced the nature of the assessments of these changes in psychosurgery patients.

THEORIES OF FRONTAL LOBE FUNCTIONS

Bricker's (1936) belief that his lobectomized patient had lost the capacity to compound simple patterns into more complex ones has already been mentioned. His work was based on the extensive study of a single case who had a bilateral removal of the frontal tissue for the extirpation of frontal neoplasms.

Goldstein (1939, 1949; Goldstein and Scheerer, 1941) initiated a widely accepted characterization of frontal lobe functioning when he concluded that his brain-damaged patients were deficient in their capacity to carry on abstract thought and tended toward a more concrete level of thinking.

Many workers, working with psychosurgery patients, have arrived at similar conclusions to those of Goldstein or have taken his hypothesis as a starting-

point. For example, Nichols and Hunt (1940) in another extensive study of a single case of frontal lobectomy, reached a position similar to Goldstein's when they described the deficit shown by their patient (in the presence of high intelligence test scores) as being composed of four aspects—

(a) the failure to supply spontaneously, fresh modes of attack on a problem, apparently resulting from an inability to abstract that aspect of the situation causing the difficulty;

(b) a rigidity of the "categorical attitude";

(c) a sharp limitation in the number of lines of endeavour able to be kept separated simultaneously;

(d) an inability to integrate several aspects of a situation.

When we come to deal with specific test results, we will mention a fairly consistently reported finding that after psychosurgical procedures there is a fall in Porteus Maze scores. Porteus has, on the basis of this, offered a theory as to the nature of frontal lobe functions. He has claimed that his test measures planning ability and has thus characterized the change in behaviour after psychosurgery as being in this function. We would like to mention two, rather lengthy, papers which treat of this proposition directly.

Porteus and Kepner (1944) reviewed the previous work on the Maze Test performance of psychosurgery patients and examined in detail the case notes of some twenty patients of mixed diagnoses who had been subjected to psychosurgical procedures. They noted that Binet scores showed no consistent changes after operation but that the lack of any increase from the pre-operative to the post-operative score on the Maze tests, indicated that the performance of the patients on the second occasion was deficient, since the Maze Test shows a large practice effect. These authors concluded that the lack of foresight and initiative, those capacities believed to be measured by the Maze Test, did indeed seem to comprise the deficit after the operations.

Porteus and Peters (1947), however, preferred to start from the other end. They observed that it is well known that psychosurgery results in a lack of foresight and initiative. This fact they perceived as a golden opportunity to validate the Maze Test which purports to measure these faculties. They compared the scores of fifty-five leucotomized patients tested on five different occasions and compared them with the scores of a group of non-operated prisoners. The post-operative patients proved once again to be inferior on this test and accordingly, the authors concluded that the Mazes do in fact measure planning ability.

The suggestions for the nature of frontal lobe

---

[1] Yokoi (1957) has summarized much of the work done on the degenerative processes after psychosurgery and he concludes, after the examination of a number of specimens himself, that widespread degeneration is evident extending to various supracortical bodies.

functionings of both Goldstein and Porteus, it can be seen, are both based on performance deficits in quite special tests and the question of what in fact the tests do measure is crucial for the acceptance of these suggestions.

Payne (see Chapter 6) has presented a most damaging set of criticisms of Goldstein's notion of abstraction and of the tests which purport to measure it. If one accepts these criticisms, it becomes evident that the matter of whether psychosurgery patients show any deficit in concept formation has never been properly tackled. It seems to the present writer that an application of the procedures described by Bruner et al. (1956) would meet Payne's criticisms, as they apply in the case of psychosurgery's effects, and could well reveal important deficits in concept formation for patients so treated.

The function measured by the Porteus Mazes is of considerable importance since, as we shall see, decreases in performance on this test do regularly follow from the introduction of frontal lobe lesions. In fact the evidence points to the Mazes not measuring some purely cognitive factor at all but rather reflecting some personality variable—probably the willingness or capacity to follow instructions. Porteus's original work was with groups of psychopaths (1923, 1933, 1942) who regularly scored below normal groups. This finding has been repeated many times (Wright, 1944; Docter and Winder, 1954; Purcell, 1956; Fooks and Thomas, 1957). That such groups should be characterized by a purely cognitive deficiency seems unlikely and in fact has never been demonstrated. That they are characterized by a high degree of extraversion has been shown a number of times (Hildebrand, 1953; Franks, 1954; Lykken, 1957). Moreover, Hildebrand (1953) has shown that the test differentiates between groups of psychiatric patients —those who would be regarded as possessing higher degrees of extraversion having lower scores (Q scores). In view of these considerations, then, we are inclined to reject the notion that the Mazes measure only foresight or planning ability and to suggest that they reflect introversion-extraversion. The consistently reported decrements on Maze scores following psychosurgery strongly support the contention that the predominant change after psychosurgery is in the direction of increased extraversion, if this interpretation of what the Maze Test measures can be accepted.

Halstead (1947a; Halstead et al., 1946) is another who has tried to specify what function is subserved by the frontal lobes in his own terms and by the employment of performance tests. He has presented the notion of "biological intelligence," a function which is measured by an "impairment index" and which was developed in view of the consistently negative findings of investigations measuring general intelligence by orthodox means in groups of brain-damaged and post-leucotomy patients.

The concept of biological intelligence is rather vague, even amongst those notions associated with the effect of psychosurgery. The function is regarded as being connected with the "ego" or with some mechanism reflecting the degree of integrity of the central nervous system. The impairment index is derived by counting how many of ten brain-damage indicators yield scores similar to those given by groups of brain-damaged patients. The battery of tests defining biological intelligence was administered to a group of brain-damaged patients including eight post-leucotomy patients (Halstead et al., 1946). According to the notion implicit in Halstead's account the operation should have interfered with the degree of integrity of the central nervous system and the psychosurgery patients should have showed a drop on the impairment index. In this study, however, they did not, although a group of lobectomized patients was differentiated from a control group.

Although Halstead's idea is an interesting one, it presents certain difficulties. For example the reliability and validity of his defining tests have never been satisfactorily established, and a number of them would seem to be intercorrelated, so that, in fact, something less than ten separate measures probably go to make up the "index." Adding the various components together, while in itself a rather dubious procedure, would at best result in a measure of a relatively narrow and undefined band of capacities.

Reitman (1955a) has attempted a validation of this notion of Halstead's in a rather strangely convoluted study. He administered the battery of index tests to fifty mixed brain-damaged cases together with ten criterion tests, culled from the literature as being good indicators of brain damage. He reported that the index tests discriminated the brain-damaged group from a control group better than did the criterion tests. The latter included a test of critical flicker fusion, a modified version of the Seguin Form Board and the rhythm subtest of the Seashore test of Musical Aptitude.

One can see that his results are favourable to the claims of the impairment index but the assumption that the criterion tests were indicators of brain damage cannot be passed undebated and, since one of these, a test of categorizing, was as good as the impairment index tests at discriminating the brain-damaged cases, one cannot see the point of employing them in its stead.

Notable physicians have frequently suggested a number of characterizations of the deficits believed to follow psychosurgery. Freeman, for example (1942) at first proposed a notion very similar to that we discussed in association with Porteus (see also Porteus,

1951, 1955), who refers to Freeman as his source in this matter. Freeman at first suggested that the frontal lobes were concerned with foresight and planning. In later writings (Freeman and Watts, 1950; Robinson and Freeman, 1954) Freeman generalized this concept somewhat and concluded that the awareness of self in time is the concern of the frontal lobes—they are concerned in the person's perception of his own continuity through the course of time.

Landis *et al.* (1950) and Mettler and Landis (Mettler 1952) have suggested two characterizations of the frontal lobe functions in cognition—

(*a*) the span of attention of the post-psychosurgery patient is decreased and he is typically "stimulus-bound";

(*b*) in the post-psychosurgery patient the most notable feature is a general weakening of stimulus bonds.

It will be noticed that (*a*) has something in common with one of the conclusions arrived at by Greenblatt and Solomon in reviewing the effects of their operated cases and could be supported by some of the findings with monkeys on delayed response tasks. In general, however, none of these formulations can command a great deal of respect. They tend either to be so narrowly associated with some specific test as to be virtually untestable other than by reference to that test or so vague, like the suggestions of Landis *et al.* or Freeman, as to be virtually incapable of disproof.

COGNITIVE CHANGES

If we now turn to data from the application of cognitive tests to psychosurgery patients, we will be impressed with the general agreement that very little change in fact ensues after these operations. This was the kind of observation that led Halstead and others to conclude that the wrong tests were being used. There is, of course, no *a priori* reason for supposing that any intellectual deficits should follow circumscribed lesions in the frontal lobes, but our view is that the matter has not been decided and, in substantial agreement with Halstead, we believe will not be decided until a thorough revision of the nature of the cognitive processes has been made. The beginnings of such a revision will be found described in chapters in this HANDBOOK by Payne and by Furneaux. We will not attempt to reproduce their arguments and the reader is referred to the relevant chapters for this information. We will simply report a selection of the findings on cognitive tests that occur in the literature on psychosurgery, without necessarily accepting the interpretation of what the tests measure usually included in these reports.

Rylander, as has been mentioned, was one of the first to administer objective tests to psychosurgery patients and he has been very much concerned with the question whether general intelligence is decreased after these operations. He has summarized his results and has illustrated his case with detailed notes on eight neurotic patients (Rylander, 1947), concluding that there is a consistent drop in intelligence as measured by the Terman and Merrill revision of the Binet Scales. Malmo (1948) reported significant drops in Wechsler-Bellevue and Stanford-Binet vocabulary scores for eight patients subjected to leucotomies and seven undergoing gyrectomies. Koskoff *et al.* (1948) reported the testing of some of ten patients subjected to a psychosurgical procedure for the alleviation of pain and found a significant decline in Wechsler-Bellevue scores. Petrie (Petrie, 1952; Petrie and Le Beau, 1956) reported a similar finding for her groups subjected to rostral procedures and standard lobotomies but found no significant changes after any of the selective procedures she examined. Tow (1955) found a significant drop in scores on Raven's Matrices and the vocabulary test from Terman's 1916 battery. Tow's patients had been subjected to a procedure similar to those employed with Petrie's earlier groups. Yacorsinski *et al.* (1948) administered a large battery of tests to a single patient and reported a drop of eighteen points on the Wechsler-Bellevue scale.

These positive findings, however, are in a minority and the more usual report is of no decrement in general intelligence as measured by orthodox means. None of the large-scale studies of the Columbia Greystone or New York Associates or those from the Boston Psychopathic Hospital contain mention of permanent deficits indicated by alterations in either Wechsler-Bellevue or Stanford-Binet scores. Likewise, the investigations of Robinson (1946), Frank (1946), Carscallen *et al.* (1951), Crown (1952), Markwell *et al.* (1953), Struckett (1953), Medina *et al.* (1954), Hirose (1954), Wideman (in Miller, 1954) and Newman (1955) were more or less negative in respect of this class of change.

A number of writers have tried to analyse putative deficits by subtests. In general, these efforts have produced no consistent findings, but a direct attack on the problem has been made by McCullough (1950). He administered Form I of the Wechsler-Bellevue Scales to twenty-one patients undergoing psychosurgery, testing on three separate occasions. McCullough reported that the most prominent changes were seen in Digit Span, Picture Arrangement and Block Design subtests while no change occurred in Vocabulary, Information and Similarities. Medina *et al.* in the study mentioned above have reported a specific deficit on the Picture Arrangement subtest. Although Wideman, also quoted above, was unable to demonstrate any deficit following operation, he reported, on analysing his subtest scores, that clinical improvement seemed to be associated with a higher Performance than Verbal score, a small degree of Performance "scatter" and relatively high scores on Picture Arrangement, Picture Completion and Similarities.

Tow's use of Raven's Matrices has already been mentioned and the fact that he found a significant deficit on this test after leucotomy operations. Previously to this study, neither Frank (1946) nor Struckett (1953) found any fall in scores on this test with psychosurgery patients.

It has been mentioned that many writers have reported utilizing Goldstein's suggestion that abstract reasoning is affected by frontal lobe damage. King (in Mettler, 1949) made an important contribution towards testing this notion in the field of psychosurgery when he administered seven different tests, purporting to measure abstract reasoning ability, to seventeen operated cases and thirteen controls. He carried out a factor analysis of the subjects' scores on these tests and on tests of general intelligence. His conclusion was that the tests of "abstract reasoning" were highly saturated with a factor of general intelligence and that no significant differences between the operated cases and the controls, could be demonstrated. Vidor (1951) also reported a high correlation between performance on sorting tests and tests of general intelligence. Sheer and Shuttleworth (in Mettler, 1952) reported a temporary deficit on the Weigl Sorting Test and on a revised Homograph test for the group of subjects of the second Columbia Greystone project, while Sheer (in Lewis et al., 1956) confirmed the finding of a deficit but once more stressed its temporary nature.

Neither of the two reports from the Boston Psychopathic Hospital made any material contribution towards this problem. Atwell in the first report (Greenblatt et al., 1950) administered Goldstein's Block Design and Colour Sorting tests, the Weigl Colour-Form Sorting Test and the Shipley Test of Abstraction. He decided that none of the tests were suitable for proper quantification and was content to make a qualitative judgement about post-operative changes. Upon the basis of these judgements he reported a slight decrement in performance on these tests. In the second report (Greenblatt and Solomon, 1953), Levinson et al. administered a number of tests of Abstract-Reasoning and of "Coherence of Association" and reported on "improvement" in their subjects, particularly in the "emotional forms of the abstraction tests" (proverbs and similarities). Supporting this claim they point out that the most clinically improved patients seen by them showed the most improvement on the test of abstraction. In so far as the interpretation of these results can be accepted, they are somewhat contrary to others in the field. King's finding mentioned previously, however,

casts doubt on all this work and suggests that tests of abstraction probably measure nothing more than general intelligence.

Certain other investigations have utilized various tests of Abstraction. Kisker (1944a) was able to demonstrate no consistent impairment on a modified version of Koh's Blocks, the Weigl and Scheerer Sorting Test and the Goldstein Colour-Form Test. Likewise Robinson (1946) reported no decrement after operation on the Shipley-Hartford Retreat Scales. Neither Berg and Grant (1948), using a Weigl type sorting test and the Weigl Colour-Form Test, nor Vidor (1951) using various tests of abstract thinking was able to demonstrate any decrement after psychosurgery. Tow (1955) administered a sorting test to his subjects and contrary to the aforementioned reports noted a large decrement after operation, significant at the 1 per cent level of confidence. Tow described the behaviour of his subjects on this test as follows—

> After operation the subject is more foolish, naïve and clumsy in his approach. He does not easily grasp the nature of the problem. If there is any plan or reason at all in his method, it is more rigid and stereotyped. The subject looks blank at the examiner's questions and he is more quickly moved to despair and abandonment of further trial. His whole performance is less directed and less purposeful. It is obvious that his ability to sort is greatly reduced. (Tow, 1955.)

Considering, then, tests of general intelligence and of abstraction together it would appear that some deficits may be expected after the more radical operations, as in the cases of Petrie and Tow, where, in addition it should also be pointed out, pre-operative performance has not been clouded by the gross cognitive defects of psychoses. For cases in which the latter defects might be expected to be considerable and for the selective operations, the position is not clear. The evidence, however, does point to there being no gross deficits following on such operations.

The evidence also most strongly suggests that the tests of abstraction are very closely related to tests of general intelligence and it is evident that where deficits are found in the latter (as in the cases of Petrie and Tow) some impairment may be expected to be evident in the scores of the former.

Many investigators have administered tests of memory and retention. Stauffer in the first report of the Columbia Greystone project (Mettler, 1949) compared the performance of nineteen operated cases with thirteen controls on learning and retention of three forms of verbal material (a) semi-meaningful paired associates, (b) meaningful paired associates and (c) verbal directions. She reported no significant impairment. In the second report of these associates (Mettler, 1952), North et al. examined memory, learning, mental set and perceptual tasks, by means of, largely, verbal tests. They reported no impairment of memory or learning. It is interesting to note that these workers attempted to duplicate the delayed-response type tasks used in comparative work but found that no deficits were evident with their human subjects. This discrepancy is not surprising, of course, when one considers the relatively much greater damage done to the primates' cortices. These workers finally suggested that "forced" tempo learning was less affected than "free." The finding is relevant to the discussions of the role of neuroticism in the performance of stressful tasks, to be found in the chapters in this Handbook by Inglis and by Jones. A relatively greater improvement under the stress of forced tempo would suggest that some decrease in the degree of neuroticism had occurred for the subjects of this study. North and Zubin (in Lewis *et al.*, 1956) repeated this investigation and in general returned negative results, only temporary deficits being evident for any of the functions they investigated. One of the few exceptions was that performance on a continuous addition task was sensitive to individual change after the operations. The impairment was not due to a decrease in accuracy but to a progressive decrease in the amount of work done over the fifteen-minute period occupied by the test. Such an increase in work decrement would be expected for a condition which heightened extraversion, by virtue of the increased liability to the effects of cortical inhibition which would be postulated as accompanying the personality change.

Kral and Durost (1953) have analysed the amnestic syndrome in a variety of different categories of brain-damaged patients, including leucotomized patients. Their findings, contrary to those listed above, are that impairment of recent memory and recall are common to all. Their conclusions have rarely been paralleled. Hirose (1954) reported no drop in memory functions in a group of ten psychopaths and five neurotic patients subjected to leucotomies—nor previous to this study did Malmo (1948) nor did Markwell *et al.* (1953) nor Medina *et al.* (1954) using the Wechsler Memory Scales and the Benton Test of Visual Retention. Contrarily again, however, Newman (1955) has reported a significant drop on Wechsler Memory Scales for his group.

Rylander (1939*a*) examined the ability of his lobectomized patients to learn a list of nonsense syllables and reported some deficits but his methods of testing were crude and his findings correspondingly equivocal. Malmo and Amsel (1949) and Malmo (1948) have examined this function more systematically.

Malmo and Amsel on the basis of the hypothesis of Malmo (1942), predicted that the characteristically bowed rote-learning curve would be more peaked for a group of patients with frontal-lobe lesions. They argued that associative interference or intraserial interference being more pronounced over the middle items of a list, the rote-learning curves of post-psychosurgery patients should be more peaked if, as Malmo suggested, such frontal lesions lead to an exaggeration of the effects of associative interference. To test the prediction they compared the rote-learning curves of six gyrectomy patients sixteen controls and sixteen

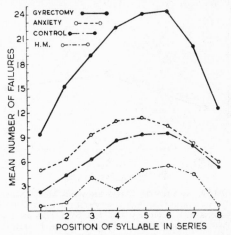

FIG. 15.3. COMPOSITE CURVES SHOWING MEAN NUMBER OF FAILURES AT VARIOUS SYLLABLES DURING LEARNING BY SIXTEEN PATIENTS WITH "CLINICAL ANXIETY," SIXTEEN CONTROLS, FIVE GYRECTOMY PATIENTS, AND H.M. (ONE GYRECTOMY PATIENT WHO APPEARED ATYPICAL)
(*From Malmo and Amsel*, 1949)

cases showing clinical anxiety, derived from the rote learning of eight syllables lists of nonsense syllables.

Fig. 15.3 illustrates the resulting data. It can be seen that the curve of the gyrectomy patients appears more peaked in accordance with the authors' prediction. Had the number of the operative cases been larger, the application of an analysis of variance device would have established this finding in a more formal way than that of inspection. Confirmatory evidence, however, is supplied by Malmo (1948)[1] from data collected on the rote learning of eight bilateral frontal lobotomy patients tested before and after their operations. The data are presented, in this study, in the form of the differential amount of behavioural oscillation evident across the segments of a nonsense syllable series. The behavioural oscillation, being measured in terms of the number of alternations from a correct to an incorrect response, is also a function of associative interference and tends also to be more pronounced over the middle items of a list. That Malmo and Amsel's prediction is confirmed is

[1] This study, appears to have succeeded that of Malmo and Amsel, although the latter appears in the literature at a later time.

suggested by the behavioural oscillation curves shown in Fig. 15.4 where it can be again seen that with the introduction of frontal lesions, the degree of peakedness over the middle items appears to have been increased.

Malmo's hypothesis is a particularization of the one we have proposed concerning the nature of the change following psychosurgery, and the data quoted

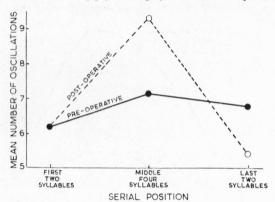

FIG. 15.4. COMPOSITE CURVES SHOWING MEAN NUMBER OF OSCILLATIONS OCCURRING BETWEEN THE FIRST CORRECT RESPONSE AND LAST FAILURE FOR SYLLABLES IN EACH POSITION FOR PRE- AND POST-OPERATIVE LEARNING
(*From Malmo*, 1948)

above strongly support our contention. Our terminology would be slightly different—we would prefer to use the term associative inhibition—but our prediction would be precisely the same. We would expect that non-brain-damaged extraverts would show evidence of exaggerated associative inhibition in an increased peakedness of the rote serial position curve by virtue of the nature of the neurological parameter postulated as underlying the dimension introversion-extraversion. Such an increase in the peakedness of the rote serial learning curves of post-psychosurgery patients would have been thus expected if the hypothesis that these patients are characterized by a high degree of extraversion is tenable. The evidence is, of course, in no way conclusive but adds weight to the body of observations supporting our hypothesis about the personality changes wrought by psychosurgery.

One further test, already mentioned in a general way, must be dealt with—the Porteus Maze Test. We have said that changes in this test are perhaps the most consistently reported of all. Apart from the

reports made by Porteus himself and his collaborators (Porteus and Kepner, 1944; Porteus and Peters, 1947; Porteus, 1951, 1955—reviews) deficits have been reported by both studies of the Columbia Greystone Associates (albeit, only temporary ones), by the New York Associates and by Greenblatt and Solomon in the second investigation from the Boston Psychopathic Hospital. Decrements in Maze performance after psychosurgery has been reported by Koskoff *et al.* (1948), Crown (1952)—an insignificant one however—Malmo (1948), Petrie (1952), Medina *et al.* (1954) and Tow (1955).

We have suggested that the function measured by the Porteus Mazes is associated with a factor of temperament—introversion-extraversion, and these consistent findings of deficits in Maze performance after psychosurgery also support our contention that it is extraversion that is altered by these procedures.

Conclusions from Studies of Cognitive Changes

Hebb (1945) in the review quoted at the commencement of this chapter, came to the conclusion that no connexion between any cognitive function and the frontal lobes had been, up to the time of his writing, demonstrated. In concluding this present review we could not presume to consider whether or not we have been dealing with frontal lobe functions, but even limiting ourselves to the more modest attempt to determine whether any purely cognitive function is disturbed after frontal surgery for the relief of psychiatric illness, we can, likewise, reach no very definite conclusions. In general it would appear that—

(*a*) there is a suggestion in the comparative work that some sort of cognitive deficit can be expected to follow extensive operations, and

(*b*) this suggestion does receive some support from the examination of cases whose pre-operative state is not so disturbed as to render psychological tests of dubious value and who are subjected to relatively radical forms of psychosurgery;

(*c*) little deficit appears to follow the more circumscribed forms of these operations;

(*d*) what functions are disturbed must wait upon the application of cognitive tests, like those described by Furneaux (Chapter 5) whose factorial composition is thoroughly known, and which are integrated with a properly formulated and tested conception of the cognitive processes.

ELECTROENCEPHALOGRAPHIC STUDIES AND MOLAR AUTONOMIC CHANGES AFTER PSYCHOSURGERY

We cannot pretend to attempt an adequate coverage of either of these areas of investigation, lying as they do, somewhat outside the limits imposed by the tech-

niques of psychological investigations, but we would like to mention certain studies which have a direct bearing on some of the points we have been making.

Electroencephalographic Studies

We have noted that the hypothesis suggested by Hebb (1949) for the action of psychosurgery, requires the presence of a hypersynchrony in the firing of cortical neurons. Hebb regards the appearance of large potentials, firing spontaneously, in the EEG records, as evidence for such a hypersynchrony and, in fact many EEG studies have reported such features in the post-operative records of psychosurgery patients. The most usual report is of slow waves of large potential appearing at first across the whole frontal cortex but becoming localized about the lesion sites with the passage of time. It should be noted that an assumption is being made about the accuracy of interpreting the EEG records in all this work, an assumption which some might query.

Reports of findings as described above have been made by Davis (1941), Hutton et al. (1941), Cohn (1945), Greville and Last (1947), Stevens and Mosovich (1947), Zigarelli (in Mettler, 1949), Bonako (in Miller, 1954) and by Walter et al. (1954). Henry (1950a) and Henry and Scoville (1952) have described analogous findings and have stressed the suppression of fast rhythms in the frontal lobes after psychosurgery and the increase in slow waves of large potential.

Somewhat different observations were made by Wada and Enko (1951), who reported the predominance of arrhythmic waves after psychosurgery and by Lennox and Coolidge (1949) who described the most characteristic change in EEG records after operation, as a $\frac{1}{2}$–1 c/s baseline sway. Henry (1950b) found no evidence of slow-wave activity in two post-operative transorbital lobotomy subjects.

That some form of hypersynchrony be present in the EEG records of post-psychosurgery patients is one necessary condition for the confirmation of Hebb's hypothesis. A second requirement is that such a hypersynchrony be concomitant with clinical improvement. The evidence here is not at all so consistent. Henry et al. (1948) found that decreased low voltage fast activity and an increase in alpha rhythm were associated with clinical improvement, a finding which supports Hebb's hypothesis. Walter et al. (1954), however, reported that their clinically improved group was characterized by the appearance of a moderate degree of slow-wave activity in post-operative EEG records but that both high and low degrees of such activity were typical of their little improved group. That the relationship between hypersynchrony and improvement should be a linear one is not a necessary implication of Hebb's hypothesis but the hypothesis would require modification if it was found to be otherwise.

Bonako (in Miller, 1954) in a well-constructed study of one hundred and twelve leucotomy patients, contrary to the above work, found no relationship between the discovery of slow waves in the post-operative EEG records of his patients and clinical improvement. Nor did he find any general change in the alpha rhythm of his post-operative patients, other than some indication of a tendency towards a concentration of the mean values of alpha rhythms. Additionally, however, Bonako did report a number of signs in the pre-operative EEG records which were statistically related to degree of clinical improvement. The favourable signs were, mean alpha indices in the slow normal range and a lower than average fast frequency content in the pre-operative records; the unfavourable signs were the obverse of these and a poorly organized alpha rhythm.

Levin et al. found no relationship between recovery rate and the occurrence of post-operative seizures. One might have expected from Hebb's hypothesis that some such relationship of a very general kind might have been found since the appearance of slow waves in EEG records tends to suggest the likelihood of seizures.

That epileptic conditions, at least of a temporary duration, are common after psychosurgery has been commented upon. The incidence of post-operative seizures is one of the usual statistics accompanying clinical reports but a number of studies which bear directly on the problem may be mentioned here.

Wayne (1952) reported that of eighty-seven leucotomy patients in her study 30 per cent developed post-operative seizures while of twenty topectomy patients 42 per cent developed seizures. Austt-Garcia et al. (1954) reported that epileptiform activation was common after Poppen-type prefrontal leucotomy and Klotz (1955) reported that of one hundred and ninety-three patients subjected to pre-frontal leucotomies, 19 per cent had grand mal seizures post-operatively whereas only 8 per cent had evidenced them pre-operatively. Klotz found no significant relationship between EEG records and the development of seizures but found that pre-operative E.C.T. treatment was associated with the post-operative development of seizures. Levin et al., quoted above, had made the same observation while Liddell and Rettersol (1957) have reported that treatment with chlorpromazine predisposed patients to develop post-operative seizures after psychosurgery.

Summary of Electroencephalographic Studies

(a) There is some suggestion from a mass of contradictory evidence that some features of the post-operative EEG records reflect a concomitant of clinical improvement, and

(b) The appearance of slow-wave activity in the EEG records would seem to be the most prominent abnormality evident and may be that feature of the records which is related to improvement. But it is also evident that the relationship is not a simple one.

(c) Certain other forms of psychiatric treatment, E.C.T. and the administration of chlorpromazine appear to predispose patients to the development of seizures after psychosurgery.

(d) The appearance of seizures does not appear to be related to clinical improvement.

Molar Autonomic Changes after Psychosurgery

Wenger (1947, 1950) has produced a considerable body of work which relates a state of autonomic imbalance to emotional lability and, as we have described earlier, Eysenck (1947, 1952) has invoked these studies in support of his notion that the neurological substructure underlying neuroticism is just such an imbalance. Apart from the work of these two writers a certain amount of independent evidence has been collected which supports Wenger's hypothesis and the relationship between autonomic imbalance and neuroticism. Granger, in his section of this HANDBOOK deals with some of this evidence, as does Martin (Chapter 11) in hers.

If a decrease in neuroticism follows psychosurgery, then we might reasonably expect evidence of a decrease in the level of autonomic activity.

The evidence collected to date is entirely equivocal. Reitman (1945) summarized the effects of Progigine, eserine, ephedrine and Benzedrine on a group of fifteen leucotomized schizophrenic patients and an equal number of controls. Reitman characterized the drug effects as suggesting that the operations resulted in a tendency to maintain autonomic equilibrium, a conclusion indicating that a decrease in neuroticism may have occurred in this group. Rinkel et al. (1947a, 1947b; and in Greenblatt et al., 1950) similarly reported that, although there was an initial heightening of autonomic responses after psychosurgery in their patients, equilibrium was re-established through readjustments within the autonomic nervous system over the passage of time.

The study of Elithorn et al. (1954) contains contradictory evidence on the question of the direction of the change, in the functions of the autonomic nervous systems after psychosurgery. On the one hand they found that their patients (twelve subjected to standard lobotomies, the others to more circumscribed operations) showed both higher surface skin temperatures and higher skin resistances and on the other, that a group of anxious patients showed reduced P.G.R. responses to a loud noise stimulus after the operation.

Ashby and Bassett (1950), however, had found the opposite results when they had compared the P.G.R. responses of a group of leucotomized psychiatric

patients to those of a control group. These authors concluded that there was no evidence of diminished emotional lability in the operated patients as shown by their P.G.R. records.

Chapman et al. (1950) reported a highly significant decrease in the tolerance of a group of post-psychosurgery patients for superficial pain (using the Hardy-Wolff Thermo-stimulator). Buck et al. reported a rapid reversion to a high rectal temperature after psychosurgery in a group of psychiatric patients who had shown this characteristic pre-operatively.

Finally, Malmo and Shagass (1950) have reported an extensive study of the effects of psychosurgery on the physiological correlates of anxiety. It should be noted that the psychiatric syndrome characterizing the patients of these authors would be held to be compounded of both introversion and of neuroticism. Malmo and Shagass proceeded from the hypothesis of Malmo (1942, 1948) (mentioned before in a different form), that the effect of psychosurgery is to reduce the capacity to maintain a set towards a goal, or to maintain an attitude of expectancy. They argued that anxiety is just such an attitude of expectancy and that psychosurgery would thus be effective when the capacity of the patient to maintain the expected attitude of anxiety was reduced.

Now, it has been argued that anxiety is a conditioned response—a conditioned fear response in fact —(cf. Chapter 13 by H. Gwynne Jones) and since we have described the extravert as being characterized by a resistance to conditioning processes and by a rapid extinction of established conditioned responses, a finding that post-psychosurgery patients were so characterized would be consistent with the contention that the post-operative change is one of increased extraversion. Describing anxiety as an attitude of expectancy, as Malmo and Shagass do, is, of course, tantamount to describing it as a conditioned response tendency, in the sense that this term is applied to human subjects.

Malmo and Shagass measured their subjects' capacity to maintain sets of expectancy in terms of the "potency of change in exteroceptive stimulation relative to the strength of internally maintained stimulation from sets and expectancies." They proceeded to test this notion by comparing the effectiveness of instructions in overcoming natural responses to painful stimuli in a group of thirteen post-operation cases and a like number of matched controls. Their subjects were instructed to keep their heads still while a heat stimulus was applied (Hardy-Wolff Thermostimulator). Measurements were taken on head movements, finger movements, respiration, P.G.R., heart rate and of muscle potentials from the head and neck.

In general Malmo and Shagass concluded that

exteroceptive stimuli showed increased potency in overcoming expectancies in their group. Moreover, they educed decreased amount of finger movement and decreased level of muscle potentials from the head and neck as further indications of a reduction in anxiety. It is significant that with the reductions in these analogues of "conditioned" responses of anxiety, there was an increase in the level of P.G.R., suggesting, if anything, an increased emotional response to the stimuli themselves.

Malmo and Shagass's work lends further support to the hypothesis we have proposed, but that the matter is a complex one is underlined by the findings of Sainsbury (1954). Sainsbury compared the autistic and communicative gestures of a group of leucotomized patients, a normal control group and a non-operated anxious group of psychiatric patients in an electromyographic study. He found that, pre-operatively, the patients made more autistic gestures than the group of normal controls and that post-operatively autistic gestures—those characterizing the mentally ill—were more decreased than the communicative gestures. He also reported that high pre-operative levels of anxiety, tension, depression and restlessness were associated with post-operative decreases in autistic movements. The implication that anxiety and tension were relieved by the operations we would have expected; that a decrease in autistic movement itself should have occurred suggests that factors other than extraversion were affected although the identification of what these factors were is not easy.

A number of studies on the rate of critical flicker fusion in psychosurgery patients have been made and are relevant to our discussion. It should be noted, first of all, that a large number of studies have associated low flicker fusion frequencies with extraversion. One can cite the studies of Madlung (1935), Washburn et al. (1930), Krugman (1947), Simonson and Brozek (1952) and Goldstone (1955). A close identification of what these authors have called extraversion and that factor we are referring to cannot

be made of course, since the same measure of intro-version-extraversion has not been used in every case. Nevertheless, these findings are suggestive.

Halstead (1947b) compared the C.F.F. rates of twenty-five post-leucotomy patients with those of twenty-one neurosurgical cases from whom had been removed equal amounts of tissue from other areas of the brain and with those of a group of thirty normal controls. He reported that the post-leucotomy patients had significantly lower C.F.F. rates than either the normal group or the operated controls. Jones (1952) made daily determinations of C.F.F. rates for twenty days before and twenty-five days after leucotomy operations in a group of psychiatric patients and reported a significant drop in these rates after the operation. Landis and Clausen (1955) in a general study of sensory and motor performances following psychosurgery also reported a significant drop in C.F.F. rates for their post-operative group.

Such findings have not been unanimous however. Young (in Mettler, 1949) and King and Clausen (in Mettler, 1952) found only irregular and temporary lowering of C.F.F. rates in their post-operative groups and were unable to point to any consistent trends.

Summary and Conclusions from Molar Autonomic Studies

(a) A number of changes in autonomic functions are suggested in the literature although there are no conclusive findings. Those most commonly reported are: changes in P.G.R., temperature regulation, response to pain stimuli, C.F.F. rates and autistic movements.

(b) There is no conclusive evidence that those measures like P.G.R. which reflect emotional lability are lower after psychosurgery.

(c) There is considerable, although also inconclusive, evidence that measures either believed to be associated with extraversion or with the predominance of the cortical inhibitory potential are altered towards suggesting an increase in both after psychosurgery.

FINAL COMMENTS AND CONCLUSIONS

In the preceding review we have attempted to give a representative cross-section of the experimental work which has been carried out on the effects of psycho-surgery. We prefaced our account with a brief summary of the clinical studies and included in it comparative investigations which seemed to be of direct interest and relevance. Without too grossly slanting our choice of studies for review towards its verification or refutation we have examined the hypothesis that an increase in extraversion is the

typical alteration in personality after psychosurgical procedures.

Summaries and conclusions have been given at the end of each section throughout the review and there seems little point in repeating them here *in extenso*, but, before concluding, we would like to offer these final comments and general summary—

(a) Psychosurgery has been based upon a set of observations of dubious validity and on a tenuous rationale.

(*b*) The most responsible and best executed studies in the field have been most cautious in associating specific surgical procedures with clinical improvements.

(*c*) Bearing the above caution in mind, the empirical evidence from the clinical studies points most regularly to psychoneurotic states of anxiety, tension and reactive depression being those relieved by psychosurgical procedures.

(*d*) When examined in terms of established dimensions of personality, the evidence, from the clinical studies, from the observations of animals, from the application of objective tests associated with these dimensions, and from the studies of molar autonomic changes, is almost entirely equivocal with respect to whether the operations reduce disease tendencies—here termed neuroticism and psychoticism—but strongly suggests that a change in the factor of temperament introversion-extraversion, towards a reduction of introversion, is the change most commonly observed.

(*e*) The systematic study of whether this hypothesis is a satisfactory one has not as yet been made, although the work of Petrie (1952; Le Beau, 1953, 1956) has laid necessary and substantial foundations for it. The methodology of such a study would require the testing of a homogeneous group of leucotomy patients of well-preserved personalities in a number of controlled laboratory experimental situations yielding measures of known relationship to the factors of temperament in question.

(*f*) Whether any purely cognitive deficits follow psychosurgical procedures also awaits systematic investigation but the available evidence from both the studies of human psychiatric patients and from comparative sources suggests that only relatively gross damage to the frontal lobes results in any deficit and even this evidence is far from conclusive.

This last comment highlights an issue which we have largely avoided—the site of the action of the operative procedures. At certain points in our discussion we have suggested that the truth of this matter may not be that superficially implied by the simple introduction of lesions into the white matter of the frontal lobes. In general we have simply attempted to relate operations to behavioural *sequelae* without concerning ourselves with the intervening processes. To have done so would have led us too far from our main purpose and field of expertise, but the issue involved here should be pointed out.

That the frontal lobes may not be as intimately concerned with higher mental processes, as has been long held, is an idea which has been filtering down from the laboratories of the neuroanatomists and neuropathologists for some time now. Fulton (1951)

has suggested that the site of action for psychosurgical procedures is in subcortical systems affected by degenerative processes and this and similar ideas have received considerable attention in the laboratories of comparative psychologists and physiologists (e.g. Chow and Hutt, 1953; Chow, 1954; French *et al.*, 1955; Peters *et al.*, 1956; Jameson *et al.*, 1957). The more technical evidence from neurology and physiology for what Penfield has called a "supracortical integrating mechanism," identified with the reticular formation, is to be found in the symposium edited by Delafresnaye (1954).

In conclusion we must also point out that the interests of psychiatrists appear, at the moment, to be turning away from psychosurgery as a treatment for their patients, and this in itself strongly suggests the inadequacies of the technique. Instead, emphasis is being placed increasingly upon pharmacological therapies. The claims of the proponents of these often seem hardly more temperate than were those of the early proponents of psychosurgery. The possibility of descriptive and systematic investigations of the effects of drugs is great and presents almost none of the mechanical difficulties, inseparable from the investigation of psychosurgery—the provision of adequate control groups has been always difficult, for example. The efforts of clinicians and psychologists investigating the effects of psychosurgery have often been repetitive and wasteful. One can only hope that those concerned with describing the behavioural effects of the many drugs now coming into psychiatric usage will profit by this example.

REFERENCES

ALDRICHT, C. K., Problems of social adjustment following lobotomy, *Amer. J. Psychiat.*, **107**, 459–462 (1950).

ALLISON, H. W. and ALLISON, S. G., Personality changes following transorbital lobotomy, *J. Abnorm. (Soc.) Psychol.*, **49**, 219–233 (1954).

ARNOT, R. E., Clinical indications for prefrontal lobotomy, *J. Nerv. Ment. Dis.*, **109**, 267–69 (1949).

ASHBY, W. R. and BASSETT, M., The effects of leucotomy on creative ability, *J. Ment. Sci.*, **95**, 418–430 (1949).

ASHBY, W. R. and BASSETT, M., The effects of prefrontal leucotomy upon the psychogalvanic response, *J. Ment. Sci.*, **96**, 458–469 (1950).

BARETTO, A. C., VELASCO, O. P., BAIROA, I. S., DA COSTA, E. M. and BERNADENELLI, P., Lobotomy in epilepsy, *Psychosurgery*, Lisbon, 1st. Inter. Congr. Psychosurgery (1949).

BECKER, W. C. and MCFARLAND, R. L., A lobotomy prognosis scale, *J. Cons. Psychol.*, **19**, 157–162 (1955).

BERG, ESTA and GRANT, D. A., The performance of topectomised patients on the University of Wisconsin Card Sorting Test, *Amer. Psychologist*, **3**, 360 (1948).

BERLINER, F., BEVERIDGE, R. L., MAYER-GROSS, W. and MOORE, J., Prefrontal leucotomy: a report on 100 cases, *Lancet*, **249**, 325–328 (1945).

BIANCHI, L., *The Mechanism of the Brain* (Edinburgh, Livingstone, 1922).

BIGELOW, N. (Ed.), Criteria for the selection of psychotic patients for psychosurgery, *Pub. Health Serv. Doc. No. 16. Fed. Sec. Agency, Washington*, (New York, 1949).

BLUM, J. S., CHOW, K. L. and BLUM, R. A., Delayed response performance of monkeys with frontal removals after excitant and sedative drugs, *J. Neurophysiol.*, **3**, 196–202 (1951).

BOCHOVEN, S. J. and HYDE, R. W., The application of a sociometric technique to the study of lobotomised patients, *J. Nerv. Ment. Dis.*, **114**, 95–105 (1951).

BONNER, F., COBB, S., SWEET, W. H. and WHITE, J. C., Frontal lobe surgery in the treatment of pain, *Psychosom. Med.*, **14**, 383–388, (1952).

BRICKNER, R. M., *The Intellectual Functions of the Frontal Lobes* (New York, Macmillan, 1936).

BRODMANN, K., *Vergleichende Lokalisationslehre der Grosshirnde* (Leipzig, Barth, 1909).

BRODY, E. B. and ROSVOLD, H. E., The influence of prefrontal lobotomy on social interaction in a monkey group, *Psychosom. Med.* **14**, 406–415 (1952).

BRUNER, J. S., GOODENOW, J. J. and AUSTEN, G. A., *A Study of Thinking* (New York, John Wiley & Sons, Inc., 1956).

BUCK, C. W., CARSCALLEN, H. B. and HOBBS, G. E., The effect of prefrontal lobotomy on temperature regulation in schizophrenic patients, *A.M.A. Arch. Neurol. Psychiat.*, **65**, 197–205 (1951).

BURKHARDT, G., Über Rindenexcisionen als Beitrag zur Operativentherapie der Psychosen, *Allg. Z. Psychiat.*, **47**, 463–548 (1890).

CAMPBELL, R. J. and HARLOW, H. F., Problem solution by monkeys following bilateral removal of the prefrontal areas: V. Spatial delayed reactions, *J. Exp. Psychol.*, **35**, 110–126 (1945).

CARSCALLEN, H. B., BUCK, C. W. and HOBBS, G. E., Clinical and pyschological investigation of prefrontal lobotomy in schizophrenia, *A.M.A. Arch. Neurol. Psychiat.*, **65**, 206–220 (1951).

CATTELL, J. P., A psychodynamic study of topectomy patients, *Amer. J. Psychiat.*, **107**, 373–377 (1950).

CATTELL, J. P., Some observations on the selection of patients for psychosurgery and psychotherapy after operation, *Amer. J. Psychiat.*, **109**, 484–491 (1953).

CHAPMAN, W. P., ROSE, A. S. and SOLOMON, H. C., A follow-up study of motor withdrawal reaction to heat discomfort in patients before and after frontal lobotomy, *Amer. J. Psychiat.*, **107**, 221–224 (1950).

CHENG, S., TAIT, H. S. and FREEMAN, W., Transorbital lobotomy vs. electroconvulsive shock therapy in the treatment of mentally ill tuberculosis patients, *Amer. J. Psychiat.*, **113**, 32–56 (1956).

CHOW, K. L., The lack of behavioural effects following destruction of some thalamic association nuclei, *A.M.A. Arch. Neurol. Psychiat.*, **71**, 762–771 (1954).

CHOW, K. L. and HUTT, P. J., The association cortex of *macaca mulata*: a review of recent contributions to its anatomy and functions, *Brain*, **76**, 625–677 (1953).

COHN, R., Electroencephalographic study of prefrontal lobotomy: a study of focal brain injury, *A.M.A. Arch. Neurol. Psychiat.*, **53**, 283–285 (1945).

CRAWFORD, M. P., FULTON, H. F., JACOBSEN, C. F. and WOLFE, J. B., Frontal lobe ablations in chimpanzee: a résumé of Becky and Lucy, Chap. I., *Res. Pub., Ass. Nerv. Ment. Dis.*, **27**, (1948) "The Frontal Lobes" (Baltimore, Williams & Wilkins, 1948).

CROOK, E. A., CULLIAN, E. R. and KUTSCHBACK-BROWNE, J. M., Anglo-American symposium on psychosurgery, neurophysiology, and physical treatments in psychiatry, *Proc. Roy. Soc. Med.*, Suppl., **42** (1949).

CROWN, S., Psychological changes following prefrontal lobotomy: a review, *J. Ment. Sci.*, **97**, 48–83 (1951).

CROWN, S., An experimental study of psychological changes following prefrontal lobotomy, *J. Gen. Psychol.*, **47**, 3–41 (1952).

DARLING, H. F. and SANDALL, J. W., A psychological concept of psychopathic personality, *J. Clin. Exp. Psychopath*, **13**, 175–80 (1952).

DAVIDSON, A., Clinical evaluation of 50 lobotomised patients, *J. Nerv. Ment. Dis.*, **115**, 180–185 (1952).

DAVIS, P. A., Electroencephalographic studies on three cases of frontal lobotomy, *Psychosom Med.*, **3**, 38–50 (1941).

DAX, E. C. and RADLEY-SMITH, E. J., The early effects of prefrontal leucotomy on disturbed patients with mental illnesses of long duration, *J. Ment. Sci.*, **39**, 182–188 (1943).

DAX, E. C., RADLEY-SMITH, E. J. and STROM-OLSEN, R., Prefrontal lobotomy: discussion, *Proc. Roy. Soc. Med.*, **39**, 448 (1946).

DELAFRESNAYE, J. F. (Ed.), *Brain Mechanisms and Consciousness* (Oxford, Blackwell, 1954).

DOCTOR, R. F. and WINDER, C. L., Delinquents' vs. non-delinquents' performance on the Porteus qualitative maze test, *J. Cons. Psychol.*, **18**, 71–73 (1954).

DORKEN, H. and KRAL, V. A., The psychological differentiation of organic brain lesions by means of the Rorschach, *Amer. J. Psychiat.*, **108**, 764–770 (1952).

DRUBIN, L., Preliminary report of 62 prefrontal lobotomies on psychotic male veterans at the veterans' hospital Northport, *J. Nerv. Ment. Dis.*, **112**, 301–310 (1950).

DUSSER DE BARENNE, J. G. and ZIMMERMAN, H. H., Changes in the cerebral cortex produced by thermocoagulation. A suggestion to neurosurgery, *A.M.A., Arch. Neurol. Psychiat.*, **33**, 123–131 (1935).

ECONOMO, C. and KOSKINAS, G. N., *Die Cytoarchitektonic der Hirnrinde des erwachsenen Menschen* (Berlin & Wien, J. Springer, 1925).

EDWARDS, A. M., Preliminary report on transorbital leucotomy, *J. Ment. Sci.*, **96**, 935–950 (1950).

EIE, N., Macroscopic investigation of 25 brains subjected to frontal leukotomy, *Acta Psychiat. Kbh.*, (1954) Suppl. 90.

ELITHORN, A., PIERCY, M. F. and CROSSBY, MARGARET, A persisting change in palmar sweating following prefrontal leucotomy, *J. Neurol. Psychiat.*, **17**, 196–203 (1954).

ELONEN, A. S. and KORNER, A. F., Pre- and post-operative psychological observations on a case of frontal lobectomy, *J. Abnorm. (Soc.) Psychol.*, **43**, 532–543 (1948).

EYSENCK, H. J., *The Dimensions of Personality* (London, Routledge & Kegan Paul, 1947).

EYSENCK, H. J., *The Scientific Study of Personality* (London, Routledge & Kegan Paul, 1952).

EYSENCK, H. J., Cortical inhibition, figural after-effect and theory of personality, *J. Abnorm. (Soc.) Psychol.*, **51**, 94–106 (1955*a*).

EYSENCK, H. J., A dynamic theory of anxiety and hysteria, *J. Ment. Sci.*, **101**, 28–51 (1955*b*).

EYSENCK, H. J., The questionnaire measurement of neuroticism and extraversion, *Rivista di Psicologia*, **50**, 113–140 (1956).

EYSENCK, H. J., *The Dynamics of Anxiety and Hysteria* (London, Routledge & Kegan Paul, 1957*a*).

EYSENCK, H. J., Drugs and personality: I. theory and methodology, *J. Ment. Sci.*, **103**, 119–131 (1957*b*).

FERNANDEZ-MORAN, H., Leucotomia e injeciones en los lobulos prefrontales por la via transorbita, *Arch. Venezol. de la Soc. de Oto-Rinol. Oftal. Neurol.*, **7**, 109 (1946).

FIAMBERI, A. M., Proposta di una tecnica operatoria modificato e semplificato per gli interventi alla Moniz sui lobi prefrontali in malati de mente, *Rassegna di studi Psychiat.*, **26**, 797 (1937).

FINAN, J., Effects of frontal lobe lesions in temporally organised behaviour in monkeys, *J. Neurophysiol.*, **2**, 208–226 (1939).

FOOKS, G. and THOMAS, R. R., Differential qualitative performance of delinquents on the Porteus mazes, *J. Cons. Psychol.*, **21**, 351–353 (1957).

FORGAYS, D. G., Reversible disturbances of function in rats following cortical insult, *J. Comp. Physiol. Psychol.*, **45**, 216–225 (1952).

FRANK, J., Clinical survey and results of 200 cases of prefrontal leucotomy, *J. Ment. Sci.*, **92**, 497–508 (1946).

FRANKL, L. and MAYER-GROSS, W. B., Personality changes after prefrontal leucotomy, *Lancet*, **2**, 820–824 (1947).

FRANKS, C. M., An experimental study of conditioning as related to mental abnormality, *Unpubl. Ph.D. Thesis, Univ. of London Lib.* (1954).

FRANKS, C. M., Conditioning and personality; a study of normal and neurotic subjects, *J. Abnorm. (Soc.) Psychol.*, **52**, 143–150 (1956).

FREEMAN, W., Transorbital lobotomy (preliminary report of first 10 cases), *Med. Ann. D. C.*, **17**, 257–261 (1948).

FREEMAN, W., Transorbital lobotomy, *Amer. J. Psychiat.*, **105**, 734–740 (1949).

FREEMAN, W., Review of psychiatric progress in 1950: Psychosurgery, *Amer. J. Psychiat.*, **107**, 524–525 (1951).

FREEMAN, W., Review of psychiatric progress in 1951: Psychosurgery, *Amer. J. Psychiat.*, **109**, 521–523 (1952).

FREEMAN, W., Review of psychiatric progress in 1952: Psychosurgery, *Amer. J. Psychiat.*, **109**, 509–511 (1953*a*).

FREEMAN, W., Prognosis in frontal lobotomy by use of the Malamud rating scale, *Amer. J. Psychiat.*, **109**, 595–602 (1953*b*).

FREEMAN, W., Review of psychiatric progress in 1953: Psychosurgery, *Amer. J. Psychiat.*, **110**, 511–512 (1954).

FREEMAN, W., Review of psychiatric progress in 1954: Psychosurgery, *Amer. J. Psychiat.*, **111**, 518–520 (1955).

FREEMAN, W., Review of psychiatric progress in 1955: Psychosurgery, *Amer. J. Psychiat.*, **112**, 529–531 (1956).

FREEMAN, W., Review of psychiatric progress in 1956: Psychosurgery, *Amer. J. Psychiat.*, **113**, 615–617 (1957*a*).

FREEMAN, W., Frontal lobotomy: a follow-up study of 3,000 patients from one to twenty years, *Amer. J. Psychiat.*, **113**, 877–886 (1957*b*).

FREEMAN, W., DAVIS, H. W., EAST., I. T. C., TAIT, H. S. and ROGERS, W. B., The West Virginia lobotomy project, *J. Amer. Med. Ass.*, **156**, 939–941 (1954).

FREEMAN, W. and WATTS, J., Psychosurgery (Springfield, Ill., C. C. Thomas, 1942).

FREEMAN, W., WATTS, J., Schizophrenia in childhood: its modification by prefrontal lobotomy, *Dig. Neurol. Psychiat.*, **15**, 202–219 (1947).

FREEMAN, W. and WATTS, J., *Psychosurgery in the Treatment of Mental Disorders and Pain* (Springfield, Ill. C.C., Thomas, 1950).

FRENCH, J. D., HERNANDEZ-PEON, R. and LIVINGSTON, R. A., Projections from cortical to cephalic brain stem (reticular formation) in monkeys, *J. Neurophysiol.*, **18**, 74–95 (1955).

FREUDENBERG, R., GLEES, P., OBRADOR, S., FOX, B. and WILLIAMS, M., Experimental studies on frontal lobe functions in monkeys related to leucotomy, *J. Ment. Sci.*, **96**, 143–156 (1950).

FREYHAN, F. A., Prefrontal lobotomy and transorbital lobotomy: a comparative study of 175 patients, *Amer. J. Psychiat.*, **111**, 22–32 (1954).

FRY, W. J., Ultrasound in neurology, *Neurology*, **6**, 693–704 (1956).

FULTON, J. F., *Frontal Lobotomy and Affective Behaviour—a Neurophysiological Analysis* (London, Chapman & Hall, 1951).

FULTON, J. F. and JACOBSEN, C. F., The functions of the frontal lobes: a comparative study in monkeys, chimpanzee and man, *Advances in Mod. Biol. (Moscow)*, **4**, 113–123, (1935) *Abstr. 2nd. Int. Neurol. Congr., London* (1935).

FURTUDO, D., Results of leucotomy: a twelve-year follow-up, *Psychosurgery*, Lisbon, 1st Inter. Congr. Psychosurgery (1949).

GARCIA-AUSTT, E., INIGUEZ, R. A., SEGUNDO, J. P., MILGLIARO, E. and PEREZ, L., Epileptic activity in isolated cortical areas in Man, *EEG & Clinical Neurophysiology*, **6**, 536–537 (1954).

GARDNER, A., Transorbital leucotomy in non-institutional cases, *Amer. J. Psychiat.*, **114**, 140–142 (1957).

GOLDSTEIN, K., *The Organism* (New York, American Book Co., 1939).

GOLDSTEIN, K., Frontal lobotomy and the impairment of abstract attitude, *J. Nerv. Ment. Dis.*, **110**, 93–112 (1949).

GOLDSTEIN, K. and SCHEERER, M., Abstract and concrete behaviour, an experimental study with special tests, *Psychol. Monogr.*, **53**, 1–151 (1941).

GOLDSTONE, S., Flicker fusion measurements and anxiety level, *J. Exp. Psychol.*, **49**, 200–202 (1955).

GRANTHAM, E. G., Prefrontal lobotomy for the relief of pain, with a report of a new operative technique, *J. Neurosurg.*, **8**, 405–410 (1951).

GREENBLATT, M., ARNOT, A. and SOLOMON, H. C., *Studies in Lobotomy* (New York, Grune & Stratton, 1950).

GREENBLATT, M. and SOLOMON, H. C., *Frontal Lobes and Schizophrenia* (New York, Springer, 1953*a*).

GREENBLATT, M. and SOLOMON, H. C., A theory of frontal lobe functioning based on eight years of lobotomy investigation, *J. Nerv. Ment. Dis.*, **117**, 170 (1953*b*).

GREENBLATT, M., WINGATE, MARIE, SOLOMON, H. C., Work adjustment 5–10 years after bilateral frontal lobotomy, *New Eng. J. Med.*, **250**, 856–860 (1954).

GREENWOOD, J., JR., Post-mortem findings in pre-frontal lobotomy, *Dis. Nerv. Syst.*, **9**, 279–282 (1948).

GREVILLE, G. D. and LAST, S. G., Leucotomy as an instrument of research in electroencephalographic studies, *Proc. Roy. Soc. Med.*, **40**, 145–147 (1947).

HALSTEAD, W. C., *Brain and Intelligence* (Chicago, Univ. of Chicago Press, 1947a).

HALSTEAD, W. C., Critical flicker fusion and prefrontal lobotomy, *Amer. Psychologist*, **2**, 337 (1947b).

HALSTEAD, W. C., CARMICHAEL, H. T. and BUCY, P. C., Prefrontal lobotomy: a preliminary appraisal of behaviour results, *Amer. J. Psychiat.*, **103**, 217–228 (1946).

HARLOW, H. F. and DAGNON, J., Problem solution by monkeys following bilateral removal of the prefrontal areas: I. The discrimination-reversal problems, *J. Exp. Psychol.*, **32**, 351–356 (1943).

HARLOW, H. F. and JOHNSON, L., Problem solution by monkeys following bilateral removal of the prefrontal areas: III. Test of the initiation of behaviour, *J. Exp., Psychol.*, **32**, 495–500 (1943).

HARLOW, H. F. and SPAET, T., Problem solution by monkeys following bilateral removal of the prefrontal areas: IV. Responses to "stimuli" having multiple sign values, *J. Exp. Psychol.*, **32**, 500–507 (1943).

HARLOW, H. F. and SETTLAGE, P. H., The effects of extirpations of frontal areas upon the learning performance of monkeys, *Res. Pub. Ass. Nerv. Ment. Dis.*, **27**, 446–459 (1948).

HARLOW, H. F., DAVIS, R. T., SETTLAGE, P. H. and MEYER, D. R., Analysis of frontal and posterior association syndromes in brain damaged monkeys, *J. Comp. Physiol. Psychol.*, **45**, 419–429 (1952).

HARROWER-ERICKSON, MOLLY, R., The value and limitations of the so-called "neurotic signs," *Rorschach Res. Exch.*, **6**, 109–114 (1942).

HEBB, D. O., Man's frontal lobes: a critical review, *A.M.A., Arch. Neurol. Psychiat.*, **54**, 10–24 (1945).

HEBB, D. O., *The Organization of Behavior, a Neuropsychological Theory* (New York, John Wiley & Sons, Inc., 1949).

HENRY, C. E., Observations on alternating burst-suppression activity of deafferented cortex, *EEG & Clinical Neurophysiology*, **2**, 232 (1950a).

HENRY, C. E., Effects on the electroencephalogram of transorbital lobotomy, *EEG & Clinical Neurophysiology*, **2**, 187–192 (1950b).

HENRY, C. E., DARROW, C. W. and BOSHES, L. D., Psychophysiological effects of prefrontal lobotomy, *Amer. Psychologist*, **3**, 360 (1948).

HENRY, C. E. and SCOVILLE, W. B., Suppression-burst activity from isolated cerebral cortex in Man, *EEG & Clinical Neurophysiology*, **4**, 1–22 (1952).

HILDEBRAND, H. P., A factorial study of introversion-extraversion by means of objective tests, *Unpubl. Ph.D. Thesis, Univ. of London Lib.* (1953).

HIROSE, SADOA, Studies on personalities of patients treated by prefrontal lobotomy, *Psychiat. Neurol. Japonica*, **56**, 379–428 (1954).

HOCH, P. H., POOL, L. G., RANSOHOFF, J., CATTELL, J. P. and PENNES, H. H., The psychosurgical treatment of pseudoneurotic schizophrenia, *Amer. J. Psychiat.*, **111**, 653–658 (1954).

HOFFMAN, J. L., A clinical appraisal of frontal lobotomy in the treatment of psychoses, *J. Nerv. Ment. Dis.*, **112**, 93–96 (1950).

HURT, J. H., Prefrontal leucotomy, *Med. J. Aust.*, **1**, 638–640 (1947).

HUTTON, E. L., Personality changes after leucotomy, *J. Ment. Sci.*, **93**, 31–42 (1947).

HUTTON, E. L. and BASSETT, M., The effect of leucotomy on creative personality, *J. Ment. Sci.*, **94**, 332–350 (1948).

HUTTON, E. L., FLEMING, G. W. T. H. and FOX, F. G., Early results of prefrontal leucotomy, *Lancet*, **2**, 3–7 (1941).

JACKSON, C. L. and JACO, E. G., Some prognostic factors in 538 transorbital lobotomy cases, *Amer. J. Psychiat.*, **111**, 353–357 (1954).

JACOBSEN, C. F., Functions of the frontal association areas in primates, *A.M.A. Arch. Neurol. Psychiat.*, **33**, 558–568 (1935).

JACOBSEN, C. F., WOLFE, J. B. and JACKSON, L. A., An experimental analysis of the functions of the frontal association areas in primates, *J. Nerv. Ment. Dis.*, **82**, 1–14 (1935).

JACOBSEN, C. F. and NISSEN, H. W., Studies of the cerebral function in primates: IV. The effects of frontal lobe lesions on the delayed alternation habit in monkeys, *J. Comp. Psychol.*, **23**, 101–112 (1937).

JAMESON, H. D., SETTLAGE, P. H. and BOGUMILL, G. P., The effect of lesions in the amygdaloid area in monkeys, *J. Gen. Psychol.*, **57**, 91–102 (1957).

JENKINS, R. S. and HOLSOPPLE, J. C., Criteria and experimental design for evaluating the results of lobotomy, *Res. Pub. Ass. Nerv. Ment. Dis.*, **31**, 319–327 (1951).

JOHNSON, O. and ERHENBERG, RUTH, A correlation of lobotomy results with basic reaction types, *Amer. J. Psychiat.*, **108**, 817–824 (1951).

JONES, D. W., An examination of the changes in the daily pattern of the critical flicker frequencies before and after bi-prefrontal leucotomy, *M.A. Thesis, Univ. of Toronto*, 1–34 (1952).

JONES, C. H. and SHANKLIN, J. G., Transorbital lobotomy in the institutional practice, *Amer. J. Psychiat.*, **107**, 120–127 (1950).

KALINOWSKI, L. B. and HOCH, P. H., *Schock Treatment, Psychosurgery and other Somatic Treatments in Psychiatry* 2nd Ed., Chapter 5 (New York, Grune & Stratton, 1952).

KANE, W. H., HURDUM, H. M. and SCHAERER, J. P., Prefrontal lobotomy: analysis of the results of 122 cases in a state hospital, *A.M.A. Arch. Neurol. Psychiat.*, **68**, 205–212 (1952).

KARPELES, LOTTA M., A further investigation of the Porteus maze test as a measure of discrimination in delinquency, *J. Appl. Psychol.*, **16**, 427–437 (1932).

KENNARD, M. A., SPENCER, S. and FOUNTAIN, G., Hyperactivity in monkeys following lesions of the frontal lobes, *J. Neurophysiol.*, **41**, 512–524 (1941).

KISKER, G. W., Abstract and categoric behaviour following therapeutic brain surgery, *Psychosom. Med.*, **6**, 146–150 (1944a).

KISKER, G. W., The Rorschach analysis of psychotics subjected to neurosurgical interruption of the thalamocortical projections, *Psychiat. Quart.*, **18**, 43–52 (1944*b*).

KLEBANOFF, S. G., Psychological changes in organic brain lesions and ablations, *Psychol. Bull.*, **42**, 585–623 (1945).

KLEBANOFF, S. G., SINGER, J. L. and WILENSKY, H., Psychological consequences of brain lesions and ablations, *Psychol. Bull.*, **51**, 1–41 (1954).

KLEIN, G. S. and KRECH, D., Cortical conductivity in the brain-injured, *J. Personality*, **21**, 118–148 (1952).

KLINE, N. S. and TENNEY, A. M., Prognosis in topectomies and lobotomies relative to body type, *A.M.A. Arch. Neurol. Psychiat.*, **65**, 323–325 (1951).

KLINE, N. S., TENNEY, A. M., DIMON, F. S. and LUTZ, W. M., Prognosis in the transorbital lobotomies relative to body type, *A.M.A., Arch. Neurol. Psychiat.*, **72**, 565–567 (1954).

KLOPFER, B., KELLEY, D. and McGLASHAN, The Rorschach Technique (New York, World Book Co., 1942, 1946).

KLOTZ, M., Incidence of siezures with E.E.G. findings in prefrontal lobotomy, *A.M.A. Arch. Neurol. Psychiat.*, **74**, 144–148 (1955).

KOHLER, W. and WALLACH, H., Figural after-effects, an investigation of visual processes, *Proc. Amer. Phil. Soc.*, **88**, 269–357 (1944).

KOLB, L. C., An evaluation of lobotomy and its potentialities for its future research in psychiatry and the basic sciences, *J. Nerv. Ment. Dis.*, **110**, 112–148 (1949).

KOLB, L. C., Clinical evaluation of prefrontal lobotomy, *J. Amer. Med. Ass.*, **152**, 1085–1089 (1953).

KOSKOFF, Y. D., DENNIS, W., LAZOVIK, D. and WHEELER, E. T., The psychological effects of prefrontal lobotomy performed for the alleviation of pain, *Res. Pub. Ass. Nerv. Ment. Dis.*, **27**, 723–753 (1948).

KOSTIC, S., Experiences and results in prefrontal leucotomy: a clinical study of 339 leucotomised patients, *J. Ment. Sci.*, **99**, 786–795 (1953).

KRAFT, T. B., The handwriting of leucotomised patients with personality changes in connection with the scientific meaning of graphology, *Ned. Tjdschr. Psychol.*, **10**, 1–38 (1955).

KRAL, V. A. and DUROST, H. B., A comparative study of the amnestic syndrome in various organic conditions, *Amer. J. Psychiat.*, **110**, 41–47 (1953).

KRAL, V. A. and ELVRIDGE, M. D., Four years' experience with prefrontal lobotomy, *Amer. J. Psychiat.*, **112**, 375–381 (1955).

KRUGMAN, H. E., Flicker fusion frequency as a function of anxiety reaction: an explanatory study, *Psychosom. Med.*, **9**, 269–272 (1947).

LANDIS, C., ZUBIN, J. and METTLER, F. A., The functions of the human frontal lobes, *J. Psychol.*, **30**, 123–138 (1950).

LANDIS, C. and ERLICK, D., Analysis of the Porteus maze test as applied to psychosurgery, *Amer. J. Psychol.*, **63**, 557–566 (1950).

LANDIS, C. and CLAUSEN, J., Changes in sensory and motor performance induced by active psychiatric treatment, *J. Psychol.*, **40**, 275–305 (1955).

LANE, MARY A., The effects of leucotomy on family life, *Brit. J. Psychiat. Soc. Work*, **3**, 18–24 (1956).

LASHLEY, K. S., *Brain Mechanisms and Intelligence: a Qualitative Study of Injuries to the Brain* (Chicago, Univ. of Chicago Press, 1929).

LE BEAU, J., *Psycho-Chirurgie et Fonctions Mentales* (Paris, Masson Cie., 1954).

LE BEAU, J. and PETRIE, A., A comparison of the personality changes after I. Prefrontal selective surgery for the relief of intractible pain and for the treatment of mental cases, II. Cingulectomy and topectomy, *J. Ment. Sci.*, **99**, 53–61 (1953).

LENNOX, MARGARET and COOLIDGE, J., Electroencephalographic changes after prefrontal lobotomy with particular reference to the effect of lobotomy upon sleep spindles, *A.M.A. Arch. Neurol. Psychiat.*, **62**, 150–161 (1949).

LEVINE, J. and ALBERT, H., Sexual behaviour after lobotomy, *J. Nerv. Ment. Dis.*, **113**, 332–341 (1951).

LEVIN, S., GREENBLATT, M., HEALEY, MARIE M. and SOLOMON, H. C., Electroencephalographic effects of bilateral prefrontal lobotomy, *Amer. J. Psychiat.*, **106**, 174–184 (1949).

LEWIS, N. D. C., LANDIS, C. and KING, H. E., *Studies in Topectomy* (New York, Grune & Stratton, 1956).

LIDDELL, D. W. and RETTERSOL, N., The occurrence of epileptic fits in leucotomised patients receiving chlorpromazine therapy, *J. Neurol. Psychiat.*, **20**, 105–107 (1957).

LICHTENSTEIN, P. E., Studies in anxiety I. The production of a feeding inhibition in dogs, *J. Comp. Physiol. Psychol.*, **43**, 16–29 (1950*a*).

LICHTENSTEIN, P. E., Studies in anxiety: II. The effects of lobotomy on a feeding inhibition in dogs, *J. Comp. Physiol. Psychol.*, **43**, 419–427 (1950*b*).

LINDSTROM, P., Prefrontal ultrasonic irradiation—a substitute for lobotomy, *A.M.A. Arch. Neurol. Psychiat.*, **72**, 399–425 (1954).

LINFORD-REES, W. and JONES, A. M., An evaluation of the Rorschach test as a prognostic aid in the treatment of schizophrenia, *J. Ment. Sci.*, **97**, 681–689 (1951).

LORR, M., Multi-dimensional scale for rating psychiatric patients, *Vet. Admin. Tech. Bull.* **10**, 507 (1953).

LORR, M., JENKINS, R. L. and HOLSOPPLE, Q., Factors descriptive of chronic schizophrenics selected for the operation of frontal lobotomy, *J. Cons. Psychol.*, **18**, 293–296 (1954).

LORR, M., HOLSOPPLE, Q., JENKINS, R. L. and O'CONNOR, P., Factors of change in lobotomised chronic schizophrenic patients, *J. Cons. Psychol.*, **19**, 39–43 (1955).

LYERLY, J. G., Transection of the deep association fibres of the prefrontal lobes in certain mental disorders, *Sth. Surg.*, **8**, 426–434 (1939).

LYERLY, J. G., Experience with prefrontal lobotomy, *Edgewood Med. Mongr.* **1**, 37–49 (1950).

LYKKEN, D. T., A study of anxiety in the sociopathic personality, *J. Abnorm. (Soc.) Psychol.*, **55**, 6–10 (1957).

MADLUNG, H., Über den Einfuss der Typologishen Veranlagung auf die Flimmergrenzen, *Untersuch. Psychol. Phil.*, **10**, 1–65 (1935).

MALMO, R. B., Interference factors in delayed response in monkeys after removal of the frontal lobes, *J. Neurophysiol.*, **5**, 295–308 (1942).

MALMO, R. B., Psychological aspects of frontal gyrectomy and frontal lobotomy in mental patients, *Res. Pub. Ass. Nerv. Ment. Dis.*, **27**, 537–563 (1948).

MALMO, R. B. and AMSEL, A., Anxiety produced interference in serial rote learning with observations on rote learning after partial frontal lobectomy, *J. Exp. Psychol.*, **38**, 440–454 (1948).

MALMO, R. B. and SHAGASS, C., Behavioural and physiologic changes under stress after operations on the frontal lobes, *A.M.A. Arch. Neurol. Psychiat.*, **63**, 113–124 (1950).

MARGOLIS, L. H., SIMON, A. and BOWMAN, K. M., Selective utilization of unilateral lobotomy, *J. Nerv. Ment. Dis.*, **116**, 392–411 (1952).

MARKWELL, E. D., WHEELER, W. M. and KITZINGER, H., Changes in Wechsler-Bellevue test performances following lobotomy, *J. Cons. Psychol.*, **17**, 229–231 (1953).

MASSERMAN, J. H. and PECHTEL, C., How brain lesions affect normal and neurotic behaviour—an experimental approach, *Amer. J. Psychiat.*, **112**, 865–872 (1956a).

MASSERMAN, J. H. and PECHTEL, C., Neurophysiologic and pharmacologic influences in experimental neuroses, *Amer. J. Psychiat.*, **113**, 510–514 (1956b).

MCCOULLOUGH, M. M., Wechsler-Bellevue changes following prefrontal lobotomy, *J. Clin. Psychol.*, **3**, 370–373 (1950).

MCFIE, J., PIERCY, M. F. and ZANGWILL, O. L., The Rorschach test in obsessional neuroses with special reference to the effects of prefrontal leucotomy, *Brit. J. Med. Psychol.*, **24**, 162–179 (1951).

MCGREGOR, J. S. and CRUMBIE, J. R., Surgical treatment of mental disease, *Lancet*, **2**, 7–8 (1941).

MCKENZIE, K. G. and PROCTOR, L. D., Bilateral frontal leucotomy in the treatment of mental disease, *J. Canad. Med. Ass.*, **55**, 433–441 (1946).

MCKISSOCK, W., Recent techniques in psychosurgery—Anglo-American symposium, *Proc. Roy. Soc. Med.*, **42**, Suppl., 13 (1949).

MCKISSOCK, W., Rostral leucotomy, *Lancet*, **2**, 91–94 (1951).

MEDINA, R. F., PEARSON, J. S. and BUCKSTEIN, R. F., The long-term evaluation of prefrontal lobotomy in chronic psychotics, *J. Nerv. Ment. Dis.*, **119**, 23–30 (1954).

METTLER, F. A., (Ed.), *Columbia-Greystone Associates—Selective Partial Ablations of the Frontal Cortex* (New York, Hoeber, 1949).

METTLER, F. A. (Ed.), *Columbia-Greystone Associates—Second Group. Psychosurgical Problems* (London, Routledge & Kegan Paul, 1952).

METTLER, F. A. and ROWLAND, L. P., *The relation of the trephine opening (Freeman and Watts lobotomy point) to the underlying cerebrum*, Presented Before the Ann. Meeting of the Amer. Neurol. Assoc. (1948).

MEYER, A. and BECK, ELIZABETH, *Prefrontal Leucotomy and Related Operations*, Henderson Trust Lecture, 17 (Edinburgh and London, Oliver & Boyd, 1954).

MILES, J. E. and ROSVOLD, H. E., The effect of prefrontal lobotomy in rhesus monkey on delayed-response performance motivated by pain-shock, *J. Comp. Physiol. Psychol.*, **49**, 286–292 (1956).

MILLER, A. (Ed.), *Lobotomy, a Clinical Study*, Monogr., 1 (Ontario Dept. Health, 1954).

MISHKIN, M., ROSVOLD, H. E. and PRIBRAM, K. H., Effects of Nembutal in baboons with frontal lesions, *J. Neurophysiol.*, **16**, 155–159 (1953).

MISHKIN, M. and HALL, MARTHA, Discrimination along a size continuum following ablation of the inferior temporal convexity in monkeys, *J. Comp. Physiol. Psychol.*, **48**, 97–101 (1955).

MISHKIN, M., PRIBRAM, K. H., Analysis of the effects of frontal lesions in monkey: I. Variations of delayed alternation, *J. Comp. Physiol. Psychol.*, **48**, 492–495 (1955).

MISHKIN, M. and PRIBRAM, K. H., Analysis of the effects of frontal lesions in monkey: II. Variations of delayed response, *J. Comp. Physiol. Psychol.*, **49**, 36–40 (1956).

MONIZ, E., *Tentatives Opératoires dans le Traitement des certaines Psychoses* (Paris, Masson Cie., 1936a).

MONIZ, E., Prefrontal leucotomy in the treatment of mental disorder, *Amer. J. Psychiat.*, **93**, 1379–1385 (1936b).

MONIZ, E., How I succeeded in performing the prefrontal leukotomy, *J. Clin. Exp. Psychopath.*, **15**, 373–379 (1954).

MOORE, M. T. and WINKELMAN, N. W., Some experiences with transorbital leucotomy, *Amer. J. Psychiat.*, **107**, 801–807 (1950).

MUNROE, R. L., Prediction of the adjustment and academic performance of college students by a modification of the Rorschach method, *Appl. Psychol. Mongr.*, No. 7 (1945).

NEWMAN, J., Prefrontal lobotomy as a means to improve the hospital adjustment of chronic psychotic patients, *J. Abnorm. (Soc.) Psychol.*, **51**, 581–584 (1955).

NICHOLS, I. C. and HUNT, J. McV., A case of partial bilateral frontal lobectomy, *Amer. J. Psychiat.*, **96**, 1063–1083 (1940).

ODY, F., Le traitement de la démence précoce par résection du lobe préfrontal, *Arch. Ital. Chir.*, **55**, 321 (1938).

OLTMAN, J. S., BRODY, B. S. and FRIEDMAN, S., Frontal lobotomy—clinical experience with 107 cases in a state hospital, *Amer. J. Psychiat.*, **105**, 742–751 (1948).

ORBACH, J., Immediate and chronic disturbances of the delayed response following transection of the frontal granular cortex, *J. Comp. Physiol. Psychol.*, **49**, 46–51 (1956).

OTENASEK, F. J., Some considerations of the total personality in prefrontal brain surgery, *Bull. Isaacs Ray Med. Lib.*, **1**, 83–95 (1953).

OVERHOLSER, W. (Ed.), Evaluation of change in patients after psychosurgery, *Proc. Second Res. Conf. on Psychosurg.*, *Pub. Health Serv. Publ.*, No. 156, Fed. Soc. Agency, Washington, (1952).

OVERHOLSER, W. (Ed.), Evaluation of psychosurgery, *Proc. Third Conf. on Psychosurgery*, *Pub. Health Serv. Publ.* No. 221, Washington, Gov. Print. Office, 1954.

PARTRIDGE, N., *Prefrontal Leucotomy* (Oxford, Blackwell, 1950).

PAUL, N. L., FITZGERALD, E. and GREENBLATT, M., The long-term comparative results of three different lobotomy procedures, *Amer. J. Psychiat.*, **113**, 808–814 (1957).

PAYNE, R. W., L'utilité du test du Rorschach en psychologie clinique, *Rev. Psychol. appl.*, **5**, 255–264 (1955).

PECHTEL, C., MASSERMAN, J. H., SCHREINER, L. R. and LEVITT, M., Differential effect of lesions in the mediodorsal nuclei of the thalamus on normal and neurotic behaviour in the cat, *J. Nerv. Ment. Dis.*, **121**, 25–33 (1955).

PETERS, R. H., ROSVOLD, H. E. and MIRSKY, A. F., The

effect of thalamic lesions upon delayed response type tests in rhesus monkeys, *J. Comp. Physiol. Psychol.*, **49**, 11–116 (1956).

PETRIE, A., *Personality and the Frontal Lobes* (London, Routledge & Kegan Paul, 1952).

PETRIE, A. and LE BEAU, J., The psychological effects of selective frontal surgery including cingulectomy, *Proc. Ve. Cong. Neurologique International, Lisbonne*, **2**, 215 (1953).

PETRIE, A. and LE BEAU, J., Psychologic changes in man after chlorpromazine and certain types of brain surgery, *J. Clin. Exp. Psychopath.*, **27**, 170–179 (1956).

PIPPARD, J., Rostral leucotomy: a report on 240 cases personally followed-up after 1½–5 years, *J. Ment. Sci.*, **101**, 756–772 (1955*a*).

PIPPARD, J., Personality changes after Rostral leucotomy: a comparison with standard prefrontal leucotomy, *J. Ment. Sci.*, **101**, 774–787 (1955*b*).

PITTMAN, A. P., BENNETT, R. E., GARBER, R. S. and WILSON, W. W., Transorbital lobotomy in chronically disturbed patients, *Welfare Reporter*, **6**, 3–5 (1951).

POOL, J. L., Topectomy, a surgical procedure for the treatment of mental illness, *J. Nerv. Ment. Dis.*, **110**, 144 (1949).

POOL, J. L., HEATH, R. G. and WEBER, J. J., Topectomy: surgical technique, psychiatric indications and post-operative management, *J. Nerv. Ment. Dis.*, **110**, 464–477 (1949).

POPPEN, J. C., Technic of prefrontal lobotomy, *J. Neurosurg.*, **5**, 514–520 (1948).

PORTEUS, S. D., Studies in mental deviation, *Training School Bull., Vineland, N. J.*, 75–116 (1923).

PORTEUS, S. D., *The Maze Test and Mental Differences* (Vineland, N. J., Smith, 1933).

PORTEUS, S. D., Qualitative Performance on the Maze Test (Vineland, N. J., Smith, 1942).

PORTEUS, S. D., The Porteus maze test and psychosurgery, *Brit. J. Med. Psychol.*, **24**, 132 (1951).

PORTEUS, S. D., Some common-sense implications of psychosurgery, *Brit. J. Med. Psychol.*, **28**, 167–176 (1955).

PORTEUS, S. D. and KEPNER, R. DE M., Mental changes after bilateral prefrontal lobotomy, *Genet. Psychol. Monogr.*, **29**, 4–115 (1944).

PORTEUS, S. D. and PETERS, H., Maze validation and psychosurgery, *Genet. Psychol. Monogr.*, **36**, 3–86 (1947).

POULL, L. E. and MONTGOMERY, R. P., The Porteus maze test as a discriminative measure in delinquency, *J. Appl. Psychol.*, **13**, 145–151 (1929).

PRIBRAM, K. H., Some physical and pharmacological factors affecting delayed response performance of baboons following frontal lobotomy, *J. Neurophysiol.*, **13**, 373–382 (1950).

PRIBRAM, K. H., Lesions of the frontal eyefields and delayed response of baboons, *J. Neurophysiol.*, **18**, 105–112 (1955).

PRIBRAM, K. H. and MISHKIN, M., Simultaneous and successive visual discrimination by monkey with inferotemporal lesions, *J. Comp. Physiol. Psychol.*, **48**, 198–202 (1955).

PRIBRAM, K. H. and MISHKIN, M., Analysis of the effect of lesions in monkey: III. Object alternation, *J. Comp. Physiol. Psychol.*, **49**, 41–45 (1956).

PUECH, P. GUILLY, P. and LAIRY BOUNES, G. C., *Introduction à la Psychochirurgie*, (Paris, Masson Cie., 1950).

PURCELL, H., A note on Porteus maze test and Wechsler-Bellevue scores as related to antisocial behaviour, *J. Cons. Psychol.*, **20**, 361–364 (1956).

REINER, E. and SANDS, S. L., Lobotomy and psychotherapy, *A.M.A. Arch. Neurol. Psychiat.*, **65**, 48–53 (1951).

REITMAN, F., Automonic responses in prefrontal lobotomy, *J. Ment. Sci.*, **91**, 318–321 (1945).

REITMAN, F., The creative spell of schizophrenics after leucotomy, *J. Ment. Sci.*, **93**, 55–61 (1947).

REITMAN, F., Evaluation of leucotomy results, *Amer. J. Psychiat.*, **105**, 86–89 (1948).

REITMAN, R. H., Investigation of the validity of Halstead's measure of biological intelligence, *A.M.A. Arch. Neurol. Psychiat.*, **73**, 28–35 (1955*a*).

REITMAN, R. H., The validity of the Rorschach test as a measure of the psychological effects of brain damage, *A.M.A. Arch. Neurol. Psychiat.*, **73**, 445–451 (1955*b*).

REITMAN, R. M., Affective disturbances in brain-damaged patients, *A.M.A. Arch. Neurol. Psychiat.*, **73**, 530–532 (1955*c*).

RICHTER, C. P. and HINES, M., Increased spontaneous activity produced in monkeys by brain lesions, *Brain*, **61**, 1–16 (1938).

RINKEL, M., GREENBLATT, M., COON, P. and SOLOMON, H.C., The effects of bilateral frontal lobotomy upon the autonomic nervous system, *Amer. J. Psychiat.*, **104**, 81–82 (1947*a*).

RINKEL, M., GREENBLATT, M., COON, P. and SOLOMON, H. C., Relationship of the frontal lobes to the autonomic nervous system, *A.M.A. Arch. Neurol. Psychiat.*, **58**, 570–581 (1947*b*).

RIZZATTI, E., L'operazione frontale bilaterale di Egas Moniz post-encephalitiche, *Schizofrenia*, **6**, 203 (1937).

RIZZATTI, E. and BORGARELLO, G., La leucotomia prefrontali di Egas Moniz in 100 casi de paicopalie gravi di cui una meta compresibili nel quando della pui completa dissociazione psichica, *Schizofrenia*, **7**, 241 (1938).

ROBIN, A. A., A controlled study of the effects of leucotomy, *J. Neurol. Psychiat.*, **21**, 262 (1958).

ROBIN, A. A., The value of leucotomy in relation to diagnosis, *J. Neurol. Psychiat.*, **22**, 132–136 (1959).

ROBINSON, MARY F., What price lobotomy?, *J. Abnorm. (Soc.) Psychol.*, **41**, 417–436 (1946).

ROBINSON, MARY F. and FREEMAN, W., *Psychosurgery and the Self* (New York and London, Grune & Stratton, 1954).

ROSENBLUM, M. P., BARNES, L. and EHRLICK, W., Pneumoencephalographic and neurological study following psychosurgery, *A.M.A. Arch. Neurol. Psychiat.*, **73**, 464–465 (1955).

ROSSVOLD, H. E. and DELAGO, J. M. R., The effect on delayed alternation test performance of stimulating or destroying electrically structures within the frontal lobes of the monkey's brain, *J. Comp. Physiol. Psychol.*, **49**, 365–372 (1956).

ROTHSCHILD, D. and KAYE, A., The effect of prefrontal lobotomy on the symptomatology of schizophrenic patients, *Amer. J. Psychiat.*, **105**, 752–759 (1948).

RYLANDER, G., *Personality Changes after Operations on*

the Frontal Lobes (London, Oxford Univ. Press, 1939a).

RYLANDER, G., Personality changes after operations on the frontal lobes, *Acta Psychiat. Kbh.* Suppl., 20, (1939b).

RYLANDER, G., Mental changes after the excision of cerebral tissue, *Acta Psychiat. Kbh.* Suppl., 25, (1943).

RYLANDER, G., Personality analysis before and after frontal surgery, *Res. Publ. Ass. Nerv. Ment. Dis.*, 27, 691–705 (1948).

RYLANDER, G., Observations on mental changes after total lobotomy and after inferior lobotomy, *Acta Psychiat. Kbh.* Suppl., 60, 82–88 (1951).

SAINSBURY, P., The measurement and description of spontaneous movements before and after leucotomy, *J. Ment. Sci.*, 100, 732–741 (1954).

SANDS, S. L. and MALAMUD, W., A rating scale analysis of the clinical effects of lobotomy, *Amer. J. Psychiat.*, 105, 760–766 (1948).

SARGANT, W., Leucotomy in psychosomatic disorders, *Lancet*, 87–91 (1951).

SCARFF, J. E., Unilateral prefrontal lobotomy with relief of ipsilateral, contralateral and bilateral pain, *Dig. Neurol. Psychiat.*, 410–413 (1948).

SCHURR, P. H., The surgical treatment of mental illness, *Mod. Treatm.*, 30, 131–134 (1956).

SCHWARZ, M. J., Lobotomy: a six-year follow-up of 45 patients, *Amer. J. Psychiat.*, 113, 224–227 (1956).

SCOVILLE, W. G., Selective cortical undercutting as a means of modifying frontal lobe function in man, preliminary report of 43 operative cases, *J. Neurosurg.*, Jan., 65 (1949).

SCOVILLE, W. B. and RYAN, G. V., Orbital undercutting in the aged, limited lobotomy in the treatment of psycho-neuroses and depressions in elderly persons, *Geriatrics*, 10, 311–317 (1955).

SCOVILLE, W. B., WILK, E. K. and PEPE, A. P., Selective cortical under-cutting results in a new method of fractional lobotomy, *Amer. J. Psychiat.*, 107, 730–738 (1950).

SHEVCHENKO, Y. G., *The Consequences of Prefrontal Leucotomy in Cases of Schizophrenia* (Moscow, "Medgyz," 1954).

SHOLL, D. A., *The Organization of the Cerebral Cortex* (London, Methuen, 1957).

SHRADER, P. J. and ROBINSON, MARY F., An evaluation of prefrontal lobotomy through ward behaviour, *J. Abnorm.* (*Soc.*) *Psychol.*, 40, 61–69 (1945).

SIMON, A., MARGOLIS, L. H., ADAMS, J. E. and BOWMAN, K. M., Unilateral and bilateral lobotomy: a controlled study, *A.M.A. Arch. Neurol. Psychiat.*, 66, 494–503 (1951).

SIMONSON, E. and BROZEK, J., Flicker fusion frequency: background and applications, *Physiol. Rev.*, 32, 349–378 (1952).

SOUPAULT, R., La place et la partée des infiltrations novo-cainiques du cerveau préfrontal, *Pr. Méd.*, 62/39, 828–829 (1954).

SOUPAULT, R. and BUCAILLE, M., Procaine injection of the prefrontal lobe of the brain, *Ann. Surg.*, 141, 388–397 (1955).

SPAET, T. and HARLOW, H. F., Problem solutions by monkeys following bilateral removal of the prefrontal areas: II. Delayed reaction problems involving the use of the matching from sample method, *J. Exp. Psychol.*, 32, 424–434 (1943).

SPIEGEL, E. A. and WYCIS, H. T., Physiological and psychological results of thalamotomy, *Proc. Roy. Soc. Med.—Anglo-American Symposium on Psychosurgery*, etc., Suppl. 42, 84–92 (1949).

SPIEGEL, E. A., WYCIS, H. and FREED, H., Thalamotomy in mental disorders, *Philad. Med.*, 43, 1524–1527 (1948).

SPRAGUE, J. M. and CHAMBERS, W. W., Regional physiology of the central nervous system, *Progr. Neurol. Psychiat.*, 10, 57–92 (1955).

STELLAR, E., Physiological psychology, *Annu. Rev. Psychol.*, 8, 415–436 (1957).

STENGEL, E., A follow-up investigation of 320 cases treated by prefrontal leucotomy, *J. Ment. Sci.*, 96, 633–662 (1950).

STEVENS, H. and MOSOVICH, A., Clinical and E.E.G. investigations of prefrontal lobotomy patients, *Amer. J. Psychiat.*, 104, 73–80 (1947).

STEVENSON, G. H. and McCAUSLAND, A., Prefrontal leucotomy for the attempted prevention of recurring manic depressive illnesses, *Amer. J. Psychiat.*, 109, 662–669 (1953).

STREB, J. M. and SMITH, K., Frontal lobotomy and the elimination of conditioned anxiety in the rat, *J. Comp. Physiol. Psychol.*, 48, 126–129 (1955).

STROM-OLSEN, R., LAST, S. L., BRODY, M. B. and KNIGHT, G. C., Results of prefrontal leucotomy in 30 cases of mental disorder, *J. Ment. Sci.*, 89, 165–181 (1943).

STRUCKETT, PAULINE, Effect of prefrontal lobotomy on intellectual functioning in chronic schizophrenia, *A.M.A. Arch. Neurol. Psychiat.*, 69, 293–304 (1953).

SUMMERFIELD, A. and STEINBERG, HANNA, Reducing interference in forgetting, *Quart. J. Exp. Psychol.*, 9, 146–154 (1957).

SWARTZLANDER, E. E., The psychological effect of prefrontal leukotomy on schizophrenics, *Psychiat. Quart.* Suppl., (1952).

THOMPSON, R. K. (Ed.), *Psychosurgery*, Chapt. V.—E. A. Walker, G. Von Bonin, J. L. Pool, R. G. Heath, "Clinical neurosurgery," *Proc. Congr. Neurological Surgeons* (Baltimore, Williams & Wilkins, 1955).

TIZARD, BARBARA, Psychological effects of frontal lesions, *Acta. Psychiat. Neurol. Scand.*, 33, 232–250 (1958).

TOW, P. MACDONALD, *Personality Changes Following Frontal Leucotomy* (London, Oxford Med. Publ., 1955).

VAN WAGENEN, W. P., Observations on changes in states of mental depression and tension following surgical section of certain frontal lobe pathways, *Surgery*, 20, 656–662 (1946).

VAN WATERS, R. O. and SACKS, J. G., Rorschach evaluation of the schizophrenic process following a prefrontal lobotomy, *J. Psychol.*, 25, 73–88 (1948).

VIDOR, MARTHA, Personality changes following prefrontal leucotomy as reflected by the M.M.P.I. and the results of psychometric testing, *J. Ment. Sci.*, 97, 159–173 (1951).

WADA, T. and ENKO, T., E.E.G. directly recorded during prefrontal lobotomy operations with description of the reaction upon barbiturate narcosis, *Toha Psychiat. Neurol. Jap.*, 5, 46–54 (1951).

WADE, MARJORIE, The effects of sedatives upon the delayed

response in monkeys, following removal of the prefrontal lobes, *J. Neurophysiol.*, **10**, 57–61 (1947).

WADE, MARJORIE, The behavioural effects of prefrontal lobectomy, lobotomy and circumsection in the monkey, *J. Comp. Neurol.*, **96**, 179–207 (1952).

WALKER, E. A., *A History of Neurological Surgery*, Chapter 11—A. G. Fisher (Baltimore, Williams & Wilkins, 1951).

WALTER, R. D., YEAGER, C. L., MARGOLIS, L. H. and SIMON, A., The E.E.G. changes in unilateral and bilateral frontal lobotomy, *Amer. J. Psychiat.*, **111**, 590–594 (1954).

WASHBURN, M. F., HUGHES, E., STEWART, C. and SLIGHT, G., Reaction time, flicker and affective sensitiveness as tests of extraversion and introversion, *Amer. J. Psychol.*, **42**, 412–413 (1930).

WARREN, J. M. and HARLOW, H. F., Learned discrimination performance by monkeys after prolonged postoperative recovery from large cortical lesions, *J. Comp. Physiol. Psychol.*, **45**, 119–126 (1951).

WATERHOUSE, I. K., The effects of prefrontal lobotomy on conditioned fear and food responses, *J. Comp. Physiol. Psychol.*, **50**, 81–88 (1957).

WAYNE, HENRIETTE L., Clinical E.E.G. observations following prefrontal lobotomy and topectomy in the treatment of chronic psychoses; a comparative study, *EEG & Clinical Neurophysiology*, **4**, 242–243 (1952).

WENGER, M. A., Preliminary study of the significance of measures of autonomic balance, *Psychosom. Med.*, **9**, No. 5 (1947).

WENGER, M. A., Mechanical emotion, *J. Psychol.*, **29**, 101–108 (1950).

WILCOX, P. H., The Gardner behaviour chart, *Amer. J. Psychiat.*, **98**, 874–880 (1942).

WILLIAMS, J. M. and FREEMAN, W., Evaluation of lobotomy with special reference to children, *Res. Publ. Ass. Nerv. Ment. Dis.*, **31**, 311–318 (1951).

WORTHING, H. J., BRILL, H. and WIDGERSON, H., Evaluation of immediate and late results of prefrontal lobotomy in 600 cases, *Amer. J. Psychiat.*, **108**, 328–336 (1951).

WRIGHT, CLARE, The qualitative performance of delinquent boys on the Porteus maze test, *J. Cons. Psychol.*, **8**, 24–26 (1944).

YACORZYNSKI, G. H., BOSHES, B. and DAVIS, L., Psychological changes produced by frontal lobotomy, *Res. Publ. Ass. Nerv. Ment. Dis.*, **27**, 642–657 (1948).

YOKOI, S., Neuropathological study of prefrontal lobotomy, *J. Neuropath.*, **16**, 251–260 (1957).

CHAPTER 16

The Psychological Effects of Cerebral Electroshock

DUGAL CAMPBELL

INTRODUCTION

ELECTRIC convulsive therapy (E.C.T.) was introduced into modern psychiatry by Cerletti and Bini in 1938 (Cerletti and Bini, 1938). Electrically induced convulsions had been used before 1938 to treat mental illness (Sargant, 1957) but they had never been generally adopted as a standard form of treatment. Since 1938 E.C.T. has become a major therapy in psychiatry. One of the principal arguments in support of the claim that psychiatry now has effective methods of treatment turns upon the results claimed for E.C.T.

The use of convulsions was initially suggested by the supposedly low incidence of schizophrenia among epileptics. Metrazol therapy was introduced by Meduna (1935) on this basis and E.C.T. was at first regarded as a more convenient way of producing convulsions. For this reason a number of the earlier reports in the psychiatric literature of the results of E.C.T. are concerned with a comparison of Metrazol therapy and E.C.T. in cases of schizophrenia. Later, one finds papers which compare the effects of various forms of E.C.T. and assess the advantages of modifying the fit by drugs. E.C.T. has rarely been examined in its own right, perhaps because it has never appeared as a wholly novel treatment which has to be proved as better than existing treatments, or than no treatment at all.

As seems to be the case for many psychiatric therapies, an initial enthusiasm for E.C.T. has now been replaced by a more moderate assessment of the efficacy of treatment. Electroconvulsions are now thought to give the most satisfactory results in the treatment of cases in which depression is either the the principal feature or among the major symptoms. Slater wrote in 1946: "Convulsion therapy has an almost specific remedial effect in one circumscribed psychiatric syndrome but as generally used in psychiatry it is a symptomatic method for the treatment of depression." The syndrome for which E.C.T. is thought to be particularly effective is involutional

melancholia. Claims have been made for recovery in up to 90 per cent of these cases (Slater, 1946).

The supposed antagonism between schizophrenic processes and physical convulsions is now thought to be unlikely as schizophrenia appears to be neither opposed to nor associated with epilepsy (Hoch, 1943). But the success of E.C.T. in alleviating depression has led to renewed speculation concerning the *modus operandi* of E.C.T. Some believe, for example, that the shock activates the autonomic nervous system to restore normal function. Others hold that the shock acts as it does because it causes damage to the brain. And it has been proposed that E.C.T. acts as a "punishment" which satisfies a patient's psychodynamic needs. None of these, or any other view, has yet been adequately demonstrated. So it may be said that E.C.T. is an entirely empirical treatment at the moment.

Given such a situation there appear to be at least four overlapping tasks which may suggest themselves to psychologists. In the first place, psychological methods may be used to estimate the efficacy of the treatment in alleviating depression and in returning patients to ordinary life. In the second, research may be concerned with the effects of E.C.T. upon measures of specific psychological functions, for example memory or intelligence. In the third place, psychological research may be of assistance in examining hypotheses concerning the mode of action of E.C.T. One might examine, for example, the notion that memories with painful associations are particularly influenced by E.C.T. And lastly, the construction of test batteries to predict the outcome of E.C.T. suggests itself as a line of investigation.

Ideally these four tasks should form part of an expanding and coherent body of knowledge. If such were the case both the prognosis in any particular instance and general psychological effects might be derived from a rational account of the action of E.C.T. and the division of the topic into four aspects would appear to be artificial. This ideal is not yet realized. The four divisions seem a reasonable way of viewing E.C.T. and may assist in assessing psychological research in this area.

In fact, psychological studies have not, for the most part, been, by design, directed at these aims, and it is more convenient in the first instance to describe the experiments by making a main division into animal and human studies. Animal subjects have been used by a number of experimenters as they make possible experimental designs which could not be applied to human subjects. In this connexion one may note that Cerletti applied electric current to his first patient only at the end of a series of experiments upon animals which culminated in his observation of the use of electricity in making pigs insensible in the Roman *abattoirs*. The majority of these experiments have been directed at describing the effects of E.C.T. upon psychological function although a few have examined aspects of explanations of E.C.T.

Other experimenters have used E.C.T. as it is ordinarily given in hospitals as an experimental variable, accepting the limitations which are thus necessarily imposed upon research design. Many experiments of this type of research, have failed to include control, or untreated, groups and consequently the results cannot be attributed unequivocally to E.C.T. None of these experiments is a direct attempt to measure the efficacy of E.C.T. The aim of the majority is to report upon the psychological effects

of E.C.T., and a few examine explanations of E.C.T.

An idea of current psychological interest in shock treatment is given by the citations in *Psychological Abstracts* for 1956. Thirty-six refer to electroconvulsive shocks but only three of these report on changes in psychological measures in human subjects. Six refer to animal subjects and the remainder treat the subject either from a psychiatric or from a physiological point of view.

At the moment there can be no doubt that the researches upon animal subjects provide information which is more reliable than do those which used human subjects. But, though many of the animal experiments use E.C.T. as a pattern it remains uncertain how the results may be applied in explaining the effects of E.C.T. in humans. Generally the experimenters who used animal subjects have been cautious in interpretation. One has said: "The greatest chances for success in discovering the secrets of the electroconvulsive shock mechanism lie in capitalizing on the advantages of research using both human and infra-human subjects." (Russell, 1948.)

The present status of work on E.C.T. is reviewed in this paper in the light of the animal experimentation as this comparison gives a clear idea of the value which can be assigned to the work with humans. The comparative psychologist has admitted advantages in experimental design but, even allowing for this, the comparison is not flattering to clinical psychology.

EXPERIMENTS USING ANIMAL SUBJECTS

Finger (1947) surveyed the several ways of inducing convulsions in rats and the various means of lowering convulsive thresholds. In common with other papers written at that time the discussion is influenced by Maier's experiments from which it appeared that convulsions could be induced by subjecting the animals to a series of insoluble trials in a Lashley jumping stand. It appeared from Finger's review that convulsions, which were behaviourally alike, had been produced by a variety of agencies, including electroshock, and that these convulsions had effects upon habits for at least some time after the convulsion. Golub and Morgan (1945), Siegel and Lacy (1946) and Stainbrook (1946) reported that electroshock produced full grand mal convulsions in the absence of any other form of stress. The course of the convulsion was described in detail by Golub and Morgan and has been consistently observed since in experiments of this type.

It therefore appeared that occurrence of convulsions could be treated as an independent variable in psychological experiments rather than merely as an effect of

some other psychological variable, such as frustration. Stainbrook made the point that the convulsion follows the electrical stimulation directly in some cases and therefore "the abnormal behaviour pattern may occur in the absence of any psychologically significant state of fear," due to pain from the passage of current.

Shock Variables and Subject Variables

When E.C.T. in human subjects and electroshock convulsions (E.S.C.) in animals were first examined attention was given to the type of electric current used. It was found that alterations in the physical characteristics of the current produced differences in the onset of the convulsion. It has been noted that rectangular current has a lower threshold than ordinary alternating current in producing shocks (Merritt and Putnam, 1938) and that such threshold differences are sensitive to slight changes in current intensity (Pierce, Russell and Patton, 1950). In individual animals the threshold for a given current is constant from day to day.

The direct physical consequences of E.S.C. also

vary with the current used. As the intensity and duration of the current used become greater, more cases of paralysis due to fractures and dislocation of vertebrae are found (Russell, Townsend, Braun and Patton, 1948).

But it is not certain how variation in current is related to subsequent psychological changes. Hayes (1948) examined the behaviour of rats in a three-choice-point T maze after petit mal convulsions and after grand mal convulsions induced by currents of either 35 milliamperes or 150 milliamperes. The results of the 35-mA and 150-mA groups were indistinguishable. From this it appears probable that the convulsion is an "all-or-nothing" reaction which proceeds independently of the stimulus once the threshold is reached. Townsend, Russell and Patton (1949) obtained similar results when they compared groups of rats given shocks of 25, 30 and 35 mA.

However Docter (1957) used square-wave d.c. current to evoke convulsions (brief stimulus therapy) and found that this had a less disruptive effect upon behaviour than 60-cycle a.c. current. This result is in agreement with those from human subjects in which the side-effects of E.C.T. are said to be avoided by using "brief stimulus therapy."

The number of shocks included in a series is related to subsequent impairment. The form of the relationship is not known but larger numbers of shocks produce greater changes (Brown and Wilbanks, 1952; McDonald and Stern, 1956).

The experiments upon shock variables have led to the use of apparatus, such as the Pittsburgh apparatus, which enables the experimenter to control the characteristics of the current, even though the load may vary. A typical shock used in experimentation with rats will have characteristics of this order: 50 mA of 60-cycle a.c., delivered for 0·2 sec through alligator clips attached to the subject's ears.

Some subject variables have also been investigated. As the weight of a rat increases the threshold for shock increases. If weight is held constant an increase in age causes a drop in threshold (Pierce and Patton, 1952). Two strain differences have been examined. No differences were found between albino and black hooded rats (Bendig and Braun, 1951), though the authors point out that finding no differences in one comparison does not imply that all genetic variables may be discounted. A comparison of tame and feral rats was made by Stone (1953). He found that feral rats showed a different shock pattern from that found in tame rats. Within the group of feral rats a non-shock group showed a decline in wild behaviour whereas a shock-group showed no change at all in emotional response during a series of shocks and remained wild despite frequent handling.

General Effects of Electroshock Convulsions

A complication which arises in assessing the results of E.S.C. in animals is that decrements in performance on a particular task may be due to some general effect of E.S.C., such as an alteration of drive, rather than being due to a specific action of E.S.C. upon the functions in question. In a number of experiments such general changes have been noted.

Page (1941) attempted unsuccessfully to condition E.S.C. He noted that repeated convulsions led to loss of weight, inactivity and passivity in his subjects. Similar results have been reported by Stone (1946) and Winder (1946). A reduction in voluntary activity occurred within twenty-four hours after shock in each case. Once the shock series had ended activity returned to the normal level again or even surpassed it.

Stern (1956) used the open field test to show changes in emotionality after E.S.C. A series of fifteen E.S.C. produced a decrease in activity and an increase in emotional behaviour which lasted for as long as one hundred days after the last shock. The disagreement of other authors on the degree and sort of emotion shown by their subjects is attributed by Stern to the varied situations in which they made their observations.

Mirsky and Rosvold (1953) suspected that activity changes might indicate loss of drive. They found that shocked rats on an *ad libitum* food schedule reduced their food intake, but that groups of rats on a deprivation schedule showed increased motivation as measured by bar-pressing to obtain food and subsequent *ad libitum* feeding. Stern (1954) had rather similar findings: an *ad libitum* feeding schedule caused shocked animals to lose weight whereas a twenty-three-hour deprivation group showed no change. Jensen and Stainbrook (1949) found a weight gain in an E.S.C. group.

Mirsky and Rosvold point out that the hunger drive and the influence of E.S.C. may cancel out in such a way that increased motivation due to deprivation may equal a drive decrement due to E.S.C. They adduce conflicting evidence from other experiments (McGinnies, 1947; Bernberg, 1951) to support this. They emphasize that the feeding schedule of animals should be specified in experiments and that the drive states of the shocked and non-shocked groups must be comparable.

In a later study, however, (Mirsky, Looney and Rosvold, 1954), no differences were found after E.S.C. in a maze habit between groups of rats, one maintained at 85 per cent of initial weight and another allowed to make a steady weight gain. It consequently appears that the variations in the results from other studies may not be attributed unequivocally to variations in hunger drive.

A number of experimenters have observed changes in specific functions or behaviours which seem to imply that E.S.C. produce quite profound changes in a variety of physical systems. These, in turn, may underlie the specific effects which are expected in maze and runway performance. The disturbance of the oestrus cycle noted by Jensen and Stainbrook (1949) is doubtful in view of Nolan's (1952) negative report. But marked disturbances of the gestatory process and subsequent maternal behaviour are produced by E.S.C. (Bacon and Rosvold, 1948; Rosvold, 1949). The disturbances in both gestation and maternal behaviour were less marked when the shocks were given later in the gestation period. Maternal behaviour was less disrupted when the shocks were not given immediately following the birth of the pups. These changes are especially interesting as other experiments have shown that maternal behaviour is largely governed, in ordinary circumstances, by the internal secretion of hormones, and by cortical centres. The prolongation of pregnancy and increased difficulty in labour are attributed to dysfunctions of the endocrine system. Rosvold notes that there are marked individual differences in the resistance of mothers to the effects of E.S.C. The number of shocks given is related to the alteration of function; one shock given twelve hours after copulation had no effect whereas six and eleven shocks given on successive days had increasing effects so that, in the eleven-shock group, the foetus was entirely resorbed (Bacon and Rosvold, 1948). Bauer (1955) also reported that E.S.C. disrupted nest-building activity.

Beach, Goldstein and Jacoby (1955) examined the effect of E.S.C. upon sexual behaviour in male rats. Various measures of sexual activity were taken before, during and after E.S.C. It was found that the subjects became less responsive to stimuli which normally set off the initiation of copulation but became more responsive to stimulation derived from the act itself; the increased reactivity to coital stimulation is retained for up to twenty-eight days. These results are explained by Gellhorn's hypothesis of shift in autonomic activity toward the sympathetic system (Gellhorn, 1953), and the additional assumption that E.S.C. temporarily reduces parasympathetic activity.

Other changes in levels of physiological function have been found. MacMahon (1929) found that electric shock caused marked and sudden pressure changes in the cardiac system. Hoyt and Rosvold (1951) showed that normal variations in rectal temperature are reduced by E.S.C.

These results indicate that E.S.C. acts not only upon individual habits but generally upon the physiological bases of behaviour. In consequence, in any particular instance one must be cautious in attributing alterations in a particular behaviour directly to the action of E.S.C. as they may be due to changes in a general physiological system. The way in which these changes are brought about is still obscure.

Retention of Habits after E.S.C.

The use of E.C.T. led to noticeable amnesias in patients immediately after the shock which, apparently, cleared up in a matter of hours. This observation naturally led to experiments concerning the retention of previously acquired habits after E.S.C.

Among the simplest responses examined have been conditioned responses. It was found that, when a conditioned response had been extinguished by a series of non-reinforced trials, the use of electroshock led to a reappearance of the initial conditioned response. (Gellhorn, Kessler and Minatoya, 1942; Gellhorn and Kessler, 1943; Gellhorn, 1945). These results suggested that E.S.C. may act specifically upon inhibited conditioned responses. Rosen and Gantt (1943) using Metrazol found that convulsions led to loss of discrimination in a conditioned response, which was made to both negative and positive stimuli. This, too, may be attributed to an alteration in inhibitory processes.

The bulk of research on habit retention after E.S.C. has used the straight runway or maze learning as a means of showing decrement in performance. Both were used to measure the consequences of audiogenic seizures, and to compare the results of audiogenic seizures and E.S.C. Stainbrook and Lowenbach (1942) reported that both "noise-fright" reactions and E.S.C. led to disorientation in rats so that they required much longer to run mazes though the error scores were unaltered. McGinnies (1947) also found great changes in maze time scores but none in error scores after E.S.C. Because of the larger variance in the results of his shocked group he suggested that individual differences in the ability to withstand stress rather than any direct neural effect might underlie the post-shock performance. Shaw, Utecht and Fullager (1953) found similar results after audiogenic seizures. They attributed the greater time scores to the time the animals spent in hiding on the way to their food-box and suggested that fear may lead to this response at the expense of goal seeking. Such results bring out the difficulties mentioned in the previous section. The increase in time scores is consonant with greater inactivity but it is uncertain, in these cases, whether or not some emotional state accounts for the changed behaviour.

A number of experiments have investigated the effects of E.S.C. upon tasks of varying difficulty. When very simple tasks of the maze variety are used it becomes more difficult to detect post-E.S.C. changes in performance. Siegel (1943) found no change in the overall speed of running through a runway. In a second experiment which measured component parts of the runway behaviour (Siegel and Siegel, 1949) E.S.C. was found to abolish the anticipatory goal reaction. In the second experiment, moreover, a control group of animals was shocked in the leg as a means of controlling for emotional change. Shock to the leg does not have the effect of E.S.C. in abolishing the anticipatory gradient.

Behaviour on more difficult tasks can more readily be shown to be influenced by E.S.C. Duncan (1945) used a Lashley type-III maze in an experiment which included an E.S.C. group, a leg-shock control group and a no-shock control group. On a relearning trial after shock the experimental shock group was significantly inferior to the controls in error scores, time scores and in the number of trials necessary to re-achieve mastery. He concluded that the effect of E.S.C. is specific to the central nervous system as shock to the legs had no effect and therefore fear might be excluded as a cause of habit decrement. Townsend, Russell and Patton (1949) showed decrements in retention of a Lashley III water-maze immediately after E.S.C. On a task at the extreme edge of the animal's capability the effect of E.S.C. may be to make it impossible for some rats to relearn the task and all have great difficulty. This has been reported for a double-alternation task (McGinnies and Schlosberg, 1945; Palmer, 1950). Cats, on the other hand, show no post-shock decrement in double-alternation problems.

Russell (1949) used a five-choice-point maze in conditions identical with those of earlier experiments. He was able to show a clear interrelationship of retention and task difficulty. The more difficult the task the less it is retained through shock.

Another feature of the effects of E.S.C. suggested by observations of human patients and the conditioned response experiments was that the effect might be greatest in the case of more recently acquired habits. Duncan (1948) trained rats first to go left in a T-maze and then to go right. The intervention of a single shock caused a significant revival of the earlier left-going habit though not all his subjects exhibited this. He pointed out the possibility that the therapeutic effect of E.C.T. may depend upon the removal of recently acquired habits which permits older ones to reappear. Braun and Patton (1950) demonstrated a limitation to this conclusion. If two tasks are of equal difficulty an earlier learned task will tend to reappear after E.S.C. and will be persisted in. But if the two tasks are of unequal difficulty then the earlier learned of the two responses will reappear only when it is also the simpler of the two.

As more recently acquired habits are often also "younger" habits in terms of the time and trials elapsed since acquisition, attention was turned to the effects of E.S.C. upon habits acquired at various time intervals before the shock series. Duncan (1949) trained rats to avoid a charged grid and gave them shocks at varying intervals after each trial; the intervals varied from twenty seconds to fourteen hours. He also used a leg-shock control group. The effect became progressively less so that animals shocked at one to fourteen hours after each trial showed no significant difference in the amount of learning impairment from the leg-shock or unshocked controls.

Worchel and Gentry (1950) compared the effects of E.S.C. given either immediately after criterion learning or four hours later. When a retest was made twenty-four hours later the immediate shock group showed the greater decrement. Worchel and Narciso (1950) repeated the experiment but included a retest four days later rather than twenty-four hours later. In these conditions the immediate shock group showed no impairment and was indistinguishable from a no-shock group. The changes caused by immediate shock appear to be temporary; in this instance six E.C.S. had been given. Thompson and Dean (1955) examined the effect on a discrimination habit of shocks given at ten seconds, two minutes, one hour and four hours after the last criterion trial. In this case, at retest forty-eight hours later, the groups with the shorter criterion-trial shock intervals showed the greater decrement.

These results are generally interpreted in terms of a neural reverberation or consolidation theory. This process is thought to be essential to retention and is disrupted, particularly in its early stages, by E.S.C.

Another line of evidence which may be related to this process is provided by experiments which investigated the relations between degree of learning and the amount of retention after electroshock. Over-learning considerably reduces the effect of E.S.C. (Worchel and Gentry, 1950; Braun and Albee, 1952). Braun and Albee compared the effects of 200 per cent and 600 per cent over-learning. The 600 per cent over-learning group did not differ significantly from the no-shock control group, and, in terms of saving scores, the 200 per cent over-learning group was also shown to be effective in resisting the consequences of E.S.C.

The effects of E.S.C. appear to lead to a permanent decrement in retention if a sufficient number of shocks are given. Worchel and Gentry found no decrement on retest four days after six shocks. But, after twenty-five convulsions, Russell and Patton (1949a; 1949b) showed larger trial, error and time scores on a water-maze in a convulsed group at one, thirty, sixty and ninety days after the last convulsion. Though an improvement in absolute performance level took place there was no reduction in degree of relative impairment shown by the shocked groups at each trial.

E.S.C. and Learning

The notion that E.C.T. may have permanent ill-effects in humans is paralleled in animal research by the idea that learning may be permanently impaired. Stainbrook (1943) trained rats in a two-choice-point T maze, gave them a course of E.S.C. and examined relearning in the maze. The shocked group took longer to relearn the mazes and made more errors than the control group. But, compared with their original learning curves, the time scores of the shocked group were better and the error scores were the same. In many studies of this type a "learning impairment" is discussed in terms of the discrepancy between the performances of a shocked experimental group and a non-shocked control group during relearning trials, following the pattern of the retention experiments. In these cases the "learning impairment" may in fact be a performance decrement due to E.S.C. which necessarily causes a longer relearning process as the shocked group begins relearning at a lower level of performance. The most informative comparison for this purpose would appear to be between relearning after shock and the original learning at the same level of proficiency.

Hayes (1948) examined this point. He found in a group of rats given grand mal shocks significantly poorer relearning curves in a three-unit T maze for both time and errors in cases where the initial relearning score happened to be very much the same as in the control group. Muhlan and Stone (1949) used a Dashiell-type water maze. They noted that, compared with a control group, a shocked group showed a weaker tendency to adopt the most economical route through the maze, covered greater distances and made more "reversals" of direction with respect to the goal. In the shocked group the evolution of an economical central path began only when the shock series ended. In a later problem, however, the convulsed group showed no certain handicap in habit formation. Rishikoff and Rosvold (1953) found impaired learning in rats on the Hebb-Williams closed field test which, they remark, provides a better analogy to human intelligence than maze problems. They found poorer initial learning thirty-five days after a series of fifteen shocks, shown by greater error scores in the shocked group. Bendig and Patton (1952) found that E.S.C. reduced latent learning.

An experiment by Horowitz and Stone (1946) is interesting as it contrasts the disorganization of a recent habit by E.S.C. and reduction in learning. They reversed a discrimination habit in shocked rats expecting that the disorganization of the previous habit by E.S.C. would facilitate learning of the new habit. In fact, the opposite result was found. The original habit was indeed disorganized after shock

but a non-shock group learned the reversed habit more readily than did the shocked group.

Rather similar results were obtained from monkeys. A "learning set" training was ended by giving a series of E.S.C. On retest for retention of the learning set, control animals had a higher rate of correct responding than the experimental animals which made only a slow approach to the level of the controls. The inferior performance of the shocked group in this case was due to a tendency to make perseverative position responses (Braun, Patton and Barnes, 1952). However, further tests of delayed responses and oddity problems given twenty-four and ninety-four days after E.S.C. showed no decrement and suggested that the previous results represented a temporary change (Braun, 1952a; 1952b).

Eriksen, Porter and Stone (1948) examined the possibility that E.S.C. produces irreversible impairment in learning ability if given in infancy. They used a split-litter technique and a multiple T-maze. They found, in rats shocked daily from twenty to twenty-nine days of age, slightly more errors and trials before mastery was attained in a T-maze than in a non-shock group. These results were found at ten, twenty and up to ninety days after the last shock. In a combined analysis of these results no decline in relative impairment could be related to the test-retest interval so it appeared that E.S.C. in infancy leads to a permanent decrement in ability which remains constant (Porter, Stone and Eriksen, 1948). Similar results were found by Braun, Pierce and Patton (1950) and Bernberg (1951). In every case the experimenters noted that the differences in actual performance were small and stiff criteria were necessary in order to demonstrate the effect. These results have been attributed to irreversible brain damage.

A contrary result is reported by Rishikoff and Rosvold (1953) on the Hebb-Williams closed field test. The shocks were given for ten days to rats aged twenty to twenty-nine days but led to no apparent increase in errors during training at one hundred and fourteen days of age.

The Effects of E.S.C. upon Emotional Responses

As the principal effect of E.C.T. is upon mood it is naturally of interest to investigate change of mood in animals. However in order to do so some marked emotion must be set up in animals and some way of measuring subsequent changes in the emotion must be found. "Anxiety" as defined by Estes and Skinner (1941) has been used in a series of experiments which have outlined the course of this response after E.S.C. Provided no alteration is made in experimental arrangements the anxiety or "conditioned emotional response" is very slow to extinguish, and shows nearly complete spontaneous recovery after extinction.

This stability of response was used to provide a useful indication of the effect of E.S.C.

Hunt and Brady (1951) used the cessation of bar-pressing in a Skinner Box as an index of "anxiety" in response to a sound which had previously been paired with an electric shock to the paws. After a course of E.S.C. the shocked animals continued to press the bar when the sound signal was presented whereas a non-shock control group retested at the same time continued to show the acquired anxiety response. In the shocking-box itself the experimental animals showed a return of exploratory behaviour whereas non-shock control animals crouched and defaecated. In a series of control experiments this result was confirmed and the possibility that it was due either to impaired hearing or to competition between the two responses of bar-pressing and crouching was excluded (Brady and Hunt, 1951; 1952). In subsequent reconditioning trials the experimental animals were all able to acquire the emotional response again. In later experiments bar-pressing was again used because of its advantages as a readily quantifiable index of anxiety. Anxiety means, in this context, a decline in rate of bar-pressing immediately following presentation of a signal which has been paired with a painful stimulus.

Brady (1951) examined the effect of E.S.C. upon the conditioned emotional response at thirty, sixty and ninety days after completion of the shock series. Four days after the shock series the emotional response had disappeared as it had done in the previous experiments. At thirty, sixty and ninety days, however, it reappeared and the effect of E.S.C. could only be detected in the smaller number of trials which the shocked group required for extinction to take place. A plausible suggestion in the light of these results was that, as time passed, the emotional response became stronger. This possibility was examined by giving E.S.C. at intervals of thirty, sixty and ninety days after the emotional conditioning and then examining for retention of the emotional response four days after the shock series. In this instance the emotional response was not abolished by the E.S.C. Only during extinction trials could the shocked animals be distinguished from the controls. But even this difference between the groups decreased as the period between emotional conditioning and the shock series grew longer. This goes to support the notion that conditioned emotional responses increase in strength as a function of elapsed time so as to offset the action of E.S.C. (Brady, 1952). Subsequently it was found that ordinary extinction procedures, applied immediately after the shock series, during the time in which the emotional response was temporarily abolished from the animals' behaviour, had the effect of permanently abolishing it. This confirms the notion that during the post-shock period the emotional response still has covert representation of some kind in the central nervous system (Hunt, Jernberg and Brady, 1952). These results recall the clinical observation that depressions of long standing are more resistant to E.C.T.

Similar results are obtained with audiogenic seizures which also abolish conditioned emotional responses (Brady, Stebbins and Galambos, 1953). An interesting additional fact was that the rank-order correlation between the number of seizures and the alteration in the rate of bar-pressing was 0·89. The "convulsive process" is assumed to be the event common to the two experimental procedures and, therefore, either it, or its effects, must be the cause of behavioural changes.

In the experiment of Brady, Stebbins and Galambos it emerged that the temporal distribution of convulsions was of importance in eliminating the emotional response. Convulsions on alternate days were not so effective as convulsions every day. This finding led to further investigation of this point. The experiments in the series initiated by Hunt and Brady had used a procedure in which the rats were given twenty-one shocks at the rate of three a day. Brady, Hunt and Geller (1954) gave twenty-one shocks at intervals ranging from one second to seventy-two hours. The emotional response was eliminated only in the groups which were shocked at intervals of one, eight and twenty-four hours, and was partially eliminated when the intervals were one-half, forty-eight and seventy-two hours. The animals given twenty-one electric shocks in twenty-one seconds had only one convulsion however, and in their case the retention of the emotional response is consistent with previous findings; similarly not all the animals shocked at half-hourly intervals had twenty-one convulsions. The partial elimination which occurred after convulsions at forty-eight and seventy-two hours suggests an interaction between the cumulative effects of E.S.C. and the gradual increase in the emotional response.

The possibility suggested by experiments in maze retention, that the emotional responses were eliminated solely because they were the most recently acquired responses was examined by Geller, Sidman and Brady (1955) who reversed the usual order of acquiring first, the bar-pressing response, and then the conditioned emotional response. In this case too the emotional response was eliminated by E.S.C.

Poschel (1957) examined both the retroactive effect, and the proactive effect of E.S.C. upon anxiety by using the approach-avoidance conflict in a runway. In his shocked groups E.S.C. acted both proactively and retroactively to reduce the fear component in the conflict. The novel element in this study is provided by the proactive effect of E.S.C. Poschel argues that these results support the notion of some physiological change caused by E.S.C. which provides a temporary basis for altered emotional behaviour.

Avoidance responses have been investigated in a similar fashion. Heistad (1955) found the E.S.C. weakened a conditioned avoidance reaction to electric shock to the paws. Carson (1957) found similar results. Hamilton and Patton (1952) examined an extinguished avoidance reaction and found that it was reactivated by the intervention of E.S.C. though not all the subjects showed this recovery on all the trials.

E.S.C. and Maladaptive Responses

Masserman and Jacques (1947) examined the effect of E.S.C. upon experimental neuroses in cats. They found that after E.S.C. the shocked animals showed a change in behaviour. Phobias and compulsions disappeared and more adaptive behaviour emerged. This did not occur in all the animals examined but, if it occurred at all, the change continued for periods of up to ten weeks. This tendency could be further improved by guidance. Later in this experiment it was found that all of the neurotic subjects and two of the controls showed an impaired ability for complex adaptation. A second experiment, using "milder" shock, led to the reduction of both normal and neurotic behaviour. In this case all but one of the neurotic subjects failed to respond to guidance as a means of restoring adaptive behaviour (Masserman, Arieff, Pechtel and Klehr, 1950). It is not entirely clear from these experiments which variable produces the alterations in behaviour: shock or subsequent guidance.

Neet and Feldman (1954) established a fixated jumping response in rats which was tested for stability during a twenty days' series of insoluble responses. They found that neither a ten-shock or a twenty-four-shock series caused the rats to abandon the fixated response. In a second experiment (Feldman and Neet, 1954) they combined shock and guidance. No significant differences were found between the shock and non-shock groups for the rate extinction of conflict-induced responses, or the number of animals able to solve the problem. In a later experiment (Feldman and Neet, 1957) they examined the possibility that their results were due to over-learning the fixated response during the many trials which permitted no consistent escape from punishment. It will be recalled that over-learning substantially reduces the effects of E.S.C. In this case too it was found that the conflict-induced fixations were not altered by E.S.C. Indeed there were consistent suggestions that E.S.C. delayed the breaking down of the stereotype; the non-shock control group learned quicker on retest.

E.S.C. and Drugs

In a number of cases E.S.C. have been given while the animal has been drugged. Porter and Stone (1947) found that E.S.C. given under ether anaesthesia produced less interference with maze learning than E.S.C. given in the ordinary way. Similarly ether anaesthesia at the time of the passage of current affords almost complete protection against the deleterious effects of E.S.C. upon gestation (Stone and Walker, 1949). Siegel, McGinnies and Box (1949) compared shock under surgical anaesthesia (Nembutal), shock and a *placebo* (saline injection), and the anaesthesia alone upon running time in a straightway. Both groups given the Nembutal were unimpaired on retest. The saline-shock group showed an increase in running time. It was concluded that anaesthesia protects the animal from the disturbing effects of E.S.C. The disturbances therefore seem to be dependent upon the convulsion and not upon the passage of the current as such. This result is analogous to the observations made of E.C.T. in human subjects, where a general anaesthesia has no apparent influence upon the beneficial changes but eliminates many of the physical risks.

The effects of E.S.C. upon emotional responses are also diminished if the convulsion is blocked by ether anaesthesia (Hunt, Jernberg and Brady, 1952).

Not all drugs have this effect. Epanutin does not modify the effects of E.S.C. upon maze performance (Broadhurst, Stone and Lawrence, 1952). Similarly E.S.C. under Epanutin or amphetamine does not prevent the usual attenuating effect of E.S.C. upon an emotional response. But E.S.C. under Phenurone does not have its usual effect upon an emotional response. These various results presumably reflect the different actions of the drugs (Hunt and Beckwith, 1956).

E.S.C. as a Cause of Brain Damage

Damage has been found in the brains of a number of animals following electric shock procedures. The most common type of damage has been haemorrhages in the meninges and within the brain (Morrison, Weeks and Cobb, 1923). The changes which occur apparently happen immediately and the evidence for them diminishes as the interval between shock and inspection increases (Heilbrunn and Liebert, 1941). The damage appeared as haemorrhages which were attributed to the sharp rise in arterial blood pressure during muscle contraction and vasospasm of peripheral arteries (Heilbrunn and Weil, 1942; Alpers and Hughes, 1942). There is additional evidence to support the view that changes in circulatory pressure during the convulsion, and not the current itself, cause the lesions because when the convulsion is prevented by ether narcosis the haemorrhages no longer occur (Heilbrunn, 1943).

The changes that occur tend to be reversible, though they are longer lasting after more intense shocks and in the current path. Hartelius (1952) found both reversible and non-reversible changes in the brains of fifty-seven cats given E.S.C. Ferraro and Helfand (1946) suggest that these reversible changes may be the basis for alterations in the mental processes of patients. However Siekert, Williams and Windle (1950) found no differences in the brains of five shocked monkeys and one control. They claimed their technique excluded post-mortem change in the brains which could give rise to the results reported by other workers.

Hypertrophy of the rat's adrenal gland has been found by Rosvold, Kaplan and Stevenson (1952) after E.S.C., though similar shocks given under anaesthesia gave no such enlargement. The coincident changes in adrenal size and behaviour provide another possible basis for the effects of E.S.C. Royce and Rosvold (1953) give further detail of endocrine changes. They found that anticonvulsant drugs given alone led to adrenal enlargement. They therefore gave additional electroshocks to animals in which further convulsions were blocked by the tonic-extension phase of the convulsion which followed the previous electroshock. In this case the current alone led to endocrine system changes (Gellhorn, 1953).

Explanations of the Consequences of E.S.C.

The experimenters who carried out the work upon animals described in the preceding sections were often led to their particular topics by considering clinical reports of the effects of E.C.T. It is natural to ask if their results are relevant to E.C.T. and if they go any distance towards providing a model for E.C.T. By and large, if one accepts the analogy between E.S.C. and E.C.T., the results are in one sense encouraging and in another discouraging. In a general sense they are encouraging as they indicate how substantial a portion of inborn and acquired psychological function survives a course of electroshock convulsions. Moreover ways in which the effects of convulsions may be reduced are also indicated. A particularly striking feature is that many of the suggestions from clinical observation have led to animal experiments whose findings, in turn, suggest further lines of research in both animal and human subjects. But in detail the results are not in close agreement. It appears that E.S.C. can have an effect upon established habits, particularly those more recently acquired, and that these effects may be permanent in certain circumstances. On the other hand, changes of emotional response are not per-manent and maladaptive habits cannot be altered more readily with the aid of E.S.C.

These conclusions run counter to clinical observations of the results of E.C.T., which is said to have no marked or permanent effect upon habits or cognitive functions, and may lead to effective permanent changes in mood and emotional tone.

Animal research has generated a number of explanations of the consequences of E.S.C. These explanations must also be thought of as candidates for the explanation of the effects of E.C.T. These explanations have turned upon either brain damage or a "consolidation" theory of neural function or Selye's general adaptation syndrome.

The brain-damage theory considers that the changes in behaviour turn upon reversible or irreversible brain changes. These have not been exactly specified but are assumed to become permanent if, either many shocks are given in a series or if they are given in infancy.

The consolidation theory supposes that E.S.C. act as they do because they break up an assumed "rever-beration" or consolidation process which is necessary to the establishment of a habit. The results which support this view most completely are those which show how E.S.C. have less effect when an interval elapses between habit training and shock administra-tion. Such reverberating circuits of the kind suggested have in fact been shown only between whole units of the central nervous system but they are assumed to exist on a local scale. Attempts have been made to provide evidence for the consolidation theory by slowing down the reverberations, so that a longer time is required to fix the habit, and then introducing E.S.C. which, if the theory is sound, should have disruptive effects as great as those generally found after shorter periods. One such attempt, which used cooling to slow the reverberatory process, showed disruption of a maze habit in hamsters after an interval of one hour as great as that ordinarily found with a training-shock interval of fifteen minutes (Gerard, 1955). Another experiment by Leukel (1957) in which Sodium pentothal was used to slow nervous activity produced results consistent with those of Gerard. A greater distribution of learning trials, which on this view should assist resistance to E.C.T., has the predicted effect (Thompson and Pennington, 1957).

The theories which evoke the general adaptation syndrome (Selye, 1950) emphasize the non-specific action of electroshock, and subsequent changes in the hormonal and central nervous systems. Riess (1948) has presented data on rats subjected to large numbers of shocks which he believes represent the three stages of the syndrome: alarm, resistance and exhaustion; in terms of maze performance the sequence was decrement, improvement and maladaptation. He also showed that dietary changes influenced the course of performance in a predicted manner. This view has been put into psychological terms by Heistad (1955) who draws on the changes in the hypothalamus and autonomic nervous system found after E.C.S. by Gellhorn (1953), and the notion of stimulus generalization to account for changes in conditioned emotional response. He suggests that the internal stimuli due to autonomic activity are altered because the autonomic activity is itself changed by shock. One will obtain different responses in accordance with stimulus generalization, depending on how unlike the original stimuli are to the altered stimuli.

In each of these three explanations the theorists have had to lean heavily upon either physiological research or upon assumptions concerning physiological processes. It is doubtful if the data at present available concerning the physiological changes following E.C.S.

are sufficient to provide an adequate basis for definitive conclusions. The "explanations" are, properly speaking, research programmes. Beach's remark is still true: " . . . [The effects of E.S.C.] are so numerous and so widespread that much additional experimentation will be necessary before any reasonably satisfactory interpretation of the present findings can be anticipated." (Beach, Goldstein and Jacoby, 1955.)

The prediction made by Harlow (1956) that work on E.S.C. will be discontinued within ten years is likely to be borne out in the sense that the psychological consequences of E.S.C. will be clearly defined. But it appears that work upon the physiological bases of the psychological effects is just beginning and much more will be necessary if E.S.C. and E.C.T. are to be satisfactorily explained.

RESEARCH USING HUMAN SUBJECTS

The experiments upon animals which were described in the preceding sections provide not only a number of suggestions for the psychological effects which may be looked for as consequences of E.C.T. They also provide a model for exact experimentation. In the best of these experiments a control group has been treated in exactly the same manner as the experimental group except for the passage of electric current. The experimental procedure was clearly specified and an appropriate statistical technique was used. If these features are sought for in the experiments which have so far used human subjects the number of studies which meet the requirements is embarrassingly small. Indeed the literature, which at first sight is large and varied, can be made to vanish altogether if one insists that a *placebo* treatment ("pseudo shock" in which the electrodes are applied but no current is passed is a common feature of animal research) should form part of an adequate experimental design. An example of an experiment using this type of control in human subjects is provided by a recent research into the efficacy of insulin shock (Ackner, Harris and Oldham, 1957). There is no reason to suppose that a similar procedure is impossible in the case of E.C.T.; it has, indeed, been used by Brengelmann (1959).

Many of the experiments which are cited as evidence for psychological changes after E.C.T. do not satisfy even less exacting requirements. Many studies have no control groups at all and, in other cases, the control subjects are not patients but normal persons. In other studies there is no statistical analysis of the data which may nevertheless be quoted as an instance of "cognitive impairment" or "greater ability to invest emotion." It is the more surprising to find this state of affairs as many experimenters have wished to

examine the retention of previously learned habits after E.C.T. It is in this area that experimental psychology has for long had a considerable technique. But from the point of view of clinical research Ebbinghaus has lived in vain.

In view of these criticisms a considerable part of the work upon human subjects has been omitted from this review. In particular studies which make no statistical analysis of the data, or which use the results of tests such as the Rorschach, whose validity is unknown or dubious, have not been discussed in great detail. The studies cited have been divided into two sections: clinical and psychological. "Clinical" studies are based upon observations made without any special techniques to measure behaviour and with no particular research design beyond the obvious comparison of "before and after" shock. A great number of observations have been made in such circumstances. Only a small number of them are cited in this paper for their relevance to psychological studies. Thus experiments which compare the use of different relaxant drugs, *glissando* shock and conventional shock and the like, have been omitted.

Clinical Studies

THE GROSS EFFECTS OF E.C.T.

Immediately following a grand mal convulsion the subject no longer reacts to any kind of stimuli. There is a gradual return of psychological functions during which signs typical of "organic" disturbance can be evoked, e.g. perseveration, retrograde amnesia (Stainbrook, 1944; Flescher, 1942). But within hours these alterations have disappeared and the individual's psychological functions are apparently at the previous level again.

RECOVERY RATES AFTER E.C.T.

A large number of studies have included figures for the recovery rate of patients following a course of E.C.T. Alexander (1944) has pointed out that, as no limit has been generally accepted for the period of time in which changes of mental state may be attributed to shock therapy, remissions occurring within two to three months of the treatment have been counted as successes. He proposed as a criterion of success a thirty-day period during which the patient must leave hospital. In fact, some reports cover periods of up to twelve months.

Many of the early papers made comparisons between various diagnostic groups or between Metrazol and electrically induced convulsions. The comparisons between diagnostic groups indicate the success of E.C.T. in treatment of affective psychoses and the comparative failure with schizophrenia. Smith, Hughes, Hastings and Alpers (1942) gave the following figures for recovery rates: involutional melancholia, 85 per cent; manic-depressive psychosis (depressive phase), 72 per cent; manic-depressive psychosis (manic phase), 70 per cent; and schizophrenia, 0 per cent. These figures were not based on large numbers but later results have generally shown close agreement with them. Smith, Hastings and Hughes (1943), for example, found that E.C.T. was most effective for involutional melancholia (recovery rate = 70 per cent) and least effective for schizophrenia (recovery rate less than 30 per cent). Alexander (1953) examined the outcome in one hundred consecutive cases treated with E.C.T. for a period of five years. The only factor which he found to be related to the final state of the patient was diagnosis; five-year remissions occurred twice as frequently in non-schizophrenic patients as among the schizophrenics. Batt (1943) found a recovery rate of 87 per cent in depressive psychosis. Kalinowsky (1943) reviewing the results of 1,500 cases found a recovery rate in the affective disorders larger than 80 per cent. He considered the duration of illness an important variable in cases of schizophrenia. The longer the illness the less likely was any improvement. Slater (1946) reported that claims have been made for a recovery rate of up to 90 per cent in involutional melancholia.

In a number of instances figures are available for both treated and untreated groups of patients. Bagchi, Howell and Schmale (1945) contrasted fifty-four neurotic and psychotic patients who were given shock therapy with sixty-four similar cases who were not shocked. Both groups also received other treatments. In the shocked group recovery was recorded in 49 per cent of the cases; 30·5 per cent of the non-shocked group recovered. These recovery rates differ significantly at the 0·02 level of confidence. Huston and Locher (1948) give figures for a shock group comprising seventy-four depressives and a similar group of eighty patients as controls. The results were as follows—

	Control (N = 80)	Experimental (N = 74)
Recovered . . .	63	65
Suicide . . .	6	1
Remained depressed . .	7	7
Died	4	1

The recovery rate favours the treatment but the difference is not significant. But though the gross recovery rates are alike the time necessary for recovery seems to be reduced by the intervention of treatment. The median time for recovery in the experimental group was nine months and, in the control group, fifteen months.

Karagulla (1950) presented an analysis of nine hundred and twenty-three cases treated both with and without E.C.T. She reported no statistical superiority for the treatment but only a greater "clinical improvement" in the treated group. Slater (1951) attacked these conclusions and using the same figures was able to show that E.C.T. led to a real improvement in the recovery rate. In a similar study Currier, Cullinan and Rothschild (1952) compared data of untreated female schizophrenics and similar treated cases. In the untreated group 30 per cent recovered and in the treated group 75 per cent recovered. Despite the differences found for the gross recovery rate it seems clear that E.C.T. shortens the course of the illness.

This type of study, in which treated and untreated groups are compared, provides a better basis for measuring the effect of E.C.T. than studies in which an E.C.T. group only is included. More work is necessary, with clear definition of time intervals and exact criteria of improvement, before the contribution E.C.T. makes to recovery over and above a natural remission rate can be assessed. The inclusion of untreated control groups, as in these studies, results in a rather more conservative estimate of the efficacy of E.C.T. than the crude recovery rate alone. It has been suggested that E.C.T. is effective only in speeding up remission which has already begun in a depressive illness. At present no definitive opinion can be passed on this possibility though the results of Huston and Locher are consistent with the idea.

CLINICAL SIGNS AND THE OUTCOME OF E.C.T.

The gross recovery rates after E.C.T. reported in the literature vary from study to study. Part of this variation might have been due to variation in the type of patient selected for treatment. Very often the treated group has included all varieties of psychotic illness. A number of researches have indicated that therapeutic outcome is also related to some clearly defined variables other than diagnosis. These factors recall features of some of the animal experiments upon retention.

Batt (1943) examined the outcome of E.C.T. in one hundred cases by dividing them into groups. He found that the recovery rate was highest if the depression treated was the first attack of the illness (96·5 per cent). In such cases he also found that a much shorter period of hospitalization was necessary even if the illness was left untreated. In other types of case, for example recurrent depression, menopausal depression, the recovery rate was rather lower. He concluded that about 90 per cent of all first treatments are successful and that 13 per cent of all cases relapse and need further treatment. The worst prognosis is for chronic cases.

Gralnick (1946) found that treatment is most effective when the patient has not had a long illness. He found a higher recovery rate in patients who had been ill for less than a year. Currier, Cullinan and Rothschild (1952) compared two groups of patients to show the effects of age, duration of illness and acuteness of onset. They found a higher recovery rate among the patients whose illness has been of short duration (less than a year), who were under forty and where the onset of the illness had been acute. Herzberg (1954) made a similar study which included an evaluation of the patient's status one year after shock treatment. He found that a short illness (less than six months) and marriage were favourable prognostic signs, but that a long illness was unfavourable; acuteness of onset was also important. Hobson (1953) examined the connexion between the outcome of treatment and one hundred and twenty-one items of clinical information. He found a suggestive or significant association for twenty items and devised a scoring scale which, in his study, gave a misclassification of outcome in only 21 per cent of his cases. Sudden onset and good insight were the main signs for a favourable prognosis; depersonalization and hypochondriasis were the principal unfavourable signs. The signs isolated in the analysis are considered, in many instances, to be relevant in cases not treated by convulsive therapy.

Retention and E.C.T.

The loss of memory shown in the period which immediately follows E.C.T. turned interest to the possibility of long-term defects in memory. Tooth and Blackburn (1939) noted that some patients complained of memory defect for periods of up to six months after treatment. A considerable number of observations of this type have been made in clinical practice.

Lowenbach and Stainbrook (1942) used the Rorschach test and Wertheimer designs to investigate memory in the period immediately following shock. They suggested that memory for remote events is less influenced by shock than memory for recent events. For example, a woman patient gave her maiden name after treatment. Levy, Serota and Grinker (1942) noted an "intellectual impairment" after shock which lasted for up to three weeks; this judgement was made on the basis of psychiatric assessment. Smith, Hughes, Hastings and Alpers (1942) noted memory defects which, though not permanent, may last for months. Brody (1944) reported on five cases in which E.C.T. appeared to have led to prolonged memory defects for familiar material.

Alexander (1953) reporting the effect of E.C.T. upon a normal subject found that post-shock amnesia was confined to an unpleasant incident which had occurred immediately before E.C.T. This he considered as evidence for the notion that E.C.T. heightens the personality's defence mechanisms, such as repression. A series of such alterations leads to recovery. Meyer (1951) considers that the post-shock amnesias have no significance for the success of therapy except in cases where there may be a total amnesia for psychotic events which permits a complete reconstruction of the personality.

Interestingly enough, some hypnotic phenomena, such as post-hypnotic suggestion and regression to earlier ages, persist, through a shock, in weakened form. The shocks were given at the end of a hypnotic trance with the patients' consent (Bowers and Berkowitz, 1953).

Physical Effects of E.C.T.

A considerable number of cases have been reported in which brain damage has been observed and could have been attributed to E.C.T. Madow (1956) summarized the data available from these observations made on thirty-eight cases and gave additional information on four further cases. As one might expect the topic is treated in the medical literature mainly for the possibility of E.C.T. causing death. The findings in the majority of cases were similar to those found in animal studies. The greatest number of changes were found in the vascular system and generally consisted of small haemorrhages. But the changes are generally held to be reversible within a fairly short period, except in cases where the patient has cardiac or vascular disease.

Changes in brain function have been examined in EEG records taken from patients in the period after treatment. Levy, Serota and Grinker (1942) found that post-shock neurological examination gave negative results but EEG records showed cerebral disturbance, which, in the most marked cases, were of an epileptoid variety. These signs disappeared, usually in a few weeks after treatment, though some patients showed them for six months. Clinical tests of mental status showed an improvement uncorrelated with EEG changes. In a similar study Pacella, Barrera and Kalinowsky (1942) noted that generalized convulsions unlike petit mal seizures, led to marked EEG changes. The longer the series of shocks the more marked and persistent were the changes. The abnormal features of the EEG record disappear in a few weeks once treatment is stopped. Roth and McClatchey (1951) obtained EEG records from post-E.C.T. patients while the patients were under the influence of the drug thiopentone. This drug reduces the activity of the midbrain. The authors conclude that the enduring and cumulative effects of E.C.T. are exerted primarily on a subcortical centre.

The EEG studies made after E.C.T. have been reviewed by Chusid and Pacella (1952). Among their conclusions they state that no correlation is found in the published reports between the post-shock EEG pattern and the clinical response to treatment, or the degree of memory disturbance.

A number of recent studies have emphasized the general effect of E.C.T. in humans (Aird, Strait, Pace, Hrenoff and Bowditch, 1956; Weil-Malherbe, 1955; Bassett and Ross Ashby, 1954). The mode of action of E.C.T. remains unclear however. Weil-Malherbe found changes in adrenaline level as a consequence of shock which he attributed to autonomic activity. Bassett and Ross Ashby found that the P.G.R. of treated patients does not habituate to sudden stimulation as it does in untreated controls. They attribute this to a direct cortical action rather than to an emotional mechanism. In this connexion an interesting case is reported by Guze, Winokur and Levin (1956) in which E.C.T. was successful even though the patient's adrenal cortex was not intact or functional.

RATIONALES FOR TREATMENT

No generally accepted explanation of the action of E.C.T. is available. Parsons, Banet, Keating and Lawrence (1955) remark in the course of a survey of the treatment: "Electroshock as a therapeutic technique is the product of accident and empiricism." The most characteristic psychiatric explanation is based, in one form or another, upon psychodynamics. Treatment is supposed to be, say, anxiety-producing, and therefore leads to more effective repression of the symptoms. This view has not led to any experimental verification up to the present though there is anecdotal evidence in support of it.

Another class of theory which is frequently put forward to explain the psychological consequences of E.C.T. has a physiological basis. E.C.T. is held to cause alterations in brain function which in turn lead to changes in mental states. It is doubtful whether enough is known at present of the physiological changes induced by E.C.T. to provide a detailed basis for such an explanation. And even if these details were available the connexions between brain function and mental states are not yet sufficiently established for one to say what changes in mood should result from any particular physiological change. Like many other psychiatric theories the view embodies an extensive programme of uncompleted research.

A typical example of this view is provided by Myerson (1943) who suggested that the convulsions and shocks "knocked out" the brain and enabled the pathological state to be "forgotten." This theory is fairly representative in its use of a simple physiological "forgetting" but, in view of the temporary nature of the changes in brain function, it would appear to need reinforcement by some account of what prevents the revival of pathology. However Kahn, Fink and Weinstein (1956) claim to have shown that the short-term response to treatment is related to signs of brain damage elicited under sodium amytal. The whole subject needs further investigation.

Psychological Studies

Experiments whose main data are taken from psychological tests are included in this section. The changes which E.C.T. is said to induce, particularly in personality and mood, would appear to provide an excellent topic for psychological investigation. In fact, very few studies have made use of psychological tests in an appropriate way and fewer still have used an experimental design which can show the intended result. Many of the references given in the literature turn out to be articles which contain no tests of significance and no control groups. It is, in fact, alarming for the reviewer to find the results so often quoted fading into insubstantiality. But such is the case and consequently no set of data analogous to that derived from animals is available for discussion.

TESTS GIVEN BEFORE AND AFTER E.C.T.

Batteries of tests given before and after E.C.T. have been used most often in attempts to show the effects of E.C.T. However, in order to establish that E.C.T. is the effective agent in producing changes in score one requires data from a control group tested at the same time or test-retest data for the battery in question obtained from comparable subjects.

For example, the Rorschach Test has been used by several experimenters in order to show post-shock personality change. An early study by Stainbrook (1941) suggested that as time elapsed after a series of shocks so the responses altered. Several studies compared results from before and after the shock treatment. In these experiments no non-shock control group was used and generally no statistical treatment is given. Even so very little is claimed for the results, though the pre- and post-treatment results are thought to be different (Kelley, Marguiles and Barrera, 1941; Beck, 1943; Pacella, Piotrowski and Lewis, 1947; Rees and Jones, 1951). Beck concluded that "shock therapy is not as effective in reaching the inner personality as either spontaneous remission or deep-searching intensive psychotherapy." In general the changes seemed to reflect little more than the customary post-shock confusion in its varying degrees.

Intellectual impairment has also been looked for. Stone (1947) proposed that each shock causes an immediate cognitive loss from which the patients recover in some three to four hours; but a series of such shocks is cumulative in effect as, each time, recovery is assumed to be a little less complete. He examined this view by using both forms of the Wechsler Memory Scale. The parallel forms of the test were given to an experimental group of patients before and after a treatment series of shocks. A control group of patients was given the test one day after a treatment series of shocks and again three weeks later. The experimental group dropped significantly on all but one subtest. The control group on the other hand showed a significant gain in score. Normal control data ordinarily show little change from Form I to Form II on retest. The Wechsler Memory Scale correlates highly with tests of intelligence (e.g. the Army Alpha test) so this finding appears to reflect a genuine cognitive impairment. These results, though consistent with Stone's view that shock leads to *gradual* decline does not in fact prove it. A complete proof would require more tests to be given during the shock series.

Summerskill, Seeman and Meals (1952) found no significant change in Wechsler I.Q., thirty minutes after a single electroshock, which suggests that the result of a single shock may be difficult to demonstrate by relying solely on a deterioration of performance. The *absence* of a significant *improvement* might emerge if there were an untreated control group for comparison. The same patients showed disorientation and impaired motor performance on the Whipple-Healy tapping test.

Huston and Strother (1948) tested patients before and after treatment. They found a slight improvement from pre-shock test to post-shock test on the Babcock and Shipley-Hartford scales but there is no data from untreated controls to aid in assessing this. At later follow-up the results of the treated group did not differ significantly from those of a set of matched normal controls, so that a long term impairment seems unlikely.

Fisher (1949) used both cognitive tests and a questionnaire to assess mood in an experimental design which depended upon the comparison of improved and unimproved patients who had been treated with E.C.T. Significant improvements in Wechsler I.Q. scores fourteen days after treatment in the group of patients who were rated as improved were mainly due to alterations in the comprehension, similarities and digit symbol subtests. The I.Q. scores in the unimproved and slightly improved groups of patients showed a small non-significant decline on retest. The pre-shock pattern of scores was similar in all three groups of patients and was of no assistance in predicting outcome of treatment. Brower and Oppenheim (1951) also report an improvement on Wechsler and Mirror Drawing scores after E.C.T. but give no details concerning tests of significance, results of a control group or the interval between tests which would enable an assessment to be made of this finding.

Beran, Perkins and Scollon (1952) compared the scores of the Wechsler Memory Scale and the Revised Beta Examination in both treated and untreated groups of neurotics and schizophrenics. The treated group was tested before and after E.C.T. and the untreated group was tested at comparable time intervals. Both the experimental and control groups showed a gain in I.Q. score on retest and the difference in the amount of gain shown by the two groups was not significant. Michael (1954) found that the Binet word naming score declined during treatment (whereas the score of a control group improved) but rose again later. Stieper, Williams and Duncan (1951) found an improvement in the abbreviated C.U.S. I.Q. but no change in Wechsler I.Q. In this case the control subjects were not mental patients, and the interval between the shock series and retest was not constant. Gurevitz and Helme (1954) examined the results of E.C.T. in sixteen child patients with schizophrenia. Tests of intellectual function (Binet, a non-language test, and the Goodenough) showed a drop in score immediately after shock (twenty-eight to forty-eight hours) but a later test showed an increase above the initial level.

A major variable in these studies (which is not always explicitly specified) appears to be the time interval between shock and test. The results of Stone and of Michael indicate that testing close after the shock tends to produce scores lower than pre-shock scores. But in other studies, where longer time intervals were allowed, either no change or a practice effect may have occurred. The general conclusion of Kalinowsky and Hoch (1952) seems valid: "Most of the psychologic investigations on human patients as well as animals are interesting scientifically, but only confirm the temporary memory impairment which is seen by the clinician."

MEMORY AND E.C.T.

The experiments upon memory and retention after E.C.T. have, on the whole, been better arranged. An early experiment by Zubin and Barrera (1941) who used paired associates showed that shock diminishes recall. Moreover, under control conditions both "remote" and "recent" associations were remembered but with a slight advantage to the recent associations. After shock the advantage of the recent associations no longer appeared which implies that shock has a greater effect on more recently acquired habits. Sherman, Mergener and Levitin (1941) on the other hand reported no significant change in memory scores but used no control tests to substantiate this finding. Rodnick (1942) trained schizophrenic patients on two incompatible habits successively. Then one group was given Metrazol shock; on retest the Metrazol group showed a significantly higher proportion of reversions to the earlier habit. Mayer-Gross (1943), who examined post-shock amnesia, found a similar retrograde effect; pictures shown early in a pre-shock series were either recognized or recalled more often than those shown later in the series. But if testing were postponed, say twenty-four hours after treatment, then this effect was very much diminished. He pointed out the similarity between these results and those found in "retroactive inhibition" experiments.

The most comprehensive experiments using human subjects were made in this area by Janis (1950). He intended to investigate specific psychological changes which persist longer than the immediate post-shock "organic syndrome." He required both experimental and control subjects to give long circumstantial accounts of their lives. On retest (which in the case of the shock group was four weeks after the shock series) the subjects were asked to repeat their histories and were then interviewed for detailed points. Every member of the E.C.T. group was unable to recall some previous memories and some, in fact, failed even to recognize descriptions of incidents from their own lives. Such failures were rare in the control group. Five cases in the experimental group which were followed up for two and a half to three and a half months showed such specific amnesias during the entire period. Janis suggests these particular circumscribed amnesias are special cases of a general retroactive inhibition which are maintained by special motivational factors. In a further study the memory of treated patients was again shown to be poorer than that of controls. An additional measure showed that the latency of even the accurate memory responses was longer in the experimental group (Janis and Astrachan, 1951). Janis, in his experiment, gave questionnaires designed to measure affective change due to E.C.T. The treated group showed its greatest change in self-deprecatory attitudes which became less marked.

Worchel and Narciso (1950) examined the effects of shock given immediately after, and one hour after, learning nonsense syllables. They were not able to demonstrate a retrograde amnesia. Carter (1953) confirmed Janis's findings. Further, by classifying the memories into "pleasant" and "painful" he was able to show that the painful memories were forgotten significantly more often than the pleasant ones. He also found that more recent memories were forgotten. The differential forgetting of pleasant and unpleasant experiences is commonly found in normal subjects under ordinary conditions. E.C.T., though it alters the amount forgotten, does not appear to alter other features of the memory process. Bogoch (1954) examined the behaviour of post-shock amnesic patients under Sodium Amytal. Seventeen out of twenty-one cases demonstrated an improvement in recall in these circumstances. Bogoch attributed the apparent inability to remember after a shock series to an inability to verbalize except under the drug.

E.C.T. AND MOTOR PERFORMANCE

Changes in motor performance have been noted after E.C.T. Generally speed, or rate of output, has been used as measures of performance. Hetherington (1952) observed changes in the motor aspects of drawing after shock. He put forward the view (1956) that E.C.T. produces an increase in the output of muscular work. This conclusion was based on a comparison of the performance of patients and normal controls on a variety of psychomotor tests given before, during and after a series of electroshocks. Since, however, the initial scores of the treated group were poorer than those of the normal controls they had more room for improvement and could display the greater practice effect which is possible in the early development of a skilled performance. Landis and Clausen (1955) found rather similar results in making a comparison of groups of patients undergoing different treatments. They offer an explanation in line with that outlined above: the improvement found in the E.C.T. group may have been a consequence of the greater benefit from practice which is possible where there is an initial retardation.

Foulds (1952) provides data upon this point. He gave a modified form of the Porteus Mazes in which the emphasis was put upon speed of performance to a group of patients undergoing E.C.T. The mazes were given twice before and twice after treatment. There was a striking improvement in speed of performance on the second trial before treatment, a decrement on the third trial given after treatment, and a further improvement on the last trial. The same procedure was used by Campbell (1957) with the addition of a control group which received no treatment between pairs of trials. In this case the decrement in speed of performance on the third trial was again found but only in the experimental group and may be attributed to E.C.T. In the same study a considerable variety of motor tests was given to both the experimental and control groups. At retest both groups showed an improvement in speed of performance on the majority of tests, no doubt the result of practice during the pre-treatment administration of the test. However, when the size of the improvements made by each group was compared it was found that the untreated group tended to show larger improvements in speed of performance and that a greater number of the subjects who had been given shock treatment showed a performance decrement. The effect occurred both in those patients who showed an improvement in clinical state and in those who did not. The results suggested that E.C.T. leads to a loss in speed of performance which may be masked by improvement from an initially retarded score unless a group of similar patients are used as control subjects to indicate the improvement which can be attributed to practice.

Callagan (1952) used a large battery of tests, including several psychomotor tasks, to examine the influence of E.C.T. in an experimental group. He gave the battery on three occasions and had an untreated control group which he tested at the same time intervals. He did not achieve his main aim of providing a prognostic scale using cognitive tests but he obtained some interesting results nevertheless. On a manual dexterity test the treated group showed a decrement in performance after shock whereas the control group showed an improvement. He also used a "slowness of writing" test as a measure of motor control. The subject is asked to write as slowly as he can; Callagan found that improved motor control after E.C.T. enables subjects to write more slowly. Campbell (1957) did not repeat this finding.

E.C.T. AND PERCEPTION

The effect of E.C.T. upon perception was examined by Williams (1950) in a well-controlled experiment. She found that responses to ambiguous stimuli were more readily aroused if some similar stimulus had been shown for identification immediately before E.C.T. That is to say, responses after E.C.T. are facilitated by previous performance even if this is not consciously remembered. In this case the previous experience has presumably served as practice and, as in the case of motor tests, the practice effect survived E.C.T. Responses to sets of stimuli which had not been presented before treatment were delayed by E.C.T. and occurred only when the "ambiguous" stimuli approximated more closely to a readily discriminable outline.

Fisichelli, Rockwell and Clarke (1955) compared spontaneous rates of reversal of perspective found in ambiguous perspective figures before and after E.C.T. The average rate of reversal was reduced in the shock group but remained unchanged in a control group. This change was largely due to the effect of E.C.T. upon those subjects whose rate of reversal was fastest in the original test. This result may be explained in terms of Kohler and Wallach's "satiation theory" (Fisichelli, 1947) which supposes that rate of reversal is determined by a neural process of "fatigue" or "inhibition" of some kind. Other researches have not found this change (Philip, 1953; Campbell, 1957); also the rate of reversal in psychiatric patients is generally slower than in normals (Eysenck, 1952). Such differences in result may depend upon the experimental conditions and procedure. Rate of reversal has been shown to be influenced by variations in both of these (Eysenck, 1952; Brown, 1954). Callagan (1952) found some significant changes before and after E.C.T. in rate of reversal of perspective when the subjects were given instructions either to maximize the rate or to take a passive attitude; but no significant changes were obtained upon a second passive trial and when the subjects were told to attempt to reduce the rate.

Brengelmann (1959) examined the effects of single and repeated electroshocks upon visual learning. He gave a test, in which the subjects were asked to reproduce designs which had been exposed briefly to them, at intervals of thirty minutes, four hours and twenty-eight hours after the first, third, fifth and seventh treatments. The first three shocks in the series produced no apparent learning deficit but five and seven shocks both led to impairment. This result appeared to be due to the creation, by repeated shock, of an organic syndrome. In a further experiment Brengelmann (1959) was able to show, by comparing a control group with his experimental group, that shock reduced the learning in the experimental group from the beginning of the experiment. The disturbance due to shock showed particularly in measures of expressive movement. Within any particular test session the electroshock did not alter the shape of the learning curve but over a series of tests the shock group either improved less than the control group or else showed an actual deterioration.

Two experiments which examined the emotional aspects of perception have been briefly reported. Teicher (1953) used tachistoscopic exposure of emotional and non-emotional words to show that an untreated group failed to differentiate the words but a treated group reacted differentially to the two categories. Korngold (1953) found that E.C.T. abolished a stimulus sensitization set up by stopping patients from completing a task. In each case the prevailing pre-shock reactions of the subjects were altered by shock.

PROGNOSIS

A number of attempts have been made (some as part of some of the experiments described earlier) to establish prognostic signs for E.C.T. Attempts using cognitive tests have been unsuccessful for the most part. The most encouraging of such experiments have used the M.M.P.I.

Pearson (1950) analysed the pre-treatment results on the M.M.P.I. of twenty-nine male schizophrenics. The treatment was a failure when extreme (high or low) scores were found in the depression scale or when high scores were found on the schizophrenia scale or any three scales together. The same results were found in a cross-validation group of fifteen cases. In a subsequent experiment, though the general tendencies held good the scoring scale did not repeat its usefulness (Pearson and Swenson, 1951). Feldman (1951) produced a prognostic scale from the M.M.P.I.

which worked well on independent groups also. Scherer (1951) found improvement after E.C.T. to be related to motor speed and "abstraction." Carpenter (1953) later found that the items of Feldman's scale were rated by "psychologically sophisticated judges" as related to "ego-alien extrapunitiveness,"

It should be pointed out that these studies of prognosis have proceeded by correlating individual test items with outcome in groups of treated cases. It is possible that they may relate to improvement as such, rather than to improvement under E.C.T. In these cases too an untreated control group is necessary for an adequate assessment of the consequences of E.C.T.

Fisher (1949) and Campbell (1957) both found that, when the Hildreth Feeling Scale was used before and after treatment there was a slight tendency for the improved patients to be those who had shown the greatest degree of pre-shock depression. This tendency also appeared in Campbell's control group which received no treatment between test and retest.

DISCUSSION

The results of the experiments carried out using human subjects may be assessed by considering the four objects of psychological research mentioned in the introduction to this chapter. No work has been done by psychologists to determine the efficacy of E.C.T. in general terms. In this respect E.C.T. is no worse off than other forms of psychiatric therapy. Investigations of this type present many opportunities for the exercise of psychological virtues such as "quantification," "objectification" and the like, which would provide alternatives to the traditional categories used to describe the outcome of a treatment. Nor have psychologists directed attention to the necessary comparison between a "natural" remission rate in depressive illness and the recovery rate following E.C.T.

The psychological changes brought about by E.C.T. have been examined by a large number of investigators. Generally speaking complex, multifactorial tests such as the Wechsler and the Rorschach have been used, and the majority of the experiments have been directed to the cognitive aspect of the changes. The results have indicated some restricted memory impairment which may be permanent, at least a temporary cognitive loss and a reduction in the benefit derived from practice on motor tasks. At present, largely because of methodological weaknesses, the psychological findings do not lend themselves to any exact specification of the changes wrought by E.C.T. It seems fair to conclude that, in this instance, the clinical observations have been confirmed but have not been refined.

Very few experiments have been designed to test explanations of the effects of E.C.T. and these have not been conclusive. Finally, the experiments concerned with prognosis, despite their initial cross-validation successes, are unlikely to be of general practical value unless a more rational basis for the results can be found in view of the differences which exist in psychiatric practice.

In view of the rather meagre results from the experiments with human subjects the best lead for further work seems to be the comparison of the animal and human experiments. It was remarked earlier that, in detail, the comparison of the two sets of results was discouraging: in contrast with clinical experience the animal experiments suggested that permanent cognitive changes may result from E.C.T. and emotional changes may be short-lasting. But the discrepant results and the variables in these experiments provide indications which may lead to more fruitful research in human subjects. For example in the case of cognitive changes it was shown in rats that the level of task difficulty used, and the measures of performance taken, had an important influence upon the results. In the case of emotional changes the time factors were shown to be of importance in a way which brings to mind the clinical observations respecting the age of an illness as a variable which influences the outcome of E.C.T.

The comparison can also be used to suggest topics in which animal research may be extended. The variables from clinical observation—age of the illness, the age of the patient, the onset of the disease, etc.—should be capable of reproduction in an animal experiment designed to provide information concerning their relative importance. A wider variety of animals should be used in experiments. The rat makes an excellent *point d'appui* but the examination of emotional changes might benefit if an animal were used which permits the construction of a better paradigm for depression than the purely situational anxiety that has been used up to the present. A variety of animals would also make more detailed physiological investigations possible. Experiments along these lines might also reduce the discontinuity which exists at present between the animal and human results.

The comparison suggests some major topics for research with human subjects. The cognitive consequences of E.C.T. may become less uncertain if two cues are taken from the animal research. The measures of impairment need to be refined and extended as the I.Q. scores which have been used may obscure the detail of the changes. In several experiments changes in subtest scores are reported which may well indicate quite specific alterations in function which deserve further investigation. Another feature of the cognitive changes which needs study is the time of the changes. No adequate data exist for the course of, and recovery from impairment. Data on this point might become of practical importance as well as being theoretically interesting in view of the large number of shocks which are given in some cases.

The simplest psychological explanation of many of the results of E.C.T. is that which likens the effect of E.C.T. to retroactive inhibition. It is supported by the observations concerning the age of the illness noted above and by the results of several experiments upon animals, but the idea has never been worked out in detail. Moreover a "gap" exists between the experiments, which have dealt with periods of a few hours, and the facts of the illness which may cover a period of months. No satisfactory large-scale experiment has tested the hypothesis in human subjects. The usual explanation of retroactive inhibition is based on the notion of "interfering" responses. In the case of E.C.T. these must presumably be older normal responses which are reactivated (in contrast to "liberated") by the treatment and supersede the abnormal state, perhaps reinforced by a relearning process of some kind. A set of experiments designed to examine specific hypotheses concerning cognitive, motor and emotional responses would be necessary to demonstrate the theory in detail.

It also seems necessary to extend the experimental measurement of affect and prevailing mood. As E.C.T. is intended to act primarily upon mood the almost universal neglect of this aspect of post-shock change is surprising. But if affect is to be subsumed under the retroactive inhibition model more exact estimates of changes in mood will be necessary. This may also remove part of the difficulty in regarding mood as sharing some of the features of a habit.

The success of research in this field appears to depend upon the adoption of techniques from experimental psychology. Clinical research requires exact hypotheses, adequate control groups and appropriate experimental design as much as any other psychological investigation. Until the example set by the minority of experimenters becomes the general rule theoretical advance will be hampered by lack of adequate data.

REFERENCES

ACKNER, B., HARRIS, A. and OLDHAM, A. J., Insulin treatment of schizophrenia, *Lancet*, 607–611 (1957).

AIRD, R. B., STRAIT, L. A., PACE, J. W., HRENOFF, M. K. and BOWDITCH, S. C., Current pathway and neurophysiologic effects of electrically induced convulsions, *J. Nerv. Ment. Dis.*, **123**, 505–512 (1956).

ALEXANDER, G. H., "Shock" therapies, *J. Nerv. Ment. Dis.*, **99**, 922–924 (1944).

ALEXANDER, G. H., Electroconvulsive therapy: a five year study of results, *J. Nerv. Ment. Dis.*, **117**, 244–250 (1953).

ALEXANDER, LEO, The effect of electroshock on a "normal" person under recent stress: an experiment elucidating the influence of electroshock on the defensive operations of the ego, *Amer. J. Psychiat.*, **109**, 696–698 (1953).

ALPERS, B. J. and HUGHES, J., Changes in the brain after electrically induced convulsions in cats, *Arch. Neurol. Psychiat. Chicago*, **47**, 385–398 (1942).

BACON, R. L. and ROSVOLD, H. E., Effects of electroconvulsive shock on pregnancy in the rat, *Proc. Soc. Exp. Biol., N.Y.*, **69**, 287–288 (1948).

BAGCHI, B. K., HOWELL, R. W. and SCHMALE, H. T., The electroencephalographic and clinical effects of electrically induced convulsions in the treatment of mental disorders, *Amer. J. Psychiat.*, **102**, 49–60 (1945).

BASSETT, M. and ROSS, ASHBY, W., The effect of electroconvulsive therapy on the psycho-galvanic response, *J. Ment. Sci.*, **100**, 632–642 (1954).

BATT, J. C., 100 depressive psychoses treated with E.I.C.s, *J. Ment. Sci.*, **89**, 289–296 (1943).

BAUER, F. J., Effects of ionised air and electroconvulsive shock on learning and innate behavior in rats, *Psychol. Monogr.*, **69**, (398), No. 13 (1955).

BEACH, F. A., GOLDSTEIN, A. C. and JACOBY, G. A., Effects of electroconvulsive shock on sexual behaviour in male rats, *J. Comp. Physiol. Psychol.*, **48**, 173–179 (1955).

BECK, S. J., Effects of shock therapy on personality—Rorschach test, *Arch. Neurol. Psychiat. Chicago*, **50**, 483 (1943).

BENDIG, A. W. and BRAUN, H. W., The influence of the genotype on the retention of a maze habit in the rat following electroshock convulsions, *J. Comp. Physiol. Psychol.*, **44**, 112–117 (1951).

BENDIG, A. W. and PATTON, R. A., Effects of electroshock convulsions on latent learning, *J. Exp. Psychol.*, **44**, 352–354 (1952).

BERAN, M., PERKINS, J. C. and SCOLLON, R. W., Psychological studies on patients undergoing non-convulsive electric-stimulation treatment, *Amer. J. Psychiat.*, **109**, 367–374 (1952).

BERNBERG, R. E., A comparison of the effects of electroconvulsive shock and electronarcosis upon the learning ability of young rats, *J. Comp. Physiol. Psychol.*, **44**, 50–60 (1951).

BOGOCH, S., A preliminary study of post-shock amnesia by Amytal interview, *Amer. J. Psychiat.*, **111**, 108–111 (1954).

BOWERS, M. K. and BERKOWITZ, B., Clinical observations on the effects of electroconvulsive therapy in the hypnotic state, *J. Nerv. Ment. Dis.*, **118**, 355–364 (1953).

BRADY, J. V., The effect of electroconvulsive shock on a conditioned emotional response: the permanence of the effect, *J. Comp. Physiol. Psychol.*, **44**, 507–511 (1951).

BRADY, J. V., The effect of electroconvulsive shock on a conditioned emotional response: the significance of the interval between the emotional conditioning and the electroconvulsive shock, *J. Comp. Physiol. Psychol.*, **45**, 9–13 (1952).

BRADY, J. V. and HUNT, H. F., A further demonstration of the effects of electroconvulsive shock on a conditioned emotional response, *J. Comp. Physiol. Psychol.*, **44**, 204–209 (1951).

BRADY, J. V. and HUNT, H. F., The effect of electroconvulsive shock on a conditioned emotional response: a control for impaired learning, *J. Comp. Physiol. Psychol.*, **45**, 180–182 (1952).

BRADY, J. V., STEBBINGS, W. C. and GALAMBOS, R., The effect of audiogenic convulsions on a conditioned emotional response, *J. Comp. Physiol. Psychol.*, **46**, 363–367 (1953).

BRADY, J. V., HUNT, H. F. and GELLER, I., The effect of electroconvulsive shock on a conditioned emotional response as a function of the temporal distribution of the treatments, *J. Comp. Physiol. Psychol.*, **47**, 454–457 (1954).

BRAUN, H. W., Effects of electroshock convulsions upon the learning performance of monkeys: II. Delayed response, *J. Comp. Physiol. Psychol.*, **45**, 352–357 (1952).

BRAUN, H. W., Effects of electroshock convulsions upon the learning performance of monkeys: III. Oddity Problems, *J. Comp. Physiol. Psychol.*, **45**, 585–588 (1952).

BRAUN, H. W. and ALBEE, G. W., The relation between retention after electroshock convulsions and degree of learning in the rat, *J. Comp. Physiol. Psychol.*, **45**, 14–17 (1952).

BRAUN, H. W. and PATTON, R. A., Habit reversal after electroshock convulsions as a function of the difficulty of the tasks, *J. Comp. Physiol. Psychol.*, **43**, 252–263 (1950).

BRAUN, H. W., PATTON, R. A. and BARNES, H. W., Effects of electroshock convulsions upon the learning performance of monkeys: I. Object quality discrimination learning, *J. Comp. Physiol. Psychol.*, **45**, 231–238 (1952).

BRAUN, H. W., PIERCE, J. F. and PATTON, R. A., Learning performance of young rats subjected to convulsive and sub-convulsive electric shocks, *J. Psychol.*, **30**, 81–84 (1950).

BRAUN, H. W., RUSSELL, R. W. and PATTON, R. A., Duration of effects of E.S.C.s on retention of a maze habit in white rats, *J. Comp. Physiol. Psychol.*, **42**, 87–106 (1949).

BRAUN, H. W., RUSSELL, R. W. and PATTON, R. A., Duration of effects of electroshock convulsions on retention of a maze habit in white rats, *J. Comp. Physiol. Psychol.*, **42**, 332–337 (1949).

BRENGELMANN, J. C., *The Effect of Repeated Electroshock on Learning in Depressives* (Heidelberg, Springer, 1959).

BROADHURST, P. L., STONE, C. P. and LAWRENCE, D. H., The effects of Epanutin and electroconvulsive shock on the maze performance of rats, *Brit. J. Psychol.*, **43**, 85–93 (1952).

BRODY, M. B., Prolonged memory defects following E.C.T., *J. Ment. Sci.*, **90**, 777 (1944).

BROWER, D. and OPPENHEIM, S., The effects of electroshock therapy on mental functions as revealed by psychological tests, *J. Gen. Psychol.*, **45**, 171–188 (1951).

BROWN, K. T., Studies on rate of apparent change as a function of observation time, using a new type of dynamic ambiguous figure, *U.S. Air Force, WADC Technical Report*, 54–139 (1954).

BROWN, W. L. and WILBANKS, W. A., The effect of different periods of electroconvulsive shock on spatial learning, *J. Genet. Psychol.*, **81**, 29–44 (1952).

CALLAGAN, J. E., Effect of E.C.T. on the test performance of depressed patients, *Unpubl. Ph.D. Thesis, Univ. of London Lib.* (1952).

CAMPBELL, D., A study of some sensory-motor functions in psychiatric patients, *Unpubl. Ph.D. Thesis, Univ. of London Lib.* (1957).

CARPENTER, L. G. JR., An experimental test of an hypothesis for predicting outcome with electroshock therapy, *J. Psychol.*, **36**, 131–135 (1953).

CARSON, R. C., The effect of electroconvulsive shock on a learned avoidance response, *J. Comp. Physiol. Psychol.*, **50**, 125–129 (1957).

CARTER, J. T., Type of personal life memories forgotten following electroconvulsive therapy, *Amer. Psychologist*, **8**, 330 (1953).

CERLETTI, V. and BINI, L., Electric shock treatment, *Boll. Accad. Med. Roma.*, **64**, 36 (1938).

CHUSID, J. G. and PACELLA, B. L., The electroencephalogram in the electric shock therapies, *J. Nerv. Ment. Dis.*, **116**, 95–107 (1952).

CURRIER, G. E., CULLINAN, C. and ROTHSCHILD, D., Results of treatment of schizophrenia in a state hospital: changing trends since advent of electroshock therapy, *A.M.A. Arch. Neurol. Psychiat.*, **67**, 80–88 (1952).

DOCTER, R. F., The effect of conventional electroconvulsive shock (E.C.S.) *v.* "Brief Stimulus Therapy" (B.S.T.) on memory and nest-building in albino rats, *J. Comp. Physiol. Psychol.*, **50**, 100–104 (1957).

DUNCAN, C. P., The effect of electroshock convulsions on the maze habit in the white rat, *J. Exp. Psychol.*, **35**, 267–278 (1945).

DUNCAN, C. P., Habit reversal induced by electroshock in the rat, *J. Comp. Physiol. Psychol.*, **41**, 11–16 (1948).

DUNCAN, C. P., The retroactive effect of electroshock on learning, *J. Comp. Physiol. Psychol.*, **42**, 32–44 (1949).

ERIKSEN, C. W., PORTER, P. B. and STONE, C. P., Learning ability in rats given electroconvulsive shocks in late infancy. Part I, *J. Comp. Physiol. Psychol.*, **41**, 144–154 (1948).

ESTES, W. K. and SKINNER, B. F., Some quantitative properties of anxiety, *J. Exp. Psychol.*, **29**, 390–400 (1941).

EYSENCK, H. J., Schizothymia-cyclothymia as a dimension of personality: II. Experimental, *J. Personality*, **20**, 345–384 (1952).

FELDMANN, M. J., A prognostic scale for shock therapy, *Psychol. Monogr.*, **65**, (10), No. 327 (1951).

FELDMANN, R. S. and NEET, C. C., The effect of electroconvulsive shock on fixated behaviour in the rat: II. The effect of E.C.S. supplemented by guidance, *J. Comp. Physiol. Psychol.*, **47**, 210–212 (1954).

FELDMAN, R. S. and NEET, C. C., The effect of electroconvulsive shock on fixated behaviour of the rat: III. The effect of E.C.S. as a function of the duration of conflict, *J. Comp. Physiol. Psychol.*, **50**, 97–99 (1957).

FERRARO, A. and HELFAND, M., Morphologic changes in the brain of monkeys following convulsions electrically induced, *J. Neuropath.*, **5**, 285–308 (1946).

FINGER, F. W., Convulsive behaviour in the rat, *Psychol. Bull.*, **44**, 201–248 (1947).

FISHER, K. A., Changes in test performance of ambulatory depressed patients undergoing E.C.T., *J. Gen. Psychol.*, **41**, 195–232 (1949).

FISICHELLI, V. R., Reversible perspective in Lissajous figures: some theoretical considerations, *Amer. J. Psychol.*, **60**, 240–249 (1947).

FISICHELLI, V. R., ROCKWELL, F. V. and CLARKE, L., The effect of electroshock therapy on the rates of reversal of ambiguous perspective figures, *Amer. J. Psychol.*, **68**, 4, 638–644 (1955).

FLESCHER, G., Retrograde amnesia following electric shock, *Schweiz. Arch. Neurol. Psychiat.*, **48**, 1 (1942).

FOULDS, G. A., Temperamental differences in maze performance: II. The effect of distraction and of electroconvulsive therapy on psychomotor retardation, *Brit. J. Psychol.*, **43**, 33–41 (1952).

GELLER, I., SIDMAN, M. and BRADY, J. V., The effect of electroconvulsive shock on a conditioned emotional response: a control for acquisition recovery, *J. Comp. Physiol. Psychol.*, **48**, 130–131 (1955).

GELLHORN, E., Further investigations on the recovery of inhibited conditioned reactions, *Proc. Soc. Exp. Biol.*, *N.Y.*, **59**, 155–161 (1945).

GELLHORN, E., *Physiological Foundations of Neurology and Psychiatry* (Minneapolis, Univ. of Minnesota Press, 1953).

GELLHORN, E. and KESSLER, M., The effect of electrically and chemically induced convulsions on conditioned reflexes, *Amer. J. Psychiat.*, **99**, 687–691 (1943).

GELLHORN, E., KESSLER, M. and MINATOYA, H., Influence of Metrazol, insulin hypoglycemia, and electrically induced convulsions on re-establishment of inhibited conditioned reflexes, *Proc. Soc. Exp. Biol.*, *N.Y.*, **50**, 260–262 (1942).

GERARD, R. W., Biological roots of psychiatry, *Science*, **122**, 225 (1955).

GOLUB, L. M. and MORGAN, C. T., Patterns of electrogenic seizures in rats: their relation to stimulus-intensity and to audiogenic seizures, *J. Comp. Psychol.*, **38**, 239–245 (1945).

GRALNICK, A., A three-year survey of electric shock therapy, *Amer. J. Psychiat.*, **102**, 583–593 (1946).

GUREVITZ, S. and HELME, W. H., Effects of electroconvulsive therapy on personality and intellectual functioning of the schizophrenic child, *J. Nerv. Ment. Dis.*, **120**, 213 (1954).

GUZE, S. B., WINOKUR, G. and LEVIN, M. E., The effect of electroshock therapy in the absence of both adrenal glands, *J. Nerv. Ment. Dis.*, **124**, 195–198 (1956).

HAMILTON, C. L. and PATTON, R. A., The effects of a series of electroshock convulsions on an inhibited conditioned response in the albino rat, *J. Comp. Physiol. Psychol.*, **45**, 600–603 (1952).

HARLOW, H. F., Current and future advances in physiological and comparative psychology, *Amer. Psychologist*, **11**, 273–277 (1956).

HARTELIUS, H., Cerebral changes following electrically induced convulsions: an experimental study on cats, *Acta Psychiat.*, *Kbh.*, Suppl. 77 (1952).

HAYES, K. J., Cognitive and emotional effects of electroconvulsive shock in rats, *J. Comp. Physiol. Psychol.*, **41**, 40–61 (1948).

HEILBRUNN, G., Prevention of hemorrhages in the brain in experimental electrical shock, *Arch. Neurol. Psychiat. Chicago*, **50**, 450–455 (1943).

HEILBRUNN, G. and LIEBERT, E., Biopsies on the brain following artificially produced convulsions, *Arch. Neurol. Psychiat. Chicago*, **46**, 548 (1941).

HEILBRUNN, G. and WEIL, A., Pathologic changes in the central nervous system in experimental electric shock, *Arch. Neurol. Psychiat. Chicago*, **47**, 918–930 (1942).

HEISTAD, G. T., An effect of electroconvulsive shock on a conditioned avoidance response, *J. Comp. Physiol. Psychol.*, **48**, 482–487 (1955).

HERZBERG, F., Prognostic variables for electroshock therapy, *J. Gen. Psychol.*, **50**, 79–86 (1954).

HETHERINGTON, R., The effects of E.C.T. on the drawings of depressed patients, *J. Ment. Sci.*, **98**, 450–453 (1952).

HETHERINGTON, R., The effects of E.C.T. on the efficiency and retentivity of depressed patients, *Brit. J. Med. Psychol.*, **29**, 258–269 (1956).

HOBSON, R. F., The prognostic factors in electric convulsive therapy, *J. Neurol. Psychiat.*, **16**, 275–281 (1953).

HOCH, P. H., Clinical and biological inter-relations between schizophrenia and epilepsy, *Amer. J. Psychiat.*, **99**, 507–512 (1943).

HOROWITZ, M. W. and STONE, C. P., The case of learning a new habit in relation to the disorganisation of an interfering habit as affected by electroconvulsive shock in the rat, *Amer. Psychologist*, **1**, 449 (1946).

HOYT, R. and ROSVOLD, H. E., Effect of electroconvulsive shock on body temperature of the rat, *Proc. Soc. Exp. Biol.*, *N.Y.*, **78**, 582–583 (1951).

HUNT, H. F. and BECKWITH, W. C., The effect of electroconvulsive shock under Phenurone, Dilantin, or amphetamine medication on a conditioned emotional response, *Amer. Psychologist*, **11**, 442, abstract (1956).

HUNT, M. F. and BRADY, J. V., Some effects of electroconvulsive shock on a conditioned emotional response ("anxiety"), *J. Comp. Physiol. Psychol.*, **44**, 88–98 (1951).

HUNT, H. F., JERNBERG, P. and BRADY, J. V., The effect of electroconvulsive shock (E.C.S.) on a conditioned emotional response: the effect of post-E.C.S. extinction on the reappearance of the response, *J. Comp. Physiol. Psychol.*, **45**, 589–599 (1952).

HUSTON, P. E. and LOCHER, L. M., Manic-depressive psychosis; course when treated and untreated with electric shock, *Arch. Neurol. Psychiat. Chicago*, **60**, 37–48 (1948).

HUSTON, P. E. and STROTHER, C. H., The effect of E.C.T. on mental efficiency, *Amer. J. Psychiat.*, **104**, 707 (1948).

JANIS, I. L., Psychological effects of electric convulsive treatments, *J. Nerv. Ment. Dis.*, **111**, 359–382, 383–397, 469–489 (1950).

JANIS, I. L. and ASTRACHAN, M., The effects of electroconvulsive treatments on memory efficiency, *J. Abnorm. (Soc.) Psychol.*, **46**, 501–511 (1951).

JENSEN, G. D. and STAINBROOK, E., The effect of electrogenic convulsions on the estrus cycle and the weight of rats, *J. Comp. Physiol. Psychol.*, **42**, 502–505 (1949).

KAHN, R. L., FINK, M. and WEINSTEIN, E. A., Relation of amobarbital test to clinical improvement in electroshock, *Arch. Neurol. Psychiat. Chicago*, **76**, 23–29 (1956).

KALINOWSY, L. B., Electric convulsive therapy with emphasis on importance of adequate treatment, *Arch. Neurol. Psychiat. Chicago*, **50**, 652 (1943).

KALINOWSKY, L. B. and HOCH, P. H., *Shock Treatments and other Somatic Treatments in Psychiatry*, 2nd ed. (New York, Grune & Stratton, 1952).

KARAGULLA, S., Evaluation of electric convulsive therapy as compared with conservative methods of treatment in depressive states, *J. Ment. Sci.*, **96**, 1,060–1,091 (1950).

KELLEY, D., MARGUILES, H. and BARRERA, S. E., The stability of the Rorschach method as demonstrated in E.C.T. cases, *Rorschach Res. Exch.*, **5**, 35 (1941).

KORNGOLD, H., An investigation of some psychological effects of electric shock treatment, *Amer. Psychologist*, **8**, 381–382 (1953).

LANDIS, C. and CLAUSEN, J., Changes in sensory and motor performances induced by active psychiatric treatment, *J. Psychol.*, **40**, 275–305 (1955).

LEUKEL, F., A comparison of the effects of E.C.S. and anesthesia on acquisition of the maze habit, *J. Comp. Physiol. Psychol.*, **50**, 300–306 (1957).

LEVY, N. A., SEROTA, H. M. and GRINKER, R. R., Disturbances in brain function following convulsive shock therapy, *Arch. Neurol. Psychiat. Chicago*, **47**, 1,009–1,029 (1942).

LOWENBACH, H. and STAINBROOK, E., Observations on mental patients after E.C.T., *Amer. J. Psychiat.*, **98**, 828–833 (1942).

MACMAHON, H. E., Electric shock, *Amer. J. Path.*, **5**, 333 (1929).

MADOW, L., Brain changes in electroshock therapy, *Amer. J. Psychiat.*, **113**, 337–347 (1956).

MASSERMANN, J. H., ARIEFF, A., PECHTEL, G. and KLEHR, H., Effects of direct interrupted E.C.T. on experimental neurosis, *J. Nerv. Ment. Dis.*, **112**, 384–392 (1950).

MASSERMANN, J. H. and JACQUES, N. G., Effects of cerebral electroshock on experimental neuroses in cats, *Amer. J. Psychiat.*, **104**, 92–99 (1947).

MAYER-GROSS, W., Retrograde amnesia, *Lancet*, **2**, 603 (1943).

McDONALD, D. G. and STERN, J. A., Cumulative effects of a series of E.C.S., *Amer. Psychologist*, **11**, 442, abstract (1956).

McGINNIES, E., Changes in the performance of albino rats subjected to electroshock convulsions, *J. Comp. Physiol. Psychol.*, **40**, 31–36 (1947).

McGINNIES, E. and SCHLOSBERG, H., The effect of E.S.C.s on double alternation lever pressing in the white rat, *J. Exp. Psychol.*, **35**, 361 (1945).

MEDUNA, L. V., Versuche über die biologische Beeinflussung des Ablaufes der Schizophrenie; Kampfer und Cardiozolkrämpfe, *Z. ges. Neurol. Psychiat.*, **152**, 235–262 (1935).

MERRITT, H. H. and PUTNAM, T. J., A new series of anticonvulsant drugs tested by experiments on animals, *Arch. Neurol. Psychiat. Chicago.*, **39**, 1,003–1,015 (1938).

MEYER, J. E., Über Schockamnesien und ihre Beziehung zum Heilverlauf der Psychosen, *Arch. Psychiat. Nervenkr.*, **186**, 254 (1951).

MICHAEL, S. T., Impairment of mental function during electric convulsive therapy, *A.M.A. Arch. Neurol. Psychiat.*, **71**, 362–366 (1954).

MIRSKY, A. F., LOONEY, E. and ROSVOLD, H. E., Maze retention deficit following electroconvulsive shock independent of feeding schedule, *J. Comp. Physiol. Psychol.*, **47**, 403–405 (1954).

MIRSKY, A. F. and ROSVOLD, H. E., The effect of electroconvulsive shock on food intake and hunger drive in the rat, *J. Comp. Physiol. Psychol.*, **46**, 153–157 (1953).

MORRISON, L. R., WEEKS, A. and COBB, S., Histopathology of different types of electric shock on mammalian brains, *J. Industr. Hyg.*, **12**, 324 (1923).

MUHLAN, G. J. and STONE, C. P., Effects of electroconvulsive shocks on rat behaviour in a Dashiell-type water maze, *J. Comp. Physiol. Psychol.*, **42**, 17–26 (1949).

MYERSON, A., Borderline cases treated by electric shock, *Amer. J. Psychiat.*, **100**, 355–357 (1943).

NEET, C. C. and FELDMAN, R. S., The effect of electroconvulsive shock on fixated behaviour of the rat. I. The effect of a ten- and of a twenty-five-day series of E.C.S. on the stability of the fixated response, *J. Comp. Physiol. Psychol.*, **47**, 124–129 (1954).

NOLAN, C. Y., Stimulational seizures without pseudopregnancy in white rats, *J. Comp. Physiol. Psychol.*, **45**, 183–187 (1952).

PACELLA, B. L., BARRERA, S. E. and KALINOWSKY, L., Variations in electroencephalogram associated with electric shock therapy of patients with mental disorders, *Arch. Neurol. Psychiat. Chicago*, **47**, 367–384 (1942).

PACELLA, B. L., PIOTROWSKI, Z. and LEWIS, N. D. C., The effects of electric convulsive therapy on certain personality traits in psychiatric patients, *Amer. J. Psychiat.*, **104**, 83 (1947).

PAGE, J. D., Studies in electrically induced convulsions in animals, *J. Comp. Psychol.*, **31**, 181–194 (1941).

PALMER, F. H., Effects of electroshock on retention of the double alternation problem in the temporal maze, *Amer. Psychologist*, **5**, 274 (1950).

PARSONS, E. H., BANET, S. R., KEATING, J. U. and LAWRENCE, G. H., Modern methods of electroshock therapy, *Amer. J. Psychiat.*, **112**, 18–22 (1955).

PEARSON, J. S., Prediction of the response of schizophrenic patients to electroconvulsive therapy, *J. Clin. Psychol.*, **3**, 285–287 (1950).

PEARSON, J. S. and SWENSON, W. M., A note on extended findings with the M.M.P.I. in predicting response to electroconvulsive therapy, *J. Clin. Psychol.*, **7**, 280–282 (1951).

PHILIP, B. R., Reversals in the perception of Lissajous figures by psychotics, *Canad. J. Psychol.*, **7**, 115–125 (1953).

PIERCE, J. F. and PATTON, R. A., Electroconvulsive thresholds of male albino rats as a function of age and weight, *J. Psychol.*, **33**, 79–86 (1952).

PIERCE, J. F., RUSSELL, R. W. and PATTON, R. A., Electroconvulsive thresholds in rats as functions of various types of stimulating currents, *J. Psychol.*, **30**, 157–170 (1950).

PORTER, P. B. and STONE, C. P., Electroconvulsive shock in rats under ether anaesthesia, *J. Comp. Physiol. Psychol.*, **40**, 441–456 (1947).

PORTER, P. B., STONE, C. P. and ERIKSEN, C. W., Learning ability in rats given E.C.S.s in late infancy. Part II, *J. Comp. Physiol. Psychol.*, **41**, 423–431 (1948).

POSCHEL, B. P. H., Proactive and retroactive effects of electroconvulsive shock on approach-avoidance conflict, *J. Comp. Physiol. Psychol.*, **50**, 392–396 (1957).

REES, W. L. and JONES, A. M., An evaluation of the Rorschach test as a prognostic aid in the treatment of schizophrenia by insulin coma therapy, electronarcosis, electroconvulsive therapy and leucotomy, *J. Ment. Sci.*, **97**, 681–689 (1951).

RIESS, B. F., The theoretical basis of convulsive therapy in relation to animal experimentation, *J. Personality*, **17**, 9–15 (1948).

RISHIKOFF, J. R. and ROSVOLD, H. E., Effects of electroconvulsive shocks on the performance of the rat in the closed-field test, *Canad. J. Psychol.*, **7**, 29–33 (1953).

RODNICK, E. H., The effect of Metrazol shock upon habit systems, *J. Abnorm. (Soc.) Psychol.*, **37**, 560–565 (1942).

ROSEN, V. H. and GANTT, W. H., Effect of Metrazol convulsions on conditioned reflexes in dogs, *Arch. Neurol. Psychiat. Chicago*, **50**, 8–17 (1943).

ROSVOLD, H. E., The effects of electroconvulsive shock on gestation and maternal behaviour: I and II, *J. Comp. Physiol. Psychol.*, **48**, 118–136, 207–219 (1949).

ROSVOLD, H. E., KAPLAN, S. J. and STEVENSON, J. A. F., Effect of electroconvulsive shock on adrenal cortex of the rat, *Proc. Soc. Exp. Biol., N.Y.*, **80**, 60–62 (1952).

ROTH, M. and McCLATCHEY, W. S., Changes in cerebral electrical activity induced by electroconvulsive treatment, *EEG & Clinical Neurophysiology*, **3**, 100–101 (1951).

ROYCE, J. R. and ROSVOLD, H. E., Electroshock and the rat adrenal cortex, *A.M.A. Arch. Neurol. Psychiat.*, **70**, 516–527 (1953).

RUSSELL, R. W., Contributions of research on infrahuman animals to the understanding of electroconvulsive shock phenomena, *J. Personality*, **17**, 16–28 (1948).

RUSSELL, R. W., Effects of electroshock convulsions on learning and retention in rats as functions of difficulty of the task, *J. Comp. Physiol. Psychol.*, **42**, 137–142 (1949).

RUSSELL, R. W., TOWNSEND, J. C., BRAUN, H. W. and PATTON, R. A., The relationships of certain instrumental variables to the occurrence of spinal lesions in rats subjected to controlled electroshock convulsions, *Amer. Psychologist*, **3**, 359–360 (1948).

SARGANT, W., *Battle for the Mind* (London, Heinemann, 1957).

SCHERER, I., Prognoses and psychological scores in electroconvulsive therapy, psychosurgery and spontaneous remission, *Amer. J. Psychiat.*, **107**, 926–931 (1951).

SHAW, W. A., UTECHT, A. J. and FULLAGER, E. A., The effects of auditory stimulation upon the immediate retention of a previously learned maze behaviour in the albino rat, *J. Comp. Physiol. Psychol.*, **46**, 212–215 (1953).

SHERMAN, I., MERGENER, J. and LEVITIN, D., The effect of convulsive treatment on memory, *Amer. J. Psychiat.*, **98**, 401–403 (1941).

SIEGEL, P. S., The effect of electroshock convulsions on the acquisition of a simple running response in the rat, *J. Comp. Psychol.*, **36**, 61–65 (1943).

SIEGEL, P. S. and LACEY, O. L., A further observation of electrically-induced "audiogenic" seizures in the rat, *J. Comp. Psychol.*, **39**, 319–320 (1946).

SIEGEL, P. S., McGINNIES, E. M. and BOX, J. C., The runway performance of rats subjected to electroconvulsive shock following Nembutal anesthesia, *J. Comp. Physiol. Psychol.*, **42**, 417–421 (1949).

SIEGEL, P. S. and SIEGEL, H. S., The effect of electroconvulsive shock on the anticipatory gradient in the rat, *J. Comp. Physiol. Psychol.*, **42**, 374–382 (1949).

SIEKERT, R. G., WILLIAMS, S. C. and WINDLE, W. F., Histologic study of the brains of monkeys after experimental electroshock, *Arch. Neurol. Psychiat. Chicago*, **63**, 79–86 (1950).

SLATER, E. T. O., Indications for electroconvulsive therapy, *Practitioner*, **157**, 403–404 (1946).

SLATER, E. T. O., Evaluation of electric convulsion therapy as compared with conservative methods of treatment in depressive states, *J. Ment. Sci.*, **97**, 567–569 (1951).

SMITH, L. H., HASTINGS, D. and HUGHES, J., Immediate and follow-up results of electroshock therapy, *Amer. J. Psychiat.*, **100**, 351 (1943).

SMITH, L. H., HUGHES, J., HASTINGS, D. W. and ALPERS, B. J., Electroshock treatment in the psychoses, *Amer. J. Psychiat.*, **98**, 558–561 (1942).

STAINBROOK, E. J., A modified Rorschach technique for the description of transitory post-convulsive personality states, *Rorschach Res. Exch.*, **5**, 192–203 (1941).

STAINBROOK, E. J., Maze behaviour of the rat after electroshock convulsions, *J. Exp. Psychol.*, **33**, 247–252 (1943).

STAINBROOK, E. J., The Rorschach description of immediate post-convulsive mental function, *Character & Pers.*, **12**, 302–322 (1944).

STAINBROOK, E. J., Experimentally induced convulsive reactions of laboratory rats: I. A comparative study of the immediate reactions, *J. Comp. Psychol.*, **39**, 243–264 (1946).

STAINBROOK, E. and LOWENBACH, H., The reorientation

and maze behaviour of the rat after noise-fright and electroshock convulsions, *J. Comp. Physiol. Psychol.*, **34**, 293–299 (1942).

STIEPER, D. R., WILLIAMS, M. and DUNCAN, C. P., Changes in impersonal and personal memory following electroconvulsive therapy, *J. Clin. Psychol.*, **7**, 361–366 (1951).

STERN, J. A., The effect of a series of electroconvulsive shocks on weight change in the albino male rat, *J. Comp. Physiol. Psychol.*, **47**, 458–461 (1954).

STERN, J. A., The permanence of effect of a series of electroconvulsive seizures on openfield behaviour, *J. Comp. Physiol. Psychol.*, **49**, 411–415 (1956).

STONE, C. P., Effects of E.C.S.s on daily activity of albino rats in revolving drums, *Proc. Soc. Exp. Biol. N.Y.*, **61**, 150 (1946).

STONE, C. P., Losses and gains in cognitive functions as related to electroconvulsive shock, *J. Abnorm. (Soc.) Psychol.*, **42**, 206–214 (1947).

STONE, C. P., Effects of electroconvulsive shocks on wildness and savageness in feral rats, *J. Comp. Physiol. Psychol.*, **46**, 373–377 (1953).

STONE, C. P. and WALKER, H. H., A note on modification of the effects of electroconvulsive shock on maternal behaviour by ether anaesthesia, *J. Comp. Physiol. Psychol.*, **42**, 429–432 (1949).

SUMMERSKILL, J., SEEMAN, W. and MEALS, D. W., An evaluation of post-electroshock confusion with the Reiter apparatus, *Amer. J. Psychiat.*, **108**, 835–838 (1952).

TEICHER, A., The effect of electroconvulsive therapy on the visual reactions of schizophrenic patients, *Amer. Psychologist*, **8**, 445 (1953).

THOMPSON, R. and DEAN, W., A further study of the retroactive effect of E.C.S., *J. Comp. Physiol. Psychol.*, **48**, 488–491 (1955).

THOMPSON, R. and PENNINGTON, D. F., Memory decrement produced by E.C.S. as a function of distribution in original learning, *J. Comp. Physiol. Psychol.*, **50**, 401–404 (1957).

TOOTH, G. and BLACKBURN, J. M., Disturbance of memory after convulsion treatment, *Lancet*, **237**, 17–20 (1939).

TOWNSEND, J. C., RUSSELL, R. W., and PATTON, R. A., Effects of electroshock convulsions on retention in rats as functions of intensity of electroshock stimulus, *J. Comp. Psychol.*, **42**, 148–155 (1949).

WEIL-MALHERBE, H., The effect of convulsive therapy on plasma adrenaline and noradrenaline, *J. Ment. Sci.*, **101**, 156–162 (1955).

WILLIAMS, M., Memory studies in electric convulsion therapy, *J. Neurol. Psychiat.*, **13**, 30–35 (1950).

WINDER, C. L., The effect of electroconvulsive shock on general activity of rats, *Amer. Psychologist*, **1**, 449 (1946).

WORCHEL, P. and GENTRY, G., Electroconvulsive shock and memory: The effect of shocks administered in rapid succession, *Comp. Psychol. Monogr.*, **20**, 95–119 (1950).

WORCHEL, P. and NARCISO, J. C., Electroshock convulsions and memory: The interval between learning and shock, *J. Abnorm. (Soc.) Psychol.*, **45**, 85–98 (1950).

WORCHEL, P. and NARCISO, J. C., The nature of the memory decrement following electroconvulsive shock, *J. Comp. Physiol. Psychol.*, **43**, 325–328 (1950).

ZUBIN, J. and BARRERA, S. E., Effect of electroconvulsive therapy on memory, *Proc. Soc. Exp. Biol. N.Y.*, **48**, 596–597 (1941).

CHAPTER 17

The Effects of Drugs on Behaviour[1]

D. TROUTON and H. J. EYSENCK

1. INTRODUCTION: PROBLEMS AND METHODOLOGY

THE experimental study of the psychological effects of drugs appears to have begun with the work of Kraepelin whose work and methods were soon taken up by other psychologists such as Rivers (1908) and Hollingworth (1912). Several reviews, such as those by Poffenberger (1914, 1916, 1917, 1919), Darrow (1927, 1929), Shock (1939), Spragg (1941), and Gray and Trowbridge (1942), have summarized the large body of work done in this field, but on the whole it cannot be said that "psychopharmacology" has received much recognition in psychological textbooks, nor is it usually represented in courses of lectures in abnormal psychology.

One of the reasons for this neglect may lie in the fact that work in this field almost inevitably must involve workers in several specialities. Several symposia on psychopharmacology have appeared recently (e.g. Abramson, 1955, 1956, *Amer. J. Psychiat.*, 1952, *Amer. Psychiat. Assoc. Res. Rep.*, 1955; *Ann. N.Y. Acad. Sci.*, 1956, *Chlorpromazine and Mental Health*, 1955; Cholden, 1955, *J. Nerv. Ment. Dis.*, 1955, *J. Pharmacol.*, 1956; Kline, 1956; Miner, 1955; Olds, 1957), and in all of these, contributions are made by a variety of different scientists including chemists, pharmacologists, biochemists, electrophysiologists and psychiatrists, as well as psychologists. The subject obviously occupies one of those borderlands between sciences which it is nobody's particular job to cultivate, but which, nevertheless, may be all the more interesting and important for that.

This review will be concerned with the behavioural effects of some of the more commonly used drugs, and we will be concerned particularly with the quantitative experimental analysis of these effects. To help to fill in some of the gaps, qualitative and clinical observations on psychiatric patients have sometimes had to be included, as are also some experiments on animals, where these are thought to contribute to our knowledge of the effects of the drugs in man.

Table XVII.1 lists some of the main factors influencing the subject's response to drugs. Most of the items will appear obvious, but nevertheless, many of them have frequently been neglected in past studies. Among the most important of these variables is the interval which is allowed to elapse between the administration of the drug and the commencement of the test; another is dosage. As regards the interval, we may wait until certain objective signs appear in the subject, or until subjective changes are reported; the other alternative is to use a fixed interval. As regards dosage, this may either be determined by reference to body weight or may be given in fixed amount; a third method, which is used particularly with intravenous barbiturates, is to continue the slow injection of the drug until certain signs occur, such as slurring of speech. Both dosage and interval may thus vary for different subjects.

Where subjects do not differ much in weight, or where the drug is selectively absorbed by certain tissues, e.g. in the brain, administration on the basis of body weight is probably less important than in the case of such drugs as alcohol, which is distributed throughout all the tissues and fluids of the body, and where a given dose would consequently be more diluted in the blood of larger subjects.

The role of variables such as age, sex, and mode of administration is fully discussed in works on pharmacology (Goodman and Gilman, 1955). Psychological factors such as those involved in the effects of *placebos*, the relation of personality to drug effects, and the

---

[1] This chapter was discussed by us in great detail before the first draft was written by Dr. D. Trouton. Several drafts followed but before the chapter could be completed Dr. Trouton's tragic death made it necessary for the editor to play a much more active role in the actual writing than had been envisaged. The whole of the first part was rewritten and much of the rest was considerably altered, usually by shortening it, occasionally by addition. An explicit statement of the dimensional hypothesis was added. It is impossible to know whether Dr. Trouton would have agreed with all the changes, and the new points added, and it seemed fairest to him that the editor should assume responsibility for his part in the chapter in a formal manner.

TABLE XVII.1
THE MAIN VARIABLES INFLUENCING DRUG EFFECTS

1. *Nature of the Drug*

Preparation (including concentration, vehicle of administration and whether disguised).

Mode (oral, intravenous injection, etc.) and rate of administration, absorption and excretion.

Dosage (according to body weight, or the same for all).

Interval before testing.

2. *The Subject*

Personality (including intelligence, extraversion-introversion, neuroticism, suggestibility, etc.).

Familiarity with the situation and the amount of stress occasioned by it.

Practice; fatigue; motivation.

Tendency to react to *placebos*.

Psychiatric state, and its duration.

Age, sex, physique, height and weight.

Present state—

General state of health, nutritional status, sleep.

Conditions of work, e.g. temperature, humidity, oxygen lack.

Diseases, disabilities (e.g. fever, thyrotoxicosis, liver or kidney damage) or effects of operations, etc. (e.g. leucotomy, concussion).

Time of day.

Interval since last meal (if drug given orally).

Recent medication with other drugs (e.g. sedation) or ingestion of drinks containing stimulants or depressants.

Previous experience of drugs—

Cumulative effect of some drugs (e.g. bromides).

Habituation, tolerance (including cross-tolerance).

Addiction.

Idiosyncracy or hypersensitivity.

3. *The Social Environment*

Interaction with other subjects.

Activities required or permitted after administration of the drug.

Suggestion.

Reinforcement of responses by the experimenter.

---

personality make-up of volunteers will be discussed below.

Placebos

In all drug experiments it is necessary to include a control group in the experimental design which is administered a "dummy" treatment, i.e. which is given pills or injections indistinguishable by sight, smell or taste from the genuine treatment, but containing only inert substances. This control treatment, often (erroneously) referred to as *placebo* treatment, is necessary because without it we could not be sure that any effects observed in the experimental group were due to the drug and not to psychological factors such as suggestibility, expectation, and so forth. Such effects are very common and may be very strong. Beecher (1955) has compared the incidence of relief provided by dummy tablets in fifteen studies involving over one thousand patients and a variety of different conditions; on the average one patient in three reported relief! He has also reported some thirty-five different "toxic" effects which have sometimes been so severe that in "double blind" studies, in which neither the doctor nor the patient knew whether the dummy or the drug treatment had been given, the code had to be broken only to disclose that the patient was merely receiving a quite innocuous mixture of sugar and flour.

Trouton (1957) quoted many studies showing that conditions such as asthma, hay-fever, coughs, headaches, tension, post-operative pain, the common cold, and daytime incontinence of psychotics have been benefited by a *placebo*. All these studies involve the comparison of the *placebo* with a supposedly effective drug, and in many instances the *placebo* was as effective as the drug under investigation. In at least three studies the *placebo* appeared slightly more effective.

These psychological effects may either add to, or subtract from, drug effect. The study of Jellinek (1946) in which he found that 52 per cent of headaches were relieved by a *placebo*, may be taken as an example of an additive effect because the psychological factor of taking a pill as such can apparently compensate for an inadequate dose of analgesic. The subtractive effect is less obvious; as an example we may quote a study by Wolf (1950). He administered ipecacuanha to a woman with *hyperemesis gravidarum* who was persuaded that her vomiting would thereby be relieved; it was, and the contractions of the stomach were also inhibited for a time.

Not all subjects of psychological experiments on the effects of drugs show reactions to dummy treatments, and it is possible that what have been called *placebo* reactors constitute a separate class of people whose presence can seriously interfere with the study of drugs. For instance, Beecher *et al.* (1953), carried out a comparative study of morphine, codeine and a *placebo*, and found that, if the *placebo* reactors were excluded, it became "possible to demonstrate significance where it had not been possible before." Jellinek (1946) appears to have been the first to advocate excluding *placebo* reactors in comparative studies of drugs.

It is not known whether the tendency to react to *placebos* is a unitary trait. It is possible that those who experience unpleasant "toxic" effects are not the same as those who are benefited by *placebos*. Jellinek (1946) claims to have found evidence for a U-shaped distribution there being "individuals who definitely tend to respond and individuals who definitely do not tend to respond to a *placebo*." But Lasagna *et al.* (1954) found that only 45 per cent (of sixty-nine patients) were consistent in their responses in a particular situation.

The question of personality correlates of *placebo* reaction is an interesting one but not one on which much work has been done. Lasagna *et al.* (1954) and Tibbetts and Hawkings (1956) have reported work suggesting greater anxiety in *placebo* reactors than in non-reactors. The possibility cannot be ruled out that primary suggestibility is operative here, particularly in view of the fact that Eysenck (1947) found this personality trait to be correlated with neuroticism and anxiety. An alternative hypothesis might be formulated in terms of learning theory. Glaser and Whittow

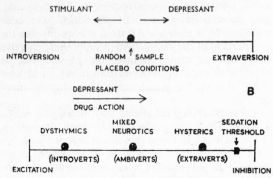

FIG. 17.1. TWO FUNDAMENTAL RESEARCH DESIGNS FOR
THE STUDY OF DRUG EFFECTS

(1953, 1954) found that if subjects were repeatedly given *placebos* and required to fill in questionnaires recording their effects, there were positive responses at first (generalization from other learning situations) but these became fewer on each occasion (lack of reinforcement); when an active drug, similar in appearance to the *placebo*, was given, more symptoms were reported when *placebos* were next administered than when subjects had not received any previous medication (response generalization). If we take these results together with Franks's (1956) demonstration that introverts form conditioned responses more quickly, it would be possible to argue that the introvert, or dysthymic, would tend to acquire *placebo* responses more readily, and to lose them less readily, than the extravert or hysteric. At present it is impossible to decide between these two hypotheses, both of which may, in fact, be valid. There appears to be an important area for research here.

The Problem of Volunteers

Much of the experimental psychological work on the effects of drugs has been done on volunteers, and there is some evidence that volunteers, particularly for drug experiments, differ in various ways from those who do not volunteer. This has been found to be the case in some studies of the personality traits of volunteers for interviews about sexual behaviour (Siegman, 1956). Riggs and Kaess (1955) compared

students who volunteered for a psychological experiment with those who had not; one of their findings was that the volunteers were significantly higher on the T and C scales of the Guilford S.T.D.C.R. questionnaire, "indicating respectively introversive thinking and moody cycloid emotionality." As Eysenck (1953) has shown, both these scales are good measures of neuroticism, so that it appears probable that more neurotic subjects are more likely to volunteer for studies of this kind. This conclusion is strengthened by a study (Lasagna *et al.*, 1954), in which a remarkably high incidence of severe maladjustment was found among fifty-six volunteers for a drug experiment at Harvard Medical School. Although the volunteers were students and supposedly normal, they included three psychotics, twelve neurotics, three psychopaths, an alcoholic, and at least four homosexuals! The authors point out that "much of the literature on marihuana, morphine, heroin, and similar drugs is derived from experience of 'volunteers' with unusual psychological orientation and imaginative, romantic proclivities. Without denying the 'reality' of responses in such people, it has proved scientifically unwise to assume that such responses are typical of those experienced by all individuals under the circumstances." Much of the literature on hallucinogens, particularly on mescaline, is subject to the same criticism. If it is not possible to use a random sample, it is clearly important to have some measure of the personality of the volunteers, and the type and degree of abnormality that may characterize them.

The Relation of Personality to Drug Effects

Drug experiments, as Eysenck (1957) has pointed out, may follow one of two paradigms. The two possibilities are illustrated in Fig. 17.1 which, for the sake of an example, deals with a particular hypothesis regarding the effects of stimulant and depressant drugs. The hypothesis, which will be discussed in more detail later, states simply that *stimulant* drugs will have *introverting* effects, whereas *depressant* drugs will have *extraverting* effects on the whole. The first and most obvious method of testing an hypothesis of this kind is clearly the one depicted in the top part of the diagram. If we are dealing with an experimental measure of extraversion-introversion which is not subject to strong learning effects, we would administer the three drugs (stimulant, depressant, and *placebo*) to the same random group of subjects on three separate occasions. Sequence effects would, of course, be controlled by some form of Latin square design, and analysis of variance would be used to sort out drug effects and practice effects. If a test had to be used which was subject to strong learning effects, it would be necessary to select three equivalent groups and to administer each of these three treatments to one of the groups; analysis of covariance could be the appropriate statistical method.

It will be noted that in this type of design no attention is paid to individual differences between subjects. In so far as these exist they are relegated to the error term of the equation. The alternative design given in the lower part of Fig. 17.1 capitalizes on these differences by making use of the prediction of different reactions for different types of people. If we are able to define a sedation threshold (Shagass, 1956, 1957) along physiological lines as a point where inhibition in the cortex has reached a given level, then it follows from the theory briefly stated above that extraverts and hysterics, who by hypothesis form inhibition potential more quickly and more strongly, would require less of the depressant drug to reach this point than would introverts. The experimental design would therefore require us in the first place to select two matched groups of extraverts and introverts respectively, and to study their behaviour with respect to our objective measure after the injection of varying amounts of, say, Sodium Amytal. Our prediction would be verified if the extraverted group required less Sodium Amytal to reach the critical point than did the introverted group. Details regarding the actual results of the experiment will be given below; it has merely been quoted here as an illustration of what, to us, appears a very powerful and useful experimental design which has unfortunately been very much neglected in the experimental literature. The importance of this type of design will be realized when it is recalled that individual differences in drug reactions are truly enormous, and may even give rise to apparently contradictory effects. By relegating them to an error term we make it very much more difficult for ourselves to find significant evidence for drug effects, and we also make it more difficult to duplicate findings in this field. When it is realized, in addition, that the relationship between dosage and drug effect may be curvilinear rather than monotonic, it will be clear that the neglect of personality factors implied in the first of the two methods discussed here carries with it a considerable waste of information. The failure of workers in the field to use the second method appears due largely to the absence of clearly formulated hypotheses relating drug effects to personality.

The Dimensional Analysis of Drug Effects

In spite of the great changes in psychological theory which have occurred during the past fifty years, the same tests appear to be used over and over again by psychologists. Reaction-time, continuous work curves, word association and time estimation were among the tests used by Kraepelin in his studies of alcohol, paraldehyde, chloral, morphine, etc. Other tests which have survived for a long time are the ergograph, the dynamometer, and tests involving tapping and steadiness (Hollingworth, 1912). Some of the assumptions made by early workers regarding psychological functions measured by such tests as these have been abandoned, but new ones have taken their place for which also no good rationale can be detected. This is a point which has such far-reaching consequences, and is so important in the design of adequate experiments in the field of psychopharmacology, that a brief discussion of modern views of psychological testing appears to be in order.

Tests which are multifactorial (i.e. the performance of which is determined by more than one ability or personality trait) cannot give results permitting of any direct psychological interpretation. This can easily be shown by writing the typical factorial equation for the variance of any particular test A—

$$\sigma_A^2 = \sigma_a^2 + \sigma_b^2 + \sigma_c^2 + \ldots \sigma_n^2 + \sigma_s^2 + \sigma_e^2$$

According to this equation, the variance of performance scores on test A is made up of the additive variance of abilities (or traits) a, b, $c \ldots n$, the specific variance (s) and the error variance (e). If we take a test such as the Complex Co-ordination Test (A), we find that performance on it is determined by the following factors: psychomotor co-ordination (a), rate of arm movement (b), spatial relations (c), perceptual speed (d), visualization (e), mechanical experience (f), numerical facility (g), and psychomotor speed (h) (Fleishman and Hempel, 1954). It will be clear that any change in performance after drug administration may be due to a change in any one, or in any combination, of these factors, and that it is impossible to assign the change in performance to any of these more fundamental psychological variables.

The position, in fact, is even more complex because the factorial composition of a given task does not remain constant during practice but changes markedly. As an example, we may quote another study by Fleishman and Hempel (1955). In Fig. 17.2 is shown the factorial composition of the Discrimination Reaction-time test at different stages of practice. It will be seen, for instance, that the factor "spatial relations" plays a far more important role in the factorial composition of test performance at the beginning than at the end of practice; the same is true of the "verbal" factor. On the other hand, "rate of movement" and "reaction-time" are factors accounting for a larger proportion of the variance towards the end of practice than at the beginning. Similar changes are indicated in Fig. 17.3, which is taken from Fleishman (1956); this demonstrates changes in proportion of variance contributed by each factor at successive stages of practice on a pursuit rotor test.

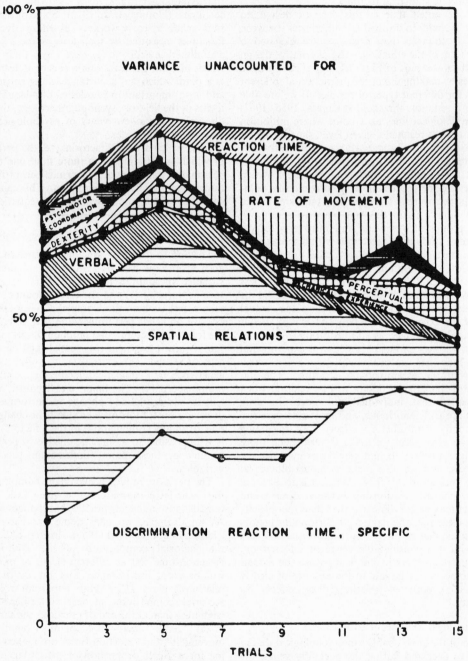

100 %

VARIANCE UNACCOUNTED FOR

REACTION TIME

RATE OF MOVEMENT

PSYCHOMOTOR COORDINATION

DEXTERITY

VERBAL

PERCEPTUAL

50 %

SPATIAL RELATIONS

DISCRIMINATION REACTION TIME, SPECIFIC

0

1　3　5　7　9　11　13　15

TRIALS

Fig. 17.2. Factorial Composition of Discrimination Reaction-time Test at Different
Stages of Practice

(*From Fleishman and Hempel,* 1955)

These considerations, which have not to our knowledge been discussed previously in this connexion, suggest quite clearly that the only approach to drug studies which can give us psychologically meaningful information is the factorial, or dimensional, approach. Instead of using single tests of a multifactorial kind, it is suggested that batteries of tests defining meaningful and experimentally demonstrated psychological factors should be employed. This would do away with arbitrary and inconclusive test results and would link drug experiments more closely to the main body of psychological knowledge. If the points here raised are as vital as we believe them to be, then we must conclude that practically all the work that has been done in the drug field is only suggestive and does not enable us to derive any firm conclusions, because it has not, in fact, been undertaken from the dimensional point of view here advocated.[1]

These considerations have a bearing on another point which we would like to stress. Much of the work summarized in this chapter has been done on the "blunderbuss" principle. A variety of tests, chosen more or less at random, or in terms of ease of administration, are given to a random group of subjects after the administration of a haphazardly chosen drug in the hope that interesting and important consequences may follow. The result of this type of approach has been disastrous. Little, if anything, is known with any degree of certainty about the psychological effects of drugs, and contradictory results are to be found on all sides. We venture to suggest that here, as elsewhere, worth-while results are more likely to follow upon clear-cut and specific theories which are stated in a sufficiently rigorous manner to make possible deductions which can be tested. If it be agreed that this is not an unreasonable proposal, then it would seem to follow that the most likely hypotheses

[1] The same point may be made from slightly different premises. Learning theorists are agreed that performance is the product of several factors, such as drive (D), habit ($_sH_R$), reactive inhibition (I_R), conditioned inhibition ($_sI_R$), and so forth. If we consider for a moment Jones's (1958) modification of Hull's equation:

$$_sH_R = (D + I_R) \times (_sH_R + _sI_R),$$

then we can see that the task score ($_sE_R$) is determined by four variables, so that modifications in $_sE_R$ produced by drugs may be due to the effect of the drug on any one, or on any combination, of these four variables. Again, therefore, any direct interpretation of the results is plainly inadmissible; what is required is a specifically designed experiment to explore these complexities.

In this connexion also, unfortunately, it must be said that hardly any of the work carried out in the field of psychopharmacology is very illuminating or has had regard to these theoretical considerations. Occasional exceptions to these general strictures will be noted (*see* also Chapter 12 of this HANDBOOK by Franks) and there are some signs that work currently going on in psychological laboratories, at least, is based on a more sophisticated view of methodological requirements. The same cannot be said of work done in psychiatric laboratories, to which even the most elementary knowledge of learning theory does not seem to have percolated.

to be testable at the present moment would be hypotheses of a dimensional character. One such hypothesis has already been mentioned, namely, that relating depressant and stimulant drugs respectively to the extraversion-introversion dimension. Other dimensional hypotheses will suggest themselves to the reader as he goes through this chapter, which has been arranged in part to summarize the evidence regarding the influence of drugs on the three major personality dimensions dealt with in this book. Thus, adrenaline

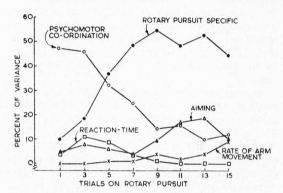

FIG. 17.3. CHANGES IN PROPORTION OF VARIANCE CONTRIBUTED BY EACH FACTOR AT SUCCESSIVE STAGES OF PRACTICE ON PURSUIT ROTOR TEST
(From Fleishman, 1956)

may be considered to be relevant to the dimension of neuroticism in the sense of increasing the emotional instability which is so characteristic of this factor. Conversely, sympatholytic drugs and some of the barbiturates would appear to have the opposite effect to adrenaline in the sense of decreasing the emotional over-response characteristic of neuroticism. Hallucinogens like LSD would appear to be related to the psychoticism dimension in the sense of increasing the thought disorders characteristic of this factor, while some, at least, of the so-called tranquillizers would appear to have the opposite effect. Hypotheses such as these, crude and over-simplified as they undoubtedly are, have one great advantage over most of the theories which we have encountered in this field. They are sufficiently clear-cut to be capable of being disproved experimentally because they give rise to rigorous deductions which do not admit of any ambiguity. It appears to us that hypotheses of this nature, even though they may turn out to be erroneous, are more fruitful in the long run than are more cautious, complex, and highly interpretive hypotheses which cannot be disproved experimentally because it is impossible to make any deductions from them which can be put to the experimental test.

This does not mean, of course, that the hypotheses

outlined above do not require certain qualifications. In the first place drugs tend to have multiple effects, and consequently it is by no means impossible that a drug exerts effects on two or all three dimensions, even though its main effect will be on one. This is not necessarily a disadvantage, nor does it make the dimensional analysis inapplicable. What we have to do, clearly, in the case of each drug is to relate it to all three dimensions and write its specification in terms of its direction cosines. (Such a procedure might have to be repeated with different dosages of the same drug in view of the fact that effects are occasionally curvilinear.) Such a set of specifications would tell us a great deal more about the psychological effects of a given drug than could be determined by any other method which is available at the present time.

Another complication which arises is due to the relatively arbitrary way in which drugs are grouped at the moment. Many quite divergent types of drugs are included under the heading "depressant" or "stimulant," and neither on pharmacological nor psychological lines can any of the present groupings be really justified. While this is true, it does not argue against the approach we suggest; quite on the contrary. It would appear that it is only by adopting whole-heartedly such a psychological method of grouping drugs along dimensional lines that we can hope to proceed further and to arrive at an appropriate biochemical and pharmacological analysis of those factors which underly uniform behavioural reactions. It may, moreover, be hypothesized that drugs whose actions are similar in terms of, say, direction cosines, will also be similar with respect to certain biochemical features which should be subject to analysis and which would make it possible to produce drugs which have some specific and precise action. Such an advance would also make possible a more rigorous determination of the site of action of the drug and thus would link up with the attempt to localize the physiological factors determining behavioural reactions concerning the three main dimensions of personality.

The factor-analytic approach suggested is probably the most generally useful when we are dealing with a dimensional problem such as the one which is now under consideration. Under certain circumstances, however, this method is faced with difficulties which suggest that an alternative should be looked for. The assumptions underlying factor-analytic work are so stringent on the mathematical side that it is sometimes doubtful whether the model is really a very suitable one for research into the relationship between drug effects and abnormal personality. It may be fruitful, then, to consider the possibility of a mathematical model which is known as *canonical*

variate analysis. Here the assumptions are less stringent and the model has particular advantages when diagnostic groups are to be used to identify the latent roots (Eysenck, 1957).

Let us consider a hypothetical experiment in which we seek to study certain hypotheses regarding the effects of Meprobamate on extraversion, neuroticism and psychoticism. We would select four groups of subjects, i.e. normals, psychotics, hysterics and dysthymics. Each of these groups would then be divided into two subgroups on a random basis, one of these two subgroups being given a *placebo*, the other Meprobamate. Subjects in all four groups would then be administered a battery of (say) ten tests which are known from previous work to be good measures of the three dimensions under investigation. Canonical variate analysis of the test scores of members of the eight groups (four diagnostic groups × two drugs) would give us three, or possibly four, significant latent roots, which after suitable rotation could be identified in terms of our three dimensions, and, if a fourth dimension was called for, as a typical drug effect dimension external to the three dimensional model. Whether or not such a fourth dimension could be found, the position of the eight groups within the three-dimensional framework would tell us (a) whether the drug had a general effect along one or more of these dimensions and (b) whether this effect was, or was not, equal for different portions of the continua in question. Such a design would overcome the obvious difficulties which are involved in calculating correlations over diagnostic groups which could not be hypothesized to give rise to a normal distribution of scores along the various continua. A modified form of such an experiment has been reported by Eysenck and Eysenck (to be published); it illustrates the uses of this method in some detail.

It seemed worth while to discuss the possibilities of the dimensional approach in some detail because the data summarized below tend on the whole to support the kind of hypothesis which was outlined earlier in the section, and because without such a theory, which produces some kind of order in this vast field, the reader would be left with nothing but a whole series of independent, unintegrated and unassimilable research findings of doubtful reliability and having little meaning.

Having discussed in some detail the methodology of drug research, and some of the difficulties attaching to any worth-while study in this field, we shall now turn to a brief consideration of the experimental literature. We shall begin by discussing stimulants and depressants, pass on to the autonomic drugs and finish up with the hallucinogens and tranquillizers.

STIMULANTS AND DEPRESSANTS

Stimulants and depressants are both very heterogeneous groups of drugs. Little purpose would be served here by attempting to define the terms; instead the major drugs in each category will be listed and some of their complexities and paradoxical effects on behaviour described.

The drugs usually classed as *depressants*, according to Goodman and Gilman (1955) are—

1. *General anaesthetics*, such as ether and cyclopropane.
2. *Sedatives-hypnotics-soporifics*, such as barbiturates, chloral hydrate, and bromides.
3. *Antiepileptics*, such as diphenylhydantoin, phenobarbital, and trimethadione.
4. *Narcotics*, such as morphine, meperidine, and methadone.
5. *Analgesics and antipyretics*, such as salicylates and aminopyrine.
6. Centrally acting *skeletal muscle relaxants*, such as mephenesin and trihexyphenidyl.

These categories overlap considerably and even within the same category there are marked differences in the effects additional to the main depressant actions, which may themselves differ.

Moreover, even chemically similar compounds may have radically different effects; for instance, there are stimulant as well as depressant barbiturates, and Meratran, which is a stimulant, is an isomer of Frenquel which, in spite of its identical chemical composition (and only a slight difference in structure), antagonizes stimulants (Brown, Feldman and Braun, 1955) and is classed as an ataractic drug, or tranquilizer (Fabing and Hawkins, 1955).

Among the central nervous *stimulants* the diversity is even greater. Here, besides the differences in the mode and site of action there is apt to be a multiplicity of side effects: "In this respect they are in marked contrast to the central depressant drugs, which, for the most part, have a selective action on the nervous system" (Goodman and Gilman, 1955). Nevertheless, depressants are far from being homogeneous, although there has been no lack of theories attempting to explain their effects in terms of a single mechanism. Toman (1952) wrote: "So diverse in chemical structure are the many substances which produce central depression or complete anaesthesia that it is hard to imagine any single mechanism of action common to all. Indeed, there is no reason to believe that a common action is essential, since there must be as many different ways of blocking central nervous activity as there are independent parameters necessary for the normal maintenance of function in the central nervous system."

Although many substances will, in toxic doses, cause central stimulation, only a few are of clinical importance. They can be arbitrarily listed as follows—

1. The *analeptics*, such as picrotoxin, nikethamide (Coramine), pentylenetetrazol (Metrazol) and strychnine. They have been chiefly used to lessen narcosis and to stimulate respiration.
2. The *xanthines*, such as caffeine and theophylline (which is present in tea).
3. Certain *sympathomimetic* substances—

(a) The amphetamines.
(b) Cocaine.

4. *Miscellaneous stimulants*, such as Meratran and Ritalin. These do not appear to be related to any of the above-mentioned compounds, nor to each other, and having only recently been introduced, their usefulness has yet to be established.

Various other drugs which act principally on the autonomic system have some central stimulant action, e.g. atropine, ephedrine, nicotine, etc.

Although stimulants and depressants have actions which are opposed in some respects, the antagonism is usually not perfect, because each drug tends to have not just one effect but a whole range of effects, which are unlikely to correspond exactly with those of the antagonist. Some effects of stimulants and depressants are even synergistic (e.g. the effects of amphetamine and amylobarbitone on mood).

Some drugs which stimulate the nervous system in small doses cause depression if larger doses are given, and depression commonly follows the stimulant effect. The effects of certain drugs are apt to be unpredictable; for example, scopolamine in therapeutic doses is usually a depressant (except on respiration, which it stimulates), but it may occasionally produce excitement, restlessness, hallucinations and delirium (Goodman and Gilman, 1955). It cannot therefore be simply classified as a stimulant or as a depressant. Likewise, "It is undecided whether marihuana is primarily a central stimulant or depressant, or both" (Goodman and Gilman, *The Pharmacological Basis of Therapeutics*, p. 171).

It is clear that few, if any, drugs are *merely* stimulant or depressant, and that most occupy some position intermediate between these two extremes, that sometimes they are inconsistent in their actions and they have a variable range of side effects. The status even of well established stimulants and depressants has been doubted. For example, Heath (1954) considers that "it is highly questionable whether amphetamine actually stimulates" and according to

Toman (1952) amphetamine appears to be primarily depressant in its action on the sciatic nerve of the frog. Gottlieb (1951) put forward the view that amylobarbitone had a stimulant effect on the central nervous system which was normally masked by the hypnotic effect. That such paradoxical effects should occur at this highly complex level is understandable when it is remembered that even at the reflex level, stimulation of the vagus may cause the stomach to relax or contract, depending on the initial state of contraction, as Gerard pointed out in the *Symposium on Sedative and Hypnotic Drugs*, p. 104 (1954). The explanation given by Heath (op. cit., pp. 103–4), is that improvement through taking sedative drugs can only happen when there is already some degree of impairment because of internal stress: "Under these circumstances, through lowering the level of activity of the total organism the stress is likewise reduced so that it no longer has the same degree of incapacitating effect or inhibition. The end result then is performance at a slightly higher level than before the administration of the drug. Here, however, the individual cannot approach what is his theoretical maximal performance."

Domino, Fox and Brody (1955), who investigated the effects of a stimulant barbiturate, point out in this context the difficulties in classifying the actions of barbiturates into stimulants and depressants on the basis of "gross observations." "The usual definition of a 'stimulant' is an agent that increases a functional activity, and that of a 'depressant' as an agent that decreases functional activity. In the complex organization of the central nervous system it is difficult to determine whether a compound is a true 'stimulant' or 'depressant' on the basis of gross observations in the intact animal. A drug may exert its effects at a variety of central sites. It may act at the neuronal level either to excite or depress; it may act at the synapse or other portions of the neuronal arc, or it may influence facilitatory or inhibitory neurons which feed into the common nervous pathway. Thus a pharmacological agent that stimulates inhibitory neurons might be an overt depressant, whereas an agent that selectively depresses inhibitory neurons may cause an overt excitatory response."

Thus, even in neurophysiology there are difficulties in ascertaining whether an agent should be classed as a stimulant or depressant, and further difficulties arise as these terms are so often used in a wider sense, e.g. to describe overt behaviour, but as Wikler (1950) points out: "The use of terminology borrowed from pharmacology or neurophysiology such as 'stimulation,' 'depression,' 'facilitation' and 'inhibition' to describe phenomena concerned with total adaptive behaviour is not only unjustified, but actually misleading." (*See also* Wikler, 1952.)

There has been much emphasis lately on the effects of drugs on the reticular activating system, and correspondingly less emphasis on Hughlings Jackson's concept of levels (e.g. Elkes, Elkes and Bradley, 1954). The importance of this system was only discovered recently, having escaped attention because the earlier experiments on the electrical activity of the nervous system had been done with the animals under general rather than local anaesthesia (Magoun, 1954). It is variously described as the mesodiencephalic activating system, the midbrain reticular formation of Moruzzi and Magoun and the thalamic diffuse projection system of Jasper. (*See* Symposium on *Brain Mechanisms and Consciousness*, edited by Delafresnaye, 1954.) If this region is stimulated electrically in a sleeping animal, arousal occurs with the characteristic EEG changes (i.e. desynchronization with disappearance of the large slow waves and spindle bursts characteristic of sleep). Its destruction in monkeys makes the animals appear as if asleep or deeply anaesthetized. The ascending reticular activating system is a multi-neuronal afferent pathway concerned with the general alertness of the animal, in contrast to the specific nature of the classical sensory pathways.

This system appears to be very sensitive to depressant drugs, such as Nembutal (pentobarbitone sodium) and ether: "Activity evoked in this subcortical mechanism by afferent stimulation shows a markedly greater susceptibility to alteration by drugs and metabolic changes than does concomitant discharge conducted to sensory areas of the cortex in direct afferent paths." (Arduini and Arduini, 1954, who confirmed the findings of French, Verzeano and Magoun, 1953.) This differential sensitivity is surprising as it has usually been assumed that the cortex was more metabolically active than the lower parts of the central nervous system and that the sensitivity was directly proportional to the metabolic activity (e.g. Himwich, 1951, 1955). It is, however, likely that the complexity of internal organization of the reticular system is at least as great as that in the cortex and that the intricacy of synaptic connexions is "of greater importance in determining sensitivity both to pharmacologic agents and to metabolic alterations than is the anatomical position of the part in a Jacksonian *schema* of serial horizontal levels." (Arduini and Arduini, 1954.)

Stimulants such as amphetamine (Elkes, Elkes and Bradley, 1954) or strychnine and Metrazol (Arduini and Arduini, 1954), increase the responsiveness of the reticular activating system. Thus, it appears that although stimulants and depressants have widespread effects, "their influence on the subcortical arousal mechanism may account in considerable measure for their generalized effects." (op. cit.)

Unfortunately the drugs usually classed as

stimulants and depressants are not the only ones which affect this system. Rinaldi and Himwich (1955*a*) suggest that this is the "specific site of action" of atropine and of cholinergic drugs, acetyl-choline producing the alerting reaction and atropine inhibiting it. There is evidence that, in therapeutic doses, chlorpromazine has a "suppressive action on the 'upward discharge' of the ascending reticular formation" (Das, Dasgupta and Werner, 1954), whereas therapeutic doses of reserpine apparently stimulate the mesodiencephalic activating system (Rinaldi and Himwich, 1955*b*). These two drugs are described as "tranquillizers" rather than as depressants because, unlike the latter, they may induce a calm state without any concomitant confusion, and if sleep occurs it is of moderate depth and the patient can easily be aroused from it. Nevertheless, they have, potentially, the effects of certain depressants. There still remains much work to be done before the different effects of these substances on the activities of the various parts of the brain are elucidated.

According to Eysenck's theory (1957) "extraverted behaviour patterns are produced by excessively strong reactive inhibition and/or excessively weak excitation, while introverted behaviour patterns are produced by excessively weak reactive inhibition and/or excessively strong excitation." He further postulates that depressant drugs increase cortical inhibition, decrease cortical excitation and thereby produce extraverted behaviour patterns, whereas stimulant drugs decrease cortical inhibition, increase cortical excitation and thereby produce introverted behaviour patterns. The evidence for this theory will be discussed later but it is worth pointing out here a possible connexion between the hypothesized (molar) basis of extraversion-introversion and the mesodiencephalic activating system. If stimulants and depressants have any common denominator this system appears to be the most likely but, at best, an action on the reticular activating system is a necessary and not a sufficient condition for stimulation or depression. It is conceivable that the reticular activating system is more active or more responsive in introverts than in extraverts. If this were the case, it would follow that any drug which increased the activity of this system would tend to be introverting, and conversely. But this is probably an oversimplification, as drugs have numerous different sites of action, and similarly, it would be surprising if the basis for a fundamental difference in personality were located in a precise region of the central nervous system.

This development of Eysenck's theory has a certain plausibility; it avoids the confusion which arises as soon as the terms "stimulant" and "depressant" are introduced, and is consistent with some of the features characteristic of introverts and extraverts. It

can be fairly[1] easily tested by studying the relationship between the effect of drugs on the reticular activating system and performance (under the influence of the drug) on the tests and questionnaires which are used to define extraversion-introversion operationally. In the course of the review any instances for and against this theory and its tentative extension will be noted. It follows from the latter that a variety of drugs, not classed as stimulants or depressants, should affect extraversion-introversion. For example, reserpine should be introverting and likewise cholinergic drugs, whereas atropine should be extraverting.[2]

The Amphetamines

Although amphetamine was introduced into clinical medicine only just over twenty years ago (Prinzmetal and Bloomberg, 1935), there is already an extensive psychological literature devoted to it and the related compounds. Amphetamine itself is a volatile liquid which was used in nasal inhaler tubes until the dangers of consuming the contents (about 325 mg) were pointed out (e.g. Monroe and Drell, 1947). It is usually administered orally in the form of its sulphate. Up to 1940, most of the work was on the racemic amphetamine sulphate (Benzedrine, Mecodrine, and Isomyn being some of the equivalent names). The dextrorotary isomer, dextro-amphetamine sulphate (*d*-amphetamine or Dexedrine) is now more commonly used, as its central effects are supposed to be relatively stronger than those of amphetamine. A related and rather similar compound is methylamphetamine (Methedrine or Pervitin, or desoxyephedrine). Chemically they resemble adrenaline and ephedrine. The drug is sympathomimetic and raises the blood-pressure. The usual oral dose for an adult is 5–20 mg of amphetamine sulphate or 2·5–10 mg of *d*-amphetamine sulphate. Absorption is rapid and, although effects may be noticed about twenty minutes later (Seifert, 1939) they do not reach their maximum until $1-2\frac{1}{2}$ hours later. Their action is prolonged, and a dose after 3 p.m. may interfere with sleep.

Among the conditions for which the amphetamines are prescribed are narcolepsy and obesity, as these

[1] This qualification is necessary, because other factors may influence the response to the drug, e.g. social factors. For example, a large dose of a moderately quick acting barbiturate may make the subject "happy, hilarious and drunk" or "gloomy, moody, depressed, weepy," according to the way the situation is manipulated.

[2] Since this view was put forward by Dr. Trouton, it has become apparent that there may be two parts of the reticular activating system: (1) an adrenaline-sensitive portion which, when stimulated produces arousal; (2) an acetylcholine-sensitive portion which, though it gives rise to EEG changes characteristic of sleep and wakefulness, does not produce the behavioural counterparts. The brain stem arousal mechanism thus appears to be truly *adrenergic* (Rothballer, 1956, 1957): hence prediction concerning the possible relationships of parasympathetic drugs and introversion-extraversion might not turn out to be as postulated.

drugs tend to increase alertness and to decrease appetite. (For further uses *see* Bett *et al.*, 1955.) In psychiatry they are given intravenously for abreactive treatment (e.g. Jonas, 1954), as an aid to psychotherapy (e.g. Schilder, 1938; Agoston, 1944) or for diagnostic purposes (e.g. Delay *et al.*, 1948; Simon and Taube, 1946).

Although intravenous amphetamine to some extent reverses barbiturate anaesthesia (Myerson *et al.*, 1939; Jacobsen *et al.*, 1938), the antagonism is by no means perfect, and the Newmans (1956) concluded that *d*-amphetamine "in ordinary therapeutic doses were ineffective in combating the depressant effect of alcohol" (*see also* Bovet and Bovet-Nitti, 1948; Koppanyi and Fazekas, 1950, and Nickerson, 1950). In some respects, the amphetamines and barbiturates are synergistic and they are commonly prescribed together orally as Drinamyl or Dexytal, or intravenously in the belief that the effects on mood are enhanced and the peripheral effects minimized; they may also be given together, intravenously (Gottleib, 1949; Delay, 1949; Gottleib *et al.*, 1952; Houston, 1952; Reznikoff, 1941; Davidoff *et al.*, 1941). Tolerance, habituation and addiction may all occur, the incidence of the last being assessed differently according to the way that addiction is defined; this is in contrast to the barbiturates which "are addicting drugs no matter how the word addicting is defined" (Isbell and Fraser, 1950). Since amphetamine is chemically related to certain hallucinogens and, like them, tends to inhibit synaptic transmission (Marrazzi and Hart, 1955b), it is not surprising that prolonged and excessive administration of it may produce a schizophrenic-like state. (For description of amphetamine craving, addiction and psychosis, *see* Norman and Shea, 1945; Wallis *et al.*, 1949; also Freyham, 1949; Knapp, 1952; Hermann and Nagler, 1954; Chapman, 1954; Connell, 1956a and b.) The early work on amphetamine was reviewed by Ivy and Goetzl (1943); a more recent review, dealing with the neurological and psychiatric aspects of these drugs, is that by Bonhoff and Lewranz (1954).

Clinical Observations

After studying the reactions of over two hundred subjects to amphetamine sulphate, Reifenstein and Davidoff (1939) characterized the actions of the drug as "variable, uncertain, unpredictable and at times paradoxic." Their table provides a convenient summary of the main effects (Table XVII.2). The "paradoxic" effects are most likely to occur with large doses. This table includes most of the symptoms which have been observed after the administration of amphetamine to normal subjects (e.g. Gwynn and Yater, 1937; Nathanson, 1937; Bahnsen *et al.*, 1938), and some of the toxic effects noted by Wand (1938).

TABLE XVII.2
EFFECTS OF AMPHETAMINE SULPHATE

(1) Stimulation of Mental Response

(a) *Major effects.* Acceleration of the stream of mental activity and increase in content of thought; increase in co-ordinate mental activity and general efficiency; increase in perception and alertness; increase in initiative; increase in attention and meticulousness; decrease in confusion; decrease in sleep requirement and insomnia; decrease in fatigue; decrease in reticence and improved performance on psychometric tests.

(b) *Paradoxic effects.* Retardation of the stream of mental activity; incapability to concentrate; forgetfulness; dullness; increase in fatigue, malaise and drowsiness; decrease in perception and alertness; decrease in attention; confusion; transitory delirium; tactile and other somatic hallucinations, paraesthesias and anaesthesias, heart consciousness, and generalized sensations of warmth.

(2) Stimulation of Speech Function

(a) *Major effects.* Increase in speech activity, disappearance of mutism, talkativeness to the point of loquaciousness; increase in accessibility with willingness to discuss personal problems, ventilation of conflicts, and elaboration of delusions and hallucinations; and increase in coherent and relevant speech.

(b) *Paradoxic effects.* Decrease in speech activity, decrease in logical progression of thought with increase in incoherent and irrelevant speech.

(3) Stimulation of Motor Functions

(a) *Major effects.* Increase in motor activity; increase in co-ordinate physical activity with increase in physical efficiency; tremulousness, restlessness, extreme hyperkinesis; and aggravation of convulsive seizures.

(b) *Paradoxic effects.* Decrease in motor activity with decrease in physical efficiency.

(4) Stimulation of Affective Function

(a) *Major effects.* Elevation of mood with cheerfulness, a feeling of well-being, exhilaration, euphoria, elation; uncontrollable laughter; facetiousness; a state of ready irritability and increased irritation; increase in drive, urge and spontaneity; decrease in shyness; increase in confidence; hair-trigger-like reactions with sudden changeability of mood; agitation, impatience, impulsiveness, and self-assertiveness approaching aggressiveness in some; aggravation of assaultiveness, and homicidal tendencies in mentally ill persons.

(b) *Paradoxic effects.* Lowering of mood with depression or melancholy; uncontrollable crying; aggravation of suicidal tendencies; resentfulness; surliness; anxiety; and increase in worry.

The reports of the effects of the amphetamines in different psychiatric disorders are somewhat conflicting. "The literature on Pervitin has consistently revealed that this drug may either relieve or exacerbate the same abnormal mental state." Normal subjects are said to be more affected by these drugs than are psychotics (Davidoff, 1936; Davidoff and Reifenstein, 1937), but even psychotics with the same diagnosis may be affected in diametrically opposite ways. For example, Delay (1949) found that catatonia was aggravated, whereas Hope, Callaway and Sands

(1951) found that catatonic patients were improved by 20 mg methylamphetamine intravenously. Acute schizophrenics were more responsive than the chronic (N = 30). Delusions and abnormal thought processes were accentuated or made more accessible. A similar effect on delusions had been observed by Levine, Rinkel and Greenblatt (1948), who compared the psychological and physiological effects of intravenous methylamphetamine, amphetamine and amylobarbitone sodium. Pennes (1954) also compared the first and last of these three drugs, together with mescaline, on fifty-five schizophrenics; he found that whereas the barbiturate was predominantly normalizing and the hallucinogen intensified the symptoms, methylamphetamine tended to produce an unstable state, with either normalization or intensification of symptoms. However, Schube et al. (1937) found that none of a group of eighty psychiatric patients were benefited by amphetamine and Wootley (1938) found that half of his group of seventy psychiatric patients were unaffected by amphetamine, even in large doses. Wilbut et al. (1937), Cameron and Kasanin (1941), Rudolph (1949), Monro and Conitzer (1950), Rudolph (1956), found little of value in the application of the drug to neurotics.

Certain types of psychopath, particularly those with a persistent theta rhythm in their EEG, tolerate the drug well and respond favourably to it. According to Hill (1947): "The personalities which respond are those showing an aggressive bad-tempered and generally hostile tendency in interpersonal relationships, which is manifested whenever frustration is met." He also states that the schizoid or paranoid personality does not respond: "The patient must be capable of some warmth and capable of emotional attachment."

The effects of amphetamine do not appear to be related to sympathotonia or vagotonia (Wootley, 1938) nor to body build (Jacobsen and Wollstein, 1939). Bett (1946) asserted: "People of pyknic build appear to tolerate it better than the asthenic. The former react with a more parasympathetic type of response . . . while the latter respond more sympathetically with palpitations and tremors. Depending on the predominance of one or other type of response, the effect of Benzedrine will be mainly beneficial or mainly unpleasant." This sounds plausible, but is not in accordance with the experiments quoted above.

Recently von Felsinger, Lasagna and Beecher (1955) have attempted to correlate the personality and the reaction to drugs in twenty healthy young male volunteers. The psychological data were based on an interview (and the inevitable Rorschach). Changes in mood and behaviour were assessed by questionnaires and by direct observation through a one-way window. The predominant reaction to amphetamine 20 mg per 70 kg bodyweight was euphoria,[1] but four experienced dysphoria, and five felt sedated. The seven subjects who showed marked stimulation were the "most responsive and expansive" and well-adjusted, whereas those responding with dysphoria were conspicuously lacking appropriate motivation in their work, and were the heaviest consumers of alcohol (being "suspected of having neurotic causes for their drinking"). Marked depressive trends and moodiness were among the "undesirable" characteristics of those who were sedated by amphetamine.

Each subject was tested on four other occasions, when he received an injection of placebo, heroin, morphine or pentobarbitone. The general conclusion was—

> The atypical responses were most frequent in the least balanced persons. It is not unreasonable to assume that such a personality structure, already inadequate to deal with everyday stresses, fraught with impulsivity and anxiety, and fearing loss of control, may be alarmed by the surge of stimulation and energy associated with amphetamine . . . A well balanced personality structure, on the other hand, could conceivably integrate such stimulation into outgoing activity without disturbance and with pleasant effect.

They interpreted the sedative effect as a "defensive reaction."

PSYCHOLOGICAL EXPERIMENTS

The most ambitious of the researches on the psychological effects of amphetamine was carried out by Carl and Turner (1939; also Turner and Carl, 1939; and Carl and Turner, 1940). They used a large battery of tests on four groups (each of about thirty-five subjects), who were tested twice, first without any drug and subsequently after a (1) placebo, or after (2) 10, (3) 20, or (4) 30 mg amphetamine. Testing was begun 75–90 min after administration of the drug. (Groups (3) and (4) received 10 mg of the dose during the session.) It is not clear how the subjects were allotted to the groups, but those under twenty-one tended to be placed in the placebo group (Turner and Carl, 1939).

The performances at the first session and early and late in the second session were compared on nearly forty different items. Some of their more definite findings are referred to subsequently but few of the intergroup differences are beyond the "realm of only very moderate statistical probability." Altogether the reports of their studies occupy about two hundred pages, but their cautious and critical interpretation leaves little which can be justifiably abstracted from

---

[1] Turner and Carl (1939) found evidence of a change from depression to elation, using an Optimism-Pessimism scale, and also a more favourable attitude towards work. The changes in the Bernreuter scale were inconsistent, but in the direction of "lowered introversion (higher extraversion), increased dominance, heightened self-confidence and greater sociability."

its context. The ratio of words to definite statements is rather high.

EFFECTS ON INTELLIGENCE TEST PERFORMANCE AND REASONING

In terms of Furneaux's (1952) analysis of intelligence (cf. Chapter 5 by W. D. Furneaux) it would be theoretically possible that amphetamine might influence the *speed* or the *level* (the latter being partly dependent upon persistence). No statistically significant improvement in score on intelligence tests appears to have been reported, although some increase was found in several of the studies (e.g. Molitch and Sullivan, 1937, *see also* Sargant and Blackburn, 1936; Peoples and Guttman, 1936; Bradley, 1937; McNamara and Miller, 1937; Wollstein, 1939;

Bradley and Green, 1940; Cutler *et al.*, 1940; Golla *et al.*, 1940). The studies by Carl and Turner (1939) are inconclusive. Neither schizophrenics (Broadhurst, 1957) nor mental defectives (Morris *et al.*, 1955) do better on intelligence tests when given an amphetamine.

It is possible that the same dose of amphetamine may improve the performance of some subjects, and impair that of others. This view was put forward by Hecht and Sargent (1941) who tested three groups of about thirty subjects each on a reasoning test and on a disarranged words test before and after receiving 10 mg amphetamine sulphate, a *placebo* or no drug. The variability was great, and none of the differences between the groups were significant. Similarly, Andrews (1940) found no statistically significant increase in scores on tests of syllogistic reasoning.

TABLE XVII.3

THE EFFECTS OF THE AMPHETAMINES ON ASSOCIATIVE TESTS

A. Arithmetic Tests

Author	Test or function	Effect
Peoples and Guttmann (1936) .	Continuous addition (Kraepelin)	Increase in speed
McNamara and Miller (1937) .	Multiplication of pairs of 3-digit numbers	No appreciable effect on speed or accuracy
Bradley (1937) . .	Arithmetic tests in children	No improvement in non-fatigued subjects working at their best
Barmack (1938) . .	Adding 6-place numbers	More problems attempted and accuracy unaffected
		Subjects less bored
	Continuous addition	No improvement in non-fatigued subjects working at their best[1]
Flory and Gilbert (1943) . .	Complex multiplication	15 mg amphetamine may impair performance
Kleemeier and Kleemeier (1947)	(*a*) Cancellation of incorrect answers to simple multiplication problems	(*a*) Marked and statistically significant increase
	(*b*) Arithmetic speed test	(*b*) Some increase
Düker and Düker (1953) . .	Continuous addition and subtraction	Improvement in speed and accuracy[1]

B. Other Associative and Psychomotor Tasks

Author	Test or function	Effect
Kleemeier and Kleemeier (1947)	(*a*) Letter cancellation (*b*) Paper and pencil motor tests (*c*) Word completion	Differences not significant but means higher in subgroups receiving amphetamine
Carl and Turner (1939) . .	Taylor number test (connecting numbers in order)	Improvement, although not demonstrated in a "thoroughly reliable manner"
	Word production test (cf. (*c*) above)	Improved by moderate doses; also by large doses in some, whereas others became confused
	Imagination test	
	Tapping test (cf. (*b*) above)	Slight improvement, especially in accuracy
Wunderle (1941) . . .	Association of ideas	Increased[1]
Welch *et al.* (1946) . .	Association to low association nonsense syllables	Significantly greater in normal subjects if 10 mg *d*-amphetamine given one hour before (but increase not comparable with that found in elated patients)

[1] Methylamphetamine was used in these experiments.

EFFECTS ON ASSOCIATIVE FUNCTIONS

These are summarized in Table XVII.3. The administration of an amphetamine may lead to a statistically significant improvement in certain associative tasks. This is clearly demonstrated in Kleemeier and Kleemeier's (1947) carefully controlled experiments (*see* Table XVII.3 A and B). In these, twenty-seven students were tested at sessions held at weekly intervals, receiving a glucose *placebo* or 10 mg amphetamine sulphate, according to the following scheme—

Session	1	2	3
Group A	practice	glucose	amphetamine
Group B	practice	amphetamine	glucose

Session		4	5
Group A		glucose	amphetamine
Group B		amphetamine	glucose

The capsules were administered ninety minutes before the beginning of the sessions, which lasted for two hours. The data were combined from sessions 2, 3, 4 and 5 to give each individual a total amphetamine score and a total *placebo* score for each test. "By combining the data in this way, practice effects were cancelled out, and equating of groups as to initial ability was unnecessary."

Their experiments cannot be described further here, but two of their findings may be of general interest. Firstly, they found no evidence that fast and slow workers were differentially affected by amphetamine. Secondly, they found evidence that the drug increased flexibility of performance or "the ability to break through 'set'," "set" being defined as "the predisposition to respond in a particular way." Most of the tests had been devised so that the mental set had to be changed several times during the course of any single one of them. For example, in the part of the Letter Series and of the Multiplication Test, the subject was required to mark correct answers or specific letters, while in another part he was required to mark wrong answers and letter groups containing none of the previously specified letters. "The latter is a considerably more difficult task," and there was a tendency for such tasks to be facilitated by amphetamine.

The discrepancies in Table XVII.3 are probably mostly explicable as a result of differences in dosage, length of work period and practice effect. Too large a dose may impair performance (e.g. Carl and Turner, 1939; Flory and Gilbert, 1943). The effects of the drug become more marked towards the end of the session, as Barmack (1938) found; he attributed the discrepancy between his findings and those of McNamara and Miller (1937) to the fact that his subjects had been required to work for ten times as long as theirs. The fact that the problems set by McNamara and Miller were more difficult than those set by Barmack or by Kleemeier and Kleemeier, and that their experimental design may have resulted in the drug effect being obscured by the practice effect, also probably contributed to their failure to find a significant improvement.

TABLE XVII.4

THE EFFECTS OF AMPHETAMINES ON LEARNING IN MAN

Author	Test	Result
Carl and Turner (1939)	Learning "Z" digit-symbol substitution (adapted from Morgenthau and Healy-Bronner)	Improved by moderate doses of amphetamine; high doses produced improvement in some and deterioration in others
Carl and Turner (1939)	Learning "D" (Healy-Bronner picture-paragraph memory test)	Little affected
Kleemeier and Kleemeier (1947)	Selective substitution test (cf. Learning "Z" test above)	Significant improvement
Lemmel and Hartwig (1940)	Nonsense syllable learning	Improved
Willet (1957)	Nonsense syllable learning (by serial anticipation method)	Improvement, but not statistically significant

EFFECTS ON LEARNING

In Man

Most of the work with the amphetamines has been concerned with the effects on performance rather than on learning and the data on the latter from human studies are scanty. The unsatisfactory evidence summarized in Table XVII.4 indicates that some improvement in learning may occur, but the most recent and the most adequate study of serial anticipation learning of nonsense syllables (Willett, 1957) did not show that the drug (10 mg *d*-amphetamine) led to a statistically significant improvement, nor were anticipatory errors increased. The serial position effect was likewise unaltered, an unexpected finding in view of the role which has been attributed to reactive inhibition (I_R). There was, however, a statistically significant decrease in the area between the curves of first success and last failure, and similarly a decrease in the number of fluctuations at the threshold of recall. As part of the same study, Franks and Trouton (1957) studied the effects of various drugs on the conditioned eyeblink response; subjects who had received d-amphetamine sulphate before acquired the responses more rapidly and lost them more slowly than those who had received a *placebo* or amylobarbitone sodium.

In Animals

There is evidence that conditioned reflexes in both rats and dogs are enhanced by amphetamine (Wentinck, 1938; Alpern *et al.*, 1943; Skinner and Heron, 1937).

Minkowski (1939) found that rats learnt a maze less readily under the influence of the drug, but the drive used was hunger, and it is well known that amphetamine reduces appetite. More recently Ewing *et al.* (1952) used thirst as the drive and found that whether the rats were injected with an amphetamine (e.g. 1 mg/kg d-amphetamine) or saline: "All groups reached a point of maximum proficiency with minimum errors on the seventh trial. . . . Thus there is no evidence that this treatment had any influence on maze-learning ability." Larger doses resulted in impairment. Ewing *et al.*, however, admit that they "have not eliminated the possibility that there might be a proper small dose that would increase the ability of rats to learn the maze."

Effects on Rote Memory

Amphetamine does not appear to improve digit span or rote memory (Carl and Turner, 1939; Wunderle, 1941).

Effects on "Attention" and Vigilance Tests

The various tests of "attention" probably measure different functions, but they are dealt with here for convenience. Barmack and Seitz (1940) found no evidence that the drug increased the "span of attention" for letters, but there was a marked practice effect. Lemmel and Hartwig (1940) found that amphetamine or methylamphetamine enabled subjects to reproduce correctly more drawings which had been exposed tachistoscopically; they claimed that there was less evidence of rational distortion but more of emotional distortion in subjects under the influence of the drug.

Mackworth (1948) reported the effects of 10 mg amphetamine sulphate on the performance of a task requiring sustained attention. In the Clock test of visual vigilance, a response is made as quickly as possible on each occasion that a clock hand gives a double jump instead of a single one. The reaction-time to these double jumps increases sharply after half an hour of watching. This increase could be prevented either by supplying the subjects with a continuous knowledge of the results of the test, or by supplying them with amphetamine. "It is clear that when Benzedrine was given, not only were the subjects able to detect more signals, but they were slightly quicker at responding to the signals they did notice." (1948, p. 43.) "There was no sign, however, that this Benzedrine level of efficiency was any better than the normal optimum without Benzedrine" (op. cit., p. 32). Incidentally, no "hangover" effects from the drug (10 mg) were observed; the control run score taken the day after a Benzedrine day was no worse than that taken the day after a control run (op. cit., p. 33).

Sensory and Perceptual Functions

There appears to have been little work done on the effects of amphetamines on sensory functions, and, therefore, the findings reported here are rather miscellaneous.

The decrease in flicker fusion threshold towards the end of the day can be more than counteracted by amphetamine (Simonson *et al.*, 1941). Roback *et al.* (1952) claimed that the increase in threshold was proportional to the dosage of d-amphetamine. Numerous other studies have shown a similar effect with amphetamine (or a decrease of F.F.T. with depressant), e.g. Landis and Zubin (1951), Seashore and Ivy (1953). (For a review of F.F.T., *see* Simonson and Brozek, 1952, and for an annotated bibliography, Landis, 1953.)

Yudkin (1941) found a transient increase in dark adaptation.

Wunderle (1941) found that subjects tended to underestimate the length of periods of time under the influence of methylamphetamine, in accordance with Turner and Carl's (1939) finding with amphetamine. The rate of fluctuation of a Necker cube did not differ significantly as a result of administration of d-amphetamine, a *placebo* or amylobarbitone sodium (Eysenck, Holland and Trouton, 1957b).

Reaction-time

Although Lemmel and Hartwig failed to find any effect on reaction-time, Thornton *et al.* (1939) found that amphetamine had a more marked effect than caffeine on the shortening of reaction-time. The drug affects the decrements produced by prolonged vigilance (Mackworth, 1948).

Effects on Motor Functions

General Activity and Speed

Using the revolving cage method, Searle and Brown (1939) found that a 3 mg/kg dose of amphetamine produced a greater increase in the activity of rats than either a 1·5 mg/kg or a 4·5 mg/kg dose. This illustrates one of the problems encountered in research with this group of drugs as, owing to wide individual variations, it is impossible to predict the optimal dose. Tainter (1943) also found a marked increase in activity with amphetamine, although caffeine had little effect. Chance (1947) reported that curious social behaviour occurred in rats after large doses, but the validity of his findings has been questioned (Ross *et al.*, 1951, and Gunn and Gurd, 1940).

Although an increase in general activity has often been observed in man clinically, this does not appear to have been quantified in relation to dosage. However, Golla *et al.* (1940) timed various familiar performances by subjects, without their knowledge. Both methylamphetamine and amphetamine increased the speed with which the majority of subjects signed their name, and similarly the speed of walking across a room and throwing darts. In the "overt" test, speed of drawing was increased, and also "speed of decision" as measured by the time taken in choosing a column of figures to add.

EFFECTS ON MOTOR TASKS

Skilled Tasks

The effects of the amphetamines on certain skilled tasks are summarized in Table XVII.5. Unless the

sional Pursuit Test. In this the subject is required "to correct for the random drift of four simulated aircraft instruments from their null positions by the timely and appropriate manipulation of four simulated aircraft controls. A timer is activated only when all four instruments are concurrently maintained in their null positions. A cycling system meters out alternate work trials (one minute) and rest periods (fifteen seconds) for any desired span of time" (Hauty and Payne, 1955). The apparatus resembles the controls of an aeroplane, but not as closely as does the Cambridge Cockpit; performance on it has a correlation of 0·3 with basic flying proficiency.

In most of the studies of work decrement, a preliminary practice period is given (fifty minutes), then a rest (ten minutes), followed by a final work period of four hours or more. "Under normal operating conditions nearly all subjects exhibit significant decrement during the first two hours of the final period" (Payne and Hauty, 1955). Various factors influencing the level of performance and its rate of decrement have been studied. Dextroamphetamine sulphate is the most effective agent for preventing or counteracting the work decrement (Fig. 17.4). The role of the drug was considered to be "that of protecting a normally progressing learning function against the cumulative burden of such factors as attitudes of aversion, boredom, physical discomfort and possibly the physiological fatigue of sensorimotor

TABLE XVII.5
THE EFFECTS OF AMPHETAMINES ON SKILLED MOTOR TASKS

Author	Test	Result
Barmack (1939)	Poffenberger pursuit meter by practised subjects for two hours	15 mg amphetamine sulphate retarded the development of inaccuracy and also "retarded the development of a condition leading to a report of boredom. . . ."
Davis (1948)	Cambridge cockpit	With doses of 10, 15 and 20 mg amphetamine: "No effects were observed in the majority of cases." (The drug tended to reduce deterioration through lack of sleep, but otherwise did not reduce errors.)
Payne and Hauty (1953, 1955*a*, 1955*b*)	USAF SAM Multidimensional pursuit test	*d*-amphetamine is the most effective agent for counteracting work decrement (*see* text)
Eysenck, Casey and Trouton (1957)	Pursuit rotor	*d*-amphetamine increased performance as compared with the *placebo* group, this effect becoming more marked as the experiment proceeded

task is prolonged, or the subject suffering from lack of sleep, there is little effect.

Several large-scale experiments, mostly utilizing a factorial design have been carried out recently by Payne (1953) and Payne and Hauty (1953, 1954, 1955), Payne and Moore (1955), and Hauty and Payne (1954, 1955), mostly utilizing the USAF SAM Multidimen-

systems" (op. cit.). However, there was some evidence that the effects of the stimulant could not be ascribed to "concomitant euphoric changes in task attitudes." That is to say, "an indoctrination designed to solicit the most favourable attitudes towards the task at hand" failed to alter the rate of decrement of performance although it did improve the feelings and attitudes (Payne and Hauty, 1953). By a combination of "conditions involving specific cue feed-back, motivation feed-back, and cerebral stimulation" a striking improvement in performance can be brought about (Payne and Hauty, 1955c).

Relatively Unskilled Tasks

Ergograph. The amphetamines can delay work decrement on various types of ergograph (Lehmann *et al.*, 1939; Alles and Fergen, 1942; Knoefel, 1943;

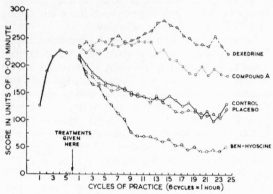

FIG. 17.4. EFFECTS OF PHARMACOLOGICAL TREATMENTS UPON TASK PERFORMANCE
(From Payne and Hauty, 1955)

Cuthbertson and Knox, 1947) and can help to counteract a moderate degree of deterioration. However, if the subject has worked to a state of exhaustion, e.g. on a bicycle ergometer until no longer able to maintain the needle on the dial in a position corresponding to 54 r.p.m., intravenous injection of amphetamine (10–15 mg) or methylamphetamine (5 mg) does not increase the rate of recovery, whereas injection of 0·5 G caffeine sodium benzoate does (Foltz *et al.*, 1943). Moreover Lehmann *et al.* (1939) considered that the drug was likely to be dangerous in heavy workers because it might lead to the "consumption of the functional reserves which the organism retains as protection against too extensive exhaustion."

Steadiness. Most of the tests of steadiness have required that the subject should place a stylus into a series of apertures of graded sizes, the number of contacts in a given period being electrically recorded. The methods used have varied and the results have been rather conflicting. The topic has recently been illuminated by the discovery that steadiness is not unitary. This conclusion is based on two very different types of evidence, factor analysis and high speed photography. Hauty (1954), who has investigated the effects of drugs on hand steadiness, describes two different components: (1) a large slow tremor involving "the co-ordinative activities of those per-

ceptual and masculature systems which determine the precision of manual movements in arriving at a fixed point in space and either maintaining this point or moving to successive fixed points. . . . Its initiation and conduct is dependent upon the integrative functions at the cortical level." Superimposed on this is (2) a fine rapid tremor "resulting from the imbalanced state of neuromuscular activity and, contrary to earlier concept, is considered as being causally dissociated from cortical activity."

There being evidence that amplitude and frequency of tremor are inversely related, it was argued that in the stylus and graded aperture type of apparatus "the score obtained at the smallest aperture of the apparatus to be used should consist, therefore, of a considerable if not predominant proportion of [fine] tremor movements," whereas the coarser "co-ordinative activities component" would be derived from the scores on the larger apertures.

Sixty-six subjects were first given three practice trials (each trial consisted of having to insert the stylus in turn into the six graded apertures and to maintain it there for thirty seconds). The score for each aperture was recorded separately. The subjects were then randomly assigned to one of six groups, receiving (*a*) 5 mg and (*b*) 10 mg dextroamphetamine sulphate; (*c*) 100 mg and (*d*) 200 mg quinalbarbitone (Seconal); (*e*) a *placebo*, (*f*) no drug. They were tested at hourly intervals. It was found that the barbiturate reduced the fine tremor but adversely affected the co-ordinative activities, whereas dextroamphetamine increased the fine tremor but did not significantly affect the latter. Doubling the dose of stimulant had no significant effect, but the larger dose of depressant led to a further significant reduction in the fine tremor and also to an increase in the coarse tremor. The *placebo* group showed significantly greater tremor ($p < 0.05$) than the group which did not receive any drug, presumably a manifestation of apprehension.

Tapping. Tapping tests usually measure not only the speed (maximal or preferred) of movement, but also varying amounts of dexterity and co-ordination. If the test is prolonged, fatigue or reactive inhibition is a further factor which is involved.

Simonson and Enzer (1941) claimed that the rapidity of pressing a button was a measure of the "maximum frequency of motor impulses," and showed that this was increased by the administration of amphetamine. Carl and Turner (1939) used a dotting test and found there was an improvement, especially in accuracy, with small doses of amphetamine, but large doses had a deleterious effect. Thornton, Holck and Smith (1939) using a test involving tapping alternately on two adjacent copper plates for three different periods, as well as tests of reaction-time, handgrip and steadiness, found that the subjects made better average scores on the days when they received amphetamine. Only three subjects were used but they had eight practice sessions followed by over twenty experimental sessions each, during which the effects of amphetamine were compared with those of caffeine and a *placebo*. Cranston, Zubin and Landis (1952) also included a tapping test in their battery,

1947; Tyler, 1947) but not necessarily the performance (e.g. Foltz *et al.*, 1943*a*; Somerville, 1946), except in lengthy or boring tests (e.g. Tyler, 1947), especially those requiring sustained alertness (e.g. Seashore and Ivy, 1953; Mackworth, 1948). Unpleasant subjective effects appear to be less common in those who are fatigued (Alwall, 1943), although various psychological disturbances may occur, even

TABLE XVII.6

THE EFFECTS OF AMPHETAMINES IN PROLONGED EXERCISE

Author	Study	Result
Alwall (1943) . . .	700 soldiers doing hard exercises for 3 nights and the intervening days, with little sleep	(a) 20 or 30 mg amphetamine or (b) 18 mg methylamphetamine mostly gave a more favourable response than the *placebo* and with no more side effects. (b) was *not* twice as potent as (a).
Foltz *et al.* (1943) . .	23 untrained subjects with heavy knapsacks on their backs had to step up and down on to a stand every 3 sec until fatigued. Tested after (a) 10 mg amphetamine (b) 0·5 G caffeine (c) *placebo*	No significant differences between (a), (b) and (c) but practice effect was marked. "It is evident, then, that training had a much greater effect on performance than did the drugs."
Somerville (1948) . .	50 soldiers and 73 officers during prolonged operations	Even 40 mg amphetamine had little effect.
Cuthbertson and Knox (1947)	Two companies of an infantry battalion, on 48-hour operations. One receiving amphetamine, the other *placebo*	70 per cent receiving the drug thought that it diminished fatigue, compared with 23 per cent in control group.
Tyler (1947) . . .	20 controlled experiments on volunteers from the Services, deprived of sleep for 24–112 hours and required to do heavy activity. Barbiturates or amphetamines given in small doses. Battery of tests administered each evening	"In general where a psychomotor test was of relatively short duration . . . no significant changes in performance occurred even after 110 hours wakefulness."
Seashore and Ivy (1953) .	Several experiments on soldiers after prolonged work or marching. Tests of speed and precision, tremor, sway and co-ordination, etc.	*Placebos*—little effect. Caffeine—improved subjective reports but motor performance little improved. Effects more marked with the amphetamines.

but analysis of variance failed to reveal any statistically significant effects of the various drugs used.[1]

EFFECTS ON MARCHING, PROLONGED WAKEFULNESS, ETC.

The full evidence concerning the usefulness of the amphetamines in military operations has presumably not been made public and the evidence that is available is conflicting (*see* Table XVII.6). From the work of the authors quoted here it appears probable that: amphetamines have beneficial effects chiefly in those who have been deprived of sleep, improving the attitude to the task[2] (e.g. Cuthbertson and Knox,

[1] Factor analysis was also used in this study, but their procedure is difficult to justify.
[2] Tyler (1947) found that a small dose of a drug, such as amphetamine, markedly decreased the proportion of men deciding to discontinue the experiment.

psychotic episodes resembling "acute schizophrenia," which were observed by Tyler (1947) in some of those who had received the *placebo*, and not amphetamine. Undesirable side effects were noted by Cuthbertson and Knox (1947), and Russell Davis (1947, 1948) has pointed out the risk of causing impairment of judgement in those who are driving cars or aeroplanes.

SUMMARY AND CONCLUSIONS

Some of Carl and Turner's conclusions (1939) remain valid—

1. "Moderate (10 mg) dosage of Benzedrine produces a tendency toward accelerated reaction in psychomotor output, so long as the execution of the actual physical movements does not require thinking or deliberation. Heavy dosage (10 mg added to 20 mg) seemingly produces a retardation in these functions

at a point following ingestion by about thirty minutes —a retardation which persists for another forty minutes.

2. "Accuracy in most of the tests seems to be relatively unaffected by doses of ordinary size (10 mg), even though speed increases."

3. The tasks most favourably affected by the amphetamines are those which are prolonged and boring, the effect of the drug tending to prevent or counteract the work decrement or loss of alertness, and becoming relatively more pronounced as the work is continued.

4. The drug usually produces a more favourable attitude towards the task, but this does not necessarily correlate with improvement.

5. Associative functions (e.g. association to nonsense syllables, continuous addition, etc.) are more liable to be improved than cognitive functions such as intelligence, or learning.

6. Individual variations are considerable, and it is possible that a given dose can have opposite effects on the same activities in different subjects.

7. The relation between the response to amphetamine and personality has not been elucidated, nor has it been established whether there are qualitative differences between the various amphetamines in their psychological effects.

In Hullian terms, the amphetamines appear both to increase drive (D) and to decrease reactive inhibition (I_R), any improvement in initial performance being largely attributable to the former and any improvement during a prolonged task being attributable to the latter effect.

Caffeine and other Stimulants

Caffeine (1,3,7-trimethylxanthine) is a central stimulant contained in several drinks such as cocoa and maté, as well as tea and coffee. In some of these dimethylxanthine, theobromine and theophylline, are also present; their properties are somewhat similar and they are all diuretics. They tend to relax smooth muscle but to improve the contraction of voluntary muscle by a direct local action in addition to their central effect. There is also a direct local action on the blood vessels and heart, which tends to be antagonistic to the effects produced by stimulation of the medulla. It is therefore difficult to predict the total effects of the drug on, for example, bloodpressure, which may remain unchanged in spite of changes in the circulating system.

Caffeine is usually administered orally or intravenously in the form of its soluble double salt, caffeine and sodium benzoate, the dosage being gr 2–10 (120–600 mg). A cup or two of tea or coffee is said to contain about 150–250 mg caffeine. Absorption is rapid and "appreciable blood levels persist for six to twelve hours" (Goodman and Gilman, 1955). Habitu-

ation and tolerance may occur, and chronic poisoning, with insomnia and restlessness, has been described.

As most of the work on the psychological effects of caffeine dates from before 1940 and is included in earlier reviews, it will only be briefly presented.

The early studies on the effects of caffeine on fatigue by Hoch, Kraepelin, Mosso and many others about sixty years ago are described by Rivers (1908), whose own experiments confirmed "in general,—the conclusion reached by all previous workers—that caffeine stimulates the capacity for muscular work; and it is clear that this increase is not due to the various psychical factors of interest, sensory stimulation, and suggestion which the experiments were specially designed to exclude" (cf. Foltz et al., 1942). He considered the chief interest of his experiments was the "clear demonstration of the very different way in which the same doses of the drug may act on different persons." It is also of interest that his earlier experiments were conducted without the use of placebos, but this deficiency was soon remedied.

Hollingworth's work, sponsored by the Coca-Cola Company, has been largely confirmed subsequently. (See Table XVII.7.) "One of the most interesting facts shown by these experiments is the complete absence of any traces of secondary depression or of any sort of secondary reaction consequent upon the stimulation which is so strikingly present in many of the tests" (Hollingworth, 1912a). As with the amphetamines, the relation between dosage and effect is not always linear, too large a dose usually resulting in impairment. The main effects are shown in Tables XVII.7 and XVII.8. The finding by Hollingworth (1912) that small doses of caffeine tended to result in retardation of the discrimination reaction-time, whereas larger doses increased the speed of reaction appears inconsistent with the effects on, for example, co-ordination which was improved by small doses and impaired by larger doses of caffeine. The explanation given by Hollingworth was that small amounts of caffeine resulted in increased briskness and an increased liability to false reactions, and that the retardation was due to caution in trying to avoid these (cf. Thornton et al., 1939).

There is evidence that caffeine improves conditioning, but Lashley (1917) found that caffeine retarded the learning of a circular maze by rats. Tolman (1917) carried out a series of experiments in which gr $1\frac{1}{2}$ of caffeine or a placebo were administered on alternate days two and a half to three hours before the subjects learned nonsense syllables. He found that there was less reactive inhibition engendered in learning the relatively pleasant lists and that the number of consonants learned was greater for the caffeine than for the non-caffeine groups. Clark Hull (1935) returned to this problem. In his controlled experiments, gr 5 of caffeine were given to eight males three and a half hours before learning a list of sixteen syllables. With caffeine there were more anticipatory displacements, but there was a mean reduction in rate of learning, amounting to 2–3 per cent (although this was not statistically reliable). The gaps in the tables reveal

Other Stimulants

Other stimulants include cocaine which, being unsuitable for psychological experimentation, will be omitted,[1] and two recently introduced drugs. One is benzhydrol, x-(2-piperidyl) benzhydrol hydrochloride or Meratran, which is isomeric with Frenquel, a

TABLE XVII.7

MAIN STUDIES ON PSYCHOLOGICAL EFFECTS OF CAFFEINE

Author	Main details of experiments	Results
Hollingworth (1912)	16 subjects were tested over a period of 40 days with and without caffeine. Tests included— 1. Tapping 2. Steadiness 3. Co-ordination (3 hole test of combined accuracy and speed) 4. Typewriting (by one subject) 5. Colour naming 6. Opposites 7. Calculation 8. Discrimination reaction times 9. Cancellation	Effects of caffeine— Improvement. Tremor. Improvement with small doses and retardation with large. Speed increased by 1–3 gr and decreased by 4–6 gr but errors decreased by both. All improved. "Small amounts . . . tend to produce retardation. . . . Larger amounts . . . produce within 2 hours after the dose a stimulation so great that retardation following small doses does not appear." Results equivocal.
Gilliland and Nelson (1939)	5 subjects given 12 practice periods on a battery of tests, before being tested 20, 100 and 140 min after coffee or a decaffeinated beverage was given. Pulse, tapping, reaction-time Adding, memory span Steadiness (Bryan tracing board)	Effects of caffeine were most marked during second testing period. All significantly decreased. Increased, but not consistently. Decreased.
Barmack (1940)	Adding 29 subjects under different conditions for 8 15-min periods	Caffeine had a negligible effect on initial rate of addition, regardless of the time of its administration, but exerted a beneficial effect when alertness would otherwise have become blunted.
Cheney (1936)	10 subjects practised for a week on pressing the key corresponding to any one of three coloured lights, testing being carried out every half hour during the mornings. Comparisons between final normal day when subject received water, the coffee day, the caffeine day and final control day (water and starch capsule)	Reaction-time decreased only if the dosage of caffeine exceeded 3 mg/kg body weight. No effect found after 24 hours. (Statistical methods not used.)
Stanley and Schlosberg (1953)	Carefully designed experiment to assess effects on (a) Simple and (b) Complex reaction-times	Decrease in both (a) and (b) immediately after drinking tea in habitual tea-drinkers. Steadiness most affected.

how unsystematically the psychological effects of caffeine have been studied. Owing to differences in tests used, some caution is necessary in attempting to compare the effects of caffeine with those of amphetamine, but it appears that the effects of small doses of caffeine are usually less marked and less consistent than those of a small dose of amphetamine.

tranquillizer (Fabing and Hawkins, 1955). The other is Ritalin or phenyl-(x-piperidyl)-acetic acid methyl ester. Both are supposed not to be sympathomimetic.

[1] Strychnine has also been studied, but no effects on Hollingworth's tests were apparent. (Poffenberger, 1914.) However, Lashley (1917) found that large doses of strychnine produced improvement in both learning and performance of a maze by rats.

Little experimental psychological work has been done on either. Drassdo and Schmidt (1954) found some evidence that Ritalin tended to counteract the effects of a barbiturate on arithmetic. Kleemeier, Rich and Justiss (1955) investigated the effects of Meratran on the performance of senile patients on tests of visual perception, sorting, tapping, verbal output, time estimation, figure drawing and hand strength. Each patient was tested weekly, twice with the drug and twice without. "Although there was a

TABLE XVII.8

A COMPARISON OF THE PSYCHOLOGICAL EFFECTS OF CAFFEINE AND AMPHETAMINE

Author	Findings on caffeine	Findings on amphetamine (*see* section on amphetamine for references)
Cognitive functions		
Cattell (1930)	Intelligence and Reasoning (*see* Jellinek and McFarland, 1940) Learning (conditioning improved as with amphetamine)	Slight but insignificant increase. No improvement.
Lashley (1917)	Caffeine retarded the learning of a circular maze by rats	Maze learning retarded except by small doses.
Tolman (1917)	Nonsense syllable learning. Less retroactive inhibition, and number of consonants learned was greater after caffeine than after a *placebo*	Slight but non-significant improvement.
Hull (1935)	Nonsense syllable learning. More anticipatory displacements after caffeine and a slight mean reduction in rate of learning	Slight but non-significant improvement in learning. No increase in anticipatory errors.
Associative functions and psychomotor tests		
Hollingworth (1912)	Colour naming improved	—
	Opposites test improved	—
	Typewriting (1 subject)—increase in speed with small doses, decrease with large	—
	Calculation test—increase in speed with small doses, decrease with large.	(*See* below)
	Cancellation test—equivocal	Probably improved.
Gilliland and Nelson (1939)	Memory span improved	No evidence of improvement.
	Rate of adding improved (neither consistently)	May be some improvement in simple calculation such as continuous adding but the
Barmack (1940)	Adding not improved initially, but only when alertness would have become blunted	discrepancy between the *placebo* and the drug performances becomes greater as the task is more prolonged.
Reaction-time (= R.T.)		
Hollingworth (1912)	Discrimination R.T. retarded by small doses, stimulated by large.	
Gilliland and Nelson (1939)	Simple auditory R.T. significantly decreased	
Cheney (1935, 1936)	Discrimination R.T. (pressing keys to coloured lights). R.T. decreased only if caffeine > 3 mg/kg body weight	
Stanley and Schlosberg (1958)	Immediate decrease in both simple and complex R.T. after drinking tea in habitual tea-drinkers	
Thornton *et al.* (1939)	Effects on R.T. not significant	
Motor functions		
Rivers (1908) (reviewing work of Hoch, Kraepelin, Mosso and others, and quoting his own)	Improves capacity for muscular work, e.g. on ergograph	Amphetamines apparently less effective in increasing rate of recovery if practised subjects have worked to exhaustion on a bicycle ergograph.
Foltz *et al.* (1943)	Confirmed the above, used more refined techniques. Co-ordination test improved with small doses, retarded with large	Co-ordination may be improved if impaired by lack of sleep.
Hollingworth 1912)	Tapping improved. Steadiness decreased	
Gilliland and Nelson (1939)	Tapping significantly decreased. Steadiness decreased	
Thornton *et al.* (1939)	Handgrip strengthened. Steadiness decreased	Amphetamine slightly more effective. Steadiness increased.

general tendency for increases in amount of production on the tests under the experimental condition, in only figure drawing, hand strength and time estimation did the group performance under the drug condition seem to be significantly altered."

One further study is of interest because it was specifically designed to test Eysenck's (1957) theory of drug action. Sinha (1957), using response alternation in rats as his measure of reactive inhibition, employed Meratran as the stimulant drug, amytal as the depressant drug, as well as a *placebo*, all drugs being administered in difference sequence to the sixty-four animals making up the experimental population. The apparatus used was a simple T maze with food always present at both ends of the maze. Runways were attached to the stem of the maze in such a way that, depending on the point of the maze where they were started, rats were required to make one, two, or three right or left turns before reaching the choice-point of the T. It was predicted (1) that the greater the number of turns in any given direction preceding the choice-point, the greater would be the tendency of the rats to turn the other way at the choice-point. On the hypothesis that this tendency was due to reactive inhibition and that reactive inhibition was increased by amytal and decreased by Meratran, it was predicted (2) that the animals' tendency to turn in the direction *opposite* to that which had been forced upon them by the maze before reaching the choice-point would be *strengthened* by amytal and *reduced* by Meratran. Fig. 17.5 shows the results of this experiment, and it will be seen that the prediction is borne out by the experimental results.

The Barbiturates

In the half century since the first barbiturate was introduced, these drugs have largely displaced the other hypnotic drugs. Chemically they are derivatives of barbituric acid, which is the product of the condensation of malonic acid and urea. Over 2,500 derivatives have been prepared by substituting various radicals for the hydrogen atoms, which has provided an opportunity to correlate the chemical structure with the pharmacological effects, but little work has been done on the differences between the psychological effects of the various compounds.

The drugs are classified according to their duration of action, e.g. (1) long-, (2) intermediate-, (3) short- and (4) ultra short-acting (Goodman and Gilman, 1955, p. 138).

Examples of these different classes are (1) phenobarbitone, (2) amylobarbitone (amytal) (3) pentobarbitone (Nembutal) and quinalbarbitone (Seconal), and (4) thiopentone (Pentothal). Terminology is confusing as even the official nomenclatures of the U.S.P. and B.P. differ, the former preferring

endings in "-al," instead of the British "-one." As sodium amylobarbitone happens to have been used more extensively than its competitors in the studies reported here the descriptions will chiefly apply to this drug. It is also known as "amobarbital sodium" U.S.P. and "Sodium Amytal" (Lilly) and should not be confused with amylobarbitone ("amytal") of which

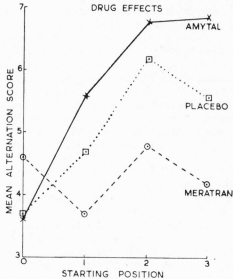

FIG. 17.5. ALTERNATION SCORES AFTER 0, 1, 2, OR 3 PREVIOUS TURNS AS AFFECTED BY DRUGS
(From Sinha, 1957)

it is the sodium salt; the effects of amylobarbitone sodium[1] (sedative dose gr 1 orally, hypnotic dose gr 3–gr 9) appear fairly soon and are of medium duration, whereas those of amylobarbitone (sedative dose gr ¼ to gr ¾, hypnotic gr 1½ to gr 3) are of medium onset and longer duration.

The main effect is, of course, depression of the central nervous system in degrees varying from mild sedation through sleep to anaesthesia. The cortex, hypothalamus and particularly the ascending reticular activating system (Magoun, 1954; Arduini and Arduini, 1954) appear to be the sites which are most sensitive to the effects of the drug.

Barbiturates do not have much effect on the pain threshold except in doses sufficient to impair consciousness (Wolff et al., 1941). "It may be inferred . . . that whatever salutary effects may follow the administration of Sodium Amytal in painful conditions, they do not stem from the blocking of pain perception. They must occur either because of alterations in the reaction of the subject to the painful experience or from interruption of the mechanism responsible for

[1] Amylobarbitone sodium will be referred to as amytal.

the noxious stimulus" (Wolf and Ripley, 1948; *see also* Beecher, 1947; Wikler, 1950; Keats *et al.*, 1950).

Much work has been done on the EEG effects: "In general, the EEG records obtained under hypnotic doses of barbiturates in animals and man are similar to those of natural sleep" (Goodman and Gilman, 1955). Brazier and Finesinger (1945) investigated the effects of intravenous barbiturates on the EEGs of thirty-two patients. In all subjects the EEG record showed the development of high voltage fast activity. In those receiving larger doses per kg body weight a second effect developed; this consisted of slow delta waves (3–4 per sec). In every subject the high voltage fast activity appeared first in the frontal leads, then in the parietal and finally in the occipital, and disappeared in the reverse order (i.e. the phylogenetically most recent were the most vulnerable). In the first few minutes, at the stage of maximal action, the patient may be unconscious without the appearance of any of the brain waves typical of sleep. These may appear later, but on arousal there is a reversion to the high voltage fast activity which is specific for barbiturates. They considered that these results were compatible with the hypothesis that the drug had two effects: (1) interference with the dehydrogenase systems and (2) a change in the permeability of the cell membrane (*see also* Brazier, 1954).

The barbiturates have peripheral as well as central effects, chiefly on the antonomic nervous system. Amylobarbitone in anaesthetic doses has a parasympatholytic action, tending to block the vagal effects; it may also interfere with "the liberation of the adrenergic mediator into the blood stream" (Goodman and Gilman, op. cit., p. 132). Hexobarbitone (Evipan) is also parasympatholytic (Emmelin, 1941) but Trewethie (1953) found that Nembutal (pentobarbitone sodium) had a blocking effect on the sympathetic nervous system peripherally. To what extent such effects contribute to the clinical diminution of anxiety is uncertain.

Not all barbiturates are depressants on anticonvulsants. For example, sodium 5-ethyl-5-(1,3-dimethyl-butyl) barbiturate has stimulant and convulsant properties. Gottleib (1951) found that this drug tended to diminish depression and to cause euphoria. He also put forward the view that amytal has a stimulating action on the central nervous system, which is masked by the hypnotic effect when larger amounts are given and that this may be responsible for the euphorogenic effect. Pennes (1954) administered the drug to schizophrenics and found it to have a beneficial effect on symptoms but also to cause convulsions. The pharmacological effects were fully investigated by Domino *et al.* (1955) who found evidence of depressant effects in addition to the other properties.

The drugs may be given by mouth or by injection, the effects of oral administration of amytal becoming apparent in twenty to fifty minutes and of intravenous injection (e.g. of Pentothal) almost immediately. The drug soon becomes distributed to all tissues, fatty tissues being of especial importance in this connexion. The slower and longer acting compounds, such as barbitone, tend to be excreted in the urine, whereas the more rapidly acting compounds (e.g. those with branched sidechains) tend to be broken down in the liver.

The chief uses of the barbiturates, besides sedation and hypnosis, are for the control of epilepsy, for inducing anaesthesia, and, in psychiatry, for narco-analysis. Habituation, tolerance and addiction may occur (Isbell and Fraser, 1950; Tichy, 1953), and there is a well marked abstinence syndrome.

CLINICAL EFFECTS

Numerous articles have appeared on the clinical effects of barbiturates, and in particular of sodium amylobarbitone; most of them are purely descriptive.

Effects of Barbiturates on Mood, etc.

One of the first to investigate the effects of an intravenous barbiturate (amytal) on the mood of normal as well as of psychiatric subjects was Lindemann (1932, 1934; Lindemann and Malamud, 1934). He found that the drug tended to cause an increase in rapport and communicativeness and also an increased interest in the outer world. "Individual differences manifested themselves in talkativeness in one subject and more quiet serenity in other subjects." There was also a "shifting of the emotional state along the depression-elation scale in the direction of elation." Among the physiological effects noted were slurring of speech, mydriasis, a fall in blood-pressure and pulse rate and an increased pain threshold (but cf. above). In neurotic subjects there is usually a diminution of any anxiety present (Delay *et al.*, 1948a) and, with larger doses, abreaction sometimes occurs.

There also appear to be differences between the effects of different barbiturates. For example, Delay *et al.* (1948a) state that Pentothal is inferior to amytal in reducing anxiety. Wendt (1954) using an adjective check-list has found consistent differences between amytal and Seconal. "First, 200 mg of amobarbital causes the subjects to describe themselves in this way: *more:* drowsy, lightheaded, tired; *less:* cheerful, contented, co-operative, earnest, easygoing, energetic, enterprising, responsive, self-confident, and sympathetic. . . . Under Secobarbital, 100 mg the *more:* amiable, courageous, decisive, elated, energetic, exultant, forceful, responsive; *less:* obedient, relaxed, quiet and satisfied." (In Wendt's studies which have been carried out in conjunction with Nowlis and others the effects of the social situation have been carefully controlled.)

There is some evidence that amytal increases the degree of extraversion (as predicted by Eysenck's theory). Laverty and Franks (1956) found that there was a significant increase in the R score of Guilford's S.T.D.C.R. after amytal, but this may be attributable to the fact that the number of "yes" replies was increased by the drug.

Effects in Relation to Psychiatric Disorders

Freyhan (1952) after investigating over two hundred patients by means of narcoanalysis with amytal concluded: "There are no similar kinds of response and there are no clear relationships to specific kinds of personality disorder." Likewise Wolf and Ripley (1948) conclude after studies on seven hundred patients: "It is clear from these data that Sodium Amytal has no direct predictable effect on the mood and attitude of the subject." In neither of these researches, however, was any adequate assessment of personality made.

Use in Diagnosis

Hoch (1946) considered that barbiturates such as amytal were reliable diagnostic agents which deserved much more widespread use. Administered intravenously, they may be of value in differentiating between—

1. organic and functional psychiatric disorders
2. functional disorders and malingering (Ludwig, 1944; Ripley and Wolf, 1947)
3. psychoses and neuroses (e.g. between hysterical amnesia and aphonia and schizophrenic mutism) (Sullivan, 1942; Hoch and Polatin, 1949)
4. "borderline" schizophrenia and psychopathic personality (Donahue *et al.*, 1948)
5. manic and catatonic stupors (Berrington, 1939).

They may also aid in diagnosis when used in psychotherapy by enabling further information to be elicited (e.g. Wedge and Moulton, 1950) or in improving contact (Smith and Schwartz, 1934). Thorner (1935a) found that 42 per cent of 207 patients "expressed ideas not previously indicated." (He does not, however, state what were the proportions of the various diagnostic groups included.) Bellak (1949) found oral barbiturates useful in overcoming resistance in psychotherapy, and in helping the patient to free-associate; he explained this facilitation as due to a decrease in anxiety with a concomitant decrease in the need for repression.

This increase in talkativeness has led to the appellation "truth drug" being applied to the barbiturates. But there is no reason to suppose that what is said under these conditions is more likely to be true than what is said in an undrugged state. The "memories" of episodes, such as alleged sexual traumata, recovered during psychoanalysis are often spurious. This is supposed not to detract from their value from the psychoanalytical point of view, but such memories are worthless from the legal point of view. It is likely that similar considerations apply to attempts at recalling past experiences after the injection of a barbiturate. Intravenous barbiturates may, of course, be of therapeutic or diagnostic value in criminals (Adatto, 1949) but Gerson and Victoroff (1948), who studied the validity of confessions obtained under the influence of a barbiturate, concluded that "there is no such thing as a 'truth serum'. . . . The validity of confessed material may be seriously limited by fantasies and delusions which are indistinguishable from truth." The chief indications appear to be for investigating cases of suspected malingering, loss of memory, and false avowals of guilt, or when great fear is present. An intravenous barbiturate, particularly if given in conjunction with an amphetamine, may also make an uncommunicative subject less cautious and more loquacious, but, to discover whether the utterances are true or false, some independent criterion is necessary.

Barbiturates and Brain Damage

The greater susceptibility to barbiturates of those with organic rather than functional psychiatric disorders was reported by Lorenze *et al.* (1934). Since then, various attempts have been made to use these drugs for detecting brain damage. It should be noted that this fact, if substantiated, would be in good agreement with Eysenck's theory (1957), as he posits increased inhibitory effects as a direct function of brain damage. (Cf. also Chapter 14 on brain damage.)

Berg (1949) gave hexobarbitone (Evipan) to normal subjects in 5, 10 and 20 per cent of the estimated narcotic dose and found that the flicker fusion threshold was unaltered; but, in patients having brain injuries, 10 per cent of the narcotic dose resulted in a decrease in flicker fusion.

Other tests have been based on the effects on the EEG: for example, Witter and Müller (1953) found a correlation between the severity of brain damage and the amount of increase of EEG activity after administration of Evipan (cf. Bergman *et al.*, 1953–4). The effects on the EEG in functional psychiatric disorders are discussed in the next section.

Weinstein and his colleagues claim that amytal is of value as a test of brain damage (Weinstein and Kahn, 1951; Weinstein *et al.*, 1953; Weinstein and Malitz, 1954; Weinstein *et al.*, 1954; and Kahn *et al.*, 1956). They found that in patients who had shown denial of illness and disorientation for time and had recovered, these phenomena could be reproduced by the intravenous injection of amytal. They compared the responses (1953) of eighty-eight neurological patients having brain disease, caused by tumours, degenerative and demyelinating diseases, etc., with those of fifty patients who had peripheral nerve lesions or neuroses. They used a standard set of questions, concerning orientation and awareness of illness, before and after the injection of amytal. "A 2·5 per cent solution was injected intravenously at the rate of 0·05 G per minute The subject was asked to count backwards from 100 to 1. At the point where nystagmus, errors in counting, dysarthria, and drowsiness were produced," the standard set of questions which had been asked immediately before the injection, was repeated (e.g. "What is your main trouble? How did it come about? Are you worried about it?" etc.) (Weinstein and Malitz, 1954). "Prior to receiving the drug, all patients expressed awareness of illness, were completely orientated for place, and identified the examiners correctly. With the drug, explicit denial of illness, disorientation for place, and gross misidentification of the examiners occurred only in some of the patients with brain damage. In the normal group, subjects talked of illness in terms of a third person, used more 'concrete' symbols, selectively misinterpreted questions about illness and misnamed the examiners in 'paraphrasic fashion.' These patients were not necessarily more communicative. Many showed no change. Some talked more, others talked less, and while some talked more, they communicated less information." The authors considered that the effects could not be adequately explained in terms of "cortical depression" or "release of repressions" or "inhibitions" (as, for example, Kubie and Margolin, 1945, postulated) but rather as an adaptive defence in a stressful situation, much of the behaviour being the manifestation of a particular observer-subject relationship. (For example, "the degree of ataxia varied greatly with the audience," and many of the defects were selective, patients being alert to some questions and giving inaudible replies to others.) However, such effects did not occur with injections of sterile water.

In a further study, Weinstein and Malitz (1954) investigated the effects of injections of amytal on a hundred general medical patients, half of them suffering from brain damage. In fifty-seven of the eighty-eight patients with brain disease who had shown no disturbances of behaviour on clinical examination, "the intravenous administration of the drug produced patterns of disorientation for time, place, and person, and denial of illness. These changes were not obtained in any of the fifty control patients."

Weinstein et al. (1954) found that the results of the amytal tests at different stages of the illnesses of thirty-four patients paralleled the improvement, and more recently Kahn et al. (1956) have found a "close

relationship between the short-term response to treatment [by E.C.T. administered to twenty-four patients] and the results of the amobarbital tests." Teng and Bender (1955) have found amytal of value in bringing out latent motor deficits due to lesions in the central nervous system. Weiner and Harlow (1952) found that in monkeys the more severe the brain damage, the greater impairment of learned performances when pentobarbitone sodium was administered.

The Sedation Threshold

Recently Shagass has developed a quantitative method using intravenous amytal for assessing manifest anxiety and tension in neurotics and the "degree of impairment of ego functioning" in psychotics (Shagass, 1954; Shagass and Naiman, 1955 and 1956; Shagass, Naiman and Mihalik, 1956; Shagass, 1956; Shagass, Mihalik and Jones, 1957). The measure obtained is termed the "sedation threshold"; this is "defined as that amount of sodium amytal (in mg per kg body weight) required to produce an inflection point in the amplitude curve of frontal 15 to 30 c/s activity, within one injection interval of onset of slurred speech. The inflexion point was defined as that point which followed an abrupt rise in the curve and preceded a tendency to flatten, or the point just preceding a clear plateau in the curve."

The procedure was for the patient to lie on a bed, while a continuous frontal EEG record was taken; 0·5 mg per kg body weight of amytal (in 1 c.c.) was injected at the beginning of every forty-second period. "Questioning was started after twenty-five seconds. The patient was asked how he felt and then asked to repeat numbers and words . . ." EEG changes similar to those observed by Brazier and Finesinger (described above) occurred. "The development of fast frequency potentials usually took place in a gradual manner. However, in most records there seemed to be a point at which relatively sudden increase in voltage and amount of frontal fast activity occurred, followed by relatively little increase thereafter. This transition point was found to coincide with the development of slurred speech . . ." (cf. Fig. 17.6).

The sedation threshold was highly and significantly correlated with the degree of "tension" as assessed psychiatrically in neurotics and in pseudoneurotic schizophrenics. Among the other schizophrenics, the correlation was not significant (Shagass, 1954) and it was considered that this was due to the influence of another factor, namely impairment of ego functioning. In a subsequent study Shagass and Naiman (1955) have produced evidence suggesting that impairment of ego functioning lowers the sedation threshold. They argued that "the chronic schizophrenic group would have higher thresholds than apparently equally tense patients with acute schizophrenia or agitated depressions." This was shown to be the case. Among normal subjects "there was a higher positive correlation between the sedation threshold and the number of symptoms of manifest anxiety elicited in a psychiatric interview." There was also a significant relationship between the threshold and the score on a self-administered symptom inventory (Saslow Screening Test). Those with organic psychoses had the lowest thresholds.

In a further study (Shagass and Naiman, 1956) the sedation thresholds for one hundred and twenty-one neurotics and forty-five normal subjects were compared. The "mean threshold for the control subjects was 3·09 mg per kg which was significantly lower than the mean for the neurotics ($p < 0.001$). The mean threshold for the hysterics (twenty-six cases) was 2·88 and for anxiety states 5·38 (twenty-nine cases). The differences between the diagnostic categories are shown in Fig. 12.6 in Chapter 12, "Conditioning and Abnormal Behaviour," by C. Franks. The test-retest reliability is high, and the results little influenced by differences in age, sex and amounts of past sedation (but alcoholics and addicts were excluded). The technique is difficult, chiefly because of the need to avoid EEG artefacts during injection. Slurring of speech is only "an adequate indicator for extremely high or low thresholds," EEG control being needed for most of the intermediate ones.

The authors note the close agreement between their findings and the dimension of extraversion-introversion as independently established by Eysenck (1947). They write: "If one assumes some kind of personality continuum, with the hysteric at one extreme and the obsessional at the other, the sedation threshold probably gives a fairly accurate indication of the position of an individual on this continuum." This personality correlate of the sedation threshold should perhaps be emphasized as much as its correlation with manifest anxiety, since it provides a link with important experimental evidence obtained by other methods. In particular, they mention the striking fact that in Hildebrand's (1953) study using objective psychological tests of introversion-extraversion the order in which the various neuroses were arranged by the test scores was "remarkably similar to the order in which they were arranged by the sedation threshold." They suggest "that these various tests probably measure different aspects of the same basic central nervous function." According to Eysenck's theory (1955) this is reactive inhibition which was predicted to be more marked in extraverts (and hysterics) than in introverts (and dysthymics).

Sodium Amytal, being a depressant drug would be postulated to increase inhibition. An extravert, whose cortex, according to . . . [Eysenck's] . . . theory, is already in a relatively inhibited state, should require comparatively little Sodium Amytal before reaching the critical sedation point; such a person should have a low sedation threshold. The introvert, on the other hand, whose cortex is in a state of considerable excitation and low inhibition, would require a considerable amount of Sodium Amytal before reaching the critical sedation point; He would be predicted to have a high sedation threshold. If he express this general hypothesis in terms of their standing on the extraversion-introversion continuum . . . then we would expect psychopaths to have the lowest threshold, followed by hysterics. Mixed neurotics would be intermediate, and anxiety states, obsessionals and reactive depressives would have high sedation thresholds.

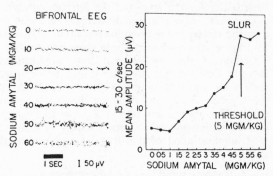

FIG. 17.6. EFFECT OF SODIUM AMYTAL ON BIFRONTAL EEG
Note progressive increase of fast-frequency amplitude. Arrow points to inflexion point in the amplitude curve, which indicates sedation threshold.
(*From Shagass, 1954*)

Referring to Shagass's work Eysenck writes: "It will be seen that these results bear out our prediction in every detail" (Eysenck, 1957).

The age and weight of the individual are not a satisfactory basis for calculating the dose of barbiturate required owing to the great individual variation (Goodman and Gilman, 1955). The work of Shagass and of Eysenck suggests that certain psychological variables may well account for some of these variations.

EXPERIMENTAL PSYCHOLOGICAL STUDIES

The Persistence of Impairment as Measured by Psychological Tests

The effects of barbiturates have been less thoroughly studied by psychological methods than have the effects of the amphetamines. This is presumably because the demonstration of impairment of a function arouses less interest than attempts to demonstrate its improvement. Nevertheless, as barbiturates are so widely used, it is of practical importance to establish the extent of impairment of various functions in relation to the different barbiturates, their dosage and the time elapsing after their administration. In order to do this adequately, especially if small doses are being used, careful experimental design and analysis are particularly necessary. This aspect will therefore be described in some detail.

Two careful experiments have been reported from the Anaesthesia Laboratory of the Harvard Medical School, using similar methods to assess the impairment of various functions following the oral administration of a hypnotic dose (100 mg) of pentobarbitone sodium (Goodnow et al., 1951; von Felsinger et al., 1953).

In the first experiments (Goodnow et al., 1951) thirty normal young men were studied in two sessions, each lasting for two days and the intervening night. After an interval of five days the subjects returned for a second session and received the preparation (placebo or drug) which they had not been given previously.

Certain of the psychological tests administered failed to show a statistically reliable effect of the drug; these were tests involving: (1) arithmetic, (2) letter-crossing, (3) coding, (4) static steadiness, (5) visual choice reaction-time and (6) C.F.F. The tests which showed statistically reliable drug effects four hours after administration of the drug were (in order of sensitivity)—

1. Tapping speed (using a telegraph key).
2. Auditory reaction-time.
3. Time taken in naming opposites.
4. Memory for digits.

There was "highly suggestive" but not statistically significant evidence of impairment as long as fourteen hours after medication.

Von Felsinger et al. (1953) were able to demonstrate significant impairment in certain tests up to eight hours after ingestion of the drug (100 mg pentobarbitone sodium). Their experiment was similar in many respects to the one described above. Twenty subjects took part and were each tested twice in the two sessions. Eight tests were used, including—

Visual perception,
Serial learning,
Recall,
Associations to nonsense syllables,
Attention,
Computation, with and without distraction, and an
Analogies test.

The tests of visual perception, attention and computation showed significant impairment after the drug. On the other hand, there was a significant increase in the number of associations to the nonsense syllables. Concerning this, the authors write that this "freer flow of internally determined ideas and associations . . . has, of course, been utilized in narcoanalytic

techniques." It is of interest that Welch et al. (1946) found a similar effect with dextroamphetamine sulphate, as these two drugs are in some respects antagonistic. Steinberg (1954) using a somewhat different association test, found that nitrous oxide produced a decline in verbal fluency, which she considered to be "of particular incidental interest . . . in view of the fact that nitrous oxide and similar drugs are often used in psychotherapy with the object of making the patient more loquacious."

Although Goodnow et al. (1951) did not find computation to be impaired by the drug, von Felsinger et al. (1953) found a statistically significant impairment, which they attributed to the fact that their subjects did not have the support to attention and concentration which is provided by pencil and paper. The effects of distraction during computation were less when the drug was given.

The tests of serial learning and analogies were unaffected by the drug, which is perhaps strange as the more complex functions are often supposed to be affected relatively more by drugs.

Von Felsinger et al. (1953) point out that their work provides "objective confirmation of the frequent complaint of 'hangover' after the use of pentobarbital sodium in ordinary hypnotic dose." Fastier (1955) concluded that 100 mg pentobarbitone sodium "was effective in inducing drowsiness and bringing about sleep more quickly than usual in less than half the subjects" who were investigated, but it was relatively more effective in causing hangover drowsiness (see also Lasagna, 1954). It is of interest that chloral hydrate (1·0G) was more effective in inducing sleep than 100 mg pentobarbitone sodium, as this drug (perhaps because it is not advertised as the barbiturates are) is "unfortunately neglected today" (Goodman and Gilman, 1955). Even half a century before Maurice Craig (Psychological Medicine, p. 449, 1905) complained that it was not used as much as it might be. Perhaps the time will come when the use of hypnotics will be based more than it is at present on careful comparative studies of their efficacy (e.g. Lasagna, 1954; Hare, 1955; Straus et al., 1955; Pollack and Takakjian, 1955).

Effects on Cognitive Functions

The effects of amytal on intelligence were investigated by Slater, Sargant and Glen (1942) and Sargant et al. (1945), using the Cattell II Intelligence Test, which has two equivalent forms A and B. In the earlier experiments they obtained a statistically significant decrease in score on the test following the administration of gr 3 amytal. This decline, which was equivalent to 3–4 I.Q. points was confirmed by Sargant et al. (1945) who compared the effects of alcohol, amytal and caffeine, using the same test. In all, three hundred and ninety-nine male psychiatric patients were tested, each receiving a *placebo* on the first day, half an hour before attempting form *A* of the test, and on the following day when form *B* was used receiving gr 3 of amytal, 20 c.c. of absolute alcohol diluted and disguised with essence of gentian or caffeine, or a *placebo*. Both alcohol and the barbiturate had a significantly deleterious effect. Although those who received alcohol only scored slightly less than those receiving amytal, their behaviour was noticeably different, the subjects often being euphoric, sleepy, inattentive and "full of backchat."

The Effects of Barbiturates on Learning

(i) *In animals*. There is some evidence which suggests that barbiturates impair conditioning (e.g. Wentinck, 1938) but conditioned reflexes may be established while the animal is under the influence of the drug to such an extent that the response is not elicited until recovery from the anaesthetic (Settlage, 1936; Headlee and Kellogg, 1941).

Dworkin *et al.* (1937) studied the effects of a variety of drugs on two dogs and two cats, which had been trained to lift the lid of a food container. Successive tests were made every two to six minutes. The animals were trained not to touch the lid during the interval ("interval inhibition") and to discriminate between two types of auditory stimuli. Five stages, corresponding to different doses of intravenous amytal, were recognized—

1. 5–7 mg per kg. Ataxia, but no effect on lid-lifting.
2. 15 mg per kg. Interval inhibition is replaced by lid-lifting.
3. 20 mg per kg. Negative stimuli now evoke responses, i.e. there is a breakdown of discrimination.
4. 25–30 mg per kg. The response to positive stimuli is delayed or lost.
5. 35 mg per kg. There is a loss of the unconditioned response, i.e. eating. Recovery occurs in 12–36 hours.

Both pentobarbitone sodium and alcohol had somewhat similar effects, their "outstanding effect" being the "decided weakening of the negative aspects of behaviour." This disinhibiting action probably accounts for the effects on mute and negativistic patients (described above), although they occur after relatively smaller doses (in terms of mg per kg).

The studies on the effects of barbiturates on learning have yielded rather discrepant results. Omwake (1933), Williams (1936), Williams and O'Brien (1937),

and Mendenhall (1940), all found that barbiturates had a detrimental effect on maze learning by rats: Coppock *et al.* (1956) found that one third of the anaesthetic dose of phenobarbitone tended either to preserve a previously established habit in rats (an avoidance response) or to interfere with the subsequent learning of an antagonistic response (i.e. in the opposite direction).

On the other hand, Fields (1935), Jones (1942) and Jones and Jones (1943) found that the drugged rats were not inferior in learning. Whereas Fields used a maze, Jones and Jones trained the rats on a discrimination problem, i.e. jumping on to one or other of two platforms having different patterns on them (an electric shock being administered if a choice was not made within ten seconds). If the wrong choice was made, the platform tipped, allowing the animal to fall into a net. The conclusion drawn from their experiments, which appear to have been well designed and carefully carried out, was "that large and prolonged doses of phenobarbital, within the limits of this experiment have no measurable effect on ability to learn a discrimination, and probably no effect on retention of what has been learned." The impaired learning which had previously been reported as a result of administration of the drug may be attributable to greater complexity of the task, ataxia (which would be a handicap in running a maze) or also to the diminution of the hunger and thirst drives, resulting from administration of the drug (Jones and Jones, 1943, but cf. O'Kelly and Weiss, 1955).

It has been claimed that repeated administration of a barbiturate can lead to a decrease in learning ability in rats which persists when the drug is no longer given (Marx and Edelstrom, 1950). Only the females were affected, and it is possible that their greater susceptibility to most barbiturates, which has been shown in several studies (Holck and Kanan, 1935; Holck *et al.*, 1937; Moir, 1937)[1] may have resulted in greater depression of eating during the four weeks when the drug was administered, and that their impaired performance was due to a dietary deficiency.

Another factor has recently been shown to be of importance by Dews (1955*a* and *b*, 1956). Using a Skinner box, he found that the effects of pentobarbitone sodium on pecking by pigeons were markedly influenced by the schedule of reinforcement, being greater on a fixed interval schedule than on the schedule according to which a reward was given for every fiftieth response. Blough (1956) has also demonstrated (in pigeons) the "insensitivity to drug effects

[1] Caution is necessary in generalizing from the rat to other animals. Holck and Kanan (1937) found no sex differences in barbiturate sensitivity in the dog, cat, rabbit, white mouse, turtle or frog; others have found women more resistant than men, resembling female guinea-pigs in this respect.

of behaviour maintained on a fixed-ratio schedule of reinforcement."

(ii) *In man*. The extent to which man resembles the rat in the characteristics of his learning is controversial, and too few studies have been carried out with barbiturates to ascertain how far the findings described above are applicable to man.

Three studies involving conditioning and learning have recently been carried out on the same group of subjects, approximately eighty female volunteers; they received at random one of four different treatments: (*a*) amytal gr 4½, (*b*) *placebo*, (*c*) Dexamphetamine sulphate, (*d*) the same drug as (*c*) but testing was begun after a longer interval (two hours instead of forty-five minutes). The tests which were given in the same sequence were (1) the acquisition of the conditioned eyeblink response (Franks and Trouton, 1958), (2) learning to operate a pursuit rotor (Eysenck *et al.*, 1957) and (3) the learning of nonsense syllables by the serial anticipation method (Willett, 1958). The experiments were carried out to test the predictions from Eysenck's theory concerning the differences between introverts and extraverts (Eysenck, 1955, 1957).

Amytal significantly impaired the number of conditioned eyeblinks acquired, but its effect on extinction was not significant (all comparisons being with the *placebo* group). (Details are given in Chapter 12, "Conditioning and Abnormal Behaviour," by Franks; cf. his Fig. 12.4 and discussion.) The curves obtained under the different conditions are similar to those obtained by Franks for dysthymics and hysterics (quoted by Eysenck, 1955; Franks, 1956) and therefore in accordance with Eysenck's theory (1957). Caution is necessary, however, in interpreting the results; the increase in activity with *d*-amphetamine has already been mentioned, and under the conditions of the experiment amytal tends to reduce the number of movements (Laverty and Franks, 1956); it also decreases action potentials from muscles (Jacobsen, 1944). In other words, the first drug tends to *decrease* and the second to *increase* the threshold for movements, and it may be this change in threshold rather than conditioning which is measured by the number of eyeblink responses (cf. Miller, 1956).

In the pursuit rotor experiment (Eysenck *et al.*, 1957), the amytal group had a significantly lower level of performance than the *d*-amphetamine group.

The study on serial anticipation learning of nonsense syllables carried out by Willett (1958) yielded few significant differences between the different conditions; the serial position effect, the number of associative errors and the number of trials to reach a criterion of one perfect repetition of the series did not differ significantly for any of the drug conditions. It is remarkable that a dose of amytal which was large enough to make many of the subjects appear as if drunk (giggling and ataxia being commonly observed) had so negligible an effect on learning.

Perception

Trent (1947) found that gr 1½ of Nembutal (pentobarbitone sodium) enhanced contour clarity. The lowering of the threshold for flicker fusion has been confirmed in several studies (e.g. Landis and Zubin, 1951; Roback *et al.*, 1952); in barbiturate addicts, the drug has less effect and may even produce an effect in the opposite direction (Ideström, 1954). Neither amytal nor *d*-amphetamine significantly affect the rate of reversal of a Necker cube (Eysenck *et al.*, 1957).

Barbiturates have sometimes been used to facilitate obtaining responses to the Rorschach cards, particularly in those who are inaccessible, reluctant to respond or frightened, uncooperative (Kelley *et al.*, 1941) or suspected of incipient schizophrenia (Zuckerman *et al.*, 1954). Mücher (1953) claimed that vague unrealistic stimulus material was perceived as more hostile, even ten hours after a barbiturate had been given.

Reaction-time

Goodnow *et al.* (1951) found a significant increase in auditory reaction-time four hours after the administration of 100 mg pentobarbitone; but Grünewald (1954) claimed that a dose of Evipan 10 per cent of the anaesthetic dose (as in Berg's 1949 study) resulted in a shorter reaction-time to visual and auditory stimuli; however, no measurements are given. Possibly the findings of Hill, Belleville and Wikler (1955, 1957) based on narcotic addicts, would be applicable to normal subjects, except that their attitude and reactions to morphine, which was used as a reward in both experiments, would be different. In the first study it was shown that pentobarbitone did not prevent the disruption of performance occasioned by electric shocks which resulted from slow visual motor reaction-times, whereas morphine prevented any significant effect on the reaction-times. In the second study (on one hundred and eighty-two former narcotic addicts), visual-motor reaction-times were measured after administration of (1) pentobarbitone, (2) morphine, and (3) no drug, under four incentive conditions (different morphine rewards). It was found that "in comparison with the control, both drugs acted either as 'stimulants' (accelerated reaction-time) or as 'depressants' (slowed reaction-time) or had no effect, depending on the particular incentives under which they were administered. The actions of these drugs, however, were 'specific' with respect to each other: the effect of pentobarbital changed from 'depressant' to 'stimulant' when conditions changed from 'Low Incentive' to 'High Incentive,' while the action of morphine changed from 'stimulant' to 'depressant' when identical changes in incentive level were made."

Slowing of reaction-time in barbiturate addicts following large doses of Seconal has been reported by Hill and Belleville (1953), and quickening of reaction-time following amytal and amphetamine has been reported in depressives (Huston and Senf, 1952).[1]

Psychological Experiments on the Effects of Barbiturates in Schizophrenia

Several studies have been carried out in an attempt to find quantitative evidence for the improvement which has been observed clinically in schizophrenics after the administration of amytal (e.g. Layman, 1940; Huston and Senf, 1952; Mainord, 1953; Ogilvie, 1954; Cohen, Senf and Huston, 1954; Huston, Cohen and Senf, 1955; Senf, Huston and Cohen, 1955; Cohen, Senf and Huston, 1956; Broadhurst, 1957). Both Layman (1940) and Mainord (1953) obtained statistically significant increases in intelligence test scores, although two more recent studies (Ogilvie, 1954 and Broadhurst, 1957) have failed to demonstrate any significant improvement. Improvement in some other tests has been observed but it appears to be less marked than the improvement in attitude (e.g. Huston and Senf, 1952).

The Effects of Barbiturates in Relation to Suggestibility and Hypnosis

The term "hypnosis" is used to describe the states produced by very different means, namely by drugs and by suggestion, and it is difficult to judge whether the similarities are merely superficial.

There appears to be agreement that barbiturates may facilitate hypnosis, but doubt concerning the resemblances between the states produced purely by one or other of these different means. Gorton (1949) maintains that the states induced by drugs "do not necessarily fulfil Hull's criteria of hypersuggestibility and it is not justifiable to place them under the heading of hypnosis. . . ." On the other hand, Wolberg (1948) points out that the drug "acts as a cortical depressant and produces the same phenomena as a hypnotically produced deadening of the cortical centers." Horsley (1943) states that several of the phenomena associated with hypnotic suggestion can be produced when the subject is merely under the influence of a barbiturate (e.g. postnarcotic amnesia, hyperamnesia and catalepsy may occur if suggested). However, the hypnotic phenomena are superimposed on the state of narcosis as a result of interaction

between the physician or experimenter and the patient, and not produced by the drug *per se* (Horsley, 1951). Furthermore an important difference is found in the EEG records; whereas the administration of a barbiturate intravenously produces certain characteristic changes in the EEG, these do not occur in hypnosis produced by suggestion and the EEG record resembles that of the normal waking state (Dynes, 1947 and Ravitz, 1951).

There is evidence that primary suggestibility and the capacity to be hypnotized are closely related (Eysenck, 1947). Numerous clinical observations testify to the increase in suggestibility which occurs with subanaesthetic amounts of anaesthetics (e.g. Starkey, 1917; Wilson, 1927) or barbiturates (Hauptmann, 1934; Stungo, 1941; Dicks, 1940; Rogerson, 1944). As different depressants appear to have similar effects on suggestibility, other drugs besides barbiturates will be included in the following account.

Baernstein (1929), using nineteen subjects, investigated the effect of subcutaneous injection of gr $\frac{1}{200}$ of scopolamine (hyoscine) hydrobromide on suggestibility, injection of saline being given as the *placebo*. The postural sway technique was employed. The subjects were tested one hour after the injection of the drug. Only eight subjects were responsive to suggestions following either the drug or the control dose. "It was found in general that subjects who were resistant to suggestion in the normal state were also resistant when under the influence of the drug. There was a fairly marked tendency, however, for those who were susceptible in the normal state to be markedly more susceptible when under the influence of scopolamine" (Hull, 1933). As Eysenck and Rees (1945) point out, Baerstein's experiment did "not include a vital control test, viz. a test of their ability to stand after the administration of the drug without any suggestion at all." Thus, all that may have been demonstrated was an increase in static ataxia.

To eliminate this factor, Eysenck and Rees (1945) used the Press-release test, for which the subject lies on a bed with his eyes closed, holding a rubber bulb, which is connected to a tambour whose movements are recorded by a kymograph. Heterosuggestion was provided by a gramophone record, and statements such as "you are squeezing the bulb . . ." were made for one minute. It had previously been shown that this test "measures essentially the same function as does the body-sway test. . . ."

Two groups of ten neurotic patients were selected on the basis of their body-sway scores, group *A* having proved to be uninfluenced by suggestion in this test, and group *B* highly influenced.

They were tested before and after the administration of the drug. Amytal was slowly injected intravenously, while the patient counted backwards from fifty;

[1] Numerous studies have been carried out, mostly on schizophrenics, using amytal and an amphetamine (e.g. Huston and Senf 1952–3, Cohen *et al.*, 1954, Cohen *et al.*, 1956, also Gottlieb *et al.*, 1952) but owing to limitations of space, the combined actions of these drugs cannot be described here.

when the counting became confused, the injection was stopped and the patient tested. The results, which were highly significant, indicated "that suggestible subjects are made more suggestible by Sodium Amytal injection, while non-suggestible subjects remain completely unaffected by the drug." (Italics omitted.)

That the results were due to the drug and not to a practice effect or suggestion was shown by injecting ten suggestible subjects with saline instead of amytal. In eight cases, there was no increase on retesting; in two cases, however, there was a marked increase.

An experiment similar to the one using the barbiturate was carried out using 45 per cent nitrous oxide in air (administered by means of a Minnitt-type apparatus), with similar results.

Eysenck and Rees give a theoretical interpretation of their findings based on Eysenck's (1947) theory of primary suggestibility.

Alcohol

Psychological experiments on the effects of alcohol have been carried out for well over half a century and the literature (much of which is in German) is vast. Fortunately, there is an excellent critical review of about forty thousand words in length and with nearly two hundred references covering the period up to 1940 by Jellinek and McFarland (1940). In the following, the account of the earlier work on alcohol is based largely on their review where further details and references may be found. As in their review, the scope here is limited to the acute psychological effects of alcohol and the chronic effects of alcohol are not discussed. Relatively little work appears to have been done on the former since 1940, most of the articles relevant to alcohol being concerned with chronic alcoholism and addiction (*see* reviews by Pullar and Strecker, 1948, 1949, 1951).

Jellinek and McFarland reanalysed the results of several of the earlier experiments and in some instances were able to show that the conclusions drawn by the original author were incorrect. As their review was approximately twice as long as this entire chapter which covers numerous other drugs it is obvious that much condensation is necessary. Only the main conclusions and the relevant references can be given here, supplemented by the seemingly scanty psychological work which has been done subsequently, some of which is reviewed by Goldberg (1943, 1949), Victor and Adams (1953). Jacobsen (1952) reviews the metabolism of alcohol. Although not yet available in this country, reference should be made to the *Classified Abstract Archives* of the literature dealing with alcohol, which was developed at Yale and is now sponsored by W.H.O. (Kellar and Efron, 1953).

As the pharmacology of alcohol is well known and described in numerous books it need only be very briefly touched on here. Such subjects as the alcoholic

TABLE XVII.9
A SCALE OF TOXIC SYMPTOMS
(*From Miles, 1932*)

Per cent alcohol in blood	Subjective state and observable changes in behaviour under conditions of heavy social drinking
0·010	Clearing of the head. Freer breathing through nasal passages. Mild tingling of mucous membranes of the mouth and throat.
0·020	Slight fullness and throbbing at back of head. Touch of dizziness. Sense of warmth and general physical well-being. Small bodily aches and fatigues relieved. Not fretful about the weather nor worried concerning personal appearance. Quite willing to talk with associates. Feeling tone of pleasantness.
0·030	Mild euphoria, "everything is all right," "very glad I came," "we will always be friends," "sure I will loan you some money," "it isn't time to go home yet!" No sense of worry. Feelings of playing a very superior game. Time passes quickly.
0·040	Lots of energy for the things he wants to do. Talks much and rather loudly. Hands tremble slightly, reaching and other movements a bit clumsy; laughs loudly at minor jokes; unembarrassed by mishaps, "you don't think I'm drunk do you, why I haven't taken anything yet." Makes glib or flippant remarks. Memories appear rich and vivid.
0·050	Sitting on top of the world, "a free human being," normal inhibitions practically cut off, takes personal and social liberties of all sorts as impulse prompts. Is long-winded and enlarges on his past exploits. "Can lick anybody in the country," but has observable difficulty in lighting a match. Marked blunting of self-criticism.
0·070	Feeling of remoteness. Odd sensations on rubbing hands together, or on touching the face. Rapid strong pulse and breathing. Amused at his own clumsiness or rather at what he takes to be the perversity of things about him. Asks others to do things for him. Upsets chair on rising.
0·100	Staggers very perceptibly. Talks to himself. Has difficulty in finding and putting on his overcoat. Fumbled long with the keys in unlocking and starting his car. Feels drowsy, sings loudly, complains that others don't keep on their side of the road.
0·200	Needs help to walk or undress. Easily angered. Shouts, groans, and weeps by turns. Is nauseated and has poor control of urination. Cannot recall with whom he spent the evening.
0·300	In a stuporous condition, very heavy breathing, sleeping and vomiting by turns. No comprehension of language. Strikes wildly at the person who tries to aid him.
0·400	Deep anaesthesia, may be fatal.

content in different drinks and the differential rates of absorption from these, the influence of food on the rate of absorption, and calculation of the blood-alcohol level, and the diagnosis of intoxication have all been intensively investigated, but the findings must be omitted here owing to lack of space.

Table XVII.9 which is taken from Miles (1932) shows the relation between the percentage of alcohol in the blood and the overt behaviour. In this connexion, it should be remembered that the effects of alcohol are very variable (Meerloo, 1947) and may even vary in the same person according to the different circumstances in which the alcohol is taken. The degree of disturbance of behaviour is affected also by the rate and direction of change of the alcohol in the blood-stream, being greater if the concentration is increasing; this is of importance because it means that a single test given a particular interval after the ingestion of alcohol may give a misleading impression of the susceptibility of the subject to alcohol, as was pointed out by Eggleton (1941) who advocated repetition of the test every ten minutes until recovery had occurred.

There are certain methodological disadvantages which are encountered in many studies of alcohol. One is that a *placebo* has rarely been used; this is partly because many of the experiments were conducted before the need for *placebo* was generally recognized, and partly because it has been widely believed that owing to the distinctive flavour of alcohol it is impossible to disguise it or to make a convincingly tasting *placebo*. Nevertheless, there are exceptions; for instance Hollingworth (1923, 1924) used de-alcoholized beer which the subjects were unable to distinguish from the ordinary beer on the basis of its taste.

PSYCHOLOGICAL EXPERIMENTS

As far as possible the main findings concerning the effects of alcohol have been condensed in tables. The references given in square brackets are taken from a review by Jellinek and McFarland (1940) whose conclusions, as was pointed out, do not always coincide with the original author. It has been necessary here to omit certain factors, which should not, however, be ignored in the studies on alcohol. Among the factors are—

1. The absolute amount of alcohol received. Probably the most commonly used dosage has been 35 c.c. of absolute alcohol given in a 20 per cent solution. If it is assumed that for every 0·01 per cent of alcohol in the blood, from 5–10 c.c. of alcohol must be ingested (Goodman and Gilman, 1941) this corresponds to a blood-alcohol concentration of about 0·04 to 0·07 per cent (i.e. 40–70 mg

of alcohol per 100 ml of blood). This results in subclinical intoxication in the majority of adults.[1]

2. (*a*) Its dilution, and (*b*) the type of beverage, e.g. whether it is diluted, absolute alcohol or beverage wine, etc. (Haggard *et al.*, 1938; Newman and Abramson, 1942).

3. The total volume of liquid consumed.

4. The speed of drinking.

5. The time after the last meal, and also the nature of the meal (e.g. fats tend to delay absorption).

6. The drinking habits of the experimental subjects, e.g. moderate, habitual, abstinent, etc.

7. The time elapsing before testing, and whether the concentration is rising or falling.

Other details, such as the experimental design, cannot be conveniently tabulated and, unless these are known, merely stating the number of subjects tested is apt to be misleading. In a remarkable number of experiments with alcohol there has been only one experimental subject and that has very often been the experimenter himself; thus a certain amount of caution is required both in the interpretation and in the attempts to generalize the results.

The main findings on the psychological effects of alcohol are summarized in Table XVII.10 (cognitive functions), Table XVII.11 (associative functions), Table XVII.12 (sensory and perceptual functions) and Table XVII.13 (*a*) and (*b*) (motor functions).

The distinction between the unskilled and the skilled motor tasks is not a fundamental one but mainly a matter of degree; even in the ergograph studies, skill and practice effects are marked and a variable amount of co-ordination is required as well as a muscular strength. It will be noticed in Table XVII.13 that small amounts of alcohol have been found to improve performance on the ergograph, at least for a short period. This is one of the very few instances where alcohol has been found to have a beneficial effect. The explanation of it given by Starling is: "In exceptional circumstances a moderate dose of alcohol may for a time abolish the sensation of fatigue, or create an emotional drive which will enable an individual to overcome temporarily the effects of fatigue, so making capable of continuing his efforts beyond the period at which they would otherwise have to come to an end. This increased work is in the nature of a call upon capital, which must be repaid later by a prolongation of the period of rest." It has sometimes been said that alcohol may have first a stimulating and then a depressing effect on the performance on the ergograph. This apparent depressant effect is due to the decrease in efficiency which occurs in any case, but

[1] For details of "The Recognition of Intoxication," *see* the *B.M.A. Special Committee Report*, 1954.

TABLE XVII.10
THE PSYCHOLOGICAL EFFECTS OF DRUGS: ALCOHOL
COGNITIVE FUNCTIONS

Function	Test	Type and number of subjects	Author and date	Effect	Comment
Intelligence		50 normal subjects	Cattell (1930)		Conclusions invalid because they depended upon the comparison of mean deviation scores. (*See* Jellinek and McFarland (1940), p. 360.)
	Naming of opposites	6 normal subjects	Hollingworth (1923-4)	Impaired	
	Colour naming	6 normal subjects	Hollingworth (1923-4)	Increase in errors	Impairment in proportion to the dose.
	Colour naming	14 normal subjects	McFarland and Barach (1936)	Increase in errors	
	Cancellation of letters	25 boys	[e.g. Erlacher and others quoted by Jellinek and McFarland Table 16, 1940][1]	Impaired	The effect on the 10-year-old boys was twice as great as on the 14-year-old boys.
Reasoning	Arithmetical reasoning	20 normal subjects	[Joss (1900)]	Impaired	
	Judgement of sorites, syllogisms and conversions	12 normal subjects	Seward and Seward (1936)		Although it was claimed that 0·75 G per kg body weight of alcohol had no effect, Jellinek and McFarland (1940, p. 360) point out that there was a marked practice effect which was lowered considerably by the alcohol.
	Artificial language test	6 normal subjects	Mead (1939)	Loss of efficiency	"An excellently devised experiment" (Jellinek and McFarland, 1940, p. 359).
Judgement of time	Driving	20 normal subjects	Vernon (1936)	Impaired	Some subjects considered that they were in fact driving more quickly.

[1] When the names of authors in Tables XVII.10, XVII.11, XVII.12 and XVII.13 are enclosed in square brackets, this indicates that the original sources have not been consulted, but the findings taken from Jellinek and McFarland (1940), where the references are also to be found.

which appears to be less marked after a moderate dose of alcohol. Larger doses of alcohol either do not influence the work output or lower it (*see* Jellinek and McFarland, 1940).

In Table XVII.13 (*b*) no attempt has been made to assess the psychological functions involved in the tasks, which are all highly complex.

Simple Reaction-time

Simple reaction-time has been extensively investigated (*see* Jellinek and McFarland). It was originally claimed by several workers, including Kraepelin, that the initial effect of alcohol on reaction-time was to shorten it. After careful reanalysis of the work upon which this conclusion was based Jellinek and McFarland concluded—

1. That tests of reaction-time involved a strong practice trend.

2. That the effects of small doses of alcohol (10 c.c.) do not overcome this practice effect in the first twenty minutes following its illustration.

3. That the effect of larger doses is to increase the reaction-time immediately.

"The oft-reported initial shortening appears to be an arithmetical artefact inherent in averages based on the entire pre-alcohol period." Jellinek and McFarland emphasize that the applicability of the laboratory tests on reaction-time to actual road conditions in driving a motor-car is "not beyond question." Hicks (1956) has also stressed that reaction-time "looks like a physiological reflex but is actually an acquired skill . . ." which is considerably influenced by the attitude of the subject (sensory or motor) and also by the "nice assessment of the proportion of errors (false reactions) one can get away with."

TABLE XVII.11

THE PSYCHOLOGICAL EFFECTS OF DRUGS: ALCOHOL
ASSOCIATIVE FUNCTIONS

Function	Test	Type and number of subjects	Author and date	Effect	Comment
	Continuous addition	7 normal subjects	[Kraepelin, 1892]	Impairment	Since confirmed in numerous other studies (see Jellinek and McFarland (1940), Table 32).
		11 psychotics	[Göring, 1911]	Great variation, 3 improving and the rest showing impairment	
		4 groups of about a dozen girls and boys each of two age groups, 10 and 14	[Erlacher, 1926, 1931]	Impairment, especially of performance by the 10-year-old girls which was twice that of the boys of that age	
	Free association to a standard list of words	One subject (Kraepelin) tested on 17 consecutive days	[Kraepelin, 1892]	Fewer new associations apart from clang associations	Alcohol was administered on 5 of the days.
	Continuous free association	1	[Kraepelin, 1892]	Incidence of superficial associations increased	
	Controlled association (supraordinates)	1	[Kraepelin, 1892]	Tendency to disregard rules and respond with synonyms, etc.	
	Continuous free association tests	6 normal subjects	[Kurka, 1928]	Kraepelin's findings largely confirmed	
Memory			e.g. Hollingworth (1923), McFarland and Barach (1936)		"There is no doubt that immediate memory is adversely affected by alcohol. . . ." (Jellinek and McFarland (1940), p. 353). Most tests have also measured learning.

TABLE XVII.12

THE PSYCHOLOGICAL EFFECTS OF DRUGS: ALCOHOL
SENSORY AND PERCEPTUAL FUNCTIONS

Function	Test	Author and date	Effect	Comment
Tactile	2-point discrimination	[Lichtenfels, 1851; Kremer, 1884]	Increase in threshold	See Jellinek and McFarland, 1940, pp. 312–317.
	Absolute threshold		No effect	
Pain	Pain threshold	[Mullin and Luckhardt, 1934]	Increased	
	Faradic threshold	[Dodge and Benedict, 1915; Miles, 1932]	Inconclusive	
Visual	Sensitivity to light	[Lange and Specht, 1914]	Increased	
	Threshold of discrimination of light intensities	[Lange and Specht, 1914]		
	Visual acuity	[Busch, 1912]	Improvement claimed but reanalysis by Jellinek and McFarland (1940) showed that impairment occurred	
		Miles (1924)	Impairment	
Auditory	Threshold of discrimination	[Specht, 1910; Hansen]	Impairment	
	Auditory sensitivity		Inconclusive	

TABLE XVII.13

THE PSYCHOLOGICAL EFFECTS OF DRUGS: ALCOHOL

MOTOR FUNCTIONS

Function	Test	Type and number of subjects	Author and date	Effect	Comment
(a) Unskilled Muscular strength	Ergograph	(see text for further details)		"Small dosages (10–20 c.c.) of alcohol have been generally found to increase the muscular output above the initial level for at least a short while. In medium dosages (30–45 c.c.) the increase is less pronounced, and large dosages (60–80 c.c.) result either in no change or in deterioration of the performance" (Jellinek and McFarland, 1940)	
Co-ordination	Velocity of eye movements	6 subjects	Dodge and Benedict (1915)	Impairment in terms of time	Co-ordination is also involved in ergograph work.
	Finger movements	6 subjects 8 subjects	Dodge and Benedict (1915) Miles (1924)		
	Tracing pathways	25 subjects	[Bahnsen and Vedel-Petersen (1934)]	Impairment in terms of errors	
	Pursuit meter	8 subjects 14 subjects	Miles (1924) McFarland and Barach (1937)	Impairment	
(b) Skilled	Typewriting	7 subjects (not professional typists)	Vernon et al. (1919)	Great increase in errors	As numerous functions are involved, only the tests are listed here.
		5 professional typists	Miles (1924)	Moderate increase in errors but slight effect on speed	Subjects were moderate drinkers
	Typesetting	4 skilled typesetters	[Aschaffenburg, 1896]	Increase in speed but no increase in errors	Subjects were habitual drinkers
	Stringing beads		[Erlacher, 1926, 1931]	Impaired	Two other experiments on 1 and 2 subjects respectively are in accordance with this (Jellinek and McFarland, 1940)
	Sewing Pin board	Various early self experiments (See Jellinek and McFarland, (1940))		Impaired performance	
	Target shooting Threading needles	20 subjects Controlled self experiments on 43 consecutive days	[Kraepelin, 1916] Tottermann (1916), quoted by Miles (1932)	Impaired performance	

668

THE EFFECTS OF ALCOHOL ON DRIVING

The role of alcohol in motor accidents is well known. Reference is made to the earlier work by Heise and Halporn (1932), Heise (1934), Vernon (1936), Cavett (1938) and others in the reviews by Jellinek and McFarland (1940) and Drew (1950).

A carefully conducted experiment on thirty-seven skilled drivers, who were mostly accustomed to drinking moderate amounts of alcohol, was carried out by Bjerver and Goldberg (1950) who also give references to much of the recent literature. They found the threshold of impairment of the driving ability of their subjects to be 0·35 to 0·40 per mille (0·035 to 0·04 per cent) in the blood. Drew (unpublished) investigated the effects of alcohol on a simulated driving problem, and found that there was a small increase in error score when the blood-alcohol level was in the range 30–50 mg per 100 ml; the speed of driving increased with small doses and fell off with larger doses, the peak speed occurring after the ingestion of about 0·35 g per kg body weight. "Statistical analysis showed that the blood-alcohol level was best for predicting . . . what the performance would be ten minutes *after* sampling; whereas the urine-alcohol level was best for estimating what the performance had been ten minutes *before* sampling.

ALCOHOL AND PERSONALITY

Although alcohol has such marked effects on the personality, these have been largely ignored, and there are remarkably few studies which are directly relevant. Hollingworth, on the basis of his studies of the effects of alcohol and caffeine on small groups of subjects, states: "There is a very striking negative correlation between final proficiency and susceptibility to the effects of alcohol . . ." and he concludes: "Drug resistance is positively correlated with general competence." (Hollingworth, 1923–4, *see also* Hollingworth, 1925 and 1931). This suggests that the neurotic may be more susceptible, and Newman (1935) found that they tended to respond differently from normal subjects following the intravenous injection of alcohol, e.g. in his series of fifty, depression and crying occurred in 34 per cent of neurotics and 45 per cent of schizophrenics but in none of the normal subjects. (The schizophrenics were differentiated from both the normal and most of the neurotic subjects by their loss of contact with reality following the injection.) According to McDougall's (1929) theory, which has been recently extended by Eysenck (1957), the extravert would be expected to be more susceptible to the effects of alcohol than the introvert, and the effects of alcohol are also claimed to be extraverting. There is as yet no direct experimental evidence for the theory based on experiments with alcohol.

There have been numerous studies of the personality traits of alcoholics; thirty-seven of these are summarized by Sutherland *et al.* (1950) who conclude: "No satisfactory evidence has been discovered that justifies a conclusion that persons of one type are more likely to become alcoholics than persons of another type. This conclusion agrees with the clinical findings of Wexberg (1949) that 'There is no alcoholic personality prior to alcoholism'." However, Parnell (1955) has found some evidence for a correlation between body build and alcohol consumption, which is greater in endomorphs than those with other physiques.

Just as the reasons for drinking are various, considerable heterogeneity is found among alcoholics, which has recently been demonstrated using factor-analytical methods (Schaefer, 1954; Markkanen, 1957).

Horton (1943) studied data from fifty-six primitive societies and found evidence in favour of the relationship between anxiety and the consumption of alcohol; this is in accordance with the findings cited in the section on the effects of alcohol in animals, and compatible with Dollard and Miller's (1950) theory. However, numerous other factors are doubtless involved, such as a low alcohol limen (Martensen-Larsen, 1950), and there is some evidence that alcoholism may be a "genetotrophic" disease, i.e. "one arising fundamentally from nutritional deficiency which in turn has its basis in a genetically controlled augmented requirement for one or more specific nutritional elements" (Williams *et al.*, 1949).

EXPERIMENTS ON THE EFFECTS OF ALCOHOL IN ANIMALS

There are numerous reports of impairment in animals as a result of alcohol (complex maze habits are disturbed more than simple ones (Varner, 1933)), and Miller and Miles (1936) found (*a*) that alcohol caused a decrease in speed and an increase in variability, and in the number of errors; (*b*) that a succession of non-rewarded trials led to similar effects and that the combination of (*a*) and (*b*) had an effect in the maze situation very much greater than the sum of the separate effects.

The effects of alcohol on conditioning are discussed in another chapter by Franks, and on "experimental neuroses" by Broadhurst. The effect on conditioning is similar to that described for barbiturates (e.g. Andreyer, 1934; Dworkin *et al.*, 1937). The conclusions from the animal experiments of Masserman (1944), Masserman and Yum (1946), Bailey and Miller (1952) and Conger (1951) may be of some relevance to the motivation of humans in taking alcohol. Masserman showed that whereas the administration of alcohol to normal cats resulted in a loss of the most complex and recently learned adaptive patterns, in some "neurotic" cats it resulted in the re-establishment of more nearly normal responses, but most of the cats developed a preference or "addiction" to alcohol until their "neuroses" were relieved by other means. Conger (1951) found that alcohol decreased the strength of avoidance motivated by fear in normal rats, and this was confirmed for cats by Bailey and Miller (1952). Dollard and Miller (1950) hypothesized that alcohol (and the barbiturates) "produce a greater reduction in the strength of fear than they do in that of other drives. Thus they lower the gradient of avoidance more than that of approach." This reduction in strength of fear and conflict reinforces the "responses" involved in drinking, which thereby become learned. These findings accord well with Eysenck's theory.

Narcotics and Analgesics

Owing to limitations of space and also the fact that morphine and similar compounds are rarely used in psychological experiments in man (except "post-addicts"), the relief of pain by drugs and the other effects caused by these drugs can only be briefly mentioned. Details of the action of morphine and related drugs on the central nervous system are given in the comprehensive and excellent review by Wikler (1950).

A new impetus was given to the experimental measurement of pain threshold and of the effects of drugs upon it, by Hardy, Wolff and Goodell (1940) who developed a thermal radiation method which has been extensively used. Hardy (1956) reports that the pain threshold obtained by this method does not differ appreciably in subjects of different sex, age, race and cultural background, but several other investigators have failed to confirm this uniformity (Beecher, 1956a and b), and the significance of the effects of narcotics and analgesics on pain threshold remains matter of controversy. Wolff, Hardy and Goodell (1940, 1941) found that morphine, aspirin and other analgesics raised the pain threshold, but Harris and Blockus (1952), using tooth pulp algesimetry, found that aspirin (0·65 G), in contrast to codeine, did not raise the threshold any more than did a *placebo*; on account of this, they even questioned whether aspirin was an analgesic. On the other hand "the existence of any dependable relationship between the effects of analgesic agents and the pain threshold" has been doubted by various workers including Beecher (1956) and his colleagues (e.g. Keats *et al.*, 1950), who have emphasized the importance of the reaction to pain rather than the pain threshold, and have argued that the potency of analgesics should be assessed in a clinical situation by measuring their effects on naturally occurring pain (Keats, Beecher and Mosteller, 1950).

That an important part of the effect of an analgesic is attributable to the influence on the reaction to pain and the diminution of anxiety has received support

from the experiments of Hill, Kornetsky, Flanary and Wikler (1952), Hill, Belleville and Wikler (1954), Kornetsky (1954) and Hill (1956). (For a recent discussion of the effects of analgesics and the nature of pain, *see* the Symposium on this subject, *J. Chronic Dis.* **4**, 1–110, 1956).

Aspirin (and Cortisone)

The psychological effects of ordinary doses of aspirin on nonsense syllable learning (Jones, 1933) and on various functions such as addition, coding, opposites test, steadiness and reaction-time (Davis, 1936) are negligible. It is of interest that a psychosis has been reported attributable to large doses of aspirin (Bowman, 1933), in view of the finding that cortisone (which may also produce a psychosis), has turned out to be like aspirin in its effects on rheumatoid arthritis, although perhaps not as satisfactory (*M.R.C. Report*, 1957). Incidentally, although there are clinical reports of the psychological effects of cortisone and ACTH (e.g. Rees, 1953; Lewis and Fleminger, 1954; Fleminger, 1955; Drake, 1954; Fox, 1955) no easily detectable changes in test performance appear to occur with cortisone (Chance and Lotsof, 1955).

Tobacco

Although Rivers (1908) observed no appreciable effect, increases (Berry, 1917) and decreases (Bush, 1914) in efficiency have been attributed to smoking, about which there has been much controversy (e.g. Earp, 1927; Hopkins, 1938). The psychological effects in smokers and non-smokers were carefully investigated by Hull (1924) who found that only three of the twelve forms of behaviour studied were definitely affected, two of which were physiological (pulse and tremor), the other being addition, which was impaired in non-smokers and improved in habitual smokers. Fay (1936) found that the smoking *situation* had little effect on simple and choice reaction-times. However, such studies appear rather trivial in comparison with the probable long-term carcinogenetic effects. (It is of interest that whereas the correlation between smoking and carcinoma of the bronchus is supposed by the tobacco manufacturers not to indicate a causal relationship, a non-causal interpretation has not apparently been suggested for the correlation between alcohol and its apparent effects.)

Anoxia

Low oxygen tension may impair performance on a variety of tasks in a manner similar to that of depressant drugs, more complex functions being impaired sooner than simpler ones (McFarland, 1932, 1939). Neurotics appear to be more susceptible than normal subjects (McFarland and Barach, 1937; Hertzman *et al.*, 1944). Impairment after alcohol is reduced by giving oxygen (McFarland and Barach, 1936) and there is some evidence that amphetamine helps to counteract the effects of oxygen lack (Seitz and Barmack, 1940) and similarly that raising the blood-glucose level tends to reduce the effects of anoxia (Richter, 1949–50). A detailed consideration of the effects of anoxia on perception will be found in Chapter 3 by G. Granger on "Abnormalities of Sensory Perception."

Nitrous Oxide

The administration of this gas, usually in the proportion of 30 per cent nitrous oxide to 70 per cent of oxygen, breathed in through a face mask, has a depressant effect on the central nervous system, and has been found by McKinney (1932) and Steinberg (1954) to affect immediate memory adversely; similarly Russell and Steinberg (1955) have found slower learning of a temporal maze. Results such as these are capable of two interpretations; the effect of the drug may be primarily on the *formation* of associations, or on their *availability*. In the studies mentioned both learning and test performance were carried out under the influence of the drug, thus confounding these two effects.

Nitrous oxide lends itself particularly well to studies in which an attempt is made to separate out these two effects because the drug is rapidly excreted, and subjects return to a normal state almost immediately after withdrawal of the drug. Two experiments of particular interest from the methodological point of view have been reported in this connexion by Steinberg and Summerfield (1957). In the first of these, nonsense syllables were learned by two groups equated for learning ability. The control group breathed air during the learning period, the experimental group breathed 30 per cent nitrous oxide. An interval of 12·5 min was introduced between the fifteenth and sixteenth trials, during which and subsequent to which the drug group reverted to breathing air. The failure of the drug group to improve their score during the interval suggests strongly that the effect of the drug is on *acquisition* rather than *performance*; that is:

"It acts so as to impede the formative processes, and does not merely obscure the progress of learning by blocking responses."

In the second experiment, Steinberg and Summerfield employed three groups. Group *C*, the control group, breathed air throughout. Group E_1 breathed air during the initial learning and nitrous oxide during the interval. Group E_2 breathed nitrous oxide throughout. The hypothesis tested in this experiment,

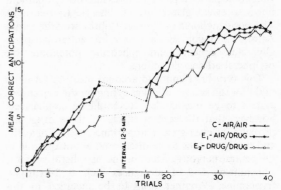

Fig. 17.7. Learning Curves for the Air/Air, Air/Drug and Drug/Drug Groups (Ten Subjects in each Group) Plotted in Terms of Mean Number of Syllables Correctly Anticipated per Trial
(From Steinberg and Summerfield, 1957)

which was identical in its general arrangement with the previous one, was as follows. According to the interference theorists, forgetting results because extraneous associations disturb the pattern built up during learning. If nitrous oxide is administered *immediately after learning*, this should reduce forgetting because, by impairing the formation of new associations, it should reduce interference. The results of the experiment are shown in Fig. 17.7. It will be seen that Group *C*, which breathed air during the interval, showed a *deterioration* of performance, while there was no such deterioration in Groups E_1 and E_2. The results therefore strongly support the general hypothesis. Quite generally these results are deducible from Eysenck's general theory (1955).

AUTONOMIC DRUGS

This section is concerned chiefly with the drugs which mimic or block the action of the peripheral autonomic nervous system, sympathetic or parasympathetic. There are thus four groups—

1. Sympathomimetic (adrenergic).
2. Sympatholytic (i.e. blocking).
3. Parasympathomimetic (cholinergic).
4. Parasympatholytic (i.e. blocking).

Several drugs already discussed have some of the properties of the drugs in these groups, for example amphetamine is sympathomimetic. Adrenaline and nor-adrenaline are the main examples of group

(1), acetylcholine and Mecholyl of group (3) and atropine of group (4). Groups (1) and (4) have some properties in common, such as dilatation of the pupil, and likewise groups (2) and (3). Hexamethonium and tetraethylammonium compounds, which have also been used in psychological experiments, are both parasympatholytic and sympatholytic.

Preganglionic nerves and nerves to voluntary muscles are cholinergic (nicotinic) whereas the post-ganglionic parasympathetic fibres and the sympathetic fibres to sweat glands are cholinergic (muscarinic). The postganglionic sympathetic fibres are adrenergic. Atropine antagonizes the muscarinic action peripherally, and cocaine and ephedrine potentiate the peripheral adrenergic actions.

This very brief and arid account must be borne in mind for the actions of drugs acting on the autonomic system to be intelligible. It should be emphasized, however, that the central effects of these drugs are probably of even greater importance psychologically, and much remains to be discovered about the role in the central nervous system of the peripheral synaptic transmitters, and of substances such as 5-hydroxy-tryptamine. Another drug to be included in this section is histamine, although it is not strictly speaking an autonomic drug; it is a substance produced peripherally by tissue damage, but its role in the central nervous system is not yet decided.

Adrenaline and Nor-adrenaline[1]

The ability of adrenaline to produce effects characteristic of stimulation of the sympathetic system has long been recognized (Langley, 1901; Elliott, 1905) and the role of this system in the emergency reactions of "fight or flight" is familiar from the work of Cannon (e.g. 1915, 1929, descriptions of which will be found in most textbooks of physiology or psychology). Recently, adrenaline and its derivatives have assumed a new importance owing to their possible role in certain psychoses.

CLINICAL DESCRIPTIONS

There has been a somewhat sterile controversy as to whether the injection of adrenaline can give rise to a "true" emotion. The difficulties are in part empirical (the solutions of adrenaline often being impure and there being large individual variations), and in part semantic. Part of the controversy arises from the ambiguity of the concept of "emotion" which, as Duffy (1951) has pointed out, is an example of a dual concept, incorporating "two aspects of behaviour which may vary independently," namely *energy mobilization* and the *direction* of behaviour. "It so happens that the administration of adrenaline affects

the energy level of behaviour but not its direction," there usually being no environmental situation towards which this additional energy could be meaningfully directed.

Maranon (1924) found that adrenaline injection sometimes resulted in an affective state in which the subjects described themselves as feeling *as if* afraid, or *as if* their emotions were aroused, etc., but in only a few instances was there evidence of genuine emotion. Cantril and Hunt (1932) concluded that "in general the injection of adrenaline is not sufficient to produce an emotion," as the intellectual content (i.e. the object or situation towards which the emotion is directed) is usually not present. Richter (1940) considered that adrenaline normally does not give rise to "true emotion but emotion with insight," and when the former does occur it is because "the subject becomes conscious of the coenaesthetic impulses arising as a result of the somatic disturbance and begins to think of emotional experiences in which he has felt a similar sensation. . . ." In current jargon, this is an example of positive feed-back. Darrow and Gellhorn (1939) demonstrated that "the secretion of adrenaline into the circulation is itself an effective damping mechanism for reducing the reactions induced by sympathetic excitation"; this might be regarded as equivalent to negative feed-back, which has also been demonstrated by Callaway and Thompson (1953). Callaway (1955) quotes evidence that procedures which evoke sympathetic activity (and stimulation of the ascending reticular system) may "create a limited sensory environment." In this way he has attempted to link up the production of hallucinations by sympathetic substances with their production by restriction of sensory stimulation.

Although Landis and Hunt (1932) maintained that the various mental disorders showed no differences in susceptibility to adrenaline, Lindemann (1935) who investigated the effect of intramuscular injection of 1 ml of 1:1,000 solution of adrenaline on forty-eight patients found that apathetic schizophrenics showed little response (cf. Freeman and Carmichael, 1935), whereas acute schizophrenics and "active psychoneurotics" showed the most marked changes. Sometimes, however, the same patient reacted differently when retested. Lindemann also noted that there was characteristically a reduction in speech and motor activity, accompanied by increased self-concern and decreased interest in the outside world. Kraines and Sherman (1940) were unable to find a significant difference in the cardiovascular effects of adrenaline between neurotic and normal groups.

Subsequently Lindemann and Finesinger (1938, 1940) studied the effects of injection of (1) saline, (2) adrenaline, (3) Mecholyl (acetyl-methylcholine chloride), a cholinergic compound. In the first study,

---

[1] "Epinephrine" and "nor-epinephrine" are synonyms for adrenaline and nor-adrenaline respectively.

they tested twenty patients who were prone to distinct attacks of anxiety but had relatively free intervals, and found that these could be divided almost evenly into four groups, those in whom—

(a) adrenaline reactivates a typical attack,
(b) Mecholyl reactivates a typical attack,
(c) both drugs reactivate a typical attack,
(d) neither drug has any effect on the anxiety state.

A marked adrenaline response was found in patients who had overwhelming attacks of distress, coming on without provocation and not related to specific situations or to a specific content. Their distress might be labelled depression, anxiety or worry . . . The markedly positive response to Mecholyl was exhibited, on the contrary, by persons who had developed definite phobias and concrete fears. Their reaction was one of panic, with alert eagerness to cope with a threatening situation, in contract to the adrenaline group, where the patient was overwhelmed by an indefinable wave of distress concerning which he does not attempt any intellectual elaboration.

Those in group (c) had a history of instability of the autonomic nervous system, and in group (d) were patients with more serious personality difficulties.

The symptoms produced by these injections were more fully described in a later article by Lindemann and Finesinger (1940). Twenty-four (out of forty) patients referred to feeling happy after Mecholyl, whereas this was never reported after adrenaline which tended to cause worry, depression and anger (cf. Jerrild and Thomas, 1931). Myerson et al. (1937) found no evidence of a change in the mental reactions of eighteen schizophrenics who received injections of Mecholyl, but Funkenstein et al. (1948) found that adrenaline or Mecholyl sometimes precipitated anxiety in schizophrenics, although not as often as in anxiety neurotics (cf. Dynes and Tod, 1940).

Lindemann and Finesinger's observations on the effects of these drugs on mood and behaviour suggest that the injection of adrenaline may make patients more dysthymic, i.e. more introverted and more neurotic. "Under the influence of adrenaline the patient appears self-absorbed, hesitant, inhibited and quite preoccupied with his symptoms," whereas with Mecholyl "the whole picture is that of vivaciousness, eagerness. There is occasional euphoria, relaxation and relief" (Lindemann and Finesinger, 1938). Similarly, under the influence of adrenaline the patient speaks little, whereas with Mecholyl the effects are just the opposite.

PSYCHOLOGICAL EXPERIMENTS

Psychological experiments on the effects of adrenaline are regrettably sparse. Jerrild and Thomas (1931) investigated the effects on performance tests by six subjects and claimed that adrenaline "did not favour mental efficiency, while the motor activities [strength of grip and tapping] were somewhat improved . . . in spite of the tremor which it caused." Landis (1935) was unable to demonstrate that it had any effect on dart throwing.

Since then a report has appeared of experiments "to explore whether prolonged intravenous adrenaline infusion at a low dose level reactivated habitual idiosyncratic anxiety patterns in normal persons." Also included were the effects "on certain cardiac indices and on psychological and motor performance known to be disturbed in anxiety" (Basowitz, Korchin and Oken, 1955; Basowitz et al., 1956).

There were twelve subjects, aged 24–28, and each was investigated on three occasions, the first being devoted to a clinical interview, and on the subsequent two visits each subject received an adrenaline or saline infusion. The following tests were administered while the infusion was in progress: (1) flicker fusion frequency, (2) hand steadiness, (3) memory for digits, (4) physical persistence, (5) the Stroop task [stressful colour-naming], (6) motor inhibition and (7) word fluency under distraction. The subjective changes and the cardiovascular effects were also studied.

Only "the more clearly motor tasks" were affected among all these tests. "Hand steadiness, physical persistence and motor inhibition showed a statistically significant decrease with adrenaline, steadiness at the 0·001 and the others at the 0·05 level of confidence. No noteworthy trends were apparent on the remaining procedures of the battery" (Basowitz et al., 1955).

In almost all subjects pulse pressure and rate were increased, and the commonest subjective response was an awareness of this. Mild apprehensiveness under adrenaline was described by seven individuals. "There was a distinct tendency for adrenalin to elicit personally-patterned symptoms consistent with the individual's past history of anxiety." In one subject with a long history of labile anxiety, they were able to turn on and off a full-blown free anxiety reaction by alternately switching in and cutting out the adrenaline infusion. "On the other hand, constricted personalities who tend to encapsulate affect failed to show appreciable subjective changes." There was a total of sixty-six symptoms in all the adrenaline sessions combined (compared with twenty-one in the saline, this figure being in part attributable to apprehensiveness occasioned by the unfamiliar surgical procedure).

Some of the effects of adrenaline infusion on psychological performance have been observed in neurotics or in normal subjects under stress (see Lazarus, Deese and Osler, 1952, for a summary of the latter). Hand steadiness and physical persistence tend to be decreased in neurotics (Eysenck, 1947) and the fact that these are also decreased by the adrenaline infusion suggests that this causes an increase in neuroticism. However, the digit span test was not affected, yet there is evidence that this is a measure of anxiety (Moldawsky and Moldawsky, 1952). In addition, there was an effect on motor inhibition, which was decreased. According to Eysenck (1947) lessened motor control is characteristic of extraversion (or hysteria).

The Differential Effects of Adrenaline and Nor-adrenaline

Some of the effects of what was thought to be adrenaline were puzzling until it was recently realized that natural adrenaline contains about 10–20 per cent of nor-adrenaline (Goodman and Gilman, 1955), a substance investigated by Barger and Dale in 1910 and strangely overlooked since.

Chemically nor-adrenaline differs from adrenaline only by the absence of the N-methyl group. There is mounting evidence that nor-adrenaline is the adrenergic transmitter substance at synapses, and not adrenaline as previously supposed. The hormone normally produced by the suprarenal medulla is, however, chiefly adrenaline. These considerations entail "a certain reorientation of our ideas on the functioning of this system. Perhaps the most important inference is that the sympathetic nervous system and the suprarenal medulla . . . should be considered as separate entities from the functional point of view" (von Euler, 1954).

Some of the contrasted effects of adrenaline and nor-adrenaline are summarized in the following table (largely based on Funkenstein et al., 1952, and Goldenberg et al., 1950).

Table XVII.14

CONTRASTED EFFECTS OF ADRENALINE AND NOR-ADRENALINE

Cardiovascular system	Adrenaline	Nor-adrenaline
Blood-pressure . . .	+++	+++
Pulse	+++	= or (−)
Cardiac output . .	+++	= or (−)
Peripheral resistance .	(−)	+++
Metabolized in body .	Quickly	Slowly
Effect on blood sugar .	+++	+
Effect of Mecholyl .	Neutralizes	Neutralizes for a short time
Stimulation of anterior pituitary to secrete ACTH	+++	0
Stimulation of C.N.S. .	+++	+
Effect of ergotamine .	Diminishes effects	Nil

+ = increase
0 = no change
− = decrease

The effects on the brain of these, and other, substances have recently been studied using a new technique (Feldberg and Sherwood, 1954a and b; Feldberg, 1955; Sherwood, 1955). The drugs are injected through an intraventricular cannula screwed into the skull where it may be kept for prolonged periods. This has been used in cats and in schizophrenic patients.

Nor-adrenaline and adrenaline in doses of less than 100 μg produced a condition resembling light Nembutal anaesthesia. This is presumably due to the stimulation of the region of the *massa intermedia* which Hess has shown to be concerned with sleep. (If dyes were injected in a similar manner, it might be easier to ascertain exactly where the injection substances reach.) A few microgrammes of acetylcholine injected in this way into the cat's lateral cerebral ventricle produced a condition resembling an akinetic seizure, after which the cat remains subdued and stuporous.

There is normally a blood cerebrospinal fluid barrier to nor-adrenaline (Richter, 1950) and other substances can rarely, if ever, reach these regions in such concentrations. Thus, fruitful as this technique may be in the study of the nervous system, the implications for psychology are obscure.

Ax (1953) has attempted to explain the differences between fear and anger in terms of adrenaline and nor-adrenaline production. He studied the reactions of forty-three subjects to fear and anger, recording the heart rate, ballistocardiogram, respiratory rate, face temperature, hand temperature, skin conductance and the integrated muscle potential. He claimed that fear was differentiated from anger by the different pattern of the reactions, and suggested that these were respectively "similar to those produced by injection of epinephrine and nor-epinephrine. However, neither are these patterns clear-cut, nor is their relationship to these hormones. Ax's view is in contrast to Arnold's (1945, 1950); she has suggested that anger involves a strong reaction of both the sympathetic and parasympathetic branches of the autonomic nervous system, whereas fear is merely a sympathetic reaction. As yet, Ax's theory is "not supported by substantial data" (Altschule, 1954). The recent work of Funkenstein et al. (1957) would appear to offer some support at least.

Funkenstein (1956) has evolved a theory which relates adrenaline and nor-adrenaline to differences in behaviour. As it is based on his work using the adrenaline-Mecholyl (Funkenstein) test, which is supposed to measure "autonomic reactivity," some of the tests of this variety will be described before proceeding to his later work.

Eppinger and Hess (1910) considered that certain symptoms could be attributed to overactivity of the parasympathetic. They therefore postulated two syndromes, sympathotonia and vagotonia, which they believed could be diagnosed on the basis of the reactions to injections of adrenaline, pilocarpine and atropine. The syndromes were supposed to have different psychological symptoms; for example, "depression, hesitation, anxiety, apathy, melancholia, liability to phobias" were attributed to the vagotonics, whereas the sympathotonics were alleged to be "impulsive, active, busy, dominating and liable to lose control over themselves" (Guillaume, 1928).

The views of Eppinger and Hess have been severely criticized (e.g. Sachs, 1936; Altschule, 1953, 1954, etc.) and there is little evidence in favour of their tests or of the idea that either the sympathetic or the parasympathetic system may predominate (e.g. Paton and Steinberg, 1956; Terry, 1953) although the work of Wenger has helped to revive interest in this subject (*see* Eysenck, 1959, Chapter 8; also Lacey, 1950, 1953, also Jacobsen *et al.*, 1955).

Numerous similar tests have been devised, which are reviewed by Cyvin *et al.* (1956). That of Funkenstein was originally used to predict the outcome of electric shock treatment (Funkenstein *et al.*, 1948, 1950). The method depends upon the blood-pressure and psychological reactions to (1) mecholyl and (2) adrenaline. Several patterns of response (I to VII) have been distinguished, according to the time for re-establishing homeostasis, and whether anxiety has been precipitated. These patterns are not specific for any diagnostic category but it is claimed (1950) that prediction of the clinical response to electric shock treatment made on the basis of the physiological reactions is more reliable than the prediction made on the basis of any single diagnostic category or group of diagnostic categories.

Funkenstein *et al.* (1952) gave the standard dose of Mecholyl intramuscularly to sixty-three patients, mostly psychotic, with raised blood-pressure. They distinguished two main patterns of response, A and B, illustrated in Fig. 17.8.

The majority of group A were improved by E.C.T. (thirty-nine out of forty-two), whereas a large majority of group B were not improved (eighteen out of twenty-one). The explanation was put forward that there was excessive secretion in group A of an adrenaline-like substance, and in group B of a nor-adrenaline-like substance. (The predominant diagnostic categories in group A were depressions and "involutional psychoses," and in group B schizophrenics.)

Funkenstein and his colleagues (e.g. Funkenstein *et al.*, 1951; Funkenstein, 1956) have also found evidence that the prognosis, irrespective of treatment (whether by insulin, lobotomy, psychotherapy) is better for Group A.

Evidence in favour of the Funkenstein test has been

obtained by Brothers and Bennett (1954), Alexander (1955), Moriarty (1956) and Geocaris and Kooiker (1956), but Sloane and Lewis (1956) were unable to confirm its value for prognosis, and Montagu and Davies (1955) concluded that the reaction to adrenaline was of no use in prognosis. The studies by Alexander (1955) and by Sloane and Lewis (1956) appear to have been carefully carried out and the results of both were evaluated statistically: the fact that one largely confirmed and the other failed to

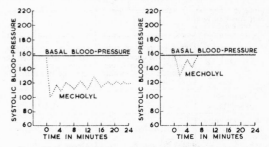

FIG. 17.8. TWO TYPES OF SYSTOLIC BLOOD-PRESSURE REACTIONS FOLLOWING THE DRUG MECHOLYL

On the left is a typical Group VI reaction interpreted on the basis of previous research as indicating excessive secretion of an epinephrine-*like* substance. On the right is a typical Group II–III reaction interpreted on the basis of previous research as indicating excessive secretion of a nor-epinephrine-*like* substance.

(*From Funkenstein*, 1956)

confirm Funkenstein's findings is therefore difficult to explain. Although Funkenstein *et al.* (e.g. 1952*a*) have emphasized that raised blood-pressure is a necessary condition for the test (and they found that only one hundred out of five hundred and eight patients were suitable subjects) this cannot explain the findings of Alexander (1955) or those of Brothers and Bennett (1954) as there was no special selection exercised, consecutive patients being tested.[1] An incidental finding in comparing five studies is that those who obtained evidence in favour of the Funkenstein test reported higher recovery rates than those who failed to confirm it.

Funkenstein and his co-workers (Funkenstein *et al.*, 1954, 1957; Funkenstein and Meade, 1954; Funkenstein, 1955, 1956; King and Henry, 1955) have carried out several studies on normal subjects under stress and on patients, which suggest that the direction of anger is related to adrenaline and nor-adrenaline, anger directed outward being associated with excessive secretion of a nor-adrenaline-like substance, whereas anger directed inwards and anxiety are supposed to be associated with excessive secretion of an adrenaline-like substance. Funkenstein (1955) wrote: "Standing

[1] It does not appear that Funkenstein rejected those with low or normal blood-pressure in his earlier studies. Moreover, if the test can only be applied to less than 20 per cent of the patients, as in his 1952 study, this must somewhat limit its value.

on the shoulders of Cannon and Freud, we have extended our view of human behaviour and discovered fertile new fields for exploration." The main characteristics which are supposed to be associated with the two different types of response to Mecholyl (shown in Fig. 17.7) are summarized in Table XVII.15.

TABLE XVII.15

FEATURES ASSOCIATED WITH THE DIFFERENT RESPONSES TO MECHOLYL, ACCORDING TO FUNKENSTEIN (1956)

Response type to mecholyl	A	B
	Marked fall of B.P., large area under curve, failure to return to pre-injection level within 25 min	Minimal fall of B.P., small area under the curve, rapid return to pre-injection B.P.
Funkenstein grouping	VI	II, III
Predominant secretion . . .	Adrenaline-like	Nor-adrenaline-like
Direction of anger .	Inwards	Outwards
Anxiety . .	May be present	Absent
Type of patient .	Depressed	Angry paranoid
Stage of development in man .	Relatively late	Characteristic of an early stage of development
Central sympathetic reactivity . .	Decreased	Normal or increased
Prognosis . .	Good response to E.C.T., insulin, lobotomy, and more spontaneous remissions and recoveries with psychotherapy	Poorer response to treatment
Social class . .	"Upper upper" (Old New England family)	Mixed

Although the terms adrenaline-*like* and nor-adrenaline-*like* are used, Funkenstein (1956) reports that Elmadjian, Hope and Freeman have confirmed, by means of a bioassay method, that the Mecholyl reaction is "an indicator of the type of preponderant adrenal medullary secretion." "Evidence of excessive secretion nor-epinephrine and epinephrine can be found in both psychotic patients and in healthy subjects, but there is a difference," namely that "in the healthy subjects, excessive secretion is found only when the subject is under stress."

Although the Mecholyl test has been interpreted by Gellhorn (*Physiological Foundations of Neurology and Psychiatry*, Chapter 20, 1953; *see also* Schneider, 1955) on the basis of his experiments on cats, as measuring central sympathetic reactivity, Altschule (1953) considers that tests of this kind do not measure the reactivity of the autonomic nervous system but merely "the activity of enzymes that inactivate or destroy the drugs; the reactivity of the end organs . . .; and, in the case of acetylcholine, the reactivity of some autonomic ganglia" (cf. Hoffer, 1954). Cyvin *et al.* (1956) who have studied the effects of adrenaline

and mecholyl on the intra-arterial blood-pressure (recorded from a punctured femoral artery by means of a Ludwig's kymograph) have also cast doubt on the Funkenstein test. Nevertheless, there appears to be a considerable amount of evidence in favour of the Mecholyl test and of some of the interpretations which have been placed upon it although these can only be provisionally accepted until confirmed by further experiments utilizing bioassay or fluorimetric methods. If the distinction between reaction types *A* and *B* is confirmed, it would be of interest to discover whether dysthymics (and introverts) were to be found in group *A*, and hysterics (and extraverts) in group *B*.

THE BLOOD LEVELS OF ADRENALINE AND NOR-ADRENALINE IN DIFFERENT CONDITIONS

It is only recently that it has become possible to estimate the amount of adrenaline and nor-adrenaline in the blood or urine. To be able to do this is obviously of considerable importance in assessing the psychological effects of these substances, e.g. to confirm or refute Funkenstein's theory. There are two main methods, biological assay and fluorimetry. Unfortunately these have sometimes resulted in widely discrepant results. Minute amounts, even one part in fifty-five million, can be detected.

A relationship between different emotions and changes in the blood has been shown by various methods of biological assay (e.g. Gagnon, 1952; Diethelm *et al.*, 1945; Fleetwood and Harrington, 1951; Fleetwood and Diethelm, 1951; Fleetwood, 1956). Fleetwood and Diethelm (1951) made repeated observations on twenty-six alcoholics whose psychological states were assessed independently by one author, while the other determined the amounts of adrenergic and cholinergic substances in their blood (the method of bioassay depending upon the contraction of the rabbit's duodenum, or the rat's colon and uterus, quantification being by comparison with the effects of adrenaline, nor-adrenaline and acetylcholine).

In states of *anxiety*, they found evidence of increased adrenergic substances, resembling nor-adrenaline, whereas in states of *tension* and *resentment* cholinergic substances were found. They claimed that "alcoholic patients had varying degrees of resentment when an urge to drink was present. Alcohol relieved the resentment and the corresponding substance in the blood declined or disappeared." (Alcohol *in vitro* did not have the same effect on the preparations.) They maintained "There are no indications that the resentment in alcoholic patients is different from that presented by other subjects." However, Fleetwood (1955) who studied a larger group of subjects, and used various drugs as well as alcohol, found that non-alcoholic patients showed considerably less resentment than alcoholics did, that they had correspondingly less of the "resentment substance" and that "the effect of alcohol on the 'resentment substance' in non-alcoholic patients was doubtful. . . ." Amytal was claimed to be more effective than alcohol in relieving tension in non-alcoholics.

Ritchie (1951) has criticized Fleetwood's technique and has failed to confirm that there is a correlation between the emotional state and the effects of the blood, and it is certainly surprising that nor-adrenaline rather than adrenaline should be the substance supposed to be related to anxiety. Independent confirmation, e.g. using fluorimetric methods, will be necessary.

HALLUCINOGENS

The drugs which have been discussed so far have recently been overshadowed by the drugs to be discussed in this and the next section, namely the hallucinogens and the tranquillizers,[1] the study of which is often equated with "psychopharmacology." The two groups of drugs tend to have opposite effects, the hallucinogens making normal subjects appear psychotic, while some of the tranquillizers tend to reduce psychotic symptoms.

Although a great variety of drugs can cause toxic psychoses, delirium (with dissociation for place and time) is usually a marked feature. The hallucinogens, on the other hand, produce symptoms which are more like those which are found in the functional psychoses. They are therefore sometimes referred to as *psychotomimetic* or, because of their effects on imagery, *phantastica*.

Mescaline

The first hallucinogen to be studied at all thoroughly was mescaline, one of the alkaloids which were isolated by Lewin (1888) from the *Lophophorus cactus* (*Anhalonium Lewinii*). The sliced-off tops of the cactus (mescal buttons or *peyotle*) have long been used by the American Indians in the region where the cactus grows, which is in North Mexico and on either side of the Rio Grande.

There have been innumerable reports on the effects of mescal buttons and of mescaline. Weir Mitchell (1896) in U.S.A. and Havelock Ellis (1897) in this country were among the first to describe their experiences with it. A few hours after taking the drug, Weir Mitchell found himself "deliciously at languid ease" and when he went into a darkened room was "enchanted" by a display such that he found it "hopeless to describe in language" which could convey to others the "beauty and splendour" of what he had seen. He supplied William James with a supply of mescal buttons, but after taking one William James was violently sick for twenty-four hours (Klüver, 1928).

During the next fifty years numerous reports of the effects of mescaline appeared, largely based on minute self descriptions by sophisticated volunteers. The work is summarized in English by Klüver (1928), in French by Routier (1927) and, at greater length, in German by Beringer (1927). An excellent description which appeared more recently is that of Stockings (1940; *see also* Guttman, 1936). For a full description of the symptoms, reference must be made to these works.

The visual phenomena have received the most attention and certain features recur in many of the studies. For example, Knauer and Maloney (1913), who investigated mescaline at Kraepelin's instigation, found that there was a characteristic sequence of the visions which began as wavy lines and mosaics and gradually became more clearly structured, so that monuments, panoramas and finally coherent scenes representing episodes appeared (*see also* Klüver, 1928, 1942). Various other phenomena have been described such as binocular diplopia or polyopia, dysmegalopsia, metamorphopsia and dysmorphopsia. The visions are chiefly noted when the subject is in the dark or closes his eyes; with his eyes open, objects may appear to move and to be of different shapes.

"The outward behaviour of the subject acutely intoxicated with mescaline is relatively normal" (Mayer-Gross, 1951). Euphoria or anxiety may be present. Aldous Huxley (1956) pointed out at an American Psychiatric Association meeting that the classic descriptions of mescaline experiences differed from those based on patients in that they were not coloured by fear of anxiety or by the subject's personal memories but were characterized by "profound impersonality."

Concerning the state of consciousness, Mayer-Gross (1951) writes "It is difficult to classify the state of consciousness during intoxication which allows such full self-observation and at times seems to foster detachment and self-scrutiny. At other times the same subject seems to have lost all clarity of consciousness, is drowsy and even close to a state of sleep."

The main effects which have been observed are listed in Table XVII.16 (from Osmond and Smythies, 1952).

Although mescaline was considered a useful research tool for the psychologist and psychiatrist, few experiments guided by any hypothesis appear to have

---

[1] In most American writings *tranquillizer* is spelt *tranquilizer* but the spelling *halucinogen* has not yet been encountered.

TABLE XVII.16

A COMPARISON BETWEEN THE PSYCHOLOGICAL EFFECTS OF MESCALINE AND THE SYMPTOMS OF ACUTE SCHIZOPHRENIA

(*From Osmond and Smythies, 1952*)

	Mescalin		Acute Schizophrenia	
	Illusions	Hallucinations	Illusions	Hallucinations
1. Sensory disorders—				
(a) Vision	× × ×	× ×	× ×	× ×
(b) Hearing	×	×	× ×	× ×
(c) Body image	× × ×	—	× ×	—
(d) Smell and taste	× × ×	× × ×	× ×	× ×
(e) Skin sense	× ×	—	× ×	—
(f) Temperature	× ×	—	× ×	—
(g) Synaesthesia	× × ×	—	0	
2. Motor disorders—				
(a) Catatonia	× ×		× × ×	
3. Behaviour disorder—				
(a) Negativism	× ×		× × ×	
(b) Withdrawal	× × (big doses)		× × ×	
(c) Antisocial violence	Reported		× ×	
4. Thought disorder—				
(a) Pressure	× ×		× ×	
(b) Disturbed association	× × ×		× × ×	
(c) Blocking	× ×		× × ×	
(d) Substitution of *primitive thinking* in the form of visual images for conceptual thought	× × ×		× × ×	
(e) Neologisms	×		× ×	
5. Disorders of interpretation—				
(a) Ideas of influence	× ×		× × ×	
(b) Paranoid ideas	× × ×		× × ×	
(c) Heightened significance of objects	× × ×		× ×	
6. Delusions	× × (time factor)		× × ×	
7. Splitting	× × (time factor)		× × ×	
8. Depersonalization (a)	× ×		× ×	
Derealization (b)	× × ×		× × ×	
9. Mood disorders—				
(a) Fear and terror	× × ×		× × ×	
(b) Depression	×		×	
(c) Indifference and apathy	× × (time factor)		× × ×	
(d) Manic symptoms	×		×	
(e) Euphoria	× × ×		× ×	
(f) Schizoid humour	× ×		× ×	
10. Insight	Sometimes absent (time factor)		Sometimes present	

0, does not occur
×, occurs
× ×, marked, when it occurs, but not always present
× × ×, marked and frequent
—, not relevant

been carried out during this period, apart from Klüver's work on the effects of mescaline on eidetic images (Klüver, 1926, 1942).

The symptoms of mescaline intoxication were often compared with those of schizophrenics. "After seeing some mescaline psychoses every investigator is at first struck by their similarity to schizophrenic states, but with more experience is disappointed when he notices the great difference" (Guttman and Maclay, 1936). Schizophrenics can usually differentiate mescaline hallunications from their endogenous ones, but tend to lay the blame for them on the same persecutors as before (Mayer-Gross, 1951; *see also* Denber and Merlis, 1955). One symptom which apparently does not occur in schizophrenia is synaesthesia (e.g. when a sound of hammering is accompanied by dots of colour).

In 1952 Osmond and Smythies drew attention (1) to the similarity of the chemical formulae of mescaline and adrenaline, and (2) to the similarity between *acute* schizophrenia and mescaline intoxication. They hypothesized that a mescaline-like (or M) substance was responsible for the genesis of schizophrenia. They argued that it was misleading to compare subacute or chronic schizophrenic reactions with the laboratory observations of trained psychiatrists taking mescaline. Although the symptoms of mescaline intoxication and of acute schizophrenia are both very diverse, "the remarkable thing is that these acute reactions have so much in common" (*see* Table XVII.16).

Although Stockings (1940) had suggested that "a toxic amine with chemical and pharmacological properties similar to those of mescaline" was the causative agent of psychoses and de Jong had pointed out the similarity of adrenaline and mescaline (1945), the implications had never been followed up.

The search for the M substance was begun in conjunction with Hoffer (1954) and it was claimed that adrenochrome, a derivative of adrenaline, induced psychotic phenomena in normal subjects, the main symptoms being overactivity, depression, hallucinations and loss of insight. Rinkel *et al.* (1954) were unable to confirm these findings and suggested (Rinkel *et al.*, 1955) that adrenoxine was the effective substance.[1] Meanwhile, Hoffer and Osmond (1955) suggested yet another oxidation product of adrenaline, adrenolution (*see also* Hoffer, 1957). Both adrenochrome and adrenolutin have indole nuclei.

Lysergic Acid Diethylamide

Meanwhile another compound, also having an indole nucleus, was being investigated, namely lysergic acid diethylamide (LSD). It is a semi-synthetic derivation of ergot, and was accidentally found to have hallucinogenic properties by the chemist Hoffmann, in 1943. Its psychological effects were first reported by Stoll (1947, 1949). Unlike mescaline, it is active in minutely small quantities (25–50 μg), but the psychological effects are rather similar, although, for example, Matefi (1952) claimed that they were

[1] Rinkel *et al.* used the inert semicarbazone of adrenochrome, not adrenochrome itself.

different. (Cf. Hoch, Cattell and Pennes, 1952; Frederking, 1955.)

There has already been a large amount of work done on LSD, and a bibliography by Cerletti (1956) lists one hundred and thirty-seven references, and a more recent one, provided by Sandoz, two hundred and fourteen. In a brief account, it is extremely difficult to select appropriate items for discussion as such a vast range is covered, from the effects of LSD on the Siamese fighting fish (Evans *et al.*, 1956), on the visual system of the cat (Evarts *et al.*, 1955), the neuroses (Sandison, 1954), the metabolism of separated mammalian cerebral tissues (Lewis and McIlwain, 1954), its affinity for wool (Fischer, 1954), to its effect on snails (Abramson and Jarvik, 1955), and on artistic expression (Tonini and Montanari, 1955). To bring together the conclusions of such disparate studies would require a longer account than can be given here. Much of the recent work is summarized by Marrazzi, Hart and Cohn (1956). For clinical reports, *see* Savage (1955), Anderson and Rawnsley (1954), Forrer and Goldner (1951), Sandison *et al.* (1954), Hoch *et al.* (1952), etc.

Comparatively few psychological studies have been carried out on the effects of LSD. Sloane and Doust (1954) used a variety of tests on normal subjects and on psychiatric patients, but concluded that "it proved difficult to obtain valid differentiating measures of clinically apparent changes." For example, in spite of "the subjective impressions of distractibility and intoxication" there were no significant changes in the tests of concentration and memory. However, Landis and Clausen (1954) give some evidence of impairment of performance on psychomotor tests by early schizophrenics who were given LSD or mescaline, but their groups were too small for "the normal tests for statistical significance" to be applied.

The most intensive studies of the psychological and other effects of LSD have been carried out by Abramson and his co-workers. So far some twenty-five articles have appeared. Some of the findings would be easier to assess if it had been practical to describe some of the experiments in a single account. "Research which can be described and published most efficiently in one unit should generally be so published, where this is practical, rather than be fractionated for multiple publication in a variety of media" (*APA Ethical Standards of Psychologists*, 1953, principle 5.34–2). It is to be hoped that a single comprehensive publication covering the entire research will eventually be published.

There is one other general criticism of the research which should be mentioned, namely that the LSD was given in tap-water instead of distilled water, as the former may contain substances which reduce or inactivate the LSD. In a personal communication

Abramson (1957) writes: "We have done many experiments on the effect of various vehicles on the administration of LSD-25 and it is rather difficult to inactivate LSD-25 unless strong oxidizing agents are present in quantity." However, Hofmann, the chemist who discovered the psychological effects of LSD disagrees with this statement as, if "25 gamma of LSD-25 are dissolved in 20 ml of tap water, a chlorine content of 1 part in 2·5 million will be sufficient to immediately destroy all the LSD," according to a personal communication from Holgate (1957). The tap water may, of course, be free from any halogen, but if it is not its use inevitably casts doubt on any quantitative relationships between dose and effect and raises the suspicion that some of the supposed drug effects may be *placebo* effects and that when effects fail to occur, it may be that the water had just been chlorinated.

In studies I and XV (Abramson *et al.*, 1955) the effects on normal subjects of varying doses of LSD and of tap water were studied by means of a questionnaire. After the *placebo*, moist palms, headache, drowsiness, anxiety, etc. were the commonest symptoms and the greatest number was recorded within half an hour of ingestion of the *placebo*. After 50 µg LSD, "unsteadiness, dream-like feelings, funny feelings on the skin, inner trembling" . . ., etc. were recorded, the peak effect occurring between one and a half and two and a half hours after ingestion of the drug.

There are seven separate articles devoted to the psychological effects of LSD (IV to X). In each of these studies, six males and six females took part, and it appears that there were the same subjects for each of the experiments.

Tests were administered at four separate testing sessions, separated by at least a week. On the first occasion the subjects received a *placebo*, tap water, and on the second and third, 50 and 100 µg respectively of LSD-25; on the fourth occasion a *placebo* was given once again, in order to measure the effects of repeated testing. Nevertheless, the design of the experiment does not make it easy to measure the extent of the practice effects in the drug sessions.

The functions studied included attention and concentration (Jarvik *et al.*, 1955), spatial relations abilities (Abramson *et al.*, 1955), recall and recognition of various stimuli (Jarvik *et al.*, 1955), motor performance (Abramson *et al.*, 1955), arithmetic test performance (Jarvik *et al.*, 1955), reaction-time to auditory and visual stimuli (Abramson *et al.*, 1955).

Simple and complex cancellation tests were used as tests of attention and concentration. Six out of eight tests showed no significant change when scores of the pre-LSD-25 zero sessions were compared with the 50 µg scores. Two tests, cancellation of "a"s and vowels showed significantly impaired performance when zero and 100 μg were compared. Cancellation of words showed a significant improvement under 100 μg of LSD. With two exceptions there was a significant increase between the first and the fourth sessions and the score decreases under the drug would probably have been more significant if the practice effect had been allowed for.

The Thurstone Hand Test and Minnesota Paper Form Board Test were used as tests of special relations. LSD-25 tended to impair the scores on these, but only a few of the changes were significant.

Nine tests of recognition and recall were used, equivalent forms being employed in the different sessions. It was found that 100 μg of LSD-25 significantly impaired the performance on six of the nine tests, compared to the *placebo*, whereas the 50 μg dose had no significant effect.

Digit span and nonsense syllable recognition showed no significant changes under the drug.

Neither the pursuit rotor test nor the steadiness test showed any significant differences between the zero dose scores and the drug scores, nor between the two drug scores, although there was a tendency for increasing impairment with increasing doses.

The arithmetic test, which involved a number of problems consisting of three numbers and required two operations to be performed appeared to one of the more sensitive tests in the battery for detecting the presence of LSD-25. It was most consistently and significantly impaired, and it was considered that LSD-25 impairs abstract thinking, ability to concentrate, and the ability to recall in normal adults.

On the average, the manual reaction-time tests were not sensitive to the drug, whereas the verbal reaction-time tests were significantly impaired, the reaction-time being longer the higher the dose.

Another test which might be mentioned here is the Bender-Gestalt test, although this was done by another group of twenty-six subjects (Abramson *et al.*, 1955). A standardized quantitative scoring system designed to differentiate psychiatrically ill persons from normal subjects was used to score the performances. There was a tendency, under the influence of the drug, for change to occur in a direction so as to resemble more closely the scores of psychiatric in-patients and out-patients. However, "the number of individual experimental subjects who shifted to predominantly or specifically psychotic modes of responding to the test stimuli was not sufficient to demonstrate statistically, in so far as the Bender-Gestalt scores furnish a measure of such change, that LSD-25 in such doses precipitates experimental psychotic-like states comparable to clinical psychotic reactions."

Using very large doses (up to 200 μg) of LSD, they found that there was impaired performance on the Wechsler-Bellevue intelligence test (Levine *et al.*, 1955).

As a result of a content analysis of the symptoms described in one hundred and forty-one experimental sessions on thirty-one subjects with LSD, Abramson *et al.* (1955) concluded: "Neurotic signs do not correlate with the magnitude of dose, while psychotic signs and distortions in perception do correlate with the magnitude of the dose." Using the category system devised by Bales they studied the effects of LSD on group communication; the drug tended to reduce the output of words of those who had received the drug, while the members of the group who had not received the drug increased their output. "The ratio of questions to answers, as well as the ratio of orientation to evaluation responses, is higher in the group under the condition 'LSD-25' than under condition 'normal' " (Lennard *et al.*, 1955).

Personality changes were assessed by various tests including the Rorschach, word association test and parts of the Thematic Apperception Test. There was a significant increase in M, an increase in the M and decrease in the FM in the M:FM ratio, an increase of Dd, increased in H, and a decrease in W and increase in M in the W:M ratio (as scored by Brown's modification of Klopfer and Kelley's method). It appears that these tests were carried out in the same session as the Wechsler-Bellevue, already reported, when very large doses were given. Five of the twenty-one subjects "showed a reaction which closely resembled paranoid schizophrenia" (Levine *et al.*, 1955*b*). Changes in handwriting after LSD were variable (Hirsch *et al.*, 1956). The remaining studies deal with the development of tolerance to LSD (Abramson *et al.*, 1956), the effect of transference (Abramson, 1956), "ego enhancement" (Abramson, 1956), and also psychotherapy (Abramson, 1955).

Other studies of normal subjects under LSD, in which psychological tests have been used are those of Rinkel *et al.* (1952 and 1955), de Shon *et al.* (1952), Bercel *et al.* (1956*a* and *b*), von Felsinger *et al.* (1956). As with mescaline, dilatation of the pupils is a constant sign and there are various autonomic changes. Visual illusions, hallucinations and other abnormalities may occur, including synaesthesiae. The time sense is distorted and the "ego boundaries" were disturbed. Euphoria or anxiety may occur and also sexual stimulation, which has rarely, if ever, been reported to occur with mescaline. Von Felsinger *et al.* (1956) report that there is "a slowing down of speech and expression." They also found that the relationship between personality and the reaction to LSD was not as marked as with certain other drugs, but they claimed that there was a correlation between the amount of induced change and the degree of pre-existing maladjustment (in ten subjects) (but cf.

Abramson *et al.*, 1955). There is probably a similar relationship of personality to drug effect as is observed with mescaline (e.g. Guttman and Maclay, 1936), although Beringer (1927) was unable to establish any such relationship.

There has been controversy as to whether the LSD-induced state resembles schizophrenia, as with mescaline. There are those in favour of the resemblance (e.g. de Shon, Rinkel and Solomon, 1952; Savage and Choldon, 1956), and those against (e.g. Hoch, Cattell and Pennes, 1952; Ebaugh, 1955; von Felsinger *et al.*, 1956). The psychological test results are of very little help in resolving this controversy, Hoagland, Rinkel and Hyde (1955) have found some biochemical evidence in favour of the similarity which, in conjunction with their previous studies (Rinkel *et al.*, 1952, 1954, 1955*a* and *b*) suggested that "an endogenous derivative of epinephrine metabolism may act in the schizophrenic patients after the manner in which LSD acts in normal persons."

Thus the work both on mescaline and on LSD converges on the adrenaline metabolism of schizophrenics (*see* Fischer, 1954; Hoffer and Osmond, 1955; Hoffer, 1957; Lea, 1955; Cowden, 1957).

Although the effects of large doses of mescaline are similar to those of minute doses of LSD, the two substances are chemically dissimilar, but it has been suggested (Fischer, 1955; cf. Jarvik, 1956), that mescaline is transformed into a substance resembling LSD before it takes effect. It would thus acquire an indole nucleus which, as Woolley and Shaw (1954) pointed out, is common to several hallucinogens such as haomine and yohimbine. They argued that these substances were antimetabolites to serotonin (5-hydroxytryptamine or 5-HT, a substance whose distribution in the brain is similar to that of adrenaline and nor-adrenaline (Amin *et al.*, 1954). Wooley and Shaw postulated that LSD might induce a serotonin deficiency and also that "naturally occurring psychiatric states such as schizophrenia might well be pictured as resulting from a deficiency of serotonin in

the brain," or possibly from an excess. The discovery by Brodie *et al.* (Shore, Silver and Brodie, 1955) that reserpine causes a release of serotonin from the brain of the rabbit appeared to link up the actions of hallucinogens and tranquillizers. However, as chlorpromazine has a reserpine-like effect but does not liberate 5-HT and, as BOL antagonizes 5-HT as markedly as LSD but does not produce any mental disturbance (Cerletti and Rothlin, 1955) this hypothesis is probably untenable.

The mode of action of hallucinogens is still a matter of speculation. According to one theory, they act by inhibiting cholinesterase or pseudocholinesterase (Thompson *et al.*, 1955; Hoffer, 1957). Another view is that they interfere with cerebral synaptic transmission: Marrazzi and Hart (1955*b*) argue "that cerebral synaptic transmission plays a part in the action of hallucinogens and other inducers of chemical psychoses of endogenous or exogenous origin, either by the direct disruption of normal patterns of synaptic activity responsible for behaviour, or indirectly by inhibiting normal restraints and thereby releasing aberrant patterns of activity as a result of alteration in the normal balance between cholinergic excitation and adrenergic inhibition at susceptible cerebral synapses."

Since hallucinations are often visual, they investigated the effects of various compounds on the transmission of impulses from the transcallosal system to the visual cortex of the cat. Adrenaline, adrenochrome, serotonin, bufotenine, amphetamine, mescaline and LSD were tested, and all produced varying degrees of inhibition of synaptic transmission. When ranked in order according to their effectiveness in this respect, it was found that this corresponded with their clinical effectiveness in producing hallucinations. Using mescaline to inhibit the evoked response in the transcallosal system of the cat, they also found that the inhibition could be reduced by chlorpromazine, reserpine and Frenquel (Marrazzi, Hart and Cohn, 1956, pp. 571–2, 574, 578).

TRANQUILLIZERS

It has yet to be shown that the various substances marketed as "tranquillizers" have enough properties in common to justify grouping them together. In theory, they are supposed to calm without inducing confusion or sleep. Some, such as chlorpromazine and reserpine (or compounds related to them) may retain a place in psychiatric treatment, but the other "tranquillizers" have been introduced too recently to justify their discussion here: should they prove to be effective this would stimulate numerous studies on them which would soon make any account written

now out of date, whereas their failure to justify the claims of their manufacturers would make such an account superfluous.

It is notorious that certain wines are ruined by being brought to this country. Sargant writes (1956): "In this respect one can expect fewer reports of good results from reserpine and chlorpromazine in this country than in the U.S.A. and France, because most of the patients are already receiving skilful treatment." Similarly, "an interesting if somewhat tendentious explanation of why American reports of the effects of tranquillizers such as reserpine are so much more enthusiastic than experience in British Hospitals would justify" is that mental hospitals in the U.S.A. have been understaffed and "their psychiatric outlook has been dominated by psychoanalytical ideas. . . ." "In consequence the American chronic mental patient has been in a state of greater neglect and the improvement he has shown when someone has taken an interest in him, and even given him a few new tablets, all the greater" (*Annotation Brit. Med. J.*, 1956).

There are four main groups of tranquillizers—

1. *Phenothiazine derivations*, e.g. chlorpromazine (Largactil, Thorazine, Megaphen), promazine (Sparine), percazine (Pacatal), etc.

2. *Rauwolfia alkaloids* (of which reserpine (Serpasil, Sandvil, Quiescin) is the best known).

3. *Benzhydrol derivations*, e.g. hydroxyzine (Atarax) benactyzine (Suavitil, Nutinal, Ludicil, Parasan and Cevanol), azacyclonal (Frenquel).

4. *Compounds related to mephenesin*, i.e. Meprobamate (Miltown, Equanil, Mepavlon) (Berger, 1957).

The main indications for tranquillizers are in the treatment of chronic agitated, excited or aggressive psychotics who can thus be subjected to chemical rather than physical restraint. Chlorpromazine appears to be more effective than reserpine, but it is not possible to predict, e.g. according to diagnosis, which is more likely to be effective. Both are liable to produce undesirable side effects; for example, chlorpromazine may cause jaundice, agranulocytosis, orthostatic hypotension, hypothermia, dryness of the mouth, photosensitivity, tachycardia, etc., whereas reserpine may result in nasal congestion, drowsiness, hypotension, nausea, vomiting, increased body weight and depression sometimes leading to suicide. Both can induce a Parkinson-like syndrome. Neither has been found to be of much use in the treatment of out-patients in this country, nor have the tranquillizers such as Meprobamate and benactyzine proved to be very effective in their treatment.

It remains difficult to explain why the use of tranquillizers by non-hospitalized patients in the U.S.A. should be criticized as seducing them into a bogus health (Cobb, 1957) and "a threat to American society" (Dickel and Dixon, 1957). It may partly be due to advertising: "Never has advertising reached such volume, such incessant repetition, nor such telling suggestions by word and picture" (Cobb, 1957). Whatever the reasons may be, the effects of tranquillizers on out-patients in this country have been remarkably unimpressive. For example, Raymond *et al.* (1957) compared amylobarbitone, benactyzine, chlorpromazine, Meprobamate, Sedaltine (a concoction including rauwolfia alkaloids) and a *placebo*, on

over fifty neurotic out-patients who had a "tension component in the symptomatology." Each patient received each drug for a fortnight, the drugs being given by the "double blind" method and the design being based on a Latin square. The patients recorded daily the effect of the drug on a 5-point scale. The cheapest, and also the smallest and least impressive of the tablets of amylobarbitone were the only ones found to be significantly superior to the *placebo* which had an average score close to zero.

Folkson and May (1955) and McGrath *et al.* (1956) found reserpine of little value in neurotics, but Davies and Shepherd (1955) and also Fergusson (1956) found some evidence in its favour in this connexion, although the latter was unable to find significant improvement in ten tests of anxiety. That deteriorated chronic psychotics may benefit from reserpine has, however, been confirmed in this country (e.g. Glynn, 1955; Wing, 1956; Foote, 1955; Moore and Martin, 1957), but chlorpromazine appears more effective and to have fewer side-effects (Vaughan *et al.*, 1955). Lomas (1957) compared Pacatal (pecazine) with chlorpromazine in schizophrenics, and concluded that there was nothing "to suggest that Pacatal has any value in the treatment of a mixed group of schizophrenic patients." Thorpe and Baker (1956) also found it inferior. Lieberman and Vaughan (1957) and Coady and Jewsbury (1956) found benactyzine had no effect on muscle tone and it gave no significant relief of symptoms; similarly Seager and Leitch (1956) found no evidence that it was of use, although Davies (1956) found that it appeared to benefit some patients.

In this country only the original tranquillizers—chlorpromazine and reserpine—have an established use, and the status of the others remains controversial. Interesting reports have been published on the effects of Meprobamate on driving tests, etc. (Marquis *et al.*, 1957), conditioned fear (Hunt, 1957), and "imprinting" in the water fowl (Hess, 1957). These are too recent to make possible any thorough-going appraisal, but suggest the worth-whileness of persevering with research on this drug. (Cf. also Eysenck *Experiments in Personality*, to be published.)

A large number of animal experiments have been done using chlorpromazine and reserpine. These drugs have been found, for example, to cause a reduction of hostility and sociability respectively in the cat (Norton and de Beer, 1956), and reserpine results in a decrease in conditioned avoidance responses in the monkey (Smith *et al.*, 1956; and Weiskrantz and Wilson, 1955) and in the rat (Brady, 1956; *see also* Sidman, 1956). Guha *et al.* (1954) found chlorpromazine relatively more effective than reserpine in decreasing the performance of a conditioned reflex in rats, and Cook *et al.* (1955), who found that chlorpromazine was effective in reducing spontaneous or d-l-amphetamine-induced activity in mice, confirmed that this drug tended to block a conditioned response in rats (*see also* Killam *et al.*, 1956; Rutledge and Doty, 1955).

Few tests have been carried out on human subjects receiving these drugs. Petrie and Le Beau (1956) claimed that chlorpromazine caused a decrease in neuroticism and an increase in introversion (the latter in contrast to leucotomy patients), but Porteus (1957) using his maze found that there was a drop in score, as after leucotomy. Several studies have utilized psychological tests or rating scales (e.g. Gaitz *et al.*, 1955; Gardner *et al.*, 1955).

Perhaps this brief and somewhat sceptical account has done less than justice to the latest "new era" in psychiatry. The reader may like to judge after consulting a recent paper by Little (1958), containing an account of a well-controlled "double-blind comparison of the effects of chlorpromazine, barbiturate and a *placebo* in one hundred and forty-two chronic psychotic in-patients." There were no significant differences between the three treatments!

GENERAL SUMMARY

The data are too divergent to permit of any useful kind of summary. With the exception of the dimensional hypothesis outlined at the beginning, little in the way of general descriptive or causal relationship between personality and drug effect has emerged. Few results have been found which stood up to replication of experiments, and few findings have achieved the status of facts on which future works may build. The reasons for this sorry state of affairs are obvious. Enthusiasm in research is no compensation for lack of competence, and few workers in the field have had the requisite training in psychological research methodology, statistical knowledge, biochemical expertise and general physiological knowhow to avoid quite elementary errors. Co-operative effort is improving the situation, but worth-while theories seldom issue from committees. Nevertheless, the promise, both for research and for applied work, held out by drugs is such that a rapid advance is likely to take place—the first for years. Of all the chapters in this book, this one is the most likely to be out of date, if any, when a new edition is called for.

REFERENCES

ABRAMSON, H. A., *Neuropharmacology. Transactions of the 2nd Conf.*, May, 1955. Sponsored by Josiah Macy (Jnr.) Foundation, N.Y. (1956).

ABRAMSON, H. A., Lysergic acid diethylamide (LSD-25): III. As an adjunct to psychotherapy with elimination of fear of homosexuality, *J. Psychol.*, 39, 127–155 (1955).

ABRAMSON, H. A., Lysergic acid diethylamide (LSD-25): XIX. As an adjunct to brief psychotherapy, with special reference to ego enhancement, *J. Psychol.*, 41, 199–229 (1956).

ABRAMSON, H. A., Lysergic acid diethylamide (LSD-25): XXII. Effect on transference, *J. Psychol.*, 42, 51–98 (1956).

ABRAMSON, H. A. and JARVIK, M. E., Lysergic acid diethylamide (LSD-25): IX. Effect on snails, *J. Psychol.*, 40, 337–340 (1955).

ABRAMSON, H. A., JARVIK, M. E., GORIN, M. H. and HIRSCH, M. W., Lysergic acid diethylamide (LSD-25):

XVII. Tolerance development and its relationship to a theory of psychosis, *J. Psychol.*, 41, 81–105 (1956).

ABRAMSON, H. A., JARVIK, M. E. and HIRSCH, M. W., Lysergic acid diethylamide (LSD-25): VII. Effect upon two measures of motor performance, *J. Psychol.*, 39, 455–464 (1955).

ABRAMSON, H. A., JARVIK, M. E. and HIRSCH, M. W., Lysergic acid diethylamide (LSD-25): X. Effect on reaction-time to auditory and visual stimuli, *J. Psychol.*, 40, 39–52 (1955).

ABRAMSON, H. A., JARVIK, M. E., HIRSCH, M. W. and EWALD, A. T., Lysergic acid diethylamide (LSD-25): V. Effect on spatial relations abilities, *J. Psychol.*, 39, 435–442 (1955).

ABRAMSON, H. A., JARVIK, M. E., KAUFMAN, M. R., KORNETSKY, C., LEVINE, A. and WAGNER, M., Lysergic acid diethylamide (LSD-25): I. Physiological and perceptual responses, *J. Psychol.*, 39, 3–60 (1955).

ABRAMSON, H. A., JARVIK, M. E., LEVINE, A., KAUFMAN, M. R. and HIRSCH, M. W., Lysergic acid diethylamide (LSD-25): XV. The effects produced by substitution of a tap water *placebo*, *J. Psychol.*, 40, 367–383 (1955).

ABRAMSON, H. A., KORNETSKY, C., JARVIK, M. E., KAUFMAN, M. R. and FERGUSON, M. W., Lysergic acid diethylamide (LSD-25): XVII. Tolerance development and its relationship to a theory of psychosis, *J. Psychol.*, 41, 81–105 (1956).

ABRAMSON, H. A., WAXENBERG, S. E., LEVINE, A., KAUFMAN, M. R. and KORNETSKY, C., Lysergic acid diethlamide (LSD-25) XIII. Effect on Bender-Gestalt Test performance, *J. Psychol.*, 40, 341–349 (1955).

ADATTO, C. P., Observations on criminal patients during narco-analysis. *Arch. Neurol. Psychiat. Chicago*, 62, 82–92 (1949).

AGOSTON, T., Benzedrine sulfate and other stimulants in psychoanalysis and psychotherapy, *Psychoanal. Rev.*, 31, No. 4, 438–452 (1944).

ALEXANDER, L., The Epinephrine-Mecholyl Test (Funkenstein Test). *A.M.A. Arch. Neurol. Psychiat.*, 73, No. 5, 496–514 (1955).

ALLES, G. A. and FERGEN, G. A., The influence of Benzedrine on work decrement and the patellar reflex, *Amer. J. Physiol.*, 136, 392–400 (1942).

ALPERN, E. B., FINKELSTEIN, N. and GANTT, W. H., Effect of amphetamine (Benzedrine) sulfate on higher nervous activity, *Johns Hopk. Hosp. Bull.*, 73, 287–299 (1943).

ALTSCHULE, M. D., *Bodily Physiology in Mental and Emotional Disorders* (New York, Grune & Stratton, 1953).

ALTSCHULE, M. D., Physiologic psychology of neurosis, *New Engl. J. Med.*, **251**, 476–483 (1954).

ALWALL, N., Frequenz und Dauer der subjektiven Wirkungen und Nebenwirkungen von Benzedrin und Pervitin bei hochgradiger Ermüdung, *Acta. med. scand.*, **114**, 6–32 (1943).

ANDERSON, E. W. and RAWNSLEY, K., Clinical studies of lysergic acid diethylamide, *Mschr. Psychiat. Neurol.*, **128**, 38–55 (1954).

ANDREWS, T. G., Effect of Benzedrine sulfate on syllogistic reasoning, *J. Exp. Psychol.*, **26**, 423–431 (1940).

ANDREYER, L. A., The effect of single and repeated doses of alcohol on the conditioned reflexes in the dog, *Arch. Int. Pharmacodyn.*, **48**, 117–124 (1934).

ARDUINI, A. and ARDUINI, M. G., Effect of drugs and metabolic alterations on brain stem arousal mechanism, *J. Pharmacol.*, **110**, 76–85 (1954).

ARNOLD, M. B., Physiological differentiation of emotional states, *Psychol. Rev.*, **20**, 725–752 (1945).

ARNOLD, M. B., An excitatory theory of emotion, in *Feelings and Emotions*, Ed. M. L. Reyment, (New York, McGraw-Hill, 1950).

AX, A. F., Physiological differentiation between fear and anger in humans, *Psychosom. Med.*, **15**, 433–443 (1953).

BAERNSTEIN, L. N., An experimental study of the effect on waking suggestibility of small doses of scopolamine hydrobromide, *M.A. Thesis, Univ. of Wisconsin*, (1929) (quoted by Hull, 1933).

BAILEY, C. J. and MILLER, N. E., The effect of Sodium Amytal on approach-avoidance conflicts in cats, *J. Comp. Physiol. Psychol.*, **45**, 205–208 (1952).

BARGER, G. and DALE, H. H., Chemical structure and sympathomimetic action of amines, *J. Physiol.*, **41**, 19–59 (1910).

BARMACK, J. E., The effect of Benzedrine sulfate (benzylmethyl carbrinamine) upon the report of boredom and other factors, *J. Psychol.*, **5**, 125–133 (1938).

BARMACK, J. E. and SEITZ, C. P., The effect of 10 mgms of Benzedrine sulfate on the span of attention for letters, *J. Gen. Psychol.*, **23**, 195–196 (1940).

BASOWITZ, H., KORCHIN, S. J. and OKEN, D., The evocation of anxiety and performance changes under minimal doses of adrenalin, *Amer. Psychologist*, **10**, p. 388 abstract.

BEECHER, H. K., Anaesthetic's second power: probing mind, *Science*, **105**, 164–166 (1947).

BEECHER, H. K., The powerful *placebo*, *J. Amer. Med. Ass.*, **159**, 1,602–1,606 (1955).

BEECHER, H. K., Evidence for increased effectiveness of *placebos* with increased stress, *Amer. J. Physiol.*, **187**, 163–169 (1956).

BEECHER, H. K., Limiting factors in experimental pain, *J. Chronic Dis.*, **4**, 11–21 (1956a).

BEECHER, H. K., Relationship of significance of wound to pain experienced, *J. Amer. Med. Ass.*, **161**, 1,609–1,613 (1956b).

BEECHER, H. K., KEATS, A. S., MOSTELLER, F. and LASAGNA, L., The effectiveness of oral analgesics (morphine, codeine, acetylsalicylic acid) and the problem of *placebo*

"reactors" and "non-reactors," *J. Pharmacol.*, **109**, 393–400 (1953).

BELLAK, L., The use of oral barbiturates in psychotherapy, *Amer. J. Psychiat.*, **105**, 849–850 (1948–9).

BERCEL, N. A., TRAVIS, L. E., OLINGER, L. B. and DREIKURS, E., Model psychoses induced by LSD-25 in normals. I. Psychophysiological investigations with special reference to the mechanism of the paranoid reaction. II. Rorschach test finding, *A.M.A. Arch. Neurol. Psychiat.*, **75**, 588–618 (1956).

BERG, O., A study of the effect of Evipan on the flicker fusion intensity in brain injuries, *Acta Psychiat. Kbh.*, **58**, 1–116 (1949).

BERGER, F. M., The chemistry and mode of action of tranquilizing drugs, *Ann. N.Y. Acad. Sci.*, **67**, 685–700 (1957).

BERGMAN, P. S., STROS, H. H. and FEINSTEIN, R., Mental and electroencephalographic changes following intravenous barbiturates in organic disease of brain, *Amer. J. Psychiat.*, **110**, 770–773 (1954).

BERINGER, K., *Der Meskalinrausch. Seine Geschichte und Erscheinungsweise* (Berlin, Springer Verlag, 1927).

BERRINGTON, W. P., Cardiazol, Sodium Amytal and alcohol in schizophrenic stupor, *J. Ment. Sci.*, **85**, 406–488 (1939).

BERRY, C. S., Effects of smoking on adding, *Psychol. Bull.*, **14**, 25–28 (1917).

BETT, W. R., Benzedrine sulphate in clinical medicine: a survey of the literature, *Post Grad. Med. J.*, **22**, 205–218 (1946).

BETT, W. R., HOWELLS, L. H. and MACDONALD, A. D., *Amphetamine in Clinical Medicine* (Edinburgh and London, Livingstone, 1955).

BJERVER, K. and GOLDBERG, L., Effect of alcohol ingestion on driving ability, Results of practical road tests and laboratory experiments, *Quart. J. Stud. Alc.*, **11**, 1–30 (1950).

BLOUGH, D. S., Techniques for studying the effects of drugs on discrimination in the pigeon, *Ann. N.Y. Acad. Sci.*, **65**, 334–344 (1956).

BONHOFF, G. and LEWRANZ, H., *Über Weckamine (Pervitin und Benzedrin). Monographien aus dem Gesamtgebiete der Neurologie und Psychiatric* (Berlin, J. Springer, 1954).

BOVET, D. and BOVET-NITTI, F., *Structure et activité pharmacodynamique des medicaments du système nerveux végétatif. Adrenaline, acetylcholic, histamine et leurs antagonistes* (Bâle, Éditions S. Karger, 1948).

BOWMAN, K. M., A case of psychosis due to large doses of acetyl salicylic acid, *J. Nerv. Ment. Dis.*, **78**, 57–60 (1933).

BRADLEY, C., The behavior of children receiving Benzedrine, *Amer. J. Psychiat.*, **94**, 577–585 (1937).

BRADLEY, C. and GREEN, E., Psychometric performance of children receiving amphetamine (Benzedrine) sulfate, *Amer. J. Psychiat.*, **97**, 388–394 (1940).

BRADY, J. V., Assessment of drug effects on emotional behaviour, *Science*, **123**, 1,033–1,034 (1956).

BRADY, J. V., A comparative approach to the evaluation of drug effects upon affective behaviour, *Ann. N.Y. Acad. Sci.*, **64**, 632–643 (1956).

BRAZIER, MARY A. B., The action of anaesthetics on the nervous system with special reference to the brain stem reticular system, in, *Brain Mechanisms and Consciousness*,

Eds. E. D. Adrian and F. Brewer (Oxford, H. H. Jasper, 1954).

BRAZIER, MARY A. B. and FINESINGER, J. E., Action of barbiturates on the cerebral cortex, *A.M.A. Arch. Neurol. Psychiat.*, **53**, 51–58 (1945).

BROADHURST, ANNE, Some variables affecting speed of mental functioning in schizophrenics, *Unpubl. Ph.D. Thesis, Univ. of London Lib.* (1956).

BROTHERS, ANITA U. and BENNETT, A. E., The Funkenstein Test as a guide to treatment in the neuroses and psychoses, *Dis. Nerv. Syst.*, **XV**, 335–339 (1954).

BROWN, B. B., FELDMAN, R. and BRAUN, D. L., Pharmacologic studies of an LSD antagonist. 4-piperidyl diphenyl carbinol hydrochloride, *Fed. Proc.*, **14**, (Pt. I), 322–329 (1955).

BUSH, A. D., Tobacco smoking and mental efficiency, *N.Y. Med. J.*, **99**, 517–527 (1914).

CALLAWAY, E., On the production of hallucinated and psychosis-like states, (Editorial) *Ann. Intern. Med.*, **42**, 721–728 (1955).

CALLAWAY, E. and THOMPSON, S. V., Sympathetic activity and perception. An approach to the relationships between autonomic activity and personality, *Psychosom. Med.*, **42**, 721–728 (1955).

CAMERON, W. M. and KASANIN, J., A pharmacologic and clinical re-evaluation of amphetamine sulphate (Benzedrine), *New Eng. J. Med.*, **224**, 544–550 (1941).

CANNON, W. B., *Bodily Changes in Pain, Hunger, Fear and Rage.* An account of recent researches into the function of emotional excitation (New York and London, Appleton, 1929).

CANTRIL, H. and HUNT, W. A., Emotional effects produced by the injection of adrenalin, *Amer. J. Psychol.*, **44**, 300–307 (1932).

CARL, G. P. and TURNER, W. D., The effects of Benzedrine sulfate (amphetamine sulphate) on performance in a comprehensive psychometric examination, *J. Psychol.*, **8**, 165–216 (1939)

CARL, G. P. and TURNER, W. D., A further report on Benzedrine sulfate (amphetamine sulphate). Psychophysical effects and supplementary results from a fifth experimental group, *J. Gen. Psychol.*, **22**, 105–191 (1940).

CATTELL, R. B., The effects of alcohol and caffeine on intelligence and association performance, *Brit. J. Psychol.*, **10**, 20–33 (1930).

CAVETT, J. W., Determination of alcohol in blood and other body fluids, *J. Lab. Clin. Med.*, **23**, 543–546 (1938).

CERLETTI, A., Literature on LSD–25. Appendix to *Neuropharmacology. 2nd Conf.*, Ed. H. A. Abramson, Sponsored by Josiah Macy, Jr., Foundation., N.Y. (1956).

CERLETTI, A. and ROTHLIN, E., Role of 5-Hydroxytryptamine in mental diseases and its antagonism to lysergic acid derivates, *Nature*, **176**, 785–786 (1955).

CHANCE, M. R. A., A peculiar form of social behaviour induced in mice by amphetamine, *Behaviour*, **1**, 64–69 (1947).

CHANCE, J. and LOTSOF, E. J., Effect of cortisone on psychological test performance, *Psychol. Rep.*, **1**, 323–330 (1955).

CHAPMAN, A. H., Paranoid psychoses associated with amphetamine usage: a clinical note, *Amer. J. Psychiat.*, **III**, 43–45 (1954).

CHENEY, R. H., Reaction-time behaviour after caffeine and coffee consumption, *J. Exp. Psychol.*, **19**, 357–369 (1936).

CHOLDEN, L., Lysergic acid diethylamide and mescaline in experimental psychiatry. Symposium held at Annual meeting of Amer. Psychiat. Ass., Atlantic City, May 12, 1955.

COADY, A. and JEWESBURY, E. C. O., A clinical trial of benactyzine hydrochloride (Suavitil) as a physical relaxant, *Brit. Med. J.*, **I**, 485–487 (1956).

COBB, S. C., Comment: peace of mind, *Amer. J. Psychiat.*, **113**, 663–664 (1957).

COHEN, B. D., SENF, R. and HUSTON, P. E., Effect of amobarbital (amytal) on affect and conceptual thinking in schizophrenia, depression and neurosis, *A.M.A. Arch. Neurol. Psychiat.*, **71**, 171–180 (1954).

COHEN, B. D., SENF, R. and HUSTON, P. E., Perceptual accuracy in schizophrenia, depression and neurosis, and effects of amytal, *J. Abnorm. (Soc.) Psychol.*, **52**, 363–367 (1956).

CONGER, J. J., The effects of alcohol on conflict behaviour in the albino rat, *Quart. J. Stud. Alc.*, **12**, 1–29 (1951).

CONNELL, P. H., Amphetamine psychosis, *M.D. Thesis, Univ. of London Lib.* (1956a).

CONNELL, P. H., Amphetamine addiction, *Dissertation for D.P.M. at Institute of Psychiatry, London* (1956b).

COOK, L., WEIDLEY, E. F., MORRIS, R. W. and MATTIS, P. A., Neuropharmacological and behavioural effects of chlorpromazine (thorazine hydrochloride), *J. Pharmacol.*, **113**, 11–12 abstract (1955).

COPPOCK, H. W. and HOOD, W. R., Retardation and retraining following phenobarbital and alcohol injections in rats, *Paper read at M.P.A. meeting, St. Louis* (1956).

COWDEN, R. C., The psychophysiology of schizophrenia, *Amer. J. Psychiat.*, **113**, 709–716 (1957).

CRAIG, M., *Psychological Medicine. A Manual on Mental Diseases for Practitioners and Students* (London, Churchill, 1905).

CRANSTON, R. E., ZUBIN, J. and LANDIS, C., The effect of small doses of thouzylamine, dexedrine and phenobarbital on test performance and self-ratings of subjective states, *J. Psychol.*, **33**, 209–215 (1952).

CUTHBERTSON, D. P. and KNOX, J. A. C., The effect of analeptics on the fatigued subject, *J. Physiol.*, **106**, 42–58 (1947).

CUTLER, M., LITTLE, J. W. and STRAUSS, A. A., The effect of Benzedrine on mentally deficient children, *Amer. J. Ment. Defic.*, **XLV**, 59–65 (1940).

CYVIN, K., JÖRSTAD, J. and RETTERSTÖL, N., Sympathomimetics as diagnostic tests in psychiatry, *Acta Psychiat. et Neurol. Scand.*, **106**, 206–220 (1956).

DARROW, C. W., Some physiological conditions of efficiency, *Psychol. Bull.*, **24**, 488–505 (1927).

DARROW, C. W., Psychological effects of drugs, *Psychol. Bull.*, **26**, 527–545 (1929).

DARROW, C. W. and GELLHORN, E., The effects of adrenalin on the reflex excitability of the autonomic nervous system, *Amer. J. Physiol.*, **127**, 243–251 (1939).

DAS, N. N., DASGUPTA, S. R. and WERNER, G., Changes of behaviour and electroencephalogram in rhesus monkeys caused by chlorpromazine, *Bull. Calcutta Sch. Trop. Med.*, **1**, 5–6 (1954).

DAVIDOFF, E., A clinical study of the effect of Benzedrine

therapy on self-absorbed patients, *Psychiat. Quart.*, **10**, 652–659 (1936).

DAVIDOFF, E. and REIFENSTEIN, E. C. (JNR.), The stimulating action of Benzedrine sulfate: a comparative study of the responses of normal persons and of depressed patients, *J. Amer. Med. Ass.*, **108**, 1,770–1,776 (1937).

DAVIDOFF, E., REIFENSTEIN, E. C. (JNR.) and GOODSTONE, G. L., Amphetamine sulfate-Sodium Amytal treatment of schizophrenia, *Arch. Neurol. Psychiat. Chicago*, **45**, 439–445 (1941).

DAVIES, D. L. and SHEPHERD, M., Reserpine in the treatment of anxious and depressed patients, *Lancet*, **11**, 117 (1955).

DAVIES, E. B., A new drug to relieve anxiety, *Brit. Med. J.*, **3**, 430–484 (1956).

DAVIS, D. R., Psychomotor effects of analeptics and their relation to fatigue phenomena in air crew, *Brit. Med. Bull.*, **5**, 1,021 (1947).

DAVIS, D. R., Pilot Error. *Some Laboratory Experiments* (London, H.M.S.O., 1948).

DAVIS, R. C., The effect of analgesic dosage of aspirin (acetyl salicylic acid) on some mental and motor performances, *J. Appl. Psychol.*, **20**, 481–487 (1936).

DELAFRESNAYE, J. F. (Ed.) *Brain Mechanisms and Consciousness. A Symposium* (Oxford, Blackwell, 1954).

DELAY, J., Pharmacological exploration of the personality narcoanalysis and methedrine shock, *Proc. Roy. Soc. Med.*, **42**, 491–496 (1949).

DELAY, J., MALLET, J. and RONBLEFF, I., Étude de l'action du sodium amytal dans les psychoses catatoniques et dépressives. I. *Encéphale*, **37**, 57–72 (1948).

DELAY, J., PICHOT, P., ROUBLEFF, I. and ROMANET, B., Le test de Rorschach après choc amphetaminique dans le diagnostic des schizophrenics, *Encéphale*, **37**, 73–98 (1948).

DENBER, H. C. B. and MERLIS, S., Studies on mescaline. I. Action in schizophrenic patients: clinical observations and brain wave patterns, showing effects before and after electric convulsive treatments, *Psychiat. Quart.*, **29**, 421–429 (1955).

DEWS, P. B., Studies on behavior: 1. Differential sensitivity to pentobarbital of pecking performance in pigeons, depending on the schedule of reward, *J. Pharmacol.*, **113**, 393–401 (1955*a*).

DEWS, P. B., Studies on behavior: 2. The effects of pentobarbital, methamphetamine and scopolamine on performances in pigeons involving discriminations, *J. Pharmacol.*, **115**, 380–383 (1955*b*).

DEWS, P. B., Modification by drugs of performance on simple schedules of positive reinforcement, *Ann. N.Y. Acad. Sci.*, **65**, Art. 4, 268–281 (1956).

DICKEL, H. A. and DIXON, H. H., Inherent dangers in use of tranquillizing drugs in anxiety states, *J. Amer. Med. Ass.*, **163**, 422 (1957).

DICKS, H. V., Hypnotics in psychotherapy, *Brit. Med. J.*, **1**, 865 (1940).

DIETHELM, O., DOTY, E. J. and MILHORAT, A. T., Emotions and adrenergic and cholinergic changes in the blood, *Arch. Neurol. Psychiat. Chicago*, **54**, 110–115 (1945).

DODGE, R., and BENEDICT, F. G., Psychological effects of alcohol, *Pub. Carneg. Inst.*, 232 (1915).

DOLLARD, J. and MILLER, N. E., *Personality and Psycho-therapy. An Analysis in Terms of Learning, Thinking and Culture* (New York, McGraw-Hill, 1950).

DOMINO, E. F., FOX, KAYE E and BRODY, T. M., Pharmacological actions of a convulsant barbiturate (sodium 5-ethyl-5- (1,3-dimethylbutyl) barbiturate). 1. Stimulant and depressant effects. *J. Pharmacol.*, **114**, 473–483 (1955).

DONAHUE, H. H., WINER, M. L. and GLAZER, N. M., Pentothal sodium; adjunct in understanding of schizophrenic reaction; preliminary report, *Psychiat. Quatr.*, **22**, 221–251 (1948).

DREW, G. C., The effect of alcohol on human efficiency with especial reference to driving, *Dept. of Sci. & Indust. Res., & M.R.C. Road Res. Lab. (restricted)* 1950 typescript.

DRASSDO, A. and SCHMIDT, M., Ritaline, a central stimulant with new chemical constitution. Part 2. Improvement in mental capacity and psychic effect produced by ritaline, *Med. Monatsschr.*, **8**, 393–395 (1954).

DRAKE, F. R., Review: Psychological responses to ACTH, cortisone and related steroid substances, *Amer. J. Ment. Sci.*, **227**, 226–229 (1954).

DUFFY, ELIZABETH, The concept of energy mobilization, *Psychol. Rev.*, **58**, 30–40 (1951).

DÜKER, H. and DÜKER, E., Über die Wirkung von Pervitin auf die psychische Leistungsfähigkeit. *Z. exp. angew. Psychol.*, **1**, 32–167 (1953).

DWORKIN, S., BOURNE, W. and RAGINSKY, B. B., Changes in conditioned responses brought about by anaesthetics and sedatives, *Canad. Med. Ass. J.*, **37**, 136–139 (1937).

DYNES, J. B., Objective methods for distinguishing sleep from the hypnotic trance, *Arch. Neurol. Psychiat. Chicago*, **57**, 84–93 (1947).

DYNES, J. B. and TODD, H., The emotional and somatic response of schizophrenic patients and normals to adrenaline and Doryl, *J. Neurol. Psychiat.*, **3**, 1–7 (1940).

EARP, J. R., The smoking habit and mental efficiency, *Lancet*, letter, **2**, 527 (1927).

EBAUGH, F. G., The Videclinic. Guest editorial, *J. A.M.A.*, **158**, 732–733 (1955).

EGGLETON, M. GRACE, The effect of alcohol on the central nervous system, *Brit. J. Psychol.*, **32**, 52–61 (1941).

ELKES, J., ELKES, C. and BRADLEY, P. B., The effect of some drugs on the electrical activity of the brain and on behaviour, *J. Ment. Sci.*, **100**, 125–128 (1954).

ELLIOTT, T. R., The action of adrenaline, *J. Physiol.*, **32**, 401–000 (1905).

ELLIS, H., A note on the phenomena of mescal intoxication, *Lancet*, **2**, 1,540–1,542 (1897).

ELMADJIAN, F., HOPE, J. M. and FREEMAN, H., Methacoline test and epinephrine and arterenal excretion, *A.M.A. Arch. Neurol. Psychiat.*, **77**, 399–405 (1957).

EMERSON, H., *Alcohol and Man* (New York, Macmillan, 1932).

EMMELIN, NILS, Evipan and parasympathetic N.S. *Acta Physiol. scand.*, **2**, 289–310 (1941).

EPPINGER, H. and HESS, L., Die Vagotonie, Berlin 1910. Trans. W. M. Kraus, and S. E. Fellippe, "Vagatonia: a study in vegetation neurology," *Nerv. & Ment. Dis. Monogr.*, No. 20 (1915).

EULER, VON, U.S., Adrenaline and nor-adrenaline, *Triangle (Sandoz) J. Med. Sci.*, **1**, No. 6, 101–109 (1954).

EVANS, J., Effect of ergot drugs on *betta splendens*, *Science*, **123**, 26–28 (1956).

EVARTS, E. V., LANDAU, W., FREYGANG, W. (JR.) and MARSHALL, W. H., Some effects of lysergic acid diethylamide and butotemic on electrical activity in the cat's visual system, *Amer. J. Physiol.*, **182**, No. 3, 594–598 (1955).

EWING, P. L., MOORE, B. M. and MOORE, W. T., The effect of amphetamine and related compounds on maze performance of white rats, *J. Pharmacol.*, **105**, 343–348 (1952).

EYSENCK, H. J., *Dimensions of Personality* (London, Routledge & Kegan Paul, 1947).

EYSENCK, H. J., La rapidité du fonctionnement mental comme mesure de l'anomalie mentale, *Rev. de Psychol. appl.*, **3**, 367–377 (1953).

EYSENCK, H. J., A dynamic theory of anxiety and hysteria, *J. Ment. Sci.*, **101**, 28–51 (1955).

EYSENCK, H. J., Drugs and personality. 1. Theory and methodology, *J. Ment. Sci.*, **103**, 119–131 (1957).

EYSENCK, H. J., *Structure of Human Personality* (London, Methuen, 1959).

EYSENCK, H. J., *Experiments in Personality* (London, Routledge and Kegan Paul, to be published).

EYSENCK, H. J. and AIBA, S., Drugs and personality: V. The effects of stimulant and depressant drugs on the suppression of the primary visual stimulus, *J. Ment. Sci.*, **103**, 661–665 (1957).

EYSENCK, H. J., CASEY, SUE and TROUTON, D. S., Drugs and personality: II. The effect of stimulant and depressant drugs on continuous work, *J. Ment. Sci.*, **103**, 645–649 (1957).

EYSENCK, H. J. and EYSENCK, S. B. G., The classification of drugs according to their behavioural effects: a new method, in *Experiments in Personality*, Ed. H. J. Eysenck (London, Routledge & Kegan Paul, to be published).

EYSENCK, H. J., HOLLAND, H. and TROUTON, D. S., Drugs and personality: III. The effects of stimulant and depressant drugs on visual after-effects, *J. Ment. Sci.*, **103**, 650–655 (1957*a*).

EYSENCK, H. J., HOLLAND, H. and TROUTON, D. S., Drugs and personality: IV. The effects of stimulants and depressant drugs on the rate of fluctuation of a reversible perspective figure, *J. Ment. Sci.*, **103**, 656–660 (1957*b*).

EYSENCK, H. J. and REES, W. L., States of heightened suggestibility: narcosis, *J. Ment. Sci.*, **91**, 301–310 (1945).

FABING, H. D. and HAWKINS, J. R., A year's experience with Frenquel in clinical and experimental schizophrenic psychoses, *Dis. nerv. Syst.*, **16**, 3–12 (1955).

FASTIER, F. N., Effects of pentobarbitone, amphetamine and lactose on healthy students, *N. Z. Med. J.*, **54**, 74–79 (1955).

FAY, P. J., The effect of cigarette smoking on simple and choice reaction-time to colored lights, *J. Exp. Psychol.*, **19**, 592–603 (1936).

FELDBERG, W., Recent experiments with injections of drugs into the ventricular system of the brain, *Proc. Roy. Soc. Med.*, **48**, No. 10, 853–855 (1955).

FELDBERG, W. and SHERWOOD, S. L., Injections of drugs into the lateral ventricle of the cat, *J. Physiol.*, **123**, 148–167 (1954*a*).

FELDBERG, W. and SHERWOOD, S. L., Behaviour of cats after intraventricular injections of eserine and DFP, *J. Physiol.*, **125**, 488–500 (1954*b*).

FELSINGER, VON, J. H., LASAGNA, L. and BEECHER, H. K., The persistence of mental impairment following a hypnotic dose of a barbiturate, *J. Pharmacol.*, **109**, 284–291 (1953).

FELSINGER, VON, J. H., LASAGNA, L. and BEECHER, H. K., Drug-induced mood changes in man. 2. Personality and reactions to drugs, *J. Amer. Med. Ass.*, **157**, 1,113–1,119 (1955).

FELSINGER, VON, J. H., LASAGNA, L. and BEECHER, H. K., The response of normal men to lysergic acid derivatives (di- and mono-ethyl-amides). Correlation of personality and drug reactions, *J. Clin. Exp. Psychopath.*, **17**, 414–428 (1956).

FERGUSON, J. T., A new therapeutic approach to abnormal behavior in geriatrics, *Geriatrics*, **11**, 217–219 (1956).

FIELDS, P. E., The effect of phenobarbital upon learning and retention of elevated T-maze patterns, *Psychol. Bull.*, **32**, 743 (1935).

FISCHER, R., Factors involved in drug-produced model psychoses, *Experientia*, **10**, 435–436 (1954). (Also *J. Ment. Sci.*, **100**, 623–631 (1954).)

FLEETWOOD, M. F., Determination of adrenergic substances in the blood related to anxiety identification as noradrenaline, *Amer. J. Physiol.*, **166**, 314–322 (1951).

FLEETWOOD, M. F., Biochemical experimental investigations of emotions and chronic alcoholism, in, *Etiology of Chronic Alcoholism*, Ed. O. Diethelm (Springfield, C. C. Thomas, 1956).

FLEETWOOD, M. F. and DIETHELM, O., Emotions and biochemical findings in alcoholism, *Amer. J. Psychiat.*, **108**, 433–438 (1951).

FLEISHMAN, E. A., Predicting advanced levels of proficiency in psychomotor skills, in *Symposium on Air force Human Engineering, Personnel, and Training Research*, Eds. G. Finch and F. Cameron. Baltimore: A.R.D.C. Technical Report, 56–58 (1956).

FLEISHMAN, E. A. and HEMPEL, W. E., Changes in factor structure of a complex psychomotor test as a function of practice, *Psychometrika*, **19**, 239–252 (1954).

FLEISHMAN, E. A. and HEMPEL, W. E., The relation between abilities and improvement with practice in a visual discrimination reaction task, *J. Exp. Psychol.*, **49**, 301–312 (1955).

FLEMINGER, J. J., The differential effect of cortisone and of ACTH on mood, *J. Ment. Sci.*, **101**, No. 422, 123–130 (1955).

FLORY, D. and GILBERT, J., The effects of benzedrine sulphate and caffeine citrate on the efficiency of college students, *J. Appl. Psychol.*, **27**, 121–134 (1943).

FOLKSON, A. and MAY, A. R., Use of reserpine and rauwolfia in psychoneuroses, *Brit. Med. J.*, **II**, 1,121–1,122 (1955).

FOLTZ, E. E., IVY, A. C. and BARBORKA, C. J., The use of double work periods in the study of fatigue and the influence of caffeine on recovery, *Amer. J. Physiol.*, **136**, 79–86 (1942).

FOLTZ, E. E., IVY, A. C. and BARBORKA, C. J., The influence of amphetamine (Benzedrine) sulfate d-desoxyephedrine hydrochloride (Pervitin) and caffeine on work output and recovery when rapidly exhausting work is done by trained subjects, *J. Lab. Clin. Med.*, **28**, 603–606 (1943).

FOLTZ, E. E., SCHRIFFIN, M. J. and IVY, A. C., The influence of amphetamine sulfate and caffeine on the performance of rapidly exhausting work by untrained subjects, *J. Lab. Clin. Med.*, **28**, 601–603 (1943).

FOOTE, E. S., Reserpine in treatment of chronic psychotics, *Brit. Med. J.*, **I**, 1,192–1,193 (1955).

FORRER, G. R. and GOLDNER, R. D., Experimental physiological studies with lysergic acid diethylamide (LSD-25), *Arch. Neurol. Psychiat. Chicago*, **65**, 581–588 (1951).

FOX, A. M., Psychological responses to the administration of ACTH and cortisone, *Ciba Found. Colloquia on Endocrin*, **VIII**, 594–606 (London, Churchill, 1955).

FRANKS, C. M., Recidivism, psychopathy and personality, *Brit. J. Delinq.*, **6**, 192–201 (1956).

FRANKS, C. M. and TROUTON, D. S., Effects of amobarbital and dexamphetamine sulfate on the conditioning of the eyeblink response, *J. Comp. Physiol. Psychol.*, **51**, 220–222 (1958).

FREDERKING, W., Intoxicant drugs (mescaline and LSD) in psychotherapy, *J. Nerv. Ment. Dis.*, **121**, No. 3, 262–266 (1955).

FREEMAN, H. and CARMICHAEL, H. T., A pharmacodynamic investigation of the autonomic nervous system in schizophrenia: 1. Effect of intravenous injections of epinephrine on the blood pressure and pulse rate, *Arch. Neurol. Psychiat. Chicago*, **33**, 342–352 (1935).

FRENCH, J. D., VERZEANO, M. and MAGOUN, H. W., A neural basis of the anaesthetic state, *A.M.A. Arch. Neurol. Psychiat.*, **69**, 519–529 (1953).

FREYHAM, F. A., Craving for Benzedrine, *Delaware Med. J.*, **21**, 151–156 (1949).

FUNKENSTEIN, D. H., The physiology of fear and anger, *Scientific American* (May, 1955).

FUNKENSTEIN, D. H., Nor-epinephrine-like and epinephrine-like substances in relation to human behavior, *J. Nerv. Ment. Dis.*, **124**, 58–68 (1956).

FUNKENSTEIN, D. H., GREENBLATT, M. and SOLOMON, H. C., Autonomic nervous system changes following electric shock treatment, *J. Nerv. Ment. Dis.*, **108**, 409–422 (1948).

FUNKENSTEIN, D. H., GREENBLATT, M. and SOLOMON, H. C., A test which predicts the clinical effects of electric shock treatment in schizophrenic patients, *Amer. J. Psychiat.*, **106**, 889–901 (1950).

FUNKENSTEIN, D. H., GREENBLATT, M. and SOLOMON, H. C., Autonomic changes paralleling psychologic changes in mentally ill patients, *J. Nerv. Ment. Dis.*, **114**, No. 1, 1–18 (1951).

FUNKENSTEIN, D. H., GREENBLATT, M. and SOLOMON, H. C., Nor-epinephrine-like and epinephrine-like substances in psychotic and psychoneurotic patients, *Amer. J. Psychiat.*, **108**, 652–661 (1952).

FUNKENSTEIN, D. H., KING, S. H. and DROLETTE, M. E., The direction of anger during a laboratory stress inducing situation, *Psychosom. Med.*, **16**, No. 5, 404–413 (1954).

FUNKENSTEIN, D. H., KING, S. H. and DROLETTE, M. E., *Mastery of Stress* (Cambridge Mass., Harvard Univ. Press, 1957).

FUNKENSTEIN, D. H. and MEADE, L. W., Nor-epinephrine-like and epinephrine-like substances and the elevation of blood pressure during acute stress, *J. Nerv. Ment. Dis.*, **119**, 380–397 (1954).

FURNEAUX, W. D., Some speed, error and difficulty relationships within a problem-solving situation, *Nature*, **170**, 37 (1952).

GAGNON, G., *The Emotions and some of their Effects on the Blood* (Washington, D.C., Catholic Univ. Amer. Press, 1952).

GAITZ, C. M., ROY, H., THOMPSON, W., KIMBELL, I., MULLEN, A. J. and POKORNY, A. D., Evaluation of chlorpromazine in comparison with other methods of treatment of hospitalized psychiatric patients, using the low multidimensional scale for rating psychiatric patients, *Psychiat. Res. Rep.*, **1**, 84–94 (1955).

GARDNER, M. J., HAWKINS, H. M., JUDAH, L. N. and MURPHREE, O. D., Objective measurement of psychiatric changes produced by chlorpromazine and reserpine in chronic schizophrenia, *Psychiat. Res. Rep.*, **1**, 77–83 (1955)

GELLHORN, E., *Physiological Foundations of Neurology and Psychiatry* (Minneapolis, Univ. of Minnesota Press, 1953).

GEOCARIS, K. H. and KOOIKER, J. E., Blood pressure responses of chronic schizophrenic patients to epinephrine and mecholyl, *Amer. J. Psychiat.*, **112**, No. 10, 808–813 (1956).

GERARD, R. W., *Psychopharmacology*. A symposium organized by the section on medical sciences of the Amer. Ass. for the Adv. of Sci., and the Amer. Psychiat. Ass. and presented at the Berkeley meeting, Dec. 30, 1954.

GILLILAND, A. R., and NELSON, D., The effects of coffee on certain mental and physiological functions, *J. Gen. Psychol.*, **21**, 339–348 (1939).

GLASER, E. M. and WHITTOW, G. C., Evidence for a nonspecific mechanism of habituation, *J. Physiol.*, **122**, 43–44 (1953).

GLASER, E. M. and WHITTOW, G. C., Experimental errors in clinical trials, *Clin. Sci.*, **13**, No. 2, 199–210 (1954).

GLYNN, J. D., *Rauwolfia serpentina* (Serpasil) in psychiatry, *J. Neurol. Psychiat.*, **18**, 225–227 (1955).

GOLDBERG, L., Quantitative studies on alcohol tolerance in man, *Acta Physiol. scand.*, **5**, Suppl., 16 (1943).

GOLDBERG, L., Alcohol research in Sweden, 1939–1948, *Quart. J. Stud. Alc.*, **10**, 278–288 (1949).

GOLLA, F. L., BLACKBURN, J. M. and GRAHAM, S., A comparison between some of the effects of isomyn (Benzedrine) and of methylisomyn, *J. Ment. Sci.*, **86**, 48–59 (1940).

GOODMAN, L. S. and GILMAN, A., *The Pharmacological Basis of Therapeutics*, 2nd ed. (New York, Macmillan, 1955).

GOODNOW, R. E., BEECHER, H. K., BRAZIER, MARY A., MOSTELLAR, F. and TAGIURI, R., Physiological performance following a hypnotic dose of a barbiturate, *J. Pharmacol.*, **102**, 55–61 (1951).

GORTON, B. E., The physiology of hypnosis, *Psychiat. Quart.*, **23**, 457–485 (1949).

GOTTLIEB, J. S., Anti-depressive action of 5-(1,3-dimethylbutyl)-5-ethyl barbituric acid, *A.M.A. Arch. Neurol. Psychiat.*, **66**, 318–328 (1951).

GOTTLEIB, J. S., BOBBIT, F. S. and FRIEDINGER, A. W., Psychopharmacologic study of schizophrenia and depressions: VI. Differences in response to sodium amytal and Benzedrine sulphate, *Psychosom. Med.*, **14**, 104–114 (1952).

GRAF, O., Influence of Pervitin on some psychic and motor functions, *Arbeitsphysiol.*, **10**, 692–705 (1939).

GRAY, M. G. and TROWBRIDGE, E. B., Methods for investigating the effects of drugs on psychological function. *Psychol. Rec.*, **5**, 127–148 (1942).

GRÜNEWALD, K., Effect of Evipan on the reaction times for light and sound in mental disorders, *Acta Psychiat. et Neurol. Scand.*, **29**, 365–368 (1954).

GUHA, G., DASGUPTA, S. R. and WERNER, G., Effects of some central depressant drugs on conditioned reflexes, *Bull. Calcutta Sch. Trop. Med.*, **2**, 46–47 (1954).

GUILLAUME, A., *Vagotonics, Sympatheticotonics, Neurotonics* (Paris, Masson et Cie, 1928).

GUNN, J. A. and GURD, M. R., Action of some amines related to adrenaline: phenylallylamine, phenylbutenylamine, diphenylethylamine, *J. Physiol.*, **98**, 424–441 (1940).

GUTTMANN, E., Artificial psychoses produced by mescaline, *J. Ment. Sci.*, **82**, 203–221 (1936).

GUTTMAN, E. and MACLAY, W. S., Mescalin-depersonalization. Therapeutic experiments, *J. Neurol. Psychopath.*, **16**, 193–212 (1936).

GWYNN, H. B. and YATER, W. M., Benzedrine sulfate as a mental stimulant, *Med. Ann. D.C.*, **6**, 356–359 (1937).

HAGGARD, H. W., GREENBERG, L. A. and COHEN, L. M., Quantitative differences: the effects of alcoholic beverages, *New Eng. J. Med.*, **219**, 466–470 (1938).

HARDY, J. D., The nature of pain, *J. Chronic. Dis.*, **4**, 22–51 (1956).

HARDY, J. D., WOLFF, H. G. and GOODELL, H., Studies on pain. A new method for measuring pain threshold: observations on spatial summation of pain, *J. Clin. Invest.*, **XIX**, 649–657 (1940).

HARE, E. H., Comparative efficacy of hypnotics. A self-controlled, self-recorded clinical trail in neurotic patients, *Brit. J. Prev. Soc. Med.*, **9**, 140–146 (1955).

HARRIS, S. C. and BLOCKUS, L. E., The reliability and validity of tooth pulp algesimetry, *J. Pharmacol.*, **104**, 135–148 (1952).

HAUPTMAN, A., Evipan Hypnose, *Klin. Wschr.*, March, 24, 438 (1934).

HAUTY, G. T., The effects of drugs upon the components of hand steadiness, *Proj. No.* 21–1,601–0004. Rep. No. 5, *Air Univ. USAF. Sch. of Aviat. Med.*, Randolph Field, Texas, June 1954.

HAUTY, G. T. and PAYNE, R. B., Effects of work prolongation upon components of a perceptual-motor task, *Proj. No.* 21–1601–0004. *Rep. No. 6, Air Univ. USAF. Sch. of Aviat. Med.*, Randolph Field, Texas, Oct. 1954.

HAUTY, G. T. and PAYNE, R. B., Mitigation of work decrement, *J. Exp. Psychol.*, **49**, 60–67 (1955).

HEADLEE, C. R. and KELLOGG, W. N., Conditioning and retention under hypnotic doses of Nembutal, *Amer. J. Psychol.*, **54**, 353–366 (1941).

HEATH, R. G., *Psychopharmacology.* A symposium organized by the section on medical sciences of the Amer. Ass. for the Adv. of Sci., and the Amer. Psychiat. Ass. and presented at the Berkeley meeting, Dec. 30, 1954.

HECHT, R. and SARGENT, S. S., Effects of Benzedrine sulfate on performance in two tests of high mental functions, *J. Exp. Psychol.*, **28**, 528–533 (1941).

HEISE, H. A., Alcohol and automobile accidents, *J. Amer. Med. Ass.*, **103**, 739–741 (1934).

HERMAN, M. and NAGLER, S. H., Psychoses due to amphetamine, *J. Nerv. Ment. Dis.*, **120**, 268–272 (1954).

HERTZMAN, M., ORLANSKY, J. and SEITZ, C. P., Personality organisation and anoxia tolerance, *Psychosom. Med.*, **6**, 317–331 (1944).

HESS, E. H., Effects of Meprobamate on imprinting in waterfowl, *Ann. N.Y. Acad. Sci.*, **67**, Art.10, 724–733 (1957).

HICK, W. E., Nystagmus and alcohol ingestion (letter), *Brit. Med. J.*, 1,541 (1956).

HILDEBRAND, H. O., A factorial study of introversion-extraversion by means of objective tests, *Ph.D. Thesis, Univ. of London, Lib.* (1953).

HILL, D., Amphetamine in psychopathic states, *Brit. J. Addict.*, **22**, 50–54 (1947).

HILL, H. E., Studies on pain and analgesics, *Psychol. Rec.*, **6**, 17–23 (1956).

HILL, H. E. and BELLEVILLE, R. E., Effects of chronic barbiturate intoxication on motivation and muscular coordination, *A.M.A. Arch. Neurol. Psychiat.*, **70**, 180–188 (1953).

HILL, H. E., BELLEVILLE, R. E. and WIKLER, A., Reduction of pain-conditioned anxiety by analgesic doses of morphine in rats, *Proc. Soc. Exp. Biol. N.Y.*, **86**, 881–884 (1954)

HILL, H. E., BELLEVILLE, R. E. and WIKLER, A., Studies on anxiety associated with anticipation of pain. Comparative effects of pentobarbital and morphine, *A.M.A. Arch. Neurol. Psychiat.*, **73**, 602–608 (1955).

HILL, H. E., BELLEVILLE, R. E. and WIKLER, A., Motivational determinants in modification of behaviour by morphine and pentobarbital, *A.M.A. Arch. Neurol. Psychiat.*, **77**, 28–35 (1957).

HILL, H. E., KORNETSKY, C. H., FLENARY, H. G. and Wikler, A., Effects of anxiety and morphine on discrimination of intensities of painful stimuli, *J. Clin. Invest.*, **31**, 473–480 (1952).

HIMWICH, H. E., *Brain Metabolism and Cerebral Disorders* (Baltimore, Williams & Wilkins, 1951).

HIMWICH, H. E., Psychopharmacology Symposium, *J. Nerv. Ment. Dis.*, **122**, 413–497 (1955).

HIRSCH, M. W., JARVIK, M. E. and ABRAMSON, H. A., Lysergic acid diethylamide (LSD-25) XVIII. Effects of LSD-25 and six related drugs upon handwriting, *J. Psychol.*, **41**, 11–22 (1956).

HOAGLAND, H., RINKEL, M. and HYDE, R. W., Adrenocortical function and urinary phosphate excretion, *A.M.A. Arch. Neurol. Psychiat.*, **73**, 100–109 (1955).

HOCH, P. H., The present status of narco-diagnosis and therapy, *J. Nerv. Ment. Dis.*, **103**, 248–259 (1946).

HOCH, P. H., CATTELL, J. P. and PENNES, H. H., Effects of mescaline and lysergic acid (d-LSD-25), *Amer. J. Psychiat.*, **108**, 579–584 (1952).

HOCH, P. H. and POLATIN, P., Pseudoneurotic forms of schizophrenia, *Psychiat. Quart.*, **23**, 248–276 (1949).

HOFFER, A., Epinephrin derivatives as potential schizophrenic factors, *J. Clin. Exp. Psychopath.*, **18**, 27–60 (1957).

HOFFER, A. and OSMOND, H., Schizophrenia: an autonomic disease, *J. Ment. Sci.*, **122**, 448–452 (1955).

HOFFER, A., OSMOND, H. and SMYTHIES, J., Schizophrenia: a new approach: II. Result of two years' research, *J. Ment. Sci.*, **100**, 29–45 (1954).

HOLCK, H. G. and KANAN, M.A., Sex difference in white rat intolerance to certain barbiturates, *Proc. Soc. Exp. Biol. N.Y.*, **32**, 700–701 (1935).

HOLCK, H. G., KANAN, M. A., MILLS, LUCILLE, M. and SMITH, E. L., Studies upon the sex difference in rats' intolerance to certain barbiturates and to nicotine, *J. Pharmacol.*, **60**, 323–346 (1937).

HOLLINGWORTH, H. L., Psychological aspects of drug action, *Psychol. Bull.*, **9**, 420–423 (1912).

HOLLINGWORTH, H. L., The influence of caffeine on the speed and quality of performance in typewriting, *Psychol. Rev.*, **19**, 66–73 (1912).

HOLLINGWORTH, H. L., The influence of alcohol, *J. Abnorm. (Soc.) Psychol.*, **18**, 204–237 (1923–4).

HOLLINGWORTH, H. L., Experiments on susceptibility to drugs, *Amer. J. Psychol.*, **43**, 139–144 (1931).

HOPE, J. M., CALLAWAY, E. and SANDS, S. L., "Methedrine" brand. Injection of d-N-Methyl-amphetamine hydrochloride. Use in schizophrenia, *Dis. Nerv. Syst.*, **12**, 67 (1951).

HOPKINS, P., *The Psychology of Social Movements. A Psychoanalytical View of Society* (London, Allen & Unwin, 1938).

HORSLEY, J. S., *Narcoanalysis* (New York, Oxford Univ. Press, 1943).

HORSLEY, J. S., Narcotic hynposis, *Brit. J. Med. Hyp.*, **2**, 2–7 (1951).

HORTON, D., The functions of alcohol in primitive societies: a cross-cultural study, *Quart. J. Stud. Alc.*, **4**, 199–320 (1943).

HOUSTON, F., A preliminary investigation into abreaction comparing Methedrine and Sodium Amytal with other methods, *J. Ment. Sci.*, **98**, 707–710 (1952).

HULL, C. L., The influence of tobacco smoking on mental and motor efficiency, *Psychol. Monogr.*, No. 150 (1924).

HULL, C. L., The influence of caffeine and other factors on certain phenomena of rote learning, *J. Gen. Psychol.*, **13**, 249–274 (1935).

HUNT, H. F., Some effects of Meprobamate on conditioned fear and emotional behavior, *Ann. N.Y. Acad. Sci.*, **67**, Art.10, 712–723 (1957).

HUSTON, P. E. and SENF, R., Psychopathology of schizophrenia and depression. 1. Effect of amytal and amphetamine sulfate on level and maintenance of attention, *Amer. J. Psychiat.*, **109**, 131–138 (1952).

HUXLEY, A., *Heaven and Hell* (London, Chatto & Windus, 1956).

IDESTRÖM, C. M., Flicker fusion in chronic barbiturate usage, *Acta Psychiat. Neurol.*, (suppl.) No. 91 (1954).

ISBELL, G. and FRASER, H., Addiction to analgesics and barbiturates, *Pharmacol. Rev.*, **2**, 355–397 (1950).

IVY, A. and GOETZL, F. R., D-desoxyephedrin. A review, *War Med.*, 60–77 (Jan. 1943).

JACOBSEN, E., Direct measurements of the effects of bromides, Sodium Amytal and of caffeine in man, *Ann. Intern. Med.*, **21**, 455–468 (1944).

JACOBSEN, E., Metabolism of ethyl alcohol, *Pharmacol. Rev.*, **4**, 107–135 (1952).

JACOBSEN, E., CHRISTENSEN, J. T., ERIKSEN, F. and HALD, J., Studien über die Weckwirkung sympathicotroper Amine, *Skand. Arch. Physiol.*, **79**, 258–281 (1938)

JACOBSEN, E., KEHLET, H. and LARSEN, K., Investigations into autonomic responses during emotion, *Acta Psychiat. Neurol., Scand.*, **30**, 607–625 (1955).

JACOBSEN, E. and WOLLSTEIN, A., Studies in the subjective effect of the cephalotropic amines in man. 1. Betaphenylisopropylaminsulphate, *Acta med. scand.*, **100**, 159–202 (1939).

JARVIK, M. E., Mechanism of action of lysergic acid diethylamide, serotonin and related drugs, *N.S. Klin. Psychopharm.*, 145–154 (1956).

JARVIK, M. E., ABRAMSON, H. A., HIRSCH, H. W. and EWALD, A. T., Lysergic acid diethylamide (LSD-25). Series of articles in *J. Psychol.*, **39**, 465–473 (1955).

JELLINEK, E. M., Clinical tests on comparative effectiveness of analgesic drugs, *Biomet. Bull.*, **2**, 87–91 (1946).

JELLINEK, E. M. and McFARLAND, R. A., Analysis of psychological experiments on the effects of alcohol, *Quart. J. Stud. Alc.*, **1**, 272–371 (1940).

JERRILD, A. T. and THOMAS, W. S., The influence of adrenal extract on behaviour and mental efficiency, *Amer. J. Psychol.*, **43**, 447–456 (1931).

JONAS, A. D., The adjunctive use of an intravenous amphetamine derivation in psychotherapy, *J. Nerv. Ment. Dis.*, **119**, 135–147 (1954).

JONES, J. R., The influence of some antipyretic drugs on learning, *J. Gen. Psychol.*, **9**, 472–475 (1933).

JONES, M. R., Effects of phenobarbital on learning and retention, *Psychol. Bull.*, **39**, 480 (1942).

JONES, M. R. and JONES, C. E., The effects of phenobarbital on learning and retention, *J. Comp. Psychol.*, **36**, 133–142 (1943).

JONG, DE, H., *Experimental Catatonia and its Implications for Human Pathology* (Baltimore, Williams & Wilkins, 1945).

KAHN, R. L., FINK, M. and WEINSTEIN, E. A., Relation of amobarbital test to clinical improvement in electroshock, *A.M.A. Arch. Neurol. Psychiat.*, **76**, 23–29 (1956).

KEATS, A. B., BEECHER, H. K. and MOSTELLAR, F. C., Measurement of pathological pain in distinction to experimental pain, *J. Appl. Physiol.*, **3**, 35–44 (1950a).

KEATS, A. B., BEECHER, H. K. and MOSTELLAR, F. C., Pain relief with hypnotic doses of barbiturates and a hypothesis, *J. Pharmacol.*, **100**, 1–13 (1950b).

KELLER, M. and EFRON, V., The classified abstract archive of the alcohol literature, *Quart. J. Stud. Alc.*, **14**, 262–284 (1953).

KELLY, D. M., LEVINE, K., PEMBERTON, W. and LILLIAN, K. K., Intravenous Sodium Amytal medication as an aid to the Rorschach method, *Psychiat. Quart.*, **15**, 68–73 (1941).

KILLAM, K. F., OLDS, J. and BACH Y RITA, P., Effect of reserpine and chlorpromazine on positive reinforcement behaviour in rats, *Fed. Proc.*, **15**, 446 (1956).

KING, S. H. and HENRY, A. F., Agression and cardiovascular reaction related to parental control over behavior, *J. Abnorm. (Soc.) Psychol.*, **50**, 206–210 (1955).

KLEEMEIER, L. B. and KLEEMEIER, R. W., Effects of Benzedrine sulfate (amphetamine) on psychomotor performance, *Amer. J. Psychol.*, **60**, 89–100 (1947).

KLEEMEIER, R. W., RICH, T. A. and JUSTISS, W. A., The effects of alpha (2-piperidyl) benzhydrol hydrochloride (Meratran) on psychomotor performance in a group of aged males, *J. Geront.*, **10**, No. 4 abstract (1955).

KLINE, N. (Ed.) *Psychopharmacology*, (1956) Amer. Ass. for the Adv. of Sci., Washington, Publ. 42, 10–165 (1956).

KLÜVER, H., Mescal visions and eidetic vision, *Amer. J. Psychol.*, **37**, 502–515 (1926).

KLÜVER, H., *Mescal: the "Divine" Plant* (London, Kegan Paul, 1928).

KLÜVER, H., Mechanisms of hallucinations; in *Studies in Personality* (New York and London, McGraw-Hill, 1942).

KNAPP, P. H., Amphetamine and addiction, *J. Nerv. Ment. Dis.*, **115**, 406–431 (1952).

KNAUER, A. and MALONEY, W. J., A preliminary note on the psychic action of mescaline with special reference to the mechanism of visual hallucinations, *J. Nerv. Ment. Dis.*, **40**, 425–438 (1913).

KNOEFEL, P. K., The influence of phenisopropyl amine and phenisopropyl methyl amine on work output, *Fed. Proc.*, **2**, 83 (1943).

KORNETSKY, C., Effects of anxiety and morphine on the anticipation and perception of painful radiant thermal stimuli, *J. Comp. Physiol. Psychol.*, **47**, 130–132 (1954).

KOPPANYI, T. and FAZEKAS, J. F., Acute barbiturate poisoning: analysis and evaluation of current therapy, *Amer. J. Med. Sci.*, **220**, 559–576 (1950).

KRAINES, S. H. and SHERMAN, I. C., Neurotic symptoms and changes in blood pressure and pulse following the injection of epinephrine, *J. Amer. Med. Ass.*, **114**, 843–845 (1940).

KUBIE, L. S. and MARGOLIN, S., The therapeutic role of drugs in the process of repression, dissociation and synthesis, *Psychosom. Med.*, **7**, 147–151 (1945).

LACEY, J. I., Individual differences in somatic response patterns, *J. Comp. Physiol. Psychol.*, **43**, 338–350 (1950).

LACEY, J. I., BATEMAN, D. E. and LEHN VAN, R., Autonomic response specificity, *Psychosom. Med.*, **15**, 8–21 (1953).

LANDIS, C., The effect of injection of adrenalin on complex muscular activity, *J. Comp. Psychol.*, **19**, 113–117 (1935).

LANDIS, C., An annotated bibliography of flicker fusion phenomena (1740–1952). Armed Forces Nat. Res. Council Vision Cttee. Secretariat. Ann Arbor, Michigan, (1953).

LANDIS, C. and CLAUSEN, J., Certain effects of mescaline and lysergic acid on psychological functions, *J. Psychol.*, **38**, 211–221 (1954).

LANDIS, C. and HUNT, W. A., Adrenalin and emotion, *Psychol. Rev.*, **39**, 467–485 (1932).

LANDIS, C. and ZUBIN, J., The effect of thouzylamine hydrochloride and phenobarbital on certain psychological functions, *J. Psychol.*, **31**, 181–200 (1951).

LANGLEY, J. N., Observations on the physiological action of extracts of the suprarenal bodies, *J. Physiol.*, **27**, 237–256 (1901).

LASAGNA, L., A comparison of hypnotic agents, *J. Pharmacol.*, **111**, 9–20 (1954).

LASHLEY, K. S., The effect of strychnine and caffeine upon rate of learning, *Psychobiology*, **1**, 141–170 (1917).

LAVERTY, S. G. and FRANKS, C. M., Sodium Amytal and behaviour in neurotic subjects, *J. Neurol. Psychiat.*, **19**, 137–143 (1956).

LAYMAN, J. W., A quantitative study of certain changes occurring under Sodium Amytal, *Psychol. Bull.*, **33**, 745 (1936).

LAYMAN, J. W., A quantitative study of certain changes in schizophrenic patients under the influence of Sodium Amytal, *J. Gen. Psychol.*, **22**, 67–86 (1940).

LAZARUS, R. S., DEESE, J. and OSLER, S. F., The effects of psychological stress upon performance, *Psychol. Bull.*, **49**, 293–301 (1952).

LEA, A. J., Adrenochrome as the cause of schizophrenia. Investigation of some deductions from this hypothesis, *J. Ment. Sci.*, **101**, 538–547 (1955).

LEHMANN, G., STRAUB, H. and SZAKALL, A., Pervitin als Leistungesteigerndes, *Mittell Arbeitsphysiologie*, **10**, 680–691 (1939).

LEIBERMAN, D. M. and VAUGHAN, G. F., The use of some new pharmacological agents in psychiatry, *J. Ment. Sci.*, **103**, 110–118 (1957).

LEMMEL, G. and HARTWIG, J., Untersuchungen über die Wirkung von Pervitin und Benzedrin auf psychischem Gebiet, *Dtsch. Arch. f. klin. Med.*, **185**, 626–639 (1940).

LENNARD, H., JARVIK, M. E. and ABRAMSON, H. A., Lysergic acid diethylamide (LSD-25): XII. A preliminary statement of its effects upon interpersonal communication, *J. Psychol.*, **41**, 185–198 (1956).

LEVINE, A., ABRAMSON, H. A., KAUFMAN, M. R. and MARKHAM, S., Lysergic acid diethylamide (LSD-25): XVI. The effect on intellectual functioning as measured by the Wechsler-Bellevue Intelligence Scale, *J. Psychol.*, **40**, 385–395 (1955a).

LEVINE, A., ABRAMSON, H. A., KAUFMAN, M. R., MARKHAM S. and KORNETSKY, C., Lysergic acid diethylamide (LSD-25): XIV. Effect on personality as observed in psychological tests, *J. Psychol.*, **40**, 351–366 (1955b).

LEVINE, A., RINKEL, M. and GREENBLATT, M., Effects of intravenous methyl amphetamine, *Amer. J. Psychiat.*, **105**, 429–434 (1948).

LEWIS, A. J. and FLEMINGER, J. J., The psychiatric risk from corticotrophin and cortisone, *Lancet*, **1**, 383–386 (1954).

LEWIS, J. L. and McILWAIN, H., The action of some ergot derivations, mescaline and dibenamine on the metabolism of separated mammalian cerebral tissues, *Biochem. J.*, **57**, 680–684 (1954).

LINDEMANN, E., Psychological changes in normal and abnormal individuals under the influence of Sodium Amytal, *Amer. J. Psychiat.*, **11**, 1,083–1,091 (1932).

LINDEMANN, E., The neurophysiological effect of intoxicating drugs, *Amer. J. Psychiat.*, **13**, 1,007–1,037 (1934).

LINDEMANN, E. and FINESINGER, J. E., The effects of adrenalin and mecholyl in states of anxiety in psychoneurotic patients, *Amer. J. Psychiat.*, **95**, 353–370 (1938).

LINDEMANN, E. and FINESINGER, J. E., The subjective response of psychoneurotic patients to adrenalin and mecholyl (acety-B-methyl-choline), *Psychosom. Med.*, **2**, 231–248 (1940).

LINDEMANN, E. and MALAMUD, W., Experimental analysis

of the psychopathological effect of intoxicating drugs, *Amer. J. Psychiat.*, **90**, 853–881 (1934).

LITTLE, J. C., A double-blind controlled comparison of the effects chlorpromazine, barbiturate and a *placebo* in one hundred and forty-two chronic psychotic in-patients, *J. Ment. Sci.*, **104**, 334–349 (1958).

LOMAS, J., Treatment of schizophrenia. Pacatal and chlorpromazine compared, *Brit. Med. J.*, **II**, 78–80 (1957).

LORENZE, W. F., REESE, H. H. and WASHBURNE, A. C., Physiological observations during intravenous Sodium Amytal medications, A preliminary report, *Amer. J. Psychiat.*, **90**, 1,205–1,213 (1934).

LUDWIG, A. O., Clinical features and diagnosis of malingering in military personnel. Use of barbiturates as an aid in detection, *War. Med.*, **5**, 378–382 (1944).

McDOUGALL, W., The chemical theory of temperament applied to introversion and extraversion, *J. Abnorm. (Soc.) Psychol.*, **24**, 293–309 (1929).

McFARLAND, R. A., The psychological effects of oxygen deprivation (anoxemia) on human behavior, *Arch. Psychol.*, No. 145, 135 (1932).

McFARLAND, R. A., The psycho-physiological effects of reduced oxygen pressure, *Res. Publ. Ass. Nerv. Ment. Dis.*, **19**, 112–143 (1939).

McFARLAND, R. A. and BARACH, A. L., Relationship between alcoholic intoxication and anoxemia, *Amer. J. Ment. Sci.*, **192**, 186–198 (1936).

McFARLAND, R. A. and BARACH, A. L., The response of psychoneurotics to variations in oxygen tension, *Amer. J. Psychiat.*, **93**, 1,315–1,341 (1937).

McGRATH, S. D., RYAN, J. P. A. and FENNELLY, J. J., The use of reserpine (Serpasil) in psychiatry, *J. Irish. Med. Ass.*, **39**, 1 (1956).

McKINNEY, F., Nitrous oxide anaesthesia as an experimental technique in psychology, *J. Gen. Psychol.*, **6**, 195–199 (1932).

McNAMARA, W. J. and MILLER, R. E., Effect of Benzedrine sulphate on mental work, *Psychol. Rec.*, **1**, 78–84 (1937).

MACKWORTH, N. H., Researches on the measurement of human performance, *M.R.C. Spec. Rep.* Ser. No. 268 (London, H.M.S.O., 1948).

MAGOUN, H. W., A neural basis for the anaesthetic state, in: *Symposium on Sedative and Hypnotic Drugs* (Baltimore, Williams & Wilkins, 1954).

MAINORD, W. A., Some effects of Sodium Amytal on deteriorated schizophrenics, *J. Cons. Psychol.*, **17**, 54–57 (1953).

MARANON, G., Contribution a l'étude de l'action émotive de l'adrenaline, *Rev. franç. Endocr.*, **2**, 301–325 (1924).

MARAZZI, A. S. and HART, E. R., Relationship of hallucinogens to adrenergic cerebral mechanisms, *Science*, **121**, 365–367 (1955a).

MARAZZI, A. S. and HART, E. R., The possible role of inhibition at adrenergic synapses in the mechanism of hallucinogenic and related drug action, *J. Nerv. Ment. Dis.*, **122**, 453–457 (1955b).

MARAZZI, A. S., HART, E. R. and COHN, V. H., Pharmacology of the nervous system, *Progr. Neurol. & Psychiat.*, **11**, 565–594 (1956).

MARKKANEN, T., An exact factor analytical approach to differences in personality structure between alcoholics

and the normal group, *Drinking and Drinkers*, Helsinki, (1957).

MARQUIS, D. G., LOWELL KELLY, E., MILLER, J. G., GERARD, R. W. and RAPOPORT, A., Experimental studies of behavioral effects of Meprobamate on normal subjects, *Ann. N.Y. Acad. Sci.*, **67**, 701–711 (1957).

MARX, M. H. and EDELSTROM, H. E., The effect of repeated pentobarbital administration on learning, *J. Comp. Physiol. Psychol.*, **43**, 428–435 (1950).

MARTENSON-LAWSON, O., The significance of a low alcohol limen *Brit. J. Addict.*, **47**, 43–47 (1950).

MASSERMAN, J. H., Neurosis and alcohol; experimental study, *Amer. J. Psychiat.*, **101**, 389–395 (1944).

MASSERMAN, H. J. and YUM, K. S., An analysis of the influence of alcohol on experimental neuroses in cats, *Psychosom. Med.*, **8**, 36–52 (1946).

MATEFI, L., Mezcalin-und lysergsäurediäthylamid Rausch. Selbstversuche mit besonderer Berücksichtigung eines Zeichentests, *Conf. Neurol.*, **12**, 146–177 (1952).

MAYER-GROSS, W., Experimental psychosis and other mental abnormalities produced by drugs, *Brit. Med. J.*, **2**, 317–321 (1951).

MEERLOO, A. M., Variable tolerance for alcohol, *J. Nerv. Ment. Dis.*, **105**, 590–597 (1947).

MENDENHALL, M. G., The effect of sodium phenobarbital on learning and reasoning in white rats, *J. Comp. Psychol.*, **29**, 257–276 (1940).

MILES, W. R., Psychological effects of alcohol in man, in *The Effect of Alcohol on Man in Health and Disease*, Ed. H. Emerson (New York, Macmillan, 1932).

MILES, W. R., Alcohol and human efficiency, *Bull. Carneg. Inst.*, 333 (1924).

MILLER, N. E., Effects of drugs on motivation: the value of using a variety of measures, *Ann. N.Y. Acad. Sci.*, **65**, 318–333 (1956).

MILLER, N. E. and MILES, W. R., Alcohol and the removal of reward. An analytical study of rodent maze behaviour, *J. Comp. Psychol.*, **21**, 179–204 (1936).

MINER, R. W., (Ed.) Reserpine in the treatment of neuropsychiatric, neurological and related clinical problems, *Ann. N.Y. Acad. Sci.*, **61**, 1–280 (1955).

MINKOWSKI, W. L., The effect of Benzedrine sulphate on learning, *J. Comp. Psychol.*, **28**, 349–360 (1939).

MITCHELL, S. W., Remarks on the effects of *Anhalonium Lewinii* (the mescal button), *Brit. Med. J.*, **2**, 1,625–1,629 (1896).

MOIR, W. M., The influence of age and sex on the repeated administration of sodium pentobarbital to ablino rats, *J. Pharmacol.*, **59**, 68–85 (1937).

MOLDAWSKY, S. and MOLDAWSKY, P. C., Digit span as an anxiety indicator, *J. Cons. Psychol.*, **16**, 115–118 (1952).

MOLITCH, M. and SULLIVAN, J. P., The effect of Benzedrine sulphate on children taking the New Stanford Achievement Test, *Amer. J. Orthopsychiat.*, **7**, 519–522 (1937).

MONRO, A. B. and CONITZER, H., A comparison of desoxyephedrine (methedrine) and electroshock in the treatment of depression, *J. Ment. Sci.*, **96**, 1,037–1,042 (1950).

MONROE, R. R. and DRELL, H. J., Oral use of stimulants obtained from inhalers, *J. Amer. Med. Ass.*, **135**, 909–915 (1947).

MONTAGU, J. D. and DAVIES, L. S., Electrical treatment of anxiety states, *J. Ment. Sci.*, **101**, 577–592 (1955).

MOORE, R. and MARTIN, S., Trial of reserpine in treatment of schizophrenia, *Brit. Med. J.*, **I**, 8 (1957).

MORIARTY, J. D., Epinephrine-mecholyl test (Funkenstein test) as a prognostic guide for various physiodynamic therapies, *Conf. Neurol.*, **16**, 105–115 (1956).

MORRIS, J. V., McGILLIVRAY, and MATHIESON, C. M., The results of the experimental administration of amphetamine sulphate in oligophrenia, *J. Ment. Sci.*, **101**, 131–140 (1955).

MÜCHER, H., Psychologische Beitrage zur Untersuchung von Schlafmittelnachwirkungen: 1. Analyse systematisch angeregter Vorstellung Statizkeit, *Psychol. Neitr.*, **1**, 81–117 (1953).

MYERSON, A., LOMAN, J. and DAMASHEK, W., Physiologic effects of acetyl-beta-methyl-choline (Mecholyl) and its relationship to other drugs affecting the autonomic nervous system, *Amer. J. Med. Sci.*, **193**, 198–214 (1937).

MYERSON, A., LOMAN, J., RINKEL, M. and LESSES, M. F., The effect of amphetamine sulphate (Benzedrine sulphate) and paredrine hydrobromide upon Sodium Amytal narcosis, *New Eng. J. Med.*, **221**, 1,015–20 (1939).

NATHANSON, M. H., The central action of beta-amino-propylbenzene (Benzedrine). Clinical observations, *J. Amer. Med. Ass.*, **108**, 528–531 (1937).

NEWMAN, H. W., Alcohol injected intravenously. Some psychological and psychopathological effects in man, *Amer. J. Psychiat.*, **91**, 1,343–1,352 (1935).

NEWMAN, H. W. and ABRAMSON, M., Some factors influencing the intoxicating effect of alcoholic beverages, *Quart. J. Stud. Alc.*, **3**, 351–370 (1942).

NEWMAN, H. W. and NEWMAN, E. J., Failure of Dexedrine and caffeine as practical antagonists of the depressant effect of ethyl alcohol, *Quart. J. Stud. Alc.*, **3**, 406–411 (1956).

NORMAN, J. and SHEA, J. T., Acute hallucinosis as a complication of addiction to amphetamine sulphate, *New Eng. J. Med.*, **30**, 233–270 (1945).

OGILVIE, B. C., A study of intellectual slowness, *Ph.D. Thesis, Univ. of London Lib.* (1954).

O'KELLY, L. I. and WEISS, H. M., The effects of ether and a barbiturate on water regulation in the rat, *J. Comp. Physiol. Psychol.*, **48**, 123–125 (1955).

OLDS, J., *Neuropharmacology. Transactions of the Third Conference.* Sponsored by Josiah Macy, Jnr., Foundation, N.Y. (1957).

OMWAKE, L., The influence of barbital on the activity and learning of white rats, *J. Comp. Physiol. Psychol.*, **16**, 317–324 (1933).

OSMOND, H. and SMYTHIES, J., Schizophrenia: a new approach, *J. Ment. Sci.*, **98**, 309–315 (1952).

PARNELL, R. W., Physique and individual alcohol consumption, *Int. J. Alc. & Alcoholism.*, **3**, 127–133 (1955).

PATON, S. and STEINBERG, H., A class experiment on ganglion block in human subjects, *Brit. Med. J.*, **1**, 622–626 (1956).

PAYNE, R. B., The effects of drugs upon psychological efficiency, *J. Aviat. Med.*, **24**, 523–529 (1953).

PAYNE, R. B. and HAUTY, G. T., The pharmacological control of work output during prolonged tasks, *Proj. No. 21–1,601–0004. Rep. No. 2. Air Univ. USAF. Sch. of Aviat. Med.*, Randolph Field, Texas (1953).

PAYNE, R. B. and HAUTY, G. T., The effects of experi-

mentally induced attitudes upon task proficiency, *J. Exp. Psychol.*, **47**, 267–273 (1954).

PAYNE, R. B. and HAUTY, G. T., Effect of psychological feedback upon work decrement, *J. Exp. Psychol.*, **50**, 343–351 (1955).

PAYNE, R. B. and HAUTY, G. T., Factors affecting the endurance of psychomotor skill, *J. Aviat. Med.*, **26**, 382–389 (1955).

PAYNE, R. B. and MOORE, E. W., The effects of some analeptic and depressant drugs upon tracking behaviour, *J. Pharmacol.*, **115**, 480–484 (1955).

PENNES, H. M., Clinical reactions of schizophrenics to Sodium Amytal, Pervitin, hydrochloride, mescaline sulfate and d-lysergic acid diethylamide (LSD-25), *J. Nerv. Ment. Dis.*, **119**, 95–112 (1954).

PEOPLES, S. A. and GUTTMAN, E., Hypertension produced with Benzedrine. Its psychological accompaniments, *Lancet*, **1**, 1,107 (1936).

PETRIE, A. and LE BEAU, J., Psychologic changes in man after chlorpromazine and certain types of brain surgery, *J. Clin. & Exp. Psychopath. & Quart. Rev. Psychiat. Neurol.*, **17**, 170–179 (1956).

POFFENBERGER, A. T., Psychological effects of drugs, *Psychol. Bull.*, **11**, 418–421 (1914); **13**, 434–436 (1916); **14**, 409–411 (1917); **16**, 291–292 (1919).

POLLACK, S. and TAKAKJIAN, M., Variables in the clinical evaluation of a hypnotic drug with a clinical evaluation of glutethimide, *J. Nerv. Ment. Dis.*, **122**, 589–594 (1955).

PORTEUS, S. D., Specific behaviour changes following chlorpromazine, *J. Cons. Psychol.*, **21**, 257 (1957).

PRINZMETAL, M. and BLOOMBERG, W., The use of Benzedrine for the treatment of narcolepsy, *J. Amer. Med. Ass.*, **105**, 2,051–2,054 (1935).

PULLAR-STRECKER, H., A review of the 1949–1950 literature of addiction, *Brit. J. Addict.*, **45**, 125 (1948); **46**, 105 (1949); **48**, 3–119 (1951).

RAVITZ, L. J., Standing potential correlates of hypnosis and narcosis, *A.M.A. Arch. Neurol. Psychiat.*, **65**, 413–436 (1951).

RAYMOND, M. J., LUCAS, C. J., BEESLEY, M. L., O'CONNELL, B. A. and ROBERTS, J. A. F., A trial of five tranquillising drugs in psychoneurosis, *Brit. Med. J.*, **II**, 63 (1957).

REES, L., Psychosomatic aspects of premenstrual tension syndrome, *J. Ment. Sci.*, **99**, 497–504 (1953).

REIFENSTEIN, E. C. (JNR.) and DAVIDOFF, E., The psychological effects of Benzedrine sulphate, *Amer. J. Psychol.*, **52**, 56–64 (1939).

REZNIKOFF, L., Effect of Benzedrine sulphate alternated with sodium amytal in schizophrenia, *Amer. J. Psychiat.*, **98**, 196–200 (1941–42).

RICHTER, D., The action of adrenalin in anxiety, *Proc. Roy. Soc. Med.*, **33**, 615–618 (1940).

RICHTER, D., Biochemistry of the nervous system In, *Recent Progress in Psychiatry*, Ed. G. W. T. H. Fleming (London, Churchill, 1950).

RIGGS, M. M. and KAESS, W., Personality differences between volunteers and non-volunteers, *J. Psychol.*, **40**, 229–245 (1955).

RINALDI, F. and HIMWICH, H. E., Alerting responses and actions of atropine and cholinergic drugs, *A.M.A. Arch. Neurol. Psychiat.*, **73**, 387–395 (1955).

RINKEL, M., DE SHON, H. J., HYDE, R. W. and SOLOMON, H. C., Experimental schizophrenia-like symptoms, *Amer. J. Psychiat.*, **108**, 572–578 (1952).

RINKEL, M., HYDE, R. W. and SOLOMON, H. C., Experimental psychiatry: III. A chemical concept of psychosis, *Dis. Nerv. Syst.*, **15**, 259–264 (1954).

RINKEL, M., HYDE, R. W. and SOLOMON, H. C., Experimental psychiatry: IV. Hallucinogens: tools in experimental psychiatry, *Dis. Nerv. Syst.*, **16**, 229–232 (1955).

RINKEL, M., HYDE, R. W., SOLOMON, H. C. and HOAGLAND, H., Experimental psychiatry: II. Clinical and physiochemical observations in experimental psychosis, *Amer. J. Psychiat.*, **111**, 881–895 (1955).

RIPLEY, H. S. and WOLF, S., The intravenous use of Sodium Amytal in psychosomatic disorders, *Psychosom. Med.*, **9**, 260–268 (1947).

RITCHIE, J. A., Adrenergic and cholinergic properties of blood. An investigation of the blood of psychiatric patients, *J. Nerv. Ment. Dis.*, **114**, 307–312 (1951).

RIVERS, W. H. R., *The Influence of Alcohol and other Drugs on Fatigue*, (London, Arnold, 1908).

ROBACK, G. S., KRASNO, L. R. and IVY, A. C., Effect of analeptic drugs on the somnifacient effect of Seconal and antihistamines as measured by flicker fusion threshold, *J. Appl. Physiol.*, **4**, 566–574 (1952).

ROGERSON, C. H., Narcoanalysis with nitrous oxide, *Brit. Med. J.*, **1**, 811–812 (1944).

ROSS, S., SMITH, W. I. and STAHL, J. E., Benzedrine and social behaviour in mice, *Behaviour*, **3**, 167–173 (1951).

ROTHBALLER, A. B., Studies on the adrenaline-sensitive component of the reticular activating system, *EEG & Clinical Neurophysiology*, **8**, 603–621 (1956).

ROTHBALLER, A. B., The effects of phenyleparine, methamphetamine, cocaine and serotonin upon the adrenalinsensitive component of the reticular activating system, *EEG & Clinical Neurophysiology*, **9**, 409–417 (1957).

ROUTIER, A., *Le Peyotl*, **12**, 371 (Paris, 1927).

RUDOLPH, G. DE M., The treatment of depression with desoxyephedrine, *J. Ment. Sci.*, **95**, 920–929 (1949).

RUDOLPH, G. DE M., The treatment of depression with methylamphetamine, *J. Ment. Sci.*, **102**, 358–363 (1956).

RUSSELL, R. W. and STEINBERG, H., Effects of nitrous oxide on reactions to "stress," *Quart. J. Exp. Psychol.*, **7**, 67–73 (1955).

RUTLEDGE, L. T. and DOTY, R. W., Differential action of chlorpromazine on conditioned responses to peripheral versus cortical stimuli, *Fed. Proc.*, **14**, 126 (1955).

SACHS, W., *The Vegatative Nervous System* (London, Cassell & Co., 1936).

SANDISON, R. A., Psychological aspects of the LSD treatment of the neuroses, *J. Ment. Sci.*, **100**, 508–515 (1954).

SANDISON, R. A., SPENCER, A. M. and WHITELAW, J. D. A., The therapeutic value of lysergic acid diethylamide in mental illness, *J. Ment. Sci.*, **100**, 491–507 (1954).

SARGANT, W., On chemical tranquillizers, *Brit. Med. J.*, **1**, 939–942 (1956).

SARGANT, W. and BLACKBURN, J. M., The effect of Benzedrine on intelligence scores, *Lancet*, **2**, 1,385–1,387 (1936).

SARGANT, W., SLATER, P., HALFSTEAD, H. and GLEN, MARGARET, Effects of alcohol and Sodium Amytal on intelligence test score, *Lancet*, **1**, 617–618 (1945).

SAVAGE, C., Varieties in ego-feeling induced by D-lsyergic acid diethylamide (LSD-25), *Psychoanal. Rev.*, **42**, 1–16 (1955).

SAVAGE, C. and CHOLDEN, L., Schizophrenia and the model psychoses, *J. Clin. Exp. Psychopath. & Quart. Rev. Psychiat.*, **17**, 405–413 (1956).

SCHAEFER, E. S., Personality structure of alcoholics in outpatient psychotherapy, *Quart. J. Stud. Alc.*, **15**, 304–319 (1954).

SCHILDER, P., The psychological effect of Benzedrine sulphate, *J. Nerv. Ment. Dis.*, **87**, 584–587 (1938).

SCHNEIDER, R. A., The acute effects of reserpine and of amytal on central sympathetic reactivity, *Ann. N.Y. Acad. Sci.*, **61**, Art.1, 160–160 (1955).

SCHUBE, P. G., MCMANAMY, M. C., TRAPP, C. E. and MYERSON. A., The effect of Benzedrine sulphate in certain abnormal mental states, *Amer. J. Psychiat.*, **94**, 27–32 (1937).

SEAGER, C. P. and LEITCH, A., Benactyzine in psychoneurosis. A controlled clinical trial in hospital patients, *Brit. Med. J.*, **2**, 1,407–1,409 (1956).

SEARLE, L. W. and BROWN, C. W., The effect of injections of Benzedrine on the activity of white rats, *Psychol. Bull.*, **34**, 558–559 (1937).

SEASHORE, R. H. and IVY, A. C., Effects of analeptic drugs in relieving fatigue, *Psychol. Mongr.*, No. 15 (1953).

SEIFERT, W., Wirkung des 1-phenyl-2-methylaminopropan (Pervitin) am Menschen, *Deutsche med. Wchschr.*, **65**, 913–916 (1939). (Also abstr. *Z. ges. Neurol.*, **95**, 56–57 (1939).

SEITZ, C. P. and BARMACK, J. E., The effects of 10 mg Benzedrine sulphate and low O_2 tension on span of attention for letters and other factors, *J. Psychol.*, **10**, 241–248 (1940).

SENF, R., HUSTON, P. E. and COHEN, B. D., Thinking deficit in schizophrenia and changes with amytal, *J. Abnorm. (Soc.) Psychol.*, **50**, 383–387 (1955).

SETTLAGE, P., The effect of Sodium Amytal on the formation and elicitation of conditioned reflexes, *J. Comp. Psychol.*, **22**, 339–343 (1936).

SEWARD, G. H. and SEWARD, J. P., Alcohol and task complexity, *Arch. Psychol.*, No. 206 1–59 (1936).

SHAGASS, C., The sedation threshold. A method for investigating tension in psychiatric patients, *EEG & Clinical Neurophysiology*, **6**, 221–233 (1954).

SHAGASS, C., Sedation threshold. A neurophysiological tool for psychosomatic research, *Psychosom. Med.*, **18**, 410–419 (1956).

SHAGASS, C., MIHALIK, J. and JONES, A. L., Clinical psychiatric studies using the sedation threshold, *J. Psychosom. Res.*, **2**, 45–55 (1957).

SHAGASS, C. and NAIMAN, J., The sedation threshold, manifest anxiety and some aspects of ego foundation, *A.M.A. Arch. Neurol. Psychiat.*, **74**, 397–406 (1955).

SHAGASS, C. and NAIMAN, J., The sedation threshold as an objective index of manifest anxiety in psychoneurosis, *J. Psychosom. Res.*, **1**, 49–57 (1956).

SHAGASS, C., NAIMAN, J. and MIHALIK, J., An objective test which differentiates between neurotic and psychotic depression, *A.M.A. Arch. Neurol. Psychiat.*, **75**, 461–471 (1956).

SHERWOOD, S. L., The response of psychotic patients to

intraventricular injections, *Proc. Roy. Soc. Med.*, **48**, 855–863 (1955).

SHOCK, N. W., Some psychophysiological relations, *Psychol. Bull.*, **36**, 447–476 (1939).

SHON, H. J. DE, RINKEL, M. and SOLOMON, H. C., Mental changes experimentally produced by LSD, *Psychiat. Quart.*, **26**, 33–53 (1952).

SHORE, P. A., SILVER, S. L. and BRODIE, B. B., Interaction of reserpine, serotonin, and lysergic acid diethylamide in brain, *Science*, **122**, 284–285 (1955).

SIDMAN, M., Drug behaviour interaction, *Ann. N.Y. Acad. Sci.*, **65**, 282–302 (1956).

SIEGMAN, A. W., Response to a personality questionnaire by volunteers and non-volunteers to a Kinsey interview, *J. Abnorm. (Soc.) Psychol.*, **52**, 280–281 (1956).

SIMON, J. L. and TAUBE, H., A preliminary study on the use of methedrine in psychiatric diagnosis, *J. Nerv. Ment. Dis.*, **104**, 593–596 (1946).

SIMONSON, E. and BROZEK, J., Flicker fusion frequency: background and applications, *Physiol. Rev.*, **32**, 349–378 (1952).

SIMONSON, E. and ENZER, N., The effect of amphetamine (Benzedrine) sulfate on the state of the motor centres, *J. Exp. Psychol.*, **29**, 517–523 (1941).

SIMONSON, E., ENZER, N. and BLANKSTEIN, S. S., Effect of amphetamine (Benzedrine) on fatigue of the C.N.S., *War Med.*, **1**, 690–695 (1941).

SINHA, S. N., The effects of an excitatory and uninhibitory drug upon reactive inhibition as measured by alternation behaviour in the rat, *M.A. Thesis, Univ. of London Lib.* (1957).

SKINNER, B. F. and HERON, W. T., Effect of caffeine and Benzedrine upon conditioning and extinction, *Psychol. Rec.*, **1**, 340–346 (1937).

SLATER, P., SARGANT, W. and GLEN, MARGARET, Influence of Sodium Amytal on intelligence test scores, *Lancet*, **1**, 676–677 (1942).

SLOANE, B. and DOUST, J. W. L., Four physiological investigations in experimental psychoses. Results of the application of D-lysergic acid diethylamide to psychiatric patients, *J. Ment. Sci.*, **100**, 129–144 (1954).

SLOANE, R. B. and LEWIS, D. J., Prognostic value of adrenaline and mecholyl responses in electroconvulsion therapy, *J. Psychosom. Res.*, **1**, 273–286 (1956).

SMITH, P. L. and SCHWARTZ, D. K., Sodium amytal as means of obtaining contact in stuporous and uncommunicative cases; preliminary report, *Psychiat. Quart.*, **8**, 748–753 (1934).

SMITH, R. P., WAGMAN, A. and RIOPELLE, A. J., Effects of reserpine on conditioned avoidance behaviour in normal and brain-operated monkeys, *J. Pharmacol.*, **117**, 136–141 (1956).

SOMERVILLE, W., The effect of Benzedrine on mental and physical fatigue in soldiers, *Canad. Med. Ass. J.*, **55**, 470–476 (1946).

SPRAGG, S. D. S., The effects of certain drugs on mental and motor efficiency, *Psychol. Bull.*, **38**, 354–363 (1941).

STANLEY, W. C. and SCHLOSBERG, H., The psychophysiological effects of tea, *J. Psychol.*, **36**, 435–448 (1953).

STEINBERG, HANNA, Selective effects of an anaesthetic drug on cognitive behaviour, *Quart. J. Exp. Psychol.*, **6**, 170–180 (1954).

STEINBERG, HANNA, and SUMMERFIELD, A., Influence of a depressant drug on acquisition in rote learning, *Quart. J. Exp. Psychol.*, **9**, 138–145 (1957).

STEINBERG, HANNA, and SUMMERFIELD, A., Reducing interference in forgetting, *Quart. J. Exp. Psychol.*, **9**, 146–157 (1957).

STOCKINGS, G. T., A clinical study of the mescaline psychosis, with special reference to the mechanism of the genesis of schizophrenia and other psychotic states, *J. Ment. Sci.*, **86**, 29–47 (1940).

STOLL, W. A., Ein neues, in sehr kleinen Mengen sirksames Phantastikum. (A new hallucinatory agent, active in very small amounts.) Proc. of 108th meeting of the Swiss Soc. Psychiat., 22nd and 23rd Nov. 1947 (Zürich), *Schweiz. Arch. Neurol.*, **64**, 483 (1949).

STRAUS, B., EISENBERG, J. and GENNIS, J., Hypnotic effects of an antihistamine; methapyrilene hydrochloride, *Ann. Intern. Med.*, **42**, 574–582 (1955).

STUNGO, E., Evipan hypnosis in psychiatric outpatients, *Lancet*, **I**, 507–509 (1941).

SULLIVAN, D. J., Psychiatric uses of intravenous sodium amytal, *Amer. J. Psychiat.*, **99**, 411–418 (1942–43).

SUTHERLAND, E. H., SCHROEDER, H. G. and TORDELLA, C. L., Personality traits and the alcoholic. A critique of existing studies, *Quart. J. Stud. Alc.*, **11**, 547–561 (1950).

TAINTER, M. L., Effects of certain analeptic drugs in spontaneous running activity of the white rat, *J. Comp. Physiol. Psychol.*, **36**, 143–155 (1943).

TENG, P. and BENDER, M. B., Effect of barbiturates on latent motor deficits, *Neurol.*, **5**, 777–786 (1955).

TERRY, R. A., Autonomic balance and temperament, *J. Comp. Physiol. Psychol.*, **46**, 454–460 (1953).

THOMPSON, R. H. S., TICKNER, A. and WEBSTER, G. R., The action of lysergic acid diethylamide on mammalian cholinesterases, *Brit. J. Pharmacol.*, **10**, 61–65 (1955).

THORNER, M. W., The psychopharmacology of Sodium Amytal, *J. Nerv. Ment. Dis.*, **81**, 161–167, **82**, 299–303 (1935).

THORNTON, G. R., HOLCK, H. G. O. and SMITH, E. L., The effect of Benzedrine and caffeine upon performance of certain psychomotor tests, *J. Abnorm. (Soc.) Psychol.*, **34**, 96–113 (1939).

THORPE, J. G. and BAKER, A. A., A research method to assess a new tranquillizing drug, *J. Ment. Sci.*, **102**, 790 (1956).

TIBBETTS, R. W. and HAWKINGS, J. R., The *placebo* response, *J. Ment. Sci.*, **102**, 60–66 (1957).

TOLMAN, E. C., Retroactive inhibition as affected by conditions of learning, *Psychol. Monogr.*, No. 107 (1917–18).

TOMAN, J. E. P., Neuropharmacology of peripheral nerves, *Pharmacol. Rev.*, **4**, 168–218 (1952).

TONINI, G. and MONTANARI, C., Effects of experimentally induced psychoses on artistic expression, *Confin. neurol.*, **15**, 225–239 (1955).

TRENT, S. E., Narcosis and visual contour clarity, *J. Gen. Psychol.*, **36**, 65–78 (1947).

TROUTON, D. S., *Placebos* and their psychological effects, *J. Ment. Sci.*, **103**, 344–354 (1957).

TURNER, W. D. and CARL, G. P., Temporary changes in affect and attitude following ingestion of various amounts of Benzedrine sulfate (amphetamine sulfate), *J. Psychol.*, **8**, 415–482 (1939).

TYLER, D. B., Effect of amphetamine sulphate and some barbiturates on the fatigue produced by prolonged wakefulness, *Amer. J. Physiol.*, **150**, 253–262 (1947).

VARNER, W. B., The effects of alcohol on two maze habits of albino rats, *Psychol. Bull.*, **30**, 616 (1933).

VAUGHAN, G. F., LEIBERMAN, D. M. and COOK, L. C., Chlorpromazine in psychiatry, *Lancet*, **I**, 1,083 (1955).

VERNON, H. M., The effects of alcohol on driving, *Hum. Factor, Lond.*, **10**, 255, (1936).

VERNON, H. M., SULLIVAN, W. C., GREENWOOD, H. and DREYER, N. R., The influence of alcohol on manual work and neuromuscular co-ordination, *M.R.C. Spec. Rep.* No. 34 (London, H.M.S.O., 1919).

VICTOR, M. and ADAMS, R. D., The effect of alcohol on the nervous system, *Proc. Ass. Res. Nerv. Ment. Dis.*, **32**, 526–573 (1953).

WALLIS, G. G., McHARG, J. F. and SCOTT, O. C. A., Acute psychosis caused by dextroamphetamine, *Brit. Med. J.*, **2**, 1,394 (1949).

WANT, S. P., The effects of toxic doses of benzyl methyl carbinamine (Benzedrine) in man, *J. Amer. Med. Ass.*, **110**, 206–207 (1938).

WEDGE, B. and MOULTON, M., Method of pharmacologic facilitation of psychiatric investigation, *J. Nerv. Ment. Dis.*, **III**, 116–121 (1950).

WEINER, R. and HARLOW, H. F., The effect of Nembutal upon learned performances of the rhesus monkey, *J. Gen. Psychol.*, **46**, 43–50 (1952).

WEINSTEIN, E. A. and KAHN, R. L., Patterns of disorientation in organic brain disease, *J. Neuropath. Clin. Neurol.*, **1**, 214–225 (1951).

WEINSTEIN, E. A., KAHN, A. L., SUGARMAN, L. A. and LINN, LOWIS, The diagnostic use of amobarbital sodium (amytal sodium) in brain disease, *Amer. J. Psychiat.*, **109**, 889–894 (1953).

WEINSTEIN, E. A., KAHN, A. L., SUGARMAN, L. A. and MALITZ, S., Serial administration of the "amytal test" for brain disease, *A.M.A. Arch. Neurol. Psychiat.*, **71**, 217–225 (1954).

WEINSTEIN, E. A. and MALITZ, S., Changes in symbolic expression with amytal sodium, *Amer. J. Psychiat.*, **III**, 198–206 (1954).

WEISKRANTZ, L. and WILSON, W. A. (JNR.), The effects of reserpine on emotional behaviour of normal and brain-operated monkeys, *Ann. N.Y. Acad. Sci.*, **61**, 36–55 (1955).

WELCH, L., DIETHELM, O. and LONG, L., Measurement of hyper-associative activity during elation, *J. Psychol.*, **21**, 113–126 (1946).

WENDT, G. R., *Psychopharmacology.* A symposium organised by the section on medical sciences of the A.A.A.S. and the American Psychiatric Association and presented at the Berkeley meeting (Dec. 1954).

WENTINCK, E. A., The effect of certain drugs and hormones upon conditioning, *J. Exp. Psychol.*, **22**, 150–163 (1938).

WEXBERG, L. E., Psychodynamics of patients with chronic alcoholism, *J. Clin. Psychopath.*, **10**, 147–157 (1949).

WIKLER, A., Sites and mechanisms of action of morphine and related drugs in the central nervous system, *Pharmacol. Rev.*, **2**, 435–506 (1950).

WIKLER, A., A critical analysis of some current concepts in psychiatry, *J. Psychosom. Med.*, **14**, 10–17 (1952).

WILBUR, D. L., MACLEAN, A. R. and ALLEN, E. V., Clinical observations on the effect of Benzedrine sulphate. Study of patients with states of chronic exhaustion, *J. Amer. Med. Ass.*, **109**, 549–554 (1937).

WILLETT, R. A., The effect of a stimulant and a depressant drug on serial rote learning of nonsense syllables (1958). (Unpubl. available at Inst. of Psychiatry, London.)

WILLETT, R. A., The effects of depressant drugs on learning and conditioning, in *Experiments in Personality*, Ed. H. J. Eysenck (London, Routledge & Kegan Paul, to be published).

WILLIAMS, G. W., The effect of sodium phenobarbital on learning of rats, *Psychol. Bull.*, **33**, 745–746 (1936).

WILLIAMS, G. W. and O'BRIEN, C., The effect of sodium phenobarbital on the learning behaviour of white rats, *J. Comp. Psychol.*, **23**, 457–474 (1937).

WILSON, S. R., The physiological basis of hypnosis and suggestion, *Proc. Roy. Soc. Med.*, **20**, 503–509 (1927–8).

WING, L., The use of reserpine in chronic patients: a controlled trial, *J. Ment. Sci.*, **102**, 530 (1956).

WITTER, H. and MÜLLER, R., Die Aktivierung des E.E.G. durch Evipan bei gedeckten traumatischen Himschadigungen, *Nervenarzt.*, **24**, 97–102 (1953).

WOLBERG, L. R., *Medical Hypnosis.* I. *The Principles of Hypnotherapy* (New York, Grune & Stratton, 1948).

WOLF, S., Effects of suggestion and conditioning on the action of chemical agents in human subjects, *J. Clin. Invest.*, **29**, 100–109 (1950).

WOLF, S. and RIPLEY, H. S., Studies in the action of intravenously administered Sodium Amytal, *Amer. J. Med. Sci.*, **215**, 56–62 (1948).

WOLFF, H. G., HARDY, J. D. and GOODELL, H., Studies on pain. Measurement of the effect of morphine, codeine, and other opiates on the pain threshold and an analysis of their relation to the pain experience, *J. Clin. Invest.*, **19**, 659–680 (1940).

WOLFF, H. G., HARDY, J. D. and GOODELL, H., Measurement of the effect on the pain threshold of acetylsalicylate acid, acetamilid, acetophenetidine, aminopyrine, ethyl alcohol, trichlorethylene, a barbiturate, quinine, ergotamine tartrate and caffeine: and analysis of their relation to the pain experience, *J. Clin. Invest.*, **20**, 63–80 (1941).

WOLLSTEIN, A., Studies on the subjective effects of the cephalotropic amines in man: III. The action of the cephalotropic amines on intelligence scores, *Acta med. scand.*, **100**, 203–207 (1939).

WOOLLEY, D. W. and SHAW, E., Some neurophysiological aspects of serotonin, *Brit. Med. J.*, **II**, 122–126 (1954).

WOOTLEY, L. F., Clinical effects of amphetamine sulfate (Benzedrine sulfate) in mental patients with retarded activity, *Psychiat. Quart.*, **12**, 66–83 (1938).

WUNDERLE, F., Experimental psychologische Untersuchungen über die Wirkung des Pervitino auf geistige Leistungen, *Arch. Psychiat. Z. Neurol.*, **113**, 504–549 (1941).

YUDKIN, S., Vitamin A and dark adaptation; effect of alcohol, Benzedrine, and vitamin C, *Lancet*, **241**, 787–791 (1941).

ZUCKERMAN, M., IZNER, S. and LEISER, R., Sodium Amytal Rorschach in incipient schizophrenia, *Dis. Nerv. Syst.*, **15**, 59–64 (1954).

CHAPTER 18

The Effects of Psychotherapy

H. J. EYSENCK

INTRODUCTION

In theory, the study of the effects of psychotherapy should be similar in methodology and experimental treatment to the study of the effects of any other therapeutic agent about which definite theories are held. In actual practice this is not so. An emotional feeling of considerable intensity has grown up in this field which makes many people regard the very questioning of its effectiveness as an attack on psychotherapy; as Teuber and Powers (1953) point out; "To some of the counselors, the whole control group idea . . . seemed slightly blasphemous, as if we were attempting a statistical test of the efficacy of prayer . . ." When the writer (1952) published a short paper summarizing the available evidence and concluding that there was little support for those who believed in the efficacy of psychotherapy, reactions ranged all the way from Sanford's (1953) opinion that "the only wise course with respect to such a challenge is to ignore it," to Meehl (1955) who said: "I cannot agree with those who consider this a foolish question or who feel little need to meet such challenges." The considerable argument aroused by this paper (Luborsky, 1954; De Charms et al., 1954; Rosenzweig, 1954; Eysenck, 1954, 1955) seems to have arisen from the conviction, well put by Shoben (1956), that "the conclusive evidence of therapeutic effectiveness must come not from argument, but from relevant and rigorous research." This chapter is an attempt to review the literature, much of which has appeared since the writer's previous review was published, in order to discover whether any new light has been thrown on this thorny problem.

To judge by their writings, some advocates of psychotherapy appear to take an attitude similar to that adopted by Galen, the father of modern medicine, in his advocacy of the wondrous powers of Samian clay: "All who drink this remedy recover in a short time, except those whom it does not help, who all die and have no relief from any other medicine. Therefore it is obvious that it fails only in incurable cases."

There are three main differences between Galen's hypothesis and that maintained by modern psychotherapists. In the first place, we have the question of *definition*. There is no disagreement about the nature of Samian clay, but as regards psychotherapy, *quot homines, tot sententiae*. In the second place there is the question of the *criterion of cure*. In Galen's case this was survival, which is easy to observe; in the case of psychotherapy, the criterion itself is in doubt, and its measurement fraught with difficulties. In the third place there is the *time factor*. Those who partook of Galen's remedy "recovered in a short time," so that the effects were easily observed; psychotherapy, particularly that of the psychoanalytic type, may go on for as many as twenty years or more, so that considerable difficulties arise in allocating responsibility for any recovery. We will now take up these points in detail, before turning to an examination of the evidence.

Definition of Psychotherapy

Raimy (1950) has characterized the confusion existing with respect to the nature of psychotherapy by defining it as, "an unidentified technique applied to unspecified problems with unpredictable outcomes. For this technique we recommend rigorous training." When we turn to definitions offered in a more serious vein, we find considerable divergences. Perhaps the most inclusive definition is one given by Levine (1948) to whom "psychotherapy means therapy by psychological means . . . it means treatment applied directly to the 'mind,' by which we mean not a separate entity, but the functioning of the person as a human being. Psychotherapy includes the direct treatment of one person, as a person, by another. It includes also the indirect treatment of one person by another, through the intermediary of other persons or situations . . . in general, psychotherapy can be defined as the provision by the physician of new life experiences which can influence a patient in the direction of health."

Similar but rather briefer is Rosanoff's (1947) definition: "Psychotherapy . . . consists in the employment of mental factors in the treatment of disease," and that of Jaspers (1918): "Psychotherapie heissen alle die Behandlungs-methoden, die auf die Seele oder den Körper mit Mitteln wirken, die über die Seele führen." (As evidence of the inclusiveness of these definitions we may quote the fact that Jasper expressly mentions "gymnastics" as one of the methods of psychotherapy!) English and Finch (1954) may also be quoted here: "Psychotherapy may be defined as the art and science of treating mental and emotional disorders and diseases through changing ideas and emotions to bring about a more favourable psychic equilibrium . . . Almost any method utilised to alleviate or remove the results of emotional conflict and improve psychic adjustment may be termed psychotherapy."

Rather more restrictive and less all-inclusive are Curran and Partridge (1955), who say that: "Psychotherapy aims at relieving symptoms of psychic origin by adjusting the attitudes that have led to their development . . . The treatment proceeds by stages which are often referred to as *explanation, suggestion, persuasion* and *re-education*." Shoben (1953) is a little more specific still. "Psychotherapy is a certain kind of social relationship between two persons who hold periodic conversations in pursuit of certain goals: namely, the lessening of emotional discomfort and the alteration of various other aspects of client behaviour . . . Therapy proceeds by virtue of communication and the therapist-patient relationship, towards the goal of alleviating symptoms and increasing the patient's affective comfort and social utility."

Most restrictive of all are certain psychoanalysts and other members of specific schools who would restrict the use of the term to procedures practised by members of their particular school. Psychotherapy would then be defined in terms of a particular theoretical system giving rise to specific methods of procedure, such as the employment of transference and counter-transference, catharsis, ego-strengthening, and so forth. Hathaway (1951) has well contrasted this narrow conception with the very broad ones quoted at the beginning of this section—

With the intention of arriving at a working definition of the term psychotherapy, at least two extremes in connotation may help in orientation. The first extreme is illustrated by those few psychoanalysts who affirm that there is only one type of psychotherapy, namely, psychoanalytic therapy, and that any other approach is a covering up or ameliorative procedure not properly so considered. Although the most brash proponents of such an extreme concept of psychotherapy are probably psychoanalytic in persuasion, there are here and there

other therapists who hold analogously restricted views. At the other extreme, psychotherapy becomes almost any predominantly psychological procedure, personal or environmental, that is assumed to be contributory to mental hygiene or personal adjustment. With this broader definition, better living conditions, better food, and the like, all become psychotherapeutic procedures in so far as they have psychological implications. One might then cite a music program in a clinic or hospital as an example of psychotherapy and the staff musician as a psychotherapist. Neither of these extreme positions is here accepted as particularly useful . . . The former connotation restricts progress by encouraging doctrinal and isolated positions antipathetic to new ideas. It inhibits active experimentation by persons who might not accept the tenets of the particular procedures defined as psychotherapy. The latter is so broad as to constitute almost a statement of the general principle that simply healthy living is therapeutic.

A decision on a definition in view of these wide divergencies must obviously be arbitrary. We shall here adopt the middle-of-the-road position not dissimilar to that defined by Winder (1957), according to which a treatment is labelled "psychotherapy" when the following conditions are fulfilled—

1. There is an interpersonal relationship of a prolonged kind between two or more people.
2. One of the participants has had special experience and/or has received special training in the handling of human relationships.
3. One or more of the participants have entered the relationship because of a felt dissatisfaction with their emotional and/or interpersonal adjustment.
4. The methods used are of a psychological nature, i.e., involve such mechanisms as explanation, suggestion, persuasion, and so forth.
5. The procedure of the therapist is based upon some formal theory regarding mental disorder in general, and the specific disorder of the patient in particular.
6. The aim of the process is the amelioration of the difficulties which cause the patient to seek the help of the therapist.

Having thus defined psychotherapy in general, we may add that it may be useful in many circumstances to specify different types of psychotherapy in terms of the particular theory adopted by the therapist. This may be done most simply by adopting a system of subscripts so that psychotherapy $_{PA}$ denotes psychotherapy carried out according to the dictates of the psychoanalytic method. Psychotherapy $_{CR}$ would denote non-directive psychotherapy carried out according to the theories of Carl Rogers. Psychotherapy $_E$ would denote eclectic psychotherapy based on the rather less formalized theories which currently pass as "orthodox" in psychiatric circles. Further types of psychotherapy can be distinguished, but there is little point in attempting any complete listing here. The device of indicating types of psychotherapy by the initials of the originators will retain its usefulness as long as there are sufficient letters of the alphabet to go round.

This question of definition does not, of course, settle the very difficult problem of whether the different methods we have distinguished by subscripts do *in fact* differ from each other in practice, nor does a definition tell us what does actually happen during treatment. Many attempts have been made to answer these questions, but the evidence is still so fragmentary, anecdotal and uncoordinated that a review of it at this point would serve little useful purpose (Ellis, 1955). It is impossible therefore to say whether the different types of therapy are in fact differentiated from each other in terms of the actual procedures adopted, or whether individual differences between therapists of the same persuasion are as great or greater than those between therapists of different persuasions. (For studies of therapeutic procedures, cf. Matarazzo, 1956; Saslow, *et al.*, 1955; Moustakas, *et al.*, 1955; Sommer, *et al.*, 1955; Danskin, 1955; Bordin, 1955; Eldred, *et al.*, 1954; Grossman, 1952; Rogers, 1951, 1942; Harway, *et al.*, 1955; Raush, *et al.*, 1956.)

Measurement of Outcome

When the method of psychotherapy has been applied to a group of patients, we obviously must have some measure to determine the initial status as well as the final status of the group. Many discussions of this problem have been reported by Zubin (1953), Knight (1941), Thorne (1952), Greenhill (1955), Watson, *et al.* (1951, 1952), and Miles, *et al.* (1951). In addition there are discussions in the books by Rogers and Dymond (1953) and by Mowrer (1953). We may summarize rather briefly in the following paragraphs the possible measures of outcome which may be used.

INTROSPECTIVE REPORTS

It is the patient who seeks our aid, and, obviously, his own judgement of any changes that have taken place is important. This may be obtained by interview, in the form of a freely written essay, by answers to a questionnaire, by means of Q-sorts, through a set of attitude endorsements, or in many similar ways. (Lipkin, 1954; Murray, *et al.*, 1954; Dollard, *et al.*, 1953; Gallagher, 1953.) It is obvious that the more objective the method used, the more trustworthy will the results be. Thus a questionnaire would be preferable to an essay. It need hardly be emphasized that, in making use of formal instruments, technical competence regarding their construction and evaluation is required. This point is mentioned only because so many experimenters have failed to take into account obvious technical difficulties arising from the method of research adopted. Thus many workers have made considerable use of Q-sorts without heeding the warning given by Cronbach and Gleser (1954) in their review of this method: "It is imperative to discourage students of personality and social psychology from copying Stephenson's designs as he presents them . . . We fear that Stephenson's book (1953) may misdirect much research effort."

RATINGS

Many of the difficulties of which the patient complains are of a kind which can be observed by outsiders. Irritability, social clumsiness, hyper-emotionality and other behaviour patterns can be rated by outside observers, and such observations should always supplement the patient's own report. Ratings can be formal or informal, and may be made by psychiatrists, social workers or the patient's family, friends or workmates. Again, it need hardly be said that these ratings are more valuable the more systematic they are, and the more they pay attention to the rules laid down by psychologists on the basis of the very large body of experimental work in this field (Eysenck, 1953). If possible, the reliability of such ratings should be established, and it should not need to be emphasized that those judges who are emotionally concerned with the particular direction of change should never be the only ones to give a rating on a particular patient. (This refers more particularly to the psychiatrist in charge of the patient, who must always be suspected of favouring the positive outcome compared with a negative one.) Sociometric measures are of value and may be listed here, as they appear to be essentially similar in their nature to ratings. (Neuburger and Schauer, 1953; Rosenburg, 1954; Parloff, *et al.*, 1954.) Rating methods are discussed in Chapter I in some detail.

PERSONALITY TESTS

This is not the place to discuss the wide variety of personality tests which may be administered to the patient in order to test specific hypotheses regarding a change that has taken place; many such tests are described in other chapters of this book. It may be necessary, however, to insist that it is useless to administer a test whose reliability and validity is either low or unknown. The writer has reviewed elsewhere the literature bearing on the reliability and validity of the so-called "projective techniques" (Eysenck, 1958), and the conclusion arrived at in that review was that these tests had failed to establish their value in any of the fields in which they had been used. Thus projective techniques should not be used as evidence to establish the outcome of psychotherapy, because any changes which might occur in the test would not be capable of interpretation. Few personality tests are characterized by a high degree of reliability and validity, but tests such as those of level of aspiration, suggestibility, and conditionability, do enable the research worker to test specific hypotheses and arrive at interpretations of his results which have a solid experimental foundation.

PHYSIOLOGICAL MEASURES

In view of the close relationship between the autonomic system and emotion, and in view also of the predominantly emotional character of so many neurotic complaints, it seems desirable that the possibility of physiological changes should not be disregarded. Much of the relevant work has been reviewed in another chapter of this book and little will, therefore, be said here about it. (Shagass and Malmo, 1954; Thetford, 1948; Di Mascio, et al., 1955; Boyd, et al., 1954; Bixenstine, 1955; Coleman, et al., 1956.)

EXPERIMENTAL INVESTIGATIONS

The most useful type of study, in our view, is that which is specifically designed to test a clear-cut hypothesis, and it will often be found that, in order to test such a hypothesis, a special experimental set-up will have to be elaborated. Thus we may hypothesize that psychotherapy of a certain type applied to a certain group will lead to an increase in frustration tolerance. In order to test this hypothesis it will be necessary to define frustration tolerance experimentally, and to design the experiment in such a way that psychotherapy is included as the independent variable. Little has been found in the literature to suggest that this method of research, in our view much the most preferable, has been used much by research workers.

SOCIAL ACTION EFFECTS

It is sometimes possible to assess the effects of treatment by reference to certain actions taken by society in relation to the patients who are being treated. Thus, for instance, certification presents us with an example of social action which can be given a numerical value and treated statistically. In the same way, we may consider the effect of psychotherapy on psychopathic behaviour, and a record of court appearances may be of relevance in assessing the value of the therapy. Here again, considerable experience and knowledge are required to evaluate the many factors liable to mislead the investigator and invalidate his conclusions; it must be assumed that the investigator is competent in such lines of research.

Each of the six methods outlined above has its own advantages and disadvantages. It may be a counsel of perfection to suggest that in any worth-while investigation more than one method should be used and that, preferably, all six methods should be included. The necessity for this, is highlighted in an experiment by Kogan, et al., (1953), who used three reliable measures of the effectiveness of therapy (client evaluation, case reader movement rating, and distress relief quotient shifts,) only to find negligible correlations between them. As Meehl (1955) points out "such a fact should make us cautious about single 'criteria' used in the evaluation of therapeutic outcome."

One other point may require to be stressed. The effects of psychotherapy, as of most other experimental manipulations of human beings, are presumably multidimensional, and consequently research should be concerned with shifts in more than one direction. The usual habit of simply rating people as "improved" or "not improved" entirely neglects to pay attention to the important and obvious fact that "improvement" is not a unidimensional concept. Under treatment a man may lose his depression, but start beating his wife; is this to be rated as "improved" or "not improved?" It is clear that research must become much more analytic before we can find out very much about the effects of psychotherapy. Further, this belief implies that progress will become much more rapid when hypotheses regarding change become more specific. It is almost impossible to prove or disprove vague and general talk about "improvement"; specific statements are much more valuable scientifically as well as easier to investigate experimentally.

GENERAL METHODOLOGY

We have now defined what we mean by psychotherapy, and have indicated the kind of measures which might be used with advantage to study the effects of therapy. What kind of design is appropriate for studies of this kind? Hunt (1952) and Watson (1952) have considered this problem, as have Greenhill (1955), Thorne (1952), Zubin (1953) and many others. A paper by Campbell (1957) which discusses the problem from a more general point of view is perhaps the most useful. A set of minimum requirements is stated by Meehl (1955) as follows: "The minimum standard for an adequate outcome study obviously includes (a) a control group, (b) pre- and post-therapy evaluation procedures which are either 'objective' or, if judgemental, are uncontaminated, (c) follow-up of both groups, preferably repeated so that exacerbation and remission rates can be estimated and the curves extrapolated." Meehl goes on to say: "I am saddened to report that perusal of over two hundred journal articles and a dozen books reveals one paper approximating these desiderata (relaxing requirements by forgetting follow-up but insisting upon controls does not change this figure)."

It would not be so necessary to insist on the need for a control group when studying the effects of psychotherapy, were it not for the fact that practically all the studies in the field have neglected to provide such a group. The one or two exceptions to this will be discussed below, but by and large it is depressing to report that this absolutely essential minimum requirement has not been met by ninety-nine out of a hundred studies in this field. It would probably be an idle exercise of ingenuity to try and describe the various possible ways in which control groups could and ought to be used; it is doubtful in any case whether much could be added to the very complete discussion given by Campbell (1957). It may be more useful to consider one or two of the reasons why control groups are so noticeably lacking in this field.

The reason most frequently given is that the effects of psychotherapy are so clear-cut and obvious that no reasonable person could doubt its effectiveness. In answer we may perhaps quote Meehl (1955)—

The history of the healing arts furnishes ample grounds for skepticism as to our nonsystematic "clinical" observations. Most of my older relatives had all their teeth extracted because it was "known" in the 1920s that the clearing up of occult focal infections improved arthritis and other disorders. No doubt the physicians who treated our ancestors by venesection had "observed" many "cures" in longitudinal study of their patients. Like all therapists, I personally experience an utter inability not to believe I effect results in individual cases: but as a psychologist I know it is foolish to take this conviction at face value. In order to bring about the needed research, it will probably be necessary for therapists and administrators to get really clear on this point. Our daily therapeutic experiences, which (on good days!) make it hard for us to take Eysenck seriously, can be explained within a crude statistical model of the patient-therapist population that assigns very little specific "power" to therapeutic intervention. If the majority of neurotics are in "unstable equilibrium" and hence tend to improve under moderately favorable régimes, those who are in therapy while improving will be talking about their current actions and feelings in the sessions. Client and therapist will naturally attribute changes to the therapy. Furthermore, neurosis often shows cyclical fluctuations, and upswing terminators will be perceived as "successful," since therapists do not automatically find out when cases relapse or enter therapy with someone else.

Another argument is the ethical one, to the effect that we are not entitled to withhold therapy from patients in need who might benefit from it. There are several answers to this point. In the first place, the benefits are merely putative, and consequently nothing is being withheld which is known to be of assistance to the patient. The argument assumes that we have already proved what is in fact the point at issue. In the second place it is a universal practice in medicine, whenever a new method of treatment is put forward, that this new method must receive clinical trials, *including a control group not treated by means of the new method.* If this is ethically admissible in the whole of medicine, even when the most serious disorders are involved and where the *a priori* probability of effectiveness in favour of the new cure may be rather high, then it is difficult to see why a different set of ethical ideals should apply in psychiatry where disorders are rather less serious and where, as we shall see, the evidence regarding the efficacy of the treatment proposed tends on the whole to be singularly negative. In the third place it is quite untrue that psychotherapy would have to be withdrawn from certain people in order to provide a control group. Of all those who are said to be able to benefit from psychotherapy only a very small number have in fact received it. In the United States, at least, there is a high correlation between the income of the patient and the choice of therapy; middle-class patients by and large get psychotherapy, working-class patients physical treatment. It would be very easy indeed to get together large groups of patients who would not in the normal way obtain psychotherapy, and to form an experimental and control group from these patients. If this were done the outcome would not be that psychotherapy was withheld from people who might otherwise benefit from it, because of the experiment; rather, the experiment would be instrumental in bringing psychotherapy to people who would not otherwise have received it. The Cambridge-Somerville Youth Study reviewed below illustrates what can be done along these lines.

A fourth argument which is sometimes put forward relates to the great difficulty in diagnosing psychiatric patients, and the difficulty in assessing the severity of illness. This, it is said, makes impossible the appropriate matching of the experimental and control groups, and thus invalidates the experimental design. This argument, which tends to be put forward by the more sophisticated psychotherapists, is clearly erroneous in that it implies that matching is an essential part of the control-group technique. It certainly is a useful adjunct, where it can be carried out with reasonable reliability, but the essential nature of the control group method implies nothing more than the random allocation of subjects to the experimental and the control groups. When this is done the appropriate statistical formulae for the assessing of sampling errors will enable us to judge the significance of any differences due to the action of the experimental variable.

One further point should be mentioned. It is

sometimes believed that if an experimental and a control group are selected on an appropriate system of random allocation or matched allocation, and if the experimental group is provided with psychotherapy while the control group is not, then any superiority of the experimental group over the control group must be due to the effects of psychotherapy. Such a result, it might then be claimed, would establish the validity of the theoretical system lying at the basis of the psychotherapeutic procedure. Nothing could be further from the truth. The experimental and the control group are differentiated in terms of a large number of variables, any one of which might be responsible for any differences that might be observed. Among the procedures to which the usual experimental group would be subjected, but which might not be experienced by the control group, are the following—

1. physical examination and the medical treatment of all sorts of minor illnesses, etc;

2. long period of rest in hospital, clinic or other institution;

3. manipulation of the environment on the part of the doctor, including attempts to change the attitudes of family, employers, etc. (Klumpner, 1955);

4. more regular and better balanced food in hospital compared with previous existence (cf. the paper by Watson and Camney, 1954, on the effects of nutritional replacement on neurotic disorders).

This list could be extended almost *ad infinitum*, and will be seen that either more than one control group would be required in order to control for these different hypothetical causal agents, or the specification of the hypothetical causal agent in psychotherapy would have to be much more precise than it usually is, so that a single group could be provided which would take care of all the possible causal agents except the one specified by the hypothesis. Thus if we were to test the hypothesis that interpretation of Oedipus material is a necessary part of psychotherapy, then our control group would have to receive an equal number of therapeutic sessions with an experienced therapist who refrained from giving any interpretation of Oedipus material, but in all other ways duplicated the treatment design of the experimental group. Thus, even if the very rough-and-ready studies summarized below had indicated some degree of effectiveness of psychotherapy, the interpretation of this finding would have been completely open. What we would have gained would have been an indication that research into the distinguishing features of psychotherapeutic treatment might be worth while and might, if accompanied by the formulation of more specific hypotheses, lead to greater understanding. On no account could such a result have been interpreted as unequivocal support for the beliefs of psychotherapists.

We have now discussed in sufficient detail the general logic of work in this field; we must next turn to the actual investigations which have been reported. This will be done in three sections, beginning with those investigations which have used a control group, going on to those investigations on adult patients which failed to use a control group, and terminating with investigations of children in which no control group was used. In the final section the findings will be summarized and the conclusions which we believe can be drawn from these studies will be indicated.

STUDIES USING A CONTROL GROUP

The Cambridge-Somerville Youth Study

Pride of place in any discussion of experiments on the effects of psychotherapy must undoubtedly go to the Cambridge-Somerville Youth Study. It is the only experiment known to us which made use of a properly chosen control group, which used large enough numbers of cases to make the results statistically convincing, which carried on both treatment and follow-up over a sufficiently long period to make the the results meaningful, which used objective methods of acknowledged social significance to assess the final outcome, and which investigated the process of therapy itself in an unbiased and properly controlled fashion. In all these ways the study can serve as an example by which to judge the deficiencies of the other work to be reviewed in this chapter.

The aim of the programme has been summed up as follows by Teuber and Powers (1953): "For approximately eight years, from 1937–1945, this large-scale treatment effort was directed at the prevention of delinquency, by guidance, counseling and therapy, in a group of over six hundred underprivileged boys . . . By setting up a control group, and by keeping unusually detailed records, the Study made provision for quantitive measurement of the effects of therapy, and for systematic attempts at an objective description of the therapeutic relationships."

The first step in the programme consisted of the selection of subjects from among underprivileged boys aged between 6 and 10 whose names had been obtained from welfare workers as being "likely to become delinquent." A list of six hundred and fifty boys having been obtained, the boys were individually matched in pairs on variables such as age, intelligence quotient, school grade, delinquency rating and ethnic and socio-economic background. The decision as to which boy in each pair should be assigned to the treatment group (*T*) and which to the untreated control group (*C*) was made by the toss of a coin. In this way two equal groups of three hundred and twenty-five boys were obtained whose chances of delinquency as far as could be ascertained were very nearly equal.

As soon as a boy had been selected as a member of the treatment group he was assigned to one of the counsellors employed by the Study and treatment was begun. Details of this treatment are given in the book by Powers and Witmer (1951) and little will be said about it here except to mention that both adherents of the psychoanalytic school and followers of Carl Rogers's non-directive approach participated in the treatment programme. "Regardless of the individual counselor's predilection all treatment consisted of individual, face-to-face contacts. These individual relationships between counselors and boys thus served as the independent variable; they represented 'treatment' . . . they were restricted to the treatment group and consistently withheld from the control group."

The follow-up extended from the end of the treatment period in 1945, when treatment had lasted for between two and eight years in individual cases, to 1948 when the outcome was evaluated. Powers (1949) gives an interesting discussion of the results which would have been reported had no control group been present. Speaking of the treatment group he points out that—

1. "There are seventy *T* boys who are now well past the age of 17, whose careers have been closely followed and who, as boys under 12, appeared to the predictors to be more likely than not to develop delinquent careers . . . after these boys had been through the treatment program, not more than one third (twenty-three boys) committed serious repeated delinquent acts, while thirty-one of them proved not to be delinquent at all."

2. "There are one hundred and sixty-three *T* boys who, when under 12, were rated . . . as probable delinquents." Of these only 14·1 per cent committed delinquent acts which led to their admission to a correctional institution. This rate seems a surprisingly low one in view of the fact that the study, it was believed, included practically all the boys in the two cities participating in the study, with a combined population of 213,000, who showed early signs of future delinquency.

3. The counselors, during the middle period of the program were asked on several different occasions to list all *T* boys who were thought to have "sub-

stantially benefited" by their contact with the study. About two-third of the boys were so listed, and about half of these were reported by the counselors as having been "outstanding" in respect of benefit received.

4. Of the boys themselves more than half (62 per cent) stated that the study had been of value to them. Many of them declared that "they help me to keep out of trouble," and this seems to have been a majority view. Powers concludes: "By such evidence at least, we might reasonably conclude that the study had been successful in preventing delinquency. Many illustrative cases could be given to 'prove' the point in the traditional manner. But the evaluation, though of the customary type, is inconclusive."

The picture changes dramatically when the control group is brought into the picture. The total number of court appearances from the beginning of treatment was recorded, and it was found that ninety-six *T* boys and ninety-two *C* boys were involved, the number of offences being two hundred and sixty-four for the *T* group and two hundred and eighteen for the *C* group. A similar picture is given by the number of appearances before the Court Prevention Bureau. Here we find that forty-nine *T* boys and forty-nine *C* boys appeared on one occasion and sixty-five *T* boys and fifty-two *C* boys two or three times. Teuber and Powers comment as follows—

Such an outcome of the delinquency prevention program of the Study appears to be not only negative, but paradoxical. Instead of confirming the expectation that the treatment group would be less delinquent than the matched control group, there is a slight difference in favour of the control group. This apparent advantage of the control group may be offset, however, by other factors which more detailed statistics seem to reveal. There is a slightly greater incidence of serious recidivism . . . in the control group, and a rating of all offences according to "seriousness" likewise shows a slight advantage of the treatment cases over the controls; there is a tendency on the part of the controls to commit a proportionately greater number of the more serious offences. None of these trends, however, are as yet significant. Unless further developments change the picture . . . the direct comparison between *T* and *C* groups fails to show that the major hypothesis can be sustained; treatment did not . . . reduce the incidence of adjudged delinquency in the treatment group.

It is not surprising that the authors, in contrasting this negative outcome of the control investigation with the enthusiastic beliefs of the counselors, conclude that "quantitative indices . . . are better than professions of faith bolstered by the therapist's prestige and the skillfull use of the illustrative case."

The reactions of the therapists themselves are of

some interest. In a detailed study of the therapist-boy relationship it was found that a number of therapists completely misinterpreted the attitudes and feelings of the boys towards themselves and that it was precisely these therapists who "considered their counseling relations as a highly effective tool in producing changes in their charges." Altogether the attitude of the therapists themselves appeared worthy of comment—

> To some of the counselors, the whole control group idea . . . seemed slightly blasphemous, . . . they insisted that the relationships established had their value in themselves, irrespective of their possible effects on the boys' behavior, and they were not perturbed when seemingly negative results of the delinquency prevention program became known. Other counselors reacted differently; they felt that research was superfluous, since all the necessary rules of conduct in therapy were already known. When they were informed of the outcome of the Study, they reacted in a characteristic fashion: those who were analytically trained and oriented asserted that the results would have been positive, had analytic principles been applied by all staff members, consistently, throughout the course of the treatment period. Conversely, those counselors, who were followers of Carl Rogers' non-directive approach averred that a systematic use of non-directive methods would have produced more definite success.

The reader may feel that, while the study failed in providing any evidence in favour of the hypothesis that treatment of the kind administered prevented delinquency, this treatment may have had many other important and desirable results. This, of course, is not impossible, but we would like to quote one final paragraph from Teuber and Powers: "We submit . . . that the data yield one definite conclusion: that the burden of proof is on anyone who claims specific results for a given form of therapy. It is admittedly difficult to provide for expensive control settings. . . . But the objective evaluation of therapeutic processes is of such importance that similar studies, in many areas of therapy, are indicated."

The Brill-Beebe Study

The data to be considered next come from *A Follow-up Study of War Neuroses* by Brill and Beebe (1955), which is essentially a statistical analysis of data collected during and after the war in connexion with soldiers discharged from the army for neurotic disorders or returned to the army as cured. The book from which the data are taken is a rather monumental account of a very large number of analyses carried out in great detail. Much of what is said in this book is relevant to the interpretation of the data to be quoted, but it would take us too far afield to go into any detail. Let it merely be said that the combination of background experience characterizing the two

authors—one of whom is a well-known psychiatrist, the other an eminent statistician—gives the book and its conclusions a unique authority and an enviable absence of the all too frequent faults of analysis usually encountered in this field.

The data relevant to this chapter come from two sources. The first relates to the improvement experienced after separation from the service by men suffering with mild or moderate neuroses at the time of separation from the service. Some of the men experienced a breakdown in combat, others outside the combat zone and before reaching it (Z/I zone). These two groups were in turn subdivided into those who received treatment after their separation from the army and those who did not. The results of the analysis are shown in Table XVIII.1. It will be seen

TABLE XVIII.1

PERCENTAGE OF MEN WITH MILD OR MODERATE NEUROSES AT SEPARATION WHO IMPROVED AFTER SEPARATION FROM SERVICE, BY LOCATION AT BREAKDOWN, AND BY TREATMENT SINCE SEPARATION

(Quoted by permission of Brill and Beebe (1955) and the V.A.)

Treatment since separation	Early Z/I breakdown		Breakdown in combat	
	Number of men	Percentage improved	Number of men	Percentage improved
None . .	82	65	58	62
Some . .	44	57	42	55
Total .	126	62	100	59

that, if anything, those who received treatment improved less than those who received no treatment. The authors summarize their findings in the following words: "Given an individual who broke down in service and who was still ill with a neurosis on discharge, any change in his condition after discharge seems to be related more to sociologic factors than anything else. What his military experience was, *what treatment he had*, and how sick he had been, seemed to make no difference. It is the poorly educated, unskilled individual of limited intelligence who was not well-adjusted before entering the service, and who was more liable to have had marital difficulty after discharge, who is least apt to improve and most apt to get worse. The overall tendency for the entire sample was to improve." We need only add that the special care taken in the follow-up study reported in this volume makes criticism of the conclusions rather less admissible than is usually the case with studies of a purely actuarial nature, and that the authors must be congratulated on the very careful work done by them to render follow-ups psychologically meaningful as well as statistically comparable. This makes the conclusion that there was no difference in remission of neuroses between those who did and those who did not receive psychiatric treatment all the more interesting.

The other type of comparison made in this book is with respect to soldiers treated in service. Table XVIII.2 shows the mean service period in months

TABLE XVIII.2

TYPE OF PSYCHIATRIC TREATMENT AT FIRST BREAKDOWN IN MILITARY SERVICE AND SUBSEQUENT LENGTH OF SERVICE

(Quoted by permission of Brill and Beebe (1955) and the V.A.)

Type of psychiatric treatment	Number of cases[1]	Mean months of service (including time in hospital) following first breakdown
None . . .	165	8·6
Rest and sedation .	150	11·0
Individual therapy .	265	10·7
Hospital routine .	328	8·4
Total . . .	908	9·5

[1] Count of cases is slightly inflated since some men receive more than one form of treatment.

following first breakdown, analysed by type of psychiatric treatment received. "Men who received individual therapy served somewhat longer, on the average, than men who received routine hospital care, or men who received essentially no psychiatric treatment. Men who received only rest and sedation also served longer than these two groups. *The differences, however, are remarkably small.*" A similar conclusion seems appropriate to the results reported in the next Table XVIII.3 showing the

TABLE XVIII.3

TYPE OF PSYCHIATRIC TREATMENT AT FIRST BREAKDOWN IN SERVICE AND RETURN TO DUTY

(Quoted by permission of Brill and Beebe (1955) and the V.A.)

Treatment	Per cent returned to duty
Essentially no treatment . . .	56
Rest and sedation only . . .	68
Individual therapy	62
Hospital routine . . .	48
Total.	57

percentage of casualties returned to duty. Here again "rest and sedation only" appears slightly superior to individual therapy, with "essentially no treatment" very close behind.

The authors find it necessary to correct the overall figures because they found that "individual therapy was given more often to combat than to non-combat cases, to men with a more adequate preservice personality (who were more apt to be in combat), and to those whose illness seemed most severe." The following summary may illustrate the results of a complex method of making the samples statistically comparable—

Although the present study provides no real basis for assessing the effects of the several forms of treatment, it was considered worth while to undertake a single controlled comparison of the several types of treatment. These treatment groups were established--

A—Not more than rest and sedation.
B—Individual therapy.
C—Hospital routine.

Matching was done on the basis of the following characteristics, so that the confounding of choice of treatment with characteristics of the patient might be minimized—

Major area of precipitating stress.
Preservice personality and impairment.
Severity of breakdown.

The three matched treatment groups (*A*, *B*, and *C*) were then compared as to health at separation and condition at follow-up with essentially negative findings. It therefore appears doubtful that there was any difference in the effectiveness of the three gross types of treatment.

In drawing conclusions from these results it may be advisable to keep in mind the warning given by the authors of the report under review: "An *ex post facto* study of different treatments is naturally hazardous; the experimentalist requires an element of physical randomization in the allocation of treatments before he is usually willing to associate differences in outcome with differential effectiveness of therapies. Here the categories of treatment are quite broad and pay little regard to intensity, but in view of the limited resources available for treatment in the military situation only a rough classification is possible." Provided that these possible sources of error are borne in mind and also that it is remembered that war neuroses may differ in many ways from civilian neuroses, the outcome of the two studies just summarized gives a reasonably clear and consistent answer to the question of the effectiveness of therapy after breakdown within the army, and after separation from the army. No evidence of such effectiveness can be found, and the main results of this comparatively well controlled and competently analysed study in so far as effectiveness of psychotherapy is concerned, must be considered to be completely negative.

The Barron-Leary Study

In this experiment one hundred and fifty psychoneurotic patients, all drawn from the same clinic population, were tested with the Minnesota Multiphasic Personality Inventory before and after an interval of time during which some of them received psychotherapy, and some of them did not. (Barron and Leary, 1955). "All one hundred and fifty patients had applied for psychotherapy in the psychiatric clinic in which the study was conducted, and all of them had been accepted for treatment; a group of twenty-three cases, however, had to be placed on a waiting list until the hospital facilities became available, and they waited some six months before beginning treatment. Of those who received psychotherapy immediately, eighty-five received group therapy, and forty-two received individual therapy; they included only those patients treated for a minimum of three months during the period of time covered by the study. The aim of the study (was) to discover what changes, if any, occurred in M.M.P.I. profiles of patients who received psychotherapy, and to compare these changes with whatever changes may be observed in the M.M.P.I. profiles of patients who during the same period of time remained untreated."

The psychotherapists carrying out the treatment included psychiatrists, social workers and psychologists; all therapists had at least three years of postdoctoral or post-graduate training and experience. The general orientation was psychoanalytic. Individual treatment consisted largely of ego-oriented psychotherapy on a once-a-week basis, whereas group therapy laid somewhat greater stress on current interpersonal relations.

The experimental and control groups were found to be quite comparable with one another in diagnosis, prognosis, severity of initial condition, age, sex and education. The interval between the initial state and terminal state was 7·00 months for the non-treatment group, 8·23 months for the individual therapy group and 8·63 months for the group-therapy group. The differences between these means fell short of significance, although it will be noted that the time interval for the non-treatment group was noticeably shorter than that for the other two groups, thus making a positive outcome of the study more likely.

None of the patients were so ill as to require hospitalization, and most were diagnosed as suffering from psychosomatic neuroses, obsessive or schizoid characters, phobias, anxiety neuroses and occasional psychopathic or hysterical disorders.

In the two psychotherapy groups significant decreases occurred in the Depression, Hysteria, Hypochondriasis and Lie scores of the M.M.P.I., whether individual or group. With group psychotherapy there was a significant decrease in the Paranoia and Psychasthenia scores as well. With both forms of therapy, there was "a significant rise in the Egostrength scores. Finally, for the individual psychotherapy patients there is also a significant rise in the K scale."

Patients of the control group, i.e. those not receiving any treatment, also had fewer complaints on second testing. "On the neurotic triad (D,Ps,Hy) the average decrease is slightly greater for the controls than for the group therapy patients. There is a significant increase in scores on Es, which would suggest that at the end of the waiting period the patients are somewhat more amenable to psychotherapy than at the beginning of that period."

We see, then, that changes in the treatment and non-treatment groups occur in very much the same fashion and in the same direction. The question arises whether the changes in the treatment group are significantly greater than those in the untreated group. The answer is that none of the differences on the psychiatric scales approach significance although in the twenty-four comparisons made altogether one would have expected one difference at least to have been significant by chance. Such a significant difference is in fact found, but it occurs in connexion with the K scale. This is not a psychiatric scale and the meaning of the difference is obscure; the authors do not attempt to interpret it. They conclude that "for the most part . . . the changes tended to be in the same direction for treatment and non-treatment groups, and of about equal magnitude." In so far as we can regard the M.M.P.I. as a reasonable measure of psychiatric status this study would appear to indicate a complete failure of psychotherapy to produce any effects whatever.

Barron and Leary add a rather curious argument. They question whether the patients on the waiting list should really be thought of as "untreated." "In a sense, of course, simply having committed oneself to participating in psychotherapy, and having had a reciprocal commitment from a clinic to afford psythotherapy, even though not immediately, represent a breaking of the neurotic circle. A force for change has already been introduced. In addition, the initial interview and the psychological testing may themselves be therapeutic events." It is, of course, possible that filling in a questionnaire and registering at a hospital may have therapeutic functions. The authors do not really give any reasons for assuming that these events were responsible for the change in the untreated group, and in any case this would not detract from the main conclusion, namely that psychotherapy adds nothing to the total situation.

It should always be possible in studies of this kind to invent *ad hoc* hypotheses to account for the improvement of the untreated group; this does not appear to be a worth-while procedure. What is required, clearly, is a method for *investigating* the factors which are believed to be responsible for the improvement, and which will tell us whether, in fact, these do or do not exert an influence. If the complex and lengthy procedure of psychotherapy cannot be shown to have any effect it does not seem likely to the present writer that filling in a questionnaire, or registering at a hospital, are likely to be so much more powerful in effecting a change.

The Rogers and Dymond Study

This study has been reported in book form under the title *Psychotherapy and Personality Change* (Rogers and Dymond, 1954). Since it is the only one of the studies reviewed here which reports a positive outcome, and since it has been widely quoted and discussed in this connexion, a review of this book obviously cannot be omitted here; the faults of the experimental design are such, however, that on the grounds of merit alone it is doubtful whether it should have been included.

The authors claim that: "This is the first thoroughly objective study of outcomes of psychotherapy in which adequate controls have been utilized. . . . We can, with a reasonable degree of assurance, sort out those changes which occur as concomitants of psychotherapy from those which occur as a result of other factors." The "objective" methods used to assess outcome are counsellor judgements, behaviour ratings by friends, questionnaires and attitude scales, T.A.T. responses and Q-Sorts. These were applied to the subjects of the experiment according to a design illustrated in Fig. 18.1.—

It will be discerned that there is a therapy, or experimental, group and a control group. A portion of the therapy group is set apart as the own-control group in which there is a sixty-day wait period, preceded and followed by the administration of the research tests, before therapy starts. This group is also matched in the so-called "wait group" of the controls. The rationale of the design is that, through the own-control group, we can control for personality factors and motivation for therapy. This is accomplished by comparing changes made during the wait and the therapy periods. The no-therapy control group provides a more precise control for the passage of time and the effects of repeated administration of the tests. If change occurs in the therapy and follow-up period which is greater than the change in the waiting period of the own-control group, or in the equivalent period for the control group, then we would have strong evidence that therapy produces change which is not accounted for on other grounds.

The therapy group consisted of twenty-nine clients whose disorders appeared to have been of a rather mild nature. The own-control group was formed by asking half of these clients to defer their therapy for sixty days. The equivalent control group was made up of twenty-three normal volunteers rather poorly matched for sex, age and social economic status with the patients.

The main criticism to be made of this arrangement is that contrary to the belief of the writers of the book, *no proper control group is in fact provided.* It is

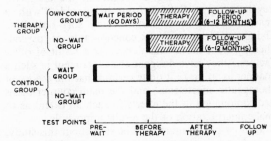

Fig. 18.1. Arrangement of Experiment by Rogers and Dymond (1954)
(Quoted by permission of Univ. of Chicago Press)

difficult to see what purpose the so-called normal control group serves. No one has, to our knowledge, advanced the hypothesis that a group of normal people not subjected to any kind of psychotherapeutic or other manipulation should change in the direction of greater integration and better mental health. The counter-hypothesis against which controls are necessary in research on the effects of psychotherapy is that spontaneous remission occurs among patients to an extent which equals the alleged effects of therapy; to this counter-hypothesis a normal control group is irrelevant.

When we come to the so-called "own-control" group it must be admitted that the logic of the design is much less susceptible to criticism *provided that the time-intervals of the waiting period and the therapy period are equal.* This is an absolutely essential proviso because the counter-hypothesis specifies that spontaneous remission would be a monotonic function of time; in other words, the longer the period of waiting, the greater the amount of spontaneous remission. If the so-called therapy period is appreciable longer than the waiting period, then we would expect on the spontaneous-remission hypothesis that more such remissions would occur in the therapy period than in the waiting period *irrespective of therapy,* so that it would be impossible to ascribe any difference in outcome between the two periods to therapy. The comparison between the waiting period and the follow-up period with respect to outcome is only meaningful if the two periods did not differ in any other variable, such as time, which is relevant to outcome. Unfortunately, it is only too obvious from what the authors say that the therapy period was in no way equated with the wait period, but was probably appreciably longer.[1] As the authors themselves admit: "The own-control plan controls motivation for therapy and, indeed, for most of the factors listed above *except passage of time* and environmental influences." The authors do not seem to realize that this admission is sufficient by itself to make the data incapable of throwing any light on the effects of psychotherapy. So far from being able "with a reasonable degree of assurance to sort out those changes which occur as concomitants of psychotherapy from those which occur as a result of other factors," they have designed the experiment in such a manner as to make it quite certain that the theory of therapeutic effectiveness and the main counter-thesis are confounded in the effects to such an extent as to make interpretation of the results impossible.

In principle no more need be said about this study, but nevertheless some of the results are interesting enough to make it desirable to say a few words about the measures used to assess the effects of therapy. Nearly all of these, it will have been noticed, are verbal in nature, calling for Q-Sorts, questionnaire responses, and other types of verbal behaviour. Even if the design of the experiment had been acceptable, verbal behaviour of this type would not be acceptable as the only evidence of improvement. There is ample evidence, from the work of Thorndike (1935), Taffel (1955), Verplanck (1955), Greenspoon (1950), Wickes (1956), Salzinger (1957), and others, that verbal responses can very easily be conditioned to indications of approval or disapproval on the part of the examiner or therapist. It requires no more than a simple nod of the head, or a repetition of the magic syllables "uh-huh" or "hmm, hmm," to produce remarkably extensive and consistent changes in verbal behaviour. It does not follow that these verbal behaviour changes are in any sense accompanied by psychological changes more directly relevant to the process of therapy. Thus we have here another alternative

hypothesis which is disregarded by Rogers and Dymond in their account, although it would again have been better able than their own to account for the actual findings. Some data are in fact provided which strongly support this alternative hypothesis. "It was found that there was no significant difference between the pre-therapy and post-therapy behaviour of our clients, on the average, according to the(ir) friends' observations. . . . When the clients' ratings of their own behaviour were compared with the ratings by their friends, it was discovered that our clients consistently rated themselves less favourably than did their friends; but this discrepancy steadily diminished, so that by the follow-up point their perception agreed much more closely with that of their friends." What appears to happen, therefore, is that there is no observable change in the behaviour of the clients, but that they become conditioned through therapy to make different responses on the purely semantic level to questions regarding their behaviour.

It is not suggested that the data prove this alternative hypothesis. We do not feel that this research was organized or analysed in a manner which makes it possible to draw any definite conclusions and we merely want to draw attention to possibilities which do not appear to have been considered by the authors. Many other such counter-hypotheses could be advanced, and would have to be eliminated before one could even begin to take the results very seriously. What strikes one most about this work is not so much its failure to be conclusive, or even the obvious faults in design and execution; it is rather that the writers appear to pride themselves on the methodological advances of their work over previous studies (among which there are such excellent prototypes of research as the Cambridge-Somerville Youth Study), and that reviewers appear to have regarded this as a major contribution without appearing to realize the crippling defects of design of the study. It would appear almost as if reviewers singled out studies giving positive results with respect to the effects of psychotherapy, while neglecting those with negative outcomes, irrespective of the quality of the work reported.

STUDIES WITHOUT CONTROL GROUPS

Psychotherapy with Adults

The experiments reviewed so far have illustrated the absolute necessity of including a control group in any experiment designed to test the efficacy of psycho-

therapy. When looking at the large body of studies without such control groups we cannot, in the nature of the case, draw any very definite conclusions. What we can do, however, is to try and provide a kind of base-line with which to compare the results of treatment, a base-line which is derived from the best available estimate of remission in the absence of psychotherapy. Our efforts along these lines will, of

---

[1] An attempt was made to obtain information on this point by writing to one of the authors, but no new information was forthcoming other than that contained on pp. 40 and 44 of the book.

course, suffer from certain obvious defects. The matching of cases is difficult enough when the same investigator selects the treatment and control groups; it becomes almost impossibly complex when all we have to go on is the usually very inadequate account given in a written report. The severity of the illness and the standards of recovery are not usually discussed in sufficient detail to make exact comparisons possible. Data on duration of treatment and the length of follow-up are not usually given in sufficient detail to enable the reader to form an accurate judgement of the time intervals involved. When all these difficulties are added to those usually implied in any actuarial comparison it will be realized that not too much faith should be placed in the results of the comparisons here given, particularly if the results should differ from those of the better-controlled studies reported earlier.

Three attempts are worth mentioning in this connexion as giving us some help in finding the requisite base-line. The first study to be quoted is a rather indirect one by Shepherd and Gruenberg (1957) in which they attempt to estimate the duration of neurotic illnesses not treated by psychotherapy by reference to the general rule stating that *the prevalence of an illness in a population is equal to the product of its incidence and duration*. They quote figures relating to both incidence and prevalence from the Health Insurance Plan of Greater New York (H.I.P.)—

From these data age-specific curves are plotted [in Fig. 18.2] for cases reported as receiving a service in any one year and for cases receiving a service for psycho-neurotic illness *for the first time* from H.I.P. in 1951, having been H.I.P. enrollees for at least three previous years without having a service for a psychoneurotic illness. While it is recognized that these are not direct estimates of momentary prevalence nor direct measures of the date of onset, they are superior to most of the other data available in that they are from a large population and that both measures derive from the same data. Because the reports stem from many different physicians trained in many different schools and practicing in diverse groups it is not possible to know just what criteria were being used to make and record these diagnoses. They undoubtedly varied widely. However, whether from accident or from consistency, both the "prevalence" curve and the "incidence" curve are similar to those obtained from other sources of data.

It will be noticed in Fig. 18.2 that the incidence and prevalence curves are not only of the same shape, but are very close to one another, running almost parallel—

From this it may be concluded that the variations in prevalence are due, predominantly, to variations in incidence, since apparently the average duration of the neuroses reported in this population does not vary

equally with age . . . since the prevalence curve here is only slightly higher than the incidence curve, it follows that the average duration of these illnesses is of between one and two years.

The authors sum up there study as follows—

While it is well known that neurotic illnesses can occur at any age and exhibit extremely long courses as

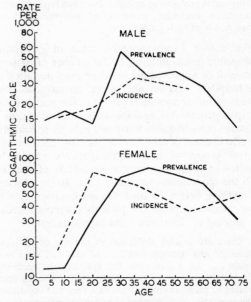

FIG. 18.2. AVERAGE ANNUAL PREVALENCE OF PSYCHO-NEUROSES IN 1948–1951 AND INCIDENCE OF NEW CASES IN 1951, FOR ENROLLEES IN H.I.P.

The prevalence curves reflect the average annual experience over the years 1948–1951 of all H.I.P. enrollees with twelve months of coverage in any one of those calendar years. There was a total of 60,302 person-years of exposure over this period; 2,714 of these person-years were characterized by the existence of one or more services related to mental illness.

The new case curves show the experience in 1951 of 6,643 enrollees who had entered H.I.P. by January 15, 1948, were still in the Plan on December 31, 1951, and had not received service related to psychoneurosis in 1948, 1949, or 1950.

(*Quoted by permission of Shepherd and Gruenberg, 1957*)

well as very brief courses, the available data are remarkably consistent in suggesting that neurotic illnesses are most characteristic of early adult life, that there is a rising incidence and prevalence during the twenties and thirties, a parallel rising prevalence continuing into the forties, and then a rapid decline in prevalence of recognized neuroses. From these data it is perfectly clear that, in the mass, neuroses must have a limited course even if untreated; in fact, the best available data would suggest an average duration between one and two years.

As a very rough-and-ready estimate of our base-line, therefore, we appear to have a figure suggesting that neurotic disorders will tend to remit spontaneously over a period of two years or so. The calculations are rather indirect, and we must next turn to two rather more direct studies.

The first of these is an evaluation by Landis (1938) who begins his discussion by pointing out that—

... before any sort of measurement can be made, it is necessary to establish a base-line and a common unit of measure. The only unit of measure available is the report made by the physician stating that the patient has recovered, is much improved, is improved or unimproved. This unit is probably as satisfactory as any type of human subjective judgement, partaking of both the good and bad points of such judgements.

For a unit Landis suggests "that of expressing therapeutic results in terms of the number of patients recovered or improved per hundred cases admitted to the hospital." As an alternative, he suggests "the statement of therapeutic outcome for some given group of patients during some stated interval of time."

Landis realized quite clearly that in order to evaluate the effectiveness of any form of therapy, data from a control group of non-treated patients would be required in order to compare the effects of therapy with the spontaneous remission rate. In the absence of anything better, he used the amelioration rate in state mental hospitals for patients diagnosed under the heading of "neuroses." As he points out—

There are several objections to the use of the consolidated amelioration rate . . . of the . . . state hospitals . . . as a base rate for spontaneous recovery. The fact that psychoneurotic cases are not usually committed to state hospitals unless in a very bad condition; the relatively small number of voluntary patients in the group; the fact that such patients do get some degree of psychotherapy especially in the reception hospitals; and the probably quite different economic, educational, and social status of the State Hospital group compared to the patients reported from each of the other hospitals —all argue against the acceptance of [this] figure . . . as a truly satisfactory base line, but in the absence of any better figure this must serve.

Actually the various figures quoted by Landis agree very well. The percentage of neurotic patients discharged annually as recovered or improved from New York state hospitals is seventy (for the years 1925–1934); for the United States as a whole it is sixty-eight (for the years 1926 to 1933). The percentage of neurotics discharged as recovered or improved within one year of admission is sixty-six for the United States (1933) and sixty-eight for New York (1914). The consolidated amelioration rate of New York state hospitals, 1917–1934, is 72 per cent. As this is the figure chosen by Landis, we may accept it in preference to the other very similar ones quoted. By and large, we may thus say that of severe neurotics receiving in the main custodial care, and very little, if any, psychotherapy, over two-thirds recovered or

improved to a considerable extent: "Although this is not, strictly speaking, a basic figure for 'spontaneous' recovery, still any therapeutic method must show an appreciably greater size than this to be seriously considered."

Another estimate of the required base-line is furnished by Denker (1946). Here is a description of his procedure—

Five hundred consecutive disability claims due to psychoneurosis, treated by general practitioners throughout the country, and not by accredited specialists or sanatoria, were reviewed. All types of neurosis were included, and no attempt made to differentiate the neurasthenic, anxiety, compulsive, hysteric, or other states, but the greatest care was taken to eliminate the true psychotic or organic lesions which in the early stages of illness so often simulate neurosis. These cases were taken consecutively from the files of the Equitable Life Assurance Society of the United States, were from all parts of the country, and all had been ill of a neurosis for at least three months before claims were submitted. They, therefore, could be fairly called "severe," since they had been totally disabled for at least a three months' period, and rendered unable to carry on with any "occupation for remuneration or profit" for at least that time.

These patients were regularly seen and treated by their own physicians with sedatives, tonics, suggestion, and reassurance, but in no case was any attempt made at anything but this most superficial type of "psychotherapy" which has always been the stock-in-trade of the general practitioner. Repeated statements, every three months or so by their physicians, as well as independent investigations by the insurance company, confirmed the fact that these people actually were not engaged in productive work during the period of their illness. During their disablement, these cases received disability benefits. . . . It is appreciated that this fact of disability income may have actually prolonged the total period of disability and acted as a barrier to incentive for recovery. One would, therefore, not expect the therapeutic results in such a group of cases to be as favourable as in other groups where the economic factor might act as an important spur in helping the sick patient adjust to his neurotic conflict and illness.

The cases were all followed up for at least a five-year period, and often as long as ten years after the period of disability had begun. The criteria of "recovery" used by Denker were as follows: (a) return to work, and ability to carry on well in economic adjustments for at least a five-year period; (b) complaint of no further or only very slight difficulties; (c) making of successful social adjustments. Using these criteria, which are very similar to those usually used by psychiatrists, Denker found that 45 per cent of the patients recovered after one year, another 27 per cent after two years, making 72 per cent in all. Another 10 per cent, 5 per cent, and 4 per cent recovered during the third, fourth, and fifth years, respectively, making a total of 90 per cent recoveries after five years.

The recovery of the patients in Denker's sample as a function of time is plotted in Fig. 18.3. An exponential curve has been fitted to these data. The formula for this curve is—

$$X = 100 \, (1 - 10^{-0.00435N})$$

where X stands for the amount of improvement achieved in per cent and N for the number of weeks elapsed. While the exact values in this formula should not be taken too seriously, its general form is of course that of the typical learning curve with which psychologists are familiar. It will be seen later that many other data are in good agreement with the generalization embodied in this formula.

The Landis and Denker studies supplement each other in a variety of ways. The patients Landis is discussing were largely working-class; those reported on by Denker almost entirely middle-class. The criterion of recovery in the Landis study was probably more lenient, that of the Denker study less lenient than the criteria usually applied by psychotherapists to their own cases. In spite of these differences the recovery figures for the two samples are not too dissimilar. If we take a period of about two years for each base-line estimate, which appears to be a reasonable figure in view of the fact that psychotherapy does not usually last very much longer than two years and may sometimes last less, we may conclude with some confidence that about two-thirds of severe neurotics show recovery or considerable improvement, without the benefit of systematic psychotherapy, after a lapse of two years from the time that their disorder is notified, or they are hospitalized. These figures are less optimistic than those given by Shepherd and Gruenberg who seem to suggest 100 per cent remission after two years; this is probably because the severity of their cases appears to have been rather less than that of those studied by Landis and Denker. When we bear in mind the different methods used by these two investigators and the very divergent samples studied, we cannot but conclude that the estimates of the rate of spontaneous remission are sufficiently similar to enable us to form a very rough-and-ready guess as to the facts of the case.[1]

We must now turn to the effects of psychothera-

[1] It may be of interest in this connexion to recall some historical comments by Bockover (1956), who points out that "early American mental hospitals recognized the importance of psychologic and social influences in what was called 'moral treatment' of the mentally ill." He points out that Worcester State Hospital showed a recovery and improvement rate of 60 per cent between 1833 and 1846, and Bloomingdale Hospital one of 65 per cent between 1821 and 1844. For the Worcester State Hospital it is claimed that between 1833 and 1946, 50 per cent of patients had no relapse.

peutic treatment. The results of nineteen studies reported in the literature, covering over seven thousand cases, and dealing with both psychoanalytic and eclectic types of treatment, are quoted in detail in Table XVIII.4. An attempt has been made to report results under the four headings: (a) cured, or

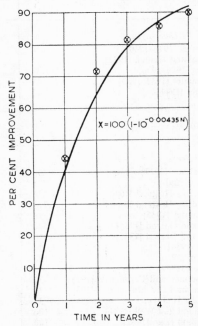

FIG. 18.3. IMPROVEMENT SHOWN BY FIVE HUNDRED SEVERE NEUROTICS, NOT RECEIVING PSYCHOTHERAPY, AFTER BETWEEN ONE AND FIVE YEARS

In the formula X denotes the proportional improvement while N denotes the number of weeks elapsing from the beginning of the experiment.

much improved; (b) improved; (c) slightly improved; (d) not improved, died, discontinued treatment, etc. It was usually easy to reduce additional categories given by some writers to these basic four; some writers give only two or three categories, and in those cases it was, of course, impossible to subdivide further, and the figures for combined categories are given. A slight degree of subjectivity inevitably enters into this procedure, but it is doubtful if it has caused much distortion. A somewhat greater degree of subjectivity is probably implied in the writer's judgement as to which disorders and diagnoses should be considered to fall under the heading of "neuroses." Schizophrenic, manic-depressive, and paranoid states have been excluded; organ neuroses, psychopathic states, and character disturbances have been included. The number of cases where there was genuine doubt is probably too small to make much change in the final figures, regardless of how they are allocated.

TABLE XVIII.4

SUMMARY OF REPORTS OF THE RESULTS OF PSYCHOTHERAPY

	N	Cured; much improved	Improved	Slightly improved	Not improved; died; left treatment	Per cent cured; much improved; improved
(A) Psychoanalytic						
1. Fenichel [1920–1930] . . .	484	104	84	99	197	39
2. Kessel and Hyman [1933] . .	34	16	5	4	9	62
3. Jones [1926–1936] . . .	59	20	8	28	3	47
4. Alexander [1932–1937] . .	141	28	42	23	48	50
5. Knight [1941]	42	8	20	7	7	67
All cases	760	335			425	44
(B) Eclectic						
1. Huddleson [1927] . . .	200	19	74	80	27	46
2. Matz [1929]	775	10	310	310	145	41
3. Maudsley Hospital Report [1931].	1,721	288	900		533	69
4. Maudsley Hospital Report [1935].	1,711	371	765		575	64
5. Neustatter [1935] . . .	46	9	14	8	15	50
6. Luff and Garrod [1935] . .	500	140	135	26	199	55
7. Luff and Garrod [1935] . .	210	38	84	54	34	68
8. Ross [1936] . . .	1,089	547	306		236	77
9. Yaskin [1936]	100	29	29		42	58
10. Curran [1937]	83	51			32	61
11. Masserman and Carmichael [1938]	50	7	20	5	18	54
12. Carmichael and Masserman [1939]	77	16	25	14	22	53
13. Schilder [1939]	35	11	11	6	7	63
14. Hamilton and Wall [1941] . .	100	32	34	17	17	66
15. Hamilton *et al.* [1942]. . .	100	48	5	17	32	51
16. Landis [1938]	119	40	47		32	73
17. Institute Med. Psychol. (quoted Neustatter)	270	58	132	55	25	70
18. Wilder [1945]	54	3	24	16	11	50
19. Miles *et al.* [1951] . . .	53	13	18	13	9	58
All cases	7,293	4,661			2,632	64

Further details regarding the method of arriving at these various figures are given by Eysenck (1952). The overall figures show that patients treated by means of psychoanalysis improved to the extent of 44 per cent; patients treated eclectically improved to the extent of 64 per cent. These figures may be compared with our base-line estimate of spontaneous remission of 72 per cent. There thus appears to be an inverse correlation between recovery and psychotherapy; the more psychotherapy, the smaller the recovery rate. The difference between eclectic treatment and no psychotherapy is probably too small to be of any significance when we bear in mind the very rough and ready methods used in arriving at these figures. As regards the psychoanalytic results we have classed those who stopped treatment together with those who have not improved. This appears to be reasonable because a patient who fails to finish his treatment, and has not improved, is surely a therapeutic failure. If we class these cases separately and deal only with the percentage of completed treatments which are successful, we find that a percentage of successful treatments of patients who finished their course must be put at approximately 66 per cent, thus bringing these figures in line with those for eclectic treatment and no psychotherapy at all.

The results have been summarized by the writer as follows (Eysenck 1952)—

In general, certain conclusions are possible from these data. They fail to prove that psychotherapy, Freudian or otherwise, facilitates the recovery of neurotic patients. They show that roughly two-thirds of a group of neurotic patients will recover or improve to a marked extent within about two years of the onset of their illness, whether they are treated by means of psychotherapy or not. This figure appears to be remarkably stable from one investigation to another, regardless of type of patient treated, standard of recovery employed, or method of therapy used. From the point of view of the neurotic, these figures are encouraging; from the point of view of the psychotherapist, they can hardly be called very favourable to his claims. The figures quoted do not necessarily disprove the possibility of therapeutic effectiveness. There are obvious shortcomings in any actuarial comparison and these shortcomings are particularly serious when there is so little agreement among psychiatrists relating even to the most fundamental concepts and definitions. Definite proof would require a special investigation, carefully planned and methodologically more adequate than these *ad hoc* comparisons.

Psychotherapy with Children

Our review here will follow very closely that published by Levitt (1957), who has summarized a large number of published and unpublished studies and arranged them in tables patterned on that published by the writer in connexion with adults. Levitt also used as the "unit of measurement" the evaluation of the degree of improvement of the patient by the clinicians concerned: "Individuals listed as 'much improved, improved, partially improved, successful, partially successful, adjusted, partially adjusted, satisfactory,' etc., will be grouped under the general heading of improved. The unimproved cases were found in groupings like 'slightly improved, unimproved, unadjusted, failure, worse,' etc."

For various good reasons Levitt refused to use the discharge rate of children's wards in state hospitals as a base-line for evaluating the effects of psychotherapy. Instead he made use of a rather different group of children—

A common phenomenon of the child guidance clinic is the patient who is accepted for treatment, but who voluntarily breaks off the clinic relationship without ever being treated. In institutions where the service load is heavy and the waiting period between acceptance and onset of treatment may range up to six months, this group of patients is often quite large. Theoretically, they have the characteristics of an adequate control group. So far as is known, they are similar to treated groups in every respect except for the factor of treatment itself. Nevertheless, the use of this type of group as a control is not common in follow-up evaluations of the efficacy of treatment. Three studies report follow-up data on such groups. Of these, the data of Morris and Soroker (1953) are not suitable for the purposes of this paper. Of their seventy-two cases, at least eleven had treatment elsewhere between the last formal contact with the clinic and the point of evaluation, while an

indeterminate number had problems too minor to warrant clinic treatment. The samples in the remaining two studies appear satisfactory as sources of base-line data. Witmer and Keller (1942) appraised their group eight to thirteen years after clinic treatment, and reported that 78 per cent were improved. In the Lehrman study (1949), a one-year follow-up interval found 70 per cent improved. The overall rate of improvement for one hundred and sixty cases in both reports is 72.5 per cent. This figure will be used as the baseline for evaluating the results of treatment of children.

It is, as will be noted, identical with that used by the writer with adults.

As regards the results of psychotherapy, Levitt, like Eysenck, rejects a number of studies for various reasons, such as peculiar or inadequate presentation of data, or because results for children and adults were inseparable. The remaining studies cover an age range from pre-school to 21 years at the time of the original clinic contact. However, very few patients were over 18 years at that time, and not many were over 17. At a rough estimate Levitt states that the median age would be about 10 years.

The data are presented in the form of two tables, the first stating the results at the close of psychotherapy. This table which is given on page 714 as Table XVIII.5 shows that the average percentage of improvement, i.e. the combined percentages in the much improved and partially improved categories is 67·05 at close. "As in the case of Eysenck's data, there is a considerable amount of consistency, considering the interstudy differences in methodology, definition, etc."

Table XVIII.6 gives the results of follow-up evaluations, and in this table the follow-up interval is given as a range of years. The average percentage of improvement in the follow-up studies is given as 78·22 per cent. Two further studies are quoted by Levitt as combining Close and Follow-up evaluation and are given in Table XVIII.7. The percentage of improvement for these studies is 73·98, roughly intermediate between the averages of the other two tables. Levitt points out that "the discrepancy between results at close and at follow-up suggests that time is a factor in improvement," and he quotes Denker's study in support of the generalization that "the rate of improvement as a function of time . . . is negatively accelerating." He then goes on to present a rank-order correlation between estimated median follow-up interval and percentage of improvement in the seventeen studies in Table XVIII.6, which turns out to be 0·48 and is statistically significant. Plotting the amount of improvement against time shows that "the curve is more or less the same as that of Denker's data, negatively accelerating with most of the improvement accomplished by $2\frac{1}{2}$ years. . . . This analysis

TABLE XVIII.5

SUMMARY OF RESULTS OF PSYCHOTHERAPY WITH CHILDREN AT CLOSE

(Quoted from Levitt (1957) by permission of the Editor, "J. Cons. Psychol.")

Study	N	Much improved	Partially improved		Unimproved		Per cent improved
Cohen, Marion, *et al.*	57	16	18	12	8	3	80·7
Hubbard, Ruth M., *et al.*	100	13	18	42	26	1	73·0
Irgens, Effie M.	70	12	29	19	10		85·7
Reid, J. H., *et al.*	250	54	82	46	68		72·8
Lehrman, L. J., *et al.*	196	76	52		68		65·3
La More, Mary T.	50	15	18		17		66·0
Christianson, Eva, *et al.*	126	25	54		47		62·7
Witmer, Helen L., *et al.*	290	75	154		61		79·0
Barbour, R. F.	814	207	398		209		74·3
Newell, N. W.	72	26	31		15		79·2
Lee, P. R., *et al.*	196	93	61		42		78·6
Brown, Marjorie	27	5	11		11		59·3
Carpenter, Jean A.	31	13	8		10		67·7
Canaday, Louise J.	23	2	9		12		47·8
Burlingham, Susan	75	35	22		18		76·0
Albright, Sue, *et al.*	80	31	21		28		65·0
Maas, H. S., *et al.*	522	225			297		43·1
Cunningham, J. M., *et al.*	420	251			169		59·8
All cases	3,399	1,174	1,105		1,120		67·05
Per cent	100·00	34·54	32·51		32·95		

TABLE XVIII.6

SUMMARY OF RESULTS OF PSYCHOTHERAPY WITH CHILDREN AT FOLLOW-UP

(Quoted from Levitt (1957) by permission of the Editor, "J. Cons. Psychol.")

Study	Interval in years	N	Much improved	Partially improved		Unimproved		Per cent improved
Lee, P. R., *et al.*	1–5	197	49	55	39	38	16	72·6
Brown, Jane L.	2	33	8	11	7	6	1	78·8
Cohen, Marion, *et al.*	2–3	57	25	17	6	6	3	84·2
Witmer, Helen L.[1]	1–10	366	81	78	106	101		72·4
Irgens, Effie M.	2–3	70	21	30	13	6		91·4
Walcott, Esther	5–8	17	7	3		4	3	58·8
Lehrman, L. J., *et al.*	1	196	99	46		51		74·0
Morris, D. P., *et al.*	16–27	34	22	11		1		97·1
Barbour, R. F.	1–20	705	358	225		122		82·7
Bronner, Augusta F.	5–18	650	355	181		114		82·5
Maberly, A., *et al.*	3–15	484	111	264		109		77·5
Fenton, N., *et al.*	1–4	732	179	398		155		78·8
Cunningham, J. M., *et al.*	5	359	228	80		51		85·8
Gollander, Barbara	1–2	25	6	12		7		72·0
Moses, Jane	1–2	25	10	6		9		64·0
Maas, H. S., *et al.*	½–1½	191	82			109		42·9
Healy W., *et al.*	1–20	78	71			7		91·0
All cases	4·8[2]	4,219	1,712	1,588		919		78·22
Per cent		100·00	40·58	37·64		21·78		

[1] Data based on thirteen studies originally reported in Witmer, Helen L., *et al.*, 1935; results of eight of these are included here.
[2] Estimated average follow-up interval per case.

TABLE XVIII.7

SUMMARY OF RESULTS OF PSYCHOTHERAPY WITH CHILDREN BASED ON COMBINED CLOSE-FOLLOW-UP EVALUATION

(Quoted from Levitt (1957) by permission of the Editor, "J. Cons. Psychol.")

Study	Interval in years	N	Much improved	Partially improved	Unimproved	Per cent improved
Jacobsen, Virginia	1–10	339	94	81 76	42 46	74·04
Johnson, Lillian J., *et al* .	1–10	30	9	13	8	73·33
All cases . . .	5·5[1]	369	103	170	96	73·98
Per cent		100·00	27·91	46·07	26·02	

[1] Estimated average follow-up interval per case.

suggests that improvement is in part a function of time, but the mechanisms involved remain purely speculative. Future comparisons of the results of psychotherapy should properly take this factor into consideration."

Levitt discusses certain features of his data at some length and finally comes to the conclusion that "the therapeutic eclecticism, the number of subjects, the results, and the conclusions of this paper are markedly similar to that of Eysenck's study. Two-thirds of the patients examined at close and about three-quarters seen in follow-up have improved. Approximately the same percentages of improvement are found for comparable groups of untreated children. . . . It now appears that Eysenck's conclusion concerning the data for adult psychotherapy is applicable to children as well; the results do not support the hypothesis that recovery from neurotic disorder is facilitated by psychotherapy."

In evaluation of Levitt's study it should perhaps be said that his control groups are less well chosen than might ideally be desired. Patients who voluntarily break off the clinic relationship while still on the waiting list are perhaps likely to be suffering from less severe and disabling disorders than those who persevere. If that were so then we would expect this group to have a higher spontaneous rating of remission than those who remain. As Levitt points out, it is not known that there are in fact any such differences between the groups, but the possibility cannot be disregarded and ought certainly to be investigated. The fact that although there have been over sixty years of psychotherapeutic work with children Levitt failed to discover in the literature a single properly controlled study, or a single investigation providing unambiguous evidence regarding a base-line figure for untreated groups, is perhaps the most eloquent testimony for the failure of clinical psychologists and psychiatrists to take seriously their task of appraising the effects of the methods they use.

The Wolpe Study

As Winder (1957) has pointed out—

In psychotherapy, it is assumed that the therapist adopts a set of ground rules which guide his behavior. Although the limiting case is probably never achieved, the ideal therapist's contribution would be completely deliberate. This is not to say that therapy cannot be effective if done intuitively, nor that the therapist can be a disinterested administrator of doses of this and that. It is to say that the ideal therapist would provide whatever is essential to therapy (warmth, empathic emotion arousal, intellectual understanding, nonjudgmental understanding, rewards, and punishments, etc.) on the basis of reason and knowledge. The next step is obviously the investigation of the effects of defined techniques, when used with particular kinds of patients, within particular contexts.

This view is also shared by Shoben, when he writes—

No matter how eclectic the counselor's manner of approach to a diagnostic judgement, it seems inevitable that he make use of some theory. Indeed, "clinical intuition" seems to represent in part this kind of utilization of theory when it has been sufficiently well practiced to occur with great rapidity. Certainly, one rarely encounters "intuitive" behavior of this kind in counselors without considerable training and experience. If this point holds in any significant degree, and if one recalls the finding of Holtzmann and Sells (1954) that that clinicians were consistently wrong in their predictions, but that they agreed remarkably well among themselves in their errors, then one can hardly escape the suspicion that something must be amiss in available theories typically employed by clinicians. Even though the situation may have been one where actuarial methods were more appropriate, the agreement in errors hints at some common stereotypes among counselors, rather than at useful theoretical constructs.

As regards the usual process of psychotherapy, some doubt has been thrown on the existence of marked differences in practice deriving from differences in theory by Fiedler (1950, 1951, 1953) whose investigations have emphasized the role of experience as opposed to that of theoretical preconception. Strupp (1955) has come to similar conclusions regarding experience as a predominant determinant. Certainly the differences between "psychoanalysis" and "psychoanalytic orientated psychotherapy" appear to be vanishing. This seems to be tacitly admitted by Alexander (1953) whose contribution is summarized by Meehl (1955) as follows: "He has been making a very convincing case to the effect that the two products are not 'essentially different,' so long as both are (a) mainly uncovering rather than supportive and (b) based on adequate dynamic formulations. It almost looks as though Alexander shares with his more orthodox colleagues the need to keep a monopoly on the prestigeful term 'psychoanalyst,' in spite of the steady breakdown, both in theory and practice, of the distinction it once really made." Certainly psychologists working in mental hospitals will have found it more and more difficult to distinguish in actual practice between adherents of different schools and different theories, and to a very real degree, therefore, it might be said that our device of distinguishing between different schools by appropriate subscripts may be a task of supererogation.

There is one outstanding exception to this general rule, and that is the kind of therapy which derives its theoretical justification not from psychoanalysis but from learning theory, and which may suitably be labelled psychotherapy$_{LT}$. A long discussion of what is implied in this has been given by the writer elsewhere (Eysenck, 1959), and several chapters in this book are concerned with an elaboration of the principles involved. Here we shall only take note of this novel departure in order to introduce the work of Wolpe (1952, 1954, 1958) who is probably the outstanding exponent of this point of view, and who has published figures on the therapeutic successes of his method and compared them with published figures of the success of psychoanalysis in similar cases. Briefly, Wolpe bases his therapy on the following hypothesis: "When fundamental psychotherapeutic effects are obtained in neuroses—no matter by what therapist—these effects are nearly always really a consequence of the occurrence of reciprocal inhibition of neurotic anxiety responses, i.e. the complete or partial suppression of the anxiety responses as a consequence of the simultaneous evocation of other responses physiologically antagonistic to anxiety." In his view, "neurotic behaviour is persistent unadaptive learned behaviour in which anxiety is almost always prominent and which is acquired in anxiety-generating situations. By 'anxiety' is meant the autonomic response pattern or patterns that are characteristically part of the given organism's response to noxious stimulation, and the term is applied irrespective of the duration of the autonomic responses or of what has led to them. Anxiety response is unadaptive when it is evoked in circumstances in which there is objectively no threat."

This theory differs radically from the psychoanalytic and has given rise to methods of treatment which also differ profoundly from those usually classified under psychotherapy.[1] Wolpe has reported on a total of one hundred and twenty-two patients treated by him, making use in his report of five criteria originally suggested by Knight (1941): "symptomatic improvement, increased productiveness, improved adjustment and pleasure in sex, improved interpersonal relationships, and ability to handle ordinary psychological conflicts and reasonable reality stresses." In addition, the patient's score on Willoughby's questionnaire is compared with his score at the beginning of treatment, and no patient is regarded as greatly benefited unless his score has dropped markedly, preferably to 20 or less.

Wolpe compared the total results of his investigations with reported results from two large psychoanalytic institutions involving almost four hundred cases. He reports that 90 per cent of his patients were either apparently cured or much improved, and only about 60 per cent of those cases treated by psychoanalysis. "If the favourable results of the present series are, to the extent of 60 per cent, regarded as due to the non-specific reciprocal inhibition that would occur in any kind of interview situation, the additional 30 per cent of good results appear to be attributable to the special measures for obtaining reciprocal inhibition described above. Furthermore, the small average number of interviews needed (four-fifths of the patients had thirty interviews or less) suggests that the use of these special measures early in treatment greatly accelerates the improvement of those patients who would have responded to the non-specific factor alone."

It is, of course, impossible to accept either Wolpe's theory or his figures without question. As regards the theory, he appears to be concerned almost exclusively with dysthymic disorders and to disregard hysterics and psychopaths. There may, as the writer has suggested (Eysenck, 1957), be other methods in addition to that of reciprocal inhibition which may lead to extinction of the faulty emotional habits which constitute the neurotic disorder. As regards the published figures it would clearly have been more

[1] Theory and method of treatment hark back to the Watson and Raynor (1920) study of "little Albert" of immortal fame, and the Jones (1924) sequel. Psychotherapy $_{LT}$ might well be renamed "behaviour therapy," because it differs so much in aim, method, and theory from traditional forms of psychotherapy. A detailed account of the principles of behaviour therapy and the many ways in which it differs from psychotherapy of the Freudian kind is given in *Behaviour Therapy and the Neuroses* by Eysenck (1959).

satisfactory if a control group had been included in the experimental design; the difficulties of using published figures as a control have been pointed out earlier in this chapter. This criticism cannot detract from the very great importance of Wolpe's work. By using the standards of recovery advocated and widely used by psychoanalysts, he has obviated the main criticism that might have been brought against him, namely that of using a more lenient criterion than the psychoanalysts. By publishing a number of his cases in considerable detail he has made it possible for the reader to judge whether the type of patient treated by him is comparable to the type of patient who usually has recourse to psychoanalytic treatment. All in all, criticism of the weaknesses of his paper would come badly from those whose theories have never been submitted to a more rigorous and well-designed test. Of all the hundreds of papers and books examined the writer has found this to be the only one to give positive evidence in favour of one specified type of psychotherapy. Obviously a repetition of the work is urgently required, preferably with two or more control groups to duplicate psychoanalytic treatment, eclectic treatment, non-psychiatric medical treatment, non-directive treatment and no treatment at all. The fact that Wolpe's treatment is so firmly anchored in a very definite theoretical framework which governs the therapeutic procedure much more directly than is usually the case, makes a test of his hypothesis very much easier than would be a similar test of the Freudian or Jungian theory. The considerable difference in approach between Wolpe and the majority of psychiatrists suggests that it may be advisable not to discard our subscripts to the term "psychotherapy" yet.

The Lakin Phillips Study

Somewhat analogous to the Wolpe Studies in the adult field is the Phillips (1957) study in the child behaviour field. Like Wolpe, Phillips declines to use methods based on psychoanalytic theories and puts forward his own "interference" theory, based on modern learning theory. Again like Wolpe, he applies this theory to actual clinical cases and compares the outcome and the duration of his treatment with psychoanalytic treatment. It might be thought that his study would deserve to be regarded as coming under our heading of "Studies using a control group"; it is included here because it did not contain an *untreated* control group, and because the psychoanalytically treated sample which constitutes his control was selected by the therapists according to different principles from those covering Phillips's own selection.

The theory involved may best be summed up in the author's own words—

Very briefly considered, interference theory constitutes the viewpoint that behavior—pathological or otherwise—is a result of various *assertions* made by the individual about himself or about his relationship with others. The person chooses now one kind of behavior, now another, depending on what kind of behavior seems likely to bring (from the environment) confirmation of his assertions. Certain behavior possibilities "interfere" with each other; that is, the person cannot do both at the same time. However, since possible behavior is always selected by a person on the basis of its appropriateness to the environment, the whole process with which we are concerned goes on "in the open." Depth views, which regard the mental life of people as having a kind of deep-going reservoir from which diabolical forces spring, are entirely anathema to the present viewpoint. The depth view is essentially untestable—an elementary, too elementaristic view, one that cannot meet the complexity of problems that we contrive in the laboratory, see in the nursery school, or meet daily in a myriad of practical situations.

The results of comparing an assertion-structured therapy with psychoanalytic therapy are given in Table XVIII.8. Before turning to this table, it should be noted that the number of interviews required by Phillips's method was less than half that required by psychoanalytic methods, a difference which was highly significant statistically. Introducing Table XVIII.8, Phillips writes as follows—

Existing follow-up research on psychotherapy deals almost exclusively with the outcomes of treatment among patients who completed (or nearly completed) therapy. Interest here is shown in the *total problem:* that is, in tracing the *efficiency* with which therapy is brought to the patients, and the *effectiveness* it was judged to have by both patient and therapist on a follow-up basis. This manner of proceeding can give us a more complete picture of the observed value of psychotherapy.

In order to do this, three groups are compared here as to their effectiveness and efficiency; a group treated by the depth-oriented, psychoanalytically-derived methods; a group treated by the assertion-structured therapy method (representing the viewpoint of this book); and a hypothetical group illustrating what one might expect under near-optimum conditions in out-patient, parent-child treatment.

As Phillips points out, "the results shown [in Table XVIII.8] suggest strongly that there are real differences in the effectiveness and efficiency of out-patient, parent-child psychotherapy, when assertion-structured therapy and psychoanalytic-derived depth methods are compared." Particularly striking, in looking at the figures for psychoanalytic therapy, is that of all those applying for therapy, only 25 per cent (forty-five out of one hundred and ninety) were actually accepted for therapy; over half of all applications were refused treatment by clinicians! "This seems like an enormously large figure and one

TABLE XVIII.8

COMPARING THE EFFICIENCY AND EFFECTIVENESS OF HYPOTHETICAL (IDEAL) THERAPY, ASSERTION-STRUCTURED THERAPY, AND DEPTH-ORIENTED THERAPY

(Quoted by permission from Phillips, 1957)

	1 Number applying for therapy	2 Number treated from among applicants	3 Number refused treatment by clinicians	4 Number who themselves refuse treatment	5 Number completing 3 or more interviews	6 Number benefited by 3 or more interviews	7 Percentage of original applicants benefited
Hypothetical group	100	90	5	5	90	90	81
Assertion-structured therapy	59	53	—	6	53	51	86·4
Psychoanalytic depth-oriented therapy	190	45	103	42	45	21[1] (patients' rating) 33[1] (therapists' rating)	11·05[1] (patients' rating) 17·3[1] (therapists' rating)

[1] Therapists' ratings were available for all forty-five patients who completed three or more interviews, Only twenty-seven of these forty-five patients returned questionnaires rating their therapy experience; the twenty-one who rated themselves as having improved somewhat supplied the figure used here.

that is not reflected in the subjective writings and appraisals of clinicians when they report on or discuss therapeutic success and failure."

Phillips has here drawn attention to a fact which is obviously important in evaluating the respective successes of different types of therapy, but which is hardly ever mentioned in the literature. Psychoanalysts are usually very selective in accepting cases for treatment, and unless the proportion of cases accepted for treatment out of the total number of the cases applying for treatment is known, it is impossible to compare the results of psychoanalytic treatment with some other treatment (or no treatment at all) where no such selection has taken place. There is a certain amount of knowledge and agreement as to good and bad prognostic signs in neurotic and psychotic disorders, and by a suitable selection of cases for treatment, it should be easy to beat the "no treatment" or "other treatment" groups not using such a process of selection. It is somewhat puzzling to the writer, in view of these considerations, that no superiority of psychoanalytic methods over others has in fact been demonstrated. Many reasons can be adduced for this; thus it might be that the total effect of psychoanalytic treatment is actually negative, thus cancelling out the effects of selection, or it might be that our principles of selection and prognosis are less valid than is commonly thought. However that might be, this is a point which should be borne in mind in all future studies.

If we disregard these considerations and concentrate on the number of patients completing three or more interviews, we find that fifty-one out of fifty-three are benefited by assertion-structure therapy, but only twenty-one out of forty-five are so benefited by psychoanalytic therapy. These figures are significantly different from each other and suggest strongly the superiority of the non-psychoanalytic method.

It is difficult not to agree with Phillips in his summing up—

One may produce certain arguments against interpreting these results as being in any way adverse so far as psychoanalytic depth-derived parent-child, out-patient treatment cases are concerned. One might say that the methods used are not "true psychoanalysis" of children. However, the record of "true" psychoanalysis of children is hardly better, if as good: witness the work of Klein and Anna Freud. The argument for depth-derived practices cannot be bolstered on the basis of probable value latent in unstudied and unreported upon therapeutic results of psychoanalysis of children. The hard reality here is that, first, there are no convincing results of a follow-up nature that can be used to support psychoanalytically derived (or "true" psychoanalysis) treatment of children; and, second, that the results that do exist fail to support any very hopeful view regarding the effectiveness and efficiency of depth-derived, parent-child, out-patient psychotherapy.

The Albert Ellis Study

A third study comparing psychoanalytic and other types of psychotherapy is reported by Ellis (1957).

He himself has used, on his patients, psychoanalytic psychotherapy of the orthodox kind; psychoanalytically oriented psychotherapy; and finally what he calls "rational psychotherapy"—

The main emphasis of the therapist who employs rational techniques is on analysing the client's current problems—especially his negative feelings of anger, depression, anxiety and guilt—and concretely showing him that these emotions arise, not from past events or external situations, but from his present irrational attitudes toward, or illogical fears about, these events and situations. . . . Where, in psychoanalytic techniques, considerable time is spent on showing the patient how he originally *became* neurotic, in rational analysis much more emphasis is placed on how he is *sustaining* his disturbance by *still* believing the nonsense, or illogical ideas, which first led him to feel and act in an aberrated fashion.

Two groups, closely matched as to diagnosis, age, sex and education were formed, each consisting of seventy-eight cases. The first group consisted of individuals treated with rational techniques over an average period of twenty-six sessions; the second group consisted of seventy-eight patients treated with psychoanalytically oriented techniques over an average of thirty-five sessions. In addition, there was a group of sixteen patients treated by orthodox psychoanalysis, and having an average of ninety-three sessions. Ellis himself treated all the patients in these three groups, and rated them soon after each case had been closed, in terms of whether he or she had made (*a*) little or no progress while being seen; (*b*) some distinct improvement; or (*c*) considerable improvement.

Ellis found "that therapeutic results appear to be best for clients treated with rational analysis and poorest for those treated with orthodox analysis . . . significantly more clients treated with rational analysis showed considerable improvement and significantly fewer showed little or no improvement than clients treated with the other two techniques." The actual proportions of cases showing distinct or considerable improvement were 90 per cent for rational psychotherapy, 63 per cent for psychoanalytically oriented psychotherapy, and 50 per cent for orthodox psychoanalysis. These figures should be seen in the light of the fact that orthodox psychoanalysis was carried on for three times as many sessions as rational psychotherapy. Ellis concludes: "While the obtained data of the study do not offer incontrovertible proof of the superiority of the technique of rational psychotherapy, they strongly indicate that neither orthodox nor liberal psychoanalytic procedures may be the very last word in effective technique."

Without the use of a non-treated control group it is difficult to say whether the patients treated by rational psychotherapy did better than those treated psychoanalytically because rational psychotherapy had a positive effect, or because psychoanalytic therapy had a negative effect. The former appears to be the more likely hypothesis, when taken in conjunction with data previously quoted, although the other hypothesis may not be altogether absurd. Ellis does not attempt to derive his rational psychotherapy from learning theory, but this should not be impossible. There are obvious similarities, as well as differences, in the approaches of Ellis, Phillips, and Wolpe, and it is to be hoped that properly controlled studies will soon be initiated to test the specific hypotheses of these authors, and compare the results of their methods of treatment.

DISCUSSION, SUMMARY AND CONCLUSIONS

In this concluding section we will first of all state very briefly the main conclusions which may be drawn from the researches outlined above, and will then go on to discuss certain theoretical points to which these conclusions are relevant. The qualifications to which the conclusions are subject have been fully stated in the text and will not be repeated. Nor will it be emphasized again that these conclusions are simply a summary of the existing literature and may have to be changed when further more adequate research is reported.

It appears that eight major conclusions can be derived from the literature—

1. When untreated neurotic control groups are compared with experimental groups of neurotic patients treated by means of psychotherapy, both groups recover to approximately the same extent.

2. When soldiers who have suffered a neurotic breakdown and have not received psychotherapy are compared with soldiers who have received psychotherapy, the chances of the two groups returning to duty are approximately equal.

3. When neurotic soldiers are separated from the Service, their chances of recovery are not affected by their receiving or not receiving psychotherapy.

4. Civilian neurotics who are treated by psychotherapy recover or improve to approximately the same extent as similar neurotics receiving no psychotherapy.

5. Children suffering from emotional disorders and treated by psychotherapy recover or improve

to approximately the same extent as similar children not receiving psychotherapy.

6. Neurotic patients treated by means of psychotherapeutic procedures based on learning theory, improve significantly more quickly than do patients treated by means of psychoanalytic or eclectic psychotherapy, or not treated by psychotherapy at all.

7. Neurotic patients treated by psychoanalytic psychotherapy do not improve more quickly than patients treated by means of eclectic psychotherapy, and may improve less quickly when account is taken of the large proportion of patients breaking off treatment.

8. With the single exception of the psychotherapeutic methods based on learning theory, results of published research with military and civilian neurotics, and with both adults and children, suggest that the therapeutic effects of psychotherapy are small or non-existent, and do not in any demonstrable way add to the non-specific effects of routine medical treatment, or to such events as occur in the patients' everyday experience.

These conclusions go a little beyond those which resulted from the writer's original survey of the literature which was published in 1952. The conclusion then was simply that published research failed to disprove the null-hypothesis with respect to psychotherapeutic effectiveness. The additional studies which have come to hand since, particularly those making use of a control group, have been so uniformly negative in their outcome that a somewhat stronger conclusion appears warranted. Methodologically, of course, it is impossible to prove that any treatment has no effect whatsoever, and no such conclusion is implied. The results do show that whatever effects psychotherapy may have are likely to be extremely small; if they were large as compared with the effects of non-specific treatments and events it seems reasonable to suppose that some effects would have been found in the studies quoted. It is possible, of course, that effects were looked for in the wrong quarter; psychotherapy may affect personality traits and behaviour patterns other than those relevant to psychiatric improvement as ordinarily understood. In the absence of specific hypotheses and experimental research there is no fruitful way of discussing such a possibility. The writer must admit to being somewhat surprised at the uniformly negative results issuing from all this work. In advancing his rather challenging conclusion in the 1952 report the main motive was one of stimulating better and more worth-while research in this important but somewhat neglected field; there was an underlying belief that while

results to date had not disproved the null-hypothesis, improved methods of research would undoubtedly do so. Such a belief does not seem to be tenable any longer in this easy optimistic form, and it rather seems that psychologists and psychiatrists will have to acknowledge the fact that current psychotherapeutic procedures have not lived up to the hopes which greeted their emergence fifty years ago.

Clearly the matter cannot be left there. It will be necessary in the first place to account for the fact that so many therapists and so many patients believe quite firmly in the efficacy of psychotherapy; this is an undoubted fact which appears to be in contradiction to our conclusion and requires explanation. In the second place it will be necessary to examine the consequences of our conclusions, in so far as they are relevant to psychological theories of neurotic disorder and breakdown; quite clearly the failure of a commonly held belief to be supported by the facts must have some repercussion on widely-held theories which have given rise to such beliefs.

To take the first point first we may perhaps take a clue from Meehl (1955). In a quotation already given he pointed out that therapeutic experiences could be explained within a crude statistical model which assigns very little specific power to therapeutic intervention. If the majority of neurotics tend to improve under moderately favourable external circumstances anyway, those who are under therapy while improving will be talking about their current actions and feelings in the sessions, and client and therapist will naturally attribute any changes to the therapy. Meehl goes on like this—

> How will such a statistical system be experienced by therapists? Very much as therapy admittedly appears to its candid practitioners. The best cases are types which seem most likely to improve anyhow. Sometimes there are temporal associations between improvement and interview events of the kind considered important, at other times such covariation is disconcertingly lacking. The therapist gradually conceptualizes the client, but there seems to be no clear-cut connection between the client's learning of this conceptualization and outcome . . . The therapist is like a Skinner-box rat on a schedule of intermittent reinforcement, which generates habits notoriously resistive to extinction. A sprinkling of even 5 or 10 per cent of "specific cures," cases whose shift towards recovery would not have occurred without intervention, could combine with the life-cures and the (unimproved) upswing terminators to yield the experiences therapists actually have in their daily work.

With this statement of the model the present writer would wholeheartedly agree, except that he can find no evidence for the "sprinkling of even 5 or 10 per cent specific cures." The fact that improvement is taking place in the whole group of patients all the time in conformity with the formula given previously will produce sufficient reinforcement for the growth of very strong beliefs in the efficacy of therapy, prayer, shock treatment, confession, or whatever else may in point of time be associated with the improvement which is taking place anyway. The fact that so many different types of treatment of neurotic disorders and so many different theories regarding neurotic disorders have found enthusiastic adherents among both therapists and patients thus finds an adequate explanation in terms of this hypothesis which is fully in conformity with the teaching of modern learning theories.

How about the repercussions which our conclusions have on modern theories of neurotic disorders? The psychoanalytic view, which is probably much the most widely accepted of all, would seem to generate certain very definite conclusions. Among these would be the following: (1) neurotic disorders have complex roots in early childhood experiences; (2) such neuroses are not self-limiting but relatively permanent; (3) they do not become extinguished in the ordinary way but require definite psychotherapy; (4) such psychotherapy requires the uncovering of the roots which lie at the base of the neurotic disorder; (5) only psychoanalysis, as a method based on Freudian theory, can carry this task to successful conclusion.

The facts summarized in this chapter contradict, in a fairly conclusive manner, all these statements.[1] We have found that neurotic disorders tend to be self-limiting, that psychoanalysis is no more successful than any other method, and that in fact all methods of psychotherapy fail to improve on the recovery rate obtained through ordinary life experiences and nonspecific treatment. What is even more conclusive, we have found that there is strong evidence to suggest that short methods of treatment based on an alternative hypothesis are significantly more successful in treating neurotic disorders than is psychotherapy of the psychoanalytic type. This alternative method is based on a point of view which regards neurotic disorders as conditioned responses or learnt habits which are non-adaptive, but which are persistent because they are constantly receiving reinforcement. Like all other habits they are subject to extinction according to rules elaborated by modern learning theory and sufficiently well understood to make possible deductions which can be tested experimentally. All the facts summarized in this chapter

fall in line with this alternative hypothesis, and there are none which contradict it. It would appear advisable, therefore, to discard the psychoanalytic model, which both on the theoretical and practical plain fails to be useful in mediating verifiable predictions, and to adopt, provisionally at least, the learning theory model which, to date, appears to be much more promising theoretically and also with regard to application. Much further evidence is available to reinforce this suggestion and will be found in other chapters of this book; all we can say in conclusion is that such work as has been done on the effects of psychotherapy not only fails to contradict, but lends strong support to this general conclusion.

The more fair-minded psychoanalysts do not appear on the whole to oppose this denial of therapeutic usefulness or theoretical and experimental appropriateness of their model and method. Glover (1955) specifically renounces therapeutic clinics, and has the following to say about psychoanalytic research (Glover, 1952, as summarized by Saslow, 1954)—

The possibility that the psychoanalysts, who gave the impetus to the enormous enrichment of psychological understanding of the last decades, will save the general situation is made to seem rather remote by the picture of psychoanalytic research presented by Glover. His address before the International Psycho-Analytical Congress on research methods in psychoanalysis is based on his own long clinical experience and his observations as Director of Research of the London Institute of Psycho-Analysis for sixteen years. He believes there has been an increasing tendency by psychoanalysts not to apply to their data such scientific controls as are available. He described vividly how hearsay evidence becomes attested conclusion (given an analyst with seniority, enthusiasm or plain dogmatism); how a student whose professional career depends on overcoming "resistance" to the satisfaction of his training analyst can hardly be expected to defend his own scientific integrity against his analyst's theories and practice, so that inherent in the training situation is a tendency to perpetuate error; how, no matter how ideal their own analysis, individual analysts tend to show at meetings and elsewhere their own conflicts and "favorite pathological mechanisms"; how these three factors lead to the stereotyped proceedings of the Psycho-Analytical Association; and how peculiarly susceptible to fashion, "canalized no doubt through a hierarchy of transferences and countertransferences" are psychoanalytic groups. He has the impression that present-day psychoanalytic teaching preserves many of the disadvantages of mid-Victorian pedagogy and few of its advantages, and that the deficiencies of such authoritarian spoon-feeding are not remedied, as is often thought, by the candidate's training analysis. He believes it is time these issues were faced, and that a first task of psychoanalysts is to settle down to the arduous task of defining terms, verifying criteria, and developing reliable statistics. His portrayal of the association

---

[1] It is interesting that Jaspers (1948), perhaps the most sophisticated and knowledgeable of modern psychiatrists, has no doubt in his own mind that, as far as therapeutic success is concerned, psychiatrists and psychoanalysts are decidedly inferior to all sorts of quacks and "headshrinkers." "Es ist selbstverständlich dass den grössten Erfolg nicht Nervenärzte, sonder—in früheren Zeiten—Schamanen, Priester und Sektenstifter, Wundermänner, Beichtväter und Seelenführer gehabt haben." He specifically quotes Ignatius Loyola, Yoga, Lourdes, and "die Gemütskurbewegung in Amerika."

between lack of scientific productivity and the psycho-analytic training procedure is that of a self-reinforcing system with tremendous internal resistance to change.

If this be true, and it is difficult to disagree with Glover on these points, then the task of those desirous of advancing to a truly scientific study of psycho-therapy will be made much more difficult than need be by the opposition of practitioners more interested in the preservation of the *status quo* than in new theories, new methods, and scientific advance generally.

REFERENCES

ALBRIGHT, S. and GAMBRELL, H., Personality traits as criteria for the psychiatric treatment of adolescents, *Smith Coll. Stud. Soc. Wk.*, **9**, 1–26 (1938).

ALEXANDER, F., *Five Year Report of the Chicago Institute for Psycho-analysis*, (1932–1937).

ALEXANDER, F., Current views on psychotherapy, *Psychiatry*, **16**, 113–123 (1953).

BARBOUR, R. F., Selected surveys prepared for the inter-clinic conference, in *Follow-up on Child Guidance Cases* Ed. J. F. Davidson, 49–59. Ninth Child Guidance Inter-Clinic Conference, London (1951).

BARRON, F. and LEARY, T. F., Changes in psychoneurotic patients with and without psychotherapy, *J. Cons. Psychol.*, **19**, 239–245 (1955).

BIXENSTINE, V. E., A case study of the use of palmar sweating as a measure of psychological tension, *J. Abnorm. (Soc.) Psychol.*, **50**, 138–143 (1955).

BOCKOVER, J. G., Moral treatment in American psychiatry, *J. Nerv. Ment. Dis.*, **124**, 107–194 (1956).

BORDIN, E. S., Ambiguity as a therapeutic variable, *J. Cons. Psychol.*, **19**, 9–15 (1955).

BOYD, R. V. and DI MASCIO, G., Social behavior and autonomic physiology. A socio-physiologic study, *J. Nerv. Ment. Dis.*, **120**, 207–212 (1954).

BRILL, N. Q., and BEEBE, G. W., A follow-up study of war neuroses, *Washington, V.A. Medical Monograph*, (1955).

BRONNER, A. F., Treatment and what happened afterward, *Amer. J. Orthopsychiat.*, **14**, 28–35 (1944).

BROWN, J. L., The follow-up procedure of an intermittent child guidance clinic, *Unpubl. Master's Thesis* (1931), quoted by Levitt.

BROWN, M., Adolescents treatable by a family agency, *Smith Coll. Stud. Soc. Wk.*, **18**, 37–67 (1947).

BURLINGHAM, S., A quantitative analysis of psychiatric social treatment carried out in seventy-five cases at the Institute for Juvenile Research, *Unpubl. Master's Thesis*, (1931), quoted by Levitt.

CAMPBELL, D. T., Factors relevant to the validity of experiments in social settings, *Psychol. Bull.*, **54**, 297–312 (1957).

CANADAY, L. J., A way of predicting the probable outcome of treatment of young children who run away, *Unpubl. Master's Thesis* (1940) quoted by Levitt.

CARMICHAEL, H. T. and MASSERMAN, T. H., Results of treatment in a psychiatric outpatients' department, *J. Amer. Ment. Ass.*, **113**, 2,292–2,298 (1939).

CARPENTER, J. A., Some factors relating to the method and outcome of case-work treatment with the adolescent girl when the girl herself is the focus of treatment, *Unpubl. Master's Thesis* (1939) quoted by Levitt.

CHRISTIANSON, E., GATES, M. and COLEMAN, F., A survey of the intake of a mental hygiene clinic with special reference to the outcome of treatment, *Smith Coll. Stud. Soc. Wk.*, **5**, 211–212 (1934).

COHEN, M. and DAVIS, E., Factors related to the outcome of treatment in a child guidance clinic, *Smith Coll. Stud. Soc. Wk.*, **5**, 212–214 (1934).

CRONBACH, L. J. and GLESER, G. C., Review: The study of behavior, *Psychometrika*, **19**, 327–330 (1957).

CUNNINGHAM, J. M. *et al.*, A follow-up study of children seen in a psychiatric clinic for children, *Paper read at Amer. Orthopsychiat. Ass., Chicago*, (1955) quoted by Levitt.

CURRAN, D., The problem of assessing psychiatric treatment, *Lancet*, **II**, 1,005–1,009 (1937).

CURRAN, D. and PARTRIDGE, M., *Psychological Medicine* (London, Livingstone, 1955).

DANSKIN, D. E., Roles played by counselors in their interviews, *J. Cons. Psychol.*, **2**, 22–27 (1955).

DE CHARMS, R., LEVY, J. and WERTHEIMER, M., A note on attempted evaluations of psychotherapy, *J. Clin. Psychol.*, **10**, 233–235 (1954).

DITTMAN, A. T., The interpersonal process in psycho-therapy: development of a research method, *J. Abnorm. (Soc.) Psychol.*, **47**, 236–244 (1952).

DOLLARD, J., AULD, F. and WHITE, A., *Steps in Psychotherapy* (New York, Macmillan, 1953).

ELDRED, S. H., *et al.*, A procedure for the systematic analysis of psychotherapeutic interviews, *Psychiatry*, **17**, 337–346 (1954).

ELLIS, A., New approaches to psychotherapy techniques, *J. Clin. Psychol.*, **11**, 208–260 (1955).

ELLIS, A., Outcome of employing three techniques of psychotherapy, *J. Clin. Psychol.*, **13**, 344–350 (1957).

ENGLISH, O. S. and FINCH, S. M., *Introduction to Psychiatry* (New York and London, Norton, 1954).

EYSENCK, H. J., The effects of psychotherapy: an evaluation, *J. Cons. Psychol.*, **16**, 319–324 (1952).

EYSENCK, H. J., *The Structure of Human Personality* (London, Methuen, 1953).

EYSENCK, H. J., A reply to Luborsky's note, *Brit. J. Psychol.*, **45**, 132–133 (1954).

EYSENCK, H. J., The effects of psychotherapy: a reply, *J. Abnorm. (Soc.) Psychol.*, **50**, 147–148 (1955).

EYSENCK, H. J., Personality tests: 1950–1955, in, *Recent Advances in Psychiatry* (London, Churchill, 1958).

EYSENCK, H. J., *The Dynamics of Anxiety and Hysteria* (London, Routledge & Kegan Paul, 1957).

EYSENCK, H. J. (Ed.) *Behaviour Therapy and the Neuroses* (London, Pergamon Press, 1959).

FENICHEL, O., *Ten years of the Berlin Psychoanalysis Institute*, 1920–1930.

FENTON, N. and WALLACE, R., Child guidance in California communities, *J. Juv. Res.*, **22**, 43–60 (1938).

FIEDLER, F. E., Quantitative studies on the role of therapists' feelings toward their patients, in *Psychotherapy: Theory and Research*, Ed. H. Mowrer, 296–315 (New York, Ronald Press, 1953).

FIEDLER, F. E., Factor analyses of psychoanalytic,

non-directive, and Adlerian therapeutic relationships, *J. Cons. Psychol.*, **15**, 32–38 (1951).

FIEDLER, F. E., A comparison of therapeutic relationships in psychoanalytic, non-directive, and Adlerian therapy, *J. Cons. Psychol.*, **14**, 436–445 (1950).

FIEDLER, F. E., The concept of the ideal therapeutic relationship, *J. Cons. Psychol.*, **14**, 239–245 (1950).

GALLAGHER, J. J., M.M.P.I. changes concomitant with client-entered therapy, *J. Cons. Psychol.*, **17**, 234–338 (1953).

GALLAGHER, J. J., Manifest anxiety changes concomitant with client-entered therapy, *J. Cons. Psychol.*, **17**, 443–446 (1953).

GLOVER, E., Research methods in psycho-analysis, *Int. J. Psycho-Anal.*, **33**, 403–409 (1952).

GLOVER, E., *The Technique of Psychoanalysis* (London, Baillière, 1955).

GOLLANDER, B., A study of overinhibited and unsocialised aggressive children: III. Later adjustment, *Unpubl. Master's Thesis* (1944) quoted by Levitt.

GREENHILL, M. H., *et al.*, Evaluation in mental health, *Publ. Hlth. Serv. Publ.* No. 413 (Washington, U.S. Gov't. Printing Off. 1955).

GREENSPOON, J., In, *Personality and Psychotherapy*, Eds. J. Dollard and N. G. Miller (New York, McGraw-Hill, 1950).

GROSSMAN, D., An experimental investigation of a psycho-therapeutic technique, *J. Cons. Psychol.*, **16**, 325–331 (1952).

HAMILTON, D. M., VANNEY, I. H. and WALL, T. H., Hospital treatment of patients with psychoneurotic disorder, *Amer. J. Psychiat.*, **99**, 243–247 (1942).

HAMILTON, D. M. and WALL, T. H., Hospital treatment of patients with psychoneurotic disorder, *Amer. J. Psychiat.*, **98**, 551–557 (1941).

HARWAY, V. I., DITTMANN, A. T., RAUSH, H. L., BORDIN, E. S. and RIGLER, D., The measurement of depth of interpretation, *J. Cons. Psychol.*, **19**, 247–253 (1955).

HATHAWAY, S. R., Clinical methods: Psychotherapy, *Annu. Rev. Psychol.*, **2**, 259–280 (1951).

HEALY, V., BRONNER, G. F., BAYLOR, E. G. and MURPHY, J. P., *Reconstructing Behavior in Youth: a Study of Problem Children in Foster Families* (New York, Knopf, 1929).

HOLTZMAN, V. V. and SELLS, G. B., Prediction of flying success by clinical analysis of test protocols, *J. Abnorm. (Soc.) Psychol.*, **99**, 485–490 (1954).

HUBBARD, R. M. and ADAMS, C. F., Factors affecting the success of child guidance treatment, *Amer. J. Orthopsychiat.*, **6**, 81–102 (1936).

HUDDLESON, J. H., Psychotherapy in two hundred cases of psychoneurosis, *Milt. Surg.*, **60**, 161–170 (1927).

HUNT, J. McV., Toward an integrated program of research on psychotherapy, *J. Cons. Psychol.*, **16**, 233–246 (1952).

IRGENS, E. M., Must parents' attitudes become modified in order to bring about adjustment in problem children? *Smith Coll. Stud. Soc. Wk.*, **7**, 17–45 (1936).

JACOBSEN, V., Influential factors in the outcome of treatment of school phobia, *Smith Coll. Stud. Soc. Wk.*, **18**, 181–202 (1948).

JASPERS, K., *Allgemeine Psychopathologie* (Berlin, Springer, 1913, 1948).

JOHNSON, L. and REID, J. N., An evaluation of ten years work with emotionally disturbed children, *Ryther Child Cent. Monogr.*, **IV**, (1947) quoted by Levitt.

JONES, E., *Decannual Report of the London Clinic of Psychoanalysis*, 1926–1936.

JONES, M. C., The elimination of children's fear, *J. Exper. Psychol.*, **7**, 382–390 (1924).

KESSEL, L. and HYMAN, H. T., The value of psychoanalysis as a therapeutic procedure, *J. Amer. Med. Ass.*, **101**, 1,612–1,615 (1933).

KLUMPNER, G. H., Army psychiatry in Korea following the cease fire agreement, *Amer. J. Psychiat.*, **112**, 260–269 (1955).

KNIGHT, R. P., Evaluation of the results of psychoanalytic therapy, *Amer. J. Psychiat.*, **98**, 434–446 (1941).

KOGAN, L. S., HUNT, J. McV. and BARTELIME, P., *A Follow-up Study of the Results of Social Casework* (New York, Family Ass. of Amer., 1953).

LA MORE, M. T., An evaluation of a state hospital child guidance clinic, *Smith Coll. Stud. Soc. Wk.*, **12**, 137–164 (1941).

LANDIS, C., Statistical evaluation of psychotherapeutic methods, in *Concepts and Problems of Psychotherapy*, Ed., S. E. Himie (London, Heinemann, 1938).

LEE, P. R. and KENWORTHY, M. G., *Mental Hygiene and Social Work* (New York, Commonwealth Fund, 1929).

LEHRMAN, L. J., SIRLUCK, H., BLACK, B. J. and GLICK, S. J., Success and failure of treatment of children in the child guidance clinics of the Jewish Branch of Guardians, New York City, *Jewish Bd. Guard. Res. Monogr.*, No. 1 (1949).

LEVINE, M., *Psychotherapy in Medical Practice* (New York, Macmillan, 1948).

LEVITT, E. E., The results of psychotherapy with children: an evaluation, *J. Cons. Psychol.*, **21**, 189–196 (1957).

LIPKIN, S., Clients' feelings and attitudes in relation to the outcome of client-centered therapy, *Psychol. Monogr.*, **68** (1954).

LUBORSKY, L., A note on Eysenck's article 'The effects of psychotherapy: an evaluation,' *Brit. J. Psychol.*, **45**, 129–131 (1954).

LUFF, M. C. and GARROD, M., The after-results of psychotherapy in five hundred adult cases, *Brit. Med. J.*, **2**, 54–59 (1935).

MAAS, H. S. *et al.*, Socio-cultural factors in psychiatric clinic services for children, *Smith Coll. Stud. Soc. Wk.*, **25**, 1–90 (1955).

MABERLY, G. and STURGE, B., After-results of child guidance, *Brit. Med. J.*, **1**, 1,130–1,134 (1939).

MASSERMAN, T. H. and CARMICHAEL, H. T., Diagnosis and prognosis in psychiatry, *J. Ment. Sci.*, **84**, 893–946 (1938).

MATARAZZO, J. D., *et al.*, The interaction chromograph as an instrument for objective measurement of interaction patterns during interviews, *J. Psychol.*, **41**, 347–367 (1956).

MATZ, P. B., Outcome of hospital treatment of ex-service patients with nervous and mental disease in the U.S. Veteran's Bureau, *U.S. Vet. Bur. Med. Bull.*, **5**, 829–842 (1929).

MEEHL, P. E., Psychotherapy, *Annu. Rev. Psychol.*, **6**, 357–378 (1955).

MILES, H., BARRABEE, E. L. and FINESINGER, J. E., Evaluation of psychotherapy, *Psychosom. Med.*, **13**, 83–105 (1951).

MORRIS, D. P. and SOROKER, E., A follow-up study of a guidance-clinic visiting list, *Ment. Hyg., N.Y.*, **37**, 84–88 (1953).

MORRIS, D. P., SOROKER, E. and BURRESS, G., Follow-up studies of shy, withdrawn children: I. Evaluation of later adjustment, *Amer. J. Orthopsychiat.*, **24**, 743–754 (1954).

MOSES, J., A study of overinhibited and unsocialised aggressive children: Part IV. The later adjustment of unsocialised aggressive children, *Unpubl. Master's Thesis* (1944) quoted by Levitt.

MOUSTAKAS, C. E. and SCHALOCK, H. D., An analysis of therapist-child interaction in child therapy, *Child Develpm.*, **26**, 143–157 (1955).

MOWRER, H., *Psychotherapy: Theory and Research* (New York, Ronald Press, 1953).

MURRAY, E. J., AULD, F. and WHITE, A. M., A psychotherapy case showing progress but no decrease in the discomfort relief quotient, *J. Cons. Psychol.*, **18**, 349–353 (1954).

NEUSTATTER, W. L., The results of fifty cases treated by psychotherapy, *Lancet*, **I**, 796–799 (1935).

NEWBURGER, H. M., The effect of group therapy upon certain aspects of the behavior and attitudes of institutionalised delinquents, *Unpubl. Ph.D. Thesis*, New York, (1952).

NEWELL, N. W., The methods of child guidance adapted to a public school system, *Ment. Hyg., N.Y.*, **18**, 362–373 (1934).

PARLOFF, M. B., KELMAN, W. C. and FRANKS, J., Comfort, effectiveness, and self-awareness as criteria of improvement in psychotherapy, *Amer. J. Psychiat.*, **110**, 343–351 (1954).

PHILLIPS, E. L., *Psychotherapy; a Modern Theory and Practice* (London, Staples, 1957).

POWERS, E., An experiment in prevention of delinquency, *Ann. Amer. Acad. Pol. Soc. Science*, 77–88 (1949).

POWERS, E. and WITMER, H., *An Experiment in the Prevention of Delinquency* (New York, Columbia Univ. Press, 1951).

RAIMY, V. (Ed.), *Training in Clinical Psychology* (New York, Prentice-Hall, 1950).

RAUSH, H. L., *et al.*, A dimensional analysis of depth of interpretation, *J. Cons. Psychol.*, **20**, 43–48 (1956).

REID, J. H. and HAGAN, H. R., *Residential Treatment of Emotionally Disturbed Children* (New York, Child Welfare League of America, 1952).

ROGER, C. A., *Counseling and Psychotherapy* (New York, Houghton Mifflin, 1942).

ROGERS, C. R. (Ed.) *Client Entered Therapy* (New York, Houghton Mifflin, 1954).

ROGERS, C. and DYMOND, R., *Psychotherapy and Personality Change* (Chicago, Univ. of Chicago Press, 1954).

ROSANOFF, A. J., *Manual of Psychiatry* (New York, John Wiley & Sons, Inc., 1947).

ROSENBERG, S., The relationship of certain personality factors to prognosis in psychotherapy, *J. Clin. Psychol.*, **10**, 341–345 (1954).

ROSENZWEIG, S., A transvaluation of psychotherapy: a reply to Hans Eysenck, *J. Abnorm. (Soc.) Psychol.*, **49**, 298–304 (1954).

ROSS, T. A., *An Enquiry into Prognosis in the Neuroses* (London, Cambridge Univ. Press, 1936).

SALZINGER, K., An experimental approach to the interview, *Résumés des Communications, XVth International Congress of Psychology*.

SANFORD, N., Clinical methods: Psychotherapy, *Annu. Rev. Psychol.*, **4**, 317–342 (1953).

SASLOW, G., Psychotherapy, *Annu. Rev. Psychol.*, **5**, 311–336 (1954).

SASLOW, G. *et al.*, The stability of interaction chronograph patterns in psychiatric interviews, *J. Cons. Psychol.*, **19**, 417–430 (1955).

SCHILDER, P., Results and problems of group psychotherapy in severe neuroses, *Ment. Hyg., N.Y.*, **23**, 87–98 (1939).

SHAGASS, C. and MALMO, R. M., Psychodynamic themes and localised muscular tension during psychotherapy, *Psychosom. Med.*, **16**, 295–314 (1954).

SHEPHERD, M. and GRUENBERG, E. M., The age for neuroses, *Millbank Mem. F. Quart. Bull.*, **35**, 258–265 (1957).

SHOBEN, E. J., Some observations on psychotherapy and the learning process, in, *Psychotherapy, Theory and Research*, Ed., O. H. Mowrer (New York, Ronald Press, 1953).

SHOBEN, E. J., Counseling, *Annu. Rev. Psychol.*, **7**, 147–172 (1956).

SOMMER, G. R., MAZO, B. and LEHNER, G. F., An empirical investigation of therapeutic "listening," *J. Clin. Psychol.*, **11**, 132–136 (1955).

STEPHENSON, W., *The Study of Behavior* (Chicago: Univ. of Chicago Press, 1953).

STRUPP, H. H., An objective comparison of Rogerian and Psychoanalytic techniques, *J. Cons. Psychol.*, **19**, 1–7 (1955).

TAFFEL, C., Anxiety and the conditioning of verbal behavior, *J. Abnorm. (Soc.) Psychol.*, **51**, 496–501 (1955).

TEUBER, N. L. and POWERS, E., Evaluating therapy in a delinquency prevention program, *Proc. Ass. Res. Nerv. Ment. Dis.*, **31**, 138–147 (1953) (Baltimore, Williams & Wilkins).

THETFORD, W. N., The measurement of physiological response to frustration before and after non-directive psychotherapy, *Amer. Psychologist*, **3**, 278 (1948).

THORNDIKE, E. L., *The Psychology of Wants, Interests and Attitudes* (New York, Appleton-Century, 1935).

THORNE, F. C., Rules of evidence in the evaluation of the effects of psychotherapy, *J. Clin. Psychol.*, **8**, 38–41 (1952).

VERPLANCK, W. S., The control of the content of conversation: reinforcement of statement of opinion, *J. Abnorm. (Soc.) Psychol.*, **51**, 668–676 (1955).

WALCOTT, G., A study of the present adjustment made by solitary children who had withdrawn into an imaginary world, *Unpubl. Master's Thesis* (1931) quoted by Levitt.

WATSON, G. and COMREY, A. L., Nutritional replacement for mental illness, *J. Psychol.*, **38**, 251–264 (1954).

WATSON, J. B. and RAYNOR, R., Conditioned emotional reactions, *J. Exp. Psychol.*, **3**, 1–4 (1928).

WATSON, R. I., Research design and methodology in evaluating the results of psychotherapy, *J. Clin. Psychol.*, **8**, 29–33 (1952).

WATSON, R. I. and MENSH, I. N., The evaluation of the effects of psychotherapy: I. Sources of material, *J. Psychol.*, **32**, 259–273 (1951).

WATSON, R. I., MENSH, I. N. and GILDEA, E. F., The evaluation of the effects of psychotherapy: III. Research design. *J. Psychol.*, **32**, 293–308 (1951).

WICKES, T. G., Examiners' influence on a testing situation, *J. Cons. Psychol.*, **20**, 23–26 (1956).

WILDER, J., Facts and figures on psychotherapy, *J. Clin. Psychopath.*, **7**, 311–347 (1945).

WINDER, C. L., Psychotherapy, *Annu. Rev. Psychol.*, **8**, 309–330 (1957).

WITMER, H. L., A comparison of treatment results in various types of child guidance clinics, *Amer. J. Orthopsychiat.*, **5**, 351–360 (1935).

WITMER, H. L. *et al.*, The later adjustment of problem children, *Smith Coll. Stud. Soc. Wk.*, **6**, 1–98 (1935).

WITMER, H. L. *et al.*, The outcome of treatment in a child guidance clinic: a comparison and an evaluation, *Smith Coll. Stud. Soc. Wk.*, **3**, 339–399 (1933).

WITMER, H. L. and KELLER, J., Outgrowing childhood problems: a study in the value of child guidance treatment, *Smith Coll. Stud. Soc. Wk.*, **13**, 74–90 (1942).

WOLPE, J., *Psychotherapy by Reciprocal Inhibition* (California, Stanford Univ. Press, 1958).

WOLPE, J., Reciprocal inhibition as the main basis of psychotherapeutic effects, *A.M.A. Arch. Neurol. Psychiat.*, **72**, 205–226 (1954).

WOLPE, J., Experimental neuroses as learned behaviour, *Brit. J. Psychol.*, **43**, 243–268 (1952).

WOLPE, J., Learning versus lesions as the basis of neurotic behavior, *Amer. J. Psychiat.*, **112**, 923–931 (1956).

WOLPE, J., Objective psychotherapy of the neuroses, *S. Afr. Med. J.*, **26**, 825–829 (1952).

YASKIN, J. C., The psychoneuroses and neuroses. A review of a hundred cases with special reference to treatment and results, *Amer. J. Psychiat.*, **93**, 107–125 (1936).

ZUBIN, J., Evaluation of therapeutic outcome in mental disorders, *J. Nerv. Ment. Dis.*, **117**, 95–111 (1953).

CHAPTER 19

Abnormal Animal Behaviour

P. L. BROADHURST

It does not seem necessary to apologize for the inclusion of the present chapter in this book. Most psychologists and many psychiatrists are by now familiar with the debt they owe to animal studies. If psychologists can point to one achievement of their infant science in which they can properly profess some pride, it is the development of modern learning theory, to which the contribution of animal studies does not need stressing. Here we are not primarily concerned with learning theory, but rather with animal studies which have been more influential in psychiatry than psychology. Since the earliest experiments involving experimental neurosis in Pavlov's laboratory before World War I, a body of work on this topic has accumulated, much of which purports to be relevant to human psychopathology. It is proposed to subject this literature to scrutiny in order to assess its worth and its relevance to the human field. In doing so, the status of the concept of experimental neurosis[1] will inevitably be called into question.

The field to be covered is somewhat arbitrarily defined. Abnormalities of behaviour produced in infrahuman animals by psychological or functional means will be included. Disorders of behaviour resulting from the ingestion of drugs, or from physical methods causing tissue damage, for example, cortical insult, and electroconvulsive shock, will be excluded, since they are treated elsewhere in this book. (*See* Chapters 17, by D. S. Trouton and H. J. Eysenck, 15, by R. A. Willett, and 16, by D. Campbell, respectively.) On the other hand, where such methods have been used in attempted therapy of abnormal behaviour,

they will be considered. Discerning readers will find other omissions: thus, audiogenic seizure phenomena —the so-called "neurotic pattern" rediscovered and described by Maier (1939), the advent of which was hailed as an alkahest for the all-too-solid problems in this field—will not be dealt with. A wealth of studies —Finger (1947), and Bevan (1955) review some two hundred papers—compels the conclusion that the convulsive phenomena observed are primarily a response to loud noise of high frequency, facilitated, in many cases, by middle-ear disease. Similarly no treatment will be found of "abnormal fixations" in learning situations. The evidence so far available (Wilcoxon, 1952) suggests that such "frustration instigated" behaviour (Maier, 1949) can be explained in terms of conventional Hullian learning theory, no new principle of the sort Maier (1956) advocates being necessary. Another omission is the neglect of the phenomena classed as "animal hypnosis." While our understanding of human hypnosis is still obscure, and it retains a flavour of the abnormal, there are no good grounds for regarding the immobility which may in some circumstances be induced in animals as examples of hypnosis. As Weitzenhoffer (1953) notes, the characteristic of hypnosis in humans is heightened suggestibility to verbal commands and statements. Even allowing for the absence of speech in lower animals, nothing remotely comparable has been reported. A fourth omission which may be detected is a lack of emphasis on those animal studies designed to confirm or refute some aspect of psychoanalytic theory. While some are superior to certain of the studies given prominence below, in that they are at least grounded in a theoretical position and so have greater heuristic potential, they are in general peripheral to the topic of this chapter. Usually they are concerned with an animal analogue of a psychoanalytic mechanism held to be operative in human development (Sears, 1943; Hilgard, 1956), and not with abnormal behaviour as such.

[1] The use of the term "experimental neurosis" is frequently avoided by authors who feel that its use, even when parenthetically protected, suggests acceptance of the implied identification of animal and human neuroses. They prefer circumlocutions such as "behaviour disorders"—seemingly innocuous, but in fact question-begging. Since much of this chapter is devoted to an attempt to examine the validity of the identification mentioned in cases where it is accepted, there is no special reason to avoid the term.

The Definition of Abnormal Behaviour in Animals

Fundamental to the topic of this chapter is the problem of the definition of abnormality in animals. One way of proceeding (Karn, 1940, 1940a) is to accept as experimental neurosis what the experimenter in question defines as experimental neurosis. This leads to the inclusion in other reviews of a paper by Carmichael (1938) which has absolutely no bearing on the topic, apparently because of the mention of the words "experimental neurosis." Some of the rats used as subjects in a maze learning study developed a resistance to running a new maze pattern: "In such cases, the animal's general behavior as indicated by head-turning, irregular movement, and the like, seemed typical of the behavior described by those who have set up so-called experimental neuroses in animals" (Carmichael, 1938, p. 162). That is all. If head turning is to be the sole criterion of neurotic behaviour, then centre-court spectators at Wimbledon would be ideal subjects for the investigation of neurosis in humans!

The alternative is to attempt to define criteria of abnormal behaviour applicable to animals, and then to apply them rigorously. This procedure is clearly superior to relying on the judgement of the individual investigator. In the absence of anything comparable to human neurosis or psychosis in animals in their natural or domesticated states, the selection of such criteria and their definition must inevitably be based on human experience. This is not to deny that bizarre behaviour is not seen in domesticated animals (Croft, 1951), but rather to stress the absence of a body of knowledge about such abnormalities, comparable with that available from human psychiatry (but *see* Melzack, 1952).

Fortunately, outstanding among studies of the problem (e.g. Hamilton, 1927; Foley, 1935; Lubin, 1943; Davis, 1954) Hebb's penetrating analysis (1947) has provided us with a set of criteria against which to evaluate behaviour thought to be indicative of experimental neurosis. For this purpose, he first defines human neurosis in behavioural terms which do not involve the use of the patient's verbal report of his subjective state, thus allowing the use of the definition at the animal level. To do so, he makes use of his concept of "associated signs" of emotion (Hebb, 1946), for the purpose of which a sharp distinction must be made between behaviour arising from a central state or event, and that central state itself— that is, between neurotic behaviour and neurosis, to which the advocate of the point of view represented by this book would add *neuroticism*, the factorial definition of the constitutional predisposition to the central state itself (*see* Chapter 1, by H. J. Eysenck). These latter two are, however, constructs designed to classify and to guide research: and it is the former,

neurotic acts, which are the associated signs of the central state. Hebb makes it plain that he is not seeking to establish what this neurotic condition essentially is; it is merely a stage in the search for criteria "to test whether a given disturbance of animal behaviour should be called neurotic."

His analysis of human neurosis along these lines leads him to advance the following definition: "Neurosis is in practice an undesirable emotional condition which is generalized and persistent; it occurs in a minority of the population and has no origin in a gross neural lesion" (Hebb, 1947, p. 11). This definition contains six elements which Hebb considers essential. Omit any one of them and the definition becomes too wide, thus—

> *undesirable* implies evaluationally abnormal— otherwise, e.g. exceptional love of sports is neurotic,
> *emotional* implies involving emotional activity— otherwise, e.g. laziness is neurotic,
> *generalized* implies shown in many ways, not solely in response to a specific excitant—otherwise, e.g. dislike of cats is neurotic,
> *persistent* implies chronic to some degree, especially persisting after the cessation of the specific excitant—otherwise, e.g. transient irritability or depression is neurotic,
> *occurs in a minority of the population* implies statistically abnormal—otherwise, e.g. emotional prudery is neurotic, and
> *no origin in a gross neural lesion* implies the absence of such physical causation as cortical insult —otherwise, e.g. emotional changes caused by brain damage are neurotic.

Hebb notes that though the first four of these criteria are inescapable, they are of different kinds. The fifth, statistical abnormality, he regards as in a sense accidental, being in fact dependent upon the current *mores*. If emotional prudery, for example, were shown to have the same origin as other aspects of neurosis, then neurosis might be said to occur in a majority of the population. The sixth criterion (absence of physical causation) resembles the previous one in being of doubtful theoretical value in the definition, but must be included because of the part both have played in clinical diagnosis of neurotic disorders.

Hebb rejects as components for inclusion in his definition—

> *neurosis has no known physiological base*—because, in his view, an aetiology dependent upon metabolic derangement does not change a diagnosis of neurosis *per se*;
> *neurosis produces a marked change of behaviour from an earlier base-line*—because this concept,

despite its profound influence on research, is not a necessary condition of neurosis; neither is

neurosis follows from some "traumatic" experience like conflict or frustration—because, though human neurosis can follow psychological strain it can also result from metabolic processes free from strain.

These three principles, Hebb feels, are not essentially true of human neurosis, though they have dominated much theorizing on the topic and have come to be accepted widely as intrinsically related to the neurotic central state. They will, nevertheless, be borne in mind so that the reader who disagrees with Hebb's estimate of their minor function will not feel cheated on that score. Another reason for the retention of these ancillary criteria is that the last two, at least, have occasionally so dominated animal research that positive evidence that the subjects' behaviour has changed after a putatively traumatic experience, has, *ipso facto*, been taken as evidence of experimental neurosis. Examples of this may be noted later.

Enough has been said to indicate that Hebb's analysis provides us with a powerful instrument for evaluating abnormal animal behaviour, especially with respect to its relevance to human studies. It is clearly of little use to argue about human abnormality on the basis of animal findings if such data are themselves not related to abnormality in the animal subjects used. True, the criteria which Hebb offers and of which extensive use will be made, are themselves derived from the human field. But no other course is at present available, and a reasonable anthropomorphism must operate in both directions, that is, not only in employing animal data to illuminate human behaviour,[1] but also in using criteria derived from our more extensive study of human behaviour to evaluate the animal data. In this way, it becomes possible to assess the suitability of such data for the constructions put upon them.

Early Russian Work on Experimental Neurosis

Priorities in science are rarely awarded accurately, and frequently what is stated to be "the first" later turns out to be "the second" or even "the third." This process appears to have started in connexion with the present topic, for, quite apart from the question of priority within Pavlov's own laboratory,

discussed below, we find that the claims of Itard to be the first to have produced an experimental neurosis are advanced (Landis and Bolles, 1949). He used colour and form matching tasks in training Victor, the wild boy of Aveyron, but had to give up when the required discriminations were made so difficult that Victor failed to respond and showed violent anger instead.

But, as is generally known, the idea of experimental neurosis originated with Pavlov. Most accounts give the name of Shenger-Krestovnikova (1921) as the first to observe an experimental neurosis. Her experiment, begun in 1914, is one of the classics of experimental psychology. A dog, conditioned to salivate to the appearance of a circle, but not to an ellipse, was trained to make finer and finer discriminations as the ellipse was made more and more circular. The disturbed behaviour which eventuated when the animal was no longer able to make the required discrimination Pavlov (1927) named experimental neurosis. But Sen (1953) points out that such behaviour had been observed previously in Pavlov's laboratory by Yerofeeva (1912, 1916, 1953), as is clear from the accounts of this early work by Pavlov himself (1927) and by his pupil, Gantt (1944). Yerofeeva's own account, though only published in abstract (1916) is therefore the pioneer report[1] of behavioural disturbances due to conditioning techniques, though, as Pavlov puts it: "The investigation of the higher nervous activity under difficult conditions, carried out in the course of M. N. Yerofeeva's experiments, unexpectedly resulted in the development for the first time of a chronic pathological state which, however, did not attract proper attention" (1927, p. 290). One might add parenthetically that the reason may have been that Pavlov's theory construction was not sufficiently advanced at that time to handle Yerofeeva's facts. On the other hand we must respect his statement that: "Possibly on account of the special nature of the stimulus used in these experiments, all these facts did not attract sufficient attention on our part" (Pavlov, 1927, p. 290).

The stimulus in question was electric shock used as a conditioned stimulus for a salivary response to meat powder, and the facts were these: the original

---

[1] This procedure implies a judicious anthropomorphism, which is inseparable from the use of animals as subjects for experimentation. It is frequently thought that the benefits deriving from such use—inevitable in, for example, selective mating, or experiments with large rewards or punishments—are only achieved at the cost of some clarity in the interpretation of the relevance of the findings to human psychology. But both Hull (1937) and Hebb (1947) have examined this problem, and conclude that cross-species identification of behaviour may properly be made if it can be shown that the principles or mechanisms governing the behaviour are the same. (*See also* Hebb and Thompson, 1954.)

[1] Available in the West, that is. For the study of much of this early Russian work on experimental neurosis, and on conditioning in general, we must rely on secondary sources and reviews—an unsatisfactory substitute for perusal of original research reports. This difficulty, which is not entirely a matter of a language barrier, has decreased recently with the publication of the English translation of Ivanov-Smolensky's important review (1954), of Liberson's review (1957), and of some further snippets of Pavlov's writings in the edition edited by Koshtoyants (1955). The writer, however, is sufficiently well aware of the difficulties preventing an adequate review of the interesting work going on in this field—*see*, for example, Zverev (1957) and Fonberg (1958)—to know that this chapter will certainly not do justice to it. He therefore apologizes for this omission and cautions the reader to bear it in mind.

unconditioned defence reaction to this shock, which Yerofeeva characterized as "strong," was abolished by training so that the shock became recognized by the subject as the signal for food, and gave rise to salivation, but when she attempted to generalize the response to other parts of the body than that originally stimulated by the shock, the defence reaction was restored, whatever area was now stimulated. The finding was confirmed on two dogs: the stimulation of new areas with the conditioned shock gives rise to general excitement "qui rend impossible tout travail de canalisation, et détruit tout le travail déjà fait" (Yerofeeva, 1916, p. 240). Note here this early hint of the Pavlovian emphasis on the abolition of previously elaborated simple conditioned responses as a criterion of the abnormal. The original state was only restored in one dog after a period of three months, and not at all in the other (Pavlov, 1927).

And there the matter was left until the well-known experiment of Shenger-Krestovnikova. What appears to have impressed Pavlov is that disordered behaviour similar to that found by Yerofeeva using electric shock was also found in an experiment employing more usual procedures. The programme of work then initiated which absorbed Pavlov's last fifteen years of life has been reported by him (1927, 1928, 1941) and by Ivanov-Smolensky (1954) on whose fuller account the following discussion is based.

The four phases in the study of experimental neurosis in Pavlov's laboratory comprise, firstly, the phase from 1922–5, in which methods used and forms of breakdown were studied and the reaction shown to depend on the dog's nervous "type"; secondly, the next phase in which the concept of overstrain of excitatory and inhibitory processes was developed, the theory of types revised, and phasic states described; thirdly, the last phase before Pavlov's death (in 1936) saw emphasis on changes in complicated patterns of conditioned responses and their inter-relationships; and, fourthly, since Pavlov's death, attention seems to have been concentrated more on the effect of experimental neurosis on other aspects of functioning—reaction to disease, or internal vegetative action—rather than on the neurotic behaviour itself.

After Shenger-Krestovnikova's experiment, the experimental work on neurosis was next taken up by Pavlov's distinguished colleague Petrova (1924, 1926), yet even her experiment appears to be only accidentally concerned with the topic. She was investigating sleep in two dogs chosen as extreme exemplars ("as judged by their general behaviour") of nervous systems based on the dominance of excitation, or of inhibition. To delay sleep on the stand, five diverse sensory conditioned stimuli were used, and delays of up to five minutes between signal and reward were achieved with the inhibitable dog. But with only two

minutes delay the excitable dog showed "general excitation," and with three "became quite crazy, unceasingly and violently moving all parts of its body, howling, barking and squealing intolerably" (Pavlov, 1927, p. 294). Practice with only one stimulus at a time restored normal responses, and delays up to three minutes were achieved: "The differences in the nervous systems of the two dogs was thus made clear," and the main object of the experiment altered to inducing abnormal behaviour by a disturbance in the "normal relations between the two antagonistic nervous processes." The technique of differentiation of positive and negative conditioned stimuli as used by Shenger-Krestovnikova, as well as others involving prolonged inhibition of the two dogs' responses, produced only transient general excitation in the excitable one. Accordingly the painful stimulus used in Yerofeeva's original work—electric shock—was employed. Again the dogs differed in their response to the shock initially but when the strength of shock was increased, delayed reflexes were "disturbed," and conditioned inhibition "incomplete." The consequent abandonment of the use of shock is surprising, if the purpose was in fact to produce disturbed behaviour: nevertheless inhibition continued to weaken so that the excitable dog gave responses to all stimuli, negative as well as positive. The same treatment led to the inhibitable dog developing responses to the shock quite easily, but with practice it led to a decrease in the salivary response to this as well as to all other stimuli. This process was repeated later, when the "ultraparadoxical" phenomenon was observed. This is Pavlov's descriptive term for the condition in which no response is made to positive stimuli, but only to previously negative ones. He clearly always regards this as evidence of abnormal cortical functioning.

Thus: ". . . in these two dogs with different types of nervous system, prolonged disturbances of the higher nervous activity which developed under precisely identical injurious influences took quite different directions. In the excitable dog the inhibitory function of the cortical elements became extremely weakened. In the quiet dog it was the excitation of the corresponding cells (since the stimuli were identical) which became extremely weak. In other words, two quite different types of neurosis were produced" (Pavlov, 1927, p. 299). Pavlov's ideas about the "type" of nervous system may be conveniently summarized as shown in Table XIX.1.

Ivanov-Smolensky notes that: "For some time after these experiments, the idea prevailed in the Pavlov laboratories that the character of the nervous breakdown as well as of the experimental neurosis evoked by it, depended mainly on the type of the animal's nervous system. However, as we shall see later, experimental facts obtained in the course of

TABLE XIX.1

PAVLOV'S TEMPERAMENTAL TYPES IN DOGS

(Adapted from Babkin, 1938)

"Type" of nervous system	Strength of nervous system		Balance of nervous system		Predominance in nervous system of		Susceptible to nervous breakdown	Type of experimental neurosis seen
	Strong	Weak	Balanced	Unbalanced	Excitation	Inhibition		
Sanguine	Yes		Yes				No	
Phlegmatic	Yes		Yes				No	
Choleric	Yes			Yes	Yes		Yes	Excitatory
Melancholic		Yes		Yes		Yes	Yes	Inhibitory

further investigations forced us considerably to revise this notion and to introduce substantial corrections" (1954, p. 100). About the same time Rosenthal (1926) precipitated in an inhibitable animal a disturbance of behaviour lasting several months and taking the form of extreme drowsiness. It followed when the inhibitory stimulus of a discrimination involving two tactile rhythms succeeded the excitatory one too closely. Kreps (1924) also produced an inhibitory breakdown by a tactile discrimination, as did Razenkov (1924) in a pioneer experiment on "phasic states" of the cerebral cortex—so called because of the display of phases of more, or less, disordered conditioned responses—by making a single transition from negative to positive conditioned stimulus. This disturbing combination was attenuated by repetition, so that by the fourth presentation no deleterious effect was observed. Siryatsky (1925) also found that discrimination of auditory stimuli occasioned the disappearance of established conditioned responses.

So far, the work in Pavlov's laboratory had been on disturbances produced by difficult discriminations or the temporal contrast of two sorts of stimulation. Rickman's work (1928) was novel because he used unusual or intense stimuli alone: "Experiments were carried out with an animal manifestly belonging to the inhibitory type of nervous system. The following stimuli were simultaneously applied to exert such unusual and intense functional influence upon the nervous system: (1) a loud rhythmic crackle produced by a rattle and resembling the crackle of gun-fire; (2) a sudden emergence in front of the dog of an unusual figure in a mask and fur coat turned inside out; (3) an explosion of powder near the stand; (4) a special swinging platform mounted on the stand and on which the dog was placed." Clearly this dog didn't like fireworks, hated swings, and didn't believe in Santa Claus, because "At the very beginning the animal started, rushed forward, instantaneously rose on its hind legs, set its forelegs against the food receptacle which was before its muzzle and became

rigid, its limbs extended, its head thrown back, its eyes wide open" (Ivanov-Smolensky, 1954, p. 102). A loud tone ended this posture and motor excitement followed for a fortnight, during which no conditioned or even unconditioned responses could be elicited. Re-introduction of the swinging platform caused excitement again: ". . . the neurosis was fully reproduced as if by the mechanism of conditioned reaction to one of the components of the initial pathogenic situation" (Ivanov-Smolensky, 1954, p. 103).

This animal was among those previously subjected to the well-known natural experiment of the Leningrad flood of 1924 so that its pre- and post-flood responses are known. The rescue from the flood exerted an inhibiting influence, judging from the animal's general behaviour (Pavlov, 1927), and this was confirmed by the performance of this particular dog in the conditioning situation. For eight months thereafter whenever the previously learned negative conditioned response was elicited it abolished all other responses. "The powerful and unusual stimuli arising from the flood increased the susceptibility of cortical elements to so great an extent that even a comparatively minute intensification of inhibition from the outside in the form of a conditioned inhibitory stimulus, rendered impossible for a long time any existence of positive conditioned reflexes under ordinary experimental conditions" (Pavlov, 1927, p. 318).

Speransky (1925) also profited by the flood. His dog, of the inhibitable type, appeared normal immediately after the flood, but a week later was restless and refused food. Though increasing the food deprivation had no effect, the presence of the experimenter had, and normal responses were restored after two months. Then, as in Rickman's experiment, a component of the traumatic situation was restored by allowing water to flow under the door of the experimental chamber. Pavlov writes vividly: "The animal jumps up quickly, gazes restlessly at the floor, tries to get off the stand and breathes heavily. The conditioned stimuli serve only to increase the general excitation, the animal declines the food" (1927, p. 315). Only several months further training restored conditioned responses to their former level. "Thus, the reproduction of a situation somewhat resembling the picture of the flood immediately evoked a new breakdown with the resulting pathological state; this convincingly proved that the first nervous breakdown in the given dog had been really caused by the flood" (Ivanov-Smolensky, 1954, p. 105). In one other dog, called "Brains" because of its facility in forming conditioned responses, Vishnevsky found disturbances of responses four months after the flood, though in this case they had also been seen before the flood (Pavlov, 1928).

Neither Pavlov, nor Frolov (1937), nor Ivanov-Smolensky review the Pavlovian work on experimental neuroses after its first phase in sufficient detail to permit independent evaluation. A further limitation is the current extension of the concept implied by the term experimental neurosis beyond Pavlov's original intention. Experimental neurosis for Pavlov appears to mean a neurosis within the experiment, or even a neurosis of the experiment (cf. Konorski's use of the term "neurotic state of the alimentary centre" (1948, p. 209) to describe the inhibition of eating, frequently met with in classical experimental neurosis); and some writers of Pavlov's school caution against an extension beyond narrow limits. Thus: "Such states were described by Pavlov as *experimental neuroses*; however, it would not be quite correct to regard them as full analogues of human neuroses and stop at that. While some of them actually are what we may call simplified models of human neuroses, others are not" (Ivanov-Smolensky, 1954, pp. 81–82), and: "The designation of these disturbances by the name of 'neurosis' does not mean that they are always of the same type or that they are the same as may be observed in human beings" (Babkin, 1938, p. 616). Nevertheless, Pavlov clearly shows in his writings that he thought them related to human psychopathology.

How then can we evaluate the experiments reviewed above, limited by our dependence upon secondary sources? It is not unreasonable to apply Hebb's criteria for abnormality, bearing in mind that deficiencies revealed may be due to faulty communication. In Table XIX.2, therefore, will be found summarized the main points of these experiments, as they relate to Hebb's criteria. To mitigate the inevitable arbitrariness in such a procedure the "benefit of the doubt" has usually been given to the Russian worker.

It is clear from the Table that a principal failing of this work in its putative relation to the abnormal is the lack of data about responses external to the experiment. Thus it is only by inference that we learn that the criterion of statistical abnormality of the responses of the dogs rescued from the flood may have been met. We are told that all the dogs were rescued from their kennels; if all had been equally affected we should no doubt have heard of it. Even more striking is the lack of information about the generalization of the abnormal behaviour—little being reported about the subject's behaviour outside the conditioning situation. This neglect throughout of the more purely behavioural aspects of the animals' response follows from Pavlov's conviction that his field of study was physiology and not psychology. For him the conditioned reflex method demonstrated the totality of the subjects' higher nervous activity, hence the paucity of detail about other aspects of behaviour. But Hebb has argued that the concept of human neurosis as a behavioural abnormality implies a response which has generalized beyond the causal stimulus. Without this, demonstrations of animal abnormality become less convincing, as they may, for example, be merely fear responses, and as such within the normal range. The available evidence suggests the verdict on this pioneer Russian work should be the Scottish one of "not proven."

American Work on Experimental Neurosis: Liddell and the Cornell Group

Several reviews of literature on the topic of this chapter already exist; in addition to Hebb's important contribution (1947), those by Babkin (1938), Cook (1939), Karn (1940; 1940a), Gantt (1944), Freeman and Watts (1944), Liddell (1947), Russell (1950), Patton (1951), Kupalov (1952), Pilgrim and Patton (1953) and Beach (1953) may be cited. The justification for adding another lies perhaps in the greater rigour of the approach adopted here, as well as in the growing recognition of the limitations of the results achieved by traditional methods (Harlow, 1956; Chance, 1957). Furthermore, the output of work appears to have passed its peak. Three major American contributions to the literature appeared in the early 1940s (Anderson and Parmenter, 1941; Masserman, 1943; Gantt, 1944). This productivity, originating in Liddell's pioneer work on conditioning in sheep (1926) and the establishment in 1929 of the Pavlovian Laboratory at Johns Hopkins University under Gantt, a translator and former student of Pavlov, has not been equalled since. It is proposed, therefore, to organize our discussion of the readily available literature around these three contributions, and pride of place, because of its range, novelty and volume, must go to the Cornell group associated with Liddell.

The story is told (in Tanner and Inhelder, 1956) of how Liddell was studying thyroidectomy in sheep and goats and found no effects on maze learning (1925, 1925a; Liddell and Simpson, 1925). He therefore

TABLE XIX.2
EARLY RUSSIAN WORK ON EXPERIMENTAL NEUROSIS

Experimenter	Date of work — Done	Date of work — Reported	Source of information	No. of cases	Techniques used — General	Techniques used — Specific	Hebb's criteria — Evaluationally abnormal	Emotional	Generalized	Chronic	Statistically abnormal	Not due to neural lesion	No known physiol. basis	Change from previous base-line	Followed trauma
Yerofeeva	1912	1916	Yerofeeva (1916), Pavlov (1927) and Ivanov-Smolensky (1954)	2, 3	Salivary conditioning to shock	Generalization of area used	1	1	?	1	?	1	?	1	1
Shenger-Krestovnikova	1914	1921	Pavlov (1927)	1	Salivary conditioning to visual stimulus	Differentiation	1	1	?	?	?	1	1	1	1
Petrova	1922–3	1924, 1926	Pavlov (1927)	2	Salivary conditioning to various stimuli, including shock later	Delayed reflexes, principally	1	1	?	?	?	1	1	1	1
Rosenthal	1922–3	1926	Ivanov-Smolensky (1954)	1	Salivary conditioning to cutaneous stimulus and "clashing"	Differentiation	1	0	?	1	?	1	1	1	1
Kreps	1923	1924	Ivanov-Smolensky (1954)	1	As above	Differentiation	?	0	?	?	?	1	1	?	1
Razenkov	1923	1924	Pavlov (1927)	1	Salivary conditioning to various stimuli	"Clashing"	?	0	?	0	?	1	1	1	1
Siryatsky	1923	1925	Ivanov-Smolensky (1954)	??	Salivary conditioning to auditory stimulus	Differentiation	?	0	?	?	?	?	?	?	1
Speransky	1924	1925	Pavlov (1927)	1	Salivary conditioning to various stimuli	Flood	1	1	?	1	?1	?	?	1	1
Vishnevsky	1924	?	Pavlov (1927)	1	Ditto	Ditto	1	0	?	1	?1	0	0	?	1
Rickman	1926	1928	Ivanov-Smolensky (1954)	1	?	Fright	1	1	?	?	?	1	1	1	1

1 means criterion apparently met
0 means criterion apparently not met
? means doubtful, or insufficient evidence to judge

turned to conditioned reflex methods for a more precise measure (Liddell and Simpson, 1926; Liddell and Bayne, 1927). This quickly led to the incidental and unintentional production of experimental neurosis in a sheep (Liddell and Bayne, 1927a), and the field of study changed. The techniques routinely used resemble the Russian, but differ in that the salivary reflex—difficult, but not impossible (Denton, 1957), with ruminants like sheep—was avoided, and the motor response to an electric shock to the foreleg, which appears as a brisk muscular flexion, used instead. This unconditioned response becomes associated in the usual way with a conditioned stimulus which then evokes it before, or in the absence of, the shock. In a study (Liddell, James and Anderson, 1934) of this motor conditioned response in the sheep, and four other species (dog, goat, pig and rabbit), it is claimed as an advance on Pavlovian procedure, because it is a more discrete event than salivation, and is easily quantified using a work accumulator (*see* Anderson, 1941 and Liddell, 1942, p. 191), though this device has not been consistently used. While physiological measures, such as respiration, heart rate and P.G.R., were recorded as well as movement of parts of the body other than that to be conditioned, only a few subjects of species other than sheep were used, and the normative data presented is inadequate, no statistic more refined than a range being given. From observations of the stressful aspects of the conditioned motor reflex procedure it is concluded that nervous strain develops when negative conditioned stimuli are introduced, restraint thus being required of the animal.

This point is developed in a paper on four cases of experimental neurosis in sheep (Anderson and Liddell, 1935). The first, briefly reported before (Liddell and Bayne, 1927), showed persistent movement of the conditioned forelimb during intervals between the stimuli when they were increased from ten to twenty during a period of six days. Moreover, contrary to its previous willingness to enter the laboratory, it now resisted and had to be forced in and on to the stand. Once there it was calm enough: "As soon, however, as the experimenter left the room the sheep began its fidgeting tentative movements of the left foreleg" (Anderson and Liddell, 1935, p. 334). Neither this sheep's thyroidectomized twin, nor two other non-operates were disturbed by comparable increases in conditioning practice. These comparisons are vitiated, however, by the operation in the first case, and the use of somewhat different conditioning signals in the second. Short periods of rest did not restore the former precision of the sheep's responses, but one and a half years away from the laboratory did. Resuming work with delayed responses precipitated further "interval activity" and resistance to experimentation. In a second sheep, the introduction of non-reinforced conditioned signals to be discriminated from the positive ones caused similar symptoms, still apparent five years later. In a third, good discrimination between different metronome rates was achieved; only when the different rates were presented in the same experimental session did the disturbed behaviour appear, and was present three years later. Rhythmical patterning of a simple discrimination caused similar restless and unmanageable behaviour in a fourth sheep, although it did not affect another similarly treated. Thus each neurosis was of an excitatory nature in Pavlov's sense, though passing through a premonitory inhibitory phase in two cases.

An apparatus devised for measuring heart rate outside the conditioning chamber, as well as inside it, represents a methodological advance by this group (Anderson, Parmenter and Liddell, 1939). By strapping to the sheep the chest-piece of a stethoscope attached to a long, flexible tube at the end of which the hidden experimenter listened, counting the beats,[1] records of heart rate of six sheep were obtained. Two of those whose experimental neurosis is described above are included in a group of four "neurotics," and there were two normals. The authors conclude: "Sheep in which an experimental neurosis has been developed reveal, upon examination, a cardiac disorder which is characterized by a rapid and irregular pulse and by extreme sensitivity of the heart's action to conditioned and other stimulation" (Anderson, Parmenter and Liddell, 1939, p. 100). Evidence for rapidity of pulse comes from a systematic though unspecified number of observations as shown in Table XIX.3, which may or may not indicate a statistically significant elevation of pulse rate. Evidence for irregularity and sensitivity comes from the experience of the observers in comparing the normal and neurotic sheep under different conditions, but since one of the "normals" became "neurotic" later (Anderson and Parmenter, 1941; Rose, Tainton-Pottberg and Anderson, 1938), the value of these comparisons is dubious. Thus recognition of the methodological advance is tempered by the absence of any satisfactory statistical treatment of the data collected. Unfortunately this criticism is also applicable to the major work of this group (Anderson and Parmenter, 1941).[2] In this monograph the series of

---

[1] In later work a cardiotachometer and a cardiograph were used.

[2] These strictures do not apply solely to the work of the Cornell group. Most of the work in this field is characterized by a poverty of experimental design, manifest in inadequate control, and the almost entire absence of quantitative data, appropriately analysed. Perhaps workers have been overinfluenced by Pavlov's manner of exposition as seen in translation. Typically, he makes a statement and then cites a detail of an experiment to support it. But not all investigators follow his manner of working, which involved scrupulously checking experimental findings (Babkin, 1951), and which to some extent renders statistical sophistication unnecessary.

TABLE XIX.3

THE PULSE RATE OF NORMAL AND NEUROTIC SHEEP UNDER NATURAL AND LABORATORY CONDITIONS

(From Anderson, Parmenter and Liddell, 1939)

	In animal quarters				In laboratory			
	Hourly diurnal observations				Observations every minute for 30 minutes		Observations every minute for 15 minutes	
	Range of pulse		Average pulse rate		Range of pulse		Range of pulse	Average pulse rate in 15-min period
	Day	Night	Day	Night	Noon	Midnight		
Normal Sheep								
Sheep 1 .	68–84	64–84	72	72	68–76	68–76	80–88	85
Sheep 11 .	56–80	56–72	70	65	60–72		74–88	80
			Average 71	. . .	compare with	. . .		Average 82
Neurotic Sheep								
Sheep 7 .	68–96	60–88	84	72	76–96	60–80	107–152	129
Sheep 8 .	80–104	72–120	87	89	76–88	80–112	88–136	111
Sheep "D" .	60–100	60–88	78	71	60–80	60–80	76–92	83
			Average 83	. . .	compare with	. . .		Average 107

cases of experimental neurosis is extended to ten (seven sheep, and three dogs) some of which had been reported before (Anderson and Liddell, 1935; Anderson, Parmenter and Liddell, 1939; Liddell, Sutherland, Parmenter and Bayne, 1936; Liddell, Sutherland, Parmenter, Curtis and Anderson, 1937; Anderson, 1939). All cases of experimental neurosis except one in a dog with whom a salivary conditioning method was used, resulted from motor conditioned reflex procedures. Three main topics are dealt with: the signs of neurosis, the methods which initiate and maintain it, and therapeutic procedures. Reproduction of polygraph recordings to illustrate the points discussed does not prevent the presentation from remaining anecdotal in flavour.

The signs of experimental neurosis are numerous. *Hyperirritability* showed as increased conditioned motor responses and startle responses. *Restlessness*, especially interval activity, is shown to be greater in a neurotic animal than in a normal, and in one sheep transferred from the reaction foreleg to the other.[1] The diurnal activity of the four sheep—two neurotic and two normal—was measured by means of a large activity platform, or a leg pedometer (Curtis, 1937a).

[1] An identical occurrence in two dogs also undergoing motor conditioning to shock (Drabovitch and Weger, 1937) hardly deserves the appellation of experimental neurosis since the authors explicitly deny any generalization—the dogs otherwise remaining normal.

The authors recognize that the resulting data are insufficient for exact comparison, principally because different breeds of sheep were used. Nevertheless, the figures suggest, not a greater total activity of the neurotics, but a decrease of the normal nocturnal rest: "The neurotic animal, like the neurotic human, is apparently a frequent sufferer from 'insomnia' " (Anderson and Parmenter, 1941, p. 37). *Postural changes* were prominent, especially among cases of inhibitory neuroses—now noted for the first time as occurring among sheep. In the conditioning situation one regularly adopted an unusual posture with concavely flexed back, and another extended the reaction limb instead of flexing it. One dog showed "pseudo-decerebrate rigidity" which allowed passive moulding of limbs into bizarre poses.

The records of *respiration* taken from many sheep suggest that the experimentally neurotic ones, as well as displaying a disordered rhythm, have an increased breathing rate, and a long-range pneumograph technique confirmed that these differences persist in the animals' living quarters. Data from systematic observation of respiration in twelve dogs suggest that the three neurotic animals had a higher breathing rate, but these data are inadequately presented for appropriate comparison. *Cardiac records* are taken as confirming previous findings, and reveal conditioning of cardiac responses. A curious inversion of the T wave (part of the P.Q.R.S.T. cardiogram complex) was observed in three sheep, but since only one was neurotic, the significance of this observation is not apparent. Another anomaly—the coupled heartbeat —seen in the cardiotachometer records of one neurotic sheep is probably an artefact to which this method of recording heart rate is prone. Another example, in this case recognized as a double recording of two (instead of one) aspects of the complex, is noted by James (1943). *Elimination* of urine and faeces in the laboratory was only observed among neurotic animals, and their *social behaviour* changed in the direction of greater solitariness, especially noticeable in the normally gregarious sheep. Neurotic animals occasionally attacked the experimenter, normal ones never. Maternal and sexual behaviour is briefly reported, but five of the seven sheep were castrated males. In later accounts of work on sheep, Liddell (1953, 1956) notes this deficiency, and characterizes the conditioning procedure as an essentially "castrating" one for the young ram, which is not tolerated by adult ones, two of whom became aggressive with a defence reaction (butting) to each stimulus (Liddell, 1951).

The conditioning procedures which gave rise to the signs of abnormal behaviour were, in order of importance, discrimination between positive and negative stimuli, experimental extinction of a positive conditioned response, and training according to a rigid time schedule. Liddell claims (1947, 1950, 1951) that this method, employing the positive conditioned stimulus only, is standard procedure for producing experimental neurosis, and even that the type of neurosis may be determined by the interval between the stimuli, five to seven minutes giving an excitatory and two minutes an inhibitory breakdown. Anderson and Parmenter only show that nervous behaviour was *maintained*—though for six years—by this method. Increasing the amount of practice as a method of producing breakdown is not now stressed.

Therapeutic procedures resemble Pavlov's, with emphasis on *rest* from experimentation and the use of *drugs*. "The periods of rest we have given our animals have ranged from one month to as long as three years. The result was somewhat beneficial. However, the improvement was of short duration once testing of the animal was resumed. The degree of improvement did not seem to be a function of the duration of the period of rest" (Anderson and Parmenter, 1941, p. 74). The effect of sedatives (sodium bromide, Sodium Amytal and ethyl alcohol) on the excitatory neurosis of one sheep is unclear from the few data presented. In a somewhat more extensive test, phenobarbital increased the magnitude of the conditioned motor responses, decreased the interval activity, and made the animal quieter in the barn. A similar effect had been found (Liddell, Anderson,

Kotyuka and Hartman, 1935, 1935a) in earlier work on four neurotic sheep in which the hormone, cortin, was used and its effect contrasted with that of adrenalin which decreased the magnitude of the response, and increased interval activity. Thyroxin is said to have no effect. These suggestive findings do not appear to have been followed up (Liddell, 1952a). *Spontaneous remission* of the neurosis in one old sheep aged twelve years may have resulted from senile changes, though in another case disordered behaviour persisted until death some thirteen years after it was first observed.

The admirable longitudinal approach of these authors is seen in the complete case histories of the subjects[1] which are appended to the monograph. The patient documentation of experimental and observational work over long periods—the shortest being two years in the dog, and five in the sheep—is unfortunately marred by the absence of any standard experimental approach. Procedures vary between subjects, and with the same subject from time to time. Considering that the subjects were of different species, and different breeds within species, it is not surprising that no new principles emerge from the plethora of observations. The need for precise standardization of experimentation on a sizeable number of subjects now appears to have been recognized (Liddell, 1950, 1950a). By means of central polygraph recording, ". . . our arrangements for conditioning six to eight sheep or goats simultaneously by automatic controls will enable us to observe and compare enough animals subjected to standard stress situations to arrive at statistically valid conclusions" (Liddell, 1950a, p. 166). Its use with four sheep of, however, varying ages and strains, led to another of the "accidental" experiments which abound in the literature on experimental neurosis. A fault in the electrical circuits caused a slight shock to be delivered to the foreleg with each click of the conditioned metronome signal in advance of the reinforcing unconditioned shock. Only after this was repaired and the "warning" shock no longer received did experimental neurosis quickly supervene in all cases (Liddell, 1950a). But no further behavioural details are given, nor have any other reports of the use of this ingenious procedure of simultaneously conditioning many subjects come to hand.

The Cornell group have also done work on two additional species, and further work on the dog. In these, strict Pavlovian techniques were not always followed. James (1943) used a conditioned avoidance technique (James, 1934); in his work on two dogs, and sought to introduce a conflict into the situation by

---

[1] The seven sheep reported to have developed experimental neurosis represent a quarter of a total population of twenty-eight tested. For the dogs, the figures are three out of twenty-six.

weighting down the foot which the dog had to with-draw to avoid shock. Thus, one Alsatian was at-tempting to lift over thirty pounds on its foreleg to avoid a shock of the maximum (unspecified) intensity. It does not seem remarkable that ". . . total flight and escape behaviour was released, signalled in the kennel by the entrance of the experimenter rather than a specific signal in the laboratory" (1943, p. 117). After six months rest, the first signal caused one dog to react so vigorously that it fell out of the harness (James, 1953). No data on other aspects of the dogs' behaviour are presented (Jensen, 1945).

The early work of this group on the pig is diffusely reported with few experimental details (Liddell, 1936; Liddell, Sutherland, Parmenter and Bayne, 1936; Curtis, 1937; Liddell, Sutherland, Parmenter, Curtis and Anderson, 1937; Liddell, 1938; Sutherland, 1939; Altmann, 1941). Liddell's own account (1942, 1944) relates how early attempts (Liddell, James and Anderson, 1934) to condition adult pigs required brute force to handle them, whereas training pigs when young succeeded. An instrumental conditioned response was used, one pig learning to lift the lid of a food box at the positive conditioned signal, and not to do so at the negative one, which was sometimes reinforced with shock to the foreleg. Only when the pig was punished with shock for opening the box before the positive signal, was abnormal behaviour precipitated. This finally took on an inhibitory nature; the pig delayed responding to the positive food signals—during which time it was unresponsive even to food on its snout (Liddell, 1938)—and finally ignored them altogether. Respiration was slow and deep (Liddell, 1951), and the pig's behaviour outside the conditioning situation ". . . showed a marked change from friendliness to irascibility, so that it was no longer to be trusted" (Liddell, 1942, p. 393).

Later Marcuse and Moore (1942, 1946; Moore and Marcuse, 1945) did careful work at Cornell on several aspects of conditioning in pigs. In only one case was abnormal behaviour observed (1944), but the authors doubt that this "tantrum behaviour" deserved the name experimental neurosis, since the pig still came to the laboratory willingly, and its heart rate during its vocal protests remained unchanged.

The interesting Cornell work on goats is even more diffusely reported than that on swine. In early work, positive and negative motor responses were con-ditioned in adult goats (Goldman, 1939), using a rigid time schedule, usually with a two-minute interval, between stimuli. Liddell (1947, 1949, 1950, 1951) notes that a "tonic immobility" was thus produced with rigid extension of the reaction foreleg. There was no cardiac conditioned response, and though respiration was disordered in the conditioning situa-tion, it was normal outside it (Liddell, 1951). The

condition persisted for seven years in one case and eight in another (Liddell, 1952). More recent work has employed the technique for conditioning in freely moving animals (Parmenter, 1940), and has been concerned with the protective effect of the presence of the mother goat against the effects of a rigid time schedule of conditioning in the young kid. The use of flexible suspensions permitted the experimenter to record activity and respiration and to shock the foreleg. At first the method of conditioned avoidance of shock appears to have been used (Liddell, 1951), the experimenter being present in the room with the kid, and turning off the shock if the leg was flexed to the conditioned signal. Later, training was begun with eight young kids, four of whom had their respective mothers with them, while their twin siblings underwent the same conditioning schedule (of ten seconds of darkness followed by shock every two minutes) alone in an adjoining room. The results reported (Liddell, 1950, 1950a, 1952, 1954; Patton, 1951; Tanner and Inhelder, 1956) show that after relatively few trials, compared with the precipitation of experimental neurosis in adult animals, a restriction of movement of the isolated kids occurred. One of the experimental isolates ceased sucking and died. Com-parable findings are reported in an experiment involv-ing twin lambs and their mother (Liddell, 1955). Liddell reports (1954) that two years later experimental neurosis was precipitated in the now adult goats from the experimental group merely by restraining them in a conditioning harness for two hours a day for twenty days, and giving signals every six minutes, whereas the adult controls were not so affected. It is to be regretted that all these suggestive findings, which have aroused widespread interest (e.g. Bowlby, 1951), do not appear to have been reported in detail, especially since the method of co-twin control is a powerful tool for the isolation of environmental effects.

How do the Cornell findings stand in relation to Hebb's criteria of abnormality? It is plain that many examples of behaviour reported are abnormal in the sense of being *evaluationally undesirable*, not only from the point of view of the experimenter and of the individual subject, but also from a broader biological standpoint. An example is the reduction in gregari-ousness in one sheep which, it is claimed (Anderson and Parmenter, 1941), led to its death when the flock was attacked by dogs. The *emotional* quality of many reactions is confirmed by the disordered physiological measures, and there is no evidence that the behaviour reported may be attributed to a *gross neural lesion*. The *persistence* of the disorders is well established. On Hebb's ancillary criteria the Cornell cases stand up well: there is usually *marked change in behaviour* from an earlier base-line, though established solely in terms of conditioned response measures, the behaviour outside the laboratory being observed casually or not at all. The selection of cases is not always beyond reproach in this respect, e.g. the use of a sheep for a study of experimental neurosis ". . . because of its atypical reactions outside the laboratory" (Anderson, Parmenter and Liddell, 1939, p. 98). The occurrence of *trauma or conflict* in most cases can be agreed, especially if Liddell's view (1942*a*) of the conditioning procedure as an essentially traumatizing one is accepted. But some difficulties arise with the important criteria of *statistical abnormality* and *generalization*, despite this group's laudable efforts in this latter direction. Two sorts of generalization may be distinguished in this connexion. Firstly, what might be termed system generalization, the involvement in the disturbed activity of segments of behaviour not specifically manipulated by the experimental procedures. This category is admittedly somewhat artificial, since the whole animal goes into the experimental situation, so all aspects of its behaviour may be modified, but one can point to certain ones unlikely to be thus modified, such as innate responses to stimuli remote from those used experimentally. Nothing in the work of the Cornell group suggests such an effect as, for example, the involvement of the urino-genital system of Gantt's dog "Nick" (*see* later). The failure of gregariousness noted in some sheep hardly qualifies, since isolation from the flock is itself a component of conditioning.[1] The emergence, or re-emergence rather, of cardiac, respiratory and motor disturbances in the experimental situation is less impressive because they are clearly components of the initial unconditioned reaction to electric shock. The fact that they re-emerged after being suppressed by adaptation to the situation is probably not of significance—change from a previous base-line not being an adequate criterion of neurosis—and on some views is exactly what one might expect, as will be shown later. The second kind of generalization may be termed situational generalization, that is, the temporal spread of disturbed behaviour to situations outside the experimental one. This Liddell has called "the subject carrying its troubles into the barn." Despite the surmounting of the difficulties involved in obtaining quantitative measures of physiological variables in the free situation, the evidence collected on this point fails to convince. The data are fragmentary, inadequately controlled and open to two fundamental objections as Hebb has noted (1947). The apparatus used to measure respiration, heart rate, etc., were themselves components of the laboratory situation, and may themselves have initiated the disturbances they

recorded by serving as conditioned stimuli for them. It may only seem that the sheep has carried its troubles to the barn because the experimenter has followed it there with part of the laboratory. This is a logical objection which can only be met by control data from longitudinal investigations of the measures in question *before* conditioning starts. It is not enough simply to compare neurotics with normals (Anderson, Parmenter and Liddell, 1939). The second objection is that the data on generalization were usually gathered during the period when the subjects were undergoing conditioning training and displaying signs of neurosis in the experimental situation. Regarding the neurotic animals' "insomnia": "Anxiety at night is not evidence of abnormal emotional functioning when the animal is exposed every morning to noxious stimuli" (Hebb, 1947, p. 13).

The evidence on the final criterion of statistical abnormality is even scantier, though it is allowed that it would be a large undertaking to establish the statistical abnormality of a behavioural response using animals larger than the rat. A reasonable quantitative expression of this criterion may be adopted from the human field: Fraser (1947) found that 10 per cent of an industrial population showed clinical signs of neurosis. Now, the evidence presented suggests that in the sheep—the species most studied—about 25 per cent developed experimental neurosis. Though the sample is still too small to allow anything less tentative, this figure seems more suggestive of a normal reaction to the stresses imposed, when the differences in its intensity and the almost certain differences in constitutional predisposition are considered. Thus, one sheep remained unaffected by conditioning procedures far more extensive and strenuous than those causing breakdown in others (Anderson and Parmenter, 1941). To sum up, it appears from the evidence reviewed that the Cornell group's efforts to establish the Pavlovian experimental neurosis on a firmer basis have produced equivocal results, and the reasons for this have been indicated. Liddell, however, believes that in some animals ". . . subjected to experimental procedures there is satisfactory evidence of a psychopathological state, i.e. a breakdown of the emotional mechanism" (1947, p. 571).

In considering Liddell's theoretical formulation of the causation of the disorders he and his colleagues have studied, it should be noted that he has consistently avoided the cross-species identification implicit in Pavlov's term experimental neurosis, which he regards as unfortunate (1950). Nevertheless, he does contend that the behaviour is abnormal, and further that it has relevance for human psychopathology: "It may be regarded as the anlage or prototype of the elaborately differentiated forms of human abnormality.

---

[1] The use of a "social sheep" during conditioning, mentioned in the early Cornell work, appears to have been dropped later, though Liddell's later work on maternal deprivation apparently begins systematic exploration of this rather obvious variable.

Like them, however, it may be self perpetuating and persist until death" (Liddell, 1947, p. 572). What then, in Liddell's view, is the origin of this disorder? It stems from the view he has developed of the conditioning procedure as in itself constituting a stress situation. "The conditioning procedure which we regarded as innocuous" (in 1927) "apparently meant murder to the sheep" (1956, p. 74) because "during the past ten years we have become convinced that all conditioning procedures which are based upon the animal's self-imposed restraint will, if long enough continued, cause that animal to become experimentally neurotic" (1956, pp. 66–67). If *all* animals broke down, then that would, *ipso facto*, be the normal reaction, of course. But Liddell probably had in mind the view that, given sufficient stress, all humans would develop neuroses.

The self-restraint of the trained animal conceals a tense expectancy. For this he uses Head's term "vigilance" which approximates to Pavlov's investigatory reflex. Vigilance, rather than the unconditioned stimuli of shock or food, ". . . supplies the power for both positive and negative conditioned reflex action. If this hypothesis proves to be sound it will lead us to another. We may then suppose that when the capacity for maintaining intense and unremitting vigilance is exceeded (for example, during long-continued and difficult regimens of conditioning) the pent-up nervous tension thereby released will disrupt the operation of the complex and delicate conditioning machinery and lead to chronic states of diffuse or congealed vigilance—experimental neurosis" (Liddell, 1950*b*, pp. 189–190). Among the further stresses which the experimenter can add to this vigilance, Liddell identifies loneliness, monotony, confusion and over-stimulation—examples of which have already been cited. The inhibitory type of neurosis—"tonic immobility"—was regarded ". . . as a state of congealed vigilance. The alarm reaction here appears to be frozen" (1951, p. 145). The excitatory type was regarded as a state of diffused vigilance, though in the most complete statements of Liddell's theory (1955, 1956) the former is now a precursor of the latter.

This brief outline probably does injustice to a theory based on a lifetime of experimental observation and experience, especially as our account of the work which nurtured it has not stressed experiments which are regarded as confirmatory, such as the accidental circuit fault which gave subjects a preliminary shock. Disorders developed only *after* the restoration of the signal to its putative role of tension arouser, unrelieved by the inadvertent shocks. Similarly a rise in tension or vigilance can be seen in indicators such as respiration rate during long conditioning sessions, even in well-trained animals (Liddell, 1951). But it must be said that the theory is not formulated in precise enough terms to have heuristic value; few testable deductions flow from it. Only Parmenter (1940, 1940*a*) has made such attempts. He showed that the absence of the restraining harness altered responses in a well-trained sheep. Among other omissions, however, he did not attempt to show whether it was more difficult to precipitate neurosis in untrained sheep by this method of no restraint. Apter (1952) claims to have done so in dogs, though Kaminsky's findings on monkeys (1939) apparently support Liddell. Secondly, Parmenter evolved a method of rapid experimental extinction in one sheep by stopping the conditioned stimulus when the response seemed imminent, thus ending the sheep's "uncertainty" sooner. But since other sheep extinguished without disturbance the support this gives to Liddell's theory is not clear.

The Work of Gantt

The work of the second major researcher in the field, Gantt, is Pavlovian, as might be expected from his training, yet, like Liddell, he is concerned with the problem of the generalization of conditioned neuroses. He, too, appears not to have been primarily concerned with abnormal behaviour at first, but in the course of his conditioning work on dogs accidentally provoked experimental neuroses which appeared to resemble those reported by Pavlov. The accumulation of data on novel aspects of the abnormal behaviour led him to organize his earlier and frequently brief reports (1936, 1938, 1940, 1940*a*, 1942; Gantt and Muncie, 1941) into his important monograph contribution (1944). This is his "monumental study of his experimentally neurotic dog, Nick (the most meticulous and complete case history of a single animal to be found in the conditioned reflex literature)" (Liddell, 1951, p. 127).

Using dogs as subjects for salivary conditioning with food or acid injected into the mouth as the unconditioned stimuli, Gantt reports on the effect of natural emotional shocks. *Parturition* in bitches disturbs differentiated conditioned responses temporarily. An *accidental disturbance*, comparable to the Leningrad flood, occurred one week-end when some fifteen dogs escaped from their quarters and roamed the building, barking and fighting. One young collie, judged of an inhibitory labile type, showed subdued behaviour and disturbed conditioned responses for a week; in two other dogs studied, the changes were short-lived. Further *fighting*, both accidental and experimentally provoked, caused temporarily altered behaviour. *Restriction* of freedom in a cage eight feet square caused a severe diminution of activity in one young bitch, who died after four months.

Experimental procedures which may give rise to disturbed conditioned responses were next considered.

Conflict of drives was studied by observing the deleterious effect of a female in oestrus on the alimentary conditioned responses of two male dogs. *Conflict of excitatory and inhibitory* conditioned stimuli is a potent source of disturbance. Unlike Liddell, Gantt does not think the restraint involved important. *Changes in conditioning routine*, e.g. the temporal patterning of stimuli (Gantt, 1940), or during experimental extinction, may cause agitated behaviour. But the major part of the work is devoted to the case histories of three dogs who reacted to approximately the same experimental procedures with different degrees of disturbance.

Fritz, a male Alsatian, was a stable, somewhat aggressive animal who developed conditioned differentiation to tones of different pitch. When the discrimination was made more difficult two years later, he showed some disturbance, barking and panting, and a loss of the conditioned responses. More radical measures, such as putting him in a swing and causing explosions, brought only temporary disturbance. After another two years a tactile differentiation was easily achieved, and the responses to auditory stimuli well retained. He died of old age in 1938, after seven years work in the laboratory. At no time did Fritz shun the experimenter or the experimental room, always ate food offered there, and displayed normal sexual activity. The second dog, Peter, was a male beagle, active and playful. In 1931 though he formed rather unstable salivary responses to the same tones as Fritz quite quickly, he barked somewhat. The initial stages of the same discrimination were successfully accomplished; when made more difficult, however, he howled, refused food in the experimental room, and had to be coaxed to enter it. Next year all conditioned responses disappeared and he had to be forced into the room. He became quieter later, resumed eating and, while the use of the swing and explosions produced disturbances, short rests from work restored normal behaviour. After a further rest of one and a half years, he was quiet and gave conditioned responses. He was killed in a fight in 1936.

The case history of the celebrated Nick is longer—he was studied for twelve years—and shows even more severe disturbance of behaviour. He was a male mongrel, about three years old, and active and playful when work began in 1932. "Nothing was noted that impressed one as remarkable; in fact he was selected with Fritz and Peter for laboratory work, as being, according to general appearances, normal" (Gantt, 1953a, p. 77). He was more restless than most dogs during adaptation to feeding in the experimental room, and slow in showing the conditioned salivary response, with restlessness and whining. When the auditory differentiation was introduced he refused food and showed defence reactions. A rest restored food acceptance, but with an increase in the difficulty of the discrimination, he refused it again (October, 1932) and he ". . . continued to refuse it practically during his whole laboratory life . . . in spite of over 10,000 presentations of (the conditioned stimulus) and food" (Gantt, 1944, p. 53). His negativism in this respect contrasts with Fritz's behaviour, and persisted despite an increase in hunger drive. The added restraint of a Pavlov harness did not affect him.

In the following year all conditioned responses failed, and a definite physical progression in the inhibitory effect of the experimental room was observed; Nick would eat the more readily the farther he was away. In the room he showed a stereotyped restlessness, frequently seen afterwards, whenever he was released from the apparatus. It consisted of rushing around, jumping up on the table and off it again, and barking at, fumbling in his mouth, and dropping, the uneaten food. The additional strain of the swing and the explosions did not exacerbate the behaviour, but neither did injections of cortin nor a three weeks rest from experimentation improve it. A further rest of two years (1934–1936) caused only a slight improvement as judged by his eating and the temporary restoration of conditioned responses. To ameliorate his condition, Nick was fed the whole of his meat ration in the experimental room every day for seven months in 1936. This attempt at therapy failed; indeed, Nick showed fresh abnormalities, involving other physiological systems. Disturbed respiration took the form of "loud, forced breathing," which was heard whenever he was excited, especially when approaching the experimental room or people connected with the experiment. The disturbance in social behaviour thus demonstrated is characteristic of Nick; Gantt repeatedly noted that he was friendlier towards strangers than towards anyone associated with the experimentation on him. Other disturbances became apparent at the end of 1936; Nick would start urinating when being brought to the experimental room where the frequency was as much as twenty-five times in thirty minutes. This exaggeration of a male canine habit was unaffected by punishment. Concurrently, abnormal sexual excitation—as judged by penile erection—was observed during conditioned stimulation, or even occasioned, apparently, by the experimental setting itself. These persistent sexual erections contrasted with the occasional short erection seen in young male dogs, especially in spring or when excited.[1] A further piece of unusual behaviour, noted around this time and which persisted for at least six

[1] Both the urinary and sexual abnormalities occurred after a bitch in oestrus had been used in the experimental situation in order to test the effect of normal sexual excitation upon Nick's other abnormal signs.

years, was Nick's habit of reacting—with defence movements, gazing, etc.—towards the place where the auditory signal *previously* came from, after its location had been changed. Pavlov (1941) mentions a similar occurrence in an experiment by Filaretov.

The rest of Nick's history—he died in a fight in 1944—was devoted to a study of his abnormalities, which did not proliferate further but fluctuated in intensity. New methods of investigation and therapy were tried. Generalization within the experimental situation was demonstrated by the prompt conditioning of Nick's responses when a new stimulus, a visual one, was given in association with the tone. Wide generalization outside the situation was observed, especially on Gantt's farm in the country, where Nick was kept for periods of two and seventeen months during 1937 and 1939–41 respectively, in that the particular food given as reinforcement in the experimental situation was consistently refused there, and sexual erection, pollakiuria, disturbed respiration and a marked increase in heart rate were sometimes observed at the approach of people previously associated with the experimentation, or even members of their families.

The rests in the country were therapeutic to the extent that afterwards the anxiety and stereotyped responses in the experimental room were lessened, though after the longer one this may have been part of a general improvement due to advancing age or to a change in method. In 1942 a motor conditioned response, using shock to the paw as the unconditioned stimulus was developed, to see if altering the response involved would prove beneficial. Unfortunately, the experimental room was also altered. The change was striking: the positive conditioned response to a tone (though not the same one as originally used) was developed readily, and some progress towards differentiation was even made. Moreover, Nick was quieter and without the sexual and respiratory disturbances which could, however, be reinstated on visits to the old experimental room. The new routine had, therefore, ". . . extinguished the pathological anxiety reactions to the specific auditory signals but it had not abolished the effect of the total environment of (the former room)" (Gantt, 1944, p. 99), which latter is hardly to be expected in view of the change in location.

The therapeutic effect of normal sexual activity outside the experimental situation was investigated by caging Nick with a female in oestrus. Less anxiety was displayed and measurement of cage activity showed a decrease. Sexual activity inside the experimental situation, however, showed a reciprocal relation with the anxiety reactions. In the presence of an oestrous female or during artificial sexual stimulation by means of electric stimulation of the external genitalia, the conditioned signal produced no reactions and its effect was diminished for some time afterwards if ejaculation had occurred. On the other hand, the experimental environment affected the sexual reflex itself. In an attempt to quantify this effect on the latency and duration of Nick's sexual response to the artificial stimulation, control measures were taken outside the experimental situation and also upon two normal dogs in both situations. The data, though inadequate for satisfactory analysis, suggest that the experimental room decreased Nick's latent period for ejaculation and duration of erection, whereas there were no marked changes in the control dogs. The effect of alcohol on Nick's disturbed behaviour was also observed (Gantt, 1940, 1952) and appeared to abolish the anxiety responses to the tone temporarily. Nick showed a greatly diminished sensitivity to the effects of adrenalin (Gantt and Freile, 1944).

In further contributions (1953; Gantt and Dykman, 1957) Gantt briefly describes another dog, V 3—"the most persistently neurotic of any dog we have had" (Gantt, 1953, p. 154). This male French poodle, born in the laboratory, had always been shy and fearful (Gantt, 1953*a*) and showed a stereotyped pattern of activity in rushing in and out of the experimental room, but a passivity on the experimental stand when limbs were retained in unusual positions in which they were placed, and the dog was apparently insensitive to pain. Since this occurred without any conditioning procedure beyond the use of restraint, it suggests a spontaneous, as opposed to an experimental, neurosis (*see* Fuller, 1947). The only experimental work reported was a study of the effects of alcohol on V 3's sexual reflexes, which, atypically, could only be elicited under the influence of this drug. His frightened behaviour was also thereby alleviated.

Gantt, though he does attempt to quantify certain behaviour, shares with the Cornell group a tendency to present inadequate data which have not been subjected to proper analysis, making unequivocal conclusions impossible. Thus most of the work reviewed here is observational or even anecdotal in character. He has a distressing technique which may be termed "evidence by appeal to the bystander." One example will suffice: he deems it worthy of report that ". . . two boys aged 7 said apropos of his (Nick's) raucous breathing, 'Gee that dog certainly does breathe funny'." (Gantt, 1944, p. 102). Moreover, the design of the experiments undertaken is not beyond criticism, as has been indicated. Gantt's use of the longitudinal approach with Fritz, Peter and Nick is a praiseworthy contribution but would have been more informative if all subjects had been from the same litter, or at least from the same breed. Again, one has the impression of an experiment turning into a study of neurosis by accident, since

Nick was originally selected for his apparent normality. Having shown disturbance, he was used, one has the further impression, mainly for demonstration purposes, and the therapeutic aspects perhaps not explored as thoroughly as otherwise might have been the case. On the other hand, Gantt in his Foreword (1944) doubts if the understanding of conditioning in physiological terms, despite the important contributions which he has made and continues to make (1957), is sufficiently advanced to evaluate abnormal behaviour in such terms. Hence his recourse to description in "behavioral terms." But there are, and indeed were in 1944, grounds for believing that behavioural measures, especially in the laboratory, may be objectified and quantified.

Hebb's criteria are easily applied to Gantt's work. Thus, Nick's behaviour was frequently *evaluationally undesirable*, e.g. his refusal of food when hungry, and was markedly *emotional*, judging by overt signs. We know from the autopsy report Gantt gives (1944) that he had *no gross neural lesion*. The persistence of disorders is strikingly well established in Nick's case, as is their *generalization* to situations other than the experimental. Their generalization to systems other than those especially concerned in the original conditioning appears as confirmation of their abnormal character, but there are dubious features about this as will be shown later. Considering two of Hebb's ancillary criteria, the *change from a previous base-line* is well seen in Nick though less well in V 3, just as is the presence of *trauma or conflict* in their history. It is in connexion with the criterion of *statistical abnormality* that reservation must be made. Gantt does not say from what total these two cases came; it is clear it must have been a substantial number, thus yielding a figure probably less than the 33 per cent implied by his presentation of the three cases of Fritz, Peter and Nick, only one of whom became neurotic. On the other hand the selection of these three for their apparent normality originally may have depressed this figure, and we are thus left in doubt. Nevertheless, we may say that Gantt's work, while not entirely satisfactory on all counts, comes closest of those so far reviewed in this chapter to meeting Hebb's criteria of abnormality which can probably be related to human neurosis.

Gantt's theoretical views (1953) employ two fundamental concepts: "schizokinesis" and "autokinesis." The former, originally called "dysfunction," implies a cleavage in response between the emotional and visceral systems and the skeletal musculature, and has its origins in observations, especially of cardiac function, suggesting that cardiac conditioned responses are formed more quickly than motor ones, are of comparatively greater intensity, and are more resistant to extinction (Gantt, 1942a, 1946, 1948; Gantt and Hoffman, 1940; Gantt and Muncie, 1941; Gantt and Traugott, 1949; Gantt and Dykman, 1952, 1957; Gantt, Hoffman and Dworkin, 1947; Gantt, Gakenheimer and Stunkard, 1951; Robinson and Gantt, 1946, 1947; Owens and Gantt, 1950). Consequently large emotional and endocrine responses may persist after the need for the appropriate accompanying motor response has passed. "Autokinesis" refers to the internal development of responses on the basis of old excitations, as seen in the spontaneous restoration of extinguished conditioned responses and the appearance of signs of experimental neurosis long after the causal conflict has been removed.

Gantt's theoretical formulation has some of the same characteristics as Liddell's. It is too imprecise to provide testable deductions, and some of the facts it endeavours to subsume are insecure. This especially applies to schizokinesis as is seen in a well-designed study with proper statistical procedures by Dykman, Gantt and Whitehorn (1956), previously reported in brief (Dykman and Gantt, 1951, 1951a). Four dogs were each given motor conditioning (leg flexion) to three intensities of shock as the unconditioned stimulus. In addition to measures of latency and amplitude of the motor response, cardiac and respiratory records were taken, though only the analysis of the former is reported. The results clearly show the development of a differential motor response—larger and swifter, usually at a satisfactory level of significance, the greater the shock stimulus, and a differential cardiac conditioned response was also detected. However, the cardiac conditioned responses did not develop more quickly than the motor ones, and the differentiation observed did not proceed faster in the cardiac than in the skeletal system. Unfortunately, no systematic study of the extinction of the conditioning was reported. The authors do say, however, that after a month two subjects showed unimpaired differentiation, presumably of both motor and cardiac responses. These findings from a well-designed and adequately analysed experiment run counter, therefore, to expectations based on the schizokinetic principle, itself elaborated from data from experiments, which, as judged by the brief reports cited above, were less well controlled. This suggests that the concept of schizokinesis itself may need revision.

The Work of Masserman

The contribution of the third major American worker in the field of abnormal animal behaviour, Masserman, is based on a psychoanalytic interpretation of behaviour, and so differs markedly from that of Gantt and Liddell, both of whom began as Pavlovians. An example of the lengths to which Masserman is prepared to go is his interpretation of Yerofeeva's experiment, in which shock was used as a conditioned stimulus (*see* page 728), as a demonstration of animal "masochism" (Masserman, 1943, pp. 176–177; Masserman and Jacques, 1948). This approach is one to which the writer is unsympathetic; the reader is therefore, cautioned against this bias. Moreover, Masserman is avowedly anthropomorphic (1942, pp. 345–346) in a way which is rightly eschewed nowadays.

Masserman's research is presented in numerous articles, but especially in his book *Behavior and Neurosis* (1943), which also reports on his work in experimental neurophysiology which will not be discussed here. For his experiments on neuroses in cats, less fully reported earlier (1942), he used a learned motor response to a warning stimulus. This response, the lifting of the lid of a food trough to secure food, had been employed by Sutherland and others in work on the pig (*see* page 736), but more extensively by Dworkin and his associates, including Sutherland, at McGill University in Montreal, in a series of experiments on the auditory capacities of the dog and the cat (Dworkin, 1935, 1935a; Dworkin, Seymour and Sutherland, 1934; Dworkin, Katzman, Hutchinson and McCabe, 1940; Davis, Dworkin, Lurie and Katzman, 1937; Dworkin, Baxt and Gross, 1942). As several cases of experimental neurosis eventuated from the use of this method, some account of Dworkin's work—itself almost a major contribution to the field—will serve as an introduction to that of Masserman.

The cats were restrained in a cage (large enough to allow free movement) in which there was a food box into which a piece of food was automatically delivered by a rotary feeder, after an auditory signal had sounded. The arrangements for dogs were similar, except that they were confined in a Pavlov harness before the food box. The lifting of the lid of the food box was regarded as the response in the trained animal, and in studies of auditory thresholds indicated that the subject had heard the tone. In discrimination studies, opening the lid indicated that the subject had recognized the positive signal—the negative one not being followed by food. Both these procedures gave rise to disturbances in both species (Dworkin, 1938, 1939). Tests of pitch discrimination involved increasingly difficult judgements as the positive and negative tones were made more alike, and in two dogs caused a progressive inhibition of the alimentary response, failure to eat the food offered, even when very hungry, and restlessness, barking and whining in the experimental situation. One dog developed a marked flexion of the left foreleg, obviously thinking it was at Cornell, not McGill! Periods of rest did not restore responses, but no unusual behaviour was observed outside the experimental situation. In cats disinhibition was observed; they responded to the negative signals as well as the positive. However, they never refused food, nor showed any other sign of disturbance.

The tests of auditory acuity involved presenting the subjects with very weak tones: four out of seven dogs showed progressive inhibition of response, first to the weak tones, but later to all stimuli, so that after four to six months two of them remained stock still in their harness, not asleep, but insensitive to all but unusual stimuli. Rest had little effect, but drugs (including alcohol, Sodium Amytal, Avertin and Nembutal) had beneficial effects in certain cases (Dworkin, Bourne and Raginsky, 1937, 1937a; Dworkin, Raginsky and Bourne, 1937). In the reactions of thirty-four cats to the same procedures, Dworkin distinguished three groups. Firstly, nine animals went through the whole experiment with no disturbances. Secondly, a group of four cats who developed inhibition to superthreshold tones after being exposed to faint ones, and showed stereotyped movements and attempts to escape. The third group, the remaining twenty-one cats, displayed a lack of restraint so that they opened the lid not only to all stimuli but constantly in between stimuli as well ("interval activity"). Rest restored the trained responses, at least temporarily. Three cases of more profound disturbances in cats are reported separately by Dworkin, Baxt and Dworkin (1942). In one cat, which had been subject to cochlear damage, the onset of the interval activity was preceded over a period of two years by restlessness and vomiting in the experimental box on at least five occasions. The absence of gastro-intestinal disorder was confirmed by necropsy, and the cat ate well elsewhere. Two further cats urinated in the box, one of them alternating with periods of interval activity, and also displaying changed behaviour outside the experimental situation. He became aggressive, and resisted coming for testing. Rest helped little, but a different experimental room and the restoration of superthreshold stimuli were beneficial. In each case bromide therapy afforded little relief. Only these last cases evidence any generalization, and so approach Hebb's criteria for abnormal behaviour. Dworkin, however, believes the disturbances of behaviour to have been more serious in dog than cat, and suggests that this supports Liddell's emphasis on the importance of restraint in the production of neurosis, since the dogs were confined in a harness whereas the cats were not. The confounding of the species difference with this variable clearly vitiates any such conclusion.

A study using the same alimentary motor reaction specifically for the production of neurosis in cats is reported by Dimmick, Ludlow and Whiteman (1939). After six cats had been trained to lift the lid of the food box on signal, they were shocked whenever they lifted it *between* the signals. They stopped feeding altogether, whereupon the presentation of the signal itself was associated with a "punishing shock." It is not clear how often this was done nor whether all subjects were treated alike or not, but the descriptive results presented show that the anxiety responses thus established generalized to the experimenters and to the cats' living quarters, and persisted despite increased motivation and a rest of ten days.

Masserman's technique (1939) is very similar, except that he also used as an aversive stimulus a blast of air to the side of the animal's head, sometimes in combination with shock, sometimes alone. It was physically harmless but made a "rather loud, sudden noise" (Wikler and Masserman, 1943), elsewhere described as "explosive" (Masserman and Jacques, 1948). Masserman's work suffers from the defects of insufficient control and inadequate quantitative analysis which it has been so frequently necessary to mention in this review, but has an ingenuity about it which compels attention. Nevertheless his description of it in his monograph (1943) is usually unsatisfactory. There is no standard experimental procedure; the intensity of the stimuli used is not specified, and the results are described in the form of a "typical" subject's reactions. Even these are sometimes internally self-inconsistent, larded with alliterative anthropomorphisms (the cat ". . . came up to the food box and muzzled it meditatively . . ." (1943, p. 69)), and contain statements for which no evidence is offered (". . . many of these animals showed chronic disturbances of pulse and respiration . . ." (1943, p. 67)). Background data—age, past experience, even sex—are lacking, and there is confusion over the number of subjects and experiments, eighty-two being mentioned in one place as the total number of cats used, though other figures relating to the number given shock, blast or both suggest a total of one hundred and six. The blast was favoured as a traumatic stimulus on the grounds that it was "psychologically more significant." Certain control observations were made which suggest that hungry cats trained to lid lifting on signal did not become neurotic if their path to the box was blocked, or the lid locked, or, what Masserman picturesquely calls "fractional frustration" (partial reinforcement) instituted. As might be expected, the feeding response was extinguished in the first two cases and very persistent in the third (Jenkins and Stanley, 1950). More crucial are the observations that the conditioned light and bell signals alone or in combination with the air blast were not disturbing, and it is claimed that the blast, after such a combination, could be used even when a cat was feeding, without ill effect, but the procedure used is unclear from the description. Even more important, in view of the criticisms of this work to be discussed, is that no such control observations involving the use of the shock are reported.

The behavioural responses to the imposition of an air blast across the food box, or the electrification of the floor or both, just as the animal opened the lid, showed individual differences. Usually there was a marked fear response, failure to feed from the box any more, and evidence of conditioned fear reactions to the signals for the delivery of food. These manifestations could be increased by pushing the cat towards the food box and persisted for months, but were, Masserman claims, at their height after three days, a time he identifies (though without supporting evidence) as coinciding with maximal hunger in the cat. The use of air blast with two dogs in a larger box gave essentially congruent results.

Evidence for the generalization of these responses is adduced from the changed "personalities" of some cats and from the fact that both dogs developed resistance to entering the apparatus. In addition, Masserman and Siever (1944) showed that the dominance order in groups of four cats—established by allowing them to compete at the food box—was disrupted by the fear conditioning. The least dominant cat could be transmogrified by successively affecting animals higher in the hierarchy. The emergence of aggression towards the competing cat is said to depend on previous experience of dominance, but this does not seem to follow from the carefully documented report on, however, only one of the groups of four.

Masserman is especially concerned with possible therapies of experimental neuroses and their relative efficacy. This enterprise is doomed to failure in any objective sense, of course, by the absence of quantification of the intensity of the disturbances induced, and of an untreated control group to assess spontaneous recovery. The techniques he applied were rest from experimentation, which had little effect, and others designed to abolish the "motivational conflicts" (between hunger and fear) which Masserman believed he had set up in his cats, thus reducing "their aberrant behavioral expression." Specifically they included: reducing the hunger drive by feeding before an experimental trial, increasing it to starvation point, reassuring and petting the cat, and forcing it towards the food box. Interestingly, it seems from Masserman's description that the movement of the barrier by which this was done developed into a conditioned signal for feeding in several animals. The technique of imitation —allowing a well-trained non-traumatized cat in the cage with the neurotic one—was ineffective as therapy, but what Masserman calls "working through," more so. This involved prior training so that the cat itself initiated the feeding signals by pressing a switch. After the fear had been induced such cats began feeding again sooner than ones not so trained.

Masserman completes his monograph on experimental neurosis with a comprehensive, if polemical, review of the pertinent literature. It is bewildering to find familiar studies being cited in support of psychoanalytic notions completely at variance with their authors intentions. Fears tend to become "phobias," repetition is always "compulsive" and the reappearance of an earlier habit, "regression." He is critical of conditioned reflex concepts, preferring a theoretical position akin to McDougall's "hormic psychology." Thus, Anderson and Parmenter's (1941) observations ". . . all but beg for more dynamic and meaningful interpretations" (1943, p. 120). His own position is expressed in four "principles of behavior," basic to his "biodynamic system." They are very general statements, some of which are widely acceptable, and comparably devoid of heuristic value. Behaviour is motivated (first principle), adaptive (second principle), symbolic (third principle) and, fourthly, subject to "vicissitudes," ". . . when the meanings of the perceptive field become confused or the motivations conflictful." Then behaviour becomes "hesitant, vacillating, inefficient, inappropriate, or excessively symbolic or substitutive," that is, neurotic. To the extent that the above adjectives fit the observed behaviour of his animals, Masserman regards that behaviour as neurotic, and the principle itself, by some naïve logic, validated. Beach's comment applies: "We do not intend to deny the possibility of a close relationship between the psychological mechanisms involved in human neurosis and the behavioral deviations which have been described in some animals. But it is very important to hold in mind the fact that this problem is unsolved and until the solution is available egregious extrapolations are unwarranted and dangerous" (1953, p. 376).

The extent to which the behaviour Masserman reports can be described as abnormal can be judged as before by reference to Hebb's criteria. It was not *statistically abnormal*, and neither its *persistence* nor its *generalization*, in terms of situations or systems, has been satisfactorily demonstrated. It is not even clear that it was *evaluationally abnormal* from the cats' point of view. The absence of *gross neural lesions* may be presumed, and the ancillary criteria of *change from a previous base-line*, and the presence of *trauma or conflict* certainly met. Indeed, the last two provide the rationale for the whole experimentation. But of all the major studies noted so far, it must be said that Masserman's least approaches the criteria adopted. The true nature of the behaviour described will be suggested, after some subsidiary work has been reviewed, and some repetitions described.

In a series of studies Masserman has investigated the therapeutic effects of various drugs, of electroconvulsive shock and of brain lesions on the disturbed behaviour. Some of the techniques used are an advance on his earlier purely observational methods. Thus, in a study of the effects of alcohol (Masserman, Yum, Nicholson and Lee, 1944; Masserman, Jacques and Nicholson, 1945; Masserman and Yum, 1946) six-point rating scales covering seventeen aspects of behaviour (e.g. reactions to experimenter, to other animals, to a caged mouse; autonomic changes; activity, etc.) were developed and applied to twenty-one cats to arrive at an "index of neurosis," said to reflect changed behaviour after air blast or shock. The use of statistical techniques such as correlation, regression and significance tests on these data cannot be unreservedly welcomed in the absence of indications of the reliability and validity of the scales. The results suggest that if given before the introduction of the aversive stimulus, alcohol prevents the development of disturbed behaviour, though the cats developed a dislike for its taste, presumably because of a conditioned association with the fear stimuli which always followed its ingestion (cf. the rationale of conditioning pharmacotherapies of alcoholism (Franks, 1958)). This contrasts with experiments where the drug was given *after* the fear responses had developed and afforded relief from feeding inhibitions, etc., in proportion to the dosage given. In this case the development of a preference for milk and alcohol as opposed to the plain milk previously preferred could be demonstrated. No "addiction" developed.[1] The preference was thus ". . . a learned adaptation contingent upon intercurrent neurotic stresses, and reversible when these stresses were resolved" (Masserman and Yum, 1946, p. 51). Macleod (1953) has criticized Masserman's interpretation, and Conger's careful work (1951) on the effect of alcohol on rats in an approach-avoidance conflict situation (Miller, 1944, 1951), which showed that the specific effect of alcohol is to reduce the avoidance response to shock, leads him to question Masserman's formulation also. However, Miller (1956) has been able to repeat neither Masserman and Yum's nor Conger's findings.

An earlier study on the effects of morphine and one not using the Masserman-Yum scales (Wikler and Masserman, 1943) gave results comparable to those found with alcohol. Four cats showed relief from anxiety and one of them did not display it again. A fifth, however, was not relieved by large, and finally fatal, doses. In studies of electroconvulsive shock using sine wave (Masserman and Jacques, 1947) and square wave (Masserman, Arieff, Pechtel and Klehr, 1950) currents, it was shown that electroconvulsive shock abolished the neurotic response as rated, but also disorganized the normal feeding responses thus

---

[1] See Stainton (1943) for a review of the literature (mostly anecdotal reports) on addiction in animals.

restored. Further work on the effect of brain lesions used twenty-three cats (Masserman and Pechtel, 1956), but a fuller report by Pechtel, Masserman, Schreiner and Levitt (1955), on the effects of lesions on nine animals operated on before being subjected to shock compared with eight operate controls not traumatized, shows that the former group had greatly diminished in their fear reactions to stimuli, including odours (Masserman, Pechtel and Schreiner, 1953), which had served as signals for shock. In most cases, however, residual muscular tension was still detectable, and the cats were rated as having become significantly more aggressive to others. For this work, the experimental box had been modified to include two upper compartments containing the switches for initiating the feeding signals, thus permitting a series of problems which, from the curves given, can be graded in difficulty. All animals had forgotten these routines post-operatively, and had to re-learn them.

Thus, Masserman has energetically applied the technique he had adopted to study a series of agents which might be expected to modify the disturbances in behaviour produced. Despite the slightly greater sophistication of the experimental methods used, the results have not been especially precise, though in most cases it has been shown that the disturbances have been attenuated (Masserman, 1951, 1953). The value these investigations have to topics other than neurosis, that is, electroconvulsive shock, and psychosurgery, has not been stressed here, and reference should be made to Chapters 16, by D. Campbell, and 15, by R. A. Willett, respectively.

Masserman's interpretation of his basic work has been challenged by Watson and by Wolpe. Watson (1954) trained seventeen cats to press a switch to activate feeding signals. Air blast or shock was applied at the moment of feeding, and the learned response was disorganized. However, one of two stable behaviour patterns soon emerged; either the cat resumed feeding or withdrew from the food altogether. No changes in behaviour in the home cages were observed. The effects of exposing ten control subjects to the aversive stimuli gave "a different acute reaction" which soon wore off, so that the stimuli were tolerated later. While noting that his work does not repeat Masserman's exactly—in particular, the cats lived in spacious group cages—Watson suggests that the behaviour observed could not be considered abnormal as it was neither chronic, nor maladaptive (Hebb's criterion of evaluationally abnormal). The two distinct patterns of behaviour which evolved are both considered adaptive—the resumption of feeding to avoid starvation, and the refusal to do so to avoid injury, which for all the cat knew may have resulted in death. Unfortunately, the value of this contribution is lessened by the serious deficiencies in the presentation of even the observational data it offers, brief descriptive statements alone being given.

Wolpe starts from a more seriously critical standpoint than is implied by Watson's simple repetition. He notes (1952) that both Masserman, and Dimmick, Ludlow and Whiteman, in using the learned alimentary response, fail to control for the effects of the noxious stimuli apart from its effects on that response, and so couch their explanations of the changed behaviour in terms of irrelevant motivational conflicts. His own experimentation is designed to remedy this deficiency. He used twelve cats in an apparatus like Masserman's; six were trained to feed on hearing a signal and then given a shock (air blast was not used) when attempting to do so. The control group of six was not trained to feed, but given only shocks, preceded by the signal, in the same box as the others. The number of shocks given was not, however, equal, the control group receiving more.

The results are presented descriptively. All animals showed resistance to being placed in the cage, and signs of anxiety especially muscular tension and mydriasis, when inside; all refused to eat there even after one to three days starvation. On occasion howling and rapid respiration were observed, and all these signs of fear were intensified by the auditory signal. One cat developed a tic reminiscent of abortive jumping which may have had its origin in his leap out of the top of the cage, left open inadvertently, when first he was shocked. An ingenious attempt was made to observe the generalization of the responses to the shock by the use of different rooms —a method used by Liddell (1944, 1956) and by Gantt (1944). Wolpe used three rooms which ". . . seemed, to the human eye and ear, to have decreasing degrees of resemblance to" the experimental room. The signs of anxiety to the conditioning signal were weaker in these rooms to the extent to which they differed from the experimental room.

In attempting therapy for five of his subjects' anxiety responses, Wolpe also used this series of rooms. A room was found in which the hungry cat's anxiety was sufficiently attenuated to allow it to feed at all. After feeding in this room, a move was made to the one next higher in the scale of resemblance to the experimental room, and so on, until the cat was feeding in the latter room itself, and, finally, in the box. Other therapies achieving the same result involved feeding the cats from the hand (four subjects), or forcing them to the food box (three subjects). Elimination of anxiety to the auditory signal was then effected in two cats by reducing the intensity of the signal to the point where it was ignored, and then gradually increasing its strength. With another seven subjects, a brief sounding of the signal was used to herald the presentation of a meat pellet. It was thus converted into a conditioned alimentary signal—for the second time in the case of the group originally trained in this way. After these procedures the auditory signal had no effect whatsoever.

Despite the lack of adequate quantification of the phenomena observed, Wolpe's experiment is superior to Masserman's because of the careful control of the variable relating to the effect of the aversive stimulus, independently of its effect on learned responses and he has replied sharply (1954) to Masserman's failure (1954; Masserman, Gross and Pechtel, 1954) to recognize this fact. He bases himself on a rational theory of learning and seeks to utilize it to devise therapies for animal and human anxiety (Wolpe, 1958) and to account for some aspects of experimental neurosis, as will be shown later. But his interpretation of the changes in behaviour produced in his cats as experimental neurosis is less satisfactory. His definition of experimental neurosis as ". . . unadaptive responses that are characterized by anxiety, that are persistent, and that have been produced by behavioural means . . ." (Wolpe, 1952, p. 243) is reminiscent of, though less comprehensive, than Hebb's. His criterion of unadaptiveness he considers to be met because the cats refused to feed even when no further shocks were to be given. But how were the subjects to know this? As Watson notes in connexion with the same problem: "It does not seem possible to regard the cats' behaviour as maladaptive without presupposing capacities to evaluate danger which cats may not possess" (1954, p. 345).

Scheflen (1957) has also studied the extinction of a fear response in cats, using air-blast as the noxious stimulus to break up a previously learned alimentary response. She used two different boxes, and showed that extinction of the fear response in one occurred sooner if the original training and aversive stimulus had occurred in the other. No suggestion that the fear responses observed are abnormal is made by this author nor by Lichtenstein (1950). He produced an inhibition of feeding in hungry dogs, who had been trained to eat in a Pavlov harness. He found that a group of ten dogs, shocked when actually eating the food, ceased feeding sooner than three dogs, shocked on the majority of occasions when only presented with it. Lichtenstein also observed catalepsy, tremors and tics (cf. Wolpe's cat[1]), and autonomic signs of fear. Some dogs always struggled and fought in the apparatus, and two dogs refused the food used in the experiment when it was offered in their home cages, one of them persistently. Excited or aggressive behaviour in their living quarters was also observed.

[1] Meige and Feindel (1907) cite other examples of tics in animals.

The feeding inhibitions were relieved in most cases by prefrontal leucotomy, while a control group subjected to sham operation maintained theirs for one to three weeks (1950a).

Lichtenstein identifies the complex of behaviour observed in his experiments, of which the actual feeding inhibition is only a part, as one of fear or anxiety, and develops a closely reasoned argument against calling it experimental neurosis (1950). Despite differences in the details of the results obtained by these workers studying feeding inhibitions,[1] it seems clear that what the investigators using alimentary responses in dogs and cats in the experiments discussed above have been observing is the conditioned emotional response or C.E.R. (Watson and Rayner, 1920; Brady and Hunt, 1955). Masserman would almost certainly disagree with this appraisal, as he has specifically denied that the responses he has elicited are conditioned fear responses (1950; Masserman and Siever, 1944), basing himself partly on the argument that ". . . the reactions of anxiety and patterned defense began to spread to other situations only remotely or 'symbolically' associated with the neurotigenic one—a process of 'irrational generalisation' that every clinician will recognize as characteristic of human neuroses" (1950, p. 56). Masserman's lack of confidence in the often demonstrated normal generalization of conditioned fear receives melodramatic expression in his claim that, in the absence of dynamic, motivational conflict, ". . . human neuroses would quite literally be confined to people who had either been caught in an electrical short-circuit or struck by lightning at the moment they were pushing an accustomed button to secure food from an automat" (1954, p. 222).

It is not possible, of course, to accept Masserman's assertions regarding the nature of the behaviour he has studied, couched as they are in subjective terms, without the backing of quantification, control and appropriate analysis. Furthermore, the appellation of experimental neurosis is especially inapposite here, since, as we have seen, there is no satisfactory evidence that the responses are abnormal, even at the level of the species in question. The application of this conceptual framework to the field of psychopharmacology (Jacobsen and Skaarup, 1955) is therefore unfortunate, especially now that the parameters of conditioned

[1] In all likelihood, many of these differences are attributable to differences in technique used. Thus, in the experiments using shock as the aversive stimulus, its strength, nowhere precisely specified, was probably weakest in Watson's case, since many of his cats resumed feeding, the next strongest in Masserman's since he does note that five cats were at first unaffected by it, and the strongest in Wolpe's and Lichtenstein's, since all animals were affected by it and the disorders were persistent. Two further repetitions of Masserman's work using cats have been reported in abstract, Yacorzynski (1946, 1948) reaching conclusions at variance with Masserman's, while Cain and Extremet (1957) do not.

fear are more fully understood and better methods of quantification available.

Masserman's further work has been on primates. It will not be reviewed in detail, not only because a promised monograph has not yet appeared, but also because the methods used and the results reported parallel those for cats. The apparatus used is a larger and more complicated version of that previously described, and the aversive stimuli used with monkeys included electric shock, a water jet, ". . . or, more significantly, the sudden appearance of a toy rubber snake in the food box" (Masserman and Pechtel, 1956). The reactions claimed as a direct and exclusive reaction to the sight of this snake, as compared with other moving toy or mechanical objects (Masserman and Pechtel, 1953, 1953a) are almost incredible. They include, as well as the feeding inhibitions met with in the cat, muscular and gastro-intestinal dysfunctions, sexual deviations, and behaviour boldly identified as "hallucinatory" in two monkeys who appeared to eat "imaginary" pieces of food. The evidence presented is neither sufficiently detailed nor well-controlled to be convincing, and the unsubstantiated claims of a psychoanalyst to have discovered in so obvious a phallic "symbol" the one object to cause persistent experimental neurosis is necessarily subject to a pardonable scepticism. This is reinforced by lack of experimental evidence for the generality of this finding. Thus, Jones and Jones (1928) showed there is no innate fear of snakes in a human infant, and Rand (1941, 1942) found that the fear of a dummy snake is soon extinguished in certain species of birds. Moreover, in monkeys the conditioned avoidance response based on shock is subject to the usual—if slow—experimental extinction (Waterhouse, 1957).

Masserman has made some use of that neglected sensory modality, smell, and has demonstrated (Masserman, Pechtel and Schreiner, 1953; Pechtel and Masserman, 1954; Masserman and Pechtel, 1956b) that odours are not so readily learned as conditioned signals for food as lights or sounds, but when associated with fear stimuli they become potent, and generalize widely to other smells. The effect of brain lesions and drugs on the monkeys' behaviour has also been reported. Again using rating scales, now said to have high reliability, Masserman and Pechtel (1956) have shown that lesions in the amygdaloid nucleus appear to have a large effect on the disturbed behaviour. The large number of variables liable to affect these findings is rightly stressed. No marked effects of drugs were found (Masserman and Pechtel, 1956a), and, indeed, this paper is more notable for the careful attempts to analyse some parameters of the behaviour observed. Thus age is shown to be important, younger monkeys being more susceptible to disturbance than older ones. The largest correlation,

however, is that between "number of traumata to produce neurosis" and "spacing of traumata," which is negative and about 0·8. Confirmation of one of the fundamentals of learning theory—the greater efficiency of spaced, as compared with massed, practice —is unexpected from such a quarter!

While the extension of Masserman's work to another species is to be welcomed, many of the criticisms made of his earlier work on cats are unfortunately still applicable. Penrose's comment that "the implications of Masserman's work do not seem to be clear at present" (1953, p. 77), still holds.

While Masserman is alone in having deliberately attempted to produce experimental neurosis in primates, several reports of the accidental or spontaneous occurrence of neurosis are found. The most celebrated of these is that of Jacobsen and his co-workers, the early reports of which (Jacobsen, 1935; Fulton and Jacobsen, 1935) inspired Moniz to initiate the technique of prefrontal leucotomy (Crawford, Fulton, Jacobsen and Wolfe, 1947). One of two chimpanzees frequently had a temper tantrum when it made a mistake on a test of delayed reaction, in which the animals were trained to choose between one of two cups under which they had seen food hidden, but which had been out of their sight in the interim. As the task was made more difficult, this behaviour became more frequent, no responses were made and the subject had to be forced into the experimental cage. "It was as complete an 'experimental neurosis' as those obtained by Pavlov's conditioned reflex procedures" (Jacobsen, Wolfe and Jackson, 1935, p. 9). Be that as it may, the disturbance was cured by feeding, petting and simplifying the problem. After one frontal area of the cortex had been removed, the same events occurred on retraining and were treated in the same way. But after the second frontal area was removed a marked change was noted. The animal no longer became upset over errors, and willingly came to the experiment despite them: "It was as if the animal had joined the 'happiness cult of Elder Micheaux,' and had placed its burdens on the Lord!" (1935, p. 10). Hence the interest of psychiatrists.

Wendt (1934) also reports " 'blow-ups' (Pavlov's 'experimental neurosis')" in one baboon during training to delay an alimentary reaction, but since they did not occur when she had been fully trained, they were probably examples of the upsets likely to disturb the smooth progress of conditioning. According to Dworkin (1939) it is difficult to distinguish such disturbances from "border-line neurosis," except by their duration. Yerkes (1943) relies heavily on this distinction: he identifies the disturbance in behaviour of a chimpanzee which bit him when she failed in a difficult problem-solving task and never applied herself to it again as a neurosis, because it was "relatively permanent." Galt (1939) found a similar change in behaviour lasting two months in a *cebus* monkey after it had been presented with an especially difficult discrimination problem, and Firsov (1952, in Liberson, 1957) reports that during operant conditioning (squeezing a bulb) to visual and auditory signals in monkeys, one broke down and became neurotic for a month when discrimination of signals was required.

Apparently spontaneous cases of neurosis in primates are also reported. Leavitt and Riggs (1942) recount the case of a young monkey who exhibited a "change of personality" after living for two and a half years with a policeman, but better authenticated are Hebb's cases of two adult chimpanzees who both showed disturbed behaviour not traceable to any discoverable trauma (1947). The first had been reared in the laboratory since birth, the second since nine months of age, so that their histories are well documented. The first showed a recurrent food phobia, occasionally associated with fear of an attendant; the second, recurrent fits of depression. In neither case was it possible to find any specific experiential cause. For example, Hebb examines and rejects the possibility that a hurtful object may have occasioned the food phobia. He considers that the disorders mentioned meet all the criteria he has laid down for animal neurosis, "as far as this can ever be possible in the absence of the verbal examination of the patient" (1947, p. 11). An apparently spontaneous case of gross self-mutilation which appears to have been associated with depression and the relationship with an attendant, is reported by Tinkelpaugh (1928), but the possibility of chronic disseminated encephalitis must be suspected in such cases (Hutyra, Marek and Manninger, 1946). Apparently abnormal motor behaviour in caged wild animals, such as stereotyped pacing movements, may be attributed (Hediger, 1950) to the interaction of the shape and size of the cage and the animal's "flight distance." Little appears to be known about abnormal behaviour in wild animals in their natural state. The apparently purposeless mass migrations occasionally reported are probably the result of ecological factors.

Later Studies, especially on the Rat

Turning to the last major section of work to be included in this review, we encounter a somewhat more rigorous methodological climate. This is perhaps because the investigators were usually trained psychologists, and frequently worked with the rat as subject. The early work of Liddell and Gantt aroused interest in the topic of experimental neuroses in the late 1930s, as may be seen by the numerous reviews of the field which appeared (Murray, 1937; Miles, 1938; Cook, 1939, 1939a; Witkin, 1939; Karn, 1940, 1940a). Interested workers tried to study the

phenomena described by using the standard laboratory animal, the rat. Advantage lay in the greater accessibility and convenience of this subject over the more esoteric species previously used, and the possibility of using larger numbers was also clearly attractive, thus avoiding the defects of lack of control and of statistical criteria, which it has been unfortunately necessary to stress time and again in this chapter. There seem to be two reasons, however, why research along these lines did not develop. Firstly, the problem proved intractable, as, looking back on it, one might have expected in view of the nature of the evidence produced. Secondly, the investigation of audiogenic seizures claimed the attention of many workers. Effort was needed to establish that the convulsive phenomena observed were not rodent parallels of the classical experimental neurosis, and they were thereafter studied for their own interest. The more basic research on the rat has never been resumed on the same scale. After reading this chapter, it may be conceded that this, perhaps, is not a bad thing.

This is not to say that early references to experimental neurosis in rats are not to be found. Some writers identify any slight deviation from what they consider to be normal performance as "neurotic" (Fields, 1931; Hall, 1933; Carmichael, 1938),[1] though others are more restrained (Miller and Stevenson, 1936; Sampson and Schneirla, 1941). However: "During the period from 1937 to 1940 there was a rather widespread effort to establish experimental neuroses in the rat with conflict as the precipitating factor. Very few of the published studies reported success, however, and it is reasonable to assume that many failures never reached print" (Finger, 1944, p. 413). Among those reported, Cook's are notable for his thoughtful analysis of the problems involved (1939, 1939a) and his painstaking attempts to overcome them (1939b). Defining experimental neurosis in terms involving Hebb's criteria of chronicity, evaluational abnormality and departure from a previous base-line, he reviews the literature to date and identifies four major factors common to the situations yielding experimental neurosis. They are the use of restraint, the development of learned responses by Pavlovian conditioning, the discrimination of similar stimuli giving rise to antagonistic responses, and the inhibition of responses during excitatory stimulation. In preliminary work he used three situations in which the first two of these elements were lacking before turning to a method of conditioning in the rat, developed by Schlosberg and his associates (1934, 1934a, 1934b, 1936, 1936a; Schlosberg and Kappauf, 1935; Kappauf and Schlosberg, 1937; Hughes and Schlosberg, 1938).

---

[1] This tendency persists; examples range from cattle (Fraser, 1957), through rodents (Green, 1958; Hansen, 1956), to the amoeba (Goldacre, 1958)!

The rat is immobilized by strapping it down in a miniature harness to a stand, and attaching an electrode to one foreleg, the withdrawal of which is automatically recorded. Cook's technique was to associate foreleg retraction first to the appearance of food in a cup near the rat's head, then to limit the movement's effectiveness in producing the food reward to the period when a bright light—the positive conditioned stimulus—shone. Next came training to inhibit the foreleg response in the presence of a dim light—the negative stimulus—by punishing such responses with shock, before the intensity of this light was increased to make the discrimination more difficult. All the six rats put through this procedure showed their dislike of it by squealing, tenseness, etc., and there were transient disturbances of the learned response, but only three rats showed some other change in behaviour such as avoiding being handled by the experimenter or becoming unresponsive to stimuli—changes which Cook thinks meet his definition of experimental neurosis: "chronic, abnormal behaviour, experimentally produced." He notes that the effectiveness of the situation involving restraint supports Liddell's view on the importance of this factor in the aetiology of experimental neurosis.

An even more thoroughgoing attempt to adapt the Pavlovian conditioning procedure to the study of experimental neurosis in the rat is due to Bijou (1942, 1943, 1947, 1951). In preliminary work (1942) he found that quicker learning was achieved by using head movement rather than leg retraction, and greater discrimination by varying the position of the stimulus lights rather than the brightness of a single panel. In a further study of eight rats differential conditioning was developed, after many trials, in five of them to the point where they were discriminating lights about one inch apart. Activity, measured before each training session, the degree of restraint used, and the subjects' emotionality, defined by defecation scores in Hall's open-field test (1934), were apparently unrelated to the speed of learning, but the use of shock to punish wrong responses "markedly increased excitable behavior." No abnormalities other than this latter were found. Later modifications to this apparatus and procedure (Bijou, 1951) and work using it to investigate other aspects of learning (Rohrer, 1947; Rigby, 1954) have been published without further attempts to precipitate experimental neurosis.

Using a more strictly Pavlovian procedure, but still employing movement as the response to be conditioned, Kawamura and Yoshii (1951) restrained thirty-six rats in a cloth holder (Cowles and Pennington, 1943) and applied an electric shock to the hind leg, preceded by an acoustic stimulus. In the absence of quantitative data it is not clear how the conditioning

developed. Tremors and tics of the hind legs are reported in five subjects, trained over two months, as well as resistance to being placed in the conditioning box and hypersensitivity to stimuli in their home cages. It is not, of course, possible to agree with the authors' identification of such behaviour as experimental neurosis, nor is their definition of phases of rats' behaviour involving hyperactivity as "acute experimental neurosis" helpful. Their use of stimulant and depressant drugs, of surgical intervention including prefrontal leucotomy, and of electroencephalography is of greater interest. Only the last is reported in any detail: Yoshii and Kawamura (1951) implanted electrodes in five rats. No abnormal wave forms were observed, and, though there is some evidence that two "neurotic" rats showed faster waves, the absence of normative data does not permit firm conclusions.

Another attempt to use Pavlovian conditioning techniques in the rat arose out of the report (Jamison, 1951) of the conditioning of a heart rate decrement which reflexly follows the inhalation of ammonia gas. A preliminary report (Broadhurst, 1954) failed to confirm the existence of this conditioned response, though a small, albeit statistically significant, conditioned cardiac response based on shock, rather than on ammonia gas, as the unconditioned stimulus was found, as well as unstable squeak and respiratory conditioning also based on the shock. No responses, however, were sufficiently definite to form the basis for differential conditioning.

It may, therefore, be said that the application of conditioning methods to the rat for the production of experimental neurosis has failed in its object. Not only have there been no reports of disturbances comparable to those reported with the use of higher animals, but the conditioning technique itself has not produced unequivocal results. It has proved just as time-consuming as with higher animals, thus frustrating the aim of employing large numbers of cheap and readily available subjects for control and statistical purposes. It is not surprising that other methods have been frequently tried.

Hunt and Schlosberg (1950) belatedly report work done in 1938–40 on the use of a "continuous conflict" situation. Of ten rats kept in stabilimeter cages to record activity, six had their water supply electrified so that every time they took a drink they received a shock from the nozzle of the water bottle, and the other four served as controls. The data presented on activity suggest that the experimental animals became more active throughout the whole day, instead of sleeping principally during the day and becoming livelier at night—the rat being a nocturnal animal: "The writers interpreted this difference to mean that continued thirst kept the animals active during the normal hours of diminished activity but did not increase the total amount of time spent in resting or sleep. Since these relatively meager results seemed to have little to do with conflict, *per se*, no further study was made of general activity" (1950, p. 150). This view reflects the search for the overt signs of abnormal behaviour in animals, which are probably not to be found. It is especially unfortunate in this case, since this same finding of increased activity during the animal's "night" is one of the few reported in other species, as mentioned in discussing the Cornell work on sheep, where thirst could not be invoked as an explanation. Hunt and Schlosberg, however, are more impressed by some incidental observations. Rats bit the nozzle of an unelectrified water bottle, apparently trying to get it into the cage, they would suddenly cease drinking from it as if shocked, and finally showed "tantrums" in which they threw food about and breathed noisily. But the latter behaviour may be observed in naïve rats never subjected to experimentation, and water-deprived ones will display the apparently aggressive behaviour towards a water nozzle with no experience of shock whatsoever. Finally, the "hallucinatory" behaviour towards the previously electrified spout may be the result of a conditioned anxiety response to it.

Only Finger (1941) appears to have taken up the suggestive findings relating to changes in activity. In a carefully controlled study, he measured general cage activity during an extended period while the subjects were also exposed to difficult discrimination problems in a Lashley jumping stand. He found a significant decrease in activity in the twenty-four-hour period following jumping sessions in which four or more errors had been made, as well as a significant increase during the following day—the rats' night. Non-jumping controls showed no change. To what extent these changes are attributable to the conflict caused by the difficult discriminations is not clear since an alternative possibility, that the incorrect jumpers were simply more tired than the others, and so slept more during the next rodent "day," is not excluded. Some data showing that the effect dissipates within twenty-four hours are not inconsistent with this explanation, though others militate against it.

King and Mavromatis (1956) used Hunt and Schlosberg's technique to study the disruptive effect on the re-learning of a conditioned avoidance response to shock of intermittently electrifying the water supply of two strains of mice. While there was a significant decrement in saving scores, as compared with appropriate control groups, the authors rightly conclude: ". . . it is impossible to assign this interference to emotional 'disturbance' experienced by the mice in the conflict situation or to a physiological adaptation to shock" (1956, p. 468). The further use of the continuous conflict technique in the production of gastro-intestinal disorders in animals will be noted later. Cook's use of it (1939*b*) in his search for a method of producing abnormal behaviour in the rat yielded no positive findings; neither did his use of a Miller-Mowrer type shuttle box in which the rats had to learn a brightness discrimination to avoid shock. Gentry and Dunlap (1942), however, forced the rat to escape from a strong shock only to meet a weak one. None of these workers found disturbed behaviour, though Gentry and Dunlap claim to have shown "atypical" learning among their twelve subjects after exposure to the shock situation and Eränkö and Muittari (1957) report changes in thyroid structure as a result of extinguishing a jumping response.

An apparatus designed to enforce wakefulness in rats might be thought provocative of disordered behaviour. Licklider and Bunch (1946) kept each subject in a cell, the floor of which was a roller surrounded by water. For control groups, the roller was locked stationary, whereas for experimental groups it was free moving, thus forming a treadmill on which animals had to move every ten to fifteen seconds in order to avoid falling off into the water. While the sleepless animals which survived became highly irritable and aggressive by the thirtieth day, no more profound disorders were reported. This was also the case in a report of enforced lack of sleep in dogs (Okazaki, 1925).

Humphrey and Marcuse's (1939, 1941) claim to have produced "neurotic behaviour" in rats by dragging the bottomless goal box of a maze across the floor after the rat had entered it cannot be entertained seriously, if only because the behaviour in question consisted principally in hesitation in entering the same goal box on subsequent trials. A very different situation has been reported to produce "psychotic" behaviour in wild rats. During toxicity tests, Richter (1950) found that wild Norway rats developed "refusal" responses after a sublethal dose of one poison, ANTU (alpha-naphthyl thiourea), presumably because they had associated its taste and smell with the respiratory distress caused. Typically, Richter used two food cups and switched the poison from one to the other. Just after this had been done, one animal developed a pseudo-catatonia, maintaining an awkward posture on its hind feet despite interruptions including the opening of the cage. This is most unusual for wild rats, which are always eager to escape. This "straphanging" behaviour lasted for two months before the rat was finally poisoned. Other rats showed similar behaviour which Richter interprets as "an ever-present fear of being poisoned." But this promising lead has petered out, as further work on over a hundred subjects has proved negative (Richter, 1953), and it is now thought that the upright posture may have resulted from the earlier experience of huddling closely when many were confined together in one cage. Moreover, wild rats sometimes show their intense fearfulness after capture by remaining motionless, even starving to death in the process, by dying of fright when handled, as Richter himself has shown (1957), or when fighting, even when uninjured (Barnett, 1955). The domesticated rats in Richter's experiments never showed comparable behaviour, and this fact alone robs the original finding of its relevance in the present connexion, since the wild rat, which needs special techniques in handling and testing (Broadhurst, 1958a), cannot be regarded as a standard laboratory animal. At this point the reader may be disposed to agree with Hebb's comment of over ten years ago: "I have seen nothing in the literature which remotely justifies calling rat behaviour neurotic" (1947, p. 14).

While examples of abnormal behaviour in animals other than the rat, or as a result of using techniques other than those discussed are worthy of mention, none of them approach the definition of neurosis adopted here. Karn (1938, 1938a; Karn and Malamud, 1939) used the double-alternation problem in a temporal maze. This is a difficult problem, the animal being required to go through the same passages of a rectangular maze four times, making different turns on the last two trials from those made on the first two. Two cases of behaviour disturbance are reported, one in a cat and one in a dog. Another animal of each species was not affected. In each case the affected animal halted at the choice-point, and cried; the cat showed a reluctance to enter the maze. Both animals failed to reach their previous performance, which fact in particular led Karn to describe the behaviour as "neurotic." However, subsequent workers using this type of problem with a larger number of cats specifically note the absence of behaviour comparable to that reported by Karn (Willoughby and Andrews, 1940; Stewart and Warren, 1957).

Cameron (1936) encased the rear legs of eighteen guinea pigs hoping to produce experimental depression by frustration of movement. This treatment did reduce the rate of respiration, but since it caused physical damage to the legs in almost all cases, the finding is on these grounds alone uninterpretable.

Despite the widespread use of birds as experimental animals, and their tendency to "superstitious behaviour" (Skinner, 1948; Morse and Skinner, 1957), there are few reports of abnormal behaviour among them. Bajandurov (1933) developed a Pavlovian conditioning procedure in doves that were restrained in a holder with an electrode attached to one foot. The response of the leg to a shock was recorded by an attached thread, and was conditioned to the appearance of illuminated shapes before the bird. The classic method of developing a positive response to a circle,

a negative one to an ellipse, and then making the ellipse progressively more circular, had the expected result. The discrimination broke down, and the previously quiet bird struggled against the restraint. A second subject became agitated with interval activity of the reaction limb, though retaining the discrimination. Brückner (1933) induced disordered behaviour in four hens by isolating them in a closed box for the first seven weeks of life. On restoration to the flock, two of them were distinguishable by their unusual behaviour for three days in one case and twelve in another. But the deprivation of visual stimulation during what probably was a "critical period" of development (see Thorpe, 1956) may be at least as important a factor as the isolation. Many studies (see Beach and Jaynes' review, 1954) indicate the importance of the effect of early experience on adult behaviour. Examples of observational accounts of abnormal behaviour in birds are Lorenz's description (1940) of depression in a grey goose after one wing was clipped, and Räber's report (1948) of the abnormal development of courting behaviour in a turkey. It would display before a mackintosh hanging on a post, which it never did before a hen bird.

These contributions have clearly not advanced a solution of the problems raised by experimental neurosis as reported by early workers. The problem has indeed proved intractable so long as it continued to be posed in terms demanding a solution by the production of overt abnormalities which would serve as convincing analogies of those seen in human neurosis, and so long as human neurosis itself continued to be regarded as a discrete disease entity, instead of the extreme of a continuum of learned, and probably overgeneralized, responses, some of which are in fact amenable to rational therapy based on learning theory (Wolpe, 1952, 1952a, 1958; Jones, 1956; Yates, 1958). This view, developed elsewhere in this book,[1] makes the study of disorders of emotional responses in animals by approaches other than that of experimental neurosis directly relevant to human problems. This is particularly true if the view is taken that cross-species identification of behaviour is permissible when it can be shown that the mechanisms giving rise to the behaviour are the same in the two cases. No attempt is made here to review all the pertinent literature, but mention of some papers will indicate the range of the possible approaches.

An interesting early attempt by Higginson (1930) sought to quantify the effect of emotional stress—a naturalistic one, the fear of cats (Curti, 1935)—on a series of measures of rats' performance in a maze. Turner (1941) amplified this approach by observing the effect of a difficult size discrimination on rats' behaviour in other situations. He confirmed Finger's

[1] See Chapters 1, by H. J. Eysenck and 20, by H. G. Jones.

finding (1941) of a depression in activity and showed a similar effect on respiration, with no effect on startle responses. Scott (1947; Scott and Marston, 1953) has also used a naturalistic stress—in this case defeats in fights—to study emotional behaviour in mice. McCleary (1954) gives a good-humoured account of a quest for cardiac measures of stress in rats. After solving the not inconsiderable difficulties associated with obtaining such records from a freely moving animal, thus avoiding the objections, both practical and theoretical (*see* page 737), to attaching electrodes, he succeeded in getting clear records of increase in heart rate when the rat heard a tone associated with shock. But control tests showed a similar increase in simple movements which apparently involved no anxiety. He doubts the value of cardiac measures of anxiety: "Maybe one would rather conclude that the rat is simply 'anxious' about everything he does. It's a moot point. Operationally, one ends up at the same place" (1954, p. 107).

The approach-avoidance model of behaviour developed by Miller (1944, 1951) offers a fruitful approach to the study of conflict between tendencies. An example is Winnick's success (1956) in giving quantitative expression to the fluctuations in anxiety, postulated as occurring in such conflict situations (Schoenfeld, 1950). She recorded the intensity with which hungry rats pushed against a panel, the release of which in order to feed would switch on a bright light—an aversive stimulus. The measurement in a readily quantified form of the conditioned emotional response or C.E.R., referred to earlier as the probable basis for feeding inhibitions, has given rise to a number of studies in which the effect on it of other variables has been examined (*see* Brady and Hunt, 1955; Brady, 1957). Another, somewhat more direct, measure of autonomic arousal in the rat—the defecation score in Hall's open-field test (1934)—has been used in the analysis of the determinants of emotionality (Broadhurst, 1957, 1958, 1958*a*) as well as providing the basis for the investigation of inherited emotional characteristics (1959*a*, 1960) and of their effect on learning (1957*a*, 1957*b*, 1958*b*). This work suggests that emotionality may be a rodent analogue of neuroticism in humans; the analogue of the orthogonal dimension of introversion-extraversion has also been tentatively identified (Sinha, Franks and Broadhurst, 1958). Factor analysis is another promising approach (Royce, 1950). Examples are seen in Royce's work on the dog (1955), Sen's on the rat (1953) and Willingham's on the mouse (1956).

The effect of psychological stress on physiological function, as seen in Pilgrim and Patton's study (1953) of growth in rats, which yielded negative results, and Ullman's (1951, 1952) on "compulsive eating," which was positive, has received new impetus with the report of the experimental production of gastric ulcers in the rat by Sawrey and Weisz (1956). A continuous-conflict technique like that used by Hunt and Schlosberg opposed severe hunger and thirst drives against fear induced by shock as the animals tried to approach food or water. Both authors have published apparently independent analyses of the variables involved (Sawrey Conger and Turrell, 1956; Weisz, 1957) which agree in assigning an important role in ulcer formation to the conflict involved, as opposed to the effect of shock or of deprivation alone. No overt behavioural changes were observed. The influence of some social factors has been demonstrated (Conger, Sawrey and Turrell, 1958), and other work showing that ulceration may be induced by direct brain stimulation (French, Porter, Cavanaugh and Longmire, 1957) suggests the possibility of identification of the cerebral mechanism involved, especially in view of the extension of the technique to primates (Porter, Brady, Conrad, Mason, Galambos and Rioch, 1958).

The approach of comparative ethologists[1] to the problems of abnormal behaviour is based on their concept of "displacement activity," the manifestation of an innate behaviour pattern in circumstances which are judged biologically inappropriate for its emergence (Tinbergen, 1952; Barnett, 1955*a*). Careful analysis of the determinants of such behaviour have been made (*see* Thorpe, 1956). Displacement activities are viewed as the basis of the phenomena of experimental neurosis (Bastock, Morris and Moynihan, 1953), as well as being related to those seen in human neurosis (Armstrong, 1950) especially psychosomatic disorders, which Barnett (1955*a*) suggests may be analogous to displacement activities in lower animals. The difficulty that the responses in lower animals are usually motor ones, whereas in man they tend, especially when pathological, to be visceral, is now less cogent in view of the work on gastric ulcers mentioned above and the development of methods for the study of asthma in lower animals (Ottenberg, Stein, Lewis, and Hamilton, 1958).

This, then, concludes the review of the factual evidence which is to be found in the experimental literature and which goes to make up our knowledge about experimental neurosis. As has been indicated, there seems very little justification for the view that

---

[1] Many ethological concepts can be criticized on various scores (Schneirla, 1952; Kennedy, 1954), and the ethologists' models may repel those accustomed to the greater sophistication of modern learning theory, which covers part of the same ground: "The gulfs between psychiatry, psychology, ethology, and physiology are both deep and wide, and the attempt to bridge them is liable to bring on fits of dizziness" (Barnett, 1955*a*, p. 1207). Such attempts are not encouraged by some ethologists' definition of their area of work as the scientific study of behaviour, thus pre-empting a field long studied by psychologists, the relevant contributions of whom many ethologists in their writings, though with certain significant exceptions, e.g. Thorpe (1956), appear to ignore.

the phenomena observed can, in all but a very few cases, be regarded as at all analogous to the phenomena observable in human neurosis. Nevertheless, it has frequently been accepted that they are so related, probably because of the lack of a theoretical framework which links them to the main body of findings in the field of animal studies. This reinforces the view, as Lichtenstein has noted (1950), that one is dealing with examples of behaviour which are strange, and thus "abnormal": it is then but a short step to defining them as "neurotic."

Theoretical Formulations of Experimental Neurosis

Two attempts have been made to describe the disturbances of behaviour experimentally produced in terms of a coherent theoretical system. These are the "vigilance" theory of Liddell, and Gantt's principles of "auto-" and "schizokinesis." Both of them, however, are *sui generis*, in that they account only for the facts of experimental neurosis as observed by their authors, and there has been very little success in demonstrating that they have any relevance beyond the situation which they were designed to illuminate. Moreover, as has been indicated in discussing them, they are not couched in terms sufficiently precise to allow testable predictions to be made from them.

To achieve the desired theoretical integration in this field, then, it seems necessary to go back to the originator of the area of study. Pavlov viewed experimental neurosis as behaviour resulting from a "clash" between cortical excitation and inhibition. This explanation in terms of a theory of brain physiology which is not widely accepted by physiologists (Liddell, 1949) in fact adds little to our understanding of the nature of the behaviour involved, and it is natural that, in seeking to encompass the problem, recourse should be had to the modern successor to Pavlovian reflex theory, that is the learning theory of Hull whose debt to Pavlov is insufficiently recognized. While recognizing the system's imperfections, it seems true to say that many, perhaps a majority, of psychologists, would acknowledge that learning theory as developed by Hull and elaborated by his pupil, Spence, and by Mowrer, Miller, and Eysenck, is at present the only coherent and consistent explanation of numerous widely differing phenomena which range from the behaviour of *paramecia* (Grosslight and Tickner, 1953) to the development of social attitudes (Eysenck, 1954). Two attempts within this general framework may be noted. Hebb's (1947) is in the nature of a series of general suggestions which might adumbrate a fuller treatment. For example, he stresses the importance of generalization in the development of disturbed behaviour outside the precipitating situation, and regards the emotional responses displayed within it as being the result of "normal emotional

conditioning." A more elaborate attempt is that of Wolpe (1952); indeed, Wolpe's whole thesis is that experimental neuroses are in fact learned behaviour, irrespective of whether one regards them as abnormal or not. To this end, he categorizes the precipitating situations into those employing severe shock, those employing mild shock, and those employing ambivalent stimulation. The behaviour resulting from the first he regards as straightforward fear conditioning in which the stimuli associated with the punishing shock become conditioned stimuli for the arousal of intense conditioned fear, that is, anxiety. With regard to the second situation in which mild shock only is used, "it is necessary to explain how a severe anxiety reaction could arise from what is apparently nothing more than the repeated conditioning of a mildly disturbing stimulus" (Wolpe, 1952, p. 265). His solution is to postulate that fear and anxiety have additive properties. To the slight amount of fear evoked by the conditioned stimulus, must be added the even smaller anxiety conditioned to it by the previous occasion on which it was used. This, however, allows a slightly larger amount of the complex of fear and anxiety to be conditioned to the stimulus, which, in turn, means a greater amount of anxiety to be added to the fear on the next occasion—and so it goes on. In this way, Wolpe suggests, anxiety can mount, so that, in time, the responses to it overwhelm other learned behaviour. With respect to the third situation, that of ambiguous stimulation, Wolpe offers this hypothesis—

> However slight and transient the anxiety produced by this conflict of tendencies may be at first, the drive reduction associated with its cessation results in the anxiety responses becoming reinforced to whatever stimuli are contiguous, and among these is the ambivalent stimulation itself. In the same way as suggested above for the case of mild noxious stimuli, the strength of the anxiety response is conceived to be gradually stepped up at each presentation of the ambivalent stimulus situation while the drive-reduction potential correspondingly grows. Eventually very powerful anxiety responses are evoked, and strong avoidance behaviour entirely replaces the approach responses to the experimental situation which were previously established by repeated feeding (1952, p. 266).

Thus, two authorities appear to support the view taken earlier in this chapter that the responses observed in the situations in which strong shock or other noxious stimuli are used (e.g. Masserman's) may be subsumed under the category of conditioned emotional responses. Hebb also appears to think that all phenomena of experimental neurosis can be so explained. Significantly, the only exception he apparently makes is the phenomenon of diminished capacity for making simple discriminations of conditioned stimuli after the application of difficult ones has caused a breakdown. It is this latter situation also which causes Wolpe most difficulty. To be sure, it is easy to see that once intense anxiety has been produced in the difficult discrimination situation, a conditioned emotional response to the stimuli used, and to the whole situation, will develop and generalize in the usual way. What is more difficult to see, is how this anxiety developed in the first place, in the absence of primary fear-producing stimuli. Wolpe's explanation, though ingenious, does not appear to the writer to be wholly satisfactory. Firstly, his assumption that fear and anxiety are additive may not be tenable. Secondly, that they do interact in the way suggested is equally hypothetical. Thirdly, even if these points are conceded, then in the discrimination situation, his explanation rests on the assumption that ambiguous stimulation gives rise to anxiety, directly. He claims that: ". . . it is a matter of everyday experience that in human subjects ambivalent stimuli arouse feelings of tension" (Wolpe, 1952, p. 266). Admittedly, there is a body of evidence which suggests that this may be in fact true, but Wolpe does not indicate how this occurs in animals. An explanation in terms of changes in difficulty level may be of assistance here; such an explanation is available in terms of the operation of the principle known as the Yerkes-Dodson law.

In 1908 Yerkes and Dodson published the results of a study of learning in mice in a brightness discrimination situation. They found that as the motivation—in this case a combination of hunger drive and electric shock punishment for wrong responses—increased, an optimum motivation was reached beyond which increases in intensity gave poorer rather than better learning. But in addition they investigated the effect of variations in the *difficulty* of the task. They discovered that the more difficult the task, the sooner the optimum motivation was reached, that is, as task difficulty increases, so the optimum motivation approaches threshold. The curvilinear relationship between performance and motivation has been confirmed in many different situations subsequently, but the relationship between it and the level of difficulty appears to have been lost sight of until recently, when the law was invoked (Eysenck, 1955) to explain the differences in performance between neurotics and normals in their accomplishment of simple tasks like conditioning, and more complex ones like maze learning (Taylor, 1956). Broadhurst (1957a) has demonstrated the action of the law itself in a factorial experiment in which it appeared as a significant interaction effect between intensity of motivation and level of task difficulty. This confirmation is thought to gain weight because a different situation, different motivation, and even a different species of subjects

from those of Yerkes and Dodson (1908) were used. In addition, the phenomena designated by the law may be explained in terms of Hullian learning theory. Thus, increasing drive level may increase the functional difficulty of a discrimination, so that objective increases in difficulty are in fact rendered more severe than the circumstances otherwise warrant. Once the optimum motivation is reached, then the decrease in task performance may be viewed as an energization of incorrect responses which are lower in the habit-family-hierarchy than the correct ones (Broadhurst, 1959). The application of this reformulation of the Yerkes-Dodson law has been shown to have relevance to such diverse fields as perceptual defence and avoidance learning, as well as experimental neuroses. (*See* Chapters 7, by J. Inglis and 13, by H. G. Jones.)

The application to the problem of how to account for the disturbed behaviour seen in experimental neurosis precipitated by difficult discriminations derives from the nature of the task imposed in this type of situation. After preliminary training in restraint, during which time the subject's fear reactions to the restraint and to the experimental situation generally are gradually inhibited and replaced by food seeking responses, the task proper begins. A feature of it is that the task becomes progressively more and more difficult—as soon as the animal masters one discrimination a start is made on the next and so on. Now, from a consideration of the action of the Yerkes-Dodson law, it is clear that the optimum performance will be achieved by the subject in this situation with a progressive *lowering* of motivation. That is to say, the optimum motivation for each new level of difficulty will be lower than that for the preceding, easier one. But it seems unlikely that experimental animals will have encountered situations before in which this principle operates, that is, in which greater reinforcement follows lower rather than higher motivation, and so will not have had the opportunity for learning which particular level of motivation will secure a desired goal. On the contrary, most of the situations they are likely to have encountered previously are simple ones in which higher drive levels have in general been more efficacious than lower ones. It is postulated, therefore, that the result of failure in the discrimination situation to receive the anticipated reinforcement when the subject responds wrongly to a negative conditioned stimulus will result in an increase of motivation, by virtue of the previously learned responses referred to above. Subjectively speaking, the natural result of failure is to try harder. Thus a conditioned increase of drive (Brown and Farber, 1951; Marx, 1956) may be added to that already existing. This, in turn, will lead to further failure to make the discrimination, and additional slight increments in drive may be expected because of the added delay in anticipated reinforcement which may occur, and because of the drive arousal cues now associated with both positive and negative stimuli, which, typically, are now both responded to equally. At this stage, it is further suggested, the increased drive level energizes incorrect responses in competition with the correct ones—responses, especially fear ones, which were suppressed early on in the training. So it is that struggling, howling, and agitated behaviour in general, which were previously characteristic of the subject's initial reactions to the situation are reinstated anew.

This formulation serves to reconcile certain phenomena frequently reported in conditioning work which do not seem to have been adequately explained hitherto. Several experimenters have mentioned the failure of the method of improving the subject's discrimination performance by increasing the hunger drive: if the above analysis is correct, the prediction might be made that reducing the hunger drive, rather than increasing it, would be more beneficial. In the same way, the observation of some workers that making the discrimination problem simpler has therapeutic value fits in with our formulation. On the other hand, the more common finding is that after the breakdown of discrimination at extreme levels of difficulty, even simple discriminations are no longer made and have to be re-learned. It seems probable that this characteristic failure of simple discrimination can be accounted for if it is recalled that even relatively simple tasks have an optimum motivation, which may well be surpassed if anxiety is added to the motivational complex.

One ubiquitous finding—Pavlov and Gantt, as well as Liddell and Masserman all mention it—is that the presence of the experimenter in the conditioning chamber with the subject appears to have a quieting effect on neurotic animals. Anderson and Liddell (1935) came nearest to a rational explanation of this fact when they observed that conditioned signals are not given when the experimenter is in the room. Now, the task this poses the animal is to distinguish between "experimenter present" and "experimenter absent"—an extremely simple perceptual discrimination. The simplicity of this task is such that it seems likely that it will be very well learned, even under the extremely high drive postulated as eventuating from the previous breakdown. Also this high drive level may be responsible for the rapid learning of any other novel feature in the experimental situation, especially if it has any drive reducing properties. Herein may lie the clue to the so-called pathological generalization of the disorder of Gantt's dog "Nick," who, it will be recalled, developed genito-urinary signs long after the original precipitating cause of the experimental neurosis had passed. They did not, however, arise spontaneously.

They followed the introduction of a bitch in oestrus into the experimental situation for therapeutic purposes. It is suggested that the pollakiuria and sexual erections noted in this dog thereafter may in fact have been conditioned responses to the experimental situation, the female acting as the original unconditioned stimulus. It should be noted that the transient abnormalities of sexual function noted in another dog (Gantt, 1944) followed attempts to develop sexual conditioned responses in the experimental situation. Two further facts about "Nick" seem to support our view; the dog learned a new association to light as a conditioned stimulus without any reward, which suggests a continuing high drive level; as does the observation that he persisted in looking towards the location of the original auditory conditioned stimulus, many years after it had been altered.

While this attempt to account for some of the facts of experimental neurosis in learning theory terms is doubtless deficient in many respects, it serves to indicate that it is likely that the phenomena observed can be brought under the rubric of conventional learning theory in a general way. More can hardly be expected at this time in view of the deficiencies in the evidence available. Significant advance in the future probably lies in the use of more strictly controlled situations for the study of the development of emotional responses—the conditioned emotional response (C.E.R.), for example—which permit detailed analysis of the stimuli and responses involved, such as that, for example, of Schoenfeld (1950). He writes: "The distance from rat to man is a long one, yet it may turn out to be filled with differences in detail rather than in principle. Most, or all, experimental psychologists are as vitally interested as the clinician in understanding man, but use the laboratory as their route to that goal in the belief that through it may be achieved a sound theory of behavior leading to widened practical successes in the field" (1950, p. 95).

REFERENCES

ALTMANN, MARGARET, A study of activity and neighbourly relations in swine, *J. Comp. Psychol.*, **31**, 473–480 (1941).

ANDERSON, O. D., Two cases of experimental neurosis in dogs of known genetic constitution, *Amer. J. Physiol.*, **126**, 421–422, abstract (1939).

ANDERSON, O. D., The role of the glands of internal secretion in the production of behavioral types in the dog, in *The Genetic and Endocrinic Basis for Differences in Form and Behavior*, Ed. C. R. Stockard, 647–747 (Philadelphia, Wistar Inst., 1941).

ANDERSON, O. D. and LIDDELL, H. S., Observations on experimental neurosis in sheep, *Arch. Neurol. Psychiat. Chicago*, **34**, 330–354 (1935).

ANDERSON, O. D. and PARMENTER, R., A long-term study

of the experimental neurosis in the sheep and dog, *Psychosom. Med. Monogr.*, **2**, 1–150 (1941).

ANDERSON, O. D., PARMENTER, R. and LIDDELL, H. S., Some cardiovascular manifestations of the experimental neurosis in the sheep, *Psychosom. Med.*, **1**, 93–100 (1939).

APTER, I. M., A contribution to the problem of the formation of experimental disruption of higher nervous activity in dogs under conditions of natural experiment, *Zh. Vyssh. Nervn. Deiatel.*, **2**, 104–112 (1952) (*Psychol. Abstr.*, **27**, No. 2,143, 1953).

ARMSTRONG, E. A., The nature and function of displacement activities, in *Physiological Mechanisms in Animal Behaviour*, Eds. J. F. Danielli and R. Brown, *Sympos. Soc. Exp. Biol.*, **4**, 361–384 (1950).

BABKIN, B. P., Experimental neuroses in animals and their treatment with bromides, *Edinb. Med. J.*, **45**, 605–619 (1938).

BABKIN, B. P., *Pavlov: a Biography* (London, Gollancz, 1951).

BAJANDUROV, B. I., Zur Physiologie des Sehenanalysators bei Vögeln, *Z. Vergl. Physiol.*, **18**, 298–306 (1933).

BARNETT, S. A., Competition among wild rats, *Nature, London*, **75**, 126–127 (1955).

BARNETT, S. A., "Displacement" behaviour and "psychosomatic" disorder, *Lancet*, **2**, 1,203–1,208 (1955a).

BASTOCK, MARGARET, MORRIS, D. and MOYNIHAN, M., Some comments on conflict and thwarting in animals, *Behaviour*, **6**, 66–84 (1953).

BEACH, F. A., Animal research and psychiatric theory, *Psychosom. Med.*, **15**, 374–389 (1953).

BEACH, F. A. and JAYNES, J., Effects of early experience upon the behavior of animals, *Psychol. Bull.*, **51**, 230–263 (1954).

BEVAN, W., Sound-precipitated convulsions: 1947–1954, *Psychol. Bull.*, **52**, 473–504 (1955).

BIJOU, S. W., The development of a conditioning methodology for studying experimental neurosis in the rat, *J. Comp. Psychol.*, **34**, 91–106 (1942).

BIJOU, S. W., A study of "experimental neurosis" in the rat by the conditioned response technique, *J. Comp. Psychol.*, **36**, 1–20 (1943).

BIJOU, S. W., A new conditioned response technique to investigate "experimental neurosis" in the rat, *Amer. Psychologist*, **2**, 319, abstract (1947).

BIJOU, S. W., A conditioned response technique to investigate "experimental neurosis" in the rat, *J. Comp. Physiol. Psychol.*, **44**, 84–87 (1951).

BOWLBY, J., *Maternal Care and Mental Health*, World Health Organisation Monogr. Ser. 2. Geneva (1951).

BRADY, J. V., A comparative approach to the experimental analysis of emotional behavior, in *Experimental Psychopathology*, Ed. P. H. Hoch and J. Zubin, 20–33 (New York, Grune & Stratton, 1957).

BRADY, J. V., and HUNT, H. F., An experimental approach to the analysis of emotional behavior, *J. Psychol.*, **40**, 313–324 (1955).

BROADHURST, P. L., Cardiac, respiratory and squeak conditioning in the rat, *Bull. Brit. Psychol. Soc.*, **23** (Inset), 3, abstract (1954).

BROADHURST, P. L., Determinants of emotionality in the rat: I. Situational factors, *Brit. J. Psychol.*, **48**, 1–12 (1957).

BROADHURST, P. L., Emotionality and the Yerkes-Dodson Law, *J. Exp. Psychol.*, **54**, 345–352 (1957a).

BROADHURST, P. L., Air deprivation as a motivational technique in the rat, and its application to the problem of emotionality as a determinant of drive, *Bull. Brit. Psychol. Soc.*, **32** (Inset), 23, abstract (1957b).

BROADHURST, P. L., Determinants of emotionality in the rat: II. Antecedent factors, *Brit. J. Psychol.*, **49**, 12–20 (1958).

BROADHURST, P. L., Determinants of emotionality in the rat: III. Strain differences, *J. Comp. Physiol. Psychol.*, **51**, 55–59 (1958a).

BROADHURST, P. L., A "Crespi effect" in the analysis of emotionality as a drive in rats, *Brit. J. Psychol.*, **49**, 56–58 (1958b).

BROADHURST, P. L., The interaction of task difficulty and motivation: the Yerkes-Dodson Law revived, *Acta Psychol.*, **16**, 321–338 (1959).

BROADHURST, P. L., Application of biometrical genetics to behaviour in rats, *Nature, London*, **184**, 1517–1518 (1959a).

BROADHURST, P. L., Studies in psychogenetics: applications of biometrical genetics to the inheritance of behaviour, in *Experiments in Personality, Vol. I, Psychogenetics and Psychopharmacology*, Ed. H. J. Eysenck (London, Routledge & Kegan Paul, 1960).

BROWN, J. S., and FARBER, I. E., Emotions conceptualized as intervening variables with suggestions toward a theory of frustration, *Psychol. Bull.*, **48**, 465–495 (1951).

BRÜCKNER, G. H., Untersuchungen zur Tiersoziologie insbesondere zur Auflösung der Familie, *Z. Psychol.*, **128**, 1–110 (1933).

CAIN, J. and EXTREMET, JOSETTE, Étude comparative des procédés de création de la névrose expérimentale chez l'animal, *Proc. XV Int. Congr. Psychol.*, Brussels, 599 abstract (1957).

CAMERON, D. E., Studies in depression, *J. Ment. Sci.*, **82**, 148–161 (1936).

CARMICHAEL, L., Learning which modifies an animal's subsequent capacity for learning, *J. Genet. Psychol.*, **52**, 159–163 (1938).

CHANCE, M. R. H., Mammalian behaviour studies in medical research, *Lancet*, **2**, 687–690 (1957).

CONGER, J. J., The effects of alcohol on conflict behavior in the albino rat, *Quart. J. Stud. Alc.*, **12**, 1–29 (1951).

CONGER, J. J., SAWREY, W. L. and TURRELL, E. S., The role of social experience in the production of gastric ulcers in hooded rats, *J. Abnorm. (Soc.) Psychol.*, **52**, 214–220 (1958).

COOK, S. W., A survey of methods used to produce "experimental neurosis," *Amer. J. Psychiat.*, **95**, 1,259–1,276 (1939).

COOK, S. W., Some theoretical considerations relating to "experimental neurosis," *Psychol. Bull.*, **36**, 516, abstract (1939a).

COOK, S. W., The production of "experimental neurosis" in the white rat, *Psychosom. Med.*, **1**, 293–308 (1939b).

COWLES, J. T. and PENNINGTON, L. A., An improved conditioning technique for determining auditory acuity of the rat, *J. Psychol.*, **15**, 41–47 (1943).

CRAWFORD, M. P., FULTON, J. F., JACOBSEN, C. F. and WOLFE, J. B., Frontal lobe ablation in chimpanzee: a résumé of "Becky" and "Lucy," in "The Frontal Lobes," Ed., J. F. Fulton, C. D. Aring and S. B. Wortis, *Assoc. Res. Nerv. Ment. Dis.* **27**, 3–58 (1947).

CROFT, PHYLLIS G., Some observations on neurosis in farm animals, *J. Ment. Sci.*, **97**, 584–588 (1951).

CURTI, MARGARET W., Native fear responses of white rats in the presence of cats, in "Studies in Psychology from Smith College," Ed. J. J. Gibson, *Psychol. Monogr.*, **46**, Whole No. 210, 78–98 (1935).

CURTIS, Q. F., Experimental neurosis in the pig, *Psychol. Bull.*, **34**, 723, abstract (1937).

CURTIS, Q. F., Diurnal variation in the free activity of sheep and pig, *Proc. Soc. Exp. Biol. N.Y.*, **35**, 566–567 (1937a).

DAVIS, D. R., Some applications of behaviour theory in psychopathology, *Brit. J. Med. Psychol.*, **27**, 216–223 (1954).

DAVIS, H., DWORKIN, S., LURIE, H. M. and KATZMAN, J., Symposium—the neural mechanism of hearing: III. Animal investigations (a) Behavioural, electrical and anatomical studies of abnormal ears, *Laryngoscope*, **47**, 435–447 (1937).

DENTON, D. A., A gregarious factor in the natural conditioned salivary reflexes of sheep, *Nature, London*, **179**, 341–344 (1957).

DIMMICK, F. L., LUDLOW, N. and WHITEMAN, A., A study of "experimental neurosis" in cats, *J. Comp. Psychol.*, **28**, 39–43 (1939).

DRABOVITCH, W. and WEGER, P., Deux cas de névrose expérimentale chez le chien, *C.R. Acad. Sci.*, **204**, 902–905 (1937).

DWORKIN, S., Pitch and intensity discriminations by cats, *Amer. J. Physiol.*, **112**, 1–4 (1935).

DWORKIN, S., Alimentary motor conditioning and pitch discrimination in dogs, *Amer. J. Physiol.*, **112**, 323–328 (1935a).

DWORKIN, S., Conditioning neurosis in the dog and cat, *Amer. J. Physiol.*, **123**, 57, abstract (1938).

DWORKIN, S., Conditioning neuroses in dogs and cats, *Psychosom. Med.*, **1**, 388–396 (1939).

DWORKIN, S., BAXT, JUDITH O. and DWORKIN, E., Behavioral disturbances of vomiting and micturition in conditioned cats, *Psychosom. Med.*, **4**, 75–81 (1942).

DWORKIN, S., BAXT, JUDITH O., and GROSS, J., Deafness "neurosis" in the cat as a special form of disinhibition, *Fed. Proc.*, **1**, 23, abstract (1942).

DWORKIN, S., BOURNE, W. and RAGINSKY, B. B., Changes in conditioned responses brought about by anaesthetics and sedatives, *Canad. Med. Ass. J.*, **37**, 136–139 (1937).

DWORKIN, S., BOURNE, W. and RAGINSKY, B. B., Action des anesthésiques, sedatifs, hypnotiques sur les centres nerveux supérieurs, *Anésth. Analgés.*, **3**, 335–349 (1937a).

DWORKIN, S., KATZMAN, J., HUTCHINSON, G. A. and McCABE, J. R., Hearing acuity of animals as measured by conditioning methods, *J. Exp. Psychol.*, **26**, 281–298 (1940).

DWORKIN, S., RAGINSKY, B. B. and BOURNE, W., Action of anaesthetics and sedatives upon the inhibited nervous system, *Curr. Res. Anesth.*, **16**, 238–240 (1937).

DWORKIN, S., SEYMOUR, S. L. and SUTHERLAND, G., A conditioned reflex method of testing hearing in cats, *Quart. J. Exp. Physiol.*, **24**, 23–30 (1934).

DYKMAN, R. A. and GANTT, W. H., A comparative study of cardiac and motor conditioned responses, *Amer. J. Physiol.*, **167**, 780, abstract (1951).

DYKMAN, R. A. and GANTT, W. H., A comparative study of cardiac conditioned responses and motor conditioned responses in controlled "stress" situations, *Amer. Psychologist*, **6**, 263–264, abstract (1951a).

DYKMAN, R. A., GANTT, W. H. and WHITEHORN, J. C., Conditioning as emotional sensitization and differentiation, *Psychol. Monogr.*, **70**, Whole No. 422 (1956).

ERÄNKÖ, M. and MUITTARI, A., Effects of experimental neurosis on the thyroid and adrenal gland of the rat, *Acta Endocrinol., Copenhagen*, **26**, 109–116 (1957).

EYSENCK, H. J., *The Psychology of Politics* (London, Routledge & Kegan Paul, 1954).

EYSENCK, H. J., A dynamic theory of anxiety and hysteria, *J. Ment. Sci.*, **101**, 28–51 (1955).

FIELDS, P. E., Contributions to visual discrimination in the white rat: II. *J. Comp. Psychol.*, **11**, 349–366 (1931).

FINGER, F. W., Quantitative studies of "conflict": II. The effect of "conflict" upon the general activity of the white rat, *J. Comp. Psychol.*, **32**, 139–152 (1941).

FINGER, F. W., Experimental behavior disorder in the rat, in *Personality and the Behavior Disorders*, Ed., J. McV. Hunt, 413–430 (New York, Ronald Press, 1944).

FINGER, F. W., Convulsive behavior in the rat, *Psychol. Bull.*, **44**, 201–248 (1947).

FOLEY, J. P., JNR., The criterion of abnormality, *J. Abnorm. (Soc.) Psychol.*, **30**, 279–291 (1935).

FONBERG, ELŻBIETA, The manifestation of the defensive reactions in neurotic states, *Acta Biol. Exp.*, **18**, 89–112 (1958).

FRANKS, C. M., Alcohol, alcoholism and conditioning: a review of the literature and some theoretical considerations, *J. Ment. Sci.*, **104**, 14–33 (1958).

FRASER, A. F., The disposition of the bull, *Brit. J. Anim. Behav.*, **5**, 110–115 (1957).

FRASER, R., *The Incidence of Neurosis among Factory Workers* (London, H.M.S.O., 1947).

FREEMAN, W. and WATTS, I. W., Physiological psychology, *Annu. Rev. Physiol.*, **6**, 517–542 (1944).

FRENCH, J. D., PORTER, R. W., CAVANAUGH, E. B. and LONGMIRE, R. L., Experimental gastroduodenal lesions induced by stimulation of the brain, *Psychosom. Med.*, **19**, 209–220 (1957).

FROLOV, Y. P., *Pavlov and his School* (London, Kegan Paul, 1937).

FULLER, J. L., Individual differences in the emotional level of dogs, *Anat. Rec.*, **99**, 621, abstract (1947).

FULTON, J. F. and JACOBSEN, C. F., The functions of the frontal lobes: a comparative study in monkeys, chimpanzee and man, *Proc. II Int. Congr. Neurol., London* (1935).

GALT, W. E., The capacity of the rhesus and *cebus* monkey and the gibbon to acquire differential response to complex visual stimuli, *Genet. Psychol. Monogr.*, **21**, 387–457 (1939).

GANTT, W. H., An experimental approach to psychiatry, *Amer. J. Psychiat.*, **92**, 1,007–1,021 (1936).

GANTT, W. H., Extension of a conflict based on food to

other physiological systems and its reciprocal relations with sexual function, *Amer. J. Physiol.*, **123**, 73–74, abstract (1938).

GANTT, W. H., Effect of alcohol on sexual reflexes in dogs, *Amer. J. Physiol.*, **129**, 360, abstract (1940).

GANTT, W. H., The role of the isolated conditioned stimulus in the integrated response pattern, and the relation of the pattern changes to psychopathology, *J. Gen. Psychol.*, **23**, 3–16 (1940a).

GANTT, W. H., The origin and development of nervous disturbances experimentally produced, *Amer. J. Psychiat.*, **98**, 475–481 (1942).

GANTT, W. H., Cardiac conditioned reflexes to painful stimuli, *Fed. Proc.*, **1**, 28, abstract (1942a).

GANTT, W. H., *Experimental Basis for Neurotic Behavior: Origin and Development of Artificially Produced Disturbances of Behavior in Dogs* (New York, Hoeber, 1944). (Also, *Psychosom. Med. Monogr.*, **3**, Nos. 3 and 4.)

GANTT, W. H., Cardiac conditional reflexes to time, *Trans. Amer. Neurol. Assoc.*, **72**, 166, abstract (1946).

GANTT, W. H., Physiological psychology, *Annu. Rev. Physiol.*, **10**, 453–478 (1948).

GANTT, W. H., Effect of alcohol on the sexual reflexes of normal and neurotic male dogs, *Psychosom. Med.*, **14**, 174–181 (1952).

GANTT, W. H., Principles of nervous breakdown in schizokinesis and autokinesis, in "Comparative conditioned neuroses," Ed. E. J. Kempf, *Ann. N.Y. Acad. Sci.*, **56**, 141–165 (1953).

GANTT, W. H., The physiological basis of psychiatry: the conditional reflex, in *Basic Problems in Psychiatry*, Ed. J. Wortis, 52–89 (New York, Grune & Stratton, 1953a).

GANTT, W. H., (Ed.) *Physiological Basis of Psychiatry* (Springfield, Ill., Thomas, 1957).

GANTT, W. H. and DYKMAN, R. A., Experimental psychogenic tachycardia, *Amer. J. Physiol.*, **171**, 725–726, abstract (1952).

GANTT, W. H. and DYKMAN, R. A., Experimental psychogenic tachycardia, in *Experimental Psychopathology*, Eds. P. H. Hoch and J. Zubin, 12–19 (New York, Grune & Stratton, 1957).

GANTT, W. H. and FREILE, M., Effect of adrenalin and acetylcholin on excitation, inhibition and neuroses, *Trans. Amer. Neurol. Assoc.*, **69**, 180–181, abstract (1944).

GANTT, W. H., GAKENHEIMER, W. A. and STUNKARD, A., Development of cardiac reflex to time intervals, *Fed. Proc.*, **10**, 47–48, abstract (1951).

GANTT, W. H. and HOFFMAN, W. C., Conditioned cardiorespiratory changes accompanying conditioned food reflexes, *Amer. J. Physiol.*, **129**, 360–361, abstract (1940).

GANTT, W. H., HOFFMAN, W. C. and DWORKIN, S., The cardiac conditional reflex, *Abstr. Comm. XVII Int. Congr. Physiol.*, *Oxford*, **15**, (1947).

GANTT, W. H. and MUNCIE, W., Rhythmic variations of muscular activity in normal and neurotic dogs correlated with secretion and with conditioned reflexes, *Amer. J. Physiol.*, **133**, 287, abstract (1941).

GANTT, W. H. and TRAUGOTT, URSULA, Retention of cardiac, salivary and motor conditional reflexes, *Amer. J. Physiol.*, **159**, 569, abstract (1949).

GENTRY, EVELYN and DUNLAP, K., An attempt to produce

neurotic behavior in rats, *J. Comp. Psychol.*, **33**, 107–112 (1942).

GOLDACRE, R. J., Polar locomotion and experimental "neurosis" in the amoeba, *Anim. Behav.*, **6**, 242, abstract (1958).

GOLDMAN, M. M., Motor conditioning in the goat, *Amer. J. Physiol.*, **126**, 504–505, abstract (1939).

GREEN, R. T., Threshold for electric shock of the laboratory rat, *Anim. Behav.*, **6**, 72–76 (1958).

GROSSLIGHT, J. H. and TICKNER, W., Variability and reactive inhibition in the mealworm as a function of determined turning sequences, *J. Comp. Physiol. Psychol.*, **46**, 35–38 (1953).

HALL, C. S., A comparative psychologist's approach to problems in abnormal psychology, *J. Abnorm. (Soc.) Psychol.*, **28**, 1–5 (1933).

HALL, C. S., Emotional behavior in the rat: I. Defecation and urination as measures of individual differences in emotionality, *J. Comp. Psychol.*, **18**, 385–403 (1934).

HAMILTON, G. V., Comparative psychology and psychopathology, *Amer. J. Psychol.*, **39**, 200–211 (1927).

HANSEN, K. H., *After Effects in the Behaviour of Mice* (Copenhagen, Munksgaard, 1956).

HARLOW, H. F., Current and future advances in physiological and comparative psychology, *Amer. Psychologist*, **11**, 273–277 (1956).

HEBB, D. O., Emotion in man and animal: an analysis of the intuitive process of recognition, *Psychol. Rev.*, **53**, 88–106 (1946).

HEBB, D. O., Spontaneous neurosis in chimpanzees: theoretical relations with clinical and experimental phenomena, *Psychosom. Med.*, **9**, 3–16 (1947).

HEBB, D. O. and THOMPSON, W. R., The social significance of animal studies, in *Handbook of Social Psychology. Vol. I, Theory and Method*, Ed. G. Lindzey, 532–561 (Cambridge, Mass., Addison-Wesley, 1954).

HEDIGER, H., *Wild Animals in Captivity* (London, Butterworth, 1950).

HIGGINSON, G. D., The after effects of certain emotional situations upon maze learning among white rats, *J. Comp. Psychol.*, **10**, 1–10 (1930).

HILGARD, E. R., *Theories of Learning*, 2nd ed. (New York, Appleton-Century-Crofts, 1956).

HUGHES, B. and SCHLOSBERG, H., Conditioning in the white rat: IV. The conditioned lid reflex, *J. Exp. Psychol.*, **23**, 641–650 (1938).

HULL, C. L., A projected integration of the conditioned-reflex and the psychoanalytic approaches to the study of psychogenic disorders, *Proc. Conference Exp. Neuroses and Allied Problems* (Washington, National Research Council, 1937).

HUMPHREY, G. and MARCUSE, F., New methods of obtaining neurotic behavior in rats, *Amer. J. Psychol.*, **52**, 616–619 (1939).

HUMPHREY, G. and MARCUSE, F., Factors influencing the susceptibility of albino rats to convulsive attacks under intense auditory stimulation, *J. Comp. Psychol.*, **32**, 285–306 (1941).

HUNT, J. McV. and SCHLOSBERG, H., Rats in continuous conflict, *J. Comp. Physiol. Psychol.*, **43**, 351–357 (1950).

HUTYRA, F., MAREK, J. and MANNINGER, R., *Special Pathology and Therapeutics of the Diseases of Domestic*

Animals, 5th Eng. ed. (London, Baillière, Tindall & Cox, 1946).

IVANOV-SMOLENSKY, A. G., *Essays on the Patho-physiology of the Higher Nervous Activity: according to I. P. Pavlov and his School* (Moscow, Foreign Languages Publishing House, 1954).

JACOBSEN, C. F., Experimental analysis of the functions of the frontal association areas in primates, *J. Nerv. Ment. Dis.*, **81**, 437–442 (1935).

JACOBSEN, C. F., WOLFE, J. B. and JACKSON, T. A., An experimental analysis of the functions of the frontal association areas in primates, *J. Nerv. Ment. Dis.*, **82**, 1–14 (1935).

JACOBSEN, E. and SKAARUP, Y., Experimental induction of conflict behaviour in cats: its use in pharmacological investigations, *Acta Pharm. Tox., Kbh.*, **11**, 117–124 (1955).

JAMES, W. T., A conditioned avoiding posture of the dog, *Psychol. Bull.*, **31**, 730, abstract (1934).

JAMES, W. T., The formation of neurosis in dogs by increasing the energy requirements of a conditioned avoiding response, *J. Comp. Psychol.*, **36**, 109–124 (1943).

JAMES, W. T., Morphological and constitutional factors in conditioning, in "Comparative conditioned neuroses," Ed. E. J. Kempf, *Ann. N.Y. Acad. Sci.*, **56**, 171–183 (1953).

JAMISON, J. H., Measurement of auditory intensity thresholds in the rat by conditioning of an autonomic response, *J. Comp. Physiol. Psychol.*, **44**, 118–125 (1951).

JENKINS, W. O. and STANLEY, J. C., JNR., Partial reinforcement: a review and critique, *Psychol. Bull.*, **47**, 193–234 (1950).

JENSEN, A. V., Identification of gun-shyness with experimental neurosis in dogs, *Fed. Proc.*, **4**, 36, abstract (1945).

JONES, H. E. and JONES, M. C., A study of fear, *Childhood Educ.*, **5**, 136–143 (1928).

JONES, H. G., The application of conditioning and learning techniques to the treatment of a psychiatric patient, *J. Abnorm. (Soc.) Psychol.*, **52**, 414–419 (1956).

KAMINSKY, S. D., Problem of experimental neurosis: the active adaptation of monkeys to difficult experimental conditions, *Arkh. Biol. Nauk.*, **53**, 69–88 (1939) (*Psychol. Abstr.*, **13**, No. 5711, 1939).

KAPPAUF, W. E. and SCHLOSBERG, H., Conditioned responses in the white rat: III. Conditioning as a function of the length of the period of delay, *J. Genet. Psychol.*, **50**, 27–45 (1937).

KARN, H. W., The behavior of cats on the double alternation problem in the temporal maze, *J. Comp. Psychol.*, **26**, 201–208 (1938).

KARN, H. W., A case of experimentally induced neurosis in the cat, *J. Exp. Psychol.*, **22**, 589–592 (1938a).

KARN, H. W., The experimental study of neurotic behavior in infrahuman animals, *J. Gen. Psychol.*, **22**, 431–436 (1940).

KARN, H. W., Experimental neurosis in infrahuman animals—a bibliography, *Psychol. Rec.*, **4**, 35–39 (1940a).

KARN, H. W. and MALAMUD, H. R., The behavior of dogs on the double alternation problem in the temporal maze, *J. Comp. Psychol.*, **27**, 461–466 (1939).

KAWAMURA, Y. and YOSHII, N., A study on the experimental neurosis of rats: behavior patterns, *Med. J. Osaka Univ.*, **2**, 133–148 (1951).

KENNEDY, J. S., Is modern ethology objective? *Brit. J. Anim. Behav.*, **2**, 12–19 (1954).

KING, J. A. and MAVROMATIS, A., The effect of a conflict situation on the learning ability in two strains of inbred mice, *J. Comp. Physiol. Psychol.*, **49**, 465–468 (1956).

KONORSKI, J., *Conditioned Reflexes and Neuron Organization* (London, Cambridge Univ. Press, 1948).

KREPS, E. M., An attempt to establish a classification of experimental animals according to type, *Coll. Papers Physiol. Lab. I. P. Pavlov*, **1**, 118–140 (1924).

KUPALOV, P. S., On experimental neuroses in animals, *Zh. Vyssh. Nervn. Deiatel*, **2**, 457–473 (1952) (*Psychol. Abstr.*, **28**, No. 8907, 1954).

LANDIS, C. and BOLLES, M. MARJORIE, *Textbook of Abnormal Psychology* (New York, Macmillan, 1949).

LEAVITT, F. H. and RIGGS, HELENA E., Pathologic study of a monkey exhibiting behavior disorder, *Arch. Neurol. Psychiat. Chicago*, **47**, 186–188 (1942).

LIBERSON, W. T., Recent advances in Russian neurophysiology, *Annu. Rev. Physiol.*, **19**, 557–588 (1957).

LICHTENSTEIN, P. E., Studies of anxiety: I. The production of a feeding inhibition in dogs, *J. Comp. Physiol. Psychol.*, **43**, 16–29 (1950).

LICHTENSTEIN, P. E., Studies of anxiety: II. The effect of lobotomy on a feeding inhibition in dogs, *J. Comp. Physiol. Psychol.*, **43**, 419–427 (1950a).

LICKLIDER, J. C. R. and BUNCH, M. E., Effects of enforced wakefulness upon growth and the maze-learning performance of white rats, *J. Comp. Psychol.*, **39**, 339–350 (1946).

LIDDELL, H. S., The behavior of sheep and goats in learning a simple maze, *Amer. J. Psychol.*, **36**, 544–552 (1925).

LIDDELL, H. S., The relation between maze learning and spontaneous activity in the sheep, *J. Comp. Psychol.*, **5**, 475–484 (1925a).

LIDDELL, H. S., A laboratory for the study of conditioned motor reflexes, *Amer. J. Psychol.*, **37**, 418–419 (1926).

LIDDELL, H. S., Nervous strain in domesticated animals and man, *Cornell Vet.*, **26**, 107–112 (1936).

LIDDELL, H. S., The experimental neurosis and the problem of mental disorder, *Amer. J. Psychiat.*, **94**, 1,035–1,043 (1938).

LIDDELL, H. S., The conditioned reflex, in *Comparative Psychology*, 2nd ed., Ed. F. A. Moss, 178–216 (New York, Prentice-Hall, 1942).

LIDDELL, H. S., The alteration of the instinctual processes through the influence of conditioned reflexes, *Psychosom. Med.*, **4**, 390–395 (1942a).

LIDDELL, H. S., Conditioned reflex method and experimental neurosis, in *Personality and the Behavior Disorders*, Ed. J. McV. Hunt, 389–412 (New York, Ronald Press, 1944).

LIDDELL, H. S., The experimental neurosis, *Annu. Rev. Physiol.*, **9**, 569–580 (1947).

LIDDELL, H. S., The nervous system as a whole: the conditioned reflex, in *Physiology of the Nervous System*, 3rd ed., Ed. J. F. Fulton, 537–568 (New York, Oxford Univ. Press, 1949).

LIDDELL, H. S., Animal origins of anxiety, in *Feelings and*

Emotions, Ed. M. L. Reymert, 181–188 (New York, McGraw-Hill, 1950).

LIDDELL, H. S., Some specific factors that modify tolerance for environmental stress, in "Life Stress and Bodily Disease," Eds. H. H. Wolff, S. G. Wolf, and C. C. Hare, *Assoc. Res. Nerv. Ment. Dis.*, **29**, 155–171 (1950a).

LIDDELL, H. S., The role of vigilance in the development of animal neurosis, in *Anxiety*, Eds. P. Hoch and J. Zubin, 183–196 (New York, Grune & Stratton, 1950b).

LIDDELL, H. S., The influence of experimental neuroses on the respiratory function, in *Somatic and Psychiatric Treatment of Asthma*, Ed. H. A. Abramson, 126–147 (Baltimore, Williams & Wilkins, 1951).

LIDDELL, H. S., Experimental induction of psychoneuroses by conditioned reflex with stress, in *The Biology of Mental Health and Disease*, 498–507, Millbank Memorial Fund (New York, Hoeber, 1952).

LIDDELL, H. S., Effect of corticosteroids in experimental psychoneurosis, in *The Biology of Mental Health and Disease*, 591–594, Millbank Memorial Fund (New York, Hoeber, 1952a).

LIDDELL, H. S., A comparative approach to the dynamics of experimental neuroses, in "Comparative Conditioned Neuroses," Ed. E. J. Kempf, *Ann. N.Y. Acad. Sci.*, **56**, 164–170, (1953).

LIDDELL, H. S., Conditioning and emotions, *Sci. Amer.*, **190**, 48–57 (1954).

LIDDELL, H. S., The natural history of neurotic behavior, in *Society and Medicine: Lectures to the Laity*, Ed. I. Galdston, No. 17, 46–69, (New York, Int. Univ. Press, 1955).

LIDDELL, H. S., *Emotional Hazards in Animals and Man* (Springfield, Ill., C. C. Thomas, 1956).

LIDDELL, H. S., ANDERSON, O. D., KOTYUKA, E. and HARTMAN, F. A., The effect of cortin on the experimental neurosis in sheep, *Amer. J. Physiol.*, **113**, 87–88, abstract (1935).

LIDDELL, H. S., ANDERSON, O. D., KOTYUKA, E. and HARTMAN, F. A., Effect of extract of adrenal cortex on experimental neurosis in sheep, *Arch. Neurol. Psychiat. Chicago*, **34**, 973–993 (1935a).

LIDDELL, H. S. and BAYNE, T. L., Auditory conditioned reflexes in the thyroidectomized sheep and goat, *Proc. Soc. Exp. Biol. N.Y.*, **24**, 289–291 (1927).

LIDDELL, H. S. and BAYNE, T. L., The development of "experimental neurasthenia" in the sheep during the formation of difficult conditioned reflexes, *Amer. J. Physiol.*, **81**, 494, abstract (1927a).

LIDDELL, H. S., JAMES, W. T. and ANDERSON, O. D., The comparative physiology of the conditioned motor reflex based on experiments with the pig, dog, sheep, goat and rabbit, *Comp. Psychol. Monogr.*, **11**, No. 51, 1–89 (1934).

LIDDELL, H. S. and SIMPSON, ETHEL D., A preliminary study of motor conditioned reflexes in thyroidectomized sheep, *Proc. Soc. Exp. Biol. N.Y.*, **23**, 720–722 (1926).

LIDDELL, H. S. and SIMPSON, S., The effects of thyroid therapy on the neuro-muscular activity of cretin sheep, *Amer. J. Physiol.*, **72**, 63–68 (1925).

LIDDELL, H. S., SUTHERLAND, G. F., PARMENTER, R. and BAYNE, T. L., A study of the conditioned reflex method for producing experimental neurosis, *Amer. J. Physiol.*, **116**, 95–96, abstract (1936).

LIDDELL, H. S., SUTHERLAND, G. F., PARMENTER, R., CURTIS, Q. F. and ANDERSON, O. D., Further analysis of the conditioned reflex method in relation to the experimental neurosis, *Amer. J. Physiol.*, **119**, 361, abstract (1937).

LORENZ, K., Durch Domestikation verursachte Störungen arteigenen verhaltens, *Z. Angew. Psychol. Charakterk.*, **59** (1940).

LUBIN, A. J., The experimental neurosis in animal and man, *Amer. J. Med. Sci.*, **205**, 269–277 (1943).

MACLEOD, L. D., "A monthly bulletin" research report, *Brit. J. Addict.*, **50**, 89–135 (1953).

MAIER, N. R. F., *Studies of Abnormal Behavior in the Rat: the Neurotic Pattern and an Analysis of the Situation which Produces it* (New York, Harper & Bros., 1939).

MAIER, N. R. F., *Frustration: the Study of Behavior Without a Goal* (New York, McGraw-Hill, 1949).

MAIER, N. R. F., Frustration theory: restatement and extension, *Psychol. Rev.*, **63**, 370–388 (1956).

MARCUSE, F. and MOORE, A. U., Conditioned reflexes in the pig, *Bull. Canad. Psychol. Assoc.*, **2**, 13–14 (1942).

MARCUSE, F. and MOORE, A. U., Tantrum behavior in the pig, *J. Comp. Psychol.*, **37**, 235–247 (1944).

MARCUSE, F. and MOORE, A. U., Motor criteria of discrimination, *J. Comp. Psychol.*, **39**, 25–27 (1946).

MARX, M. H., Some relations between frustration and drive, in *Nebraska Symposium on Motivation*, 1956, Ed. M. R. Jones, 92–130 (Lincoln, Univ. of Nebraska Press, 1956).

MASSERMAN, J. H., An automatic apparatus for the central conditioning of small animals, *J. Comp. Psychol.*, **28**, 201–205 (1939).

MASSERMAN, J. H., Psychobiologic dynamisms in behaviour: an experimental study of neuroses and therapy, *Psychiatry*, **5**, 341–347 (1942).

MASSERMAN, J. H., *Behavior and Neurosis: an Experimental Psychoanalytic Approach to Psychobiologic Principles* (Chicago, Univ. of Chicago Press, 1943).

MASSERMAN, J. H., A biodynamic psychoanalytic approach to the problems of feeling and emotions, in *Feelings and Emotions*, Ed. M. L. Reymert, 49–75 (New York, McGraw-Hill, 1950).

MASSERMAN, J. H., La création des névroses expérimentales, *Psyche, Paris*, **6**, 799–808 (1951).

MASSERMAN, J. H., Psycho-analysis and biodynamics—an integration, *Int. J. Psycho-Anal.*, **34**, (Suppl.) 13–42 (1953).

MASSERMAN, J. H., Letter to the editor, *Brit. J. Psychol.*, **45**, 221–222 (1954).

MASSERMAN, J. H., ARIEFF, A., PECHTEL, C. and KLEHR, H., Effects of direct interrupted electroshock on experimental neuroses, *J. Nerv. Ment. Dis.*, **112**, 384–392 (1950).

MASSERMAN, J. H., GROSS, Z. and PECHTEL, C., Abnormalities of behavior, *Annu. Rev. Psychol.*, **5**, 263–280 (1954).

MASSERMAN, J. H. and JACQUES, MARY G., Effects of cerebral electro-shock on experimental neurosis, *Amer. J. Psychiat.*, **104**, 92–99 (1947).

MASSERMAN, J. H. and JACQUES, MARY G., Experimental masochism, *Arch. Neurol. Psychiat. Chicago*, **60**, 402–404 (1948).

MASSERMAN, J. H., JACQUES, MARY G. and NICHOLSON,

MARY R., Alcohol as preventive of experimental neuroses, *Quart. J. Stud. Alc.*, **6**, 281–299 (1945).

MASSERMAN, J. H. and PECHTEL, C., Neuroses in monkeys: a preliminary report of experimental observations, in "Comparative conditioned neuroses," Ed. E. J. Kempf, *Ann. N.Y. Acad. Sci.*, **56**, 253–265 (1953).

MASSERMAN, J. H. and PECHTEL, C., Conflict-engendered neurotic and psychotic behavior in monkeys, *J. Nerv. Ment. Dis.*, **118**, 408–411 (1953a).

MASSERMAN, J. H. and PECHTEL, C., How brain lesions affect normal and neurotic behavior: an experimental approach, *Amer. J. Psychiat.*, **112**, 865–872 (1956).

MASSERMAN, J. H. and PECHTEL, C., Neurophysiologic and pharmacologic influences on experimental neuroses, *Amer. J. Psychiat.*, **113**, 510–514 (1956a).

MASSERMAN, J. H. and PECHTEL, C., Normal and neurotic olfactory behavior in monkeys: a motion picture, *J. Nerv. Ment. Dis.*, **124**, 518–519 (1956b).

MASSERMAN, J. H., PECHTEL, C. and SCHREINER, L., The role of olfaction in normal and neurotic behavior in animals: preliminary report, *Psychosom. Med.*, **15**, 396–404 (1953).

MASSERMAN, J. H. and SIEVER, P. W., Dominance, neurosis, and aggression: an experimental study, *Psychosom. Med.*, **6**, 7–16 (1944).

MASSERMAN, J. H. and YUM, K. S., An analysis of the influence of alcohol on experimental neuroses in cats, *Psychosom. Med.*, **8**, 36–52 (1946).

MASSERMAN, J. H., YUM, K. S., NICHOLSON, MARY R. and LEE, S., Neurosis and alcohol: an experimental study, *Amer. J. Psychiat.*, **101**, 389–395 (1944).

McCLEARY, R. A., Measurement of experimental anxiety in the rat: an attempt, *J. Genet. Psychol.*, **84**, 95–108 (1954).

MEIGE, H. and FEINDEL, E., *Tics and their Treatment* (London, Appleton, 1907).

MELZACK, R., Irrational fears in the dog, *Canad. J. Psychol.*, **6**, 141–147 (1952).

MILES, W. R. (Ed.) *Problems of Neurotic Behavior: the Experimental Production and Treatment of Behavior Derangement* (Washington, National Research Council, 1938).

MILLER, N. E., Experimental studies of conflict, in *Personality and the Behavior Disorders*, Ed. J. McV. Hunt, 431–465 (New York, Ronald Press, 1944).

MILLER, N. E., Learnable drives and rewards, in *Handbook of Experimental Psychology*, Ed. S. S. Stevens, 435–473 (New York, John Wiley & Sons, Inc., 1951).

MILLER, N. E., Effects of drugs on motivation : the value of using a variety of measures, in "Techniques for the behavioral study of drugs," Ed. P. B. Dews, *Ann. N.Y. Acad. Sci.*, **65**, 318–333 (1956).

MILLER, N. E. and STEVENSON, S. S., Agitated behavior of rats during experimental extinction and a curve of spontaneous recovery, *J. Comp. Psychol.*, **21**, 205–231 (1936).

MOORE, A. U. and MARCUSE, F. L., Salivary, cardiac and motor indices of conditioning in two sows, *J. Comp. Psychol.*, **38**, 1–16 (1945).

MORSE, W. H. and SKINNER, B. F., A second type of superstition in the pigeon, *Amer. J. Psychol.*, **70**, 308–311 (1957).

MURRAY, H. A., JNR., The available procedures for the production of neurotic-like phenomena, *Proc. Conference Exp. Neuroses and Allied Problems*, (Washington, National Research Council, 1937).

OKAZAKI, S., An experimental study of the lack of sleep, *Shinsei Gaku Zatshi*, **25** (1925) (*Psychol. Abstr.*, **2**, No. 2773, 1928).

OTTENBERG, P., STEIN, M., LEWIS, J. and HAMILTON, C., Learned asthma in the guinea pig, *Psychosom. Med.*, **20**, 395–400 (1958).

OWENS, OLGA and GANTT, W. H., Does the presence of a person act on the cardiac rate of the dog as an unconditional stimulus? *Amer. J. Physiol.*, **163**, 740, abstract (1950).

PARMENTER, R., The influence of degrees of freedom upon stereotyped conditioned motor reflexes in the sheep, *J. Gen. Psychol.*, **23**, 47–54 (1940).

PARMENTER, R., Avoidance of nervous strain in experimental extinction of the conditioned motor reflex, *J. Gen. Psychol.*, **23**, 55–63 (1940a).

PATTON, R. A., Abnormal behavior in animals, in *Comparative Psychology*, 3rd ed., Ed. C. P. Stone, 458–513 (New York, Prentice-Hall, 1951).

PAVLOV, I. P., *Conditioned Reflexes: an Investigation of the Physiological Activity of the Cerebral Cortex* (London, Oxford Univ. Press, 1927).

PAVLOV, I. P., *Lectures on Conditioned Reflexes: Twenty-five Years of Objective Study of the Higher Nervous Activity (Behavior) of Animals*, Vol. I. (New York, Int. Publishers, 1928).

PAVLOV, I. P., *Lectures on Conditioned Reflexes: Vol. II. Conditioned Reflexes and Psychiatry* (London, Lawrence & Wishart, 1941).

PAVLOV, I. P., *Selected Works*, Ed. Kh. S. Koshtoyants (Moscow, Foreign Languages Publishing House, 1955).

PECHTEL, C. and MASSERMAN, J. H., The osmotic responses of normal and neurotic monkeys, *Ann. N.Y. Acad. Sci.*, **58**, 256–260 (1954).

PECHTEL, C., MASSERMAN, J. H., SCHREINER, L. and LEVITT, M., Differential effects of lesions of the mediodorsal nuclei of the thalamus on normal and neurotic behavior in the cat, *J. Nerv. Ment. Dis.*, **121**, 26–33 (1955).

PENROSE, L. S., Psycho-analysis and experimental science, *Int. J. Psycho-Anal.*, **34**, (Suppl.), 74–82 (1953).

PETROVA, M. K., Different kinds of internal inhibition under a particularly difficult situation, *Coll. Papers Physiol. Lab. I. P. Pavlov*, **1**, 61–70 (1924).

PETROVA, M. K., Pathological deviations of the inhibitory and excitatory process in a case of their clashing, *Coll. Papers Physiol. Lab. I. P. Pavlov*, **1**, 199–211 (1926).

PILGRIM, F. J. and PATTON, R. A., Food consumption and growth of the rat as a measure of motivational stress, *J. Genet. Psychol.*, **83**, 89–119 (1953).

PORTER, R. W., BRADY, J. V., CONRAD, D., MASON, J. W., GALAMBOS, R. and RIOCH, D. McK., Some experimental observations on gastrointestinal lesions in behaviorally conditioned monkeys, *Psychosom. Med.*, **20**, 379–394 (1958).

RÄBER, H., Analyse des Balzerhaltens eines domestizierten Truthahns (*Meleagris*), *Behaviour*, **1**, 237–266 (1948).

RAND, A., Development and enemy recognition of

Curve-billed Thrasher *Toxostoma curvirostre*, *Bull. Amer. Mus. Nat. Hist.*, **78**, 213–242 (1941).

RAND, A., Some notes on bird behavior, *Bull. Amer. Mus. Nat. Hist.*, **79**, 517–524 (1942).

RAZENKOV, I. P., Modifications of the excitatory process in the cortex under some complex conditions, *Coll. Papers Physiol. Lab. I. P. Pavlov*, **1**, 103–117 (1924).

RICHTER, C. P., Psychotic behavior produced in wild Norway and Alexandrine rats apparently by the fear of food poisoning, in *Feelings and Emotions*, Ed. M. L. Reymert, 189–202 (New York, McGraw-Hill, 1950).

RICHTER, C. P., Experimentally produced behavior reactions to food poisoning in wild and domesticated rats, in "Comparative conditioned neuroses," Ed. E. J. Kempf, *Ann. N.Y. Acad. Sci.*, **56**, 225–239 (1953).

RICHTER, C. P., On the phenomenon of sudden death in animals and man, *Psychosom. Med.*, **19**, 191–198 (1957).

RICKMAN, V. V., Disturbance of the normal nervous activity in the dog, effected by powerful extraneous stimuli, *Coll. Papers Physiol. Lab. I. P. Pavlov*, **3**, 19–34 (1928).

RIGBY, W. K., Approach and avoidance gradients and conflict behavior in a predominantly temporal situation, *J. Comp. Physiol. Psychol.*, **47**, 83–89 (1954).

ROBINSON, JANICE and GANTT, W. H., The cardiac component of the orienting reflex, *Fed. Proc.*, **5**, 87–88, abstract (1946).

ROBINSON, JANICE and GANTT, W. H., The orienting reflex (questioning reaction): cardiac, respiratory, salivary and motor components, *Johns Hopk. Hosp. Bull.*, **80**, 231–253 (1947).

ROHRER, J. H., Experimental extinction as a function of the distribution of extinction trials and response strength, *J. Exp. Psychol.*, **37**, 473–493 (1947).

ROSE, J. A., TAINTON-POTTBERG, A. and ANDERSON, O. D., Effects of insulin shock on behavior and conditioned reflex action in the well trained sheep, *Proc. Soc. Exp. Biol. N.Y.*, **38**, 653–655 (1938).

ROSENTHAL, O. S., The mutual interactions of the excitatory and inhibitory processes (a new type of differentiation of tactile conditioned stimuli), *Coll. Papers Physiol. Lab. I. P. Pavlov*, **1**, 141–160 (1926).

ROYCE, J. R., The factorial analysis of animal behavior, *Psychol. Bull.*, **47**, 235–259 (1950).

ROYCE, J. R., A factorial study of emotionality in the dog, *Psychol. Monogr.*, **69**, Whole No. 407 (1955).

RUSSELL, R. W., The comparative study of "conflict" and "experimental neurosis," *Brit. J. Psychol.*, **41**, 95–108 (1950).

SAMPSON, B. H. and SCHNEIRLA, T. C., The appearance of nail-biting in a rat: a fixation in a frustrating problem situation, *J. Comp. Psychol.*, **32**, 437–510 (1941).

SAWREY, W. L., CONGER, J. J. and TURRELL, E. S., An experimental investigation of the role of psychological factors in the production of gastric ulcers in rats, *J. Comp. Physiol. Psychol.*, **49**, 457–461 (1956).

SAWREY, W. L. and WEISZ, J. D., An experimental method of producing gastric ulcers, *J. Comp. Physiol. Psychol.*, **49**, 269–270 (1956).

SCHEFLEN, NORMA, Generalization and extinction of experimentally induced fear in cats, in *Experimental Psychopathology*, Eds. P. H. Hoch and J. Zubin, 1–11 (New York, Grune & Stratton, 1957).

SCHLOSBERG, H., A preliminary description of the behavior of the white rat in a simple conditioned response situation, *Psychol. Bull.*, **31**, 615–616, abstract (1934).

SCHLOSBERG, H., A quantitative study of certain factors influencing the rate and depth of conditioning in the white rat, *Psychol. Bull.*, **31**, 732, abstract (1934a).

SCHLOSBERG, H., Conditioned responses in the white rat, *J. Genet. Psychol.*, **45**, 303–335 (1934b).

SCHLOSBERG, H., Conditioned responses in the white rat: II. Conditioned responses based on shock to the foreleg, *J. Genet. Psychol.*, **49**, 107–138 (1936).

SCHLOSBERG, H., Comparison of the conditioned and unconditioned responses based on foreleg shock in the rat, *Psychol. Bull.*, **33**, 782, abstract (1936a).

SCHLOSBERG, H. and KAPPAUF, W. E., The role of "effect" in conditioned leg withdrawal, *Psychol. Bull.*, **32**, 562, abstract (1935).

SCHNEIRLA, T. C., A consideration of some conceptual trends in comparative psychology, *Psychol. Bull.*, **49**, 559–597 (1952).

SCHOENFELD, W. N., An experimental approach to anxiety, escape and avoidance behavior, in *Anxiety*, Eds. P. H. Hoch and J. Zubin, 70–99 (New York, Grune & Stratton, 1950).

SCOTT, J. P., "Emotional" behavior of fighting mice caused by conflict between stimulatory and weak inhibitory training, *J. Comp. Physiol. Psychol.*, **40**, 275–282 (1947).

SCOTT, J. P. and MARSTON, MARY-'VESTA, Nonadaptive behavior resulting from a series of defeats in fighting mice, *J. Abnorm. (Soc.) Psychol.*, **48**, 417–428 (1953).

SEARS, R. R., Survey of objective studies of psychoanalytic concepts, *Soc. Sci. Res. Council Bull.*, No. 51 (1943).

SEN, N. N., Behavioural traits associated with experimental neurosis in rats, *Unpubl. Doctor's Dissertation, Univ. of London Lib.* (1953).

SHENGER-KRESTOVNIKOVA, N. R., Contributions to the question of differentiation of visual stimuli and the limits of differentiation by the visual analyser of the dog, *Bull. Lesgaft Inst. Petrograd*, **3**, 1–43 (1921).

SINHA, S. N., FRANKS, C. M. and BROADHURST, P. L., The effect of a stimulant and a depressant drug on a measure of reactive inhibition, *J. Exp. Psychol.*, **56**, 349–354 (1958).

SIRYATSKY, V. V., Pathological deviations in the activity of the central nervous system in the case of clashing of excitation and inhibition, *Russ. J. Physiol.*, **8**, (1925).

SKINNER, B. F., "Superstition" in the pigeon, *J. Exp. Psychol.*, **38**, 168–172 (1948).

SPERANSKY, A. D., Modifications of the interrelations between the excitatory and inhibitory processes in a dog after a flood, *Russ. J. Physiol.*, **8**, (1925).

STAINTON, H., Addiction in animals, *Brit. J. Inebr.*, **41**, 24–31 (1943).

STEWART, C. N. and WARREN, J. M., The behavior of cats on the double-alternation problem, *J. Comp. Physiol. Psychol.*, **50**, 26–28 (1957).

SUTHERLAND, G. F., Salivary conditioned reflexes in swine, *Amer. J. Physiol.*, **126**, 640–641, abstract (1939).

TANNER, J. M. and INHELDER, BÄRBEL, (Eds.) *Discussions*

on Child Development: Vol. II. (London, Tavistock Publ., 1956).

TAYLOR, JANET A., Drive theory and manifest anxiety, *Psychol. Bull.*, **53**, 303–320 (1956).

THORPE, W. H., *Learning and Instinct in Animals* (Cambridge, Mass., Harvard Univ. Press, 1956).

TINBERGEN, N., "Derived" activities; their causation, biological significance, origin, and emancipation during evolution, *Quart. Rev. Biol.*, **27**, 1–32 (1952).

TINKELPAUGH, O. L., The self-mutilation of a male macacus rhesus monkey, *J. Mammal.*, **9**, 293–300 (1928).

TURNER, R. H., An approach to the problem of neurosis through the study of respiration, activity, and startle in the rat as influenced by the difficulty of visual size discrimination, *J. Comp. Psychol.*, **32**, 389–405 (1941).

ULLMAN, A. D., The experimental production and analysis of a "compulsive eating symptom" in rats, *J. Comp. Physiol. Psychol.*, **44**, 575–581 (1951).

ULLMAN, A. D., Three factors involved in producing compulsive eating in rats, *J. Comp. Physiol. Psychol.*, **45**, 490–496 (1952).

WATERHOUSE, I. K., Effects of prefrontal lobotomy on conditioned fear and food responses in monkeys, *J. Comp. Physiol. Psychol.*, **50**, 81–88 (1957).

WATSON, J. B. and RAYNER, ROSALIE, Conditioned emotional responses, *J. Exp. Psychol.*, **3**, 1–14 (1920).

WATSON, R. E., Experimentally induced conflict in cats, *Psychosom. Med.*, **16**, 340–347 (1954).

WEISZ, J. D., The etiology of experimental gastric ulceration, *Psychosom. Med.*, **19**, 61–73 (1957).

WEITZENHOFFER, A. M., *Hypnotism: an Objective Study in Suggestibility* (New York, John Wiley & Sons, Inc., 1953).

WENDT, G. R., Auditory acuity of monkeys, *Comp. Psychol. Monogr.*, **10**, No. 3 (1934).

WIKLER, A. and MASSERMAN, J. H., Effects of morphine on learned adaptive responses and experimental neurosis in cats, *Arch. Neurol. Psychiat. Chicago*, **50**, 401–404 (1943).

WILCOXON, H. C., "Abnormal fixation" and learning, *J. Exp. Psychol.*, **44**, 324–331 (1952).

WILLINGHAM, W. W., The organization of emotional behavior in mice, *J. Comp. Physiol. Psychol.*, **49**, 345–348 (1956).

WILLOUGHBY, R. R. and ANDREWS, R. C., Stimulation interval as a possible psychopathogenic factor, *J. Comp. Psychol.*, **30**, 137 (1940).

WINNICK, WILMA A., Anxiety indicators in an avoidance response during conflict and non-conflict, *J. Comp. Physiol. Psychol.*, **49**, 52–59 (1956).

WITKIN, H. A., Abnormal behavior in animals, *Psychol. League J.*, **3**, 75–83 (1939).

WOLPE, J., Experimental neuroses as learned behaviour, *Brit. J. Psychol.*, **43**, 243–268 (1952).

WOLPE, J., Objective psychotherapy of the neuroses, *S. Afr. Med. J.*, **26**, 825–829 (1952a).

WOLPE, J., Letter to the editor, *Brit. J. Psychol.*, **45**, 220–221 (1954).

WOLPE, J., *Psychotherapy by Reciprocal Inhibition* (Stanford, Stanford Univ. Press, 1958).

YACORZYNSKI, G. K., Necessary and facilitating conditions in producing experimental neurosis in cats, *Amer. Psychologist*, **1**, 245, abstract (1946).

YACORZYNSKI, G. K., Etiologic factors in experimental neurosis from the standpoint of behavior, *Arch. Neurol. Psychiat. Chicago*, **60**, 323–324, abstract (1948).

YATES, A. J., The application of learning theory to the treatment of tics, *J. Abnorm. (Soc.) Psychol.*, **56**, 175–182 (1958).

YERKES, R. M., *Chimpanzees: a Laboratory Colony* (New Haven, Yale Univ. Press, 1943).

YERKES, R. M. and DODSON, J. D., The relation of strength of stimulus to rapidity of habit-formation, *J. Comp. Neurol. Psychol.*, **18**, 459–482 (1908).

YEROFEEVA, M. N., Electrical stimulation of the skin of the dog as a conditioned salivary stimulus, Thesis, St. Petersburg, (1912). (Also; *Moscow: Akad. Med. Nauk. S.S.S.R.* (1953) (*Psychol. Abstr.*, **29**, No. 443, 1955).

YEROFEEVA, M. N., Contribution à l'étude des réflexes conditionnels distructifs, *C.R. Soc. Biol.*, **79**, 239–240, abstract (1916).

YOSHII, N. and KAWAMURA, Y., A study on experimental neurosis of rats: II. Electroencephalography of experimentally induced neurotic rats, *Jap. J. Physiol.*, **2**, 125–129 (1951).

ZVEREV, A. T., On the mechanism of some experimental neuroses in dogs, *Zh. Vyssh. Nervn. Deiatel.*, **7**, 434–441 (1957) (*Psychol. Abstr.*, **32**, No. 4427, 1958).

CHAPTER 20

Applied Abnormal Psychology: the Experimental Approach

H. GWYNNE JONES

INTRODUCTION

THIS chapter, unlike those preceding, does not include a review of literature but merely expresses a point of view concerning the practice of clinical psychology and based on a particular conception of the role of a psychologist in a psychiatric institution. This point of view is not peculiar to, nor was it originated by the writer. In general, it is shared by his colleagues of the Psychology Department at the University of London Institute of Psychiatry and has been advocated in earlier papers by Shapiro (1951, 1957), and also by Eysenck (1952, 1955) and Payne (1953, 1957). The section on treatment, for which the writer assumes a greater measure of personal responsibility, is largely based on two previous papers (Jones, 1956a, 1958). Each single aspect described has figured in the writings of psychologists from many clinics but a consistent application of this general approach seems rare in practice.

The aim and concern of the clinical psychologist, like that of the physician, social worker, or nurse, is to foster the welfare of individual patients. In order to justify his separate professional existence, he must, by virtue of his particular qualifications, make some independent contribution to the furtherance of this aim. Moreover, in so far as he insists on professional status, this contribution should be at a responsible level and he bears the onus not only of practising but of developing his techniques. Despite the varying content of courses of training in clinical psychology, graduate status in academic psychology is a universal pre-training requirement. Thus, it seems clear that the special contribution of the psychologist should be the application of the findings and techniques of general psychology to the problems involved in the investigation and treatment of psychiatric patients.

This might seem a statement of the obvious but, in practice, many factors influence the psychologist into accepting other roles. Not least among these is the low status of psychology as a scientific discipline, both in terms of its reputation among representatives of other disciplines and in terms of actual achievement as represented by a coherent body of knowledge, codified in terms of clearly defined concepts and laws concerning the interrelationships between these concepts, which have been verified empirically and are generally accepted as valid. As a consequence of this lack of status, psychology, as taught academically, does not bear the same fundamental relationship to psychiatry as, for example, physiology bears to physical medicine. Faced with the problems of treating dysfunctions of behaviour, psychiatrists have evolved their own "psychologies" to explain behaviour and, despite deficiencies at least as serious as those appertaining to academic psychology, these tend to acquire the status granted to medicine in general.

In these circumstances, it is not surprising if a psychologist entering a clinic is less confident than a biochemist or physiologist that he has a science to apply and seeks other means of justifying his employment. Mental hospitals and similar institutions are frequently under-staffed and the needs of patients are many. Occasionally a psychologist of humane outlook makes a major contribution in such a setting by virtue of his personal qualities rather than his psychological training; a contribution which, given equal opportunity and equal calibre, could be made equally well by a social worker, minister of religion, or intelligent layman with some experience of mental disorder. Others take over the concepts and methods of psychiatry and become assistant psychiatrists, but with some special knowledge of certain test procedures, which derive from psychiatric theory, and which are validated against psychiatric opinion and are administered routinely or by specific request.

The deficiencies of psychology as a science are not,

764

however, so great as to render its application impossible or even inadvisable. Though thoroughly validated theories embracing broad aspects of behaviour are lacking, there are many more satisfactory miniature theoretical systems and empirical generalizations concerning a wide range of phenomena. Even in the restricted field of abnormal psychology, there are sufficient data to have enforced a handbook of this magnitude, though much that would be apt to discussions of many psychiatric problems has been omitted. The more speculative broad theories are also of value if they are testable in the sense that they mediate predictions which can be subjected to empirical verification. This does not necessarily imply that a simple direct test of a single unequivocal prediction can be made. The more complex a theory the greater its susceptibility of disproof, in that it generates predictions over a wider range of phenomena, but each single prediction refers to more variables, which may then exceed the possibilities of control in a single experiment. Application in the clinical field may serve as a complex test of a complex theory, leading to refinement of the theory and improvement of clinical techniques.

Apart from its *content*, general psychology may contribute much in terms of *method*. The use of standardized validated test procedures, derived from differential psychology, is common in clinical practice but far less use is made of experimental techniques though, for many purposes, their utility is immensely greater. Thus an individual may present or complain of an apparent psychological abnormality for which no general explanation is available. Whether or not similar abnormalities are displayed by other individuals, this may be investigated as a miniature research problem in its own right. First the abnormality is described in terms of the concepts of general psychology by eliciting and observing relevant behaviour in a standard controlled situation. This observation is objectively recorded and, ideally, takes the form of quantitative measurement. Hypotheses are then formulated concerning more basic factors and processes contributing to the abnormality and predictions from these tested experimentally. If, during this procedure, independent variables are discovered which enable the psychologist to bring the abnormality under experimental control, therapeutic procedures may be devised around these variables.

In many such investigations no external control data are necessary as the predictions tested are concerned entirely with variations in the subject's performance from situation to situation. Provided that the experimental design allows for the effects of such factors as practice, the subject may then be used as his own control. Maxwell (1958) discusses at length many such experimental designs and various statistical procedures applicable to experiments with a single subject. Frequently, however, a hypothesis cannot be adequately tested without obtaining data concerning control subjects. The collection of such data is extremely time-consuming but it is often possible to make use of published data such as norms for tests or scores reported in research papers. When this is impossible, it is sometimes useful to employ a single control subject. Thus it may be postulated that, for a certain individual, an abnormality of some complex function, A, results directly from impairment of some simpler, more basic function, B. If this individual and another, not displaying a dysfunction of A, are both tested in respect of B and the experimental subject scores no lower than the control subject, the hypothesis is then shown to be untenable. If, however, the control subject's score is superior extended control data will be required.

Our insistence on the independence of the psychologist's contribution to psychiatric practice is not meant to imply competition with the psychiatrist. On the contrary, it is suggested that the most appropriate role for a clinical psychologist, while not that of an assistant or technician, is that of an auxiliary scientist akin to a medical physicist or biochemist. The essential similarity with the latter professions tends to become obscured by the psychologist's much more extensive personal contacts with patients, which make his functions appear more truly clinical. Novel techniques in physical medicine, involving the use of radioactive materials, have recently had similar effects on the physicist's functions.

Psychiatric procedure may be conveniently considered in terms of the following stages—

1. The routine collection of data concerning the patient and his illness.
2. The evaluation of these data and the specification of further data required, hypotheses to be tested and problems to be investigated.
3. The carrying out of these additional investigations.
4. Diagnostic and prognostic evaluation, and making decisions concerning treatment or disposal.
5. Treatment.
6. Assessment of the effects of treatment.

These stages all refer to activity related to single patients, but it is important that, from experience with individual patients, generalizations of wider implication are formulated. Thus research must be included as a further category of psychiatric activity. It is claimed that the psychologist can be of assistance at each of these stages and the remainder of this chapter will be devoted to a description and exemplification of his role as here conceived.

THE PSYCHOLOGICAL DESCRIPTION OF PSYCHIATRIC PATIENTS

Routine Description

Relative status in terms of certain psychological functions is so frequently relevant to a patient's mode of adjustment that its routine measurement is advisable. Intellectual status is one such variable for most types of patient. For a child, the demands of his formal educational environment are so great, and play such an important role in his emotional adjustment, that knowledge of his levels of scholastic attainment is essential for a realistic appraisal of his difficulties. For this type of description, involving comparisons with people in general or with specific groups of people in terms of relatively well-defined dimensions, the use of standardized validated tests is both economical and efficient, provided that care is taken to ascertain that the standardization sample is representative of the relevant population. This is particularly important in Britain where many of the tests in common use were originally standardized in the U.S.A. The standardization data for several of these have been shown to apply fairly well to British populations but this cannot be assumed to be true of all. Ingham (1951), for example, found that a child patient achieved a very low score on Thurstone's Primary Mental Abilities test and a relatively high score on Raven's Matrices. Testing the hypothesis that this discrepancy resulted from slow speed of performance, Ingham administered both tests to the patient's classmates and found a large mean discrepancy in the same direction. When a test is administered deliberately out of its standardization context, common-sense judgements as to the implications of the score may be seriously in error. Thus Shapiro (1951) describes a young man who, though achieving a score well above the average on the Wechsler Intelligence Test, obtained almost zero scores on two oral reading comprehension tests standardized on young children. Further investigation showed, however, that large discrepancies in the same direction, though not to the same extent, were characteristic of a group of graduate psychologists.

With psychiatric patients, mental testing also presents difficulties related to the standardization of administration procedures. Such patients frequently co-operate badly or display emotional or other reactions which make it difficult to obtain responses in the usual manner. It is permissible, and an expression of his skill, for the psychologist to employ any appropriate devices, verbal or otherwise, in an attempt to allay the patient's anxieties and enlist his co-operation before the actual testing is commenced. If the standard procedure is modified during the actual test administration, the score obtained cannot be assessed in terms of the published norms. Minimal changes sometimes have to be made in order to obtain a response at all. Thus a patient with speech difficulties may be required to point, instead of speak, in order to indicate his selections from among groups of multiple-choice responses. More gross and unsystematic modifications should be avoided until a normal administration of the test has given an indication of the patient's actual level of performance under standard conditions, though not necessarily of his potential. Readministration under altered conditions is essentially a test of an implicit hypothesis and, as such, belongs to the third procedural stage described earlier.

Error is inherent in all measurement and the errors of measurement resulting from imperfect reliability, validity and standardization, associated with even the most satisfactory tests, may be quite extensive. The resultant misclassification may be sufficiently small to be relatively unimportant for some group selection procedures but the clinician is, at any one time, concerned with only one individual for whom the results of misclassification may be serious. Of those individuals obtaining a median score on a test with a validity coefficient as high as 0·9, which is rare, some 10 per cent would be more correctly assigned at above the 70th or below the 30th percentile, without considering errors of sampling during the standardization of the test. Sometimes, errors in one direction may be more serious than those in the opposite direction as, for example, when incorrect inclusion within a "mental defective" category has more serious consequences for a patient's welfare than incorrect exclusion from the same category. Thus it is important that the psychologist considers not only the obtained score but the whole range of assessments consistent with this score and the probabilities associated with them. Payne and Jones (1957) discuss at length the statistical computations necessary for such consideration.

Many psychologists would include among their routine descriptive procedures some technique of personality assessment. If, however, objective procedures are used for this purpose they only provide measures of certain very restricted traits or, if of wider connotation, the errors of measurement are generally too large for individual assessment. Large claims are made by the proponents of the less objective "projection" techniques, such as the Rorschach, but the available evidence does little to substantiate these claims (cf. Payne, 1955). Whatever the merits of the techniques employed, there would be considerable overlap with the inquiries being carried out by the psychiatrist and the psychiatric social worker at this stage of investigation. It is more economical and probably more efficient to confine the psychological investigations of personality factors to later attempts at solving specific problems.

For similar reasons it is considered inadvisable to employ a battery of tests covering a wide range of attributes at the routine descriptive stage of an investigation. Even if sufficient standardized validated tests were available, it would be virtually impossible to include measures of all the variables which might be relevant to the patient's disorder. In the field of learning alone, in which, as illustrated by later examples, psychiatric patients frequently display abnormalities of a rather specific nature, it would require at least sixty-four separate tests to vary at all adequately the sensory modality of presentation, the nature of the material in terms of verbal–non-verbal and sense–nonsense dichotomies, the difficulty level of the task and recognition and recall methods of testing. Increased time can only be granted to routine measurement at the expense of later specific investigations. One unfortunate consequence of this is the temptation to "over-interpret" one's test results, by deriving from them inferences additional to those justified by the validation data. Thus an individual's responses to items of the Terman-Merrill Binet test may suggest conclusions concerning his spatial ability, memory, or some other "partial" ability, but McNemar (1942) shows that the reliability of items is low and, even when both forms of the test are combined, no valid subscales, except for vocabulary, may be derived from the total scale. Similarly unjustified conclusions are frequently drawn from the degree of scatter or pattern of scores on many tests (cf. Jones, 1956b). Inferences concerning orectic factors may be suggested by the verbal content of a response, irrespective of its accuracy. All such inferences, however, are of the nature of hypotheses and require further validation.

Specific Investigations

After the collection of the limited quantity of data advocated in the last section, the psychologist meets with the psychiatrist, the social worker, and others concerned, for discussion and joint evaluation of all the available data concerning the patient and his problems. The broader theories of general and abnormal psychology will be the frame of reference for his contribution to this discussion. In all but cases of a most routine nature, and these are rare in psychiatry owing to the multiplicity of factors affecting symptomatology, discussion results in the specification of problem areas requiring further investigation before firm decisions can be made as to the treatment of the patient.

Descriptive measurement by means of standardized tests may again be necessary to assess the statistical abnormality of a patient's level in respect of some function such as "manual dexterity," "extraversion," or "level of aspiration." This is easily determined if suitable tests are available with adequate norms for a population comparable with the patient in respect of such variables as age, sex and intelligence. Questions of validity, particularly the avoidance of "faculty error," are, however, especially important when using tests of relatively "narrow" functions of doubtful status in psychological theory. For example, if it is proposed to use a test of "perseveration," it is necessary to consider the evidence as to whether a general factor, several group factors, many relatively specific factors, or some combination of these, best accounts for the intercorrelations between tests of this function. When there is no evidence of a relevant general factor from intercorrelations within a normal population, it may still be reasonable to postulate that, for a particular patient, some pathological process has resulted in a tendency to respond in a particular way in a variety of test situations, but this hypothesis cannot be adequately tested by obtaining a score from any one standardized test. It is frequently necessary to compare the patient's performance, not with general norms, but with those for some specific population. For example, the patient may have suffered a neurotic breakdown during the early stages of a university course and questions are raised as to the adequacy of his intellectual or other equipment and his prospects of ultimate success. Earlier routine testing will have provided data relevant to these questions but much more precise information may be obtained from tests of attributes, interests, aptitudes and abilities shown to be relevant to the course in question, standardized on specific university populations and validated against criteria of success. Another patient might have developed a psychiatric illness shortly after the successful completion of such a course and the nature of his symptoms may be such as to suggest some deterioration of intellectual functions. The same tests might then be employed to assess whether the patient is now abnormal when compared with a population of which he was earlier a member.

Frequently, at this stage of an investigation, no standardized validated tests are available, which are capable of supplying the requisite information, or the hypotheses under consideration may refer, not to descriptive attributes, but to dynamic interrelationships between variables, which cannot be verified by simple measurement. Procedures of a more experimental nature must then be adopted and these are best described by exemplification. The descriptions of experimental investigations which follow include several concerned with abnormalities of learning in order to illustrate the wide range of specific disabilities which may occur within a single functional category and to provide a link with the writer's earlier chapter concerned with this function.

Bartlet and Shapiro (1956) describe the investigation of a ten-year-old child with severe psychiatric symptoms including paranoid reactions, temper tantrums, lack of sociability, encopresis and enuresis. Despite adequate though below average scores on intelligence tests and special remedial treatment by competent teachers, he was very backward scholastically and, in particular, was unable to read the simplest of words. The reading disability assumed considerable clinical importance in that the patient continually expressed a strong desire to be able to read but displayed marked signs of anxiety in a teaching situation. The psychological investigations were focused on this abnormality.

The more usual diagnostic reading tests were of little value owing to the extreme nature of the disability but errors made in naming letters of the alphabet were suggestive of both auditory and visual discrimination difficulties. Specially designed tests of these functions, however, gave no indication of gross disability. It was then postulated that the dysfunction was basically one of learning or retention. This was tested in a situation, closely analogous to learning to read, by setting the patient and a single control subject (matched for age and intelligence but able to read) the task of associating spoken nonsense syllables with visually presented nonsense shapes, e.g. $\int^-$ -REZ Three series of three such pairs were learned to a criterion on successive days until no relearning was necessary. Retention was then tested after an interval of five days. There was a large and significant difference in favour of the control subject in terms of the number of trials required on the first day of testing, a similar but insignificant difference on the second day, but no differences on subsequent days. The control group was then extended by applying the first day's procedure for one of the series to a group of ten backward children. The scores obtained fell into two distinct groups, a low scoring group equivalent to the original control subject and a high scoring group equivalent to the patient. The latter group were all non-readers and all, like the patient, made errors in reading the alphabet. There was a clear difference between the two groups in the latter respect. Initial learning disabilities thus seem more widespread than would be judged from the literature.

The patient's disability was explored further in a second experiment, with the aim of providing indications as to the most suitable method for remedial teaching. Paired associates were again used but included visual, auditory and tactile-kinaesthetic material, associations being formed both within and between these modalities. The same control subject was employed and eight associations of each type were learned according to a complex experimental design, which ensured that the daily task was small, and retention was tested over twenty-four hours. The results showed no difference between the patient and control subject in respect of learning visual-visual pairs, but there were highly significant differences, in favour of the control, within both other modalities. All cross-modality pairs produced significant differences, the probabilities ranking as would be predicted from the intra-modality results. During the retention phase, differences were insignificant for the intra-modality pairs but significant, though smaller than during the learning phase, for the cross-modality associations. Thus the results of the second experiment confirmed those of the first, in that initial learning difficulties were again evident, but these were shown not to apply to purely visual material. Unlike the first, the second experiment suggests difficulties of retention but, in this study, overlearning was prevented by use of interpolated material whereas, during the first experiment, the criterion applied to a series as a whole and allowed considerable overlearning of some pairs by the patient. The descriptive investigation was discontinued at this stage and the findings applied to the remedial treatment of the patient.

Inglis (1956) described the investigation of two cases along similar lines. One, a young woman referred for investigation as an "illiterate mental defective," achieved, in fact, a full scale Wechsler I.Q. of 82 but with a marked discrepancy between the Verbal (I.Q. 75) and performance (I.Q. 94) scales. Paired-associate learning tests gave evidence of a gross dysfunction but confined to the auditory modality. The second, an old lady of 72, was presented clinically as a case of "memory disorder." Although this term suggests a defect of retention, an experimental investigation demonstrated that the primary weakness lay in the process of acquisition and was common to the modalities tested and to both the recall and recognition methods of reproduction. Although tests of "immediate memory," such as digit span, are commonly used clinically with this type of patient, she achieved normal scores on tests of this function.

The investigation (Payne, 1957) of a young woman with a history of encephalitis and a severe "memory disorder" also indicated a disability of learning rather than one of retention, but this was confined to the learning of meaningful material such as words and pictures. Her ability to learn meaningless paired associates such as nonsense syllables or nonsense drawings was no worse than that of control subjects. It required a long series of experiments, controlling various other factors, before this generalization could be considered reliable and valid. The labour was reduced by the employment of tasks previously used in a research study and for which control data were available in published form.

In all these investigations the results indicated greater difficulties of acquisition than of retention. The reverse tended to be true of another case (Jones, 1957), a boy of eleven with a marked arithmetic disability. The discrepancy between his scores on verbal and performance tests of intelligence was abnormally large, with verbal ability little below average and performance ability little above the "defective" level. His scores on non-verbal tests appeared to be negatively correlated with the contributions of "spatial" and motor factors to the tests used. Investigations also gave evidence of a marked learning disability and this was maximal when the task was selected to include motor and spatial aspects (a stylus maze). Most striking, however, were his retention difficulties, which are best illustrated by data from the records of attempted remedial treatment over a period of four years. One of his major difficulties in making arithmetical computations was lack of knowledge of the multiplication tables. He could recite some of the tables in order, but only by making a series of mental additions. After two year's coaching for one hour a week, except for school holidays, he was still uncertain of forty-five of the hundred multiplication facts concerning numbers below ten. These were then arranged in random order to form nine series of five problems to be learned by the anticipation method. Two such series were learned to a criterion of three successive correct responses during each coaching session and no series was eliminated until the criterion was reached, without relearning, on three successive occasions. Results with the first series ($4 \times 5, 6 \times 3, 5 \times 6, 8 \times 4, 9 \times 5$) are typical of his performance in general. He never required more than nine trials to achieve the criterion and, after five or six sessions, seldom more than four. It required a year's such practice, however, to achieve the criterion of retention, and deterioration in performance was noted immediately following a holiday period. When, at school leaving age, the patient stopped attending the clinic his knowledge of the multiplication tables was still far from complete.

Though the disabilities investigated during the studies outlined above have all been described as dysfunctions of learning, in only two instances was there a general impairment of learning for all the situations employed. The remainder might better be described in terms of the modality or other factor crucial to the demonstration of impairment, the learning nature of the task being considered merely as a convenient expression of the patient's ability in these conditions. This distinction is illustrated by an investigation of an adolescent girl who achieved a verbal I.Q. of 99 on the W.I.S.C. and a performance I.Q. of only 46. This is the largest discrepancy of this nature observed by the writer and, from the standard-ization data, would only occur once in some 5,000 cases. A series of experimental results suggested that the patient's perceptual functioning was adequate for all modalities, and that mechanisms concerned with such functions as problem-solving and connexion forming were unimpaired but, whenever she was required to make an overt motor response relevant to these functions, its execution was inaccurate. Among the experiments performed was one involving the administration of "digit span" tasks to the patient and a control subject in the following ways: (1) digits presented orally for repetition by the subject; (2) printed digits presented visually for oral repetition by the subject; (3) visual presentation by patterns of dots, oral responses by the subject; (4) Knox cube presentation by tapping a sequence on four wooden blocks, motor repetition by the subject; (5) Knox cube presentation, as before, but with prior verbal allocation of numbers to the blocks, oral responses by the subject. Consistent with the other findings, the only appreciable difference in score resulted from the fourth condition but this cannot then be considered as evidence of some dysfunction of "memory span."

Beech (1957) made use of learning tasks for the experimental investigation of more dynamic hypotheses concerning a young man with apparently psychosomatic symptoms and a history of failure to complete a Science degree course at two universities. One of these institutions reported that he was lazy and pleasure-seeking, the other that he lacked ability. In fact, on tests of various relevant abilities, his scores were above average for a university population. Questionnaire measurement showed him to be highly introverted and his performance was entirely adequate on simple paired-associate learning tasks of the type described above. After an interview with the patient it was postulated that one reason for his academic failure was a tendency to set unrealistically high goals and to overestimate his ability. This was confirmed by use of "level of aspiration" techniques during performance of a laboratory "tracking" task. His overt emotional disturbance ("catastrophic reaction"), when he repeatedly failed to achieve his target, suggested the additional hypothesis that he was exceptionally susceptible to stress, particularly stress resulting from threat of failure. Given the mildly stressful task of learning, by serial anticipation, a list of nonsense syllables presented by means of a memory drum, the patient achieved a score 0.7 S.D. below the mean for a group of University students employed in a research project. When then told that his performance had been inferior but that the psychologist's evaluation would depend upon a second test, his score fell to -4.0 S.D. for an equivalent series. The hypothesis was further supported by the patient's differential performance on tasks which, though of equal objective difficulty, were presented by the psychologist as of varying difficulty, and on tasks truly varying in objective difficulty.

Krikler and Shapiro (1957) found evidence of similar abnormal susceptibility to stress in a young male neurotic patient with study difficulties. Though achieving high scores relative to a university population on the Nufferno level and speed tests (cf. Chapters 5 by D. Furneaux and 6 by R. W. Payne), his relative speed of problem-solving declined appreciably, both when instructed to work fast and when presented with more difficult problems. Repetition of these and other intellectual tests resulted in improvements beyond those expected from practice. This suggested the hypothesis that, for this patient, novelty of the task was an additional stressor factor and this was confirmed in later experiments. The nature of some tests is such that the correctness of a subject's solution to a problem can be checked for accuracy before proceeding to the next problem. Other tests are essentially ambiguous in this respect, there being no external check on the correctness of a solution. It was noted and verified that the patient's performance was consistently superior on tests of the former type. Thus, while this patient and the previous one both reacted adversely to stress, the specific situations inducive of stress were different in the two cases.

In terms of the theories and empirical studies discussed at length in the chapter on learning, both these patients would be described as exhibiting high levels of drive. The reverse is true of an adolescent patient investigated by the writer (Jones, 1957). This boy was an inveterate truant and thief and his scholastic attainment, particularly in reading, was well below that predicted from his age and test intelligence, which was average. In view of his backwardness and generally extraverted pattern of behaviour, a learning disability was postulated but not confirmed by appropriate tests. Further experiments, however, gave evidence of other factors tending to reduce his cognitive efficiency. Compared with a group of adolescents tested during a research project, his speed of performance was slow but more striking was his relative lack of persistence when tested with Raven's progressive Matrices. His persistence fluctuated considerably: with relatively easy items he persisted a few seconds only and consequently made many errors. Thus, for the entire Matrices test his score was equivalent to an I.Q. of 87 but, when only the more difficult items were considered, his performance was at least average. This pattern of relatively worse performance with less difficult tasks was also evident from the learning tasks. He required five trials to learn a fairly simple stylus maze path and only six trials to learn a path of considerably greater complexity. The control group, on the average, required more than twice as many trials with the second than with the first path.

Experimental methods may also be applied for the testing, by the psychologist, of hypotheses formulated by the psychiatrist and derived from psychiatric data. Walton (1957a) describes the application of "perceptual defence" techniques (cf. Chapter 7 by J. Inglis) in investigations of this nature. The psychiatric examination of one patient had produced evidence of three major sources of emotional disturbance; parent-child relationships, sexual adjustment and vocational adjustment. Before planning treatment it was important to decide which of these areas of difficulty was most relevant to the patient's illness and, to aid in reaching this decision, Walton carried out an experiment with the patient based on Rosenstock's (1951) technique. Eight sentences were constructed relating directly to the known emotional difficulties of the patient and two matched neutral sentences for use as controls. These were projected with three-second exposures at seven graded values of illumination. It was postulated that the control sentences would be perceived at lower levels of illumination and with fewer errors and distortions than the affectively loaded sentences. Among the latter, those related to the most disturbing area were expected to be differentiated by the same criteria operating in the reverse direction. There was no significant difference between scores for the neutral sentences and the total group of affective sentences but the difference in error scores between the neutral and parent-child sentences was highly significant. This suggested that the parent-child relationship might be the source of greatest disturbance, a conclusion supported by subsequent psychiatric and psychological investigations.

Beech (1957) has applied similar techniques to the testing of specific "psychodynamic" hypotheses concerning relationships between symptomatology and psychopathology. Thus anorexia nervosa is a condition considered by some to result from a rejection by the patient of her sexuality. Starving herself, such a patient denies her femininity by not allowing her figure to acquire feminine curves. This hypothesis implies the development of an association between stimuli concerned with food and those concerned with sexuality. Beech sought to verify such an association in his investigation of a young anorexic patient. After establishing the patient's auditory threshold, tones 5 db above that threshold were presented and immediately followed by the auditory presentation, 5 db below threshold, of words of either neutral or sexual connotation. The patient was instructed to respond to each tone by writing down the first word that came to mind, however foolish it seemed. It was predicted that words related to eating would occur more frequently during the presentation of subliminal sexual stimulation than during the neutral subliminal stimulation. Such a trend was in fact observed to a degree just short of significance at the 5 per cent level.

Two investigations by Metcalfe illustrate a more direct experimental approach to problems of this nature. One (Metcalfe, 1956) was designed to test the hypothesis that a patient's asthmatic condition was related to emotional difficulties deriving from her relationship with her mother, and that individual attacks were precipitated by contacts with her mother. From a log including records of all the patient's attacks of asthma and her main day-to-day activities, it was possible to demonstrate a highly significant statistical relationship between the attacks and the patient's meetings with her mother, but the experimental presentation of stimuli associated with her mother had no similar effect. The second patient (*see* Shapiro, 1957) was a tiqueur and the hypothesis was tested that the frequency of the tics was increased in situations of specific stress defined by the psychiatrist. The actual frequency was recorded in such situations and in control situations of minimal stress. It was shown that the patient in fact produced the tic far more frequently in the latter situations.

Nosological Description

Psychiatrists, following the well-established procedures of general medicine, are much concerned to apply diagnostic labels to their patients and consequently, their descriptive investigations are largely directed to this end. Thus many of the specific problems presented to the psychologist for investigation refer to questions of diagnosis or, more frequently, questions of differential diagnosis between certain alternative nosological categories. In response to demands of this nature, many diagnostic tests have been developed and validated in terms of their power to differentiate between groups of patients selected, on psychiatric grounds, as typical of the categories to which they are assigned.

Payne (1958) has critically examined the rationale for diagnostic testing and points out that it is based on the assumption that, as in physical medicine, the diagnostic categories refer to qualitatively different and mutually incompatible disease entities. Much evidence, however, indicates that patients suffering from many of the so-called functional diseases are characterized by certain combinations of loci along unrelated psychological continua, equally applicable to the description of normal subjects (cf. Chapter 1 by H. J. Eysenck). Even if this basic assumption is considered valid, there remain various difficulties of a statistical nature in interpreting a particular diagnostic test score. Antecedent probabilities, deriving from differential "base rates" (cf. Meehl and Rosen, 1955), need to be taken into account before assigning a patient to a particular category and these are usually impossible to assess for any particular clinic population. The magnitude of a particular test score may be used to determine the probability of correct assignment to a particular group but the nature of the validation procedure is seldom such that variations in score imply varying severities of disorder within that group: the scores of two patients may imply that one is more likely to be depressed than the other, but not that he is more depressed. A related difficulty arises from the fact that validation is based on typical patients, whereas psychologists are usually asked to test atypical patients with disorders difficult to diagnose by psychiatric criteria. The reliability of the criterion, psychiatric opinion, is itself low, and there is considerable variation among psychiatrists from different clinics as to the signs and symptoms indicative of a particular diagnostic category.

The value of a diagnostic label, Payne argues, lies in its practical implications. Unlike diagnoses in physical medicine, psychiatric diagnoses rarely imply a specific aetiology, because the aetiology of most psychiatric conditions is still a matter of speculation. They do, however, bear implications concerning prognosis and methods of treatment. They are also descriptive in that they imply the presence of at least some members of a specific cluster of symptoms. The reliabilities of and intercorrelations between tests and diagnoses, and the intercorrelations between diagnoses and their inferred consequences are, however, generally low. Thus the inference that a test score carries the same implications as the diagnosis against which it was validated is by no means certain. Payne therefore argues that tests should be validated directly against practical criteria related to such factors as specific symptomatology, prognosis, or the success of specific methods of treatment. Diagnostic tests, at their present stage of development, may be considered comparable with intelligence tests when validated against such criteria as teachers' ratings. Later developments in intelligence testing involved methods of internal validation and external validation against more objective criteria, such as success in examinations. Internal validation procedures applied to diagnostic tests have produced results incompatible with the use of the present external criterion and Payne advocates a change to external criteria of the second type.

Quite apart from such considerations, the employment by psychologists of diagnostic tests, derived from and interpreted within a framework of psychiatric concepts, is a violation of the principle of independent contribution described earlier, and unlikely to advance the development of psychological techniques and theory. A psychologist, examining the case-history of a neurotic patient, and adopting as his frame of reference the type of aetiological theory described in the chapter on learning, will be less interested in the precise nosological category applicable to the patient than in such variables as his degree of neuroticism, his position on the introversion-extraversion dimension, the nature and amount of stress to which he has been subjected, the conditioned stimuli which evoke the abnormal reactions and the patient's characteristic emotional and instrumental responses to these stimuli and to situations of direct stress. This type of diagnostic evaluation by a formulation of the relevant characteristics of the patient, his past history and his environment is, in fact, advocated by many psychiatrists, and is common practice in child guidance clinics. Few objective techniques are available for the evaluation of these factors and practically none of sufficient reliability and validity for use with individual cases. Recourse must then be made to more experimental investigations, such as those described earlier. These may furnish leads for improved methods of routine measurement.

Frequently, description in terms of psychological variables may be more helpful than nosological information in terms of relevance to practical problems of prognosis, treatment or disposal. The first group of experimental investigations, described earlier, which gave evidence of specific disabilities confined to narrow zones of functioning were all suggestive of some form of cerebral damage or agenesis, and one of the patients concerned had a clear history of such a condition. It is doubtful, however, that a positive indication from a test of brain damage would have assisted the psychiatrist to any extent in his treatment of these cases. Frequently, too, problems posed by a psychiatrist in nosological terms cannot be solved by diagnostic tests, however efficient. This is illustrated by the investigation (Beech and Jones, 1957) of a middle-aged woman who complained of memory defect following a head injury received in a motor accident. She was suing for damages from the owner of the offending vehicle and there existed a strong possibility that the disability was simulated. She achieved very low scores on the Wechsler-Bellevue and Wechsler Memory Scales but her co-operation was suspect. Neither a test score indicative of brain damage nor, for example, a pattern of responses to the Rorschach cards, considered typical for malingerers, would have decided the issue.

If the patient was in fact falsifying her responses this should be evident in a situation where the information necessary for falsification was itself acquired within that situation. The learning of a serial T maze is a task of this nature. During the first trial the subject cannot know which of each pair of possible responses is correct but, during the course of successive trials, he gradually learns the correct and, equally, the

incorrect responses. A malingerer might then be expected to achieve scores significantly worse than those expected from chance selection of responses or, if extremely sophisticated, which this patient was not, to maintain an artificially equal frequency of correct and incorrect responses, or show gradual but slow improvement which does not follow the usual curve of learning, nor display the usual serial position effects. Thus the patient was told that her memory was to be tested and was presented with a series of ten cards, each with its central area painted either red or green in colour, the succession of colours to be learned by serial anticipation. Though relatively slow in learning this simple series, she achieved the criterion of one correct reproduction and her pattern of improvement was in no way abnormal. It was therefore considered unlikely that the disability was simulated.

Assessment of the Effects of Treatment

The discussion so far has been concerned with the psychological description of patients as they present themselves at a clinic but the main function of a clinic is treatment. It is, therefore, important to develop objective methods of describing relevant changes in a patient's modes of functioning in order to assess the efficacy of the treatment applied. An earlier chapter was devoted to a consideration of the evidence concerning the effects of psychotherapy and the discussion there illustrated the difficulties of establishing satisfactory criteria of improvement and cure. These difficulties are even greater when a single patient is considered in isolation, and a thorough evaluation of all the effects of a particular treatment is scarcely possible. It is frequently possible, however, to trace changes in status in terms of specific measures shown to reflect changes in a patient's general clinical condition or related to specified aims of the therapist. Earlier investigations will often suggest such measures as in the cases, described previously, of patients shown to react abnormally to various stresses of a specific nature. Effective therapy with these patients should modify these reactions and such a modification could be demonstrated by measuring performance during fresh presentations of the original stress situations.

Soueif, Shapiro and Martin (1957) attempted to measure the effects of leucotomy on a depressed, anxious and obsessional patient, who also complained of excessive and persistent muscular tension. Before the operation, scores on the Hildreth Scale for Feelings and Attitudes, the Taylor Manifest Anxiety Scale and a specially designed questionnaire, based on the patient's case-notes, were all consistent with extreme anxiety and depression. An experimental measure of the frequency and duration of "obsessional" thoughts was taken during rest and when carrying out a mental arithmetic task. Measures of muscular tension were obtained during rest and when the patient was responding orally to very simple arithmetical questions and to questions concerned with her symptomatology. Her initial resting level of tension was not significantly higher than that of control subjects but showed an abnormally large increase in both activity conditions, and remained high when the questioning ended. When retested after the operation, the scores related to anxiety, depression and obsessional thinking were well within normal ranges, but the muscle tension measures showed no significant change for the activity conditions and a significant rise under the initial rest conditions. An intended retest some months after the operation could not be carried out owing to the patient's refusal to co-operate.

Payne (1956) studied an interesting side-effect of treatment with Antabuse on a man with a history of delirium tremens and polyneuritis. A psychiatric colleague had noted that an earlier patient, with possible organic impairment, had shown signs of intellectual deterioration when treated in this way and postulated that in a patient already brain-damaged, Antabuse produced further deterioration. Before treatment, the second patient achieved scores within the average range on several tests of intelligence and tests of paired-associate learning in various modalities: he was below average in numerical and motor abilities. He was retested after receiving Antabuse treatment for three weeks and showed a marked decline in learning ability, especially for learning new verbal material in the auditory modality. There was no deterioration evident in the other abilities tested, his scores increasing to a degree consistent with normal practice effects. The patient was discharged and readmitted a few weeks later with peripheral neuritis. His learning ability was retested six weeks following the first retest and three days after his last dose of Antabuse. His scores were equivalent to those on the second occasion but, when tested seven weeks later, his learning ability was again normal. Similar investigations of other patients has confirmed this temporary effect of Antabuse treatment on learning ability.

PSYCHOLOGICAL TREATMENT

The methods, generalizations and theories of psychology are as applicable to the treatment of psychiatric disorders as to their description. Each of the descriptive investigations reported in the previous section resulted in generalizations concerning aspects of the patient's functioning, with implications for his treatment or appropriate disposal: if the original hypotheses had not carried such implications they would not have been tested. Frequently the methods of treatment suggested by such descriptions of patients' abnormalities in psychological terms involve essentially psychological techniques, and the psychologist may then be the most appropriate therapist.

This is well illustrated by the treatment, by Bartlet, of the boy with severe psychiatric symptoms and a gross reading disability, the investigation of which was described earlier. Owing to his strong motivation, treatment was directed towards teaching him to read and was carried out by the psychologist. The results of the experimental investigation implied that the remedial method should maximize the use of visual material and foster the development of visual associations. It also seemed important that the initial units learned should be small, few of these should be presented during any one session, and overlearning should be encouraged by plentiful revision. For the latter reasons an analytic method was employed, the sounds of letters being learned first and then larger phonograms. Irregular words were introduced relatively late and these were also analysed into smaller units. Such a method is not usually predominantly visual in nature but the Moxon method (cf. Bartlet and Shapiro, 1956) is essentially analytic-synthetic and yet depends largely on the association of letter sounds with pictorial material. An adaptation of this method was used in the remedial treatment, which took place during daily half-hour sessions over a period of six months. His score on a graded word reading test was then equivalent to a reading age of 7 years 1 month and equivalent to 9 years for a simple prose comprehension test. His psychiatric condition had improved remarkably and, towards the end of this period, though living in the hospital, he attended a normal day school. He then returned home and attended the local school, where he continued to make good scholastic progress and his behaviour created no difficulties.

Specific remedial techniques of this nature, based on careful behavioural analyses of dysfunctions, should find ready application in the re-education of patients displaying psychological deficits caused by brain lesions resulting from injury, disease, or surgical intervention. Many such deficits involve symbolic functions such as language and recovery is then generally considered to imply the transfer of functions to the equivalent anatomical areas in the nondominant cerebral hemisphere. If so, it should be possible to facilitate this transfer by appropriate techniques. Thus a patient with an acquired alexia, but no hemianopsia, might well recover more rapidly if reading material was at first presented only in one half of the visual field, or even in the form of mirror writing.

Stammering is a dysfunction generally considered to be symptomatic of a primary emotional disorder and, therefore, best treated psychotherapeutically. An alternative approach derives from the work of Cherry and Sayers (1956) who assume that speech production involves a closed-cycle feed-back system, enabling the speaker to monitor his own speech. They postulate that stammering is a form of relaxation oscillation resulting from instability of the feed-back loop. Consistent with this hypothesis, they find that prevention of the self-monitoring process by a masking continuous tone inhibits stammering but agree with earlier workers that inhibition in this way is temporary only and unlikely to be of therapeutic value. They obtained similar effects by forcing the stammerer to listen to the voice of another speaker while speaking himself. This is most easily achieved by a "shadowing" technique, the experimenter reading from a book while the stammerer shadows him without seeing the text. Practice at shadowing has the effect of training stammerers into new perceptual habits and may be of great therapeutic value. Marland, in an appendix to the paper cited, reports promising results with a wide range of patients during preliminary clinical trials and Meyer (1956) found the technique similarly effective for the treatment of two psychiatric patients with severe chronic stammers.

Patients with perceptual dysfunctions of an "hysterical" nature fail to become consciously aware of certain classes of stimuli but these stimuli do in fact initiate various involuntary responses, frequently physiological in nature, of which the patient is unaware. Implicit in many reports, and of considerable importance from a therapeutic viewpoint, is the generalization that, if these patients are made aware of such responses, and thereby presented with a demonstration of the fact that the stimulation does in some way affect them, they may recover the lost perceptual function. A technique of this nature was utilized by members of the Psychology Department of the University of Minnesota for the treatment of a patient with hysterical deafness and was described in a broadcast, of which the writer was privileged to hear a recording. The critical stage of this treatment involved the demonstration to the patient of her own galvanic skin responses in response to speech sounds. Unfortunately, however, the situation was so manipulated as to induce in the patient a simultaneous emotional abreaction and the independent effects of these two factors cannot be evaluated.

Complicating factors of this nature are less evident in the ingenious treatment of a patient with an hysterical glove paralysis and anaesthesia of one arm described by Hilgard and Marquis (1940). They attached electrodes to both hands of the patient and, during the first phase of treatment, repeatedly applied shock to the normal hand as the unconditioned stimulus for finger withdrawal. These shocks were preceded by similar shocks applied to the anaesthetic hand and which acted as conditioned stimuli. The patient could observe the conditioned responses and sensitivity returned gradually to the affected hand. The conditioning procedure was then reversed, a conditioned stimulus of very weak shock being applied to the normal hand and followed by an unconditioned stimulus of strong shock to the paralysed hand. During the course of successive stimulations the affected arm gradually recovered powers of movement and conditioned withdrawal responses occurred. Theoretical explanations of this type of phenomenon are lacking but there is no reason why they should not be utilized for empirical treatments.

The examples of treatments so far described have been based on generalizations concerning the malfunctions of single patients or restricted groups of patients. Similar use may be made of broad psychological theories applicable to a wide range of patients. In the chapter on learning the writer discussed at length a theory concerning the aetiology of neurosis based on theories of learning. In terms of this type of theory, neuroses are behavioural abnormalities which include ideational response components but do not derive from some psychic entity lying behind the symptomatic manifestations. If this analysis is valid all treatment must be symptomatic: if all symptoms are removed so is the neurosis. It is true that, if only instrumental acts mediated by a conditioned avoidance drive (C.A.D.) are removed, the aversive drive tendencies will remain and, from the theory, one would predict that new instrumental acts would be reinforced and become habitual. This may be the foundation of the clinical belief in symptom substitution. In these instances the elimination of the C.A.D. responses themselves is also necessary. Some instrumental acts are themselves, however, the stimuli from which these responses derive. In writer's cramp, for example, the origin of the tremor may have been the result of a transient emotional disturbance. The disturbed writing behaviour could, however, lead to embarrassment and stress and, therefore, generate increased anxiety which would become conditioned to the various stimuli associated with preparation for writing. Liversedge (1957) has described a method by which this condition was symptomatically treated in a group of patients with no evidence of symptom substitution (see also Liversedge and Sylvester, 1955). The same is true of certain other well defined symptom entities such as nocturnal enuresis when treated symptomatically.

As to techniques of treatment, as modification of

behaviour is the aim, the generalizations of learning theory should provide the necessary guidance. Indeed, from one point of view, treatment may be considered as a problem in eliminating specific behaviour as presented and without reference to the causes and circumstances of their development and, where there is a circumscribed symptomatic entity with clear-cut stimuli defined by the situation, as in the example quoted of writer's cramp, this approach may be adequate. In other instances, however, various remote stimuli are of such importance that a knowledge of the history of the condition is important. In either case the emphasis is placed on observable behaviour rather than on underlying forces of a psychic nature and the treatments suggested may be better described as "behaviour therapy" than "psychotherapy" (cf. Chapter 1 by H. J. Eysenck and Eysenck, 1959).

Various experimental circumstances result in the decrement or elimination of responses. Each may provide an analogous therapeutic situation.

Punishment. Thorndike postulated a negative law of effect as well as a positive, and punishment is frequently used in everyday life to control disapproved behaviour. The work of Estes (1944) and others suggests, however, that punishment merely produces a temporary interference with ongoing behaviour and does not reduce the probability of its evocation on future occasions. In this connexion we need to distinguish between punishment and escape from punishment, a rewarding situation often confused with punishment. Even if effective, punishment would be an undesirable technique for dealing with responses mediated by a C.A.D. as the punishment itself would produce further stress and anxiety, which would summate with that already present.

Removal of unconditioned and conditioned stimuli. In the absence of the relevant stimuli, potential responses are not evoked and, in the long term, a process of forgetting or decay of habit strength may occur. This is precisely the rationale of Meyerian treatment by environmental manipulation, illustrated by the extensive social and educational modification carried out in child guidance clinics.

Satiation. Massed evocation of a response without reinforcement results in extinction of that response. After an interval, the response reappears owing to the phenomenon of reminiscence. Repeated massed extinction trials ultimately eliminate the response. This technique was adapted to the treatment of tics by Dunlap (1932), but his work has been largely ignored. Recently the writer has collaborated with Yates (1957) in attempting to eliminate a set of multiple tics in a young woman by this method. These tics are allied to respiratory movements and appear to have started following traumatic experiences while undergoing anaesthesia. During treatment sessions the patient voluntarily reproduces the tics as accurately as possible, and over prolonged periods of massed practice. Predictions on the basis of learning theory have been verified in this situation, but it has required considerable experimentation to establish the optimal conditions for the development of conditioned inhibition. At the present time her voluntary responses have been much affected by inhibition, and there is a concomitant decline in her involuntary tics and a general improvement in her clinical condition. The questions still remain as to whether her tics will entirely disappear before or when conditioned inhibition of the voluntary responses is complete, and whether their disappearance, if it occurs, will still leave her with anxiety symptoms. This patient's pattern of tics is extremely complex and was arbitrarily divided into components for separate massed practice. Since the completion of the initial experiments, Pickersgill (1957), adopting the same method, has successfully treated two patients with severe and chronic tics but less complex in form and more easily reproducible.

The modification of expectations. Contemporary learning theories take into account the mediation of responses by goal expectancies built up from experience of the reinforcing situations. When expectations are not fulfilled, as when the reinforcement situation is altered, new expectancies are developed and new instrumental behaviour mediated. Thus it might be thought that, if the neurotic individual was forced or persuaded to remain in feared situations or to carry out feared acts, he would discover that the feared consequences no longer occurred. He would, however, meet the painful consequences of the unchecked arousal of the C.A.D., a response which it is extremely difficult to extinguish. When traumatically trained animals are forced to reality test in this way, little modification of avoidance responses occurs. This is consistent with the fact that a patient with a severe phobia or obsession is quite well aware that his anxieties are unrealistic.

The strengthening of incompatible reactions. If one response, incompatible with another, is conditioned to the same stimulus as the latter, and the new connexion progressively strengthened, the probability of evocation of the old response is progressively decreased, and will ultimately reach zero. This is the most promising method of response decrement for clinical application because emotional responses incompatible with anxiety and similar states are available in addition to incompatible instrumental responses.

One form of incompatible response is the opposite of the one to be eliminated. Actual inhibition of a muscular response is an example of this and is the principle underlying the well-known conditioning treatment of enuresis (Mowrer and Mowrer, 1938; Davidson and Douglass, 1950). The enuretic responds by urinating to the stimulus of a full bladder. During treatment the same stimulus, the full bladder, is linked with a waking stimulus, a bell operated electrically at the commencement of urination. Urination responses are spontaneously inhibited on waking, and this inhibition, by a conditioning process, ultimately occurs spontaneously without waking and without sounding the bell.

Of a similar nature is Liversedge's method for the treatment of writer's cramp mentioned previously. He considers this symptom to be a form of conditioned response and the treatment is essentially a process of counter-conditioning. The cramp includes both tremor and spasm components and these are treated separately. During the "tremor" stage the patient repeatedly inserts a stylus into the progressively smaller holes of a steadiness tester. If contact is made with the edge of a hole, a circuit is completed which applies shock to the patient's *free* hand. After training with the steadiness tester the patient traces straight, curved and zigzag shapes with the stylus, deviations from the pattern resulting in shock as before. To counteract the spasm component the patient writes with a specially constructed pen. Excessive pressure with the thumb of the writing hand completes a circuit and the usual shock to the free hand is experienced. In the paper cited, Liversedge reports excellent results with a large series of patients.

Therapeutic techniques based on relaxation (cf. Jacobson, 1938) have an essentially similar rationale, as has Meige and Feindel's (1907) technique for the treatment of tics, employing graduated exercises involving the immobilization of the muscles contracted during the tic. These exercises are combined, however, with others involving active muscular responses incompatible with the execution of the tic. Such use of responses essentially different from the one treated, but chosen so that the same response systems are involved and the two responses cannot occur simultaneously, considerably extend the possibilities of this approach, especially for the modification of emotional responses.

Extensive use of treatment of this nature has been made by Wolpe (1954, 1958) who claims a high degree of therapeutic success for a wide range of neurotic conditions. It is doubtful whether all the methods he describes, which include such diverse techniques as carbon dioxide inhalation and emotional abreaction, may legitimately be included within his general category of "reciprocal inhibition" but many certainly do and clearly illustrate the rationale described above. Thus one of his subsidiary techniques is based on the expectation that, if an unpleasant emotional state comes to an end immediately following the presentation of some stimulus, that stimulus will become conditioned to the "relief" responses following and incompatible with the unpleasant emotions. In this way the stimulus should acquire the capacity to inhibit unpleasant emotions arising in new situations. In practice Wolpe applies a continuous shock to the patient's left forearm, instructing him to tolerate it for as long as possible and then to say "calm." Immediately following this utterance, the current is disconnected and the process repeated some ten to twenty times in a session. Wolpe claims that most subjects report a strong feeling of relief with the cessation of shock, out of proportion to the disturbance produced by the shock. After several sessions, the patient's use of the word "calm" when emotionally disturbed in everyday life decreases the anxiety experienced and this effect becomes progressively stronger.

When, however, a response mediated by a strong C.A.D. is involved it is extremely difficult to initiate and sustain alternative behaviour. Even if this were possible, intense conflicts would ensue which might themselves be the source of additional anxiety. It is in these instances that use needs to be made of the generalization continuum in order to reduce the response potential of the undesirable response. At the same time, stimulation and motivation associated with the alternative response is enhanced. In these circumstances the alternative reaction becomes prepotent and, owing to its own generalization gradient, the process can be repeated nearer the centre of activity of the response to be treated. By moving along the generalization gradient in this way, the alternative response ultimately becomes prepotent in all circumstances. This technique has an experimental foundation in Wolpe's (1952) animal experiments and is essentially the method advocated by Jersild and Holmes (1935) for treating children's fears. Thus a child, afraid of dogs, is given a puppy. The puppy is sufficiently unlike a grown dog to elicit the fear to a small degree only. The puppy's antics create pleasurable responses and, as the puppy grows into a dog, this attitude spreads to all dogs. Desensitization procedures fit this pattern. Thus a certain concentration of allergen may inevitably result in an asthmatic attack. With practice at tolerating a concentration just below the threshold, however, the concentration can be gradually increased without precipitating an attack.

An interesting modification of desensitization procedures was involved in the treatment of a case described fully elsewhere (Jones, 1956). A young professional dancer had been forced to give up her stage career by reason of a disabling frequency of mucturition with associated secondary fears and lack of confidence. Bykov (1953) reports a study in which warm water was introduced into the bladder of human subjects, the pressure changes being displayed on a manometer placed before the subject. This manometer could be disconnected without the subject's knowledge. Subjects rapidly developed a conditioned "connexion" between the manometer reading equivalent to their original threshold pressure and the actual urge to urinate. An intense urinary urge and a galvanic skin response could be elicited merely by calling out the critical manometer reading. Conversely, if the manometer was disconnected, far greater quantities of fluid than normally produced urination could be introduced without evoking the urgency response. In the light of this report a similar apparatus was constructed and, by a combination of desensitization procedures and conditioned inhibition of the urgency response achieved by falsification of the manometer readings, the patient's bladder responses were greatly modified and her urinary symptoms disappeared. No other symptoms were then evident in the hospital, which she attended on a day-to-day basis, but the prospect of venturing into the street still induced a strong anxiety reaction, which was treated on the lines described above by instituting a daily programme in several stages. In a secluded roof-garden, the patient first embarked alone on a training course of limbering-up exercises to make her fit for dancing. She then devised and rehearsed a dance routine, first concentrating on the movements and then on acting as if before an audience. She was encouraged to imagine such an audience and to live the part as actively as possible. She then acted before the writer and finally performed successfully in a public non-professional stage show. Parallel with this training she made unrehearsed and progressively more extensive outdoor expeditions. A successful outcome has now survived a follow-up period of several years.

Another example (Carpenter and Jones, 1956), illustrating the separate treatment of somatic and emotional symptoms, concerns a male patient who exhibited a marked tremor, associated with anxiety, and particularly evident when the patient had to write in front of others, especially his superiors at work, where he was a pay clerk. The tremor also occurred when holding a cup or glass in public, and in other similar situations. At the time the patient was first seen, the tremor was almost chronic. As the main symptom was somewhat akin to writer's cramp, the conditioning treatment described by Liversedge was applied. At the beginning of treatment the tremor was very marked, and the patient was unable to place the stylus in the largest hole of the tester. A regular learning curve was produced, and at the end of this phase the patient's skill with this apparatus was well above that of an untrained normal person. There was also a general improvement in his condition.

Even so, on those occasions when he had to sign documents in the office of his superior, his anxiety was intense and the tremor reappeared. The generalization technique was employed with considerable success. Each day the patient carried out a task involving writing behaviour in public, but where the social consequences of failure were not serious and withdrawal to privacy was possible. Thus, for example, he might take a cheque to pay into his bank account and deliberately fail to endorse it. When the cashier pointed this out and requested his signature, the patient would be prepared and could, if overwhelmed with anxiety, retire to a writing booth. This case has been followed up for well over a year without relapse.

Walton (1958) combined the generalization technique with that of Cherry and Sayers in treating a stammerer who became very anxious and increased his stammer when forced to use a telephone, especially at work. The patient was taught to "shadow" and, when competent, repeated, by shadowing, to one psychologist in the room with him, the message received by telephone from a second psychologist. At a later stage this procedure was reversed, the psychologist in the room dictating the message and the patient shadowing, via the telephone, to the other psychologist. The final stage involved a graded series of unshadowed telephone conversations. Throughout this training objective records showed a steady improvement in the patient's speech with temporary partial relapses after the introduction of each new stage.

The treatment of two phobic cases by Meyer (1957) demonstrates the importance of individual differences in personality structure and the manner in which such differences dictate modifications of this type of therapeutic technique. One patient, suffering from blackouts and under investigation for suspected temporal lobe epilepsy, also complained of fear of going out on her own and occasionally with others. The latter symptom responded well to a graded re-education programme over a period of five weeks, similar to that during the later phases of the treatment of the dancer, described earlier. The second patient, a man, also suffered from blackouts and complained of excessive tension and various fears mainly related to entering enclosed and crowded places such as cinemas. As his fears seemed less specific than those of the other patient, he was treated by Wolpe's method for conditioning anxiety-relief responses to the word "calm," and concurrently embarked on a graded programme involving short daily visits to the local cinema at progressively later hours so that the cinema became progressively more crowded. After seven days he showed no improvement and continued to feel anxious in the cinema. Despite the similarity of symptomatology this response was very different from that of the first patient. In terms of Eysenck's theory concerning the relationships between personality and learning (cf. Chapters 12 by C. Franks and 13 by H. Gwynne Jones) it was postulated that, though both patients would score high on tests of neuroticism, the second, compared with the first, would be considerably more extraverted and condition less readily in a laboratory situation. This was confirmed by scores on appropriate personality inventories and a measure of eye-blink conditionability. On the basis of the theory that excitant drugs increase condition-ability, the second patient was then given 10 mg of Dexedrine each day and, after four days, the earlier procedure was repeated and achieved rapid success. The dosage of Dexedrine was reduced progressively, being replaced with *placebo*. *Placebo* tablets were taken until his discharge after some five weeks of treatment.

Herzberg (1941, 1945) reports good results with a large group of patients treated by a technique involving graduated everyday tasks of a similar nature but real life situations may not be necessary in all cases, at least during the early stages of treatment. Psychodrama may well be adapted to this theoretical formulation. Unlike psychotherapeutically orientated psychodrama, this will not involve the "acting out" of existing attitudes and responses but their suppression by alternative incompatible responses from the earliest stages.

In chronic and widely generalized conditions it may be extremely difficult to find a situation in which an adverse emotional response is sufficiently weak to be superseded. This is true of a female patient at present being treated by the writer and with a long history of intractable fears, obsessions and compulsions. Despite hospitalization, pharmacological treatment and protracted attempts to treat this condition along lines similar to those described, progress was extremely slow and no situation could be discovered in which the patient was truly "at ease." Much better progress is now being made after the adoption of a procedure combining two of Wolpe's techniques. During each treatment session the patient is hypnotized and, being a good subject, does achieve a truly relaxed state. When in a deep trance it is suggested that she is in various situations known to be traumatic for her. If possible, situations are chosen which she is likely to experience in actuality within a short time. When she shows signs of disturbance she is instructed to say "calm" and suggestions of appropriate sensations of tranquillity and ease are made. The only post-hypnotic suggestion made is that, when she wakes up, she will not remember the traumatic situations but only the calmness and how, when she says "calm," she does in fact become calm. Her use of this word

in life situations is now becoming progressively more effective but she is still vulnerable to many such situations.

Removal of "manipulanda." Another possible method of response decrement, essentially similar to the last, is to eliminate from the stimulus situation those aspects necessary for the performance of the undesired response, while the remainder of the stimulation remains intact. Thus, if a rat spends much time in a Skinner box, from which the bar is removed, earlier learned bar-pressing responses will be eliminated (Hurwitz, 1955). Similarly, if the tremulous patient, previously described, had been able to spend a considerable period each day with his employer, but without being required to write, a later demand for his signature might have produced no marked effect.

Throughout this discussion fairly obvious and rather mechanical applications of therapeutic principles have been stressed but verbal interactions between therapist and patient may equally well be manipulated along these lines. The concept of "transference" might well fit into this conceptual framework: the therapist will presumably lie somewhere along the stimulus generalization continuum derived from, for example, the patient's father, and will therefore elicit responses learned in relation with the father. In so far as these responses become modified, the new responses generalize back to the father. Shoben (1949) claims that all psychotherapeutic procedures make use of three interrelated psychological processes: (1) the lifting of repression and the development of insight through the symbolic reinstatement of stimuli producing anxiety; (2) the diminution of anxiety by counter-conditioning from the attachment of these stimuli to "comfort" reactions induced by the therapeutic relationship; (3) re-education by helping the patient to form rational goals and develop appropriate behavioural methods for their achievement. The last two of these processes are clearly involved in the procedures described here and the main difference between "behaviour therapy" and "psychotherapy" lies in the emphasis placed on the first. The principles outlined here tend to indicate more active treatment than is usual in psychotherapy and would focus attention on the development of new responses rather than on the "understanding" of old responses.

It needs to be stated that, though the apparently successful treatment of a few cases has been described, other cases, treated on similar lines, have not been successful. It is not claimed that the remainder necessarily improved as a result of the treatment received, nor that behavioural retraining techniques are superior to psychotherapeutic procedures. What is claimed is the possibility of devising treatments derived from the findings of experimental psychology, in line with the view here expressed concerning the role of the psychologist. Large-scale controlled studies involving such treatments would be necessary to establish their efficacy and the limits of their application. The reported results of workers such as Wolpe and Herzberg encourage some optimism as to the results of such an investigation.

No specific mention has been made of the treatment of psychotic patients because neither the writer nor any of his colleagues has direct experience of such treatment. Though the aetiology of these conditions may not involve learning processes, many forms of treatment will involve such principles of learning as the graduation and spacing of practice. These principles are clearly operative in the work described in recent reports on the rehabilitation of chronic psychotic patients by vocational and other training programmes within hospitals. There is also evidence that practice with tasks of graduated difficulty has a generalized therapeutic effect on psychotic patients, as shown by the work of Peters and Jenkins (1954).

Two recent reports illustrate the specific treatment of non-neurotic symptoms by techniques closely akin to those described here. Cowden and Brown (1956) were interested in the relationship between hypochondriasis and schizophrenia and the various psychological advantages gained by schizophrenics from the possession of a physical symptom. To test their hypotheses concerning this relationship, they attempted to relieve a schizophrenic patient of his psychotic symptoms by replacing them with a physical symptom. The symptom chosen was a backache, consistent with an earlier injury to the patient's back. For a period of three months all members of the staff who had contact with the patient focused his attention on his injured back, which was "investigated" and "treated" with great care. At the end of this period, though showing little change in personality, the patient was convinced that his difficulties derived from his back injury and was free of psychotic symptoms.

Efron (1957) describes a patient whose uncinate seizures could be arrested by a strong olfactory stimulus applied at a certain stage during the development of the aura. Conditioned inhibition to a non-specific stimulus was then established by presenting an appropriate odour simultaneously with a visual stimulus in the form of a silvered bracelet. After eight days' training, the bracelet, when presented alone, produced a vivid experience of the odour. Thereafter, the bracelet was as effective in inhibiting the seizures as the olfactory stimulus had been previously and, at a later stage, the mere act of "thinking about the bracelet" was equally effective. Still later, there was evidence that fits were spontaneously inhibited and, for some time, this inhibition coincided with a spontaneous hallucination of the specific odour used for the treatment.

RESEARCH

The type of experimental clinical investigation advocated earlier is, in essence, a form of research carried out on a single patient and producing results which are then applied in further procedures with that patient. Patients seldom display unique abnormalities, however, and generalizations found to be applicable to a single patient may apply equally to a large group of patients. The testing of hypotheses with general implications may well be carried out as and when appropriate patients present themselves in the course of clinical work, the assessment of results being postponed until a group sufficiently large has been collected. The slow pace of research of this nature may even be advantageous in that it allows time for the careful matching of control subjects. Generalizations established in this way, not only furnish data relevant to theories of abnormal psychology, but enable clinical investigations to be made with greater economy of effort in that standard techniques of testing hypotheses are provided and control data is made available.

An example of such clinical research developing from one of the single case investigations described in this chapter is provided by Inglis (1957). His (1956) findings concerning the elderly woman with "memory disorder" were later shown to have a considerable degree of generality. Other similar patients were tested, together with control patients, carefully matched in age and verbal intelligence but *not* showing any memory disorder. Three major findings emerge from this study: (1) scores on tasks akin to digit span are not affected by memory disorder; (2) failure in the acquisition of material is at least as important in memory disorder as poor retention; (3) disorders of learning in elderly people appear to be associated with disturbances of some intellectual functions. A further investigation is now in progress with the aim of confirming these findings and relating memory failure to disturbances of conceptual usage in elderly psychiatric patients (Inglis, 1959).

Apart from research of this nature, closely related to his practical clinical work, a clinical psychologist may be usefully employed in more formal research projects. One type of project, entirely appropriate to his function, may well fit the term "operational research." Projects in this category would be concerned with such matters as the validation of some diagnostic procedure or the assessment of the effects of some form of therapy.

Other projects would be more of the nature of "pure" research in the field of abnormal psychology. Advances in the practice of clinical psychology are largely dependent upon advances in fundamental research and many would claim that, in the present state of knowledge, the most useful function of a psychologist in a psychiatric institution is the prosecu-

tion of basic research. Practical clinical work, if allied with appropriate reading of the research literature, can be one of the most fruitful sources of hypotheses concerning the nature of psychological abnormalities and clinical psychologists can and have contributed much to research in this area.

From the nature of his training, a psychologist may also contribute to the research carried out by psychiatrists, by advising on such matters as the design of experiments and the statistical evaluation of results.

CONCLUDING DISCUSSION

One characteristic of the approach to clinical psychology advocated in this chapter is the stress placed on objective methods of observation and the testing of hypotheses. This is not meant to imply that the psychologist should refrain from making a judgement on the basis of inadequate data. Time and other economic factors are of considerable importance in clinical work, and decisions of importance may have to be made when hypotheses are untested or partially tested. The hypothesis which seems most likely to prove useful then becomes a working hypothesis, on the basis of which action is planned or an opinion given. This does not imply a violation of scientific procedure as research can only demonstrate the falsity of a generalization and never its truth.

Many of the investigations and treatment procedures described here were extremely time-consuming. Apart from that spent with the patients, much time was frequently required for the preparation of apparatus and material, the collection of control data, the reading of relevant reports and the assessment of results. It is not suggested that the bulk of a psychologist's clinical work should be of this nature, nor that he should make a major contribution to the investigation or treatment of every patient: many will present few problems relevant to his functions. Even so, it is unfortunate that, with normal staff complements and the usual pressure of routine commitments, a psychologist can rarely undertake more than one or two long-term investigations at any one time. In ideal circumstances, a clinical unit dealing with some twenty neurotic patients would fully occupy the working time of one psychologist.

Another characteristic of this approach is its apparent disregard of the holistic nature of a patient's personality. The investigations and treatments described were all concerned with partial aspects of the patient's functioning and, in several instances, the aspect studied was apparently unrelated to the complaint which brought the patient to hospital. This is not to deny that an individual is unique nor that, in certain respects, one deals with and "knows" another

individual in holistic terms. Description and certainly measurement are, however, impossible without attempting to analyse the personality into its partial aspects, as is evident from the personality reports of clinical psychologists of holistic persuasion. Equally, to treat a patient's difficulties, one must consider partial aspects of his functioning, related though they be to other aspects, and attempt to bring them under control. Indeed, by very reason of these interrelationships, modification of partial aspects results in modification of the whole individual. The art of a psychologist may lie in his ability to deal with individuals but his science consists in analysing the complexities which go to make up individuality.

REFERENCES

BARTLET, DEONE and SHAPIRO, M. B., Investigation and treatment of a reading disability in a dull child with severe psychiatric disturbances, *Brit. J. Educ. Psychol.*, **26**, 180–190 (1956).

BEECH, H. R., Unpublished case data, Maudsley Hospital (1957).

BEECH, H. R. and JONES, H. G., Unpublished clinical investigation (1957).

BYKOV, K. M., New data on the physiology and pathology of the cerebral cortex, *Communication at the XIXth International Physiological Congress, Montreal* (1953).

CARPENTER, GENEVIEVE L. and JONES, H. G., Unpublished case data, Maudsley Hospital (1956).

CHERRY, C. and SAYERS, B. McA., Experiments upon the total inhibition of stammering by external control and some clinical results, *J. Psychosom. Res.*, **1**, 233–246 (1956).

COWDEN, R. C. and BROWN, J. E., The use of a physical symptom as a defense against psychosis, *J. Abnorm. (Soc.) Psychol.*, **53**, 133–135 (1956).

DAVIDSON, J. R. and DOUGLASS, E., Nocturnal enuresis: A special approach to treatment, *Brit. Med. J.*, **1**, 1,345–1,350 (1950).

DUNLAP, K., *Habits: their Making and Unmaking* (New York, Liveright, 1932).

EFRON, R., The conditioned inhibition of uncinate fits, *Brain*, **80**, 251–262 (1957).

ESTES, W. K., An experimental study of punishment, *Psychol. Monogr.*, **57**, Whole No. 263 (1944).

EYSENCK, H. J., The role of the psychologist in psychiatric practice, *Proc. R. Soc. Med.*, **45**, 447–449 (1952).

EYSENCK, H. J., *Psychology and the Foundations of Psychiatry* (London, H. K. Lewis, 1955).

EYSENCK, H. J. (Ed.) *Behaviour Therapy and the Neuroses* (London, Pergamon, 1959).

HERZBERG, A., Short treatment of neuroses by graduated tasks, *Brit. J. Med. Psychol.*, **19**, 19–36 (1941).

HERZBERG, A., *Active Psychotherapy* (New York, Grune & Stratton, 1945).

HILGARD, E. R. and MARQUIS, D. M., *Conditioning and Learning* (New York, Appleton-Century-Crofts, 1940).

HURWITZ, H. M. B., Response elimination without performance, *Quart. J. Exp. Psychol.*, **7**, 1–7 (1955).

INGHAM, J. G., Unpublished case data, Maudsley Hospital (1951).

INGLIS, J., Unpublished case data, Maudsley Hospital (1956).

INGLIS, J., An experimental study of learning and "memory function" in elderly psychiatric patients, *J. Ment. Sci.*, **103**, 796–803 (1957).

INGLIS, J., Learning, retention and conceptual usage in elderly patients with memory disorder, *J. Abnorm. (Soc.) Psychol.*, **59**, 210–215 (1959).

JACOBSON, E., *Progressive Relaxation* 2nd ed. (Chicago, Univ. of Chicago Press, 1938).

JERSILD, A. T. and HOLMES, F. B., Methods of overcoming children's fears, *J. Psychol.*, **1**, 75–104 (1935).

JONES, H. G., The application of conditioning and learning techniques to the treatment of a psychiatric patient, *J. Abnorm. (Soc.) Psychol.*, **52**, 414–419 (1956a).

JONES, H. G., The evaluation of the significance of differences between scaled scores on the WAIS: the perpetuation of a fallacy, *J. Cons. Psychol.*, **20**, 319–320 (1956b).

JONES, H. G., Unpublished case data, Maudsley Hospital (1957).

JONES, H. G., Neurosis and experimental psychology, *J. Ment. Sci.*, **104**, 55–62 (1958).

KRIKLER, B. and SHAPIRO, M. B., Unpublished case data, Maudsley Hospital (1957).

LIVERSEDGE, L. A., Conditioning treatment of writer's cramp, *Paper presented at the 3rd European Conference on Psychosomatic Research, Copenhagen* (1957).

LIVERSEDGE, L. A. and SYLVESTER, J. D., Conditioning techniques in the treatment of writer's cramp, *Lancet*, **1**, 1,147–1,149 (1955).

MAXWELL, A. E., *Experimental Design in Psychology and the Medical Sciences* (London, Methuen, 1958).

MCNEMAR, Q., *The Revision of the Stanford-Binet Scale* (Boston, Houghton Mifflin, 1942).

MEEHL, P. E. and ROSEN, A., Antecedent probability and the efficiency of psychometric signs, patterns or cutting scores, *Psychol. Bull.*, **52**, 194–216 (1955).

MEIGE, H. and FEINDEL, E., *Tics and their Treatment.*

Translated and edited by S. A. K. Wilson (London, Sidney Appleton, 1907).

METCALFE, MARYSE, Demonstration of a psychosomatic relationship, *Brit. J. Med. Psychol.*, **29**, 63–66 (1956).

MEYER, V., Unpublished case data, Maudsley Hospital (1956).

MEYER, V., The treatment of two phobic patients on the basis of learning principles, *J. Abnorm. (Soc.) Psychol.*, **55**, 261–266 (1957).

MOWRER, O. H. and MOWRER, W. M., Enuresis. A method for its study and treatment, *Amer. J. Orthopsychiat.*, **8**, 436–459 (1938).

PAYNE, R. W., The role of the clinical psychologist at the Institute of Psychiatry, *Rev. Psychol. appl.*, **3**, 150–160 (1953).

PAYNE, R. W., L'utilité du test de Rorschach en psychologie clinique, *Rev. Psychol. appl.*, **5**, 255–264 (1955).

PAYNE, R. W., Unpublished case data, Maudsley Hospital (1956).

PAYNE, R. W., Experimental method in clinical psychological practice, *J. Ment. Sci.*, **103**, 189–196 (1957).

PAYNE, R. W., Diagnostic and personality testing in clinical psychology, *Amer. J. Psychiat.*, **115**, 25–29 (1958).

PAYNE, R. W. and JONES, H. G., Statistics for the investigation of individual cases, *J. Clin. Psychol.*, **13**, 115–121 (1957).

PETERS, H. N. and JENKINS, R. L., Improvement of chronic schizophrenic patients with guided problem solving, motivated by hunger, *Psychiat. Quart. Suppl.*, **28**, 84–101 (1954).

PICKERSGILL, MARY J., Personal communication (1957).

ROSENSTOCK, I. M., Perceptual aspects of repression, *J. Abnorm. (Soc.) Psychol.*, **46**, 304–315 (1951).

SHAPIRO, M. B., An experimental approach to diagnostic psychological testing, *J. Ment. Sci.*, **97**, 748–764 (1951).

SHAPIRO, M. B., Experimental method in the psychological description of the individual psychiatric patient, *Internat. J. Soc. Psychiat.*, **3**, 89–103 (1957).

SHOBEN, E. J., JR., Psychotherapy as a problem in learning theory, *Psychol. Bull.*, **46**, 366–392 (1949).

SOUEIF, M. I., SHAPIRO, M. B. and MARTIN, IRENE, Unpublished case data, Maudsley Hospital (1957).

WALTON, D., A further experimental study of using perceptual errors as an aid to diagnosis, *J. Ment. Sci.*, **103**, 556–580 (1957).

WALTON, D., The application of learning theory to the treatment of stammering, *J. Psychosom. Res.*, **3**, 170–179 (1958).

WOLPE, J., Experimental neuroses as learned behaviour, *Brit. J. Psychol.*, **43**, 243–268 (1952).

WOLPE, J., Reciprocal inhibition as the main basis of psychotherapeutic effects, *A.M.A. Arch. Neurol. Psychiat.*, **72**, 205–226 (1954).

WOLPE, J., *Psychotherapy by Reciprocal Inhibition* (Stanford, Calif., Stanford Univ. Press, 1958).

YATES, A. J., The application of learning theory to the treatment of tics, *J. Abnorm. (Soc.) Psychol.*, **56**, 175–182 (1958).

Index of Authors

782

Index of Subjects